The
AMERICAN PEOPLE

The
AMERICAN
PEOPLE

 CREATING A NATION
AND A SOCIETY

fifth edition

General Editors

GARY B. NASH
University of California, Los Angeles

JULIE ROY JEFFREY
Goucher College

JOHN R. HOWE
University of Minnesota

PETER J. FREDERICK
Wabash College

ALLEN F. DAVIS
Temple University

ALLAN M. WINKLER
Miami University of Ohio

Longman

New York   San Francisco   Boston
London   Toronto   Sydney   Tokyo   Singapore   Madrid
Mexico City   Munich   Paris   Cape Town   Hong Kong   Montreal

Publisher:	Priscilla McGeehon
Senior Acquisitions Editor:	Jay O'Callaghan
Development Manager:	Lisa Pinto
Development Editor:	Karen Helfrich
Executive Marketing Manager:	Sue Westmoreland
Supplement Editor:	Jennifer Ackerman
Media Supplement Editor:	Mark Toews
Senior Production Manager:	Valerie Zaborski
Project Coordination, Text Design, and Electronic Page Makeup:	Elm Street Publishing Services, Inc.
Cover Designer/Manager:	Nancy Danahy
Cartographer:	Magellan Geographix, Inc.
Photo Researcher:	PhotoSearch, Inc.
Senior Manufacturing Buyer:	Dennis J. Para
Printer and Binder:	Quebecor-World-Taunton
Cover Printer:	The Lehigh Press, Inc.

For permission to use copyrighted material, grateful acknowledgment is made to the following copyright holders:

p. 321 "Land Sales Chart (1800–1860)" from *America Moves West,* Fifth Edition by Robert E. Riegel and Robert G. Athearn, copyright © 1971 by Holt, Rinehart and Winston, Inc., reprinted by permission of the publisher.

p. 353 William J. Faulkner, *The Days When the Animals Talked.* Copyright © 1977 by William J. Faulkner. Used by permission of Marie Brown Associates.

Library of Congress Cataloging-in-Publication Data

The American people : creating a nation and a society / general editors, Gary B. Nash . . . [et al.]. —
5th ed.
p.   cm.
Includes bibliographical references and index.
ISBN 0-321-07106-9 (volume one)
1. United States—History.   I. Nash, Gary B.
E178.1 .A49355 2001
973—dc21   99-087019

Please visit our website at http://www.awl.com

ISBN 0-321-08167-6 (NASTA version)

3 4 5 6 7 8 9 10—QWT—03 02

Brief
CONTENTS

Detailed
CONTENTS

Specialized CONTENTS

MAPS

FIGURES

TABLES

PREFACE

The Yoruba people of West Africa have an old saying, "However far the stream flows, it never forgets its source." Why, we wonder, do such ancient societies as the Yoruba find history so important, whereas today's American students question its relevance? This book aims to end such skepticism about the usefulness of history.

As we begin the twenty-first century, in an ethnically and racially diverse society caught up in an interdependent global society, history is of central importance in preparing us to exercise our rights and responsibilities as free people. History cannot make good citizens, but without history we cannot understand the choices before us and think wisely about them. Lacking a collective memory of the past, we lapse into a kind of amnesia, unaware of the human condition and the long struggles of men and women everywhere to deal with the problems of their day and to create a better society. Unfurnished with historical knowledge, we deprive ourselves of knowing about the huge range of approaches people have taken to political, economic, and social life; to solving problems; and to conquering the obstacles in their way.

History has a deeper, even more fundamental importance: the cultivation of the private person whose self-knowledge and self-respect provide the foundation for a life of dignity and fulfillment. Historical memory is the key to self-identity, to seeing one's place in the long stream of time, in the story of humankind. "It is true that history cannot satisfy our appetite when we are hungry, nor keep us warm when the cold wind blows," says the New York Chinatown History Project. "But it is also true that if younger generations do not understand the hardships and triumphs of their elders, then we will be a people without a past. As such, we will be like water without a source, a tree without roots."

When we study our own history, that of the American people, we see a rich and extraordinarily complex human story. This country, whose written history began with a convergence of Native Americans, Europeans, and Africans, has always been a nation of diverse peoples—a magnificent mosaic of cultures, religions, and skin shades. This book explores how American society assumed its present shape and developed its present forms of government; how as a nation we have conducted our foreign affairs and managed our economy; how as individuals and in groups we have lived, worked, loved, married, raised families, voted, argued, protested, and struggled to fulfill our dreams and the noble ideals of the American experiment.

Several ways of making the past understandable distinguish this book from most textbooks written in the last twenty years. The coverage of public events like presidential elections, diplomatic treaties, and economic legislation is integrated with the private human stories that pervade them. Within a chronological framework, we have woven together our history as a nation, as a people, and as a society. When, for example, national political events are discussed, we analyze their impact on social and economic life at the state and local level. Wars are described not only as they unfolded on the battlefield and in the salons of diplomats but also on the home front, where they are history's greatest motor of social change. The interaction of ordinary Americans with extraordinary events runs as a theme throughout this book.

Above all, we have tried to show the "humanness" of our history as it is revealed in people's everyday lives. The authors have often used the words of ordinary Americans to capture the authentic human voices of those who participated in and responded to epic events such as war, slavery, industrialization, and reform movements.

GOALS AND THEMES OF THE BOOK

Our primary goal is to provide students with a rich, balanced, and thought-provoking treatment of the American past. By this, we mean a history that treats the lives and experiences of Americans of all national origins and cultural backgrounds, at all levels of society, and in all regions of the country. It also means a history that seeks connections between the many factors—political, economic, technological, social, religious, intellectual, and biological—that have molded and remolded American society over four centuries. And, finally, it means a history that encourages students to think about how we have all inherited a complex past filled with both notable achievements and thorny problems. The only history befitting a democratic nation is one that inspires students to initiate a frank and searching dialogue with their past.

To speak of a dialogue about the past presumes that history is always under revision and is always interpretive rather than simply an agreed-upon account of what happened in the past. Historians continually revise their understanding of what happened in the past. This is true in every country and has been true since Herodotus and Thucydides wrote the first histories of ancient Greece. Historians reinterpret history both because they find new evidence on old topics and also because new sensibilities inspire them to ask questions about the past that did not interest earlier historians. It is this continual questioning of the past that has led to historical research and writing on many topics previously ignored or scanted.

Through this book, we also hope to promote class discussions, which can be organized around seven questions that we see as basic to the American historical experience:

1. How has this nation been peopled, from the first inhabitants to the many groups that arrived in slavery or servitude during the colonial period down to the voluntary immigrants of today? How have these waves of newcomers contributed to the American cultural mosaic? To what extent have different immigrant groups preserved elements of their ethnic, racial, and religious heritages? How have the tensions between cultural assimilation and cultural preservation been played out, in the past and today?

2. To what extent have Americans developed a stable, democratic political system flexible enough to address the wholesale changes occurring in the last two centuries and to what degree has this political system been consistent with the principles of our nation's founding?

3. How have economic and technological changes affected daily life, work, family organization, leisure, sexual behavior, the division of wealth, and community relations in the United States?

4. How did the European settlement of the Americas alter the landscape? How have environmental factors shaped American society, and how have Americans changed in their attitudes and policies concerning the natural environment?

5. Has American religion served more to promote or retard social reform in our history? Whatever their varied sources, how have the recurring reform movements in our history dealt with economic, political, and social problems in attempting to square the ideals of American life with the reality?

6. What has been the role of our nation in the world? To what extent has the United States served as a model for other peoples, as an interventionist savior of other nations around the globe, and as an interfering expansionist in the affairs of other nations?

7. How have American beliefs and values changed over more than four hundred years of history,

and how have they varied between different groups—women and men; Americans of many colors and cultures; people of different regions, religions, sexual orientations, ages, and classes?

In writing a history that revolves around these themes, we have tried to convey two dynamics that operate in all societies. First, we observe people continuously adjusting to new developments, such as industrialization and urbanization, over which they seemingly have little control; yet we realize that people are not paralyzed by history but are the fundamental creators of it. They retain the ability, individually and collectively, to shape the world in which they live and thus in considerable degree to control their own lives.

Second, we emphasize the connections that always exist among social, political, economic, and cultural events. Just as our individual lives are never neatly parceled into separate spheres of activity, the life of a society is made up of a complicated and often messy mixture of forces, events, and accidental occurrences. In this text, political and economic, technological and cultural factors are intertwined like strands in a rope.

STRUCTURE OF THE BOOK

Part Organization

The chapters of this book are grouped into six parts that relate to major periods in American history. The title of each part suggests a major theme that helps to characterize the period.

Chapter Structure

Every chapter begins with a *personal story* recalling the experience of an ordinary or lesser-known American. Chapter 1, for example, is introduced with the tragic account of Opechancanough, a Powhatan tribesman whose entire life of nearly ninety years was consumed by a struggle for his land and against hunger and alien values brought by Spanish and English newcomers. This brief anecdote introduces the overarching themes and major concepts of the chapter, in this case the meeting of three societies—Native American, European, and African—in the North American wilderness, each with different cultural values, life-styles, and aspirations. In addition, the personal story launches the chapter by engaging the student with a human account, suggesting that history was shaped by ordinary as well as extraordinary people. Following the personal story and easily identifiable by its visual separation from the anecdote and the body of the chapter, a *brief chapter overview* links the biographical sketch to the text. Students should read these crucial transition paragraphs carefully for two reasons: first, to identify the three or four major themes of the chapter; and second, to understand the organizational structure of the chapter.

We aim to facilitate the learning process for students in other ways as well. Every chapter ends with pedagogical features to reinforce and expand the presentation. A *Timeline* reviews the major events and developments covered in the chapter. A *Conclusion* briefly summarizes the main concepts and developments elaborated in the chapter and serves as a bridge to the following chapter. A list of *Recommended Readings* provides supplementary sources for further study or research; an annotated selection of novels and films is included. Finally, a special annotated section of *Suggested Web Sites* follows the print sources, offering students information on electronic sources relating to chapter themes. Each map, figure, and table has been chosen to relate clearly to the narrative.

SPECIAL FEATURES

A distinctive feature of this book is the two-page *Recovering the Past* presented in each chapter. These RTPs, as the authors affectionately call them, introduce students to the fascinating variety of evidence—ranging from household inventories, folk tales, and diaries to tombstones, advertising, and popular music—that historians have learned to employ in reconstructing the past. Each RTP gives basic information about the source and its use by historians and then raises questions for students to consider as they study the example reproduced for their inspection.

In addition to the "Recovering the Past" sections, we have provided other elements that will facilitate learning for students.

- *Technology Changes the American People* is a new feature that helps students understand the ways in which scientific and technological changes have come about and the impact they have had on the character of American life. The feature shows that the process of invention and change is not confined by national boundaries; technological and scientific innovations in the United States have often been connected with and dependent on developments elsewhere in the world. While many of the ideas and technological advances discussed came from outside the United States, each feature highlights the ways in which innovations have affected and often transformed the daily life of ordinary Americans. The flush toilet, the bicycle, plastic, and more recently the World Wide Web are some of the innovations discussed in the new feature. All have changed the way Americans lived in their homes, spent their free time, worked at their jobs, and did their shopping.

- In a series of *Diagraphics* we bring together, in visually engaging ways, economic data that portrays how political, social, and technological changes are closely intertwined at particular moments in American history. One diagraphic, for example, suggests the broad impact of new methods of steel production during the nineteenth century on the ways in which Americans worked, travelled, constructed their buildings, and waged war.

- The program of *color illustrations*—paintings, cartoons, photographs, maps, and figures—amplifies important themes while presenting visual evidence for student reflection and analysis. Captions on all photographs, maps, and figures are designed to help students understand and interpret the information presented. Summary tables, which we refer to as "talking boxes," recap points discussed in the narrative, pulling the material together in a format designed for ease of student study. Examples of such "talking boxes" include "Significant Factors Promoting Economic Growth, 1820–1860" in Chapter 10 and "Conflicting Aims During the Cold War" in Chapter 27.

- The comprehensive timeline developed for this edition includes the important political, diplomatic, social, economic, cultural, and technological events of the past 400 years. This six-page, full-color timeline, with illustrations as well as a listing of significant events, is designed to be hung on a wall and used throughout the semester. It is available free with every purchase of a new copy of the book.

THE FIFTH EDITION

The fifth edition of *The American People* has benefited from both the helpful comments of scholars and the experience of teachers and students who used previous editions of the book. While some of the modifications are small, others, like the revision and updating of Chapter 30, are substantial. Another major effort of this edition has been the coverage of science and technology. Aware of the importance of this aspect of our history, we have paid careful attention not only to the process and character of scientific and technological change but also to its social consequences. Much of the treatment of science and technology has been woven into the text, but the new feature, *Technology Changes the American People*, provides detailed analyses of significant developments that have had a substantial impact on

American life. This edition also features several substantially revised and some entirely new RTPs, a feature of the book that has been one of the favorites over the years. An expanded map program as well as carefully selected new visual materials provide students with additional ways of understanding chapter discussions. Revised bibliographies with new annotated sections on film and fiction and a list of helpful Web sites provide avenues for further explorations outside of the classroom. The foldout timeline, described above, is also a new feature of this edition.

Major Changes in the Fifth Edition

- *Chapter 3* revises the discussion of African slavery and the Atlantic slave trade and features a new section on slavery in the French and British colonies of North America
- *Chapter 4* includes the RTP on household inventories, moved from Chapter 5; *Technology Changes the American People* discusses the lightning rod
- *Chapter 5* has a new RTP that focuses on poetry and the work of African American writer, Phillis Wheatley; small pox inoculation is the subject of the new feature, *Technology Changes the American People*
- *Chapter 6* has been shortened and reorganized; the discussion of the American Revolution has been enriched by placing it within the larger context of the other Democratic revolutions of the period; a revised RTP on Patriotic Paintings (moved from Chapter 8) appears in this chapter with a discussion of artist John Trumbull and his painting *The Death of General Warren at the Battle of Bunker's Hill*
- *Chapter 7* blends material on revolutionary politics, once part of Chapter 6, into the analysis of the continuing ambiguities of politics in the post-war 1780s, thus making Chapters 6 and 7 more balanced in length; the analysis of the republican community makes clear the hardening of racial attitudes
- *Chapter 8* treats domestic events, like the American response to the French Revolution and the Alien and Sedition Acts, in the context of the broad theme of trans-Atlantic Democratic revolutions; highlights the contributions made by radical Irish, among them ardent Irish nationalists, and other immigrants to the Jeffersonian opposition during the hectic politics of the 1790s; a significantly revised RTP on European Travel Journals (moved from Chapter 12) now appears in this chapter, with a substantial journal selection from the French visitor,

Moreau de Saint Mery; a *Technology Changes the American People* essay focuses on the development of wooden machinery and the role of this early technology in the first stirrings of the industrial revolution
- *Chapter 9* concludes the new theme of the age of Democratic revolutions in the discussion of the domestic fallout over the Haitian revolution and the emotional, ideological, and diplomatic connections between the United States and Latin American independence movements; the chapter now emphasizes the hardening of northern racial attitudes as northerners ended slavery in that region; an analysis of Eli Whitney and the Cotton Gin is the focus of the new section, *Technology Changes the American People*
- *Chapter 11* includes more material on the importance of outwork during the early industrial period
- *Chapter 12* has a new RTP on slave narratives that not only provides an introduction to slave narratives as an historical source but also places them in the context of the abolitionist campaign to end slavery; the development of a practical sewing machine and its impact are the basis for the section *Technology Changes the American People*
- *Chapter 14* has changes, especially in terminology, that reflect the contributions of the New Western History
- *Chapter 18* includes an expanded analysis of the technological advances of the industrial age and provides insight into the factors that helped to spark change; the flush toilet is the focus of *Technology Changes the American People*
- *Chapter 19* looks at the bicycle in the section *Technology Changes the American People*
- *Chapter 21* shows the link between scientific theories and racism
- *Chapter 22* features a new discussion of the great Flu Epidemic of 1918 and has included some new material on scientific and technical research during the war
- *Chapter 23* includes new material on the technology of flood control to accompany the new section on the Great Mississippi flood of 1927 and enriched sections on household technology and the impact of the automobile; the development and impact of the wireless radio is the subject of *Technology Changes the American People*
- *Chapter 24* points out the limitations of the New Deal for African Americans
- *Chapter 25* has a new RTP on historical monuments and their relationship to history and

memory and discusses the development of plastics in *Technology Changes the American People*

- *Chapter 26* has increased coverage of computers in connection with the edition's goal of highlighting technology; features new material on the experiences of Native American, Latino, and African American communities in the postwar United States; the chapter also focuses on the development and significance of air conditioning in the new feature, *Technology Changes the American People*

- *Chapter 27* refocuses the analysis of the Cold War as a result of new materials now available to scholars; provides additional material on Eisenhower and on anti-Communism at home, including the ways in which an anti-homosexual effort played a part in the anti-Communist crusade

- *Chapter 29* has stronger coverage of the Civil Rights Movement and additional material on Native American rights; as part of the effort to highlight the importance of science and technology, there is an expanded discussion of birth control and the development of the pill and

more material on nuclear regulation

- *Chapter 30* has been significantly revised and updated; it opens with a new anecdote, revealing the experience of a working-class family in the 1990s; the section on the economy discusses the recent boom period and notes the significance of the merger movement and the soaring stock market; sections on foreign policy (including Kosovo) and the Clinton presidency (including impeachment efforts) have been updated; new materials have been added on declining voter turnouts, the end of Affirmative Action, the environmental movement, and immigration laws; in keeping with the emphasis on science and technology this chapter features the World Wide Web as the subject for *Technology Changes the American People*

Our aim has been to write a balanced and vivid history of the development of the American nation and its society. We have also tried to provide the support materials necessary to make teaching and learning enjoyable and rewarding. The reader will be the judge of our success. The authors welcome your comments.

Gary B. Nash
Julie Roy Jeffrey

NOTE *to the* STUDENT

FEATURES OF THIS BOOK

The authors have included a number of tools to help you in your study of American history.

- Each chapter begins with a *personal story* recalling the experience of an ordinary or lesser-known American. A *brief chapter overview* links this opening story to the major themes of the chapter.
- An *outline* provides an overview of the chapter topics and organization.
- *Summary* tables ("talking boxes") recap points discussed in the chapter for easy reference.
- Special icons in every chapter mark general and specific topics also addressed on *The History Place Web Site* that you have access to with the purchase of this text: http://www.ushistoryplace.com. This teaching and learning Web-based resource for students and instructors of American history provides interactive maps; timelines; a rich collection of primary sources, secondary sources, and links to related American history sites; an Op-Ed forum to spark classroom discussion; and Updated News presented with historical perspective.
- *Recovering the Past* essays in each chapter examine different kinds of historical evidence ranging from household inventories, folktales, and diaries to tombstones, advertising, and popular music.
- Eleven *Technology Changes the American People* essays focus on the development of science and new technologies (such as the cotton gin and the flush toilet) and their impact on peoples' everyday lives.
- A carefully selected program of *illustrations*—paintings, cartoons, photographs, maps, and figures—amplifies important themes while presenting visual evidence for your reflection and analysis.
- A *timeline* reviews the major events and developments covered in the chapter.
- Also included with this text is a full-color *timeline poster*, designed to be hung on a wall and used throughout the semester. This comprehensive timeline includes numerous important political, diplomatic, social, economic, cultural, and technological events of the past 400 years of American history.

- A *Conclusion* briefly summarizes the main concepts and developments discussed in the chapter.
- *Recommended Readings* are included at the end of every chapter, offering you research suggestions for scholarly resources, as well as a brief list of fiction and film (feature films and documentaries) related to chapter topics and themes.
- At the end of each chapter there is also an annotated list of *Suggested Web Sites* that relate to chapter topics and themes. Though these Web addresses were checked for accuracy before publication of this text, the changing nature of Web sites suggests that at least a few might be outdated links by the time you investigate them. These and additional Web suggestions will be updated regularly on the text's Web site (*http://www.awl.com/nash*) and The History Place site.

In addition to the specific Web sites recommended for the chapters, you may also want to visit some of the following *major history Web sites* that have content that relates to all periods of American history.

Smithsonian Institution—National Museum of American History
http://americanhistory.si.edu/

Library of Congress Web Site
http://www.loc.gov/

Library of Congress American Memory Project
http://memory.loc.gov/ammem/amhome.html

National Archives and Records Administration Home Page
http://www.nara.gov

"The Digital Classroom"
http://www.nara.gov/education/teaching/teaching.html

"The Exhibit Hall"
http://www.nara.gov/exhall/

Documents for the Study of American History (AMDOCS)
http://www.ukans.edu/carrie/docs/amdocs_index.html

United States Census Bureau
http://www.census.gov/

The African-American Mosaic—A Library of
    Congress Resource Guide
http://lcweb.loc.gov/exhibits/african/intro.html

National Women's History Project
http://www.nwhp.org

National Gallery of Art
http://www.nga.gov/home.htm

Historical Maps: The Perry Castaneda Library
    Map Collection
http://www.lib.utexas.edu/Libs/PCL/
    Map_collection/historical/history_main.html

University of California—Berkeley Library
    Digital Map Collection
http://www.lib.berkeley.edu/EART/digital/
    tour.html

SUPPLEMENTS

FOR QUALIFIED COLLEGE ADOPTERS

Companion Web Site, Nash Online, http://www. awl.com/nash. This online course companion provides a wealth of resources for both students and instructors using *The American People,* Fifth Edition. Instructors will find the instructor's manual, teaching links, downloadable figures and photos, animated maps, thematic timelines, and narrated photo essays.

The History Place Premium Web Site, http://www. ushistoryplace.com. Available at no additional cost for students who purchase a new copy of the textbook, the site is a continually updated American history Web site of extraordinary breadth and depth, which features unmatched interactive maps, timelines, and activities; hundreds of source documents, images, and audio clips; a powerful TestFlight student self-assessment tool; and much more.

Instructor's Manual. Neal Brooks and Ingrid Sabio, Essex Community College. This guide was written based on ideas generated in "active learning" workshops and is tied closely to the text. In addition to suggestions on how to generate lively class discussion and involve students in active learning, this supplement also offers a file of exam questions and lists of resources, including films, slides, photo collections, records and audiocassettes.

Comprehensive American History Transparency Set. This vast collection of American history map transparencies includes over two hundred map transparencies ranging from the first Native Americans to the end of the Cold War, covering wars, social trends, elections, immigration and demographics. Also included are a reproducible set of student map exercises, teaching tips, and correlation charts.

American Impressions: A CD-ROM for U.S. History. This unique CD-ROM for the U.S. History course is organized in a topical and thematic framework which allows in-depth coverage with a media-centered focus. Hundreds of photos, maps, works of art, graphics, and historical film clips are organized into narrated vignettes and interactive activities to create a tool for both professors and students. Topics include "The Encounter Period," "Revolution to Republic," "A Century of Labor and Reform," and "The Struggle for Equality." A guide for instructors provides teaching tips and suggestions for using advanced media in the classroom. The CD-ROM is available in both Macintosh and Windows formats.

Visual Archives of American History, 2/e. This two-sided video laserdisc explores history from the meeting of three cultures to the present. It is an encyclopedic chronology of U.S. history offering hundreds of photographs and illustrations, a variety of source and reference maps—several of which are animated—plus fifty minutes of video. For ease in planning lectures, a manual listing barcodes for scanning and frame numbers for all the material is available.

Discovering American History Through Maps and Views. Created by Gerald Danzer, University of Illinois at Chicago, the recipient of the AHA's 1990 James Harvey Robinson Prize for his work in the development of map transparencies—this set of 140 four-color acetates is a unique instructional tool. It contains an introduction on teaching history through maps and a detailed commentary on each transparency. The collection includes cartographic and pictorial maps, views and photos, urban plans, building diagrams, and works of art.

A Guide to Teaching American History Through Film. Written by Randy Roberts, Purdue University, this guide provides instructors with a creative and practical tool for stimulating classroom discussion. The sections include "American Films: A Historian's Perspective," a list of films, practical suggestions and bibliography. The film listing is presented in narrative form, developing connections between each film and the topics being discussed.

Video Lecture Launchers. Prepared by Mark Newman, University of Illinois at Chicago, these video lecture launchers (each two to five minutes in duration) cover key issues in American history from 1877 to the present. The launchers are accompanied by an *Instructor's Manual.*

Transparencies. A set of 40 map transparencies drawn from the text.

"This Is America" Immigration Video. Produced by the American Museum of Immigration, this video tells the story of American immigrants, relating their personal stories and accomplishments. By showing how the richness of our culture is due to the contributions of millions of immigrant Americans, the videos make the point that America's strength lies in the ethnically and culturally diverse backgrounds of its citizens.

Telecourse Package. America in Perspective: U.S. History Since 1877—produced and distributed by the LeCroy Center for Educational Telecommunications, Dallas Country Community College District—are designed as a component of a comprehensive learning package consisting of the 26-lesson telecourse program, *The American People,* and a telecourse study guide. *Telecourse Study Guide for America in Perspective* contains numerous study aids, self-tests, enrichment ideas, and suggested readings, all keyed to specific pages in *The American People.* The study guide can be ordered through your Longman representative. In addition, *The American Adventure Telecourse Study Guide* has been updated to include a new pagination key to better correlate to this new edition of *The American People.*

Test Bank. This test bank, prepared by Jeanne Whitney, Salisbury State University, contains more than 3,500 objective, conceptual, and essay questions. All questions are keyed to specific pages in the text.

Test Gen Computerized Testing System. This flexible, easy-to-master computer test bank includes all the test items in the printed test bank. The software allows you to edit existing questions and add your own items. Tests can be printed in several different formats and can include figures such as graphs and tables.

➣ FOR STUDENTS

Companion Web Site, Nash Online, http://www. awl.com/nash. This online course companion provides a wealth of resources for both students and instructors using *The American People,* Fifth Edition. Students will find chapter summaries, test questions, interactive Web exercises, animated maps, primary sources, and thematic timelines.

The History Place Premium Web Site, http://www. ushistoryplace.com. Available at no additional cost for students who purchase a new copy of the textbook, the site is a continually updated American history Web site of extraordinary breadth and depth, which features unmatched interactive maps, timelines, and activities; hundreds of source documents, images, and audio clips; a powerful TestFlight student self-assessment tool; and much more.

Interactive Edition CD-ROM. This unique CD-ROM offers students a complete multimedia learning experience. It contains the full text of the book, plus photos, figures, maps, video, web links, practice tests, and primary sources. The easy-to-use navigation makes it simple to search the text, take notes, and highlight key sections. *Free* when packaged with the text.

Study Guide. This two-volume study guide, created by Neal Brooks and Ingrid Sabio, Essex Community College, includes chapter outlines, significant themes and highlights, a glossary, learning enrichment ideas, sample test questions, exercises for identification and interpretation, and geography exercises based on maps in the text.

Study Wizard Computerized Tutorial. Prepared by J. Patrick McCarthy, University of Georgia, this interactive program features chapter outlines and multiple-choice, true-false, and short-answer questions. It also contains a glossary and gives users immediate test scores and answer explanations.

Longman American History Atlas. This full color historical atlas includes more than 100 maps, all designed especially for this volume. This valuable reference tool is available shrinkwrapped with *The American People* at low cost.

America Through the Eyes of Its People: Primary Sources in American History, Second Edition. This one-volume collection of primary documents portrays the rich and varied tapestry of American life. It contains documents by women, Native Americans, African Americans, Hispanics, and others who helped to shape the course of U.S. history along with student study questions and contextual headnotes.

Sources of the African American Past. Edited by Roy Finkenbine, University of Detroit at Mercy, this collection of primary sources covers key themes in the African-American experience from the West African background to the present. Balanced between political and social history, it offers a vivid snapshot of the lives of African Americans in different historical periods, and includes documents representing women and different regions of the United States. Available at a minimum cost when bundled with the text.

Women and the National Experience. Edited by Ellen Skinner, Pace University, this primary source reader contains both classic and unusual documents describing the history of women in the United States. The documents provide dramatic evidence that outspoken women attained a public voice and participated in the development of national events and policies long before they could vote. Chronologically organized and balanced between social and political history, this reader offers a striking picture of the lives of women across American history. Available at a minimum cost when bundled with the text.

Reading the American West. Edited by Mitchel Roth, Sam Houston State University, this primary source reader uses letters, diary excerpts, speeches, interviews, and newspaper articles to let students experience how historians research and how history is written. Every document is accompanied by a contextual headnote and study questions. The book is divided into chapters with extensive introductions. Available at a minimum cost when bundled with the text.

Retracing the Past, Third Edition. This two-volume set of readers is edited by Ronald Schultz, University of Wyoming, and Gary B. Nash. These secondary source readings cover economic, political, and social history with special emphasis on women, racial and ethnic groups, and working-class people.

Learning to Think Critically: Films and Myths About American History. Randy Roberts and Robert May, Purdue University, use well-known films such as *Gone with the Wind* and *Casablanca* to explore some common myths about America and its past. This short handbook subjects some popular beliefs to his-

torical scrutiny in order to help students develop a method of inquiry for approaching the subject of history in general.

Mapping America: A Guide to Historical Geography. This workbook by Ken Weatherbie, Del Mar College, was revised specifically for this new edition. Each volume contains 18 exercises corresponding to the map program in the text; each exercise concludes with interpretive questions about the role of geography in American history. This free item is designed to be packaged with *The American People.*

Mapping American History: Student Activities. Written by Gerald Danzer, University of Illinois at Chicago, this free map workbook for students features exercises designed to teach students to interpret and analyze cartographic materials as historical documents. This free item is designed to be packaged with *The American People.*

ACKNOWLEDGMENTS

The authors wish to thank the following reviewers who gave generously of their time and expertise and whose thoughtful and constructive work have contributed greatly to this edition:

Cara Anzilotti, *Loyola Marymount University*

Virginia H. Bellows, *Tulsa Community College*

S. Charles Bolton, *University of Arkansas at Little Rock*

William Furdell, *University of Great Falls*

David J. Grettler, *Northern State University*

David Gutzke, *Southwest Missouri State University*

Craig Hendricks, *Long Beach City College*

Anne Klejment, *University of St. Thomas*

Larry Lowther, *Central Washington University*

Robert F. Marcom, *San Antonio College*

Thomas M. McLuen, *Spokane Falls Community College*

Cassandra L. Newby-Alexander, *Norfolk State University*

Sean O'Neill, *Grand Valley State University*

Gene B. Preuss, *Texas Tech University*

Dale J. Schmitt, *East Tennessee State University*

John A. Trickel, *Richland College*

Michael P. White, *Temple College*

Over the years, as previous editions of this text were being developed, many of our colleagues read and criticized the various drafts of the manuscript. For their thoughtful evaluations and constructive suggestions, the authors wish to express their gratitude to the following reviewers:

Richard H. Abbott, *Eastern Michigan University*

John Alexander, *University of Cincinnati*

Kenneth G. Alfers, *Mountain View College*

Terry Alford, *North Virginia Community College*

Gregg Andrews, *Southwest Texas State University*

Robert Asher, *University of Connecticut, Storrs*

Harry Baker, *University of Arkansas at Little Rock*

Michael Batinski, *Southern Illinois University*

Gary Bell, *Sam Houston State University*

Virginia Bellows, *Tulsa Community College*

Spencer Bennett, *Siena Heights College*

Jackie R. Booker, *Western Connecticut State University*

James Bradford, *Texas A&M University*

Neal Brooks, *Essex Community College*

Jeffrey P. Brown, *New Mexico State University*

Dickson D. Bruce, Jr., *University of California, Irvine*

David Brundage, *University of California, Santa Cruz*

Colin Calloway, *Dartmouth University*

D'Ann Campbell, *Indiana University*

Jane Censer, *George Mason University*

Vincent A. Clark, *Johnson County Community College*

Neil Clough, *North Seattle Community College*

Matthew Ware Coulter, *Collin County Community College*

David Culbert, *Louisiana State University*

Mark T. Dalhouse, *Northeast Missouri State University*

Bruce Dierenfield, *Canisius College*

John Dittmer, *DePauw University*

Gordon Dodds, *Portland State University*

Richard Donley, *Eastern Washington University*

Dennis B. Downey, *Millersville University*

Robert Downtain, *Tarrant County Community College*

Robert Farrar, *Spokane Falls Community College*

Bernard Friedman, *Indiana University–Purdue University at Indianapolis*

Bruce Glasrud, *California State University, Hayward*

Brian Gordon, *St. Louis Community College*

Richard Griswold del Castillo, *San Diego State University*

Carol Gruber, *William Paterson College*

Colonel Williams L. Harris, *The Citadel Military College*

Robert Haws, *University of Mississippi*

Jerrold Hirsch, *Northeast Missouri State University*

Frederick Hoxie, *University of Illinois*

John S. Hughes, *University of Texas*

Link Hullar, *Kingwood College*

Donald M. Jacobs, *Northeastern University*

Delores Janiewski, *University of Idaho*

David Johnson, *Portland State University*

Richard Kern, *University of Findlay*

Robert J. Kolesar, *John Carroll University*

Monte Lewis, *Cisco Junior College*

William Link, *University of North Carolina, Greensboro*

Patricia M. Lisella, *Iona College*

Paul K. Longmore, *San Francisco State University*

Rita Loos, *Framingham State College*

Ronald Lora, *University of Toledo*

George M. Lubick, *Northern Arizona University*

Suzanne Marshall, *Jacksonville State University*

John C. Massman, *St. Cloud State University*

Vern Mattson, *University of Nevada at Las Vegas*

Art McCoole, *Cuyamaca College*

John McCormick, *Delaware County Community College*

Sylvia McGrath, *Stephen F. Austin University*

James E. McMillan, *Denison University*

Otis L. Miller, *Belleville Area College*

Walter Miszczenko, *Boise State University*

Norma Mitchell, *Troy State University*

Gerald F. Moran, *University of Michigan, Dearborn*

William G. Morris, *Midland College*

Marian Morton, *John Carroll University*

Roger Nichols, *University of Arizona*

Paul Palmer, *Texas A&I University*

Al Parker, *Riverside City College*

Judith Parsons, *Sul Ross State University*

Carla Pestana, *Ohio State University*

Neva Peters, *Tarrant County Community College*

James Prickett, *Santa Monica College*

Noel Pugash, *University of New Mexico*

Juan Gomez-Quiñones, *University of California, Los Angeles*

George Rable, *Anderson College*

Joseph P. Reidy, *Howard University*

Leonard Riforgiato, *Pennsylvania State University*

Randy Roberts, *Purdue University*

Mary Robertson, *Armstrong State University*

David Robson, *John Carroll University*

Jud Sage, *Northern Virginia Community College*

Phil Schaeffer, *Olympic College*

Sylvia Sebesta, *San Antonio College*

Herbert Shapiro, *University of Cincinnati*

David R. Shibley, *Santa Monica College*

Ellen Shockro, *Pasadena City College*

Nancy Shoemaker, *University of Connecticut*

Bradley Skelcher, *Delaware State University*

Kathryn Kish Sklar, *State University of New York at Binghampton*

James Smith, *Virginia State University*

John Snetsinger, *California Polytechnic State University, San Luis Obispo*

Jo Snider, *Southwest Texas State University*

Stephen Strausberg, *University of Arkansas*

Katherine Scott Sturdevant, *Pikes Peak Community College*

Nan M. Sumner-Mack, *Hawaii Community College*

Cynthia Taylor, *Santa Rosa Junior College*

Tom Tefft, *Citrus College*

John A. Trickel, *Richland College*

Donna Van Raaphorst, *Cuyahoga Community College*

Morris Vogel, *Temple University*

Michael Wade, *Appalachian State University*

Jackie Walker, *James Madison University*

Paul B. Weinstein, *University of Akron—Wayne College*

Joan Welker, *Prince George's Community College*

Kenneth H. Williams, *Alcorn State University*

Mitch Yamasaki, *Chaminade University*

Charles Zappia, *San Diego Mesa College*

ABOUT *the* AUTHORS

GARY B. NASH received his Ph.D. from Princeton University. He is currently Director of the National Center for History in the Schools at the University of California, Los Angeles, where he teaches colonial and revolutionary American history. Among the books Nash has authored are *Quakers and Politics: Pennsylvania, 1681–1726* (1968); *Red, White, and Black: The Peoples of Early America* (1974, 1982, 1992, 2000); *The Urban Crucible: Social Change, Political Consciousness, and the Origins of the American Revolution* (1979); and *Forging Freedom: The Black Urban Experience in Philadelphia, 1720–1840* (1988). A former president of the Organization of American Historians, his scholarship is especially concerned with the role of common people in the making of history. He wrote Part I and served as a general editor of this book.

JULIE ROY JEFFREY earned her Ph.D. in history from Rice University. Since then she has taught at Goucher College. Honored as an outstanding teacher, Jeffrey has been involved in faculty development activities and curriculum evaluation. She was Fulbright Chair in American Studies at the University of Southern Denmark, 1999–2000. Jeffrey's major publications include *Education for Children of the Poor* (1978); *Frontier Women: The Trans-Mississippi West, 1840–1880* (1979, 1997); *Converting the West: A Biography of Narcissa Whitman* (1991); and *The Great Silent Army of Abolitionism: Ordinary Women in the Antislavery Movement* (1998). She is the author of many articles on the lives and perceptions of nineteenth-century women. Her research continues to focus on abolitionism as well as on history and film. She wrote Parts III and IV in collaboration with Peter Frederick and acted as a general editor of this book.

JOHN R. HOWE received his Ph.D. from Yale University. At the University of Minnesota, his teaching interests include early American politics and relations between Native Americans and whites. His major publications include *The Changing Political Thought of John Adams* (1966) and *From the Revolution Through the Age of Jackson* (1973). He is presently completing a book on conceptions of language in American Revolutionary political writing, and has launched a project dealing with the social politics of verbal discourse in revolutionary America. Howe wrote Part II of this book.

PETER J. FREDERICK received his Ph.D. in history from the University of California, Berkeley. His career has focused on innovative student-centered teaching in American history at California State University, Hayward, and since 1970 at Wabash College (1992–1994 at Carleton College). Recognized nationally as a distinguished teacher and for numerous articles and workshops for faculty on learning and teaching, Frederick has also written several articles on biography and autobiography, and a book, *Knights of the Golden Rule: The Intellectual as Christian Social Reformer in the 1890s*. He coordinated and edited all the "Recovering the Past" sections and coauthored Parts III and IV.

ALLEN F. DAVIS earned his Ph.D. from the University of Wisconsin. A former president of the American Studies Association, he is a professor of history at Temple University and editor of *Conflict and Consensus in American History* (9th edition, 1997). He is the author of *Spearheads for Reform: The Social Settlements and the Progressive Movement* (1967) and *American Heroine: The Life and Legend of Jane Addams* (1973). He is coauthor of *Still Philadelphia* (1983), *Philadelphia Stories* (1987), and *One Hundred Years at Hull-House* (1990). He is currently working on a book on masculine culture in America. Davis wrote Part V of this book.

ALLAN M. WINKLER received his Ph.D. from Yale University. He has taught at Yale and the University of Oregon, and is now Distinguished Professor of History at Miami University of Ohio. An award-winning teacher, he has also published extensively about the recent past. His books include *The Politics of Propaganda: The Office of War Information, 1942–1945* (1978); *Modern America: The United States from the Second World War to the Present* (1985); *Home Front U.S.A.: America During World War II* (1986, 2000); and *Life Under a Cloud: American Anxiety About the Atom* (1993, 1999.). His research centers on the connections between public policy and popular mood in modern American history. Winkler wrote Part VI of this book.

The
AMERICAN PEOPLE

1

THREE WORLDS MEET

F. Maij

In the late 1550s, a few years after Catholic King Philip II and Protestant Queen Elizabeth assumed the thrones in Spain and England, respectively, Opechancanough was born in Tsenacommacah. In the Algonquian language, the word *tsenacommacah* meant "densely inhabited land." Later, English colonizers would rename this place Virginia after their monarch, the virgin queen Elizabeth. Before he died in the 1640s, in the ninth decade of his life, Opechancanough had seen light-skinned, swarthy, and black-skinned newcomers from a half-dozen European nations and African kingdoms swarm into his land. Like thousands of other Native Americans, he was witnessing the early moments of European expansion across the Atlantic Ocean.

Opechancanough was only an infant when Europeans first reached the Chesapeake Bay region. A small party of Spanish had explored the area in 1561, but they found neither gold nor silver nor anything else of value. Upon departing, they took with them the brother of one of the local chieftains, who was a member of Opechancanough's clan. They left behind something of unparalleled importance in the history of contact between the peoples of Europe and the Americas: a viral infection that spread like wildfire through a population that had no immunity against it. Many members of Opechancanough's tribe died, although their casualties were light compared with those of other tribes that caught the deadly European diseases.

In 1570, when Opechancanough was young, the Spanish returned and established a Jesuit mission near the York River. Violence occurred, and before the Spanish abandoned the Chesapeake in 1572, they put to death a number of captured Indians, including a chief who was Opechancanough's relative. The Native Americans learned that Europeans, even when they came bearing the crosses of their religion, were a volatile and dangerous people.

Opechancanough was in his forties when three ships of fair-skinned settlers disembarked in 1607 to begin the first permanent English settlement in the New World. For several months, he watched his half brother Powhatan, high chief of several dozen loosely confederated tribes in the region, parry and fence with the newcomers. Then Powhatan sent him to capture the English leader John Smith and escort him to the Indians' main village. Smith was put through a mock execution but then released. He later got the best of Opechancanough, threatening him with a pistol, humiliating him in front of his warriors, and assaulting one of his sons, whom Smith "spurned like a dog."

Opechancanough nursed his wounds for years while Powhatan grew old and the English settlements slowly spread in the Chesapeake region. Then, in 1617, he assumed leadership of the Powhatan Confederacy. Two years later, a Dutch trader sold 20 Africans to the settlers after docking at Jamestown. Three years after that, Opechancanough led a determined assault on the English plantations that lay along the rivers and streams emptying into the bay. The Indians killed nearly one-third of the intruders. But they paid dearly in the retaliatory raids that the colonists mounted in succeeding years.

As he watched the land-hungry settlers swarm in during the next two decades, Opechancanough's patience failed him. Finally, in 1644, now in his eighties, he galvanized a new generation of warriors and led a final desperate assault on the English. It was a suicidal attempt, but the "great general" of the Powhatan Confederacy, faithful to the tradition of his people, counseled death over enslavement and humiliation. Though the warriors inflicted heavy casualties, they could not overwhelm the colonizers, who vastly outnumbered them. For two years, Opechancanough was kept prisoner by the Virginians. Nearly blind and "so decrepit that he was not able to walk alone," he was fatally shot in the back by an English guard in 1646.

Over a long lifetime, Opechancanough painfully experienced the meeting of people from three continents. His land was one of many that would be penetrated by Europeans over the next three centuries, as Christian civilization girdled the globe. On the Chesapeake Bay, this clash of cultures formed the opening chapter of what we know as American history. That history, in turn, was one scene in a much broader drama of European colonization and exploitation of many indigenous cultures thousands of miles from the Old World. The nature of this violent intermingling of Europeans, Africans, and Native Americans is an essential part of early American history. But to understand how the destinies of red, white, and black people became intertwined in Opechancanough's land, we must look at the precontact history and cultural foundations of life in the homelands of each of them.

The French, under Jean Ribault, discovering the River of May in Florida on May 1, 1564. Engraving by Theodore De Bry, 1591, after a painting by Jacques Le Moyne, who accompanied the expedition in 1564. (*The Granger Collection, New York*)

THE PEOPLE OF AMERICA BEFORE COLUMBUS

Thousands of years before the European voyages of discovery, the history of humankind in North America began. Nomadic bands from Siberia, hunting big game animals such as bison, caribou, and reindeer, began to migrate across a land bridge connecting northeastern Asia with Alaska. Geologists believe that this land bridge, perhaps 600 miles wide, existed most recently between 25,000 and 14,000 years ago, when massive glaciers locked up much of the earth's moisture and left part of the Bering Sea floor exposed. Ice-free passage through Canada was possible only briefly at the beginning and end of this period, however. At other times, melting glaciers flooded the land bridge and blocked foot traffic to Alaska. Scholars are divided on the exact timing, but the main migration apparently occurred between 11,000 and 14,000 years ago, although possibly much earlier. Some new archaeological finds suggest multiple migrations, both by sea and land, from several regions of Asia and even from Europe.

Hunters and Farmers

For thousands of years, the early hunters trekked southward and eastward, following vegetation and game. In time, they reached the tip of South America and the eastern edge of North America. Thus did people from the "Old World" discover the "New World" thousands of years before Columbus.

Archaeologists have excavated ancient sites of early life in the Americas, unearthing tools, ornaments, and skeletal remains that can be scientifically dated. In this way, they have tentatively reconstructed the dispersion of these first Americans over an immense land mass. Although much remains unknown, archaeological evidence suggests that as centuries passed and population increased, the earliest inhabitants evolved into separate cultures, adjusting to various environments in distinct ways. Europeans who rediscovered the New World thousands of years later would lump together the myriad societies they found. But by the 1500s, the "Indians" of the Americas were enormously diverse in the size and complexity of their societies, the languages they spoke, and their forms of social organization.

Archaeologists and anthropologists have charted several phases of "Native American" history. The Beringian period of initial migration ended about 14,000 years ago. During the Paleo-Indian era, 14,000 to 10,000 years ago, big-game hunters flaked hard stones into spear points and chose "kill sites" where they slew herds of Pleistocene mammals. This more reliable food source allowed population growth, and

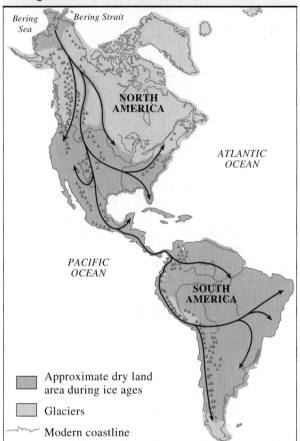

Migration Routes from Asia to the Americas

- Approximate dry land area during ice ages
- Glaciers
- Modern coastline

The red arrows indicate the general flow of migrating societies over thousands of years before Europeans reached the Americas. Based on fragile archaeological evidence, these migratory patterns are necessarily tentative, and new discoveries support early Stone Age arrivals by boat.

nomadism began to give way to settled habitations or local migration within limited territories.

Then during the Archaic era, from about 10,000 to 2,500 years ago, great geological changes brought further adaptations to the land. As the massive Ice Age glaciers slowly retreated, a warming trend turned vast grassland areas from Utah to the highlands of Central America into desert. The Pleistocene mammals were weakened by more arid conditions, but human populations ably adapted. They learned to exploit new sources of food, especially plants. In time, a second technological breakthrough, the "agricultural revolution," occurred.

We have sometimes imagined that these early people lived in a primordial paradise in harmony with their surroundings. But recent archaeological evidence points to examples of environmental devastation that severely damaged the biodiversity of the Americas. The first wave of intruders found a wilderness teeming with so-called megafauna: saber-toothed tigers, woolly mammoths, gigantic ground sloths, huge bison, and monstrous bears. But by about 10,000 years ago, these animals were almost extinct. Both overhunting and a massive shift of climate that deprived the huge beasts of their grazing environment were to blame.

The depletion of the megafauna left the hemisphere with a much restricted catalogue of animals. Left behind were large animals such as elk, buffalo, bear, and moose. But the extinction of the huge beasts forced people to prey on new sources of food such as turkeys, ducks, and guinea pigs. Their reduced food supply may have gradually reduced their population.

Over many centuries in the Americas, salinization and deforestation put the environment under additional stress. For example, in what is today central Arizona, the Hohokam civilization collapsed hundreds of years ago, much like that in ancient Mesopotamia, when the irrigation system became too salty to support agriculture. At New Mexico's Chaco Canyon, the fast-growing Anasazi denuded a magnificently forested region in their search for firewood and building materials. This, in turn, led to the erosion of rich soil that impoverished the region for the Anasazi.

When Native Americans learned to domesticate plant life, they began the long process of transforming their relationship to the physical world. Learning how to plant, cultivate, and harvest allowed them certain control over once-ungovernable natural forces. Anthropologists believe that this process began independently in widely separated parts of the world—Africa, Asia, Europe, and the Americas—about 9,000 to 7,000 years ago. Though agriculture developed very slowly, it eventually brought dramatic changes in human societies everywhere.

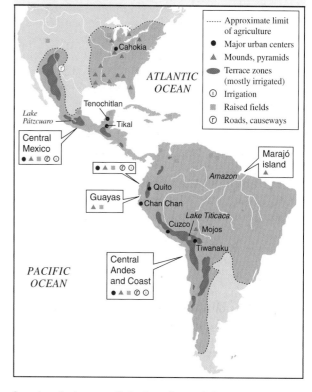

Pre-Columbian Societies of the Americas

Legend:
- ‑‑‑‑‑ Approximate limit of agriculture
- ● Major urban centers
- ▲ Mounds, pyramids
- ▨ Terrace zones (mostly irrigated)
- ⓘ Irrigation
- ▪ Raised fields
- ⓕ Roads, causeways

ATLANTIC OCEAN

Cahokia

Lake Pátzcuaro

Tenochitlan

Tikal

Central Mexico
● ▲ ▪ ⓕ ⓘ

● ▲ ▪ ⓕ ⓘ

Quito

Guayas
▲ ▪

Chan Chan

Amazon

Marajó island
▲

Lake Titicaca

Cuzco

Mojos

Tiwanaku

Central Andes and Coast
● ▲ ▪ ⓕ ⓘ

PACIFIC OCEAN

Once described as nomadic hunter-gatherers, indigenous peoples in the Americas were agriculturalists and urban dwellers in many areas and populated the land as densely as did people in many other parts of the world.

Over the millennia, humans progressed from doorside planting of a few wild seeds to systematic clearing and planting of bean and maize fields. As

The ruins of Pueblo Bonita in Chaco Canyon, New Mexico, mark the center of Anasazi culture in the twelfth century A.D. This San Juan River basin town may have contained 1,000 people living in apartment-like structures larger than any built in North America until the late nineteenth century. (© *David Muench*)

the production of domesticated plant food ended dependence on gathering wild plants and pursuing game, settled village life began to replace nomadic existence. Increases in food supply brought about by agriculture triggered other major changes. As more ample food fueled population growth, large groups split off to form separate societies. Greater social and political complexity developed because not everyone was needed as before to secure the society's food supply. Men cleared the land and hunted game, and women planted, cultivated, and harvested crops. Many societies empowered religious figures, who organized the common followers, directed their work, and exacted tribute as well as worship from them. In return, the community trusted them to ward off hostile forces.

Everywhere in the Americas, regional trading networks formed. Along trade routes carrying commodities such as salt for food preservation, obsidian rock for projectile points, and copper for jewelry also traveled technology, religious ideas, and agricultural practices. By the end of the Archaic period, about 500 B.C., hundreds of independent kin-based groups, like

people in other parts of the world, had learned to exploit the resources of their particular area and to trade with other groups in their region.

Native Americans in 1600

The last epoch of pre-Columbian development, the post-Archaic phase, occurred during the 2,000 years before contact with Europeans. It involved a complex process of growth and environmental adaptation among many distinct societies—and crisis in some of them. In the American Southwest, for example, the ancestors of the present-day Hopi and Zuni developed carefully planned villages composed of large, terraced, multistoried buildings, each with many rooms. By the time the Spanish arrived in the 1540s, the indigenous Pueblo people were using irrigation canals, dams, and hillside terracing to water their arid maize fields. In their agricultural techniques, their skill in ceramics, their use of woven textiles for clothing, and their village life, Pueblo society resembled that of peasant communities in many parts of Europe and Asia.

Far to the east were the mound-building societies of the Mississippi and Ohio valleys. When European

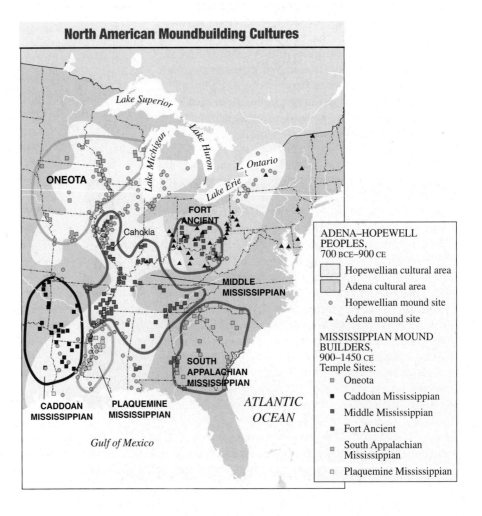

Plows, shovels, and bulldozers have obliterated many of the earthworks created at hundreds of moundbuilding sites in the eastern half of North America.

One of the hundreds of symbolic mounds built by people of the Hopewell culture, this one, in the shape of a serpent, is near present-day Cincinnati. *(National Museum of the American Indian, New York)*

settlers first crossed the Appalachian Mountains a century and a half after arriving on the continent, they were amazed to find hundreds of ceremonial mounds and gigantic sculptured earthworks in geometric designs or in the shapes of huge humans, birds, or writhing serpents. Believing all "Indians" to be forest primitives, they reasoned that these were the remains of an ancient civilization that had found its way to North America—perhaps Phoenicians, survivors of the sunken island of Atlantis, or the Lost Tribes of Israel spoken of in European mythology.

The mound-building societies of the Ohio valley declined many centuries before Europeans reached the continent, perhaps attacked by other tribes or damaged by severe climatic changes that undermined agriculture. But about A.D. 600, another mound-building agricultural society arose in the Mississippi valley. Its center, the city of Cahokia with perhaps 40,000 inhabitants, stood near present-day St. Louis. Great ceremonial plazas, flanked by a temple that rose in four terraces to a height of 100 feet, marked this first metropolis in America. This was the urban center of a far-flung Mississippi culture that encompassed hundreds of villages from Wisconsin to Louisiana and from Oklahoma to Tennessee.

Before the mound-building cultures of the continental heartlands mysteriously declined, their influence was already transforming the woodlands societies along the Atlantic coastal plain. The numerous small tribes that settled from Nova Scotia to Florida never equaled the larger societies of the midcontinent in earthwork sculpture, architectural design, or development of large-scale agriculture. But they were far from the "savages" that the first European explorers described. They had added limited agriculture to their skill in using natural plants for food, medicine, dyes, and flavoring and had developed food procurement strategies that exploited all the resources around them—cleared land, forests, streams, shore, and ocean.

Most of the eastern woodlands tribes lived in waterside villages. Locating their fields of maize near fishing grounds, they often migrated seasonally between inland and coastal village sites or situated themselves astride two ecological zones. In the Northeast, their birchbark canoes, light enough to be carried by a single man, helped them trade and communicate over immense territories. In the Southeast, population was denser and social and political organization more elaborate.

On the eve of European exploration of the Americas, the continent north of the Rio Grande contained at least 3 to 4 million people, of whom perhaps 500,000 lived along the eastern coastal plain and in the piedmont region accessible to the early European settlers. Though estimates vary widely, perhaps 40 to 60 million people lived in the entire hemisphere when Europeans first arrived. This contrasted with some 70 to 90 million in Europe about 1500 and about 50 to 70 million in Africa. The colonizers were not coming to a "virgin wilderness," as they often described it, but to a land inhabited for thousands of years by people whose village existence in many ways resembled that of the arriving Europeans.

In some important ways, however, Indian culture differed sharply from that of Europeans. Horses and oxen, for example, did not exist in the New World. Without large draft animals, Indians had no incentive to develop wheeled vehicles or, for that matter, the

Recovering the Past

ARCHAEOLOGICAL ARTIFACTS

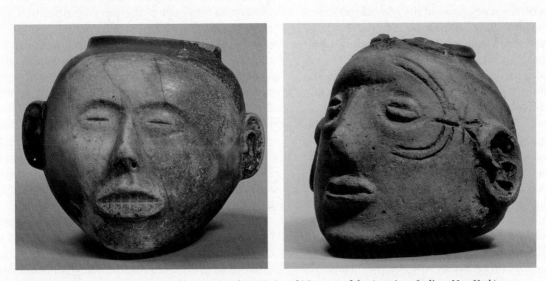

The recovery of the past before there were extensive written records is the domain of archaeology. Virtually our entire knowledge of Indian societies in North America before the arrival of European colonizers is drawn from the work of archaeologists who have excavated the ancient living sites of the first Americans. Many Native Americans today strongly oppose this rummaging in the ancient ancestral places; they particularly oppose the unearthing of burial sites. But the modern search for knowledge about the past goes on.

Archaeological data have allowed us to overcome the stereotypic view of Native Americans as a primitive people whose culture was static for thousands of years before Europeans arrived in North America. This earlier view allowed historians to argue that the tremendous loss of Native American population and land accompanying the initial settlement and westward migration of white Americans was more or less inevitable. When two cultures, one dynamic and forward-looking and the other static and backward, confronted each other, historians have frequently main-

tained, the more advanced or "civilized" culture almost always prevailed.

Much of the elaborate early history of people in the Americas is unrecoverable. But many fragments of this long human history are being recaptured through archaeological research. Particularly important are studies that reveal how Indian societies were changing during the few centuries immediately preceding the European arrival in the New World. These studies give us a much better chance to interpret the seventeenth-century interaction of Native Americans and Europeans because they provide an understanding of Indian values, social and political organization, material culture, and religion as they existed when the two cultures first met.

One such investigation has been carried out over the last century at the confluence of the Mississippi and Missouri Rivers near modern-day East St. Louis, Illinois. Archaeologists have found the center of a vast Mississippi culture that began about A.D. 600, reached its peak about 300 years before Columbus's voyages, and then declined through a combination of drought, dwindling food supplies, and internal tensions. Cahokia is the name given to

Pottery effigy vessels in the shape of human heads. *(National Museum of the American Indian, New York)*

A reconstructed view of Cahokia, the largest town in North America before European arrival, painted by William R. Iseminger. An estimated 50 million cubic feet of earth was used to construct the ceremonial and burial mounds. *(Cahokia Mounds State Historic Site)*

the urban center of a civilization that at its height dominated an area as large as New York State. At the center of Cahokia stood one of the largest earth constructions built by ancient man anywhere on the planet. Its base covering 15 acres, this gigantic earthen temple rises in four terraces to a height of 100 feet, as tall as a ten-story modern office building. The drawing shown above indicates some of the dozens of smaller geometric mounds discovered near this major temple. Notice the outlying farms, a sure sign of the settled (as opposed to nomadic) existence of the people who flourished ten centuries ago in this region. How does this depiction of ancient Cahokia change your image of Native American life before the arrival of Europeans?

By recovering artifacts from Cahokia burial mounds, archaeologists have pieced together a picture, still tentative, of a highly elaborate civilization along the Mississippi bottomlands. Cahokian manufacturers mass-produced salt, knives, and stone hoe blades for both local consumption and export. Cahokian artisans made sophisticated pottery, ornamental jewelry, metalwork, and tools. They used copper and furs from the Lake Superior region, black obsidian stone from the Rocky Mountains, and seashells from the Gulf of Mexico, demonstrating that the people at Cahokia were involved in long-distance trade. In fact,

Cahokia was a crucial crossroads of trade and water travel in the heartland of North America.

The objects shown on page 8, unearthed from graves by archaeologists, are an example of the culture of the Mississippi Mound Builders. The round-faced pottery bottles in the form of heads, each about 6 inches tall and wide, show a sense of humor in early Mississippi culture. Holes in the ears of the bottles once held thongs so that the objects could be hung or carried. Other objects, such as a figure of a kneeling woman found in Tennessee, had holes under the arms for a similar purpose. What other conclusions about Cahokian culture can you draw from figures such as these? Are there archaeological sites in your area that contain evidence of Native American civilization?

The fact that some graves uncovered at Cahokia contain large caches of finely tooled objects and that other burial mounds contain many skeletons unaccompanied by any artifacts leads archaeologists to conclude that this was a more stratified society than those the first settlers encountered along the Atlantic seaboard. Anthropologists believe that some of the Mississippi culture spread eastward before Cahokia declined, but much mystery still remains concerning the fate and cultural diffusion of these early Americans.

potter's wheel. Many inventions—such as the technology for smelting iron, which had diffused widely in the Old World—had not crossed the ocean barrier to reach the New World. The opposite was also true: Valuable New World crops, such as corn and potatoes, which had been developed by Indian agriculturists, were unknown in the Old World before Columbus.

Contrasting Worldviews

Colonizing Europeans called themselves "civilized" and typically described the people they met in the Americas as "savage," "heathen," or "barbarian." The gulf separating people in Europe and North America was defined not only by their material cultures but also by the way they viewed their relationship to the environment and defined social relations in their communities. Having evolved in complete isolation from each other, European and Indian cultures exhibited a wide difference in values.

Regarding land as a resource to be exploited for human benefit, Europeans believed that it should be privately possessed. From this belief developed much that Europeans took for granted: property lines often demarcated by fences, inheritance customs for transmitting land from one generation to another within the same family, and courts to settle resulting disputes. Property was the basis not only of sustenance but also of independence, wealth, status, and identity. The social structure directly mirrored patterns of land ownership, with a land-wealthy elite at the apex of the social pyramid and a propertyless mass at the bottom.

Native Americans also had concepts of property and boundaries. But they believed that land had sacred qualities and should be held in common. As one German missionary explained the Indian view in the eighteenth century, the Creator "made the Earth and all that it contains for the common good of mankind. Whatever liveth on the land, whatsoever groweth out of the earth, and all that is in the rivers and waters . . . was given jointly to all and everyone is entitled to his share."

Communal ownership sharply limited social stratification and increased a sense of sharing in most Indian communities, much to the amazement of Europeans accustomed to wide disparities of wealth. Observing the Iroquois of the eastern woodlands in 1657, a French Jesuit noted with surprise that they had no almshouses because "their kindness, humanity and courtesy not only makes them liberal with what they have, but causes them to possess hardly anything except in common. A whole village must be without corn, before any individual can be obliged to endure privation." Not all Europeans were acquisitive, competitive individuals. The majority were peasants scratching a subsistence living from the soil, living in kin-centered villages with little contact with the outside world, and exchanging goods and labor through barter. But in Europe's cities, a wealth-conscious, ambitious individual who valued and sought wider choices and greater opportunities to enhance personal status was coming to the fore. In contrast, Native American traditions stressed the group rather than the individual and valor rather than wealth.

There were exceptions. The empires of the Aztec in Central America and the Inca in South America were highly developed, populous, and stratified. So, in North America, were a few tribes such as the Natchez. But on the eastern and western coasts of the continent and in the Southwest—the regions of contact in the sixteenth and seventeenth centuries—the European newcomers encountered a people whose cultural values differed strikingly from theirs.

European colonizers in North America also found disturbing the matrilineal organization of many tribal societies. Contrary to European practice, family membership among most tribes was determined through the female line. A typical family consisted of an old woman, her daughters with their husbands and children, and her unmarried granddaughters and grandsons. When a son or grandson married, he moved from this female-headed household to one headed by the matriarch of his wife's family. Divorce was also the woman's prerogative. If she desired it, she merely set her husband's possessions outside their dwelling door. Clans were composed of several matrilineal kin groups related by a blood connection on the mother's side. To Europeans, this was a peculiar and dangerous reversal of their male-dominated sexual hierarchy.

In Native American societies, women also held subordinate positions, but not nearly to the extent found among European women. For example, European women were almost entirely excluded from political affairs. But in many Native American villages, designated men sat in a circle to deliberate and make decisions, and the senior women of the village stood behind them, lobbying and instructing. Village chiefs were male, but they were often chosen by the elder women of their clans, as was the case with the Iroquois. If they moved too far from the will of the women who appointed them, these chiefs were removed—or "dehorned." "Our ancestors," the Oneida chief Giod Peter explained, "considered it a great transgression to reject the counsel of their women, particularly the female governesses. Our ancestors considered them mistresses of the soil. . . . The women, they are the life of the nation."

The role of women in the tribal economy reinforced the sharing of power between male and female.

Indian Societies During the Period of Early European Settlement

The great number of Indian societies within the present-day boundaries of the United States—each with its own language—indicates the cultural diversity of the first peoples of North America at the time Europeans arrived.

Men hunted, fished, and cleared land, but women controlled the cultivation, harvest, and distribution of crops, supplying probably three-quarters of their family's nutritional needs. When the men were away hunting, women directed village life. Europeans, imbued with the idea of male superiority and female subordination, perceived such sexual equality as another mark of "savagery."

In economic relations, Europeans and Indians differed in ways that sometimes led to misunderstanding and conflict. Over vast stretches of the continent, Indians had built trading networks for centuries before Europeans arrived, making it easy for them to trade with arriving Europeans and incorporate new metal and glass trade items into their culture. But trade for Indian peoples was also a way of preserving interdependence and equilibrium between individuals and communities. This principle of reciprocity displayed itself in elaborate ceremonies of gift giving and pipe smoking that preceded the exchange of goods. Europeans saw trade largely as economic exchange, with the benefit of building good will between two parties sharply limited in comparison with Indians.

In the religious beliefs of Native Americans, the English saw a final damning defect. Europeans built their religious life around the belief in a single divinity, written scriptures, a trained and highly literate clergy, and churches with structured ceremonies. Native American societies, sharing no literary tradition, had less structured religious beliefs. Believing that human life could be affected, positively or negatively, by the mysterious power pervading everything in nature—in rocks, water, the sun, the moon, and animals—Indian people sought to conciliate these spirits and maintain proper relationships with them, even the spirits of the fish, beaver, and deer they hunted. Pueblo people, for example, living in arid lands where rainfall dictated their well-being, expressed their thanks for rain by performing frequent ritual dances.

For Europeans, the Indians' polytheism was pagan and devilish. Europeans understood that Indians had religious leaders called shamans, who used medicinal plants and magical chants to heal the sick and facilitated the people's quests to communicate with the spiritual world. But Europeans regarded the shamans as especially dangerous because they occupied powerful roles among a spiritually misled people. Their fear and hatred of infidels intensified by the Protestant Reformation, Europeans saw a holy necessity to convert—or destroy—these enemies of their God.

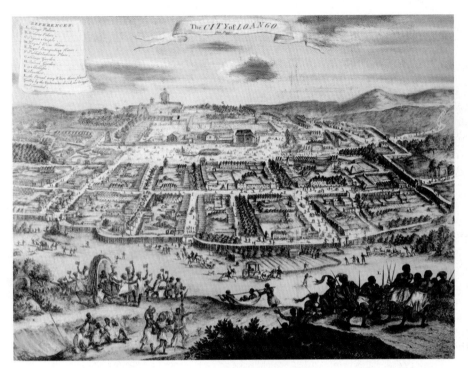

The city of Loango, at the mouth of the Congo River on the west coast of Africa, was larger at the time of this drawing in the mid-eighteenth century than all but a few seaports in the British colonies in North America. *(The Granger Collection, New York)*

AFRICA ON THE EVE OF CONTACT

Half a century before Columbus reached the Americas, a Portuguese sea captain, Antam Gonçalves, made the first European landing on the west coast of sub-Saharan Africa. If he had been able to travel the length and breadth of the immense continent, he would have encountered a rich variety of African states, peoples, and cultures. African "backwardness" and cultural impoverishment was a myth perpetuated after the slave trade had begun transporting millions of Africans to the New World. During the period of early contact with Europeans, Africa, like pre-Columbian America, was recognized as a diverse continent with a long history of cultural evolution.

The Kingdoms of Africa

The estimated 50 million peoples in fifteenth-century Africa lived in vast deserts, grasslands, and tropical forests. As in Europe and the Americas at that time, most people tilled the soil. Part of their skill in farming derived from the development of iron production, which began in present-day Nigeria about 450 B.C., long before it reached Europe. More efficient iron implements increased agricultural productivity, in turn spurring population growth. The pattern was repeated in other parts of the world—the Americas, Europe, the Far East, and the Middle East—when the agricultural revolution began.

Before fifteenth-century Europeans reached the west coast of Africa, a number of large empires had risen there. The first was the kingdom of Ghana, which embraced an immense territory between the Sahara and the Gulf of Guinea and stretched from the Atlantic Ocean to the Niger River.

The development of large towns, skillfully designed buildings, elaborate sculpture and metalwork, long-distance commerce, and a complex political structure marked the Ghanaian kingdom from the sixth to eleventh centuries. A thriving caravan trade with Arab peoples across the Sahara to Morocco and Algeria brought extensive Muslim influence by the eleventh century, when the king of Ghana boasted an army of 200,000, maintained trading contacts as far east as Cairo and Baghdad, and was furnishing, through Muslim middlemen in North Africa, two-thirds of the gold supply for the Christian Mediterranean region.

An invasion of North African Muslim warriors beginning in the eleventh century introduced a period of religious strife that eventually destroyed the kingdom of Ghana. But in the same region arose the Islamic kingdom of Mali. Prospering through its control of the gold trade, Mali flourished until the early sixteenth century. Its city of Timbuktu contained a distinguished faculty of scholars to whom North Africans and even southern Europeans came to study. Traveling there in the 1330s, the Arab geographer Ibn-Battuta wrote admiringly of "the discipline of its officials and provincial governors, the excellent condition of public finance, and . . . the respect accorded to the decisions of justice and to the authority of the sovereign."

Elsewhere along the Atlantic coast, other kingdoms such as Kongo, Songhay, and Benin grew in the centuries before seaborne Europeans reached Africa.

In their towns, rivaling those of Europe in size, lived people skilled in metalworking, weaving, ceramics, architecture, and aesthetic expression. Codes of law, regional trade, and effective political organization all developed by the fifteenth century. Finding their way to Africa south of the Sahara, Europeans encountered not a backward area but a densely settled region with an ancient history of long-distance trade and cultural exchange with other peoples.

Population growth and cultural development in Africa, as elsewhere in the world, proceeded at different rates in different regions. Where soil was rich, rainfall adequate, and minerals abundant, as in western Sudan, population grew and cultures changed rapidly. Where inhospitable desert or impenetrable forest ruled, societies remained small and changed very slowly. Isolation from other cultures retarded development, whereas contact with other regions encouraged change. For example, cultural innovation accelerated in East African Swahili-speaking societies facing the Indian Ocean after trading contacts began with the Eastern world in the ninth century. Around the same time, traders from Arabia, India, and the East Indies began to spread Muslim influence in West Africa.

The African Ethos

The many peoples of Africa, who were to supply at least two-thirds of all the immigrants who crossed the ocean to the Western Hemisphere in the three centuries after Europeans began colonizing there, came from a rich diversity of cultures. But most of them shared certain ways of life that differentiated them from Europeans.

As in Europe, the family was the basic unit of social organization. Unlike European societies, however, African societies were organized in a variety of kinship and political systems. In many African societies, like many Native American ones, the family was matrilineal. Property rights and political inheritance descended through the mother rather than the father. The son of a chief's sister inherited his position, and a married man joined his bride's people.

West Africans believed in a Supreme Creator and in lesser deities associated with natural forces such as rain, fertility, and animal life. Because these deities could intervene in human affairs, they were elaborately honored. Like most North American Indian societies, West Africans held that spirits dwelt in the trees, rocks, and rivers around them, and hence they exercised care in the treatment of these natural objects.

Africans also worshiped ancestors, who were believed to mediate between the Creator and the living. Because the dead played such an important role for the living, relatives held elaborate funeral rites to ensure the proper entrance of a deceased relative into the spiritual world. The more ancient an

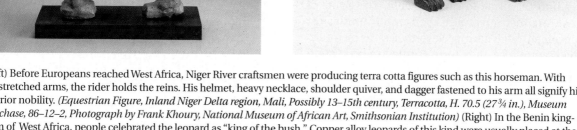

(Left) Before Europeans reached West Africa, Niger River craftsmen were producing terra cotta figures such as this horseman. With outstretched arms, the rider holds the reins. His helmet, heavy necklace, shoulder quiver, and dagger fastened to his arm all signify his warrior nobility. (*Equestrian Figure, Inland Niger Delta region, Mali, Possibly 13–15th century, Terracotta, H. 70.5 (27¾ in.), Museum purchase, 86–12–2, Photograph by Frank Khoury, National Museum of African Art, Smithsonian Institution*) (Right) In the Benin kingdom of West Africa, people celebrated the leopard as "king of the bush." Copper alloy leopards of this kind were usually placed at the king's side when he sat in state to symbolize the king's ominous power combined with prudent reserve. (© *Dirk Bakker, 1978*)

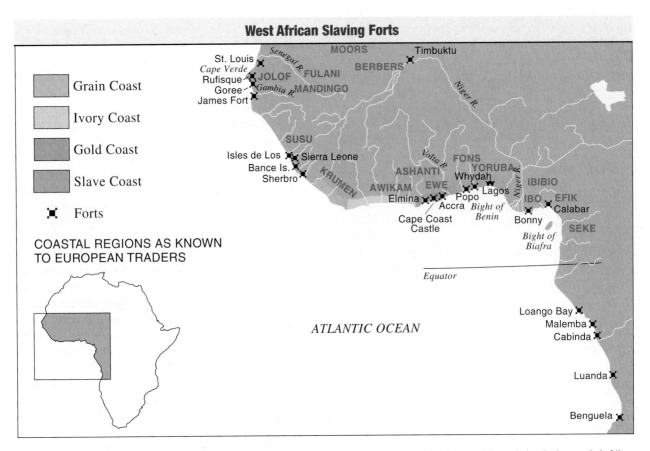

Europeans fought lustily for control of slaving forts on the West African coast, and many forts changed hands several times during the long period of the Atlantic slave trade.

ancestor, the greater was this person's power to affect the living; thus the "ancient ones" were devoutly worshiped. Deep family loyalty and regard for family lineage flowed naturally from ancestor worship. Finally, West Africans believed in spirit possession, where gods spoke to men and women through priests and other religious figures.

Social organization in much of West Africa by the time Europeans arrived was as elaborate as in fifteenth-century Europe. At the top of society stood nobles and priests, usually elderly men. Beneath them were the great masses of people, mostly farmers, but also some craftsmen, traders, teachers, and artists. At the bottom of society resided slaves. As in ancient Greece and Rome, they were "outsiders"—war captives, criminals, or sometimes people who sold themselves into servitude to satisfy a debt. The rights of slaves were restricted, and their opportunities for advancement were narrow. Nevertheless, as members of the community, they were entitled to protection under the law and allowed the privileges of education, marriage, and parenthood. Their servile condition was not permanent, nor was it automatically inherited by their children, as would be the fate of Africans enslaved in the Americas.

EUROPE IN THE AGE OF EXPLORATION

In the ninth century, about the time that the mound builders of the Mississippi valley were constructing their urban center at Cahokia and the kingdom of Ghana was rising in West Africa, western Europe was an economic and cultural backwater. The center of political power and economic vitality in the Old World had shifted eastward to Christian Byzantium, which controlled Asia Minor, the Balkans, and parts of Italy. The other dynamic culture of this age, Islam, had spread through the Middle East, spilled across North Africa, and penetrated Spain and West Africa south of the Sahara.

Over the next six centuries, an epic revitalization of western Europe occurred, creating the conditions that enabled its leading maritime nations vastly to extend their oceanic frontiers. By the late fifteenth century, a 400-year epoch of militant European expansion was under way. Only in the twentieth century was this process of Europeanization reversed, as colonized people regained their autonomy and cultural identity through wars of national liberation.

The Rise of Europe

The rebirth of western Europe, which began around A.D. 1000, owed much to a revival of long-distance trading from Italian ports on the Mediterranean and the rediscovery of ancient knowledge that these contacts permitted. The once mighty cities of the Roman Empire had stagnated for centuries, but now Venice, Genoa, and other Italian ports began trading with peoples facing the Adriatic, the Baltic, and the North Seas. These new contacts brought wealth and power to the Italian commercial cities, which gradually evolved into merchant-dominated city-states that freed themselves from the rule of feudal lords in control of the surrounding countryside.

While merchants led the emerging city-states, western Europe's feudal system was gradually weakening. For centuries, feudal lords, not kings, had exercised the normal powers of the state—the power to tax, wage war, and administer the law. In the thirteenth and fourteenth centuries, however, kings began to reassert their political authority and to undertake efforts to unify their realms. One of their primary goals was to curb the power of the great lords who dominated entire regions and to force lesser nobles into dependence on and obedience to the crown.

The Black Death (bubonic plague), which devastated western Europe and Africa from 1348 to 1354, promoted the unification of old realms into early modern states. The plague killed one-third of the population, a blow from which Europe did not recover demographically for centuries. The nobilities with which monarchs had to contend were reduced in size, for the plague defied class distinction. Ironically, feudal lords treated their peasants better for a time because their labor, tremendously reduced by the plague, became more valuable.

Early developments in England led to a distinctive political system. In 1215, the English aristocracy curbed the powers of the king when they forced him to accept the Magna Carta. On the basis of this charter, a parliament composed of elective and hereditary members eventually gained the right to meet regularly to pass money bills. Parliament was thus in a position to act as a check on the crown, an arrangement unknown on the Continent. During the sixteenth century, the crown and Parliament worked together toward a more unified state, with the English kings wielding less political power than their European counterparts.

Economic changes of great significance also occurred in England during the sixteenth century. To practice more profitable agriculture, great landowners began to "enclose" (consolidate) their estates, throwing peasant farmers off their plots and turning many of them into wage laborers. The formation of this working class was the crucial first step toward industrial development.

Continental Europe lagged behind England in two respects. First, it was far less affected by the move to "enclose" agricultural land. Part of the explanation lies in the values of continental aristocrats, who regarded the maximization of profit as unworthy of gentlemen. French nobles could lose their titles for commercial activities. Second, continental rulers were less successful in engaging the interests of their nobilities, and these nobles never shared governance with their king, as did English aristocrats through their participation in Parliament. In France, a noble faction assassinated Henry III in 1589, and the nobles remained disruptive for nearly another century. In Spain, the final conquest of the Muslims and expulsion of the Jews, both in 1492, strengthened the monarchy's hold, but regional cultures and leaders remained strong. The continental monarchs would thus warmly embrace doctrines of royal absolutism developed in the sixteenth century.

The New Monarchies and the Expansionist Impulse

In the second half of the fifteenth century, ambitious monarchs coming to power in France, England, and Spain sought social and political stability in their kingdoms. Louis XI in France, Henry VII in England, Isabella of Castile, and Ferdinand of Aragon all created armies and bureaucratic state machinery strong enough to quell internal conflict, such as the English War of the Roses, and to raise taxes sufficient to support their regimes. In these countries, and in Portugal as well, economic revival and the reversal of more than a century of population decline and civil disorder nourished the impulse to expand. This impulse was also fed by Renaissance culture. Ushering in a new, more secular age, the Renaissance (Rebirth) encouraged freedom of thought, richness of expression, and an emphasis on human abilities. Beginning in Italy and spreading northward through Europe, the Renaissance peaked dramatically in the late fifteenth century when the age of exploration began.

The exploratory urge had two initial objectives: first, to circumvent Muslim traders by finding an eastward oceanic route to Asia; and second, to tap the African gold trade at its source. Since the tenth century, Muslim middlemen in North Africa had brought the precious metal to Europe from Guinea. Now the possibility arose of bypassing these non-Christian traffickers. Likewise, Christian Europeans dreamed of eliminating Muslim traders from the commerce with Asia. Since 1291, when Marco Polo returned to Venice with

European Exploration of the Americas, 1492–1610

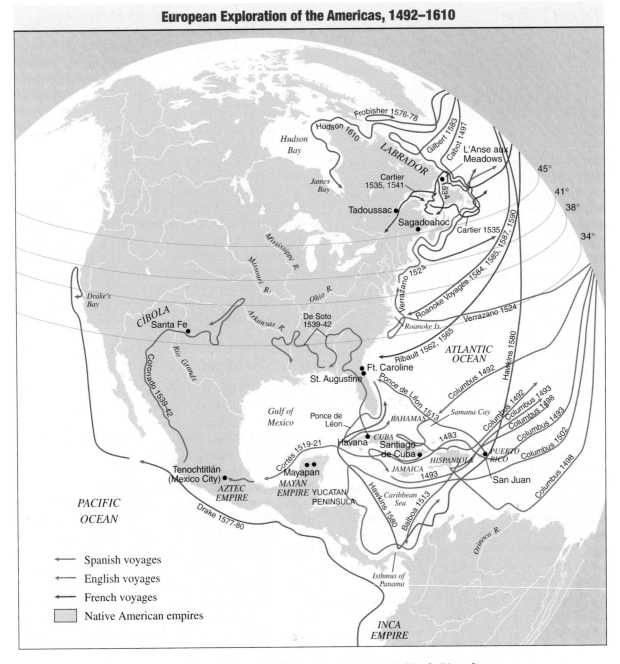

Within one century, Europeans had mapped most of the coasts of the Americas and the islands of the Caribbean Sea.

tales of Eastern treasures—spices, silks, perfumes, drugs, and jewels—Europeans had bartered with the Orient. But the difficulties of the long eastward overland route through the Muslim world kept alive the hopes of Christian Europeans that an alternative water route existed. Eventually, Europe's mariners found they could voyage to Cathay by both eastward and westward water routes.

Portugal seemed the least likely of the rising nation-states to lead the expansion of Europe outside its continental boundaries, yet it forged into the lead at the end of the fifteenth century. A poor and insignificant country of only one million inhabitants, Portugal had gradually overcome Moorish control in the twelfth and thirteenth centuries and, in 1385, had wrenched itself free of domination by neighboring Castile. Led by Prince Henry the Navigator, for whom trade was secondary to the conquest of the Muslim world, Portugal breached the unknown. In the 1420s, Henry began dispatching Portuguese mariners to probe the unknown Atlantic "sea of darkness." His intrepid sailors were aided by important improvements in navigation, mapmaking, and ship design, all promoted by the prince.

Portuguese captains operated at sea on three ancient Ptolemaic principles: that the earth was round, that distances on its surface could be measured by degrees, and that navigators could "fix" their position on a map by measuring the position of the stars. The invention in the 1450s of the quadrant, which allowed a precise measurement of star altitude necessary for determining latitude, represented a leap forward from the chart-and-compass method of navigation. Equally important was the design of a lateen-rigged caravel, adapted from a Moorish ship design. Its triangular sails permitted ships to sail into the wind, allowing them to beat southward along the African coast—a feat the square-rigged European vessels could never perform—and return northward against prevailing winds.

By the 1430s, the ability of Prince Henry's captains to break through the limits of the world known to Europeans had carried them to Madeira, the Canaries, and the Azores, lying off the coasts of Portugal and northwestern Africa. These were soon developed as the first European agricultural plantations, located on the continent's periphery. From there, the Portuguese sea captains pushed farther south.

By the time of Prince Henry's death in 1460, Portuguese mariners had reached the west coast of Africa, where they began a profitable trade in ivory, slaves, and especially gold. By 1500, they had captured control of the African gold trade monopolized for centuries by North African Muslims. The gleaming metal now traveled directly to Lisbon by sea rather than by camel caravan across the Sahara to North African Muslim ports such as Tunis and Algiers. In 1497, Vasco da Gama became the first European to sail around the Cape of Africa, allowing the Portuguese to colonize the Indian Ocean and to reach modern Indonesia and south China by 1513. By forcing trade concessions in the islands and coastal states of the East Indies, the Portuguese unlocked the fabulous Asian treasure houses that since Marco Polo's time had whetted European appetites.

Reaching the Americas

The marriage of Ferdinand and Isabella in 1469 united the independent states of Aragon and Castile and launched the Spanish nation into its golden age. Leading the way for Spain was an Italian sailor, Christopher Columbus. The son of a poor Genoese weaver, Columbus had married into a prominent family of Lisbon merchants, thus making important contacts at court.

Celebrated for hundreds of years as the intrepid explorer who initiated permanent contact between Europe and the Americas, Columbus is attacked by some today as the ruthless exploiter of Indian peoples and lands. But Columbus is best understood in the context of his own times—an age of great brutality and violence and also an age in which Catholic Spain was engaged in the final stages of expelling the Moorish people who had controlled southern Spain for centuries. Columbus's urge to explore was nourished by ideas and questions about the geographic limits of his world, and he was inspired by notions of contributing to the reconquest of Moorish Spain. The Latin inscription on the tomb of his monarchs, Isabella and Ferdinand, captures the mood of the era: "Overthrowers of the Mahometan sect and repressors of heretical stubbornness."

Like many sailors, Columbus had listened to sea tales about lands to the west. He may have heard Icelandic sagas about the voyages of Leif Eriksson and several thousand Norse immigrants who reached Newfoundland five centuries before. Other ideas circulated that the Atlantic Ocean stretched to India and eastern Asia. Could one reach the Indies by sailing west rather than by sailing east around Africa, as the Portuguese were attempting? Columbus hungered to know.

For nearly ten years, Columbus tried unsuccessfully to secure financial backing and royal sanction in Portugal for exploratory voyages. Many mocked his modest estimates of the distance westward from Europe to Japan. Finally, in 1492, Queen Isabella of Spain commissioned him, and he sailed west with three tiny ships and a crew of about 90 men. Strong winds, lasting ten days, blew the ships far into the Atlantic. There they were becalmed. In the fifth week at sea—longer than any European sailors had been out of the sight of land—mutinous rumblings swept through the crews. But Columbus pressed on. On the seventieth day, long after Columbus had calculated he would reach Japan, a lookout sighted land. On October 12, 1492, the sailors clambered ashore on a tiny island in the Bahamas, which Columbus named San Salvador (Holy Savior). Grateful sailors "rendered thanks to Our Lord, kneeling on the ground, embracing it with tears of joy."

Believing he had reached Asia, Columbus explored the island-speckled Caribbean for ten weeks. After landing on a heavily populated island that he named Hispaniola (shared today by Haiti and the Dominican Republic) and on Cuba (which he thought was the Asian mainland), he set sail for Spain with cinnamon, coconuts, a bit of gold, and several kidnapped natives. Homeward bound, he penned a report of what he believed were his Asian discoveries: hospitable people, fertile soils, magnificent harbors, and gold-filled rivers.

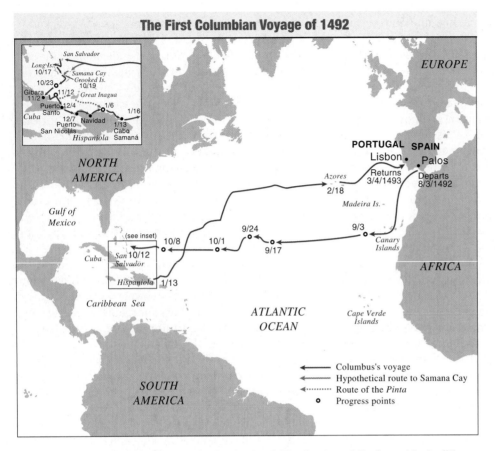

The First Columbian Voyage of 1492

In Columbus's 70-day voyage from Spain to San Salvador, it took thirty days to reach the Canary Islands off the coast of West Africa.

Quickly printed and distributed throughout Europe, Columbus's report brought him financing between 1494 and 1504 for three much larger expeditions to explore the newfound lands. The second voyage, carrying over 1,200 Spanish in 17 ships, initiated the first extended contact between Europeans and Native Americans. In an ominous display of what was to come, Columbus's men captured some 1,600 Tainos on Hispaniola and carried 550 of them back to Spain as slaves in 1495. Only 350 survived the stormy voyage to Spain. Here began the Atlantic slave trade that would alter the history of the world, though it began in the reverse direction of what would soon become its dominant flow. Although his discoveries seemed less significant than the Portuguese exploits in the South Atlantic, Columbus led Spain to the threshold of a mighty empire. He reaped few rewards, however, dying unnoticed and penniless in 1506. To the end, he believed that he had found the water route to Asia.

The expansion of Spain and Portugal into new areas of the world profoundly affected patterns of economic activity in Europe. Its commercial center now shifted away from the ports of the Mediterranean to the Atlantic ports facing the New World.

The New World also beckoned as a field of religious contest. The heavily populated Americas offered millions of potential Christian converts. But the Catholic-Protestant division within Christianity complicated Christian dreams of converting a "heathen" continent. The people of western Europe, just as they were unlocking the secrets of the new worlds to the east and west in the sixteenth century, were torn by religious schisms that magnified national rivalries.

Religious Conflict During the Reformation

At the heart of Europe's religious strife was a continental movement to cleanse the Christian church of corrupt practices and return it to the purer ways of early Christianity. Criticism of the worldliness of the Catholic church mounted during the Renaissance. Then a German friar, Martin Luther, became the first to break successfully with Rome, initiating a Protestant Reformation of theology and practice. As Protestant sects multiplied, a Catholic Reformation grew up within the church, and the two groups began a long battle for the souls of Europeans.

Luther was preparing for a legal career in 1505 when a bolt of lightning nearly struck him during a violent thunderstorm. Trembling with fear, he vowed to become a monk. But in the religious order of Saint Augustine, he lost faith in the power of the age-old rituals of the church—prayer, the Mass, confession, pilgrimages to holy places, even crusades against Muslim infidels. He reasoned that salvation came through an inward faith, or "grace," that God conferred on those he chose. Good works, Luther believed, did not earn grace but were only the external evidence of grace won through faith. Luther had taken the revolutionary step of rejecting the church's elaborate hierarchy of officials, who presided over the rituals intended to guide individuals along the path toward salvation.

Luther's doctrine of private "justification by faith" did not immediately threaten the church. But in 1517, he openly attacked the sale of "indulgences" for sins by which the pope raised money for the building of St. Peter's in Rome. By purchasing indulgences, individuals had been told, they could reduce their time (or that of a deceased relative) in purgatory. Luther drew up 95 arguments against this practice and called on Christians to practice true repentance. The spread of printing, invented less than 70 years before, allowed the rapid circulation of his ideas. The printed word and the ability to read it were to become revolutionary weapons throughout the world.

Luther's cry for reform soon inspired Germans of all classes. He denounced five of the seven sacraments of the church, calling for a return to baptism and communion alone. He attacked the upper clergy for luxurious living and urged priests, who were nominally celibate but were often involved in irregular sexual relations, to marry respectably. He railed against the "detestable tyranny of the clergy over the laity" and called for a priesthood of all believers. He urged people to seek faith individually by reading the Bible, which he translated into German and made widely available for the first time in printed form. Most dangerously, he called on the German princes to assume control over religion in their states, directly challenging the authority of Rome and further undermining the functions of its clergy.

The basic issue dividing Catholics and Protestants thus centered on the source of religious authority. To Catholics, religious authority resided in the organized Church, headed by the pope. To Protestants, the Bible was the sole authority, and access to God's word or God's grace did not require the mediation of the Church.

Building on Luther's redefinition of Christianity, John Calvin, a Frenchman, brought new intensity and meaning to the Protestant Reformation. In 1536, at

John Calvin (1509–1564), painted by Hans Holbein the Younger, is portrayed as a man of letters, books, and solemn religiosity. "What I have taught and written," wrote Calvin, "did not grow in my brain, but that I hold it from God." *(The Granger Collection, New York)*

age 26, he published a ringing appeal to every Christian to form a direct, personal relationship with God. By Calvin's doctrine, God had saved a few souls at random before Creation and damned the rest. Human beings could not alter this predestination, but those who were good Christians must struggle to understand and accept God's saving grace if he chose to import it. Without mediation of ritual or priest but by "straight-walking," one was to behave as one of God's elect, the "saints." This radical theology, even more insistent on individual godliness than Luther's, spread among all classes throughout Europe.

Calvin proposed reformed Christian communities structured around the elect few. To remake the corrupt world and follow God's will, communities of "saints" must control the state, rather than the other way around. Elected bodies of ministers and dedicated laymen, called presbyteries, were to govern the church, directing the affairs of society down to the last detail so that all, whether saved or damned, would work for God's ends.

Calvinism, as a fine-tuned system of self-discipline and social control, was first put into practice in the

1550s in the city-state of Geneva, near the French border of Switzerland. Here the brilliant and austere leader established what he intended to be a model Christian community. A council of 12 elders drove non-believers from the city, rigidly disciplined daily life, and stripped the churches of every appeal to the senses—images, music, incense, and colorful clerical gowns. Religious reformers from all over Europe flocked to the new holy community, and Geneva soon became the continental center of the reformist Christian movement and a haven for refugee Protestant leaders. The city was, wrote John Knox of Scotland in 1556, "the most perfect school of Christ that ever was in the earth since the days of the apostles."

Calvin's radical program converted large numbers of people to Protestantism throughout Europe. Like Lutheranism, it recruited most successfully among the privileged classes of merchants, landowners, lawyers, and the nobility and among the rising middle class of master artisans and shopkeepers.

Sixteenth-century monarchs initially regarded attacks on the Catholic Church with horror. But many local princes adopted some version of the reformed faith. The most important monarch to break with Catholicism was Henry VIII of England. When Pope Clement VII refused him permission to divorce and remarry, Henry declared himself head of the Church of England, or Anglican church. Although it retained many Catholic features, the Church of England moved further in a Protestant direction under Henry's son Edward. But when Mary, Henry's older Catholic daughter, came to the throne, she vowed to reinstate her mother's religion by suppressing Protestants. Her policy created Protestant martyrs, and many were relieved when she died in 1558, bringing Henry's younger Protestant daughter, Elizabeth, to the throne. During her long rule, the flinty Elizabeth steered Anglicanism along a middle course between the radicalism of Geneva and the Catholicism of Rome.

The countries most affected by the Reformation—England, Holland, and France—were slow in trying to colonize the New World, so Protestantism did not gain an early foothold in the Americas. Catholicism in Spain and Portugal remained almost immune from the Protestant Reformation. Thus, even while under attack, Catholicism swept across the Atlantic almost unchallenged during the century after Columbus's voyages.

⬠ THE IBERIAN CONQUEST OF AMERICA

From 1492 to 1518, Spanish and Portuguese explorers opened up vast parts of Asia and the Americas to European knowledge. Yet during this age of explo-ration, only modest attempts at settlement were made, mostly by the Spanish on the Caribbean islands of Cuba, Puerto Rico, and Hispaniola. The three decades after 1518, however, became an age of conquest. In some of the bloodiest chapters in recorded history, the Spanish nearly exterminated the native peoples of the Caribbean islands, toppled and plundered the great inland empires of the Aztec and Inca in Mexico and Peru, discovered fabulous silver mines, and built an oceanic trade of enormous importance to all of Europe. This short era of conquest had immense consequences for global history.

Portugal, meanwhile, restricted by one of the most significant lines ever drawn on a map, concentrated mostly on building an eastward oceanic trade to south-eastern Asia. In 1493, to settle a dispute, the pope had demarcated Spanish and Portuguese spheres of explo-ration in the Atlantic. Drawing a north–south line 100 leagues (about 300 miles) west of the Azores, the pope confined Portugal to the eastern side. One year later, in the Treaty of Tordesillas, Portugal obtained Spanish agreement to move the line 270 leagues farther west. Nobody knew at the time that a large part of South America, as yet undiscovered by Europeans, bulged east of the new demarcation line and therefore fell within the Portuguese sphere. In time, Portugal would develop this region, Brazil, into one of the most prof-itable areas of the New World.

The Spanish Onslaught

Within a single generation of Columbus's death in 1506, Spanish conquistadores explored, claimed, and conquered most of South America (except Brazil), Central America, and the southern parts of North America from Florida to California. Led by audacious explorers and military leaders, and usually accompa-nied by enslaved Africans, they established Spanish authority and Catholicism over an area that dwarfed their homeland in size and population. They were motivated by religion, growing pride of nation, and dreams of personal enrichment. "We came here," explained one Spanish foot soldier in Cortés's legion, "to serve God and the king, and also to get rich."

In two bold and bloody strokes, the Spanish over-whelmed the ancient civilizations of the Aztec and Inca. In 1519, Hernando Cortés set out with 600 sol-diers from coastal Veracruz and marched over rugged mountains to attack Tenochtitlán (modern-day Mexico City), the capital of Montezuma's Aztec empire. At its height, centuries before, the ancient city in the valley of Mexico had contained perhaps 200,000 people. But in 1521, following two years of tense rela-tions between the Spanish and Aztec, it fell before Cortés's assault. The Spanish use of horses and firearms provided an important advantage; so did a

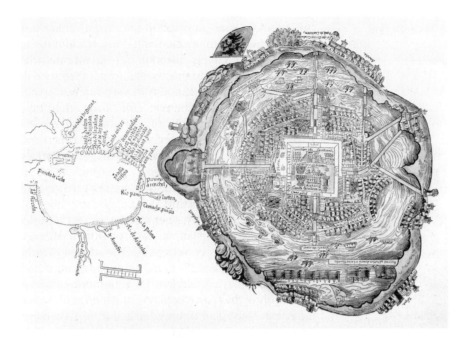

The plan of Tenochtitlán, later Mexico City, is from the Latin edition of Cortés's "Second Letter," on his conquest of the Aztec. Cortés's account was widely published in Europe, where Germans, French, and English were astounded to hear of such an extraordinary Aztec metropolis with floating gardens, causeways, and monumental architecture.
(The Granger Collection, New York)

murderous smallpox epidemic in 1520 that felled thousands of Aztec. Support from local peoples oppressed by Montezuma's tyranny was also indispensable in overthrowing the Aztec ruler. From the valley of Mexico, the Spanish extended their dominion over the Mayan people of the Yucatán and Guatemala in the next few decades.

In the second conquest, the intrepid Francisco Pizarro, marching from Panama through the jungles of Ecuador and into the towering mountains of Peru with a mere 168 men, most of them not even soldiers, toppled the Inca empire. Like the Aztec, the populous Inca lived in a highly organized social system. But also like the Aztec, they were riddled by smallpox and weakened by violent internal divisions. This ensured Pizarro's success in capturing their capital at Cuzco in 1533. From there, Spanish soldiers marched farther afield, plundering other gold- and silver-rich Inca cities. Further expeditions into Chile, New Granada (Colombia), Argentina, and Bolivia in the 1530s and 1540s brought under Spanish control an empire larger than any in the Western world since the fall of Rome.

By 1550, Spain had overwhelmed the major centers of native population throughout the Caribbean, Mexico, Central America, and the west coast of South America. Spanish ships carried gold, silver, dyewoods, and sugar east across the Atlantic and transported African slaves, colonizers, and finished goods west. In a brief half century, Spain had exploited the advances in geographic knowledge and marine technology of its Portuguese rivals and brought into harsh but profitable contact with each other the people of three continents. The triracial character of the Americas was already firmly established by 1600.

For nearly a century after Columbus's voyages, Spain enjoyed almost unchallenged dominion over the fabulous hemisphere newly revealed to Europeans. Greedy buccaneers of various nations snapped at the heels of homeward-bound Spanish treasure fleets with cargoes of silver, but this was only a nuisance. France made gestures of contesting Spanish or Portuguese control by planting small settlements in Brazil and Florida in the mid-sixteenth century, but they were quickly wiped out. England remained island-bound until the 1580s. Until the seventeenth century, only Portugal, which staked out important claims in Brazil in the 1520s, challenged Spanish domination of the New World.

The Great Dying

Spanish conquest of major areas of the Americas set in motion two of the most far-reaching processes in modern history. One involved microbes; the other, silver.

Spanish contacts with the natives of the Caribbean basin, central Mexico, and Peru in the early sixteenth century triggered the most dramatic and disastrous population decline in recorded history. The population of the Americas on the eve of European arrival had grown to an estimated 50 to 60 million or more. In some areas, such as central Mexico, the highlands of Peru, and certain Caribbean islands, population density exceeded that of most of Europe. But though they were less populous than the people of the Americas, the European colonizers had one extraordinary biological

Spanish and Portuguese Conquests in the Americas

Santa Fe (1609)
St. Augustine (1565)
Gulf of Mexico
ATLANTIC OCEAN
Mexico City (1521)
Carribbean Sea
Caracas (1567)
Panama City (1519)
NEW GRENADA
PACIFIC OCEAN
PERU
Lima (1535)
Rio de Janeiro (1555)
São Paulo (1554)
LA PLATA
Santiago (1541)
Buenos Aires (1535)
TO SPAIN / TO PORTUGAL

Spanish
Portuguese
Disputed
(1555) Date city founded

Never before the Spanish and Portuguese arrived in the Americas had such small numbers of people established their dominance over such a large and populous area.

advantage: for centuries Old World peoples had been exposed to nearly every lethal microbe that infects humans on an epidemic scale in the temperate zone. Over the centuries, Europeans had built up immunities to these diseases. Such biological defenses did not eliminate smallpox, measles, diphtheria, and other afflictions, but they limited their deadly power. Geographic isolation, however, had kept these diseases from the peoples of the Americas. So, too, did the Native Americans' lack of large domesticated animals, which were the major disease carriers. Arriving Europeans therefore unknowingly encountered a huge component of the human race that was utterly defenseless against the "domesticated" infections the Europeans and their animals carried inside their bodies.

The results were catastrophic. On Hispaniola, a population of about one million that had existed when Columbus arrived had only a few thousand survivors by 1530. Of some 15 million inhabitants in central Mexico before Cortés's arrival, nearly half perished within fifteen years. Demographic disaster also struck the populous Inca peoples of the Peruvian Andes, speeding ahead of Pizarro's conquistadores. Smallpox "spread over the people as great destruction," an old

Indian told a Spanish priest in the 1520s. "There was great havoc. Very many died of it. They could not stir, they could not change position, nor lie on one side, nor face down, nor on their backs. And if they stirred, much did they cry out. . . . And very many starved; there was death from hunger, [for] none could take care of [the sick]." Such terrifying sickness led many natives to believe that their gods had failed them, and this belief left them ready to acknowledge the greater power of the Spainards' God.

In most areas where Europeans intruded in the hemisphere for the next three centuries, the catastrophe repeated itself. Whether Protestant or Catholic, whether French, English, Spanish, or Dutch, whether male or female, every newcomer from the Old World participated accidentally in the spread of disease that typically eliminated, within a few generations, at least two-thirds of the native population. Millions of Native Americans who had never seen a European died of European diseases, which swept like wildfire through densely populated regions.

The enslavement and brutal treatment of the native people intensified the lethal effects of European diseases. After their spectacular conquests of the Inca and Aztec, the Spanish enslaved thousands of native people and assigned them work regimens that severely weakened their resistance to disease. Some priests like Bartolomé de Las Casas waged lifelong campaigns to reduce the exploitation of the Indians, but they had only limited power to control the actions of their colonizing compatriots.

Silver, Sugar, and Their Consequences

The small amount of gold that Columbus brought home from the West Indies raised hopes that this metal, which along with silver formed the standard of wealth in Europe, might be found in the transatlantic paradise. Some gold was gleaned from the Caribbean islands and later from Colombia, Brazil, and Peru. But though men pursued it fanatically to the far corners of the hemisphere, more than three centuries would pass before they found gold in windfall quantities in North America. Silver proved most abundant—so plenteous, in fact, that when bonanza strikes were made in Bolivia in 1545 and then in northern Mexico in the next decade, much of Spain's New World enterprise focused on its extraction. The Spanish empire in America, for most of the sixteenth century, was a vast mining community.

Native people, along with some African slaves, provided the first labor supply for the mines. The Spaniards permitted the highly organized Indian societies to maintain control of their own communities but exacted from them huge labor drafts for mining. By imposing themselves at the top of a highly stratified

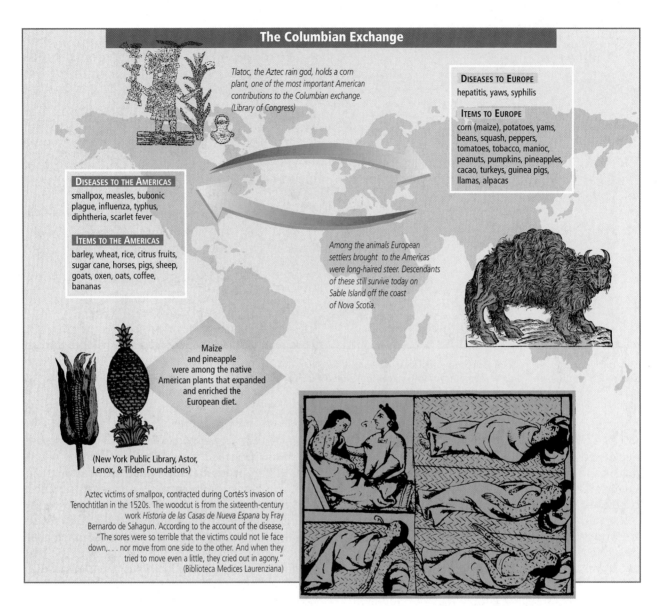

The Columbian Exchange

Tlatoc, the Aztec rain god, holds a corn plant, one of the most important American contributions to the Columbian exchange. (Library of Congress)

DISEASES TO EUROPE
hepatitis, yaws, syphilis

ITEMS TO EUROPE
corn (maize), potatoes, yams, beans, squash, peppers, tomatoes, tobacco, manioc, peanuts, pumpkins, pineapples, cacao, turkeys, guinea pigs, llamas, alpacas

DISEASES TO THE AMERICAS
smallpox, measles, bubonic plague, influenza, typhus, diphtheria, scarlet fever

ITEMS TO THE AMERICAS
barley, wheat, rice, citrus fruits, sugar cane, horses, pigs, sheep, goats, oxen, oats, coffee, bananas

Among the animals European settlers brought to the Americas were long-haired steer. Descendants of these still survive today on Sable Island off the coast of Nova Scotia.

Maize and pineapple were among the native American plants that expanded and enriched the European diet.

(New York Public Library, Astor, Lenox, & Tilden Foundations)

Aztec victims of smallpox, contracted during Cortés's invasion of Tenochtitlan in the 1520s. The woodcut is from the sixteenth-century work *Historia de las Casas de Nueva Espana* by Fray Bernardo de Sahagun. According to the account of the disease, "The sores were so terrible that the victims could not lie face down, . . . nor move from one side to the other. And when they tried to move even a little, they cried out in agony."
(Biblioteca Medices Laurenziana)

social order that had previously been organized around tributary labor, the Spanish enriched themselves beyond the dreams of even the most visionary explorers. At Potosí, in Bolivia, 58,000 workers labored at elevations of up to 13,000 feet to extract the precious metal from a fabulous sugarloaf "mountain of silver." The town's population reached 120,000 by 1570, making it larger than any in Spain at the time. Thousands of other workers toiled in the mines of Zacatecas, Taxco, and Guanajuato. By 1660, they had scooped up more than 7 million pounds of silver from the Americas, tripling the entire European supply.

The massive flow of bullion from the Americas to Europe triggered profound changes. It financed further conquests and settlement in Spain's American empire, spurred long-distance trading in luxury items such as silks and spices from East Asia, and capitalized agricultural development in the New World of sugar, coffee, cacao, and indigo. The bland diet of Europeans gradually changed as items such as sugar and spices, previously luxury articles for the wealthy, became accessible to ordinary people.

The enormous increase of silver in circulation in Europe after the mid-sixteenth century also caused a "price revolution." As the supply of silver increased faster than the volume of goods and services that Europeans could produce, the value of the metal declined. Put differently, prices rose. Between 1550 and 1600, they doubled in many parts of Europe and then rose another 50 percent in the next half century. Land-owning farmers got more for their produce, and merchants thrived on the increased circulation of goods. But artisans, laborers, and landless agricultural workers (the vast majority of the population) suffered

This 1823 lithograph by William Clark romanticizes gang labor in the sugar fields of the British West Indies by decorously clothing men and women in trousers, jackets, and skirts. In reality, enslaved Africans worked semi-naked under the punishing sun. However, this depiction accurately reflects the use of female labor in the harvesting of sugar cane. *(By Permission of the British Library)*

because their wages did not keep pace with rising prices. Skilled artisans, lamented one of the first English immigrants to America, "live in such a low condition as is little better than beggary."

Overall, the price revolution brought a major redistribution of wealth and increased the number of people in western Europe living at the margins of society. It thus built up the pressure to emigrate to the Americas, Europe's new frontier. At the same time, rising prices stimulated commercial development. Expansion overseas fed expansion at home and intensified changes toward capitalist modes of production already under way in the sixteenth century.

While the Spaniards organized their overseas empire around the extraction of silver from the highlands of Mexico, Bolivia, and Peru, the Portuguese staked their future on sugar production in the lowlands of Brazil. Spanish colonial agriculture supplied the huge mining centers, but the Portuguese, adapting techniques of cultivation worked out earlier on their Atlantic islands, produced sugar for export markets.

Whereas the Spanish mining operations rested primarily on the backs of the native labor force, the lowland Portuguese sugar planters scattered the indigenous people and replaced them with platoons of African slaves. By 1570, this regimented work force was producing nearly 6 million pounds of sugar annually; by the 1630s, output had risen to 32 million pounds per year. High in calories but low in protein, the sweet "drug food" revolutionized the tastes of millions of Europeans and stimulated the oceanic transport of millions of African slaves across the Atlantic.

From Brazil, sugar production jumped to the island-speckled Caribbean. Here, in the early seventeenth century, England, Holland, and France challenged Spain and Portugal for the riches of the New World. Once they secured footholds in the West Indies, Spain's enemies stood at the gates of the Hispanic New World empire. This ushered in a long period of conflict "beyond the line"—where European treaties had no force. Through contraband trading with Spanish settlements, piratical attacks on Spanish treasure fleets, and outright seizure of Spanish-controlled islands, the Dutch, French, and English in the seventeenth century gradually sapped the strength of the first European empire outside of Europe.

Spain's Northern Frontier

The crown jewels of Spain's New World empire were silver-rich Mexico and Peru, with the islands and coastal fringes of the Caribbean representing lesser, yet valuable, gemstones. Distinctly third in importance were the northern borderlands of New Spain—the present-day Sun Belt of the United States. Yet the early Spanish influence in Florida, the Gulf region, Texas, New Mexico, Arizona, and California indelibly marked the history of the United States. Spanish control of the southern fringes of North America began in the early 1500s and did not end for three centuries, when Mexico wrested independence from Spain in 1821. Far outlasting Spanish rule were the plants and animals they introduced to North America, ranging from sheep, cattle, and horses to various grasses and weeds that crowded out native plants.

Spanish explorers began charting the southeastern region of North America in the early sixteenth century, beginning with Juan Ponce de León's expeditions to Florida in 1515 and 1521 and Lucas Vasquez d'Ayllon's short-lived settlement at Winyah Bay in South Carolina in 1526. For the next half century, Spaniards planted small settlements along the coast as far north as the Chesapeake Bay, where their temporary encampment included many enslaved Africans. The Spanish traded some with the natives, but the North American coast, especially Florida, was chiefly important to the Franciscan priests, who attempted to gather the local tribes into mission villages and convert them to Catholicism.

The Spanish made several attempts to bring the entire Gulf of Mexico region under their control. From 1539 to 1542, Hernando de Soto, a veteran of Pizarro's conquest of the Inca, led a military expedition deep into the homelands of the Creeks and Choctaws and explored westward from Tampa Bay across the Mississippi to Arkansas.

De Soto's expedition at first found receptive natives, but his men could not provide what the Spanish most wanted—gold. Pillaging Indian villages and seizing food supplies, de Soto's men cut a brutal swath as far north as North Carolina and as far west as Arkansas. Disease followed the Spanish explorers everywhere they went. Little could the English know that their Spanish enemies were paving the way for them in North America's southeastern sector by spreading lethal microbes that devastated Indian societies and broke up the great chiefdoms of the lower South.

In 1559, Spaniards again marched northward from Mexico in an attempt to establish their authority in the lower Gulf region. Everywhere they went, they enslaved Indians to carry provisions. In 1565, they sought to secure Florida. Building a fort at St. Augustine, they evicted their French rivals at Fort Caroline, 40 miles to the north. St. Augustine became the center of Spain's northeastern frontier, and Florida remained a Spanish possession for more than two centuries.

The Southwest became a more important region of early Spanish activity in North America. Francisco Vásquez de Coronado explored the region from 1540 to 1542, leading an expedition of several hundred Spanish soldiers, a number of Africans, and a baggage train of 1,300 friendly Indians, servants, and slaves. Coronado never found the Seven Cities of Cíbola, reported by earlier Spanish explorers to be fabulously decorated in turquoise and gold. But he opened much of Arizona, New Mexico, and Colorado to eventual Spanish control, happened upon the Grand Canyon, and probed as far north as the Great Plains. His interior explorations, together with the nearly simultaneous expedition of de Soto in the Southeast, established Spanish claims to the southern latitudes of North America and gave them contacts, often bloody, with the populous corn-growing Indian societies of the region.

The Southwest, like Florida and the Gulf region, had no golden cities. In New Mexico, however,

James Walker's *Vaqueros in a Horse Corral* speaks beautifully of the Spanish origins of the cowboy in the American West. *(Gilcrease Museum of American Art, Tulsa, OK)*

Franciscan priests tried to harvest souls. A half century after Coronado's exploratory intrusions, Juan de Onate led 400 Spanish soldiers and ten Franciscan friars up the Rio Grande in 1598 to find some 60,000 Pueblo gathered in scores of settled towns where they had practiced agriculture for centuries. For the next 80 years, the Franciscans tried to graft Catholicism onto Pueblo culture by building churches on the edges of ancient native villages. As long as the priests were content to overlay Indian culture with a veneer of Catholicism, they encountered little resistance because the Pueblo found advantage in Spanish military protection from their Apache enemies and valued access to mission livestock and grain during years of drought. So, outwardly, they professed the Christian faith. But secretly the Pueblo still practiced their traditional religion in the underground Pueblo ceremonial chambers called kivas.

ENGLAND LOOKS WEST

By the time England awoke to the promise of the New World, Spain and Portugal were firmly entrenched there. But by the late sixteenth century, the conditions necessary to propel England overseas had ripened. During the seventeenth century, the English, as well as the Dutch and French, began overtaking their southern European rivals. The first challenge came in the Caribbean, where between 1604 and 1640 the English planted several small colonies producing tobacco and later sugar. Few guessed that some secondary and relatively unproductive settlements then being planted on the North American mainland would in time be among England's most prized possessions.

England Challenges Spain

England was the slowest of the Atlantic powers to begin exploring and colonizing the New World. Although far more numerous than the Portuguese, the English in the fifteenth century had little experience with long-distance trade and few contacts with cultures beyond their island aside from the French, against whom they had waged the Hundred Years' War (1337–1453). Only the voyages of John Cabot (the Genoa-born Giovanni Caboto) gave England any claim in the New World sweepstakes. But Cabot's voyages to Newfoundland and Nova Scotia a few years after Columbus's first voyage—the first northern crossing of the Atlantic since the Vikings—were never followed up.

At first, England's interest in the far side of the Atlantic centered primarily on fish. This high-protein food, basic to the European diet, was the gold of the North Atlantic. Early North Atlantic explorers found the waters off Newfoundland and Nova Scotia teeming with fish—not only the ordinary cod but also the delectable salmon. But the fishermen of Portugal, Spain, and France, more than those of England, began making annual spring trips to the offshore fisheries in the 1520s. Not until the end of the century would the French and English drive Spanish and Portuguese fishermen from the Newfoundland Banks.

Exploratory voyages along the eastern coast of North America hardly interested the English. It was for the French that Cartier and Verrazano sailed between 1524 and 1535. Looking for straits westward to India, through the northern land mass that was still thought to be a large island, they made contact with many Indian tribes and charted the coastline from the St. Lawrence River to the Carolinas. They established the northern latitudes as a suitable place for settlement but found nothing of immediate value to take home. The time had not yet arrived when Europeans would leave their homelands to resettle in America rather than go there merely to extract its riches.

Changes in the late sixteenth century, however, propelled the English overseas. The rising production of woolen cloth, a mainstay of the English economy, had sent merchants scurrying for new markets after 1550. Their success in establishing trading companies in Russia, Scandinavia, the Middle East, and India vastly widened England's commercial orbit and raised hopes for developing still other spheres. Meanwhile, population growth and rising prices depressed the economic conditions of ordinary people and made them look across the ocean for new opportunities.

The cautious policy of Queen Elizabeth I, who ruled from 1558 to 1603, did not include promoting overseas colonies. She favored Protestantism partly as a vehicle of national independence. Ambitious and talented, she had to contend with Philip II, king of Spain and her fervently Catholic brother-in-law, whose long reign nearly coincided with hers. Regarding Elizabeth as a Protestant heretic, Philip plotted incessantly against her. The pope added to Catholic–Protestant tensions in England by excommunicating Elizabeth in 1571 and absolving her subjects from paying her allegiance—in effect, inciting them to overthrow her.

The smoldering conflict between Catholic Spain and Protestant England broke into open flames in 1587. Two decades before, Philip II had sent 20,000 Spanish soldiers into his Netherlands provinces to suppress Protestantism. Then, in 1572, he had helped arrange the massacre of thousands of French Protestants. By the 1580s, Elizabeth was providing covert aid to the Protestant Dutch revolt against Catholic rule. Philip vowed to crush the rebellion and

Under the leadership of Elizabeth I, here displayed in royal finery and resting her hand on the globe, England challenged and ultimately overturned Spain's domination of worldwide sea trade. Behind the placid face was a determined and sometimes ruthless ruler. *(By kind permission of the Marquess of Tavistock and Trustees of the Bedford Estate)*

decided as well to launch an attack on England to wipe out this growing center of Protestant power.

Elizabeth fed the flames of the international Catholic–Protestant conflict in 1585 by sending 6,000 English troops to aid the Dutch Protestants. Three years later, Philip dispatched a Spanish armada of 130 ships carrying 30,000 men and 2,400 artillery pieces. Sails blazing with crusaders' crosses, the fleet set forth to conquer Elizabeth's England. For two weeks in the summer of 1588, a sea battle raged off the English coast. A motley collection of smaller English ships, with the colorful sea dog Francis Drake in the lead, defeated the Armada, sinking many of the lumbering Spanish galleons and then retiring as the legendary "Protestant wind" blew the crippled Armada into the North Sea.

The Spanish defeat prevented a crushing Catholic victory in Europe and brought a temporary stalemate in the religious wars. It also solidified Protestantism in England and brewed a fierce nationalistic spirit there. Shakespeare's love of "this other Eden, this demi-paradise" spread among the people; and with Spanish naval power checked, both the English and the Dutch found the seas more open to their rising maritime and commercial interests.

The Westward Fever

In the last decades of the sixteenth century, the idea of overseas expansion captured the imagination of important elements of English society. Urging them on were two Richard Hakluyts, uncle and nephew. In the 1580s and 1590s, they devoted themselves to advertising the advantages of colonizing on the far side of the Atlantic. For nobles at court, colonies

offered new baronies, fiefdoms, and estates. For merchants, the New World promised exotic produce to sell at home and a new outlet for English cloth and other goods. For militant Protestant clergy, there awaited a continent filled with heathen people to be saved from devilish savagery and Spanish Catholicism. For the commoner, opportunity beckoned in the form of bounteous land, almost for the taking. The Hakluyts' pamphlets publicized the idea that the time was ripe for England to break the Iberian monopoly on the riches of the New World.

England first attempted colonizing, however, in Ireland. In the 1560s and 1570s, the English gradually extended control over the island through brutal military conquest. Ireland became a turbulent frontier for thousands of career-hungry younger sons of gentry families as well as landless commoners. Many of the leaders first involved in New World colonizing served in Ireland, and many of their ideas of how to deal with a "savage" and "barbaric" people stemmed from their Irish experience.

The first English attempts at overseas settlement were small, feeble, and ill-fated. Whereas the Spanish encountered unheard-of wealth and scored epic victories over ancient and populous civilizations, the English at first met only failure in relatively thinly settled lands. Beginning in 1583, they mounted several unsuccessful attempts to settle Newfoundland. Other settlers, organized by Walter Raleigh, planted a settlement from 1585 to 1588 at Roanoke Island, off the North Carolina coast. They apparently perished in attacks by a local tribe after killing a tribal leader and displaying his head on a pike. Small groups of men sent out to establish a tiny colony in Guiana, off the

South American coast, failed in 1604 and 1609, and another group that set down in Maine in 1607 lasted only a year. Even the colonies founded in Virginia in 1607 and Bermuda in 1612, although they would flourish in time, floundered badly for several decades.

English merchants, sometimes supported by gentry investors, undertook these first tentative efforts. They risked their capital hoping that small-scale ventures in North America might produce the profits of their other overseas commercial ventures. They had their queen's blessing though little royal backing in subsidies, ships, and naval protection. The Spanish and Portuguese colonizing efforts were national enterprises, sanctioned, capitalized, and coordinated by the crown. The English colonies were private ventures, organized and financed by small partnerships of merchants who pooled their slender resources.

English colonization could not succeed until these first merchant adventurers solicited the wealth and support of the prospering middle class. This support grew steadily in the first half of the seventeenth century, but even then, investors were drawn far more to the quick profits promised in West Indian tobacco production than to the uncertainties of mixed farming, lumbering, and fishing on the North American mainland. In the 1620s and 1630s, most of the English capital invested overseas went into establishing tobacco colonies in tiny Caribbean islands, including St. Christopher (1624), Barbados (1627), Nevis (1628), Montserrat (1632), and Antigua (1632).

Apart from the considerable financing required, the vital element in launching a colony was a suitable body of colonists. About 80,000 streamed out of England between 1600 and 1640, as economic, political, and religious developments pushed them from their homeland at the same time that dreams of opportunity and adventure pulled them westward. In the next 20 years, another 80,000 departed.

Economic difficulties in England prompted many to try their luck in the New World. The changing agricultural system, combined with population growth and the unrelenting increase in prices caused by the influx of New World silver, produced a surplus of unskilled labor, squeezed many small producers, and spread poverty and crime. By the late 1500s, the roads, wrote Richard Hakluyt, were swarming with "valiant youths rusting and hurtful for lack of employment," and the prisons were "daily pestered and stuffed full of them."

A generation later, beginning in 1618, the renewed European religious wars between Protestants and Catholics devastated the continental market for English woolen cloth, bringing unemployment and desperate conditions to the textile regions. Probably half of England's households lived on the edge of poverty. "This land grows weary of her inhabitants,"

John White, governor of the second expedition to Virginia in 1587, rendered the first pictorial records of native life in the Americas. This watercolor of a tattooed noblewoman of Pomeiock shows her right arm resting in a chain of pearls or copper beads. Her young daughter holds a prized English doll in an Elizabethan dress. *(Copyright The British Museum)*

wrote John Winthrop of East Anglia, "so as a man, which is the most precious of all creatures, is near more vile among us than a horse or a sheep."

Religious persecution and political considerations intensified the pressure to emigrate from England in the early seventeenth century. How this operated in specific situations will be considered in the next chapter. The largest number of emigrants went to the West Indies. The North American mainland colonies attracted perhaps half as many, and the Irish plantations in Ulster and Munster still fewer. For the first time in their history, large numbers of English people were abandoning their island homeland to carry their destinies to new frontiers.

Anticipating North America

The early English settlers in North America were far from uninformed about the indigenous people of the New World. Beginning with Columbus's first description of the New World, published in several European cities in 1493 and 1494, reports and promotional accounts circulated among the participants in early voyages of discovery, trade, and settlement. This literature became the basis for anticipating the world that had been discovered beyond the setting sun.

Colonists who read or listened to these accounts got a dual image of the native people. On the one hand, the Indians were depicted as a gentle people who eagerly received Europeans. Columbus had written of the "great amity toward us" that he encountered in San Salvador in 1492 and had described the Arawaks there as "a loving people" who "were greatly pleased and became so entirely our friends that it was a wonder to see." Verrazano, the first European to touch the eastern edge of North America, wrote optimistically about the native people in 1524. The natives, graceful of limb and tawny-colored, he related, "came toward us joyfully uttering loud cries of wonderment, and showing us the safest place to beach the boat."

This positive image of the Native Americans reflected both the friendly reception that Europeans often actually received and the European vision of the New World as an earthly paradise where war-torn, impoverished, and persecuted people could build a new life. The strong desire to trade with the native people also encouraged a favorable view because only a friendly Indian could become a suitable partner in commercial exchange.

A counterimage of a savage, hostile Indian, however, also entered the minds of settlers coming to North America. Like the positive image, it originated in the early travel literature. As early as 1502, Sebastian Cabot had paraded in England three Eskimos he had kidnapped on an Arctic voyage. They were described as flesh-eating savages and "brute beasts" who "spake such speech that no man could understand them." Many other accounts portrayed the New World natives as crafty, brutal, loathsome halfmen, who lived, as Amerigo Vespucci put it, without "law, religion, rulers, immortality of the soul, and private property."

The English had another reason for believing that all would not be friendship and amiable trading when they came ashore. For years they had read accounts of the Spanish experience in the Caribbean, Mexico, and Peru—and the story was not pretty. Many books described in gory detail the wholesale violence that occurred when Spaniard met Mayan, Aztec, or Inca. Accounts of Spanish cruelty, even genocide, were useful to Protestant pamphleteers, who labeled the Catholic Spaniards "hell-hounds and wolves." Immigrants embarking for North America wondered whether similar violent confrontations awaited them.

Timeline

	Pre-Columbian Epochs
12,000 B.C.	Beringian epoch ends
6000 B.C.	Paleo-Indian phase ends
500 B.C.	Archaic era ends
500 B.C.–c. 1000	Post-Archaic era in North America
	Norse seafarers establish settlements in Newfoundland
A.D. 1000–1500	Kingdoms of Ghana, Mali, Songhay in Africa
1420s	Portuguese sailors explore west coast of Africa
1492	Christopher Columbus lands on Caribbean islands
	Spanish expel Moors (Muslims) and Jews
1494	Treaty of Tordesillas
1497–1585	French and English explore northern part of the Americas
1498	Vasco da Gama reaches India after sailing around Africa
1513	Portuguese explorers reach China
1515–1565	Spanish explore Florida and southern part of North America
1520s	Luther attacks Catholicism
1521	Cortés conquers the Aztec
1530s	Calvin calls for religious reform
1533	Pizarro conquers the Inca
1540–1542	Coronado explores the Southwest
1558	Elizabeth I crowned queen of England
1585	Roanoke Island settlement
1588	English defeat the Spanish Armada
1603	James I succeeds Elizabeth I
1607	English begin settlement at Jamestown, Virginia

Another factor nourishing negative images of the Indian stemmed from the Indians' possession of the land necessary for settlement. For Englishmen, rooted in a tradition of the private ownership of property, this presented moral and legal, as well as practical, problems. As early as the 1580s, George Peckham, an early promoter of colonization, had admitted that the English doubted their right to take the land of others. In 1609, Anglican minister Robert Gray wondered, "By what right can we enter into the land of these savages, take their rightful inheritance from them, and plant ourselves in their places, being unwronged or unprovoked by them?"

The problem could be partially solved by arguing that English settlers did not intend to take the Indians' land but wanted only to share it with them. In return, they would offer the natives the advantages of a more advanced culture and, most important, the Christian religion. This argument would be repeated for generations. As the governing council in Virginia put it in 1610, the settlers "by way of merchandizing and trade, do buy of [the Indians] the pearls of earth, and sell to them the pearls of heaven."

A more ominous argument arose to justify English rights to native soil. By denying the humanity of the Indians, the English, like other Europeans, claimed that the native possessors of the land disqualified themselves from rightful ownership of it. "Although the Lord hath given the earth to children of men," one Englishman reasoned, "the greater part of it [is] possessed and wrongfully usurped by wild beasts and unreasonable creatures, or by brutish savages, which by reason of their godless ignorance and blasphemous idolatry, are worse than those beasts which are of the most wild and savage nature."

Defining the Native Americans as "savage" and "brutish" did not give the English arriving in Opechancanough's land the power to dispossess his people of their soil, but it armed them with a moral justification for doing so when their numbers became sufficient. Few settlers arriving in North America doubted that their technological superiority would allow them to overwhelm the indigenous people. For their part, people like Opechancanough probably perceived the arriving Europeans as impractical, irreligious, aggressive, and strangely intent on accumulating material wealth.

Conclusion

Converging Worlds

The English immigrants who began arriving on the eastern edge of North America in the early seventeenth century came late to a New World that other Europeans had been colonizing for more than a century. The first English arrivals, the immigrants to Virginia, were but a small advance wave of the large, varied, and determined fragment of English society that would flock to the western Atlantic frontier during the next few generations. Like Spanish, Portuguese, and French colonizers before them, they would establish new societies in the newfound lands in contact with the people of two other cultures— one made up of ancient inhabitants of the lands they were settling and the other composed of those brought across the Atlantic against their will. We turn now to the richly diverse founding experience of the English latecomers in the seventeenth century.

Recommended Reading

The People of America Before Columbus

Brian M. Fagan, *The Great Journey: The Peopling of Ancient America* (1987) and *Ancient North America: The Archaeology of a Continent* (1991); Alvin M. Josephy, Jr., *America in 1492: The World of the Indian Peoples Before the Arrival of Columbus* (1992); Philip Kopper, *The Smithsonian Book of North American Indians: Before the Coming of Europeans* (1986); Kenneth Macgowan and Joseph A. Hester, Jr., *Early Man in the New World* (1983); Lynne Sebastian, *The Chaco Anasazi: Sociopolitical Evolution in the Prehistoric Southwest* (1994); Lynda N. Shaffer, *Native Americans Before 1492: The Moundbuilding Centers of the Eastern Woodlands* (1992); Dean Snow, *The Archaeology of North America: American Indians and Their Origins* (1976).

Africa on the Eve of Contact

George E. Brooks, *Landlords and Strangers: Ecology, Society, and Trade in Western Africa, 1000–1630* (1993); Basil Davidson, *The African Genius* (1969); Paul E. Lovejoy, *Transformations in Slavery: A History of Slavery in Africa* (1983); Roland Oliver and Anthony Atmore, *The African Middle Ages, 1400–1800* (1981); John Thornton, *Africa and Africans in the Making of the Atlantic World, 1400–1600* (1992).

Europe in the Age of Exploration

Carlo M. Cipolla, *Guns, Sails, and Empires: Technological Innovations and the Early Phases of European Expansion, 1400–1700* (1966) and *Before the Industrial Revolution: European Society and Economy, 1000–1700* (1976); Ralph Davis, *The Rise of the Atlantic Economies* (1973); J. H. Elliot, *The Old World and the New, 1492-1650* (1970); W. H. McNeill, *The Rise of the West* (1963); William D. Phillips, Jr., and Carla Rahn Phillips, *The Worlds of Christopher Columbus* (1992); Eric Wolf, *Europe and the People without History* (1982).

The Iberian Conquest of America

Inga Clendinnen, *The Aztecs* (1991); Alfred Crosby, Jr., *The Columbian Exchange: Biological and Cultural Consequences of 1492* (1972); Charles Gibson, *The Aztecs Under Spanish Rule* (1964); Charles Hudson, *Knights of Spain, Warriors of the Sun: Hernando de Soto and the South's Ancient Chiefdoms* (1997); James Lockhart and Stuart B. Schwartz, *Early Latin America* (1983); R. C. Padden, *The Hummingbird and the Hawk: Conquest and Sovereignty in the Valley of Mexico, 1503–1541* (1962); M. Leon Portilla, *The Broken Spears: The Aztec Account of the Conquest of Mexico* (1962); David E. Stannard, *American Holocaust: Columbus and the Conquest of the New World* (1992).

England Looks West

Kenneth R. Andrews, *Trade, Plunder, and Settlement: Maritime Enterprise and the Genesis of the British Empire, 1480–1630* (1985); Nicholas P. Canny, *The Elizabethan Conquest of Ireland* (1976); De Lamar Jensen, *Reformation Europe, Age of Reform and Revolution* (1981); Karen Kupperman, *Roanoke: The Abandoned Colony* (1984); Peter Laslett, *The World We Have Lost* (1971); David B. Quinn, *England and the Discovery of America, 1481–1620* (1974) and *Set Fair for Roanoke: Voyages and Colonies, 1584–1606* (1985); A. L. Rowse, *The Expansion of Elizabethan England* (1955); Keith Wrightson, *English Society, 1580–1680* (1982).

Fiction and Film

Search of the First Americans (1992), part of the Nova series produced by the Public Broadcasting System (PBS), provides a fascinating introduction to the peopling of the Americas before the Columbian voyages. *Secrets of the Lost Red Paint People,* also in this series, shows how archaeologists have reconstructed—always tentatively—the ancient world of the Americas. In a feature film titled *Conquest of Paradise* (1992) Gerard Depardieu plays Christopher Columbus, but Boston's WGBH seven-part *Columbus and the Age of Discovery* (1991) is much more comprehensive and more authentic. In *Roanoke,* a miniseries, PBS has also explored the friction between Indians and colonizers in the first attempt of the English to plant a North American settlement.

Suggested Web Sites

http://www.anthro.mankato.msus.edu/prehistory/vikings/vikhome.html

Vikings in the New World. This site explores the history of some of the earliest European visitors to America.

http://www.mcn.org/2/oseeler/drake.htm

Sir Francis Drake. This comprehensive site covers much of Drake's life and voyages.

http://lcweb.loc.gov/exhibits/1492/intro.html

1492: An Ongoing Voyage. An exhibit of the Library of Congress, Washington DC, this site provides brief essays and images about early civilizations and contact in the Americas.

http://marauder.millersv.edu/~columbus/

The Computerized Information Retrieval System on Columbus and the Age of Discovery. The History Department and Academic Computing Services of Millersville University of Pennsylvania provide this text retrieval system containing over 1,000 text articles from various magazines, journals, newspapers, speeches, official calendars, and other sources relating to various encounter themes.

http://www.angelfire.com/ca/humanorigins/index.html

Ancient Mesoamerican Civilizations. Kevin L. Callahan of the University of Minnesota Department of Anthropology maintains this page that supplies information regarding Mesoamerican civilizations with well-organized essays and photos.

http://medicine.wustl.edu/~mckinney/cahokia/cahokia.html

Cahokia Mounds. The Cahokia Mounds state historical site gives information about a fascinating pre-Columbian culture in North America.

http://www.mexonline.com/precolum.htm

Mexico Pre-Columbian History. This site provides information on the Aztec, Maya, Mexica, Olmec, Toltec, Zapotec, and other pre-European cultures, as well as information on museums, archaeology, language, and education.

http://www.acs.ucalgary.ca/HIST/tutor/eurvoya/

The European Voyages of Exploration. This University of Calgary site has images and texts for nearly every facet of European exploration.

http://www.ushistoryplace.com

A richly detailed on-line learning environment complete with interactive maps, timelines, history activities, primary source documents, and links to related American history sites.

COLONIZING *a* CONTINENT

CHAPTER OUTLINE

By 1637, after five years in New England, John Mason knew both the prospects and perils of England's new overseas frontier. In his early thirties, Mason had emigrated from southeastern England. He was part of the flock of John Warham, a Puritan minister from the village of Dorchester. In Massachusetts, the group commemorated their origins by giving the name Dorchester to the area assigned to them. Here, six miles south of Boston, they built a simple church, assigned town lots and outlying farms, and began the work of serving their God in the wilderness of North America.

Like many Puritans, Mason had thrilled at the sight of southern New England's game-filled forests and fish-filled streams, the fields cleared and tilled by Algonquian agriculturists, the lush meadows available for grazing stock. Though the winters were inhospitable, it seemed this might be the Promised Land where Puritan refugees could plant their New World Zion. But Mason also recognized that these lands were not vacant. From the earliest days of the Pilgrim settlers at Plymouth in 1620, it was evident that the native occupiers of the region, whose claim went back a hundred generations, stood in the way of the Puritan "errand into the wilderness."

In the fall of 1636, Mason followed many of his Dorchester friends out of Massachusetts. Desirous of better land and restless with the political squabbling in the Massachusetts Bay Colony, the Dorchester settlers set out for the Connecticut River, 100 miles to the west. For 14 days, nipped by the frost of late autumn, they trekked wearily along Indian paths, carrying their meager possessions. At their journey's end, they founded the town of Windsor, on the west bank of the Connecticut.

Six months later, when his new village was no more than a collection of crude lean-tos, militia captain John Mason marched south against the Pequots. He owed his officership to military experience in the Netherlands, where thousands of English soldiers had gone in the 1620s to help the Protestant Dutch break the yoke of Catholic Spain in the Lowlands. Now he commanded several hundred men whom the fledgling Connecticut River towns had dispatched to drive the Pequots from the area. In the

years before the English arrival, the powerful Pequots had formed a network of tributary tribes. Finding it impossible to placate the English as they swarmed into the Connecticut River valley, the Pequots chose resistance.

At dawn on May 26, 1637, Captain Mason and his troops approached a Pequot village on the Mystic River. Supported by Narragansett allies, the English slipped into the town. After a few scuffles in the half-light, Mason cried out, "We must burn them," and his men began torching the Pequot wigwams. Then they rushed from the fortified village. As flames engulfed the huts, the Pequots fled the inferno, only to be cut down with musket and sword by the English soldiers, who had ringed the community. Most of the terrified victims were noncombatants—old men, women, and children—for the Pequot warriors were preparing for war at another village about five miles away.

Before the sun rose, a major portion of the Pequot tribe had been exterminated. The resistance of the others crumbled when they learned the fate of their families. "It was a fearful sight to see them thus frying in the fire," wrote one Puritan, "and horrible was the stink and scent thereof; but the victory seemed a sweet sacrifice, and they gave the praise thereof to God, who had wrought so wonderfully for them." Mason himself wrote that God had "laughed at his enemies and the enemies of his people, . . . making them as a fiery oven."

Captain John Mason was a God-fearing Puritan and a man highly esteemed by his fellow colonists. His actions at the Mystic River, just seven years after the great Puritan migration to New England had begun in 1630, testify that the European colonization of America involved a violent confrontation of two cultures. We often speak of the "discovery" and "settlement" of North America by English and other European colonists. But the penetration of the eastern edge of what today is the United States might more accurately be called the "invasion of America."

Yet mixed with violence was utopian idealism. In the New World, Puritans—and countless waves of immigrants who followed them—sought both spiritual and economic renewal. Settlement in America represented a chance to escape European war, despotism, material want, and religious corruption. The New World was a place to rescue humankind from the ruins of the Old World. This chapter reconstructs the manner of settlement and the character

Cecil Calvert grasping a map of Maryland held by his grandfather, the second Lord Baltimore; detail of a painting by Gerard Soest, court painter to Charles II. (*Enoch Pratt Free Library, Baltimore*)

of immigrant life in six areas of early colonization: the Chesapeake Bay, southern New England, the French and Dutch area from the St. Lawrence River to the Hudson River, the Carolinas, Pennsylvania, and the Spanish toeholds on the south-ern fringe of the continent. A comparison of these various colonies will show how the colonizers' backgrounds, ideologies, goals, and modes of settlement produced distinctly different soci-eties in North America in the seventeenth century.

THE CHESAPEAKE TOBACCO COAST

In 1585, England gained a first foothold in a hemisphere dominated by Spanish and Portuguese colonizers. A reconnaissance expedition organized by Walter Raleigh, one of Queen Elizabeth's favorite courtiers, scouted the Carolina coast and hastened homeward carrying two natives and a string of tales about rich soil, friendly Indians, and mineral wealth. A second voyage in 1585 and a third in 1587, composed of 91 men, 17 women, and 9 children, planted a small colony on Roanoke Island. But the enterprise failed. The voyages to Roanoke were too small and poorly financed to establish successful settlements. They served only as tokens of England's rising challenge to Spain in North America and as a source of valuable information for colonists later settling the area.

The Roanoke colony also failed resoundingly as the first sustained contact between English and Native American peoples. Although one member of the first expedition reported that "we found the people most gentle, loving, and faithful, void of all guile and trea-son," relations with the local tribes quickly soured and then turned violent. Charges flew back and forth, the English believing that the local Indians had stolen a silver cup and the Indians angered by English raids on their winter supply of corn. Aware of their numerical disadvantage and afraid of a coordinated attack against them, the English turned their muskets on a local leader to intimidate the natives with their supe-rior technology. In 1591, when a relief expedition reached Roanoke, none of the settlers could be found. Most likely these "lost colonists" succumbed to Indian attacks. It was an ominous beginning for England's overseas ambitions.

Jamestown

In 1607, a generation after the first Roanoke expedition, a group of merchants established England's first permanent colony in North America at Jamestown, Virginia. Under a charter from James I, they operated as a joint-stock compa-ny, an early form of a modern corporation that allowed them to sell shares of stock in their company and use the pooled investment capital to outfit and supply overseas expeditions. Although the king's charter to the Virginia Company of London began with a concern for bringing Christian religion to native people who "as yet live in darkness and miser-able ignorance of the true knowledge of God," most of the settlers probably agreed with Captain John Smith, who emerged as their strongest leader. "We did admire," he wrote, "how it was possible such wise men could so torment themselves with such absur-dities, making religion their colour, when all their aim was profit."

Profits in the early years proved elusive, however. Expecting to find gold and other minerals, anticipat-ing a rewarding trade with Indians for beaver and deer skins, and, best of all, hoping to discover the fabled passage through the North American continent to China, the original investors and settlers received a rude shock. Rather than duplicating the remarkable success of the Spanish and Portuguese in Mexico, Peru, and Brazil, the early Virginia colonists died mis-erably of dysentery, malaria, and malnutrition. More than 900 settlers, mostly men, arrived in the colony between 1607 and 1609; only 60 survived.

Seeking occupational diversity, the Virginia Company sent French silk artisans, Italian glassmak-ers, and Polish potash burners to Jamestown. But one-third of the first three groups of immigrants were gold-seeking adventurers with unroughened hands, a proportion of gentlemen six times as great as in the English population. Many others were unskilled ser-vants, some with criminal backgrounds, who "never did knowe what a days work was," observed John Smith. Both types adapted poorly to wilderness con-ditions, leaving Smith begging for "but thirty carpen-ters, husbandmen, gardeners, fishermen, and black-smiths" rather than "a thousand such gallants as were sent to me, that would do nothing but complain, curse and despair, when they saw . . . all things contrary to the report in England."

The Jamestown colony was also hampered by the common assumption that Englishmen could exploit the Indians of the region. Cortés and Pizarro had con-quered the mighty Aztec and Inca empires with a few hundred soldiers and then turned the labor of thou-sands of natives to Spanish advantage. Why not, the early settlers mused, in Virginia?

The Great English Migration, 1630–1660

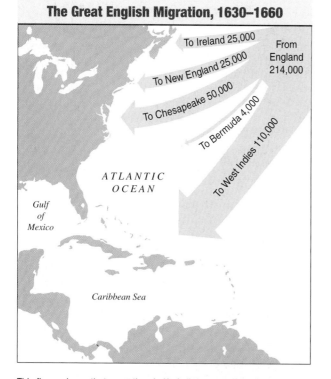

To Ireland 25,000

From England 214,000

To New England 25,000

To Chesapeake 50,000

To Bermuda 4,000

To West Indies 110,000

ATLANTIC OCEAN

Gulf of Mexico

Caribbean Sea

This figure shows that more than half of all the early English immigrants to the Americas went to the West Indies. Even a larger proportion of the Africans brought to the English colonies found themselves sold in England's Caribbean islands.

But the English found that the indigenous peoples were not densely settled and could not be easily subjugated. Contrary to expectations, no wealthy Indian empire lay waiting to be conquered. Nor could the Virginians mold the 20,000 Powhatan Indians of the region into a servile labor force, because, unlike the Spanish, the English settlers brought neither an army of conquistadores nor an army of priests to subdue the natives.

Instead, relations with some 40 small groups that the able Powhatan had united into a confederacy turned bitter almost from the beginning. Powhatan brought supplies of corn to the sick and starving Jamestown colony during the first autumn. However, John Smith, whose military experience in eastern Europe had schooled him in dealing with people he regarded as "barbarians," raided Indian corn supplies and tried to cow the local tribes by shows of force. In response, Powhatan withdrew from trade with the English and sniped at their flanks. Many settlers died in the "starving times" of the first years.

Despite these early failures, the Virginia Company of London poured more money and settlers into the venture. Understanding the need for ordinary farmers who could raise the food necessary to sustain the colony, they reorganized the company in 1609. They enticed many new settlers by promising free land at the end of seven years' labor for the company. In 1618, they sweetened the terms by offering 50 acres of land outright to anyone journeying to Virginia. To thousands of people on the margins of English society, such an offer was irresistible. More than 9,000 crossed the Atlantic between 1610 and 1622 to begin life anew in Virginia. Yet only 2,000 remained alive at the end of that period. "Instead of a plantation," wrote one English critic, "Virginia will shortly get the name of a slaughter house."

No one knows exactly what the Jamestown settlement looked like in its early years; this twentieth-century mural by Stanley King is a conjectured rendering based on archaeological evidence. New archaeological findings at the site of the Jamestown fort are adding to our knowledge of the first English Virginians. *(National Park Service, Colonial National Historical Park)*

Sot Weed and Indentured Servants

Even though the colony proved a burial ground for most immigrants within a few years of arrival, the promise of free land lured a steady stream of settlers to Virginia. Also crucial to the continued migration was the discovery that tobacco grew splendidly in Chesapeake soil. Frenchmen had first brought tobacco from Florida to Portugal in the 1560s. But it was Francis Drake's boatload of the "jovial weed" (so named for its intoxicating effect), procured in the West Indies in 1586, that popularized it among the upper class and launched a long history of addiction that still ravages the world.

Even James I's denunciation of smoking as "loathsome to the eye, hateful to the nose, harmful to the brain, and dangerous to the lungs" failed to halt the smoking craze. The "sot weed" became Virginia's salvation. Planters shipped the first crop in 1617, and tobacco cultivation spread rapidly. Commanding the handsome price of three shillings per pound in England, tobacco allowed a profit sufficient for settlers to plant it even in the streets and marketplace of Jamestown. By

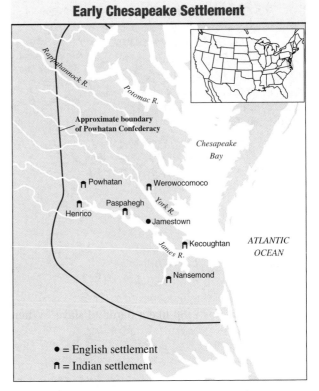

Early Chesapeake Settlement

Rappahannock R.

Potomac R.

Approximate boundary of Powhatan Confederacy

Chesapeake Bay

Powhatan   Werowocomoco

Henrico   Paspahegh   York R.

Jamestown

Kecoughtan   ATLANTIC OCEAN

James R.

Nansemond

● = English settlement

⌂ = Indian settlement

Only the major Indian villages in the early 1600s are indicated on this map. Note that the town sites are all oriented to the rivers—the source of both food and transportation.

By the end of the 1600s, most young European males were addicted to tobacco. Like the young Dutchmen shown in this painting, they practiced various tricks such as the "ring," "whiffle," "gulp," and "retention" as part of the smoking cult. (*Adriaen Brouwer, "The Smokers," The Metropolitan Museum of Art, Bequest of Michael Friedsam, 1931, The Friedsam Collection*)

1624, Virginia exported 200,000 pounds of the "stinking weed"; by 1638, though the price had plummeted, the crop exceeded three million pounds. Tobacco became to Virginia in the 1620s what sugar was to the West Indies and silver to Mexico and Peru. In London, men gibed that Virginia was built on smoke.

While launching Virginia on an era of sustained growth, the cultivation of tobacco also obliged Virginia's planters to find a reliable supply of cheap labor. Tobacco required intensive care through the various stages of planting, weeding, thinning, suckering, worming, cutting, curing, and packing. To fill their need, planters recruited immigrants in England and Ireland and a scattering from Sweden, Portugal, Spain, Germany, and even Turkey and Poland. Such people, called indentured servants, willingly sold a portion of their working lives in exchange for free passage to America. About four of every five seventeenth-century immigrants to Virginia—and later, Maryland—were indentured. Nearly three-quarters of them were male, and mostly between 15 and 24 years old.

Many of the indentured servants came from the armies of the unemployed. Others were orphans, political prisoners, or common criminals who escaped the gallows by going abroad. Some were of the "middling sort," younger sons unlikely to inherit a father's farm or shop, or young men eager to leave behind an unfortunate marriage. Others were drawn simply by the prospect of adventure in a "strange new land." But overwhelmingly, indentured servants came from the lower rungs of the social ladder at home.

Life for indentured servants often turned into a nightmare. Only a handful, perhaps one in 20, realized the dream of achieving freedom and acquiring land. If malarial fevers or dysentery did not quickly kill them, servants often succumbed to the brutal work routine imposed by harsh masters. Even by the middle of the seventeenth century, when the starving times were only a memory, about half died during the first few years of "seasoning." Masters bought and sold their servants as property, gambled for them at cards, and worked them to death because there was little motive for keeping them alive beyond their term of labor. "My Master Adkins," wrote one servant in 1623, "hath sold me for £150 like a damned slave." When servants neared the end of their contract, masters found ways to add time and were backed by courts that they controlled.

Contrary to English custom, masters often put women servants to work at the hoe. Sexual abuse by masters was common, and servant women paid dearly for illegitimate pregnancies. The courts fined them heavily and ordered them to serve an extra year or two to repay the time lost during pregnancy and childbirth. They also deprived mothers of their illegitimate children, indenturing them out at an early age. For many servant women, marriage was the best release from this hard life. Many willingly accepted the purchase of their indenture by any man who suggested marriage.

Expansion and Indian War

As Virginia's population increased, spurred by the growth of tobacco production, violence mounted between white colonizers and the Powhatan tribes. In 1614, the sporadic hostility of the early years ended temporarily with the arranged marriage of Powhatan's daughter, the fabled Pocahontas, to planter John Rolfe. However, the profitable cultivation of tobacco created an intense demand for land. As more and more settlers pushed up the rivers flowing into Chesapeake Bay, the local tribes worried that the previous abrasive and sometimes bloody contact might become a disastrous one.

In 1617, when Powhatan retired, the leadership of the Chesapeake tribes fell to Opechancanough. This proud and talented leader began building military strength for an all-out attack on his English enemies. The English murder of Nemattanew, a Powhatan war captain and religious prophet, triggered a fierce Indian

Robert Vaughan's scenes for John Smith's memoirs (1624) get some of the story right but are fanciful in some respects. Here, Smith takes the gigantic Powhatan by the scalplock. The close combat between Indians and Englishmen in the background is dramatic but hardly accurate. (*From* The Generall Historie of Virginia, *1624, by Captain John Smith/Library of Congress*)

assault on Good Friday in 1622 that dealt Virginia a staggering blow. More than one-quarter of the white population fell before the marauding tribesmen; the casualties in cattle, crops, and buildings were equally severe.

The devastating attack bankrupted the Virginia Company. As a result, the king annulled its charter in 1624 and established a royal government, which allowed the elected legislative body established in 1619, the House of Burgesses, to continue lawmaking in concert with the royal governor and his council.

The Indian assault of 1622 fortified the determination of the surviving planters to pursue a ruthless new Indian policy. John Smith, writing from England two years later, noted the grim satisfaction that had followed the Indian attack. Many, he reported, believed that it "will be good for the plantation, because now we have just cause to destroy them by all means possible." Bolstered by instructions from London to "root out [the Indians] from being any longer a people," the Virginians conducted annual military expeditions

Painted at the time she was presented to the court of King James I, Pocahontas appears in a red velvet jacket over a dark dress with gold buttons. She holds a fan of three ostrich feathers. We can only imagine how her elaborate shoulder collar of white lace must have felt for a 22-year-old woman accustomed to loose-fitting, comfortable clothes. *(National Portrait Gallery, Smithsonian Institution/Art Resource, NY)*

against the native villages west and north of the settled areas. The "flood of blood," as the English poet John Donne called it in 1622, had cost the colony dearly and doomed the Virginia Company of London. Yet it justified a policy of "perpetual enmity," even though several leaders admitted that the Indians had attacked in 1622 because of "our own perfidious dealing with them."

Population growth after 1630 and the recurrent need for fresh acreage by settlers who planted soil-exhausting tobacco intensified the pressure on Indian land. The tough, ambitious planters soon encroached on Indian territories, provoking war in 1644 and again in 1675. In each of these conflicts, the colonizers proved superior. Greatly outnumbering their opponents, they reduced the native population of Virginia to less than 1,000 by 1680. The Chesapeake tribes, Virginians came to believe, were merely obstacles to be removed from the path of English settlement.

Proprietary Maryland

By the time Virginia had achieved commercial success in the 1630s, another colony on the Chesapeake took root. The founder's main aim was not profit but a refuge for Catholics and a New World version of the English manorial countryside.

George Calvert, an English nobleman, designed and promoted Virginia's Chesapeake neighbor. Closely connected to the royal family, he had received a huge grant of land in Newfoundland in 1628, just three years after James I had elevated him to the peerage as Lord Baltimore. In 1632, Charles I, James's son, prepared to grant him a more hospitable domain of 10 million acres. Calvert named it Terra Maria after the king's Catholic wife, Queen Henrietta Maria. In English it became Maryland.

Catholics were an oppressed minority in England, and Lord Baltimore planned his colony as a haven for them. But knowing that he needed more than a small band of Catholic settlers, the proprietor invited others too. Catholics, never a majority in his colony, were quickly overwhelmed by Protestants who jumped at the offer of free land with only a modest yearly fee to the Calverts.

Lord Baltimore died while the charter for his colony was being drawn up in 1632, leaving his 26-year-old son, Cecilius, to carry out his plans. The charter guaranteed the proprietor control over all branches of government, but young Calvert learned that his colonists

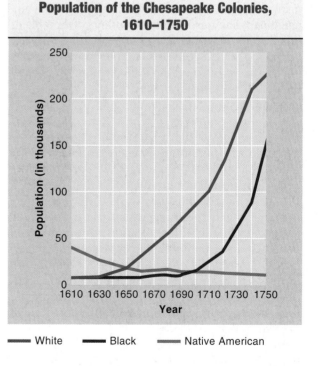

As indicated in this chart, it was not until the 1690s, when Chesapeake planters began turning to Africa for their labor, that the black population in the Chesapeake colonies began to rise rapidly. Source: U.S. Bureau of the Census.

would not be satisfied with fewer political liberties than they enjoyed at home or could find in other colonies. Hence, the Lords Baltimore were obliged to give up their charter-given right to initiate all colonial laws, subject only to the advice and consent of the people.

In land policy, Calvert's heirs found it impossible to carry out his plan for establishing feudalism in the woodlands of eastern North America. Arriving in 1634, immigrants blithely ignored his design of 6,000-acre manors for his relatives and 3,000-acre manors for lesser aristocrats, each to be ruled by provincial nobles and worked by flocks of serflike tenants. The settlers took up their free land, imported as many indentured servants as they could afford, maintained generally peaceful relations with local Indian tribes, grew tobacco on scattered riverfront plantations like their Virginia neighbors, and governed themselves locally as much as possible. In time, they created their own social hierarchy, not with assigned social roles but with status determined by the ability of some to rise above others in the competitive tobacco economy. Although Maryland grew slowly at first—in 1650, it had a population of only 600—it developed rapidly in the second half of the seventeenth century. By 1700, its population of 33,000 was half that of Virginia.

Daily Life on the Chesapeake

Though immigrants to the Chesapeake Bay region dreamed of bettering the life they had known in England, existence for most of them was dismally difficult. Only a minority could expect to marry and rear a family, because marriage had to be deferred until the indenture was completed; also, there were three times more men than women. Once made, marriages were fragile. Either husband or wife was likely to suc-cumb to disease within about seven years. The vulnerability of pregnant women to malaria frequently terminated marriages in the first few years, and death claimed half the children born before they reached adulthood. Few children had both parents alive while growing up. Grandparents were almost unknown.

In a society so numerically dominated by men, widows were prized and remarried quickly. Such conditions produced complex families, full of stepchildren and stepparents, half-sisters and half-brothers. In the common case of marriage between a widow and a widower, each with children from a previous marriage, the web of family life became particularly complex, and the tensions attending child rearing unusually thick.

The household of Robert Beverley of Middlesex County illustrates the tangled family relationships in this death-filled society. When Beverley married Mary Keeble in 1666, she was a 29-year-old widow who had borne seven children during her first marriage. At least four of them were still alive to join the household of their mother's new husband. They gained five half-brothers and half-sisters during their mother's 12-year marriage to Beverley. When Mary Keeble Beverley died at age 41, her husband quickly remarried a recent widow, Katherine Hone. Beverley's second wife brought her son into the household and in the next nine years produced four more children with Beverley before his death in 1687. Thus, between 1666 and 1687, Beverley had married two widows who bore him nine children and had been stepfather to the eight children his two wives had produced with previous husbands. Not one of these 17 children, from an interlocking set of four marriages, reached adulthood with both a living mother and father.

We think of the churches of the colonial South as handsome, steepled, red brick buildings, but this unpainted clapboard church is typical of the rudimentary buildings erected by early colonists in the Chesapeake region. (*Harold Wickliffe Rose Papers, Yale University Library, New Haven, CT*)

Plagued by such mortality, the Chesapeake remained, for most of the seventeenth century, a land of immigrants rather than a land of settled families. Churches and schools took root very slowly amid such fluidity. The large number of indentured servants further destabilized community life. Strangers in a household, they served their time and moved on, replaced by other strangers, purchased as they clambered off boats fresh from England.

The fragility of life in the tobacco-growing Chesapeake world showed clearly in the region's architecture. As in most New World colonies, the settlers at first erected only primitive huts and shanties, hardly more than windbreaks. After establishing crops, planters improved their habitats but still built ramshackle one-room dwellings. "Their houses," it was observed in 1623, "stand scattered one from another, and are only made of wood . . . so as a firebrand is sufficient to consume them all." Even as Virginia and Maryland matured, cheaply built and cramped houses, usually no larger than 16 by 24 feet, remained the norm. Life was too uncertain, the tobacco economy too volatile, and the desire to invest every available shilling in field labor too great for men to build grandly. In England, solidly framed buildings erected on stone foundations had become the rule several centuries before. But throughout the Chesapeake, settlers erected "earthfast" flimsy cabins and houses directly on the ground or on posts.

Even by the early eighteenth century, most Chesapeake families were "pigg'd lovingly together," as one planter said, in a crude house without interior partitions. Eating, dressing, working, and loving all took place with hardly a semblance of privacy. For nearly two centuries, most ordinary Virginians and Marylanders lived in such quarters. "Like a flock of sheep in a fold," an eighteenth-century traveler described the family he bedded down with, 16 to a room, on the Virginia frontier. Even prosperous planters did not begin constructing fully framed, substantial homesteads until a century after the colony was founded.

The crudity of life also showed in the household possessions of the Chesapeake colonists. Struggling farmers and tenants were likely to own only a straw mattress, a simple storage chest, and the tools for food preparation and eating—a mortar and pestle to grind corn, knives for butchering, a pot or two for cooking stews and porridges, wooden trenchers and spoons for eating. Most ordinary settlers owned no chairs, no dressers, no plates or silverware. Among middling planters, the standard of living was raised only by possession of a flock mattress, coarse earthenware for milk and butter, a few pewter plates and porringers, a frying pan or two, and a few rough tables and chairs.

Even one of Virginia's wealthiest planters, the prominent Robert Beverley, had "nothing in and about his house but what was necessary . . . good beds . . . but no curtains, and instead of cane chairs, he hath stools made of wood." To be near the top of Chesapeake society meant having three or four rooms, sleeping more comfortably, sitting on chairs rather than squatting on the floor, and acquiring such ordinary decencies as chamber pots, candlesticks, bed linen, a chest of drawers, and a desk. Only a few boasted such luxury items as clocks, books, punch bowls, wine glasses, and imported furniture. Four generations elapsed in the Chesapeake settlements before the frontier quality of life slowly gave way to more refined living.

MASSACHUSETTS AND ITS OFFSPRING

While some English settlers in the reign of James I (1603–1625) scrambled for wealth on the Chesapeake, others in England looked to the wilds of North America as a place to build a tabernacle to God. The society they fashioned aimed at unity of purpose and utter dedication to reforming the corrupt world. American Puritanism would powerfully affect the nation's history, especially in planting the seeds of a belief in America's special mission in the world. Yet the "New England way" only partially prefigured the pathways of American development because Puritanism represented a visionary attempt to banish diversity on a continent where the arrival of streams of immigrants from around the globe was destined to become a primary phenomenon.

Puritanism in England

England had been officially Protestant since 1558. Many English in the late sixteenth century, however, thought the Church of England was still ridden with Catholic vestiges. Detesting such remnants of Catholicism as vestments and rituals that lingered on in the reign of Elizabeth (1558–1603), some demanded the end of every taint of "the Bishop of Rome and all his detestable enormities." Because they wished to purify the Church of England, they were dubbed Puritans.

The people attracted to the Puritan movement were not only religious reformers but also men and women who hoped to find in religion an antidote to the changes sweeping over English society. Many feared for the future, as they witnessed the growth of turbulent cities, the increase of wandering poor, rising prices, and accelerating commercial activity. In general, they disapproved of the growing freedom from the restraints of gentry-dominated medieval institutions such as the church, guilds, and local government.

The concept of the individual operating as freely as possible, maximizing both opportunities and personal potential, is at the core of our modern system of beliefs and behavior. But many in Elizabethan England dreaded the crumbling of traditional restraints. They worried that individualistic behavior would undermine the notion of community—the belief that people were bound together by reciprocal rights, obligations, and responsibilities. Especially they decried the "degeneracy of the times," which they saw in the defiling of the Sabbath by maypole dancing, card playing, fiddling, bowling, and all the rest of the roistering and erotic behavior reflected in Shakespeare's dramatic portrayals of "Merrie England." Puritans vowed to reverse the march of disorder, wickedness, and disregard for community by imposing a new discipline.

One part of their plan was a social ethic stressing work as a primary way of serving God. Derived from the Calvinist concept of "calling," this emphasis on work made the religious quest of every member of society equally worthy. The labor of a mason was just as valuable in God's sight as that of a merchant, and so was his soul. The "work ethic" would banish idleness and impart discipline throughout the community. Second, Puritans organized themselves into religious congregations where each member hoped for personal salvation but also supported all others in their quest. Third, Puritans assumed responsibility for the "unconverted" people around them. They were convinced that others who could not find Christian truth in their hearts might have to be coerced and controlled, as in Calvin's Geneva. Religious reform and social vision were in this way interlocked.

When King James VI of Scotland succeeded the childless Elizabeth as James I of England in 1603, he spoke stridently for the divine right of the monarch and his own role as head of the church. Claiming responsibility only to God, James collided with the rising power of the Puritans. They had occupied the pulpits in hundreds of churches, gained control of several colleges at Oxford and Cambridge, and recruited many followers. Translating their religious appeal into political power, the Puritans obtained many seats in Parliament and aggressively challenged the king's power. James responded by harassing them, removing dozens of Puritan ministers from their pulpits, and threatening many others. "I will harry them out of the land," he vowed, "or else do worse."

When Charles I succeeded to the throne in 1625, the situation worsened for Puritans. Determined to strengthen the monarchy and stifle dissent, the king summoned a new Parliament in 1628 and one year later adjourned this venerable body (which was the Puritans' main instrument of reform) when it would

not accede to royal demands. The king then appointed William Laud, the bishop of London, to high office and turned him loose on the Puritans, whom Laud called "wasps" and the "most dangerous enemies of the state."

By 1629, when the king began ruling without Parliament, many Puritans were turning their eyes to northern Ireland, Holland, the Caribbean islands, and, especially, North America. They were convinced that God intended them to carry their religious and social reforms beyond the reach of persecuting authorities. A declining economy added to their discouragement about England, for the depression in the cloth trades was most severe in Puritan strongholds. To some distant shore, many Puritans decided, they should transport a fragment of English society and complete the Protestant Reformation. As they understood history, God had assigned them a special task in his plan for the redemption of humankind.

Puritan Predecessors in New England

Puritans were not the first Europeans to reach northeastern North America. Fishermen of various European nations had been working the fishing banks off Newfoundland and drying the cod they caught on the coast of Cape Cod and Maine since the early 1500s. They frequently made contact with the Algonquian-speaking tribes of the area. A short-lived attempt at settlement on the coast of Maine had also been made in 1607. Seven years later, the aging Chesapeake war dog John Smith, hired to hunt whales off the North American coast, coined the term "New England" after visiting the area. In his *Description of New England*, published in 1616, he excited considerable interest in the "Paradise of these parts."

No permanent settlement took root, however, until the Pilgrims—actually outnumbered by non-Pilgrims—arrived in Plymouth in 1620. Unlike the Puritans who followed, these humble Protestant farmers did not expect to convert a sinful world. Rather, they wanted to be left alone to realize their radical vision of a pure and primitive life. Instead of reforming the Church of England, they left it and hence were called Separatists. They had first fled from England to Amsterdam in 1608, then to Leyden when they found the commercial capital of Holland too corrupt, and, finally, in 1620, to North America.

When they arrived at the northern tip of Cape Cod in November 1620, the Pilgrims were weakened by a stormy nine-week voyage and ill-prepared for the harsh winter ahead. Misled by John Smith's glowing report of a warm, fertile country, they discovered instead a severe climate and a rockbound coast. By the following spring, half the Mayflower passengers were dead, including 13 of the 18 married women.

Recovering the Past

HOUSES

Homesteading is central to our national experience. For 300 years after the founding of the first colonies, most Americans were involved in taming and settling the land. On every frontier, families faced the tasks of clearing the fields, beginning farming operations, and building shelter for themselves and their livestock. The kinds of structures they built depended on available materials, their resources and aspirations, and their notions of a "fair" dwelling. The plan of a house and the materials used in its construction reveal much about the needs, resources, priorities, and values of the people who built it.

By examining archaeological remains of early ordinary structures and by studying houses that are still standing, historians are reaching new understandings of the social life of pioneering societies. Since the 1960s, archaeologists and architectural historians have been studying seventeenth-century housing in the Chesapeake Bay and New England regions. They have discovered a familiar sequence of house types—from temporary shanties and lean-tos to rough cabins and simple frame houses to larger and more substantial dwellings of brick and finished timber. This hovel-to-house-to-home pattern existed on every frontier, as sodbusters, gold miners, planters, and cattle raisers secured their hold on the land and then struggled to move from subsistence to success.

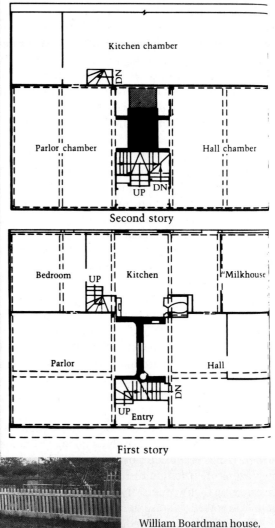

William Boardman house, Saugus, Massachusetts, c. 1687; a floor plan of the house is shown above. (*The Society for the Preservation of New England Antiquities*)

Reconstructed Chesapeake planter's house, typical of such simply built and unpainted structures in the seventeenth century. *(Photograph by Julie Roy Jeffrey)*

What is unusual in the findings of the Chesapeake researchers is the discovery that the second phase in the sequence—the use of temporary, rough-built structures—lasted for more than a century. Whereas many New Englanders had rebuilt and extended their temporary clapboard houses into timber-framed, substantial dwellings by the 1680s, Chesapeake settlers continued to construct small, rickety buildings that had to be repaired continually or abandoned altogether every 10 to 15 years.

The William Boardman house shown at left, built around 1687, is an example of the "orderly, fair, and well-built" houses of late-seventeenth-century Massachusetts. Its plan shows a typical arrangement of space: the hall, used for cooking, eating, working, and socializing; the parlor; a sleeping room for the parents; and a lean-to for kitchen chores and activities such as dairying. The great central chimney warmed the main downstairs room. Upstairs were two rooms used for both storage and sleeping. As you examine the exterior of the building, note the materials that have been used and the arrangement and treatment of windows, doors, and chimney. What impression of the Boardman family might visitors have as they approached the house? What kind of privacy and comfort did the house provide for family members?

The house shown above is a typical reconstructed tobacco planter's house. It has some of the same features as the Boardman house, for both are products of an English building tradition. But there are some major differences between the two. In the Chesapeake house, the chimney is not built of brick but of mud and wood; there is no window glass, only small shutters. The exterior is rough, unfinished planking. The placement of doors and windows and the overall dimensions indicate that this house has only one room downstairs and a loft above. The builders of this house clearly enjoyed less privacy and comfort than the Boardmans.

Historians have puzzled over this contrast between the architecture of the two regions. Part of the explanation may lie in the different climatic conditions and different immigration patterns of New England and the Chesapeake. In the southern region, disease carried off thousands of settlers in the early decades. The imbalance of men and women produced a stunted and unstable family life, hardly conducive to an emphasis on constructing fine homes. In New England, good health prevailed almost from the beginning, and the family was at the heart of society. It made more sense, in this environment, to make a substantial investment in larger and more permanent houses. Some historians argue, moreover, that the Puritan work ethic impelled New Englanders to build solid homes—a compulsion unknown in the culturally backward, "lazy" South.

Archaeological evidence combined with data recovered from land, tax, and court records, however, suggests another reason for the impermanence of housing in the Chesapeake region. Living in a labor-intensive tobacco world, it is argued, planters large and small economized on everything possible in order to buy as many indentured servants and slaves as they could. Better to live in a shanty and have ten slaves than to have a handsome dwelling and nobody to cultivate the fields. As late as 1775, the author of *American Husbandry* calculated that in setting up a tobacco plantation, five times as much ought to be spent on purchasing 20 black fieldhands as on the "house, offices, and tobacco-house."

Only after the Chesapeake region had emerged from its prolonged era of mortality and gender imbalance and a mixed economy of tobacco, grain, and cattle had replaced the tobacco monoculture did the rebuilding of the region begin. Excavated house sites indicate that this occurred in the period after 1720. New research is revealing that the phases of home building and the social and economic history of a society were closely interwoven. What do houses today reveal about the resources, economic livelihood, priorities, and values of contemporary Americans? Do class and regional differences in house design continue?

The survivors, led by the staunch William Bradford, settled at Plymouth. Squabbles soon erupted with local Indians, whom Bradford considered "savage and brutish men, which range up and down, little otherwise than the wild beasts." In 1622, they found themselves nearly overwhelmed by the arrival of 60 non-Pilgrims, sent out by the London Company, which had helped the Pilgrims finance their colony. For two generations, the Pilgrims tilled the soil, fished, and tried to keep intact their religious vision. But with the much larger Puritan migration that began in 1630, the Pilgrim villages nestled on the shores of Cape Cod Bay became a backwater of the thriving, populous Massachusetts Bay Colony, which absorbed them in 1691.

Errand into the Wilderness

In 11 ships, about a thousand Puritans set out from England in 1630 for the Promised Land. They were the vanguard of a movement that by 1642 brought about 18,000 colonizers to New England. Led by John Winthrop, a talented Cambridge-educated member of the English gentry, they operated under a charter from the king to the Puritan-controlled Massachusetts Bay Company. The Puritans set about building their utopia convinced they were carrying out a divine task. "God hath sifted a nation," wrote one Puritan, "that he might send choice grain into this wilderness."

Their intention was to establish communities of pure Christians who collectively swore a covenant with God to work for his ends. To accomplish this, the Puritan leaders agreed to employ severe means. Civil and religious transgressors must be rooted out and severely punished. They emphasized homogeneous communities where the good of the group outweighed individual interests. "We must delight in each other, make others' conditions our own, rejoice together, mourn together, labor and suffer together," counseled Winthrop.

To realize their utopian goals, the Puritans willingly gave up freedoms that their compatriots sought. An ideology of rebellion in England, Puritanism in North America became an ideology of control. Much was at stake, for as Winthrop reminded the first settlers, "we shall be as a city upon a hill [and] the eyes of all people are upon us." That visionary sense of mission would help to shape a distinctive American self-image in future generations.

As in Plymouth and Virginia, the first winter tested the strongest souls. More than 200 of the first 700 settlers perished, and 100 others, disillusioned and sickened by the forbidding climate, returned to England the next spring. But Puritans kept coming. They "hived out" along the Back Bay of Boston, the port capital of

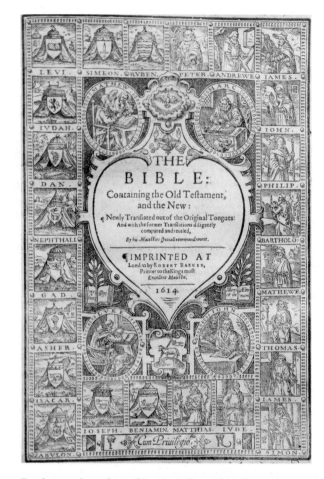

Fundamental to reformed Protestantism was each person having direct access to the Gospel. Literacy was therefore widespread in New England. London printers turned out thousands of Bibles in a variety of sizes and forms. John Winthrop carried this Bible across the Atlantic. The engraved title page shown here presents the emblems of the chiefs of the twelve tribes of Israel and the twelve apostles of Christ. *(Courtesy of the Massachusetts Historical Society)*

the colony, along the rivers that emptied into the bay, south into what became Connecticut and Rhode Island a few years later, and north along the rocky Massachusetts coast.

Motivated by their militant work ethic and sense of mission, and led by men experienced in local government, law, and exhortation, the Puritans thrived almost from the beginning. The early leaders of Virginia were soldiers of fortune or roughneck adventurers with predatory instincts, men who had no families or had left them at home. The ordinary Chesapeake settlers were mostly young men with little stake in English society who sold their labor to cross the Atlantic. But the early leaders in Massachusetts were university-trained ministers, experienced members of the lesser gentry, and men with a compulsion to fulfill God's prophecy for New England. Most ordinary settlers came as freemen in families. Trained artisans and farmers from the middle rank of English society, they established tight-knit communities in which, from the outset, the brutal exploitation of labor rampant in the Chesapeake had no place.

An Elusive Utopia

The Puritans built a sound economy based on agriculture, fishing, timbering, and trading for beaver furs with local Indians. Even before leaving England, the directors of the Massachusetts Bay Company transformed their commercial charter into a rudimentary government and transferred the charter to New England. There they laid the foundations of self-government. Free male church members annually elected a governor and deputies from each town, who formed one house of a colonial legislature, the General Court. The other house was composed of the governor's assistants, later to be called councillors. Consent of both houses was required to pass laws.

The Puritans also established the first printing press in the English colonies and planted the seed of a university, Harvard College, which opened its doors in 1636 to train clergymen. The Puritan leaders also launched a brave attempt in 1642 to create a tax-supported school system so that all children might gain the "ability to read and understand the principles of religion and the capital laws of this country." In 1647, the government ordered every town with 50 families to establish an elementary school and every town with 100 families a secondary school as well, open to all who wanted an education.

In spite of these accomplishments, the Puritan colony suffered many of the tensions besetting people bent on human perfection. Nor did Puritans prove any better than their less religious countrymen on the Chesapeake at reaching an accommodation with the Native Americans. Surrounded by seemingly boundless land, Puritans found it difficult to stifle acquisitive instincts and to keep families confined in compact communities. Restless souls looked to more distant valleys. "An over-eager desire after the world," wrote an early leader, "has so seized on the spirits of many as if the Lord had no farther work for his people to do, but every bird to feather his own nest." Those remaining at the nerve center in Boston agitated for broader political rights and even briefly ousted Winthrop as governor in 1635, when the colony's clergy backed the stiff-necked Thomas Dudley. After a few years, Governor Winthrop wondered if the Puritans had not gone "from the snare to the pit."

Winthrop's troubles multiplied in 1633 when Salem's Puritan minister, Roger Williams, began to voice disturbing opinions on church and government policies. Now the colony's leaders faced a contentious and visionary young man who argued that the Massachusetts Puritans were not truly pure because they would not completely separate from the polluted Church of England (which most Puritans still hoped to reform). Williams also denounced mandatory worship, which he said "stinks in God's nostrils," and argued that government officials should not interfere with religious matters but confine themselves to civil affairs. "Coerced religion," he warned, "on good days produces hypocrites, on bad days rivers of blood." Today honored as the earliest spokesman for the separation of church and state, Williams seemed in 1633 to strike at the heart of the Bible commonwealth, whose leaders regarded civil and religious affairs as inseparable. Williams also charged the Puritans with illegally intruding on Indian land.

Winthrop and others spent two years plying Williams alternately with sweet reason and threats, but they could not quiet the determined young man. Convinced that he would split the colony into competing religious groups and undermine authority, the magistrates vowed to deport him to England. Warned by Winthrop, Williams fled southward through winter snow with a small band of followers to found Providence, a settlement on Narragansett Bay in what would become Rhode Island.

Even as they were driving Williams out, the Puritan authorities confronted another threat: a magnetic woman of extraordinary talent and intellect. Anne Hutchinson was as devoted a Puritan as any who came to the colony. Arriving in 1634 with her husband and seven children, she gained great respect among Boston's women as a midwife, healer, and spiritual counselor. She soon began to discuss religion, suggesting that the "holy spirit" was absent in the preaching of some ministers. Before long Hutchinson was leading a movement labeled "antinomianism," an interpretation of Puritan doctrine that stressed the mystical nature of God's free gift of grace while discounting the efforts the individual could make to gain salvation.

By 1636, Boston was dividing into two camps—those who followed the male clergy and those who cleaved to the theological views of a gifted though untrained woman with no official standing. Her followers included most of the community's malcontents—merchants who chafed under the price controls the magistrates imposed in 1635, young people resisting the rigid rule of their elders, women disgruntled by male authority, and artisans who resented wage controls designed to arrest growing inflation. Hutchinson doubly offended the male leaders of the colony because she boldly stepped outside the subordinate position expected of women. "The weaker sex" set her up as a "priest" and "thronged" after her, wrote one male leader. Another described a "clamour"

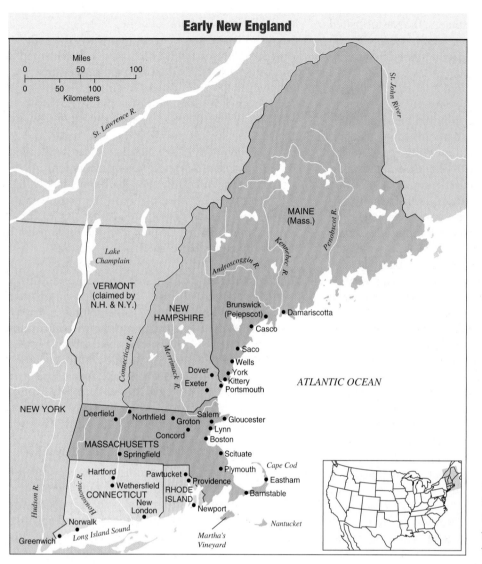

Early New England

Maine and New Hampshire became the frontier to which New England settlers migrated when their towns and farmlands became too crowded.

in Boston that "New England men . . . usurp over their wives and keep them in servile subjection."

Determined to remove this thorn from their sides, the clergy and magistrates put Hutchinson on trial in 1637. After two long interrogations, they convicted her of sedition and contempt in a civil trial and banished her from the colony "as a woman not fit for our society." Six months later, the Boston church excommunicated her for preaching 82 erroneous theological opinions. She had "highly transgressed and offended and troubled the church," intoned the presiding clergyman, and "therefore in the name of our Lord Jesus Christ, I do cast you out and deliver you up to Satan and account you from this time forth to be a heathen and a leper." In the last month of her eighth pregnancy, Hutchinson, with a band of supporters, followed Roger Williams's route to Rhode Island, the catch basin for Massachusetts Bay's dissidents.

Ideas proved harder to banish. The magistrates could never enforce uniformity of belief nor curb the appetite for land. Growth, geographic expansion, and commerce with the outside world all eroded the ideal of integrated, self-contained communities filled with piety. Leaders never wearied of reminding Puritan settlers that the "care of the public must oversway all private respects." But they faced the nearly impossible task of containing land-hungry immigrants in an expansive region. By 1636, groups of Puritans had swarmed not only to Rhode Island but also to Hartford and New Haven, where Thomas Hooker and John Davenport led new Puritan settlements in what became Connecticut.

New Englanders and Indians

The charter of the Massachusetts Bay Company proclaimed that the "principal end of this plantation" was

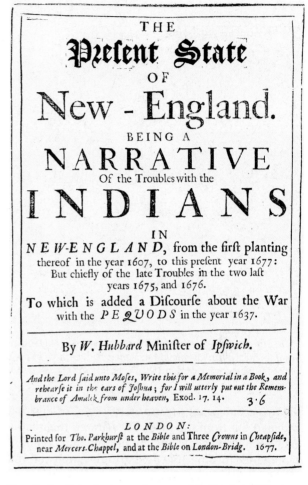

"to win and incite the natives to the knowledge and obedience of the only true God and Saviour of mankind and the Christian faith." But the instructions that Governor John Winthrop carried from England reveal other Puritan thoughts about the native inhabitants. According to Winthrop's orders, all men were to receive training in the use of firearms, a reversal of the sixteenth-century English policy of disarming the citizenry in order to quell public disorders. New England magistrates prohibited Indians from entering Puritan towns and threatened to deport any colonist selling arms to an Indian or instructing one in their use.

Only sporadic conflict with local tribes occurred at first because disease had catastrophically struck the Native Americans of New England, who may have numbered 125,000 in 1600, and left much of their land vacant. English fishermen, stopping along the coast in 1616, triggered a ferocious outbreak of respiratory viruses and smallpox that wiped out three-quarters of the population. Five years later, an Englishman exploring the area wrote that the Indians "died on heapes, as they lay in their houses" and described walking through a forest where human skeletons covered the ground.

When smallpox returned in 1633, killing thousands more natives, it again relieved pressure for land. The Puritans saw the disease as proof that God had intervened on their side, just when a flood of new settlers was causing trouble over rights to land. "Without this remarkable and terrible stroke of God upon the natives," reported the Charlestown settlers, "[we] would with much more difficulty have found room, and at far greater charge have obtained and purchased land." Many surviving Indians welcomed the Puritans because they now had surplus land and through trade hoped to gain English protection against tribal enemies to the north.

The settler pressure for new land, however, soon reached into areas untouched by disease. Land hunger mingled with the Puritan sense of mission made an explosive mix. To a people brimming with messianic zeal, the heathen Indians represented a mocking challenge to the building of a religious commonwealth that would "shine as a beacon" back to decadent England. A failure to convert the natives to civility and Christianity would have represented a failure by the Puritans to control the land to which God had directed them. God, they knew, would punish them with his wrath for this failure.

Making the "savages" of New England strictly accountable to the ordinances that governed white behavior was part of this quest for fulfilling their mission. The Puritans succeeded with the smaller, disease-ravaged tribes of eastern Massachusetts. But

New England's leaders were always troubled by their difficult relations with the native inhabitants of the region. Histories of these tensions, like this one published in Boston and London in 1677, often appeared after Indian wars and usually defended the colonists' actions. (*The New York Public Library*)

their attempts to control the stronger Pequots led to the bloody war in 1637 in which John Mason was a leader. The Puritan victory in that war assured English domination over all the tribes of southern New England except the powerful Wampanoags and Narragansetts of Rhode Island and removed the last obstacle to expansion into the Connecticut River valley. Missionary work, led by John Eliot, began among the remnant tribes in the 1640s. After a decade of effort, about 1,000 Indians had been settled in four "praying villages," learning to live according to the white man's ways.

The Web of Village Life

The village was the vital center of Puritan life. Unlike the Chesapeake tobacco planters, who dispersed along the streams and rivers of their area, the Puritans established small, tightly settled villages. Most pursued "open field" agriculture, trudging out from the

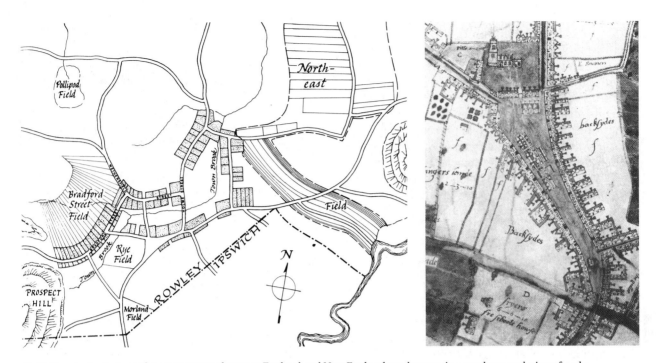

(Left) The similarity in settlement patterns between England and New England can be seen in a modern rendering of early seventeenth-century Rowley, Massachusetts (*Reprinted by permission of David Grayson Allen, ©1981. All rights reserved*), and (right) a plan of Chelmsford, Essex, in 1591 (*Essex Record Office, Essex, England*).

village each morning to farm narrow strips of land that radiated out from the town. They grazed their cattle on common meadow and cut firewood on common woodland. In other towns, Puritans employed the "closed field" system of self-contained farms that they had known at home. Both systems re-created agricultural life in many parts of England.

In either system, families lived close together in compact towns built around a common, with its meetinghouse and tavern. These small, communal villages kept families in close touch so that each could be alert not only to its own transgressions, but also to those of its neighbors. "In a multitude of counsellors is safety," Puritan ministers were fond of advising, and the little villages of 50 to 100 families perfectly served the need for moral surveillance, or "holy watching." To achieve godliness and communal unity, Puritans also prohibited single men and women from living by themselves, beyond patriarchal authority and group observation. Left to themselves, men and women would stray from the path, for, as Thomas Hooker put it, "every natural man and woman is born full of sin, as full as a toad of poison." Virginia planters counted the absence of restraint as a blessing. New Englanders feared it as the Devil.

At the center of every Puritan village stood the meetinghouse. These plain wooden structures, sometimes called "Lord's barns," gathered in every soul in the village, not just once but twice a week—on the Lord's day and during midweek as well. No man stood higher in the community than the minister. He was the spiritual leader in these small, family-based, community-oriented settlements, which viewed life as a Christian pilgrimage.

The unique Puritan mixture of strict authority and incipient democracy, of hierarchy and equality, can be seen in the way the Massachusetts town distributed land and devised local government. Each town was founded by a grant of the colony's General Court, sitting in Boston. Only groups of Puritans who had signed a compact signifying their unity of purpose received settlement grants. "We shall by all means," read the town of Dedham's covenant, "labor to keep off from us such as are contrary minded, and receive only such unto us as may be probably of one heart with us."

After receiving a grant, townsmen met to parcel out land. They awarded individual grants according to the size of a man's household, his wealth, and his usefulness to the church and town. Such a system perpetuated existing differences in wealth and status. Yet some towns wrote language into their covenants that to the modern ear has an almost socialistic ring. "From each according to his ability to each as need shall require," read one. It was not socialism that the Puritans had in mind. Rather, they believed that the community's welfare transcended individual ambitions or accomplishments and that unity demanded limits on the accumulation of wealth. Every family should have enough land to sustain it, and prospering men were expected to use their wealth for the community's benefit, not for conspicuous consumption. Repairing the meetinghouse, building a school, aiding a widowed neighbor—such were the proper uses of wealth.

Having felt the sting of centralized power in church and state, Puritans emphasized local exercise of authority. Until 1684, only male church members could vote, and as the proportion of males who were church members declined, so did the proportion of men who could vote. These voters elected selectmen, who allocated land, passed local taxes, and settled disputes. Once a year, all townsmen gathered for the town meeting, called later by Thomas Jefferson the "wisest invention ever devised by the wit of man for the perfect exercise of self-government." At the town meeting, the citizens selected town officers for the next year and decided matters large and small: Should the playing of football in the streets be prohibited? Might Widow Thomas be allowed £10 for a kidney stone operation for her son? What salary should the schoolteacher be paid?

The appointment of many citizens to minor offices—surveyors of hemp, informers about deer, purchasers of grain, town criers, measurers of salt, fence viewers, and many others—bred the tradition of local government. Complaints about officialdom rarely grew into political bitterness in such a system. All officeholders were annually subject to electoral approval, and about one out of every ten adult males in many towns was selected each year for some office, large or small. In New England, nobody could acquire a reputation for sobriety and industry without finding himself elected to a local post.

The predominance of families also lent cohesiveness to Puritan village life. Strengthening this family orientation was the remarkably healthy environment of the Puritans' "New Israel." Whereas the germs carried by English colonizers devastated neighboring Indian societies, the effect on the newcomers of entering a new environment was the opposite. The low density of settlement prevented infectious diseases from spreading, and the isolation of the New England villages from the avenues of Atlantic commerce, along which diseases as well as cargo flowed, minimized biological hazards.

The result was a spectacular natural increase in the population and a life span unknown in Europe. At a time when the population of western Europe was barely growing—deaths almost equaled births—the population of New England, discounting new immigrants, doubled every 27 years. The difference was not due to a higher birthrate. New England women typically bore about seven children during the course of a marriage, but this barely exceeded the European

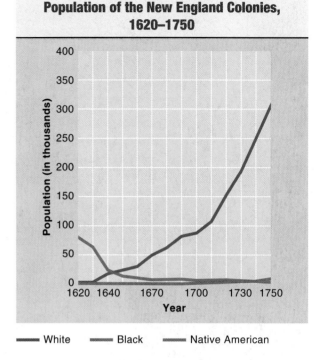

Population of the New England Colonies, 1620–1750

White — Black — Native American

The far more rapid white population growth in New England than in the Chesapeake region reflected higher birthrates, a healthier environment, and a reliance on free labor. Source: U.S. Bureau of the Census.

norm. The crucial factor was that chances for survival after birth were far greater than in England because of the healthier climate and better diet. In most of Europe, only half the babies born lived long enough to produce children themselves. Life expectancy for the population at large was less than 40 years. In New England, nearly 90 percent of the infants born in the seventeenth century survived to marriageable age, and life expectancy exceeded 60 years—longer than for the American population as a whole at any time until the early twentieth century. About 25,000 people immigrated to New England in the seventeenth century, but by 1700, they had produced a population of 100,000. By contrast, some 75,000 immigrants to the Chesapeake colonies had yielded a population of only about 70,000 by the end of the century.

Women played a vital role in this family-centered society. The Puritan woman was not only wife, mother, and housekeeper; she also kept the vegetable garden; salted and smoked meats; preserved vegetables and dairy products; and spun yarn, wove cloth, and made clothes.

The presence of women and a stable family life strongly affected New England's regional architecture. As communities formed, the Puritans converted early economic gains into more substantial housing rather than investing in bound labor as Chesapeake colonists

Three of Arthur and Joanna Mason's five children were captured in this 1670 painting. The nine-year-old boy on the left holds a silver-headed walking stick, signifying his status as male heir. His six-year-old sister in the middle holds a yellow fan and red and yellow ribbons. The four-year-old sister to the right holds a rose, which Puritans used as a symbol of innocence associated with childhood. (*Fine Arts Museum of San Francisco, Gift of Mr. and Mrs. John Rockefeller 3rd, 1979 .7.3*)

did, retarding family formation and rendering the economy unstable. In New England, well-constructed one-room houses with sleeping lofts quickly replaced the early "wigwams, huts, and hovels." Families then added parlors and lean-to kitchens as soon as they could. Within a half century, New England immigrants accomplished a general rebuilding of their living structures, whereas the Chesapeake lagged far behind.

A final binding element in Puritan communities was the stress on literacy and education, eventually to become a hallmark of American society. Placing religion at the center of their lives, Puritans emphasized the ability to read catechisms, psalmbooks, and especially the Bible. Literacy could instill the basic precepts of life. "Thy life to mend, this book attend" went one verse in a children's schoolbook. In literacy, Puritans saw guarantees that they would not succumb to the savagery they perceived all around them in the new land. Through education, they could preserve the central values of their struggle to redeem humankind in the North American wilderness.

An event in England in 1642 affected the future development of the New England colonies. King Charles I pushed his people into revolution by violating the country's customary constitution and continuing earlier attacks against Puritans. By 1649, the ensuing civil war climaxed with the trial and behead-

ing of the king. Thereafter, during the so-called Commonwealth period (1649–1660), Puritans in England could complete the reform of religion and society at home. Meanwhile, migration to New England abruptly ceased.

The 20,000 English immigrants who had come to New England by 1649 were scattered from Maine to Long Island. Governor Winthrop of Massachusetts lamented the dispersion, and Roger Williams condemned the "depraved appetite" for new and better land. Yet, in a terrain so rock-strewn that its pastures were said to produce Yankee sheep with sharpened noses, it was natural that farmers should seek better plow land.

To combat the problems of dispersion, Puritan leaders established a broad intercolony political structure in 1643 called the Confederation of New England. Designed to coordinate government among the various Puritan settlements (Rhode Island was pointedly excluded) and especially to provide greater defense against the French, the Dutch, and the Indians, the pact bound together Massachusetts, Plymouth, the small colony of New Haven, and the river towns of Connecticut. This first American attempt at federalism managed to function fitfully for a generation, though Massachusetts, the strongest and largest member, often refused to abide by group decisions when they ran counter to its objectives.

Although the Puritans fashioned stable communities, developed the economy, and constructed effective government, their leaders, as early as the 1640s, complained that the founding vision of Massachusetts Bay was faltering. Material concerns seemed to transcend religious commitment; the individual prevailed over the community. In 1638, the General Court declared a day of humiliation and prayer to atone for the colony's "excess idleness and contempt of authority." A generation later, the synod of 1679—a convention of Puritan Churches—cried out that the "church, the commonwealth and the family are being destroyed by self-assertion." By this time, Puritans rarely mentioned the work of salvaging English Protestantism by example. Instead, they concentrated on keeping their children on the straight and narrow road.

But despite such complaints about moral laxness, New England had achieved economic success and political stability by the end of the seventeenth century. Towns functioned efficiently, poverty was uncommon, public education had been mandated, and family life was stable. If social diversity increased and the religious zeal of the founding generation waned, that was only to be expected. One second-generation Bay colonist put the matter bluntly. His minister had noticed his absence in church and found him late that day at the docks, unloading a boatload of cod. "Why were you not in church this morning?" asked the clergyman. Back came the reply: "My father came here for religion, but I came for fish."

⤳ FROM THE ST. LAWRENCE TO THE HUDSON

The New Englanders were not the only European settlers in the northern region, for both France and Holland created colonies there. While English settlers founded Jamestown, the French were settling Canada, where they had failed in the 1540s.

France's America

Henry IV, the first strong French king in half a century, sent Samuel de Champlain to explore deep into the territory even before the English had obtained a foothold on the Chesapeake. Champlain established a small settlement in Port Royal, Acadia (later Nova Scotia), in 1604 and another at Quebec, in 1608. Already established French fish-drying stations in Newfoundland had initiated trading with Indians for furs, and Champlain's settlers hoped for easy profits on beaver. But the holders of the fur monopoly in France did not encourage immigration to the colony, because settlement would reduce the forests from which the furs were harvested. New France therefore

remained so lightly populated that English marauders easily seized and held Quebec from 1629 to 1632.

In 1609–1610, Champlain allied with the Algonquian Indians of the St. Lawrence region in attacking their Iroquois enemies to the south, earning their eternal enmity. This drove the Iroquois to trade furs for European goods with the Dutch on the Hudson River, and when the Iroquois exhausted the furs of their own territory, they turned north and west, determined to seize the forest-rich resources from the Hurons, French allies in the Great Lakes region.

When the fury of the Iroquois descended on them in the 1640s, the Hurons were a people already decimated by a decade of epidemics that had spread among them as they accepted Jesuit priests in their villages. In the "beaver wars" of the 1640s and 1650s, the Iroquois used Dutch guns to attack Huron parties carrying beaver pelts to the French. By mid-century, Iroquois attacks had scattered the Hurons, all but ending the French fur trade and reducing the Jesuit influence to a few villages of Christianized Hurons.

The bitterness bred in these years colored future colonial warfare, driving the Iroquois to ally with the English against the French. But for the time being, in the mid-seventeenth century, the English remained unhindered by the beleaguered French colonists, who numbered only about 400.

England Challenges the Mighty Dutch

By 1660, the Chesapeake and New England regions each contained about 30,000 settlers. Between them lay the mid-Atlantic area controlled by the Dutch, who had planted a small colony named New Netherland at the mouth of the Hudson River in 1624 and in the next four decades had extended their control to the Connecticut and Delaware river valleys. South of the Chesapeake lay a vast territory where only the Spanish, on their mission frontier in Florida, challenged the power of Native American tribes.

These two areas, north and south of the Chesapeake, became strategic zones of English colonizing activity after the end of England's civil war in 1660 brought the restoration of the English monarchy. Commercial rival of the Dutch and religious and economic enemy of the Spanish, England moved to cement its claims on the North American coast.

Although for generations they had been the Protestant bulwarks in a mostly Catholic Europe, England and Holland became bitter commercial rivals in the mid-seventeenth century. By the time the Puritans arrived in New England, the Dutch had become the mightiest carriers of seaborne commerce in western Europe. By one contemporary estimate, Holland owned 16,000 of Europe's 20,000 merchant ships. The Dutch had also muscled in on Spanish and

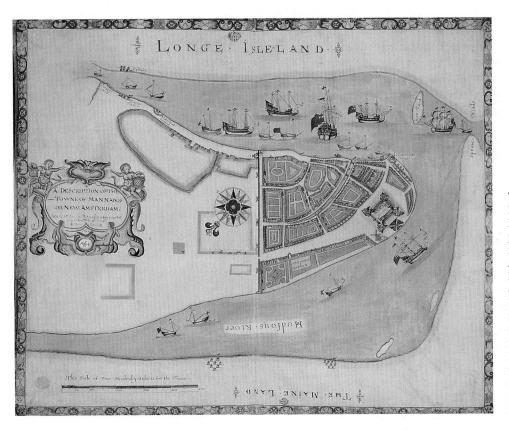

The fort at the tip of Manhattan, flying an English flag, shows prominently in this 1664 map of Dutch New Amsterdam just after it had been bloodlessly conquered by a small English fleet. The park-filled city and the Governor's garden fronting on the Hudson River were separated by a wall from the farmlands of "upper" Manhattan. (*By Permission of the British Library*)

Portuguese transatlantic commerce, trading illegally with Iberian colonists who gladly violated their government's commercial policies to obtain cloth and slaves more cheaply.

By 1650, the Dutch had temporarily overwhelmed the Portuguese in Brazil, and soon their vast trading empire reached the East Indies, Ceylon, India, and Formosa. The best shipbuilders, mariners, and businessmen in western Europe, they validated the dictum of Sir Walter Raleigh that "whosoever commands the sea commands the trade; whosoever commands the trade of the world commands the riches of the world, and consequently the world itself."

In North America, the Dutch West India Company's New Netherland colony was small but profitable. Agents fanned out from Fort Orange (Albany) and New Amsterdam (New York City) into the Hudson, Connecticut, and Delaware river valleys. There they established a lucrative fur trade with local tribes by hooking into the sophisticated trading network of the Iroquois Confederacy, which stretched to the Great Lakes. The Iroquois welcomed the Dutch presence. The newcomers were few in number, they did not have voracious appetites for land, and they were willing to exchange desirable goods for the pelts of animals that were abundant in the vast Iroquois territory. At Albany, the center of the Dutch–Iroquois trade,

relations remained peaceful and profitable for several generations because both peoples admirably served each other's needs.

Although the Dutch never settled more than 10,000 people in their mid-Atlantic colonies, their commercial and naval powers were impressive. The Virginians learned as much in 1667 when brazen Dutch raiders captured 20 tobacco ships on the James River and confiscated virtually the entire tobacco crop for that year.

By 1650, England was ready to challenge Dutch maritime supremacy. Three times between 1652 and 1675, war broke out between the two Protestant competitors for control of the emerging worldwide capitalist economy. In the second and third wars, the Dutch colony on the Hudson River became an easy target for the English. They captured it in 1664 and then, after it fell to the Dutch in 1673, recaptured it almost immediately. By 1675, the Dutch had been permanently dislodged from the North American mainland. But they remained mighty commercial competitors of the English around the world.

New Netherland—where from the beginning Dutch, French Huguenots, Walloons from present-day Belgium, Swedes, Portuguese, Finns, English, refugee Portuguese Jews from Brazil, and Africans had commingled in a babel of languages and religions—now

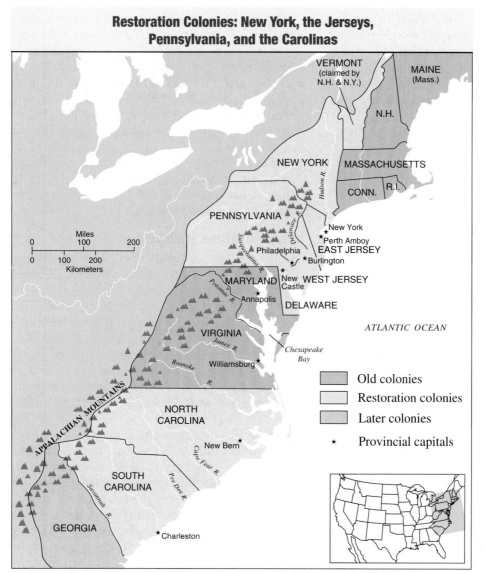

Restoration Colonies: New York, the Jerseys, Pennsylvania, and the Carolinas

Old colonies
Restoration colonies
Later colonies
★   Provincial capitals

After founding the Restoration colonies from the 1660s to the 1680s, England's colonists claimed the entire seaboard between Spanish Florida and French Canada.

became New York. It was so named because Charles II made a proprietary grant of the territory, along with the former Dutch colonies on the Delaware River, to James, duke of York, his brother and heir to the English throne.

Under English rule, the Dutch colonists remained ethnically distinct for several generations, clinging to their language, their Dutch Reformed Calvinist churches, and their architecture. In time, however, English immigrants overwhelmed the Dutch, and gradual intermarriage among the Dutch, French Huguenots (Protestants), and the English—the three main groups—diluted ethnic loyalties. But New York retained its polyglot, religiously tolerant character, and its people never allowed religious concerns or utopian plans to interfere with the pragmatic conduct of business.

⌖ PROPRIETARY CAROLINA: A RESTORATION REWARD

In 1663, three years after he was restored to his father's throne, England's Charles II granted a vast territory named Carolina to a group of supporters during his years of exile. Its boundaries extended from Virginia southward to central Florida and westward to the Pacific. Within this potential empire, eight proprietors, including several involved in Barbados sugar plantations, gained large powers of government and semifeudal rights to the land. For settling their royal reward, they constructed a system of government with both feudal and modern features. To lure settlers, they promised religious freedom and offered land free for the asking. But onto this generous land offer they grafted plans for a semimedieval government in which they, their deputies, and a few noblemen would monopolize political power. Reacting to a generation of violence and radical social experiments during the English civil war (1642–1649), they designed Carolina as a model of social and political stability in which a hereditary aristocracy would check boisterous small landholders.

Carolina realities bore faint resemblance to these hopes. The rugged sugar and tobacco planters who streamed in from Barbados and Virginia, where depressed economic conditions made a new beginning in Carolina seem attractive, claimed their 150 acres of free land (and additional acreage for each family member or servant they brought). But they ignored proprietary regulations about settling in compact rectangular patterns and reserving two-fifths of every county for an appointed nobility. In government, they also did as they pleased. Meeting in assembly for the first time in 1670, they refused to accept the proprietors' Fundamental Constitutions of 1667 and ignored the orders of the governor appointed in London. Most of the settlers already knew how to run a slave society from having lived in Barbados, and from that experience they shaped local government.

The Indian Debacle

Carolina was the most elaborately planned colony in English history but the least successful in achieving amicable relations with the natives. The proprietors in London had intended otherwise. Mindful of the violence that had plagued other settlements, they projected a well-regulated Indian trade run exclusively by their appointed agents. But the aggressive settlers from the West Indies and the Chesapeake flouted all this. Those from Barbados, accustomed to exploiting African slave labor, saw that if the major tribes of the Southeast—the Cherokee, Creek, and Choctaw—could be drawn into trade, the planters might reap vast wealth. The Spanish in Florida had done little to tap this potential gold mine; their main goal was to protect their territorial claim by establishing missions that gathered local Indians into a sedentary, agricultural life.

It was not the beaver that beckoned in the Indian trade, as in the North, but the deerskin, much desired in Europe for making warm and durable clothing. In the villages of the southeastern tribes, where natives farmed as well as hunted, the Carolina colonies found a people eager to obtain European trade goods. But what began as a trade for the skins of deer soon became a trade for the skins of Indians. To the consternation of the London proprietors, capturing Indians for sale in New England and the West Indies became the cornerstone of commerce in Carolina in the early years.

The Indian slave trade plunged Carolina into a series of wars. Planters and merchants selected a tribe, armed it, and rewarded it handsomely for bringing in enemy captives. Even strong tribes that allied for trade with the Carolinians found that after they had used English guns to enslave their weaker neighbors, they themselves were sometimes scheduled for elimination. The colonists claimed that "thinning the barbarous Indian natives" was necessary to make room for white settlement. The "thinning" was so thorough that by the early eighteenth century the two main tribes of the coastal plain, the Westos and the Savannahs, were nearly extinct.

Early Carolina Society

Carolina's fertile land and warm climate convinced many that it was a "Country so delicious, pleasant, and fruitful that were it cultivated doubtless it would prove a second Paradize." In came Barbadians, Swiss, Scots, Irish, French Huguenots, English, and even migrants from New England, New York, and New Jersey. But far from creating paradise, this ethnically and religiously diverse people clashed abrasively in an atmosphere of fierce competition, ecological exploitation, brutal race relations, and stunted social institutions.

For the land-hungry white cattle raisers and rice growers of coastal South Carolina, the Indian slave trade had no direct benefits, because the profits flowed entirely to the merchants of Charleston, the main port and seat of government. They reaped important secondary advantages, however. As the Indian population of the coastal region fell sharply, expansion from the initial settlements around Charleston became easier. Along the twisting rivers that flowed to the coast, planters staked out claims and experimented with a variety of exotic crops, including sugar, indigo, tropical fruits, tobacco, and rice. After much experimentation, planters found that rice was the staple crop on which a flourishing economy could be built.

Rice cultivation required backbreaking labor to drain the swampy lowlands, build dams and levees, and hoe, weed, cut, thresh, and husk the crop. Many early settlers had owned African slaves in Barbados, so their early reliance on slave labor came naturally. On widely dispersed plantations, black labor came to predominate. In 1680, four-fifths of South Carolina's population was white. But by 1720, when the colony had grown to 18,000, black slaves outnumbered whites two to one.

As in Virginia and Maryland, the low-lying areas of coastal Carolina were so disease-ridden that population grew only slowly in the early years. "In the spring a paradise, in the summer a hell, and in the autumn a

This painting of Mulberry Plantation in South Carolina shows the mansion house, built in 1708, and rows of slave huts constructed in an African style. Most enslaved Africans lived in far more primitive structures in the eighteenth century. (*Gibbes Museum/Carolina Art Association*)

hospital," remarked one traveler. Malaria and yellow fever, especially dangerous to pregnant women, were the main killers that retarded population growth, and the scarcity of women further limited natural increase. Like the West Indies, the rice-growing region of Carolina was at first more a place to accumulate a fortune than to rear a family.

In healthier northern Carolina, a different kind of society emerged amid pine barrens along a sandy coast. Settled largely by small tobacco farmers from Virginia seeking free land, the Albemarle region developed a mixed economy of livestock grazing, tobacco and food production, and the extraction of naval stores—lumber, turpentine, resin, pitch, and tar. Slavery took root only slowly in North Carolina, which was still 85 percent white in 1720. A land of struggling white settlers (called "Lubberland" by one prosperous Virginia planter), its healthier climate and settlement by families rather than by single men with servants and slaves gave it a greater potential for sustained growth.

In 1701, North and South Carolina became separate colonies, their distinctiveness having already divided them. But in North as well as South Carolina, several factors inhibited the growth of a strong corporate identity: the pattern of settlement, ethnic and religious diversity, and a lack of shared assumptions about social and religious goals.

THE QUAKERS' PEACEABLE KINGDOM

Of all the utopian dreams imposed on the North American landscape in the seventeenth century, the most remarkable was the Quakers'. During the English civil war, the Society of Friends, as the Quakers called

themselves, had sprung up as one of the many radical sects searching for a juster society and a purer religion. Their visionary ideas and defiance of civil authority cost them dearly in fines, brutal punishment, and imprisonment. After Charles II and Parliament stifled radical dissent in the 1660s, they, too, sent many converts across the Atlantic. The society they founded in Pennsylvania foreshadowed more than any other colony the future religious and ethnic pluralism of the United States.

The Early Friends

Like Puritans, the Quakers regarded the Church of England as corrupt and renounced its formalities and rituals, which smacked of Catholicism. They also foreswore all Church officials and institutions, persuaded that every believer could find grace through the "inward light," a redemptive spark in every human soul. Rejecting original sin and eternal predestination, Quakers offered a radical alternative to the reigning Calvinist doctrine.

Quakers were persecuted in England after their movement, led by George Fox and Margaret Fell, gathered momentum in the 1650s. Other Protestants regarded them as dangerous fanatics, for the Quakers' egalitarian doctrine of the "light within" took precedence even over scripture and elevated all lay people to the position of the clergy.

Garbing themselves in plain black cloth and practicing civil disobedience, the Quakers also threatened social hierarchy and order. They refused to observe the customary marks of deference, such as doffing one's hat to a superior, believing that God made no social distinctions. They used the familiar "thee" and "thou" instead of the formal and deferential "you," they resisted taxes supporting the Church of England,

and they refused to sign witnesses' oaths on the Bible, regarding this as profane. Most shocking, they renounced the use of force in human affairs and therefore refused to perform militia service.

Quakers also affronted traditional views when they insisted on the spiritual equality of the sexes and the right of women to participate in church matters on an equal, if usually separate, footing with men. Quaker leaders urged women to preach and to establish separate women's meetings. Among Quakers who fanned out from England to preach the doctrine of the inward light, 26 of the first 59 to cross the Atlantic were women. All but four of them were unmarried or without their husbands and therefore living, traveling, and ministering outside the bounds of male authority.

Intensely committed to converting the world, Quakers ranged westward to North America and the Caribbean in the 1650s and 1660s. Nearly everywhere, they were reviled, mutilated, imprisoned, and deported. Puritan Massachusetts warned them that their liberty in that colony consisted of "free liberty to keep away from us and such as will come to be gone as fast as they can, the sooner the better." Hungering to serve in what they called "the Lamb's War" (the crusade of the meek), the Quakers vowed to test the Puritans' resolve and kept coming.

The Bay Colony magistrates were desperate to eliminate this dangerous threat to religious conformity and civil authority. Finally, in 1659, they hanged two Quaker men on the Boston Common and threatened to hang Mary Dyer, an old woman who had followed Anne Hutchinson a quarter century before. Escorted from the colony, she returned the next year, undaunted, to meet her death at the end of a rope.

Early Quaker Designs

By the 1670s, the English Quakers were looking for a place in the New World to carry out their millennial dreams. In England, royal fears of a Catholic conspiracy led to severe religious repression of all dissenting groups in the late 1670s. Thousands of Quakers were jailed and fined heavily for practicing their faith.

Emerging as their leader in this dark period was William Penn, the son of Admiral Sir William Penn, who by capturing Jamaica from the Spanish in 1654 had placed in English hands one of the most productive sugar-growing sites in the world. Young William had been groomed for life in the English aristocracy, but he rebelled against his parents' designs for him in one of the professions. At age 23, he was converted by a spellbinding speech about the power of the Quaker inward light. After joining the Society of Friends in 1666, Penn devoted himself to their cause.

In 1674, Penn joined other Friends in establishing their own colony, on former Dutch territory, between the Hudson and Delaware rivers. They purchased the land, known as West Jersey, from Lord John Berkeley. Penn now helped fashion a constitution, extraordinarily liberal for its time, that allowed virtually all free males to vote annually for legislators and local officials. Settlers were guaranteed freedom of religion and trial by jury. As Penn and the other trustees of the colony explained, "We lay a foundation for [later] ages to understand their liberty as men and Christians, that they may not be brought in bondage, but by their own consent; for we put the power in the people."

The last phrase, summing up the document, would have shocked anyone of property and power in England or America at the time. Most regarded "the people" as ignorant, dangerous, and certain to bring society to a state of anarchy if entrusted with the right to rule themselves. Nowhere in the English world had ordinary citizens, especially those who owned no land, enjoyed such extensive privileges. Nowhere had a popularly elected legislature received such broad authority.

Despite these idealistic plans, West Jersey sputtered at first. Only 1,500 immigrants arrived in the first five years, and the colony for several decades was caught up in legal complications caused by the tangled claims to the land and government. The center of Quaker hopes lay across the Delaware River, where in 1681, Charles II granted William Penn a territory almost as large as England itself. The grant extinguished a large royal debt to Penn's father, but the crown also benefited by getting the pesky Quakers out of England. To the Quakers' great fortune, the territory granted to Penn, the last unassigned segment of the eastern coast of North America, was also one of the most fertile.

Pacifism in a Militant World: Quakers and Indians

On the day Penn received his royal charter for Pennsylvania, he wrote a friend, "My God that has given it to me will, I believe, bless and make it the seed of a nation." The nation that Penn envisioned was unique among colonizing schemes. Penn intended to make his colony an asylum for the persecuted, a refuge from arbitrary state power. Puritans had striven for social homogeneity and religious uniformity, excluding all not of like mind. In the Chesapeake and Carolina colonies, aggressive, nonidealistic men sought to exploit the region's resources and bondspeople. But Penn dreamed of inviting to his forested colony people of all religions and national backgrounds and blending them together in peaceful coexistence. His state would claim no authority over the consciences of its citizens nor demand military service of them.

The Quakers who began streaming into Pennsylvania in 1682 quickly absorbed earlier Dutch,

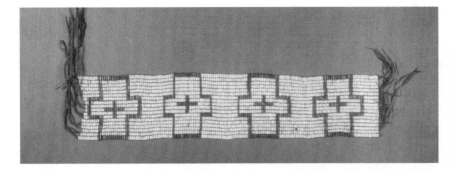

Just as a deed finalized a land exchange to Europeans, the wampum belt signified an agreement to the Indians. This Lenape belt, made of leather and simple shell beads, is said to have been given to William Penn at the signing of the Treaty of Shackamaxon in 1682. (*National Museum of the American Indian, New York*)

Finnish, and Swedish settlers. They participated in the government by electing representatives who initiated laws. They were primarily farmers, and like colonists elsewhere they avidly acquired land, which Penn sold at reasonable rates. But unlike other colonizers, the Quakers practiced pacifism, holding the ethic of love and nonresistance embodied in the Sermon on the Mount as literally binding on them.

Even before arriving, Penn laid the foundation for peaceful relations with the Delaware tribe inhabiting his colony. "The king of the Country where I live, hath given me a great Province," he wrote to the Delaware chiefs, "but I desire to enjoy it with your Love and Consent, that we may always live together as Neighbors and friends." In this single statement Penn dissociated himself from the entire history of European colonization in the New World and from the widely held negative view of Indians. Recognizing the Indians as the rightful owners of the land included in his grant, Penn pledged not to sell one acre until he had first purchased it from local chiefs. He also promised strict regulation of the Indian trade and a ban on the sale of alcohol.

The Quaker accomplishment is sometimes disparaged with the claim that there was little competition for land in eastern Pennsylvania between the natives and the newcomers. However, a comparison between Pennsylvania and South Carolina, both established after the restoration of Charles II to the English throne in 1660, shows the power of pacifism. A quarter century after initial settlement, Pennsylvania had a population of about 20,000 whites. Penn's peaceful policy had so impressed Native American tribes that Indian refugees began migrating into Pennsylvania from all sides. During the same 25 years, South Carolina had grown to only about 4,000 whites, while becoming a cauldron of violence. Carolinians spread arms through the region to facilitate slave dealing, shipped some 10,000 members of local tribes off to New England and the West Indies as slaves, and laid waste to the Spanish mission frontier in Florida.

As long as the Quaker philosophy of pacifism and friendly relations with the Delawares and Susquehannocks held sway, interracial relations in the Delaware River valley contrasted sharply with those in other parts of North America. But ironically, the Quaker policy of toleration, liberal government, and exemption from military service attracted to the colony, especially in the eighteenth century, thousands of immigrants whose land hunger and disdain for Indians undermined Quaker trust and friendship. Germans and Scots-Irish flooded in, swelling the population to 31,000 by 1720. Neither shared Quaker idealism about racial harmony. Driven from their homelands by hunger and war, they pressed inland and, sometimes encouraged by the land agents of Penn's heirs, encroached on the lands of the local tribes. This created conflict with the natives who had sought sanctuary in Pennsylvania. By the mid-eighteenth century, a confrontation of displaced people, some red and some white, was occurring in Pennsylvania.

Building the Peaceable Kingdom

Although Pennsylvania came closer to matching its founder's goals than any other European colony, Penn's dreams never completely materialized. Nor could he convince people to settle in compact villages, which he believed necessary for his "holy experiment." The plain Quaker farmers scattered across the countryside and built simple farmsteads. Instead of agricultural villages with meetinghouses at their centers, as in New England, they created open country networks without any particular centers or boundaries. Yet a sense of common endeavor persisted.

Quaker farmers prized family life and emigrated almost entirely in kinship groups. This helped them maintain their distinctive identity. So did other practices such as allowing marriage only within their society, carefully providing land for their offspring, and guarding against too great a population increase (which would cause too rapid a division of farms) by limiting the size of their families.

Settled by religiously dedicated farming families and favored by rich grainlands, Pennsylvania's countryside blossomed. The colony's port capital of Philadelphia also grew rapidly. By 1700, it overtook

Edward Hicks painted *Penn's Treaty with the Indians* in the nineteenth century. It is a romanticized version of the Treaty of Shackamaxon by which the Lenape chiefs ceded the site of Philadelphia to Penn. The treaty was actually made in 1682, but Hicks was correct in implying that the Lenape held Penn in high regard for his fair treatment of them. (*Hicks, Edward,* Penn's Treaty with the Indians, *Gift of Edgar William and Bernice Chrysler Garbisch, ©2000 Board of Trustees, National Gallery of Art, Washington, c. 1840/1844, canvas, .617 x .765 [24¼ x 30⅛])*

New York City in population, and a half century later it was the largest city in the colonies, bustling with a wide range of artisans, merchants, and professionals.

The Limits of Perfectionism

Despite commercial success and peace with Native Americans, not all was harmonious in early Pennsylvania. Politics were often turbulent, in part because of Pennsylvania's weak leadership. Penn was a much-loved proprietor, but he did not tarry long in his colony to guide its course. He returned to England in 1684, visited his colony briefly in 1700, and then left forever. The leadership vacuum he left was never filled.

A more important cause of disunity resided in the Quaker attitude toward authority. In England, balking at authority was almost a daily part of Quaker life. To be a Quaker was to refuse to bear arms, to disobey the law prohibiting nonconformists to hold religious services, to deny the Bible as revealed truth, to reject the traditional role assigned women, and to violate social custom obliging inferiors to defer to their superiors. But in Pennsylvania, the absence of persecution eliminated a crucial binding element. The factionalism that developed among them demonstrated that people never unify so well as when under attack. Rather than looking inward and banding together, they looked outward to an environment filled with opportunity. Their squabbling filled Penn with dismay.

Why, he asked, were his settlers so "governmentish, so brutish, so susceptible to scurvy quarrels that break out to the disgrace of the Province?"

Meanwhile, Quaker industriousness and frugality led to such material success that after a generation, social radicalism and religious evangelicalism began to fade. As in other colonies, settlers discovered the door to prosperity wide open, and in they surged.

Where Pennsylvania differed from New England and the South was in its relations with Native Americans, at least for the first few generations. It also departed from the Puritan colonies in its immigration policy. Pennsylvania, it is said, was the first community since the Roman Empire to allow people of different national origins and religious persuasions to live together under the same government on terms of near equality. English, Highland Scots, French, Germans, Irish, Welsh, Swedes, Finns, and Swiss all settled in Pennsylvania. This ethnic mosaic was further complicated by a medley of religious groups, including Mennonites, Lutherans, Dutch Reformed, Quakers, Baptists, Anglicans, Presbyterians, Catholics, Jews, and a sprinkling of mystics. Their relations may not always have been friendly, but few attempts were made to discriminate against dissenting groups. Pennsylvanians thereby laid the foundations for the pluralism that was to become the hallmark of American society.

☙ NEW SPAIN'S NORTHERN FRONTIER

Spain's outposts in Florida and New Mexico, preceding all English settlements on the eastern seaboard, fell into disarray between 1680 and the early eighteenth century just as the English colonies were sinking deep roots. Trying to secure a vast northern frontier with only small numbers of settlers, the Spanish relied on forced Indian labor. This reliance proved to be their undoing in Florida and New Mexico.

Popé's Revolt

During the 1670s, when the Franciscan priests developed a new zeal to root out traditional Indian religious ceremonies, the Pueblo people turned on the Spanish intruders. In years of harsh rule, the Spanish had extracted tribute labor from the Pueblo, who at the same time suffered the ravaging effects of European diseases. Both of these punishing long-term effects contributed to Pueblo alienation. But pushing the Pueblo to the edge was an assault on their religion. Launching a campaign to restrict native religious ceremonies in the 1670s, the Spanish friars began to seize the Pueblo kivas (underground ceremonial religious chambers), to forbid native dances, and to destroy priestly Indian masks and prayer sticks. In August 1680, led by Popé, a much-persecuted medicine man from San Juan pueblo, about two dozen Pueblo villages scattered over several hundred miles rose up in fury. They burned Spanish ranches and government buildings, systematically destroyed Spanish churches, lay waste to Spanish fields, and killed half of the friars. As the Spanish governor in Santa Fe watched the church go up in flames, he reported his shock at the "scoffing and ridicule which the wretched and miserable Indian rebels made of the sacred things, intoning . . . prayers of the church with jeers."

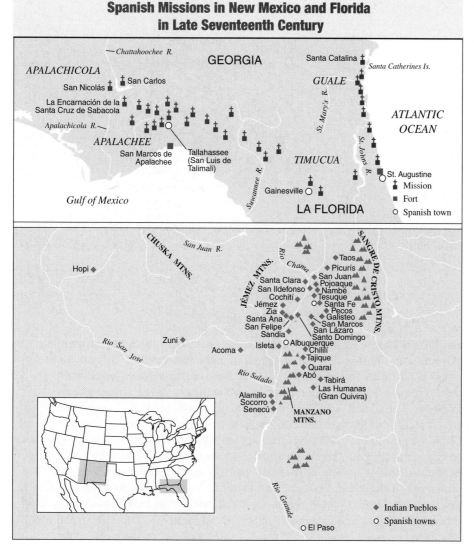

Spanish Missions in New Mexico and Florida in Late Seventeenth Century

The extensive Spanish missionary activity in Florida and New Mexico had no English parallel.

Spanish settlers, soldiers, and friars streamed back to El Paso, abandoning their northern frontier in the Southwest for more than a decade. Only in 1694 did a new Spanish governor, the intrepid Diego de Vargas, regain Santa Fe and gradually subdue most of the Pueblo. Learning from Popé's rebellion, the Spanish declared a kind of cultural truce, easing their demands for Pueblo labor tribute and tolerating certain Pueblo rituals in return for nominal acceptance of Christianity. Periodic tension and animosity continued, but the Pueblo had to come to terms with the Spanish because of their need for defense against their old enemies—the Navajo, Ute, and Apache.

Decline of Florida's Missions

The Franciscan missions in Florida were as severely pummeled as those in New Mexico in the late seventeenth and early eighteenth centuries. Rapidly settling in South Carolina, the English were eager to use Indian allies to attack the Spanish Indian villages and sell the captives into slavery. The resentment of missionized Indians, wearying under demands on their labor, further weakened the tenuous Spanish hold on them. The attacks of Carolinians in the early 1680s destroyed a number of Spanish missions. When England and Spain went to war in 1701—called Queen Anne's War in the colonies—the Carolinians attacked St. Augustine by land and sea. Burning mission villages to the ground, they slaughtered the Spanish friars and captured some 4,000 women and children to be sold as slaves. The Spanish mission frontier was thoroughly devastated, with only St. Augustine remaining as a Spanish stronghold. Unlike New Mexico, no Spanish reconquest of the territory occurred. From this time forward, English and French traders, with more attractive trade goods to offer, would have the main influence over Florida Indians.

Timeline

1590	Roanoke Island colony fails
1607	Jamestown settled
1616–1621	Native American population in New England decimated by European diseases
1617	First tobacco crop shipped from Virginia
1619	First Africans arrive in Jamestown
1620	Pilgrims land at Plymouth
1622	Powhatan tribes attack Virginia settlements
1624	Dutch colonize mouth of Hudson River
1630	Puritan immigration to Massachusetts Bay
1632	Maryland grant to Lord Baltimore (George Calvert)
1633–1634	Native Americans in New England again struck by European diseases
1635	Roger Williams banished and flees to Rhode Island
1636	Anne Hutchinson exiled to Rhode Island
1637	New England wages war against the Pequot people
1642–1649	English civil war ends great migration to New England
1643	Confederation of New England
1659–1661	Puritans hang two Quaker men and one Quaker woman on Boston Common
1660	Restoration of King Charles II in England
1663	Carolina charter granted to eight proprietors
1664	English capture New Netherland and rename it New York
	Royal grant of the Jersey lands to proprietors
1680	Popé's revolt in New Mexico
1681	William Penn receives Pennsylvania grant

Conclusion

The Achievement of New Societies

Nearly 200,000 immigrants who had left their European homelands reached the coast of North America in the seventeenth century. Coming from a variety of social backgrounds and spurred by different motives, they represented the rootstock of distinctive societies that would mature in the North American colonies of England, France, Holland, and Spain. For three generations, North America served as a social laboratory for religious and social visionaries, political theorists, fortune seekers, social outcasts, and, most of all, ordinary men and women seeking a better life than they had known in their European homelands.

Nearly three-quarters of them came to the Chesapeake and Carolina colonies. Most of them found this region a burial ground rather than an arena of opportunity. Disease, stunted family life, and the harsh work regimen imposed by the planters who commanded the labor of the vast majority ended the dreams of most who came. Yet population inched upward, and the bone and sinew of a workable economy formed. In the northern colonies, to which the fewest immigrants came, life was more secure. Organized around family and community, favored by a healthier climate, and motivated by religion and social vision, the Puritan and Quaker societies thrived. Utopian expectations were never completely fulfilled. But nowhere else in the

Western world at that time could they even have been attempted. What did succeed was the rooting of agricultural life based on family farms and the establishment of locally oriented political institutions marked by widespread participation. Thus, as the seventeenth century progressed, the scattered settlements along the North American coast, largely isolated from one another, as well as a few inland French and Spanish settlements, pursued their separate paths of development.

Recommended Reading

The Chesapeake Tobacco Coast

Philip D. Morgan and Jean Russo, eds., *Colonial Chesapeake Society* (1989); Edmund S. Morgan, *American Slavery, American Freedom: The Ordeal of Colonial Virginia* (1975); David B. Quinn, ed., *Early Maryland in a Wider World* (1982); Darrett B. Rutman and Anita H. Rutman, *A Place in Time: Middlesex County, Virginia, 1650–1750* (1984); Karen Kupperman, *Settling with the Indians: The Meeting of English and Indian Cultures in America, 1580–1640* (1980); Kathleen M. Brown, *Good Wives, Nasty Wenches, and Anxious Patriarchs: Gender, Race, and Power in Colonial Virginia* (1996); Alden Vaughan, *American Genesis: Captain John Smith and the Founding of Virginia* (1975).

Massachusetts and Its Offspring

Christopher Hill, *Society and Puritanism in Pre-Revolutionary England*, 2d ed. (1967); Perry Miller, *Errand into the Wilderness* (1956); David Cressy, *Coming Over: Migration and Communication Between England and New England in the Seventeenth Century* (1987); David D. Hall, *Worlds of Wonder, Days of Judgment: Popular Religious Belief in Early New England* (1989); John Demos, *A Little Commonwealth: Family Life in Plymouth Colony* (1970); Kenneth Lockridge, *A New England Town* (1970); Stephen Innes, *Labor in a New Land* (1983); Darrett B. Rutman, *Winthrop's Boston* (1965); Edmund S. Morgan, *The Puritan Dilemma: The Story of John Winthrop* (1958); Robert Middlekauff, *The Mathers* (1971); Roger Thompson, *Sex in Middlesex: Popular Mores in a Massachusetts County, 1649–1699* (1986); Stephen Innes, *Creating the Commonwealth: The Economic Culture of Puritan New England* (1995); Virginia D. Anderson, *New England's Generation: The Great Migration and the Formation of Society and Culture in the Seventeenth Century* (1991).

From the St. Lawrence to the Hudson

Robert C. Ritchie, *The Duke's Province: A Study of Politics and Society in Colonial New York, 1660–1691* (1977); Daniel K. Richter and James H. Merrell, eds., *Beyond the Covenant Chain: The Iroquois and Their Neighbors in Indian North America, 1600–1800* (1987); Joyce Goodfriend, *Before the Melting Pot: Society and Culture in Colonial New York City, 1664–1730* (1992); Daniel K. Richter, *The Ordeal of the Longhouse: The Peoples of the Iroquois League in the Era of European Colonization* (1992); Bruce G. Trigger, *Children of the Aataentsic: A History of the Huron People, 1600–1664* (1976); James Axtell, *The Invasion Within: The Contest of Cultures in Colonial North America* (1985).

Proprietary Carolina

M. Eugene Sirmans, *Colonial South Carolina* (1966); Verner Crane, *The Southern Frontier, 1670–1732* (1929); Robert M. Weir, *Colonial South Carolina* (1983); Richard Waterhouse, *A New World Gentry: The Making of a Merchant and Planter Class in South Carolina, 1670–1770* (1989); Daniel C. Littlefield, *Rice and Slaves: Ethnicity and the Slave Trade in Colonial South Carolina* (1981).

The Quakers' Peaceable Kingdom

Frederick B. Tolles, *Meeting House and Counting House: The Quaker Merchants of Colonial Philadelphia* (1948); Gary B. Nash, *Quakers and Politics: Pennsylvania, 1681–1726* (1968); J. William Frost, *The Quaker Family in Colonial America* (1972); Sharon V. Salinger, *"To Serve Well and Faithfully": Labor and Indentured Servitude in Pennsylvania* (1987); Sally Schwartz, *A Mixed Multitude: The Struggle for Toleration in Colonial Pennsylvania* (1987); Barry J. Levy, *Quakers and the American Family* (1988).

New Spain's Northern Frontier

David J. Weber, *The Spanish Frontier in North America* (1992); Ramon A. Gutiérrez, *When Jesus Came, the Corn Mothers Went Away: Marriage, Sexuality, and Power in New Mexico, 1500–1846* (1991); Marvin T. Smith, *Archaeology of Aboriginal Culture Change in the Interior Southeast: Depopulation During the Early Historical Period* (1987); Andrew L. Knout, *The Pueblo Revolt of 1680* (1995); Jerald T. Milanich, *Florida Indians and the Invasion of Europe* (1995); Jane Landers, *Black Society in Spanish Florida* (1999).

Fiction and Film

Nathaniel Hawthorne's *The Scarlet Letter* (1850) is an American classic on Puritan love, infidelity, and morality; Hollywood's version, by the same title, features Demi Moore and Gary Oldman (1995). John Barth's *The Sotweed Factor* (1960) is a rollicking and ribald novel about indentured servitude, tobacco planting, love, and brutishness in seventeenth-century Maryland. *Black Robes* (1991), a gripping film made in Canada, evokes all the cruelty of the contact between early French Jesuit missionaries and the Iroquois people. The film is based on Brian Manning's novel of the same name. Werner Herzog's *Aguirre: The Wrath of God* (1972) is a surreal film about the early Spanish conquest of much of the Americas in the sixteenth century. A much milder film on early Indian–European contact is *Squanto: A Warrior's Tale* (1994), featuring Adam Beach.

Suggested Web Sites

http://www.apva.org.

Jamestown Rediscovery. This site mounted by the Association for the Preservation of Virginia Antiquity has excellent material on archaeological excavations at Jamestown.

http://etext.virginia.edu/users/deetz

The Plymouth Colony Archive Project at the University of Virginia. This site contains comprehensive and fairly extensive information about late seventeenth-century Plymouth Colony.

http://xroads.virginia.edu/~CAP/PENN/pnhome.html

William Penn, Visionary Proprietor. William Penn had an interesting life, and this site is a good introduction to the man and some of his achievements.

http://www.hanksville.org/NAresources

Index of Native American Resources on the Internet. A comprehensive source for Native American history and art.

http://www.ushistoryplace.com

A richly detailed on-line learning environment complete with interactive maps, timelines, history activities, primary source documents, and links to related American history sites.

3

MASTERING *the* NEW WORLD

CHAPTER OUTLINE

**A**nthony Johnson, an African, arrived in Virginia in 1621 with only the name Antonio. Caught as a young man in the Portuguese slave-trading net, he had passed from one trader to another in the New World until he reached Virginia. There he was purchased by Richard Bennett and sent to work at Warrasquoke, Bennett's tobacco plantation situated on the James River. In the next year, Antonio was brought face-to-face with the world of triracial contact and conflict that would shape the remainder of his life. On March 22, 1622, the Powhatan tribes of tidewater Virginia fell on the white colonizers in a determined attempt to drive them from the land. Of the 57 people on the Bennett plantation, only Antonio and four others survived.

Antonio—his name anglicized to Anthony—labored on the Bennett plantation for some 20 years, slave in fact if not in law, for legally defined bondage was still in the formative stage. During this time, he married Mary, another African trapped in the labyrinth of servitude, and fathered four children. In the 1640s, Anthony and Mary Johnson gained their freedom after half a lifetime of servitude. Probably at this point they chose a surname, Johnson, to signify their new status. Already past middle age, the Johnsons began carving out a niche for themselves on Virginia's eastern shore. By 1650, they owned 250 acres, a small herd of cattle, and two black servants. In a world in which racial boundaries were not yet firmly marked, the Johnsons had entered the scramble of small planters for economic security.

By schooling themselves in the workings of the English legal process, carefully cultivating white patronage, and working industriously on the land, the Johnsons gained their freedom, acquired property, established a family, warded off contentious neighbors, and hammered out a decent existence. But by the late 1650s, as the lines of racial slavery tightened, the customs of the country began closing in on Virginia's free blacks.

In 1664, convinced that ill winds were blowing away the chances for their children and grandchildren in Virginia, the Johnsons began selling their land to white neighbors. The following spring, most of the clan moved north to Maryland, where they rented land and again took up farming and cattle

Slave Deck of the Albanoz, watercolor done by a young naval officer in a Spanish slave ship captured by the *HMS Albanoz*. (*National Maritime Museum, Greenwich, England*)

raising. Five years later, Anthony Johnson died, leaving four children and his wife. The growing racial prejudice of Virginia followed Johnson beyond the grave. A jury of white men in Virginia declared that because Johnson "was a Negroe and by consequence an alien," the 50 acres he had deeded to his son Richard before moving to Maryland should be awarded to a local white planter.

Johnson's children and grandchildren, born in America, could not duplicate the modest success of the African-born patriarch. By the late seventeenth century, people of color faced much greater difficulties in extricating themselves from slavery. When they did, they found themselves forced to the margins of society. Anthony's sons never rose higher than the level of tenant farmer or small freeholder. John Johnson moved farther north into Delaware in the 1680s, following a period of great conflict with Native Americans in the Chesapeake region. Members of his family married local Indians and became part of a triracial community that has survived to the present day. Richard Johnson stayed behind in Virginia. When he died in 1689, just after a series of colonial insurrections connected with the overthrow of James II in England, he had little to leave his four sons. They became tenant farmers and hired servants, laboring on plantations owned by whites. By now, in the early eighteenth century, slave ships were pouring Africans into Virginia and Maryland to replace white indentured servants, the backbone of the labor force for four generations. To be black had at first been a handicap. Now it became a fatal disability, an indelible mark of degradation and bondage.

Mastering the North American environment involved several processes that would echo down the corridors of American history. Prominent among them were the molding of an African labor force and the gradual subjection of Native American tribes who contested white expansion. Both developments occurred in the lifetimes of Anthony and Mary Johnson and their children. Both involved a level of violence that made this frontier of European expansion not a zone of pioneer equality and freedom but one of growing inequality and servitude.

This chapter surveys the fluid, conflict-filled era from 1675 to 1715, a time when five overlapping struggles for mastery occurred. First, in determining to build a slave labor force, the colonists struggled to establish their mastery over resistant African captives. Second, the settlers sought mastery over Native American tribes, both those that stood in the way of white expansion and those that were their trading and military partners. Third, the colonists resisted the attempts of English imperial administrators to bring them into a more depen-

dent relationship. Fourth, within colonial societies, emerging elites struggled to establish their claims to political and social authority. Finally, the colonizers, aided by England, strove for mastery over French, Dutch, and Spanish contenders in North America.

AFRICAN BONDAGE

For almost four centuries after Columbus's voyages to the New World, European colonizers transported Africans out of their homelands in the largest forced migration in history. Estimates vary widely, but the number of Africans brought to the New World was probably not less than 12 million. Millions more perished while being marched from the African interior to coastal trading forts or during the passage across the Atlantic. Nearly as many were traded across the Sahara to Red Sea and Indian Ocean slave markets during the centuries from 650 to 1900.

African peoples, fed into the merciless slave trade, were crucially important in building the first trans-oceanic European colonial empires. Once the slave trade began, locales for producing desired commodities such as sugar, coffee, rice, and tobacco moved from the Old World to the Americas. This gradually shifted Europe's orientation from the Mediterranean Sea to the Atlantic Ocean. Africa became an essential part of the Atlantic-basin system of trade and communication by providing Europeans with the human labor needed to unlock the profits buried in productive American soils. Without African labor, the overseas colonies of European nations would never have flourished as they did.

While the economic importance of enslaved Africans can hardly be overstated, it is equally important to understand the cultural interchange that occurred when some 12 million Africans arrived in the Western hemisphere. Of all the newcomers who peopled the New World between the late fifteenth and early nineteenth centuries, the Africans were by far the most numerous, probably outnumbering Europeans two or three to one. As a result, African slavery became the context in which European life would evolve in many parts of the Americas. At the same time, the slave trade etched lines of communication for the movement of crops, agricultural techniques, diseases, and medical knowledge among Africa, Europe, and the Americas.

European slave traders carried most Africans to the West Indies, Brazil, and Spanish America. Fewer than one out of every 20 reached North America, which remained a fringe area for slave traders until

the early eighteenth century. Yet those who came to the American colonies, about 10,000 in the seventeenth century and 350,000 in the eighteenth, profoundly affected the destiny of North American society. In a prolonged period of labor scarcity, their labor and skills were indispensable to colonial economic development while their African customs mixed continuously with that of their European masters. Moreover, the racial relations that grew out of slavery so deeply marked society that the problem of race has continued to be one of this nation's most difficult problems.

The Slave Trade

The African slave trade did not begin as a part of the colonization of the Americas but as an attempt to fill a labor shortage in the Mediterranean world. As early as the eighth century, Arab and Moorish traders had driven slaves across Saharan caravan trails for delivery to Mediterranean ports. Seven centuries later, Portuguese merchants became the first European slave traders. For Africans, the Portuguese were nothing more than a new trading partner who could provide guns, horses, copper and brass, rum, and especially textiles.

When Portuguese ship captains reached the west coast of Africa by water, they tapped into a slave-trading network that had operated in central and west Africa for many generations. Slaveholding was deeply rooted in African societies, regarded as a natural part of human organization, and was important in enhancing one's status and augmenting one's ability to produce wealth. However, slaves were employed in a wide variety of occupations, often serving as soldiers, administrators, and even occasionally as royal advisors.

Many Africans were relegated to slavery by judicial decree for crimes they had committed, but far more were victims of military enslavement, captives in the wars between the numerous states of central and west Africa. For example, Songhay—the largest state in Africa in the 1500s—waged wars of territorial conquest recurrently, capturing slaves as it expanded its empire. The economy of the kingdom of Dahomey leaned heavily for several centuries on commerce in slaves. One former slave, Francisco Feliz de Sousa, came to own a fleet of slave ships. But the carrying trade was mainly in the hands of Europeans.

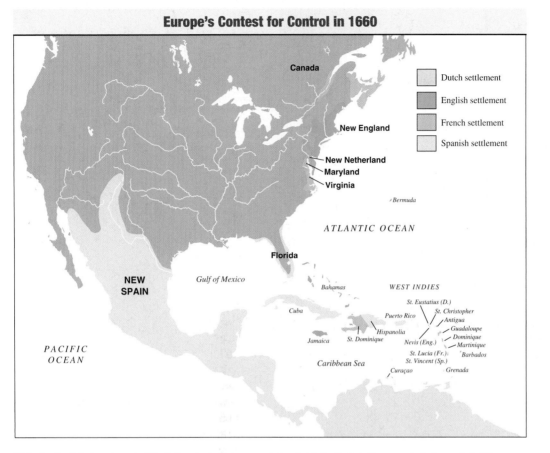

Europe's Contest for Control in 1660

Dutch settlement

English settlement

French settlement

Spanish settlement

Canada

New England

New Netherland

Maryland

Virginia

Bermuda

ATLANTIC OCEAN

Florida

NEW SPAIN

Gulf of Mexico

Bahamas

WEST INDIES

Cuba

St. Eustatius (D.)

St. Christopher

Puerto Rico

Antigua

Guadaloupe

Hispanolia

Dominique

Jamaica

St. Dominique

Nevis (Eng.)

Martinique

St. Lucia (Fr.)

Barbados

St. Vincent (Sp.)

Caribbean Sea

Curaçao

Grenada

PACIFIC OCEAN

While the English clung to part of North America's eastern coast, they battled with their European rivals for control of the more valuable Caribbean.

More than anything else, sugar transformed the African slave trade. For centuries, sugarcane had been grown in the Mediterranean countries to sweeten the diet of the wealthy. As sugar's popularity grew, the center of production shifted to Portugal's Atlantic island of Madeira, off the coast of Africa. Here in the sixteenth century, a European nation for the first time established an overseas colony organized around slave labor. From Madeira, the cultivation of sugar spread to Portuguese Brazil and Spanish Santo Domingo. By the seventeenth century, with Europeans developing a taste for sugar almost as insatiable as their craving for tobacco, they vied fiercely for the tiny islands dotting the Caribbean and for control of the trading forts on the West African coast. African kingdoms, eager for European trade goods, fought each other to supply the "black gold" demanded by white ship captains.

Many European nations competed for trading rights on the West African coast. In the seventeenth century, when slave traders brought about one million Africans to the New World, the Dutch replaced the Portuguese as the major supplier. The English, meanwhile, hardly counted in the slave trade. Not until the 1690s, when they began their century-long rise to maritime greatness, did the English challenge the Dutch. But by the 1790s, the English were the foremost European slave traders.

In the eighteenth century, European traders carried at least six million Africans to the Americas. By this time African slave labor figured so importantly in the colonial world that one Englishman called slavery the "strength and the sinews of this western world."

Once established on a large scale, the Atlantic slave trade dramatically altered slave recruitment in Africa. When criminals and "outsiders" were insufficient in number to satisfy the growing European demand, African kings waged war against neighboring tribes. European guns abetted the process. By 1730, Europeans were providing some 180,000 weapons a year, spreading kidnapping and organized violence while strengthening the most militarily effective kingdoms. Again and again, coastal and interior kings invaded the hinterlands of western and central Sudan to procure slaves. Perhaps three-quarters of the slaves transported to English North America came from the part of western Africa that lies between the Senegal and Niger rivers and the Gulf of Biafra.

The pain of a slave coffle, in which enslaved Africans were tied together with forked branches and bark rope, shows in this eighteenth-century print. About one-eighth of the slaves marched toward coastal holding pens were children. (*The Mansell Collection*)

In this forcible recruitment of slaves, young males—most of them 10 to 24 years old—were preferred over women. This was the preference of New World plantation owners for male field laborers, but it also reflected the decision of vanquished African villagers to yield up more men than women to raiding parties because women were the chief agriculturists in their society and, in matrilineal and matrilocal kinship systems, were too valuable to be sacrificed.

Even the most vivid accounts of the slave trade cannot convey the pain and demoralization that accompanied the initial capture and subsequent march to slave-trading forts on the West African coast or the dreaded "middle passage" across the Atlantic. Olaudah Equiano, an eighteenth-century Ibo from what is now Nigeria, described how raiders from another tribe kidnapped him and his younger sister when he was only 11 years old. He passed from one trader to another while being marched to the coast. Many slaves attempted suicide or died from exhaustion or hunger on these forced marches. But Equiano survived. Reaching the coast, he encountered the next humiliation, confinement in barracoons, fortified enclosures on the beach, where a surgeon from an English slave ship inspected him. Equiano was terrified by the light skins, language, and

long hair of the English and was convinced that he "had got into a world of bad spirits and that they were going to kill me."

More cruelties followed. European traders often branded the African slaves they purchased with a hot iron to indicate which company had procured them. The next trauma came with the ferrying of slaves in large canoes to the ships anchored in the harbor. An English captain recounted the desperation of Africans who were about to lose touch with their ancestral homeland and embark on a vast unknown ocean. "The Negroes are so loath to leave their own country," he wrote, "that they have often leaped out of the canoes, boat and ship, into the sea, and kept under the water till they were drowned."

Conditions aboard the slave ships were miserable, even though the traders' goal was to deliver alive as many slaves as possible to the other side of the Atlantic. Equiano recounted the scene below decks, where manacled slaves were crowded together like corpses in coffins. "With the loathsomeness of the stench, and crying together, I became so sick and low that I was not able to eat, nor had I the least desire to taste anything." The refusal to take food was so common that ship captains devised special techniques to cope with slaves who were determined to starve themselves to death rather than reach the New World in chains. Slavers flogged their captives brutally and applied hot coals to their lips. If this did not suffice, they force-fed the slaves with a mouth wrench.

The Atlantic passage usually took four to eight weeks, so physically depleting and psychologically wrenching that one of every seven captives died en route. Many others arrived in the Americas deranged or near death. In all, the relocation of any African may have averaged about six months from the time of capture to the time of arrival at the plantation of a colonial buyer. During this protracted personal crisis, the slave was completely cut off from the moorings of a previous life—language, family and friends, tribal religion, familiar geography, and status in a local community. Still awaiting these victims of the European demand for cheap labor was adaptation to a new physical environment, a new language, a new work routine, and a life of unending bondage for themselves and their children.

Slavery in the Spanish and French Borderlands

Before a single enslaved African touched soil in the English colonies, thousands of slaves were already present in North America. They came first with fifteenth-century Spanish explorers such as Ponce de Leon, Vasquez de Ayllon, de Soto, and Coronado. Estevancio, born in Morocco, was indispensable to Coronado's expedition in North America's Southwest, serving as guide, healer, linguist, and diplomat to Indian tribes. The importance of Africans on these arduous expeditions gave slavery a distinct character in the early Spanish colonies. Laboring in fields, in fort and church construction, and on supply trains, they were also valuable as soldiers, guides, and linguistic go-betweens with Indian people. In this way, slavery had little of the castelike character it developed in the English colonies. Also contributing to the greater flexibility of Spanish slavery was the frequent crossing of blood among Spaniards, Indians, and Africans.

French slaves were as important to the development of Louisiana as they were to Spanish Florida and New Mexico. Arriving with skills as rice growers, indigo processors, metal workers, river navigators, herbalists, and cattle keepers, West Africans became the backbone of the economy. Like male slaves in the Spanish colonies, they mingled extensively with Indian women, producing mixed-race children known locally as *grifs*. African women sometimes made interracial liaisons with French immigrants, often soldiers in search of partners. Always precariously in charge of limited numbers of French settlers, French governors in Louisiana used enslaved Africans extensively as militiamen and sometimes granted them freedom for

military service. All in all, the chance of gaining freedom in fluid French Louisiana exceeded that of any other colony in North America's Southeast, and the absorption of free blacks into white society, particularly if they were of mixed-race descent, was shockingly common from the English point of view.

The Southern Transition to Black Labor

Although they were familiar with Spanish, Dutch, Portuguese, and French use of black slaves, English colonists on the mainland of North America turned only slowly to Africa to solve their labor problem. Like other Europeans, they first regarded Native Americans as the obvious source of labor. But European diseases ravaged native societies, and Indians, more at home in the environment than the white colonizers, proved difficult to subjugate. Indentured white labor proved the best way to meet the demand for labor during most of the seventeenth century. Beginning in 1619, a small number of Africans entered Virginia and Maryland to labor in the tobacco fields alongside white servants. But as late as 1671, when some 30,000 slaves toiled in English Barbados, fewer than 3,000 served in Virginia. They were still outnumbered there at least three to one by white indentured servants.

Only in the last quarter of the seventeenth century did the southern labor force begin to change into one in which black slaves performed most of the field labor. Three reasons explain this shift. First, the rising commercial power of England, at the expense of the Spanish and Dutch, swelled English participation in the African slave trade. Beginning in the 1680s, southern planters could purchase slaves more readily and cheaply than before. Second, the supply of white servants from England began drying up, and those who did arrive fanned out among a growing number of colonies. Third, white servant unrest and a growing population of landless, discontented, and potential rebellious former servants led white planters to seek a more pliable labor force. Consequently, by the 1730s, the number of white indentured servants had dwindled to insignificance. Black hands, not white, tilled and harvested Chesapeake tobacco and Carolina rice. Nothing had greater priority in starting a plantation than procuring slave labor. "If any one designs to make a plantation in this province," wrote Thomas Nairne from South Carolina in 1710, "the first thing to be done is, after having cut down a few trees, to split palisades or clapboards and therewith make small houses or huts to shelter the slaves."

In enslaving Africans, English colonists merely copied their European rivals in the New World. Making it all the more natural for American planters to adopt this labor system was the precedent their countrymen had set in the English West Indies. From

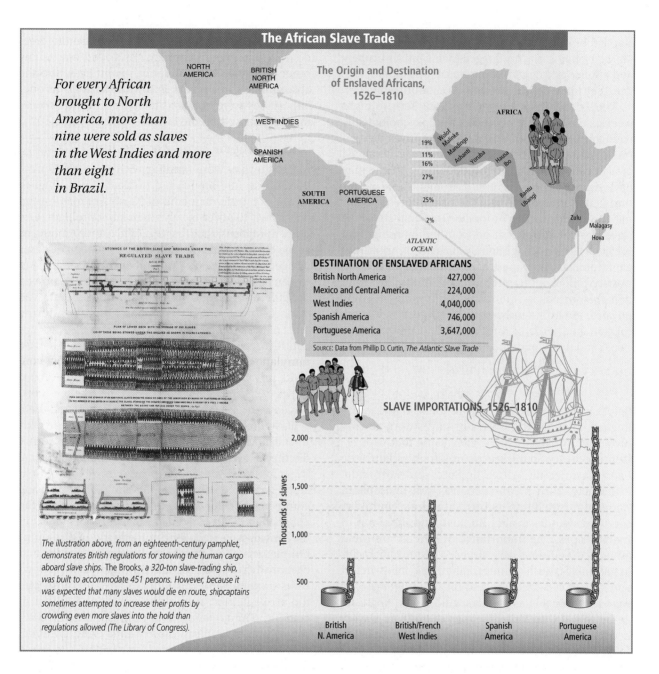

The African Slave Trade

For every African brought to North America, more than nine were sold as slaves in the West Indies and more than eight in Brazil.

The Origin and Destination of Enslaved Africans, 1526–1810

DESTINATION OF ENSLAVED AFRICANS	
British North America	427,000
Mexico and Central America	224,000
West Indies	4,040,000
Spanish America	746,000
Portuguese America	3,647,000

SOURCE: Data from Phillip D. Curtin, *The Atlantic Slave Trade*

SLAVE IMPORTATIONS, 1526–1810

The illustration above, from an eighteenth-century pamphlet, demonstrates British regulations for stowing the human cargo aboard slave ships. The Brooks, a 320-ton slave-trading ship, was built to accommodate 451 persons. However, because it was expected that many slaves would die en route, shipcaptains sometimes attempted to increase their profits by crowding even more slaves into the hold than regulations allowed (The Library of Congress).

---

the 1630s onward, the English imported Africans in droves in Barbados, Jamaica, and the Leeward Islands. Through brutal repression, they molded them into a sugar-producing slave labor force. Human bondage would later become the subject of intense moral debate, but in the seventeenth century, all but a few whites accepted it without question.

Slavery in the Northern Colonies

Slavery never became the foundation of the northern colonial workforce, for labor-intensive crops such as sugar and rice would not grow in colder climates. On the smaller family farms, household labor and occasional hired hands sufficed. Only in the cities, where

slaves worked as artisans and domestic servants, and in a few scattered rural areas did slavery take substantial root.

Although the northern colonists employed few slaves, their economies became enmeshed in the Atlantic commercial network, which depended on slavery and the slave trade. New England's merchants eagerly pursued profits in the slave trade as early as the 1640s, when their ships began supplying Barbados with Africans. By 1676, New England slavers were packing their holds with slaves from Madagascar, off the coast of East Africa, and transporting them 6,000 miles to the western side of the Atlantic. By 1750, half the merchant fleet of Newport, Rhode Island, reaped profits from carrying human cargo. In New York and Philadelphia, building and outfitting slave vessels proved profitable.

New England's involvement in the international slave trade deepened with the growth of its seaports as centers for the distilling of rum—the "hot, hellish and terrible liquor." Made from West Indian sugar, rum became one of the principal commodities traded for slaves on the African coast. As the number of slaves to be fed in the Caribbean multiplied—from about 50,000 in 1650 to 500,000 in 1750—the West Indies became a favorite market for the codfish hauled in by New England's extensive fishing fleet. Wheat from the middle colonies and barrel staves and hoops from North Carolina also fed into the slave-based West Indies economy. Hence, as the plantation South became most directly involved in an international system of racial exploitation, every other North American colony also participated in it.

The System of Bondage

The first Africans brought to the American colonies came as bound servants. They served their term, and if (like Anthony and Mary Johnson) they survived, they gained their freedom. Once released, they could own land, hire out their labor, and move as they pleased. Their children, like those of white indentured servants, were born free.

But gradually, seventeenth-century, Chesapeake planters began to draw tighter lines around the activities of black servants. By the 1640s, Virginia forbade blacks, free or bound, to carry firearms. In the 1660s, marriages between white women and black servants were called "shameful matches" and the "disgrace of our Nation." Bit by bit, white settlers strengthened the association between black skin and slave status.

By the mid-seventeenth century, most white colonists were convinced that perpetual bondage was the appropriate status for black servants. By the end of the century, when incoming Africans increased from a trickle to a torrent, even the small number of free blacks found themselves pushed to the margins of society. Slavery, which had existed for centuries in many societies as the lowest social status, was in the Americas becoming a caste reserved for those with black skin. Step by step, white society was turning the black servant from a human being into a chattel.

In this dehumanization of Africans, which the English largely copied from their colonial rivals, the key step was instituting hereditary lifetime service. Once servitude became perpetual, relieved only by death, all other privileges quickly vanished. When a mother's slave condition legally passed on to her newborn black infant (not the case in other forms of slavery, such as in Africa), slavery became self-perpetuating, passing automatically from one generation to the next.

Slavery was not only a system of forced labor but also a pattern of human relationships legitimated by law. By the early eighteenth century, most provincial legislatures were enacting laws for limiting black rights and controlling black activities. Borrowed largely from England's Caribbean colonies, "black codes" forced Africans into an ever narrower world. Slaves were forbidden to testify in court, engage in commercial activity, hold property, participate in the political process, congregate in public, travel without permission, and legally marry or be parents. Nearly stripped of human status, they became defined as property; gradually all legal restraints on the master's treatment of them disappeared.

Eliminating slave rights had both pragmatic and psychological dimensions. With every African in chains a potential rebel, the rapid increase in the slave population brought anxious demands for strict control. The desire to stifle black rebelliousness mingled with a need to justify brutal behavior toward slaves by defining them as less than human. "The planters," wrote one Englishman in Jamaica, "do not want to be told that their Negroes are human creatures. If they believe them to be of human kind, they cannot regard them as no better than dogs or horses."

Dehumanizing slaves involved one of the great paradoxes of modern history. Many Old World immigrants imagined the Americas as a liberating and regenerating arena. Yet the opportunity to exploit its resources led to a historic world process by which masses of people were wrenched from their homelands and forced into a system of slavery that could be maintained only by increasing intimidation and brutality.

SLAVE CULTURE

The basic struggle for Africans toiling on plantations 5,000 miles from their homes was to create strategies for living as satisfactorily as possible despite horrifying treatment. The master hoped to convert the slave into a mindless drudge who obeyed every command and worked efficiently for his profit. But the attempt to cow slaves rarely succeeded completely. Masters could set the external boundaries of existence for their slaves, controlling physical location, work roles, diet, and shelter. But the authority of the master class impinged far less on how slaves established friendships, fell in love, formed kin groups, reared children, worshiped their gods, buried their dead, and organized their leisure time.

In these aspects of daily life, slaves in America drew on their African heritage to shape their existence to some degree. In doing so, they laid the foundations for an African American culture. At first, this culture had many variations because slaves came from many areas in Africa and lived under different conditions in the colonies. But common elements emerged, led by developments in the South, where about 90 percent of American slaves labored in the colonial period.

The Growth of Slavery

Arriving in North America, Africans entered a relatively healthy environment compared with other areas of the New World. The West Indies became a graveyard for both whites and blacks. In South America, tropical diseases swept away slaves like leaves in a windstorm. In the southern colonies, where the ghastly mortality of the early decades had subsided by the time Africans were arriving in large numbers, their chances for survival were much better. A simple comparison makes the point. Colonizers in Virginia and Jamaica each owned about 200,000 slaves in 1775. But to attain that number, more than three times as many Africans had been imported into Jamaica as into Virginia during the eighteenth century.

This environmental advantage, combined with a more even sex ratio, led to a natural increase in the North American slave population unparalleled elsewhere. In 1675, about 4,000 slaves were scattered across Virginia and Maryland. Most were men. They toiled with their masters and a larger number of white indentured servants, clearing the land, planting, hoeing, and harvesting tobacco. A half century later, with the decline of white servitude, 45,000 slaves labored on Chesapeake plantations. By 1760, when the number of slaves exceeded 185,000, the Chesapeake plantations relied almost entirely on black labor.

Although slave codes severely restricted the lives of slaves, the possibility for family life increased as the southern colonies matured. Larger plantations employed dozens and even hundreds of slaves, many of the men laboring in skilled crafts, and the growth of roads and market towns permitted them greater opportunities to forge relationships beyond their own plantation. By the 1740s, a growing proportion of Chesapeake slaves were American-born, had established families, and lived in plantation outbuildings where from sundown to sunup they could fashion personal lives—and a distinct black culture—of their own.

In South Carolina, African slaves drew on agricultural skills they had practiced on the other side of the Atlantic and made rice the keystone of the coastal economy by the early eighteenth century. Their numbers increased rapidly, from about 4,000 in 1708 to 90,000 by 1760. Working mostly on large plantations in

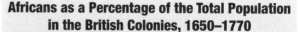

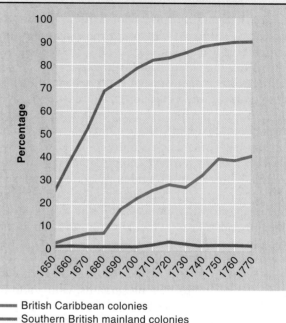

Variations in the racial composition of Britain's American colonies led to distinct differences in cuisine, dress, language, music, and other cultural characteristics. Source: Robert W. Fogel and Stanley L. Engerman, *Time on the Cross* (Boston: Little, Brown, 1974), 21.

swampy lowlands, they endured the most life-sapping conditions on the continent. But in the coastal low country, they outnumbered whites three to one by 1760 and hence were able to maintain more of their African culture than slaves in the Chesapeake region. South Carolina, one European observed in 1737, "looks more like a negro country than like a country settled by white people." Many slaves spoke Gullah, a "pidgin" mixing several African languages. They often gave African names to their children—names like Cudjoe, Cuffe, Quashey, and Phibbi—and kept alive their African religious customs.

In the northern colonies, where no labor shortage existed and the climate did not allow the cultivation of staple crops, slaves made up less than 10 percent of the population. They typically worked as artisans, farmhands, or personal servants. Mingled among them were occasional Indian slaves. Whereas about two-thirds of all southern slaves worked on plantations with at least ten of their fellows by the 1720s, in the North the typical slave labored alone or with only a few others. Living in the same house as the master, slaves adapted to European ways much faster than in the South, where the slave quarters were places for perpetuating African folkways. Slavery was also less repressive in the North. Slaves were more widely dispersed among the white population, and black–white contact was so extensive that African culture faded more quickly.

Slavery spread more extensively in the northern ports than across the countryside. Artisans found it profitable to invest in slaves whom they could work on a year-round basis. Ship captains purchased them for maritime labor. And an emerging urban elite of merchants, lawyers, and landlords displayed its wealth and status by employing slaves as liveried coachmen and house servants. By the beginning of the eighteenth century, more than 40 percent of New York City's households owned slaves. Even in Quaker Philadelphia, slaveholding increased sharply in the eighteenth century. Struggling white artisans resented slave workers for undercutting their wages, and the white citizenry felt threatened by potential black arsonists and rebels. Yet where labor demand was high, the desire for lifelong servants, who could be purchased for a mere two years of a free white laborer's wages, outweighed these reservations.

Resistance and Rebellion

While struggling to adapt to bondage in various regions of British America, slaves also resisted and rebelled in ways that constantly reminded their masters that slavery's price was eternal vigilance. Slaveowners preferred to interpret rebelliousness as evidence of the "barbarous, wild savage natures" of Africans, as a South Carolina law of 1712 phrased it. Some planters, like Virginia's Landon Carter, believed that "slaves are devils and to make them free is to set devils free." But from the African point of view, the struggle against enslavement was essential to maintaining meaning and dignity in a life of degrading toil. Resisters' goals varied: to rejoin family members, to flee, to convince masters to improve their condition, or to avenge sadistic overseers.

"Saltwater" Africans, those fresh from their homelands, often resisted slavery fiercely. "You would really be surprised at their perseverance," wrote one observer. "They often die before they can be conquered." Commonly, this initial resistance took the form of escaping to the frontier to begin renegade settlements, to Indian tribes in the interior that sometimes offered refuge, or to Spanish Florida. Open rebellions, such as those in New York City in 1712 and at Stono, South Carolina, in 1739, mostly involved newly arrived slaves.

There was no North American parallel, however, for the massive slave uprisings that erupted periodically in the West Indies and Brazil. Nor was there an American parallel to the semistates in the South Atlantic sugar world, where runaway slaves built their own communities and resisted periodic assaults by colonial troops. Slaves had far better chances to mount successful rebellions in these areas because they vastly outnumbered their masters and, in the case of Brazil, could flee to the rugged interior to join unconquered Indian tribes. "The greater number of blacks which a frontier has," remarked one colonist, "and the greater the disproportion is between them and her white people, the more danger she is liable to."

In North America, slaves rarely outnumbered whites except in South Carolina, and the master class tried to cultivate tension between local Indians and slaves so that they would be a "check upon each other," as one worried planter explained. When rebellion did occur, white colonizers stopped at nothing to quell it. They tried to intimidate all slaves by torturing, hanging, dismembering, and even burning captured rebels at the stake. After an uprising was disclosed near Charleston, South Carolina, in 1739, for example, city officials tortured and hanged 50 blacks. Their decapitated heads, impaled on posts, gave warning to other potential insurrectionists. In New York City a year later, officials responded to a rumored insurrection by hanging 18 slaves and four white allies and burning 13 other slaves at the stake.

Open rebelliousness often gave way to more subtle forms of resistance as slaves learned English; adjusted to the routines of shop, farm, and plantation; and began forming families. Dragging out the job, shamming illness, pretending ignorance, and breaking tools were strategies for avoiding physical exhaustion and also indirect forms of opposing slavery itself.

Slaves resisted more directly through truancy, arson directed against the master's barns and houses, crop destruction, pilfering to supplement their food supply, and direct assaults on masters, overseers, and drivers. Slave masters extracted labor and obedience from their slaves in an overall sense. If they had not, the slave system would have collapsed. But they did so only with difficulty. Masters learned that to push slaves too hard could be costly. One South Carolina planter drove his slaves late into the night cleaning and barreling a rice crop in 1732. When he awoke in the morning, he found his barn, with the entire harvest in it, reduced to ashes.

Black Religion and Family

Resistance and rebellion represented attacks on the institution of slavery. But the balance of power was always massively stacked against the slaves. Only the most desperate were willing to challenge the system directly. Of greater importance was the struggle of black slaves to find meaning and worth in their existence, no matter how brutal and discouraging the slave system that manacled them. In this quest, religion and family played a central role—one destined to continue far into the postslavery period.

Africans brought a complex religious heritage to the New World. No amount of desolation or physical abuse could wipe out these deeply rooted beliefs. People enduring the daily travail that accompanied slavery typically turned for relief to their deepest emotional sources. Coming from cultures where the division between sacred and secular activities was less clear than in Europe, slaves made religion central to their existence. But until the mid-eighteenth century, most slaves died strangers to Christianity. Only slowly would slaves blend African religious practices with the religion of the master class. Partly this was because slave masters were not eager to see their slaves exposed to Christianity because of its potentially dangerous notions of brotherhood and its prohibition against enslaving other Christians. Yet Christianity's emphasis on meekness and obedience might restrain black rebelliousness. Gradually slaves gained exposure to Christianity, using it both to light the spark of resistance and to find comfort from oppression.

The religious revival that began in the 1720s in the northern colonies and spread southward thereafter made important contributions to African American religion. Evangelicalism stressed personal rebirth, used music and body motion, and caught individuals up in an intense emotional experience. The dancing, shouting, rhythmic clapping, and singing that came to characterize slaves' religious expression represented a creative mingling of West African and Christian religions.

Besides religion, the slaves' greatest refuge from their dreadful fate lay in their families. In West Africa, all social relations were centered in kinship, which stretched backward to include dead ancestors. Torn from their native societies, slaves placed great importance on rebuilding extended kin groups.

Most English colonies prohibited slave marriages. But in practice, domestic life was an area in which slaves and masters struck a bargain. Masters found that slaves would work harder if they were allowed to form families. Moreover, family ties stood in the way of escape or rebellion, for few slaves wanted to leave loved ones at the mercy of an angry master. For their part, slaves valued family life so highly that they were willing to risk almost everything to secure the right to marry and parent children.

Slaves fashioned a family life only with difficulty, however. The general practice of importing three male slaves for every two females stunted family formation. Female slaves, much in demand, married in their late teens, but males usually had to wait until their mid- to late twenties. As natural increase swelled the slave population in the eighteenth century, however, the sex ratio became more even.

Slave marriages were rarely secure because they could be abruptly severed by the sale of either party. This happened repeatedly, especially when a deceased planter's estate was divided among his heirs or his slaves were sold to his creditors to satisfy debts. Young children usually stayed with their mothers until about age eight; then they were frequently torn from their families through sale, often to small planters needing

This eighteenth-century watercolor depicts slaves in South Carolina dancing the "juba," a West African dance. The gourdlike banjo and the twisted leather drumsticks are of African design, reflecting the cultural heritage of Africa transplanted to the American colonies. *(Abby Aldrich Rockefeller Folk Art Center, Williamsburg, VA)*

This portrait, painted about 1780 after Equiano had purchased his freedom, shows him as a successful Londoner with hair and clothes in the style of a fashionable Englishman. In 1792, Equiano married an English woman and had two daughters with her. He died five years later. *(Robert Albert Memorial Museum, Exeter, Devon England/The Bridgeman Art Library)*

only a hand or two. Few slaves escaped separation from family members at some time during their lives.

White male exploitation of black women represented another assault on family life. How many black women were coerced or lured with favors into sexual relations with white masters and overseers cannot be known. But the sizable mulatto (racially mixed) population at the end of the eighteenth century indicates that the number was large. Interracial liaisons, frequently forced, were widespread, especially in the Lower South. In 1732, the *South-Carolina Gazette* called racial mixing an "epidemical disease." It was a malady that had traumatic effects on slave attempts to build stable relationships.

In some interracial relationships, the coercion was of a more subtle nature. In some cases, black women sought the liaison to gain advantages for themselves or their children. These unions nonetheless threatened both the slave community and the white plantation ideal. They bridged the supposedly unbridgeable gap between slave and free society and produced children who plagued whites because they did not fit into the separate racial categories that the colonists wished to maintain.

Despite such obstacles, slaves fashioned intimate ties as husband and wife, parent and child. If monogamous relationships did not last as long as in white society, much of the explanation lies in the conditions of slave life: the shorter life span of African Americans, the shattering of marriage through sale of one or both partners, and the call of freedom that impelled some slaves to run away.

Whereas slave men struggled to preserve their family role, many black women assumed a position in the family that differed from that of white women. Plantation mistresses usually worked hard in helping manage estates, but nonetheless the ideal grew that they should remain in the house to guard white virtue and set the standards for white culture. In contrast, the black woman remained indispensable to both the work of the plantation and the functioning of the slave quarters. She toiled in the fields and worked in the slave cabins. Paradoxically, black women's roles, which required constant labor, made them more equal to men than was the case of women in white society.

Above all, slavery was a set of power relationships designed to extract the maximum labor from its victims. Hence, it regularly involved cruelties that filled family life with tribulation. But slaves in America were unusually successful in establishing families because they lived in a healthier environment; toiled in less physically exhausting circumstances than slaves on sugar and coffee plantations; and were better clothed, fed, and treated than Africans in the West Indies, Brazil, and other parts of the hemisphere. In these more tropical areas, plantation owners imported large numbers of male slaves, literally worked them to death, and then purchased replacements from Africa. Family life in the American colonies brimmed with uncertainty and sorrow, but slaves nonetheless made it the greatest monument to their will to endure captivity and eventually gain their freedom.

THE STRUGGLE FOR LAND

As slavery became entrenched in North America, New England, Virginia, and, later, South Carolina fought major wars against Native Americans. All resulted from settler desire for land, and all left legacies of widespread destruction, heavy casualties, and bitterness. The coastal tribes suffered disastrous defeat and decline; for the colonists, the wars added to the turbulence of the late seventeenth and early eighteenth centuries. Sometimes, as in Virginia, Indian war overlapped with a power struggle within white society.

King Philip's War in New England

Following the Pequot War of 1637 in New England, the Wampanoags and Narragansetts, whose fertile land lay within the boundaries of Plymouth and Rhode Island, tried to keep their distance from the New England colonists. But the New Englanders coveted

The Wampanoags led New England tribes in a tenacious campaign of resistance against the white settlers. Paul Revere engraved this picture of the Wampanoag chief Metacomet, called King Philip by the English. The musket held by Metacomet bespeaks the Indian adoption of European weaponry. (*American Antiquarian Society*)

Indian territories. As they quarreled among themselves over provincial boundaries, they gradually reduced the Indians' land base.

By the 1670s, when New England's population had grown to about 50,000, younger Indians began brooding over their situation. Their leader, Metacomet (named King Philip by the English), was the son of Massasoit, the Wampanoag chief who had allied with the first Plymouth settlers in 1620. Metacomet had watched his older brother preside over the deteriorating position of his people after their father's death in 1661. A year later, Metacomet's brother died mysteriously while Plymouth officials questioned him about a rumored Indian conspiracy. Becoming chief in his turn, Metacomet faced one humiliating challenge after another, climaxing in 1671, when Plymouth forced him to surrender a large stock of guns and accept his people's subjection to English law. Convinced that more setbacks would follow and humiliated by the discriminatory treatment of

Indians brought before English courts, Metacomet began recruiting for a resistance movement.

The triggering incident of King Philip's War was the trial of three Wampanoags who were dragged before a Puritan court for an act of tribal revenge against John Sassamon, a Christianized Indian educated at Harvard and Metacomet's aide. Sassamon was a man caught between two cultures. Though he had fled white society after his college years, he warned the Plymouth government in 1675 that the Wampanoags were preparing a general attack on the English settlements. When Sassamon was found murdered shortly afterward, Plymouth officials produced an Indian who claimed he had witnessed the murder and could identify the felons. As a result, three Wampanoags swung at the end of English ropes in June 1675.

The execution of the three tribesmen was the catalyst, but the root cause of the war that erupted was the rising anger of the young Wampanoag males. As would happen repeatedly in the next two centuries as Americans pushed westward, younger Native Americans refused to imitate their fathers, who had tolerated the colonizers' encroachments and abridgment of their sovereignty. Rather than submit further, they attempted a pan-Indian offensive against an intruder with far greater numbers and a much larger arsenal of weapons. For the young tribesmen, revitalization of their ancient culture through war became as important a goal as defeating the enemy.

In the summer of 1675, the Wampanoags unleashed daring hit-and-run attacks on villages in the Plymouth colony. By autumn, many New England tribes, including the powerful Narragansetts, had joined Metacomet's warriors. Towns all along the frontier reeled under Indian attacks. "We were too ready to think that we could easily suppress that flea," confessed John Eliot, who had worked to convert the Indians to Christianity, "but now we find that all the craft is in catching them, and that in the meantime they give us many a sore nip." By the time the first snow fell in November, mobile Indian warriors had devastated the entire upper Connecticut River valley.

By March 1676, Metacomet's forces were attacking less than 20 miles from Boston and Providence. Assumptions about English military superiority faded. Desperate to reverse the course of the war, New England officials passed America's first draft laws. Evasion was widespread, however, with eligible men—all those between ages 16 and 60—"skulking from one town to another." Political friction among the New England colonies also hampered a united counteroffensive.

Metacomet's offensive faltered in the spring of 1676. Food shortages and disease sapped Indian strength, and the powerful Mohawks, with their own

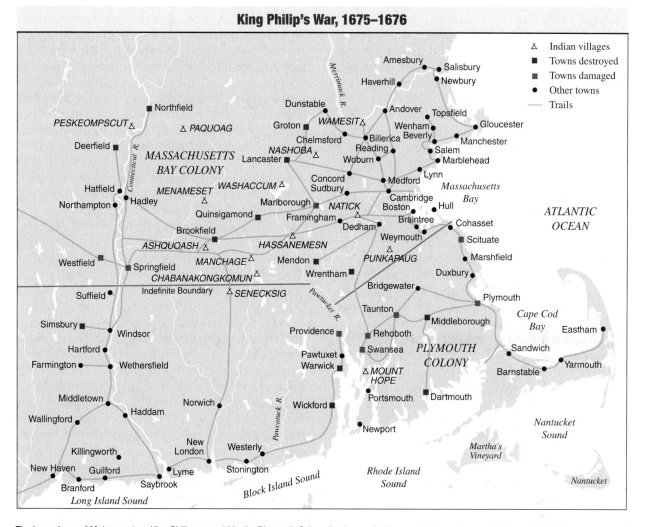

King Philip's War, 1675–1676

The home base of Metacomet, or King Philip, was within the Plymouth Colony, but he carried the war to the westernmost Massachusetts towns.

advantages in the fur trade to protect, refused to support the New England tribes. By summer, groups of Indians were surrendering, while some moved westward seeking shelter among other tribes. Then Metacomet fell in a battle near the Wampanoag village in Rhode Island where the war had begun. The head of this "hell-hound, fiend, serpent, caitiff and dog," as one colonial leader branded him, was carried triumphantly back to Plymouth, where it remained on display for 25 years.

At war's end, several thousand colonists and perhaps twice as many Indians lay dead. Of some 90 Puritan towns, 52 had been attacked and 13 completely destroyed. Some 1,200 homes lay in ruins and 8,000 cattle were dead. The estimated cost of the war exceeded the value of all personal property in New England. Not for 40 years would the frontier advance beyond the line it had reached in 1675. Indian towns were devastated even more completely, including several inhabited by "praying Indians" who had con-

verted to Christianity and allied with the whites. An entire generation of young men had been nearly annihilated. Many of the survivors, including Metacomet's wife and son, were sold into slavery in the West Indies.

Bacon's Rebellion Engulfs Virginia

While New Englanders fought local tribes in 1675 and 1676, the Chesapeake colonies became locked in a struggle involving both a war between the red and white populations and civil war among the colonizers. Before it ended, hundreds of whites and Indians lay dead in Virginia and Maryland, Virginia's capital of Jamestown lay smoldering, and English troops were crossing the Atlantic to suppress what the king labeled an outright rejection of his authority. This deeply tangled conflict was called Bacon's Rebellion after the headstrong Cambridge-educated planter Nathaniel Bacon, who arrived in Virginia at age 28.

Bacon and many other ambitious young planters detested the Indian policy of Virginia's royal governor, Sir William Berkeley. In 1646, after the second Indian uprising against the Virginians, the Powhatan tribes had accepted a treaty granting them exclusive rights to territory north of the York River, beyond the limits of white settlement. Stable Indian relations suited the established planters, some of whom traded profitably with the Indians, but became obnoxious to new settlers. Nor did the harmonious conditions please the white indentured servants who had served their time and were hoping to find cheap frontier land.

Land hunger and dissatisfaction with declining tobacco prices, rising taxes, and lack of opportunity erupted into violence in the summer of 1675. A group of frontiersmen used an incident with a local tribe as an excuse to attack the Susquehannocks, whose rich land they coveted. Governor Berkeley denounced the attack, but few supported his position. He faced, he said, "a people where six parts of seven at least are poor, indebted, discontented, and armed."

Although badly outnumbered, the Susquehannocks prepared for war. Virginians girded themselves for the southern version of what they heard was occurring in New England. Rumors swept the colony that the Susquehannocks were offering large sums to gain western Indian allies, or that King Philip would support them.

Thirsting for revenge, the Susquehannocks attacked during the winter of 1675–1676 and killed 36 Virginians. That spring, the hot-blooded Nathaniel Bacon became the frontiersmen's leader. Joined by hundreds of runaway servants and some slaves, he attacked friendly and hostile Indians alike. When Governor Berkeley refused to sanction these attacks, Bacon ignored his authority. The governor then declared Bacon a rebel and sent out 300 militiamen to drag him to Jamestown for trial. Bacon headed into the wilderness for "a more agreeable destiny" and recruited more followers, including many substantial planters. Frontier skirmishes with Indians had turned into civil war.

During the summer of 1676, Bacon's and Berkeley's troops maneuvered around each other, while Bacon's men continued their forays against local Indian tribes. In one bold move, Bacon and his followers captured the capital at Jamestown. They razed the statehouse, church, and other buildings and put Governor Berkeley to flight across Chesapeake Bay.

Virginians at all levels had chafed under Berkeley's rule. High taxes, an increase in the governor's powers at the expense of local officials, and the monopoly that Berkeley and his friends held on the Indian trade were especially unpopular. This opposition surfaced in the summer of 1676 as Berkeley's and Bacon's troops pursued each other through the wilderness. Berkeley tried to rally public support by holding new assembly elections and extending the vote to all freemen, whether they owned property or not. But the new assembly turned on the governor, passing a set of reform laws intended to make government more responsive to the common people and to end rapacious officeholding. It also made legal the enslaving of Native Americans.

Time was on the governor's side, however. Having crushed the Indians, Bacon's followers began drifting home to tend their crops. Meanwhile, Berkeley's reports of the rebellion brought the dispatch of 1,100 royal troops from England. By the time they arrived in January 1677, Nathaniel Bacon lay dead of swamp fever and most of his followers had melted back into the frontier. After Bacon's death in October 1676, Berkeley rounded up 23 rebel leaders and hanged them without benefit of trial.

Royal investigators who arrived in 1677 remarked on the genocidal mentality of Bacon's followers, whom they denounced as the "inconsiderate sort of men who so rashly and causelessly cry up a war and seem to wish and aim at an utter extirpation of the Indians." Even a royal governor could not restrain such men, bent on pursuing their hopes of land ownership and independence. To them, Indians were only "wolves, tigers, and bears," as Bacon charged, "which daily destroyed our harmless and innocent lambs."

Hatred of Indians, bred into white society during the war, became a permanent feature of Virginia life. A generation later, in 1711, the legislature spurned the governor's plea for quieting the Indian frontier with educational missions and regulated trade, instead voting military appropriations of £20,000 "for extirpating all Indians without distinction of Friends or Enemys." The remnants of the once populous Powhatan Confederacy lost their last struggle for the world they had known. Now they moved farther west or submitted to a life on the margins of white society as tenant farmers, day laborers, or domestic servants.

After Bacon's Rebellion, an emerging planter aristocracy annulled most of the reform laws of 1676. But the war relieved much of the social tension among white Virginians. Newly available Indian land created fresh opportunities for small planters and former servants. Equally important, Virginians with capital to invest were turning from the impoverished rural villages of England and Ireland to the villages of West Africa to supply their labor needs. This halted the influx of poor white servants who, once free, had formed a discontented mass at the bottom of Chesapeake society. A racial consensus, uniting whites of different ranks in the common pursuit of a prosperous, slave-based economy, began to take shape.

Bacon's Rebellion caused insurrectionary rumblings north and south of Virginia. Many of Bacon's followers took refuge after his death in North Carolina's Albemarle County, the "backside of Virginia." There they joined dissident tobacco farmers, who were distressed by recent Indian uprisings, export duties on tobacco, and quitrents controlled by a mercenary elite. Led by George Durant and John Culpeper, they drove the governor from office and briefly seized the reins of power.

In Maryland, Protestant settlers chafed under high taxes; quitrents; and officeholders regarded as venal, Catholic, or both. Declining tobacco prices and a fear of Indian attacks increased their touchiness. A month after Bacon razed Jamestown, insurgent small planters tried to seize the Maryland government. Two of their leaders were hanged for the attempt. In 1681, Josias Fendall and John Coode, "two rank Baconists" according to Lord Baltimore, led another abortive uprising. After their attempt to kidnap the Catholic proprietor failed, the authorities executed Fendall and banished Coode from the colony.

In all three southern colonies, the volatility of late-seventeenth-century life owed much to the region's peculiar social development. Where family formation was retarded by imbalanced sex ratios and fearsome mortality, and where geographic mobility was high, little social cohesion or attachment to community could grow. Missing in the southern colonies were the stabilizing power of mature local institutions, a vision of a larger purpose, and the presence of experienced and responsive political leaders.

AN ERA OF INSTABILITY

A dozen years after the major Indian wars in New England and Virginia, a series of insurrections and a major witchcraft incident convulsed colonial society. The rebellions were triggered by the Revolution of 1688, known thereafter to Protestants in England as the Glorious Revolution because it ended forever the notion that kings ruled by a God-given "divine right" and marked the last serious Catholic challenge to Protestant supremacy. But these colonial disruptions also signified a struggle for social and political dominance in the expanding colonies. So did the Salem witchcraft trials in Massachusetts.

Organizing the Empire

From the beginning of colonization, the English assumed that overseas settlements existed to promote the national interest at home. According to this mercantilist theory, colonies served as outlets for English manufactured goods, provided foodstuffs and raw materials, stimulated trade (and hence pro-

moted a larger merchant navy), and filled royal coffers by exporting commodities such as sugar and tobacco on which duties were paid. In return, colonists benefited from English military protection and guaranteed markets.

England proceeded slowly in the seventeenth century to regulate its colonies and mold them into a unified empire. A first small step was taken in 1621, when the king's council forbade tobacco growers to export their crop to anywhere but England. Three years later, when the Virginia Company of London plunged into bankruptcy, the crown made Virginia a royal colony, the first of many. However, not until 1651, when the colonists traded freely with the commercially aggressive Dutch, did Parliament consider regulating colonial affairs. It passed a navigation act requiring that English or colonial ships, manned by English or colonial sailors, carry all goods entering England, Ireland, and the colonies, no matter where those goods originated. These first steps toward a regulated empire were also the first steps to place England's power behind national economic development.

In 1660, after the monarchy was restored, Parliament passed a more comprehensive navigation act that listed colonial products (tobacco, sugar, indigo, dyewoods, and cotton) that could be shipped only to England or other English colonies. Like its predecessor, the act took dead aim at Holland's domination of Atlantic commerce while increasing England's revenues by imposing duties on the enumerated articles. Later navigation acts closed loopholes in the 1660 law and added other enumerated articles. Nevertheless, this regulation bore lightly on the colonists because the laws lacked enforcement mechanisms.

After 1675, international competition and war led England to impose greater imperial control. That year marked the establishment of the Lords of Trade, a committee of the king's privy council vested with power to make and enforce decisions regarding the management of the colonies. Their chief goal was to create more uniform governments in North America and the West Indies that would do the crown's will. Although this movement toward the central administration of empire often sputtered, the trend was unmistakable, especially to colonists who felt the sting of royal customs agents sent to enforce the navigation acts. England was becoming the shipper of the world, and its state-regulated policy of economic nationalism, duplicating that of the Dutch, was essential to this rise to commercial greatness.

The Glorious Revolution in New England

When Charles II died in 1685, his brother, the duke of York, became King James II. This set in motion a chain

Recovering the Past

TOMBSTONES

Historians have used funeral orations, gravestone designs and inscriptions, and handbooks on how to die to gain insight into early American culture. Tombstone markings—"graven images," they have been called—provide a particularly fascinating body of evidence. At first, Puritans in New England marked their graves only with wooden rails and posts. But in the 1670s, carved headstones filled with symbolic images began to appear, and they became a regular feature of New England graveyards after that. Hardly any Puritan family thereafter, one historian noted, was "ready to commit its loved ones to the cold earth without an appropriate cluster of symbols hovering protectively over the grave." How the symbols carved on tombstones changed tells much about how people's attitudes and values shifted. "There is no better place in all New England to stand face to face with the past," it has been said, "than in the old burying grounds."

The tombstone shown below shows vividly the intensity with which Puritans faced death. To die was to be called to final account by a just and merciful God, and the way one died gave evidence of one's self-discipline and faith. The scrolled pediment on this gravestone signifies the doorway between earthly life and spiritual rebirth through which Joseph Tapping's relatives hoped he passed. The grim winged skull represents the soul of the dying man in transition. This death's-head motif was widely used on seventeenth-century gravestones. It conveys much of the Puritans' intense concern that life is transitory (note the hourglass above the skull) and that salvation is not automatically granted to those who believe in Christ. This emphasis on life as a preparation for afterlife is reinforced by the Latin mottoes on the right side of the stone: *Vive memor loethi* ("Live mindful of death") and *Fugit hora* ("The hour flies"). At bottom center of the stone is an image of Time fending off Death as Death tries to snuff out the candle of Life.

The Puritans' fixation on death has also been noted in the elaborate and expensive funerals they often conducted and in the content of funeral sermons and handbooks on how to die well. In a popular book on advice for the young, *Token for Children*, published first in England in 1671 and in an American edition in 1700, James Janeway described the "Joy and holy Triumph" of a 12-year-old girl's death. As a model of faith in God's mercy, without yielding to pride or certainty of salvation in her last hours, this young girl

> spake with a holy Confidence in the Lord's Love to her Soul, and was not in the least daunted when she spake of her Death, but seemed greatly delighted in the Apprehension of her nearness to her Father's House: And it was not long before she was fill'd with Joy unspeakable in believing.

Also obsessed with death, but with a less joyful view, was Michael Wigglesworth's *Day of Doom* (1662), an account of the Judgment Day in verse intended to reinvigorate Puritan spirituality. *Day of Doom* was New England's first best-seller. The verses reprinted here may suggest why.

By the second quarter of the eighteenth century, attitudes toward death were changing, as the gravestone iconography after about 1730 attests. The epitaphs stressing mortality appeared much less frequently, and

Joseph Tapping headstone, Boston, 1678. (*From the Daniel and Jessie Lie Farber Collection of Gravestone Photographs, American Antiquarian Society*)

Betsy Shaw headstone, Plymouth, 1795. (*From the Daniel and Jessie Lie Farber Collection of Gravestone Photographs, American Antiquarian Society*)

the ever-present foreboding death's-head, shovels, and hourglass symbols of the seventeenth century began to be replaced by smiling cherubs, angels, natural objects, and sentimentalized willow and urn motifs.

Note the details shown above from an eighteenth-century gravestone compared with those on the Tapping stone. A winged image of Mrs. Betsy Shaw (Plymouth, Massachusetts, 1795) optimistically represents the flight of her soul heavenward. This romantic design tells us much about the secularization of New England society and the passing of the early Puritans' intense seriousness about their godly mission in America to redeem humankind.

As the funerary handiwork of stonecarvers reveals, the Puritans' early providential self-image had been transformed. Less piety and morbid introspection, more worldliness and individual hopefulness had spread through the Puritan Holy Commonwealth. Can you point out how these changes are reflected on the Shaw and Tapping gravestones? What do the markings, inscriptions, and design of tombstones in cemeteries near you reveal about the changing experience and values of later Americans?

Day of Doom
Michael Wigglesworth (1662)

56

*Now it comes in, and every sin unto men's
 charge doth lay;
It judgeth them and doth condemn, though all
 the world say nay.*

*It so stingeth and tortureth, it worketh such
 distress,
That each man's self against himself is forced
 to confess.*

57

*It's vain moreover for men to cover the least
 iniquity;
The Judge hath seen, and privy been to all
 their villainy.
He unto light and open sight the work of
 darkness brings;
He doth unfold both new and old, both known
 and hidden things.*

58

*All filthy facts and secret acts, however closely
 done
And long concealed, are there revealed before
 the mid-day sun.
Deeds of the night, shunning the light, which
 darkest corners sought,
To fearful blame and endless shame are there
 most justly brought.*

59

*And as all facts and grosser acts, so every word
 and thought,
Erroneous notions and lustful motion, are
 unto judgment brought,
No sin so small and trivial but hither it must
 come,
Nor so long past, but now at last it must
 receive a doom....*

188

*The Judge is strong; doers of wrong cannot his
 power withstand.
None can be flight run out of sight nor 'scape out
 of his hand.
Sad is their state, for advocate to plead their
 cause there's none–
None to prevent their punishment, or misery
 bemoan.*

189

*O dismal day! wither shall they for help and
 succor flee?
To God above, with hopes to move their
 greatest enemy?
His wrath is great, whose burning heat no
 floods of tears can slake:
His word stands fast, that they be cast into the
 burning lake.*

of events that nearly led to civil war. Like his brother, James II professed the Catholic faith. But unlike Charles II, who had disclosed this only on his deathbed, the new king announced his faith immediately on assuming the throne. Consternation ensued. Protestant England recoiled when James issued the Declaration of Indulgence, which granted liberty of worship to all. Although religious toleration is cherished today, it was unacceptable to most English Protestants 300 years ago. Belief that the declaration was primarily a concession to Catholics hardened when the king began creating Catholic peerages to fill the House of Lords; appointed Catholics to high government posts, including command of the English navy; and demanded that Oxford and Cambridge open their doors to Catholic students. In 1687, the king dismissed a resistant Parliament. When his wife, believed to be too old for further childbearing, gave birth to a son in 1688, a Catholic succession loomed.

Convinced that James was trying to seize absolute power and fearing a Catholic conspiracy, a group of Protestant leaders secretly plotted the king's downfall. In 1688, led by the earl of Shaftesbury, they invited William of Orange, a prince of the Netherlands, to invade England and take the throne with his wife, Mary, James's Protestant daughter. James abdicated rather than fight. It was a bloodless victory for Protestantism, for parliamentary power and the limitation of kingly prerogatives, and for the propertied merchants and gentry of England who stood behind the revolt.

The response of New Englanders to these events stemmed from their previous experience with royal authority and their fear of "papists." In 1676, New England became a prime target for efforts to reorganize the empire and crack down on smuggling, which had prevailed there for two generations. In 1684, Charles II had annulled the Massachusetts charter. Two years later, James II appointed Sir Edmund Andros, a crusty professional soldier and former governor of New York, to rule over the newly created Dominion of New England. Soon the Dominion gathered under one government the colonies of New Hampshire, Massachusetts, Connecticut, Plymouth, Rhode Island, New York, New Jersey, and part of Maine. Puritans now had to swallow the bitter fact that they were subjects of London bureaucrats who cared more about shaping a disciplined empire than about the special religious vision of one group of overseas subjects.

At first, New Englanders accepted Andros, though coolly. But he soon earned their hatred by invading freedoms they had come to cherish. He imposed taxes without legislative consent, ended trial by jury, abolished the General Court of Massachusetts (which had met annually since 1630), muzzled Boston's town meeting, and challenged the validity of all land titles. He mocked the Puritans by converting a Boston Puritan church into an Anglican chapel, held services there on Christmas Day—a gesture that to Puritans stank of popery—and overturned their practice of suppressing religious dissent.

When news reached Boston in April 1689 that William of Orange had landed in England, ending James II's hated Catholic regime, Bostonians streamed into the streets to the beat of drums. They imprisoned

BOSTON'S FIRST TOWN-HOUSE
1657~1711

The center of government and official news in colonial New England was Boston's town house, built in 1657. Note the stocks and whipping post at lower left. (*From* Boston's First Town House, 1657–1711, *1930, by Charles A. Lawrence/ The Bostonian Society*)

Andros, a suspected papist, and overwhelmed the fort in Boston harbor, which held most of the governor's small contingent of red-coated royal troops. Andros escaped, disguised in women's clothing, but was quickly recaptured. Boston's ministers, along with merchants and former magistrates, led the rebellion, but city folk of the lower orders supplied the foot soldiers. For three years, an interim government ruled Massachusetts while the Bay colonists awaited a new charter and a royal governor.

Although Bostonians had dramatically rejected royal authority, which to them represented the "bloody Devotees of Rome" as well as arbitrary power, no internal revolution occurred. However, growing social stratification and the emergence of a political elite led some citizens to argue that men of modest means but common sense might better be trusted with power. "Anarchy" was the word chosen by Samuel Willard, minister of Boston's Third Church, to tar the popular spirit he saw unloosed in Boston in the aftermath of Andros's ouster. But such egalitarian rumblings came to little.

Leisler's Rebellion in New York

In New York, the Glorious Revolution was similarly bloodless at first but far more disruptive. It was not necessary to overthrow royal government when news arrived of James II's abdication. It simply melted away. When a local militia captain, the German-born Jacob Leisler, appeared at Fort James at the lower tip of Manhattan, Governor Francis Nicholson made only a token show of resistance before quietly stepping down. Displacing the governor's "popishly affected dogs and rogues," Leisler established an interim government and ruled with an elected Committee of Safety for 13 months until a governor appointed by King William arrived.

Leisler's government enjoyed popularity among small landowners and urban laboring people. Most of the upper echelon, however, detested him. They remembered that he had come to New Amsterdam in 1660 as a common foot soldier of the Dutch West India Company and three years later had leapfrogged into the merchant class by marrying a wealthy widow. After the English took over the Dutch colony in 1664, he was often at odds with New Yorkers of the upper rank. "Up jump into the saddle hott brain'd Capt. Leisler," sneered one aristocrat after Leisler's takeover. Thereafter, the Leislerians were often labeled as people of "mean birth, and sordid education and desperate fortunes."

Such antipathy was returned in kind by lower- and middle-class Dutch inhabitants, who felt a smoldering resentment toward the town's English elite. Many Dutch merchants had readily adjusted to the English conquest of New Netherland in 1664, and many incoming English merchants had married into Dutch families. But beneath the upper class, where economic success softened ethnic friction, incidents of Anglo-Dutch hostility were common. Ordinary Dutch families felt that the English were crowding them out of the society they had built.

The Glorious Revolution was the spark igniting this smoldering social conflict. Leisler shared Dutch hostility toward New York's English elite, and his sympathy for the common people, mostly Dutch, earned him the hatred of the city's oligarchy. Leisler freed imprisoned debtors, planned a town-meeting system of government for New York City, and replaced merchants with artisans in important offices. By the autumn of 1689, Leislerian mobs were attacking the property of some of New York's wealthiest merchants. Two merchants, refusing to recognize Leisler's authority, were jailed.

Leisler's opponents, accustomed to controlling government, were horrified at the power of what they called the "rabble" or the "tumultuous multitude." They believed that ordinary people had no right to rebel against authority or to exercise political power. When a new English governor arrived in 1691, the anti-Leislerians embraced him and charged Leisler and seven of his assistants with treason for assuming the government without royal instructions.

In the ensuing trial, Leisler and Jacob Milbourne, his son-in-law and chief lieutenant, were convicted of treason by an all-English jury and hanged. Leisler's popularity among the artisans of the city was evident when his wealthy opponents could find no carpenter in the city who would furnish a ladder to use at the scaffold. After his execution, peace gradually returned to New York, but for years provincial and city politics reflected the deep rift between Leislerians and anti-Leislerians.

Southern Rumblings

The Glorious Revolution also focused dissatisfactions in several southern colonies. Because Maryland was ruled by a Catholic proprietor, the Protestant majority seized power on word of the Glorious Revolution and used it for their own purposes. Lord Baltimore had returned to England in 1684. In 1688, when his instructions to his colony to honor William and Mary were delayed, leading officials and planters formed a Protestant Association. Seizing control of the government in July 1689, they vowed to cleanse Maryland of popery and to reform a corrupt customs service, cut taxes and fees, and extend the rights of the representative assembly. The militant Protestant John Coode, formerly a fiery Anglican minister who, as we have seen, had been involved in a brief rebellion in 1681, assumed the reins of government and held them until the arrival of Maryland's first royal governor in 1692.

In neighboring Virginia, the wounds of Bacon's Rebellion were still healing when word of the Glorious Revolution arrived. The fact that Virginia lived under a Catholic governor, Lord Howard of Effingham, and a number of Catholic officials he had installed fostered rumors of a Catholic plot. News of the revolution in England led a group of planters, suffering a prolonged drop in tobacco prices, to attempt an overthrow of the governor. The uprising quickly faded when the governor's council asserted itself and took its own measures to remove Catholics from positions of authority.

The Glorious Revolution brought lasting political changes to several colonies. The Dominion of New England collapsed. Connecticut and Rhode Island regained the right to elect their own governors, but Massachusetts (now including Plymouth) and New Hampshire became royal colonies with governors appointed by the king. In Massachusetts, a new royal charter in 1691 eliminated Church membership as a voting requirement. The Maryland proprietorship was abolished (to be restored in 1715 when the Calverts became Protestant), and Catholics were barred from office. Everywhere Protestant Englishmen celebrated their liberties.

The Social Basis of Politics

Although the colonial insurrections associated with the Glorious Revolution sought primarily to overthrow arbitrary royal governors and foil papist plots (most of them imaginary), they revealed social and political tensions that accompanied the transplanting of English society to the North American wilderness. Still hardly beyond the frontier stage, the immature societies along the coast were fluid, unruly, and competitive. They lacked the stable political systems and acknowledged leadership class thought necessary for maintaining social order.

The colonial elite tried, of course, to foster social and political stability. The best insurance of this, they believed, was the maintenance of a stratified society where children were subordinate to parents, women to men, servants to masters, and the poor to the rich. Amid the barbarizing conditions of the New World, where anarchy lurked just beyond every threshold, it was especially vital—in the eyes of the upper echelon—to reproduce the social arrangements of the Old World.

Hence, in every settlement, leaders tried to maintain a system of social gradations and subordination. Puritans did not file into church on Sundays and occupy the pews in random fashion. Rather, the seats were "doomed," or assigned according to customary yardsticks of respectability—age, parentage, social position, wealth, and occupation. Even in fluid Virginia, lower-class people were hauled before courts for horse racing because this was a sport by law reserved for men of social distinction.

But this social ideal proved difficult to maintain. Regardless of previous rank, settlers rubbed elbows so frequently and faced such raw conditions together that those without pedigrees often saw little reason to defer to men of superior rank. "In Virginia," explained John Smith, "a plain soldier that can use a pickaxe and spade is better than five knights." Colonists everywhere gave respect not to those who claimed it by birth, but to those who earned it by deed.

Adding to the difficulty of reproducing a traditional social order in the colonies was the social fluidity in frontier society. A native elite gradually formed, but it had no basis, as in Europe, in legally defined and hereditary social rank. Planters and merchants, accumulating large estates, aped the English gentry by cultivating the arts, building fine houses, and acquiring symbols of respectability such as libraries, coaches, and racehorses. Yet their place was rarely secure. In the race to drag wealth from the resource-rich environment, new competitors nipped constantly at their heels.

Amid such social flux, the elite could never command general allegiance to the ideal of a fixed social structure. Ambitious men on the rise such as Nathaniel Bacon and Jacob Leisler, and thwarted men below them who followed their lead, rose up against the constituted authorities, which they almost certainly would not have dared to do so in their homelands. When they gained power during the Glorious Revolution, in every case only briefly, the leaders of these uprisings linked themselves with a tradition of English struggle against tyranny and oligarchical power. They vowed to make government more responsive to the ordinary people, who composed most of their societies.

In both North and South, this earned parvenu leaders the epithet "Masaniello," after the peasant fish seller of Naples who in 1647 had mobilized ordinary people against exploitation by the rich. Masaniello briefly controlled the city, momentarily stood the political order on its head, and became an Italian Robin Hood. In America, Virginia's royal governor likened Bacon's Rebellion to Masaniello's revolt. In New York, Leisler was labeled a local Masaniello by his wealthy enemies. In Maryland, John Coode proudly called himself a Chesapeake Masaniello. The comparisons were far from exact, but references to the Italian folk hero indicate that colonists from all ranks recognized that social relations in their competitive and open society were subject to violent alterations that violated the ideal of a fixed, orderly social system.

Witchcraft in Salem

The ordinary people in the colonies, for whom Bacon and Leisler tried to speak, could sometimes be misled, as the tragic events of the Salem witch hunts demonstrated. In Massachusetts, the deposing of Governor Andros left the colony in political limbo for three years, and this allowed what might have been a brief outbreak of witchcraft in the little community of Salem to escalate into a bitter and bloody battle. The provincial government, caught in transition, reacted only belatedly.

On a winter's day in 1692, 9-year-old Betty Parris and her 11-year-old cousin Abigail Williams began to play at magic in the kitchen of a small house in Salem, Massachusetts. They enlisted the aid of Tituba, the slave of Betty's father, Samuel Parris, the minister of the small community. Tituba told voodoo tales handed down from her African past and baked "witch cakes." The girls soon became seized with fits and began making wild gestures and speeches. Soon other young girls in the village were behaving strangely. Village elders extracted confessions that they were being tormented by Tituba and two other women, both social outcasts.

What began as the innocent play of young girls turned into a ghastly rending of a farm community capped by the execution of 20 villagers accused of witchcraft. In the seventeenth century, people still took literally the biblical injunction "Thou shalt not suffer a witch to live." For centuries throughout western Europe, people had believed that witches followed Satan's bidding and did evil to anyone he designated. Communities had accused and sentenced women to death for witchcraft far more often than men. In Massachusetts, more than 100 people, mostly older women, had been accused of witchcraft before 1692, and more than a dozen had been hanged.

In Salem, the initial accusations against three older women quickly multiplied. Within weeks, dozens had been charged with witchcraft, including several prominent members of the community. But formal prosecution of the accused witches could not proceed because neither the new royal charter of 1691 nor the royal governor to rule the colony had yet arrived. For three months, while charges spread, local authorities could only jail the accused without trial. When Governor William Phips arrived from England in May 1692, he ordered a special court to try the accused. By then events had careened out of control.

All through the summer, the court listened to testimony. By September it had condemned about two dozen villagers. The authorities hanged 19 of them on barren "Witches Hill" outside the town and crushed 80-year-old Giles Corey to death under heavy stones. The trials rolled on into 1693, but by then, colonial leaders, including many of the clergy, recognized that a feverish fear of one's neighbors, rather than witchcraft itself, had possessed the little village of Salem.

Many factors contributed to the hysteria. Among them were generational differences between older Puritan colonists and the sometimes less religiously motivated younger generation, old family animosities, population growth and pressures on the available farmland, and tensions between agricultural Salem Village and the nearby commercial center called Salem Town. An outbreak of food poisoning may also have caused hallucinogenic behavior. Probably nobody will ever fully understand the exact mingling

Witch hangings, usually of women, were numerous in Europe as well as the colonies; this woodcut appeared in *England's Grievance Discovered* (1655), a book on injustices in England's coal industry. Identified by letter in the picture are the hangman (A), town crier (B), sheriff (C), and magistrate (D).

of causes, but the fact that most of the individuals charged with witchcraft were women underscores the relatively weak position of women in Puritan society. The relentless spread of witchcraft accusations reflects the anxiety of this tumultuous era. War, economic disruption, the political takeover of the colony by Andros and then his overthrow, and erosion of the early generation's utopian vision all became a deadly mix.

CONTENDING FOR A CONTINENT

At the end of the seventeenth century, Indian wars and internal upheaval gave way to protracted international war. The smoldering struggle for mastery of the New World among four contending European powers—Holland, Spain, France, and England—now became overt. North America was less an arena of armed rivalry among the European powers than were the Carribbean sugar islands. Nonetheless, the global struggle for control of land and sea that erupted late in the seventeenth century—beginning nearly 100 years of conflict—reached the doorsteps of those who thought that in immigrating to North America they had left war behind.

Anglo-French Rivalry

In 1661, the French king, Louis XIV, ushered in a new era for New France. Determined to make his country the most powerful in Europe, the king regarded North America and the Caribbean with renewed interest. New France's timber resources would build the royal navy, its fish would feed the growing mass of slaves in the French West Indies, and its fur trade, if greatly expanded, would fill the royal coffers.

Under able governors such as Count Frontenac, New France grew in population, economic strength, and ambition in the late seventeenth century. In the 1670s, Louis Jolliet and Father Jacques Marquette, a Jesuit priest, explored an immense territory watered by the Mississippi and Missouri rivers, previously unknown to Europeans. A decade later, military engineers and priests began building forts and missions, one complementing the other, throughout the Great Lakes region and the Mississippi valley.

Visions of a mighty inland empire grew in the 1680s when René Robert de La Salle canoed down the Mississippi all the way to the Gulf of Mexico and planted a settlement in Texas at Matagorda Bay. The dream of connecting Canada and Louisiana by a chain of forts and trading posts would not be realized for another half century. But it was the French, with a colonial population of only 12,000, rather than the English, with colonies inhabited by 200,000, whom the Indian tribes permitted to settle in the interior of

North America. Traders and missionaries from France seemed very different in Indian villages than land-hungry, expansionist English settlers.

The growth of French strength and ambitions brought New England and New France into deadly conflict for a generation, beginning in the late seventeenth century. Religious hostility overlaid commercial rivalry. Protestant New Englanders regarded Catholic New France as a satanic challenge to their divinely sanctioned mission. When the European wars began in 1689, precipitated by Louis XIV's territorial aggression in western and central Europe, armed conflict between England and France quickly extended into every overseas theater where the two powers had colonies. In North America, the battle zone was New York, New England, and eastern Canada.

In two wars, from 1689 to 1697 and 1702 to 1713, the English and French, while fighting in Europe, also sought to oust each other from the New World. The zone of greatest importance was the Caribbean, where slaves produced huge sugar fortunes. Both home governments understood that the North American colonies were important chiefly as a source of the timber and fish that sustained the sugar-producing tropical economy of the West Indies. On the North American mainland, problems of weather, disease, transport, and supply were so great that only irregular warfare was possible.

The English struck three times at the centers of French power—Port Royal, which commanded the access to the St. Lawrence River, and Quebec, the administrative center of New France. In 1690, during King William's War (1689–1697), their small flotilla captured Port Royal, the hub of Acadia (which was returned to France at the end of the war). The English assault on Quebec, however, failed disastrously. In Queen Anne's War (1702–1713), New England attacked Port Royal three times before finally capturing it in 1710. A year later, when England sent a flotilla of 60 ships and 5,000 men to conquer Canada, the land and sea operations foundered before reaching their destinations.

With European-style warfare miserably unsuccessful in America, both England and France attempted to subcontract military tasks to their Indian allies. Here was a new aspect of the meeting of cultures—the use of Native Americans as mercenaries in an international conflict. This policy occasionally succeeded, especially with the French, who gladly sent their own troops into the fray alongside Indian partners. The French and their Indian allies wiped out the frontier outpost of Schenectady, New York, in 1690; razed Wells, Maine, and Deerfield, Massachusetts, in 1703; and battered other towns along the New England frontier during both wars.

Visiting French Louisiana in 1735, Alexander de Batz painted members of the Illinois tribe who traded at New Orleans. Note the hatted African, who apparently has been adopted by the Illinois. (*Alexander de Batz, Desseins de Sauvages de Plusieurs Natims, 1735, Peabody Museum, Harvard University, Photograph by: Hillel Burger*)

In retaliation, the Iroquois, supplied by the English, stung several French settlements and left New France "bewildered and benumbed" after a massacre near Montreal in 1689. Assessing their own interests, and too powerful to be bullied by either France or England, the Iroquois sat out the second war in the early eighteenth century. Convinced that neutrality served their purposes better than acting as mercenaries for the English, they held to the principle that "we are a free people uniting ourselves to whatever sachem [chief] we wish."

The Results of War

The Peace of Utrecht in 1713, which ended Queen Anne's War, capped the century-long rise of England and the decline of Spain in the rivalry for the sources of wealth outside Europe. England, the big winner, received Newfoundland and Acadia (renamed Nova Scotia), and France recognized English sovereignty over the fur-rich Hudson Bay territory. France retained Cape Breton Island, controlling the entrance to the St. Lawrence River. In the Caribbean, France yielded St. Kitts and Nevis to England. Spain lost its provinces in Italy and the last of its holdings in the Netherlands to the Austrian Habsburgs. Spain also surrendered Gibraltar and Minorca to England and awarded the English the lucrative privilege of supplying the Spanish empire in America with African slaves, a favor formerly enjoyed by the French Senegal Company.

The French were the big losers in these wars, but they did not abandon their New World ambitions. Soon after Louis XIV died in 1715, his successors tried to regain lost time in America by mounting a huge

Timeline

1600–1700	Dutch monopolize slave trade
1619	First Africans imported to Virginia
1637	Pequot War in New England
1640s	New England merchants enter slave trade
	Virginia forbids blacks to carry firearms
1650–1670	Judicial and legislative decisions in Chesapeake colonies solidify racial lines
1651	Parliament passes first navigation act
1664	English conquer New Netherland
1673–1685	French expand into Mississippi valley
1675–1677	King Philip's War in New England
1676	Bacon's Rebellion in Virginia
1682	La Salle canoes down Mississippi River and claims Louisiana for France
1684	Massachusetts charter recalled
1688	Glorious Revolution in England, followed by accession of William and Mary
1689	Overthrow of Governor Andros in New England
	Leisler's Rebellion in New York
1689–1697	King William's War
1690s	Transition from white indentured servant to black slave labor begins in Chesapeake region
1692	Witchcraft hysteria in Salem
1700	Spanish establish first mission in Arizona
1702–1713	Queen Anne's War
1713	Peace of Utrecht

North American Cultural Regions

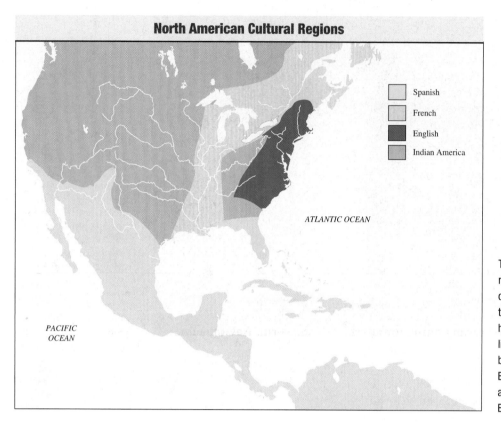

Spanish

French

English

Indian America

ATLANTIC OCEAN

PACIFIC OCEAN

This map of European cultural regions in mid-eighteenth-century North America disguises the cultural influence of hundreds of Indian societies that lived among, between, and beyond the sparsely settled European settlements. Only along the eastern seaboard was European dominance secure.

expedition to settle Louisiana. Because France deported many undesirables to the colony and because the French aristocracy destroyed by wild speculation the stock that financed the project, few French immigrants joined the settlement of New Orleans. French colonies expanded only in the Caribbean, where by 1750, the islands of Hispaniola, Martinique, and Guadeloupe counted 46,000 whites and 250,000 slaves. Although the islands enriched a few, they strengthened the empire little, because slaves could not be armed and the islands were expensive to defend.

After the Peace of Utrecht, Spain still retained—on paper—a vast empire in North America. However, its hold on the southern tier of the continent was very tenuous, and it had learned how easily its thinly peopled missions and frontier outposts could be crippled or destroyed by chafing Native Americans and invading English. In the first half of the eighteenth century, the Spanish settlements stagnated, suffering from Spain's colonial policy that regarded them as marginal, money-losing affairs worth the trouble only as essentially defensive outposts.

Spain's priority was not to expand its presence in North America but to preserve what it had by keeping others away. That in itself would prove to be difficult, for this garrison mentality had to compete with the commercially minded English and French, whose

colonial population, especially the former's, was growing rapidly. Small, impoverished Spanish frontier outposts could do little to halt the expansion of British and French America.

Though England had rebuffed France after a generation of war, New England suffered grievous economic and human losses. In time, Nova Scotia would provide a new frontier for Puritan farmers. But the two wars between 1689 and 1713 struck hard at New England's economy. Massachusetts bore the brunt of the burden. Probably one-fifth of all able-bodied males in the colony participated in the Canadian campaigns, and of these, about one-quarter never lived to tell of the terrors of New England's first major experience with international warfare. At the end of the first war, in 1697, one leader bemoaned that Massachusetts was left "quite exhausted and ready to sink under the calamities and fatigue of a tedious consuming war." The war debt was £50,000 sterling in Massachusetts alone, a greater per capita burden than the national debt today.

At the end of the second conflict, in 1713, war widows were so numerous that the Bay Colony faced its first serious poverty problem. In addition, wartime taxes had "much impoverished and enfeebled" the people, and price inflation had eaten deeply into the pocketbooks of most working families. Pamphleteers in New England's principal port wrote of the "present melancholy circumstances" and the "distressed state of the Town of Boston."

The colonies south of New England remained on the sidelines during most of the war. But war at sea between European rivals affected even those who sat out the land war. In Queen Anne's War, New York lost one of its best grain markets when Spain, allied with France, outlawed American foodstuffs in its West Indian colonies. The French navy plucked off nearly 30 New York merchant vessels, about one-quarter of the port's fleet, and disrupted the vital sea lanes between the mainland and the Caribbean to the detriment of Philadelphia's grain merchants.

The burdens and rewards fell unevenly on the participants, as usually happens in wartime. Some low-born men could rise spectacularly. William Phips, the twenty-sixth child in his family, had been a poor sheep farmer and ship's carpenter in Maine who seemed destined to go nowhere. Then he won a fortune by recovering a sunken Spanish treasure ship in the West Indies in 1687. For that feat, he was given command of the expedition against Port Royal in 1690. Victory there catapulted him to the governorship of Massachusetts in 1691; thereafter his status was secure.

Other men, already rich, got richer. Andrew Belcher of Boston, who had grown wealthy on provisioning contracts during King Philip's War (1675–1677), combined patriotism with profit in King William's and Queen Anne's wars by supplying warships and outfitting the New England expeditions to Canada. As one of the favored recipients of the fruits of war, Belcher became a local titan, riding through Boston's crooked streets in London-built coaches, erecting a handsome mansion on State Street, and purchasing slaves to symbolize his rise to the pinnacle of New England society.

Most men, especially those who did the fighting, gained little, however, and many lost all. The least securely placed New Englanders—indentured servants, apprentices, recently arrived immigrants, unskilled laborers, fishermen, and ordinary farmers—supplied most of the voluntary or involuntary troops, and they died in numbers that seem staggering today. Antipopery, dreams of glory, and promises of plunder in French Canada lured most of them into uniform. Having achieved no place on the paths leading upward, they grasped at straws. A hefty percentage of those who sailed in the naval expeditions against Port Royal or plodded overland to attack Montreal and Quebec never lived even to collect their meager wages. None found the advertised booty, which turned out to be only a sugarplum dangled by military recruiters.

Conclusion

Controlling the New Environment

By the second decade of the eighteenth century, the 12 English colonies on the eastern edge of North America had secured footholds in the hemisphere and erected the basic scaffolding of colonial life. With the aid of England, they had ousted the Dutch from their mid-Atlantic perch. They had fought the French to a draw and held their own against the Spanish. The coastal Indian tribes were reeling from disease and a series of wars that secured the colonists' land base along 1,000 miles of coastal plain. Though never controlling the powerful Indian tribes of the interior, the colonists had established a profitable trade with them. The settlers had overcome a scarcity of labor by copying the other European colonists in the hemisphere, who had linked the west coast of Africa to the New World through the ghastly trade in human flesh. Finally, the colonists had engaged in insurrections against what they viewed as arbitrary and tainted governments imposed by England.

The embryo of British America carried into the eighteenth century contained peculiarly mixed features. Still physically isolated from Europe, the colonists developed of necessity a large measure of self-reliance. Slowly, they began to identify themselves as the permanent inhabitants of a new land rather than as transplanted English, Dutch, or Scots-Irish. Viewing land and labor as the indispensable elements of a fruitful economy, they learned to exploit without apologies the land of one dark-skinned people and the labor of another. Yet even as they attained a precarious mastery in a triracial society, they were being culturally affected by the very people to which whose land and labor they laid claim. Although utopian visions of life in America still reverberated in the heads of some, most colonists had awakened to the reality that life in the New World was a puzzling mixture of unpredictable opportunity and sudden turbulence, unprecedented freedom and debilitating wars, racial intermingling and racial separation. It was a New World in much more than a geographic sense, for the people of three cultures who now inhabited it had remade it; and, while doing so, they were remaking themselves.

Recommended Reading

African Bondage

Philip Curtin, *The Atlantic Slave Trade: A Census* (1969) and *The Rise and Fall of the Plantation Complex* (1990); David B. Davis, *The Problem of Slavery in Western Culture* (1966); Carl N. Degler, *Neither Black nor White: Slavery and Race Relations in Brazil and the United States* (1971); Richard S. Dunn, *Sugar and Slaves: The Rise of the Planter Class in the English West Indies, 1624–1713* (1972); H. Hoetink, *Slavery and Race Relations in the Americas* (1973); Patrick Manning, *Slavery and African Life: Occidental, Oriental, and African Slave Trades* (1990); James A. Rawley, *The Transatlantic Slave Trade* (1981); Walter Rodney, *West Africa and the Atlantic Slave Trade* (1969); Frank Tannenbaum, *Slave and Citizen (1956);* Hugh Thomas, *The Slave Trade* (1997); John Thornton, *Africa and Africans in the Making of the Atlantic World, 1440–1680* (1992); Lorena Walsh, *From Calabar to Carter's Grove: The History of a Virginia Slave Community* (1997).

Slave Culture

Ira Berlin, *Many Thousands Gone: The First Two Centuries of Slavery in North America* (1998); T. H. Breen and Stephen Innes, *"Myne Owne Ground": Race and Freedom on Virginia's Eastern Shore, 1640–1676* (1980); Thomas J. Davis, *A Rumor of Revolt: The "Great Negro Plot" in Colonial New York* (1985); Michael A. Gomez, *Exchanging Our Country Marks: The Transformation of African Identities in the Colonial and Antebellum South* (1998); Gwendolyn Midlo Hall, *Africans in Colonial Louisiana* (1992); Winthrop D. Jordan, *White Over Black* (1968); Marvin L. Michael Kay and Lorin Lee Cary, *Slavery in North Carolina, 1748–1775* (1995); Allan Kulikoff, *Tobacco and Slaves: The Development of Southern Cultures in the Chesapeake, 1680–1800* (1986); Philip D. Morgan, *Slave Counterpoint: Black Culture in the Eighteenth-Century Chesapeake and Low-Country* (1998); Gerald Mullin, *Flight and Rebellion: Slave Resistance in Eighteenth-Century Virginia* (1972); Michael Mullin, *Africa in America: Slave Acculturation and Resistance in the American South* (1992); William Piersen, *Black Yankees: The Development of an African-American Subculture in Eighteenth-Century New England* (1988); Mechal Sobel, *The World They Made Together: Black and White Relations in Eighteenth-Century Virginia* (1987); Betty Wood, *Slavery in Colonial Georgia, 1730–1775* (1984); Peter H. Wood, *Black Majority: Negroes in South Carolina from 1670 Through the Stono Rebellion* (1974); Michael A. Gomez, *Exchanging Our Country Marks: The Transformation of African Identities in the Colonial and Antebellum South* (1998); Lorena S. Walsh, *From Calabar to Carter's Grove: The History of a Virginia Slave Community* (1997); Graham Russell Hodges, *Root and Branch: African Americans in New York and East Jersey, 1613–1863* (1999).

The Struggle for Land

James Axtell, *The European and the Indian* (1981); Colin G. Calloway, *New Worlds for All: Indians, Europeans, and the Remaking of Early America* (1997); Francis Jennings, *The Ambiguous Iroquois Empire* (1984); Jill Lepore, *The Name of the War: King Philip's War and the Origins of American Identity* (1998); Calvin Martin, *Keepers of the Game: Indian-Animal Relationships and the Fur Trade* (1978); Gary B. Nash, *Red, White, and Black*, 4th ed. (2000); Daniel Usner, Jr., *Indians, Settlers, and Slaves in a Frontier Exchange Economy: The Lower Mississippi Valley Before 1783* (1992); Wilcomb Washburn, *The Governor and the Rebel* (1957); J. Leitch Wright, *The Only Land They Knew: The Tragic Story of the American Indians in the Old South* (1981).

An Era of Instability

Paul Boyer and Steven Nissenbaum, *Salem Possessed: The Social Origins of Witchcraft* (1974); John P. Demos, *Entertaining Satan: Witchcraft and the Culture of Early New England* (1982); Carol F. Karlsen, *The Devil in the Shape of a Woman* (1987); David Lovejoy, *The Glorious Revolution in America* (1972); Mary Beth Norton, *Founding Mothers and Fathers: Gendered Power and the Forming of American Society* (1996); Richard Weisman, *Witchcraft, Magic, and Religion in 17th-Century Massachusetts* (1984).

Contending for a Continent

Ramon A. Gutiérrez, *When Jesus Came, the Corn Mothers Went Away: Marriage, Sexuality, and Power in New Mexico, 1500–1846* (1992); A. H. Johns, *Storms Brewed in Other Men's Worlds: The Confrontation of Indians, Spanish, and French in the Old Southwest* (1975); Oakah L. Jones, Jr., *Los Paisanos: Spanish Settlers on the Northern Frontier of New Spain* (1979); D. W. Meinig, *The Shaping of America: Atlantic America, 1492–1800* (1986); Edward Spicer, *Cycles of Conquest: The Impact of Spain, Mexico, and the United States on the Indians of the Southwest, 1533–1960* (1962); Ian K. Steele, *Warpaths: Invasions of North America* (1994); David J. Weber, *The Spanish Frontier in North America* (1992); Richard White, *The Middle Ground: Indians, Empires, and Republics in the Great Lakes Region, 1650–1815* (1991).

Fiction and Film

Louise Erdrich's poem titled "Captivity," which can be found in her *Jacklight* collection (1984), is a valuable Indian-centered reading of one of the most popular Indian captivity accounts ever published—Mary Rowlandson's *A Narrative of the Captivity, Sufferings and Removes of Mrs. Mary Rowlandson,* first published in 1682. Boston's WGBH has produced a superb four-part video series on *Africans in America* (1998). The first two parts cover slavery and slave culture in the seventeenth and eighteenth centuries. Much shorter is *A Son of Africa: The Slave Narrative of Olaudah Equiano,* a half-hour video, produced by the BBC, of the only eighteenth-century slave who wrote an autobiography. *Three Sovereigns for Sarah* (1985), a PBS miniseries starring Vanessa Redgrave, stunningly dramatizes the Salem witchcraft trials. Arthur Miller's play, *The Crucible* (1953) is on the same topic and is as engaging today as it was three decades ago when it played on stages around the country.

Suggested Web Sites

http://etext.virginia.edu/salem/witchcraft

Witchcraft in Salem Village. Extensive archive of the 1692 trials and life in late seventeenth-century Massachusetts.

http://dpls.dacc.wisc.edu/slavedata/index.html

DPLS Archive: Slave Movement During the Eighteenth and Nineteenth Centuries (Wisconsin). This site explores the slave ships and the slave trade that carried millions of Africans to the New World.

http://vi.uh.edu/pages/mintz/primary.htm

Excerpts From Slave Narratives. The seventeenth- through nineteenth-century accounts of slavery housed in this site speak volumes about the many impacts of slavery.

http://www.thc.state.tx.us/belle/index.html

La Salle Shipwreck Project. This Texas Historical Commission site is about the archaeological dig to recover the ship of one of America's famous early explorers.

http://www.law.umkc.edu/faculty/projects/ftrials/salem/salem.htm

Salem Witchcraft Trials (1692). Images, chronology, court, and official documents by Dr. Doug Linder at University of Missouri—Kansas City Law School.

http://www.yale.edu/lawweb/avalon/18th.htm

Colonial Documents. The key documents of the Colonial Era are reproduced here, as are some of the important documents from earlier and later time periods in American history.

http://members.aol.com/jeworth/gboindex.htm

Georgia Before Oglethorpe. This resources guide informs the viewer about Native American Georgia in the seventeenth century.

http://www.ushistoryplace.com

A richly detailed on-line learning environment complete with interactive maps, timelines, history activities, primary source documents, and links to related American history sites.

The MATURING of COLONIAL SOCIETY

s a youth, Devereaux Jarratt knew only the isolated life of the small southern planter. Born in 1733 on the Virginia frontier, he was the third son of an immigrant yeoman farmer. In New Kent County, where Jarratt grew up, class status showed in a man's dress, his leisure habits, his house, even in his religion. A farmer's "whole dress and apparel," Jarratt recalled later, "consisted in a pair of coarse breeches, one or two shirts, a pair of shoes and stockings, an old felt hat, and a bear skin coat." In a maturing colonial society that was six generations old by the mid-eighteenth century, such simple folk stepped aside and tipped their hats when prosperous neighbors went by. "A periwig, in those days," recollected Jarratt, "was a distinguishing badge of gentle folk, and when I saw a man riding the road, near our house, with a wig on, it would so alarm my fears . . . that, I dare say, I would run off, as for my life."

As the colonies grew rapidly after 1700, economic development brought handsome gains for some, opened modest opportunities for many, but produced disappointment and privation for others. Jarratt remembered that his parents "neither sought nor expected any title, honors, or great things, either for themselves or their children. They wished us all brought up in some honest calling that we might earn our bread, by the sweat of our brow, as they did." But Jarratt was among those who advanced. His huge appetite for learning was apparent to his parents when as a small child he proved able to repeat entire chapters of the Bible before he had learned to read. That earned him some schooling. But at age 8, when his parents died, he had to take his place behind the plow alongside his brothers. Then, at 19, Jarratt was "called from the ax to the quill" by a neighboring planter's timely offer of a job tutoring his children.

Tutoring put Jarratt in touch with the world of wealth and status. Gradually, he advanced to positions in the households of wealthy Virginia planters. His modest success also introduced him to the world of evangelical religion. In the eighteenth century, an explosion of religious fervor dramatically reversed the growing secularism of the settlers. Jarratt first encountered evangelicalism in the published sermons of George Whitefield, an English clergyman.

But it was later, at the plantation of John Cannon, "a man of great possessions in lands and slaves," that he personally experienced conversion under the influence of Cannon's wife. Jarratt later became a clergyman in the Anglican Church, which was dominated in the South by wealthy and dignified planters. He never lost his religious zeal and desire to carry religion to the common people. In this commitment to spiritual renewal, he participated in the first mass religious movement to occur in colonial society.

Colonial North America in the first half of the eighteenth century was a thriving, changing set of regional societies that had developed from turbulent seventeenth-century beginnings. New England, the mid-Atlantic colonies, the Upper and Lower South, New France, and the northern frontier of New Spain were all distinct regions. Even within regions, diversity increased in the eighteenth century as incoming streams of immigrants, mostly from Africa, Germany, Ireland, and France, added new pieces to the emerging American mosaic.

Despite their bewildering diversity and lack of cohesion, the colonies along the Atlantic seaboard were affected similarly by population growth and economic development. Everywhere except on the frontier, class differences grew. A commercial orientation spread from north to south, especially in the towns, as local economies matured and forged links with the network of trade in the Atlantic basin. The exercise of political power of elected legislative assemblies and local bodies produced seasoned leaders, a tradition of local autonomy, and a widespread belief in a political ideology stressing the liberties that freeborn Englishmen should enjoy. All regions experienced a deep-running religious awakening that was itself connected to secular changes. All these themes will be explored as we follow the way scattered frontier settlements developed into mature provincial societies.

Joseph Beekman Smith, *Wesley Chapel on John Street, New York City—1768* (detail), completed 1817–1844 (based on earlier sketches). *(Old John Street United Methodist Church, New York)*

AMERICA'S FIRST POPULATION EXPLOSION

In 1680, some 150,000 colonizers clung to the eastern edge of North America. By 1750, they had swelled sevenfold to top one million. This growth rate, never experienced in Europe, staggered English policymakers. Perceptive observers understood that the population gap between England and its American colonies was closing rapidly. Benjamin Franklin's prediction in 1751—that before his grandchildren died, the colonies would outstrip the mother country in population—proved correct.

The population boom was fed from both internal and external sources. Among the white colonial population, a high marriage rate, large families, and lower mortality than in Europe prevailed by the 1720s. Natural increase accounted for much of the population boom in all the colonies and nearly all of it in New England, where immigrants arrived only in a trickle in the eighteenth century. The black population also began to increase naturally by the 1720s. American-born slaves, forming families and producing as many children as white families, soon began to outnumber slaves born in Africa. The 15,000 Africans in 1690 grew to 80,000 in 1730 and 325,000 in 1760. By then, when they composed one-fifth of the colonial population, their numbers were growing far more from natural increase than from importation.

The New Immigrants

While expanding through natural increase, the colonial population also absorbed waves of new immigrants. They were not English, however. The last sizable group of settlers from England had arrived at the end of the seventeenth century. The eighteenth-century newcomers, who far outnumbered those emigrating before 1700, came overwhelmingly from Germany, Switzerland, Ireland, and Africa, and they were mostly indentured servants and slaves. Of all the groups arriving in the eighteenth century, the Africans were the largest.

German-speaking settlers, about 90,000 strong, flocked to the colonies in the eighteenth century. Many were Protestant farmers of Swiss and French extraction, fleeing "God's three arrows"—famine, war, and pestilence. Drifting down the Rhine to Rotterdam, they crowded onto ships and began the long voyage to America. Once in the colonies, they hurried to areas where promoters promised them cheap and fertile land, low taxes, and freedom from military duty. Most settled between New York and South Carolina, with Pennsylvania claiming the largest number of them. Coming mostly in families, they turned much of the mid-Atlantic hinterland into

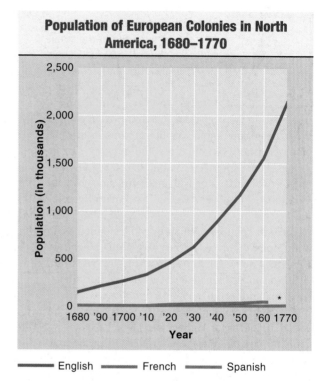

Whereas the population of French and Spanish colonies in North America inched upward (the result of few arriving immigrants and a low birthrate in settlements dominated by males), the population of English colonies soared.

a German-speaking region. Place names still mark their zone of settlement: Mannheim, New Berlin, and Herkimer, New York; Bethlehem, Ephrata, Nazareth, and Hanover, Pennsylvania; Hagerstown and Frederick, Maryland; Mecklenberg and New Hanover, North Carolina.

Even more Protestant Scots-Irish arrived. Several thousand from northern Ireland arrived each year after the Peace of Utrecht in 1713 reopened the Atlantic sea lanes. Mostly poor farmers, they streamed into the same backcountry areas where Germans were settling, though more of them followed the mountain valleys south into the Carolinas and Georgia. Occasionally mingling with the Germans, these Ulster families washed over the ridges of Appalachia until their appetite for land brought them face-to-face with the ancient occupiers of the land. No major Indian wars occurred between 1715 and 1754, but the frontier bristled with tension as the new settlers pushed westward.

In the enormous population growth occurring after 1715, the region southward from Pennsylvania increased most spectacularly. New England nearly tripled in population, but the middle and southern colonies quadrupled, though in the South the fast-growing slave population accounted for much more of

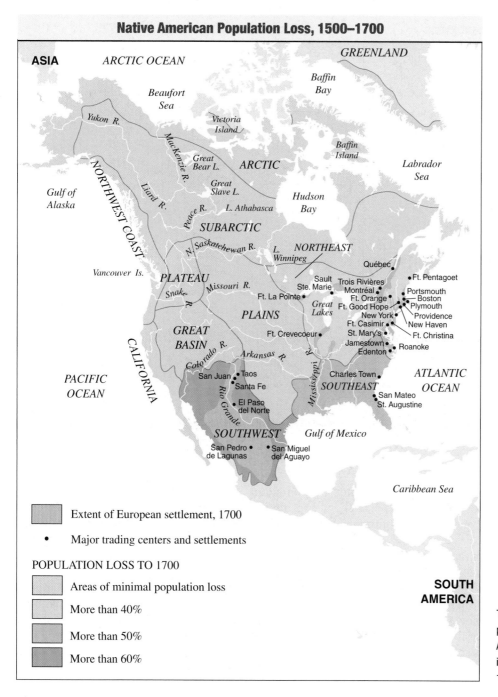

Native American Population Loss, 1500–1700

Extent of European settlement, 1700

• Major trading centers and settlements

POPULATION LOSS TO 1700

Areas of minimal population loss

More than 40%

More than 50%

More than 60%

This map does not show Indian population loss in Central America and the West Indies, but in most of this region the loss by 1700 was at least 80 percent.

the growth than in the mid-Atlantic. Pennsylvania, with its fertile lands and open door policy, grew fastest of all. Between 1720 and 1760, its population mushroomed from 30,000 to 180,000. Virginia, with a population of nearly 340,000 by 1760, remained by far the largest colony.

The social background of these new European immigrants differed substantially from that of their seventeenth-century predecessors. The early settlers included a number of men from the upper levels of the English social pyramid: university-trained Puritan

ministers, sons of wealthy gentry, and merchants. In the eighteenth century, few such men arrived.

The seventeenth-century immigrants had also included many from the middle rungs of the English social ladder—yeomen farmers, skilled craftsmen, and shopkeepers. They formed the backbone of the provincial churches and participated actively in community politics. Through "shipboard mobility," they moved up a notch or two on the western side of the Atlantic. Many lived to see their sons enter the professions or embark on a mercantile career in a society

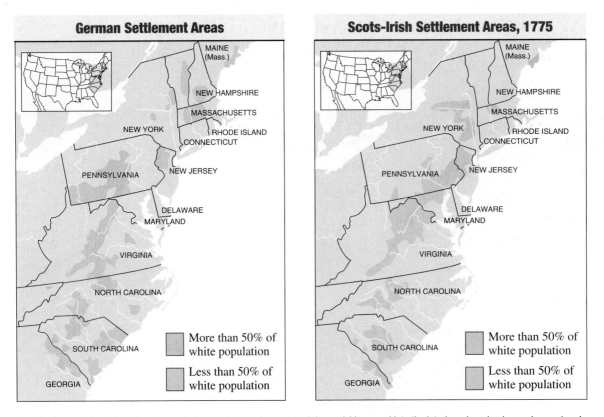

Most German and Scots-Irish immigrants in the 1700s were farmers, and they quickly moved into the interior, where land was cheapest and most available.

with plenty of room at the top. Such people came rarely in the eighteenth century, for religious persecution had waned in England, and material conditions had improved.

Slaves and indentured servants made up most of the incoming human tide after 1713. The traffic in servants became a regular part of the commerce linking Europe and America. Shipowners made their profits fetching sugar, fish, furs, rice, tobacco, and forest products eastward. On the westbound voyages, plenty of room remained for human cargo after loading the less bulky textiles and manufactured products desired by colonists.

Shipboard conditions for servants worsened in the eighteenth century and were hardly better than on slave ships. The wretchedness of the passage can be judged by the attempt at reform in the 1720s, when the British government required an increase in horizontal space to 6 feet by 18 inches per passenger, with no allowance for children.

Such attempts to reduce "tight packing" did little to improve shipboard life. Crammed between decks in stifling air, servants suffered from smallpox and fevers, rotten food, impure water, cold, and lice. "Children between the ages of one and seven seldom survive the sea voyage," bemoaned one German immigrant, "and parents must often watch their offspring suffer miserably, die, and be thrown into the ocean." One expedition of 3,000 Palatinate immigrants in 1717 lost 470 en route; on another, 250 succumbed shortly after reaching port. "I never see such parcels of poor wretches," one Virginia observer remarked of an incoming troop of servants in 1758, "some almost naked and what had clothes was as black as chimney sweepers and almost starved." The misery would be repeated thousands of times in the next two centuries. The shipboard mortality rate of about 15 percent in the colonial era made this the most unhealthy of all times to seek American shores.

Like indentured servants in the seventeenth century, servant immigrants who poured ashore after 1715 came mostly from the bottom of society. As earlier, some were petty criminals, political prisoners, and the castoffs of the cities. Yet they were bold and ambitious souls. "Men who emigrate," an Englishman commented, "are from the nature of their circumstances, the most active, hardy, daring, bold and resolute spirits, and probably the most mischievous also."

Once ashore, most indentured servants, especially males, found the labor system harsh. Merchants sold them, one shocked Britisher reported in 1773, "as they do their horses, and advertise them as they do their

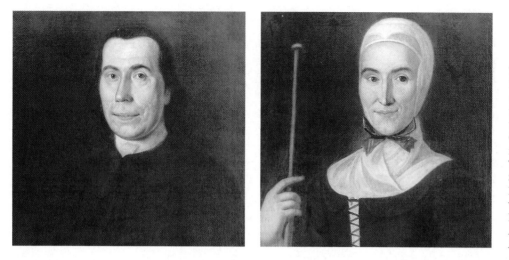

The communalistic Moravian immigrants who came to Pennsylvania in the 1740s dedicated themselves, like the Quakers, to peaceful relations with the Indians. The Prussian John Jacob Schmick and his Norwegian wife, Johanna, were missionaries to the Delawares. *(Moravian Historical Society, Nazareth, PA)*

beef and oatmeal." Facing cruel treatment, thousands of servants ran away. Advertisements for them filled the colonial newspapers alongside notices for escaped slaves. Servants knew the penalties if they were caught: whipping and additional service, usually reckoned at twice the time lost to the master, but sometimes calculated at a 5-to-1 or 10-to-1 ratio, as in Pennsylvania and Maryland. When war came in the mid-eighteenth century, hundreds of servants fled to the British army, not known for its kindly treatment of soldiers but preferable in many servants' eyes to four or five years under a harsh colonial master.

The goal of every servant was to secure a foothold on the ladder of opportunity. "The hope of buying land in America," a New Yorker noted, "is what chiefly induces people into America." However, many servants died before serving out their time. Others won freedom only to toil for years as poor day laborers and tenant farmers. Only a small proportion achieved the dream of becoming independent landholders. The indentured servants in the seventeenth-century Chesapeake world suffered fearful mortality rates, but those who survived often rose in society. Among the eighteenth-century servants, ironically, the chances of living long enough to complete the labor contract were much better, but the opportunity to climb into the propertied ranks became less favorable. The chief beneficiaries of the system of bound white labor were not the laborers but their masters.

Africans in Chains

The most numerous of the thousands of ships crossing the Atlantic in the eighteenth century were those fitted out as seagoing dungeons for slaves. The slave trade to the southern colonies after the Peace of Utrecht expanded so sharply that within two generations what had been a society with many slaves became a society built on slavery. From 1690 to 1715,

annual importations rarely exceeded 1,000, but in the next 15 years, the number probably doubled. The generation after 1730 witnessed the largest influx of African slaves in the colonial period, averaging about 5,000 a year. In the entire period from 1700 to 1775, more than 350,000 African slaves entered the American colonies.

Most of these miserable captives were auctioned off to southern planters, but some landed in the northern cities, especially New York and Philadelphia.

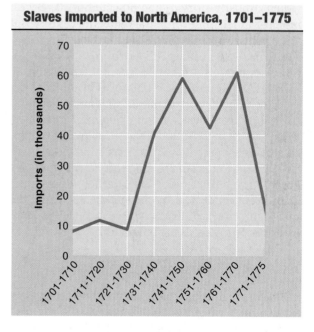

Slaves Imported to North America, 1701–1775

Overwhelmingly, Africans transported to the American colonies arrived from the 1730s to the 1770s. Rapid natural increase, as well as importation, swelled the African population to about 500,000 by the outbreak of the American Revolution. Source: R. C. Simmons, *The American Colonies: From Settlement to Independence*, 1976.

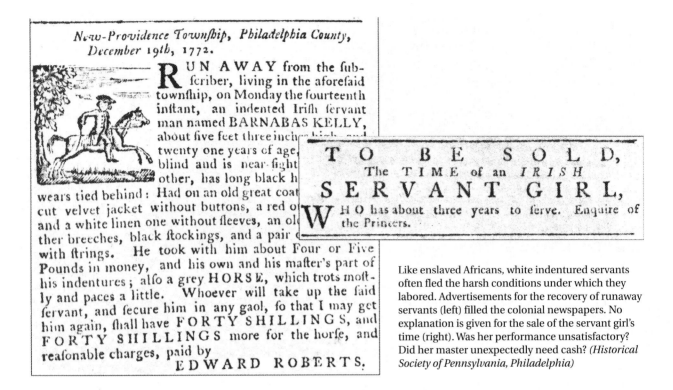

New-Providence Township, Philadelphia County, December 19th, 1772.

RUN AWAY from the subscriber, living in the aforesaid township, on Monday the fourteenth instant, an indented Irish servant man named BARNABAS KELLY, about five feet three inch~~es high, and~~ twenty one years of age, ~~is~~ blind and is near-sight~~ed in one~~ other, has long black h~~air which he~~ wears tied behind: Had on an old great coat, ~~a~~ cut velvet jacket without buttons, a red o~~ne,~~ and a white linen one without sleeves, an ol~~d lea-~~ ther breeches, black stockings, and a pair ~~of shoes~~ with strings.   He took with him about Four or Five Pounds in money, and his own and his master's part of his indentures; also a grey HORSE, which trots mostly and paces a little.   Whoever will take up the said servant, and secure him in any gaol, so that I may get him again, shall have FORTY SHILLINGS, and FORTY SHILLINGS more for the horse, and reasonable charges, paid by
EDWARD ROBERTS.

TO BE SOLD, The TIME of an *IRISH* SERVANT GIRL, WHO has about three years to serve. Enquire of the Printers.

Like enslaved Africans, white indentured servants often fled the harsh conditions under which they labored. Advertisements for the recovery of runaway servants (left) filled the colonial newspapers. No explanation is given for the sale of the servant girl's time (right). Was her performance unsatisfactory? Did her master unexpectedly need cash? *(Historical Society of Pennsylvania, Philadelphia)*

Merchants sold them there to artisans, farmers, and upper-class householders seeking domestic servants.

Even as the traffic in slaves peaked, religious and humanitarian opposition to slavery arose. A few individuals, mostly Quaker, had objected to slavery on moral grounds since the late seventeenth century. But the idea grew in the 1750s that slavery contradicted the Christian concept of brotherhood and the Enlightenment notion of the natural equality of all humans. Abolitionist sentiment was also fed by the growing belief that a slave master's authority "depraved the mind," as the Quaker John Woolman argued. An introspective tailor from New Jersey, Woolman dedicated his life in the 1750s to a crusade against slavery. He traveled thousands of miles on foot to convince every Quaker slaveholder of his or her wrongdoing. Only a few hundred masters freed their slaves in the mid-eighteenth century, but men such as Woolman had planted the seeds of abolitionism.

BEYOND THE APPALACHIANS

By the mid-eighteenth century, the American colonists, though increasing rapidly in number, still occupied only a narrow strip of coastal plain in eastern North America. Of about 1.2 million settlers and slaves in 1750, only a tiny fraction lived farther than 100 miles from the Atlantic Ocean. But between them and the Pacific Ocean lay rich soils in the river valleys of the Ohio and Mississippi and beyond that a vast domain that they had not even imagined. Beginning in the 1750s, westward-moving colonists in pursuit of more land would encounter four other groups already established to their west: the populous interior Native American tribes and smaller groups of French Americans, Spanish Americans, and African Americans. Changes already occurring among these groups would affect settlers breaching the Appalachian barrier and, in the third quarter of the eighteenth century, would even reach eastward to the original British settlements.

Cultural and Ecological Changes Among Interior Tribes

During the first half of the eighteenth century, the inland tribes proved their capacity to adapt to the contending European colonizers in their region while maintaining their political independence. Yet extensive contact with the French, Spanish, and English slowly brought ominous changes to Indian ways of life.

The introduction of European trade goods, especially iron implements, textiles, firearms and ammunition, and alcohol, inescapably changed Indian lifeways. Subsistence hunting, limited to satisfying tribal food requirements, turned into commercial hunting, restricted only by the quantity of trade goods desired. Indian males, gradually exhausting the population of deer and beaver east of the Mississippi River, spent far more time away from the villages trapping and hunting.

Women were also drawn into the new economic activities, threatening the matrilineal basis of society. Once killed, the beaver, deer, marten, and fox had to be skinned and the pelts then scraped, dressed, trimmed, and sewn into robes by women. Among some tribes, all this became so time-consuming that they had to procure food resources from other tribes.

The fur trade altered much in traditional Native American life. Spiritual beliefs that the destinies of humans and animals were closely linked eroded when trappers and hunters declared all-out war on the beaver and other fur-bearing animals to provide pelts for the European traders who offered attractive trade goods. Competition for furs sharpened intertribal tensions, often to the point of war. As fur traders of different nationalities competed for client tribes in the fur trade, the tribes were sucked into their patron's rivalry. Also, tribes came to depend on certain trade articles. When furs became depleted in their hunting grounds, they could maintain trade only by conquering more remote tribes with fertile hunting grounds or by forcibly intercepting the furs of other tribes on their way to European trading posts. The introduction of European weaponry, which Indians quickly mastered, further intensified intertribal conflict.

Tribal political organization in the interior also changed in the eighteenth century. Earlier, most tribes had been loose confederations of villages and clans, each exercising local autonomy. The Creek, Cherokee, and Iroquois gave primary loyalty to the village, not to the tribe or confederacy. But trade, diplomatic contact, and war with Europeans required coordinated policies, so villagers gradually adopted more centralized leadership.

Cherokee political organization in the eighteenth century illustrates the changes overcoming tribal societies. Early in the century, the nearly autonomous village formed the basic unit of political authority. But tension with Creek neighbors and intermittent hostilities with English traders and settlers pressed home the need for coordinated decision making. By 1750, the Cherokee had formed an umbrella political organization that under the leadership of Chief Old Hop gathered together the fragmented authority of the villages and formed a more centralized tribal "priest state." When even this proved inadequate, warriors began to assume the dominant role in tribal councils, replacing the civil chiefs. By this process, the Cherokee reorganized their political structure so that dozens of scattered villages could pool their strength.

While incorporating trade goods into their material culture and adapting their economies and political structures to new situations, the interior tribes held fast to tradition in many ways. They saw little reason to replace what they valued in their own culture. What they saw of the colonists' systems of law and justice, religion, education, family organization, and child rearing usually convinced Native Americans that their own ways were superior.

The Indians' refusal to accept the superiority of white culture frustrated English missionaries, eager to win Native Americans from "savage" ways. Some colonists understood that the white behavior observed by natives cast doubts on the notion that Indians were of an inferior race. A Carolinian admitted that "they are really better to us than we are to them. We look upon them with scorn and disdain, and think them little better than beasts in human shape, though if well examined, we shall find that, for all our religion and education, we possess more moral deformities and evils than these savages do."

Despite maintaining many cultural practices, the interior Indian tribes suffered from the commercial, diplomatic, and military contact with the British colonizers. Decade by decade, the fur trade spread epidemic diseases, intensified warfare, depleted game animals, and drew Native Americans into a market economy where their trading partners gradually became trading masters.

France's Inland Empire

While the powerful Iroquois, Cherokee, Creek, and Choctaw tribes interacted with British colonists to their east, they also faced a growing French presence to their west. Between 1699 and 1754, the French developed a system of small forts, trading posts, and agricultural villages throughout the central area of the continent. The aim was to connect French Canada to the Gulf of Mexico and pin the English to the seaboard. French success in this vast region hinged partly on shrewd dealing with the Indian tribes, which retained sovereignty over the land but gradually succumbed to French diseases, French arms, and French-promoted intertribal wars.

Because France's interior empire was organized primarily as a military, trading, and missionizing operation, male French settlers arrived with few French women. This led to a long period when French men encountered Indians in a state of need—not only for trading partners, allies, and souls to be converted but also for wives. From this need came the mingling of French and Indian peoples—what the French called *metissage*—in the vast North American interior. It was almost unthinkable for a French fur trader to do business without an Indian wife who could pave the way for his trading with the Ojibway, Menominee, or any other Great Lakes tribe.

Such interracial marriages, soon to be called "the custom of the country," were desired by the Indians as well as the French. Marital alliances cemented

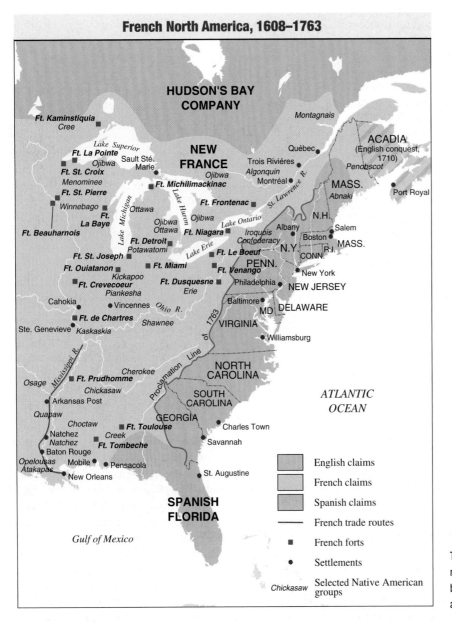

French North America, 1608–1763

HUDSON'S BAY
COMPANY

Montagnais

Ft. Kaminstiquia
Cree

ACADIA
(English conquest, 1710)

Lake Superior
Ft. La Pointe
Ojibwa   Sault Sté.
Ft. St. Croix   Marie
Menominee
Ft. St. Pierre

NEW
FRANCE

Québec

Trois Riviéres
Algonquin
Montréal

Penobscot

St. Lawrence R.

MASS.
Abnaki

Port Royal

Winnebago
Ft.
La Baye

Lake Michigan

Ft. Michilimackinac

Ojibwa

Ft. Frontenac

N.H.

Lake Huron   Ojibwa   Lake Ontario
Ojibwa
Ottawa

Albany
Salem

Ft. Beauharnois

Ottawa

Ft. Niagara

Iroquois
Confederacy

Boston   MASS.

Ft. Detroit
Potawatomi

Lake Erie

Ft. Le Boeuf

N.Y.   CONN.   R.I.

Ft. St. Joseph

Ft. Miami

PENN.

New York

Ft. Ouiatanon
Kickapoo
Ft. Crevecoeur
Piankesha

Ft. Venango
Ft. Dusquesne
Erie

Philadelphia   NEW JERSEY

Cahokia   Vincennes   Ohio R.
Ft. de Chartres   Shawnee

Baltimore
MD   DELAWARE

Ste. Genevieve   Kaskaskia

Line of 1763

VIRGINIA

Williamsburg

Mississippi R.

Cherokee
Ft. Prudhomme
Chickasaw

Proclamation Line

NORTH
CAROLINA

Osage

SOUTH
CAROLINA

ATLANTIC
OCEAN

Arkansas Post

Quapaw
Choctaw
Natchez
Natchez
Ft. Tombeche
Baton Rouge

GEORGIA
Ft. Toulouse
Creek

Charles Town

Savannah

Opelousas
Atakapas

Mobile
New Orleans

Pensacola

St. Augustine

SPANISH
FLORIDA

Gulf of Mexico

	English claims
	French claims
	Spanish claims
——	French trade routes
■	French forts
•	Settlements
Chickasaw	Selected Native American groups

Though thinly settled by colonists, the vast region west of the Proclamation Line claimed by France was held by a combination of forts and trading posts.

trade relations and military alliances. French traders entered Indian kinship circles, making trade flow smoothly, while Indians gained protection against their enemies and access to provisions at the French trading posts. Though the French sometimes descended into fierce warfare with Indian peoples, the North American heartland was a cultural merging ground and marrying ground, as well as marketplace and battleground.

For a full century after 1650, the French Jesuits and fur traders had been building a crescent of settlements and military posts extending down the St. Lawrence River basin, through the Great Lakes, and southward down the Mississippi valley to the Gulf of Mexico. Even though farming communities such as Kaskaskia and Prairie du Chien were thinly dotted,

this French presence in the continent's heartland created an effective shield against the expansion-minded British to the east. As the French population grew to about 70,000 by 1750, they demonstrated uniquely how European settlers could coexist with Indian peoples by negotiating incessantly with Indian leaders, respecting Indian ways of conducting trade, and—above all—mingling so thoroughly that almost all French settlements in North America's interior were mixed-race communities. French Louisiana, for example, though thinly populated, had more mixed-race children and more white and black men who lived with Native Americans than any Anglo-American colony.

In 1718, the few hundred early French pioneers of the interior were suddenly inundated when France

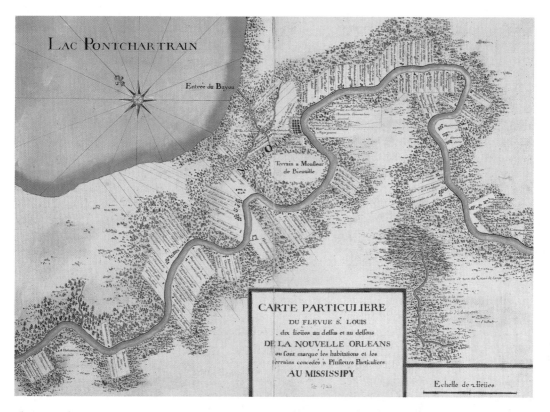

This map of New Orleans Parish in 1723, when the colony was still struggling, shows every plantation fronting on the Mississippi River. *(The Newberry Library)*

settled New Orleans at great cost by transporting almost 7,000 whites and 5,000 African slaves to the mouth of the Mississippi River. Disease rapidly whittled down these numbers, and an uprising of the powerful Natchez in 1729 discouraged further French immigration. Most of the survivors settled around the little town of New Orleans in long, narrow plantations stretching back from the Mississippi River to the endless cypress swamps. Slaves made wood products from cypress and pine for the West Indies and produced indigo, rice, and other crops for France. New Orleans merchants also marketed wheat from the little farming villages taking root in Illinois; bear oil and tobacco from settlements around the western post of Natchitoches; beef from herds in the Mobile River valley; produce from the small upriver German village Les Allemandes; and tens of thousands of deer skins and other pelts delivered annually by Indians for trade goods.

In its economy and society, New Orleans much resembled early Charleston, South Carolina. By contrast, however, French New Orleanians knew nothing of representative political institutions. Ruled by a governor, a commissary and chief judge, and a small appointed council, the people had no elections, no assembly, no newspapers, and no taxes. Because the French king paid dearly to keep the town's troops sup-

plied, he would share power with no one, although he granted planters many favors. A mid-century English observer noted that the planter "is considered as a Frenchman venturing his life, enduring a species of banishment, and undergoing great hardships for the benefit of his country, for which reason he has great indulgence shown." This could not have been said of English planters in Georgia, South Carolina, or Virginia.

From its first introduction in Louisiana in 1719, French plantation slavery grew so rapidly that blacks outnumbered whites by 1765. Most slaves and a majority of whites lived in the New Orleans area. The conditions of life for slaves differed little from the southern English colonies, for slaves also lived in simple cabins and worked under the sun and the lash in a master's fields and swamps. But the French had a paternalistic legal code that gave slaves some protection in courts. When the Spanish took over the colony in 1769, they instituted their own law guaranteeing slaves the right to buy freedom with money earned in their free time. Soon a large free black class emerged, headed by substantial people like Simon Calfat, who ran various enterprises, helped other slaves pay for their freedom, and headed a company of free black militia. When Americans acquired the colony in 1803, they suppressed freedom purchase and discouraged manumission.

Most blacks who lived outside the British colonies labored in New Orleans, but a few could be found pioneering elsewhere beyond the Appalachians. By the early eighteenth century, slaves who escaped Spanish, French, or English masters formed bands in the interior allied with Indian tribes. The Spanish settlers in Texas and California carried a few blacks with them. A supreme expression of the range of possibilities occurred just before the American Revolution when a free black of West Indian parentage, Jean-Baptiste Point du Sable, with his Potawatomi wife, planted the first settlement in what became Chicago. A few years later, the British army arrested Point du Sable and his fellow pioneers as sympathizers with the American rebels.

Spain's America

In the first half of the eighteenth century, the Spanish still possessed by far the largest empire in the Americas. But in North America, the Spanish had great difficulty defending their Florida mission network and military posts, while trying on a shoestring to counter French expansion in the Mississippi River watershed with only a few military posts in Texas and New Mexico. Hispanics, mestizos, and detribalized Indians began to increase modestly in Texas, New Mexico, and California in the first half of the eighteenth century, but they were falling further and further behind in relation to the English and French. The English in South Carolina were ten times as numerous as the Spanish in Florida by 1745, and the gap kept widening. New Mexico's Hispanic population of about 10,000 at mid-century could defend the vast region only because no European challenger appeared.

As in New France, racial intermixture and social fluidity were more extensive in New Spain than in the English colonies. Precisely how much is uncertain because the Spanish never defined racial groups as distinctly as the English. The word *Spaniard* on a census might mean a white immigrant from Mexico or a part-Indian person who "lived like a Spaniard." Social mobility was considerable because the crown was willing to raise even a common person to the status of hidalgo (minor nobleman) as an inducement to settle in New Spain's remote northern frontier. Most of the immigrants became small ranchers, producing livestock, corn, and wheat for export to southward Spanish provinces.

Native Americans had mixed success in resisting Spanish domination in different colonies. In New Mexico, an early nineteenth-century Spanish investigator saw the key to Pueblo cultural autonomy as the underground kivas, which were "like impenetrable temples, where they gather to discuss mysteriously their misfortunes or good fortunes, their happiness or grief. The doors of these *estufas* are always closed to us." The tribes of California, though, were less successful in maintaining cultural cohesion. In the 1770s, the Spanish rapidly completed their western land and sea routes from San Diego to Yerba Buena (San Francisco) to block Russian settlement south of their base in northern California. California's Spanish pioneers were Franciscan missionaries, accompanied by royal soldiers. The priests would choose a good location and then attract a few Indians to be baptized and resettled around the missions, which they helped build. Visiting relatives would then be induced to stay. These Indians lived under an increasingly harsh regimen until they were reduced to a condition of virtual slavery. The California mission, with its extensive and profitable herds and grain crops, theoretically belonged to the Indian converts, but they did not enjoy the profits. Priests even hired them out to immigrant Spaniards. Ironically, the spiritual motives of the priests produced the same reduction and degradation of tribal Americans as elsewhere.

A LAND OF FAMILY FARMS

Population growth and economic development gradually transformed the landscape of eighteenth-century British America. Three variations of colonial society emerged: the farming society of the North, the plantation society of the South, and the urban society of the seaboard commercial towns. Although they shared some important characteristics, each was distinct.

Northern Agricultural Society

In the mid-eighteenth-century northern colonies, especially New England, tightknit farming families, organized in communities of several thousand people, dotted the landscape. New Englanders staked their future on a mixed economy. They cleared forests for timber used in barrels, ships, houses, and barns. They plumbed the offshore waters for fish that fed both local populations and the ballooning slave population of the West Indies. And they cultivated and grazed as much of the thin-soiled, rocky hills and bottomlands as they could recover from the forest.

The farmers of the middle colonies—Pennsylvania, Delaware, New Jersey, and New York—drove their wooden plows through much richer soils than New Englanders. They enjoyed the additional advantage of settling an area cleared by Native Americans who had relied more on agriculture than New England tribes. Thus favored, mid-Atlantic farm families produced modest surpluses of corn, wheat, beef, and pork. By the mid-eighteenth century, New York and Philadelphia ships were carrying these foodstuffs not only to the West Indies, always a primary market, but also to areas that could no longer feed themselves—England, Spain, Portugal, and even New England.

In the North, the broad ownership of land distinguished farming society from every other agricultural region of the Western world. Although differences in circumstances and ability led gradually toward greater social stratification, in most communities, few were truly rich or abjectly poor, and the gap between them was small compared with European society. Except for indentured servants, most men lived to purchase or inherit a farm of at least 50 acres. With their family's labor, they earned a decent existence and provided a small inheritance for each of their children. Settlers valued land highly, for freehold tenure ordinarily guaranteed both economic independence and political rights.

Amid widespread property ownership, a rising population pressed against a limited land supply by the eighteenth century, especially in New England. Family farms could not be divided and subdivided indefinitely, for it took at least 50 acres (of which only a quarter could usually be cropped) to support a family. In Concord, Massachusetts, for example, the founders had worked farms averaging about 250 acres. A century later, in the 1730s, the average farm had shrunk by two-thirds, as farm owners struggled to provide an inheritance for the three or four sons that the average marriage produced.

Decreasing soil fertility compounded the problem of dwindling farm size. When land had been plentiful, farmers planted crops in the same field for three years and then let it lie fallow in pasturage seven years or more until it regained its fertility. But on the smaller farms of the eighteenth century, farmers had reduced fallow time to only a year or two. Such intense use of the soil reduced crop yields, forcing farmers to plow marginal land or shift to livestock production. Such was the process that led Jaret Eliot, New England's first agricultural essayist, to refer to "our old land which we have worn out."

The diminishing size and productivity of family farms drove many New Englanders to the frontier or out of the area altogether in the eighteenth century. "Many of our old towns are too full of inhabitants for husbandry, many of them living on small shares of land," bemoaned one Yankee. In Concord, one of every four adult males migrated from town every decade from the 1740s on, and in many towns out-migration was even greater. Some drifted south to New York and Pennsylvania. Others sought opportunities as artisans in the coastal towns or took to the sea. More headed for the colony's western frontier or north to New Hampshire and the eastern frontier of Maine. Several thousand New England families migrated even farther north, to the Annapolis valley of Nova Scotia. Throughout New England after the early eighteenth century, most farmers' sons knew that their destiny lay elsewhere.

Wherever they took up farming, northern cultivators engaged in agricultural work routines that were far less intense than in the South. The growing season was much shorter, and cereal crops required incessant labor only during spring planting and autumn harvesting. This less burdensome work rhythm led many northern cultivators to fill out their calendars with intermittent work as clockmakers, shoemakers, carpenters, and weavers.

Changing Values

Boston's weather on April 29, 1695, began warm and sunny, noted the devout merchant Samuel Sewall in his diary. But by afternoon, thunder, lightning, and hailstones "as big as pistol and musket bullets" pummeled the town. Sewall dined that evening with Cotton Mather, New England's most prominent Puritan clergyman. Mather wondered why "more ministers' houses than others proportionately had been smitten with lightning." The words were hardly out of his mouth before hailstones began to shatter the windows of Sewall's house, "flying to the middle of the room or farther." Sewall and Mather fell to their knees and broke into prayer together "after this awful Providence."

These two third-generation Massachusetts Puritans understood that God was angry with them as leaders of a people whose piety and moral rectitude were being overtaken by worldliness. Even if farms were getting smaller and open land scarcer, growth and success had undermined early utopian dreams and made Massachusetts "sermon-proof," as one dejected minister put it.

In other parts of the North, the expansive environment and the Protestant emphasis on self-discipline and hard work were also breeding qualities that would become hallmarks of American culture: an ambitious outlook, individualistic behavior, and a love of material things. In Europe, most tillers of the soil expected little from life. With no frontier lands ripe for exploitation, impoverished peasant farmers viewed life not as a quest for achievement but as a perpetual struggle against famine and disease. In America, starvation was almost unknown, and few obstacles held people back from uncharted expanses of land once they had overwhelmed the Native Americans. "Every man," one colonist remarked, "expects one day or another to be upon a footing with his wealthiest neighbor."

Commitment to religion, family, and community did not disappear, but fewer men and women saw daily existence as a preparation for the afterlife. They began to regard land not simply as a source of livelihood but

A proud and prosperous Rhineland immigrant, Martin Van Bergen, had this mural painted over the mantelpiece of his New York farmhouse, giving us a rare view of a colonial farm. *(New York State Historical Association, Cooperstown)*

as a commodity to be bought and sold for profit. "Every man is for himself," sighed a Philadelphia leader only a generation after Penn had planted his "holy experiment." A few decades later, a New Yorker wrote that "the only principle of life propagated among the young people is to get money, and men are only esteemed according to what they are worth, that is, the money they are possessed of."

A slender almanac, written by the twelfth child of a poor Boston candlemaker, captured the new outlook with wit and charm. Born in 1706, Benjamin Franklin had climbed the

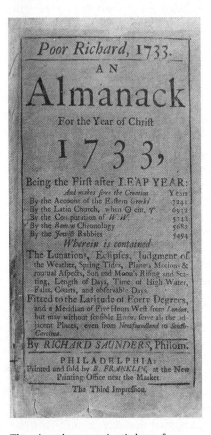

The wit and pragmatic wisdom of Boston-born Benjamin Franklin made his *Poor Richard's Almanack* the most widely read book in the colonies after the Bible. *(Historical Society of Pennsylvania, Philadelphia)*

ladder of success spectacularly. Running away from a harsh apprenticeship to an older brother when he was 16, he abandoned a declining Boston for a rising Philadelphia. By 23, he had learned the printer's trade and was publishing the *Pennsylvania Gazette.* Three years later, he began *Poor Richard's Almanack,* next to the Bible the most widely read book in the colonies.

Franklin spiced his annual almanac—the ordinary person's guide to weather and useful information—with quips, adages, and homespun philosophy. Eventually, this homely material added up to a primer for success published in 1747 as *The Way to Wealth.* "The sleeping fox gathers no poultry" and "Lost time is never found again," advised Poor Richard, emphasizing that time is money. "It costs more to maintain one vice than to raise two children," he counseled, advocating not morality but practicality. "Sloth makes all things difficult but industry all easy," he assured his readers. Ever cocky, Franklin caught the spirit of the rising secularism of the eighteenth century. He embodied the growing utilitarian doctrine that good is whatever is useful and the notion that the community is best served through individual self-improvement and accomplishment.

Women and the Family in Northern Colonial Society

In 1662, Elnathan Chauncy, a Massachusetts schoolboy, copied into his writing book that the soul "consists of two portions, inferior and superior; the superior is masculine and eternal; the feminine inferior and mortal." This lesson had been taught for generations on both sides of the Atlantic. It was part of a larger conception of God's design that assigned degrees of status and stations in life to all individuals. In such a world, women were subordinate, taught from infancy to be modest, patient, and compliant. Regarded by men as weak of mind and large of heart, they existed for and through men. As daughters they were subject to their fathers, as wives to their husbands. John Winthrop reflected the common view that such submission was natural, and hence "a true wife accounts her subjection her honor."

European women usually accepted these narrowly circumscribed roles. Few complained, at least openly, that their work was generally limited to housewifery and midwifery. They silently accepted exclusion from the early public schools and laws that transferred to their husbands any property or income they brought into a marriage. Nor could women speak in their churches or participate in governing them (except in Quaker meetinghouses), and they had no legal voice in political affairs. Most women did not expect to choose a husband for love; parental guidance prevailed in a society in which producing legal heirs was the means of transmitting property. Once wed, women expected to remain so until death, for they could rarely obtain a divorce.

On the colonial frontier, women's lives changed in modest ways. In Europe, about one of ten women did not marry. But in the colonies, where men outnumbered women for the first century, a spinster was almost unheard of, and widows remarried with astounding speed. "A young widow with 4 or 5 children, who among the middling or inferior ranks of people in Europe would have little chance for a second husband," observed one Englishman, "is in America frequently courted as a sort of fortune." *Woman* and *wife* thus became nearly synonymous.

A second difference concerned property rights. Single women and widows in the colonies, as in England, could make contracts, hold and convey property, represent themselves in court, and conduct business. Under English common law, a woman forfeited these rights, as well as all property, when she married. In the colonies, however, legislatures and courts gave wives more control over property brought into marriage or left at their husbands' death. They also enjoyed broader rights to act for and with their husbands in business transactions. In addition, young colonial women slowly gained the right to consent to a marriage partner—a right that came by default to the thousands of female indentured servants who completed their labor contracts and had no parents within 3,000 miles to dictate to them.

Although colonial society did not encourage or reward female individuality and self-reliance, women worked alongside their husbands in competent and complementary ways. Women had limited career choices and rights but broad responsibilities. The work spaces and daily routines of husband and wife overlapped and intersected far more than today. Farm women as well as men worked at planting, harvesting, and milking cows. Women also made candles and soap, butter and cheese, and smoked meat; they made cloth and sometimes marketed farm products. A merchant's wife kept shop, handled accounts when her husband voyaged abroad, and helped supervise the servants and apprentices. "Deputy husbands" and "yoke mates" were revealing terms used by New Englanders to describe eighteenth-century wives.

Despite conventional talk of inferiority, women within their families and neighborhoods nevertheless shaped the world around them. Older women modeled the behavior of young women, aided the needy, and subtly affected menfolk, who held the formal reins of authority. In church life, where they outnumbered men, women worked privately in their families to promote religion in outlying areas, to seat and unseat ministers, and to influence the community's moral life. Periodically, they appeared as visionaries and mystics.

Women held vital responsibilities as midwives. Until the late eighteenth century, the "obstetrick art" was almost entirely in their hands. Midwives such as Anne Hutchinson counseled pregnant women, delivered babies, supervised postpartum recovery, and participated in infant baptism and burial ceremonies. Mrs. Phillips, an immigrant to Boston in 1719, was a familiar figure as she hurried through the streets to attend the lying-in of about 70 women each year. In her 42-year career, she delivered more than 3,000 infants. Because colonial women were pregnant or nursing infants for about half their years between the ages 20 and 40 and because childbirth was dangerous, the circle of female friends and relatives attending childbirth created strong networks of mutual assistance.

In her role as wife and mother, the eighteenth-century northern woman differed somewhat from her English counterpart. Whereas English women married in their mid-twenties, American women typically took husbands a few years earlier. This head start increased their childbearing years. Hence, the average colonial family included five children (two others typically died in infancy), whereas the English family contained fewer than three. Gradually, as the coastal plain filled up in the eighteenth century and older family farms were divided and subdivided among descendants of the early settlers, marriage age crept up and the number of children per family inched down.

Northern child-rearing patterns differed considerably. In the seventeenth century, stern fathers dominated Puritan family life, and few were reluctant to punish unruly children. "Better whip'd than damn'd," advised Cotton Mather, the minister who served as the Puritan conscience of New England. Many parents believed that breaking the young child's will created a pious and submissive personality. In Quaker families, however, mothers played a more active role in child rearing. More permissive, they relied on tenderness and love rather than guilt to mold their children. Attitudes toward choosing a marriage partner also

Childbirth was an oft-repeated event in the lives of most colonial wives. In this portrait of the Cheney family, the older woman is a nanny or mother-in-law; the younger woman holding a baby is Mr. Cheney's second wife. (The Cheney Family, *Gift of Edgar and Bernice Chrysler Garbisch, ©2000 Board of Trustees, National Gallery of Art, Washington, c. 1795, canvas, .490 x .650 [19¼ x 25⅝])*

separated early Puritan and Quaker approaches to family life. Puritan parents usually arranged their children's marriages but allowed them the right to veto. Young Quaker men and women made their own matches, subject to parental veto.

Despite this initial diversity in child rearing, the father-dominated family of New England gradually declined in the eighteenth century. In its place rose the mother-centered family, in which affectionate parents encouraged self-expression and independence in their children. This "modern" approach, on the rise in Europe as well, brought the colonists closer to the methods of parenthood found among the coastal Native Americans, who initially had been widely disparaged for their lax approach to rearing their young.

ECOLOGICAL TRANSFORMATION

Wherever Europeans settled in the Americas, they brought with them animals, plant life, diseases, and ways of viewing the natural resources—all with enormous consequences for the ecosystems they were entering. In New Spain, the introduction of grazing animals—cattle, horses, pigs, sheep, and goats—profoundly altered the landscape. Breeding prolifically in an environment generally free of animal predators, pigs and cattle devoured the tall grasses and most palatable plant species. Within a half century, the domesticated animals left huge areas with little or no ground cover. In this rearranged landscape, new unwelcome plant species took hold—stinging nettle, nightshade, and dandelion.

In England's North American colonies, the rapid increase of settlers after 1715 had different environmental effects. Two were of special importance. First, the demand for wood—for building and heating houses, for producing the charcoal necessary for ironmaking, for shipbuilding and barrelmaking—swiftly depleted coastal forests. Just for heating and cooking, the typical northern farmhouse required an acre of trees each year. An iron furnace needed 20,000 acres of forest to produce a thousand tons of iron. A 40-acre field required 8,000 fence rails. With the population explosion of the eighteenth century, the price of firewood quickly rose as woodcutters ventured farther and farther inland.

Rapid and often wasteful harvesting of the forests had many effects. As the colonists chopped down the forest canopy that had previously moderated the weather, the summers became hotter and winters colder. In deforested areas, snow melted sooner, and, as the winter's melting snow ran off more quickly, watersheds emptied faster. This, in turn, caused soil erosion and periods of drought.

A second ecological transformation occurred when animals brought by Europeans began to replace animals already in North America. European colonists were a livestock people, skilled in mixed farming and herding of domesticated cattle, horses, pigs, sheep, and goats. Such animals provided food, leather, fibers for clothmaking, and the sheer pulling and carrying power relied on by a people who had no other source of energy than their own muscles. Multiplying rapidly in a favorable environment, pigs and cattle "swarm like vermin upon the earth," reported one Virginia account as early as 1700. In some areas, the animals multiplied so rapidly and denuded the native grasses and shrubs so quickly that they actually ate themselves out of subsistence and began to die for lack of grazing land.

While European livestock filled the land, the native fur-bearing animals—beaver, deer, bear, wolf, raccoon, and marten—rapidly became extinct in the areas of settlement. Prized for their skins or hated as predators of domesticated animals, these species were hunted relentlessly as the colonists offered trade goods to Native Americans in exchange for pelts. One broken link in the ecological chain affected others. For example, the dams and ponds of the beaver, which had been breeding grounds for many species of wild ducks, soon were drained and converted to grazing meadows for cattle.

Animals prized for dinner table fare also quickly reached extinction along the East Coast. Wild turkeys were a rarity in Massachusetts by the 1670s. Deer disappeared by the early 1700s in settled areas. "Hunting with us exists chiefly in the tales of other times," wrote Yale's president in the late eighteenth century.

All these environmental changes were linked not only to the numbers of Europeans arriving in North America but also to their ways of thinking about nature. Looking out over wooded hills and fertile valleys, transplanted Europeans could only imagine the possibility of raising valuable crops as if the ecosystem was composed of unconnected elements, each ripe for exploitation. Land, lumber, fish, and fur-bearing animals could be converted into sources of cash that would buy imported commodities that improved one's material condition. The New England writer Edward Johnson described the process perceptively as early as 1653: Who would have imagined, he mused, "that this wilderness should turn a mart for merchants in so short a space, Holland, France, Spain, and Portugal coming hither for trade?" Supplying these Europeans were the farmers, woodcutters, and fishermen who consigned to the marketplace huge portions of the ecosystem that in the world of Native Americans were all-important for sustaining life but not part of a transoceanic system of commercial exchange.

Coming from homelands where land was scarce, the settlers viewed their ability to reap nature's abundance in North America as proof of their success. From their perspective, they were correct because, in fact, colonial agriculture was abundantly successful in terms of what the settlers obliged the land to yield up. Yet the "rage for commerce" and for an improved life produced wasteful practices on farms and in forests and fisheries. "The grain fields, the meadows, the forests, the cattle, etc.," wrote a Swedish visitor in the 1750s, "are treated with equal carelessness." Accustomed to the natural abundance once the native peoples had been driven from the land, and seeing no limits to the land that was available, the colonists embarked on ecologically destructive practices that over a period of many generations profoundly altered the natural world of North America.

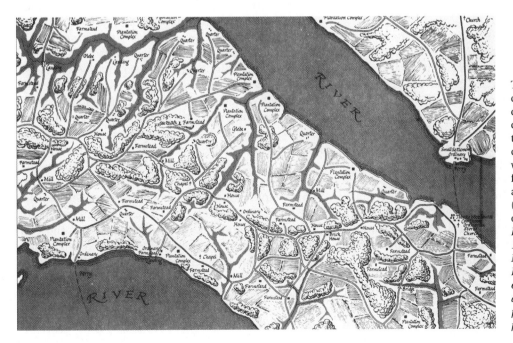

The distribution of cultivated fields, dwellings, and commercial buildings in the tidewater landscape created "communities" without towns (rendered from historical and archaeological evidence). (*From* The Transformation of Virginia, 1740–1790 *by Rhys Isaac. Copyright © 1982 by the University of North Carolina Press. Published for the Institute of Early American History and Culture. Used by permission of the publisher.*)

☙ THE PLANTATION SOUTH

Between 1680 and 1750, the white tidewater settlements of the southern colonies changed from a frontier society marked by high immigration, a surplus of males, and an unstable social organization to a settled society composed mostly of native-born families. After 1715, Scots-Irish and German immigrants flooded into the backcountry of Virginia, the Carolinas, and Georgia, this last intended as a debtors' haven but designed in 1732 as a buffer between Spanish Florida and the Carolinas. But between the piedmont region and the ocean, a mature southern culture took form.

The Tobacco Coast

Tobacco production in Virginia and Maryland expanded rapidly in the seventeenth century, with exports reaching 25 million pounds annually during the 1680s. But then two decades of war in Europe and the Americas, bridging the turn of the century, drove up transportation costs and dampened the demand for tobacco. Stagnation in the tobacco market lasted from the mid-1680s until about 1715.

Yet in this period the Upper South underwent a profound social transformation. First, slaves replaced indentured servants so rapidly that by 1730 the unfree labor force was overwhelmingly black. Second, the planters responded to the depressed tobacco market by diversifying their crops. They shifted some tobacco fields to grain, hemp, and flax; increased their herds of cattle and swine; and became more self-sufficient by developing local industries to produce iron, leather, and textiles. By the 1720s, when a profitable tobacco trade with France created a new period of prosperity, the economy was much more diverse and resilient than a generation before.

Third, the population structure changed rapidly. Black slaves grew from about 7 percent to more than 40 percent of the region's population between 1690 and 1750, and the drastic imbalance between white men and women disappeared. Families rather than single men now predominated. The earlier frontier society of white immigrants who mostly lived short and unrewarding lives as indentured servants grew into an eighteenth-century plantation society of native-born freeholder families.

Notwithstanding the influx of Africans, slave owning was far from universal. As late as 1750, a majority of families owned no slaves at all. Among slave owners, not more than one-tenth held more than 20 slaves. Nonetheless, the common goal was the large plantation where black slaves made the earth yield up profits to support an aristocratic life for their masters. As one Virginia minister observed, "The custom of the country is such that without slaves a man's children stand but a poor chance to marry in reputation."

The Chesapeake planters who acquired the best land and accumulated enough capital to invest heavily in slaves created a gentry lifestyle that set them apart from ordinary farmers such as Devereaux Jarratt's father. By the eighteenth century, the development of the northern colonies had produced prosperous farmers worth several thousand pounds. But such wealth paled alongside the estates of men such as Charles Carroll of Maryland and Robert "King" Carter and William Byrd of Virginia. These Chesapeake planters counted their slaves by the hundreds, their acres by the thousands, and their fortunes by the tens of thousands of pounds.

Ritual display of wealth marked southern gentry life. Racing thoroughbred horses and gambling on them recklessly, sometimes for purses of £100 (at a time when a laboring man earned £40 per year), became common sport for young gentlemen, who had often been educated in England. Planters began to construct stately brick Georgian mansions, some designed by imported English architects. These "greathouses," similar in style to the houses of English gentry, were filled with imported furniture, attended by liveried black slaves, and graced by formal gardens and orchards.

Some observers saw the cultivated aristocratic lifestyle as a veneer. "If a [man] has Money, Negroes, and Land enough," scoffed a Scottish newcomer, "he is a complete Gentleman. These hide all his defects, usher him into the best of company, and draw upon him the smiles of the fair Sex." Affected or not, the emerging Chesapeake planter elite controlled the county courts, officered the local militia, ruled the parish vestries of the Anglican Church, and made law in their legislative assemblies. To their sons, they passed the mantle of political and social leadership.

For all their airs, these southern squires were essentially agrarian businessmen. They spent their days haggling over credit, dealing in land and slaves, scheduling planting and harvesting routines, conferring with overseers, disciplining slaves, and arranging leases with tenants. Cultivating tobacco was a particularly demanding enterprise and a highly personal one. Whereas other staple crops such as wheat and corn required intensive labor only during the planting and harvesting seasons, tobacco demanded the planter's attention throughout the year as the crop moved through the many stages of planting, transplanting, topping, cutting, curing, and packing. A planter's reputation rose and fell with the quality of his crop. So personalized was the culture of tobacco that planters stamped their hogsheads of leaf with their initials or emblem. "Question a planter on the subject," explained one observer, "and he will tell you that he cultivates such or such a kind [of tobacco], as for example, Colonel Carter's sort, John Cole's sort or [that of] some other leading crop master."

Planters' wives also shouldered many responsibilities. They superintended cloth production and the processing and preparation of food while ruling over households crowded with children, slaves, and visitors. An aristocratic veneer gave the luster of gentility to plantations from Maryland to North Carolina, but this could not disguise the fact that these were large working farms, often so isolated from one another that the planter and his wife lived a "solitary and unsociable existence," as one phrased it. With only infrequent contact with the outside world, they learned to be independent as they managed their own little communities of servants, slaves, and family members. Patriarchs on their estates, southern planters were "haughty and jealous of their liberties, impatient of restraint, and can scarcely bear the thought of being controlled by any superior power," noted a mid-eighteenth-century visitor.

The Rice Coast

The plantation economy of the Lower South in the eighteenth century rested on the production of rice and indigo. Rice exports surpassed 1.5 million pounds per year by 1710 and reached 80 million pounds by the eve of the Revolution. Indigo, a smelly blue dye obtained from plants for use in textiles, became a staple crop in the 1740s after Eliza Lucas Pinckney, a wealthy South Carolina planter's wife, experimented successfully with its cultivation. Within a generation, indigo production had spread into Georgia. It soon ranked among the leading colonial exports.

The expansion of rice production transformed the swampy coastal lowlands. In the rice-producing region radiating out from Charleston, planters imported thousands of slaves after 1720; by 1740, slaves composed nearly 90 percent of the region's inhabitants. White population declined as wealthy planters left their estates in the hands of resident overseers. They wintered in cosmopolitan Charleston and summered in Newport, Rhode Island, their refuge from seasonal malaria along the rice coast. Rice converted the eighteenth-century Carolina coast into a tropical plantation regime similar to that of the sugar-producing West Indies. At mid-century, a shocked New England visitor described it as a society "divided into opulent and lordly planters, poor and spiritless peasants, and vile slaves."

Throughout the plantation South, the courthouse became a central gathering place for men. On court days, all classes came to settle debts, dispute land boundaries, sue and be sued. When court was over, a

Rice and Indigo Exports from South Carolina and Georgia, 1698–1775

Just as Virginia had been built on tobacco, South Carolina and Georgia were built on rice. Much of it was sent to the West Indies to feed the huge population of enslaved Africans there. Source: U.S. Bureau of the Census.

multitude lingered on, drinking, gossiping, and staging horse races, cockfights, wrestling matches, footraces, and fiddling contests. Competition and assertiveness lay at the heart of all these demonstrations of male prowess.

The church, almost always Anglican in the South before 1750, also became a center of community gathering. A visiting northerner described the animated socializing before worship, men "giving and receiving letters of business, reading advertisements, consulting about the price of tobacco and grain, and settling either the lineage, age, or qualities of favourite horses." Then, as the hour of service approached, people filed into church. Reaffirming the social gradation of their rank-conscious society, the lower and middling planters entered first. They stood attentively until the wealthy gentry, striding in together "in a body," took their pews at the front. After church, socializing continued, with young people strolling together and older ones extending invitations to Sunday dinner. The pious Sabbath atmosphere perpetuated in New England was little in evidence.

The Backcountry

While the southern gentry matured along the tobacco and rice coasts, settlers poured into the upland backcountry. As late as 1730, only hunters and Indian fur traders had known this vast expanse of hilly red clay and fertile limestone soils, stretching from Pennsylvania to Georgia. Over the next four decades, it attracted some 250,000 inhabitants, nearly half the southern white population.

Thousands of land-hungry German and Scots-Irish settlers spilled into the interior valleys running along the eastern side of the Appalachians. They squatted on land, lived tensely with neighboring Indians in a region where boundaries were shadowy, and created a subsistence society of small farms. Gradually acquiring slaves, this "mixed medley from all countries and the off scouring of America," as one colonist described them, pursued mixed farming and cattle raising. Their enclaves remained isolated from the coastal region for several generations, which helped these pioneers cling fiercely to the folkways they had brought across the Atlantic.

Crude backcountry life appalled many visitors from the more refined seaboard. In 1733, William Byrd described a large Virginia frontier plantation as a "poor, dirty hovel, with hardly anything in it but children that wallowed about like so many pigs." Charles Woodmason, a stiff-necked Anglican minister who spent three years tramping between settlements in the Carolina upcountry, could hardly find words to express his shock. "Through the licentiousness of the people," he wrote, "many hundreds live in concubinage—swopping their wives as cattle and living in a state of nature more irregularly and unchastely than the Indians."

What Byrd and Woodmason were really observing was the poverty of frontier life and the lack of schools, churches, and towns. Most families plunged into the backcountry with only a few crude household possessions and farm tools, perhaps a pair of oxen, a few chickens and swine, and the clothes on their backs. They lived in rough-hewn log cabins—"cold cabins, unfloored and almost open to the sky," Woodmason observed—and planted their corn, beans, and wheat between the stumps of trees they had felled. Women toiled alongside men, in the fields, forest, and homestead. For a generation, these settlers endured a poor diet, endless work, and meager rewards.

By the 1760s, the southern backcountry had begun to emerge from the frontier stage. Small marketing towns such as Camden, South Carolina; Salisbury, North Carolina; Winchester, Virginia; and Fredericktown, Maryland, became centers of craft activity, church life, and local government. Farms began producing surpluses for shipment east. Density of settlement increased, creating a social life known for harvest festivals, log-rolling contests, horse races, wedding celebrations, dances, and prodigious drinking bouts during which hard cider,

whiskey, and apple and peach brandy flowed freely. Class distinctions remained narrow compared with the older seaboard settlements, as many backcountry settlements acquired the look of permanence.

Family Life in the South

As the South emerged from the early era of withering mortality and stunted families, male and female roles gradually became more physically and functionally separated. In most areas, the white gender ratio reached parity by the 1720s, depriving women of their former leverage in the marriage market. The growth of slavery also changed the work role of white women with the wealthy planter's wife becoming the domestic manager in "the great house." In a description of his daughters' daily routine, William Byrd II pointed to the emerging female identity: "They are every day up to their elbows in housewifery, which will qualify them effectually for useful wives and if they live long enough for notable women."

The balanced sex ratio and the growth of slavery also brought changes for southern males. The planter's son had always been trained to operate in the world beyond the plantation-house doors. Learning horsemanship, the use of a gun, and the rhythms of agricultural life was as important a part of a young man's education as lessons with tutors such as Devereaux Jarratt. Ordering and disciplining slaves also became a part of the southern youth's education. Many had slaves of their own before reaching adulthood. Some planters worried that this would lead, as Thomas Jefferson would later write, to "odious peculiarities" in the character of southern men, because slavery involved a "perpetual exercise of the most boisterous passions" by white masters "nursed, educated, and daily exercised in tyranny." But bred to command, southern planters' sons also developed a self-confidence and authority that propelled many of them into leadership roles during the American Revolution.

On the small farms of the tidewater region and throughout the back settlements, women's roles closely resembled those of northern women. Women labored in the fields alongside their menfolk. "She is a very civil woman," noted an observer of a southern frontierswoman, "and shows nothing of ruggedness or immodesty in her carriage; yet she will carry a gun in the woods and kill deer and turkeys, shoot down wild cattle, catch and tie hogs, knock down beeves with an ax, and perform the most manful exercises as well as most men in those parts."

Marriage and family life were more informal in the backcountry. With vast areas unattended by ministers of any religion and courthouses out of reach, most couples married or "took up" with each other in matches unsanctioned by state or church. The arrival of an itinerant clergyman on horseback typically brought forth dozens of couples living in common-law marriage who asked to have vows performed and their children legitimized by baptism. Respectable clergymen saw the frontier settlers living in lascivious abandon. But the poor upcountry hunters and farmers were really only the first of many generations of pioneers who made do as best they could on the forest's edge, where the institutions of settled society had not yet arrived.

THE URBAN WORLD OF COMMERCE AND IDEAS

Only about 5 percent of the eighteenth-century colonists lived in towns as large as 2,500, and none of the commercial centers boasted a population greater than 16,000 in 1750 or 30,000 in 1775. Yet the urban societies were at the leading edge of social change. Almost all the alterations associated with the advent of "modern" life occurred first in the seaport towns and then radiated outward to the villages, farms, and plantations of the hinterland. In the seaboard centers, the transition first occurred from a barter to a commercial economy, from a social order based on achievement rather than assigned status, from rank-conscious and deferential politics to participatory and contentious politics, and from small-scale craftsmanship to factory production. In addition, the cities were the centers of intellectual life and the conduits through which European ideas flowed into the colonies.

Sinews of Trade

In the half century after 1690, Boston, New York, Philadelphia, and Charleston blossomed from urban waterside villages into thriving commercial centers. Their growth accompanied the development of the agricultural interior, to which the seaports were closely linked. As the colonial population rose and spread out, minor seaports such as Salem, Newport, Providence, Annapolis, Norfolk, and Savannah gathered 5,000 or more inhabitants.

Trade was indispensable to colonial economic life, and cities were trade centers. Through them flowed colonial export staples such as tobacco, rice, furs, wheat, timber products, and fish as well as the imported goods that colonists needed: manufactured and luxury goods from England such as glass, paper, iron implements, and cloth; wine, spices, coffee, tea, and sugar from other parts of the world; and the human cargo to fill the labor gap. In these seaports, the pivotal figure was the merchant. Frequently engaged in both retail and wholesale trade, the merchant was also moneylender (for no banks yet existed), shipbuilder,

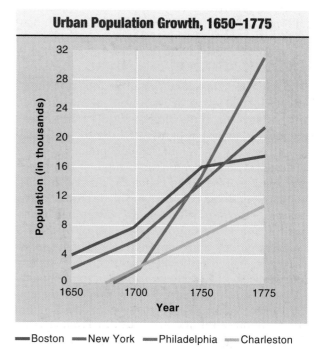

Urban Population Growth, 1650–1775

— Boston — New York — Philadelphia — Charleston

By 1755, Boston had lost its lead as British North America's largest city. Plagued by costly wars and economic difficulties, its population leveled off, whereas that of other cities grew. Source: Gary B. Nash, *The Urban Crucible,* 1979.

insurance agent, land developer, and often coordinator of artisan production.

By the eighteenth century, the American economy was integrated into an Atlantic basin trading system that connected settlers to Great Britain, western Europe, Africa, the West Indies, and Newfoundland. The rulers of Great Britain, like those of other major trading nations of western Europe, pursued mercantilist trade policies. Mercantilism's core idea was that a country must gain wealth by increasing exports, levying duties on imports, regulating production and trade, and exploiting colonies. The British followed these principles by controlling their colonies' trade; requiring their colonies to supply them with foodstuffs, lumber, and other nonmanufactured products; and selling the colonists British manufactured goods.

The colonists could never produce enough exportable raw materials to pay for the imported goods they craved, so they had to earn credits in England by supplying the West Indies and other areas with foodstuffs and timber products. They also accumulated credit by providing shipping and distribution services. New Englanders became the most ambitious participants in the carrying trade. Sailing from Boston, Salem, Newport, and Providence, Yankee merchant seamen, manning Yankee-built ships, dominated the traffic along the Atlantic seaboard, the Caribbean trade, and the transatlantic commerce. A much higher proportion of New England's population made its living in maritime enterprise than in any other colonial region.

The Artisan's World

Though merchants stood first in wealth and prestige in the colonial towns, artisans were far more numerous. About two-thirds of urban adult males (slaves excluded) labored at handicrafts. By the mid-eighteenth century, the colonial cities contained scores of specialized "leather apron men," not only the proverbial butcher, baker, and candlestick maker but also the carpenters and coopers (who made barrels); shoemakers and tailors; silver-, gold-, pewter-, and blacksmiths; mast and sail makers; masons, plasterers, weavers, potters; and many more. Handicraft specialization increased as the cities matured, but every artisan worked with hand tools, usually in small shops.

Work patterns for artisans were irregular, dictated by weather, hours of daylight, erratic delivery of raw materials, and shifting consumer demand. When ice blocked northern harbors, mariners and dockworkers endured slack time. If prolonged rain delayed the slaughter of cows in the country or made impassable the rutted roads into the city, the tanner and the shoemaker laid their tools aside. The hatter depended on the supply of beaver skins, which could stop abruptly if disease struck an Indian tribe or war disrupted the fur trade. Every urban artisan knew "broken days," slack spells, and dull seasons. Ordinary laborers dreaded winter, for it was a season when cities had "little occasion for the labor of the poor," and firewood to heat even a small house could cost several months' wages.

Urban artisans took fierce pride in their crafts. While deferring to those above them, they saw themselves as the backbone of the community, contributing essential products and services. "Our professions rendered us useful and necessary members of our community," the Philadelphia shoemakers asserted; "proud of that rank, we aspired to no higher." This self-esteem and desire for community recognition sometimes jostled with the upper-class view of artisans as "mere mechanicks," part of the "vulgar herd."

Striving for respectability, artisans placed a premium on achieving economic independence. Every craftsman began as an apprentice, spending five or more teenage years learning the "mysteries of the craft" in a master's shop. After fulfilling his contract, the young artisan became a "journeyman," selling his labor to a master craftsman and frequently living in his house, eating at his table, and sometimes marrying his daughter. The journeyman hoped to complete within a few years the three-step climb from servitude to self-employment. After setting up his own shop, he could control his work hours and acquire the respect that

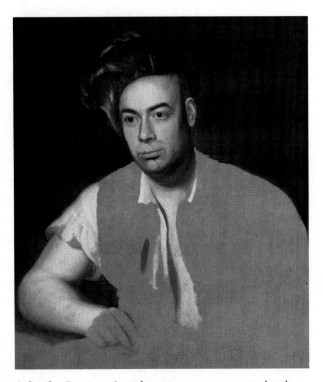

Only a few Boston artisans became prosperous enough to have their portrait painted. But a few did, including Paul Revere and Nathaniel Hurd, the engraver shown here. Hurd came from a long line of artisans: his great-grandfather was a tailor, his grandfather a joiner, and his father a silversmith. Hurd's open collar and rolled-up sleeves show him in his working outfit. This unfinished portrait was probably a study for a more elegant portrait that showed Hurd in an embroidered silk blouse. *(Memorial Art Gallery of the University of Rochester, Marion Stratton Gould Fund)*

came from economic independence. But in trades requiring greater organization and capital, such as distilling and shipbuilding, the rise from journeyman to master proved impossible for many artisans. Nonetheless, the ideal of the independent craftsman prevailed.

In good times, urban artisans did well. They expected to earn a "decent competency" and eventually to purchase a small house. But success was far from automatic, even for those following Poor Richard's advice about hard work and frugal living. An advantageous marriage, luck in avoiding illness, and the size of an inheritance were often the critical factors in whether an artisan moved up or down the ladder of success. In Philadelphia, about half the artisans in the first half of the eighteenth century died leaving enough personal property to have ensured a comfortable standard of living. Another quarter left more, often including slaves and indentured servants. New England's artisans did not fare so well, for their economy was weaker in the eighteenth century. But in all cities, artisans took pride in their life of productive labor. "The meanest [of them] thinks he has a right of civility from the greatest" person in the city, wrote one city dweller.

One of the few contemporary paintings of social activity in colonial taverns, this colorful portrayal of a tavern in Surinam, a Dutch island on the northeastern coast of South America, shows carousing sea captains. American ships went there frequently to trade illegally for shipments of sugar that were quickly transformed into rum—the alcohol of choice in many North American taverns. (*John Greenwood,* Sea Captains Carousing in Surinam, 1758, *The Saint Louis Art Museum*)

URBAN SOCIAL STRUCTURE

Population growth, economic development, and a series of wars that punctuated the period from 1690 to 1765 altered the urban social structure. Stately townhouses rose as testimony to the fortunes acquired in trade, shipbuilding, war contracting, and—probably the most profitable of all—urban land development. "It is almost a proverb," a Philadelphian observed in the 1760s, "that every great fortune made here within these 50 years has been by land." Some merchants amassed fortunes. A merchant's estate of £2,000 sterling was counted impressive in the early eighteenth century. Two generations later, some commercial titans had become North America's first millionaires by accumulating estates of £10,000 to £20,000 sterling.

The rise of Thomas Hancock, on whose fortune his less commercially astute nephew, John Hancock, would later construct a shining political career, provides a glimpse of how war could catapult an enterprising trader to affluence. Hancock, a minister's son, became a bookseller in Boston. An opportune marriage to the daughter of a prosperous merchant provided a toehold in commerce and enough capital to invest in several vessels. By 1735, Hancock had made enough money, much of it from smuggling tea, to build a mansion on Beacon Hill.

When war broke out with Spain in 1739, Hancock used his connections with the governor to obtain lucrative supply contracts for military expeditions to the Caribbean and Nova Scotia. He also invested heavily in privateers, who engaged in private warfare against enemy shipping and auctioned the enemy vessels they overpowered. When peace returned in 1748, all Boston witnessed what war had done for a well-connected merchant. The man who had sold books from a tiny shop on Drawbridge Street 15 years before now imported a four-horse chariot from London with the interior lined in scarlet and the doors emblazoned with a heraldic shield.

Alongside urban wealth grew urban poverty. From the beginning, every city had its disabled, orphaned, and widowed who required aid. But after 1720, poverty marred the lives of many more city dwellers. Many were war widows with numerous children and no means of support. Others were rural migrants seeking opportunities in the city. Some were recent immigrants, who found fewer chances for employment than earlier. Boston was hit especially hard. Its economy stagnated in the 1740s, and taxpayers groaned under the burden of paying for heavy war expenditures. The overseers of the poor lamented that their relief expenditures were double the outlays of any town of equal size "upon the face of the whole earth."

Burdened with mounting poor taxes, cities devised new ways of helping the needy. Rather than support the impoverished in their homes with "outrelief" payments, officials built large almshouses where the poor could be housed and fed more economically. Many of the indigent preferred "to starve in their homes" rather

Recovering the Past

HOUSEHOLD INVENTORIES

Historians use probate records to examine social changes in American society. They include wills, the legal disposition of estates, and household inventories taken by court-appointed appraisers that detail the personal possessions left at death. Inventories have been especially valuable in tracing the transformation of colonial communities.

Like tax lists, inventories can be used to show changes in a community's distribution of wealth. But they are far more detailed than tax lists, providing a snapshot of how people lived at the end of their life. Inventories list and value almost everything a person owned—household possessions, equipment, books, clothes and jewelry, cash on hand, livestock and horses, crops and stored provisions. Hence, through inventories, we can measure the quality of life at different social levels. We can also witness how people made choices about investing their savings—in capital goods of their trade such as land, ships, and equipment; in personal goods such as household furnishings and luxury items; or in real property such as land and houses.

Studied systematically (and corrected for biases, which infect this source as well as others), inventories show that by the early 1700s, ordinary householders were improving their standard of living. Finished furniture such as cupboards, beds, tables, and chairs turn up more frequently in inventories. Pewter dinnerware replaces wooden bowls and spoons, bed linen makes an appearance, and books and pictures are sometimes noted.

Among an emerging elite before the Revolution, much more fashionable articles of consumption appear. The partial inventory of Robert Oliver, a wealthy merchant and officeholder living in a Boston suburb, is reproduced here. You can get some idea of the dignified impression Oliver wished to make by looking at his furniture and dishes and by noticing that he owned a mahogany tea table, damask linen, and a bed with curtains. The inventory further suggests the spaciousness of Oliver's house and shows how he furnished each room.

It is helpful when studying inventories to categorize the goods in the following way: those that are needed to survive (basic cooking utensils, for example); those that make life easier or more comfortable (enough plates and beds for each member of the family, for example); and those that make life luxurious (slaves, silver plates, paintings, mahogany furniture, damask curtains, spices, wine, and so forth). Oliver had many luxury goods as well as items that contributed to his use of leisure time and his personal enjoyment. Which items in his inventory do you think were needed only to survive comfortably? Which were luxuries? What other conclusions can you draw about the lifestyle of rich colonial merchants like Oliver?

Beyond revealing a growing social differentiation in colonial society, the inventories help the historian understand the reaction during the Great Awakening to what many ordinary colonists regarded as sinful pride and arrogance displayed by the elite. By the 1760s, this distrust of affluence among simple folk had led to outright hostility toward men who surrounded themselves with the trappings of aristocratic life. Even the ambitious young John Adams, a striving lawyer, was shocked at what he saw at the house of a wealthy merchant in Boston. "Went over the House to view the Furniture, which alone cost a thousand Pound sterling," he exclaimed. "A seat it is for a noble Man, a Prince. The Turkey Carpets, the painted Hangings, the Marble Tables, the rich Beds with crimson Damask Curtains . . . are the most magnificent of any Thing I have ever seen."

Such a description takes on its full meaning only when contrasted with what inventories tell us about life at the bottom of society. The hundreds of inventories for Bostonians dying in the decade before the American Revolution show that fully half of them died with less than £40 personal wealth and one-quarter with £20 or less. The inventories and wills of Jonathan and Daniel Chandler of Andover, Massachusetts, show the material circumstances of less favored Americans who suffered from the economic distress afflicting New England since the 1730s. Note that Daniel Chandler was a shoemaker. How do the possessions of these brothers compare with Oliver's partial inventory? An examination of these contrasting inventories helps explain the class tension that figured in the revolutionary experience.

Household Inventory of Robert Oliver, Wealthy Merchant

Dorchester Jan.ry 11th 1763.

Inventory of what Estates Real & Personall, belonging to Coll.o Robert Oliver [Esquire] late of Dorchester Deceased, that has been Exhibited to us the Subscribers, for Apprizement. Viz.t

In the Setting Parlour Viz.t

Item		£
a looking Glass		£4.—
a Small Ditto	@ 6/	0.6.0
12 Metzitens pictures Glaz'd		3.12.—
8 Cartoons D.o Ditto		4.—
11 small Pictures		.4.—
4 Maps		.10.—
1 Prospect Glass		.10.—
2 Escutchons Glaz'd		.4.—
1 pair small hand Irons		.6.—
1 Shovel & Tongs		.8.—
1 Tobacco Tongs		.1.—
1 pair Bellowes		.2.—
1 Tea Chest		.2.—
2 Small Waters		.1.—
1 Mehogony Tea Table		1.—
8 China Cups & Saucers		.2.—
1 Earthen Cream Pott		.—.1
1 Ditto. Sugar Dish		.—.4
1 Black Walnut Table		1.—
1 Black Ditto Smaller		0.6.—
1 Round painted Table		0.1.—
7 Leather Bottom Chairs	@ 6/	2.2.—
1 Arm.d Chair Common		1.3.—
1 Black Walnut Desk		1.12.—
1 pair Candlesticks snuffers & Stand Base Mettle		
		.4.— .1.—
6 Wine Glasses 1 Water Glass		1.—.—
a parcell of Books		0.4.—
a Case with Small Bottles		22.1.5

In the Entry & Stair Case Viz.t

Item	£
17 pictures	£0.10.—
	0.10.0

In the Kitchen Chamber Viz.t

Item		£
a Bedstead & Curtains Compleat		£4.—.—
a Bed Bolster & 2 pillows		5.—
a Under Bed & 1 Chair	@ 6/	0.1.—
2 Rugs & 1 Blankett		0.18.—
		09.19.0

In the Dining Room Viz.t

Item	£
1 pair of andirons	£0.3.—
7 Bass Bottoms Chairs	0.7.—
1 Large Wooden Table	0.3.—
1 Small Ditto Oak	0.1.—
1 Small looking Glass	0.6.—
1 Old Desk	0.6.—
1 Case with 2 Bottles	0.2.—
1 Warming pan	0.12.—
	2. 0. 0

In the Marble Chamber Viz.t

Item		£
1 Bedstead & Curtains Compleat		£8.—
1 feather Bed, Bolster & 2 pillows		8.—
1 Chest of Drawers		2.8.—
1 Buroe Table	@ 6/	4.—
6 Chairs Leather'd Bottoms		1.16.—
1 Small dressing Glass		.6.—
1 Small Carpett		1.—.—
1 White Cotton Counterpin		.18.—
1 pair Blanketts		1.12.—
1 pair holland Sheets	@ 12/ p.r	1.4.—
3 pair Dowlases D.o New	@ 4/	1.16.—
3 pair & 1 Ditto Coarser	@ 3/	0.14.—
3 pair Cotton & Linnen D.o	@ 2/	0.9.—
4 pair Servants Ditto	@ 1/	0.8.—
4 Coarse Table Cloths	@ 1/	0.4.—
10 Ditto Kitchen Towels	@ 12/	0.1.—
5 Diaper Table Cloths	@ 18/	3.—.—
6 Damask Table Cloths	@ 3	5.8.—
4 N. England Diaper D.o	@ 2/	0.12.—
4 pair Linnen pillow Cases	@ 1/	0.8.—
5 Coarser Ditto	@ 6.d	0.5.—
6 Diaper Towels	@ 2/	0.3.—
7 Damask Ditto	@ 24/ doz.n	0.14.—
2 doz.n & 9 Damask Napkins		3.6.—
1 Gauze Tea Table Cover		0.1.—
		£43.13.0

Household Inventory of Jonathan Chandler

(d. 1745)

Cash	£18p
Gun	1p
Psalmbook	8p
	£19p
Debts	£5p
Total	£14p

Household Inventory of Daniel Chandler

(d. 1752), Shoemaker

Bible	
Shoe knife	
Hammer	Total £12
Last (shoe shaper)	
Various notes	

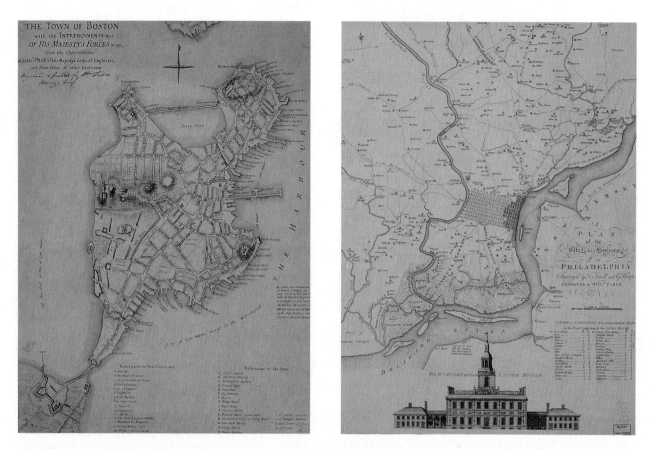

The grid pattern of Philadelphia's straight streets contrasts sharply with Boston's crooked and irregular roads and alleys. Topography had everything to do with this. Surrounded by water creating an irregular shoreline and dominated by three high hills, leveled in the nineteenth century, Boston's streets were laid out in the manner of goat paths. *(Library of Congress Geography & Maps Division)*

than leave their neighborhoods to suffer the discipline and indignities of the poorhouse. Boston's poor women also resisted laboring in the linen factory that was built in 1750 to enable them to contribute to their own support through spinning and weaving. Despite the warnings of Boston's ministers that "if any would not work, neither should they eat," they refused to leave their children at home to labor in America's first textile factory.

The increasing gap between the wealthy and the poor was recorded in the urban eighteenth-century tax lists. The top 5 percent of taxpayers increased their share of the cities' taxable assets from about 30 to 50 percent between 1690 and 1770. The bottom half of the taxable inhabitants saw their share of the wealth shrink from about 10 to 4 percent. Except in Boston, the urban middle classes continued to gain ground. But the growth of princely fortunes amid increasing poverty made some urban dwellers reflect that Old World ills were reappearing in the New.

The Entrepreneurial Ethos

As the cities grew, new values took hold. In the traditional "corporate" view of society, economic life ideally operated according to what was fair, not what was

profitable. Citizens usually agreed that government should provide for the general welfare by regulating prices and wages, setting quality controls, licensing providers of service such as tavernkeepers and ferrymen, and supervising public markets where all food was sold. Such regulation seemed natural because a community was defined not as a collection of individuals, each entitled to pursue separate interests, but as a single body of interrelated parts where individual rights and responsibilities formed a seamless web.

But as cities and commerce grew, new values about economic life took hold. Subordinating private interests to the commonweal became viewed as a lofty but unrealistic ideal. Prosperity required the encouragement of acquisitive appetites rather than self-denial, for ambition would spur economic activity as more people sought more goods. The new view held that, if people were allowed to pursue their material desires competitively, they would collectively form a natural, impersonal market of producers and consumers that would operate to everyone's advantage.

As the colonial port towns took their places in the Atlantic world of commerce, merchants became accustomed to making decisions according to the

WEALTH DISTRIBUTION IN COLONIAL AMERICA

Percentage of wealth held by the richest 10% and the poorest 30% of the population in two cities and one rural area

Year	Richest 10%	Poorest 30%
Boston		
1684–1699	41.2	3.3
1700–1715	54.5	2.8
1716–1725	61.7	2.0
1726–1735	65.6	1.9
1736–1745	58.6	1.8
1746–1755	55.2	1.8
1756–1765	67.5	1.4
1766–1775	61.1	2.0
Philadelphia		
1684–1699	36.4	4.5
1700–1715	41.3	4.9
1716–1725	46.8	3.9
1726–1735	53.6	3.7
1736–1745	51.3	2.6
1746–1755	70.1	1.5
1756–1765	60.3	1.1
1766–1775	69.9	1.0
Chester County, Pennsylvania		
1693	23.8	17.4
1715	25.9	13.1
1730	28.6	9.8
1748	28.7	13.1
1760	29.9	6.3
1782	33.6	4.7

Source: Gary B. Nash, *The Urban Crucible*, 1979.

emerging commercial ethic that rejected traditional restraints on entrepreneurial activity. If wheat fetched 8 shillings a bushel in the West Indies but only 5 in Boston, a grain merchant felt justified in sending all he could purchase from local farmers to the more distant buyer. Indifferent to individuals and local communities, the new transatlantic market responded only to the invisible laws of supply and demand.

Tension between the new economic freedom and the older concern for the public good erupted only with food shortages or galloping inflation. Because the American colonies experienced none of the famines that ravaged Europe in this period, such crises occurred rarely, usually during war, when demand for provisions rose sharply.

Such a moment struck in Boston during Queen Anne's War. Merchant Andrew Belcher contracted to ship large quantities of wheat to the Caribbean, where higher prices would yield greater profit than in Boston. Ordinary neighbors, threatened with a bread shortage and angered that a townsman would put profit ahead of community needs, attacked one of Belcher's grain-laden ships in 1710. They sawed through the rudder and tried to run the vessel aground in order to seize the grain. Invoking the older ethic that the public welfare outweighed private interests, they took the law into their own hands. Even the grand jury, composed of substantial members of the community, hinted its approval of the violent action against Belcher by refusing to indict the rioters.

The two conceptions of community and economic life rubbed against each other for many decades. Urban merchants, shopkeepers, land speculators, and ambitious artisans—participants in England's rising commercial empire—cleaved more and more to the new economic formulas, although they continued to voice respect for the old precepts of the corporate community. The clergy continued to preach the traditional message: "Let no man seek his own, but every man another's wealth." But by the mid-eighteenth century, the pursuit of a profitable livelihood, not the social compact of the community, animated most city dwellers.

The American Enlightenment

Ideas about not only economic life but also the nature of the universe and the improvement of the human condition filtered across the Atlantic. In the eighteenth century, an American version of the European intellectual movement called the Enlightenment occurred, and the cities became centers for disseminating these new ideas.

In what is called the Age of Reason, European thinkers rejected the pessimistic Calvinist concept of innate human depravity, replacing it with the optimistic notion that a benevolent God had blessed humankind with the supreme gift of reason. Thinkers like John Locke, in his influential *Essay Concerning Human Understanding* (1689), argued that God had not predetermined the content of the human mind but had instead given it the capacity to acquire knowledge. All Enlightenment thinkers prized this acquisition of knowledge, for it allowed humankind to improve its condition. As the great scientific thinkers Galileo and Isaac Newton demonstrated, systematic investigation could unlock the secrets of the physical universe. Moreover, scientific knowledge could be applied to human institutions to improve society.

The scientific and intellectual advances of the seventeenth and eighteenth centuries encouraged a belief in "natural law" and fostered debate about the "natural" human rights. In Europe, French philosophers Voltaire and Denis Diderot explored the issue of equality. From 1750 to 1772, Diderot published his *Encyclopedia,* which treated such topics as equality,

The American bison, unknown in Europe, was common east of the Mississippi River when European settlers arrived. *(Colonial Williamsburg Foundation)*

liberty, reason, and rights. The ideas of the Enlightenment spread in Europe and the Americas and eventually found expression in movements for reform, democracy, and liberation—all of deep interest to those who were beginning to oppose slavery and the slave trade as abominations.

Though only a small number of educated colonists read the Enlightenment authors, they began in the eighteenth century to make significant contributions to the advancement of science. Naturalists such as John Bartram of Philadelphia gathered and described American plants from all over the eastern part of the continent as part of the transatlantic attempt to classify all plant life into one universal system. Professor John Winthrop III of Harvard made an unusually accurate measurement of the earth's distance from the sun. Standing above them all was Benjamin Franklin, whose spectacular (and dangerous) experiments with electricity, the properties of which were just becoming known, earned him an international reputation.

Franklin's true genius as a figure of the Enlightenment came in his practical application of scientific knowledge. Among his inventions were the lightning rod, which nearly ended the age-old danger of

fires when lightning struck wooden buildings; bifocal spectacles; and an iron stove that heated rooms—in an age when firewood was a major item in the household budget—far more efficiently than the usual open fireplace. Franklin also made his adopted city of Philadelphia a center of the American Enlightenment. He led the founding of America's first circulating library in 1731, an artisans' debating club for "mutual improvement" through discussion of the latest ideas from Europe, and an intercolonial scientific association that in 1769 became the American Philosophical Society.

Though most colonists were not educated enough to participate actively in the American Enlightenment, the efforts of men such as Franklin exposed thousands, especially in the cities, to new currents of thought. This led to the growing sense that the colonists, blessed by their abundant environment, might achieve the Enlightenment ideal of a perfect society.

THE GREAT AWAKENING

Many of the social, economic, and political changes occurring in the eighteenth-century colonies converged in the Great Awakening, the first of many religious revivals that would sweep American society during the next two centuries. The timing and character of the Awakening varied from region to region. But everywhere, this quest for spiritual renewal challenged old sources of authority and produced patterns of thought and behavior that helped fuel a revolutionary movement in the next generation.

Fading Faith

Colonial America in the early eighteenth century remained an overwhelmingly Protestant culture. The Puritan, or Congregational, Church dominated all of New England except Rhode Island. Anglicanism held sway in much of New York and throughout the South except the backcountry. In the mid-Atlantic and in the back settlements, German Mennonites, Dunkers, Moravians, and Lutherans; Scots-Irish Presbyterians; and English Baptists and Quakers all mingled.

Yet these diverse groups commanded the allegiance of only about one-third of the colonists. Those who went to no church at all remained the majority. In many areas, ministers and churches were simply unavailable. In Virginia, the most populous colony, only 60 clergymen in 1761 served a population of 350,000—one for every 5,800 people.

Most colonial churches were voluntary or gathered ("congregated") groups, formed for reasons of conscience, not because of government compulsion. Catholics, Jews, and nonbelievers could not vote or hold office. But the persecution of Quakers and Catholics had largely passed, and some dissenting groups by 1720 had gained the right to use long-obligatory church taxes to support their own congregations.

The clergy often administered their congregations with difficulty. Anglicans and several German sects maintained close ties to mother churches across the Atlantic, whereas other denominations attempted to centralize authority. However, most efforts to tighten organization and discipline failed. For example, Anglican ministers had to be ordained in England and regularly report to the bishop of London. But once installed in a Chesapeake parish, an Anglican priest faced wealthy planters who controlled the vestry (the local church's governing body), set his salary, and would drive him out if he challenged them too forcefully. In Connecticut, the Saybrook Platform of 1708 created a network, or "consociation," of Congregational Churches, but individual churches still preserved much of their autonomy.

Though governing their churches frustrated many clergymen, religious apathy was a far more pressing problem in the early eighteenth century. As early as the 1660s, the Congregational clergy of New England had attempted to return wandering sheep to the fold by adopting the Half-Way Covenant. It allowed children of church members, if they adhered to the "forms of godliness," to join the church even if they could not demonstrate that they had undergone a conversion experience. They could not, however, vote in church affairs or take communion.

Adopted in 1662, this compromise kept in the church many children of the founders, and they in turn could pass church membership on to their children. Some ministers took other measures to increase their flocks. Solomon Stoddard, for 60 years patriarch of the Congregational Church in Northampton, Massachusetts, gave communion to every professing Christian and used an emotional style of preaching to reap annual "harvests" of souls.

Despite compromises and innovations, most church leaders saw creeping religious apathy when they surveyed their towns. An educated clergy, its energies often drained by doctrinal disputes within denominations, appealed too much to the mind and not enough to the heart. In such a state, as one Connecticut leader remembered it, "the spirit of God appeared to be awfully withdrawn."

The Awakeners' Message

The Great Awakening was not a unified movement but rather a series of revivals that swept different regions between 1720 and 1760 with varying degrees of intensity. The first stirrings came in the 1720s in New Jersey and Pennsylvania. Theodore Frelinghuysen, a Dutch Reformed minister, excited his congregation through emotional preaching. Avoiding theological abstractions, he concentrated on arousing a need to be "saved." A neighboring Presbyterian, Gilbert Tennent, soon took up the Dutchman's techniques, with similar success.

From New Jersey, the Awakening spread to Pennsylvania in the 1730s, especially among Presbyterians, and then broke out in the Connecticut River valley. There it was led by Jonathan Edwards, who had succeeded his grandfather, Solomon Stoddard, in Northampton's Church. Later a philosophical giant in the colonies, Edwards as a young man gained renown by frightening his parishioners with the fate of "sinners in the hands of an angry God." "How manifold have been the abominations of your life!" Edwards preached. "Are there not some here that have debased themselves below the dignity of human nature, by allowing in sensual filthiness, as swine in the mire . . . ?" Edwards paraded one sin after another before his trembling congregants: "God and your own consciences know what abominable lasciviousness you have practised in things not fit to be named, when you have been alone; when you ought to have been reading, or meditating, or on your knees before God in secret prayer."

After cataloging his parishioners' sins, Edwards drew such graphic pictures of the hell awaiting the unrepentant that his Northampton neighbors were soon preparing frantically for the conversion by which they would be "born again." His *Faithful Narrative of the Surprizing Work of God* (1736), which described his town's awakening, was the first published revival narrative. This literary form would be used many times in the future to fan the flames of evangelical religion.

In 1739, these regional brushfires of evangelicalism were drawn together by a 24-year-old Anglican priest from England, George Whitefield. Inspired by John Wesley, the founder of English Methodism, Whitefield became a master of emotional open-air preaching. Whitefield made seven barnstorming tours along the American seaboard, the first in 1739 and 1740. Thousands turned out to see him, and with each success, his fame and influence grew. In the cities, people fought for places in the churches when he spoke and gathered by the thousands in open fields to hear his message. Even in sedate Philadelphia, he turned skeptics into true believers, "so that one could not walk thro' town, in an evening," claimed the unreligious Benjamin Franklin, "without hearing psalms sung in different families of every street." In Boston, Whitefield preached to 19,000 in three days. Then, at a farewell sermon, he left 25,000 writhing in fear of damnation. In his wake came American preachers, mostly young men like Devereaux Jarratt, whom he had inspired.

Technology Changes the American People

LIGHTNING RODS

✦

In 1746, Benjamin Franklin, already a successful printer, newspaper editor, and civic organizer in Philadelphia, began experimenting with electricity, at that time a mysterious force. Franklin had read about the experiments of Dutchman Pieter van Musschenbroek, who had learned how to condense electricity in a glass bottle (called a Leyden jar) and to produce electrical sparks by attaching a conductor to the two sides of the bottle. Throughout Europe, amateur scientists began to play with Leyden jars, but nobody really understood the source or nature of the mysterious electrical "fluid."

By 1748, Franklin had constructed a number of experiments for producing brilliant sparks from Leyden jars and for measuring the intensity of the sparks. His *Experiments and Observations on Electricity,* published in London three years later, put his name on the lips of scientists all over Europe. His achievements catapulted Franklin to the forefront of the world's scientists and earned him a coveted medal from the Royal Society of London, one of the most advanced scientific bodies in the world. Scientific knowledge had traveled westward across the Atlantic from Europe for two centuries but now went eastward from North America to the amazed Europeans.

In practical terms, Franklin's most important discovery was that lightning produced by thunderstorms was a form of electricity. Devising a common kite of silk stretched across sticks of wood with a thin wire at the top and a metal key tied to the end of the kite string, he proved that "electric fire" would "stream plentifully from the key." His experiment constituted a breakthrough of one of the most formidable barriers of the unknown and opened up an entirely new field of controlled study.

Franklin personified the eighteenth-century Enlightenment in his desire to understand the laws that govern the natural world. He was also an Enlightenment figure in his determination to use these ideas, or what we would call scientific theory, to harness nature. Electricity, in the form of lightning, was a terrifying destructive natural force that for centuries had destroyed buildings, ships, and people with awful regularity. Once Franklin learned the properties of electricity

Franklin's global influence reached as far as Japan, as shown in this Japanese electrical parlor game in 1813. *(The Burndy Library, Dibner Institute for the History of Science and Technology)*

Benjamin Franklin's fame in "capturing" the lightning of violent thunderstorms led to dramatic representations of his kite experiment. Here Franklin holds a metal key; through it passes a silk string that leads to the high-flying kite.
(West, Benjamin—Benjamin Franklin Drawing Lightning from the Sky, *Philadelphia Museum of Art: Gift of Mr. and Mrs. Wharton Sindler)*

and had established that lightning was a form of it, he found it relatively easy to contrive a metal rod, coated to prevent rusting, that would "throw off" the electricity and render it harmless.

By 1753, convinced that he had mastered the theory of electricity and lightning, Franklin went public with an essay that was to make life better for millions of people around the world. In "How to Secure Houses from Lightning" he provided a practical essay that took the terror out of a natural phenomenon and taught people how to use a simple and inexpensive device to protect their lives and property. Soon lightning rods shot up on houses and barns all over the American colonies—and soon all over Europe and other parts of the world. Farmers, homeowners, mariners, and church wardens could soon rest easier, knowing that their barns, houses, ships, and churches were safe. What had seemed to be the wrathful work of an angry God now became a force within the power of humans to control.

In Franklin's premodern world, scientific breakthroughs proceeded slowly. Usually individuals rather than research teams conducted research, and they did so without government sponsorship, without highly capitalized corporate research facilities, even—at least in America—without university laboratories. Franklin conducted his research at home and in the fields surrounding the city of Philadelphia. His was a one-man operation, and his success emanated from what was later called "an ingenious mind and a contriving hand." If the power of Lightning could be harnessed by the son of a Boston candlemaker far from the centers of learning in Europe, what other forces of nature might be understood and brought under rein?

Why do you think Franklin's *Experiments and Observations on Electricity* (1751) were published in London instead of Philadelphia? Do you think that it was advantageous that in the era before patents Franklin's lightning rod could easily be made, leaving him only with honor but no profits from his remarkable invention?

Readings: I. Bernard Cohen, *Benjamin Franklin: Scientist and Statesman* (New York, 1963); Brooke Hindle, *The Pursuit of Science in Revolutionary America, 1735–1789* (Chapel Hill, NC, 1956).

Jonathan Edwards (1703–1758) was the first major philosopher in the American colonies. A leader of the Great Awakening in Massachusetts, he was ousted by his congregation for reprimanding the children of church members for reading *The Midwife Rightly Instructed*, an obstetric guide that was as close as curious children could come to learning about sex. *(Yale University Art Gallery, Bequest of Eugene Phelps Edwards)*

Samson Occom, a Mohegan born in Connecticut, was attracted to Christianity, like so many others who were "outsiders," by the emotional and populistic appeal of the Great Awakening preachers. On a trip to England, Occom raised £12,000 for an evangelical school for Indians, later to become Dartmouth College. *(Courtesy of the Boston Public library, Print Department)*

George Whitefield, who first toured the American colonies in 1739 and 1740, sent thousands of souls "flying to Christ" with his emotional sermons. More Americans heard Whitefield on his many seaboard itineracies, than any other figure in the eighteenth century. *(National Portrait Gallery, London)*

Some of Whitefield's appeal lay in his genius for dramatic performance and some in his ability to simplify theological doctrine and focus people's attention on one facet of religious life, the conversion experience. In electrifying performances, he cast away the conventional written sermons in favor of spontaneous preaching. Using wild body movements and his magnificent voice, he filled thousands with the desire to "fly to Christ."

The appeal of the Awakeners lay both in the medium and the message. They preached that the established, college-trained clergy was too intellectual and tradition-bound to bring faith and piety to a new generation. Congregations were dead, Whitefield declared, "because dead men preach to them." "The sapless discourses of such dead drones," cried another Awakener, were worthless. The fires of Protestant belief could be reignited only if individuals assumed responsibility for their own conversion.

An important form of individual participation was "lay exhorting." "Exhorting" meant that anyone—young or old, female or male, black or white—might spontaneously recount a conversion experience and preach "the Lord's truth." This horrified most established clergymen. Lay exhorting shattered their monopoly on religious discourse and gave new importance to the oral culture of common people, whose spontaneous outpourings contrasted sharply with the controlled literary culture of the gentry. Through lay exhorting, ordinary men and women, and even children, servants, and slaves, crossed class lines and defied assigned roles.

How religion, social change, and politics became interwoven in the Great Awakening can be seen by examining two regions swept by revivalism. Both Boston, the heartland of Puritanism, and interior Virginia, a land of struggling small planters and slave-rich aristocrats, experienced the Great Awakening, but in different ways and at different times.

The Urban North

In Boston, Whitefield-inspired revivalism blazed up amid political controversy. Since 1739, the citizens had argued strenuously about remedies for the severe depreciation of the province's paper currency, which had been issued for years to finance military expeditions against French Canada. The English government insisted that Massachusetts retire all paper money by 1741. Searching for a substitute circulating medium, one group proposed a land bank to issue private bills of credit backed by land. Another group proposed a silver bank to distribute bills of credit backed by silver. Controversy over the land and silver banks swept politics in 1740 and 1741, pitting large merchants, who preferred the fiscally conservative silver bank, against local traders, artisans, and the laboring poor, who preferred the land bank.

Whitefield's arrival in Boston coincided with the currency furor. His stay in Boston overlapped with attacks on merchants as "gripping and merciless usurers" who "heaped up vast estates" at the expense of the common people. At first, Boston's elite applauded Whitefield's ability to call the masses to worship. The master evangelist, it seemed, might restore social harmony by redirecting people from earthly matters such as the currency dispute to concerns of the soul.

When Whitefield left Boston in 1740, he was succeeded by others who were more critical of the "unconverted" clergy and the self-indulgent accumulation of wealth. One was James Davenport, who arrived in 1742. His great-grandfather had been a founder of New Haven, and his father was a respected Congregational minister in Connecticut. But the 25-year-old Davenport, who had been inspired by Whitefield, appeared anything but respectable to the elite.

Finding every church closed to him, even those whose clergy had embraced the Awakening, Davenport preached daily on the Boston Common, aroused religious ecstasy among thousands, and stirred up feeling against Boston's leading figures. Respectable people grew convinced that revivalism had gotten out of hand, for by this time ordinary people were verbally attacking opponents of the land bank in the streets as "carnal wretches, hypocrites, fighters against God, children of the devil, cursed Pharisees." A revival that had begun as a return to religion among backsliding Christians had overlapped with political affairs. Hence, it threatened polite culture, which stressed order and discipline from ordinary people.

The Rural South

The Great Awakening was ebbing in New England and the middle colonies by 1744, although aftershocks continued for years. But in Virginia, where the initial religious earthquake was barely felt, tremors of enthusiasm rippled through society from the mid-1740s onward. As in Boston, the Awakeners challenged and disturbed the gentry-led social order.

Whitefield stirred some religious fervor during his early trips through Virginia. Traveling "New Light" preachers, led by the brilliant orator Samuel Davies, were soon gathering large crowds both in the backcountry and in the traditionally Anglican parishes of the older settled areas. By 1747, worried Anglican clergyman convinced the governor to issue a proclamation restraining "strolling preachers." As in other colonies, Virginia's leaders despised traveling evangelists, for like lay exhorters, these roving Awakeners conjured up a world without properly constituted authority. As one critic put it in 1745, the wandering preachers "have turned the world upside down." When the Hanover County court gave the fiery James Davenport a license to preach in 1750, the governor ordered the suppression of all circuit riders.

New Light Presbyterianism, which challenged the religious monopoly of the gentry-dominated Anglican Church, spread in the 1750s. Then, in the 1760s, came the Baptists. Renouncing finery, attacking ostentatious display, and addressing each other as "brother" and "sister," the Baptists reached out to thousands of unchurched people. Like northern revivalists, they focused on the conversion experience. Many of their preachers were uneducated farmers and artisans who called themselves "Christ's poor." They stressed equality in human affairs and insisted that heaven was always populated more by the humble poor than by the purse-proud rich. Among the poorest of all, Virginia's 140,000 slaves in 1760, the evangelical message began to take hold.

The insurgent Baptist movement in rural Virginia became both a quest for a personal, emotionally satisfying religion among ordinary folk and a rejection of the gentry's social values. Established Anglican pulpits denounced the Awakeners as furiously as had respectable New England divines. In both regions, social changes had weakened the cultural authority of the upper class and, in the context of religious revival, produced a vision of a society drawn along more equal lines.

Legacy of the Awakening

By the time George Whitefield returned to America for his third tour in 1745, the revival had burned out in the North. Its effects, however, were long-lasting. Notably, the Awakening promoted religious pluralism and nourished the idea that all denominations were equally legitimate; none had a monopoly on the truth. Whitefield had anticipated this tendency when he sermonized: "Father Abraham, whom have you in heaven? Any Episcopalians? And the answer came back, No! Any Presbyterians? No! Any Independents or Methodists? No, no, no! Whom have you there? And the final answer came down from heaven, We don't know the names here. All who are here are Christians."

By legitimizing the dissenting Protestant groups that had sprung up in seventeenth-century England, the Great Awakening gave them all a basis for living together in relative harmony. From this framework of denominationalism came a second change—the separation of church and state. Once a variety of churches gained legitimacy, it was hard to justify one denomination claiming special privileges. In the seventeenth century, Roger Williams had tried to sever church and state because he believed that ties with civil bodies would corrupt the church. But during the Awakening, groups such as the Baptists and Presbyterians in Virginia constituted their own religious bodies and broke the Anglican monopoly as *the* Church in the colony. This undermining of the church–state tie would be completed during the revolutionary era.

A third effect of the revival was to legitimate community diversity. Almost from their beginnings, Rhode Island, the Carolinas, and the middle colonies had recognized this. But homogeneity had been prized elsewhere, especially in Massachusetts and Connecticut. There, the Awakening split Congregational Churches into New Lights and Old Lights, and mid-Atlantic Presbyterian Churches were similarly beset by schisms. In hundreds of rural communities by the 1750s, two or three churches existed where only one had stood

before. People learned that the fabric of community could be woven from threads of many hues.

New eighteenth-century colonial colleges reflected the religious pluralism symbolized by the Great Awakening. Before 1740, there existed only Puritan Harvard (1636) and Yale (1701) and Anglican William and Mary (1693). To these small seats of higher education were added six new colleges between 1746 and 1769—Dartmouth, Brown, Princeton, and what are now Columbia, Rutgers, and the University of Pennsylvania.

In spite of ties to particular denominations, none of the new colleges was controlled by an established church, all had governing bodies composed of men of different faiths, and all admitted students regardless of religion. Eager for students and funds, they made nonsectarian appeals and constructed classical curricula mixed with natural sciences and natural philosophy.

Last, the Awakening nurtured a subtle change in values that crossed over into politics and daily life. Especially for ordinary people, the revival experience created a new feeling of self-worth. People assumed new responsibilities in religious affairs and became skeptical of dogma and authority. Many, especially the fast-growing Baptists, decried the growing materialism and deplored the new acceptance of self-interested behavior. He who was "governed by regard to his own private interest," Gilbert Tennent preached, was "an enemy to the public," for in true Christian communities, "mutual love is the band and cement." By learning to oppose authority and to take part in creating new churches, thousands of colonists unknowingly rehearsed for revolution.

POLITICAL LIFE

"Were it not for government, the world would soon run into all manner of disorders and confusions," wrote a Massachusetts clergyman early in the eighteenth century. "Men's lives and estates and liberties

COLONIAL COLLEGES			
Name	**Colony**	**Founding Date**	**Denominational Affiliation**
Harvard College	Massachusetts	1636	Congregational
College of William and Mary	Virginia	1693	Anglican
Yale College	Connecticut	1701	Congregational
College of New Jersey (Princeton)	New Jersey	1746	Presbyterian
College of Philadelphia (University of Pennsylvania)	Pennsylvania	1754	Secular
King's College (Columbia)	New York	1754	Anglican
College of Rhode Island (Brown)	Rhode Island	1764	Baptist
Queen's College (Rutgers)	New Jersey	1766	Dutch Reformed
Dartmouth College	New Hampshire	1769	Congregational

would soon be prey to the covetous and the cruel," and every man would be "as a wolf" to his neighbors. Few colonists would have disagreed. On both sides of the Atlantic, people believed that government existed to protect life, liberty, and property.

A less easily resolved matter was how political power should be divided—in England, between the English government and the American colonies, and within each colony. Colonists naturally drew heavily on inherited political ideas and institutions, almost entirely English ones, for it was English charters that sanctioned settlement, English governors who ruled, and English common law that governed the courts. But meeting unexpected circumstances in a new environment, colonists modified familiar political forms to suit their needs.

Structuring Colonial Governments

All societies consider it essential to determine the final source of political authority. In England, the notion of the God-given supreme authority of the monarch was crumbling even before the planting of the colonies. In its place arose the belief that stable and enlightened government depended on blending and balancing the interests of monarchy, aristocracy, and democracy. Unalloyed, each of these forms of government would degenerate into oppression. Monarchy, the rule of one, would become despotism. Aristocracy, the rule of the few, would turn into corrupt oligarchy. Democracy, the rule of the many, would descend into anarchy or mob rule. Most colonists believed that the Revolution of 1688 in England, by thwarting the king's pretensions to greater power, had vindicated and strengthened a carefully balanced political system.

In the colonies, political balance was achieved somewhat differently. The governor was the king's agent (or, in proprietary colonies, the agent of the proprietor to whom the king delegated authority). The council, composed of wealthy appointees of the governor in most colonies, was a pale equivalent of the English House of Lords. The assembly, elected by white male freeholders, functioned as a replica of the House of Commons. "The concurrence of these three forms of government," wrote a Bostonian in 1749, "seems to be the highest perfection that human civil government can attain to."

COLONIAL FOUNDATIONS OF THE AMERICAN POLITICAL SYSTEM

1606	Virginia companies of London and Plymouth granted patents to settle lands in North America.
1619	First elected colonial legislature meets in Virginia.
1634	Under a charter granted in 1632, Maryland's proprietor is given all the authority "as any bishop of Durham" ever held—more than the king possessed in England.
1635	The council in Virginia deports Governor John Harvey for exceeding his power, thus asserting the rights of local magistrates to contest authority of royally appointed governors.
1643	The colonies of Massachusetts, Plymouth, Connecticut, and New Haven draw up articles of confederation and form the first intercolonial union, the United Colonies of New England.
1647	Under a charter granted in 1644, elected freemen from the Providence Plantations draft a constitution establishing freedom of conscience, separating church and state, and authorizing referenda by the towns on laws passed by the assembly.
1677	The Laws, Concessions, and Agreements for West New Jersey provide for a legislature elected annually by virtually all free males, secret voting, liberty of conscience, election of justices of the peace and local officeholders, and trial by jury in public so that "justice may not be done in a corner."
1689	James II deposed in England in the Glorious Revolution and royal governors, accused of abusing their authority, ousted in Massachusetts, New York, and Maryland.
1701	First colonial unicameral legislature meets in Pennsylvania under the Frame of Government of 1701.
1735	John Peter Zenger, a New York printer, acquitted of seditious libel for printing attacks on the royal governor and his faction, thus widening the freedom of the press.
1754	First congress of all the colonies meets at Albany (with seven colonies sending delegates) and agrees on a Plan of Union (which is rejected by the colonies and the English government).
1765	The Stamp Act Congress, the first intercolonial convention called outside England's authority, meets in New York.

Bicameral legislatures developed in most of the colonies in the seventeenth century. The lower houses, or assemblies, represented the local interests of the people at large. The upper houses, or councils (which usually also sat as the highest courts), represented the nascent aristocracy. Except in Rhode Island and Connecticut, every statute required the governor's assent, and all colonial laws required final approval from the king's privy council. This royal check on colonial lawmaking operated imperfectly, however. Laws took months to reach England, and months more passed before word of their final approval or rejection returned. In the meantime, the laws set down in the colonies took force.

Behind the formal structure of politics stood the rules governing who could participate in the political process. In England since the fifteenth century, the ownership of land had largely defined electoral participation (women and non-Christians were uniformly excluded). Only men with property sufficient to produce an annual rental income of 40 shillings could vote or hold office. The colonists closely followed this principle, except in Massachusetts, where until 1691 church membership was the basic requirement. As in England, the poor and propertyless were excluded, for they lacked the "stake in society" that supposedly transformed unpredictable, ignorant creatures into thoughtful and responsible voters.

Whereas in England, the 40-shilling freehold requirement was intended to restrict the size of the electorate, in the colonies, because of the cheapness of land, it conferred the vote on a large proportion of adult males—between 50 and 75 percent in most colonies. As the proportion of landless colonists increased in the eighteenth century, however, the franchise slowly contracted.

Though voting rights were broadly based, most men assumed that only the wealthy and socially prominent should hold positions of political power. Lesser men, it was held, ought to defer to their betters. Balancing this elitist conception of politics, however, was the notion that the entire electorate should periodically judge the performance of those entrusted with political power and reject those who represented them inadequately. Unlike the members of the English House of Commons, who by the seventeenth century thought of themselves as representing the entire nation, the colonial representatives were expected to reflect the views of those who elected them locally. Believing this, their constituents judged them accordingly.

When were citizens entitled to defy those who ruled them? The answer to this vexing question followed English precedent: The people were justified in badgering their leaders, protesting openly, and, in extreme cases of abuse of power, assuming control in order to put things right. The uprisings in the colonies associated with England's Glorious Revolution represented such moments when the deferential mass transformed itself into a purposeful crowd to overthrow those who trampled on their traditional English liberties.

The Crowd in Action

Crowd action, frequently effective, gradually achieved a kind of legitimacy. What gave special power to the common people when they assembled to protest oppressive authority was the general absence of effective police power. In the countryside, where most colonists lived, only the county sheriff, with an occasional deputy, insulated civil leaders from angry farmers. In the towns, the sheriff had only the frail night watch to safeguard public order. As late as 1757, the night watch of New York was described as a "parcell of idle, drinking vigilant snorers, who never quelled any nocturnal tumult in their lives." In theory, the militia stood ready to suppress public disturbances, but both urban and rural crowds usually included many of the very people who composed the militia. Thus, the assembled people became perceived as the watchdog of government, ready to chastise or drive from office those who violated the collective sense of what was right and proper.

Boston's impressment riot of 1747 vividly illustrates the people's readiness to defend their inherited privileges and the weakness of law enforcement. It began when Commodore Charles Knowles brought his Royal Navy ships to Boston for provisioning—and to replenish the ranks of mariners thinned by desertion. When Knowles sent press gangs out on a chill November evening to fill the crew vacancies from Boston's waterfront population, they scooped up artisans, laborers, servants, and slaves, as well as merchant seamen from ships riding at anchor in the harbor.

But before the press gangs could hustle their victims back to the British men-of-war, a crowd of angry Bostonians seized several British officers, surrounded the governor's house, and demanded the release of their townsmen. When the sheriff and his deputies tried to intervene, the mob mauled them. The militia, called to arms by the governor to "suppress the mob by force, and if need be to fire upon 'em with ball," refused to respond. By dusk, a crowd of several thousand defied the governor's orders to disperse, stoned the windows of the governor's house, and dragged a royal barge from one of the British ships into the courtyard of his house, where they burned it amid cheers.

Enraged by the defiant Bostonians, Commodore Knowles threatened to bombard the town. Negotiations averted a showdown, and Knowles released the impressed Bostonians. After the riot, a young politician named Samuel Adams defended Boston's defiance of royal authority. The people, he argued, had a "natural right" to band together against press gangs that deprived them of their liberty. Local magnates who supported the governor in this incident were labeled "tools to arbitrary power."

The Growing Power of the Assemblies

Incidents such as the impressment riot of 1747 demonstrated the touchiness of England's colonial subjects. But a more gradual and restrained change—the growing ambition and power of the legislative assemblies—was far more important. For most of the seventeenth century, royal and proprietary governors had exercised greater power in relation to the elected legislatures than did the king in relation to Parliament. Governors could dissolve the lower houses and delay their sitting, control the election of their speakers, and in most colonies initiate legislation with their appointed councils. Governors also had authority to appoint and dismiss judges at all levels of the judiciary and to create chancery courts, which sat without juries. They also controlled the expenditure of public monies and had authority to grant land to individuals and groups, which they sometimes used to confer vast estates on their favorites.

By the 1730s, royal governments had replaced many of the proprietary governments. In the seventeenth century, Virginia, Massachusetts, and New York had become royal colonies, with governors appointed by the crown. In the eighteenth century, royal government came to New Jersey (1702), South Carolina (1719), and North Carolina (1729), replacing proprietary regimes.

Many royal governors were competent military officers or bureaucrats, but often they were simply recipients of patronage posts. They were rewarded for whom they knew, not what they had done or might accomplish. A few were psychologically damaged, like Sir Danvers Osborn, who committed suicide a week after arriving in New York in 1753. Many were corrupt. Some governors never took up their posts at all, preferring, like the earl of Orkney, Virginia's royal governor from 1705 to 1737, to pocket the salary and pay a part of it to other men who went to the colony as lieutenant governors. But most governors were not crazy, corrupt, or absent; they were merely mediocre.

In the eighteenth century, elected colonial legislatures challenged the swollen executive powers of these colonial governors. The governors lacked the exten-sive patronage power that enabled ministers of government in England to manipulate elections and buy off opposition groups. They could therefore contest but not prevent encroachments on their power. Bit by bit, the representative assemblies won new rights—to initiate legislation, to elect their own speakers, to settle contested elections, to discipline their membership, and to nominate provincial treasurers who disbursed public funds. Most important, they won the "power of the purse"—the authority to initiate money bills, specifying how much money should be raised by taxes and how it should be spent. Thus the elected assemblies gradually transformed themselves into governing bodies reflecting the interests of the electorate. Governors complained bitterly about the "levelling spirit" and "mutinous and disorderly behavior" of the assemblies, but they could not stop their rise.

Local Politics

Binding elected officeholders to their constituents became an important feature of the colonial political system. In England, the House of Commons was filled with representatives from "rotten boroughs" (ancient places left virtually uninhabited by population shifts) and with men whose vote was in the pocket of the ministry because they had accepted crown appointments, contracts, or gifts. The American assemblies, by contrast, contained mostly representatives sent by voters who instructed them on particular issues and held them accountable for serving local interests.

Royal governors and colonial grandees who sat as councillors often deplored this localist, popular orientation of the people's representatives. The assemblies, sniffed one aristocratic New Yorker, were crowded with "plain, illiterate husbandmen [small farmers], whose views seldom extended farther than the regulation of highways, the destruction of wolves, wildcats, and foxes, and the advancement of the other little interests of the particular counties which they were chosen to represent." In actuality, the voters mostly sent merchants, lawyers, and substantial planters and farmers to represent them in the lower houses, and by the mid-eighteenth century in most colonies, these men had formed political elites. But it was true that they represented the local interests of their constituents. They prided themselves on doing so, for they saw themselves as bulwarks against oppression and arbitrary rule, which history taught them were most frequently imposed by monarchs and their appointed agents.

Local government was usually more important to the colonists than provincial government. In the North, local political authority generally rested in the towns. The New England town meeting decided a

When frontier farmers marched on Philadelphia in 1763 to demand more protection on the frontier, a miniature civil war almost broke out. Philadelphians had little use for the "Paxton Boys," who had murdered 20 harmless Christian Indians in retaliation for frontier raids. (*The Library Company of Philadelphia*)

wide range of matters. In making decisions, the meeting strived for consensus, searching and arguing until it could express itself as a single unit. "By general agreement" and "by the free and united consent of the whole" were phrases denoting a decision-making process that sought participatory assent rather than a democratic competition among differing interests and points of view.

In the South, the county was the primary unit of government. No equivalent of the town meeting existed for placing local decisions before the populace. The planter gentry ruled the county courts and the legislature, and substantial farmers served in minor offices such as road surveyor and deputy sheriff. At court sessions, usually four times a year, deeds were read aloud and then recorded, juries impaneled and justice dispensed, elections held, licenses issued, and proclamations read aloud. On election days, gentlemen treated their neighbors (on whom they depended for votes) to "bumbo," "kill devil," and other alcoholic treats. By the mid-eighteenth century, a landed squirearchy of third- and fourth-generation families had achieved political dominance.

The Spread of Whig Ideology

Whether in local or provincial affairs, a political ideology called Whig, or "republican," had spread widely by the mid-eighteenth century. This body of thought,

inherited from England, rested on the belief that concentrated power was historically the enemy of liberty and that too much power lodged in any person or group usually produced corruption and tyranny. The best defenses against concentrated power were balanced government, elected legislatures adept at checking executive authority, prohibition of standing armies (almost always controlled by tyrannical monarchs to oppress the people), and vigilance by the people in watching their leaders for telltale signs of corruption.

Much of this Whig ideology reached the people through the newspapers that began appearing in the seaboard towns in the early eighteenth century. The first was the *Boston News-Letter*, founded in 1704. By 1763, some 23 papers circulated in the colonies. Though limited to a few pages and published only once or twice a week, the papers passed from hand to hand and were read aloud in taverns and coffeehouses. In this way, their contents probably reached most households in the towns and a substantial minority of farmsteads in the countryside.

By the 1730s, newspapers had become an important conduit of Whig ideology. Many reprinted material from English Whig writers who railed against corruption and creeping despotism in the reign of George II (1727–1760). Particularly popular were the essays of John Trenchard and Thomas Gordon, whose *Cato's Letters* and *Independent Whig* found their way into the private libraries of many colonists and were widely reprinted in the newspapers.

The new power of the press and its importance in guarding the people's liberties against would-be tyrants (such as abrasive royal governors) were vividly illustrated in the Zenger case in New York. Young John Peter Zenger, a printer's apprentice, had been hired in 1733 by the antigovernment faction of Lewis Morris to start a newspaper that would publicize the tyrannical actions of Governor William Cosby. In Zenger's *New-York Weekly Journal,* the Morris faction fired salvos at Cosby's interference with the courts and his alleged corruption in giving important offices to his henchmen. New Yorkers believed, said one essay published by Zenger, "that their LIBERTIES and PROPERTIES are precarious, and that SLAVERY is like to be tailed on them and their posterity if some things past are not amended."

Arrested for seditious libel, Zenger was brilliantly defended by Andrew Hamilton, a Philadelphia lawyer hired by the Morris faction to convince the jury that Zenger had been simply trying to inform the people of attacks on their liberties. Although the jury acquitted Zenger, the libel laws remained very restrictive. But the acquittal did reinforce the notion that the government was the people's servant, and it brought home the point that public criticism could keep people with political authority responsible to the people they ruled. Such ideas about liberty and corruption, raised in the context of local politics, would shortly achieve a much broader significance.

Timeline

1662	Half-Way Covenant in New England
1685–1715	Stagnation in tobacco market
1704	*Boston News-Letter,* first regular colonial newspaper, published
1713	Beginning of Scots-Irish and German immigration
1715–1730	Volume of slave trade doubles
1718	French settle New Orleans
1720s	Black population begins to increase naturally
1732	Benjamin Franklin publishes first *Poor Richard's Almanack*
	Impressment riot in Boston
1734–1736	Great Awakening begins in Northampton, Massachusetts
1735	Zenger acquitted of seditious libel in New York
1739–1740	Whitefield's first American tour spreads Great Awakening
	Slaves compose 90 percent of population on Carolina rice coast
1740s	Indigo becomes staple crop in Lower South
1760	Africans compose 20 percent of American population
1760s–1770s	Spanish establish California mission system
1769	American Philosophical Society founded at Philadelphia

Conclusion

America in 1750

The American colonies, robust and expanding, matured rapidly between 1700 and 1750. Transatlantic commerce linked them closely to Europe, Africa, and other parts of the New World. Churches, schools, and towns—the visible marks of the receding frontier—appeared everywhere. A balanced sex ratio and stable family life had been achieved throughout the colonies. Seasoned political leaders and familiar political institutions functioned from Maine to Georgia.

Yet the sinew, bone, and muscle of American society had not yet fully knit together. The polyglot population, one-fifth of it bound in chattel slavery and its Native American component still unassimilated and uneasily situated on the frontier, was a kaleidoscopic mixture of ethnic and religious groups. Its economy, while developing rapidly, showed weaknesses, particularly in New England, where land resources had been strained. The social structure reflected the colonizers' emergence from a frontier stage, but the consolidation of wealth by a landed and mercantile elite was matched by pockets of poverty appearing in the cities and some rural areas. Full of strength, yet marked by awkward incongruities, colonial America in 1750 approached an era of strife and momentous decisions.

Recommended Reading

America's First Population Explosion

Bernard Bailyn, *Voyagers to the West: A Passage in the Peopling of America on the Eve of the American Revolution* (1986); Jon Butler, *The Huguenots in Colonial America* (1983); R. J. Dickson, *Ulster Immigration to Colonial America, 1718–1775* (1966); Aaron S. Fogleman, *Hopeful Journeys: German Immigration, Settlement, and Political Culture, 1717–1775* (1996); James A. Henretta and Gregory Nobles, *Evolution and Revolution: American Society: 1620–1820* (1987); Ned Landsman, *Scotland and Its First American Colony* (1985); John J. McCusker and Russell R. Menard, *The Economy of British America, 1607–1789* (1985); Edwin J. Perkins, *The Economy of Colonial America*, 2d ed. (1988); Stephanie G. Wolf, *Urban Village: Population, Community, and Family Structure in Germantown, Pennsylvania* (1977).

Beyond the Appalachians

Kathryn E. Holland Braund, *Deerskins and Duffels: The Creek Indian Trade with Anglo-America, 1685–1815* (1993); Thomas Ingersoll, *Mammon and Manon in Early New Orleans: The First Slave Society in the Deep South, 1717–1819* (1999); Robert H. Jackson and Edward Castillo, *Indians, Franciscans, and Spanish Colonization* (1995); Marc Simmons, *Coronado's Land: Essays on Daily Life in Colonial New Mexico* (1991); Richard White, *The Middle Ground: Indians, Empires, and Republics in the Great Lakes Region, 1650–1815* (1991); Daniel H. Usner, Jr., *Indians, Settlers, and Slaves in a Frontier Exchange Economy: The Lower Mississippi Valley before 1783* (1992).

A Land of Family Farms

John L. Brooke, *The Heart of the Commonwealth: Society and Political Culture in Worcester County, Massachusetts, 1713–1861* (1989); Richard Bushman, *From Puritan to Yankee* (1967); David W. Conroy, *In Public Houses: Drink and the Revolution of Authority in Colonial Massachusetts* (1995); Cornelia Hughes Dayton, *Women Before the Bar: Gender, Law, and Society in Connecticut, 1639–1789* (1995); Christopher M. Jedrey, *The World of John Cleaveland: Family and Community in Eighteenth-Century New England* (1979); Sung Bok Kim, *Landlord and Tenant in the Colony of New York: Manorial Society, 1664–1775* (1976); James Lemon, *The Best Poor Man's Country: A Geographical Study of Early Southeastern Pennsylvania* (1972); Laurel T. Ulrich, *Good Wives: Image and Reality in the Lives of Women in Northern New England, 1650–1750* (1982); Daniel Vickers, *Farmers and Fishermen: Two Centuries of Work in Essex County, Massachusetts, 1630–1850* (1994).

Ecological Transformation

Alfred Crosby, *Ecological Imperialism: The Biological Expansion of Europe, 900–1900* (1986); Carolyn Merchant, *Ecological Revolutions: Nature, Gender, and Science in New England* (1989); Anthony Penna, *Nature's Bounty: Historical and Modern Environmental Perspectives* (1999); Timothy Silver, *A New Face on the Countryside: Indians, Colonists, and Slaves in South Atlantic Forests, 1500–1800* (1990); Christopher Vecsey and Robert W. Venables, eds., *American Indian Environments: Ecological Issues in Native American History* (1980).

The Plantation South

T. H. Breen, *Tobacco Culture: The Mentality of the Great Tidewater Planters on the Eve of the Revolution* (1985); Joyce E. Chaplin, *An Anxious Pursuit: Agricultural Innovation and Modernity in the Lower South, 1730–1815* (1993); Paul G. E. Clemens, *The Atlantic Economy and Colonial Maryland's Eastern Shore: From Tobacco to Grain* (1980); Carville Earle, *The Evolution of a Tidewater Settlement System* (1975); Rhys Isaac, *The Transformation of Virginia, 1740–1790* (1982); Allan Kulikoff, *Tobacco and Slaves: The Development of Southern Culture in the Chesapeake, 1680–1800* (1986); Daniel Blake Smith, *Inside the Great House: Planter Family Life in Eighteenth-Century Chesapeake Society* (1980); Gregory Stiverson, *Poverty in the Land of Plenty: Tenancy in Eighteenth-Century Maryland* (1980).

The Urban World of Commerce and Ideas

Bernard Bailyn, *The New England Merchants in the Seventeenth Century* (1955); Gary B. Nash, *The Urban Crucible: Social Change, Political Consciousness, and the Origins of the American Revolution* (1979); Billy G. Smith, *The "Lower Sort": Philadelphia's Laboring People, 1750–1800* (1990); G. B. Warden, *Boston, 1687–1776* (1970); Esmond Wright, *Franklin of Philadelphia* (1986).

The Great Awakening

Patricia Bonomi, *Under the Cope of Heaven: Religion, Society, and Politics in Colonial America* (1986); Alan Heimert, *Religion and the American Mind: From the Great Awakening to the Revolution* (1966); Susan Juster, *Disorderly Women: Sexual Politics and Evangelicalism in Revolutionary New England* (1994); Frank J. Lambert, *"Pedlar in Divinity": George Whitefield and the Transatlantic Revivals* (1994); Henry May, *The American Enlightenment* (1976); Perry Miller, *From Colony to Province* (1953); Harry S. Stout, *The Divine Dramatist: George Whitefield and the Rise of Modern Evangelicalism* (1991); Patricia Tracy, *Jonathan Edwards, Pastor* (1979).

Political Life

Bernard Bailyn, *The Origins of American Politics* (1968); Patricia Bonomi, *A Factious People: Politics and Society in Colonial New York* (1977); William Pencak, *War, Politics, and Revolution in Provincial Massachusetts* (1981); Charles Sydnor, *American Revolutionaries in the Making: Political Practices in Washington's Virginia* (1965); Alan Tully, *Forming American Politics: Ideas, Interests, and Institutions in Colonial New York and Pennsylvania* (1994); Robert Zemsky, *Merchants, Farmers, and River Gods: An Essay on Eighteenth-Century American Politics* (1971).

Fiction and Film

Kenneth Roberts, king of historical novelists on eighteenth-century America, movingly describes the Seven Years' War in *Northwest Passage* (1937); Spencer Tracy starred in the Hollywood version with the same title. James Fenimore Cooper's *The Last of the Mohicans* (1836) is another American classic, but much more to the taste of today's students is Hollywood's movie by the same title (1992), starring Daniel Day-Lewis and Madeleine Stowe.

Suggested Web Sites

http://www.historybuff.com/library/refseventeen.html

History Buff's Reference Library. Brief journalistic essays on newspaper coverage of sixteenth- to eighteenth-century American history.

http://www.virginia.edu/~econ/brock.html

The Leslie Brock Center for the Study of Colonial Currency. This site includes both useful primary and secondary documents on early American currency.

http://www.whiteoak.org/

White Oak Fur Post. This site documents an eighteenth-century fur trading post among the Indians in what would become Minnesota.

http://www.english.udel.edu/lemay/franklin/

Benjamin Franklin Documentary History Website. University of Delaware professor J. A. Leo Lemay tells the story of Franklin's varied life in seven parts on this intriguing site.

http://www.civilization.ca/index1e.html

Canada History. Canada and the United States shared a colonial past but developed differently in the long run. This site is a part of the virtual museum of the Canadian Museum of Civilization Corporation.

http://www.jonathanedwards.com/

Jonathan Edwards. Speeches by this famous preacher of the Great Awakening are on this site.

http://www.ushistoryplace.com

A richly detailed on-line learning environment complete with interactive maps, timelines, history activities, primary source documents, and links to related American history sites.

BURSTING *the* COLONIAL BONDS

CHAPTER OUTLINE

In 1758, when he was 21 years old, Ebenezer MacIntosh of Boston laid down his shoemaker's awl and enlisted in the Massachusetts expedition against the French on Lake Champlain. The son of a poor Boston shoemaker who had fought against the French in a previous war, MacIntosh had known poverty all his life. Service against the French offered the hope of plunder or at least an enlistment bounty worth half a year's wages. One among thousands of colonists who fought against the "Gallic menace" in the Seven Years' War, MacIntosh contributed his mite to the climactic Anglo-American struggle that drove the French from North America.

But a greater role lay ahead for the poor Boston shoemaker. Two years after the Peace of Paris in 1763, England imposed a stamp tax on the American colonists. In the massive protests that followed, MacIntosh emerged as the street leader of the Boston crowd. In two nights of the most violent attacks on private property ever witnessed in America, a Boston crowd nearly destroyed the houses of two of the colony's most important officials. On August 14, they tore through the house of Andrew Oliver, a wealthy merchant and the appointed distributor of stamps for Massachusetts. Twelve days later, MacIntosh led the crowd in attacking the mansion of Thomas Hutchinson, a wealthy merchant who served as lieutenant governor and chief justice of Massachusetts. "The mob was so general," wrote the governor, "and so supported that all civil power ceased in an instant."

For the next several months, the power of the poor Boston shoemaker grew. Called "General" MacIntosh and "Captain-General of the Liberty Tree" by his townspeople, he soon sported a militia uniform of gold and blue and a hat laced with gold. Two thousand townsmen followed his commands on November 5, when they marched in orderly ranks through the crooked streets of Boston to demonstrate their solidarity in resisting the hated stamps.

Five weeks later, a crowd publicly humiliated stamp distributor Oliver. Demanding that he announce his resignation before the assembled citizenry, they marched him across town in a driving December rain. With MacIntosh at his elbow, he finally reached the "Liberty Tree," which had become a symbol of resistance to England's new colonial policies. There the aristocratic Oliver ate humble pie.

A View of the Town of Concord (April 1775), attributed to Ralph Earle. *(Courtesy Concord Museum, Concord, MA)*

He concluded his resignation remarks with bitter words, hissing sardonically that he would "always think myself very happy when it shall be in my power to serve the people."

"To serve the people" was an ancient idea embedded in English political culture, but it assumed new meaning in the American colonies during the epic third quarter of the eighteenth century. Few colonists in 1750 held even a faint desire to break the connection with England, and fewer still might have predicted the form of government that 13 independent states in an independent nation might fashion. Yet in a whirlwind of events, two million colonists moved haltingly toward a showdown with mighty England. Little-known men like Ebenezer MacIntosh as well as his well-known and historically celebrated townsmen Samuel Adams, John Hancock, and John Adams were part of the struggle. Collectively, ordinary people such as MacIntosh influenced—and in fact sometimes even dictated—the revolutionary movement in the colonies. Though we read and speak mostly of a small group of "founding fathers," the wellsprings of the American Revolution can be fully discovered only among a variety of people from different social groups, occupations, regions, and religions.

This chapter addresses the tensions in late colonial society, the imperial crisis that followed the Seven Years' War (in the colonies often called the French and Indian War), and the tumultuous decade that led to the "shot heard round the world" fired at Concord Bridge in April 1775. It portrays the origins of a dual American Revolution. Ebenezer MacIntosh, in leading the Boston mob against crown officers and colonial collaborators who tried to implement a new colonial policy after 1763, helped set in motion a revolutionary movement to restore ancient liberties thought by the Americans to be under deliberate attack in England. This movement eventually escalated into the war for American independence.

But MacIntosh's Boston followers were also venting years of resentment at the accumulation of wealth and power by Boston's aristocratic elite. Behind every swing of the ax, every shattered crystal goblet and splintered mahogany chair, lay the fury of a Bostonian who had seen the city's conservative elite try to dismantle the town meeting, suffered economic hardship, and lost faith that opportunity and just relations still prevailed in his town. This sentiment, which called for the reform of a colonial society that had become corrupt, self-indulgent, and dominated by an elite, fed an idealistic commitment to reshape American

society even while severing the colonial bond. As distinguished from the war for independence, this was the American Revolution.

THE CLIMACTIC SEVEN YEARS' WAR

After a brief period of peace following King George's War (1744–1748), France and England fought the fourth, largest, and by far most significant of the wars for empire that had begun in the late seventeenth century. Known variously as the Seven Years' War, the French and Indian War, and the Great War for Empire, this global conflict in part represented a showdown for control of North America between the Atlantic Ocean and the Mississippi River. In North America, the Anglo-American forces ultimately prevailed, and their victory dramatically affected the lives of all the diverse people living in the huge region east of the Mississippi—English, German, and Scots-Irish settlers in the English colonies; French and Spanish colonizers in Canada, Florida, and interior North America; African slaves in a variety of settlements; and, perhaps most of all, the powerful Native American tribes of the interior.

War and the Management of Empire

After the Glorious Revolution of 1688, England began constructing a more coherent imperial administration. In 1696, a professional Board of Trade replaced the old Lords of Trade; the Treasury strengthened the customs service; and Parliament created overseas vice-admiralty courts, which functioned without juries to prosecute smugglers who evaded the trade regulations set forth in the Navigation Acts. Parliament began playing a more active role after the reign of Queen Anne (1702–1714) and continued to do so when weak, German-speaking King George I came to the throne. Royal governors received greater powers and more detailed instructions and came under more insistent demands from the Board of Trade to enforce British policies. England was quietly installing the machinery of imperial management and a corps of colonial bureaucrats.

The best test of an effectively organized state is its ability to wage war. Four times between 1689 and 1763, England matched its strength against France, its archrival in North America and the Caribbean. These wars of empire had tremendous consequences for all involved—the home governments, their colonial subjects, and the Indian tribes drawn into the bloody conflicts.

We have already seen (in Chapter 3) how the Peace of Utrecht, which ended Queen Anne's War (1702–1713), brought victor's spoils of great importance to England. The generation of peace that followed was really only a time-out, which both England and France used in the years until 1739 to strengthen their war-making capacity. Britain's productive and efficiently governed New World colonies made important contributions. Though known as a period of "salutary neglect," this was actually an era when king and Parliament increased their control over colonial affairs.

Concerned mainly with economic regulation, Parliament added new articles such as fur, copper, hemp, tar, and turpentine to the list of items produced in America that had to be shipped to England before being exported to another country. Parliament also curtailed colonial production of articles important to England's economy: woolen cloth (1699), beaver hats (1732), and finished iron products (1750). Most important, Parliament passed the Molasses Act in 1733. Attempting to stop the trade between New England and the French West Indies, where Yankee traders exchanged fish, beef, and pork for molasses to convert into rum, Parliament imposed a prohibitive duty of 6 pence per gallon on French slave-produced molasses. This turned many of New England's largest merchants and distillers into smugglers and schooled them for a generation—along with their ship captains, crews, and allied waterfront artisans—in defying royal authority.

The generation of peace ended abruptly in 1739 when England declared war on Spain. The immediate cause was the ear of an English sea captain, Robert Jenkins. Spanish authorities had deprived him of that appendage eight years before for smuggling in their colonies. Encouraged by his government, Jenkins publicly displayed his pickled ear in 1738 to whip up war fever against Spain, which English policymakers wanted to chasten for transferring certain commercial privileges from England to France. The real cause of the war, however, was England's determination to continue its drive toward commercial domination of the Atlantic basin.

Five years after the war with Spain began in 1739, it merged into a much larger conflict between England and France, in Europe called the War of Austrian Succession (1744–1748). Its scale far exceeded that of previous conflicts. As military priorities became paramount, the need increased for discipline within the empire. In addition, unprecedented military expenditures led Britain to ask its West Indian and American colonies to share in the costs of defending—and extending—the empire and to tailor their behavior to the needs of the home country.

Outbreak of Hostilities

The tension between English and French colonists in North America, which reached back to the early seventeenth century, was intensified by the spectacular population growth of the English colonies: from 250,000 in 1700 to 1.25 million in 1750, and to 1.75 million in the next decade. Three-quarters of the increase came in the colonies south of New York, propelling thousands of land-hungry settlers toward the mountain gaps in the Appalachians in search of farmland.

Promoting this westward rush were fur traders and land speculators. The fur traders were penetrating a French-influenced region, where they offered native trappers and hunters better prices and higher-quality goods than the French. In the 1740s and 1750s, speculators (including many future revolutionary leaders) formed land companies to capitalize on the seaboard population explosion. The farther west the settlement line moved, the closer it came to the western trading empire of the French and their Indian allies.

Colonial penetration of the Ohio valley in the 1740s established the first English outposts in the continental heartland. This challenged the French where their interest was vital. While the English controlled most of the eastern coastal plain of North America, the French had nearly encircled them to the west by building a chain of trading posts and forts along the St. Lawrence River, through the Great Lakes, and southward into the Ohio and Mississippi valleys all the way to New Orleans.

Challenged by the English, the French resisted. They attempted to block further English expansion by constructing new forts in the Ohio valley and by prying some tribes loose from their new English connections. The English, a French emissary warned a western tribe in the 1750s, "are much less anxious to take away your peltries than to become masters of your lands, and your blindness is so great that you do not perceive that the very hand that caresses you will scourge you like negroes and slaves, so soon as it will have got possession of your lands."

By 1755, the French had driven the English traders out of the Ohio River valley and established forts as far east as the fork of the Ohio River, near present-day Pittsburgh. There, at Fort Duquesne, the French smartly rebuffed an ambitious young Virginia militia colonel named George Washington, dispatched by his colony's government to expel them from the region.

The Iroquois warrior depicted here shows the blending of Indian and European weaponry. His snowshoes and the war club held in his right hand are native in origin. His English musket, slung over his shoulder, and the steel axe fastened at his belt are European trade items. (© *Collection of the New-York Historical Society*)

Men in the capitals of Europe, not in the colonies, made the decision to force a showdown in the interior of North America. England's powerful merchants, supported by American clients, had been emboldened by English success in the previous war against the French. Now, they argued, the time was ripe to destroy the French overseas trade. Convinced, the English ministry ordered several thousand troops to America in 1754; in France, 3,000 regulars embarked to meet the English challenge.

With war looming, the colonial governments attempted to coordinate efforts. Representatives of seven colonies met with 150 Iroquois chiefs at Albany, New York, in June 1754 to woo the powerful Iroquois out of their neutrality and plan a colonial union. Both failed. The Iroquois left the conference with 30 wagonloads of gifts but made no firm commitment to fight against the French. Benjamin Franklin designed a plan for an intercolonial government to manage Indian affairs, provide for defense, and have the power to pass laws and levy taxes. But even the clever woodcut displayed in the *Pennsylvania Gazette* that pictured a chopped-up snake with the insignia "Join or Die" failed to overcome the long-standing jealousies

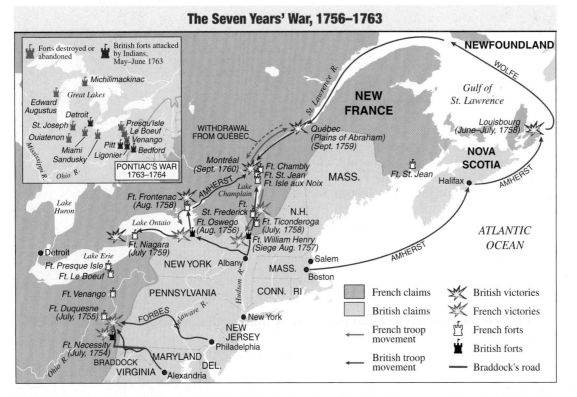

The British-American victory over France and its Indian allies in the Seven Years' War did not bring peace on the western frontier. After the war, Pontiac lead pan-Indian attacks on settlers and British forts. As the map shows, the war began in 1754, two years ahead of the usual date given.

that had thwarted previous attempts at intercolony cooperation. "Everyone cries a union is necessary," sighed Franklin, "but when they come to the manner and form of the union, their weak noodles are perfectly distracted."

With his British army and hundreds of American recruits, General Edward Braddock slogged across Virginia in the summer of 1755, each day cutting a few miles of road through forests and across mountains. A headstrong professional soldier who regarded his European battlefield experience as sufficient for war in the American wilderness, Braddock had contempt for the woods-wise French regiments and their stealthy Indian allies.

As Braddock neared Fort Duquesne, the entire French force and the British suddenly surprised one another in the forest. The French had 218 soldiers and militiamen and 637 Indian allies, while Braddock commanded twice that many redcoats but few Indians. Pouring murderous fire into Braddock's tidy lines, the French and Indians won. Just before he fell, mortally wounded (perhaps by one of his own angry men), Braddock presumably learned that Indians were essential allies and fully capable of pitched battle. Two-thirds of the British and Americans were killed or wounded, and Washington, his uniform pierced by four bullets, had two horses shot from

beneath him. Although they had 1,000 men in reserve down the road, the Anglo-American force beat a hasty, ignominious retreat.

Throughout the summer, French-supplied Indian raiders torched the Virginia and Pennsylvania backcountry. "The roads are full of starved, naked, indigent multitudes," observed one officer. One French triumph followed another during the next two years. The victory over Braddock's army had brought almost every tribe north of the Ohio River to the French side. Never was disunity within the English colonies so painfully evident. With its Indian allies, French Canada, only 70,000 inhabitants strong, had badly battered a million and a half colonists supported by the British army.

The turning point in the war came after the energetic William Pitt became England's secretary of state in 1757. "I believe that I can save this nation and that no one else can," he boasted, abandoning Europe as the main theater of action against the French and throwing his nation's military might into the American campaign. The forces he dispatched to America in 1757–1758 dwarfed all preceding commitments: about 23,000 British troops and a huge fleet with 14,000 mariners. But even forces of this magnitude, when asked to engage the enemy in the forests of North America, were not necessarily sufficient to the task

CHAPTER 5   BURSTING THE COLONIAL BONDS

without Indian support, or at least neutrality. "A doubt remains not," proclaimed one English official in the colonies, "that the prosperity of our colonies on the continent will stand or fall with our interest and favour among them."

Tribal Strategies

Anglo-American leaders knew that the support of the Iroquois Confederacy and their tributary tribes was crucial. Iroquois allegiance could be secured in only two ways: through purchase or by a demonstration of power that would convince the tribes that the English would prevail with or without their assistance. The Iroquois understood that their interest lay in playing off one European power against the other. "To preserve the balance between us and the French," wrote a New York politician, "is the great ruling principle of modern Indian politics."

The first English stratagem for securing Iroquois support failed in 1754 when colonial negotiators heaped gifts on the Iroquois chiefs at the Albany Congress but received in return only tantalizing half-promises of support against the French. The second alternative fizzled because the English proved militarily inferior to the French in the first three years of the war. Hence, the westernmost of the Iroquois Six Nations, the Seneca, fought on the side of the French in

the campaigns of 1757 and 1758, while the Delaware, a tributary tribe, harassed the Pennsylvania frontier.

In 1758, the huge English military buildup began to produce victories. The largest army ever assembled in North America to that point, some 15,000 British and American soldiers, including the Bostonian Ebenezer MacIntosh, suffered terrible casualties and withdrew from the field after attempting to storm Fort Ticonderoga on Lake Champlain in June 1758. Then the tide turned. Troops under Sir Jeffrey Amherst captured Louisbourg, on Cape Breton Island, and Fort Duquesne fell to another army of 6,000 led by General John Forbes. The resolute Pitt had mobilized the fighting power of the English nation and put more men in the field than existed in all of New France. The colonists, in turn, had put aside intramural squabbling long enough to overwhelm the badly outnumbered French.

The victories of 1758 finally moved the Iroquois away from neutrality. Added incentive to join the Anglo-American side came when the English navy bottled up French shipping in the St. Lawrence River, cutting the Iroquois off from French trade goods. By early 1759, foreseeing a French defeat in North America, the Iroquois pledged 800 warriors for an attack on Fort Niagara, the strategic French trading depot on Lake Ontario.

The storming of French Quebec in 1759 was the decisive blow in England's campaign to end the French domination of Canada and the lands west of the Appalachians. The heroic exploits of General James Wolfe made him a hero throughout England and the colonies. (A View of the Taking of Quebec, September 13, 1759, *National Army Museum, London*)

Even dramatic Anglo-American victories did not always guarantee Indian support. In the South, back-country skirmishes with the Cherokee from Virginia to South Carolina turned into a costly war from 1759 to 1761. In 1760, the Cherokee mauled a British army of 1,300 under Amherst. The following summer, a much larger Anglo-American force invaded Cherokee country, burning towns and food supplies. By this time, English control of the sea had interrupted the Indians' supply of French arms. Beset by food shortages, lack of ammunition, and a smallpox epidemic, the Cherokee finally sued for peace.

Other Anglo-American victories in 1759, the "year of miracles," decided the outcome of the bloodiest war yet known in the New World. The capture of Fort Niagara, the critical link in the system of forts that joined the French inland empire with the Atlantic, was followed by the conquest of sugar-rich Martinique in the West Indies. The culminating stroke came with a dramatic victory at Quebec. Led by 32-year-old General James Wolfe, 5,000 troops scaled a rocky cliff and overcame the French on the Plains of Abraham. The capture of Montreal late in 1760 completed the shattering of French power in North America. The theater of operations shifted to the Caribbean, where fighting continued, as in Europe, for three years longer. But in the American colonies, the old English dream of ridding the continent of the Gallic menace had finally come true.

Consequences of War

The strokes of a few diplomats' pens in 1762–1763 brought astounding changes to European and Indian peoples who for decades had been involved in dizzying complex and shifting relationships that alternated between conflict and cooperation over vast stretches of North American territory. The Spanish, who had tried to check the expansive French southern influence directed from Louisiana, now acquired New Orleans and all of the vast Louisiana territory west of the Mississippi. Although this could provide a buffer against English aspirations in the continent's heartland, Spain's king surrendered Spanish Florida to the British—a pragmatic decision because England agreed to compensate Spain with Havana, which the British had captured during the war.

For the interior Indian tribes, the Treaty of Paris ending the Seven Years' War in 1763 dealt a harsh blow. Unlike the coastal Native Americans, whose population and independence had ebbed rapidly through contact with the colonizers, the inland tribes had maintained their strength and sometimes even grown more unified through relations with settlers. Although they came to depend on European trade goods, Native Americans had turned this commercial connection to their advantage so long as more than one source of trade goods existed.

The Indian play-off system came to a crashing halt when the French ceded Canada and all territory east of the Mississippi, except for New Orleans, to England in the Treaty of Paris. For the interior tribes, only one source of trade goods remained. Two centuries of European rivalry for control of eastern North America ended abruptly. Iroquois, Cherokee, Creek, Ojibway, Shawnee, and scores of other interior tribes were now forced to adjust to this reality.

After making peace, the English government launched a new policy designed to separate Native Americans and colonizers by creating a racial boundary roughly following the crestline of the Appalachian Mountains from Maine to Georgia. The Proclamation of 1763 reserved all land west of the line for Indian nations. White settlers already living beyond the Appalachians were told to withdraw to the east.

Though well intended, this attempt to legislate interracial accord failed completely. Even before the proclamation was issued, the Ottawa chief Pontiac, concerned that the elimination of the French threatened the old treaty and gift-giving system, had gathered together many of the northern tribes that had aided the French assaults on the English forts during the Seven Years' War. Although Pontiac's pan-Indian movement to drive the British out of the Ohio valley collapsed in 1764, it served notice that the interior tribes would not passively watch the invasion of their lands after the French withdrawal from North America.

The English government could sternly command colonial governors to observe the Proclamation of 1763, but it could not enforce its policy. Staggering under an immense wartime debt, England decided to maintain only small army garrisons in America to regulate the interior. Nor could royal governors stop land speculators and settlers from privately purchasing land from trans-Appalachian tribes or from simply encroaching on their land. Under such circumstances, the western frontier seethed after 1763.

Although the epic Anglo-American victory redrew the map of North America, the war also had important social and economic effects on colonial society. It convinced the colonists of their growing strength, yet left them debt-ridden and weakened in manpower. The wartime economy spurred economic development and poured British capital into the colonies, yet rendered them more vulnerable to cyclic fluctuations in the British economy.

Military contracts, for example, brought prosperity to most colonies during the war years. Huge orders for ships, arms, uniforms, and provisions enriched northern merchants and provided good prices for farmers as well. Urban artisans enjoyed full employment and high

North America After 1763

At the Treaty of Paris in 1763, France surrendered huge claims west of the Mississippi River to Spain and east of the river to England. England also acquired Florida from Spain.

wages, as tailors' needles flashed to meet clothing contracts, shoemakers stitched for an unprecedented demand for shoes, and bakers found armies clamoring for bread. Privateers—privately outfitted ships licensed by colonial governments to attack enemy shipping—enriched the fortunate few. On a single voyage in 1758, John MacPherson snared 18 French ships. The prize money was lavish enough to allow this son of a Scottish immigrant to pour £14,000 into creating a country estate outside Philadelphia, to which he retired in splendor.

The war, however, required heavy taxes and took a huge human toll. Privateering carried many fortune seekers to a watery grave, and the wilderness campaigns from 1755 to 1760 claimed thousands of lives. Garrison life brought wracking fevers (which claimed more victims than enemy weapons), and battlefield medical treatment was too primitive to save many of the wounded. Boston's Thomas Hancock accurately predicted at the beginning of the war that "this province is spirited to [send] every third man to do the work of the Lord." But the Lord's work was expensive. Thomas Pownall, assuming the governorship of

Massachusetts in August 1757, found not the "rich, flourishing, powerful, enterprizing" colony he expected but a province "ruined and undone."

The magnitude of human loss in Boston indicates the war's impact. The wartime muster lists show that nearly every working-class Bostonian tasted military service at some point during the long war. When peace came, Boston had a deficit of almost 700 men in a town of about 2,000 families. The high rate of war widowhood feminized poverty and required expanded poor relief to maintain husbandless women and fatherless children.

Peace ended the amount of new casualties but also brought depression. The British forces in the American theater numbered about 40,000 at the conclusion of the North American campaigns. With their departure for the Caribbean in 1760, the economy slumped badly, especially in the coastal towns. "The tippling soldiery that used to help us out at a dead lift," mused a New York merchant, "are gone to drink [rum]in a warmer region, the place of its production."

The greatest hardships after 1760 fell on laboring people, although even some wealthy merchants went

Recovering the Past

POETRY

Poetry is one of the most ancient and universal of the arts. Making its effect by the rhythmic sound and imagery of its language, poetry often expresses romantic love, grief, and responses to nature. But other kinds of poetry interest historians: reflections of human experience, often expressed with deep emotion; and political verses often written to serve propagandistic goals. For generations, American historians have drawn on poetry to recapture feelings, ideas, and group experiences. For example, American Indian creation myths have often taken poetic form; the poems of Anne Bradstreet and Michael Wigglesworth in seventeenth-century Massachusetts tell us much about Puritan mentality and attitudes on topics running from marriage to death; the poetry of the American Transcendentalists tells us about nineteenth-century notions of heroism and who was admired; and Langston Hughes, Arno Bontemps, and other poets of the Harlem Renaissance have expressed through poetry the bittersweet nature of the African American experience. All this material is grist for the historian's mill.

The revolutionary generation created poetry of great interest to historians. The newspapers of several port cities published weekly "Poet's Corner" satires, drinking songs, and versed commentary on the issues of the day. Verse was widely used to provoke public discussion; in 1767 poets prompted the boycott of British goods to obtain Parliament's reversal of the hated Townshend duties.

A year later, Philadelphia's John Dickinson composed a "Liberty Song" that became the first set of verses learned in all the colonies. Boston's Sons of Liberty began using this "Liberty Song" in annual ceremonies celebrating their resistance to the Stamp Act. Soon the verses were printed in newspapers throughout the colonies and widely used in public gatherings. Set to music and easily learned, the verses cultivated anti-British feeling and a sense of the need for intercolonial cooperation:

> COME join Hand in Hand, brave AMERICANS all,
> And rouse your bold Hearts at fair LIBERTY'S Call;
> No tyrannous Acts shall suppress your just Claim,
> Or stain with Dishonor AMEÏRICA's Name.

Of all the poets of the revolutionary era, none has fascinated today's historians more than Phillis Wheatley, a young slave in Boston who wrote her first poem at age fourteen in 1767. Within six years, she became North America's first published black poet. Boston's "Ethiopian poetess" had been brought from Africa to Boston at age seven and purchased by a prospering tailor named John Wheatley. Soon her master and his wife discovered that she was a prodigy. Learning English in sixteen months so well that she could read the most difficult passages of the Bible, she soon showed an uncanny gift for writing. Much of her writing was inspired by deep religious feelings, but she soon was caught up in the dramatic events in Boston that were bringing revolution closer and closer. In "To the King's Most Excellent Majesty," she saluted King George III in poetry for repealing the Stamp Act; in "On the Death of Mr. Snider [Seider], Murder'd by Richardson," she lambasted the British customs officer who murdered a teenage member of a crowd protesting the British soldiers who occupied Boston in 1768.

Wheatley was anything but radical. She had so thoroughly imbibed Christianity from her master and mistress that she wrote in one of her first poems that "Twas mercy brought me from my *Pagan* land." Many times she used poetry to implore slaves to "fly to Christ." But by 1772, she was inserting a muffled plea for an end of slavery in her odes to American rights and American resistance to British policies.

That Wheatley's poems were published in London in 1773 is remarkable. Women were not supposed to write publicly in the eighteenth century, and certainly not black women. Nonetheless, her master, supported by Boston friends and proud of his slave prodigy, shipped a sheaf of poems to a bookseller in England, who obtained the support of the Countess of Huntingdon for publishing them. They appeared under the title *Poems on Various Subjects, Religious and Moral*. Even more remarkable was that Wheatley, only 20 years old, took ship to London to see her book come off the press. Her master and mistress financed the trip, hoping that sea air would clear her clogged lungs. There she was introduced to important reformers and public dignitaries, received a copy of Milton's *Paradise Lost* from the lord mayor of London, and met with Benjamin Franklin. She returned to Boston in 1774.

Read the two poems below: Wheatley's "On the Death of Mr. Snider [Seider], Murder'd by Richardson," composed

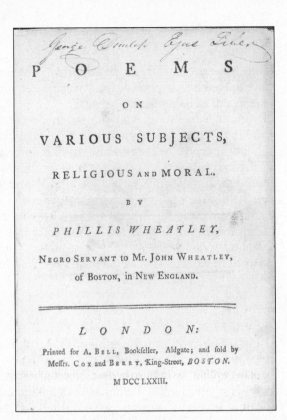

(Left) Wheatley worshiped at Old South Meeting House, which held some 5,000 people. In the 1770s, people frequently gathered there for political rallies and deliberations. This partly explains Wheatley's growing interest in the political battles raging in Boston. (Right) Wheatley's patroness in England specifically requested a drawing of Phillis for the frontispiece of this volume of poetry. Scipio Moorhead, slave of Boston's Presbyterian minister, did the drawing. Wheatley's mistress, Susannah Wheatley, called it a fine likeness. *(From the copy in the Rare Book Collection, The University of North Carolina at Chapel Hill)*

in 1770; and her poem addressed to the King's minister in charge of colonial affairs, penned two years later. As modern readers, you may find the poetry stilted, but Wheatley's style was modeled on poetic conventions of the eighteenth century. What change can you discern in Wheatley's political consciousness between 1770 and 1772? Do you consider her poem on Seider's murder by a British customs officer propagandistic? How does she relate the plight of enslaved Africans to the American colonists' struggle? More generally, how effective do you think poetry is in arousing sentiment and mobilizing political energy? Can you think of verse serving as lyrics in popular protest music today?

On the Death of Mr. Snider, Murder'd by Richardson (1770)

In heaven's eternal court it was decreed
How the first martyr for the cause should bleed
To clear the country of the hated brood
We whet his courage for the common good.
Long hid before, a vile infernal here
Prevents Achilles in his mid career
Wherev'r this fury darts his Poisonous breath
All are endanger'd to the shafts of death

To the Right Honourable William,
  Earl of Dartmouth, His Majesty's Principal
  Secretary of State for North America (1772)

HAIL, happy day, when, smiling like the morn,
Fair Freedom *rose* New-England *to adorn:*
The northern clime beneath her genial ray,
Dartmouth, *congratulates thy blissful sway:*
Elate with hope her race no longer mourns,
Each soul expands, each grateful bosom burns,
While in thine hand with pleasure we behold
The silken reins, and Freedom's *charms unfold.*
No more, America, *in mournful strain*
Of wrongs, and grievance unredress'd complain,
No longer shalt thou dread the iron chain,
Which wanton Tyranny with lawless hand
Had made, and with it meant t' enslave the land.
Should you, my lord, while you peruse my song,
Wonder from whence my love of Freedom *sprung,*
Whence flow these wishes for the common good,
By feeling hearts alone best understood,
I, young in life, by seeming cruel fate
Was snatch'd from Afric's *fancy'd happy seat:*
What pangs excruciating must molest,
What sorrows labour in my parent's breast?
Steel'd was that soul and by no misery mov'd
That from a father seiz'd his babe belov'd :
Such, such my case. And can I then but pray
Others may never feel tyrannic sway?

bankrupt. Those with the smallest wages had the thinnest savings to cushion them against hard times. How quickly their security could evaporate showed in Philadelphia, where early in the contractionary cycle many poor people, unable to pay their property taxes, were "disposing of their huts and lots to others more wealthy than themselves." The economic security of the middle sector of society also slipped, as established craftsmen and shopkeepers were caught between rising prices and reduced demand for their goods and services. A New York artisan expressed a common lament in 1762. Thankfully, he still had employment, he wrote in the *New-York Gazette*. But despite every effort at unceasing labor and frugal living, he had fallen into poverty and found it "beyond my ability to support my family . . . [which] can scarcely appear with decency or have necessaries to subsist." His situation, he added, "is really the case with many of the inhabitants of this city."

The Seven Years' War paved the way, though not foreseen at the time, for a far larger conflict in the next generation. The legislative assemblies, for example, which had been flexing their muscles at the expense of the governors in earlier decades, accelerated their bid for political power. During wartime, knowing that their governors must obtain military appropriations, they extracted concessions as the price for raising revenues. The war also trained a new group of military and political leaders. In carrying out military operations on a scale unknown in the colonies and in shouldering heavier political responsibilities, men such as George Washington, Samuel Adams, Benjamin Franklin, Patrick Henry, and Christopher Gadsden acquired the experience that would serve them well in the future.

The Seven Years' War, in spite of the severe costs, left many of the colonists buoyant. New Englanders rejoiced at the final victory over the "Papist enemy of the North." Frontiersmen, fur traders, and land speculators also celebrated the French withdrawal, for the West now appeared open for exploitation. This "Garden of the World," trumpeted a Boston almanac publisher, was larger than France, Germany, and Poland combined, "and all well provided with rivers, a very fine wholesome air, a rich soil, . . . and all things necessary for the conveniency and delight of life." A new frontier now seemed to await those whom opportunity had passed by on the crowded seaboard.

The colonists also felt a new sense of identity after the war. Surveying a world free of French and Spanish threats, they could not help but reassess the advantages and disadvantages of subordination to England. The colonists would soon discover, a French diplomat predicted at the war's end, "that they stand no longer in need of your protection. You will call on them to contribute towards supporting the burden which they have helped to bring on you; they will answer you by shaking off all dependence."

Although the American colonists inched toward thinking of themselves as a people capable of standing alone, the British viewed the matter differently at the end of the Seven Years' War. From their perspective, the colonists were unreliable and had fought poorly. Many royal army officers who had fought alongside the Americans had little but contempt for the "martial virtue" of the colonists. "He could take a thousand grenadiers to America," boasted one officer, "and geld all the males, partly by force and partly by a little coaxing."

THE CRISIS WITH ENGLAND

George Grenville became the chief minister of England's 25-year-old king, George III, at the end of the Seven Years' War. He inherited a national debt that had billowed from £75 million to £145 million and a nation of wearied taxpayers. To reduce the debt, Grenville proposed new taxes in England and others in America, asking the colonists to bear their share of running the empire. Grenville's particular concern was financing the 10,000 British regulars left in North America after 1763 to police French-speaking Canada and the frontier and to remind the unruly American subjects that they were still beholden to the crown. Grenville's revenue program initiated a rift between England and its colonies that a dozen years later would become a revolution.

Sugar, Currency, and Stamps

In 1764, Grenville pushed through Parliament several bills that in combination pressed hard on colonial economies. First came the Revenue Act (or Sugar Act) of 1764. While reducing the tax on imported French molasses from six to three pence per gallon, it added a number of colonial products to the list of commodities that could be sent only to England. It also required American shippers to post bonds guaranteeing observance of the trade regulations before loading their cargoes. Finally, it strengthened the vice-admiralty courts, where violators of the trade acts were prosecuted.

Many colonial legislatures grumbled about the Sugar Act because a strictly enforced duty of three pence per gallon on molasses pinched more than the loosely enforced six-pence duty. But only New York objected that any tax by Parliament to raise revenue (rather than to control trade) violated the rights of overseas English subjects who were unrepresented in Parliament.

Next came the Currency Act. In 1751, Parliament had forbidden the New England colonies to issue paper money as legal tender, and now it extended that prohibition to all the colonies. In a colonial economy chronically short of hard cash, this constricted trade.

The move to tighten up the machinery of empire confused the colonists because many of the new regulations came from Parliament. Before, Parliament had let the king, his ministers, and the Board of Trade run overseas affairs. In a world where history taught that power and liberty were perpetually at war, generations of colonists had viewed Parliament as a bastion of English liberty, the bulwark against despotic political rule. Now Parliament began to seem like a violator of colonial rights.

In protesting new parliamentary regulations, colonial leaders were hobbled by uncertainty concerning where Parliament's authority began and ended in administering the colonies. The colonists had always implicitly accepted parliamentary power overseas because it was easier to evade distasteful trade regulations than to contest this power. But the exact limits of that authority were vague.

After Parliament passed the Sugar Act in 1764, Grenville announced his intention to extend to America the stamp duties—already imposed in England—but he gave the colonies a year to suggest alternative ways of raising revenue. The colonies objected strenuously to the proposed stamp tax, but none provided another plan. Knowing that colonial property taxes were slight compared with those in England, Grenville dismissed the petitions that poured in from the colonies and drove the bill through Parliament. The Stamp Act became effective in November 1765. It required revenue stamps on every newspaper, pamphlet, almanac, legal document, liquor license, college diploma, pack of playing cards, and pair of dice.

Colonial reaction to the Stamp Act ranged from disgruntled submission to mass defiance. The breadth of the reaction shocked the British government—and many Americans as well. Lieutenant Governor Hutchinson of Massachusetts believed that "there is not a family between Canada and Pensacola that has not heard the name of the Stamp Act and but very few . . . but what have some formidable apprehensions of it." In many cases, resistance involved not only discontent over England's tightening of the screws on the American colonies but also internal resentments born out of local events. Especially in the cities, the defiance of authority and destruction of property by people from the middle and lower ranks redefined the dynamics of politics, setting the stage for a ten-year internal struggle for control among the various social elements alarmed by the new English policies.

Stamp Act Riots

The Virginia House of Burgesses was the first legislature to react to the news of the Stamp Act, which arrived in April 1765. Virginians were already on edge because a severe decline in tobacco prices and heavy war-related taxes had mired most planters in debt. In late 1764, the burgesses had strenuously objected to the proposed stamp tax, citing the economic hardship it would cause and arguing that it was their "inherent" right to be taxed only by their own consent.

The Stamp Act enraged a group of Virginia's young burgesses. Led by 29-year-old Patrick Henry, a fiery lawyer newly elected from a frontier county, the House of Burgesses in May 1765 debated seven strongly worded resolutions. Old-guard burgesses regarded some of them as treasonable. The legislature finally adopted the four more moderate resolves, including one proclaiming Virginia's right to impose taxes. But they rejected the other resolves, which declared it "illegal, unconstitutional, and unjust" for anybody outside Virginia to lay taxes; asserted that Virginians did not have to obey any externally imposed tax law; and labeled as an "enemy to this, his Majesty's colony" anyone denying Virginia's exclusive right to tax its inhabitants.

Many burgesses had left for home before Henry introduced his resolutions, so less than a quarter of Virginia's legislators voted for the four moderate resolves. But within a month, all seven resolutions were broadcast in the newspapers of other colonies. Henry and the aggressive young burgesses had hurled words of defiance at Parliament for other colonies to reflect on and match.

Governor Francis Bernard of Massachusetts called the Virginia resolves an "alarm bell for the disaffected." Events in Boston in August 1765 amply confirmed his view. On August 14, Bostonians awoke to find an effigy of stamp distributor Andrew Oliver, dressed in rags, hanging from an elm tree in the south end of town. When the sheriff tried to remove it at the order of Lieutenant Governor Thomas Hutchinson, Oliver's brother-in-law, a hostile crowd intervened. In the evening, working men began gathering for a mock funeral. Led by Ebenezer MacIntosh, they cut down Oliver's effigy and boisterously carried it through the streets. Then they leveled Oliver's new brick office on the wharves, rumored to be the distribution point for the hated stamps.

As night fell, the crowd reduced Oliver's luxurious mansion to a shambles. The stamp distributor promptly asked to be relieved of his commission. Twelve days later, MacIntosh led the crowd again in an all-night bout of destruction of the handsomely appointed homes of two British officials and

From the time of his election to the Virginia House of Burgesses at the age of 29, Patrick Henry was an outspoken proponent of American rights. In this portrait, he pleads a case at a county courthouse crowded with local planters. (*Virginia Historical Society, Richmond, VA*)

Hutchinson, a haughty man, who was as unpopular with the common people as his great-great-grandmother, Anne Hutchinson, had been popular. Military men "who have seen towns sacked by the enemy," one observer reported, "declare they never before saw an instance of such fury."

In attacking the property of men associated with the stamp tax, the Boston crowd demonstrated not only its opposition to parliamentary policy but also its resentment of a local elite that for years had disdained lower-class political participation and had publicly denounced the working poor for their supposed lack of industry and frugality. For decades, ordinary Bostonians had aligned politically with the Boston "caucus," which led the colony's "popular party" against conservative aristocrats such as Hutchinson and Oliver. They had also read in the *Boston Gazette* that the new parliamentary legislation had been proposed by "mean mercenary hirelings among yourselves, who for a little filthy lucre would at any time betray every right, liberty, and privilege of their fellow subjects."

But the "rage-intoxicated rabble" had suddenly broken away from the leaders of the popular party and gone further than they had intended. Hutchinson was one of their main targets. Characterized by young lawyer John Adams as "very ambitious and avaricious," Hutchinson was, in the popular view, chief among the "mean mercenary hirelings" of the British. In the aftermath of the destruction of his house—what Governor Bernard called "a war of plunder, of taking away the distinction between rich and poor"—the more cautious political leaders knew that they would have to struggle to regain control of the protest movement.

Violent protests against the Stamp Act also wracked New York and Newport, Rhode Island. Leading the resistance were groups calling themselves the Sons of Liberty, composed mostly of artisans, shopkeepers, and ordinary citizens. Protest took a more dignified form at the Stamp Act Congress, called by Massachusetts and attended by representatives of nine colonies, who met in New York in October 1765. English authorities branded this first self-initiated intercolonial convention a "dangerous tendency." The delegates formulated 12 restrained resolutions that accepted Parliament's right to legislate for the colonies but denied its right to tax them directly.

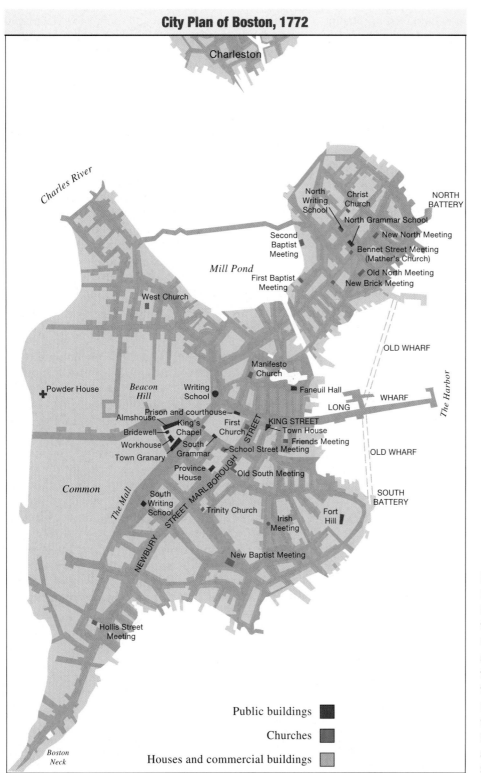

City Plan of Boston, 1772

Charleston

Charles River

NORTH
BATTERY

North
Writing
School

Christ
Church

North Grammar School

New North Meeting

Second
Baptist
Meeting

Bennet Street Meeting
(Mather's Church)

Mill Pond

First Baptist
Meeting

Old North Meeting

New Brick Meeting

West Church

OLD WHARF

Manifesto
Church

The Harbor

Faneuil Hall

WHARF

Powder House

Beacon
Hill

Writing
School

LONG

Prison and courthouse

KING STREET

Almshouse

King's
Chapel

First
Church

Town House

STREET

Bridewell

South
Grammar

Friends Meeting

OLD WHARF

Workhouse

School Street Meeting

Town Granary

Province
House

Old South Meeting

Common

SOUTH
BATTERY

The Mall

South
Writing
School

Trinity Church

Irish
Meeting

Fort
Hill

NEWBURY STREET MARLBOROUGH

New Baptist Meeting

Hollis Street
Meeting

Boston
Neck

Public buildings ▮

Churches ▮

Houses and commercial buildings ▮

Boston's many churches became important political meeting places in the tumultuous decade leading to the outbreak of war in 1775. Old South Meeting House, holding as many as 5,000 people, became the gathering place of "body of the people." Faneuil Hall was the usual site of town meetings, but when crowds exceeded its capacity of 1,200, meetings were adjourned and reconvened at Old South Meeting House.

By late 1765, effigy-burning crowds all over America were convincing stamp distributors to resign. Colonists defied English authority even more directly by forcing most customs officers and court officials to open the ports and courts for business after November 1 without using the hated stamps required after that date. This often took months of pressure and sometimes mob action, but the Sons of Liberty, often led by new faces in local politics, ultimately got their way by going outside the law.

In March 1766, Parliament debated the surprising American reaction to the Stamp Act. Lobbied by many merchant friends of the Americans, Parliament voted to repeal it. Some members warned that to retreat before colonial defiance of the law would ultimately be fatal. But the legislators bowed to expediency. They satisfied themselves with passing the Declaratory Act, which asserted Parliament's power to enact laws for the colonies in "all cases whatsoever."

The crisis had passed, yet nothing was really solved. Americans had begun to recognize a grasping government trampling its subjects' rights. The Stamp Act, one New England clergyman foresaw, "diffused a disgust through the colonies and laid the basis of an alienation which will never be healed." Stamp Act resisters had politicized their communities as never before. The established leaders, generally cautious in their protests, were often displaced by those beneath them on the social ladder. Men such as New York ship captains Alexander McDougall and Isaac Sears mobilized common citizens and raised political consciousness, employing mass demonstrations and street violence to humble stamp distributors and force open the courts and seaports. Scribbled John Adams in his diary: "The people have become more attentive to their liberties, . . . and more determined to defend them. . . . Our presses have groaned, our pulpits have thundered, our legislatures have resolved, our towns have voted; the crown officers have everywhere trembled, and all their little tools and creatures been afraid to speak and ashamed to be seen."

An Uncertain Interlude

Ministerial instability in England hampered the quest for a coherent, workable American policy. Attempting to be a strong king, George III chose ministers who commanded little respect in Parliament. This led to strife between Parliament and the king's chief ministers; that in turn led to a shuffling of chief ministers and a chaotic political situation at the very time that the king was attempting to overhaul the empire's administration.

To manage the colonies more effectively, the Pitt-Grafton ministry that the king had appointed in 1767 obtained new laws to reorganize the customs service, establish a secretary of state for American affairs, and install three new vice-admiralty courts in the port cities. Still hard-pressed for revenue—for at home the government faced severe unemployment, tax protests, and riots over the high price of grain—the ministry also pushed through Parliament the relatively small Townshend duties on paper, lead, painters' colors, and tea. A final law suspended New York's assembly until that body ceased defying the Quartering Act of 1765, which required public funds for support of British troops garrisoned in the colony since the end of the Seven Years' War. New York knuckled under to save its legislature.

Colonial protests against the Townshend Acts, centered in Massachusetts, were more restrained than in 1765. But the Massachusetts House of Representatives sent a circular letter to each colony objecting to the new Townshend duties, small though they were. Written by Samuel Adams, the letter attacked as unconstitutional the plan to underwrite salaries for royal officials in America from customs duties. Under instructions from England, Governor Bernard dissolved the legislature after it refused to rescind the circular letter. "The Americans have made a discovery," declared Edmund Burke before Parliament, "that we mean to oppress them; we have made a discovery that they intend to raise a rebellion. We do not know how to advance; they do not know how to retreat."

This wood engraving, published in 1829 in a history of the United States, recalls a New Hampshire riot in which townspeople lynched and stoned a stamp distributor in effigy. Cobblestones pried loose from the street seemed to provide the crowd's arsenal. (*The Metropolitan Museum of Art, New York, Bequest of Charles Allen Munn*)

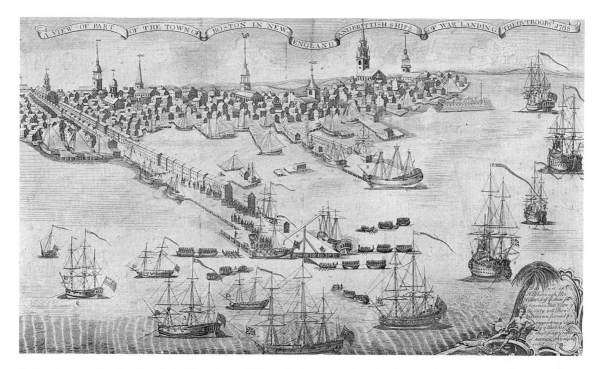

Rather than quelling the disorder as King George III hoped, the occupation of Boston by British troops in 1768 increased tensions. In this engraving by Paul Revere, the red-coated troops are debarking at the Long Wharf. (*Courtesy the Henry Francis du Pont Winterthur Museum*)

Although most colonists only grumbled and petitioned, Bostonians protested stridently. In the summer of 1768, after customs officials seized a sloop owned by John Hancock for a violation of the trade regulations, an angry crowd mobbed them. They fled to a British warship in Boston harbor and remained there for months. Newspapers hounded overeager revenue officers who extracted money for the maintenance of "swarms of officers and pensioners, and an enormous train of underlings and dependents"; they also warned of new measures designed to "suck the life blood" from the people and predicted that troops would be sent to "dragoon us into passive obedience." To many, the belief grew that the English were plotting "designs for destroying our constitutional liberties."

Troops indeed came. The attack on the customs officials brought a resolute response from England, where the government regarded the Bostonians' action as insubordinate and selfish. The ministry dispatched two regiments from England and two more from Nova Scotia. The intention was to bring the Bostonians to a proper state of subordination and make them an example to the rest of the colonies. Now cries went up against maintaining standing armies in peacetime, but radical Bostonians who proposed force to prevent the troops from landing got little support from delegates called to a special provincial convention. On October 1, 1768, red-coated troops marched into Boston without resistance.

After the troops occupied Boston, the colonists' main tactic of protest against the Townshend Acts became economic boycott. First in Boston and then in New York and Philadelphia, merchants and consumers adopted nonimportation and nonconsumption agreements, pledging neither to import nor to use British goods. These measures promised to bring the politically influential English merchants to their aid, for half of British shipping was engaged in commerce with the colonies, and one-quarter of all English exports were consumed there. When the southern colonies also adopted nonimportation agreements in 1768, a new step toward intercolonial union had been taken.

Many colonial merchants, however, especially those tied to the government's interest, saw nonimportation agreements as lacking legal force and refused to be bound by them. They had to be persuaded otherwise by street brigades, usually composed of artisans who warmly supported nonimportation as a boon to home manufacturing. Crowd action welled up again in the seaports, as determined patriot bands attacked the homes and warehouses of offending merchants and "rescued" incoming contraband goods seized by zealous customs officials.

England's attempts to discipline its American colonies and oblige them to share the costs of governing an empire lay in shambles by the end of the 1760s. Using troops to restore order undermined the respect for the mother country on which colonial acceptance of its authority ultimately depended. American newspapers denounced new extensions of British authority. Colonial governors quarreled with their legislatures. Customs officials met with determined opposition and were widely accused of arbitrary actions and excessive zeal in enforcing the Navigation Acts. The Townshend duties had failed miserably, yielding less than £21,000 by 1770 while costing British business £700,000 through the colonial nonimportation movement.

On March 5, 1770, Parliament repealed all the Townshend duties except the one on tea (which the new minister of state, Lord North, explained was retained "as a mark of the supremacy of Parliament and an efficient declaration of their right to govern the colonies"). On that same evening in Boston, British troops fired on an unruly crowd of heckling citizens. For months, Bostonians had been baiting the "lobsterbacks," as they dubbed the red-coated British soldiers. They hated them for competing with townspeople for menial jobs when off duty, as well as for their military presence. On this evening, a taunting crowd had first hurled insults and snowballs and then surged toward a sentry. After a squad of redcoats joined the sentry, someone cried, "Fire!" When the smoke cleared, five bloody bodies, including that of Ebenezer MacIntosh's brother-in-law, stained the snow-covered street. Bowing to furious popular reaction, Thomas Hutchinson, recently appointed governor, ordered the British troops out of town and arrested the commanding officer and the soldiers involved. They were later acquitted, with two young patriot lawyers, John Adams and Josiah Quincy, Jr., providing a brilliant defense.

In spite of the potential of the "Boston massacre" for galvanizing the colonies into further resistance, opposition to English policies, including boycotts, subsided in 1770. Popular leaders such as Samuel Adams in Boston and Alexander McDougall in New York, who had made names for themselves as the standard-bearers of American liberty, had few issues left to exploit. They were further handicapped by the end of the depression that had previously helped sow discontent. Yet the fires of revolution had been not extinguished but merely dampened.

The Growing Rift

From 1770 to 1772, relative quiet descended over the colonies. Then in June 1772, England created a new furor by announcing that it, rather than the provincial legislature, would henceforth pay the salaries of the royal governor and superior court judges in Massachusetts. Even though the measure saved the colony money, it looked like a scheme, undermining a right set forth in the colony's charter, to impose a despotic government on the colony. Judges paid from London presumably would obey London.

Paul Revere was not only a noted silversmith and political activist but also a man who put art to work in the cause of revolutionary politics. This engraving became known throughout the colonies and convinced many people to involve themselves in what had been mainly New England's cause. The smiling British redcoats are reviled in verse: "While faithless P[resto]n and his savage Bonds, / With murd'rous Rancour stretch their bloody Hands, / Like fierce Barbarians grinning o'er their Prey, / Approve the Carnage and enjoy the Day." (*American Antiquarian Society*)

Boston's town meeting protested loudly and created a Committee of Correspondence "to state the rights of the colonists . . . and to communicate and publish the same to the several towns and to the world." Crown supporters called the committee "the foulest, subtlest, and most venomous serpent ever issued from the egg of sedition." By the end of 1772, another 80 towns in Massachusetts had created committees. In the next year, all but three colonies established Committees of Correspondence in their legislatures.

Samuel Adams was by now the leader of the Boston radicals, for the influence of laboring men like Ebenezer MacIntosh had been quietly reduced. Adams was an experienced caucus politicker and a skilled political journalist, and (despite his Harvard degree) he had deep roots among the laboring people. He organized the working ranks through the taverns, clubs, and volunteer fire companies and secured the support of wealthy merchants such as John Hancock, whose ample purse financed patriotic celebrations and feasts that kept politics on everyone's mind and helped build interclass bridges. In England, Adams became known as one of the most dangerous firebrands in America.

In 1772, Rhode Islanders gave Adams new material to work with when they attacked a royal warship. The British commander of the *Gaspee* was roundly hated for hounding the fishermen and small traders of Narragansett Bay. When his ship ran aground while pursuing a suspected smuggler, Rhode Islanders took their revenge, burning the stranded vessel to the waterline. Adding insult to injury, a Rhode Island court convicted the *Gaspee*'s captain of illegally seizing what he was convinced was smuggled sugar and rum. London reacted with cries of high treason. Finding the lips of Rhode Islanders sealed regarding the identity of the arsonists, an investigating committee could do little. The event was tailor-made for Samuel Adams, who used it to "awaken the American colonies, which have been too long dozing upon the brink of ruin."

The final plunge into revolution began when Parliament passed the Tea Act in early 1773. The act allowed the East India Company, which was on the verge of bankruptcy, to ship its tea directly to North America. By eliminating English middlemen and English import taxes, this provided Americans with the opportunity to buy their tea cheaply from the company's agents in the colonies. Even with the small tax to be paid in the colonies, Indian tea would now undersell smuggled Dutch tea. The Americans would get inexpensive tea, the crown would derive a modest revenue, and the East India Company would obtain a new lease on life. The company soon had 600,000 pounds of tea in 2,000 chests ready for shipment to America.

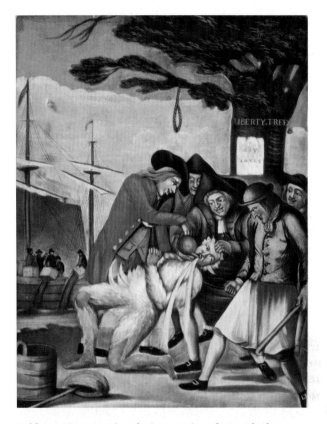

Public sentiment against the importation of tea and other British goods often found expression in a coat of tar and feathers applied to the bare skin of the offending importer. Note the symbols in *The Bostonians Paying the Excise-Man:* the Liberty Tree with a hangman's noose and the overturned copy of the Stamp Act. In the background, Bostonians dump chests of tea into the harbor. (*Library of Congress*)

Parliament monumentally miscalculated the American response. For several years, merchants in Philadelphia and New York had been flagrantly smuggling Dutch tea. As a consequence, imports of English tea in the two seaports plummeted from 500,000 pounds in 1768 to a mere 650 pounds in 1772. The merchants bitterly denounced the new act for giving the East India Company a monopoly on the American tea market. Other monopolies would follow, they predicted, and middlemen of all kinds would be eliminated. The colonists also objected that the government was shrewdly trying to gain acceptance of Parliament's taxing power. As Americans drank the taxed tea, they would also be swallowing the English right to tax them.

The colonists quickly demonstrated that their principles were not entirely in their pocketbooks. Mass meetings in the port towns soon forced the resignation of the East India Company's agents, and citizens vowed to stop the obnoxious tea at the water's edge.

Governor Hutchinson of Massachusetts brought the tea crisis to a climax, convinced that to yield again to popular pressure would forever cripple English sovereignty in America. The popular party led by Samuel Adams had been urging the citizens to demonstrate that they were not yet prepared for the "yoke of slavery" by sending the tea back to England. Hutchinson's refusal to grant the tea ships clearance papers to return to England with their cargoes finally led to dramatic action. Buoyed by resolutions from surrounding towns, 5,000 Bostonians packed Old South Church on December 16, 1773, noisily passing resolutions urging the governor to clear the ships. But Hutchinson was not swayed by the Bostonians' determination to resist what they regarded as another affront to their liberties. "This meeting," despaired Samuel Adams, "can do no more to save the country."

At nightfall, a band of Bostonians, dressed as Indians, boarded the tea ships, broke open the chests of tea, and flung £10,000 worth of the East India Company's property into Boston harbor. George Hewes, a 31-year-old shoemaker, recalled how he had garbed himself as a Mohawk, blackened "face and hands with coal dust in the shop of a blacksmith," and joined men of all ranks in marching stealthily to the wharves to do their work. In time, this would be remembered as The Boston Tea Party.

Now the die was cast. Lord North, the king's chief minister, called the Bostonians "fanatics" and argued that the dispute was no longer about taxes but about whether England had any authority over the colonies. George III put it succinctly: "We must master them or totally leave them to themselves and treat them as aliens."

Thoroughly aroused, Parliament passed the Coercive Acts, stern laws that Bostonians promptly labeled the "Intolerable Acts." The acts closed the port of Boston to all shipping until the colony paid for the destroyed tea. They barred local courts from trying British soldiers and officials for acts committed while suppressing civil disturbances. To hamstring the colony's truculent political assemblies, Parliament amended the Massachusetts charter to transform the council from an upper legislative chamber, elected by the lower house, to a body appointed by the governor. This stripped the council of its veto power over the governor's decisions.

The act also struck at local government by authorizing the governor to prohibit all town meetings except for one annual meeting to elect local officers of government. Finally, General Thomas Gage, commander in chief of British forces in America, replaced Thomas Hutchinson as governor. "This is the day, then," declared Edmund Burke in the House of Commons, "that you wish to go to war with all America, in order to conciliate that country to this."

Royal Governor Thomas Hutchinson called Sam Adams "[the greatest] incendiary in the King's dominion" whereas his cousin, John Adams, called him "a plain, simple, decent citizen of middling stature, dress, and manners." Boston's premier painter, John Singleton Copley, painted Adams in just this way—in a simple wool suit with no embroidery and a partially unbuttoned waistcoat suggesting the patriot leader's disdain for proper appearances. *(Samuel Adams, about 1772; John Singleton Copley, American (1738–1815), Oil on canvas; 49½ x 39½ in. (125.7 x 100.3 cm), Deposited by the city of Boston, 30.76c. Courtesy of the Museum of Fine Arts, Boston. Reproduced with permission. © 1999 The Museum of Fine Arts, Boston. All Rights Reserved.)*

Lord North's plan to strangle Massachusetts into submission and hope for acquiescence elsewhere in the colonies proved popular in England. Earlier, the colonies had gained supporters in Parliament for their resistance to what many regarded as attacks on their fundamental privileges. Now this support evaporated. After a decade of debating constitutional rights and mobilizing sentiment against what many believed was a systematic plot to enslave freeborn citizens, the Americans found their maneuvering room severely narrowed.

When the Intolerable Acts arrived in May 1774 aboard the *Harmony*, Boston's town meeting reacted belligerently. It dispatched a circular letter to all the colonies urging an end to trade with England. This met with faint support. But a second call, for a meeting in Philadelphia of delegates from all colonies, received a better response. The Continental Congress, as it was called, now began to transform a ten-year debate conducted by separate colonies into a unified American cause.

Fifty-five delegates from all the colonies except Georgia converged on Carpenter's Hall in Philadelphia in September 1774. The discussions centered not on how to prepare for a war that many sensed was inevitable but on how to resolve sectional differences that most delegates feared were irreconcilable. Overcoming prejudices and hostilities was as important as the formal debates. New Englanders were especially eyed with suspicion for their reputed intolerance and self-interest. "We have numberless prejudices to remove here," wrote John Adams from Philadelphia. "We have been obliged to keep ourselves out of sight, and to feel pulses, and to sound the depths; to insinuate our sentiments, designs, and desires by means of other persons, sometimes of one province, and sometimes of another."

The Continental Congress was by no means a unified body. Some delegates, led by cousins Samuel and John Adams from Massachusetts and Richard Henry Lee and Patrick Henry of Virginia, argued for outright resistance to Parliament's Coercive Acts. Moderate delegates from the middle colonies, led by Joseph Galloway of Pennsylvania and James Duane of New York, urged restraint and further attempts at reconciliation. After weeks of debate, the delegates agreed to a restrained Declaration of Rights and Resolves. It attempted to define American grievances and justify the colonists' defiance of English policies and laws by appealing to the "immutable laws of nature, the principles of the English constitution, and the several [colonial] charters and compacts" under which they lived. More concrete was the Congress's agreement on a plan of resistance. If England did not rescind the Intolerable Acts by December 1, 1774, a ban would take effect on all imports and exports between the colonies and Great Britain, Ireland, and the British West Indies. Some exceptions were made for the export of southern staple commodities to keep reluctant southern colonies in the fold.

By the time the Congress adjourned in late October, leaders from different colonies had transformed what had been primarily Boston's cause into a national movement. "Government is dissolved [and] we are in a state of nature," Patrick Henry argued dramatically. "The distinctions between Virginians, Pennsylvanians, New Yorkers, and New Englanders are no more. I am not a Virginian, but an American." Many other delegates were a long way from feeling this way, but still the Congress agreed to reconvene in May 1775.

Even before the Second Continental Congress met, the fabric of government had been badly torn in most colonies. Revolutionary committees, conventions, and congresses, entirely unauthorized by law, were replac-

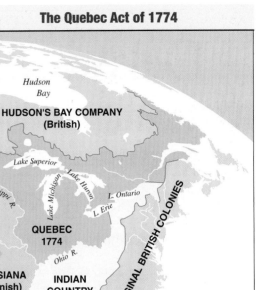

The Quebec Act of 1774

Most colonists hated the Quebec Act, which attached the trans-Appalachian interior north of the Ohio River to the British government in Quebec, because they believed this act passed by Parliament, like others during the prewar years, was aimed at the heart of colonial liberty. It not only sealed off the western lands from colonial speculators but guaranteed the right of French Catholics to practice their religion freely—an offense, especially, to New England Puritans.

ing legal governing bodies. Assuming authority in defiance of royal governors, who suspended truculent legislatures in many colonies, they often operated on instructions from mass meetings where the legal franchise was ignored. These extralegal bodies created and armed militia units, bullied merchants and shopkeepers refusing to conform to popularly authorized boycotts, levied taxes, operated the courts, and obstructed the work of English customs officials. By the end of 1774, all but three colonies defied their own charters by appointing provincial assemblies without royal authority. In the next year, this independently created power became evident in the nearly complete cessation of trade with England.

The Final Rupture

The final spark to the revolutionary powder keg was struck in early 1775. General Gage had assumed the governorship of Massachusetts 11 months earlier and

TO THE

Delaware Pilots.

WE took the Pleasure, some Days since, of kindly admonishing you *to do your Duty*; if perchance you should meet with the *(Tea,)* Ship Polly, Captain Ayres; a Three Decker which is hourly expected,

We have now to add, that Matters ripen fast here; and that *much is expected from those Lads who meet with the Tea Ship.*----There is some Talk of a handsome Reward for the Pilot who gives the first good Account of her.----How that may be, we cannot *for certain* determine: But all agree, that Tar and Feathers will be his Portion, who pilots her into this Harbour. And we will answer for ourselves, that, whoever is committed to us, as an Offender against the Rights of *America*, will experience the utmost Exertion of our Abilities; as

THE COMMITTEE FOR TARRING AND FEATHERING.

Not only Bostonians took action against the Tea Act. This Philadelphia broadside from "The Committee for Tarring and Feathering," issued several weeks before the Boston Tea Party, exhorts pilots on the Delaware River to watch for an arriving tea ship. *(Rare Book Collection, New York Public Library, Astor, Lenox and Tilden Foundations)*

occupied Boston with 4,000 troops—one for every adult male in the town. In April 1775, the government in London ordered Gage to arrest "the principal actors and abettors" of insurrection in Massachusetts. Under cover of night, he sent 700 redcoats out of Boston to seize colonial arms and ammunition in nearby Concord. But Americans learned of the plan. When the troops reached Lexington at dawn, 70 "Minutemen"—townsmen available on a minute's notice—were waiting. In the skirmish that ensued, 18 Massachusetts farmers fell, 8 of them mortally wounded.

Marching six miles west, the British entered Concord, where another firefight broke out. Withdrawing, the redcoats made their way back to Boston, harassed by militiamen firing from farmhouses and barns and from behind stone walls. Before the bloody day ended, 273 British and 95 Americans lay dead or wounded. News of the bloodshed swept through the colonies. Within weeks, thousands of men besieged the British troops in Boston. One colonist reported that wherever one traveled, "you see the inhabitants training, making firelocks, casting mortars, shells, and shot."

The outbreak of fighting vastly altered the debates of the Second Continental Congress, which assembled in Philadelphia in May 1775. The Congress had the same slim powers as its predecessor, but it acquired awesome new responsibilities. Many delegates knew one another from the earlier Congress. But fresh faces appeared, including Boston's wealthy merchant, John Hancock; a tall, young planter-lawyer from Virginia, Thomas Jefferson; and the much-applauded Benjamin Franklin, who had arrived from London only four days before the Congress convened.

The Congress had no power to legislate or command; it could only request and recommend. Delegate John Adams worried that such a body could

form a constitution "for a great empire," and "at the same time they have a country of 1,500 miles to fortify, millions to arm and train, a naval power to begin, an extensive commerce to regulate, numerous tribes of Indians to negotiate with, a standing army of 27,000 men to raise pay, victual, and officer."

Another 14 months elapsed before the Congress issued a formal declaration of independence, but the war with England—and a civil war in America—had already begun. Meeting in the statehouse in Philadelphia, where the king's arms hung over the entrance and the inscription on the tower bell read "Proclaim liberty throughout the land unto all the inhabitants thereof," the Second Congress set to work. It authorized a continental army of 20,000 and, partly to cement Virginia to the cause, chose George Washington as commander in chief. It issued a "Declaration of Causes of Taking-up Arms," sent the king an "Olive Branch Petition" humbly begging him to remove the obstacles to reconciliation, made moves to secure the neutrality of the interior Indian tribes, issued paper money, erected a postal system, and approved plans for a military hospital.

While debate continued over whether the colonies ought to declare themselves independent, military action grew hotter. Hotheaded Ethan Allen and his Green Mountain Boys from eastern New York captured Fort Ticonderoga, controlling the Champlain valley, in May 1775. On New Year's Day in 1776, the British shelled Norfolk, Virginia. In March 1776, Washington's army forced the British to evacuate Boston. In spite of these acts of aggression, many members of the Congress dreaded a final rupture and still hoped for reconciliation with England. Such hopes crumbled at the end of 1775 when news arrived that the king, rejecting the Olive Branch Petition, had dispatched 20,000 additional British troops to quell the American insurrection and had proclaimed the colonies in "open and avowed rebellion." Those fatal

STEPS ON THE ROAD TO REVOLUTION

1763	Treaty of Paris ends Seven Years' War between England and France; France cedes Canada to England.
	Proclamation of 1763 forbids white settlement west of Appalachian Mountains.
1764	Sugar Act sets higher duties on imported sugar and lower duties on molasses and enlarges the power of vice-admiralty courts.
	Currency Act prohibits issuance of paper money by colonies.
1765	Stamp Act requires revenue-raising stamps purchased from British-appointed stamp distributors on printed documents.
	Stamp Act Congress meets in New York.
	Quartering Act requires colonies to furnish British troops with housing and certain provisions.
	Sons of Liberty formed in New York City and thereafter in many towns.
1766	Declaratory Act asserts Parliament's sovereignty over the colonies after repealing Stamp Act.
	Rent riots by New York tenant farmers.
1767	Townshend Revenue Acts impose duties on tea, glass, paper, paints, and other items.
	South Carolina Regulators organize in backcountry.
1768	British troops sent to Boston.
1770	British troops kill four and wound eight American civilians in Boston Massacre.
1771	Battle of Alamance pits frontier North Carolina Regulators against eastern militia led by royal governor.
1772	British schooner *Gaspee* burned in Rhode Island.
	Committee of Correspondence formed in Boston and thereafter in other cities.
1773	Tea Act reduces duty on tea but gives East India Company right to sell directly to Americans.
	Boston Tea Party dumps £10,000 of East India Company tea into Boston harbor.
1774	Coercive Acts close port of Boston, restrict provincial and town governments in Massachusetts, and send additional troops to Boston.
	Quebec Act attaches trans-Appalachian interior north of Ohio River to government of Quebec.
	First Continental Congress meets and forms Continental Association to boycott British imports.
1775	Battles of Lexington and Concord cause 95 American and 273 British casualties; Americans take Fort Ticonderoga.
	Second Continental Congress meets and assumes many powers of an independent government.
	Dunmore's Proclamation in Virginia promises freedom to slaves and indentured servants fleeing to British ranks.
	Prohibitory Act embargoes American goods.
	George III proclaims Americans in open rebellion.
1776	Thomas Paine publishes *Common Sense*.
	British troops evacuate Boston.
	Declaration of Independence.

words made all the Congress's actions treasonable and turned all who obeyed them into traitors.

By the time Thomas Paine's hard-hitting pamphlet *Common Sense* appeared in Philadelphia on January 9, 1776, members of the Congress were talking less gingerly about independence. Paine's blunt words and compelling rhetoric smashed through the remaining reserve. "O ye that love mankind! Ye that dare oppose not only the tyranny, but also the tyrant, stand forth!" wrote Paine. Within weeks, the pamphlet was in bookstalls all over the colonies. "The public sentiment which a few weeks before had shuddered at the tremendous obstacles, with which independence was envisioned," declared Edmund Randolph of Virginia, now "overleaped every barrier."

The Continental Congress continued to debate independence during the spring of 1776, even as the war became bloodier. While the delegates talked, men under arms acted. Washington's army forced the British to withdraw from Boston, but an American assault on Quebec failed in May 1776. England embargoed all trade to the colonies and ordered the seizure of American ships. That convinced the Congress to declare its ports open to all countries. "Nothing is left now," Joseph Hewes of North Carolina admitted, "but to fight it out." It was almost anticlimactic when Richard Henry Lee introduced his congressional resolution on June 7 calling for a declaration of independence. After two days of debate, the Congress ordered a committee chaired by Jefferson to begin drafting the document.

Though it would become revered as the new nation's birth certificate, the declaration was not a highly original statement. It drew heavily on the Congress's earlier justifications of American resistance, and its theory of government had already been set forth in scores of pamphlets over the previous decade. The ringing phrases that "all men are created equal, that they are endowed by their Creator with certain unalienable Rights, that among these are Life, Liberty and the pursuit of Happiness" were familiar in the writing of many pamphleteers, including John Adams, Thomas Paine, and James Wilson.

Jefferson's committee presented the declaration to the Congress on June 28. The proposals were read and ordered to "lie on the table" until the following Monday, July 1. "This morning is assigned for the greatest debate of all," noted John Adams, when the Congress reconvened. "May Heaven prosper the new-born republic, and make it more glorious than any former republics have been." At the end of the day, nine colonies voted to adopt the declaration, two voted against, one delegation split, and one abstained. The next day, July 2, twelve delegations voted yes, with New York's abstaining, thus allowing the Congress to say that the vote for independence was unanimous. Two days more were spent cutting and polishing the document. The major change was the elimination of a long argument blaming the king for slavery in America.

On July 4, Congress sent the Declaration of Independence to the printer. Four days later,

Philadelphians thronged to the statehouse to hear it read aloud. They "huzzahed" the reading, tore the king's arms from above the statehouse door, and later that night, amid cheers, toasts, and clanging church bells, hurled this symbol of more than a century and a half of colonial dependency on England into a roaring bonfire.

THE IDEOLOGY OF REVOLUTIONARY REPUBLICANISM

Since 1763, the colonists responded to a variety of ideas that gave meaning to the events and conditions they were experiencing. Mostly these ideas took the form of newspaper articles and pamphlets written by educated lawyers, clergymen, merchants, and planters. But the middling and lower ranks of society had also expressed themselves in printed broadsides, appeals in the newspapers, and also street demonstrations where ordinary people carried out ideologically laden rituals of humiliation against their enemies such as tarring and feathering and burnings in effigy. Gradually, the colonists pieced together a political ideology, borrowed partly from English political thought, partly from the theories of the Enlightenment, and partly from their own experiences. Historians call this new ideology "revolutionary republicanism." But because the colonists varied widely in interests and experiences, no single coherent ideology united them all.

The able Doctor, or America Swallowing the Bitter Draught.

Liberty always had to struggle against power, as American colonists saw it. In this cartoon, England (power) forces Liberty (America in the form of a woman) to drink the "Bitter Draught" of tea. Uncompliant, America spits the tea into England's face while another corrupt Englishman peeks under her petticoat. (*Massachusetts Historical Society*)

A Plot Against Liberty

Many American colonists agreed with earlier English Whig writers who charged that corrupt and power-hungry men were slowly extinguishing the lamp of liberty in England. The so-called country party represented by these Whig pamphleteers proclaimed itself the guardian of the true principles of the English constitution and opposed the "court" party representing the king and his appointees.

When the king's ministers began a new program for disciplining the empire after 1763, American Whig writers were intellectually prepared to view the new laws and policies as attacks on such traditional English liberties as balanced government, representative rights, and disestablishment of standing armies in peacetime. Even Parliament, traditionally the preserver of the people's rights against tyrannical executive power, seemed to threaten a despotism of its own in its alliance with the monarchy. Every ministerial policy and parliamentary act in the decade after the Stamp Act appeared as a subversion of English liberties. Most Americans regarded resistance to such blows against liberty as wholly justified.

The belief that England was carrying out "a deep-laid and desperate plan of imperial despotism . . . for the extinction of all civil liberty," as the Boston town meeting expressed it in 1770, spread rapidly in the next few years. By 1774, John Adams was writing of the "conspiracy against the public liberty [that] was first regularly formed and begun to be executed in 1763 and 1764." From London, America's favorite writer, Benjamin Franklin, described the "extreme corruption prevalent among all orders of men in this old rotten state." Another pamphleteer reached the conclusion that England was no longer "in a condition at present to suckle us, being pregnant with vermin that corrupt her milk and convert her blood and juices into poison."

Among many Americans, especially merchants, the attack on constitutional rights blended closely with the threats to their economic interests contained in the tough new trade policies. Merchants saw a coordinated attack on their "lives, liberties, and property," as they frequently phrased it. If a man was not secure in his property, he could not be secure in his citizenship, for it was property that gave a man the independence to shape his identity.

Revitalizing American Society

The continuing crisis over the imperial relationship by itself inspired many colonists to resist impending tyranny. But for others, the revolutionary mentality was also fed by a belief that an opportunity was at hand to revitalize American society. They believed that the colonies had been undergoing a silent transfor-

mation and that the growing commercial connections with the decadent and corrupt mother country had injected poison into the American bloodstream. They worried about the luxury and vice they saw around them and came to believe that resistance to England would return American society to a state of civic virtue, spartan living, and godly purpose.

The fervent support of the patriot movement by much of the colonial clergy, especially in New England, and the clergy's importance in writing protest pamphlets helped give a high-toned moral character to colonial protest. Such appeals resonated most strongly in New England, where even so secular a man as John Adams groaned at the "universal spirit of debauchery, dissipation, luxury, effeminacy and gaming." As in most revolutionary movements, talk of moral regeneration, of a society-wide rebirth through battle against a corrupt enemy, ennobled the cause, inspiring people in areas that had been stirred a generation before by the Great Awakening.

The growth of a revolutionary spirit among ordinary people also owed much to the plain style of polemical writers such as Thomas Paine and Patrick Henry. Paine's *Common Sense* transformed the terms of the imperial argument by attacking monarchy itself. Its astounding popularity—it went through 25 editions in 1776 and sold more copies than any printed piece in colonial history—stemmed not only from its argument but also from its style. Paine wrote for the common people who knew nothing more than the Bible. Using biblical imagery and plain language, he appealed to their Calvinist heritage and their belief in their providential destiny. After savagely attacking the king, whom he called "a royal brute," Paine appealed to millennial yearnings: "We have it in our power to begin the world over again. The birthday of a new world is at hand," if only the Americans would stand up for liberty, the goddess whom "Europe regards . . . like a stranger, and England hath given . . . warning to depart."

Paine avoided the elaborate legalistic style of most of the pamphlets written by lawyers and clergymen in the preceding decade. His language could be understood on the docks, in the taverns, on the streets, and in the farmyards. Many Whig leaders found his pungent language and egalitarian call for ending hereditary privilege and concentrated power too strong. They denounced the disheveled immigrant with "genius in his eyes" as a "crack-brained zealot for democracy" and a dangerous man who appealed to "every silly clown and illiterate mechanic." But thousands who read or listened to *Common Sense* were radicalized by it and came to believe not only that independence could be wrested from England but also that a new social and political order could be created in North America.

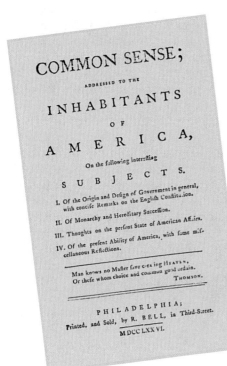

In *Common Sense,* Thomas Paine dared to articulate, in plain but muscular language, the thoughts of rebellion and independence that others had only alluded to. Note that Paine did not put his name on the title page of Common Sense, though he was quickly identified as the author. *(Left, Library of Congress; Right, National Portrait Gallery, London)*

✑ THE TURMOIL OF REVOLUTIONARY SOCIETY

The long struggle with England over colonial rights between 1764 and 1776 did not occur in a unified society. Social and economic change, which accelerated in the late colonial period, brought deep unrest and calls for reform from many quarters. By the end of the Seven Years' War, faith in the internal social systems of the colonies had waned among many colonists, just as allegiance to the mother country and to the British mercantile system had worn thin.

Many of the colonists who struggled for security in the aftermath of the Seven Years' War hoped that migration to frontier land would improve their fortunes. A flood of new immigrants from Ireland and Germany after the Treaty of Paris in 1763 added to the pressure to reach the trans-Appalachian river valleys. However, the western option involved much violence with Indian tribes unreceptive to encroaching settlers. So most colonists chose to work out their destinies at home or in other communities along the coastal plain to which they migrated in search of opportunity.

As agitation against English policy intensified, previously passive people took a more active interest in politics. In this charged atmosphere, the constitutional struggle with England spread quickly into uncharted territory. Groups emerged—slaves, urban laboring people, backcountry farmers, evangelicals, women—who enunciated goals of their own that were sometimes only loosely connected to the struggle with England. The stridency and potential power of these groups raised for many upper-class leaders the frightening specter of a radically changed society. Losing control of the protests they had initially led, many would abandon the resistance movement against England.

Urban People

Although the cities contained only about 5 percent of the colonial population, they formed the vital cores of revolutionary agitation. As centers of communications, government, and commerce, they led the way in protesting English policy, and they soon contained the most politicized citizens in America. Local politics could be rapidly transformed as the struggle against England became enmeshed with calls for internal reform.

Philadelphia offers a good example of popular empowerment. Before the Seven Years' War, craftsmen had usually acquiesced in politics to the merchant and lawyer politicos. But economic difficulties in the 1760s and 1770s led them to band together within their craft and community. Artisans played a central role in forging and—equally important—enforcing a nonimportation agreement in 1768, calling public meetings, publishing newspaper appeals, organizing secondary boycotts against foot-dragging merchants, and ferreting out and tarring and feathering opponents to their policies. Cautious merchants complained that mere artisans had "no right to give their sentiments respecting an importation" and called the craftsmen a "rabble." But artisans, casting off their customary deference, forged ahead.

By 1772, artisans were filling elected municipal positions and insisting on their right to participate equally with their social superiors in nominating assemblymen and other important officeholders. They also began lobbying for reform laws. The craftsmen called for elected representatives to be more accountable to their constituents. Genteel Philadelphians muttered, "It is time the tradesmen were checked—they ought not to intermeddle in state affairs—they will become too powerful."

By 1774, the Philadelphia working-class's meddling in state affairs reached a bold new stage—the de facto assumption of governmental powers by committees created by the people at large. Craftsmen had first assumed such extralegal authority in policing the nonimportation agreement in 1769. Five years later, responding to the Intolerable Acts, they proposed a radical slate of candidates for a committee to enforce a new economic boycott. Their ticket drubbed one nominated by conservative merchants.

As the impasse with England reached a climax in 1775, the political mobilization and heightened consciousness of laboring Philadelphians continued. By then, many pacifist Quaker leaders of the city had abandoned politics, and other conservative merchants had concluded that mob rule had triumphed. Into the leadership vacuum stepped a group of radicals from the middling ranks: the fiery Scots-Irish doctor Thomas Young, who had agitated in Boston and Albany before migrating to Philadelphia; Timothy Matlack, a hardware retailer who was popular with the lower class for matching his prize bantam cocks against those of New York's aristocratic James Delancy; James Cannon, a young schoolteacher; Benjamin Rush, whose new medical practice took him into the garrets and cramped rooms of the city's poor; and Thomas Paine, a recent immigrant seeking something better in America than he had found as an ill-paid excise officer in England.

The political support of the new radical leaders centered in the 31 companies of the Philadelphia militia, composed mostly of laboring men, and in the extralegal committees now controlling the city's economic life. Their leadership helped overcome the conservatism of the regularly elected Pennsylvania legis-

Benjamin Rush, a young Philadelphia doctor, was one of the revolutionary radicals who wanted to reform American society as well as win independence. Among the reforms Rush promoted were abolishing slavery and establishing free public schools that would teach women as well as men. (*Charles Willson Peale*, Portrait of Benjamin Rush, 1783/ *The Henry Francis duPont Winterthur Museum*)

lature, which was resisting the movement of the Continental Congress toward independence. In addition, the new radical leaders demanded internal reforms: curbing the accumulation of wealth by "our great merchants" who were "making immense fortunes at the expense of the people"; abolishing the property requirement for voting; allowing militiamen to elect their officers; and imposing stiff fines, to be used for the support of the families of poor militiamen, on men who refused militia service.

Philadelphia's radicals never controlled the city. They always jostled for position with prosperous artisans and shopkeepers of more moderate views and with cautious lawyers and merchants. But mobilization among artisans, laborers, and mariners, in other cities as well as Philadelphia, became part of the chain of events that led toward independence. Whereas most of the patriot elite fought only to change English colonial policy, the people of the cities also struggled for internal reforms and raised notions of how an independent American society might be reorganized.

Patriot Women

Women also played a vital role in the relentless movement toward revolution, and they drew upon

Technology Changes the American People

SMALLPOX INOCULATION

✦

When thinking about the dangers early settlers in North America faced, Indian attacks and war with the French and Spanish capture the popular imagination. But the greatest threat by far was disease. Recurring epidemics swept through the colonies decade after decade. They ravaged the budding urban centers especially, where dense settlement made communicable diseases much more lethal than in rural areas, where people settled thinly.

The greatest killer of all was smallpox. In Boston alone, it struck with fury four times between 1640 and 1690 and four times again in 1702, 1721, 1730, and 1751. For half the population to contract smallpox and for half of those to die of it was not unusual. Smallpox claimed 848 Bostonians in 1721 (equivalent to 240,000 dying in Chicago today in a single year) and 569 in 1751.

For more than a century after settling Massachusetts in 1630 most Puritans thought of smallpox and other ravaging diseases such as influenza, diphtheria, and scarlet fever as visitations from an omnipotent and angry God. In view of this, prayer and fasting days were the Puritans' main defense against infection. Less religious persons, who thought contagion originated in a corruption of the air, believed that the chance of escaping a horrid disease, once an outbreak was discovered, depended on retreating from the city to the countryside.

In trying to combat disease, the colonists relied on medical knowledge imported from Europe and other places because the colonies had no schools of medicine or research capabilities. In Boston, the smallpox center of North America, such an attempt to use imported medical knowledge led to the first important experiment in America to use preventative medicine. Borrowing from experiments on "buying" the disease—introducing a mild case of smallpox that would give immunity to the patient—several doctors and ministers in Boston began to inoculate family members and friends in 1721. Learning of the success in greatly limiting the lethal character of smallpox in Turkey and Greece, Boston doctors also heard from the slave of Puritan minister Cotton Mather that he had been inoculated in Africa, where introducing the virus by placing pus from an infected patient under the skin of a healthy person had warded off lethal cases of the disease.

Philadelphia Mortality Bill, 1793 (*The Library Company of Philadelphia*)

Several REASONS

Proving that Inoculating or Transplanting the *Small Pox*, is a Lawful Practice, and that it has been Blessed by GOD for the Saving of many a Life.

By *Increase Mather*, D. D.

Exod. XX. 13. *Thou shalt not kill.*
Gal. I. 10. *Do I seek to please Men? if I please Men, I should not be a Servant of* CHRIST.

It has been Questioned, Whether *Inoculating* the *Small Pox* be a Lawful Practice. I incline to the Affirmative, for these Reasons.

I. Because I have read, that in *Smyrna, Constantinople*, and other Places, Thousands of Lives have been saved by Inoculation, and not one of Thousands has miscarried by it. This is related by Wife & Learned Men who would not have imposed on the World a false Narrative. Which also has been published by the *Royal Society*; therefore a great Regard is due to it.

II. WE hear that several *Physicians* have Recommended the Practice hereof to His *Majesty*, as a Means to preserve the Lives of his Subjects, and that His Wife and Excellent *Majesty* King GEORGE, as also his Royal Highness the *Prince* have approved hereof, and that it is now coming into practice in the Nation. In one of the Publick Prints are these Words, " *Inoculating the Small Pox is a safe and " universally Useful Experiment.* Several Worthy Persons lately arrived from *England* inform us, that it is a successful Practice there: If Wife & Learned Men in *England*, declare their Approbation of this *Practice*, for us to declare our Disapprobation will not be for our Honour.

III. GOD has graciously owned the *Practice of Inoculation*, among us in *Boston*, where some Scores, yea above an hundred have been *Inoculated*, & not one miscarried; but they Bless GOD, for His discovering this Experiment to them. It has been objected, that one that was Inoculated, died, viz. Mrs. D———ll: but she had the *Small Pox*, in the common way before, & her Friends and nearest Relations declare that she received no hurt by Inoculation, but was by a fright put into Fits that caused her Death. It is then a wonderful Providence of GOD, that all that were Inoculated should have their Lives preserved; so that the Safety and Usefulness of this Experiment is confirmed to us by Ocular Demonstration: I confess I am afraid, that the Discouraging of this Practice, may cause many a Life to be lost, which for my own part, I should be loth to have any hand in, *because of the Sixth Commandment.*

IV. IT cannot be denied but that some Wife and Judicious Persons among us, approve of Inoculation, both *Magistrates and Ministers*; Among Ministers I am One, who have been a poor Preacher of the Gospel in *Boston* above Threescore Years, and am the most Aged, Weak and unworthy Minister now

in *New-England*. My Sentiments, and my Son's also, about this *Matter* are well known. Also we hear that the Reverend and Learned Mr. *Solomon Stoddard* of *Northampton* concurs with us; so doth the Reverend Mr. *Wise* of *Ipswich*, and many other younger Divines, not only in *Boston*, but in the Country, joyn with their Fathers. Furthermore, I have made some Enquiry, Whether there are many Persons of a Prophane Life and Conversation, that do Approve and Defend *Inoculation*, and I have been answered, that they know but of very few such. This is to me a weighty Consideration. But on the other hand, tho' there are some Worthy Persons, that are not clear about it; nevertheless, it cannot be denied, but that the known Children of the Wicked one, are generally fierce Enemies to Inoculation. It is a grave saying of Old *Seneca*, *Pessimi Argumentum Turba est.* For my part I should be ashamed to joyn with such Persons; *O my Soul come not thou into their Secret, unto their Assembly be not thou United.* I am far from reflecting upon all that are against *Inoculation.* I know there are very worthy Persons (with whom I desire to Live and Die) that are not clear in their Judgments for it, and they are greatly to be commended and honoured in that they will not act against a doubting Conscience; yet it may be some of them might change their minds, if they would advise with those who are best able to afford them Scripture Light in this as well as in other Cases of Conscience.
Novemb. 20. 1721.

That the Cause may have Two Witnesses, here are subjoyned the Sentiments of another, well known in our Churches, of which I declare my hearty Approbation.

Sentiments on the Small Pox Inoculated.

A most Successful, and Allowable Method of preventing Death, and many other grievous Miseries, by the Small Pox, is not only Lawful but a Duty, to be used by those who apprehend their Lives immediately endanger'd by the terrible Distemper.

But the Method of managing and governing the Small Pox in the way of Inoculation, is a most successful and allowable Method of preventing Death, and many other grievous Miseries by this dreadful Distemper. Therefore, 'tis not only Lawful, but also

Pamphlet by Increase Mather in the debate over inoculation, 1721 *(The University of Virginia Library, Special Collection)*

A furious religious and scientific debate erupted in Boston over inoculation in 1721. Some thought that introducing mild cases of smallpox would spread the disease even further. Others, believing that God sent epidemics to chasten sinful people, argued that it was blasphemous to challenge providence. Yet the public was won over slowly as experiments in Philadelphia and Charleston showed that the inoculated rarely died of the disease while the uninoculated died in alarming numbers. By 1763, when smallpox broke out in Boston again, almost all the nonimmune stepped forward to receive inoculation (with only 46 deaths among 4,977 inoculated). Free inoculation for the poor at public dispensaries in several cities on the eve of the American Revolution sharply arrested the disease. Smallpox was all but eliminated as a killer disease after 1798 when an English doctor discovered that vaccination with cowpox gave almost foolproof immunity to the disease.

In conquering smallpox, Americans were only beginning to use science to win the war for public health. Repeated outbreaks of yellow fever, traveling from Africa to the West Indies to North America, caused terror in Philadelphia, New York, and other cities in the 1790s. The ghastly death tolls, reaching 5,000 in Philadelphia in 1793 and some 4,000 in New York in 1799, represented biological holocausts never experienced since. Almost all cities established boards of health in the early nineteenth century to improve sanitation, contain epidemic diseases, and urge vaccination against them when medical knowledge brought about effective procedures. But this did not prevent cholera epidemics that swept through American cities like a hurricane from the 1830s to the 1860s or stop a vicious wave of influenza in 1918 that moved like an avenging angel through military camps and civilian populations alike (killing ten times as many Americans as in World War I). As late as the 1940s, several million Americans were struck down or paralyzed by polio.

Before the twentieth century, few American families escaped untimely death through epidemic disease. As in the colonial period, terrifying epidemic diseases disrupted and disfigured family life and often brought local economies to their knees. Americans relied primarily on imported medical knowledge to combat epidemic diseases for a long time, but gradually after World War I, university schools of medicine, pharmaceutical company laboratories, and the National Institutes of Health (founded in 1930) put the United States in the forefront of disease control and research medicine.

How has religion remained a factor in medical intervention? What explains American preeminence in medical research after World War II?

Reading: Charles E. Rosenberg, *Explaining Epidemics and Other Studies in the History of Medicine* (Cambridge, Eng., 1992); J. H. Powell, *Bring Out Your Dead: The Great Plague of Yellow Fever in Philadelphia in 1793* (Philadelphia, 1949).

revolutionary arguments to define their own goals. They signed nonimportation agreements, harassed noncomplying merchants, and helped organize "fast days," on which communities prayed for deliverance from English oppression. But the women's most important role was to facilitate the boycott of English goods. The success of the nonconsumption pacts depended on substituting homespun cloth for English textiles on which colonists of all classes had always relied. From Georgia to Maine, women and children began spinning yarn and weaving cloth. "Was not every fireside, indeed a theatre of politics?" John Adams remembered after the war. Towns often vied patriotically in the manufacture of cotton, linen, and woolen cloth, the women staging open-air spinning contests to publicize their commitment. In 1769, the women of tiny Middletown, Massachusetts, set the standard by weaving 20,522 yards of cloth, about 160 yards each.

After the Tea Act in 1773, the interjection of politics into the household economy increased as patriotic women boycotted their favorite drink. Newspapers

As marketgoers and consumers, urban women played a crucial role in applying economic pressure on England during the prerevolutionary decade. This British cartoon, published in 1775, derisively depicts a group of North Carolina women signing an anti-tea agreement. A slave woman looks on while a bewigged Whig focuses on something other than tea. (*Library of Congress*)

carried recipes for tea substitutes and recommendations for herbal teas. In Wilmington, North Carolina, women paraded solemnly through the town and then made a ritual display of their patriotism by burning their imported tea. Many women agreed with one Rachel Wells: "I have done as much to carry on the war as many that set now at the helm of government."

Women's perception of their role was also changed by colonial protests and petitions against England's arbitrary uses of power. The more male leaders talked about England's intentions to "enslave" the Americans and England's callous treatment of its colonial "subjects," the more American women began to rethink their own domestic situations. The language of protest against England reminded many American women that they too were badly treated "subjects" of their husbands, who often dealt with them cruelly and exercised power over them arbitrarily. If there was to be independence, new laws must be passed, Abigail Adams reminded her husband John in March 1776. As they did their work, the male lawmakers should think about the rights of women and their enslavement by men. Choosing words and phrases that had been used over and over in the protests against England, she wrote: "Do not put such unlimited power into the hand of the husbands. . . . Put it out of the power of the vicious and the lawless to use us with cruelty and indignity," she insisted. "Remember, all men would be tyrants if they could." Borrowing directly from the republican ideology used to protest Parliament's attempts to tax the Americans, Abigail Adams warned that American women "will not hold ourselves bound by any laws in which we have no voice, or representation" and even promised that women would "foment a rebellion" if men did not heed their rightful claims.

Many American women, still bound by the social conventions of the day, were not ready to occupy such new territory. But the protests against England had stirred up new thoughts about what seemed "arbitrary" or "despotic" in their own society. Hence, many agendas for change appeared and with them a new feeling that what had been endured in the past was no longer acceptable. "We have it in our power," warned Abigail Adams to her husband, "not only to free ourselves but to subdue our masters, and without violence throw both your natural and legal authority at our feet."

Protesting Farmers

In most of the agricultural areas of the colonies, where many settlers made their livelihoods, passions over English policies awakened only slowly. After about 1740, farmers had benefited from a sharp rise in the demand for foodstuffs in England, southern Europe, and the West Indies. Rising prices and brisk markets brought a higher standard of living to thousands of rural colonists, especially south of New England. Living far from harping English customs officers, impressment gangs, and occupying armies, the colonists of the interior had to be drawn gradually into the resistance movement by their urban cousins. Even in Concord, Massachusetts, only a dozen miles from the center of colonial agitation, townspeople found little to protest in English policies until England closed the port of Boston in 1774. They concerned them-selves with local issues—roads, schools, the location of churches—but rarely with the frightful offenses to American liberty that Bostonians perceived.

Yet some parts of rural America seethed with social tension in the prewar era. The dynamics of conflict, shaped by the social development of particular regions, eventually became part of the momentum for revolution. In three western counties of North Carolina and in the Hudson River valley of New York, for example, widespread civil disorder marked the prerevolutionary decades. The militant rhetoric and tactics small farmers used to combat exploitation formed rivulets that fed the mainstream of revolu-tionary consciousness.

For years, the small farmers of western North Carolina had suffered exploitation by corrupt county court officials appointed by the governor and a legis-lature dominated by eastern planter interests. Sheriffs and justices, allied with land speculators and lawyers, seized property when farmers could not pay their taxes and sold it, often at a fraction of its worth, to their cronies. The legislature rejected western peti-tions for lower taxes, paper currency, and lower court fees. In the mid-1760s, frustrated at getting no satis-faction from legal forms of protest, the farmers formed associations of so-called Regulators that forcibly closed the courts, attacked the property of their enemies, and whipped and publicly humiliated judges and lawyers. When their leaders were arrested, the Regulators stormed the jails and released them.

In 1768 and again in 1771, Governor William Tryon led troops against the Regulators. Bloodshed was avert-ed on the first occasion, but on the second, at the Battle of Alamance, two armies of more than 1,000 opened fire on each other. Nine men died on each side before the Regulators fled the field. Seven leaders were exe-cuted in the ensuing trials. Though the Regulators lost on the field of battle, their protests became part of the larger revolutionary struggle. They railed against the self-interested behavior of a wealthy elite and asserted the necessity for people of humble rank to throw off deference and assume political responsibilities.

Rural insurgency in New York flared up in the 1750s, subsided, and then erupted again in 1766. The

Timeline

1696	Parliament establishes Board of Trade
1701	Iroquois set policy of neutrality
1702–1713	Queen Anne's War
1713	Peace of Utrecht
1733	Molasses Act
1744–1748	King George's War
1754	Albany conference
1755	Braddock defeated by French and Indian allies
1756–1763	Seven Years' War
1759	Wolfe defeats the French at Quebec
1759–1761	Cherokee War against the English
1760s	Economic slump
1763	Treaty of Paris ends Seven Years' War
	Proclamation line limits westward expansion
1764	Sugar and Currency acts
	Pontiac's Rebellion in Ohio valley
1765	Colonists resist Stamp Act
	Virginia House of Burgesses issues Stamp Act resolutions
1766	Declaratory Act
	Tenant rent war in New York
	Slave insurrections in South Carolina
1767	Townshend duties imposed
1768	British troops occupy Boston
1770	"Boston Massacre"
	Townshend duties repealed (except on tea)
1771	North Carolina Regulators defeated
1772	*Gaspee* incident in Rhode Island
1773	Tea Act provokes Boston Tea Party
1774	"Intolerable Acts"
	First Continental Congress meets
1775	Second Continental Congress meets
	Battles of Lexington and Concord
1776	Thomas Paine publishes *Common Sense*
	Declaration of Independence

conditions under which land was held precipitated the violence. The Hudson River valley had long been controlled by a few wealthy families with enormous landholdings, which they leased to small tenant farm-ers. The Van Rensselaer manor, for example, totaled a million acres, the Phillipses' manor nearly half as much. Hundreds of tenants with their families paid substantial annual rents for the right to farm on these lands, which had been acquired as virtually free gifts from royal governors. When tenants resisted rent increases or purchased land from Indians who swore that manor lords had extended the boundaries of their manors by fraud, the landlords began evicting them.

As the wealthiest men of the region, the landlords had the power of government, including control of the courts, on their side. Organizing themselves and going outside the law became the tenants' main strategy, as with the Carolina Regulators. By 1766, while New York City was absorbed in the Stamp Act furor, tenants led by William Prendergast began resisting sheriffs who tried to evict them from lands they claimed. The militant tenants threatened landlords with death and broke open jails to rescue their friends. British troops from New York were used to break the tenant rebellion. Prendergast was tried and sentenced to be hanged, beheaded, and quartered. Although he was pardoned, the bitterness of the Hudson River tenants endured through the Revolution. Most of them, unlike the Carolina Regulators, fought for the British because their landlords had joined the patriot cause

Conclusion

Forging a Revolution

The colonial Americans who lived in the third quarter of the eighteenth century participated in an era of political tension and conflict that changed the lives of nearly all of them. The Seven Years' War removed French and Spanish challengers and nurtured the colonists' sense of separate identity. Yet it left them with difficult economic adjustments, heavy debts, and growing social divisions. The colonists heralded the Treaty of Paris in 1763 as the dawning of a new era, but it led to a reorganization of England's triumphant yet debt-torn empire that had profound repercussions in America.

In the prerevolutionary decade, as England and the colonies moved from crisis to crisis, a dual disillusionment penetrated ever deeper into the colonial consciousness. Pervasive doubt arose concerning both the colonies' role, as assigned by England, in the economic life of the empire and the sensitivity of the government in London to the colonists' needs. At the same time, the colonists began to perceive British policies—instituted by Parliament, the king, and his advisors—as a systematic attack on the fundamental liberties and natural rights of British citizens in America.

The fluidity and diversity of colonial society and the differing experiences of Americans during and after the Seven Years' War evoked varying responses to the disruption that accompanied the English reorganization of the empire. In the course of resisting English policy, many previously inactive groups entered public life to challenge gentry control of political affairs. Often occupying the most radical ground in the opposition to England, they simultaneously challenged the growing concentration of economic and political power in their own communities.

When the Congress turned the 15-month undeclared war into a formally declared struggle for national liberation in July 1776, it steered its compatriots onto turbulent and unknown seas. Writing to his wife Abigail from his Philadelphia boardinghouse, the secularized Puritan John Adams caught some of the peculiar blend of excitement and dread that thousands shared. "You will think me transported with enthusiasm but I am not. I am well aware of the toil and blood and treasure that it will cost us to maintain this Declaration, and support and defend these States. Yet through all the gloom I can see the rays of ravishing light and glory. I can see that the end is more than worth all the means. And that posterity will triumph in that day's transactions, even though we should rue it, which I trust in God we shall not."

Recommended Reading

The Climactic Seven Years' War

Fred Anderson, *A People's Army: Massachusetts Soldiers and Society in the Seven Years' War* (1984); Gregory Dowd, *A Spirited Resistance: The North American Indian Struggle for Unity, 1745–1815* (1992); Tom Hatley, *The Dividing Paths: Cherokees and South Carolinians through the Era of Revolution* (1993); Francis Jennings, *Empire of Fortune: Crowns, Colonies, and Tribes in the Seven Years' War in America* (1988); Howard H. Peckham, *Pontiac and the Indian Uprising* (1947); Fred Anderson, *Crucible of War: The Seven Years' War and the Fate of Empire in British North America, 1754–1766* (2000).

The Crisis with England

John Brewer, *Party Ideology and Popular Politics at the Accession of George III* (1976); Ian R. Christie, *Crisis of Empire: Great Britain and the American Colonies, 1754–1783* (1966); Michael Kammen, *Empire and Interest* (1970); John Shy, *Toward Lexington: The Role of the British Army in the Coming of the American Revolution* (1965); Peter D. G. Thomas, *Tea Party to Independence: The Third Phase of the American Revolution* (1991).

The Ideology of Revolutionary Republicanism

Bernard Bailyn, *The Ideological Origins of the American Revolution* (1967); Ruth Bloch, *Visionary Republic: Millennial Themes in American Thought, 1750–1800* (1985); Richard Bushman, *King and People in Provincial Massachusetts* (1985); Jay Fliegelman, *Prodigals and Pilgrims: The American Revolution Against Patriarchal Authority, 1750–1800* (1982); Nathan O. Hatch, *The Sacred Cause of Liberty: Republican Thought and the Millennium in Revolutionary New England* (1977); Pauline

Maier, *From Resistance to Revolution: Colonial Radicals and the Development of American Opposition to Britain, 1765–1776* (1972); Edmund S. Morgan, *Inventing the People: The Rise of Popular Sovereignty in England and America* (1988); Gary B. Nash, *The Urban Crucible: Social Change, Political Consciousness, and the Origins of the American Revolution* (1979); Alfred F. Young, *The Shoemaker and the Tea Party: Memory and the American Revolution* (1999).

The Turmoil of Revolutionary Society

Edward Countryman, *A People in Revolution* (1981); David Hackett Fischer, *Paul Revere's Ride* (1994); Eric Foner, *Tom Paine and Revolutionary America* (1976); Robert Gross, *The Minutemen and Their World* (1976); Dirk Hoerder, *Crowd Action in Revolutionary Massachusetts, 1765–1780* (1977); Linda K. Kerber, *Women of the Republic: Intellect and Ideology in Revolutionary America* (1980); Henry Mayer, *A Son of Thunder: Patrick Henry and the American Republic* (1991); Mary Beth Norton, *Liberty's Daughters: The Revolutionary Experience of American Women, 1750–1800* (1980); Steven Rosswurm, *Arms, Country, and Class: The Philadelphia Militia and the "Lower Sort" During the American Revolution* (1987); Alfred E. Young, ed., *The American Revolution: Essays in the History of American Radicalism* (1976).

Suggested Web Sites

http://www.lib.virginia.edu/exhibits/lewis_clark/home.html

Exploring the West from Monticello: An Exhibition of Maps and Navigational Instruments. Maps and charts reveal knowledge and conceptions about the known and the unknown. This site includes a number of eighteenth-century maps.

http://scarlett.libs.uga.edu/darchive/hargrett/maps/colamer.html

http://scarlett.libs.uga.edu/darchive/hargrett/maps/revamer.html

Georgia's Rare Map Collection. These two sites contain maps of Colonial and Revolutionary America.

http://digitalhistory.org

The French and Indian War. Digital History LTD provides extensive archives in this site not intended for an exclusively academic audience.

Fiction and Film

Americans have written novels about the American Revolution almost from the day the firing stopped. James Fenimore Cooper's *The Spy: A Tale of the Neutral Ground* (1822) is the best of the early ones. Historian Paul Leicester Ford's *Janice Meredith: A Story of the American Revolution* (1899) is absorbing a century after its publication. In the modern period, Kenneth Roberts's four novels on the Revolution have entertained American readers for two generations: *Arundel* (1933); *Oliver Wiswell* (1940); *Rabble in Arms* (1953); and *The Battle of Cowpens: The Great Morale-Builder* (1958). *Oliver Wiswell* is especially notable for its recreation of a Loyalist's view of the Revolution. *Mary Silliman's War* (Heritage Film and Citadel Film, 1993) shows the Revolution through the eyes of a Connecticut family where husband and wife must reconcile their differing views on the Patriots and Loyalists. The English film on George III, *The Madness of King George* (1994), brings alive the era of the American Revolution and turns the king into the deeply psychotic ruler that some at the time believed he was. *Liberty* (Middlemarch Films, 1997) is a docudrama produced for television that has many high moments but neglects the internal struggles within the Patriot ranks for reforming American society.

http://web.syr.edu/~laroux/

The French and Indian War. This site is about French soldiers who came to New France between 1755 and 1760 to fight in the French and Indian War.

http://www.dpipc.com/cdadesign/paine/home.html

Thomas Paine National Historical Association. This official site contains a large archive of Paine's works and information about the association.

http://www.ushistoryplace.com

A richly detailed on-line learning environment complete with interactive maps, timelines, history activities, primary source documents, and links to related American history sites.

A PEOPLE
in REVOLUTION

CHAPTER OUTLINE

Among the Americans wounded and captured at the Battle of Bunker Hill in the spring of 1775 was Lieutenant William Scott of Peterborough, New Hampshire. Asked by his captors how he had come to be a rebel, "Long Bill" Scott replied:

The case was this Sir! I lived in a Country Town; I was a Shoemaker, & got [my] living by my labor. When this rebellion came on, I saw some of my neighbors get into commission, who were no better than myself. . . . I was asked to enlist, as a private soldier. My ambition was too great for so low a rank. I offered to enlist upon having a lieutenant's commission, which was granted. I imagined my self now in a way of promotion. If I was killed in battle, there would be an end of me, but if my Captain was killed, I should rise in rank, & should still have a chance to rise higher. These Sir! were the only motives of my entering into the service. For as to the dispute between Great Britain & the colonies, I know nothing of it; neither am I capable of judging whether it is right or wrong.

Scott may have been trying to gain the sympathy of his captors, but people fought in America's Revolutionary War for a variety of reasons—fear and ambition as well as principle among them. We have no way of knowing whether Long Bill Scott's motives were typical. Certainly many Americans knew more than he about the colonies' struggle with England, but many did not.

In the spring of 1775, the Revolutionary War had just begun. So had Long Bill's adventures. When the British evacuated Boston a year later, Scott was transported to Halifax, Nova Scotia. After several months' captivity, he managed to escape and make his way home to fight once more. He was recaptured in November 1776 near New York City, when its garrison fell to a surprise British assault. Again Scott escaped, this time by swimming the Hudson River at night with his sword tied around his neck and his watch pinned to his hat.

William Mercer, *Battle of Princeton*, c. 1786–1790. Because infantry weapons were inaccurate at long distances, lines formed in close proximity, where weapons were more deadly and combat was intensely personal. Here, General Washington directs the American force. (*Historical Society of Pennsylvania*)

During the winter of 1777, he returned to New Hampshire to recruit his own militia company. It included two of his eldest sons. In the fall, his unit helped defeat Burgoyne's army near Saratoga, New York, and later took part in the fighting around Newport, Rhode Island. When his light infantry company was ordered to Virginia in early 1778, Scott's health broke, and he was permitted to resign from the army. After only a few months' recuperation, however, he was at it again. During the last year of the war, he served as a volunteer on a navy frigate.

For seven years, the war held Scott in its harsh grasp. Scott's oldest son died of camp fever after six years of service. In 1777, Long Bill sold his New Hampshire farm to meet family expenses. He lost a second farm in Massachusetts shortly afterward. After his wife died, he turned their youngest children over to relatives and set off to beg a pension or job from the government.

Long Bill's saga was still not complete. In 1792, he rescued eight people when their boat capsized in New York harbor. Three years later, General Benjamin Lincoln took Scott with him to the Ohio country, where they surveyed land that was opening for white settlement. At last he had a respectable job and even a small government pension as compensation for his nine wounds. But trouble would still not let him go. While surveying on the Black River near Sandusky, Scott and his colleagues contracted "lake fever." Though ill, he guided part of the group back to Fort Stanwix in New York, then returned for the others. It was his last heroic act. A few days after his second trip, on September 16, 1796, he died.

American independence and the Revolutionary War that accompanied it were not as hard on everyone as they were on Long Bill Scott, yet together they transformed the lives of countless Americans. The war lasted seven years, longer than any other of America's wars until Vietnam, nearly two centuries later. And unlike the nation's twentieth-century contests, it was fought on American soil, among the American people. It called men by the thousands from shops and fields, disrupted families, destroyed communities, spread diseases, and made a shambles of the economy.

Amid this struggle for independence, the American people also mounted a political revolution of profound importance. Politics and government were transformed in keeping with republican principles and the rapidly changing circumstances of public life. What did republican liberty entail? How should government power be organized? Who should be considered republican citizens? How democratic could American society safely be? These were among the questions with which the American people wrestled at the nation's beginning.

As the tempo of political activity increased under the pressures of war and revolution, people clashed repeatedly over new state constitutions and the shape of a national government. Seldom has America's political agenda been more troubled.

The American Revolution dominated the lives of all who lived through it. But it had different consequences for men than for women, for black slaves than for their white masters, for Native Americans than for frontier settlers, for overseas merchants than for urban workers, for northern businessmen than for southern planters. Our understanding of the experience out of which the American nation emerged must begin with the Revolutionary War, for liberty came at a high cost.

THE WAR FOR AMERICAN INDEPENDENCE

The war began in Massachusetts in 1775, but within a year its focus shifted to the middle states. After 1779, the South became the primary theater. Why did this geographic pattern develop, what was its significance, and why did the Americans win?

The War in the North

For a brief time following Lexington and Concord, British officials thought of launching forays out from Boston into the surrounding countryside. They soon reconsidered, however, for the growing size of the continental army and the absence of significant Loyalist strength in the New England region urged caution. Even more important, Boston became untenable after the Americans placed artillery on the strategic Dorchester Heights. On March 7, 1776, the British commander, General William Howe, decided to evacuate.

People worried that Howe would set fire to the city as he departed. Fearing retaliation against Loyalist property and wishing not to destroy any lingering hopes of reconciliation, Howe spared the city from the torch. The town, however, had been treated badly enough. British officers had taken over the homes of John Hancock, James Bowdoin, and others, while dragoons had used the Old South Meeting House as a riding school, after tearing out the pews, and the Old North Church had been demolished for firewood. All around lay trampled gardens, uprooted trees, and filth. "Almost everything here, appears Gloomy and Melancholy," lamented one returning resident.

For a half dozen years after Boston's evacuation, British ships prowled the New England coast, confiscating supplies and attacking coastal towns. Yet away from the coast, there was little fighting. Most New Englanders had reason to be thankful for their good fortune.

After evacuating Boston, British officials established their military headquarters in New York City. Their decision was strategically sound, for New York offered important strategic advantages. It was centrally located, and its spacious harbor lay at the mouth of the Hudson River, the major water route northward into the interior. Control of New York would, in addition, ensure access to the abundant grain and livestock of the Middle Atlantic states. Finally, Loyalist sentiment ran deep among the inhabitants of the city and its environs.

In the summer of 1776, Washington moved his troops south from Boston, determined to challenge the British for control of New York City. It proved a terrible mistake. Outmaneuvered and badly outnumbered, he suffered defeat at the Battle of Long Island and then in Manhattan itself. By late October, the city was firmly in British hands. It would remain so until the war's end.

In the fall of 1776, King George III instructed his two chief commanders in North America—General Howe and his brother, Admiral Richard Howe—to make a final effort at reconciliation with the colonists. They carried authority to pardon all Americans who acknowledged allegiance to the king and to negotiate with any colony that dissolved its revolutionary committees. In early September, the Howes met with three delegates from the Congress on Staten Island, in New York harbor. The outcome was not long in doubt, for when the Howes demanded revocation of the Declaration of Independence before negotiations could begin, all hope of reconciliation vanished.

For the next two years, the war swept back and forth across New Jersey and Pennsylvania. Reinforced by German mercenaries hired in Europe, the British moved virtually at will. Neither the state militias nor the continental army—weakened by losses, low morale, and inadequate supplies—offered serious opposition. At Trenton in December 1776 and again at Princeton the following month, Washington surprised the British and scored victories that prevented the

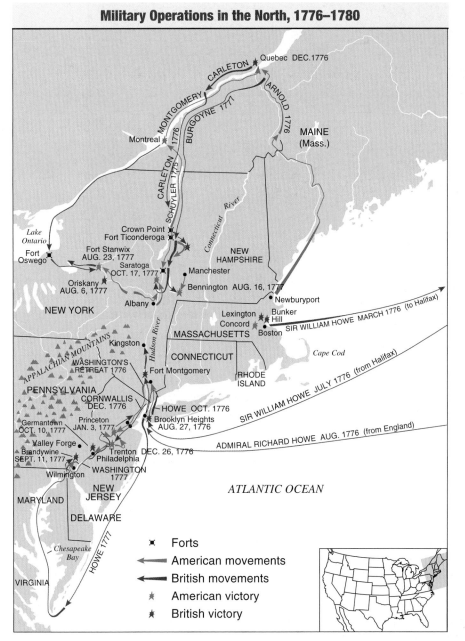

Military Operations in the North, 1776–1780

During the early years of the war, fighting was most intense in upper New York and the mid-Atlantic states. Note the importance of water routes to military strategies.

Americans' collapse. For the rebels, however, survival remained the primary goal.

American efforts during the first year of the war to invade Canada and bring that British colony into the rebellion also fared badly. In November 1775, American forces under General Richard Montgomery had taken Montreal. But the subsequent assault against Quebec ended with almost 100 Americans killed or wounded and more than 300 taken prisoner. The American cause could not survive many such losses.

Washington had learned the painful lesson at New York that his troops were no match for the British in frontal combat. He realized, moreover, that if the con-

tinental army was defeated, American independence would certainly be lost. Thus, he decided on a strategy of harassing the British, making the war as costly for them as possible, and protecting the civilian population as best he could while avoiding major battles. He would follow that strategy for the rest of the war.

As a consequence, the war's middle years turned into a deadly chase that neither side proved able to win. In September 1777, the British took Philadelphia, sending the Congress fleeing into the countryside, but then hesitated to press their advantage. On numerous occasions British commanders failed to act decisively, either reluctant to move through the hostile countryside or uncertain of their instructions. Offsetting

This watercolor painting offers a humorous, even mocking, depiction of the variety of uniforms worn by American troops. *(Anne S. K. Brown Military Collection, Brown University)*

British domination of the Middle Atlantic region was the American victory in October at Saratoga, New York, where General Burgoyne surrendered with 5,700 British soldiers. That victory prompted France to join the struggle against England.

Congress and the Articles of Confederation

As the war erupted, the Continental Congress turned to the task of creating a more permanent and effective national government. It was a daunting assignment, for prior to independence the colonies had quarreled repeatedly over colonial boundaries, control of the Indian trade, and commercial advantage within the empire. The crisis with England had forced them together, and the Congress was the initial embodiment of that tenuous union. The first Continental Congress had met for only seven weeks, limiting itself to protesting English policies and urging support for the Continental Association.

The Second Continental Congress, convening in May 1775, in the midst of the war crisis, began to exercise some of the most basic responsibilities of a sovereign government: raising an army and establishing diplomatic relations. Its powers, though, were unclear; its legitimacy, uncertain. As long as hopes of reconciliation with England lingered, these limitations posed no serious problems. But as independence and the prospects of an extended war loomed, pressure to establish a more durable central government increased. On June 20, 1776, shortly before independence was declared, Congress appointed a committee, chaired by John Dickinson of Pennsylvania, to draw up a plan of perpetual union. So urgent was the crisis that the committee responded in a month's time, and debate on its proposed Articles of Confederation quickly began.

The delegates promptly clashed over whether to form a strong, consolidated government or a loosely joined confederation of sovereign states. Those differences sharpened as the discussion proceeded. The Dickinson draft outlined a government of considerable power. Although each state was to retain "the . . . exclusive regulation . . . of its internal police," that was to be only in matters that did not interfere with the Articles of Confederation. The only unqualified restriction on the Congress was that it might never impose taxes or duties except in managing the post office. Dickinson's proposals met determined opposition. Experience with the "tyrannous" actions of the English king and Parliament had revealed how dangerous central governments, unmindful of the people's liberties, could be. Expressing fears widely held among congressional delegates, North Carolina's Thomas Burke warned that one oppressive government should not be substituted for another and insisted that Congress be subordinate to the states.

As finally approved, the Articles of Confederation represented a compromise. Article 9 gave the Congress sole authority to regulate foreign affairs, declare war, mediate boundary disputes between the states, manage the post office, and administer relations with Indians living outside state boundaries. The Articles also stipulated that the inhabitants of each state were to enjoy the "privileges and immunities" of the citizens of every other state. Embedded in that clause was the basis for national, as distinguished from state, citizenship.

At the same time, the Articles sharply limited what the Congress could do and reserved broad governing powers to the states. For example, the Congress could neither raise troops nor levy taxes but only ask the states for such support. Article 2 stipulated that each state was to "retain its sovereignty, freedom and independence," as well as "every power, jurisdiction, and right which is not by this confederation expressly delegated to the United States in Congress assembled." Nor could the Congress's limited powers be easily expanded, because the Articles could be amended only by the agreement of all 13 states.

Though the Congress sent the Articles to the states for approval in November 1777, they were not ratified until March 1781. For one thing, ratification required unanimous approval, and that was hard to obtain. The biggest impediment was a bitter dispute over control of the lands west of the Appalachian Mountains that pitted states such as Virginia, South Carolina, and New York, which had western claims tracing back to their colonial charters, against states such as Maryland and New Jersey, which had no such claims. In December 1778, the Maryland assembly announced that it would not ratify until all the western lands had been ceded to the Congress. For several years, ratification hung in the balance while politicians and land speculators jockeyed for advantage. In 1780 New York and Virginia finally agreed to transfer their western lands to the Congress. Those decisions paved the way for Maryland's ratification in early 1781. Approval of the Articles was now assured.

Meanwhile, Congress managed the war effort as best it could, using the unratified Articles as a guide. Events quickly proved its inadequacy, because Congress could do little more than pass resolutions and implore the states for support. If they refused, as they frequently did, the Congress could only protest and urge cooperation. Its ability to function was further limited by the stipulation that each state's delegation cast but one vote. On a number of occasions, disagreements within state delegations prevented them from voting at all. That could paralyze the Congress,

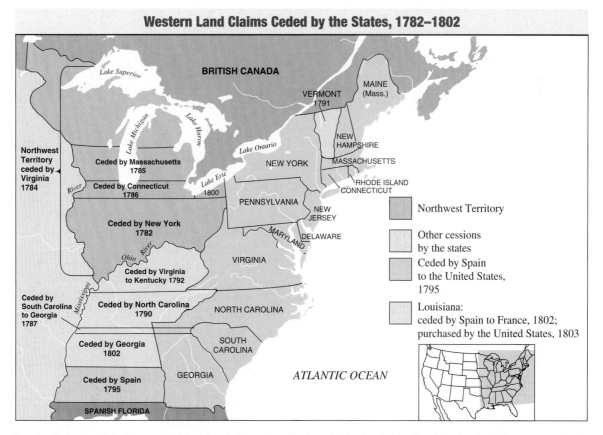

Western Land Claims Ceded by the States, 1782–1802

Based on their colonial charters, seven of the original states claimed land west of the Appalachian Mountains. Eventually those states ceded their western claims to the Congress, making ratification of the Articles of Confederation and the creation of new western states possible.

because most important decisions required a nine-state majority.

As the war dragged on, Washington repeatedly criticized the Congress for its failure to support the army. Acknowledging its own ineffectiveness, the Congress in 1778 temporarily granted Washington extraordinary powers and asked him to manage the war on his own. In the end, the Congress survived because enough of its members realized that disaster would follow its collapse.

The War Moves South

As the war in the North bogged down in a costly stalemate, British officials adopted an alternative strategy: invasion and pacification of the South. Royal officials in the South encouraged the idea with reports that thousands of Loyalists would rally to the British standard. The southern coastline with its numerous rivers, moreover, offered maximum advantage to British naval strength. Then there were the slaves, that vast but imponderable presence in southern society. If they could be lured to the British side, the balance might tip in Britain's favor. In any case, the threat of slave rebellion would weaken white southerners' will to resist. Persuaded by these arguments, British policymakers made the southern states the primary theater of military operations during the final years of the war.

Georgia—small, isolated, and largely defenseless—was the initial target. In December 1778, Savannah, the state's major port, fell before a seaborne attack of 3,500 men. For nearly two years, the Revolution in the state virtually ceased. Encouraged by their success, the British turned to the Carolinas, with equally impressive results. On May 12, 1780, Charleston surrendered after a month's siege. At a cost of only 225 casualties, the British captured the entire 5,400-man American garrison. It was the costliest American defeat of the war.

Military Operations in the South, 1778–1781

The war in the South was fought both along the coast and in the interior.

After securing Charleston, the British quickly extended their control north and south along the coast. At Camden, South Carolina, the British commander Cornwallis, aided by a corps of mounted dragoons, killed nearly 1,000 Americans and captured 1,000 more, temporarily destroying the southern continental army. With scarcely a pause, the British pushed on into North Carolina. There, however, British officers quickly learned the difficulty of extending their lines into the interior: distances were too large, problems of supply too great, the reliability of Loyalist troops too uncertain, and support among the people for the revolutionary cause too strong.

In October 1780, Washington sent Nathanael Greene south to lead the continental forces. It was a fortunate choice, for Greene knew the region and the kind of war that had to be fought. Determined, like Washington, to avoid large-scale encounters, Greene divided his army into small, mobile bands. Employing what today would be called guerrilla tactics, he harassed the British and their Loyalist allies at every opportunity, striking by surprise and then disappearing into the interior. Nowhere was the war more fiercely contested than through the Georgia and Carolina countryside. Neither British nor American authorities could restrain the violence. Bands of private marauders, roving the land and seizing advantage from the war's confusion, compounded the chaos.

In time, the tide began to turn. At Cowpens, South Carolina, in January 1781, American troops under General Daniel Morgan won a decisive victory, suffering fewer than 75 casualties to 329 British deaths, and taking 600 men prisoner. In March, at Guilford Court House in North Carolina, Cornwallis won, but at a cost that forced his retreat to Wilmington, near the sea.

In April 1781, convinced that British authority could not be restored in the Carolinas while the rebels continued to use Virginia as a supply and staging area, Cornwallis moved north. With a force of 7,500, he raided deep into Virginia, sending Governor Jefferson and the Virginia legislature fleeing from Charlottesville into the mountains. But again Cornwallis found the costs of victory high, and again he turned toward the coast for protection and resupply. On August 1, he reached Yorktown.

Cornwallis's position was secure as long as the British fleet controlled the waters of Chesapeake Bay. That advantage, however, did not last long. In 1778, the French government, still smarting from its defeat by England in the Seven Years' War and buoyed by the American victory at Saratoga in 1777, had signed an alliance with the American Congress, promising to send its naval forces into the war. Initially, the French concentrated their fleet in the West Indies, where they hoped to seize some of the British sugar islands. After repeated American urging, however, the French finally sailed north, and on August 30, 1781, the French admiral, Comte de Grasse, arrived off Yorktown. Reinforced by a second French squadron from the North, de Grasse established naval superiority in the region.

As Washington had foreseen, French entry turned the tide of war. Cut off from the sea and pinned down on a peninsula between the York and James Rivers by 17,000 French and American troops, Cornwallis's fate was sealed. On October 19, 1781, near the Virginia hamlet of Yorktown, he surrendered to General Washington. While a military band played "The World Turned Upside Down" and hundreds of civilians looked on, nearly 7,000 British troops laid down their arms.

Learning the news of Yorktown in London a month later, Lord North, the king's chief minister, exclaimed, "Oh, God! It is all over." On February 27, 1782, the House of Commons cut off further support of the war. The next month, Lord North resigned. In Philadelphia,

At Yorktown, Cornwallis asserted he was ill and sent a subordinate, Brigadier General Charles O'Hara, to yield the symbolic sword of surrender. (*Library of Congress*)

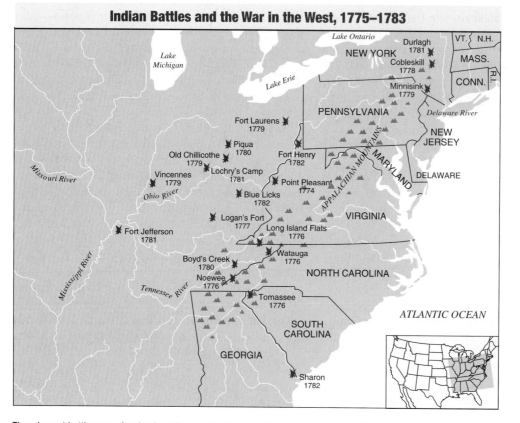

Indian Battles and the War in the West, 1775–1783

Though most battles were fought along the coastal plain, the British and their Indian allies opened a second front far to the west.

citizens poured into the streets to celebrate while the Congress assembled for a solemn ceremony of thanksgiving. Though the preliminary articles of peace were not signed until November 1782, everyone knew after Yorktown that the Americans had won their independence.

Native Americans in the Revolution

The Revolutionary War involved countless Native Americans as well as colonists and Englishmen. It could hardly have been otherwise, for the lives of all three peoples had been intertwined since the first English settlements more than a century and a half before.

Though small tribes still struggled to maintain their identities along the eastern seaboard and though Indians still roamed the streets of America's port cities, the coastal tribes—their villages displaced by white settlement and their numbers thinned by warfare and disease—no longer challenged white hegemony. Powerful tribes, however, still dominated the vast interior region between the Appalachian Mountains and the Mississippi River. The Iroquois Six Nations, a confederation numbering 15,000 people, controlled a huge area stretching westward from Albany, New York, and dominated the "western tribes" of the Ohio valley—the Shawnee, Delaware, Wyandotte, and Miami. In the Southeast, five tribes—the Choctaw, Chickasaw, Seminole, Creek, and Cherokee, 60,000 people in all—dominated the interior.

Though England's victory over France in the Seven Years' War had ended the Indians' "play-off game" and made them solely dependent on their Anglo-American trading partners, the interior tribes still retained their distinctive ways of life. Far outnumbering the few white settlers that had pushed across the Appalachians, they were more than a match, militarily and diplomatically, for the Anglo-Americans. As the imperial crisis between England and its colonies deepened, Native and European Americans eyed each other warily across this vast "middle ground."

When the Revolutionary War began, British and American officials urged neutrality on the Indians. The British, expecting the conflict to be short, wished to disrupt the interior as little as possible, while the Americans worried about Indian attacks from the west when confronting British power along the coast. The Native Americans, however, were too important militarily to ignore for long. By the spring of 1776, both sides were actively seeking Indian alliances.

Recognizing their immense stake in the imperial conflict, Native Americans up and down the interior debated their options. Alarmed by encroaching white settlement and eager to take advantage of the colonists' troubles with England, a band of Cherokee, led by the warrior Dragging Canoe, launched a series of raids in July 1776 in what is today eastern Tennessee. In a devastating response, the Virginia and Carolina militias laid waste a group of Cherokee towns. Thomas Jefferson expressed satisfaction at the outcome. "I hope that the Cherokees will now be driven beyond the Mississippi," he wrote. "Our contest with Britain is too serious, and too great to permit any possibility of [danger] . . . from the Indians." Though the Cherokee raided sporadically throughout the war, they never again mounted a sustained military effort against the rebels. Seeing what had befallen their neighbors, the Creek stayed aloof. Their time for resistance would come in the early nineteenth century, when white settlers began to push onto their lands.

In the Ohio country, the struggle lasted longer. For several decades before the Revolution, explorers such as Daniel Boone had contested with the Shawnee and others for control of the region bordering the Ohio River. The Revolutionary War intensified these conflicts. In February 1778, George Rogers Clark led a ragtag band of Kentuckians through icy rivers and across 180 miles of forbidding terrain to attack a British outpost at Vincennes, in present-day Indiana. Though outnumbered nearly four to one by the 500 British regulars and their Indian allies, Clark fooled the fort's defenders into believing that his force was much larger, and the British commander surrendered without a shot. Though skirmishes between Indians and marauding American forces continued for several years, Clark's victory tipped the balance in the war's western theater.

The Devastation of the Iroquois

To the northeast, a similar but even more deadly scenario unfolded. At a council in Albany, New York, in August 1775, representatives of the Iroquois Six Nations listened while American commissioners urged them to remain at home and keep the hatchet buried deep. "The determination of the Six Nations," replied Little Abraham, a Mohawk leader, "[is] not to take any part; but as it is a family affair, to sit still and see you fight it out." Iroquois neutrality, however, did not last long.

As the war spread throughout the Northeast in 1776, U.S. troops raided deep into Mohawk territory west of Albany. Alarmed, the British argued with words, rum, and trade goods that the Iroquois should join them against the rebels. At the Oswego Council in the summer of 1777, most of the Iroquois abandoned neutrality and took up arms against the Americans. They did so at the urging of Joseph Brant, a Mohawk warrior who had visited England several years before and argued England's value as an ally against American expansion.

It was a fateful decision for Indians and whites alike. Over the next several years, the Iroquois and their British allies devastated large areas in central New York and Pennsylvania, destroying property and terrorizing the inhabitants. An officer of the Pennsylvania militia reported somberly, "Our country is on the eve of breaking up. There is nothing to be seen but disolation, fire & smoak."

The Americans' revenge came swiftly. During the summer of 1779, General John Sullivan led a series of punishing raids into the Iroquois country, burning villages; killing men, women, and children; and destroying fields of corn. His motto for the campaign was blunt: "Civilization or death to all American savages." By war's end, the Iroquois had lost as many as a third of their people as well as countless towns. Their domination of the northeastern interior was permanently shattered.

Not all the Eastern Woodland tribes sided with England in the Revolutionary War. The Oneida and the Tuscarora, members of the Iroquois confederation, fought with the Americans, their decision driven by intertribal politics and effective diplomacy by emissaries of the Continental Congress. In New England, the Stockbridge, a small tribe surrounded by a sea of white settlement, contributed warriors and scouts, while farther to the south the Catawba, similarly dependent on the Americans for trade and diplomacy, also signed on. The Indians who fought for American independence, however, reaped little benefit from their efforts. Though General Sullivan spared the Oneida and Tuscarora villages, the British and their Iroquois allies destroyed them in turn. And although a number of Indian warriors were compensated by grateful state governments once the war was over, tribes allied with the victorious American cause enjoyed no protection from the accelerating spread of white settlement.

Most Indians had good reason for opposing American independence, because England provided them with trade goods, arms, and markets for their furs. England, moreover, had promised protection against colonial expansion, as the Proclamation Line of 1763 had demonstrated. At the peace talks that ended the Revolutionary War, however, the British ignored their Indian allies. They received neither

Mohawk chief Joseph Brant (Thayendanegea) played a major role in the Iroquois's decision to enter the war on the side of Britain. (*The National Gallery of Canada, Ottawa*)

compensation for their losses nor guarantees of their land, for the boundary of the United States was set far to the west, at the Mississippi River.

Though the Indians' struggle against white expansion would continue, their own anticolonial war of liberation had failed. The American Revolution, declared a gathering of Indian chiefs to the Spanish governor at Saint Louis in 1784, had been "the greatest blow that could have been dealt us."

Negotiating Peace

In September 1781, formal peace negotiations began in Paris between the British commissioner, Richard Oswald, and the American emissaries, Benjamin Franklin, John Adams, and John Jay. The negotiations were complicated by the involvement in the war of several European countries seeking to weaken Great Britain. The Americans' main ally, France, had entered the war in February 1778. Eight months later, Spain declared war on England, though it declined to recognize American independence. Between 1780 and 1782, Russia, the Netherlands, and six other European countries joined in a League of Armed Neutrality aimed at protecting their maritime trade against British efforts to control it. America's Revolutionary War had quickly become internationalized. It could

hardly have been otherwise, given England's centrality to the European balance of power and the long-standing competition among European powers for colonial dominance in North America.

Dependent on French economic and military support, the Congress instructed the American commissioners to follow the advice of the French foreign minister, Charles Grannier de Vergennes. The American commissioners, however, soon learned that he was prepared to let the exhausting war continue in order to weaken England and tighten America's dependence on France. Even more alarming, Vergennes suggested that the new nation's western boundary should be set no farther west than the crest of the Appalachian Mountains and hinted that the British might retain areas they controlled at the war's end. That proposal threatened to leave New York City and other coastal enclaves in British hands.

In the end, the American commissioners ignored Congress's instructions and, without a word to Vergennes, arranged a provisional peace agreement with the British emissaries. It was fortunate that they did so, for the British were prepared to be generous. In the Treaty of Paris signed in September 1783, England recognized American independence and agreed to place the western boundary of the United States at the Mississippi River. Moreover, Britain promised that U.S. fishermen would have access to the waters off Newfoundland and that British forces would evacuate American territory "with all convenient speed" once hostilities had ended. In return, the Congress agreed to recommend that the states restore the civil rights and property of the Loyalists. Both sides agreed that prewar debts owed the citizens of one country by the citizens of the other would remain valid. Each of these issues would trouble Anglo-American relations in the years ahead, but for the moment it seemed a splendid outcome to a long and difficult struggle.

The Ingredients of Victory

How were the weak and disunited American states able to defeat Great Britain, the most powerful nation in the Atlantic world? Certainly Dutch and French loans, as well as French war supplies and military forces, were crucially important. More decisive, though, was the American people's determination not to submit. Often the Americans were disorganized and uncooperative. Repeatedly, it seemed that the war effort was about to collapse as continental troops drifted away, state militias refused to march, and military supplies failed to materialize. Neither the Congress nor the states proved capable of providing consistent direction to the struggle. Yet as the war progressed, the people's estrangement from England deepened and their commitment to the "glorious

John Jay, John Adams, and Benjamin Franklin (the three figures on the left in the unfinished painting by Benjamin West) meet with the British commissioners in Paris to negotiate preliminary conditions of peace in 1783. *(Benjamin West,* Commissioners of the Preliminary Peace Negotiations with Great Britain, *c. 1783/Courtesy, The Henry Francis du Pont Winterthur Museum)*

cause" grew stronger. To subdue the colonies, England would have had to occupy the entire eastern third of the continent, and that it could not do.

Even though state militias frequently refused to go beyond their own borders and, after the first months of the war, engaged in relatively few battles, they provided a vast reservoir of manpower capable of intimidating Loyalists, gathering intelligence, and harassing British forces that would otherwise have been free to engage the continental army. And though Washington frequently disparaged the militia's fighting qualities and complained that their independent maneuvers threatened to disrupt his own plans, he gradually learned to utilize their strengths in the war effort.

The American victory owed much as well to the administrative and organizational talents of Washington. Against massive odds, he held the continental army together, often by the sheer force of his will. Facing inadequate supplies, high rates of turnover among the troops, ineffective support from the Congress, and lack of cooperation from the states, he created a military force capable of winning selected encounters and, more important, of surviving over time. Had he failed, the Americans could not possibly have succeeded.

In the end, however, it is as accurate to say that Britain lost the war as that the United States won it. With vast economic and military resources, Britain enjoyed clear military superiority over the American states. Its troops were more numerous, better armed and supplied, and more professionally trained. Until the closing months of the contest, Britain enjoyed naval superiority as well. As a consequence, its forces moved up and down the coast virtually at will.

Britain, however, could not capitalize on its advantages. It had difficulty extending command structures and supply routes across several thousand miles of ocean. Because information flowed erratically across the water, strategic decisions made in London were often based on faulty or outdated intelligence. Given the difficulties of supply, British troops often had to live off the land, reducing their mobility and increasing the resentment of Americans whose crops and animals they commandeered.

Faced with these circumstances, British leaders were often overly cautious. Burgoyne's attempt in 1777 to isolate New England by invading from Canada failed because Sir William Howe decided to attack Philadelphia rather than move northward up the Hudson River to join him. Similarly, neither Howe nor Cornwallis pressed his advantage in the central states during the middle years of the war, when more aggressive action might have crushed the continental force.

Just as important, British commanders generally failed to adapt their battlefield tactics to the realities of the American war. They continued to fight in the

European style, during specified times of the year and using formal battlefield formations when the rough, wooded American terrain was better suited to the use of smaller units and irregular tactics.

Washington and Greene were more flexible, often employing a patient strategy of raiding, harassment, and strategic retreat. Behind this strategy lay a willingness, grounded in necessity, to allow England control of territory along the coast. But it was based as well on the conviction that popular support for the revolutionary cause would grow and that the costs of subduing the colonial rebellion would become greater than the British government could bear. As a much later American war, in Vietnam, would also reveal, a guerrilla force can win if it does not lose, while a regular army loses if it does not consistently win.

The American strategy proved sound. As the war dragged on and its costs escalated, Britain's will began to waver. After France and Spain entered the conflict, Britain had to worry about Europe and the Mediterranean as well as North America, while unrest in Ireland and food riots in London tied down additional English troops. As the cost in money and lives increased and prospects of victory dimmed, opposition to the war mounted. It was spearheaded by long-time critics of imperial policy such as Edmund Burke and given popular voice by the followers of John Wilkes and other English radicals who saw in America's rebellion the promise of political reform at home. With the defeat at Yorktown, support for the war collapsed. Britain's effort to hold onto its 13 North American colonies had failed.

⤳ THE EXPERIENCE OF WAR

In terms of loss of life and destruction of property, the Revolutionary War pales by comparison with America's more recent wars. Yet modern comparisons are misleading, for the War of American Independence proved terrifying to the people caught up in it.

Recruiting an Army

Estimates vary, but on the American side as many as 250,000 men may at one time or another have borne arms. That amounted to about one out of every two or three adult white males. Though a majority of recruits were native born, many who fought for American freedom came from the thousands of British and European immigrants who streamed into North America during the middle decades of the eighteenth century. Of the 27 men enrolled in Captain John Wendell's New York company, for example, over half had been born abroad, the majority in Ireland but others in Germany and the Netherlands as well.

And while the motives of these laborers and farmers, carpenters and coppersmiths were as various as those of native born soldiers, many had come to America seeking to better their lives and eagerly embraced the Revolution's democratic promise. They were the vanguard of a transatlantic political network that, over the final quarter of the eighteenth century, would tie the new American republic to English reformers and French radicals during what historians have called the age of democratic revolution.

As the war began, most state militias were not effective fighting forces. This was especially true in the South, where Nathanael Greene complained that the men came "from home with all the tender feelings of domestic life" and were not "sufficiently fortified . . . to stand the shocking scenes of war, to march over dead men, [or] to hear without concern the groans of the wounded." The militia did, however, serve as a convenient recruiting system, for men were already enrolled, and arrangements were in place for calling them into the field on short notice. This was of special importance before the continental army took shape. Given its grounding in local community life, the militia also legitimated the war among the people and secured their commitment to the revolutionary cause. What better way, as well, to separate Patriots from Loyalists than by mustering the local company and seeing who turned out?

During the early years of the war, when enthusiasm ran high, men of all ranks—from the rich and middle classes as well as the poor—volunteered to fight the British. But as the war went on, casualties increased, enlistment terms grew longer, and military discipline became stiffer, so the army filled with conscripts. Eventually, the war was transformed, as wars so often are, into a poor man's fight as wealthier men hired substitutes and communities filled their quotas with strangers lured by enlistment bonuses or dragooned by laws that subjected "vagrants" and men with "no family . . . or visible means of support" to impressment. Convicts, out-of-work laborers, free and unfree blacks, even occasional British deserters filled the continental army with an array of "Tag, Rag, and Bobtail" soldiers.

For the poor and the jobless, whose ranks the war rapidly swelled, military bonuses and the promise of board and keep proved attractive. But often the bonuses failed to materialize, and pay was long overdue. Moreover, life in the camps was harsh, and soldiers' families at home were frequently in distress. As the war dragged on, desertion rose as high as 25 percent, while Washington imposed harsher discipline in an effort to hold his troops in line.

Occasionally, frustration spilled over into open revolt. In 1779, Sergeant Samuel Glover and a group of

As this painting suggests, military recruiting was a community affair in the eighteenth century. What do you suppose the man with upraised arms is doing? What role might the women be playing in the recruitment process? *(William T. Ranney & Charles F. Blauvelt,* Recruiting for the Continental Army, *c. 1857–59, oil on canvas, 53¾ x 82¼ in, Munson-Williams-Proctor Institute, Museum of Art, Utica, New York, Gift of T. Proctor Eldred)*

soldiers from the North Carolina line, who had been unpaid for 15 months, refused to obey the commands of their superior officer "until they had justice done them." Glover was executed for insubordination. His widow later apologized to the North Carolina assembly for her husband's conduct but asked sorrowfully, "What must the feeling of the man be who . . . with poverty staring him full in the face, was denied his pay?" Soldiers, she protested, possessed the same affection for their families as those in command.

Throughout the war, soldiers suffered from shortages of supplies. At Valley Forge during the terrible winter of 1777–1778, men went without shoes or coats. In the midst of that winter's gloom, Washington wrote, "There are now in this army 4,000 men wanting blankets, near 2,000 of which have never had one, altho' some of them have been 12 months in service." "I am sick, discontented, and out of humour," declared one despairing soul. "Poor food, hard lodging, cold weather, fatigue, nasty cloathes, nasty cookery, vomit half my time, smoaked out of my senses. The Devil's in't, I can't Endure it. Why are we sent here to starve and freeze?"

The states possessed food and clothing enough but were often reluctant to strip their own people of wagons and livestock, blankets and shoes for use elsewhere. Moreover, mismanagement often stood in the way. Neither the state governments nor the Congress could effectively administer a war of such magnitude. Wagon transport was slow and costly, and the British fleet made water travel along the coast perilous. Though many individuals served honorably as supply officers, others took advantage of the army's distress.

Washington commented bitterly on the "speculators, various tribes of money makers, and stock-jobbers" whose "avarice and thirst for gain" threatened the country's ruin.

Swarms of camp followers further complicated army life. Wives and prostitutes, personal servants and slaves, con men and official sutlers swarmed around the continental army. While often providing essential services, they slowed its movement and threatened its discipline as well.

The Casualties of Combat

The death that soldiers dispensed to each other on the battlefield was intensely personal. Because the effective range of muskets was little more than 100 yards, soldiers came virtually face-to-face with the men they killed. According to eighteenth-century practice, armies formed on the battlefield in ranks and fired in unison. After massed volleys, the lines often closed for hand-to-hand combat with knives and bayonets. Such encounters were indelibly etched in the memory of individuals who survived them. Partisan warfare in the South, with its emphasis on ambush and cyclic patterns of revenge and counterrevenge, personalized combat even more. British officers expressed shock at the "implacable ardor" with which the Americans fought.

The Americans' ferocity is attributable to the fact that this was a civil war. Not only did Englishmen fight Americans, but American Loyalists and Patriots confronted each other as well. As many as 50,000 colonists fought for the king in some of the war's bitterest encounters. They figured importantly in Burgoyne's invasion from Canada and in the attacks on Savannah and Charleston. Benedict Arnold, the American traitor who was then fighting for the British, led a force of Loyalists on raids through the Connecticut and James River valleys, and Loyalist militia units joined Indian allies in destructive sweeps through central New York, Pennsylvania, and the backcountry of the Carolinas. The passion with which American Patriots fought derived as well from their belief that the very future of human liberty depended on their success. In such a historic crusade, nothing was to be spared that might bring victory.

Medical treatment, whether for wounds or the diseases that raged through military camps, frequently did little good and often did harm. Casualties poured into hospitals, overcrowding them beyond capacity. Dr. Jonathan Potts, the attending physician at Fort George in New York, reported that "we have at present upwards of one thousand sick crowded into sheds & labouring under the various and cruel disorders of dysentaries, bilious putrid fevers and the effects of a confluent smallpox. . . ." The entire medical staff consisted of "four seniors and four mates" in addition to Potts himself.

Surgeons, operating without anesthetics and with the crudest of instruments, threatened life as often as they preserved it. Few understood the causes or proper treatment of infection. Doctoring consisted of bleeding, blistering, and vomiting (which was "deemed of excellent use, by opening and squeezing all the glands of the body, & then shaking from the nervous system, the contaminating poison"). One doctor reported that "we lost no less than from 10 to 20 of camp diseases, for one by weapons of the enemy."

How many soldiers actually died we do not know, for no one kept accurate records. But the most conservative estimate runs to over 25,000, a higher percentage of the total population than for any other American conflict except the Civil War. For Revolutionary War soldiers, death was an imminent reality.

Civilians and the War

While the experience of war varied from place to place depending on people's proximity to battle, vulnerability to economic disruption, and racial and ethnic makeup, it touched the lives of virtually every American in one way or another. Noncombatants experienced the realities of war with greatest immediacy in densely settled areas along the coast. The British concentrated most of their military efforts there because the coastal communities were the political and economic centers of American life and were vulnerable to England's naval power. At one time or

another, British troops occupied every major port city: Boston for a year at the war's start, New York from 1777 to 1783, Philadelphia over the winter and spring of 1777–1778, Charleston in 1780–1781, and Savannah two years earlier.

The disruptions of urban life were profound. In September 1776, a fire consumed 500 houses, nearly a quarter of the dwellings, in New York City. About half the town's inhabitants fled when the British occupation began and were replaced by an equal number of Loyalists who streamed in from the surrounding countryside. Ten thousand British and German troops added to the crowding. Makeshift shelters of sailcloth and timber, patched together by the growing number of the poor, stretched along Broadway. An American officer somberly reported what he found as his troops entered New York at the war's end: "Close on the eve of an approaching winter, with an heterogeneous set of inhabitants, composed of almost ruined exiles, disbanded soldiery, mixed foreigners, disaffected Tories, and the refuse of the British army, we took possession of a ruined city."

In Philadelphia, the occupation was shorter and the disruptions less severe, but the shock of invasion was no less real. Elizabeth Drinker, living alone after local Patriots had exiled her Quaker husband, found herself the unwilling landlady of a British officer and his friends. Though the major's presence may have protected her from the plundering that went on all around, she was constantly anxious, confiding to her journal that "I often feel afraid to go to Bed." During the occupation, British soldiers frequently tore down fences for their campfires and confiscated food to supplement their own tedious fare. Even the Loyalists commented on the "dreadful consequences" of British occupation.

Along the entire coastal plain, British landing parties descended without warning, seizing supplies and terrorizing the inhabitants. In 1780 and 1781, the British mounted a punishing attack along the Connecticut coast. Over 200 buildings in Fairfield were burned, and much of nearby Norwalk was destroyed. The southern coast, with its broad, navigable rivers, was even more vulnerable. In December 1780, Benedict Arnold ravaged Virginia's James River valley, uprooting tobacco, confiscating slaves, and creating panic among whites. Similar devastation befell the coasts of Georgia and the Carolinas.

Such punishing attacks sent civilians fleeing into the interior. During the first years of the war, the port cities lost nearly half their population, and inland communities struggled to cope with the thousands of refugees who streamed into them. At one point, so many Bostonians had crowded into Concord, Massachusetts, that they decided to hold a town

In September 1776, as American troops fought unsuccessfully for control of New York, nearly a quarter of the city was destroyed by a fire apparently set by a defiant Patriot woman. Not until the war ended did cleanup of the ruins and reconstruction of the city begin. *(Library of Congress)*

meeting there! By March 1776, Concord's population had grown by 25 percent, creating problems of housing, social order, and public health.

Not all the refugee traffic moved inland, away from the coast. In western New York, Pennsylvania, Virginia, and the Carolinas, frontier settlements collapsed under British and Indian assaults. By 1783, the white population along the Mohawk River west of Albany, New York, had declined from 10,000 to 3,500. According to one observer, after nearly five years of warfare in Tryon County, 12,000 farms had been abandoned, 700 buildings burned, thousands of bushels of grain destroyed, nearly 400 women widowed, and perhaps 2,000 children orphaned. The destruction in western New York was duplicated up and down the backcountry from Maine to Georgia as Loyalist rangers, their Indian allies, and Patriot militias joined in a violent, often chaotic struggle.

Wherever the armies went, they generated a swirl of refugees, who spread vivid tales of the war's devastation. This refugee traffic, together with the constant movement of soldiers back and forth between army and civilian life, brought the war home to countless people who did not experience it at first hand. Moreover, disease followed the armies like an avenging angel, ravaging soldiers and civilians alike.

As they moved across the countryside, the armies lived off the land, impressing the supplies they needed. In an effort to protect the surrounding population during the desperate winter of 1777–1778, Washington prohibited his troops from roaming more than a half mile from camp. In New Jersey, Britain's German mercenaries raised additional fears, particularly among women. In April 1777, a committee of the Congress, taking affidavits from women who had been raped, reported that it had "authentic information of many instances of the most indecent treatment, and actual ravishment of married and single women." Such was the nature of that "most irreparable injury," however, that the persons suffering it, "though perfectly innocent, look upon it as a kind of reproach to have the facts related and their names known." Whether the report had any effect is unknown.

The Loyalists

No Americans suffered greater personal losses during the revolution than those who remained loyal to the crown. Although we do not know how many Loyalists there actually were, we do know that tens of thousands evacuated with British troops from New York, Charleston, and Savannah at the end of the war. At least as many slipped away to

Loyalists, or "Tories," as the Patriots called them, often suffered the indignities of tarring, feathering, and public humiliation for their loyalty to England. *(Corbis-Bettmann)*

England, Canada, or the West Indies while fighting was still under way. Additional thousands who wished that the Revolution had never occurred stayed on in the new nation, trying to keep out of trouble and struggling to rebuild their lives. The incidence of loyalism differed from region to region. There were fewest Loyalists in New England and most in and around New York City, the center of British authority throughout the war.

Emotions ran high between Patriots and Loyalists. "The rage of civil discord," lamented one individual, "hath advanced among us with an astonishing rapidity. The son is armed against the father, the brother against the brother, family against family." Many Patriots were determined to exact revenge against those who had rejected the revolutionary cause.

In each state, revolutionary assemblies enacted laws depriving Loyalists of the vote, confiscating their property, and banishing them from their homes. In 1778, the Georgia assembly declared 117 persons guilty of treason, expelled them from the state on pain

of death, and declared their possessions forfeit. Two years earlier, the Connecticut assembly had passed a remarkably punitive law threatening anyone who criticized either the assembly or the Continental Congress with immediate fine and imprisonment. Probably not more than a few dozen Loyalists actually died at the hands of the revolutionary regimes, but thousands found their livelihoods destroyed, their families ostracized, and themselves subject to physical attack.

Punishing Loyalists—or people accused of loyalism, a distinction that was often unclear in the confusion of the times—was politically popular. Most Patriots argued that such "traitors" had put themselves outside the protection of American law. Others, however, argued that republics were intended to be "governments of law and not of men" and worried that no one's rights would be safe when the rights of any were disregarded. No other war-time issue raised so starkly the nettlesome question of balancing individual liberty against the requirements of public security. That issue would return to trouble the nation in the years ahead.

Though many Loyalist émigrés established successful lives in England, the Maritime Provinces of Canada, and the British West Indies, others found the uprooting an ordeal from which they never recovered. On September 8, 1783, Thomas Danforth, formerly a prosperous lawyer from Cambridge, Massachusetts, appeared in London before the King's Commission of Enquiry into the Losses and Services of the American Loyalists. Like others who appealed to the commission, Danforth began by explaining the consequences of his loyalty to the crown. Having devoted his whole life to "preparing himself for future usefulness," he now found himself "near his fortieth year, banished under pain of death, to a distant country, where he has not the most remote family connection . . . cut off from his profession, from every hope of importance in life, and in a great degree from social enjoyments." Without assistance he would sink to "a station much inferior to that of a menial servant."

The commission's response to Danforth's plea is unknown, but many of the several thousand Loyalists who appeared before the commission recovered no more than a third of their losses, meager compensation for the loss of house and property, expulsion from their communities, and relocation in an unfamiliar land. Along with countless others, Danforth found himself relegated to the fringes of English society, his financial affairs in disarray, his future uncertain.

Why did so many Americans remain loyal, often at the cost of personal danger and loss? Customs officers, members of the governors' councils, and Anglican clergy—all appointed to office in the king's name—often sided with England. Loyalism was common as well among groups dependent on British authority—for example, settlers on the Carolina frontier who believed themselves mistreated by the planter elite along the coast; ethnic minorities, such as Germans in the middle states who feared domination by the Anglo-American majority; and tenants on large estates along the Hudson River, who had struggled for years with Patriot landlords over the terms of their leaseholds. Many Loyalists made their choice because they believed it futile to oppose English military power or doubted the ability of a new nation to survive in an Atlantic world dominated by competing empires, even if independence could be won.

Loyalism often had a principled grounding as well, as Samuel Seabury made clear. "Every person owes obedience to the laws of the government," Seabury insisted, "and is obliged in honour and duty to support them. Because if one has a right to disregard the laws of the society to which he belongs, all have the same right; and then government is at an end." William Eddis wondered what kind of society independence would bring when revolutionary crowds showed no respect for the rights of Loyalist dissenters such as he. "If I differ in opinion from the multitude," he asked, "must I therefore be deprived of my character, and the confidence of my fellow-citizens; when in every station of life I discharge my duty with fidelity and honour?" Loyalists such as Eddis and Seabury claimed to be upholding reason and the rule of law against revolutionary disorder.

After the war ended and passions had cooled, most states repealed their anti-Loyalist legislation. In 1786, the Connecticut assembly went so far as to invite its émigrés to return, hoping that their skills and experience would contribute to postwar recovery. In a number of instances, former Loyalists even reentered public life. Still, the permanent departure of so many colonists committed to monarchy, with its values of social and political hierarchy, weakened the forces of conservatism in America and facilitated revolutionary change.

African Americans and the Revolutionary War

The American Revolution was more than a struggle between white belligerents, for it caught up American blacks in its toils as well. In the northern states, both free and enslaved blacks were enlisted in support of the revolutionary cause. In the South nearly 400,000 slaves constituted a vast and uncertain force, viewed by the British as a resource to be exploited and by southern whites as a source of great vulnerability and danger. Sizing up the opportunities provided by the war's confusion, southern blacks struck out for their own freedom by seeking liberty behind English lines or fleeing to mixed-race, maroon settlements in the interior. Before the war was over, the conflict provoked the largest slave rebellion in American history prior to the Civil War.

Hearing their masters talk excitedly about liberty, increasing numbers of black Americans questioned their own oppression. In the North, slaves petitioned state legislatures for their freedom, while in the South pockets of insurrection appeared. In 1765, more than 100 South Carolina slaves, most of them young men in their 20s and 30s, fled their plantations. The next year, slaves paraded through the streets of Charleston chanting, "Liberty, liberty!"

In November 1775, the royal governor of Virginia, Lord Dunmore, issued a proclamation offering freedom to all slaves and servants, able and willing to bear arms, who would leave their masters and join the British forces at Norfolk. Within weeks, 500 to 600 slaves had responded. Among them was Thomas Peters, of Wilmington, North Carolina.

Kidnapped from the Yoruba tribe in what is now Nigeria and brought to North America by a French slave trader, Peters had been purchased in Louisiana about 1760. He resisted enslavement so fiercely that his master sold him into the English colonies. By 1770, Peters belonged to William Campbell, an immigrant Scots planter on North Carolina's Cape Fear River. Here Peters toiled while the storm brewed between England and the colonies.

Peters's plans for his own declaration of independence may have ripened as a result of the rhetoric of liberty he heard around his master's house, for William Campbell was a leading member of Wilmington's Sons of Liberty and talked excitedly about inalienable rights. By mid-1775, the Cape Fear region, like many areas from Maryland to Georgia, buzzed with rumors of slave uprisings. The importation of new slaves was banned, and patrols were dispatched to disarm all blacks in the area. In July, the state's revolutionary government imposed martial law when the British commander of Fort Johnston, near Wilmington, encouraged Negroes to "elope from their masters." When 20 British ships entered the Cape Fear River in March 1776 and disembarked royal troops, Peters seized the moment to redefine himself as a man, instead of William Campbell's property, and escaped. Before long, he would fight with the British-officered Black Pioneers.

How many African Americans sought liberty behind British lines is unknown, but as many as 20 percent may have done so. Unlike their white masters, blacks saw in England the promise of freedom, not tyranny. As the war dragged on, English commanders pressed blacks into service. A regiment of black soldiers, formed from Virginia slaves who responded to

James Armistead Lafayette, a Virginia slave, served as a spy against the British for the French general Lafayette. In recognition of his service, the Virginia General Assembly granted him his freedom in 1786. (*Valentine Museum, Richmond, VA*)

Dunmore's proclamation, marched into battle, their chests covered by sashes emblazoned with the slogan "Liberty to Slaves."

Some of the blacks who joined England achieved their freedom. At the war's end, several thousand were evacuated with the British to Nova Scotia. Their reception by the white inhabitants, however, was generally hostile. By 1800, most had left Canada to settle in the free black colony of Sierra Leone on the west coast of Africa. Thomas Peters was a leader among them.

Many of the slaves who fled behind British lines, however, never won their freedom. Under the terms of the peace treaty, hundreds were returned to their American owners. Several thousand others, their value as field hands too great to be ignored, were transported to the harsher slavery of the sugar plantations in the British West Indies. England had not entered the war to abolish slavery.

Other blacks took advantage of the war's confusion to slip away from their masters in pursuit of a new life. Some made their way north, following rumors that slavery had been abolished there, while others sought refuge among the Indians in the southern interior. The Seminole of Georgia and Florida generally welcomed black runaways and through intermarriage absorbed them into tribal society. Blacks met a more uncertain reception, however, among the Cherokee and Creek.

While some were taken in, others were returned to their white owners in return for bounties, and still others were held in slavelike conditions by new Indian masters. Whatever their destination, thousands of African Americans acted to throw off the bonds of slavery.

Fewer blacks fought on the American side than on England's, in part because neither the Congress nor the states were eager to see them armed. Faced with the increasing need for troops, however, the Congress and each of the states except Georgia and South Carolina eventually relented and pressed blacks into service. Of those who served the Patriot cause, many received the freedom they were promised. The patriotism of countless others, however, went unrewarded.

THE FERMENT OF REVOLUTIONARY POLITICS

The Revolution altered people's lives in countless ways that reached beyond the sights and sounds of battle. No areas of American life were more powerfully changed than politics and government. Who would have a voice in revolutionary politics, and who would be excluded? How vigorously would notions of political equality be pursued, or how tenaciously would people cling to the more traditional belief that ordinary citizens should defer to their political betters? And how would the new state governments balance the need for order and the security of property against demands for democratic openness and accountability? These were some of the explosive questions that had to be addressed. Seldom has American politics been more heated; seldom has it struggled with more fundamental or more daunting problems than during the years of the nation's founding.

Mobilizing the People

Under the pressure of revolutionary events, politics absorbed people's energies as never before. The politicization of American society was evident in the flood of printed material that streamed from American presses. While newspapers multiplied in number, pamphlets by the thousands fanned the political debate. Declared one contemporary in amazement, it was

> a spectacle . . . without a parallel on earth. . . . Even a large portion of that class of the community which is destined to daily labor have free and constant access to public prints, receive regular information of every occurrence, [and] attend to the course of political affairs. [Never were political writings] so cheap, so universally diffused, so easy of access.

Ordinary men and women took to the streets in political rallies, such as this mock parade of 1780 in Philadelphia, in which Benedict Arnold, an American general who deserted to the British, was burned in effigy. Such rallies were filled with powerful symbols. *(American Antiquarian Society)*

Pulpits rocked with political exhortations as well. Religion and politics had never been sharply separated in colonial America, but the Revolution drew them more tightly together. Some believed that God had designated revolutionary America as the place of Christ's Second Coming and that independence foretold that glorious day. Others of a less millennial persuasion thought of America as a "New Israel," a covenanted people specially chosen by God to preserve liberty in a threatening world. Giving the metaphor a classical twist, Samuel Adams called on Bostonians to join in creating a "Christian Sparta."

In countless sermons, Congregational, Presbyterian, and Baptist clergy exhorted the American people to repent the sins that had brought English tyranny upon them and urged them to rededicate themselves to God's purposes by fighting for American freedom. It was language that people nurtured in Puritan piety and the Great Awakening instinctively understood.

The belief that God sanctioned their revolution strengthened Americans' resolve. It also encouraged them to identify their own political interests with divine intent and thus offered convenient justification for whatever they believed necessary to do. This was not the last time Americans would make that dangerous equation.

By contrast, Loyalist clergy, such as Maryland's Jonathan Boucher, urged their parishioners to support the king as head of the Anglican Church. During the months preceding independence, as the local Committee of Safety interrupted worship to harass him, Boucher carried a loaded pistol into the pulpit while he preached submission to royal authority.

Belief in the momentous importance of what they were doing increased the intensity of revolutionary politics. John Adams, writing to his wife, Abigail, as the Congress moved toward its fateful declaration, exalted independence as "the greatest question . . . which ever was debated in America." This moment, he continued,

ought to be solemnized with pomp and parade, with shows, games, sports, guns, bells, bonfires, and illuminations, from one end of this continent to the other, from this time forward forevermore.

As independence was declared, people in towns and hamlets throughout the land raised toasts to the great event: "Liberty to those who have the spirit to preserve it," and "May Liberty expand sacred wings, and, in glorious effort, diffuse her influence o'er and o'er the globe." Inspired by the searing experience of rebellion, war, and nation building, they believed they held the future of human liberty in their hands. Small wonder that they took their politics so seriously.

The expanding array of extralegal committees and spontaneous public gatherings that erupted during the 1770s and 1780s provided the most dramatic evidence of the people's newly awakened political commitment. Prior to independence, crowds had taken to the streets to protest measures like the Stamp Act (see Chapter 5). After 1776, direct political action accelerated as people gathered to intimidate Loyalists, enforce price and wage controls, administer rough-hewn justice, and, as one individual protested, even direct "what we shall eat, drink, wear, speak, and think"—all on behalf of the Revolution.

Patriots of more radical temperament defended these activities as essential expressions of the popular will. More conservative republicans, however, worried that such behavior threatened political stability. Direct

Recovering the Past

PATRIOTIC PAINTINGS

The work that historians do is limited only by their own curiosity and the evidence left behind for them to study. In addition to written evidence such as household inventories and Indian treaties and material artifacts like tombstones and the archaeological residue of burial mounds, historians also examine paintings and other forms of visual evidence for information about the past.

While revealing the development of artistic styles and techniques, paintings also provide important windows into past eras for social and cultural historians by revealing how people looked and did their work, as well as what the landscape and built environment were like. Paintings offer insights additionally into the values and attitudes of past times, for they are often intended to enlighten and instruct, as well as please the viewer's eye.

So it was with Charles Willson Peale, who, as a member of the Pennsylvania militia, carried paint kits and canvas along with his musket as he followed George Washington during the Revolutionary War. Before it was over, he had completed four portraits of the general.

And so it was, even more spectacularly, with the artist John Trumbull, who recorded on canvas some of the most dramatic events of the nation's founding. Slighted for promotion during the Rhode Island campaign early in the war, Trumbull resigned his commission to become a painter. After a frustrating start, he sailed for London, where he studied with the artist Benjamin West, another transplanted American. Imprisoned briefly at the urging of angry American Loyalists, Trumbull was deported to the United States. Returning to England at the war's end, he was urged by West and Thomas Jefferson to paint an ambitious series of "national history" canvases. Over the next four decades, in addition to numerous portraits, religious subjects, and landscapes, Trumbull fashioned the most famous sequence of patriotic paintings ever undertaken by an American artist.

Included were four canvases, depicting crucial military and civil turning points in the struggle for American independence, commissioned by Congress in the early nineteenth century and now hanging in the capitol rotunda in Washington, D.C.—*The Surrender of General Burgoyne at Saratoga, The Surrender of Lord Cornwallis at Yorktown, The Declaration of Independence,* and *The Resignation of General Washington* as commander of the continental army. In addition to those monumental works, Trumbull fashioned a number of heroic battle scenes, including *The Death of General Warren at the Battle of Bunker Hill,* shown opposite.

Though Trumbull knew Warren and others who fought at Bunker Hill, had witnessed the battle from a distance, and was familiar with the techniques of military combat from his own months in the army, he was not primarily concerned with literal accuracy as he composed his painting. Guided by the canons of classical aesthetics popular at the time, he was more interested in the power of artistic "invention" to impart "ideal" truths through the use of brush and pigment.

Examine the painting carefully. How has the artist arranged the figures in relationship to each other? What facial expressions and postures has he given to the people depicted? In what ways do the banners, clouds, and uses of light and color contribute to the painting's overall effect? What messages about the Revolutionary War did Trumbull want viewers to carry away from the canvas?

In all his historical canvases, Trumbull was intent on promoting national pride and constructing a usable public memory. How does this painting serve those purposes? Why was the creation of a shared public memory so important during the early years of the new republic? Might Trumbull have had future generations of Americans as well as his own contemporaries in mind as he did his work?

Art and politics have been intimately related throughout our history, for painting and theater, music, and other forms of performance art have been employed to challenge as well as celebrate political leaders and their policies. Think for a moment about the connections between art and politics in our own time. Why have controversies recently swirled around the National Endowments for the Arts and the Humanities? Should the government provide financial assistance for the arts? If so, should such assistance be accompanied by restrictions on the political messages such art might convey? Is art ever nonpolitical?

John Trumbull, *The Death of General Warren at the Battle of Bunker Hill. (Yale University Art Gallery, Trumbull Collection)*

In celebration of American independence, Patriots and their slaves toppled the statue of King George III that stood at Bowling Green in New York City. *(Library of Congress)*

action by the people had been necessary in the struggle against England, but why such restlessness now, after the yoke of English tyranny had been cast aside? Even Thomas Paine expressed concern. "It is time to have done with tarring and feathering," he wrote in 1777. "I never did and never would encourage what may properly be called a mob, when any legal mode of redress can be had."

This dramatic expansion of popular politics resulted from an explosive combination of circumstances: the momentous events of revolution and war; the efforts of Patriot leaders to mobilize popular support for the desperate struggle against England; and the determination of artisans, workingmen, farmers, and other common folk to apply the principles of liberty to the conditions of their own lives.

A Republican Ideology

Throughout history, as people have moved from colonial subordination to independence, they have struggled to define their identities as free and separate nations. It was no different with the American Revolutionary generation. No longer English, they struggled to understand what it meant to be American. "Our style and manner of thinking," observed Thomas Paine in amazement, "have undergone a revolution. . . . We see with other eyes, we hear with other ears, and think with other thoughts than those we formerly used." The ideology of revolutionary republicanism, pieced together from English political thought, Enlightenment doctrine, and assorted religious beliefs, constituted that revolution in thought. Many of its tenets were broadly shared among the American

people, but its larger meanings were sharply contested throughout the revolutionary era.

The rejection of monarchy was one basic component of America's new republican faith. "The word *republic,*" explained Paine, "means the public good of the whole, in contradistinction to the despotic form which makes the good of the sovereign, or of one man, the only object of government." It was Paine's unsparing rejection of monarchy that made his pamphlet *Common Sense* seem so radical. "Of more worth is one honest man to society, and in the sight of God," he scoffed, "than all the crowned ruffians that ever lived."

In rejecting monarchy, the American people also rejected the system of hierarchical authority on which monarchy rested, a system that promised protection by the crown in return for obedience by the people. Under a republican system, by contrast, public authority was created by the people contracting together for their mutual good. In that fundamental change lay much of the American Revolution's radical promise.

No doctrine was more basic to republican belief than the notion that government power, when removed from the people's close oversight and control, threatened to expand at the expense of liberty. The recent experience with England had burned that lesson indelibly into people's consciousness. Although too much liberty might degenerate into political chaos, history seemed to demonstrate that trouble arose most often from too much government, not too little. "It is much easier to restrain the people from running into licentiousness," went a typical refrain, "than power from swelling into tyranny and oppression."

Given the need to limit government power, how could political order be maintained? The revolutionary generation offered an extraordinary answer to that question. Order was not to be imposed from above through traditional agencies of central control such as monarchies, standing armies, and state churches. In a republic, political discipline had to flow upward from the self-regulated behavior of citizens, especially from their willingness, whenever necessary, to put the public good ahead of their own interests. In a republic, explained one pamphleteer, "each individual gives up all private interest that is not consistent with the general good." This radical principle of "public virtue" was an essential ingredient of the republican ideology.

By contrast, political "faction," or organized self-interest, constituted the "mortal disease" to which popular governments throughout history had succumbed. Given the absence in republics of a strong central government capable of imposing political order, factional conflict could easily spin out of control. This fear of "party faction" added to the intensity of political conflict in revolutionary America by inclining people to attribute the most selfish motives to their political opponents.

The idea of placing responsibility for political order with the people and counting on them to act selflessly for the good of the whole, alarmed countless Americans, for what if the people proved unworthy? If the attempt was made, warned one individual darkly, "the bands of society would be dissolved, the harmony of the world confused, and the order of nature subverted." A strong incentive toward loyalism lurked in such concerns.

Few Patriots were so naive as to believe that the American people were altogether virtuous. During the first years of independence, when revolutionary enthusiasm ran high, however, many believed that public virtue was sufficiently widespread to support republican government, while others argued that the American people would learn public virtue by its necessary practice. The revolutionary struggle would serve as a "furnace of affliction," refining the American character as it strengthened people's capacity for virtuous behavior. It was an extraordinarily hopeful but risk-filled undertaking.

The principle of political equality was another controversial touchstone of republicanism. It was broadly assumed that republican governments must be grounded in popular consent, that elections should be frequent, and that citizens must be vigilant in defense of their liberties. There, however, agreement often ended.

Some Americans took literally the principle of political equality by arguing that every citizen should have an equal voice and that public office should be open to all. This position was most forcefully articulated by tenants and small farmers in the interior, as well as workers and artisans in the coastal cities who had long struggled to claim a political voice. More cautious citizens emphasized the need for order as well as liberty, arguing that stable republics required leadership by men of ability and experience, an "aristocracy of talent" that could give the people clear direction. Merchants, planters, and large commercial farmers who were used to providing such leadership saw no need for radical changes in the existing distribution of political power.

Creating Republican Governments

These competing differences of ideology and self-interest burst through the surface of American political life during the debates over new state constitutions that occurred immediately following independence. Fashioning new, republican governments would not be easy, for the American people had no experience with government making on such a scale and had to make the attempt in the midst of a disruptive war. In addition, there were sharp divisions over the kinds of "new modelled" governments they wished to create. One person thought it the "most difficult and dangerous business" that was to be done. Events proved those words prophetic.

Connecticut and Rhode Island continued under their colonial charters, simply deleting all reference to the British crown. The other 11 states set their charters aside and started anew. Within two years following independence, all but Massachusetts had completed the task. By 1780, it had done so as well.

Given their recent experience with England and the prompting of republican theory, constitution makers began with two overriding concerns: to limit the powers of government and to make public officials accountable. The only certain way of accomplishing these goals was by establishing a fundamental law, in the form of a written constitution, that could serve as a standard for regulating government behavior.

In most states, the provincial congresses, extralegal successors to the defunct colonial assemblies, wrote the first constitutions. But this made people increasingly uneasy. If government bodies wrote the documents, they could change them as well, and what would then protect liberty against the abuse of government power? Some way had to be found of grounding the fundamental law, not in the actions of government but directly in the people's sovereign will.

Massachusetts was the first state to solve the problem. In 1779, its citizens elected a special convention

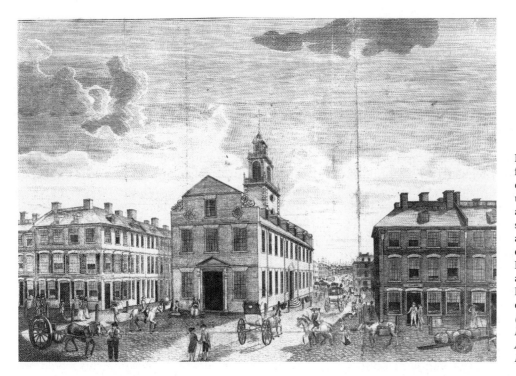

Massachusetts was the first state to elect a special convention to draw up a new constitution and then return that constitution to the people for approval. The new government—along with Boston's officials, courts, and the Merchants' Exchange—met in the old colonial statehouse. *(Stokes Collection, The New York Public Library, Astor, Lenox and Tilden Foundations)*

for the sole purpose of preparing a new constitution. The convention did its work, and the resulting document was returned to the people for ratification.

Through trial and argumentation, the revolutionary generation gradually worked out a clear understanding of what a constitution was and how it should be developed. In the process, it established some of the most basic doctrines of American constitutionalism: that sovereignty resides in the people; that written constitutions, produced by specially elected conventions and then ratified by the people, embody their sovereign will; and that governments must function within clear constitutional limits. No principles have been more important to the preservation of American liberty.

The new constitutions redefined American government in fundamental and lasting ways. For one thing, the new governments were considerably more democratic than the colonial regimes had been. Most state officials were now elected, many of them annually rather than every two or three years as before. The assemblies, moreover, were now larger and more representative than they had been prior to 1776, and many of the powers formerly held by colonial governors—such as control over the budget, veto power over legislation, and the right to appoint various state officials—were either stripped away or reallocated to the assemblies.

Different Paths to the Republican Goal

At the same time, constitution making generated considerable controversy, especially over how democratic the new governments should be. In Pennsylvania, a coalition of western farmers, Philadelphia artisans, and radical leaders such as Thomas Paine, Timothy Matlack, and Thomas Young pushed through the most democratic state constitution of all. Drafted less than three months after independence, during the most intense period of political reform, it rejected the familiar English model of two legislative houses and an independent executive. Republican governments, the radicals insisted, should be simple and easily understood. The constitution thus provided for a single, all-powerful legislative house, its members annually elected and its debates open to the public. There was to be no governor; legislative committees would handle executive duties. A truly radical assumption underlay this unitary design: that only the "common interest of society" and not "separate and jarring private interests" should be represented in public affairs. Property-holding requirements for public office were abolished, and the franchise was opened to every taxpaying, white male over 21. A bill of rights guaranteed every citizen religious freedom, trial by jury, and freedom of speech.

The most radical proposal of all called for the redistribution of property. "An enormous proportion of property vested in a few individuals," declared the proposed constitution, "is dangerous to the rights, and destructive of the common happiness of mankind." Alarmed conservatives just managed to have the offending language removed.

Debate over the constitution divided the state deeply. Men of wealth condemned the document's

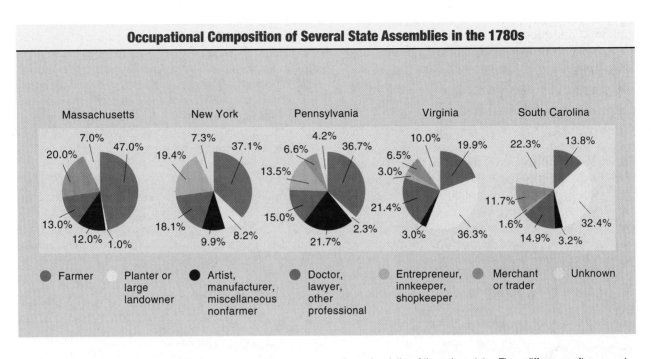

Occupational Composition of Several State Assemblies in the 1780s

Membership in the revolutionary assemblies reflected differences in the economies and societies of the various states. Those differences often generated political conflict throughout the revolutionary era. What are the major differences between northern and southern state assemblies, and how do you explain them? Source: Jackson T. Main, *Political Parties Before the Constitution,* 1973.

supporters as "coffee-house demagogues" seeking to introduce a "tyranny of the people." The constitution's proponents—tradesmen, farmers, and other small producers—shot back that their critics were "the rich and great men" who had no "common interest with the body of the people."

In 1776, the radicals had their way, and the document was approved. The Pennsylvania constitution, together with its counterparts in Vermont and Georgia, represented the most radical thrust of revolutionary republicanism. Its guiding principle, declared Thomas Young, was that "the people at large [are] the true proprietors of governmental power." As later events would reveal, the struggle for political control in Pennsylvania was not over, for in 1790 a new and more conservative constitution would be approved. For the moment, however, the lines of political power in Pennsylvania had been decisively redrawn.

In Massachusetts, constitution making followed a different and more cautious course. There the disruptions of war were less severe and the continuity of political leadership was greater. John Adams, the main architect of the constitution, readily admitted that the new government had to be firmly grounded in the people. Yet he warned against "reckless experimentation" and regarded the Pennsylvania constitution as far too democratic. He thought a balance between two legislative houses and an independent executive was essential to preserving liberty.

Believing that society was inescapably divided between "democratic" and "aristocratic" forces, Adams sought to isolate them in separate legislative houses where they could guard against each other. The lower house or assembly, he explained, should be "an exact portrait, in miniature," of the people; it should "think, feel, act, and reason" like them. The senate, by contrast, should constitute a "natural aristocracy" of wealth, talent, and good sense. Following Adams's advice, the Massachusetts convention provided for a popular, annually elected assembly and a senate based on wealth, its members apportioned according to the amount of taxes paid in special senatorial districts. The constitution also provided for an independent governor with the power to veto legislation, make appointments, serve as commander in chief of the militia, and oversee state expenditures. The convention endorsed as well an escalating scale of property requirements for assemblymen, senators, and the governor as a way of ensuring that only the better sort would qualify for public office.

When the convention sent the document to the town meetings for approval on March 2, 1780, farmers and Boston artisans attacked it as "aristocratic." The citizens of Dorchester warned that the property requirement for the franchise would exclude "half the people of this commonwealth" from participation in the choice of their elected officials, while the inhabitants of Petersham feared that "rich and powerful men" would control the proposed government. Despite these and other objections, the convention reconvened in June, declared the document approved, and the constitution went into effect four months later.

Women and the Limits of Republican Citizenship

While men of the revolutionary generation battled among themselves over the degree of political equality appropriate for themselves, they were virtually unanimous in the belief that women could not be full republican citizens. Though women participated in revolutionary crowds and other political activities, they continued to be denied the franchise. Except on scattered occasions, women had neither voted nor held public office during the colonial period. Nor, with rare exceptions, did they do so in revolutionary America.

The New Jersey constitution of 1776 opened the franchise to "all free inhabitants" meeting property and residency requirements. During the 1780s, numerous women took advantage of that opening and cast their votes, leading one disgruntled male to protest, "It is evident that women, generally, are neither by nature, nor habit, nor education . . . fitted to perform this duty with credit to themselves, or advantage to the public." Reflecting that widely held, male sentiment, the New Jersey assembly passed a bill in 1807 specifically disenfranchising women. Its author, John Condict, had narrowly escaped defeat several years earlier when women voted in conspicuous numbers for his opponent. In no other state did women even temporarily secure the vote. Not until the twentieth century would women secure the franchise, the most fundamental attribute of citizenship.

Prior to independence, most women had accepted the principle that political debate fell outside the feminine sphere. The Revolution altered that attitude, for women felt the urgency of the revolutionary crisis as intensely as men. "How shall I impose a silence upon myself," wondered Anne Emlen in 1777, "when the

Though women were discouraged from public writing, Mercy Otis Warren, related by both birth and marriage to leading Massachusetts Patriots, published pamphlets and plays dealing with revolutionary politics. *(Courtesy, Museum of Fine Arts, Boston. Reproduced with permission ©1999 The Museum of Fine Arts, Boston. All Rights Reserved.)*

Timeline

1775	Lord Dunmore's proclamation to slaves and servants in Virginia
	Iroquois Six Nations pledge neutrality
	Continental Congress urges "states" to establish new governments
1776	British evacuate Boston and seize New York City
	Declaration of Independence
	Eight states draft constitutions
	Cherokee raids and American retaliation
1777	British occupy Philadelphia
	Most Iroquois join the British
	Americans win victory at Saratoga
	Washington's army winters at Valley Forge
1778	War shifts to the South
	Savannah falls to the British
	French treaty of alliance and commerce
1779	Massachusetts state constitutional convention
	Sullivan destroys Iroquois villages in New York
1780	Massachusetts constitution ratified
	Charleston surrenders to the British
	Pennsylvania begins gradual abolition of slavery
1780s	Virginia and Maryland debate abolition of slavery
	Destruction of Iroquois Confederacy
1781	Cornwallis surrenders at Yorktown
	Articles of Confederation ratified by states
1783	Peace treaty with England signed in Paris
	Massachusetts Supreme Court abolishes slavery
	King's Commission on American Loyalists begins work

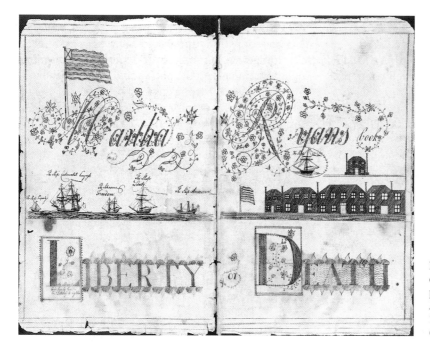

Martha Ryan, a young North Carolina girl, decorated the cover of her copybook with political themes. *(from the Ryan Cipher Book, #1940, Southern Historical Collection, The Library of the University of North Carolina at Chapel Hill)*

subject is so very interesting, so much engrossing conversation & what every member of the community is more or less concerned in?" With increasing frequency, women wrote and spoke to each other about public events, especially as they affected their own lives. Declared Eliza Wilkerson of South Carolina during the British invasion of 1780, "None were greater politicians than the several knots of ladies, who met together. All trifling discourses of fashions, and such low chat were thrown by, and we commenced perfect statesmen."

As the war progressed, increasing numbers of women spoke out publicly. A few, such as Esther DeBerdt Reed of Philadelphia, published essays explaining women's urgent desire to contribute to the Patriot cause. In her 1780 broadside "The Sentiments of an American Woman," she declared that women wanted to serve like "those heroines of antiquity, who have rendered their sex illustrious," and she called on women to renounce "vain ornament" as they had earlier renounced English tea. The money thus saved would be the "offering of the Ladies" to Washington's army. In Philadelphia, women responded by collecting $300,000 in continental currency from over 1,600 individuals. Refusing Washington's proposal that the money be mixed with general funds in the national treasury, they insisted on using it to purchase materials for shirts so that each soldier might know he had received a contribution directly from the women.

Even women's traditional roles took on new political meaning. With English imports cut off and the army badly in need of clothing, spinning and weaving assumed patriotic significance. Coming together as Daughters of Liberty, women made shirts and other items of clothing. Charity Clarke, a New York teenager, acknowledged that she "felt Nationaly" as she knitted stockings for the soldiers. Though "heroines may not distinguish themselves at the head of an army," she informed an English cousin, a "fighting army of amazons . . . armed with spinning wheels" would emerge in America.

The most traditional of all female roles, the care and nurture of children, took on special political resonance during the revolutionary era. How could the republic be sustained once independence had been won? Only by a rising generation of republican citizens schooled in the principles of public virtue and ready to assume the task. How would they be prepared? During their formative years by their "Republican Mothers," the women of the Revolution.

Most women did not press for full political equality, since the idea flew in the face of long-standing social convention and its advocacy exposed a person to public ridicule. Some women did make the case to each other or their husbands. "I cannot say, that I think you are very generous to the ladies," Abigail Adams chided her husband, John. "For whilst you are proclaiming peace and good will to men, emancipating all nations, you insist upon retaining an absolute power over all wives." John consulted Abigail on many things but turned this admonition quickly aside.

While women developed new ties to the public realm during the revolutionary years, the assumption that politics and government were an exclusively male domain did not easily die. Indeed, the republican ideology, so effectively invoked in support of American liberty against the English king and

Parliament, actually sharpened political distinctions between women and men. The independence of judgment required of republican citizens assumed a level of economic self-sufficiency denied married women by the long-established principle of *coverture*, a legal doctrine that transferred women's property to their husbands and designated them as political dependents as well.

Republican virtue, moreover, was understood to encompass such "manly" qualities as rationality, self-discipline, and public sacrifice, qualities believed inconsistent with "feminine" attributes of passion and self-indulgence. Finally, the desperate struggle against England emphasized the patriarchal values of the military hero and classic lawgiver.

In time, further challenges to male political hegemony would emerge. When they did, women would find guidance in the principles enshrined in the Declaration of Independence that the women of the Revolution had helped to defend.

Conclusion
The Crucible of Revolution

Independence and war redrew the contours of American life and changed the destinies of the American people. Though the Revolutionary War ended in victory, liberty had its costs. Lives were lost, property was destroyed, and local economies were deranged. The war altered relationships between Indians and whites, for it left the Iroquois and Cherokee severely weakened and opened the floodgates of western expansion. For African Americans, the revolution had paradoxical results. It produced an ideology that decried slavery, generated efforts to end the slave trade, and marked the first general debate over abolishing the oppressive institution. Yet slavery was eradicated only where it was least important, in the North, while in the South, where slavery had the strongest hold, its future was guaranteed. In spite of the political ferment generated by the Revolution, women reaped few clear advantages. Though they participated in many revolutionary activities and achieved enhanced status as "Republican Mothers," they were still denied the franchise, the critical right of full republican citizenship.

By 1783, a new nation had come into being where none had existed before, a nation based not on age-encrusted principles of monarchy and aristocratic privilege but on the doctrines of republican liberty. That was the greatest change of all. The political transformations set in motion, however, generated angry disputes whose outcomes could be only dimly foreseen. Thomas Paine put the matter succinctly: "The answer to the question, can America be happy under a government of her own, is short and simple—as happy as she pleases; she hath a blank sheet to write upon." The years immediately ahead would determine whether America's republican experiment, launched with such hopefulness in 1776, would succeed.

Recommended Reading

The War for American Independence

John Ferling, ed., *The World Turned Upside Down: The American Victory in the War of Independence* (1988); Don Higginbotham, *The War of Independence* (1983); Ronald Hoffman and Peter Albert, eds., *Arms and Independence: The Military Character of the American Revolution* (1984); Mark Kwasney, *Washington's Partisan War, 1775–1783* (1996); Holly Mayer, *Belonging to the Army: Camp Followers and Community During the American Revolution* (1996); Robert Middlekauff, *The Glorious Cause* (1982).

Colin Calloway, *The American Revolution in Indian Country* (1995); Tom Hatley, *The Dividing Paths: Cherokees and South Carolinians Through the Revolutionary Era* (1993); Isabel Kelsey, *Joseph Brant, 1743–1807: Man of Two Worlds* (1984); Max Mintz, *Seeds of Empire: The American Revolutionary Conquest of the Iroquois* (1999); Anthony Wallace, *The Death and Rebirth of the Seneca* (1969).

Jonathan Dull, *A Diplomatic History of the American Revolution* (1985); Ronald Hoffman and Peter Albert, eds., *Peace and the Peacemakers: The Treaty of 1783* (1986); Reginald Horsman, *Diplomacy of the New Republic, 1775–1815* (1985).

The Experience of War

E. Wayne Carp, *To Starve the Army at Pleasure: Continental Army Administration and American Political Culture, 1775–1783* (1984); Lawrence Cress, *Citizens in Arms: The Army and the Militia in American Society to the War of 1812* (1982); Sylvia Frey, *The British Soldier in America: A Social History of Military Life in the Revolutionary Period* (1981); Charles Neimeyer, *America Goes to War: A Social History of the Continental Army* (1996); Charles Royster, *A Revolutionary People at War: The Continental Army and American Character, 1775–1783* (1979).

John Buchanan, *The Road to Guilford Courthouse: The American Revolution in the Carolinas* (1997); John Franz and William Pencak, eds., *Beyond Philadelphia: The American Revolution in the Pennsylvania Hinterland* (1998); James Leamon, *Revolution Downeast: The War for American Independence in Maine* (1993); John Pancake, *This Destructive War: The British Campaign in the Carolinas, 1780–1782* (1985).

Bernard Bailyn, *The Ordeal of Thomas Hutchinson* (1974); Robert Calhoon, *The Loyalists in Revolutionary America, 1760–1781* (1973); Mary Beth Norton, *The British Americans: The*

Loyalist Exiles in England, 1774–1789 (1972); Janice Potter, *Liberty We Seek: Loyalist Ideology in Colonial New York and Massachusetts* (1983).

Ira Berlin and Ronald Hoffman, eds., *Slavery and Freedom in the Age of the American Revolution* (1983); David B. Davis, *The Problem of Slavery in the Age of the Democratic Revolution* (1975); Sylvia Frey, *Water from the Rock: Black Resistance in a Revolutionary Age* (1991); Sidney Kaplan, *The Black Presence in the Era of the American Revolution, 1770–1800* (1973); Gary B. Nash, *Race and Revolution* (1990).

The Ferment of Revolutionary Politics

Bernard Bailyn, *Faces of Revolution* (1991); Edward Countryman, *A People in Revolution: The American Revolution and Political Society in New York, 1760–1790* (1981); Eric Foner, *Tom Paine and Revolutionary America* (1976); Ronald Hoffman, *A Spirit of Dissension: Economics, Politics, and the Revolution in Maryland* (1973); Norman Risjord, *Representative Americans: The Revolutionary Generation* (1980); John Selby, *The Revolution in Virginia, 1775–1783* (1988); Robert Shalhope, *Bennington and the Green Mountain Boys: The Emergence of Liberal Democracy in Vermont, 1760–1850* (1996); Alan Taylor, *Liberty Men and Great Proprietors: The Revolutionary Settlement on the Maine Frontier, 1760–1820* (1990); Peter Thompson, *Rum, Punch, and Revolution: Taverngoing and Public Life in Eighteenth Century Philadelphia* (1999); Gordon Wood, *The Creation of the American Republic, 1776–1787* (1969) and *The Radicalism of the American Revolution* (1992); Al Young, ed., *Beyond the American Revolution: Explorations in the History of American Radicalism* (1993).

Willi Paul Adams, *The First American Constitutions: Republican Ideology and the Making of the State Constitutions in the Revolutionary Era* (1980); Mark Kruman, *Between Authority and Liberty: State Constitution Making in Revolutionary America* (1997); Donald Lutz, *Popular Consent and Popular Control: Whig Political Thought in the Early State Constitutions* (1980); Edmund Morgan, *Inventing the People: The Rise of Popular Sovereignty in England and America* (1988); John Phillip Reid, *Constitutional History of the American Revolution* (1995).

Joy Day Buel and Richard Buel, Jr., *The Way of Duty: A Woman and Her Family in Revolutionary America* (1995); Edith Gelles, *Portia: The World of Abigail Adams* (1992); Joan Gunderson, *To Be Useful to the World: Women in Revolutionary America* (1996); Ronald Hoffman and Peter Albert, eds., *Women in the Age of the American Revolution* (1989); Mark Kann, *A Republic of Men: The American Founders, Gendered Language, and Patriotic Politics* (1998); Linda Kerber, *Women of the Republic* (1980); Cynthia Kerner, *Southern Women in Revolution, 1776–1800* (1998); Mary Beth Norton, *Liberty's Daughters* (1980); Jeffrey Richards, *Mercy Otis Warren* (1995).

Fiction and Film

The Broken Chain, a made-for-television historical drama produced and aired in 1994, tells the story of the Mohawk war chief Joseph Brant, who fought with England during the Revolutionary War and then led many of his people to Canada following the peace of 1783.

The Way of Duty, a PBS documentary drama based on a book by the historians Richard and Joy Buel, traces the challenging experiences of a Connecticut woman and her family during the American Revolution.

James Fenimore Cooper's dramatic novel *The Pilot* (1824) offers an imaginative account of naval warfare and seafaring life during the Revolution. In the more recently published novel *Oliver Wiswell* (1940), Kenneth Roberts depicts the Revolution as seen through the eyes of an American Loyalist.

Suggested Web Sites

http://nwta.com/main.html

Northwest Territory Alliance. This Revolutionary era reenactment organization site contains several links and offers an interesting look at historical reenactment.

http://users.erols.com/candidus/index.htm

Maryland Loyalism and the American Revolution. This look at Maryland's Loyalists promotes the book Maryland Loyalists in the American Revolution, but it also has good information about an underappreciated phenomenon, including Loyalist songs and poems.

http://www.geocities.com/Athens/Forum/9061/USA/revolution/rev.html

Revolution Era Documents. The Historical Text Archive has numerous useful documents for the period of the revolution.

http://revolution.h-net.msu.edu/

The American Revolution. This site accompanies the PBS series Liberty! with essays and resource links to a rich array of sites containing information on the American Revolution. Included are the Bill of Rights, slave documents, and maps of the era.

http://earlyamerica.com/

Archiving Early America. Via this site students can access writings, maps, and images of leading men and women reproduced from newspapers and magazines of the revolutionary era.

http://www.colonialhall.com/index.asp

Colonial Hall: Biographies of America's Founding Fathers. This site provides interesting information about the men who signed the Declaration of Independence and includes a trivia section.

http://www.ushistoryplace.com

 A richly detailed on-line learning environment complete with interactive maps, timelines, history activities, primary source documents, and links to related American history sites.

7

CONSOLIDATING *the* REVOLUTION

CHAPTER OUTLINE

Timothy Bloodworth of New Hanover County, North Carolina, knew what the American Revolution was all about, for he had experienced it firsthand. A man of humble origins, Bloodworth had known poverty as a child. Lacking any formal education, he had worked hard during the middle decades of the eighteenth century as an innkeeper and ferry pilot, self-styled preacher and physician, blacksmith and farmer. By the mid-1770s, he owned nine slaves and 4,200 acres of land, considerably more than most of his neighbors.

His unpretentious manner and commitment to political equality earned Bloodworth the confidence of his community. In 1758, at the age of 22, he was elected to the North Carolina colonial assembly. Over the next three decades, he was deeply involved in the political life of his home state.

When the colonies' troubles with England drew toward a crisis, Bloodworth spoke ardently of American rights and mobilized support for independence. In 1775, he helped form the Wilmington Committee of Safety. Filled with revolutionary fervor, he urged forward the process of republican political reform and, as commissioner of confiscated property for the district of Wilmington, pressed the attack on local Loyalists.

In 1784, shortly after the war ended, the North Carolina assembly named Bloodworth one of the state's delegates to the Confederation Congress. There he learned for the first time about the problems of governing a new nation. As the Congress struggled through the middle years of the 1780s with the intractable problems of foreign trade, war debt, and control of the trans-Appalachian interior, Bloodworth shared the growing conviction that the Articles of Confederation were too weak. He supported the Congress's call for a special convention to meet in Philadelphia in May 1787 for the purpose of taking action necessary "to render the constitution of the federal government adequate to the exigencies of the Union."

Like thousands of other Americans, Bloodworth eagerly awaited the convention's work. And like countless Americans, he was stunned by the result, for the proposed constitution described a govern-

ment that seemed to him certain not to preserve republican liberty but to endanger it.

Once again sniffing political tyranny on the breeze, Bloodworth resigned his congressional seat and in August 1787 hurried back to North Carolina to help organize opposition to the proposed constitution. Over the next several years, he worked tirelessly for its defeat.

Alarmed by the prospect of such a powerful central government, Bloodworth protested that "we cannot consent to the adoption of a Constitution whose revenues lead to aristocratic tyranny, or monarchical despotism, and open a door wide as fancy can point, for the introduction of dissipation, bribery and corruption to the exclusion of public virtue." Had Americans so quickly forgotten the dangers of consolidated power? Were they already prepared to turn away from their brief experiment in republicanism?

Alarmed by a variety of provisions in the document, Bloodworth demanded the addition of a federal bill of rights to protect individual liberties. Echoing the language of revolutionary republicanism, he warned the North Carolina ratifying convention that "without the most express restrictions, Congress may trample on your rights. Every possible precaution should be taken when we grant powers," he continued, for "Rulers are always disposed to abuse them."

Bloodworth also feared the sweeping authority Congress would have to make "all laws which shall be necessary and proper" for carrying into execution "all other powers vested . . . in the government of the United States." That language, he insisted, "would result in the abolition of the state governments. Its sovereignty absolutely annihilates them."

In North Carolina, the arguments of Bloodworth and his Anti-Federalist colleagues carried the day. By a vote of 184 to 84, the ratifying convention declared that a bill of rights "asserting and securing from encroachment the great Principles of civil and religious Liberty, and the unalienable rights of the People" must be approved before North Carolina would concur. The convention was true to its word. Not until November 1789, well after the new government had gotten under way and Congress had forwarded a national bill of rights to the states for approval, did North Carolina, with Timothy Bloodworth's cautious endorsement, finally enter the new union.

Ratification of the U.S. Constitution by the states in 1788 brought an end to the revolutionary years and ushered in a dramatically new era in the nation's history. *(John Feingersh/Stock Boston)*

Just as Timothy Bloodworth knew the difficulties of achieving American independence, so he learned the problems of preserving American liberty once independence had been won. As a member of the Confederation

Congress, Bloodworth confronted the continuing vestiges of colonialism: the patronizing attitudes of England and France, their continuing imperial ambitions in North America, and the republic's ongoing economic dependence on Europe. He also observed the Congress's inability to pay off the war debt, pry open foreign ports to American commerce, and persuade the states to join in a common tariff policy against England. As a southerner, Bloodworth was equally alarmed by the willingness of a congressional majority to forgo free navigation of the Mississippi River, deemed essential for development of the southern backcountry, in exchange for northern commercial advantages in Europe. Finally, he worried about political turmoil in the states as issues of taxation, debt, and paper money led discontented citizens openly to challenge public authority.

By 1786, Bloodworth, like countless other Americans, was caught up in an escalating debate between the Federalists, who believed that the Articles of Confederation were fatally deficient and must be replaced by a stronger national government, and the Anti-Federalists, who were deeply troubled by the dangers consolidated power posed to individual liberties.

That debate over the future of America's republican experiment came to a head in the momentous Philadelphia convention of 1787, which produced not reform but revolutionary change in the national government. With ratification of the new Constitution, the revolutionary era came to an end, and the American people opened a portentous new chapter in their history.

STRUGGLING WITH THE PEACETIME AGENDA

As the war ended, problems of demobilization and adjustment to the conditions of independence troubled the new nation. Whether the Confederation Congress could effectively deal with the problems of the postwar era remained unclear.

Demobilizing the Army

Demobilizing the army presented the Confederation government with some difficult moments, for when the fighting stopped, many of the troops refused to go home until the Congress redressed their grievances. Trouble first arose in early 1783 when officers at the continental army camp in Newburgh, New York, sent a delegation to the Congress to complain about arrears in pay and other benefits that had been promised them during the dark days of the war. When Congress called on the army to disband, an anonymous address circulated among the officers, attacking the "coldness and severity" of the Congress, calling for "a last remonstrance," and hinting darkly at more direct action if their grievances were not met.

Several Congressmen encouraged the officers' muttering, hoping the crisis would add urgency to their own calls for a stronger central government. Most, however, found the challenge to Congress's authority alarm-ing. Washington moved quickly to calm the situation. Promising that Congress would treat the officers justly, he counseled patience and urged his comrades not to tarnish the victory they had so recently won. His efforts succeeded, for the officers reaffirmed their confidence in the Congress and agreed to disband.

Military officers were not the only ones to take action. In June, several hundred disgruntled continental soldiers and Pennsylvania militiamen gathered in front of Philadelphia's Independence Hall, where both Congress and Pennsylvania's executive council were meeting. When the state authorities would not guarantee the Congress's safety, it fled to Princeton, New Jersey. Once there, tension eased when Congress issued the soldiers three months' pay and furloughed them until they could be fully discharged. By early November, the crisis was over, but congressional authority had been seriously damaged.

Over the next several years, the country's governing body shuffled between Princeton and Annapolis, Trenton and New York City, its transience visible evidence of its steadily eroding authority. A hot-air balloon, scoffed the *Boston Evening Herald,* would "exactly accommodate the itinerant genius of Congress," because it could then "float along from one end of the continent to the other . . . and when occasion requires . . . suddenly pop down into any of the states they please." Never had the Congress been so openly mocked.

Opening the West

The Congress was not without important accomplishments during the postwar years. Most notable were the two great land ordinances of 1785 and 1787. The first provided for the systematic survey and sale of the region west of New York and Pennsylvania and north of the Ohio River. The area was to be laid out in townships 6 miles square, which were in turn to be subdivided into lots of 640 acres each. Thus began the rectangular grid pattern of land survey and settlement that to this day characterizes the Midwest and distin-

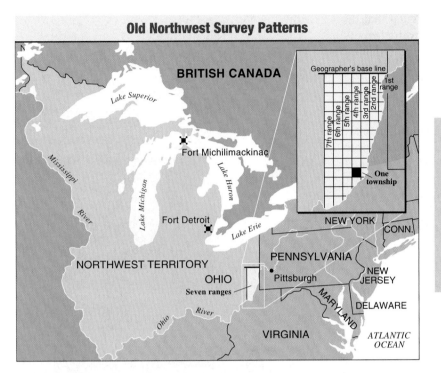

Old Northwest Survey Patterns

The Land Ordinance passed by Congress in 1785 provided for townships divided into lots of 640 acres. Its purpose was to promote the rapid and orderly settlement of the Old Northwest.

guishes it so markedly from the irregular settlement patterns of the older, colonial areas to the east.

Two years later, Congress passed the Northwest Ordinance. It provided for the political organization of the same interior region, first under congressionally appointed officials, then under popularly elected territorial assemblies, and ultimately as new states to be incorporated into the Union "on an equal footing with the original states in all respects whatsoever." Together these laws represented a conception of empire dramatically different from the one that had guided England's colonial domain. Rather than seeking to restrain white settlement on behalf of England's national interest as Parliament had attempted to do in the Proclamation Line of 1763, the central government in America's "empire of liberty" would actively promote its citizens' well-being by making land available via land laws and Indian policies. In addition, settlements established in the American West would not remain permanent colonies but would be fully incorporated into the expanding American nation. These changes carried profound importance for the future.

Both bills enjoyed broad political support, for they opened land to settlers and profits to speculators. The income from land sales, moreover, promised to help reduce the Revolutionary War debt. While permitting slave owners already living north of the Ohio River to retain their chattels, the Ordinance of 1787 prohibited the importation of new slaves into the region. This

made the area more attractive to white farmers who worried about competing with slave labor and living among blacks. Southern delegates in the Congress accepted the restriction because they could look forward to slavery's expansion south of the Ohio. During the 1780s, the country's interior seemed large enough to accommodate everyone's needs.

Despite these accomplishments, however, the Congress could neither get British troops out of the western posts south of the Great Lakes nor guarantee free navigation of the Mississippi. Nor was it able to clear the tribes of the Ohio region out of the white settlers' way. These failings led growing numbers of Americans to question whether the Confederation government was capable of promoting the nation's westward expansion.

During the immediate postwar years, the Congress operated as if the Native Americans of the interior were "conquered" peoples—allies of England who had lost the war and had thus come under U.S. control. Since the Treaty of Paris gave the United States ownership of all land east of the Mississippi River, Americans insisted that it gave the U.S. political sovereignty over the tribes living there.

Such claims were grounded as well in notions of Indian inferiority. Even the most sympathetic whites believed that Native Americans would have to become "civilized" and "Christianized" before they could coexist with white society. Many whites doubted that such "improvements" were possible, and argued that the Indians must simply be driven out of white settlers' way. George Washington gave blunt expression to the prevailing view. "The gradual extension of our settlements," he explained, "will as certainly cause the savage as the wolf to retire; both being beasts of prey though they differ in shape."

For a few years, the conquest strategy appeared to work. During the mid-1780s, Congress imposed several important land treaties on the interior tribes, among them the Iroquois. Their numbers reduced and their confederation shattered, many Iroquois had fled into Canada. Pressured by both Congress and the New York government, those who remained deeded away much of their land. At the Treaty of Fort Stanwix in 1784, the first treaty between the newly independent government and an Indian tribe, the Six Nations officially made peace, ceded most of their lands to the United States, and retreated to small reservations. By the 1790s, little remained of the once imposing Iroquois domain but a few islands in a spreading sea of white settlement. On those islands—"slums in the wilderness" they have been called—the Iroquois struggled for survival against disease and poverty, their traditional lifeways gone, their self-confidence broken. The Iroquois were not the only tribe to lose their land. In January 1785, representatives of the Wyandotte, Chippewa, Delaware, and Ottawa tribes relinquished claim to most of present-day Ohio.

Often exacted under the threat of force, many of the treaties generated resentment. At Fort Stanwix negotiations were held at gunpoint, and hostages were

The symbolic figure of Columbia, often presented in the form of an Indian maiden embodying the innocence and freedom of the new republic, first became popular during the Revolution. This began to change as Americans moved west across the Appalachians. By the time this French engraving appeared in the early nineteenth century, Columbia was usually garbed in classical attire and had lost her Indian headdress. *(Library of Congress)*

"Utmost Good Faith" Clause from the Northwest Ordinance (1787)

The following articles shall be considered as articles of compact between the original States and the people and States in the said territory and forever remain unalterable, unless by common consent, to wit:

> The utmost good faith shall always be observed towards the Indians; their land and property shall never be taken from them without their consent; and, in their property, rights, and liberty, they shall never be invaded or disturbed, unless in just and lawful wars authorized by Congress, but laws founded in justice and humanity, shall from time to time be made for preventing wrongs being done to them, and for preserving peace and friendship with them.

taken to coerce the Indian delegates. Two years later the Iroquois openly repudiated the treaty, asserting that they were still sovereigns of their own soil and "equally free as . . . any nation under the sun." The Revolution, moreover, left behind a legacy of bitterness: among Indians because they had suffered betrayal and defeat, among white Americans because the Indians had sided with England and thus threatened the Revolution's success. Such bitterness would trouble Indian–white relations for years to come.

By the mid-1780s, tribal groups in the Ohio Valley were actively resisting white expansion. North of the river, the Shawnee, Delaware, and Miami moved to strengthen their Western Confederacy and prepare for the defense of their homeland. In the fall of 1786, the confederacy rejected congressional claims of conquest and asserted that the Ohio River was the proper boundary between them and the United States. When white settlers continued to press into the region, Native Americans launched a series of devastating raids, bringing white settlement to a virtual halt. By the end of 1786, the entire region from the Great Lakes

British and Spanish Possessions in Eastern North America, 1783

* Military and administrative centers

British Canada

United States

Spanish possessions

Though victorious in its struggle for independence, the United States remained surrounded on three sides by British and Spanish possessions. North America continued to be a focus of European colonial ambitions after 1783.

to the Gulf of Mexico was embroiled in warfare. With the continental army disbanded, there was little that the Congress could do.

Congress's inability to open the interior to white settlement alarmed countless Americans: speculators facing the loss of their investments; farmers wanting to leave the crowded lands of the East; revolutionary soldiers eager to start afresh on the rich soil of Kentucky and Ohio that they had been promised as payment for military service; and leaders such as Thomas Jefferson who believed that republican liberty depended on an ever expanding frontier. With the Confederation Congress unable to implement the promised "empire of liberty," there was growing reason to question its adequacy.

Settling the interior, the indispensable land reserve for the fast-growing nation, involved delicate negotiations with European nations as well. Here, too, the Congress proved ineffective. In June 1784, Spain—still in possession of Florida, the Gulf Coast, and the trans-Mississippi West—closed the mouth of the Mississippi

River at New Orleans to American shipping. Spain's action raised a storm of protest among western settlers who counted on floating their produce downstream to New Orleans for transshipment to markets along the East Coast and in Europe. Land speculators were angered as well, for closure of the Mississippi would discourage development of the southern backcountry and reduce their profits. Rumors spread, moreover, that Spanish agents were urging American frontiersmen to break away from the new nation and seek affiliation with Spain. Washington commented uneasily that settlers were "on a pivot" throughout the West. "The touch of a feather," he feared, "would turn them away."

For more than a year, Foreign Secretary John Jay negotiated with the Spanish ambassador to the United States, Don Diego de Gardoqui, in an effort to reopen the vital Mississippi River outlet. When Gardoqui held firm, Jay offered to relinquish American claims to free transit of the Mississippi in return for a commercial treaty opening Spanish ports to American shipping. Excited by the prospect of Spanish trade, northern merchants supported the bargain, but the southern delegates in Congress, angry at Jay's betrayal of their interests, refused to go along. Stalemated, the Congress took no action at all.

Wrestling with the National Debt

The Congress's inability to deal effectively with the nation's war debt, estimated at $35 million, offered further evidence of the Confederation government's weakness. Much of the debt was held by French and Dutch bankers. Unable to make regular payment against the loan's principal, the Congress had to borrow additional money abroad simply to pay the accumulating interest. At home, things were no better. In response to the incessant demands of its creditors, the government could only delay and try to borrow more.

In 1781, the Congress appointed Robert Morris, a wealthy Philadelphia merchant, superintendent of finance and gave him broad authority to deal with the nation's troubled affairs. Morris urged the states to stop issuing paper money and persuaded the Congress to demand that the states pay their requisitions in specie. In addition, he secured a Congressional charter for the Bank of North America and took steps to make federal bonds more attractive to investors.

Though Morris made considerable progress, the government's finances remained shaky. Lacking the power to tax, the Congress continued to depend on the states' willingness to meet their financial obligations. This arrangement, however, proved unworkable. Desperate for resources, the Congress, in October 1781, requested $8 million from the states. Two and a half years later, less than $1.5 million of that amount had come in. In January 1784, Morris resigned, partly in despair over the government's financial situation and partly to recoup his personal fortunes.

By 1786, total federal revenue amounted to no more than $370,000 a year, not enough, as one official lamented, to provide for "the bare maintenance of the federal government [even] on the most economical establishment." Declared a congressional committee, Americans "must decide whether they will support their rank as a nation, by maintaining the public faith at home and abroad; or whether, for want of . . . a general revenue . . . they will hazard . . . the great and invaluable privileges for which they have so arduously and so honorably contended."

Not all Americans were alarmed. Some pointed out approvingly that several state governments, having brought their own financial affairs under control, were beginning to assume responsibility for portions of the national debt. Others, however, saw that as additional evidence of the Congress's weakening condition and wondered how a government unable to maintain its credit could long endure.

Surviving in a Hostile Atlantic World

The Congress's difficulties in dealing with its creditors abroad and countering Spain's closure of the Mississippi River at home pointed to a broader problem in American foreign relations. Even after the United States had formally won independence, England, France, and Spain continued to threaten the new republic.

The Revolutionary War had dramatically transformed America's relationships with other nations. England, once the nurturing "mother country," had become the enemy, while France, long the mortal foe of England and the colonies alike, had proved a vital ally. Yet France was at best an uncertain friend. With an empire of its own, it feared colonial rebellions. In addition, the French king and aristocracy regarded republicanism as deeply subversive, and France's efforts to manipulate the peace process for its own advantage had taught the Americans a hard lesson in the realities of power diplomacy.

Independence, moreover, did not end European ambitions in North America. Though France had lost its North American possessions in the Seven Years' War (see Chapter 5), it would gain title to most of the trans-Mississippi west by 1800. Meanwhile, Great Britain's Union Jack continued to fly over eastern Canada, while British troops retained possession of strategic outposts on American soil at Detroit, Michilimackinac, and Niagara. And as alarmed reaction to the Jay–Gardoqui affair made evident, Spain still conjured up grim memories of past New World conquests. The reason for America's diplomatic troubles was clear: the country was new, weak, and republican in an Atlantic world dominated by strong, monarchical governments and divided into warring empires.

Nothing revealed the difficulties of national survival more starkly than the Congress's futile efforts to rebuild America's crucially important overseas commerce. As we have seen, the Revolutionary War brought American trade virtually to a halt. Once the war was over, American merchants eagerly sought to reopen commerce with England. While highly desired English goods once again flooded American markets, few American goods flowed the other way. John Adams learned why. In 1785, he arrived in London as the first American minister to England. The Congress had assigned him the task of negotiating a commercial treaty, but he soon discovered how difficult that would be. After endless rebuffs, he reported in frustration that England had no intention of reopening the empire's ports to American shipping. English officials testily reminded him that Americans had desired independence and must now live with its consequences. Moreover, British goods could command the American market, they pointed out, without England's needing to grant trade concessions in return.

Progress was slow as American merchants searched for new commercial arrangements during the 1780s. Not only did England remain intractable, but France and Spain also withdrew wartime trading privileges and returned to a policy of maritime restrictions. In an effort to rebuild American commerce, the Congress tried to secure the states' cooperation in a program of economic recovery. Its efforts, however, were unavailing. In 1784, it failed to obtain authorization from the states to regulate the nation's foreign trade because each state was preoccupied with its own commercial advantage. As a consequence, American overseas trade continued to languish.

The result was deepening economic hardship. In Philadelphia, only 13 ships were built in 1786, one-third as many as just two years before. By the late 1780s, the per capita value of American exports had fallen a startling 30 percent from the 1760s. No wonder that merchants and artisans, carpenters and shopkeepers, sailors and dock workers—all directly dependent on shipbuilding and overseas commerce—suffered. In an Atlantic world divided into exclusive, imperial trading spheres, the United States lacked both the political unity and the economic muscle to protect its interests.

REVOLUTIONARY POLITICS IN THE STATES

Revolutionary politics took different forms in each state, depending on the impact of the war, the extent of

Loyalism, patterns of social conflict, and the disruptions of economic life. Throughout the nation, though, citizens struggled with an often intractable array of issues that arose during the war years but continued to trouble American politics well into the 1780s.

Separating Church and State

Among the most explosive issues was determining the proper relationship between church and state. Prior to independence, only Rhode Island, New Jersey, Pennsylvania, and Delaware had allowed full religious liberty. In the other colonies one or another religious group benefited from endorsement by the government and public tax support for its clergy. There civil authorities grudgingly tolerated "dissenters" such as the Methodists and Baptists, whose numbers were growing among the lower classes of the city and countryside and who were noisily pressing their case for full religious liberty.

With independence, pressure built for severing all ties between church and state. Such arguments were strengthened by the belief that alliances between government and church authorities had resulted in religious oppression throughout history and that voluntary choice was the only safe principle of religious association.

In Massachusetts, Connecticut, and New Hampshire, Congregationalists fought to retain their long-established privileges. Separating church and state, they argued, risked the growth of infidelity and disorder. Isaac Backus, the most outspoken of New England's Baptists, protested that "many, who are filling the nation with the cry of *liberty* and against *oppressors* are at the same time themselves violating that dearest of all rights, *liberty of conscience.*"

Massachusetts's new constitution guaranteed everyone the right to worship God "in the manner and season most agreeable to the dictates of his own conscience." But as Backus pointed out, it also empowered the legislature to require that towns tax their residents to support the public worship of God. Such support, Backus argued, should be ended completely, since religious toleration fell far short of true religious freedom. Not until the early nineteenth century—in Massachusetts not until 1833—were the laws linking church and state finally repealed.

In Virginia, the Baptists pressed their cause against the Protestant Episcopal Church, successor to the Church of England. The adoption in 1786 of Thomas Jefferson's Bill for Establishing Religious Freedom, rejecting all connections between church and state and removing all religious tests for public office, decisively settled the issue. Three years later, that statute served as a model for the First Amendment to the new federal Constitution.

Even most supporters of religious freedom, however, were not prepared to extend it universally. While the wartime alliance with Catholic France together with congressional efforts to entice Catholic settlers in Quebec to join the resistance against England had weakened long-established prejudices, anti-Catholic biases remained strong, especially in New England.

This nineteenth-century print says it gives "A Correct View of the Old Methodist Church in John Street, New York. The first erected in America. Founded A.D. 1768." Methodists and Baptists were among the "dissenting" groups pressing for full religious freedom during the revolutionary era. (*The Metropolitan Museum of Art, Bequest of Edward W. C. Arnold, 1954. The Edward W. C. Arnold Collection of New York Prints, Maps and Pictures. (54.90.168))*

Recovering the Past

INDIAN TREATIES

uring the 1780s, the new American government contracted its first treaties with Native Americans of the trans-Appalachian interior, including the Wyandotte, the Delaware, and the Cherokee. The treaties were necessary to complete the peacemaking process at the end of the Revolutionary War, because most of the interior tribes had sided with England. The treaties were also intended to open trans-Appalachia to white settlement.

The treaty texts, like the agreement between the Congress and the Cherokee signed at Hopewell in November 1785, presented here, tell us a great deal about the issues that lay at the center of Indian–white relations during the 1780s. What major issues did the treaty of 1785 attempt to resolve? Why were these issues important to the Congress and the Native Americans?

A careful reading of the treaty language can also tell us much about the attitudes and values that white negotiators brought to the treaty-making process and provide hints of how that process functioned. Which phrases in the treaty reveal how the Congress's negotiators viewed their Cherokee counterparts? From the evidence of the treaty text, how would you characterize the treaty negotiations?

Most of the treaties arranged during the 1780s failed to last, and by the end of the decade trans-Appalachia, both north and south of the Ohio River, was embroiled in Indian–white warfare. Why did these agreements prove so fragile?

Treaty with the Cherokee, 1785

Articles concluded at Hopewell, on the Keowee, between Benjamin Hawkins, Andrew Pickens, Joseph Martin, and Lachlan M'Intosh, Commissioners Plenipotentiary of the United States of America, of the one Part, and the Head-Men and Warriors of all the Cherokees of the other.

The Commissioners Plenipotentiary of the United States, in Congress assembled, give peace to all the Cherokees, and receive them into the favor and protection of the United States of America, on the following conditions:

Article I

The Head-Men and Warriors of all the Cherokees shall restore all the prisoners, citizens of the United States, or subjects of their allies, to their entire liberty: They shall also restore all the Negroes, and all other property taken during the late war from the citizens, to such person, and at such time and place, as the Commissioners shall appoint.

Article II

The Commissioners of the United States in Congress assembled, shall restore all prisoners taken from the Indians, during the late war, to the Head-Men and Warriors of the Cherokees, as early as is practicable.

Article III

The said Indians for themselves and their respective tribes and towns do acknowledge all the Cherokees to be under the protection of the United States of America, and of no other sovereign whosoever.

Article IV

The boundary allotted to the Cherokees for their hunting grounds, between the said Indians and the citizens of the United States, within the limits of the United States of America, is, and shall be the following. . . .

Article V

If any citizen of the United States, or other person not being an Indian, shall attempt to settle on any of the lands westward or southward of the said boundary which are hereby allotted to the Indians for their hunting grounds, or having already settled and will not remove from the same within six months after the ratification of this treaty, such person shall forfeit the protection of the United States, and the Indians may punish him or not as they please. . . .

Article VI

If any Indian or Indians, or person residing among them, or who shall take refuge in their nation, shall commit a robbery, or murder, or other capital crime, on any citizen of the United States, or person under their protection, the nation, or the tribe to which such offender or offenders may belong, shall be bound to deliver him or them up to be punished according to the ordinances of the United States; Provided, that the punishment shall not be greater than if the robbery or murder, or other capital crime had been committed by a citizen on a citizen.

Article VII

If any citizen of the United States, or person under their protection, shall commit a robbery or murder, or other capital crime, on any Indian, such offender or offenders shall be punished in the same manner as if the murder or robbery, or other capital crime, had been committed on a citizen of the United States; and the punishment shall be in presence of some of the Cherokees, if any shall attend at the time and place. . . .

Article VIII

It is understood that the punishment of the innocent under the idea of retaliation, is unjust, and shall not be practiced on either side, except where there is a manifest violation of this treaty; and then it shall be preceded first by a demand of justice, and if refused, then by a declaration of hostilities.

Article IX

For the benefit and comfort of the Indians, and for the prevention of injuries or oppressions on the part of the citizens or Indians, the United States in Congress assembled shall have the sole and exclusive right of regulating the trade with the Indians, and managing all their affairs in such manner as they think proper. . . .

Article XI

The said Indians shall give notice to the citizens of the United States, of any designs which they may know or suspect to be formed in any neighboring tribe, or by any person whosoever, against the peace, trade or interest of the United States.

Article XII

That the Indians may have full confidence in the justice of the United States, respecting their interests, they shall have the right to send a deputy of their choice, whenever they think fit, to Congress.

Article XIII

The hatchet shall be forever buried, and the peace given by the United States, and friendship re-established between the said states on the one part, and all the Cherokees on the other, shall be universal; and the contracting parties shall use their utmost endeavors to maintain the peace given as aforesaid, and friendship re-established.

In witness of all and every thing herein determined, between the United States of America and all the Cherokees, we, their underwritten Commissioners, by virtue of our full powers, have signed this definitive treaty, and have caused our seals to be hereunto affixed.

Done at Hopewell, on the Keowee, this twenty-eighth of November, in the year of our Lord one thousand seven hundred and eighty-five.

Benjamin Hawkins,
And'w Pickens,
Jos. Martin,
Lach'n McIntosh,
Koatohee, or Corn Tassel of Toquo, his x mark,
Scholauetta, or Hanging Man of Chota, his x mark,
Tuskegatahu, or Long Fellow of Chistohoe, his x mark,
Ooskwha, or Abraham of Chilkowa, his x mark,
Kolakusta, or Prince of Noth, his x mark,
Newota, or the Gritzs of Chicamaga, his x mark,
Konatota, or the Rising Fawn of Highwassay, his x mark,
Tuckasee, or Young Terrapin of Allajoy, his x mark,
Toostaka, or the Waker of Oostanawa, his x mark,
Untoola, or Gun Rod of Seteco, his x mark,
Unsuokanail, Buffalo White Calf New Cussee, his x mark,
Kostayeak, or Sharp Fellow Wataga, his x mark,
Chonosta, of Cowe, his x mark,
Chescoonwho, Bird in Close of Tomotlug, his x mark,
Tuckasee, or Terrapin of Hightowa, his x mark,
Chesetoa, or the Rabbit of Tlacoa, his x mark. . . .
Witness:
Wm. Blount,
Sam'l Taylor, Major.,
John Owen,
Jess. Walton,
Jno. Cowan, capt. comm'd't,
Thos. Gregg, 4
W. Hazzard,
James Madison,
Arthur Cooley, Sworn interpreters.

Source: Charles Kapple, ed., *Indian Affairs: Laws and Treaties* (Washington, D.C.: U.S. Government Printing Office, 1904–1941), vol. 2, pp. 8–11.

The people of Northbridge, Massachusetts, wanted to exclude "Roman Catholics, pagons, or Mahomitents" from public office. Disestablishment did not end religious discrimination. But it implanted the principle of religious freedom firmly in American law.

Slavery under Attack

Whether human slavery was tolerable in a republican society committed to the inalienable right to life, liberty, and the pursuit of happiness also vexed the revolutionary generation. During the several decades preceding independence, the trade in human chattels had flourished. While the 1760s had witnessed the largest importation of slaves in colonial history, the Revolutionary War halted the slave trade almost completely. Though southern planters talked of replacing their lost chattels once the war ended, a combination of revolutionary principles, a reduced need for field hands in the depressed Chesapeake tobacco economy, the continuing natural increase among the slave population, and anxiety over black rebelliousness argued for the slave trade's permanent extinction. By 1790, every state except South Carolina and Georgia had outlawed slave importations.

Ending the slave trade had powerful implications, for it reduced the infusion of new Africans into the black population. As a result, an ever higher proportion of blacks was American born, thus speeding the cultural transformation by which Africans became African Americans.

Slavery itself came under attack during the revolutionary era, with immense consequences for blacks and for the nation's future. As the crisis with England heated up, catchwords such as *liberty* and *tyranny*, mobilized by colonists against British policies, reminded citizens that one-fifth of the colonial population was in chains. Samuel Hopkins, a New England clergyman, accosted his compatriots for "making a vain parade of being advocates for the liberties of mankind, while . . . continuing this lawless, cruel, inhuman, and abominable practice of enslaving your fellow creatures." Following independence, the antislavery attacks intensified.

In Georgia and South Carolina, where blacks outnumbered whites more than two to one, slavery escaped significant challenge. Committed to the doctrine of racial superiority and fearing the black majority, whites shuddered at the prospect of black freedom. Moreover, slave labor remained essential to the still prosperous rice economy. In response to the dangers generated by the war, whites wound the local slave codes even tighter.

In Virginia and Maryland, by contrast, whites openly argued whether slavery was compatible with republicanism, and in these states significant change did occur. The weakened demand for slave labor posed by the depressed tobacco economy facilitated the debate. Though neither state abolished slavery, both passed laws making it easier for owners to manumit (that is, to free) their slaves without continuing to be responsible for their behavior. Moreover, increasing numbers of blacks purchased freedom for themselves and their families or simply ran away. By 1800, more than one of every ten blacks in the Chesapeake region was no longer enslaved, a dramatic increase from 30 years before. Not all were genuinely free, since many found their lives constrained as indentured servants obligated to work for others. For them, true freedom was postponed.

The majority of free blacks lived and worked in Baltimore, Richmond, and other towns, where they formed communities that served as centers of an expanding African American society as well as havens for slaves escaping from the countryside. In the Chesapeake region, the conditions of life for black Americans slowly changed for the better.

The most dramatic breakthrough occurred in the North. There slavery was either abolished or put on the road to gradual extinction. Abolition was possible in the North because blacks were a numerical minority—in most areas, blacks constituted no more than 4 percent of the population—and slavery had neither the economic nor social importance that it did in the South.

Northern blacks joined in the attacks on slavery. Following independence, they eagerly petitioned state assemblies for their freedom. "Every Principle from which America has acted in the course of their unhappy difficulties with Great Britain," declared one group of Philadelphia blacks, "pleads stronger than a thousand arguments in favor of our petition." In 1780, the Pennsylvania assembly passed a law stipulating that all newborn blacks were to be free when they reached age 21. It was a cautious but decisive step. Other northern states adopted similar policies of gradual emancipation.

In scattered instances, free blacks participated actively in revolutionary politics. When the first draft of the Massachusetts constitution, explicitly excluding blacks and mulattoes from the franchise, was made public, William Gordon, a white clergyman, voiced his protest. "Would it not be ridiculous . . . and unjust to exclude freemen from voting . . . though otherwise qualified, because their skins are black?" he questioned. "Why not . . . for being long-nosed, short-faced, or . . . lower than five feet nine?" In the end, Massachusetts's constitution made no mention of race, and there, as well as in Pennsylvania and New York, African Americans occasionally cast their ballots.

If civic participation by blacks was scattered and temporary in the North, it was almost totally absent in the South. With the brief exception of North Carolina, African Americans in the South could neither vote nor enjoy such basic rights of citizenship as protection of their persons and property under the law. Here, blacks remained almost entirely without political voice, except in the petitions against slavery and mistreatment that they pressed upon the state regimes. Even as freemen, blacks continued to encounter pervasive discrimination.

Still, remarkable progress had been made. Prior to the Revolution, slavery had been an accepted fact of northern life. After the Revolution, it no longer was. That change made a vast difference in the lives of countless black Americans. The abolition of slavery in the North, moreover, widened the sectional divergence between North and South, with enormous consequences for the years ahead. In addition, there now existed a coherent, publicly proclaimed antislavery ideology that was closely linked in Americans' minds to the nation's founding. The first antislavery organizations had been created as well. Although another half century would pass before antislavery became a significant force in American politics, the groundwork for slavery's final abolition had been laid.

Politics and the Economy

The devastating economic effects of independence and the Revolutionary War continued to plague the American people throughout the 1780s. The cutoff of long-established patterns of overseas trade with England sent American commerce into a tailspin from which it did not recover for nearly 20 years. While English men-of-war prowled the coast, American ships rocked idly at empty wharves, New England's once booming shipyards grew quiet, and communities whose livelihood depended on the sea sank into depression. Virginia tobacco planters, their English markets gone and their plantations open to seaborne attack, struggled to survive. Farmers in the middle and New England states often prospered while hungry armies were nearby but saw their profits plummet when the armies moved on.

Not everyone suffered equally. With British goods excluded from American markets and wearing homespun clothes deemed patriotic, American artisans often prospered. (The familiar slogan "Buy American" has a long tradition.) Handsome profits from government contracts, moreover, were enjoyed by people with the right political connections. Henry Knox, sometime merchant and commander of the continental artillery, observed that he was "exceedingly anxious to effect something in these fluctuating times, which may make . . . [me] easy for life." In the eight-

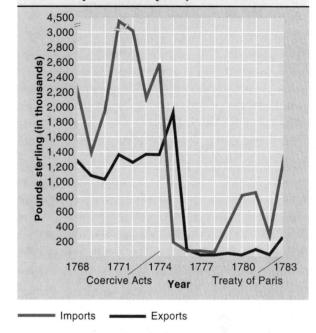

Nonimportation affected colonial commerce during the late 1760s and early 1770s, but exports as well as imports plummeted with the Coercive Acts and the outbreak of war. Source: U.S. Bureau of the Census.

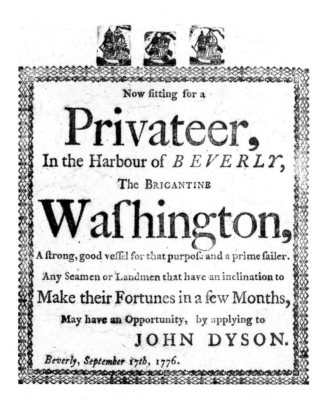

As this Massachusetts broadside suggests, the lure of adventure and hope for quick profits enticed countless young men into dangerous but exciting service aboard American privateers. *(American Antiquarian Society)*

eenth century, as now, the boundary between private interest and public duty was often unclear.

But even as some prospered, countless others saw their affairs fall into disarray. Intractable issues such as price and wage inflation, skyrocketing taxation, and mushrooming debt set people sharply against each other. Heated debates arose over whether the states' war debts should be funded at face value or at some reduced rate. Arguing for full value were creditors—merchants and other persons of wealth who had loaned money to the states and had bought up large amounts of government securities at deep discounts. These people spoke earnestly of upholding the public honor and giving fair return to those who had risked their personal resources in the revolutionary cause. Opposed were common folk angered by the speculators' profits. No one, they argued, should reap personal advantage from public distress.

The issue of taxation, seared into Americans' consciousness by their troubles with England, generated similarly heated controversy. As the costs of the war mounted, so did taxes. Between 1774 and 1778, Massachusetts levied more than £400,000 in taxes, a stunning increase over colonial days. Complained one anguished soul, taxes siphoned off nearly one-third of the inhabitants' incomes. Massachusetts was not unique.

As taxes skyrocketed, farmers, artisans, and others of modest means argued that taxes should be

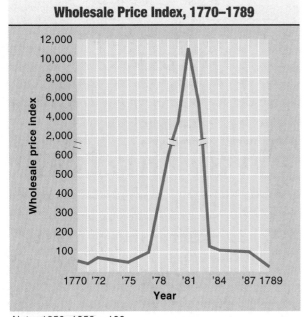

Wholesale Price Index, 1770–1789

Note: 1850–1859 = 100

Prices skyrocketed as Congress and the state governments printed huge amounts of paper money in a desperate effort to cover the costs of the war. Source: U.S. Bureau of the Census.

payable in depreciated paper money or government securities rather than only in specie (gold or silver coin), as some state laws required. Lacking specie, they faced foreclosure of their property when they could not meet their obligations. Government officials responded that allowing payment in depreciated paper would deprive the government of critically needed revenue.

Controversy swirled as well around efforts to control soaring prices. Every state experimented with price controls at one time or another. Seldom were such efforts effective; frequently, they generated political firestorms. In general, the poor and those not yet integrated into the market economy supported controls. Faced with escalating prices, they had difficulty making ends meet. They also believed that goods should carry a "just price" that was fair to buyer and seller alike. In keeping with these principles, a crowd in New Windsor, New York, seized a shipment of tea bound for Albany in 1777 and sold it for what they deemed a fair offering.

Merchants, shopkeepers, and others accustomed to a commercial economy, however, believed that the laws of supply and demand should regulate economic transactions. "It is contrary to the nature of commerce," observed Benjamin Franklin, "for government to interfere in the prices of commodities." Attempts to regulate prices only created a disincentive to labor, which was "the principal part of the wealth of every country."

Disputes over paper money divided the American people as well. Faced with the uncontrollable escalation of wartime expenses, Congress and the states did what colonial governments had done before and American governments have done ever since: they printed money. In the first year of the war alone, they issued more than $400 million in various kinds of paper, and that was just the beginning. Only the citizens' willingness to accept such paper supported its value. That willingness rapidly disappeared as the flood of paper increased. Congressional bills of credit that in 1776 were pegged against gold at the ratio of 1.5 to 1 had slipped five years later to 147 to 1. State currencies depreciated just as alarmingly. In 1780, New York exchanged its old currency for new at the rate of 128 to 1.

Immense quantities of counterfeit currency produced by unscrupulous Americans out to make a profit as well as by British agents intent on disrupting the American war effort added to the monetary confusion. So worthless did American currency become that a crowd paraded the streets of Philadelphia in 1781 with paper money stuck in their hats as cockades and leading a dog plastered with congressional dollars.

Lacking sufficient gold and silver to cover the escalating costs of war, Congress printed massive amounts of paper money, which, in spite of the printed pledge, rapidly depreciated in value. *(Smithsonian Institution)*

The upward spiral of prices was staggering. In Massachusetts, a bushel of corn that sold for less than a dollar in 1777 went for nearly $80 two years later, and in Maryland the price of wheat increased several thousandfold. In Boston, a crowd of women, angered by the escalating costs of food, tossed a merchant suspected of monopolizing commodities into a cart and dragged him through the city's streets while "a large concourse of men stood amazed."

The disastrous monetary depreciation threatened to disrupt long-established social arrangements. James Lovell reported nervously that "sailors with clubs" were parading the streets of Boston "instead of working for paper." With property values in disarray, it seemed at times as if the very foundations of society were coming unhinged. "The war," wrote Thomas Paine,

> has thrown property into channels where before it never was.... Monies in large sums ... enable ... [profiteers] to roll the snow ball of monopoly and forestalling ... [and] while these people are heaping up wealth ... the remaining part are jogging on in their old way, with few or no advantages.

The poor suffered most severely, for they were most vulnerable to losses in the purchasing power of wages and military pay. They, however, were not alone. Farmers and merchants, planters and artisans also faced the burden of growing debt and uncertainty.

Rarely has the American economy been in such disarray as at the nation's founding. There were no ready solutions to the problems of debt, taxation, price control, and paper money for such issues often exceeded the capacity of politics for compromise and resolution. Divisive and intractable, they continued to heighten political tensions during the postwar years.

POLITICAL TUMULT IN THE STATES

Among the many issues embroiling state politics, debt relief, paper money, and arguments over equality came together with particularly explosive force in the mid-1780s. The political crisis that resulted spurred demands for a new and more powerful national government.

The Limits of Republican Experimentation

In a pattern that would frequently recur in American history, the postwar era witnessed growing social and political conservatism. Exhausted by the war's ordeal, many Americans turned their energies toward solving the problems troubling their personal lives. With the patriotic crusade against England successfully concluded, the initial surge of republican reform subsided. As a consequence, political leadership fell increasingly to men convinced that republican experimentation had gone too far, that the balance between order and liberty had to be reestablished, and that the "better sort" of men, not democratic newcomers, should occupy public office.

The most dramatic change occurred in Pennsylvania, where the democratic constitution of

1776 was replaced by a far more conservative document in 1790. The new constitution provided for a strong governor who could veto legislation and control the militia and a conservative senate designed to balance the more democratic assembly. Gaining a legislative majority by the mid-1780s, the conservatives dismantled much of the radicals' program by repealing revolutionary test oaths, stopping the issuance of paper money, and rechartering the Bank of North America. Pennsylvania's experiment in radical republicanism was over.

Shays's Rebellion

The conservative resurgence generated surprisingly little controversy in Pennsylvania. Elsewhere, however, popular opposition to hard money and high-tax policies produced vigorous protest. Nowhere was the situation more volatile than in Massachusetts. The controversy that erupted there in 1786 echoed strongly of equal rights and popular consent, staples of the rhetoric of 1776.

Given the war's disruption of economic affairs, increasing numbers of Massachusetts citizens found that they had to borrow money just to pay their taxes and support their families. Others who were more fortunate borrowed in order to speculate in western land or government securities. Because there were no commercial banks, people borrowed from each other in a complicated and highly unstable pyramid of credit and debt that reached from wealthy merchants along the coast to shopkeepers and farmers in the interior.

Trouble began when English goods glutted the American market, forcing down prices. In 1785, a number of English banking houses, heavily overcommitted in the American trade, began calling in loans they had extended to American importers. In a desperate effort to survive, these wholesalers demanded payment of the debts due them from retail storekeepers, sending a credit crisis surging through the state's economy.

Hardest hit were laboring people and farmers in town and countryside. Caught in a tightening financial bind, they turned to the state government for "stay laws" suspending the collection of private debts and thus easing the threat of foreclosure against their farms and shops. They also demanded new issues of paper money with which to pay both private debts and public taxes. The largest creditors, most of whom lived in commercial areas along the coast, fought such proposals because they wanted to collect the sums owed them promptly and in hard money. They also feared that paper money would quickly depreciate and further confound economic affairs.

By 1786, Massachusetts farmers, desperate in the face of mounting debt and a lingering agricultural depression, were petitioning the Massachusetts assembly for relief in words that echoed the colonial protests of the 1760s. Their appeals, however, fell on deaf ears, for commercial and creditor interests now controlled the government. Turning aside appeals for tax relief, the government passed a law calling for full repayment of the state debt and levied a heavy new round of taxes that would make such payment possible. No matter that, as one angry citizen reported, "there was not . . . the money in possession or at command among the people . . . to discharge their taxes." Between 1784 and 1786, 29 towns defaulted on their tax obligations.

This woodcut from *Bickerstaff's Genuine Boston Almanack* of 1787 depicts a county convention framing a petition for redress of grievances to the Massachusetts government. *(Library of Congress)*

Shays's Rebellion generated considerable alarm throughout Massachusetts. Grateful citizens of Springfield commissioned Paul Revere to make this silver punch bowl for General William Shepard, who was credited with defeating the insurgents. *(Yale University Art Gallery, The Mabel Brady Garvan Collection)*

As frustrated citizens had done before and would do again when the law proved unresponsive to their needs, Massachusetts farmers took matters into their own hands. A Hampshire County convention of delegates from 50 towns condemned the state senate, court fees, and the tax system. It advised against violence, but mobs soon began to form.

The county courts drew much of the farmers' wrath because they issued the writs of foreclosure that state and private creditors demanded. On August 31, 1786, armed men prevented the county court from sitting at Northampton, and on September 5 angry citizens closed down the court at Worcester. When farmers threatened similar actions elsewhere, an alarmed Governor James Bowdoin dispatched 600 militiamen to protect the state Supreme Court, then on circuit at Springfield.

About 500 insurgents had gathered nearby under the leadership of Daniel Shays, a popular Revolutionary War captain recently fallen on hard times. A "brave and good soldier," Shays had returned home in 1780, tired and frustrated, to await payment for his military service. Like thousands of others, he had a long wait. Meanwhile, his farming went badly, his debts accumulated, and, as he later recalled, "the spector of debtor's jail . . . hovered close by." Most of the men who gathered around Shays were also debtors and veterans.

The Continental Congress, urged by the Massachusetts delegates to take action and worried about a possible raid on the federal arsenal at Springfield, authorized 1,300 troops, ostensibly for service against the Indians but actually to be ready for use against Shays and his supporters. For a few weeks, Massachusetts teetered on the brink of civil conflict.

The insurrection collapsed in eastern Massachusetts in late November but was far from over

in the west. When several insurgent groups refused Governor Bowdoin's order to disperse, he called out a force of 4,400 men, financed and led by worried eastern merchants. On January 26, 1787, Shays led 1,200 men toward the federal arsenal at Springfield. Its frightened defenders opened fire, killing four of the attackers and sending the Shaysites into retreat.

Over the next several weeks, the militia chased the remnants of Shays's followers across the state and sent Shays himself fleeing into Vermont for safety. By the end of February, the rebellion was over. In March, the legislature pardoned all but Shays and three other leaders; in another year, they too were forgiven.

Similar challenges to public authority, fired by personal troubles and frustration over unresponsive government, erupted in six other states. In Charles County, Maryland, a "tumultuary assemblage of the people" rushed into the courthouse in June 1786 and closed it down. Like the Massachusetts rebels, they demanded paper money and the suspension of debt proceedings. In Cecil County, farmers circulated

Following the war, hundreds of women petitioned state legislatures to recover property and seek redress for other war related grievances. In this petition, Mary Moore seeks compensation from the North Carolina Assembly. *(Courtesy of the North Carolina Division of Archives and History)*

unsigned handbills threatening state officers if they seized people's property for unpaid taxes. The governor condemned the "riotous and tumultuous" proceedings and warned against further "violence and outrages." In South Carolina in May 1785, an incensed Hezekiah Mayham, "being served by the sheriff with a writ [of foreclosure], obliged him to eat it on the spot." Warned Judge Aedanus Burke, not even "5,000 troops, the best in America or Europe, could enforce obedience" to the court under such conditions.

Across the states, politics was in turmoil. While some felt betrayed by the Revolution's promise of equal rights and were angered by the "arrogant unresponsiveness" of government leaders, others were alarmed by the "democratic excesses" that the revolution appeared to have unleashed. What the immediate future might hold seemed exceedingly uncertain.

TOWARD A NEW NATIONAL GOVERNMENT

By 1786, belief was spreading among members of Congress and other political leaders that the nation was in crisis and that the experiment in republicanism was in danger of foundering. Explanations for the crisis and prescriptions for its resolution varied, but attention focused on the inadequacies of the Articles of Confederation. Within two years, following a raucous and deeply divisive political struggle, a new constitution had replaced the Articles, altering forever the course of American history.

The Rise of Federalism

The supporters of a stronger national government called themselves Federalists (leading their opponents to adopt the name Anti-Federalists). Led by men such as Washington, Hamilton, Madison, and Jay, whose experiences in the continental army and Congress had strengthened their national vision, the Federalists believed that the nation was in the midst of a political crisis that threatened its survival. Such men had never been comfortable with the democratic impulses of the Revolution. While committed to moderate republicanism, they believed that democratic change had been carried too far, property rights needed to be secured, and an aristocracy of talent should lead the country.

The Revolution, lamented John Jay, "laid open a wide field for the operation of ambition," especially for "men raised from low degrees to high stations and rendered giddy by elevation." It was time, he insisted, to find better ways of protecting "the worthy against the licentious."

Federalist leaders feared the loss of their own social and political power, but they were concerned as well about the collapse of the orderly world they believed essential to the preservation of republican liberty. In 1776, American liberty had required protection from overweening British power. Now, however, danger arose from an excess of liberty that threatened to degenerate into license. "We have probably had too good an opinion of human nature," concluded Washington somberly. "Experience has taught us, that men will not adopt and carry into execution measures the best calculated for their own good, without the intervention of a coercive power." What America now needed was a "strong government, ably administered."

The Federalists regarded outbursts such as Shays's uprising in Massachusetts not as evidence of genuine social distress but as threats to social and political order. Although they were reassured by the speed with which the Shaysites had been dispatched, the episode persuaded them of the need for a stronger national government managed by the "better sort."

Congress's inability to handle the national debt, establish public credit, and restore overseas trade also troubled the Federalists. Sensitive to America's economic and military weakness, smarting from French and English arrogance, and aware of continuing Anglo-European designs on North America, the Federalists called for a new national government capable of extending American trade, spurring economic recovery, and protecting national interests.

Beyond that, the Federalists shared a vision of an expanding commercial republic, its people spreading across the rich lands of the interior, its merchant ships connecting America with the markets of Europe and beyond. That vision, so rich in national promise, seemed also at risk.

The Grand Convention

The first step toward government reform came in September 1786, when delegates of five states who had gathered in Annapolis, Maryland, to discuss interstate commerce issued a call for a larger, more ambitious convention to convene in Philadelphia in May 1787. In February, the Confederation Congress cautiously endorsed the idea of a convention to revise the Articles of Confederation. Before long, it became clear that substantially more than a revision of the Articles was afoot.

During May, delegates representing every state except Rhode Island began assembling in Philadelphia. Eventually, 55 delegates would participate in the convention's work, though daily attendance hovered between 30 and 40. The city bustled with excitement as they gathered, for the Grand Convention's roster read like an honor roll of the Revolution. From Virginia came the distinguished lawyer George Mason, chief author of Virginia's trailblazing bill of rights, and the already legendary George Washington. Proponents of the convention had held their breath while Washington considered whether to attend. His presence vastly increased the prospect of success. James Madison was there as well. No one, with perhaps the single exception of Alexander Hamilton, was more committed to nationalist reform. Certainly, no one had worked harder to prepare for the convention than he. Poring over treatises on republican government and natural law that his friend Thomas Jefferson sent from France, Madison brought to Philadelphia his own design for a new national government. That design, presented to the convention as the Virginia Plan, would serve as the basis for the new constitution. Nor did anyone rival the diminutive Madison's contributions to the convention's work. Tirelessly, he took the convention floor to argue the nationalist cause or buttonhole wavering delegates to strengthen their resolve. Somehow, he also found the energy to keep extensive notes in his personal shorthand. Those notes constitute our essential record of the convention's proceedings.

Two distinguished Virginians were conspicuously absent. Thomas Jefferson was abroad serving as minister to France, and the old patriot Patrick Henry, an ardent champion of state supremacy, feared what the convention might do and wanted no part of it.

From Pennsylvania came the venerable Franklin, too old to contribute significantly to the debates but still able to call quarreling members to account and reinspire them in their work. His colleagues from Pennsylvania included the erudite Scots lawyer James Wilson, whose nationalist sympathies had been inflamed when a democratic mob, resentful of privileged lawyers and merchants, attacked his elegant Philadelphia townhouse in 1779. Robert Morris, probably the richest man in America, was there as well. Massachusetts was ably represented by Elbridge Gerry and Rufus King, while South Carolina sent John Rutledge and Charles Pinckney. Roger Sherman led Connecticut's contingent.

The New York assembly sent a deeply divided delegation. Governor George Clinton, long a personal enemy of Alexander Hamilton and determined to protect New York's autonomy as well as his own political power, saw to it that several Anti-Federalist skeptics made the trip to Philadelphia. They were no match for Hamilton, however.

Born in the Leeward Islands, the "bastard brat of a Scots-peddlar" and a strong-willed woman with a troubled marriage, Hamilton used his immense intelligence and ingratiating charm to rise rapidly in the world. Sent to New York by wealthy sponsors, he quickly established himself as a favorite of the city's mercantile community. While still in his early twenties, he became Washington's wartime aide-de-camp.

James Madison of Virginia, only 36 years old when the Philadelphia convention met, worked tirelessly between 1786 and 1788 to replace the Articles of Confederation with a new and more effective national constitution. *(Mead Art Museum, Amherst Collection, Bequest of Herbert L. Pratt, 1895, 1945.82)*

That relationship served Hamilton well for the next 20 years. Returning from the war, he married the wealthy Elizabeth Schuyler, thereby securing his personal fortune and strengthening his political connections. Together with Madison, Hamilton had promoted the abortive Annapolis convention. At Philadelphia, he was determined to drive his nationalist vision ahead.

Meeting in Independence Hall, where the Declaration of Independence had been proclaimed little more than a decade earlier, the convention elected Washington as its presiding officer, adopted rules of procedure, and, after spirited debate, voted to close the doors and conduct its business in secret.

Debate focused first on the Virginia Plan, introduced on May 29 by Edmund Randolph. It outlined a potentially powerful national government and effectively set the convention's agenda. According to its provisions, there would be a bicameral Congress, with the lower house elected by the people and the upper house, or senate, chosen by the lower house from nominees proposed by the state legislatures. The plan also called for a president who would be named by the Congress, a national judiciary, and a Council of Revision, whose task was to review the constitutionality of federal laws.

The smaller states quickly objected to the Virginia Plan's call for proportional rather than equal representation of the states. On June 15, William Paterson introduced a counterproposal, the New Jersey Plan. It urged retention of the Articles of Confederation as the basic structure of government while conferring on Congress the long-sought powers to tax and regulate foreign and interstate commerce. After three days of heated debate, by a vote of seven states to three, the delegates adopted the Virginia Plan as the basis for further discussions. It was now clear that the convention would set aside the Articles for a much stronger national government. The only question was how powerful the new government would be.

At times over the next four months, it seemed that the Grand Convention would collapse under the weight of its own disagreements and the oppressive summer heat. How were the sharply conflicting interests of large and small states to be reconciled? How should the balance of power between the national and state governments be struck? Could an executive branch be created that was strong enough to govern but not so strong as to endanger republican liberty? And what, if anything, would the convention say about slavery and the slave trade, issues on which northerners and southerners, antislavery and proslavery advocates so passionately disagreed?

At one extreme was Hamilton's audaciously conservative proposal, made early in the convention's deliberations, for a Congress and president elected for life and a national government so powerful that the states would survive as little more than administrative agencies. Finding his plan under attack and his influence rapidly eroding, Hamilton withdrew from the convention in late June. He would return a month later but make few additional contributions to the convention's work.

At the other extreme stood the ardent Anti-Federalist Luther Martin of Maryland. Rude and unkempt, Martin voiced his uncompromising opposition to anything that threatened state sovereignty or smacked of aristocracy. Increasingly isolated by the convention's nationalist inclinations, Martin also returned home, in his case to spread the alarm.

By early July, with tempers frayed and frustration growing over the apparent deadlock, the delegates agreed to recess, ostensibly for Independence Day but actually to let Franklin, Roger Sherman of Connecticut, and others make a final effort at compromise. All agreed that only a bold stroke could prevent a collapse.

That stroke came on July 12, as part of what has become known as the Great Compromise. The reassembled delegates settled one major point of controversy by agreeing that representation in the lower house should be based on the total of each state's white population plus three-fifths of its blacks. Though African Americans were not accorded citizenship and

This painting by Thomas Rossiter, done in the early nineteenth century, provides an imaginative portrayal of the Philadelphia convention, with George Washington presiding and a rising sun, symbolic of the new nation, shining behind him. *(Independence National Historical Park Collection)*

could not vote, the southern delegates argued that they should be fully counted for this purpose. Delegates from the northern states, where relatively few blacks lived, did not want them counted at all, but the bargain was struck. As part of this compromise, the convention agreed that direct taxes would also be apportioned on the basis of population and that blacks would be counted similarly in that calculation. On July 16, the convention accepted the principle that each state should have an equal vote in the senate. Thus the interests of both large states and small were effectively accommodated.

The convention then submitted its work to a committee of detail for drafting in proper constitutional form. That group reported on August 6, and for the next month the delegates hammered out the exact language of the document's seven articles. On several occasions, differences seemed so great that it was uncertain whether the convention could proceed. In each instance, however, agreement was reached, and the discussion continued.

Determined to give the new government the stability that state governments lacked, the delegates created an electoral process designed to bring only persons of experience and reputation into national office. An Electoral College of wise and experienced leaders would meet to choose the president. The process functioned exactly that way during the first several presidential elections.

Selection of the Senate would be similarly indirect, for its members were to be named by the state legislatures. (Not until 1913, with ratification of the Seventeenth Amendment, would the American people begin electing their senators.) Even the House of Representatives, the only popularly elected branch of the new government, was to be filled with people of standing and wealth, for the Federalists were confident that only well-established leaders would be able to attract the necessary votes.

The delegates' final set of compromises touched the fate of black Americans. At the insistence of southerners, the convention agreed that the slave trade would not formally end for another 20 years. The delegates never used the words *slavery* or *slave trade*, but spoke more vaguely about not prohibiting the "migration or importation of such persons as any of the states now existing shall think proper to admit." Their meaning, however, was entirely clear.

Despite an impassioned charge by Gouverneur Morris of New York that slavery was a "nefarious institution" that would bring "the curse of Heaven on the states where it prevails," the delegates firmly rejected a proposal to abolish slavery, thereby acknowledging its legitimacy. More than that, they guaranteed slavery's protection, by writing in Section 2 of Article 4 that "No person held to service or labour in one state, . . . [and] escaping into another, shall, in consequence of any law . . . therein, be discharged from such service, but shall be delivered up on claim of the party to whom such service or labour may be due." The delegates thus provided federal sanction for the capture and return of runaway slaves. This fugitive slave clause would return to haunt northern consciences in the years ahead. At the time, however, it seemed a small price to pay for sectional harmony and a new government. Northern accommodation to the demands of the southern delegates was eased, moreover, by knowledge that southerners in the Confederation Congress had just agreed to prohibit new slaves from entering the Northwest Territory.

Although the Constitution's unique federal system of governance called for shared responsibilities between the nation and the states, it decisively strengthened the national government. Among the extensive list of powers granted to Congress were the authority to levy and collect taxes, regulate commerce with foreign nations and between the states, devise uniform rules for naturalization, administer national patents and copyrights, and control the federal district in which it would eventually be located. Conspicuously missing was any statement reserving to the states all powers not explicitly conferred on the central government. Such language had proved crippling in the Articles of Confederation. On the contrary, the Constitution contained a number of clauses bestowing vaguely defined grants of power on the new government. Section 8 of Article 1, for example, granted Congress the authority to "provide for the . . . general welfare of the United States" as well as to "make all laws . . . necessary and proper for carrying into execution . . . all . . . powers vested by this Constitution in the government of the United States." Later generations would call these phrases "elastic clauses" and would use them to expand the federal government's activities.

In addition, Section 10 of Article 1 contained a litany of powers now denied the states, among them issuing paper money, passing laws impairing the obligation of contracts, and entering into agreements with foreign powers other than by the consent of Congress. A final measure of the Federalists' determination to make the new government supreme over the states was the assertion in Article 6 that the Constitution and all laws passed under it were to be regarded as the "supreme Law of the Land."

When the convention had finished its business, 3 of the 42 remaining delegates refused to sign the document. The other 39 affixed their names and forwarded it to the Confederation Congress along with the request that it be sent on to the states for approval. On September 17, the Grand Convention adjourned.

Federalists versus Anti-Federalists

Ratification presented the Federalists with a more difficult problem than they had faced at Philadelphia, for the debate now shifted to the states, where sentiment was sharply divided and the political situation was more difficult to control. Recognizing the unlikelihood of gaining quick agreement from all 13 states, the Federalists stipulated that the Constitution should go into effect when any 9 agreed to it. Other states could then enter the Union as they were ready. Ratification was to be decided by specially elected conventions rather than by the state assemblies, because under the Constitution the assemblies would lose substantial amounts of power. Ratification by such conventions would also give the Constitution greater legitimacy by grounding it directly in the people.

In the Confederation Congress, opponents of the new Constitution charged that the Philadelphia Convention had exceeded its authority. But after a few days' debate, the Congress dutifully forwarded the document to the states for consideration. Word of the dramatic changes being proposed spread rapidly. In each state, Federalists and Anti-Federalists, the latter now actively opposing the Constitution, prepared to debate the new articles of government.

Although levels of Federalist and Anti-Federalist strength differed from state to state, opposition to the Constitution was widespread and vocal. Some critics feared that a stronger central government would threaten state interests or their own political power. Others, like Timothy Bloodworth, charged the Federalists with betraying revolutionary republicanism. Like all "energetic" governments, they warned, the new one would be corrupted by its own power. Far from the watchful eyes of the citizenry, its officials would behave as power wielders always had, and American liberty, so recently preserved at such high cost, would once again come under attack.

The Anti-Federalists were aghast at the Federalists' vision of an expanding "republican empire." "The idea of . . . [a] republic, on an average of 1,000 miles in length, and 800 in breadth, and containing 6 millions of white inhabitants all reduced to the same standards of morals, . . . habits . . . [and] laws," exclaimed one critic incredulously, "is itself an absurdity, and contrary to the whole experience of mankind." Such an extended republic would quickly fall prey to factional conflict and internal disorder. The Anti-Federalists continued to believe that republican liberty could be preserved only in small, homogeneous societies, where the seeds of faction were few and public virtue guided citizens' behavior.

Nor did the Anti-Federalists believe that either the proposed separation of executive, legislative, and judicial branches or the balancing of state and national governments would prevent power's abuse.

Gradually, a white woman clothed in the flowing robes of classical attire replaced the Indian Columbia. In this painting by Samuel Jennings, Columbia offers the promise of education to a group of black Americans. *(The Library Company of Philadelphia)*

Government, they insisted, must be kept simple, for complexity only confused the people and cloaked selfish ambition.

Not all the Anti-Federalists were democrats. In the South, many held slaves, and their appeals to local authority did not always mean support for political equality, even among whites. Yet along with their warnings against centralized power, they often spoke fervently of democratic principles. Certainly, they believed more firmly than their Federalist opponents that if government was to be safe, it must be tied closely to the people.

Federalist spokesmen moved quickly to counter the Anti-Federalists' attack, for many of those criticisms carried the sanction of the revolutionary past. Their most important effort was a series of essays penned by James Madison, Alexander Hamilton, and John Jay and published in New York under the pseudonym Publius. *The Federalist* essays, as they were called, were written to promote ratification in New York but were quickly reprinted by Federalists elsewhere.

Madison, Hamilton, and Jay moved systematically through the Constitution, explaining its virtues and responding to the Anti-Federalists' attacks. In the process, they described a political vision fundamentally at odds with that of their Anti-Federalist opponents.

No difference was more dramatic than the Federalists' treatment of government power. Power, the Federalists now argued, was not the enemy of liberty but its guarantor. Where government was not sufficiently "energetic" and "efficient" (these were favorite

Federalist words), demagogues and disorganizers would find space to do their nefarious work. It is far better, Hamilton wrote in *Federalist No. 26,* "to hazard the abuse of . . . confidence than to embarrass the government and endanger the public safety by impolitic restrictions of . . . authority."

The authors of the *Federalist* also countered the Anti-Federalists' warning that a single, extended republic encompassing the country's economic and social diversity would lead inevitably to factional conflict that would destroy republican liberty. Turning the Anti-Federalists' classic, republican argument on its head, they explained that factional divisions were the inevitable accompaniment of human liberty. Wrote Madison in *Federalist No. 10:* "Liberty is to faction what air is to fire, an aliment without which it instantly expires." To suppress faction would require the destruction of liberty itself.

Earlier emphasis on public virtue as the guarantor of political order, the Federalists explained, had been naive, for few people would consistently put the public good ahead of their own interests. Politics had to heed this harsh fact of human nature and provide for peaceful compromise among conflicting groups. That could be best accomplished by expanding the nation so that it included innumerable factions. Out of the clash and accommodation of multiple social and economic interests would emerge compromise and the best possible approximation of the public good.

The Federalists' argument established the basic rationale for modern democratic politics, but it left the Anti-Federalists sputtering in frustration. Where in the

The eagle, an important symbol of the new nation, appeared on water pitchers, whiskey bottles, flags, newspaper mastheads, and fabrics of all kinds. The flag also became an important icon. While its red and white stripes represented the 13 original states, its blue field of stars was modified as new states entered the Union. (quilt: *Magnette, Edith,* Quilt, *Index of American Design, ©2000 Board of Trustees, National Gallery of Art, Washington, c. 1941, watercolor and graphite on paperboard, .759 x .506 [29⅞ x 19¹⁵⁄₁₆]; pine chest: formerly in the Collection of The Henry Ford Museum and Greenfield Village)*

Federalists' scheme was there a place for that familiar abstraction, the public good? What would become of public virtue in a system built on the notion of competing interests? In such a free market of competition, the Anti-Federalists warned, the wealthy and powerful would thrive while ordinary folk would suffer.

As the ratification debate revealed, the Federalists and Anti-Federalists held sharply contrasting visions of the new republic. The Anti-Federalist vision remained much closer to the original republicanism of 1776, with its suspicion of power and wealth, its emphasis on the primacy of local government, and its fears of national development. The Anti-Federalists envisioned a decentralized republic filled with self-reliant citizens, limited in personal ambition and guided by public virtue, whose destiny was determined primarily by what happened in the states rather than the nation. Anxious about the future, they longed to preserve the political world much as it had been.

The Federalists, on the other hand, persuaded that America's situation had changed dramatically since 1776, embraced the idea of nationhood and looked forward with anticipation to the development of a rising "republican empire," based on commercial development and led by men of wealth and talent. Both Federalists and Anti-Federalists claimed to be heirs of the Revolution, yet they differed fundamentally in what they understood that heritage to be.

The Struggle over Ratification

No one knows what most Americans thought of the proposed Constitution, for no national plebiscite on it was ever taken. Probably no more than several hundred thousand people participated in the elections for the state ratifying conventions, and many of the delegates carried no binding instructions from their constituents on how they should vote. A majority of the people probably opposed the document, either out of indifference or alarm. Fortunately for the Federalists, they did not have to persuade most Americans but needed only to secure majorities in nine of the state ratifying conventions, a much less formidable task.

They set about it with determination. As soon as the Philadelphia Convention adjourned, its members hurried home to organize the ratification movement in their states. In Delaware and Georgia, New Jersey and Connecticut, where the Federalists were confident of their strength, they pressed quickly for a vote. Where the outcome was uncertain, as in New York, Massachusetts, and Virginia, they delayed, hoping that word of ratification elsewhere would work to their benefit.

It took less than a year to secure approval of the necessary nine states. Delaware, Pennsylvania, and New Jersey ratified first, in December 1787. Approval came a month later in Georgia and Connecticut. Massachusetts ratified in February 1788, but only after considerable political maneuvering. In an effort to woo Anti-Federalist delegates and persuade the uncommitted, Federalist leaders there agreed to forward a set of amendments outlining a federal "bill of rights" along with notice of ratification. The strategy worked, for it brought Samuel Adams and John Hancock into line. They brought with them the crucial convention votes that were needed.

Maryland and South Carolina were the seventh and eighth states to approve. That left New Hampshire and Virginia as the most likely candidates for the honor of being ninth and putting the Constitution over the top. There was staunch opposition in both states. The New Hampshire convention met on February 13. Sensing that they lacked the necessary votes, the Federalists adjourned the convention until mid-June and worked feverishly to build support. When the convention reconvened, it took but three days to secure a Federalist majority. New Hampshire ratified on June 21.

Two massive gaps in the new Union remained—Virginia and New York. The nation clearly could not endure without them. In Virginia, Madison gathered support by promising that the new Congress would immediately consider a federal bill of rights. Other Federalists spread the rumor that Patrick Henry, one of the most ardent Anti-Federalist leaders, had changed sides, a charge that Henry angrily denied. His eloquence, however, proved no match for the careful politicking of Madison and others. On June 25, the Virginia convention voted to ratify by the narrow margin of ten votes.

The New York convention gathered on June 17 at Poughkeepsie, with the Anti-Federalist followers of

RATIFICATION OF THE CONSTITUTION			
Votes of State Ratifying Conventions			
State	**Date**	**For**	**Against**
Delaware	December 1787	30	0
Pennsylvania	December 1787	46	23
New Jersey	December 1787	38	0
Georgia	January 1788	26	0
Connecticut	January 1788	128	40
Massachusetts	February 1788	187	168
Maryland	April 1788	63	11
South Carolina	May 1788	149	73
New Hampshire	June 1788	57	47
Virginia	June 1788	89	79
New York	July 1788	30	27
North Carolina	November 1789	194	77
Rhode Island	May 1790	34	32

Governor Clinton firmly in command. Hamilton worked for delay, hoping that news of the results in New Hampshire and Virginia would turn the tide. For several weeks, approval hung in the balance while the two sides maneuvered for support. On July 27, approval squeaked through, 30 to 27. That left two states still uncommitted. North Carolina (with Timothy Bloodworth's skeptical approval) finally ratified in November 1789. Rhode Island did not enter the Union until May 1790, more than a year after the new government had gotten under way.

The Social Geography of Ratification

A glance at the geographic pattern of Federalist and Anti-Federalist strength reveals their very different sources of political support. Federalist strength was concentrated in areas along the coast and navigable rivers and was strongest in cities and towns. Merchants and businessmen supported the Constitution most ardently. Enthusiasm also ran high among urban laborers, artisans, and shopkeepers—surprisingly so, given the Anti-Federalists' criticism of wealth and power and their emphasis on democratic equality. While city artisans and workers had been in the vanguard of democratic reform during the Revolution, in the troubled circumstances of the late 1780s they worried primarily about their livelihoods and believed that a stronger government could promote overseas trade and better protect American artisans from foreign competition.

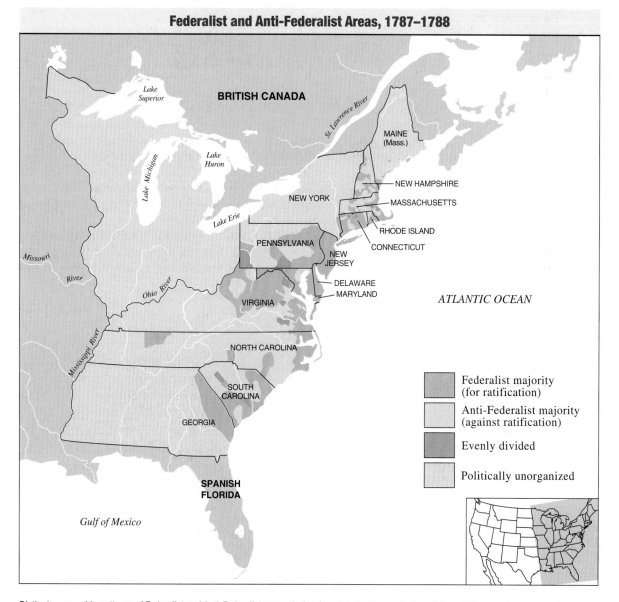

Federalist and Anti-Federalist Areas, 1787–1788

Federalist majority (for ratification)

Anti-Federalist majority (against ratification)

Evenly divided

Politically unorganized

Distinct geographic patterns of Federalist and Anti-Federalist strength developed during the ratification debate. This map shows areas whose delegates to the state ratifying conventions voted for and against the Constitution.

The federal ship *Hamilton* formed the centerpiece of a grand procession in New York City celebrating the successful ratification of the new Constitution.

On July 4, 1788, a grand procession celebrating the Constitution's ratification wound through the streets of Philadelphia. Seventeen thousand strong, it graphically demonstrated the breadth of support for the Constitution. At the head of the line marched lawyers, merchants, and others of the city's elite. Close behind them came representatives of virtually every trade in the city, from ship's carpenters to shoemakers, each with its own floats, flags, and mottoed banners. "May commerce flourish and industry be rewarded," declared the mariners and shipbuilders. "May the federal government revive our trade," exclaimed the bakers. "Home-brewed is best," insisted the maltsters. For the moment, declared Benjamin Rush in amazement, "rank . . . forgot all its claims. Hand in hand marched merchants and sea-men, lawyers and artisans." Within a few years, political disputes would divide them once again. For the moment, however, people of all ranks joined in celebrating the new Constitution.

Elsewhere class differences and geographic location separated people more clearly. The Constitution found support among commercial farmers and southern planters eager for profit and anxious about overseas markets, but Federalist enthusiasm waned and Anti-Federalist sentiment grew in the interior. The centers of Anti-Federalism lay away from the coast in central New England, upstate New York, the Virginia Piedmont and southside, and western Carolina. Among ordinary farmers living outside the market economy, local loyalties outweighed their interest in national affairs. Federalist visions of a growing "American empire" they found strange and alarming.

Why did the Federalists finally prevail? After all, their opponents had only to tap into people's deep-seated fears of central government. The Federalists, by contrast, had to explain how republicanism had suddenly become compatible with a powerful government and an expanding empire. Moreover, they faced the complicated task of coordinating ratification in the various states.

The Federalists' task was simplified by the widely shared belief that the Articles of Confederation needed strengthening. The troubled events of the

Timeline

1784	Treaty of Fort Stanwix with the Iroquois
	Spain closes the Mississippi River to American navigation
1785	Treaty of Hopewell with the Cherokee
	Land Ordinance for the Northwest Territory
	Jay–Gardoqui negotiations
1786	Virginia adopts "Bill for Establishing Religious Freedom"
	Annapolis Convention calls for revision of the Articles of Confederation
1786–1787	Shays's Rebellion
1787	Northwest Ordinance
	Constitutional Convention
	Federalist Papers published by Hamilton, Jay, and Madison
1788	Constitution ratified

1780s supported Federalist arguments that America's experiment in republican independence was doomed unless decisive action was taken. More than anything, however, the Federalists succeeded because of their determination and political skill. Most of the Revolution's major leaders were Federalists. Time and again these worthies spoke out for the Constitution, and time and again their support proved decisive.

Their experience as army officers and as members of the Continental and Confederation Congresses caused them to identify with the nation and imagine what it might become. They brought their vision to the ratification process and asked others to share it. Altogether, it was an impressive political performance. With their success, the Federalists turned the American republic in a new and fateful direction.

Conclusion

Completing the Revolution

Only five years had passed between England's acknowledgment of American independence in 1783 and ratification of the new national Constitution, yet to many Americans it seemed far longer. At war's end, the difficulties of sustaining American liberty were evident. The experience of the next half decade added to them. While struggling to survive in a hostile Atlantic environment and coping with economic distress and political turmoil at home, Americans continued to argue about their experiment in republicanism. Above all, they wondered how democratic it could safely be, and even whether it would survive.

At the same time, the American people retained an immense reservoir of optimism about the future. Had they not defeated mighty England? Was not their Revolution destined to change the course of history and provide a model for all mankind? Did not America's wonderfully rich interior contain a limitless promise of economic and social opportunity? Most Americans, still filled with the enthusiasm of their new beginning, answered with a resounding "Yes." Much would depend, of course, on their new Constitution and the government soon to be created under it. As the ratification debate subsided and the Confederation Congress prepared for the transition, the American people looked eagerly and anxiously ahead.

Recommended Reading

Struggling with the Peacetime Agenda

Ira Berlin and Ronald Hoffman, eds., *Slavery and Freedom in the Age of the American Revolution* (1983); Richard Buel, Jr., *In Irons: Britain's Naval Supremacy and the American Revolutionary Economy* (1998); Thomas Curry, *The First Freedoms: Church and State in America to the Passage of the First Amendment* (1986); Eric Hinderaker, *Elusive Empires: Constructing Colonialism in the Ohio Valley, 1673–1800* (1997).

Ronald Hoffman and Peter Albert, eds., *Religion in a New Age* (1994) and *Sovereign States in an Age of Uncertainty* (1778); James Hutson, *Religion in a Revolutionary Age* (1994); Merrill Jensen, *The New Nation: A History of the United States During the Confederation, 1781–1789* (1950); Susan Juster, *Disorderly Women: Sexual Politics and Evangelicalism in Revolutionary New England* (1994); Jackson T. Main, *Political Parties Before the Constitution* (1973); Frederick Marks, *Independence on Trial: Foreign Affairs and the Making of the Constitution* (1973); Cathy Matson and Peter Onuf, *A Union of Interests: Political and Economic Thought in Revolutionary America* (1990); William McLaughlin, *Soul Liberty: The Baptists' Struggle in New England, 1630–1833* (1991); Gary B. Nash and Jean Soderlund, *Freedom By Degrees: Emancipation in Pennsylvania and Its Aftermath* (1991); Robert Olwell, *Masters, Slaves, and Subjects: The Culture of Power in the South Carolina Low Country, 1740–1790* (1998).

Peter Onuf, *The Origins of the Federal Republic: Jurisdictional Controversies in the United States, 1775–1787* (1983) and *Statehood and Union: A History of the Northwest Ordinance* (1987); Merrill Peterson and Robert Vaughan, eds., *The Virginia Statute for Religious Freedom* (1988); Jack Rakove, *The Beginnings of National Politics: An Interpretive History of the Continental Congress* (1979); T. Stephen Whitman, *The Price of*

Freedom: Slavery and Manumission in Baltimore and Early National Maryland (1997).

Political Tumult in the States

Robert Gross, ed., *In Debt to Shays: The Bicentennial of an Agrarian Rebellion* (1993); Ronald Hoffman et al., *An Uncivil War: The Southern Backcountry During the American Revolution* (1985); David Szatmary, *Shays's Rebellion: The Making of an Agrarian Rebellion* (1988); Robert Taylor, *Western Massachusetts in the Revolution* (1954); Albert Tillson, Jr., *Gentry and Commonfolk: Political Culture on a Virginia Frontier, 1740–1789* (1991).

Toward a New National Government

Lance Banning, *The Sacred Fire of Liberty: James Madison and the Founding of the Federal Republic* (1995); Richard Beeman et al., *Beyond Confederation: Origins of the Constitution and American National Identity* (1987); Stephen Boyd, *The Politics of Opposition: Antifederalists and the Acceptance of the Constitution* (1979); Patrick Conley and John Kaminsky, eds., *The Constitution and the States* (1988); Jack Greene, *Peripheries and Center: Constitutional Development in the Extended Polities of the British Empire and the United States, 1687–1788* (1986); Jackson T. Main, *The Antifederalists: Critics of the Constitution, 1781–1788* (1961); Frederick Marks III, *Independence on Trial: Foreign Affairs and the Making of the Constitution* (1973); Forrest McDonald, *Novus Ordo Seclorum: The Intellectual Origins of the Constitution* (1985); Richard Morris, *Witnesses at the Creation: Hamilton, Madison, Jay, and the Constitution* (1985); Jack Rakove, *Original Meanings: Politics and Ideas in the Making of the Constitution* (1996); Gary Wills, *Explaining America: The*

"Federalist" (1981); Gordon Wood, *The Creation of the American Republic, 1776–1787* (1969).

Fiction and Film

The visually lush commercial film *Jefferson in Paris* (1995) combines a depiction of Jefferson's years as U.S. minister to France (1785–1789) with commentaries on themes of liberty and slavery involving events leading to the French Revolution and Jefferson's controversial liaison with his slave girl Sally Hemmings.

The documentary film *Unearthing the Slave Trade* (1994) uses the recent discovery and excavation of an old black bury-ing ground near Wall Street in New York City, where deceased slaves were interred from about 1712 to 1790, to depict the life of urban slaves in eighteenth-century America.

Herman Melville's novel *Israel Potter* (1855) tells the story of a fictitious Revolutionary War sailor who encounters Benjamin Franklin, Ethan Allen, and John Paul Jones during his adventures and ends up in England as a gardener to King George III.

In *Those Who Love: A Biographical Novel of Abigail and John Adams* (1965), Irving Stone traces the life story of this remarkable couple, largely through Abigail's eyes, as they move from early courtship through the end of John's presidency in 1800.

Suggested Web Sites

http://lcweb.loc.gov/exhibits/religion/religion.html

Religion and the Founding of the American Republic. This Library of Congress site is an on-line exhibit about religion and the creation of the United States.

http://www.nara.gov/fedreg/ec-hmpge.html

The Electoral College. This National Archives and Records Administration site explains how the Electoral College works.

http://www.taxhistory.org/federalists/

Taxing Federalism. This site, provided by the Tax History Project, offers information on the history of U.S. federal taxation by describing several of the *Federalist Papers* related to federal taxing power.

http://www.law.emory.edu/FEDERAL/federalist/

The Federalist. This site is a collection of the most important *Federalist Papers,* a series of documents designed to convince people to support the new Constitution and the Federalist party.

http://www.pbs.org/jefferson/

Thomas Jefferson Online. This companion site to the PBS series on Jefferson is especially important because it contains a fine collection of other people's views of Jefferson.

http://www.law.emory.edu/FEDERAL/usconst.html

The Constitution of the United States. This is a searchable site to the Constitution, especially useful for its information about the Bill of Rights and other constitutional amendments.

http://rs6.loc.gov/ammem/bdsds/bdsdhome.html

Continental Congress and the Constitutional Convention Home Page. This site, presented by the Library of Congress, allows access to the Continental Congress Broadside Collection (253 titles) and the Constitutional Convention Broadside Collection (21 titles), containing documents relating to the work of Congress and the drafting and ratification of the Constitution. Items include extracts of the journals of Congress, resolutions, proclamations, committee reports, treaties, and early printed versions of the U.S. Constitution and the Declaration of Independence.

http://www.americanhistory.si.edu/hohr/springer

Smithsonian Institution. Part of the Smithsonian's on-line museum, this exhibit enables students to examine artifacts from the home of New Castle, Delaware, residents Thomas and Elizabeth Springer and interpret the lives of a late eighteenth-century American family.

http://www.ushistoryplace.com

A richly detailed on-line learning environment complete with interactive maps, timelines, history activities, primary source documents, and links to related American history sites.

CREATING
a NATION

CHAPTER OUTLINE

In October 1789, David Brown arrived in Dedham, Massachusetts. Born about 50 years earlier in Bethlehem, Connecticut, Brown served in the revolutionary army. After the war was over, he shipped out on an American merchantman to see the world. His travels, as he later reported, took him to "nineteen different . . . Kingdoms in Europe, and nearly all the United States." For two years before settling in Dedham, he visited scores of Massachusetts towns, supporting himself as a day laborer while discussing the troubled state of public affairs with local townspeople.

Initially, the people of Dedham took little notice of Brown, but he soon made his presence felt. Though he had little formal schooling, he was a man of powerful opinions and considerable natural ability. His reading and personal experience had persuaded him that government was a conspiracy of the rich to exploit farmers, artisans, and other common folk, and he was quick to make his opinions known.

The object of his wrath was the central government recently established under the new national constitution. Though he could cite no evidence, he accused government leaders of engrossing the nation's western lands for themselves. "Five hundred [people] out of the union of five millions receive all the benefit of public property and live upon the ruins of the rest of the community," he wrote in one of his numerous pamphlets. Brown warned that no government could survive "after the confidence of the people was lost."

In the highly charged political climate of the 1790s, Brown's radical language and exaggerated attacks on the new government's leaders brought a sharp response. In 1798, John Davis, the federal district attorney in Boston, issued a warrant for Brown's arrest on charges of sedition, while government-supported newspapers attacked him as a "rallying point of insurrection and disorder." Fearing arrest, Brown fled to Salem on the Massachusetts coast, but there he was caught and charged with intent to defame the government and aid the country's enemies. For want of $400 bail, he was clapped in prison.

Prior to 1799, when the national government moved to the new capital in the District of Columbia, it shared the State House in Philadelphia with the Pennsylvania assembly. In this image, a variety of people, including several Indians, mingle informally in the State House yard. *(William Birch,* The State House, *Philadelphia, 1800, Historical Society of Pennsylvania)*

In June 1799, Brown came before the U.S. Circuit Court, Justice Samuel Chase presiding. Chase's behavior was anything but judicious. Persuaded that critics of the administration were also enemies of the republic, Chase was determined to make Brown an example. Confused and hoping for leniency, Brown pleaded guilty to the charges against him.

Ignoring Brown's plea, Chase directed the federal prosecutor to "examine the witness . . . that the degree of his guilt might be duly ascertained." Before sentencing him, Chase demanded that Brown provide the names of his accomplices and a list of subscribers to his writings. When Brown refused, protesting that he would "lose all my friends," Chase sentenced him to a fine of $480 and 18 months in jail. That Brown could not pay the fine and faced the prospect of indefinite imprisonment did not matter.

In rendering judgment, Chase castigated Brown for his "disorganizing doctrines and . . . falsehoods, and the very alarming and dangerous excesses to which he attempted to incite the uninformed part of the community." Not all citizens, Chase thought, should be allowed to comment so brashly on public affairs. For nearly two years, Brown languished in prison. Not until the Federalist party was defeated in the election of 1800 and the Jeffersonian Republicans had taken office was he freed.

David Brown discovered how easy it was for critics of the government to get into trouble during the 1790s, one of the most tumultuous decades in American political history. Though independence had been won, the struggle over control of the revolutionary heritage continued. As Benjamin Rush, Philadelphia physician and revolutionary patriot, explained: "The American War is over, but this is far from being the case with the American Revolution. On the contrary, nothing but the first act of the great drama is closed. It remains [for us] . . . to establish and perfect our new forms of government."

Those efforts proceeded differently in the states than at the center of the new, national government in Philadelphia. In the states, government and politics remained close to the people. There the fires of political controversy, fanned to a white heat over taxes and paper money, slavery and the separation of church and state, as well as issues of political democracy continued to burn.

In the new Congress, the Senate and House of Representatives were filled with men of distinction, heroes of the Revolution, exactly as the Constitution's Federalist architects had intended. Though they would soon divide into competing Federalist and Jeffersonian coalitions over an array of foreign and domestic policies, they were united in the belief that the nation's well-being depended on the leadership of gentlemen such as themselves, men of wisdom and accomplishment who were ultimately responsible to the people but who were at the same time obligated to govern according to their own, independent judgment.

At first, the gentry-led politics of congressional elites and the more rapidly evolving, democratic politics of the states proceeded along parallel trajectories. Before long, however, the decade's events began to force them together. As a result, by 1800 a distinctly new form of American politics was becoming visible.

Controversy first erupted in the Congress over a series of economic policies designed to stabilize the new government's finances. Within a few years, foreign policy issues generated by the French Revolution and the accompanying European war further inflamed congressional politics and began to rouse the

people at large. By the last years of the decade, accumulating political divisions, intensified by the Alien and Sedition Acts and other Federalist measures, brought the nation to the brink of political upheaval, a prospect narrowly avoided by the Federalists' defeat and Thomas Jefferson's election to the presidency in 1800.

A number of additional circumstances added to the political volatility of the 1790s: the still unproven nature of America's unprecedented "experiment" in an extended republican empire; fundamental disagreements over the proper course of the nation's development; threats to the nation's security posed by a hostile international environment; and the absence of political parties capable of forging political compromise.

As political controversy grew, it caught up countless people like David Brown in its toils. By decade's end, it was apparent how fragile, and yet how resilient, America's new government had proven to be.

⬄ LAUNCHING THE NATIONAL REPUBLIC

Once the Constitution had been ratified, its Anti-Federalist critics seemed ready to give the new experiment a chance. They were determined, however, to watch it closely for the first signs of danger. It was not many months before they sounded the alarm.

Beginning the New Government

On April 16, 1789, George Washington started north from Virginia toward New York City to be inaugurated as the first president of the United States. The Electoral College had unanimously elected him to the nation's highest office. Washington's feelings were mixed as he set forth. "I bade adieu to Mount Vernon, to private life, and to domestic felicity," he confided to his diary, "and with a mind oppressed with more anxious and painful sensations than I have words to express, set out for New York . . . with the best disposition to render service to my country in obedience to its call, but with less hope of answering its expectations." Events would soon show that he had good reason for such foreboding.

Washington's journey resembled a royal procession, for he was the object of constant adulation along the way. In villages and towns, guns boomed their salutes, children danced in the streets, church bells

pealed, and dignitaries toasted his arrival. On April 23, the president-elect and his entourage reached the New Jersey shore, where he climbed aboard an elegant barge festooned with flowers. Accompanied by a flotilla of boats, he was rowed across the harbor to New York City, where throngs of citizens and newly elected members of Congress greeted the weary traveler. Over the streets of the city stretched gaily decorated arches. During the parade uptown to the governor's mansion, young women in white, flowing robes strewed flowers in his path. That night, bonfires illuminated the city.

On October 10, the old Confederation Congress had transacted its last official business and adjourned *sine die* after setting March 4, 1789, as the day for the new government to assemble. Inaugural day was April 30. Shortly after noon on that day, on a small balcony overlooking Wall Street thronged with people, Washington took the oath of office. "It is done," exulted New York's chancellor, Robert Livingston. "Long live George Washington, President of the United States!" With the crowd roaring its approval and 13 guns booming in the harbor, the president bowed his way off the balcony and into Federal Hall. Late into the night, celebrations filled the air.

Though hopefulness and excitement attended those first weeks, it was important that the new government begin properly. "Things which appear of

This imaginative scene of President-elect Washington's reception in Trenton, New Jersey, during his trip from Virginia to New York City for his first inauguration depicts the popular adulation that surrounded him, as well as the sharply different political roles of men and women. *(Library of Congress)*

little importance in themselves and at the beginning," the president warned, "may have great and durable consequences" from having been established at the commencement of the new government.

When Washington addressed the first Congress, it prompted republican purists to complain that the ceremony smacked too much of the English monarch's speech from the throne at the opening of Parliament. The occasion also raised the question of how the president should be addressed. Several congressmen pointed out that state governors and foreign ambassadors carried the title of "Excellency" and argued that the American president should be more exalted than that. Vice President Adams proposed "His Most Benign Highness," while others offered the even gaudier suggestion: "His Highness, the President of the United States, and Protector of the Rights of the Same." Both proposals elicited howls of outrage from those who thought titles had no place in a republican government. Good sense finally prevailed, and Congress settled on the simple and now familiar "Mr. President." Every decision seemed filled with significance, for people believed they were setting the new government's direction for years to come. That belief gave special intensity to the politics of the time.

The Bill of Rights

Among the Congress's first tasks was consideration of the constitutional amendments that several states had made conditions of their ratification. Although Madison, Hamilton, and other Federalists had argued that a national bill of rights was unnecessary, they

President Washington took the oath of office on the balcony of Federal Hall in New York City, where the new national government first met. The shield of the United Sates and thirteen stars emblazoned its cornice, while arrows (symbolizing war) and olive branches (symbolizing peace) appeared above the windows. *(Museum of the City of New York)*

were prepared to keep their promise that such amendments would be considered. That would reassure the fearful, head off calls for a second constitutional convention, and build support for the new regime. "We have in this way something to gain," Madison observed, "and if we proceed with caution, nothing to lose."

From the variety of proposals offered by the states, Madison culled a set of specific propositions for Congress to consider. After extensive debate, Congress reached agreement in September 1789 on twelve amendments and sent them to the states for approval. By December 1791, ten had been ratified and became the national Bill of Rights. Among other things, they guaranteed freedom of speech, press, and religion; pledged the right of trial by jury and due process of law; forbade "unreasonable searches and seizures"; and protected individuals against self-incrimination in criminal cases. The Bill of Rights was the most important achievement of these early years, for it has protected individuals' democratic rights throughout the nation's history.

The People Divide

During its first months in office, Washington's administration enjoyed almost universal support. The honeymoon did not last long, however, for criticism of the administration's policies soon appeared. First in Congress and then increasingly among the people, the growing opposition coalesced in a political party known as the Jeffersonian Republicans. As that occurred, the administration's supporters rallied under the name of Federalists.

Disagreement began in January 1790, when Secretary of the Treasury Alexander Hamilton submitted to Congress the first of several major policy statements on the country's economic future. Seldom in the nation's history has a single official so dominated public affairs as Hamilton did during these early years. A man of extraordinary intelligence and ambition, Hamilton preferred to act behind the scenes, where he could shape events beyond the public eye. His instincts for locating and seizing the levers of political power were unerring.

An ardent proponent of America's economic development, Hamilton foresaw the country's future strength and was determined to promote its growth through government efforts to foster domestic manufacturing and overseas trade. The United States, he was fond of saying, was a "Hercules in the cradle." The people he most admired were men of wealth and ambition, entrepreneurs eager to tie their fortunes to America's rising empire. A close alliance between such people and government officials he regarded as essential to achieving American greatness.

Alexander Hamilton used the office of secretary of the treasury and his personal relationship with President Washington to shape national policy during the early 1790s. (*White House Collection*)

If Hamilton's economic policies were liberal in looking forward to enhanced economic opportunity, his politics were profoundly conservative. Deeply impressed by the stability of the British monarchy and the confident governing style of the British upper class, Hamilton distrusted the people's wisdom and feared their purposes. "The people," he asserted, "are turbulent and changing; they seldom judge or determine right." That stark belief guided his public career.

While Hamilton thought the Constitution not "high-toned" enough, he was anxious to give it proper direction. His opportunity came when Washington named him secretary of the treasury. Recognizing the potential importance of his office, he determined to use it to build the kind of nation he envisioned.

In his first "Report on the Public Credit," Hamilton recommended funding the remaining Revolutionary War debt by allowing the government's creditors to exchange their depreciated public securities at face value for new, interest-bearing bonds. The foreign-held debt Hamilton set at $11.7 million; the domestic debt, including back interest, he fixed at $40.4 million. Second, he proposed that the federal government assume responsibility for the $21.5 million in remaining state war debts. These actions were intended to stabilize the government's finances, establish its credit, build confidence in the new nation at home and abroad, and tie business and commercial interests firmly to the new administration.

The proposal to fund the foreign debt aroused little controversy, but Hamilton's plans for handling the government's domestic obligations generated immediate opposition. In the House of Representatives, James Madison, Hamilton's recent ally in the ratification process, protested the unfairness of funding depreciated securities at face value because speculators, some anticipating Hamilton's proposals, had acquired many of them at a fraction of their initial worth. In addition, Madison and his southern colleagues knew that northern businessmen held most of the securities and that funding would bring little benefit to the South.

Hamilton was not impressed. Speculators, he observed, "paid what the commodity was worth in the market, and took the risks"—they should therefore "reap the benefit." If his plan served the interests of the wealthy, that was exactly as he intended, for it would further strengthen the ties between personal wealth and national power. After a bit of grumbling, Congress endorsed the funding plan.

Federal assumption of the remaining state debts, another important part of Hamilton's program, aroused greater criticism. States with the largest unpaid obligations, such as Massachusetts, thought assumption a splendid idea. But others, such as Virginia and Pennsylvania, which had already retired much of their debt, were adamantly opposed. Critics also warned that assumption would strengthen the central government at the expense of the states, since wealthy individuals would look to it rather than the states for a return on their investments. Moreover, with its increased need for revenue to pay off the accumulated debt, the federal government would have additional reason to exercise its newly acquired power of taxation. That was exactly what Hamilton intended.

Once again, Congress supported Hamilton's bill, in good measure because Madison and Jefferson approved it as part of an agreement to relocate the seat of government from New York to Philadelphia and then finally to a permanent federal district on the Potomac River. Southerners hoped that moving the government away from northern commercial centers would enable them to control its development and keep it more closely aligned with their own agrarian interests.

Opposition to the funding and assumption scheme, however, did not die. In December 1790, the Virginia assembly passed a series of resolutions, framed by that old Anti-Federalist Patrick Henry, warning that southern agriculture was being subordinated to the interests of northern commerce, and that the government's powers were expanding in dangerous fashion. Hearing of the Virginia resolutions,

Hamilton wrote privately that "This is the first symptom of a spirit which must either be killed, or will kill the Constitution." The contest for control of the new government was now vigorously joined.

As controversy grew, Hamilton introduced the second phase of his financial program in December 1790—establishment of a national bank capable of handling the government's financial affairs and pooling private investment capital for economic development. Though he was careful not to mention it publicly, he considered the Bank of England and its mutually beneficial ties to the royal government as a model.

Congressional opposition to the bank came almost entirely from the South (only one northern delegate voted against it), since it seemed clear that the bank would serve the needs of northern merchants and manufacturers far better than of southern agrarians. Still, in February 1791, Congress approved the bank bill.

Before signing it, Washington asked his cabinet for advice. Hamilton urged him to sign the legislation, following the constitutional doctrine of "implied powers," the principle that the government possessed the authority to make any laws "necessary and proper" for exercising the powers specifically granted [the history place] it by the Constitution. He argued that the authority to charter such a bank followed from Congress's power to collect taxes and regulate trade. Secretary of State Jefferson, however, advised a presidential veto. He saw in Hamilton's argument a blueprint for the indefinite expansion of federal authority and insisted that the government possessed only those powers specifically itemized in the Constitution. Because the Constitution said nothing about chartering banks, the bill was unconstitutional and should be rejected. Jefferson also feared the rapid development of commerce and domestic manufacturing that the bank was intended to promote. To Jefferson's distress, Washington followed Hamilton's advice and signed the bank bill into law.

In December 1790, in his second "Report on the Public Credit," Hamilton proposed a series of excise taxes, including one on the manufacture of distilled liquor. By this so-called Whiskey Tax, he intended to signal the government's intention to use its taxing authority to increase federal revenue. The power to tax and spend, Hamilton knew, was the power to govern. The Whiskey Tax became law in March 1791.

Finally, in a "Report on Manufactures" issued in December 1791, Hamilton called for a schedule of tariffs (i.e., taxes) on imported European goods as a way of protecting American industries; bounties to encourage the expansion of commercial agriculture; and a network of federally sponsored internal

The revolutionary generation found inspiration in the republican eras of ancient Greece and Rome. This bust of Thomas Jefferson, cast in the classical style, was completed in 1789 by the French sculptor Jean-Antoine Houdon. *(Collection of the New-York Historical Society)*

improvements such as roadways and lighthouses, intended to stimulate commerce and bind the nation more tightly together. Because of opposition from southern agrarians and northern merchants who feared that such tariffs would reduce overseas trade and raise the cost of living, Congress never endorsed this report.

All the while, criticism of Hamilton's ambitious program continued to mount. In October 1791, opposition leaders in Congress established a newspaper, the *National Gazette,* that vigorously attacked the administration's policies. Hamilton responded with a series of anonymous articles in the administration's paper, *The Gazette of the United States,* accusing Jefferson (inaccurately) of having opposed the Constitution and charging him (also inaccurately) of fomenting opposition to the government. Alarmed at the division within his administration, Washington pleaded for restraint.

Congressional criticism of Hamilton's policies reached a climax in January 1793, when Representative William Branch Giles of Virginia introduced a series of resolutions calling for an inquiry into the condition of the Treasury, accusing Hamilton of using the office for his own benefit, and urging censure of the secretary's conduct. Hamilton vigorously defended both his policies and his behavior and none of Giles's accusations passed the House. The month-long

debate, however, showed just how acrimonious politics at the nation's capital had already become.

Political conflict was now spreading beyond the circle of governing officials in Philadelphia. Among ordinary Americans, Hamilton's financial program drew a mixed response. In northern towns and cities, artisans and other working people generally approved his efforts to improve credit and stimulate economic development. With their own economic circumstances now improving, they seemed undisturbed by the special benefits that funding, assumption, and the bank brought to a few. Within several years, many of them would move into the Jeffersonian opposition, but for the moment, their support of the government was secure.

The Whiskey Rebellion

The farmers of western Pennsylvania provided the most dramatic expression of popular discontent over government policies. Their anger focused on the Whiskey Tax. Ever since the trouble with England 30 years before, Americans had been sensitive to taxation and suspicious of its connections with government power. The farmers of western Pennsylvania had special reason to dislike this particular tax. Their livelihood depended on transporting surplus grain eastward across the mountains to market. Shipping it in bulk was prohibitively expensive, so they distilled the grain and moved it far more efficiently as whiskey. Hamilton's tax threatened to make this unprofitable. They also objected that people charged with tax evasion had to stand trial in federal court hundreds of miles away in Philadelphia.

The farmers' frustration, however, went deeper than that. Although they frequently turned to state authorities for help against Indians and depended on eastern markets for their grain, they resented the loss of control over their own lives as their communities were absorbed in the expanding market economy and fell under the control of a political system dominated by more populous areas to the east. In southern states like South Carolina, the integration of coastal and interior regions occurred more smoothly because of their similar agricultural interests and a white racial alliance against blacks. In the more economically diverse and racially homogenous states of the north, however, conflicts between coastal and backcountry regions sharpened.

Hamilton cared little what the farmers thought either about the Whiskey Tax or local self-reliance. The government needed revenue, and the farmers would have to bear the cost. George Clymer, federal supervisor of revenue for Pennsylvania, was equally unsympathetic. Referring to the "moral and personal weakness" of "lesser folk," Clymer publicly castigated the "sordid shopkeepers" who retailed Pennsylvania whiskey and the "depraved" farmers who produced it. Westerners resented such official arrogance as much as the tax and quickly made their resentment known.

Trouble was brewing by the summer of 1792 as angry farmers gathered in mass meetings across western Pennsylvania. In August, a convention at Pittsburgh denounced the Whiskey Tax and declared that the people would prevent its collection. Like opponents of the Stamp Act in 1765, they concluded that liberties would be lost if resistance did not soon begin.

Alarmed, Washington issued a proclamation warning against such "unlawful" gatherings and insisting that the Excise Tax would be enforced. As tax collections began, the farmers took matters into their own hands.

In July 1794, when federal marshal David Lennox, in company with John Neville, a local excise inspector, attempted to serve papers on several recalcitrant farmers near Pittsburgh, an angry crowd gathered and stood in the way. Soon 500 armed men surrounded Neville's home demanding his resignation. Learning that Neville had fled, they ordered the dozen soldiers trapped in the house to lay down their arms and come out. Fearing for their safety, the soldiers refused, and for several hours the two sides exchanged gunfire. After several men had been wounded, the soldiers finally surrendered, whereupon Neville's house was put to the torch. Similar episodes involving angry

crowds, the erection of liberty poles reminiscent of the Revolution, and the hoisting of banners bearing slogans such as "Liberty and No Excise. O Whiskey!" erupted across the state. At Parkinson's Ferry, a convention of over 200 delegates debated armed resistance and talked ominously about secession from the state.

Alarmed that the protests might spread through the entire backcountry region from Maine to Georgia, Washington ordered the insurgents home and called out troops from eastern Pennsylvania and surrounding states to restore order. For more than a year, Hamilton had been urging the use of force against the protesters. He viewed the insurrection not as indication of an unjust policy needing change but as a test of the administration's ability to govern. Suppressing the rebellion, Hamilton explained, "will . . . add to the solidity of everything in this country." He eagerly volunteered to accompany the federal army west.

In late August, a force of nearly 13,000 men, larger than the average strength of the continental army during the Revolutionary War, moved into western Pennsylvania. At its center was Colonel William McPherson's "Pennsylvania Blues," an upper-class, strongly Federalist cavalry regiment. At its head rode the president of the United States and the secretary of the treasury. Washington soon returned to Philadelphia, persuaded by his aides of the danger to his safety, but Hamilton pressed ahead. When later criticized for accompanying the army to Pittsburgh,

President Washington and Treasury Secretary Hamilton led a federal army of nearly 13,000 troops into western Pennsylvania in 1794. Rebellious farmers, protesting the government's excise tax on whiskey, dispersed as the army approached. *(The Metropolitan Museum of Art, Gift of Edgar William and Bernice Chrysler Garbisch, 1963)*

he replied that he had "long since . . . learned to hold public opinion of no value." The battle that Hamilton had anticipated, however, never materialized, for as the federal army approached, the "Whiskey Rebels" dispersed, two of their leaders fleeing across the Ohio River. Of the 20 men taken prisoner, two were convicted of treason and sentenced to death. Later, in a calmer mood, Washington pardoned them both.

As people quickly realized, the "Whiskey Rebellion" had never threatened the government's safety. "An insurrection was . . . proclaimed," Jefferson scoffed, "but could never be found." Hamilton was merely pursuing his "favorite purpose of strengthening government" under the sanction of Washington's name. Even such an ardent Federalist as Fisher Ames was uneasy at the sight of federal troops marching against American citizens. Though a government "by overcoming an unsuccessful insurrection becomes stronger," he warned, "elective rulers can scarcely ever employ the physical force of a democracy without turning the moral force, or the power of public opinion, against the government." Americans would soon have additional reason to ponder Ames's warning.

Although the Pennsylvania rebels were promptly dispersed, their outburst pointed toward broader patterns of disaffection within the extended backcountry, revealed in rumors that Spanish emissaries and American adventurers were plotting secession among settlers in Kentucky and the western Carolinas. The whiskey affray gave indication as well that the gentry-led politics of Congress and the locally based politics of the people were becoming more closely joined.

THE REPUBLIC IN A THREATENING WORLD

Because the nation was so new and the outside world so threatening, foreign policy issues generated extraordinary excitement during the 1790s. This was especially so after the tumultuous events of the French Revolution and the accompanying European war burst on the international scene. In their disputes over the revolution in France and its implications for the United States, the American people revealed once again how sharply they differed and how deeply engaged in national politics they were becoming.

The Promise and Peril of the French Revolution

France's revolution began in 1789 as an effort to reform a monarchy weakened by debt and administrative decay. Pent-up demands for social justice, however, quickly outran initial attempts at moderate, constitutional reform, and by 1793 France was embroiled in a genuinely radical revolution. In January the monarch, Louis XVI, was beheaded. While the rest of Europe watched in horrified fascination, the forces of revolution and reaction struggled for the nation's soul.

As the revolution extended its attack on the aristocracy, the monarchy, and the Catholic Church, conservatives across the European Continent gathered in opposition, their fears fueled by the frantic accounts of fleeing French aristocrats. Finding itself surrounded and facing assault by Austria and Prussia, France's revolutionary government launched a series of military thrusts triggering a general declaration of war. By the end of 1793, Europe was locked in a deadly struggle between revolutionary France and a counterrevolutionary coalition led by Prussia and Great Britain.

For more than a decade, the French Revolution dominated European affairs. Before it was finished, it would transform the course of Western history. The revolution also cut like a plowshare through the surface of American politics, not only threatening the nation's security but also capturing people's imaginations and setting them against each other.

The outbreak of European war posed thorny diplomatic problems for Washington's administration. Under international law, neutral nations could continue to trade with warring powers as long as such trade did not include goods directly related to the war effort. American merchants eagerly took advantage of that opportunity because it promised handsome profits. Within a few years, American commerce was booming. For the first time since the Revolutionary War, prosperity returned to the nation's coastal cities. By 1800, American exports had more than doubled, and American ships were carrying an astonishing 92 percent of all commerce between America and Europe. Though the benefits were most evident in coastal cities, they radiated as well into the surrounding countryside, where cargoes of agricultural and forest goods as well as the provisions required by ships' crews were produced.

America's expanding commerce, however, quickly encountered problems, for while both England and France sought access to American goods, each was determined to keep those goods from reaching the other, if necessary by stopping American ships and confiscating their cargoes. Neither belligerent was willing to tie itself down with legal formalities when locked in such a deadly struggle.

America's relations with England were further complicated by the Royal navy's practice of impressing American sailors into service aboard its warships to meet its growing demand for seamen. Washington faced the dilemma of upholding the country's neutral rights and protecting its citizens without getting drawn into the European conflict.

This scene of bustling commercial activity in New York City in 1797 reveals the benefits that expanded neutral trade brought to the nation's major seaports. (*The New-York Historical Society*)

The French alliance of 1778 compounded the government's troubles because it seemed to require the United States to come to France's aid, much as France had assisted the American states a decade and a half before. Those sympathetic to the French cause argued that America's commitment still held. Others, fearing the consequences of American involvement and the political infection that closer ties with revolutionary France might bring, insisted that the treaty had lapsed when the French monarchy was overthrown.

The American reaction to the European drama further complicated the situation. At first the revolution in France had seemed an extension of America's own struggle for liberty and thus was to be celebrated as an event linking France and America in a universal struggle for liberty. Even the swing toward genuine social revolution did not immediately dampen American enthusiasm.

By the mid-1790s, however, especially after France's revolutionary regime launched an attack on organized Christianity, many Americans pulled back in alarm. What connection could there possibly be between the principles of 1776 and the chaos of revolutionary France? Insisted the *Gazette of the United States,* a staunchly Federalist newspaper, "In America no barbarities were perpetrated—no men's heads were stuck upon poles—no mangled ladies' bodies were carried thro' the streets in triumph. . . . Whatever blood was shed, flowed gallantly in the field." The writer conveniently ignored the violence meted out by supporters of the French monarchy and betrayed a selective memory of America's own revolution. Even so, the differences were indeed profound.

For the Federalists, revolutionary France now symbolized social anarchy and threatened the European order on which America's commercial and diplomatic security depended. With increasing vehemence, they castigated the revolution, championed England as the defender of European civilization, and sought ways of linking England and the United States more closely together.

Other Americans, however, continued to support France. While decrying the revolution's excesses, they noted how difficult it was to uproot deeply entrenched forces of reaction. Though Jefferson regretted the shedding of innocent blood, he thought it necessary if true liberty was to be achieved. John Bradford, editor of the *Kentucky Gazette,* agreed. "Instead of reviling the French republicans as monsters," he wrote, "the friends of royalty in this country should rather admire their patience in so long deferring the fate of their perjured monarch." In Bradford's judgment, England was not a bastion of civilization and order but of privilege and political oppression.

Citizen Genêt and the Democratic-Republican Societies

Popular associations known as Democratic-Republican societies—political and philosophical heirs of the Sons of Liberty and Committees of Correspondence (see Chapter 5) that had mobilized patriots against England twenty years earlier—provided the most vocal support for the revolution in France, as well as for political democracy at home. As early as 1792, ordinary citizens began to form "constitutional societies" dedicated to "watching over the rights of the people, and giving an early alarm in case of governmental encroachments." During the government's first years, several dozen societies had formed in opposition to Hamilton's financial program. The French Revolution stoked the fires of democratic enthusiasm and stimulated the societies' growth.

The arrival in April 1793 of Citizen Edmund Genêt, minister from the French republic to the United States, sparked a firestorm of democratic enthusiasm. Genêt landed at Charleston, South Carolina, to a tumultuous reception. His instructions were to court popular support and negotiate a commercial treaty. Shortly after his arrival, however, he began commissioning American privateers to prey on British shipping in the Caribbean and enlisting American seamen for expeditions against Spanish Florida. Both were clear violations of American neutrality.

The enthusiastic receptions he encountered as he traveled north toward Philadelphia soon led him astray. Despite a warning from Secretary of State Jefferson and in open defiance of diplomatic protocol, he urged Congress to reject Washington's recently issued neutrality proclamation and side with revolutionary France. That was the final straw. On August 2, the president demanded Genêt's recall, charging that his conduct threatened "war abroad and anarchy at home." Washington's decision drew sharp cries of protest.

As the Genêt controversy escalated, other circumstances added to the sense of anxiety gripping politicians at the Philadelphia capital. Through the summer of 1793 an unrelenting heat wave descended on southeastern Pennsylvania, searing trees and gardens, threatening supplies of potable water, and raising a stench in the refuse-filled streets. Even more alarming, from early August to mid-October a deadly epidemic of yellow fever gripped the city, sending those able to escape fleeing to the countryside for safety and taking a terrible toll on those forced to stay behind. Before early frosts finally destroyed the swarms of mosquitoes that carried the deadly pestilence through the city's crowded streets, well over 4,000 black and white Philadelphians had died, a full 10 percent of the city's 35,000 people. Yellow fever was not new to Philadelphia, and it would return again before the decade was out. But never did it reap such a destructive harvest as in 1793.

If Genêt failed as a diplomat, he succeeded in fanning popular enthusiasm for revolutionary France. In June 1793, with his open encouragement, the largest and most influential of the new societies, the Democratic Society of Pennsylvania, was founded in Philadelphia. It immediately called for the formation of similar societies elsewhere to join in supporting France and promoting the "spirit of freedom and equality" at home. People across the land, it declared, should join in "erecting the temple of liberty on the ruins of palaces and thrones." Washington and his Federalist colleagues had reason to wonder if that challenge was aimed at them.

Although a full network of popular societies never developed, about 40 organizations scattered from Maine to Georgia sprang up during the next several years. Working people—artisans and laborers in the cities, small farmers and tenants in the countryside—provided the bulk of membership. Federalist critics derided them as "the lowest orders of . . . draymen . . . broken hucksters, and trans-Atlantic traitors." That final canard was in reference to a growing tide of Irish immigrants, fleeing hard times and English oppression at home, who voiced not only demands for Irish independence but a commitment to political equality as well, together with a relish for an in-your-face, rough-and-tumble style of politics. Many of them soon enlisted as foot soldiers in the growing opposition to Federalist rule.

The societies' leaders were generally individuals of acknowledged respectability, such as doctors, lawyers, and tradesmen. But leaders and followers were united by a dedication to the "principles of '76" and a determination to preserve those principles against the "royalizing" tendencies of Washington's administration.

Lamenting the threats to egalitarianism at home, the societies urged citizens to be vigilant in the face of Federalist behavior. Asserted the Newark, New Jersey, society, "members of the government are nothing more than the agents of the people," and "have no right to prevent their employers from inspecting into their conduct." Committed to an awakened citizenry, the societies organized public celebrations, issued ringing addresses filled with democratic principles, and sent petitions sharply critical of administration policies to the president and Congress. Washington's proclamation of neutrality they labeled a "pusillanimous truckling to Britain, despotically conceived and unconstitutionally promulgated." Several of the societies openly urged the United States to enter the war on France's behalf. Declared the New York society: "We firmly believe that he who is an enemy to the French revolution cannot be a firm republican; and therefore . . . ought not to be entrusted with the guidance of any part of the machine of government."

West of the Appalachians, local societies agitated against England's continuing occupation of the frontier posts around the Great Lakes and berated Spain for closing the Mississippi River. In the Northeast, they castigated England for its "piracy" against American shipping. In the Carolinas, they demanded greater representation for the growing backcountry in the state's assembly. And everywhere they protested the

Excise Tax, opposed the administration's overtures to England, and demanded that public officials attend to the people's wishes.

Finally, they campaigned for a press free from control by Federalist "aristocrats." Declared William Manning, a Massachusetts farmer who had marched to the "Concord fight" in 1775 and who continued to praise the principles for which he had fought: "A labouring man may as well hunt for pins in a haymow as to try to collect the knowledge necessary for him to have from such promiscuous piles of contradictions" as appeared in the Federalist press.

President Washington and other Federalists were incensed by the societies' support of Genêt and criticism of the government. The "real design" of these "nurseries of sedition," thundered Fisher Ames, was to revolutionize America as the Jacobins had revolutionized France. Writing in the *Virginia Chronicle* of January 17, 1794, a Federalist author berated Kentucky's Democratic Society as "that horrible sink of treason, that hateful synagogue of anarchy, that

odious conclave of tumult, that frightful cathedral of discord, that poisonous garden of conspiracy, that hellish school of rebellion and opposition to all regular and well-balanced authority!" Such breathless expressions of alarm gave evidence of how inflamed public discourse had become.

Jay's Controversial Treaty

The uproar over Jay's Treaty with England further heightened tensions at mid-decade. Alarmed by the deteriorating relations with England, Washington sent Chief Justice John Jay to London in the spring of 1794 with instructions to negotiate a wide range of troublesome issues carried over from the Revolutionary War. Notable among them were continued British occupation of the western posts, interference with American neutral shipping, and impressment of American seamen.

Early in 1795, Jay returned home with a treaty that resolved almost none of these grievances. England finally agreed to vacate the western posts, but not for

Cartoons became powerful weapons in the superheated politics of the 1790s. This Jeffersonian cartoon lampoons William Cobbett, one of the Federalists' most acid-penned pamphleteers who wrote under the pseudonym Peter Porcupine. While Columbia swoons over the political division, the English Lion urges Cobbett to "sow the seeds of discord." *(The Historical Society of Pennsylvania (HSP)*, "Caricature against William Cobbett, editor of the Porcupine Gazette," 1796, *[Accession #Bb612Se31])*

Recovering the Past

FOREIGN TRAVEL JOURNALS

Historians utilize many different kinds of sources in their quest to recover the American past. Among the most revealing are travel accounts penned by foreign visitors eager to learn about the United States and record their impressions of it. From the days of earliest explorations to our own time, travelers have been fascinated by the people, customs, institutions, and physical setting of North America. Out of this continuing interaction between America and its foreign visitors has emerged a rich and fascinating travel literature that reveals much not only about America but about the travelers who have visited it as well.

During the second quarter of the nineteenth century, a stream of perceptive European visitors—Alexis de Tocqueville, Harriet Martineau, and Francis Grund among them—toured the United States, eager to record their impressions of what Jacksonian America was like. Fifty years earlier, the American Revolution fanned similar interest in the minds of Europeans fascinated by the newly independent nation and anxious to discern its implications for them. Among the most opinionated and engaging of these earlier commentators was the Frenchman Moreau de Saint Méry.

Born on the French island of Martinique in January 1750, de Saint Méry established a successful legal practice before moving to France, where relatives introduced him to polite, Parisian society. In the late 1780s, he became an ardent champion of political reform during the early days of the French Revolution. As the revolution entered its radical phase, however, he was forced to flee to the United States for safety. Arriving at Norfolk, Virginia, with his wife and two children, de Saint Méry settled in Philadelphia, where he remained from October 1794 to August 1798. While there, he mingled with civic and cultural leaders, opened a bookstore that served as a rendezvous for French émigrés who also had fled the revolution's turmoil, and published a French-language paper that reported the latest news from home. In the late summer of 1798, de Saint Méry returned safely to France.

As with all such travel accounts, de Saint Méry's commentary must be read with a critical eye, for travelers disagreed over what they thought important and worth reporting, and interpreted what they saw in very different ways. In nearly 400 pages of commentary, de Saint Méry touched on numerous aspects of American life, but none in more frank and compelling fashion than relations between the sexes. The selections that follow (somewhat rearranged for greater continuity) provide tantalizing insights into the behavior and sexual mores of American men and women in the early years of the republic.

What did de Saint Méry find most interesting about gender relations in Philadelphia? How did religion, class, and ethnicity shape men's and women's behavior? What forms of behavior did he approve and disapprove?

de Saint Méry's explicit commentary is virtually unique among the numerous accounts left by foreign travelers in the early republic, most of whom showed far more interest in America's racial makeup, political practices, and physical environment. de Saint Méry's observations may thus be idiosyncratic and should be approached with caution.

What other kinds of sources might enable us to evaluate the accuracy of such travel accounts? In what ways is a traveler's own nationality, gender, religion, or class likely to shape his or her impressions of the United States? Similarly, how important is it to know travelers' motives for coming, how long they stayed, which parts of the country they visited, and with whom they associated while here?

Does the gendered world of late eighteenth-century Philadelphia, as described by de Saint Méry, seem strange or familiar, attractive or distasteful to your own sensibilities? If you were to visit another country today, how accurate do you think you could be in assessing the social behavior and cultural values of its people? To what extent would your values, perhaps like those of Moreau de Saint Méry, color your impressions? Might it be more difficult to understand some foreign cultures than others? Why?

Moreau de Saint Méry's American Journal

American men, generally speaking, are tall and thin . . . [and] seem to have no strength. . . . They are brave, but they lack drive. Indifferent toward almost everything, they sometimes behave in a manner that suggests real energy; then follow it with a "Oh-to-hell-with-it" attitude which shows that they seldom feel genuine enthusiasm.

Their dinner consists of . . . English roast surrounded by potatoes. Following that are boiled green peas . . . baked or fried eggs, boiled or fried fish, salad which may be thinly sliced cabbage . . . [and] sweets to which they are excessively partial. . . . For dessert, they have a little fruit, some cheese, and a pudding. The entire meal is washed down with cider, weak or strong beer . . . [and] wine . . . which they keep drinking right through dessert, toward the end of which any ladies who are at the dinner leave the table and withdraw by themselves, leaving the men free to drink as much as they please. . . . Toasts are drunk, cigars are lighted, diners run to the corners of the room hunting night tables and vases which will enable them to hold a greater amount of liquor. . . . Finally the dinner table is deserted because of boredom, fatigue or drunkenness. . . .

American women are pretty, and those of Philadelphia are prettiest of all. . . . Girls ordinarily mature in Philadelphia at the age of fourteen, and reach that period without unusual symptoms. . . . But they soon grow pale. . . . After eighteen years old they lose their charms. . . . Their hair is scanty, their teeth bad. . . . In short, while charming and adorable at fifteen, they are faded at twenty-three, old at thirty-five, decrepit at forty or forty-five. . . .

American women carefully wash their faces and hands, but not their mouths, seldom their feet and even more seldom their bodies. . . . They are greatly addicted to finery and have a strong desire to display themselves—a desire . . . inflamed by their love of adornment. They cannot, however, imitate that elegance of style possessed by Frenchwomen. . . .

One is struck by the tall and pretty young girls one sees in the streets, going and coming from school. They wear their hair long, and skirts with closed seams. But when nubility has arrived they put up their hair with a comb, and the back of the skirt has a placket. At this time, they . . . become their own mistresses, and can go walking alone and have suitors. . . .

They invariably make their own choice of a suitor, and the parents raise no objection because that's the custom of the country. The suitor comes into the house when he wishes; goes on walks with his loved one whenever he desires. On Sunday he often takes her out in a cabriolet, and brings her back in the evening without anyone wanting to know where they went. . . . Although in general one is conscious of widespread modesty in Philadelphia, the customs are not particularly pure, and the disregard . . . of some parents for the manner in which their daughters form relationships to which they . . . have not given their approval is an encouragement to indiscretions . . .

A young woman trusts in her suitor's delicacy and charges him with maintaining for her a respect which she is not always able to command. Each day both of them are entrusted to no one but each other. . . . Her servant . . . leaves the house as soon as night as arrived. . . . Her father, her mother, her entire family have gone to bed. The suitor and his mistress remain alone; and sometimes, when the servant returns, she finds them asleep and the candle out, such is the frigidity of love in this country. . . . [American women] endure the company of their lovers for whole hours without being sufficiently moved to change their expression.

When one considers the unlimited liberty which young ladies enjoy, one is astonished by their universal eagerness to be married. . . . When a young woman marries, she enters a wholly different existence. She is no longer a . . . butterfly who denies herself nothing and whose only laws are her whims and her suitor's wish. She now lives only for her husband, and to devote herself without surcease to the care of her household and her home. . . . The more her husband is capable of multiplying . . . the pleasures of matrimony . . . the more her health may suffer, most of all when she has a child; for sometimes while nursing it, or as soon as it is weaned, she has already conceived another. . . .

One very remarkable and important thing is the respect in which married women are held, and the virtuous conduct of almost all. . . . In spite of conjugal customs which would seem to indicate a state of happiness, they do not produce the happiness which would be expected to result. . . . This is evidenced by the multiplicity of second marriages. . . . The men in particular remarry oftenest. . . . Divorce is obtained with scandalous ease. From this alone one can judge the extent of loose habits. . . .

Bastards are extremely common in Philadelphia. There are two principal reasons for this. In the first place, the city is full of religious sects, but none of them give their clergymen any authority to enforce obedience. Consequently there is no way of inspiring shame in women who become mothers for no reason except the pleasure they get out of it. In the second place, once an illegitimate child is twelve months old, a mother can disembarrass herself of him by farming him out for twenty-one years. This makes it possible for her to commit the same sin for a second time. It never occurs to her that her child can never know her, and that the whole business is shameful. . . .

There are streetwalkers . . . in Philadelphia. These are very young and very pretty girls, elegantly dressed, who promenade two by two, arm in arm and walking very rapidly, at an hour which indicates that they aren't just out for a stroll. . . . Anyone who accosts them is taken to their home . . . [where] they fulfill every desire for two dollars, half of which is supposed to pay for the use of the room. Quaker youths are frequent visitors in the houses of ill fame, which have multiplied in Philadelphia and are frequented at all hours. There is even a well-known gentleman who leaves his horse tied to the post outside one of these houses, so that everyone knows when he is there and exactly how long he stays. . . .

Source: Moreau de St. Mery's American Journey, 1793–1798, trans. and ed., Kenneth Roberts and Anna M. Roberts. (New York: Doubleday & Co., 1947), pp. 265, 281–283, 312–313.

another year and then only if it was guaranteed continued access to the fur trade on American soil south of the Great Lakes. Jay failed as well to secure compensation for American slaves carried off by the British at the end of the Revolutionary War. Nor would the British foreign minister offer assurances against the future impressment of American seamen, compromise on the issue of neutral rights, or agree to open the British West Indies to American shipping.

When the terms of Jay's treaty were made public, they triggered an explosion of protest. The administration's pleas that the agreement headed off an open breach with England and was the best that could be obtained failed to pacify its critics. In New York City, Hamilton was stoned when he defended the treaty at a noonday mass meeting. The "rabble," sniffed one disgusted Federalist, attempted "to knock out Hamilton's brains to reduce him to an equality with themselves." Southern planters were angry because the agreement brought no compensation for their lost slaves. Westerners complained that the British were not evacuating the posts, while merchants and sailors railed against Jay's failure to open the West Indies trade or stop impressment. After a long and acrimonious debate, the Senate ratified the treaty by the narrowest of margins.

The administration made better progress on the still volatile issue of free transit of the Mississippi River at New Orleans. In the Treaty of San Lorenzo, negotiated by Thomas Pinckney in 1795, Spain for the first time recognized the United States' boundaries under the peace treaty of 1783 (the Mississippi River to the west and the 31st parallel to the south) and thus gave up all claim to U.S. territory. Spain also granted American shippers free navigation of the Mississippi and the right to unload goods for transshipment at New Orleans, though only for three years.

By mid-decade, political harmony had disappeared both in Congress and the country more generally, as divisions deepened on virtually every important issue of foreign and domestic policy. Increasingly estranged from Washington's administration, Jefferson resigned as secretary of state in July 1793. He soon joined politicians such as Madison and Albert Gallatin of Pennsylvania in open opposition.

In September 1796, in what came to be called his Farewell Address, Washington announced that he would not accept a third term as president. He had long been contemplating retirement, for he was now 64 and was exhausted by the controversies swirling around him. Even the Great Patriot was no longer immune to personal attack. "As to you, sir," fumed Thomas Paine in an open letter to the Philadelphia *Aurora,* "treacherous in private friendship . . . and a hypocrite in public life, the world

will be puzzled to decide, whether you are an apostate or an impostor; whether you have abandoned good principles, or whether you ever had any." Seldom has an American president been subjected to such public abuse as was Washington during his final year in office.

THE POLITICAL CRISIS DEEPENS

By 1796, bitter controversy surrounded the national government. That controversy intensified during the last half of the 1790s until the very stability of the country seemed threatened.

The Election of 1796

The presidential election of 1796 reflected the political storms buffeting the nation. Four years earlier, Washington and Adams had been reelected without significant opposition. The situation now was vastly different.

With Washington out of the picture, the contest quickly narrowed to Adams and Jefferson. Both were elder statesmen; Adams was 61 years old, while

John Adams, Washington's vice president, won a narrow victory over Jefferson for the presidency in 1796. His administration foundered on conflicts over foreign policy abroad and the suppression of political dissent at home. *(Adams National Historic Site/U.S. Department of the Interior, National Park Service)*

PRESIDENTIAL ELECTIONS, 1788–1800			
Year	Candidate	Party	Electoral Votes
1788	GEORGE WASHINGTON	None	69
1792	GEORGE WASHINGTON	Federalist	132
1796	JOHN ADAMS	Federalist	71
	Thomas Jefferson	Democratic-Republican	68
	Thomas Pinckney	Federalist	59
	Aaron Burr	Democratic-Republican	30
	Minor Candidates	—	48
1800	THOMAS JEFFERSON	Democratic-Republican	73
	Aaron Burr	Democratic-Republican	73
	John Adams	Federalist	65
	Charles C. Pinckney	Federalist	64
	John Jay	Federalist	1

Note: Winners' names are in capital letters.

Jefferson was eight years his junior. They had become friends and earned each other's respect years earlier, during the Revolution. Sharing first in the electrifying task of drafting the Declaration of Independence, they joined forces abroad during the 1780s when Adams served as first U.S. minister to Great Britain while Jefferson was minister to France. They came together a third time in the early 1790s, Adams as vice president (a position he regarded as "wholly insignificant") and Jefferson as secretary of state.

Though they had worked closely together, they differed in many ways. Short, rotund, and fastidiously neat, Adams contrasted sharply in physical appearance with the tall, frequently disheveled Jefferson. At once intensely ambitious and deeply insecure about the judgments of both his contemporaries and history, Adams struggled self-consciously to construct his public career. Jefferson, by contrast, charted his course more quietly and repeatedly sought the solace of private life. They differed in intellect and vision as well. Jefferson's mind was more expansive and his interests more encompassing. Politician and political theorist, he was also an avid naturalist, architect, and philosopher. Adams's interests were more tightly focused on legal and constitutional affairs.

By the mid-1790s, the two statesmen differed also in their visions of the nation's future. Though fearing Hamilton's ambition and distrusting his infatuation with England, Adams was a committed Federalist. He believed in a vigorous national government, was appalled by the French Revolution, and was persuaded that the impulses of popular democracy must be counterbalanced by a stable and propertied elite. Jefferson, while firmly supporting the Constitution, was alarmed by Hamilton's financial program, viewed France's revolution as a logical if chaotic extension of America's struggle for freedom, and sought the expansion of political democracy. By 1796, he had become the vocal leader of an increasingly articulate political opposition, the Jeffersonian Republicans.

The election that year bound Jefferson and Adams together in a deeply strained and ill-fated alliance. With Washington gone, Adams became the Federalists' candidate for president. Though Jefferson did not openly oppose Adams, he sanctioned a vigorous campaign on his own behalf. In the election, Adams received 71 electoral votes and won the presidency. Jefferson came in second with 68 and, as the Constitution then specified, assumed the vice presidency. The narrowness of Adams's majority—his enemies gleefully reminded him that he was only a "President of three votes"—foreshadowed the troubles that lay ahead.

Adams later recalled his inaugural day. "A solemn scene it was indeed, and it was made more affecting by the presence of the General [Washington], whose countenance was as serene and unclouded as the day. He seemed to enjoy a triumph over me. Methought I heard him say, 'Ay! I am fairly out and you fairly in! See which of us will be the happiest.'" The answer was not long in coming.

The War Crisis with France

Adams had no sooner taken office than he confronted a deepening crisis with France that would push the nation to the brink of civil conflict. Hoping to ease relations between the two countries, he sent three commissioners to Paris to negotiate an accord. When they arrived, agents (identified only as "X," "Y," and "Z") of the French foreign minister, Talleyrand, made it clear that the success of their mission depended on a substantial loan to the French government and a

$240,000 gratuity for themselves. The two staunchly Federalist commissioners, John Marshall and Charles Pinckney, indignantly rejected the demands and sailed for home. The third commissioner, Elbridge Gerry, stayed behind, hoping for an accommodation and alarmed by Talleyrand's intimation that if all three Americans left, France would declare war.

When Adams reported to Congress on the so-called XYZ Affair, American opinion was outraged. The Federalists quickly exploited the French blunder. Secretary of State Pickering urged an immediate declaration of war, while Federalist congressmen thundered against the insult to American honor and promised "millions for defense, but not one cent for tribute." Adams now found himself an unexpected hero. When he attended the theater in Philadelphia, audiences cheered themselves hoarse with shouts of "Adams and Liberty!" Caught up in the anti-French furor and emboldened by the petitions of support that flooded in from around the country, the president lashed out at "enemies" at home and abroad. The nation, he warned ominously, had never been in greater danger from "traitors" ready to "unite with the invading enemy and fly within their lines." Emotions were further inflamed by the so-called Quasi War, a series of naval encounters between American and French ships on the high seas.

As tensions with France increased, the government built men-of-war to defend American commerce on the high seas and in anticipation of a French invasion that never materialized. (*William Russell Birch,* Preparation for War to Defend Commerce, *1800, Free Library of Philadelphia*)

For the moment, the Republicans were in disarray. Publicly, they deplored the French government's behavior and pledged to uphold the nation's honor. But among themselves, they talked with alarm about the Federalists' intentions. They had good reason for concern, because the Federalists soon mounted a crash program to repel foreign invaders and roust out traitors in the country's midst.

The Alien and Sedition Acts

In May 1798, Congress created a Navy Department and called for the development of a naval force capable of defending the American coast against French attack. In July, Congress moved closer to an open breach with France by unilaterally repealing the treaty of 1778 and calling for the formation of a 10,000-man army. (The Federalists' original goal had been 50,000 men.) The army's stated mission was to repel an anticipated French invasion. Given France's desperate struggle in Europe, however, such an attack seemed exceedingly unlikely. The Jeffersonians, remembering the speed with which Federalist troops had been deployed against the Whiskey Rebels only a few years earlier, feared the army would be used against them.

As criticism of the army bill mounted, Adams had second thoughts. He was still enough of an old revolutionary to worry about the domestic dangers of a standing army. "This damned army," he burst out, "will be the ruin of the country." The navy, he believed, should be America's first line of defense. He was further angered when members of his party sought to put Hamilton in command of the army. To the dismay of hard-line Federalists, Adams issued only a few of the officers' commissions that Congress had authorized. Without officers, the troops could not be mobilized.

Fearful of foreign subversion and aware that French as well as Irish immigrants were active in the Jeffersonian opposition, the Federalist-dominated Congress moved in the summer of 1798 to curb the flow of aliens into the country. The Naturalization Act raised the residence requirement for citizenship from 5 to 14 years, while the Alien Act authorized the president to expel aliens whom he judged "dangerous to the peace and safety of the United States." Imprisonment and permanent exclusion from citizenship awaited individuals who were warned to leave but refused to go. Another bill, the Alien Enemies Act, empowered the president in time of war to arrest, imprison, or banish the subjects of any hostile nation without specifying charges against them or providing opportunity for appeal. The Federalist Congressman Harrison Gray Otis explained that there was no need "to invite hordes of Wild Irishmen, nor the turbulent and disorderly of all

A fight erupted in the House of Representatives in 1798 when Matthew Lyon, a Jeffersonian from Vermont, spat on the Federalist Roger Griswold. As the two congressmen battle, other representatives and a dog look on. *(Print Collection, Miriam and Ira D. Wallach Division of Art, Prints and Photographs, The New York Public Library, Astor, Lenox and Tilden Foundations)*

parts of the world, to come here with a view to distract our tranquility."

The implications of these acts for basic political liberties were ominous enough, but the Federalists were not yet finished. In July 1798, Congress passed the Sedition Act, aimed directly at the Jeffersonian opposition. The bill made it punishable by fine and imprisonment for anyone to conspire in opposition to "any measure or measures of the government" or to aid "any insurrection, riot, unlawful assembly, or combination." Fines and imprisonment also awaited those who dared "write, print, utter, or publish . . . any false, scandalous and malicious writing" bringing the government, Congress, or the president into disrepute.

The Federalist moves stunned the Jeffersonians, for they threatened to smother all political opposition. The Federalists left no room for doubts on the matter. With an open declaration of war, predicted Congressman James Lloyd of Delaware, "traitors and sedition mongers who are now protected and tolerated, would . . . be easily restrained or punished." The Federalists had come to equate their own political control with the nation's survival.

Under the terms of the Alien Act, Secretary of State Pickering launched investigations intended to force all foreigners to register with the government. The act's chilling effects were immediate and widespread. In July, Pickering noted approvingly that large numbers of aliens, especially people of French ancestry, were leaving the country. As prosecutions under the Sedition Act went forward, 25 people, among them

David Brown of Dedham, were arrested. Fifteen were indicted, and 10 were ultimately convicted, the majority of them Jeffersonian printers and editors.

Representative Matthew Lyon, a cantankerous, acid-tongued Jeffersonian from Vermont, learned the consequences of political indiscretion, even for members of Congress. Born in Ireland, Lyon had come to America as a young indentured servant harboring undying enmity toward England and disrespect for privilege of every sort. A veteran of the War for Independence, he took his revolutionary principles seriously.

During a particularly heated debate over the Sedition Act, Lyon spat in the face of a Federalist opponent, Roger Griswold of Connecticut, thus earning the derisive sobriquet of the "Spitting Lion." Two weeks later, Griswold exacted revenge by caning Lyon on the House floor. Later that year, Lyon was hauled into court, fined $1,000, and sentenced to four months in prison. His crime? Making reference in a personal letter to President Adams's "unbounded thirst for ridiculous pomp, foolish adulation, and selfish avarice."

Local Reverberations

David Brown was not the only ordinary citizen to experience the enmity of Federalist authorities, for the political conflict that was brewing penetrated deeply into American communities. Luther Baldwin of Newark, New Jersey, discovered how little it took to get into trouble. On July 27, 1798, President and Mrs.

Adams passed through Newark on their way from Philadelphia to their home in Quincy, Massachusetts. As the nation's first couple moved along Broad Street around 11 o'clock that morning, they were greeted by firing cannon, ringing church bells, and the cheers of the citizenry.

Not all Newark's residents shared in the moment's enthusiasm. Luther Baldwin happened to be coming toward John Burnett's dram shop when one of the tavern's customers, noting that the cannon continued to fire after the president had passed by, commented acidly, "There goes the President and they are firing at his a — —." Already "a little merry with drink," Baldwin replied that "he did not care if they fired thro' his a — —." Whereupon, the Federalist tavern keeper cried out that Baldwin had spoken sedition and must be punished. Within two months, a local grand jury indicted him, and the following year he was hauled before the federal Circuit Court, where he was convicted of speaking "seditious words tending to defame the President and Government of the United States," fined, and committed to jail until both fine and court fees were paid.

Local Jeffersonians made a field day of Baldwin's trial. The New York *Argus* wondered in mock astonishment whether the "most enthusiastic Federalists and Tories" supposed that anyone "would feel . . . justification in firing at such a disgusting target as the a— — of J. A.?" The Jeffersonians, however, saw danger as well as humor in the Federalists' zealous overreaction. When so much is made of such a "ridiculous expression" as Baldwin's, the *Argus* warned, the "malignancy of the federal faction" was evident.

With little prospect of reversing the actions of the Federalist-dominated Congress, the Jeffersonians turned to the states for support. Building on the firestorm of protest that greeted the Alien and Sedition Acts, the Virginia and Kentucky assemblies mounted a direct challenge to the Federalist laws. The Kentucky Resolutions, drafted by Jefferson and passed on November 16, 1798, declared that the national government had violated the Bill of Rights. Faced with the arbitrary exercise of federal power, the resolutions continued, each state "has an equal right to judge [of infractions] by itself . . . [and] the mode and measure of redress." Nullification (declaring a federal law invalid within a state's borders) was the "rightful remedy" for such unconstitutional laws. The Virginia Resolutions, written by Madison and passed the following month, asserted that when the central government threatened the people's liberties, the states "have the right and are in duty bound to interpose for arresting the progress of the evil." It would not be the last time in American history that state leaders would claim authority to set aside a federal law.

The Kentucky and Virginia resolutions received little support in either the North or South, and neither state actually attempted to obstruct enforcement of the Alien and Sedition Acts. Still, the resolutions indicated the depth of opposition to the Federalists' program.

As Federalists pressed ahead, some Jeffersonians prepared for open conflict. The Virginia assembly called for the formation of a state arsenal at Harpers Ferry, reorganization of the militia, and a special tax to pay for these preparations. In Philadelphia, Federalist patrols walked the streets to protect government officials from angry crowds. As a precaution, President Adams smuggled arms into his residence. As 1799 began, the country seemed on the brink of upheaval.

Within a year, however, the political cycle turned again, this time decisively against the Federalists. The break came with Adams's dramatic decision to send a new emissary to France. From Europe, the president's son, John Quincy Adams, sent assurances that Talleyrand was now ready to negotiate an honorable accord. Alarmed at the political furor consuming the nation and fearful that war with France "would convulse the attachments of the country," Adams eagerly seized the opening. "The end of war is peace," he explained, "and peace was offered me." Moreover, he had concluded that his only chance of reelection lay in fashioning a peace coalition out of both parties.

Adams's cabinet was enraged when they learned of the new mission, for the legitimacy of the Federalist war program depended on the continuation of the French crisis. After Secretary of State Pickering repeatedly ignored the president's orders to send the new commissioners on their way, Adams dismissed him and personally ordered the commissioners to depart. By year's end, the envoys had secured an agreement releasing the United States from the 1778 alliance and restoring peaceful relations between the two nations.

The "Revolution of 1800"

As the election of 1800 approached, the Federalists were in disarray, having squandered the political advantage handed them by the XYZ Affair in 1798. With peace now a reality, they stood before the nation charged with the unconstitutional exercise of federal power, the suppression of political dissent, and the intention of using the federal army against American citizens. The Federalists, moreover, were bitterly divided. Followers of Hamilton were furious at Adams's "betrayal." When the president announced his intention of standing for reelection, they plotted his defeat.

The Presidential Election of 1800

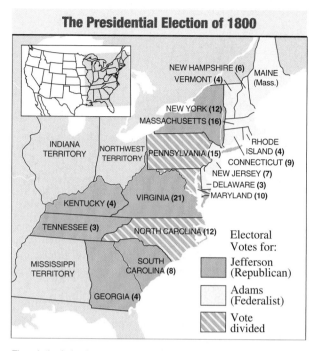

NEW HAMPSHIRE (6)
VERMONT (4)
MAINE (Mass.)
NEW YORK (12)
MASSACHUSETTS (16)
INDIANA TERRITORY
NORTHWEST TERRITORY
PENNSYLVANIA (15)
RHODE ISLAND (4)
CONNECTICUT (9)
NEW JERSEY (7)
DELAWARE (3)
MARYLAND (10)
VIRGINIA (21)
KENTUCKY (4)
TENNESSEE (3)
NORTH CAROLINA (12)
MISSISSIPPI TERRITORY
SOUTH CAROLINA (8)
GEORGIA (4)

Electoral Votes for:

Jefferson (Republican)

Adams (Federalist)

Vote divided

Though the federal government was little more than a decade old, the electoral vote in 1800 revealed the sectional divisions that already troubled national politics.

Emotions were running high as the election approached. In Philadelphia a group of young men showing their sympathy with England by wearing black cockades in their caps confronted another group sporting the tricolored cockade of France. "A fray ensued," Jefferson reported, "the light horse were called in, and the city was so filled with confusion from about 6 to 10 o'clock . . . that it was dangerous going out."

The arch-Federalist Fisher Ames berated the Jeffersonians as "fire-eating salamanders" and "poison-sucking toads," while the Jeffersonians returned the abuse in kind. Both sides believed that the republic's survival depended on their own political triumph and the destruction of their political enemies. In the heat of the moment, no compromise seemed possible. This election, Jefferson declared, will "fix our national character" and "determine whether republicanism or aristocracy" will prevail. In Virginia, rumors of a slave insurrection briefly interrupted the feuding, but the scare passed and soon Federalists and Jeffersonians were at each others' throats once again.

Election day was tense throughout the nation but passed without serious interruption. As the results were tallied, it became clear that the Jeffersonians had handed the Federalists a decisive defeat. The two Republican candidates for president, Jefferson, the Republicans' first choice, and Aaron Burr, their other

nominee, each had 73 electoral votes while Adams followed with 65.

Because of the tie vote, the election was thrown into the House of Representatives, as provided in the Constitution. There a deadlock quickly developed. In spite of pressure from Jefferson's supporters, Burr refused to give way. The Federalist caucus decided to back Burr, believing him less dangerous than Jefferson. After a bitter struggle, the House finally elected Jefferson, 10 states to 4, on the thirty-sixth ballot. (Seeking to prevent a recurrence of such a crisis, the next Congress passed and the states ratified the Twelfth Amendment, providing for separate Electoral College ballots for president and vice president.) The magnitude of the Federalists' defeat was even more evident in the congressional elections, where they lost their majority in both House and Senate.

The election's outcome revealed the strong sectional divisions now evident in the country's politics. The Federalists dominated New England because of regional loyalty to Adams, the area's commercial ties with England, and fears, fed by local ministers and politicians alike, that the Jeffersonians intended to import social revolution from France. From Maryland south, Jeffersonian control was almost as complete. In the middle states, where issues of foreign and domestic policy cut across society in more complicated ways, the election was more closely contested. In the years ahead, sectional differences would continue to shape American politics.

The conflict between Federalists and Jeffersonians was deeply rooted as well in socioeconomic divisions among the American people. Federalist strength was strongest among merchants, manufacturers, and commercial farmers situated within easy reach of the coast—groups that had supported the Constitution in 1787 and 1788. Connecticut Federalists claimed the support of "men of talents, information, and property." In New York City and Philadelphia, Federalists were most numerous in wards where assessments were highest, houses largest, and addresses most fashionable.

By contrast, the Jeffersonian opposition included most of the old Anti-Federalists as well as agriculturalists in both North and South. They marshaled significant support as well among urban workers and artisans, many of whom had once been staunch Federalists. An important reason for their shift in political allegiance was illustrated by an episode that occurred in New York City in 1795.

Thomas Burke and Timothy Crady, two recent Irish immigrants, operated a ferry across the East River between lower Manhattan and Brooklyn. One day in

Technology Changes the American People

INDUSTRIAL TECHNOLOGY
IN THE WOODEN AGE

The decades between 1790 and 1830 witnessed the first stirring of a revolution in industrial technology that would eventually transform the American economy and shape the working lives of millions of Americans. The nation's earliest experiments in industrial technology were fashioned out of wood, not iron. Though wooden machinery often broke down, required continuous maintenance, and frequently caught fire from friction, it was cheap to construct, easily repaired, and readily fabricated by experienced craftsmen. Wooden machinery, moreover, was especially well suited to the small scale of American manufacturing. The early republic was still part of the "wooden age," when, in addition to tools and machines, wood was the major source of fuel, construction material for ships and wagons, fences and houses, and important chemicals such as potash and turpentine.

Many Americans in the young republic were enthusiastic about technology's promise for the nation's future. Robert Fulton, inventor of one of the earliest steamboats, explained how technological progress would strengthen American republicanism. "Every order of things which has a tendency to remove oppression and meliorate the condition of man, by directing his ambition to useful industry," he proclaimed in a speech before Congress in 1810, "is, in effect, republican." Fulton's comments reflected a widely held belief that technology, representing the application of reason and science to practical, everyday needs, would foster the betterment of mankind.

In 1789, an enterprising English mechanic named Samuel Slater arrived in New York. Familiar with British textile technology, he brought with him detailed knowledge of mechanical carding machines that combed cotton fibers into alignment suitable for spinning, as well as the Arkwright spinning frame, capable of fashioning 48 uniform cotton threads at a time. Slater wasn't the only immigrant who made valuable contributions to technological development in the early republic, for much American technical know-how was borrowed from Europe. Powered by waterwheels and placed in the fledgling textile factories that sprung up in increasing numbers along New England's fast-flowing rivers from the 1790s on, the new wooden machines spurred a startling growth in the American textile industry. In 1800, an estimated 1,000 wage earners labored in the nation's textile factories. By 1830, the number had climbed to 55,000.

Thought they vastly increased the output of cotton cloth, the new machines also created a dangerous environment for the workers who tended them. Not only were the early textile factories deafeningly noisy because of the pounding motion and clacking wooden gears, but also cotton dust filled the air, and the

Within a few years, young women joined children as workers in many of the nations' textile mills. (*The Slater Mill Historic Site*)

Samuel Slater's textile mill at Pawtucket Falls in Rhode Island was among the first to employ new wooden machinery. *(Courtesy The Rhode Island Historical Society)*

leather belts that transmitted power from the factories' waterwheels frequently snared workers' hair or clothing, with awful results. Tending the machines, moreover, required repetitious, deadening labor far different from the traditionally slower-paced and more varied work of artisan shops.

Enterprising factory managers quickly learned to fill their workforce with children whose nimble fingers, greater docility, and lower wages promised high profits. Samuel Slater staffed his first factory entirely with youngsters between the ages of 7 and 12. By 1820, children comprised an estimated 47 percent of the labor force in Connecticut and 55 percent in Rhode Island. The children's workweek in the Connecticut mills ranged from 72 to 84 hours. In response to such obvious exploitation, the Connecticut legislature passed a law requiring instruction in reading, writing, and arithmetic for all children working in facto-

ries. The law, however, simply made child labor more productive and thus acceptable.

Not until the middle of the nineteenth century would factories replace homes and shops as producers of most American textiles. The awesome transformation of manufacturing technology and the conditions of American industrial labor, however, had its beginning many years earlier, in the primitive wooden machinery of early America.

Many of the goods sold today in American stores are manufactured by children and other laborers in underdeveloped countries. Defenders of such practices argue that child labor provides desperately needed income for poor families and enables American manufacturers to compete with foreign producers. Similar arguments were made in the early nineteenth century. What do you think of the nineteenth-century arguments? What do you think of similar arguments today?

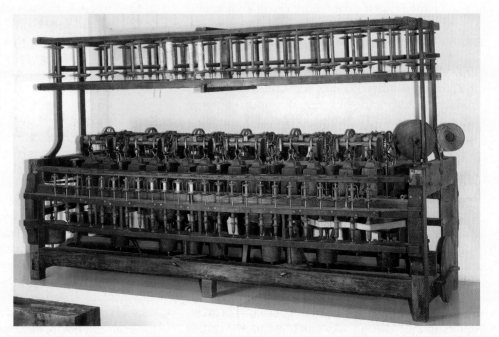

A 48-spindle frame built by Samuel Slater in Pawtucket, 1790. *(Courtesy National Museum of History and Technology, Smithsonian Institution, Washington, D.C.)*

early November, Gabriel Furman, a merchant and Federalist alderman, arrived on the Brooklyn shore a bit before the scheduled departure time. Impatient to get across, Furman instructed the ferrymen to leave early. When they refused, he upbraided the "rascals" for their disrespect and threatened to have them arrested. Crady was especially angered by the alderman's arrogance. He and Burke, Crady exploded, "were as good as any buggers," and he threatened to use his boathook on anyone who tried to arrest him.

When the ferry landed on the Manhattan shore, Furman had the two arrested, brandishing his cane at them as they were taken off to jail, where they were charged with vagrancy. Their employer offered bail, but Furman refused to allow it, and so the boatmen remained 12 days in Bridewell prison awaiting trial.

Crady and Burke were eventually hauled before Mayor Varick and three other Federalist aldermen, sitting as the Court of General Sessions. The judges quickly decided to make examples of the two insolent Irishmen. "You rascals, we'll trim you," Varick allegedly said; "we'll learn you to insult men in office." The two ferrymen were not allowed to speak on their own behalf, nor were friendly witnesses permitted to testify. The magistrates found the two guilty on charges of insulting an alderman and threatening the constable, sentenced them to two months at hard labor, and ordered that 25 lashes be laid on Crady for good measure.

Within a month, the two ferrymen bolted from jail and disappeared into the woods of Pennsylvania, never to be heard from again. The episode, however, was not yet over, for a young Jeffersonian lawyer named William Keteltas publicly castigated the "tyranny and partiality of the court," arguing that Burke and Crady had been punished to "gratify the pride, the ambition and insolence of men in office." The authorities had supposedly acted to protect the mayor's reputation. But what, he asked, about the reputation of the ferrymen? After Keteltas was upbraided for his insolence, 2,000 citizens carried him through the streets chanting "The Spirit of '76" and waving a banner sardonically inscribed "What, you rascal, insult your superiors?"

In the politically charged setting of the 1790s, tensions between social privilege and democratic equality suffused American political life. As things turned out, the Jeffersonians' opposition to Federalist arrogance, support for revolutionary France, and challenge to the Alien and Sedition Acts worked steadily to their political advantage.

The political alignment evident in the election of 1800 resembled but did not duplicate the Federalist/Anti-Federalist division of 1787–1788. The Jeffersonian coalition was much broader than the

Timeline

1789	George Washington inaugurated as first president
	Outbreak of the French Revolution
1790	Slave trade outlawed in all states except Georgia and South Carolina
	Hamilton's "Reports on the Public Credit"
1791	Bill of Rights ratified
	Whiskey Tax and national bank established
	Hamilton's "Report on Manufactures"
1792	Washington reelected
1793	Outbreak of war in Europe
	Washington's Neutrality Proclamation
	Jefferson resigns from cabinet
	Controversy over Citizen Genêt's visit
1794	Whiskey Rebellion in Pennsylvania
1795	Controversy over Jay's Treaty with England
1796	Washington's Farewell Address
	John Adams elected president
1797	XYZ Affair in France
1798	Naturalization Act
	Alien and Sedition Acts
	Virginia and Kentucky Resolutions
1798–1800	Undeclared naval war with France
1799	Trials of David Brown and Luther Baldwin
1801	Jefferson elected president by House of Representatives

Anti-Federalists' had been, for it included countless individuals, from urban workers to leaders such as Madison and Jefferson, who had supported the Constitution and had helped set the new government on its feet. Unlike the Anti-Federalists, the Jeffersonians were ardent supporters of the Constitution but insisted that it be implemented in ways consistent with political liberty and a strong dependence on the states.

The Jeffersonians differed even more dramatically from their Federalist opponents. Suspicious of central government, they placed their political faith in the states. And far more than the Federalists, they believed that government should be closely accountable to the people. While some Jeffersonian leaders continued to argue the importance of leadership by a "natural aristocracy of talent," and while southern Jeffersonians continued to reconcile black slavery and white liberty, the Jeffersonian coalition numbered countless individuals committed to the creation of a democratic political society. Motivated by a combination of electoral self-interest, political principle, and the determination of ordinary men to claim their rights as republican citizens, the Jeffersonians mounted elaborate parades, organized voters, and exploited the popular press to mobilize the people. And when Jeffersonian leaders hesitated, they found themselves pushed ahead by the growing tide of popular politics.

Conclusion

Toward the Nineteenth Century

The election of 1800 proved a remarkable outcome to more than a decade of political crisis. It had begun in the late 1780s with the intensifying debate over the Articles of Confederation and the movement toward a stronger central government. Then had come the heated contest over ratification of the new Constitution. Scarcely had the new government gotten under way than divisions began to form, first among political leaders in Congress but increasingly among the American people as well. Hamilton's domestic policies generated the first outburst of political conflict, but it was the French Revolution, the European war, Jay's Treaty, and the Federalist war program that galvanized political energies and set Federalists and Jeffersonians so adamantly against each other.

By 1800, the system of gentry-led politics centered in Congress and the more popular, democratic politics brewing in the states had drawn more closely together. The years ahead would bring them into even closer alignment, with dramatic consequences for the nation's political future.

In the election of 1800, control of the federal government passed for the first time from one political party to another, not easily but peacefully and legally. "The Revolution of 1800," the Jeffersonians claimed, was "as real a revolution in the principles of our government as that of 1776 was in its form." The future would show whether they were correct. But for the moment, the crisis had passed, the Federalists had been defeated, and the government was securely in the hands of the Jeffersonians.

Recommended Reading

Launching the National Republic

Richard Beeman, *Evolution of the Southern Backcountry* (1988); David Currie, *The Constitution in Congress: The Federal Period, 1789–1801* (1997); Stanley Elkins and Eric McKitrick, *The Age of Federalism* (1993); Ronald Hoffman and Peter Albert, eds., *Launching the "Extended Republic"* (1996); Rachel Klein, *The Unification of a Slave State* (1990); Norman Risjord, *Chesapeake Politics, 1781–1800* (1978); Robert Rutland, *The Birth of the Bill of Rights, 1776–1791* (1983); Stephen Schechter and Richard Bernstein, eds., *Contexts of the Bill of Rights* (1990); Bernard Schwartz, *The Great Rights of Mankind* (1977); Thomas Slaughter, *The Whiskey Rebellion* (1986); Alan Taylor, *Liberty Men and Great Proprietors: The Revolutionary Settlement of the Maine Frontier* (1990); Patricia Watlington, *The Partisan Spirit: Kentucky Politics, 1779–1792* (1972).

The Republic in a Threatening World

Albert Bowman, *The Struggle for Neutrality: Franco-American Diplomacy During the Federalist Era* (1974); Jerald Combs, *The Jay Treaty* (1970); Michael Durey, *Transatlantic Radicals and the Early American Republic* (1997); J. Worth Estes and Billy G. Smith, eds., *A Melancholy Scene of Devastation: The Public Response to the 1793 Yellow Fever Epidemic* (1997); Daniel Lang, *Foreign Policy in the Early Republic* (1985); David Wilson, *United Irishmen, United States: Immigrant Radicals in the Early Republic* (1998).

The Political Crisis Deepens

Stuart Andrews, *The Rediscovery of America: Transatlantic Crosscurrents in an Age of Revolution* (1998); Joyce Appleby, *Capitalism and the New Social Order: The Republican Vision of the 1790s* (1984); Aliene Austin, *Matthew Lyon: "New Man" of the Democratic Revolution, 1749–1800* (1981); Doron Ben-Atar and Barbara Oberg, eds., *Federalists Reconsidered* (1998); Joseph Ellis, *Passionate Sage: The Character and Legacy of John Adams* (1993); John Hoadley, *Origins of American Political Parties, 1789–1803* (1986); John Howe, *The Changing Political Thought of John Adams* (1966); Richard Kohn, *Eagle and Sword: The Federalists and the Creation of a Military Establishment in America, 1783–1802* (1975); Leonard Levy, *Freedom of the Press from Zenger to Jefferson* (1966); Simon Newman, *Parades and the Politics of the Street* (1997); James Roger Sharp, *American Politics in the Early Republic* (1998); James Morton Smith, *Freedoms's Fetters: The Alien and Sedition Laws and American Civil Liberties* (1956); Charles Steffen, *The Mechanics of Baltimore: Workers and Politics in the Age of Revolution, 1763–1812* (1984); William Stinchcomb, *The XYZ Affair* (1981).

Fiction and Film

Adapted from Laurel Thatcher Ulrich's prize-winning book, the docudrama *A Midwife's Tale* (1997) depicts the daily life of nurse-midwife Martha Ballard, who delivered a thousand babies and served her New England community during the closing years of the eighteenth century.

The initial installment of C-SPAN's *American Presidents: Life Portraits* series (1999) effectively portrays the challenges and accomplishments of the nation's first president, George Washington.

In the novel *Fever* (1996), John Weidman offers a vivid account of the yellow fever plague that killed hundreds of people and threatened social chaos in Philadelphia in 1793.

The essayist and novelist Gore Vidal explores the tangled politics and personalities of the early republic via a largely sympathetic portrayal of Aaron Burr (who killed Alexander Hamilton in a duel in 1804), in *Burr: A Novel* (1973).

Suggested Web Sites

http://www.virginia.edu/~gwpapers/

The Papers of George Washington Papers Homepage. This site is a wealth of information on a project that aims to publish a complete edition of Washington's correspondence. You can view selected documents, essays, and an index of the published volumes.

http://www.mountvernon.org/

Historic Mount Vernon. This is a vast site about Mount Vernon, the home of George Washington. Take a tour, visit the library, even see a reenactment of Washington's funeral.

http://www.nps.gov/inde/visit.html

Independence Hall National Historical Park. This site includes images and historical accounts of Independence Hall and other Philadelphia buildings closely associated with the nation's founding.

http://www.whitehousehistory.org/whha/default.asp

White House Historical Association. This interactive site contains a timeline of the history of the White House and several interesting photos and links.

http://www.whitehouse.gov/WH/glimpse/presidents/html/ja2.html

John Adams. This site contains biographical information about the second president and links to his inaugural address, his more quotable phrases, and information about his wife, Abigail.

http://www.DoHistory.org/

DoHistory, Harvard University Film Study Center. Focusing on the life of Martha Ballard, a late eighteenth-century New England woman, this site employs selections from her diary, excerpts from a book and film of her life, and other primary documents to enable students to conduct their own historical investigation.

http://www.ushistoryplace.com

 A richly detailed on-line learning environment complete with interactive maps, timelines, history activities, primary source documents, and links to related American history sites.

9

SOCIETY *and* POLITICS *in the* EARLY REPUBLIC

CHAPTER OUTLINE

In May 1809, Mary and James Harrod gathered their five children, loaded a few belongings (tools, seeds for the summer planting, and several prized pieces of furniture) on a wagon, closed the door on their four-room cabin, fell in line with a dozen other families, and headed west from Spotsylvania County, Virginia, toward a new life in Kentucky. They left behind 15 years of wearying effort trying to wring a modest living from 10 acres of marginal upland, and a family cemetery that held two of their other children and Mary's parents.

Beyond the Appalachian Mountains, 450 difficult miles ahead, lay additional hard work and uncertainty. Though central Kentucky where the Harrods would settle contained few Indian villages, powerful tribes from north and south of the Ohio River hunted there and fought over its control. They also fought the growing tide of white settlers. The first years would be especially hard for James and Mary as they "opened up" the land, planted the first crops, and erected a cabin. They would be lonesome as well, for the Harrods would be unlikely to see even the chimney smoke of their nearest neighbors.

James and Mary were hopeful, though, as they trudged west. The land agent who had sold them their claim had promised rich, fertile soil that in time would support a good life. And they had been excited at the prospect of joining the swelling stream of migrants seeking new lives in the trans-Appalachian West. They looked forward as well to escaping Virginia's slave society with its arrogant planters and oppressed slaves. That was no place for poor whites to live. Once in Kentucky, they settled on their own plot of land, joined with others in fashioning a new community, and took responsibility for their own lives.

In April 1795, Ben Thompson started north from Queen Anne's County, Maryland, for New York City. Ben knew little beyond farming, but he was ambitious and when he arrived in New York he listened carefully to the ship's captains who talked about life at sea while they recruited men for their crews. Ben was lucky, for he arrived just as American overseas commerce, stimulated by renewed war in Europe, was entering a decade of unprecedented prosperity. Sailors were in demand, pay was good, and few questions were asked. For five years, Ben sailed the seas. Having enough of travel, he returned to New York and hired out as an apprentice to a ship's carpenter.

About the same time, Phyllis Sherman left her home in Norwalk, Connecticut. She also headed for New York, where she took a job as a maid in the household of one of the city's wealthy merchants. As fate would have it, Phyllis and Ben met, fell in love, and in the spring of 1802 were married.

There is little of note in this except that Ben and Phyllis were former slaves and were married in the African Methodist Episcopal Zion Church. Ben had cast off his slave name, Cato, as a sign of liberation, while Phyllis kept the name her master had given her. Ben was doubly fortunate, for he had purchased his freedom just as cotton production began to expand through the Chesapeake region. In another decade, he would have faced greater difficulty securing his independence. Phyllis had been freed as a child when slavery ended in Connecticut. As she grew up, she tired of living as a servant with her former owner's family and longed for the companionship of other blacks. She had heard that there were people of color in New York City, and she was correct. In 1800, it contained 6,300 African Americans, more than half of them free.

Though life in New York was better than either Ben or Phyllis had known before, it was hardly easy. They shared only marginally in the city's commercial prosperity. In 1804, they watched helplessly as yellow fever carried off their daughter and many of their friends. And while they found support in newly established African American churches and the expanding black community, they had to be constantly on guard because slave ships still moved in and out of the port and slave catchers pursued southern runaways in the city's streets.

During the early years of the nineteenth century, thousands of people like Mary and James and Ben and Phyllis seized whatever opportunities they could find to improve their lives. In doing so, they helped strengthen America's commitment to social equality, individual opportunity, political democracy, and personal autonomy—doctrines that would gradually transform the nation.

This transformation—some have called it the "opening" of American society—was driven in part by the accelerating expansion of white settlement out of long-settled areas along the Atlantic coast onto new lands in the trans-Appalachian interior. That expansion disrupted families and disorganized older communities even as it

Detail from Thomas Coke Ruckle, *Fairview Inn or Three Mile House on Old Frederick Road* (near Baltimore), 1829. At country inns, people on the move bought supplies, exchanged goods, and secured information about the routes that lay ahead. *(Maryland Historical Society, Baltimore, Maryland)*

generated new settlements and social relationships. At work as well was an increasingly dynamic market economy with its relentless discipline of supply and demand, individual profit, and impersonal, contractual relationships. As the market economy expanded, long-standing commitments to notions of a "just price" and the social good, staples of an earlier, "moral economy," weakened.

Contributing also to the promotion of individualism and equality was the wave of religious revivalism known as the Second Great Awakening that swept through American society beginning about 1800. The Gospel message, carried by swarms of untutored, itinerant Methodist and Baptist preachers, stressed universal salvation, the equality of all believers before God, and the individual's responsibility for her or his own soul.

The transformation of American society was spurred finally by the accelerating challenge of locally based democratic forces to a more conservative, gentry-led politics centered in the national Congress. Those democratic forces, energized initially during the revolutionary struggle against England and strengthened during the tumultuous politics of the 1790s, were promoted as well by younger political leaders eager to supplant the revolutionary generation and claim their place in shaping the nation's future.

Not all Americans benefited equally from the changes of these early nineteenth-century years. Doctrines of equality, opportunity, and individual autonomy resonated far more powerfully in the lives of white men than of white women, while numerous Americans were actually disadvantaged by the changes that were under way. In the South, African Americans found their lives more harshly constrained by a revitalized system of slavery, while in the North free blacks faced an increasingly racialized society. West of the Appalachians, Native Americans confronted a swelling tide of white settlement sweeping across their homeland.

As the nineteenth century progressed, these processes of social, economic, and political change would radically transform the American nation. The beginnings of that transformation were clearly evident by the 1820s.

The years of the early republic witnessed as well a diplomatic revolution of major importance as the American people broke free from their centuries-old dependence on Europe and focused their energies on exploiting the vast North American continent. At the same time, the United States asserted a bold, new role among the emerging nations of Latin America as they also threw off the yoke of colonialism.

RESTORING AMERICAN LIBERTY

The Jeffersonians took office in 1801 determined to rescue the national government from Federalist mismanagement. They had several objectives in mind: calming the political storms that had threatened to tear the country apart, purging the government of Federalist influences, and consolidating their recent political victory.

The Jeffersonians Take Control

In November 1800, while John Adams was still president, the government had moved from Philadelphia to the new capital in the District of Columbia. When the politicians arrived there, they were stunned by its primitiveness and isolation. New York and Philadelphia, seats of the national government since 1789, had offered comfortable accommodations, sophisticated surroundings, and direct contact with the Atlantic world. By contrast, the new capital was little more than a swampy village of 5,000 inhabitants on the banks of the Potomac River.

Boasting that Washington would become the "Rome of the New World," Congress had commissioned a Frenchman, Pierre L'Enfant, to develop a plan for the capital city's development. Aided by a black American mathematician and surveyor, Benjamin Banneker, L'Enfant produced a magnificent design, replete with central plazas and broad boulevards radiating outward from a government center anchored by the Capitol and the presidential mansion. Little of that grand design, however, had materialized by 1800. The Capitol wing containing the House chamber had been completed, but the Senate chamber was still under construction, and the president's mansion remained unfinished.

As a symbolic gesture intended to rid the government of Federalist pomp, Jefferson planned a simple inauguration. Shortly before noon on March 4, he walked to the Capitol from his nearby boardinghouse. "His dress," noted one observer, "was . . . that of a plain citizen, without any distinctive badge of office." The president-elect read his short inaugural address, Chief Justice John Marshall (a fellow Virginian but a staunch Federalist) administered the oath of office, and a militia company fired a 16-gun salute. That was it.

Unlike highly commercial, cosmopolitan centers such as New York and Philadelphia that had served as earlier capitals, Washington seemed lost in the woods of southern Maryland and northern Virginia. *(Library of Congress)*

Though fleeting, the moment was filled with significance. For the first time in the nation's brief history, control of the government had shifted from one political party to another. Mrs. Samuel Harrison Smith, Washington resident and political observer, described the occasion's drama. "I have this morning witnessed one of the most interesting scenes a free people can ever witness," she wrote to a friend. "The changes of administration, which in every . . . age have most generally been epochs of confusion, villainy, and bloodshed, in this our happy country take place without any species of distraction or disorder." Many Americans shared her sense of pride and relief.

In his inaugural speech, Jefferson enumerated the "essential principles" that would guide his administration: "equal and exact justice to all," support of the states as "the surest bulwarks against antirepublican tendencies," "absolute acquiescence" in majority rule, supremacy of civil over military authority, reduction of government spending, "honest payment" of the public debt, freedom of the press, and "freedom of the person under the protection of the habeas corpus." Though Jefferson never mentioned the Federalists by name, his litany of principles reverberated with the dark experience of the 1790s.

The president spoke also of political reconciliation. "Every difference of opinion," he declared, "is not a difference of principle. We have called by different names brethren of the same principles. We are all republicans—we are all federalists." Not all his follow-

ers welcomed that final flourish, for many were eager to scatter the Federalists to the political winds. Jefferson eventually agreed that a "general sweep" of Federalist officeholders was necessary. By 1808, virtually all government offices were in Republican hands.

Politics and the Federal Courts

Having lost Congress and the presidency, the Federalists turned to the judiciary for protection against the expected Jeffersonian onslaught. In the last months of the Adams administration, the lame duck Congress had passed a new Judiciary Act increasing the number of circuit courts, complete with judges, marshals, and clerks. Before leaving office, Adams filled many of those offices with staunch Federalists. Our opponents, observed Jefferson bitterly, "defeated at the polls, have retired into the Judiciary, and from that barricade . . . hope to batter down all the bulwarks of Republicanism." Something had to be done. In January 1802, the new Congress repealed the Federalist Judiciary Act by a strict party vote.

As Federalists spluttered in anger, the Jeffersonians prepared to purge several highly partisan Federalist judges from the bench. In March 1803, the House of Representatives impeached District Judge John Pickering of New Hampshire. The grounds were not "high crimes and misdemeanors," as the Constitution required, but the Federalist diatribes with which Pickering regularly assaulted both juries and defendants. Impeachment, declared Representative William Branch Giles of Virginia, is nothing more than a decla-

Only the wing housing the House of Representatives had been completed when Congress first met in the new capitol in 1800. *(Library of Congress)*

ration by Congress that an individual holds "dangerous opinions," which appear to threaten the union. Although Giles's speech echoed the language of repression used by Federalists only a few years earlier, the Jeffersonian-controlled Senate convicted Pickering handily.

Spurred on by their success, the Jeffersonians next brought impeachment charges against Supreme Court Justice Samuel Chase, one of the most notorious Republican baiters. The indictment charged Chase with "intemperate and inflammatory political harangues," delivered "with intent to excite the fears and resentment of the . . . people . . . against the Government of the United States." When the trial revealed that Chase had committed no impeachable offense, he was acquitted and returned triumphantly to the bench.

Chase was a sorry hero, but constitutional principles are often established in the defense of less than heroic people. Had Chase's impeachment succeeded, Chief Justice Marshall would almost certainly have been next, and that would surely have precipitated a serious constitutional crisis. Sensing the danger, the Jeffersonians pulled back, content to allow time and the regular turnover of personnel to cleanse the courts of Federalist control. The vital principle of judicial independence had been narrowly preserved.

In two trailblazing decisions, the Supreme Court shortly laid down some of the most fundamental doctrines of American constitutional law. 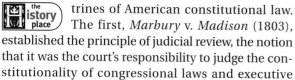 The first, *Marbury* v. *Madison* (1803), established the principle of judicial review, the notion that it was the court's responsibility to judge the constitutionality of congressional laws and executive

John Marshall, appointed chief justice of the United States by President Adams in 1801, served in that position for 34 years. Under his leadership, the Supreme Court established some of the most basic principles of American constitutional law. *(Boston Atheneum)*

behavior. In the majority opinion, Chief Justice Marshall declared that "It is emphatically the province and duty of the judicial department to say what the law is." Sixteen years later, in another landmark decision, *McCulloch* v. *Maryland,* the court struck down a Maryland law taxing the Baltimore branch of the Second Bank of the United States. No state, Marshall ruled, possessed the right to tax a nationally chartered bank, for "the power to tax involves the power to destroy." In the McCulloch decision, Marshall also established the constitutional basis for broad congressional authority. Let congressional intent "be within the scope of the Constitution," he wrote, "and all means which are appropriate . . . which are not prohibited, but consist with the letter and spirit of the Constitution, are constitutional."

Dismantling the Federalist War Program

The Jeffersonians had regarded the Federalists' war program as a threat to public liberty, so they moved quickly to dismantle it. Jefferson ended prosecutions under the Sedition Act, freed its victims, and silently let it lapse in 1802. Neither Jefferson nor most of his followers were consistent civil libertarians, for a number of opposition editors felt the sting of government displeasure. Still, Jefferson never duplicated the Federalists' attempts to stifle dissent.

The president undercut the Alien Acts by dismantling the hated inspection system. In 1802, Congress passed a new naturalization law, restoring the requirement of 5 rather than 14 years before a foreigner could be naturalized. The Federalists' provisional army also fell victim to the Jeffersonian assault and was quickly disbanded. Federal troops would no longer intimidate American citizens.

Finally, Jefferson acted to reduce the size of the federal government. Tiny by modern standards, the government had fewer than 3,000 civilian employees, only 300 of them, including the cabinet and members of Congress, located in Washington. That amounted to one federal public official for every 1,914 citizens, compared with one for approximately every 68 citizens today. Even so, Jefferson wrote that he was "hunting out and abolishing multitudes of useless offices, striking off jobs, etc., etc." The "principal care of our persons and property," he declared, should be left to the states because they were more closely attuned to the people's needs and could be held more closely accountable. Under Jefferson's administration, the federal government did little

FEDERAL REVENUES AND EXPENDITURES, 1790–1820 (IN THOUSANDS OF DOLLARS)

Year	Revenues		Expenditures	
1790	Customs	4,399	Military	634
	Other	19	Interest on public debt	2,349
		4,418	Other	1,426
				4,409
1800	Customs	9,081	Military	6,010
	Internal revenue	809	Interest on public debt	3,375
	Other	793	Other	1,466
		10,683		10,851
1810	Customs	8,583	Military	3,948
	Internal revenue	7	Interest on public debt	2,845
	Sale of public lands	697	Other	1,447
	Other	793		8,240
		10,080		
1820	Customs	15,006	Military	7,018
	Internal revenue	106	Interest on public debt	5,126
	Sale of public lands	1,636	Other	9,324
	Other	2,769		21,468
		19,517		

Note: In constant dollars, the revenue of the federal government in 1998 was $1,658 trillion and its expenditures were $1,668 trillion.

Source: U.S. Bureau of the Census

more than deliver the mail, deal with Indians on federal land, and administer the public domain. In addition to cutting jobs, the Jeffersonians reduced the national debt from $83 million in 1801 to $57 million a decade later.

Not everything the Jeffersonians did was consistent with limited government. As the nation grew, so did pressures for a federal program of internal improvements, especially from the new states forming beyond the Appalachians that sought closer ties with the East. Before many years, the government responded by constructing several western routes, including the National Road (1811) connecting Cumberland, Maryland, with Wheeling on the Ohio River. The states, however, continued to carry the major responsibility for internal improvements. Though the Jeffersonians may not have "revolutionized" the government as they claimed, they reduced its size and pointed it in a new direction.

⤳ BUILDING AN AGRARIAN NATION

The Jeffersonians did far more than reverse Federalist initiatives, for they were committed to implementing their own vision of an expanding, agrarian nation. That vision was mixed and inconsistent, because the Jeffersonian party embraced an array of often conflicting groups: southern patricians like Jefferson himself, determined to maintain a gentry-led, slavery-based agrarian order; lower- and middle-class southern whites committed to black servitude but ardent proponents of political equality among whites; northern artisans who brought to the Jeffersonian party an aversion to slavery (though rarely a commitment to racial equality) together with a fierce dedication to honest toil and their own economic interests; western farmers devoted to personal self-sufficiency on the land; and northern intellectuals ideologically committed to political democracy. In time, such diversity would splinter the Jeffersonian coalition. For the moment, however, these groups found unity not only in opposing their Federalist enemies but also in a set of broadly shared principles that guided Jeffersonian policies through the presidential administrations of Jefferson (1801–1808), James Madison (1809–1816), and James Monroe (1817–1824).

The Jeffersonian Vision

Political liberty, the Jeffersonians believed, could survive only under conditions of broad economic and social equality. They placed their faith in a nation filled with independent, yeoman farmers who were self-reliant, industrious, and filled with concern for the public good. Such people exemplified the qualities essential to democratic citizenship.

The Jeffersonian vision was clouded, however, by the realization that industriousness and self-discipline generated personal wealth, that wealth bred social inequality, and that inequality threatened to destroy the very foundation of a democratic society. The solution to that dilemma, they believed, was to be found in rapid territorial expansion that would provide land for the nation's yeoman citizens, draw restless people out of the cities and off the crowded lands of the East, and preserve the social equality that democratic liberty required. The expansion of white settlement across the North American continent would delay, perhaps even prevent, the cyclical process of growth, maturity, and decay that had been the fate of all past societies.

Calls for expanding white settlement were strengthened by the somber writings of an English clergyman and political economist named Thomas Malthus. In 1798, Malthus published an essay that jolted Europeans and Americans alike. Observing the increasingly crowded conditions of his native England, Malthus argued that "the power of population" was "greater than the power in the earth to produce subsistence for man." Enlightenment hopes for a steadily improving quality of life, he warned, were a delusion, for the future would be filled with increasing misery as population outran the supply of food.

Jefferson took Malthus's warnings seriously but believed that the Englishman failed to understand that America's vast reservoir of land would enable its people to escape Europe's fate. Differences of circumstance, Jefferson explained, would produce a different result. "There . . . the quantity of food is fixed . . . [while] supernumerary births add only to mortality. Here the immense extent of uncultivated and fertile lands enables every one who will labor, to marry young, and to raise a family of any size. Our food, then, may increase geometrically with our laborers, and our births, however multiplied, become effective." Rapid and continuing territorial expansion was thus indispensable to the Jeffersonian vision of the nation's future.

There were more immediate reasons for promoting American expansion, too, for occupation of the West would secure America's borders against continuing threats from England, France, and Spain. Finally, the Jeffersonians calculated that the creation of new, western states, committed to democratic forms of politics, would strengthen their own political control and assure the Federalists' permanent demise.

Time would reveal that American exceptionalism—the idea that America could avoid Europe's woes by continental expansion—was more limited than Jefferson imagined. Yet from the perspective of the early nineteenth century, the Jeffersonians offered a hopeful, indeed compelling, vision of the nation's future.

The Windfall Louisiana Purchase

Efforts to ensure agrarian democracy through territorial expansion lay behind Jefferson's most dramatic 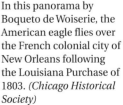 accomplishment, buying the Louisiana Territory in 1803. The purchase nearly doubled the nation's size.

In 1800, Spain ceded the vast trans-Mississippi region called Louisiana to France. Jefferson was profoundly disturbed by such clear evidence that European nations still coveted North American territory. His fears were well grounded, for in October 1802, the Spanish commander at New Orleans, which Spain had retained, once again closed the Mississippi River to American commerce.

In January 1803, the president sent his young associate James Monroe to Paris with instructions to purchase New Orleans and West Florida (which contained Mobile, the only good harbor on the Gulf Coast). When Monroe arrived, he was surprised to find French officials prepared to sell all of Louisiana (though not West Florida). The successful black rebellion against French rule in Haiti and the renewed threat of war with England made the French ruler, Napoleon Bonaparte, eager to concentrate French troops in Europe. In addition, he feared American designs on Louisiana and knew that he would not be able to defend it. In April, the deal was struck. For $15 million, the United States obtained all of Louisiana, nearly 830,000 square miles of land.

Federalists reacted with alarm to news of the acquisition, fearing with good reason that the states to be carved from Louisiana would be staunchly Jeffersonian. In addition, they worried that a rapidly expanding frontier would "decivilize" the entire nation.

Expansion did not stop with Louisiana. In 1810, American adventurers fomented a revolt in Spanish West Florida, proclaimed an independent republic, and sought annexation by the United States. Two years later, over vigorous Spanish objections, Congress annexed the region. In 1819, Spain ceded East Florida as well. As part of that agreement, the United States extended its territorial claims beyond Louisiana to include the Pacific Northwest. These impressive accomplishments set the stage for the final surge of continental expansion that would come during the 1840s.

Opening the Trans-Mississippi West

If America's vast domain was to serve the needs of the agrarian nation, it would have to be explored and prepared for white settlement. In the summer of 1803, Jefferson dispatched an expedition led by his secretary, Meriwether Lewis, and a young army officer named William Clark to explore the Far Northwest, make contact with Native Americans there, open the fur trade, and bring back scientific information about the area. For nearly two and a half years, the intrepid band of explorers, assisted by the Shoshoni woman Sacajawea, made its way across thousands of miles of unmapped and hostile terrain—up the Missouri River, through the

In this panorama by Boqueto de Woiserie, the American eagle flies over the French colonial city of New Orleans following the Louisiana Purchase of 1803. *(Chicago Historical Society)*

Recovering the Past

MAPS

O f the several exploring ventures President Jefferson sent into the trans-Mississippi West, the Lewis and Clark expedition (1803–1806) was the most important. It proved the feasibility of an overland route to the Pacific, produced scientific information about the fauna and flora of the Far Northwest, established contact with the Native Americans of the area, and helped stimulate westward expansion. Many of the place names the explorers gave to rivers and other natural features are still in use today.

During their travels, Meriwether Lewis, William Clark, and others in their party kept extensive journals in which they recorded their experiences and observations. These journals provide a vivid account of the expedition, including information on the landscape through which the explorers passed and the people they encountered. The journals also reveal a great deal about the attitudes and expectations of the explorers themselves. As they moved across the continent, the explorers produced detailed trail maps as well. These cartographic records also tell us a great deal about the experience and perceptions of the explorers, as well as about the regions through which they passed.

Examine the map shown here. It is an example of the sketch maps that William Clark drew as the expedition made its way across the land. The map represents about a 30-mile stretch along the Missouri River in what is today west-central North Dakota. After the expedition was over, these detailed studies were used to prepare large, composite maps of the entire region that were far more accurate than any that had been made before.

Mapmaking has changed dramatically since Clark's early efforts. Over the years, as surveying technology and map design have changed, we have vastly improved our knowledge of the earth's topography, as well as our ability to represent the earth's rounded surface on a map's flat plane. Today, the most detailed and accurate maps are drawn from high-resolution photos taken by satellites.

To imagine Clark's mapmaking difficulties, as well as to appreciate his accomplishment, try this experiment. Without consulting anything but your own memory, try to draw a map of the region you passed through on your way to college. Include the major topographical and other interesting features on the route. Also indicate the groups of people you met or passed near. Alternatively, draw a map of the area around your hometown, including the major features, inhabitants, and travel routes. Make your map as accurate as possible to aid others who might depend on it for their own travels.

Now consider Clark's map carefully. How accurate do you suppose it is? How accurate would it have had to be to be useful? What does the map reveal about the explorers' rate of travel through this region? Why do you suppose they traveled along the winding course of the Missouri River rather than overland?

Cartographers, or mapmakers, have to decide what to include and what to omit from their maps. Those decisions depend on the purposes the map is intended to serve. Under what circumstances and for what purposes was Clark's map created? How many different kinds of information does it contain? What are its dominant features, and why are they emphasized? Imagine yourself in the role of Clark. As you observe your surroundings, what do you see but decide not to record on the map? How would a modern map of the same region differ?

Finally, think about the significance of the maps, written journals, and oral accounts generated by the Lewis and Clark expedition. How did they help change the map of the United States?

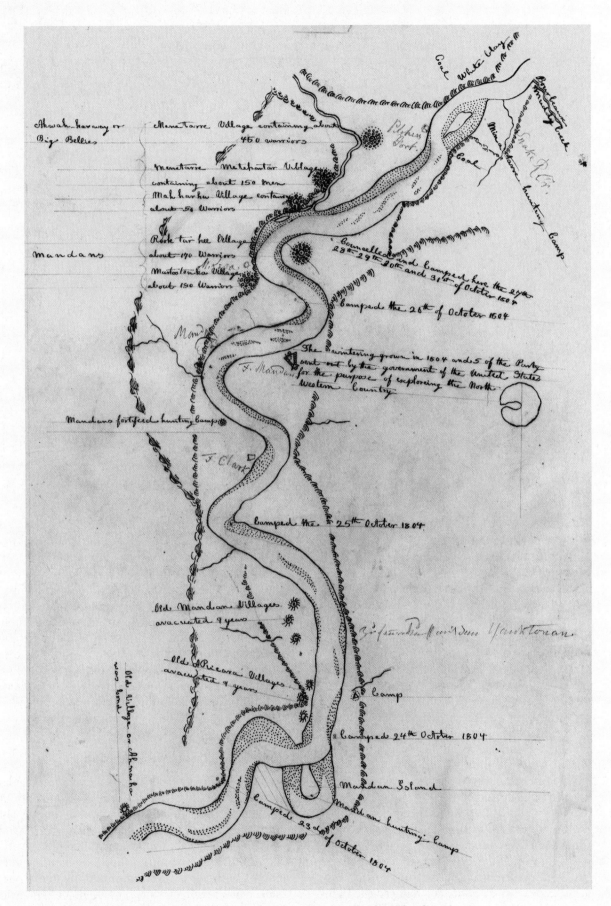

Lewis and Clark's map of the Missouri River, 1804. (*Joslyn Art Museum, Omaha, Nebraska*)

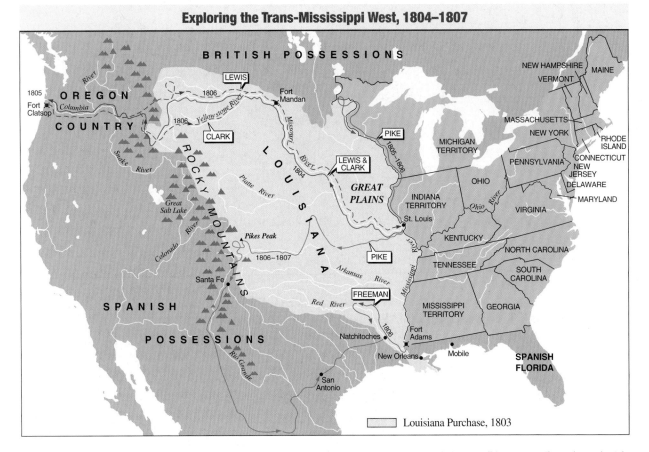

Exploring the Trans-Mississippi West, 1804–1807

With the nation nearly doubled in size following the Louisiana Purchase, President Jefferson sent out exploring expeditions to map the region and establish an American presence there.

Rockies via the Bitterroot Valley and Lolo Pass, down the Columbia to the Pacific coast, and back again, finally reemerging at St. Louis in September 1806. Lewis and Clark's journey fanned American interest in the trans-Mississippi West and demonstrated the feasibility of an overland route to the Pacific.

In 1805 and 1806, Lieutenant Zebulon Pike explored the sources of the Mississippi River in northern Minnesota, then followed that trek with an equally bold venture into the southern Rocky Mountains, where he explored the peak that still bears his name. In the following decade, the government established a string of military posts from Fort Snelling, at the confluence of the Minnesota and Mississippi Rivers, to Fort Smith on the Arkansas. They were intended to secure the American frontier, promote the fur trade, and support white settlement.

The Jeffersonians' blueprint for an agrarian democracy also guided changes in federal land policy. While Federalists had viewed the sale of public land as a source of government revenue, the Jeffersonians were primarily concerned to speed white settlement. Accordingly, the Land Act of 1801 reduced the minimum purchase from 640 to 320 acres, established a

generous credit system, and offered 8 percent discounts for cash sales. Over the next year and a half, settlers, speculators, and land companies bought nearly four times as much land as during the entire 1790s. In the years ahead, principles of preemption (which enabled squatters to secure title to land simply by occupying it) and pricing graduation (whereby lands that did not readily sell were offered at discounted prices or given away) were added. Though Jeffersonian land policy fostered widespread speculation and contributed to the Panic of 1819, it speeded the transfer of public land into private hands.

A NATION OF REGIONS

During the early years of the republic, the vast majority of Americans drew their living from the land. In 1800, fully 83 percent of the labor force was engaged in agriculture; that figure had hardly changed 25 years later. Yet people occupied the land differently in various regions of the country. While long-standing differences between the Northeast and the South persisted, a new region of white settlement took shape in the nation's interior.

AGRICULTURAL PRODUCTIVITY IN 1800 AND 1997				
	Wheat		Cotton	
	Worker-Hours per Acre	Yield per Acre	Worker-Hours per Acre	Yield per Acre
1800	56.0	15 bushels	185	147 pounds
1997	2.4	40 bushels	4.6	686 pounds

Source: U.S. Bureau of the Census.

The Northeast

In the region stretching from eastern Pennsylvania and New Jersey through New England, family farms dominated the landscape. Because much of New England's land was poor, farmers there often abandoned crop agriculture for the greater profits to be made from dairying and livestock. By contrast, on the richer agricultural lands of New York and Pennsylvania, farmers cultivated the land intensively, planting crops year after year rather than following the customary practice of allowing worn-out fields to lie fallow and recover their fertility. Before 1776, much of the mid-Atlantic landscape had looked cluttered and unkempt, with wide areas still covered by timber and fallow lands lapsing back into brush. Fifty years later, the countryside appeared clean and orderly, its cultivated fields clearly marked by hedges and stone walls.

Farmers in New York's Hudson River valley and southeastern Pennsylvania produced an agricultural surplus, which they exchanged in nearby towns for commodities such as tea, sugar, window glass, and tools. Even there, however, most farmers marketed only what was left over after they had met their own family's needs. "The great effort," reported a European visitor, "was for every farmer to produce anything he required within his own family; and he was esteemed the best farmer, to use a phrase of the day, 'who did everything within himself.'"

Across large areas of the rural Northeast, cash played a small part in economic exchanges. Declared an observant Frenchman, people "supply their needs in the countryside by direct reciprocal exchanges. The tailor and the bootmaker go and do the work of their calling at the home of the farmer . . . who . . . provides the raw material for it and pays for the work in goods. . . . They write down what they give and receive on both sides, and at the end of the year they settle a large variety of exchanges with a very small quantity of coin."

Most farms were not large. By 1800, the average farm in the longer-settled areas of New England and the mid-Atlantic states was no more than 100 to 150 acres, down substantially from half a century before,

as a result of the continued division of farm property across generations of fathers and sons. Even in southeastern Pennsylvania, probably the most productive agricultural region in the entire Northeast, economic opportunity was declining. Long and continuous cropping had robbed the soil of its fertility, forcing farmers to bring more marginal land under cultivation. By 1800, nearly 20 percent of the area's male taxpayers were single, clear evidence that young men were finding it harder to establish themselves on the land before taking a wife.

Frustrated at the backwardness of much American agriculture, some individuals called for more "scientific" practices. Leading citizens like John Adams joined in creating agricultural associations such as the Massachusetts Society for Promoting Agriculture that established agricultural libraries and issued publications. Others, such as Elkanah Watson, a prosperous businessman turned gentleman farmer, urged farmers to turn their attention to raising the fine-fleeced merino sheep that agricultural reformers promised would bring newfound prosperity.

Watson was instrumental as well in creating the nation's first agricultural fairs in western Massachusetts. Part visionary, part huckster, and part enthusiast for scientifically based farming, Watson intended the fairs' displays of equipment, animals, and produce not only to educate farmers but to "excite a lively spirit of competition" and thus energize them as well. His efforts succeeded beyond his fondest hopes, for within a few years rural folk by the thousands were converging on the annual Berkshire gatherings. In a short while, these precursors to the county fairs that have remained a staple of rural and small town American life had spread from Maine to Virginia and as far west as Illinois. In addition to farming, growing numbers of rural folk also worked as artisans or day laborers in surrounding towns or toiled in the small-scale manufactories—grain and saw mills, potash works, and iron forges—that dotted the rural landscape. It would be another generation, however, before urban factories began luring large numbers of young men off the land.

Though this Pennsylvania scene features cattle rather than merino sheep, it reveals the interests of farmers and more elegantly attired gentlemen in the commercial benefits of "scientific" livestock breeding. Note what appear to be plowing contests in the background. (*John A. Woodside,* A Country Fair in Pennsylvania, *1824, from the Collection of Harry T. Peters, Jr.*)

By 1830, the relentless demands of the Northeast's expanding population for land and a wide variety of wood products had significantly transformed the region's once heavily forested landscape. Iron furnaces dotting the countryside consumed firewood voraciously. The Union Furnace in New Jersey exhausted a forest of nearly 20,000 acres in less than 15 years and had to be abandoned, a fate duplicated at the Sterling Ironworks in southern New York, as well as at Stockbridge and Pittsfield in Massachusetts. The production of pot and pearl ash, turpentine, and planking for wooden houses and fencing further depleted forest ranges.

More than anything, though, it was the demand for heating fuel during the long winter months that made the woodcutter's axe ring. "So much of the comfort and convenience of our life," observed Benjamin Franklin, "depends on the article of *fire.*" Rural households consumed from 20 to 30 cords of firewood annually in the highly inefficient open fireplaces that warmed their homes. As the region's coastal cities grew and nearby woodlots were exhausted, wood had to be fetched from as far away as 100 miles. By 1800, Bostonians were dependent on wood shipped in from Maine and New Hampshire. Although deserted farmlands here and there lapsed into new growth, thus contributing a bit of ecological renewal, the northeastern coastal plain had been largely denuded of forest.

The Nation's Cities

Though most Northeasterners lived on the land or in the small towns dotting the countryside, increasing numbers of people dwelt in the region's cities. Between 1790 and 1830, the nation's population increased by nearly 230 percent. During those same years, urban places of more than 2,500 residents grew almost twice as fast. In 1790, there were only five cities holding more than 10,000 inhabitants. By 1810 there were 23 such places, including four cities of over 50,000 and one, New York, with well over 100,000 people. Though fledgling cities such as Pittsburgh, Cincinnati, and Saint Louis dotted river valleys of the western interior, the majority of the nation's burgeoning urban centers were located along the northeastern coast.

Though increasing rapidly in population, these urban places were small in area, "walking cities" in which residents could easily stroll from one side of town to the other. The result was increasing crowding and congestion. Asa Greene, a New York physician, observed ruefully that to cross Broadway "you must button your coat tightly about you . . . settle your hat firmly on your head, look up street and down street . . . to see what carts and carriages are upon you, and then run for your life."

Along with crowding came serious problems of public health and safety. While Philadelphia led the way in street paving, dust in dry weather and mud when it rained were constant sources of complaint. One alarmed citizen, finding a man embedded up to his neck in a mud hole following a violent downpour, offered to help pull him out. "No need to worry," replied the man, "I have a horse underneath me." So, at least, went a popular fable.

More than dirt clogged urban streets in the early nineteenth century, for residents dumped their garbage there, privies leached into open drains, and kitchen waste was tossed out the door. Untethered cows, goats, and sheep left their droppings as well.

Francis Guy, *Winter Scene in Brooklyn,* c. 1817–1820. Many areas of early nineteenth-century cities retained a small-town, neighborhood atmosphere, as this Brooklyn scene reveals. *(The Brooklyn Museum, 97.13, Gift of the Brooklyn Institute of Arts and Sciences)*

Though one urban dweller regarded the hogs that scavenged off such refuse as "disgusting," she acknowledged that without them the streets would soon be choked with filth.

Under such conditions, diseases like typhoid and dysentery, which spread via contaminated water supplies, took a continuous human toll. The aristocratic John Pintard attributed the 1832 cholera epidemic in New York City to "the lower classes of intemperate dissolute & filthy people huddled together like swine in their polluted habitations." Nothing, he concluded, could be done to help them. "The . . . quicker . . . [their] dispatch," he concluded, "the sooner the malady will cease." Such attitudes, combined with ignorance about the causes and etiology of disease, put urban populations continuously at risk.

Though buildings and streets were virtually devoid of the commercial signage that would emblazon American cities by the middle of the nineteenth century, the urban economies of these northeastern cities hummed with activity. As during the colonial era, economic life continued to center on the wharves where sailing ships from around the world tied up and the warehouses where overseas cargoes were unloaded. Sailors and ships' captains, often speaking unfamiliar tongues, filled the harbor-front taverns with colorful stories of far-off lands, adding raucous behavior and at times an edge of danger to urban life.

Though true industrialization would not become evident in the cities of the northeast until the second half of the nineteenth century, large-scale manufacturing was beginning to transform their economies by 1830. The expansion of southern cotton production was turning Philadelphia into a textile manufacturing center, while places like New York City and Newark, New Jersey, were producing shoes and other manufactured products. As these enterprises expanded, artisanal production began to give way to factory-based wage labor.

As these urban places evolved, the gap between richer and poorer inhabitants widened. Prosperous merchants, reaping the rewards of overseas trade and investing much of their profit in budding manufacturing enterprises, rested securely at the top. Below them came an aspiring middle class of shopkeepers and professional men whose families shared modestly in the general prosperity. At the bottom of the human pyramid lay a spreading underclass of common laborers, dock workers, and the unemployed, their lives taken up with a continuing struggle for survival. Though rich and poor had often lived close together in colonial cities, rising land values now forced the lower classes into crowded alleys and tenements, while more prosperous urban dwellers congregated in separate, fashionable neighborhoods.

By 1830, the living standard of many middle- and upper-class families had significantly improved. As wills and estate inventories show, such households were now more likely to possess table linens and china bowls, store-bought furniture, and tailor-made clothes, the artifacts of an expanding consumer economy. Material prosperity, however, passed most urban folk by.

The South

Life was very different in the American South, a region stretching from Maryland to Georgia, and west across the southern interior. As the nineteenth century began, much of southern agriculture was in disarray. Falling prices, worn-out land, and the destruction wrought by the Revolutionary War had left the Chesapeake's tobacco economy in shambles. One English traveler reported that throughout much of the upper Shenandoah Valley crops were "so intermixed with extensive tracts of waste land, worn out by the culture of tobacco . . . that on the whole the country had the appearance of barrenness." The extensive loss of slaves added to the region's economic woes.

Southern planters experimented with wheat and other grains in an effort to bolster their sagging fortunes, but regional recovery began in earnest when they turned to a new staple crop—cotton. Especially valuable was the hardier short-staple variety that could be successfully cultivated across large areas of the southern interior. While its fibers could be separated from the plant's sticky, green seeds only with

great difficulty, Eli Whitney's cotton gin effectively solved that problem.

In 1790, the South had produced only 3,135 bales of cotton. By 1820, output had mushroomed to 334,378 bales. In 1805, cotton accounted for 30 percent of the nation's agricultural exports; by 1820, it exceeded half. Across both the old coastal South and the newly developing states of Alabama, Mississippi, and Tennessee, cotton was becoming king. The growing demand of textile mills in England and the American Northeast provided the essential stimulus, but a portentous combination of other factors made possible the South's dramatic response: wonderfully productive virgin soil; a long, steamy growing season; an ample supply of slave labor; and southern planters with long experience in the production and marketing of staple crops.

As we shall see in later chapters, the swing to cotton marked a momentous turning point for both the South and the nation. Not only did it raise the value of prime southern land and open economic opportunity for countless southern whites, but it also increased the demand for black field hands and breathed new life into the institution of slavery. Some of the escalating demand for slave labor was met from overseas. In 1803 alone, Georgia and South Carolina imported 20,000 new slaves, as southern planters and northern suppliers rushed to fill the need before the slave trade ended in 1807. Much of the demand for agricultural labor, however, would be met by the internal slave trade that moved African Americans from the worn-

Slave labor, provided by women as well as men, followed the spread of cotton cultivation into new lands of the southern interior. This Benjamin Latrobe sketch is of *An Overseer Doing His Duty. (Maryland Historical Society, Baltimore, Maryland)*

out lands of the Chesapeake to the lush cotton fields of the Deep South.

Trans-Appalachia

West of the Appalachian Mountains a third, distinctive region of settlement was forming as the nineteenth century began. In the eighteenth century, European Americans had called the interior beyond the area of white settlement the "backcountry," because their lives were still dominated by the centers of economic and political activity along the coast. As attention began to shift toward settlement of the trans-Appalachian West, however, people spoke increasingly of an ever expanding "frontier."

Trans-Appalachia extended west from the Appalachian Mountains to the Mississippi River and south from the Great Lakes to the Gulf of Mexico. In 1790, scarcely 100,000 white settlers lived there. By 1810, their number had swollen to nearly a million. A decade later, augmented by people like Mary and

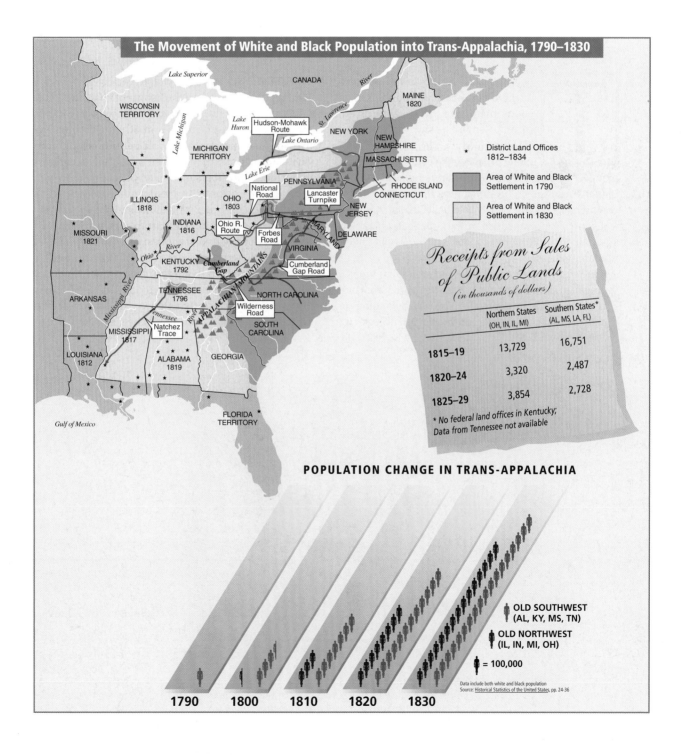

The Movement of White and Black Population into Trans-Appalachia, 1790–1830

★ District Land Offices 1812–1834

Area of White and Black Settlement in 1790

Area of White and Black Settlement in 1830

Receipts from Sales of Public Lands (in thousands of dollars)

	Northern States (OH, IN, IL, MI)	Southern States* (AL, MS, LA, FL)
1815–19	13,729	16,751
1820–24	3,320	2,487
1825–29	3,854	2,728

* No federal land offices in Kentucky; Data from Tennessee not available

POPULATION CHANGE IN TRANS-APPALACHIA

OLD SOUTHWEST (AL, KY, MS, TN)

OLD NORTHWEST (IL, IN, MI, OH)

= 100,000

1790   1800   1810   1820   1830

Data include both white and black population
Source: *Historical Statistics of the United States*, pp. 24-36

Technology Changes the American People

ELI WHITNEY AND THE COTTON GIN

Though the technological innovations of the early American republic may seem primitive, they generated intense enthusiasm at the time. Observed Tench Coxe, an ardent promoter of American economic development, "Machines, ingeniously constructed, will give . . . immense assistance" in developing the nation. Coxe's comment echoed the widely held belief that technological genius was embedded in the American character and that commitment to applied science would foster human progress.

One of the most significant technological breakthroughs in the early republic was Eli Whitney's cotton gin. By the 1790s, cotton cultivation was beginning to expand across the American South, as planters began to experiment with the short-staple variety of the crop. Though its fibers were less luxuriant than the long-staple cotton that flourished in the hot coastal lowlands and sea islands of Georgia and South Carolina, the hardier short-staple variety could be successfully cultivated in large areas of the southern interior. In contrast to the long, silky fibers of long-staple cotton, however, short-staple cotton clung tenaciously to the plant's sticky, green seeds, making it difficult to prepare the raw cotton for manufacturing into cloth. A slave could clean no more than a pound of short-staple cotton a day.

During these same years, demand for cotton of all sorts was growing in England and the American Northeast, where the weaving and spinning machines of new textile factories created an insatiable appetite for the crop. Demand and supply began to converge in

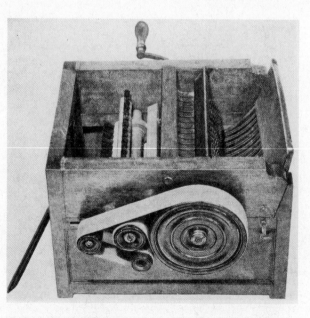

This model of the original cotton gin was deposited in the Smithsonian Museum by Whitney's son in 1884. *(National Museum of American History, Smithsonian Institution)*

Though others had tinkered with mechanical devices for stripping cotton fibers from their seeds, Whitney was the first to develop a successful gin. *(Library of Congress)*

1793 when Eli Whitney, a Yale graduate then supporting himself as a teacher on a Georgia plantation, turned his mind to the problem of short-staple cotton and its seeds. Within a short time he had designed a functioning model of a machine he called a "cotton gin." In conception it was disarmingly simple, nothing more than a wooden box containing a roller, equipped with wire teeth, designed to pull the fibers through a comblike barrier, thus stripping them from the seeds. A hand crank activated the mechanism. The implications of Whitney's invention were immediately apparent, for with this crude device a slave could clean up to 50 pounds of short-staple cotton in a day.

As Chapter 9 explains, a variety of circumstances combined to produce the cotton boom that exploded across the American South during the first half of the nineteenth century, a boom that held profound implications for black and white Americans (and in the Civil War crisis, for the nation at large). The cotton gin, fashioned by hand in a plantation shed and then improved by other craftsmen in succeeding decades, played a major role in that fateful development.

Whitney patented his device under the first federal Patent Law of 1794 but exhausted most of the profit it produced protecting his patent rights against infringement. Better times, however, lay ahead. Though he reaped little financial advantage from his invention, he opened a factory in Connecticut manufacturing firearms by an ingenious system of interchangeable parts. A government contract finally brought him financial success.

By the late nineteenth and twentieth centuries, successful technological innovations would require large amounts of venture capital, sophisticated engineering know-how, and large-scale organizational support. In the early years of the republic, however, the tinkering of lone inventors could produce dramatic results.

Historians frequently disagree over the extent to which heroic inventors are able to alter the course of history. Some assert that men and women capable of thinking beyond the conventional wisdom of their time and envisioning solutions to complicated technological problems can move history decisively in new directions. Others argue that broad economic and social forces determine the basic path that technology takes and that most inventions are as much the result of chance or simple trial and error as of individual genius.

How do you think Eli Whitney should be regarded? Did his cotton gin transform the nation's history, or did it represent little more than the work of a clever craftsman with the patience to solve a bothersome problem? Was his work pivotal, or is it likely that someone else would have come along to solve the problem of short-staple cotton if Whitney had never traveled into the South? Think about comparable technological breakthroughs in your own time.

Sources: Constance Green, *Eli Whitney and the Birth of American Technology* (1956); Brooke Hindle, ed., *Material Culture in the Wooden Age* (1981).

As settlers moved west, they cleared the land of trees for agriculture and produced lumber for houses and fences, as this sketch of a sawmill in upstate New York suggests. *(Library of Congress)*

James Harrod, there were over a million more. There, in a broad and constantly shifting "middle ground," resident Indians and white intruders engaged in intricate patterns of cultural, economic, sexual, and military exchange.

White settlers entered the region by wagon along Zane's Trace and other tortuous, overland routes into Kentucky and Tennessee and clambered aboard flatboats at Pittsburgh every spring when the water was high enough to float down the Ohio River to destinations at Wheeling, Cincinnati, and Louisville. The human tide appeared to grow with each passing year. "Genessee fever" brought thousands of settlers surging into the river country of western New York. "The woods are full of new settlers," wrote an amazed observer near Batavia, New York, in 1805. "Axes are resounding, and the trees literally falling around us as we passed." By 1812, 200,000 souls lived in the western part of the state, where scarcely 30,000 whites had resided only 20 years before. "America is breaking up and going west!" exclaimed the British traveler Morris Birkbeck in wonder. At the time, it seemed literally true.

Settlers were drawn by the promotions of speculators seeking their fortunes in the sale of western land. Between 1790 and 1820, land companies hawked vast areas of New York, Ohio, and Kentucky to prospective settlers like James and Mary Harrod. The most extravagant ventures often failed, but countless others succeeded, returning handsome profits to their investors. Individual settlers shared in the speculative fever, often

going deeply into debt to buy extra land for resale when population increased and land prices rose.

North of the Ohio River, settlement followed the grid pattern prescribed in the Land Ordinance of 1785. There mixed, free-labor agriculture took hold and towns such as Columbus and Cincinnati emerged to provide services and cultural amenities for the surrounding population. South of the Ohio, people distributed themselves more randomly across the land, much as their ancestors had done back east. In Kentucky and Tennessee, free-labor agriculture was soon challenged by the spread of slavery-based cotton.

As people poured into the region, they established churches, schools, and colleges. Transylvania University, founded in Lexington, Kentucky, in 1780, was the first college west of the Appalachians. Even so, trans-Appalachia retained a reputation for its rough and colorful ways. While life could be depressingly lonesome for families lost in the hollows of the Cumberland Mountains of eastern Tennessee, in towns along the Ohio River boatmen and gamblers, con men and speculators gave civic life a raucous quality. And everywhere the transience, youthfulness, and predominant maleness of the population kept society unsettled.

The constant drama of migration together with the grandeur of the natural surroundings stoked people's imaginations. No characters were more famous in popular folklore than western adventurers such as Daniel Boone. None was more colorful than the mythical riverman Mike Fink, "half man, half alligator," who could "whip his weight in grizzly bears." And nothing revealed more graphically the West's rawness than the eye-gouging, ear-biting, no-holds-barred, "rough and tumble" brawls that regularly erupted.

As settlers arrived, they began the long process of transforming the region's heavily forested land. In the mountainous areas of western Pennsylvania, entire hillsides were denuded of trees that anxious travelers dragged behind their wagons as makeshift brakes during the jolting rides downhill. Believing, erroneously, that the unforested "oak openings" scattered through the woods of Ohio and southern Michigan were infertile, many farmers staked their claims where the trees grew thickest and set about the arduous task of clearing the land. They followed the time-honored practice of cutting a girdle of bark off the trees and then setting them on fire or leaving them to die in place while planting crops around the decaying hulks. "The scene is truly savage," observed an English traveler used to the orderly landscape of his own country. "Immense trees stripped of their foliage, and half consumed by fire extend their sprawling limbs . . . now bleached by the weather." By this method, a family could clear 3 to 5 acres a year for cultivation.

The relentless demands for wood generated by the growing white population added to the assault on the region's forests. As expanding areas of trans-Appalachia came under the farmers' plows, forests and wildlife gave way.

INDIAN–WHITE RELATIONS IN THE EARLY REPUBLIC

The years from 1790 to the end of the 1820s witnessed a dramatic turning point in Indian–white relations. As the era began, Native American tribes still controlled vast areas of the trans-Appalachian interior. North of the Ohio River, the Shawnee, Delaware, and Miami formed a western confederacy capable of mustering several thousand warriors. South of the river lived five major tribal groups: the Cherokee, Creek, Choctaw, Chickasaw, and Seminole. Together, these southern tribes totaled nearly 60,000 people. By 1830, however, the balance of power between Indians and European Americans had shifted decisively as white settlers streamed into the region (bringing black slaves with them south of the Ohio River) to occupy the land.

As white expansion increased, Indian tribes devised various strategies of resistance and survival. Among the Cherokee, many followed a path of peaceful accommodation, while others like the Shawnee and the Creek rose in armed resistance. Neither strategy was altogether successful, for by 1830 the Indians

faced a future of continued acculturation, military defeat, and forced migration to lands west of the Mississippi River.

Less dramatic but no less important, during these years the social and cultural separation of Indians and white Americans increased sharply. As late as the 1780s, Native Americans still walked the streets of Boston and Philadelphia, while Indians and white Americans interacted regularly as allies and antagonists, traders and marriage partners. By 1830, such contacts were much less common. East of the Appalachians, whites now regarded Indians as exotic curiosities, while west of the mountains the Indians' increasing confinement on reservations, together with the forced removal of northern tribes to areas west of the Mississippi River, began a similar process of racial separation.

The Initial Goals of Indian Policy

During the years from 1790 to 1830, the federal government established a set of Indian policies that would govern Indian–white relations through much of the nineteenth century. Intended initially to promote the eventual assimilation of Native Americans into white society, those policies speeded the transfer of Indian land to white settlers and helped set the stage for a later, more dramatic program of Indian removal.

With the government's initial "conquest" theory rendered ineffective by the Indians' refusal to regard themselves as a conquered people (see Chapter 7), government officials shifted course by recognizing Indian rights to the land they inhabited and declaring that future land transfers be accomplished by treaty agreements.

Henry Knox, Washington's first secretary of war, laid out the government's new position in 1789. The Indians, he explained, "being the prior occupants of the soil, possess the right of the soil." It should not be taken from them "unless by their free consent, or by the right of conquest in case of just war." To dispossess them for other reasons "would violate the fundamental laws of nature and . . . justice." Though Knox helped establish a more humane Indian policy, the acquisition of Indian land for white settlement remained the overarching goal.

The new treaty-based strategy proved effective, as Native American leaders agreed to cede land in return for trade goods, yearly annuity payments, and assurances that no further demands would be made on them. Reluctant tribal leaders could often be persuaded to cooperate by warnings about the inevitable spread of white settlement, or more tractable chieftains could be found. In these ways, vast areas of trans-Appalachia passed into the possession of white settlers.

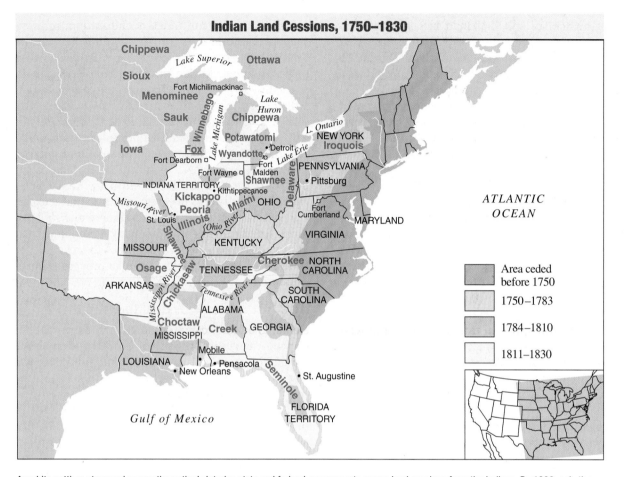

Indian Land Cessions, 1750–1830

As white settlers streamed across the nation's interior, state and federal governments wrung land cessions from the Indians. By 1830, only the southeastern tribes still controlled significant areas of their ancestral land east of the Mississippi River. Labels in red indicate the major Native American tribes.

Federal policy also attempted to regulate the fur trade. Both Native Americans and whites found benefit in the trade. The Indians, in return for their abundant furs, secured goods such as blankets, guns, rum, and ironware that they valued highly. White traders, by contrast, acquired highly desired furs in exchange for inexpensive trade goods.

While the fur trade brought handsome profits to private companies such as John Jacob Astor's American Fur Company (1808), it often worked to the Indians' disadvantage. Trade goods frequently transmitted diseases such as measles and smallpox. Indians, moreover, became dependent on the trade because it provided the only certain supplies of coveted goods such as rum and firearms. As the demand for furs and pelts increased, moreover, Native Americans overtrapped their hunting grounds, forcing them to compete with other tribes for access to fresh sources of furs farther to the west.

In 1796, in an effort to reduce fraud and its attendant conflict, Congress created government trading posts, or "factories," where Indians could come for fair treatment. The system lasted until 1822 but never supplanted private traders as Congress had intended.

A third objective of federal Indian policy was to civilize and Christianize the Native Americans, then assimilate them into white society. In the trans-Appalachian West, most settlers regarded Indians as savages to be moved out of white settlement's way. In the East, however, clergymen and government officials displayed greater concern over the Native Americans' well-being. While uneasy over Indian "savagery," easterners admired the Native Americans' "bravery," "independence," and "simplicity of life," qualities resembling highly valued democratic virtues.

Following the revolution, Moravians, Quakers, and Baptists sent scores of missionaries to live among the Indians, preach the Gospel, and teach the benefits of white civilization. John Stewart, a freeborn, part-Indian mulatto, was one such missionary. From 1815 to his death in 1821, he preached to the Wyandotte near Sandusky, Ohio. Among the most selfless were Quaker missionaries who labored with the Iroquois in New York, attempting to inspire conversion and improve the conditions of Iroquois life. In spite of the missionaries' best efforts, however, most Native Americans remained aloof, because the chasm between Christianity and their own religion was wide (see Chapter 1), and the missionaries' denigration of Indian culture was clearly apparent.

Education was another weapon of the assimilationists. In 1793, Congress appropriated $20,000 to promote literacy, agriculture, and vocational instruction. With government encouragement, missionaries established schools in which Indian children were taught reading, writing, and vocational skills. The vast majority of Indian children never attended the mission schools. Among those who did, many stayed but a short while, they and their parents preferring the education offered by family and tribe over the culturally threatening environment of the white-run schools.

Although the assimilationists cared deeply about the physical and spiritual fate of Native American people, they showed little sympathy for Indian culture, for they demanded that Native Americans give up their language, religion, dress, and extended family arrangements—that is, cease being Indian and adopt the ways of white society. Assimilation or removal were the alternatives posed by even the most benevolent whites.

Strategies of Survival: The Iroquois and the Cherokee

Faced with the steady loss of land and tribal autonomy, Native Americans devised various strategies of resistance and survival. Among the Iroquois, a prophet named Handsome Lake, who had fought with England during the Revolutionary War and then succumbed to the despair of military defeat and reservation life, led his people through a process of cultural revitalization. In 1799, following a series of trancelike visions, he preached a combination of Indian and white ways that included temperance, peace, land retention, and the rituals of *Gaiwiio*, a new religion combining elements of Christianity and traditional Iroquois belief. His vision, providing a new definition of what it meant to be an Indian, offered hope and renewed pride for the Iroquois in the midst of their radically transformed lives.

Far to the south, the Cherokee followed a different path of accommodation. As the nineteenth century began, the Cherokee still controlled millions of acres in Tennessee, Georgia, and the western Carolinas. Their land base, however, was shrinking. By 1800, more than 40 Cherokee towns had disappeared.

Southern state governments, responding to white demands for Indian land, sought ways to undercut tribal autonomy. In 1801, Tennessee unilaterally brought Cherokee territory under state authority. As violence escalated along the borders between white and Indian settlements, state officials demanded that Native Americans accused of horse stealing and other crimes stand trial in state courts. The Cherokee, who had their own system of justice and distrusted the state courts with their all-white juries and exclusion of Indian testimony, rejected Tennessee's demands.

In Cherokee councils, a group of full-blood leaders called for armed resistance. Better to stand and fight, they argued, than follow the false path of accommodation. Others, however, including mixed-bloods such as John Ross, insisted that accommodation offered the best hope for survival. After a bitter struggle, the accommodationists won out. Soon they began to bring the tribe's scattered villages under a common government, the better to defend their freedom and prevent the further loss of land. In 1808, the Cherokee National Council adopted a written code combining elements of American and Indian law, and in 1827 it devised a written constitution patterned after those of nearby states. Members of the council accompanied it with a bold declaration that the Cherokee constituted an independent nation with full sovereignty over their lands. In 1829, the Cherokee government made it an offense punishable by death for any member of the tribe to transfer land to white ownership without the consent of tribal authorities.

Meanwhile, the process of social and cultural accommodation, encouraged by Cherokee leaders such as Ross and promoted by white missionaries and

Sequoyah, who sat for this portrait in 1838, devised the Cherokee alphabet, which formed the basis for the first written Indian language in North America. *(The Newberry Library, Chicago)*

government agents, went forward. Missionaries opened a school for Cherokee youth in 1804 on the Hiwasee River on the Tennessee–Georgia boundary and established a boarding school near present-day Chattanooga 12 years later. They stepped up their religious activities as well, baptizing Cherokee into the Christian faith.

As the Cherokee turned from their traditional hunting, gathering, and farming economy to settled agriculture, many moved from town settlements onto individual farmsteads, while others established sawmills, country stores, and blacksmith shops. In contrast to traditional Cherokee practices of sharing and the communal ownership of property, notions of private property took hold.

The majority of Cherokee people continued to inhabit crude log cabins and live a hand-to-mouth existence. Some mixed-bloods, however, like Joseph Vann who learned English and understood how to deal with white authorities, accumulated hundreds of acres of fertile land and scores of black slaves. Since the mid-eighteenth century, the Cherokee had held a few runaway blacks in slavelike conditions. During the early nineteenth century, Cherokee slavery expanded and became more harsh. By 1820, there were nearly 1,300 black slaves in the Cherokee nation. A Cherokee law of 1824 forbade intermarriage with blacks. The accelerating spread of cotton cultivation increased demand for slave labor among Cherokee as well as southern whites. As accommodation increased, slave ownership became a mark of social standing.

By 1820, the strategy of peaceful accommodation had brought clear rewards. Tribal government was stronger, and the sense of Cherokee identity was reasonably secure. Before long, however, the Cherokee's success would prove their undoing, for as their self-confidence grew, so did the hostility of neighboring whites impatient to gain possession of their land. That hostility would erupt in a final campaign to remove the Cherokee from their land forever (see Chapter 12).

Patterns of Armed Resistance: The Shawnee and the Creek

Not all tribes proved so accommodating to white expansion. Faced with growing threats to their political and cultural survival, the Shawnee and Creek nations rose in armed resistance. Conflict was smoldering as the nineteenth century began; it burst into open flame during the War of 1812.

In the late 1780s, chieftains such as Little Turtle of the Miami and Blue Jacket of the Shawnee had led a series of devastating raids across Indiana, Ohio, and western Pennsylvania, creating panic among white settlers and challenging the federal government's control of the Old Northwest. After two efforts to quell the

uprising had failed, President Washington determined to smash the Indians' resistance once and for all. In 1794, a federal army led by the old Revolutionary War general Anthony Wayne defeated 2,000 Indian warriors in the Battle of Fallen Timbers. Shortly after, in the Treaty of Greenville, the assembled chiefs ceded the southern two-thirds of Ohio. That cession opened the heart of the Old Northwest to white control. In subsequent years, additional treaties further reduced the Indians' land base, driving the tribes more tightly in upon each other.

By 1809, two Shawnee leaders, the brothers Tecumseh and Elskwatawa, the latter known to whites as "the Prophet," were traveling among the region's tribes attempting to forge an alliance against the invading whites. They established headquarters at an ancient Indian town named Kithtippecanoe in northern Indiana. Soon it became a gathering point for Native Americans from across the region responding to the messages of cultural pride, land retention, and pan-Indian resistance presented by the Shawnee brothers.

Between 1809 and 1811, Tecumseh carried his message of Indian nationalism and military resistance south to the Creek and Cherokee. His speeches rang with bitterness. "The white race is a wicked race," he told his listeners. "Since the days when the white race first came in contact with the red men, there has been a continual series of aggressions. The hunting grounds are fast disappearing, and they are driving the red men farther and farther to the west. . . . The only hope . . . is a war of extermination against the paleface." Though the southern tribes refused to join, by 1811 over 1,000 fighting men had gathered at Kithtippecanoe.

Alarmed, the governor of the Indiana Territory, William Henry Harrison, surrounded the Indian stronghold with a force of 1,000 soldiers. At dawn on November 7, 1811, 400 Indian warriors assaulted Harrison's lines. After a furious encounter, the victorious Harrison counted over 150 warriors dead. Before retiring to the territorial capital at Vincennes, he burned Kithtippecanoe to the ground.

Over the next several months, Tecumseh's followers, taking advantage of the recent outbreak of the War of 1812 and aided by British troops from Canada, carried out devastating raids across Indiana and southern Michigan. Together, they crushed American armies at Detroit and Fort Nelson and followed up with forays against Fort Wayne. The tide turned, however, at the Battle of the Thames near Detroit, where Harrison inflicted a grievous defeat on a combined British and Indian force. Among those slain was Tecumseh.

The American victory at the Thames signaled an end to Indian resistance in the Old Northwest.

Beginning in 1815, American settlers surged once more across Ohio and Indiana and pressed on into Illinois and Michigan.

To the south, the Creek challenged white intruders with similar militancy. By 1800, white settlers were pushing onto Creek lands in northwestern Georgia and central Alabama. Although some Creek leaders urged accommodation, others, called Red Sticks, prepared to fight. The embers of this smoldering conflict were fanned into flame by an aggressive Tennessee militia commander named Andrew Jackson. Citing Creek atrocities against "defenseless women and children," Jackson in 1808 urged President Jefferson to endorse a campaign against the "ruthless foe."

He got his chance in the summer of 1813, when the Red Sticks carried out a series of frontier raids, killing and scalping two white families and capping their campaign with an assault on Fort Mims on the Alabama River where they killed as many as 500 people, women and children among them. News of the tragedy raised bitter cries for revenge. "When the tomahawk and the scalping knife are drawn in the cabins of our peaceful and unsuspecting citizens," declared the Tennessee legislature, "it is time, high time to prepare . . . for defense."

At the head of 5,000 Tennessee and Kentucky militia, augmented by Cherokee, Choctaw, and Chickasaw warriors eager to punish their traditional Creek enemies, Jackson launched his long-awaited attack. As he moved south, the ferocity of the fighting increased. Davey Crockett later reported that the militia volunteers shot the Red Sticks down "like dogs." The Indians gave like measure in return.

The climactic battle of the Creek War came in March 1814 at Horseshoe Bend, on the Tallapoosa River in central Alabama. There, in the fortified town of Tohopeka, 1,000 Creek warriors made their stand against fourteen hundred state troops and 600 Cherokee allies. While American cannon fire raked the Creek defenses, the allied Cherokee crossed the river to cut off retreat. In the battle that followed, over 800 Native Americans died, more than in any other Indian–white battle in American history.

Jackson followed up his victory with a scorched-earth sweep through the remaining Red Stick towns. With no hope left, Red Eagle, one of the few remaining Red Stick leaders, walked alone into Jackson's camp and addressed the American commander: "General Jackson, I am not afraid of you. I fear no man, for I am a Creek warrior. I have nothing to request in behalf of myself; you can kill me if you desire. But I come to beg you to send for the women and children of the war party, who are now starving in the woods. . . . I am now done fighting."

Jackson allowed Red Eagle and his followers to return home, but in August 1814 he exacted his final revenge by constructing Fort Jackson on the Hickory Ground, the most sacred spot of the Creek nation. Over the following months, he seized 22 million acres, nearly two-thirds of the Creek domain. Before his Indian-fighting days were over, Jackson would acquire for the United States, through treaty or military conquest, nearly three-fourths of Alabama and Florida, a third of Tennessee, and a fifth of Georgia and Mississippi.

Just as Tecumseh's death had signaled the end of Indian resistance in the North, so Jackson's defeat of the Creek at Horseshoe Bend broke the back of Indian defenses in the South. With all possibility of armed resistance gone, Native Americans gave way before the swelling tide of white settlement.

PERFECTING A DEMOCRATIC SOCIETY

Throughout our nation's history, the American people have launched a variety of reform movements aimed at achieving social justice and bringing the conditions of daily life into conformity with the nation's democratic ideals. The first of those reform eras occurred in the early nineteenth century.

The Revolutionary Heritage

Reform was inspired in part by democratic ideals fostered during the Revolution and still fresh in Americans' minds. Preeminent among them was the principle of social equality. In part, this meant equality of opportunity, the notion that people should have a chance to rise as far as ability and ambition would carry them. Such an idea appealed to social democrats, for it spoke of setting privilege aside and giving everyone an equal chance. Social conservatives could embrace it as well, for it could be used to justify the social inequalities that individual effort often produced. The doctrine of social equality had a powerful moral dimension as well, because it implied an equality of worth among individuals, no matter their social standing. Though Americans generally accepted differences of wealth and social position, they were less willing to tolerate social pretension or the assumption that such differences made some people better than others.

The Evangelical Impulse

More than revolutionary idealism lay behind the concern over social justice, for a surge of evangelical religion inspired the reform impulse also. Throughout our history, religion has been a major force in American public life. This was true during the years of the early republic, when a wave of religious revivalism known as the Second Great Awakening swept across the American nation. From its beginnings in the 1790s through much of the nineteenth century, and in settings as different as the Cane Ridge district of backwoods Kentucky and the sophisticated cities of the Northeast, Americans by the tens of thousands sought personal salvation and found a sense of social belonging in the shared experience of religious enthusiasm.

Displayed most spectacularly among ordinary folk gathered in Methodist and Baptist camp meetings, the revivals reached across boundaries of class and race. Rough-hewn itinerant preachers, black as well as white, many of them theologically untrained but all of them afire with religious conviction, carried the Gospel message from place to place, in the process knitting networks of believers closely together.

In 1809, Benjamin Latrobe, principal architect of the new Capitol building in Washington, D.C., and shrewd observer of the American scene, visited a Methodist camp meeting on the Leesburg Road in northern Virginia, just outside the nation's capital. "As we approached the meeting ground. . . ," Latrobe reported, "we could distinguish among the trees, half concealed by the underwood, houses, chaises, light wagons, hacks, & a crowd of men and women, in the midst of whom we presently arrived. . . . Crowds of negroes & mullatoes tastily dressed stood among the trees, & the groups looked as if any motives but religious ones had assembled them."

Positioning himself at the head of the clearing, Latrobe watched in fascination as "Mr. Bunn, a blacksmith of G[eorge] Town . . . spoke [with] immense rapidity & exertion . . . of the judgement to come." As Bunn exhorted the assembled throng, "a general groaning & shrieking was . . . heard from all Quarters" while the preacher "threw out both his arms sideways at full length, & shook himself violently." Every time Bunn pronounced "the stroke of grace," Latrobe continued, he brought his hands together so as to produce an astonishing clap. "The stroke again," Bunn shouted, "and another stroke, and another . . . and now it works, it works. . . . There it is, now she has it, glory! glory! glory!"

Though the salvation of souls was the camp meeting's central purpose, Latrobe perceived that it ministered to a variety of other human needs as well. "The illumination of the woods, the novelty of a camp especially to the women and children, the dancing and singing, & the pleasure of a crowd, so tempting to the most fashionable," generated a powerful sense of social belonging at such gatherings.

Offering a simple message that ordinary folks could readily grasp, itinerant preachers such as Bunn emphasized the equality of all believers before God

and declared each individual responsible for his or her own soul. The power and inclusiveness of that message was revealed in the explosive growth of Methodist and Baptist churches. By mid-century, they would constitute the nation's largest religious denominations.

The Awakening had additional implications, for it called on believers to demonstrate their faith by going into the world to lift up the downtrodden and do good works. That religious impulse would provide much of the energy for later antebellum reforms such as temperance and abolition (see Chapter 12). Its influence was evident as well in earlier efforts at perfecting American society.

Alleviating Poverty and Distress

In the early republic, as at other times in the nation's history, ideals jarred awkwardly against social reality. One source of tension was the contrast between the doctrine of democratic equality and the reality of deepening class distinctions.

As the nineteenth century began, women still held far less property than men. For black slaves, ownership of more than the most basic personal possessions

The Hot Corn Seller

Women as well as men among the urban poor peddled food and other commodities on the streets in an effort to make ends meet. *(Niccolino Calyo,* The Hot Corn Seller, *c. 1840. Museum of the City of New York)*

The American Revolution together with broader humanitarian impulses prompted various efforts at social reform in early America. Pictured here, from left to right, are the Philadelphia Almshouse, House of Employment, and Prison. *(Will Brown, Philadelphia, PA/The Dietrich American Foundation)*

was beyond reach. Though the condition of free blacks such as Ben Thompson and Phyllis Sherman was considerably better, they, too, enjoyed little of the country's bounty.

Among white males, property was most broadly shared in rural areas of the North, where free labor and family-farm agriculture predominated, and least so in the South, where the planters' control of slave labor and the best land permitted them to monopolize the region's wealth. The most even distribution of wealth existed on the edges of white settlement in trans-Appalachia, but it was little more than an equality of want. As the frontier developed, differences in wealth appeared there as well.

Though America, unlike Europe, contained no permanent, destitute underclass (at least among its white citizens), poverty was real and increasing. In the South, it was most evident among poor whites living on the sandy pine barrens of the backcountry. In the North, the port cities held growing numbers of poor. Boston artisans and shopkeepers who together had owned 20 percent of the city's wealth in 1700, for example, held scarcely half as much a century later.

Recurring recessions hit the urban poor with particular force, while winter added to hard times as shipping slowed and jobs disappeared. During the winter of 1805, New York's Mayor DeWitt Clinton worried publicly about the disruptive behavior of 10,000 impoverished New Yorkers and asked the state legislature for help. During the winter of 1814–1815, relief agencies assisted nearly one-fifth of the city's population.

In rural New England and southeastern Pennsylvania, a transient, propertyless underclass was growing. The "strolling poor," they were called—men, and sometimes women, unable to secure land of their own, and thus forced to roam the countryside searching for work.

Three other groups were conspicuous among the nation's poor. One consisted of old Revolutionary War veterans like Long Bill Scott, who had found poverty as well as adventure in the war. State and federal governments were peppered with petitions from grizzled veterans and their widows, detailing their misery and seeking relief. Women and children also suffered disproportionately from poverty. Annual censuses of almshouse residents in New York City from 1816 to 1821 consistently listed more women and children than men.

For every American who actually suffered poverty's effects, several others struggled to get by, living just beyond its reach. The thinness of their margin of safety became clear during the depression of 1819–1822. Triggered by a financial panic created by the unsound practices of hundreds of newly chartered state banks, a deep depression settled over the land, causing bankruptcies and sending unemployment soaring. In upstate New York, the pay of turnpike workers sank from 75 to 12 cents a day. In Ohio, the governor reported that "the greater part of our mercantile citizens are in a state of bankruptcy," while "the citizens of every class are . . . delinquent in discharging even the most trifling of debts." In the South, farms and plantations were abandoned as cotton and tobacco exports fell. By the early 1820s, the depression was lifting, but it left behind broken fortunes and shattered dreams.

Alleviating poverty was a central goal of the early reformers. In New York City, private and public authorities established over 100 charitable and relief agencies to aid orphans and widows, aged women and young prostitutes, imprisoned debtors and poverty-stricken seamen. Across the nation, a "charitable revolution" increased benevolent institutions from 50 in 1790 to nearly 2,000 by 1820. Most of these ventures drew a distinction between the "worthy poor," respectable folk who were victims of circumstance and merited assistance, and the "idle" or "vicious poor," who were deemed to lack character and thus deserved their fate. Many Americans believed such distinctions were clearly discoverable. No matter that a New York commission in 1823 found only 46 able-bodied adults (37 women and 9 men) among the 851 inmates of the city's almshouses or that a similar listing of supposed ne'er-do-wells included disabled Revolutionary War veterans, abandoned infants, and indigent immigrants recently arrived from Europe. New Yorkers had not yet made the connection between pauperism and the changing conditions of urban life.

Poverty was not the only target of public and private reform. Municipal authorities and private charities also established orphanages for children, asylums for the insane, and hospitals for the sick. Many such efforts were limited and shortlived, but they attested to the continuing strength of both revolutionary and religious ideals. Moreover, they provided a foundation for more ambitious reform efforts several decades later.

Women's Lives

Women's lives were not markedly altered during these early nineteenth-century years. Changes, however, did occur that helped set the stage for later, more dramatic breakthroughs.

Divorce was one area where women achieved greater equality. When a neighbor asked John Backus, a silversmith in Great Barrington, Massachusetts, why he kicked and struck his wife, John replied that it was partly because his father had treated his mother in the same way. We do not know whether John's mother tolerated such abuse, but his wife did not. She complained of cruelty and secured a divorce. More and more women followed her example.

Divorce was not easy to come by for women, since most states allowed it only on grounds of their husband's adultery. South Carolina did not permit it at all. Moreover, women typically faced the discomfort of presenting detailed evidence of their husbands' infidelities to an all-male court. Accusations of a wife's transgressions, by contrast, were more easily proven.

Still, divorce was becoming more available to women. In Massachusetts during the decade after independence, 50 percent more women than men filed for divorce, with almost identical rates of success. Part of the explanation for the increase lay in the war's disruptions, which led large numbers of men to desert their families and thus encouraged their wives to take action. It seems just as certain, however, that women's firmer commitment to individualism and equality led them to expect more of marriage.

Changes also occurred in women's education. Given their special role as Republican Mothers, women would have to prepare for their responsibilities as keepers of public morality and nurturers of republican citizens. Judith Sargeant Murray, along with other women, however, demanded even more of women's education. In a series of essays published in the 1790s, Murray criticized parents who "pointed their daughters" exclusively toward marriage and dependence. "They should be enabled to procure for themselves the necessaries of life; independence should be placed within their grasp," she wrote. "A woman should reverence herself."

Between 1790 and 1820, a number of female academies were established. Most, such as Susanna Rowson's Young Ladies Academy in Philadelphia, were located in northeastern cities. Timothy Dwight, the future president of Yale, opened his academy at Greenfield Hill in Connecticut to girls and taught them the same subjects he taught boys. Dwight, however, was the exception. Most proposals for female education assumed that girls should be taught separately from boys and that the curriculum should be less demanding. Though Benjamin Rush prescribed book-keeping, reading, geography, music ("because it soothes cares and is good for the lungs"), and history as proper elements of a girl's education, traditionalists such as the Boston minister John Gardiner were more conservative. Warning that intellectual activity would unsex women, he declared that "Women of masculine minds have generally masculine manners, and a robustness of person ill calculated to inspire the tender passions." Even the most ardent supporters of female learning, like Murray, insisted that education was primarily important so that women might function more effectively within the domestic sphere. The happiness of the nation, she explained, was based on the happiness of families, and that depended in turn on "daughters of Columbia," educated women who would "fill with honor the parts allotted to them."

The evangelical impulse to which so many women were drawn actually reduced women's place in the churches. Whereas women had previously served as religious exhorters and participated in Baptist and Methodist church governance, they found themselves

Female academies in the early republic provided young middle- and upper-class women with the knowledge and skills necessary for their roles as Republican Mothers. (*Jacob Marling,* The Crowning of Flora, *1816/The Chrysler Museum of Art, Norfolk, VA, Gift of Edgar William and Bernice Chrysler Garbisch 80.118.20*)

increasingly marginalized as evangelical churches strove for social acceptance and adopted the rigidly gendered rules that Presbyterians and Congregationalists had always followed. In matters of church discipline, women were more frequently charged with "disorderliness" and condemned by their male brethren for "disobedience", thus calling into question a once robust tradition of piety in which men and women shared spiritual truth and ministered to each other's souls.

Race, Slavery, and the Limits of Reform

As we have seen (Chapter 7), the Revolution initiated the end of slavery in the northern states and challenged its continued existence in the Upper South. As the new century began, however, private manumissions were declining across Maryland and Virginia, while antislavery sentiment was weakening and more rigid categories of racial exclusiveness were appearing in the North.

In the southern states, the accelerating spread of cotton increased the value of slave labor, while revolutionary idealism faded with the passage of time. Equally important were two slave rebellions that generated intense alarm among southern whites. Panic-stricken refugees fleeing the Caribbean island of Saint Domingue beginning in 1791 carried word to the North American mainland of the black Haitians' rebellion against French colonial authority. Inspired by Toussaint L'Ouverture and other black leaders, the

island's slaves struggled for 13 years against a French army of 25,000 before finally throwing off their French oppressors. By the time that struggle was finished, it achieved the first mass emancipation of a slave society and establishment of the first black republic in the Americas.

While Thomas Jefferson, as secretary of state, initially applauded the Haitian independence movement, he refused as president to extend diplomatic recognition to the new Haitian republic and sought to quarantine it within the Americas. He had solid political reasons for doing so, for news of the revolution spread terror through the South, where rumors abounded that Haitian incendiaries would soon be landing. In response, southern whites tightened their "black codes," cut the importation of new slaves from the Caribbean, and sought out malcontents among their own chattels. Colonial rebellions were admirable, but not when they set blacks against their white masters.

A second shock occurred in the summer of 1800, when a rebellion just outside Richmond, Virginia, was nipped in the bud. A 24-year-old slave named Gabriel had devised a plan to arm 1,000 slaves for an assault on the city. Gabriel and his accomplices were American-born blacks who spoke English, worked at skilled jobs that allowed them considerable personal freedom (and thus opportunity to lay their plans), and had fashioned their own ideology of liberation and racial justice by appropriating Virginia's revolutionary tradition and applying it to the circumstances of their own lives. A drenching downpour delayed the attack, providing time for several house servants (subsequently granted their freedom by the Virginia Assembly) to sound the alarm before the conspirators could act. No white lives were lost, but authorities arrested scores of slaves and free blacks, while 25 suspects, including Gabriel, were hanged at the order of Governor James Monroe. The carnage both alarmed and saddened Jefferson. "There is strong sentiment that there has been hanging enough," he confided to Monroe. "The other states and the world at large will forever condemn us if we . . . go one step beyond absolute necessity." In the midst of panic, however, the line between necessity and revenge was hard to find.

In the early nineteenth century, antislavery appeals all but disappeared from the South. Even religious groups that had once denounced slavery now grew quiet. "A majority of the people of the southern states," declared Congressman Peter Early of Georgia in 1806, "do not consider . . . it immoral to hold human flesh in bondage. Many deprecate slavery as an evil, as a political evil," he continued, "but not as a crime." At the time of the American Civil War, Confederate spokesmen would be saying much the same thing.

In the North, where the gradual abolition of slavery soothed white consciences, sentiment was increas-ingly conciliatory toward southern slave owners. At the same time, the conviction grew that immutable racial differences, grounded in nature, differentiated whites from blacks and that the two races existed in a hierarchical relationship to each other.

In the eighteenth century, ideas of racial exclusiveness had competed with Enlightenment beliefs in the common humanity of all mankind. American independence, however, dramatized for white Americans the contrast between their own successful struggle to throw off the threatened yoke of English "slavery" and the perpetual slavery of black Americans in their midst. That contrast seemed explainable by racial differences. The Revolution, moreover, focused the attention of white Americans on the essential attributes of republican citizenship—civic responsibility, economic self-sufficiency, and independence of judgment—qualities clearly lacking among the slave population. Even the gains achieved by free blacks as slavery was abolished appeared to harden white racial attitudes in the North. With racial domination no longer enforced by law, northern whites more readily invoked doctrines of black racial inferiority to assure their own continued predominance.

The hardening of white racial attitudes was clearly evident in the strengthening calls for colonizing free

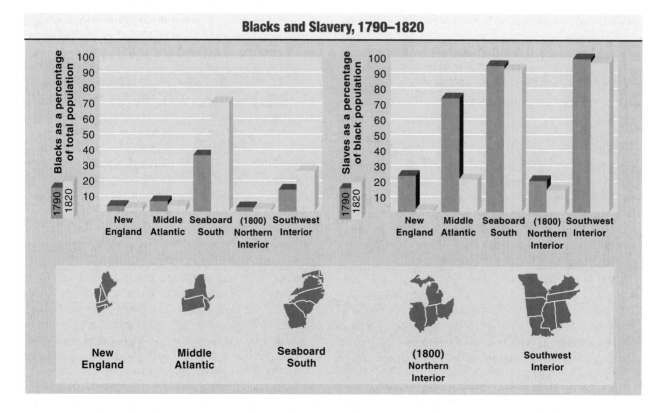

Though regions had differed in the importance of slavery and the number of blacks in their population as the Revolutionary War ended, those differences increased significantly over the next 30 years. Source: U.S. Bureau of the Census.

blacks outside the United States, in areas of western Africa that would become Liberia and Sierre Leone. The American Colonization Society, founded in 1816, typified these attitudes. Its supporters, while detesting slavery, believed that the two races could not peacefully coexist. That position was affirmed by many southern slaveholders who saw in colonization a convenient way of reducing the free black population and eliminating troublesome bondsmen. In the end, the Colonization Society never sent many freedmen and women abroad, but it did help to allay white anxieties.

Although some blacks were sympathetic to colonization, believing it offered the best promise of true freedom, most black spokesmen vigorously opposed it, condemning the ideology of black racial inferiority upon which colonization was based and demanding their full rights as Americans. In joining together in active opposition to colonization, American blacks gained experience in forging a more effective political voice. That experience would prove valuable training for the abolitionist crusade that lay ahead.

Not all northern whites succumbed to the new racism, for the states of Massachusetts, Rhode Island, and Pennsylvania would soon become hotbeds of a resurgent, multiracial abolition movement. Blacks, moreover, enjoyed greater liberty in the cities of the Northeast than elsewhere in the nation. Nonetheless, during the early years of the republic the revolutionary promise of equality rang hollow for most black Americans.

Forming Free Black Communities

During the half century following independence, vibrant black communities appeared in the port cities. As the lives of Ben Thompson and Phyllis Sherman revealed, emancipation in the North and the increase of freedmen in the Upper South enabled growing numbers of African Americans to seek the companionship of people of color in places such as Boston, New York, Philadelphia, and Baltimore. On the eve of independence, 4,000 slaves and a few hundred free blacks had called these four port cities home; 50 years later, more than 30,000 African Americans did so.

The men sought employment as laborers or sailors, the women as domestics. There were hundreds like Alexander Giles, a free black Philadelphia seaman who had been born in 1777 in nearby Kent County, Delaware, and Randall Shepherd, who had made his way north from Nansemond County, Virginia, in 1798. In rural areas, free blacks such as Phyllis Sherman had lived in isolation. In the port cities, black communities provided a higher measure of security and better chances of finding a marriage partner, establishing a family, and participating in community organizations.

Family formation was eased because many of the migrants were women, thus correcting a long-standing urban imbalance in the black population. Former slaves often created extended households that included relatives, friends, and boarders. As circumstances allowed, single-family units were formed. By 1820, most blacks in the northern cities lived in autonomous households.

As their numbers grew, African Americans created institutions independent of white control and capable of serving the needs of the black community. Schools educated children excluded from white academies, while mutual-aid societies offered help to the down and out and fraternal associations, such as the first African American Masonic Lodge established in Boston in 1797, provided fellowship and mutual support. It was black churches, however, that emerged as the institutional cornerstones of black community life, a position they would occupy throughout the nation's history.

In the years following the Revolution, free blacks joined integrated Methodist and Baptist congregations in cities such as Philadelphia and New York, drawn by their strongly biblical theology, enthusiastic forms of worship, and opposition to slavery. By 1790, 20 percent of Methodist church members were black. As the numbers of black communicants grew, however, they found themselves increasingly segregated in church galleries, excluded from leadership roles, and even denied communion. Whereas Christianity often comforted blacks by promising equality in the eyes of God, empowering them to adapt Christian beliefs to their own cultural and religious needs, and at times inspiring them to rebellion, the Christianity of white churches served increasingly to legitimize white supremacy and racial separation. Although many black Christians were reluctant to withdraw from biracial congregations, others sought opportunity to control their religious lives by breaking away.

In 1794, a small group of black Methodists led by Richard Allen, a slave-born, itinerant preacher, organized the Bethel African American Methodist Church in Philadelphia. Originally established as an integral part of American Methodism, Allen's congregation moved toward separatism by requiring that only "Africans and descendants of the African race" be admitted to membership. In 1816, it joined with a similar congregation in Baltimore to form the African Methodist Episcopal Church—the first independent black denomination in the United States. Though never as numerous as black Methodists, black Baptists established their own separate churches during the early nineteenth century in places such as Boston (1805), Philadelphia (1810), New Orleans (1826), and St. Louis (1827).

In his watercolor of a black Methodist church meeting, Paul Svinin, a traveler from Russia, reveals his amazement at the physical emotion displayed by the worshippers. "African" churches and other organizations were rare before 1800 but grew steadily in the ensuing decades. *(The Metropolitan Museum of Art, Rogers Fund, 1942 (42.95.19))*

Located in the heart of black communities, these churches not only nurtured distinctive, African American forms of worship but also provided education for black children and burial sites for families excluded from white cemeteries. Equally important, black churches offered secure sites where the basic rituals of family and community life—marriages and birth announcements, funerals and anniversaries—could be celebrated and where community norms could be enforced. By the 1830s, a rich cultural and institutional life had taken root in the black neighborhoods of American cities.

White hostility, however, remained a reality of black urban life, especially during hard times when free blacks competed with white laborers for scarce jobs. Working-class whites were unnerved as well by the growing competition for cheap housing. Overt violence against free blacks was infrequent during the early decades of the century, but even so, blacks found themselves increasingly segregated in residence, employment, and social life.

In response, leaders such as Richard Allen, Prince Hall, and Absolom Jones, through speeches, pamphlets, and public meetings, explored the meaning of black "freedom" in a white republic. In the process, they struggled to create a sense of civic identity for Americans of African descent.

A FOREIGN POLICY FOR THE NEW NATION

During the early decades of the nineteenth century, the Jeffersonians struggled to fashion a foreign policy appropriate for the expanding agrarian nation. Several goals guided their efforts: protecting American interests on the high seas, clearing the West of foreign troops, and breaking free from the country's historic dependence on Europe. The goals were not easily accomplished, yet by the 1820s the Jeffersonians had fashioned a new relationship with Europe. In the Monroe Doctrine of 1823, they projected a momentous new role for the United States within the Americas as well.

Jeffersonian Principles

Jeffersonian foreign policy was based on the doctrine of "no entangling alliances" with Europe that Washington had articulated in his Farewell Address of 1796. In the Jeffersonians' minds, England was still the principal enemy, but France was now suspect as well. By the time the Jeffersonians took office, the French Revolution had run its course. Although some Jeffersonians continued to harbor hopes for French liberty, most were sobered by Napoleon's dictatorial rule.

Second, the Jeffersonians emphasized the importance of overseas commerce for the nation's well-being. Foreign trade would provide markets for America's agricultural produce and fetch manufactured goods in return. The Federalists had nurtured domestic manufacturing by offering tariff protection against European competition. The Jeffersonians hoped to keep large-scale manufacturing in Europe, because they feared the concentrations of wealth and dependent working classes that domestic manufacturing would bring.

The Jeffersonians' third goal was maintaining peace. They feared war's effects on democratic liberty because it stifled free speech, increased the public debt, and expanded government power. Although seeking peace, the Jeffersonians understood the dangers lurking throughout the Atlantic world and knew that protecting the nation's interests might require force. Between 1801 and 1805, Jefferson dispatched naval vessels to the Mediterranean to defend American commerce against the Barbary States (Algiers, Morocco, Tripoli, and Tunis) of North Africa. War, however, was to be a policy of last resort. The Jeffersonians' handling of the crisis leading into the War of 1812 against Great Britain illustrates how eagerly, and in this case how futilely, they sought to avoid conflict.

Struggling for Neutral Rights

After a brief interlude of peace, European war resumed in 1803. Once again Britain and France seized American shipping. Britain's overwhelming naval superiority made its attacks especially serious, while its continuing refusal to negotiate on issues of impressment, occupation of the fur-trading posts, and reopening the West Indian trade increased Anglo-American tension.

In response to British seizures of American shipping, Congress passed the Non-Importation Act in April 1806, banning British imports that could be produced domestically or acquired elsewhere. A month later, Britain blockaded the European coast. Threatened by Britain's action, Napoleon answered by forbidding all commerce with the British Isles.

Tension between Britain and the United States reached the breaking point in June 1807, when the British warship *Leopard* stopped the American frigate *Chesapeake* off the Virginia coast and demanded that four crew members be handed over as British deserters. When the American commander refused, protesting that the sailors were Americans, the *Leopard* opened fire, killing 3 and wounding 18. After the *Chesapeake* limped back into port with the story, cries of outrage rang across the land.

Knowing that the United States was not prepared to confront Britain, Jefferson withdrew American ships from the Atlantic. In December 1807, Congress passed the Embargo Act, forbidding all American vessels from sailing for foreign ports. Urging the embargo was one of Jefferson's most ill-fated decisions.

The embargo had relatively little effect. British shipping actually profited from the withdrawal of American competition, and British importers effectively supplied the country's agricultural needs from Latin America. The measure's domestic impact, however, was immediate and far-reaching. American

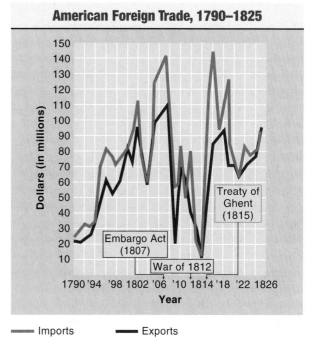

American overseas trade fluctuated dramatically as tensions with England and France ebbed and flowed. Source: U.S. Bureau of the Census.

exports plummeted 80 percent in a year, while imports dropped by more than half. New England was hardest hit. In ports such as Salem, Boston, and Providence, ships rocked idly at the wharves and thousands of workers were unemployed as depression settled in.

Up and down the coast, communities dependent on overseas commerce openly ignored the embargo's restrictions. Attempts to police it proved futile, for the government could not close off either the Atlantic coast or the northern border across which large quantities of American goods were smuggled into Canada. In the area of Lake Champlain, federal officials declared martial law and sent in troops in an effort to control the situation. Guerrilla skirmishing resulted as local citizens fired on U.S. revenue boats and recaptured confiscated goods.

Throughout the Federalist Northeast, bitterness threatened to escalate into open rebellion. Connecticut's governor, in words reminiscent of the Virginia and Kentucky Resolutions, warned that if Congress exceeded its authority, the states were duty-bound "to interpose their protecting shield between the rights and liberties of the people and the assumed power of the general government."

In the election of 1808, the Federalists rebounded after nearly a decade's decline. James Madison handily succeeded Jefferson in the presidency, but the Federalist candidate, C. C. Pinckney, garnered 47

The tranquillity of Crowninshield wharf in Salem, Massachusetts, reveals ships idled and docks emptied by Jefferson's embargo. *(George Ropes, Crowninshield Wharf/The Essex Institute, Salem, Massachusetts)*

electoral votes. The Federalists made gains in Congress and recaptured several state legislatures as well.

Faced with the embargo's ineffectiveness abroad and disastrous consequences at home, Congress repealed the measure in 1809. Over the next several years, Congress tried more limited trade restrictions aimed at reducing British and French attacks on American shipping. When these failed as well, war fever continued to mount.

The War of 1812

The loudest calls for war came from the West and South. The election of 1810 brought to Congress a new group of western and southern leaders, firmly Republican in party loyalty but impatient with the administration's bumbling policy and insistent that tougher measures were needed. These "War Hawks"—including Henry Clay and Richard Johnson of Kentucky, John Calhoun and Langdon Cheves of South Carolina, Felix Grundy of Tennessee, and Peter Porter from western New York— were an impressive group.

For too long, the War Hawks cried, the United States had tolerated Britain's presence on American soil, encouragement of Indian raids, and attacks on American commerce. They talked openly of expanding the nation north into Canada and south into Spanish Florida. Most of all, these young nationalists resented British arrogance and America's continuing humiliation. No government and no political party, they warned, could survive unless it protected its people's interests and upheld the nation's honor.

Responding to the growing pressure, President Madison finally asked Congress for a declaration of war on June 1, 1812. Opposition came entirely from the New England and Middle Atlantic states—ironi-

cally, the regions British policies affected most adversely—whereas the South and West voted solidly for war. Rarely had sectional alignments been more sharply drawn.

Rarely also had American foreign policy proven less effective. Madison decided to abandon economic coercion just as the British government suspended its European blockade. Three days later, unaware of Britain's action, the Congress declared war.

The war itself was a curious affair. Britain beat back several American forays into Canada and launched a series of attacks along the Gulf Coast. As it had done during the Revolutionary War, the British navy blockaded American coastal waters, while landing parties launched punishing attacks up and down the Atlantic Coast. On August 14, a British force occupied Washington, torched the Capitol and the president's mansion (which became known as the White House after being repaired and whitewashed), and sent the president and Congress fleeing into Virginia. Britain, however, did not press its advantage, for it was preoccupied with Napoleon's armies in Europe and wanted to end the American quarrel.

On the American side, emotions ran high among the war's Federalist critics and Republican supporters. On the night of June 22, 1812, a Republican crowd in Baltimore demolished the printing office of a local Federalist newspaper. The attack was inspired by partisan politics, but even more by working-class animosity toward Federalist "aristocrats" and the eagerness of working people to support the job-creating war. In late July, after copies of the *Federal-Republican* again appeared on Baltimore's streets, a crowd of 1,000 men and women once more surrounded the paper's office. When Federalist defenders opened fire, the crowd rolled up a cannon and sent a round of

A British cartoon shows President Madison spilling official papers as he flees the burning capital, while citizens react with sarcastic comments during the British attack on Washington in 1814. *(Anne S. K. Brown Military Collection, Brown University Library)*

grapeshot into the building. Several people lay dead on both sides before the militia finally carted the Federalists off to the safety of jail.

The bloody encounter was not over yet, for the following night, a crowd assembled in front of the city jail, brushed aside the mayor's pleas to disperse, and seized ten prisoners, including James Lingan, an old Revolutionary War general. The enraged mob beat Lingan and several others to death and left the bodies, stripped of their fine clothing, sprawling in the street.

Though fortunately the Baltimore riots were not duplicated elsewhere, emotions continued to run high throughout the country. In Federalist New England, opposition to the war veered toward outright disloyalty. In December 1814, delegates from the five New England states met at Hartford, Connecticut, to debate proposals for secession. Cooler heads prevailed, but before adjourning, the Hartford Convention asserted the right of a state "to interpose its authority" against "unconstitutional" acts of the government. Now it was New England's turn to play with the nullification fire. As the war dragged on, Federalist fortunes soared in the Northeast, while elsewhere bitterness grew over New England's disloyalty.

Before the war ended, American forces won several impressive victories, among them Commander Oliver Hazard Perry's defeat of the British fleet on Lake Erie in 1813. That victory proved a turning point of the war in the Old Northwest, for it secured American dominance on the Great Lakes, ended the threat of a British invasion of Michigan, and weakened the British–Indian alliance that had menaced American interests in the region. The most dramatic American triumph was Andrew Jackson's smashing victory in 1815 over an attacking British force at New Orleans. It had little to do with the war's outcome, however, for it occurred after preliminary terms of peace had already been signed.

Increasingly concerned about the balance of power in Europe, Britain's foreign secretary, Lord Castlereagh, offered to negotiate peace. Madison eagerly accepted, and on Christmas Eve in 1814, at Ghent, Belgium, the two sides reached agreement. The treaty resolved almost nothing, for it ignored impressment, blockades, neutral rights, and American access to Canadian fisheries. Britain did agree to evacuate the western posts, but other than that, the agreement did little more than declare the conflict over, provide for an

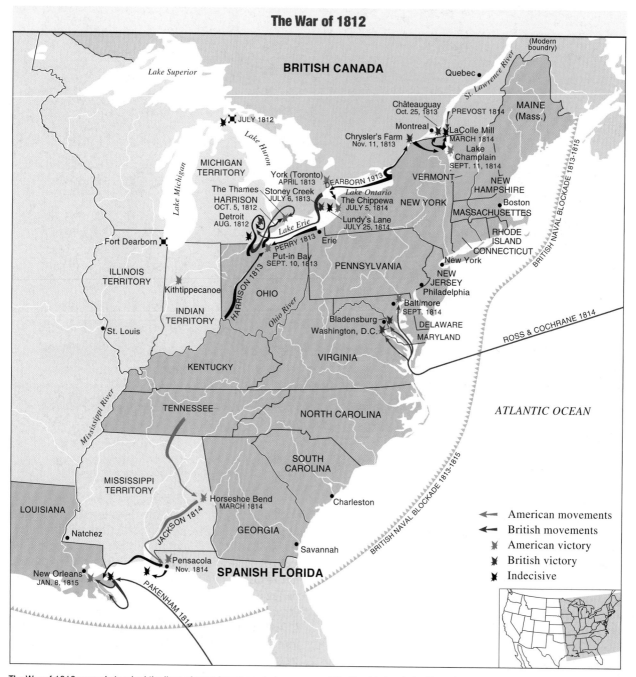

The War of 1812 scarcely touched the lives of most Americans, but areas around the Great Lakes, Lake Champlain, Chesapeake Bay, and the Gulf Coast witnessed significant fighting.

exchange of prisoners and the restoration of conquered territory, and call for the appointment of joint commissions to resolve lingering disputes.

Still, the war left its mark on the American nation. Nearly 20 percent of American seamen during the war were black, seafaring offering one of the few occupations commonly available to black men. Altogether, 4,000 African Americans served in the struggle against England, further strengthening black claims for full American citizenship. In addition, the war made

Andrew Jackson a national hero and established him as a political figure of major importance. The American people, moreover, regarded the contest as a "Second War of American Independence," another twisting of the English lion's tail that finally secured the country against outside interference. In the years following 1815, the nation turned its primary energies toward the task of internal development—occupying the continent, strengthening the economy, and perfecting American society.

Perry's victory at the Battle of Lake Erie turned the tide of naval warfare on the Great Lakes. *(U.S. Capitol Historical Society)*

At the same time, European nations, increasingly occupied with their own problems of unification and economic development, began what would prove to be nearly a century free of general war. In the past, European wars had drawn in the American people; in the twentieth century, they would do so again. For the remainder of the nineteenth century, however, that fateful link was broken. In addition, the focus of European colonial competition was shifting to Africa and Asia, and that diverted European attention from the Americas as well.

The United States and the Americas

While disengaging from Europe, the president and Congress fashioned new policies for Latin America that would guide the nation's hemispheric relations for years to come. Americans cheered when Spain and Portugal's Latin American colonies began their struggles for independence in 1808. Though some were skeptical that the racially mixed populations of Latin America, with their history of brutal colonialism, were capable of orderly self-government, it was flattering to have leaders such as Simón Bolívar hold the United States up as a model for Latin American liberation. North Americans, moreover, were happy to see European colonialism weakened and believed that independent nations in Latin America offered the promise of increased trade.

Both the president and Congress were initially reluctant to recognize the governments of Colombia, Mexico, Chile, and Argentina. In part, that reflected a fear of disrupting delicate efforts then under way to secure Florida from Spain. There was concern as well that the newly independent countries might attempt to form their own united confederacy. "In a single mass," the aged Jefferson mused, "they would be a very formidable neighbor." Far better if they remained separate nations, enabling the United States to act as a dominant, "balancing" power.

Eventually, President Monroe sent Congress a message proposing formal recognition of the new republics. Congress quickly agreed, and over the next several years the United States established diplomatic relations with seven Latin American nations.

Trouble arose, however, in November 1822, when the major European powers talked of helping Spain regain its American possessions. Such prospects alarmed Great Britain as well as the United States, and in August 1823, British Foreign Secretary George Canning broached the idea of Anglo-American cooperation to thwart Spain's intentions.

Secretary of State John Quincy Adams opposed the idea. Son of the former president, Adams had joined the Jeffersonian camp some years before as part of the continuing exodus from the Federalist party. Filled with nationalist fervor generated by the War of 1812 and suspicious, like his father, of British intentions, Adams declared that the United States would not "come in as a cockboat in the wake of the British man-of-war." He called instead for independent action based on two principles: a sharp separation between the Old World and the New, and U.S. dominance in the Western Hemisphere.

Monroe agreed that the United States should issue its own policy statement. In his annual message of December 1823, he outlined a new Latin American policy. Though known as the Monroe Doctrine, it was of Adams's devising.

The doctrine asserted four basic principles: (1) the American continents were closed to new European colonization, (2) the political systems of the Americas were separate from those of Europe, (3) the United States would consider as dangerous to its peace and safety any attempts to extend Europe's political influence into the Western Hemisphere, and (4) the United States would neither interfere with existing colonies in the New World nor meddle in European affairs.

Monroe's declaration had little immediate effect, for the United States possessed neither the economic nor the military power to enforce it. By the end of the nineteenth century, when the nation's might had increased, however, it would become clear what a fateful moment in the history of the Americas Monroe's declaration had been.

POLITICS IN TRANSITION

For two decades following the election of 1800, the Jeffersonian Republicans monopolized the presidency and dominated Congress. Though Federalists for a while kept up a drumfire of attack on their political opponents, including the charge published by a Federalist editor in 1803 that Jefferson had sired several children by his slave girl Sally Hemmings, the Federalist party gradually collapsed, its reputation soiled by charges of disloyalty during the War of 1812 and its "aristocratic" image. Even so, by the late 1820s the Jeffersonian ascendancy was at an end and the Federalist-Jeffersonian party system was in disarray.

As the old, gentry-based politics declined, a new, more democratic system emerged to take its place. The new politics appeared first in the states, for it was there that government acted decisively on people's lives, claimed their attention, and lured them in extraordinary numbers to the polls. It was there as well that vestiges of gentry elitism came under sharpest attack and assertions of political equality were most forcefully put forward. And it was in the states that a younger generation of political leaders, uninhibited by their elders' fears of "party faction," first learned how to create political parties capable of managing democratic electoral politics. By the end of the 1820s, America stood poised on the threshold of an entirely new political era.

Division Among the Jeffersonians

With the Federalists in disarray following the War of 1812, the Jeffersonian Republicans stood triumphant, their ranks swollen by fresh recruits in the East and the admission of new states in the West. The

Jeffersonians' success, however, proved their undoing, for no single party could contain the nation's swelling diversity of economic and social interests, its increasing sectional differences, or the personal ambitions of a new generation of political leaders.

In response to growing pressures from both West and Northeast, as well as to nationalist sentiment stimulated by the War of 1812, Madison's administration launched a Federalist-like program of national development. In March 1816, President Madison signed a bill creating a second Bank of the United States (the first bank's charter had expired in 1811), intended to stimulate economic expansion and regulate the loose currency-issuing practices of the country's countless state-chartered banks. At Madison's urging, the Congress also passed America's first protective tariff, a set of duties on imported woolen and cotton goods, iron, hats, and sugar.

The administration's program of national development drew sharp criticism from so-called Old Republicans, southern politicians who regarded themselves as guardians of the Jeffersonian conscience. Speaking in opposition to the bank bill in 1816, Congressman John Randolph of Virginia warned that "the question is whether . . . the state governments are to be swept away; or whether we . . . still . . . regard their integrity and preservation as part of our policy." Over the following decade, the Old Republicans continued to sound the alarm, even as their numbers dwindled.

Madison also recommended construction of a federally subsidized network of roads and canals to speed economic development and enhance national security. He counseled that a constitutional amendment authorizing such action should first be passed, but Representatives John Calhoun and Henry Clay, unwilling to delay, pushed an internal improvements bill through Congress. True to his principles, Madison vetoed the bill, temporarily stopping the project. Schemes for federal programs of national development, however, would not die. By the early 1820s, Clay and others, calling themselves National Republicans, were proposing an even more ambitious program of tariffs and internal improvements under the name the American System.

American Nationality and the Specter of Sectionalism

During the years of the early republic, sectional identities, deeply rooted in the long colonial experience, competed with an emerging sense of national identity for the loyalty of the American people. Among the circumstances strengthening American nationalism were the second War of Independence against England; the constitution uniting the 13 original states and promising to embrace America's expanding western empire; a shared English language and system of laws; the galvanizing experience of the Second Great Awakening that strengthened belief in America as God's chosen nation; and a rapidly expanding postal service that by 1830 was carrying nearly 14 million letters annually, a 136 percent increase since the new government began.

Shared rituals of patriotic celebration on occasions such as Washington's birthday and the Fourth of July helped unify the nation as well. Although Federalists and Jeffersonian-Republicans, northerners and southerners, black and white Americans competed to fill these celebratory occasions with political meaning, those very clashes revealed the sense of urgency with which all Americans sought to stake their claim to a common heritage. Moreover, the printed reports of local celebrations, carried throughout the land via the expanding circulation of newspapers, knitted communities together in a national conversation of patriotism.

Even as the construction of a shared national identity went forward, however, the Virginia and Kentucky Resolutions of the 1790s and Federalist talk of disunion during the War of 1812 revealed how fragile national unity continued to be. Though congressional

debates over the tariff, internal improvements, and the national bank echoed with sectional tensions, it was the Missouri crisis of 1819–1820 that jolted the nation's consciousness.

Ever since 1789, politicians had labored to keep the explosive issue of slavery tucked safely beneath the surface of political life, for they recognized how quickly it could jeopardize national unity. Their fears were borne out in 1819 when Missouri's application for admission to the Union raised anew the question of slavery's expansion. The Northwest Ordinance of 1787 had limited slavery north of the Ohio River while allowing its expansion to the south. But Congress had said nothing about slavery's place in the vast new territory west of the Mississippi River.

Seizing the opportunity to deal with that question, Senator Rufus King of New York demanded that Missouri prohibit slavery before entering the Union. His proposal triggered a fierce debate over Congress's authority to regulate the spread of slavery. Southerners were adamant that the trans-Mississippi West remain open to their slave property and were determined to maintain the Senate's equal balance between slave and free states. Already by 1819, the North's more rapidly growing population had given it a 105-to-81 advantage in the House of Representatives. Equality in the Senate

In the early republic, celebrations of Independence Day mingled military processions with patriotic displays and neighborhood conviviality. *(The Historical Society of Pennsylvania (HSP), "Fourth of July Celebration," India ink and watercolors on paper by Lewis Krimmel, Accession #Bc882K897)*

The House of Representatives, depicted in this 1821 painting by Samuel F. B. Morse, later inventor of the telegraph, rang with debate over the Missouri Compromise and other explosive issues. *(Samuel F. B. Morse,* The Old House of Representatives, *1882, 86½ x 130¾ in, oil on canvas. In the Collection of the Corcoran Gallery of Art, Washington, D.C., Museum Purchase, Gallery Fund 11.14)*

offered the only sure protection of southern interests. Northerners, however, vowed to keep the trans-Mississippi West open to free labor, which meant closing it to slavery.

For nearly three months, Congress debated the issue. During much of the time, free blacks, listening intently to northern antislavery speeches, filled the House gallery. "This momentous question," worried the aged Jefferson, "like a fire-bell in the night, [has] awakened and filled me with terror." Northerners were similarly alarmed. The Missouri question, declared the editor of the New York *Daily Advertiser,* "involves not only the future character of our nation, but the future weight and influence of the free states. If now lost—it is lost forever."

In the end, compromise prevailed. Missouri gained admission as a slave state, while Maine came in as a counterbalancing free state, and a line was drawn west from Missouri at latitude 36° 30' to the Rocky Mountains, dividing the lands that would be open to slavery from those that would not. For the moment, the issue had been put to rest. It would not be long, however, before the problem of slavery's expansion would set North and South even more violently against each other.

Collapse of the Federalist-Jeffersonian Party System

The final collapse of the Federalist-Jeffersonian system of politics was triggered by the presidential election of 1824. For the first time since 1800, when the "Virginia dynasty" of Jefferson, Madison, and

Monroe began, there was competition for the presidency from every major wing of the Jeffersonian party. Of the five candidates, John Quincy Adams of Massachusetts and Henry Clay of Kentucky advocated active federal programs of economic development. William Crawford of Georgia and Andrew Jackson of Tennessee clung to traditional Jeffersonian principles of limited government, agrarianism, and states' rights. In between stood John Calhoun of South Carolina, just beginning his fateful passage from nationalism to southern nullification.

Attracting limited support, Calhoun withdrew to become the vice-presidential partner of both Adams and Jackson. When none of the remaining candidates received an electoral majority, the election, as in 1800, moved into the House of Representatives. There, an alliance of Adams and Clay supporters gave the New Englander the election, even though he trailed Jackson in electoral votes, 84 to 99. The Jacksonians' charges of a "corrupt bargain" gained credence when Adams appointed Clay secretary of state.

Adams's ill-fated administration revealed the disarray in American politics. His stirring calls for federal road and canal building, standardization of weights and measures, establishment of a national university, and government support for science and the arts quickly fell victim to sectional conflicts, political factionalism, and his own open scorn for the increasingly democratic politics of the day. Against the urging of his political advisers, Adams declined an invitation from the Maryland Agricultural Society to attend its annual cattle show, explaining that the president

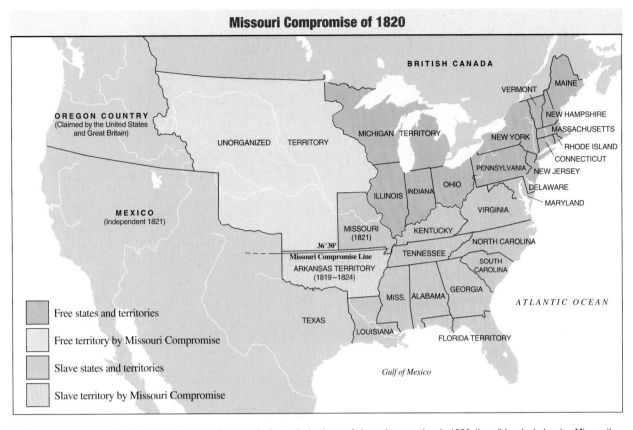

Missouri Compromise of 1820

Legend:
- Free states and territories
- Free territory by Missouri Compromise
- Slave states and territories
- Slave territory by Missouri Compromise

In the early nineteenth century, politicians struggled to contain the explosive issue of slavery's expansion. In 1820, they did so by balancing Missouri's admission as a slave state with Maine's as a free state and drawing the Missouri Compromise line, separating free territories from slave territories.

should stand above such efforts to court popular favor. In the increasingly raucous, democratic political climate of the 1820s, such an attitude amounted to political suicide. Within a year of his inauguration, Adams's administration had foundered. For the rest of his term, politicians jockeyed for position in the political realignment that was under way.

A New Style of Politics

At the same time, political energies continued to stir in the states, most dramatically in the surge of voter participation in state elections. Women, blacks, and Native Americans were still excluded, but white men flocked to the polls in unprecedented numbers. In the New Hampshire gubernatorial election of 1814, participation soared as high as 81 percent of eligible voters. On one occasion in Alabama, voter turnout topped 90 percent.

The flood of voters resulted in part from the removal of long-established, property-holding restrictions on the franchise. The constitutions of new states such as Indiana (1816), Illinois (1818), and Alabama (1819) provided for universal white, male suffrage. Older states such as Connecticut and New York abolished property requirements as well.

Voters' intensifying interest in politics was stimulated as well by the active role of state governments in their daily lives. While the domestic policies of the national government remained limited, state legislatures buzzed with activity over building highways, bridges, and ferries; regulating banks, lotteries, stray cattle, and insane asylums; enforcing Sunday blue laws and temperance; passing regulations providing consumer protection; and regulating relief for the poor. Electoral politics provided the essential connections between public demands and legislative behavior in the spirited civic arenas of the states.

Just as important was the emergence of a post-Revolutionary generation of political leaders—men such as Martin Van Buren of New York, Levi Woodbury of New Hampshire, and Lewis Cass of Ohio—ready to set aside old worries about "party faction" and eager to experiment with the techniques of mass, democratic politics. Even some of the younger Federalists, learning from the disastrous consequences of their elders' elitist behavior, changed their political ways. By the 1820s, successful politicians of every persuasion vied for voters' support through registration drives, party conventions, and popular campaigning.

Election days were often raucous affairs in the increasingly democratic, male-dominated politics of the early republic, as this Philadelphia scene (c. 1815) amply testifies. *(The Historical Society of Pennsylvania (HSP), India ink and watercolors on paper of* "Election Day at the State House, 1816" *by John Lewis Krimmel, Accession #Bc47K897)*

While the conduct of mass, democratic politics was first evident in the states where the new party machinery could be most easily developed, the election of Andrew Jackson to the presidency in 1828 would bring the techniques of mass politics to presidential electioneering as well. When that happened, American politics would change forever.

Timeline

1789	Knox's report on Indian affairs
1790s	Second Great Awakening begins
1794	Battle of Fallen Timbers
1795	Treaty of Greenville
1796	Congress establishes Indian Factory System
1800	Capital moves to Washington
1801	Thomas Jefferson elected president
	Judiciary Act
	New Land Act
1802	Judiciary Act repealed
1803	*Marbury* v. *Madison*
	Louisiana Purchase
1803–1806	Lewis and Clark expedition
1803–1812	Napoleonic wars resume
	British impress American sailors
1804	Jefferson reelected
1805–1807	Pike explores the West
1806	Non-Importation Act
1807	Embargo Act
	Chesapeake–Leopard affair
	Congress prohibits slave trade
1808	James Madison elected president
	Cherokee legal code established
1809	Tecumseh's confederacy formed

1811	Battle of Kithtippecanoe
1812	Madison reelected
	West Florida annexed
	War declared against Great Britain
1813	Battle of the Thames
1813–1814	Creek War
1814	Treaty of Ghent
	Battle of Horseshoe Bend
1814–1815	Hartford Convention
1815	Battle of New Orleans
	U.S. establishes military posts in trans-Mississippi West
1816	James Monroe elected president
	Second Bank of the United States chartered
1819	Adams–Onis Treaty with Spain
	Spain cedes East Florida to United States
	McCulloch v. *Maryland*
1819–1822	Bank panic and depression
1820	Missouri Compromise
1822	Diplomatic recognition of Latin American republics
1823	Monroe Doctrine proclaimed
1824	John Quincy Adams elected president
1827	Cherokee adopt written constitution

Conclusion
The Passing of an Era

During the first quarter of the nineteenth century, Americans reshaped the social, territorial, and political dimensions of their republic. Safely in control of the federal government, the Jeffersonians labored to set it on a new, more democratic course. In the process, they fashioned domestic policies designed to promote the country's agrarian expansion and foreign policies that transformed the nation's relations with Europe and the Americas. They also sought, less successfully, to reconcile Native American rights with national growth. By the end of the 1820s, an earlier system of politics divided between gentry domination in the Congress and popular politics in the states was in its final throes. In the years immediately ahead, its place would be taken by a new and dramatically different national system of democratic politics.

The events of the early republic testified to the strength, as well as limitations, of America's democratic faith. The nation's continuing task was to bring that faith into closer alignment with the lives of the American people.

During the decade of the 1820s, the American people turned from an earlier era of founding, when the national government was new and the outcome of the republican experiment uncertain, to a new era of national expansion. That transition was dramatized on July 4, 1826, the fiftieth anniversary of American independence, when two of the remaining revolutionary patriarchs, John Adams and Thomas Jefferson, died within a few hours of each other. "The sterling virtues of the Revolution are silently passing away," mused George McDuffie of South Carolina, "and the period is not distant when there will be no living monument to remind us of those glorious days of trial." As the anniversary celebrations ended and memories of the revolutionary founders died away, the American people had reason to ponder what the future would bring.

Recommended Reading

Restoring American Liberty

Noble Cunningham, *The Process of Government Under Jefferson* (1978); Joseph Ellis, *American Sphinx: The Character of Thomas Jefferson* (1997); Richard Ellis, *The Jeffersonian Crisis: Courts and Politics in the Young Republic* (1971); Annette Gordon-Reed, *Thomas Jefferson and Sally Hemmings: An American Controversy* (1997); Herbert Johnson, *The Chief Justiceship of John Marshall, 1801–1835* (1997); Merrill Peterson, *Thomas Jefferson and the New Nation* (1970); Francis Stites, *James Madison, Defender of the Constitution* (1981).

Building an Agrarian Nation

Lance Banning, *The Jeffersonian Persuasion: The Evolution of a Party Ideology* (1978); Donald Jackson, *Thomas Jefferson and the Stony Mountains: Exploring the American West from Monticello* (1981); Drew McCoy, *The Elusive Republic* (1980); James Ronda, *Lewis and Clark Among the Indians* (1984).

A Nation of Regions

Jeremy Atack and Fred Bateman, *To Their Own Soil: Agriculture in the Antebellum North* (1987); Jeanne Boydston, *Home and Work: Housework, Wages, and the Ideology of Labor in the Early Republic* (1990); Stephen Hahn and Jonathan Prude, *The Countryside in the Age of Capitalist Transformation* (1985); James Lemon, *The Best Poor Man's Country* (1972); Howard Rock et al., *American Artisans: Crafting Social Identity* (1995); Daniel Vickers, *Farmers and Fishermen: Two Centuries of Work in Essex County, Massachusetts, 1630–1850* (1994).

Robert Doherty, *Society and Power: Five New England Towns, 1800–1860* (1977); Richard Wade, *The Urban Frontier: The Rise of Western Cities, 1790–1830* (1959).

Daniel Dupre, *Transforming the Cotton Frontier: Madison County, Alabama, 1800–1840* (1997); Allan Kulikoff, *The Agrarian Origins of American Capitalism* (1992).

Michael Allen, *Western Rivermen, 1763–1861* (1990); Andrew R. L. Cayton and Fredrika Teute, eds., *Contact Points: American Frontiers from the Mohawk Valley to the Mississippi, 1750–1830* (1998); William C. David, *A Way Through the Wilderness: The Natchez Trace and the Civilizing of the Southern Frontier* (1995); John Mack Farragher, *Daniel Boone: The Life and Legend of an American Pioneer* (1992); Robert Mitchell, ed., *Appalachian Frontiers: Settlement, Society, and Development in the Preindustrial Era* (1991); Malcolm Rohrbough, *The Trans-Appalachian Frontier* (1978).

Indian–White Relations in the Early Republic

Gregory Dowd, *Spirited Resistance: The North American Indian Struggle for Unity, 1745–1815* (1992); R. David Edmunds, *Tecumseh and the Quest for Indian Leadership* (1984); William McLaughlin, *Cherokee Renascence in the New Republic* (1986); Theda Perdue, *Cherokee Women: Gender and Culture Change, 1700–1835* (1998); Francis Paul Prucha, *American Indian Policy in the Formative Years* (1970); Bernard Sheehan, *Seeds of Extinction: Jeffersonian Philanthropy and the American Indian* (1973); Wiley Sword, *President Washington's Indian War, 1790–1795* (1985); Richard White, *The Middle Ground: Indians, Empires, and Republics in the Great Lakes Region, 1650–1815* (1991).

Perfecting a Democratic Society

Paul Conkin, *Cane Ridge: American Pentacost* (1990); Nathan Hatch, *The Democratization of American Christianity* (1989); Jean Mathews, *Toward a New Society: American Thought and Culture, 1800–1830* (1990); Randolph Roth, *The Democratic Dilemma: Religion, Reform, and the Social Order in the Connecticut River Valley of Vermont, 1791–1850* (1987); John Wigger, *Taking Heaven by Storm: Methodism and the Rise of Popular Christianity in America* (1998).

Robert Cray, Jr., *Paupers and Poor Relief in New York City and Its Rural Environs, 1700–1830* (1988); Michael Meranze, *Laboratories of Virtue: Punishment, Revolution, and Authority in Philadelphia, 1760–1835* (1996); Conrad Wright, *The*

Transformation of Charity in Post-Revolutionary New England (1992).

Norma Basch, *Framing American Divorce: From the Revolutionary Generation to the Victorians* (1999); Lee Chambers-Schiller, *Liberty, A Better Husband* (1984); Nancy Cott, *The Bonds of Womanhood: "Women's Sphere" in New England, 1780–1835* (1977); Cathy Davidson, *Revolution and the Word: The Rise of the Novel in America* (1986); Joan Jensen, *Loosening the Bonds: Mid-Atlantic Farm Women, 1750–1850* (1986); Susan Juster, *Disorderly Women: Sexual Politics and Evangelicalism in Revolutionary New England* (1994); Mark Kann, *A Republic of Men: The American Founders, Gendered Language, and Patriotic Politics* (1998); Cynthia Kierner, *Beyond the Household: Women's Place in the Early South, 1700–1835* (1998).

Sylvia Frey and Betty Wood, *Come Shouting to Zion: African-American Protestantism in the American South and British Caribbean to 1830* (1998); Kimberly Hanger, *Bounded Lives, Bounded Places: Free Black Society in New Orleans, 1769–1803* (1997); Joanne Pope Melish, *Disowning Slavery: Gradual Emancipation and "Race" in New England, 1780–1860* (1998); Gary B. Nash, *Forging Freedom: The Formation of Philadelphia's Black Community, 1720–1840* (1988); James Sidbury, *Plowshares into Swords: Race, Rebellion, and Identity in Gabriel's Virginia, 1730–1810* (1997); T. Stephen Whitman, *The Price of Freedom: Slavery and Manumission in Baltimore and Early National Maryland* (1997).

A Foreign Policy for the New Nation

Lawrence Kaplan, *"Entangling Alliances With None": American Foreign Policy in the Age of Jefferson* (1987); James Lewis, Jr., *The American Union and the Problem of Neighborhood: The United States and the Collapse of the Spanish Empire, 1783–1829* (1998); Ernest May, *The Making of the Monroe Doctrine* (1975); Robert Rutland, *The Presidency of James Madison* (1990); David C. Skaggs and Gerard Altoff, *A Signal Victory: The Lake Erie Campaign, 1812–1813* (1997); Burton Spivak, *Jefferson's English Crisis: Commerce, Embargo, and the Republican Revolution* (1974); J. C. A. Stagg, *Mr. Madison's War* (1983).

Politics in Transition

Andrew Cayton, *The Frontier Republic: Ideology and Politics in the Ohio Country, 1780–1825* (1986); Donald Cole, *Martin Van Buren and the American Political System* (1984); Evan Cornog, *The Birth of Empire: DeWitt Clinton and the American Experience, 1769–1828* (1998); Richard John, *Spreading the News: The American Postal System from Franklin to Morse* (1995); David Konig, ed., *Devising Liberty: Preserving and Creating Freedom in the New American Republic* (1995); Drew McCoy, *The Last of the Fathers: James Madison and the Republican Legacy* (1989); Paul Nagel, *John Quincy Adams: A Public Life, A Private Life* (1997); Ronald Schultz, *The Republic of Labor: Philadelphia Artisans and the Politics of Class, 1720–1830* (1993); Alan Taylor, *William Cooper's Town: Power and Persuasion on the Frontier in the Early American Republic* (1995); Len Travers, *Celebrating the Fourth: Independence Day and the Rites of Nationalism in the Early Republic* (1997); David Waldstreicher, *In the Midst of Perpetual Fetes: The Making of American Nationalism, 1776–1820* (1997); Steven Watts, *The Republic Reborn: War and the Making of Liberal America, 1790–1820* (1987).

Fiction and Film

Scandalmonger (2000), a novel by the *New York Times* columnist William Safire, describes personal intrigue within high political circles in the early republic. *Tecumseh: The Last Warrior* (1995), a made-for-television historical drama, offers an imaginative rendering of the Shawnee leader who sought to unite tribes north and south of the Ohio River against invading white settlers in the early nineteenth century. *Lewis and Clark: The Journey of the Corps of Discovery* (1997), a PBS documentary by Ken Burns, tells the story of this path-breaking expedition and reveals the dramatic landscape through which it passed.

In the classic American novel *Rip Van Winkle* (1829), Washington Irving explores the transiency of historical memory via the story of an eighteenth-century New Yorker who mysteriously falls asleep during the American Revolution and awakes decades later to find his community radically changed and himself the object of intense curiosity.

Suggested Web Sites

http://www.lcweb.loc.gov/exhibits/us.capitol/s0.html

Temple of Liberty—Building the Capitol for a New Nation. Compiled from holdings in the Library of Congress, this site contains detailed information on the design and early construction of the capitol building in Washington, D.C.

http://etext.virginia.edu/jefferson/

Thomas Jefferson Online Resources at the University of Virginia. Mr. Jefferson's University—the University of Virginia—houses this site, with numerous resources about Jefferson and his times.

http://www.syracuse.com/features/eriecanal

Erie Canal Online. This site, built around the diary of a fourteen-year-old girl who travelled from Amsterdam to Syracuse, New York, in the early nineteenth century, explores the construction and importance of the Erie Canal.

http://www.pbs.org/lewisandclark/

PBS Online—Lewis and Clark. This is a companion site to Ken Burns's site, containing a timeline of the expedition, a collection of related links, a bibliography, and over eight hundred minutes of unedited, full-length RealPlayer interviews with seven experts featured in the film.

http://www.indianapolis.in.us/cp/stories.html

Prairietown Stories. This fictional model of a town (Prairietown, Indiana) and its inhabitants on the early frontier says much about America's movement westward and the everyday lives of Americans.

http://members.tripod.com/~war1812/index.html

War of 1812–1814. This site offers in-depth and varied information about the War of 1812.

http://www.seminoletribe.com/

Indians—Seminole Tribe of Florida. This site is dedicated to the rich history and culture of the Seminole, a tribe against which Andrew Jackson began a war before he was president.

http://www.ushistoryplace.com

 A richly detailed on-line learning environment complete with interactive maps, timelines, history activities, primary source documents, and links to related American history sites.

10

CURRENTS *of* CHANGE *in the* NORTHEAST *and the* OLD NORTHWEST

For her first 18 years, Susan Warner was little touched by the far-reaching economic and social changes that were transforming the character of the country and her own city of New York. Whereas some New Yorkers toiled to make a living by taking in piecework and others responded to unsettling new means of producing goods by joining trade unions to agitate for wages that would enable them to "live as comfortable as others," Susan was surrounded by luxuries and privilege. Much of the year was spent in the family's townhouse in St. Mark's Place, not far from the home of the enormously rich real estate investor and fur trader John Jacob Astor. There Susan acquired the social graces and skills appropriate for a girl of her position and background. She had dancing and singing lessons, studied Italian and French, and learned the etiquette involved in receiving visitors and making calls. When hot weather made life in New York unpleasant, the Warners escaped to the cooler airs of Canaan, where they had a summer house. Like any girl of her social class, Susan realized that her carefree existence could not last forever. With her marriage, which she confidently expected some time in the future, would come significant new responsibilities as a wife and mother but not the end of the comfortable life to which she was accustomed.

It was not marriage and motherhood that disrupted the pattern of Susan's life but financial disaster. Sheltered as she had been from the unsettling economic and social changes of the early nineteenth century, Susan discovered that she, too, was at the mercy of forces beyond her control. Her father, heretofore so successful a provider and parent, lost most of his fortune during the financial Panic of 1837. Like others experiencing a sharp economic reversal, the Warners had to make radical adjustments. The fashionable home in St. Mark's Place and the pleasures of New York were exchanged for a more modest existence on an island in the Hudson River. Susan turned "housekeeper" and learned how to do tasks once relegated to others: sewing and making butter, pudding sauces, and johnny cake.

The change of residence and Susan's attempt to master domestic skills did not halt the family's financial decline. Prized possessions, including the

This picture of an 1845 fair suggests the cornucopia of goods made available in the early stages of industrialization. *(B. J. Harrison,* Fair of the American Institute at Niblo's Garden, *1845/Museum of the City of New York)*

piano and engravings, all symbols of the life the Warners had once taken for granted, eventually went up for auction. "When at last the men and the confusion were gone," Susan's younger sister, Anna, recalled, "then we woke up to life."

Waking up to life meant facing the necessity of making money. But what could Susan do to reverse sliding family fortunes? True, some women labored as factory operatives, domestics, seamstresses, or schoolteachers, but it was doubtful Susan could even imagine herself in any of these occupations. Her Aunt Fanny, however, had a suggestion that was more congenial to the genteel young woman. Knowing that the steam-powered printing press had revolutionized the publishing world and created a mass readership, much of it female, Aunt Fanny told her niece, "Sue, I believe if you would try, you could write a story." "Whether she added 'that . . . would sell,' I am not sure," recalled Anna later, "but of course that was what she meant."

Taking Aunt Fanny's advice to heart, Susan started to write a novel that would sell. She constructed her story around the trials of a young orphan girl, Ellen Montgomery. As Ellen suffered one reverse after another, she learned the lessons that allowed her to survive and eventually triumph over adversity: piety, self-denial, discipline, and the power of a mother's love. Entitled *The Wide, Wide World,* the novel was accepted for publication only after the mother of the publisher, George Putnam, read it and told her son, "If you never publish another book, you must make *The Wide, Wide World* available for your fellow men." A modest 750 copies were printed. Much to the surprise of the cautious Putnam, if not to his mother, 13 editions were published within two years. *The Wide, Wide World* became the first American novel to sell more than a million copies. It was one of the best-sellers of the century.

Long before she realized the book's success, Susan, now much aware of the need to make money, was working on a new story. Drawing on her own experience of economic and social reversal, Susan described the spiritual and intellectual life of a young girl thrust into poverty after an early life of luxury in New York. Entitled *Queechy,* this novel was also a great success.

Though her fame as a writer made Susan Warner unusual, her books' popularity suggested how well they spoke to the concerns and interests of a broad readership. The background of social and financial uncertainty, with its sudden changes of fortune, so prominent in several of the novels, captured the reality and fears of a fluid society in the process of transformation. While one French writer was amazed that "in America a three-volume novel is devoted to the history of the moral progress of a girl of thirteen," pious heroines like Ellen Montgomery, who struggled to master their passions and urges toward independence, were shining exemplars of the new norms for middle-class women. Their successful efforts to mold themselves heartened readers who believed that the future of the nation depended on virtuous mothers and who struggled to live up to new ideals. Susan's novels validated their efforts and spoke to the importance of the domestic sphere. "I feel strongly impelled to pour out to you my most heartful thanks," wrote one woman. None of the other leading writers of the day had been able to minister "to the highest and noblest feelings of my nature *so much as yourself.*"

Susan Warner's life and her novels serve as an introduction to the far-reaching changes that this chapter explores. Between 1820 and 1860, as Susan Warner discovered, economic transformations in the Northeast and the Old Northwest reshaped economic, social, cultural, and political life. Though most Americans still lived in rural settings rather than in factory towns or cities, economic growth and the new industrial mode of production affected them through the creation of new goods, opportunities, and markets. In urban communities and factory towns, the new economic order ushered in new forms of work, new class arrangements, and new forms of social strife.

After discussing the factors that fueled antebellum growth, the chapter turns to the industrial world, where so many of the new patterns of work and life appeared. An investigation of urbanization reveals shifting class arrangements and values as well as rising social and racial tensions. Finally, an examination of rural communities in the East and on the frontier in the Old Northwest highlights the transformation of these two sections of the country. Between 1840 and 1860, industrialization and economic growth increasingly knit them together.

ECONOMIC GROWTH

Between 1820 and 1860, the American economy entered a new and more complex stage of development as it moved away from its reliance on agriculture as the major source of growth toward an industrial and technological future. In this period of general national expansion, real per capita output grew an average of 2 percent annually between 1820 and 1840 and slightly less between 1840 and 1860. This doubling of per capita income over a 40-year period suggests that many Americans were enjoying a rising standard of living.

Though expanding, the economy was also unstable, as the Warners discovered so dramatically. Periods of boom (1822–1834, mid-1840s–1850s) alternated with periods of bust (1816–1821, 1837–1843). As never before, Americans faced dramatic and recurrent shifts in the availability of jobs and goods and in prices and wages. Particularly at risk were working-class Americans, a third of whom lost their jobs during years of depression. Moreover, because regional economies were increasingly linked, problems in one area tended to affect conditions in others.

Factors Fueling Economic Development

What accounted for this new phase of growth and economic development? As the table nearby suggests, the abundance of natural resources and an expanding population provided the raw materials and the human brawn and brains that supported growth and transformation. Because the size of American families gradually shrank—in 1800, the average white woman bore seven children; by 1860, the number had declined to five—immigration from Europe (discussed in detail later in the chapter) played an important part in providing the new workers, new households, and new consumers so essential to economic development as well as the capital and technological ideas that helped to shape American growth.

Improved transportation played a key role in bringing about economic and geographic expansion. Early in the century, high freight rates discouraged production for distant markets and the exploitation of resources, and primitive transportation hindered western settlement. As one disgruntled Senate committee pointed out, "A coal mine may exist in the United States not more than ten miles from valuable ores of iron and other materials, and both of them be useless . . . as the price of land carriage is too great to be borne by either." During the 1820s and 1830s, however, canal-building projects dramatically transformed this situation. The 363-mile-long Erie Canal, the last link in a chain of waterways binding New York City to the Great Lakes and the Northwest, was the most impressive of these new canals. The volume of goods and people it carried at low cost, the economic advantages it conferred on those within its reach (suggested by both the figure on inland freight rates and the table on economic growth) prompted the construction of over 3,000 miles of canals by 1840, primarily in eastern and midwestern states.

SIGNIFICANT FACTORS PROMOTING ECONOMIC GROWTH, 1820–1860

Factor	Important Features	Contribution to Growth
Abundant natural resources	Acquisition of new territories (Louisiana Purchase, Florida, trans-Mississippi West); exploitation and discovery of eastern resources	Provided raw materials and energy vital to economic transformation
Substantial population growth	Increase from 9 million in 1820 to over 30 million in 1860—due to natural increase of population and, especially after 1840, to rising immigration; importance of immigration from Ireland, Germany	Provided workers and consumers necessary for economic growth; immigration increased diversity of workforce with complex results, among them supply of capital and technological know-how
Transportation revolution	Improvement of roads; extensive canal building, 1817–1837; increasing importance of railroad construction thereafter; by 1860, 30,000 miles of tracks; steamboats facilitate travel on water	Facilitated movement of peoples, goods, and information; drew people into national economy market; stimulated agricultural expansion, regional crop specialization; decreased costs of shipping goods; strengthened ties between Northeast and Midwest
Capital investment	Investments by European investors and U.S. interests; importance of mercantile capital and banks, insurance companies in funneling capital to economic enterprises	Provided capital to support variety of new economic enterprises, improvements in transportation
Government support	Local, state, and national legislation; loans favoring enterprise; judicial decisions	Provided capital, privileges, and supportive climate for economic enterprises
Industrialization	New methods of producing goods, with and without involvement of machinery	Produced more numerous, cheaper goods for mass market; transformed classes and nature of work; affected distribution of wealth and individual opportunity

Even at the height of the canal boom, politicians, promoters, and others, impressed with Britain's success with railways, also supported the construction of railroads. Railroads, unlike canals that might freeze during the winter, were capable of operating year-round. Nor did they need large amounts of water to operate, as canals did. They could be built almost anywhere, an advantage that encouraged Baltimore merchants, envious of New York's water link to the Northwest, to begin the Baltimore & Ohio Railroad in 1828.

Despite the interest in and advantages of railroads, there were technical problems to resolve; for example, the first trains jumped their tracks and spewed sparks, setting nearby fields ablaze. But such difficulties were quickly overcome. By 1840, there were 3,000 miles of track, most in the Northeast. Another 5,000 miles were laid during the 1840s, and by the end of the 1850s, total mileage soared to 30,000. Like the canals, the new railroads strengthened the links between the Old Northwest and the East.

Improved transportation had such a profound influence on American life that some historians use the term *transportation revolution* to refer to its impact. Canals and railroads bound the country together in a new way. They provided farmers, merchants, and manufacturers with cheap and reliable access to distant markets and goods and encouraged Americans to settle the frontier and cultivate virgin lands. The economic opportunities they opened fostered technological innovations that might increase production. Eventually, the strong economic and social ties the waterways and then the railways fostered between the Northwest and the East led people living in the two regions to share political outlooks.

Especially in terms of the pattern of western settlement, railroads exerted enormous influence. As the railroads followed—or led—settlers westward, their routes could determine whether a city, town, or even homestead survived. The railroad transformed Chicago from a small settlement into a bustling commercial and transportation center. In 1850, the city contained not one mile of track, but within five years, 2,200 miles of track serving 150,000 square miles terminated in Chicago.

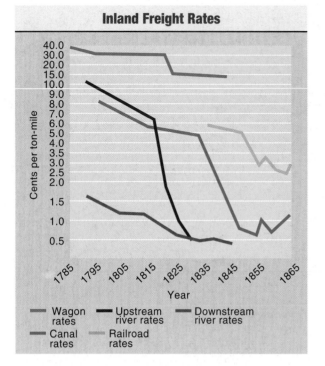

Inland Freight Rates

Cents per ton-mile

40.0
30.0
20.0
15.0
10.0
9.0
8.0
7.0
6.0
5.0
4.0
3.5
3.0
2.5
2.0

1.5

1.0

0.5

1785 1795 1805 1815 1825 1835 1845 1855 1865
Year

— Wagon rates   ▬ Upstream river rates   — Downstream river rates
— Canal rates   — Railroad rates

As this chart makes dramatically clear, the transportation revolution had a tremendous impact on the cost of shipping goods and materials to markets and factories.

The dramatic rise in railroad construction in the two decades before the Civil War contributed to faster economic growth after 1839. Goods, people, commercial information, and mail flowed ever more predictably, rapidly, and cheaply. In 1790, an order from Boston took two weeks to reach Philadelphia; in 1836, it took only 36 hours.

Improved transportation stimulated agricultural expansion and regional specialization. Farmers began to plant larger crops for the market, concentrating on those most suited to their soil and climate. By the late 1830s, the Old Northwest had become the country's granary, and New England farmers turned to dairy or produce farming. By 1860, American farmers were producing four to five times as much wheat, corn, cattle, and hogs as they had in 1810. Their achievements meant plentiful, cheap food for American workers and more income for farmers to spend on the new consumer goods.

Capital and Government Support

Internal improvements, the exploitation of natural resources, and the cultivation of new lands all demanded capital. Much of it came from European investors. Between 1790 and 1861, over $500 million

This view of the junction of the Erie and Champlain Canals around 1830 suggests the ambitious construction efforts that lay behind the improvement of transportation. The Erie Canal stretched for 363 miles and was the last link in a chain of waterways connecting New York to the Great Lakes and the Northwest. Irish immigrants who flooded into the country during the antebellum period provided the muscle power for building the Erie Canal and worked on many other transportation projects. One of the laborers' songs captures the pride and magnitude of "such a great undertaking. . . . To dig through the vallies so level, through rocks for to cut a canal." *(© Collection of the New-York Historical Society)*

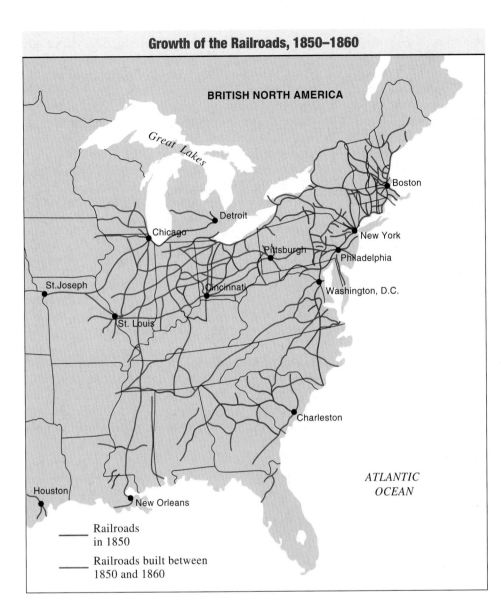

Growth of the Railroads, 1850–1860

BRITISH NORTH AMERICA

Great Lakes

Boston

Detroit

Chicago

New York

Pittsburgh

Philadelphia

St. Joseph

Cincinnati

Washington, D.C.

St. Louis

Charleston

ATLANTIC OCEAN

Houston

New Orleans

_____ Railroads in 1850

_____ Railroads built between 1850 and 1860

This map shows the tremendous surge of railroad building between 1850 and 1860 and the ways the railroad strengthened the ties between the Northeast and the Midwest. Notice that the railroad has crossed the Mississippi River. Because of the transportation revolution, almost the entire area east of the Mississippi was within a week's journey of New York City by 1860.

flowed into the United States from Europe. Foreign investors from Europe, adding to funds brought by immigrant families, financed as much as a third of all canal construction and bought about a quarter of all railroad bonds.

American mercantile capital fueled growth as well. As Chapter 9 suggested, the merchant class prospered in the half century after the Revolution. Now merchants invested in schemes ranging from canals to textile factories. Many ventured into the production of goods and became manufacturers themselves.

Prosperous Americans, like Arthur Bronson and Charles Butler, eagerly sought opportunities to put their capital to work. Intrigued by the Northwest's investment possibilities, the two New Yorkers toured the region in 1833. Despite primitive conditions, both men saw wonderful opportunities. Detroit, Butler concluded, "is destined to be a very great city," and

Chicago "presents one of the finest fields in America for industry & enterprise." Each man channeled funds into western projects. Bronson's investments included Ohio banks; farmland in Wisconsin territory, Illinois, Michigan, Ohio, and Indiana; and real estate in Chicago and Detroit, all in addition to his holdings in New York ironworks and banks.

Bronson's investment in banks indicated his understanding of their role in stimulating economic growth. He also actively promoted life insurance companies, which, unlike commercial banks, lent money on a long-term basis. These financial institutions, he realized, served as intermediaries, funneling into economic enterprises the capital of people with neither the time nor the expertise to invest their money themselves.

Local and state government played their part by enthusiastically supporting economic growth. States often helped new ventures raise capital by passing laws of incorporation, by awarding entrepreneurs special privileges such as tax breaks or monopolistic control, by underwriting bonds for improvement projects, which increased their investment appeal, and by providing loans for internal improvements. New York, Pennsylvania, Ohio, Indiana, Illinois, and Virginia publicly financed almost 75 percent of the canal systems in their states between 1815 and 1860.

The national government also encouraged economic expansion by cooperating with states on some internal improvements, such as the National Road linking Maryland and Illinois. Federal tariff policy shielded American products, and the second U.S. Bank provided the financial stability investors required. So widespread was the enthusiasm for growth that the line separating the public sector from the private often became unclear.

The law also helped promote aggressive economic growth. Judicial decisions created a new understanding of property rights. The case of *Palmer* v. *Mulligan,* decided by the New York State Supreme Court in 1805, laid down the principle that property ownership included the right to develop property for business purposes. Land was increasingly defined as a productive asset for exploitation, not merely subsistence, as earlier judicial rulings had suggested.

Investors and business operators alike wanted to increase predictability in the conduct of business. Contracts lay at the heart of commercial relationships, but contract law hardly existed in 1800. A period of rapid development ensued. A series of important Supreme Court decisions between 1819 and 1824 established the basic principle that contracts were binding. In *Dartmouth College* v. *Woodward,* the Court held that a state charter could not be modified unless both parties agreed, and it declared in *Sturges* v. *Crowninshield* that a New York law allowing debtors to repudiate their debts was unconstitutional.

A New Mentality

As the discussion of the links between law and economic growth suggests, economic expansion depends on intangible factors as well as more obvious ones such as improved transportation. When a farmer decided to specialize in apples for the New York market rather than to concentrate on raising food for his family, he was thinking in a new way just as was Arthur Bronson when he invested in banks that would, in turn, finance a variety of economic enterprises. The entrepreneurial outlook, the *"universal desire,"* as one newspaper editor put it, *"to get forward,"* was shared by millions of Americans. By encouraging investment, new business and agricultural ventures, and land speculation, entrepreneuri-

alism played a vital role in antebellum economic development.

Europeans often recognized another intangible factor when they described Americans as energetic and open to change. As one Frenchman explained in 1834, "All here is circulation, motion, and boiling agitation. Experiment follows experiment; enterprise succeeds to enterprise." An American observer agreed. "Every man seems born with some steam engine within him, driving him into an incessant and restless activity of body and mind . . . every head and every hand busy, with a thousand projects, and only one holiday—the 4th of July—working from morning till night with the most intense industry."

Others described an American mechanical "genius." The American was "a mechanic by nature," one Frenchman insisted. "In Massachusetts and Connecticut, there is not a labourer who had not invented a machine or tool." This observer exaggerated the uniqueness of American inventiveness. Many American innovations drew on British precedents and were introduced by immigrants well acquainted with the British originals. Nor was every ordinary laborer an inventor. Many of the changes that improved efficiency came from machinists as they made adjustments to British equipment or tinkered with malfunctioning mill machines to get them back in working order. But every invention and improvement attracted scores of imitators. In 1854, the government patent office issued 56 patents for harvesting implements and 39 for seed planters; the next year, it issued 40 for sewing machines.

Mechanically minded Americans prided themselves on developing efficient and productive tools and machines. The McCormick harvester was the product of two generations of the McCormick family who dreamed of replacing scythes and sickles with a horsedrawn reaping machine and worked for years to realize that dream. Like the McCormicks, John Jervis experimented for years to modify the heavy rigid English railroad engine into a lighter, more flexible engine suited to American conditions. The Colt revolver, Goodyear vulcanized rubber products, and the sewing machine were developed, refined, and developed further. Such improvements cut labor costs and increased efficiency. By 1840, the average American cotton textile mill was about 10 percent more efficient and 3 percent more profitable than its British counterpart.

Although the shortage of labor in the United States stimulated technological innovations that replaced humans with machines, the rapid spread of education after 1800 also contributed to innovation and increased productivity. By 1840, most whites were literate. In that year, public schools nationwide were

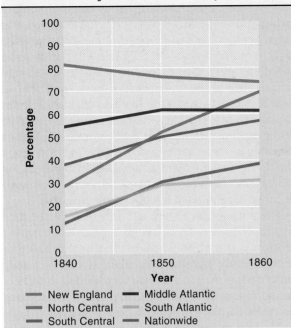

White Secondary School Enrollment, 1840–1860*

Legend:
— New England
— North Central
— South Central
— Middle Atlantic
— South Atlantic
— Nationwide

*Note the regional difference in school enrollment and changes over time. Source: Albert W. Niemi, *U.S. Economic History* (1975).

educating 38.4 percent of white children between the ages of five and nineteen. The belief that education spurred economic growth helped foster enthusiasm for public education, particularly in the Northeast. The development of the Massachusetts common school illustrates the connections many saw between education and progress.

Although several states had decided to use tax monies for education by 1800, Massachusetts moved first toward mass education by mandating in 1827 that taxes pay the whole cost of the state's public schools. Several years later, the state set up a permanent elementary education fund and in 1836 forbade factory managers to hire children who had not spent three of the previous twelve months in school. Despite the legislation, the Massachusetts school system limped along. School buildings were often run-down, even unheated. Because school curricula were virtually nonexistent, students often lounged idly at their desks.

Under the leadership of Horace Mann, the reform of state education for white children began in earnest in 1837. Mann intended to regularize the operation of schools and attract more students to them. He and others pressed for graded schools, uniform curricula, and teacher training. Believing that the power of local districts over their schools presented a barrier against improvement, he sought to reduce local control. Mann's success

inspired reformers everywhere. For the first time in American history, primary education became the rule for most children outside the South between five and nineteen. The expansion of education created a whole new career of schoolteaching, a career that attracted mostly young women.

Mann believed that education promoted inventiveness. It "had a market value." Businessmen often agreed. Prominent industrialists in the 1840s were convinced that education produced workers who could handle complex machinery without undue supervision and were superior employees—reliable, punctual, industrious, and sober. Manufacturers valued education not merely because of its intellectual content but also because it encouraged habits essential to a disciplined and productive workforce.

Ambivalence Toward Change

While supporting education as a means to economic growth, many Americans also firmly believed in its social value. They expected the public schools to mold student character and promote "virtuous habits" and "rational self-governing" behavior. Many school activities sought to instill good habits. Students learned facts by rote because memory work and recitation taught them discipline and concentration. Nineteenth-century schoolbooks reinforced classroom goals. "It is a great sin to be idle," children read in one 1830 text, and another encouragingly pointed out, "He who rises early and is industrious and temperate will acquire health and riches." A third warned of the consequences of ignoring the message: "Poverty is the fruit of idleness."

The concern with education and character indicates that as much as Americans welcomed economic progress, they also feared its results. The much-heralded improvements in transportation that encouraged trade and emigration, for example, created anxieties that civilization might disintegrate as people moved far from their place of birth and from familiar institutions. Others worried that rapid change undermined the American family and would turn children into barbarians. Schools, which taught students to be deferential, obedient, and punctual, could counter the worst by-products of change. The schools served as much as a defense against change as they did its agent. Fear and confidence were two sides of the coin of economic transformation.

Other signs of cultural uneasiness appeared. In the eighteenth century, Benjamin Franklin emphasized the importance of hard work in his celebrated *Poor Richard's Almanack*. In the 1830s, popularizers restated Franklin's message. As the publishing revolution lowered costs and speeded the production of printed material, these authors poured out tracts, stories, and

This photograph of the Emerson School for Young Ladies was taken sometime between 1840 and 1862. An examination of the way the classroom was organized—the relative position of students and teacher and the prominent role of the clock—begins to suggest the emphasis schools placed on obedience, deference, order, and punctuality. The varied clothing of the students also highlights the impact of the manufacturing revolution on everyday life. *(The Metropolitan Museum of Art, Gift of I. N. Phelps Stokes, Edward S. Hawes, Alice Mary Hawes, Marion Augusta Hawes, 1937)*

manuals on how to get ahead. Claiming that hard work and good character led to success, they touted the virtues of diligence, punctuality, temperance, and thrift. These habits probably did assist economic growth. Slothful workers are seldom productive. Industry and perseverance often pay off. But the success of early nineteenth-century economic ventures frequently depended on the ability to take risks, to think daringly. The emphasis these publicists gave to the safe but stolid virtues and to responsible behavior suggests their fear of social disintegration. Their books and tracts aimed to counter unsettling effects of change and ensure the dominance of middle-class values.

The Advance of Industrialization

Significant economic growth between 1820 and 1860 resulted from the reorganization of production. Before industrialization, individual artisans fashioned goods with hand tools. Many American families also fabricated necessary articles; as late as 1820, Americans made two-thirds of all their clothes at home.

Factory production moved away from this decentralized system of artisan or family-based manufacturing and reorganized work by breaking down the manufacture of an article into discrete steps. Initially, early manufacturers often relied on what came to be called the "putting-out" system. Their strategy was to gain control of the raw materials from which goods were fashioned—leather in the case of shoes; cotton, flax, and wool for textiles—and arrangements for marketing the finished products. Some steps in the manufacturing process they farmed out to workers in shops and homes, paying them on a piecework basis, for the pieces they were able to "put out." Other steps manufacturers consolidated in their own central shops.

The putting-out system not only reorganized production but also entangled rural families in the market economy and affected their relationships to one another. Early pieceworkers might labor as a family unit, leaving men to exercise their power as fathers and husbands. But by the 1830s, men were moving into the workplace while wives and daughters continued to take in piecework. Unless they were driven by poverty, the women usually worked only intermittently. They took in shoes or made palm-leaf hats to pay off a family debt or to earn some cash for a desirable new good like cotton cloth or an iron cook stove. While most outworkers were not highly paid, they enjoyed earning their own cash and store credit. Piecework provided them with a new kind of independence even as they continued to stay at home.

The putting-out system persisted even as some manufacturers moved to consolidate all the steps of production under one roof. Hand labor gradually gave way to power-driven machinery such as wooden "spinning jennies." Often manufacturers sought the help of British immigrants who had the practical experience and technical know-how that few Americans possessed.

In 1789, William Ashley and Moses Brown, Rhode Island merchants, hired 21-year-old Samuel Slater, a former apprentice with an English cotton textile firm, to devise a water-powered, yarn-spinning machine. Slater did that, but he also developed a machine capable of carding, or straightening, the cotton fibers. Within a year, Ashley and Brown's spinning mill had begun operations in Pawtucket, Rhode Island. Its initial workforce consisted of nine children, ranging in age from seven to twelve. Ten years later, their number had grown to over 100. As factory workers replaced artisans and home manufacturers, the volume of goods rose, and prices dropped dramatically. The price of a yard of cotton cloth fell from 18 to 2 cents over the 45 years preceding the Civil War.

The transportation improvements that provided the opportunity to reach large markets after 1820

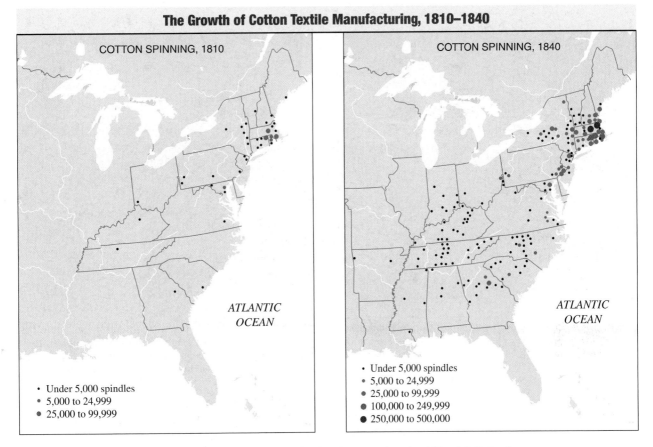

The Growth of Cotton Textile Manufacturing, 1810–1840

COTTON SPINNING, 1810

ATLANTIC OCEAN

- Under 5,000 spindles
- 5,000 to 24,999
- 25,000 to 99,999

COTTON SPINNING, 1840

ATLANTIC OCEAN

- Under 5,000 spindles
- 5,000 to 24,999
- 25,000 to 99,999
- 100,000 to 249,999
- 250,000 to 500,000

The concentration of textile manufacturing in New England suggests the changing economic and social trends in that region.

encouraged the reorganization of the production process and the use of machinery. The simple tastes and rural character of the American people suggested the wisdom of manufacturing inexpensive everyday goods like cloth and shoes rather than luxuries for the rich.

Between 1820 and 1860, textile manufacturing became the country's leading industry. Textile mills sprang up across the New England and Middle Atlantic states, regions that contained swift-flowing streams to power the mills, capitalists eager to finance the ventures, children and women to tend the machines, and numerous cities and towns with ready markets for cheap textiles. Early mills were small affairs, containing only the machines for carding and spinning. The thread was then put out to home workers to be woven into cloth. The early mechanization of cloth production did not replace home manufacture but supplemented it.

Already under way, however, were experiments that would further transform the industry. Closeted in the attic of a Boston house in 1813, Francis Cabot Lowell, a merchant, and Paul Moody, a mechanic, worked to devise a power loom capable of weaving cloth. Lowell's study of mechanical looms during his earlier

tour of English and Scottish cotton factories guided their work. Eventually, they succeeded, and the loom they devised was soon installed in a mill at Waltham, Massachusetts, capitalized at $300,000 by Lowell and his Boston Associates.

The most important innovation of the Waltham operation was Lowell's decision to bring all the steps of cotton cloth production together under one roof. The Waltham mill thus differed from mills in Rhode Island and Great Britain, where spinning and weaving were separate operations. Through this centralizing of the entire manufacturing process and workforce in one factory, cloth for the mass market could be produced more cheaply and more profitably. The work of maintaining the equipment in good order encouraged machinists to improve upon existing machines. Constant innovation thus helped mills to make cloth ever more cheaply and quickly. In 1823, the Boston Associates expanded their operations to East Chelmsford on the Merrimack River, a town they renamed Lowell.

Most New England mills followed the Lowell system. In the Middle Atlantic states, the textile industry was more varied. Philadelphia became a center for fine textiles, and Rhode Island factories produced less

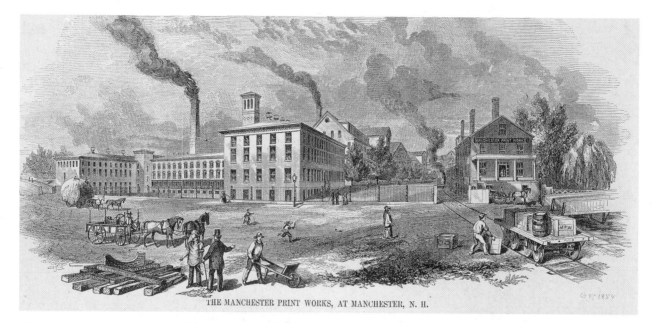

THE MANCHESTER PRINT WORKS, AT MANCHESTER, N. H.

Gleason's Pictorial, one of the many modestly priced publications that the introduction of steam-powered printing presses put within reach of the reading public, pictures the Manchester Print Works in New Hampshire in 1854. Although the smokestacks spewing forth black clouds of smoke hint at the pollution that accompanied the Industrial Revolution, nineteenth-century viewers most likely were impressed by the dignified mill building and the seemingly spacious surroundings. Men appear in the foreground, but over half the workers in this calico factory were female. *(Library of Congress)*

expensive materials. Maryland manufacturers, like those in Philadelphia, focused on quality goods. The cumulative impact of the rise of the textile industry was to supplant the home production of cloth, even though some women would continue to spin and weave for their families for some years to come, and hand-loom weavers would survive for another generation. In the process, Americans were transformed from a people clad in earth-colored homespun into a nation decked out in gayer, more colorful clothing.

Textile mills were an important component of the increasingly industrial character of the Northeast. The majority of the South's cotton still went to England, but an increasing share flowed to northeastern mills. Other manufacturing concerns, such as shoemaking, also contributed to the Northeast's economy. By 1860, fully 71 percent of all manufacturing workers lived in this region of the country. Still other important manufacturing operations reached west and south from New England. The processing of wheat, timber, and hides using power-driven machinery was common in most communities of 200 families or more. Although a third of them were clustered in Philadelphia, paper mills were widespread. The ironworking and metalworking industry stretched from Albany, New York, south to Maryland and west to Cincinnati.

Environmental Consequences

Although canals, railroads, steamboats, and the growth of industry undergirded economic growth,

their impact on the environment was far-reaching and often harmful. Steamboats and early railroads, for example, depended on wood for fuel. So, too, did the heating stoves that were keeping American families warm. Armed with new steel axes, lumbermen and farmers kept up with the increased demand for wood, and the eastern forest and the wildlife that lived there rapidly disappeared. Better transportation, which encouraged western settlement, also promoted forest clearance as individual settlers cleared land for crops and cut wood for housing. Sawmills and milldams interfered with spawning habits of fish, clogged their gills with sawdust, and even changed the flow of rivers. The process of ecological change, spurred by the desire for wood, recurred as lumber companies and entrepreneurs moved from the East to exploit the forests of the Great Lakes and of the Gulf states.

As late as 1840, wood was the main source for the country's energy needs. But the high price of wood and the discovery of anthracite coal in Pennsylvania signaled the beginning of a shift to coal as the major source of power. While the East gradually regained some of its forest cover, the heavy use of coal resulted in air pollution. Steam engines and heating stoves poured out dirty fumes into the air. In New York City, one could see the evidence of pollution everywhere— in the gray cloud hanging over the city; in the smoke rising from its machine shops, refineries, and private houses; in the acrid smells and black soot that were a part of daily life. Pittsburgh, considered by some the dirtiest city in the United States, was surrounded by "a dense black smoke" and rained down "flakes of soot" on houses and people alike.

Textile mills located along rivers and streams might present a prettier picture than the shops and refineries of New York because they used water as the source of power. But mills also adversely affected the environment. Dams and canals supporting industrial activities contributed to soil erosion. "Industrial operations," declared the Vermont fish commissioner in 1857, are "destructive to fish that live or spawn in fresh water. . . . The thousand deleterious mineral substances, discharged into rivers from metallurgical, chemical, and manufacturing establishments, poison them by shoals."

Some Americans were aware of the environmental consequences of rapid growth and change. Author James Fenimore Cooper had one of his characters in his novel *The Pioneers* condemn those who destroyed nature "without remorse and without shame." The popularity in the 1820s of a song with the lines "Woodman, / Spare that Tree / Touch not a single bough" suggested sympathy for that point of view. Yet most Americans accepted the changing environment as an inevitable part of progress.

ꙮ EARLY MANUFACTURING

Industrialization created a more efficient means of producing more goods at much lower cost than had been possible in the homes and small shops of an earlier day. Philadelphian Samuel Breck's diary reveals some of the new profusion and range of goods. "Went to town principally to see the Exhibition of American Manufactures at the Masonic Hall," he noted in 1833. "More than 700 articles have been sent. Among this great variety, I distinguished the Philadelphia porcelains, beautiful Canton cotton, made at York in this state, soft and capacious blankets, silver plate, cabinet ware, marble mantels, splendid pianos and centre tables, chymical drugs, hardware, saddlery, and the most beautiful black broadcloth I ever saw."

The Impact of Industrialization

Two examples illustrate how industrialization transformed American life in both simple and complex ways. Before the nineteenth century, local printing shops depended on manual labor to produce books, newspapers, and journals. The cost of reading material was high enough to make a library a sign of wealth. Many literate families of moderate means had little in their homes to read other than a family Bible and an almanac.

Between 1830 and 1850, however, adoption and improvement of British inventions revolutionized the printing and publishing industries. Like other changes in production, the transformation of publishing involved not only technological but also managerial and marketing innovations. A $2.5 million market in 1830, the book business quintupled by 1850.

As books and magazines dropped in cost and grew in number, far more people could afford them. Without this new mass market of readers, Susan Warner's literary success would hardly have been possible. But the implications of the changes in publishing went beyond best-sellers. The presence of inexpensive reading material inspired and nourished literacy. Easy access to reading material also encouraged a new sort of independence. No longer needing to rely solely on the words of the "better sort" for information, people could form their own views on the basis of what they read. At the same time, however, readers everywhere were exposed repeatedly to the mainstream norms, values, and ideas expressed in magazines and books. Even on the frontier, pioneer women could study inexpensive ladies' magazines and books of domestic advice or be inspired by the pious example of Ellen Montgomery in *The Wide, Wide World*. Their husbands could follow the latest political news, market prices, or theories about scientific farming while the children learned their letters and the moral lesson in McGuffey readers. The proliferation of printed matter had an enormous impact on people's stock of information, values, tastes, and use of leisure time.

Just as printed materials wrought great changes in American life, the making of inexpensive timepieces affected its pace and rhythms. Before the 1830s, when few Americans could afford a clock, it was difficult to make exact plans or to establish rigid schedules. But the production of timepieces soared in the 1830s, and by mid-century, peddlers had carried inexpensive mass-produced wooden clocks everywhere. Even on the frontier, "in Kentucky, in Indiana, in Illinois, in Missouri, and here in every dell in Arkansas, and in cabins where there was not a chair to sit on," according to one observer, "there was sure to be a Connecticut clock." Free of nature's irregular divisions of the day, Americans could decide how to use their time and coordinate their activities. Clocks encouraged a more disciplined use of time and undergirded the economic changes taking place. Timepieces, for example, were essential for the successful operation of steamboats and railroads, which ran on schedules.

Clocks also imposed a new rhythm in many workplaces. For some Americans, the clock represented a form of oppression rather than liberation. An early mill song put it directly: "The factory bell begins to

This simple thirty-hour clock was the result of successful technological innovations by Eli Terry. As a boy, when Terry learned the trade, each clock was made by hand and was far too expensive for ordinary people to purchase. Terry experimented with replacing brass parts with wooden ones and developed machinery capable of mass producing clocks with the assistance of unskilled workers. His modestly priced timepieces, carried by peddlers into the countryside, helped to transform the ways Americans contemplated and used their time. *(National Museum of American History, Smithsonian Institution)*

ring / And we must all obey, / And to our old employment go / Or else be turned away."

🖝 A NEW ENGLAND TEXTILE TOWN

The process of industrialization and its impact on work and the workforce are ably illustrated by Lowell, the "model" Massachusetts textile town, and Cincinnati, a bustling midwestern industrial center. Though there were similarities between the process of industrialization in these two communities, significant differences also existed. The example of Lowell points out the importance of women in the early manufacturing workforce, whereas Cincinnati shows that industrialization was often an uneven and complex process.

Lowell was a new town, planned and built expressly for industrial purposes in the 1820s. Planners gave most attention to the shops, mills, and workers' housing, but the bustling town had a charm that prompted visitors to see it as a model factory community. In 1836, Lowell, with 17,000 inhabitants, aspired to become the "Manchester of America." It was the country's most important textile center.

By 1830, women composed nearly 70 percent of the Lowell textile workforce, with men and children filling the remaining positions. The women who came to Lowell for jobs were the first women to labor outside their homes in large numbers. Some had already labored for wages by taking in piecework. Now they became some of the first Americans to experience the full impact of the factory system.

Lowell's planners realized the difficulty of persuading men to leave farming for millwork, but saw that they might recruit unmarried women relatively cheaply for a stint. Unlike mill owners farther south, they decided not to depend on child labor. By hiring women who would work only until marriage, they hoped to avoid the depraved and depressed workforce so evident in Great Britain. New England factory communities, they hoped, because of their special arrangements, would become models for the world.

Working and Living in a Mill Town

At the age of 15, Mary Paul wrote to her father asking him "to consent to let me go to Lowell if you can." This young woman from Vermont was typical of those drawn to work in Lowell and other New England textile towns. As the planners had anticipated, the bulk of the workforce was made up of young unmarried women. In 1830, more than 63 percent of Lowell's population was female, and most were between the ages of 15 and 29.

These women, from New England's middling rural families, came to the mills for a variety of reasons, but desperate poverty was not one of them. The decline of home manufacture deprived many women, especially daughters in farming families, of their traditional productive role. Some rural young women took in piecework to replace or supplement regular chores. Millwork offered them more money than piecework and the possibility of independence. As Sally Rice from Vermont explained, "I am almost nineteen years old. I must of course have something of my own before many more years have passed over my head.

This recruiting poster, if read carefully, reveals the ways young women were brought to the mills and the conditions of their employment. What might a young woman find attractive about millwork if she read this poster? Are there any statements that might make her reluctant to work in the mills? *(Courtesy of Baker Library, Harvard Graduate School of Business Administration, Boston, Mass.)*

And where is that something coming from if I go home and earn nothing." Millwork paid women relatively well in the 1820s and 1830s. Domestic servants' weekly wages hovered around 75¢, and seamstresses' 90¢, whereas in the mid-1830s women could make between $2.40 and $3.20 a week in the mill. The lure of the "privileges" of the new environment also drew young women to Lowell.

Few considered their decision to come to Lowell a permanent commitment. Most young women were like Mary Paul and Sally Rice. They came to work for a few years, felt free to go home or to school for a few months, and then returned to millwork. Once married—and the majority of women did marry—they left the millwork force forever.

New manufacturing work was regimented and exhausting. The day began at dawn or even earlier and ended about 7 in the evening. The standard schedule was 12 hours a day, six days a week, with only a half-hour for breakfast and lunch. The clock tower atop the attractive four- to six-story brick mills symbolized the new control of work.

Within the factory, the organization of space facilitated production. In the basement was the waterwheel, the source of power. Above, successive floors were completely open, each containing the machines necessary for the different steps of cloth making: carding, spinning, weaving, and dressing. Elevators moved materials from one floor to another. On a typical floor, rows of machines stretched the length of the low room, tended by operatives who might watch over several machines at the same time. From his elevated

This depiction of Lowell workers, engraved in the 1850s by the American Banknote company, shows neatly dressed young women carefully tending to their machines. Their concentration on their task suggests that they had to pay close attention to their repetitive work. The engraving gives little idea of the tedium, noise, and other difficulties of millwork that the young women often mentioned in their letters. *(Print Collection, Miriam and Ira D. Wallach Division of Art, Prints and Photographs, The New York Public Library, Astor, Lenox and Tilden Foundations)*

desk at the end of the room, the overseer watched the workers. The male supervisor and two or three children roamed the aisles to survey the work and to help out. The rooms were noisy, poorly lit, and badly ventilated. Overseers, believing that humidity would prevent threads from breaking, often nailed the windows shut.

Although machines, not operatives, did the basic work of production, workers had to ensure that their machines worked properly. The lowest-paid women workers who watched over the spinning frames and drawing frames were responsible for piecing together broken yarn once the machines had automatically halted. The better-paid weavers made skillful interventions in the production process, repairing warp yarns and rapidly replacing shuttle bobbins when they ran out of yarn so that production would slow down for only a moment. "I can see myself now," recalled Harriet Robbins, "racing down the alley, between the spinning frames, carrying in front of me a bobbin-box bigger than I was . . . so as not to keep the spinning-frames stopped long."

Involving an adaptation to a new work situation, millwork also entailed a new living situation for women operatives. The companies provided substantial quarters for their overseers and housing for male workers and their families. Hoping to attract respectable females to Lowell and to avoid the kind of slums found in English industrial cities, the mill owners constructed company boardinghouses for women workers. Headed by female housekeepers, the boardinghouse maintained strict rules, including a 10 o'clock curfew. Owners wanted a respectable and well-rested work force. Little personal privacy was possible. Normally, four or six women shared a small room, which contained little more than the double beds in which they slept together.

Amid such intimate working and living conditions, young women formed close ties with one another and developed a strong sense of community. Strong group norms dictated acceptable behavior, clothing, and speech and shared leisure activities at lectures, night classes, sewing and literary circles, and church. At work, experienced operatives initiated newcomers into the mysteries of tending machines, stood in for each other, and shared work assignments.

Female Responses to Work

Although millwork offered better wages than other occupations open to women, all female workers had limited job mobility. The small number staying in the mills for more than a few years did receive increases in pay and promotions to more responsible positions. A top female wage earner took home 40 percent more

than a newcomer. But she never could earn as much as male employees, who at the top of the job ladder earned 200 percent more than men at the bottom. Because only men could hold supervisory positions, economic and job discrimination were an integral part of the early American industrial system.

Job discrimination generally went unquestioned, for most female operatives accepted sexual differences as part of life. But the sense of sisterhood, so much a part of the Lowell work experience, supported open protest, most of it focused against a system that workers feared was turning them into a class of dependent wage earners. Lowell women's critique of the new industrial order drew on both the sense of female community and the revolutionary tradition.

Trouble broke out when hard times hit Lowell in February 1834. Falling prices, poor sales, and rising inventories prompted managers to announce a 15 percent wage cut. This was their way of protecting profits—at the expense of their employees. The mill-workers sprang into action. Petitions circulated, threatening a strike. Meetings followed. At one lunchtime gathering, the company agent, hoping to end the protests, fired an apparent ringleader. But, as the agent reported, "she declared that every girl in the room should leave with her," then "made a signal, and . . . they all marched out & few returned the ensuing morning." The strikers roamed the streets appealing to other workers and visited other mills. In all, about a sixth of the town's workforce turned out.

Though this work stoppage was brief and failed to prevent the wage reduction, it demonstrated women workers' concern about the impact of industrialization on the labor force. Strikers, taunted as unfeminine for their "amazonian display," refused to agree that workers were inferior to bosses. Pointing out that they were daughters of free men, strikers, as the words of their song suggest, sought to link their protest to their fathers' and grandfathers' efforts to throw off the bonds of British oppression during the Revolution.

> Let oppression shrug her shoulders,
> And a haughty tyrant frown,
> And little upstart Ignorance,
> In mockery look down.
> Yet I value not the feeble threats
> Of Tories in disguise,
> While the flag of Independence
> O'er our noble nation flies.

The women viewed threatened wage reductions as an unjust attack on their economic independence and also on their claim to equal status with their employers. Revolutionary rhetoric that once held only political meaning took on economic overtones as Lowell women confronted industrial work.

During the 1830s, wage cuts, long hours, increased workloads, and production speedups, mandated by owners' desires to protect profits, constantly reminded Lowell women and other textile workers of the possibility of "wage slavery." In Dover, New Hampshire, 800 women turned out and formed a union in 1834 to protest wage cuts. In the 1840s, women in several New England states agitated for the ten-hour day, and petitions from Lowell prompted the Massachusetts legislature to hold the first government hearing on industrial working conditions.

The Changing Character of the Workforce

Most protest efforts met with limited success. The short tenure of most women millworkers prevented permanent labor organizations. Protests mounted in hard times often failed because mill owners could easily replace striking workers. Increasingly, owners found that they could do without the Yankee women altogether. The waves of immigration that deposited so many penniless foreigners in northeastern cities in the 1840s and 1850s created a new pool of labor. The newcomers were desperate for jobs and would accept lower wages than New England farm girls. Gradually, the Irish began to replace Yankee women in the mills. Representing only 8 percent of the Lowell workforce in 1845, the Irish composed nearly half the workers by 1860.

As the example of Lowell suggests, the reality of massive immigration had a far-reaching effect on American life in the antebellum period. Immigration, of course, had been a constant part of the country's experience from the early seventeenth century. But it occurred on an unprecedented scale after 1845, the nearby figure makes clear. What had been a trickle in the 1820s—some 128,502 foreigners came to U.S. shores during that decade—became a torrent in the 1850s, with more than 2.8 million migrants to the United States. Although families and single women emigrated, the majority of the newcomers were young European men of working age.

This vast movement of people, which began in the 1840s and continued throughout the nineteenth century, resulted from dramatic changes in European life: a population explosion between 1750 and 1845 and the introduction of new farming and industrial practices that undermined or ended traditional means of livelihood. Agricultural disaster also played a major role in uprooting the Irish from their homeland. Potatoes were the staple of the Irish diet. In 1845, a terrible blight attacked and destroyed the potato crop. Years of devastating famine followed. One million Irish starved to death between 1841 and 1851; another million and a half emigrated. Although not all chose the United States as their destination, the Irish were the most numerous of all newcomers to America in the two decades preceding the Civil War. They usually arrived almost penniless in eastern port cities without the skills needed for good jobs. With only their raw labor to sell, employers, as one observer noted, "will engage Paddy as they would a dray horse."

German immigrants, who made up the second largest group of newcomers during this period (1,361,506 arrived between 1840 and 1859), were not driven to the United States by the kind of desperate circumstances forcing the Irish to leave their homeland. Some even arrived with sufficient resources to go west and buy land. (The significance of this German midwestern presence is suggested by the fact that as late as 1940, German was one of the most common "street" languages in Minnesota.) Others had the training to join the urban working class as shoemakers, cabinetmakers, and tailors.

The arrival of so many non-British newcomers made American society more diverse than it had ever been. The consequences of this diversity were complex, as discussions in this and subsequent chapters will make clear. Because over half of the Irish and German immigrants were Roman Catholics, a religion long feared and disliked by Protestants, religious differences acerbated economic and ethnic tensions.

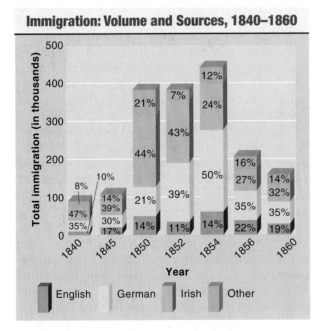

Immigration: Volume and Sources, 1840–1860

This chart captures the growing ethnic diversity of the country in the years before the Civil War. What is only implied is the element of religious diversity that immigration also introduced. Most of the Irish immigrants and half of the Germans were Roman Catholics. The presence of immigrants who differed so dramatically from Protestant Americans in background and culture contributed to the tensions of the period.

The impact of the Irish presence in Lowell was far-reaching. As the ethnic makeup of the workforce changed in the city, so did its gender composition. More men came to work in the mills. By 1860, some 30 percent of the Lowell workers were male. All these changes made the Yankee women expendable and increased the costs of going "against the mill."

It was easy for New England women to blame the Irish for declining pay and deteriorating conditions. Gender no longer unified women workers, not only because there were more men in the mills but also because Irish women and New England women had little in common. The Irish mill girl who started working as early as age 13 to earn money for her family's survival had a different perspective on work than the older Yankee woman who was earning money for herself. Segregated living conditions further divided the workforce and undermined the likelihood of united worker actions in the 1850s.

Lowell itself changed as the Irish crowded into the city and New England women gradually left the mills. With owners no longer feeling the need to continue paternalistic practices, boardinghouses disappeared. A permanent workforce, once a nightmare to owners, had become a reality by 1860, and Lowell's reputation as a model factory town faded away.

Factories on the Frontier

Cincinnati, a small Ohio River settlement of 2,540 in 1810, grew to be the country's third-largest industrial center by 1840. With a population of 40,382, it contained a variety of industries at different stages of development. Cincinnati manufacturers who turned out machines, machine parts, hardware, and furniture were quick to mechanize for increased volume and profits. Other trades like carriage making and cigar making moved far more slowly toward mechanization

before 1860. Alongside these concerns, artisans like coopers, blacksmiths, and riverboat builders still labored in small shops, using traditional hand tools. The new and the old ways coexisted in Cincinnati, as they did in most manufacturing communities.

No uniform work experience prevailed in Cincinnati. The size of the shop, the nature of work, the skills required, and the rewards all varied widely. In 1850, most Cincinnati workers worked in small or medium-sized shops, but almost 20 percent labored in factories with over 100 employees. Some craftsmen continued to use a wide array of skills as they produced goods in time-honored ways. Others used their skills in new factories, but they tended to focus on more specialized and limited tasks. In furniture factories, for example, machines did the rough work of cutting, boring, and planing, while some artisans worked exclusively as varnishers, others as carpenters, and still others as finishers. No single worker made a chair from start to finish. But all used some of their skills and earned steady wages. Though in the long run, machines threatened to replace them, these skilled factory workers often had reason in the short run to praise the factory's opportunities.

Less fortunate was the new class of unskilled factory laborers who performed limited operations at their jobs either with or without the assistance of machinery. In the meatpacking industry, for example, workers sat at long tables. Some cleaned the ears of the hogs, others scraped the bristles, others had the unenviable task of gutting the dead animals. Whereas owners in the industry profited from efficient new operations, workers received low wages and had little job security. Because they had no skills to sell, they were easily replaced and casually dismissed during business slowdowns.

The experience of Cincinnati's working women differed from that of their male counterparts. Cincinnati's large black community was so economically marginal that a majority of black women labored as washerwomen, cooks, or maids. Many white women were earning money as "outworkers" for the city's growing ready-to-wear clothing industry. Manufacturers purchased the cloth, cut it into basic patterns, and then contracted the work out to be finished by the women in small workshops or at home. Like many other urban women, Cincinnati women sought employment of this kind because they could not count on their husbands or fathers earning enough to support the family and because outwork allowed them to labor at home. Middle-class domestic ideology prescribed that home was the proper sphere for women, not the workplace. Many working men supported these views because they feared female labor would undercut their wages and destroy order in

CHANGING OCCUPATIONAL DISTRIBUTION, 1820–1860*			
	1820	**1840**	**1860**
Agriculture	78.8%	63.1%	52.9%
Mining	0.4	0.6	1.6
Construction	—	5.1	4.7
Manufacturing	2.7	8.8	13.8
Trade	—	6.2	8.0
Transport	1.6	1.8	2.0
Service	4.1	5.0	6.4
Other	12.4	9.4	10.6

*The decline of agriculture and the increased involvement in industrial pursuits are represented in this table.

Source: U.S. Bureau of the Census.

In 1848, an unknown photographer took this picture of Cincinnati. The prominence of steamboats in the picture suggests the role that location and improvements in transportation played in the city's growth. Although the countryside is visible in the background, the rows of substantial commercial and industrial buildings make Cincinnati's status as a bustling urban center clear. *(Public Library of Cincinnati and Hamilton County, Ohio)*

the family. Outwork, then, allowed poor married women to supplement their family income while honoring social norms.

Paid by the piece, female outworkers were among the most exploited of Cincinnati's workers. Long days spent sewing in darkened rooms not only often failed to bring an adequate financial reward but also led to health problems—ruined eyes and curved spines.

The successful marketing of sewing machines in the 1850s contributed to worsening working conditions and lower pay. The sewing machine made stitching easier, so the pool of potential workers increased and the volume of work that bosses expected grew. As tasks were further subdivided, work also became more monotonous. As one Cincinnati citizen observed, "As many as 17 hands" were employed on a single pair of pants.

Cincinnati employers claimed that the new industrial order offered great opportunities to most of the city's male citizens. Manufacturing work encouraged the "manly virtues" so necessary to the "republican citizen." Not all Cincinnati workers agreed. Like workers in Lowell and other manufacturing communities, Cincinnati's laborers rose up against their bosses in the decades before the Civil War.

The workingman's plight, as Cincinnati labor leaders analyzed it, stemmed from his loss of independence. Even though a manufacturing job provided a decent livelihood for some people, the new industrial order was changing the nature of the laboring class itself. A new kind of worker had emerged. Rather than selling the products of his skills, he had only his raw labor to sell. His "wage slavery," or dependence on wages, promised to be lifelong. The reorganization of work signaled the end of the progression from apprentice to journeyman to master and undermined traditional skills. Few workers could expect to rise to the position of independent craftsman. Most would labor only for others, just as slaves labored for their masters. Nor would wages bring to most that other form of independence, the ownership of shop and home. The expression "wage slavery" contained a deep truth about the changed conditions of many American workingmen.

Workers also resented the masters' attempts to control their lives. In the new factories, owners insisted on a steady pace of work and uninterrupted production. Artisans who were used to working in spurts, stopping for a few moments of conversation or a drink, disliked the new routines. Those who took a dram or two at work found themselves discharged. Even outside the workplace, manufacturers attacked Cincinnati's working-class culture. Crusades to abolish volunteer fire companies and to close down saloons, both attacked as nonproductive activities, suggested how little equality the Cincinnati worker enjoyed in an industrializing society.

The fact that workers' wages in Cincinnati, as in other cities, rose more slowly than food and housing costs compounded discontent over changing working conditions. The working class sensed it was losing ground at the very time the city's rich were visibly growing richer. In 1817, the top tenth of the city's taxpayers owned over half the wealth, whereas the bottom half possessed only 10 percent. In 1860, the share of the top tenth had increased to two-thirds, while the bottom half's share had shrunk to 2.4 percent. Cincinnati workers may not have known these exact percentages, but they could see growing social and economic inequality in the luxurious mansions the city's rich were building and in the spreading blight of slums.

In the decades before the Civil War, Cincinnati workers formed unions, turned out for fair wages, and rallied in favor of the ten-hour day. Like the Lowell mill girls, they cloaked their protest with the mantle of the Revolution. Striking workers staged parades with fifes and drums and appropriated patriotic symbols to bolster their demands for justice and independence. Although they did not see their bosses as a separate or hostile class, labor activists insisted that masters were denying workers a fair share of profits. This unjust distribution doomed them to economic dependency. Because the republic depended on a free and independent citizenry, the male workers warned that their bosses' policies threatened to undermine the republic itself.

Only in the early 1850s did Cincinnati workers begin to suspect that their employers formed a distinct class of parasitic "nonproducers." Although most strikes still revolved around familiar issues of better hours and wages, signs appeared of the more hostile labor relations that would emerge after the Civil War.

As elsewhere, skilled workers were in the forefront of Cincinnati's labor protest and union activities. But their victories proved temporary. Depression and bad times always harmed labor organizations and canceled out employers' concessions. Furthermore, Cincinnati workers did not readily unite to protest new conditions. The uneven pace of industrialization meant that these workers, unlike the Lowell mill women, had no common working experience. Moreover, growing cultural, religious, and ethnic diversity compounded differences in the workplace. By 1850, almost half the people in the city were foreign-born, most of them German, whereas only 22 percent had been in 1825.

As the heterogeneity of the American people increased, ethnic and religious tensions simmered.

Immigrants, near the bottom of the occupational ladder, faced limited job choices and suspicion of their faith, habits, and culture. Protestant workers frequently felt that they had more in common with their Protestant bosses than with Catholic Irish or German fellow workers. These tensions exploded in Cincinnati in the spring of 1855. Americans attacked barricades erected in German neighborhoods, crying out death threats. Their wrath visited the Irish as well. Ethnic, cultural, and social differences often drove workers apart and concealed their common grievances. In many cases, disunity served economic progress by undermining workers' efforts for higher pay, shorter hours, and better working conditions, thus enabling businesses to maximize productivity and profits while minimizing the cost of labor.

URBAN LIFE

Americans experienced the impact of economic growth most dramatically in the cities. In the four decades before the Civil War, the rate of urbanization in the United States was faster than ever before or since. In 1820, about 9 percent of the American people lived in cities (defined as areas containing a population of 2,500 or more). Forty years later, almost 20 percent of them did. Older cities like Philadelphia and New York mushroomed, while new cities like Cincinnati, Columbus, and Chicago sprang up "as if by enchantment." Although urban growth was not confined to the East, it was most dramatic there. By 1860, more than a third of the people living in the Northeast were urban residents, compared with only 14 percent of westerners and 7 percent of southerners. Although the majority of northerners still lived on farms or in small farm towns, the region was clearly urbanizing.

The Process of Urbanization

Three distinct types of cities—commercial centers, mill towns, and transportation hubs—emerged during these years of rapid economic growth. Although the lack of water power limited industrial development, commercial seaports like Boston, Philadelphia, and Baltimore expanded steadily and developed diversified manufacturing to supplement the older functions of importing, exporting, and providing services and credit. New York replaced Philadelphia as the country's largest and most important city. The completion of the Erie Canal allowed New York merchants to gain control of much of the trade with the West. By 1840, they had also seized the largest share of the country's import and export trade.

Access to water power fueled the development of a second kind of city, exemplified by Lowell,

The balloon frame, the most important technological improvement in building in the years before the Civil War, allowed the rapid construction of housing in new and old sections of the country. First introduced in 1839 in Chicago, the balloon frame was made of small, light, mill-cut pieces of lumber joined by factory-produced nails. Unlike the older forms of building construction that had used heavy timbers joined by hand-made pegs and mortise-and-tenon joints, balloon frames were easy to put together and demanded only a few workers. Since this construction is still used today, you have probably seen examples of the balloon frame. (*Engraving by W. W. Wilson, From Edward Shaw,* The Modern Architect, *1855, Constructing a Balloon Frame House, The Metropolitan Museum of Art, Harris Brisbane Dick Fund, 1934. [34.46.9])*

Massachusetts; Trenton, New Jersey; and Wilmington, Delaware. Situated inland along the waterfalls and rapids that provided the power to run their mills, these cities burgeoned, as American industry, especially the production of textiles, expanded in the decades before the Civil War.

Between 1820 and 1840, one-quarter of the increase in urban population occurred west of the Appalachian Mountains, where a third type of city arose. Louisville, Cleveland, and St. Louis were typical of cities that had served as transportation service and distribution centers from the earliest days of frontier settlement. Chicago acted as "grand depot, exchange, counting-house, and metropolis" for its hinterlands. Like most of these western cities, Chicago was a commercial rather than an industrial center. In the 1850s, selling lumber to prairie farmers who needed it for fences and housing was one of Chicago's most significant commercial activities.

As the number of urban dwellers grew, their needs helped generate economic growth. City dwellers rarely had gardens or animals, so they had to purchase their food. This encouraged farmers to turn to commercial farming. Cities also provided a growing market for other products, including shoes, clothing, furniture, and carriages. The iron industry sold more than a half million cast-iron stoves yearly, mainly to city dwellers, and city governments purchased cast-iron pipes for sewers and the water supply and city merchants erected cast-iron buildings.

Until 1840, the people eagerly crowding into cities came mostly from the American countryside. Then ships began to spill their human cargoes into seaboard cities, and a growing number of immigrants began their lives anew in the United States. Immigrants who could afford to leave the crowded port cities for the interior, many of them Germans and Scandinavians, did so. But the penniless had little choice but to remain in eastern cities and search for work there. By 1860, fully 20 percent of the people living in the Northeast were immigrants; in some of the largest cities, they and their children made up more than half the population. The Irish, fleeing famine and poverty at home, were the largest foreign group in the Northeast.

A look at Philadelphia reveals the character, rhythms, rewards, and tensions of urban life during the antebellum period. The city was one of the giants of the age. An inland port, a bustling mercantile city, a center of shops producing textiles, metals, and a host of other products, Philadelphia stood second only to New York. Though William Penn's "green country town" boasted an attractive appearance and an orderly plan, the expanding nineteenth-century city merited little praise. Speculators interested only in profit relied on the grid pattern as the cheapest and most efficient way to divide land for development. They built monotonous miles of new streets, new houses, new alleys, with "not a single acre left for public use, either for pleasure or health," as merchant Samuel Breck observed.

A few cities, like New York and Boston, did lay aside areas where residents could escape from the noises, sights, and smells of urban life. Frederick Law Olmsted and Calvert Vaux designed New York's picturesque Central Park, adorning it with grass, trees, and tranquil lakes. Olmsted envisioned the park as a place where all classes of New Yorkers could come together to enjoy themselves in a "quiet and orderly" manner. As with so much else of urban life, however, it was mainly the middle and upper classes who had the time to spend in the park and the money to pay for transportation to it.

As the example of Central Park suggests, not all citizens enjoyed the benefits of urban life. Overwhelmed by rapid growth, city governments provided few of the

Although this panoramic view of Philadelphia in about 1855 shows individual buildings and empty lots, it is the grid street pattern that stands out as the main feature of the city. By imposing the grid pattern on varied landscapes, Americans created similar types of urban spaces all over the country. This picture does not hint at the underside of Philadelphia life; its purpose seems to be to highlight the importance of the nation's second-largest city. *(The Historical Society of Pennsylvania)*

services we consider essential today, and usually only to those who paid for them. Poor families devoted many hours to securing necessities that affluent citizens had at their fingertips. Water is a case in point. By 1801, Philadelphia had constructed a system of waterworks that drew water from the Schuylkill River and then pumped it through wooden pipes to street hydrants. Only by paying a special fee could Philadelphians have water brought into their homes, so most of the city's residents went without. In the 1820s, the city expanded the water system by constructing the Fairmount waterworks, but the more abundant supply of water again benefited those who could afford to pipe it into their homes.

In 1849, Isaac Parrish's report on the sanitary conditions in Philadelphia lamented some of the consequences. "There is . . . a general absence of bathing apparatus, and even of hydrants," he wrote, "in the houses of the poorer classes, and especially in confined courts and alleys of the populous districts of the city." An earlier inspection, carried out by Mathew Carey in 1837, had pointed to an even more basic problem: 253 persons crowded into 30 tenements without even one privy. The ability to pay for services determined not only comfort but health.

Class Structure in the Cities

The drastic differences in the quality of urban life reflected social fluidity and the growing economic inequality that characterized Philadelphia and other American cities. In sharp contrast to the colonial period, the first half of the nineteenth century witnessed a dramatic rise in the concentration of wealth in the United States. The pattern was most extreme in cities.

Because Americans believed that capitalists deserved most of their profits, the well-to-do profited handsomely from this period of growth, whereas workers lost ground. The merchants, brokers, lawyers, bankers, and manufacturers of Philadelphia's upper class gained control of more and more of the city's wealth. By the late 1840s, the wealthiest 4 percent of the population held about two-thirds of the wealth. The economic pattern was similar in other American cities, as the nearby table on wealth distribution indicates. The houses of the city's elite were spacious and filled with new conveniences. Samuel Breck's house in 1839 was elegant and luxurious, with "parlours 14 feet high, . . . furnaces, water closet and shower and common bath up stairs, marble mantels and fireplaces in dressing rooms." Costing $22,500, Breck's "splendid house" represented the sum an ordinary Philadelphia textile factory operative might expect to earn in 75 years of work.

The widening gap between the upper class and the working class did not translate into mass suffering, because more wealth was being generated. But the growing inequality hardened class lines, nourished social tensions, and contributed to the labor protests of the antebellum period.

Between 1820 and 1860, a new working and middle class were in the process of formation in Philadelphia

WEALTH DISTRIBUTION IN THREE EASTERN CITIES IN THE 1840S*			
Level of Wealth	Percentage of Population	Approximate Noncorporate Wealth Owned	Percentage Noncorporate Wealth
Brooklyn in 1841			
$50,000 or more	1	$10,087,000	42
$15,000 to $50,000	2	$14,000,000	17
$4,500 to $15,000	9	$15,730,000	24
$1,000 to $4,500	15	$12,804,000	12
$100 to $1,000	7	$11,000,000	4
Under $100	66	—	—
New York City in 1845			
$50,000 or more	1	$85,804,000	40
$20,000 to $50,000	3	$55,000,000	26
Boston in 1848			
$90,000 or more	1	$47,778,500	37
$35,000 to $90,000	3	$34,781,800	27
$4,000 to $35,000	15	$40,636,400	32
Under $4,000	81	$16,000,000	4

*Americans and foreign visitors often commented on the rough equality they believed characterized American life. Wealth distribution figures, although incomplete, suggest a different picture of American society.

Source: Edward Pessen, *Riches, Class, and Power Before the Civil War* (1973).

and elsewhere. As preindustrial ways of producing goods yielded to factory production and as the pace of economic activity quickened, some former artisans and skilled workers took advantage of newly created opportunities. Perhaps 10 to 15 percent of Philadelphians in each decade before the Civil War were able to improve their occupations and places of residence. They became businessmen, factory owners, mill supervisors, clerks, bookkeepers, engineers, or shopkeepers. Increasingly, membership in this middle class meant having a nonmanual occupation and a special place of work suited to activities that demanded brainpower rather than brawn. But as new opportunities opened up for some, downward occupational mobility increased. Former artisans or journeymen became part of a new class of permanent manual workers, dependent on wages for their livelihood. Fed by waves of immigrants, the lower class was growing at an accelerating rate. Moreover, within the working class itself, the percentage of unskilled wage earners living in poverty or on its brink increased from 17 to 24 percent between 1820 and 1860. At the same time, the proportion of craftsmen, once the heart of the laboring class, shrank from 56 to 47 percent.

The Urban Working Class

As with so much else in urban life, housing patterns reflected social and economic divisions. The poorest rented quarters in crowded, flimsily constructed shacks, shanties, and two-room houses. Because renters moved often, from one cramped lodging to another, it was difficult for them to create close-knit neighborhoods that might offer the fellowship and assistance to offset the harsh conditions of daily life.

Substantial houses fronting the main streets concealed the worst urban housing, which was in back alleys or even in backyards. Many visitors did not even realize slums lay behind the rows of brick housing, nor did they know of the uncollected garbage, privy runoffs, and fetid decay in the dark, unpaved alleys. In his diary, Philadelphia shopkeeper Joseph Sill left a description of living conditions at the bottom. "In the afternoon," he wrote, "Mrs. S & I went to the lowest part of the City to see some poor persons who had call'd upon us for Charity. We found one woman, with two children, & expecting soon to be confined, living in a cellar, part of which was unfloored, & exhibited much wretchedness; but it was tolerably clean. Her husband is a Weaver, & had his loom in the Cellar, but has only occasional work."

What the Sills witnessed during their visit to the weaver's family was not just poverty but the transformation of working-class family life. Men could no longer be sure of supporting their wives and children, even when they were employed. Women, who had once been able to feed their families by raising food on small garden plots and by keeping pigs and chickens, were forced to use scarce cash to buy food at urban markets now that overcrowding and city regulations made keeping gardens and animals impossible. Making ends meet was a struggle that colored family relations. Men felt they had lost much of their authority and power, and some thought their wives no longer subservient or seemingly careless with their hard-earned money. When one woman failed to explain clearly what she had done with the grocery money, her angry husband "said if she did not give him a full account . . . he would kill her or something like that." The squabble ended in murder. This family was an extreme case, but family violence that spilled out onto the streets was not uncommon in working-class quarters.

Middle-Class Life and Ideals

Although the Sills ventured into the world of the working class, their life could not have been more different. Members of the new middle class like the Sills profited from the dramatic increase in wealth in antebellum America. They lived in pleasantly furnished houses, enjoying more peace, more privacy, and more comfort than the less affluent. Franklin stoves gave warmth in winter, and iron cookstoves made cooking easier. Conveniences like Astral lamps made it possible to read after dark. Bathing stands and bowls ensured higher standards of cleanliness. Rugs muffled sounds and kept in the heat.

Material circumstances were one badge of middle-class status, but there were others as well. The acceptance of certain norms and values also identified a person as a member of the new middle class. Genteel behavior and the careful observance of elaborate rules of etiquette (a gentleman was expected to back out of a parlor after making a call upon a lady), the appropriate clothes and conversation, an elegantly furnished parlor for the entertainment of visitors—all served to establish the standing of the members of a middle-class family.

New expectations about the roles of men and women, prompted partly by economic change, also shaped middle-class life. In the seventeenth and eighteenth centuries, the labor of men and women, adults and children, all contributed to the family's economic welfare. But improved transportation, new products, and the rise of factory production and large businesses changed the family economy. Falling prices for processed and manufactured goods like soap, candles, clothing, and even bread made it unnecessary for women, except on the frontier, to continue making these items at home.

As men increasingly involved themselves in a money economy, whether through commerce or market farming, women's and children's contributions to the family welfare became relatively less significant. Although middle-class women and children still worked in their homes as their husbands left to "bring home the bacon," they often neither produced vital goods nor earned money. Even the rhythm of their lives, oriented to housework rather than the demands of the clock, separated them from the bustling commercial world where their husbands now labored. By 1820, the notion that the sexes occupied separate spheres emerged to express the new reality. Men's sphere was the public world, whereas women's was the domestic.

Men were charged with the task of financial support, a responsibility that, as Susan Warner's family experience suggested, was a heavy one in a changing economy. Women's duties included working at home—not as producer but as housekeeper. As a popular book, *Whisper to a Bride*, counseled readers, "For his sake . . . acquaint thyself with the knowledge that appertaineth unto a wife and housekeeper. If thou art deficient in this knowledge, rest not, till thou hast acquired it. It cometh readily to an attentive mind, and groweth with experience."

The role of housekeeper had both pleasure and frustration built into it. Susan Warner's celebration of domestic life in her novels suggested the satisfactions derived from a cozy household. Yet it was sometimes impossible to achieve the new standards of cleanliness, order, and beauty. Catharine Beecher's "Words of Comfort for a Discouraged Housekeeper" listed just a few of the problems—an inconvenient house, sick children, poor domestics—that undermined efforts to create a perfect harmonious home.

Although women were expected to become "systematic, neat and thorough" housekeepers, whatever the personal costs might be, they were also given more elevated responsibilities as moral and cultural guardians of their own families and, by extension, of society as a whole. Believing that women were innately pious, virtuous, unselfish, and modest (all characteristics that men lacked), publicists built on the argument developed during the revolutionary era. By training future citizens and workers to be obedient, moral, patriotic, and hardworking, mothers ensured the welfare of the republic. Just as important, they preserved important values in a time of rapid change. Because men had none of women's virtues and were daily caught up in the fast-paced world of business, wives were responsible for helping husbands cope with temptations and tensions. A wife was, in the words of one preacher, the "guardian angel" who "watches over" her husband's interests, "warns him against dangers, comforts him under trial; and by . . . pious, assiduous, and attractive deportment, constantly endeavors to render him more virtuous, more useful, more honourable, and more happy."

This view, characterizing women as morally superior to and different from men, had important conse-

This illustration, entitled "Maternal Instruction," from an 1845 issue of *Godey's Lady's Book and Magazine* not only suggests the importance of the printing revolution in spreading the new middle-class norms but also emphasizes the importance attached to women's role as guides for their children. *(The Newberry Library, Chicago)*

quences for female life. Because women thought they had a unique nature and because their husbands spent much of their time away from home working, friendship with other women often became central. Women felt that they shared more with one another than with men, even their husbands. Similar social experiences and perspectives made female friendships a source of comfort, security, and happiness.

Although the concept of domesticity seemed to confine women to their homes and to emphasize the private nature of family life, it actually prompted women to take on activities in the outside world. If women were the guardians of morality, why should they not carry out their tasks in the public sphere? "Woman," said Sarah Hale, editor of the popular magazine *Godey's Lady's Book,* was "God's appointed agent of *morality.*" Such reasoning lay behind the tremendous growth of voluntary female associations in the early decades of the nineteenth century. Initially, most involved religious and charitable activities. Women supported orphanages, paid for and distributed religious tracts and Bibles, established Sunday schools, and ministered to the poor. The associations provided women with congenial companions and suitable tasks for their "moral charac-

ter." Sometimes the women recognized special interests that men did not share. In the 1830s, as we shall see in Chapter 12, women added specific moral concerns like the abolition of slavery to their missionary and benevolent efforts. As these women took on more active and controversial tasks, they often clashed with men and with social conventions about "woman's place."

Domesticity described norms, not the actual conduct of middle-class women. Obviously, not all women were pious, disinterested, selfless, virtuous, cheerful, and loving. But these ideas, expressed so movingly by novelists like Susan Warner, influenced how women thought of themselves, promoted "female" behavior by encouraging particular choices, and helped many women make psychological sense of their lives. New norms, effectively spread by the publishing industry, also influenced rural and urban working women. The insistence on marriage and service to family discouraged married women from entering the workforce. Many took in poorly paid piecework so that they could remain at home. Those who had to work often bore a burden of guilt. Though the new feminine ideal may have suited urban middle-class women, it created difficult tensions in the lives of working-class women.

As family roles were reformulated, a new view of childhood emerged. Working-class children still worked or scavenged for goods to sell or use at home, but middle-class children were no longer expected to contribute economically to the family. Middle-class parents now came to see childhood as a special stage of life, a period of preparation for adulthood. In a child's early years, mothers were to impart important values, including the necessity of behaving in accordance with gender prescriptions. Harsh punishments lost favor. As Catharine Beecher explained, "Affection can govern the human with a sway more powerful than the authority of reason or [even] the voices of conscience." Schooling also prepared a child for the future, and urban middle-class parents supported the public school movement.

Children's fiction, which poured off the printing presses, also socialized children. Stories pictured modest youngsters happily making the correct choices of playmates and activities, obeying their parents, and being dutiful, religious, loving, and industrious. Occasionally, as in *The Child at Home* (1833), the reader could discover the horrible consequences of wrongdoing. The young girl who refused to bring her sick mother a glass of water saw her promptly die. Heavy-handed moralizing made sure that children got the proper message.

The growing publishing industry helped spread new ideas about family roles and appropriate family

Recovering the Past

FAMILY PAINTINGS

Although paintings are often admired and studied for artistic reasons alone, their value as historical documents should not be overlooked. In an age before the camera, paintings, sketches, and even pictures done in needlework captured Americans at different moments of life and memorialized their significant rituals. Paintings of American families in their homes, for example, reveal both an idealized conception of family life and the details of its reality. In addition, the paintings provide us with a sense of what the houses of the middle and upper classes (who could afford to commission art) were like.

Artists trained in the European tradition of realism painted family scenes and portraits, but so did many painters who lacked formal academic training, the so-called primitive artists. Their art was abstract in the sense that the artists tended to emphasize what they knew or felt rather than what they actually saw.

Some primitive artists were women who had received some drawing instruction at school. They often worked primarily for their own pleasure. Other artists were craftsmen, perhaps house or sign painters, who painted pictures in their leisure time. Some traveling house decorators made a living by making paintings and wall decorations. Many primitive paintings are unsigned, and even when we know the painter's identity, we rarely know more than a name and perhaps a date. Primitive artists flourished in the first three-quarters of the nineteenth century, eventually supplanted by the camera and inexpensive prints.

We see here a painting of the Sargent family done by an unknown artist around 1800. Though not an exact representation of reality, it does convey what the artist and the buyer considered important. Like any piece of historical evidence, this painting must be approached critically and carefully. Our questions focus on four areas: (1) the individual family members and their treatment, (2) the objects associated with each, (3) the

implied or apparent relationship between family members, and (4) the domestic environment. The painting gives us an idealized version of what both the painter and the subjects felt ought to be as well as what actually was. First, study the family itself. Describe what you see. How many family members are there, and what is each one doing? What seems to be the relationship between husband and wife? Why do you think Mr. Sargent is painted with his hat on? Who seems to dominate the painting, and how is this dominance conveyed (positioning, attitude or facial expression, eye contact, clothing)? What can you conclude about different "spheres" and roles for men and women?

Why do you think the artist painted two empty chairs and included a ball and a dog in this scene of family life? What do these choices suggest about attitudes toward children and their upbringing? What seems to be the role of the children in the family? What does the painting suggest about how this family wished to be viewed? How do your conclusions relate to information discussed in this chapter?

Take a look at the room in which the Sargents are gathered. Make an inventory of the objects and furnishings in it. The room seems quite barren in comparison with present-day interiors. Why? Why do you think the chairs are placed near the window and door? What kind of scene does the window frame?

The *Family at Home*, painted by H. Knight in 1836, is a more detailed painting showing a larger family gathering almost 40 years later. Similar questions can be asked about this painting, particularly in relationship to the different treatment of boys and girls and the positioning and objects associated with each sex. There are many clues about the different socialization of male and female children. The family's living room can be contrasted with the Sargent family's room to reveal some of the changes brought about by industrialization.

Finally, how do these nineteenth-century homes and sex roles differ from those in colonial New England and the Chesapeake?

Anonymous, *The Sargent Family*, 1800. *(National Gallery of Art)*

H. Knight, *The Family at Home*, 1836. *(Private collection)*

behavior. Novels, magazines, etiquette and child-rearing manuals, and schoolbooks all carried the message from northern and midwestern centers of publishing to the South, to the West, and to the frontier. Probably few Americans lived up to the new standards established for the model parent or child, but the standards increasingly influenced them.

New notions of family life supported the widespread use of contraception for the first time in American history. Because children required so much loving attention and needed careful preparation for adulthood, many parents desired smaller families. The declining birthrate was evident first in the Northeast, particularly in cities and among the middle class. Contraceptive methods included abortion, which was legal in many states until 1860. This medical procedure terminated perhaps as many as a third of all pregnancies. Other birth control methods included coitus interruptus and abstinence. The success of these methods for family limitation suggests that many men and women adopted the new definitions of the female sex as naturally affectionate but passionless and sexually restrained.

Mounting Urban Tensions

The social and economic changes transforming U.S. cities in the half century before the Civil War produced urban violence on a scale never before witnessed in the United States, not even during the Revolution. Festering ethnic and racial tensions often triggered mob actions that lasted for days. American cities were slow to establish a modern police force (London had organized one in 1829). Most still had the traditional constable-and-watch system. The night watch lit city streetlights and patrolled the streets to preserve order and arrest suspicious characters. During the day, constables investigated health hazards, carried out court orders, and apprehended criminals against whom complaints had been lodged. Neither group tried to prevent crimes or discover offenses. Neither wore uniforms. Certainly, neither was able to "prevent a tumult." Each chaotic event made the London model more attractive.

Racial tensions contributed to Philadelphia's disorders. An unsavory riot in August 1834 revealed other important sources of social antagonism as well as the inability of its police force to control disorder.

One hot August evening, several hundred white Philadelphians wrecked a building on South Street that contained a merry-go-round patronized by both blacks and whites. A general melee followed. As the *Philadelphia Gazette* reported, "At one time it is supposed that four or five hundred persons were engaged in the conflict, with clubs, brickbats, paving stones, and the materials of the shed in which the flying

horses were kept." Spurred by the taste of blood, the white mob moved into the center of the crowded, racially mixed neighborhood, where they continued their orgy of destruction, looting, and intimidation of black residents. Similar mayhem followed on the next two nights. Intermittent rioting broke out the succeeding night as well, but the presence of 300 special constables, a troop of mounted militia, and a company of infantry prevented the violence from reaching the pitch of the previous nights.

An investigation following the riots revealed at least $4,000 of damage to two black churches and more than 36 private homes. At least one black had been killed, and numerous others were injured. As one shocked eyewitness reported, "The mob exhibited more than fiendish brutality, beating and mutilating some of the old, confiding and unoffending blacks with a savageness surpassing anything we could have believed men capable of."

Many rioters bragged that they were "hunting the nigs." Riots, however, are complicated events, and this racial explanation does not reveal the range of causes underlying the rampage of violence and destruction. The rioters were young and generally of low social standing. Many were Irish. Some had criminal records. A number of those arrested, however, were from a "class of mechanics of whom better things are expected": weavers, house painters, a cabinetmaker, a carpenter, a blacksmith, and a plasterer. No professional people or businessmen seem to have been involved. Accompanying the rioters, however, were onlookers who egged the mob on. As one paper reported, these onlookers "countenanced" the operations of the mob "and in one or two instances coincided with their conduct by clapping." The rioters revealed that in the event of an "attack by the city police, they confidently counted" on the assistance of these bystanders.

The mob's composition hints at some of the reasons for participation. Many of the rioters were at the bottom of the occupational and economic ladder and competed with blacks for jobs. This was particularly true of the newly arrived Irish immigrants, who were attempting to replace blacks in low-status jobs. Subsequent violence against blacks suggested that economic rivalry was an important component of the riot. "Colored persons, when engaged in their usual vocations," the *Niles Register* observed, "were repeatedly assailed and maltreated. . . . Parties of white men have insisted that no blacks shall be employed in certain departments of labor."

If blacks threatened the dream of advancement of some whites, this was not quite the complaint of the skilled workers. These men were more likely to have experienced the negative impact of a changing economic system that was undermining the small-scale mode of production. The dream of a better life seemed increasingly illusory as their declining wages drew them closer to unskilled workers than to the middle class. Like other rioters, they were living in one of the poorest and most crowded parts of the city. Their immediate scapegoats were blacks, but for them, the real but intangible villain was the economic system itself. Trade union organizing and a general strike a year later would highlight the grievances of this group.

Urban expansion also contributed to the racial violence. Most of the rioters lived either in the riot area or nearby. All had experienced the overcrowded and inadequate living conditions caused by the city's rapid growth. The racial tensions generated by squalid surroundings and social proximity go far to explain the outbreak of violence. The same area would later become the scene of race riots and election trouble and became infamous for harboring criminals and juvenile gangs. The absence of middle- and upper-class participants did not mean that these groups were untroubled during times of growth and change, but their material circumstances cushioned them from some of the more unsettling forces.

The city's police proved unable to control the mob, thus prolonging the violence. Philadelphia, like other eastern cities, was in the midst of creating its police force. In 1833, a small force had been added to the constable-and-watch system. Its task was to deter crime by walking the city streets. But the police were too few to cope with the angry mob. Only continued rowdiness, violence, and riots would convince residents and city officials in Philadelphia (and in other large cities) to support an expanded, quasi-military, preventive, and uniformed police force. By 1855, most sizable eastern cities had established such forces.

Finally, the character of the free black community itself was a factor in producing those gruesome August events. Not only was the community large and visible, but it also had created its own institutions and its own elite. Whites resented "dressy blacks and dandy coloured beaux and belles" returning from "their proper churches." The mob vented its rage against black affluence by targeting the solid brick houses of middle-class blacks and robbing them of silver and watches. Black wealth threatened the notion of the proper social order held by many white Philadelphians and seemed unspeakable when whites could not afford life's basic necessities or lacked jobs.

The Black Underclass

Events in Philadelphia showed how hazardous life for free blacks could be. Although a small elite group of blacks emerged in Philadelphia and in other cities as well, most African Americans did not enjoy the rewards of economic expansion and industrial progress. Black men, often with little or no education, held transient and frequently dangerous jobs. Black women, many of whom headed their households because men were away working or had died, held jobs before and after marriage. In Philadelphia in 1849, almost half of the black women washed clothes for a living. Others took boarders into their homes and thereby added to their domestic chores.

Northern whites, like southerners, believed in black inferiority and depravity and feared black competition for jobs and resources. Although northern states had passed gradual abolition acts between 1780 and 1803 and the national government had banned slaves from entering new states to be formed out of the Northwest Territory, nowhere did any government extend equal rights and citizenship or economic opportunities to free blacks in their midst.

For a time in the early nineteenth century, some blacks living in the North were permitted to vote, but they soon lost that right. Beginning in the 1830s, in part because of the influx of fugitive slaves and manumitted blacks without property or jobs, Pennsylvania, Connecticut, and New Jersey disenfranchised blacks. New York allowed only those with three years' residence and property valued at $250 or more to vote. Only the New England states (with the exception of Connecticut), which had tiny black populations, preserved the right to vote regardless of color. By 1840, fully 93 percent of the northern free black population lived in states where law or custom prevented them from voting.

Other black civil rights were also restricted. In five northern states, blacks could not testify against whites or serve on juries. In most states, the two races were thoroughly segregated. Blacks increasingly endured separate and inferior facilities in railway cars, steamboats, hospitals, prisons, and other asylums. In some states, they could enter public buildings only as personal servants of white men. They sat in "Negro pews" in churches and took communion only after whites had left the church. Although most Protestant religious denominations in the antebellum period split into northern and southern branches over the issue of slavery, most northern churches were not disposed to welcome blacks as full members.

As the Philadelphia riot revealed, whites were driving blacks from their jobs. In 1839, *The Colored American* blamed the Irish. "These impoverished and destitute beings . . . are crowding themselves into every place of business . . . and driving the poor colored American citizen out." Increasingly after 1837, these "white niggers" became coachmen, stevedores, barbers, cooks, house servants—all occupations blacks had once held.

Educational opportunities for blacks were also severely limited. Only a few school systems admitted blacks, in separate facilities. The case of Prudence Crandall illustrates the lengths to which northern whites would go to maintain racial segregation. In 1833, Crandall, a Quaker schoolmistress in Canterbury, Connecticut, announced that she would admit "young colored ladies and Misses" to her school. The outraged townspeople, fearful that New England would become the "Liberia of America," tried all sorts of persuasion and intimidation to induce Crandall to abandon her project.

Nonetheless, Crandall opened the school. Hostile citizens harassed and insulted students and teachers, refused to sell them provisions, and denied them medical care and admission to churches. Ministers preached against Crandall's efforts, and local residents poured manure in the school's well, set the school on fire, and knocked in walls with a battering ram. Crandall was arrested, and after two trials—in which free blacks were declared to have no citizenship rights—she finally gave up and moved to Illinois.

Crandall likely did not find the Old Northwest much more hospitable. The fast-growing western states were intensely committed to white supremacy and black exclusion. In Ohio, the response to talk of freeing the slaves was to pass "black laws" excluding them from the state. Said one Ohioan, "The banks of the Ohio would be lined with men with muskets to keep off the emancipated slaves." In 1829 in Cincinnati, where evidence of freedom papers and $500 bond were demanded of blacks who wished to live in the city, white rioters ran nearly 2,000 blacks out of town.

As an Indiana newspaper editor observed in 1854, informal customs made life dangerous for blacks. They were "constantly subject to insults and annoyance in traveling and the daily avocations of life; [and] are practically excluded from all social privileges, and even from the Christian communion." An Indiana senator proclaimed in 1850 that a black could "never live together equally" with whites because "the same power that has given him a black skin, with less weight or volume of brain, has given us a white skin with greater volume of brain and intellect." A neighboring politician, Abraham Lincoln of Illinois, would not have disagreed with this assessment.

⧉ RURAL COMMUNITIES

Although the percentage of families involved in farming fell from 72 to 60 percent between 1820 and 1860, Americans remained a rural people. Agriculture persisted as the country's most significant economic activity, and farm products still made up most of the

nation's exports. The small family farm still characterized eastern and western agriculture.

Even though farming remained the dominant way of life, agriculture changed in the antebellum period. Vast new tracts of land came under cultivation in the West. Railroads, canals, and better roads pulled rural Americans into the orbit of the wider world. Some crops were shipped to regional markets; others, like grain, hides, and pork, stimulated industrial processing. Manufactured goods, ranging from cloth to better tools, flowed in return to farm families. Like city dwellers, farmers and their families read books, magazines, and papers that exposed them to new ideas. Commercial farming encouraged different ways of thinking and acting and lessened the isolation so typical before 1820.

Farming in the East

During the antebellum period, economic changes created new rural patterns in the Northeast. Marginal lands in New England, New York, and Pennsylvania, cultivated as more fertile lands ran out, yielded discouraging returns. Gradually, after 1830, farmers abandoned these farms, forest reclaimed farmland, and the New England hill country began a slow decline. By 1860, almost 40 percent of people who had been born in Vermont had left their native state. A popular song of the 1840s captured the pattern of flight: "Come, all ye Yankee farmers who wish to change your lot, / Who've spunk enough to travel beyond your native spot. / And leave behind the village where Pa and Ma do stay, / Come follow me, and settle in Michigan, yea, yea."

Farmers who did not migrate west had to transform their production. By the 1830s, eastern farmers, realizing that they could not compete with western grain, sought new agricultural opportunities created by better transportation and growing urban markets. One demand was for fresh milk. By the 1830s, some eastern cities had grown so large that milk was turning sour before it reached central marketplaces. As a result, several cities, including New York, started urban dairies, where cows often fed on garbage and slop from distilleries and breweries. When railroad lines extended into rural areas, however, farmers living as far away as Vermont and upper New York State discovered that they could ship cooled milk to urban centers. In 1842 and 1843, the Erie Railroad carried 750,000 gallons of milk to New York City. New dairy farmers eventually drove the unsavory city dairies out of business. City residents had fresher and cheaper milk and drank more of it as a result.

Urban appetites encouraged other farmers to cultivate fruit and vegetables. Every city was surrounded by farmers growing produce for urban consumption.

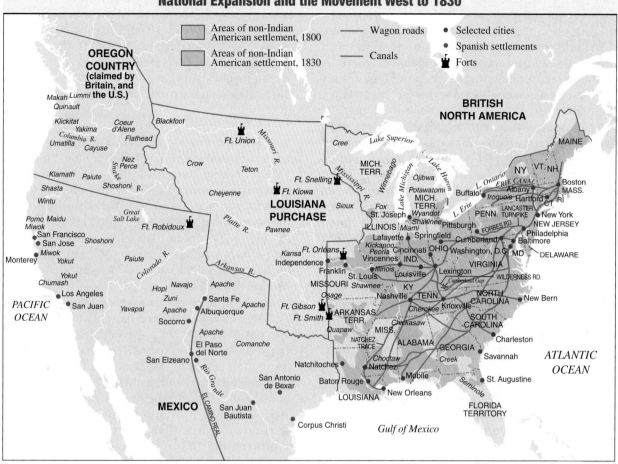

National Expansion and the Movement West to 1830

This map shows the expansion of American settlement in the first decades of the nineteenth century as well as the expanding transportation network that facilitated the movement of people and goods.

Railroads also prompted farmers miles away to turn to specialized farming. Upper New York State farmers began to raise and ship apples, while New Jersey and Delaware farmers became famous for their peaches. Thus, in July 1837, a Boston housewife could buy at the central market a wide variety of fresh vegetables and fruits, ranging from peas, summer squash, and cauliflower to grapes, cherries, and raspberries. Cookbooks began to include recipes calling for fresh ingredients.

As northern farmers adopted new crops, they began to consider farming as a scientific endeavor. After 1800, northern farmers started using manure as fertilizer rather than disposing of it as a smelly nuisance. By the 1820s, some farmers were rotating their crops and planting new grasses and clover to restore fertility to the soil. These techniques recovered worn-out wheat and tobacco lands in Maryland and Delaware for livestock farming. Calculation began to replace "habit and prejudice . . . the powerful opponents of improvement."

Farmers in the Delaware River valley were leaders in adopting new methods, but interest in scientific farming was widespread. By 1860, American farmers had developed thousands of special varieties of plants for local conditions. Many improvements resulted from experimentation, but farmers also enjoyed more and better information. New journals like the *New England Farmer*, the *Farmers' Register*, and the *Cultivator* informed readers of modern farming practices, fertilizers, scientific breeding, and methods for treating fruits and vegetables. Following New York's lead in 1819, many states established agricultural agencies to propagate new ideas. Although wasteful farming practices did not disappear, they became less characteristic of the Northeast. Improved farming methods contributed to increased agricultural output and helped reverse a two-hundred-year decline in farm productivity in some of the oldest areas of settlement. The increased use of a tool called the cradle increased farmers' ability to harvest grain and made it possible to cultivate more acres than before. A "scientific" farmer in 1850 could often produce two to four times as much per acre as in 1820.

Farmers in the fertile area around Northampton, Massachusetts, illustrate the American farmer's adjustment to new economic conditions. As early as 1800, better roads, a turnpike, and stage routes reduced rural isolation. Canal improvements and then railroads strengthened new contacts. With markets ever more accessible, farmers began to change agricultural patterns. Rather than raising crops and animals for home use or for local barter, farmers started to cultivate crops "scientifically" to increase profits. Farming was becoming a business. At home, women found themselves freed from many of their traditional tasks. Peddlers brought goods to the door. The onerous duty of making cloth and clothing disappeared with the coming of inexpensive ready-made cloth and even ready-made clothes in the 1820s. Daughters liberated from the chores of home manufacturing went off to the mills or earned money by taking in piecework from local merchants.

As the rhythms of rural life in the Connecticut River valley quickened, attitudes also changed. Cash transactions replaced the exchange of goods. Country stores became more reluctant to accept wood, rye, corn, oats, and butter as payment for goods instead of cash. Some farmers adopted the ethic of getting ahead, although their motive was not entrepreneurship but rather a desire to provide for family material comfort.

Traditional attitudes did not disappear completely, however. Some farmers contented themselves with making a living rather than chasing a profit. "Reason's whole pleasure, all the joys of sense / Lie in three words, health, peace and competence" remained their motto. The desire to just get along rather than becoming involved in the market economy helps explain why wealth inequality increased near Northampton, as it did elsewhere in the rural Northeast.

Frontier Families

Many people who left the North during these years headed for the expanding frontier. After the War of 1812, Americans flooded into the Old Northwest. Early communities dotted the Ohio River, the link to the South. Concentrating on corn and pork, settlers sent their products down the Ohio and Mississippi Rivers to southern buyers. In 1820, less than one-fifth of the American population lived west of the Appalachians; by 1860, almost half did, and Ohio and Illinois had become two of the nation's most populous states.

By 1830, Ohio, Indiana, and southern Illinois were heavily settled, but Michigan, northern Illinois, Wisconsin, and parts of Iowa and Missouri were still frontier. Chicago had only 250 residents. Conditions were often primitive, as Charles Butler and Arthur Bronson discovered during their 1833 trip. Their hotel in Michigan City, Indiana, was "a small log house, a single room . . . [where] some eleven or twelve persons lodged in beds & on the floor."

During the 1830s, land sales and settlement boomed in the Old Northwest. Changes in federal land policy, which reduced both prices and the minimum acreage a settler had to buy, helped stimulate migra-

This 1856 print titled "Preparing for Market" shows the farm as a center of human and animal activity and suggests the shifts in eastern agriculture that took place in the East as competition from the Midwest stimulated farmers to raise new crops for the market. The rise of commercial farming also encouraged technological innovation—The McCormick reaper was patented in 1834. *(Yale University Art Gallery, New Haven. CT/Mabel Brady Garvan Collection)*

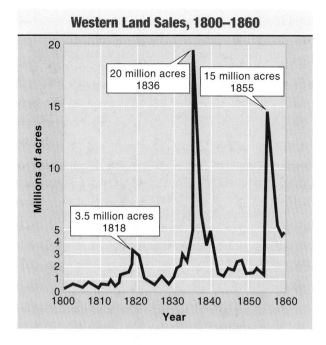

Changing prices for federal lands and the reduction in the number of acres a settler had to buy stimulated migration and land purchases.

tion, as the nearby figure on western land sales shows. Eastern capital also contributed to the boom with loans, mortgages, and speculative buying. Speculators frequently bought up large tracts of land from the government and then subdivided them and sold parcels off to settlers.

Internal improvement schemes after 1830 also contributed to new settlement patterns and tied the Old Northwest firmly to the East. Erasmus Gest, who as a 17-year-old had worked on canal projects in Indiana, recalled the settlers' enthusiasm for improvements: "We Engineers were favorites with the People wherever we went."

Wheat for the eastern market rather than corn and hogs for the southern market became increasingly important with the transportation links eastward. Between 1840 and 1860, Illinois, southern Wisconsin, and eastern Iowa turned into the country's most rapidly growing grain regions. In the 1850s, these three states accounted for 70 percent of the increase in national wheat production.

Although the Old Northwest passed rapidly through the frontier stage between 1830 and 1860, its farming families faced severe challenges. Catharine Skinner, who moved from New York to Indiana with her husband when she was 24, described her rigorous existence. "We are poor and live in the woods where deers roam plentifully and the wolf is occasionally heard," she wrote to her sister in 1849. "We are employed in honest business and trying to do the best

we can; we have got 80 acres of land in the woods of Indiana, a very level country; we have got two acres cleared and fenced and four more pirty well under way; we have got about five acres of wheat in the ground; we raised corn enough for our use and to fat our pork . . . we have a cow so that we have milk and butter and plenty of corn bread but wheat is hard to be got in account of our not having mony."

The Skinners were typical. Western farms were small, for there were limits to what a family with hand tools could manage. A family with two healthy men could care for about 50 acres. In wooded areas, it took several years to get even that much land under cultivation, for only a few acres could be cleared in a year. The Skinners' target was to clear 10 acres during the first 12 months, if, as Catharine said, "health permit." At this rate, it could take ten years for settlers in forested areas to get a farm in full operation. On the prairies, the typical settler would need only half that time.

Catharine Skinner mentioned the shortage of money and described her family as "poor." Although money was in short supply in the Northwest, she probably overstated her family's poverty. It took capital to begin farming—a minimum initial investment of perhaps $100 for 80 acres of government land, $300 for basic farming equipment, and another $100 or $150 for livestock. To buy an already "improved" farm cost more, and free bidding at government auctions could drive the price of unimproved federal land far above the minimum price. Once farmers moved onto the prairies of Indiana and Illinois, they needed an initial investment of about $1,000 because they had to buy materials for fencing, housing, and expensive steel plows. If farmers invested in the new horse-drawn reapers, they could cultivate more land, but all their costs also increased.

Opportunities in the Old Northwest

It was possible to begin farming with less, however. Some farmers borrowed from relatives, banks, or insurance companies like the Ohio Life Insurance and Trust Company. Others rented land from farmers who had bought more acres than they could manage. Tenants who furnished their own seeds and animals could expect to keep about a third of the yield. Within a few years, some saved enough to buy their own farms. Even those without any capital could work as hired hands. Labor was scarce, so they earned good wages. In Indiana, German settler Jacob Schramm hired men "to help with heavy labors of lumbering and field work, ditch-digging, and so on." Five to ten years of frugal living and steady work for men like Schramm would bring the sum needed to get started.

Probably about a quarter of the western farm population consisted of young men laboring as tenants or hired hands. Although they stood on the bottom rung of the agricultural ladder, their chances of moving up and joining the rural middle class were favorable. Widespread ownership of land characterized western rural communities. Lucinda Easteen knew as much when she told her younger sister to come to Illinois, where "you can have a home of your own, but never give your hand or heart to a lazy man."

Rural communities, unlike the cities, had no growing class of propertyless wage earners, but inequalities nevertheless existed in the Old Northwest. In Butler County, Ohio, for example, 16 percent of people leaving wills in the 1830s held half the wealth. By 1860, the wealthiest 8 percent held half the wealth. In a Wisconsin frontier county in 1860, the richest tenth owned 40 percent of all property. Although wealth was not as concentrated in rural areas as in the cities, a few residents benefited more from rapid economic development than others.

Nevertheless, the Northwest offered many American families the chance to become independent producers and to enjoy a "pleasing competence." The rigors of frontier life faded with time. As Catharine Skinner wrote to her sister from her new Illinois home in 1850, "We here have meetings instead of hearing the hunters gun and the woo[d]man's ax on the sabbath."

Commercial farming brought new patterns of family life. As one Illinois farmer told his wife and daughter, "Store away your looms, wheels, [and] warping bars . . . all of your utensils for weaving cloth up in the loft. The boys and I can make enough by increasing our herds." Many farm families had money to spend on new goods. As early as 1836, the *Dubuque Visitor* was advertising the availability of ready-made clothing and "Calicoes, Ginghams, Muslins, Cambricks, Laces and Ribbands." The next year the *Iowa News* told of the arrival of "Ready Made Clothing from New York."

Agriculture and the Environment

Shifting agricultural patterns in the East and expanding settlement into the Old Northwest contributed to the changing character of the American landscape. As naturalist John Audubon mused in 1826, "A century hence," the rivers, swamps, and mountains "will not be here as I see them. Nature will have been robbed of many brilliant charms, the rivers will be tormented and turned astray from their primitive course, the hills will be levelled with the swamps, and perhaps the swamps will have become a mount surmounted by a fortress of a thousand guns." His sense of the consequences of the movement of peoples and the exploitation of land was shared by one French visitor who

remarked that Americans would never be satisfied until they had subdued nature.

More than the subjugation of nature was involved, however. When eastern farmers changed their agricultural practices as they became involved in the market economy, their decisions left an imprint on the land. Selling wood and potash stimulated clearing of forests, as did the desire for new tools, plow castings, threshing machines, and wagon boxes, which were produced in furnaces fueled by charcoal. As forests disappeared, so, too, did their wildlife. Even using mineral manures like gypsum or lime or organic fertilizers like guano to revitalize worn-out soil and increase crop yields meant the depletion of land elsewhere.

When farmers moved into the Old Northwest, they used new steel plows, like the one developed in 1837 by Illinois blacksmith John Deere. Unlike older eastern plows, the new ones could cut through the dense, tough prairie cover. Deep plowing and the intensive

Timeline

1805	*Palmer* v. *Mulligan*
1816	Second U.S. Bank chartered
1817	New York Stock Exchange established
1819	*Dartmouth College* v. *Woodward*
1820	City of Lowell, Massachusetts, founded by Boston Associates
	Land Act of 1820
	The expression "woman's sphere" becomes current
1824	*Sturges* v. *Crowninshield*
1824–1850	Construction of canals in the Northeast
1825–1856	Construction of canals linking the Ohio, the Mississippi, and the Great Lakes
1828	Baltimore & Ohio Railroad begins operation
1830	Preemption Act
1830s	Boom in the Old Northwest
	Increasing discrimination against free blacks
	Public education movement spreads
1833	Philadelphia establishes small police force
1834	Philadelphia race riots
	Lowell work stoppage
	Cyrus McCormick patents his reaper
1837	Horace Mann becomes secretary of Massachusetts Board of Education
1837–1844	Financial panic and depression
1840	Agitation for ten-hour day
1840s–1850s	Rising tide of immigration
1841	Distributive Preemption Act

cultivation of large cash crops had immediate benefits. But these practices could result in robbing the soil of necessary minerals like phosphorous, carbon, and nitrogen. When farmers built new timber houses as frontier conditions receded, they helped fuel the destruction of the country's forests.

Conclusion
The Character of Progress

Between 1820 and 1860, the United States experienced tremendous growth and economic development. Transportation improvements facilitated the movement of people, goods, and ideas. Larger markets stimulated both agricultural and industrial production. There were more goods and ample food for the American people. Cities and towns were established and thrived. Visitors constantly remarked on the amazing bustle and rapid pace of American life. The United States was, in the words of one Frenchman, "one gigantic workshop, over the entrance of which there is the blazing inscription 'NO ADMISSION HERE, EXCEPT ON BUSINESS.'"

Although the wonders of American development dazzled foreigners and Americans alike, economic growth had its costs. Expansion was cyclic, and financial panics and depression punctuated the era. Industrial profits were based partly on low wages to workers. Time-honored routes to economic independence disappeared, and a large class of unskilled, impoverished workers appeared in U.S. cities. Growing inequality characterized urban and rural life, prompting some labor activists to criticize new economic and social arrangements. But workers, still largely unorganized, did not speak with one voice. Ethnic, racial, and religious diversity divided Americans in new and troubling ways.

Yet a basic optimism and sense of pride also characterized the age. To observers, however, it frequently seemed as if the East and the Old Northwest were responsible for the country's achievements. During these decades, many noted that the paths between the East, Northwest, and South seemed to diverge. The rise of King Cotton in the South, where slave rather than free labor formed the foundation of the economy, created a new kind of tension in American life, as the next chapter will show.

Recommended Reading

Economic Growth

Thomas C. Cochran, *Frontiers of Change: Early Industrialism in America* (1981); Robert F. Dalzell Jr., *Enterprising Elite: The Boston Associates and the World They Made* (1987); David Freeman Hawke, *Nuts and Bolts of the Past: A History of American Technology, 1776–1860* (1988); David A. Hounshell, *From the American System to Mass Production, 1800–1832: The Development of Manufacturing Technology in the United States* (1984); David J. Jeremy, *Transatlantic Industrial Revolution: The Diffusion of Textile Technology Between Britain and America, 1790–1830* (1981); Nathan Rosenberg, *Technology and American Economic Growth* (1972); Charles G. Sellers, *The Market Revolution: Jacksonian America, 1815–1848* (1991); Carol Sheriff, *The Artificial River: the Erie Canal and the Paradox of Progress, 1817–1862* (1996).

Early Manufacturing

Mary H. Blewett, *Men, Women, and Work: Class, Gender, and Protest in the New England Shoe Industry, 1780–1910* (1988); Alan Dawley, *Class and Community: The Industrial Revolution in Lynn* (1976); Thomas Dublin, *Women at Work: The Transformation of Work and Community in Lowell, Massachusetts, 1826–1860* (1979), and ed., *Farm to Factory: Women's Letters, 1830–1860* (1981); Bruce Laurie, *Artisans into Workers: Labor in Nineteenth-Century America* (1989); Steven J. Ross, *Workers on the Edge: Work, Leisure, and Politics in Industrializing Cincinnati, 1788–1890* (1985); Richard B. Stott, *Workers in the Metropolis: Class, Ethnicity, and Youth in Antebellum New York City* (1990); Sean Wilentz, *Chants Democratic: New York City & The Rise of the American Working Class, 1788–1850* (1984).

Urban Life

Stuart M. Blumin, *The Emergence of the Middle Class: Social Experience in the American City, 1760–1900* (1989); Tamara K. Hareven, ed., *Family and Kin in Urban Communities, 1700–1930* (1977); John F. Kasson, *Rudeness and Civility: Manners in Nineteenth-Century America* (1990); Gary B. Nash, *Forging Freedom: The Formation of Philadelphia's Black Community, 1720–1840* (1988); Edward Pessen, *Riches, Class, and Power Before the Civil War* (1973); Christopher Phillips, *Freedom's Port: The African-American Community of Baltimore, 1780–1860* (1997); Mary P. Ryan, *Cradle of the Middle Class: The Family in Oneida County, New York, 1790–1865* (1981); Christine Stansell, *City of Women: Sex and Class in New York, 1789–1860* (1986).

Rural Communities

Jeremy Atack and Fred Bateman, *To Their Own Soil: Agriculture in the Antebellum North* (1987); Christopher Clark, *The Roots of Rural Capitalism: Western Massachusetts, 1780–1860* (1992); Don H. Doyle, *The Social Order of a Frontier Community: Jacksonville, Illinois, 1825–1870* (1978); John Mack Faragher, *Sugar Creek: Life on the Illinois Prairies* (1986); Susan E. Gray, *The Yankee West: Community Life on the Michigan Frontier* (1996); John Denis Haeger, *The Investment Frontier: New York Businessmen and the Economic Development of the Old Northwest* (1981); Joan M. Jensen, *Loosening the Bonds: Mid-Atlantic Farm Women, 1750–1850* (1986); Robert Leslie Jones, *History of Agriculture in Ohio to 1880* (1983); Donald H. Parkerson, *The Agricultural Transition in New York State: Markets and Migration in Mid-Nineteenth Century America* (1995).

Fiction and Film

Nathaniel Hawthorne's novel *The Scarlet Letter* (1850, but use any edition), although set in the Puritan period, reveals more about the attitudes and controversies of the antebellum period than it does about the seventeenth century. The novels of James Fenimore Cooper provide a picture of the impact of social and economic change on the frontier. Susan Warner's *The Wide, Wide World* (any edition) as well as her other popular novels provide an excellent picture of female interests and concerns in this period (although certainly not all her readers were women).

Little Women (1994) is a feature film presenting a moving picture of the domestic and family life so idealized by the middle class. It also suggests the struggle of the middle class to maintain its status in difficult times. Some critics have pointed out that this adaptation of Louisa May Alcott's novel has strong overtones of contemporary feminism. *Out of Ireland: The Story of Irish Emigration to America,* (1994) gives a vivid picture of Irish emigration between 1840 and 1920.

Suggested Web Sites

http://www.si.edu/lemelson/centerpieces/whole_cloth/

Whole Cloth: Discovering Science and Technology Through American History. The Jerome and Dorothy Lemelson Center for the Study of Invention and Innovation/Society for the History of Technology put together this site, which includes excellent activities and sources concerning early American manufacturing and industry.

http://www.connerprairie.org/ntlroad.html

Road Through the Wilderness. The National Road was a hot political topic in the early republic and was part of the beginning of the development of America's infrastructure. This site tells the history of the building of the National Road.

http://www.history.rochester.edu/Scientific_American/

19th Century Scientific American Online. Magazines and journals are windows through which we can view society. This site provides on-line editions of one of the more interesting nineteenth-century journals.

http://www.indianapolis.in.us/cp/jmed.html

Jacksonian Medicine. Survival was far from certain in the Jacksonian era. This site discusses some of the reasons and some of the possible cures of the times.

http://www.upenn.edu/AR/1830/

Penn 1830: A Virtual Tour. This "virtual tour" shows what a fairly typical campus looked like and what student life was like at one of the larger universities in the antebellum era.

http://www.connerprairie.org/clothing.html

Clothing of the 1830s. Visit this site to see how clothing worn in the early republic was quite different from what you are wearing now.

http://www.ushistory

A richly detailed on-line learning environment complete with interactive maps, timelines, history activities, primary source documents, and links to related American history sites.

SLAVERY *and the* OLD SOUTH

CHAPTER OUTLINE

Engraved by J. C. Buttre from a Daguerreotype

As a young slave boy, Frederick Douglass was sent by his master to live in Baltimore. When he first met his mistress, Sophia Auld, she appeared to be a "woman of the kindest heart and finest feelings." He was "astonished at her goodness" as she began to teach him to read. Her husband, however, ordered her to stop because Maryland law forbade teaching slaves to read. A literate slave was "unmanageable," utterly "unfit . . . to be a slave." From this episode Douglass learned to set inverse goals from Master Auld's wishes. "What he most dreaded, that I most desired . . . and the argument which he so warmly urged, against my learning to read, only served to inspire me with a desire and determination to learn."

In the seven years he lived with the Aulds, young Frederick used "various stratagems" to teach himself to read and write. In the narrative of his early life, written after his dramatic escape to the North, Douglass acknowledged that his master's "bitter opposition" had been as beneficial to him as Mrs. Auld's "kindly aid" in achieving his eventual freedom.

Most slaves did not, like Douglass, escape to freedom. But all were as inextricably tied to their masters as Douglass was to the Aulds. Nor could whites in antebellum America escape the pervasive influence of slavery. Otherwise decent people were often compelled by the "peculiar institution" to act inhumanely. After her husband's interference, Sophia Auld, Douglass observed, was transformed from an angel into a demon by the "fatal poison of irresponsible power." Her formerly tender heart turned to "stone" when she ceased teaching him. "Slavery proved as injurious to her," Douglass wrote, "as it did to me."

Such was also the case in Douglass's relationship with Mr. Covey, a slavebreaker to whom he was sent in 1833 to have his will broken. Covey succeeded for a time, Douglass reported, in breaking his "body, soul, and spirit" by brutal hard work and discipline. But one hot August day in 1833, the two men fought a long, grueling battle, which Douglass won. His victory, he said, "rekindled the few expir-ing embers of freedom, and revived within me a sense of my own manhood." Although it would be four more years before his escape to the North, the young man never again felt like a slave. The key to Douglass's successful resistance to Covey's power was not just his strong will, or even the magical root he carried in his pocket, but rather his knowledge of how to jeopardize Covey's reputation and livelihood as a slavebreaker. The oppressed survive by knowing their oppressors.

As Mrs. Auld and Covey discovered, as long as some people were not free, no one was free. Douglass observed, "You cannot outlaw one part of the people without endangering the rights and liberties of all people. You cannot put a chain on the ankle of the bondsman without finding the other end of it about your own necks." After quarreling with a house servant, one plantation mistress complained that she "exercises dominion over me—or tries to do it. One would have thought . . . that I was the Servant, she the mistress." Many whites lived in constant fear of a slave revolt. A Louisiana planter recalled that he had "known times here when there was not a single planter who had a calm night's rest; they then never lay down to sleep without a brace of loaded pistols at their sides." In slave folktales, the clever Brer Rabbit usually outwitted the more powerful Brer Fox or Brer Wolf, thus reversing the roles of oppressed and oppressor.

Slavery, then, was an intricate web of human relationships as well as a labor system. After showing the economic growth and development of the Old South, in which slavery and cotton played vital roles, this chapter will emphasize the daily lives and relationships of masters and slaves who, like Douglass and the Aulds, lived, loved, learned, worked, and struggled with one another in the years before the Civil War.

Perhaps no issue in American history has generated quite as many interpretations or as much emotional controversy as that of slavery. As American attitudes toward that institution have changed over the years, three interpretive schools have developed, each adding to our knowledge of the peculiar institution. The first saw slavery as a relatively humane and reasonable institution in which plantation owners took care of helpless, childlike slaves. The second depicted slavery as a harsh and cruel system of oppressive exploitation. The third, and most recent, interpretation described the slavery experience from the perspective of the slaves, who did indeed suffer brutal

The young Frederick Douglass, shown here in a photograph from about 1855, understood as well as any American the profound human, social, and political complexities and consequences of slavery. *(New York Public Library, Schomburg Center for Research in Black Culture)*

treatment in slavery yet nevertheless survived with integrity, self-esteem, and a sense of community and culture.

The first and second interpretive schools emphasized workaday interactions among masters and mostly passive, victimized slaves, while the third focused on the creative energies and survival of life in the slave quarters from sundown to sunup. In a unique structure, this chapter follows these masters and slaves through their day, from morning in the Big House through hot afternoon in the fields to the slave cabins at night. Although slavery was the crucial institution in defining the Old South, many other social groups and patterns contributed to the tremendous economic growth of the South from 1820 to 1860. We will look first at these diverse aspects of antebellum southern life.

🐚 BUILDING THE COTTON KINGDOM

Many myths obscure our understanding of the vast region of the antebellum South. It was not a monolithic society filled only with large cotton plantations worked by hundreds of slaves. The realities of the South and slavery were much more complex. Large-plantation agriculture was dominant in the antebellum South, but most southern whites were not even slaveholders, much less large planters. Most southern farmers lived not in mansions but in dark, cramped, two-room cabins. Cotton was a key cash crop in the South, but it was not the only crop grown there. Some masters were kindly, but many were not; some slaves were contented, but most were not.

There were many Souths, encompassing several geographic regions, each with different economic bases and social structures and each reflecting its own cultural and political values. The older Upper South of Virginia, Maryland, North Carolina, and Kentucky grew different staple crops from those grown in the newer, Lower or "Black Belt" South that stretched from South Carolina to eastern Texas. Within each state, moreover, the economies of flat coastal areas, inland upcountry forests, and pine barrens all differed. A still further diversity existed between these areas and the Appalachian highlands of northern Alabama and Georgia, eastern Tennessee and Kentucky, and western Virginia and North Carolina. Finally, the cultural and economic life of New Orleans, Savannah, Charleston, and Richmond differed dramatically from rural areas of the South.

Although the South was diverse, agriculture dominated its industry and commerce. In 1859, a Virginia planter complained about a neighbor who was considering abandoning his farm to become a merchant. "To me it seems to be a wild idea," the planter wrote in his diary, hoping that his friend would "give it up and be satisfied to farm." Southerners placed a high value on agricultural labor. Slavery was primarily a labor system intended to produce wealth for landowners. Although slavery in older areas was paternalistic, with masters and slaves owing mutual obligations to each other, increasingly it became a capitalistic enterprise intended to maximize productivity and profits.

Economic Expansion

In the 20 years preceding the Civil War, the South's economy grew slightly faster than the North's. Personal income in 1860 was 15 percent higher in the South than in the prosperous states of the Old Northwest. If the South had become an independent nation in 1860, it would have ranked as one of the wealthiest countries in the world in per capita income. One dramatic technological breakthrough, the cotton gin, was fundamental to this economic growth. The cotton gin had two momentous effects: first, it tied the southern economy to cotton production for a century; second, it allowed the expansion of slavery into vast new territories.

As we learned in Chapter 9, most cotton farmers planted "long-staple" cotton before the invention of Eli Whitney's cotton gin in 1793. After the cotton gin, the "short-staple" variety, which could grow anywhere in the South, predominated. But only large-plantation owners could afford to buy gins and purchase the fertile bottomlands of the Gulf states. Thus, the plantation system spread with the rise of cotton.

Because cotton could be grown all over the South after the perfection of the cotton gin, men rushed westward to fresh, fertile lands. Large-scale farming increased, demanding more and more slave labor. As a valuable capital resource, slaves received a degree of care and protection. But despite the abolition of slavery in the North and occasional talk of emancipation in the South, slavery became more deeply entrenched, seemingly a permanent part of southern life. Any doubts whispered about ending it could be dispelled by one word: cotton.

Although corn was a larger crop than cotton in total acreage, cotton was the largest cash crop and for that reason was called "king." In 1820, the South became the world's largest producer of cotton, and from 1815 to

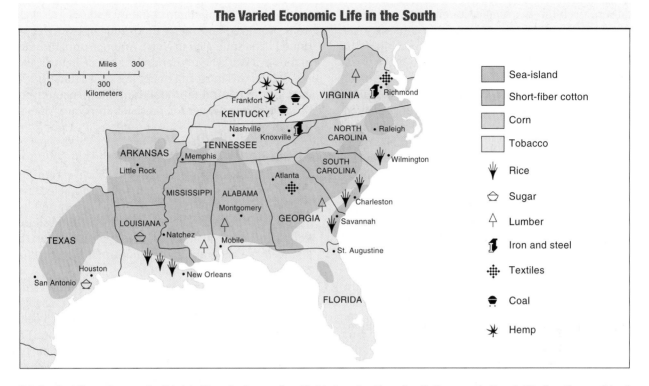

The Varied Economic Life in the South

Note the short-fiber, cotton-growing "black belt" running from southern Virginia to eastern Texas. Despite the economically varied South, cotton was "king."

1860, cotton represented more than half of all American exports. The economic growth spurred by cotton helped not only the South but also the North and the Midwest. Northern merchants gained by shipping, insuring, and marketing southern cotton. Western farmers found a major market for their foodstuffs. Cotton was the mainstay of the southern economy, but it was also a crucial link in the national economy.

The supply of cotton from the South grew at an astonishing rate. Cotton production soared from 461,000 bales in 1817 to 1.35 million bales in 1840. A cotton "boom" started in 1849 when output reached 2.85 million bales and continued until 1860, when production peaked at 4.8 million bales. In the period from 1817 to 1860, cotton production jumped over tenfold. This rapid growth was stimulated by world demand, especially from English textile mills. The availability of new lands, a self-reproducing supply of cheap slave labor, and low-cost steamboat transportation down the Mississippi River to New Orleans helped keep cotton king.

White and Black Migrations

Southerners migrated southwestward in huge numbers between 1830 and 1860 to grow more and more cotton. Seeking profits from the worldwide demand for cotton, they pushed the southeastern Indians and the Mexicans in Texas out of the way and were still moving into Texas as the Civil War began.

Southern cotton growers, like northern grain farmers, followed parallel migration paths westward. Whereas New Englanders moved into the upper Midwest, southerners migrated from the coastal states westward into the lower Midwest and the Lower South. By the 1830s, the center of cotton production had shifted from South Carolina and Georgia to Alabama and Mississippi. This process continued in the 1850s as southerners forged into Arkansas, Louisiana, and eastern Texas. As they moved, they carried their values and institutions, including slavery, with them. Usually, a father and his sons would go west first, find land and clear it, plant some corn, and begin to raise a cabin. Leaving the sons to finish, the father would return east, where his wife and daughters had been managing the farm, pack up the household, and bring it to the new home. Thus, in November 1835, one extended family of nearly 50 people left South Carolina for Alabama. "We bade adieu to friends," a daughter wrote, "and left the old homestead never to look upon it again."

Not only were these migrating southern families attracted by the pull of fresh land and cheap labor, but they also were pushed westward by deteriorating economic conditions and other pressures in the older Atlantic states. Beginning in the 1820s, the states of the Upper South underwent a long depression affecting tobacco and cotton prices. Moreover, years of constant use had exhausted their lands, and families with numerous children struggled to give each child an inheritance or financial help to start a family or a career. In a society that valued land ownership, farm families had several choices. One was to move west. Another was to stay and diversify. Therefore, the older states of the Upper South continued to shift to grains, mainly corn and wheat. Because these crops required less labor than tobacco, slave owners, especially those with pressing debts, began to sell some of their slaves.

The internal slave trade from Virginia "down the river" to the Old Southwest thus became a multimillion-dollar "industry" in the 1830s. Between 1830 and 1860, an estimated 300,000 Virginia slaves were transported south for sale. One of the busiest routes was from Alexandria, Virginia, almost within view of the nation's capital, to a huge depot near Natchez, Mississippi. Although most southern states attempted occasionally to outlaw or control the traffic in slaves, these efforts were poorly enforced and usually short-lived. Besides, the reason for outlawing the slave trade was generally not humanitarian but rather originated in a fear of a rapid increase in the slave population, especially of "wicked" slaves sent south because they were considered unmanageable. Alabama, Mississippi, and Louisiana all banned the importation of slaves after the Nat Turner revolt in Virginia in 1831 (described later in this chapter). But all three states permitted the slave trade again during the profitable 1850s.

Congress formally ended the external slave trade on January 1, 1808, the earliest time permitted by the Constitution. Enforcement by the United States was weak, however, and many thousands of blacks continued to be smuggled to North America until the end of the Civil War. The tremendous increase in the slave population was the result not of this illegal trade, however, but of natural reproduction, often encouraged by slave owners eager for more laborers and salable human property.

The Dependence on Slavery

The rapid increase in the number of slaves, from 1.5 million in 1820 to 4 million in 1860, paralleled the growth of the southern economy and its dependence on the slave labor system. Economic growth and migration southwestward changed the geographic distribution of slaves, thus hindering the cause of abolition.

Although most slaves worked on plantations and medium-size farms, they could be found in all segments of the southern economy. In 1850, some 75 percent of all slaves were engaged in agricultural labor: 55 percent growing cotton, 10 percent tobacco, and 10 percent rice, sugar, and hemp. Of the remaining one-fourth, about 15 percent were domestic servants, and the remainder were in mining, lumbering, construction, and industry.

The 300,000 slaves in 1850 who were not domestics or agricultural laborers worked as lumberjacks and turpentine producers in Carolina and Georgia forests; gold, coal, and salt miners in Virginia and Kentucky; boiler stokers and deckhands on

Slaves were found not just on plantations doing agricultural labor but in nearly every kind of labor in the South. These Virginia dockworkers were photographed about 1860 in Alexandria, Virginia, by Mathew Brady. *(National Archives)*

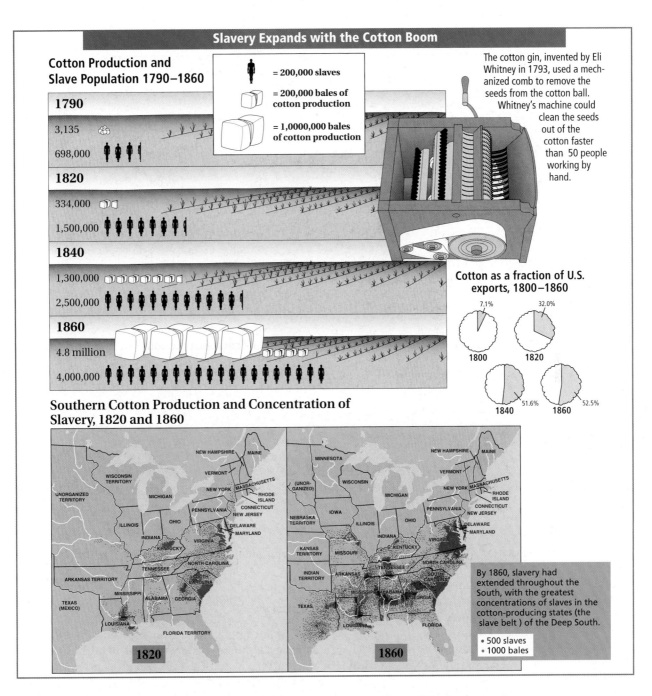

Slavery Expands with the Cotton Boom

Cotton Production and Slave Population 1790–1860

= 200,000 slaves

= 200,000 bales of cotton production

= 1,0000,000 bales of cotton production

1790
3,135
698,000

1820
334,000
1,500,000

1840
1,300,000
2,500,000

1860
4.8 million
4,000,000

The cotton gin, invented by Eli Whitney in 1793, used a mechanized comb to remove the seeds from the cotton ball. Whitney's machine could clean the seeds out of the cotton faster than 50 people working by hand.

Cotton as a fraction of U.S. exports, 1800–1860

7.1% 1800
32.0% 1820
51.6% 1840
52.5% 1860

Southern Cotton Production and Concentration of Slavery, 1820 and 1860

1820

1860

By 1860, slavery had extended throughout the South, with the greatest concentrations of slaves in the cotton-producing states (the slave belt) of the Deep South.

• 500 slaves
• 1000 bales

Mississippi River steamships; toilers on road and railroad construction gangs in Georgia and Louisiana; textile laborers in Alabama cotton mills; dockworkers in Savannah and Charleston; and tobacco and iron workers in Richmond factories. A visitor to Natchez in 1835 observed slaves working as "mechanics, draymen, hostelers, labourers, hucksters, and washwomen, and the heterogeneous multitude of every other occupation, who fill the streets of a busy city—for slaves are trained to every kind of manual labour."

Masters also used slaves in industry. The Tredegar Iron Company of Richmond decided in 1847 to shift from white labor "almost exclusively" to slave labor to destroy the potential power of organized white workers to strike. Tredegar's decision foreshadowed the similar strategy of many future employers to exploit black laborers as a means of eliminating or putting an economic squeeze on organized white laborers.

Whether in iron factories, coal mines, or cotton fields, slavery was profitable as a source of labor and as a capital investment. In 1859, the average plantation slave produced $78 in cotton earnings for his master annually while costing only about $32 to be fed, clothed, and housed. Despite maintenance costs, debts from the purchase of land and more slaves, and

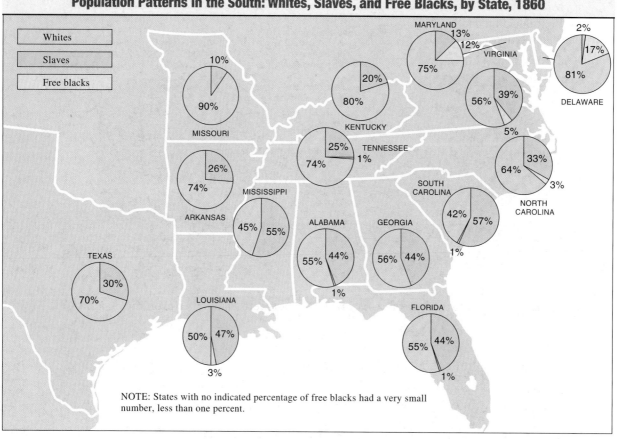

Population Patterns in the South: Whites, Slaves, and Free Blacks, by State, 1860

Whites

Slaves

Free blacks

MISSOURI — 90%, 10%

KENTUCKY — 80%, 20%

MARYLAND — 75%, 13%, 12%

VIRGINIA — 56%, 39%, 5%

DELAWARE — 81%, 17%, 2%

TENNESSEE — 74%, 25%, 1%

NORTH CAROLINA — 64%, 33%, 3%

ARKANSAS — 74%, 26%

MISSISSIPPI — 45%, 55%

SOUTH CAROLINA — 42%, 57%, 1%

ALABAMA — 55%, 44%, 1%

GEORGIA — 56%, 44%

TEXAS — 70%, 30%

LOUISIANA — 50%, 47%, 3%

FLORIDA — 55%, 44%, 1%

NOTE: States with no indicated percentage of free blacks had a very small number, less than one percent.

Note how the largest proportions of free blacks were in the older Upper South and in Louisiana (mostly in New Orleans). Note also the two states with more slaves than whites.

the unstable price of cotton, the "crop value per slave" increased from about $15 in 1800 to $125 in 1860. Slaves were also a good investment. In 1844, a "prime field hand" sold for $600. A cotton boom beginning in 1849 raised this price by 1860 to $1800. A slave owner could prosper by buying slaves, working them for several years, and then selling them for a profit. The rising price of slaves reflected the optimism of the planter class.

The economic growth of the slaveholding South was impressive, but slavery still limited it. Generally, agricultural growth leads to the rise of cities and industry, facilitating sustained economic growth. In the planter-dominated antebellum South, however, agricultural improvements did not lead to industrialization and urbanization. In 1860, the South had 35 percent of the country's population and only 15 percent of its manufacturing establishments. On the eve of the Civil War, 1 southerner in 14 was a city dweller, compared with 1 of every 3 people in the North. The South would continue its economic backwardness as long as whites with capital insisted on putting all their business energies toward cotton production.

Some southerners were aware of the dangers of following a single path to wealth. J. D. B. De Bow created a journal in 1846 dedicated to trade, commerce, and manufacturing. De Bow's *Review* called for greater economic independence in the South through the diversification of agriculture, the development of industry, and an improved transportation system. A believer in slavery, De Bow thought that slave labor could fuel the Industrial Revolution in the South. But the planter class had little enthusiasm for such plans. As long as money could be made through an agricultural slave system, plantation owners saw no reason to risk capital in new areas.

Slavery and Class in the South

Slavery also served social purposes. Although the proportion of southern white families that owned slaves slowly declined from 40 to 25 percent as some families sold off their slaves to cotton planters, the ideal of slave ownership still permeated all classes and determined the hierarchical character of the southern social structure. At the top stood the planter aristocracy, much of it new wealth, elbowing its way among

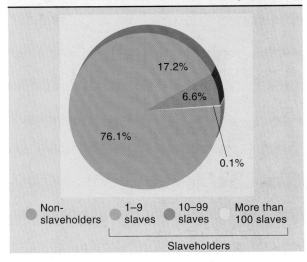

White Class Structure in the South, 1860

17.2%

6.6%

76.1%

0.1%

● Non-slaveholders ● 1–9 slaves ● 10–99 slaves ○ More than 100 slaves

Slaveholders

In a pyramidal class structure, the richest southerners were those few with the largest number of slaves. As the chart shows, three-fourths of antebellum southerners held no slaves at all.

the old established families like the Byrds and Carters of Virginia. Some 10,000 rich families owned 50 or more slaves in 1860; about 3,000 of these owned over 100. Below them was a slightly larger group of small planters who held from 10 to 50 slaves. But the largest group, 70 percent of all slaveholders in 1860, comprised 270,000 middle-level farm families with fewer than 10 slaves. The typical slaveholder worked a small family farm of about 100 acres with 8 or 9 slaves, perhaps members of the same family. The typical slave, however, was more likely to be in a group of 20 or more other slaves on a large farm or small plantation.

In 1841, a young white North Carolinian, John Flintoff, went to Mississippi to fulfill his dream of wealth and prestige. Beginning as an overseer managing an uncle's farm, he bought a "negro boy 7 years old" even before he owned any land. After several years of unrewarding struggle, Flintoff married and returned to North Carolina. There he finally bought 124 acres and a few more cheap, young blacks, and by 1860, he had a modest farm with several slaves growing corn, wheat, and tobacco. Although he never became as prosperous as he had dreamed, his son went to college, and his wife, he reported proudly, "has lived a Lady."

Slavery was a powerful force in the lives of middle-level farmers like John Flintoff, who had only a few slaves, and even for those who owned none. Economic, social, and political standing depended on owning slaves. Whites like John Flintoff hoped to purchase one slave, perhaps a female who would bear children, and then climb the economic and social

ladder of southern society. White southerners therefore supported slavery whether they owned slaves or not.

They also defended the institution because it gave them a sense of superiority over at least one group and a sense of kinship, if not quite equality, with other whites. Although there was always a small element of southern society that believed in emancipation, most southerners did not. A small Alabama farmer told a northern visitor in the 1850s that if the slaves were given their freedom, "they'd all think themselves just as good as we. . . . How would you like to hev a nigger feelin' just as good as a white man?" Another said that he wished "there warn't no niggers here" and did not know anybody who favored freeing them.

The Nonslaveholding South

Below Flintoff and other middling farmers lived the majority of white southerners, who owned no slaves but were equally, or even more, antiblack. Newton Knight, for example, worked a harsh piece of land cut out of the pines of southern Mississippi. He and his wife lived in a crude log cabin, scratching out their livelihood by growing corn and sweet potatoes and raising chickens and hogs. A staunch Baptist given to fits of violence, Knight had once killed a black.

The 75 percent of southern whites who, like Newton Knight and his family, owned no slaves were scattered throughout the South. Many were Scots-Irish. Most lived in the foothills of the mountains and worked generally poorer land than the large planters. They did not need to be near commercial centers because they were largely self-sufficient. Working together as a family, they raised mostly corn and wheat, hogs, enough cotton for their own clothes and a little cash, and subsistence vegetable crops. These farmers maintained a household economy, making soap, shoes, candles, whiskey, coarse textiles, and ax handles and trading hogs, eggs, small game, or homemade items for cash and other goods. They lived in two-room log houses separated by a "dog run." Cooperation with neighbors brightened the yeoman farmer's drab and isolated life. Families gathered at corn huskings and quilting parties, logrolling and wrestling matches, and political stump and revivalist camp meetings.

In many ways, the yeoman farmers were the solid backbone of the South. In 1860 in North Carolina, 70 percent of the farmers held fewer than 100 acres; in Mississippi and Louisiana, reputedly large plantation states, more than 60 percent of the farms were under 100 acres. Fiercely proud of their independence, the yeoman farmers had a share of political power, voting overwhelmingly for Andrew Jackson. Although some resented the tradition of political deference to "betters,"

Southern yeoman farm families lived self-sufficient lives in cabins such as this one on the edge of a clearing. The isolation of the woman drawing water from a well was partly relieved by gatherings such as quilting parties, which created not only social contact but also a uniquely female American work of useful art. Note that men were also at the party, talking (politics, perhaps) by the stove, bouncing a baby, carrying food, and courting a young woman by the quilt. *(Above, Abby Aldrich Rockefeller Folk Art Center; right, North Wind Picture Archives)*

these farmers were not yet ready to challenge planters for political power. Yeoman farmers fought with the Confederacy during the Civil War; but some, like Newton Knight, refused to fight against the Union and ended up organizing a guerrilla band of Unionists in southern Mississippi.

Another little-known group of southern whites included the herdsmen who raised hogs and other livestock. Living among the plantations and small farms, they supplied bacon and pork to local slave-holders (who often thought hog growing was beneath their dignity) and drove herds of hogs to stockyards in Nashville, Louisville, and Savannah. The South raised two-thirds of the nation's hogs. In 1860, the value of southern livestock was $500 million, twice that of cotton. Although much of the corn crop fed the hogs, many herdsmen preferred to let their stock roam loose in the woods. As one South Carolinian explained, "We raise our hogs by allowing them to range in our woods, where they get fat . . . on acorns," which he and others considered a better diet for bacon and pork than corn. However valuable the total size of the hog business, individual hog herdsmen did not stand very high on the southern social ladder.

Below them were the poor whites of the South, about 10 percent of the population. Often sneeringly called "hillbillies," "dirt eaters," "crackers," or "poor white trash," they eked out a living in isolated, inhospitable areas. Although they grew a little corn and vegetables, their livelihood came mostly from fishing, hunting small game, and raising a few pigs. Some made corn whiskey, and many hired themselves out as farmhands for an average wage, with board, of about $14 per month. Because of poor diet and bad living conditions, these poor whites often suffered from hookworm and malaria. This, and the natural debilitation of heat and poverty, gave them a reputation as lazy, shiftless, and illiterate. An English visitor, Fanny Kemble, described them as "the most degraded race of human beings claiming an Anglo-Saxon origin that can be found on the face of the earth."

The poor whites stayed poor partly because the slave system allowed the planter class to accumulate a disproportionate amount of land and political power. High slave prices made entry into the planter class increasingly difficult, increasing class tensions within the South. Because the larger planters dominated southern life and owned the most slaves, an understanding of the character of slavery and the relationships between masters and slaves is best accomplished by looking at plantation life during a typical day from morning to night.

MORNING: MASTER IN THE BIG HOUSE

It is early morning in the South. Imagine four scenes. In the first, William Waller of Virginia and a neighbor are preparing to leave with 20 choice slaves on a long trip to the slave market in Natchez, Mississippi. Waller is making this "intolerable" journey, as he calls it, to sell some of his slaves to ease his heavy debts. Although he "loaths the vocation of slave trading," he must recover some money out of a "sense of duty" to see his family "freed from my bondage" of indebtedness. To ease his conscience, he intends to supervise the sale personally, thus securing the best possible deal not only for himself but also for his departing slaves.

On another plantation, owned by James Hammond of South Carolina, the horn blows an hour before daylight to awaken the slaves for work in the fields. Hammond rises soon after, ever aware that "to continue" as a wealthy master, he must "draw the rein tighter and tighter" to hold his slaves "in complete check." He is as good as his word, recommending that "in general 15 to 20 lashes will be sufficient flogging" for most offenses but that "in extreme cases," the punishment "must not exceed 100 lashes in one day."

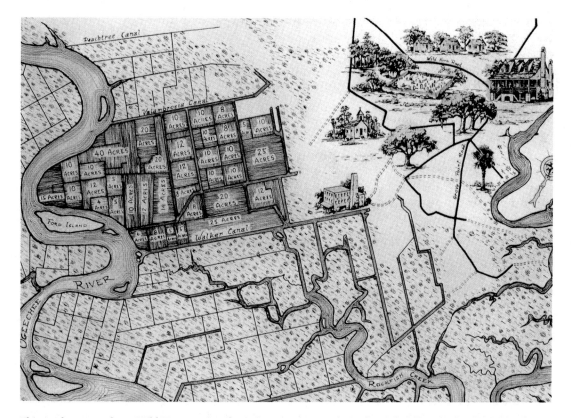

This modern map shows Wild Heron, a rice plantation near Savannah similar to the Allston's. Note the elaborate system of canals, roads, and paths connecting the rice fields with the mill, plantation house, slave quarters, cemetery, and chapel. *(Danzer Map Collection/University of Tennessee Press)*

On an Alabama plantation, Hugh Lawson is up early, writing a sorrowful letter to Susanna Clay, telling her of the death of a "devotedly attached and faithful" slave, Jim. "I feel desolate," Hugh writes, "my most devoted friend is gone and his place can never be supplied by another." As Lawson pens his letter, a female slave has already awakened and "walked across a frosty field in the early morning and gone to the big house to build a fire" for her mistress. As the mistress wakes up to a warming house, she says to the slave, a grown woman responsible for the welfare of two families, "Well, how's my little nigger today?"

In a fourth household, this one a medium-size farm in upcountry Georgia, not far from Hammond's huge plantation, Charles Brock wakes up at dawn and joins his two sons and four slaves to work his modest acreage of grains and sweet potatoes, while Brock's wife and a female slave tend the cows that provide milk and butter. On small and medium-size family farms with five or fewer slaves, blacks and whites commonly worked together, as one observer noted, with the "axe of master and man [slave] falling with alternate strokes . . . [and] ploughing side by side."

As these diverse scenes suggest, slavery thoroughly permeated the lives of southern slaveholders. For the slaves, morning was a time for getting up and going to work. But for white slaveholders, morning involved contact with slaves in many ways: as burdens of figuring profit and loss, as objects to be kept obedient and orderly, as intimates and fellow workers, and as ever-present reminders of fear, hate, and uncertainty.

The Burdens of Slaveholding

Robert Francis Withers Allston (1801–1864) was a major rice planter in the Georgetown district of South Carolina, a low, swampy, mosquito-infested tidal area where four rivers empty into Winyah Bay. It was a perfect spot for growing rice, but so unhealthy that few whites wanted to live there. The death rate among slaves was appallingly high. In 1840, a total of 18,274 slaves toiled in the Georgetown district, but only 2,193 whites, many for only part of the year. Robert was the fifth generation of Allstons to live in this inhospitable land. By 1860, he owned seven plantations along the Peedee River, totaling some 4,000 acres, in addition to another 9,500 acres of pasture and timberland. He held nearly 600 slaves, 236 of whom worked at the home plantation, Chicora Wood. The total value of his land and slaves in the 1850s was approximately $300,000. Rich in land and labor, he nevertheless had large mortgages and outstanding debts.

Allston was an enlightened, talented, public-spirited man. Educated at West Point but also trained in the law, he did far more than practice agriculture. He

served as a state senator in South Carolina for 24 years and as governor from 1856 to 1858. His political creed, he wrote in 1838, was one of "virtue and purity" based on "the principles of Thomas Jefferson." The core of his conviction was a "plain, honest, commonsense reading of the Constitution," which for Allston clearly meant the constitutionality of slavery and nullification and the illegitimacy of abolitionism and the United States Bank.

Allston also reflected Jefferson's humane side. He was an ardent reformer, advocating liberalization of South Carolina's poor laws; an improved system of public education open to rich and poor alike; humanitarian care of the deaf, blind, insane, and other disabled people; and the improvement of conditions on the reservations of the Catawba Indians. He was active in the Episcopal Church and gave money generously to support ministerial students.

In 1832, Allston married Adele Petigru, an equally enlightened and hardworking person. She participated fully in the management of the plantation and ran it while Robert was away on politics. In a letter to her husband, written in 1850, Adele demonstrated her diverse interests by reporting on family affairs and the children's learning, sickness among the slaves, the status of spring plowing, the building of a canal and causeway, her supervision of the bottling of some wine, and current politics. After Robert's death during the Civil War, she assumed control of the Allston plantations, which had been abandoned when Union troops moved through the area. Eventually, she had to sell most of the estate at auction, holding on only to Chicora Wood, which she managed with a daughter until her death in 1896.

State politics lured Robert from his land for part of each year, but he was by no means an absentee owner. Except when away to escape the worst periods of mosquitoes and heat, the Allstons were fully engaged in the operation of their plantations. Managing thousands of acres of rice required not only an enormous investment in labor and equipment but also careful supervision of both the slaves and an elaborate irrigation system. Although Robert Allston's acreage and slave population were larger than those of most big planters and he grew rice rather than cotton, his concerns were typical.

Allston's letters frequently expressed the serious burdens of owning slaves. Although he was careful to distribute enough cloth, blankets, and shoes to his slaves and to give them sufficient rest, the sickness and death of slaves, especially young field workers, headed his list of concerns. "I lost in one year 28 negroes," Allston complained, "22 of whom were task hands." He tried to keep slave families together but sold slaves when necessary. In a letter to his son, Benjamin, he

Agreement To Purchase Slaves, January 25, 1859

Robert Allston bought these slaves for his son, Benjamin, who was then 25 years old and taking charge of one of his father's many plantations, Guendalos. Note that in this (not unusual) case, slave families were kept together in the transaction.

Agreed to purchase from Dr. Forster Forty one Negroes of Mrs. Withers of the "remainder" from the Estate of the late Francis Withers, to be deliver'd in all this week at $500. Titles to Ben Allston his Bond and mine payable in 8, 10, 12 yrs. secured by mortgage of the property, viz

$1,000	1	Andrew	38	yrs.
800	2	Serena	36	
400	3	Jos.	10	
300	4	Judy	8	
200	5	Henry	5	
1,000	6	Jack	30	
800	7	Patience	27	pregnant
400	8	Daniel	11	
300	9	Prince	9	
250	10	Phyllis	5	
200	11	Bess	3½	
800	12	James*	28	carpenter, Drinks, delicate
800	13	Hagar	24	pregnant, near time of delivery
200	14	Joe	39	carpenter and cooper
800	15	Levi	50	
500	16	Betsey†	40	delicate
400	17	Murria‡	18	
400	18	Toby	14	
$1,000	19	Paris	35	
800	20	Hannah	33	
800	21	Frank	16½	
500	22	William	14	
350	23	Caty	9	
300	24	Michael	6	
150	25	Eleanor	3½	
50	26	Dandy	1	
800	27	Strophon	50	
700	28	Lucy	18	
500	29	Judy	14	
1,000	30	Toney	38	an indifferent carpenter
800	31	Betty	35	
800	32	Daniel	16½	3 years with Bricklayers to mix mortar
200	33	Francis	4½	
100	34	Caesar	1½	
500	35	O Sary	50	cook and washer
1,000	36	Israel	31	
800	37	Esther	28	
100	38	William	1½	
800	39	Dinah	18½	
500	40	Quash	14½	
300	41	William	9	

*Has Epileptic attacks produced by drink, would be valuable if kept from drink.
†With this family there is the incumbrance of an old man of 80 years, father of Betsey.
‡Murria is half witted.
Note: Prices are from a second list, as are some of the remarks concerning individuals. The horizontal lines probably separate family groups.

Source: This and other material on the Allstons is from *The South Carolina Rice Plantation as Revealed in the Papers of Robert F. W. Allston*, ed., J. H. Easterby (1945).

Adele and Robert F. W. Allston shared the work and burdens of managing their rice plantations, while their slaves, many of them women, as seen in these drawings, planted rice seeds by covering them with their feet (as was done in Africa), and later carried the harvested rice to flatboats, where it was taken to the threshing yard. *(Portraits, South Carolina Library, Columbia; Drawings, From Down by the Riverside, Charles Joyner, 1984, sketch by Alice R. Huger Smith, c. 1914; photograph from Photographs and Prints Division, Schomburg Center for Research in Black Culture, The New York Public Library, Astor, Lenox and Tilden Foundations)*

expressed concern over the bad example set by a slave driver who was "abandon'd by his hands" because he had not worked with them the previous Sunday. In the same letter, Allston urged Benjamin to keep up the "patrol duty," less to guard against runaway slaves, he said, than to restrain the excesses of "vagabond whites." Clearly, the planter class felt a duty to control lower-class whites as well as black slaves.

Other planters shared Allston's concerns, seeing slavery as both a duty and a burden. A Louisiana planter, in financial difficulty, wrote how much he dreaded the "miserable occupation of seeing to negroes, and attending to their wants and sickness and to making them do their duty—and after all have no prospect of being paid for my trouble." Many planters insisted that they worked harder than their slaves to feed and clothe them and to make their lives "as comfortable as possible." Some accepted this as part of their responsibility, and others complained loudly. R. L. Dabney of Virginia exclaimed: "There could be no greater curse inflicted on us than to be compelled to manage a parcel of Negroes." Curse or not, Dabney and other planters profited from their burdens, a point they seldom admitted.

Their wives experienced other kinds of burdens. "The mistress of a plantation," wrote Susan Dabney Smedes, "was the most complete slave on it." Southern women were expected to adhere to the cult of domesticity both by improving their husbands' morals, which often meant restraining them from excessive cruelty toward slaves, and by beautifying their parlors. Moreover, plantation mistresses suffered under a double standard of morality. They were expected to act as chaste ladies, whereas their husbands had virtually unrestricted sexual access to slave women. "God forgive us, but ours is a monstrous system," Mary Boykin Chesnut wrote in her diary. "Like the patriarchs of old, our men live all in one house with their wives and their concubines; and the mulattoes one sees in every family partly resemble the white children. Any lady is ready to tell you who is the father of all the mulatto children in everybody's household but her own. Those, she seems to think, drop from the clouds."

Chesnut called the sexual dynamics of slavery "the sorest spot." There were others. Together with female slaves, plantation mistresses had to tend to the food, clothing, health, and welfare of not just their husbands and children, but the plantation slave population as well. Adele Allston, we saw, added plantation management to these duties. The son of a Tennessee slaveholder remembered his mother and grandmother as "the busiest women I ever saw." One woman, who spent the night sitting up to attend a slave birth,

complained to a northern visitor: "It is the slaves who own me. Morning, noon, and night, I'm obliged to look after them, to doctor them, and attend to them in every way." The plantation mistress, then, served many roles: as a potential humanizing influence on men; as a tough, resourceful, responsible manager of numerous plantation affairs; as a coercer of slaves and perpetuator of the system; and sometimes as a victim herself.

Justifying Slavery

The behavior of Douglass's mistress suggests that the institution of slavery pressured well-intentioned people, women and men alike, to act inhumanely. Increasingly attacked as immoral, slaveholders felt compelled to justify their institution. Until the 1830s, they explained slavery as a "necessary evil." After abolitionists stepped up their attack in that decade, however, they shifted to justifying slavery, in John C. Calhoun's words, as a "positive good." Various arguments were used: biblical, historical, constitutional, scientific, and sociological.

The biblical justification was based in part on the curse that had fallen upon the son of Ham, one of Noah's children, and in part on Old and New Testament admonishments to servants to obey their masters. As a historical justification, southerners claimed that slavery had always existed and that great ancient civilizations—Egypt, Greece, and Rome—had built their grandeur in part on slave labor.

The legal justification rested on the U.S. Constitution's acceptance of slavery. In fact, although slavery was not mentioned specifically, three passages in the original document clearly implied its constitutionality. First, slaves, called "all other Persons," were counted as three-fifths of a person for purposes of representation. Second, the overseas slave trade was protected from congressional abolition for 20 years. Third, the Constitution mandated the return of runaway slaves from one state to another.

A fourth justification was scientific. Until the 1830s, most white southerners believed that blacks were degraded not by nature but by African climate and their slave condition. As a result of books on cranial shapes and sizes written by northern writers (or scholars), scientists maintained that in the black "the animal parts of the brain preponderate over the moral and intellectual, which explains why he is deficient in reason, judgement and forecast." Southerners bought the argument, increasingly insisting that blacks had been created separately as an inherently inferior race, which justified their argument that they were destined to labor for the superior Caucasians. This led to the "positive good" defense of slavery in which the patriarchal slave system would tame and domesticate the uncivilized Africans. As Allston put it, "The educated master is the negro's best friend upon earth."

Allston's point suggested a paternalistic sociological defense of slavery. George Fitzhugh, a leading advocate of this view, argued that "the Negro is but a grown child and must be governed as a child." Therefore, he needed the paternal guidance, restraint, and protection of his white masters. Many southerners believed that chaos and race mixing would ensue if slaves were freed. Allston wrote that emancipation "cannot be contemplated," for it would lead to "giving up our beautiful country to the ravages of the black race and amalgamation with savages." Fitzhugh was a little less direct. He compared the treatment of southern slaves favorably with that of free blacks and of free laborers working in northern factories. These "wage slaves," he argued, worked as hard as slaves, yet with their paltry wages they had to feed, clothe, and shelter themselves. Southern masters took care of all these necessities. Emancipation, therefore, would be heartless and unthinkable, a burden to both blacks and whites.

Southern apologists for slavery faced the difficult intellectual task of justifying a system that ran counter to the main ideological directions of nineteenth-century American society: the expansion of individual liberty, mobility, economic opportunity, and democratic political participation. Moreover, the southern defense of slavery had to take into account the 75 percent of white families who owned no slaves and who envied those who did. Because of the potential for class antagonisms among whites, wealthy planters developed a justification of slavery that deflected class differences by maintaining that all whites were superior to all blacks but equal to one another. The theory of democratic equality among whites, therefore, was made consistent with racism and the holding of slaves.

However couched in the language of science, law, history, or religion, the underlying motive of these various justifications, though rarely admitted, was that slavery was profitable. As the southern defense of slavery intensified in the 1840s and 1850s, it aroused greater opposition from northerners and from slaves themselves. Although slavery was cruel in many ways, perhaps its worst feature was not physical but psychological: to be enslaved at all and barred from participation in a nation that put a high value on freedom and equality of opportunity. "One of the grossest frauds committed upon the down-trodden slave," Douglass wrote, was to encourage drunkenness during holidays so that the slaves would be disgusted with freedom and would look forward to marching back to the fields.

NOON: SLAVES IN HOUSE AND FIELDS

It is two o'clock on a hot July afternoon on the plantation. The midday lunch break is over, and the slaves are returning to their work in the fields. Lunch was the usual fare of cornmeal and pork. The slaves return to work slowly and listlessly, not because of innate laziness but because of a lack of stamina resulting from deficient diet and the suffocating heat and humidity. Douglass remembered that "we worked all weathers. . . . It was never too hot, or too cold" for toiling in the fields. Mary Reynolds of Louisiana recalled that she hated most having to pick cotton "when the frost was on the bolls," which made her hands "git sore and crack open and bleed."

Daily Toil

The daily work schedule for most slaves, whether in the fields or the Big House, was long and demanding. Aroused by a bell or horn before daybreak, they worked on an average day 14 hours in the summer and 10 hours in the winter. During harvest time, it was not uncommon to work for 18 hours. Depending on the size of the workforce and the crop, the slaves were organized either in gangs or according to tasks. The gangs, usually of 20 to 25, worked their way along the cotton rows under the watchful eye and quick whip of a driver. Ben Simpson, a Georgia slave, remembered vividly how his master would use a "great, long whip platted out of rawhide" to hit a slave in the gang who would "fall behind or give out."

Under the task system, each slave had a specific task to complete daily. This system gave slaves the incentive to work hard enough to finish early, but it meant that the quality of their work was scrutinized constantly. An overseer's weekly report to Robert Allston in 1860 noted that he had "flogged for hoeing corn bad Fanny 12 lashes, Sylvia 12, Monday 12, Phoebee 12, Susanna 12, Salina 12, Celia 12, Iris 12." The black slave driver, George Skipwith, was no less rigorous in his expectations of work from fellow slaves. In 1847, he reported to his master that several slaves working under him "at a reasonable days work" should have plowed 7 acres apiece but had done only 1½. Therefore, George proudly reported, "I gave them ten licks a peace upon their skins [and] I gave Julyann eight or ten licks for misplacing her hoe."

An average slave was expected to pick 130 to 150 pounds of cotton per day. The work on sugar and rice plantations was even harder. Sugar demanded constant cultivation and the digging of drainage ditches in snake-infested fields. At harvest time, cutting, stripping, and carrying the cane to the sugar house for boiling was exhausting. In addition, huge quantities

---

An Overseer's Report

W. Sweet to Adele Petigru Allston N[ightin]gale hall, 14th September, 1864.

Dear madam I comence my harvest on last saterday on Boath Plantations the weather is very fin for harvest so far I will Bring some Rice in to the Barn yard at N[ightin]gale hall to Day and at ganderloss to morrow. I think that I will make about 2 Barrels of Syrrup on Each Place I finish grinding at ganderloss to Day I will not finish at Nightingale hall until the last of next weeak. litle Dianah was confined with a boy child on the 9 I am very sorry to say to you that one of Prisilia children a boy name July Dide on 12th with fits a[nd] fever I have had a grea[t] deal of fever among the children But not much among the grone negroes. old Rose is Stil quite sick mr Belflowers sent toney to mee on friday last I have concluded to let toney wife stay whare she is for a while as I understand that she is Pregnant and will not Be much survice in the harvest if I am Rong for soe Doing Pleas let mee know. the negroes all sends thare love to you an family my self and family is very un well.

N[ightin]gale hall

8th September	all hands hoing Bancks and grinding shugar cain no sick
9th September	all hands hoing Bancks grind shugar cain no sick
10th September	all hands cu[tt]ing Rice grinding shugar cain no sick
12th September	all hands harvesting grinding shugar cain 3 women with sick children
13th September	all hands harvesting grinding shugar cain 3 women with sick children
14th September	all hands harvesting grinding shugar cain 1 woman with sick child

Source: *The South Carolina Rice Plantation as Revealed in the Papers of Robert F. W. Allston*, ed., J. H. Easterby (1945).

---

of firewood had to be cut and carried. Working in the low-country rice fields was worse: slaves spent long hours standing in water up to their knees.

House slaves, most of them women, had relatively easier assignments than the field slaves, though they were usually called on to help with the harvest. Their usual work was in or near the Big House as housemaids, cooks, seamstresses, laundresses, coachmen, drivers, gardeners, and mammies. Slaves did most of the artisanal work on the plantation; many became skilled carpenters, blacksmiths, stonemasons, weavers, mechanics, and millers. More intimacy between whites and blacks occurred near the house. House slaves ate and dressed better than their fellow slaves in the fields.

But there were also disadvantages. House slaves were watched more closely, were on call at all hours of the day and night, and were more often involved in personality conflicts in the white household. As one house servant put it, "We were constantly exposed to the whims and passions of every member of the family." This meant everything from assignment to petty jobs to insults, spontaneous angry whippings, and sexual assault. The most feared punishment for a house slave, however, other than sale to the Deep South, was to be sent to the fields.

Slave Health

Although slave owners had an interest in keeping their slaves healthy, slaves led sickly lives. Home was a crude one-room log cabin with a dirt floor and a fireplace; some such houses were well made, others were not. Cracks and holes allowed mosquitoes easy entry, disturbing sleep. Typical furnishings included a table, some stools or boxes to sit on, an iron pot and wooden dishes, and perhaps a bed. Some slaves slept on the ground on mattresses of corn shucks, using burlap bags for blankets. Cabins were crowded, with usually more than one family. Clothing was shabby and uncomfortable. Usually, each man was issued two cotton shirts and two pairs of cotton or woolen pants each fall and spring and a pair of stout shoes once a year. Women were given cotton and woolen cloth twice a year with which to make their own and their children's clothes.

Studies disagree on the adequacy of slave diet, some showing that the food most slaves ate was deficient in calories and vitamins, others claiming that the energy value of the slave diet exceeded that of free whites in the general population. Compared with Latin American slavery, where the ratio of male slaves to white residents was much higher than in the United States, American slaves were well fed. Once a week,

Slaves survived nobly despite hard work, ill health, a deficient diet, and poor living conditions. Female slaves had a double burden of work and caring for their families, as seen in the photograph of the woman picking cotton with her child and of the woman cooking in her cabin while her children look out from the doorway. But female slaves also managed to develop networks of support while working, as seen to the left in the drawing of the three women winnowing rice. *(top left,* From Down by the Riverside, *Charles Joyner, 1984, sketch by Alice R. Huger Smith, c. 1914; top right, photograph from* Photographs and Prints Division, Schomburg Center for Research in Black Culture, The New York Public Library, Astor, Lenox and Tilden Foundations; *directly above, Private Collection)*

each slave was issued an average ration of a peck of cornmeal, three to four pounds of salt pork or bacon, some molasses, and perhaps some sweet potatoes. The mainstay was corn. This bland fare was supplemented for some slaves, with the master's permission, by growing vegetables in a small garden and by fishing or hunting small game.

Most slaves, however, rarely enjoyed fresh meat, dairy products, fruits, or vegetables. The limitations of their diet led to theft from the master's kitchen, gardens, and barnyard. Such offenses were frequent, and just as frequently punished. A Louisiana planter told a neighbor, "I beg to regrets that two of my men have been found guilty of killing one of your calves," and another complained of many acts of theft committed by "famished negroes." Inadequate diet, moreover, led some slaves to become dirt eaters, which gave them worms and "swollen shiny skin, puffy eyelids, pale palms and soles." Others suffered regularly from skin disorders, cracked lips, and sore eyes. Many children were malnourished, and, like poor whites, slaves came down with vitamin deficiency diseases and even mental illness.

Women slaves especially suffered weaknesses caused by vitamin deficiency, hard work, and disease, as well as those associated with the menstrual cycle and childbirth. Women were expected to do the same tasks in the fields as the men, in addition to cooking, sewing, child care, and traditional female jobs in the quarters when the fieldwork was finished. "Pregnant women," the usual rule stated, "should not plough or lift but must be kept at moderate work until the last hour" and were given a three-week recovery period after giving birth. But these guidelines were more often violated than honored. Infant mortality of slave children under five years of age was twice as high as for white children.

Life expectancy for American slaves was longer than for those in Latin America and the Caribbean, but not very high for either blacks or whites in the antebellum South (21.4 for blacks and 25.5 for whites in 1850). In part because of poor diet and climate, slaves were highly susceptible to epidemic diseases. Despite some resistance as a result of the sickle-cell trait, many slaves still contracted and died from malaria, yellow fever, cholera, and other diseases caused by mosquitoes or bad water, especially in the dangerous low-lying rice fields of the Georgia coast and the sugar fields of Louisiana. Slaves everywhere suffered and died from intestinal ailments in the summer and respiratory diseases in the winter. An average of 20 percent (and sometimes 50 to 60 percent) of the slaves on a given plantation would be sick at one time, and no overseer's report was complete without an account of sickness and the number of days of lost labor.

The relatively frequent incidence of whippings and other physical punishments aggravated the poor physical condition of the slaves. Many slaveholders offered rewards—a garden plot, an extra holiday, hiring oneself out, or passes—as inducements for faithful labor, which helped some slaves to build a supplemental livelihood for themselves and their family. For punishments, some whites would withhold these privileges rather than resort to the lash. Southern court records, plantation diaries, and slave memoirs, however, also reveal that sadistic slave punishments were frequent and harsh.

The slave William Wells Brown reported that on his plantation, the whip was used "very frequently and freely" for inadequate or uncompleted work, stealing, running away, and even insolence and lying. Whippings ranged from 10 to 100 strokes of the lash, occasionally even more. Former slaves described a good owner as one who did not "whip too much" and a bad owner as one who "whipped till he'd bloodied you and blistered you." Slaveholders had many theories on the appropriate kind of lash to inflict sufficient pain and punishment without damaging a valuable laborer. Other forms of punishment included isolation and confinement in stocks and jails during leisure hours, chains, muzzles, salt on lash wounds, brands, burns, and castration.

Nothing testifies better to the physical brutality of slavery than the advertisements for runaways that slaveholders printed in antebellum newspapers. In searching for the best way to describe the physical characteristics of a missing slave, slave owners unwittingly condemned their own behavior. One Mississippi slave had "large raised scars . . . in the small of his back and on his abdomen nearly as large as a person's finger." Another, a Georgia female, was "considerably marked by the whip." Still another, who according to his North Carolina master had a "remarkably bad temper," was described by the "marks of the lash upon his back." Slaves who were branded were even easier to identify in these advertisements. One fugitive, Betty, was described as recently "burnt . . . with a hot iron on the left side of her face." "I tried to make the letter M," her master admitted in his diary. One can almost imagine Betty's master agonizingly applying his brand.

Slave Law and the Family

Complicating master–slave relationships was the status of slaves as both human beings and property, a legal and psychological ambiguity the South never resolved. On the one hand, the slaves had names, personalities, families, and wills of their own. This required dealing with them as fellow humans. On the other hand, they were items of property, purchased and maintained to perform specific profit-making tasks. As a Kentucky court put the problem in 1836, "Although the law of this state considers slaves as property, . . . it recognizes their personal existence, and, to a qualified extent, their natural right."

This ambiguity led to confusion in the laws governing treatment of slaves. Until the early 1830s, some southern abolitionist activity persisted, primarily in the Upper South, and slaves had slight expectations that they might be freed, if not by state action then by individual manumission. But along with this ray of hope, they suffered careless and often brutal treatment in matters of food, housing, work load, and punishments. This confusion changed with

The breakup of families and friendships was an ever-present fear for slaves, who might be sold for purely economic reasons as well as in retribution for uncooperative behavior. In this painting of a slave market by an unidentified artist in the 1850s, note the varied colors of the African Americans (a sad light-skinned young woman in the center, a mulatto male in the left foreground staring longingly at her, and dark-skinned women clutching their children to the right) and the diverse social class of the whites (the suave merchant leaning back in a chair on the porch, nattily attired slave auctioneers and buyers, and a gaudily dressed lower-class overseer cracking the whip over the separation of child from mother). All southern social classes perpetuated slavery, and African Americans of all hues were victimized by it. *(Anonymous American, Slave Market, c. 1860/The Carnegie Museum of Art, Gift of Mrs. W. Fitch Ingersoll)*

the threatening convergence in 1831 of Nat Turner's revolt and William Lloyd Garrison's publication of the abolitionist *Liberator*. After 1831, the South tightened up the slave system. Laws prohibiting manumission were passed, and the slaves' expectation of freedom other than by revolt or escape vanished. At the same time, laws protecting them from overly severe treatment were strengthened, and material conditions generally improved.

But whatever the law said, the practice was always more telling. Treatment varied with individual slaveholders and depended on their mood and other circumstances. This was especially true with regard to the slave family. Most planters, like Robert Allston, generally encouraged their slaves to marry and did all they could to keep families intact. They believed that families made black males more docile and less inclined to revolt or run away. But some masters failed to respect slave marriages or broke them up because of financial problems. This tendency was supported by southern courts and legislatures, which did not legally recognize slave marriages or the right to family

unity. As a North Carolina Supreme Court justice said in 1853, "Our law required no solemnity or form in regard to the marriage of slaves."

Adding to the pain of forced breakup of the slave family was the sexual abuse of black women. Although the frequency of such abuse is unknown, the presence of thousands of mulattoes in the antebellum era is testimony to this practice. White men in the South abused black slave women in several ways: by offering gifts for sexual "favors," by threatening those who refused sex with physical punishment or the sale of a child or loved one, by purchasing concubines, and by outright rape. As Frederick Douglass put it, "The slave woman is at the mercy of the fathers, sons or brothers of her master."

Because of the need to obtain cheap additional slaves for the workforce, slaveholders encouraged young slave women to bear children, whether married or not. If verbal prodding and inducements such as less work and more rations did not work, masters would choose mates and foist them on slave women. Massa Hawkins, for example, selected Rufus to live

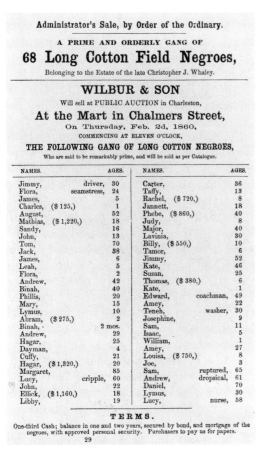

Administrator's Sale, by Order of the Ordinary.

A PRIME AND ORDERLY GANG OF

68 Long Cotton Field Negroes,

Belonging to the Estate of the late Christopher J. Whaley.

WILBUR & SON

Will sell at PUBLIC AUCTION in Charleston,

At the Mart in Chalmers Street,

On Thursday, Feb. 2d, 1860,

COMMENCING AT ELEVEN O'CLOCK,

THE FOLLOWING GANG OF LONG COTTON NEGROES,

Who are said to be remarkably prime, and will be sold as per Catalogue.

NAMES.		AGES.	NAMES.		AGES.
Jimmy,	driver,	30	Carter,		36
Flora,	seamstress,	24	Taffy,		13
James,		5	Rachel,	($ 720,)	8
Charles,	($ 125,)	1	Jannett,		18
August,		52	Phebe,	($ 860,)	40
Mathias,	($ 1,220,)	18	Judy,		8
Sandy,		16	Major,		40
John,		13	Lavinia,		30
Tom,		70	Billy,	($ 550,)	10
Jack,		38	Tamor,		6
James,		6	Jimmy,		52
Leah,		5	Kate,		46
Flora,		2	Susan,		25
Andrew,		42	Thomas,	($ 380,)	6
Binah,		40	Kate,		1
Phillis,		20	Edward,	coachman,	49
Mary,		15	Amey,		22
Lymus,		10	Teneh,	washer,	30
Abram,	($ 275,)	2	Josephine,		9
Binah,		2 mos.	Sam,		11
Andrew,		29	Isaac,		5
Hagar,		25	William,		1
Dayman,		4	Amey,		27
Cuffy,		21	Louisa,	($ 750,)	8
Hagar,	($1,320,)	20	Joe,		3
Margaret,		85	Sam,	ruptured,	65
Lucy,	cripple,	60	Andrew,	dropsical,	61
John,		22	Daniel,		70
Ellick,	($1,160,)	18	Lymus,		30
Libby,		19	Lucy,	nurse,	58

TERMS.

One-third Cash; balance in one and two years, secured by bond, and mortgage of the
negroes, with approved personal security.   Purchasers to pay us for papers.

29

Announcement of slave sale in Charleston, 1860.
(Public Domain)

with 16-year-old Rose Williams, as she recalled many years later. She resisted the attempted liaison with unmistakable clarity: "I puts de feet 'gainst him and give him a shove and out he go on de floor 'fore he knew what I's doin'." When Rufus persisted, Rose took a poker and "lets him have it over de head." Hawkins then threatened Rose with a "whippin' at de stake" or sale away "from my folks." This was too much for her. "What am I's to do? So I 'cides to do as de massa wish and so I yields."

Unlike the case of Rose and Rufus, however, slaves usually chose their own mates on the basis of mutual attraction during an uneasy courtship complicated by the threat of white interference. As among poor whites, premarital intercourse was frequent, but promiscuous behavior was rare. Most couples maintained affectionate, lasting relationships. This, too, led to numerous sorrows in slavery. Members of slave families had to witness the flogging or physical abuse of loved ones and were powerless to intervene. William Wells Brown remembered that "cold chills ran over me and I wept aloud" when he saw his mother whipped for being late into the fields for work. For this reason, some slaves preferred to marry a spouse from a plantation other than their own.

Although motherhood was the key event in a slave woman's life, bearing children and the double burden of work and family responsibilities challenged her resourcefulness. New mothers often had to choose between taking their babies into the fields to be fed or leaving them to the care of others. Some masters would provide time off for nursing mothers, but the more common practice was for them to work in the fields with their newborn infants lying nearby, wrapped in cloth to protect them from the sun. Although children were sometimes denied proper physical care and emotional support by the absence of their parents during the working day, the slaves adapted. Women developed networks of mutual support, looking after one another's children; meeting together to sew, quilt, cook, or do laundry; and attending births, caring for the sick and dying, and praying together.

The most traumatic problem for slaves was the separation of families, a haunting fear rarely absent from slave consciousness. Although many slaveholders had both moral and economic reasons to maintain families, inevitably they found themselves destroying them. One study, compiling 30 years of data from three Deep South states, shows that masters dissolved one-third of all slave marriages. Even then, the slaves tried to maintain contact. When Abream Scriven informed his wife, Dinah, of his sale to a trader in New Orleans, he had no idea where he would be sold but promised to "write and let you know where I am. . . . My Dear Wife for you and my Children my pen cannot Express the griffe I feel to be parted from you all." Two Missouri slave women, when told they might be sent to Texas, begged their master to reconsider, pleading that "to be separated from our husbands forever in this world would make us unhappy for life."

There was a sound basis in fact for the abolitionists' contention that slavery was a harsh, brutal system. However, two points need to be emphasized. First, although slavery was a barbarous institution that led otherwise decent human beings to commit inhumane acts, many slaveholders throughout the South were neither sadistic nor cruel; they did what they could for their slaves, out of both economic self-interest and Christian morality. Second, whether under kind or cruel masters, the slaves endured with dignity, communal sensitivity, and even some joy. If daytime in the fields describes a view of slavery at its worst, nighttime in the quarters, examined from the black perspective, reveals the slaves' survival powers and their capacity to mold an African American culture even under slavery.

NIGHT: SLAVES IN THEIR QUARTERS

It is near sundown, and the workday is almost over. Some of the slaves begin singing the gentle spiritual "Steal Away to Jesus," and others join in. Or perhaps they sing "Dere's a Meeting Here Tonight." To the unwary overseer or master, the humming, soothing sound of the song suggests happy slaves, content with their earthly lot and looking forward to deliverance in heaven, "in the sweet bosom of Jesus." To the slaves, however, the songs are a signal that, as a former slave, Wash Wilson, put it, they are to "steal away to Jesus" because "dere gwine be a 'ligious meetin' dat night." When evening arrived on the plantation, after a hard day of work in the hot sun or in the Big House, the slaves returned to their own quarters. There, as Wilson said, "sometimes us sing and pray all night."

In the slave quarters, away from white masters, overseers, and the burdens of daily work, an elaborate black community helped the slaves make sense out of their lives. In family life, religion, song, dance, the playing of musical instruments, and the telling of stories, the slaves both described their experiences and sought release from hardship and suffering. However burdensome their lives from sunup to sundown, after work the slaves experienced enjoyment and a sense of self-worth, hope, and group identity in their quarters.

Black Christianity

As suggested by the scene described by Wash Wilson, Christian worship was an indispensable part of slave life in the quarters. The revivals of the early nineteenth century led to an enormous growth of Christianity among black Americans. Some independent black Baptist and Methodist churches, especially in border states and cities, served both slaves and free blacks and occasionally even whites. These separate churches had to steer a careful path to maintain their freedom and avoid white interference. But the vast majority of southern blacks were slaves, attending plantation missions set up by their masters.

Robert Allston built a prayer house for his slaves, reporting with pride that they were "attentive to religious instruction, and greatly improved in intelligence and morals." For the slaveholders, religion often represented a form of social control. Despite the presence of illiterate but eloquent slave preachers on the plantation, who frequently played a prominent role in administering baptisms, weddings, and funerals, white masters sought to direct the purposes of religion to their own ends. Black religious gatherings were usually forbidden unless white observers were present or white preachers led them. Whether in slave or white churches (where blacks sat in the back), preachers often delivered sermons from the text "Servants, obey your masters." These sermons emphasized the importance of work, obedience, honesty, and respect for the master's property. One former slave complained that "all that preacher talked about was for us slaves to obey our masters and not to lie and steal."

There were limits, however, to the effectiveness of white control. Although some slaves accommodated themselves to the master's brand of Christianity and patiently waited for heavenly deliverance, others rebelled and sought earthly liberty. Not far from Allston's plantation, several slaves were discovered (and imprisoned) for singing "We'll soon be free / We'll fight for liberty / When de Lord will call us home." Douglass had an illegal Sabbath school on one plantation, where he and others risked being whipped while learning about Christianity and how to read. "The work of instructing my dear fellow-slaves," he wrote, "was the sweetest engagement with which I was ever blessed."

In religious schools and meetings like these, the slaves created an "invisible" church. On Sunday morning, they sat dutifully through the master's service and waited for the "real meetin'" and "real preachin'" later that night. Sarah Fitzpatrick, an Alabama slave, recalled that the slaves wanted so much to "go to church by de'selves" that they were willing to sit through the "white fo'ks' . . . service in de mornin'." But when evening came, "a'ter dey clean up, wash de dishes, an' look a'ter ever'thing," the slaves would "steal away" to the nearby woods for their own service.

Long into the night, they would sing, dance, shout, and pray. "Ya' see," Sarah explained, "niggers lack ta shout a whole lot an' wid de white fo'ks al'round 'em, dey couldn't shout jes' lack dey want to." But at night they could, taking care to deaden the sound to keep the whites away. One method was to hang a curtain from the trees. Another, an African custom, was to turn over a pot to "catch the sound." Another African practice, the frenetic dancing of the ring shout, survived in adapted form. Dance, forbidden by Methodists, was transformed into the "ecstatic shout," praising the Lord. The religious ceremony itself, with its camp meeting features, relieved the day's burdens and expressed communal religious values. "At night," another former slave recalled with pride, "was when the darkies really did have they freedom of spirit."

Although many of the expressive forms were African, the message reiterated over and over in the invisible slave church was the Christian theme of suffering and deliverance from bondage. Slaves identified with the children of Israel and with the Exodus story, as well as with the suffering of Jesus and the inner turmoil of an unconverted "trebbled spirit." "We prayed a lot to be free," Anderson Edwards recalled, but the freedom the slaves sought was a complex blend of a peaceful soul and escape from slavery. Nothing illustrated both the communal religious experience and these mixed Christian themes of suffering and redemption better than slave spirituals.

The Power of Song

A group of slaves gathers in the dark of night in the woods behind their quarters to sing and shout together:

> *O brothers, don't get weary*
> *O brothers, don't get weary*
> *O brothers, don't get weary*
> *We're waiting for the Lord.*
> *We'll land on Canaan's shore*
> *We'll land on Canaan's shore*
> *When we land on Canaan's shore*
> *We'll meet forever more.*

Then, after moaning of being stolen from Africa and sold in Georgia, with families "sold apart," they sing:

> *There's a better day a-coming,*
> *Will you go along with me?*
> *There's a better day a-coming,*
> *Go sound the jubilee!*

Music was a crucial form of expression in the slave quarters on both secular and religious occasions. The slaves were adept at creating a song, as one slave woman recalled, "on de spurn of de moment." Jeanette Robinson Murphy described a process of spontaneous creation that, whether in rural church music or urban jazz, describes black music to this day. "We'd all be at the 'prayer house' de Lord's day," she said, when all of a sudden, perhaps even in the midst of a white preacher's sermon, "de Lord would come a-shinin' thoo dem pages and revive dis ole nigger's heart, and I'd jump up dar and den and holler and shout and sing and pat, and dey would all cotch de words and I'd sing it to some ole shout song I'd heard 'em sing from Africa, and dey'd all take it up and keep at it, and keep a-addin' to it, and den it would be a spiritual."

Although the spirituals were composed for many purposes, they reiterated one basic Judeo-Christian theme: a chosen people, the children of God, were held captive in bondage but would be delivered. The titles and lyrics reveal the message: "We Are de People of de Lord," "To the Promised Land I'm Bound to Go," "Go Down, Moses," "Who Will Deliver Po' Me?" What they meant by deliverance was not always clear and

After sundown, when the work was done, slaves often gathered in "hush arbors" deep in the woods away from the overseer's and master's interference. There they danced the "ring shout" and "praised de Lord" in ways that combined African and Christian forms of spiritual expression. This painting by John Antrobus shows a "Negro Burial." *(The Historic New Orleans Collection)*

often had a double meaning: freedom in heaven and freedom in the North. Where, exactly, was the desired destination of "Oh Canaan, sweet Canaan / I am bound for the land of Canaan"? Was it heaven? A vague symbol for freedom "anyplace else but here"? A literal reference to the terminus of the underground railroad? For different slaves, and at different times for the same person, it meant all of these.

"The songs of the slave," Douglass wrote, "represent the sorrows of his heart." Indeed, they often expressed the sadness of broken families and the burdens of work and were filled with images of trouble, toil, and homelessness. But they also expressed joy, triumph, and deliverance. Each expression of sorrow usually ended in an outburst of eventual affirmation and justice. "O nobody knows a who I am" resolved itself on "judgment morning" when one heard the "bells a-ringing in my soul." The sadness of "Nobody knows the trouble I've seen" was lightened by happening upon some juicy berries hanging down "just as sweet as de honey in de comb." And the deep sorrow of "Sometimes I feel like a motherless chile," as terrible a situation as any person could endure, was transformed later in the song into "Sometimes I feel like / A eagle in de air. . . . / Gonna spread my wings an' / Fly, fly, fly."

Slave songs did not always contain hidden meanings. Sometimes slaves gathered simply for music, to play fiddles, drums, and other instruments fashioned by local artists in imitation of West African models.

In the quarters at night, slave men, women, and children created a vibrant black community, socializing outdoors amid the physical objects typical of their daily life. *(© Collection of the New-York Historical Society)*

Some musicians were so talented that whites invited them to perform at ceremonies and parties. Most, however, played for the slave community. Sacred and secular events such as weddings, funerals, holiday celebrations, family reunions, and a successful harvest were all occasions for a communal gathering, usually with music. So, too, was news of external events that affected their lives—a crisis in the master's situation, a change in the slave code, the outcome of a battle during the Civil War, or emancipation itself.

The Enduring Family

The role of music in milestones of family life suggests that the family was central to life in the slave quarters. Although sexual abuse and family separation happened all too often during slavery, many families maintained remarkable continuity. Naming practices, for example, show that children were connected to large extended families. In the records of one plantation for the century from 1760 to the eve of the Civil War, some 175 men, women, and children were linked by blood and marital ties, respecting taboos against marrying first cousins.

The benefits of family cohesion were those of any group: love, protection, education, moral guidance, the transmission of culture, and the providing of status, role models, and basic support. All of these existed in the slave quarters. As the slaves gathered together at the end of the working day, parents passed on to their children the family story, language patterns and words, recipes, folktales, religious and musical traditions, and strong impressions of strength and beauty. In this way, they preserved cultural traditions, which enhanced the identity and self-esteem of parents and children alike. Parents taught their children how to survive in the world and how to cope with life under slavery. As the young ones neared the age when they would work full time in the fields, their parents instructed them in the best ways to pick cotton or corn, how to avoid the overseer's whip, whom to trust and learn from, and ways of fooling the master.

Opportunities existed on many plantations for slave parents to improve the welfare of the family by working extra to earn money to buy scarce items like sugar or clothing, by hunting and fishing to add protein to the diet, or by working a small garden to grow vegetables. J. W. C. Pennington proudly recalled helping his "father at night in making straw hats and willow-baskets, by which means we supplied our family with little articles of food, clothing and luxury."

Slaves were not always totally at the mercy of abusive masters and overseers. Occasionally, one family member could intervene to prevent the abuse of another. Harriet Jacobs successfully fended off her master's lustful advances partly by her own cleverness

Despite separation, sale, and sexual abuse by white masters, many slave families endured and provided love, support, and self-esteem to their members. This 1862 photograph shows five generations of a slave family, all born on the plantation of J. J. Smith of Beaufort, South Carolina. *(Library of Congress)*

and sass: "I . . . openly expressed my contempt for him." She also threatened to use her free black grandmother's considerable influence in the community against him: "I told him that I must and would apply to my grandmother for protection." That enraged but always stopped him.

When family intervention, emotional appeals for mercy, or the magic effects of the conjurer's bag of herbs hung around the neck did not work, some slaves resorted to physical force. In 1800, a slave called Ben shot and killed a white man for living with Ben's wife, and another slave killed an overseer in 1859 for raping his wife. Female slaves, too, risked the consequences of resistance to protect themselves or family members from harm. When Cherry Loguen was attacked by a knife-wielding rapist, she knocked him out with a large branch. When an Arkansas overseer tried to make an example of a slave woman named Lucy, according to her son, "she jumped on him and like to tore him up."

Despite numerous incidents of mutual support, the love and affection that slaves had for each other was sometimes a liability. Many slaves, women especially, were reluctant to run away because they did not want to leave their families. Others were reluctant to give up a private means of modest income and supplemental diet from hiring out and growing food for trade. Those who fled were easily caught because, as

an overseer near Natchez, Mississippi, told a northern visitor, they "almost always kept in the neighborhood, because they did not like to go where they could not sometimes get back and see their families."

As these episodes suggest, violence, sexual abuse, and separation constantly threatened slave families. Despite these serious obstacles, slave parents served as protectors, providers, comforters, transmitters of culture, and role models for their children. The slave family, though constantly endangered, played a crucial role in helping blacks adapt to slavery and achieve a sense of self-esteem.

RESISTANCE AND FREEDOM

Songs, folktales, and other forms of cultural expression enabled slaves to articulate their resistance to slavery. For example, Old Jim was going on a "journey" to the "kingdom," and, as he invited others to "go 'long" with him, he taunted his owner: "O blow, blow, Ole Massa, blow de cotton horn / Ole Jim'll neber wuck no mo' in de cotton an' de corn." From refusal to work, it was a short step to outright revolt. In another song, "Samson," the slaves clearly stated their determination to abolish the house of bondage: "An' if I had-'n my way / I'd tear the buildin' down! / . . . And now I got my way / And I'll tear this buildin' down." Every hostile song, story, or event, like Douglass's victory over Covey, was an act of resistance by which the slaves asserted their dignity and gained a measure of freedom. Some escaped slavery altogether to achieve such autonomy as was possible for free blacks in the antebellum South.

Forms of Black Protest

One way slaves protested the burdensome demands of continuous forced labor was in various "day-to-day" acts of resistance. These ranged from breaking tools to burning crops, barns, and houses, from stealing or destroying animals and food to defending fellow slaves from punishment, from self-mutilation to deliberate work slowdowns, and from poisoning masters to feigning illness. Two favorite techniques were to pretend sickness during periods when the overseers were driving the hardest and to misplace tools or deliberately leave them in the fields so that they would have to be "hunted all over the place when wanted."

Slave women, aware of their childbearing value, were adept at missing work on account of "disorders and irregularities," as a frustrated Virginia planter put it, "which cannot be detected by exterior symptoms." He went on to complain that "you dare not set her to work, and so she will lay up till she feels like taking the air again; and plays the lady at your expense." They established networks of support while winnowing and pounding rice or shucking corn, sharing miseries but also encouraging each other in private acts of subtle defiance and resistance such as ruining the master's meals and faking sickness.

Overseers also suffered from these acts of disobedience, for their job depended on productivity, which in turn depended on the goodwill of the slave workers. No one knew this better than the slaves themselves, who cleverly played on the frequent struggle between overseer and master. Often, conflicts were ended by firing a bad overseer and hiring a more suitable replacement. Many slaveholders eventually resorted to using black drivers rather than overseers, but this created other problems.

The black slave drivers were "men between," charged with the tricky job of getting the master's work done without alienating fellow slaves or compromising their own values. Although some drivers were as brutal as white overseers, many became leaders and role models for other slaves. A common practice of the drivers was to appear to punish without really doing so. Solomon Northrup reported that he "learned to handle the whip with marvellous dexterity and precision, throwing the lash within a hair's breadth of the back, the ear, the nose, without, however, touching either of them." As he did this, the "punished" slave would howl in pretended pain and complain loudly to his master about his harsh treatment.

Another form of resistance was to run away. So many blacks ran off that a southern doctor coined a new word, *drapetomania,* which meant "the disease causing negroes to run away." The typical runaway was a young male, who ran off alone and hid out in a nearby wood or swamp. He left to avoid a whipping or because he had just been whipped, to protest excessive work demands, or, as one master put it, for "no cause" at all. But there was a cause—the need to experience a period of freedom away from the restraints and discipline of the plantation. Many runaways would sneak back to the quarters at night for food, and after a few days, if not tracked down by hounds, they would return, perhaps to be whipped, but also perhaps with some concessions for better treatment in the future.

Some slaves left again and again. Remus and his wife, Patty, ran away from their master, James Battle, in Alabama. They were caught and jailed three times, but each time they escaped again. Battle urged the next jailer to "secure Remus well." Some runaways, called "Maroons," hid out for months and years at a time in communities of runaway slaves. Several Maroon colonies were located in the swamps and mountains of the South, especially in Florida, where Seminole and other Indians befriended them. In these areas, blacks and Indians, sharing a common hostility to local whites, frequently intermarried, though sometimes southeastern Indians were hired to track down runaway slaves.

The means of escape were manifold: forging passes, posing as master and servant, disguising one's sex, sneaking aboard ships, and pretending loyalty until taken by the master on a trip to the North. One slave even hid in a large box and had himself mailed to the North. The Underground Railroad, organized by abolitionists, was a series of safe houses and stations where runaway slaves could rest, eat, and spend the night before continuing. Harriet Tubman, who led some 300 slaves out of the South on 19 separate trips, was the railroad's most famous "conductor." It is difficult to know exactly how many slaves actually escaped to the North and Canada, but the numbers were not large. One estimate suggests that in 1850, about 1,000 slaves (out of over 3 million) attempted to run away, and most of them were returned. Nightly patrols by white militiamen, an important aspect of southern life, reduced the chances for any slave to escape and probably deterred many slaves from even trying to run away.

Slaves also sought their freedom by petitioning Congress and state legislatures, bringing suit against their masters that they were being held in bondage illegally, persuading masters to provide for emancipation in their wills, and purchasing their own freedom by hiring out to do extra work at night and on holidays.

Slave Revolts

The ultimate act of resistance, of course, was rebellion. Countless slaves committed individual acts of revolt. In addition, there were hundreds of conspiracies whereby slaves met to plan a group escape and often the massacre of whites. Most of these conspiracies never led to action, either because circumstances changed or the slaves lost the will to follow through or, more often, because some fellow slave—perhaps planted by the master—betrayed the plot. Such spies thwarted the elaborate conspiracies of Gabriel in Virginia in 1800 and Denmark Vesey in South Carolina in 1822. Gabriel and Vesey were both skilled, knowledgeable blacks who planned their revolts in hopes that larger events (a possible war with France in 1800 and the Missouri debates in 1820) would support their efforts. They planned to seize, respectively, Richmond and Charleston, but both were discovered and put down before the revolts could begin. Both resulted in severe reprisals by whites, including mass executions of leaders and the random killing of innocent blacks. The severity and intensity of the white response indicated the enormous fear southern whites had of a slave revolt.

Only a few organized revolts, in which slaves threatened white lives and property, ever actually took place. Latin American slaves challenged their masters more often than their North American counterparts. Weaker military control, easier escape to rugged interior areas, the greater imbalance of blacks to whites, and the continued dependence of Latin American slaveholders on the African slave trade for their supply of mostly male workers explain this pattern. Nearly 80 percent of the Africans imported into Brazil in the 1830s and 1840s were male, and as late as 1875, only one in six Brazilian slaves was recorded as married. The imbalance of males to females (156 to 100 in Cuba in 1860, for example, compared with a near one-to-one ratio in the United States) weakened family restraints on violent revolts.

The most famous slave revolt in North America, led by Nat Turner, occurred in Southampton County, Virginia, in 1831. Turner was an intelligent, skilled, unmarried, religious slave who had experienced many visions of "white spirits and black spirits engaged in battle." He believed that he was "ordained for some great purpose in the hands of the Almighty."

On a hot August night, Turner and a small band of fellow slaves launched their revolt. They intended, as Turner said, "to carry terror and devastation" throughout the country. They crept into the home of Turner's

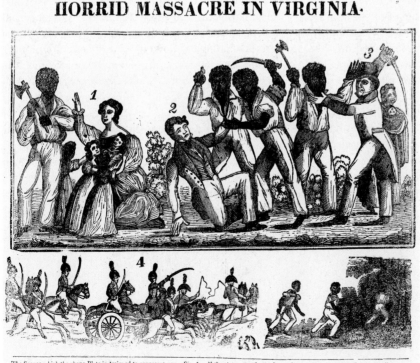

HORRID MASSACRE IN VIRGINIA.

The Scenes which the above Plate is designed to represent, are—Fig 1. a Mother intreating for the lives of her children.—2. Mr. Travis, cruelly murdered by his own Slaves.—3. Mr. Barrow, who bravely defended himself until his wife escaped.—4. A comp. of mounted Dragoons in pursuit of the Blacks.

Nat Turner's revolt, in 1831, the most famous American slave uprising, killed 55 whites in Southampton County, Virginia, before overwhelming white forces drove Turner to a hiding place in the woods. *(Library of Congress)*

Recovering the Past

FOLKTALES

A frequent activity of family life in the slave quarters was telling stories. The folktale was an especially useful and indirect way in which older slaves could express hostility toward their masters, impart wisdom to the young, teach them how to survive, portray and mock their own weaknesses, and entertain themselves. Thus, folktales reveal to historians a great deal about the slaves' view of their experience.

Although the tales took many forms, perhaps the best known were the "Brer Rabbit" animal stories. The trickster rabbit, who existed originally in African folklore, was weak and careless, and was looked down on by the other animals. Like the slaves, he was a victim. But he was also clever, boastful, and full of mischief, and he knew how to use his cunning to outwit stronger foes, usually by knowing them better than they knew him, a psychological necessity for all who are oppressed.

In one story, the powerful Brer Tiger took all the water and food for himself during a time of famine, leaving the weaker animals miserable. Brer Rabbit, however, turned things around. He played on Brer Tiger's fears that he would be blown away by a "big wind," secretly manufactured by the rabbit. The tiger was so afraid of the wind (perhaps the winds of revolt?) that he begged Brer Rabbit to tie him "tightly" to a tree to keep from being blown away. Brer Rabbit was happy to oblige, after which all the creatures of the forest were able to share the cool water and juicy pears.

In another folktale, Brer Rabbit fell into a well, but then got out by tricking Brer Wolf into thinking it was better to be in the cool bottom of the well than outside where it was hot. As the wolf lowered himself down in one bucket, Brer Rabbit rose up in the other, laughingly saying as he passed Brer Wolf, "Dis am life; some go up and some go down." In these stories, the slaves vicariously outwitted their more powerful masters and even reversed roles, thus revealing much about their experience under slavery and their aspirations for freedom.

The accompanying excerpt is from perhaps the most famous animal tale, "The Tar Baby Tricks Brer Rabbit." This version is by William J. Faulkner, who, after he retired as minister and dean of men at Fisk University, gathered and recorded the folktales he had heard in his youth in South Carolina as told by a former slave, Simon Brown. Rev. Faulkner opposed telling the stories in dialect because he believed readers formed stereotyped judgments from the dialect and missed the significance of the tale itself. We enter the story as an angry Brer Wolf has decided on a plan to catch the lazy Brer Rabbit, who refused to help the wolf build a well and has been fooling him by drinking from the well while Brer Wolf was asleep.

When you have finished reading the story, ask yourself what you learned about slavery from this story. Did violence work for Brer Rabbit or did it only make things worse? What finally worked? How do you interpret the ending? Brer Rabbit is returned to the briar patch, "the place where I was born." But is the briar patch, with all its thorns, scratches, and roots, Africa or slavery? Or what?

Finally, reflect on the stories you heard as a child or now find yourself telling others. How do they express the realities, flaws, values, and dreams of the American people? The same question applies to the songs we sing, the art we make, the rhythms we move to, and the jokes we tell: What do they tell us about ourselves and our values? In answering these questions, we deepen the knowledge of our own history.

Tar Baby

Brer Wolf studied and studied to find a way to catch Brer Rabbit. He scratched his head, and he pulled his chin whiskers until by and by he said, "I know what I'll do. I'll make me a tar baby, and I'll catch that good-for-nothing rabbit.'"

And so Brer Wolf worked and worked until he had made a pretty little girl out of tar. He dressed the tar baby in a calico apron and carried her up to the well, where he stood her up and fastened her to a post in the ground so that nobody could move her. Then Brer Wolf hid in the bushes and waited for Brer Rabbit to come for some water. But three days passed before Brer Rabbit visited the well again. On the fourth day, he came with a bucket in his hand. When he saw the little girl, he stopped and looked at her. Then he said, "Hello. What's your name? What are you doing here, little girl?"

The little girl said nothing.

This made Brer Rabbit angry, and he shouted at her, "You no-mannered little snip, you! How come you don't speak to your elders?"

The little girl still said nothing.

"I know what to do with little children like you. I'll slap your face and teach you some manners if you don't speak to me," said Brer Rabbit.

Still the little girl said nothing.

And then Brer Rabbit lost his head and said, "Speak to me, I say. I'm going to slap you." With that, Brer Rabbit slapped the tar baby in the face, and his right hand stuck.

"A-ha, you hold my hand, do you? Turn me loose, I say. Turn me loose. If you don't, I'm going to slap you with my left hand. And if I hit you with my left hand, I'll knock the daylights out of you."

But the little girl said nothing. So Brer Rabbit drew back his left hand and slapped the little girl in her face, bim, and his left hand stuck.

"Oh, I see. You're going to hold both my hands, are you? You better turn me loose. If you don't, I'm going to kick you. And if I kick you, it's going to be like thunder and lightning!" With that, Brer Rabbit drew back his right foot and kicked the little girl in the shins with all his might, blap! Then his right foot stuck.

"Well, sir, isn't this something? You better turn my foot loose. If you don't, I've got another foot left, and I'm going to kick you with it, and you'll think a cyclone hit you." Then Brer Rabbit gave that little girl a powerful kick in the shins with his left foot, blip! With that, his left foot stuck, and there he hung off the ground, between the heavens and the earth. He was in an awful fix. But he still thought he could get loose.

So he said to the little girl, "You've got my feet and my hands all stuck up, but I've got one more weapon, and that's my head. If you don't turn me loose, I'm going to butt you! And if I butt you, I'll knock your brains out." Finally then, Brer Rabbit struck the little girl a powerful knock on the forehead with his head, and it stuck, and there he hung. Smart old Brer Rabbit, he couldn't move. He was held fast by the little tar baby.

Now, Brer Wolf was hiding under the bushes, watching all that was going on. And as soon as he was certain that Brer Rabbit was caught good by his little tar baby, he walked over to Brer Rabbit and said, "A-ha, you're the one who wouldn't dig a well. And you're the one who's going to catch his drinking water from the dew off the grass. A-ha, I caught the fellow who's been stealing my water. And he isn't anybody but you, Brer Rabbit. I'm going to fix you good."

"No, sir, Brer Wolf, I haven't been bothering your water. I was just going over to Brer Bear's house, and I stopped by here long enough to speak to this little no-manners girl," said Brer Rabbit.

"Yes, you're the one," said Brer Wolf. "You're the very one who's been stealing my drinking water all this time. And I'm going to kill you."

"Please, sir, Brer Wolf, don't kill me," begged Brer Rabbit. "I haven't done anything wrong."

"Yes, I'm going to kill you, but I don't know how I'm going to do it yet," growled Brer Wolf. "Oh, I know what I'll do. I'll throw you in the fire and burn you up."

"All right, Brer Wolf," said Brer Rabbit. "Throw me in the fire. That's a good way to die. That's the way my grandmother died, and she said it's a quick way to go. You can do anything with me, anything you want, but please, sir, don't throw me in the briar patch."

"No, I'm not going to throw you in the fire, and I'm not going to throw you in the briar patch. I'm going to throw you down the well and drown you," said Brer Wolf.

"All right, Brer Wolf, throw me down the well," said Brer Rabbit. "That's an easy way to die, but I'm surely going to smell up your drinking water, sir."

"No, I'm not going to drown you," said Brer Wolf. "Drowning is too good for you." Then Brer Wolf thought and thought and scratched his head and pulled his chin whiskers. Finally he said, "I know what I'm going to do with you. I'll throw you in the briar patch."

"Oh, no, Brer Wolf," cried Brer Rabbit. "Please, sir, don't throw me in the briar patch. Those briars will tear up my hide, pull out my hair, and scratch out my eyes. That'll be an awful way to die, Brer Wolf. Please, sir, don't do that to me."

"That's exactly what I'll do with you," said Brer Wolf all happy-like. Then he caught Brer Rabbit by his hind legs, whirled him around and around over his head, and threw him way over into the middle of the briar patch.

After a minute or two, Brer Rabbit stood up on his hind legs and laughed at Brer Wolf and said to him, "Thank you, Brer Wolf, thank you. This is the place where I was born. My grandmother and grandfather and all my family were born right here in the briar patch."

And that's the end of the story.

*Tar was often spread on fences by masters to catch slaves who, out of hunger or mischief, would sneak into field and orchards to steal food. Tar stuck on the hands would betray the "guilty" slave.

Source: William J. Faulkner, *The Days When the Animals Talked.* Copyright © 1977 by William J. Faulkner. Used by permission of Modern Curriculum Press, Inc.

master, Joseph Travis, who Nat said was a "kind master" with "the greatest confidence in me," and killed the entire family. Before the revolt was finally put down, 55 white men, women, and children had been murdered and as many blacks killed in the aftermath. Turner hid in the woods for two weeks before he was apprehended and executed, but not before dictating a chilling confession to a white lawyer who may have exaggerated his role. The Turner revolt was a crucial moment for southern whites. A Virginia legislator said that he suspected there was "a Nat Turner . . . in every family." Rarely thereafter would slaveholders go to sleep without the Southampton revolt in mind.

The fact that Turner was an intelligent and trusted slave, with "no cause to complain" of his master's treatment, yet led such a terrible revolt suggests again how difficult it is to generalize about slavery and slave behavior. Slaves, like masters, had diverse personalities and changeable moods, and their behavior could not be easily predicted. Sometimes humble and deferential, at other times obstinate and rebellious, the slaves made the best of a bad situation and did what they needed to do to survive and achieve a measure of self-worth.

Free Blacks: Becoming One's Own Master

No matter how well they coped with their bondage, the slaves obviously preferred freedom. As Frederick Douglass said of the slave, "Give him a bad master, and he aspires to a good master; give him a good master, and he wishes to become his own master." When Douglass himself had successfully forged a free black's papers as a seaman and sailed from Baltimore to become his own master in the North, he found "great insecurity and loneliness." Apart from the immediate difficulties of finding food, shelter, and work, he realized that he was a fugitive in a land "whose inhabitants are legalized kidnappers" who could at any moment seize and return him to the South. Apart from this fear, which haunted blacks in the North, what was life like for the 11 percent of the total African American population who in 1860 were not slaves?

Between 1820 and 1860, the number of free blacks in the United States doubled, from 233,500 to 488,000. This rise resulted from natural increase, successful escapes, "passing" as whites, purchasing of freedom, and a continuation of occasional manumissions despite legal restriction in most states after the 1830s. Some free blacks passed into the white population, and others migrated to Canada or the West Indies. The free African American population actually decreased from 13.2 percent in 1820 to a little more than 11 percent in 1860. Thus, the percentage of American blacks who were slaves grew faster than those who were free.

Many slaves were able to acquire a degree of autonomy and self-esteem, and occasionally new skills and some money of their own, by hiring out, as seen in these two advertisements in the *Paris Western Citizen* in 1852. *(Audio-Visual Archives, Special Collections and Archives, University of Kentucky Libraries)*

More than half the free blacks lived in the South, most (85 percent in 1860) in the Upper South, where the total number of slaves had declined slightly.

Because free African Americans represented a constant reminder of freedom to slaves and feared reenslavement themselves, they were found least frequently in the Black Belt of the Lower South. They lived, rather, away from the dense plantation centers, scattered on impoverished rural farmlands and in small towns and cities. Still, fully one-third of the southern free African American population lived in cities or towns (compared with only 15 percent of whites and 5 percent of slaves). In part, because it took a long time to buy their freedom, they tended to be older, more literate, and lighter-skinned than other African Americans. In 1860, over 40 percent of free blacks were mulattoes (compared with 10 percent of the slaves). With strong leadership, Baltimore, Richmond, Charleston, New Orleans, and other southern cities developed vibrant African American communities, as free blacks formed churches, schools, and benevolent societies in the midst of white hostility and restrictions.

Most African Americans in the antebellum South were poor, laboring as farmhands, day laborers, or woodcutters. In the cities, they worked in factories and lived in appalling poverty. A few skilled jobs,

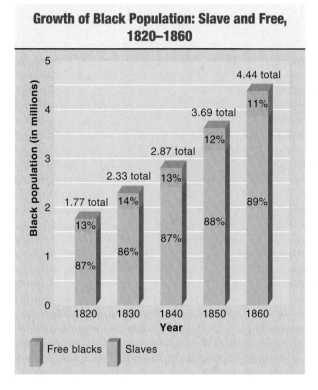

Growth of Black Population: Slave and Free, 1820–1860

Although the number of free African Americans doubled in size between 1820 and 1860, their proportion relative to the total black population actually decreased. This indicates that the institution of slavery seemed unlikely to be ended voluntarily by southerners.

such as barbering, shoemaking, and plastering, were reserved for black men; they were barred from more than 50 other trades. Women worked as cooks, laundresses, and domestics. The 15 percent of free African Americans who lived in the Lower South were divided into two distinct castes. Most were poor. But in New Orleans, Charleston, and other southern cities, a small, mixed-blood class of free blacks emerged as an elite group, closely connected to white society and removed from the mass of poor blacks. A handful even owned land and slaves. One white observed that these blacks were "respectable" and enjoyed "their rights."

Most free blacks, however, had no such privileges. "We reside among you . . . surrounded by the freest people and most republican institutions in the world," a Baltimore black paper said in 1826, pointing out that African Americans were not yet citizens: "Though we are not slaves, we are not free." Southern state laws seriously limited the mobility, rights, and opportunities of free blacks. In most states, they could not vote, bear arms, buy liquor, assemble, speak in public, form societies, or testify against whites in court. Nevertheless, the African American persistence to gather together and support each other in prayer

meetings, back alleys, burial societies, and grocery stores was stronger than white efforts to impede it.

One reason urban whites sought to restrain African American contact was their fear of free black influence as they mixed with whites in working-class grogshops, gambling halls, and brothels. Richmond police closed one house of ill fame where "men and women of diverse colors . . . congregate for most unhallowed purposes." Efforts were made to confine the free blacks to certain sections of the city or, increasingly by the 1850s, to compel them to leave the city, county, or state altogether. Those who stayed had trouble finding work, were required to carry licenses and freedom papers to be surrendered on demand, and often needed a white guardian to approve their actions. Southern whites were especially afraid of contact between free blacks and slaves, who often worked together, attended the same churches and places of entertainment in the city, occasionally got married, and developed strong bonds of mutual protection and identity.

The key institution in these developments was the African American Church. "As among our people generally," Martin Delaney wrote to Douglass in 1849, "the church is the Alpha and Omega of all things." Welcoming the freedom from white control, independent urban black churches grew enormously in the two decades before the Civil War. The African Methodist Episcopal (AME) Church in Baltimore doubled its membership between 1836 and 1856, with the overflow from the first congregation creating a second. By 1860, Baltimore had 15 African churches representing five different denominations. In Richmond the First African Church opened in 1841, soon followed by another; 20 years later, there were four! In the same period, 14 new black Baptist churches were founded in Virginia. These institutions not only performed the usual ritual functions and guarded moral discipline and community values but also provided and promoted education, social insurance, self-help benevolent societies, picnics, concerts, and other forms of recreation.

The growth of African American churches resulted from the overflow of successful institutions, doctrinal differences, the vital role the urban church played in black community life, and conversions. White southerners were trapped by their need to convert Africans to Christianity and then not wanting them in their own churches. Besides, blacks were unwilling parishioners. As one Baptist observed about those forced to attend white churches: "The usual African resort is a loud, comfortable snoring nap."

Nor were African American Catholics left out. Baltimore and New Orleans had strong black Catholic adherents made up of Creoles, converts, former

Churches for free blacks, rare before 1800, became a major source of social as well as religious activity by the 1840s. *(Library of Congress)*

slaves, and refugees from Haiti. The first ordained African American priests were three Georgia sons, born of a mulatto slave mother and an Irish immigrant father and educated at Holy Cross in the 1850s. The next black priest, however, was ordained three decades later. In the absence of African American priests, black sisterhoods took on special importance. The Sisters of the Holy Family and other communities of Catholic black women, begun in eastern cities, started schools and ministered to the aged and infirm as they spread with black Catholic communities westward to Louisville and St. Louis.

The African American churches not only were centers of vital urban black community activities but also were springboards for activist black preachers seeking larger changes in American society. The Reverend James W. C. Pennington, an escaped slave (see Chapter 12, "Recovering the Past: Slave Narratives,"), attended lectures at Yale Divinity School, though he was denied the right to enroll or borrow books. Licensed to preach in 1838, he headed prominent black churches in New Haven, Hartford, and finally New York City. Pennington started several schools, was an abolitionist leader of the National Negro Convention movement (see Chapter 12), and founded the Union Missionary Society in 1841, a black organization that focused on African missions and eventually merged with the American Missionary Society in 1846.

Charles Bennett Ray was educated at Wesleyan University in Connecticut and, as minister of Bethesda Church in New York City for 20 years, was involved

Timeline

1787	Constitution adopted with proslavery provisions
1793	Eli Whitney invents cotton gin
1800	Gabriel conspiracy in Virginia
1808	External slave trade prohibited by Congress
1820	South becomes world's largest cotton producer
1822	Denmark Vesey's conspiracy in Charleston
1830s	Southern justification of slavery changes from a necessary evil to a positive good
1831	Nat Turner's slave revolt in Virginia
1845	*Narrative of the Life of Frederick Douglass* published
1850s	Cotton boom
1851	Indiana state constitution excludes free blacks
1852	Harriet Beecher Stowe publishes best-selling *Uncle Tom's Cabin*
1860	Cotton production and prices peak

with the Underground Railroad and for four years was the editor of *The Colored American*. These and other black religious leaders prepared the way not only for Civil War but also for an unprecedented further growth of African American churches in the postwar years.

A young minister, Henry M. Turner, later an AME bishop, proudly proclaimed in the 1850s, "We, as a race, have a chance to be Somebody, and if we are ever going to be a people, now is the time." Turner's exhortations were heralded 20 years earlier by Maria Stewart, the first African American woman to give published public speeches. Stewart's religious conversion gave her the confidence to brave censure and ridicule in speaking out not only against slavery and northern racism but also in opposition to those who cited St. Paul in defending the established order. "Did Saint Paul but know of our wrongs and deprivations," Stewart said, "I presume he would make no objections to our pleading in public for our rights."

In part because free blacks were becoming more of a "people," they faced a crisis of extinction in the 1850s. Growing prosperity and the worsening conflict between North and South over slavery in the territories caused many white southerners to be even more concerned than usual with the presence of free blacks in their midst. North Carolina whites complained in 1852 that free blacks were "a perfect nuisance" because they attempted "in divers ways to equalize themselves with [the] white population." Pressures increased in the late 1850s, either to deport the free blacks or to enslave them. In the wake of increasing threats to their already precarious free status, some black leaders not surprisingly began to look more favorably on migration to Africa. That quest was interrupted, however, by the outbreak of the Civil War, rekindling in Douglass and others the "expiring embers of freedom."

Conclusion

Douglass's Dream of Freedom

Frederick Douglass eventually won his freedom by forging a free black sailor's pass and escaping through Chesapeake Bay to New York. In a real sense, he wrote himself into freedom. *The Narrative of the Life of Frederick Douglass*, "written by himself" in 1845, was a way both of exposing the many evils of slavery and of creating his own identity, even to the point of choosing his own name. Ironically, Douglass had learned to value reading and writing, we recall, from his Baltimore masters, the Aulds. This reminds us again of the intricate and subtle ways in which the lives of slaves and masters were tied together in the antebellum South. Our understanding of the complexities of this relationship is enhanced as we consider the variations of life in the Big House in the morning, in the fields during the afternoons, in the slave quarters at night, and in the degrees of freedom blacks achieved through resistance, revolt, and free status.

In a poignant moment in his *Narrative*, Douglass described his dreams of freedom as he looked out at the boats on the waters of Chesapeake Bay as a boy. Contrasting his own enslavement with the boats he saw as "freedom's swift-winged angels," Douglass vowed to escape: "This very bay shall yet bear me into freedom. . . . There is a better day coming." As we will see later, southern white planters also bemoaned their lack of freedom relative to the North and made their own plans to achieve independent status through secession. Meanwhile, as that struggle brewed beneath the surface of antebellum life, many other Americans were dismayed by various evil aspects in their society, slavery among them, and sought ways of shaping a better America. We turn to these other dreams in the next chapter.

Recommended Reading

Building the Cotton Kingdom

Charles Bolton, *Poor Whites of the Antebellum South: Tenants and Laborers in Central North Carolina and Northeast Mississippi* (1994); Bruce Collins, *White Society in the Antebellum South* (1985); Charles Dew, *Bond of Iron: Master and Slave at Buffalo Forge* (1994); Clement Eaton, *The Growth of Southern Civilization* (1961); Robert Fogel, *Without Consent or Contract: The Rise and Fall of American Slavery* (1989); John Hope Franklin, *The Militant South* (1966); Peter Kolchin, *American Slavery, 1619–1877* (1993); Grady McWhiney, *Cracker Culture: Celtic Folkways in the Old South* (1988); James Oakes, *Slavery and Freedom: An Interpretation of the Old South* (1990); Frank Owsley, *Plain Folk in the Old South* (1949); Harold Woodman, *Slavery and the Southern Economy* (1966); Gavin Wright, *The Political Economy of the Cotton South: Households, Markets, and Wealth in the Nineteenth Century* (1978).

Morning: Master in the Big House

Victoria E. Bynum, *Unruly Women: The Politics of Social and Sexual Control in the Old South* (1990); Catharine Clinton, *Plantation Mistress* (1983); J. H. Easterby, ed., *The South Carolina Rice Plantation as Revealed in the Papers of Robert F. W. Allston*

(1945); Drew Faust, *James Henry Hammond and the Old South: A Design for Mastery* (1982); Elizabeth Fox-Genovese, *Within the Plantation Household: Black and White Women of the Old South* (1988); George Fredrickson, *The Black Image in the White Mind: The Debate on Afro-American Character and Destiny, 1817–1914* (1971); Eugene Genovese, *The Slaveholder's Dilemma: Freedom and Progress in Southern Conservative Thought, 1820–1860* (1992); Suzanne Lebsock, *The Free Women of Petersburg: Status and Culture in a Southern Town, 1784–1860* (1984); Stephanie McCurry, *Masters of Small Worlds: Yeoman Households, Gender Relations & the Political Culture of the Antebellum South Carolina Lowcountry, 1850–1890* (1995); James Oakes, *The Ruling Race: A History of American Slaveholders* (1982); Steven Stowe, *Intimacy and Power in the Old South: Rituals in the Lives of the Planters* (1987).

Noon: Slaves in House and Fields

Edward Ball, *Slaves in the Family* (1998); John Blassingame, ed., *Slave Testimony* (1977); Paul David et al., *Reckoning with Slavery: A Critical Study of the Quantitative History of American Negro Slavery* (1976); Carl Degler, *Neither Black Nor White: Slavery and Race Relations in Brazil and the United States* (1971); Eugene Genovese, *Roll, Jordan, Roll: The World the Slaves Made* (1974); Larry E. Hudson Jr., *To Have and to Hold: Slave Work and Family Life in Antebellum South Carolina* (1997); Peter Kolchin, *American Slavery, 1619–1877* (1993); Ulrich B. Phillips, *American Negro Slavery* (1919) and *Life and Labor in the Old South* (1929); Kenneth Stampp, *The Peculiar Institution* (1956).

Night: Slaves in Their Quarters

William L. Andrews, *To Tell a Free Story: The First Century of Afro-American Autobiography, 1760–1865* (1986); John Blassingame, *The Slave Community*, rev. ed. (1979); Jacqueline Jones, *Labor of Love, Labor of Sorrow: Black Women, Work, and the Family from Slavery to the Present* (1985); Herbert Gutman, *The Black Family in Slavery and Freedom, 1750–1925* (1976); James Oliver Horton, *Free People of Color: Inside the African-American Community* (1993); Charles Joyner, *Down by the Riverside: A South Carolina Slave Community* (1984); Lawrence Levine, *Black Culture and Black Consciousness: Afro-American Folk Thought from Slavery to Freedom* (1977); Anne Patton Malone, *Sweet Chariot: Slave Family and Household Structure in Nineteenth Century Louisiana* (1992); George Rawick, *From Sundown to Sunup: The Making of a Black Community* (1972); Albert Roboteau, *Slave Religion: The "Invisible Institution" in the Ante-bellum South* (1978); Sterling Stuckey, *Slave Culture: Nationalist Theory and the Foundation of Black America* (1987); Thomas L. Webber, *Deep Like Rivers: Education in the Slave Quarters, 1831–1865* (1978); Deborah Gray White, *Arn't I a Woman?* (1985).

Resistance and Freedom

William L. Andrews, ed., *The Oxford Frederick Douglass Reader* (1996); Herbert Aptheker, *Nat Turner's Slave Rebellion* (1966); Ira Berlin, *Slaves Without Masters: The Free Negro in the Antebellum South* (1976); Leonard Curry, *The Free Black in Urban America, 1800–1850: The Shadow of the Dream* (1981); Merton L. Dillon, *Slavery Attacked: Southern Slaves and Their Allies, 1619–1865* (1990); Douglass R. Egerton, *He Shall Go Out Free: The Lives of Denmark Vesey* (1999); John Hope Franklin, *Runaway Slaves: Rebels on the Plantation* (1999); Michael P. Johnson and James L. Roark, *No Chariot Down: Charleston's Free People of Color on the Eve of the Civil War* (1984) and *Black Masters: A Free Family of Color in the Old South* (1984); Norrece R. Jones Jr., *Born a Child of Freedom, Yet a Slave: Mechanisms of Control and Strategies of Resistance in Antebellum South Carolina* (1990); Robert S. Levine, *Martin Delany, Frederick Douglass, and the Politics of Representative Identity* (1997); Waldo Martin Jr., *The Mind of Frederick Douglass* (1984); William S. McFeely, *Frederick Douglass* (1991).

Fiction and Film

Charles Johnson's *Middle Passage* (1990) is a novel about antebellum life in New Orleans and on slave trade ships between West Africa and the Caribbean. Toni Morrison's novel *Beloved* (1988), a powerful and challenging account of African American life both during and after slavery, is based on the historical case of infanticide by a runaway slave mother near Cincinnati who killed her baby girl, Beloved, rather than allow her to be taken back to the South. Harriet Beecher Stowe's *Uncle Tom's Cabin* (1852), the novel that captivated northern readers in the 1850s, follows various black and white lives in antebellum Kentucky and the deep South. Harriet Wilson's novel *Our Nig; or, Sketches from the Life of a Free Black* (1859), the first known novel written by an African American woman, combines Victorian sentimentalism in the tradition of *Uncle Tom's Cabin* with conventions of the slave narrative.

Amistad, is a 1997 Hollywood film based on a successful mutiny on a slave ship in 1839 near Cuba and the subsequent capture and trial of the mutineers in Connecticut, where they were defended by ex-President John Quincy Adams. The film contains gripping scenes aboard slave ships. *Beloved* is a 1998 film version of Toni Morrison's 1988 novel of the same name.

Suggested Web Sites

http://newdeal.feri.org/asn/index.htm

"Been Here So Long." This site offers selections from the Works Progress Administration (WPA) slave narratives, some of the more interesting primary sources about slavery.

http://amistad.mysticseaport.org/main/welcome.html

Exploring Amistad: Race and the Boundaries of Freedom in Antebellum Maritime America. Mystic Seaport, a maritime museum in Mystic, Connecticut, runs this site, which includes extensive collections of historical resources relating to the Amistad Revolt and the subsequent trial of enslaved Africans.

http://www.pbs.org/wgbh/aia/home.html

Africans in America. This PBS site contains images and documents recounting slavery in America.

http://www.law.umkc.edu/faculty/projects/ftrials/amistad/AMISTD.HTM

Amistad Trial Home Page. Images, chronology, and court and official documents make up this site by Dr. Douglas Linder at University of Missouri—Kansas City Law School.

http://metalab.unc.edu/docsouth/neh/neh.html

North American Slave Narratives, Beginnings to 1920. This site, part of *Documenting the American South,* presents the telling narratives of the African American struggle for freedom.

http://www.loc.gov/exhibits/african/perstor.html

Personal Stories and ACS New Directions. This site contains images and text relating to the colonization movement to return African Americans to Africa.

http://www.cr.nps.gov/delta/under.htm

The Underground Railroad. This is perhaps the best and most extensive National Park Service site, telling the story of the Underground Railroad, with special reference to the Lower Mississippi river valley.

http://www.ushistoryplace.com

A richly detailed on-line learning environment complete with interactive maps, timelines, history activities, primary source documents, and links to related American history sites.

SHAPING AMERICA *in the* ANTEBELLUM AGE

CHAPTER OUTLINE

On November 19, 1836, as the second term of President Andrew Jackson neared its end, 30-year-old Marius Robinson and Emily Rakestraw were married near Cincinnati, Ohio. Two months after their wedding, he went on the road to speak against slavery and to organize abolitionist societies throughout Ohio. Emily stayed in Cincinnati to teach in a school for free blacks. During their ten-month separation, they exchanged affectionate letters that reflected their love and work.

Writing after midnight from Concord, Ohio, Marius complained of the "desolation of loneliness" he felt without her. Emily responded that she felt "about our separation just as you do" and confessed that her "womanish nature" did not much enjoy self-denial. In their letters, each imagined the "form and features" of the other and chided the other for not writing more often. Each voiced concern for the responsibilities and burdens of the other's work. Each expressed comfort and support, doubted his or her own abilities ("a miserable comforter I am"), and agreed that in their separation, as Marius put it, "we must look alone to God."

With such love for each other, what prompted this painful separation so early in their marriage? Emily wrote of their duty "to labor long in this cause so near and dear to us both," together if they could, but apart if so decreed by God. Marius, who had experienced a series of conversions inspired by the revivalist Charles G. Finney and his abolitionist disciple Theodore Dwight Weld, described the reason for their separation: "God and humanity bleeding and suffering demand our services apart." Thus motivated by a strong religious commitment to serve others, these two young reformers dedicated themselves to several social causes: the abolition of slavery, equal rights and education for free blacks, temperance, and women's rights.

Their commitments cost more than separation. When Emily went to Cincinnati to work with other young reformers, her parents disapproved. When she married Marius, who already had a reputation as a "rebel," her parents disowned her altogether. Emily wrote with sadness that her sisters and friends also "love me less . . . than they did in by-gone days." Marius responded that he wished he could dry her tears and sought to heal the rift. Although Emily's family eventually accepted their marriage, there were other griefs. Teaching at the school in Cincinnati was demanding, and Emily could not get rid of a persistent cough. Furthermore, the white citizens of the city resented the school and the young abolitionists in their midst, treating them with contempt. Earlier in the year, Marius had escaped an angry mob by disguising himself and mingling with the crowd that came to sack the offices of a reformist journal edited by James G. Birney. Emily, meanwhile, tirelessly persisted in the work of "our school" while worrying about the health and safety of her husband on the road.

She had good reason for concern, for Marius's letters were full of reports of mob attacks, disrupted meetings, stonings, and narrow escapes. At two lectures near Granville, Ohio, he was "mobbed thrice, once most rousingly," as he faced crowds of "the veriest savages I ever saw," armed with clubs, cudgels, and intense hatred for those speaking against slavery. In June, he was dragged from the home of his Quaker host and beaten, tarred, and feathered. Never quite recovering his health, Marius spent half a year in bed, weak and dispirited. For nearly ten years after that, the Robinsons lived quietly on an Ohio farm, only slightly involved in the abolitionist movement. Despite the joyous birth of two daughters, they felt lonely, restless, and guilt-ridden, "tired of days blank of benevolent effort and almost of benevolent desires."

The work of Emily and Marius Robinson represents one response by the American people to the rapid social and economic changes of the antebellum era described in chapters 10 and 11. In September 1835, a year before the Robinsons' marriage, the *Niles Register* commented on some 500 recent incidents of mob violence and social upheaval. "Society seems everywhere unhinged, and the demon of 'blood and slaughter' has been let loose upon us. . . . [The] character of our countrymen seems suddenly changed." How did Americans adapt to these changes? In a world that seemed everywhere "unhinged" and out of control, in which old rules and patterns no longer provided guidance, how did people maintain some sense of control over their lives? How did they seek to shape their altered

---

Marius and Emily Robinson, like other Americans, sought to find goodness and order in a society that seemed "everywhere unhinged." (*Anonymous,* Moving Day in the City, *c. 1829, Photo by Eric Schaal/LIFE Magazine © Time Inc.*)

world? How could they both adopt the benefits of change and reduce the accompanying disruptions?

One way was to embrace the changes fully. Thus, some Americans became entrepreneurs in new industries; invested in banks, canals, and railroads; bought more land and slaves; and invented new machines. Others went west or to the new textile mills, enrolled in common schools, joined trade unions, specialized their labor in both the workplace and the home, and celebrated the practical benefits that resulted from modernization. Marius Robinson eventually went into life insurance, though he and Emily never fully abandoned their reformist efforts and idealism.

But many Americans were uncomfortable with the character of the new era. Some worried about the unrestrained power and selfish materialism symbolized by the slavemaster's control over his slaves. Others feared that institutions like the U.S. Bank represented a "monied aristocracy" capable of undermining the country's honest producers. Seeking positions of leadership and authority, these critics of the new order tried to shape a nation that retained the benefits of economic change without sacrificing humane principles of liberty, equality of opportunity, and community virtue. This chapter examines four ways the American people responded to change by attempting to influence their country's development: religious revivalism, party politics, utopian communitarianism, and social reform.

RELIGIOUS REVIVAL AND REFORM PHILOSOPHY

When the Frenchman Alexis de Tocqueville visited the United States in 1831 and 1832, he observed that he could find "no country in the whole world in which the Christian religion retains a greater influence over the souls of men than in America." What de Tocqueville was describing was a new and powerful religious enthusiasm among American Protestants. Fired by the power of religious rebirth, some discovered that religion provided them with moorings in a fast-changing world. Others were inspired by revivalism to refashion American society, working through new political parties to shape an agenda for the nation or through reform associations organized to eliminate a particular social evil. Although not all evangelicals agreed about politics or even about what aspects of American society needed to be reformed, religion was the lens through which they viewed contemporary events and through which they sought to effect change.

Finney and the Second Great Awakening

From the late 1790s until the late 1830s, a wave of religious revivals that matched the intensity of the Great Awakening in the 1730s and 1740s swept through the United States. The camp meeting revivals of the frontier at the turn of the century and the New England revivals sparked by Lyman Beecher took on a new emphasis and location after 1830. Led by the spellbinding Charles G. Finney, under whose influence Marius Robinson had been converted, revivalism shifted to upstate New York and the Old Northwest. Both areas had been experiencing profound economic and social changes, as the example of Rochester, New York, suggests.

By the 1830s, Rochester, like Lowell and Cincinnati, was a rapidly growing American city. Located on the recently completed Erie Canal, it was a flour-milling center for the rich wheatlands of western New York. The canal changed Rochester from a sleepy little village of 300 in 1815 to a bustling commercial and milling city of nearly 20,000 inhabitants by 1830. As in other cities, economic growth affected relationships between masters and workers, distancing them both physically and psychologically. As the gulf widened, the masters' control over their laborers weakened. Saloons and unions sprang up in workingmen's neighborhoods, and workers became more transient, following the canal and other opportunities westward.

Prominent Rochester citizens therefore invited Charles Finney to come to town in 1830 to deliver some sermons. What followed was one of the most successful revivals of the Second Great Awakening. "You could not go upon the streets," a convert recalled, "and hear any conversation, except upon religion." Finney preached nearly every night and three times on Sundays, converting first the city's business elite, often through their wives, and then many workers. For six months, Rochester went through a citywide prayer meeting in which one conversion led to another.

The Rochester revival was part of the wave of religious enthusiasm in America that contributed to the tremendous growth of Methodists, Baptists, and other evangelical denominations in the first half of the nineteenth century. By 1844, for example, the

This 1839 painting of a camp meeting captures the religious fervor that many Americans turned to in the face of social and economic upheavals. These mass conversions led some believers to individual salvation and others to social reform. *(Old Dartmouth Historical Society-New Bedford Whaling Museum)*

Methodist church had become the largest denomination in America, with over a million members. To bring large masses of people to accept Christ as their savior, revivalist preachers deemphasized doctrine in favor of emotion, softening strict Calvinist tenets such as predestination, original sin, and limited atonement.

Unlike Jonathan Edwards, who believed that revivals were God's miracles, Finney understood that the human "agency" of the minister was crucial in causing a revival. He even published a do-it-yourself manual for other revivalists. Few, however, could match Finney's powerful preaching style. The hypnotic effect of his eyes and voice carried such power that he could dissolve an audience into tears. When he threw an imaginary brick at the Devil, people ducked. When his finger pointed the descent of a sinner into hell, people in the back row stood up to see the final disappearance. A former lawyer, Finney used logic as well as emotion to bring about conversions.

Many revivalists, especially in the South, sought individual salvation. American Catholics also caught the revival fervor in the 1830s. Scattered in small but growing numbers in eastern cities like Baltimore, Philadelphia, and New York and in western cities such as Cincinnati, St. Louis, Louisville, and New Orleans, Catholic leaders recognized that survival as a small and often despised religion depended on constant reinvigoration and evangelism. Focusing on the parish mission, energetic retreats and revivals gathered Catholics from miles around to preserve a religious heritage seriously threatened by life in Protestant America.

The Finney revivals differed from Catholic and southern revivalism because they insisted that conversion and salvation were not the end of religious experience but the beginning. Finney believed that humans were not passive objects of God's predestined plan but moral free agents who could choose good over evil, convince others to do the same, and thereby eradicate sin from the world. Finney's idea of the "utility of benevolence" meant not only individual reformation but also the commitment to do one's sacred duty in reforming one's society.

The Transcendentalists

No one knew this better than Ralph Waldo Emerson, a Concord, Massachusetts, essayist who was the era's foremost intellectual figure. Emerson's essays of the 1830s—"Nature," "American Scholar," and "Divinity School Address," among others—influenced the generation of reformist American intellectuals coming of age in mid-century and helped inspire artists and writers. The small but influential group of New England intellectuals who lived near Emerson were called Transcendentalists because of their belief that truth was found in intuition beyond sense experience. Casting off the European intellectual tradition, Emerson urged Americans to look inward and to nature for self-knowledge, self-reliance, and the spark of divinity burning within all people. "To acquaint a man with himself," he wrote, would inspire a "reverence" for self and others, which would then lead outward to social reform. "What is man born for," Emerson wrote, "but to be a Reformer?"

Inspired by self-reflection, the Transcendentalists asked troublesome questions about the quality of American life. They questioned not only slavery, an obvious evil, but also the obsessive competitive pace of economic life, the overriding concern for materialism, and the restrictive conformity of social life.

Although not considered Transcendentalists, Nathaniel Hawthorne and Herman Melville, two giants of mid-century American literature, also reflected these concerns in their fiction. Like Emerson, they were romantic in spirit, celebrating emotion over reason, nature over civilization, and virtue over self-interest. Hawthorne's great subject was the "truth of the human heart," which he portrayed as more authentic than the calculating minds of scientists and their schemes. In his greatest novel, *The Scarlet Letter* (1850), Hawthorne sympathetically told the story of a courageous Puritan woman's adultery and her eventual loving triumph over the narrowness of both cold intellect and intolerant social conformity.

Herman Melville dedicated his epic novel *Moby Dick* (1851) to Hawthorne. At one level, a rousing story of whaling on the high seas in pursuit of the great white whale, *Moby Dick* was actually an immense allegory of good and evil, bravery and weakness, innocence and experience. In Melville's other novels, he continued this sea voyage setting to make a powerful statement on behalf of the lowly seaman's claims for freedom and just social relations against the tyranny of the ship captain. Like Emerson, Hawthorne and Melville mirrored the tensions of the age as they explored issues of freedom and control.

When Emerson wrote, "Whoso would be a man, must be a nonconformist," he described his friend Henry David Thoreau. No one thought more deeply about the virtuous natural life than Thoreau. On July 4, 1845, he went to live in a small hut by Walden Pond, near Concord. There he planned to confront the "essential facts of life"—to discover who he was and how to live well. When Thoreau left Walden two years later, he protested against slavery and the Mexican War by refusing to pay his taxes. He went to jail briefly and wrote an essay, "On Civil Disobedience" (1849), and a book, *Walden* (1854), which are still considered classic statements of what one person can do to protest unjust laws and wars and live a life of principle.

THE POLITICAL RESPONSE TO CHANGE

Transcendentalism touched only a few elite New Englanders, but perhaps as many as 40 percent of the American people were affected by the winds of evangelical Protestantism. Although economic, ethnic, and even regional factors played a part in shaping political loyalties, evangelical values and religious loyalties colored many people's understanding of the appropriate role of government and influenced their involvement in political activities. As politics became more of a popular than elite interest, it was not surprising that religious commitments spilled over into the political sphere.

At the heart of American politics was the concern for the continued health of the republican experiment. As American society changed, so, too, did the understanding of what was needed to maintain that health. In the late 1850s, a Maine newspaper warned that the preservation of the nation's freedom depended on the willingness of its citizens to go to the polls. It was, in fact, the "positive duty of every citizen of a Republic to vote." This insistence on voting as crucial to the well-being of the country was new. Before the 1820s, politics was primarily for the social and economic elite. Even though many states were removing voting restrictions in the early nineteenth century, the majority of white men did not trouble themselves with political matters. But the trauma of the Panic of 1819 and the spirited presidential campaigns for Andrew Jackson helped create widespread interest in politics. For many Americans, political participation became an important way of asserting and supporting important values and promoting their vision of the republic.

Changing Political Culture

Jackson's presidency was crucial in bringing politics to the center of many Americans' lives. Styling himself as the people's candidate in 1828, Andrew Jackson derided the Adams administration as corrupt and aristocratic and promised a more democratic political system. He told voters that he intended to "purify" and "reform the Government," purging all "who have been appointed from political considerations or against the will of the people." Unlike in our own age, most Americans then believed the campaign rhetoric. Four times more men turned out to vote in the election of 1828 than had four years earlier. They gave Jackson a resounding 56 percent of their ballots. No other president in the century would equal that percentage of popular support.

Despite campaign rhetoric and his image as a democratic hero, Jackson was not personally very democratic, nor did the era he symbolized involve any significant redistribution of wealth. Jackson himself owned slaves, defended slavery, and condoned mob attacks on abolitionists like Marius Robinson. He disliked Indians and ordered the forcible removal of the southeastern Indian nations to west of the Mississippi River in blatant disregard of the treaty rights and a Supreme Court decision. Belying promises of widening opportunity, the rich got richer during the Jacksonian era, and most farming and urban laboring families did not prosper.

But the nation's political life had changed in important ways. The old system of politics, based on elite coalitions bound together by ties of family and friendship and dependent on the deference of voters to their "betters," largely disappeared. In its place emerged a competitive party system, begun early in the republic but now oriented toward widespread voter participation. The major parties grew adept at raising money, selecting and promoting candidates, and bringing voters to the polls. A new "democratic" style of political life emerged as parties sponsored conventions, rallies (much like evangelical revivals in their flavor and fervor), and parades to encourage political participa-

tion and identification. Party politics became a central preoccupation for many adult white males. In the North, even women turned out for political hoopla, riding on floats at party parades.

Parties appealed to popular emotions, religious views, and ethnic prejudices. Party-subsidized newspapers regularly indulged in scurrilous attacks on political candidates. The language of politics became contentious and militaristic. Jackson's rhetoric exemplified the new trends. He described an opponent as an "enemy" who waged "war against the cause of the people." He reminded Americans that "those who are not for us are against us." Politicians talked of elections as battles and party members as their disciplined "rank and file." Strong party identification was part of the new national political culture. James Buchanan complained in 1839 about a colleague who urged politicians "to rise above mere party, and to go for our country." Instead, Buchanan said, "in supporting my party, I honestly believe I am . . . promoting the interest of my country."

Jackson's Path to the White House

The early career of Andrew Jackson gave few hints of his future political importance. Orphaned at 14, young Jackson was rowdy, indecisive, and often in trouble. As a law student, he was "a most roaring, rollicking, game-cocking, horse-racing, card-playing, mischievous fellow." Despite these preoccupations, which included dueling, Jackson passed the bar and set out at the age of 21 to seek his fortune in the West. Settling in frontier Nashville, the tall, red-headed young man built up a successful law practice in Tennessee and went on to become state attorney general, a substantial landowner, and a prominent citizen of Nashville.

Jackson's national reputation stemmed mainly from his military exploits, primarily against American Indians. As major general of the Tennessee militia, he proved able and popular. Jackson's troops admired his toughness and nicknamed him "Old Hickory." His savage victory over the Creek nation in the South in 1813 and 1814 brought notoriety and an appointment as major general in the U.S. Army. His victory at New Orleans in 1815 made him a national hero. His tour of the country after the war suggested political ambitions. As early as 1817, resolutions supporting a Jackson bid for the presidency began to appear in several states.

Although Jackson's aggressive military forays into Spanish Florida in 1818 bothered rival politicians and added to his reputation for scandal, they increased his popularity and his interest in the presidency. Jackson recognized that his greatest appeal lay with ordinary

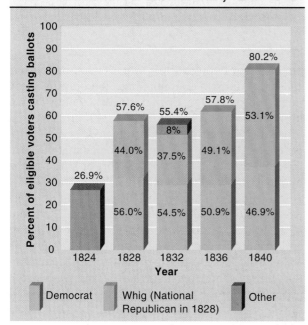

More Americans Vote for President, 1824–1840

The single-party system (Jeffersonian Democratic Republican) that existed in 1824 collapsed with the intense personal rivalries and ideological differences of the 1820s and 1830s. The emergence of a two-party system in the Jacksonian era dramatically increased (white male) voter participation to percentages far exceeding those of modern U.S. presidential elections.

people, whom he cultivated. But he also secured effective political backing. Careful political maneuvering in Tennessee in the early 1820s brought him election as U.S. senator and nomination for the presidency in 1824.

In the 1824 election, Jackson won both the popular and the electoral votes but lost in the House of Representatives to John Quincy Adams. When Henry Clay threw his support to Adams and was named secretary of state, Jackson condemned this deal as a "corrupt bargain." Jackson's loss convinced him of the importance of having an effective political organization. He felt confident of his strength in the West, and support by Adams's vice president, John C. Calhoun, helped him in the South. Jackson organized his campaign by setting up loyal committees and newspapers in many states and by encouraging efforts to undermine Adams and Clay.

A loose coalition promoting Jackson's candidacy began to call itself the Democratic party. Politicians of diverse views from all sections of the country were drawn to it, including Martin Van Buren of New York. Jackson masterfully waffled on controversial issues. He concealed his dislike of banks and paper money and vaguely advocated a "middle and just course" on the tariff. And he promised to cleanse government of corruption and privileged interests.

The Jackson–Adams campaign in 1828 degenerated into a nasty but entertaining contest. The Democrats whipped up enthusiasm with barbecues, mass rallies, and parades and gave out buttons and hats with hickory leaves attached. Amid the hoopla, few people discussed issues. Both sides made slanderous personal attacks. Supporters of Adams and Clay, who called themselves National Republicans, branded Jackson "an adulterer, a gambler, a cockfighter, a brawler, a drunkard, and a murderer." His wife, Rachel, was maligned as common and immoral.

The Jacksonians in turn charged Adams with bribing Clay for his support in 1824. They described him as a "stingy, undemocratic" aristocrat determined to destroy the people's liberties. Worse yet, Adams was an intellectual. Campaign slogans emphasized the differences between the hero of New Orleans, "a man who can fight," and the wimpy Adams, "a man who can write." "Who do you want," one slogan asked, "John Quincy Adams, who quotes law, or Andy Jackson, who makes law?" The question left little doubt as to how proud Americans would vote.

Jackson's supporters in Washington worked to ensure his election by devising a tariff bill to win necessary support in key states. Under the leadership of Van Buren, who hoped to replace Calhoun as Jackson's heir apparent, the Democrats in Congress

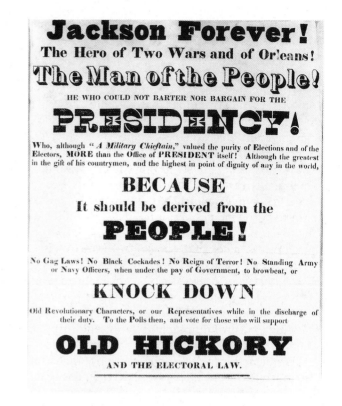

Unlike his rivals, J. Q. Adams and Henry Clay, who deprived Jackson of the presidency in 1824, Jackson, nicknamed "old Hickory" after America's toughest hardwood, claimed to honor the constitutional electoral system and the will of the people. (© *Collection of the New-York Historical Society*)

put together enough votes to pass what opponents called the "Tariff of Abominations." It arbitrarily raised rates to protect New England textiles, Pennsylvania iron, and some agricultural goods, winning voters in those states where the Democrats needed more support. John Randolph of Virginia sneered that the tariff "referred to manufactures of no sort or kind but the manufacture of a President of the United States."

The efforts of Jackson and his party paid off as he won an astonishing 647,286 ballots, about 56 percent of the total. Organization, money, effective publicity, and a popular style of campaigning had brought the 60-year-old Jackson to the presidency. His inauguration, however, horrified many Americans. Washington was packed for the ceremonies. Daniel Webster noted that "persons have come five hundred miles to see General Jackson, and they really seem to think that the country is to be rescued from some dreadful danger." When Jackson stood to take the oath of office, wild cheering broke out. Few in the crowd heard him, but many hoped to shake the new president's hand, and Jackson was all but mobbed as he tried to make his way to his horse.

As depicted in the Robert Cruikshank lithograph, *All Creation Going to the White House,* the first inauguration of Andrew Jackson in 1829 was the scene of wild festivities, a harbinger of the excesses in American life and politics in the ensuing years. *(Library of Congress)*

The White House reception soon got completely out of hand. A throng of people, "from the highest and most polished, down to the most vulgar and gross," Justice Joseph Story observed, poured into the White House with muddy boots to overturn furniture in a rush for food and punch. Jackson was forced to leave by a side door. When wine and ice cream were carried out to the lawn, many guests followed by diving through the windows. The inauguration, Story concluded, meant the "reign of King Mob." Another observer called it a "proud day for the people." These contrasting views on the events of the inauguration captured the essence of the Jackson era. For some, they symbolized the excesses of democracy; for others, they represented democratic fulfillment.

Old Hickory's Vigorous Presidency

Although Jackson had taken vague positions on important issues during the campaign, as president he needed to confront many of them. His decisions, often controversial, helped sharpen what it meant to be a Democrat and what it meant to be Democracy's opponent.

A few key convictions—the principle of majority rule, the limited power of the national government, the obligation of the national government to defend the interests of the nation's average people against the "monied aristocracy"—guided Jackson's actions as president. Seeing himself as the people's most authentic representative (only the president was elected by all the people), Jackson intended to be a vigorous executive. More than any previous president, Jackson

used presidential power in the name of the people and justified his actions by appeals to the people.

Jackson asserted his power most dramatically through the veto. His six predecessors had cast only nine vetoes, mostly against measures that they had believed unconstitutional. Jackson, however, argued that he had "undoubted right . . . to withhold . . . assent from bills on other grounds than their constitutionality." Jackson vetoed 12 bills during his two terms, often because they conflicted with his political agenda.

One of the abuses Jackson had promised to correct was what he described as an undemocratic and corrupt system of government officeholding. Too often "unfaithful or incompetent" men clung to government jobs for years. Jackson proposed to throw these scoundrels out and establish a system of rotation of office. The duties of public office were so "plain and simple," he said, that ordinary men could fulfill them.

Jackson's rhetoric was more extreme than his actions. He did not replace officeholders wholesale. In the first year and a half of his presidency, he removed 919 officeholders of a total of 10,093, fewer than one in ten. Most of these were for good reason—corruption or incompetence. Nor were the new Democratic appointees especially plain, untutored, or honest; they were in fact much like their predecessors. Still, Jackson's rhetoric helped create a new kind of democratic political culture that would prevail for most of the nineteenth century.

His policy on internal improvements—roads, canals, and other forms of transportation—was less far-seeing. Like most Americans, Jackson recognized their economic importance and as president wished "to see them extended to every part of the country." But Jackson was against infringement on states' rights. When proposals for federal support for internal improvements seemed to rob local and state authorities of their proper function, he opposed them. In 1830, he vetoed the Maysville Road bill, which proposed federal funding for a road in Henry Clay's Kentucky. But projects of national significance, like river improvements or lighthouses, were different. During his presidency Jackson supported an annual average of $1.3 million in internal improvements.

In a period of rapid economic change, tariffs stirred heated debate. New England and the Middle Atlantic states, the center of manufacturing operations, favored protective tariffs. The South had long opposed them because they made it more expensive to buy manufactured goods from the North or abroad and threatened to provoke foreign retaliation against southern cotton and tobacco exports. Feelings against the "Tariff of Abominations" ran particularly high in South Carolina. Some of that state's leaders mistakenly believed the tariff was the prime reason for the economic depression that hung over their state. In addition, some worried that the federal government might eventually interfere with slavery, a frightening prospect in a state where slaves outnumbered whites.

Vice President Calhoun, a brilliant political thinker and opponent of the tariff, provided the appropriate theory to check federal power and to protect minority rights. "We are not a nation," he once remarked, "but a Union, a confederacy of equal and sovereign states." In 1828, the same year as the hateful tariff, Calhoun anonymously published *Exposition and Protest,* presenting the doctrine of nullification as a means by which southern states could protect themselves from harmful national action. He argued that when federal laws overstepped the limits of constitutional authority, a state had the right to declare that legislation null and void and to refuse to enforce it.

Two years later, Calhoun's doctrine was aired in a Senate debate over public land policy. South Carolina's Robert Hayne defined nullification and, in the name of liberty, urged western states to adopt the doctrine. Daniel Webster responded. The federal government, he said, was no mere agent of the state legislatures. It was "made for the people, made by the people, and answerable to the people." No state legislature, therefore, could ever be sovereign over the people. Aware that nullification raised the specter of a "once glorious Union . . . drenched . . . in fraternal blood," Webster cried out in his powerful closing words that the appropriate motto for the nation was not "Liberty

With references to the still-hated British royalty, this cartoon, widely distributed by Whigs (a name chosen with antimonarchical British politics in mind), shows President Jackson, with a vetoed bill in one hand and kingly scepter in the other, trampling on the Constitution, the U.S. Bank, and internal improvements. *(Collection of The New-York Historical Society)*

first and Union afterwards, but Liberty and Union, now and forever, one and inseparable!"

The drama was repeated a month later at a birthday dinner in memory of Thomas Jefferson, when President Jackson declared himself on the issue. Despite his support of states' rights, Jackson did not believe that any state had the right to reject the will of the majority or to destroy the Union. Knowing that the supporters of nullification hoped to use the gathering to win adherents, Jackson rose for a toast, held high his glass, and said, "Our Union—it must be preserved." Thus challenged, Calhoun followed: "The Union—next to our liberty most dear." The split between them widened over personal as well as ideological issues, and in 1832 Calhoun resigned as vice president. Final rupture came in a collision over the tariff and nullification.

In 1832, hewing to Jackson's "middle course," Congress modified the tariff of 1828 by retaining high duties on goods such as wool, woolens, iron, and hemp but lowering other rates to an earlier level. Many southerners felt injured. A South Carolina convention later that year adopted an Ordinance of Nullification, voiding the tariffs of 1828 and 1832 in that state. The South Carolina legislature funded a volunteer army and threatened secession if the federal government tried to force the state to comply.

South Carolina's actions represented a direct attack on the concepts of federal union and majority rule. Jackson responded forcefully. To the "ambitious malcontents" in South Carolina, as he called the nullifiers, he proclaimed emphatically that "the laws of the United States must be executed. . . . Disunion by armed force is treason. . . . The Union will be preserved and treason and rebellion promptly put down."

Jackson's proclamation stimulated an outburst of patriotism all over the country. South Carolina stood alone, abandoned even by other southern states. Jackson asked Congress for legislation to enforce tariff duties (the Force Bill of 1833), and new tariff revisions, engineered by Henry Clay and supported by Calhoun, called for reductions over a ten-year period. South Carolina quickly repealed its nullification of the tariff laws but saved face by nullifying the Force Bill, which Jackson ignored. The crisis was over, but left unresolved were the constitutional issues it raised. Was the Union permanent? Was secession a valid way to protect minority rights? Such questions would trouble Americans for three decades.

Jackson's Indian Policy

Although Jackson only threatened force on South Carolina, he used it on the southeastern Indians. His policy of forcible removal and relocation westward and on reservations defined white American practice toward the Native American Indians for the rest of the century. In the opening decades of the nineteenth century, the vast landholdings of the five "civilized nations" of the Southeast (the Cherokee, Choctaw, Chickasaw, Seminole, and Creek) had been seriously eroded by the pressures of land-hungry whites supported by successful military campaigns led by professional Indian fighters like Jackson.

The Creek lost 22 million acres in southern Georgia and central Alabama after Jackson defeated them at Horseshoe Bend in 1814. Land cessions to the government and private sales accounted for even bigger losses: Cherokee tribal holdings, for example, of more than 50 million acres in 1802 had dwindled to only 9 million 20 years later.

The trend was bolstered by a Supreme Court decision in 1823 declaring that Indians could occupy but not hold title to land in the United States. Recognizing that their survival was threatened, Indian nations acted to end the pattern. By 1825, the Creek, Cherokee, and Chickasaw had each resolved to restrict land sales to government agents. The Cherokee, who had already assimilated many elements of white culture including clothing, agricultural practices, and slaveholding (see Chapter 9), established a police force to prevent local leaders from selling off tribal lands. Indian determination to resist pressure confronted white resolve to gain these southern lands for cotton planting and mining. Jackson's election in 1828 boosted efforts to relocate the Indians west of the Mississippi.

In his first annual message to Congress in 1829, Jackson recommended removal of the southeastern tribes. Appealing at first more to sympathy than to force, Jackson argued that because the Indians were "surrounded by the whites with their arts of civilization," it was inevitable that the "resources of the savage" would be destroyed, dooming the Indians to "weakness and decay." Removal was justified, Jackson claimed, by both "humanity and national honor." He also endorsed the paramount right of state laws over the claims of either Indians or the federal government (thus contradicting his tariff policy).

The crisis soon came to a head in Georgia. In 1829, the Georgia legislature declared the Cherokee tribal council illegal and its laws null and void in Cherokee territories and announced that the state had jurisdiction over both the tribe and its lands. In the following year, the Cherokee were forbidden to defend their interests by bringing suits against whites into the Georgia courts or even by testifying in such cases. Without legal recourse on the state level, the Cherokee carried their protests to the Supreme Court. In 1832, Chief Justice Marshall supported their position in *Worcester* v. *Georgia*, holding that the Georgia law was "repugnant to the Constitution" and did not apply to the Cherokee nation.

Legal victory could not, however, suppress white land hunger. With Jackson's blessing, Georgians defied the Court ruling. By 1835, harassment, intimidation, and bribery had persuaded a minority of chiefs to sign a removal treaty. That year, Jackson informed the

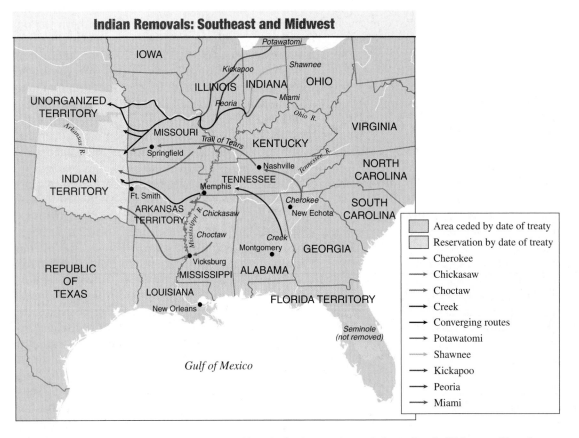

Indian Removals: Southeast and Midwest

▨	Area ceded by date of treaty
▨	Reservation by date of treaty
→	Cherokee
→	Chickasaw
→	Choctaw
→	Creek
→	Converging routes
→	Potawatomi
→	Shawnee
→	Kickapoo
→	Peoria
→	Miami

This map shows the westward routes of Indians removed from the Southeast to the new Indian territory in Oklahoma and from the Midwest (Old Northwest Territory) to present day Kansas. See the painting on the next page.

Cherokee, "You cannot remain where you are. Circumstances . . . render it impossible that you can flourish in the midst of a civilized community." Despite the president's pronouncement and the treaty, many Cherokee refused to leave their lands, and the Cherokee people divided into two factions over what to do. In 1837 and 1838, the U.S. Army searched out and seized those opposed to migration westward and gathered them in stockades before herding them west to the "Indian Territory" in Oklahoma. An eyewitness described how the Cherokee trek began:

> Families at dinner were startled by the sudden gleam of bayonets in the doorway and rose to be driven with blows and oaths along the weary miles of trail that led to the stockade. Men were seized in their fields, or going along the road, women were taken from their [spinning] wheels and children from their play. In many cases, on turning for one last look as they crossed the ridge they saw their homes in flames, fired by the lawless rabble that followed on the heels of the soldiers to loot and pillage.

The removal, whose $6 million cost was deducted from the $9 million awarded the Cherokee for its east-

ern lands, killed perhaps a quarter of the 15,000 who set out. The Cherokee "Trail of Tears" followed those of other southeastern Indian nations. Tribal communities in the Old Northwest between 1821 and 1840 were also forced westward to Kansas and Oklahoma. The Chickasaw suffered as high a death rate as the Cherokee during their removal, while the Seminole and the Sac and Fox fought back. Although Jackson and the Removal Act of 1830 had promised to protect and forever guarantee the Indian lands in the West, within a generation those promises, like others before and since, would be broken. Indian removal left the eastern United States open for the enormous economic expansion described in Chapter 10.

Jackson's Bank War and "Van Ruin's" Depression

As the (white) people's advocate, Jackson could not ignore the Second Bank of the United States, which in 1816 had received a charter for 20 years. The bank generated intense feelings. Jackson called it a "monster" that threatened the people's liberties. But it was not as irresponsible as Jacksonians imagined.

Guided since 1823 by the aristocratic Nicholas Biddle, the Philadelphia bank and its 29 branches gen-

Their attempts at assimilating into white society having failed, the Cherokee finally succumbed to white pressures and their own internal divisions and were forced to travel along the "Trail of Tears" to Oklahoma in 1838. About 4,000 died along the way. The Cherokee removal was actually the last major Indian group east of the Mississippi forced west. Upper midwestern Indian nations such as the Shawnee, Potawatomi, Miami, Kickapoo, and Peoria had been removed to Missouri, Kansas, and Oklahoma in the 1810s and 1820s; the migration of southeastern nations began with the Choctaw in 1830. *(Woolaroc Museum, Bartlesville, Oklahoma)*

erally played a responsible economic role in an expansionary period. As the nation's largest commercial bank, the U.S. Bank could shift funds around the country as necessary and could influence state banking activity. It restrained state banks from making unwise loans by insisting that they back their notes with specie (gold or silver coin) and by calling in its own loans to these institutions. The bank accepted federal deposits, made commercial loans, and bought and sold government bonds. Businessmen, state bankers needing credit, and nationalist politicians such as Webster and Clay, who were on the bank's payroll, all favored it.

Other Americans, however, led by the president, distrusted the bank. Businessmen and speculators in western lands resented its careful control over state banking and wanted cheap, inflated money. Some state bankers resented its power. Southern and western farmers regarded it as immoral because it dealt with paper, not landed property. Others simply thought it was unconstitutional and should be abolished.

Jackson had long opposed the Bank of the United States. He hated banks in general because of a near financial disaster in his own past and also because he and his advisers considered the bank the chief example of a special privilege monopoly that hurt the common man—farmers, craftsmen, and debtors. Jackson called the bank an "irresponsible power" and

a threat to the Republic. Its power and financial resources, he thought, allowed the bank to become a "vast electioneering engine" with the "power to control the Government and change its character."

Aware of Jackson's hostility, Clay and Webster persuaded Biddle to ask Congress to recharter the bank in 1832, four years ahead of schedule. They reasoned that in an election year, Jackson would not risk a veto. The bill to recharter the bank swept through Congress and landed on the president's desk one hot, muggy day in July. Jackson took up the challenge. Rather than implement the "milk & water half way veto" recommended by his advisers, Jackson forcefully said: "The bank . . . is trying to kill me, but I will kill it."

Jackson determined not only to veto the bill but also to carry his case to the public. His veto message, condemning the bank as undemocratic, un-American, and unconstitutional, was meant to stir up voters. He presented the bank as a dangerous monopoly that gave the rich special privileges and harmed "the humble members of society." He also pointed to the high percentage of foreign investors in the bank. Jackson's veto message turned the rechartering issue into a struggle between the people and the aristocracy. His oversimplified analysis made the bank into a symbol of everything that worried Americans in a time of change.

The bank furor helped to clarify party differences. In the election of 1832, the National Republicans, now calling themselves Whigs to show their opposition to "King Andrew," nominated Henry Clay. Biddle and the Whigs spent thousands of dollars trying to ensure Clay's election over Jackson, whom they labeled a "tyrant." Democratic campaign rhetoric pitted Jackson, the people, and democracy against Clay, the bank, and aristocracy. The Anti-Masons, the first third party in American political life and the first to hold a nominating convention, expressed popular resentments against the elitist Masonic order (Jackson was a member) and other secret societies.

Jackson won handsomely, with 124,000 more popular votes than the combined total for Clay and the Anti-Mason candidate, William Wirt. "He may be President for life if he chooses," said Wirt of Jackson.

Jackson saw the election as a victory for his bank policy and made plans to finish his war with Biddle. The bank still had four years before the charter expired. Jackson announced that "the hydra of corruption is only scotched, not dead" and declared that it must be killed. He and his advisers decided to weaken the bank by transferring $10 million in government funds to state banks. Although two secretaries of the treasury balked at the removal request as financially unsound, Jackson persisted until he found one, Roger Taney, willing to do it. When Chief Justice John Marshall died in 1835, Jackson replaced him with Taney.

Jackson's war with Biddle and the bank had serious economic consequences. A wave of speculation in western lands and ambitious new state internal improvement schemes in the mid-1830s produced inflated land prices and a flood of paper money. Even Jackson was concerned, and he tried to curtail irresponsible economic activity. In July 1836, he issued the Specie Circular, announcing that the government would accept only gold and silver in payment for public lands. Panicky investors rushed to change paper notes into specie, while banks started calling in loans. The result was the Panic of 1837. Jackson was blamed for this rapid monetary expansion followed by sudden deflation, but international trade problems with Britain and China probably contributed more to the panic and to the ensuing seven years of depression.

Whatever the primary cause, Jackson left his successor, Martin Van Buren, who was elected in 1836 over a trio of Whig opponents, with an economic crisis. Van Buren had barely taken the oath of office in 1837 when banks and businesses began to collapse. "Martin Van Ruin's" presidency was dominated by a severe depression. As New York banks suspended credit and began calling in loans, some $6 million was lost on defaulted debts. In 1838, wealthy merchant and New York mayor Philip Hone wrote in his diary that half his friends were deeply in debt. By 1840, he noted, his three grown sons were out of work and "business of all kinds [was] completely at a stand."

As Hone knew well, however, the laboring poor suffered most in a depression. By the fall of 1837, one-third of America's workers were unemployed, and thousands of others found only sporadic part-time work. For those fortunate enough to retain their jobs, wages fell by 30 to 50 percent within two years. Meanwhile, the price of necessities like flour, pork, and coal nearly doubled. As winter neared in late 1837, a journalist estimated that 200,000 in New York City were "in utter hopeless distress with no means of surviving the winter but those provided by charity." Not surprisingly, they took to the streets, demanding, "Bread! Meat! Rent! Fuel! Their prices must come down!" One worker told newspaperman Horace Greeley that most laborers called "not for the bread and fuel of charity, but for Work!"

The pride of workers was dampened as soup kitchens and bread lines grew faster than jobs. Laboring families found themselves defenseless, for the depression destroyed the trade union movement begun a decade earlier. Many employers hastened the process of killing trade unionism by imposing longer hours, cutting wages and piece rates, and dividing workers. One New England hat manufacturer offered to hire only those untouched by the "moral gangrene of Trades' Union principles." As the hardships of the depression grew worse, violence increased. In 1842, when Philadelphia textile employers lowered wages below subsistence levels, angry hand-loom weavers broke machinery, destroyed cloth, and wrecked the homes of Irish strikebreakers. Job competition, poverty, and ethnic animosities led to violent clashes in other eastern cities as well, as we saw in Chapter 10.

"How is it," a Philadelphia mechanic asked in 1837, that in a country as rich as the United States so many people were "pinched for the common necessaries of life . . . [and] bowed down with gloom and despair?" President Van Buren's responses to the social misery behind this question were sympathetic but limited and even made things worse. An executive order in 1840 declaring a ten-hour day for federal employees affected few workers. Despite inadequate measures, political participation, as well as church membership, reached new heights during the depression, as Americans sought to alleviate their "gloom and despair."

The Second American Party System

By the mid-1830s, a new two-party system and a lively participatory national political culture had emerged

THE SECOND AMERICAN PARTY SYSTEM

	Democrats	Whigs
Leaders	Andrew Jackson John C. Calhoun Martin Van Buren Thomas Hart Benton	Henry Clay Daniel Webster John Quincy Adams William Henry Harrison
Political tradition	Republican party (Jefferson, Madison	Federalist party (Hamilton, John Adams
Major Political Beliefs		
	State and local autonomy Opposition to monopoly and privilege Low land prices and tariffs Freedom from government interference	National power Support for U.S. Bank, high tariff Internal improvements Broad government role in reforming America
Primary Sources of Support		
Region	South and West	New England, Middle Atlantic, Upper Midwest
Class	Middle-class and small farmers, northeastern urban laborers and artisans	Big southern planters and wealthy businessmen, pockets of middling farmers in Midwest and South, artisans
Ethnicity	Scots-Irish, Irish, French, German, and Canadian immigrants	English, New England old stock
Religion	Catholics, frontier Baptists and Methodists, free thinkers	Presbyterians, Congregationalists, Quakers, moralists, reformers

in the United States. The parties had taken shape amid the conflicts of Jackson's presidency and the religious fervor of the Second Great Awakening. Although both parties included wealthy and influential leaders and mirrored the growing diversity of a changing nation, the Democrats had the better claim that they were the party of the common man with strength in all sections of the country.

Whigs represented greater wealth than Democrats and were strongest in New England and in areas settled by New Englanders across the Upper Midwest. In an appeal to businessmen and manufacturers, Whigs generally endorsed Clay's American System, which meant that they favored a national bank, federally supported internal improvements, and tariff protection for industry. Many large southern cotton planters joined the Whig party because of its position on bank credit and internal improvements. Whigs ran almost evenly with Democrats in the South for a decade, and artisans and laborers belonged equally to each party. The difficulty in drawing clear regional or class distinctions between Whigs and Democrats suggests that other factors, such as ethnic, religious, and cultural background, also influenced party choice. Because each party offered its own vision of the good society and notions on the role of government in private lives, broad cultural and social perspectives helped to determine party affiliation.

In the Jeffersonian tradition, the Democrats espoused liberty and local rule. They wanted freedom from legislators of morality, from religious tyranny, from special privilege, and from too much government. For them, the best society was one in which all Americans were free to follow their own individual interests. Those who wanted to maintain religious or ethnic traditions found a home in the Democratic party. So, too, did many members of denominations that had suffered discrimination in the colonies and states that had had an established church. The Scots-Irish, German, French, and Irish Catholic immigrants, as well as free thinkers and labor organizers, tended to be Jacksonians. Although they zealously promoted their social vision, Democrats were less moralistic than Whigs. Especially on matters like temperance and slavery, their religious background generally taught the inevitability of sin and evil in the world. Therefore, Democrats sought to keep politics separate from moral issues.

By contrast, for many Whigs, the line between reform and politics was hazy. Indeed, politics seemed an appropriate arena for cleansing society of sin. Calling themselves the party of law and order, most Whigs did not think Americans needed more freedom, but rather they needed to learn to use the freedom they already had. If all men were to vote, they required a "system of general education" that would teach them to use their political privileges. Old-stock New England Yankee Congregationalists and Presbyterians were usually Whigs. So were Quakers and evangelical Protestants, who believed that positive government action could change moral behavior and eradicate sin. Whigs supported a wide variety of reforms, such as temperance, antislavery, public education, and strict observance of the Sabbath, as well as government action to promote economic development.

Party identification played an increasingly large part in the lives of American men. The flamboyant new electioneering styles and techniques were designed to recruit new voters into the political process and to ensure continued loyalty. Party activities offered excitement, entertainment, and camaraderie. They offered a way to shape the changing world.

The election of 1840 illustrated the new style of political culture. Passing over Henry Clay, the Whigs nominated William Henry Harrison of Indiana, the aging hero of the Battle of Tippecanoe (Kithtippecanoe), fought nearly 30 years earlier. A Virginian, John Tyler, was nominated as vice president to underline the regional diversity of the party. The Democrats had no choice but to renominate Van Buren, who conducted a quiet campaign. The Whig campaign, however, featured every form of popularized appeals for votes—barbecues, torchlight parades, songs, and cartoons. Political symbolism was exploited by posing Harrison (who lived in a mansion) in front of a rural log cabin with a barrel of hard cider. Jugs of cider and coonskin caps inscribed with clever slogans were lavishly dispensed to grateful voters.

(Left) In the election of 1840, the Whigs "out-Jacksoned the Jacksonians" by playing to the popular political style of slogans, songs, and cider. They touted their candidate as a backwoodsy Indian fighter, the hero of the battle of Tippecanoe who lived in a log cabin and drank hard cider. *(Cincinnati Historical Society)* (Below) Louisiana Democrats responded to the Whig use of the log cabin and cider campaign with this cartoon, titled the "Federal-Abolition-Whig Trap to Catch Voters In," which shows an unwary voter, a member of the "industrious laboring classes," being lured under the log cabin by the promise of hard cider. "Just let him get a taste, " the text said, "and they come down at once upon him, hard and heavy, swig after swig, until they get him in a ranting way, shouting and bawling for Tip. and Ty." *(Library of Congress)*

A DROP OF
HARD CIDER
OR THE
TIPPECANOE
ROARER,
EMBODYING THE SOUL OF ALL THE
NORTH-BEND MELODIES, WHIG SONGS, &c,
PUBLISHED UNDER THE PATRONAGE OF THE GLORIOUS
Seventeen Tippecanoe Clubs of this City.
New-York,
ELTON: SONG-BOOK EMPORIUM,
108 Nassau, Corner of Ann-street, and 290 Bowery.

FEDERAL BANK WHIG MOTTO.
"WE STOOP TO CONQUER."

HARD CIDER

FEDERAL-ABOLITION-WHIG TRAP,
TO CATCH VOTERS IN.

The Whigs reversed conventional images by labeling Van Buren an aristocratic dandy and contrasting him with their simple candidate sitting in front of his cabin. Harrison reminded voters of General Jackson, and they swept him into office, 234 electoral votes to Van Buren's 60. In one of the largest turnouts in American history, over 80 percent of eligible voters marched to the polls. Commenting on the defeat, a Democratic party journal acknowledged that the Whigs had out-Jacksoned the Jacksonians: "We taught them how to conquer us."

Concern over the new politics outlasted Harrison, who died only a month after taking office. One man complained during the campaign that he was tired of all the hoopla over "the Old Hero. Nothing but politics . . . mass-meetings are held in every groggery." His comment about the combination of politics and drinking was especially telling. For many Americans, usually Whigs and often women, it was precisely the excesses of Jacksonian politics, most notably intemperance and the inherent violence of slavery, that led them to seek other ways than politics of imposing order and morality on American society. To gain a measure of control over their lives and reshape their changing world, the American people turned also to religion, social reform, and utopianism.

⤳ PERFECTIONIST REFORM AND UTOPIANISM

"Be ye therefore perfect even as your Father in heaven is perfect," commanded the Bible. Mid-nineteenth-century reformers, inspired by the Finney revivals, took the challenge seriously. Eventually, a perfected millennial era of 1,000 years of peace, harmony, and Christian brotherhood on earth would bring the Second Coming of Christ.

The perfectionist thrust in religion fit America's sense of itself as a redeemer nation chosen by God to reform the entire world. Religious commitment fused with patriotic duty. The motivating impulse to reform in the 1830s, then, had many deep-rooted causes. These included the Puritan idea of American mission;

the secular examples of founding fathers like Benjamin Franklin to do good, reinforced by Republican ideology and romantic beliefs in the natural goodness of human nature; the social activist tendencies in Whig political ideology; anxiety over shifting class relationships and the need to achieve some control over one's life as a result of the socioeconomic changes of recent years; family influence and the desire of young people to choose careers of principled service; and the direct influence of the Finney revivals in the early 1830s.

The Dilemmas of Reform

Religious reformers and Whig politicians both faced timeless dilemmas about how best to effect change. Does one, for example, try to change attitudes first and then behavior, or the reverse? Which is more effective, to appeal to people's minds and hearts to change bad institutions, or to change institutions first, assuming that altered behavior will then change attitudes? Taking the first path, the reformer relies on education, on the moral suasion of sermons, tracts, literature, argument, and personal testimony. Following the second, the reformer acts politically and institutionally, seeking to pass laws, win elections, form unions, boycott tainted goods, and create or abolish institutions.

Reformers, moreover, have to decide whether to attempt to bring about limited, piecemeal practical change on a single issue or go for perfection. Should they improve on a partly defective system or tear down the entire system to build a utopian new one? Reformers must further decide whether to use or recommend force and whether to enter into coalitions with less principled potential allies. They also face the difficult challenge of making sure that their own attitudes and actions are thoroughly consistent with the principles of behavior they would urge on others, as Thoreau had demonstrated.

These challenging problems fill the lives of reformers with turmoil. Advocates of change in the status quo experience enormous pressures, recriminations, and economic or physical persecution from the majority. As Marius and Emily Robinson understood,

---

MOTIVATIONS AND CAUSES OF REFORM IN AMERICA, 1830–1850

- Changing relationships between men and women, masters and workers as a result of the market economy, growth of cities, and increasing immigration
- Finney and other religious revivals in the Second Great Awakening
- Social activist and ethical impulses of the Whig party
- Psychological anxieties over shifting class and ethnic relationships
- Family traditions and youthful idealism
- Puritan and Revolutionary traditions of the American mission to remake the world
- Republican ideology and Enlightenment emphasis on virtue and good citizenship
- Romantic literary influences such as Transcendentalism

promoting change has its costs. What is more, reformers invariably do not agree on appropriate ideology and tactics, so they end up quarreling with one another as well as with representatives of the established order they wish to change. Although reformers suffer pressure to conform and to cease questioning things, their duty to themselves, their society, and their God sustains their commitment.

Utopian Communities: Oneida and the Shakers

Thoreau tried to lead an ideal solitary life. Other reformers sought to create perfect communities. Emerson noted in 1840 that he hardly met a thinking, reading man who did not have "a draft of a new community in his waistcoat pocket." One way to redeem a flawed society, one that seemed to be losing the cohesion and traditional values of small community life, was to create miniature utopian societies. These would offer alternatives to a world characterized by factories, foreigners, flawed morals, and greedy entrepreneurship.

In 1831, as President Jackson and South Carolina approached their confrontation over the tariff and nullification, as Nat Turner planned his slave revolt in Virginia, and as the citizens of Rochester sought ways of controlling their workers' drinking habits, a young man in Putney, Vermont, heard Charles Finney on one of his whirlwind tours of New England. John Humphrey Noyes was an instant, if unorthodox, convert.

Noyes believed that the act of final conversion led to absolute perfection and complete release from sin. However spiritually blessed, Noyes's earthly happiness was soon sorely tested. In 1837, a woman he loved rejected both his doctrine and his marriage offer. Despondent, Noyes wrote a friend that "when the will of God is done on earth as it is in heaven there will be no marriage." Among those who were perfect, he argued, all men and women belonged equally to each other. For Noyes, complete sharing in family relationships was a step toward perfect cooperation, as was shared wealth in socioeconomic relationships. Others called his heretical doctrines "free love" and socialism. Noyes recovered from his unhappy love affair and married a loyal follower. When she delivered four stillborn children within six years, Noyes revised even further his unconventional ideas about sex.

In 1848, Noyes and 51 devoted followers founded a "perfectionist" community at Oneida, New York. Under his strong leadership, Oneida grew and prospered. Sexual life at the commune was subject to many regulations, including sexual restraint and male continence except under carefully prescribed conditions. In a system of

In this sacred Shaker dance, sin is being shaken out of the body through the fingertips. Note the separation of women and men. *(Shakertown at Pleasant Hill, Kentucky)*

planned reproduction, only certain spiritually advanced males (usually Noyes) were allowed to father children. Other controversial practices included communal child rearing, sexual equality in work, the removal of the competitive spirit from both work and play, and an elaborate program of "mutual criticism" at community meetings presided over by "Father" Noyes.

Though creating considerable tension, these unorthodox sexual and social rules gave Oneidans a sense of uniqueness. Wise economic decisions also bound community members in mutual prosperity. Forsaking the nostalgic agricultural emphasis that typified most other communes, Noyes opted for modern manufacturing. Oneida specialized at first in the fabrication of steel animal traps and later diversified into making silverware. Eventually abandoning religion to become a joint-stock company in which individual members held shares, Oneida thrived for many years and continues today as a silverware company.

Noyes greatly admired another group of communitarians, the Shakers, who also believed in perfectionism, surrendering worldly property to the community, and the devotion of one's labor and love to bringing about the millennial kingdom of heaven. Unlike the Oneidans, Shakers condemned sexuality and demanded absolute chastity, so that only conversions could bring in new members. Founded by an Englishwoman, Mother Ann Lee, Shaker conversions grew in the Second Great Awakening and peaked around 6,000 souls by the 1850s, with communities from Maine to New York to Kentucky. They believed that God had a dual personality, male and female, and that Ann Lee was the female counterpart to the masculine Christ. The Shaker worship service featured frenetic dancing intended to release (or "shake") sin out through the fingertips. Shaker communities, some of which survived long into the twentieth century, were known for their communal ownership of property, equality of women and men, simplicity, and beautifully crafted furniture.

Other Utopias

Over 100 utopian communities like Oneida and the Shaker colonies were founded. Some were religiously motivated; others were secular. Most were small and lasted only a few months or years. All eventually collapsed, though giving birth to significant social ideas.

Pietist German-speaking immigrants founded the earliest utopian communities in America, to preserve their language, spirituality, and ascetic lifestyle. The most notable of these were the Ephrata colonists in Pennsylvania, the Harmonists in Indiana, the Zoar community in Ohio, and the Amana Society in Iowa. Some antebellum utopian communities focused less on otherworldly contemplation than on the regenera-

tion of this world. In 1840, Adin Ballou founded Hopedale in Massachusetts as a "miniature Christian republic" based on the ethical teachings of Jesus. Hopedale's newspaper, *The Practical Christian*, advocated temperance, pacifism, women's rights, and other reforms.

Other communities, founded on the secular principles of reason inherited from the Enlightenment, responded more directly to the social misery and wretched working conditions accompanying the Industrial Revolution. These communities differed from religious ones in assuming that evil came from bad environments rather than individual acts of sin. They consequently believed that altered environ-

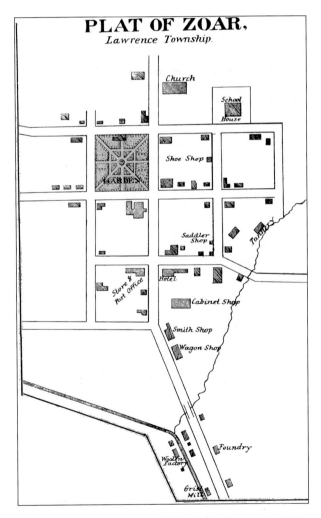

The Zoar community was founded by Pietist Germans in 1817 and lasted until 1898. This type of map, or plat, shows the ordered plan for the town, the prominence of the public gardens (land was not held individually but in common), and the artisan and commercial shops built along the river and the Ohio and Erie Canal, which passed through Zoar in 1832. Note that despite the importance of religion, the church is on the edge of town, while commercial sites, including a hotel welcoming visitors, are in the center. *(Danzer Map Collection)*

ments rather than new morals would eliminate or reduce poverty, ignorance, intemperance, and other ugly by-products of industrialism.

Robert Owen was the best known of the secular communalists. A Scottish industrialist who saw the miserable lives of cotton millworkers, he envisioned a society of small towns—"Agricultural and Manufacturing Villages of Unity and Mutual Cooperation"—with good schools and healthy work for all citizens. Unemployment, poverty, and vice would be unknown in Owen's model communities. In 1824, he established his first town in America at New Harmony, Indiana, a former Pietist community. But little harmony prevailed, and it failed within three years.

Brook Farm, founded by two Concord friends of Emerson, tried to integrate "intellectual and manual labor." Residents would hoe in the fields and shovel manure for a few hours each day and then study literature and recite poetry. Although the colony lasted less than three years, it produced some notable literature in a journal, *The Dial,* edited by Margaret Fuller. Nathaniel Hawthorne briefly lived at Brook Farm and wrote a novel, *The Blithedale Romance* (1852), criticizing the utopians' naive optimism.

The utopian communities all failed for similar reasons. Americans seemed ill-suited to communal living and work responsibilities and were unwilling to share either their property or their spouses. Nor did celibacy arouse much enthusiasm. Other recurring problems included unstable leadership, financial bickering, local hostility toward sexual experimentation and other unorthodox practices, the indiscriminate admission of members, and waning enthusiasm. Emerson pinned the failure of the communities on their inability to confront the individualistic impulses of human nature. As he said of Brook Farm, an epitaph suitable for all utopian communities: "It met every test but life itself."

Millerites and Mormons

If utopian communities failed to bring about the millennium, an alternative hope was to leap directly past the thousand years of peace and harmony to the Second Coming of Christ. William Miller, a shy farmer from upstate New York, became so absorbed with the idea of the imminent coming of Christ that he figured out mathematically the exact time of the event in March 1843. A religious sect, the Millerites, gathered around him to prepare for Christ's return and the Day of Judgment.

A mixture of excitement and fear grew as the day of the predicted return came closer. Some people gave away all their worldly belongings, neglected business,

put on robes, and flocked to high hills and rooftops to be nearest the blessed event. When 1843 passed without the expected end, Miller and his followers recalculated and set a series of alternative dates. Each new disappointment diminished Miller's followers, and he died in 1848 a discredited man. But a small Millerite sect, the Seventh-Day Adventists, had already taken root and continues to this day.

Other groups that emerged from the same religiously active area of upstate New York were more successful. As Palmyra, New York, was being swept by Finney revivalism, young Joseph Smith, a recent convert, claimed to be visited by the angel Moroni. According to Smith, Moroni led him to golden tablets buried in the ground near his home. On these plates were inscribed more than 500 pages of *The Book of Mormon,* which described the one true church and a "lost tribe of Israel" missing for centuries. The book also predicted the appearance of an American prophet who would establish a new and pure kingdom of Christ in America. Smith published his book in 1830 and soon founded the Church of Jesus Christ of Latter-Day Saints (the Mormons). His visionary leadership attracted thousands of ordinary people trying to escape what they viewed as social disorder, religious impurity, and commercial degradation in the 1830s.

Smith and a steadily growing band of converts migrated successively to Ohio and Missouri and then back to Illinois, where they met ridicule, persecution, and violence. The hostility stemmed in part from their active missionary work, in part from their beliefs and support for local Indian tribes, and in part from rumors of unorthodox sexual practices.

Despite external persecution and internal dissension caused by Smith's strong leadership style, the Mormons prospered and increased. Converts from England and northern Europe added substantially to their numbers. By the mid-1840s, Nauvoo, Illinois, with a thriving population of nearly 15,000, was the showplace of Mormonism. Smith petitioned Congress for separate territorial status and ran for the presidency in 1844. This was too much for the citizens of nearby towns. Violence escalated and culminated in Smith's trial for treason and his murder by a mob. Under the brilliant leadership of Smith's successor, Brigham Young, the Mormons headed westward in 1846 in their continuing search for the "land of promise."

REFORMING SOCIETY

The Mormons and the utopian communitarians had as their common goal, in Brigham Young's words, "the spread of righteousness upon the earth." Most people,

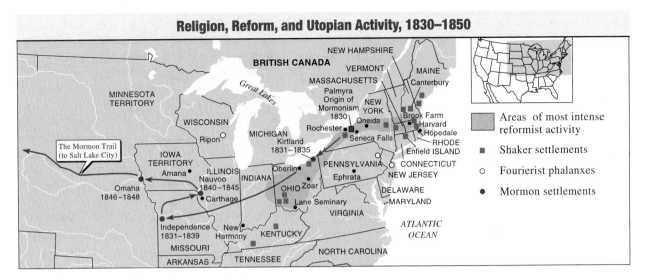

Religion, Reform, and Utopian Activity, 1830–1850

Reformist activity followed both religious revival areas and the Erie Canal into the growing states of the Old Northwest.

however, preferred to spread righteousness by focusing on a specific social evil rather than embracing whole new religions or joining utopian colonies.

"We are all a little wild here," Emerson wrote in 1840, "with numberless projects of social reform." Mobilized in part by their increased participation in the political parties of Jacksonian America, the reformers created and joined all kinds of societies for social betterment. The reform ranks were swelled by thousands of women, stirred to action by the religious revivals and freed from domestic burdens by delayed marriage and smaller families. Organized in hundreds of voluntary societies, women such as

Emily Rakestraw joined men such as Marius Robinson in directing their energies to numerous social issues. These included alcohol consumption; diet and health; sexuality; institutional treatment of the mentally ill, the disabled, paupers, and criminals; education; the rights of labor; slavery; and women's rights.

Temperance

On New Year's Eve in 1831, a Finney disciple, Theodore Dwight Weld, delivered a four-hour temperance lecture in Rochester. In graphic detail, he described the awful fate of those who

The temperance movement of the 1830s and 1840s used the tactics of religious revivalists to scare drinkers into taking the "teetotal" pledge. Who could resist this poignant 1846 portrayal of *The Drunkard's Progress*? *(Library of Congress)*

refused to stop drinking and urged his audience not only to cease their tippling but also to stop others. Several were converted to abstinence on the spot. The next day, Elijah and Albert Smith, the largest providers of whiskey in Rochester, rolled their barrels out onto the sidewalk and smashed them. Cheering Christians applauded as the whiskey ran out into Exchange Street.

Americans in the nineteenth century drank heavily. One man observed that "a house could not be raised, a field of wheat cut down, nor could there be a log rolling, a husking, a quilting, a wedding, or a funeral without the aid of alcohol." The corrosive effects of drinking were obvious: poverty, crime, illness, insanity, battered and broken families, and corrupt politics.

Early efforts at curbing alcohol consumption emphasized moderation. Forming local societies, groups of people agreed to limit how much they drank or to imbibe only beer and wine. Some societies even met in local taverns to toast their commitment to moderation. But under the influence of the Beecher and Finney revivals, the movement achieved better organization and clearer goals. The American Temperance Society, founded in 1826, was dedicated not just to moderation but to total abstinence. Within a few years, thousands of local and state societies had formed, though some refused to prohibit drinking of hard cider and communion wine.

Temperance advocates copied successful revival techniques. Fiery lecturers expounded on the evil consequences of drink and urged group pressure on the weak-willed. Mass meetings were accompanied by a deluge of graphic and sometimes gory temperance tracts. Who would not cringe at descriptions of drinkers: "Some are killed instantly; some die a lingering, gradual death; some commit suicide in fits of intoxication; and some are actually burnt up." One "intemperate man," it was claimed, died when his "breath caught fire by coming in contact with a lighted candle." The accumulated pressure of both written and oral testimony, capped off by a sermon like Weld's, was intended to convince people to take the "teetotal" pledge.

By 1840, disagreements over goals and methods split the temperance movement into many separate organizations. In depression times, when jobs and stable families were harder to find than whiskey and beer, laboring men and women moved more by practical concerns than religious fervor joined the crusade. The Washington Temperance Society, founded in a Baltimore tavern in 1840, was enormously popular with unemployed young workers and grew to an estimated 600,000 members in three years. The Washingtonians, arguing that alcoholism was a disease rather than moral failure, changed the shape of the temperance movement. They replaced revivalist techniques with those of the new party politics by organizing parades, picnics, melodramas, and festivals to encourage people to take the pledge.

Tactics in the 1840s also shifted away from moral suasion to political action. Temperance societies lobbied for local option laws, allowing communities to prohibit the sale, manufacture, and consumption of alcohol. The first such law in the nation was passed in Maine in 1851. Fifteen other states followed with similar laws before the Civil War. Despite weak enforcement, the per capita drinking fell dramatically in the 1850s. Interrupted by the Civil War, the movement reached its ultimate objective with passage of the Eighteenth Amendment in 1919.

The temperance crusade reveals the many practical motivations for Americans to join reform societies. For some, as in Rochester, temperance provided an opportunity for the Protestant middle classes to exert some control over laborers, immigrants, and Catholics. Perfectionists saw abstinence as a way of practicing self-control. For many women, the temperance effort was a respectable way to control the behavior of drunken men who beat wives and daughters. For many young men, especially after the onset of the depression of 1837, a temperance society provided entertainment, fellowship, and contacts to help their careers. In temperance societies as in political parties, Americans found jobs, purpose, support, spouses, and relief from the loneliness and uncertainty of a changing world.

Health and Sexuality

It was a short step from the physical and psychological ravages of drink to other potentially harmful effects on the body. Reformers were quick to attack too much eating, too many stimulants, and, above all, too much sex. Many endorsed a variety of special diets and exercise programs for maintaining good health. Some promoted panaceas. One of these was hydropathy: clients sojourned at one of 70 special resorts for bathing and water purges of the body. Many of these resorts especially attracted women who not only found an escape from daily drudgery in the home but also found cures for chronic and untreated urogenital infections. Other panaceas, including hypnotism, phrenology (the study of bumps on the head), and various "spiritualist" seances, sought to cure problems of the mind.

Sylvester Graham, inventor of the Graham cracker, combined all these enthusiasms into a focus on sexual purity. In 1834 he delivered a series of lectures on chastity, later published as an advice book. To those "troubled" by sexual desire, he recommended "cold baths" and "more active exercise in the open air. Graham advised women, apparently not as "passionless" as the Victorian stereotype suggested, to "have intercourse only for procreation." Although females learned to control sexuality for their own purposes, as we shall see, male "sexual purity" advocates urged sexual restraint to protect various male interests. One doctor argued that women ought not to be educated because blood needed for the womb would be diverted to the head, thus breeding "puny men."

The authors of antebellum "health" manuals advocated abstinence from sexual activity as vehemently as from alcohol. The body, they argued, was a closed energy system in which each organ had particular and limited functions to perform. Semen must be saved for reproductive purposes and should not be wasted in masturbation or intercourse only for pleasure. Such waste would cause enervation, disease, insanity, and death. Some argued further that the "expenditure" of sperm meant a loss of needed energy from the economy.

Humanizing the Asylum

In their effort to restore order to American society, some reformers preferred to work not for private influence over individuals but toward public changes in institutions. They wanted to transform such social institutions as asylums, almshouses, prisons, schools, and even factories. Horace Mann, who led the struggle for common schools in Massachusetts (see Chapter 10), was a typical antebellum reformer. He blended dedicated idealism with a canny, practical sense of how to institutionalize educational improvements in one state: teacher training schools, higher teachers' salaries, and compulsory attendance laws.

Other reformers were less successful in achieving their goals. This was especially true in the treatment of society's outcasts. In the colonial era, the family or the local community cared for orphans, paupers, the insane, and even criminals. Beginning early in the nineteenth century, various states built asylums, houses of refuge, reform schools, jails, and other institutions to uplift and house social victims. In some of these institutions, such as prisons and almshouses, the sane and insane, children and hardened adult criminals were thrown together in terrible conditions. In 1843, Dorothea Dix, a frail New Englander, horrified the Massachusetts legislature with her famous report that imprisoned insane people in the state were subject to the "extremest state of degradation and misery." They were confined in "cages, closets, stalls, pens! Chained, naked, beaten with rods, and lashed into obedience!" Dix recommended special hospitals, or asylums, where the insane could be "humanly and properly controlled" by trained attendants.

Many perfectionist reformers like Dix believed that asylums could reform society's outcasts. Convinced

With strong religious roots, the frail Dorothea Dix tirelessly waged a courageous and creative campaign to improve conditions for the insane throughout the nation. "I encounter nothing which a determined will created by the necessities of the cause does not enable me to vanquish," she wrote, reflecting her irrepressible spirit on behalf of public support for humane hospitals for "hundreds of wailing, suffering creatures." *(The Granger Collection, New York)*

that bad institutions corrupted basically good human beings, they reasoned that reformed institutions could rehabilitate them. In 1853, Charles Loring Brace started a Children's Aid Society in New York City that was a model of change through effective education and self-help. Reformers like Dix and Brace, as well as Samuel Gridley Howe and Thomas Gallaudet, who founded institutions for the care and education of the blind and deaf, achieved remarkable results.

But all too often, results were disappointing. Prison reformers believed that a properly built and administered penitentiary could bring a hardened criminal "back to virtue." They argued intensely over the most appropriate structural design for rehabilitating criminals. Some preferred the rectangular prison at Auburn, New York, with its tiny cells and common workrooms, whereas others pointed to the Pennsylvania star-shaped system, where each inmate was in solitary confinement, though in a fairly modern cell. Whichever system was preferred, prison reformers assumed that if "penitents" were put into isolated cells to study the Bible and reflect on their wrongdoing,

A popular workingmen's form of entertainment was the minstrel show, where whites would blacken their faces with burnt cork and perform songs and skits that negatively stereotyped blacks. Two oft-depicted types were thick-lipped, dim-witted slavish clowns and faithful "old Darkies," both incapable of coping with plantation life. Another was the northern pseudo-suave dandy like "Zip Coon," shown here who, despite his airs, was always humiliated so as to reassure white workers that free blacks posed no threat to take either their women or their jobs. *(The Harvard Theatre Collection, The Houghton Library)*

they would eventually decide to become good citizens. In practice, many criminals simply went mad or committed suicide. The institutions built by well-intentioned reformers became dumping places for society's outcasts. By mid-century, American prisons and mental asylums had become sadly impersonal, understaffed, overcrowded institutions.

Working-Class Reform

Efforts to improve the institutional conditions of American life were not all top-down movements initiated and led by middle-class reformers. For working-class Americans, the social institution most in need of transformation was the factory. Workers, many of whom were involved in other issues such as temperance, peace, and abolitionism, tried to improve their own lives. As labor leader Seth Luther told a meeting of New England mechanics and laborers, "We must take our business into our own hands. Let us awake."

And awake they did, forming both trade unions and workingmen's parties as Andrew Jackson neared the presidency.

Between 1828 and 1832, dozens of workingmen's parties arose. They advocated free, tax-supported schools, free public lands in the West, equal rights for the poor, and elimination of monopolistic privilege. Trade union activity began in Philadelphia in 1827 as skilled workers organized journeymen carpenters, plasterers, printers, weavers, tailors, and other tradesmen. That same year, 15 unions combined into a city-wide federation, a process followed in other cities. The National Trades Union, founded in 1834, was the first attempt at a national labor organization.

Trade unions fared better than labor parties, as Jacksonian Democrats siphoned off workers' votes. Union programs set more practical goals, including shorter hours, wages that would keep pace with rising prices, and ways (such as the closed shop) of warding off the competitive threat of cheap labor. In addition, both workers and their middle-class supporters called for the abolition of imprisonment for debt and of compulsory militia duty (both of which often cost workers their jobs), free public education, improved living conditions in workers' neighborhoods, and the right to organize. Discouraged by decisions of New York State courts, which denied the right to organize in 1835 and again in 1836, workers argued that unions were necessary to "resist the oppressions of avarice" and compared themselves with the Americans who dumped British tea in Boston's harbor in 1773.

Fired by revolutionary tradition, by increasing political influence, and by a union membership of near 300,000, workers struck some 168 times between 1834 and 1836. Over two-thirds of the strikes were over wages (see Chapter 10); the others were for shorter hours. Identifying with the "blood of our fathers" shed on the battlefields of the American Revolution, Boston tradesmen struck in 1835 for a ten-hour day. They failed, but their attempt heralded the subsequent resurgence of a successful ten-hour-day movement in the 1850s. The Panic of 1837 ushered in a depression that dashed the hopes and efforts of American workers. But the organizational work of the 1830s promised that the labor movement would reemerge, strengthened, later in the century.

ABOLITIONISM AND THE WOMEN'S RIGHTS MOVEMENT

As American workers struggled in Lowell and other eastern cities for better wages and hours in 1834, Emily and Marius Robinson arrived in Cincinnati to fight for their causes. They and many other young idealists had been attracted by the newly founded Lane Seminary, a school to train abolitionist leaders. Financed by two wealthy New York brothers, Arthur and Lewis Tappan, Lane soon became a center of reformist activity. When nervous local residents persuaded President Lyman Beecher to crack down on the students, 40 "Lane rebels," led by Theodore Weld, fled to Oberlin in northern Ohio. The rebels turned Oberlin College into the first institution in the United States open to women and men, blacks and whites. Thus, the movements to abolish slavery and for equal rights to women and free blacks were joined.

The goals of the struggle against slavery and subtle forms of racism and sexism often seemed as distant and unrealizable as the millennium itself. Yet antislavery and feminist advocates persisted in their efforts to abolish what they believed were concrete, visible, institutionalized social wrongs. Whether seeking to eliminate coercion in the cotton fields or in the kitchen, they faced the dual challenge of pursuing elusive goals while achieving practical changes in everyday life.

Tensions within the Antislavery Movement

Although the antislavery movement was smaller than temperance advocacy, it revealed more clearly the difficulties of pursuing significant social change in America. As a young man of 22, William Lloyd Garrison passionately desired to improve, if not to perfect, the flawed world in which he lived. He was also ambitious and said that his name would "one day be known to the world." He was right. On January 1, 1831, eight months before Nat Turner's revolt, Garrison published the first issue of *The Liberator*, soon to become the leading antislavery journal in the United States. "I am in earnest," he wrote. "I will not equivocate—AND I WILL BE HEARD." After first organizing the New England Anti-Slavery Society with a group of blacks and whites in a church basement in Boston, in 1833 Garrison and 62 others established the American Anti-Slavery Society.

Before Garrison, most antislavery whites, dominated by southerners like Henry Clay, had advocated gradual emancipation by individual slave owners. Many joined the American Colonizationist Society, founded in 1816, which sent a few former slaves to Liberia, on the West Coast of Africa. But these efforts were woefully inadequate and were racist, the main goal being to rid the country of free blacks rather than slavery itself.

Garrison furiously opposed the colonizationists. "I do not wish to think, or speak, or write, with moderation," he wrote. "No! no! tell a man whose house is on fire to give a moderate alarm; tell him to moderately rescue his wife from the hands of the ravisher." For Garrison, compromise was unthinkable. There would be "no Union with slaveholders," he cried, condemning the Constitution that perpetuated slavery as "a covenant with death, an agreement with Hell." The American Anti-Slavery Society called for the immediate and total abolition of slavery. After escaping slavery, Frederick Douglass agreed: "Power concedes nothing without a demand. It never did and it never will." But the abolitionists did not always agree, splitting into colonizationists, gradualists, and immediatists.

Abolitionists also differed over the tactics of ending slavery. Their primary method was moral suasion, by which they sought to convince slaveholders and their supporters that slavery was a sin. In an outpouring of sermons, petitions, resolutions, pamphlets, and speeches, abolitionists tried to overwhelm slaveholders with moral guilt so that, repentant, they would free their slaves. But as Marius wrote to Emily Robinson, "The spirit of slavery is not confined to the South." His Ohio trip suggests that northerners were equally guilty in providing the support necessary to maintain the slave system.

The abolitionists by 1837 flooded the nation with over a million pieces of antislavery literature. Their writing described slave owners as "mansteaiers" who gave up all claim to humanity. A slaveholder, Garrison wrote, led a life "of unbridled lust, . . . of haughty domination, of cowardly ruffianism, of boundless dissipation, of matchless insolence, of infinite self-conceit, of unequalled oppression, of more than savage cruelty." In 1839, Weld published *American Slavery as It Is*, which described in the goriest possible detail the inhumane treatment of slaves.

Other abolitionists preferred more direct methods. The main alternative lay in political action by bringing antislavery petitions before Congress and forming third parties. Boycotting goods made by slave labor was a third tactic.

A fourth approach was to call for slave rebellion, as did two northern blacks, David Walker in a pamphlet in 1829 and Henry Highland Garnet in a speech at a convention of black Americans in 1843. Walker, a North Carolina free black living in Boston, published a powerful essay, "Walker's Appeal." He called upon other free blacks to "enlighten your brethren" to their ignorant "wretched condition" and upon slaves themselves to cease their submissiveness and rise up and throw off the yoke of slavery. "Now I ask you," Walker wrote, "had you not rather be killed than to be a slave to a tyrant, who takes the life of your mother, wife, and dear little children? Look upon your mother, wife and children, and answer God almighty; and believe this,

Recovering the Past

SLAVE NARRATIVES

⬚

In the 1840s and 1850s, male and female abolitionists eagerly sought out, subsidized, and published book-length accounts of slavery written by runaway slaves themselves. These chilling stories of captivity and successful escapes, in the voices of former slaves, had enormous emotional power and were instrumental by abolitionists in their effort to influence public opinion and end slavery. According to one estimate, nearly 100 book-length "slave narratives" have been published, selections from two of which are included here.

The slave narratives combined three American autobiographical traditions: spiritual confessionals characteristic of Puritans such as Jonathan Edwards; the rags-to-riches individualistic success story of Benjamin Franklin; and Indian captivity narratives. The last tradition, popular reading in the early nineteenth century, described the adventures of white captives who were dragged away from their villages by Indians; suffered the trials, tortures, and sometimes harmonious adaptations to living in an Indian village; and were finally freed and returned ("redeemed") home to white civilization.

The African American slave narratives followed a similar three-stage pattern, beginning either with an idyllic childhood in a West African village or the relative innocence of childhood on a southern plantation. Aimed at northern white readers, the bulk of the story described, in vivid detail, the brutal oppressions of captivity and slavery, dwelling on the horrors of the slave ships, slave sales and the breakup of families, and the daily beatings, punishments, and harsh rigors of life on the plantation. But the narratives also described heroic struggles to survive and even "sass" one's owners and cunning strategies for avoiding work, connecting with loved ones, and learning how to read and write. The narratives concluded with the story of escape and the taking on of a new identity—and often a new name as well—in freedom.

In fact, for many former slaves, the actual process of writing the narrative marked the attainment of their identity and freedom, often involving a ritual of self-naming. As William L. Andrews put it in *To Tell a Free Story*, for blacks to write their story was "in some ways uniquely self-liberating, the final, climactic act in the drama of their lifelong quests for freedom." Other typical themes included poignant appeals to white readers to agitate for the abolition of slavery; contrasts between the slaveholder's use of religion to justify slavery and the simple, spiritually based Christianity of the slaves themselves; and the supportive strength of the slave community and the white and black underground network in facilitating a successful runaway.

Although not the first, the prototypical slave narrative was that of Frederick Douglass, whose story is told in Chapter 11. You have seen how he grew up witnessing the horrors of slavery on a Maryland plantation and as an urban slave in Baltimore, learned to read and write, successfully defied the cruel Mr. Covey's efforts to break his will as a slave, and finally escaped to become a leading abolitionist. Similar stories were told by Henry Bibb, William Welles Brown, Olaudah Equiano, Josiah Henson, Harriet Jacobs, Mattie Jackson, Solomon Northup, Sojourner Truth, and many many others, all of whom provided gory details of whippings and the wrenching loss of loved ones.

The two short selections here—from James W. C. Pennington's *Fugitive Blacksmith* (1849) and Harriet Jacobs's *Incidents in the Life of a Slave Girl* (1861)—focus not on white oppression but on the initial process of planning an escape. Jacobs wrote under the pseudonym Linda Brent and as background to this passage discovers that her two children are to be brought to her master's plantation to be "broke in." As you read, look for restraints on running away, anticipated difficulties, sources of support, and the intelligent cleverness of the runaways. What role does religion play in their efforts? What about issues of family, trust, safety, and self-reliance? What do you learn about slavery in these brief descriptions of the first moments of self-emancipation? Can you imagine the impact they had on northern readers, and why abolitionists avidly used the narratives as part of their attack on slavery?

The Flight

It was the Sabbath: the holy day which God in his infinite wisdom gave for the rest of both man and beast. In the state of Maryland, the slaves generally have the Sabbath, except in those districts where the evil weed, tobacco, is cultivated; and then, when it is the season for setting the plant, they are liable to be robbed of this only rest.

It was in the month of November, somewhat past the middle of the month. It was a bright day, and all was quiet. Most of the slaves were resting about their quarters; others had leave to visit their friends on other plantations, and were absent. The evening previous I had arranged my little bundle of clothing, and had secreted it at some distance from the house. I had spent most of the forenoon in my workshop, engaged in deep and solemn thought.

It is impossible for me now to recollect all the perplexing thoughts that passed through my mind during that forenoon; it was a day of heartaching to me. But I distinctly remember the two great difficulties that stood in the way of my flight: I had a father and mother whom I dearly loved,——I had also six sisters and four brothers on the plantation. The question was, shall I hide my purpose from them?

moreover, how will my flight affect them when I am gone? Will they not be suspected? Will not the whole family be sold off as a disaffected family, as is generally the case when one of its members flies? But a still more trying question was, how can I expect to succeed, I have no knowledge of distance or direction. I know that Pennsylvania is a free state, but I know not where its soil begins, or where that of Maryland ends? Indeed, at this time there was no safety in Pennsylvania, New Jersey, or New York, for a fugitive, except in lurking-places, or under the care of judicious friends, who could be entrusted not only with liberty, but also with life itself.

With such difficulties before my mind, the day had rapidly worn away; and it was just past noon. One of my perplexing questions I had settled——I had resolved to let no one into my secret; but the other difficulty was now to be met. It was to be met without the least knowledge of its magnitude, except by imagination. Yet of one thing there could be no mistake, that the consequences of a failure would be most serious. Within my recollection no one had attempted to escape from my master; but I had many cases in my mind's eye, of slaves of other planters who had failed, and who had been made examples of the most cruel treatment, by flogging and selling to the far South, where they were never to see their friends more. I was not without serious apprehension that such would be my fate. The bare possibility was impressively solemn; but the hour was now come, and the man must act and be free, or remain a slave for ever. How the impression came to be upon my mind I cannot tell; but there was a strange and horrifying belief, that if I did not meet the crisis that day, I should be self-doomed——that my ear would be nailed to the door-post for ever. The emotions of that moment I cannot fully depict. Hope, fear, dread, terror, love, sorrow, and deep melancholy were mingled in my mind together; my mental state was one of most painful distraction. When I looked at my numerous family—a beloved father and mother, eleven brothers and sisters, &c.; but when I looked at slavery as such; when I looked at it in its mildest form, with all its annoyances; and above all, when I remembered that one of the chief annoyances of slavery, in the most mild form, is the liability of being at any moment sold into the worst form; it seemed that no consideration, not even that of life itself, could tempt me to give up the thought of flight. And then when I considered the difficulties of the way——the reward that would be offered——the human blood-hounds that would be set upon my track——the weariness——the hunger——the gloomy thought, of not only losing all one's friends in one day, but of having to seek and to make new friends in a strange world. But, as I have said, the hour was come, and the man must act, or for ever be a slave.

Harriet Jacobs—from Incidents in the Life of a Slave Girl

Again and again I had traversed those dreary twelve miles, to and from the town; and all the way, I was meditating upon some means of escape for myself and my children. My friends had made every effort that ingenuity could devise to effect our purchase, but all their plans had proved abortive. Dr. Flint was suspicious, and determined not to loosen his grasp upon us. I could have made my escape alone; but it was more for my helpless children than for myself that I longed for freedom. Though the boon would have been precious to me, above all price, I would not have taken it at the expense of leaving them in slavery. Every trial I endured, every sacrifice I made for their sakes, drew them closer to my heart, and gave me fresh courage to beat back the dark waves that rolled and rolled over me in a seemingly endless night of storms. . . .

My plan was to conceal myself at the house of a friend, and remain there a few weeks till the search was over. My hope was that the doctor would get discouraged, and, for fear of losing my value, and also of subsequently finding my children among the missing, he would consent to sell us; and I knew somebody would buy us. I had done all in my power to make my children comfortable during the time I expected to be separated from them. . . .

Mr. Flint was hard pushed for house servants, and rather than lose me he had restrained his malice. I did my work faithfully, though not, of course, with a willing mind. They were evidently afraid I should leave them. Mr. Flint wished that I should sleep in the great house instead of the servants' quarters. His wife agreed to the proposition, but said I mustn't bring my bed into the house, because it would scatter feathers on her carpet. I knew when I went there that they would never think of such a thing as furnishing a bed of any kind for me and my little one. I therefore carried my own bed, and now I was forbidden to use it. I did as I was ordered. But now that I was certain my children were to be put in their power, in order to give them a stronger hold on me, I resolved to leave them that night. I remembered the grief this step would bring upon my dear old grandmother; and nothing less than the freedom of my children would have induced me to disregard her advice. I went about my evening work with trembling steps. Mr. Flint twice called from his chamber door to inquire why the house was not locked up. I replied that I had not done my work. "You have had time enough to do it," said he. "Take care how you answer me!"

I shut all the windows, locked all the doors, and went up to the third story, to wait till midnight. How long those hours seemed, and how fervently I prayed that God would not forsake me in this hour of utmost need! I was about to risk every thing on the throw of a die; and if I failed, O what would become of me and my poor children? They would be made to suffer for my fault.

At half past twelve I stole softly down stairs. I stopped on the second floor, thinking I heard a noise. I felt my way down into the parlor, and looked out of the window. The night was so intensely dark that I could see nothing. I raised the window very softly and jumped out. Large drops of rain were falling, and the darkness bewildered me. I dropped on my knees, and breathed a short prayer to God for guidance and protection. I groped my way to the road, and rushed towards the town with almost lightning speed. I arrived at my grandmother's house, but dared not see her. She would say, "Linda, you are killing me;" and I knew that would unnerve me. I tapped softly at the window of a room, occupied by a woman, who had lived in the house several years. I knew she was a faithful friend, and could be trusted with my secret. I tapped several times before she heard me. . . . I told her I had a hiding-place, and that was all it was best for her to know.

. . . The tidings made the old doctor rave and storm at a furious rate. It was a busy day for them. My grandmother's house was searched from top to bottom. As my trunk was empty, they concluded I had taken my clothes with me. Before ten o'clock every vessel northward bound was thoroughly examined, and the law against harboring fugitives was read to all on board. At night a watch was set over the town. Knowing how distressed my grandmother would be, I wanted to send her a message; but it could not be done. Every one who went in or out of her house was closely watched. The doctor said he would take my children, unless she became responsible for them; which of course she willingly did. The next day was spent in searching. Before night, the following advertisement was posted at every corner, and in every public place for miles round:——

$300 Reward! Ran away from the subscriber, an intelligent, bright, mulatto girl, named Linda, 21 years of age. Five feet four inches high. Dark eyes, and black hair inclined to curl; but it can be made straight. Has a decayed spot on a front tooth. She can read and write, and in all probability will try to get to the Free States. All persons are forbidden, under penalty of law, to harbor or employ said slave. $150 will be given to whoever takes her in the state, and $300 if taken out of the state and delivered to me, or lodged in jail.

Dr. Flint

Note: James Pennington successfully escaped to New York, where he became a Presbyterian minister and later performed Frederick Douglass's marriage rites. Harriet Jacobs hid for seven years in a cramped, tiny garret in her grandmother's house before finally escaping in disguise by ship; she eventually was reunited with her children. To mislead Dr. Flint as to her location, she wrote letters to him secreted to and postmarked from the North begging him to free her children.

that it is no more harm for you to kill a man, who is trying to kill you, than it is for you to take a drink of water when thirsty." It was Walker, however, who was mysteriously found dead on a Boston street a year after the publication of his "Appeal." Garnet's call for rebellion was clear: "Brethren arise, arise! Strike for your lives and liberties. Now is the day and the hour. . . . You cannot be more oppressed than you have been—you cannot suffer greater cruelties than you have already. RATHER DIE FREEMEN, THAN LIVE TO BE SLAVES. Remember that you are THREE MILLIONS!"

Abolitionists' tactical disagreements helped splinter the movement. Garrison's unyielding personal style and his commitment to even less popular causes such as women's rights offended many abolitionists. In 1840, at its annual meeting in New York, intended as a unity convention to heal growing divisions, the American Anti-Slavery Society split. Several delegates walked out when a woman, Abby Kelley, was elected to a previously all-male committee. One group, which supported multiple issues and moral suasion, stayed with Garrison; the other followed James Birney and the Tappans into the Liberty party and political action.

Class differences and race further divided abolitionists. Northern workers, though fearful of the potential job competition implicit in emancipation, nevertheless saw their "wage slavery" as similar to chattel slavery. Both violated fundamental republican values of freedom and equality. Strains between northern labor leaders and middle-class abolitionists, who minimized the seriousness of workingmen's concerns, were similar to those between white and black

antislavery forces. Whites like Wendell Phillips decried slavery as a moral blot on American society, and blacks like Douglass were more concerned with the effects of slavery and discrimination on black people. Moreover, white abolitionists tended to see slavery and freedom as absolute moral opposites: a person was either a slave or free. Blacks, however, knew that there were degrees of freedom and that discriminatory restrictions on freedom existed for blacks in the North just as did relative degrees of servitude in the South.

Furthermore, black abolitionists themselves experienced prejudice, not just from ordinary northern citizens but also from their white abolitionist colleagues. Many antislavery businessmen refused to hire blacks. The antislavery societies usually provided less than full membership rights for blacks, permitted them to do only menial tasks rather than form policy, and perpetuated black stereotypes in their literature. One free black, in fact, described a white abolitionist as one who hated slavery, "especially that slavery which is 1,000 to 1,500 miles away," but who hated even more "a man who wears a black skin."

The celebrated conflict between Garrison and Douglass reflected these tensions. The famous runaway slave was one of the most effective orators in the movement. But after a while, rather than simply describing his life as a slave, Douglass began skillfully to analyze abolitionist policies. Garrison warned him that audiences would not believe he had ever been a slave, and other whites told him to stick to the facts and let them take care of the philosophy.

It was dangerous to be a public abolitionist in this period. In this Winslow Homer engraving for *Harper's Weekly*, titled "Expulsion of Negroes and Abolitionists from Tremont Temple, Boston, Massachusetts, on December 3, 1860," Homer shows Frederick Douglass being forced from the stage by pro-southern demonstrators, who interrupted the meeting called to debate "How can American slavery be Abolished?" The policeman removing Douglass for his safety was reported to have told him that he "must instantly leave," thus ending the debate and meeting before it had hardly begun. *(The Museum of Fine Arts, Houston; The Mavis P. Wilson Kelsey Collection of Winslow Homer Graphics)*

Douglass gradually moved away from Garrison's views, endorsing political action and sometimes even slave rebellion. Garrison's response, particularly when Douglass came out for the Liberty party, was to denounce his independence as "ungrateful . . . and malevolent in spirit." In 1847, Douglass started his own journal, the *North Star,* later called *Frederick Douglass's Paper.* In it, he expressed his appreciation for the help of that "noble band of white laborers" but declared that it was time for those who "suffered the wrong" to lead the way in advocating liberty.

Moving beyond Garrison, a few black nationalists, like the fiery Martin Delany, totally rejected white American society and advocated emigration and a new destiny in Africa. Most blacks, however, agreed with Douglass to work to end slavery and discrimination in the United States. They believed that for better or worse, their home was America and not some distant land they had not known for generations.

These black leaders were practical. David Ruggles in New York and William Still in Philadelphia led black vigilance groups that helped fugitive slaves escape to Canada or to safe northern black settlements. Ministers, writers, and orators such as Douglass, Henry Highland Garnet, William Wells Brown, Samuel Cornish, Lewis Hayden, and Sojourner Truth lectured and wrote journals and slave narratives on the evils of slavery. They also organized a National Negro Convention movement, which began annual meetings in 1830. These blacks met not only to condemn slavery but also to discuss concrete issues of discrimination facing free blacks in the North.

Flood Tide of Abolitionism

Black and white abolitionists, however, agreed more than they disagreed and usually worked together well. They supported each other's publications. The first subscribers to Garrison's *Liberator* were nearly all black, and an estimated 80 percent of the readers of Douglass's paper were white. Weld and Garrison often stayed in the homes of black abolitionists when they traveled. Black and white "stations" cooperated on the Underground Railroad, too, passing fugitives on from hiding places in a black church to a white farmer's barn to a Quaker meetinghouse to a black carpenter's shop.

The two races worked together fighting discrimination as well as slavery. When David Ruggles was dragged from the "white car" of a New Bedford, Massachusetts, railway in 1841, Garrison, Douglass, and 40 other protesters organized what may have been the first successful integrated "sit-in" act of civil disobedience in American history. Blacks and whites also worked harmoniously in protesting segregated schools. After several years of joint boycotts and legal challenges in Massachusetts, in 1855 that state became the first to outlaw segregated public education. Almost exactly 100 years later, the Supreme Court would begin the desegregation of schools throughout the country.

White and black abolitionists were united perhaps most closely by defending themselves against the attacks of people who regarded them as dangerous fanatics bent on disrupting an orderly society. As abolitionists organized to rid the nation of slavery, they aroused many, northerners as well as southerners, who were eager to rid the nation of abolitionists. Mob attacks like the one on Marius Robinson in Ohio in 1836 occurred frequently in the mid-1830s. Abolitionists were stoned, dragged through streets, ousted from their jobs and homes, and reviled by northern mobs, often led or encouraged by leading citizens. Theodore Weld, known as "the most mobbed man in the United States," could hardly finish a speech without disruption. Douglass endured similar attacks, and Garrison was saved from a Boston mob only by being put in jail. In 1837, an antislavery editor in Illinois, Elijah Lovejoy, was murdered and his printing press destroyed.

Anti-abolitionists were as fervid as the abolitionists themselves and equally determined to publicize their cause. "I warn the abolitionists, ignorant and infatuated barbarians as they are," growled one South Carolinian, "that if chance shall throw any of them into our hands, they may expect a felon's death." One widely circulated book in 1836 described opponents of slavery, led by the "gloomy, wild, and malignant" Garrison, as "crack-brained enthusiasts" and "female fanatics" with "disturbed minds." President Jackson joined in, denouncing the abolitionists in his annual message in 1835 as "incendiaries" who deserved to have their "unconstitutional and wicked" activities broken up by mobs. The president went on to urge Congress to ban antislavery literature from the U.S. mails. A year later, southern Democratic congressmen, with the crucial support of Van Buren, succeeded in passing a "gag rule" to stop the flood of abolitionist petitions in Congress.

By the 1840s, despite factionalism and opposition, the antislavery movement had gained significant strength in American life. Many northerners, including many workers otherwise unsympathetic to the goal of ending slavery, decried the mob violence, supported the right of free speech, and denounced the South and its northern defenders as undemocratic. The gag rule, interference with the mails, and the killing of Lovejoy seemed proof of the growing pernicious influence of slave power. Former president John Quincy Adams, who had returned to Washington as a congressman, devoted himself for several years to the

This marriage certificate from 1848, detailing the respective marital requirements of husband and wife, makes clear male dominance and female subservience ("the wife hath not power of her own body"). In that same year, however, women's rights activists began their long struggle for equality at Seneca Falls, New York. (*Library of Congress*)

repeal of the gag rule, which he finally achieved in 1844. In this way, he kept the matter in the public eye until the question of slavery in the territories became the dominant national political issue of the 1850s (see Chapter 14). Meanwhile, black and white abolitionists continued their struggle, using many different tactics without knowing that the only one that would work, and indirectly at that, would be civil war.

Women's Rights

As a young teacher in Massachusetts in 1836, Abby Kelley circulated petitions for the local antislavery society. She came to reform from revivalism and in 1837 wrote, "'Tis a great joy to see the world grow better. . . . Indeed I think endeavors to improve mankind is the only object worth living for." A year later, she braved the threats of an angry crowd in Philadelphia by delivering an abolitionist speech to a convention of antislavery women. Her speech was so eloquent that Weld told her that if she did not join the movement full-time, "God will smite you." Before the convention was over, a mob, incensed by both abolitionists and women speaking in public, attacked with stones and torches and burned the hall to the ground.

After a soul-searching year, Kelley left teaching to devote all her efforts to the antislavery movement and women's rights. When she married Stephen Foster, she retained her own name and went on lecture tours of the West while her husband stayed home to care for their daughter. Other young women were also defining unconventional new relationships while illustrating the profound difficulty of both fulfilling traditional roles and speaking out for change. Angelina and Sarah Grimké, two demure but outspoken Quaker sisters from Philadelphia who had grown up in slaveholding South Carolina, went to New England in 1837 to lecture to disapproving audiences on behalf of abolitionism and the rights of women. After the tour, Angelina married Theodore Weld and stopped her public speaking to show that she could also be a good wife and mother. At the same time, she and Sarah, who moved in with her, undertook the task of compiling most of the research and doing most of the writing for Weld's book attacking American slavery.

Young white couples like the Robinsons, Kelley and Foster, and Grimké and Weld, while pursuing reform, also experimented with equal private relationships in an age that assigned distinctly unequal roles to husbands and wives. The cult of domesticity told women that their sphere was the home, where they served as guardians of piety and virtue, influencing their husbands and children to lead morally upright lives in a harsh, changing economic world. As one clergyman said, although women were not expected to "step beyond the threshold" of the home, their ethical influence would be "felt around the globe." Given moral responsibilities like this, it is not surprising that many women joined the perfectionist movement to cleanse

(Far Left) Elizabeth Cady Stanton (1815–1902) and (Left) Lucretia Mott (1793–1880) were the leaders of the 1848 gathering for women's rights at Seneca Falls, New York. "The acquaintance of Lucretia Mott, who was a broad, liberal thinker on politics, religion, and all questions of reform," Stanton wrote in her autobiography, "opened to me a new world of thought." *(Sophia Smith Collection, Smith College, Northampton, Massachusetts)*

America of its sins. Active in every reform movement, women discovered the need to improve their own condition.

To achieve greater personal autonomy in the antebellum era, American women pursued several paths. The choice depended on class, cultural background, and situation. Thus, in 1834, the Lowell textile workers went on strike to protest wage reductions while looking to marriage as an escape from millwork. Catharine Beecher argued that it was by accepting marriage and the home as a woman's sphere and by mastering domestic duties there that women could best achieve power and autonomy. In another form of "domestic feminism," American wives exerted considerable control over their own bodies by convincing their husbands to practice abstinence, coitus interruptus, and other forms of birth control.

Other women found an outlet for their role as moral guardians by attacking the sexual double standard. In 1834, a group of Presbyterian women formed the New York Female Moral Reform Society. Inspired by revivalism, they visited brothels and opened up a house of refuge in an effort to convert prostitutes to evangelical Protestantism. They went even further, seeking to limit men's sexual behavior by trying to close houses of prostitution and by publicly identifying men who visited them. Within five years, 445 auxiliaries of the Female Moral Reform Society had blossomed.

The Lowell millworkers and New York moral reformers generally accepted the duties—and attractions—of the cult of female domesticity. Other women, usually from upper-middle-class families, did not. They sought control over their lives by working directly for more legally protected equal rights with men. Campaigns to secure married women's control of their property and custody of their children involved many of them. Others, like Kelley and the Grimkés, labored in the abolitionist movement and garnered not only valuable experience in organizational tactics but also a growing awareness of the striking similarities between the oppression of women and that of slaves. As they collected antislavery signatures and spoke out in churches and public meetings, they continually faced denials of their right to speak or act politically. American women "have good cause to be grateful to the slave," Kelley wrote, for in "striving to strike his iron off, we found most surely, that we were manacled *ourselves*."

The more active women became in antislavery activities, the more hostility they encountered, especially from clergymen, who quoted the Bible to justify female inferiority and servility. Sarah Grimké was criticized once too often for her outspoken views. She struck back in 1837 with a series called *Letters on the Condition of Women and the Equality of the Sexes,* claiming that "men and women were created equal" and that "whatever is right for man to do, is right for woman." Arguing that men ought to be satisfied with 6,000 years of dominion based on a false interpretation of the creation story, Grimké concluded that she sought "no favors for my sex. I surrender not our claim to equality. All I ask of our brethren is, that they will take their feet from off our necks and permit us to stand upright on that ground which God designed us to occupy."

Technology Changes the American People

THE SEWING MACHINE

Probably no technological innovation changed everyday life for American women in the second half of the nineteenth century more than the sewing machine. In 1860, *Godey's Lady's Book* hailed the sewing machine as the "queen of invention," crediting it not only with the power to transform the work of American women but also with the ability to "do a hundred times more toward clothing the indigent and feeble than the united fingers of all the [world's] charitable and willing ladies." Like many innovations, the marvelous machine that could fasten two pieces of cloth or leather together using either one thread (the chain stitch) or two (the lock stitch), resulted from 50 years of experimentation on both sides of the Atlantic. The first successful machine may have been one devised by a French tailor, Barthelemy Thimonnier, in 1829. Constructed mostly of wood, the machine had a hooked needle and made a chain stitch. Thimonnier, with the backing of the French government, established a factory with 80 machines. His success in the garment industry, however, was short lived; outraged Paris tailors, who rightly saw that Thimonnier's enterprise threatened their livelihood, attacked the factory and destroyed all the machines.

In the United States, experiments started at least as early as 1818. One of the first significant American technological breakthroughs came in the 1840s. Elias Howe, a former worker at a Massachusetts textile mill, and an apprentice to a Boston maker of precision instruments devised a machine that used an eye-pointed needle that pulled one thread through the cloth to make a loop through which a shuttle with another thread passed, thus producing a lock stitch. Both the eye-pointed needle and the moving shuttle became standard features of the commercial sewing machine.

Howe's first sewing machines were extremely expensive ($300 when the yearly wage of a fully employed and well-paid factory girl might be only $165). Despite his successful demonstration of the machine's abilities (using it, he was able to sew faster than five able seamstresses), he was not able to sell any in the United States. While Howe was in England trying to promote his invention there, Isaac Singer, a one-time mechanic and cabinetmaker, was trying to solve some of the problems connected with the new machine. Securing a patent in 1851, Singer began to manufacture and market his machines.

The basic Singer machine was both practical and complex. Special features made the machine relatively easy to operate but also contributed to its cost. Clothing and shoe manufacturers quickly acquired the machines because they

Singer came up with a device in which the needle moved vertically rather than horizontally (as Howe's machine had done) and where power came from a treadle rather than a handcrank. *(The Granger Collection, New York)*

could afford to pay the high prices and recognized the obvious benefits of using them. The introduction of the sewing machine stimulated a period of expansion. By 1858, in Troy, New York, alone 3,000 machines were turning out men's shirts and collars. Larger and more important than the clothing industry, the shoe industry had an immense demand for sewing machines, the first application of technology to the shoe manufacturing process. By 1860, one female worker, using a machine, was able to stitch together enough shoe uppers to keep 20 shoemakers busy.

Despite their marketing success with clothing and shoe manufacturers, sewing machine makers dreamed of selling their wares to the many thousands of women who were sewing by hand for their families. But the purchase price was too high for most family budgets. In 1856, Singer's partner, Edward Clark, came up with the idea of allowing buyers to pay for their machines in installments. The plan succeeded brilliantly. The very next year, sales of Singer machines almost tripled. Clark then hit upon another marketing concept—the trade-in. The Singer Company offered $50 for "old Sewing Machines of any kind" that could be used to finance a new machine. Sales took another leap upward. Profits produced by these innovative schemes allowed improvements in the production of sewing machines that halved prices by 1859. Technological and marketing innovations combined to put machines into the hands of ordinary Americans.

As sewing machines entered American households, they relieved women of their most time-consuming domestic chore: sewing by hand. Harriet Kidder, mother of five, welcomed her new "very valuable household article," which made "sewing a pleasure rather than a toil." The calico dress that once demanded over six hours of hand sewing now could be finished in less than an hour.

Some women ended up doing more and fancier sewing than they had done without their new machines. If one calico dress took only an hour, why not make several? Ruffles, pleats, tucks, and other embellishments could all be made with the machine, and women's fashions reflected the ornamental possibilities now within reach. Sewing machines also transformed other sewing tasks. Quilting became more elaborate, and many quilters during the second half of the nineteenth century used their machines to create complex works of art.

Many women did not have the luxury of using their machines to create elaborate clothes or colorful quilts. Instead, sewing machines became their means of support, as they labored as machine operators in factories or as piece workers at home.

Like most successful innovations, the development of the sewing machine had some surprising consequences. In what ways could you argue that the sewing machine improved women's lives? In what ways could you suggest that it did not? Did the sewing machine have effects on all members of the family or just the women of the household? In what ways did the sewing machine have an impact on the larger society? What does the development of the sewing machine reveal about the process of technological change?

In this competition with five New York seamstresses, Elias Howe demonstrated the superiority of his machine over hand sewing. (© *Collection of the New-York Historical Society*)

Male abolitionists were divided about women's rights. At the World Anti-Slavery Convention in 1840, attended by many American abolitionists, the delegates refused to let women participate. Two upstate New Yorkers, Elizabeth Cady Stanton and Lucretia Mott, were compelled to sit behind curtains and not even be seen, much less be permitted to speak. When they returned home, they resolved to "form a society to advocate the rights of women." In 1848, in Seneca Falls, New York, their intentions, though delayed, were fulfilled in one of the most significant protest gatherings of the antebellum era.

In preparing for the meeting, Mott and Stanton drew up a list of women's grievances. They discovered that even though some states had award-ed married women control over their property, they still had none over their earnings. Modeling their "Declaration of Sentiments" on the

Declaration of Independence, the women at Seneca Falls proclaimed it a self-evident truth that "all men and women are created equal" and that men had usurped women's freedom and dignity. A man, the Declaration of Sentiments charged, "endeavored in every way he could, to destroy [woman's] confidence in her own powers, to lessen her self-respect, and to make her willing to lead a dependent and abject life." The remedy was expressed in 11 resolutions calling for equal opportunities in education and work, equality before the law, and the right to appear on public platforms. The most controversial resolution called for women's "sacred right to the elective franchise." The convention approved Mott and Stanton's list of resolutions.

Throughout the 1850s, led by Stanton and Susan B. Anthony, women continued to meet in annual conventions, working by resolution, persuasion, and petition

Timeline

1824	New Harmony established
1825	John Quincy Adams chosen president by the House of Representatives
1826	American Temperance Society founded
1828	Calhoun publishes "Exposition and Protest"
	Jackson defeats Adams for the presidency
	Tariff of Abominations
1828–1832	Rise of workingmen's parties
1830	Webster–Hayne debate and Jackson–Calhoun toast
	Joseph Smith, *The Book of Mormon*
	Indian Removal Act
1830–1831	Charles Finney's religious revivals
1831	Garrison begins publishing *The Liberator*
1832	Jackson vetoes U.S. Bank charter
	Jackson reelected
	Worcester v. *Georgia*
1832–1833	Nullification crisis
1832–1836	Removal of funds from U.S. Bank to state banks
1833	Force Bill
	Compromise tariff
	Calhoun resigns as vice president
	American Anti-Slavery Society founded
1834	New York Female Moral Reform Society founded
	National Trades Union founded
	Whig party established
1835–1836	Countless incidents of mob violence
1836	"Gag rule"

	Specie Circular
	Van Buren elected president
1837	Financial panic and depression
	Sarah Grimké, *Letters on the Equality of the Sexes*
	Emerson's "American Scholar" address
1837–1838	Cherokee "Trail of Tears"
1840	William Henry Harrison elected president
	American Anti-Slavery Society splits
	World Anti-Slavery Convention
	Ten-hour day for federal employees
1840–1841	Transcendentalists found Hopedale and Brook Farm
1843	Dorothea Dix's report on treatment of the insane
1844	Joseph Smith murdered in Nauvoo, Illinois
1846–1848	Mormon migration to the Great Basin
1847	First issue of Frederick Douglass's *North Star*
1848	Oneida community founded
	First women's rights convention at Seneca Falls, New York
1850	Nathaniel Hawthorne's *Scarlet Letter* is published
1851	Maine prohibition law
	Herman Melville's *Moby Dick* is published
1853	Children's Aid Society established in New York City
1854	Thoreau's *Walden* is published
1855	Massachusetts bans segregated public schools

campaign to achieve equal political, legal, and property rights with men. The right to vote, however, was considered the cornerstone of the movement. It remained so for 72 years of struggle until 1920, when passage of the Nineteenth Amendment made woman suffrage part of the Constitution. The Seneca Falls convention was crucial in beginning the campaign for equal public rights. The seeds of psychological autonomy and self-respect, however, were sown in the struggles of countless women like Abby Kelley, Sarah Grimké, and Emily Robinson. The struggle for that kind of liberation continues today.

Conclusion

Perfecting America

Inspired by religious revivalism, advocates for women's rights and temperance, abolitionists, and other reformers carried on very different crusades from those waged by Andrew Jackson against Indians, nullificationists, and the U.S. Bank. In fact, Jacksonian politics and antebellum reform were often at odds. Most abolitionists and temperance reformers were anti-Jackson Whigs. Jackson and most Democrats repudiated the passionate moralism of reformers.

Yet both sides shared more than either side would admit. Reformers and political parties were both organized rationally. Both mirrored new tensions in a changing, growing society. Both had an abiding faith in change and the idea of progress yet feared that sinister forces jeopardized that progress. Whether ridding the nation of alcohol or the national bank, slavery or nullification, mob violence or political opponents, both forces saw these responsibilities in terms of patriotic duty. Whether inspired by religious revivalism or political party loyalty, both believed that by stamping out evil forces, they could shape a better America. In this effort, they turned to politics, religion, reform, and new lifestyles. Whether politicians like Jackson and Clay, religious community leaders like Noyes and Ann Lee, or reformers like Garrison and the Grimkés, these antebellum Americans sought to remake their country politically and morally as it underwent social and economic change.

As the United States neared mid-century, slavery emerged as the most divisive issue. Against much opposition, the reformers had made slavery a matter of national political debate by the 1840s. Although both major political parties tried to evade the question, westward expansion and the addition of new territories to the nation would soon make avoidance impossible. Would new states be slave or free? The question increasingly aroused the deepest passions of the American people. For the pioneer family, who formed the driving force behind the westward movement, however, questions involving their fears and dreams seemed more important. We turn to this family and that movement in the next chapter.

Recommended Reading

Religious Revival and Reform Philosophy

Robert Abzug, *Cosmos Crumbling: American Reform and the Religious Imagination* (1994); Richard J. Carwardine, *Evangelicals and Politics in Antebellum America* (1993); Jay P. Dolan, *Catholic Revivalism: The American Experience, 1830–1890* (1978); Charles E. Hambrick-Stowe, *Charles G. Finney and the Spirit of American Evangelicalism* (1996); Mark Y. Hanley, *Beyond a Christian Commonwealth: The Protestant Quarrel with the American Republic, 1830–1860* (1994); Paul Johnson, *A Shopkeeper's Millennium: Society and Revivals in Rochester, New York, 1815–1837* (1978); William McLoughlin, *Revivals, Awakenings, and Reform: An Essay on Religion and Social Change in America* (1980); Stephen Mintz, *Moralists and Modernization: American Pre–Civil War Reformers* (1995); Richard Rabinowitz, *The Spiritual Self in Everyday Life: The Transformation of Personal Religious Experience in 19th Century New England* (1989); Mary Ryan, *Cradle of the Middle Class: The Family in Oneida County, New York, 1790–1865* (1981).

The Political Response to Change: Politics and Parties in the Age of Jackson

Jean Baker, *Affairs of Party* (1983); Donald B. Cole, *The Presidency of Andrew Jackson* (1993); Richard Ellis, *The Union at Risk: Jacksonian Democracy, States Rights, and the Nullification Crisis* (1987); Ronald Formisano, *The Transformation of Political Culture* (1983); Lawrence F. Kohl, *The Politics of Individualism: Parties and the American Character in the Jackson Era* (1989); Richard Latner, *The Presidency of Andrew Jackson: White House Politics, 1829–1837* (1979); Theda Perdue and Michael D. Green, eds., *The Cherokee Removal: A Brief History with Documents* (1995); Michael Paul Rogin, *Fathers and Children: Andrew Jackson and the Subjugation of the American Indian* (1975); Arthur M. Schlesinger, Jr., *The Age of Jackson* (1945); Charles Sellers, *The Market Revolution: Jacksonian America, 1815–1846* (1992); Joel H. Silbey, *The Partisan Imperative: The Dynamics of American Politics Before the Civil War* (1985); Harry L. Watson, *Liberty and Power: The Politics of Jacksonian America* (1990); Major L. Wilson, *The Presidency of Martin Van Buren* (1984).

The Political Response to Change: Political Biographies of the Jacksonian Era

Maurice G. Baxter, *One and Inseparable: Daniel Webster and the Union* (1984); Richard Current, *Daniel Webster and the Rise of National Conservatism* (1955); Clement Eaton, *Henry Clay and the Art of American Politics* (1957); John Niven, *John C. Calhoun and the Price of Union* (1988); Merrill O. Peterson, *The Great*

Triumvirate: Webster, Clay, and Calhoun (1987); Robert Remini, *Life of Andrew Jackson* (1988), *Andrew Jackson and the Course of American Freedom, 1822–1832* (1981), and *Andrew Jackson and the Course of American Democracy* (1984); John William Ward, *Andrew Jackson: Symbol for an Age* (1955).

Perfectionist Reform and Utopianism

Arthur Bestor, *Backwoods Utopias* (1950); Priscilla Brewett, *Shaker Communities, Shaker Lives* (1986); Michael Fellman, *The Unbounded Frame: Freedom and Community in Nineteenth-Century American Utopianism* (1973); Robert Fogarty, ed., *American Utopianism* (1972); Lawrence Foster, *Women, Family, and Utopia: Communal Experiments of the Shakers, the Oneida Community, and the Mormons* (1991); William Kephart and William Zellner, *Extraordinary Groups: An Examination of Unconventional Life Styles*, 4th ed. (1991); Carol A. Kolmerten, *Women in Utopia: The Ideology of Gender in the American Owenite Communities* (1990); Grant Underwood, *The Millenarian World of Early Mormonism* (1993); Kenneth H. Winn, *Exiles in a Land of Liberty* (1989).

Reforming Society

Susan Cayleff, *Wash and Be Healed: The Water-Cure Movement and Women's Health* (1987); Teresa Anne Murphy, *Ten Hours' Labor: Religion, Reform, and Gender in Early New England* (1992); Stephen Nissenbaum, *Sex, Diet, and Debility in Jacksonian America: Sylvester Graham and Health Reform* (1980); W. J. Rorabaugh, *The Alcoholic Republic: An American Tradition* (1979); David Rothman, *The Discovery of the Asylum: Social Order and Disorder in the New Republic* (1971); Alice Felt Tyler, *Freedom's Ferment* (1944); Ian Tyrrell, *Sobering Up: From Temperance to Prohibition in Antebellum America, 1800–1860* (1979); Ronald Walters, *American Reformers, 1815–1860* (1978); Sean Wilentz, *Chants Democratic: New York City and the Rise of the American Working Class, 1788–1850* (1983).

Abolitionism and the Women's Rights Movement

Robert Abzug, *Passionate Liberator: Theodore Dwight Weld and the Dilemma of Reform* (1980); Ellen DuBois, *Feminism and Suffrage: The Emergence of an Independent Women's Movement in America, 1848–1869* (1978); Lawrence Friedman, *Gregarious Saints: Self and Community in American Abolitionism, 1830–1870* (1982); Paul Goodman, *Of One Blood: Abolitionism and the Origins of Racial Equality* (1998); Elisabeth Griffith, *In Her Own Right: The Life of Elizabeth Cady Stanton* (1984); Julie Roy Jeffrey, *The Great Silent Army of Abolitionism: Ordinary Women in the Antislavery Movement* (1998); Gerda Lerner, *The Grimké Sisters from South Carolina: Rebels Against Slavery* (1967); Henry Mayer, *All on Fire: William Lloyd Garrison and the Abolition of Slavery* (1998); Keith Melder, *Beginnings of Sisterhood: The American Woman's Rights Movement, 1800–1850* (1977); Jane A. and William H. Pease, *They Who Would Be Free: Blacks' Search for Freedom, 1830–1861* (1974).

Fiction and Film

Nathaniel Hawthorne's *Blithedale Romance* (1852), a novel set in a utopian community much like Brook Farm, reveals the challenges of perfecting America through socialistic communal experiments and other reforms such as woman suffrage, spiritualism, and prison reform. Hawthorne's *Celestial Railroad and Other Stories* (1963 edition, reprinting stories written in the 1830s and 1840s)—in particular, "The Birthmark," "Rappaccini's Daughter," and the title story—and *The Scarlet Letter* (1850) show the author's struggles to balance the head and the heart, scientific and romantic perfectionism. *The Scarlet Letter* is also a 1995 Hollywood film, but not a particularly good adaptation of Hawthorne's novel. A better version is a four-episode *Scarlet Letter* produced in 1979 by Boston public television station WGBH and available from PBS. Although not fiction, *Walden* (1854), Henry David Thoreau's account of living for two years in a small cabin by Walden Pond, is one of the great creative, imaginative, and naturalistic expressions of the age, exemplifying the transcendentalist message of Ralph Waldo Emerson's "Self-Reliance," "Nature," "The American Scholar," and other essays. *Not for Ourselves Alone: The Story of Elizabeth Cady Stanton and Susan B. Anthony* is a superb documentary produced by Ken Burns for PBS in 1999.

Suggested Web Sites

http://memory.loc.gov/ammem/daghtml/daghome.html

America's First Look into the Camera: Daguerreotype Portraits and Views, 1839–1864. The Library of Congress' daguerreotype collection consists of more than 650 photographs. Portraits, architectural views, and some street scenes make up most of the collection.

http://memory.loc.gov/ammem/naw/nawshome.html

NAWSA Home Page. This Library of Congress site is called "Votes for Women: Selections from the National American Woman Suffrage Association Collection, 1848–1921." It contains 167 books, pamphlets, and other artifacts documenting the suffrage campaign.

http://memory.loc.gov/ammem/vfwhtml/vfwhome.html

Votes for Women: 1850–1920. Portraits, suffrage parades, picketing suffragists, an anti-suffrage display, and cartoons commenting on the movement make up this Library of Congress site.

http://xroads.virginia.edu/~HYPER/DETOC/FEM/home.htm

Women in America. This University of Virginia site takes a look at women in antebellum America, 1820–1842.

http://www.history.rochester.edu/godeys/

Godey's Lady's Book Online Home Page. Here is on-line text of this interesting nineteenth-century journal.

http://www.loc.gov/exhibits/african/influ.html

Influence of Prominent Abolitionists. This Library of Congress exhibit site, with pictures and text, discusses some key African American abolitionists and their efforts to end slavery.

http://www.tocqueville.org/

In Search of Tocqueville's Democracy in America. Text, images, and teaching suggestions are part of this companion site to C-SPAN's recent programming on de Tocqueville.

http://www.ushistoryplace.com

 A richly detailed on-line learning environment complete with interactive maps, timelines, history activities, primary source documents, and links to related American history sites.

MOVING WEST

CHAPTER OUTLINE

By the 1840s, the frontier was retreating across the Mississippi. As Americans contemplated the lands west of the great river, they debated the question of expansion. Some, like Michigan's senator Lewis Cass, saw the Pacific Ocean as the only limit to territorial expansion. Cass believed that the West represented not only economic opportunity for Americans but also political stability for the nation as well. People crowded into cities and confined to limited territories endangered the Republic, he told fellow senators in a speech. But if they headed west to convert the "woods and forests into towns and villages and cultivate fields" and to extend the "dominion of civilization and improvement over the domain of nature," they would find rewarding personal opportunities that would ensure political and social harmony.

Cass's arguments supporting the righteousness and necessity of westward expansion were echoed again and again in the 1840s. Thousands of men seconded his sentiments by volunteering to join American forces in the war against Mexico in the summer of 1845. Largely untrained, dressed in fanciful uniforms, and called by names like Eagles, Avengers, and Tigers, the companies hurried south. But before long, these supporters of expansion saw the ugly side of territorial adventures: insects, bad weather, poor food, and unsanitary conditions. They discovered that such illnesses as the "black vomit" (yellow fever), dysentery, and diarrhea could kill more men than Mexican bullets. As a member of the American occupying army, Henry Judah also experienced the hostility of conquered peoples. In his diary, he reported, "It is dangerous to go out after night. . . . Four of our men were stabbed today." Not only, he wrote, was a man "by the name of Brown" stabbed in the back, but an "infernal villain cut his throat."

Like Henry Judah, Thomas Gibson, a captain of Indiana volunteers, also paid some of the costs of winning new territories. Less than a month after Cass's speech, he wrote to his wife, Mary, in Charlestown, Indiana. Although glad to report news of an American victory, he described a battlefield "still covered with [Mexican] dead" where "the stench is most horrible." Indiana friends had been killed, and Gibson himself had narrowly escaped. "The ball struck me a glancing blow on the head and knocked me down, but it did not harm me." As for the rest, the weather was foul, and so too was the food—"hard biscuit full of bitter black bugs."

Despite the harsh realities of war, Gibson did not challenge the enterprise. He bragged to Mary that "our little army could go out tomorrow in a fair field of battle and whip fifty thousand of the best Mexican troops that ever were on a field of battle. One thing is certain, we would be willing to try it."

Like other wives and family members at home, Mary was less interested in heroics than in the simple truth: Was Tommy dead or alive? As she anxiously awaited news, she wrote of her great hope: "May God bless you and send you home." Yet even with all her worries and prayers for the war's rapid conclusion, she could not escape the heady propaganda for national expansion. She had heard that Indiana soldiers had "shode themselves great cowards by retreating during battle," and she disapproved. "We all would rather you had stood like good soldiers," she told her husband.

Lewis Cass, Henry Judah, Thomas and Mary Gibson, and thousands of other Americans played a part in the nation's expansion into the trans-Mississippi West. The differences and similarities in their perspectives and in their responses to territorial growth unveil the complex nature of the western experience. Lewis Cass's speech illustrates the hold the West had on people's imagination and shows how some linked expansion to the American belief in individual opportunity and national progress. His reference to its riches reminds us of the gigantic contribution western resources made to national development and wealth. Yet his assumption that the West was vacant points to the costs of white expansion for Mexican Americans and Native Americans and the challenge non-Anglo groups would pose to the inclusiveness of American ideals. The Gibsons' letters show similar preconceptions and racial prejudices. They also portray the winning of the West on a human level: the anxieties, deprivation, enthusiasm, and optimism felt by those who fought for and settled in the West.

This chapter concerns movement into the trans-Mississippi West between 1830 and 1865. First we will consider how and when Americans moved west, by what

This painting by Albert Bierstadt captures the majesty of the western landscape, which dwarfs the Native Americans depicted in the foreground. (*The Rocky Mountains, Lander's Peak, 1863, The Metropolitan Museum of Art, Rogers Fund, 1907 (07.123) Photograph by Geoffrey Clements*)

means the United States acquired the vast territories that in 1840 belonged to other nations, and the meaning of "Manifest Destiny," the slogan used to defend the conquest of the continent west of the Mississippi River. Then we explore the nature of life on the western farming, mining, and urban frontiers. Finally, the chapter examines responses of Native Americans and Mexican Americans to expansion and illuminates the ways different cultural traditions intersected in the West.

PROBING THE TRANS-MISSISSIPPI WEST

Until the 1840s, most Americans lived east of the Mississippi. The admission of new states between 1815 and 1840 symbolized the steady settlement of the eastern half of the continent. As frontier log cabins gave way to brick and clapboard houses, farmers cleared and planted land earlier settlers had ignored. Roads replaced tracks, and new churches, schools, stores, and banks attested to the march of settlement toward the Mississippi. By 1860, some 4.3 million Americans had moved west of the great river.

Foreign Claims and Possessions

With the exception of the Louisiana Territory, Spain held title to most of the trans-Mississippi region in 1815. For hundreds of years, explorers, soldiers, settlers, and missionaries had marched north from Mexico to explore and settle the lands lying beyond the Rio Grande and to spread Spanish culture to native peoples. Eventually, Spanish holdings included present-day Texas, Arizona, New Mexico, Nevada, Utah, western Colorado, California, and small parts of Wyoming, Kansas, and Oklahoma. Spanish rulers had tried to keep foreigners out of its northern frontier areas, but increasingly they found this policy difficult to enforce. When Mexico won its independence from Spain in 1821, it inherited this vast area with 75,000 Spanish-speaking inhabitants and numerous Native Americans living there. These people confronted the avid American appetite for expansion that Spain had tried to curb.

To the north of California was the Oregon country, a vaguely defined area extending from California to Alaska. Both Great Britain and the United States claimed the Oregon country on the basis of explorations in the late eighteenth century and fur trading in the early nineteenth. Joint occupation, agreed on in the Convention of 1818 and the Occupation Treaty of 1827, temporarily avoided settling the boundary question.

Early Interest in the West

Americans penetrated the trans-Mississippi West long before the great migrations of the 1840s and 1850s and were familiar with some of its people and terrains. Commercial goals fueled early interest as traders first sought beaver skins in Oregon territory and then bison robes prepared by the Plains tribes in the area around the upper Missouri River and its tributaries.

As early as 1811, Americans engaged in the fur trade in Oregon, and within ten years, fur trappers and traders were actively exploiting the resources of the Rocky Mountain region. Many of the men in the fur business married Indian women, thereby making valuable connections with Indian tribes involved in trapping. They and their wives occupied a cultural middle ground, adopting elements from both American and native ways of life. When the beaver was all but exterminated in the mid-1830s, some of the early traders and trappers acted as guides for Americans who would have little tolerance for the hybrid ways of the mountain men and their families.

Religious idealism also drew some Americans to the West. Two Presbyterian missionary couples, Marcus and Narcissa Whitman and Henry and Eliza Spalding, were among the first to travel to Oregon territory with help from fur traders. Like Methodist and Roman Catholic missionaries (sent from Europe), the Presbyterians hoped to convert Oregon Indians to Christianity. Their fervor drew strength from the fires of the Second Great Awakening and their conviction that without conversion, the Indians were doomed to everlasting torment in hell. Less successful initially in converting the Indians than their Catholic counterparts who were more tolerant of Indian culture, American missionaries also tried to teach Indians how to live like white people. Their missions became early outposts of Americanism.

In the Southwest, the collapse of the Spanish Empire in 1821 gave American traders an opportunity they had long sought. Each year, caravans from "the States" followed the Santa Fe Trail over the plains and mountains, loaded with weapons, tools, and brightly colored calicoes. New Mexico's 40,000 inhabitants proved eager buyers, exchanging precious metals and furs for manufactured goods. Eventually, some "Anglos" settled there. Their economic activities prepared the way for military conquest.

To the south, in Texas, land for cotton rather than trade or missionary fervor attracted settlers and squatters in the 1820s at the very time that the Hispanic population of 2,000 was adjusting to their country's new independence. The lure of cheap land drew more Americans to that area than to any other. By 1835, almost 30,000 Americans were living in Texas. As the largest group of Americans living outside the nation's boundaries at that time, their numbers dwarfed that of Tejanos.

On the Pacific, a handful of New England traders carrying sea otter skins to China anchored in the harbors of Spanish California in the early nineteenth century. By the 1830s, as the near extermination of the animals ruined this trade, a commerce based on California cowhides and tallow developed. New England ships tied up in California ports while hides were collected from local ranches in exchange for clothes, boots, hardware, and furniture manufactured in the East.

Among the earliest easterners to settle in the trans-Mississippi West were tribes from the South and the Old Northwest whom the American government forcibly relocated in present-day Oklahoma and Kansas. Ironically, some of these eastern tribes acted as agents of white civilization by introducing cotton, the plantation system, black slavery, and schools. Other tribes triggered conflicts that weakened the western tribes with whom they came into contact. The Cherokee, Shawnee, and Delaware forced the Osage out of their Missouri and Arkansas hunting grounds, and tribes from the Old Northwest successfully claimed hunting areas long used by Kansas plains tribes. These disruptions foreshadowed white incursions later in the century.

The facts that much of the trans-Mississippi West lay outside U.S. boundaries and that the government had guaranteed Indian tribes permanent possession of some western territories did not curtail American economic or missionary activities. By the 1840s, a growing volume of published information fostered dreams of possession. Government reports by explorers Zebulon Pike and John C. Frémont, among others, provided detailed information about the interior, and guidebooks and news articles described the routes that such fur trappers as Jim Bridger, Kit Carson, and Jedediah Smith had mapped out. Going west was clearly possible. Lansford Hastings's *Emigrants' Guide to Oregon and California* (1845) provided not only the practical information that emigrants would need but also the encouragement that heading for the frontier was the right thing to do.

In his widely read guide, Hastings minimized the importance of Mexican and British sovereignty. California, as a Mexican possession, presented a problem, he conceded, but Oregon did not. "So far from having any valid claim to any portion of it," Hastings

argued, Great Britain "had no right even to occupy it." Furthermore, American settlers were already trickling into the Pacific Northwest, bringing progress with them. Surely the day could not be far distant, he wrote approvingly, "when genuine Republicanism and unsophisticated Democracy shall be reared up . . . upon the now wild shores, of the great Pacific," to replace "ignorance, superstition, and despotism."

Hastings's belief that Americans would obtain rights to foreign holdings in the West came true within a decade. In the course of the 1840s, the United States, through war and diplomacy, acquired Mexico's territories in the Southwest and on the Pacific (1,193,061 square miles, including Texas) as well as title to the Oregon country up to the 49th parallel (another 285,580 square miles). Later, with the Gadsden Purchase in 1853, the country incorporated another 29,640 square miles of Mexican territory.

Manifest Destiny

What explained the feverish desire to expand? Bursts of florid rhetoric accompanied territorial growth, and Americans used the slogan "Manifest Destiny" to justify and account for it. The phrase, coined in 1845 by John L. O'Sullivan, editor of the *Democratic Review*, expressed the conviction that the country's superior institutions and culture gave Americans a God-given right, even an obligation, to spread their civilization across the entire continent. Lewis Cass, Henry Judah, the Gibsons, Lansford Hastings, and most other Americans agreed.

This sense of uniqueness and mission was a legacy of early Puritan utopianism and the republicanism of the Revolutionary era. By the 1840s, however, an argument for territorial expansion merged with the belief that the United States possessed a unique civilization. The successful absorption of the Louisiana Territory, rapid population growth, and advances in transportation, communication, and industry bolstered the idea of national superiority and the notion that the United States could successfully absorb new territories. Publicists of Manifest Destiny proclaimed that the nation must do so.

WINNING THE TRANS-MISSISSIPPI WEST

Manifest Destiny justified expansion but did not cause it. Concrete events in Texas triggered the national government's determination to acquire territories west of the Mississippi River. The Texas question originated in the years when Spain held most of the Southwest. Although some settlements such as Santa Fe, founded in 1609, were almost as old as Jamestown, the Spanish considered the sparsely populated and underdeveloped Southwest primarily a buffer zone for Mexico. The main centers of Spanish settlement were geographically distant from one another and thousands of miles from Mexico City. Although these northern borderlands formed a weak defensive perimeter of the Spanish Empire that was increasingly vulnerable as Spain weakened, their legal status was recognized internationally in the Transcontinental Treaty. Moreover, in its treaty negotiations with Spain in 1819, the United States, in return for Florida, accepted a southern border excluding Texas, to which the Americans had vague claims stemming from the Louisiana Purchase.

Annexing Texas, 1845

By the time the treaty was ratified in 1821, Mexico had won its independence from Spain but had scarcely had the opportunity to cope effectively with the borderlands, their people, and their problems or to develop powerful bonds of national identity. Mexicans soon had reason to wonder whether the American disavowal of any claim to Texas in the Transcontinental Treaty would last, for political leaders like Henry Clay began to cry out for "reannexation." Fear about American expansionism, fueled by several attempts to buy Texas and by continuing aggressive American statements, permeated Mexican politics.

In 1823, the Mexican government resolved to strengthen border areas by increasing population. To attract settlers, it offered land in return for token payments and pledges to become Roman Catholics and Mexican citizens. Stephen F. Austin, whose father had gained rights from Spain to bring 200 families into Texas two years earlier, was among the first of the American impresarios, or contractors, to take advantage of this opportunity from the new Mexican government. His call for settlers brought an enthusiastic response, as Mary Austin Holley recalled. "I was a young thing then, but 5 months married, my husband . . . failed in Tennessee, proposed to commence business in New Orleans. I ready to go anywhere . . . freely consented. Just then Stephen Austin and Joe Hawkins were crying up Texas—beautiful country, land for nothing, etc.—Texas fever rose then . . . there we must go. There without much reflection, we did go." Like the Holleys, most of the American settlers came from the South, and some brought slaves. By the end of the decade, some 15,000 white Americans and 1,000 slaves lived in Texas, far outnumbering the 5,000 Tejano inhabitants.

Mexican officials soon questioned the wisdom of their invitation. Although Stephen Austin converted to Roman Catholicism, few settlers gave signs of honoring their bargain with the Mexican government. Most remained far more American than Mexican. Some were malcontents who disliked Mexican laws and customs and limitations on their economic and commercial opportunities. In late 1826, a small group of them raised the flag of rebellion and declared the Republic of

This 1872 painting by John Gast—with its large, goddesslike figure trailing telegraph lines, its parade of settlers, its depiction of technological progress— captures the confidence of white Americans that the acquisition of the West was a positive and inevitable event. It also presents the conventional picture of the settlement of the frontier as a process generated by the movement of people from east to west. In fact, the West was also settled by emigrants moving from Mexico northward and by Indian tribes moving south. *(The Museum of the City of New York)*

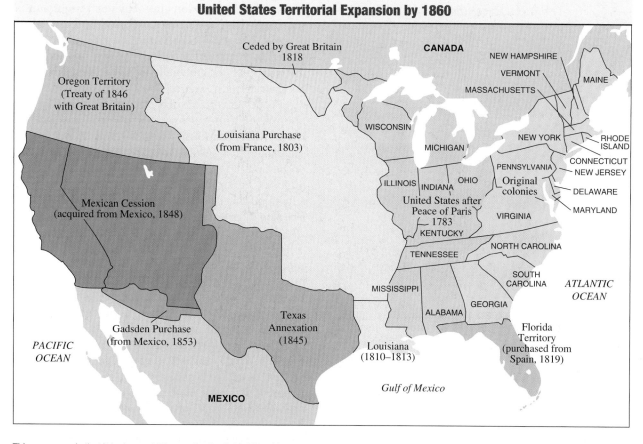

United States Territorial Expansion by 1860

Ceded by Great Britain 1818

CANADA

Oregon Territory (Treaty of 1846 with Great Britain)

Louisiana Purchase (from France, 1803)

Mexican Cession (acquired from Mexico, 1848)

United States after Peace of Paris 1783

Original colonies

NEW HAMPSHIRE
VERMONT
MAINE
MASSACHUSETTS
WISCONSIN
NEW YORK
RHODE ISLAND
MICHIGAN
CONNECTICUT
NEW JERSEY
PENNSYLVANIA
ILLINOIS   INDIANA   OHIO
DELAWARE
MARYLAND
VIRGINIA
KENTUCKY
TENNESSEE
NORTH CAROLINA
SOUTH CAROLINA
MISSISSIPPI
GEORGIA
ALABAMA

ATLANTIC OCEAN

Gadsden Purchase (from Mexico, 1853)

PACIFIC OCEAN

Texas Annexation (1845)

Louisiana (1810–1813)

Florida Territory (purchased from Spain, 1819)

MEXICO

Gulf of Mexico

This map reveals that it took over 100 years for the United States to expand from the original 13 colonies to Mississippi. You can see the substantial gains Americans won as a result of the Revolution. Then, as the map shows, within the span of a lifetime, the United States acquired the vast territories across the Mississippi River.

Fredonia. Although Stephen Austin and others assisted in putting down the brief uprising, American newspapers hailed the rebels as "apostles of democracy" and called Mexico an "alien civilization."

Mexican anxiety grew apace. Secretary of Foreign Relations Lucas Aláman accused American settlers of being advance agents of the United States. "They commence by introducing themselves into the territory which they covet," he told the Mexican Congress, "grow, multiply, become the predominant party in the population. . . . These pioneers excite . . . movements which disturb the political state of the country . . . and then follow discontents and dissatisfaction."

In 1829, the Mexican government altered its Texas policy. Determined to curb American influence, the government abolished slavery in Texas in 1830 and forbade further emigration from the United States. Officials began to collect customs duties on goods crossing the Louisiana border. But little changed in Texas. American slave owners freed their slaves and then forced them to sign life indenture contracts. Emigrants still crossed the border and continued to outnumber Mexicans.

Tensions escalated to the brink of war. In October 1835, a skirmish between the colonial militia and Mexican forces signaled the beginning of hostilities. Sam Houston, onetime governor of Tennessee and army officer, became commander in chief of the Texas forces. Although Texans called the war with Mexico a revolution, a Vermont soldier perhaps more accurately observed, "It is in fact a rebellion."

Mexican dictator and general Antonio López de Santa Anna hurried north to crush the rebellion with an army of 6,000 conscripts. Although he had a numerical advantage, many of his soldiers were Mayan Indians who had been drafted unwillingly, spoke no Spanish, and were exhausted by the long march. Supply lines were spread thin. Nevertheless, Santa Anna and his men won the initial engagements of the war: the Alamo at San Antonio fell to him, taking Davy Crockett and Jim Bowie with it. So, too, did the fortress of Goliad, to the southeast.

As he pursued Houston and the Texans toward the San Jacinto River, carelessness proved Santa Anna's undoing. Although fully anticipating an American attack, the Mexican general and his men settled down

The Texas Revolution, 1836

KANSAS

UNORGANIZED TERRITORY

DISPUTED TERRITORY

ARKANSAS

Jonesborough

Sabine R.

Red R.

Mississippi River

REPUBLIC OF TEXAS

Nacogdoches

Natchitoches

Colorado R.

Brazos R.

Washington-on-the-Brazos

Harrisburg

LOUISIANA

Fredericksburg

The Alamo
Feb. 24, 1836
San Antonio

HOUSTON

Lynchburg
San Jacinto
April 21, 1836
New Washington

Presidio del Rio Grande

Gonzales
Victoria

Brazoria

Matagorda

Gulf of Mexico

SANTA ANNA

Rio Grande

Goliad

MORALES & MONTOYA

Refugio

COAHUILA   Laredo

Corpus Christi

Monclova

URREA

NUEVO LEON

Matamoros

Saltillo   Monterrey

TAMAULIPAS

MEXICO

	Anglo settlements
	Predominantly Mexican settlements
	Native American settlements
	European settlements

→ Mexican forces
→ Texan forces
✳ Major battles
≈ Major roads

This map shows the significance of the American settlement in Texas and the major military engagements of the war. The map also suggests how far the Mexican army had traveled before meeting the Texans on the battlefield.

to their usual siesta on April 21, 1836, without posting an adequate guard. As the Mexicans dozed, the Americans attacked. With cries of "Remember the Alamo! Remember Goliad!" the Texans overcame the army, captured its commander in his slippers, and won the war within 20 minutes. Their casualties were minimal: 8 or 9 dead, 17 wounded. But 630 Mexicans lay dead.

With the victory at San Jacinto, Texas gained its independence. Threatened with lynching, Santa Anna saw little choice but to sign the treaty of independence setting the republic's boundary at the Rio Grande. When news of the disastrous events reached Mexico City, however, the Mexican Congress repudiated an "agreement carried out under the threat of death." Mexico maintained that Texas was still part of Mexico.

The new republic started off shakily. It was financially unstable, unrecognized by its enemy, rejected by its

friends. Although Texans immediately sought admission to the Union, their request failed. Jackson, whose agent in Texas had reported that the republic was so weak that "her future security must depend more upon the weakness and imbecility of her enemy than upon her own strength," was reluctant to act quickly and run the risk of war with Mexico. Many northerners violently opposed annexation of another slave state. The Union was precariously balanced, with 13 free and 13 slave states. Texas would upset that equilibrium in favor of the South. Petitions poured into Congress in 1837 opposing annexation, and John Quincy Adams repeatedly denounced the idea. Annexation was too explosive a political issue to pursue; debate finally died down and then disappeared.

For the next few years, the Lone Star Republic led a precarious existence. Mexico refused to recognize its independence but could send only an occasional raiding party across the border. Texans skirmished with Mexican bands, did their share of border raiding, and suffered an ignominious defeat in an ill-conceived attempt to capture Santa Fe in 1841. Diplomatic maneuvering in European capitals for financial aid and recognition was only moderately successful. Financial ties with the United States increased, however, as trade grew and many Americans invested in Texas bonds and lands.

Texas became headline news again in 1844. "It is the greatest question of the age," an Alabama expansionist declared, "and I predict will agitate the country more than all the other public questions ever have." He was right. Although President John Tyler (who assumed office after Harrison's sudden death) reopened the question of annexation hoping that Texas would ensure his reelection, the issue exploded. It brought to life powerful sectional, national, and political tensions and demonstrated how divisive the questions connected to the expansion of slavery into the West could be. Southern Democrats insisted that the South's future hinged on the annexation of Texas. "Now is the time to vindicate and save our institutions," John C. Calhoun insisted. His supporters hoped that by exploiting the Texas issue, Calhoun would win the White House.

Other wings of the Democratic party capitalized more successfully on the issue, however. Lewis Cass, Stephen Douglas of Illinois, and Robert Walker of Mississippi vigorously supported annexation, not because it would expand slavery, a topic they carefully avoided, but because it would spread the benefits of American civilization. Their arguments, classic examples of the basic tenets of Manifest Destiny, put the question into a national context of expanding American freedom. So powerfully did they link Texas to Manifest Destiny and avoid sectional issues that their candidate, James Polk of Tennessee, secured the Democratic nomination in 1844. Polk called for "the reannexation of Texas at the earliest practicable period" and the occupation of the Oregon Territory. Manifest Destiny had come of age.

Whigs tended to oppose annexation, fearing slavery's expansion and the growth of southern power with the addition of another slave state. They accused the Democrats of exploiting Manifest Destiny, more as a means of securing office than of bringing freedom to Texas.

The Whigs were right that the annexation issue would bring victory to the Democrats. Polk won a close election in 1844. But by the time he took the oath of office in March 1845, Tyler had resolved the question of annexation. In his last months in office, Tyler pushed through Congress a joint resolution admitting Texas to the Union. Unlike a treaty, which required the approval of two-thirds of the Senate and which Tyler had failed to win in 1844, a joint resolution needed only majority support. Nine years after its revolution, Texas finally became part of the Union. The agreement gave Texas the unusual right to divide into five states if it chose to do so.

War with Mexico, 1846–1848

When Mexico learned of Texas's annexation, it promptly severed diplomatic ties with the United States. It was easy for Mexicans to interpret the events from the 1820s on as part of a gigantic American plot to steal Texas. During the war for Texas independence, American papers, especially those in the South, had enthusiastically hailed the efforts of the rebels, while southern money and volunteers had aided the Texans in their struggle. Now that the Americans had gained Texas, would they want still more?

In his inaugural address in 1845, President Polk pointed out "that our system may easily be extended to the utmost bounds of our territorial limits, and that as it shall be extended the bonds of our Union, so far from being weakened will become stronger." What were those territorial limits? Did they extend into the territory the Mexican government considered its own?

Polk, like many other Americans, failed to appreciate how the annexation of Texas humiliated Mexico and increased pressures on its government to respond belligerently. Aware of its weakness, the president anticipated that Mexico would grant his grandiose demands: a Texas bounded by the Rio Grande rather than the Nueces River 150 miles to its north, as well as California and New Mexico.

Even before the Texans could accept the long-awaited invitation to join the Union, rumors of a Mexican invasion were afloat. As a precautionary move, Polk ordered General Zachary Taylor to move "on or near the Rio Grande." By October 1845, Taylor and 3,500 American troops had reached the Nueces River. The positioning of an American army in Texas did not mean that Polk actually expected war. Rather, he hoped that a show of military force, coupled with secret diplomacy, would bring the desired concessions. In November, the president sent his secret agent, John L. Slidell, to Mexico City with instructions to secure the Rio Grande border and to buy Upper California and New Mexico. When the Mexican government refused to receive Slidell, an angry Polk decided to force Mexico into accepting American terms. He ordered Taylor south of the Rio Grande. To the Mexicans, who insisted that the Nueces River was the legitimate boundary, their presence constituted an act of war. Democratic newspapers and expansionists enthusiastically hailed Polk's provocative decision; the Whigs opposed it.

It was only a matter of time before an incident occurred to serve as the American justification for hostilities. In late April, the Mexican government declared a state of defensive war. Two days later, a skirmish broke out between Mexican and American troops, resulting in 16 American casualties. When Polk received Taylor's report, he quickly drafted a war message for Congress. The president claimed that Mexico had "passed the boundary of the United States . . . invaded our territory and shed American blood upon American soil." "War exists," he claimed, and, he added untruthfully, "notwithstanding all our efforts to avoid it, exists by act of Mexico."

Although Congress declared war, the conflict bitterly divided Americans. Many Whigs, including Abraham Lincoln, questioned the accuracy of Polk's initial account of the events, and their opposition grew more vocal as time passed. Lincoln called the war one "of conquest brought into existence to catch votes." The American Peace Society revealed sordid examples of army misbehavior in Mexico, and Frederick Douglass accused the country of "cupidity and love of dominion." Many workers also were critical of the war.

Debate continued as American troops swept into Mexico and advanced toward the capital. Although the Mexicans were also fighting Indian tribes on their northern border, the government refused to admit defeat and negotiate an end to the hostilities. The war dragged on and on. The *American Review,* a Whig paper, proclaimed that the conflict was a "crime over which angels may weep." In 1847, a month after General Winfield Scott took Mexico City, Philadelphian Joseph Sills wrote in his diary, "There is a widely spread conviction . . . that it is a wicked & disgraceful war."

In February 1847, American forces, depleted by the departure of 9,000 troops for the Vera Cruz campaign, met Santa Anna's much larger army several miles north of the hacienda of Buena Vista. The Americans, largely inexperienced volunteers, dug themselves into the valley's gullies and ravines. After bitter conflict, the Americans won the day with far fewer casualties than their Mexican opponents. This victory secured northeastern Mexico for the Americans and helped make General Zachary Taylor into a popular hero and potential political candidate. *(Frances Flora Bond Palmer after Joseph H. Eaton,* Battle of Buena Vista. View of the Battle-Ground of "The Angostura" fought near Buena Vista, Mexico February 23rd. 1847. (Looking S. West) *Amon Carter Museum, Fort Worth, Texas 1971.48)*

Yet Polk enjoyed the enthusiastic support of expansionists. Thomas Gibson's men, like most other soldiers, were eager volunteers. Some expansionists even urged permanent occupation of Mexico. Illinois Democratic Senator Sidney Breese told the Senate, "The avowed objects of the war . . . [were] to obtain redress of wrongs, a permanent and honorable peace, and indemnity for the past and security for the future." To secure these goals, Breese could even contemplate permanent occupation with "great ultimate good" to the United States, to Mexico, "and to humanity."

Inflated rhetoric did not win the war, however. In the end, chance helped draw hostilities to a close. Mexican moderates approached Polk's diplomatic representative, Nicholas Trist, who accompanied the American army in Mexico. In Trist's baggage were detailed, though out-of-date, instructions outlining Polk's requirements: the Rio Grande boundary, Upper California, and New Mexico. Although the president had lost confidence in Trist and had ordered him home in chains, Trist stayed in Mexico to negotiate an end to the war. Having obtained most of Polk's objectives, Trist returned to Washington to an ungrateful president. Apparently Polk had wanted more territory from Mexico for less money. Firing him from his job at the State Department, Polk denounced Trist as an "impudent and unqualified scoundrel."

California and New Mexico

Although Texas and Mexico dominated the headlines, Polk made it clear from the early days of his presidency that California and New Mexico were part of any resolution of the Mexico crisis. Serious American interest in California dated only from the late 1830s. A few Americans, mostly traders and shopkeepers, had settled in California during the 1820s and 1830s, but they constituted only a small part of the Spanish-speaking Californio population that had reached 3,200 by 1821. Many had married into Californio families and taken Mexican citizenship. But gradual recognition of California's fine harbors, its favorable position for the China trade, and the suspicion that other countries, especially Great Britain, had designs on the region nourished the conviction that it must become part of the United States.

In 1842, a comic dress rehearsal for rebellion occurred when a U.S. naval commodore, Thomas

The Mexican-American War

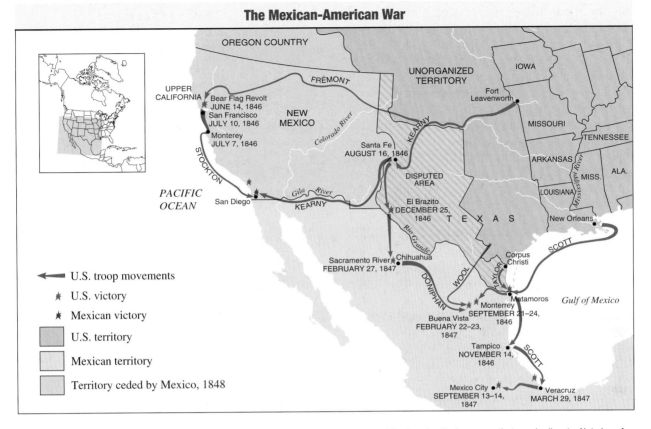

This map shows not only the movements of American troops during the Mexican-American War but also the large area that was in dispute. Note how far into Mexico American troops penetrated during the conflict.

Catsby Jones, believing that war had broken out with Mexico, sailed into Monterey, forced the Mexican commander to surrender, and proclaimed California's annexation. When Jones learned of his error, he apologized and watched the Mexican flag hoisted once more. Yet the arrival of 1,500 American overland emigrants in a three-year period intensified the friction. These newcomers had little interest in blending into Californio society. They and their families wanted an American California. As one resident realized, "The American population will soon be sufficiently numerous to play the Texas game."

In 1845, Polk appointed Thomas Larkin, a successful American merchant in Monterey, as his confidential agent. Larkin had clear instructions should Californians decide to break with Mexico. "While the President will make no effort and use no influence to induce California to become one of the free and independent states of the Union," wrote Polk's secretary of state, James Buchanan, to Larkin, "yet if the people should desire to unite their destiny with ours, they would be received as brethren." Polk's efforts to purchase California suggested that he was sensitive to the fragility of American claims to the region. But Santa Anna, who bore the burden of having lost Texas, was

in no position to sell. Thus, in 1846, a few armed American settlers rose up against Mexican "tyranny" and established the "Bear Flag Republic."

New Mexico was also on Polk's list. Ties with the United States began in the 1820s, when American traders began to bring their goods to Santa Fe. Economic profits stimulated American territorial appetites. As the oldest and largest Mexican group in North America (60,000 out of 75,000), however, New Mexicans had little desire for annexation. The unsuccessful attempt by the Texans to capture Santa Fe in 1841 and border clashes in the two following years did not enhance the attractiveness of their Anglo neighbors. But, standing awkwardly in the path of westward expansion and further isolated from Mexico by the annexation of Texas in 1846, New Mexico had an uncertain future as a Mexican province.

In June 1846, shortly after the declaration of war with Mexico, the Army of the West, led by Colonel Stephen W. Kearney, left Fort Leavenworth, Kansas, for New Mexico. Kearney had orders to occupy Mexico's northern provinces and to protect the lucrative Santa Fe trade. Two months later, the army took Santa Fe without a shot, although one eyewitness noticed the "surly countenances" and the "wail of grief . . . above the din of our horses' tread." New Mexico's upper class, who had already begun to intermarry with American merchants and send some sons to colleges in the United States, readily accepted the new rulers. However, ordinary Mexicans and Pueblo Indians did not take conquest so lightly. After Kearney departed for California, resistance erupted in New Mexico. Californios also fought the American occupation force. Kearney was wounded, and the first appointed American governor of New Mexico was killed. In the end, however, superior American military strength won the day. By January 1847, both California and New Mexico were firmly in American hands.

The Treaty of Guadalupe Hidalgo, 1848

Negotiated by Trist and signed on February 2, 1848, the Treaty of Guadalupe Hidalgo dictated the fate of most people living in the Southwest. The United States absorbed the region's 75,000 Spanish-speaking inhabitants and its 150,000 Native Americans and increased its territory by 529,017 square miles, almost a third of Mexico's extent. Mexico received $15 million and in 1853 would receive another $10 million for large tracts of land in southern Arizona and New Mexico (the Gadsden Purchase). In the treaty, the United States guaranteed the civil and political rights of former Mexican citizens and their rights to land and also agreed to satisfy all American claims against Mexico.

If the territorial gains were immense, some costs were equally huge: 13,000 American lives lost, mostly to diseases such as measles and dysentery, and $97 million expended for military operations. Although sporadic violence would continue for years in the Southwest as Mexicans protested the new status quo, the war was over, and the Americans had won.

The Oregon Question, 1844–1846

Belligerence and war secured vast areas of the Southwest and California for the United States. In the Pacific Northwest, the presence of mighty Great Britain rather than the weak, crisis-ridden Mexican government suggested more cautious tactics. There diplomacy became the means for territorial gains. Despite the disputed nature of claims to the Oregon Territory, Polk assured the inauguration day crowd huddled under umbrellas that "our title to the country of Oregon is 'clear and unquestionable,' . . . already our people are preparing to perfect that title by occupying it with their wives and children." Polk's words reflected American confidence that settlement carried the presumption of possession. But the British did not agree. As the *London Times* warned, "Ill regulated, overbearing, and aggressive . . . [Polk's] pretensions amount, if acted upon, to the clearest

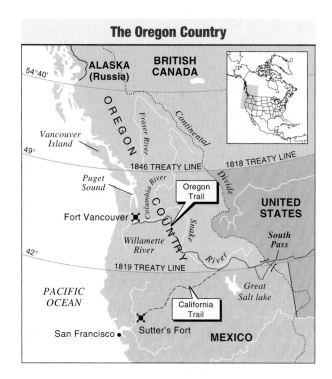

This map highlights the extravagant claims to Oregon voiced during the election of 1844 and the eventual boundaries established with Great Britain. The major trails that brought American settlers to the West suggest the population movements that lay behind the Oregon controversy.

causa belli which has yet arisen between Great Britain and the American Union."

Though the British considered the president's speech belligerent, Polk was correct in saying that Americans had not hesitated to settle the disputed territories. Between 1842 and 1845, the number of Americans in Oregon grew from 400 to over 5,000. Most located south of the Columbia River in the Willamette valley. By 1843, these settlers had written a constitution and soon after elected a legislature. At the same time, changing conditions set the stage for an eventual compromise. British interests in the area were declining as the near destruction of the beaver caused the fur trade to dwindle. Attractive commercial opportunities elsewhere were opening up; New Zealand and other colonies lured English settlers away from the Pacific Northwest.

Polk's flamboyant posture and the expansive American claims made mediation difficult, however. The Democratic platform and the slogan that had helped elect Polk laid claim to a boundary of 54°40'. In fact, Polk was not willing to go to war with Great Britain for Oregon. Privately, he considered reasonable a boundary at the 49th parallel, which would extend the existing Canadian-American border to the Pacific and secure the harbors of Puget Sound for the United States. But Polk could hardly admit this to his

Democratic supporters, who had so enthusiastically shouted "Fifty-four forty or fight" during the recent campaign.

Soon after his inaugural, Polk offered his compromise to Great Britain. But his tone offended the British minister, who rejected the offer at once. Polk compounded his error by gracelessly withdrawing the suggestion. In his year-end address to Congress in 1845, the president created more diplomatic difficulties. Urging the protection of American settlers in Oregon, he again publicly claimed that Oregon belonged to the United States. In addition, he asked Congress to give Britain the one-year notice required by previous agreements to terminate joint occupation there.

Discussions about Oregon occupied Congress for months in early 1846. Debate, however, gradually revealed deep divisions about Oregon and the possibility of war with Great Britain. Despite slogans, most Americans did not want to fight for Oregon and preferred to resolve the crisis diplomatically. As war with Mexico loomed, this task became more urgent.

The British, too, were eager to settle. In June 1846, the British agreed to accept the 49th-parallel boundary if Vancouver Island remained British. Polk took the unorthodox step of forwarding this proposal to the Senate for a preliminary response. Within days, the Senate overwhelmingly approved the compromise. Escaping some of the responsibility for retreating from slogans by sharing it with the Senate, Polk ended the crisis just a few weeks before the declaration of war with Mexico.

As these events show, Manifest Destiny was an idea that supported and justified expansionist policies. It corresponded, at the most basic level, to what Americans believed, that expansion was both necessary and right. As early as 1816, American geography books pictured the nation's western boundary at the Pacific and included Texas. Poems, essays, and stories about winning the West, enlivened with illustrations of covered wagons and Indian fighters, were standard reading fare. Popular literature typically described Indians as a dying race that had failed in the basic tasks of cultivating the soil and conquering the wilderness. Mexicans were dismissed as "unjust and injurious neighbor[s]." Only whites could make the wilderness flower. Thus, as lands east of the Mississippi filled up, Americans automatically called on familiar ideas to justify expansion.

GOING WEST

After diplomacy and war clarified the status of the western territories, Americans lost little time in moving there. What had been a trickle of emigrants became a flood. During the 1840s, 1850s, and 1860s, thousands of Americans left their homes for the frontier. By 1860, California alone had 380,000 settlers.

Some chose to migrate by sea. Although the trip was expensive, one could sail from Atlantic or Gulf Coast ports around South America to the West Coast or embark for Panama, cross the isthmus by land, and then continue by sea. Most emigrants, however, chose land routes. In 1843, the first large party succeeded in crossing the plains and mountains to Oregon. More followed. Between 1841 and 1867, some 350,000 traveled the overland trails to California or Oregon, while others trekked part of the way to intermediate points like Colorado and Utah.

The Emigrants

Most of the emigrants who headed for the Far West, where slavery was prohibited, were white and American-born. They came from the Midwest and the Upper South. A few free blacks made the trip as well. Pioneer Margaret Frink remembered seeing a "Negro woman . . . tramping along through the heat and dust, carrying a cast iron black stove on her head, with her provisions and a blanket piled on top . . . bravely pushing on for California." Emigrants from the Deep South usually selected Arkansas or Texas as their destination, and many took their slaves with them. By 1840, over 11,000 slaves toiled in Texas and 20,000 in Arkansas.

The many pioneers who kept journals during the five- to six-month overland trip captured the human dimension of emigrating. Their journals, usually their only contribution to the historical record, focused on day-to-day events and expressed some of the thoughts and emotions experienced on the long journey west. One migrant, Lodisa Frizzell, described her feelings at parting in 1852:

> Who is there that does not recollect their first night when started on a long journey, the well known voices of our friends still ring in our ears, the parting kiss feels still warm upon our lips, and that last separating word farewell! sinks deeply into the heart! It may be the last we ever hear from some or all of them, and to those who start . . . there can be no more solemn scene of parting only at death.

Most emigrants traveled with family and relatives. Only during the gold rush years did large numbers, usually young men, travel independently. Migration was a family experience, mostly involving men and women from their late twenties to early forties. A sizable number of them had recently married. And for most, migration was a familiar experience. Like other geographically mobile Americans, emigrants to the Far West had earlier moved to other frontiers, often as children or as newlyweds. The difference was the vast distance to this frontier and the seemingly final separation from home.

Migrants' Motives

What led so many Americans to sell most of their possessions and embark on an unknown future thousands of miles away? Many believed that frontier life would offer rich opportunities. A popular folk song expressed this widespread conviction:

Since times has been hard, I'll tell you sweetheart,
I've a notion to leave off my plow and my cart,
Away to Californy a journey pursue,
To double my fortunes as other men do.

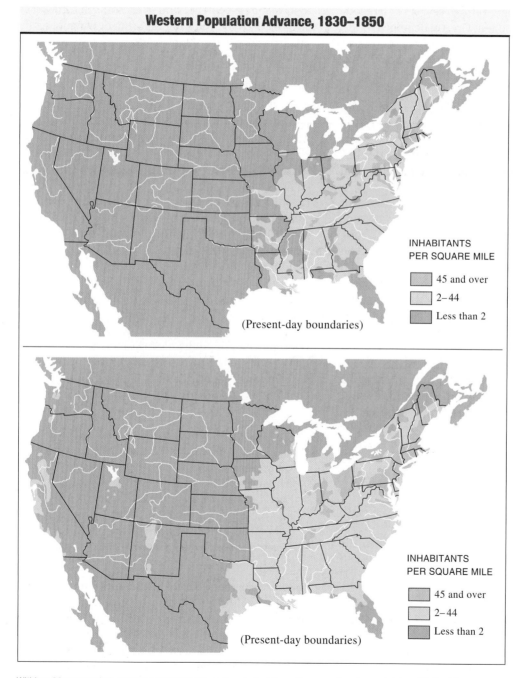

Western Population Advance, 1830–1850

INHABITANTS PER SQUARE MILE

- 45 and over
- 2–44
- Less than 2

(Present-day boundaries)

INHABITANTS PER SQUARE MILE

- 45 and over
- 2–44
- Less than 2

(Present-day boundaries)

Within a 20-year period, as this map shows, the eastern half of the nation was almost completely settled, while some areas of the trans-Mississippi West acted as magnets for emigrants. Despite the considerable disruption to nature and the peoples living near the overland trails caused by emigrant trains, many parts of the West were little touched by white settlement until after the Civil War.

The kinds of opportunities emigrants expected varied widely. Thousands sought riches in the form of gold. Others anticipated making their fortune as merchants, shopkeepers, and peddlers. Some intended to speculate in land, acquiring large blocks of public lands and then selling them later to settlers at a handsome profit. The possibility of professional rewards gained from practicing law or medicine on the frontier attracted still others.

Most migrants dreamed of bettering their life by cultivating the land. As one settler explained, "The motive that induced us to part with pleasant associates and dear friends of our childhood days, was to obtain from the government of the United States a grant of land that 'Uncle Sam' had promised." Federal and state land policies made the acquisition of land increasingly alluring. Preemption acts during the 1830s and 1840s gave "squatters" the right to settle public lands before the government offered them for sale and then allowed them to purchase these lands at the minimum price once they came on the market. At the same time, the amount of land a family had to buy shrank to only 40 acres. In 1862, the Homestead Act went further by offering 160 acres of government land free to citizens or future citizens over 21 who lived on the property, improved it, and paid a small registration fee. Oregon's land policy, which predated the Homestead Act, was even more generous. It awarded a single man 320 acres of free land and a married man 640 acres provided he occupied his claim for four years and made improvements.

Some emigrants hoped the West would restore them to health. Settlers from the Mississippi valley wished to escape the region's debilitating agues and fevers. Doctors advised those suffering the dreaded tuberculosis that the long out-of-doors trip and the western climate might cure them. Even invalids grasped at the advice offered by one doctor in 1850, who urged them to "attach themselves to the companies of emigrants bound for Oregon or Upper California."

Others pursued religious or cultural missions in the West. Missionary couples like David and Catherine Blaine, who settled in Seattle when it was a frontier outpost, determined to bring Protestantism and education west. Stirred by the stories they had heard of the "deplorable morals" on the frontier, they willingly left the comforts of home to evangelize and educate westerners. Still others, like the Mormons, made the long trek to Utah to establish a society in conformity with their religious beliefs.

Not everyone who dreamed of setting off for the frontier could do so, however. Unlike the moves to earlier frontiers, the trip to the Far West involved considerable expense. The sea route, while probably the

This illustration of a young woman being carried away by a Comanche chief came from a book entitled *Thrilling Adventures Among the Indians*, published in 1850. An increasingly racist view of Native Americans, nourished by popular accounts of Indians as "savage brute[s]," colored emigrants' views of Indians they encountered in the trans-Mississippi West and seemed to justify disregarding native rights. *(The Newberry Library)*

most comfortable, was the most costly. Guidebooks estimated that the trip around Cape Horn came to $600 per person. For the same sum, four people could make the overland trip. And if the emigrants sold their wagons and oxen at the journey's end, the final expenses might amount to only $220. Clearly, however, the initial financial outlay was considerable enough to rule out the trip for the very poor. Despite increasingly liberal land policies, migration to the Far West (with the exception of group migration to Utah) was a movement of middle-class Americans.

The Overland Trails

The trip started for most emigrants in the late spring when they left their homes and headed for starting points in Iowa and Missouri: Council Bluffs, Independence, Westport, St. Joseph. There, companies of wagons gathered, and when grass was up for the stock, usually by the middle of May, they set out. Emigrant trains first followed the valley of the Platte

Recovering the Past

PERSONAL DIARIES

 ineteenth-century journals kept by hundreds of ordinary men and women traveling west on the overland trails constitute a rich source for exploring the nature of the westward experience. They are also an example of how private sources can be used to deepen our understanding of the past. Diaries, journals, and letters all provide us with a personal perspective on major happenings. These sources tend to focus on the concrete, so they convey the texture of daily life in the nineteenth century, daily routines and amusements, clothing, habits, and interactions with family and friends. They also provide evidence of the varied concerns, attitudes, and prejudices of the writers, thus providing a test of commonly accepted generalizations about individual and group behavior.

Like any historical source, personal documents must be used carefully. It is important to note the writer's age, sex, class, and regional identification. Although this information may not be available, some of the writer's background can be deduced from what he or she has written. It is also important to consider for what purpose and for whom the document was composed. This information will help explain the tone or character of the source and what has been included or left out. It is, of course, important to avoid generalizing too much from one or even several similar sources. Only after reading many diaries, letters, and journals is it possible to make valid generalizations about life in the past.

Here we present excerpts from two travel journals of the 1850s. Few of the writers considered their journals to be strictly private. Often, they were intended as a family record or as information for friends back home. Therefore, material of a personal nature has often been excluded. Nineteenth-century Americans referred to certain topics, such as pregnancy, only indirectly or not at all.

One excerpt comes from Mary Bailey's 1852 journal. Mary was 22 when she crossed the plains to California with her 32-year-old doctor husband. Originally a New Englander, Mary had lived in Ohio for six years before moving west. The Baileys were reasonably prosperous and were able to restock necessary supplies on the road west. The other writer, Robert Robe, was 30 when he crossed along the same route a year earlier than the Baileys, headed for Oregon. Robert was a native of Ohio and a Presbyterian minister.

As you read these excerpts, notice what each journal reveals about the trip west. What kinds of challenges did the emigrants face on their journey? Do these correspond to the picture you may have formed from novels, television, and movies? What kinds of work needed to be done, and who did it? Can you see any indication of a division of work based on sex? What kinds of interactions appear to have occurred between men and women on the trip? What does the pattern tell us about nineteenth-century society? How does the painting of the "emigrant train" reinforce the journal accounts of men's and women's roles?

Even these short excerpts suggest that men and women, as they traveled west, may have had different concerns and different perspectives on the journey. In what ways do the two accounts differ, and in what ways are they similar?

(Benjamin Reinhardt, The Emigrant Train Bedding Down for the Night, *1867, 40 x 70 in. oil on canvas. In the Collection of the Corcoran Gallery of Art, Washington, D.C., Gift of Mr. and Mrs. Landsell K. Christie, 59.21)*

Journal of Mary Stuart Bailey

Wednesday, April 13, 1852 Left our hitherto happy home in Sylvania amid the tears of parting kisses of dear friends, many of whom were endeared to me by their kindness shown to me when I was a stranger in a strange land, when sickness and death visited our small family & removed our darling, our only child in a moment, as it were. Such kindness I can never forget. . . .

Friday, 21st [May] Rained last night. Slept in the tent for the first time. I was Yankee enough to protect myself by pinning up blankets over my head. I am quite at home in my tent.

12:00 Have traveled in the rain all day & we are stuck in the mud. I sit in the wagon writing while the men are at work doubling the teams to draw us out. . . .

Sunday, 23rd. Walked to the top of the hill where I could be quiet & commune with nature and nature's God. This afternoon I was annoyed by something very unpleasant & shed many tears and felt very unhappy. . . .

Thursday, 4th [June] Very cold this morning after the shower. . . . We stopped on the banks of the Platte to take dinner. I am sitting on the banks of the Platte with my feet almost in the water. Have been writing to my Mother. How I wish I had some of my own relations with me. . . .

Sunday, 4th [July] Started at 3 o'clock to find feed or know where it was. Had to go 4 or 5 miles off the road.

Found water & good grass. Camped on the sand with sage roots for fuel. It is wintery, cold & somewhat inclined to rain, not pleasant. Rather a dreary Independence Day. We speak of our friends at home. We think they are thinking of us. . . .

Monday, 12th. Stayed in camp another day to get our horse better. He is much improved. It is cold enough. Washed in the morning & had the sick headache in the afternoon. . . .

Thursday, 12th [August] Very warm. Slept until we stopped to take breakfast. Mr. Patterson starts as soon as light & stops in the heat of the day to rest the animals. We do not have much time to do anything except 4 or 5 hours in the middle of the day. . . .

Friday, 17th [September] Have been confined ever since Monday with ague in my face which is very much swollen. Have suffered very much. We are now in Carson Valley. Plenty of trees but the country is very barren.

Saturday, 18th. Very pleasant, delightful weather. Feel much better today. We are not stirring this afternoon. We have heard to a great deal of suffering, people being thrown our on the desert to die & being picked up & brought to the hospital. . . .

Source: Sandra L. Myers, ed., *Ho for California! Women's Overland Diaries from the Huntington Library* (San Marino, CA: Henry F. Huntington Library, 1980).

Journal of Robert Robe

[May] 19, [1851] A fine day. The first spent in travelling on the plains of the Platte river.

20. Continue our journey up the Platte valley which I would judge to be here some 12 miles wide on this side of the river. The only game seen here are the antelope and wolf beside some wild fowl.

21. A rainy morning started early passed an old Pawnee village in ruins. The houses are constructed by placing timbers in forks and upon these without placing upright poles then rushes bound with [illegible] and finally earth. Chimney in center. Day became more & more rainy and wound up with a storm which beggared description.

22. Bluff approach the river—travelling less monotonous river finely skirted with timber.

23. Roads very muddy in afternoon. Today our wagon severed itself from our former companions & joined a company of Californians.

24. Before starting a trader direct from Ft. Kearney arrived at our camp. He informs us it is yet 25 miles thither. Travelling is by no means dangerous a waggon of provisions passing with only three guards. In the afternoon passed the entrance of the Independence Weston & St. Jo. roads. Emigrants became more numerous.

25. Passed Fort Kearney this morning and after a short drive encamped. Having conversed with some of the soldiers I find they consider life very monotonous.

26. Roads heavy—short drive—a storm.

27. High Bluffs on the opposite side of river approach and present a beautiful appearance. At night a fearful storm.

28. Roads heavy nothing singular.

29. Have arrived in the region abounding in Buffalo. At noon a considerable herd came in sight. The first any of us had ever seen. Thus now for the chase—the horsemen proved too swift in pursuit and frightened them into the Bluffs without capturing any—the footmen pursued however and killed three pretty good success for the first.

30. Nothing remarkable today.

31. Game being abundant we resolved to rest our stock and hunt today—Started in the morning on foot. Saw probably 1,000 Buffalo. Shot at several and killed one. Where ever we found them wolves were prowling around as if to guard them. Their real object is however no doubt to seize the calves as their prey. Saw a town of Prairie dogs, they are nearly as large as a gray squirrel. They bark fiercely when at a little distance but on near approach flee to their holes. Wherever we see numerous owls. After a very extensive ramble and having seen a variety of game we returned at sunset with most voracious appetites.

June 1. The Bluffs became beautifully undulating losing their precipitous aspect and the country further back is beautifully rolling prairie.

2. In the evening camped beside our old friends Miller and Dovey. They had met with a great loss this morning their 3 horses having taken fright at a drove of buffalo and ran entirely away. Some of our company killed more buffalo this evening & a company went in the night with teams to bring them in.

Source: *Pacific Northwest Quarterly* 19 (January 1928): 52–63.

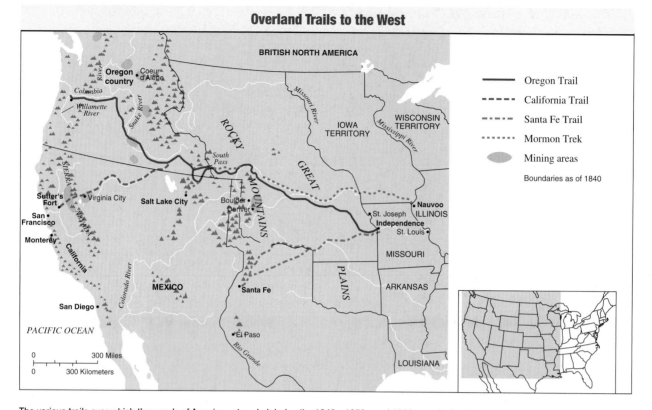

Overland Trails to the West

The various trails over which thousands of Americans traveled during the 1840s, 1850s, and 1860s are depicted on this map. The geographic features begin to suggest the increasing number of natural obstacles that travelers faced during the last months of their trip.

River. Making only 15 miles a day, they slowly wound their way through the South Pass of the Rockies, heading for destinations in California or Oregon.

Emigrants found the first part of the trip novel and even enjoyable. The Indians, one woman noted, "proved better than represented"; some even helped emigrants cross rivers swollen by spring rains. The scenery, with its spring and early summer flowers, was new. Familiar chores were a challenge out in the open. The traditional division of labor known at home persisted. Generally, men did the "outdoor" work. They drove and repaired the wagons, ferried cattle and wagons across rivers, hunted, and stood guard at night. Women labored at domestic chores, caring for children, cooking meals, and washing clothes. As they had at home, women procured small treats, trading with each other and with Indians for buffalo meat, fish, or moccasins. During travel, young children stayed out of the way in the wagons, while older brothers and sisters walked alongside and lent a hand to their elders. Many of the children later remembered the trip as an exciting adventure. Sometimes a day off from traveling provided a chance for fun. Wagon trains might stop to observe the Sabbath, allowing men and animals time to rest and women an opportunity to catch up on the laundry.

As the trip lengthened, difficulties multiplied. Cholera often took a heavy toll. Conflict with Indians became a problem only in the 1850s and made emigrants jumpy during the second half of the trip. (Between 1840 and 1860, Indians killed about 400 emigrants, most during the second half of the trip; the emigrants themselves killed at least that many Indians.) Traveling grew more arduous as deserts and mountains replaced rolling prairies.

Emigrants had to cross the final mountain ranges of the Sierras and the Cascades before the first snowfall, so there was a pressing need to push ever onward. Animals weakened by constant travel, poor feed, and bad water sickened, collapsed, and often died. As families faced the harsh realities of travel, they had to lighten their wagons by throwing out possessions lovingly brought from home. Food grew scarce.

The familiar division of responsibilities often broke down. Women found themselves driving wagons, loading them, even helping to drag them over rocky mountain trails. Their husbands worked frantically with the animals and the wagons as the time of the first snowfall drew closer. Tempers frayed among tired, overworked, and anxious families. Finally, five or six months after setting out, emigrants arrived, exhausted and often penniless, in Oregon or

This view of a Mormon wagon train in the 1850s gives some idea of the rough terrain that emigrant families encountered as they went west. The Mormon migrations were the most organized of the migrations into the trans-Mississippi West, although not all Mormons were lucky enough to travel by wagon. Some emigrants to Utah pushed handcarts across the plains to their destination. *(Used by permission, Utah State Historical Society, all rights reserved. Photo no. 10077)*

California. As one wrote on a September day in 1854, her journey had ended, "which for care, fatigue, tediousness, perplexities and dangers of various kinds, can not be excelled."

The strains of the trip led some groups to draw up rules and elect officers. This did not prevent dissension, however. Many companies split because of arguments over the pace of travel or the number of rest stops or because some changed their minds about their eventual destination. Family harmony often collapsed under the strain of increased workloads, the irritations of travel, and crises of sickness and even death. Mary Power, who with her husband and three children crossed in 1853, revealed exasperation and depression in her journal: "I felt my courage must fail me, for there we were in a strange land, almost without anything to eat, [with] a team that was not able to pull an empty wagon." In a letter she was even more candid: "I felt as though myself and the little ones were at the mercy of a madman." Men, too, lost nerve as they confronted the hazards of travel. Oregon-bound John Minto described coming upon a father of four, "lying on his back upon a rock, taking the rain in his face, seemingly given up all thought of manly struggle," while the cry of Indians sent some men in another train into their wagons to hide.

LIVING ON THE FRONTIER

When emigrants finally reached their destinations, their feelings ranged from acute disappointment to buoyant enthusiasm. But whether elated or depressed, they had no choice but to start anew. As they turned toward building a new life, they naturally drew on their experiences back East. "Pioneers though we are, and proud of it, we are not content with the wilds . . . with the idleness of the land, the rudely construct[ed] log cabin," one Oregon settler explained. "Pioneers are not that kind of folks."

Farming on the Frontier

Pioneer farmers faced the urgent task of establishing their homesteads and beginning farming. First, the family had to locate a suitable claim. Clearing the land and constructing a crude shelter followed. Only then could crops be planted.

As farmers labored "to get the land subdued and the wilde nature out of it," they repeated a process that had occurred on earlier frontiers. Felling timber, pulling out native plants that seemed to have no value, and planting familiar crops began a transformation of the landscape (see the final section of Chapter 10). The results were often unanticipated. When they planted their crops, for example, farmers unknowingly introduced weeds whose seeds were mixed in with plant seeds from home. Some of the weeds, like the Canadian thistle, might do even better than the intended crops. Over time, the weeds could become much more than a nuisance to be pulled out of the ground. The Canadian thistle, for example, moved from field to pasture, where it gradually displaced grass and rendered the land useless for livestock grazing.

As they began their agricultural operations, emigrants did not recognize the ecological patterns that seem so clear to us today. The goal of taming nature was so central and the task so challenging that there was little time or inclination to question long-range consequences.

Because emigrants brought so few of their possessions west, the work of getting started was even more difficult than it would have been in the East. A young Oregon bride who set up housekeeping in the 1840s with only a stew kettle and three knives was not unusual. A letter from Sarah Everett to her sister-in-law in the East told the tale of hardship. Pleased with a gift of pretty trimmings, Sarah confessed, "I am a very old woman. My face is thin sunken and wrinkled, my hands bony and withered and hard—I shall look strangely I fear with your nice undersleeves and coquettish cherry bows." Sarah was 29 years old.

After months of intense interaction with other travelers, families were now alone on their claims. The typical frontier household consisted of parents with one to four children. Although frontier families might interact with nearby Indians, cultural biases made close friendships difficult. No wonder the pioneers often felt lonely and thought longingly of old friends. No wonder either that women helped men with their work and men assisted their wives in domestic chores such as washing.

For several years, such isolation was the rule. One pioneer remembered, "We were . . . 'all told,' eleven families within a radius of six or eight miles, widely separated by our holdings and three hundred and twenty acres to each family. In those days anyone residing within twenty miles was considered a neighbor." But the isolation usually ended within a few years as most areas attracted new emigrants and old settlers seeking better claims.

As rural communities grew, settlers worked to establish schools, churches, and clubs. These organizations drew together people from different places and backgrounds and helped mold them into a new community. They also served to redefine acceptable forms of behavior and remind members of conventional standards and beliefs.

The determination to reestablish familiar institutions was most apparent in politics and law. In Oregon, for example, the pioneers set up a political system based on eastern models before the status of the territory was resolved. Before permanent schools or churches existed, men resumed the familiar political rituals of voting, electioneering, and talking politics. They were also going to court to resolve controversies and to ensure law and order. Although modern movies and novels suggest that violence was a part of everyday life on the frontier, this was not true on the farming frontier. Courts, rather than rough-and-ready vigilante groups, usually handled the occasional violence.

Setting up a common school system was more difficult and less urgent in the eyes of many frontier communities than beginning political life. Few settlers initially thought education important enough to tax themselves for permanent public schools. There were some schools, of course. But most operated sporadically and only for students who could pay at least part of the fees.

Various obstacles hindered organized religion. Although settlers often attended early church services no matter what the denomination, community growth proved a mixed blessing. When confirmed believers gathered in their own churches, they often discovered to their dismay that the congregation was too small to sustain the new church financially. Nor were converts plentiful, for many settlers had grown out of the habit of regular churchgoing. In early Seattle, Catherine and David Blaine were shocked. "Observation and experience have taught us since we left home," David remarked, "the unwelcome lesson that separation from gospel influences has rendered them quite indifferent to gospel truth." Catherine believed, "This is an awfully wicked country."

The chronic shortage of cash on the frontier retarded the growth of both schools and churches. Until farmers could send their goods to market, they had little cash to spare. Geographic mobility also contributed to institutional instability. Up to three-quarters of the population of a frontier county might vanish within a ten-year period as emigrants left to seek better land. Some farmed in as many as four locations until they found a satisfactory claim. Institutions relying on continuing personal and financial support suffered accordingly.

Yet even if their efforts to re-create familiar institutional life often faltered, settlers did not lose sight of their goals. Newspapers, journals, and books, which circulated early on the frontier, reinforced familiar values and norms and kept determination strong. As more and more settlers arrived, the numbers willing to support educational, religious, and cultural institutions grew. In the end, as one pioneer pointed out, "We have a telegraph line from the East, a daily rail road train, daily mail and I am beginning to feel quite civilized. And here ended my pioneer experience." Only 16 years had passed since she had crossed the Plains.

Although the belief in the frontier's special economic and social opportunities encouraged emigration, the dream was often illusory. Western society rapidly acquired a social and economic structure similar to that of the East. Frontier newspapers referred to leading settlers as the "better" sort, giving voice to an emerging world of social and economic distinctions. The appearance of workers for hire and tenant farmers also pointed to real economic differences and hinted at the difficulties those on the bottom would face as they tried to improve their situation.

Their widespread geographic mobility also indicates that many found it difficult to capitalize on the benefits of homesteading. Census data show that those who moved were generally less successful than the core of stable residents, who became the community's economic and social leaders. Of course, those on the move may have believed that fortune would finally smile on them at their next stop. But one wife was not so hopeful. When her husband announced that they were to move once again, she commented, "Perhaps I was not quite so enthusiastic as he. I seemed to have heard all this before."

Mining Western Resources

The mineral riches of the trans-Mississippi West prompted people to leave their ordinary lives behind and set out to make their fortunes. News of the discovery of gold in 1848 in California swept the country like "wildfire," according to one Missouri emigrant. Thousands raced to cash in on the bonanza. Within a year, California's population ballooned from 14,000 to almost 100,000. By 1852, that figure had more than doubled.

Like migrants who planned to establish farms in the West, the "forty-niners" were mostly young (in 1850, over half the people in California were in their twenties). Unlike pioneers headed for the rural frontier, however, the gold seekers were unmarried, predominantly male, and heterogeneous. Of those pouring into California in 1849, about 80 percent came from the United States, 8 percent from Mexico, and 5 percent from South America. The rest came from Europe and Asia. Few were as interested in settling the West as they were in extracting its precious metals and returning home rich.

California was the first and most dramatic of the western mining discoveries. But others followed. Rumors of gold propelled between 25,000 and 30,000 emigrants, many from California, to British Columbia

Charles Nalil's 1856 painting *Saturday Night at the Mines* creates a rather cozy picture of the men. But the presence of the bottle, the miners' rough clothing and beards, all show that the miners made little pretense of upholding eastern manners. Miners went west to get rich, not to advance civilization. *(Stanford University Museum of Art, 12083, Gift of Jane Lathrop Stanford)*

in Canada in 1858. A year later, news of gold strikes in Colorado set off another frantic rush for fortune. Precious metals unearthed in the Pacific Northwest early in the decade and in Montana and Idaho a few years later kept dreams alive and prospectors moving. In the mid-1870s, more gold, this time in the Black Hills of North Dakota, attracted hordes of fortune seekers.

In contrast to the agricultural settlements, where early residents were isolated and the community expanded gradually, the discovery of gold or silver spurred rapid, if usually short-lived, growth. Mining camps, ramshackle and often hastily constructed, soon housed hundreds or even thousands of miners and people serving them. Merchants, saloonkeepers, cooks, druggists, gamblers, and prostitutes hurried into boom areas as fast as prospectors. Usually, about half the residents of any mining camp were there to prospect the miners rather than the mines.

Given the motivation, character, and ethnic diversity of those flocking to boomtowns and the feeble attempts to set up local government in what were perceived as temporary communities, it was hardly surprising that mining life was often disorderly. Racial antagonism between American miners and foreigners, whom they labeled "greasers" (Mexicans), "chinks" (Chinese), "keskedees" (Frenchmen), and lesser "breeds," led to ugly riots and lynchings. Miners had few qualms about eliminating those who interfered with the race for riches. Fistfights, drunkenness, and murder occurred often enough to become part of the lore of the gold rush. Wrote one woman, "In the short space of twenty four days, we have had murders, fearful accidents, bloody deaths, a mob, whippings, a hanging, an attempt at suicide, and a fatal duel."

If mining life was usually not this violent, it tolerated behavior that would have been unacceptable farther east. Miners were not trying to re-create eastern communities but to get rich. Married men, convinced of the raucous and immoral character of mining communities, hesitated to bring wives and families west. As one declared, "I would much prefer that a wife of mine should board in a respectable bawd house in the city of New York than live anywhere in the city of San Francisco."

Although the lucky few struck it rich or at least made enough money to return home with pride intact, miners' journals and letters reveal that many made only enough to keep going. Wrote one, "Everybody in the States who has friends here is always writing for them to come home. Now they all long to go home. . . . But it is hard for a man to leave . . . with nothing. . . . I have no pile yet, but you can bet your life I will never come home until I have something more than when I started." The problem was that easily mined silver and gold deposits soon ran out. Although Chinese miners proved adept at finding what early miners overlooked, the remaining rich deposits lay deeply embedded in rock or gravel. Extraction required cooperative efforts, capital, technological experience, and expensive machinery. Eventually, mining became a corporate industrial concern, with miners as wage earners. As early as 1852, the

This 1852 photograph of miners and the constructions they built on the American River hints at some of the environmental consequences of mining activity. The formal clothing of the woman contrasts sharply with that worn by the men and suggests that she has not forgotten the standards of civilized life. *(California State Library)*

This picture of the near ghost town of Ophir City, Nevada, taken in the 1870s, points to the way the mining frontier left its mark on the landscape and suggests the unstable nature of such a frontier. *(Denver Public Library, Western History Department)*

changing nature of mining in California had transformed most of the shaggy miners into wage workers.

Probably 5 percent of early gold rush emigrants to California were women and children. Many of the women also anticipated getting "rich in a hurry." Because there were so few of them, the cooking, nursing, laundry, and hotel services women provided had a high value. When Luzena Wilson arrived in Sacramento, a miner offered to pay her $10 for a biscuit. That night, Luzena dreamt she saw "crowds of bearded miners striking gold from the earth with every blow of the pick, each one seeming to leave a share for me." Yet it was wearying work, and some wondered if the money compensated for the exhaustion. As Mary Ballou thought it over, she decided, "I would not advise any Lady to come out here and suffer to toil and fatigue I have suffered for the sake of a little gold." As men's profits shrank, so, too, did those of the women who served them.

Some of the first women to arrive on the mining frontier were prostitutes. They rejected the hard labor of cooking and washing that "respectable" women performed, hoping that the sex ratio would make their profession especially profitable. Prostitutes may have constituted as much as 20 percent of California's female population in 1850, and they probably vastly outnumbered other women in early mining camps. During boom days, they made good money and sometimes won a recognized place in society. But prostitutes always ran risks in a disorderly environment. They were more often the victims of murder and violence than the recipients of courtesy.

The Mexicans, South Americans, Chinese, and small numbers of blacks seeking their fortunes in California soon discovered that although they contributed substantially to California's growth, racial discrimination flourished vigorously in the land of golden promise. At first, American miners hoped to force foreigners out of the gold fields altogether. But an attempt to declare mining illegal for all foreigners failed. A high tax on foreign miners proved more successful. Thousands of Mexicans left the mines, while the Chinese found other jobs in San Francisco and Sacramento. As business stagnated in mining towns, however, white miners had second thoughts about the levy and reduced it. By 1870, when the tax was declared unconstitutional, the Chinese, who had paid 85 percent of it, had "contributed" $5 million to California for the right to prospect. The hostility that led to this legislation also fed widespread violence against the Chinese and Mexicans.

Black Americans found that their skin color placed them in a situation akin to that of foreigners. Deprived of the vote, forbidden to testify in civil or criminal cases involving whites, excluded from the bounties of the state's homestead law, blacks led a precarious existence. When news arrived of the discovery of gold in British Columbia in the late 1850s, hundreds of blacks as well as thousands of Chinese left the state, hoping that the Canadian frontier would be more hospitable than California.

For the Native American tribes of the interior, the mining frontier was a disaster. Used to foraging for food, they found fish and game increasingly scarce as miners diverted streams, hunted game, or drove it from mining areas altogether. When Indians responded by raiding mining camps, miners erupted with fury. They stalked and killed native men and women, sometimes collecting bounties offered by some mining communities for their scalps. Indian women were raped; children were kidnapped and offered as apprentices. As one miner pointed out, "Indians seven or eight years old are worth $100 . . . [and] it is a damn poor Indian that's not worth $50." Without legal recourse because of their skin color, Native Americans could not withstand the onslaught of white society. Subjected not only to violence but to white disease, Indians died by the thousands. In 1849, there had been about 150,000 Indians in California. In just over 20 years, numbers had tumbled to fewer than 30,000.

Although the mining frontier was never as brutal for whites as for people of color, white men's and women's fantasies of dazzling riches rarely came true. The ghost towns of the West testify to the typical pattern: boom, bust, decay, death. The empty streets and rotting buildings stood as symbols of dashed hopes and disappointed dreams. Also left behind were other physical signs recalling the presence and passing of the mining frontier. Mining operations left an indelible mark on the land. Forests were decimated to provide timber for the flumes miners constructed to divert rivers from their channels in the hopes of exposing rich gold deposits in the dry river beds. They built slurries and ditches and created mounds of debris that during floods or heavy rains oozed over fields and choked rivers and streams. Consumed by visions of glittering metal, miners were blind to the realities of eroding soil, deforested mountains, diverted waterways, and silt.

It was difficult, however, to recognize some of the negative consequences of the discovery of gold, for it had many positive effects on the West as a whole. Between 1848 and 1883, California mines supplied two-thirds of the country's gold. Gold transformed San Francisco from a sleepy town into a bustling metropolis. It fueled the agricultural and commercial development of California and Oregon, as miners provided a market for goods and services. Gold built harbors, railroads, and irrigation systems not just in California and Oregon but all over the West. Though few people made large fortunes, both the region and the nation profited from gold.

The Mormon Frontier

In the decades before 1860, many emigrants heading for the Far West stopped to rest and buy supplies in Salt Lake City, the heart of the Mormon state of Deseret. There they encountered a society that seemed familiar and orderly, yet foreign and shocking. Visitors admired the attractively laid out town with its irrigation ditches, gardens, and tidy houses. But as they noted the decorous nature of everyday life, they gossiped about polygamy and searched for signs of rebellion in the faces of Mormon women. Emigrants who opposed slavery were fond of equating the position of the Mormon wife with that of the black slave. They were amazed that so few Mormon women seemed interested in escaping from the bonds of plural marriage.

Violent events had driven the Mormons to the arid Great Basin area. Joseph Smith's murder in 1844 marked no end to the persecution of his followers. By the fall of 1846, angry mobs had chased the last of the "Saints" out of Nauvoo, Illinois. As they struggled to join their advance groups at temporary camps in Iowa, Smith's successor, Brigham Young, realized that flight from the United States represented the best hope for survival. The Saints must create the kingdom of God anew, somewhere in the West, far removed from the United States, that "Babylon" of corruption and injustice.

The Mexican-American war unexpectedly furthered Mormon plans. At first, most Mormons probably agreed with Hosea Stout, who was glad "to learn of the war," hoping it "might never end until the States were entirely destroyed, for they had driven us into the wilderness, and now were laughing at our calamities." But Brigham Young realized that war might provide capital needed for the new Mormon kingdom. By raising 500 Mormon young men for Kearney's Army of the West, Young acquired vital resources. The battalion's advance pay bought wagonloads of supplies for starving and sick Mormons strung out along the trail between Missouri and Iowa and helped finance the impending great migration.

Young selected the Great Basin area, technically part of Mexico, as the best site for his future kingdom. It was arid and remote, 1,000 miles from its nearest "civilized" neighbors. But if irrigated, Mormon leaders concluded it might prove as fertile as the fields and vineyards of ancient Israel.

In April 1847, Young led an exploratory expedition of 143 men, 3 women, and 2 children to this promised land. In late July, after reaching Salt Lake, Young exclaimed, "This is the place." Before returning to Iowa to prepare Mormons for the trip to Utah, he announced his land policy. Settlers would receive virtually free land on the basis of a family's size and its

C. A. A. Christensen painted this picture of the Mormon Temple in Nauvoo, Illinois, in 1844. Despite the dignified and substantial nature of the building, which almost could be an academy or a New England church, the Mormons appeared to their neighbors to harbor unacceptable and un-American ideas. *(Museum of Art, Brigham Young University)*

ability to cultivate it. After Young left, the expeditionary group followed his directions to construct irrigation ditches and begin planting.

The following months and years tested Young's organizational talents and his followers' cooperative abilities. By September 1847, fully 566 wagons and 1,500 of the Saints had made the arduous trek to Salt Lake City. Still more Mormons came the next year, inspired by visions of a new Zion in the West. Their trip was also a collective venture, planned and directed by Church leaders. By 1850, the Mormon frontier had attracted over 11,000 settlers. Missionary efforts in the United States and abroad, especially in Great Britain and Scandinavia, drew thousands of converts to the Great Basin. The Church emigration society and a loan fund facilitated the journey for many who could never have otherwise undertaken the trip. By the end of the decade, over 30,000 Saints lived in Utah, not only in Salt Lake City but also in more than 90 village colonies Young had planned. Though hardship marked these early years, the Mormons thrived. As one early settler remarked, "We have everything around us we could ask."

Non-Mormon, or "Gentile," emigrants passing through Utah found much that was recognizable. The government had familiar characteristics. Most Mormons were farmers; many of them came originally from New England and the Midwest and shared many of the same customs and attitudes. But outsiders perceived profound differences, for the heart of Mormon society was not the individual farmer living on his own homestead but the cooperative village.

Years of persecution had nourished a strong sense of group identity and acceptance of Church leadership. Organized by the Church leaders, who made the

essential decisions, farming became a collective enterprise. All farmers were allotted land. All had irrigation rights, for water did not belong to individuals but to the community. During Sunday services, the local bishop might give farming instructions to his congregation along with his sermon. As Young explained, "I have looked upon the community of Latter-day Saints in a vision and beheld them organized as the great family of heaven, each person performing his several duties in his line of industry, working for the good of the whole more than for individual aggrandizement." In this vast communal effort, every Mormon was expected to work for success, men and women alike. "We do not believe in having any drones in the hive," one woman said tartly.

The Church was omnipresent in Utah; in fact, nothing separated Church and state. Despite familiar government forms, Church leaders occupied all important political posts. Brigham Young's Governing Quorum contained the high priests of the Church, who made both religious and political decisions.

When it became clear that Utah would become a territory, Mormon leaders drew up a constitution that divided religious and political power. But once in place, powers overlapped. As one Gentile pointed out, "This intimate connection of church and state seems to pervade everything that is done. The supreme power in both being lodged in the hands of the same individuals, it is difficult to separate their two official characters, and to determine whether in any one instance they act as spiritual or merely temporal officers."

The Treaty of Guadalupe Hidalgo officially incorporated Utah into the United States, but little affected political and religious arrangements. Brigham Young became territorial governor. Local bishops continued to act as spiritual leaders as well as civil magistrates in Mormon communities. Mormons had come to Utah to establish a kingdom rather than a republic. Their motives dictated the unique politicoreligious nature of the Utah experience.

Other aspects of the Mormon frontier were distinctive. Mormon policy toward the Indian tribes was remarkably enlightened. As one prominent Mormon pointed out, "It has been our habit to shoot Indians with tobacco and bread biscuits rather than with powder and lead, and we are most successful with them." After two expeditions against the Timpanago and Shoshone in 1850, Mormons concentrated on converting rather than killing Native Americans. Mormon missionaries learned Bannock, Ute, Navajo, and Hopi languages to bring the faith to these tribes. They also encouraged Native Americans to ranch and farm.

Although most Gentiles could tolerate some of the differences they encountered on the Mormon frontier, few could accept polygamy and the seemingly immoral extended family structure that plural marriage entailed. Although Joseph Smith and other Church leaders had secretly practiced polygamy in the early 1840s, Brigham Young publicly revealed the doctrine only in 1852, when the Saints were safely in Utah. Smith believed that the highest or "celestial" form of marriage brought special rewards in the afterlife. Because wives and children contributed to these rewards, polygamy was a means of sanctification. From a practical standpoint, polygamy served to incorporate into Mormon society single female converts who had left their families to come to Utah.

Although most Mormons accepted the doctrine and its religious justification, some found it hard to follow. One woman called it a "great trial of feelings." Actually, relatively few families were polygamous. During the 40-year period in which Mormons practiced plural marriage, only 10 to 20 percent of Mormon families were polygamous. Few men had more than two wives. Because of the expense of maintaining several families and the personal strains involved, usually only the most successful and visible Mormon leaders practiced polygamy.

Polygamous family life was a far cry from the lascivious arrangement outsiders fantasized. Jealousy among wives could destroy the institution of plural marriage, so Mormon leaders minimized the role of romantic love and sexual attraction in courtship and marriage. Instead, they encouraged marriages founded on mutual attachment, with sex for the purposes of procreation rather than pleasure.

To the shock of outsiders, Mormon women did not consider themselves slaves but rather highly regarded members of the Mormon community. Whether plural wives or not, they saw polygamy as the cutting edge of their society and defended it to the outside world. Polygamy was preferable to monogamy, which left the single woman without the economic and social protection of family life and forced some of them into prostitution, Brenda Pratt explained. "Polygamy . . . tends directly to the chastity of women, and the sound health and morals . . . of their children."

Although they faced obvious difficulties, many plural wives found rewards in polygamy. Without the constant presence of husbands, they had an unusual opportunity for independence. Many treated husbands when they visited as revered friends; their children, not their spouses, provided them with day-to-day emotional satisfaction. Occasionally, plural wives lived together and shared domestic work, becoming close friends. As one such wife put it, "We three . . . loved each other more than sisters" and would "go hand in hand together down till eternity."

Although the Mormon frontier seemed alien to outsiders, it succeeded in terms of its numbers, its growing economic prosperity, and its group unity. Long-term threats loomed for this community, however, once the area became part of the United States. Attacks on Young's power as well as heated verbal denunciations of polygamy proliferated. Efforts began in Congress to outlaw polygamy. In the years before the Civil War, Mormons withstood these assaults on their way of life. But as Utah became more connected to the rest of the country, the tide would turn against them.

Cities in the West

Many emigrants went west not to claim farmland or to pan for gold but rather to settle in cities like San Francisco, Denver, and Portland. There they hoped to find business and professional opportunities or, perhaps, the chance to make a fortune by speculating in town lots.

Cities were an integral part of frontier life and, in some cases, preceded agricultural settlement. Some communities turned into bustling cities as they catered to the emigrant trade. St. Joseph, Missouri, outfitted families setting out on the overland journey. Salt Lake City offered weary pioneers headed for California an opportunity to rest and restock. Portland was the destination of many emigrants and became a market and supply center for homesteaders.

Some cities grew so rapidly that they have been called "instant cities." San Francisco and Denver turned into cities almost overnight; in a mere 12 years, San Francisco's population zoomed from 812 to 56,802. The discovery of precious metals sent thousands of miners with diverse demands and desires to and through these places. And once the strike ran out, many miners returned to these cities to make a new start. Still other places supplied frontier farmers and

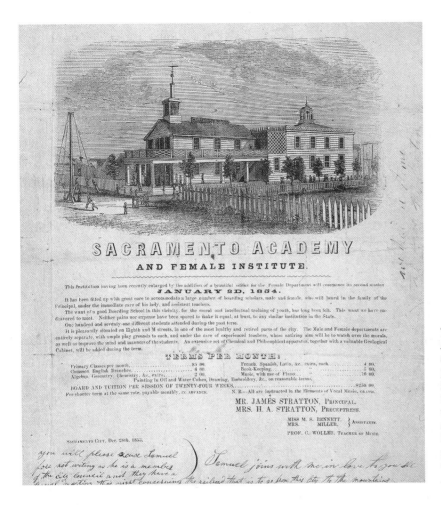

This circular advertising Sacramento Academy and Female Institute shows settlers' desire to re-create familiar patterns of life. The circular informs interested parents that the school's teachers would watch over "the morals, as well as improve the minds and manners of our students." It was possible to study French, Latin, and Spanish and to study piano for an extra fee. *(Courtesy of the California History Room, California State Library, Sacramento, California)*

served as their markets. They only gradually acquired urban characteristics.

Commercial life bustled on the urban frontier, offering residents a wide range of occupations and services. As a Portland emigrant remarked in 1852, only a few years after that community's beginning, "In many ways life here . . . was more primitive than it was in the early times in Illinois and Missouri. But in others it was far more advanced. . . . We could get the world's commodities here which could not be had then, or scarcely at all, in the interior of Illinois or Missouri."

Young, single men seeking their fortunes made up a disproportionate share of the urban population. Frontier Portland had more than three men for every woman. Predictably, urban life was often noisy, rowdy, and occasionally violent. The presence of so many young men could not help but affect urban family life. Mothers worried that their children would fall into bad company. Some attempted to reform the atmosphere by pressing for Sunday store closings or prohibition. Other women, of course, enjoyed all the attention that came with the presence of so many young men. As one observed with gusto, "There is plenty of men here. They cast sheeps eyes at Lib and Lucy's girl but have not popt

the question yet." Eventually, the sex ratio became balanced, but as late as 1880, fully 18 of the 24 largest western cities had more men than women.

Although western cities began with distinctive characters, they soon resembled eastern cities. As a western publication boasted, "Transport a resident of an Eastern city and put him down in the streets of Portland, and he would observe little difference between his new surroundings and those he beheld but a moment before in his native city."

The history of Portland suggests the common pattern of development. In 1845, Portland was only a clearing in the forest, large enough for four streets and 16 blocks. Speculation in town lots was lively. By the early 1850s, Portland had grown into a small trading center with a few rough log structures and muddy tracks for streets. As farmers poured into Oregon, the city became a regional commercial center. More permanent structures were built, giving the city an "eastern" appearance.

The belief that urban life in the West abounded with special opportunities initially drew many young men to Portland and other western cities. Many of them did not find financial success there.

This 1853 view of San Francisco reveals the rapid transformation of the city. Brick buildings, several stories high, with elaborate cornices, board sidewalks, kerosene street lamps, and the inevitable grid street pattern give San Francisco the appearance of an eastern city rather than a raw western community, only four years after the gold rush. (*The Bancroft Library, University of California, Berkeley*)

Opportunities were greatest for newcomers who brought assets with them. These residents became the elite of the community. By the 1860s, when the city's population had reached 2,874, Portland's Social Club symbolized the emergence of that city's elite. Portland's businessmen, lawyers, and editors controlled an increasing share of the community's wealth and set its social standards. Their elaborate parties, summer trips, and exclusive clubs showed how far Portland had come from its raw frontier beginnings.

CULTURES IN CONFLICT

Looking at westward expansion through the eyes of white emigrants provides only one view of the frontier experience. An entry from an Oregon Trail journal suggests other perspectives. On May 7, 1864, Mary Warner, a bride of only a few months, described a frightening event. That day, a "fine-looking" Indian had visited the wagon train and tried to buy her. Mary's husband, probably uncertain how to handle the situation, played along, agreeing to

trade his wife for two ponies. The Indian generously offered three. "Then," wrote Mary, "he took hold of my shawl to make me understand to get out [of the wagon]. About this time I got frightened and really was so hysterical [that] I began to cry." Everyone laughed at her, she reported, though surely the Indian found the whole incident no more amusing than she had.

This ordinary encounter on the overland trail only begins to hint at the social and cultural differences separating white Americans moving west and the peoples with whom they came in contact. Confident of their values and rights, emigrants had little regard for those who had lived in the West for centuries and no compunction in seizing their lands. Many even predicted that the Indian race would disappear from the continent, a just reward for tribal "degeneracy."

Confronting the Plains Tribes

During the 1840s, white Americans, for the first time, came into extensive contact with the powerful Plains tribes, whose culture differed from that of the more familiar eastern Woodlands tribes. Probably a quarter million Native Americans occupied the area from the Rocky Mountains to the Missouri River and from the Platte River to New Mexico. Nearest the Missouri and Iowa frontier lived the "border" tribes—the Pawnee, Omaha, Oto, Ponca, and Kansa. These Indians, unlike other Plains tribes, lived in villages and raised crops, though they supplemented their diet with buffalo meat during the summer months. On the Central Plains lived the Brulé and Oglala Sioux, the Cheyenne, the Shoshone, and the Arapaho, aggressive tribes who followed the buffalo and often raided the border tribes. In the Southwest were the Comanche, Ute, Navajo, and some Apache bands; the Kiowa, Wichita, Apache, and southern Comanche claimed northern and western Texas as their hunting grounds. Many of the southwestern tribes had adopted aspects of Spanish culture and European domestic animals like cattle, sheep, and horses.

Although there were differences between the Plains tribes, they shared certain characteristics. Most had adopted a nomadic way of life after the introduction of Spanish horses in the sixteenth century increased their seasonal mobility from 50 to 500 miles. Horses allowed Indian braves to hunt the buffalo with such success that tribes (with the exclusion of the border groups) came to depend on the beasts for food, clothing, fuel, teepee dwellings, and trading purposes. Because women were responsible for processing buffalo products, some men had more than one wife to tan skins for trading.

Mobility also increased tribal contact and conflict. War played a central part in the lives of the Plains tribes. No male became a fully accepted member of

Indian Land Cessions in 1840

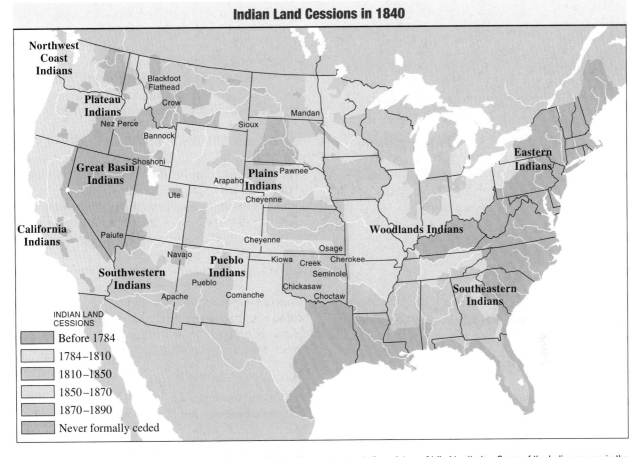

This map of Indian tribes and groupings reveals locations in 1840, but it presents too static a picture of tribal territories. Some of the Indian groups in the West had been forced across the Mississippi by events in the Midwest. What the map does make obvious, however, is the rapid pace of Indian land cessions in the nineteenth century, especially in the trans-Mississippi West.

his tribe until he had proved himself in battle. But tribal warfare was not like the warfare of white men. Indians sought not to exterminate their enemies or to claim territory but rather to steal horses and to prove individual prowess. They considered it braver to touch an enemy than to kill or scalp him. This pattern of conflict on the Plains discouraged political unity. Moreover, individual tribes were loosely organized. Chiefs enjoyed only limited authority over their followers. As Chief Low Horn, a Blackfoot, explained, chiefs "could not restrain their young men . . . their young men were wild, and ambitious, in their turn to be braves and chiefs. They wanted by some brave act to win the favor of their young women, and bring scalps and horses to show their prowess."

Armed with guns, mounted on fast ponies, and skilled in warfare and raiding, the Plains tribes, though disunified, posed a fearsome obstacle to white expansion. They had signed no treaties with the United States and had few friendly feelings toward whites. Their contact with white society had brought gains through trade in skins, but the trade had also brought

alcohol and destructive epidemics of smallpox and scarlet fever.

When the first emigrants drove their wagons across the plains and prairies in the early 1840s, relations between Indians and whites were peaceable. But the intrusion of whites set in motion an environmental cycle that eventually drew the two groups into conflict. Indian tribes depended on the buffalo but respected this source of life. The Teton Sioux performed rituals to ensure a continuing supply of the animals, while hunters often ritualistically apologized to the Great Unseen Buffalo for slaughtering what the tribe needed. The grasses that nourished the buffalo also sustained the Indians' own ponies and the animals that supported horse traders like the Cheyenne.

Whites, however, fed their oxen and horses on the grass both the Indians' ponies and the buffalo needed. And they adopted the "most exciting sport," the buffalo hunt. As the great herds began to shrink, Native American tribes began to battle one another for hunting grounds and food. The powerful Sioux swooped down into the hunting grounds of their enemies and

This drawing, done by an unknown Indian artist sometime in the 1840s, contrasts the traditionally clad Indians and the wild animals they hunted with the formally dressed white men and their stock animals. Has the artist depicted whites in a sympathetic manner? *(Archives de Jesuites, St. Jerome Quebec)*

mounted destructive raids against the Pawnee and other smaller tribes. In an 1846 petition to President Polk, the Sioux explained that "for several years past the Emigrants going over the Mountains from the United States, have been the cause that Buffalo have in great measure left our hunting grounds, thereby causing us to go into the Country of Our Enemies to hunt, exposing our lives daily for the necessary subsistence of our wives and Children and getting killed on several occasions." Despite their difficulties, the Sioux had "all along treated the Emigrants in the most friendly manner, giving them free passage through our hunting grounds."

The Sioux requested compensation for damages caused by whites. When the president denied their request, they tried to extract taxes from the emigrants passing over their lands. Emigrants were outraged at what they considered Indian effrontery. After all, the

United States had won these lands. Frontier newspapers printed letters denouncing the Sioux, demanding adequate protection for travelers and some chastening of the "savages." However, little was done to relieve the suffering of the tribes bearing the brunt of Sioux aggression, the dismay of the Sioux at the white invasion, or the fears of the emigrants themselves.

The discovery of gold in California, which lured over 20,000 across the Plains in 1849 alone, became the catalyst for federal action. The vast numbers of gold seekers and their animals wrought such devastation in the Platte valley that it rapidly became a wasteland for the Indians. The dreaded cholera that whites carried with them spread to the Indians, killing thousands.

To meet the crisis, government officials devised a two-pronged plan. The government would construct a chain of forts to protect emigrants and, simultaneously, call the tribes to a general conference. Officials expected that in return for generous presents, Indians would end tribal warfare and limit their movements to prescribed areas. They instructed tribes to select chiefs to speak for them at the conference.

The Fort Laramie Council, 1851

In 1851, the tribal council convened at Fort Laramie. As many as 10,000 Indians, hopeful of ending the destruction of their way of life and eager for the promised presents, gathered at the fort. Tribal animosities simmered, however. Skirmishes occurred on the way to the fort, and the border tribes, fearful of the Sioux, declined to participate. The Comanche, Kiowa, and Apache also refused to come, because their enemies, the Sioux and the Crow, were to be there.

At the conference, whites told the gathered tribes that times had changed. In the past, "you had plenty of buffalo and game . . . and your Great Father well knows that war has always been your favorite amusement and pursuit. He then left the question of peace and war to yourselves. Now, since the settling of the districts West . . . by the white men, your condition has changed." There would be compensation for the destruction of their grass, timber, and buffalo and annual payments of goods and services. But in return, the tribes had to give up their rights of free movement. The government drew tribal boundaries, and chiefs made promises to stay within them. In most cases, some tribal lands were sold.

The Fort Laramie Treaty was the first agreement between the Plains tribes and the U.S. government. It expressed the conviction of whites that Indians must stay in clearly defined areas apart from white civilization.

But this system of isolation and its purported benefits were still in the future. During the conference, ominous signs appeared that more trouble would precede any "resolution" of Indian–white affairs. Sioux Chief Black Hawk told whites, "You have split the country and I do not like it." His powerful tribe refused to be restricted to lands north of the Platte, for south of the river lay their recently conquered lands. "These lands once belonged to the Kiowas and the Crows," one Sioux explained, "but we whipped those nations out of them and in this we did what the white men do when they want the lands of the Indians." The words suggested that Indians, despite agreements, would not willingly abandon their traditional way of life for confinement. In the following years, it would become evident that Americans and Sioux had conflicting interests south of the Platte. Elsewhere in the trans-Mississippi West, other tribes, like the fierce Navajo of New Mexico, also resisted white attempts to confine them.

Overwhelming the Mexicans

In the Southwest, in Texas, and in California, Americans encountered a Spanish-speaking population and Hispanic culture. Expansionist Lewis Cass expressed Americans' scorn for both. Speaking in a congressional debate on the annexation of New Mexico, Cass stated, "We do not want the people of Mexico, either as citizens or as subjects. All we want is a portion of territory . . . with a population, which would soon recede, or identify itself with ours." Americans regarded Mexicans as lazy, ignorant, and cunning, the "dregs of society." Although Mexicans easily recognized such cultural arrogance, they lacked the numbers to fend off American aggression.

Although Anglo–Mexican interaction differed from place to place, few Anglos heeded the Treaty of Guadalupe Hidalgo's assurances that Mexicans would have citizens' rights and the "free enjoyment of their liberty and property." The greatest numbers of Spanish-speaking people lived in New Mexico, and, of all former Mexican citizens, they probably fared best. Most were of mixed blood, living marginally as ranch hands for rich landowners or as farmers and herdsmen in small villages dominated by a *patron,* or headman. As the century wore on, Americans produced legal titles and took over lands long occupied by peasant farmers and stock raisers. But despite economic reversals, New Mexicans survived, carrying their rural culture well into the twentieth century.

Light-skinned, upper-class landowners fared better. Even before the conquest, rich New Mexicans had protected their future by establishing contracts with American businessmen and by sending their sons east to American schools. When the United States annexed New Mexico, this substantial and powerful class contracted strategic marriage and business alliances with the Anglo men who slowly trickled into the territory. During the 1850s, they maintained their influence and prestige and their American connections. Only rarely did they bother with the plight of their poor countrymen. Class outweighed ethnic or cultural considerations.

In Texas, the Spanish-speaking residents, only 10 percent of the population in 1840, shrank to a mere 6 percent by 1860. Although the upper class also intermarried with Americans, they lost most of their power, as Germans, Irish, French, and Americans poured into the state. Poor, dark-skinned Hispanics clustered in low-paying and largely unskilled jobs.

In California, the discovery of gold radically changed the situation for the Californios. In 1848, there were 7,000 Californios and about twice as many Anglos. By 1860, the Anglo population had ballooned to 360,000. Hispanic-Americans were hard-pressed to cope with the rapid influx of outsiders. At first, Californios and several thousand Mexicans from Sonora joined Anglos and others in the gold fields. But competition there fed antagonism and finally open conflict. Posters warned foreigners out of the gold fields. In Anglo eyes, one Hispanic was much like another, even if one claimed to be a Californio with political rights and another a Sonoran. Taxes and terrorism ultimately succeeded in forcing most Spanish speakers out of the mines and established the racial contours of the new California.

Other changes were even more disastrous. In 1851, Congress passed the Gwinn Land Law, supposedly a measure for validating Spanish and Mexican land titles. The law violated the pledge contained in a Statement of Protocol accompanying the Treaty of Guadalupe Hidalgo that stated the government "did not in any way" intend to annul the grants of lands made by Mexico, for it forced California landowners to defend what was already theirs and encouraged squatters to settle on land in the hopes that the Californios' titles would prove false. The process was slow—it took an average of 17 years to establish clear title to land—and unfamiliar. As one woman explained, her mother had been "totally unprepared for the problems that came with American rule. Not only was the language foreign to her, but also the concept of property taxes, mortgages and land title regulations." Landowners found themselves paying American lawyers large fees, often in land, and borrowing at high interest rates to pay for court proceedings. A victory at court often turned into a defeat when legal expenses forced owners to sell their lands to pay debts. In the South, where Anglos judged land less valuable than in the mining North, the process of dispossession was slower. But by the early 1860s, the ranching class there had also lost most of its extensive holdings and slid into relative poverty.

This painting presents an idyllic picture of the lives of the elite Mexican landowners. Their way of life would disappear with the arrival of hordes of American settlers. Both the former elite and more ordinary Mexicans would find themselves, in the words of Pablo la Guerra, "foreigners in their own land." *(Charles Christian Nahl,* The Fandango, *1873/Crocker Art Museum, E. B. Crocker Collection, Sacramento, California,)*

For working-class Hispanic-Americans, who became laborers for Anglo farmers or mining or railroad companies, the arrival of Anglos was the start of a steadily deteriorating situation. Whatever their employment, Hispanic-Americans earned less and did more unpleasant jobs than Anglo workers. By 1870, the average Hispanic-American worker's property was worth only about a third of its value of 20 years earlier. As newspaper editor and champion of the Mexican–American cause, Francisco Ramírez pointed out in the Los Angeles newspaper *El Clamor Publico* in 1856, "California has fallen into the hands of the ambitious sons of North America who will not stop until they have satisfied their passions, by driving the first occupants of the land out of the country, villifying their religion and disfiguring their customs."

Western movies and novels, with their images of sheriffs in hot pursuit of outlaws and bandits, some wearing sombreros, hint at the reality of resistance to American expansion into the Southwest. The exploits of Tiburcio Vásquez, a notorious *bandido* in southern California, reveal that some Hispanics responded to events through violence:

My career grew out of the circumstances by which I was surrounded. . . . As I grew to manhood I was in the habit of attending balls and parties given by the native Californians, into which the Americans, then beginning to become numerous, would force themselves and shove the native born men aside, monopolizing the dance and the women. This was about 1852. A spirit of hatred and revenge took possession of me. I had numerous fights in defense of my countrywomen. The officers were continually in pursuit of me. I believed we were unjustly and wrongfully deprived of the social rights that belonged to us.

Other Hispanics tried different tactics. In New Mexico, members of Las Gorras Blancas ripped up railroad ties and cut the barbed-wire fences of Anglo ranchers and farmers. The religiously oriented Penitentes tried to work through the ballot box. Ordinary men, women, and children resisted efforts to convert them to Protestantism and clung to familiar customs and beliefs even as they learned some of the skills needed to survive in a changing culture.

Timeline

1803–1806	Lewis and Clark expedition
1818	Treaty on joint U.S.–British occupation of Oregon
1819	Spain cedes Spanish territory in United States and sets transcontinental boundary of Louisiana Purchase, excluding Texas
1821	Mexican independence
	Opening of Santa Fe Trail
	Stephen Austin leads American settlement of Texas
1821–1840	Indian removals
1830	Mexico abolishes slavery in Texas
1836	Texas declares independence
	Battles of the Alamo and San Jacinto
1840s	Emigrant crossings of Overland Trail
1844	James Polk elected president

1845	"Manifest Destiny" coined
	United States annexes Texas and sends troops to the Rio Grande
	Americans attempt to buy Upper California and New Mexico
1846	Mexico declares defensive war
	United States declares war and takes Santa Fe
	Resolution of Oregon question
1847	Attacks on Veracruz and Mexico City
	Mormon migration to Utah begins
1848	Treaty of Guadalupe Hidalgo
1849	California gold rush begins
1850	California admitted to the Union
1851	Fort Laramie Treaty
1853	Gadsden Purchase
1862	Homestead Act

Conclusion
Fruits of Manifest Destiny

Like Lewis Cass, many nineteenth-century Americans were convinced that the country had merely gained western territories to which it was entitled. Although the process of acquiring the western half of the continent was swift, the prospect of winning the West loomed large in the imagination of the American people for many years. A number of western settlers became folk heroes. All white Americans could be thankful for the special opportunities, the new chance for success, that the West seemed to offer.

The expanding nation did gain vast natural wealth in the trans-Mississippi West. But only a small fraction of the hopeful emigrants heading for the frontier realized their dreams of success. And the move west had a dark side, as Americans clashed with Mexicans and Native Americans in their drive to fulfill their "Manifest Destiny" and as the acquisition of new territories fueled the controversy over the future of slavery.

Recommended Reading

Probing the Trans-Mississippi West

Norman A. Graebner, ed., *Manifest Destiny* (1968); Theodore J. Karamanski, *Fur Trade and Exploration: Opening the Far Northwest, 1821–1852* (1983); Patricia Nelson Limerick, *The Legacy of Conquest: The Unbroken Past of the American West* (1987); Anders Stephanson, *Manifest Destiny: American Expansionism and the Empire of Right* (1995).

Winning the Trans-Mississippi West

Gene Brack, *Mexico Views Manifest Destiny, 1821–1846* (1975); Robert H. Ferrell, ed., *Monterrey Is Ours! The Mexican War Letters of Lieutenant Dana, 1845–1847* (1990); Neal Harlow, *California Conquered* (1982); Robert W. Johanssen, *To the Halls of Montezuma: The Mexican War in the American Imagination* (1985); Ernest M. Lander Jr., *Reluctant Imperialists: Calhoun, the South Carolinians, and the Mexican War* (1980); David Pletcher, *The Diplomacy of Annexation: Texas, Oregon, and the Mexican War* (1973); Cecil Robinson, ed., *The View from Chapultepec: Mexican Writers on the Mexican-American War* (1989); David J. Weber, *The Mexican Frontier, 1821–1846* (1982).

Going West

John Mack Faragher, *Women and Men on the Overland Trail* (1978); Sandra Myres, ed., *Ho for California! Women's Overland Diaries from the Huntington Library* (1980); John D. Unruh Jr., *The Plains Across: The Overland Emigrants and the Trans-Mississippi West, 1840–1860* (1979).

Living on the Frontier

Peter G. Boag, *Environment and Experience: Settlement Culture in Nineteenth-Century Oregon* (1992); Richard L. Bushman, *Joseph Smith and the Beginnings of Mormonism* (1984); Arrell Morgan Gibson, *Yankees in Paradise: The Pacific Basin Frontier* (1993); Julie Roy Jeffrey, *Frontier Women: "Civilizing" the West? 1840–1880* (1998); William Loren Katz, *The Black West* (1971); Lawrence H. Larson, *The Urban West at the End of the Frontier* (1978); Laurie F. Maffly-Kipp, *Religion and Society in Frontier California* (1994); Dean L. May, *Three Frontiers: Family, Land, and Society in the American West, 1850–1900* (1994); Adolf E. Schroeder and Carla Schulz-Geisberg, eds., *Hold Dear, As Always: Jette, a German Immigrant Life in Letters* (1988).

Cultures in Conflict

Albert Camarillo, *Chicanos in a Changing Society: From Mexican Pueblos to American Barrios in Santa Barbara and Southern California, 1848–1930* (1979); Albert L. Hurtado, *Indian Survival on the California Frontier* (1988); Julie Roy Jeffrey, *Converting the West: A Biography of Narcissa Whitman* (1991); Timothy M. Marovina, *Tejano Religion and Ethnicity: San Antonio, 1821–1860* (1995); M. S. Meir and Feliciano Rivera, *The Chicanos: A History of Mexican-Americans* (1972); Alfredo Mirande and Evangeline Enriquez, *La Chicana: The Mexican-American Woman* (1979); Peter Nabakov, ed., *Native American Testimony: An Anthology of Indian and White Relations* (1978); Jacqueline Peters, *Sacred Encounters: Father DeSmet and the Indians of the Rocky Mountain West* (1993); Leonard Pitt, *The Decline of the Californios: A Social History of the Spanish-Speaking Californians, 1846–1890* (1970); Robert J. Rosenbaum, *Mexicano Resistance in the Southwest: "The Sacred Right of Self-Preservation"* (1981); Theodore Stern, *Chiefs & Chief Traders: Indian Relations at Fort Nez Perces, 1818–1855 (1993);* Sylvia Van Kirk, *Many Tender Ties: Women in the Fur Trade Society, 1670–1870* (1983); David J. Wishart, *An Unspeakable Sadness: The Dispossession of the Nebraska Indians* (1994).

Fiction and Film

Mark Twain's *Roughing It* is often humorous, but through the humor you can see Twain's insightful comments about westerners' values and standards. James C. Work's *Gunfight!* (1996) contains a selection of gunfight stories originally printed in popular magazines. For an example of an early dime novel, see Ann Sophia Winterbotham Stephens's *Malaeska: Indian Wife of the White Hunter* (1861, but use any edition).

The West is a nine-part series by Ken Burns, first shown on television. The films provide a sympathetic and critical account of the settlement of the West and its impact on Native Americans. *The Donner Party* (1992) is a PBS video of the disastrous experience of a party of emigrants who were caught in the Sierra Nevadas during the winter of 1846–1847. One critic notes a dark tone to the film, which is characteristic of the New Western History.

Suggested Web Sites

http://memory.loc.gov/ammem/umhtml/umhome.html

Pioneering the Upper Midwest: Books from Michigan, Minnesota, and Wisconsin, ca. 1820–1910. This Library of Congress site looks at first-person accounts, biographies, promotional literature, local histories, ethnographic and antiquarian texts, colonial archival documents, and other works from the seventeenth to the early twentieth century. It covers many topics and issues that affected Americans in the settlement and development of the Upper Midwest.

http://sunsite.unam.mx/revistas/1847

The Mexican-American War Memorial Homepage. Images and text at this site explain the causes, courses, and outcomes of the Mexican-American War.

http://www.ukans.edu/carrie/kancoll/galtrl.htm

Gallery: On the Trail . . . This Kansas Collection site holds several good primary sources with images concerning the Oregon Trail and America's early movement westward.

http://www.xmission.com/~drudy/amm.html

Mountain Men and the Fur Trade. Private letters can speak volumes about the concerns and environment of the writers and recipients. Letters from early settlers west of the Mississippi River are offered on this site, which is an on-line research center devoted to the trappers, explorers, and traders known as the Mountain Men.

http://members.aol.com/danmrosen/donner/index.htm

The Donner Party. This site includes logs from the infamous party that resorted to extreme measures to survive. It also has images of the region.

http://www.si.edu/organiza/museums/amerind/start.htm

National Museum of the American Indian. The Smithsonian Institution maintains this site, providing information about the museum. The museum is dedicated to everything about Native Americans.

http://www.ushistoryplace.com

 A richly detailed on-line learning environment complete with interactive maps, timelines, history activities, primary source documents, and links to related American history sites.

The UNION *in* PERIL

CHAPTER OUTLINE

The autumn of 1860 was a time of ominous rumors and expectations. The election was held on November 6 in an atmosphere of crisis. In Springfield, Illinois, Abraham Lincoln, taking coffee and sandwiches prepared by the "ladies of Springfield," waited as the telegraph brought in the returns. By 1 A.M., victory was certain. He reported later, "I went home, but not to get much sleep, for I then felt, as I never had before, the responsibility that was upon me." And with good cause. He and the American people faced the most serious crisis since the founding of the Republic.

Lincoln won an unusual four-party election with only 39 percent of the popular vote. He had appealed almost exclusively to northern voters in a blatantly sectional campaign, defeating his three opponents by carrying every free state except New Jersey. Of the candidates, only Illinois Senator Stephen Douglas campaigned actively in every section of the country. For his efforts, he received the second-highest number of votes. Douglas's appeal, especially in the closing days of the campaign, was "on behalf of the Union," which he feared—correctly—was in imminent danger of splitting apart.

Other Americans sensed the mood of crisis that fall and faced their own fears and responsibilities. A month before the election, plantation owner Robert Allston wrote his oldest son, Benjamin, that "disastrous consequences" would follow from a Lincoln victory. Although his letter mentioned the possibility of secession, he dealt mostly with plantation concerns: a new horse, the mood of the slaves, ordering supplies from the city, instructions for making trousers on a sewing machine. After Lincoln's election, Allston corresponded with a southern colleague about the need for an "effective military organization" to resist "Northern and Federal aggression." In his shift from sewing machines to military ones, Robert Allston prepared for what he called the "impending crisis."

Frederick Douglass greeted the election of 1860 with characteristic optimism. Not only was this an opportunity to "educate . . . the people in their moral and political duties," he said, but "slaveholders know that the day of their power is over when a Republican President is elected." But no sooner had Lincoln's victory been determined than Douglass's hopes turned sour. He noted that Republican leaders, in their desire to keep southern border states from seceding, sounded more antiabolitionist than antislavery. They vowed not to touch slavery in areas where it already existed, which included the District of Columbia, and they promised to enforce the hated Fugitive Slave Act and to put down slave rebellions. Slavery would, in fact, Douglass bitterly concluded, "be as safe, and safer" with Lincoln than with a Democrat.

Michael Luark, an Iowa farmer, was not so sure. Born in Virginia, Luark was a typically mobile nineteenth-century American. After growing up in Indiana, he followed the mining booms of the 1850s to Colorado and California before returning to the Midwest to farm. Luark sought a good living and resented all the furor over slavery. He could not, however, avoid the issue. Writing in his diary on the last day of 1860, Luark looked ahead to 1861 with a deep sense of fear. "Startling" political changes would occur, he predicted, perhaps even the "Dissolution of the Union and Civil War with all its train of horrors." He blamed abolitionist agitators, perhaps reflecting his Virginia origins. On New Year's Day, he expressed his fears that Lincoln would let the "most ultra sectional and Abolition" men disturb the "vexed Slavery question" even further, as Frederick Douglass wanted. But if this happened, Luark warned, "then farewell to our beloved Union of States."

Within four months of this diary entry, the guns of the Confederate States of America fired on a federal fort in South Carolina, and the Civil War began. Luark's fears, Douglass's hopes, and Lincoln's and Allston's preparations for responsibility all became realities. The explanation of the peril and dissolution of the Union forms the theme of this chapter.

Such a calamitous event as Civil War had numerous causes, large and small. The reactions of Allston, Douglass, and Luark to Lincoln's election suggest some of them: moral duties, sectional politics, growing apprehensions over emotional agitators, and a concern for freedom and independence on the part of blacks, white southerners, and western farmers. But as Douglass understood, by 1860, it was clear that "slavery is the real issue, the single bone of contention between all parties and sections. It is the one disturbing force, and explains the confused and irregular motion of our political machine."

George Caleb Bingham's *Stump Speaking* (1856) captures the democratic energy of politics at mid-century. Note the Lincolnlike figure sitting to the right. *(From the Art Collection of Bank of America)*

This chapter analyzes how the momentous issue of slavery disrupted the political system and eventually the Union itself. We will look at how four major developments between 1848 and 1861 contributed to the Civil War: first, a sectional dispute over the extension of slavery into the western territories; second, the breakdown of the political party system; third, growing cultural differences in the views and lifestyles of southerners and northerners; and fourth, intensifying emotional and ideological polarization between the two regions over losing their way of life and sacred republican rights at the hands of the other. A preview of civil war, bringing all four causes together, occurred in 1855-1856 in Kansas. Eventually, emotional events, mistrust, and irreconcilable differences made conflict inevitable. The election of Lincoln was the spark that touched off the conflagration of civil war, with all its "train of horrors."

SLAVERY IN THE TERRITORIES

Senator Lewis Cass (chapter 13) had been wrong when he predicted that the western territories were areas of individual freedom where civilization would advance and political and social harmony would prevail. As many migrants and residents discovered, personal costs attended the American march westward. White migrations threatened both the safety and the cultural integrity of Native Americans and Mexicans whose land stood in the way. They also caused a collision of Yankees and slaveholders.

The North and the South had contained their differences over slavery, with only occasional difficulties, during the 60 years after the Constitutional Convention. Compromise in 1787 had resolved questions of the slave trade and the matter of counting slaves for congressional representation. Although slavery threatened ("like a fireball in the night," Jefferson had said) the uneasy sectional harmony in 1820, the Missouri Compromise had established a workable balance of free and slave states and had defined a geographic line (36°30') to determine future decisions. In 1833, compromise had defused South Carolina's attempt at nullification, and the gag rule in 1836 had kept the abolitionists' petitions off the floor of Congress.

Each apparent resolution, however, raised the level of emotional conflict between North and South and postponed ultimate settlement of the slavery question. One reason why these compromises temporarily worked was the two-party system, with Whigs and Democrats in both North and South. Party loyalties served as an "antidote," as Van Buren put it, to sectional allegiance. The parties differed over cultural and economic issues, but the volatile issue of slavery was largely kept out of political campaigns and congressional debates. This changed in the late 1840s, and the change would prove catastrophic to the Union.

Free Soil or Constitutional Protection?

When the war with Mexico broke out in 1846, it seemed likely that the United States would acquire new territories in the Southwest. Would they be slave or free? To an appropriations bill to pay for the war, David Wilmot, a congressman from Pennsylvania, added a short amendment declaring that "neither slavery nor involuntary servitude shall ever exist" in any territories acquired from Mexico. The debates in Congress over the Wilmot Proviso were significant because legislators voted not as Whigs and Democrats but as northerners and southerners.

A Boston newspaper prophetically observed that Wilmot's resolution "brought to a head the great question which is about to divide the American people." When the Mexican-American War ended, several solutions were presented to deal with this question of slavery in the territories. The first was the "free soil" idea of preventing any extensions of slavery. But did Congress have the power or right to do so? Two precedents suggested that it did. One was the Northwest Ordinance, which had prohibited the entry of slaves into states created in the Upper Midwest; the other was the Missouri Compromise.

Supporters of free soil had mixed motives. For some, slavery was a moral evil to be attacked and destroyed because it trampled on principles of liberty and equality. But for many northern white farmers looking to move westward, the threat of economic competition with an expanding system of large-scale slave labor was even more serious. Neither did they wish to compete for land with free blacks. As Wilmot put it, his proviso was intended to preserve the area for the "sons of toil, of my own race and own color." Other northerners supported the Wilmot Proviso as a means of restraining what seemed to them the growing political power and "insufferable arrogance" of the "spirit and demands of the Slave Power."

Opposed to the free-soil position were the arguments of Senator John C. Calhoun of South Carolina, expressed in several resolutions introduced in the Senate in 1847. Not only did Congress lack the constitutional right to exclude slavery from the territories, Calhoun argued, but it had a positive duty to protect it. The Wilmot Proviso, therefore, was unconstitutional, as was the Missouri Compromise, and any other federal act that prevented slaveholders from taking their slave property into the territories of the United States.

Economic, political, and moral considerations stood behind the Calhoun position. Many southerners hungered for new cotton lands in the West and Southwest, even in Central America and the Caribbean. Politically, southerners feared that northerners wanted to trample on their liberties—namely, the right to protect their institutions against abolitionism. Southern leaders saw the Wilmot Proviso as a moral issue that raised questions about basic republican principles. One congressman called it "treason to the Constitution," and Senator Robert Toombs of Georgia warned that if Congress passed the proviso, he would favor disunion rather than "degradation."

Popular Sovereignty and the Election of 1848

With such divisive potential, it was natural that many Americans sought a compromise solution to keep slavery out of politics. Polk's secretary of state, James

Buchanan of Pennsylvania, proposed that the Missouri Compromise line be extended through the lands acquired from Mexico to the Pacific Ocean, avoiding thorny questions about the morality of slavery and the constitutionality of congressional authority. So would "popular sovereignty," Senator Cass's proposal to leave decisions about permitting slavery to the local territorial legislature, avoid these issues. The idea appealed to the American democratic belief in local self-government but left many details unanswered. At what point in the progress toward statehood could a territorial legislature decide about slavery? Cass preferred to leave such questions ambiguous, reasoning that both northern and southern politicians would conclude that popular sovereignty favored their interests.

The Democratic party, liking popular sovereignty because it could mean all things to all people, nominated Cass for president in 1848. Cass denounced abolitionists and the Wilmot Proviso but otherwise avoided the issue of slavery. The Democrats, however, cleverly printed two campaign biographies of Cass, one for the South and one for the North.

The Whigs found an even better way to hold the party together by evading the slavery issue. Rejecting

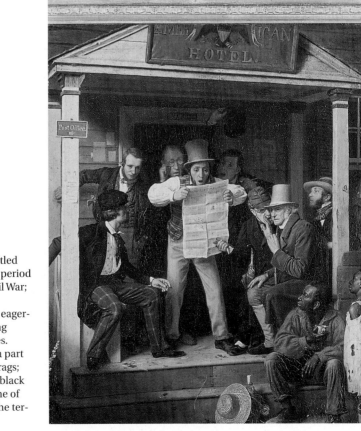

This 1848 painting by Richard Caton Woodville, titled *War News from Mexico,* captures the mood of the period from the Mexican-American War through the Civil War; in towns across the country, outside of countless "American Hotels," the American people listened eagerly to the latest news in an era of steadily worsening political, socioeconomic, and constitutional crises. Separate from the men on the porch, but clearly a part of the picture, are a black father and daughter in rags; they await the war news with special interest, for black Americans would have most to lose by an outcome of the war that led to the expansion of slavery into the territories. *(National Academy of Design, New York)*

Recovering the Past

SENATE SPEECHES

The history of average, anonymous Americans can be recovered in letters, diaries, folktales, and other nontraditional sources. But in times of political conflict with enormous implications for all Americans, as in the years before the Civil War, historians turn to more conventional sources such as congressional speeches. Recorded in the *Congressional Globe,* these speeches are a revealing means of recovering the substance, tone, and drama of political debate.

Despite the cynical view of American politics held by some European visitors, the mid-nineteenth century was an era of giants in the U.S. Senate: Daniel Webster, Henry Clay, Thomas Hart Benton, John C. Calhoun, William Seward, and Stephen Douglas. When Congress debated a major issue, such as the tariff, nullification, or the extension of slavery, large crowds would pack the Senate galleries. The speeches would then be quickly printed and widely distributed. These spectacular oratorical encounters provided mass entertainment and political instruction. Such was the case with the Senate speeches over the Compromise of 1850. The three principal figures early in the debates were Clay (Kentucky), Calhoun (South Carolina), and Webster (Massachusetts), each of whom delivered a great address crowning a long, distinguished career.

Born within five years of each other as the American Revolution was ending (1777–1782), each man began his political career in the House of Representatives in the era of the War of 1812. Each served a term as secretary of state; in addition, Clay was speaker of the House and Calhoun secretary of war and vice president. Each served for over a decade in the Senate (Clay, 13 years; Calhoun, 15 years; Webster, 19 years). Each was a party leader, Clay and Webster of the Whigs and Calhoun of the Democrats. During their 40 years of public service, they represented strong nationalistic positions as well as their various states and sections. All three were candidates for presi-dent between 1824 and 1844. All three spent most of their careers in the political shadow of Andrew Jackson, and all three had serious conflicts with him.

Many years of political and ideological conflict with each other not only sharpened their oratorical skills but also led to mutual respect. Webster said of Calhoun that he was "the ablest man in the Senate. He could have demolished Newton, Calvin, or even John Locke as a logician." Calhoun said of Clay, "He is a bad man, but by god, I love him." And "Old Man Eloquent" himself, John Quincy Adams, said of Webster that he was "the most consummate orator of modern times."

It was therefore a momentous event when they each prepared speeches and met for one last encounter early in 1850. Clay was over 70 years old and in failing health, but he came out of retirement to try to keep the Union together. He defended his compromise proposals in a four-hour speech spread over two days, February 5 and 6. The Senate galleries were so packed that listeners were pushed into hallways and even into the rotunda of the Capitol. Copies of his speech were in such demand that over 100,000 were printed.

A month later, on March 7, the scene was repeated as Webster rose to join Clay in defending the compromise. Three days earlier, although too ill to deliver the speech himself, Calhoun had "tottered into the Senate" on the arm of a friend to hear James Mason of Virginia read his rejection of the compromise. Within a month, Calhoun was dead. Clay and Webster followed him to the grave two years later, and Senate leadership passed on to Seward, Douglas, and a new generation of Senate giants.

As you read the excerpts from each speech, try to imagine yourself sitting in the gallery overlooking the Senate floor, listening to each man and absorbing the drama of the moment. How do the oratorical styles differ? Which passages convey the most emotional power? Which speaker is most persuasive to you? Why? To what extent do the three agree on the fugitive slave issue?

John C. Calhoun

March 4, 1850
Having now, Senators, explained what it is that endangers the Union, and traced it to its cause, and explained its nature and character, the question again recurs—How can the Union be saved? To this I answer, there is but one way by which it can be—and that is—by adopting such measures as will satisfy the States belonging to the Southern section, that they can remain in the Union consistently with their honor and their safety....

But will the North agree to this? It is for her to answer the question. But, I will say, she cannot refuse, if she has half the love of the Union which she professes to have, or without justly exposing herself to the charge that her love of power and aggrandizement is far greater than her love of the Union. At all events, the responsibility of saving the Union rests on the North, and not on the South....

Henry Clay

February 5–6, 1850
I have seen many periods of great anxiety, of peril, and of danger in this country, and I have never before risen to address any assemblage so oppressed, so appalled, and so anxious; and sir, I hope it will not be out of place to do here, what again and again I have done in my private chamber, to implore of Him who holds the destinies of nations and individuals in His hands, to bestow upon our country His blessing, to calm the violence and rage of party, to still passion, to allow reason once more to resume its empire....

Mr. President, it is passion, passion-party, party, and intemperance—that is all I dread in the adjustment of the great questions which unhappily at this time divide our distracted country. Sir, at this moment we have in the legislative bodies of this Capitol and in the States, twenty old furnaces in full blast, emitting heat, and passion, and intemperance, and diffusing them throughout the whole extent of this broad land. Two months ago all was calm in comparison to the present moment. All now is uproar, confusion, and menace to the existence of the Union, and to the happiness and safety of this people....

Sir, when I came to consider this subject, there were two or three general purposes which it seemed to me to be most desirable, if possible, to accomplish. The one was, to settle all the controverted questions arising out of the subject of slavery.... I therefore turned my attention to every subject connected with this institution of slavery, and out of which controverted questions had sprung, to see if it were possible or practicable to accommodate and adjust the whole of them....

We are told now, and it is rung throughout this entire country, that the Union is threatened with subversion and destruction. Well, the first question which naturally rises is, supposing the Union to be dissolved,—having all the causes of grievance which are complained of,—How far will a dissolution furnish a remedy for those grievances? If the Union is to be dissolved for any existing causes, it will be dissolved because slavery is interdicted or not allowed to be introduced into the ceded territories; because slavery is threatened to be abolished in the District of Columbia, and because fugitive slaves are not returned, as in my opinion they ought to be, and restored to their masters. These, I believe, will be the causes; if there be any causes, which can lead to the direful event to which I have referred....

Mr. President, I am directly opposed to any purpose of secession, of separation. I am for staying within the Union, and defying any portion of this Union to expel or drive me out of the Union.

Daniel Webster

March 7, 1850
Mr. President: I wish to speak to-day, not as a Massachusetts man, nor as a Northern man, but as an American, and a member of the Senate of the United States....

I speak to-day for the preservation of the Union. "Hear me for my cause." I speak to-day, out of a solicitous and anxious heart, for the restoration to the country of that quiet and that harmony which make the blessing of this Union so rich, and so dear to us all.... I shall bestow a little attention, Sir, upon these various grievances existing on the one side and on the other. I begin with complaints of the South ... and especially to one which has in my opinion just foundation; and that is, that there has been found at the North, among individuals and among legislators, a disinclination to perform fully their constitutional duties in regard to the return of persons bound to service who have escaped into the free States. In that respect, the South, in my judgment, is right, and the North is wrong. Every member of every Northern legislature is bound by oath, like every other officer in the country, to support the Constitution of the United States; and the article of the Constitution which says to these States they shall deliver up fugitives from service is as binding in honor and conscience as any other article....*

Where is the line to be drawn? What States are to secede? What is to remain American? What am I to be? An American no longer? Am I to become a sectional man, a local man, a separatist, with no country in common with the gentlemen who sit around me here, or who fill the other house of Congress? Heaven forbid! Where is the flag of the republic to remain? Where is the eagle still to tower? or is he to cower, and shrink, and fall to the ground?

Henry Clay, they nominated the Mexican-American War hero, General Zachary Taylor, a Louisiana slaveholder. Taylor compared himself with Washington as a "no party" man above politics. This was about all he stood for. Southern Whigs supported Taylor because they thought he might understand the burdens of slaveholding, and northern Whigs were pleased that he took no stand on the Wilmot Proviso.

The evasions of the two major parties disappointed Calhoun, who tried to create a new unified southern party. His "Address to the People of the Southern States" threatened secession and called for a united stand against further attempts to interfere with the southern right to extend slavery. Although only 48 of 121 southern representatives signed the address, Calhoun's argument raised the specter of secession and disunion.

Warnings also came from the North. A New York Democratic faction bolted to support Van Buren for president. At first, the split had more to do with internal state politics than moral principles, but it soon involved the question of slavery in the territories. Disaffected "conscience" Whigs from Massachusetts, unhappy with a slaveholder as their party standard-bearer, also explored a third-party alternative. These groups met in Buffalo, New York, to form the Free-Soil party and nominate Van Buren for president. The platform of the new party, an uneasy mixture of ardent abolitionists and opponents of free blacks moving into

western lands, pledged to fight for "free soil, free speech, free labor and free men."

General Taylor won easily, largely because defections from Cass to the Free-Soilers cost the Democrats New York and Pennsylvania. Although weakened, the two-party system survived. Purely sectional parties had failed. The Free-Soilers took only about 10 percent of the popular vote, and no electoral votes.

The Compromise of 1850

Taylor won by avoiding slavery questions. But as president he had to deal with them. As he was inaugurated in 1849, four compelling issues faced the nation. First, the rush of some 80,000 unruly gold miners to California qualified it for statehood. But California's entry as a free state would upset the balance between slave and free states in the Senate that had prevailed since 1820.

The unresolved status of the Mexican cession in the Southwest posed a second problem. The longer the area remained unorganized, the louder local inhabitants called for an application of either the Wilmot Proviso or the Calhoun doctrine. The Texas–New Mexico boundary was also disputed, Texas claiming everything east of Santa Fe. Northerners feared that Texas might split into five or six slave states.

A third problem, especially for abolitionists, was the existence of slavery and one of the largest slave markets in North America in the nation's capital.

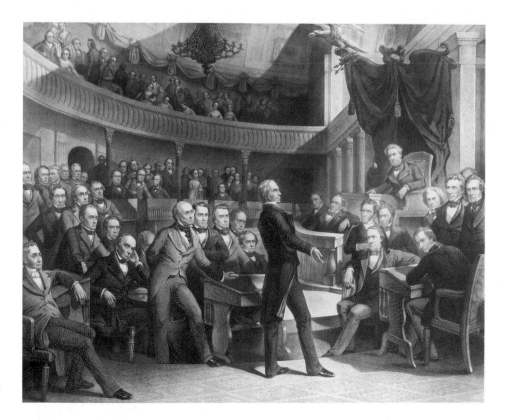

Henry Clay argues for the compromise package of 1850 in this painting by R. Whitechurch, titled *The United States Senate, 1850.* Clay warned that failure to adopt his bill would lead to "furious" and "bloody" civil war. *(Library of Congress)*

Fourth, southerners resented the lax federal enforcement of the Fugitive Slave Act of 1793. They called for a stronger act that would end protection for runaways fleeing along the Underground Railroad to Canada.

Although Taylor was a newcomer to politics (he had never even voted in a presidential election before 1848), he tackled these problems in a statesmanlike, if evasive, manner. Sidestepping the issue of slavery in the territories, he invited California and New Mexico to apply immediately for statehood, presumably as free states. But soon he alienated both southern supporters like Calhoun and mainstream Whig leaders like Clay and Webster.

Early in 1850, the old compromiser Henry Clay sought to regain control of the Whig party by proposing solutions to the divisive issues before the nation. With Webster's support, Clay introduced a series of resolutions in an omnibus package intended to settle these issues once and for all. The stormy debates, great speeches, and political maneuvering that followed provided a crucial and dramatic moment in American history. Yet despite some 70 speeches on behalf of the compromise, the Senate defeated Clay's Omnibus Bill. The tired and disheartened 73-year-old Clay left Washington, hoping to regain his strength. He never did, and soon died. Into the gap stepped a new compromiser, Senator Stephen Douglas of Illinois, who saw that Clay's resolutions had a better chance of passing if voted on individually. Under Douglas's leadership, and with the support of Millard Fillmore, who succeeded to the presidency upon Taylor's sudden death, a series of bills was finally passed.

The so-called Compromise of 1850 put Clay's resolutions, slightly altered, into law. First, California entered the Union as a free state, ending the balance of free and slave states, 16 to 15. Second, territorial governments were organized in New Mexico and Utah, letting the people there decide whether to permit slavery. The Texas–New Mexico border was settled, denying Texas the disputed area. In return, the federal government gave Texas $10 million to pay debts owed to Mexico. Third, the slave trade, but not slavery, was abolished in the District of Columbia.

The fourth and most controversial part of the compromise was the Fugitive Slave Act, containing many provisions that offended northerners. One denied alleged fugitives a jury trial, leaving special cases for decision by commissioners (who were paid $5 for setting a fugitive free but $10 for returning a fugitive). An especially repugnant provision compelled northern citizens to assist in the enforcement of the act by hunting down runaway slaves and turning them in.

Consequences of Compromise

The Compromise of 1850 was the last attempt to keep slavery out of politics. How well it succeeded in doing so is debatable. Voting behavior on the several bills

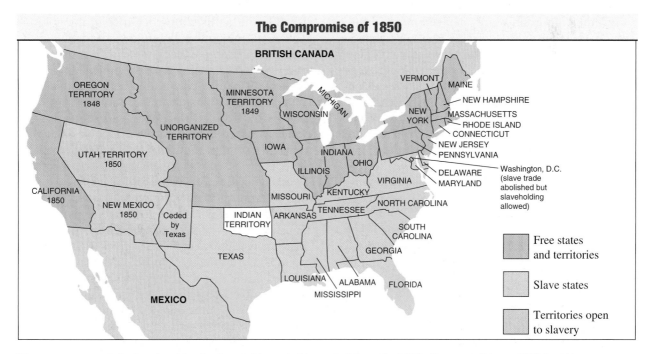

The Compromise of 1850

"I have seen many periods of great anxiety, of peril, and of danger in this country," Henry Clay told the Congress in February 1850, "and I have never before risen to address any assemblage so oppressed, so appalled, and so anxious." What followed were the debates that led eventually to the passage of his great compromise. Can you find three of the four major parts of the bill on the map?

As a group of runaways makes its way north in this painting by Theodor Kaufmann, *On to Liberty* (1867) *(The Metropolitan Museum of Art, gift of Erving and Joyce Wolf, 1982 (1982.443.3)),* the peril of the journey, even if successful, is reflected in this broadside published by Boston abolitionist Theodore Parker, which alerted the city's black community in 1851 to the dangers posed by the Fugitive Slave Act. *(Chicago Public Library)*

varied, with legislators following sectional lines on some issues and party lines on others. Douglas had good reason to feel pleased, celebrating the acts of 1850 as a "final settlement" of the slavery question.

But the compromise only delayed more serious sectional conflict, and it added two new ingredients to American politics. First, political realignment along sectional lines moved closer. Second, although repudiated by most ordinary citizens, ideas like secessionism, disunion, and a "higher law" than the Constitution entered political discussions. People wondered whether the question of slavery in the territories could be compromised away the next time it arose.

Others were immediately upset. The new fugitive slave law angered many northerners because it brought the evils of slavery right into their midst. The owners of runaway slaves hired agents, labeled "kidnappers" in the North, to hunt down fugitives. In a few dramatic episodes, most notably in Boston, literary and religious intellectuals led mass protests to resist slave hunters' efforts to return alleged fugitives to the South. When Senator Webster supported the law, New England abolitionists denounced him as "indescribably base and wicked." Theodore Parker called the new law a "hateful statute of kidnappers," and Ralph Waldo Emerson said it was a "filthy law" that he would not obey.

Frederick Douglass would not obey it either. As a runaway slave himself, he was threatened with arrest and return to the South until friends overcame his objections and purchased his freedom. Douglass still risked harm by his strong defiance of the Fugitive Slave Act. Arguing the "rightfulness of forcible resistance," he urged free blacks to arm themselves and even wondered whether it was justifiable to kill kidnappers. "The only way to make the Fugitive Slave Law a dead letter," he said in Pittsburgh in 1853, "is to make a half dozen or more dead kidnappers." Douglass raised money for black fugitives, hid runaways in his home, and helped hundreds escape to Canada.

Other northerners, white and black, stepped up their work for the Underground Railroad in response to the fugitive slave law. Several states passed "personal liberty laws" that prohibited the use of state officials and institutions in the recovery of fugitive slaves. But most northerners complied. Of some 200 blacks arrested in the first six years of the law, only 15 were rescued, and only 3 of these by force. Failed rescues, in fact, had more emotional impact than successful ones. In two cases in the early 1850s (Thomas Sims in 1851 and Anthony Burns in 1854), angry mobs of abolitionists in Boston, reminiscent of the Revolutionary days of the Tea Party, failed to prevent the forcible return of blacks to the South. These celebrated cases aroused antislavery emotions in more northerners than the abolitionists had been able to do in all their tracts and speeches. Amos Lawrence, a textile tycoon in Massachusetts, wrote of the trial of Anthony Burns that sent him back to the South: "We went to bed one night old fashioned, conservative Compromise Union Whigs and waked up stark mad abolitionists."

Longtime abolitionists escalated their rhetoric, fueling emotions over slavery in the aftermath of the Fugitive Slave Act. In an Independence Day speech in 1852, Frederick Douglass wondered, "What, to the American slave, is your 4th of July?" It was, he said, the day that revealed to the slave the "gross injustice and cruelty to which he is the constant victim." To a slave, the American claims of national greatness were vain and empty; the "shouts of liberty and equality" were "hollow mockery, . . . mere bombast, fraud, deception, impiety, and hypocrisy." Douglass's speeches, like those of another former slave, Sojourner Truth, took on an increasingly strident tone in the early 1850s.

At a women's rights convention in Akron, Ohio, in 1851, Truth made one of the decade's boldest statements for minority rights. The convention was attended by some clergymen who kept interrupting the pro-

ceedings to heckle female speakers. Up stood Sojourner Truth to speak in words still debated by historians. She pointed to her many years of childbearing and hard, backbreaking work as a slave, crying out in a repetitive refrain, "And ar'n't I a woman?" Referring to Jesus, she asked where he came from: "From God and a woman: Man had nothing to do with Him." Referring to Eve, she concluded, "If the first woman God ever made was strong enough to turn the world upside down all alone, these women together ought to be able to turn it back, and get it right side up again! And now they is asking to do it, the men better let them." Her brief speech silenced the hecklers.

As Truth spoke, another American woman, Harriet Beecher Stowe, was finishing a novel, *Uncle Tom's Cabin*, that would go far toward turning the world upside down and trying to right it again. As politicians were hoping the American people would forget slavery, Stowe's novel brought it to the attention of thousands. She gave readers an absorbing indictment of the horrors of slavery and its immoral impact on both northerners and southerners. Published initially in serial form, each month's chapter ended at a nail-biting dramatic moment. Readers throughout the North cheered Eliza's daring

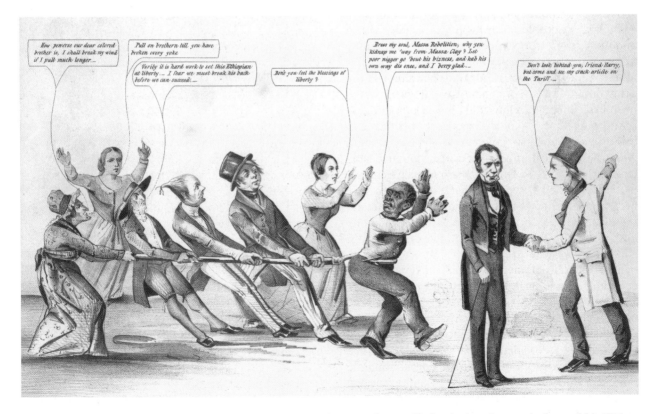

The hypocrisy of the Fugitive Slave Act (part of the Compromise of 1850) and Henry Clay's mixed motives are the focus of this 1851 cartoon. Whites preach the "blessings of liberty" at a free black man they are holding back from freedom as Clay turns his back on the fugitive slave and talks to a northerner about the tariff. *(Library of Congress)*

escape across the ice floes on the Ohio River, cried over Uncle Tom's humanity and Little Eva's death, suffered under the lash of Simon Legree, and rejoiced in the reuniting of black family members.

Although outraging the South when published in full in 1852, *Uncle Tom's Cabin* became one of the all-time best-sellers in American history. In the first year, over 300,000 copies were printed, and Stowe's novel was eventually published in 20 languages. When President Lincoln met Stowe in 1863, he is reported to have said to her: "So you're the little woman who wrote the book that made this great war!"

🖋 POLITICAL DISINTEGRATION

The response to *Uncle Tom's Cabin* and the Fugitive Slave Act indicated that politicians had congratulated themselves too soon for saving the Republic in 1850. Political developments, not all dealing with slavery, were already weakening the ability of political parties—and ultimately the nation—to withstand the passions slavery aroused.

The Apathetic Election of 1852

Political parties, then and now, thrive on their ability to convince voters that their party stands for moral values and economic policies crucially different from those of the opposition. In the period between 1850 and 1854, these differences were blurred, thereby undermining party loyalty. First, both parties scrambled to convince voters that they had favored the Compromise of 1850. In addition, several states rewrote their constitutions and remodeled their laws in the early 1850s, standardizing many political and economic procedures. One effect of these changes was to reduce the number of patronage jobs available for party victors to dispense. Another effect was to regularize the process, begun in the 1830s, for securing banking, railroad, and other corporate charters, removing the role formerly played by the legislature. Both of these weakened the importance of the party in citizens' lives.

The third development that weakened parties was economic. For almost a quarter of a century, Whigs and Democrats had disagreed over such issues as the tariff, money and banking systems, and government support for internal improvements. But economic conditions improved markedly in the early 1850s. In a time of prosperity, party distinctions over economic policies seemed less important. An ample money supply made the revenues of a high tariff less necessary. Moreover, in the rush for railroad charters during the boom of the early 1850s, local connections were more important than national party politics.

Economic issues persisted, but the battles were fought at the local rather than national level. Thus Georgia voters in 1851 disagreed over commercial banking laws, taxes for internal improvements, and, as an Augusta newspaper put it, "the jealousies of the poor who owned no slaves, against the rich slaveholder." In Indiana, where Congressman George Julian observed that people "hate the Negro with a perfect if not a supreme hatred," legislators rewrote the state constitution in 1851, depriving blacks of the rights to vote, attend white schools, and make contracts. Those who could not post a $500 bond were expelled from the state, and an 1852 law made it a crime for blacks to settle in Indiana. In Massachusetts, temperance reform and a law limiting the working day to ten hours were hot issues. Fleeting political alliances developed around particular issues and local personalities. As a Baltimore businessman said, "The two old parties are fast melting away."

CHANGING POLITICAL PARTY SYSTEMS AND LEADERS

It is characteristic of American politics that when the two major parties fail to respond to the pressing issues of the day, third parties are born and major party realignment occurs. This happened in the 1850s over the issue of slavery and its extension into the territories, which resulted in the collapse of the Whigs and the emergence of the Republican party. Note that the "Republican" party begins in one tradition and ends up in the other. Is political realignment happening again in American politics?

First Party System: 1790s–1820s

Republican	Federalist
Jefferson	Hamilton
Madison	John Adams
Monroe	

Transition: 1824 and 1828

Democrat-Republican	National Republican
Jackson	J. Q. Adams

Second Party System: 1830s–1850s

Democrat	Whig
Jackson	Clay
Van Buren	Webster
Calhoun	W. H. Harrison
Polk	

Third Party System: 1856–1890s

Democrat	Republican
Douglas	Lincoln
Pierce	Seward
Buchanan	Grant

The election of 1852 illustrated the lessening significance of political parties. The Whigs nominated General Winfield Scott, another Mexican-American War hero, whom they hoped would repeat Taylor's success four years earlier. With Clay and Webster both dead, party leadership had passed to Senator William Seward of New York, who wanted a president he could influence more successfully than the pro-southern Fillmore. Still, it took 52 ballots to nominate Scott over Fillmore, with serious costs to the party allegiance of southern Whigs. Democrats had their own problems deciding on a candidate. After 49 ballots, in which Cass, Douglas, and Buchanan each held the lead for a time, the party turned to the lackluster Franklin Pierce of New Hampshire as a compromise candidate.

The two parties offered little choice. Both played down issues so as not to widen intraparty divisions. Voter interest diminished. "Genl. Apathy is the strongest candidate out here," was the report from Ohio, while the Baltimore *Sun* remarked that "there is no issue that much interests the people." Democratic prospects were aided by thousands of new Catholic immigrants from Ireland and Germany. Eligible for naturalization and, therefore, the right to vote after only three years, they were influenced by party officials, usually Democrats, who bought their votes with bribes and drinks. Internal conflicts and defections seriously weakened the Whigs, and Pierce won easily, 254 to 42 electoral votes.

The Kansas-Nebraska Act

The Whig party's final disintegration came on a February day in 1854 when southern Whigs stood to support Stephen Douglas's Nebraska bill, thus choosing to be more southern than Whig. The Illinois senator had many reasons for introducing a bill organizing the Nebraska Territory (which included Kansas). As an ardent nationalist and chairman of the Committee on Territories, he was concerned for the continuing development of the West. As a solid citizen of Illinois in a period of explosive railroad building, he wanted the eastern terminus for a transcontinental railroad in Chicago rather than in rival St. Louis. This meant organizing the lands west of Iowa and Missouri.

Politics also played a role. Douglas wanted to recapture the party leadership he had held when he led the fight to pass the Compromise of 1850. He also harbored presidential ambitions. Although he had replaced Cass as the great advocate of popular sovereignty, which won him favor among northern Democrats, he needed the support of southern Democrats. Many southerners, especially slaveholders from Missouri, just east of the Nebraska Territory, opposed the organization of the territory unless it were open to slavery. The problem, as Douglas knew well, was that the entire Nebraska Territory lay north of the line where slavery had been prohibited by the Missouri Compromise.

In George Caleb Bingham's *Verdict of the People* (after 1855), the American flag flies proudly over a happy throng celebrating the outcome of the political process. However, the process of deciding the Kansas-Nebraska Act marked the collapse of the second party system and moved the Union a step closer to disruption and civil war. In an earlier version of the painting, the women on a hotel balcony in the upper right display a banner announcing (ironically?) "Freedom for Virtue." *(Courtesy of the R.W. Norton Art Gallery, Shreveport, Louisiana)*

Douglas's bill, introduced early in 1854, recommended using the principle of popular sovereignty in organizing the Kansas and Nebraska territories. This meant that inhabitants could vote slavery in, thereby violating the Missouri Compromise. Douglas reasoned, however, that the climate and soil of the prairies in Kansas and Nebraska would never support slavery-based agriculture, and the people would decide to be a free state. Therefore, he could win the votes he needed for the railroad without also getting slavery. His bill, then, ignored the Missouri Compromise, simply stating that the state or states created out of the Nebraska Territory would enter the Union "with or without slavery, as their constitution may prescribe at the time of their admission."

Douglas miscalculated. Northerners from his own party immediately attacked him and his bill as a "criminal betrayal of precious rights" and as part of a plot promoting his own presidential ambitions by turning free Nebraska over to "slavery despotism." The outrage among Whigs and abolitionists was even greater. Frederick Douglass branded the act a "hateful" attempt to extend slavery, the result of the "audacious villainy of the slave power."

But Stephen Douglas was a fighter. The more he was attacked, the harder he fought. Eventually his bill passed, but not without seriously damaging the political party system. What began as a railroad measure ended in reopening the question of slavery in the territories that Douglas and others had thought was finally settled in 1850. What began as a way of avoiding conflict ended up in violence over whether Kansas would enter the Union slave or free. What began as a way of strengthening party lines over issues ended up destroying one party (the Whigs), planting deep, irreconcilable divisions in another (the Democrats), and creating two new ones (Know-Nothings and Republicans).

Expansionist "Young America"

The Democratic party was weakened in the early 1850s not only by the Kansas-Nebraska Act but also by an ebullient, expansive energy that led Americans to adventures far beyond Kansas. As republican revolutions erupted in Europe in 1848, Americans greeted them as evidence that the American model of free republican institutions was the wave of the future. Those dedicated to the idea of this continuing national mission, which ironically included the spread of slavery, were called "Young America." An early expression of the spirit of Young America was the enthusiastic reception given the exiled Hungarian revolutionary Louis Kossuth while on a tour of the United States in 1851.

Pierce's platform in 1852 recalled the successful expansionism of the Polk years, declaring that the war with Mexico had been "just and necessary." Many Democrats took their overwhelming victory as a mandate to continue adding territory to the Republic. A Philadelphia newspaper in 1853 described the United States as a nation bound on the "East by sunrise, West by sunset, North by the Arctic Expedition, and South as far as we darn please." Southward expansion into Latin America looked most attractive.

Many of Pierce's diplomatic appointees were southerners interested in adding new cotton-growing lands to the national domain. As ambassador to Mexico, for example, Pierce sent James Gadsden of South Carolina to negotiate with Mexican President Santa Anna for the acquisition of large parts of northern Mexico. Gadsden failed to get all the land he wanted, but he did manage to purchase a strip of desert along the southwest border to build a transcontinental railroad linking the Deep South with the Pacific Coast.

The failure to acquire more territory from Mexico legally did not discourage expansionist Americans from pursuing illegal means. During the 1850s, Texans and Californians staged dozens of raids (called "filibusters") into Mexico. The most daring adventurer of the era was William Walker, a 100-pound Tennessean with a zest for danger and power. After migrating to southern California, Walker made plans to add slave lands to the country. In 1853, he invaded Lower California (the Baja Peninsula) with fewer than 300 men and declared himself president of the independent Republic of Sonora. Although eventually arrested and tried in the United States, he was acquitted after eight minutes of deliberation.

Back Walker went, invading Nicaragua two years later. He overthrew the government, proclaimed himself to have been elected dictator, and issued a decree legalizing slavery. When the Nicaraguans, with British help, acted to regain control of their country, the U.S. Navy rescued Walker. After a triumphant tour in the South, he tried twice more to conquer Nicaragua. Walker came to a fitting end in 1860 when he was captured and shot by a Honduran firing squad after invading that country.

Undaunted by failures in the Southwest, the Pierce administration looked to the acquisition of Cuba, a Spanish colony many Americans thought destined to be a part of their country. One expansionist even suggested that Cuba physically belonged to the United States because it had been formed by alluvial deposits from the Mississippi River. "What God has joined together let no man put asunder," he said. The acquisition of Cuba was necessary, many maintained, as an extension of America's Manifest Destiny and as an ideal place for expanding the slave-based economy of the southern states.

A decade earlier, the Polk administration had offered $10 million for Cuba, but Spain had refused the offer. Unsuccessful efforts were then made to foment a revolution among Cuban sugar planters, who would then request annexation by the United States. One Latin adventurer organized an invasion of Cuba, launched from New Orleans in 1850. When his attempt failed, he was executed, and hundreds of captured comrades were sent to Spain. The citizens of New Orleans rioted in protest, storming the Spanish consulate, which forced an embarrassed Congress to pay an indemnity. A few years later, a former governor of Mississippi, with the support of his friend, Secretary of War Jefferson Davis, planned to raise $1 million and 50,000 troops to invade the island. The proposed expedition, intended to carve Cuba into several new slave states, was aborted.

Although President Pierce did not support these illegal efforts, his administration did want Cuba. Secretary of State William Marcy instructed the emissary to Spain, Pierre Soulé, to offer $130 million for Cuba. If that failed, Marcy suggested stronger measures. In 1854, the secretary arranged for Soulé and the American ministers to France and England to meet in Belgium to consider options. The result was the Ostend Manifesto, a document intended to pressure Spain to sell Cuba to the United States. It also provides a fascinating glimpse of American expansionist attitudes.

The manifesto argued that Cuba "belongs naturally" to the United States. Both geographically and eco-nomically, the fortunes and interests of Cubans and southerners were so "blended" that they were "one people with one destiny." Trade and commerce in the hemisphere would "never be secure" until Cuba was part of the United States. Moreover, southern slave-holders feared that a slave rebellion would "Africanize" Cuba, like Haiti, suggesting all kinds of "horrors to the white race" in the nearby southern United States. The American acquisition of Cuba was necessary, there-fore, to "preserve our rectitude and self-respect."

If Spain refused to sell the island, the ministers threatened a revolution in Cuba with American sup-port. If that should fail, the manifesto warned, "we should be justified in wresting it from Spain." Even Secretary Marcy was shocked when he received the document from Belgium, and he quickly rejected it. Like the Kansas-Nebraska Act, Democrats who advo-cated the expansion of slavery urged approval of the Ostend Manifesto. The outraged reaction of northern-ers in both cases divided and further weakened the Democratic Party.

Nativism, Know-Nothings, and Republicans

Foreign immigration damaged an already enfeebled Whig party and created concern among many native-born Americans. To the average hardworking Protestant American, the foreigners pouring into the cities and following the railroads westward spoke

The American (Know-Nothing) party campaign against the immigrants is dramatically shown in this cartoon of a whiskey-drinking Irishman and beer-barreled German stealing the ballot box while native-born Americans fight at the election poll in the background. The Know-Nothing flag (right) makes starkly clear the origin of the danger. One can only imagine what American Indians thought of this banner. *(New York Public Library, Astor, Lenox & Tilden Foundations)*

unfamiliar languages, wore funny clothes, drank alcohol freely in grogshops, and increased crime and pauperism. Moreover, they seemed content with a lower standard of living and would work for lower wages than American workers, thus threatening their jobs.

Still worse, these Irish and German immigrants were part of an unprecedented growth in the Catholic Church. By the 1850s, there were nearly three million Catholics in the United States, not only in eastern cities but expanding westward into the Ohio valley (Germans in Wheeling, Cincinnati, and St. Louis) and south along old French Canadian trade routes through Detroit, Green Bay, and Vincennes. A surprising and, to many, disturbing development was the Catholic success in converting Protestants. As one Catholic put it, it was "a time when great throngs of Americans began to flock to the Roman Catholic Church despite bitterly intense propaganda and overt opposition." Although overstated, two notable conversions in 1844 compelled Protestant Americans to take the threat seriously. Orestes Brownson, a lifelong Jacksonian Democrat and spiritual seeker, moved successively through Congregationalism, Presbyterianism, Unitarianism, and Transcendentalism until finally converting to a Catholicism he argued was fully compatible with democracy. His disciple, the Methodist German immigrant Isaac Hecker, converted to Catholicism two months earlier in 1844. Joining the Redemptorist order, Hecker served poor German immigrants and, with papal permission, shifted in the 1850s to the active recruiting of Protestants.

Led by the Redemptorists and Jesuits, over 400 parish mission revivals and retreats were held in the 1850s in an aggressive effort to convert urban American Protestants to Roman Catholicism. "All America can be reformed," one religious superior told a group of seminarians in 1856, calling them "instruments in the hands of God which He will use to effect a wonderful change—a spiritual revolution in this country." Sending their children to Catholic schools offended Protestants. Perhaps worst of all, many charged that Catholic immigrants corrupted American politics.

Most Catholics preferred the Democratic party out of traditional loyalties and because Democrats were less inclined than Whigs to interfere with religion, schooling, drinking, and other aspects of personal behavior. It was mostly former Whigs, therefore, who in 1854 founded the American party to oppose the new immigrants. Members wanted a longer period of naturalization to guarantee the "vital principles of Republican Government" and pledged themselves never to vote for Irish Catholics for public office, because it was assumed that their highest loyalty was to the pope in Rome. They also agreed to keep information about their order secret. If asked, they would say, "I know nothing." Hence, they were dubbed the Know-Nothing party.

The Know-Nothings were overwhelmingly a party of the middle and lower classes, workers who worried about their jobs and wages and farmers and small-town Americans who worried about disruptive new forces in their lives. As one New Yorker put it in 1854, "Roman Catholicism is feared more than American slavery." It was widely believed that Catholics slavishly obeyed the orders of their priests, who represented a Church associated with European despotism. The opposition of the Catholic Church to the revolutionary movements of 1848 in Europe intensified the fears of many Protestant Americans that Catholic voters and the Catholic revivals deeply threatened their democratic order. The call to parish missions by Hecker to "make Yankeedom the Rome of the modern world" confirmed their fears. In the 1854 and 1855 elections, the Know-Nothings gave anti-Catholicism a national political focus for the first time.

Although nativists argued that papism would subvert freedom and other republican values, others maintained that the slave power of the South was the chief danger. No sooner had the debates over Nebraska ended than a group of former Whigs and Free-Soilers met and formed the nucleus of another new party, called the Republican party. Concerned about southern expansionism, as reflected in the Kansas-Nebraska Act debates, the Ostend Manifesto, and plans to build a transcontinental railroad from the South to California on land acquired in the Gadsden Purchase, the party sought to respond to popular sentiments by mobilizing sectional fears and ethnic and religious concerns.

Composed almost entirely of northerners, former "conscience" Whigs, and disaffected Democrats, the Republican party combined four main elements. The first group—led by William Seward, Senators Charles Sumner of Massachusetts and Salmon P. Chase of Ohio, and Congressmen Joshua Giddings of Ohio and George Julian of Indiana—was fired by a moral fervor to prohibit slavery in the territories. They also sought to divorce the federal government from the support of slavery by freeing slaves in the District of Columbia, repealing the Fugitive Slave Act, and eliminating the internal slave trade. There were, however, limits to the idealism of most Republicans. A more moderate and larger group, typified by Abraham Lincoln of Illinois, opposed slavery in the western territories only but would not interfere with it where it already existed. This group also indicated that it would not support efforts to achieve equal rights for northern free blacks.

Republicans were anti-Catholic as well as antislavery. This third element of the party, reflecting the tra-

THE EMERGING THIRD PARTY SYSTEM: PRESIDENTIAL ELECTIONS, 1852–1860				
Year	Candidates	Party	Popular Vote	Electoral Vote
1852	FRANKLIN PIERCE	Democrat	1,601,474 (51%)	254
	Winfield Scott	Whig	1,386,578 (44%)	42
	John P. Hale	Free-Soil	156,149 (5%)	0
1856	JAMES BUCHANAN	Democrat	1,838,169 (45%)	174
	John C. Frémont	Republican	1,335,264 (33%)	114
	Millard Fillmore	American	874,534 (22%)	8
1860	ABRAHAM LINCOLN	Republican	1,866,352 (40%)	180
	Steven A. Douglas	Democrat	1,375,157 (29%)	12
	John C. Breckinridge	Democrat	847,953 (18%)	72
	John Bell	Constitutional Union	589,581 (13%)	39

Note: Winners' names appear in capital letters.

ditional Whig reformist impulse, felt responsible for cleansing America of its sins of intemperance, impiety, parochial schooling, and other forms of immorality. Another sin included voting for Democrats, who were accused of catering to the "grog shops, foreign vote, and Catholic brethren" by combining the "forces of Jesuitism and Slavery."

The fourth element of the Republican party, a Whig legacy from the American System of Henry Clay, included those who wanted the federal government to

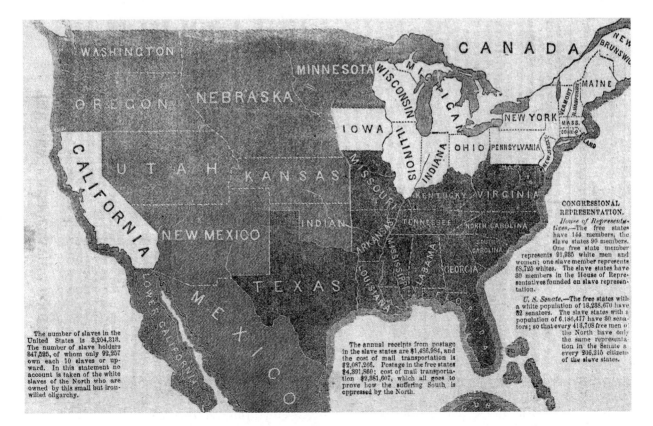

This map was part of a Frémont campaign handbill in 1856, which contrasted the white "free soil" states (including Canada) with the slave states shown in black. Frémont and the Republicans advocated "the extension of free labor" in contrast to his rival, James Buchanan, who championed the extension of slavery. The use of gray for all of the U.S. territories (and Mexico and Cuba) seems to anticipate the Dred Scott decision in 1857, which opened those areas to slavery. Although Minnesota and Oregon would soon come into the Union as "white" free states, taken together, the vastness of the black and the gray areas posed an ominous threat to liberty, according to Republican northerners. The written messages, which are difficult to read, reinforce the Republican point that the slave states, because of the 3/5s rule (which counted slaves in figuring representatives in the House), were overrepresented in Congress. *(Danzer Map Collection)*

promote commercial and industrial development and the dignity of labor. This fourth group, like the anti-slavery and anti-Catholic elements, had a strong ideological faith that a system of free labor led to progress. At the heart of both the new party and the future of America were hardworking, middle-class, mobile, free white laborers—farmers, small businessmen, and independent craftsmen. As the Springfield *Republican* said in 1856, the Republican party's strength came from "those who work with their hands, who live and act independently, who hold the stakes of home and family, of farm and workshop, of education and freedom—these as a mass are enrolled in the Republican ranks."

The strengths of the Republican and Know-Nothing (American) parties were tested in 1856. Which party could best oppose the Democrats? The American party nominated Fillmore, who had strong support in the Upper South and border states. The Republicans chose John C. Frémont, a Free-Soiler from Missouri with virtually no political experience. The Democrats nominated James Buchanan of Pennsylvania, commonly known as a "northern man with southern principles." Frémont's strength in the North helped him carry several free states, while Fillmore won only Maryland. Buchanan, taking advantage of the divided opposition, won the election, but with only 45 percent of the popular vote.

After 1856, the Know-Nothings died out, largely because Republican leaders cleverly redirected nativist fears—and voters—into their broader program, but also because Know-Nothing secrecy, hatreds, and occasional violent attacks on Catholic voters damaged their image. The Know-Nothings represented a powerful current in American politics that would return each time social and economic changes seemed to threaten the nation. It became convenient to label certain people "un-American" and seek to root them out. Thus, the Know-Nothing party disappeared after 1856, but nativism did not.

⌒ KANSAS AND THE TWO CULTURES

However appealing nativist issues were for many Americans, the problem of slavery was the issue that would not disappear. As Democrats sought ways of expanding slavery and other American institutions westward across the Plains and south into Cuba in the mid-1850s, Republicans wanted to halt the advance of slavery to prove to the world, as Seward said, that the American "experiment in self-government" still worked. In 1854, Lincoln worried that it was slavery that "deprives our republican example of its just influence in the world." The specific cause of his concern was the likelihood that slavery might be extended into

Kansas as a result of the passage that year of Stephen Douglas's Kansas-Nebraska Act.

Competing for Kansas

During the congressional debates over the Kansas-Nebraska bill, Seward had accepted the challenge of slave-state senators to "engage in competition for the virgin soil of Kansas." The passage of the Kansas-Nebraska Act in 1854 opened the way for proslavery and antislavery forces to meet physically and to compete over whether Kansas would become a slave or free state. No sooner had the bill passed Congress than Eli Thayer founded the Massachusetts Emigrant Aid Society to recruit free-soil settlers to go to Kansas. From New York, Frederick Douglass called for "companies of emigrants from the free states . . . to possess the goodly land." By the summer of 1855, about 1,200 New England colonists had migrated to Kansas.

One of the migrants was Julia Louisa Lovejoy, a Vermont minister's wife. As a Mississippi riverboat carried her into a slave state for the first time, she described the dilapidated plantation homes of the monotonous Missouri shore as reflecting the "blighting mildew of slavery." By the time Julia and her husband arrived in the Kansas Territory, she had concluded that the "inhabitants and morals" of slaveholding Missourians who had moved into Kansas were of an "*undescribably repulsive* and undesirable character." To Julia Lovejoy, northerners came to bring the "energetic Yankee" virtues of morality and economic enterprise to the drunken, unclean slaveholders of the Southwest.

Perhaps she had in mind David Atchison, Democratic senator from Missouri. Atchison believed that Congress had an obligation to protect slavery in the territories, thereby permitting Missouri slaveholders to move into Kansas. As early as 1853, he pledged himself "to extend the institutions of Missouri over the Territory at whatever sacrifice of blood or treasure." He described New England migrants as "negro thieves" and "abolition tyrants." He recommended to fellow Missourians that they defend their property and interests "with the *bayonet* and with *blood*" and, if need be, "to kill every God-damned abolitionist in the district."

Under Atchison's inflammatory leadership, secret societies sprang up in the Missouri counties adjacent to Kansas. They vowed to combat the Free-Soilers. One editor exclaimed that northerners came to Kansas "for the express purpose of stealing, running off and hiding runaway negroes from Missouri [and] taking to their own bed . . . a stinking negro wench." It was not slaveholders but New Englanders, he said, who were immoral, uncivilized, and hypocritical. Rumors of 20,000 such Massachusetts migrants spurred Missourians to action. Thousands poured across the border late in 1854 to vote on whether to permit slavery in the territory. Twice as many ballots were cast as the number of registered voters, and in one polling place only 20 of over 600 voters were legal residents.

The proslavery forces overreacted to their fear of the New England migrants and their intentions. The permanent population of Kansas consisted primarily of migrants from Missouri and other border states who were more concerned with land titles than slavery. They opposed any blacks—slave or free—moving into their state. As one clergyman put it, "I kem to Kansas to live in a free state and I don't want niggers a-trampin' over my grave."

In March 1855, a second election was held to select a territorial legislature. The pattern of border crossings, intimidation, and illegal voting was repeated. Atchison himself, drinking "considerable whiskey" along the way, led a band of armed men across the state line to vote and frighten would-be Free-Soil voters away. Not surprisingly, a small minority of eligible voters elected a proslavery territorial legislature. Free-Soilers, meanwhile, staged their own constitutional convention in Lawrence and created a Free-Soil government at Topeka. It banned blacks from the state. The proslavery legislature settled first in

Shawnee Mission and then in Lecompton, giving Kansas two governments.

The struggle shifted to Washington, where President Pierce, who could have nullified the illegal election, did nothing. Congress debated the wrongs in Kansas and sent an investigating committee, which further inflamed passions. Throughout 1855, the call to arms grew more strident. One proslavery newspaper invited southerners to bring their weapons and "send the scoundrels" from the North "back to whence they came, or . . . to hell, it matters not which." In South Carolina, Robert Allston wrote his son Benjamin that he was "raising men and money . . . to counteract the effect of the Northern hordes. . . . We are disposed to fight the battle of our rights . . . on the field of Kansas."

Both sides saw Kansas as a holy battleground for their version of moral right. An Alabaman, Colonel Jefferson Buford, sold his slaves to raise money to hire an army of 300 men to fight for slavery in Kansas, promising free land to his recruits. A Baptist minister blessed their departure from Montgomery, promised them God's favor, and gave each man a Bible. Northern Christians responded in kind. At Yale University, the noted minister Henry Ward Beecher presented 25 Bibles and 25 Sharps rifles to young men who would go fight for the Lord in Kansas. "There are

Led by Senator David Atchison, thousands of gun-toting Missourians crossed into Kansas in 1854 and 1855 to vote illegally for a proslavery territorial government. The ensuing bloodshed made Kansas a preview of the Civil War. *(The Newberry Library, Chicago)*

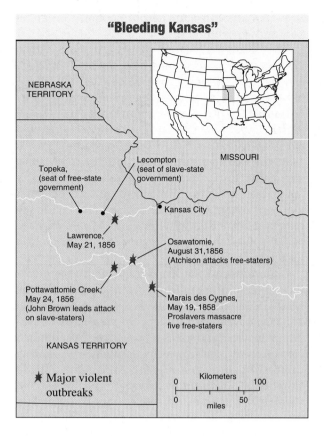

"Bleeding Kansas"

NEBRASKA TERRITORY

MISSOURI

Topeka, (seat of free-state government)

Lecompton (seat of slave-state government)

Kansas City

Lawrence, May 21, 1856

Osawatomie, August 31,1856 (Atchison attacks free-staters)

Pottawattomie Creek, May 24, 1856 (John Brown leads attack on slave-staters)

Marais des Cygnes, May 19, 1858 Proslavers massacre five free-staters

KANSAS TERRITORY

✦ Major violent outbreaks

Kilometers
0   100
0   50
miles

times," he said, "when self-defense is a religious duty. If that duty was ever imperative it is now, and in Kansas." Beecher suggested that rifles would be of greater use than Bibles. Missourians dubbed them "Beecher's Bibles" and vowed, as one newspaper put it, "Blood for Blood! . . . for each drop spilled, we shall require one hundred fold!"

"Bleeding Kansas"

As civil war threatened in Kansas, a Brooklyn poet, Walt Whitman, heralded American democracy in his epic poem *Leaves of Grass* (1855). Whitman identified himself as the embodiment of average Americans "of every hue and caste, . . . of every rank and religion." Ebulliently, Whitman embraced urban mechanics, southern woodcutters, planters' sons, runaway slaves, mining camp prostitutes, and a catalog of others in his poetic celebration of "the word Democratic, the word En-Masse." At the same time, Whitman's faith in the American masses faltered in the mid-1850s. He worried that a knife plunged into the "breast" of the Union would bring on the "red blood of civil war."

As Whitman feared, blood flowed in Kansas. In May 1856, supported by a prosouthern federal marshal, a mob entered Lawrence, smashed the offices and presses of a Free-Soil newspaper, fired several cannonballs into the Free State Hotel, and destroyed homes and shops. Three nights later, motivated by vengeance and a feeling that he was doing God's will, John Brown led a small New England band, including four of his sons, to a proslavery settlement near Pottawatomie Creek. There they dragged five men out of their cabins and despite the terrified entreaties of their wives, hacked them to death with swords.

Violence also entered the halls of Congress. That same week, abolitionist Senator Charles Sumner delivered a tirade that became known as "The Crime Against Kansas." He lashed out at the "murderous robbers" and "incredible atrocities of the Assassins and . . . Thugs" from the South. With nasty invective, he accused proslavery Senate leaders, especially Atchison and Andrew Butler of South Carolina, of cavorting with the "harlot, Slavery." Two days later, Butler's nephew, Congressman Preston Brooks, avenged the honor of his colleague by beating Sumner senseless with his cane as he sat at his Senate desk.

The sack of Lawrence, the massacre at Pottawatomie Creek, and the caning of Sumner set off a minor civil war, which historians have called "Bleeding Kansas." It lasted throughout the summer. Crops were burned, homes were destroyed, fights broke out in saloons and streets, and night raiders tortured and murdered their enemies. For residents like Charles Lines, who just wanted to farm his land in peace, it was impossible to remain neutral. Lines hoped his neighbors near Lawrence would avoid "involving themselves in trouble." But when proslavery forces seized a mild-mannered neighbor, bound him, tortured him, and left him to die, Lines joined the battle. He wrote to a friend that "blood must end in the triumph of the right."

Even before the bleeding of Kansas began, the New York *Tribune* warned, "We are two peoples. We are a people for Freedom and a people for Slavery. Between the two, conflict is inevitable." As the moral rhetoric and violence in Kansas demonstrated, competing visions of two separate cultures for the future destiny of the United States were at stake. Despite many similarities between the North and the South, the gap between the two sides widened as the hostilities of the 1850s increased.

Northern Views and Visions

The North saw itself, as Julia Lovejoy suggested, as a prosperous land of bustling commerce and expanding, independent agriculture. Northern farmers and workers were self-made free men who believed in individualism and democracy. The "free labor system" of the North, as both Seward and Lincoln often said, offered equality of opportunity and upward mobility. Both generated more wealth. Although the North contained many growing cities, northerners revered the values of the small towns that spread from New England across the Upper Midwest. These values included a respect for the rights of the people, tempered by the rule of law; individual enterprise, balanced by a concern for one's neighbors; and a fierce morality rooted in Calvinist Protestantism. Northerners would regulate morality—by persuasion if possible but by legislation if necessary—to remove the sins of irreligion, illiteracy, and intemperance from American society. It was no accident that the ideas of universal public education and laws against the sale and consumption of alcohol both began in New England.

Northerners valued the kind of republican government that guaranteed the rights of free men, enabling them to achieve economic progress. Specifically, this meant supporting government action to promote free labor, industrial growth, some immigration, foreign trade (protected by tariffs), and the development of railroads and free farm homesteads westward across the continent. Energetic mobility both westward and upward would dissolve state, regional, and class loyalties and increase the sense of nationhood. A strong Union could achieve national and even international greatness. These were the conditions, befitting a chosen people, that would, as Seward put it, spread American institutions around the world and "renovate the condition of mankind." These were also the ideological principles of the Republican party.

Only free men could achieve economic progress and moral society. Therefore, the worst sin in the northerner's view was the loss of one's freedom. Slavery was the root of all evil. It was, Seward said, "incompatible with all . . . the elements of the security, welfare, and greatness of nations." The South, then, represented the antithesis of everything that northerners saw as good. Southerners were unfree, backward, economically stagnant, uneducated, lawless, immoral, and out of harmony with the values and ideals of the nineteenth century. Julia Lovejoy's denunciation of slaveholding Missourians was mild. Her fellow migrants to Kansas described southerners as subhuman, unclean, and uncivilized. They were, as one put it, "drunken ourangoutans," "wild beasts" who drank whiskey, ate dirt, uttered oaths, raped slave women, and fought or dueled at the slightest excuse. In the popular language of the day, they were known as "Pukes."

The Southern Perspective

Epithets aside, southerners were a diverse people who, like northerners, shared certain broad values, general-ly those of the planter class. If in the North the values of economic enterprise were most important, southerners revered social values most. Like the English gentry they sought to emulate, they saw themselves as courteous, refined, hospitable, and chivalrous. By contrast, they saw northerners as coarse, ill-mannered, aggressive, materialistic "Yankees." In a society where one person in three was a black slave, racial distinctions and paternalistic relationships were crucial in maintaining order and white supremacy. Fear of slave revolt was ever present. The South had five times more military schools than the North. Northerners educated the many for economic utility, but southerners educated the few for grace and character. In short, the South saw itself as a genteel, ordered society guided by the aristocratic code of the gentleman planter.

Southerners agreed with northerners that sovereignty in a republic rested in the people, who created a government of laws to protect life, liberty, and property. But unlike people in the North, southerners believed that the democratic principle of self-government was best preserved in local political units such as the state. Southerners were ready to fight to defend their sacred rights against any tyrannical encroachment on their liberty, as they had in 1776. They saw themselves, in fact, as true revolutionary patriots. Like northerners, southerners cherished the Union. But they preferred the loose confederacy of the Jeffersonian past to the centralized nationalism Seward kept invoking.

To southerners, Yankees were in too much of a hurry—to make money, to reform the behavior of others, to put dreamy theories (like racial equality) into practice. Two images dominated the South's view of northerners: either they were stingy, hypocritical, moralizing Puritans, or they were grubby, slum-dwelling, Catholic immigrants. A Georgia paper combined both images in an 1856 editorial: "Free society! we sicken at the name. What is it but a conglomeration of greasy mechanics, filthy operatives, small-fisted farmers, and moon-struck theorists?" These northerners, the paper said, "are devoid of society fitted for well-bred gentlemen."

Each side, then, saw the other threatening its freedom and infringing on its view of a proper republican society. Each saw the other imposing barriers to its vision for America's future, which included the economic systems described in Chapters 10 and 11. As hostilities increased, the views each section had of the other grew steadily more rigid and conspiratorial. Northerners saw the South as a "slave power," determined to foist the slave system on free labor throughout the land. Southerners saw the North as full of "black Republicanism," determined to destroy the southern way of life.

These scenes illustrate the contrasting socioeconomic cultures of the antebellum North and South. Chicago (top) was a rapidly growing, bustling northern city in the 1850s; situated on the Great Lakes and a developing railroad hub, Chicago became the distribution center for industrial and agricultural goods throughout the Midwest. The vital unit of southern commerce was, by contrast, the individual plantation (bottom), with steamboats and flatboats carrying cotton and sugar to port cities for trade with Europe. *(top: Corbis; bottom: Library of Congress)*

POLARIZATION AND THE ROAD TO WAR

Because of the national constituencies of the two major political parties, northern and southern cultural stereotypes and conspiratorial accusations had been largely held in check. But events in Kansas solidified the image of the Republicans as a northern party and seriously weakened the Democrats. Further events, still involving the question of slavery in the territories, split the Democratic party irrevocably into sectional halves: the Dred Scott decision of the

Supreme Court (1857), the constitutional crisis in Kansas (1857), the Lincoln–Douglas debates in Illinois (1858), John Brown's raid in Virginia (1859), and Lincoln's election (1860). These incidents further polarized the negative images each culture held of the other and set the nation on the final road to civil war.

The Dred Scott Case

The events of 1857 reinforced the arguments of those who believed in a slave power conspiracy. Two days after James Buchanan's inauguration, the Supreme Court finally ruled in *Dred Scott* v.

Sandford. The case had been pending before the Court for nearly three years, but the slave family of Dred Scott had been waiting longer for the decision. In 1846, Dred and Harriet Scott had filed suit in Missouri for their freedom. They argued that their master had taken them into Minnesota, Wisconsin, and other territories where the Missouri Compromise prohibited slavery, and therefore they should be freed. By the time the case reached the Supreme Court, the issue of slavery in the territories had become a heated political issue.

When the Court, with a majority of southern judges, issued its decision, by a vote of 7 to 2, it made three rulings. First, because blacks were, as Chief Justice Roger Taney put it, "beings of an inferior order [who] had no rights which white men were bound to respect," Dred Scott was not a citizen and had no right to sue in federal courts. Justice Peter Daniel of Virginia was even more indelicate in his consenting opinion, saying that the "African Negro race" did not belong "to the family of nations," but rather was a subject for "commerce or traffic." The second ruling stated that the Missouri Compromise was unconstitutional because Congress did not have the power to ban slavery in a territory. And third, the fact that the Scotts had been taken in and out of free states did not affect their status. Despite two eloquent dissenting opinions, Dred and Harriet Scott remained slaves.

The implications of these decisions went far beyond the Scotts' personal freedom. The arguments about black citizenship infuriated many northerners. Frederick Douglass called the ruling "a most scandalous and devilish perversion of the Constitution, and a brazen misstatement of the facts of history." Many citizens worried about the few rights free blacks still held. Even more troublesome was the possibility hinted at in the decision that slavery might be permitted in the free states of the North, where it had long been banned. People who suspected a conspiracy were not calmed when Buchanan endorsed the Dred Scott decision as a final settlement of the right of citizens to take their "property of any kind, including slaves, into the common Territories . . . and to have it protected there under the Federal Constitution." Rather than settling the political issue of slavery in the territories, as Buchanan had hoped, the Dred Scott decision threw it back into American politics. It opened up new questions and increased sectional hostilities.

Douglas and the Democrats

The Dred Scott decision and Buchanan's endorsement fed northern suspicions of a slave power conspiracy to impose slavery everywhere. Events in Kansas, which still had two governments, heightened these fears. In the summer of 1857, Kansas had still another election, with so many irregularities that only 2,000 out of a possible 24,000 voters participated. They elected a proslavery slate of delegates to a constitutional convention meeting at Lecompton as a preparation for statehood. The convention decided to exclude free blacks from the state, to guarantee the property rights of the few slaveholders in Kansas, and to ask voters to decide in a referendum whether to permit more slaves.

The proslavery Lecompton constitution, clearly unrepresentative of the wishes of the majority of the people of Kansas, was sent to Congress for approval. Eager to retain the support of southern Democrats, Buchanan endorsed it. Stephen Douglas challenged the president's power and jeopardized his own standing with southern Democrats by opposing it. Facing reelection to the Senate from Illinois in 1858, Douglas needed to hold the support of the northern wing of his party. Congress sent the Lecompton constitution back to the people of Kansas for another referendum. This time they defeated it, which meant that Kansas remained a territory rather than becoming a slave state. While Kansas was left in an uncertain status, the larger political effect of the struggle was to split the Democratic party almost beyond repair.

No sooner had Douglas settled the Lecompton question than he faced reelection in Illinois. Douglas's opposition to the Lecompton constitution had restored his prestige in the North as an opponent of the slave power. This cut some ground out from under the Republican party claim that it was the only force capable of stopping the spread of southern power. Republican party leaders from the West, however, had a candidate who understood the importance of distinguishing Republican moral and political views from those of the Democrats.

Lincoln and the Illinois Debates

Although he was relatively unknown nationally and had not held elected office in several years, by 1858, Abraham Lincoln of Illinois had emerged to challenge William Seward for leadership of the Republican party. Lincoln's character was shaped on the Midwestern frontier, where he had educated himself, developed mild abolitionist views, and dreamed of America's greatness.

Douglas was clearly the leading Democrat, so the Senate election in Illinois appeared to be a preview of the presidential election of 1860. The other Douglass, Frederick, observed that "the slave power idea was the ideological glue of the Republican party." Lincoln's handling of this idea would be crucial in distinguishing him from Stephen Douglas. The Illinois campaign featured a series of seven debates between Lincoln and Douglas in different cities. With a national as well

The overwhelming stress of leading the nation through the Civil War is evident in these two images of Abraham Lincoln. To the left is a portrait from 1860 *(Chicago Historical Society)* and on the right is an April 1865 photograph taken just before his assassination. *(Library of Congress)*

as a local audience, the debates provided a remarkable opportunity for the two men to state their views on the heated racial issues before the nation.

Lincoln set a solemn tone when he accepted the Republican senatorial nomination in Chicago in June. The American nation, he said, was in a "crisis" and building toward a worse one. "A House divided against itself cannot stand. I believe this government cannot endure, permanently half *slave* and half *free*." Lincoln said he did not expect the Union "to be dissolved" or "the house to fall," but rather that "it will become *all* one thing, or *all* the other." Then he rehearsed the history of the South's growing influence over national policy since the Kansas-Nebraska Act, which he blamed on Douglas. Lincoln stated his firm opposition to the Dred Scott decision, which he believed part of a conspiracy involving Pierce, Buchanan, Taney, and Douglas. People like himself, who opposed this conspiracy, wished to place slavery, he said, on a "course of ultimate extinction."

In the ensuing debates with Douglas, Lincoln reiterated these controversial themes. He also expressed his views on race and slavery, formed from a blend of experience, principle, and politics. Although far from a radical abolitionist, in these debates Lincoln skillfully staked out a moral position not only in advance of Douglas but well ahead of his time.

Lincoln was also very much a part of his time. He believed that whites were superior to blacks and opposed granting specific equal civil rights to free blacks. He believed, furthermore, that the physical and moral differences between whites and blacks would "forever forbid the two races from living together on terms of social and political equality" and recommended "separation" and colonization in Liberia or Central America as the best solution to racial differences.

Lincoln, however, differed from most contemporaries in his deep commitment to the humane principles of the equality and essential dignity of all human beings, including blacks. Douglas, by contrast, arguing against race mixing in a blatant bid for votes, continually made racial slurs. Lincoln believed not only that blacks were "entitled to all the natural rights . . . in the Declaration of Independence" but also that they had many specific economic rights as well, like "the right to put into his mouth the bread that his own hands have earned." In these rights, blacks were, Lincoln said, "my equal and the equal of Judge Douglas, and the equal of every living man."

Unlike Douglas, Lincoln hated slavery. At Galesburg, he said, "I contemplate slavery as a moral, social, and political evil." In Quincy, he said that the difference between a Republican and a Democrat was quite simply whether one thought slavery wrong or right. Douglas was more equivocal and dodged the issue in Freeport by pointing out that slavery would not exist if favorable local legislation did not support it. Douglas's moral indifference to slavery was clear in his admission that he did not care if a territorial legislature voted it "up or down." A white supremacist, Douglas was democratic enough to want white people to be able to create whatever type of society they wanted. Republicans did care, Lincoln affirmed, sounding a warning that by stopping the expansion of slavery, the course toward "ultimate extinction" had begun. Although barred by the Constitution from doing anything about slavery where it already existed, Lincoln said that because Republicans believed slavery to be wrong, "we propose a course of policy that shall deal with it as a wrong."

What Lincoln meant by "policy" was not yet clear, even to himself. However, in the debates, he did succeed in affirming that the Republican party was the only moral and political force capable of stopping the slave power. It seems ironic now, though not at the time, that Douglas won the election. When he and Lincoln met again two years later, the order of their finish would be reversed. Elsewhere, in 1858, however, Democrats did poorly, losing 18 congressional seats to the Republicans.

John Brown's Raid

Unlike Lincoln, John Brown was prepared to act decisively against slavery. On October 16, 1859, he and a band of 22 men attacked a federal arsenal at Harpers Ferry, Virginia (now West Virginia). He hoped that the action might provoke a general uprising of slaves throughout the Upper South or at least provide the arms by which slaves could make their way to freedom. Although he seized the arsenal, federal troops soon overcame him. Nearly half his men were killed, including two sons. Brown himself was captured, tried, and hanged for treason. So ended a lifetime of failures.

In death, however, Brown was not a failure. His daring if foolhardy raid, and his impressively dignified behavior during his trial and speedy execution, unleashed powerful passions, further widening the gap between North and South. Northerners responded to his death with an outpouring of sympathy; memorial rallies, parades, and prayer meetings were

This modern mural captures both the madness and passionate larger-than-life commitment of John Brown against a backdrop of flag-covered wagon trains across the Great Plains, a raging tornado and angry sky (God's wrath?), struggling slaves (by his left knee), and a violent confrontation between those for and against slavery. *(Kansas State Historical Society)*

In the aftermath of John Brown's raid, passions fed by fear were unleashed throughout the South against northern sympathizers, and vice versa. A year later, the editor of a Massachusetts newspaper who expressed Democratic, southern sympathies found himself the victim of the time-honored mob punishment of tarring and feathering. *(The New York Public Library, Astor, Lenox & Tilden Foundations)*

held. Admirers wrote poems, songs, and speeches in Brown's honor. Thoreau compared him to Christ and called him an "angel of light." Abolitionist William Lloyd Garrison, though a pacifist, was moved to wish "success to every slave insurrection" in the South. Ministers called slave revolt a "divine weapon" and glorified Brown's treason as "holy."

Brown's raid, Frederick Douglass pointed out, showed that slavery was a "system of brute force" that would only be ended when "met with its own weapons." Southerners were filled with "dread and terror" over the possibility of a wave of slave revolts led by hundreds of imaginary John Browns and Nat Turners and concluded that northerners would stop at nothing to free the slaves. This atmosphere of suspicion eroded freedom of thought and expression. A North Carolinian described a "spirit of terror, mobs, arrests, and violence" in his state. Twelve families in Berea, Kentucky, were evicted from the state for their mild abolitionist sentiments. A Texas minister who criticized the treatment of slaves in a sermon was given 70 lashes.

In response to the Brown raid, southerners also became more convinced, as the governor of South Carolina put it, that a "black Republican" plot in the

North was "arrayed against the slaveholders." In this atmosphere of mistrust, southern Unionists lost their influence, and power became concentrated in the hands of those favoring secession. Only one step remained to complete the southern sense of having become a permanent minority within the United States: withdrawal to form a new nation. Senator Robert Toombs of Georgia, insistent that northern "enemies" were plotting the South's ruin, warned fellow southerners late in 1859, "Never permit this Federal government to pass into the traitorous hands of the black Republican party."

The Election of 1860

The conflict between Buchanan and Douglas took its toll on the Democratic party. When the nominating convention met in Charleston, South Carolina, a hotbed of secessionist sentiments, it sat for a record ten days and went through 59 ballots without being able to name a candidate. Twice, southern delegates withdrew, forcing adjournments. Reconvening in Baltimore, the Democrats acknowledged their irreparable division by choosing two candidates at two separate conventions: Douglas for northern Democrats and John C. Breckinridge, Buchanan's vice

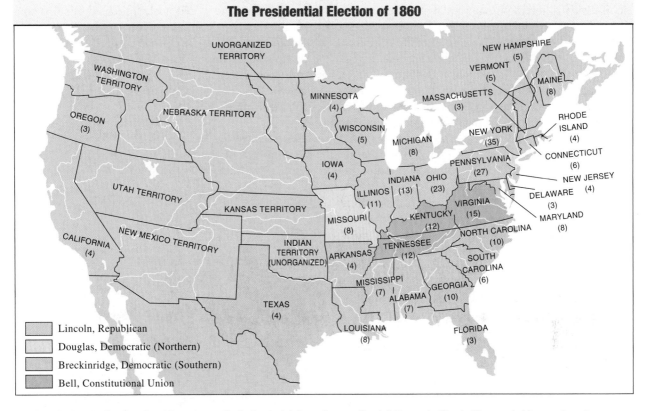

The Presidential Election of 1860

UNORGANIZED TERRITORY

WASHINGTON TERRITORY

OREGON (3)

NEBRASKA TERRITORY

MINNESOTA (4)

WISCONSIN (5)

IOWA (4)

MICHIGAN (8)

NEW HAMPSHIRE (5)

VERMONT (5)

MAINE (8)

MASSACHUSETTS (3)

NEW YORK (35)

RHODE ISLAND (4)

CONNECTICUT (6)

NEW JERSEY (4)

UTAH TERRITORY

KANSAS TERRITORY

ILLINIOS (11)

INDIANA (13) OHIO (23)

PENNSYLVANIA (27)

DELAWARE (3)

MARYLAND (8)

CALIFORNIA (4)

NEW MEXICO TERRITORY

INDIAN TERRITORY (UNORGANIZED)

MISSOURI (8)

KENTUCKY (12)

VIRGINIA (15)

NORTH CAROLINA (10)

ARKANSAS (4)

TENNESSEE (12)

SOUTH CAROLINA (6)

MISSISSIPPI (7)

ALABAMA (7)

GEORGIA (10)

TEXAS (4)

LOUISIANA (8)

FLORIDA (3)

- Lincoln, Republican
- Douglas, Democratic (Northern)
- Breckinridge, Democratic (Southern)
- Bell, Constitutional Union

Lincoln's election, the first by a Republican, was on the basis of a totally northern sectional victory, and with only 40 percent of the popular vote.

president, for the proslavery South. The Constitutional Union party, made up of former southern Whigs and border-state nativists, claimed the middle ground and nominated John Bell, a slaveholder from Tennessee favoring compromise.

With Democrats split and a new party in contention, the Republican strategy aimed at keeping the states carried by Frémont in 1856 and adding Pennsylvania, Illinois, and Indiana. Seward, the leading candidate for the nomination, had been tempering his antislavery views to appear more electable. So had Abraham Lincoln, who seemed more likely than Seward to carry those key states. After shrewd maneuvers emphasizing his "availability" as a moderate with widespread appeal, Lincoln was nominated.

The Republican platform also reflected moderation, opposing only slavery's extension. Most of it spoke of tariff protection, subsidized internal improvements, free labor, and a homestead bill. Above all, the Republicans, like southern Democrats, defended their view of what republican values meant for America's future. It did not include the equal rights envisioned by Frederick Douglass. An English traveler in 1860 observed that in America "we see, in effect, two nations—one white and another black—growing up together within the same political circle, but never mingling on a principle of equality."

The Republican moderate strategy worked as planned. Lincoln was elected by sweeping the entire Northeast and Midwest. Although he got less than 40 percent of the popular vote nationwide, his triumph in the North was decisive. Even a united Democratic party could not have defeated him. With victory assured, Lincoln finished his sandwich and coffee on election night in Springfield and prepared for his awesome new responsibilities. They came even before his inauguration.

THE DIVIDED HOUSE FALLS

The Republicans overestimated the extent of Unionist sentiment in the South. They could not believe that the secessionists would prevail after Lincoln's victory. A year earlier, some southern congressmen had walked out in protest of the selection of an antislavery speaker of the House. A Republican leader, Carl Schurz, recalling this act, said that the southerners had taken a drink and then come back. Now, Schurz predicted, they would walk out, take two drinks, and come back again. He was wrong.

Secession and Uncertainty

On December 20, 1860, South Carolina seceded from the Union, declaring the "experiment" of putting people with "different pursuits and institutions" under one government a failure. By February 1, the other six Deep South states (Mississippi, Florida, Alabama, Georgia, Louisiana, and Texas) had seceded. A week later, delegates met in Montgomery, Alabama, created the Confederate States of America, adopted a constitution, and elected Jefferson Davis, a Mississippi senator and cotton planter, its provisional president. The divided house had fallen, as Lincoln had predicted it would. What was not yet certain, though, was whether the house could be put back together or whether disunion necessarily meant civil war.

The government in Washington had three options. The first was compromise, but the emotions of the time ruled out that possibility. Most proposed compromises were really concessions to the secessionist states. The second option, suggested by Horace Greeley, editor of the New York *Tribune,* was to let the seven states "go in peace," taking care not to lose the border states. But this was opposed by northern businessmen, who would lose profitable economic ties with the South, and by those who believed in an indissoluble Union. The third option was to compel secessionist states to return, which probably meant war.

Republican hopes that southern Unionism would assert itself and make none of these options necessary seemed possible in February 1861. The momentum toward disunion slowed, and no other southern states seceded. The nation waited and watched, wondering what Virginia and the border states would do, what outgoing President Buchanan would do, and what Congress would do. Prosouthern and determined not to start a civil war in the last weeks of his already dismal administration, Buchanan did nothing. Congress made some feeble efforts to pass compromise legislation, waiting in vain for the support of the president-elect. And as Union supporters struggled with secessionists, Virginia and the border states, like the entire nation, waited for Abraham Lincoln.

Frederick Douglass waited, too, without much hope. He wanted nothing less than the "complete and universal *abolition* of the whole slave system," as well as equal suffrage and other rights for free blacks. His momentary expectation during the presidential campaign, that Lincoln and the Republicans had the will to do this, had been thoroughly dashed. In November, the voters of New York State had defeated a referendum for black suffrage by more votes than a similar measure 14 years earlier. Moreover, Douglass saw northern politicians and businessmen "granting the most demoralizing concessions to the Slave Power."

In his despair, Douglass began to explore possibilities for emigration and colonization in Haiti, an idea he had long opposed. To achieve full freedom and citizenship in the United States for all blacks, he said in January 1861, he would "welcome the hardships consequent upon a dissolution of the Union." In February, Douglass said, "Let the conflict come." He opposed all compromises, hoping that with Lincoln's inauguration in March it would "be decided, and decided forever, which of the two, Freedom or Slavery, shall give law to this Republic."

Lincoln and Fort Sumter

As Douglass penned these thoughts, Lincoln began a long, slow train ride from Springfield, Illinois, to

Timeline

1832	Nullification crisis
1835–1840	Intensification of abolitionist attacks on slavery
	Violent retaliatory attacks on abolitionists
1840	Liberty party formed
1846	Wilmot Proviso
1848	Free-Soil party founded
	Zachary Taylor elected president
1850	Compromise of 1850, including Fugitive Slave Act
1850–1854	"Young America" movement
1851	Women's rights convention in Akron, Ohio
1852	Harriet Beecher Stowe publishes *Uncle Tom's Cabin*
	Franklin Pierce elected president
1854	Ostend Manifesto
	Kansas-Nebraska Act nullifies Missouri Compromise
	Republican and Know-Nothing parties formed
1855	Walt Whitman publishes *Leaves of Grass*
1855–1856	Thousands pour into Kansas, creating months of turmoil and violence
1856	John Brown's massacre in Kansas
	Sumner–Brooks incident in Senate
	James Buchanan elected president
1857	Dred Scott decision legalizes slavery in territories
	Lecompton constitution in Kansas
1858	Lincoln–Douglas debates
1859	John Brown's raid at Harpers Ferry
1860	Democratic party splits
	Four-party campaign
	Abraham Lincoln elected president
1860–1861	Seven southern states secede
1861	Confederate States of America founded
	Attack on Fort Sumter begins Civil War

THE CAUSES OF THE CIVIL WAR

Date	Issues and Events	Deeper, Underlying Causes of Civil War
1600s–1860s	Slavery in the South	Major underlying pervasive cause
1700s–1860s	Development of two distinct socioeconomic systems and cultures	Further reinforced slavery as fundamental socioeconomic, cultural moral issue
1787–1860s	States' rights, nullification doctrine	Ongoing political issue, less fundamental as cause
1820	Missouri Compromise (36°30')	Background for conflict over slavery in territories
1828–1833	South Carolina tariff nullification crisis	Background for secession leadership in South Carolina
1831–1860s	Antislavery movements, southern justification	Thirty years of emotional preparation for conflict
1846–1848	War with Mexico (Wilmot Proviso, Calhoun, popular sovereignty)	Options for issue of slavery in territories

Date	Issues and Events	Specific Impact on the Road to War
1850	Compromise of 1850	Temporary and unsatisfactory "settlement" of divisive issue
1851–1854	Fugitive slaves returned and rescued in North; personal liberty laws passed in North; Harriet Beecher Stowe's *Uncle Tom's Cabin*	Heightened northern emotional reactions against the South and slavery
1852–1856	Breakdown of Whig party and national Democratic party; creation of a new party system with sectional basis	Made national politics an arena where sectional and cultural differences over slavery were fought
1854	Ostend Manifesto and other expansionist efforts in Central America	Reinforced image of Democratic party as favoring slavery
	Formation of Republican party	Major party identified as opposing the extension of slavery
	Kansas-Nebraska Act	Reopened "settled" issue of slavery in the territories
1856	"Bleeding Kansas"; Senator Sumner physically attacked in Senate	Foretaste of Civil War (200 killed, $2 million in property lost) inflamed emotions and polarized North and South
1857	Dred Scott decision; proslavery Lecompton constitution in Kansas	Made North fear a "slave power conspiracy," supported by President Buchanan and the Supreme Court
1858	Lincoln-Douglas debates in Illinois; Democrats lose 18 seats in Congress	Set stage for election of 1860
1859	John Brown's raid and reactions in North and South	Made South fear a "black Republican" plot against slavery; further polarization and irrationality
1860	Democratic party splits in half; Lincoln elected president; South Carolina secedes from Union	Final breakdown of national parties and election of "northern" president; no more compromises
1861	Six more southern states secede by February 1; Confederate Constitution adopted February 4; Lincoln inaugurated March 4; Fort Sumter attacked April 12	Civil War begins

Washington, writing and rewriting his inaugural address. Lincoln's quietness in the period between his election and his inauguration had led many to wonder if he were not weak and indecisive. He was not. Lincoln was firmly opposed to secession and to any compromises with the principle of stopping the exten-sion of slavery. He would neither conciliate secession-ist southern states nor force their return.

But Lincoln believed in his constitutional responsi-bility to uphold the laws of the land, and on this signif-icant point he would not yield. The focus of his atten-tion was a federal fort in the harbor of Charleston,

South Carolina. Major Robert Anderson, the commander of Fort Sumter, was running out of provisions and had requested new supplies from Washington. Lincoln would enforce the laws and protect federal property at Fort Sumter.

As the new president rose to deliver his inaugural address on March 4, he faced a tense and divided nation. Federal troops, fearing a Confederate attack on the nation's capital, were everywhere. Lincoln asserted his unequivocal intention to enforce the laws of the land, arguing that the Union was constitutionally "perpetual" and indissoluble. He reminded the nation that the "only substantial dispute" was that "one section of our country believes slavery is *right*, and ought to be extended, while the other believes it is *wrong*, and ought not to be extended." Still hoping to appeal to Unionist strength among southern moderates, Lincoln indicated that he would make no attempts to interfere with existing slavery or the law to return fugitive slaves.

Nearing the end of his address, Lincoln urged against rash actions and put the burden of initiating a civil war on the "dissatisfied fellow-countrymen" who had seceded. As if aware of the horrible events that might follow, he said in an eloquent conclusion:

I am loath to close. We are not enemies, but friends. We must not be enemies. Though passion may have strained, it must not break our bonds of affection. The mystic chords of memory, stretching from every battlefield, and patriot grave, to every living heart and hearthstone, all over this broad land, will yet swell the chorus of the Union, when again touched, as surely they will be, by the better angels of our nature.

Frederick Douglass was not impressed with Lincoln's "honied phrases" and accused him of "weakness, timidity and conciliation." Also unmoved, Robert Allston wrote his son from Charleston, where he was watching the developing crisis over Fort Sumter, that the Confederacy's "advantage" was in having a "much better president than they have."

On April 6, Lincoln notified the governor of South Carolina that he was sending "provisions only" to Fort Sumter. No effort would be made "to throw in men, arms, or ammunition" unless the fort were attacked. On April 10, Jefferson Davis directed General P. G. T. Beauregard to demand the surrender of Fort Sumter. Davis told Beauregard to reduce the fort if Major Anderson refused.

On April 12, as Lincoln's relief expedition neared Charleston, Beauregard's batteries began shelling Fort Sumter, and the Civil War began. Frederick Douglass was about to leave for Haiti when he heard the news. He immediately changed his plans: "This is no time . . . to leave the country." He announced his readiness to help end the war by aiding the Union to organize freed slaves "into a liberating army" to "make war upon . . . the savage barbarism of slavery." The Allstons had changed places, and it was Benjamin who described the events in Charleston harbor to his father. On April 14, Benjamin reported exuberantly the "glorious, and astonishing news that Sumter has fallen." With it fell America's divided house.

Conclusion

The "Irrepressible Conflict"

Lincoln had been right. The nation could no longer endure half-slave and half-free. The collision between North and South, William Seward said, was not an "accidental, unnecessary" event but an "irrepressible conflict between opposing and enduring forces." Those forces had been at work for many decades, but they developed with increasing intensity after 1848 in the conflict over the extension of slavery into the territories. Although economic, cultural, political, constitutional, and emotional forces all contributed to the developing opposition between North and South, slavery was the fundamental, enduring force that underlay all others, causing what Walt Whitman called the "red blood of civil war."

Recommended Reading

Overviews of the Imperiled Union and Crises of the 1850s

Eric Foner, ed., *Politics and Ideology in the Age of the Civil War* (1980); James McPherson, *Ordeal by Fire: The Civil War and Reconstruction* (1982); David Potter, *The Impending Crisis, 1848–1861* (1976); Brian Holden Reid, *The Origins of the American Civil War* (1996); Richard Sewall, *A House Divided: Sectionalism and Civil War, 1848–1865* (1988); Kenneth Stampp, *The Imperilled Union: Essays on the Background of the Civil War*

(1980); Kenneth Stampp, ed., *The Causes of the Civil War, rev. ed.* (1974); Mark Summers, The Plundering Generation: Corruption and the Crisis of the Union, 1849–1861 *(1987).*

Slavery in the Territories

Eugene Berwanger, *The Frontier Against Slavery: Western Anti-Negro Prejudice and the Slavery Extension Controversy* (1967); William W. Freehling, *The Road to Disunion: I. Secessionists at*

Bay, 1776–1854 (1990); Hamilton Holman, *Prologue to Conflict: The Crisis and Compromise of 1850* (1964); Willard C. Klunder, *Lewis Cass and the Politics of Moderation* (1996); Michael A. Morrison, *Slavery and the American West: The Eclipse of Manifest Destiny and the Coming of the Civil War* (1997); Mark J. Stegmaier, *Texas, New Mexico, and the Compromise of 1850: Boundary Dispute & Sectional Crisis* (1996); Albert J. Von Frank, *The Trials of Anthony Burns* (1998).

Political Disintegration and Realignment

Eric Foner, *Free Soil, Free Labor, Free Men: The Ideology of the Republican Party Before the Civil War* (1970); William E. Gienapp, *The Origins of the Republican Party, 1852–1856* (1987); William E. Gienapp, Thomas B. Alexander, Michael F. Holt, Stephen E. Mazlish, and Joel H. Silbey, *Essays on American Antebellum Politics, 1840–1860* (1982); Anthony Gronowicz, *Race and Class Politics in New York City Before the Civil War* (1997); Michael Holt, *The Political Crisis of the 1850s* (1978); Robert W. Johannsen, *The Frontier, the Union, and Stephen A. Douglas* (1989); Robert Remini, *Daniel Webster: The Man and His Time* (1997); E. Smith, *The Presidencies of Zachary Taylor and Millard Fillmore* (1988); Geoffrey Wolff, *The Kansas-Nebraska Bill: Party, Section and the Origin of the Civil War* (1977).

Kansas, Two Cultures, and Polarized Emotions

William J. Cooper, *The South and the Politics of Slavery* (1978) and *Liberty and Slavery: Southern Politics to 1860* (1983); Donald Fehrenbacher, *Slavery, Law, and Politics: The Dred Scott Case in Historical Perspective* (1981); Thomas F. Gossett, *Uncle Tom's Cabin and American Culture* (1985); David S. Heidler, *Pulling the Temple Down: The Fire-Eaters and the Destruction of the Union* (1994); Nell Irvin Painter, *Sojourner Truth: A Life, A Symbol* (1996); James Rawley, *Race and Politics: "Bleeding Kansas" and the Coming of the Civil War* (1969); Richard Sewell, *Ballots for Freedom: Antislavery Politics in the United States, 1837–1865* (1976).

Lincoln and the Divided House: The Road to Civil War

David H. Donald, *Lincoln* (1995); Don Fehrenbacher, ed., *Abraham Lincoln: A Documentary Portrait Through His Speeches and Writings* (1977); Maury Klein, *Days of Defiance: Sumter, Secession, and the Coming of the Civil War* (1997); Mark E. Neely, *The Last Best Hope of Earth: Abraham Lincoln and the Promise of America* (1993); Kenneth Stampp, *America in 1857: A Nation on the Brink* (1990) and *And the War Came* (1950); David Zarefsky, *Lincoln, Douglas and Slavery in the Crucible of Public Debate* (1990).

Fiction and Film

Russell Banks's *Cloudsplitter* (1998) is an exciting novel on John Brown's antislavery activities in the 1850s. Ken Burns's *Civil War*, part 1, sets the slavery and 1850s background for his haunting documentary portrayal of the Civil War. Herman Melville's *Moby Dick* (1850), an immense novel published at the time of the Senate debates over the disposition of slavery in the territories, tells the story of Ahab's pursuit of the great white whale. *Moby Dick* is about giant polar forces facing each other, good and evil, nature and man, and, perhaps, North and South. Harriet Beecher Stowe wrote *Uncle Tom's Cabin* (1852) in serial form, with each episode stopping at a nail-biting moment. Stowe's romantic novel strongly influenced northern readers and had an impact on the antislavery politics of the 1850s. Walt Whitman's collection of poems, *Leaves of Grass* (1855), celebrates not only the poet's own ego but also the common people and democratic American values in a decade that sorely tested those values.

Suggested Web Sites

http://history.furman.edu/~benson/docs/

Furman: Secession Era Editorials Project. Furman University is digitizing editorials about the secession crisis and already includes scores of them on this site.

http://www.law.umkc.edu/faculty/projects/ftrials/Brown.html

John Brown Case. For information about the trial of John Brown, this site provides a list of excellent links.

http://grid.let.rug.nl/~usa/H/1990/ch5_p6.htm

USA: Lincoln Attacks Slavery. This site discusses Lincoln's views and action concerning slavery, especially the Lincoln–Douglas debate.

http://www.ukans.edu/carrie/kancoll/galbks.htm

Gallery: Bleeding Kansas. Contemporary and later accounts of America's rehearsal for the Civil War make up this University of Kansas site.

http://www.pbs.org/wgbh/aia/part4

The Compromise of 1850 and the Fugitive Slave Act. From the series on Africans in America, an analysis of the Compromise of 1850 and of the effects of the Fugitive Slave Act on black Americans.

http://nac.gmu.edu/mmts/50proto.html

The 1850s: An Increasingly Divided Union. A tutorial skills development site focusing on the events in the 1850s leading to the Civil War; from MMTS, the Multi-Media Thinking Skills project.

http://lcweb2.loc.gov/ammem/mcchtml/corhome.html

Words and Deeds in American History. A Library of Congress site containing links to Frederick Douglass, the Compromise of 1850, speeches by John C. Calhoun, Daniel Webster and Henry Clay, and other topics from the Civil War era.

http://www.ushistoryplace.com

 A richly detailed on-line learning environment complete with interactive maps, timelines, history activities, primary source documents, and links to related American history sites.

The UNION SEVERED

CHAPTER OUTLINE

In his remarks to Congress in 1862, Abraham Lincoln reminded congressmen that, "We cannot escape history. We of this Congress and this administration will be remembered in spite of ourselves. No personal significance, or insignificance, can spare . . . us. The fiery trial through which we pass, will light us down, in honor or dishonor, to the latest generation." Lincoln's conviction that Americans would long remember him and other major actors of the Civil War was correct. Jefferson Davis, Robert E. Lee, Ulysses S. Grant—these are the men whose characters, actions, and decisions have been the subject of continuing discussion and analysis, whose statues and memorials dot the American countryside and grace urban squares. Whether seen as heroes or villains, great men have dominated the story of the Civil War.

Yet from the earliest days, the war touched the lives of even the most uncelebrated Americans. From Indianapolis, 20-year-old Arthur Carpenter wrote to his parents in Massachusetts begging for permission to enlist in the volunteer army: "I have always longed for the time to come when I could enter the army and be a military man, and when this war broke out, I thought the time had come, but you would not permit me to enter the service . . . now I make one more appeal to you." The pleas worked, and Carpenter enlisted, spending most of the war fighting in Kentucky and Tennessee.

In that same year, in Tennessee, George and Ethie Eagleton faced anguishing decisions. Though not an abolitionist, George, a 30-year-old Presbyterian preacher, was unsympathetic to slavery and opposed to secession. But when his native state left the Union, George felt compelled to follow and enlisted in the 44th Tennessee Infantry. Ethie, his 26-year-old wife, despaired over the war, George's decision, and her own forlorn situation.

Mr. Eagleton's school dismissed—and what for? O my God, must I write it? He has enlisted in the service of his country—to war—the most unrighteous war that ever was brought on any nation that ever lived. Pres. Lincoln has done what no other Pres. ever dared to do—he has divided these once peaceful and happy United States. And Oh! the dreadful dark cloud that is now hanging over our country—'tis enough to sicken the heart of any one. . . . Mr. E. is gone. . . . What will become of me, left here without a home and relatives, a babe just nine months old and no George.

Both Carpenter and the Eagletons survived the war, but the conflict transformed each of their lives. Carpenter had difficulty settling down. Filled with bitter memories of the war years in Tennessee, the Eagletons moved to Arkansas. Ordinary people such as Carpenter and the Eagletons are historically anonymous. Yet their actions on the battlefield and behind the lines helped to shape the course of events, as their leaders realized, even if today we tend to remember only the famous and influential.

For thousands of Americans, from Lincoln and Davis to Carpenter and the Eagletons, war was both a profoundly personal and a major national event. Its impact reached far beyond the four years of hostilities. The war that was fought to conserve two political, social, and economic visions ended by changing familiar ways of life in both North and South. War was a transforming force, both destructive and creative in its effect on the structure and social dynamics of society and on the lives of ordinary people. This theme underlies this chapter's analysis of the war's three stages: the initial months of preparation, the years of military stalemate between 1861 and 1865, and, finally, resolution.

Artist Winslow Homer captured a Union sharpshooter in one of his early paintings. *(Portland Museum of Art, Maine. Gift of Barbro and Bernard Osher, 3.1993.3)*

ORGANIZING FOR WAR

The Confederate bombardment of Fort Sumter on April 12, 1861, and the surrender of Union troops the next day ended the uncertainty of the secession winter. The North's response to Fort Sumter was a virtual declaration of war as President Lincoln called for state militia volunteers to crush southern "insurrection." His action pushed several slave states (Virginia, North Carolina, Tennessee, Arkansas) off the fence and into the southern camp. Other states (Maryland, Kentucky, and Missouri) agonizingly debated which way to go. The "War Between the States" was now a reality.

Many Americans were unenthusiastic about the course of events. Southerners like George Eagleton only reluctantly followed Tennessee out of the Union. When he enlisted, he complained of the "disgraceful cowardice of many who were last winter for secession and war . . . but are now refusing self and means for the prosecution of war." Robert E. Lee of Virginia was equally hesitant to resign his federal commission but finally decided that he could not "raise [a] hand against . . . relatives . . . children . . . home." Whites living in the southern uplands (where blacks were few and slaveholders were heartily disliked and envied), yeomen farmers in the Deep South (who owned no slaves), and many residents of border states were dismayed at secession and war. Many would eventually join the Union forces.

In the North, large numbers had supported neither the Republican party nor Lincoln. Irish immigrants who feared the competition of free black labor and southerners now living in Illinois, Indiana, and Ohio harbored misgivings about the war. Indeed, northern Democrats at first blamed Lincoln and the Republicans almost as much as the southern secessionists for the nation's crisis.

Nevertheless, the days following Fort Sumter and Lincoln's call for troops saw an outpouring of support on both sides, fueled in part by relief at decisive action, in part by patriotism and love of adventure, in part by unemployment. Northern blacks and even some southern freedmen proclaimed themselves "ready to go forth and do battle," while whites like Carpenter enthusiastically flocked to enlist. In some places, workers were so eager to join up that trade unions collapsed. Sisters, wives, and mothers set to work making uniforms. A New Yorker, Jane Woolsey, described the drama of those early days "of terrible excitement."

> Outside the parlor windows the city is gay and brilliant with excited crowds, the incessant movement and music of marching regiments and all the thousands of flags, big and little, which suddenly came fluttering out of every window and door. . . . In our little circle of friends, one mother has just sent away an idolized son; another, two; another, four. . . . One sweet young wife is packing

In May 1861, the first Michigan Regiment mustered in Detroit before boarding the train to Washington. The people crowded in the square, on the porches of the Rail-Road Hotel and on rooftops suggest the patriotic enthusiasm of the send-off. Many women shared the fervor for the coming conflict. Thousands of them would be involved in war work at home or in army hospitals or camps. As one explained, "As the soldiers went from among us, there came the yearning wish to lessen somewhat the hardships of their lonely camp life, especially when sick in hospital or wounded." *(Courtesy of the Burton Historical Collection, Detroit Public Library)*

a regulation valise for her husband today, and doesn't let him see her cry.

The war fever produced so many volunteers that neither northern nor southern officials could handle the throng. Northern authorities turned aside offers from blacks to serve. Both sides sent thousands of white would-be soldiers home. The conviction that the conflict would rapidly come to a glorious conclusion fueled the eagerness to enlist. "We really did not think that there was going to be an actual war," remembered Mary Ward, a young Georgia woman. "We had an idea that when our soldiers got upon the ground and showed, unmistakably that they were really ready and willing to fight . . . the whole trouble would be declared at an end." Lincoln's call for 75,000 state militiamen for only 90 days of service, and a similar enlistment term for Confederate soldiers, supported the notion that the war would be short.

The Balance of Resources

Despite the bands, parades, cheers, and confidence, the outcome of the approaching civil conflict was much in doubt. Statistics of population and industrial development suggested that the North would win. But Great Britain had also enjoyed enormous statistical advantages in 1775 and yet had lost the War of American Independence. Many of the North's assets would become effective only with time. The military stalemate in 1861 and 1862 proved that in the short term, North and South were evenly matched.

In the North, state militia volunteers called up in April 1861 supplemented the small federal army of 16,000. Probably a quarter of the regular army officers, however, had followed Lee's example and resigned. The Confederate Army, authorized in March 1861, could count on the service of able military men like Robert E. Lee, Joseph E. Johnston, and Albert Sidney Johnston. Its president, Jefferson Davis, was an 1828 graduate of West Point.

The North's white population greatly exceeded that of the South, giving the appearance of a military advantage. Yet in the early days of war, the armies were not unevenly matched. Almost 187,000 Union troops bore arms in July 1861, while just over 112,000 men marched under Confederate colors. Even if numerically inferior, southerners believed that their population would prove the superior fighting force because it was more accustomed to outdoor life and the use of firearms. Many northerners feared that southerners were better natural warriors. True or not, slaves could carry on vital work behind the lines, freeing most adult white males to serve the Confederacy. Slavery, southerners thought, would prove to be a "tower of strength . . . at the present crisis."

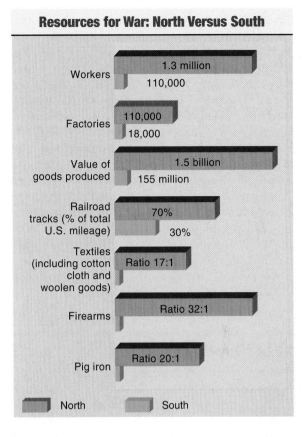

This chart shows the long-range advantages the North enjoyed in the war, but the length and destruction of the conflict suggest that the North was not able to capitalize on its strengths effectively to bring the war to a quick end.

The Union also enjoyed impressive economic advantages. In the North, 1.3 million workers in 110,000 manufacturing concerns produced goods valued at $1.5 billion annually, while 110,000 southern workers in 18,000 manufacturing concerns produced goods valued at only $155 million a year. The North had one factory for every southern industrial worker, and 70 percent of the nation's railroad tracks were in the North. Producing 17 times as much cotton cloth and woolen goods, 32 times as many firearms, and 20 times as much pig iron as the South, the North could clothe and arm troops and move them and their supplies on a scale that the South could not match. But to be effective, northern industrial resources had to be mobilized for war. That would take time, especially because the government did not intend to direct production. Furthermore, the depleted northern treasury made the government's first task the raising of funds to pay for military necessities.

The South traditionally depended on imported manufactured goods from the North and from Europe. If Lincoln cut off that trade, the South would face the enormous task of creating its industry almost from scratch. Moreover, its railroad system was organized to move cotton, not armies and supplies. Yet the agricultural South did have important resources of food, draft animals, and, of course, cotton, which southerners believed would secure British and French support. Finally, in choosing to wage a defensive war, the South could tap regional loyalty and would enjoy protected lines of supply and support.

Union forces, however, were embarked on an expensive and difficult war of conquest. Because many parts of the South raised cotton and tobacco rather than food crops, Union armies could not forage for necessary food and fodder. Supplying northern forces in the South presented significant logistic problems and dangers. Extended supply lines were always vulnerable to attack, rendering northern armies less mobile and secure than southern troops. The Union had to win a war of conquest and occupation. The South merely had to survive until its enemy tired and gave up.

The Border States

Uncertainty over the war's outcome and divided loyalties produced indecision in the border states. When the seven states of the Deep South seceded during the winter of 1860–1861, the border states adopted a wait-and-see attitude. Delaware identified with the Union camp, but the others vacillated. Their decisions were critically important to both North and South.

The states of the Upper South could provide natural borders for the Confederacy along the Ohio River, access to its river traffic, and vital resources, wealth,

and population. The major railroad link to the West ran through Maryland and western Virginia. Virginia boasted the South's largest ironworks, and Tennessee was the region's principal source of grain. Missouri provided the road to Kansas and the West and was strategically placed to control Mississippi River traffic. It was difficult to imagine the long- or short-term success of the Confederacy without the border states.

For the North, every border state that elected to remain loyal represented a psychological triumph for the idea of Union. Nor was the North indifferent to the economic and strategic advantages of keeping the border states with the Union. Lincoln's call for troops precipitated decisions in several states, however. Between April 17 and May 20, 1861, Virginia, Arkansas, Tennessee, and North Carolina joined the Confederacy.

The significance of border state loyalty was soon dramatized in Maryland. Slave-owning tobacco and wheat planters from the state's southern counties and eastern shore favored secession. Confederate enthusiasts abounded in Baltimore. But in the western and northern parts of the state, small farmers, often of German background, opposed slavery and supported the Union cause.

On the morning of April 19, the 6th Massachusetts Regiment arrived in Baltimore headed for Washington. Because the regiment had to change railroad lines, the soldiers set out across the city on foot and in horsecars. As they marched through the streets, a mob of some 10,000 southern sympathizers, flying Confederate flags, attacked them with

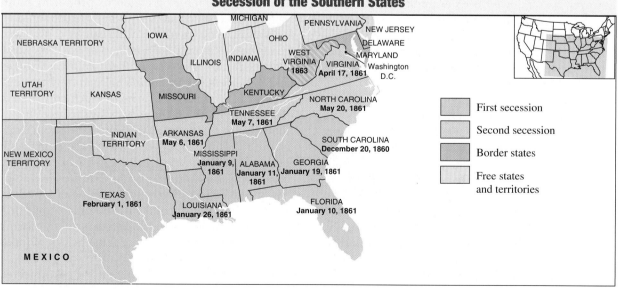

Secession of the Southern States

This map provides a chronology of secession and shows the geographic importance of the border states. The map also highlights the vulnerable position of Washington and explains many of Lincoln's actions in the early days of the war.

paving stones, then bayonets and bullets. Finally, as a contemporary explained, the "patience of their commander was . . . exhausted. He cried out in a voice, which was heard even above the yells of the mob, 'Fire!' . . . A scene of bloody confusion followed." In the commotion, would-be secessionists burned the railroad bridges connecting Baltimore to the North and to the South. Washington found itself cut off from the rest of the Union, an island in the middle of hostile territory.

Lincoln took stern measures to secure Maryland. The president agreed temporarily to route troops around Baltimore. In return, the governor called the state legislature into session at Frederick, a center of Union sentiment in western Maryland. This action and Lincoln's swift violation of civil rights damped secessionist enthusiasm. Hundreds of southern sympathizers, including 19 state legislators and Baltimore's mayor, were arrested and languished in prison without trial. Although the chief justice of the United States, Roger B. Taney, challenged the legality of the president's action and issued a writ of habeas corpus for the release of John Merryman, a southern supporter, Lincoln ignored him. A month later, Taney ruled in *Ex parte Merryman* that if the public's safety was endangered, only Congress had the right to suspend a writ of habeas corpus. By then, Lincoln had secured Maryland for the Union.

Though Lincoln's quick and harsh response ensured Maryland's loyalty, he was more cautious elsewhere. Above all, he had to deal with slavery prudently, for any hasty action would push border states into the waiting arms of the Confederacy. Thus, when General John C. Frémont, in a burst of enthusiasm, issued an unauthorized declaration of emancipation in Missouri in August 1861, Lincoln revoked the order and recalled the general. As the president explained, he expected a chain reaction if certain key states left the Union. "I think to lose Kentucky is nearly the same as to lose the whole game. Kentucky gone, we cannot hold Missouri, nor, as I think, Maryland. These all against us, and the job on our hands is too large for us." In the end, after some fighting and much maneuvering, Kentucky and Missouri, like Maryland, stayed in the Union.

Challenges of War

The tense weeks after Fort Sumter spilled over with unexpected challenges. Neither North nor South could handle the floods of volunteers. Both faced enormous organizational problems as they readied for war. In the South, a nation-state had to be created and its apparatus set in motion. Everything from a constitution and government departments to a flag and postage stamps had to be devised. As one onlooker observed, "The whole country was new. Everything was to be done—and to be made."

In February 1861, the original seceding states sent delegates to Montgomery, Alabama, to begin work on a provisional framework and to select a provisional president and vice president. The delegates swiftly wrote a constitution, much like the federal constitution of 1787 except in its emphasis on the "sovereign and independent character" of the states and its explicit recognition of slavery. The provisional president, Jefferson Davis of Mississippi, tried to put together a geographically and politically balanced cabinet with a moderate face for the outside world. He succeeded in creating a balanced cabinet, but it had few of his friends and, more serious, few men of political stature. As time passed, it turned out to be unstable as well. In a four-year period, 14 men held six positions.

Davis's cabinet appointees faced the formidable challenge of creating government departments from scratch. They had to hire employees and initiate administrative procedures with woefully inadequate resources. The president's office was in a hotel parlor. The Confederate Treasury Department was housed in a room in an Alabama bank "without furniture of any kind; empty . . . of desks, tables, chairs or other appliances for the conduct of business." Treasury Secretary Christopher G. Memminger bought furniture with his own money; operations lurched forward in fits and starts. In those early days, when an army captain came to the treasury with a warrant from Davis for blankets, he found only one clerk. After reading the warrant, the clerk offered the captain a few dollars of his own, explaining, "This, Captain, is all the money that I will certify as being in the Confederate Treasury at this moment." Other departments faced similar difficulties.

Inheriting the federal government, Lincoln did not have to set up a postal system or decide whether laws passed before 1861 were valid. Without administrative experience, however, the new president, like his Confederate counterpart, faced organizational problems. Military officers and government clerks daily left the capital for the South. The treasury was empty. The Republicans had won their first presidential election, and floods of office seekers who had worked for Lincoln now thronged into the White House looking for rewards.

Nor could Lincoln, who did not know many of the "prominent men of the day," easily select a cabinet. Finally, he appointed important Republicans from different factions of the party to cabinet posts whether they agreed with him or not. Most were almost strangers to the president. Several scorned him as a bumbling backwoods politician. Treasury Secretary Salmon P. Chase actually hoped to replace Lincoln as president in four years' time. Soon after the inauguration, Secretary of State William Seward sent Lincoln a memo condescendingly offering to oversee the formulation of presidential policy.

Lincoln and Davis

A number of Lincoln's early actions illustrated that he was no malleable backcountry bumbler. As his Illinois law partner, William Herndon, pointed out, Lincoln's "mind was tough—solid—knotty—gnarly, more or less like his body." In his reply to Seward's memo, the president firmly indicated that he intended to run his own administration. After Sumter, he swiftly called up the state militias, expanded the navy, and suspended habeas corpus. He ordered a naval blockade of the South and approved the expenditure of funds for military purposes, all without congressional sanction, because Congress was not in session. As Lincoln told legislators later, "The dogmas of the quiet past are inadequate to the stormy present. . . . As our case is new, so must we think anew, and act anew . . . and then we shall save our country." This willingness to "think anew" was a valuable personal asset, even though some critics called his expansion of presidential power despotic.

By coincidence, Lincoln and his rival, Jefferson Davis, were born only 100 miles apart in Kentucky. However, the course of their lives diverged radically. Lincoln's father had migrated north and eked out a simple existence as a farmer in Indiana and Illinois. Abraham had only a rudimentary formal education and was largely self-taught. Davis's family, however, had moved south to Mississippi and become cotton planters. Davis grew up in comfortable circumstances, went to Transylvania University and West Point, and fought in the Mexican-American War before his election to the U.S. Senate. In recognition of his social, political, and economic prominence, Davis served as secretary of war under Franklin Pierce (1853–1857). Tall, distinguished-looking, and very rich, he appeared every inch the aristocratic southerner.

Although Davis had not been eager to accept the presidency, he had loyally responded to the call of the provisional congress in 1861 and worked tirelessly as the chief executive of the Confederacy until the war's end. His wife, Varina, observed that "the President hardly takes time to eat his meals and works late at night." Some contemporaries suggested that Davis's inability to let subordinates handle details explained this schedule. Others observed that he was sickly, reserved, humorless, too sensitive to criticism, and hard to get along with. But Davis, like Lincoln, found it necessary to "think anew." He reassured southerners in his inaugural address that his aims were conservative, "to preserve the Government of our fathers in

spirit." Yet under the pressure of events, he moved toward creating a new kind of South.

⤳ CLASHING ON THE BATTLEFIELD, 1861–1862

The Civil War was the most brutal and destructive conflict in American history. Much of the bloodshed resulted from changing military technology coupled with inadequate communications. By the opening of hostilities, the range of rifles had increased from 100 to 500 yards, in part owing to the new French minié bullet, which traveled with tremendous velocity and accuracy. The greater reach of the new rifles meant that it was no longer possible to position the artillery close enough to enemy lines to allow it to support an infantry charge. During the Civil War, then, attacking infantry soldiers faced a final, often fatal, dash of 500 yards in the face of deadly enemy fire.

As it became clear that infantry charges resulted in horrible carnage, military leaders increasingly valued the importance of the strong defensive position. Although Confederate soldiers criticized General Lee as "King of Spades" when he first ordered them to construct earthworks, the epithet evolved into one of affection as it became obvious that earthworks saved lives. Union commanders followed suit. By the end of 1862, both armies dug defensive earthworks and trenches whenever they interrupted their march.

War in the East

The war's brutal character only gradually revealed itself. The Union commanding general, 70-year-old Winfield Scott, at first pressed for a cautious, long-term strategy, known as the Anaconda Plan. Scott proposed weakening the South gradually through blockades on land and at sea until the northern army was strong enough for the kill. The excited public, however, hungered for action and quick victory. So did Lincoln, who knew that the longer the war lasted, the more embittered the South and the North would both become, making reunion ever more difficult. Under the cry of "Forward to Richmond!" 35,000 partially trained men led by General Irwin McDowell headed out from Washington in sweltering July weather.

On July 21, 1861, only 25 miles from the capital at Manassas Creek, or Bull Run, as it is also called, inexperienced northern troops confronted 25,000 raw Confederate soldiers commanded by Brigadier General P. G. T. Beauregard, a West Point classmate of McDowell's. Although sightseers, journalists, and politicians accompanied the Union troops, expecting only a Sunday outing, the encounter at Bull Run was no picnic. The course of battle swayed back and forth before the arrival of 2,300 fresh Confederate troops, brought by trains, decided the day. Union soldiers and sightseers fled toward Washington in terror and confusion. An English journalist, William Russell, described the troops as they poured into Washington on July 22:

> I saw a steady stream of men covered with mud, soaked through with rain . . . pouring irregularly, without any semblance of order, up Pennsylvania Avenue toward the Capitol. . . . I perceived they belonged to different regiments . . . mingled pell-mell together. . . . Hastily [I] . . . ran downstairs and asked an officer . . . a pale young man who looked exhausted to death and who had lost his sword . . . where the men were coming from. "Where from? Well, sir, I guess we're all coming out of Virginny as far as we can, and pretty well whipped too. . . . I know I'm going home. I've had enough of fighting to last my lifetime."

"Pretty well whipped" the Union forces certainly were. Yet inexperienced Confederate troops had lost their chance to turn the rout into the quick and decisive victory they sought. As General Joseph E. Johnston pointed out, his men were disorganized,

confused by victory, and not well enough supplied with food to chase the Union army back toward Washington.

In many ways, the Battle of Bull Run was prophetic. Victory would be neither quick nor easy. As the disorganization and confusion of both sides suggested, the armies were unprofessional. And it was becoming obvious that bravado would not win the war. Then, too, both sides faced problems with short-term enlistments. Finally, logistic problems connected with mass armies plagued both sides. The Civil War put more men in the field than any previous American engagement. Supplying and moving so many men and ensuring adequate communication, especially during battle, were tasks of an unprecedented kind. It was hardly surprising that the armies floundered trying to meet these logistic challenges.

Robert Allston, the prominent South Carolina rice planter, viewed the battlefield at Bull Run and decided it had been a "glorious tho bloody" day. For the Union, however, the loss at Bull Run was sobering. Replacing McDowell with 34-year-old General George McClellan, Lincoln began his search for a northern commander capable of winning the war. McClellan, formerly an army engineer, confronted the task of

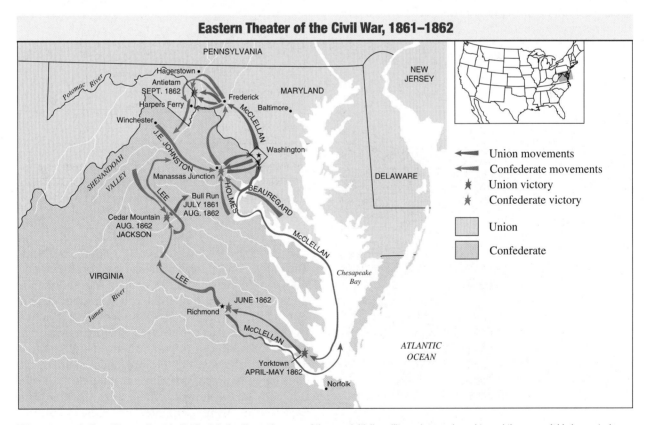

Eastern Theater of the Civil War, 1861–1862

This map reveals the military actions in the East during the early years of the war. Initially, military planners hoped to end the war quickly by capturing Richmond. They soon discovered that the Confederate army was too powerful to allow them an easy victory. Eventually, Lincoln decided to combine military pressure on Virginia with an effort in the West aimed at cutting the Confederacy in two.

transforming the Army of the Potomac into a fighting force. Short-term militias went home. When Scott retired in the fall of 1861, McClellan became general in chief of the Union armies.

McClellan had considerable organizational ability but no desire to be a daring leader on the battlefield. Convinced that the North must combine military victory with efforts to persuade the South to return to the Union, he sought to avoid unnecessary and embittering loss of life and property. He intended to win the war "by maneuvering rather than fighting."

In March 1862, pushed by an impatient Lincoln, McClellan finally led his army of 130,000 toward Richmond, now the Confederate capital. By late June, his army was close enough to hear Richmond's church bells pealing. But just as it seemed that victory was within grasp, Lee counterattacked and slowly drove the Union forces away from the city. Finally, orders came from Washington: abandon the Peninsula campaign.

Other Union defeats followed in 1862 as commanders came and went. In September, the South took the offensive with a bold invasion of Maryland. But after a costly defeat at Antietam, in which more than 5,000 soldiers were slaughtered and another 17,000 wounded on the grisliest day of the war, Lee withdrew his army to Virginia. Victory eluded both sides. The war in the East was stalemated.

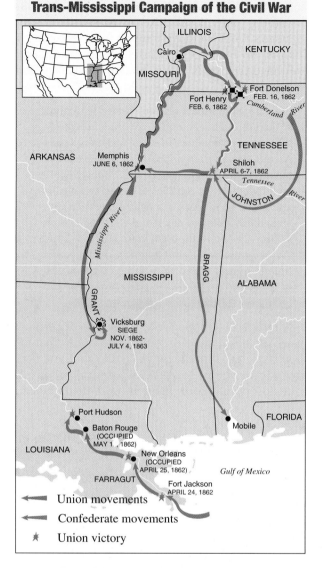

Trans-Mississippi Campaign of the Civil War

← Union movements

← Confederate movements

✴ Union victory

The military movements in the trans-Mississippi West appear here. Union forces operating in the Mississippi valley were attempting to separate Texas, Arkansas, and Louisiana from other southern states as part of an attempt to squeeze the Confederacy.

War in the West

The early struggle in the East focused on Richmond, the Confederacy's capital and one of the South's most important railroad, industrial, and munitions centers. But the East was only one of three theaters of action. Between the Appalachian Mountains and the Mississippi lay the western theater, the states of Kentucky, Tennessee, Mississippi, and Alabama. At its edge lay the Mississippi, with its vital river trade and its great port, New Orleans. Here both George Eagleton and Arthur Carpenter served. Beyond lay the trans-Mississippi West—Louisiana, Arkansas, Missouri, Texas, and the Great Plains—where Native American tribes joined the conflict on both sides.

This dying horse, stripped of saddle and bridle, was the mount of a Confederate officer killed during the battle of Antietam. The stark character of the picture reveals the devastating nature of the Civil War battlefield. *(Library of Congress)*

This photograph taken at a field hospital in Virginia during a battle in the summer of 1862 shows surgeons trying to attend to the crowds of wounded lying on the ground. Many deaths resulted from inadequate care for the wounded and sick of both armies. Although there was initial resistance to the idea of women becoming nurses in such hospitals, the dreadful shortage of qualified medical men and the huge workload that they faced eventually resulted in allowing women nurses into hospitals. One described her first reaction to the scene that greeted her eyes: "A strange sense of suffocation oppressed me, as the air by which I was surrounded was filled with poisonous vapors, and for a few minutes I doubted my own strength." *(Library of Congress)*

In the western theater, the Union had two strategic objectives: the domination of Kentucky and eastern Tennessee, the avenues to the South and West, and control of the Mississippi River to split the South in two. Major campaigns sought strategic points along rivers and railroads.

It was in the western theater that Ulysses S. Grant rose to prominence. His modest military credentials included a West Point education, service in the Mexican-American war, and an undistinguished stint in the peacetime army. After his resignation, he went bankrupt. At the war's opening, he was working in his family's leather store in Illinois. Soon after Fort Sumter, Grant enlisted as a colonel in an Illinois militia regiment. Within two months, he was a brigadier general.

Grant's military genius consisted of an ability to see beyond individual battles to larger goals. In 1862, he realized that the Tennessee and Cumberland Rivers were the paths for the successful invasion of Tennessee. A premature Confederate invasion of Kentucky allowed Grant to bring his forces into that state without arousing sharp local opposition. Assisted by gunboats, Grant was largely responsible for the capture of Fort Henry and Fort Donelson, key points on the rivers, in February 1862. His successes there raised fears among Confederate leaders that southern mountaineers, loyal to the Union, would rush to Grant's support.

Despite Grant's grasp of strategy, his army was nearly destroyed by a surprise Confederate attack at Shiloh Church in Tennessee. The North won this battle, but victory proved enormously costly. In that two-day engagement, the Union suffered over 13,000 casualties, while 10,000 Confederates lay dead or wounded. More men fell in this single battle than in the American Revolution, the War of 1812, and the Mexican-American War combined. Because neither army offered sufficient care on the battlefield, untreated wounds caused many of the deaths. A full day after the battle had ended, nine-tenths of the wounded still lay in the rain. Many died of exposure; others drowned in the downpour. Those who survived the weather had infected wounds by the time they received medical attention. Though more successful than efforts in the East, such devastating Union campaigns failed to bring decisive results. Western plans were never coordinated with eastern military activities. Victories there did not force the South to its knees.

The war in the trans-Mississippi West was a sporadic, far-flung struggle for control of the manpower and natural resources of this vast area. California was one prize that lured both armies into the Southwest. Confederate troops from Texas held Albuquerque and Santa Fe briefly in 1862. Volunteer soldiers from the Colorado mining fields, joined by Mexican Americans and other soldiers, drove the Texas Confederates from New Mexico. A Union force recruited in California arrived after the Confederates were gone. They spent the remainder of the Civil War years fighting the Apache and the Navajo and with brutal competence crushed both Native American nations.

Farther east was another prize, the Missouri River, which flowed into the Mississippi River, bordered Illinois, and affected military campaigns in Kentucky and Tennessee. Initially, Confederate troops were successful here, as they had been in New Mexico. But in March 1862, at Pea Ridge in northern Arkansas, the balance tilted in favor of the Union. There the Union forces defeated a Confederate army of 16,000 that included a brigade of Native Americans from the Five Civilized Nations. Missouri entered the Union camp for the first time in the war, and fierce guerrilla warfare continued in the region.

Naval Warfare

At the beginning of the war, Lincoln had decided to strangle the South with a naval blockade. But an effective blockade proved elusive. With no more than 33 ships, the Union navy tried to close up 189 ports along a 3,500-mile coastline. In 1861, the navy intercepted only about one blockade runner in ten and in 1862 one in eight. In the short run, the blockade did little damage to the South.

More successful were operations to gain footholds along the southern coast. In November 1861, a Union expedition took Port Royal Sound, where it freed the first slaves, and the nearby South Carolina sea islands. A few months later, the navy defeated a Confederate force on Roanoke Island, North Carolina. By gaining fueling stations and other important coastal points, the navy increased the possibility of making the blockade effective. The Union's greatest naval triumph in the early war years was the capture of New Orleans in 1862. The loss of the South's greatest port seriously weakened the Confederacy. The success of this amphibious effort stimulated other joint attempts to cut the South in two.

The Confederate leadership, recognizing that the South could not match the Union fleet, concentrated on developing new weapons like torpedoes and formidable ironclad vessels, a concept already successfully tested by the French navy. Because the Union fleet consisted primarily of wooden ships, iron ships might literally crash through the Union blockade.

The *Merrimac* was one key to southern naval strategy. Originally a U.S. warship sunk as the federal navy hurriedly abandoned the Norfolk Navy Yard early in the war, the Confederates raised the vessel and covered it with heavy iron armor. Rechristened the *Virginia*, the ship steamed out of Norfolk in March 1862, heading directly for the Union ships blocking the harbor. Using its 1,500-pound ram and guns, the *Virginia* drove a third of the ships aground and destroyed the squadron's largest ships. Victory was short-lived. The next day, the *Virginia* confronted the *Monitor*, a newly completed and better designed Union iron vessel. While the *Virginia* survived the crash, it withdrew and was burned during the evacuation of Norfolk that May. Southern attempts to buy and produce ironclad ships failed and southern hopes of evading the northern noose faded.

Though technological innovation failed to break the blockade, the Confederate navy's policy of harming northern commerce brought some success. Confederate raiders, many of them built in England, wreaked havoc on northern shipping. In its two-year career, the raider *Alabama* destroyed 69 Union mer-

This painting of the battle between the Confederate *Virginia* (stubbornly called the *Merrimac* by northerners) and the Union *Monitor* captures the dramatic impact of the new iron ships. During this engagement, the *Monitor* showed it could manuever more easily than the Confederate vessel. Both navies eventually used these innovative iron ships, but the Confederacy could never match the pace of northern production. *(Chicago Historical Society)*

chant vessels valued at more than $6 million. But while such blows were costly to the North, they did not seriously damage its overall war effort.

Throughout the first two years of conflict, both sides achieved victories, but the war remained deadlocked. Although the South was far from being defeated, the North was as far from giving up or accepting southern independence. The costs of war, in manpower and supplies, far exceeded what either side had anticipated. The need to replace lost men and supplies thus loomed ever more serious at the end of 1862.

Cotton Diplomacy

Both sides in the Civil War realized that attitudes in Europe could be critical. European diplomatic recognition of the Confederacy would give the nation credibility in the eyes of the rest of the world. Furthermore, European loans and assistance might bring the South victory just as French and Dutch aid had helped the American colonies win their independence. If the European nations refused to recognize the South, however, the fiction of the Union was kept alive, undermining Confederate chances for long-term survival. The European powers, of course, consulted their own national interests. Neither England nor France, the two most important nations, wished to back the losing side. Nor did they wish to upset Europe's delicate balance of power by hasty intervention in American affairs. One by one, therefore, the European states declared a policy of neutrality.

Southerners were sure that cotton would be their trump card. English and French textile mills needed cotton, and southerners believed that their owners would eventually force government recognition of the Confederacy and an end to the North's blockade. But a glut of cotton in 1860 and 1861 left foreign mill owners oversupplied. As stockpiles dwindled, European industrialists found cotton in India and Egypt. The conviction that cotton was "the king who can shake the jewels in the crown of Queen Victoria" proved false.

Union Secretary of State Seward sought above all else to prevent diplomatic recognition of the Confederacy. The North had its own economic ties with Europe, so the Union was not as disadvantaged as southerners thought. Seward daringly threatened Great Britain with war if it interfered in what he insisted was an internal matter. Some called his boldness reckless, even mad. Nevertheless, his policy succeeded. Even though England allowed the construction of Confederate raiders in its ports, it did not intervene in American affairs in 1861 or 1862. Nor did the other European powers. Unless the military situation changed dramatically, the Europeans were willing to sit on the sidelines.

Common Problems, Novel Solutions

As the conflict dragged on into 1863, unanticipated problems appeared in both the Union and the Confederacy, and leaders devised novel approaches to solve them. War acted as a catalyst for changes that no one could have imagined in the heady spring days of 1861.

The problem of fighting a long war was partly monetary. Both treasuries had been empty initially, and the war proved extraordinarily expensive. Neither side considered trying to finance the war by imposing direct taxes. Such an approach violated custom and risked alienating support. Nevertheless, each side was so starved for funds that it initiated taxation on a small scale. Ultimately, taxes financed 21 percent of the North's war expenses (but only 1 percent of southern expenses). Both treasuries also tried borrowing. Northerners bought over $2 billion worth of bonds, but southerners proved reluctant to buy their government's bonds.

As in the American Revolution, the unwelcome solution was to print paper money. In August 1861, the Confederacy put into circulation $100 million in

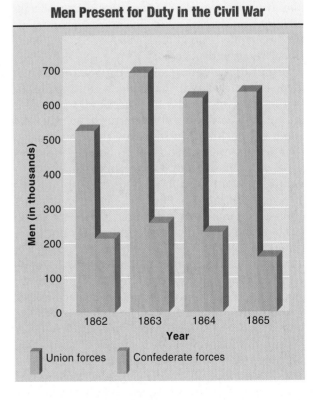

Men Present for Duty in the Civil War

Men (in thousands) — Union forces / Confederate forces, by Year (1862, 1863, 1864, 1865)

This chart demonstrates the growing superiority of the North in terms of manpower and the impact of draft laws. After 1863, blacks, like native-born Americans and Irish and German immigrants, served in the armed forces.

crudely engraved bills. Millions more followed the next year. Five months later, the Union issued $150 million in paper money, soon nicknamed "greenbacks" because of their color. Although financing the war with paper money was unexpected, the resulting inflation was not. Inflation was particularly troublesome in the Confederacy, but a "modest" 80 percent increase in food prices brought Union city families near starvation and contributed to urban unhappiness during the war.

Both sides confronted similar manpower problems as initial enthusiasm for the war evaporated. Soldiering, it turned out, was nothing like the militia parades and outings familiar to most American males. Young men were shocked at the deadliness of diseases that accompanied the army wherever it went and were unprepared for the boredom of camp life. As one North Carolina soldier explained, "If anyone wishes to become used to the crosses and trials of this life, let him enter camp life." None was prepared for the vast and impersonal destruction of the battlefield, which made a mockery of values like courage and honor. It was with anguish that Robert Carter of Massachusetts saw bodies tossed into trenches "with not a prayer, eulogy or tear to distinguish them from so many animals." Those in the service longed to go home. The swarm of volunteers disappeared. Rather than fill their military quotas from within, rich northern communities began offering bounties of $800 to $1,000 to outsiders who would join up.

Arthur Carpenter's letters give a good picture of life in the ranks and a young man's growing disillusionment with the war. As Carpenter's regiment moved into Kentucky and Tennessee in the winter of 1862, his enthusiasm for army life evaporated. "Soldiering in Kentucky and Tennessee," he complained, "is not so pretty as it was in Indianapolis. . . . We have been half starved, half frozen, and half drowned. The mud in Kentucky is awful." Soldiering often meant marching over rutted roads carrying 50 or 60 pounds of equipment with insufficient food, water, or supplies. One blanket was not enough in the winter. In the summer, stifling woolen uniforms attracted lice and other vermin. Poor food, bugs, inadequate sanitation, and exposure invited disease. Carpenter marched through Tennessee suffering from diarrhea and then fever. His regiment left him behind in a convalescent barracks in Louisville, which he fled as soon as he could. He feared the hospital at least as much as the sickness. "99 Surgeons out of a hundred," he wrote his parents, "would not know whether his patient had the horse distemper, lame toe, or any other disease."

Confederate soldiers, even less well supplied than their northern counterparts, complained similarly. In 1862, a Virginia captain described what General Lee called the best army "the world ever saw":

> During our forced marches and hard fights, the soldiers have been compelled to throw away their knapsacks and there is scarcely a private in the army who has a change of clothing of any kind. Hundreds of men are perfectly barefooted and there is no telling when they can be supplied with shoes.

In such circumstances, desertion was common. An estimated one of every nine men enlisting in the Confederate armies and one of every seven in the Union armies deserted.

As the manpower problems became critical, both governments resorted to the draft. Despite the sacrosanct notion of states' rights, the Confederate Congress passed the first conscription act in American history in March 1862. Four months later, the Union Congress also approved a draft measure. Both laws sought to encourage men already in the army to reenlist and to stimulate volunteers rather than to force men to serve. Ultimately, over 30 percent of the Confederate army and 6 percent of the Union forces were draftees.

The Confederacy relied more heavily on the draft than the Union did because the North's initial manpower pool was larger and growing. During the war, 180,000 foreigners of military age poured into the northern states. Some came specifically to claim bounties and fight. Immigrants made up at least 20 percent of the Union army.

Necessary though they were, draft laws were very unpopular. The first Confederate conscription declared all able-bodied men between 18 and 35 eligible for military service but allowed numerous exemptions and the purchase of substitutes. Critics complained that the provision entitling every planter with more than 20 slaves to one exemption from military service favored rich slave owners. Certainly, the legislation fed class tension in the South and encouraged disloyalty and desertion among the poorer classes, particularly among southern mountaineers. The advice one woman shouted after her husband as he was dragged off to the army was hardly unique. "You desert again, quick as you kin. . . . Desert, Jake!" The law, as one southerner pointed out, "aroused a spirit of rebellion."

Northern legislation was neither more popular nor fair. The 1863 draft allowed the hiring of substitutes, and $300 bought an exemption from military service. Workers, already suffering from inflation, resented the ease with which moneyed citizens could avoid army duty. In July 1863, the resentment boiled over in New York City in the largest civil disturbance of the nineteenth century.

These advertisements from a Virginia newspaper include two for substitutes, indicating the advantages money provided for those who wished to avoid military service. (*Virginia Historical Society, Richmond*)

The three-day riot came only a month after a work stoppage on the New York waterfront. The process of selecting several thousand conscripts began on a weekend in early July. By Monday, workers opposed to the draft were parading through the streets. Several Irish members of the Black Joker Volunteer Fire Company whose names had been listed were determined to go further than peaceful protest by destroying draft records and the Enrollment Office. Events spun out of control as a mob also burned the armory, plundered the houses of the rich, and looted jewelry stores. Blacks, whom the Irish hated as economic competitors and the cause of the war, became special targets. Mobs shouting, "Vengeance on every nigger in New York," beat and lynched blacks and even burned the Colored Orphan Asylum. More than 100 people died in the violence. There was much truth in the accusation that the war on both sides was a rich man's war but a poor man's fight.

Political Dissension, 1862

As the war continued, rumbles of dissension grew louder. On February 24, 1862, the *Richmond Examiner* summarized many southerners' frustration. "The Confederacy has had everything that was required for success but one, and that one thing it was and is supposed to possess more than anything else, namely Talent." As victory proved elusive, necessitating unpopular measures like the draft, criticism of Confederate leaders mounted. Jefferson Davis's vice president, Alexander Stephens of Georgia, became one of the administration's bitterest accusers. Public criticism reflected private disapproval. Wrote one southerner to a friend, "Impeach Jeff Davis for incompetency & call a convention of the States. . . . West Point is death to us & sick Presidents & Generals are equally fatal."

Because the South had no party system, dissatisfaction with Davis and his handling of the war tended to be factional, petty, and personal. No party mechanism existed to channel or curb irresponsible criticism. Detractors rarely felt it necessary to offer programs in place of Davis's policies. Davis suffered personally from the carping comments of his detractors. More important, the Confederacy suffered. Without a party leader's traditional weapons and rewards, Davis had no mechanism to generate enthusiasm for his war policies.

Although Lincoln has since become a folk hero, at the time, many northerners derided his performance and eagerly looked forward to a new president in 1864. Peace Democrats, called Copperheads, claimed that Lincoln betrayed the Constitution and that working-class Americans bore the brunt of his policy of conscription. New York Democrats warned the city's Irish residents that freed blacks would "steal the work and bread of honest Irish." Immigrant workers in eastern cities and those who lived in the southern parts of the Midwest had little sympathy for abolitionism or blacks, and they supported the antiwar stance of the Copperheads. Even Democrats favoring the war effort found Lincoln arbitrary and tyrannical. Fearing his expansion of presidential power, they also worried that extreme Republicans would push Lincoln into making the war a crusade for the abolition of slavery.

Republicans were themselves divided. Moderates favored a cautious approach toward winning the war, fearing the possible consequences of emancipating the slaves, confiscating Confederate property, or arming blacks. The radicals, however, urged Lincoln to make emancipation a wartime objective. They hoped for a victory that would revolutionize southern social and racial arrangements.

Lincoln had been moderate on the issue of slavery before the war, advocating the end of its expansion in the West but not its abolition in the South. He began changing his mind in early 1862. The reduction of the congressional Republican majority in the fall elections of 1862 made it imperative that Lincoln listen not only to both factions of his party but also to the Democratic opposition.

∼ THE TIDE TURNS, 1863–1865

Hard political realities as well as Lincoln's sense of the public's mood help explain why he delayed an emancipation proclamation until 1863. Like congressional Democrats, many northerners supported a war for the Union but not one for emancipation. Not only did many, if not most, whites see blacks as inferior, but they also suspected that emancipation would trigger a massive influx of former slaves who would steal white men's jobs and political rights. Race riots in New York, Brooklyn, Philadelphia, and Buffalo dramatized white attitudes. In Cincinnati, Irish dockworkers attacked blacks who were offering to work for less pay with the cry, "Let's clear out the niggers." Arthur Carpenter's evaluation of blacks was typical of many northern soldiers confronting blacks for the first time. In December 1861, he wrote to his parents:

> No one who has ever seen the nigger in all its glory on the southern plantations . . . will ever vote for emancipation. . . . If emancipation is to be the policy of the war (and I think it will not) I do not care how quick the country goes to pot. The negro never was intended to be equal with the white man.

The Emancipation Proclamation, 1863

If the president moved too fast on emancipation, he risked losing the allegiance of people like Carpenter, offending the border states, and increasing the Democrats' chances for political victory. Moreover, he had at first hoped that pro-Union sentiment would emerge in the South and compel its leaders to abandon their rebellion. But if Lincoln did not move at all, he would alienate abolitionists and lose the support of radical Republicans, which he could ill afford.

For these reasons, Lincoln proceeded cautiously. At first, he hoped the border states would take the initiative. In the early spring of 1862, he urged Congress to pass a joint resolution offering federal compensation to states beginning a "gradual abolishment of slavery." Border state opposition killed the idea and indicated reluctance to believe, as Lincoln did, that the "friction and abrasion" of war would finally end slavery. Abolitionists and northern blacks, however, greeted Lincoln's proposal with a "thrill of joy."

That summer, Lincoln told his cabinet he intended to emancipate the slaves. Secretary of State Seward urged the president to delay any general proclamation until the North won a decisive military victory. Otherwise, he warned, Lincoln would appear to be urging racial insurrection behind the Confederate lines to compensate for northern military bungling.

Lincoln followed Seward's advice, using that summer and fall to prepare the North for the shift in the war's purpose. To counteract white racial fears of free blacks, he promoted various schemes for establishing free black colonies in Haiti and Panama. Seizing unexpected opportunities, he lay the groundwork for the proclamation itself. In August, Horace Greeley, the influential abolitionist editor of the New York *Tribune*, printed an open letter to Lincoln attacking him for failing to act on slavery. In his reply, Lincoln linked the idea of emancipation to military necessity. His primary goal, he wrote, was to save the Union:

> If I could save the Union without freeing any slave, I would do it; and if I could save it by freeing all the slaves, I would do it; and if I could do it by freeing some and leaving others alone, I would also do that. What I do about Slavery and the colored race, I do because I believe it helps to save this Union.

If Lincoln attacked slavery, then, it would be only because emancipation would save white lives, preserve the democratic process, and win the conflict for the Union.

In September 1862, the Union victory at Antietam gave Lincoln the opportunity to issue a preliminary emancipation proclamation. It stated that unless rebellious states (or parts of states in rebellion) returned to the Union by January 1, 1863, the president would declare their slaves "forever free." Although supposedly aimed at bringing the southern states back into the Union, Lincoln never expected the South to lay down arms after two years of bloodshed. Rather, he was preparing northerners to accept the eventuality of emancipation on the grounds of necessity. Frederick Douglass greeted the president's action with jubilation. "We shout for joy," he wrote, "that we live to record this righteous decree."

Not all northerners shared Douglass's joy. In fact, the September proclamation probably harmed Lincoln's party in the fall elections. As one Democratic ditty put it:

> *"De Union!" used to be de cry—*
> *For dat we want it strong;*
> *But now de motto seems to be,*
> *"De nigger, right or wrong."*

Although the elections of 1862 weakened the Republicans' grasp on the national government, they did not destroy it. Still, cautious cabinet members begged Lincoln to forget about emancipation. His refusal demonstrated his vision and humanity, as did his efforts to reduce racial fears. "Is it dreaded that the freed people will swarm forth and cover the whole land?" he asked. "Are they not already in the land? Will liberation make them any more numerous? Equally distributed among the whites of the whole country, and there would be but one colored to seven whites. Could the one, in any way, greatly disturb the other?"

Finally, on New Year's Day, 1863, Lincoln issued the final Emancipation Proclamation as he had promised. It was an "act of justice, warranted by the Constitution upon military necessity." Thus, what had started as a war to save the Union now also became a struggle that, if victorious, would free the slaves. Yet the proclamation had no immediate impact on slavery. It affected only slaves living in the unconquered portions of the Confederacy. It was silent about slaves in the border states and in parts of the South already in northern hands. These limitations led Elizabeth Cady Stanton and Susan B. Anthony to establish the woman's Loyal National League to lobby Congress to emancipate all southern slaves.

Though the Emancipation Proclamation did not immediately liberate southern slaves from their masters, it had a tremendous symbolic importance. On New Year's Day, blacks gathered outside the White House to cheer the president and tell him that if he would "come out of that palace, they would hug him to death." They realized that the proclamation had changed the nature of the war. For the first time, the government had committed itself to freeing slaves. Jubilant blacks could only believe that the president's action heralded a new era for their race. More immediately, the proclamation sanctioned the policy of accepting blacks as soldiers into the military. Blacks also hoped that the news would reach southern slaves, encouraging them either to flee to Union lines or to subvert the southern war effort by refusing to work for their masters.

Diplomatic concerns also lay behind the Emancipation Proclamation. Lincoln and his advisers anticipated that the commitment to abolish slavery would favorably impress foreign powers. European statesmen, however, did not abandon their cautious stance toward the Union. The English prime minister called the proclamation "trash." But important segments of the English public who opposed slavery now came to regard any attempt to help the South as immoral. Foreigners could better understand and sympathize with a war to free the slaves than they could with a war to save the Union. In diplomacy, where image is so important, Lincoln had created a more attractive picture of the North. The Emancipation Proclamation became the North's symbolic call for human freedom.

Unanticipated Consequences of War

The Emancipation Proclamation was but another example of the war's surprising consequences. Innovation was necessary for victory. In the final two years of the war, both North and South experimented on the battlefields and behind the lines in desperate efforts to conclude the conflict successfully.

One of the Union's experiments involved using black troops for combat duty. Blacks had offered

This depiction of African Americans celebrating the Emancipation Proclamation appeared in the French publication *Le Monde Illustre.* The artist has provided a triumphant and sympathetic picture of rejoicing freed people. The appearance of such a picture in France points to the importance of the Emancipation Proclamation in legitimizing the Union cause in Europe. *(Public Domain)*

themselves as soldiers in 1861 but had been turned away. They were serving as cooks, laborers, teamsters, and carpenters in the army, however, and composed as much as a quarter of the navy. But as white casualties mounted, so did the interest in black service on the battlefield. The Union government allowed states to escape draft quotas if they enlisted enough volunteers, and they allowed them to count southern black enlistees on their state rosters. Northern governors grew increasingly interested in black military service. One piece of doggerel reflected changing attitudes:

> Some tell us 'tis a burnin' shame
> To make the naygers fight;
> And that the thrade of bein' kilt
> Belongs but to the white:
> But as for me, upon my soul!
> So liberal are we here.
> I'll let Sambo be murthered instead of myself
> On every day in the year.

Beyond white self-interest lay the promises of the Emancipation Proclamation and the desire to prove blacks' value to the Union. Black leaders like Frederick Douglass pressed for military service. "Once let the black man get upon his person the brass letter, U.S., let him get an eagle on his button, and a musket on his shoulder and bullets in his pocket," Douglass believed that "there is no power on earth that can deny that he has earned the right to citizenship." By the war's end, 186,000 blacks (10 percent of the army) had served the Union cause, 134,111 of them escapees from slave states.

Enrolling blacks in the Union army was an important step toward citizenship and acceptance of blacks by white society. But the black experience in the army highlighted some of the obstacles to racial acceptance. Black soldiers, usually led by white officers, were second-class soldiers for most of the war, receiving lower pay ($10 a month as compared with $13), poorer food, often more menial work, and fewer benefits than

Newspaper engravings provided civilians with images of the conflict. This colored lithograph by Currier & Ives was produced a generation after the war, but it is very much like the journalistic images of the time. The picture shows a famous black regiment, the 54th Massachusetts, valiantly storming Fort Wagner, South Carolina. James Gooding, a member of the volunteer regiment and a free black from New Bedford, Massachusetts, described the assault. "We went at it, over the ditch and on to the parapet through a deadly fire; but we could not get into the fort. We met the foe on the parapet of Wagner with the bayonet—we were exposed to a murderous fire. . . . Mortal men could not stand such a fire, and the assault on Wagner was a failure." The experiences of the 54th form the basis for the Hollywood movie *Glory*. (*Library of Congress*)

whites. Even whites who were working to equalize black and white pay often considered blacks inferior. Many white soldiers, including an entire regiment from Illinois, quit the service rather than fight alongside blacks.

The army's racial experiment had mixed results. But the faithful and courageous service of black troops helped modify some of the most demeaning white racial stereotypes of blacks. The black soldiers, many of them former slaves, who conquered the South felt a sense of pride and dignity as they performed their duties. Wrote one, "We march through these fine thoroughfares where once the slave was forbid being out after nine P.M. . . . Negro soldiers!—with banners floating."

As the conflict continued, basic assumptions about how it should be waged weakened. One wartime casualty was the courtly idea that war involved only armies. Early in the war, many officers tried to protect civilians and their property. In the Richmond campaign, General McClellan actually posted guards to prevent stealing. Such concern for rebel property soon vanished, and along with it went chickens, corn, livestock, and, as George Eagleton noted with disgust, even the furnishings of churches, down to the binding of the Bible in the pulpit. Southern troops, on the few occasions when they came North, also lived off the land. War touched all of society, not just the battlefield participants.

Changing Military Strategies, 1863–1865

In the early war years, the South's military strategy combined defense with selective maneuvers. Until the summer of 1863, the strategy seemed to be succeeding, at least in the eastern theater. But an occasional

victory over the invading northern army, such as at Fredericksburg in December 1862, did not change the course of the war. Realizing this, Lee reviewed his strategy and concluded, "There is nothing to be gained by this army remaining quietly on the defensive." Unless the South won victories in the North, he believed, it could not gain the peace it so desperately needed.

In the summer of 1863, Lee led the Confederate army of Northern Virginia across the Potomac into Maryland and southern Pennsylvania. His goal was a victory that would threaten both Philadelphia and Washington. He even dreamed of capturing a northern city. Such spectacular feats would surely bring diplomatic recognition and might even force the North to sue for peace.

At Gettysburg on a hot and humid July 1, Lee came abruptly face-to-face with a Union army led by General George Meade. During three days of fighting, the fatal obsession with the infantry charge returned as Lee ordered costly assaults that probably lost him the battle. On July 3, Lee sent three divisions, about 15,000 men in all, against the Union center. The assault, known as Pickett's Charge, was as futile as it was gallant. At 700 yards, the Union artillery opened fire. One southern officer described the scene: "Pickett's division just seemed to melt away in the blue musketry smoke which now covered the hill. Nothing but stragglers came back."

Lee's dreams of victory died that hot week, with grave consequences for the southern cause. Fighting in the eastern theater dragged on for another year and a half, but Lee's Gettysburg losses were so heavy that he could never mount another southern offensive. Instead, the Confederacy committed itself to a

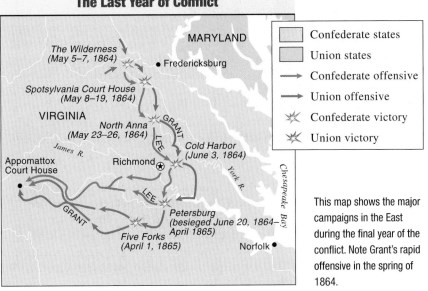

This map shows the major campaigns in the East during the final year of the conflict. Note Grant's rapid offensive in the spring of 1864.

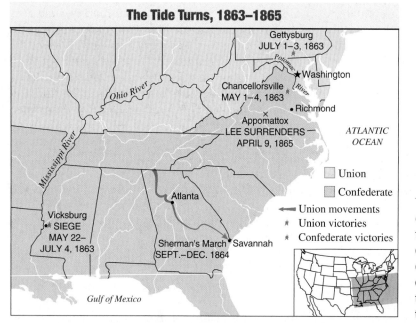

The Tide Turns, 1863–1865

This map highlights important military events during the war's final two years. In the West, Union forces took Vicksburg, and in the East at the battle of Gettysburg they defeated the Confederacy's final effort to bring the war north. During the final stages of the war, Sherman and his army cut a swath through Georgia and then marched north through the Carolinas.

desperate defensive struggle. Gettysburg marked the turn of the military tide in the East.

Despite the Gettysburg victory, Lincoln was dissatisfied with General Meade, who had failed to finish off Lee's demoralized and exhausted army as it retreated. His disappointment soon faded with news of a great victory at Vicksburg in the western theater. The commander, Ulysses S. Grant, would soon solve Lincoln's leadership problem. His July 4 triumph at Vicksburg was thus doubly significant. Vicksburg represented the completion of the Union campaign to gain control of the Mississippi River and to divide the South. Grant's successful capture of the city illustrated the boldness and flexibility that Lincoln sought in a commander.

By the summer of 1863, the military situation finally looked promising for the North. The Union controlled much of Arkansas, Louisiana, Mississippi, Missouri, Kentucky, and Tennessee. In March 1864, Lincoln recognized Grant as the commander to conclude the war and appointed him general in chief of the Union armies. Grant planned for victory within a year. "The art of war is simple enough," he reasoned. "Find out where your enemy is. Get at him as soon as you can. Strike at him as hard as you can, and keep moving on."

As an outsider to the prewar military establishment, Grant had no difficulty rejecting conventional military wisdom. "If men make war in slavish observance of rules, they will fail," he asserted. He sought not one decisive engagement but rather a grim campaign of annihilation, using the North's superior resources of men and supplies to wear down and defeat the South. Although Grant's plan entailed large casualties on both sides, he justified the strategy by

arguing that "now the carnage was to be limited to a single year."

A campaign of annihilation involved the destruction not only of enemy armies but also of the resources that fueled the southern war effort. Although the idea of cutting the enemy off from needed supplies was implicit in the naval blockade, economic or "total" warfare was a relatively new and shocking idea. Grant, however, "regarded it as humane to both sides to protect the persons of those found at their homes, but to consume everything that could be used to support or supply armies." Following this policy, he set out after Lee's army in Virginia. General William Tecumseh Sherman, who pursued General Joseph Johnston from Tennessee toward Atlanta, further refined this plan.

The war, Sherman believed, must also be waged in the minds of civilians. His desire was to make southerners "fear and dread" their foes. Therefore, his campaign to seize Atlanta and his march to Savannah spread destruction and terror. Ordered to forage "liberally" on the land, his army left desolation in its wake. "Reduction to poverty," Sherman asserted, "brings prayers for peace." A Georgia woman described in her diary the impact of Sherman's march:

> There was hardly a fence left standing all the way from Sparta to Gordon. The fields were trampled down and the road was lined with carcasses of horses, hogs and cattle that the invaders, unable either to consume or to carry away with them, had wantonly shot down, to starve out the people. . . .

This albumen print by Timothy H. O'Sullivan is entitled "A Harvest of Death, Gettysburg, Pennsylvania, July, 1863." It captures the quiet and misery of the battlefield and suggests the important role photography was coming to play in recording the sweep of American life. *(Rare Books Division, The New York Public Library, Astor, Lenox and Tilden Foundations)*

The dwellings that were standing all showed signs of pillage, and on every plantation we saw . . . charred remains.

This destruction, with its goal of total victory, showed once more how conflict produced the unexpected. The war that both North and South had hoped would be quick and relatively painless was ending after four long years with great cost to both sides. But the bitter nature of warfare during that final year threatened Lincoln's hopes for reconciliation.

CHANGES WROUGHT BY WAR

As bold new tactics emerged both on and off the battlefield, both governments took steps that changed their societies in surprising ways. Of the two, the South, which had left the Union to conserve a traditional way of life, experienced the more radical transformation.

A New South

The expansion of the central government's power in the South, starting with the passage of the 1862 Conscription Act, continued in the last years of the war. Secession grew out of the concept of states' rights, but, ironically, winning the war depended on central direction and control. Many southerners denounced Davis as a tyrant and a despot because he recognized the need for the central government to take the lead. Despite the accusations, the Confederate Congress cooperated with him and

established important precedents. In 1863, it enacted a comprehensive tax law and an impressment act that allowed government agents to requisition food, horses, wagons, and other necessary war materials, often for only about half their market price. These were prime examples of the central government's power to interfere with private property. Government impressment of slaves for war work in 1863 affected the very form of private property that had originally driven the South from the Union.

The Conscription Act of 1862 did not solve the Confederate army's manpower problems. By 1864, the southern armies were only a third the size of the Union forces. Hence, in February 1864, an expanded conscription measure made all white males between the ages 17 and 50 subject to the draft. By 1865, the necessities of war had led to the unthinkable: arming slaves as soldiers. Black companies were recruited in Richmond and other southern towns. However, because the war soon ended, no blacks actually fought for the Confederacy.

In a message sent to Congress in November 1864, Davis speculated on some of the issues involved in arming slaves. "Should a slave who had served his country" be retained in servitude, he wondered, "or should his emancipation be held out to him as a reward for faithful service, or should it be granted at once on the promise of such service . . . ?" The war fought by the South to preserve slavery ended in the contemplation of emancipation.

Recovering the Past

PHOTOGRAPHY

The invention of photography in 1839 expanded the visual and imaginative world of nineteenth-century Americans. For the first time, Americans could visually record events in their own lives and see the images of people and incidents from far away. Photographs, of course, also expand the boundaries of the historian's world. As photographic techniques became simpler, more and more visual information about the nineteenth century was captured. Historians can use photographs to discover what nineteenth-century Americans wore, how they celebrated weddings and funerals, and what their families, houses, and cities looked like. Pictures of election campaigns, parades, strikes, and wars show the texture of public life. But historians can also study photographs, as they do paintings, to glean information about attitudes and norms. The choice of subjects, the way people and objects are arranged and grouped, and the relationships between people in photographs are all clues to the social and cultural values of nineteenth-century Americans.

Some knowledge of the early history of photography helps place the visual evidence in the proper perspective. The earliest type of photograph, the daguerreotype, was not a print but the negative itself on a sheet of silver-plated copper. The first daguerreotype required between 15 and 30 minutes for the proper exposure. This accounts for the stiff and formal quality of many of these photographs. Glass ambrotypes (negatives on glass) and tintypes (negatives on gray iron bases), developed after the daguerreotype, were easier and cheaper

Mathew Brady, *Confederate Captives, Gettysburg. (National Archives)*

Mathew Brady, *Burial Party at Cold Harbor. (Chicago Historical Society)*

to produce. But both techniques produced only one picture and required what to us would seem an interminable time for exposure.

A major breakthrough came in the 1850s with the development of the wet-plate process. In this process, the photographer coated a glass negative with a sensitive solution, exposed the negative (i.e., took the picture), and then quickly developed it. The new procedure required a relatively short exposure time of perhaps five seconds out of doors and one minute inside. Action shots, however, were still not feasible. The entire process tied the photographer to the darkroom. Traveling photographers carried their darkrooms with them. The advantage of the wet-plate process was that it was possible to make many paper prints from one negative, opening new commercial vistas for professional photographers.

Mathew Brady, a fashionable Washington photographer, realizing that the camera was the "eye of history," asked Lincoln for permission to record the war with his camera. He and his team of photographers left about 8,000 glass negatives, currently stored in the Library of Congress and the National Archives, as their record of the Civil War. Shown here are two photographs, one of three Confederate soldiers captured at Gettysburg, the other of the battlefield of Cold Harbor in Virginia.

In the first photograph, study and describe the three soldiers. How are they posed? What kind of clothes are they wearing? What about their equipment? What seems to be their physical condition? Using this photograph as evidence, what might you conclude about the southern soldier—his equipment, uniforms, shoes? How well fed do the men in the picture appear? What attitudes are conveyed through their facial expressions and poses? Finally, what kind of mood was the northern photographer trying to create? What might a northern viewer conclude about the South's war effort after looking at this picture?

The second picture was taken in April 1865, about a year after the battle at Cold Harbor. In the background, you can see two Union soldiers digging graves. In the foreground are the grisly remains of the battle. What do you think is the intent of the photograph? The choice of subject matter shows clearly that photography reveals attitudes as well as facts. What attitude toward war and death is conveyed in this picture? Why is the burial taking place a full year after the battle? What does this tell us about the nature of civil warfare? Notice that the soldiers ordered to undertake this ghastly chore are black, as was customary. What might this scene suggest about the experience of black soldiers in the Union army?

These photographs just begin to suggest what can be discovered from old photographs. Your local historical society and library probably have photograph collections available to you. In addition, at home or in a relative's attic you may find visual records of your family and its history.

Southern agriculture also changed under the pressure of war. Earlier, the South had imported food from the North, concentrating on the production of staples such as cotton and tobacco for market. Now, more and more land was turned over to food crops. Some farmers voluntarily shifted crops, but others responded only to state laws reducing the acreage permitted for cotton and tobacco cultivation. These measures never succeeded in raising enough food to feed southerners adequately. But they contributed to a dramatic decline in the production of cotton, from 4.5 million bales in 1861 to 300,000 bales in 1864.

The South had always depended on imported manufactured goods. Even though some blockade runners were able to evade the Union ships, the noose tightened after 1862. The Confederacy could not, in any case, rely on blockade runners to arm and equip the army. Thus, war triggered the expansion of military-related industries in the South. Here, too, the government played a crucial role. The war and navy offices directed industrial development, awarding contracts to private manufacturing firms like Richmond's Tredegar Iron Works and operating other factories themselves. The number of southerners working in industry rose dramatically. In 1861, the Tredegar Iron Works employed 700 workers; two years later, it employed 2,500, more than half of them black. The head of the Army Ordnance Bureau reflected on the amazing transformation. "Where three years ago we were not making a gun, pistol nor a sabre, no shot nor shell . . . we now make all these in quantities to meet the demands of our large armies." At the end of the war, the soldiers were better supplied with arms and munitions than with food.

Although the war did not transform the southern class structure, relations between the classes began to change. The pressures of the struggle undermined the solidarity of whites, which was based on racism and supposed political unanimity. Draft resistance and desertion reflected growing alienation from a war perceived as serving only the interests of upper-class plantation owners. More and more yeoman families suffered grinding poverty as the men went off to war and government officials and armies requisitioned needed resources. A poor farmer from Georgia, Harlan Fuller, explained his family's situation in the spring of 1864. Fuller was 50 but now eligible for the draft. "I am liable at any time to be taken away from my little crops leaving my family almost without provisions & no hope of making any crop atal. I have sent six sons to the war & now the seventh enrolled he being the last I have no help left atal." This new poverty was an ominous hint of the decline of the yeoman farming class in postwar years.

The Victorious North

Although changes in the South were more noticeable, the Union's government and economy also responded to the demands of war. Like Davis, Lincoln was accused of being a dictator. Although he rarely tried to control Congress, veto its legislation, or direct government departments, Lincoln did use executive power freely. He violated the writ of habeas corpus by suspending the civil rights of over 13,000 northerners, who languished in prison without trials; curbed the freedom of the press because of supposedly disloyal and inflammatory articles; established conscription; issued the Emancipation Proclamation; and removed army generals. Lincoln argued that this vast extension of presidential power was temporarily justified because, as president, he was responsible for defending and preserving the Constitution.

Many of the wartime changes in government proved more permanent than Lincoln had imagined. The financial necessities of war helped revolutionize the country's banking system. Ever since Andrew Jackson's destruction of the Bank of the United States, state banks had served American financial needs. Treasury Secretary Chase found this banking system inadequate and chaotic and proposed to replace it. In 1863 and 1864, Congress passed banking acts that established a national currency issued by federally chartered banks and backed by government bonds. The country had a federal banking system once again.

The northern economy also changed under wartime demands. The need to feed soldiers and civilians stimulated the expansion of agriculture and new investment in farm machinery. With so many men off soldiering, farmers were at first short of labor. McCormick reapers performed the work of four to six men, and farmers began to buy them. During the war, McCormick sold 165,000 of his machines. Northern farming, especially in the Midwest, was well on the way to becoming mechanized. Farmers not only succeeded in growing enough grain to feed civilians and soldiers but also gathered a surplus to export as well.

The war also selectively stimulated manufacturing. Although it is easy to imagine that northern industry as a whole expanded during the Civil War, in fact, the war retarded overall economic growth. War consumed rather than generated wealth. Between 1860 and 1870, the annual rate of increase in real manufacturing value added was only 2.3 percent, in contrast with 7.8 percent for the years between 1840 and 1860 and 6 percent for the period 1870 to 1900. Some important prewar industries, like cotton textiles, languished without a supply of southern cotton.

However, industries that produced for the war machine, especially those with advantages of scale, expanded and made large profits. Each year, the Union army required 1.5 million uniforms and 3 million pairs of shoes; the woolen and leather industries grew accordingly. Meatpackers and producers of iron, steel, and pocket watches all profited from wartime opportunities. Cincinnati was one city that flourished from supplying soldiers with everything from pork to soap and candles.

On the Home Front, 1861–1865

In numerous, less tangible ways, the war transformed northern and southern society. The very fact of conflict established a new perspective for most civilians. War news vied with local events for their attention. They read newspapers and national weekly magazines with a new eagerness. The use of the mails increased dramatically as they corresponded with faraway relatives and friends. Wrote one North Carolina woman, "I never liked to write letters before, but it is a pleasure as well as a relief now." Distant events became almost as real and vivid as those at home. The war helped make Americans less parochial, integrating them into the larger world.

For some Americans, like John D. Rockefeller and Andrew Carnegie, war brought army contracts and unanticipated riches. The New York *Herald* reported that New York City had never been "so gay, . . . so crowded, so prosperous," as it was in March 1864. Residents of Cincinnati noted people who "became suddenly immensely wealthy, and in their fine equipages, with liveried servants, rolled in magnificence along the city streets." In the South, blockade runners made fortunes slipping luxury goods past Union ships.

For the majority of Americans, however, war meant deprivation. The war effort gobbled up a large part of each side's resources, and ultimately ordinary people suffered. To be sure, the demand for workers ended unemployment and changed employment patterns. Large numbers of women and blacks entered the workforce, a phenomenon that would be repeated in all future American wars. But whereas work was easy to get and wages appeared to increase, real income actually declined. Inflation, especially destructive in the South, was largely to blame. By 1864, eggs sold in Richmond for $6 a dozen; butter brought $25 a pound.

This photograph of workers in front of a Washington, D.C., shop points to the vital role the home front workers played in the war. The manpower advantages enjoyed by the North are suggested here. *(Library of Congress)*

The dislocations caused by the war were many. These southerners, forced to leave their home by invading troops, have packed what few belongings they could transport and stand ready to evacuate their homestead. *(Library of Congress)*

Strikes and union organizing pointed to working-class discontent.

Low wages compounded the problem of declining income and particularly harmed women workers. Often forced into the labor market because husbands could save little or nothing from small army stipends, army wives and other women took what pay they could get. As more women entered the workforce, employers cut costs by slashing wages. In 1861, the Union government paid Philadelphia seamstresses 17 cents per shirt. At the height of inflation, three years later, the government reduced the piecework rate to 15 cents. Private employers paid even less, about 8 cents a shirt. Working women in the South fared no better. War may have brought prosperity to a few Americans, North and South, but for most it meant trying to survive on an inadequate income.

Economic dislocation caused by the war reduced the standard of living for civilians. Shortages and hardships were severe in the South, which bore the brunt of the fighting. Most white southerners did without food, manufactured goods, and medicine during the war. Farming families who had no slaves to help with work in the fields fared poorly. As one Georgia woman explained, "I can't manage a farm well enough [alone] to make a suporte." Conditions were most dismal in cities, where carts brought in vital supplies, because trains were reserved for military use. Hunger was rampant. Food riots erupted in Richmond and other cities; crowds of hungry whites broke into stores to steal food. The very cleanliness of southern cities pointed to urban hunger. As one Richmond resident noted, everything was so "cleanly consumed that no garbage or filth can accumulate."

Thousands of southerners who fled as Union armies advanced suddenly found themselves home-less. "The country for miles around is filled with refugees," noted an army officer in 1862. "Every house is crowded and hundreds are living in churches, in barns and tents." Caught up in the effort of mere survival, worried about what had happened to homes and possessions left behind and whether anything would remain when they returned, these southerners must have wondered if the cause was worth their sacrifices. Life was probably just as agonizing for those who chose to stay put when Union troops arrived. Virginia Gray, an Arkansas woman, wrote in her diary of her fear of the "Feds" and the turmoil they caused when they suddenly appeared and then disappeared.

White flight also disrupted slave life. Even the arrival of Union forces could prove a mixed blessing. One slave described the upsetting behavior of the Yankees at his plantation in Arkansas: "Them folks stood round there all day. Killed hogs . . . killed cows . . . . Took all kinds of sugar and preserves. . . . Tore all the feathers out of the mattresses looking for money. Then they put Old Miss and her daughter in the kitchen to cooking." So frightened was this slave's mother that she hid in her bed, only to be roused by the lieutenant, who told her, "We ain't a-going to do you no hurt. . . . We are freeing you." But the next day, the Yanks were gone and the Confederates back. During Sherman's march through Georgia in 1864, his troops stole not only from whites but from slaves as well. Indeed some soldiers flogged blacks who tried to stop the looting.

Wartime Race Relations

The journal kept by Emily Harris in South Carolina conveys some of the character of life behind the lines. She revealed not only the predictable story of shortages, hardships, and the psychological burdens of those at home but also the subtle social changes the war stimulated. Emily and her husband David lived on a 500-acre farm with their seven young children and ten slaves. When David went to war, Emily had to manage the farm, even though David worried that she would be "much at a loss with the . . . farm and the negroes."

Emily's early entries establish two themes that persist for the years she kept her diary. She was worried about how David would survive the "privation and hardships" of army life and was also anxious about her own "load of responsibilities." Her December 1862 entry provides a poignant picture of a wife's thoughts. "All going well as far as I can judge but tonight it is raining and cold and a soldier's wife cannot be happy in bad weather and during a battle." The dozens of tasks she had to do depressed her. "I shall never get used to being left as the head of affairs," she wrote in January 1863. "I am not an independent woman nor ever shall be." As time passed and the war went badly, the dismal news and mounting list of casualties heightened her concern about David's safety.

Her relations with her slaves compounded Emily's problems. As so many southerners discovered, war transformed the master–slave relationship. Because Emily was not the master David had been, her slaves gradually began to take unaccustomed liberties. At Christmas in 1864, several left the farm without her permission; others stayed away longer than she allowed. "Old Will" boldly requested his freedom. Worse yet, she discovered that her slaves had helped three Yankees who had escaped from prison camp.

The master–slave relationship was crumbling, and Emily reported in her journal the consequences for whites. "It seems people are getting afraid of negroes." Although not admitting to fear, she revealed that she could no longer control the blacks, who were increasingly unwilling to play a subservient role.

Understanding what was at stake, slaves, in their own way, often worked for their freedom. Said one later, "Us slaves worked den when we felt like it, which wasn't often." Emily's journal entry for February 22 confessed a "painful necessity." "I am reduced," she said, "to the use of a stick but the negroes are becoming so impudent and disrespectful that I cannot bear it." A mere two weeks later she added, "The Negroes are all expecting to be set free very soon and it causes them to be very troublesom."

Similar scenes occurred throughout the South. Insubordination, refusal to work, and refusal to accept punishment marked the behavior of black slaves, especially those who worked as fieldhands. Thousands of blacks (probably 20 percent of all slaves), many of them women who had been exploited

as workers and as sexual objects, fled toward Union lines after the early months of the war. Their flight pointed to the changing nature of race relations and the harm slaves could do to the southern cause. Reflected one slaveowner, "The 'faithful slave' is about played out."

Women and the War

If Emily Harris's journal reveals that she was sometimes overwhelmed by her responsibilities and shocked by the changes in dealings with her slaves, it also illustrates how the war affected women's lives. Nineteenth-century ideology promoted women's domestic role and minimized their economic importance. But the war made it impossible for many women to live according to conventional norms of behavior. So many men on both sides had gone off to fight that women had to find jobs and carry on farming operations. During the war years, southern women who had no slaves to help with the farmwork and northern farm wives who labored without the assistance of husbands or sons carried new physical and emotional burdens.

Women also participated in numerous war-related activities. In both North and South, they entered government service in large numbers. In the North, hundreds of women became military nurses. Under the supervision of Drs. Emily and Elizabeth Blackwell; Dorothea Dix, superintendent of army nurses; and Clara Barton, northern women nursed the wounded and dying for low pay or even for none at all. They also attempted to improve hospital conditions by attacking red tape and bureaucracy. The diary of a volunteer, Harriet Whetten, revealed the activist attitude of many others:

> I have never seen such a dirty disorganized place as the Hospital. The neglect of cleanliness is inexcusable. All sorts of filth, standing water, and the embalming house near the Hospital. . . . No time had to be lost. Miss Gill and I set the contrabands at work making beds & cleaning.

Although men largely staffed southern military hospitals, Confederate women also played an important part in caring for the sick and wounded in their homes and in makeshift hospitals behind the battle lines. Grim though the work was, many women felt that they were participating in the real world for the first time in their lives.

Women moved outside the domestic sphere in other forms of volunteer war work. Some women gained administrative experience in soldiers' aid societies and in the U.S. Sanitary Commission. Many others made bandages and clothes, put together packages for soldiers at the front, and helped army wives and disabled soldiers find jobs. Fund-raising activities realized substantial sums. By the end of the war, the Sanitary Commission had raised $50 million for medical supplies, nurses' salaries, and other wartime necessities.

Many of the changes women experienced during war years ended when peace returned. Jobs in industry and government disappeared when the men came to reclaim them. Women turned over the operation of farms to returning husbands. But for women whose men came home maimed or not at all, the work had not ended. Nor had the discrimination. Trying to pick up the threads of their former lives, they found it impossible to forget what they had done to help the war effort. At least some of them were sure they had equaled their men in courage and commitment.

The Election of 1864

In the North, the election of 1864 brought some of the transformations of wartime into the political arena. The Democrats, seeking to regain power by capitalizing on war weariness, nominated General George McClellan for president. The party proclaimed the war a failure and demanded an armistice with the South. During the campaign, Democrats accused Lincoln of arbitrarily expanding executive power and denounced sweeping economic measures such as the banking bills. Arguing that the president had transformed the war from one for Union into one for emancipation, they tried to inflame racial passions by insinuating that if the Republicans won, a fusion of blacks and whites would result.

Although Lincoln easily gained the Republican renomination because of his tight control over party machinery and patronage, his party did not unite behind him. Lincoln seemed to please no one. His veto of the radical reconstruction plan for the South, the Wade-Davis bill, led to cries of "usurpation." The Emancipation Proclamation did not sit well with conservatives. In August 1864, a gloomy Lincoln told his cabinet that he expected to lose the election. As late as September, some Republicans actually hoped to reconvene the convention and select another candidate.

Sherman's capture of Atlanta in September 1864 and the march through Georgia to Savannah helped swing voters to Lincoln. In the end, Republicans had no desire to see the Democrats oust their party. Lincoln won 55 percent of the popular vote and swept the electoral college.

Why the North Won

In the months after Lincoln's reelection, the war drew to an agonizing conclusion. Sherman moved north from Atlanta to North Carolina, while Grant pummeled Lee's forces in Virginia. The losses Grant would sustain were staggering: 18,000 in the Battle of the Wilderness, over 8,000 at Spotsylvania, and another 12,000 at Cold Harbor. New recruits stepped forward to replace the dead. On April 9, 1865, Grant accepted Lee's surrender at Appomattox. Southern soldiers and officers were allowed to return home with their personal equipment after promising to remain there peaceably. The war was finally over.

Technically, the war was won on the battlefield and at sea. But Grant's military strategy succeeded because the Union's manpower and economic resources could survive staggering losses of men and equipment while the Confederacy's could not. As Union armies pushed back the borders of the Confederacy, the South lost control of territories essential for their war effort. Finally, naval strategy eventually paid off because the North could build enough ships to make its blockade work. In 1861, fully 90 percent of the blockade runners were slipping through the naval cordon. By the war's end, only half made it.

The South had taken tremendous steps toward meeting war needs. But despite the impressive growth of manufacturing and the increasing acreage devoted to foodstuffs, the southern army and the southern people were poorly fed and poorly clothed. As one civilian realized, "The question of bread and meat . . . is beginning to be regarded as a more serious one even than that of War." Women working alone or with disgruntled slaves on farms could not produce enough food. Worn-out farm equipment was not replaced. The government's impressment of slaves and animals cut production. The half million blacks who fled to Union lines also played their part in pulling the South down in defeat.

New industries could not meet the extraordinary demands of wartime, and advancing Union forces destroyed many of them. A Confederate officer in northern Virginia observed, "Many of our soldiers are thinly clothed and without shoes and in addition to this, very few of the infantry have tents. With this freezing weather, their sufferings are indescribable." Skimpy rations, only a third of a pound of meat for each soldier a day by 1864, weakened the Confederate force, whose trail was "traceable by the deposit of dysenteric stool" it left behind. By that time, the Union armies were so well supplied that soldiers often threw away heavy blankets and coats as they advanced.

The South's woefully inadequate transportation system also contributed to defeat. Primitive roads deteriorated and became all but impassable without repairs. The railroad system, geared to the needs of cotton, not war, was inefficient. When tracks wore out or were destroyed, they were not replaced. Rails were too heavy for blockade runners to bother with, and as the Confederate railroad coordinator observed in

This photograph of the South Side Railroad at Appomattox Station, Virginia, shows the condition of a southern railroad at the end of the war. You can see the poor condition of the tracks and the destroyed train lying beside the tracks. The breakdown of the Confederate transportation system through battle, sabotage, and simple wear and tear contributed to the defeat of the Confederacy. *(Library of Congress)*

1865, "Not a single bar of railroad iron has been rolled in the Confederacy since the war, nor can we hope to do better." Thus, food intended for the army rotted awaiting shipment. Supplies were tied up in bottlenecks and soldiers went hungry. Food riots in southern cities pointed to the hunger, anger, and growing demoralization of civilians.

Ironically, measures the Confederacy took to strengthen its ability to win the war, as one Texan later observed, "weakened and paralyzed it." Eventually, the Confederacy could no longer "command and control its moral resources." Conscription, impressment, and taxes all contributed to resentment and sometimes open resistance. They fueled class tensions already strained by the poverty war brought to many yeoman farmers and led some of them to assist the invaders or to join the Union army. The proposal to use slaves as soldiers called into question the war's purpose. The many southern governors who refused to contribute men, money, and supplies on the scale Davis requested implicitly condoned disloyalty to the cause. The belief in states' rights and the sanctity of private property that gave birth to the Confederacy also helped kill it.

By the final months of the war, Jefferson Davis had recognized how dangerous opposition to government measures and defeatist attitudes were to the Confederacy's cause. "The malcontents, seizing on the restlessness consequent upon long and severe pressure," he pointed out, "have created a feeling hostile to the execution of the rigorous laws which were necessary to raise and feed our armies, then magnifying every reverse and prophesying ruin, they have produced public depression and sown the seeds of disin-

tegration." But such realization did not result in any vigorous attempts to influence public opinion or to control internal dissent.

It is tempting to compare Lincoln and Davis as war leaders. There is no doubt that Lincoln's humanity, his awareness of the terrible costs of war, his determination to save the Union, and his eloquence set him apart as one of this country's most extraordinary presidents. Yet the men's personal characteristics were probably less important than the differences between the political and social systems of the two regions. Without the support of a party behind him, Davis failed to engender enthusiasm or loyalty. Even though the Republicans rarely united behind Lincoln, they uniformly wanted to keep the Democrats from office. Despite all the squabbles, Republicans tended to support Lincoln's policies in Congress and back in their home districts. Commanding considerable resources of patronage, Lincoln was able to line up federal, state, and local officials behind his party and administration.

Just as the northern political system provided Lincoln with more flexibility and support, its social system also proved more able to meet the war's extraordinary demands. Although both societies adopted innovations in an effort to secure victory, northerners were more cooperative, disciplined, and aggressive in meeting the organizational and production challenges of wartime. In the southern states, old attitudes, habits, and values impeded the war effort. Southern governors, wedded to states' rights, refused to cooperate with the Confederate government. North Carolina, the center of the southern textile industry, actually kept back most uniforms for its own regiments. At the war's end, 92,000 uniforms and thousands of blankets, shoes, and tents still lay in its warehouses. When Sherman approached Atlanta, Georgia's governor would not turn over the 10,000 men in the state army to Confederate commanders. Even slaveholders, whose property had been the cause for secession, resisted the impressment of their slaves for war work.

In the end, the Confederacy collapsed, exhausted and bleeding. Hungry soldiers received letters from their families revealing desperate situations at home. They worried and then slipped away. By December 1864, the Confederate desertion rate had passed 50 percent. Replacements could not be found. Farmers hid livestock and produce from tax collectors. Many southerners felt their cause was lost and resigned themselves to defeat. But some fought on till the end. One northerner described them as they surrendered at Appomattox:

> Before us in proud humiliation stood the embodiment of manhood: men whom neither toils and sufferings, nor the fact of death, nor disaster, nor hopelessness could bend from their resolve; standing before us now, thin, worn, and famished, but erect, and with eyes looking level into ours, waking memories that bound us together as no other bond.

The Costs of War

The long war was over, but the memories of that event would fester for years to come. About 3 million American men, a third of all free males between the ages of 15 and 59, had served in the army. Each would remember his own personal history of the war. For George Eagleton, who had worked in army field hospitals, the history was one of "Death and destruction! Blood! Blood! Agony! Death! Gaping flesh wounds, broken bones, amputations, bullet and bomb fragment extractions." Of all wars Americans have fought, none has been more deadly. The death rate during this war was over five times as great as the death rate during World War II. About 360,000 Union soldiers and another 258,000 Confederate soldiers died, about a third of them because their wounds were either improperly treated or not treated at all. Disease claimed more lives than combat. Despite the efforts of men like Eagleton and the women army nurses, hospitals could not handle the scores of wounded and dying. "Glory is not for the private soldier, such as die in the hospitals," reflected one Tennessee soldier, "being eat up with the deadly gangrene, and being imperfectly waited on."

Thousands upon thousands of men would be reminded of the human costs of war by the injuries they carried with them to the grave, by the missing limbs that marked them as Civil War veterans. About

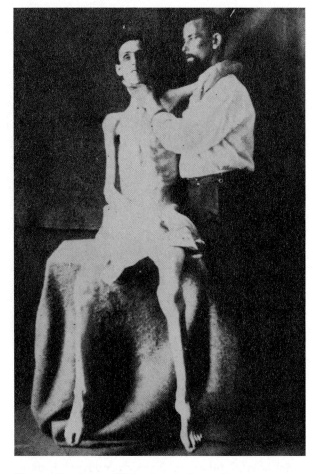

The emaciated state of this prisoner of war, who was incarcerated in Belle Isle Prison, Richmond, shows the fearsome conditions experienced by some Union prisoners. A Union surgeon who inspected the prison's inmates claimed that 90 percent weighed less than 90 pounds when freed. *(Library of Congress)*

275,000 on each side were maimed. Another 410,000 (195,000 northerners and 215,000 southerners) would recall their time in wretchedly overcrowded and unsanitary prison camps. The lucky ones would remember only the dullness and boredom. The worst memory was of those who rotted in prison camps, such as Andersonville in Georgia, where 31,000 Union soldiers were confined. At the war's end, over 12,000 graves were counted there.

Some Americans found it hard to throw off wartime experiences and adjust to peace. As Arthur Carpenter's letters suggest, he gradually grew accustomed to army life. War provided him with a sense of purpose. When it was over, he felt aimless. A full year after the war's end, he wrote, "Camp life agrees with me better than any other." Many others had difficulty returning to civilian routines and finding a new focus for life. Even those who adjusted successfully discovered that they looked at life from a different perspective. The experience of fighting, of mixing with all sorts of people from many places, of traveling far from home had lifted former soldiers out of their familiar local world and widened their vision. Fighting the war made the concept of national union real.

Unanswered Questions

What, then, had the war accomplished? On the one hand, death and destruction. Physically, the war devastated the South. Historians have estimated a 43 percent decline in southern wealth during the war years, exclusive of the value of slaves. Great cities like Atlanta, Columbia, and Richmond lay in ruins. Fields lay weed-choked and uncultivated. Tools were worn out. A third or more of the South's stock of mules, horses, and swine had disappeared. Two-thirds of the railroads had been destroyed. Thousands were hungry, homeless, and bitter about their four years of what now appeared a useless sacrifice. Over four million slaves, a vast financial investment, were free.

On the other hand, the war had resolved the question of union and ended the debate over the relationship of the states to the federal government. During the war, Republicans seized the opportunity to pass legislation that would foster national union and economic growth: the Pacific Railroad Act of 1862, which set aside huge tracts of public land to finance the transcontinental railroad; the Homestead Act of 1862, which was to provide yeoman farmers cheaper and easier access to the public domain; the Morrill Act of 1862, which established support for agricultural (land-grant) colleges; and the banking acts of 1863 and 1864.

The war had also resolved the issue of slavery, the thorny problem that had so long plagued American life. Yet uncertainties outnumbered certainties. What would happen to the former slaves? When blacks had fled to Union lines during the war, commanders had not known what to do with them. Now the problem became even more pressing. Were blacks to have the same civil and political rights as whites? In the Union army, they had been second-class soldiers. The behavior of Union forces toward liberated blacks in the South showed how deep the stain of racism went. One white soldier, caught stealing a quilt by a former slave, shouted, "I'm fighting for $14 a month and the Union"—not to end slavery. Would blacks be given land, the means for economic independence? What would be their relations with their former owners?

What, indeed, would be the status of the conquered South in the nation? Should it be punished for the rebellion? Some people thought so. Should southerners keep their property? Some people thought not. There were clues to Lincoln's intentions. As early as December 1863, the president had announced a gen-

Timeline

1861	Lincoln calls up state militia and suspends habeas corpus
	First Battle of Bull Run
	Union blockades the South
1862	Battles at Shiloh, Bull Run, and Antietam
	Monitor and *Virginia* battle
	First black regiment authorized by Union
	Union issues greenbacks
	South institutes military draft
	Pacific Railroad Act
	Homestead Act
	Morrill Land-Grant College Act
1863	Lincoln issues Emancipation Proclamation
	Congress adopts military draft
	Battles of Gettysburg and Vicksburg
	Union Banking Act
	Southern tax laws and impressment act
	New York draft riots
	Southern food riots
1864	Sherman's march through Georgia
	Lincoln reelected
	Union Banking Act
1865	Lee surrenders at Appomattox
	Lincoln assassinated; Andrew Johnson becomes president
	Congress passes Thirteenth Amendment, abolishing slavery

erous plan of reconciliation. He was willing to recognize the government of former Confederate states established by a group of citizens equal to 10 percent of those voting in 1860, as long as the group swore to support the Constitution and to accept the abolition of slavery. He began to restore state governments in three former Confederate states on that basis. But not all northerners agreed with his leniency, and the debate continued.

In his 1865 inaugural address, Lincoln urged Americans to harbor "malice towards none . . . and charity for all." "Let us strive," he urged, "to finish the work we are in; to bind up the nation's wounds . . . to do all which may achieve a just and lasting peace." Privately, the president said the same thing. Generosity and goodwill would pave the way for reconciliation. On April 14, he pressed the point home to his cabinet. His wish was to avoid persecution and bloodshed. That same evening, only five days after the surrender at Appomattox, the president attended a play at Ford's Theatre. There, as one horri-fied eyewitness reported,

> a pistol was heard and a man . . . dressed in a black suit of clothes leaped onto the stage apparently from the President's box. He held in his right hand a dagger whose blade appeared about 10 inches long. . . . Every one leaped to his feet, and the cry of "the President is assassinated" was heard—Getting where I could see into the President's box, I saw Mrs. Lincoln . . . in apparent anguish.

John Wilkes Booth, a southern sympathizer, had killed the president.

Conclusion

An Uncertain Future

As the war ended, many Americans grieved for the man whose decisions had so marked their lives for five years. "Strong men have wept tonight & the nation will mourn tomorrow," wrote one eyewitness to the assassination. Many more wept for friends and relations who had not survived the war but whose actions had in one way or another contributed to its outcome. Perhaps not all Americans realized how drastical-ly the war had altered their lives, their futures, their nation. It was only as time passed that the war's impact became clear to them. And it was only with time that they recognized how many problems the war had left unsolved. It is to these years of Reconstruction that we turn next.

Recommended Reading

Organizing for War

David Donald, *Liberty and Union* (1978); Joseph T. Glatthatt, *Partners in Command: The Relationship between Leaders in the Civil War* (1994); James McPherson, *Battle Cry of Freedom: The Civil War Era* (1988); Phillip S. Paludan, *"A People's Contest": The Union and the Civil War, 1861–1865* (1989); Peter J. Parrish, *The American Civil War* (1985); Emory M. Thomas, *The Confederate Nation, 1861–1865* (1979).

Clashing on the Battlefield, 1861–1862

Thomas B. Buell, *The Warrior Generals Combat Leadership in the American Civil War* (1996); Benjamin Frankling Colling, *Fort Donelson's Legacy: War and Society in Kentucky and Tennessee, 1862–1863* (1997); Perry D. Jamieson, *Attack and Die: Civil War Tactics and the Southern Heritage* (1982); Russell F. Weigley, *The American Way of War: A History of U.S. Military Strategy and Policy* (1973); T. Harry Williams, *The History of American Wars* (1981).

The Tide Turns, 1863–1865

Richard E. Beringer, Herman Hattaway, Archer Jones, and William N. Still, Jr., *Why the South Lost the Civil War* (1986) and *The Elements of Confederate Defeat: Nationalism, War Aims, and Religion* (1988); Robert F. Durden, *The Gray and the Black: The Confederate Debate on Emancipation* (1972); Laurence M. Hauptman, *The Iroquois in the Civil War: From Battlefield to Reservation* (1993); Randall C. Jimerson, *The Private Civil War* (1988); Gerald F. Linderman, *Embattled Courage: The Experience of Combat in the American Civil War* (1987); Malcolm C. McMillan, *The Disintegration of a Confederate State* (1986); James M. McPherson, *For Cause and Comrades: Why Men Fought in the Civil War* (1997); Reid Mitchell, *The Vacant Chair: The Northern Soldier Leaves Home* (1993).

Changes Wrought by War

Ira Berlin, ed., *Freedom: A Documentary History of Emancipation, 1861–1867*, Series I and II (1979, 1982); David W. Blight and Brooks D. Simpson., eds., *Union & Emancipation: Essays on Politics and Race in the Civil War Era* (1997); Michael Burlingame, *The Inner World of Abraham Lincoln* (1994); Catherine Clinton, *Tara Revisited: Women, War, and the Plantation Legend* (1995); Catherine Clinton and Nina Silber, *Divided Houses: Gender and the Civil War* (1992); Mary A. Decredico, *Patriotism for Profit: Georgia's Urban Entrepreneurs and the Confederate War Effort* (1990); David Donald, *Lincoln* (1995); Wayne K. Durrell, *War of Another Kind: A Southern Community in the Great Rebellion* (1990); Drew Gilpin Faust, *Mothers of Invention: Women of the Slaveholding South in the American Civil War* (1997); Eric Foner, *Politics and Ideology in the Age of Civil War* (1980); J. Matthew Gallman, *Mastering Wartime: A Social History of Philadelphia During the Civil War* (1990); Theodore J. Karamanski, *Rally 'Round the Flag: Chicago and the Civil War* (1993); Elizabeth D. Leonard, *Yankee Women: Gender Battles in the Civil War* (1994); Glenn M. Lindend and Thomas J. Pressly, eds., *Voices from the House Divided* (1995); Leon F. Litwack, *Been in the Storm So Long: The Aftermath of Slavery* (1979); David E. Long, *The Jewel of Liberty: Abraham Lincoln's Re-Election and the End of Slavery* (1994); Clarence L. Mohr, *On the Threshold of Freedom* (1986); John L. Thomas, ed., *Abraham Lincoln and the American Political Tradition (1986)*; Wendy Hamand Venet, *Neither Ballots Nor Bullets: Women Abolitionists and the Civil War* (1991).

Fiction and Film

Stephen Crane's *The Red Badge of Courage* (any edition) exam-ines the soldier's experience during the war, while MacKinlay Kantor's novel, *Andersonville* (1955), provides an insight into the Civil War's worst prison camp.

The film *Glory,* a feature film, focuses on a black regiment, the 54th Massachusetts, that demonstrated its heroism in the midst of battle. You will get a better sense of the character of warfare and race relations if you see this film. The classic *Gone with the Wind* offers a romanticized but powerful picture of southern life before, during, and after the Civil War. Ken Burns's famous series, *The Civil War,* is a powerful evocation of that period with ample use of period photographs and documents.

Suggested Web Sites

http://sunsite.utk.edu/civil-war/warweb.html

The American Civil War Homepage. This site has a great collection of hypertext links to the most useful identified electronic files about the American Civil War.

http://jefferson.village.virginia.edu/vshadow/vshadow.html

The Valley of the Shadow: Living the Civil War in Pennsylvania and Virginia. This project tells the histories of two communities on either side of the Mason-Dixon line during the Civil War. It includes narrative and an electronic archive of sources.

http://www.awod.com/gallery/probono/cwchas/cwlayout.html

Civil War @ Charleston. This site covers the history of the Civil War in and around Charleston, South Carolina.

http://www.alincolnassoc.com/

Abraham Lincoln Association. This site allows you to search digital versions of Lincoln's papers.

http://www.ruf.rice.edu/~pjdavis/jdp.htm

The Papers of Jefferson Davis Home Page. This site tells about the collection of Jefferson Davis Papers and includes a chronology of his life, a family genealogy, some key Davis documents on-line, and a collection of related links.

http://www.tulane.edu/~latner/CrisisMain.html

Crisis at Fort Sumter. This well-crafted use of hypermedia with assignments and problems explains and explores the events in and around the start of the Civil War.

http://www.cwc.lsu.edu/

U.S. Civil War Center. This is a site whose mission is to "locate, index, and make available all appropriate private and public data on the Internet regarding the Civil War" and to promote the study of the Civil War from the perspectives of all professions, occupations, and academic disciplines.

http://scriptorium.lib.duke.edu/collections/civil-war-women.html

Civil War Women—On-line Archival Exhibits at Duke University. This site includes original documents, links, and biographical information about several women and their lives during the Civil War.

http://www.itd.nps.gov/cwss/history/aa_history.htm

History of African-Americans in the Civil War. This National Park Service site explores the history of the United States Colored Troops.

http://memory.loc.gov/ammem/alhtml/alrintr.html

Mr. Lincoln's Virtual Library. Part of the American Memory series, this site explores the assassination of Abraham Lincoln, with introduction, timeline, and gallery.

http://lcweb2.loc.gov/ammem/cwphome.html

Selected Civil War Photographs Home Page. This is a Library of Congress site, with over 1,000 photographs, many from Mathew Brady.

http://www.historyplace.com/civilwar/index.html

The History Place—U.S. Civil War 1861–1865. This gives a complete timeline of the Civil War, well-illustrated with photographs.

http://www.ushistoryplace.com

 A richly detailed on-line learning environment complete with interactive maps, timelines, history activities, primary source documents, and links to related American history sites.

16

The UNION RECONSTRUCTED

CHAPTER OUTLINE

In April 1864, one year before Lincoln's assassination, Robert Allston died of pneumonia. His daughter, Elizabeth, was left with a "sense of terrible desolation and sorrow" as the Civil War raged around her, and she and her mother took over the affairs of their many rice plantations. With Yankee troops moving through coastal South Carolina in the late winter of 1864–1865, Elizabeth's sorrow turned to "terror" as Union soldiers arrived seeking liquor, firearms, and hidden valuables. The Allston women endured an insulting search and then fled. In a later raid, Yankee troops encouraged the Allston slaves to take furniture and other household goods from the Big Houses, some of which the blacks returned when the Yankees were gone. But before they left, the Union soldiers, in their role as liberators, gave the keys to the crop barns to the semifree slaves.

When the war was over, Adele Allston took an oath of allegiance to the United States and secured a written order commanding the blacks to relinquish these keys. She and Elizabeth made plans to return in the early summer of 1865 to resume control of the family plantations, thereby reestablishing white authority. She was assured that although the blacks had guns and were determined to have the means to a livelihood, "no outrage has been committed against the whites except in the matter of property." But property was the key issue. Possession of the keys to the barns, Elizabeth wrote, would be the "test case" of whether former masters or their former slaves would control land, labor and its fruits, and even subtle aspects of interpersonal relations.

Not without some fear, Adele and Elizabeth Allston rode up in a carriage to their former home, Nightingale Hall, to confront their former slaves. To their surprise, a pleasant reunion took place. The Allston women greeted the blacks by name, inquired after their children, and caught up on the affairs of those with whom they had lived closely for many years. A trusted black foreman handed over the keys to the barns. This harmonious scene was repeated elsewhere.

In this Winslow Homer painting, *A Visit from the Old Mistress,* imagine Adele Allston returning to her plantation to reunite with former slaves. What kind of new relationships would they form in the transformed world after a wrenching Civil War? *(National Museum of American Art, Smithsonian Institution)*

But at Guendalos, a plantation owned by a son absent during most of the war fighting with the Confederate army, the Allston women met a very different situation. As their carriage arrived and moved slowly toward the crop barns, a defiant group of armed former slaves lined both sides of the road, following the carriage as it passed by. Tension grew when the carriage stopped. A former black driver, Uncle Jacob, was unsure whether to yield the keys to the barns full of rice and corn, put there by black labor. Mrs. Allston insisted. As Uncle Jacob hesitantly began to hand the keys to her, an angry young man shouted out: "Ef yu gie up de key, blood'll flow." Uncle Jacob slowly slipped the keys back into his pocket.

The tension increased as the blacks sang freedom songs and brandished hoes, pitchforks, and guns in an effort to discourage anyone from going to town for help. Two blacks, however, left the plantation to find some Union military officers to come settle the issue of the keys, most likely on the side of the Allstons. As Adele and Elizabeth waited, word finally arrived that the Union officers, who were difficult to locate, would no doubt be found the next day and would come to Guendalos. The Allstons spent the night safely, if restlessly, in their house. Early the next morning, they were awakened by a knock at the unlocked front door. Adele slowly opened the door, and there stood Uncle Jacob. Without a word, he gave her the keys.

The story of the keys reveals most of the essential human ingredients of the Reconstruction era. Despite defeat and surrender, southern whites were determined to resume control of both land and labor. Rebellion aside, the law, property titles, and federal enforcement were generally on the side of the original owners of the land. The Allston women were friendly to the blacks in a genuine but maternal way and insisted on the restoration of the deferential relationships that existed before the war. Adele and Elizabeth, in short, both feared and cared about their former slaves.

The black freedmen likewise revealed mixed feelings toward their former owners. At different plantations, they demonstrated a variety of emotions: anger, loyalty, love, resentment, and pride. Respect was paid to the person of the Allstons but not to their property and crops. The action of the blacks indicated that what they wanted was not revenge but economic independence and freedom.

In this encounter between former slaves and their mistresses, the role of the northern federal officials is also revealing. The Union soldiers, literally and symbolically, gave the keys of freedom to the blacks but did not stay around long enough to guarantee that freedom. Although encouraging the freedmen to plunder the master's house and take possession of the crops, in the crucial encounter, northern officials had disappeared. Understanding the limits of northern help, Uncle Jacob handed the keys to land and liberty back to his former owner. The blacks at Guendalos knew that if they wanted to ensure their freedom, they had to do it themselves.

The theme of this chapter is the story of what happened to the conflicting goals and dreams of three groups as they sought to form new social, economic, and political relationships during the Reconstruction era. Amid devastation and divisions of class and race, Civil War survivors sought to put their lives back together again. Victorious but variously motivated northern officials, defeated but defiant southern planters, and impoverished but hopeful black freedmen—all had strong needs and dreams. In no way could all fulfill their conflicting goals, yet each had to try. This situation guaranteed that the Reconstruction era would be divisive, leaving a mixed legacy of human gains and losses.

☞ THE BITTERSWEET AFTERMATH OF WAR

"There are sad changes in store for both races," the daughter of a Georgia planter wrote in her diary early in the summer of 1865, adding, "I wonder the Yankees do not shudder to behold their work." To understand the bittersweet nature of Reconstruction, we must look at the state of the nation in the spring of 1865, shortly after the assassination of President Lincoln.

The United States in 1865

The "Union" faced constitutional crisis in April 1865. What was the status of the 11 former Confederate states? The North had denied the South's constitutional right to secede but needed four years of civil war and over 600,000 deaths to win the point. Were the 11 southern states part of the Union or not? Lincoln's official position had been that they had never left the Union, which was "constitutionally indestructible." As a result of their rebellion, they were only "out of their proper relation" with the United States. The president, therefore, as commander in chief, had the authority to decide how to set relations right again.

Lincoln's congressional opponents argued that by declaring war on the Union, the Confederate states had broken their constitutional ties and reverted to a kind of pre-statehood status, like territories or "conquered provinces." Congress, therefore, which decided on the admission of new states, should resolve the constitutional issues and assert its authority over the reconstruction process. Differences between Congress and the White House mirrored a wider struggle between two branches of the national government. During war, as has usually been the case, the executive branch assumed broad powers necessary for rapid mobilization of resources and domestic security. Many believed, however, that Lincoln had far exceeded his constitutional authority. As the war ended, Congress sought to reassert its authority, as it would do after every subsequent war.

In April 1865, the Republican party ruled virtually unchecked. Only 11 years old, the Republicans had made immense achievements in the eyes of the northern public: winning the war, preserving the Union, and freeing the slaves. The party had enacted sweeping economic programs on behalf of free labor and free enterprise. These included a high protective tariff, a national banking system, broad use of the power to tax and to borrow and print money, generous federal appropriations for internal improvements, the Homestead Act, and an act to establish land-grant colleges to teach agricultural and mechanical skills. Alexander Hamilton, John Quincy Adams, and Henry Clay might all have applauded. Despite these achievements, the Republican party was still an uneasy grouping of former Whigs, Know-Nothings, Unionist Democrats, and antislavery idealists.

The Democrats, by contrast, were in shambles. Republicans depicted southern Democrats as rebels, murderers, and traitors, and they blasted northern Democrats as weak-willed, disloyal, and opposed to economic growth and progress. Nevertheless, in the elections of 1864 the Republicans, needing to show that the war was a bipartisan effort, nominated a Unionist Tennessee Democrat, Andrew Johnson, as Lincoln's vice president. Now the tactless Johnson headed the government.

The United States in the spring of 1865 presented stark contrasts. Northern cities hummed with productive activity; many southern cities were piles of rubble. Northern factories produced railroad tracks and

CONFLICTING GOALS DURING RECONSTRUCTION

Victorious Northern ("Radical") Republicans

- Justify the war by remaking southern society in the image of the North
- Inflict political but not physical or economic punishment on Confederate leaders
- Continue programs of economic progress begun during the war: high tariffs, railroad subsidies, national banking
- Maintain the Republican party in power
- Help the freedmen make the transition to full freedom by providing them with the tools of citizenship (suffrage) and equal economic opportunity

Northern Moderates (Republicans and Democrats)

- Quickly establish peace and order, reconciliation between North and South
- Bestow on the southern states leniency, amnesty, and merciful readmission to the Union
- Perpetuate land ownership, free labor, market competition, and other capitalist ventures
- Promote local self-determination of economic and social issues; limit interference by the national government
- Provide limited support for black suffrage

Old Southern Planter Aristocracy (Former Confederates)

- Ensure protection from black uprising and prevent excessive freedom for former slaves
- Secure amnesty, pardon, and restoration of confiscated lands
- Restore traditional plantation-based, market-crop economy with blacks as cheap labor force
- Restore traditional political leaders in the states
- Restore traditional paternalistic race relations as basis of social order

New "Other South": Yeoman Farmers and Former Whigs (Unionists)

- Quickly establish peace and order, reconciliation between North and South
- Achieve recognition of loyalty and economic value of yeoman farmers
- Create greater diversity in southern economy: capital investments in railroads, factories, and the diversification of agriculture
- Displace the planter aristocracy with new leaders drawn from new economic interests
- Limit the rights and powers of freedmen; extend suffrage only to the educated few

Black Freedmen

- Secure physical protection from abuse and terror by local whites
- Achieve economic independence through land ownership (40 acres and a mule) and equal access to trades
- Receive educational opportunity and foster the development of family and cultural bonds
- Obtain equal civil rights and protection under the law
- Commence political participation through the right to vote

engines, steel, textiles, farm implements, and building materials; southern factory chimneys stood silent above the rubble. Roadways and railroad tracks laced the North; southern railroads and roads lay in ruins. Northern banks flourished; southern financial institutions were bankrupt. Increasingly mechanized northern farms were more productive than ever before, and free farmers took pride that they had amply fed the Union army and urban workers throughout the war. They saw the Union victory as evidence of the superiority of free over slave labor. By contrast, southern farms and plantations, especially those that had lain in the path of Sherman's march, were like a "howling waste." Said one resident, "The Yankees came through . . . and just tore up everything."

Despite pockets of relative wealth, the South was largely devastated as soldiers demobilized and returned home in April 1865. Rare was the family, North or South, that had not suffered a serious casualty in the war. Missing limbs and suffering from hunger (a half-million southern whites faced starvation), the ragtag remains of the Confederate army experienced widespread sickness and social disorder as they traveled home. Yet, as a later southern writer, Wilbur Cash, explained, "If this war had smashed the Southern world, it had left the essential Southern mind and will . . . entirely unshaken." Many white southerners braced to resist Reconstruction and restore their former life, but the minority who had remained quietly loyal to the Union dreamed of reconciliation.

Whatever the extremes of southern white attitudes, the dominant social reality in the spring of 1865 was that nearly four million former slaves were on their own, facing the challenges of freedom. After an initial

THE UNITED STATES IN 1865: CRISES AT THE END OF THE CIVIL WAR

- **Military Casualties**

  360,000 Union soldiers dead
  260,000 Confederate soldiers dead
  620,000 Total dead
  375,000 Seriously wounded and maimed
  995,000 Casualties nationwide in a total male population of 15 million (nearly 1 in 15)

- **Physical and Economic Crises**

  The South devastated; its railroads, industry, and some major cities in ruins; its fields and livestock wasted

- **Constitutional Crisis**

  Eleven former Confederate states not a part of the Union, their status unclear and future states uncertain

- **Political Crisis**

  Republican party (entirely of the North) dominant in Congress; a former Democratic slaveholder from Tennessee, Andrew Johnson, in the presidency

- **Social Crisis**

  Nearly four million black freedmen throughout the South facing challenges of survival and freedom, along with thousands of hungry demobilized white southern soldiers and displaced white families

- **Psychological Crisis**

  Incalculable stores of resentment, bitterness, anger, and despair throughout North and South

reaction of joy and celebration, expressed in jubilee songs, the freedmen quickly became aware of their continuing dependence on former owners. A Mississippi woman stated the uncertainty of her new status this way:

> I used to think if I could be free I should be the happiest of anybody in the world. But when my master come to me, and says—Lizzie, you is free! it seems like I was in a kind of daze. And when I would wake up in the morning I would think to myself, Is I free? Hasn't I got to get up before day light and go into the field of work?

For Lizzie and four million other blacks, everything—and nothing—had changed.

Hopes Among the Freedmen

Throughout the South in the summer of 1865, optimism surged through the old slave quarters. As Union soldiers marched through Richmond, prisoners in slave-trade jails chanted: "Slavery chain done broke at last! Gonna praise God till I die!" The slavery chain, however, was not broken all at once but link by link. After Union soldiers swept through an area, Confederate troops would follow, or master and overseer would return, and the slaves learned not to rejoice too quickly or openly. "Every time a bunch of No'thern sojers would come through," recalled one slave, "they would tell us we was free and we'd begin celebratin'. Before we would get through somebody else would tell

us to go back to work, and we would go." Another slave recalled celebrating emancipation "about twelve times" in one North Carolina county. So former slaves became cautious about what freedom meant.

Gradually, though, freedmen began to test the reality of freedom and express a vision of what life beyond bondage and the plantation might be like. Typically, the first test was to leave the plantation, if only for a few hours or days. "If I stay here I'll never know I am free," a South Carolina woman said, and off she went to work as a cook in a nearby town. Some former slaves cut their ties entirely, leaving cruel and kindly masters alike. Some returned to an earlier master, but others went to towns and cities to work and to find schools, churches, and association with other blacks, where they would be safe from whippings and retaliation.

Many freedmen left the plantation in search of members of their families. The quest for a missing spouse, parent, or child, sold away years before, was a powerful force in the first few months of emancipation. Advertisements detailing these sorrowful searches filled black newspapers. For those who found a spouse and those who had been living together in slave marriages, freedom meant getting married legally. Wedding ceremonies involving many couples were common in the first months of emancipation. Legal marriage was important morally, but it also served such practical purposes as establishing the legitimacy of children and gaining access to land titles and other

Both white southerners and their former slaves suffered in the immediate aftermath of the Civil War, as illustrated by this engraving from *Frank Leslie's Illustrated Newspaper,* February 23, 1867. *(The Granger Collection, New York)*

economic opportunities. Marriage also meant special burdens for black women who took on the now familiar double role as housekeeper and breadwinner. For many newly married blacks, however, the initial goal was to create a traditional family life, resulting in the widespread withdrawal of women from plantation field labor.

Freedmen also demonstrated their new status by choosing surnames. Names connoting independence, such as Washington, were common. As an indication of the mixed feelings the freedmen had toward their former masters, some would adopt their master's name, and others would pick "any big name 'ceptin' their master's." Emancipation changed black manners around whites as well. Masks were dropped, and old expressions of humility—tipping a hat, stepping aside, feigning happiness, addressing whites with titles of deference—were discarded. For the blacks, these were necessary symbolic expressions of selfhood; they

proved that things were now different. To whites, these behaviors were seen as acts of "insolence," "insubordination," and "puttin' on airs."

However important were choosing names, dropping masks, moving around, getting married, and testing new rights, the primary goal for most freedmen was the acquisition of their own land. "All I want is to git to own fo' or five acres ob land, dat I can build me a little house on and call my home," a Mississippi black said. Only through economic independence, the traditional American goal of controlling one's own labor and land, could former slaves prove to themselves that emancipation was real.

During the war, some Union generals had placed liberated slaves in charge of confiscated and abandoned lands. In the Sea Islands off the coast of South Carolina and Georgia, blacks had been working 40-acre plots of land and harvesting their own crops for several years. Farther inland, most freedmen who

In the early months of freedom, the daily life of former slaves was both changed and unchanged. Here (above) we see a photograph of freedmen, led by a crew leader much like during slavery days, leaving the cotton fields after a full day of gang labor carrying cotton on their heads, and a sketch (below) of a Freedmen's Bureau school in 1866, which many men, women, and children attended at night. *(Above, © Collection of The New-York Historical Society; Below, The Newberry Library)*

The Promise of Land: 40 Acres

Note the progression in the various documents in this chapter from promised lands (this page), to lands restored to whites (page 501), to work contracts (page 508), to semiautonomous tenant farms (page 510). Freedom came by degrees to the freedmen.

To All Whom It May Concern

Edisto Island, August 15th, 1865

George Owens, having selected for settlement forty acres of Land, on Theodore Belab's Place, pursuant to Special Field Orders, No. 15, Headquarters Military Division of the Mississippi, Savannah, Ga., Jan. 16, 1865; he has permission to hold and occupy the said Tract, subject to such regulations as may be established by proper authority; and all persons are prohibited from interfering with him in his possession of the same.

By command of   R. SAXTON
                     Brev't Maj. Gen.,
                     Ass't. Comm.
                     S.C., Ga., and Fla.

---

received land were the former slaves of Cherokees and Creeks. Some blacks held title to these lands. Northern philanthropists had organized others to grow cotton for the Treasury Department to prove the superiority of free labor over slavery. In the Davis Bend section of Mississippi, thousands of former slaves worked 40-acre tracts on leased lands formerly owned by Jefferson Davis. In this highly successful experiment, they made profits sufficient to repay the government for initial costs, then lost the land to Davis's brother.

Many freedmen expected a new economic order as fair payment for their years of involuntary work on the land. "It's de white man's turn ter labor now," a black preacher in Florida told a group of fieldhands. Whites would no longer own all the land, he went on, "fur de Guverment is gwine ter gie ter ev'ry Nigger forty acres of lan' an' a mule." Other freedmen were willing to settle for less: One in Virginia offered to take only one acre of land—"Ef you make it de acre dat Marsa's house sets on." Another was more guarded, aware of how easy the power could shift back to white planters: "Gib us our own land and we take care ourselves; but widout land, de ole massas can hire us or starve us, as dey please." However cautiously expressed, the freedmen had every expectation, fed by the intensity of their dreams, that the promised "40 acres and a mule" was forthcoming. Once they obtained land, reunited families, and education, they looked forward to civil rights and the vote.

The White South's Fearful Response

White southerners had equally mixed goals and expectations at the war's end. Yeoman farmers and poor whites stood side by side with rich planters in bread lines, as together they looked forward to the restoration of their land and livelihood. Suffering from "extreme want and destitution," as a Cherokee County, Georgia, resident put it, white southerners responded to the immediate postwar crises with feelings of outrage, loss, and injustice. "I tell you it is mighty hard," said one man, "for my pa paid his own money for our niggers; and that's not all they've robbed us of. They have taken our horses and cattle and sheep and everything." Others felt the loss more personally, as former slaves whom they thought were faithful or for whom they felt great affection suddenly left. "Something dreadful has happened dear Diary," a Florida woman wrote in May 1865. "My dear black mammy has left us. . . . I feel lost, I feel as if someone is dead in the house. Whatever will I do without my Mammy?"

A more dominant emotion than sorrow, however, was fear. The entire structure of southern society was shaken, and the semblance of racial peace and order that slavery had provided was shattered. Many white southerners could hardly imagine a society without blacks in bondage. It was the basis not only of social order but of a lifestyle the larger slaveholders, at least, had long regarded as the perfect model of gentility and civilization. Having lost control of all that was familiar and revered, whites feared everything from losing their cheap labor supply to having to sit next to blacks on trains.

The mildest of their fears was the inconvenience of doing various jobs and chores they had rarely done before, like housework. A Georgia woman, Eliza Andrews, complained that it seemed to her a "waste of time for people who are capable of doing something better to spend their time sweeping and dusting while scores of lazy negroes that are fit for nothing else are

The black codes, widespread violence against freedmen, and President Johnson's veto of the Civil Rights Bill gave rise to the sardonic question "Slavery Is Dead?" Note the irony of blind justice presiding over two violations of the freedmen's rights (described in the newspaper headings at the bottom on either side of a death's head encircled by "state rights"). *(The Newberry Library, Chicago)*

lying around idle." Worse yet was the "impudent and presumin'" new manners of former slaves, as a North Carolinian put it, worrying, with others, that blacks wanted social equality.

The worst fears of southern whites were of rape and revenge. Impudence and pretensions of social equality, some thought, would lead to legal intermarriage, which in turn would produce mulattoes, "Africanization," and the destruction of the purity of the white race. The presence of black soldiers touched off fears of violence and revenge. Although demobilization occurred rapidly after Appomattox, a few black militia units remained in uniform, parading with guns in southern cities. Acts of violence by black soldiers against whites, however, were extremely rare.

Believing that their world was turned upside down, the former planter aristocracy tried to set it right again. Their goal was to restore the old plantation order and appropriate racial relationships. The key to reestablishing white dominance was in the

"black codes" that state legislatures passed in the first year after the end of the war. Many of the codes granted freedmen the right to marry, sue and be sued, testify in court, and hold property. But these rights were qualified. Complicated passages in the codes explained under exactly what circumstances blacks could testify against whites or own property (mostly they could not) or exercise other rights of free people. Some rights were denied, including racial intermarriage and the right to bear arms, possess alcoholic beverages, sit on trains except in baggage compartments, be on city streets at night, or congregate in large groups.

Many of the qualified rights guaranteed by the black codes—testimony in court, for example—were passed only to induce the federal government to withdraw its remaining troops from the South. This was a crucial issue, for in many places marauding groups of whites were assaulting and terrorizing virtually defenseless freedmen. In one small district in Kentucky, for example, a government agent reported in 1865:

> Twenty-three cases of severe and inhuman beating and whipping of men; four of beating and shooting; two of robbing and shooting; three of robbing; five men shot and killed; two shot and wounded; four beaten to death; one beaten and roasted; three women assaulted and ravished; four women beaten; two women tied up and whipped until insensible; two men and their families beaten and driven from their homes, and their property destroyed; two instances of burning of dwellings, and one of the inmates shot.

Freedmen clearly needed protection and the right to testify in court against whites.

For white planters, the violence was another sign of social disorder that could be eased only by restoring a plantation-based society. More significant, they needed the freedmen's labor. The crucial provisions of the black codes were thus intended to regulate the freedmen's economic status. "Vagrancy" laws provided that any blacks not "lawfully employed," which usually meant by a white employer, could be arrested, jailed, fined, or hired out to a man who would assume responsibility for their debts and future behavior. The codes regulated the work contracts by which black laborers worked in the fields for white landowners, including severe penalties for leaving before the yearly contract was fulfilled and rules for proper behavior, attitude, and manners. Thus, southern leaders sought to reestablish their dominance. Although thwarted in perpetuating slavery or even in a program for gradual emancipation, many southerners believed, like this Texan, that "we will be enabled to adopt a coercive system of labor." A Kentucky newspaper was more direct: "The tune . . . will not be 'forty acres and a mule,' but . . . 'work nigger or starve.'"

NATIONAL RECONSTRUCTION

The black codes directly challenged the national government in 1865. How would it use its power—to uphold the codes and impose racial intimidation in the South, or to defend the newly sought rights of the freedmen? Would the federal government stress human liberty and the democratic reform impulse in American history, or would it emphasize property rights, order, and self-interest? Although the primary drama of Reconstruction pitted white landowners against black freedmen over land and labor in the South, in the

background of these local struggles raged the debate over Reconstruction policy among politicians in Washington. This dual drama would extend well into the twentieth century.

The Presidential Plan

After initially demanding that the defeated Confederates be punished for "treason," President Johnson soon adopted a more lenient policy. On May 29, 1865, he issued two proclamations setting forth his reconstruction program. Like Lincoln's, it rested on

---

Promised Land Restored to Whites

Richard H. Jenkins, an applicant for the restoration of his plantation on Wadmalaw Island, S. C., called "Rackett Hall," the same having been unoccupied during the past year and up to the 1st of Jan. 1866, except by one freedman who planted no crop, and being held by the Bureau of Refugees, Freedmen and Abandoned Lands, having conformed to the requirements of Circular No. 15 of said Bureau, dated Washington, D. C., Sept. 12, 1865, the aforesaid property is hereby restored to his possession.

. . . The Undersigned, Richard H. Jenkins, does hereby solemnly promise and engage, that he will secure to the Refugees and Freedmen now resident on his Wadmalaw Island Estate, the crops of the past year, harvested or unharvested; also, that the said Refugees and Freedmen shall be allowed to remain at their present houses or other homes on the island, so long as the responsible Refugees and Freedmen (embracing parents, guardians, and other natural protectors) shall enter into contracts, by leases or for wages, in terms satisfactory to the Supervising Board.

Also, that the undersigned will take the proper steps to enter into contracts with the above described responsible Refugees and Freedmen, the latter being required on their part to enter into said contracts on or before the 15th day of February, 1866, or surrender their right to remain on the said estate, it being understood that if they are unwilling to contract after the expiration of said period, the Supervising Board is to aid in getting them homes and employment elsewhere.

the claim that the southern states had never left the Union.

Johnson's first proclamation continued Lincoln's policies by offering "amnesty and pardon, with restoration of all rights of property" to most former Confederates who would take an oath of allegiance to the Constitution and the Union of the United States. Johnson revealed his Jacksonian hostility to "aristocratic" planters by exempting former Confederate government leaders and rich rebels with taxable property valued over $20,000. Any southerners not covered by the amnesty proclamation, however, could apply for special individual pardons, which Johnson granted to nearly all applicants.

In his second proclamation, Johnson accepted the reconstructed government of North Carolina and prescribed the steps by which other southern states could reestablish state governments. First, the president would appoint a provisional governor, who would call a state convention representing "those who are loyal to the United States," including persons who took the oath of allegiance or were otherwise pardoned. The convention must ratify the Thirteenth Amendment, which abolished slavery; void secession; repudiate all Confederate debts; and elect new state officials and members of Congress.

Under this lenient plan, all southern states successfully completed Reconstruction and sent representatives to the Congress that convened in December 1865. Southern voters defiantly elected dozens of former officers and legislators of the Confederacy, including a few not yet pardoned. Some state conventions hedged on ratifying the Thirteenth Amendment, and some asserted former owners' right to compensation for the loss of slave property. No state convention provided for black suffrage, and most did nothing to guarantee civil rights, schooling, or economic protection for the freedmen.

Less than eight months after Appomattox, the southern states were back in the Union, former slaves were returning to work for their former masters under annual contracts, and the new president seemed firmly in charge. Reconstruction of the southern states seemed to be over. But northern Republicans were far from satisfied with President Johnson's efforts. Georges Clemenceau, a young French newspaper reporter covering the war, wondered if the North, having made so many "painful sacrifices," would "let itself be tricked out of what it had spent so much trouble and perseverance to win."

Congressional Reconstruction

Late in 1865, northern leaders painfully saw that almost none of their postwar goals—moral, political, or psychological—were being fulfilled. The South seemed far from reconstructed and was taking advantage of the president's program to restore the power of the prewar planter aristocracy. The freedmen were receiving neither equal citizenship nor economic independence. And the Republicans were not likely to maintain their political power and stay in office. Would Democrats and the South gain by postwar elections what they had been unable to achieve by civil war?

A song popular in the North in 1866 posed the question: "Who shall rule this American Nation?"—those who would betray their country and "murder the innocent freedmen" or those "loyal millions" who had shed their "blood in battle"? The answer was obvious. Congressional Republicans, led by Congressman Thaddeus Stevens of Pennsylvania and Senator Charles Sumner of Massachusetts, decided to assert their own policies for reconstruction. Although labeled "radicals," the vast majority of Republicans were moderates on the issues of the economic and political rights of the freedmen.

Rejecting Johnson's notion that the South had already been reconstructed, Congress exercised its constitutional authority to decide on its own membership. It refused to seat the new senators and representatives from the old Confederate states. It also established the Joint Committee on Reconstruction to investigate conditions in the South. Its report documented disorder, resistance, and the appalling treatment and conditions of the freedmen.

Even before the report came out in 1866, Congress passed a civil rights bill to protect the fragile rights of the blacks and extended for two more years the Freedmen's Bureau, an agency providing emergency assistance at the end of the war. Johnson vetoed both bills and called his congressional opponents "traitors." His actions drove moderates into the radical camp, and Congress passed both bills over his veto—both, however, watered down by weakening the power of enforcement. Southern courts, therefore, regularly disallowed black testimony against whites, acquitted whites charged with violence against blacks, and sentenced blacks to compulsory labor. In this judicial climate, racial violence erupted with discouraging frequency.

In Memphis, for example, a race riot occurred in May 1866 that typified race relations during the Reconstruction period. In the months before the riot, local Irish policemen frequently unleashed unprovoked brutality on black Union soldiers stationed at nearby Fort Pickering. A Memphis newspaper suggested that "the negro can do the country more good in the cotton field than in the camp" and criticized what it called the "dirty, fanatical, nigger-loving Radicals of this city" who thought otherwise.

A white mob burned this freedmen's school during the Memphis riot of May 1866. *(Library Company of Philadelphia)*

In this inflamed atmosphere, a street brawl erupted between the police and some recently discharged but armed black soldiers. After some fighting and an exchange of gunfire, the soldiers went back to their fort. That night, white mobs, led by prominent local officials (one of whom urged the mob to "go ahead and kill the last damned one of the nigger race"), invaded the black section of the city. With the encouragement of the Memphis police, the mobs engaged in over 40 hours of terror, killing, beating, robbing, and raping virtually helpless residents and burning houses, schools, and churches. When it was over, 48 people, all but two of them black, had died in the riot. The local Union army commander took his time intervening to restore order, arguing that his troops had a "large amount of public property to guard [and] hated Negroes too." A congressional inquiry found that in Memphis, blacks had "no protection from the law whatever."

A month later, Congress sent to the states for ratification the Fourteenth Amendment, the single most significant act of the Reconstruction era. The first section of the amendment sought to provide permanent constitutional protection of the civil rights of freedmen by defining them as citizens. States were prohibited from depriving "any person of life, liberty, or property, without due process

of law," and all people were guaranteed the "equal protection of the laws." In Section 2, Congress granted black male suffrage in the South by making blacks whole people eligible to vote (thus canceling the Constitution's "three-fifths" clause). States that denied this right would have their "basis of representation reduced" proportionally. Other sections of the amendment denied leaders of the Confederacy the right to hold national or state political office (except by act of Congress), repudiated the Confederate debt, and denied claims of compensation to former slave owners. Johnson urged the southern states to reject the Fourteenth Amendment, and ten states immediately did so.

The Fourteenth Amendment was the central issue of the 1866 midterm election. Johnson barnstormed the country asking voters to throw out the radical Republicans and trading insults with hecklers in a nasty campaign of low forms of electioneering. Democrats north and south appealed openly to racial prejudice in attacking the Fourteenth Amendment. The nation would be "Africanized," they charged, with black equality threatening both the marketplace and the bedroom.

Republicans responded in kind, calling Johnson a drunkard and a traitor. Bitter Civil War memories were revived as Republicans "waved the bloody shirt," reminding voters of Democrats' treason and draft

RECONSTRUCTION AMENDMENTS		
Constitutional Seeds of Dreams Deferred for 100 Years (or More)		
Substance	Outcome of Ratification Process	Final Implementation and Enforcement
Thirteenth Amendment—Passed by Congress January 1865		
Prohibited slavery in the United States	Ratified by 27 states, including 8 southern states, by December 1865	Immediate, although economic freedom came by degrees
Fourteenth Amendment—Passed by Congress June 1866		
(1) Defined equal national citizenship; (2) reduced state representation in Congress proportional to number of disenfranchised voters; (3) denied former Confederates the right to hold office	Rejected by 12 southern and border states by February 1867; radicals made readmission depend on ratification; ratified in July 1868	Civil Rights Act of 1964
Fifteenth Amendment—Passed by Congress February 1869		
Prohibited denial of vote because of race, color, or previous servitude	Ratification by Virginia, Texas, Mississippi, and Georgia required for readmission; ratified in March 1870	Voting Rights Act of 1965

dodging. Governor Oliver P. Morton of Indiana described the Democratic party as a "common sewer and loathsome receptacle, into which is emptied every element of treason . . . inhumanity and barbarism which has dishonored the age." Although voters were moved more by self-interest and local issues rather than by such speeches, the result was an overwhelming Republican victory. The mandate was clear. The presidential plan for reconstruction had not worked, and Congress must suggest another.

Early in 1867, Congress passed three Reconstruction acts. The southern states were divided into five military districts, whose military commanders had broad powers to maintain order and protect civil and property rights. Congress also defined a new process for readmitting a state. Qualified voters—including blacks but excluding unreconstructed rebels—would elect delegates to state constitutional conventions that would write new constitutions guaranteeing black suffrage. After the new voters of the states had ratified these constitutions, elections would be held to choose governors and state legislatures. When a state ratified the Fourteenth Amendment, its representatives to Congress would be accepted, completing readmission to the Union.

The President Impeached

Congress also restricted presidential powers and established legislative dominance over the executive branch. The Tenure of Office Act, designed to prevent Johnson from removing the outspoken Secretary of War Edwin Stanton, limited the president's appointment powers. Other measures trimmed his power as commander in chief.

Johnson responded exactly as congressional Republicans had anticipated. He vetoed the Reconstruction acts, limited the activities of military commanders in the South, and removed cabinet officers and other officials sympathetic to Congress. The House Judiciary Committee investigated, charging the president with "usurpations of power" and of acting in the "interests of the great criminals" who had led the southern rebellion. It was evident, however, that Johnson was guilty only of holding principles, policies, and prejudices different from those of congressional leaders, and moderate House Republicans defeated the impeachment resolutions.

In August 1867, Johnson dismissed Stanton and asked for the consent of the Senate. When the Senate refused, the president ordered Stanton to surrender his office, which he refused, barricading himself inside. Now the House quickly approved impeachment resolutions, charging the president with "high crimes and misdemeanors," mostly alleged violations of the Tenure of Office Act. The three-month trial in the Senate early in 1868 featured impassioned oratory, similar to that heard in the Clinton impeachment and trial proceedings in 1998–1999. Evidence was skimpy, however, that Johnson had committed any crime justifying his removal. With seven moderate Republicans joining Democrats against conviction, the effort to find the president guilty fell exactly one vote short of the required two-thirds majority. Not until Nixon in the 1970s would a president again face removal from office through impeachment.

Moderate Republicans, satisfied with the changes wrought by the Civil War, may have feared the consequences of removing Johnson, for the next man in line for the presidency, Senator Benjamin Wade of Ohio, was a leading radical Republican. Wade had endorsed woman suffrage, rights for labor unions, and civil rights for blacks in both southern and northern states. As moderate Republicans gained strength in 1868 through their support of the presidential election winner, Ulysses S. Grant, radicalism lost much of its power within Republican ranks.

Congressional Moderation

The impeachment crisis revealed that most Republicans were more interested in protecting themselves than the freedmen and in punishing Johnson rather than the South. Congress's political battle against the president was not matched by an idealistic resolve on behalf of the rights and welfare of the freedmen. As early as the state and local elections of 1867, it was clear that voters preferred moderate reconstruction policies. It is important to look not only at what Congress did during Reconstruction but also at what it did not do.

With the exception of Jefferson Davis, Congress did not imprison Confederate leaders, and only one person, the commander of the infamous Andersonville prison camp, was executed. Congress did not insist on long probation before southern states could be readmitted to the Union. It did not reorganize southern local governments. It did not mandate a national program of education for the four million former slaves. It did not confiscate and redistribute land to the freedmen, nor did it prevent President Johnson from taking land away from freedmen who had gained titles during the war. It did not, except indirectly, provide economic help to black citizens.

What Congress did do, and that only reluctantly, was grant citizenship and suffrage to the freedmen. Northerners were no more prepared than southern-

ers to make blacks equal citizens. Between 1865 and 1869, several states held referendums proposing black suffrage. Voters in Kansas, Ohio, Michigan, Missouri, Wisconsin, Connecticut, New York, and the District of Columbia (by a vote of 6,521 to 35!) all turned the proposals down. Only in Iowa and Minnesota (on the third try, and then only by devious wording) did northern whites grant the vote to blacks.

Proposals to give black men the vote gained support in the North only after the election of 1868, when General Grant, a military hero regarded as invincible, barely won the popular vote in several states. To ensure grateful black votes, congressional Republicans, who had twice rejected a suffrage amendment, took another look at the idea. After a bitter fight, the Fifteenth Amendment, forbidding all states to deny the vote to anyone "on account of race, color, or previous condition of servitude," became part of the Constitution in 1870. A black preacher from Pittsburgh observed that "the Republican party had done the Negro good, but they were doing themselves good at the same time."

Congress, therefore, gave African Americans the vote but not the land, the opposite priority of what the freedmen wanted. Almost alone, Thaddeus Stevens argued that "forty acres . . . and a hut would be more valuable . . . than the . . . right to vote." But Congress never seriously considered his plan to confiscate the land of the "chief rebels" and to give a small portion of it, divided into 40-acre plots, to the freedmen. This would have violated deeply held beliefs of the Republican party and the American people in the sacredness of private property. Moreover, northern business interests looking to develop southern industry and invest in southern land liked the prospect of a large pool of propertyless black workers.

Most Americans, North and South, opposed land confiscation and the right of independent blacks to own land. Congress did, however, pass the Southern Homestead Act of 1866, proposed by George Julian of Indiana, making public lands available to blacks and loyal whites in five southern states. But the land was

PRESIDENTIAL ELECTIONS, 1864–1868

Year	Candidate	Party	Popular Vote	Electoral Vote
1864	ABRAHAM LINCOLN	Republican	2,206,938 (55.0%)	212
	George B. McClellan	Democratic	1,803,787 (45.0%)	21
1868	ULYSSES S. GRANT	Republican	3,013,421 (52.7%)	214
	Horatio Seymour	Democratic	2,706,829 (47.3%)	80

Note: Winners' names are in capital letters.

poor and inaccessible; no transportation, tools, or seed was provided; and most blacks were bound by contracts that prevented them from moving onto claims before the deadline. Only about 4,000 black families even applied for the Homestead Act lands, and fewer than 20 percent of them saw their claims completed. White claimants did little better. Congressional moderation, therefore, left the freedmen economically weak as they faced the challenges of freedom.

Women and the Reconstruction Amendments

One casualty of the Fourteenth and Fifteenth Amendments was the goodwill of women who had been petitioning and campaigning for suffrage for two decades. They had hoped that grateful male legislators would recognize their wartime service in support of the Union effort and the willing temporary suspension of their own campaign for rights in order to work on behalf of blacks. They would be deeply disappointed.

During the war the Woman's Loyal League, headed by Elizabeth Cady Stanton and Susan B. Anthony, gathered nearly 400,000 signatures on petitions asking Congress to pass the Thirteenth Amendment. They were therefore shocked when the Fourteenth Amendment, in referring to a citizen's right to vote, for the first time inserted the word *male* into the Constitution. To one senator who supported adding woman suffrage at the same time, a colleague said that for "negroes" the ballot "is necessary for their protection; but to extend the right of suffrage to women is not necessary."

Some suffragists such as Lucy Stone were willing to accept delay, recognizing the plea of Frederick Douglass, a longtime proponent of woman suffrage, that this was "the Negro's hour." But Stanton, Anthony, and other women campaigned against an amendment that left them out, arguing against having to continue to rely on their fathers and husbands to protect their rights. Anthony vowed to "cut off this right arm of mine before I will ever work for or demand the ballot for the Negro and not the woman." Largely abandoned by Reconstruction social activists, women had few champions in Congress, and their efforts were put off for half a century.

Disappointment over the suffrage issue helped split the women's movement in 1869. Anthony and Stanton continued their fight for a national amendment for woman suffrage and a long list of property, educational, and sexual rights, while other women focused their hopes on securing the vote state by state. But African Americans would also be disappointed. Events in coming decades showed that the Reconstruction amendments did not change the fact that specific requirements for the suffrage were still in the hands of states, and that southern states would find many ingenious ways to prevent blacks from voting.

⤳ LIFE AFTER SLAVERY

Union army major George Reynolds boasted to a friend late in 1865 that in the area of Mississippi under his command, he had "kept the negroes at work, and in a good state of discipline." Clinton Fisk, a well-meaning white who helped found a black college in Tennessee, told freedmen in 1866 that they could be "as free and as happy" working again for their "old master . . . as any where else in the world." Such pronouncements reminded blacks of white preachers' exhortations during slavery to work hard and obey their masters. Ironically, Fisk and Reynolds were agents of the Freedmen's Bureau, the agency intended to ease the transition from slavery to freedom for the four million former slaves.

The Freedmen's Bureau

Never in American history has one small agency—underfinanced, understaffed, and undersupported—been given a harder task than was the Bureau of Freedmen, Refugees and Abandoned Lands. Its purposes and mixed successes epitomized the tortuous course of Reconstruction.

The Freedmen's Bureau performed many essential services. It issued emergency food rations, clothed and sheltered homeless victims of the war, and established medical and hospital facilities. It provided funds to relocate thousands of freedmen and white refugees. It helped African Americans search for relatives and get legally married, and it served as a friend in local civil courts to ensure that the freedmen got fair trials. Although not initially empowered to do so, the agency was responsible for educating the former slaves in schools staffed by other blacks and idealistic northerners.

The bureau's largest task was to serve as an employment agency, tending to blacks' economic well-being. This included settling them on abandoned lands and getting them started with tools, seed, and draft animals, as well as arranging work contracts with white landowners. As we shall see, in the area of work contracts, the Freedmen's Bureau served more to "reenslave" the freedmen as impoverished fieldworkers than to set them on their way as independent farmers.

The Freedmen's Bureau had fewer resources in relation to its purpose than any agency in the nation's history. *Harper's Weekly* published this engraving of freedmen lining up for aid in Memphis in 1866. *(Library of Congress)*

Although some agents were idealistic young New Englanders eager to help slaves adjust to freedom, others were Union army officers more concerned with social order than social transformation. Working in a postwar climate of resentment and violence, Freedmen's Bureau agents were constantly accused of partisan Republican politics, corruption, and partiality to blacks by local white residents. But even the best-intentioned agents would have agreed with General O. O. Howard, commissioner of the bureau, in a belief in the traditional nineteenth-century American values of self-help, minimal government interference in the marketplace, the sanctity of private property, contractual obligations, and white superiority. The bureau's work served to uphold these values.

On a typical day, these overworked and underpaid agents would visit courts and schools in their district, supervise the signing of work contracts, and handle numerous complaints, most involving contract violations between whites and blacks or property and domestic disputes among blacks. One agent sent a man who had complained of a severe beating back to work with the advice, "Don't be sassy [and] don't be lazy when you've got work to do." Another, reflecting

his growing frustrations, complained that the freedmen were "disrespectful and greatly in need of instruction." Although helpful in finding work for the freedmen, more often than not the agents found themselves defending white landowners by telling the blacks to obey orders, to trust their employers, and to sign and live by disadvantageous contracts.

Despite mounting pressures to support white landowners, personal frustrations, and even threats on their lives, the agents accomplished a great deal. In little more than two years, the Freedmen's Bureau issued 20 million rations (nearly one-third to poor whites); reunited families and resettled some 30,000 displaced war refugees; treated some 450,000 people for illness and injury; built 40 hospitals and hundreds of schools; provided books, tools, and furnishings—and even some land—to the freedmen; and occasionally protected their economic and civil rights. Black historian W. E. B. Du Bois's epitaph for the bureau might stand for the whole of Reconstruction: "In a time of perfect calm, amid willing neighbors and streaming wealth," he wrote, it "would have been a herculean task" for the bureau to fulfill its many purposes. But in the midst of hunger, sorrow, spite, suspicion, hate, and cruelty, "the work of any instrument of social regeneration was . . . foredoomed to failure."

Economic Freedom by Degrees

The economic failures of the Freedmen's Bureau, symbolic of the entire congressional program, forced the freedmen into a new economic dependency on their former masters. Although the planter class did not lose its economic and social power in the postwar years, the character of southern agriculture went through some major changes. First, a land-intensive system replaced the labor intensity of slavery. Land ownership was concentrated into fewer and even larger holdings than before the Civil War. From South Carolina to Louisiana, the wealthiest tenth of the population owned about 60 percent of the real estate in the 1870s. Second, these large planters increasingly concentrated on one crop, usually cotton, and were tied into the international market. This resulted in a steady drop in food production (both grains and livestock) in the postwar period. Third, reliance on one-crop farming meant that a new credit system emerged whereby most farmers—black and white—depended on local merchants for renting seed, farm implements and animals, provisions, housing,

A Freedman's Work Contract

As you read this rather typical work contract defining the first economic relationship between whites and blacks in the early months of the postwar period, note the regulation of social behavior and deportment, as well as work and "pay" arrangements. How different is this from slavery? As a freedman or freedwoman, would you have signed such an agreement? Why or why not? What options did you have?

State of South Carolina
Darlington District
Articles of Agreement

This Agreement entered into between Mrs. Adele Allston Exect of the one part, and the Freedmen and Women of The Upper Quarters plantation of the other part Witnesseth:

That the latter agree, for the remainder of the present year, to reside upon and devote their labor to the cultivation of the Plantation of the former. And they further agree, that they will in all respects, conform to such reasonable and necessary plantation rules and regulations as Mrs. Allston's Agent may prescribe; that they will not keep any gun, pistol, or other offensive weapon, or leave the plantation without permission from their employer; that in all things connected with their duties as laborers on said plantation, they will yield prompt obedience to all orders from Mrs. Allston or his *[sic]* agent; that they will be orderly and quiet in their conduct, avoiding drunkenness and other gross vices; that they will not misuse any of the Plantation Tools, or Agricultural Implements, or any Animals entrusted to their care, or any Boats, Flats, Carts or Wagons; that they will give up at the expiration of this Contract, all Tools & c., belonging to the Plantation, and in case any property, of any description belonging to the Plantation shall be willfully or through negligence destroyed or injured, the value of the Articles so destroyed, shall be deducted from the portion of the Crops which the person or persons, so offending, shall be entitled to receive under this Contract.

Any deviations from the condition of the foregoing Contract may, upon sufficient proof, be punished with dismissal from the Plantation, or in such other manner as may be determined by the Provost Court; and the person or persons so dismissed, shall forfeit the whole, or a part of his, her or their portion of the crop, as the Court may decide.

In consideration of the foregoing Services duly performed, Mrs. Allston agrees, after deducting Seventy five bushels of Corn for each work Animal, exclusively used in cultivating the Crops for the present year; to turn over to the said Freedmen and Women, one half of the remaining Corn, Peas, Potatoes, made this season. He *[sic]* further agrees to furnish the usual rations until the Contract is performed.

All Cotton Seed Produced on the Plantation is to be reserved for the use of the Plantation. The Freedmen, Women and Children are to be treated in a manner consistent with their freedom. Necessary medical attention will be furnished as heretofore.

Any deviation from the conditions of this Contract upon the part of the said Mrs. Allston or her Agent or Agents shall be punished in such manner as may be determined by a Provost Court, or a Military Commission. This agreement to continue till the first day of January 1866.

Witness our hand at The Upper Quarters this 28th day of July 1865.

Sharecroppers and tenant farmers, though more autonomous than contract laborers, remained dependent on the landlord for their survival. *(Brown Brothers)*

and land. These changes affected race relations and class tensions among whites.

This new system, however, took a few years to develop after emancipation. At first, most freedmen signed contracts with white landowners and worked in gangs in the fields as farm laborers very much as during slavery. Watched over by superintendents, who still used the lash, they toiled from sunrise to sunset for a meager wage and a monthly allotment of bacon and meal. All members of the family had to work to receive their rations. The freedmen resented this new form of semiservitude, preferring small plots of land of their own to grow vegetables and grains. Moreover, they wanted to be able to send their children to school and insisted on "no more outdoor work" for women. What the freedmen wanted, a Georgia planter correctly observed, was "to get away from all overseers, to hire or purchase land, and work for themselves."

Many blacks therefore broke contracts, ran away, engaged in work slowdowns or strikes, burned barns, and otherwise expressed their displeasure with the contract labor system. One white landowner expressed his frustration over having "to bargain and haggle with our servants about wages." In the Sea Islands and rice-growing regions of coastal South Carolina and Georgia, where slaves had long held a degree of autonomy, resistance was especially strong. On the Heyward plantations, near those of the Allstons, the freedmen "refuse work at any price," a

Freedman's Bureau agent reported, and the women "wish to stay in the house or the garden all the time." The Allstons' former slaves also refused to sign their contracts, even when offered livestock and other favors, and in 1869, Adele Allston was forced to sell much of her vast landholdings.

Blacks' insistence on autonomy and land of their own was the major impetus for the change from the contract system to tenancy and sharecropping. As a South Carolina freedman put it, "If a man got to go crost de riber, and he can't git a boat, he take a log. If I can't own de land, I'll hire or lease land, but I won't contract." Families would hitch a team of mules to their old slave cabin to drag it to their assigned plot of land as far away from the Big House as possible. Sharecroppers received seed, fertilizer, implements, food, and clothing. In return, the landlord (or a local merchant) told them what to grow and how much and he took a share—usually half—of the harvest. The half retained by the cropper usually went to pay for goods bought on credit (at high interest rates) at the landlord's store. Thus, sharecroppers remained only semiautonomous, tied to the landlord's will for economic survival.

Tenant farmers had only slightly more independence. Before a harvest, they promised to sell their crop to a local merchant in return for renting land, tools, and other necessities. From the merchant's store they also had to buy goods on credit (at a higher price than whites paid) against the harvest. At "settling up" time, income from sale of the crop was compared with debts accumulated at the store. It was possible, especially after an unusually bountiful season, to come out ahead and eventually to own one's own land. But tenants rarely did; in debt at the end of each year, they had to pledge the next year's crop. World cotton prices remained low, and whereas big landowners still generated profits through their large scale of operation, sharecroppers rarely made much money. When they were able to pay their debts, landowners frequently altered loan agreements. Thus, a system of debt peonage replaced slavery, ensuring a continuing cheap labor supply to grow cotton and other staples in the South. Only a very few blacks became independent landowners—about 2 to 5 percent by 1880, but closer to 20 percent in some states by 1900.

These changes in southern agriculture affected yeoman and poor white farmers as well, and planters worried about a coalition between poor black and pro-Unionist white farmers. As a yeoman farmer in Georgia said in 1865, "We should tuk the land, as we did the niggers, and split it, and giv part to the niggers and part to me and t'other Union fellers." But confiscation and redistribution of land was no more likely for white farmers than for the freedmen. Whites, too, were forced to concentrate on growing staples, to pledge their crops against high-interest credit from local merchants, and to face the inevitability of perpetual indebtedness. In the upcountry piedmont area of Georgia, for example, the number of whites who worked their own land dropped from nine in ten before the Civil War to seven in ten by 1880. During the same period, the production of cotton doubled.

Larger planters' reliance on cotton meant fewer food crops, which necessitated greater dependence on local merchants for provisions. In 1884, Jephta Dickson of Jackson County, Georgia, purchased over $50 worth of flour, meal, meat, syrup, peas, and corn

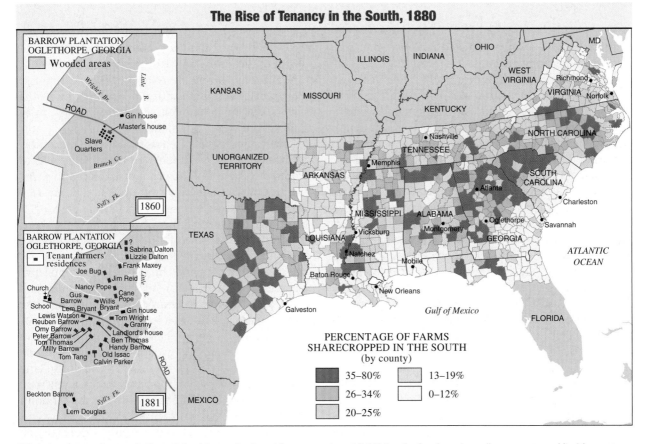

Although no longer slaves and after resisting labor contracts and the gang system of field labor, the freedmen (as well as many poor whites) became tenant farmers, working on shares, in the New South. The former slaves on the Barrow Plantation in Georgia, for example, moved their households to individual 25–30 acre tenant farms, which they rented from the Barrow family in annual contracts requiring payment in cotton and other cash crops. Note that the highest percentage of tenants were in the "black belt."

from a local store, an almost unthinkable situation 25 years earlier, when he would have needed to buy almost no food to supplement his homegrown fare. Fencing laws seriously curtailed the livelihood of poor whites raising pigs and hogs, and restrictions on hunting and fishing reduced the ability of poor whites and blacks alike to supplement their income and diet.

In the worn-out flatlands and barren mountainous regions of the South, poor whites faced diminishing fortunes in the era of Reconstruction. Their antebellum heritage of poverty, ill health, and isolation worsened in the years after the war. A Freedmen's Bureau agent in South Carolina described the poor whites in his area as "gaunt and ragged, ungainly, stooping and clumsy in build." They lived a marginal existence, hunting, fishing, and growing corn and potato crops that, as a North Carolinian put it, "come up puny, grow puny, and mature puny." Many poor white farmers, in fact, were even less productive than black sharecroppers. Some became farmhands at $6 a month and board. Others fled to low-paying jobs in cotton mills, where they would not have to compete against blacks.

The cultural life of poor southern whites reflected both their lowly position and their pride. Their emotional religion centered on camp meeting revivals. Their ballads and folklore told of debt, chain gangs, and deeds of drinking prowess. In backwoods clearings and bleak pine barrens, men and women told tall tales of superhuman feats and exchanged folk remedies for poor health. In Alabama, there were over 90 superstitious sayings for calling rain. Aesthetic expression, in quilt making and house construction, for example, reflected a marginal culture in which everything was saved and reused.

In part because their lives were so hard, poor whites persisted in their belief in white superiority. As a federal officer reported in 1866, "The poorer classes of white people . . . have a most intense hatred of the Negro, and swear he shall never be reckoned as part of the population." Many poor whites, therefore, joined the Ku Klux Klan and other southern white terror groups that emerged between 1866 and 1868. But however hard life was for poor whites, blacks were far more often sentenced to chain gangs for the slightest crimes and were bound to a life of debt, degradation, and dependency. The high hopes with which the freedmen had greeted emancipation turned slowly to resignation and disillusionment. Felix Haywood, a former Texas slave, recalled:

We thought we was goin' to be richer than white folks, 'cause we was stronger and knowed how to

work, and the whites . . . didn't have us to work for them anymore. But it didn't turn out that way. We soon found out that freedom could make folks proud but it didn't make 'em rich.

Black Self-Help Institutions

Felix Haywood understood the limitations of government programs and efforts on behalf of the freedmen. It was clear to many black leaders, therefore, that because white institutions could not fulfill the promises of emancipation, black freedmen would have to do it themselves. Fortunately, the tradition of black community self-help survived in the organized churches and schools of the antebellum free Negro communities and in the "invisible" cultural institutions of the slave quarters. Religion, as usual, was vital. Emancipation brought an explosion in the growth of membership in black churches. The Negro Baptist Church grew from 150,000 members in 1850 to 500,000 in 1870. The various branches of the African Methodist Episcopal Church increased fourfold in the decade after the Civil War, from 100,000 to over 400,000 members.

Black ministers continued their tradition of community leadership. Many led efforts to oppose discrimination, some by entering politics. Over one-fifth of the black officeholders in South Carolina were ministers. Most preachers, however, focused on traditional religious themes of sin, conversion, and salvation. An English visitor to the South in 1867 and 1868, after observing a revivalist preacher in Savannah arouse nearly 1,000 people to "sway, and cry, and groan," noted the intensity of black "devoutness." Despite some efforts by urban elite blacks to restrain the emotionalism characteristic of black worship, most congregations preferred their traditional forms of religious expression. One black woman, when urged to pray more quietly, complained: "We make noise 'bout ebery ting else . . . I want ter go ter Heaben in de good ole way."

The freedmen's desire for education was as strong as for religion. A school official in Virginia echoed the observation of many when he said that the freedmen were "down right crazy to learn." A Mississippi farmer vowed, "If I nebber does do nothing more, I shall give my children a chance to go to school, for I consider education next best ting to liberty." The first teachers of these black children were unmarried northern women, the legendary "Yankee schoolmarms." Sent by groups such as the American Missionary Association, these idealistic young women sought to convert blacks to Congregationalism and to white moral values of cleanliness, discipline, and dutiful

Along with equal civil rights and land of their own, what the freedmen wanted most was education. Despite white opposition and limited facilities for black schools, one of the most positive outcomes of the Reconstruction era was education in freedmen's schools. *(Valentine Museum, Richmond, Virginia)*

work. In October 1865, Esther Douglass found "120 dirty, half naked, perfectly wild black children" in her schoolroom near Savannah, Georgia. Eight months later, she reported that "their progress was wonderful." They could read, sing hymns, and repeat Bible verses and had learned "about right conduct which they tried to practice."

Glowing reports like this one changed as white teachers grew frustrated with crowded facilities, limited resources, local opposition, and the absenteeism that resulted from the demands of fieldwork. In Georgia, for example, only 5 percent of black children went to school for part of any one year between 1865 and 1870; this contrasted with 20 percent of white children. Furthermore, blacks increasingly preferred their own teachers, who could better understand former slaves. To ensure the training of black preachers and teachers, northern philanthropists founded Howard, Atlanta, Fisk, Morehouse, and other black universities in the South between 1865 and 1867.

Black schools, like churches, became community centers. They published newspapers, provided training in trades and farming, and promoted political participation and land ownership. A black farmer in

Mississippi founded both a school and a society to facilitate land acquisition and better agricultural methods. These efforts made black schools objects of local white hostility. A Virginia freedman told a congressional committee that in his county, anyone starting a school would be killed and that blacks were "afraid to be caught with a book." In 1869, in Tennessee alone, 37 black schools were burned to the ground.

White opposition to black education and land ownership stimulated black nationalism and separatism. In the late 1860s, Benjamin "Pap" Singleton, a former Tennessee slave who had escaped to Canada, observed that "whites had the lands and . . . blacks had nothing but their freedom." Singleton urged them to abandon politics and migrate westward. He organized a land company in 1869, purchased public property in Kansas, and in the early 1870s took several groups from Tennessee and Kentucky to that prairie state to establish separate black towns. In following years, thousands of "exodusters" from the Lower South bought some 10,000 infertile acres in Kansas. But natural and human obstacles to self-sufficiency often proved insurmountable. By the 1880s, despairing of ever finding economic independence in the United States, Singleton and other nationalists urged emigration to Canada and Liberia. Other black leaders, notably Frederick Douglass, continued to press for full citizenship rights within the United States.

⤳ RECONSTRUCTION IN THE STATES

Douglass's confidence in the power of the ballot seemed warranted in the enthusiastic early months under the Reconstruction Acts of 1867. With President Johnson neutralized, national Republican leaders were finally in a position to accomplish their political goals. Local Republicans, taking advantage of the inability or refusal of many southern whites to vote, overwhelmingly elected their delegates to state con-

stitutional conventions in the fall of 1867. With guarded optimism and a sense of the "sacred importance" of their work, black and white Republicans turned to the task of creating new state governments.

Republican Rule

Despite popular belief, the southern state governments under Republican rule were not dominated by illiterate black majorities intent on "Africanizing" the South by passing compulsory racial intermarriage laws, as many whites feared. Nor were these governments unusually corrupt or financially extravagant. Nor did they use massive numbers of federal troops to enforce their will. By 1869, only 1,100 federal soldiers remained in Virginia, and most federal troops in Texas were guarding the frontier against Mexico and hostile Indians. Without the support of a strong military presence, then, these new state governments tried to do

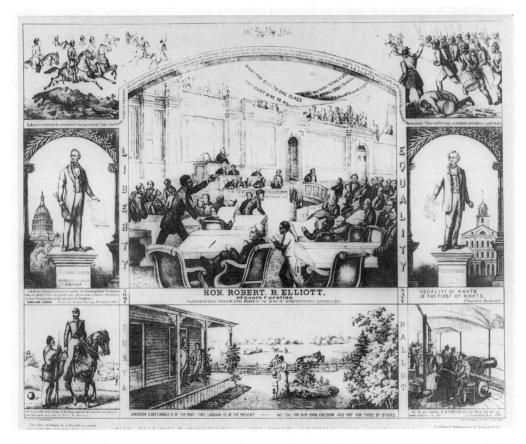

A talented, articulate, well-educated lawyer and Civil War veteran, Robert B. Elliott was elected to the South Carolina legislature in 1868, where he later was Speaker of the House, and served two terms in the U.S. Congress, from 1871 to 1874. This 1874 lithograph is titled "The Shackle Broken by the Genius of Freedom." The banner quotes Elliott, saying: "What you give to one class you must give to all. What you deny to one class you shall deny to all." *(Chicago Historical Society)*

their work in a climate of economic distress and increasingly violent harassment.

A diverse combination of political groups made up the new governments elected under congressional Reconstruction. Labeled the "black and tan" governments by their opponents to suggest domination by former slaves and mulattoes, they were actually predominantly white, with the one exception of the lower house of the South Carolina legislature. One part of the new leadership consisted of an old Whiggish elite class of bankers, industrialists, and others interested far more in economic growth and sectional reconciliation than in radical social reforms. A second group consisted of northern Republican capitalists who headed south for investments in land, railroads, and new industries. Others included retired Union veterans seeking a warmer climate for health purposes and missionaries and teachers pursuing an outlet for their idealism in the Freedmen's Bureau schools. Such people were unfairly labeled "carpetbaggers."

Moderate blacks made up a third group participating in the Republican state governments. A large percentage of black officeholders were mulattoes, many of them well-educated preachers, teachers, and soldiers from the North. Others, such as John Lynch of Mississippi, were self-educated tradesmen or representatives of the small landed class of southern blacks. In South Carolina, for example, of some 255 black state and federal officials elected between 1868 and 1876, two-thirds were literate and one-third owned real estate. Only 15 percent owned no property at all. This class composition meant that black leaders often supported land policies that largely ignored the economic needs of the black masses.

These black politicians were more interested in pursuing a political agenda of gaining access to government influence and education than an economic agenda of land redistribution or state aid to black peasants. They fashioned their political goals squarely in the American republican tradition. Black leaders reminded whites that they, too, were southerners and Americans, attached both to the land of the South and to the white families they had lived with for generations: "The dust of our fathers mingles with yours in the same grave yards. . . . This is your country, but it is ours too." Because of this intermingled past, blacks sought no revenge or reversal of power, only, as an 1865 petition said, "that the same laws which govern white men shall govern black men [and that] we be dealt with as others are—in equity and justice."

The primary accomplishment of Republican rule in the South was in eliminating the undemocratic features of earlier state constitutions. All states provided universal men's suffrage and loosened requirements for holding office. The basis of state representation was made fairer by apportioning more legislative seats to the interior regions of southern states. Social legislation included the abolition of automatic imprisonment for debt and laws for the relief of poverty and for the care of the handicapped. The first divorce laws in many southern states were passed, as were laws granting property rights to married women. Penal laws were modernized by reducing the list of crimes punishable by death, in one state from 26 to 5.

Republican governments undertook the task of financially and physically reconstructing the South, overhauling tax systems, and approving generous railroad and other capital investment bonds. Harbors, roads, and bridges were rebuilt. Hospitals, asylums, and other state institutions were established. Most important, the Republican governments provided for a state-supported system of public schools, absent before in most of the South. As in the North, these schools were largely segregated, but for the first time, rich and poor, black and white alike had access to education. As a result, black school attendance increased from 5 to over 40 percent, and white from 20 to over 60 percent by the 1880s. All this cost money, and the Republicans did indeed greatly increase tax rates and state debts. All in all, the Republican governments "dragged the South, screaming and crying, into the modern world."

These considerable accomplishments were achieved in the midst of opposition like that expressed at a convention of Louisiana planters, which labeled the Republican leaders the "lowest and most corrupt body of men ever assembled in the South." There was some corruption, to be sure, but mostly in land sales, fraudulent railway bonds, and construction contracts, the kind of graft that had become a way of life in American politics, South and North, in the aftermath of the Civil War. Given their lack of experience with politics, the black role was remarkable. As Du Bois put it, "There was one thing that the White South feared more than negro dishonesty, ignorance, and incompetence, and that was negro honesty, knowledge, and efficiency."

Despite its effectiveness in modernizing southern state governments, the Republican coalition did not last very long. In fact, as the map nearby indicates, Republican rule lasted for different periods of time in different states. In some states—Virginia, for example—the Republicans ruled hardly at all. Situated in the shadow of Washington, conservatives in Virginia professed their agreement with Congress's Reconstruction guidelines while doing as they pleased. As one of the states most devastated by the war, Virginia looked almost immediately to northern

The Return of Conservative Democratic Control in Southern States During Reconstruction

VIRGINIA 1870/1869

NORTH CAROLINA 1868/1870

TENNESSEE 1866/1869

ARKANSAS 1868/1874

SOUTH CAROLINA 1868/1876

MISSISSIPPI 1870/1876

GEORGIA 1870/1871

ALABAMA 1868/1874

TEXAS 1870/1873

LOUISIANA 1868/1877

FLORIDA 1868/1877

1870 Date readmitted to the Union

1870 Date of reestablishment of conservative government

Note that the length of time Republican governments were in power to implement even moderate Reconstruction programs varied from state to state. In North Carolina and Georgia, for example, Republican rule was very brief, while in Virginia it never took place at all. "Redemption," the return of conservative control, took longest in the three Deep South states where electoral votes were hotly contested in the election of 1876.

investors to rebuild its cities and to develop industry. Blacks and whites alike flocked to the cities for work. In South Carolina, the unwillingness of black leaders to use their power to help black laborers contributed to their loss of political control to the Democrats. Class tensions and divisions among blacks in Louisiana helped to weaken that Republican regime as well.

Republican rule lasted the longest in the black belt states of the Deep South, where the black population was equal to or greater than the white. In Louisiana, Reconstruction began with General Ben Butler's occupation of New Orleans in 1862. Although he insisted on granting civil rights to blacks, he was quickly replaced by a succession of Republican governors in the late 1860s more interested in graft, election laws, and staying in office than in the rights and welfare of poor black Louisianans. Alabama received a flood of northern capital to develop the rich coal, iron ore, and timber resources of the northern third of the state. Republican rule in Alabama, as in other states, involved a greater role for towns and merchants, the endorsement of generous railroad bonds, and an emergent class structure that replaced the old planter aristocracy with a new industrial one.

Violence and "Redemption"

A Georgia newspaper in 1868 charged that Republican rulers would "see this fair land drenched in blood from the Potomac to the Rio Grande rather than lose their power." In fact, it was the Democrats who used racial violence, intimidation,

and coercion to restore their power. As one southern editor put it, "We must render this either a white man's government, or convert the land into a Negro man's cemetery." The Ku Klux Klan was only one of several secret organizations that used force and violence against black and white Republicans to drive them from power. The cases of North Carolina and Mississippi are representative in showing how conservative Democrats were able to regain control.

After losing a close election in North Carolina in 1868, conservatives waged a concentrated campaign of terror in several counties in the piedmont area. If the Democrats could win these counties in 1870, they would most likely win statewide. In the year before the election, several prominent Republicans were killed, including a white state senator, whose throat was cut, and a leading black Union League organizer, who was hanged in the courthouse square with a sign pinned to his breast: "Bewar, ye guilty, both white and black." Scores of citizens were flogged, tortured, fired from their jobs, or forced to flee in the middle of the night from burning homes and barns. The courts consistently refused to prosecute anyone for these crimes. Local papers, in fact, charged that "disgusting negroes and white Radicals" had committed the crimes. The conservative campaign worked. In the election of 1870, some 12,000 fewer Republicans voted in the two crucial counties than had voted two years earlier, and the Democrats swept back into power.

In the state election in Mississippi in 1875, Democrats used similar tactics, openly announcing that "the thieves . . . robbers, and scoundrels, white

As shown in this Thomas Nast cartoon, "Worse Than Slavery," to restore a "white man's government" and redeem the noble "lost cause," white groups such as the Ku Klux Klan and the White League used every form of terror, violence, and intimidation. (Harper's Weekly, *October 24, 1874*)

and black," in power "deserve death and ought to be killed." In what was called the Mississippi Plan, local Democratic clubs organized themselves into armed militias, marching defiantly through black areas, breaking up Republican meetings, and provoking riots to justify the killing of hundreds of blacks. Armed men were posted during voter registration to intimidate Republicans. At the election itself, anyone still bold enough to attempt to vote was either helped by gun-toting whites to cast a Democratic ballot or driven away from the polls with cannon and clubs. Counties that had earlier given Republican candidates majorities in the thousands in 1875 managed a total of less than a dozen votes!

Democrats called their victory "redemption." As conservative Democratic administrations resumed control of each state government, Reconstruction came to an end. Redemption resulted from a combination of the persistence of white southern resistance, including violence and other coercive measures, and a loss of will to persist in the North. Albion Tourgée summed up the Reconstruction era in his novel *A*

Fool's Errand (1879): "The spirit of the dead Confederacy was stronger than the mandate of the nation to which it had succumbed in battle."

Congress and President Grant did not totally ignore the violence in the South. Three force acts, passed in 1870 and 1871, gave the president strong powers to use federal supervisors to make sure that citizens were not prevented from voting by force or fraud. The third act, known as the Ku Klux Klan Act, declared illegal secret organizations that used disguise and coercion to deprive others of equal protection of the laws. Congress created a joint committee to investigate Klan violence, which reported in 1872 in 13 huge volumes of horrifying testimony. Grant, who had supported these measures, delivered special messages to Congress proclaiming the importance of the right to vote, issued proclamations condemning lawlessness, and sent some additional troops to South Carolina. However, as reform Republicans realized that black voters supported Grant, they lost interest in defending those voters. Regular Republicans were also not very supportive, because many felt that they could do

"The negroes of the South are free—
ree as air," says the parliamentary Wat-
erson. This is what the *State*, a well-
known Democratic organ of Tennessee,
says, in huge capitals, on the subject :
' Let it be known before the election that
the farmers have agreed to spot every
leading Radical negro in the county, and
treat him as an enemy for all time to come.
The rotten ring must and shall be broken
at any and all costs. The Democrats have
determined to withdraw all employment
from their enemies. Let this fact be
known."

Although the Fourteenth and Fifteenth Amendments gave African American males the right to vote in the late 1860s, by the 1870s white southerners opposed to black suffrage found many illegal ways of influencing and eventually depriving that vote, thus returning white Democrats to office. In this cartoon, titled "Of course he wants to vote the Democratic Ticket," one of the two pistol-wielding men is saying: "You're as free as air, ain't you? Say you are, or I'll blow your black head off!" Note that another freedmen is being led down the street to the polling place, no doubt to vote Democratic also. *(Corbis)*

without black voters. Both groups were much more concerned with northern issues. In 1875, Grant's advisers told him that Republicans might lose important Ohio elections if he continued to protect blacks. Thus, he decided that year to reject appeals by Mississippi blacks that troops be stationed in their state to guarantee free elections. Grant declared instead that he and the nation "had tired of these annual autumnal outbreaks."

The success of the Mississippi Plan in 1875, imitated a year later in South Carolina and Louisiana, indicated that congressional reports and presidential proclamations did little to stop the reign of terror against black and white Republicans throughout the South. The force acts were wholly inadequate and weakly enforced. Although there were hundreds of arrests, all-white juries were reluctant to find their fellow citizens guilty of crimes against blacks. The U.S. Supreme Court backed them. In two decisions in 1874, the Court threw out cases against whites found guilty of preventing blacks from voting and declared key parts of the force acts unconstitutional.

In Hamburg, South Carolina, in 1876, several blacks were killed in a riot that started in a courtroom when a white mob came to provide its own form of "justice" to some black militiamen who had been arrested for parading on Independence Day. Although the Ku Klux Klan's power was officially ended, the attitudes (and tactics) of Klansmen would continue long into the next century.

Reconstruction, Northern Style

Most northerners, like their leaders, were never committed to the principle of guaranteeing constitutional rights to African Americans. It was easy, therefore, to shift their attention to other matters than helping the freedmen. Frustrated with the difficulties of trying to transform an unwilling South, the easiest course was to give blacks citizenship and the vote, and wash their hands of the whole thing. Americans of increasing ethnic diversity were interested primarily in starting families, finding work, and making money. Thus, German immigrants fired furnaces in new steel plants in Wheeling, West Virginia; Chinese men pounded in

These two scenes vividly contrast family life during Reconstruction in the North and South. For most white northerners, as shown in this 1868 Currier & Ives print (top), the end of the Civil War meant renewing the good life of genteel middle-class values. *(Museum of the City of New York, The Harry T. Peters Collection)* For many black freedmen, however, family life was constantly threatened by the intrusion of Klan violence. *(The Granger Collection, New York)*

railroad ties for the Central Pacific over the Sierra Nevada mountains and across the Nevada desert; female teachers struggled to teach in one-room schoolhouses in Vermont for $23 a month; Mexican vaqueros drove Texas cattle herds to Kansas; and Scandinavian families battled heat, locusts, and high railroad rates on farmsteads in the Dakotas.

At both the individual and national levels, Reconstruction, northern style, meant the continuation of the enormous economic revolution of the nineteenth century. Northern Republicans were able to accelerate and solidify their program of economic growth and industrial and territorial expansion. The sad, practical consequence of this focus, however, was the abandonment of efforts to help four million freedmen to secure their freedom.

Thus, as the Central Pacific and Union Pacific railroads met at Promontory Point, Utah, in 1869, linking the Atlantic and the Pacific by rail, Klansmen met in dark forests to plan their next raid in North Carolina. As southern cotton production revived, northern iron and steel manufacturing and western settlement of the mining, cattle, and agricultural frontiers also surged. As black farmers were "haggling" over work contracts with white landowners in Georgia, white workers were organizing the National Labor Union in Baltimore. As Elizabeth and Adele Allston demanded the keys to their crop barns in the summer of 1865, the Boston Labor Reform Association was demanding that "our . . . education, morals, dwellings, and the whole Social System" needed to be "reconstructed." If the South would not be reconstructed, labor relations might be.

The years between 1865 and 1875 featured not only the rise (and fall) of Republican governments in the South but also the spectacular rise of working-class activity and organization. Stimulated by the Civil War to improve working conditions in northern factories, trade unions, labor reform associations, and labor parties flourished, culminating in the founding of the National Labor Union in 1866. Before the depression of 1873, an estimated 300,000 to 500,000 American workers enrolled in some 1,500 trade unions, the largest such increase in the nineteenth century.

This growth inevitably stirred class tensions. In 1877, thousands of railroad workers in Pittsburgh, St. Louis, Omaha, and other northern cities went out in a nationwide wave of strikes over wage cuts, clashing with local police and the National Guard. As we will see in Chapter 18, union activity and strikes exploded in the last two decades of the century. But southern black workers also protested worsening labor conditions. A year before the northern railroad strikes, hundreds of freedmen in the rice region along the Combahee River in South Carolina had organized a strike to protest a 40-cent-per-day wage cut. They clashed not only with local sheriffs but also with unofficial white Democratic rifle clubs, and no friendly Union troops were there to defend them.

As economic relations changed, so did the Republican party. Heralded by the moderate tone of the state elections of 1867 and Grant's election in 1868, the Republicans changed from a party of moral reform to one of material interest. In the continuing struggle in American politics between "virtue and commerce," commercial self-interest was again winning.

Abandoning the Freedmen's Bureau, Republican politicians had no difficulty handing out huge grants of money and land to the railroads. As blacks were told to go to work and help themselves, the Union Pacific was getting subsidies of between $16,000 and $48,000 for each mile of track laid across western plains and mountains. As Susan B. Anthony and others tramped through the snows of Upstate New York with petitions for rights of suffrage and citizenship, Boss Tweed and other machine politicians defrauded New York taxpayers of millions of dollars. As Native Americans in the Great Plains struggled to preserve their sacred Black Hills from greedy gold prospectors and U.S. soldiers, government officials in the East "mined" public treasuries by various forms of graft.

By 1869, the year financier Jay Gould almost succeeded in cornering the gold market, the nation was increasingly defined by materialistic "go-getters" and by sordid grasping for wealth and power. Henry Adams, descendant of two presidents, was living in Washington, D.C., during this era. As he wrote later in his autobiography, *The Education of Henry Adams* (1907), he had high expectations in 1869 that Grant, like another "great soldier" and president, George Washington, would restore moral order and peace. But when Grant announced the members of his cabinet, a group of army cronies and rich friends to whom he owed favors, Adams felt betrayed, complaining that "a great soldier might be a baby politician."

Ulysses Grant himself was an honest man, but his judgment of others was flawed. The scandals of his administration touched his relatives, his cabinet, and two vice presidents. Under Grant's appointments, outright graft, as well as loose prosecution and generally negligent administration, flourished in a half dozen departments. Most scandals involved large sums of public money. The Whiskey Ring affair, for example, cost the public millions of dollars in lost tax revenues siphoned off to government officials. Gould's gold scam received the unwitting aid of Grant's Treasury Department and the knowing help of the president's brother-in-law.

Nor was Congress pure. Crédit Mobilier, a dummy corporation supposedly building the transcontinental

Recovering the Past

NOVELS

We usually read novels, short stories, and other forms of fiction for pleasure, for the enjoyment of plot, style, symbolism, and character development. "Classic" novels such as *Moby Dick, Huckleberry Finn, The Great Gatsby, The Invisible Man,* and *Beloved,* to name a few American examples, are not only written well but also explore timeless questions of good and evil, innocence and knowledge, noble dreams fulfilled and shattered. Often, we enjoy novels because we find ourselves identifying with one of the major characters. Through that person's problems, joys, relationships, and search for identity, we gain insights about our own.

We can also read novels as historical sources, for they reveal much about the attitudes, dreams, fears, and ordinary everyday experiences of human beings in a particular historical period. They also show how people reacted to and felt about the major events of that era. The novelist, like the historian, is a product of time and place and has an interpretive point of view. Consider the two novels about Reconstruction quoted here. Neither is reputed for great literary merit, yet both reveal much about the various interpretations and impassioned attitudes of the post–Civil War era. *A Fool's Errand* was written by Albion Tourgée, a northerner; *The Clansman,* by Thomas Dixon, Jr., a southerner.

Tourgée was a young northern teacher and lawyer who fought with the Union army at several major battles during the Civil War. After the war, he moved to North Carolina, partly for health reasons and partly to begin a legal career. He became a judge and was an active Republican, supporting black suffrage and helping shape the new state constitution and the codification of North Carolina laws in 1868. With jurisdiction over eight counties, Tourgée earned a reputation as one of the fairest judges in the state. Because he boldly criticized the Ku Klux Klan for its campaign of terror against blacks, his life was threatened many times. When the fearless judge finally left North Carolina in 1879, he published an autobiographical novel about his experiences.

The "fool's errand" in the novel is that of the northern veteran, Comfort Servosse, who like Tourgée seeks to fulfill humane goals on behalf of both blacks and whites in post–Civil War North Carolina. His efforts are thwarted, however, by threats, intimidation, a campaign of violent "outrages" against Republican leaders in the county, and a lack of support from Congress. Historians have verified the accuracy, down to the smallest details, of the events in Tourgée's novel. While exposing the brutality of the Klan, Tourgée features loyal southern Unionists, respectable planters ashamed of Klan violence, and even guilt-ridden poor white Klansmen who try to protect or warn intended victims.

In the year of Tourgée's death, 1905, another North Carolinian published a novel with a very different analysis of Reconstruction and its fate. Thomas Dixon was born during the Civil War. He was a lawyer, North Carolina state legislator, Baptist minister, lecturer, and novelist. *The Clansman,* subtitled *A Historical Romance of the Ku Klux Klan,* reflects turn-of-the-century attitudes most white southerners still had about Republican rule during Reconstruction. According to Dixon, once the "Great Heart" Lincoln was gone, a power-crazed, vindictive radical Congress, led by scheming Austin Stoneman (Thaddeus Stevens), sought to impose corrupt carpetbagger and brutal black rule by bayonet on a helpless South. Only through the inspired leadership and redemptive role of the Ku Klux Klan was the South saved from the horrors of rape and revenge.

Dixon dedicated *The Clansman* to his uncle, a Grand Titan of the Klan in North Carolina during the time when two crucial counties were being transformed from Republican to Democratic through intimidation and terror. No such violence shows up in Dixon's novel. When the novel was made the basis of D. W. Griffith's film classic, *Birth of a Nation,* in 1915, the novel's attitudes were firmly imprinted on the twentieth-century American mind.

Both novels convey the events and attitudes of the era by creating clearly defined heroes and villains. Both include exciting chase scenes, narrow escapes, daring rescues, and tragic, heart-rending deaths. Both include romantic subplots in which a young white southern man falls in love with a young white northern woman. In each novel, however, the author's primary purpose was to convey his views of the politics of Reconstruction. Examining brief excerpts is a poor substitute for reading the novels in their entirety. Notice the obvious differences of style and attitude in the descriptions of Uncle Jerry and Old Aleck.

When the second Christmas came, Metta wrote again to her sister:

"The feeling is terribly bitter against Comfort on account of his course towards the colored people. There is quite a village of them on the lower end of the plantation. They have a church, a sabbath school, and are to have next year a school. You can not imagine how kind they have been to us, and how much they are attached to Comfort. . . . I got Comfort to go with me to one of their prayer-meetings a few nights ago. I had heard a great deal about them, but had never attended one before. It was strangely weird. There were, perhaps, fifty present, mostly middle-aged men and women. They were singing in a soft, low mono-tone, interspersed with prolonged exclamatory notes, a sort of rude hymn, which I was surprised to know was one of their old songs in slave times. How the chorus came to be endured in those days I can not imagine. It was

'Free! free! free, my Lord, free!
An' we walks de hebben-ly way!'

"A few looked around as we came in and seated our-selves; and Uncle Jerry, the saint of the settlement, came forward on his staves, and said, in his soft voice,

"'Ev'nin', Kunnel! Sarvant, Missus! Will you walk up, an' hev seats in front?'

"We told him we had just looked in, and might go in a short time; so we would stay in the back part of the audience.

"Uncle Jerry can not read nor write; but he is a man of strange intelligence and power. Unable to do work of any account, he is the faithful friend, monitor, and director of others. He has a house and piece of land, all paid for, a good horse and cow, and, with the aid of his wife and two boys, made a fine crop this season. He is one of the most promising colored men in the settle-ment: so Comfort says, at least. Everybody seems to have great respect for his character. I don't know how many people I have heard speak of his religion. Mr. Savage used to say he had rather hear him pray than any other man on earth. He was much prized by his master, even after he was disabled, on account of his faithfulness and character."

THE CLANSMAN

THOMAS DIXON, JR. (1905)

At noon Ben and Phil strolled to the polling-place to watch the progress of the first election under Negro rule. The Square was jammed with shouting, jostling, perspiring negroes, men, women, and children. The day was warm, and the African odour was supreme even in the open air. . . .

The negroes, under the drill of the League and the Freedman's Bureau, protected by the bayonet, were voting to enfranchise themselves, disfranchise their former masters, ratify a new constitution, and elect a legislature to do their will. Old Aleck was a candidate for the House, chief poll-holder, and seemed to be in charge of the movements of the voters outside the booth as well as inside. He appeared to be omnipresent, and his self-importance was a sight Phil had never dreamed. He could not keep his eyes off him. . . .

[Aleck] was a born African orator, undoubtedly descended from a long line of savage spell-binders, whose eloquence in the palaver houses of the jungle had made them native leaders. His thin spindle-shanks supported an oblong, protruding stomach, resembling an elderly monkey's, which seemed so heavy it swayed his back to carry it.

The animal vivacity of his small eyes and the flexibil-ity of his eyebrows, which he worked up and down rapidly with every change of countenance, expressed his eager desires.

He had laid aside his new shoes, which hurt him, and went barefooted to facilitate his movements on the great occasion. His heels projected and his foot was so flat that what should have been the hollow of it made a hole in the dirt where he left his track.

He was already mellow with liquor, and was dressed in an old army uniform and cap, with two horse-pistols buckled around his waist. On a strap hanging from his shoulder were strung a half-dozen tin canteens filled with whiskey.

railroad, received generous bonds and contracts in exchange for giving congressmen gifts of money, stocks, and railroad lands. An Ohio congressman described the House of Representatives in 1873 as an "auction room where more valuable considerations were disposed of under the speaker's hammer than any place on earth." Henry Adams spoke for many Americans when he said that Grant's administration "outraged every rule of decency."

In *Democracy* (1880), a novel written by Henry Adams about Washington life during this period, Adams's main character, Mrs. Madeleine Lee, sought to uncover "the heart of the great American mystery of democracy and government." What she found were corrupt legislators and lobbyists in an unprincipled pursuit of power and wealth. "Surely something can be done to check corruption?" Mrs. Lee asked her friend one evening, "Are we forever to be at the mercy of thieves and ruffians? Is a respectable government impossible in a democracy?" The answer she heard was hardly reassuring: "No responsible government can long be much better or much worse than the society it represents."

The election of 1872 marked the decline of public interest in moral issues. A "liberal" faction of the Republican party, unable to dislodge Grant and disgusted with his administration, formed a third party with a reform platform and nominated Horace Greeley, editor of the New York *Tribune,* for president. The liberal Republicans advocated free trade, which meant lower tariffs and fewer grants to railroads; honest government, which meant civil service reform; and noninterference in southern race relations, which meant the removal of federal troops from the South. Democrats, lacking notable presidential candidates, also nominated Greeley, even though he had spent much of his earlier career assailing Democrats as "rascals." Despite his wretched record, Grant easily won a second term. Greeley was beaten so badly, he said, that "I hardly knew whether I was running for the Presidency or the Penitentiary."

The End of Reconstruction

Soon after Grant's second inauguration, a financial panic, caused by railroad mismanagement and the collapse of some eastern banks, started a terrible depression that lasted throughout the mid-1870s. In these times of hardship, economic issues dominated politics, further diverting attention from the freedmen. As Democrats took control of the House of Representatives in 1874 and looked toward winning the White House in 1876, politicians talked about new

Grant scandals, unemployment and public works projects, the currency, and tariffs.

No one, it seemed, said much about the rights and conditions of southern freedmen. In 1875, a guilt-ridden Congress passed Senator Charles Sumner's civil rights bill, intended to put teeth into the Fourteenth Amendment. But the act was not enforced and after eight years was declared unconstitutional by the Supreme Court. Congressional Reconstruction, long dormant, had ended. The election of 1876 sealed the conclusion.

As their presidential candidate in 1876, the Republicans nominated a former governor of Ohio, Rutherford B. Hayes. Hayes had a reputation for honesty and had been an officer in the Union army, a necessity for post–Civil War candidates. But he was also, as Henry Adams put it, "obnoxious to no one." The Democrats nominated Governor Samuel J. Tilden of New York, who achieved national recognition as a civil service reformer in breaking up the corrupt Tweed ring.

Tilden won a majority of the popular vote and appeared to have enough electoral votes for victory. Twenty more electoral votes were disputed, all but one in the Deep South states of Louisiana, South Carolina, and Florida, where some federal troops still remained on duty and where Republicans still controlled the voting apparatus. Democrats, however, had applied various versions of the Mississippi Plan to intimidate voters. To settle the disputed electoral votes, Congress created a special electoral commission of five senators, five representatives, and five Supreme Court justices—eight of whom were Republicans and seven Democrats. The vote in each disputed case was eight to seven along party lines. Hayes was given all 20 votes, enough to win, 185 to 184.

Outraged Democrats threatened to stop the Senate from officially counting the electoral votes, thus preventing Hayes's inauguration. The country was in a state of crisis, and some Americans wondered if civil war might break out again. But unlike the 1850s, when passions over slavery erupted, this time a compromise was drawn between northerners and southerners mutually interested in modernization of the southern economy through capital investments. They focused on a Pacific railroad linking New Orleans with the West Coast. Northern investors wanted the government to help pay for the railroad. Southerners wanted northern dollars but not northern political influence—no social agencies, no federal enforcement of the Fourteenth and Fifteenth Amendments, and no military occupation, not even the small symbolic presence left in 1876.

As the March 4 inauguration date approached and newspapers echoed outgoing President Grant's call for "peace at any price," the forces of mutual self-interest concluded the "compromise of 1877." Democrats agreed to suspend resistance to the counting of the electoral votes, and on March 2, Rutherford B. Hayes was declared president. After his inauguration, he ordered the last federal troops out of the South, appointed a former Confederate general to his cabinet, supported federal aid for economic and railroad development in the South, and promised to let southerners handle race relations themselves.

On a goodwill trip to the South, Hayes told blacks in Atlanta that "your rights and interests would be safer if this great mass of intelligent white men were let alone by the general government." The message was clear: Hayes would not enforce the Fourteenth and Fifteenth Amendments, thus initiating a pattern of presidential inaction and white northern abandonment of African Americans that would last for nearly a hundred years. Thus ended the era of Reconstruction.

Under a caption quoting a Democratic party newspaper, "This is a white man's government," this Thomas Nast cartoon from 1868 shows three white groups, stereotyped as apelike northern Irish workers, unrepentant former Confederates, and rich northern capitalists, joining hands to bring Republican Reconstruction to an end almost before it began. The immigrant's vote, the Kluxer's knife, and the capitalist's dollars would restore a "white man's government" on the back of the freedman, still clutching the Union flag and reaching in vain for the ballot box. No single image better captures the story of the end of Reconstruction. (Harper's Weekly, *September 5, 1868/ The Granger Collection, New York*)

Timeline

1865	Civil War ends
	Lincoln assassinated; Andrew Johnson becomes president
	Johnson proposes general amnesty and reconstruction plan
	Racial confusion, widespread hunger, and demobilization
	Thirteenth Amendment ratified
	Freedmen's Bureau established
1865–1866	Black codes
	Repossession of land by whites and freedmen's contracts
1866	Freedmen's Bureau renewed and Civil Rights Act passed over Johnson's veto
	Southern Homestead Act
	Ku Klux Klan formed
	Tennessee readmitted to Union
1867	Reconstruction Acts passed over Johnson's veto
	Impeachment controversy
	Freedmen's Bureau ends
1868	Fourteenth Amendment ratified
	Senate fails to convict Johnson of impeachment charges
	Ulysses Grant elected president

1868–1870	Ten states readmitted under congressional plan
1869	Georgia and Virginia reestablish Democratic party control
1870	Fifteenth Amendment ratified
1870s–1880s	Black "exodusters" migrate to Kansas
1870–1871	Force acts
	North Carolina and Georgia reestablish Democratic control
1872	Grant reelected president
1873	Crédit Mobilier scandal
	Panic causes depression
1874	Alabama and Arkansas reestablish Democratic control
1875	Civil Rights Act passed
	Mississippi reestablishes Democratic control
1876	Hayes–Tilden election
1876–1877	South Carolina, Louisiana, and Florida reestablish Democratic control
1877	Compromise of 1877; Rutherford B. Hayes assumes presidency and ends Reconstruction
1880s	Tenancy and sharecropping prevail in the South
	Disfranchisement and segregation of southern blacks begins

Conclusion

A Mixed Legacy

In the 12 years between Appomattox and Hayes's inauguration, victorious northern Republicans, defeated white southerners, and hopeful black freedmen each wanted more than the others would give. But each saw some fulfillment of their dreams. The compromise of 1877 cemented the reunion of South and North, providing new opportunities for economic development in both regions. The Republican party achieved its economic goals and preserved its political hold on the White House, though not Congress, until 1932. The former Confederate states came back into the Union, and southerners retained their firm grip on southern lands and black labor, though not without struggle and some changes.

And the freedmen? In 1880, Frederick Douglass wrote:

> Our Reconstruction measures were radically defective. . . . To the freedmen was given the machinery of liberty, but there was denied to them the steam to put it in motion. They were given the uniform of soldiers, but no arms; they were called citizens, but left subjects; they were called free, but left almost slaves. The old master class . . . retained the power to starve them to death, and wherever this power is held there is the power of slavery.

The wonder, Douglass said, was "not that freedmen have made so little progress, but, rather, that they have made so much; not that they have been standing still, but that they have been able to stand at all."

The freedmen had made admirable gains in education and economic and family survival. Despite sharecropping and tenancy, black laborers organized themselves to achieve a measure of autonomy and opportunity in their lives that could never be diminished. The three great Reconstruction amendments to the Constitution, despite flagrant violation over the next 100 years, held out the promise of equal citizenship and political participation.

And yet, there was still an underlying tragedy to Reconstruction, as a short story by W. E. B. Du Bois, written a few years later, makes sadly clear. Two boyhood playmates, both named John, one black and one white, are sent from the fictional town of Altamaha, Georgia, north to school to prepare for leadership of their respective communities, the black John as a teacher and the white John as a judge and possible governor of the state. While they were away, the black and white people of Altamaha, each race thinking of its own John and not of the other, waited for "the coming of two young men, and dreamed . . . of new things that would be done and new thoughts that all would think."

After several years, both Johns returned to Altamaha, but a series of tragic events shattered the hopes and dreams of a new era of racial justice and harmony. Neither John understood the people of the town, and each was in turn misunderstood. Black John's school was closed because he was teaching ideals of liberty. Heartbroken and discouraged as he walked through the forest near town, he surprised the white John in an attempted rape of his sister. Without a word, black John picked up a fallen limb, and with "all the pent-up hatred of his great black arm," killed his boyhood friend. Within hours he was lynched.

Du Bois's story captures the human cost of the Reconstruction era. The black scholar's hope for reconciliation by a "union of intelligence and sympathy across the color-line" was smashed in the tragic encounter between the two Johns. Both young men, each once filled with glorious dreams, lay dead under the pines of the Georgia forest. Dying with them were hopes that interracial harmony, intersectional trust, and equal opportunities and rights for the freedmen might be the legacies of Reconstruction. Conspicuously absent in the forest scene was the influence of the victorious northerners. They had turned their attention to other, less noble, causes.

Recommended Reading

The Bittersweet Aftermath of War

Dan T. Carter, *When the War Was Over: The Failure of Self-Reconstruction in the South* (1985); W. E. B. Du Bois, *Black Reconstruction* (1935); Laura Edwards, *Gendered Strife & Confusion: The Political Culture of Reconstruction* (1997); Eric Foner, *Nothing but Freedom: Emancipation and Its Legacy* (1983) and *Reconstruction: America's Unfinished Revolution, 1863–1877* (1988); John Hope Franklin, *Reconstruction after the Civil War* (1961); Leon Litwack, *Been in the Storm So Long: The Aftermath of Slavery* (1980).

National Reconstruction

Richard H. Abbott, *The Republican Party and the South, 1855–1877* (1986); Michael Les Benedict, *A Compromise of Principle: Congressional Republicans and Reconstruction, 1863–1869* (1974); Frederick J. Blue, *Charles Sumner and the Conscience of the North* (1994); James E. Bond, *No Easy Walk to Freedom: Reconstruction and the Ratification of the Fourteenth Amendment* (1997); David Donald, *The Politics of Reconstruction* (1965); William Gillette, *Retreat from Reconstruction, 1869–1879* (1979); Brooks D. Simpson, *Let Us Have Peace: Ulysses S. Grant and the Politics of War and Reconstruction, 1861–1868* (1991); Hans Trefousse, *Thaddeus Stevens: Nineteenth-Century Egalitarian* (1997); C. Vann Woodward, *The Strange Career of Jim Crow* (1974) and *Reunion and Reaction* (1956).

Life After Slavery

W. E. B. Du Bois, *The Souls of Black Folk* (1903); Jacqueline Jones, *Soldiers of Light and Love: Northern Teachers and Georgia Blacks, 1865–1873* (1980); Leon Litwack, *Been in the Storm So Long: The Aftermath of Slavery* (1980); William E. Montgomery, *Under Their Own Vine and Fig Tree: The African-American Church in the South, 1865–1900* (1993); Donald Nieman, *To Set the Law in Motion: The Freedmen's Bureau and the Legal Rights of Blacks, 1865–1868* (1979); Claude Oubré, *Forty Acres and a Mule: The Freedmen's Bureau and Black Land Ownership* (1978); Nell I. Painter, *Exodusters: Black Migration to Kansas after Reconstruction* (1977); Roger Ransom and Richard Sutch, *One Kind of Freedom: The Economic Consequences of Emancipation* (1977); Edward Royce, *The Origins of Southern Sharecropping* (1993); Julie Saville, *The Work of Reconstruction: From Slave to Wage Laborer in South Carolina, 1860–1870* (1994).

Reconstruction in the States

W. Fitzhugh Brundage, *Lynching in the New South: Georgia and Virginia, 1880–1930* (1993); Paul Cimbala, *Under the Guardianship of the Nation: The Freedmen's Bureau and the Reconstruction of Georgia, 1865–1870* (1997); Thomas Holt, *Black over White: Negro Political Leadership in South Carolina During Reconstruction* (1977); Edward Miller, *Gullah Statesman: Robert Smalls from Slavery to Congress, 1839–1915* (1995); George C. Rable, *But There Was No Peace: The Role of Violence in the Politics of Reconstruction* (1984); Allen Trelease, *White Terror: The Ku Klux Klan Conspiracy and Southern Reconstruction* (1971); Richard Zuczek, *State of Rebellion: Reconstruction in South Carolina* (1996).

Fiction and Film

Toni Morrison's *Beloved* (1988), an extraordinary novel set near Cincinnati in 1873, is about the lasting traumas of slavery and the trials of blacks putting new lives together and pursuing their dreams in freedom. The film by the same name, though long and slow moving, follows the time disconnections of the novel well, with some powerfully effective acting. *Birth of a Nation,* the classic 1913 film by D. W. Griffith portraying heroically the rise of the Ku Klux Klan as the defender of white supremacy, is based on Thomas Dixon's *The Clansman* (1905), described in the "Recovering the Past" section of this chapter. A quite different film portrayal is seen in Oscar Micheaux's *Within Our Gates* (1919), the first feature film by an African American, available from the Library of Congress early American film collection. W. E. B. Du Bois's *The Quest of the Silver Fleece* (1911) is a little-known novel by the sociologist-historian about the lives of sharecroppers during Reconstruction. Howard Fast's *Freedom Road* (1944) is a novel about the heroic but ultimately failed efforts of poor whites and blacks to unite politically during the Reconstruction era. Ernest Gaines's *The Autobiography of Miss Jane Pittman* (1971), framed as an autobiography, is actually a gripping fictional account of a proud centenarian black woman who lived from the time of the Civil War to the era of civil rights. Albion Tourgée in *A Fool's Errand* (1879), as described in the "Recovering the Past" section of this chapter, takes the viewpoint of a sympathetic white judge toward helping the freedmen in North Carolina during Reconstruction.

Suggested Web Sites

http://www.ohiohistory.org/places/hayes/search/index.cfm

Hayes Diary Search. The Rutherford B. Hayes Presidential Center in Fremont, Ohio, maintains this searchable database of Hayes's writing.

http://digital.nypl.org/schomburg/images_aa19/

Images of African Americans from the 19th Century. The New York Public Library–Schomburg Center for Research in Black Culture site contains visuals by artists, engravers, and photographers capturing elements of African-American life in the nineteenth century.

http://www.inform.umd.edu/ARHU/Depts/History/Freedman/home.html

Freedmen and Southern Society Project. This site contains a chronology and sample documents from several print collections and primary sources about emancipation and freedom in the 1860s.

http://www.whitehouse.gov/WH/glimpse/presidents/html/aj17.html

Andrew Johnson. This is a White House web site that presents a history of Andrew Johnson.

http://www.whitehouse.gov/WH/glimpse/presidents/html/ug18.html

Ulysses S. Grant. This White House site gives a history of Ulysses Grant.

http://www.ncwa.org/info.html

National Civil War Association Home Page. The NCWA is one of the many Civil War reenactment organizations in the United States. Its site includes a Civil War and history links page.

http://www.ushistoryplace.com

 A richly detailed on-line learning environment complete with interactive maps, timelines, history activities, primary source documents, and links to related American history sites.

17

The REALITIES *of* RURAL AMERICA

CHAPTER OUTLINE

In 1873, Milton Leeper, his wife, Hattie, and their baby, Anna, climbed into a wagon piled high with their possessions and set out to homestead in Boone County, Nebraska. Once on the claim, the Leepers dreamed confidently of their future. Wrote Hattie to her sister in Iowa, "I like our place the best of any around here." "When we get a fine house and 100 acres under cultivation," she added, "I wouldn't trade with any one." But Milton had broken in only 13 acres when disaster struck. Hordes of grasshoppers appeared, and the Leepers fled their claim and took refuge in the nearby town of Fremont.

There they stayed for two years. Milton worked first at a store and then hired out to other farmers. Hattie sewed, kept a boarder, and cared for chickens and a milk cow. The family lived on the brink of poverty but never gave up hope. "Times are hard and we have had bad luck," Hattie acknowledged, but "I am going to hold that claim . . . there will [be] one gal that won't be out of a home." In 1876, the Leepers triumphantly returned to their claim with the modest sum of $27 to help them start over.

The grasshoppers were gone, there was enough rain, and preaching was only half a mile away. The Leepers, like others, began to prosper. Two more daughters were born and cared for in the comfortable sod house—"homely" on the outside but plastered and cozy within. As Hattie explained, the homesteaders lived "just as civilized as they would in Chicago."

Their luck did not last. Hattie, pregnant again, fell ill and died in childbirth along with her infant son. Heartbroken, Milton buried his wife and child and left the claim. The last frontier had momentarily defeated him, although he would try farming in at least four other locations before his death in 1905.

The same year that the Leepers established their Boone County homestead, another family tried their luck in a Danish settlement about 200 miles west of Omaha. Rasmus and Ane Ebbesen and their eight-year-old son, Peter, had arrived in the United States from Denmark in 1868, lured by the promise of an "abundance" of free land "for all willing to cultivate it." By 1870, they had made it as far west as Council Bluffs, Iowa. There they stopped to earn the capital that would be necessary to begin farming. Rasmus dug ditches for the railroad, Ane worked as a cleaning woman in a local boardinghouse, and young Peter brought drinking water to thirsty laborers who were digging ditches for the town gas works.

Like the Leepers, the Ebbesens eagerly settled on their homestead and began to cultivate the soil. Peter later recalled that the problems that the family had anticipated never materialized. Even the rumors that the Sioux, "flying demons" in the eyes of settlers, were on the rampage proved false. The real problems the family faced were unexpected: rattlesnakes, prairie fires, and an invasion of grasshoppers. The grasshoppers were just as devastating to the Ebbesen farm as they had been to the Leeper homestead. But unlike the Leepers, the Ebbesens stayed on the claim. Although the family "barely had enough" to eat, they survived the three years of grasshopper infestation.

In the following years, the Ebbesens thrived. Rasmus had almost all the original 80 acres under cultivation and purchased an additional 80 acres from the railroad. A succession of sod houses rose on the land and finally even a two-story frame house, paid for with money Peter earned teaching school. By 1873, Rasmus and Ane were over 50 and could look with pride at their "luxurient and promising crop." But once more natural disaster struck: a "violent hailstorm . . . which completely devastated the whole lot."

The Ebbesens were lucky, however. A banker offered to buy them out, for $1,000 under what the family calculated was the farm's "real worth." But it was enough for the purchase of a "modest" house in town. Later, there was even a "dwelling of two stories and nine rooms . . . with adjacent park."

The stories of the Leepers and the Ebbesens, though different in their details and endings, hint at some of the problems confronting rural Americans in the last quarter of the nineteenth century. As a mature industrial economy transformed agriculture and shifted the balance of economic power permanently away from America's farmlands to the country's cities and factories, many farmers found it impossible to realize the traditional dream of rural independence and prosperity. Even bountiful harvests no longer guaranteed success. "We were told two years ago to go to work and raise a big crop; that was all we needed," said one farmer. "We went to work and plowed and planted; the rains fell, the sun shone, nature smiled,

The flat landscape disappearing into the horizon, the picture of a hardworking and determined woman—these suggest some of the geographic and physical realities of rural life in the West. *(Harvey Dunn,* The Homesteader's Wife, *1916/South Dakota Memorial Art Center Collection, Brookings)*

and we raised the big crop they told us to; and what came of it? Eight cent corn, ten cent oats, two cent beef and no price at all for butter and eggs—that's what came of it." Native Americans also discovered that changes in rural life threatened their values and dreams. As the Sioux leader Red Cloud told railroad surveyors in Wyoming, "We do not want you here. You are scaring away the buffalo."

This chapter explores the agricultural transformation of the late nineteenth century and highlights the ways in which rural Americans—red, white, and black—joined the industrial world and responded to new economic and social conditions. The rise of large-scale agriculture in the West, the exploitation of its natural resources, and the development of the Great Plains form a backdrop for the discussion of the impact of white settlement on western tribes and their reactions to white incursions. In an analysis of the South, the efforts of whites to create a "New South" form a contrast to the underlying realities of race and cotton. Although the chapter shows that discrimination and economic peonage characterized the lives of most black southerners during this period, it also describes the rise of new black protest tactics and ideologies. Finally, the chapter highlights the ways in which agricultural problems of the late nineteenth century, which would continue to characterize much of agricultural life in the twentieth century, led American farmers to become reformers and to form a new political party.

⤳ MODERNIZING AGRICULTURE

Between 1865 and 1900, the nation's farms more than doubled in number as Americans eagerly took up virgin land west of the Mississippi River. In both newly settled and older areas, farmers raised specialized crops with the aid of modern machinery and relied on the expanding railroad system to send them to market. The character of agriculture became increasingly capitalistic. Farmers, as one New Englander pointed out, "must understand farming as a business; if they do not it will go hard with them."

Rural Myth and Reality

The number of Americans still farming the land suggested the vigor of a rural tradition that pictured the farmer as a central figure for the nation. In Thomas Jefferson's words, the farmer was the "deposit for substantial and genuine virtue" and therefore fundamental to the health of the republic.

The notion that the farmer and the farm life symbolized the essence of America persisted as the United States industrialized. The popularity of inexpensive Currier & Ives prints, like the one pictured nearby, testifies to the powerful appeal of an idealized view of country life. Other prints implied harmony between the new technological industrial world and rural America. Trains, representing the new order, chug peacefully through fertile farmlands, bringing progress and prosperity.

The prints obscured the reality of American agriculture. However much Americans wanted to believe that no tension existed between technological progress and rural life, it did. Farmers were slipping from their dominant position in the workforce. In 1860, they represented almost 60 percent of the labor force; by 1900, less than 37 percent of employed Americans farmed. At the same time, farmers' contribution to the nation's wealth declined from a third to a quarter.

Nor were farmers the independent yeomen of the rural myth, for the industrial and urban world increasingly affected them. Reliable, cheap transportation allowed them to specialize. Farmers on the Great Plains now grew most of the country's wheat, whereas those in the Midwest replaced that crop with corn used to feed hogs and cattle. Eastern farmers turned to vegetable, fruit, and dairy farming. Some, like Milachi Dodge from New Hampshire, gave up farming altogether. As he explained, when his "boys came home" from the Civil War, "they did not want to work on a farm, and I sold my farm out." Cotton continued to dominate the economy of the South, although farmers also raised tobacco, wheat, and rice. In the Far West, grain, fruits, and vegetables predominated.

As farmers specialized in cash crops for national and international markets, their success depended increasingly on outside forces and demands. Bankers and loan companies provided capital to expand farm operations, middlemen stored and sometimes sold produce, railroads carried farm goods to market. A prosperous American economy put money into laborers' pockets for food purchases. Even international conditions affected the American farmer. After 1870, exports of wheat, flour, and animal products rose, with wheat becoming the country's chief cash crop. Thus, the cultivation of wheat in Russia and Argentina meant fewer foreign buyers for American grain; the opening of the Canadian high plains in the

This Currier & Ives print provides an idyllic view of rural life. Happy children greet hunters loaded down with game, while the woman of the family looks out from her cozy cabin at the cheerful sight. This image looked more to an idealized frontier past than to the reality of rural life after the Civil War. American agriculture was tied increasingly to national and international markets. Settlers on the Plains frontier lived in dugouts or shacks rather than in cozy log cabins like the one pictured here. *(Museum of the City of New York, The Harry T. Peters Collection)*

1890s added another competitor. When several European countries banned American pork imports between 1879 and 1883, fearing trichinosis, American stock raisers suffered.

Farming was becoming a modern business calling for particular attitudes and skills. "Watch and study the markets and the ways of marketmen [and] learn the art of 'selling well,'" one rural editor advised in 1887. "The work of farming is only half done when the crop is out of the ground."

Like other businesses of the post–Civil War era, farming stimulated technological innovation. Farmers increasingly desired and depended upon improved machinery. Inventors and manufacturers met the demand. "It is no longer necessary for the farmer to cut his wheat with sickle or cradle, nor to rake it and bind it by hand; to cut his cornstalks with a knife and shock the stalks by hand; to thresh his grain with a flail," reported one observer. Harvesters, binders, and other new machines, pulled by work animals, performed such tasks.

These machines diminished much of the drudgery of farming life, making the production of crops easier, more efficient, and cheaper. Moreover, they allowed a farmer to cultivate far more land than possible with hand tools. By 1900, more than twice as much land was in cultivation as in 1860. But machinery was expensive, and many American farmers borrowed to buy it. In the decade of the 1880s, mortgage indebtedness grew two and a half times faster than agricultural wealth.

New Farmers, New Farms

As farmers used machinery, brought new land into cultivation, raised specialized crops, and sent them to faraway markets, they operated much like other nineteenth-century businessmen. Some even became large-scale entrepreneurs. Small family farms still typified American agriculture, but vast mechanized operations devoted to the cultivation of one crop appeared, especially west of the Mississippi River. These farms with huge barns for storage of machinery and only a handful of other buildings had few gardens, trees, or outbuildings. No churches or villages interrupted the monotony of the new agricultural landscape.

The bonanza farms, established in the late 1870s on the northern plains, symbolized the trend to large-scale agriculture. Thousands of acres in size, these wheat farms required large capital investments; in fact, corporations owned many of them. Like factories, they depended on machinery, hired workers, and efficient managers. The North Dakota farm that Oliver Dalrymple operated for two Northern Pacific Railroad directors used 200 pairs of harrows and 125 seeders for planting and required 155 binders and 26 steam threshers for harvesting. At peak times, the farm's workforce numbered 600 men. The results were impressive: 600,000 bushels of wheat harvested in 1882. Although bonanza farms were not typical, they dramatized the agricultural changes that were occurring everywhere on a smaller scale.

George Inness's *Lackawanna Valley*—with the reclining figure in the foreground, the train, and puffing smokestacks in the background—suggests that there need be no conflict between technology and agriculture. *(Inness, George, The Lackawanna Valley, Gift of Mrs. Huttleston Rogers, © 2000 Board of Trustees, National Gallery of Art, Washington, c. 1856, oil on canvas, .860 x 1.275 [33⅞ x 50¼])*

Overproduction and Falling Prices

Subscribing wholeheartedly to the rural myth Currier & Ives pictured so winningly, farmers only gradually realized that technology might backfire. As they cultivated more land with the help of machinery, they began to discover unanticipated consequences. Productivity rose 40 percent between 1869 and 1899. Almost every crop showed impressive statistical gains. But the yields for some crops like wheat were so large that the domestic market could not absorb them.

The prices farm products commanded steadily declined. In 1867, corn sold for 78 cents a bushel. By 1873, it had tumbled to 31 cents, and by 1889, to 23 cents. Wheat similarly plummeted from about $2 a bushel in 1867 to only 70 cents a bushel in 1889. Cotton profits also spiraled downward, the value of a bale depreciating from $43 in 1866 to $30 in the 1890s.

Falling prices did not automatically hurt all farmers. Because the supply of money rose more slowly than productivity, all prices declined—by more than half between the end of the Civil War and 1900 (for a discussion of the money issue, see Chapter 19). In a deflationary period, farmers were receiving less for their crops but also paying less for their purchases.

Deflation may have encouraged overproduction, however. To make the same amount of money, many farmers believed they had to raise larger and larger crops. As they did, prices fell even lower. Furthermore, deflation increased the real value of debts. In 1888, it took 174 bushels of wheat to pay the interest on a

$2,000 mortgage at 8 percent. By 1895, it took 320 bushels. Falling prices thus had their greatest impact on farmers in newly settled areas who had borrowed heavily to finance their new operations.

Price of Wholesale Wheat Flour, 1865–1900

Dollars per barrel (y-axis, 0 to 14)

Year (x-axis, 1865 to 1900)

The plummeting price of wheat flour was just one indication of the difficulties farmers faced in the late nineteenth century. Source: U.S. Bureau of the Census.

Farming on the Western Plains, 1880s–1890s

Between 1870 and 1900, the acreage devoted to farming tripled west of the Mississippi as settlers flocked to the Great Plains (North and South Dakota, Kansas, Nebraska, Oklahoma, and Texas). In the mid-nineteenth century, emigrants headed for the Far West, believing the plains unsuitable for cultivation. Views of the farming potential of this vast area changed after the Civil War, however. Railroads, town boosters, land speculators, hoping to make their Great Plains investments profitable, launched extravagant promotional campaigns. "This is the sole remaining section of paradise in the western world," promised one newspaper. "All the wild romances of the gorgeous orient dwindle into nothing when compared to the everyday realities of Dakota's progress." Addressing the fear that

the Plains lacked adequate rain, the article suggested, "All that is needed is to plow, plant and attend to the crops properly; the rains are abundant." The rainfall, above average for the region in the 1880s, lent strength to the claim of adequate moisture.

Late-nineteenth-century industrial innovations helped settlers overcome the natural obstacles that made farming on the plains so problematic at mid-century. Because there was so little timber for fencing and housing on the plains, early emigrants had chosen to settle elsewhere. But in the 1870s, Joseph Glidden developed barbed wire as a cheap alternative to timber fencing. During a visit to a country fair, Glidden had seen a simple wooden device with protruding points that was intended to keep animals away from fences. The device suggested the possibility of making fencing wire with similar protruding barbs. Before long, he and a partner were producing

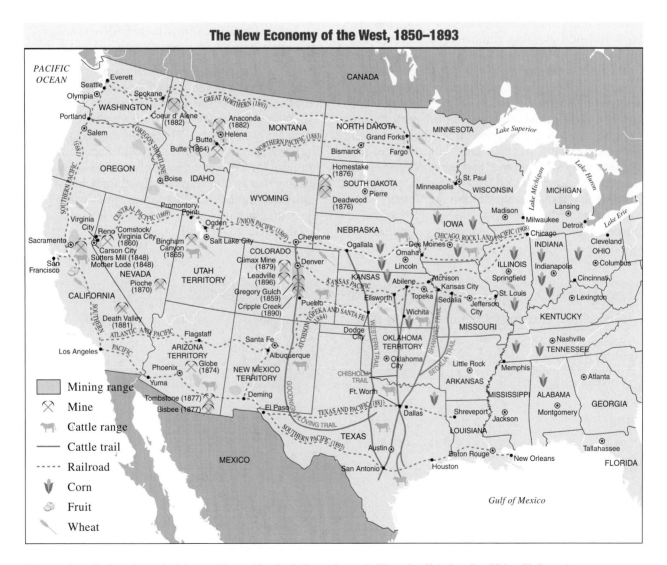

The New Economy of the West, 1850–1893

This map shows the importance of mining, ranching, and farming in the western part of the nation. Note the railroad links with the east.

hundreds of miles of barbed wire fencing that could be used to enclose fields on the Plains. Other innovations overcame some of the remaining challenges to successful agriculture. Twine binders, which speeded up grain harvesting, reduced the threat of losing crops to the unpredictable weather. And mail-order steel windmills for pumping water from deep underground wells relieved water shortages by the 1890s.

In the first boom period of settlement, lasting from 1879 to the early 1890s, tens of thousands of eager families like the Leepers and Ebbesens moved onto the Great Plains and began farming. Some made claims under the Homestead Act, which granted 160 acres to any family head or adult who lived on the claim for five years or who paid $1.25 an acre after six months of residence. Because homestead land was frequently less desirable than land held by railroads and speculators, however, most settlers bought land outright rather than taking up claims.

The costs of getting started were thus more substantial than the Homestead Act would suggest. Western land was cheap compared with farmland in the East, but an individual farmer was fortunate if he could buy a good quarter section for under $500. The costs of machinery would often reach $700. Although some farmers thought it made better economic sense to lease rather than buy land, many rented only because they lacked the capital to purchase land and set up operations. In 1880, some 20 percent of the Plains farmers were tenants, and this percentage rose over time.

Like the Ebbesens, many of the new settlers were immigrants, making the Great Plains the second most important destination for them. The most numerous arrived from Germany, the British Isles, and Canada. Many Scandinavians, Czechs, and Poles also moved to the new frontier. Unlike the single male immigrants flocking to American cities for work, these newcomers came with their families. From the beginning, they intended to put down roots in the new country.

Life on the Plains frontier often proved difficult. Wrote Miriam Peckham, a Kansas homesteader:

> I tell you Auntie no one can depend on farming for a living in this country. Henry is very industrious and this year had in over thirty acres of small grain, 8 acres of corn and about an acre of potatoes. We have sold our small grain . . . and it come to $100; now deduct $27.00 for cutting, $16.00 for threshing, $19.00 for hired help, say nothing of boarding our help, none of the trouble of drawing 25 miles to market and 25 cts on each head for ferriage over the river and where is your profit. I sometimes think this a God forsaken country, the [grass]hopper hurt our corn and we have 1/2 a crop and utterly destroyed our garden. If one wants trials, let them come to Kansas.

Peckham's letter highlights the uncertainties of frontier life: the costs of machinery, the vagaries of crops and markets, the threat of pests and natural disasters, the shortage of cash. Unlike earlier emigrants to the Far West, who had to have the means to finance the six-month trip, many Plains pioneers took up their homesteads with only a few dollars in their pockets. Frontier diaries often revealed the marginality of early frontier operations, the loans from family in the East, the debts. Survival often depended on how well families managed to do during the crucial first years and

AGRICULTURAL PRODUCTIVITY, 1800–1900				
Crop and Productivity Indicator	1800	1840	1880	1900
Wheat				
Worker-hours/acre	56	35	30	15
Yield/acre (bushels)	15	15	13	14
Worker-hours/100 bushels	373	233	152	108
Corn				
Worker-hours/acre	86	69	46	38
Yield/acre (bushels)	25	25	26	26
Worker-hours/100 bushels	344	276	180	147
Cotton				
Worker-hours/acre	185	135	119	112
Yield/acre (bushels)	147	147	179	191
Worker-hours/bale	601	439	318	280

The astonishing gains in the productivity of wheat farmers points to the use of reapers that cut and bound the wheat and thrashers that knocked the grain off the stalks. The combine integrated both operations and also cleared and bagged the grain.

Source: U.S. Bureau of the Census.

how much work each member of the family, including women and children, could perform. If they succeeded in raising and selling their crops, they might accumulate the capital needed to continue. But if nature was harsh or their luck or health bad, or if they were unable to adjust to new conditions or to do the hard labor that was necessary to get the farm going, the chances of failure were great.

Many settlers recoiled from a landscape without trees and the other natural markings that might make it familiar or provide a human scale. As one New England visitor observed, "It has been terrible on settlers, on the women especially, for there is no society and they get doleful and feel almost like committing suicide for want of society." This was the point many authors chose to emphasize. O. E. Rölvaag's novel *Giants in the Earth* (1927) depicts the wife of a Norwegian immigrant farmer driven to madness and death. Hamlin Garland's *Main-Travelled Roads* (1891), inspired by a "mood of resentment" after a visit to his mother "on a treeless farm," pictures overworked, hopeless women whom the frontier defeats.

Life on the Plains was not always so discouraging, however. Willa Cather, who grew up in Nebraska, showed both the harshness and the appeal of the prairie in her novels. Alexandra Bergson, the main character of *O Pioneers!* (1913), loves the land: "It seemed beautiful to her, rich and strong and glorious." The thousands of letters and diaries that survive from the period also provide a more positive picture of farming life. One woman reflected on the way she had softened the harsh landscape. "Our flower garden was

such a vision of beauty . . . the dreary, desolate place was blossoming in all the gorgeous beauty that God has promised to those who try." Elam Bartholomew's diary shows a life filled with human contacts and social events. In 1880, only six years after he had settled in northern Kansas, Elam's journal reveals that 1,081 people stopped at his home. His wife served 783 meals to visitors. Trips to church, parties, sings, and neighborhood get-togethers brightened family life.

The Plains frontier required many adjustments. Scarce water and violent changes in temperature called for resourcefulness and new modes of behavior. Without firewood, farmers learned to burn corncobs and twisted straw for warmth. The log cabin, long the symbol of frontier life, disappeared as inventive settlers discovered how to build houses of sod "bricks." Although from a distance such houses often looked like mounds of earth—"homely old things," as Hattie Leeper described them—they frequently had glass windows, wooden shingles, and even plastered interiors. Dark and gloomy to our eyes, they were comfortable, cozy, and practical for the settlers. Walls two to three feet thick kept out the scorching summer heat and fierce cold of winter, the moaning winds, and the prairie fires. The solidity of the sod house provided a welcome contrast to the impersonal power and scale of nature.

The first boom on the Great Plains halted abruptly in the late 1880s and early 1890s. Falling agricultural prices cut profits. Then, the unusual rainfall that had lured farmers into the semiarid region near the hundredth meridian vanished. A devastating drought fol-

This photograph of immigrant women settlers, probably in North Dakota, shows some of the hard physical labor involved in homesteading. The presence of immigrants also reminds us that the West was the home of diverse peoples including Asians, European newcomers, Native Americans, black migrants, and Hispanics whose families had lived in the West for generations. *(The Fred Hulstrand History in Pictures Collection, NDSU, Fargo, ND)*

The combination of graphics and text provided a persuasive message about the excellence of the Gold Medal Threshing-Machine. The picture gave prospective purchasers an idea of the machine's appearance and size, and the text emphasized its award-winning status and included testimonials about its performance. Manufacturers of farm machinery used many strategies, including mass advertising, to sell their products. In one Kansas county, farm families increased their spending for machinery by an average of 250 percent between 1870 and 1890. *(Corbis-Bettmann)*

lowed. One farmer reported in 1890 that he had earned $41.48 from his wheat crop, yet his expenses for seed and threshing amounted to $56.00. The destitute survived on boiled weeds, a few potatoes, and a little bread and butter. Although cash was scarce on the frontier, credit had not been. Many farmers had accumulated debts they now could not repay. Thousands lost their farms to creditors. Some stayed on as tenants. Homesteaders like the Leepers gave up. By 1900, two-thirds of homesteaded farms had failed. Many homesteaders fled east. In western Kansas, the population declined by half between 1888 and 1892. The wagons of those who retreated bore the epitaph of their experience: "In God We Trusted: In Kansas We Busted."

Whether individual farmers remained on the Great Plains or retreated to more promising climates, collectively these new agricultural efforts had a significant long-term impact on the region's environment. When farmers removed sod to build their sod houses and broke the prairies with their plows to plant their crops, they were removing the earth's protective covering. The heavy winds so common on the prairies could lift exposed topsoil and carry it miles away. Deep plowing, which was essential for dry farming techniques introduced after the drought of the 1880s, worsened this situation. The dust bowl of the 1930s was the eventual outcome of these agricultural interventions. Other less obvious consequences of farming and settlement on the Great Plains included a lowering of the water table level as mail-order steel windmills provided the power for pumping water from deep underground. Far from the Plains, the pine forests around the Great Lakes fell to satisfy the settlers' need for wood and the railroads' voracious appetite for railroad ties.

The Early Cattle Frontier, 1860–1890

In the mid-1870s, a clash between John Duncan, a cattleman, and Peter Schmidt, a German farmer, sym-

This 1880 photo highlights the role of machine and animal power rather than human power during the wheat harvest. With more land under cultivation, there was a strong impetus to develop larger and/or more efficient harvesting machines. *(Corbis-Bettmann)*

This sod house, surrounded by wooden planks, was the home of a Norwegian family. Note that the family are dressed in their good clothes, and have posed with some of their furniture, their houseplants, and an elaborate baby carriage. One of the children holds her doll. This scene suggests the pride the family felt in their homestead. *(The Fred Hulstrand History in Pictures Collection, NDSU, Fargo, ND)*

bolized the meeting of the farming and cattle frontiers. Duncan allowed his cattle to roam; some wandered onto Schmidt's property and destroyed his garden. An outraged Schmidt ran Duncan's cattle off. For many years, such incidents had been rare, for few farmers were living on the Plains. As settlement increased in the 1880s and 1890s, they became more common.

Although cattle raising dated back to Spanish mission days, the commercial cattle frontier was an unexpected by-product of Union military strategy. During the war, the North had split the South and cut Texas off from Confederate cattle markets. By the war's end, millions of longhorns were roaming the Texas range. The postwar burst of railroad construction provided a way of turning these cattle into dollars. If Texas ranchers drove their steers north to towns like Abilene, Wichita, or Dodge City, they could be loaded on railroad cars for slaughtering and packinghouses in cities like Chicago and Kansas City. In the cattle drives of the late 1860s and 1870s, cowboys herded thousands of longhorns north with hefty profits for owners and investors.

Ranchers on the Great Plains, where grasses were ripe for grazing, bought some of the cattle and bred them with Hereford and Angus cows to create cattle able to withstand the region's severe winters. In the late 1870s and early 1880s, huge ranches appeared in

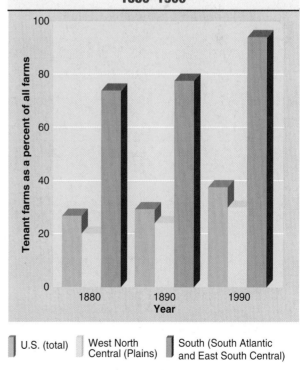

The rise in tenancy, most pronounced in the South, suggests the problems American farmers were experiencing. Source: U.S. Bureau of the Census.

eastern Colorado, Wyoming, and Montana and in western Kansas, Nebraska, and the Dakotas. These ventures, many owned by outside investors, paid off handsomely. Because the cattle could roam at will over the public domain, they cost owners little as they fattened up but commanded good prices at the time of sale. The cowboys (a third of them Mexican and black) who herded the steers, however, shared few of the profits. Their meager wages of $25 to $40 a month were just enough to pay for a fling in the saloons, dance halls, and gambling palaces in Dodge City or Abilene when taking the cattle to market.

By the mid-1880s, the first phase of the cattle frontier was ending as farmers moved onto the Plains, bought up public lands once used for grazing, and fenced them in. But the struggle between cattle ranchers and farmers was only one factor in the cattle frontier's collapse. Eager for fat profits, ranchers overstocked their herds in the mid-1880s. European investors added to the rush of capital into herding. Hungry cattle ate everything in sight, then grew weak as grass became scarce. As was often the case on the

Plains, the weather had a part to play. A winter of memorable blizzards followed the very hot summer of 1886. Cattle, usually able to forage for themselves during the winter months, could not dig through the deep snow to the grass and died from starvation. By spring, 90 percent of the cattle were dead. Frantic owners dumped their remaining cattle on the market, getting $8 or even less per animal.

In the aftermath, the ranchers who remained stock raisers adopted new techniques. Experimenting with new breeds, they began to fence in their herds and to feed them grain during the winter. Moreover, consumers were hungering for tender beef rather than the tough flesh of animals who roamed the land, and these new methods satisfied the market. Ranching, like farming, was becoming a modern business rather than the colorful adventure portrayed in popular culture.

Just as the plows and windmills of the agriculturist disrupted Plains ecology, so, too, did the herds of the cattle frontier. As one Texan realized, "Grass is what counts. It's what saves us all—as far as we get saved. . . . Grass is what holds the earth together." Seeing native species as either competing with cattle for nourishment or threatening them, ranchers hunted and killed antelope, elk, wolves, and other wildlife. When cattlemen overstocked the range, their herds devoured the perennial grasses. In their place, tough, less nutritious annual grasses sprang up, and sometimes even these grasses disappeared. Lands once able to support large herds of cattle eventually were transformed into deserts of sagebrush, weeds, and dust.

Cornucopia on the Pacific

When gold was discovered in California, Americans rushed west to find it. But as one father told his eager son, "Plant your lands; these be your best gold fields." He was right; with the completion of a national railroad system, farming eventually became California's greatest asset. But farming in California neither resembled the rural life Currier & Ives depicted nor fulfilled the dreams of the framers of the Homestead Act.

Although federal and state land policies supposedly promoted "homes for the homeless," little of California's land was actually homesteaded or developed as small family farms. When California entered the Union, Mexican ranchers had vast landholdings that never became part of the public domain. Because most Mexican Americans impoverished themselves in legal efforts to establish the legitimacy of their claims, speculators eventually acquired much of their land. Consequently, small farmers needed substantial sums to buy land. As Charles Reed observed in 1869, "Land which but two years ago could have been bought . . . for from $1 to $1.25 per acre cannot now be bought for less than $10 to $15 per acre."

Frederick Remington's 1888 painting of a cowboy in the midst of a stampede provides a dashing picture of cowboy life that became a mainstay of American popular culture. The reality was less colorful than popular culture suggested. *(The Granger Collection, New York)*

By 1871, reformer Henry George described California as "not a country of farms but a country of plantations and estates." California farms were indeed substantially larger than farms in the rest of the country. In 1870, the average California farm was 482 acres, whereas the national average farm was only 153 acres. By 1900, farms of 1,000 acres or more made up two-thirds of the state's farmland. This landscape reflected the advent of large-scale farming. As one California visitor reported to the *New York Times* in 1887, "You go through miles and miles of wheat fields, you see the fertility of the land and the beauty of the scenery, but where are the hundreds of farm houses . . . that you would see in Ohio or Iowa?"

Small farmers and ranchers did exist, of course, but they found it difficult to compete with large, mechanized operators using cheap migrant laborers, usually Mexican or Chinese. One wheat farm in the San Joaquin Valley was so vast that workers started plowing in the morning at one end of the 17-mile field, ate lunch at its halfway point, and camped at its end that night.

The value of much of California's agricultural land, especially the southern half of the Central Valley, depended on water. Many gold rush immigrants were stunned by the brown and yellow grasses, the parched earth. By the 1870s, however, water, land, and railroad companies, using the labor and expertise of Chinese workers, were taking on the huge costs of building dams, headgates, and canals. They passed on the costs of construction to settlers now eager to acquire hitherto barren lands along with water rights. By 1890, over a quarter of California's farms benefited from irrigation. The irrigation ditches were a fitting symbol of the importance of technology and a managerial attitude toward the land that characterized late-nineteenth-century agriculture, particularly in California.

Although grain was initially California's most valuable crop, it faced stiff competition from farmers on the Plains and in other parts of the world. Some argued that land capable of raising luscious fruits "in a climate surpassing that of Italy, is too valuable for the cultivation of simple cereals." But high railroad rates and lack of refrigeration limited the volume of fresh fruit and vegetables sent to market. As railroad managers in the 1880s realized the potential profit California's produce represented, they lowered rates and introduced refrigerated railroad cars. Fruit and vegetable production rose, benefiting from the agricultural expertise of Chinese laborers. In June 1888, fresh apricots and cherries successfully survived the trip from California to New York. Two years later, 9,000 carloads of navel oranges headed east. Before long, California fruit was available in London. Some travel-ers even began to grumble that the railroads treated produce better than people. Perhaps the complaint was true. The daily eastern express contained "two sleeping cars, two or three passenger cars, and twenty cars loaded with green fruit." The comments highlighted the fact that successful agriculture in California depended on the railroad system, irrigation, and the use of machinery.

Exploiting Natural Resources

The perspective that led Americans to treat farming as a business was also evident in the ways in which they dealt with the country's abundant natural resources. Gold had been the precious metal originally drawing prospectors to California, but the discovery of some other precious materials—silver, iron, copper, coal, lead, zinc, tin—lured thousands west to Colorado, Montana, Idaho, and Nevada as well as to states like Minnesota. The popular conception of the miner as a hardy "forty-niner" searching for loose placer deposits of gold captures the early days of mining. But it does not describe the reality of late-nineteenth-century mining that relied on machinery, railroads, engineers, and a large workforce for the discovery and extraction of the earth's metals and minerals. Mining was a big business with high costs and a basic dynamic that encouraged rapid and thorough exploitation of the earth's resources.

The decimation of the nation's forests went hand in hand with large-scale mining and the railroads that provided the links to markets. Both railroads and mining depended on wood—railroads for wooden ties, mines for shaft timber and ore reduction. The impact of these demands is captured by the California State Board of Agriculture's estimate in the late 1860s that one-third of the state's forests had already disappeared.

When lumber companies cut down timber, they affected the flow of streams and destroyed the habitat supporting birds and animals. Like the activities of farmers and cattle owners, the companies that stripped the earth of its forest cover were also contributing to soil erosion. The idea that the public lands belonging to the federal government ought to be rapidly developed supported such exploitation of the nation's natural resources. Often, in return for royalties, the government leased parts of the public domain to companies that hoped to extract valuable minerals, not to own the land permanently. In other cases, companies bought land, but not always legally. In 1878, Congress passed the Timber and Stone Act, which initially applied to Nevada, Oregon, Washington, and California. This legislation allowed the sale of 160-acre parcels of the public domain that were "unfit for cultivation" and "valuable chiefly for timber." Timber companies were quick to see the possibilities in the new law. They hired men willing to register for claims and then to turn them over to timber interests. By the end of the century, more than 3.5 million acres of the public domain had been acquired under the legislation, and most of it was in corporate hands.

The rapacious and rapid exploitation of resources combined with the increasing pace of industrialization to make some Americans uneasy. Many believed that forests played a part in causing rainfall and that their destruction would have an adverse impact on the climate. Others, like John Muir, lamented the destruction of the country's great natural beauty. In 1868, Muir came upon the Great Valley of California, "all one sheet of plant gold, hazy and vanishing in the distance . . . one smooth, continuous bed of honey-bloom." He soon realized, however, that a "wild, restless agriculture" and "flocks of hoofed locusts, sweeping over the ground like a fire" would destroy this vision of loveliness. Muir became a conservation champion. He played a part in the creation of Yosemite National Park in 1890 and participated in a successful effort to allow President Benjamin Harrison to classify certain parts of the public domain as forest reserves (the Forest Reserve Act of 1891). In 1892, Muir established the Sierra Club. Conservation ideas were more popular in the East, however, than in the West, where the seeming abundance of natural resources and the profit motive diminished support.

⟲ THE SECOND GREAT REMOVAL

Black Elk, an Oglala Sioux, listened to a story his father had heard from his father.

> A long time ago . . . there was once a Lakota [Sioux] holy man, called Drinks Water, who dreamed what was to be; and this was long before the coming of the Wasichus [white men]. He dreamed . . . that a strange race had woven a spider's web all around the Lakotas. And he said: "When this happens, you shall live in square gray houses, in a barren land, and beside those square gray houses you shall starve."

So great was the wise man's sorrow that he died soon after his strange dream. But Black Elk lived to see it come true.

As farmers settled the western frontier and became entangled in a national economy, they clashed with the Indian tribes who lived on the land. In California, disease and violence killed 90 percent of the Native American population in the 30 years following the gold rush. Elsewhere, the struggle among Native Americans, white settlers, the U.S. Army, and government officials and reformers was prolonged and bitter. Although some tribes moved onto government reservations with little protest, most tribes, including the Nez Percé in the Northwest, the Apache in the Southwest, and the Plains Indians, resisted the attempts to curb their way of life and to transform their culture.

Background to Hostilities

As Chapter 13 suggested, the lives of most Plains Indians revolved around the buffalo. Increased emigration to California and Oregon in the 1840s and 1850s disrupted tribal pursuits and animal migration patterns. Initially, the federal government tried, without much success, to persuade the Plains tribes to stay away from white wagon trains and white settlers. As Lone Horn, a Miniconjou chief, explained when American commissioners at the 1851 Fort Laramie Council asked him if he would be satisfied to live on

Black Elk, pictured here on the left, was perceptive of the deleterious changes experienced by Indians during the latter part of the nineteenth century. Although Black Elk was one of the holy men of Oglala Sioux, he became a convert to Roman Catholicism in the early twentieth century. (*Smithsonian Institution*)

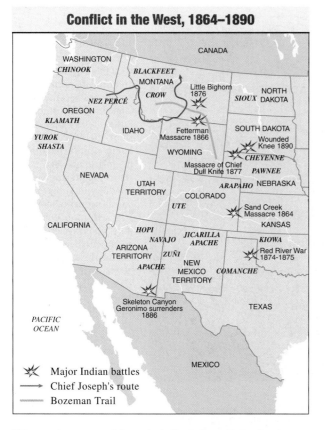

Conflict in the West, 1864–1890

Major Indian battles

→ Chief Joseph's route

Bozeman Trail

This map shows some of the major battles between Native American tribes and the U.S. army in the post–Civil War period. Americans were determined to change Native American life, and many Indians were equally determined to resist these attempts to force them to adopt white ways.

the Missouri River, "When the buffalo comes close to the river, we come close to it. When the buffaloes go off, we go off after them."

During the Civil War, the eastern tribes that were forced to relocate in Oklahoma divided, some, especially the slaveholders, supporting the Confederacy and others the Union. After the war, however, all were branded as "traitors." The federal government callously nullified earlier pledges and treaties, leaving Indians defenseless against further incursions on their lands. As settlers pushed into Kansas, the tribes living in Kansas were shunted into Oklahoma.

The White Perspective

When the Civil War ended, red and white men on the Plains were already at war. In 1864, the Colorado militia had massacred a band of friendly Cheyenne at Sand Creek, Colorado, despite the fact that Chief Black Kettle waved both a white flag of truce and an American flag. Militia leader John Chivington urged his men on. "Kill and scalp all, big and little." Before long, Cheyenne, Sioux, and Arapaho were responding in kind. The Plains wars had begun.

Although not all whites condoned the militia's butchery, the deliberations of the congressional commission authorized to make peace revealed a constricted vision of the future of Native Americans. The commission, which included the commander of the army in the West, Civil War hero General William T. Sherman, accepted as fact that the future of the West lay in an "industrious, thrifty, and enlightened population" of whites. All Native Americans, the commission believed, must relocate in one of two areas: Oklahoma and the western half of present-day South Dakota. There they would learn the ways of white society and agricultural and mechanical arts. Annuities, food, and clothes would placate the Indians and ease their transition from a "savage" to a "civilized" life.

At two major conferences in 1867 and 1868, Native American chiefs listened to these drastic proposals that spelled out the end of the traditional native life. Some agreed with the terms. Others, like Satanta, a Kiowa chief, insisted, "I don't want to settle. I love to roam over the prairies." In any case, the agreements extracted were not binding, because no chief had authority to speak for his tribe. For its part, the U.S. Senate dragged its feet in approving the treaties. Supplies promised to Indians who settled in the arid reserved areas failed to materialize, and wildlife proved too sparse to support them. These Indians soon drifted back to their former hunting grounds.

As General Sherman had warned, however, "All who cling to their old hunting ground are hostile and will remain so till killed off." When persuasion failed, the U.S. Army adopted militant tactics. "The more we can kill this year," Sherman remarked, "the less will have to be killed the next war." In 1867, Sherman entrusted General Philip Sheridan with the duty of dealing with the tribes. Sheridan introduced winter campaigning, aimed at seeking out the Indians who divided into small groups during the winter and exterminating them.

The completion of the transcontinental railroad in 1869 added yet another pressure for "solving" the Indian question. Transcontinental railroads wanted rights-of-way through tribal lands and needed white settlers to make their operations profitable. They carried not only thousands of hopeful settlers to the West, but miners and hunters as well. Few thought Native Americans had any right to the lands whites wanted.

In his 1872 annual report, the commissioner for Indian affairs, Francis Amasa Walker, addressed the two fundamental questions troubling whites: how to prevent Indians from blocking white migration to and settlement in the Great Plains and what to do with Native Americans once they had been controlled. Because they could mount 8,000 warriors, Walker sug-

As the plains and prairies of the trans-Mississippi West filled up with farms and rural communities, Americans became nostalgic for the recent past. Buffalo Bill's Wild West show offered a colorful but inaccurate picture of the migration west. Native Americans were hired for the show to take part in scenes where they attacked "innocent settlers" and travelers. White audiences loved the clear picture the show provided of villains and heroes, while ironically Native Americans were often grateful for the opportunity to escape the confines of reservation life and to earn money. *(The Granger Collection, New York)*

gested buying off the "savages." With promises of food and gifts, he hoped to lure them onto reservations and there impose a "rigid reformatory discipline."

Coercion would be necessary, because Indians, according to Walker, were "unused to manual labor, and physically unqualified for it by the habits of the chase . . . without forethought and without self control . . . with strong animal appetites and no intellectual tastes or aspirations to hold those appetites in check." The grim reservations he proposed resembled prisons more than schools. Indians could not leave without permission and could be arrested if they tried to do so. Though Walker considered himself a "friend of humanity" and, like many reformers, wished to save the Indians from destruction, he said that there was only one choice: "yield or perish."

The Tribal View

Native Americans defied such attacks on their ancient way of life and protested the wholesale violation of treaties. Black Elk remembered that, in 1863, when he was only three, his father had his leg broken in a fierce battle against the white men. "When I was older," he recalled,

> I learned what the fighting was about. . . . Up on the Madison Fork the Wasichus had found much of the yellow metal that they worship and that makes them crazy, and they wanted to have a road up through our country to the place where

the yellow metal was; but my people did not want the road. It would scare the bison and make them go away, and also it would let the other Wasichus come in like a river. They told us that they wanted only to use a little land, as much as a wagon would take between the wheels; but our people knew better.

Black Elk's father and many others soon realized that fighting was the only "way to keep our country." But "wherever we went, the soldiers came to kill us."

Broken promises fired Indian resistance. In 1875, the federal government allowed gold prospectors into the Black Hills, part of the Sioux reservation and one of their sacred places. Chiefs Sitting Bull, Crazy Horse, and Rain-in-the-Face led the angry Sioux on the warpath. At the Battle of Little Big Horn in 1876, they vanquished General George Custer. But their bravery and skill could not permanently withstand the power of the well-supplied, well-armed, and determined U.S. Army. Elsewhere, the pattern of resistance and ultimate defeat was repeated. In Texas, General Sherman vanquished Native American tribes, and in the Pacific Northwest, Nez Percé Chief Joseph surrendered in 1877.

The wholesale destruction of the buffalo was an important element in white victory. The animals were central to Indian life, culture, and religion. As one Pawnee chief explained, "Am afraid when we have no

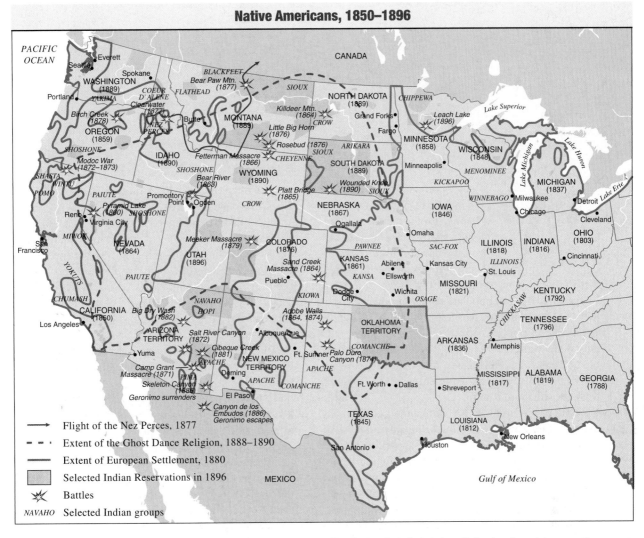

Native Americans, 1850–1896

Flight of the Nez Perces, 1877

Extent of the Ghost Dance Religion, 1888–1890

Extent of European Settlement, 1880

Selected Indian Reservations in 1896

Battles

NAVAHO   Selected Indian groups

This map reveals the widespread appeal of the Ghost Dance movement as well as the result of efforts to force Native Americans into reservations.

meat to offer, Great Spirit . . . will be angry & punish us." Although Plains Indians could be wasteful of buffalo in areas where the animals were abundant, white miners and hunters ultimately destroyed the herds. Sportsmen shot the beasts from train windows. Railroad crews ate the meat. Ranchers' cattle competed for grass. And demand for buffalo bones for fertilizer and hides for robes and shoes encouraged the decimation.

The slaughter, which had claimed 13 million animals by 1883, was in retrospect disgraceful. The Indians considered white men demented. "They just killed and killed because they like to do that," said one, whereas when "we hunted the bison . . . [we] killed only what we needed." But the destruction of the herds pleased whites who were determined to curb the movements of Native Americans. As Secretary of the Interior Columbus Delano explained

in 1872, "I cannot regard the rapid disappearance of the game from its former haunts as a matter prejudicial to our management of the Indians." Rather, he said, "as they become convinced that they can no longer rely upon the supply of game for their support, they will return to the more reliable source of subsistence furnished at their agencies."

The Dawes Act, 1887

Changing federal policy was aimed at ending Indian power and culture. In 1871, Congress abandoned the practice, in effect since the 1790s, of treating the tribes as sovereign nations. Other measures supplemented this attempt to undermine both tribal integrity and the prestige of tribal leaders, whom negotiators would no longer recognize as speaking for their tribes. The government urged

Recovering the Past

MAGAZINES

Weekly and monthly magazines constitute a rich primary source for the historian, offering a vivid picture of the issues of the day and useful insights into popular tastes and values. With advances in the publishing industry and an increasingly literate population, the number of these journals soared in the years following the Civil War. In 1865, only 700 periodicals were published. Twenty years later there were 3,300. As the *National Magazine* grumbled, "Magazines, magazines, magazines! The newsstands are already groaning under the heavy load, and there are still more coming."

Some of these magazines were aimed at the mass market. *Frank Leslie's Illustrated Newspaper,* established in 1855, was one of the most successful. At its height, circulation reached 100,000. Making skillful use of pictures (sometimes as large as two by three feet and folded into the magazine), the weekly covered important news of the day as well as music, drama, sports, and books. Although Leslie relied more heavily on graphics and sensationalism than do modern news weeklies, his publication was a forerunner of *Newsweek* and *Time.*

Another kind of weekly magazine was aimed primarily at middle- and upper-class readers. Editors like the oft-quoted Edwin Lawrence Godkin of *The Nation,* with a circulation of about 30,000, hoped to influence those in positions of authority and power by providing a forum for the discussion of reform issues. In contrast, *Scribner's* revealed a more conservative, middle-of-the-road point of view. Both magazines, however, exuded a confident, progressive tone characteristic of middle-class Americans.

Harper's Weekly was one of the most important magazines designed primarily for middle- and upper-class readers. Established in 1857, this publication continued in print until 1916. The success of *Harper's Weekly,* which called itself a "family newspaper," rested on a combination of its moderate point of view and an exciting use of illustrations and cartoons touching on contemporary events. The popular cartoons of Thomas Nast appeared in this magazine. In large part because of

the use of graphics, in 1872 the circulation of *Harper's Weekly* reached a peak of 160,000.

Illustrated here is a page from the January 16, 1869, issue of *Harper's Weekly.* The layout immediately suggests the importance of graphics. Most of the page is taken up with the three pictures. The top and bottom pictures are wood engravings based on drawings by Theodore R. Davis, one of *Harper's* best-known illustrator-reporters. The center picture was derived from a photograph.

The story featured on this page concerns a victory of General George Custer in the war against the Cheyenne tribe that the U.S. Army was waging that winter. Davis had been a correspondent in the West covering Custer's actions in 1867. But when news of Custer's victory arrived, Davis was back in New York. He thus drew on his imagination for the two scenes reproduced on the next page. What kind of characterization of Native Americans does Davis give in the picture at the top of the page? What view of American soldiers does he suggest? At the bottom of the page, you can see soldiers slaughtering "worthless" horses while Cheyenne teepees burn in the background. Would the average viewer have any sympathy for the plight of the Cheyenne by looking at this picture? This "victory," in fact, involved the slaughter not only of horses but also of all males over age eight.

The editors' decision to insert a picture that had nothing to do with the incident being reported was obviously significant. As you can see, the subject in the center illustration is a white hunter who had been killed and scalped by Indians. What kind of special relationship were the editors suggesting by placing the picture of one dead white hunter in the center of a page that primarily covered a specific conflict between the Indians and the U.S. Army? How might the reader respond to the group of pictures as a whole? How do you? How does the text contribute to the overall view of the Indian–white relationship that the pictures suggest? By considering the choice of graphics and text, you can begin to discover how magazines provide insight, not only into the events of the day but also into the ways magazines shaped the values and perspectives of nineteenth-century men and women.

UPPER — INDIAN SCOUTS CELEBRATING THE VICTORY OVER BLACK KETTLE. [SKETCHED BY THOS. R. DAVIS.]

THE INDIAN WAR

THE SCALPED HUNTER.—[PHOTOGRAPHED BY WM. S. SOULE.]

CUSTER — COMMAND SHOOTING DOWN WORTHLESS HORSES.—[SKETCHED BY THOS. R. DAVIS.]

Harper's Weekly delivered powerful messages about the Native Americans in its choice of illustrations. *(The New York Public Library, Astor, Lenox & Tilden Foundations)*

tribes to replace tribal justice with a court system and extended federal jurisdiction to the reservations. Tribes were also warned not to gather for religious ceremonies.

The Dawes Severalty Act of 1887 pulled together the strands of federal Indian policy that emerged after the Civil War and set its course for the rest of the century. Believing that tribal bonds kept Indians in savagery, reformers intended to destroy them. As Theodore Roosevelt noted approvingly, the bill was a "mighty pulverizing engine to break up the tribal mass." Rather than allotting reservation lands to tribal groups, the act allowed the president to distribute these lands to individuals. Private property, the framers of the bill reasoned, would undermine communal norms and tribal identity and encourage Indians to settle down and farm as white men did. Although Indian agents explained that Native Americans opposed the Dawes Act, Congress, convinced that white people knew what was best for Indians, did not hesitate to legislate on their behalf.

The fact that speculators as well as reformers lobbied for the legislation betrayed another motive at work. Even if each Indian family head claimed a typical share of 160 acres, millions of "surplus" acres would remain for sale to white settlers. Within 20 years of the Dawes Act, Native Americans had lost 60 percent of their lands. The federal government held the profits from land sales "in trust" and used them for the "civilizing" mission.

The Ghost Dance: An Indian Renewal Ritual

By the 1890s, the grim reality of their plight made many Native Americans responsive to the message of Paiute prophet Wovoka. Wovoka did not urge Native Americans to strike out against whites, for his revelations predicted that natural disasters would eliminate the white race. Indians would enter a new period of happiness as ancestors and wild game returned to life. Wovoka's prophecies spread rapidly. Believers expressed their faith and hope through the new rituals of ghost or spirit dancing, hypnosis, and meditation. The more frequently they danced, the quicker whites would vanish.

Although Wovoka's prophecies discouraged hostile actions against whites, American settlers were uneasy. Indian agents tried to prevent the ghost dances and filed hysterical reports. "Indians are dancing in the snow and are wild and crazy. . . . We need protection, and we need it now." One agent identified the Sioux medicine man Sitting Bull, who had strenuously opposed American expansion, as a leading troublemaker and decided to arrest him. In the confusion of arrest, Indian police killed Sitting Bull.

Bands of Sioux fled the reservation with the army in swift pursuit. In late December 1890, the army overtook the Sioux at Wounded Knee Creek. Although the Sioux had raised a flag of

In connection with the Dawes Act, the federal government supported educational and missionary work with Indians. This Roman Catholic boarding school tried to introduce the children to "the habits of civilized life," and eliminate "the blighting influence" of a "savage environment." As students learned to speak English and to observe white norms of behavior, some lost touch with their own cultures. When they returned to the reservations, they could no longer speak their native language and communicate with family and friends. *(78-35, William Farr Collection, K. Ross Toole Archives, University of Montana, Missoula)*

truce, a scuffle as they were turning over their weapons led to a bloody massacre. Using the most up-to-date machine guns and Hotchkiss cannons, the army killed over 200 men, women, and children. An eyewitness described the desolate scene a few days later. "Among the fragments of burned tents . . . we saw the frozen bodies lying close together or piled one upon another."

Thus arose the lament of Black Elk, who saw his people diminished, starving, despairing:

> Once we were happy in our own country and we were seldom hungry, for then the two-leggeds and the four-leggeds lived together like relatives, and there was plenty for them and for us. But then the Wasichus came, and they have made little islands for us . . ., and always these islands are becoming smaller, for around them surges the gnawing flood of the Wasichus; . . .dirty with lies and greed.

As Black Elk recognized, white Americans had finally defeated the western tribes. Once independent, proud, and strong, Native Americans suffered dependency, poverty, and social and cultural disorganization on the reservations, in grim Indian schools, and in the slums of America's cities.

THE NEW SOUTH

Of all the nation's agricultural regions, the South was the poorest. In 1880, southerners' yearly earnings were only half the national average. But despite poverty and backwardness, some southerners during the late nineteenth century dreamed of making the agricultural South the rival of the industrial North.

The vision of a modern, progressive, and self-sufficient South had roots in the troubled decade of the 1850s. At that time, southern intellectuals and writers had argued that the South must throw off its dependence on the North and on cotton. "The smoke of the steam engine should begin to float over the cotton fields, and the hum of spindles and the click of looms make music on all our mountain streams," insisted the editor of the New Orleans *Picayune*.

Postwar Southerners Face the Future

Too few southerners had listened. Now, after the painful war and Reconstruction, the cry for regional self-sufficiency grew sharper. Publicists of the movement for a "New South" argued that southern backwardness did not stem from the war itself, as so many southerners wished to believe, but from basic conditions in southern life, a rural economy based on cotton foremost among them. The defeat only made clearer the reality of the nineteenth century. Power and wealth came not from cotton but from factories, machines, and cities.

Henry Grady, editor of the Atlanta *Constitution* and the New South's most famous spokesman, dramatized the need for change with his story of a southerner's funeral:

> They buried him in the midst of a marble quarry; they cut through solid marble to make his grave; and yet a little tombstone they put above him was from Vermont. They buried him in the heart of a pine forest, and yet the pine coffin was imported from Cincinnati. They buried him within touch of an iron mine, and yet the nails in his coffin and the iron in the shovel that dug his grave were imported from Pittsburgh. . . . They put him away . . . in a New York coat and a Boston pair of shoes and a pair of breeches from Chicago and a shirt from Cincinnati, leaving him nothing to carry into the next world with him to remind him of the country in which he lived and for which he fought for four years, but the chill of blood in his veins and the marrow in his bones.

Regional pride and self-interest dictated a new course. As Grady told a Boston audience in 1886, industrial advances would allow the South to match the North in another, more peaceful contest. "We are going to take a noble revenge," he said, "by invading every inch of your territory with iron, as you invaded ours twenty-nine years ago."

In hundreds of speeches, editorials, pamphlets, articles, and books, spokesmen for the New South tried to persuade fellow southerners of the need for change. Southerners must abandon prewar ideals that glorified leisure and gentility and adopt the ethic of hard work. To lure northern capital, critical because the South was short of capital, New South advocates held out attractive investment possibilities. Thus, said one beckoning New South advocate, "the profits to be reaped from investments in the South . . . appear to be fabulous." The South would be the "El Dorado of the next half century."

In a bid to draw manufacturers, several southern state governments offered tax exemptions and cheap labor based on leasing state prison convicts. Texas and Florida awarded the railroads land grants, and cities like Atlanta and Louisville mounted huge industrial exhibitions as incentives to industrial progress. Middle-class southerners increasingly accepted new entrepreneurial values. The most startling example of commitment to the vision of a New South may have come in 1886 when southern railroad companies decided to bring their tracks into line with the "standard" northern gauges. On a Sunday in May, 8,000 men equipped with sledgehammers and crowbars attacked the 2,000 miles of track belonging to the Louisville and Nashville Railroad Company and moved the western rail three inches to the east. On that same day, they also adjusted the iron wheels of 300 locomotives and 10,000 pieces of rolling stock to fit the new gauge.

During the late nineteenth century, northern money flowed south as dollars replaced the moral fervor and political involvement of the Civil War and Reconstruction years. In the 1880s, northerners increased their investment in the cotton industry sevenfold and financed the expansion of the southern railroad system. Northern capital helped southern cities to embark on an extended period of expansion. By 1900, some 15 percent of all southerners lived in cities, whereas only 7 percent had in 1860. (The national averages for these years were 40 and 20 percent, respectively.)

The city of Birmingham, Alabama, symbolized the New South. In 1870, the site of the future city was a peaceful cornfield. The next year, two northern real estate speculators arrived on the scene, attracted by the area's rich iron deposits. Despite a siege of cholera and the depression of the 1870s, Birmingham rapidly became the center of the southern iron and steel industry. By 1890, a total of 38,414 people lived in the city. Coke ovens, blast furnaces, rolling mills, iron foundries, and machine shops belched forth polluting smoke into the air where once there had been only fields. Millions of dollars of finished goods poured forth from the city's mills and factories, and eight railroad lines carried them away.

Other southern cities flourished as well. Memphis prospered from its lumber industry and the manufacturing of cottonseed products, and Richmond became the country's tobacco capital even as its flour mills and iron and steel foundries continued to produce wealth. Augusta, Georgia, was the "Lowell of the South," a leader in the emerging textile industry that blossomed in Georgia, North and South Carolina, and Alabama. Augusta's eight cotton mills employed about 2,800 workers, many of them women and children.

The Other Side of Progress

New South leaders—a small group of merchants, industrialists, and planters—bragged about the growth of the iron and textile industries and paraded statistics to prove the success of efforts to modernize. The South, one writer boasted, was "throbbing with industrial and railroad activity." But despite such optimism about matching or even surpassing the North's economic performance, the South made slow progress.

Older values persisted. Indeed, New South spokesmen paradoxically kept older, chivalric values alive by romanticizing the recent past. "In the eyes of Southern people," one publication asserted, "all Confederate veterans are heroes." Loyalty to the past impeded full acceptance of a new economic order. It was significant that despite the interest in modernization, the southern school system lagged far behind that of the North.

Although new industries and signs of progress abounded, two of the new industries depended on tobacco and cotton, traditional crops long at the center of rural life. Moreover, the South did not better its position relative to the North. Whereas in 1860, the South had 17 percent of the country's manufacturing concerns, by 1904, it had only 15 percent. During the same period, the value of its manufactures grew from 10.3 percent of the total value of manufactures in the United States to only 10.5 percent. Commerce and government work still were responsible for urban growth, as they had been before the Civil War. The South's achievements were not insignificant during a period in which northern industry and cities rapidly expanded, but they could not make the South the equal of the North.

Moreover, the South failed to reap many benefits from industrialization. Southern businessmen like Richmond banker and railroad president John Skelton Williams hoped "to see in the South in the not distant future many railroads and business institutions as great as the Pennsylvania Railroad, the Mutual Life Insurance Company, the Carnegie Steel Company or the Standard Oil Company." This was not to happen. As in the antebellum period, the South remained an economic vassal of the North.

Southern businessmen grew in number, but with the exception of the American Tobacco Company no great southern corporations arose. Instead, southerners worked for northern companies and corporations, which absorbed southern businesses or dominated them financially. By 1900, for example, five corporations directed three-quarters of the railroad mileage in the South (excluding Texas), and northern bankers controlled all five. Northerners also took over the southern steel industry.

As this happened, profits flowed north. "Our capitalists are going into your country," the Lowell *Manufacturers' Record* noted, "because they see a chance to make money there, but you must not think that they will give your people the benefit of the money they make. That will come North and enrich their heirs, or set up public libraries in our country towns." As dollars fled north, so, too, went the power to make critical decisions. In many cases, northern directors determined that southern mills and factories could handle only the early stages of processing, while northern factories finished the goods. Thus, southern cotton mills sent yarn and coarse cloth north for completion. Southern manufacturers who did finish their products, hoping to compete in the marketplace, found that railroad rate discrimination robbed their goods of any competitive edge.

Individual workers in the new industries may have found factory life preferable to sharecropping, but their rewards were meager. The thousands of women and children in factories were silent testimony to the fact their husbands and fathers could not earn sufficient wages to keep them at home. As usual, women and children earned lower wages than men. Justifying these policies, one Augusta factory president claimed that the employment of children was "a matter of charity with us; some of them would starve if they were not given employment. . . . Ours are not overworked. The work we give children is very light." Actually, many children at his factory were doing the same work as adults, for children's pay.

In general, all workers earned lower wages and worked longer hours in the South than elsewhere. Per capita income was the same in 1900 as it had been in 1860—and only half the national average. In North Carolina in the 1890s, workers were paid an average of 50 cents a day and toiled 70 hours a week. Black workers, who made up 6 percent of the southern manufacturing force in 1890 (but who were excluded from textile mills), usually had the worst jobs and the lowest wages.

Cotton Still King

Although New South advocates envisioned the South's transformation from a rural to an industrial society, they always recognized the need for agricultural change. "It's time for an agricultural revolution," Henry Grady proclaimed. "When we once decide that southern lands are fit for something else besides cotton, and then go to work in earnest to multiply and diversify our products and industries, independence and wealth will be the certain reward of our intelligent and industrious farmers."

The overdependence on "King Cotton" hobbled southern agriculture by making farmers the victims of faraway market forces and an oppressive credit system. Subdivide old cotton plantations into small diversified farms, Grady urged. Truck farming could produce "simply wonderful profits" and

> would give employment throughout the entire season, and at the end of it the fortunate farmer would have before him the assurance that diversified crops and a never-failing market alone afford, with no [fertilizer] . . . bills to settle, and no liens past or to come to disturb his mind.

A new agricultural South with new class and economic arrangements did emerge, but it was not the one Grady and others envisioned. Despite the breakup of some plantations following the Civil War, large landowners proved resourceful in holding on to their property and in dealing with postwar conditions, as Chapter 16 showed. As they adopted new agricultural arrangements, former slaves sank into debt peonage.

White farmers on small- and medium-size holdings fared only slightly better than black tenants and sharecroppers. Immediately after the war, high cotton prices tempted them to raise as much cotton as they could. Then prices began a disastrous decline, from 11 cents a pound in 1875 to less than 5 cents in 1894. "At the close of the war a 500 lb. bale of cotton would bring $100," a Cherokee County, Georgia, tenant complained in 1891, "and today it will bring $32.50." Yeoman farmers became entangled in debt. Each year, farmers found themselves buying supplies on credit from merchants so that they could plant the next year's crop and support their families until harvest time. In return, merchants demanded their exclusive business and acquired a lien (or claim) on their crops. But when farmers sold their crops at declining prices, they usually discovered that they had not earned enough to settle with the merchant, who had charged dearly for store goods and whose annual interest rates might exceed 100 percent. Each year, thousands of farmers fell further behind.

The story of S. R. Simonton was typical. Between 1887 and 1895, the South Carolina farmer spent $2,681 at T. G. Patrick's furnishing house. But he could manage to pay back only $687. Like many others, Simonton lost his land and became a tenant farmer. The number of tenants inched upward, whereas the number of small independent farmers fell. By 1900, over half the South's white farmers and three-quarters of its black farmers were tenants. Although tenancy was increasing all over rural America, nowhere did it rise more rapidly than in the Deep South.

These patterns had baneful results for individual southerners and for the South as a whole. Caught in a cycle of debt and poverty, few farmers could think of improving agricultural techniques or diversifying crops. In their desperate attempt to pay off debts, they concentrated on cotton, despite falling prices. "Cotton brings money, and money pays debt," was the small farmer's slogan. Landowners also pressured tenants to raise a market crop. Far from diversifying, as Grady had hoped, farmers increasingly limited the number of crops they raised. By 1880, the South was not growing enough food to feed its people adequately. Poor nutrition contributed to chronic bad health and sickness.

Black dockworkers load bales of cotton in this undated photograph, which is evidence not only of the kinds of jobs that free blacks could secure but also of the continuing dominance of cotton in southern life. *(Library of Congress)*

The Nadir of Black Life

Grady and other New South advocates painted a picture of a strong, prosperous, and industrialized South, a region that could deal with the troublesome race issue without the interference of any "outside power." Grady had few regrets over the end of slavery, which he thought had contributed to southern economic backwardness. Realizing that black labor would be crucial to the transformation he sought, he advocated racial cooperation.

But racial cooperation did not mean equality. Grady assumed that blacks were racially inferior and supported an informal system of segregation. "The negro is entitled to his freedom, his franchise, to full and equal legal rights," Grady wrote in 1883. But "social equality he can never have. He does not have it in the north, or in the east, or in the west. On one pretext or another, he is kept out of hotels, theatres, schools and restaurants."

By the time of Grady's death in 1889, a much harsher perspective on southern race relations was replacing his view. In 1891, at a national assembly of women's clubs in Washington, D.C., a black woman, Frances Ellen Watkins Harper, anticipated efforts to strip the vote from blacks and appealed to the white women at the meeting not to abandon black suffrage. "I deem it a privilege to present the negro," she said, "not as a mere dependent asking for Northern sympathy or Southern compassion, but as a member of the body politic who has a claim upon the nation for justice, simple justice." This claim, she continued, was for "protection to human life," for "the rights of life and liberty," and for relief from charges of ignorance and poverty. These were "conditions which men outgrow." Women, of all people, should understand this and not seek to achieve their own right to vote at the expense of the vote for black men, Harper suggested. "Instead of taking the ballot from his hands, teach him how to use it, and add his quota to the progress, strength, and durability of the nation."

The decision by congressional leaders in 1890 to shelve a proposed act for protecting black civil rights and the defeat of the Blair bill providing federal assistance for educational institutions left black Americans vulnerable, as Frances Harper realized. The traditional sponsor of the rights of freedmen, the Republican party, left blacks to fend for themselves as a minority in the white South. The courts also abandoned blacks. In 1878, the Supreme Court declared unconstitutional a Louisiana statute banning discrimination in transportation. In 1882, the Court voided the Ku Klux Klan Act of 1871 that had been passed to break the power of the clan. In 1883, the provisions of the Civil Rights Act of 1875, which assured blacks of equal rights in public places, were declared unconstitutional on the grounds that the federal government did not have the right to involve itself in the racial relations between individuals.

Northern leaders did not oppose these actions. In fact, northerners increasingly promulgated negative stereotypes, picturing blacks as either ignorant, lazy, childlike fools or lying, stealing, raping degenerates. Obviously, they could not be left to themselves or given the same rights and freedoms whites enjoyed. Instead, blacks needed the paternal protection of the superior white race. These stereotypes filled the magazines and newspapers and were perpetuated in cartoons, advertisements, "coon songs," serious art and theater, and the minstrel shows that dominated northern entertainment.

The *Atlanta Monthly* in 1890 anticipated a strong current in magazine literature when it expressed doubts that this "lowly variety of man" could ever be brought up to the intellectual and moral standards of whites. Other magazines openly opposed suffrage as wasted on people too "ignorant, weak, lazy and incompetent" to make good use of it. *Forum* magazine suggested that "American Negroes" had "too much liberty." When this freedom was combined with natural "race traits" of stealing and hankering after white women, the *Forum* advised in 1893, black crime increased. Only lynching and burning would deter the "barbarous" rapist and other "sadly degenerated" Negroes corrupted since the Civil War by independence and too much education. The author concluded that the Negro question was "more vital" than gold, silver, or the tariff. Encouraged by northern public opinion, and with the blessing of Congress and the Supreme Court, southern citizens and legislatures sought to make blacks permanently second-class members of southern society.

In the political sphere, white southerners amended state constitutions to disenfranchise black voters. By various legal devices—the poll tax, literacy tests, "good character" and "understanding" clauses administered by white voter registrars, and all-white primary elections—blacks lost the right to vote. The most ingenious method was the "grandfather clause," which specified that only citizens whose grandfathers were registered to vote on January 1, 1867, could cast their ballots. This virtually excluded blacks. Although the Supreme Court outlawed such blatantly discriminatory laws as grandfather clauses, a series of other constitutional changes, like those mentioned above, beginning in Mississippi in 1890 and spreading to all 11 former Confederate states by 1910, effectively excluded the black vote. The results were dramatic. Louisiana, for example, contained 130,334 registered black voters in 1896. Eight years later, there were only 1,342.

In a second tactic in the 1890s, state and local laws legalized informal segregation in public facilities. Beginning with railroads and schools, "Jim Crow" laws were extended to libraries, restaurants, hospitals, prisons, parks and playgrounds, cemeteries, toilets, drinking fountains, and nearly every other place where blacks and whites might mingle. The Supreme Court upheld these laws in 1896 in *Plessy* v. *Ferguson* by declaring that "separate but equal" facilities did not violate the equal protection clause of the Fourteenth Amendment because separation did not necessarily mean the inferiority of a group. The Court's decision opened the way for as many forms of legal segregation as southern lawmakers could devise.

Political and social discrimination made it ever more possible to keep blacks permanently confined to agricultural and unskilled labor. While extended families—aunts, uncles, cousins, and other kin—all helped blacks to cope with their dire situation, the truth was that all too often blacks were dependent on whites for their material welfare. In 1900, nearly 84 percent of black workers nationwide engaged in some form of agricultural labor as farmhands, overseers, sharecroppers, or tenant or independent farmers or in service jobs, primarily domestic service and laundry work. These had been the primary slave occupations. The remaining 16 percent worked in forests, sawmills, mines, and, with northward migration, in northern cities.

Gone were the skilled black tradesmen of slavery days. At the end of the Civil War, at least half of all skilled craftsmen in the South had been black. But by the 1890s, the percentage had decreased to less than 10 percent, as whites systematically excluded blacks from the trades. Such factory work as blacks had been doing was also reduced, largely to drive a wedge between poor blacks and whites to prevent unionization. In Greensboro, North Carolina, for example, where in 1870 some 30 percent of all blacks worked in skilled trades or factory occupations, by 1910, blacks in the skilled trades had been reduced to 8 percent, and not a single black worked in a Greensboro factory. The exclusion of blacks from industry prevented them from acquiring the skills and habits that would enable them to rise into the middle class as would many European immigrants and their children by the mid-twentieth century.

Blacks did not accept their declining position passively. In the mid-1880s, they enthusiastically joined the mass worker organization the Knights of Labor (discussed in Chapter 18), first in cities such as Richmond and Atlanta, and then in rural areas. As one South Carolina black explained, "We are [bound] to join something what will lead to better rights than we have." Blacks made up at least a third of the Knights' membership in the South. But southern whites feared that the Knights' policies of racial and economic coop-

In 1896, an African American, William Biggerstaff, was hung for what was labeled the murder of a white man. The picture cannot reveal the innocence or guilt of the accused. Lynching and violence aimed at blacks became common in the late nineteenth century. As the crowd suggests, lynchings were often well attended events. *(Montana Historical Society, Helena, MT)*

as fire . . . can inflict" could other blacks "be deterred from the commission of like crimes." Ed Coy was one of more than 1,400 black men lynched or burned alive during the 1890s. About a third were charged with sex crimes. The rest were accused of a variety of "crimes" related to not knowing their place: marrying or insulting a white woman, testifying in court against whites, having a "bad reputation."

Diverging Black Responses

White discrimination and exploitation nourished new protest tactics and ideologies among blacks. For years, Frederick Douglass had been proclaiming that blacks should remain loyal Americans and count on the promises of the Republican party. But on his deathbed in 1895, his last words were allegedly, "Agitate! Agitate! Agitate!"

Among black expressions of protest, one was a woman's. In Memphis, Tennessee, Ida B. Wells, the first woman editor of an important newspaper, launched a campaign against lynching in 1892. So hostile was the response from the white community that Wells carried a gun to protect herself. When white citizens finally destroyed the press and threatened her partner, Wells left Memphis to pursue her activism elsewhere.

Other voices called for black separatism within white America. T. Thomas Fortune wrote in the black New York *Freeman* in 1887 that "there will one day be an African Empire." Three years later, he organized the Afro-American League (a precursor of the NAACP), insisting that blacks must join together to fight the rising tide of discrimination. "Let us stand up," he urged, "in our own organization where color will not be a brand of odium." The League encouraged independent voting, opposed segregation and lynching, and urged the establishment of black institutions like banks to support black businesses. As a sympathetic journalist explained, "The solution of the problem is in our own hands. . . . The Negro must preserve his identity."

Although some promoted black nationalism, most blacks worked patiently but persistently within white society for equality and social justice. In 1887, J. C. Price formed the Citizens Equal Rights Association, which supported various petitions and direct-action campaigns to protest segregation. The association also called for state laws to guarantee equal rights in the aftermath of the Supreme Court's 1883 ruling. Other blacks boycotted streetcars in southern cities, and Daniel Payne, a Methodist bishop, got off the Jim Crow car on a Florida train and, rather than riding in the segregated car, with great ceremony walked to a church conference. Other blacks petitioned Congress, demanding reparations for unpaid labor as slaves.

eration might lead to social equality. "The forcing of a colored man among the white people here . . . knocked me out of the order," reported one. The Charleston *News and Courier* warned of the dangers of "miscegenation" and the possibility that the South would be left "in the possession of . . . mongrels and hybrids." As blacks continued to join it, whites abandoned the order in growing numbers. The flight of whites weakened the organization in the South, and a backlash of white violence finally smashed it.

Against this backdrop, incidents of lynchings and other forms of violence against blacks increased. On February 21, 1891, the *New York Times* reported that in Texarkana, Arkansas, a mob apprehended a 32-year-old black man, Ed Coy, charged with the rape of a white woman, tied him to a stake, and burned him alive. As Coy proclaimed his innocence to a large crowd, his alleged victim herself somewhat hesitatingly put the torch to his oil-soaked body. The *Times* report concluded that only by the "terrible death such

Efforts to escape oppression in the South, like "Pap" Singleton's movement to found black towns in Tennessee and Kansas, continued. In the 1890s, black leaders lobbied to make the Oklahoma Territory, recently opened to white settlement, an all-black state. Blacks founded 25 towns there, as well as in other states and even Mexico. But these attempts, like earlier ones, were short-lived, crippled by limited funds and the hostility of white neighbors. Singleton eventually recommended migration to Canada or Liberia as a final solution, and later black nationalist leaders also looked increasingly to Africa. Bishop Henry McNeal Turner, a former Union soldier and prominent black leader, despaired of ever securing equal rights for blacks in the United States. He described the Constitution as "a dirty rag, a cheat, a libel" and said that it ought to be "spit upon by every Negro in the land." In 1894, he organized the International Migration Society to return blacks to Africa, arguing that "this country owes us forty billions of dollars" to help. He succeeded in sending two boatloads of emigrants to Liberia, but this colonization effort worked no more successfully than those earlier in the century.

As Douglass had long argued, no matter how important African roots might be, blacks had been in the Americas for generations and would have to win justice and equal rights here. W. E. B. Du Bois, the first black to receive a Ph.D. from Harvard, agreed. Yet in 1900, he attended the first Pan-African Conference in London, where he argued that blacks must lead the struggle for liberation both in Africa and in the United States. It was at this conference that Du Bois first made his prophetic comment that "the problem of the Twentieth Century" would be "the problem of the color line."

Despite these vigorous voices of militant anger and nationalistic fervor, most black Americans continued to follow the slow, moderate, self-help program of Booker T. Washington, the best-known black leader in America. Born a slave, Washington had risen through hard and faithful work to become the founder (in 1881) and principal of Tuskegee Institute in Alabama, which he personally and dramatically built into the nation's largest and best-known industrial training school. At Tuskegee, young blacks received a highly disciplined education in scientific agricultural techniques and vocational skilled trades. Washington believed that economic self-help and the familiar Puritan virtues of hard work, frugality, cleanliness, and moderation would lead to success for African Americans despite the realities of racism. He spent much of his time traveling through the North to secure philanthropic gifts to support Tuskegee. In time, he became a favorite of the American entrepreneurial elite whose capitalist assumptions he shared.

In 1895, Washington was asked to deliver a speech at the Cotton States and International Exposition in Atlanta, celebrating three decades of industrial and agricultural progress since the Civil War. He took advantage of that invitation, a rare honor for a former slave, to make a significant statement about the position of blacks in the South. Without a hint of protest, Washington decided "to say something that would cement the friendship of the races." He therefore proclaimed black loyalty to the economic development of the South while accepting the lowly status of southern blacks. "It is at the bottom of life we must begin, and not at the top," he declared. "In all things that are purely social we can be as separate as the fingers, yet one as the hand in all things essential to mutual progress." Although Washington worked actively behind the scenes for black civil rights, in Atlanta, he publicly renounced black interest in either the vote or civil rights as well as social equality with whites. Whites throughout the country enthusiastically acclaimed Washington's address, but many blacks called his "Atlanta Compromise" a serious setback in the struggle for black rights.

Washington has often been charged with conceding too quickly that political rights should follow rather than precede economic well-being. In 1903, Du Bois confronted Washington directly in *The Souls of Black Folk*, arguing instead for the "manly assertion" of a program of equal civil rights, suffrage, and higher education in the ideals of liberal learning. A trip through the black belt of Dougherty County, Georgia, showed Du Bois the "forlorn and forsaken" condition of southern blacks. The young sociologist saw that most blacks were confined to dependent agricultural labor, "fighting a hard battle with debt" year after year. Although "here and there a man has raised his head above these murky waters . . . a pall of debt hangs over the beautiful land." Beneath all others was the cotton picker, who, with his wife and children, would have to work from sunup to sundown to pick 100 pounds of cotton to make 50 cents. The lives of most blacks were still tied to the land of the South. If they were to improve their lives, rural blacks would have to organize.

FARM PROTEST

During the post–Civil War period, many farmers, both black and white, began to realize that only by organizing could they hope to ameliorate the conditions of rural life. Not all were dissatisfied with their lot, however. Farmers in the Midwest and near city markets successfully adjusted to new economic conditions and had little reason for discontent. Farmers in the South and West, by contrast, faced new problems and difficulties that led to the first mass organization of farmers in American history.

The Grange in the 1860s and 1870s

The earliest effort to organize white farmers came in 1867 when Oliver Kelley founded the Order of the Patrons of Husbandry. At first, the organization emphasized social and cultural goals. More aggressive goals soon evolved. Dudley Adams, speaking to an Iowa group in 1870, emphasized the powerlessness of the "immense helpless mob" of farmers, victims of "human vampires." Salvation, Adams maintained, lay in organization.

More and more farmers, especially those in the Midwest and the South, agreed with Adams. The depression of the 1870s (discussed in Chapter 18) sharpened discontent. By 1875, an estimated 800,000 had joined Kelley's organization, now known as the National Grange. The "Farmers' Declaration of Independence," read before local granges on July 4, 1873, captured the new activist spirit. The time had come, the declaration announced, for farmers suffering from "oppression and abuse" to rouse themselves and, by "all lawful and peaceful means," to cast off the "tyranny of monopoly." Although the declaration clearly expressed rural discontent, it gave few indications that Grangers recognized the complex changes that had created their problems.

Grangers were looking for culprits close to home. Middlemen seemed obvious oppressors. They gouged farmers by raising the prices of finished goods farmers needed to buy and by lowering the prices they received for their products. Some of the Granger "reforms" attempted to bypass middlemen by establishing buying and selling cooperatives. Although many of the cooperatives failed, they indicated that farmers realized that they could not respond to new conditions on an individual basis but needed to act collectively.

Operators of grain elevators also drew fire. Midwestern farmers claimed that these merchants often misgraded their wheat and corn and paid less than its worth. But they pointed to the railroads, America's first big business, as the greatest offenders. As Chapter 18 will show, cut-throat competition among railroad companies generally brought lower rates. But even though rates dropped nationwide, the railroads often set high rates in rural areas. Moreover, railroads awarded discriminatory rebates to large shippers and put small operators at a disadvantage.

Although the Grange was originally nonpolitical, farmers recognized that confronting the mighty rail-roads demanded political action. Other groups also wished to see some controls imposed on the railroads. Railroad policies that favored large Chicago grain terminals and long-distance shippers over local concerns victimized many western businessmen. Between 1869 and 1874, both businessmen and farmers in Illinois, Iowa, Wisconsin, and Minnesota lobbied for state railroad laws. The resulting Granger laws (an inaccurate name because the Grangers do not deserve complete credit for them) established the maximum rates railroads and grain elevators could charge. Other states passed legislation setting up railroad commissions with power to regulate railroad rates. In some states, legislators outlawed railroad pools, rebates, passes, and other practices that seemed to represent "unjust discrimination and distortion."

Railroad companies and grain elevators quickly challenged the new laws. In 1877, the Supreme Court upheld the legislation in *Munn* v. *Illinois* on the grounds that railroads could be regulated for the common good even though they were privately owned because their operation affected the public interest. Even so, it soon became apparent that although state commissions had authority over local rates and fares, they could not control long-haul rates. To make up for the money lost on local hauls, railroads often raised long-haul charges, thus frustrating the intent of the laws. Other complicated issues involved determining what was a fair rate, who was competent to decide that rate, and what was a justifiable return for the railroad. The tangle of questions that state regulation raised proved difficult to resolve at the local level.

Although the Granger laws failed to solve the questions involved in attempts to control the railroads, they established an important principle. The Supreme Court decision made clear that state legislatures had the power to regulate businesses of a public nature like the railroads. But the failure of the Granger laws and the Supreme Court's reversal of *Munn* v. *Illinois* in its 1886 decision *Wabash* v. *Illinois* led to greater pressure on Congress to continue the struggle against big business.

The Interstate Commerce Act, 1887

In 1887, Congress responded to farmers, railroad managers who wished to regulate the fierce competition that threatened to bankrupt their companies, and shippers who objected to transportation rates by passing the Interstate Commerce Act. That legislation required that railroad rates be "reasonable and just," that rate schedules be made public, and that practices such as rebates be discontinued. The act also set up the first federal regulatory agency, the Interstate Commerce Commission (ICC). The ICC had the power

"The Purposes of the Grange: Gift for the Grangers," done in 1873, not surprisingly makes a sturdy farmer its focus. The scenes around the border picture rural life as farmers wished it to be rather than as it was. *(Library of Congress)*

to investigate and prosecute lawbreakers, but the legislation limited its authority to control over commerce conducted between states.

Like state railroad commissions, the ICC found it difficult to define a reasonable rate. Moreover, thousands of cases overwhelmed the tiny staff in the early months of operation. In the long run, the lack of enforcement power was most serious. The ICC's only recourse was to bring offenders into the federal courts and engage in lengthy legal proceedings. Few railroads worried about defying ICC directions on rates. When they appeared in court four or five years later, they often won their cases from judges suspicious of new federal authority. Between 1887 and 1906, a total of 16 cases made their way to the Supreme Court, which decided 15 of them in the railroads' favor. As one railroad executive candidly admitted, "There is not a road

in the country that can be accused of living up to the rules of the Interstate Commerce Law."

The Southern Farmers' Alliance in the 1880s and 1890s

The Grange declined in the late 1870s as the nation recovered from depression. But neither farm organizations nor farm protest died. Depression struck farmers once again in the late 1880s and worsened as the 1890s began. Official statistics told the familiar, dismal story of falling prices for cereal crops grown on the plains and prairies. A bushel of wheat that had sold for $1 in 1870 was worth 60 cents in the 1890s. Kansas farmers, in 1889, were selling their corn for a mere 10 cents a bushel. The national currency shortage, which usually reached critical proportions at harvest time, helped push agricultural prices ever lower.

And whereas prices declined, the load of debt climbed. Mortgage rates ranged between 18 and 36 percent, and shipping rates were high. It sometimes cost a farmer as much as one bushel of corn to send another one to market.

A Kansas farmer's letter reveals some of the human consequences of such trends:

> At the age of 52 years, after a long life of toil, economy and self-denial, I find myself and family virtually paupers. With hundreds of cattle, hundreds of hogs, scores of good horses, and a farm that rewarded the toil of our hands with 16,000 bushels of golden corn, we are poorer by many dollars than we were years ago. What once seemed a neat little fortune and a house of refuge for our declining years . . . has been rendered valueless.

Under these pressures, farmers turned again to organization, education, and cooperation. The Southern Farmers' Alliance became one of the most important reform organizations of the 1880s as it launched an ambitious organizational drive, sending lecturers throughout the South and onto the western plains. Eventually, alliance lecturers reached 43 states and territories, bringing their message to two million farming families and organizing a far-reaching agrarian network.

An article in their newspaper, the *National Economist,* pointed out some of the alliance's fundamental beliefs. "The agricultural population of today is becoming rapidly aroused to the fact that agriculture, as a class, can only be rendered prosperous by radical changes in the laws governing money, transportation, and land." The economic and social position of farmers had slipped, even though as producers the farming class was critical to national well-being. The farmer's condition was, in the words of an alliance song, a "sin," the result of the farmer's forgetting that "he's the man that feeds them all." Alliance lecturers proposed various programs that would help realize their slogan: "Equal rights to all, special privileges to none."

On the one hand, the alliance experimented with buying and selling cooperatives to free farmers from the clutches of supply merchants, banks, and other credit agencies. Although these efforts often failed in the long run, they taught the value of cooperation to achieve common goals. On the other hand, the alliance supported legislative efforts to regulate powerful monopolies and corporations, which they believed gouged the farmer. Many alliance members also felt that increasing the money supply was critical to improving the position of farmers and supported a national banking system empowered to issue paper money.

The alliance also called for a variety of measures to improve the quality of rural life: better public schools for rural children, state agricultural colleges, and an improvement in the status of women. "This order has the good sense, magnanimity and moral courage," declared Hattie Huntingdon of Louisiana, "to lay aside deeply-rooted prejudices handed down from the barbaric past and admit women into its fold and proclaim to the world that it believes in equal rights to all."

By 1890, rural discontent was spreading. In the Midwest, where farmers were prospering by raising hogs and cattle on cheap grain, and in the East, where farmers were growing fruit and vegetables for urban markets, discontent was muted. But that summer in Kansas, hundreds of farmers packed their families into wagons to set off for alliance meetings or to parade in long lines through the streets of nearby towns and villages. Floats garnished with evergreens proclaimed that the farmers' new organization focused on live issues, not the dead ones Congress debated.

Similar scenes occurred through the West and the South. A farmer's wife, Zenobia Wheeless, captured the hopeful spirit of the protest in her letter to North Carolina alliance leader Leonidas Polk. "We rode sixteen miles . . . to hear Brother Tracy [an organizer from Texas]—started about sun-up and trotted all the way . . . . Brother Tracy's lecture was very interesting . . . it seemed that all eyes were riveted upon him." Never had there been such a wave of organizational activity in rural America. In 1890, more than a million farmers counted themselves as alliance members.

The alliance network also included black farmers. In 1888, black and white organizers established the Colored Farmers' Alliance, headed by a white Baptist minister, R. M. Humphrey. The Colored Farmers' Alliance recognized that black and white farmers faced common economic problems and must cooperate to ameliorate their shared plight. Few initially confronted the fact that many southern cotton farmers depended on black labor and had a different perspective from that of blacks. In 1891, however, cotton pickers working on plantations near Memphis, Tennessee, went on strike. White posses chased the strikers, lynched 15 of them, and demonstrated that racial tensions simmered just below the surface.

The Ocala Platform, 1890

In December 1890, the National Alliance gathered in Ocala, Florida, to develop an official platform. Most delegates felt that the federal government had failed to address the farmers' problems. "Congress must come nearer the people or the people will come nearer the Congress," warned the alliance's president. Both parties were far too subservient to the "will of corporation and money power."

The platform called for the direct election of U.S. senators. Alliance members supported lowering the tariff, a much debated topic in Congress, but their justification, emphasizing the need to reduce prices for the "poor of our land," had a radical ring. Their money plank went far beyond what any national legislator was likely to consider. Rejecting the notion that only gold had value or, indeed, that precious metals had to be the basis for currency, alliance leaders boldly envisioned a new banking system controlled by the federal government. They demanded that the government take an active economic role by increasing the amount of money in circulation in the form of treasury notes and silver. More money would lead to inflation, higher prices, and a reduction in debt, they believed.

The platform also called for the creation of subtreasuries (federal warehouses) in agricultural regions where farmers could store their produce at low interest rates until market prices favored selling. To tide farmers over until that time, the federal government would lend farmers up to 80 percent of the current local price for their products. Thus, the plan would free farmers from the twin evils of the credit merchant and depressed prices at harvest time. Other demands included a graduated income tax and support for the regulation of transportation and communication networks. If regulation failed, the government was called on to take over both networks and run them for the public benefit.

In the context of late-nineteenth-century political life, almost all these planks represented radical departures from political norms. They demanded aggressive government action to assist the country's farmers at a time when the government favored big business (see Chapter 19). Even though a minority of farmers belonged to the alliance, many Americans feared that the organization was capable of upsetting political arrangements.

The New York *Sun* reported that the alliance had caused a "panic" in the two major parties. The alliance's warning that the people would replace their representatives unless they were better represented was already coming true. Although the alliance was not formally in politics, it had supported sympathetic candidates in the fall elections of 1890. A surprising number of these local and state candidates had won. Alliance victories in the West harmed the Republican party enough to cause President Harrison to refer to "our election disaster."

Before long, many alliance members were pressing for an independent political party, as legislators who had courted alliance votes conveniently forgot their pledges once elected. Alliance support did not necessarily bring action on issues of interest to farmers, or

even respect. One Texas farmer reported that the chairman of the state Democratic executive committee "calls us all skunks" and observed that "anything that has the scent of the plowhandle smells like a polecat" to the Democrats. On the national level, no one had much interest in the Ocala platform. As one North Carolinian observed, "I am not able to perceive any very great difference between the two parties."

Among the first to realize the necessity of forming an independent third party was Georgia's Tom Watson. "We are in the midst of a great crisis," he argued. "We have before us three or four platforms . . . [and] the Ocala platform is the best of all three. It is the only one that breathes the breath of life." Watson also realized that electoral success in the South would depend on unity between white and black farmers.

The People's Party, 1892

In February 1892, the People's, or Populist, party was established, with almost 100 black delegates in attendance. Leonidas Polk, president of the alliance and promoter of a political coalition between the South and the West, became the party's presidential candidate that fall. "The time has arrived," he thundered, "for the great West, the great South, and the great Northwest, to link their hands and hearts together and march to the ballot box and take possession of the government, restore it to the principles of our fathers, and run it in the interest of the people." But by the time the party met at its convention in July in Omaha, Polk had died. The party nominated James B. Weaver, Union army veteran from Iowa, as its presidential candidate, and James G. Field, a former Confederate soldier, for vice president.

The platform preamble, written by Ignatius Donnelly, a Minnesota farmer, author, and politician, caught much of the urgent spirit of the agrarian protest movement in the 1890s:

> We meet in the midst of a nation brought to the verge of moral, political and material ruin. Corruption dominates the ballot box, the legislatures, the Congress, and touches even the ermine of the bench. The people are demoralized. . . . The fruits of the toil of millions are boldly stolen to build up colossal fortunes . . . we breed two great classes—paupers and millionaires.

The charge was clear: "The controlling influences dominating the old political parties have allowed the existing dreadful conditions to develop without serious effort to restrain or prevent them."

The Omaha platform demands, drawn from the Ocala platform of 1890, were greatly expanded. They included more means of direct democracy (direct election of senators, direct primaries, the initiative, referendum, and the secret ballot) and several planks intended to enlist the support of urban labor (eight-hour workday, immigration restriction, and condemnation of the use of Pinkerton agents as an "army of mercenaries . . . a menace to our liberties"). The People's party also endorsed a graduated income tax, the free and unlimited coinage of silver at a ratio of 16 to 1 (meaning that the U.S. Mint would have to buy silver for coinage at one-sixteenth the current official price of the equivalent amount of gold), and, rather than regulation, government ownership of railroads, telephone, and telegraph. "The time has come," the platform said, "when the railroad corporations will either own the people or the people must own the railroads."

The Populist party attempted to widen the nature of the American political debate by promoting a new vision of the government's role with respect to farmers' problems. But the tasks the party faced in attempting to win power were monumental. Success at the polls meant weaning the South away from the Democratic party, encouraging southern whites to work with blacks, and persuading voters of both parties to abandon familiar political ties. Nor were all Alliance members eager to follow their leaders into the third party. At the most basic level, the Populists had to create the political machinery necessary to function in the 1892 electoral campaign.

Despite these obstacles, the new party pressed forward. Unlike the candidates of the major parties in 1892, Benjamin Harrison and Grover Cleveland, Weaver campaigned actively. In the South, he faced rowdy audiences, rotten eggs, and rocks from hostile Democrats, who disapproved of attempts to form a biracial political coalition. The results of the campaign were mixed. Although Weaver won over a million popular votes (the first third-party candidate to do so), he carried only four states (Kansas, Colorado, Idaho, and Nevada) and parts of two others (Oregon and North Dakota), for a total of 22 electoral votes.

The attempt to break the stranglehold of the Democratic party on the South had failed. Democrats raised the cry of "nigger rule" and fanned racial fears. White farmers who viewed the alliance with blacks as one of necessity voted Democratic. Intimidation tactics and violence frightened off others.

Just as important, Weaver failed to appeal to city workers, who were suspicious of the party's antiurban tone and its desire for higher agricultural prices (which meant higher food prices). Nor did it appeal to people living east of the Mississippi or to farmers in the Great Lakes states. Their families enjoyed better farming weather, owed fewer debts, and were relatively prosperous. They saw little of value in the Omaha platform. Their disinterest was significant, for the growing population of the industrial northern cities, combined with the populous and prosperous Great Lake states, constituted an electoral majority by the 1890s.

Although the People's party failed to recruit a cross-section of American voters in 1892, it gained substantial support. Miners and mine owners in states like Montana and Colorado and in territories like New Mexico favored the demand for coinage of silver. Most Populists, however, were rural Americans in the South

Timeline

1860s	Cattle drives from Texas begin
1865–1867	Sioux wars on the Great Plains
1867	National Grange founded
1869	Transcontinental railroad completed
1869–1874	Granger laws
1873	Financial panic triggers economic depression
1874	Barbed wire patented
1875	Black Hills gold rush incites Sioux war
1876	Custer's last stand at Little Big Horn
1877	*Munn* v. *Illinois*
	Bonanza farms in the Great Plains
1878	Timber and Stone Act
1880s	Attempts to create a "New South"
1881	Tuskegee Institute founded
1883–1885	Depression
1884	Southern Farmers' Alliance founded
1886	Severe winter ends cattle boom
	Wabash v. *Illinois*
1887	Dawes Severalty Act
	Interstate Commerce Act
	Farm prices plummet
1888	Colored Farmers' Alliance founded
1890	Afro-American League founded
	Sioux ghost dance movement
	Massacre at Wounded Knee
	Ocala platform
	Yosemite National Park established
1890s	Black disenfranchisement in the South
	Jim Crow laws passed in the South
	Declining farm prices
1891	Forest Reserve Act
1892	Populist party formed
	Sierra Club founded
1895	Booker T. Washington's "Atlanta Compromise" address
1896	*Plessy* v. *Ferguson*

and West who stood outside the mainstream of American life. Economic grievances sharpened political discontent. But Populists were often no poorer or more debt-ridden than other farmers. They did tend to lead more isolated lives, however; often their farms were far from towns, villages, and railroads. They felt powerless to affect the workings of their political, social, and economic world. Thus, they responded to a party offering to act as their advocate.

Farmers who were better integrated into their world tended to believe they could work through existing political parties. In 1892, when thousands of farmers and others were politically and economically discontented, they voted for Cleveland and the Democrats, not the Populists.

Yet the Populists did not lose heart in 1892, as Chapter 19 will show. Populist governors were elected in Kansas and North Dakota, and the party swept Colorado. It was obvious that the showing of the party in the South, where even Tom Watson lost his bid for a congressional seat, stemmed from violent opposition and fraud on the part of the Democrats. For example, returns in Richmond County, Georgia, revealed a Democratic majority of 80 percent in a total vote twice the size of the actual number of legal voters.

Conclusion
Farming in the Industrial Age

The late nineteenth century brought turbulence to rural America. The "Indian problem," which had plagued Americans for 200 years, was tragically solved for a while, but not without resistance and bloodshed. Few whites found these events troubling. Most were caught up in the challenge of responding to a fast-changing world. Believing themselves to be the backbone of the nation, white farmers brought Indian lands into cultivation, modernized their farms, and raised bumper crops. But success and a comfortable competency eluded many of them. Some, like Milton Leeper, never gave up hope or farming. Many were caught in a cycle of poverty and debt. Others fled to the cities, where they joined the industrial workforce described in the next chapter. Many turned to collective action and politics. Their actions demonstrate that they did not merely react to events but attempted to shape them.

Recommended Reading

Modernizing Agriculture

Rodman W. Paul, with Martin Ridge, *The Far West and the Great Plains in Transition, 1859–1900* (1988); William G. Robbins, *Colony & Empire: The Capitalist Transformation of the American West* (1994); Donald Worster, *Rivers of Empire: Water, Aridity, and the Growth of the American West* (1985) and *An Unsettled Country: Changing Landscapes of the American West* (1994).

The Second Great Removal

John G. Neihardt, *Black Elk Speaks* (1932); Robert M. Utley, *The Indian Frontier of the American West* (1984) and *The Lance and the Shield: The Life and Times of Sitting Bull* (1993); Richard White, *The Roots of Dependency: Subsistence, Environment, and Social Change Among the Choctaws, Pawnees, and Navajos* (1983).

The New South

W. Fitzhugh Brundage, *Lynching in the New South; Georgia and Virginia, 1880–1930* (1993); Orville Vernon Burton and Robert C. McMath, Jr., eds., *Toward a New South?: Post–Civil War Southern Communities* (1982); Paul M. Gaston, *The New South Creed: A Study in Southern Mythmaking* (1970); Glenda Elizabeth Gilmore, *Gender and Jim Crow: Women and the Politics of White Supremacy in North Carolina, 1896–1920* (1996); Jacquelyn Jones, *Labor of Love, Labor of Sorrow: Black Women, Work, and the Family from Slavery to the Present* (1985); Lawrence H. Larsen, *The Rise of the Urban South* (1985); William E. Montgomery, *Under Their Own Vine and Fig Tree: The African-American Church in the South, 1865–1900* (1993); Edward Royce, *The Origins of Southern Sharecropping* (1993); C. Vann Woodward, *The Origins of the New South, 1877–1913* (1951).

Farm Protest

Lawrence Goodwyn, *The Populist Moment: A Short History of the Agrarian Revolt in America* (1978); Steven Hahn, *The Roots of Southern Populism: Yeoman Farmers and the Transformation of the Georgia Upcountry, 1850–1890* (1983); Robert W. Larson, *Populism in the Mountain West* (1986); Jeffrey Ostler, *Prairie Populism: The Fate of Agrarian Radicalism in Kansas, Nebraska, and Iowa, 1880–1892* (1993); Bruce Palmer, *"Men over Money": The Southern Populist Critique of American Capitalism* (1980).

Fiction and Film

Willa Cather's novels *My Antonia* and *O Pioneers!* emphasize the energy and determination of those farming in the post–Civil War West as well as the presence of immigrants there. O. E. Rölvaag's *Giants in the Earth* deals with immigrant families but gives a very grim picture of their adjustment to farming life in the United States. Written in 1885 by Maria Amparo Ruiz de Burton, *The Squatter and the Don* provides an insight into the views of Mexican Americans.

High Noon, a classic film from the 1950s, depicts what happens in a small western town in the trans-Mississippi area when a convicted criminal returns to kill the sheriff who put him in jail. (The film's treatment of gender and race owe much to the period in which it was made.) *Dances with Wolves* (1990) is Kevin Costner's indictment of the white assault on Native American life and culture. His depiction of Indian life is sympathetic although overly romantic and bears the mark of the 1990s consciousness. *Ethnic Notions* (1987), an Emmy-winning documentary by Marlon Riggs, traces the evolution of negative stereotypes of African Americans and the ways these stereotypes have been embodied in popular culture.

Suggested Web Sites

http://memory.loc.gov/ammem/award97/ndfahtml/ngphome.html

The Northern Great Plains, 1880–1920. This American Memory site from the Library of Congress contains 900 photographs of rural and small town life at the turn of the century, including images of sod homes, farms and machinery, and one-room schools.

http://memory.loc.gov/ammem/cbhtml/cbhome.html

"California as I Saw It": First-Person Narratives of California's Early Years, 1849–1900. This site is part of the American Memory series and contains texts and illustrations of nearly 200 works, covering the gold rush, the interaction of various groups, and the settling of the region.

http://history.cc.ukans.edu/heritage/old_west/cowboy.html

Home on the Range/Cowboy Heritage. This site tells the history of the cattle trails and towns like Dodge City with useful text, links, documents, and maps.

http://www.library.okstate.edu/kappler

Kappler's Indian Affairs: Laws and Treaties. This digitized text from Oklahoma State University includes preremoval treaties with the "Five Civilized Tribes" and other tribes.

http://www.ukans.edu/carrie/kancoll/galhero.htm

Heroes and Villains. This site is part of the Kansas Collection Gallery, which offers glimpses of books, letters, diaries, photos, and other materials from the past.

http://www.csusm.edu/projects/nadp/nadp.htm

Native American Documents Project. California State University at San Marcos has several digital documents relating to Native Americans on this site.

http://odur.let.rug.nl/~usa/B/geronimo/geronixx.htm

USA: Geronimo, His Own Story. This site contains biographical and autobiographical information about this famous Native American who resisted European American domination.

http://www.ushistoryplace.com

A richly detailed on-line learning environment complete with interactive maps, timelines, history activities, primary source documents, and links to related American history sites.

18

The RISE of SMOKESTACK AMERICA

CHAPTER OUTLINE

By 1883, Thomas O'Donnell, an Irish immigrant, had lived in the United States for over a decade. He was 30 years old, married, with two young children. His third child had died in 1882, and O'Donnell was still in debt for the funeral. Money was scarce, for O'Donnell was a textile worker in Fall River, Massachusetts, and not well educated. "I went to work when I was young," he explained, "and have been working ever since." However, O'Donnell worked only sporadically at the mill. New machines needed "a good deal of small help," and the mill owners preferred to hire man-and-boy teams. Because O'Donnell's children were only one and three, he often saw others preferred for day work. Once, when he was passed over, he recalled, "I said to the boss . . . what am I to do; I have got two little boys at home . . . how am I to get something for them to eat; I can't get a turn when I come here. . . . I says, 'Have I got to starve; ain't I to have any work?'"

O'Donnell and his family were barely getting by, even though he worked with pick and shovel when he could. He estimated that he had earned only $133 the previous year. Rent came to $72. The family spent $2 for a little coal but depended for heat on driftwood that O'Donnell picked up on the beach. Clams were a major part of the family diet, but on some days there was nothing to eat at all.

The children "got along very nicely all summer," but it was now November, and they were beginning to "feel quite sickly." It was hardly surprising. "One has one shoe on, a very poor one, and a slipper, that was picked up somewhere. The other has two odd shoes on, with the heel out." His wife was healthy, but not ready for winter. She had two dresses, one saved for church, and an "undershirt that she got given to her, and . . . an old wrapper, which is about a mile too big for her; somebody gave it to her."

O'Donnell was describing his family's marginal existence to a Senate committee that was gathering testimony in Boston in 1883 on the relations between labor and capital. As the senators heard the tale, they asked him why he did not go west. "It would not cost you over $1,500," said one senator.

The gap between the worlds of the senator and the worker could not have been more dramatic. O'Donnell replied, "Well, I never saw over a $20 bill . . . if some one would give me $1,500 I will go." Asked by the senator if he had friends who could provide him with the funds, O'Donnell sadly replied no.

The senators, of course, were far better acquainted with the world of comfort and leisure than with the poverty of families like the O'Donnells. From their vantage point, the fruits of industrial progress were clear. As the United States became a world industrial leader in the years after the Civil War, its factories poured forth an abundance of ever-cheaper goods ranging from steel rails and farm reapers to mass-produced parlor sets. These were years of tremendous growth and broad economic and social change. Manufacturing replaced agriculture as the leading source of economic growth between 1860 and 1900. By 1890, a majority of the American workforce held nonagricultural jobs; over a third lived in cities. A rural nation of farmers was becoming a nation of industrial workers and city dwellers.

As O'Donnell's appearance before the senatorial committee illustrates, industrial and technological advances profoundly changed the nature of American life. For O'Donnell and others like him, the benefits of this transformation were hard to see. Although no nationwide studies of poverty existed, estimates suggest that perhaps half the American population was too poor to take advantage of the new goods of the age. Eventually, the disparity between the reality of life for humble families like the O'Donnells and American ideals would give rise to attempts to improve conditions for working-class Americans, but it is unlikely that O'Donnell ever profited from such efforts.

This chapter examines the new order that resulted from the maturing of the American industrial economy. Focusing on the years between 1865 and 1900, it describes the rise of heavy industry, the organization and character of the new industrial workplace, and the emergence of big business. It then examines the locus of industrial life, the fast-growing city, and its varied people, classes, and social inequities. The chapter's central theme grows out of O'Donnell's story: As the United States built up its railroads, cities, and factories, its production and profit orientation resulted in the maldistribution of wealth

This anxious scene of a strike hints at the tensions between workers and owners during the industrial era. (*Robert Koehler,* The Strike *(detail), 1886, Courtesy of District 1199, National Union of Hospital and Health Care Employees, RWDSW/AFL-CIO and Lee Baxandall)*

and power. Although many Americans were too exhausted by life's daily struggles to protest new inequalities, strikes and other forms of working-class resistance punctuated the period. The social problems that accompanied the country's industrial development would capture the attention of reformers and politicians for decades to come.

THE TEXTURE OF INDUSTRIAL PROGRESS

When Americans went to war in 1861, agriculture was the country's leading source of economic growth. Forty years later, manufacturing had taken its place. During these years, the production of manufactured goods outpaced population growth. By 1900, three times as many goods per person existed as in 1860. Per capita income increased by over 2 percent a year. But these aggregate figures disguise the fact that many people did not win any gains at all.

As the nature of the American economy changed, big businesses became the characteristic form of economic organization. Big businesses, with large amounts of capital, could afford to build huge factories, buy and install the latest and most efficient machinery, hire hundreds of workers, and use the most up-to-date methods. The result was more goods at lower prices. Machines costing thousands of dollars mass-produced goods costing pennies.

With the expansion of manufacturing, new regions grew in industrial importance. From New England to the Midwest lay the country's industrial heartland. New England remained a center of light industry, while the Midwest still processed natural resources. Now, however, the production of iron, steel, and transportation equipment joined older manufacturing operations there. In the Far West, manufacturers concentrated on processing the region's natural resources, but heavy industry made strides as well. In the South, the textile industry put down roots by the 1890s, although the South as a whole was far less industrialized than either the North or the Midwest.

Although many factors contributed to dramatically rising industrial productivity, the changing nature of the industrial sector itself played an important role. Manufacturers before the Civil War had produced textiles, clothing, and leather products or processed agricultural and natural resources. Although these operations continued, heavy industry, which turned out goods like steel, iron, petroleum, and machinery, grew rapidly. The manufacturing of these goods intended for other producers rather than consumers fueled economic growth. Farmers, who purchased machinery for their farms; manufacturers, who installed new equipment in their factories; and railroads, which bought steel rails for their tracks—all contributed to rising productivity figures and encouraged the technological innovations that revolutionized production.

Technological Innovations

An accelerating pace of technological change contributed to and was shaped by the industrial transformation of the late nineteenth century. Technological breakthroughs allowed more efficient production that, in turn, helped to generate new needs and stimulated further innovation. Developments in the steel and electric industries exemplify this interdependent process as well as the role played by entrepreneurs and the important new ways of organizing research and innovation.

Iron production before the Civil War was slow and expensive. Skilled, highly paid workers turned iron ore into wrought iron, which farmers and mechanics could easily shape into tools and machines. But the iron was soft; heavy trains wore out iron rails in a matter of years. The need for a more durable metal supported the development and introduction of new technologies capable of producing hard steel. The Bessemer converter (named after its English inventor) transformed iron into steel by forcing air through the liquid iron, thus reducing the carbon (see the diagraphic on page 566). The process had the added advantage of reducing the need for so many skilled workers.

Andrew Carnegie was neither an inventor nor an engineer, but he recognized the possibilities in the new processes and the methods of organizing industry that it made possible. Steel companies like Carnegie's acquired access to raw materials and markets and brought all stages of steel manufacturing, from smelting to rolling, into one mill. Production soared and prices fell. When Andrew Carnegie introduced the Bessemer process in his plant in the mid-1870s, the price of steel plummeted from $100 a ton to $50. By 1900, steel cost only $12 a ton.

This cheaper, stronger, more durable material stimulated the development of new goods, new demands, new markets, and then further technological change. Bessemer furnaces, geared toward making steel rails, did not produce steel for building. Experimentation with the open-hearth process that used very high temperatures resulted in steel used by bridge builders, engineers, architects, and even designers of subways. Supporters of a new foreign policy lobbied success-

The Homestead Steel Works, pictured here in about 1890, were located near Pittsburgh, Pennsylvania. The vast scale of the enterprise suggests the ways in which technological innovation stimulated the expansion of the steel industry in the late nineteenth century. Although the two small figures in the foreground humanize the picture, the extent and size of the steel mills created a workplace that was anything but humane. *(Courtesy of Rivers of Steel Archives)*

fully for an expanded navy of steel vessels. Countless Americans bought steel in more humble forms: wire, nails, bolts, needles, and screws.

Electricity provided a new source of power that, in the twentieth century, would replace the steam engine as the major provider of the nation's industrial energy. Experiments in generating electricity dated back to the middle of the eighteenth century and had made possible the development of the telegraph in 1844. Thomas Edison, in 1878, decided that he would be the one to solve the problem of electric lighting.

Edison had already developed the ticker tape (by which information could be sent directly from the stock exchange to the offices of investors) and a telegraph capable of simultaneously transmitting four messages along the wires before he turned his attention to electric lighting. Edison's success with the electric light stemmed not only from his own inventiveness but his realization that successful innovation was fostered by professional collaboration. In 1876, he set up a research lab with a range of specialists and facilities that included an advanced library, a chemical lab, and eventually even a glassblowing lab. His work with the ticker tape ensured generous support from the business and financial community.

By 1880, Edison had not only developed a workable and safe lightbulb but also created a company in New York to build the electric generating station to provide electricity to the city's customers. Since people used their electric lights mainly at night, there was a built-in incentive to find a way to use generators during the day. Electric traction trolley cars using steel tracks provided one way to maximize the potential of the generating station. Experimenting with electric generators also led to the development of the electric machine, which has transformed American life.

Railroads: Pioneers of Big Business

The completion of a national transportation and communications network was intricately linked with economic growth. Mass production and distribution depended on fast, efficient, and regular transportation and communication, while the completion of the national system both encouraged and supported the adoption of mass production and mass marketing.

In 1860, most railroads were located in the East and the Midwest. From 1862 on, the federal and state governments vigorously promoted railroad construction with generous land grants from the public domain. Similarly, counties and cities donated land for stations and terminals, bought railroad stock, made loans and grants, and gave tax breaks to railroads.

With such incentives, the first transcontinental railroad was completed in 1869. A burst of railroad

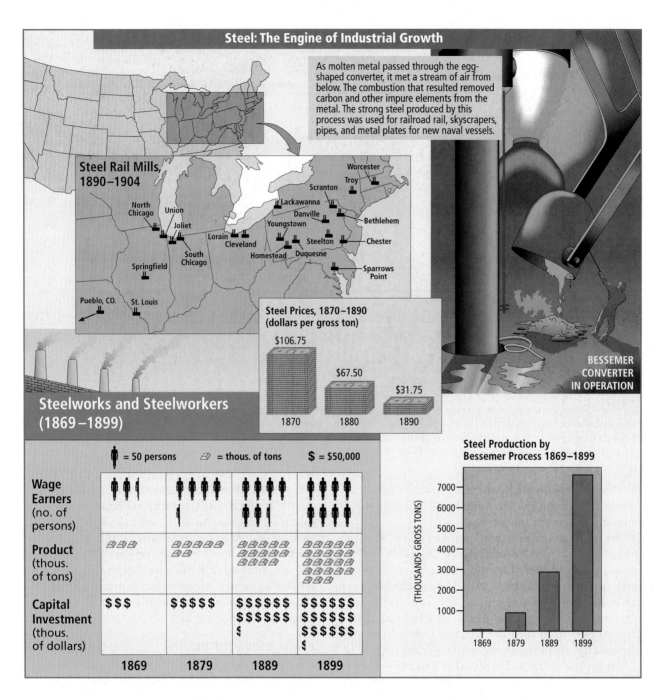

Steel: The Engine of Industrial Growth

As molten metal passed through the egg-shaped converter, it met a stream of air from below. The combustion that resulted removed carbon and other impure elements from the metal. The strong steel produced by this process was used for railroad rail, skyscrapers, pipes, and metal plates for new naval vessels.

Steel Rail Mills, 1890–1904

Worcester
Troy
Scranton
North Chicago
Union
Joliet
Lackawanna
Danville
Bethlehem
Youngstown
Lorain
Cleveland
Steelton
Chester
Homestead
Duquesne
South Chicago
Springfield
Sparrows Point
Pueblo, CO.
St. Louis

Steel Prices, 1870–1890 (dollars per gross ton)

$106.75 — 1870
$67.50 — 1880
$31.75 — 1890

BESSEMER CONVERTER IN OPERATION

Steelworks and Steelworkers (1869–1899)

👤 = 50 persons   ▱ = thous. of tons $ = $50,000

	1869	1879	1889	1899
Wage Earners (no. of persons)				
Product (thous. of tons)				
Capital Investment (thous. of dollars)				

Steel Production by Bessemer Process 1869–1899

(THOUSANDS GROSS TONS)

7000
6000
5000
4000
3000
2000
1000

1869 1879 1889 1899

construction followed. By 1890, trains were rumbling across 165,000 miles of tracks with Western Union lines running alongside them.

The railroads were the pioneers of big business. As railroads expanded after the Civil War, railroad companies grew in size. In 1888, a medium-size Boston railroad company had three times as many employees and received six times as much income as the Massachusetts state government.

The size of railroads; the huge costs of construction, maintenance, and repair; and the complexity of operations required unprecedented amounts of capital and new management techniques. No single person could finance a railroad or hope to supervise its operations involving hundreds of miles of track and hundreds of employees. Nor could any one person resolve the thorny questions such a large enterprise raised. How should the operations and employees be organized? What were the long- and short-term needs of the railroad? What were proper rates? What share of the profits did workers deserve?

Unlike small businesses with modest overhead costs, railroads faced high constant costs of maintaining equipment and lines. In addition, railroads carried a heavy load of debt, incurred to pay for construction and expansion. The burden of regular

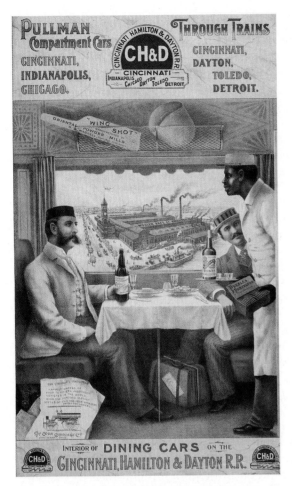

This depiction emphasizes the luxury, comfort, and attentive service (note the smiling black attendant who offers the diners cigars and drinks) available in a Pullman dining car. Through the window a large factory is visible. The image as a whole suggests the pride many Americans felt in industrial development and their realization of the importance of railroads to economic progress. (*The Granger Collection, New York*)

interest payments and expenses encouraged railroads to adopt aggressive business practices and to use their equipment as intensively as possible. If 20 cars were almost as expensive to pull as 25, why not haul 25? If lower rates would lure customers, why not offer them? Railroad freight charges dropped steadily during the last quarter of the century. When two or more lines competed for the same traffic, railroads often offered lower rates than their rivals or offered secret rebates (cheaper fares in exchange for all of a company's business). Rate wars helped customers, but they could plunge a railroad into bankruptcy. Instability plagued the railroad industry even as it expanded.

In the 1870s, railroad leaders sought stability through eliminating ruinous competition. As George Perkins of the Chicago, Burlington, and Quincy Railroad explained, "The struggle for existence and the survival of the fittest is a pretty theory, but it is also a law of nature that even the fittest must live." Railroad leaders established "pools," informal agreements that set uniform rates or divided up the traffic. Yet pools never completely succeeded. Too often, individual companies disregarded their agreements, especially when the business cycle took a downturn.

Railroad leaders often tried to control costs and counter the late-nineteenth-century pattern of falling prices by slashing their workers' wages. Owners justified this strategy by reasoning that they had taken all the business risks. As a result, railroads faced powerful worker unrest (described later in this chapter).

The huge scale and complexity of the railroads required new management techniques. In 1854, the directors of the Erie Railroad hired engineer and inventor Daniel McCallum to devise a system to make railroad managers and their employees more accountable. In his report, McCallum highlighted the differences between large and small organizations. In a small organization, one could pay personal attention to all the details of operation. But, McCallum argued, "any system that might be applicable to the business and extent of a short road would be found entirely inadequate to the wants of a long one."

McCallum's system, emphasizing division of responsibilities and a regular flow of information, attracted widespread interest, and railroads became pioneers in rationalized administrative practices and management techniques. Their procedures became models for other businesses in decision making, scheduling, and engineering. The steel industry emulated the practices of the railroads that had fostered their development. Other large-scale businesses also adopted the new procedures that effectively distributed responsibilities and separated management from operations. Because they faced similar economic conditions, big businesses also emulated the behavior of the railroads—their competitiveness, their attempts to underprice one another, their eventual interest in merger, and their tendency to cut workers' wages.

Growth in Other Industries

By the last quarter of the century, the textile, metal, and machinery industries equaled the railroads in size. In 1870, the typical iron and steel firm employed under 100 workers. Thirty years later, the average workforce was four times as large. By 1900, more than 1,000 American factories had giant labor forces ranging between 500 and 1,000. Almost 450 others employed more than 1,000 workers. Big business had come of age.

Business expansion was accomplished in one of two ways (or a combination of both). Some owners, like steel magnate Andrew Carnegie, integrated their businesses vertically. Vertical integration meant adding operations either before or after the production process. Even though he had introduced the most up-to-date innovations in his steel mills, Carnegie realized he needed his own sources of pig iron, coal, and coke. This was "backward" integration, away from the consumer, to avoid dependence on suppliers. When Carnegie acquired steamships and railroads to transport his finished products, he was integrating "forward," toward the consumer. Companies that integrated vertically frequently achieved economies of scale through more efficient management techniques.

Other companies copied the railroads and integrated horizontally by combining similar businesses. They did not intend to control the various stages of production, as was the case with vertical integration, but rather to gain a monopoly of the market to eliminate competition and to stabilize prices. Horizontal integration sometimes, though not always, brought economies and thus greater profits. The control over prices that monopoly provided did boost earnings.

John D. Rockefeller used the strategy of horizontal integration to gain control of the oil market. By a combination of astute and ruthless techniques, Rockefeller bought or drove out competitors of his Standard Oil of New Jersey. Although the company never achieved a complete monopoly, by 1898 it was refining 84 percent of the nation's oil. Rockefeller reflected, "The day of individual competition [in the oil business] . . . is past and gone."

Rockefeller accurately characterized the new economic conditions. As giant businesses competed intensely, often cutting wages and prices, they absorbed or eliminated smaller and weaker producers. Business ownership became increasingly concentrated. In 1870, some 808 American iron and steel firms competed in the marketplace. By 1900, the number had dwindled to fewer than 70.

Like the railroads, many big businesses chose to incorporate. Although corporations were not new, most manufacturing firms were unincorporated in 1860. By 1900, corporations turned out two-thirds of the country's industrial goods.

Business gained many advantages by incorporating. Through the sale of stock, they could raise funds for their large-scale operations. The principle of limited liability protected investors, whereas the corporation's legal identity ensured its survival after the death of original and subsequent shareholders. Longevity suggested a measure of stability that heightened the attractiveness of a corporation as an investment.

Financing Postwar Growth

Such changes demanded huge amounts of capital and the willingness to accept financial risks. The creation

of the railroad system alone cost over $1 billion by 1859 (the canal system's modest price tag was less than $2 million). The completion of the national railroad network required another $10 billion. British, French, and German investors saw American railroads as a good investment; ultimately, foreigners contributed a third of the sum needed to complete the system. Americans also eagerly supported new ventures and began to devote an increasing percentage of the national income to investment rather than consumption.

Although savings and commercial banks continued to invest their depositors' capital, investment banking houses like Morgan & Co. played a new and significant role in matching resources with economic enterprises. Investment bankers marketed investment opportunities. They bought up blocks of corporate bonds (which offered set interest rates and eventually the repayment of principal) at a discount for interested investors and also sold stocks (which paid dividends only if the company made a profit). Because stocks were riskier investments than bonds, buyers were at first cautious. But when John Pierpont Morgan, a respected investment banker, began to market stocks, they became more popular. The market for industrial securities expanded rapidly in the 1880s and 1890s. Although some Americans feared the power of investment bankers and distrusted the financial market, both were integral to the economic expansion of the late nineteenth century.

The Erratic Economic Cycle

The transformation of the economy, however, was neither smooth nor steady. Rockefeller, describing his years in the oil business as "hazardous," confessed that he did not know "how we came through them."

Two depressions, one from 1873 to 1879 and the other from 1893 to 1897, surpassed the severity of economic downturns before the Civil War. Collapsing land values, unsound banking practices, and changes in the supply of money had caused antebellum depressions. The depressions of the late nineteenth century, when the economy was larger and more interdependent, were industrial, intense, and accompanied by widespread unemployment, a phenomenon new to American life.

During expansionary years, manufacturers flooded markets with goods. The pattern of falling prices that characterized the postwar period and fierce competition between producers combined to encourage overproduction. When the market was finally saturated, sales and profits declined and the economy spiraled downward. Owners slowed production and laid off workers. Industrial workers, now an increasing percentage of the American workforce,

INCREASE IN SIZE OF INDUSTRIES, 1860–1900

Industry	Average Number of Workers per Establishment	
	1860	**1900**
Cotton goods	112	287
Glass	81	149
Iron and steel	65	333
Hosiery and knit goods	46	91
Silk and silk goods	39	135
Woolen goods	33	67
Carpets and rugs	31	213
Tobacco	30	67
Slaughtering and meatpacking	20	61
Paper and wood pulp	15	65
Shipbuilding	15	42
Agricultural implements	8	65
Leather	5	40
Malt liquors	5	26

This table highlights the dramatic changes in the workplace over a 40-year period. Think about what the figures suggest about the experience of work.
Source: U.S. Bureau of the Census

depended solely on wages for their livelihood. As they economized and bought less food, farm prices also plummeted. Farmers, like wage workers, cut back on purchases. Business and trade stagnated, and the railroads were finally affected. Eventually, the cycle bottomed out, but in the meantime, millions of workers lost employment, thousands of businesses went bankrupt, and many Americans suffered deprivation and hardship.

Pollution

Another by-product of the industrial age, widespread pollution, was less dramatic and worrisome to most Americans than the vagaries of the economic cycle. But industrial processes everywhere had an adverse impact on the environment. In the iron and steel city of Birmingham, Alabama, for example, the coke ovens poured smoke, soot, and ashes into the air. Coal tar, a by-product of the coking process, was dumped, and it made the soil so acid that nothing would grow on it.

When industrial, human, and animal wastes were disposed of in rivers, they killed off fish and other forms of marine life and the plants that were part of that ecosystem. By the late nineteenth century, major pollution of eastern and midwestern rivers as well as lakes had become pronounced.

The intellectual rationale stressed growth, development, and the rapid exploitation of the country's resources rather than conservation. As the last chapter pointed out, there were some steps taken toward protecting the environment. Presidents Grover Cleveland and Benjamin Harrison both set aside forest reserves, and there was growing interest in creating national parks. But these sorts of actions were limited in scope and impact and did not begin to touch the problems created by the rise of heavy industry and the rapid urban expansion that it stimulated.

URBAN EXPANSION IN THE INDUSTRIAL AGE

Before the Civil War, manufacturers had relied on water power and chosen rural sites for their factories. Now as they shifted to steam power, most favored urban locations that offered them workers, specialized services, local markets, and railroad links to materials and to distant markets. Although technological innovations like electric lights (invented in 1879) and telephones (1876) were still not widespread, they further increased the desirability of urban sites. Industry, rather than commerce or finance, fueled urban expansion between 1870 and 1900.

Cities of all sizes grew. The population of New York and Philadelphia doubled and tripled. Smaller cities, especially those in the industrial Midwest like Omaha, Duluth, and Minneapolis, boasted impressive growth rates. Southern cities, as we saw in Chapter 17, also shared in the dramatic growth. In the Far West during the 1880s, Spokane exploded from 350 to 20,000, and Tacoma from 1,100 to 36,000. In 1870, some 25 percent of Americans lived in cities; by 1900, fully 40 percent of them did.

A Growing Population

The American population as a whole was growing at a rate of about 2 percent a year, but cities were expanding far more rapidly. What accounted for the dramatic increase in urban population?

Certainly not a high birthrate. Although more people were born than died in American cities, births contributed only modestly to the urban population explosion. The general pattern of declining family size that had emerged before the Civil War continued. By 1900, the average woman bore only 3.6 children, in contrast to 5.2 in 1860. Urban families, moreover, tended to have fewer children than their rural counterparts. And urban children faced a host of health hazards like tuberculosis, diarrhea, and diphtheria. All city residents were vulnerable, but children especially so. The death rate for infants was twice as high in cities as in the countryside. In the 1880s, half the children born in Chicago did not live to celebrate their fifth birthday.

The real cause of urban growth was the special ability to attract newcomers from the nation's small towns and farms and from abroad. For foreigners and Americans alike, a combination of pressures, some encouraging them to abandon their original homes, others attracting them to the urban environment, prompted the decision to relocate.

For rural Americans, the "push" came from the modernization of agricultural life. Factories poured out farm machines that replaced human hands. By 1896, one man with machinery could harvest 18 times as much wheat as a farmer working with hand tools in 1830.

The City's Appeal

Work in the industrial city was the prime attraction. Although urban jobs were often dirty, dangerous, and

This 1896 picture of Chicago shows how the appearance of cities changed when structural steel became available for skyscrapers. Once the national rail system was complete, steelmakers turned to new urban markets to maintain profits. *(Chicago Historical Society)*

exhausting, so was farmwork. Moreover, by 1890, manufacturing workers were earning hundreds of dollars more a year than farm laborers. Some industrial workers, like miners in the Far West, earned even more. Part of the difference between rural and urban wages was eaten up by the higher cost of living in the city, but not all of it.

TEN LARGEST CITIES IN THE UNITED STATES, 1810, 1850, 1860, 1890			
1810	**1850**	**1860**	**1890**
1. New York	1. New York	1. New York	1. New York
2. Philadelphia	2. Philadelphia	2. Philadelphia	2. Chicago
3. Baltimore	3. Baltimore	3. Baltimore	3. Philadelphia
4. Boston	4. Boston	4. Boston	4. St. Louis
5. Charleston	5. New Orleans	5. New Orleans	5. Boston
6. New Orleans	6. Cincinnati	6. Cincinnati	6. Baltimore
7. Salem	7. Brooklyn	7. St. Louis	7. Pittsburgh
8. Providence	8. St. Louis	8. Chicago	8. San Francisco
9. Richmond	9. Albany	9. Buffalo	9. Cincinnati
10. Albany	10. Pittsburgh	10. Newark	10. Cleveland

By 1890, only four cities that had been among the nation's largest in 1810 retained their position. Cities in the Midwest and West assumed new importance at the end of the century.
Source: U.S. Bureau of the Census

An intangible but important lure was the glitter of city life. Rural life was often monotonous and drab. The young man who saw Kansas City as a "gilded metropolis" filled with "marvels," a veritable "round of joy," found the excitement of urban life, its culture, its amusements dazzling. Shops, theaters, restaurants, churches, department stores, newspapers, ballgames, and the urban throng all amazed young men and women who had grown up on farms and in small towns.

Southern blacks, often single and young, also fed the migratory stream into the cities. In the West and the North, blacks constituted only a tiny part of the population: 3 percent in Denver in the 1880s and 1890s, 2 percent in Boston. In southern cities, however, they were more numerous. About 44 percent of Atlanta's and 38 percent of Nashville's residents in the late nineteenth century were black.

The New Immigration, 1880–1900

In 1870, a "brokenhearted" Annie Sproul stole away from her parents' home in Londonderry, Ireland, to seek a new future in Philadelphia. She took all the money in the house, "leaving not the price of a loaf" behind. Probably the disgrace of a love affair prompted Annie's desperate flight, but the young woman was one of many who left their homelands in the nineteenth century in the hope of making a fortune in the New World. In the 40 years before the Civil War, five million immigrants poured into the United States;

from 1860 to 1900, that volume almost tripled. Three-quarters of the newcomers stayed in the Northeast, and many of the rest settled in cities across the nation, where they soon outnumbered native-born whites. The American mosaic of differing cultures and races assumed new complexities.

As the flow of immigration increased, the national origin of immigrants shifted. Until 1880, three-quarters of the immigrants, often called the "old immigrants," hailed from the British Isles, Germany, and Scandinavia. Irish and Germans were the largest groups. Then the pattern slowly changed in ways that increased the ethnic and religious heterogeneity of the American people and changed the composition of the laboring class. By 1890, old immigrants composed only 60 percent of the total number of newcomers, and the "new immigrants" from southern and eastern Europe (Italy, Poland, Russia, Austria-Hungary, Greece, Turkey, and Syria) made up most of the rest. Italian Catholics and eastern European Jews were the most numerous, followed by Slavs.

Cheaper, faster, and better transportation facilitated the great tide of migration. Trains reached far into eastern and southern Europe. On transatlantic vessels, even steerage passengers could now expect a bed with blankets, cooked meals, and a communal washroom. But dissatisfaction with life at home was basic to the decision to migrate. Overpopulation, famine, and disease drove people to leave. "We could have eaten each other had we stayed," explained one Italian immigrant.

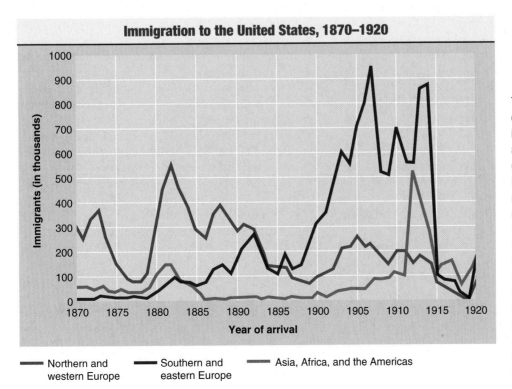

Immigration to the United States, 1870–1920

Immigrants (in thousands) — vertical axis: 0, 100, 200, 300, 400, 500, 600, 700, 800, 900, 1000

Year of arrival — horizontal axis: 1870, 1875, 1880, 1885, 1890, 1895, 1900, 1905, 1910, 1915, 1920

— Northern and western Europe   — Southern and eastern Europe   — Asia, Africa, and the Americas

This chart shows the changing pattern of immigration between 1870 and 1920. You can see the growing importance of immigration from southern and eastern Europe as well as a period of intensive immigration from China. Newcomers made the United States not only more ethnically diverse but more religiously diverse as well. The new European immigration contained large numbers of Jews and Roman Catholics. Source: U.S. Bureau of the Census.

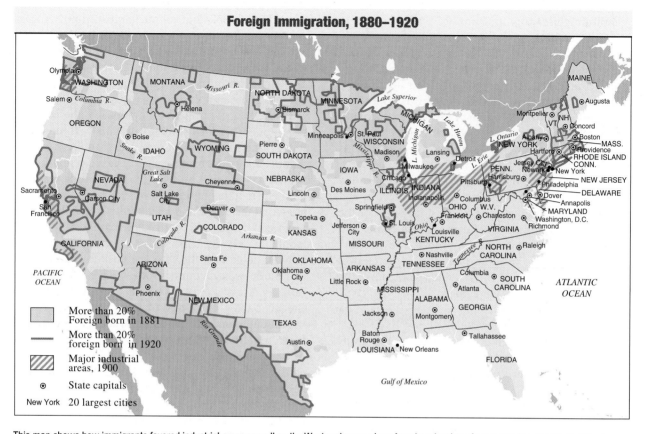

Foreign Immigration, 1880–1920

This map shows how immigrants favored industrial areas as well as the West and areas along American borders. As you can see, the South did not attract large numbers of foreigners.

Efforts to modernize European economies also stimulated immigration. New agricultural techniques led landlords to consolidate their land, evicting long-time tenants. Younger European farmers traveled in increasingly wide circles searching for work. Some emigrated to cities elsewhere in Europe. Many set out for Canada or South America. The largest share went to the United States. Similarly, artisans and craftsmen whose skills were made obsolete by the introduction of machinery pulled up stakes and headed for the United States and other destinations. Government policies pushed others to leave. In eastern Europe, especially in Russia, the official persecution of minorities and the expansion of the draft for the czar's army led millions of Jewish families and others to emigrate.

Opportunity in the "golden land" of America also lured thousands to American shores. State commissioners of immigration and American railroad and steamship companies, eager for workers and customers, wooed potential immigrants. Friends and relatives wrote letters describing favorable living and working conditions and promising to help newcomers find work. American cities were great places for "blast frnises and Rolen milles," explained one unskilled worker." Often passage money or pictures of friends in

alluringly fashionable clothes were slipped between the pages. The phenomenon of immigrants being recruited through the reports and efforts of their predecessors has come to be known as "chain migration."

Like rural and small-town Americans, Europeans came primarily to work. Most were young, single men who, in contrast to pre–Civil War immigrants, had few skills. Jews, however, came most often in family groups, and women predominated among the Irish. When times were good and American industry needed large numbers of unskilled laborers, migration was heavy. When times were bad and letters warned that "work is dull all over . . . no work to be got except by chance or influence," numbers fell off. Immigrants hoped to earn enough money in America to realize their ambitions at home. A surprising number, perhaps as many as a third, eventually returned to their native lands.

Although the greatest influx of Mexicans would come in the twentieth century, Mexican laborers added to the stream of foreigners migrating to the United States. Like many European countries, Mexico was in the throes of modernization. Overpopulation and new land policies uprooted many inhabitants, including Gonzalo Plancarte. In the 1890s, Gonzalo

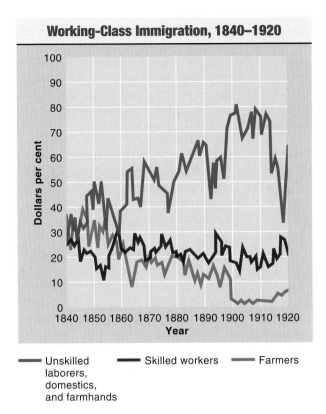

Working-Class Immigration, 1840–1920

Dollars per cent (y-axis: 0, 10, 20, 30, 40, 50, 60, 70, 80, 90, 100)

Year (x-axis: 1840, 1850, 1860, 1870, 1880, 1890, 1900, 1910, 1920)

— Unskilled laborers, domestics, and farmhands
— Skilled workers
— Farmers

The large numbers of unskilled workers coming to the United States were responding to the need for unskilled labor during the second industrial revolution. Source: U.S. Bureau of the Census.

and his father supported themselves by raising cattle in central Mexico. When the owner of the hacienda determined to turn his land over to producing goods for export, he ended the family's grazing privileges. The two men took to the road with their herd but failed to find sufficient grazing for their animals. Eventually, they sold the cattle, and after his father died, a desperately poor Gonzalo headed north. In 1895, the construction of a railroad from the Texas border 900 miles into Mexico facilitated migration. Many of these newcomers found work in the Southwest and West, often on the railroads and in mines.

Overpopulation, depressed conditions, unemployment, and crop failures brought Asians, most of them from southern China, to the "Land of the Golden Mountains." "We were very much in debt because of the local warfare," explained one immigrant. "We planted each year, but we were robbed. We had to borrow. When news about the Gold Rush in California was spread by the shippers, my father decided to take the big chance."

Although only 264,000 Chinese came to the United States between 1860 and 1900, they constituted a significant minority on the West Coast. Most were unskilled male contract laborers who promised to work for a number of years and then return to their wives and families at home. They performed some of the hardest, dirtiest, and least desirable jobs in the West, including mining, railroad and levee construction, and factory and laundry work. To serve these men, often away from their wives for years, contractors brought in Chinese women to serve as prostitutes. Virtually enslaved, some of these women were able to pay off the costs of their passage or escape from brothel life. But a Cantonese saying captured the

Although not one of the largest immigrant groups in the late nineteenth century, Chinese made up a sizable proportion of foreign workers in California. The overwhelming male nature of this immigration is apparent in this photograph. Because many of the Chinese women coming to the United States were prostitutes, Congress passed a law in 1873 curtailing Asian female immigration on moral grounds. (*Asian American Studies Library, University of California, Berkeley*)

sexual imbalance in the Chinese life: "Pathetic the lonely bachelors stranded in a foreign land."

🔊 THE INDUSTRIAL CITY, 1880–1900

The late-nineteenth-century industrial city had new physical and social arrangements that attracted widespread comment. James Bryce, a Scottish visitor, noted that urban "monotony haunts one like a nightmare." Slums, which were not new, seemed disturbing because so many people lived in them. Yet these same cities also boasted of grand mansions, handsome business and industrial buildings, grandiose civic monuments, and acres of substantial middle-class homes.

By the last quarter of the nineteenth century, the jumbled arrangements of the antebellum "walking city," whose size and configuration had been limited by the necessity of walking to work, disappeared. Where once substantial houses, businesses, and small artisan dwellings had stood side by side, central business districts emerged. Here were banks, shops, theaters, professional firms, and businesses. Few people lived downtown, although many worked or shopped there. Surrounding the business center were areas of light manufacturing and wholesale activity with housing for workers. Beyond these working-class neighborhoods stretched middle-class residential areas. Then came the suburbs, with "pure air, peacefulness, quietude, and natural scenery." Scattered throughout the city were pockets of industrial activity surrounded by crowded working-class housing.

This new pattern, with the poorest city residents clustered near the center, is familiar today. However, it reversed the early nineteenth-century urban form, when much of the most desirable housing was in the heart of the city. New living arrangements were also more segregated by race and class than those in the preindustrial walking city. Homogeneous social and economic neighborhoods emerged, and it became more unusual than before for a poor, working-class family to live near a middle- or upper-class family.

The changing urban geography reflected the dense development of the central business district, the rise of heavy industry, and improvements in transportation. Better transportation increasingly allowed middle- and upper-class residents to live away from their work and from grimy industrial districts.

The urban transportation revolution started modestly in the 1820s and 1830s with the horse-drawn omnibus. This slow-moving vehicle accommodated only 10 to 12 passengers. Its expensive fares obliged most people to live within walking distance of their work. In the 1850s, many cities introduced horse railways. Pulling cars over rails with as many as 25 passengers, horses could cover 5 to 6 miles an hour. The horse railways, which radiated from city centers like the spokes of a wheel, allowed the city to expand outward about four miles. The cost of a fare limited ridership to the middle and upper classes. The introduction of cable cars, trolley cars, and subways after 1880 further extended city boundaries and broadened residential choices for the middle class.

Neighborhoods and Neighborhood Life

Working-class neighborhoods clustered near the center of most industrial cities. Here lived newcomers from the American countryside and, because most immigrants settled in cities, crowds of foreigners as well.

Ethnic groups frequently chose to gather in particular neighborhoods, often located near industries requiring their labor. In Detroit in 1880, for example, 37 percent of the city's native-born families lived in one area, whereas 40 percent of the Irish inhabited the "Irish West Side." Over half the Germans and almost three-quarters of the Poles settled on the city's east side. Although such neighborhoods often had an ethnic flavor, with small specialty shops and foreign-language signs, they were not ethnic ghettos. Immigrants and native-born Americans often lived in the same neighborhoods, on the same streets, and even in the same houses. Toward the end of the century, when ethnic enclaves emerged, they were just that—enclaves within a neighborhood. Italians might live on one block, Jews on the next.

Working-class neighborhoods were often what would be called slums today. They were crowded and unsanitary and had inadequate public services. Many workers lived in houses once occupied by middle- and upper-class residents, now divided and subdivided to accommodate more people than the original builders had intended. Others crowded into tenements, specially constructed to house as many families as possible. Outdoor privies, often shared by several families, were the rule. Water came from outdoor hydrants, and women had to carry it inside for cooking, washing, and cleaning. When there were indoor fixtures, they frequently emptied waste directly into unpaved alleys and courts served by inadequate sewage systems or none at all. Piles of garbage and waste stank in the summer and froze in the winter. Even when people kept their own living quarters clean, their outside environment was unsanitary and unhealthy. It was no surprise that urban death rates were so high. Only at the turn of the century did the public health movement, particularly the efforts to treat water supplies with germ-killing chemicals, begin to ameliorate these living conditions.

Not every working-class family lived in abject circumstances. Skilled workers might rent comfortable

Downtown New York City in 1890 hosted a mixture of horse-drawn vehicles and the new "horseless carriages." The non-residential character of the central business district gave a special character to the late nineteenth century city. *(Brown Brothers)*

quarters, and a few even owned their own homes. A study of working-class families in Massachusetts found the family of one skilled worker living "in a tenement of five rooms in a pleasant and healthy locality, with good surroundings. The apartments are well furnished and [the] parlor carpeted." The family even had a sewing machine. But the unskilled and semiskilled workers were not so fortunate. The Massachusetts survey describes the family of an unskilled ironworker crammed into a tenement of four rooms,

> in an overcrowded block, to which belong only two privies for about fifty people. When this place was visited the vault had overflowed in the yard and the sink-water was also running in the same place, and created a stench that was really frightful. . . . The house inside, was badly furnished and dirty, and a disgrace to Worcester.

Drab as their neighborhoods usually were, working families created a community life that helped alleviate some of their dreary physical surroundings. The expense of moving around the city helped encourage a neighborhood and family focus. Long working hours meant that precious free time was apt to be spent close to home.

A wide range of institutions and associations came to life in urban neighborhoods and demonstrate that working-class men and women were not just victims of their environment. Frequently rooted in religious and ethnic identities, these organizations helped residents feel at home in the city. But they also could separate ethnic groups from one another and from native-born Americans. Irish associational life, for example, focused around the Roman Catholic parish church, its Irish priest, and its many religious services, clubs, and group activities. Catholicism had fused

with nationalism in an Ireland dominated by Protestant English landlords. In the new country, it provided comfort and a shared sense of identity. Irish nationalist organizations, ward politics, and Irish saloons gave men opportunities to meet, socialize, drink, and talk politics. Jews gathered in their synagogues, Hebrew schools, and Hebrew- and Yiddish-speaking literary groups. Germans had their family saloons and educational and singing societies. Although such activities may have slowed assimilation into American society and discouraged intergroup contact, they provided companionship, a social network, spiritual consolation, and a bridge between life in the "old country" and life in America.

Black Americans faced the most wretched living conditions of any group in the city. In the North, they often lived in segregated black neighborhoods. In southern cities, they gathered in back alleys and small streets. Many could afford only rented rooms.

However, a rich religious and associational life tempered the suffering. Black churches enjoyed phenomenal growth. Black members of mainline Protestant denominations separated from their white counterparts to establish autonomy and self-respect. The African Methodist Episcopal Church, with a membership of 20,000 in 1856, founded churches in every city and sizable town, and by 1900 claimed more than 400,000 members. Black worship continued to express the emotional exuberance that had characterized slave religion. Energetic preaching and expressive music helped make churchgoing a fulfilling spiritual experience. Often associated with churches were mutual-aid and benevolent societies that helped needy members of the community. Outreach activities also included support for black missionaries in Africa.

This photograph of a middle-class house in River Forest, Illinois, suggests the comfort available to those who could afford it and the ways suburban life shielded them from the squalor and ugliness of industrial life. *(Culver Pictures)*

Some urban blacks in the late nineteenth century rose into the middle class. In spite of the heavy odds against them, they created the nucleus of professional and artistic life. Henry Ossawa Tanner gained international recognition as a painter and sculptor, black educators such as George Washington Williams wrote some of the first African American histories, and novelists such as Charles W. Chesnutt, William Wells Brown, and Paul Laurence Dunbar produced noteworthy novels and short stories.

Beyond working-class neighborhoods and pockets of black housing lay streets of middle-class houses. Here lived the urban lower middle class: clerks, shopkeepers, bookkeepers, salesmen, and small tradesmen. Their salaries allowed them to buy or rent houses with some privacy and comfort. Separate spaces for cooking and laundry work kept hot and often odorous housekeeping tasks away from other living areas. Many houses boasted up-to-date gas lighting and bathrooms. Outside, the neighborhoods were cleaner and more attractive than in the inner city. Residents could pay for garbage collection, gaslights, and other improvements.

Streetcar Suburbs

On the fringes of the city were houses for the substantial middle class and the rich, who made their money in business, commerce, and the professions or inherited family fortunes. Public transportation sped them downtown to their offices and then home. For example, Robert Work, a modestly successful cap and hat merchant, moved his family to a $5,500 house in West Philadelphia in 1865 and commuted more than four miles to work.

The 1880 census revealed the Work family's comfortable lifestyle. The household contained two servants, two boarders, Robert's wife, and their eldest son, who was still in school. The Works' house had running hot and cold water, indoor bathrooms, central heating, and other modern conveniences of the age. Elaborately carved furniture, rugs, draperies, and lace curtains probably graced the downstairs, where the family entertained and gathered for meals. Upstairs, comfortable bedrooms provided a maximum of privacy for family members. The live-in servants, who did most of the housework, shared little of this space or privacy, however. They were restricted to the kitchen, the pantry, and bedrooms in the attic.

The Social Geography of the Cities

In industrial cities of this era, people were sorted by class, income, occupation, and race. Their circumstances not only dictated who would live comfortably with access to some of the conveniences and improvements industrial development had made possible but also affected family size and domestic life. Although the size of the middle-class family was shrinking over the course of the century, working-class and immigrant families remained large. In Buffalo, New York, in 1900, for example, middle-class families had 3.5 children while laboring families had 5.7. Because working-class children went out to work, large families made economic sense and represented one means of improving a family's wellbeing.

Upper- and middle-class neighborhoods and working-class neighborhoods were physically separated, so city dwellers often had little firsthand knowledge of people different from themselves. Ignorance led to distorted views and social disapproval. Reformers criticized working-class families for encouraging their children to leave school and work. Middle-class newspapers unsympathetically described laboring men as "loafing" and criticized the "crowds of idlers, who, day and night, infect Main Street." Yet those "idlers" were often men who could not find employment. The comments of a working-class woman to her temperance visitors in 1874 suggest the critical view from the bottom of society up: "When the rich stopped drinking, it would be time to speak to the poor about it."

⟆ THE LIFE OF THE MIDDLE CLASS

The sharp comments made by different classes of Americans suggest the economic polarization and social conflict that late-nineteenth-century industrialization spawned. Middle-class Americans found much to value in the new age: job and education opportunities, material comforts, and leisure time. Between 1865 and 1890, the average middle-class

This 1869 advertisement for a home washing machine shows an elegantly attired matron supervising her maids, who do the laundry in a well-equipped kitchen that includes a hot-water heater. Doing laundry was one of the most hated household chores, and even with this machine, wet clothes had to be put through a wringer. It was not until the 1930s that washers had the capacity to spin clothes dry. The arduous nature of laundering clothes accounted for the proliferation of laundries, often operated by the Chinese, in the nineteenth century. Although only a minority could afford washing machines in 1869, by 1941 a majority of American households owned a power-driven washer. *(The Granger Collection, New York)*

income had risen about 30 percent. Although the cost of living rose even faster than income, the difference was met by more family members holding jobs and by taking in lodgers. By 1900, fully 36 percent of urban families owned their homes.

The expansion of American industry raised the living standard for increasing numbers of Americans, who were better able to purchase consumer products manufactured, packaged, and promoted in an explosion of technological inventions and shrewd marketing techniques. Among the still familiar products and brands invented or mass-produced for the first time in the 1890s were Del Monte canned fruits and vegetables, National Biscuit Company (Nabisco) crackers, Van Camp's pork and beans, Wesson oil, Lipton tea, Wrigley's Juicy Fruit chewing gum, the Hershey bar, Aunt Jemima pancake mix, Jell-O, Campbell's soup, Coca-Cola, Pepsi-Cola, and Michelob beer. Cooked chopped meat put between two pieces of bread was first sold (for 7 cents) and called a "hamburger" in 1899.

More time for recreation like bicycling or watching professional baseball and greater access to consumer goods signaled the power of industrialism to transform the lives of middle-class Americans. Once favored with greater buying power, middle-class Americans sought to organize efficient ways of producing, purchasing, and consuming the newfound wealth. American women, agents of the rise in consumer spending, were themselves often on display as stylish objects of leisure and ostentatious wealth.

Shopping for home furnishings, clothes, and other items in the new department stores that began to appear in central business districts in the 1870s became an integral part of many middle-class women's lives. A plentiful supply of immigrant servant girls relieved urban middle-class wives of many housekeeping chores, and smaller families lessened the burdens of motherhood.

New Freedoms for Middle-Class Women

At the same time that many middle-class women enjoyed more leisure time and enhanced purchasing power, they won new freedoms. Several states granted women more property rights in marriage, adding to their growing sense of independence. Women, moreover, finally cast off confining crinolines and bustles. The new dress, a shirtwaist blouse and ankle-length skirt, was more comfortable for working, school, and sports. The *Ladies' Home Journal* recommended bicycling, tennis, golf, gymnastics—even having fewer babies—to women in the early 1890s. This "new woman," celebrated as *Life* magazine's active, healthy, slightly rebellious "Gibson girl," differed dramatically from the frail ideals of beauty admired earlier in the century.

Using their new freedom, women joined organizations of all kinds. Literary societies, charity groups, and reform clubs like the Women's Christian Temperance Union gave women organizational experience, awareness of their talents, and contact with people and problems away from their traditional family roles. The

Technology Changes the American People

THE FLUSH TOILET

✦

In the early nineteenth century, a resident of York, Pennsylvania, described a practice that most of us today regard with horror. Yet the scene he described could happen all too easily in the days before flush toilets. In York's North George Street, a Mr. Day indulged in "a bad practice by pouring out of the upper window his filthiness." Perhaps most of his neighbors were aware of Day's practice of emptying his chamber pot out of his window. But others were not prepared. Certainly, the bride and groom hurrying to their wedding did not know of Day's habits and, to their dismay, they were caught in the odorous discharge that "fouled" the bride's silk dress.

This small incident, surely not so small in the minds of the couple on their way to be married, reminds us of the realities of everyday American life in the first three centuries. For some rural Americans the elimination of waste was no problem. They just gravitated to a convenient spot outdoors when they felt the need. But in crowded places or areas where the weather was problematical, privies and chamber pots were common. Privies, called "necessary houses" or "outhouses," were used during the day. On farms, necessary houses were located in a convenient location, sometimes one connected to the house. In cities, the most common site was in the backyard. No matter where it was placed, the principle of the privy was simple: waste material passed directly into a pit (which might overflow and seep into the yard), or even into a nearby body of water. The most sanitary arrangement was the privy that channeled the waste into a special container that could be emptied from time to time. At night, people used chamber pots located in their bedroom. Sometimes enclosed in a wooden box and called a commode, the chamber pot was convenient. But for the servant or housewife who was responsible for emptying all the bedroom chamber pots, the chore of carrying them to

This elaborate victorian bathroom shows the importance given to the new room that gathered activities once performed separately into one space. *(Culver Pictures)*

the privy (or perhaps like Mr. Day taking the easy way out) was an unpleasant duty.

In 1849, Catharine Beecher, author of a series of widely read domestic advice books, urged her audience to consider installing an earth closet in their homes. The earth closet, as the name suggests, dumped earth on the waste and allowed it to decompose naturally. Although eventually the earth had to be carted away, the earth closet offered certain advantages: it worked without any water supply and saved the householder from the expense of pipes and other hardware.

Rapid development of a system depending on water occurred during the final decades of the nineteenth century. The water closet—although it needed a reliable water supply, fittings, and pipes, depended on municipal investment and decisions and, until technological problems were solved, could threaten health and safety (through poisonous sewer gases or the possibility of contamination, for example)—potentially offered the quickest and cleanest way to dispose of human waste. Flush toilets drew upon technological innovations connected with the development of steam power in the mid-eighteenth century. The many improvements that were necessary before flush toilets became a standard feature of American homes, however, resulted from years of experimentation by inventors on both sides of the Atlantic as well as by the unknown plumbers who came up with improvements through a process of trial and error. The development of a successful venting system stemmed from one American plumber's idea that vent pipes would work if the air pressure in the system was adjusted to the pressure of the air outside of the house. While the system he installed in 1874 reduced the odors, the pipes soon clogged. Other plumbers experimented with increasing the size of the vent pipes until eventually they solved the problem.

Some early luxury hotels had their own water and removal systems and installed working water closets for their guests. But until cities constructed adequate water and sewer systems,

real improvements in American sanitary arrangements would be slow. By 1875, most large American cities provided municipal water to at least some urban neighborhoods, and a few years later they began building sewer systems. The possibility of a large domestic market stimulated invention and experimentation. By 1900, innovations and the manufacturing of the essential components were common.

A description of some of the stages in the development of the flush toilet will provide an idea of some of the technological advances during the nineteenth century. The pan closet featured an earthenware bowl sitting on top of a copper pan holding several inches of water. When the user pushed a lever, the copper pan dumped the waste into a cast iron container connected to the drainage system. The siphonic closet, developed by John Randall Mann, in 1870, used water from three pipes. One provided water for the basin's flushing rim, another deposited water into the basin to start the action, while the other brought in new water after the flush. Many others made refinements to the siphonic closet in the last decades of the nineteenth century, while twentieth-century inventors offered improvements like placing the tank on top of the bowl, the arrangement with which we are familiar today.

For much of the nineteenth century, water closets were just that—toilets in closets. Gradually, first in elite and then in middle-class households, the bathtub, sink, and toilet came to be placed in one room. While we take this room for granted, think about the ways the flush toilet, along with the sink and bathtub, changed everyday life. What were the most important consequences of a working flush toilet? How did the toilet affect personal and family habits? Did the innovation influence the patterns and rhythms of each family member's daily routine equally? Do you think that the introduction of the toilet, bathtub, and sink into middle-class and upper-class homes may have contributed to tensions between class? Why or why not?

THE KELLY
SELF-ACTING
WATER CLOSET,
FOR HIGH OR LOW PRESSURES.

The valve is closed by a weighted lever and opened by a rod connecting the seat with the lever, while a pressure is brought to bear on the seat.

Sectional cut, showing how simple and substantial the valve is made. Preferred above all others by those who are acquainted with its merits.

Send for descriptive catalogue of Self-acting Urinals, Self-closing Hopper Cocks, etc.

THOS. KELLY & BROS.,
186 Dearborn Street, Chicago,

The washdown closet used water, stored in a tank above, to provide the needed power. When the user pulled a handle, a valve opened to release the water and to flush the waste away. *(Culver Pictures)*

In the late nineteenth century, middle-class women joined many different types of women's clubs that provided them with valuable educational and social experiences and even the opportunity to help solve public problems. The young women pictured here were members of the Saturday Morning Club formed in 1871. You see them in classical clothing. After hearing a lecture by a Harvard professor on the Greek play *Antigone,* the women decided to perform the play themselves. *(Schlesinger Library, Radcliffe Institute, Harvard University)*

General Federation of Women's Clubs, founded in 1890, boasted one million members by 1920. The depression of 1893 stimulated many women to become socially active, investigating slum and factory conditions, but some began this work even earlier. Jane Addams told her graduating classmates at the Rockford, Illinois, Female Seminary in 1881 to lead lives "filled with good works and honest toil," then went off herself to found Hull House, a social settlement that did more than its share of good works.

Job opportunities for these educated middle-class women were generally limited to the social services and teaching. Still regarded as a suitable female occupation, teaching was a highly demanding job as urban schools expanded under the pressure of a burgeoning population. Women teachers, frequently hired because they accepted lower pay than men, often faced classes of 40 to 50 children in poorly equipped rooms. In Poughkeepsie, New York, teachers earned the same salaries as school janitors. By the 1890s, the willingness of middle-class women to work for low pay opened up new forms of employment in office work, nursing, and clerking in department stores. In San Francisco, the number of clerical jobs doubled between 1852 and 1880. But moving up to high-status jobs proved difficult, even for middle-class women.

After the Civil War, educational opportunities for women expanded. New women's colleges such as Smith, Vassar, Bryn Mawr, and Goucher offered programs similar to those at competitive men's colleges, while state schools in the Midwest and the West dropped prohibitions against women. The number of women attending college rose. In 1890, some 13 percent of all college graduates were women; by 1900, this had increased to nearly 20 percent.

Higher education prepared middle-class women for conventional female roles as well as for work and public service. A few courageous graduates succeeded in joining the professions, but they had to overcome numerous barriers. Many medical schools refused to accept women students. As a Harvard doctor explained in 1875, a woman's monthly period "unfits her from taking those responsibilities which are to control questions often of life and death." Despite the obstacles, 2,500 women managed to become physicians and surgeons by 1880 (constituting 2.8 percent of the total). Women were less successful at breaking into the legal world. In 1880, fewer than 50 female lawyers practiced in the entire country, and as late as 1920, only 1.4 percent of the nation's lawyers and judges were women. George Washington University did not admit women to law school because mixed classes would be an "injurious diversion of attention of the students." Despite such resistance, by the early twentieth century the number of women professionals (including teachers) was increasing at three times the rate for men.

One reason for the greater independence of American middle-class women, especially those who were educated, is that they were having fewer babies. Advances in birth control technology (the modern diaphragm was developed in 1880) in addition to

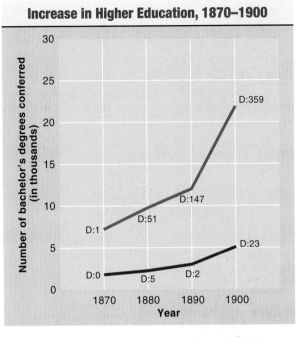

Increase in Higher Education, 1870–1900

Male graduates ▬ Female graduates **D** Recipients of doctorates

Note the rising pattern of college graduation, which suggests the professionalization of middle-class life. Source: U.S. Department of Commerce.

older devices like condoms and the use of abstinence helped make new patterns possible. Between 1850 and 1900, the number of live children born to white women fell from 5.42 to 3.56. In 1900, nearly one married woman in five was childless. Decreasing family size and an increase in the divorce rate (one out of 12 marriages in 1905) fueled men's fears that the new woman threatened the family, traditional sex roles, and social order. Theodore Roosevelt called this "race suicide," arguing that the falling white birthrate endangered national self-interest.

Arguments against the new woman intensified as many men reaffirmed Victorian stereotypes of the "woman's sphere." Magazine editors and ministers borrowed from biology, sociology, and theology to find "scientific" proof that a woman's place was at home. One male orator in 1896 attacked the new woman's public role because "a woman's brain involves emotions rather than intellect." This fact "painfully disqualifies her for the sterner duties to be performed by the intellectual faculties. The best wife and mother and sister would make the worst legislator, judge and police."

Many men worried about female independence because it threatened their own masculinity. Male campaigns against prostitution and for sex hygiene, as well as efforts to reinforce traditional sex roles, reflected their deeper fears that female passions

might weaken male vigor. The intensity of men's opposition to the new woman put limits on her emerging freedom.

Male Mobility and the Success Ethic

As middle-class women's lives were changing, so were men's. As the postwar economy expanded and the structure of American business changed, many new job opportunities opened up for middle-class men. The growing complexity of census classifications attests to some of them. Where once the census taker had noted only the occupation of "clerk," now were listed "accountant," "salesman," and "shipping clerk." As the lower ranks of the white-collar world became more specialized, the number of middle-class jobs increased.

To prepare for these new careers, Americans required more education. The number of public high schools in the United States increased from 160 in 1870 to 6,000 in 1900. By 1900, a majority of states and territories had compulsory school attendance laws.

Higher education also expanded in this period. The number of students in colleges and universities nearly doubled, from 53,000 in 1870 to 101,000 in 1900. Charles Eliot, president of Harvard from 1869 to 1909, led that university through a period of dynamic growth, introducing reforms such as higher faculty salaries and sabbatical leaves as well as the elective system of course selection for students. Harvard's growth reflected the rise of the university to a new stature in American life. As the land-grant state universities (made possible by the Morrill Act of 1862) continued to expand, generous gifts from wealthy businessmen helped found leading research universities such as Stanford, Johns Hopkins, and the University of Chicago.

These developments led to greater specialization and professionalism in education, medicine, law, and business. Before the Civil War, a Swedish pioneer in Wisconsin described a young mason who "laid aside the trowel, got himself some medical books, and assumed the title of doctor." But by the 1890s, with government licensing and the rise of professional schools, the word *career* began to take on its modern meaning. No longer were tradesmen likely to read up on medicine and become doctors. In this period, organizations like the American Medical Association and the American Bar Association were regulating and professionalizing membership. The number of law schools doubled in the last quarter of the century, and 86 new medical schools were founded in the same period. Dental schools increased from 9 to 56 between 1875 and 1900.

The need for lawyers, bankers, architects, and insurance agents to serve business and industry expanded career opportunities. Between 1870 and 1900, the number of engineers, chemists, metallurgists, and architects grew rapidly. As large companies formed and became bureaucratized, business required many more managerial positions. As the public sector expanded, new careers in social services and government opened up as well. Young professional experts with graduate training in the social sciences filled many of them. The professional disciplines of history, economics, sociology, psychology, and political science all date from the last 20 years of the nineteenth century.

The social ethic of the age stressed that economic rewards were available to anyone who fervently sought them. Many people argued that, unlike Europe, where family background and social class determined social rank, in America, few barriers held back those of good character and diligent work habits. Anyone doubting this opportunity needed only be reminded of the rise of two giants of industry. John D. Rockefeller had worked for a neighboring farmer and raised turkeys as a boy. Andrew Carnegie's mother was a washerwoman, and his father had worked himself to death in the mills within five years of reaching the United States. Both had risen spectacularly through their own efforts. Writers, lecturers, clergymen, and politicians zealously propagated the rags-to-riches tradition of upward mobility. Self-help manuals that outlined the steps to success for self-made men became widely available.

The best-known popularizer of the myth of the self-made man was Horatio Alger, Jr. Millions of boys read his 119 novels, with titles like *Luck and Pluck, Strive and Succeed,* and *Bound to Rise.* In a typical Alger novel, *Ragged Dick,* the story opens with the hero leading the low life of a shoeshine boy in the streets. Dressed in rags, he sleeps in packing crates and unwisely spends what little money he has on tobacco, liquor, gambling, and the theater. A chance opportunity to foil an attempt to cheat a gentleman results in the reward of a new suit of clothes for Dick. Before long, Dick aspires to become an office boy, "learn the business and grow up 'spectable." As he begins the process of becoming respectable, good fortune intervenes again. Dick is able to rescue a child who tumbles into the icy waters of the harbor. Her father completes the hero's transformation from Ragged Dick to Richard Hunter, Esq., by offering him a job as a clerk in his counting house. Although moralists pointed to virtuous habits as crucial in Alger's heroes, success often depended as much on luck as on pluck.

Unlimited and equal opportunity for upward advancement in America has never been as easy as the "bootstraps" ethic maintains. But the persistence of the success myth owes something to the fact that many Americans, particularly those who began well, did rise rapidly. Native-born, middle-class whites tended to have the skills, resources, and connections that opened up the most desirable jobs. Financier Jay Gould overstated the case in maintaining that "nearly every one that occupies a prominent position has come up from the ranks." In fact, the typical big businessman was a white, Anglo-Saxon Protestant from a middle- or upper-class family whose father was most likely in business, banking, or commerce.

INDUSTRIAL WORK AND THE LABORING CLASS

David Lawlor, an Irish immigrant who came to the United States in 1872, might have agreed with Jay Gould on the opportunities for mobility. As a child, he worked in the Fall River textile mills and read Horatio Alger in his free time. Like Alger's heroes, he went to night school and rose in the business world, eventually becoming an advertising executive.

But Lawlor's success was exceptional. Most working-class Americans labored long hours on dangerous factory floors, in cramped sweatshops, or in steamy basement kitchens for meager wages. As industrialization transformed the nature of work and the composition of the workforce, traditional opportunities for mobility and even for a secure livelihood slipped away from the grasp of many working-class Americans.

The Impact of Ethnic Diversity

Immigrants made up a sizable portion of the urban working class in the late nineteenth century. They formed 20 percent of the labor force and over 40 percent of laborers in the manufacturing and extractive industries. In cities, where they tended to settle, they accounted for more than half the working-class population.

The fact that more than half the urban industrial class was foreign and unskilled and often had only a limited command of English influenced industrial work, urban life, labor protest, and local politics. Eager for the unskilled positions rapidly being created as mechanization and mass production took hold, immigrants often had little in common with native-born workers or even with one another. Because of immigration, American working-class society was a mosaic of nationalities, cultures, religions, and interests, a patchwork where colors clashed as often as they complemented one another.

The ethnic diversity of the industrial workforce helps explain its occupational patterns. Although every city offered somewhat different employment opportunities, generally occupation was related to ethnic background and experience.

The picture of a puddler at work makes the physical demands of his job and the harsh environment of his workplace clear. While we might be dismayed by the nature of the puddler's job, puddling was an occupation that demanded skill and paid well. *(Courtesy of Rivers of Steel Archives)*

At the top of the working-class hierarchy, native-born Protestant whites held a disproportionate share of well-paying skilled jobs. They were the aristocrats of the working class. Their jobs demanded expertise and training, as had been true of skilled industrial workers in the pre–Civil War period. But their occupations bore the mark of late-nineteenth-century industrialism. They were machinists, iron puddlers and rollers, engineers, foremen, conductors, carpenters, plumbers, mechanics, and printers.

Beneath native-born whites, skilled northern European immigrants filled most of the positions in the middle ranks of the occupational structure. The Germans, who arrived with training as tailors, bakers, brewers, and shoemakers, moved into similar jobs in

this country, and Cornish and Irish miners secured skilled jobs in western mines. The Jews, who had tailoring experience in their homelands, became the backbone of the garment industry (where they faced little competition from American male workers, who considered it unmanly to work on women's clothes).

But most of the "new immigrants" from southern and central Europe had no urban industrial experience. They labored in the unskilled, dirty jobs near the bottom of the occupational ladder. They relined blast furnaces in steel mills, carried raw materials or finished products from place to place, or cleaned up after skilled workers. Often, they were carmen or day laborers on the docks, ditchdiggers, or construction workers. Hiring was often on a daily basis, often arranged through middlemen like the Italian padrone. Unskilled work provided little in the way of either job stability or income.

At the bottom, blacks occupied the most marginal positions as janitors, servants, porters, and laborers. Racial discrimination generally excluded them from industrial jobs, even though their occupational background differed little from that of rural white immigrants. There were always plenty of whites eager to work, so it was not necessary to hire blacks except occasionally as scabs during a labor strike. "It is an exceptional case where you find any colored labor in the factories, except as porters," observed one white. "Neither colored female . . . nor male laborer is engaged in the mechanical arts."

The Changing Nature of Work

The rise of big business, which relied on mechanization for the mass production of goods, changed the size and shape of the workforce and the nature of work itself. More and more Americans were wage

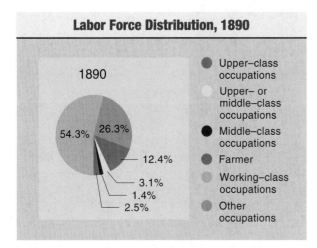

Labor Force Distribution, 1890

1890

54.3%   26.3%

12.4%

3.1%

1.4%

2.5%

● Upper–class occupations
○ Upper– or middle–class occupations
● Middle–class occupations
● Farmer
● Working–class occupations
● Other occupations

Whereas a majority of Americans in the twentieth century defined themselves as middle-class, in the nineteenth century most Americans held working-class jobs. Source: U.S. Bureau of the Census.

earners rather than independent artisans. The number of manufacturing workers doubled between 1880 and 1900, with the fastest expansion in the unskilled and semiskilled ranks.

But the need for skilled workers remained. New positions, as in steam fitting and structural ironwork, appeared as industries expanded and changed. Increasingly, older skills became obsolete, however. And all skilled workers faced the possibility that technical advances would eliminate their favored status or that employers would eat away at their jobs by having unskilled helpers take over parts of them. In industries as different as shoemaking, cigar making, and iron puddling, new methods of production and organization undermined the position of skilled workers.

Work Settings and Experiences

The workplace could be a dock or cluttered factory yard, a multistoried textile mill, a huge barnlike steel mill with all the latest machinery, or a mine tunnel hundreds of feet underground. A majority of American manufacturing workers now labored in factories (rather than the shops of an earlier age), and the numbers of those working in large plants dominated by the unceasing rhythms of machinery increased steadily.

Some Americans, however, still toiled in small shops and sweatshops tucked away in basements, lofts, or immigrant apartments. Even in these smaller settings, the pressure to produce was almost as relentless as in the factory, for volume, not hours, determined pay. When contractors cut wages, workers had to speed up to earn the same pay.

The organization of work divided workers from one another. Those paid by the piece competed against the speed, agility, and output of other workers. It was hard to feel any bonds with these unknown and unseen competitors. In large factories, workers separated into small work groups and mingled only rarely with the rest of the workforce. The clustering of ethnic groups in certain types of work also undermined working-class solidarity.

All workers had one thing in common: a very long working day. Although the workday had fallen from the 12 hours expected in factories before the Civil War, people still spent over half their waking hours on the job—usually ten hours a day, six days a week. Different occupations had specific demands. Bakers worked 65 hours a week; canners, 77. Sweatshop workers might labor far into the night long after factory workers had gone home.

Work was usually unhealthy, dangerous, and comfortless. Although a few states passed laws to regulate work conditions, enforcement was spotty. Few owners paid attention to regulations on toilets, drinking facil-

ities, or washing areas. Poorly ventilated mines, for example, stank of human waste and spoiled garbage. Nor did owners concern themselves with the health or safety of their employees. Women bent over sewing machines developed digestive illnesses and curved spines. In some mines, workers labored in temperatures of over 120 degrees, handled dynamite, and died in cave-ins caused by inadequate timber supports in the mine shafts. When new drilling machinery was introduced into western mines, the shafts were filled with tiny stone particles that caused lung disease.

Accident rates in the United States far exceeded those of Europe's industrial nations. Each year, 35,000 workers died from industrial mishaps. Iron and steel mills were the big killers, although the railroads alone accounted for 6,000 fatalities a year during the 1890s. Nationwide, nearly one-quarter of the men reaching the age of 20 in 1880 would not live to see 44 (compared with 7 percent today). American business owners had little legal responsibility—and some felt none—for employees' safety or health. The law placed the burden of avoiding accidents on workers, who were expected to quit if they thought conditions were unsafe.

Industrial workers labored at jobs that were also increasingly specialized and monotonous. The size of many firms allowed a kind of specialization that was impossible in a small enterprise. Even skilled workers did not produce a complete product, and the range of their skills was narrowing. "A man never learns the machinist's trade now," one New Yorker grumbled.

Factory work was usually uncomfortable and hazardous. Here workers in the Stetson hat factory, none of them with proper back support, cut fur hats to be sewn together by hand. The sexual division of labor is clear in the picture. *(Philadelphia Commercial Museum, Pennsylvania State Archives)*

"The different branches of the trade are divided and subdivided so that one man may make just a particular part of a machine and may not know anything whatever about another part of the same machine." Cabinetmakers found themselves not crafting cabinets but putting together and finishing pieces made by others. In such circumstances, many skilled workers complained that they were being reduced to drudges and wage slaves.

Still, industrial work provided some personal benefits. New arrangements helped humanize the workplace. Workers who obtained their jobs through family and friends found themselves in the same departments with them. In most industries, the foreman controlled day-to-day activities. He chose workers from the crowds at the gate, fired those who proved unsatisfactory, selected appropriate materials and equipment, and determined the order and pace of production. Because the foreman was himself a member of the working class who had climbed his way up, he might sympathize with subordinates. Yet the foreman could also be authoritarian and harsh, especially if the workers he supervised were unskilled or belonged to another ethnic group.

The Worker's Share in Industrial Progress

The huge fortunes accumulated by famous industrialists like Andrew Carnegie and John D. Rockefeller during the late nineteenth century dramatized the pattern of wealth concentration that had begun in the early period of industrialization. In 1890, the top 1 percent of American families possessed over a quarter of the wealth, whereas the share held by the top 10 percent was about 73 percent. Economic growth still benefited people who influenced its path, and they claimed the lion's share of the rewards.

But what of the workers who tended the machines that lay at the base of industrial wealth? Working-class Americans made up the largest segment of the labor force (more than 50 percent), so their experience reveals important facets of the American social and economic system and American values.

Statistics of increasing production, of ever more goods, tell part of the story. Figures on real wages also reveal something important. Industry still needed skilled workers and paid them well. Average real wages rose over 50 percent between 1860 and 1900. Skilled manufacturing workers, about a tenth of the nonagricultural working class in the late nineteenth century, saw their wages rise by about 74 percent. But wages for the unskilled increased by only 31 percent. The differential was substantial and widened as the century drew to a close.

Taken as a whole, the working class accrued substantial benefits in the late nineteenth century, even if its share of the total wealth did not increase. American workers had more material comforts than their European counterparts. But the general picture conceals the realities of working-class economic life. A U.S. Bureau of Labor study of working-class families in

TWO NINETEENTH-CENTURY BUDGETS

	Monthly budget of a laborer, his wife and one child in 1891; his income is $23.67	Monthly budget of a married bank accountant with no children in 1892; his income is about $66.50
Food	$6.51	$13.22
Rent	9.02	9.88
Furniture	3.61	0.30
Taxes and insurance	3.32	7.11
Utilities	2.94	4.99
Sundries	1.09	2.10
Liquor and tobacco	0.66	0.42
Medicine	0.29	0.27
Clothes	0.21	0.19
Dry goods	0.16	2.45
Postage	0.10	
Transportation	0.08	1.71
Reading material		0.53
	$27.99	$43.17

The differences between these two family budgets capture different standards of living and different consumption choices. In 1999 dollars, the laborer took home $426 a month while the accountant earned almost $2000 a month.
Source: Olivier Zunz, *The Changing Face of Inequality* (1982).

1889 revealed great disparities of income: a young girl in a silk mill made $130 a year; a laborer earned $384 a year; a carpenter took home $686. The carpenter's family lived in a four-room house. Their breakfast usually included meat or eggs, hotcakes, butter, cake, and coffee. The silk worker and the laborer, by contrast, ate bread and butter as the main portion of two of their three daily meals. Their yearly income fell far short of the $600 to $800 that was necessary for a family to survive in any comfort.

For workers without steady employment, rising real wages were meaningless. Workers, especially those who were unskilled, often found work only sporadically. When times were slow or conditions depressed, as they were between 1873 and 1879 and 1893 and 1897, employers, especially in small firms, laid off both skilled and unskilled workers and reduced wages. Even in a good year like 1890, one out of every five men outside of agriculture had been unemployed at least a month. One-quarter lost four months or more.

Unemployment insurance did not exist, so workers had no cushion against losing their jobs. One woman grimly recalled, "If the factory shuts down without warning, as it did last year for six weeks, we have a growing expense with nothing to counterbalance." Older workers who had no social security or those who had accidents on the job but no disability insurance had severely reduced incomes. Occasionally, kindhearted employers offered assistance in hard times, but it was rarely enough. The Lawrence Manufacturing Company compensated one of its workers $50 for the loss of a hand and awarded another $66.71 for a severed arm.

Although nineteenth-century ideology pictured men as breadwinners, many working-class married men could not earn enough to support their families alone. A working-class family's standard of living thus often depended on its number of workers. Today, two-income families are common. But in the nineteenth century, married women did not usually take outside employment, although they contributed to family income by taking in sewing, laundry, and boarders. In 1890, only 3.3 percent of married women were to be found in the paid labor force.

The Family Economy

If married women did not work for pay outside their homes, their children did. The laborer whose annual earnings amounted to only $384 depended on his 13-year-old son, not his wife, to go out and earn an extra $196, critical to the family's welfare. Sending children into the labor market was an essential survival strategy for many working-class Americans. In 1880, one-fifth of the nation's children between the ages of 10 and 14 held jobs.

UNEMPLOYMENT RATES, 1870–1899			
Period	Average Percent Unemployed	Peak Year	Percent Unemployed in Peak Year
1870–1879	10	1876	12–14
1880–1889	4	1885	6–8
1890–1899	10	1894	15+

These figures are only estimates because national unemployment statistics were not kept.

Child labor was closely linked to a father's income, which in turn depended on skill, ethnic background, and occupation. Immigrant families more frequently sent their young children out to work (and also had more children) than native-born families. Middle-class reformers sentimentalized childhood and thus disapproved of parents who put their children to work. As one investigator of working-class life reported, "Father never attended school, and thinks his children will have sufficient schooling before they reach their tenth year, thinks no advantage will be gained from longer attendance at school, so children will be put to work as soon as able." Reformers believed that such fathers condemned their children to future poverty by taking them out of school. Actually, sending children to work was a means of coping with the immediate threat of poverty, of financing the education of one of the children, or paying off the mortgage.

Many more young people over 14 were working for wages than was the case for children. Half of all Philadelphia's students had quit school by that age. Daughters as well as sons were expected to take positions, although young women from immigrant families were more likely to work than young American women. As *Arthur's Home Magazine* for women pointed out, a girl's earnings would help "to relieve her hard-working father of the burden of her support, to supply home with comforts and refinements, to educate a younger brother." By 1900, nearly 20 percent of American women were in the labor force.

Employed women earned far less than men. An experienced female factory worker might be paid between $5 and $6 a week, whereas an unskilled male laborer could make about $8. Discrimination, present from women's earliest days in the workforce, persisted. Still, factory jobs were desirable because they often paid better than other kinds of work open to women.

Employment opportunities for women were narrow, and ethnic taboos and cultural traditions helped shape choices. About a quarter of working women secured factory jobs. Italian and Jewish women (whose cultural backgrounds virtually forbade

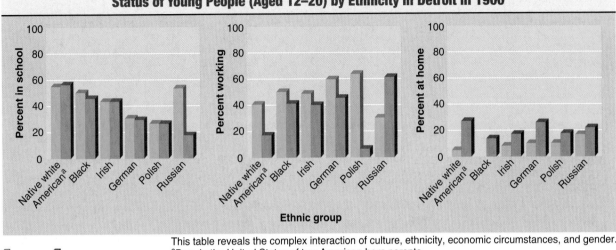

Status of Young People (Aged 12–20) by Ethnicity in Detroit in 1900

male   female

This table reveals the complex interaction of culture, ethnicity, economic circumstances, and gender.
[a]Born in the United States of two American-born parents.
Source: Olivier Zunz, *The Changing Face of Inequality* (1982)

their going into domestic service) clustered in the garment industry, and Poles and Slavs went into textiles, food processing, and meatpacking. In some industries, like textiles, women composed an important segment of the workforce. But about 40 percent of them, especially those from Irish, Scandinavian, and black families, took jobs as maids, cooks, laundresses, and nurses.

Domestic service was arduous, with few machines to lighten the labor. A Minneapolis housemaid described an exhausting routine. "I used to get up at four o'clock every morning and work till ten P.M. every day of the week. Mondays and Tuesdays, when the washing and ironing was to be done, I used to get up at two o'clock and wash or iron until breakfast time." Nor could domestics count on much sympathy from their employers. "Do not think it necessary to give a hired girl as good a room as that used by members of the family," said one lady of the house. "She should sleep near the kitchen and not go up the front stairs or through the front hall to reach her room."

A servant received room and board plus $2 to $5 a week. The fact that so many women took domestic work despite the job's disadvantages speaks clearly of their limited opportunities.

The dismal situation facing working women drove some, like Rose Haggerty, into prostitution. Burdened with a widowed and sickly mother and four young brothers and sisters, Rose was only 14 when she started work at a New York paper bag factory. She earned $10 a month, but $6 went for rent. Her fortunes improved when a friend helped her buy a sewing machine. Rose then sewed shirts at home, often working as long as 14 hours a day, to support her family. Suddenly, the piecework rate for shirts was slashed in half. In desperation, Rose contemplated suicide. But

when a sailor offered her money for spending the night with him, she realized she had an alternative. Prostitution meant food, rent, and heat for her family. "Let God Almighty judge who's to blame most," the 20-year-old Rose reflected, "I that was driven, or them that drove me to the pass I'm in."

Prostitution appears to have increased in the late nineteenth century, although there is no way of knowing the actual numbers of women involved. Probably most single women accepted the respectable jobs open to them. They tolerated discrimination and low wages because their families depended on their contributions. They also knew that when they married, they would probably leave the paid workforce forever.

Marriage hardly ended women's work, however. Like colonial families, late-nineteenth-century working-class families operated as cooperative economic units. The unpaid domestic labor of working-class wives was critical to family survival. With husbands away for 10 to 11 hours a day, women bore the burden and loneliness of caring for children. They did all the domestic chores. Because working-class families could not afford labor-saving conveniences, housework was time-consuming and arduous. Without a refrigerator, a working-class woman spent part of each day shopping for food (more expensive in small quantities). The washing machine, advertised to do the "ordinary washing of a family in only one or two hours," was out of the question with a price tag of $15. Instead, women carried water from outside pumps, heated it on the stove, washed clothes, rinsed them with fresh water, and hung them up to dry. Ironing was a hot and unpleasant job in small and stuffy quarters. Keeping an apartment or house clean when the atmosphere was grimy and unpaved roads were littered with refuse and horse dung was a challenge.

Recovering the Past

CONGRESSIONAL HEARINGS

Students of history can discover fascinating materials on nineteenth-century life by exploring the published records of the American political system. The *Congressional Globe,* the proceedings of the Senate and the House, privately published from 1833 to 1873, reveals the nature of congressional deliberations in an era when debate, such as that over the Compromise of 1850 in the Senate, was the focus of the national political process. After 1873, the government published these proceedings in the *Congressional Record.* The *Record* is not a literal transcription of debate, for members can edit their remarks, insert speeches, and add supporting materials. Still, it gives a good sense of the proceedings of both the Senate and the House.

Much of the serious work of government, past and present, takes place in congressional committees. One foreign observer called Congress "not so much a legislative assembly as a huge panel from which committees are selected." The committee system is almost as old as the constitutional system itself and is rooted in the Constitution's granting of the lawmaking power to Congress. From the start, Congress divided into assorted committees to gather information, enabling members to evaluate legislative proposals intelligently.

Two kinds of committees existed in the House and Senate. Standing committees had permanent responsibility for reviewing legislative proposals on a host of financial, judicial, foreign, and other affairs. By 1892, the Senate had 44 standing committees, and the House had 50. Select committees were temporary, often charged with investigating specific problems. In the late nineteenth century, congressional committees investigated such problems as Ku Klux Klan terrorism, the sweatshop system, tenement house conditions, and relations between labor and capital. In each case, extensive hearings were held.

Congressional hearings have become increasingly important sources of historical evidence in recent years. They show the Senate and the House of Representatives in action as they seek to translate popular sentiment into law. But they also reveal public attitudes themselves as they record the voices of Americans testifying in committee halls. Because one function of legislative hearings is to enable diverse groups to express their frustrations and desires, they often contain the testimony of witnesses drawn from many different social and economic backgrounds. Included here is the partial testimony of a Massachusetts laborer who appeared before the Senate Committee on Education and Labor in 1883. Because working-class witnesses like this man usually left no other record of their experiences or thoughts, committee reports and hearings provide valuable insight into the lives and attitudes of ordinary people.

Hearings also reveal the attitudes and social values of committee members. Hence, caution is needed in the use of hearings. Witnesses often have vested interests and are frequently coached and cautious in what they communicate on the stand. Committee members often speak and explore questions for other reasons, usually political, than to illuminate issues.

Despite these limitations, committee hearings are rich sources of information. In this excerpt, what can you learn about the life of the witness testifying before the committee? In what way are the values of the committee members in conflict with those of the witness? Why is the chairman so harsh toward the witness? Is he entirely unsympathetic? Why do you think the questioner overemphasizes the relationship between moral beliefs and economic realities? What kind of social tensions does the passage reveal?

Have you observed any recent hearings of congressional investigating committees on television? Are moral behavior and hunger still topics of concern for Americans? How is the interaction between modern haves and have-nots similar to and different from those between this laborer and the committee members in 1883? Do ethical beliefs and economic realities still separate social classes?

Hearings on the Relations Between Labor and Capital

Q. You get a dollar a day, wages?—A. That is the average pay that men receive. The rents, especially in Somerville, are so high that it is almost impossible for the working men to live in a house.

Q. What rent do you pay?—A. For the last year I have been paying $10 a month, and most of the men out there have to pay about that amount for a house—$10 a month for rooms.

Q. For a full house, or for rooms only?—A. For rooms in a house.

Q. How many rooms?—A. Four or five.

Q. How much of your time have you been out of work, or idle, for the last full year, say?—A. I have not been out of work more than three weeks altogether, because I have been making a dollar or two peddling or doing something, when I was out of work, in the currying line.

Q. Making about the same that you made at your trade?—A. Well, I have made at my trade a little more than that, but that is the average.

Q. Are you a common drunkard?—A. No, sir.

Q. Do you smoke a great deal?—A. Well, yes, sir; I smoke as much as any man.

The CHAIRMAN. I want to know how much you have got together in the course of a year, and what you have spent your money for, so that folks can see whether you have had pay enough to get rich on.

The WITNESS. A good idea.

The CHAIRMAN. That is precisely the sort of idea that people ought to know. How much money do you think you have earned during this last year; has it averaged a dollar a day for three hundred days?

The WITNESS. I have averaged more than that; I have averaged $350 or $400. I will say, for the year.

Q. You pay $10 a month rent; that makes $120 a year?—A. Yes, sir.

The CHAIRMAN. I have asked you these questions in this abrupt way because I want to find out whether you have spent much for practices that might have been dispensed with. You say you smoke?

The WITNESS. Yes, sir.

Q. How much a week do you spend for that?—A. I get 20 cents worth of tobacco a week.

Q. That is $10.40 a year?—A. Yes, sir.

Q. And you say you are not a common drunkard?—A. No, sir.

Q. Do you imagine that you have spent as much more for any form of beer, or ale, or anything of that kind, that you could have got along without?—A. No, sir.

Q. How much do you think has gone in that way?—A. About $1 or $2.

Q. During the whole year?—A. Yes, sir.

Q. That would make $11.40 or $12.40—we will call it $12—gone for wickedness. Now, what else, besides your living, besides the support of your wife and children?—A. Well, I don't know as there is anything else.

Q. Can you not think of anything else that was wrong?—A. No, sir.

Q. Twelve dollars have gone for sin and iniquity; and $120 for rent; that makes $132?—A. Yes.

Q. How many children have you?—A. Two.

Q. Your family consists of yourself, your wife, and two children?—A. Yes.

Q. One hundred and thirty-two dollars from $400 leaves you $268, does it not?—A. Yes, sir.

Q. And with that amount you have furnished your family?—A. Yes, sir.

Q. You have been as economical as you could, I suppose?—A. Yes.

Q. How much money have you left?—A. Sixty dollars in debt.

Q. How did you do that?—A. I don't know, sir.

Q. Can you not think of something more that you have wasted?—A. No, sir.

Q. Have you been as careful as you could?—A. Yes, sir.

Q. And you have come out at the end of the year $60 in debt?—A. Yes, sir.

Q. Have you been extravagant in your family expenses?—A. No, sir; a man can't be very extravagant on that much money. . . .

Q. And there are four of you in the family?—A. Yes, sir.

Q. How many pounds of beefsteak have you had in your family, that you bought for your own home consumption within this year that we have been speaking of?—A. I don't think there has been five pounds of beefsteak.

Q. You have had a little pork steak?—A. We had a half a pound of pork steak yesterday; I don't know when we had any before.

Q. What other kinds of meat have you had within a year?—A. Well, we have had corn beef twice I think that I can remember this year—on Sunday, for dinner.

Q. Twice is all that you can remember within a year?—A. Yes—and some cabbage.

Q. What have you eaten?—A. Well, bread mostly, when we could get it; we sometimes couldn't make out to get that, and have had to go without a meal.

Q. Has there been any day in the year that you have had to go without anything to eat?—A. Yes, sir, several days.

Q. More than one day at a time?—A. No.

Q. How about the children and your wife—did they go without anything to eat too?—A. My wife went out this morning and went to a neighbor's and got a loaf of bread and fetched it home, and when she got home the children were crying for something to eat.

Q. Have the children had anything to eat to-day except that, do you think?—A. They had that loaf of bread—I don't know what they have had since then, if they have had anything.

Q. Did you leave any money at home?—A. No, sir.

Q. If that loaf is gone, is there anything in the house?—A. No, sir; unless my wife goes out and gets something; and I don't know who would mind the children while she goes out.

These domestics, in their best clothes, pose with the symbol of their work in what appears to be the parlor. Although there is no way to ascertain the background of these young women, a majority of domestic servants were Irish or Irish American. Domestic work was often exhausting and provided little privacy or free time, but many women were attracted by the opportunity to live in a middle-class home and to have regular meals. In addition, domestic work often paid better than factory work. Still, some young women avoided service, explaining that "it's freedom that we want when the day's work is done." *(State Historical Society of Wisconsin, neg. #WHi (V22) 1387)*

As managers of family resources, married women had important responsibilities. What American families had once produced for themselves now had to be bought. It was up to the working-class wife to scour secondhand shops to find cheap clothes for her family. Here small domestic economies were vital to survival. "In summer and winter alike," one woman explained, "I must try to buy the food that will sustain us the greatest number of meals at the lowest price."

Women also supplemented family income by taking in work. Jewish and Italian women frequently did piecework and sewing at home. In the Northeast and the Midwest, between 10 and 40 percent of all working-class families kept boarders. Immigrant families in particular often made ends meet by taking single young countrymen into their homes. The cost was the added burden of work (providing meals and clean laundry), the need to juggle different work schedules, and the sacrifice of privacy. But the advantages of extra income far outweighed the disadvantages for many working-class families.

Black women's working lives reflected the obstacles blacks faced in late-nineteenth-century cities. Although few married white women worked outside the home, black women did so both before and after marriage. In southern cities in 1880, about three-quarters of single black women and one-third of married women worked outside the home. This contrasted to rates for white women of 24 and 7 percent, respectively. Because industrial employers would not hire black women, most of them had to work as domestics or laundresses. The high percentage of married black

women in the labor force reflected the marginal wages their husbands earned. But it may also be explained partly by the lesson learned during slavery that children could thrive without the constant attention of their mothers.

CAPITAL VERSUS LABOR

Class conflict characterized late-nineteenth-century industrial life. Although workers welcomed the progress the factory made possible, many rejected their employers' values, which emphasized individual gain at the expense of collective good. While owners reaped most of the profits, bad pay, poor working conditions, and long hours were turning workers into wage slaves. Fashioning their arguments from their republican legacy, workers claimed that the degradation of the country's citizen laborers threatened to undermine the republic itself.

On-the-Job Protests

Workers and employers engaged in a struggle over who would control the workplace. Many workers staunchly resisted unsatisfactory working conditions and the tendency of bosses to treat them "like any other piece of machinery, to be made to do the maximum amount of work with the minimum expenditure of fuel." Skilled workers, like iron puddlers and glassblowers, had indispensable knowledge about the production process and practical experience and were in a key position to direct on-the-job actions. Sometimes their goal was to retain control over critical work decisions.

Detroit printers, for example, struggled to hold on to the privilege of distributing headlines and white space (the "fat") rather than letting their bosses hand out the fat as a special reward and means of increasing competition among workers. Others hoped to humanize work. Cigar makers clung to their custom of having one worker read to others as they performed their tedious chores. Often, workers sought to control the pace of production.

Workers also resisted owners' attempts to grasp large profits through unlimited production. Too many goods meant an inhuman pace of work and might result in overproduction, massive layoffs, and a reduction in the prices paid for piecework. Thus, workers established informal production quotas. An experienced worker might whisper to a new hand, "See here, young fellow, you're working too fast. You'll spoil our job for us if you don't go slower."

A newspaper account of a glassblower's strike in 1884 illustrates the clash between capital and labor. With an eye toward bigger profits, the boss tried to increase production. "He knew if the limit was taken off, the men could work ten or twelve hours every day in the week; that in their thirst for the mighty dollar they would kill themselves with labor; they would 'black sheep' their fellows by doing the labor of two men." But his employees resisted his proposal, refusing to drive themselves to exhaustion for a few dollars more. Their goal was not riches but a decent pace of work and a respectable wage. Thus "they thundered out no. They even offered to take a reduction that would average ten percent all around, but they said, 'We will keep the forty-eight box limit.' Threats and curses would not move them."

In attempting to protect themselves and preserve the dignity of their labor, workers devised ways of combating employer attempts to speed up the production process. Denouncing fellow workers who refused to honor production codes as "hogs," "runners," "chasers," and "job wreckers," they ostracized and even injured them. As the banner of the Detroit Coopers' Union proudly proclaimed at a parade in 1880: "Each for himself is the bosses' plea/ [but] Union for all will make you free."

Absenteeism, drunkenness at work, and general inefficiency were other widespread worker practices that contained elements of protest. In three industrial firms in the late nineteenth century, one-quarter of the workers stayed home at least one day a week. Some of these lost days were due to layoffs, but not all. The efforts of employers to impose stiff fines on absent workers suggested their frustration at uncooperative workers.

To a surprising extent, workers made the final protest by quitting their jobs altogether. Most employers responded by penalizing workers who left without giving sufficient notice—to little avail. A Massachusetts labor study in 1878 found that although two-thirds of them had been in the same occupation for more than ten years, only 15 percent of the workers surveyed were in the same job. A similar rate of turnover occurred in the industrial workforce in the early twentieth century. Workers unmistakably and clearly voted with their feet.

Strike Activity After 1876

The most direct and strenuous attempts to change conditions in the workplace came in the form of thousands of strikes punctuating the late nineteenth century. In 1877, railroad workers staged the first and most violent nationwide industrial strike of the nineteenth century. The immediate cause of the disturbance was the railroad owners' decision to reduce wages. But the rapid spread of the strike from Baltimore to Pittsburgh and then to cities as distant as San Francisco, Chicago, and Omaha, as well as the violence of the strikers, who destroyed railroad property and kept trains idle, indicated more fundamental discontent.

An erratic economy, high unemployment rates, and the lack of job security all contributed to the conflagration. Over 100 people died before federal troops ended the strike. The frenzied response of the propertied class, which saw the strike as the beginning of revolution and favored the intervention of the military, forecast the pattern of later conflicts. Time and time again, middle- and upper-class Americans would turn to the power of the state to crush labor activism.

A wave of confrontations followed the strike of 1877. Between 1881 and 1905, a total of 36,757 strikes erupted, involving over six million workers—three times the strike activity in France.

These numbers indicate that far more than the "poorest part" of the workers were involved. Many investigations of this era found evidence of widespread working-class discontent. When Samuel M. Hotchkiss, commissioner of the Connecticut Bureau of Labor Statistics, informally surveyed the state's workers in 1887, he was shocked by the "feeling of bitterness," the "distrust of employers," the "discontent and unrest." These sentiments exploded into strikes, sabotage, and violence, most often linked to demands for higher wages and shorter hours.

Nineteenth-century strike activity underwent important changes, however, as the consciousness of American workers expanded. In the period of early industrialization, discontented laborers rioted in their neighborhoods rather than at their workplaces. The Lowell protests of the 1830s (Chapter 10) were not typical. Between 1845 and the Civil War, however, strikes at the workplace began to replace neighborhood riots.

This depiction of working-class unrest appeared in *Harper's Weekly* in 1894. Note the prominence of the destruction wrought by the enraged workers and the artist's decision to place the National Guardsmen in the foreground. Contrast the individualized guardsmen with the faceless mob in the background. The artist's choices convey his sympathy with the forces of order. *(The Granger Collection, New York)*

Although workers showed their anger against their employers by turning out and often calling for higher wages, they had only a murky sense that the strike could be a weapon to force employers to improve working conditions.

As industrialization transformed work and an increasing percentage of the workforce entered factories, collective actions at the workplace spread. Local and national unions played a more important role in organizing protest, conducting 60 percent of the strikes between 1881 and 1905. As working-class leaders realized more clearly the importance of collective action in dealing with their opponents and perceived that transportation had knit the nation together, they also tried to coordinate local and national efforts. By 1891, more than one-tenth of the strikes called by unionized workers were sympathy strikes. Coordination among strikers employed by different companies improved as workers tried to order capitalism by making the same wage demands. Finally, wages among the most highly unionized workers became less of an issue. Workers sought more humane conditions. Some attempted to end subcontracting and the degradation of skills. Others, like the glassblowers, struggled to enforce work rules. Indeed, by the early 1890s, over one-fifth of strikes involved the rules governing the workplace.

Labor Organizing, 1865–1900

The Civil War experience colored labor organizing in the postwar years. As one working-class song pointed out, workers had borne the brunt of that struggle.

> *You gave your son to the war*
> *The rich man loaned his gold*
> *And the rich man's son is happy to-day,*
> *And yours is under the mold.*

Now workers who had fought to save the Union argued that wartime sacrifices justified efforts to gain justice and equality in the workplace.

Labor leaders quickly realized the need for national as well as local organizations to protect the laboring class against "despotic employers." In 1866, several craft unions and reform groups formed the National Labor Union (NLU). Claiming 300,000 members by the early 1870s, the organization supported a range of causes, including temperance, women's rights, and the establishment of cooperatives to bring the "wealth of the land" into "the hands of those who produce it," thus ending "wage slavery."

The call for an eight-hour day reveals some of the basic assumptions of the organized labor movement. Few workers saw employers as a hostile class or felt it necessary to overturn the economic system. But they did believe bosses were often dangerous tyrants whose time demands threatened to turn citizens into slaves. The eight-hour day would curb the power of owners and allow workers the time to cultivate the qualities necessary for republican citizenship.

Many of the NLU's specific goals survived, although the organization did not. An unsuccessful attempt to create a political party and the depression of 1873 decimated the NLU and many local unions as well. Survival and the search for a job took precedence over union causes.

The Knights of Labor and the AFL

As the depression wound down, a new mass organization, the Noble and Holy Order of the Knights of Labor, rose to national importance. Founded as a secret society in 1869, the order became public and national when Terence V. Powderly, an Irish American, was elected Grand Master Workman in 1879. The Knights of Labor sought "to secure to the workers the full enjoyment of the wealth they create." Because the industrial system denied workers their fair share as producers, the Knights of Labor proposed to mount a cooperative system of production alongside the existing system. "There is no reason," Powderly believed, "why labor cannot, through cooperation, own and operate mines, factories and railroads." Cooperative efforts would give workers the economic independence necessary for citizenship, and an eight-hour day would provide them with the leisure for moral, intellectual, and political pursuits.

The Knights of Labor opened its ranks to all American "producers," defined as all contributing members of society—skilled and unskilled, black and white, men and women. Only the idle and the corrupt (bankers, speculators, lawyers, saloonkeepers, and gamblers) were to be excluded. Membership was even open to sympathetic merchants and manufacturers. In fact, many shopkeepers joined the order and advertised their loyalty as "friend of the workingman."

This inclusive membership policy meant that the Knights potentially had the power of great numbers. The organization grew in spurts, attracting miners between 1874 and 1879 and skilled urban tradesmen between 1879 and 1885. Masses of unskilled workers joined thereafter.

Although Powderly frowned on using the strike as a labor weapon, the organization reaped the benefits of grassroots strike activity. Local struggles proliferated after 1883. In 1884, unorganized workers of the Union Pacific Railroad walked off the job when management announced a wage cut. Within two days, the company caved in, and the men joined the Knights of Labor. The next year, a successful strike against the Missouri Pacific Railroad brought in another wave of members.

Then, in 1886, the Haymarket Riot in Chicago led to such a growth in labor militancy that in that single year, the membership of the Knights of Labor ballooned from 100,000 to 700,000.

The "riot" at Haymarket was, in fact, a peaceful protest meeting connected with a lockout at the McCormick Reaper Works. When the Chicago police arrived to disperse the crowd, a bomb exploded. Seven policemen were killed. Although no one knows who planted the bomb, eight anarchists were tried and convicted. Four were executed, one committed suicide, and the others served prison terms. Overheated newspaper accounts put the blame on "long-haired, wild-eyed, bad-smelling, atheistic, reckless foreign wretches, who never did an honest hour's work in their lives."

Labor agitation and turbulence spilled over into politics. In 1884 and 1885, the Knights of Labor lobbied to secure a national contract labor law that would demand work contracts and state laws outlawing the use of convict labor. The organization also pressed successfully for the creation of a federal Department of Labor. As new members poured in, however, direct political action became increasingly attractive. Between 1885 and 1888, the Knights of Labor sponsored candidates in 200 towns and cities in 34 states and 4 territories. They achieved many electoral victories. In Waterloo, Iowa, a bank janitor ousted a successful attorney to become the town's mayor. Despite local successes, no national labor party emerged. But in the 1890s, the Knights cooperated with the Populists in their attempt to reshape American politics and society.

Despite the dramatic surge in membership, the Knights of Labor could not sustain their momentum as the voice for the American laboring people. Employers, alerted by the Haymarket riot, were determined to break the power of the organization. A strike against Jay Gould's southwestern railroad system in 1886 failed, tarnishing the Knights' reputation. Consumer and producer cooperatives fizzled; the policy of accepting both black and white workers led to strife and discord in the South. The two major parties proved adept at co-opting labor politicians. As labor politicians became respectable, they left the rank and file to fend for themselves.

The failure of national leaders paralleled the failure of local leadership. Powderly was never able to unify or direct his diverse following. His concern with general reform issues and political action dissatisfied members pressing for better wages and work conditions. Nor could Powderly control the militant elements who opposed him. Local, unauthorized strike actions were often ill-considered and violent. Lawlessness helped neither the organization nor its

This handbill in both German and English denouncing the "atrocious act of the police" highlights the importance of immigrants in the labor movement.

members. By 1890, the membership had dropped to 100,000, although the Knights continued to play a role well into the 1890s.

In the 1890s, the American Federation of Labor (AFL), founded in 1886, replaced the Knights of Labor as the nation's dominant union. The history of the Knights pointed up the problems of a national union that admitted all who worked for wages, but officially rejected strike action in favor of the ballot box and arbitration. The leader of the AFL, Samuel Gompers, had a different notion of effective worker organization. Gompers's experience as head of the Cigarmakers' Union in the 1870s and as a founder of the Federation of Organized Trades and Labor Unions in 1881 convinced him that skilled workers should put their specific occupational interests before the interests of workers as a whole. By so doing, they could control the supply of skilled labor and keep wages up.

Gompers organized the AFL as a federation of skilled trades—cigar makers, iron molders, ironworkers, carpenters, and others—each one autonomous, yet linked through an executive council to work together for prolabor national legislation and mutual support during boycott and strike actions. Gompers was a practical man. He repudiated the notion of a

cooperative commonwealth and dreams of ending the wage system, accepting the fact that workers "are a distinct and practically permanent class of modern society." Thus, he focused on immediate, realizable "bread and butter" issues, particularly higher wages, shorter hours, industrial safety, and the right to organize.

Although Gompers rejected direct political action as a means of obtaining labor's goals, he did believe in the value of the strike. He told a congressional hearing in 1899 that unless working people had "the power to enter upon a strike, the improvements will all go to the employer and all the injuries to the employees." A shrewd organizer, he knew from bitter experience the importance of dues high enough to sustain a strike fund through a long, tough fight.

Under Gompers's leadership, the AFL grew from 140,000 in 1886 to nearly one million by 1900. Although his notion of a labor organization was elitist, he succeeded in steering his union through a series of crises, fending off challenges from socialists on his left and corporate opposition to strikes from his right. But there was no room in his organization for the unskilled or for blacks, in whom he claimed to see an "abandoned and reckless disposition."

The AFL made a brief and halfhearted attempt to unionize women in 1892. Hostile male attitudes constituted a major barrier against organizing women. Men resented women as coworkers and preferred them to stay in the home. The AFL stood firmly for the principle that "the man is the provider" and that women who work in factories "bring forth weak children." The Boston Central Labor Union declared in 1897 "the demand for female labor an insidious assault upon the home. . . . It is the knife of the assassin, aimed at the family circle." Change was slow in coming. In 1900, the International Ladies' Garment Workers Union (ILGWU) was established. Although women were the backbone of the organization, men dominated the leadership.

Working-Class Setbacks

Despite the growth of working-class organizations, workers lost many of their battles with management. Some of the more spectacular clashes reveal why working-class activism often ended in defeat and why so many workers lived precariously on the edge of poverty.

In 1892, silver miners in Coeur d'Alene, Idaho, went on strike when their employers installed machine drills in the mines, reduced skilled workers to shovelmen, and announced a wage cut of a dollar a day. The owners, supported by state militiamen and the federal government, successfully broke the strike by using scabs, but not without armed fighting. Several hundred union men were arrested, herded into huge bull pens, and eventually tried and found guilty of a wide variety of charges. Out of the defeat emerged the Western Federation of Miners (WFM), whose chief political goal was an eight-hour law for miners. The pattern of struggle in Coeur d'Alene was followed in many subsequent strikes.

Determined mine owners characteristically met strikes by shutting off credit to union men, hiring strikebreakers and armed guards, and paying spies to infiltrate unions. Violence was frequent, and confrontations usually ended with the arrival of state militia, the erection of bull pens, incarceration or intimidation of strikers and their local sympathizers, legal action, and elaborate blacklisting systems. In spite of this, the WFM won as many strikes as it lost.

The Homestead and Pullman Strikes of 1892 and 1894

The most serious setback to labor occurred in 1892 at the Homestead steel mills near Pittsburgh, Pennsylvania. Andrew Carnegie had recently purchased the Homestead plant and put Henry Clay Frick in charge. Together, they wanted to eliminate the Amalgamated Association of Iron, Steel, and Tin Workers, which threatened to increase its organization of the steel industry. After three months of stalemated negotiations over a new wage contract, Frick issued an ultimatum. Unless the union accepted wage decreases, he would lock them out and replace them. As the deadline passed, Frick erected a formidable wood and barbed wire fence around the entire plant, with searchlight and sentry stands on it, and hired 300 armed Pinkerton agents to guard the factory. As they arrived on July 6, they engaged armed steelworkers in a daylong gun battle. Several men on both sides were killed, and the Pinkertons retreated.

Frick telegraphed Pennsylvania's governor, who sent 8,000 troops to crush both the strike and the union. Two and a half weeks later, Alexander Berkman, a New York anarchist sympathetic to the plight of the oppressed Homestead workers, attempted to assassinate Frick. The events at Homestead dramatized the lengths to which both labor and capital would go to achieve their ends.

Observing these events, Eugene Victor Debs of Terre Haute, Indiana, for many years an ardent organizer of railroad workers, wrote, "If the year 1892 taught the workingmen any lesson worthy of heed, it was that the capitalist class, like a devilfish, had grasped them with its tentacles and was dragging them down to fathomless depths of degradation." Debs saw 1893 as the year in which organized labor would "escape the prehensile clutch of these monsters." But 1893 brought a new depression and even

worse challenges and setbacks for labor. Undaunted, Debs succeeded in combining several of the separate railroad brotherhoods into a united American Railway Union (ARU). Within a year, over 150,000 railroadmen joined the ARU, and Debs won a strike against the Great Northern Railroad, which had attempted to slash workers' wages.

Debs faced his toughest crisis at the Pullman Palace Car Company in Chicago. Pullman was a model company town where management controlled all aspects of workers' lives. "We are born in a Pullman house, fed from the Pullman shop, taught in the Pullman school, catechized in the Pullman church, and when we die we shall be buried in the Pullman cemetery and go to the Pullman hell," said one worker wryly.

Late in 1893, as the depression worsened, Pullman cut wages by one-third and laid off many workers but made no reductions in rents or prices in the town stores. Forced to pay in rent what they could not recover in wages, working families struggled to survive the winter. Some parents kept their children home from school because they had no shoes or coats and could keep warm only in bed. Those still at work suffered speedups, intimidating threats, and further

In this 1892 engraving of the Homestead strikers surrendering, done for *Harper's Weekly*, the sympathy of the artist lies with the detectives in the foreground. The strikers appear as an unruly crowd in the distance, whereas the detectives' kindly faces are highlighted. *(Library of Congress)*

wage cuts. Desperate and "without hope," the Pullman workers joined the ARU in the spring of 1894 and went out on strike.

In late June, after Pullman refused to submit the dispute to arbitration, Debs led the ARU into a sympathy strike in support of the striking Pullman workers. Remembering the ill-fated railroad strike of 1877, Debs advised his lieutenants to "use no violence" and "stop no trains." Rather, he sought to boycott trains handling Pullman cars throughout the West. As the boycott spread, the General Managers Association, which ran the 24 railroads centered in Chicago, came to Pullman's support, convinced that "we have got to wipe him [Debs] out." After hiring some 2,500 strikebreakers, the GMA appealed to the state and federal governments for military and judicial support in stopping the strike.

Governor Richard Altgeld of Illinois, sympathizing with the workers and believing that local law enforcement was sufficient, opposed the use of federal troops. But Richard Olney, a former railroad lawyer and U.S. attorney general, persuaded President Cleveland that only federal troops could restore law and order. On July 2, Olney obtained a court injunction to end the strike as a "conspiracy in restraint of trade." Two days later, Cleveland ordered federal troops in to support the injunction and crush the strikers.

Violence now escalated rapidly. Local and federal officials hired armed guards, and the railroads paid them to help the troops. Within two days, strikers and guards were fighting bitterly, freight cars were burned, and over $340,000 worth of railroad property was destroyed. The press reported "Unparalleled Scenes of Riot, Terror and Pillage" and "Frenzied Mobs Still Bent on Death and Destruction." As troops poured into Chicago, the violence worsened, leaving scores of workers dead.

Debs's resources were near an end unless he could enlist wider labor support. "Capital has combined to enslave labor," he warned other labor groups. "We must all stand together or go down in hopeless defeat." When Samuel Gompers refused his support, the strike collapsed. Debs and several other leaders were arrested for the contempt of the court injunction of July 2 and found guilty. A lifelong Democrat, Debs soon became a confirmed socialist. His arrest and the defeat of the Pullman strike provided a deathblow to the American Railway Union. In 1895, the Supreme Court upheld the legality of using an injunction to stop a strike and provided management with a powerful weapon to use against unions in subsequent years. Most unions survived the difficult days of the 1890s, but the labor movement emerged with distinct disadvantages in its conflicts with organized capital.

Although in smaller communities strikes against outside owners might receive support from the local middle class, most labor conflicts ran up against the widespread middle- and upper-class conviction that unions and their demands were un-American. Many people claimed to accept the idea of worker organizations, but they would not concede that unions should participate in making economic or work decisions. Most employers violently resisted union demands as infringements of their rights to make production decisions, to hire and fire, to lock workers out, to hire scabs, or to reduce wages in times of depression. The sharp competition of the late nineteenth century, combined with a pattern of falling prices, stiffened employers' resistance to workers' demands. State and local governments and the courts frequently supported them in their battles to curb worker activism.

The severe depressions of the 1870s and 1890s also undermined working-class activism. Workers could not focus on union issues when survival itself was in question. They could not afford union dues or turn down offers of work, even at wages below union standards. Many unions collapsed during hard times. Of the 30 national unions in 1873, fewer than one-third managed to survive the depression.

A far more serious problem was the reluctance of most workers to organize even in favorable times. In 1870, less than one-tenth of the industrial workforce belonged to unions, about the same as on the eve of the Civil War. Thirty years later, despite the expansion of the workforce, only 8.4 percent (mostly skilled workers) were union members.

Why were workers so slow to join unions? Certainly, diverse work settings and ethnic differences made it difficult for workers to recognize common bonds. Moreover, many unskilled workers sensed that labor aristocrats did not have their interest at heart. Said one Cleveland Pole, "The [union] committee gets the money, 'Bricky' Flannigan [a prominent Irish striker] gets the whiskey, and the Polack gets nothing."

Moreover, many native-born Americans still clung to the tradition of individualism. "The sooner working-people get rid of the idea that somebody or something is going to help them," one Massachusetts shoemaker declared, "the better it will be for them." Others continued to nourish dreams of escaping from the working class and entering the ranks of the middle class. The number of workers who started their own small businesses attests to the power of that ideal, which prevented an identification with working-class causes.

The comments of an Irish woman highlight another important point. "There should be a law . . . to give a job to every decent man that's out of work," she declared, "and another law to keep all them I-talians from comin' in and takin' the bread out of the mouths of honest people." The ethnic and religious diversity of the workforce made it difficult to forge a common front. No other industrial country depended so heavily on immigrants for its manufacturing labor force. The lack of common cultural traditions and goals created friction and misunderstandings. In addition, immigrants clustered in certain jobs and were insulated from other workers, both foreign-born and American. Skill differences related to ethnic group membership also clouded common class concerns.

The perspective of immigrant workers contributed to their indifference to unions and to tension with native-born Americans. Many foreigners planned to return to their homeland and had limited interest in changing conditions in the United States. Moreover, because their goal was to work, they took jobs as scabs. Much of the violence that accompanied working-class actions erupted when owners brought in strikebreakers. Some Americans blamed immigrants for both low wages and failed worker actions. Divisions among workers were often as bitter as those between strikers and employers. When workers divided, employers benefited.

The tension within laboring ranks appeared most dramatically in the anti-Chinese campaign of the 1870s and 1880s as white workers in the West began to blame the Chinese for economic hardships. A meeting of San Francisco workers in 1877 in favor of the eight-hour day exploded into a rampage against the Chinese. In the following years, angry mobs killed Chinese workers in Tacoma, Seattle, Denver, and Rock Springs, Wyoming. "The Chinese must go! They are stealing our jobs!" became a rallying cry for American workers.

Hostility was also expressed at the national level with the Chinese Exclusion Act of 1882. The law, which had the support of the Knights of Labor in the West, prohibited the immigration of both skilled and unskilled Chinese workers for a ten-year period. It was extended in 1892 and made permanent in 1902. Although both middle- and working-class Americans supported sporadic efforts to cut off immigration, working-class antipathy exacerbated the deep divisions that undermined worker unity.

At the same time, many immigrants, especially those who were skilled, did support unions and cooperate with native-born Americans. Irish Americans played important roles in the Knights of Labor and the AFL. British and Germans also helped build up the unions. Often ethnic bonds served labor causes by tying members to one another and to the community. For example, in the 1860s and 1870s, as the Molders' Union in Troy, New York, battled with manufacturers, its Irish membership won sympathy and support from the Irish-dominated police force, the Roman Catholic Church, fraternal orders, and public officials.

The importance of workers' organizations lay not so much in their successful struggles and protests as in the implicit criticism they offered of American society. Using the language of republicanism, many workers lashed out at an economic order that robbed them of their dignity and humanity. As producers of wealth, they protested that so little of it was theirs. As members of the working class, they rejected the middle-class belief in individualism and social mobility.

The Balance Sheet

Except for skilled workers, most laboring people found it impossible to earn much of a share in the material bounty industrialization created. Newly arrived immigrants especially suffered from low pay and economic uncertainty. Long hours on the job and the necessity of walking to and from work left workers little free time. Family budgets could include, at best, only small amounts for recreation. Even a baseball game ticket was a luxury.

Yet this view of the harshness of working-class life partly grows out of our own standards of what is acceptable today. Because so few working-class men or women recorded their thoughts and reactions, it is hard to know just what they expected or how they viewed their experiences. But culture and background influenced their perspectives. The family tenement, one Polish immigrant remarked, "seemed quite advanced when compared with our home" in Poland. American poverty was preferable to Russian pogroms. A ten-hour job in the steel mill might be an improvement over dawn-to-dusk farmwork that brought no wages.

Studies of several cities show that nineteenth-century workers achieved some occupational mobility. One worker in five in Los Angeles and Atlanta during the 1890s, for example, managed to climb into the middle class. Most immigrant workers were stuck in ill-paid, insecure jobs, but their children ended up doing better. The son of an unskilled laborer might move on to become a semiskilled or skilled worker as new immigrants took the jobs at the bottom. Second-generation Irish made progress, especially in the West and the Midwest. Even in Boston, 40 percent of the children of Irish immigrants obtained white-collar jobs.

Mobility, like occupation, was related to background. Native-born whites, Jews, and Germans rose more swiftly and fell less often than Irish, Italians, or Poles. Cultural attitudes, family size, education, and group leadership all contributed to different ethnic mobility patterns. Jews, for example, valued education and sacrificed to keep children in school. By 1915, Jews represented 85 percent of the free City College student body in New York City, 20 percent of New York

This photograph of a store in San Francisco's Chinatown suggests that even though many of the immigrants originally planned to return home, many stayed and created a lively culture in this country. The presence of only men in the picture highlights the male character of the Chinese immigration. *(Collection University of Oregon Library)*

University's student body, and one-sixth of those studying at Columbia University. With an education, they moved upward. The Slavs, however, who valued a steady income over mobility and education, took their children out of school and sent them to work at an early age. This course of action, they believed, not only helped the family, but gave the child a head start in securing reliable, stable employment. The southern Italian proverb "Do not make your child better than you are" suggests the value Italians placed on family rather than individual success. Differing attitudes and values led to different aspirations and career patterns.

Two groups enjoyed little mobility: African Americans and Hispanic Americans. African Americans were largely excluded from the industrial occupational structure and restricted to unskilled jobs. Unlike immigrant industrial workers, they did not have the opportunity to move to better jobs as new unskilled workers took the positions at the bottom. A study in Los Angeles suggests that Hispanic residents made minimal gains. Their experiences elsewhere may have been much the same.

Although occupational mobility was limited for immigrants, other kinds of rewards often compensated for the lack of success at the workplace. Home ownership loomed important for groups like the Irish, for in their homeland, home ownership had been all but impossible. Ownership of a home also allowed a family to earn extra income by taking in boarders and provided some protection against the uncertainties of industrial life and the coming of old age. The Irish also

proved adept politicians and came to dominate big-city government in the late nineteenth century. Their political success opened up city jobs, particularly in the police force, to the Irish. In 1886, one-third of Chicago's police force was Irish-born; many more were second-generation Irish Americans. The Irish were also successful in the construction industry and dominated the hierarchy of the Catholic Church. Irish who did not share this upward mobility could nevertheless benefit from ethnic connections and take pride in their group's achievements.

Likewise, participation in social clubs and fraternal orders compensated in part for lack of advancement at work. Ethnic associations, parades, and holidays provided a sense of identity and security that offset the limitations of the job world.

Moreover, a few rags-to-riches stories always encouraged the masses who struggled. The family of John Kearney, in Poughkeepsie, New York, for example, achieved modest success. After 20 years as a laborer, John started his own business as a junk dealer and even bought a simple house. His sons started off in better jobs than their father. One became a grocery store clerk, later a baker, a policeman, and, finally, at the age of 40, an inspector at the waterworks. Another was an iron molder, and the third son was a post office worker and eventually the superintendent of city streets. If this success paled next to that of industrial giants like Andrew Carnegie and John D. Rockefeller, it was still enough to keep the American dream alive.

Timeline

1843–1884	"Old immigration"
1844	Telegraph invented
1850s	Steam power widely used in manufacturing
1859	Value of U.S. industrial production exceeds value of agricultural production
1866	National Labor Union founded
1869	Transcontinental railroad completed
	Knights of Labor organized
1870	Standard Oil of Ohio formed
1870s–1880s	Consolidation of continental railroad network
1873	Bethlehem Steel begins using Bessemer process
1873–1879	Depression
1876	Alexander G. Bell invents telephone
	Thomas Edison establishes his "invention factory" at Menlo Park, New Jersey
1877	Railroad workers hold first nationwide industrial strike

1879	Thomas Edison invents incandescent light
1882	Chinese Exclusion Act
1885–1914	"New immigration"
1886	American Federation of Labor founded
	Haymarket Riot in Chicago
1887	Interstate Commerce Act
1890	Sherman Anti-Trust Act
1892	Standard Oil of New Jersey formed
	Coeur d'Alene strike
	Homestead steelworkers strike
1893	Chicago World's Fair
1893–1897	Depression
1894	Pullman railroad workers strike
1900	International Ladies' Garment Workers Union founded
	Corporations responsible for two-thirds of U.S. manufacturing

Conclusion

The Complexity of Industrial Capitalism

The rapid growth of the late nineteenth century made the United States one of the world's industrial giants. Many factors contributed to the "wonderful accomplishments" of the age. They ranged from sympathetic government policies to the rise of big business and the emergence of a cheap industrial workforce. But it was also a turbulent period. Many Americans benefited only marginally from the new wealth. Some of them protested by joining unions, by walking out on strike, or by initiating on-the-job actions. Most lived their lives more quietly and never had the opportunity that Thomas O'Donnell did of telling their story to others. But middle-class Americans began to wonder about the O'Donnells of the country. It is to their concerns, worries, and aspirations that we now turn.

Recommended Reading

The Texture of Industrial Progress

Alfred D. Chandler, Jr., *The Visible Hand: The Managerial Revolution in American Business* (1977); Robert L. Heilbroner, *The Economic Transformation of America* (1977); Thomas P. Hughes, *American Genius* (1989); Thomas J. Misa, *A Nation of Steel* (1995); James D. Norris, *Advertising and the Transformation of American Society, 1865–1920* (1990); William G. Roy, *Socializing Capitalism: The Rise of the Large Industrial Corporation in America* (1997); Douglas Steeples, *Democracy in Desperation: The Depression of 1893* (1998); Olivier Zunz, *Making America Corporate, 1870–1929* (1990).

Urban Expansion in the Industrial Age

James Borchert, *Alley Life in Washington: Family, Community, Religion, and Folklife in the City, 1850–1970* (1980); William Cronon, *Nature's Metropolis: Chicago and the Great West* (1991); David Goldfield, *Cotton Fields and Skyscrapers: Southern City and Region* (1989); William E. Montgomery, *Under Their Own Fig Tree: The African-American Church in the South, 1865–1900* (1993); David Nasaw, *Going Out: The Rise and Fall of Public Amusements* (1993); Carl Smith, *Urban Disorder and the Shape of Belief: The Great Chicago Fire, the Haymarket Bomb, and the Model Town of Pullman* (1993); Sam Bass Warner, Jr., *Streetcar Suburbs: The Process of Growth in Boston, 1870–1900* (1962).

The Life of the Middle Class

Gunther Barth, *The Rise of Modern City Culture in Nineteenth-Century America* (1980); Anne Ruggles Geere, *Intimate Practices: Literacy and Cultural Work in U.S. Women's Clubs, 1880–1992* (1997); Thomas Goebel, *The Children of Athena: Chicago Professionals and the Creation of a Credentialing Society* (1996); Judy Hilkey, *Character in Capital: Success Manuals and Manhood in Gilded Age America* (1997).

Industrial Work and the Laboring Class

Thomas J. Archdeacon, *Becoming American: An Ethnic History* (1983); David M. Gordon, Richard Edwards, and Michael Reich, *Segmented Work, Divided Workers: The Historical Transformation of Labor in the United States* (1982); Herbert G. Gutman, *Work, Culture, and Society in Industrializing*

America (1976); Christiane Harrig et. al., *Peasant Maids—City Women: From the European Countryside to Urban America* (1997); David M. Katzman, *Seven Days a Week: Women and Domestic Service in Industrializing America* (1978); Alice Kessler-Harris, *Out to Work: A History of Wage-Earning Women in the United States* (1982); Kerby A. Miller, *Emigrants and Exiles: Ireland and the Irish Exodus to North America* (1985); Madelon Powers, *Faces along the Bar: Lore and Order in the Working-Man's Saloon, 1870–1920* (1998).

Capital Versus Labor

Leon Fink, *Workingmen's Democracy: The Knights of Labor and American Politics* (1983); David Montgomery, *Workers' Control in America: Studies in the History of Work, Technology, and Labor Struggles* (1970) and *The Fall of the House of Labor: The Workplace, the State, and American Labor Activism, 1865–1925* (1987); Ronald Takaki, *A Different Mirror: A History of Multicultural America* (1993); Daniel J. Walkowitz, *Worker City, Company Town: Iron and Cotton-Worker Protest in Troy and Cohoes, New York, 1855–84* (1978); Robert E. Weit, *Beyond Labor's Veil: the Culture of the Knights of Labor* (1996); James Whiteside,

Regulating Danger: The Struggle for Mine Safety in the Rocky Mountain Coal Industry (1990).

Fiction and Film

Theodore Dreiser tells the story of a young rural woman who comes to Chicago and violates its social norms to acquire some of the city's offerings in *Sister Carrie* (1900). Stephen Crane's novel *Maggie: A Girl of the Streets* (1893) gives a grim picture of life in the urban slums. Thomas Bell follows several generations of the same immigrant family whose American life is entwined with steel in *Out of This Furnace* (1976 ed.).

The Richest Man in the World: Andrew Carnegie, a 1997 film made for PBS, analyzes the personal and professional life of Carnegie and makes good use of interviews with business and labor historians. It offers extended treatment of the Homestead strike, for which the film holds Carnegie largely responsible. *The Age of Innocence*, which takes place in 1870s New York, offers a splendid picture of the sumptuous lives of the rich and the norms and values to which they were supposed to adhere. This 1993 Martin Scorsese film is based on the novel by the same name by Edith Wharton.

Suggested Web Sites

http://memory.loc.gov/ammem/bellhtml/bellhome.html

Alexander Graham Bell Family Papers. This Library of Congress site contains papers from 1862 to 1939 and includes a chronology, images, selected documents, and interpretive essays about Bell.

http://www.pbs.org/wgbh/pages/amex/carnegie

The American Experience: Andrew Carnegie. This American Experience/PBS site provides images and text about Carnegie's life and activities.

http://memory.loc.gov/ammem/aap/aaphome.html

African American Pamphlets Home Page. This collection includes writings of famous African Americans, including Frederick Douglass, Booker T. Washington, Ida B. Wells-Barnett, Benjamin W. Arnett, Alexander Crummel, and Emanuel Love.

http://www.pitzer.edu/~dward/Anarchist_Archives/archivehome.html

Anarchy Archives. This site offers classic anarchist texts, including information and graphics for the Haymarket Riot.

http://www.micheloud.com/FXM/SO/

John D. Rockefeller and the Standard Oil Company. This study, with accompanying images by François Micheloud, tells of the rise of Rockefeller and his mammoth company.

http://www.unionweb.org/history.htm

A Short History of American Labor. This brief essay is adapted from the AFL-CIO's *American Federationist*, March 1981.

http://www.geocities.com/CollegePark/Quad/6460/AmLabHist/index.html

American Labor History. This site takes a general look at the history of labor in America.

http://www.enarco.com/

ENARCO, The History of the National Refining Company. This positive history of the company reflects the industrial changes of late-nineteenth-century America.

http://www.inform.umd.edu/HIST/Gompers/web1.html

Samuel Gompers Papers at the University of Maryland. This site includes information about the papers project and also has a photo gallery, selected documents, and a brief history of the first president of the American Federation of Labor (AFL).

http://www.ushistoryplace.com

 A richly detailed on-line learning environment complete with interactive maps, timelines, history activities, primary source documents, and links to related American history sites.

POLITICS *and* REFORM

CHAPTER OUTLINE

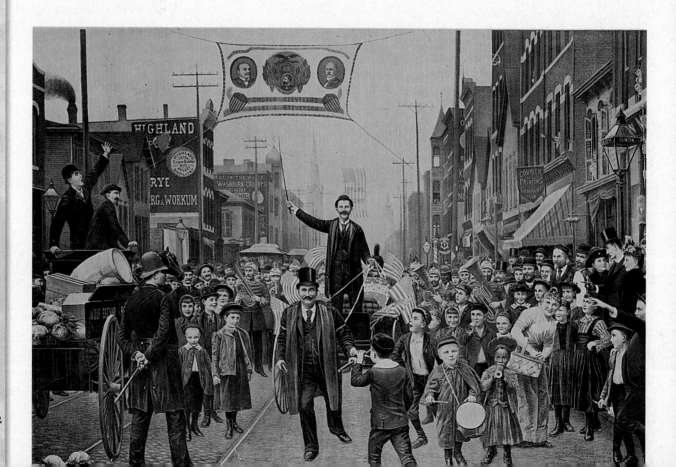

At the start of his best-seller *Looking Backward* (1888), Edward Bellamy likened the American society of his day to a huge stagecoach. Dragging the coach along sandy roads and over steep hills were the "masses of humanity." While they strained desperately "under the pitiless lashing of hunger" to pull the coach, at the top sat the favored few, riding well out of the dust in breezy comfort. The fortunate few, however, were constantly fearful that they might lose their seats from a sudden jolt, fall to the ground, and have to pull the coach themselves.

Bellamy's famous coach allegory introduced a utopian novel in which the class divisions and pitiless competition of the nineteenth century were replaced by a classless, caring, cooperative new society. Economic anxieties and hardships were supplanted by satisfying labor and leisure. In place of the coach, all citizens in the year 2000 walked together in equal comfort and security under a huge umbrella over the sidewalks of the city. Bellamy's outlook on American life was a middle-class reformist one. His book had enormous appeal, not only because of his humane economic analysis but also because he clothed it in the form of a novel, complete with futuristic technological wonders, such as television and credit cards, a double-dream surprise ending, and a love story.

The novel opens in 1887. The hero, Julian West, a wealthy Bostonian, falls asleep worrying about the effect local labor struggles might have on his upcoming wedding. When he wakes up, it is the year 2000. In the new society, he discovers, through his genial guide, Dr. Leete, that all citizens live in material comfort and happiness. Utopia had been achieved peacefully through the development of one gigantic trust, owned and operated by the national government. All citizens between 21 and 45 work in an industrial army with equalized pay and work difficulty. Retirement after 45 is devoted to hobbies, reading, culture, and such minimal political and judicial leadership as is needed in a society without crime, poverty, graft, vice, lawyers, or war.

Although this 1892 painting by John Klir shows the outcome of a "Lost Bet" in the election that year, note the ethnic, racial, and class diversity of the street crowds, momentarily united in enjoyment of watching the humiliated loser pulling his victorious opponent (and a wagon full of American flags). Will a more diverse America hold together? *(Library of Congress)*

Bellamy's treatment of the role of women in the world of 2000 reflected his own era's struggle with changing gender and class relationships. On the one hand, new labor-saving gadgets relieved women of housework, and they served, like men, in the industrial army. Women married not for dependence but for love and could even initiate romantic relationships. On the other hand, the women Bellamy portrayed were still primarily responsible for shopping, supervising domestic and aesthetic matters, and nurturing the young. In the women's division of the industrial army, women worked shorter hours in "lighter occupations." The purpose of equality of the sexes and more leisure, the novel made clear, was to enable women to cultivate their "beauty and grace" and, by extension, to feminize culture and politics.

Bellamy's book was popular with educated middle-class Americans, who were attracted by his vision of a society in which humans were both morally good and materially well off. Readers were intrigued not only by all that was new but also by how much of the old society was preserved. The traditional male view of woman's place and purpose was one example. But Bellamy also retained such familiar values as individual taste and incentive, private property, and rags-to-riches presidents. Like most middle-class Americans of his day, he disapproved of European socialism. Although the collectivist features of Bellamy's utopia were socialistic, he and his admirers called his system "nationalism." This appealed to a new generation of Americans who had put aside Civil War antagonisms to embrace the greatness of a growing, if now economically divided, nation. In the early 1890s, with Americans buying nearly 10,000 copies of *Looking Backward* every week, over 160 Nationalist clubs were formed to crusade for the adoption of Bellamy's ideas.

The inequalities of wealth described in Bellamy's coach scene reflected a political life in which many participated but only a few benefited. The wealthiest 10 percent, who rode high on the social coach, dominated national politics, whereas untutored bosses held sway in governing cities. Except for token expressions of support, national political leaders ignored the cries of factory workers, immigrants, farmers, African Americans, Native Americans, and other victims of the vast transformation of American industrial, urban, and agrarian life in the late nineteenth century. But as the century closed, middle-class Americans like Bellamy, as well as labor, agrarian, and ethnic leaders themselves, proposed various reforms. Their concern was never more appropriate than during the depression of the mid-1890s, a real-life social upheaval that mirrored the worst features and fears of Bellamy's fictional coach.

In this chapter, we will examine American politics at the national and local level from the end of Reconstruction to the 1890s, a period that for the most part bolstered the rich and neglected the corrosive human problems of urban industrial life. Then we will look at the growing social and political involvement of educated middle-class reformers who, despite their distaste for mass politics, now acted to effect change both locally and nationally. We will conclude with an account of the pivotal importance of the 1890s, highlighted by the Populist revolt, the depression of 1893–1897, and the election of 1896. In an age of strong national identity and pride, the events of the 1890s shook many comfortable citizens out of their apathy and began the reshaping of American politics.

POLITICS IN THE GILDED AGE

In a satirical book in 1873, Mark Twain, with Charles Dudley Warner, used the expression "Gilded Age" to describe the political corruption of Grant's presidency. The phrase, with its suggestion of shallow glitter, has come to characterize social and political life in the last quarter of the nineteenth century. Ironically, although Gilded Age politics were tainted by corruption and tinted by more color than substance, the period was one of high party vitality. Politicians avoided fundamental issues in favor of the politics of mass entertainment—pomp, parades, penny beer, pennants, and the prattle of three-hour speeches. As a result, voter participation in national elections between 1876 and 1896 hovered at an all-time high of 73 to 82 percent of all registered voters.

Behind the glitter of Gilded Age politics, though, two gradual changes occurred that would greatly affect twentieth-century politics. First was the development of a professional bureaucracy. In congressional committees and executive branch offices, elite specialists and experts emerged as a counterfoil to the perceived dangers of majority rule represented by high voter participation, especially by new immigrants. How else, New England poet James Russell Lowell wondered, could the culturally "better" classes temper the excesses of equality "when interpreted and applied politically by millions of newcomers alien to our traditions?" Second, after a period of close elections and party stalemate based on Civil War divisions between Democrats and Republicans, new issues and concerns fostered a party realignment in the 1890s.

Politics, Parties, Patronage, and Presidents

American government in the 1870s and 1880s clearly supported the interests of riders atop Bellamy's coach. Few nineteenth-century Americans would have agreed that the national government should tackle problems of poverty, unemployment, and trusts. They mistrusted organized power and believed in harmony of interests and laissez-faire, a doctrine that argued that all would benefit from an economic life free of government interference. After the traumas of the Civil War era, when a strong centralized state pursued high moral causes, late-nineteenth-century political leaders favored a period of government passivity. This would permit the continuing pursuit of industrial expansion and wealth. As Republican leader Roscoe Conkling explained, the primary role of government was "to clear the way of impediments and dangers, and leave every class and every individual free and safe in the exertions and pursuits of life."

The Gilded Age, Henry Adams observed, was the most "thoroughly ordinary" period in American politics since Columbus. "One might search the whole list of Congress, Judiciary, and Executive during the twenty-five years 1870–95 and find little but damaged reputation." Few eras of American government were so corrupt, and Adams was especially sensitive to this decline in the quality of democratic politics. His autobiography, *The Education of Henry Adams* (1907), contrasted the low political tone of his own age with the exalted political morality of his grandfather John Quincy Adams and great-grandfather John Adams.

During the weakened Johnson and Grant presidencies, Congress and its committee system emerged as the dominant branch of government. Senators James G. Blaine (Maine) and Roscoe Conkling (New York) typified the low moral quality of legislative leadership. Despite lying about having been paid off by favors to railroads, Blaine was probably the most popular Republican politician of the era. Charming, intelligent, witty, and able, he served twice as secretary of state and was a serious contender for the presidency in every election from 1876 to 1892.

Conkling was even more typical. The *New York Times* described him as "a man by whose career and character the future will judge of the political standards of the present." A stalwart Republican who controlled the rich patronage jobs of the New York customhouse, Conkling spent most of his career in patronage conflicts with fellow party leaders. He quarreled even more with liberal Republican civil service reformers, who believed that government jobs should be dispersed for expertise and merit rather than party loyalty. Conkling could imagine no other purpose of politics than party loyalty and accused these genteel "mugwump" reformers of wanting the jobs for themselves. "Their real object is office and plunder." Fittingly, his career ended when he resigned from the Senate in a patronage dispute with President Garfield. Though he served in Congress for over two decades, Conkling never drafted a bill. His career was unharmed, for legislation was not Congress's primary purpose.

In 1879, a disgusted student of legislative politics, Woodrow Wilson, described the degradation of Gilded Age politics: "No leaders, no principles; no principles, no parties." Little differentiated the two major parties. They diverged not over principles but patronage, not over issues but the spoils of office. At stake in elections were not laws but the thousands of government jobs at the disposal of the winning candidate and his party. In a shrewd analysis of the American political system in the late nineteenth century, an English observer, Lord James Bryce, concluded that the most cohesive force in American politics was the "desire for office and for office as a means of gain." The two parties, like two bottles of liquor, Bryce said, bore different labels, yet "each was empty."

The clear ideological party positions taken during the Civil War and Reconstruction had all but disappeared. Party affiliation generally reflected interest in important cultural, religious, and ethnic questions. Republican votes still came from northeastern Yankee industrial interests and from New England migrants and Scandinavian Lutherans across the Upper Midwest. Democrats depended on southern whites, northern workers, and Irish Catholic and other urban immigrants. Because the Republican Party had proved its willingness in the past to mobilize the power of the state to reshape society, people who wished to regulate moral life but not economic development were attracted to it. White southerners and Irish and German Catholics preferred the Democratic party because it opposed government efforts to regulate morals. Said one Chicago Democrat, "A Republican is a man who wants you t' go t' church every Sunday. A Democrat says if a man want t' have a glass of beer on Sunday he can have it."

For a few years, Civil War and Reconstruction issues generated party differences, as Republicans reminded voters of its role in winning the Civil War and preserving the Union. But after 1876, on national issues at least, party labels did indeed mark "empty" bottles. Because the two parties were evenly matched, it made sense to avoid controversial stands. In three of the five presidential elections between 1876 and 1892, a mere 1 percent of the vote separated the two major candidates. In 1880, James Garfield defeated his Democratic opponent, General Winfield Hancock, a Reconstruction moderate and Union war hero, by only 7,018 votes. In 1884, Grover Cleveland squeaked by James G. Blaine by a popular vote margin of 48.5 to 48.2 percent. In two elections (1876 and 1888), the electoral vote winner had fewer popular votes. Further evidence of political stalemate was that only twice, and for only two years, did one party control the White House and both houses of Congress. Although all the presidents in the era except Cleveland were Republicans, the Democrats controlled the House of Representatives in eight of the ten sessions of Congress between 1875 and 1895.

Gilded Age presidents were an undistinguished group. Like Washington, D.C., itself, they played only a minor role in national life, especially when compared with industrial entrepreneurs like Carnegie and Rockefeller. None of them—Rutherford B. Hayes (1877–1881), James Garfield (1881), Chester A. Arthur (1881–1885), Grover Cleveland (1885–1889 and 1893–1897), and Benjamin Harrison (1889–1893)—served two consecutive terms. None was strongly identified with any particular issue. None has been highly regarded by historians. The only Democrat in the group, Cleveland differed little from the Republicans. Upon his election in 1884, financier Jay Gould sent him a telegram stating his confidence that "the vast business interests of the country will be entirely safe in your hands." When Cleveland actually initiated a strong policy by calling for a lower tariff in his annual message in 1887, Congress listened politely and did nothing. Voters turned him out of office a year later.

Most Americans expected their presidents to take care of party business by rewarding the faithful with government positions. The scale of patronage was enormous. Garfield complained of having to dispense thousands of jobs as he took office in 1881, worrying, he said, "whether A or B should be appointed to this or that office." He is remembered primarily for being shot early in his administration by a disappointed office seeker. He achieved heroic stature only by hanging on for two and a half months before he died. Garfield's successor, Chester Arthur, was so closely identified with Conkling's patronage operation that when the shooting of the president was announced, a friend said with shocked disbelief, "My God! Chet Arthur in the White House!"

PRESIDENTIAL ELECTIONS, 1872–1892

Year	Candidate	Party	Popular Vote	Electoral Vote
1872	ULYSSES S. GRANT	Republican	3,596,745 (56%)	286
	Horace Greeley	Democrat	2,843,446 (44%)	0*
1876	Samuel J. Tilden	Democrat	4,284,020 (51%)	184
	RUTHERFORD B. HAYES	Republican	4,036,572 (48%)	185
1880	JAMES A. GARFIELD	Republican	4,449,053 (48.5%)	214
	Winfield S. Hancock	Democrat	4,442,035 (48.1%)	155
	James B. Weaver	Greenback-Labor	308,578	0
1884	GROVER CLEVELAND	Democrat	4,911,017 (48.5%)	219
	James G. Blaine	Republican	4,848,334 (48.2%)	182
	Minor parties		325,739 (03.3%)	0
1888	Grover Cleveland	Democrat	5,540,050 (48.6%)	168
	BENJAMIN HARRISON	Republican	5,444,337 (47.9%)	233
	Minor parties		396,441 (03.5%)	0
1892	GROVER CLEVELAND	Democrat	5,554,414 (46%)	277
	Benjamin Harrison	Republican	5,190,802 (43%)	145
	James B. Weaver	Populist	1,027,329 (9%)	22

A British observer of American politics, James Bryce, said in 1888 that "the American usually votes with his party, right or wrong, and the fact that there is little distinction of view between the parties makes it easier to stick to your old friends." American voters stayed with their "old friends," as this table of the evenly matched presidential elections of the Gilded Age shows. Except for 1872, the popular vote was never wider than 3 percent and in three elections was less than 1 percent.

* Greeley died before the electoral college met.

Note: Winners' names appear in capital letters.

National Issues

Four issues were important at the national level in the Gilded Age: the tariff, currency, civil service, and government regulation of railroads (see Chapter 17). In confronting these issues, legislators tried to serve both their own self-interest and the national interest of an efficient, productive economy.

The tariff was one issue where party as well as regional attitudes toward the use of government power made some difference. Republicans wanted government to support business interests and stood for a high tariff to protect businessmen, wage earners, and farmers from the competition and products of foreign labor. By contrast, Democrats demanded a low tariff because "the government is best which governs least." But in practice, politicians accommodated local interests when it came to tariffs. Democratic senator Daniel Vorhees of Indiana explained, "I am a protectionist for every interest which I am sent here by my constituents to protect."

Tariff revisions were bewilderingly complex as legislators catered to these many special interests. As one senator knowingly said, "The contest over a revision of the tariff brings to light a selfish strife which is not far from disgusting." Most tariffs included a mixture of higher and lower rates that defied understanding. The federal government depended on tariffs and excise taxes (primarily on tobacco and liquor) for most of its revenue, so there was little chance that the tariff would be abolished or substantially lowered. Moreover, surpluses produced by the tariff during the Gilded Age helped the parties finance patronage jobs and government programs.

The money question was even more complicated. During the Civil War, the federal government had circulated paper money (greenbacks) that could not be exchanged for gold or silver (specie). In the late 1860s and 1870s, politicians debated whether the United States should return to a metallic standard, which would allow paper money to be exchanged for specie. "Hard-money advocates supported either withdrawing all paper money from circulation or making it convertible to specie. They opposed increasing the volume of money, fearing inflation. Greenbackers argued that there was not enough currency in circulation for an expanding economy and urged increasing the supply of paper money to raise farm prices and cut interest rates.

Hard-money interests had more power and influence. In 1873, Congress stopped using silver for coinage. In 1875, it passed the Specie Resumption Act, gradually retiring greenbacks from circulation and putting the nation firmly on the gold standard. But as large supplies of silver were discovered and mined in the West, pressure was resumed for increasing the money supply by coining silver. Soft-money advocates

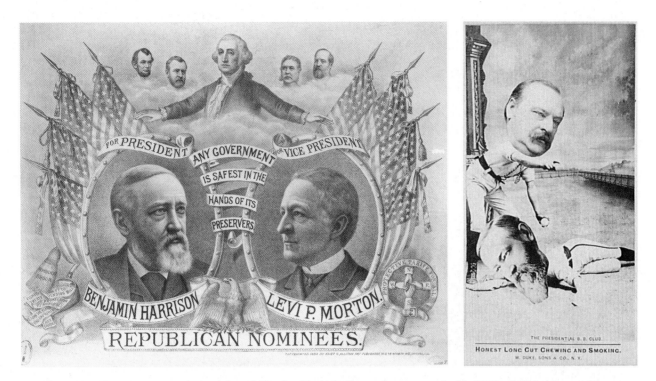

Although the tariff protectionist Harrison defeated Cleveland in 1888 (the results were reversed in 1892), all Gilded Age presidents were essentially "preservers" rather than innovators. None had approached the greatness of Washington, Lincoln, and the other Republican presidents hovering over Harrison and Morton in this illustration. *(Library of Congress)* In a second image from 1888, titled "The Presidential B.B. Club," politics and business are merged in a tobacco advertisement, which shows Cleveland the fielder tagging out Harrison the batter—true enough for the election of 1892 but not for 1888, which Harrison won. *(From the collection of David J. and Janice L. Frent)*

pushed for the unlimited coinage of silver in addition to gold. In an 1878 compromise, the Treasury was required to buy between $2 million and $4 million of silver each month and to coin it as silver dollars. Despite the increase in the money supply, the period was not inflationary. Prices fell, disappointing supporters of soft money. Their response was to push for more silver, continuing the controversy into the 1890s.

The issue of civil service reform was, Henry Adams observed, a "subject almost as dangerous in political conversation in Washington as slavery itself in the old days before the war." The worst feature of the spoils system was that parties financed themselves by assessing holders of patronage jobs, often as much as 1 percent of their annual salaries. Reformers, most of them genteel native-born white Protestants, pressed for competitive examinations, allegedly to ensure the creation of a professional, honest, nonpartisan permanent civil service. But they were motivated as well by a desire to provide "barriers against the invasion of modern barbarism and vulgarity," as Harvard culture guardian Charles Eliot Norton put it, describing the threat of dividing the spoils of office among immigrants and their urban political machine bosses.

Civil service reform had first been raised under Grant, but little came of it. Garfield's assassination by a

crazed office-seeker, however, created enough public support to force Congress to take action, and "Chet" Arthur surprised doubters by being responsive to the issue. The Pendleton Act of 1883 mandated merit examinations for about one-tenth of federal offices. Gradually, more bureaucrats fell under its coverage, but parties became no more honest. As campaign contributions from government employees dried up, parties turned to huge corporate contributions, which, in 1888, helped elect Benjamin Harrison.

The Lure of Local Politics

The fact that the major parties agreed substantially on issues such as money and civil service does not mean that nineteenth-century Americans found politics dull. Far more eligible voters turned out in the late nineteenth century than at any time since. The 78.5 percent average turnout to vote for president in the 1880s contrasts sharply with the near–50 percent of eligible Americans who vote today.

American men were drawn to the polls in part by the hoopla of party parades, buttons, and banners but also by emotional local issues. Voters may have been cool toward the tariff and civil service, but they expressed strong interest in issues of race, religion, nationality, and alcohol, which often overrode economic self-inter-

Women, often targets of drunken male violence, campaigned for temperance as well as for equal rights. Here Victoria Claflin Woodhull reads a suffrage proposal to the House Judiciary Committee in 1871. If denied the vote, she vowed that women "mean secession, and on a thousand times grander scale than was that of the South. We are plotting a revolution; we will overthrow this bogus Republic and plant a government of righteousness in its stead." *(Library of Congress)*

est. Iowa farmers favored curbing the power of the rail-roads to set high grain-shipping rates, but they also turned out to vote for temperance and compulsory education laws. Irish Catholics in New York sought political support for parochial schools, while third-generation, middle-class American Protestants from Illinois and Connecticut voted for laws that would compel attendance at public schools. Nashville whites supported laws that established segregated railroad cars and other public facilities. Ohio and Indiana Protestants pushed for laws against drinking to protect social order and morality against hard-drinking Catholics, while German Catholic Milwaukee brewery workers, cherishing both their jobs and their beer, voted against local temperance laws.

The new urban immigrants played a large role in stimulating political participation. As traditional native-born elites left local government for more lucrative and higher-status business careers, urban bosses stepped in. Their control rested on an ability to deliver the immigrant vote, which they secured by operating informal welfare systems. Bosses like "Big Tim" Sullivan of New York and "Hinky Dink" Kenna of Chicago handed out jobs and money for rent, fuel, and bail. Sullivan gave new shoes as birthday presents to all poor children in his district, as well as turkeys to poor families at Thanksgiving. Above all, party bosses provided a personal touch in a strange and forbidding environment. As one boss explained, "I think that there's got to be in every ward somebody that any bloke can come to—no matter what he's done—and get help."

New York City's Tammany Hall boss, George Washington Plunkitt, perfected the relationship of mutual self-interest with his constituents. The favors he provided in return for votes ranged from attending weddings and funerals to influencing police and the courts. His clients included not only Jewish brides, Italian mourners, and burned-out tenants but also job seekers, store owners, saloon-keepers, and madams, all of whom needed favors. State party leaders were no less effective than urban bosses in mobilizing voters. An Indiana Republican state chairman appointed 10,000 district workers in 1884 to ferret out the "social and political affiliation" of every single voter.

Party leaders also won votes by making politics exciting. The parades, rallies, buttons, songs, and oratory of late-nineteenth-century campaigns generated excitement even when substantive issues were not at stake. In the election of 1884, for example, emotions ran high over the moral lapses of the opposition candidate. The Democrats made much of Blaine's record of dishonesty, chanting in election eve parades and rallies: "Blaine! Blaine! James G. Blaine! / Continental liar from the state of Maine!" Republicans mocked Cleveland's illegitimate child with their own chant: "Ma! Ma! Where's my pa? / Gone to the White House, Ha! Ha! Ha!" Cleveland won in part because an unwise Republican clergyman called the Democrats the party of "rum, Romanism, and rebellion" on election eve in New York. The remark backfired, and the Republicans lost both New York, which should have been a safe state, and the election.

Race, religion, and class often played a strong role in local politics. New Mexico, for example, was marked for 20 years by the corrupt land grabs of the Santa Fe ring, a small group of Anglo-Protestant Republican bankers, lawyers, and politicians who exploited anti-Mexican and anti-Catholic sentiments. The ring controlled judges, legislators, and the business interests of the state, as well as many Spanish-speaking voters. In the late 1880s, desperate Mexican American tenant farmers turned to violence, which the ring manipulated to dispossess Mexican Americans, Indians, and even white squatters from enormous tracts of land. The New Mexico events showed the power of race and religion in local politics.

Prohibition also provoked spirited local contests. Many Americans considered drinking a serious social problem. Annual consumption of brewery beer had risen from 2.7 gallons per capita in 1850 to 17.9 in 1880. Although this increase could have been the result of changes in drinking habits, many people feared that alcoholism was on the increase. Certainly, the number of saloons ballooned. In one city, saloons outnumbered churches 31 to 1. Such statistics shocked those who believed that drinking corrupted politics and led to poverty, crime, and unrestrained sexuality. Because they were often the targets of violent drunken men, women especially supported temperance. Rather than try to persuade individuals to give up drink, as the pre–Civil War temperance movement had done, many now sought to stop drinking by making it illegal.

The battle in San Jose, California illustrates the strong passions such efforts aroused. In the 1870s, temperance reformers put on the ballot a local option referendum to ban the sale of liquor in San Jose. Women, using their influence as guardians of morality, erected a temperance tent, where they held conspicuous daily meetings. Despite denunciations from some clergymen and heckling from some of the town's drinkers, the women refused to retreat to their homes. On election eve, a large crowd appeared at the temperance tent, but a larger one turned up at a pro-liquor rally. In the morning, women roamed the streets, urging men to adopt the referendum. Children were marched around to the polls and saloons, singing, "Father, dear father, come home with me now." By afternoon, the mood grew ugly, and the women were harassed and threatened by drunken men. The prohibition proposal lost by a vote of 1,430 to 918.

Similarly, emotional conflicts occurred in the 1880s at the state level over other issues, especially education. In Iowa, Illinois, and Wisconsin, Republicans sponsored laws mandating that children attend "some public or private day school" where instruction was in English, an early but not the last movement for English-only education. These laws aimed to undermine parochial schools, which taught in the language of the immigrants. In Iowa, where a state prohibition law also passed, the Republican slogan was "A schoolhouse on every hill, and no saloon in the valley." Confident in their cause, Protestant Iowa Republicans proclaimed that "Iowa will go Democratic when hell goes Methodist," and indeed they won. But in Wisconsin, a law for compulsory school attendance was so strongly anti-Catholic that it backfired. Many voters, disillusioned with Republican moralism, shifted to the Democrats. Campaigns like these both reflected and nourished ethnic tension and helped draw the middle class into a more active engagement with politics.

MIDDLE-CLASS REFORM

Most middle-class Americans were not reformers. But urban corruption, poverty, and labor violence frightened many out of their aversion to politics. They worried that their absence from political discourse was having a negative affect on the morality of American life.

Frances Willard and the Women's Christian Temperance Union (WCTU) is an example. As president of the WCTU from 1879 until her death in 1898, Willard headed the largest women's organization in the country. Most WCTU members were churchgoing, white Protestant women who believed drunkenness caused poverty and family violence. But after 1886, the WCTU reversed its position, attributing drunken-

Grover Cleveland's hypocrisy as "Grover the Good" is lampooned by this cartoon from the election of 1884 showing a tearful mother with Cleveland's "illegitimate" child. The people elected him anyway. *(The Granger Collection, New York)*

ness to poverty, unemployment, and bad labor conditions. Willard joined the Knights of Labor in 1887 and took a greater interest in politics. By the 1890s she had influenced the WCTU to extend its programs in a "do-everything" policy to alleviate the problems of workers, particularly women and children.

The Gospel of Wealth

Frances Willard called herself a Christian socialist because she believed in applying the ethical principles of Jesus to economic life. For Willard and many other educated middle-class reformers, Christianity called for a cooperative social order designed to reduce inequalities of wealth. But for most Americans in the Gilded Age, Christianity supported the competitive individualistic ethic that justified the lofty place of those who were at the top.

This ethic was endorsed by leading ministers and others, who preached sermons and wrote treatises justifying class divisions and the moral superiority of the wealthy. Episcopal Bishop William Lawrence wrote that it was "God's will that some men should attain great wealth." Philadelphia Baptist preacher Russell Conwell's famous sermon "Acres of Diamonds," delivered 6,000 times to an audience estimated at 13 million listeners, praised riches as a sure sign of "godliness" and stressed the power of money to "do good."

Industrialist Andrew Carnegie expressed the ethic most clearly. In an article, "The Gospel of Wealth" (1889), Carnegie celebrated competition for producing better goods at lower prices. The concentration of wealth in the hands of a few leading industrialists, he concluded, was "not only beneficial but essential to the future of the race." Those most fit would bring order and efficiency out of the chaos of rapid industrialization. Carnegie's defense of the new economic order in his article and in a book, *Triumphant Democracy* (1886), found as many supporters as Bellamy's ideas in *Looking Backward*. This was partly because Carnegie insisted that the rich must spend some of their wealth to benefit their "poorer brethren." Carnegie built hundreds of libraries, most still operating in large and small towns throughout the United States, and in later years turned his attentions to other projects, including world peace.

Carnegie's ideas about wealth were drawn from an ideology known as social Darwinism, based on the work of naturalist Charles Darwin, whose famous *Origin of Species* was published in 1859. Darwin had concluded that plant and animal species had evolved through natural selection. In the struggle for existence, some species managed to adapt to their environment and survived; others failed to adapt and perished. Herbert Spencer, an English social philosopher,

adopted this "survival of the fittest" notion to human society. Progress, Spencer said, resulted from relentless competition in which the weak were eliminated and the strong climbed to the top. He believed that "the whole effort of nature is to get rid of such as are unfit, to clear the world of them, and make room for better."

When Spencer visited the United States in 1882, leading men of business, science, religion, and politics thronged to honor him with a lavish banquet at Delmonico's restaurant in New York City. Here was the man whose theories justified their amassed fortunes because they were men of "superior ability, foresight, and adaptability." Spencer warned against any interference in the economic world by tampering with the natural laws of selection. The select at the dinner heaped their praise on Spencer as founder of not only a new sociology but also a new religion.

Spencer's American followers, like Carnegie and Yale political economist William Graham Sumner, familiarized the American public with the basic ideas of social Darwinism. They emphasized that poverty was the inevitable consequence of the struggle for existence and that attempts to end it were pointless, if not immoral. Sumner's emotional hero was the middle-class "forgotten man," but his writings defended the material accumulations of the wealthy. To take power or money away from millionaires, Sumner scoffed, was "like killing off our generals in war." It was "absurd," he wrote, to pass laws permitting society's "worst members" to survive or to "sit down with a slate and pencil to plan out a new social world."

The scientific vocabulary of social Darwinism injected scientific rationality into what often seemed a baffling economic order. Sumner and Spencer argued that underlying laws of political economy, like those of the natural world, dictated economic affairs. Social Darwinists also believed in the superiority of the Anglo-Saxon race, which they maintained had reached the highest stage of evolution. Their theories were used to justify race supremacy and imperialism as well as the monopolistic efforts of American businessmen. Railroad magnate James J. Hill said that the absorption of smaller railroads by larger ones was the industrial analogy of the victory in nature of the fit over the unfit. John D. Rockefeller, Jr., told a YMCA class in Cleveland that "the growth of a large business is merely a survival of the fittest." Like the growth of a beautiful rose, "the early buds which grow up around it" must be sacrificed. This was, he said, "merely the working out of a law of nature and a law of God."

Others questioned this rosy outlook. Brooks Adams, Henry's brother, wrote that social philosophers like Spencer and Sumner were "hired by the comfortable classes to prove that everything was all

The luxury of a fashionable bedroom with chandelier, elegant furniture, and fancy curtains was accessible to anyone who worked hard, according to advocates of the gospel of wealth and social Darwinism. The successful, illustrated here by the bedroom in Alexander Stewart's Fifth Avenue mansion, represented society's "fittest" element. *(Brown Brothers)* This contrasted with poor immigrants forced to live in crowded, filthy, unhealthy, one-room tenements on New York's Lower East Side. *(International Museum of Photography/George Eastman House)*

right." Fading aristocrats like the Adams family, increasingly displaced by a new industrial elite, may have felt a touch of envy for the new rich. They succeeded, however, in suggesting that possibilities for social change were not as closed as the social Darwinists claimed.

Reform Darwinism and Pragmatism

A number of intellectual reformers directly challenged the gloomy social Darwinian notion that nothing could be done to alleviate poverty and injustice. With roots in antebellum abolitionism, women's rights, and other crusades for social justice, men like Wendell Phillips, Frederick Douglass, and Franklin Sanborn and women like Elizabeth Cady Stanton and Susan B. Anthony transferred their reform fervor to postbellum issues. Sanborn, for example, an Emersonian Transcendentalist, founded the American Social Science Association in 1865 to "treat wisely the great social problems of the day." As the Massachusetts inspector of charities in the 1880s, he earned a reputation as the "leading social worker of his day," doing good deeds informed by a developing professional body of social scientific research.

Reformer Henry George, who was not a social scientist, nevertheless observed that wherever the highest degree of "material progress" had been realized, "we find the deepest poverty." George's book, *Progress*

and Poverty (1879), was an early statement of the contradictions of American life. With Bellamy's *Looking Backward*, it was the most influential book of the age, selling 2 million copies by 1905. George admitted that economic growth had produced wonders but pointed out the social costs and the loss of Christian values. His remedy was to break up landholding monopolists who profited from the increasing value of their land, which they rented to those who actually did the work. He proposed a "single tax" on the unearned increases in land value received by landlords. In 1886, on a United Labor party ticket supported by workers, clergymen, and middle-class reformers, George ran well but unsuccessfully for mayor of New York City.

George's solution may seem simplistic, but his religious tone and optimistic faith in the capacity of humans to effect change appealed to many middle-class intellectuals. Some went beyond George's ideas to develop social scientific models to justify active reform. Sociologist Lester Frank Ward and economist Richard T. Ely both found examples of cooperation in nature and demonstrated that competition and laissez-faire had proved both wasteful and inhumane. Reform Darwinists like Ely urged instead an economic order marked by cooperation and social regulation.

Two pragmatists, John Dewey and William James, established a philosophical foundation for reform. James, a Harvard professor, argued that while environment was important, so also was human will. People could influence the course of human events. "What is the 'cash value' of a thought, idea, or belief?" James asked. What was its result? "The ultimate test for us of what a truth means," he said, was in the "consequences" of an idea and what kind of moral "conduct it dictates." He argued that expressions of human sympathy and aversion to both economic and international war were appropriate examples of conduct with ethical consequences.

James and young social scientists such as Ward and Ely gathered statistics documenting social wrongs and rejected the social determinism of Spencer and Sumner. They argued that the application of intelligence and human will could change the "survival of the fittest" into the "fitting of as many as possible to survive." Their position encouraged educators, economists, and reformers of every stripe, giving them an intellectual justification to struggle against misery and inequalities of wealth.

Settlements and Social Gospel

Jane Addams saw the gap between progress and poverty in the streets of Chicago in the winter of 1893. "The stream of laboring people goes past you," she wrote, and "your heart sinks with a sudden sense of futility." Addams had long been aware that life in big cities for working-class families was bitter and hard. Born in rural Illinois, Addams founded Hull House in Chicago in 1889 "to aid in the solution of the social and industrial problems which are engendered by the modern conditions of life in a great city." Young Wellesley literature professor Vida Scudder also "felt the agitating and painful vibrations" of the depression. Scudder returned from study at Oxford resolved to do something to alleviate the suffering of the poor. She and six other Smith College graduates formed an organization of college women in 1889 to work in settlement houses.

Middle-class activists like Addams and Scudder worried about social conditions, particularly the degradation of life and labor in America's cities, factories, and farms. They were mostly professionals—lawyers, ministers, teachers, journalists, and academic social scientists. Influenced by European social prophets like Karl Marx, Leo Tolstoy, and Victor Hugo and by Americans such as Emerson, Whitman, George, and Bellamy, most drew upon the ethical teachings of Jesus for inspiration in solving social problems.

The message Addams and Scudder began to preach in the 1890s was highly idealistic, ethical, and Christian. They preferred a society marked by cooperation rather than competition, where self-sacrifice rather than self-interest held sway and, as they liked to

say, where people were guided by the "golden rule rather than the rule of gold." Like Frances Willard, they meant to apply the ethics of Jesus to industrial and urban life to bring about the kingdom of heaven on earth. Some preferred to put their goals in more secular terms; they spoke of radically transforming American society. Most, however, worked within existing institutions. As middle-class intellectuals, they tended to stress an educational approach to problems. But they were also practical, seeking tangible improvements by running for public office, crusading for legislation, mediating labor disputes, and living in the poor neighborhoods of the people they helped.

The settlement house movement typified the blend of idealism and practicality characteristic of middle-class reformers in the 1890s. Addams opened Hull House, and Scudder started Denison House in Boston. A short time later, on New York's Lower East Side, Lillian Wald opened her "house on Henry Street." The primary purpose of the settlement houses was to help immigrant families, especially women, adapt Old World rural styles of childbearing and child care, housekeeping, and cooking to American urban life. They launched day nurseries, kindergartens, and boarding rooms for working women; they offered classes in sewing, cooking, nutrition, health care, and English; and they tried to keep young people out of saloons by organizing sports clubs and coffeehouses.

A second purpose of the settlement house movement was to give college-educated women meaningful work at a time when they faced professional barriers and to allow them to preserve the strong feelings of sisterhood they had experienced at college. Settlement house workers, Scudder wrote, were like "Early Christians" in their renunciation of worldly goods and dedication to a life of service. Living in a settlement was in many ways an extension of woman's traditional role as nurturer of the weak.

A third goal was to gather data exposing social misery to spur legislative action—developing city building codes for tenements, abolishing child labor, and improving factory safety. Hull House, Addams said, was intended in part "to investigate and improve the conditions in the industrial districts of Chicago."

The settlement house movement, with its dual emphasis on the scientific gathering of facts and spiritual commitment, nourished the new academic study of sociology, first taught in divinity schools. Many organizations were founded to blend Christian belief and academic study in an attempt to change society along Christian collectivist lines. One was the American Institute of Christian Sociology, founded in 1893 by Josiah Strong, a Congregational minister, and economist Richard T. Ely. Similar organizations were the Christian Social Union, the Church Association for

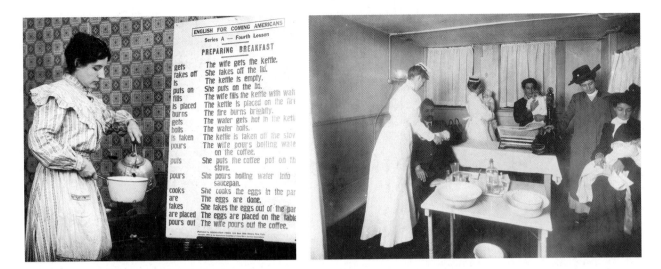

In the settlement houses, immigrant women learned English along with proper cooking, hygiene, child care, and other American domestic practices. *(U.S. Government Education Bureau of the National Geographic Image Collection)* The settlements also included public health clinics, like this one at Vida Scudder's Denison House in Boston. Settlement house work, Scudder wrote, fulfilled "a biting curiosity about the way the Other Half lived, and a strange hunger for fellowship with them." *(Schlesinger Library, Radcliffe Institute, Harvard University)*

the Advancement of the Interests of Labor, and the Society of Christian Socialists.

Dwight Moody preached a more traditional Christianity in American cities, where he led hundreds of urban revivals in the 1870s. The revivals appealed to lower-class rural folk who were either drawn to the city by their hopes or pushed there by economic ruin. Supported by businessmen, who felt that religion would make workers and immigrants more docile, revivalists battled sin through individual conversion. The revivals helped to nearly double Protestant Church membership in the last two decades of the century. Although some urban workers drifted into secular faiths like socialism, most remained conventionally religious.

Unlike Moody, many Protestant ministers embraced the Social Gospel movement of the 1890s, which tied salvation to social betterment. Like the settlement house workers, these religious leaders sought to make Christianity relevant to industrial and urban problems. In Columbus, Ohio, Congregational minister Washington Gladden advocated collective bargaining and various forms of corporate profit sharing in books such as *Working Men and Their Employers, Social Salvation,* and *Applied Christianity.* A young Baptist minister in the notorious Hell's Kitchen area of New York City, Walter Rauschenbusch, raised an even louder voice. Often called on to conduct funeral services for children killed by the airless, diseased tenements and sweatshops, Rauschenbusch scathingly attacked the selfishness of capitalism and church ignorance of socioeconomic issues. His progressive ideas for social justice and a welfare state were later published in two landmark Social Gospel books,

Christianity and the Social Crisis (1907) and *Christianizing the Social Order* (1912).

Perhaps the most influential book promoting social Christianity was a best-selling novel, *In His Steps,* published in 1897 by Charles Sheldon. The novel portrayed the dramatic changes in business relations, tenement life, and urban politics made possible by the work of a few community leaders who resolved to base all their actions on a single question: "What would Jesus do?" For a minister, this meant seeking to "bridge the chasm between the church and labor." For the idle rich, it meant settlement house work and the reform of prostitutes. For landlords and factory owners, it meant improving the living and working conditions of tenants and laborers. Although streaked with naive sentimentality characteristic of much of the Social Gospel, Sheldon's novel prepared thousands of influential middle-class Americans for progressive civic leadership after 1900.

Reforming the City

The crucial event in *In His Steps* was a city election pitting moral middle-class reformers against seedy saloon interests and corrupt urban political machines. No late-nineteenth-century institution needed reforming more than urban government. The president of Cornell University described American city governments as "the worst in Christendom—the most expensive, the most inefficient, and the most corrupt." A Philadelphia committee found "inefficiency, waste, badly paved and filthy streets, unwholesome and offensive water, and slovenly and costly management" to have been the rule for years. Conditions in New York and Chicago, where cholera

Technology Changes the American People

THE BICYCLE

✦

At the Centennial Exhibition in Philadelphia in 1876, a Boston merchant, Albert A. Pope, was so intrigued by the display of an English high-wheeled bicycle that he went to England to study its manufacture. Two years later, "the father of the bicycle in America" began making a model called the "Columbia," in Hartford, Connecticut. In 1887, the Pope Manufacturing Company shifted its production to the even more popular "safety" bicycle, a chain-driven model with two wheels of equal size very much like those we ride today. Within a decade, more than 300 companies were producing over a million bicycles a year, and millions of Americans, mostly middle-class but increasingly including working-class riders, were finding a new mobility and freedom.

The bicycle craze peaked in 1896 and 1897, but the importance of this innovation in transportation—the link between the horse and the automobile—was far-reaching, for the bicycle heralded several major technological and marketing developments of the twentieth century. As Joseph Woodworth wrote in *American Tool Making and Interchangeable Manufacturing* in 1907, "The manufacture of the bicycle . . .brought out the capabilities of the American mechanic as nothing else had ever done. It demonstrated to the world that he and his kind were capable of designing and making special machinery, tools, fixtures, and devices for economic manufacturing in a manner truly marvelous." Moreover, Woodworth went on, the bicycle led to "the installation of the interchangeable system of manufacturing in a thousand and one shops where it was formerly thought to be impractical."

In an 1898 *Atlantic Monthly* article, reviewing 50 years of developments in modern science, W. J. McGee stated that the bicycle was a typical American invention because it not only stimulated inventiveness and new production techniques but also "developed individuality, judgement, and prompt decision on the part of its users." It is revealing that Pope began his manufacture of bicycles in a sewing machine company, which itself had started as a rifle plant, for the manufacturing techniques were virtually identical for all three products. Following the established New England armory principles of machine-produced interchangeable parts, bicycle parts were drop-forged and then machine-tooled and finished. In a noteworthy innovation, again heralding twentieth-century techniques, a Chicago firm, the Western Wheel Works, developed presses for stamping out parts from large sheets of steel. This technique was superior to drop-forging because it was more precise and required less machine tooling. The devel-

The social implications of a new technology—bicycling on Riverside Drive, New York City, 1895. (*The Granger Collection, New York*)

opment of the pneumatic tire completed the crucial technological improvements.

The social implications of the bicycle were as great as the technological ones. The availability of cheaper bicycles was an economic, gender, and even racial leveler, as bicycle riding became accessible to women and working-class Americans. "The bicycle," McGee wrote, "has broken the pernicious differentiation of the sexes" by making available a model for women that opened up areas of freedom, mobility, sport, and good health practices previously unknown. The bicycle even changed "the bonds of fashion" and was "daily impressing Spartan strength and grace, and more than Spartan intelligence, on the mothers of coming generations."

A 17-year-old African American, Marshall "Major" Taylor, who worked in a bicycle shop in Indianapolis ("a beehive of cycling industry"), shocked the cycling world by winning a 75-mile race in Indiana in 1895. Although the League of American Wheelmen (LAW) had excluded "colored persons" from membership at its annual convention in Louisville in 1894, competitive racing, in the North anyway, was generally open to all. As a debate raged in LAW over exclusion, young "Major" Taylor kept winning races and eventually became the American and world sprint champion in 1899. Taylor made a triumphant tour of Europe in 1901 and broke several world records in an era when bicycle racing was as popular a spectator sport as baseball and boxing.

One of W. J. McGee's insights was that the bicycle was shaping national character by "transforming itself and its rider into a single thing," thus providing autonomy of movement and prefiguring the development of the automobile. In 1895, Albert Pope predicted "the advent of the motor-carriage" and employed Hiram Percy Maxim to begin building experimental automobiles. As Maxim put it later, the bicycle "created a new demand which it was beyond the ability of the railroad to supply." Thus, "the bicycle could not satisfy the demand which it had created. A mechanically propelled vehicle was wanted instead of a foot-propelled one, and we now know that the automobile was the answer." With the principles and practice of mass production, interchangeable parts, sheet metal presswork, and democratic use already established, the bicycle almost literally "paved the road" for Henry Ford.

What other mass-produced inventions did bicycle manufacturing lead to that made life easier for Americans in the twentieth century? As a result of the availability of bicycle riding to women, African Americans, and working-class Americans, what other social implications do you think were caused by the invention of the bicycle? How has the bicycle influenced gender and family relations, dress, recreation, health, sexuality, and sports? What do you think about McGee's claims that the bicycle not only transformed gender relations but also shaped American national character?

Andrew Ritchie, *Major Taylor: The Extraordinary Career of a Champion Bicycle Racer* (San Francisco, 1988). Robert A. Smith, *A Social History of the Bicycle: Its Early Life and Times in America* (New York, 1972).

Left, Preautomobile mass production *(Bettmann/CORBIS)*. Right, An early Jackie Robinson. Twenty years old in 1898, Marshall "Major" Taylor appears on the cover of the premier French sports magazine as an international racing star. *(Public Domain)*

615

and typhoid epidemics resulting from raw sewage that was poured into Lake Michigan, were even worse.

While settlement house women sought to reform the city by working in poor immigrant neighborhoods, urban planners and landscape architects attempted to counteract pollution and reshape the larger environment by creating the "city beautiful." Thus, they put in sewers and water mains, planted trees along broadened boulevards, expanded city parks, and erected monumental public buildings—libraries, museums, theaters, and music halls—to establish centers of culture. Boston filled in over 500 acres of tidal flats in the Back Bay, as well as elsewhere around the core of the city, and along tree-lined Commonwealth Avenue created an elegant upper-class neighborhood.

Such environmental transformations of urban space, however beautiful, rarely reached the squalid sections of the city inhabited by the urban masses, who lived in crowded tenement house districts on narrow, dirty streets filled with people, garbage, and animals pulling streetcars and food and clothing carts. Although the "city beautiful" movement was intended to benefit poor as well as rich, it hardly touched these slums, which looked worse by contrast, especially as the influx of European immigrants increased.

Rapid urban growth swamped city leaders with new demands for service. Flush toilets, thirsty horses pulling street railways, and industrial users of water, for example, all exhausted the capacity of municipal waterworks built for an earlier age. As city governments struggled to respond to new needs, they raised taxes and incurred vast debts. This combination of rapid growth, indebtedness, and poor services in crowded immigrant neighborhoods prepared fertile ground for graft and "bossism."

The rise of the boss was directly connected to the growth of the city. As immigrant voters appeared, traditional native-born ruling groups left city government for business, where more money and status beckoned. Into the resulting power vacuum stepped the boss. In an age of urban expansion, bosses dispensed patronage jobs in return for votes and contributions to the party machine. They awarded street railway, gas line, and other utility franchises and construction contracts to local businesses in return for kickbacks and other favors. They also passed on tips to friendly real estate men about the location of projected city improvements. Worse yet, the bosses received favors from the owners of saloons, brothels, and gambling clubs in return for their help with police protection, bail, and influence with the courts. These institutions were vital to the urban economy and played

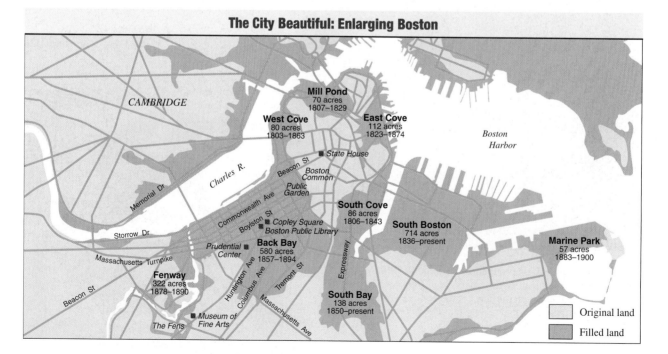

As part of the "city beautiful" movement, Boston filled in coastal swampy lowlands with gravel, thus adding the fashionable Back Bay along Commonwealth Avenue.

THE
BALLOT

IN
COUNTIN
THERE IS
STRENGT

As critically portrayed in many cartoons by Thomas Nast, William "Boss" Tweed was head of New York City's corrupt Democratic Party organization, Tammany Hall. Tweed typified bossism in its cynical disregard for morality, truth, and accurate ballot counting. Here he is saying: "As long as I count the Votes, what are you going to do about it? say?" Well, Nast did a lot about it in his cartoons. (Harper's Weekly, *September 5, 1868*)

an important role in easing the immigrants' way into American life. For many young women, prostitution was a means of economic survival. For men, the saloon was the center of social life and a source of cheap meals and job leads.

Bossism deeply offended middle-class urban reformers, who were unkindly dubbed "goo-goos" for their insistence on purity and good government. They opposed not only graft and vice but also the perversion of democracy by the exploitation of ignorant immigrants. As one explained, the immigrants "follow blindly leaders of their own race, are not moved by discussion, and exercise no judgment of their own." Indeed, he concluded, they were "not fit for the suffrage."

Urban reformers' programs were similar in most cities. They not only worked for the "Americanization" of immigrants in public schools (and opposed parochial schooling) but also formed clubs and voters' leagues to discuss the failings of municipal government. They delighted in making spectacular exposures of electoral irregularities and large-scale graft. These discoveries led to strident calls for replacing the mayor, often an Irish Catholic, with an Anglo-Saxon Protestant reformer.

Political considerations pervaded every reform issue. Many Anglo-Saxon men favored prohibition partly to remove ethnic saloon owners from politics and supported woman suffrage partly to gain a middle-class political advantage against male immigrant voters. Most urban reformers could barely hide their distaste for the "city proletariat mob," as one put it. They proposed to replace the bosses with expert city managers, who would bring honest professionalism to city government. They hoped to make government less costly and thereby lower taxes. One effect of their emphasis on cost efficiency was to cut services to the poor. Another was to disfranchise working-class and ethnic groups, whose political participation depended on the old ward-boss system.

All urban reformers were not elitist managerial types. Samuel Jones of Toledo, Ohio, opposed bossism and passionately advocated political participation by urban immigrants. He had himself begun as a poor Welsh immigrant in the Pennsylvania oil fields. In the rags-to-riches tradition, Jones worked his way up to the ownership of several oil fields and a factory in Toledo. Once successful, however, Jones espoused a different ethic from Carnegie's "Gospel of Wealth." Jones described himself as a "Golden Rule man," converted by a combination of firsthand contact with the "piteous appeals" of people put out of work by the depression and by his reading of Emerson, Whitman, Tolstoy, and the New Testament.

In 1894, Jones resolved that he would "apply the Golden Rule as a rule of conduct" in his factory. He instituted an eight-hour day for his employees. In addition, he gave them $2 minimum wage per day (50 to 75 cents higher than the Toledo average for ten hours), a cooperative insurance program, and an annual 5 percent Christmas dividend. Plastering the Golden Rule over his factory walls, Jones hired former criminals and social outcasts. He anticipated twentieth-century industrial reforms by creating a company cafeteria and offering a hot lunch for 15 cents, a Golden Rule park for workers and their families, employee music groups, and a Golden Rule Hall, where he invited social visionaries to speak.

In 1897, Jones decided to extend his notions of cooperation and brotherhood to city government (much as Hazen Pingree had been doing in nearby Detroit) and was elected to the first of an unprecedented four terms as mayor as a maverick Republican. As mayor, Jones antagonized prominent citizens and was adored by ordinary people. He advocated municipal ownership of natural gas, street railways, and other utilities; public works jobs and housing for the unemployed; more civic parks and playgrounds; and free municipal baths, pools, skating rinks, sleigh rides, vocational education, and kindergartens (few of which were implemented). A pacifist, he did not believe in violence or coercion of any kind and took away policemen's sidearms and heavy clubs. In police court, he regularly dismissed most cases of petty theft and drunkenness on grounds that the accused were victims of social injustice, and he usually released prostitutes after fining every man in the room 10 cents—and himself a dollar—for condoning prostitution. Crime in notoriously sinful Toledo fell during his term. When he died in 1904, nearly 55,000 people, "tears streaming down their faces," filed past his coffin.

The Struggle for Woman Suffrage

Women served, in Jane Addams's phrase, as "urban housekeepers" in the settlement house and good government movements, which reflected the tension many women felt between their public and private lives, between their obligations to self, family, and society. This tension was not usually expressed openly. A few women writers, however, began to vent the frustrations and restraints of middle-class domestic life. In her novel *The Awakening* (1899), Kate Chopin portrayed a young woman who, in awakening to her own sexuality and life's possibilities beyond being a "mother-woman," defied conventional expectations of woman's role. Her sexual affair and eventual suicide prompted a St. Louis newspaper to say of the novel that it was "too strong drink for moral babes and should be labeled 'poison.'"

Some middle-class women, Addams and Scudder, for example, avoided marriage altogether, preferring the nurturing relationships found in the female settlement house community. "Married life looks to me . . . terribly impoverished for women," a Smith College graduate observed, declaring that "most of my deeper friendships have been with women." A few women boldly advocated free love or, less openly, formed lesbian relationships. Although most women preferred traditional marriages and chose not to work outside the home, the generation of women that came of age in the 1890s married less—and later—than any other in American history.

One way women reconciled the conflicting pressures between their private and public lives, and deflected male criticism, was to see their work as maternal. Addams called Hull House the "great mother breast of our common humanity." Frances Willard told Susan B. Anthony in 1898 that "government is only housekeeping on the broadest scale," a job men had botched, thus requiring women's saving participation. One of the leading female organizers of coal workers was "Mother" Jones, and the fiery feminist anarchist Emma Goldman titled her monthly journal *Mother Earth*. By using maternal language to describe their work, women furthered the very arguments used against them. Many, of course, remained economically dependent on men, and all women still lacked the essential rights of citizenship. How could they be municipal housekeepers if they could not yet even vote?

After the Seneca Falls Convention in 1848, women's civil and political rights advanced very slowly. Although several western states gave women the right to vote in municipal and school board elections, before 1890 only the territory of Wyoming (1869) granted full political equality. Colorado, Utah, and Idaho enfranchised women in the 1890s, but no other states granted suffrage until 1910. This slow pace resulted in part from an antisuffrage movement led by an odd combination of ministers, saloon interests, and men threatened in various ways by women's voting rights. "Equal suffrage," said a Texas senator, "is a repudiation of manhood."

In the 1890s, leading suffragists reexamined the situation. The two wings of the women's rights movement, split since 1869, combined in 1890 as the National American Woman Suffrage Association (NAWSA). Although Elizabeth Cady Stanton and Susan B. Anthony continued to head the association, both were in their seventies. Effective leadership passed to younger, more moderate women who, unlike Stanton and Anthony, concentrated on the single issue of the vote. Moderate leaders were also embarrassed by Stanton's *Woman's Bible* (1895), a devastating attack

The young Jane Addams was one of the college-educated women who chose to remain unmarried and pursue a career as an "urban housekeeper" and social reformer, serving immigrant families in the Chicago neighborhood near her Hull House. *(The University of Illinois at Chicago, The University Library, Jane Addams Memorial Collection)*

on the religious argument against woman suffrage. At the NAWSA convention in 1896, despite the pleas of Anthony not to "sit in judgment" on her good friend, a resolution renouncing any NAWSA connection with Stanton's book passed by a vote of 53 to 41.

Changing leadership meant a shift from principled to expedient arguments for the suffrage. Since 1848, suffragists had made their argument primarily from principle, citing, as Stanton argued at a congressional hearing in 1892, "our republican idea, individual citizenship." But as Stanton's leadership waned, younger leaders shifted to three expedient arguments. The first was that women needed the vote to pass self-protection laws to guard against rapists and unsafe industrial work. The second argument, Addams's notion of urban housekeeping, pointed out that political enfranchisement would further women's role in cleaning up immoral cities and corrupt politics.

The third expedient argument reflected urban middle-class reformers' prejudice against non-

Protestant immigrants. Machine bosses saw to it that immigrant men got to vote, sometimes several times in a day. Suffragists argued that educated, native-born American women should be given the vote to counteract the undesirable influence of what they saw as ignorant, illiterate male immigrants. In an Iowa speech in 1894, Carrie Chapman Catt, who would succeed Anthony as president of NAWSA in 1900, argued that the "Government is menaced with great danger . . . in the votes possessed by the males in the slums of the cities." This danger, she argued, could be averted by taking away the immigrant male vote and giving it instead to women. In the new century, under the leadership of women like Catt, suffrage would finally be secured.

THE PIVOTAL 1890S

Americans mistakenly think of the last decade of the nineteenth century as the "gay nineties," symbolized by mustached baseball players, sporty Gibson girls, and the opulent dinners of rich entrepreneurs. The 1890s was, indeed, a decade of sports and leisure, the electrification of the city, and the enormous wealth of the few. But for many more Americans, as we have seen, it was also a decade of dark tenements and grinding work or desperate unemployment and poverty. The early 1890s were marked by Populism and protesting farmers; Wounded Knee and the "second great removal" of Native Americans; lynchings, disfranchisement, and the "nadir of black life"; and the "new immigration," a changing workplace, and devastating labor defeats at Coeur d'Alene, Homestead, and Pullman (Chapters 17 and 18).

The 1890s, far from gay, were years of contrasts and crises. The obvious contrast, as Bellamy had anticipated, was between the rich and the poor. As the Populist Omaha platform put it, "We breed two great classes—paupers and millionaires." Supreme Court Justice John Harlan saw a "deep feeling of unrest" everywhere among people worrying that the nation was in "real danger from . . . the slavery that would result from aggregations of capital in the hands of a few." Populist "Sockless" Jerry Simpson simply saw a struggle between "the robbers and the robbed." On the one side, Simpson saw "the allied hosts of monopolies, the money power, great trusts, and railroad corporations, who seek the enactment of laws to benefit them and impoverish the people." On the other, he put those "who produce wealth and bear the burdens of taxation. Between these two there is no middle ground."

Although Simpson was wrong about the absence of a middle ground, the gap was indeed huge between the rich and poor. The fiery Kansas orator Mary E.

The contrasts between rich and poor and the threat of social upheaval are dramatically illustrated in this turn-of-the-century work, called "From the Depths." *(Culver Pictures)*

Lease said in 1890, "What you farmers need to do is to raise less corn, and more Hell"; by contrast, a wealthy Indianapolis woman told her husband, "I'm going to Europe and spend my money before these crazy people take it." The pivotal nature of the 1890s hinged on this feeling of polarizing unrest and upheaval as the nation underwent the traumas of change from a rural to an urban society. The new immigration from Europe and the northward, westward, and cityward internal migrations of blacks and farmers added to the "great danger" against which Carrie Catt warned. The depression of 1893 widened the gap between rich and poor and accelerated demands for reform. The federal government bureaucracy slowly began to adapt to the needs of governing a complex specialized society, and Congress toyed with abandoning laissez-faire to confront national problems.

Republican Legislation in the Early 1890s

Harrison's election in 1888 was accompanied by Republican control of both houses of Congress. The Republicans moved forward in the first six months of 1890 with legislation in five areas: pensions for Civil War veterans and their dependents, trusts, the tariff, the money question, and rights for blacks. A bill providing generous support of $160 million a year for Union veterans and their dependents sailed through Congress.

The Sherman Anti-Trust Act passed with only one nay vote. It declared illegal "every contract, combination . . . or conspiracy in restraint of trade or commerce." Although the Sherman Act was vague and not really intended to break up big corporations, it was an initial attempt to restrain large business combinations. But in *United States* v. *E. C. Knight* (1895), the Supreme Court ruled that the American Sugar Refining Company, which controlled more than 90 percent of the nation's sugar-refining capacity, was not in violation of the Sherman Act

A tariff bill introduced in 1890 by Ohio Republican William McKinley stirred more controversy. McKinley's bill raised tariff rates to higher levels than ever before. Despite heated opposition from agrarian interests, whose products were generally not protected, the bill passed the House and, after nearly 500 amendments, also the Senate.

Silver was trickier. Recognizing the appeal of free silver to agrarian debtors and the new Populist party, Republican leaders feared their party might be destroyed by the issue. Senator Sherman proposed a compromise that momentarily satisfied almost everyone. The Sherman Silver Purchase Act ordered the Treasury to buy 4.5 million ounces of silver monthly and to issue Treasury notes for it. Silverites were pleased by the proposed increase in the money supply. Opponents felt they had averted the worst—free coinage of silver. The gold standard remained secure.

Republicans were also prepared to confront violations of the voting rights of southern blacks in 1890. President Harrison told the editor of the New York *Tribune,* "I feel very strong upon the question of a free ballot." As usual, political considerations paralleled moral ones. Since 1877, the South had become a Democratic stronghold, where party victories could be traced to fraud and intimidation of black Republican voters. "To be a Republican . . . in the South," one Georgian noted, "is to be a foolish martyr." Republican legislation, then, would honor old commitments to the freedmen and improve party fortunes in the South. An elections bill, proposed by Massachusetts Senator Henry Cabot Lodge, tried to ensure African American voter registration and fair elections. But Democrats disapproved, calling Lodge's measure the "Force Bill." Former president Cleveland called it a "dark blow at the freedom of the ballot," and the Mobile *Daily Register* claimed that it "would deluge the South in blood." Senate Democrats delayed action with a filibuster.

Meanwhile, Republican leaders, to secure passage of the McKinley Tariff, bargained away the elections bill. The ploy marked the end of major party efforts to protect African American voting rights in the South until the 1960s. In a second setback for black southerners, the Senate defeated a bill to provide federal aid to schools in the South, mostly black, that did not receive their fair share of local and state funds. These two failed measures were the last gasp of the Republican party's commitment to the idealistic principles of Reconstruction. "The plain truth is," said the New York *Herald,* "the North has got tired of the negro," foreshadowing a similar abandonment in the 1980s and 1990s.

The legislative efforts of the summer of 1890, impressive by nineteenth-century standards, fell far short of solving the nation's problems. Trusts grew more rapidly after the Sherman Act than before.

Union veterans were pleased by their pensions, but southerners were incensed that Confederate veterans were left out. Others, seeing the pension measure as extravagant, labeled the 51st Congress the "billion-dollar Congress." Despite efforts to please farmers, many still viewed tariff protection as a benefit primarily for eastern manufacturers. Farm prices continued to slide, and gold and silver advocates were only momentarily silenced. African American rights were put off to another time. Polarizing inequalities of wealth remained. Nor did Republican legislative activism lead the Republicans to a "permanent tenure of power," as party leaders had hoped. Voters abandoned the party in droves in the 1890 congressional elections, dropping the Republican contingent in the House from 168 to 88.

Two years later, Cleveland won a presidential rematch with Harrison. "The lessons of paternalism ought to be unlearned," he said in his inaugural address, "and the better lesson taught that while the people should . . . support their government, its functions do not include the support of the people."

The Depression of 1893

Cleveland's philosophy soon faced a difficult test. No sooner had he taken office than began one of the worst depressions ever to grip the American economy, lasting from 1893 to 1897. Its severity was heightened by the growth of a national economy and economic interdependence. The depression started in Europe and spread to the United States as overseas buyers cut back on their purchases of American products. Shrinking markets abroad soon crippled American manufacturing. Foreign investors, worried about the stability of American currency after passage of the Sherman Silver Purchase Act, dumped some $300 million of their securities in the United States. As gold left the country to pay for these securities, the nation's money supply declined. At the same time, falling prices hurt farmers, many of whom discovered that it cost more to raise their crops and livestock than they could make in the market. Workers fared no better, as wages fell faster than the price of food and rent.

The collapse in 1893 was also caused by serious over-extensions of the domestic economy, especially in railroad construction. Farmers, troubled by falling prices, planted more and more crops, hoping that the market would pick up. As the realization of overextension spread, confidence faltered and then gave way to financial panic. When Wall Street crashed early in 1893, investors frantically sold their shares, companies plunged into bankruptcy, and disaster spread. People rushed to exchange paper notes for gold, reducing gold reserves and confidence in the econo-

MAJOR LEGISLATIVE ACTIVITY OF THE GILDED AGE

In the table, notice the kinds of issues dealt with at the different levels: mostly money, tariff, immigration, and civil service legislation at the national level and emotional "hot button" social and value issues in the states and localities.

Date	National
1871	National Civil Service Commission created
1873	Coinage Act demonetizes silver
	"Salary Grab" Act (increased salaries of Congress and top federal officials) partly repealed
1875	Specie Resumption Act retires greenback dollars
1878	Bland-Allison Act permits partial coining of silver
1882	Chinese Exclusion Act
	Federal Immigration Law restricts certain categories of immigrants and requires head tax of all immigrants
1883	Standard time (four time zones) established for the entire country
	Pendleton Civil Service Act
1887	Interstate Commerce Act sets up Interstate Commerce Commission
	Dawes Act divides Indian tribal lands into individual allotments
1890	Dependent Pension Act grants pensions to Union army veterans
	Sherman Anti-Trust Act
	Sherman Silver Purchase Act has government buy more silver
	McKinley Tariff sets high protective tariff
	Federal elections bill to protect black voting rights in South fails in Senate
	Blair bill to provide support for education defeated
1891	Immigration law gives federal government control of overseas immigration
1893	Sherman Silver Purchase Act repealed
1894	Wilson-Gorman Tariff lowers duties slightly
1900	Currency Act puts United States on gold standard

Date	State and Local
1850s–1880s	State and local laws intended to restrict or prohibit consumption of alcoholic beverages
1871	Illinois Railroad Act sets up railroad commission to fix rates and prohibit discrimination
1874	Railroad regulatory laws in Wisconsin and Iowa
1881	Kansas adopts statewide prohibition
1882	Iowa passes state prohibition amendment
1880s	Massachusetts, Connecticut, Rhode Island, Montana, Michigan, Ohio, and Missouri all pass local laws prohibiting consumption of alcohol
	Santa Fe ring dominates New Mexico politics and land grabbing
1889	New Jersey repeals a county-option prohibition law of 1888
	Laws in Wisconsin and Illinois mandate compulsory attendance of children at schools in which instruction is in English
	Kansas, Maine, Michigan, and Tennessee pass antitrust laws
1889–1890	Massachusetts debates bill on compulsory schooling in English
1899–1902	Eleven former Confederate states amend state constitutions and pass statutes restricting the voting rights of blacks
1890–1910	Eleven former Confederate states pass segregation laws
1891	Nebraska passes eight-hour workday law
1893	Colorado adopts woman suffrage
1894–1896	Woman suffrage referenda defeated in Kansas and California

my even further. Banks called in loans, which by the end of the year led to 16,000 business bankruptcies and 500 bank failures.

The decrease in available capital and diminished buying power of rural and small-town Americans (still half the population) forced massive factory closings. Within a year, an estimated three million Americans—20 percent of the workforce—lost jobs. People fearfully watched tramps wandering from city to city looking for work. "There are thousands of homeless and starving men in the streets," one young man reported from Chicago, indicating that he had seen "more misery in this last week than I ever saw in my life before."

As in Bellamy's coach image, the misery of the many was not shared by the few, which only increased discontent. While unemployed men foraged in garbage dumps for food, the wealthy gave lavish parties sometimes costing $100,000. At one such affair, diners ate their meal while seated on horses; at another, many guests proudly proclaimed that they had spent over $10,000 on their attire. While poor families shivered in poorly heated tenements, the very rich built million-dollar summer resorts at Newport, Rhode Island, or grand mansions on New York's Fifth Avenue and Chicago's Gold Coast. While Lithuanian immigrants walked or rode streetcars to Buffalo steel factories to work, wealthy men skimmed across lakes and oceans in huge pleasure yachts. J. P. Morgan owned three, one with a crew of 85 sailors.

Nowhere were these inequalities more apparent than in Chicago during the World's Columbian Exposition, which opened on May 1, 1893, five days before a plummeting stock market began the depression. The Chicago World's Fair was designed, as President Cleveland said in an opening-day speech, to show off the "stupendous results of American enterprise." When he pressed an ivory telegraph key, he started electric current that unfurled flags, spouted water through gigantic fountains, lit 10,000 electric

lights, and powered huge steam engines, 37 in one building alone. For six months, some 27 million visitors strolled around the White City, admiring its wide lagoons, its neoclassical white plaster buildings, and its exhibit halls filled with inventions. Built at a cost of $31 million, the fair celebrated the marvelous mechanical accomplishments of American enterprise and of the "city beautiful" movement to make cities more livable.

But as fairgoers sipped pink champagne, in immigrant wards less than a mile away people drank contaminated water, crowded into packed tenements, and looked in vain for jobs. The area around Jane Addams's Hull House was especially disreputable, with saloons, gambling halls, brothels, and pawnshops dotting the neighborhood. "If Christ came to Chicago," a British journalist, W. T. Stead, wrote in a book of that title in

The depression of 1893 accentuated contrasts between rich and poor. While middle-class Americans enjoyed visiting the Palace of Electricity and boating on the lagoons of the Chicago World's Columbian Exposition (above) *(Corbis/Bettman)*, slum children played in filthy streets nearby, Jane Addams's Hull House less than a mile away (left). *(Library of Congress)*

1894, this would be "one of the last precincts into which we should care to take Him." Stead's book showed readers the "ugly sight" of corruption, poverty, and wasted lives in a city with 200 millionaires and 200,000 unemployed men.

Despite the magnitude of despair during the depression, national politicians and leaders were reluctant to respond. Only mass demonstrations forced city authorities to provide soup kitchens and places for the homeless to sleep. When an army of unemployed led by Jacob Coxey marched on Washington in the spring of 1894 to press for public work relief, its leaders were arrested for stepping on the Capitol grass. Cleveland's reputation for callousness worsened later that summer when he sent federal troops to Chicago to crush the Pullman strike.

The president focused on tariff reform and repeal of the Silver Purchase Act, which he blamed for the depression. Although repeal was ultimately necessary to reestablish business confidence, in the short run, Cleveland only worsened the financial crisis, focused attention further on silver as a panacea, and hurt conservative Democrats. With workers, farmers, and wealthy silver miners alienated, in the midterm elections of 1894, voters abandoned the Democrats in droves, giving both Populists and Republicans high hopes for 1896.

The Crucial Election of 1896

The campaign of 1896, waged during the depression and featuring a climactic battle over the currency, was one of the most critical in American history. Although Cleveland was in disgrace for ignoring depression woes, few leaders in either major party thought the federal government was responsible for alleviating the suffering of the people. But unskilled Slavic workers tending Pennsylvania blast furnaces, unemployed Polish meatpackers in Chicago, railway firemen in Terre Haute, Italian immigrant women in New Haven tenements, and desperate white and black tenant farmers in Georgia all wondered where relief might be found. Would either major party respond to the pressing human needs of the depression? Would the People's party succeed in setting a new national agenda for politics? Or would the established order prevail? These questions were raised and largely resolved in the election of 1896.

As the election approached, Populist leaders emphasized the silver issue and debated whether to fuse with one of the major parties by agreeing on a joint ticket, which meant abandoning much of the Populist platform. Influenced by silver mine owners, many Populists became convinced that the hope of the party lay in a single-issue commitment to the free and unlimited coinage of silver at the ratio of 16 to 1. Populist candidate James Weaver expected both parties to nominate gold candidates, which he thought would send silverites to the Populist standard.

In the throes of the depression in the mid-1890s, silver took on enormous importance as the symbol of the many grievances of downtrodden Americans. Popular literature captured the rural, moral dimen-

William Jennings Bryan, surprise nominee at the 1896 Democratic Convention, was a vigorous proponent of the "cause of humanity." His nomination threw the country into a frenzy of fear and the Populist party into a fatal decision over "fusion." *(Library of Congress)*

sions of the silver movement. Although William Harvey's highly popular *Coin's Financial School* (1894) was more timely, L. Frank Baum's *Wonderful Wizard of Oz* (1900), written as a "modernized fairy tale," has had an enduring claim on the hearts of all Americans. Baum's classic was a free-silver moral allegory of rural values (Kansas, Auntie Em, the uneducated but wise scarecrow, and the goodhearted tin woodsman) and Populist policies (the wicked witch of the East and the magical silver shoes in harmony with the yellow brick road, in "Oz"—ounces).

The Republicans, holding their convention first, nominated William McKinley on the first ballot. A congressman from 1877 to 1891 and twice governor of Ohio, McKinley was happily identified with the high protective tariff that bore his name. Citing the familiar argument that prosperity depended on the gold standard and protection, Republicans blamed the depression on Cleveland's attempt to lower the tariff.

The excitement of the Democratic convention in July contrasted with the staid, smoothly organized Republican gathering. State after state elected delegates pledged to silver, thus repudiating Cleveland's policies. Gold Democrats, however, had enough power left to wage a close battle for the platform plank on money. The Democrats' surprise nominee was an ardent young silverite, William Jennings Bryan, a 36-year-old former congressman from Nebraska. Few saw him as presidential material, but Bryan arranged to give the closing argument for a silver plank himself. His dramatic speech swept the convention for silver and ensured his own nomination. "I come to speak to you," Bryan cried out, "in defense of a cause as holy as the cause of liberty—the cause of humanity." At the conclusion of what was to become one of the most famous political speeches in American history, Bryan attacked the "goldbugs" and promised,

> having behind us the producing masses of this nation . . . and toilers everywhere, we will answer their demand for a gold standard by saying to them: "You shall not press down upon the brow of labor this crown of thorns, you shall not crucify mankind upon a cross of gold."

Bryan stretched out his arms as if on a cross, and the convention exploded with applause.

Populist strategy lay in shambles when the Democrats named a silver candidate. Some party leaders favored fusion with the Democratic ticket (whose vice presidential candidate was a goldbug), but antifusionists were outraged. Unwisely, the Populists nominated Bryan with Georgia Populist Tom

In his 1896 campaign, William McKinley periodically spoke to visitors gathered at his home, flailing free silver and flaunting the flag. His landslide electoral victory represented Americans' endorsement of the Republican party as the party of prosperity, tariff protection, thriving factories, and the gold standard. *(The Granger Collection, New York)*

Recovering the Past

POLITICAL CAMPAIGN ARTIFACTS: BUTTONS AND POSTERS

istorians recover the past, as we have seen, in printed sources such as books, diaries, magazines, and government documents as well as in visual records such as paintings, photographs, and the artifacts of material culture. Throughout American history, presidential political campaigns have produced, in addition to the streams of speeches, words and sound bites, mountains of material objects: buttons, badges, banners, bumper stickers, yard signs, posters, cartoons, and other campaign paraphernalia pointing out why voters should support one candidate or another.

The election of 1896 was no exception and, in fact, produced a plethora of political campaign artifacts on behalf of William McKinley and William Jennings Bryan. The fervor of that pivotal political contest led to the production of thousands and thousands of lapel pins, buttons, ribbons, bandanas, shirts, teacups, paper cutout and soap dolls, posters, and other articles intended to influence American voters to cast their ballot for Bryan or McKinley. Although some of it seems silly, symbolic imagery was important. The examination of just two kinds of material paraphernalia—buttons and posters—reveals a great deal about the issues, values, symbolism, and style of the election of 1896.

Examine the buttons pictured here (as well as the "goldbug" and other stickpins). What issues are voters reminded of, and how complex is the message? How many different ways is the message, reinforced by recurring symbols, repeated on these buttons? Now compare the buttons and pins with the two posters. Do not worry that you cannot read most of the words; focus instead on the visual imagery and such words as you can make out. How do the posters reinforce key symbols, slogans, and substantive issues associated with each candidate?

What images do the posters add? What audience do you think these campaign artifacts had in mind? What summary statements would you make about the 1896 campaign on the basis of these material items? Do these artifacts suggest that voters were more or less involved with political issues and party identification than they are today? Do campaigners today use buttons and posters, or their equivalents? What would modern campaign artifacts tell future historians about presidential elections and parties at the dawn of the twenty-first century?

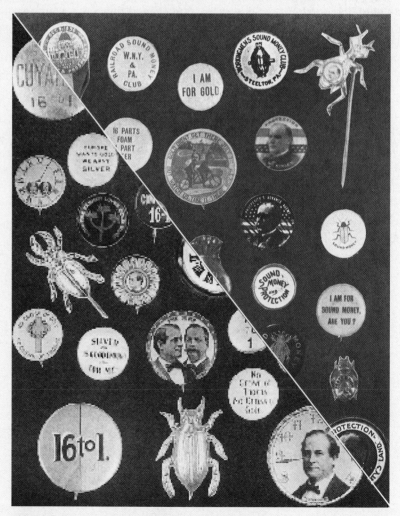

Below left, Bryan campaign artifacts (*Courtesy Rodger Fischer*). Above right, McKinley campaign artifacts (*Courtesy Michael Kelly*).

Campaign poster showing William McKinley and his running mate, Garret Hobart. *(Library of Congress)*

Campaign poster showing William Jennings Bryan, his wife and children, and the text of the "Cross of Gold" speech. *(The Granger Collection, New York)*

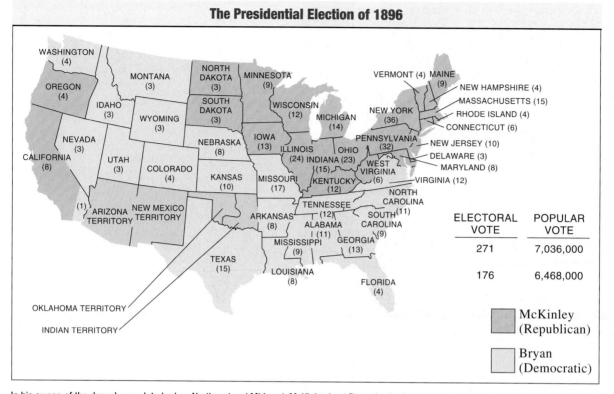

The Presidential Election of 1896

ELECTORAL VOTE	POPULAR VOTE
271	7,036,000
176	6,468,000

■ McKinley (Republican)

□ Bryan (Democratic)

In his sweep of the densely populated urban Northeast and Midwest, McKinley beat Bryan by the largest popular vote margin since 1872. In his cabled congratulations, the first ever by a loser, Bryan, ever the "democrat," said: "We have submitted the issues to the American people and their will is law." Note that California's nine electoral votes (few compared with today) were split. As was then legal, one elector, from the Imperial Valley bordering the Arizona Territory, voted for Bryan and the Democrats.

Watson as his running mate. Running on competing silverite slates damaged Bryan's electoral hopes.

During the campaign, McKinley stayed at his home in Canton, Ohio, where some 750,000 admirers came to visit him, brought by low excursion rates offered by the railroads. The republicans made an unprecedented effort to reach voters through a highly sophisticated media campaign, heavily financed by such major corporations as Standard Oil and the railroads. Party leaders hired thousands of speakers to support McKinley and distributed over 200 million pamphlets in 14 languages to a voting population of 15 million, all advertising McKinley as the "advance agent of prosperity."

From his front porch in Canton, McKinley responded to Bryan's challenge by aiming his appeal not only at the business classes but also at unemployed workers, to whom he promised a "full dinner pail." He also spoke about the money issue, declaring that "our currency today is . . . as good as gold." Free silver, he maintained, would lead to inflation and more economic disaster. Recovery depended not on money but on tariff reform to stimulate industry and provide jobs—"not open mints for the unlimited coinage of the silver of the world," he said, "but open mills for

the full and unrestricted labor of American workingmen."

In sharp contrast to the Republican stay-at-home policy, Bryan took his case to the people. Three million people in 27 states heard him speak as he traveled over 18,000 miles, giving as many as 30 speeches a day. Bryan's message was simple. Prosperity required free coinage of silver. Government policies should attend to the needs of the producing classes rather than the vested interests that believed in the gold standard. "That policy is best for this country," Bryan proclaimed, "which brings prosperity first to those who toil." But his rhetoric favored rural toilers. "The great cities rest upon our broad and fertile prairies," he had said in the "Cross of Gold" speech. "Burn down your cities and leave our farms, and your cities will spring up again as if by magic; but destroy our farms and the grass will grow in the streets of every city in the country." Urban workers were not inspired by this rhetoric, nor immigrants by Bryan's prairie moralizing.

To influential easterners, the brash young Nebraskan represented a threat to social harmony. Theodore Roosevelt wrote: "This silver craze surpasses belief. Bryan's election would be a great calamity." A

Brooklyn minister declared that the Democratic plat-form was "made in Hell." One newspaper editor said of Bryan that he was just like Nebraska's Platte River: "six inches deep and six miles wide at the mouth." Others branded him a "madman" and an "anarchist." The New York *Mail* wrote, "No wild-eyed and rattle-brained horde of the red flag ever proclaimed a fiercer defiance of law, precedent, order, and government."

With such intense interest in the election, voters turned out in record numbers. In key states like Illinois, Indiana, and Ohio, 95 percent of those eligible to vote went to the polls. McKinley won 271 electoral votes to Bryan's 176. Millionaire Mark Hanna jubilant-ly wired McKinley: "God's in his heaven, all's right with the world." Bryan was defeated by the largest popular majority since Grant trounced Greeley in 1872.

Although Bryan won over six million votes (47 per-cent of the total), more than any previous Democratic winner, he failed to carry the Midwest or the urban middle classes and industrial masses, who had little confidence that the Democrats could stimulate eco-nomic growth or cope with industrialism. McKinley's promise of a "full dinner pail" was more convincing than the untested formula for free silver. Northern laborers feared that inflation would leave them even poorer—that prices and rents would rise faster than their wages. Catholic immigrants distrusted Populist Protestantism. In the Great Lakes states, prosperous farmers felt less discontent than farmers elsewhere. But chance also played a part in Bryan's defeat. Bad wheat harvests in India, Australia, and Argentina drove up world grain prices, and many of the com-plaints of American farmers evaporated with a better price for their crops.

The New Shape of American Politics

The landslide Republican victory broke the stalemate that had characterized American politics since the end of the Civil War. Republicans dropped their identifi-cation with the politics of piety and strengthened their image as the party of prosperity and national great-ness, which gave them a party dominance that lasted until the 1930s. The Democrats, under Bryan's leader-ship until 1912, put on the mantle of Populist moral-ism but were largely reduced to a sectional party, reflecting narrow southern views on money, race, and national power. The 1896 election demonstrated that the Northeast and Great Lakes states had acquired so many immigrants that they now controlled the nation's political destiny. The demoralized Populists disappeared. Within the next 20 years, however, many Populist issues were taken over and adopted by the two major parties.

Another result of the election of 1896 was a change in the pattern of political participation. Because the Republicans were so dominant outside of the South, and Democrats so powerful in the South, few states had vigorous two-party political battles and less reason to mobilize large numbers of voters. With elec-tion results so often a foregone conclusion, voters had little motivation to cast a ballot. Many black voters in the South, moreover, were disfranchised, and middle-class good government reformers succeeded in reduc-ing the high voter turnout achieved by urban party bosses. Thus, the tremendous rate of political partici-pation that had characterized the nineteenth century

Timeline

1873	Congress demonetizes silver
1875	Specie Resumption Act
1877	Rutherford B. Hayes becomes president
1878	Bland-Allison Act
1879	Henry George, *Progress and Poverty*
1880	James A. Garfield elected president
1881	Garfield assassinated; Chester A. Arthur succeeds to presidency
1883	Pendleton Civil Service Act
1884	Grover Cleveland elected president
1887	College Settlement House Association founded
1888	Edward Bellamy, *Looking Backward*
	Benjamin Harrison elected president
1889	Jane Addams establishes Hull House
	Andrew Carnegie promulgates "The Gospel of Wealth"
1890	Sherman Anti-Trust Act
	Sherman Silver Purchase Act
	McKinley Tariff
	Elections bill defeated
1890s	Wyoming, Colorado, Utah, and Idaho grant women suffrage
1892	Cleveland elected president for the second time; Populist party wins over a million votes
	Homestead steel strike
1893	World's Columbian Exposition, Chicago
1893–1897	Financial panic and depression
1894	Pullman strike
	Coxey's march on Washington
1895	*United States* v. *E. C. Knight*
1896	Populist party fuses with Democrats
	William McKinley elected president
1897	"Golden Rule" Jones elected mayor of Toledo, Ohio
	Economic recovery begins
	Charles Sheldon, *In His Steps*

since the Jackson era gradually declined. In the twentieth century, political involvement among poorer Americans lessened considerably, a phenomenon unique among Western industrial countries.

McKinley had promised that Republican rule meant prosperity, and as soon as he took office, the economy recovered. Discoveries of gold in the Yukon and the Alaskan Klondike increased the money supply, ending the silver mania until the early 1930s. Industrial production returned to full capacity. Touring the Midwest in 1898, McKinley spoke to cheering crowds about the hopeful economic picture. "We have gone from industrial depression to industrial activity," he told citizens of Clinton, Iowa, who burst into enthusiastic applause.

McKinley's election marked not only the return of economic health but also the emergence of the executive as the preeminent focus of the American political system. Just as McKinley's campaign set the pattern for the extravagant efforts to win office that have dominated modern times, his conduct as president foreshadowed the twentieth-century presidency. McKinley rejected traditional views of the president as the passive executor of laws, instead playing an active role in dealing with Congress and the press. His frequent trips away from Washington showed an increasing regard for public opinion. Some historians see McKinley as the first modern president in his emphasis on the role of the chief executive in contributing to industrial growth and national power. As we shall see in Chapter 20, he began the transformation of the presidency into a potent force, not only in domestic life, but in world affairs as well.

Conclusion

Looking Forward

This chapter began with Edward Bellamy's imaginary look backward from the year 2000 at the grim economic realities and unresponsive politics of American life in the late nineteenth century. McKinley's triumph in 1896 indicated that in a decade marked by depression, Populist revolt, and cries for action to close the inequalities of wealth—represented by Bellamy's coach—the established order remained intact and politics remained as unresponsive as ever. Calls for change did not necessarily lead to change. But in the areas of personal action and the philosophical bases for social change, intellectual middle-class reformers like Edward Bellamy, Henry George, William James, Jane Addams, "Golden Rule" Jones, and many others were showing the way to progressive reforms in the new century. More Americans were able to look forward to the kind of cooperative, caring, and cleaner world envisioned in Bellamy's utopian novel.

As 1900 approached, people took a predictably intense interest in what the new century would be like. Henry Adams, still the pessimist, saw an ominous future, predicting the explosive and ultimately destructive energy of unrestrained industrial development, symbolized by the "dynamo" and other engines of American power. Such forces, he warned, would overwhelm the gentler, moral forces represented by art, woman, and religious symbols like the Virgin. But others were more optimistic, preferring to place their confidence in America's historic role as an exemplary nation, demonstrating to the world the moral superiority of its economic system, democratic institutions, and middle-class Protestant values. Surely the new century, most thought, would see not only the continued perfection of these values and institutions but also the spread of American influence throughout the world. Such confidence resulted in foreign expansion by the American people even before the old century had ended. We turn to that in the next chapter.

Recommended Reading

Politics in the Gilded Age

John Allswang, *Bosses, Machines, and Urban Voters* (1977); Charles W. Calhoun, *The Gilded Age: Essays on the Origins of Modern America* (1996); Sean Dennis Cashman, *America and the Gilded Age: From the Death of Lincoln to the Rise of Theodore Roosevelt* (1984); Morton Keller, *Affairs of State: Public Life in Late Nineteenth Century America* (1977); Paul Kleppner, *The Third Electoral System, 1853–1892: Parties, Voters, and Political Cultures* (1979); H. Wayne Morgan, *From Hayes to McKinley: National Party Politics, 1877–1896* (1969); Nell I. Painter, *Standing at Armageddon in the United States, 1877–1919* (1987); William Riordon, *Plunkitt of Tammany Hall* (1963); Richard E. Welch, Jr., *The Presidencies of Grover Cleveland* (1988).

Middle-Class Reform

Jane Addams, *Twenty Years at Hull House* (1910); Ruth Bordin, *Frances Willard: A Biography* (1986) and *Women and Temperance: The Quest for Power and Liberty, 1873–1900* (1981); Mina Carson, *Settlement Folk: Social Thought and the American Settlement Movement, 1885–1930* (1990); Susan Curtis, *A Consuming Faith: The Social Gospel and Modern American Culture* (1991); Allen F. Davis, *American Heroine: The Life and Legend of Jane Addams* (1973) and *Spearheads for Reform: The Social Settlements and the Progressive Movement, 1890–1914* (1967); Richard Digby-Junger, *The Journalist as Reformer: Henry Demarest Lloyd and Wealth Against Commonwealth* (1996); Peter J. Frederick, *Knights of the Golden Rule: The Intellectual as Christian Social Reformer in the 1890s* (1976); Marnie Jones, *Holy Toledo: Religion and Politics in the Life of "Golden Rule" Jones* (1998); Aileen Kraditor, *The Ideas of the Woman's Suffrage Movement, 1890–1920* (1965); Arthur Mann, *Yankee Reformers in an Urban Age: Social Reform in Boston, 1880–1900* (1954); Daphne Pata, ed., *Looking Backward, 1988–1888: Essays on Edward Bellamy* (1988); Kathryn Kish Sklar, *Florence Kelly and the Nation's Work: The Rise of Women's Political Culture, 1830–1900* (1995); John L. Thomas, *Alternative America: Henry George, Edward Bellamy, Henry Demarest Lloyd and the Adversary Tradition* (1983); Marjorie Spruill Wheeler, ed., *One Woman, One Vote: Rediscovering the Woman Suffrage Movement* (1995).

The Pivotal 1890s

Peter Argersinger, *The Limits of Agrarian Radicalism: Western Populism and American Politics* (1995); Gene Clanton, *Populism: The Humane Preference in America, 1890–1900* (1991); Robert F. Durden, *The Climax of Populism: The Election of 1896* (1965); Paul Glad, *McKinley, Bryan and the People* (1964); Lawrence Goodwyn, *Democratic Promise: The Populist Movement in America* (1976); Charles Hoffman, *The Depression of the Nineties:*

An Economic History (1970); R. Hal Williams, *Years of Decision: American Politics in the 1890s* (1978).

Fiction and Film

Henry Adams's *Democracy: An American Novel* (1880) uses an ironic title to capture the elitist nature of politics and life in Washington in the Gilded Age. Edward Bellamy's *Looking Backward* (1888) is the utopian novel that began this chapter and that stimulated much late-nineteenth-century reform. Upper-class life in the late nineteenth century is portrayed in the Hollywood film *The Bostonians* (1998), based on a novel by Henry James. Kate Chopin's *The Awakening* (1899), set in New Orleans in the 1890s, tells a modern-style story of a woman's discovery of self. Edgar L. Doctorow's *Ragtime* (1975) is an innovative novel that plays fast and loose with the history and historical figures of turn-of-the-century America; it was also made into a recent Broadway play. Theodore Dreiser's *Sister Carrie* (1900), influenced by social Darwinian determinism and set in Chicago and New York, shows the life of a young farm girl who rises to fame and fortune in the city. *Hester Street* is a wonderfully teachable film about Jewish immigrants in New York City and the process of Americanization.

Two novels by William Dean Howells, *A Hazard of New Fortunes* (1889) and *The Rise of Silas Lapham* (1885), capture the social life of the new rich in the 1880s. Frank Norris's *The Octopus* (1901), set in the San Joaquin Valley of California, is an immense novel showing the struggle not only between farmers and railroads but also between rich and poor, commercial wheat farmers and sheep herders, city and country, and native-born and immigrant Americans. Gore Vidal's *1876: A Novel* (1976) is a modern fictional look at America in the centennial year. Mark Twain and Charles D. Warner's *The Gilded Age* (1873) spares no one in its satirical criticism of the social, political, and economic life of the late nineteenth century. Anzia Yezierska's *Bread Givers* (1925), similar to *Hester Street*, reveals the struggles between an Old World Jewish father and his Americanized daughter.

Suggested Web Sites

http://www.history.ohio-state.edu/projects/mckinley/default.htm

The Era of William McKinley. This site contains numerous images from various stages of McKinley's career, along with a brief biographical essay. This Ohio State University site also has a section with an excellent collection of cartoons from the era.

http://xroads.virginia.edu/~MA96/WCE/title.html

World's Columbian Exposition: Idea, Experience, Aftermath. This site has a virtual tour of the fair, along with contemporary reactions and modern analysis.

http://www.emayzine.com/lectures/Gilded~1.htm

United States History: The Gilded Age (1890) to World War I. This site consists of a good overview essay of the era.

http://www.wm.edu/~srnels/gilded.html

The Gilded Page. This site has links to scores of Gilded Age and Progressive Era documents.

http://www.vineyard.net/vineyard/history/pdgech3.htm

Chapter Three: American Socialists and Reformers. This site includes a fine essay about Edward Bellamy and some of the movements and ideas he inspired.

http://jefferson.village.virginia.edu/seminar/unit8/home.htm

Election of 1896. This University of Virginia site contains biographical information, images, cartoons, and related links about the pivotal 1896 election.

http://www.ushistoryplace.com

A richly detailed on-line learning environment complete with interactive maps, timelines, history activities, primary source documents, and links to related American history sites.

20

BECOMING *a* WORLD POWER

In January 1899, the U.S. Senate was locked in a dramatic debate over whether to ratify the Treaty of Paris concluding the recent war with Spain over Cuban independence. At the same time, American soldiers uneasily faced Filipino rebels across a neutral zone around the outskirts of Manila, capital of the Philippines. Until recent weeks, the Americans and Filipinos had been allies, together defeating the Spanish to liberate the Philippines. The American fleet under Admiral George Dewey had destroyed the Spanish naval squadron in Manila Bay on May 1, 1898. Three weeks later, an American ship brought from exile the native Filipino insurrectionary leader Emilio Aguinaldo to lead rebel forces on land while U.S. gunboats patrolled the seas.

At first, the Filipinos looked on the Americans as liberators. Although the intentions of the United States were never clear, Aguinaldo believed that, as in Cuba, the Americans had no territorial ambitions. They would simply drive the Spanish out and then leave themselves. In June, therefore, Aguinaldo declared the independence of the Philippines and began setting up a constitutional government. American officials pointedly ignored the independence ceremonies. When an armistice ended the war in August, American troops denied Filipino soldiers an opportunity to liberate their own capital city and shunted them off to the suburbs. The armistice agreement recognized American rights to the "harbor, city, and bay of Manila," while the proposed Treaty of Paris gave the United States the entire Philippine Island archipelago.

Consequently, tension mounted in the streets of Manila and along 14 miles of trenches separating American and Filipino soldiers. Taunts, obscenities, and racial epithets were shouted across the neutral zone. Barroom skirmishes and knifings pervaded the city at night; American soldiers searched houses without warrants and looted stores. Their behavior was not unlike that of English soldiers in Boston in the 1770s.

On the night of February 4, 1899, Privates William Grayson and David Miller of Company B, 1st Nebraska Volunteers, were on patrol in Santa Mesa, a Manila suburb surrounded on three sides by insurgent trenches. The Americans had orders to shoot any Filipino soldiers found in the neutral area. As the two Americans cautiously worked their way to a

Dewey at Manila Bay, May 1, 1898 (painting by Rufus Zogbaum): American Expansionism Triumphant. *(Courtesy of The Vermont State House)*

bridge over the San Juan River, they heard a Filipino signal whistle, answered by another. Then a red lantern flashed from a nearby blockhouse. The two froze as four Filipinos emerged from the darkness on the road ahead. "Halt!" Grayson shouted. The native lieutenant in charge answered, "Halto!," either mockingly or because he had similar orders. Standing less than 15 feet apart, the two men repeated their commands. After a moment's hesitation, Grayson fired, killing his opponent with one bullet. As the other Filipinos jumped out at them, Grayson and Miller shot two more. Then they turned and ran back to their own lines shouting warnings of attack. A full-scale battle followed.

The next day, Commodore Dewey cabled Washington that the "insurgents have inaugurated general engagement" and promised a hasty suppression of the insurrection. The outbreak of hostilities ended the Senate debates. On February 6, the Senate ratified the Treaty of Paris, thus formally annexing the Philippines and sparking a war between the United States and Filipino nationalists.

In a guerrilla war similar to those fought later in the twentieth century in Asia, Filipino nationalists tried to undermine the American will by hit-and-run attacks. American soldiers, meanwhile, remained in heavily garrisoned cities and undertook search-and-destroy missions to root out rebels and pacify the countryside. The Filipino-American War lasted until July 1902, three years longer than the Spanish-American War that caused it and involving far more troops, casualties, and monetary and moral costs.

How did all this happen? What brought Private Grayson to "shoot my first nigger," as he put it, halfway around the world in distant Asia? For the first time in history, regular American soldiers found themselves fighting outside North America. The "champion of oppressed nations," as Aguinaldo said, had turned into an oppressor nation itself, imposing the American way of life and American institutions on faraway peoples against their will.

The war in the Philippines marked a critical transformation of America's role in the world. Within a few years at the turn of the century, the United States acquired an empire, however small by European standards, and established itself as a world power. In this chapter, we will review the historical dilemmas of America's role in the world, especially those of the expansionist nineteenth century. Then we will examine the motivations for the intensified expansionism of the 1890s and how they were manifested in Cuba, the

Philippines, and elsewhere. Finally, we will look at how the fundamental patterns of modern American foreign policy were established for Latin America, Asia, and Europe in the early twentieth century. Throughout this discussion, we will see that the tension between idealism and self-interest that has permeated America's domestic history has guided its foreign policy as well.

STEPS TOWARD EMPIRE

The circumstances that brought Privates Grayson and Miller from Nebraska to the Philippines originated deep in American history. As early as the seventeenth-century Puritan migration from England to Massachusetts Bay, Americans worried about how to do good in a world that does wrong. John Winthrop sought to set up a "city on a hill" in the New World, a model community of righteous living for others in the world to behold and imitate. "Let the eyes of the world be upon us," Winthrop said. That wish, reaffirmed during the American Revolution, became a permanent goal of American policy toward the outside world.

America as a Model Society

Nineteenth-century Americans continued to believe in the nation's special mission. The Monroe Doctrine in 1823 pointed out moral differences between the monarchical, arbitrary governments of Europe and the free republican institutions of the New World. As Spanish colonies in South and Central America followed the American Revolutionary model, Monroe warned Europe to stay out. In succeeding decades, a number of distinguished European visitors came to study "democracy in America," to see for themselves the "great social revolution" at work. They found widespread democracy, representative and responsive political and legal institutions, a religious commitment to the notion of human perfectibility, unlimited energy, and the ability to apply unregulated economic activity and inventive genius to produce more things for more people.

The model seemed irresistible. In a world that was evil, Americans believed that they stood as a transforming force for good. But how could a nation committed to isolationism do the transforming? One way was to encourage other nations to observe and imitate the good example set by the United States. Often, however, other nations preferred their own society or were attracted to competing models of modernization, such as fascism or socialism. This implied the need for a more aggressive foreign policy.

Americans have rarely focused just on perfecting the good example at home, waiting for others to copy it. This requires patience and passivity, two traits not characteristic of Americans. Rather, throughout history, the American people have actively and sometimes forcefully imposed their ideas and institutions on others. The international crusades of the United States, well intentioned if not always well received, as recently as in Somalia, Kosovo, and the Gulf War have usually been motivated by a mixture of idealism and self-interest. Hence, the effort to spread the exemplary American model to an imperfect world has been both a blessing and a burden, both for others and for the American people themselves.

Early Expansionism

Persistent expansionism marked the first century of American independence. Jefferson's purchase of the Louisiana Territory in 1803 and the grasping for Florida and Canada by War Hawks in 1812 signaled an intense American interest in territorial growth. Although the United States remained "unentangled" in European affairs for most of the century, as both Washington and Jefferson had advised, the American government and people were much entangled elsewhere. To the Cherokee, Seminole, Lakota, Apache, Cheyenne, and other American Indian nations, the United States was far from isolationist. Nor did the Canadians, the Spanish in Florida, nor Mexicans in Texas and California consider the Americans nonexpansionist. Until mid-century, the United States pursued its "Manifest Destiny" (see Chapter 13) by expanding across the North American continent. In the 1850s, Americans began to look beyond their own continent as Commodore Perry in 1853 "opened" Japan and southerners sought more cotton lands in the Caribbean and a canal connecting the two oceans.

After the Civil War, Secretary of State William Seward spoke of an America that would hold a "commanding sway in the world," destined to exert commercial domination "on the Pacific ocean, and its islands and continents." He purchased Alaska from Russia in 1867 for $7.2 million and acquired a coaling station in the Midway Islands near Hawaii, where missionaries and merchants were already active. This paved the way for American commercial expansion in Korea, Japan, and China. Seward also advocated annexing Cuba and other islands of the West Indies and tried to negotiate a treaty securing an American-built canal through the isthmus of Panama. Seward dreamed of "possession" of the entire North and Central American continent and ultimately "control

When the United States went to war against Spain in 1898, partly to help the Cubans win their independence from imperial Spanish rule, no one could have imagined the ironic outcomes. Within a year, Americans would impose imperial rule over the Philippines, marching through and burning villages (as the 20th Kansas Volunteers are doing here) and waging war against civilians in a faraway Asian land. *(Above, The Newberry Library; Right, Keystone-Mast Collection (24039), URL/California Museum of Photography, University of California at Riverside)*

of the world." Although his larger dreams went unrealized, his interest in expansion into the Caribbean persisted among business interests and politicians to the end of the century and beyond.

Expansion After Seward

In 1870, foreshadowing the Philippine debates 30 years later, supporters of President Grant tried to force the Senate to annex Santo Domingo on the island of Hispaniola. They cited the strategic importance of the Caribbean and argued forcefully for the economic value of raw materials and markets that Santo Domingo would bring. Opponents responded that expansionism violated the American principle of self-determination and government by consent of the governed. They claimed that the native peoples of the Caribbean were brown-skinned, culturally inferior, non-English-speaking, and therefore unassimilable. Expansionism might also involve foreign entanglements, a large and expensive navy, bigger government, and higher taxes. So the Senate rejected the annexation treaty.

Although reluctant to add territory outright, American interests eagerly sought commercial dominance in Latin America and Asia. A number of statesmen asserted U.S. influence in these areas. President Hayes dismissed a treaty with England agreeing to joint construction and control of a canal across either Panama or Nicaragua. If such a canal were built, he said, it was sure to be "under American control" and would be considered "virtually a part of the coast line of the United States." But nothing came of diplomatic efforts with Nicaragua for an American-built canal except to cause Nicaraguan suspicions of U.S. intentions.

In 1881, Secretary of State James G. Blaine sought to convene a conference of American nations to promote hemispheric peace and trade. Latin Americans may have wondered what Blaine intended, for in 1881 he intervened in three separate border disputes in Central and South America, in each case at the cost of goodwill and trust. Ten years later, relations with Chile were harmed when several American sailors on shore leave were involved in a barroom brawl in Valparaiso. Two Americans were killed and several others injured. American pride was also injured, and President Benjamin Harrison sent an ultimatum calling for a "prompt and full reparation." After threats of war, Chile complied.

American expansion produced other incidents in the Pacific. In the mid-1870s, American sugar-growing interests in the Hawaiian Islands were strong enough to put whites in positions of influence over the native monarchy. In 1875, they obtained a reciprocity treaty admitting Hawaiian sugar duty-free to the United States, and in 1877 the United States also won exclusive rights to build a naval base at Pearl Harbor. Hawaiians resented the growing influence of American sugar interests, especially as they brought in Japanese to replace native people—many of whom died by white diseases—in the sugarcane fields. Between 1885 and 1924, 200,000 Japanese workers,

Attracted to sugar and the mid-Pacific location of the Hawaiian Islands, American imperial interests sought to tie Hawaii more closely to the faraway U.S. mainland. The Iolani Palace, former home of Queen Liliuokalani, was the scene of annexation ceremonies in 1898, when Hawaii became a U.S. territory. "We need Hawaii just as much as and a good deal more than we did California," President McKinley said. "It is manifest destiny." *(Library of Congress)*

pursuing "huge dreams of fortune . . . across the ocean," migrated to Hawaii, and nearly another 200,000 went to the West Coast of the United States.

In 1891, the strongly nationalist Queen Liliuokalani assumed the throne in Hawaii and sought to establish control over whites in the name of "Hawaii for the Hawaiians." So in 1893, white planters, fearful that the queen might turn to Japan for support, staged a coup with the help of U.S. gunboats and marines. With the success of their bloodless coup, called one "of sugar, by sugar, for sugar," the whites sought formal annexation by the friendly Harrison administration. But then Grover Cleveland, who opposed imperial expansion, returned to the presidency for his second term and stopped the move. He was, however, unable to remove the white sugar growers from power in Hawaii. They waited patiently for a more desirable time for annexation, which came during the war in 1898.

Moving ever closer toward the fabled markets of the Far East, the United States acquired a naval station at Pago Pago in the Samoan Islands in 1878, sharing the port with Great Britain and Germany. In an incident in 1889, American and German naval forces almost fought each other, but a typhoon ended the crisis by wiping out both navies. Troubles in the Pacific also occurred in the late 1880s over the American seizure of several Canadian ships in seal fur and fishing disputes in the Bering Sea. This issue was settled only by the British threat of naval action and with the ruling of an international arbitration commission, which ordered the United States to pay damages.

The United States confronted the English closer to home as it sought to replace Britain as the most influential nation in Central American affairs. In 1895, a boundary dispute between Venezuela and British Guiana threatened to bring British intervention against the Venezuelans. President Cleveland, needing a popular political issue to deflect attention from the depression, asked Secretary of State Richard Olney to send a message to Great Britain. Olney's note, which was stronger than Cleveland had intended, invoked the Monroe Doctrine, declared the United States as "practically sovereign on this continent," and demanded British acceptance of international arbitration to settle the dispute. The British ignored the note, and war loomed. But then both sides realized that war between the two English-speaking nations would be an "absurdity." The dispute was settled by agreeing to an impartial American commission to settle the boundary.

These increasing conflicts in the Caribbean and the Pacific signaled the rise of American presence beyond the borders of the United States. Yet as of 1895, the nation had neither the means nor a consistent policy for enlarging its role in the world. The diplomatic service was small, inexperienced, and unprofessional. Around the world, American emissaries kept sloppy records, issued illegal passports, involved themselves in petty local issues and frauds, and exhibited insensitive behavior toward indigenous cultures. No U.S. embassy official in Beijing spoke Chinese. The U.S. Army, with about 28,000 men, was ranked 13th in the world, behind Bulgaria. The navy, dismantled after the Civil War and partly rebuilt under President Arthur, ranked no higher than 10th and included many dangerously obsolete ships. These limited and backward instruments of foreign policy could not support the aspirations of an emerging world power, especially one whose rise to power had come so quickly.

EXPANSIONISM IN THE 1890S

In 1893, the historian Frederick Jackson Turner wrote that for three centuries, "the dominant fact in American life has been expansion." Turner observed that the "extension of American influence to outlying islands and adjoining countries" indicated that expansionism would continue. Turner struck a responsive chord in a country that had always been restless, mobile, and optimistic. With the western frontier closed, Americans would surely look for new frontiers, for mobility and markets as well as for morality and missionary activity. The motivations for the expansionist impulse of the late 1890s resembled those that had prompted people to settle the New World in the first place: greed, glory, and God. We will examine expansionism as a reflection of profits, patriotism, piety (moral mission), and politics.

Profits: Searching for Overseas Markets

Albert Beveridge of Indiana bragged in 1898 that "American factories are making more than the American people can use; American soil is producing more than they can consume. Fate has written our policy for us; the trade of the world must and shall be ours." Americans like Beveridge revived older dreams of an American commercial empire in the islands and adjoining countries of the Caribbean Sea and the Pacific Ocean. With a strong belief in free enterprise and open markets for investing capital and selling products, American businessmen saw huge profits beckoning in the heavily populated areas of Latin America and Asia and wanted to get their share of these markets to stay competitive with European countries. The attraction was enhanced by the availability in those lands of abundant raw materials such as sugar, coffee, fruits, oil, rubber, and minerals.

Understanding that commercial expansion required a stronger navy and coaling stations and colonies, business interests began to shape diplomatic and military strategy. Senator Orville Platt of Connecticut said in 1893, "A policy of isolation did well enough when we were an embryo nation, but today things are different." By 1901, the economic adviser for the State Department described overseas commercial expansion as a "natural law of economic and race development." But not all businessmen in the 1890s liked commercial expansion backed by a vigorous foreign policy. Some preferred traditional trade with Canada and Europe rather than risky new ventures in Asia and Latin America. Securing colonies and developing faraway markets and investment opportunities would not only require high expenses but also might involve the United States in wars with commercial rivals or native peoples in distant places. Some thought it more important to recover from the depression than to annex islands.

But the drop in domestic consumption during the depression also encouraged businessmen to expand into new markets to sell surplus goods. The tremendous growth of American industrial and agricultural production in the post–Civil War years made expansionism more attractive than drowning in overproduction. Many businessmen preferred new markets to cutting prices, which would redistribute wealth by allowing the lower classes to buy excess goods, or to laying off workers, which would increase social unrest. Commercial expansion was led by the newly formed National Association of Manufacturers, which emphasized in 1896 "that the trade centres of Central and South America are natural markets for American products."

Despite the depression of the 1890s, products spewed from American factories at a staggering rate. The United States moved from fourth in the world in manufacturing in 1870 to first in 1900, doubling the number of factories and tripling the value of farm output—mainly cotton, corn, and wheat. The United States led the world not only in railroad construction (206,631 miles of tracks in 1900, four times more than in 1870) but also in agricultural machinery and mass-produced technological products such as sewing machines, electrical implements, telephones, cash registers, elevators, and cameras. Manufactured goods grew nearly fivefold between 1895 and 1914.

Correspondingly, the total value of American exports tripled, jumping from $434 million in 1866 to nearly $1.5 billion in 1900. By 1914, exports had risen to $2.5 billion, a 67 percent increase over 1900. The increased trade continued to go mainly to Europe rather than Asia. In 1900, for example, only 3 to 4 percent of U.S. exports went to China and Japan. Nevertheless, interest in Asian markets grew, especially as agricultural production continued to increase

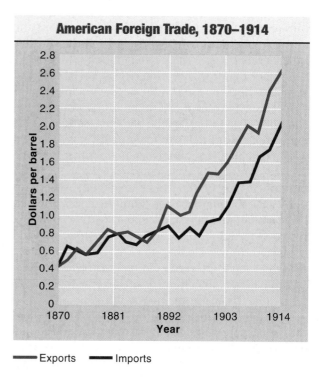

American Foreign Trade, 1870–1914

—— Exports   —— Imports

Note, after a rather gradual increase in trade through the boom-and-bust cycles of the 1870s and 1880s and an actual dip during the depression of 1893–1895, the spectacular increases during the Republican era of Presidents McKinley, Roosevelt, and Taft. Source: U.S. Bureau of the Census.

and prices remained low. Farmers dreamed of selling their surplus wheat to China. James J. Hill of the Great Northern Railroad promoted their hopes by printing wheat cookbooks in various Asian languages and distributing them in the Far East, hoping to fill his westward-bound boxcars and merchant ships with wheat and other grains.

Investment activity followed a similar pattern. American direct investments abroad increased from about $634 million to $2.6 billion between 1897 and 1914. Although investments were largest in Britain, Canada, and Mexico, most attention focused on actual and potential investment in Latin America and Asia. Central American investment increased from $21 million in 1897 to $93 million by the eve of World War I, mainly in mines, railroads, and banana and coffee plantations. At the turn of the century came the formation and growth of America's biggest multinational corporations—the United Fruit Company, Alcoa Aluminum, Amalgamated Copper, Du Pont, American Tobacco, and others. Although slow to respond to investment and market opportunities abroad, these companies soon supported an aggressive foreign policy, expanding America's world presence.

Patriotism: Asserting National Power

American interest in investments, markets, and raw materials abroad reflected a determination not to be left out of the international competition among European powers and Japan for commercial spheres of influence and colonies in Asia, Africa, and Latin America. In 1898, a State Department memorandum stated that "we can no longer afford to disregard international rivalries now that we ourselves have become a competitor in the world-wide struggle for trade." The national state, then, should support commercial interests.

More Americans, however, saw national glory and greatness as legitimate motivations for expansionism. In the late 1890s, a group of men centered on Assistant Secretary of the Navy Theodore Roosevelt and Senator Henry Cabot Lodge of Massachusetts emerged as highly influential leaders of a changing American foreign policy. These vigorous and intensely nationalistic young men successfully shifted official policy from "continentalism" to what Lodge called the "large policy." By 1899, Assistant Secretary of State John Bassett Moore wrote that the United States had finally

Citing the Monroe Doctrine and Senator Lodge's "large policy" as justification, U.S. imperial interests at the turn of the century spread American economic, political, and military influence from Alaska across the Caribbean to South America and into the islands of the Pacific Ocean. Note Uncle Sam's determined gaze westward.

moved "into the position of what is commonly called a world power. . . . Where formerly we had only commercial interests, we now have territorial and political interests as well." Roosevelt agreed that economic interests should take second place to questions of what he called "national honor."

The writings of Alfred Thayer Mahan, a naval strategist and author of several books on the importance of sea power to national greatness, greatly influenced the new foreign policy elite. Mahan argued that in a world of Darwinian struggle for survival, national power depended on naval supremacy, control of sea lanes, and vigorous development of domestic resources and foreign markets. He advocated colonies in both the Caribbean and the Pacific, linked by a canal built and controlled by the United States. Strong nations, Mahan wrote, had a special responsibility to dominate weak ones. In a world of constant "strife," where "everywhere nation is arrayed against nation," it was imperative that Americans begin "to look outward." National pride and glory would surely follow.

Piety: The Missionary Impulse

As Mahan's and Roosevelt's statements suggest, a strong sense of duty and the missionary ideal of doing good for others also motivated expansionism. A statesman once boasted that "with God's help, we will lift Shanghai up and up, ever up, until it is just like Kansas City." Richard Olney agreed, saying in 1898, "the mission of this country is . . . to forego no fitting opportunity to further the progress of civilization." Motivated by America's sense of itself as a model nation, such statements sometimes rationalized the exploitation and oppression of weaker peoples. Although the European countries had their own justifications for imperialism, Americans such as Roosevelt, Lodge, and Mahan all would have agreed with the following summary of expansionist beliefs:

Certain nations are more civilized than others, especially those peopled by English-speaking, white, Protestant Anglo-Saxons. They enjoy free enterprise and republican political institutions, meaning representative government, shared power, and the rule of law. Further evidence of the civilized nature of such nations includes their advanced technological and industrial development, large middle classes, and high degree of education and literacy. The prime examples in the world are England, Germany, and the United States.

In the natural struggle for existence, the races and nations that survive and prosper, such as these, prove their fitness and superiority over others. The United States, as a matter of history, geographic location, and political genius, is so favored and fit that God has chosen it to take care of and uplift less favored peoples. This responsibility cannot be avoided. It is a national duty, or burden—the "white man's burden"—that civilized nations undertake to bring peace, progressive values, and ordered liberty to the world.

These ideas, widespread in popular thought, described America's providential sense of itself. As a missionary put it in 1885, "The Christian nations are subduing the world in order to make mankind free." Josiah Strong, a Congregational minister, was one of the most ardent advocates of American missionary expansionism. Although his book *Our Country* (1885) focused on internal threats to American social order, in a long chapter titled "The Future of the Anglo-Saxon Race," Strong made his case for an outward thrust. He argued that in the struggle for survival among nations, the United States had emerged as the center of Anglo-Saxonism and was "divinely commissioned" to spread the blessings of political liberty, Protestant Christianity, and civilized values over the earth. "This powerful race," he wrote, "will move down upon Mexico, down upon Central and South America, out upon the islands of the sea, over upon Africa and beyond." In a cruder statement of the same idea, Albert Beveridge said in 1899 that God had prepared English-speaking Anglo-Saxons to become the "master organizers of the world to establish and administer governments among savages and senile peoples."

If not so crudely, missionaries carried similar Western values to non-Christian lands around the world. China was a favorite target. The number of American Protestant missionaries in China increased from 436 in 1874 to 5,462 in 1914. The largest increase came in the 1890s. Although the missionaries were not as effective as they had hoped to be, the estimated number of Christian converts in China jumped from 5,000 in 1870 to nearly 100,000 in 1900. This tiny fraction of the Chinese population included many young reformist intellectuals who absorbed Western ideas in Christian mission colleges and went on to lead the Revolution of 1912 that ended the Manchu dynasty. Economic relations between China and the United States increased at approximately the same rate as missionary activity. The number of American firms in China grew from 50 to 550 between 1870 and 1930, while trade increased 1,500 percent.

Politics: Manipulating Public Opinion

These figures suggest how economic, religious, moral, and nationalistic motivations became interwoven in American expansionism in the late 1890s. Although less significant than the other motives, politics also played a role. For the first time in American history, public opinion over international issues loomed large in presidential politics. The psychological tensions and economic hardships of the depression of the 1890s jarred national self-confidence. Foreign adventures and the glories of expansionism provided an emotional release from domestic turmoil and promised to restore patriotic pride—and maybe even win votes.

This process was helped by the growth of a highly competitive popular press, the penny daily newspaper, which brought international issues before a mass readership. When several newspapers in New York City, notably William Randolph Hearst's *Journal* and Joseph Pulitzer's *World,* competed to see which could stir up more public support for the Cuban rebels in their struggle for independence from Spain, politicians ignored the public outcry at their peril. Daily reports of Spanish atrocities in 1896 and 1897 kept public moral outrage constantly before President McKinley as he considered his course of action. His Democratic opponent, William Jennings Bryan, entered the fray. Although in principle a pacifist, Bryan advocated U.S. intervention in Cuba on moral grounds of a holy war to help the oppressed. He even raised a regiment of Nebraska volunteers to go off to the war, but the Republican administration kept him far from battle and therefore far from the headlines.

Politics, then, joined profits, patriotism, and piety in motivating the expansionism of the 1890s. These four impulses interacted to influence the Spanish-American War, the annexation of the Philippine Islands, and the foreign policy of President Theodore Roosevelt.

CUBA, THE SPANISH-AMERICAN WAR, AND THE PHILIPPINES

Lying 90 miles off the southern tip of Florida, Cuba had been the object of intense American interest for a half century. Although successful in thwarting American adventurism in Cuba in the 1850s (see Chapter 14), Spain was unable to halt the continuing struggle of the Cuban people for relief from exploitive labor in the sugar plantations, even after slavery itself ended, and for a measure of autonomy. The most recent uprising, which lasted from 1868 to 1878, had raised tensions between Spain and the United States, just as it whetted the Cuban appetite for complete independence.

The Road to War

When the Cuban revolt flared up anew in 1895, the Madrid government again failed to implement reforms but instead sent General "Butcher" Weyler with 50,000 troops to quell the disturbance. When Weyler began herding rural Cuban citizens into "reconcentration" camps, Americans were outraged. An outpouring of sympathy swept the nation, especially as reports came back of the horrible suffering in the camps, with thousands dying of malnutrition, starvation, and disease. Sensationalist newspapers in the United States, competing for readers, stirred up sentiment with pages of bloody stories of atrocities. "The old, the young, the weak, the crippled—all are butchered without mercy," wrote the New York *World*.

The Cuban struggle appealed to a country convinced of its role as protector of the weak and defender of the right of self-determination. One editorial deplored Spanish "injustice, oppression, extortion, and demoralization," while describing the Cubans as heroic freedom fighters "largely inspired by our glorious example of beneficent free institutions and successful self-government." Motivated by genuine humanitarian concern and a sense of duty, many Americans held Cuba rallies to raise money and food for famine relief. They called for land reforms, and some advocated armed intervention, but neither President Cleveland nor President McKinley wanted a war over Cuba.

Self-interested motives also played a role. For many years, Americans had noted the profitable resources and strategic location of the island. American companies had invested extensively in Cuban sugar plantations. By 1897, trade with Cuba reached $27 million per year. Appeals for reform had much to do with ensuring a stable environment for further investments, as well as for the protection of sugar fields against the ravages of civil war.

The election of 1896 diverted attention from Cuba to the issues of free silver and jobs, but only temporarily. A new government in Madrid recalled Weyler and seemed ready to grant a degree of self-government to the Cubans. But these concessions were half-hearted. Conditions worsened in the reconcentration camps, and the American press kept the plight of the Cuban people before the public. McKinley, eager not to take any action that might upset business recovery from the depression, skillfully resisted the pressure for war. But his skill could not control Spanish misrule or Cuban aspirations for freedom. The fundamental causes of the war—Spanish intransigence in the face

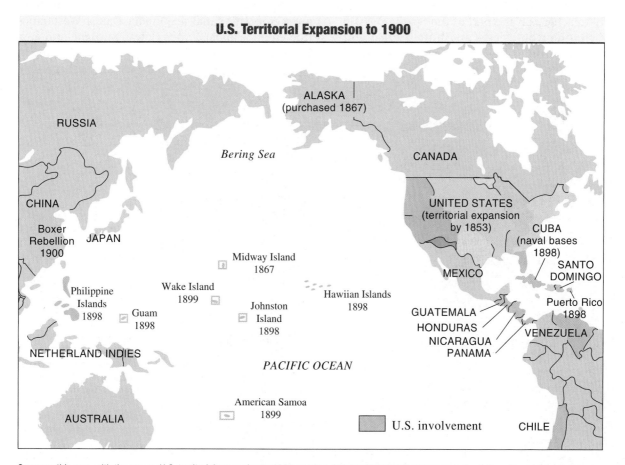

U.S. Territorial Expansion to 1900

RUSSIA

Bering Sea

ALASKA (purchased 1867)

CANADA

CHINA

Boxer Rebellion 1900

JAPAN

Midway Island 1867

UNITED STATES (territorial expansion by 1853)

MEXICO

CUBA (naval bases 1898)

SANTO DOMINGO

Philippine Islands 1898

Guam 1898

Wake Island 1899

Johnston Island 1898

Hawiian Islands 1898

GUATEMALA
HONDURAS
NICARAGUA
PANAMA

Puerto Rico 1898

VENEZUELA

NETHERLAND INDIES

PACIFIC OCEAN

AUSTRALIA

American Samoa 1899

U.S. involvement

CHILE

Compare this map with the one on U.S. territorial expansion to 1860 on page 401 (represented in miniature in the U.S. portion of this map).

of persistent Cuban rebellion and American sugar interests and sympathies for the underdog—were seemingly unstoppable.

Events early in 1898 sparked the outbreak of hostilities. Rioting in Havana intensified both Spanish repression and American outrage. As pressures for war increased, a letter from the Spanish minister to the United States, Depuy de Lôme, calling McKinley a "weak" hypocritical politician, was intercepted by spies and made public. The American populace became enraged as Hearst's New York *Journal* called De Lôme's letter "the worst insult to the United States in its history."

A second event was more serious. When the rioting broke out, the U.S. battleship *Maine* was sent to Havana harbor to protect American citizens. Early in the evening on February 15, a tremendous explosion blew up the *Maine*, killing 262 men. American advocates of war, who assumed Spanish responsibility, called immediately for intervention. Newspaper publishers offered rewards for discovery of the perpetrators of the crime and broadcast slogans like "Remember the *Maine!* To hell with Spain!"

Assistant Secretary of the Navy Theodore Roosevelt, who had been preparing for war for some time, said that he believed the *Maine* had been sunk "by an act of dirty treachery on the part of the Spaniards." He added that he would "give anything if President McKinley would order the fleet to Havana tomorrow." When the president did not, Roosevelt privately

declared that McKinley had "no more backbone than a chocolate éclair" and continued to ready the navy for action. Although an official board of inquiry concluded that an external submarine mine caused the disaster, probably a faulty boiler or some other internal problem set off the explosion, a possibility even Roosevelt later conceded.

After the sinking of the *Maine*, Roosevelt took advantage of Secretary of the Navy John D. Long's absence from the office one day to send a cable to Commodore George Dewey, commander of the U.S. Pacific fleet at Hong Kong. Roosevelt's message ordered Dewey to fill his ships with coal and, "in the event" of a declaration of war with Spain, to sail to the Philippines and make sure "the Spanish squadron does not leave the Asiatic coast." Roosevelt wrote in his diary that night that "the Secretary is away and I am having immense fun running the Navy."

Roosevelt's act was not impetuous, as Long thought, but consistent with naval policies he had been urging on his more cautious superior for more than a year. As early as 1895, the navy had formulated plans for attacking the Philippines. Influenced by Mahan and Lodge, Roosevelt wanted to enlarge the navy, whose growth had been restricted for years. He also believed that the United States should construct an interoceanic canal, acquire the Danish West Indies (the Virgin Islands), annex Hawaii outright, and oust Spain from Cuba. As Roosevelt told McKinley late in 1897, he was putting the navy in "the best possible

The artist has captured here the horror of the sinking of the *Maine*, with scenes before and after the explosion. Secretary of the Navy John Long, on returning to his office to discover that Assistant Secretary Roosevelt had cabled Admiral Dewey to prepare for war in the aftermath of the *Maine* explosion, wrote in his diary, "I find that Roosevelt has come very near causing more of an explosion than happened to the *Maine*." (*The Granger Collection, New York*)

shape" for "when war began." His order to Dewey, then, reflected a well-thought-out strategy to implement the "large policy" necessary for the advance of civilization.

The public outcry over the *Maine* drowned out McKinley's efforts to calm the populace and avoid war. The issues had become highly political, especially with midterm elections in the fall and a presidential race only two years away. Fellow Republican Senator Lodge warned McKinley, "If war in Cuba drags on through the summer with nothing done we shall go down to the greatest defeat ever known." McKinley hoped that the Madrid government would make the necessary concessions in Cuba and sent some tough demands in March. But the Spanish response was delayed and inadequate, refusing to grant full independence to the Cubans.

On April 11, 1898, President McKinley sent an ambiguous message to Congress that seemed to call for war. Two weeks later, Congress authorized the use of troops against Spain and passed a resolution recognizing Cuban independence, actions amounting to a declaration of war. In a significant additional resolution, the Teller Amendment, Congress stated that the United States had no intentions of annexing Cuba, guaranteeing the Cubans the right to determine their own destiny. Senator George F. Hoar of Massachusetts, who later assailed the United States for its war against the Filipinos, declared that intervention in Cuba would be "the most honorable single war in all history," undertaken without "the slightest thought or desire of foreign conquest or of national gain or advantage."

"A Splendid Little War"

As soon as war was declared, Theodore Roosevelt resigned his post in the Navy Department and prepared to lead a cavalry unit in the war. African American regiments as well as white headed to Tampa, Florida, to be shipped to Cuba. One black soldier, noting the stark differences in the southern reception of the segregated regiments, commented, "I

The celebrated charge of "Teddy's Rough Riders" up Kettle Hill, shown in this heroic picture (left) *(The Granger Collection, New York)*, was made possible (and safe) because Spanish resistance was neutralized by African American troops like these from the 9th U.S. Cavalry (above). *(Library of Congress)*

am sorry that we were not treated with much courtesy while coming through the South." Blacks were especially sympathetic to the Cuban people's struggle. As one soldier wrote in his journal, "Oh, God! at last we have taken up the sword to enforce the divine rights of a people who have been unjustly treated." On arriving in Puerto Rico, a white soldier wrote that it was a "wonderful sight how the natives respect us." As the four-month war neared its end in August, John Hay wrote Roosevelt that "it has been a splendid little war; begun with the highest motives, carried on with magnificent intelligence and spirit."

It was a "splendid" war also because, compared with the long, bloody Civil War or even the British fight with the Boers in South Africa going on at the same time, the war with Spain was short and relatively easy. Naval battles were won almost without return fire. At both major naval engagements, Manila Bay and Santiago Bay, only two Americans died, one of them from heat prostration while stoking coal. The islands of Guam and Puerto Rico were taken virtually without a shot. Only 385 men died from Spanish bullets, but over 5,000 succumbed to tropical diseases.

The Spanish-American War was splendid in other ways, as letters from American soldiers suggest. One young man wrote that his comrades were all "in good spirits" because oranges and coconuts were so plentiful and "every trooper has his canteen full of lemonade all the time." Another wrote his mother that he found Cuba better than Texas in many ways: "Our money is worth twice as much as Spanish money. We do not want for anything." And another wrote his brother that he was having "a lot of fun chasing Spaniards."

But for many men, the war was anything but splendid. One soldier wrote: "Words are inadequate to express the feeling of pain and sickness when one has the fever. For about a week every bone in my body ached and I did not care much whether I lived or not." Another wrote:

> One of the worst things I saw was a man shot while loading his gun. The Spanish Mauser bullet struck the magazine of his carbine, and . . . the bullet was split, a part of it going through his scalp and a part through his neck. . . . He was a mass of blood.

The "power of joy in battle" that Roosevelt felt "when the wolf rises in the heart" was not a feeling shared by other American soldiers. Roosevelt's brush with death at Las Guásimas and his celebrated charge up Kettle Hill near Santiago, his flank protected by African American troops, made three-inch headlines and propelled him toward the New York governor's mansion. "I would rather have led that charge," he

said later, "than served three terms in the U.S. Senate." No one did as much during the war as Roosevelt to advance not only his political career but also the cause of expansion and national glory.

The Philippines Debates and War

Roosevelt's ordering Dewey to Manila initiated a chain of events that led to the annexation of the Philippines. The most crucial battle of the Spanish-American War occurred on May 1, 1898, when Dewey destroyed the Spanish fleet in Manila Bay and cabled McKinley for additional troops. The president said later that when he received Dewey's cable, he was not even sure "within two thousand miles" where "those darned islands were." Actually, McKinley had approved Roosevelt's policies and knew what course of action to pursue. He sent twice as many troops as Dewey had asked for and began the process of shaping American public opinion to accept the "political, commercial [and] humanitarian" reasons for annexing all 7,000 Philippine islands. The Treaty of Paris gave the United States all of them in exchange for a $20 million payment to Spain.

The treaty was sent to the Senate for ratification during the winter of 1898–1899. Senators for and against annexation hurled arguments at each other across the floor of the Senate as American soldiers hurled oaths and taunts across the neutral zone at Aguinaldo's insurgents near Manila. Private Grayson's encounter, as we have seen, led to the passage of the treaty in a close Senate vote and began the Filipino-American War and the debates over what to do with the Philippines. These debates took place in a wider arena than the Senate, as the entire nation joined the argument. At stake were two very different views of foreign policy and of America's vision of itself. After several months of quietly seeking advice and listening to public opinion, McKinley finally recommended annexation.

Many Democrats supported the president out of fear of being labeled disloyal. At a time when openly racist thought flourished in the United States, fellow Republicans confirmed McKinley's arguments for annexation, adding even more insulting ones. Filipinos were described as childlike, savage, stunted in size, dirty, and backward. Unflattering comparisons were made to blacks and Native Americans, and policies were proposed befitting the inferior condition in which white Americans saw the Filipinos. "The country won't be pacified," a Kansas veteran of the Sioux wars told a reporter, "until the niggers are killed off like the Indians." Roosevelt called Aguinaldo a "renegade Pawnee" and said that the Filipinos had no right "to administer the country which they happen to be occupying." The attitudes favoring annexation, there-

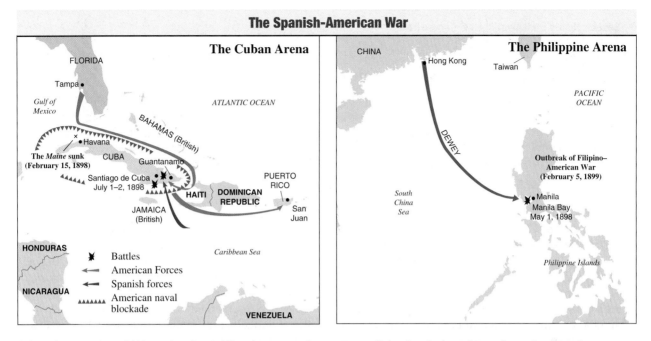

Refer to the map on page 641 to see how far apart these two war zones were; as a result, American foreign policy was forever transformed.

fore, asserted Filipino inferiority and incapacity for self-rule while also reflecting America's proud sense of itself in 1900 as a nation of civilized order and progress.

Other Americans were not so positive about such "progress." A small but vocal group organized in the Anti-Imperialist League vigorously opposed war and annexation. Many felt displaced by the younger generation of modern expansionists. By attacking imperialism, the anti-imperialists struck out against the forces of modernism that they felt threatened their elite social position. They included a cross-section of

American dignitaries: former presidents Harrison and Cleveland, Samuel Gompers and Andrew Carnegie, William James, Jane Addams, and many others.

The major anti-imperialist arguments pointed out how imperialism in general and annexation in particular contradicted American ideals. First, the annexation of territory without immediate or planned steps toward statehood was unprecedented and unconstitutional. Second, to occupy and govern a foreign people without their consent violated the ideals of the Declaration of Independence. A third argument was that social reforms needed at home demanded

President McKinley's Annexation Argument

In a speech to a group of expansionist Methodist ministers and missionaries in 1900, President McKinley explained his reasons for recommending annexation of the Philippines. His statement summarizes most of the reasons for expansionism. It also offers a fascinating glimpse into the inner process of presidential decision making (or at least of a president who later sought to justify a decision).

The truth is I didn't want the Philippines and when they came to us as gift from the gods, I did not know what to do about them. . . . And one night it came to me this way—(1) that we could not give them back to Spain—that would be cowardly and dishonorable; (2) that we could not turn them over to France or Germany—our commercial rivals in the Orient—that would be bad business and discreditable; (3) that we could not leave them to themselves—they were unfit for self-government—and they would soon have anarchy and misrule over there worse than Spain's was; and (4) that there was nothing left for us to do but to take them all, and to educate the Filipinos, and uplift and civilize and Christianize them, and by God's grace do the very best we could by them, as our fellowmen for whom Christ also died. And then I went to bed, and went to sleep, and slept soundly, and the next morning I sent for the chief engineer of the War Department (our map-maker), and I told him to put the Philippines on the map of the United States, and there they are, and there they will stay while I am President!

Senator Hoar's Statement Against Imperialism

In one of the strongest anti-imperialist statements, Senator George F. Hoar of Massachusetts, who had called the war in Cuba "honorable," described the war in the Philippines in the following way.

We changed the Monroe Doctrine from a doctrine of eternal righteousness and justice, resting on the consent of the governed, to a doctrine of brutal selfishness looking only to our own advantage. We crushed the only republic in Asia. We made war on the only Christian people in the East. We converted a war of glory to a war of shame. We vulgarized the American flag. We introduced perfidy into the practice of war. We inflicted torture on unarmed men to extort confession. We put children to death. We devastated provinces. We baffled the aspirations of a people for liberty.

American energies and money before foreign expansionism. "Before we attempt to teach house-keeping to the world," one writer put it, we needed "to set our own house in order."

Not all anti-imperialist arguments were so noble. Some were practical or downright racist. One position alleged that because the Filipinos were nonwhite, Catholic, and inferior in size and intelligence, they were unassimilable. Annexation would lead to miscegenation and contamination of Anglo-Saxon blood. Senator Ben Tillman of South Carolina argued that although whites could "walk on the necks of every colored race," he still opposed "incorporating any more colored men into the body politic." The practical argument suggested that once in possession of the Philippines, the United States would have to defend them, possibly even acquiring more territories. This would require higher taxes and bigger government to build and support a navy that holding such possessions demanded. Some saw the Philippines as a burden that would require American troops to fight distant Asian wars.

The last argument became fact when Private Grayson's encounter started the Filipino-American War. Before it was over in 1902, some 126,500 American troops served in the Philippines, 4,234 died there, and 2,800 more were wounded. The cost was $400 million. Filipino casualties were much worse. In addition to the 18,000 killed in combat, an estimated 200,000 Filipinos died of famine and disease as American soldiers burned villages and destroyed crops and livestock to disrupt the economy and deny rebel fighters their food supply. General Jacob H. Smith ordered his troops to "kill and burn and the more you kill and burn, the better you will please me." Atrocities on both sides increased with the frustrations of a lengthening war, but the American "water cure" and other tortures were especially brutal.

As U.S. treatment of the Filipinos during the war became more and more like Spanish mistreatment of

Bringing "civilization" to the Filipinos, American soldiers stand guard over captured guerrillas in 1899. Finley Peter Dunne quipped, "Twud be a disgrace f'r to lave befure we've pounded these frindless an' ongrateful people into insinsibility." (Library of Congress)

the Cubans, the hypocrisy of American behavior became even more evident. This was especially true for black American soldiers who fought in the Philippines. They identified with the dark-skinned insurgents, whom they saw as tied to the land, burdened by debt, and pressed by poverty like themselves. They were also called "nigger" from morning to night. "I feel sorry for these people," a sergeant in the 24th Infantry wrote. "You have no idea the way these people are treated by the Americans here."

The war starkly exposed the hypocrisies of shouldering the white man's burden. On reading a report that 8,000 Filipinos had been killed in the first year of the war, Carnegie wrote a letter, dripping with sarcasm, congratulating McKinley for "civilizing the Filipinos. . . . About 8,000 of them have been completely civilized and sent to Heaven. I hope you like it." Another writer penned a devastating one-liner: "Dewey took Manila with the loss of one man—and all our institutions." One of the most active anti-imperialists, Ernest Howard Crosby, wrote a parody of Rudyard Kipling's "White Man's Burden," which he titled "The Real 'White Man's Burden'":

> *Take up the White Man's burden.*
> *Send forth your sturdy kin,*
> *And load them down with Bibles*
> *And cannon-balls and gin.*
> *Throw in a few diseases*
> *To spread the tropic climes,*
> *For there the healthy niggers*
> *Are quite behind the times.*
>
> *They need our labor question, too.*
> *And politics and fraud—*
> *We've made a pretty mess at home,*
> *Let's make a mess abroad.*

The anti-imperialists failed either to prevent annexation or to interfere with the war effort. However prestigious and sincere, they had little or no political power. They were seen as an older, conservative, elite group of Americans opposed to the kind of dynamic progress represented by Teddy Roosevelt and other expansionists. They were out of tune with the period of exuberant national pride, prosperity, and promise.

Expansionism Triumphant

By 1900, Americans had ample reason to be patriotic. Within a year, the United States had acquired several island territories, thereby joining the other great world powers. But several questions arose over what to do with the new territories. What was their status? Were they colonies? Would they be granted statehood or would they develop gradually from colonies to constitutional parts of the United States? Moreover, did

the indigenous peoples of Hawaii, Puerto Rico, Guam, and the Philippines have the same rights as American citizens on the mainland? Were they protected by the U.S. Constitution? The answers to these difficult questions emerged in a series of Supreme Court cases, congressional acts, and presidential decisions.

Although slightly different governing systems were worked out for each new territory, the solution in each was to define its status somewhere between subject colony and candidate for statehood. Territorial status came closest. The native people were usually allowed to elect their own legislature for internal lawmaking, but governors and other judicial and administrative officials were appointed by the American president. A provincial governor, George Curry, was subsequently made governor of the New Mexico Territory, a step indicating that both the Philippines and New Mexico remained somewhere between colonies and equal states. The first full governor of the Philippines, McKinley appointee William Howard Taft, effectively moved the Filipinos toward self-government. Final independence did not come until 1946, however, and elsewhere the process was equally slow.

The question of constitutional rights was resolved by deciding that Hawaiians and Puerto Ricans, for example, would be treated differently from Texans and Oregonians. In the "insular cases" of 1901, the Supreme Court ruled that these people would achieve citizenship and constitutional rights only when Congress said they were ready. To the question "Does the Constitution follow the flag?" the answer, as Secretary of State Elihu Root put it, was, "Ye-es, as near as I can make out the Constitution follows the flag—but doesn't quite catch up with it."

McKinley's resounding defeat of Bryan in 1900 clearly revealed the optimistic, nationalistic spirit of the American people. Bryan's intentions to make imperialism the "paramount issue" of the campaign failed, in part because the country strongly favored annexation of the Philippines. A rising sense of nationhood made the Filipino-American War a popular one, and it was politically unwise to risk being branded a traitor by opposing it. In the closing weeks of the campaign, Bryan and the Democrats shied away from imperialism and the war as a "paramount issue" and focused more on economic issues—trusts, the labor question, and free silver.

But Bryan fared no better on those issues. Prosperity returned with the discovery of gold in Alaska, and cries for reform fell on deaf ears. The McKinley forces rightly claimed that under four years of Republican rule, more money, jobs, thriving factories, and manufactured goods had been created. Moreover, McKinley pointed to the tremendous growth in American prestige abroad. Spain had been

This 1900 campaign poster for McKinley makes a compelling case that four years of Republican party leadership had brought prosperity and humanity both at home and abroad. Note not only that McKinley and Roosevelt have wrapped themselves in the American flag but also the dramatic contrasts after four years of Republican rule compared with the condition of the United States and Cuba when the Democrats left office in 1896. *(From the collection of David J. and Janice L. Frent)*

kicked out of Cuba, and the American flag flew in many places around the globe. It had been a triumphant four years. As a disappointed Tom Watson put it, noting the end of the Populist revolt with the war fervor over Cuba, "The Spanish war finished us. The blare of the bugle drowned out the voice of the reformer."

He was more right than he knew. Within one year, the expansionist Theodore Roosevelt went from assistant secretary of the navy to colonel of the Rough Riders to governor of New York. For some Republican politicos, who thought he was too vigorous, unorthodox, and independent, this quick rise as McKinley's potential rival came too fast. One way to eliminate Roosevelt politically, or at least slow him down, was to make him vice president, which they did in 1900. But six months into McKinley's second term, the president was killed by an anarchist, the third presidential assassination in less than 40 years. "Now look," exclaimed party boss Mark Hanna, who had opposed putting Roosevelt on the ticket, "that damned cowboy is President of the United States!"

THEODORE ROOSEVELT'S ENERGETIC DIPLOMACY

At a White House dinner party in 1905, a guest told a story about visiting the Roosevelt home when he had been a baby. "You were in your bassinet, making a good deal of fuss and noise," the guest reported, "and your father lifted you out and asked me to hold you." Secretary of State Elihu Root looked up from his plate and asked, "Was he hard to hold?" Whether true or not, the story reveals much about President Roosevelt's principles and policies on foreign affairs. As president from 1901 to 1909, and as the most dominating American personality for the 15 years between 1897 and 1912, Roosevelt made much fuss and noise about the activist role he thought the United States should play in the world. As he implemented his policies, he often seemed "hard to hold." Roosevelt's energetic foreign policy in Latin America, Asia, and Europe paved the way for the vital role as a world power the United States would play for the entire twentieth century.

Foreign Policy as Darwinian Struggle

Roosevelt's personal principles and presidential policies went together. He was an advocate of both individual physical fitness and collective national strength. An undersized boy, he was physically humiliated by schoolmates and therefore pursued a rigorous program of bodybuilding. During summers spent on his ranch in the North Dakota Badlands, Roosevelt learned to value the "strenuous life" of the cowboy. Reading Darwin taught him that life was a constant struggle for survival.

Roosevelt extended his beliefs about strenuous struggle from individuals to nations. His ideal was a "nation of men, not weaklings." To be militarily prepared and to fight well were the tests of racial superiority and national greatness. "All the great masterful races," he said, "have been fighting races." Although he believed in Anglo-Saxon superiority, he admired—and feared—Japanese military prowess. Powerful nations, like individuals, Roosevelt believed, had a duty to cultivate qualities of vigor, strength, courage, and moral commitment to civilized values. In practical terms, this meant developing natural resources, building large navies, and being ever prepared to fight. "I never take a step in foreign policy," he wrote, "unless I am assured that I shall be able eventually to carry out my will by force."

Although famous for saying "speak softly and carry a big stick," Roosevelt often not only wielded a large stick but spoke loudly as well. In a speech in 1897, he used the word *war* 62 times, saying, "no triumph of peace is quite so great as the supreme triumphs of war." But despite his bluster, Roosevelt was usually restrained in the exercise of force. He won the Nobel Peace Prize in 1906 for helping end the Russo-Japanese War. The purpose of the big stick and the loud talk was to preserve order and peace in the world. "To be prepared for war," he said, "is the most effectual means to promote peace."

Roosevelt divided the world into civilized and uncivilized nations, the former usually defined as Anglo-Saxon and English-speaking. The civilized nations had a responsibility to "police" the uncivilized, not only maintaining order but also spreading superior values and institutions. This "international police power," as Roosevelt called it, was the "white man's burden." As part of this burden, civilized nations sometimes had to wage war on the uncivilized, as the British did against the Boers in South Africa and the Americans did in the Philippines. These wars were justified because the victors bestowed the blessings of culture and racial superiority on the vanquished.

A war between two civilized nations, however, as between Germany and England, would be wasteful and foolish. Above all, Roosevelt believed in the balance of power. Strong, advanced nations like the United States had a duty to use their power to preserve order and peace. The United States had "no choice," Roosevelt said, but to "play a great part in the world." Americans could no longer "avoid responsibilities" that followed

The "big stick" became a memorable image in American diplomacy as Teddy Roosevelt sought to make the United States a policeman not only of the Caribbean basin but also of the whole world. "As our modern life goes on," Roosevelt said, "and the nations are drawn closer together for good and for evil, and this nation grows in comparison with friends and rivals, it is impossible to adhere to the policy of isolation." *(Puck, 1901)*

from "the fact that on the east and west we look across the waters at Europe and Asia." The 1900 census showed that the United States, with 75 million people, was much more populous than Great Britain, France, or Germany. These nations had many colonies in Asia and Africa, so it seemed time for Americans to exercise a greater role in world affairs.

As Roosevelt looked across the oceans, he developed a highly personal style of diplomacy. Bypassing the Department of State, he preferred face-to-face contact and personal exchange of letters with foreign ambassadors, ministers, and heads of state. Roosevelt made foreign policy while horseback riding with the German ambassador and while discussing history with the ambassador from France. A British emissary observed that Roosevelt had a "powerful personality" and a commanding knowledge of the world. As a result, ministries from London to Tokyo respected both the president and the power of the United States.

When threats of force failed to accomplish his goals, Roosevelt used direct personal intervention. "In a crisis the duty of a leader is to lead," he said. Congress was too slow and deliberate to play a significant role in foreign affairs. When he wanted Panama, Roosevelt bragged later, "I took the Canal Zone" rather than submitting a long "dignified State Paper" for congressional debate. And while Congress debated his actions, he was fond of pointing out, the building of the canal began. Roosevelt's energetic executive activism in foreign policy set a pattern for nearly every twentieth-century American president.

Taking the Panama Canal

In 1906, 2,600 American troops were sent into Honduras and Nicaragua. Philander Knox, secretary of state from 1909 to 1913, justified these interventions: "We are in the eyes of the world, and because of the Monroe Doctrine, held

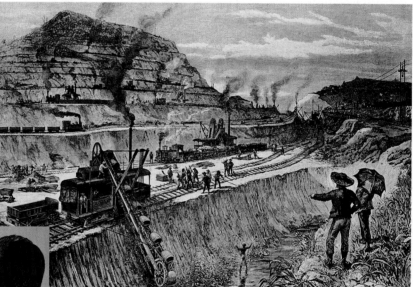

(Above) In 1903, despite protests from the Panamanian government, the United States acquired the right to begin the enormous engineering feat of building the Panama Canal. *(The Granger Collection)* (Left) A year later, a cartoonist showed the American eagle celebrating "his 128th birthday" with wings spanning the globe from Panama to the Philippines. In a prophetic anticipation of American overexpansion in the twentieth century, the eagle says, "Gee, but this is an awful stretch." *(The Granger Collection, New York)*

responsible for the order of Central America, and its proximity to the Canal makes the preservation of peace in that neighborhood particularly necessary." The Panama Canal was not yet finished when Knox spoke, but it had already become a cornerstone of U.S. policy in the region.

Three problems had to be surmounted to dig an interoceanic connection. First, an 1850 treaty bound the United States to build a canal jointly with Great Britain. But in 1901, John Hay, secretary of state between 1901 and 1905, convinced the British to cancel the treaty in exchange for an American guarantee that the canal would be "free and open to the vessels of commerce and of war of all nations." A second problem was where to dig it. American engineers rejected a long route through Nicaragua in favor of a shorter, more rugged path across the isthmus of Panama, where a French firm, the New Panama Company, had already begun work.

The third problem was that Panama was a province of Colombia and thus could not negotiate with the United States. The Colombian government was unimpressed with the share of a likely settlement the Americans would provide in buying up the New Panama Canal Company's $40 million in assets. Indeed, in 1903, the Colombian senate rejected a treaty negotiated by Hay, but mostly on nationalistic, not financial, grounds. Roosevelt, angered by this rebuff, called the Colombians "Dagoes" and "foolish and homicidal corruptionists" who tried to "hold us up" like highway robbers.

Aware of Roosevelt's fury, encouraged by hints of American support, and eager for the economic benefits the building of a canal would bring, Panamanian nationalists in 1903 staged a revolution led by several rich families and a Frenchman, Philippe Bunau-Varilla of the New Panama Canal Company. The Colombian army dispatched to quell the revolt was deterred by the presence of an American warship; local troops were separated from their officers, who were bought off. A bloodless revolution occurred on November 3; the next day, Panama declared its independence, and on November 6 the United States recognized the new government. Although Roosevelt did not formally encourage the revolution, it would not have occurred without American money and support.

On November 18, Hay and Bunau-Varilla signed a treaty establishing the American right to build and operate a canal through Panama and to exercise "titular sovereignty" over the ten-mile-wide Canal Zone. The Panamanian government protested the treaty, to no avail, and a later government called it the "treaty that no Panamanian signed." Roosevelt, in his later boast that he "took the canal," claimed that his diplomatic and engineering achievement, completed in 1914, would "rank . . . with the Louisiana Purchase and the acquisition of Texas." Panama did not gain control of the canal until January 1, 2000.

Policeman of the Caribbean

As late as 1901, the Monroe Doctrine was still regarded, according to Roosevelt, as the "equivalent to an open door in South America." To the United States, this meant that although no nation had a right "to get territorial possessions," all nations had equal commercial rights in the Western Hemisphere south of the Rio Grande. But as American investments poured into Central America and the Caribbean, the policy changed to one asserting U.S. dominance in the Caribbean basin.

This change was demonstrated in 1902, when Germany and Great Britain seized several Venezuelan gunboats and blockaded Venezuela's ports to force the government to pay defaulted debts. Roosevelt was especially worried that German influence would replace the British. He insisted that the European powers accept arbitration of the disputed financial claims and threatened to "move Dewey's ships" to the Venezuelan coast to enforce his intentions. The crisis passed, largely for other reasons, but Roosevelt's threat of force made very clear the paramount presence and self-interest of the United States in the Caribbean.

After the Spanish were expelled from Cuba, the United States supervised the island under Military Governor General Leonard Wood until 1902, when the Cubans elected their own congress and president. The United States honored Cuban independence, as it had promised to do in the Teller Amendment. But through the Platt Amendment, which Cubans reluctantly were forced to attach to their constitution in 1902, the United States obtained many economic rights in Cuba, a naval base at Guantanamo Bay, and the right to intervene if Cuban sovereignty were ever threatened. Newspapers in Havana assailed this violation of their newfound independence. One cartoon, titled "The Cuban Calvary," showed a figure representing the "Cuban people" crucified between two thieves, Wood and McKinley.

American policy intended to make Cuba a model of how a newly independent nation could achieve orderly self-government with only minimal guidance. Cuban self-government, however, was shaky. When in 1906 an internal political crisis threatened to plunge the infant nation into civil war, Roosevelt expressed his fury with "that infernal little Cuban republic." At Cuba's request, he sent warships to patrol the coastline and special commissioners and troops "to restore order and peace and public confidence." As he left office in 1909, Roosevelt proudly proclaimed that "we

Recovering the Past

POLITICAL CARTOONS

One of the most enjoyable ways of recovering the values and attitudes of the past is through political cartoons. Ralph Waldo Emerson once said, "Caricatures are often the truest history of the times." A deft drawing of a popular or unpopular politician can freeze ideas and events in time, conveying more effectively than columns of type the central issues of the day and creating an immediate response in the viewer. It is this freshness that makes caricatures such a valuable source when attempting to recover the past. Cartoonists are often at their best when they are critical, exaggerating a physical feature of a political figure or capturing public sentiment against the government.

The history of political cartoons in the United States goes back to Benjamin Franklin's "Join or Die" cartoon calling for colonial cooperation against the French in 1754. But political cartoons were rare until Andrew Jackson's presidency. Even after such cartoons as "King Andrew the First" in the 1830s, they did not gain notoriety until the advent of Thomas Nast's cartoons in *Harper's Weekly* in the 1870s. Nast drew scathing cartoons exposing the corruption of William "Boss" Tweed's Tammany Hall, depicting Tweed and his men as vultures and smiling deceivers. "Stop them damn pictures," Tweed ordered. "I don't care so much what the papers write about me. My constituents can't read. But, damn it, they can see pictures." Tweed sent some of his men to Nast with an offer of $100,000 to "study art" in Europe. The $5000-a-year artist negotiated up to a half million dollars before refusing Tweed's offer. "I made up my mind not long ago to put some of those fellows behind bars," Nast said, "and I'm going to put them there." His cartoons helped drive Tweed out of office.

The emergence of the United States as a world power and the rise of Theodore Roosevelt gave cartoonists plenty to draw about. An impetus to political cartoons was given by the rise of cheap newspapers such as William Randolph Hearst's *Journal* and Joseph Pulitzer's *World*. When the Spanish-American War broke out, newspapers whipped up public sentiment by having artists draw pictures of Spaniards stripping American

"The Spanish Brute Adds Mutilation to Murder," by Grant Hamilton, in *Judge*, July 9, 1898. *(Culver Pictures)*

women at sea and encouraging cartoonists to depict the "Spanish brute." Hearst used these tactics to increase his paper's daily circulation to one million copies. But by the time of the Philippines debates, many cartoonists took an anti-imperialist stance, pointing out American hypocrisy. Within a year, cartoonists shifted from depicting "The Spanish Brute Adds Mutilation to Murder" (1898) to "Liberty Halts American Butchery in the Philippines" (1899). The cartoons are very similar in condemning "butchery" of native populations, but the target has of course changed. Although Uncle Sam as a killer is not nearly as menacing as the figure of Spain as an ugly gorilla, both cartoons share a similarity of stance, the blood-covered swords, and a trail of bodies behind.

When Theodore Roosevelt rose to the presidency, cartoonists rejoiced. His physical appearance and personality made him instantly recognizable, a key factor in the success of a political cartoon. His broad grin, eyeglasses, and walrus mustache were the kind of features that fueled the cartoonist's imagination. A man of great energy, Roosevelt's style was as distinctive as his look.

"Liberty Halts American Butchery in the Philippines," from *Life*, 1899.

Other factors, such as the "Rough Rider" nickname, the symbol of the "big stick," and policies like "gunboat diplomacy" made Teddy the perfect target for political cartoons.

To understand and appreciate the meaning of any cartoon, certain facts must be ascertained, such as the date, artist, and source of the cartoon; the particular historical characters, events, and context depicted in it; the significance of the caption; and the master symbols employed by the cartoonist. The two remaining cartoons, "Panama or Bust" (1903) and "For President!" (1904), were both printed in American daily newspapers. Aside from the context and meaning of each cartoon, which should be obvious, note how the cartoonists use familiar symbols from Roosevelt's life and American history to underline the ironic power of their point. How many can you identify, and how are they used?

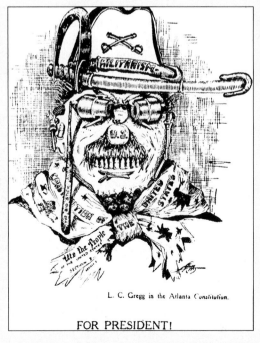

L. C. Gregg in the Atlanta Constitution.

FOR PRESIDENT!

"Panama or Bust," from the *New York Times*, 1903 (above). "For President!" by L. C. Gregg, in the *Atlanta Constitution*, 1904 (right).

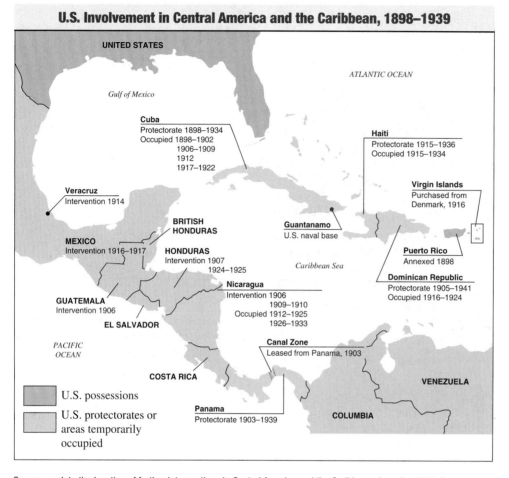

U.S. Involvement in Central America and the Caribbean, 1898–1939

Can you update the location of further interventions in Central America and the Caribbean since the 1950s?

have done our best to put Cuba on the road to stable and orderly government." The road was paved with sugar. U.S. trade with Cuba increased from $27 million in the year before 1898 to an average of $43 million per year during the following decade. Along with economic development, American political and even military involvement in Cuban affairs continued throughout the century.

The pattern repeated throughout the Caribbean. The Dominican Republic, for example, suffered from unstable governments and great poverty. In 1904, as a revolt erupted, European creditors pressured the Dominican government for payment of $40 million in defaulted bonds. Sending its warships to discourage European intervention, the United States took over the collection of customs in the republic. Two years later, the United States intervened in Guatemala and Nicaragua, where American bankers controlled nearly 50 percent of all trade, the first of several twentieth-century interventions in those countries.

Roosevelt clarified his policy that civilized nations should "insist on the proper policing of the world" in

his annual message in 1904. The goal of the United States, he said, was to have "stable, orderly and prosperous neighbors." A country that paid its debts and kept order "need fear no interference from the United States." A country that did not, but rather committed "chronic wrong-doing" and loosened the "ties of civilized society," would require the United States to intervene as an "international police power." This doctrine became known as the Roosevelt Corollary to the Monroe Doctrine. Whereas Monroe's doctrine had warned European nations not to intervene in the Western Hemisphere, Roosevelt's corollary justified American intervention. Starting with a desire to protect property, loans, and investments, the United States wound up supporting the brutal regimes of elites who owned most of the land, suppressed the poor, blocked reform, and acted as American surrogates.

After 1904, the Roosevelt Corollary was invoked in several Caribbean countries. Intervention usually required the landing of U.S. Marines to counter a threat to American property. Occupying the capital and major seaports, marines, bankers, and customs officials usually remained for several years, until they were satisfied that stability had been reestablished. Roosevelt's successors, William Howard Taft and Woodrow Wilson, pursued the same interventionist policy. So would later presidents, most recently Ronald Reagan (Grenada and Nicaragua), George Bush (Panama), and Bill Clinton (Haiti).

Opening the Door to China

Throughout the nineteenth century, American relations with China were restricted to a small but profitable trade. The British, in competition with France, Germany, and Russia, took advantage of the crumbling Manchu dynasty to force treaties on China creating "treaty ports" and granting exclusive trading privileges in various parts of the country. After 1898, Americans with dreams of exploiting the seemingly unlimited markets of China wanted to join the competition and enlarge their share. Moral interests, however, including many missionaries, reminded Americans of their revolutionary tradition against European imperialism. They made clear their opposition to crass U.S. commercial exploitation of a weak nation and supported the preservation of China's political integrity as the other imperial powers partitioned the country.

The United States' imperial role in China is supported in this cartoon showing President McKinley and Uncle Sam leading the charge against the Boxer Rebellion in 1900. What do you think is the point of view of the cartoonist? *(The Granger Collection, New York)*

American attitudes toward the Chinese people reflected this confusion of motives. Some Americans held an idealized view of China as the center of Eastern wisdom and saw a "special relationship" between the two nations. But the dominant American attitude viewed the Chinese as heathen, exotic, backward, and immoral. The Exclusion Act of 1882 and the riots in western states against Chinese workers in the 1870s and 1880s reflected this negative stereotype. The Chinese, in turn, regarded the United States with a mixture of admiration, curiosity, resentment, suspicion, and disdain.

The annexation of Hawaii, Samoa, and the Philippines in 1898–1899 convinced Secretary of State Hay that the United States should announce its own policy for China. He did so in the Open Door notes of 1899–1900, which became the cornerstone of U.S. policy in Asia for half a century. The first note demanded an open door for American trade by declaring the principle of equal access to commercial rights in China by all nations. The second note, addressing Russian movement into Manchuria, called on all countries to respect the "territorial and administrative integrity" of China. This second principle opened the way for a larger American role in Asia, offering China protection from foreign invasions and preserving an East Asian balance of power.

An early test of this new role came during the Boxer Rebellion in 1900. The Boxers were a society of young traditionalist Chinese in revolt against both the Manchu dynasty and the growing Western presence and influence in China. During the summer of 1900, Boxers killed some 242 missionaries and other foreigners and besieged the western quarter of Peking. Eventually, an international military force of 19,000 troops, including some 3,000 Americans sent from the Philippines, marched on Peking to end the siege.

The relationship with China was plagued by America's exclusionist immigration policy. Despite the barriers and riots, Chinese workers kept coming to the United States, entering illegally through Mexico and British Columbia. In 1905, Chinese nationalists at home boycotted American goods and called for a change in immigration policy. Roosevelt, contemptuous of the Chinese as a "backward" people, bristled with resentment and sent troops to the Philippines as a threat. Halfheartedly, he also asked Congress for a modified immigration bill, but nothing came of it.

Despite exclusion and insults, the idea that the United States had a unique guardian relationship with China persisted well into the twentieth century. Japan had ambitions in China, so this created a rivalry between Japan and the United States, testing the American commitment to preserve the Open Door in China and the balance of power in Asia. Economic motives, however, proved to be less significant. Investments there developed very slowly, as did the dream of the "great China market" for American grains and textiles. Although textile exports to China increased from $7 to nearly $24 million in a decade, the China trade always remained larger in imagination than in reality.

Japan and the Balance of Power

Population pressures, war, and a quest for economic opportunities caused Japanese immigration to the United States to increase dramatically around the turn of the century. Coming first as unmarried males working on western railroads and in West Coast canneries, mines, and logging camps, immigrants from Japan increased from 25,000 in the 1890s to 125,000 between 1901 and 1908. Like the earlier Chinese immigrants, they met nativist hostility and discrimination. Japanese workers were barred from factory jobs and shunted off to agricultural labor in California fields and orchards. Many Japanese immigrants, however, became successful independent farmers despite the prejudice against them. In 1906, the San Francisco

school board, claiming that Japanese children were "crowding the whites out of the schools," segregated them into separate schools and asked Roosevelt to persuade Japan to stop the emigration of its people. The insulted Japanese agreed to limit the migration of unskilled workers to the United States in a "gentleman's agreement" signed in 1907. In return, the segregation law was repealed, but not without costs in relations between the two nations.

Roosevelt worked hard to maintain the balance of power in East Asia. The Boxer Rebellion of 1900 left Russia with 50,000 troops in Manchuria, making it the strongest regional power. Roosevelt's admiration for the Japanese as a "fighting" people and valuable factor in the "civilization of the future" contrasted with his low respect for the Russians, whom he described as "corrupt," "treacherous," and "incompetent." As Japan moved into Korea, and Russia into Manchuria, Roosevelt hoped that each would check the growing power of the other.

Roosevelt welcomed news in 1904 that Japan had successfully mounted a surprise attack on Port Arthur in Manchuria, beginning the Russo-Japanese

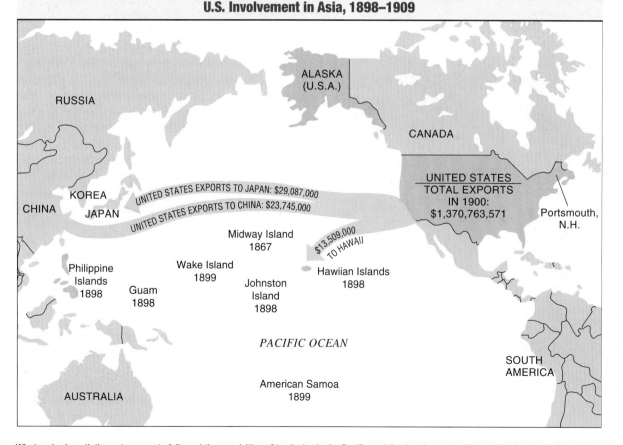

What major twentieth-century events followed the acquisition of territories in the Pacific and the development of intensified trade with East Asian countries?

Despite facing enormous prejudice from white Californians, Japanese immigrants to the West Coast of the United States around the turn of the century worked hard, irrigated the valleys of California, Oregon, and Washington, and became independent and highly productive farmers. *(Pat Hathaway Collection of California Views)*

War. He was "well pleased with the Japanese victory," he told his son, "for Japan is playing our game." But as Japanese victories continued, many Americans worried that Japan might play the game too well, shutting the United States out of Far Eastern markets. Roosevelt shifted his support toward Russia. When the Japanese expressed interest in an end to the war, the American president was pleased to exert his influence.

Roosevelt's goal was to achieve peace and leave a balanced situation. "It is best," he wrote, that Russia be left "face to face with Japan so that each may have a moderative action on the other." The negotiations and resulting treaty were carried out in the summer of 1905 near Portsmouth, New Hampshire. Nothing better symbolized the new American power and presence in the world than the signing of a peace treaty ending a war in Manchuria between Russia and Japan halfway around the globe in New Hampshire!

The Treaty of Portsmouth left Japan dominant in Manchuria and established the United States as the major balance to Japan's power. Almost immediately, the Japanese developed a naval base at Port Arthur, built railroads, and sought exclusive rights of investment and control in the Chinese province. In part because of his lack of respect for the Chinese, Roosevelt willingly recognized Japan's "dominance in Manchuria," as well as its control in Korea. But in return, in the Root-Takahira Agreement of 1908, he got Japan's promise to honor U.S. control in the Philippines and to make no further encroachments into China.

These agreements over territorial divisions barely covered up the tensions in Japanese–American relations. Some Japanese were angry that they had not received in the Portsmouth Treaty the indemnities they had wanted from Russia, and they blamed Roosevelt. American insensitivity on the immigration issue also left bad feelings. In Manchuria, U.S. Consul General Willard Straight aggressively pushed an anti-Japanese program of financing capital investment projects in banking and railroads. This policy, later known as "dollar diplomacy" under Roosevelt's successor, William Howard Taft, like the pursuit of markets, was larger in prospect than results. Nevertheless, the United States was in Japan's way, and rumors of war circulated.

It was clearly a moment for Roosevelt's "big stick." In 1907, he told Secretary of State Root that he was "more concerned over the Japanese situation than almost any other. Thank Heaven we have the navy in good shape." Although the naval buildup had begun over a decade earlier, under Roosevelt, the U.S. Navy had developed into a formidable force. From 1900 to 1905, outlays to the Navy rose from $56 to $117 million. Such a naval spending binge was without precedent in peacetime. In 1907, to make it clear that "the Pacific was as much our home waters as the Atlantic," Roosevelt sent his new, modernized "Great White Fleet" on a goodwill world tour. The first stop was the Japanese port of Yokohama. Although American sailors were greeted warmly, the act may have stimulated navalism in Japan, which came back to haunt the United States in 1941. But for the time being, the balance of power in Asia was preserved.

Preventing War in Europe

The United States was willing to stretch the meaning of the Monroe Doctrine to justify sending Marines and engineers to Latin America and the Navy and dollars to Asia. Treaties, agreements, and the protection of territories and interests entangled the United States with foreign nations from Panama and the Dominican Republic to the Philippines and Manchuria. Toward Europe, however, the traditional policies of neutrality continued.

Roosevelt believed that the most serious threats to world peace and civilized order lay in the relationships among Germany, Great Britain, and France. He established two fundamental policies toward Europe that would define the U.S. role throughout the century. The first was to make friendship with Great Britain the cornerstone of U.S. policy. As Roosevelt told King Edward VII in 1905, "In the long run the English people are more apt to be friendly to us than any other." Second, the crucial goal of a neutral power like the United States was to prevent a general war in Europe among strong nations. Toward this end, Roosevelt depended on his personal negotiating skills and began the twentieth-century practice of summit diplomacy.

It is difficult now to think of England as anything other than the most loyal friend of the United States outside North America. Yet throughout most of the nineteenth century, England was America's chief enemy and commercial rival. From the War of 1812 to the Venezuelan border crisis of 1895, conflict with Great Britain developed in squabbles over old debts and trade barriers, disputes over Canadian borders and fishing jurisdictions, and British interference in the American Civil War.

The Venezuelan crisis and a number of other events at the turn of the century shocked the United States and England into an awareness of their mutual interests. Both nations appreciated the neutrality of the other in their respective wars shouldering the white man's burden against the Filipinos and the Boers. Roosevelt supported British imperialism because he believed that England was "fighting the battle of civilization." Furthermore, both nations worried about growing German power in Europe, Africa, and the Far East. As German naval power increased, England had to bring its fleet closer to home. Friendly allies were needed to police parts of the world formerly patrolled by the British navy. England therefore concluded a mutual-protection treaty with Japan in 1902 and willingly let the Americans police Central America and the Caribbean Sea.

Similarities of language and cultural traditions, as well as strategic self-interest, drew the two countries together. Roosevelt's personal style furthered the con-

President Roosevelt stands proudly between Russian and Japanese representatives as they negotiated an end to the Russo-Japanese War in 1905 in, of all places, Portsmouth, New Hampshire. No image better captured the expanding role of the United States in global affairs than this photograph of Teddy Roosevelt helping to negotiate the end of war fought in Manchuria halfway around the world from the East Coast of the United States. *(Corbis-Bettmann)*

nection. He was clearly and unashamedly pro-British, and his most intimate circle of friends included many Englishmen. Although Roosevelt sometimes criticized English policies, his British bias was never in doubt. He knew, as he wrote to Lodge in 1901, that the United States had "not the least particle of danger to fear" from England and that German ambitions and militarism represented the major threat to peace in Europe. As Roosevelt left the presidency in 1909, one of his final acts was to proclaim the special American friendship with Great Britain.

German Kaiser Wilhelm II often underestimated the solidity of Anglo-American friendship and thought that Roosevelt was really pro-German, an illusion the American president skillfully cultivated. Wilhelm, therefore, sought Roosevelt's support on several diplomatic issues between 1905 and 1909. In each case, Roosevelt flattered the Kaiser while politely rejecting his overtures. The relationship gave Roosevelt a unique advantage in influencing affairs in Europe to prevent the outbreak of war.

The Moroccan crisis in 1905 and 1906 is illustrative. European powers competed for colonies and spheres of influence in Africa as well as in Asia. Germany in particular resented French dominance along the North African coast in Morocco and feared the recent Anglo-French entente. The Kaiser precipitated a crisis in the summer of 1905 by delivering a bellicose speech in Casablanca, intended to split the British and French and to force an opening of commercial doors in Morocco. In this endeavor, he sought help from Roosevelt. The French were outraged at Wilhelm's boldness, and war threatened. Roosevelt intervened, arranging a conference in Algeciras, Spain, to head off the conflict. The treaty signed in 1906 peacefully settled the Moroccan issue favorably for the French.

Roosevelt's successful countering of meddlesome German policies continued, as did his efforts in preventing war. At the Hague conference on disarmament in 1907, the Kaiser sought an agreement to reduce British naval supremacy, a superiority Roosevelt thought "quite proper." The German emperor also tried to promote German-Chinese-American entente to balance the Anglo-Japanese Treaty in Asia. Roosevelt rebuffed all these efforts. While on a European tour in 1910, the retired American president was warmly entertained and celebrated by Wilhelm, who continued to misunderstand him. Roosevelt, meanwhile, kept on urging his English friends to counter the German naval buildup to maintain peace in Europe.

In 1911, Roosevelt wrote that there would be nothing worse than that "Germany should ever overthrow England and establish the supremacy in Europe she aims at." A German attempt "to try her hand in America," he thought, would surely follow. To avert it, Roosevelt's policy for Europe included cementing friendship with England and, while maintaining official neutrality, using diplomacy to prevent hostilities among European powers. The relationship between Great Britain and Germany continued to deteriorate, however, and by 1914, a new American president, Woodrow Wilson, would face the terrible reality that Roosevelt had skillfully sought to prevent. When World War I finally broke out, no American was more eager to fight on the British side against the Germans than the leader of the Rough Riders.

Timeline

1823	Monroe Doctrine
1857	Trade opens with Japan
1867	Alaska purchased from Russia
1870	Failure to annex Santo Domingo (Hispaniola)
1875	Sugar reciprocity treaty with Hawaii
1877	United States acquires naval base at Pearl Harbor
1878	United States acquires naval station in Samoa
1882	Chinese Exclusion Act
1889	First Pan-American Conference
1890	Alfred Mahan publishes *Influence of Sea Power upon History*
1893	Hawaiian coup by American sugar growers
1895	Cuban revolt against Spanish
	Venezuelan boundary dispute
1896	Weyler's reconcentration policy in Cuba
	McKinley-Bryan presidential campaign
1897	Theodore Roosevelt's speech at Naval War College
1898	
January	De Lôme letter
February	Sinking of the battleship *Maine*
April	Spanish-American War
	Teller Amendment
May	Dewey takes Manila Bay
July	Annexation of Hawaiian Islands
August	Americans liberate Manila; war ends
December	Treaty of Paris; annexation of the Philippines
1899	Senate ratifies Treaty of Paris
	Filipino-American War begins
	American Samoa acquired
1899–1900	Open Door notes
1900	Boxer Rebellion in China
	William McKinley reelected president
1901	Supreme Court insular cases
	McKinley assassinated; Theodore Roosevelt becomes president
1902	Filipino-American War ends
	U.S. military occupation of Cuba ends
	Platt Amendment
	Venezuela debt crisis
1903	Panamanian revolt and independence
	Hay-Bunau-Varilla Treaty
1904	Roosevelt Corollary
1904–1905	Russo-Japanese War ended by treaty signed at Portsmouth, New Hampshire
1904–1906	United States intervenes in Nicaragua, Guatemala, and Cuba
1905–1906	Moroccan crisis
1906	Roosevelt receives Nobel Peace Prize
1907	Gentleman's agreement with Japan
1908	Root-Takahira Agreement
1909	U.S. Navy ("Great White Fleet") sails around the world
1911	United States intervenes in Nicaragua
1914	Opening of the Panama Canal
	World War I begins
1916	Partial home rule granted to the Philippines

Conclusion:

The Responsibilities of Power

Since the earliest settlements at Massachusetts Bay, Americans had struggled with the dilemma of how to do good in a world that did wrong. The realities of power in the 1890s brought increasing international responsibilities. Roosevelt said in 1910 that because of "strength and geographical situation," the United States had itself become "more and more, the balance of power of the whole world." This ominous responsibility was also an opportunity to extend American economic, political, and moral influence around the globe.

As president in the first decade of the twentieth century, Roosevelt established aggressive American policies toward the rest of the world. The United States dominated and policed Central America and the Caribbean Sea to maintain order and protect its investments and other economic interests. In the Far East, Americans marched through Hay's Open Door with treaties, troops, navies, missionaries and dollars to protect the newly annexed Philippine Islands, to develop markets and investments, and to preserve the balance of power in Asia. In Europe, the United States sought to remain neutral and uninvolved in European affairs and at the same time to cement Anglo-American friendship and prevent "civilized" nations from going to war.

How well these policies worked would be seen later in the twentieth century. Whatever the particular judgment, the fundamental ambivalence of America's sense of itself as a model "city on a hill," an example to others, remained. As widening involvements around the world—the Filipino-American War, for example—painfully demonstrated, it was increasingly difficult for the United States to be both responsible and good, both powerful and loved. The American people thus learned to experience both the satisfactions and burdens, both the profits and costs, of the missionary role.

Recommended Reading

Steps Toward Empire and American Expansionism in the 1890s

Robert Beisner, *From the Old Diplomacy to the New, 1865–1900* (1986); Charles Campbell, *The Transformation of American Foreign Relations, 1865–1900* (1976); John Dobson, *Reticent Expansionism: The Foreign Policy of William McKinley* (1988); David Healy, *U.S. Expansion: Imperialist Urge in the 1890s* (1970); Walter La Feber, *The Cambridge History of Foreign Relations: The Search for Opportunity, 1865–1913* (1993); Ernest May, *Imperial Democracy: The Emergence of America as a Great Power* (1961); H. Wayne Morgan, *America's Road to Empire: The War with Spain and Overseas Expansion* (1965); Emily Rosenberg, *Spreading the American Dream: American Economic and Cultural Expansion, 1890–1945* (1982); William Widenor, *Henry Cabot Lodge and the Search for an American Foreign Policy* (1980).

Cuba, the Spanish-American War, and the Philippines

Robert Beisner, *Twelve Against Empire: The Anti-Imperialists, 1898–1900* (1968); Michael Blow, *A Ship to Remember: The Maine and the Spanish-American War* (1992); James C. Bradford, ed., *Crucible of Empire: The Spanish-American War and Its Aftermath* (1993); Frank Freidel, *The Splendid Little War* (1958); Willard Gatewood, Jr., *Black Americans and the White Man's Burden* (1975) and *"Smoked Yankees" and the Struggle for Empire: Letters from Negro Soldiers, 1898–1902* (1971); Stanley Karnow, *In Our Image: America's Empire in the Philippines* (1989); Stuart Creighton Miller, *"Benevolent Assimilation": The American Conquest of the Philippines, 1899–1903* (1982); John L. Offner, *An Unwanted War: The Diplomacy of the United States and Spain over Cuba, 1895–1898* (1992); Louis A. Perez, Jr., *The War of 1898: The United States and Cuba in History and Historiography* (1998); David Trask, *The War with Spain in 1898* (1981); Richard Welch, *Response to Imperialism: The United States and the Philippine-American War, 1899–1902* (1979).

Theodore Roosevelt's Energetic Diplomacy

Howard Beale, *Theodore Roosevelt and the Rise of America to World Power* (1956); Richard Collin, *Theodore Roosevelt's Caribbean: The Panama Canal, the Monroe Doctrine, and the Latin American Context* (1990); Roger Daniels, *Asian Americans: Chinese and Japanese in the United States Since 1850* (1988); Michael Hunt, *The Making of a Special Relationship: The United States and China to 1914* (1983); Walter La Feber, *Inevitable Revolutions: The United States in Central America* (1983); Frederick Marks II, *Velvet on Iron: The Diplomacy of Theodore Roosevelt* (1979); David McCollough, *The Path Between the Seas: The Creation of the Panama Canal, 1870–1914* (1977); Ronald Takaki, *Strangers from a Different Shore: A History of Asian Americans* (1989).

Fiction and Film

Mariano Azuela's *The Underdogs* (1915), written and published in El Paso, Texas, is a gripping novel of the Mexican revolution in 1911 by an ardent Mexican patriot. Frank Chinn's *Donald Duk* (1991) is a fanciful story of San Francisco's Chinatown, with flashbacks to the history of Chinese railroad workers in the late nineteenth century. Ernest Howard Crosby's *Captain Jinks, Hero* (1902), is an anti-imperialist novel set in the Philippines. Maxine Hong Kingston's *The Woman Warrior* (1975) faithfully reflects Chinese culture in the coming-of-age story of a young Chinese woman in California. Robert Michener's *Hawaii* (1959) is an immense saga of the multicultural history of the islands annexed by the United States in 1898. Four PBS videos on *The American Experience* depict the history of the era: *America 1900*, which focuses on the year 1900, including the second presidential race between McKinley and Bryan; *Hawaii's Last Queen* (1997), an account of the clash between native Hawaiians and U.S. business interests and Marines; a 1999 series on *Crucible of Empire: The Spanish-American War;* and an earlier video, *In Our Image: The United States and the Philippines.*

Suggested Web Sites

http://www.history.ohio-state.edu/projects/mckinley/SpanAmWar.htm

William McKinley and the Spanish-American War. Part of Ohio State University's site about William McKinley, this part highlights the Spanish-American War with an essay and photos.

http://www.boondocksnet.com/centennial/index.html

Sentenaryo/Centennial: The Philippine Revolution and Philippine-American War. The editor of this site, Jim Zwick, organizes primary documents, images, and essays focusing upon the Philippines and American involvement in the war.

http://www.boondocksnet.com/ail98-35.html

Anti-Imperialism in the United States, 1898–1935. Jim Zwick edits this extensive site, collating a large number of primary documents about anti-imperialism in America.

http://www.geocities.com/djmabry/USA/twenty/filipino.html

Images from the Philippine-United States War. The Philippine-American War is one of the least discussed military engagements in American History. Many tactics employed then were later used in the Vietnam War. This site is an archive of historical texts.

http://www.smplanet.com/imperialism/toc.html

The Age of Imperialism. Focusing on the period around the turn of the century, this site puts much information about American imperialism in one place.

http://www.ushistoryplace.com

A richly detailed on-line learning environment complete with interactive maps, timelines, history activities, primary source documents, and links to related American history sites.

21

The PROGRESSIVES CONFRONT INDUSTRIAL CAPITALISM

CHAPTER OUTLINE

Frances Kellor, a young woman who grew up in Ohio and Michigan, received her law degree in 1897 from Cornell University and became one of the small but growing group of professionally trained women in the United States. Deciding that she was more interested in solving the nation's social problems than in practicing law, she moved to Chicago, studied sociology, and trained herself as a social reformer. Kellor believed passionately that poverty and inequality could be eliminated in America. She also had the progressive faith that if Americans could only hear the truth about the millions of people living in urban slums, they would rise up and make changes. She was one of the experts who provided the evidence to document what was wrong in industrial America.

Like many progressives, Kellor believed that environment was more important than heredity in determining ability, prosperity, and happiness. Better schools and better housing, she thought, would produce better citizens. Even criminals, she argued, were simply victims of environment. Kellor demonstrated that poor health and deprived childhoods explained the only differences between criminals and college students. If it were impossible to define a criminal type, then it must be possible to reduce crime by improving the environment.

Kellor was an efficient professional. Like the majority of the professional women of her generation, she never married but devoted her life to social research and social reform. She lived for a time at Hull House in Chicago and at the College Settlement in New York, centers not only of social research and reform but also of lively community. For many young people, the settlement, with its sense of commitment and its exciting conversation around the dinner table, provided an alternative to the nuclear family or the single apartment.

While staying at the College Settlement, Kellor researched and wrote a muckraking study of employment agencies, published in 1904 as *Out of Work*. She revealed how employment agencies exploited immigrants, blacks, and other recent arrivals in the city. Kellor's book, like the writing of most progressives, spilled over with moral outrage. But Kellor went beyond moralism to suggest corrective legislation at the state and national levels. She became one of the leaders of the movement to Americanize the immigrants pouring into the country in unprecedented numbers. Between 1899 and 1920, over eight million people came to the United States, most from southern and eastern Europe. Many feared that this flood of immigrants threatened the very basis of American democracy. Kellor and her coworkers represented the side of progressivism that sought state and federal laws to protect the new arrivals from exploitation and to establish agencies and facilities to educate and Americanize them. Another group of progressives, often allied with organized labor, tried to pass laws to restrict immigration. Kellor did not entirely escape the ethnocentrism that was a part of her generation's worldview, but she did maintain that all immigrants could be made into useful citizens.

Convinced of the need for a national movement to push for reform legislation, Kellor helped to found the National Committee for Immigrants in America, which tried to promote a national policy "to make all these people Americans," and a federal bureau to organize the campaign. Eventually, she helped establish the Division of Immigrant Education within the Department of Education. A political movement led by Theodore Roosevelt excited her most. More than almost any other single person, Kellor had been responsible for alerting Roosevelt to the problems the immigrants faced in American cities. When Roosevelt formed the new Progressive party in 1912, she was one of the many social workers and social researchers who joined him. She campaigned for Roosevelt and directed the Progressive Service Organization, to educate voters in all areas of social justice and welfare after the election. After Roosevelt's defeat and the collapse of the Progressive party in 1914, Kellor continued to work for Americanization. She spent the rest of her life promoting justice, order, and efficiency and trying to find ways for resolving industrial and international disputes.

George Bellows, *Cliff Dwellers*, 1913. Bellows was one of many talented artists who migrated from the Midwest to New York early in the century. In this painting he captures some of the life and excitement in a tenement district on a hot summer night. To Bellows this was romantic; to the progressive reformers it was a problem to be solved. (*Los Angeles County Museum of Art, Los Angeles County Funds*)

Frances Kellor's life illustrates two important aspects of progressivism, the first nationwide reform movement of the modern era: first, a commitment to promote social justice, ensure equal opportunity, and preserve democracy; and second, a search for order and efficiency in a world complicated by rapid industrialization, immigration, and spectacular urban growth. But no one person can represent all facets of so complex a movement. Borrowing from populism and influenced by a number of reformers from the 1890s, progressivism reached a climax in the years from 1900 to 1914. Like most American reform movements, the progressive movement did not plot to overthrow the government; rather, it sought to reform the system to ensure the survival of the American way of life.

This chapter traces the important aspects of progressivism. It examines the social justice movement, which sought to promote reform among the poor and to improve life for those who had fallen victim to an urban and industrial civilization. It surveys life among workers, a group the reformers sometimes helped but often misunderstood. Then it traces the reform movements in the cities and states, where countless officials and experts tried to reduce chaos and promote order and democracy. Finally, it examines progressivism at the national level during the administrations of Theodore Roosevelt and Woodrow Wilson, the first thoroughly modern presidents.

THE SOCIAL JUSTICE MOVEMENT

Historians write of a "progressive movement," but actually there were a number of movements, some of them contradictory, but all focusing on the problems created by a rapidly expanding urban and industrial world. Some reformers, often from the middle class, sought to humanize the modern city. They hoped to improve housing and schools and to provide a better life for the poor and recent immigrants. Others were concerned with the conditions of work and the rights of labor. Still others pressed for changes in the political system to make it more responsive to their interests. Progressivism had roots in the 1890s, when many reformers were shocked by the devastation caused by the depression of 1893, and they were influenced by reading Henry George's *Progress and Poverty* (1879) and Edward Bellamy's *Looking Backward* (1888). They were also influenced by the Social Gospel movement, which sought to build the kingdom of God on earth by eliminating poverty and promoting equality (see Chapter 19).

The Progressive Worldview

Intellectually, the progressives were influenced by the Darwinian revolution. They believed that the world

John Sloan (1871–1951) was one of the leading members of the "ash can school," a group of artists who experimented with new techniques and painted ordinary scenes of urban life, such as this 1912 painting: *Sunday, Women Drying Their Hair.* His paintings offended many because he flouted genteel codes of propriety and decorum, and he showed working-class women in ways that were just as shocking as progressive era reports on child labor and prostitution. (*© Addison Gallery of American Art, Phillips Academy, Andover, Massachusetts. All Rights Reserved.*)

was in flux, and they rebelled against the fixed and the formal in every field. One of the philosophers of the movement, John Dewey, wrote that ideas could become instruments for change. William James, in his philosophy of pragmatism, denied that there were universal truths; ideas should be judged by their usefulness. Most of the progressives were environmentalists who were convinced that environment was much more important than heredity in forming character. Thus, if one could build better schools and houses, one could make better people and a more perfect society. Yet even the more advanced reformers thought in racial and ethnic categories. They believed that some groups could be molded and changed more easily than others. Thus, progressivism did not usually mean progress for blacks.

In many ways, progressivism was the first modern reform movement. It sought to bring order and efficiency to a world that had been transformed by rapid growth and new technology. Yet elements of nostalgia infected the movement as reformers tried to preserve the handicrafts of a preindustrial age and to promote small-town and farm values in the city. The progressive leaders were almost always middle class, and they quite consciously tried to teach their middle-class values to the immigrants and the working class. Often, the progressives seemed more interested in control than in reform; frequently, they betrayed a sense of paternalism toward those they tried to help.

The progressives were part of a statistics-minded, realistic generation. They conducted surveys, gathered facts, wrote reports about every conceivable problem, and usually had faith that their reports would lead to change. Their urge to document and record came out in haunting photographs of young workers taken by Lewis Hine, in the stark and beautiful city paintings by John Sloan, and in the realist novels of Theodore Dreiser and William Dean Howells.

The progressives were optimistic about human nature, and they believed that change was possible. In retrospect, they may seem naive or bigoted, but they wrestled with many social questions, some of them old but fraught with new urgency in an industrialized society. What is the proper relation of government to society? In a world of large corporations, huge cities, and massive transportation systems, how much should the government regulate and control? How much responsibility does society have to care for the poor and needy? The progressives could not agree on the answers, but they struggled with the questions.

The Muckrakers

One group of writers who exposed corruption and other evils in American society were labeled "muckrakers" by Theodore Roosevelt. Not all muckrakers were reformers—some merely wanted to profit from the scandals—but the reformers learned from their techniques of exposé.

In part, the muckrakers were a product of the journalistic revolution of the 1890s. Nineteenth-century magazines such as *Atlantic, Century,* and *Scribner's* had small, highly educated audiences. The new magazines, among them *American, McClure's,* and *Cosmopolitan,* had slick formats, carried more advertising, and sold more widely. Several had circulations of more than 500,000 in 1910. Competing for readers, editors eagerly published the articles of investigative reporters who wanted to tell the public what was wrong in American society.

Lincoln Steffens, a young California journalist, wrote articles for *McClure's* exposing the connections between respectable urban businessmen and corrupt politicians. When published in 1904 as *The Shame of the Cities,* Steffens's account became a battle cry for people determined to clean up the graft in city government. Ida Tarbell, a teacher turned journalist, had grown up in western Pennsylvania, almost next door to the first oil well in the United States. She published several successful books before turning her attention to the Standard Oil Company and John D. Rockefeller. Her outraged exposé, based on years of research, revealed Rockefeller's ruthless ways and his unfair business practices.

After Steffens and Tarbell achieved popular success, many others followed. Ray Stannard Baker exposed the railroads' corrupt tactics, while Frank Norris dramatized the railroad's stranglehold on the farmers in his novel *The Octopus.* Robert Hunter, a young settlement worker, shocked Americans in 1904 with his book *Poverty;* setting the poverty line at $460 for a family of five, he found ten million people living below that level. David Graham Phillips revealed the alliance of politics and business in *The Treason of the Senate* (1906), while Upton Sinclair's novel *The Jungle* (1906) described the horrors of the Chicago meatpacking industry.

Working Women and Children

Nothing disturbed the social justice progressives more than the sight of children, sometimes as young as eight or ten, working long hours in dangerous and depressing factories. Young people had worked in factories since the beginning of the Industrial Revolution, but that did not make the practice any less repugnant to the reformers. "Children are put into industry very much as we put in raw material," Jane Addams objected, "and the product we look for is not better men and women, but better manufactured goods."

Florence Kelley was one of the most important leaders in the crusade against child labor. Kelley had grown up in an upper-class Philadelphia family and graduated from Cornell in 1882—like Addams and Kellor she was a member of the first generation of college women in the United States. When the University of Pennsylvania refused her admission as a graduate student because she was a woman, she went to the University of Zurich in Switzerland. There she married and became a socialist. The marriage failed, and some years later, Kelley moved to Chicago with her children, became a Hull House resident, and poured her considerable energies into the campaign against child labor. A friend described her as "explosive, hot-tempered, determined . . . a smoking volcano that at any moment would burst into flames." When she could find no attorney in Chicago to argue child labor cases against some of the prominent corporations, she went to law school, passed the bar exam, and argued the cases herself.

Although Kelley and the other child labor reformers won a few cases, they quickly recognized the need for state laws if they were going to have any real influence. Child labor was an emotional issue. Many businesses made large profits by employing children, and many legislators and government officials, remembering their own rural childhoods, argued that it was good for the children's character to work hard and take responsibility. Reformers, marshaling their evidence about the tragic effects on growing children of long working hours in dark and damp factories, pressured the Illinois state legislature into passing an anti–child

labor law. A few years later, however, the state supreme court declared the law unconstitutional.

Judicial opposition was one factor leading reformers to the national level in the first decade of the twentieth century. Florence Kelley again led the charge. In 1899, she had become secretary of the National Consumers League, an organization that enlisted consumers in a campaign to lobby elected officials and corporations to ensure that products were produced under safe and sanitary conditions. It was not Kelley, however, but Edgar Gardner Murphy, an Alabama clergyman, who suggested the formation of the National Child Labor Committee. Like many other Social Gospel ministers, Murphy believed that the church should reform society as well as save souls. He was appalled by the number of young children working in southern textile mills, where they were exposed to great danger and condemned to "compulsory ignorance" (because they dropped out of school).

The National Child Labor Committee, headquartered in New York, drew up a model state child labor law, encouraged state and city campaigns, and coordinated the movement around the country. Although two-thirds of the states passed some form of child labor law between 1905 and 1907, many had loopholes that exempted a large number of children, including newsboys and youngsters who worked in the theater. The committee also supported a national bill introduced in Congress by Indiana Senator Albert Beveridge in 1906 "to prevent the employment of children in factories and mines." The bill went down to defeat. However, the child labor reformers convinced

Nothing tugged at the heartstrings of the reformers more than the sight of little children, sullen and stunted, working long hours in factory, farm, and mine. These children, breaker boys who spent all day sorting coal in western Pennsylvania, were carefully posed by documentary photographer Lewis Hine while he worked for the National Child Labor Committee in 1911. *(Records of the Children's Bureau, The National Archives, Office of the Chief Signal Officer)*

Congress in 1912 to establish a children's bureau in the Department of Labor. Despite these efforts, compulsory school attendance laws did more to reduce the number of children who worked than federal and state laws, which proved difficult to pass and even more difficult to enforce.

The crusade against child labor was a typical social justice reform effort. Its origins lay in the moral indignation of middle-class reformers. But reform went beyond moral outrage as reformers gathered statistics, took photographs documenting the abuse of children, and used their evidence to push for legislation first on the local level, then in the states, and eventually in Washington.

Like other progressive reform efforts, the battle against child labor was only partly successful. Too many businessmen, both small and large, were profiting from employing children at low wages. Too many politicians and judges were reluctant to regulate the work of children or adults because work seemed such an individual and personal matter. And some parents, who often desperately needed the money their children earned in the factories, opposed the reformers and even broke the law to allow their children to work.

The reformers also worried over the young people who got into trouble with the law, often for pranks that in rural areas would have seemed harmless. They feared for young people tried by adult courts and thrown into jail with hardened criminals. Almost simultaneously in Denver and Chicago, reformers organized juvenile courts, where judges had the authority to put delinquent youths on probation, take them from their families and make them wards of the state, or assign them to an institution. The juvenile court often helped prevent young delinquents from adopting a life of crime. Yet the juvenile offender was frequently deprived of all rights of due process, a fact that the Supreme Court finally recognized in 1967, when it ruled that children were entitled to procedural rights when accused of a crime.

Closely connected with the anti–child labor movement was the effort to limit the hours of women's work. It seemed inconsistent to protect a girl until she was 16 and then give her the "right to work from 8 A.M. to 10 P.M., 13 hours a day, 78 hours a week for $6." Florence Kelley and the National Consumers League led the campaign. It was foolish and unpatriotic, they argued, to allow the "mothers of future generations" to work long hours in dangerous industries. "Adult females," a Pennsylvania superior court stated, "are so constituted as to be unable to endure physical exertion and exposure."

The most important court case on women's work came before the U.S. Supreme Court in 1908. Josephine Goldmark, a friend and coworker of Kelley's at the Consumers League, wrote the brief for *Muller* v. *Oregon* that her brother-in-law, Louis Brandeis, used when he argued the case. The Court upheld the Oregon ten-hour law largely because Goldmark's sociological argument detailed the danger and disease that factory women faced. Brandeis opposed laissez-faire legal concepts, arguing that the government had a special interest in protecting the health of its citizens. Most states fell into line with the Supreme Court decision and passed protective legislation for women, though many companies found ways to circumvent the laws. Even the work permitted by the law seemed too long to some women. "I think ten hours is too much for a woman," one factory worker stated. "I have four children and have to work hard at home. Make me awful tired. I would like nine hours. I get up at 5:30. When I wash, I have to stay up till one or two o'clock."

By contending that "women are fundamentally weaker than men in all that makes for endurance: in muscular strength, in nervous energy, in the powers of persistent attention and application," the reformers won some protection for women workers. But their arguments that women were weaker than men would eventually be used to reinforce gender segregation of the workforce for the next half century.

In addition to working for protective legislation for working women, the social justice progressives also campaigned for woman suffrage. Unlike some supporters who argued that middle-class women would offset the ignorant and corrupt votes of immigrant men, these social reformers supported votes for all women. Addams argued that urban women not only could vote intelligently but also needed the vote to protect, clothe, and feed their families. Women in an urban age, she suggested, needed to be municipal housekeepers. Through the suffrage, they would ensure that elected officials provided adequate services—pure water, uncontaminated food, proper sanitation, and police protection. The progressive insistence that all women needed the vote helped to push woman suffrage toward the victory that would come after World War I.

Much more controversial than either votes for women or protective legislation was the movement for birth control. Even many advanced progressives could not imagine themselves teaching immigrant women how to prevent conception, especially because the Comstock Law of 1873 made it illegal to promote or even write about contraceptive devices.

Margaret Sanger, a nurse who had watched poor women suffer from too many births and even die from dangerous illegal abortions, was one of the founders of the modern American birth control movement. Middle-class Americans had limited family size in the

While the poor lived in overcrowded tenements, the middle and upper classes surrounded themselves with overstuffed abundance. The piano became a symbol of middle-class status for many, and the draped, cluttered interiors a sign of success. The elegantly clad wife and daughter, who had the leisure time to play the piano, were additional ornaments in the crowded decor. Many progressive reformers rebelled against this opulent style and urged a leaner, Arts and Crafts look. (*Museum of The City of New York*)

nineteenth century through abstinence, withdrawal, and abortion, as well as through the use of primitive birth control devices, but much ignorance and misinformation remained, even among middle-class women. Sanger obtained the latest medical and scientific European studies and in 1914 explained in her magazine, *The Woman Rebel*, and in a pamphlet, *Family Limitation,* that women could separate sex from procreation. She was promptly indicted for violation of the postal code and fled to Europe to avoid arrest.

Birth control remained controversial, and in most states illegal, for many years. Yet Sanger helped to bring the topic of sexuality and contraception out into the open. When she returned to the United States in 1921, she founded the American Birth Control League, which became the Planned Parenthood Federation in 1942.

Home and School

The reformers believed that better housing and education could transform the lives of the poor and create a better world. Books such as Jacob Riis's *How the Other Half Lives* (1890) horrified them. With vivid language and haunting photographs, Riis had documented the overcrowded tenements, the damp, dark alleys, and the sickness and despair that affected people who lived in New York's slums. Reformers had been trying to improve housing for the poor for years. They had constructed model tenements and housing projects and had sent "friendly visitors" to the residents to collect the rent and teach them how to live

like the middle class. Riis labored to replace New York's worst slums with parks and playgrounds.

In the first decade of the twentieth century, the progressives took a new approach toward the housing problems. They collected statistics, conducted surveys, organized committees, and constructed exhibits to demonstrate the effect of urban overcrowding. Then they set out to pass tenement house laws in several cities, but the laws were often evaded or modified. In 1910, they organized the National Housing Association, and some of them looked ahead to federal laws and even to government-subsidized housing.

The housing reformers combined a moral sense of what needed to be done to create a more just society with practical ability to organize public opinion and get laws passed. They also took a paternalistic view toward the poor. Many reformers disapproved of the clutter and lack of privacy in immigrant tenements. One reformer's guide, *How to Furnish and Keep House in a Tenement Flat*, recommended "wood-stained and uncluttered furniture surfaces, iron beds with mattresses, and un-upholstered chairs. . . . Walls must be painted not papered. Screens provide privacy in the bedrooms; a few good pictures should grace the walls." But often immigrant family ideals and values differed from those of the middle-class reformers. The immigrants actually did not mind the clutter and lack of privacy. Despite the reformers' efforts to separate life's functions into separate rooms, most immigrants still crowded into the kitchen and hung religious objects rather than "good pictures" on the walls.

Ironically, many middle-class women reformers who tried to teach working-class families how to live in their tenement flats had never organized their own homes. Often they lived in settlement houses, where they ate in a dining hall and never had to worry about cleaning, cooking, or doing laundry. Some of them, however, began to realize that the domestic tasks expected of women of all classes kept many of them from taking their full place in society. Charlotte Perkins Gilman, author of *Women and Economics* (1898), dismantled the traditional view of "woman's sphere" and sketched an alternative. Suggesting that entrepreneurs ought to build apartment houses designed to allow women to combine motherhood with careers, she advocated shared kitchen facilities and a common dining room, a laundry run by efficient workers, and a roof-garden day nursery with a professional teacher.

Gilman, who criticized private homes as "bloated buildings, filled with a thousand superfluities," was joined by a few radicals in promoting new living arrangements. Most Americans, however, of all political persuasions continued to view the home as sacred space where the mother ruled supreme and created an atmosphere of domestic tranquillity for the husband and children.

Next to better housing, the progressives stressed better schools as a way to produce better citizens. Public school systems were often rigid and corrupt. Far from producing citizens who would help transform society, the schools seemed to reinforce the conservative habits that blocked change. A reporter who traveled around the country in 1892 discovered mindless teachers who drilled pupils through repetitive rote learning. A Chicago teacher advised her students, "Don't stop to think; tell me what you know." When

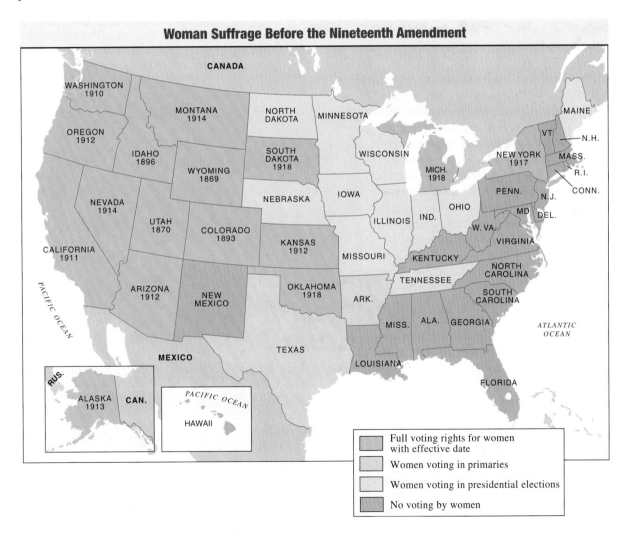

Woman Suffrage Before the Nineteenth Amendment

Western states led the battle for women's right to vote, but key victories in New York (1917) and Michigan (1918), and a carefully organized campaign in all parts of the country, finally led to the ratification of the Nineteenth Amendment. It was a triumph of progressive reform.

Recovering the Past

DOCUMENTARY PHOTOGRAPHS

As we saw in Chapter 15, photographs are a revealing way of recovering the past visually. But when looking at a photograph, especially an old one, it is easy to assume that it is an accurate representation of the past. Photographers, however, like novelists and historians, have a point of view. They take their pictures for a reason and often to prove a point. As one photographer remarked, "Photographs don't lie, but liars take photographs."

To document the need for reform in the cities, progressives collected statistics, made surveys, described settlement house life, and even wrote novels. But they discovered that the photograph was often more effective than words. Jacob Riis, the Danish-born author of *How the Other Half Lives* (1890), a devastating exposure of conditions in New York City tenement house slums, was also a pioneer in urban photography. Others had taken pictures of dank alleys and street urchins before, but Riis was the first to photograph slum conditions with the express purpose of promoting reform. At first he hired photographers, but then he bought a camera and taught himself how to use it. He even tried a new German flash powder to illuminate dark alleys and tenement rooms to record the horror of slum life.

Riis made many of his photographs into lantern slides and used them to illustrate his lectures on the need for housing reform. Although he was a creative and innovative photographer, his pictures were often far from objective. His equipment was awkward, his film slow. He had to set up and prepare carefully before snapping the shutter. His views of tenement ghetto streets and poor children now seem like clichés, but they were designed to make Americans angry, to arouse them to reform.

Another important progressive photographer was Lewis Hine. Trained as a sociologist, like Riis, he taught himself photography. Hine used his camera to illustrate his lectures at the Ethical Culture School in New York. In 1908, he was hired as a full-time investigator by the National Child Labor Committee. His haunting photographs of children in factories helped convince many Americans of the need to abolish child labor. Hine's children were appealing human beings. He showed them eating, running, working, and staring wistfully out factory windows. His photographs avoided the pathos that Riis was so fond of recording, but just as surely they documented the need for reform.

Lewis Hine, Carolina Cotton Mill, 1908. *(George Eastman House)*

Another technique that the reform photographer used was the before-and-after shot. The two photographs shown here of a one-room apartment in Philadelphia early in the century illustrate how progressive reformers tried to teach immigrants to imitate middle-class manners. The "before" photograph shows a room cluttered with washtubs, laundry, cooking utensils, clothes, tools, even an old Christmas decoration. In the "after" picture, much of the clutter has been cleaned up. A window has been installed to let in light and fresh air. The wallpaper, presumably a haven for hidden bugs and germs, has been torn off. The cooking utensils and laundry have been put away. The woodwork has been stained, and some ceremonial objects have been gathered on a shelf.

What else can you find that has been changed? How well do you think the message of the photographic combinations like this one worked? Would the immigrant family be happy with the new look and condition of their room? Could anyone live in one room and keep it so neat?

As you look at these, or any photographs, ask yourself: What is the photographer's purpose and point of view? Why was this particular angle chosen for the picture? And why center on these particular people or objects? What does the photographer reveal about his or her purpose? What does the photographer reveal unintentionally? How have fast film and new camera styles changed photography? On what subjects do reform-minded photographers train their cameras today?

The reality of one-room tenement apartments (right) contrasted with the tidiness that reformers saw as the ideal (above). *(Temple University Libraries/Urban Archives)*

671

asked why the students were not allowed to move their heads, a New York teacher replied, "Why should they look behind when the teacher is in front of them?"

Progressive education, like many other aspects of progressivism, opposed the rigid and the formal in favor of flexibility and change. John Dewey was the key philosopher of progressive education. Having grown up in Vermont, he tried throughout his life to create a sense of the small rural community in the city. In his laboratory school at the University of Chicago, he experimented with new educational methods. He replaced the school desks, which were bolted down and always faced the front, with seats that could be moved into circles and arranged in small groups. The movable seat, in fact, became one of the symbols of the progressive education movement.

Dewey insisted that the schools be child-centered, not subject-oriented. Teachers should teach children rather than teach history or mathematics. Dewey did not mean that history and math should not be taught but that those subjects should be related to the students' experience. Students should learn by doing. They should actually build a house, not just study how others constructed houses. Students should not just learn about democracy; the school itself should operate like a democracy.

Dewey also maintained, somewhat controversially, that the schools should become instruments for social reform. But like most progressives, Dewey was never quite clear whether he wanted the schools to help the students adjust to the existing world or to turn out graduates who would change the world. Although he wavered on that point, the spirit of progressive education, like the spirit of progressivism in general, was optimistic. The schools could create more flexible, better-educated adults who would go out to improve society.

Crusades Against Saloons, Brothels, and Movie Houses

Given their faith in the reforming potential of healthy and educated citizens, it was logical that most social justice progressives opposed the sale of alcohol. Some came from Protestant homes where the consumption of liquor was considered a sin, but most favored prohibition for the same reasons they opposed child labor and favored housing reform. They saw eliminating the sale of alcohol as part of the process of reforming the city and conserving human resources.

Americans did drink great quantities of beer, wine, and hard liquor, and the amount they consumed rose rapidly after 1900, peaking between 1911 and 1915. An earlier temperance movement had achieved some success in the 1840s and 1850s (see Chapter 12), but

only three states still had prohibition laws in force. The modern antiliquor movement was spearheaded in the 1880s and 1890s by the Women's Christian Temperance Union and after 1900 by the Anti-Saloon League and a coalition of religious leaders and social reformers. During the progressive era, temperance forces had considerable success in influencing legislation. Seven states passed temperance laws between 1906 and 1912.

The reformers were appalled to see young children going into saloons to bring home a pail of beer for the family and horrified by tales of alcoholic fathers beating wives and children. But most often progressives focused on the saloon and its social life. Drug traffic, prostitution, and political corruption all seemed linked to the saloon. "Why should the community have any more sympathy for the saloon . . . than . . . for a typhoid-breeding pool of filthy water, . . . a swarm of deadly mosquitoes, or . . . a nest of rats infected with bubonic plague?" an irate reformer asked.

Although they never quite understood the role alcoholic drinks played in the social life of many ethnic groups, Jane Addams and other settlement workers appreciated the saloon's importance as a neighborhood social center. Addams started a coffeehouse at Hull House in an attempt to lure the neighbors away from the evils of the saloon. In his study *Substitutes for the Saloon*, Raymond Caulkins, a young social worker, suggested parks, playgrounds, municipal theaters, and temperance bars as replacements for the saloons, where so many men gathered after work.

The progressives never found an adequate substitute for the saloon, but they set to work to pass local and state prohibition laws. As in many other progressive efforts, they joined forces with diverse groups to push for change. Their combined efforts led to victory on December 22, 1917, when Congress sent to the states for ratification a constitutional amendment prohibiting the sale, manufacture, and import of intoxicating liquor within the United States. The spirit of sacrifice for the war effort facilitated its rapid ratification.

The progressives saw, in addition to the saloon, the urban dance hall and the movie theater as threats to the morals and well-being of young people, especially young women. The motion picture, invented in 1889, developed as an important form of entertainment only during the first decade of the twentieth century. At first, the "nickelodeons," as the early movie theaters were called, appealed mainly to a lower-class and largely ethnic audience. In 1902, New York City had 50 theaters; by 1908, there were over 400 showing 30-minute dramas and romances.

Not until World War I, when D. W. Griffith produced long feature films, did the movies begin to attract a

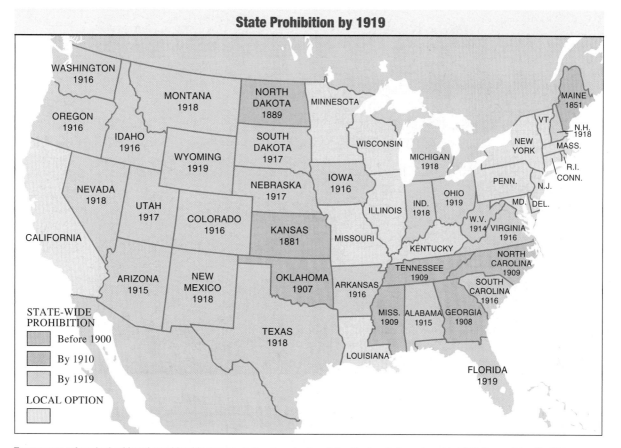

State Prohibition by 1919

WASHINGTON
1916

OREGON
1916

IDAHO
1916

MONTANA
1918

NORTH
DAKOTA
1889

MINNESOTA

SOUTH
DAKOTA
1917

WYOMING
1919

NEVADA
1918

UTAH
1917

COLORADO
1916

NEBRASKA
1917

IOWA
1916

WISCONSIN

MICHIGAN
1918

MAINE
1851

VT

N.H.
1918

MASS.

NEW
YORK

R.I.

CONN.

PENN.

N.J.

KANSAS
1881

MISSOURI

ILLINOIS

IND.
1918

OHIO
1919

MD. DEL.

W.V.
1914 VIRGINIA
1916

CALIFORNIA

ARIZONA
1915

NEW
MEXICO
1918

OKLAHOMA
1907

ARKANSAS
1916

KENTUCKY

TENNESSEE
1909

NORTH
CAROLINA
1909

SOUTH
CAROLINA
1916

MISS.
1909

ALABAMA
1915

GEORGIA
1908

TEXAS
1918

LOUISIANA

FLORIDA
1919

STATE-WIDE
PROHIBITION

Before 1900

By 1910

By 1919

LOCAL OPTION

Temperance reform had achieved considerable success before the adoption of the Nineteenth Amendment in 1919. Some states like Maine, Kansas, and North Dakota had voted dry since the middle of the nineteenth century, while other states joined the anti-liquor crusade during the progressive era. Anti-German hysteria during World War I helped to close breweries (most with German names), setting the stage for national prohibition in 1919.

middle-class audience. The most popular of these early films was Griffith's *Birth of a Nation* (1915), a blatantly racist and distorted epic of black debauchery during Reconstruction. Many early films were imported from France, Italy, and Germany; because they were silent, it was easy to use subtitles in any language. But one did not need to know the language, or even be able to read, to enjoy the action. That was part of the attraction of the early films. Many had plots that depicted premarital sex, adultery, and violence, and, unlike later films, many attacked authority and had tragic endings. *The Candidate* (1907) showed an upper-class reform candidate who gets dirt thrown at him for his efforts to clean up the town. The film *Down with Women* (1907) showed well-dressed men denouncing woman suffrage and the incompetence of the weaker sex, but throughout the film, only strong women are depicted. In the end, when the hero is arrested, a female lawyer defends him.

Some of the films stressed slapstick humor or romance and adventure; others bordered on pornography. The reformers objected not only to the plots

and content of the films but also to the location of the theaters (near saloons and burlesque houses) and to their dark interiors. "In the dim auditorium which seems to float on the world of dreams . . . an American woman may spend her afternoon alone," one critic wrote. "She can let her fantasies slip through the darkened atmosphere to the screen where they drift in rhapsodic amours with handsome stars." It was these fantasies, in addition to the other things they imagined were going on in the dark, that disturbed the reformers. But for young immigrant women, who made up the bulk of the audience at most urban movie theaters, the films provided rare exciting moments in their lives. One daughter of strict Italian parents remarked, "The one place I was allowed to go by myself was the movies. I went to the movies for fun. My parents wouldn't let me go anywhere else, even when I was twenty-four."

Saloons, dance halls, and movie theaters all seemed dangerous to progressives interested in improving life in the city, because all appeared to be somehow connected with the worst evil of all, prostitution.

This is an amusement park near Long Beach, California, one of hundreds around the country that marked the rise of a new, mass, urban culture and the commercialization of leisure in the first two decades of the twentieth century. This postcard shows a well-dressed crowd waiting to go on the Whip and the Crazy House Slide. They were typical of the people from all walks of life who flocked to the amusement parks to enter a world of fantasy and make believe for a day. But it was a fantasy based on electricity and a new technology. The visitors arrived by electric streetcar, and the rides were all powered by electricity and illuminated by thousands of lightbulbs. *(Postcard from the author's collection)*

Campaigns against prostitution had been waged since the early nineteenth century, but they were nothing compared with the progressives' crusade to wipe out what they called the "social evil." All major cities and many smaller ones appointed vice commissions and made elaborate studies of prostitution. The reports, which often ran to several thick volumes, were typical progressive documents. Compiled by experts, they were filled with elaborate statistical studies and laced with moral outrage.

The progressive antivice crusade attracted many kinds of people, for often contradictory reasons. Racists and immigration restrictionists maintained that inferior people—blacks and recent immigrants, especially those from southern and eastern Europe— became prostitutes and pimps. Others had a variety of motives. Most progressives, however, stressed the environmental causes of vice. They viewed prostitution, along with child labor and poor housing, as evils that education and reform could eliminate.

Most progressive antivice reformers stressed the economic causes of prostitution. "Is it any wonder,"

Mary Pickford, one of the stars of the silent movies, played the heroine in a film that outraged the reformers because it dealt with the subject of unwed motherhood. *(The Everett Collection)*

the Chicago Vice Commission asked, "that a tempted girl who receives only six dollars per week working with her hands sells her body for twenty-five dollars per week when she learns there is a demand for it and men are willing to pay the price?" "Do you suppose I am going back to earn five or six dollars a week in a factory," one prostitute asked an investigator, "when I can earn that amount any night and often much more?"

Despite all their reports and all the publicity, the progressives failed to end prostitution and did virtually nothing to address its roots in poverty. They wiped out a few red-light districts, closed a number of brothels, and managed to push a bill through Congress (the Mann Act of 1910) that prohibited the interstate transport of women for immoral purposes. Perhaps more important, in several states they got the age of consent for women raised, and in 20 states they made the Wassermann test for syphilis mandatory for both men and women before a marriage license could be issued.

THE WORKER IN THE PROGRESSIVE ERA

Progressive reformers sympathized with industrial workers who struggled to earn a living for themselves and their families. The progressives sought protective legislation—particularly for women and children—unemployment insurance, and workers' compensation. But often they had little understanding of what it was really like to sell one's strength by the hour. For example, they supported labor's right to organize at a time when labor had few friends, yet often opposed the strike as a weapon against management. And neither organized labor nor the reformers, individually or in shaky partnership, had power over industry. Control was in the hands of the owners and managers, and they were determined to strengthen their grip on the workplace as the nature of industrial work was being transformed.

Adjusting to Industrial Labor

John Mekras arrived in New York from Greece in 1912 and traveled immediately to Manchester, New Hampshire, where he found a job in the giant Amoskeag textile mill. He did not speak a word of English. "The man who hands out the jobs sent me to the spinning room," he later remembered. "There I don't know anything about the spinning. I'm a farmer. . . . I don't know what the boss is talking about." Mekras didn't last long at the mill. He was one of the many industrial workers who had difficulty adjusting to factory work in the early twentieth century.

Many workers—whether they were from Greece, eastern Europe, rural Vermont, or Michigan—confronted a bewildering world based on order and routine. Unlike farm or craft work, factory life was dominated by the clock, the bell tower, and the boss. The workers continued to resist the routine and pace of factory work, and they subtly sabotaged the employers' efforts to control the workplace, as they had done in earlier periods (see Chapters 10 and 18). They stayed at home on holidays when they were supposed to work, took unauthorized breaks, and set their own informal productivity schedules. Often they were fired or quit. In the woolen industry, the annual turnover of workers between 1907 and 1910 was more than 100 percent. In New York needleworker shops in 1912 and 1913, the turnover rate was over 250 percent. Overall in American industry, one-third of the workers stayed at their jobs less than a year.

This industrial workforce, still composed largely of immigrants, had a fluid character. Many migrants, especially those from southern and eastern Europe, expected to stay only for a short time and then return to their homeland. "Italians come to America with the sole intention of accumulating money," one Italian American writer complained in 1905. "Their dreams, their only care is the bundle of money . . . which will give them, after 20 years of deprivation, the possibility of having a mediocre standard of living in their native country." Many men came alone—70 percent in some years. They saved money by living in boardinghouses. In 1910, two-thirds of the workers in Pittsburgh made less than $12 a week, but by lodging in boarding houses and paying $2.50 a month for a bed, they could save perhaps one-third of their pay. "Here in America one must work for three horses," one immigrant wrote home. "The work is very heavy, but I don't mind it," another wrote; "let it be heavy, but may it last without interruption."

About 40 percent of those who immigrated to America in the first decade of the twentieth century returned home, according to one estimate. In years of economic downturn, such as 1908, more Italians and Austro-Hungarians left the United States than entered it. For many immigrants, the American dream never materialized. But these reluctant immigrants provided the mass of unskilled labor that American industry exploited and sometimes consumed, much the way other Americans exploited the land and the forests. The great pool of immigrant workers meant profits for American industry.

The nature of work continued to change in the early twentieth century as industrialists extended late-nineteenth-century efforts to make their factories and their workforces more efficient, productive, and profitable. In some industries, the introduction of new machines revolutionized work and eliminated highly paid skilled jobs. Glassblowing machines (invented

Immigrants from Eastern and Southern Europe came to the United States in great numbers from 1890 to 1914. The women were often employed in textile factories and the men in construction. They provided the labor that drove the American economy. This photograph by Lewis Hine captures the moment of arrival of an immigrant family. *(Courtesy George Eastman House)*

about 1900), for example, replaced thousands of glass-blowers or reduced them from craftsmen to workers. Power-driven machines, better-organized operations, and, finally, the moving assembly line, perfected by Henry Ford, transformed the nature of work and turned many laborers into unskilled tenders of machines.

Coal miner John Brophy recalled his father's pride in his work as a miner. "The skill with which you undercut the vein, the judgment in drilling the coal after it has been undercut and placing the exact amount of explosive so that it would do an effective job of breaking the coal from the solid . . . indicated the quality of his work." But by the beginning of the twentieth century, undercutting machines and the mechanization of mining operations diminished miners' pride and independence.

The influence of the machine was uneven, having a greater impact in some industries than in others. Although some skilled weavers and glassblowers were transformed into unskilled operators, the introduction of the machines themselves created the need for new skilled workers. In the auto industry, for example, the new elite workers were the mechanics and tool and die men who kept the assembly line running. Although these new skilled artisans survived, the trend toward mechanization was unstoppable, and even the most skilled workers were eventually removed from making decisions about the production process.

More than machines changed the nature of industrial work. The principles of scientific management,

which set out new rules for organizing work, were just as important. The key figure was Frederick Taylor, the son of a prominent Philadelphia family. Taylor had a nervous breakdown while at a private school. When his physicians prescribed manual labor as a cure, he went to work as a laborer at the Midvale Steel Company in Philadelphia. Working his way up rapidly while studying engineering at night, he became chief engineer at the factory in the 1880s. Later he used this experience to rethink the organization of industry.

Taylor was obsessed with efficiency. He emphasized centralized planning, systematic analysis, and detailed instructions. Most of all, he studied all kinds of workers and timed the various components of their jobs with a stopwatch. "The work of every workman is fully planned out by the management at least one day in advance," Taylor wrote in 1898, "and each man receives in most cases complete written instructions, describing in detail the task which he is to accomplish, as well as the means to be used in doing the work."

Many owners enthusiastically adopted Taylor's concepts of scientific management, seeing an opportunity to increase their profits and to take firmer control of the workplace. As Taylor himself explained, scientific management meant the "deliberate gathering in on . . . management's side of all of the great mass of traditional knowledge, which in the past has been in the heads of the workmen, and in the physical skill and knack of the workman which he has acquired through years of experience." Not surprisingly, many workers resented the drive for efficiency and control. "We don't want to work as fast as we are able to," one machinist remarked. "We want to work as fast as we think it comfortable for us to work."

Union Organizing

The progressive reformers had little understanding of the revolution going on in the factory. Samuel Gompers, head of the American Federation of Labor, however, was quick to recognize that Taylorism would reduce workers to "mere machines." Under his guidance, the AFL prospered during the progressive era. Between 1897 and 1904, union membership grew from 447,000 to over two million, with three out of every four union members claimed by the AFL. By 1914, the AFL alone had over two million members. Gompers's "pure and simple unionism" was most successful among coal miners, railroad workers, and the building trades. As we saw in Chapter 18, Gompers ignored the growing army of unskilled and immigrant workers and concentrated on raising the wages and improving the working conditions of the skilled craftsmen who were members of unions affiliated with the AFL.

For a time, Gompers's strategy seemed to work. Several industries negotiated with the AFL as a way of avoiding disruptive strikes. But cooperation was short-lived. Labor unions were defeated in a number of disastrous strikes, and the National Association of Manufacturers (NAM) launched an aggressive counterattack. NAM and other employer associations provided strikebreakers, used industrial spies, and blacklisted union members to prevent them from obtaining other jobs.

The Supreme Court came down squarely on management's side, ruling in the Danbury Hatters case in 1908 that trade unions were subject to the Sherman Anti-Trust Act. Thus, union members themselves could be held personally liable for money lost by a business during a strike. Courts at all levels sided overwhelmingly with employers. They often declared strikes illegal and were quick to issue restraining orders, making it impossible for workers to interfere with the operation of a business.

Although many social justice progressives sympathized with the working class, they spent more time promoting protective legislation than strengthening organized labor. Often cast in the role of mediators during industrial disputes, they found it difficult to comprehend what life was really like for people who had to work six days a week.

Working women and their problems aroused more sympathy among progressive reformers than the plight of working men. The number of women working outside the home increased steadily during the progressive era, from over 5 million in 1900 to nearly 8.5 million in 1920. But few belonged to unions—only a little over 3 percent in 1900—and the percentage declined by half by 1910 before increasing a little after that date with aggressive organizing in the textile and clothing trades.

Many upper-class women reformers tried to help these working women in a variety of ways. The settlement houses organized day care centers, clubs, and classes, and many reformers tried to pass protective legislation. Tension and misunderstanding often cropped up between the reformers and the working women, but one organization in which there was genuine cooperation was the Women's Trade Union League. Founded in 1903, the league was organized by Mary Kenney and William English Walling, a socialist and reformer, but it also drew local leaders from the working class, such as Rose Schneiderman, a Jewish immigrant cap maker, and Leonora O'Reilly, a collar maker. The league established branches in most large eastern and midwestern cities and served for more than a decade as an important force in helping to organize women into unions. The league forced the AFL to pay more attention to women, helped out in time of strikes, put up bail money for the arrested, and publicized the plight of working women.

Garment Workers and the Triangle Fire

Thousands of young women, most of them Jewish and Italian, were employed in the garment industry in New York City. Most were between 16 and 25; some lived with their families, and others lived alone or with a roommate. They worked a 56-hour, 6-day week and made about $6 for their efforts. New York was the center of the garment industry, with over 600 shirtwaist (blouse) and dress factories employing more than 30,000 workers.

Like other industries, garment manufacturing had changed in the first decade of the twentieth century. Once conducted in thousands of dark and dingy tenement rooms, now all the operations were centralized in large loft buildings in lower Manhattan. These buildings were an improvement over the sweating labor of the tenements, but many were overcrowded, and they had few fire escapes or safety features. In addition, the owners applied scientific management techniques to increase their profits, making life miserable for the workers. Most of the women had to rent their sewing machines and even had to pay for the electricity they used. They were penalized for mistakes or for talking too loudly. They were usually supervised by a male contractor who badgered and sometimes even sexually harassed them.

In 1909, some of the women went out on strike to protest the working conditions. The International Ladies' Garment Workers Union (ILGWU) and the

The Triangle fire shocked the nation, and dramatic photographs, such as this candid shot showing bodies and bystanders waiting for more young women to jump, helped stimulate the investigation that followed. *(Brown Brothers)*

Women's Trade Union League supported them. But strikers were beaten and sometimes arrested by unsympathetic policemen and by strikebreakers on the picket lines. At a mass meeting held at Cooper Union in New York on November 22, 1909, Clara Lemlich, a young shirtwaist worker who had been injured on the picket line and was angered by the long speeches and lack of action, rose and in an emotional speech in Yiddish demanded a general strike. The entire audience pledged its agreement. The next day, all over the city, the shirtwaist workers went out on strike.

"The uprising of the twenty thousand," as the strike was called, startled the nation. One young worker wrote in her diary, "It is a good thing, that strike is. It makes you feel like a grown-up person." The Jews learned a little Italian and the Italians a little Yiddish so that they could communicate. Many social reformers, ministers, priests, and rabbis urged the strikers on. Mary Dreier, an upper-class reformer and president of the New York branch of the Women's Trade Union League, was arrested for marching with the strikers. A young state legislator, Fiorello La Guardia, later to become a congressman and mayor of New York, was one of the many public officials to aid the strikers.

The shirtwaist workers won, and in part, the success of the strike made the garment union one of the most powerful in the AFL. But the victory was limited. Over 300 companies accepted the union's terms, but others refused to go along. The young women went back to work amid still oppressive and unsafe condi-

tions. That became dramatically obvious on Saturday, March 25, 1911, when a fire broke out on the eighth floor of the ten-story loft building housing the Triangle Shirtwaist Company near Washington Square in New York. There had been several small fires in the factory in previous weeks, so no one thought much about another one. But this one was different. Within minutes, the top three floors of the factory were ablaze. Many exit doors were locked. The elevators broke down. There were no fire escapes. Forty-six women jumped to their deaths, some of them in groups of three and four holding hands. Over 100 died in the flames.

Shocked by the Triangle fire, the state legislature appointed a commission to investigate working conditions in the state. One investigator for the commission was a young social worker, Frances Perkins, who in the 1930s would become secretary of labor. She led the politicians through the dark lofts, filthy tenements, and unsafe factories around the state to show them the conditions under which young women worked. The result was state legislation limiting the work of women to 54 hours a week, prohibiting labor by children under 14, and improving safety regulations in factories. One supporter of the bills in Albany was a young state senator named Franklin Delano Roosevelt.

The investigative commission was a favorite progressive tactic. When there was a problem, reformers often got a city council, a state legislature, or the federal government to appoint a commission. If they could not find a government body to give them a mandate, they made their own studies. They brought in experts, compiled statistics, and published reports.

The federal Industrial Relations Commission, created in 1912 to study the causes of industrial unrest and violence, conducted one of the most important investigations. As it turned out, the commission spent most of its time exploring a dramatic and tragic incident of labor–management conflict in Colorado, known as the Ludlow Massacre. A strike broke out in the fall of 1913 in the vast mineral-rich area of southern Colorado, much of it controlled by the Colorado Fuel and Iron Industry, a company largely owned by the Rockefeller family. It was a paternalistic empire where workers lived in company towns and sometimes in tent colonies. They were paid in company scrip and forced to shop at the company store. When the workers, supported by the United Mine Workers, went on strike demanding an eight-hour day, better safety precautions, and the removal of armed guards, the company refused to negotiate. The strike turned violent, and in the spring of 1914, strikebreakers and national guardsmen fired on the workers. Eleven children and two women were killed in an attack on a tent city near Ludlow, Colorado.

The Industrial Relations Commission called John D. Rockefeller, Jr., to testify and implied that he was personally guilty of the murders. The commission decided in its report that violent class conflict could be avoided only by limiting the use of armed guards and detectives, by restricting monopoly, by protecting the right of the workers to organize, and, most dramatically, by redistributing wealth through taxation. The commission's report, not surprisingly, fell on deaf ears. Most progressives, like most Americans, denied the commission's conclusion that class conflict was inevitable.

Radical Labor

Not everyone accepted the progressives' faith in investigations and protective labor legislation. Nor did everyone approve of Samuel Gompers's conservative tactics or his emphasis on getting better pay for skilled workers. A group of about 200 radicals met in Chicago in 1905 to form a new union as an alternative to the AFL. They called it the Industrial Workers of the World (IWW) and talked of one big union. Like the Knights of Labor in the 1880s, the IWW would welcome all workers: the unskilled, and even the unemployed, women, African Americans, Asians, and all other ethnic groups.

Daniel De Leon of the Socialist Labor party attended the organizational meeting, and so did Eugene Debs. Debs, who had been converted to socialism after the Pullman strike of 1894, had already emerged by 1905 as one of the outstanding radical leaders in

the country. Also attending was Mary Harris Jones, who dressed like a society matron but attacked labor leaders "who sit on velvet chairs in conferences with labor's oppressors." In her sixties at the time, everyone called her "Mother" Jones. She had been a dressmaker, a Populist, and a member of the Knights of Labor. During the 1890s, she had marched with miners' wives on the picket line in western Pennsylvania. She was imprisoned and denounced, and by 1905 she was already a legend.

Presiding at the Chicago meeting was "Big Bill" Haywood. He had been a cowboy, a miner, and a prospector. Somewhere along the way, he had lost an eye and mangled a hand, but he had a booming voice and a passionate commitment to the workers. "This is

The way art and politics sometimes combined in the progressive era is illustrated by this poster for a performance at Madison Square Garden in New York by a group of political radicals. They reenacted the IWW supported silk workers' strike, then going on in Patterson, New Jersey. Many of the actual strikers took part in the performance. But the play lost money, and the strike ultimately failed. Still, this impressively designed program cover reminds of a time when radical artists and labor leaders sought to transform the world. *(The Tamiment Institute Library, New York University)*

the Continental Congress of the working class," he announced, adopting the rhetoric of the American Revolution. "We are here to confederate the workers of this country into a working-class movement that shall have for its purpose the emancipation of the working class from the slave bondage of capitalism." Denouncing Gompers and the AFL, he talked of class conflict. "The purpose of the IWW," he proclaimed, "is to bring the workers of this country into the possession of the full value of the product of their toil."

The IWW remained a small organization, troubled by internal squabbles and disagreements. Debs and De Leon left after a few years. Haywood dominated the movement, which played an important role in organizing the militant strike of textile workers in Lawrence, Massachusetts, in 1912 and the following year in Paterson, New Jersey, and Akron, Ohio. The IWW had its greatest success organizing itinerant lumbermen and migratory workers in the Northwest. But in other places, especially in times of high unemployment, the Wobblies, as they were called, helped the unskilled workers vent their anger against their employers.

Many American workers still did not feel, as European workers did, that they were engaged in a perpetual class struggle with their capitalist employers. Some immigrant workers, intent on earning enough money to go back home, had no time to join the conflict. Most of those who stayed in the United States were consoled by the promises of the American dream. Thinking they might secure a better job or move up into the middle class, they avoided organized labor militancy. They knew that even if they failed, their sons and daughters would profit from the American way. The AFL, not the IWW, became the dominant American labor movement. But for a few, the IWW represented a dream of what might have been. For others, its presence, though small and largely ineffective, meant that perhaps someday a European-style, working-class movement might develop in America.

REFORM IN THE CITIES AND STATES

The reform movements of the progressive era usually started at the local level, then moved to the state, and finally to the nation's capital. Progressivism in the cities and states had roots in the depression and discontent of the 1890s. The reform banners called for more democracy, more power for the people, and legislation regulating railroads and other businesses. Yet often the professional and business classes were the movement's leaders. They intended to bring order out

of chaos and to modernize the city and the state during a time of rapid growth.

Municipal Reformers

American cities grew rapidly in the last part of the nineteenth and the first part of the twentieth centuries. New York, which had a population of 1.2 million in 1880, grew to 3.4 million by 1900 and 5.6 million in 1920. Chicago expanded even more dramatically, from 500,000 in 1880 to 1.7 million in 1900 and 2.7 million in 1920. Los Angeles was a town of 11,000 in 1880 but multiplied ten times by 1900, and then increased another five times, to more than a half million, by 1920.

The spectacular and continuing growth of the cities caused problems and created a need for housing, transportation, and municipal services. But it was the kind of people who were moving into the cities that worried many observers. Americans from the small towns and farms continued to throng to the urban centers, as they had throughout the nineteenth century, but immigration produced the greatest surge in population. Fully 40 percent of New York's population and 36 percent of Chicago's was foreign-born in 1910; if one included the children of the immigrants, the percentage approached 80 percent in some cities. The new immigrants from eastern and western Europe, according to Francis Walker, the president of MIT, were "beaten men from beaten races, representing the worst failures in the struggle for existence." They seemed to threaten the American way of life and the very tenets of democracy.

Fear of the city and its new inhabitants motivated progressive municipal reform efforts. Urban problems seemed to have reached a crisis stage. The twentieth-century reformers, mostly middle-class citizens like those in the nineteenth century, wanted to regulate and control the sprawling metropolis, restore democracy, reduce corruption, and limit the power of the political bosses and their immigrant allies. When these reformers talked of restoring power to the people, they usually meant ensuring control for people like themselves. The chief aim of municipal reform was to make the city more organized and efficient for the business and professional classes who were to control its workings.

Municipal reform movements varied from city to city. In Boston, the reformers tried to strengthen the power of the mayor, break the hold of the city council, and eliminate council corruption. They succeeded in removing all party designations from city election ballots, and they extended the term of the mayor from two to four years. But to their chagrin, in the election of 1910, John Fitzgerald, grandfather of John F. Kennedy and foe of reform, defeated their candidate.

Cities grew so rapidly that they often ceased to work. This 1909 photograph shows Dearborn Street looking south from Randolph Street in Chicago. Horse-drawn vehicles, streetcars, pedestrians, and even a few early autos clogged the intersection and created the urban inefficiency that angered municipal reformers. *(Chicago Historical Society)*

In other cities, the reformers used different tactics, but they almost always conducted elaborate studies and campaigned to reduce corruption.

The most dramatic innovation was the replacement of both mayor and council with a nonpartisan commission of administrators. This innovation began quite accidentally when a hurricane devastated Galveston, Texas, in September 1900. In one of the worst natural disasters in the nation's history, over 6,000 people died. The existing government was helpless to deal with the crisis, so the state legislature appointed five commissioners to run the city during the emergency.

The idea spread to Houston, Dallas, and Austin and to cities in other states. It proved most popular in small to medium-size cities in the Midwest and the Pacific Northwest. By World War I, more than 400 cities had adopted the commission form. Dayton, Ohio, went one step further: after a disastrous flood in 1913, the city hired a city manager to run the city and to report to the elected council. Government by experts was the perfect symbol of what most municipal reformers had in mind.

The commission and the expert manager did not replace the mayor in most large cities. One of the most flamboyant and successful of the progressive mayors was Tom Johnson of Cleveland. Johnson had made a fortune by investing in utility and railroad franchises before he was 40. But Henry George's *Progress and Poverty* so influenced him that he began a second career as a reformer. After serving in Congress, he was elected mayor of Cleveland in 1901. During his two terms in city hall, he managed to reduce transit fares and to build parks and municipal bath houses throughout the city. Johnson also broke the connection between the police and prostitution in the city by promising the madams and the brothel owners that he would not bother them if they would be orderly and not steal from their customers or pay off the police.

His most controversial move, however, was to advocate city ownership of the street railroads and utilities (sometimes called municipal socialism). "Only through municipal ownership," he argued, "can the gulf which divides the community into a small dominant class on one side and the unorganized people on the other be bridged." Johnson was defeated in 1909 in part because he alienated many powerful business interests, but one of his lieutenants, Newton D. Baker, was elected mayor in 1911 and carried on many of his programs. Cleveland was one of many cities that began to regulate municipal utilities or to take them over from the private owners.

The way much of municipal reform and the progressive social justice movement was closely tied to religion, especially to the Protestant Social Gospel movement, can be illustrated by The Men and Religion Forward Movement. Led by the YMCA, The Federal Council of Churches, and a coalition of Protestant agencies, The Men and Religion Forward Movement conducted a whirlwind campaign in 1911–1912, not only to reform the cities but also to bring men back into the churches. Believing that religion, like much of American life, had become too effeminate, too dominated by women, the leaders of the movement tried to bring "3,000,000 missing men" back to Christianity. Teams of men consisting of Social Gospel ministers and lay experts fanned out across the country, stopping a week in each city. They held rallies and revival meetings; they met with clergy, labor leaders, and urban reformers. They tried to stimulate an interest in the churches and at the same time to wipe out child labor, slum housing, gambling dens, and houses of prostitution. They also tried to promote cleaner streets and better government. One of the leaders of the movement, Raymond Robins, had been a settlement worker and a coworker with Jane Addams in many reform crusades in Chicago. When the Men and Religion Forward campaign was finished, he moved directly to work for Theodore Roosevelt and the Progressive party. The movement failed to bring a great many men back to religion, and it did not appreciably improve the cities, but it does suggest how religion and politics became intertwined during the progressive era.

City Beautiful

In Cleveland, both Tom Johnson and Newton Baker promoted the arts, music, and adult education. They also supervised the construction of a civic center, a library, and a museum. Most other American cities during the progressive era set out to bring culture and beauty to their centers. They were influenced at least in part by the great, classical White City constructed for the Chicago World's Fair of 1893 and by the grand European boulevards such as the Champs-Élysées in Paris.

The architects of the "city beautiful" movement preferred the impressive and ceremonial architecture of Rome or the Renaissance for libraries, museums, railroad stations, and other public buildings. The huge Pennsylvania Station in New York (now replaced by Madison Square Garden) was modeled after the imperial Roman baths of Caracalla, and the Free Library in Philadelphia was an almost exact copy of a building in Paris. The city beautiful leaders tried to make the city more attractive and meaningful for the middle and upper classes. The museums and the libraries were closed on Sundays, the only day the working class could possibly visit them.

The social justice progressives, especially those connected with the social settlements, were more concerned with neighborhood parks and playgrounds than with the ceremonial boulevards and grand buildings. Hull House established the first public playground in Chicago. Jacob Riis, the housing reformer, and Lillian Wald of the Henry Street Settlement campaigned in New York for small parks and for the opening of schoolyards on weekends. Some progressives looked back nostalgically to their rural childhoods and desperately tried to get urban children out of the city in the summertime to rural camps. But they also tried to make the city more livable as well as more beautiful.

Most progressives had an ambivalent attitude toward the city. They feared it, and they loved it. Some saw the great urban areas filled with immigrants as a threat to American democracy, but one of Tom Johnson's young assistants, Frederic C. Howe, wrote a book called *The City: The Hope of Democracy* (1905). Hope or threat, the progressives realized that the United States had become an urban nation and that the problems of the city had to be faced.

Reform in the States

The progressive movements in the states had many roots and took many forms. In some states, especially in the West, progressive attempts to regulate railroads and utilities were simply an extension of Populism. In other states, the reform drive bubbled up from reform efforts in the cities. Most states passed laws during the progressive era designed to extend democracy and give more authority to the people. Initiative and referendum laws allowed citizens to originate legislation and to overturn laws passed by the legislature, and recall laws gave the people a way to remove elected officials. One important success for progressive reform was finally achieved in 1913 with the ratification of the Seventeenth Amendment to the Constitution, which provided for the direct election of U.S. senators, rather than their appointment by the legislatures. Most of these "democratic" laws worked better in theory than in practice, but their passage in many states did represent a genuine effort to remove special privilege from government.

Much progressive state legislation concerned order and efficiency, but many states passed social justice measures as well. Maryland enacted the first workers' compensation law in 1902, paying employees for days missed because of job-related injuries. Illinois approved a law aiding mothers with dependent children. Several states passed anti–child labor bills, and Oregon's ten-hour law restricting women's labor became a model for other states.

The states with the most successful reform movements elected strong and aggressive governors: Charles Evans Hughes in New York, Hoke Smith in Georgia, Hiram Johnson in California, Woodrow Wilson in New Jersey, and Robert La Follette in Wisconsin. After Wilson, La Follette was the most famous and in many ways the model progressive governor. Born in a small town in Wisconsin, he graduated from the University of Wisconsin in 1879 and was admitted to the bar. Practicing law during the 1890s in Madison, the state capital, he received a large retainer from the Milwaukee Railroad and defended the railroad against both riders and laborers who sued the company.

The depression of 1893 hit Wisconsin hard. More than a third of the state's citizens were out of work, farmers lost their farms, and many small businesses went bankrupt. At the same time, the rich seemed to be getting richer. "Men are rightly feeling that a social order like the present, with its enormous wealth side by side with appalling poverty, . . . cannot be the final form of human society," a Milwaukee minister announced. As grassroots discontent spread, a group of Milwaukee reformers attacked the giant corporations and the street railways. Several newspapers joined the battle and denounced special privilege and corruption. Everyone could agree on the need for tax reform, railroad regulation, and more participation of the people in government.

La Follette, who had had little interest in reform, took advantage of the general mood of discontent to win the governorship in 1901. It seemed ironic that La Follette, who had once taken a retainer from a railroad, owed his victory to his attack on the railroads. But La Follette was a shrewd politician. He used professors from the University of Wisconsin, in the capital, to prepare reports and do statistical studies. Then he worked with the legislature to pass a state primary law and an act regulating the railroads. "Go back to the first principles of democracy; go back to the people" was his battle cry. The "Wisconsin idea" attracted the attention of journalists like Lincoln Steffens and Ray Stannard Baker, and they helped to popularize the "laboratory of democracy" around the country. La Follette became a national figure and was elected to the Senate in 1906.

The progressive movement did improve government and made it more responsible to the people in states like Wisconsin. For example, the railroads were brought under the control of a railroad commission. But by 1910, the railroads no longer complained about the new taxes and restrictions. They had discovered that it was to their advantage to make their operations more efficient, and often they were able to convince the commission that they should raise rates or abandon the operation of unprofitable lines. Progressivism in the states, like progressivism everywhere, had mixed results. But the spirit of reform that swept the country was real, and progressive movements on the local level did eventually have an impact on Washington, especially during the administrations of Theodore Roosevelt and Woodrow Wilson.

THEODORE ROOSEVELT AND THE SQUARE DEAL

President William McKinley was shot in Buffalo, New York, on September 6, 1901, by Leon Czolgosz, an anarchist. McKinley died eight days later, making Theodore Roosevelt, at 42, the youngest man ever to become president. The nation mourned its fallen leader, and in many cities, anarchists and other radicals were rounded up for questioning.

No one knew what to expect from Roosevelt. Some politicians thought he was too radical, but a few social justice progressives remembered his suggestion that the soldiers fire on the strikers during the 1894 Pullman strike. Nonetheless, under his leadership, progressivism reshaped the national political agenda. Although early progressive reformers had attacked problems that they saw in their own communities, they gradually understood that some problems could not be solved at the state or local level. The emergence of a national industrial economy had spawned conditions that demanded national solutions.

Progressives at the national level turned their attention to the workings of the economic system. They scrutinized the operation and organization of the railroads and other large corporations. They examined the threats to the natural environment. They reviewed the quality of the products of American industry. As they fashioned legislation to remedy the flaws in the economic system, they vastly expanded the power of the national government.

A Strong and Controversial President

Roosevelt came to the presidency with considerable experience. He had run unsuccessfully for mayor of New York, served a term in the New York state assembly, spent four years as a U.S. civil service commissioner, and served two years as the police commissioner of New York City. His exploits in the Spanish-American War brought him to the public's attention, but he had also been an effective assistant secretary of the navy and a reform governor of New York. While police commissioner and governor, he had been influenced by a number of progressives. Jacob Riis, the housing reformer, became one of his friends and led him on nighttime explorations of the slums of New York City. Roosevelt had also impressed a group of New York settlement workers with his genuine concern for human misery, his ability to talk to all kinds of people, and his willingness to learn about social problems.

But no one was sure how he would act as president. He came from an upper-class family and had associated with the important and the powerful all over the world. He had written a number of books and was one of the most intellectual presidents since Thomas Jefferson. But none of these things assured that he would be a progressive in office.

Roosevelt loved being president. He called the office a "bully pulpit," and he enjoyed talking to the people and the press. His appealing personality and sense of humor made him a good subject for the new mass-market newspapers and magazines. The American people quickly adopted him as their favorite. They called him "Teddy" and named a stuffed bear after him. Sometimes his exuberance got a little out of hand. On one occasion, he took a foreign diplomat on a nude swim in the Potomac River. You have to understand, another observer remarked, that "the president is really only six years old."

Roosevelt was much more than an exuberant six-year-old. He was the strongest president since Lincoln. By revitalizing the executive branch, reorganizing the army command structure, and modernizing the consular service, he made many aspects of the federal government more efficient. He established the Bureau of Corporations, appointed independent commissions staffed with experts, and enlisted talented and well-trained men to work for the government. "TR," as he became known, called a White House conference on the care of dependent children, and in 1905 he even summoned college presidents and football coaches to the White House to discuss ways to limit violence in football. He angered many social justice progressives by not going far enough. In fact, on one occasion, Florence Kelley was so furious with him that she walked out of the Oval Office and slammed the door. But he was the first president to listen to the pleas of the progressives and to invite them to the White House. Learning from experts like Frances Kellor, he became more concerned with social justice as time went on. In 1904, running on a platform of a "Square Deal" for the American people, he was reelected by an overwhelming margin.

Dealing with the Trusts

One of Roosevelt's first actions as president was to attempt to control the large industrial corporations. He took office in the middle of an unprecedented wave of business consolidation. Between 1897 and 1904, some 4,227 companies combined to form 257 large corporations. U.S. Steel, the first billion-dollar corporation, was formed in 1901 by joining Carnegie

Theodore Roosevelt was a dynamic public speaker who used his position to influence public opinion. Despite his high-pitched voice, he could be heard at the back of the crowd in the days before microphones. Note the row of reporters decked out in their summer straw hats writing their stories as the president speaks. *(Brown Brothers)*

Steel with its eight main competitors. In one stroke, the new company controlled two-thirds of the market, and J. P. Morgan made $7 million for supervising the operation.

The Sherman Anti-Trust Act of 1890 had been virtually useless in controlling the trusts, but a new outcry from muckrakers and progressives called for regulation. Some even demanded the return to the age of small business. Roosevelt opposed neither bigness nor the right of businessmen to make money. "Our aim is not to do away with corporations," he remarked in 1902; "on the contrary, these big aggregations are the inevitable development of modern industrialism." But he thought some businessmen arrogant, greedy, and irresponsible. "We draw the line against misconduct, not against wealth," he said.

To the shock of much of the business community, he directed his attorney general to file suit to dissolve the Northern Securities Company, a giant railroad monopoly put together by James J. Hill and financier J. P. Morgan. Morgan came to the White House to tell Roosevelt, "If we have done anything wrong, send your man to my man and they can fix it up." Roosevelt was furious, and he was determined to let Morgan and other businessmen know that they could not deal with the president of the United States as just another tycoon.

The government won its case and proceeded to prosecute some of the largest corporations, including Standard Oil of New Jersey and the American Tobacco Company. However, Roosevelt's antitrust policy did not end the power of the giant corporations or even alter their methods of doing business. More disturbing to consumers, it did not force down the price of kerosene, cigars, or railroad tickets. But it did breathe some life into the Sherman Anti-Trust Act, and it increased the role of the federal government as regulator. It also caused large firms such as U.S. Steel to diversify to avoid antitrust suits.

Roosevelt sought to strengthen the regulatory powers of the federal government in other ways. He steered the Elkins Act through Congress in 1903 and the Hepburn Act in 1906, which together increased the power of the Interstate Commerce Commission (ICC). The first act eliminated the use of rebates by railroads, a method that many large corporations had used to get favored treatment. The second act broadened the power of the ICC and gave it the right to investigate and enforce rates. Opponents in Congress weakened both bills, however, and the legislation neither ended abuses nor satisfied the farmers and small businessmen who had always been the railroads' chief critics.

Roosevelt firmly believed in corporate capitalism. He detested socialism and felt much more comfortable around business executives than labor leaders. Yet he saw his role as mediator and regulator. His view of the power of the presidency was illustrated in 1902 during the anthracite coal strike. Led by John Mitchell of the United Mine Workers, the coal miners went on strike to protest low wages, long hours, and unsafe working conditions. In 1901, a total of 513 coal miners had died in industrial accidents. The mine owners refused to talk to the miners. They hired strikebreakers and used private security forces to threaten and intimidate the workers. George F. Baer of the Reading Railroad articulated the most extreme form of the employers' position. He argued that workingmen had no right to strike or to say anything about working conditions.

> The rights and interests of the laboring man will be protected and cared for, not by the labor agitators, but by the Christian man to whom God in His infinite wisdom has given the control of the property interests of the country, and upon the successful management of which so much depends.

Although Roosevelt had no particular sympathy for labor, he would certainly not have gone as far as Baer. In the fall of 1902, however, schools began closing for lack of coal, and it looked like many citizens would suffer through the winter. Coal, which usually sold for $5 a ton, rose to $14. Roosevelt called the owners and representatives of the union to the White House even

Business Mergers, 1895–1905

Business mergers did decline during the Roosevelt years, but they did not cease entirely, and they even rose again during his second term.
Source: U.S. Bureau of the Census.

though the businessmen protested that they would not deal with "outlaws." Finally, the president appointed a commission that included representatives of the union as well as the community. Within weeks, the miners went back to work with a 10 percent raise.

Meat Inspection and Pure Food and Drugs

Roosevelt's first major legislative reform began almost accidentally in 1904 when Upton Sinclair, a 26-year-old muckraking journalist, started research on the Chicago stockyards. Born in Baltimore, Sinclair had grown up in New York, where he wrote dime novels to pay his tuition at City College. He was converted to socialism by his reading and by his association with a group of idealistic young writers in New York. Though he knew little about Chicago, he was driven by a desire to expose the exploitation of the poor and oppressed in America. He boarded at the University of Chicago Settlement while he did research, conducted interviews, and wrote the story that would be published in 1906 as *The Jungle*.

Sinclair's novel told of the Rudkus family, who emigrated from Lithuania to Chicago filled with ambition and hope. But the American dream failed for them. Sinclair documented exploitation in his fictional account, but his description of contaminated meat drew more attention. He described spoiled hams treated with formaldehyde and sausages made from rotten meat scraps, rats, and other refuse. Hoping to convert his readers to socialism, Sinclair instead turned their stomachs and caused a public outcry for better regulation of the meatpacking industry.

Selling 25,000 copies in its first six weeks, *The Jungle* disturbed many people, including Roosevelt, who, it was reported, could no longer enjoy his breakfast sausage. Roosevelt ordered a study of the meatpacking industry and then used the report to pressure Congress and the meatpackers to accept a bill introduced by Albert Beveridge, the progressive senator from Indiana.

In the end, the Meat Inspection Act of 1906 was a compromise. It enforced some federal inspection and mandated sanitary conditions in all companies selling meat in interstate commerce. The meatpackers defeated a provision that would have required the dating of all meat. Some of the large companies supported the compromise bill because it gave them an advantage in their battle with the smaller firms. But the bill was a beginning. It illustrates how muckrakers, social justice progressives, and public outcry eventually led to reform legislation. It also shows how Roosevelt used the public mood and manipulated the political process to get a bill through Congress. Many

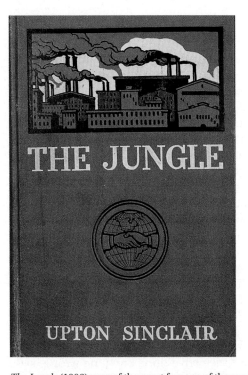

The Jungle (1906), one of the most famous of the muckraking novels, was written by the young, radical journalist Upton Sinclair (1878–1966) when he was only twenty-eight years old. He documented the plight of immigrant workers and the horrible and unsanitary conditions in the meat packing plants in Chicago. He failed to convert many readers to socialism (one of his goals), but he did alert them to the dangers of contaminated meat. *(The Berg Collection, The New York Public Library, Astor, Lenox and Tilden Foundations)*

of the progressive reformers were disappointed with the final result, but Roosevelt was always willing to settle for half a loaf rather than none at all. Ironically, the Meat Inspection Act restored the public's confidence in the meat industry and helped the industry increase its profits.

Taking advantage of the publicity that circulated around *The Jungle*, a group of reformers, writers, and government officials supported legislation to regulate the sale of food and drugs. Americans consumed an enormous quantity of patent medicines, which they purchased through the mail, from traveling salesmen, and from local stores. One article pointed out in 1905:

> Gullible Americans will spend this year some seventy-five million dollars in the purchase of patent medicines. In consideration of this sum it will swallow huge quantities of alcohol, an appalling amount of opiates and narcotics, a wide assortment of varied drugs ranging from powerful and dangerous heart depressants to insidious liver stimulants; and, far in excess of all other ingredients, undiluted fraud. For fraud exploited by the skillfullest of advertising bunco men is the basis of the trade.

Many packaged and canned foods contained dangerous chemicals and impurities. One popular remedy, Hosteter's Stomach Bitters, was revealed on analysis to contain 44 percent alcohol. Coca-Cola, a popular soft drink, contained a small amount of cocaine, and many medicines were laced with opium. Many people, including women and children, became alcoholics or drug addicts in their quest to feel better. The Pure Food and Drug Act, which passed Congress on the same day in 1906 as the Meat Inspection Act, was not a perfect bill, but it corrected some of the worst abuses, including eliminating the cocaine from Coca-Cola.

Conservation

Although Roosevelt was pleased with the new legislation for regulating the food and drug industries, he always considered his conservation program his most important domestic achievement. An outdoorsman, hunter, and amateur naturalist since his youth, he announced soon after he became president that the planned protection of the nation's forests and water

resources would be one of his most vital concerns. Using his executive authority, he more than tripled the land set aside for national forests, bringing the total to more than 150 million acres.

Because he had traveled widely in the West, Roosevelt understood, as few easterners did, the problems created by limited water in the western states. In 1902, with his enthusiastic support, Congress passed the Newlands Act, named after Francis Newlands, its most ardent advocate from the arid state of Nevada. The National Reclamation Act (as it was officially called) set aside the proceeds from the sale of public land in sixteen western states to pay for the construction of irrigation projects in those states. Although it tended to help big farmers more than small producers, the Newlands Act federalized irrigation for the first time.

More important than conservation bills passed during Roosevelt's presidency, however, were his efforts to raise the public consciousness about the need to save the nation's natural resources. He convened a White House Conservation Conference in

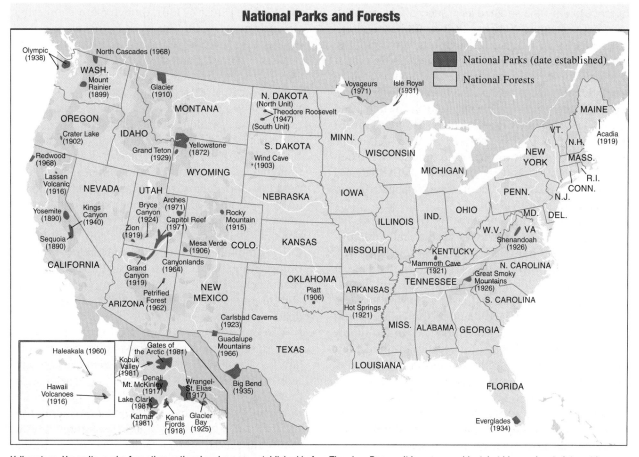

National Parks and Forests

Yellowstone, Yosemite, and a few other national parks were established before Theodore Roosevelt became president, but his passionate interest in conservation led to a movement to set aside and preserve thousands of acres of the public domain. Despite disagreements over the proper goals for the management of federal land, the movement continues to this day.

1908 that included among its delegates most of the governors and representatives of 70 national organizations. A direct result of the conference was Roosevelt's appointment of a National Conservation Commission charged with making an inventory of the natural resources in the entire country. To chair the commission Roosevelt appointed Gifford Pinchot, probably the most important conservation advocate in the country.

A graduate of Yale, Pinchot had studied scientific forestry management in Germany and France before becoming the forest manager of the Vanderbilt's Biltmore estate in North Carolina. In 1898, he was appointed chief of the U.S. Division of Forestry, and in 1900 he became the head of the Bureau of Forestry in the Department of Agriculture. An advocate of selective logging, fire control, and limited grazing on public lands, he became a friend and adviser to Roosevelt.

Pinchot's conservation policies pleased many in the timber and cattle industries; at the same time, they angered those who simply wanted to exploit the land. But his policies were denounced by the followers of John Muir, who believed passionately in preserving the land in a wilderness state. Muir had founded the Sierra Club in 1862 and had led a successful campaign to create Yosemite National Park in California. With his shaggy gray beard, his rough blue work clothes, and his black slouch hat, Muir seemed like an eccentric to many, but thousands agreed with him when he argued that to preserve the American wilderness was a spiritual and psychological necessity for overcivilized and overstimulated urban dwellers. Muir was one of the leaders in a "back to nature" movement at the turn of the century. Many middle-class Americans took up hiking, camping, and other outdoor activities, and children joined the Boy Scouts (founded in 1910) and the Camp Fire Girls (1912).

The conflicting conservation philosophies of Pinchot and Muir were most dramatically demonstrated by the controversy over Hetch-Hetchy, a remote valley deep within Yosemite National Park. It was a pristine wilderness area, and Muir and his followers wanted to keep it that way. But in 1901, the mayor of San Francisco decided the valley would make a perfect place for a dam and reservoir to supply his growing city with water for decades to come. Muir argued that wilderness soon would be scarcer than water and more important for the moral strength of the nation. Pinchot, on the other hand, maintained that it was foolish to pander to the aesthetic enjoyment of a tiny group of people when the comfort and welfare of the great majority was at stake.

The Hetch-Hetchy affair was fought out in the newspapers and magazines as well as in the halls of Congress, but in the end, the conservationists won out over those who wanted only to preserve the wilderness. Roosevelt and Congress sided with Pinchot and eventually the dam was built, turning the valley into a lake. But the debate over how to use the nation's land and water would continue throughout the twentieth century.

Progressivism for Whites Only

Like most of his generation, Roosevelt thought in stereotyped racial terms. He called Indians "savages" and once remarked that blacks were "wholly unfit for the suffrage." He believed that blacks, Asians, and Native Americans were inferior, and he feared that massive migrations from southern and eastern Europe threatened the United States. This kind of racism was supported by scientific theories accepted by many experts in the universities. In 1916 Madison Grant summarized these theories in his book *The Passing of the Great Race,* in which he argued against the dangers of "mongrelization," and he urged the protection of the purity of the Anglo-Saxon race. Roosevelt was influenced by these theories, but he was first of all a politician, so he made gestures of goodwill to most groups. He even invited Booker T. Washington to the White House in 1901, though many southerners viciously attacked the president for his breach of etiquette. Roosevelt also appointed several qualified blacks to minor federal posts, notably Dr. William D. Crum to head the Charleston, South Carolina, customs house in 1905.

At other times, however, Roosevelt seemed insensitive to the needs and feelings of black Americans. This was especially true in his handling of the Brownsville, Texas, riot of 1906. Members of a black army unit stationed there, angered by discrimination against them, rioted one hot August night. Exactly what happened no one was sure, but one white man was killed and several wounded. Waiting until after the midterm elections of 1906, Roosevelt ordered all 167 members of three companies dishonorably discharged. It was an unjust punishment for an unproven crime, and 66 years later, the secretary of the army granted honorable discharges to the men, most of them by that time dead.

The progressive era coincided with the years of greatest segregation in the South, but even the most advanced progressives seldom included blacks in their reform schemes. Hull House, like most social settlements, was segregated, although Jane Addams more than most progressives struggled to overcome the racist attitudes of her day. She helped found a settlement that served a black neighborhood in Chicago, and she spoke out repeatedly against lynching. Addams also supported the founding of the National Association for the Advancement of Colored People

(NAACP) in 1909, the most important organization of the progressive era aimed at promoting equality and justice for blacks.

The founding of the NAACP is the story of cooperation between a group of white social justice progressives and a number of courageous black leaders. Even in the age of segregation and lynching, blacks in all parts of the country—through churches, clubs, and schools—sought to promote a better life for themselves. In Boston, William Monroe Trotter used his newspaper to oppose Washington's policy of accommodation. In Chicago, Ida B. Wells, a large woman with flashing eyes, launched a one-woman crusade against lynching, organized a women's club for blacks, and founded the Negro Fellowship League to help black migrants.

The most important black leader who argued for equality and opportunity for his people was W. E. B. Du Bois. As discussed in Chapter 17, Du Bois differed dramatically from Booker T. Washington on the proper position of blacks in American life. Whereas Washington advocated vocational education, Du Bois

argued for the best education possible for the most talented tenth of the black population. Whereas Washington preached compromise and accommodation to the dominant white society, Du Bois increasingly urged aggressive action to ensure equality.

Denouncing Washington for accepting the "alleged inferiority of the Negro," Du Bois called a meeting of young and militant blacks in 1905. They met in Canada, not far from Niagara Falls, and issued an angry statement. "We want to pull down nothing but we don't propose to be pulled down," the platform announced. "We believe in taking what we can get but we don't believe in being satisfied with it and in permitting anybody for a moment to imagine we're satisfied." The Niagara movement, as it came to be called, was small, but it was soon augmented by a group of white liberals concerned with violence against blacks and race riots in Atlanta and even in Springfield, Illinois, the home of Abraham Lincoln. Jane Addams joined the new organization, as did Oswald Garrison Villard, grandson of abolitionist William Lloyd Garrison.

Tuskegee Institute followed Booker T. Washington's philosophy of black advancement through accommodation to the white status quo. Here students study white American history, but most of their time was spent on more practical subjects. This photo was taken in 1902 by Frances Benjamin Johnson, a pioneer woman photographer. *(Library of Congress)*

In 1910, the Niagara movement combined with the NAACP, and Du Bois became editor of its journal, *The Crisis*. He toned down his rhetoric, but he tried to promote equality for all blacks. The NAACP was a typical progressive organization, seeking to work within the American system to promote reform. But to Roosevelt and many others who called themselves progressives, the NAACP seemed dangerously radical.

William Howard Taft

After two terms as president, Roosevelt decided to step down. "I believe in a strong executive," he remarked in 1908. "I believe in power, but I believe that responsibility should go with power, and that it is not well that the strong executive should be a perpetual executive." But he soon regretted his decision. He was only 50 years old and at the peak of his popularity and power. Because the U.S. system of government provides little creative function for former presidents, Roosevelt decided to travel and to go big-game hunting in Africa. But before he left, he hand-picked his successor.

William Howard Taft, Roosevelt's personal choice for the Republican nomination in 1908, was a distinguished lawyer, federal judge, and public servant. Born in Cincinnati, he had been the first civil governor of the Philippines and Roosevelt's secretary of war. After defeating William Jennings Bryan for the presidency in 1908, he quickly ran into difficulties. In some ways, he seemed more progressive than Roosevelt. His administration instituted more suits against monopolies in one term than Roosevelt had in two. He supported the eight-hour workday and legislation to make mining safer and urged the passage of the Mann-Elkins Act in 1910, which strengthened the ICC by giving it more power to set railroad rates and extending its jurisdiction over telephone and telegraph companies. Taft and Congress also authorized the first tax on corporate profits. He also encouraged the process that eventually led to the passage of the federal income tax, which was authorized under the Sixteenth Amendment, ratified in 1913. That probably did more to transform the relationship of the government to the people than all other progressive measures combined.

Taft's biggest problem was his style. He was a huge man, weighing over 300 pounds. Rumors circulated that he had to have a special oversize bathtub installed in the White House. Easily made fun of, the president wrote ponderous prose and spoke uninspiringly. He also lacked Roosevelt's political skills and angered many of the progressives in the Republican party, especially the midwestern insurgents led by Senator Robert La Follette of Wisconsin. Many progressives were annoyed when he signed the Payne-Aldrich Tariff, which midwesterners thought left rates on cotton and wool cloth and other items too high and played into the hands of the eastern industrial interests.

Even Roosevelt was infuriated when his successor reversed many of his conservation policies and fired Chief Forester Gifford Pinchot, who had attacked Secretary of the Interior Richard A. Ballinger for giving away rich coal lands in Alaska to mining interests. Roosevelt broke with Taft, letting it be known that he was willing to run again for president. This set up one of the most exciting and significant elections in American history.

The Election of 1912

Woodrow Wilson won the Democratic nomination for president in 1912. Born two years before Roosevelt, Wilson came from a very different background and would be cast in opposition to the former president during most of his political career. Wilson was the son and grandson of Presbyterian ministers. Growing up in a comfortable and intellectual southern household, he very early seemed more interested in politics than in religion. After graduating from Princeton University in 1879, he studied law at the University of Virginia and practiced law briefly before entering graduate school at Johns Hopkins University in Baltimore. Soon after receiving his Ph.D. he published a book, *Congressional Government* (1885), that established his reputation as a shrewd analyst of American politics. He taught history briefly at Bryn Mawr College near Philadelphia and at Wesleyan in Connecticut before moving to Princeton. Less flamboyant than Roosevelt, he was an excellent public speaker with the power to convince people with his words.

In 1902, Wilson was elected president of Princeton University, and during the next few years he established a national reputation as an educational leader. Wilson had never lost interest in politics, however, so when offered a chance by the Democratic machine to run for governor of New Jersey, he took it eagerly. In his two years as governor, he showed courage as he quickly alienated some of the conservatives who had helped elect him. Building a coalition of reformers, he worked with them to pass a direct primary law and a workers' compensation law. He also created a commission to regulate transportation and public utility companies. By 1912, Wilson not only was an expert on government and politics but had also acquired the reputation of a progressive.

Roosevelt, who had been speaking out on a variety of issues since 1910, competed with Taft for the Republican nomination, but Taft, as the incumbent president and party leader, was able to win it. Roosevelt then startled the nation by walking out of

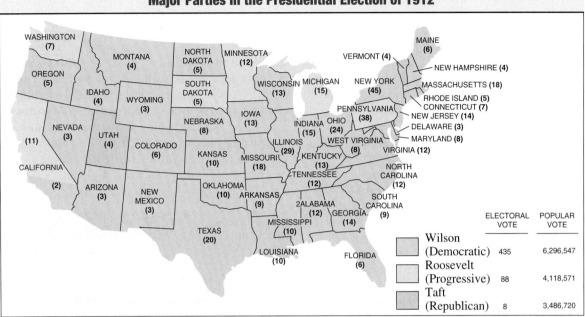

Major Parties in the Presidential Election of 1912

	ELECTORAL VOTE	POPULAR VOTE
Wilson (Democratic)	435	6,296,547
Roosevelt (Progressive)	88	4,118,571
Taft (Republican)	8	3,486,720

Even though Roosevelt ran one of the most successful third-party campaigns in American history, the American electoral system made it almost impossible for him to win. But Taft's overwhelming defeat was humiliating for an incumbent president. Notice how much of the electoral vote was concentrated in states east of the Mississippi.

the convention and forming a new political party, the Progressive party. The new party would not have been formed without Roosevelt, but it was always more than Roosevelt. It appealed to progressives from all over the country who had become frustrated with the conservative leadership in both major parties.

Many social workers and social justice progressives supported the Progressive party because of its platform, which contained provisions they had been advocating for years. The Progressives supported an eight-hour day, a six-day week, the abolition of child labor under age 16, and a federal system of accident, old age, and unemployment insurance. Unlike the Democrats, the Progressives also endorsed woman suffrage. "Just think of having all the world listen to our story of social and industrial injustice and have them told that it can be righted," one social worker exclaimed.

Most supporters of the Progressives in 1912 did not realistically think they could win, but they were convinced that they could organize a new political movement that would replace the Republican party, just as the Republicans had replaced the Whigs after 1856. To this end, Progressive leaders, led by Kellor, set up the Progressive Service, designed to apply the principles of social research to educating voters between elections.

The Progressive convention in Chicago seemed to many observers more like a religious revival meeting or a social work conference than a political gathering. The delegates sang "Onward Christian Soldiers," "The Battle Hymn of the Republic," and "Roosevelt, Oh Roosevelt" (to the tune of "Maryland, My Maryland"). They waved their bandannas, and when Jane Addams rose to second Roosevelt's nomination, a large group of women marched around the auditorium with a banner that read "Votes for Women." The Progressive cause "is based on the eternal principles of righteousness," Roosevelt announced. "In the end the cause itself shall triumph."

The enthusiasm for Roosevelt and the Progressive party was misleading, for behind the unified facade lurked many disagreements. Roosevelt had become more progressive on many issues since leaving the presidency. He even attacked the financiers "to whom the acquisition of untold millions is the supreme goal of life, and who are too often utterly indifferent as to how these millions are obtained." But he was not as committed to social reform as some of the delegates. Perhaps the most divisive issue was the controversy over seating black delegates from several southern states. A number of social justice progressives fought hard to include a plank in the platform supporting equality for blacks and for seating the black delegation. Roosevelt, however, thought he had a realistic chance to carry several southern states, and he was not convinced that black equality was an important progressive issue. In the end, no blacks sat with the southern delegates, and the platform made no mention of black equality.

The political campaign in 1912 became a contest primarily between Roosevelt and Wilson, with Taft, the Republican candidate and incumbent, ignored by most reporters who covered the campaign. On one level, the campaign became a debate over political philosophy, the proper relationship of government to society in a modern industrial age. Roosevelt borrowed some of his ideas from a book, *The Promise of American Life* (1909), written by Herbert Croly, a young journalist. But he had also been working out his own philosophy of government. He spoke of the "new nationalism." In a modern industrial society, he argued, large corporations were "inevitable and necessary." What was needed was not the breakup of the trusts but a strong president and increased power in the hands of the federal government to regulate business and industry and to ensure the rights of labor, women and children, and other groups. The government should be the "steward of the public welfare." He argued for using Hamiltonian means to ensure Jeffersonian ends, for using strong central government to guarantee the rights of the people.

Wilson responded with a slogan and a program of his own. Using the writings of Louis Brandeis, he talked of the "new freedom." He emphasized the need for the Jeffersonian tradition of limited government with open competition. He spoke of the "curse of bigness" and argued against too much federal power. "If America is not to have free enterprise, then she can have freedom of no sort whatever." "What I fear is a government of experts," Wilson declared, implying that Roosevelt's New Nationalism would lead to regulated monopoly and even collectivism.

The level of debate during the campaign was impressive, making this one of the few elections in American history when important ideas were actually discussed. It also marked a watershed for political thought for liberals who rejected Jefferson's distrust of a strong central government. It is easy to exaggerate the differences between Roosevelt and Wilson. There was some truth in the charge of William Allen White, the editor of the Emporia *Gazette* in Kansas, when he remarked, "Between the New Nationalism and the New Freedom was that fantastic imaginary gulf that always had existed between Tweedle-dum and Tweedle-dee." Certainly, in the end, the things that Roosevelt and Wilson could agree on were more important than the issues that divided them. Both Roosevelt and Wilson urged reform within the American system. Both defended corporate capitalism, and both opposed socialism and radical labor organizations such as the IWW. Both wanted to promote more democracy and to strengthen conserva-

tive labor unions. Both were very different in style and substance from the fourth candidate, Eugene Debs, who ran on the Socialist party ticket in 1912.

Debs, in 1912, was the most important socialist leader in the country. Socialism has always been a minority movement in the United States; it had its greatest success in the first decade of the twentieth century. Thirty-three cities, including Milwaukee, Wisconsin; Reading, Pennsylvania; Butte, Montana; Jackson, Michigan; and Berkeley, California, chose socialist mayors. Socialists Victor Berger from Wisconsin and Meyer London from New York were

The Armory Show held in New York in 1913 introduced modern art to the American public. It was a cultural moment of great importance during the progressive era. Marcel Duchamp's *Nude Descending a Staircase* illustrates the impact of technology on painting as well as the beginning of cubism and abstract construction. It was denounced by many critics as "an explosion in a shingle factory," and as "a rude descending a staircase." But it was one of the most popular paintings in the show, and it has remained a symbol of modernism in America. *(Marcel Duchamp.* Nude Descending Staircase, No. 2. *1912. Oil on canvas, 58" x 35". Philadelphia Museum of Art: The Louise and Walter Annenberg Collection)*

elected to Congress. The most important socialist periodical, *Appeal to Reason,* published in Girard, Kansas, increased its circulation from about 30,000 in 1900 to nearly 300,000 in 1906. Socialism appealed to a diverse group. In the cities, some who called themselves socialists merely favored municipal ownership of street railways. Some reformers, such as Florence Kelley and William English Walling, joined the party because of their frustration with the slow progress of reform. The party also attracted many recent immigrants, who brought with them a European sense of class and loyalty to socialism.

A tremendously appealing figure and a great orator, Debs had run for president in 1900, 1904, and 1908, but in 1912 he reached much wider audiences in more parts of the country. His message differed radically from that of Wilson or Roosevelt. Unlike the progressives, socialists argued for fundamental change in the American system. The Socialist party is "organized and financed by the workers themselves," Debs announced, "as a means of wresting control of government and industry from the capitalists and making the working class the ruling class of the nation and the world." Debs polled almost 900,000 votes in 1912 (6 percent of the popular vote), the best showing ever for a socialist in the United States. Wilson received 6.3 million votes; Roosevelt, a little more than 4 million; and Taft, 3.5 million. Wilson garnered 435 electoral votes; Roosevelt, 88; and Taft, only 8.

WOODROW WILSON AND THE NEW FREEDOM

Wilson was elected largely because Roosevelt and the Progressive party split the Republican vote. But once elected, Wilson became a vigorous and aggressive chief executive who set out to translate his ideas about progressive government into legislation. Wilson was the first southerner elected president since Zachary Taylor in 1848 and only the second Democrat since the Civil War. Wilson, like Roosevelt, had to work with his party, and that restricted how progressive he could be. But he was also constrained by his own background and inclinations. Still, like Roosevelt, Wilson became more progressive during his presidency.

Tariff and Banking Reform

Wilson was not as charismatic as Roosevelt. He had a more difficult time relating to people in small groups, but he was an excellent public speaker who dominated through the force of his intellect. He probably had an exaggerated belief in his ability to persuade and a tendency to trust his own intuition too much. Ironically, his early success in getting his legislative agenda through Congress contributed to the overconfidence that would get him into difficulty later in foreign affairs. But his ability to push his legislative program through Congress during his first two years in

Woman suffrage advocates, dressed fashionably in their long skirts and hats, gathered in Washington in 1913 to try to convince Congress and President Wilson to support a suffrage amendment. *(Corbis-Bettmann)*

office was matched only by Franklin Roosevelt during the first months of the New Deal and by Lyndon Johnson in 1965.

Within a month of his inauguration, Wilson went before a joint session of Congress to outline his legislative program. He recommended reducing the tariff to eliminate favoritism, freeing the banking system from Wall Street control, and restoring competition in industry. By appearing in person before Congress, he broke a precedent established by Thomas Jefferson. First on Wilson's agenda was tariff reform. The Underwood Tariff, passed in 1913, was not a free-trade bill, but it did reduce the schedule for the first time in many years.

Attached to the Underwood bill was a provision for a small and slightly graduated income tax, which had been made possible by the passage of the Sixteenth Amendment. It imposed a modest rate of 1 percent on income over $4,000 (thus exempting a large portion of the population), with a surtax rising to 6 percent on high incomes. The income tax was enacted to replace the money lost from lowering the tariff. Wilson seemed to have no interest in using it to redistribute wealth in America.

The next item on Wilson's agenda was reform of the banking system. A financial panic in 1907 had revealed the need for a central bank, but few people could agree on the exact nature of the reforms. The progressive faction of the Democratic party, armed with the findings of the Pujo Committee's investigation of the money trust, argued for a banking system and a currency controlled by the federal government. The congressional committee, led by Arsène Pujo of Louisiana, had revealed a massive consolidation of banks and trust companies and a system of interlock-

ing directorates and informal arrangements that concentrated resources and power in the hands of a few firms, such as the J. P. Morgan Company. But talk of banking reform raised the specter among conservative Democrats and the business community of socialism, populism, and the monetary ideas of William Jennings Bryan.

The bill that passed Congress was a compromise. In creating the Federal Reserve System, it was the first reorganization of the banking system since the Civil War. The bill provided for 12 Federal Reserve banks and a Federal Reserve Board appointed by the president. The bill also created a flexible currency, based on Federal Reserve notes, that could be expanded or contracted as the situation required. The Federal Reserve System was not without its flaws, as later developments would show, and it did not end the power of the large eastern banks; but it was an improvement, and it appealed to the part of the progressive movement that sought order and efficiency.

Despite these reform measures, Wilson was not very progressive in some of his actions during his first two years in office. In the spring of 1914, he failed to support a bill that would have provided long-term rural credit financed by the federal government. He opposed a woman suffrage amendment, arguing that the states should decide who could vote. He also failed to support an anti–child labor bill after it had passed the House. Most distressing to some progressives, he ordered the segregation of blacks in several federal departments.

Booker T. Washington had remarked on Wilson's election, "Mr. Wilson is in favor of the things which

PRESIDENTIAL ELECTIONS OF THE PROGRESSIVE ERA				
Year	Candidate	Party	Popular Vote	Electoral Vote
1900	WILLIAM MCKINLEY	Republican	7,218,039 (51.7%)	292
	William Jennings Bryan	Democratic, Populist	6,358,345 (45.5%)	155
1904	THEODORE ROOSEVELT	Republican	7,628,834 (56.4%)	336
	Alton B. Parker	Democratic	5,084,401 (37.6%)	140
	Eugene V. Debs	Socialist	402,460 (3.0%)	0
1908	WILLIAM H. TAFT	Republican	7,679,006 (51.6%)	321
	William J. Bryan	Democratic	6,409,106 (43.1%)	162
	Eugene V. Debs	Socialist	420,820 (2.8%)	0
1912	WOODROW WILSON	Democratic	6,296,547 (41.9%)	435
	Theodore Roosevelt	Progressive	4,118,571 (27.4%)	88
	William H. Taft	Republican	3,486,720 (23.2%)	8
	Eugene V. Debs	Socialist	897,011 (6.0%)	0
1916	WOODROW WILSON	Democratic	9,129,606 (49.4%)	277
	Charles E. Hughes	Republican	8,538,221 (46.2%)	254
	Allan L. Benson	Socialist	585,113 (3.2%)	0

Note: Winners' names appear in capital letters.

tend toward the uplift, improvement, and advancement of my people, and at his hands we have nothing to fear." But when southern Democrats, suddenly in control in many departments, began dismissing black federal officeholders, especially those "who boss white girls," Wilson did nothing. When the NAACP complained that the shops, offices, rest rooms, and lunchrooms of the post office and treasury departments and the Bureau of Engraving were segregated, Wilson replied, "I sincerely believe it to be in their [the blacks'] best interest." When the president endorsed the blatantly racist movie *Birth of a Nation*, others doubted that he believed in justice for the Afro-American people. "Have you a 'new freedom' for white Americans and a new slavery for your African-American fellow citizens?" William Monroe Trotter, a Boston journalist, asked.

Moving Closer to a New Nationalism

How to control the great corporations in America was a question Wilson and Roosevelt debated extensively during the campaign. Wilson's solution was the Clayton Act, submitted to Congress in 1914. The bill prohibited a number of unfair trading practices, outlawed the interlocking directorate, and made it illegal for corporations to purchase stock in other corporations if this tended to reduce competition. It was not clear how the government would enforce these provisions and ensure the competition that Wilson's New Freedom doctrine called for, but the bill became controversial for another reason.

Labor leaders protested that the bill had no provision exempting labor organizations from prosecution under the Sherman Anti-Trust Act. When a section was added exempting both labor and agricultural organizations, Samuel Gompers hailed it as labor's Magna Carta. It was hardly that, because the courts interpreted the provision so that labor unions remained subject to court injunctions during strikes despite the Clayton Act.

More important than the Clayton Act, which both supporters and opponents realized was too vague to be enforced, was the creation of the Federal Trade Commission (FTC), modeled after the ICC, with enough power to move directly against corporations accused of restricting competition. The FTC was the idea of Louis Brandeis, but Wilson accepted it even though it seemed to move him more toward the philosophy of New Nationalism.

The Federal Trade Commission and the Clayton Act did not end monopoly, and the courts in the next two decades did not increase the government's power to regulate business. The success of Wilson's reform agenda appeared minimal in 1914, but the outbreak of war in Europe and the need to win the election of 1916

Timeline

1901	McKinley assassinated; Theodore Roosevelt becomes president
	Robert La Follette elected governor of Wisconsin
	Tom Johnson elected mayor of Cleveland
	Model tenement house bill passed in New York
	U.S. Steel formed
1902	Anthracite coal strike
1903	Women's Trade Union League founded
	Elkins Act
1904	Roosevelt reelected
	Lincoln Steffens writes *The Shame of the Cities*
1905	Frederic C. Howe writes *The City: The Hope of Democracy*
	Industrial Workers of the World formed
1906	Upton Sinclair writes *The Jungle*
	Hepburn Act
	Meat Inspection Act
	Pure Food and Drug Act
1907	Financial panic
1908	*Muller* v. *Oregon*
	Danbury Hatters case
	William Howard Taft elected president
1909	Herbert Croly writes *The Promise of American Life*
	NAACP founded
1910	Ballinger–Pinchot controversy
	Mann Act
1911	Frederick Taylor writes *The Principles of Scientific Management*
	Triangle Shirtwaist Company fire
1912	Progressive party founded by Theodore Roosevelt
	Woodrow Wilson elected president
	Children's Bureau established
	Industrial Relations Commission founded
1913	Sixteenth Amendment (income tax) ratified
	Underwood Tariff
	Federal Reserve System established
	Seventeenth Amendment (direct election of senators) passed
1914	Clayton Act
	Federal Trade Commission Act
	AFL has over two million members
	Ludlow Massacre in Colorado

would influence him in becoming more progressive in the next years (see Chapter 22).

Neither Wilson nor Roosevelt satisfied the demands of the advanced progressives. Most of the efforts of the two progressive presidents were spent trying to regulate economic power rather than to promote social justice. Yet the most important legacy of these two fascinating and powerful politicians was their attempts to strengthen the office of president and the executive branch of the federal government. The nineteenth-century American presidents after Lincoln had been relatively weak, and much of the federal power had resided with Congress. The progressive presidents reasserted presidential authority, modernized the executive branch, and began the creation of the federal bureaucracy, which had had a major impact on the lives of Americans in the twentieth century.

Both Wilson and Roosevelt used the presidency as a bully pulpit to make pronouncements, create news, and influence policy. For example, both presidents called White House conferences and appointed committees and commissions. Roosevelt strengthened the Interstate Commerce Commission and Wilson created the Federal Trade Commission, both of which were the forerunners of many other federal regulatory bodies. And by breaking precedent and actually delivering his annual message in person before a joint session of Congress, Wilson symbolized the new power of the presidency.

More than the increased power of the executive branch changed the nature of politics. The new bureaus, committees, and commissions brought to Washington a new kind of expert, trained in the universities, at the state and local level, and in voluntary organizations. Julia Lathrop, a coworker of Jane Addams at Hull House, was one such expert. Appointed by President Taft in 1912 to become chief of the newly created Children's Bureau, she was the first woman ever appointed to such a position. She used her post not only to work for better child labor laws but also to train a new generation of women experts who would take their positions in state, federal, and private agencies in the 1920s and 1930s. Other experts emerged in Washington during the progressive era to influence policy in subtle and important ways. The expert, the commission, the statistical survey, and the increased power of the executive branch were all legacies of the progressive era.

Conclusion
The Limits of Progressivism

The progressive era was a time when many Americans set out to promote reform because they saw poverty, despair, and disorder in the country transformed by immigration, urbanism, and industrialism. The progressives, unlike the socialists, however, saw nothing fundamentally wrong with the American system. Progressivism was largely a middle-class movement that sought to help the poor, the immigrants, and the working class. Yet the poor were rarely consulted about policy, and many groups, especially African Americans, were almost entirely left out of reform plans. Progressives had an optimistic view of human nature and an exaggerated faith in statistics, commissions, and committees. They talked of the need for more democracy, but they often succeeded in promoting bureaucracy and a government run by experts. They believed there was a need to regulate business, promote efficiency, and spread social justice, but these were often contradictory goals. In the end, their regulatory laws tended to aid business and strengthen corporate capitalism, while social justice and equal opportunity remained difficult to achieve. By contrast, most of the industrialized nations of western Europe, especially Germany, Austria, France, and Great Britain, passed legislation during this period providing for old-age pensions and health and unemployment insurance.

Progressivism was a broad, diverse, and sometimes contradictory movement that had its roots in the 1890s and reached a climax in the early twentieth century. It began with many local movements and voluntary efforts to deal with the problems created by urban industrialism and moved to the state and finally the national level. Women played important roles in organizing reform, and many became experts at gathering statistics and writing reports. Eventually they began to fill positions in the new agencies in the state capitals and in Washington. Neither Theodore Roosevelt nor Woodrow Wilson was an advanced progressive, but during both their administrations, progressivism achieved some success. Both presidents strengthened the power of the presidency, and both promoted the idea that the federal government had the responsibility to regulate and control and to promote social justice. Progressivism would be altered by World War I, but it survived, with its strengths and weaknesses, to affect American society through most of the twentieth century.

Recommended Reading

The Social Justice Movement

Paul Boyer, *Urban Masses and Moral Order in America, 1820–1920* (1978); George Cotkin, *Reluctant Modernism: American Thought and Culture, 1880–1900* (1992); Mark Connelly, *The Response to Prostitution in the Progressive Era* (1980); Robert Crunden, *Ministers of Reform* (1982); Susan Curtis, *Consuming Faith: The Social Gospel and Modern American Culture* (1991); Allen F. Davis, *Spearheads For Reform: The Social Settlements and the Progressive Movement* (1967); Alan Dawley, *Struggle for Justice: Social Responsibility and the Liberal State* (1991); Steven J. Diner, *A Very Different Age: America in the Progressive Era* (1998); Louis Filler, *The Muckrakers* (1976); Ellen Fitzpatrick, *Endless Crusade: Women Social Scientists and the Progressive Era* (1990); David Kennedy, *Birth Control in America* (1970); Aileen Kraditor, *The Ideas of the Woman Suffrage Movement* (1965); Daniel Levine, *Poverty and Society: The Growth of the American Welfare State in International Perspective* (1988); Rivka Shpak Lissak, *Pluralism and Progressivism* (1989); Robin Muncy, *Creating a Female Dominion in American Reform* (1991); Daniel T. Rodgers, *Atlantic Crossings: Social Politics in a Progressive Age* (1998); Ruth Rosen, *The Lost Sisterhood: Prostitutes in America: 1900–1918* (1982); James H. Timberlake, *Prohibition and the Progressive Movement* (1963); Robert C. Westbrook, *John Dewey and American Democracy* (1989).

The Worker in The Progressive Era

David Brody, *Workers in Industrial America* (1980); Melvin Dubofsky, *We Shall Be All* (1969); Julie Green, *Pure and Simple Politics: The American Federation of Labor and Political Activism* (1998); Michael Kazin, *Barons of Labor* (1981); Alice Kessler-Harris, *Out to Work* (1982); Lary May, *Screening Out the Past: The Birth of Mass Culture and the Motion Picture Industry* (1980); David Montgomery, *Workers Control in America* (1979); David Nasaw, *Going Out* (1993); Daniel Nelson, *Managers and Workers* (1975); Kathy Peiss, *Cheap Amusements: Working Women and Leisure at Turn of the Century New York* (1986).

Reform in the Cities and States

John D. Buenker, *Urban Liberalism and Progressive Reform* (1973); James J Connolly, *The Triumph of Ethnic Progressivism* (1998); Dewey Grantham, *Southern Progressivism* (1983); Melvin G. Holli, *Reform in Detroit: Hazen Pingree and Urban Politics* (1969); Mamie Jones, *Holy Toledo: Religion and Politics in the Life of "Golden Rule" Jones* (1998); George Mowry, *California Progressives* (1951); Zane Miller, *Boss Cox's Cincinnatti* (1968); Bradley R. Rice, *Progressive Cities* (1977); David P. Thelen, *Robert M. LaFollette and the Insurgent Spirit* (1976); Robert Wiebe, *The Search for Order, 1877–1920* (1967).

Theodore Roosevelt and the Square Deal

John Morton Blum, *The Progressive Presidents* (1980); John Milton Cooper Jr., *The Warrior and the Priest* (1983); George Mowry, *The Era of Theodore Roosevelt* (1958); Lewis L Gould, *The Presidency of Theodore Roosevelt* (1991); James Penick Jr., *Progressive Politics and Conservation: The Ballinger–Pinchot Affair* (1968).

Woodrow Wilson and the New Freedom

John Morton Blum, *Woodrow Wilson and the Politics of Morality* (1956); Kendrick A. Clements, *The Presidency of Woodrow Wilson* (1992); Paolo E. Coletta, *The Presidency of William Howard Taft* (1973); Arthur Link, *Woodrow Wilson and the Progressive Era* (1954); Nick Salvatore, *Eugene V. Debs* (1982).

Fiction and Film

Three books written in the early 1900s help readers understand what life was like during the Progressive era. Theodore Dreiser's *Sister Carrie* (1900) is a classic of social realism that was controversial at the time it was published. Upton Sinclair's *The Jungle* (1906) is about the meatpacking industry and the failure of the American dream. *Susan Lenox* (1917), written by David Graham Phillips, is an epic of slum life and political corruption.

Birth of A Nation (1915) is an important film not only because of its innovative technique but also because it is a mirror of the racism of the Progressive era. *Hester Street* (1975), a later film, creates a realistic picture of the immigrant experience and the conflict between husbands and wives created by assimilation.

Suggested Web Sites

http://www.pbs.org/wgbh/pages/amex/1900/

The American Experience: America 1900. This is the companion site to the PBS documentary *America 1900.* It includes audio clips of respected historians on the economics, politics, and culture of 1900; a primary-source database; a timeline of the year, downloadable software to compile your family tree; and other materials.

http://memory.loc.gov/ammem/amrvhtml/conshome.html

The Evolution of the Conservation Movement, 1850–1920. This Library of Congress site brings together scores of primary sources and photographs about "the historical formation and cultural foundations of the movement to conserve and protect America's natural heritage."

http://www.ilr.cornell.edu/trianglefire/

Triangle Fire. The Kheel Center for Labor-Management Documentation and Archives at Cornell University has put together this excellent site composed of oral histories, cartoons, images, and essays about the shirtwaist factory fire of March 1911.

http://www.nyu.edu/projects/sanger

Margaret Sanger Papers Project: Home Page. This site from New York University contains much information about Margaret Sanger and digital versions of several of her works.

http://www.history.ohio-state.edu/projects/laborconflict/

Labor-Management Conflict in American History. This Ohio State University site includes primary accounts of some of the major events in the history of labor–management conflict in the late 19th and early 20th centuries.

http://lcweb2.loc.gov/ammem/papr/west/westhome.html

Westinghouse Works Home Page. Part of the American Memory Project at the Library of Congress, this site provides a glimpse inside a turn-of-the-century factory.

http://digital.nypl.org/schomburg/writers_aa19/

NYPL Digital Schomburg African American Women Writers of the 19th Century. The New York Public Library's Schomburg Center for Research in Black Culture maintains this site, which contains a large number of digital texts by African American women of the 19th century.

http://memory.loc.gov/ammem/detroit/dethome.html

Detroit Publishing Company Photographs Home Page. This Library of Congress collection has thousands of photographs from turn-of-the-century America.

http://www.law.umkc.edu/faculty/projects/ftrials/ haywood/haywood.htm

The Trial of Bill Haywood. This site contains images, chronology, and court and official documents maintained by Dr. Doug Linder at the University of Missouri—Kansas City Law School. Bill Haywood was a labor radical accused of ordering the assassination of former governor of Idaho Frank Steunenberg in 1907.

http://www.theodoreroosevelt.org/

Theodore Roosevelt Association. This site contains much biographical and research information about this famous American.

http://www.ipl.org/ref/POTUS/wwilson.html

IPL POTUS—Woodrow Wilson. This Internet Public Library—Presidents of the United States site contains basic factual data about Wilson's election and presidency, speeches, and on-line biographies.

http://www.ushistoryplace.com

A richly detailed on-line learning environment complete with interactive maps, timelines, history activities, primary source documents, and links to related American history sites.

The GREAT WAR

CHAPTER OUTLINE

On April 7, 1917, the day after the United States officially declared war on Germany, Edmund P. Arpin, Jr., a young man of 22 from Grand Rapids, Wisconsin, decided to enlist in the army. The war seemed to provide a solution for his aimless drifting. It was not patriotism that led him to join the army but his craving for adventure and excitement. A month later, he was at Fort Sheridan, Illinois, along with hundreds of other eager young men, preparing to become an army officer. He felt a certain pride and sense of purpose, and especially a feeling of comradeship with the other men, but the war was a long way off.

Arpin finally arrived with his unit in Liverpool on December 23, 1917, aboard the *Leviathan*, a German luxury liner that the United States had interned when war was declared and pressed into service as a troop transport. In England, he discovered that American troops were not greeted as saviors. Hostility against the Americans simmered partly because of the previous unit's drunken brawls. Despite the efforts of the U.S. government to protect its soldiers from the sins of Europe, drinking seems to have been a preoccupation of the soldiers in Arpin's outfit. Arpin also learned something about French wine and women, but he spent most of the endless waiting time learning to play contract bridge.

Arpin saw some of the horror of war when he went to the front with a French regiment as an observer, but his own unit did not engage in combat until October 1918, when the war was almost over. He took part in the bloody Meuse-Argonne offensive, which helped end the war. But he discovered that war was not the heroic struggle of carefully planned campaigns that newspapers and books described. War was filled with misfired weapons, mix-ups, and erroneous attacks. Wounded in the leg in an assault on an unnamed hill and awarded a Distinguished Service Cross for his bravery, Arpin later learned that the order to attack had been recalled, but word had not reached him in time.

When the armistice came, Arpin was recovering in a field hospital. He was disappointed that the war had ended so soon, but he was well enough to go to Paris to take part in the victory celebration and to explore some of the famous Paris restaurants and nightclubs. In many ways, the highlight of his war experiences was not a battle or his medal but his adventure after the war was over. With a friend, he went absent without leave and set out to explore Germany. They avoided the military police, traveled on a train illegally, and had many narrow escapes, but they made it back to the hospital without being arrested.

Edmund Arpin was in the army for two years. He was one of 4,791,172 Americans who served in the army, navy, and marines. He was one of the two million who went overseas and one of the 230,074 who were wounded. Some of his friends were among the 48,909 who were killed. When he was mustered out of the army in March 1919, he felt lost and confused. Being a civilian was not nearly as exciting as being in the army and visiting new and exotic places.

In time, Arpin settled down. He became a successful businessman, married, and reared a family. A member of the American Legion, he periodically went to conventions and reminisced with men from his division about their escapades in France. Although the war changed their lives in many ways, most would never again feel the same sense of common purpose and adventure. "I don't suppose any of us felt, before or since, so necessary to God and man," one veteran recalled.

For Edmund P. Arpin, Jr., the Great War was the most important event of a lifetime. Just as war changed his life, so, too, did it alter the lives of most Americans. Trends begun during the progressive era accelerated. The power and influence of the federal government increased. Not only did the war promote woman suffrage, prohibition, and public housing, but it also helped to create an administrative bureaucracy that blurred the lines between public and private, between government and business—a trend that would continue throughout the twentieth century.

In this chapter, we examine the complicated circumstances that led the United States into the war and share the wartime experiences of American men and women overseas and at home. We will study not only military actions but also the impact of the war on domestic policies and on the lives of ordinary Americans, including the migration of African Americans into northern cities. The war left a legacy of prejudice and hate and raised the basic question: could the tenets of American democracy, such as freedom of speech, survive participation in a major war? The chapter concludes with a look at the

A 1918 painting of German and American wounded and exhausted soldiers after the Meuse-Argonne offensive captures some of the horror and pathos of war. *(Harvey Dunn, Argonne, 1918/Smithsonian Institution)*

idealistic efforts to promote peace at the end of the war and the disillusion that followed. The Great War thrust the United States into the role of leadership on the world scene, but many Americans were reluctant to accept that role.

THE EARLY WAR YEARS

Few Americans expected the Great War that erupted in Europe in the summer of 1914 to affect their lives or alter their comfortable world. When a Serbian student terrorist assassinated Archduke Franz Ferdinand of Austria-Hungary in Sarajevo, the capital of the province of Bosnia, a place most Americans had never heard of, it precipitated a series of events leading to the most destructive war the world had ever known.

The Causes of War

Despite Theodore Roosevelt's successful peacekeeping attempts in the first decade of the century (see Chapter 20), relationships among the European powers had not improved. Intense rivalries for empire turned minor incidents in Africa, Asia, and the Balkans into events that threatened world peace. A growing sense of nationalism and pride in being French or British or German was fanned by a popular press, much the way Hearst's *Journal* and Pulitzer's *World* had increased American patriotism in the years before the Spanish-American War. National rivalry, especially between Great Britain and Germany, led to military competition and a race to build bigger battleships.

As European nations armed, they drew up a complex series of treaties. Austria-Hungary and Germany (the Central Powers) became military allies, and Britain, France, and Russia (the Allied Powers) agreed to assist one another in case of attack. Despite peace conferences and international agreements, many promoted by the United States, the European balance of power rested precariously on layers of treaties that barely obscured years of jealousy and distrust.

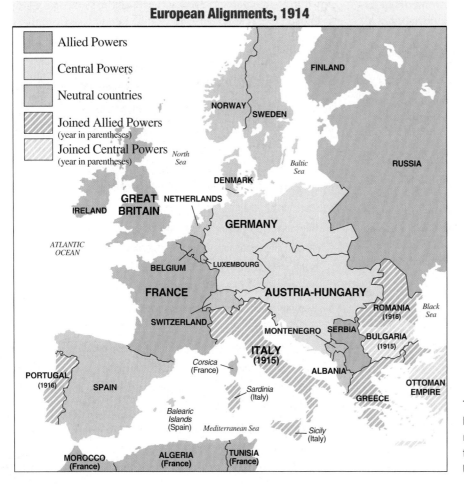

European Alignments, 1914

- Allied Powers
- Central Powers
- Neutral countries
- Joined Allied Powers (year in parentheses)
- Joined Central Powers (year in parentheses)

The Great War had an impact on all of Europe, even on the few countries that managed to remain neutral. Russia left the war in 1917, the same year that the United States joined the fight.

The incident in Sarajevo destroyed that balance. The leaders of Austria-Hungary determined to punish Serbia for the assassination. Russia mobilized to aid Serbia. Germany, supporting Austria-Hungary, declared war on Russia and France. England hesitated, but when Germany invaded Belgium to attack France, England declared war and the slaughter began.

Despite much evidence to the contrary, many intelligent people on both sides of the Atlantic believed that education, science, social reform, and negotiation had replaced all-out war as a way of solving international disputes. "It looks as though we are going to be the age of treaties rather than the age of wars, the century of reason rather than the century of force," a leader of the American peace movement had declared only two years before. But as news of the German invasion of Belgium and reports of the first bloody battles began to reach the United States in late summer, it seemed to most Americans that madness had replaced reason. Europeans "have reverted to the condition of savage tribes roaming the forests and falling upon each other in a fury of blood and carnage," the *New York Times* announced.

The American sense that the nation would never succumb to the barbarism of war, combined with the knowledge that the Atlantic Ocean separated Europe from the United States, contributed to a great sense of relief after the first shock of the war began to wear off. Woodrow Wilson's official proclamation of neutrality on August 4, 1914, reinforced the belief that the United States had no major stake in the outcome of the war and would stay uninvolved. The president was preoccupied with his own personal tragedy. His wife, Ellen Axson Wilson, died of Bright's disease the day after his proclamation. Two weeks later, still engulfed by his own grief, he urged all Americans to "be neutral in fact as well as in name, . . . impartial in thought as well as in action." The United States, he argued, must preserve itself "fit and free" to do what "is honest and disinterested . . . for the peace of the world." But it was obvious that it was going to be difficult to stay uninvolved, at least emotionally, with the battlefields of Europe.

American Reactions

Many social reformers despaired when they heard the news from Europe. Even during its first months, the war seemed to deflect energy away from reform. "We are three thousand miles away from the smoke and flames of combat, and have not a single regiment or battleship involved," remarked John Haynes Holmes, a liberal New York minister. "Yet who in the United States is thinking of recreation centers, improved housing or the minimum wage?" Settlement worker Lillian Wald responded to the threat of war by helping to lead 1,500 women in a "woman's peace" parade down Fifth Avenue. Jane Addams of Hull House helped to organize the American Woman's Peace party. Drawing on traditional conceptions of female character, she argued that women had a special responsibility to work for peace and to speak out against the blasphemy of war because women and children suffered most in any war, especially in a modern war where civilians as well as soldiers became targets.

Although many people worked to promote an international plan to end the war through mediation, others could hardly wait to take part in the great adventure. Hundreds of young American men, most of them students or recent college graduates, volunteered to join ambulance units, to take part in the war effort without actually fighting. Among the most famous of them were Ernest Hemingway, John Dos Passos, and E. E. Cummings, who later turned their wartime adventures into literary masterpieces. Others volunteered for service with the French Foreign Legion or joined the Lafayette Escadrille, a unit of pilots made up of well-to-do American volunteers attached to the French army. Many of these young men were inspired by an older generation who pictured war as a romantic and manly adventure. One college president talked of the chastening and purifying effect of armed conflict, and Theodore Roosevelt projected an image of war that was something like a football game where red-blooded American men could test their idealism and manhood.

Alan Seeger, a graduate of Harvard in 1910, was one of those who believed in the romantic and noble purpose of the war. He had been living in Paris since 1912, and when the war broke out, he quickly joined the French Foreign Legion. For the next two years, he wrote sentimental poetry, articles, and letters describing his adventures. "You have no idea how beautiful it is to see the troops undulating along the road . . . with the captains and lieutenants on horse back at the head of the companies," he wrote his mother. When Seeger was killed in 1916, he became an instant hero. Some called him "America's Rupert Brooke," after the gallant British poet who died early in the war.

Many Americans visualized war as a romantic struggle for honor and glory because the only conflict they remembered was the "splendid little war" of 1898. For them, war meant Theodore Roosevelt leading the charge in Cuba and Commodore Dewey destroying the Spanish fleet in Manila harbor without the loss of an American life. Many older Americans recalled the Civil War, but the horrors of those years had faded, leaving only the memory of heroic triumphs. As Oliver Wendell Holmes, the Supreme Court justice who had been wounded in the Civil War, remarked, "War, when you are at it, is horrible and dull. It is only when time has passed that you see that its message was divine."

Part of the American delegation to the International Congress of Women at The Hague, The Netherlands, April 28–May 1, 1915. The American women braved submarine-infested waters to join women from the neutral countries and from those at war to try to stop the war through mediation. Jane Addams (behind the peace banner facing right) was elected president of the congress. The women were ridiculed by the press on both sides of the Atlantic, but they represented an important part of an idealistic American peace movement. *(The Swarthmore College Peace Collection)*

The reports from the battlefields, even during the first months of the war, should have indicated that the message was anything but divine. This would be a modern war in which men died by the thousands, cut down by an improved and efficient technology of killing.

The New Military Technology

The German Schlieffen plan called for a rapid strike through Belgium to attack Paris and the French army from the rear. However, the French stopped the German advance at the Battle of the Marne in September 1914, and the fighting soon bogged down in a costly and bloody routine. Soldiers on both sides dug miles of trenches and strung out barbed wire to protect them. Thousands died in battles that gained only a few yards or nothing at all. Rapid-firing rifles, improved explosives, incendiary shells, smokeless bullets, and tracer bullets all added to the destruction. Most devastating of all, however, was the improved artillery, sometimes mounted on trucks and directed by spotters using wireless radios, that could fire over the horizon and hit targets many miles behind the lines.

The technology of defense, especially the machine gun, neutralized the frontal assault, the most popular military tactic since the American Civil War. As one writer explained: "Three men and a machine gun can stop a battalion of heroes." But the generals on both

sides continued to order their men to charge to their almost certain deaths.

The war was both a traditional and a revolutionary struggle. It was the last war in which cavalry was used and the first to employ a new generation of military technologies. By 1918, airplanes, initially used only for observation, were creating terror below with their bombs. Tanks made their first tentative appearance in 1916, but it was not until the last days of the war that this new offensive weapon began to neutralize the machine gun. Poison gas, first used in 1914, added a new element of fear to a war of already unspeakable horror. But then military technicians on both sides developed the gas mask, allowing the defense to counter the new offensive weapon.

Despite the reports of carnage from the battlefields, some Americans could hardly wait to join the fighting. Theodore Roosevelt and his friend Leonard Wood, the army chief of staff, led a movement to prepare American men for war. Wood was determined that upper-class and college-educated men be ready to lead the nation into battle. In 1913, he established a camp for college men at Plattsburgh, New York, to give them some experience with military life, with order, discipline, and command. By 1915, thousands had crowded into the camp; even the mayor of New York enrolled. The young men learned to shoot rifles and to endure long marches and field exercises. But most of all, they associated with one another. Gathered around the campfire at night, they heard Wood and other veterans tell of winning glory and honor on the battlefield. In their minds at least, they were already leading a bayonet charge against the enemy, and the enemy was Germany.

Difficulties of Neutrality

Despite Wilson's efforts to promote neutrality, most Americans favored the Allied cause. About eight million Austrian Americans and German Americans lived in the United States, and some supported the cause of the Central Powers. They viewed Kaiser Wilhelm II's Germany as a progressive parliamentary democracy. The anti-British sentiment of some Irish Americans led them to take sides not so much for Germany as against England. A few Swedish Americans distrusted Russia so vehemently that they had difficulty supporting the Allies. A number of American scholars, physicians, and intellectuals fondly remembered studying in Germany. To them, Germany meant great universities and cathedrals, music and culture. It also represented social planning, health insurance, unemployment compensation, and many programs for which the progressives had been fighting.

For most Americans, however, the ties of language and culture tipped the balance toward the Allies. After all, did not the English-speaking people of the world have special bonds and special responsibilities to promote civilization and ensure justice in the world? American connections with the French were not so close, but they were even more sentimental. The French, everyone remembered, had supported the American Revolution, and the French people had given the Statue of Liberty, the very symbol of American opportunity and democracy, to the United States.

Other reasons made real neutrality nearly impossible. The fact that export and import trade with the Allies was much more important than with the Central Powers favored the Allies. Wilson's advisers, especially Robert Lansing and Edward House, openly supported the French and the British. Most newspaper owners and editors had close ethnic, cultural, and sometimes economic ties to the British and the French. The newspapers were quick to picture the Germans as barbaric Huns and to accept and embellish the atrocity stories that came from the front, some of them planted by British propaganda experts. Gradually for Wilson, and probably for most Americans, the perception that England and France were fighting to preserve civilization from the forces of Prussian evil replaced the idea that all Europeans were barbaric and decadent. But the American people were not yet willing to go to war to save civilization. Let France and England do that.

Woodrow Wilson also sympathized with the Allies for practical and idealistic reasons. He wanted to keep the United States out of the war, but he did not object to using force to promote diplomatic ends. "When men take up arms to set other men free, there is something sacred and holy in the warfare," he had written. Moreover, Wilson believed that by keeping the United States out of the war, he might control the peace. The war, he hoped, would show the futility of imperialism and would usher in a world of free trade in products and ideas. The United States had a special role to play in this new world and in leading toward an orderly international society. "We are the mediating nation of the world [and] we are therefore able to understand all nations."

Remaining neutral while maintaining trade with the belligerents became increasingly difficult. Remaining neutral while speaking out about the peace eventually became impossible. The need to trade and the desire to control the peace finally led the United States into the Great War.

World Trade and Neutrality Rights

The United States was part of an international economic community in 1914 in a way that it had not been a hundred years earlier during the Napoleonic Wars. The outbreak of war in the summer of 1914 caused an immediate economic panic in the United States. On July 31, 1914, the Wilson administration closed the stock exchange to prevent the unloading of European securities and panic selling. It also adopted a policy discouraging loans by American banks to belligerent nations. Most difficult was the matter of neutral trade. Wilson insisted on the rights of Americans to trade with both the Allies and the Central Powers, but Great Britain instituted an illegal naval blockade, mined the North Sea, and began seizing American ships, even those carrying food and raw materials to Italy, the Netherlands, and other neutral nations. The first crisis that Wilson faced was whether to accept the illicit British blockade. To do so would be to surrender one of the rights he supported most ardently, the right of free trade.

Wilson eventually backed down and accepted British control of the sea. His conviction that the destinies of the United States and Great Britain were intertwined outweighed his idealistic belief in free trade and caused him to react more harshly to German violations of international law than he did to British violators. Consequently, American trade with the Central Powers declined between 1914 and 1916 from $169 million to just over $1 million, whereas with the Allies it increased during the same period from $825 million to over $3 billion. At the same time, the U.S. government eased restrictions on private loans to belligerents. In March 1915, the House of Morgan loaned the French government $50 million, and in the fall of 1915, the French and British obtained an unsecured loan of $500 million from American banks. With dollars as well as sentiments, the United States gradually ceased to be neutral.

Germany retaliated against British control of the seas with submarine warfare. The new weapon, the U-boat *(Unterseeboot),* created unprecedented problems. Nineteenth-century international law obligated a belligerent warship to warn a passenger or merchant ship before attacking, but the chief advantage of the submarine was surprise. Rising to the surface to issue a warning would have meant being blown out of the water by an armed merchant ship.

On February 4, 1915, Germany announced a submarine blockade of the British Isles. Until Britain gave up its campaign to starve the German population, the Germans would sink even neutral ships. Wilson warned Germany that it would be held to "strict accountability" for illegal destruction of American ships or lives.

In March 1915, a German U-boat sank a British liner en route to Africa, killing 103 people, including one American. How should the United States respond? Wilson's advisers could not agree. Robert Lansing, a legal counsel at the State Department, urged the president to issue a strong protest, charging a breach of international law. William Jennings Bryan, the secretary of state, argued that an American traveling on a British ship was guilty of "contributory negligence" and urged Wilson to prohibit Americans from traveling on belligerent ships in the war zone. Wilson never did settle the dispute, for on May 7, 1915, a greater crisis erupted. A German U-boat torpedoed the British luxury liner *Lusitania* off the Irish coast. The liner, which was not armed but was carrying war supplies, sank in 18 minutes. Nearly 1,200 people, including many women and children, drowned. Among the dead were 128 Americans. Suddenly Americans confronted the horror of total war fought with modern weapons, a war that killed civilians, including women and children, just as easily as it killed soldiers.

The sinking of the *Lusitania* shocked Americans and illustrated the complexity and horror of modern warfare. In the days before radio, most Americans received their news through the newspapers. New York had fifteen daily papers in 1915, and all produced "Extra" editions to announce such dramatic events as the sinking of the *Lusitania.* (New York Tribune, *May 8, 1915*)

The tragedy horrified most Americans. Despite earlier warnings by the Germans in American newspapers that it was dangerous to travel in war zones, the same newspapers denounced the act as "mass murder." Some called for a declaration of war. Wilson and most Americans had no idea of going to war in the spring of 1915, but the president refused to take Bryan's advice and prevent further loss of American lives by simply prohibiting all Americans from traveling on belligerent ships. Instead, he sent a series of protest notes demanding reparation for the loss of American lives and a pledge from Germany that it would cease attacking ocean liners without warning.

Bryan resigned as secretary of state over the tone of the notes and charged that the United States was not being truly neutral. Some denounced Bryan as a traitor, but others charged that if the United States really wanted to stay out of the war, Bryan's position was more logical, consistent, and humane than Wilson's. The president replaced Bryan with Robert Lansing, who was much more eager than Bryan to oppose Germany, even at the risk of war.

The tense situation eased late in 1915. After a German U-boat sank the British steamer *Arabic*, which claimed two American lives, the German ambassador promised that Germany would not attack ocean liners without warning (the *Arabic* pledge). But the *Lusitania* crisis caused an outpouring of books and articles urging the nation to prepare for war. The National Security League, the most effective of the preparedness groups, called for a bigger army and navy, a system of universal military training, and "patriotic education and national sentiment and service among the people of the United States."

Organizing on the other side was a group of progressive reformers who formed the American Union Against Militarism. They feared that those urging preparedness were deliberately setting out to destroy liberal social reform at home and to promote imperialism abroad.

Wilson sympathized with the preparedness groups to the extent of asking Congress on November 4, 1915, for an enlarged and reorganized army. The bill met great opposition, especially from southern and western congressmen, but the Army Reorganization Bill that Wilson signed in June 1916 increased the regular army to just over 200,000 and integrated the National Guard into the defense structure. Few Americans, however, expected those young men to go to war. One of the most popular songs of 1916 was "I Didn't Raise My Boy to Be a Soldier." Even before American soldiers arrived in France, however, Wilson used the army and the marines in Mexico and Central America.

Intervening in Mexico and Central America

Woodrow Wilson came to office in 1913 planning to promote liberal and humanitarian ends, not only in domestic policies but also in foreign affairs. He had a vision of a world purged of imperialism, a world of free trade, but a world where American ideas and American products would find their way. Combining the zeal of a Christian missionary with the conviction of a college professor, he spoke of "releasing the intelligence of America for the service of mankind" and of enriching the world "with the products of our mines, our farms, and our factories, with the creations of our thought and the fruits of our character." With his secretary of state, William Jennings Bryan, Wilson denounced the "big stick" and "dollar diplomacy" of the Roosevelt and Taft years. Yet in the end, Wilson's administration used force more systematically than those of his predecessors. The rhetoric was different, yet just as much as Roosevelt, Wilson tried to maintain stability in the countries to the south in order to promote American economic and strategic interests.

At first, Wilson's foreign policy seemed to reverse some of the most callous aspects of dollar diplomacy in Central America. Bryan signed a treaty with Colombia in 1913 that agreed to pay $5 million for the loss of Panama and virtually apologized for the Roosevelt administration's treatment of Colombia. The Senate, not so willing to admit that the United States had been wrong, refused to ratify the treaty.

The change in spirit proved illusory. After a disastrous civil war in the Dominican Republic, the United States offered in 1915 to take over the country's finances and police force. But when the Dominican leaders rejected a treaty making their country virtually a protectorate of the United States, Wilson ordered in the marines. They took control of the government in May 1916. Although Americans built roads, schools, and hospitals, people resented their presence. In neighboring Haiti, the situation was different, but the results were similar. The marines landed at Port-au-Prince in the summer of 1915 to prop up a pro-American regime. In Nicaragua, the Wilson administration kept the marines sent by Taft in 1912 to keep the pro-American regime of Adolfo Díaz in place and acquired the right, through treaty, to intervene at any time to preserve order and protect American property. Except for a brief period in the mid-1920s, the marines remained until 1933.

Wilson's policy of intervention ran into greatest difficulty in Mexico, a country that had been ruled by dictator Porfirio Díaz, who had long welcomed American investors. By 1910, more than 40,000 American citizens lived in Mexico, and more than

$1 billion of American money was invested in the country. Americans controlled 75 percent of the mines, 70 percent of the rubber, and 60 percent of the oil. In 1911, however, Francisco Madero, a reformer who wanted to destroy the privileges of the upper classes, overthrew Díaz. Two years later, Madero was deposed and murdered by order of Victoriano Huerta, the head of the army. This was the situation when Wilson became president.

To the shock of many diplomats and businessmen, Wilson refused to recognize the Huerta government. Everyone admitted that Huerta was a ruthless dictator, but diplomatic recognition, the exchange of ambassadors, and the regulation of trade and communication had never meant approval. In the world of business and diplomacy, it merely meant that a particular government was in power. But Wilson set out to remove what he called a "government of butchers." "The United States Government intends not merely to force Huerta from power," he wrote to a British diplomat, "but also to exert every influence it can to secure Mexico a better government under which all contracts and business concessions will be safer than they have ever been."

At first, Wilson applied diplomatic pressure. Then, using a minor incident as an excuse, he asked Congress for power to involve American troops if necessary. Few Mexicans liked Huerta, but they liked even less the idea of North American interference. Hence, they rallied around the dictator. As it had in 1847, the United States landed troops at Veracruz. Angry Mexican mobs destroyed American property wherever they could find it. Wilson's action outraged many Europeans and Latin Americans as well as Americans.

Wilson's military intervention succeeded in forcing Huerta out of power, but a civil war between forces led by Venustiano Carranza and those led by General Francisco "Pancho" Villa ensued. The United States sent arms to Carranza, who was considered less radical than Villa, and Carranza's soldiers defeated Villa's. When an angry Villa led what was left of his army in a raid on Columbus, New Mexico, in March 1916, Wilson sent an expedition commanded by Brigadier General John Pershing to track down Villa and his men. The strange and comic scene developed of an American army charging 300 miles into Mexico unable to catch the retreating villain. Not surprisingly, given the history of Mexican-American relations, the Mexicans feared that Pershing's army was planning to occupy northern Mexico. Even Carranza shot off a bitter note to Wilson, accusing him of threatening war, but Wilson refused to withdraw the troops. Tensions rose. An American patrol attacked a Mexican garrison, with loss of life on both sides. Just as war seemed inevitable, Wilson agreed to recall the troops and to recognize the Carranza government. But this was in January 1917, and if it had not been for the growing crisis in Europe, it is likely that war would have resulted.

The tragedy was that Wilson, who idealistically wanted the best for the people of Mexico and Central America and who thought he knew exactly what they needed, managed to intervene too often and too bla-

Pancho Villa on horseback leading the rebel Mexican army that clashed with the American army in Mexico in 1916. President Wilson sent American forces over 300 miles into Mexico to arrest Villa, who allegedly had murdered a number of Americans, but the Americans were not able to catch him. *(Brown Brothers)*

tantly to protect the strategic and economic interests of the United States. In the process, his policy alienated one-time friends of the United States. His policies would contribute to future difficulties in both Latin America and Europe.

THE UNITED STATES ENTERS THE WAR

A significant minority of Americans opposed going to war in 1917, and that decision would remain controversial when it was reexamined in the 1930s. But once involved, the government and the American people made the war into a patriotic crusade that influenced all aspects of American life.

The Election of 1916

American political campaigns do not stop even in times of international crisis. As 1915 turned to 1916, Wilson had to think of reelection as well as of preparedness, submarine warfare, and the Mexican campaign. At first glance, the president's chances of reelection seemed poor. He had won in 1912 only because Theodore Roosevelt and the Progressive party had split the Republican vote. If supporters of the Progressives in 1912 returned to the Republican fold, Wilson's chances were slim indeed. Because the Progressive party had done very badly in the 1914 congressional elections, Roosevelt seemed ready to seek the Republican nomination.

Wilson was aware that he had to win over voters who had favored Roosevelt in 1912. In January 1916, he appointed Louis D. Brandeis to the Supreme Court. The first Jew ever to sit on the High Court, Brandeis was confirmed over the strong opposition of many legal organizations. His appointment pleased the social justice progressives because he had always championed reform causes. They made it clear to Wilson that the real test for them was whether he supported the anti–child labor and workers' compensation bills pending in Congress.

In August, Wilson put heavy pressure on Congress and obtained passage of the Workmen's Compensation Bill, which gave some protection to federal employees, and the Keatings-Owen Child Labor Bill, which prohibited the shipment in interstate commerce of goods produced by children under 14 and in some cases under 16. This bill, later declared unconstitutional, was a far-reaching proposal that for the first time used federal control over interstate commerce to dictate the conditions under which businesspeople could manufacture products.

To attract farm support, Wilson pushed for passage of the Federal Farm Loan Act, which created 12 Federal Farm Loan banks to extend long-term credit to farmers.

Urged on by organized labor as well as by many progressives, he supported the Adamson Act, which established an eight-hour day for all interstate railway workers. Within a few months, Wilson reversed the New Freedom doctrines he had earlier supported and brought the force of the federal government into play on the side of reform. The flurry of legislation early in 1916 provided one climax to the progressive movement. The strategy seemed to work, for progressives of all kinds enthusiastically endorsed the president.

The election of 1916, however, turned as much on foreign affairs as on domestic policy. The Republicans ignored Theodore Roosevelt and nominated instead the staid and respectable Charles Evans Hughes, a former governor of New York and future Supreme Court justice. Their platform called for "straight and honest neutrality" and "adequate preparedness." In a bitter campaign, Hughes attacked Wilson for not promoting American rights in Mexico more vigorously and for giving in to the unreasonable demands of labor. Wilson, on his part, implied that electing Hughes would guarantee war with both Mexico and Germany and that his opponents were somehow not "100 percent Americans." As the campaign progressed, the peace issue became more and more important, and the cry "He kept us out of war" echoed through every Democratic rally. It was a slogan that would soon seem strangely ironic.

The election was extremely close. In fact, Wilson went to bed on election night thinking he had lost the presidency. The election was not finally decided until the Democrats carried California (by fewer than 4,000 votes). Wilson won by carrying the West as well as the South.

Deciding for War

Wilson's victory in 1916 seemed to be a mandate for staying out of the European war. But the campaign rhetoric made the president nervous. He had tried to emphasize Americanism, not neutrality. As he told one of his advisers, "I can't keep the country out of war. They talk of me as though I were a god. Any little German lieutenant can put us into war at any time by some calculated outrage."

People who supported Wilson as a peace candidate applauded in January 1917 when he went before the Senate to clarify the American position on a negotiated settlement of the war. The German government had earlier indicated that it might be willing to go to the conference table. Wilson outlined a plan for a negotiated settlement before either side had achieved victory. It would be a peace among equals, "a peace without victory," a peace without indemnities and annexations. The peace agreement Wilson outlined contained his idealistic vision of the postwar world as an open marketplace, and it could have worked only if Germany and the Allies were willing to settle for a draw.

The German government refused to accept a peace without victory, probably because early in 1917, the German leaders thought they could win. On January 31, 1917, the Germans announced that they would sink on sight any ship, belligerent or neutral, sailing toward England or France. A few days later, in retaliation, the United States broke diplomatic relations with Germany. But Wilson—and probably most Americans—still hoped to avert war without shutting off American trade. As goods began to pile up in warehouses and American ships stayed idly in port, however, pressure mounted to arm American merchant ships. An intercepted telegram from the German foreign secretary, Arthur Zimmermann, to the German minister in Mexico increased anti-German feeling. If war broke out, the German minister was to offer Mexico the territory it had lost in Texas, New Mexico, and Arizona in 1848. In return, Mexico would join Germany in a war against the United States. When the Zimmerman note was released to the press on March 1, 1917, many Americans demanded war against Germany. Wilson still hesitated.

As the country waited on the brink of war, news of revolution in Russia reached Washington. That event would prove as important as the war itself. The March 1917 revolution in Russia was a spontaneous uprising of the workers, housewives, and soldiers against the government of Tsar Nicholas II and its inept conduct of the war. The army had suffered staggering losses at the front. The civilian population was in desperate condition. Food was scarce, and the railroads and industry had nearly collapsed. At first, Wilson and other Americans were enthusiastic about the new republic led by Alexander Kerensky. The overthrow of the feudal aristocracy seemed in the spirit of the American Revolution. Kerensky promised to continue the struggle against Germany. But on November 6, 1917, the revolution took a more extreme turn. Vladimir Ilyich Ulyanov, known as Lenin, returned from exile in Switzerland and led the radical Bolsheviks to victory over the Kerensky regime. He immediately signed an armistice with Germany that released thousands of German troops, who had been fighting the Russians, to join the battle against the Allies on the western front

Lenin, a brilliant lawyer and revolutionary tactician, was a follower of Karl Marx (1818–1883). Marx was a German intellectual and radical philosopher who had described the alienation of the working class under capitalism and predicted a growing split between the proletariat (the unpropertied workers) and the capitalists. Lenin extended Marx's ideas and

argued that capitalist nations eventually would be forced to go to war over raw materials and markets. Believing that capitalism and imperialism went hand in hand, Lenin, unlike Wilson, argued that the only way to end imperialism was to end capitalism. The new Soviet Union, not the United States, was the model for the rest of the world to follow; communism, Lenin predicted, would eventually dominate the globe. The Russian Revolution posed a threat to Wilson's vision of the world and to his plan to bring the United States into the war "to make the world safe for democracy."

More disturbing than the first news of revolution in Russia, however, was the situation in the North Atlantic, where German U-boats sank five American ships between March 12 and March 21, 1917. Wilson no longer hesitated. On April 2, he urged Congress to declare war. His words conveyed a sense of mission about the country's entry into the war, but Wilson's voice was low and somber. "It is a fearful thing," he concluded, "to lead this great, peaceful people into war, into the most terrible and disastrous of all wars." The war resolution swept the Senate 82 to 6 and the House of Representatives 373 to 50.

Once war was declared, most Americans forgot their doubts. Young men rushed to enlist; women volunteered to become nurses or to serve in other ways. Towns were united by patriotism.

A Patriotic Crusade

Not all Americans applauded the declaration of war. Some pacifists and socialists opposed the war, and a black newspaper, *The Messenger,* decried the conflict. "The real enemy is War rather than Imperial Germany," wrote Randolph Bourne, a young New York intellectual. "We are for peace," Morris Hillquit, a socialist leader, announced. "We are unalterably opposed to the killing of our manhood and the draining of our resources in . . . a pursuit which begins by suppressing the freedom of speech and press and public assemblage, and by stifling legitimate political criticism." "To whom does war bring prosperity?" Senator George Norris of Nebraska asked on the Senate floor.

> Not to the soldier, . . . not to the broken hearted widow, . . . not to the mother who weeps at the death of her brave boy. . . . War brings no prosperity to the great mass of common patriotic citizens. We are going into war upon the command of gold. . . . I feel that we are about to put the dollar sign on the American flag.

For most Americans in the spring of 1917, the war seemed remote. A few days after the war was declared, a Senate committee listened to a member of the War

GEE !!
I WISH I WERE
A MAN

I'd JOIN
The NAVY

BE A MAN AND DO IT
**UNITED STATES NAVY
RECRUITING STATION**
34 East 23rd Street, New York

Recruiting posters helped to create a sense of purpose and patriotism and often used pictures of attractive women to make their point. To be a soldier was to be a real man; to avoid service was to be something less than a man. *(The Granger Collection, New York)*

Department staff list the vast quantities of materials needed to supply an American army in France. One of the senators, jolted awake, exclaimed, "Good Lord! You're not going to send soldiers over there, are you?"

To convince senators and citizens alike that the war was real and that American participation was just, Wilson appointed a Committee on Public Information, headed by George Creel, a muckraking journalist from Denver. The Creel Committee launched a gigantic propaganda campaign to persuade the American public that the United States had gone to war to promote the cause of freedom and democracy and to prevent the barbarous hordes from overrunning Europe and eventually the Western Hemisphere.

The patriotic crusade soon became stridently anti-German and anti-immigrant. Most school districts banned the teaching of German, a "language that disseminates the ideals of autocracy, brutality and hatred." Anything German became suspect. Sauerkraut was renamed "liberty cabbage," and

German measles became "liberty measles." Many families Americanized their German surnames. Several cities banned music by German composers from symphony concerts. South Dakota prohibited the use of German on the telephone, and in Iowa, a state official announced, "If their language is disloyal, they should be imprisoned. If their acts are disloyal, they should be shot." Occasionally, the patriotic fever led to violence. The most notorious incident occurred in East St. Louis, Illinois, which had a large German population. A mob seized Robert Prager, a young German American, in April 1918, stripped off his clothes, dressed him in an American flag, marched him through the streets, and lynched him. The eventual trial led to the acquittal of the ringleaders on the grounds that the lynching was a "patriotic murder."

The Wilson administration, of course, did not condone domestic violence and murder, but heated patriotism led to irrational hatreds and fears of subversion. Suspect were not only German Americans but also radicals, pacifists, and anyone who raised doubts about the American war efforts or the government's policies. In New York, the black editors of *The Messenger* were given two-and-a-half-year jail sentences for the paper's article "Pro-Germanism Among Negroes." The Los Angeles police ignored complaints that Mexicans were being harassed, because after learning of the Zimmermann telegram they believed that all Mexicans were pro-German. In Wisconsin, Senator Robert La Follette, who had voted against the war resolution, was burned in effigy and censured by the faculty of the University of Wisconsin. At a number of universities, professors were dismissed, sometimes for as little as questioning the morality or the necessity of America's participation in the war.

On June 15, 1917, Congress, at Wilson's behest, passed the Espionage Act, which provided imprisonment of up to 20 years or a fine of up to $10,000, or both, for people who aided the enemy or who "willfully cause . . . insubordination, disloyalty, mutiny or refusal of duty in the military . . . forces of the United States." The act also authorized the postmaster general to prohibit from the mails any matter he thought advocated treason or forcible resistance to U.S. laws. The act was used to stamp out dissent, even to discipline anyone who questioned the administration's policies. Using the act, Postmaster General Albert S. Burleson banned the magazines *American Socialist* and *The Masses* from the mails.

Congress later added the Trading with the Enemy Act and a Sedition Act. The latter prohibited disloyal, profane, scurrilous, and abusive remarks about the form of government, flag, or uniform of the United States. It even prohibited citizens from opposing the purchase of war bonds. In the most famous case tried under the act, Eugene Debs was sentenced to ten years in prison for opposing the war. In 1919, the Supreme Court upheld the conviction, even though Debs had not explicitly urged the violation of the draft laws. Not all Americans agreed with the decision, for while still in prison, Debs polled close to one million votes in the presidential election of 1920. Ultimately, the government prosecuted 2,168 people under the Espionage and Sedition Acts and convicted about half of them. But these figures do not include the thousands informally persecuted and deprived of their liberties and their right of free speech.

A group of amateur loyalty enforcers, called the American Protective League, cooperated with the Justice Department. League members often reported nonconformists and anyone who did not appear 100 percent loyal. People were arrested for criticizing the Red Cross or a government agency. One woman was sentenced to prison for writing, "I am for the people and the government is for the profiteers." Ricardo Flores Magon, a leading Mexican American labor organizer and radical in the Southwest, was sentenced to 20 years in prison for criticizing Wilson's Mexican policy and violating the Neutrality Acts. In Cincinnati, a pacifist minister, Herbert S. Bigelow, was dragged from the stage where he was about to give a speech, taken to a wooded area by a mob, bound and gagged, and whipped. The attorney general of the United States, speaking of opponents of government policies, said, "May God have mercy on them for they need expect none from an outraged people and an avenging government."

The Civil Liberties Bureau, an outgrowth of the American Union Against Militarism, protested the blatant abridgment of freedom of speech during the war, but the protests fell on deaf ears at the Justice Department and in the White House. Rights and freedoms have been reduced or suspended during all wars, but the massive disregard for basic rights was greater during World War I than during the Civil War. This was ironic because Wilson had often written and spoken of the need to preserve freedom of speech and civil liberties. During the war, however, he tolerated the vigilante tactics of his own Justice Department, offering no more than feeble protest. Wilson was so convinced his cause was just that he ignored the rights of those who opposed him.

Raising an Army

How should a democracy recruit an army in time of war? The debate over a volunteer army versus the draft had been going on for several years before the United States entered the war. People who favored some form of universal military service argued that college graduates, farmers, and young men from the slums of east-

ern cities could learn from one another as they trained together. The opponents of a draft pointed out that people making such claims were most often the college graduates, who assumed they would command the boys from the slums. The draft was not democratic, they argued, but the tool of an imperialist power bent on ending dissent. "Back of the cry that America must have compulsory service or perish," one opponent charged, "is a clearly thought out and heavily backed project to mold the United States into an efficient, orderly nation, economically and politically controlled by those who know what is good for the people." Memories of massive draft riots during the Civil War also led some to fear a draft.

Wilson and his secretary of war, Newton Baker, both initially opposed the draft. In the end, both concluded that it was the most efficient way to organize military manpower. Ironically, it was Theodore Roosevelt who tipped Wilson in favor of the draft. Even though his health was failing and he was blind in one eye, the old Rough Rider was determined to recruit a volunteer division and lead it personally against the Germans. The officers would be Ivy League graduates and men trained at the Plattsburgh camp, with some places reserved for the descendants of prominent Civil War generals and a few French officers, in memory of Lafayette. There would be a German American regiment and a black regiment (led by white officers). Roosevelt pictured himself leading this mixed but brave and virile group to France to restore the morale of the Allied troops and win the war.

The thought of his old enemy Theodore Roosevelt blustering about Europe so frightened Wilson that he supported the Selective Service Act in part, at least, to prevent such volunteer outfits as Roosevelt planned. Yet controversy filled Congress over the bill, and the House finally insisted that the minimum age for draftees should be 21, not 18. On June 5, 1917, some 9.5 million men between the ages of 21 and 31 registered, with little protest. In August 1918, Congress extended the act to men 18 to 45. In all, over 24 million men registered and over 2.8 million were inducted, making up over 75 percent of soldiers who served in the war.

The draft worked well, but it was not quite the perfect system that Wilson claimed. Most Americans took seriously their obligation of "service" during time of war. But because local draft boards had so much control, favoritism and political influence allowed some to stay at home. Draft protests erupted in a few places, the largest in Oklahoma, where a group of tenant farmers planned a march on Washington to take over the government and end the "rich man's war." The Green Corn Rebellion, as it came to be called, died before it got started. A local posse arrested about 900 rebels and took them off to jail.

Some men escaped the draft. Some were deferred because of war-related jobs, and others resisted by claiming exemption for reasons of conscience. The Selective Service Act did exempt men who belonged to religious groups that forbade members from engaging in war, but religious motivation was often difficult to define, and nonreligious conscientious objection was even more complicated. Thousands of conscientious objectors were inducted. Some served in noncombat positions; others went to prison. Roger Baldwin, a leading pacifist, was jailed for refusing military service. But Norman Thomas, a socialist, urged young men to register for the draft and to express their dissent within the democratic process.

〜 THE MILITARY EXPERIENCE

Family albums in millions of American homes contain photographs of young men in uniform, some of them stiff and formal, some of them candid shots of soldiers on leave in Paris or Washington or Chicago. These photographs testify to the importance of the war to a generation of Americans. For years afterward, the men and women who lived through the war sang "Tipperary," "There's a Long, Long Trail," and "Pack Up Your Troubles" and remembered rather sentimentally what the war had meant to them. For some, the war was a tragic event, as they saw the horrors of the

battlefield firsthand. For others, it was a liberating experience and the most exciting period in their lives.

The American Soldier

The typical soldier, according to the U.S. Medical Department, stood 5 feet 7½ inches tall, weighed 141½ pounds, and was about 22 years old. He took a physical exam, an intelligence test, and a psychological test, and he probably watched a movie called *Fit to Fight,* which warned him about the dangers of venereal disease. The majority of the American soldiers had not attended high school. The median amount of education for native whites was 6.9 years and for immigrants 4.7 years but was only 2.6 years for southern blacks. As many as 31 percent of the recruits were declared illiterate, but the tests were so primitive that they probably tested social class more than anything else. More than half the recent immigrants from eastern Europe ranked in the "inferior" category. Fully 29 percent of the recruits were rejected as physically unfit for service, which shocked the health experts.

Most World War I soldiers were ill-educated and unsophisticated young men, quite different from Ernest Hemingway's heroes or even from Edmund Arpin. They came from farms, small towns, and urban neighborhoods. They came from all social classes and ethnic groups, yet most were transformed into soldiers. In the beginning, however, they didn't look the part, because uniforms and equipment were in short

Many women joined the great adventure by serving overseas as nurses with the Red Cross or as volunteers with the Salvation Army, but they could not join the Army or Navy as women did in World War II. This woman is serving coffee to soldiers behind the lines in France. *(National Archives)*

Recovering the Past

GOVERNMENT PROPAGANDA

All governments produce propaganda. Especially in time of war, governments try to convince their citizens that the cause is important and worthwhile even if it means sacrifice. Before the United States entered the war, both Great Britain and Germany presented their side of the conflict through stories planted in newspapers, photographs, and other devices. Some historians argue that the British propaganda depicting the Germans as barbaric Huns who killed little boys and Catholic nuns played a large role in convincing Americans of the righteousness of the Allied cause.

When the United States entered the war, a special committee under the direction of George Creel did its best to persuade Americans that the war was a crusade against evil. The committee organized a national network of "four-minute men," local citizens with the proper political views, who could be used to whip up a crowd into a patriotic frenzy. These local rallies, enlivened by bands and parades, urged people of all ages to support the war effort and buy war bonds. The Creel Committee also produced literature for the schools, much of it prepared by college professors who volunteered their services. One pamphlet, titled *Why America Fights Germany*, described in lurid detail a possible German invasion of the

Liberty Bond propaganda. *(The Granger Collection, New York)*

United States. The committee also used the new technology of motion pictures, which proved to be the most effective propaganda device of all.

There is a narrow line between education and propaganda. As early as 1910, Thomas Edison made films instructing the public about the dangers of tuberculosis, and others produced movies that demonstrated how to avoid everything from typhoid to tooth decay. However, during the war, the government quickly realized the power of the new medium and adopted it to train soldiers, instill patriotism, and help the troops avoid the temptations of alcohol and sex.

After the United States entered World War I, the Commission of Training Camp Activities made a film called *Fit to Fight* that was shown to almost all male servicemen. It was an hour-long drama following the careers of five young recruits. Four of them, by associating with the wrong people and through lack of willpower, caught venereal disease. The film interspersed a simplistic plot with grotesque shots of men with various kinds of venereal disease. The film also glorified athletics, especially football and boxing, as a substitute for sex. It emphasized the importance of patriotism and purity for America's fighting force. In one scene, Bill Hale, the only soldier in the film to remain pure, breaks up a peace rally and beats up the speaker. "It serves you right," the pacifist's sister remarks, "I'm glad Billy punched you."

Fit to Fight was so successful that the government commissioned another film, *The End of the Road,* to be shown to women who lived near military bases. The film is the story of Vera and Mary. Although still reflecting progressive attitudes, the film's message is somewhat different from that of *Fit to Fight.* Vera's strict mother tells her daughter that sex is dirty, leaving Vera to pick up "distorted and obscene" information about sex on the street. She falls victim to the first man who comes along and contracts a venereal disease. Mary, in contrast, has an enlightened mother who explains where babies come from. When Mary grows up, she rejects marriage and becomes a professional woman, a nurse. In the end, she falls in love with a doctor and gets married. *The End of the Road* has a number of subplots and many frightening shots of syphilitic sores. Several illustrations show the dangers of indiscriminate sex. Among other things, the film preached the importance of science and sex education and the need for self-control.

What do the anti-VD films tell us about the attitudes, ideas, and prejudices of the World War I period? What images do they project about men, women, and sex roles? Would you find the same kind of moralism, patriotism, and fear of VD today? How have attitudes toward sex changed? Were you shown sex education films in school? Were they like these? Who sponsored them? What can historians learn from such films? Does the government produce propaganda today?

Anti-VD poster issued by the U.S. Commission on Training Camp Activities. *(Army Educational Commission)*

Scene from *Fit to Fight. (War Department, Commission on Training Camps)*

supply. Many men had to wear their civilian clothes for months, and they often wore out their shoes before they were issued army boots. "It was about two months or so before I looked really like a soldier," one recruit remembered.

The military experience changed the lives and often the attitudes of many young men. Women also contributed to the war effort as telephone operators and clerk typists in the navy and the marines. Some went overseas as army and navy nurses. Others volunteered for a tour of duty with the Red Cross, the Salvation Army, or the YMCA. Yet the military experience in World War I was predominantly male. Even going to training camp was a new and often frightening experience. A leave in Paris or London, or even in New York or New Orleans, was an adventure to remember for a lifetime. Even those who never got overseas or who never saw a battle experienced subtle changes. Many soldiers saw their first movie in the army or had their first contact with trucks and cars. Military service changed the shaving habits of a generation because the new safety razor was standard issue. The war also led to the growing popularity of the cigarette rather than the pipe or cigar because a pack of cigarettes fit comfortably into a shirt pocket and a cigarette could be smoked during a short break. The war experience also caused many men to abandon the pocket watch for the more convenient wristwatch, which had been considered effeminate before the war.

The Black Recruit

Blacks had served in all American wars, and many fought valiantly in the Civil War and the Spanish-American War. Yet black soldiers had most often performed menial work and belonged to segregated units. Most black leaders supported American participation in the war. An exception was William Monroe Trotter, a Boston editor, who argued that German atrocities were no worse than the lynching of black men in America. Instead of making the world safe for democracy, he suggested, the government should make "the South safe for Negroes " But W. E. B. Du Bois, the editor of *The Crisis,* urged blacks to close ranks and support the war. He predicted that the war experience would cause the "walls of prejudice" to crumble gradually before the "onslaught of common sense." But the walls did not crumble, and the black soldier never received equal or fair treatment during the war.

The Selective Service Act made no mention of race, and African Americans in most cases registered without protest. Many whites, especially in the South, feared having too many blacks trained in the use of arms. But this fear diminished as the war progressed. In some areas, draft boards exempted single white men but drafted black fathers. The most notorious situation existed in Atlanta, where one draft board inducted 97 percent of the African Americans registered but exempted 85 percent of the whites. Still, most southern whites found it difficult to imagine a black man in the uniform of the U.S. Army.

Assigned to segregated units, black soldiers were also excluded from white recreation facilities. Here black women from Newark, New Jersey, aided by white social workers, entertain black servicemen. *(National Archives)*

White attitudes toward African Americans sometimes led to conflict. In August 1917, violence erupted in Houston, Texas, involving soldiers from the regular army's all-black 24th Infantry Division. Harassed by the Jim Crow laws, which had been tightened for their benefit, a group of soldiers went on a rampage, killing 17 white civilians. Over 100 soldiers were court-martialed; 13 were condemned to death. Those convicted were hanged three days later before any appeals could be filed.

This violence, coming only a month after a race riot in East St. Louis, Illinois, brought on in part by the migration of southern blacks to the area, caused great concern about the handling of African American soldiers. Secretary of War Baker made it clear that the army had no intention of upsetting the status quo. The basic government policy was of complete segregation and careful distribution of black units throughout the country.

Some African Americans were trained as junior officers and were assigned to the all-black 92nd Division, where the high-ranking officers were white. But a staff report decided that "the mass of colored drafted men cannot be used for combatant troops." Most of the black soldiers, including about 80 percent of those sent to France, worked as stevedores and common laborers under the supervision of white noncommissioned officers. "Everyone who has handled colored labor knows that the gang bosses must be white if any work is to be done," remarked Lieutenant Colonel U. S. Grant, the grandson of the Civil War general. Other black soldiers acted as servants, drivers, and porters for the white officers. It was a demeaning and ironic policy for a government that advertised itself as standing for justice, honor, and democracy.

Over There

The conflict that Wilson called the war "to make the world safe for democracy" had become a contest of stalemate and slaughter. Hundreds of thousands had died on both sides, but victory remained elusive. To this ghastly war, Americans made important contributions. In fact, without their help, the Allies might have lost. But the American contribution was most significant only in the war's final months.

When the United States entered the conflict in the spring of 1917, the fighting had been dragging on for nearly three years. After a few rapid advances and retreats, the war in western Europe had settled down to a tactical and bloody stalemate. The human costs of trench warfare were horrifying. In one battle in 1916, a total of 60,000 British soldiers were killed or wounded in a single day, yet the battle lines did not move an inch. By the spring of 1917, the British and French armies were down to their last reserves. Italy's army had nearly collapsed. In the East, the Russians were

engaged in a bitter internal struggle, and in November, the Bolshevik Revolution would cause them to sue for a separate peace, freeing the German divisions on the eastern front to join in one final assault in the West. The Allies desperately needed fresh American troops, but those troops had to be trained, equipped, and transported to the front. That took time.

A few token American regiments arrived in France in the summer of 1917 under the command of General John J. "Black Jack" Pershing, a tall, serious, Missouri-born graduate of West Point. He had fought in the Spanish-American War and led the Mexican expedition in 1916. When the first troops marched in a parade in Paris on July 4, 1917, the emotional French crowd shouted, *"Vive les Américains"* and showered them with flowers, hugs, and kisses. But the American commanders worried that many of their soldiers were so inexperienced they did not even know how to march, let alone fight. The first Americans saw action near Verdun in October 1917. By March 1918, over 300,000 American soldiers had reached France, and by November 1918, more than two million.

One reason that the United States forces were slow to see actual combat was Pershing's insistence that they be kept separate from the French and British divisions. An exception was made for four regiments of black soldiers who were assigned to the French army. Despite the American warning to the French not to "spoil the Negroes" by allowing them to mix with the French civilian population, these soldiers fought so well that the French later awarded three of the regiments the Croix de Guerre, their highest unit citation.

In the spring of 1918, with Russia out of the war and the British blockade becoming more and more effective, the Germans launched an all-out, desperate offensive to win the war before full American military and industrial power became a factor in the contest. By late May, the Germans had pushed to within 50 miles of Paris. American troops were thrown into the line and helped stem the German advance at Château-Thierry, Belleau Wood, and Cantigny, place names that proud survivors would later endow with almost sacred significance. Americans also took part in the Allied offensive led by General Ferdinand Foch of France in the summer of 1918.

In September, over a half million American troops fought near St. Mihiel in the first battle where large numbers of Americans were pressed into action. One enlisted man remembered that he "saw a sight which I shall never forget. It was zero hour and in one instant the entire front as far as the eye could reach in either direction was a sheet of flame, while the heavy artillery made the earth quake." The Americans suffered over 7,000 casualties, but they captured more than 16,000 German soldiers. The victory, even if it

American airplane pilots were the most popular heroes of the war. Many young Americans volunteered to fly for the British or the French before the United States entered the war. The war in the air seemed much more romantic than the trench warfare on the ground. One of the popular American aces was Eddie Rickenbacker (in the center), a former auto racer, who was credited with shooting down 26 German aircraft. *(Corbis)*

came against exhausted and retreating German troops, seemed to vindicate Pershing's insistence on a separate American army. The British and French commanders were critical of what they considered the disorganized, inexperienced, and ill-equipped American forces. They especially denounced the quality of the American high-ranking officers. One French report in the summer of 1918 suggested that it would take at least a year before the American army could become a "serious fighting force."

In the fall of 1918, the combined British, French, and American armies drove the Germans back. Faced with low morale among the German soldiers and finally the mutiny of the German fleet and the surrender of Austria, Kaiser Wilhelm II abdicated on November 8, and the armistice was signed on November 11. More than a million American soldiers took part in the final Allied offensive near the Meuse River and the Argonne forest. It was in this battle that Edmund Arpin was wounded. Many of the men were inexperienced, and some, who had been rushed through training as "90-day wonders," had never handled a rifle before arriving in France. There were many disastrous mistakes and bungled situations. The most famous blunder was the "lost battalion." An American unit advanced beyond its support and was cut off and surrounded. The battalion suffered 70 percent casualties before being rescued.

The performance of the all-black 92nd Division was also controversial. The 92nd had been deliberately dispersed around the United States and had never trained as a unit. Its higher officers were white, and they repeatedly asked to be transferred. Many of its men were only partly trained and poorly equipped, and they were continually being called away from their military duties to work as stevedores and common laborers. At the last minute during the Meuse-Argonne offensive, the 92nd was assigned to a particularly difficult position on the line. They had no maps and no wire-cutting equipment. Battalion commanders lost contact with their men, and on several occasions, the men broke and ran in the face of enemy fire. The division was withdrawn in disgrace, and for years politicians and military leaders used this incident to point out that black soldiers would never make good fighting men, ignoring the difficulties under which the 92nd fought and the valor shown by black troops assigned to the French army.

The war produced a few American heroes. Joseph Oklahombie, a Choctaw, overran several German machine gun nests and captured more than 100 German soldiers. Sergeant Alvin York, a former conscientious objector from Tennessee, single-handedly killed or captured 160 Germans using only his rifle and pistol. The press made him a celebrity, but his heroics were not typical. Artillery, machine guns, and, near the end, tanks, trucks, and airplanes won the war. "To be shelled when you are in the open is one of the most terrible of human experiences," one American soldier wrote. "You hear this rushing, tearing sound as the thing comes toward you, and then the huge explosion as it strikes, and infinitely worse, you see its hideous work as men stagger, fall, struggle, or lie quiet and unrecognizable."

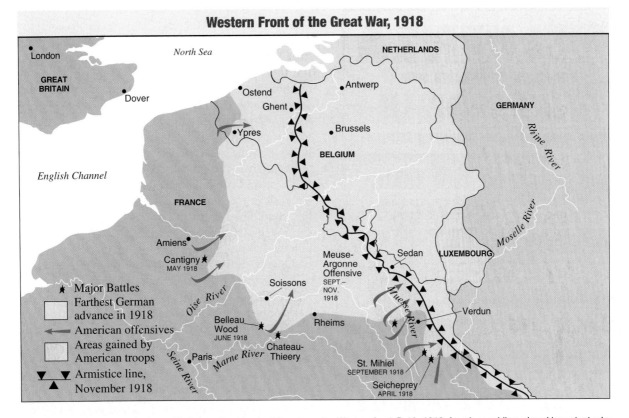

Western Front of the Great War, 1918

For more than three years, the war settled down to a bloody stalemate on the Western front. But in 1918, American soldiers played important roles in the Allied offensive that finally ended the war.

With few exceptions, the Americans fought hard and well. Although the French and British criticized American inexperience and disarray, they admired their exuberance, their "pep," and their ability to move large numbers of men and equipment efficiently. One British officer, surveying the abundance of American men and supplies, remarked, "For any particular work they seem to have about five times as much of both as we do." Sometimes it seemed that Americans simply overwhelmed the enemy with their numbers. They suffered over 120,000 casualties in the Meuse-Argonne campaign alone. One officer estimated that he lost ten soldiers for every German his men killed in the final offensive.

The United States entered the war late but still lost more than 48,000 service personnel and had many more wounded. Disease claimed 15 of every 1,000 soldiers each year (compared with 65 per 1,000 in the Civil War). But the British lost 900,000 men, the French 1.4 million, and the Russians 1.7 million. American units fired French artillery pieces; American soldiers were usually transported in British ships and wore helmets and other equipment modeled after the British. The United States purchased clothing and blankets, even horses, in Europe. American fliers, including heroes like Eddie Rickenbacker, flew French and British planes. The United States contributed huge amounts of men

and supplies in the last months of the war, and that finally tipped the balance. But it had entered late and sacrificed little compared with France and England. That would influence the peace settlement.

The end of the Great War brought relief and joy to many, but in the fall of 1918 an influenza pandemic swept around the world, killing at least 30 million people, with 675,000 deaths in the United States in a little more than a year. The Spanish Flu, as it was called, although there is no evidence that it originated in Spain, started with a cough and sore throat, then developed into pneumonia; its victims were often dead within a few days. Only a small percentage of those who caught the disease died from it, but, unlike most epidemics, it hit hardest among young adults. Over 43,000 American servicemen died from the flu (almost as many as died on the battlefield.) Early in the epidemic, rumors blamed German germ warfare for the disease, but the German army was infected as well. There were no antibiotics or shots that could prevent or cure the disease, and the surgical masks required in some cities did no good. Even President Wilson came near death from the disease in the spring of 1919. The flu of 1918–1919 killed more people in a short time than any event in human history. The virus that caused the outbreak has never been identified.

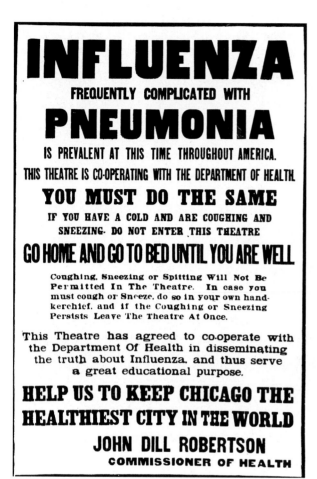

A poster distributed in 1918 to movie theaters in Chicago by the Commissioner of Health. The language of the poster reveals the fear and near panic that many Americans felt in the face of the deadly flu epidemic. *(National Library of Medicine)*

🖎 DOMESTIC IMPACT OF THE WAR

For at least 30 years before the United States entered the Great War, a debate raged over the proper role of the federal government in regulating industry and protecting people who could not protect themselves. Controversy also centered on the question of how much power the federal government should have to tax and control individuals and corporations and the proper relation of the federal government to state and local governments. Even within the Wilson administration, advisers disagreed on the proper role of the federal government. In fact, Wilson had only recently moved away from what he defined in 1912 as the New Freedom. But the war and the problems it raised increased the power of the federal government in a variety of ways. The wartime experience did not end the debate, but the United States emerged from the war a more modern nation, with more power residing in Washington.

Financing the War

The war, by one calculation, cost the United States over $33 billion. Interest and veterans' benefits bring the total to nearly $112 billion. Early on, when an economist suggested that the war might cost the United States $10 billion, everyone laughed. Yet many in the Wilson administration knew the war was going to be expensive, and they set out to raise the money by borrowing and by increasing taxes.

Secretary of the Treasury William McAdoo, who, like Wilson, had moved from the South to the North because of the lure of greater economic opportunities, shouldered the task of financing the war. Studying the policies that Treasury Secretary Salmon Chase had followed during the Civil War, he decided that Chase had made a mistake in not appealing to the emotions of the people. A war must be a "kind of crusade," he remarked. His campaign to sell liberty bonds to ordinary American citizens at a very low interest rate called forth patriotic sentiment. "Lick a Stamp and Lick the Kaiser," one poster urged. Celebrities such as film stars Mary Pickford and Douglas Fairbanks promoted the bonds, and McAdoo employed the Boy Scouts to sell them. "Every Scout to Save a Soldier" was the slogan. He even implied that people who did not buy bonds were traitors. "A man who can't lend his government $1.25 per week at the rate of 4% interest is not entitled to be an American citizen," he announced. A banner flew over the main street in Gary, Indiana, that made the point of the campaign clear: "ARE YOU WORTHY TO BE FOUGHT AND DIED FOR? BUY LIBERTY BONDS."

The public responded enthusiastically, but they discovered after the war that their bonds had dropped to about 80 percent of face value. Because the interest on the bonds was tax exempt, well-to-do citizens profited more from buying the bonds than did ordinary men, women, and children. But the wealthy were not as pleased with McAdoo's other plan to finance the war by raising taxes. The War Revenue Act of 1917 boosted the tax rate sharply, levied a tax on excess profits, and increased estate taxes. Another bill the next year raised the tax on the largest incomes to 77 percent. The wealthy protested, but a number of progressives were just as unhappy with the bill, for they wanted to confiscate all income over $100,000 a year. Despite taxes and liberty bonds, however, World War I, like the Civil War, was financed in large part by inflation. Food prices, for example, nearly doubled between 1917 and 1919.

Increasing Federal Power

At first, Wilson tried to work through a variety of state agencies to mobilize the nation's resources. The need for more central control and authority soon led Wilson to create a series of federal agencies to deal with the war emergency. The first crisis was food. Poor grain crops for two years and an increasing demand for American food in Europe caused shortages. To solve the problem, Wilson appointed Herbert Hoover, a young engineer who had won great prestige as head of the Commission for Relief of Belgium, to direct the Food Administration. Hoover set out to meet the crisis not so much through government regulation as through an appeal to the patriotism of farmers and consumers alike. He instituted a series of "wheatless" and "meatless" days and urged housewives to cooperate. In Philadelphia, a large sign announced, "FOOD WILL WIN THE WAR; DON'T WASTE IT."

Women emerged during the war as the most important group of consumers. The government urged them to save, just as later it would urge them to buy. *The Ladies' Home Journal* announced, "To lose the war because we were unwilling to make the necessary efforts and the required sacrifices in regard to the food supply would be one of the most humiliating spectacles in history."

The Wilson administration used the authority of the federal government to organize resources for the war effort. The National Research Council and the National Advisory Committee on Aeronautics helped mobilize scientists in industry and the universities to produce strategic materials formerly imported from Germany, especially optical glass and chemicals to combat poison-gas warfare. American companies also tried to reproduce German color lithography that had dominated the market for postcards, posters, and magazine illustrations before the war. Perhaps most valuable were the efforts of scientists in industry to improve radio, airplanes, and instruments to predict the weather and detect submarines. The war stimulated research and development and made the United States less dependent on European science and technology.

The War Industries Board, led by Bernard Baruch, a shrewd Wall Street broker, used the power of the government to control scarce materials and, on occasion, to set prices and priorities. The government itself went into the shipbuilding business. The largest shipyard, at Hog Island, near Philadelphia, employed as many as 35,000 workers, but the yard did not launch its first ship until the late summer of 1918. But cooperation among government, business, and university scientists and technical experts to promote research and develop new products was one legacy of the war.

The government also got into the business of running the railroads. When a severe winter and a lack of coordination brought the rail system near collapse in December 1917, Wilson put all the nation's railroads under the control of the United Railway Administration. The government spent more than $500 million to improve the rails and equipment, and in 1918, the railroads did run more efficiently than they had under private control. Some businessmen complained of "war socialism" and resented the way government agencies forced them to comply with rules and regulations. But most came to agree with Baruch that a close working relationship with government could improve the quality of their products, promote efficiency, and increase profits.

War Workers

The Wilson administration sought to protect and extend the rights of organized labor during the war, while mobilizing the workers necessary to keep the factories running. The National War Labor Board insisted on adequate wages and reduced hours, and it tried to prevent the exploitation of women and children working under government contracts. On one occasion, when a munitions plant refused to accept the War Labor Board's decision, the government simply took over the factory. When workers threatened to strike for better wages or hours or for greater control over the workplace, the board often ruled that they either work or be drafted into the army.

The Wilson administration favored the conservative labor movement of Samuel Gompers and the AFL, and the Justice Department put the radical Industrial Workers of the World "out of business." Beginning in September 1917, federal agents conducted massive raids on IWW offices and arrested most of the leaders.

Samuel Gompers took advantage of the crisis to strengthen the AFL's position to speak for labor. He lent his approval to administration policies by making clear that he opposed the IWW as well as socialists and communists. Convincing Wilson that it was important to protect the rights of organized labor during wartime, he announced that "no other policy is compatible with the spirit and methods of democracy." As the AFL won a voice in home front policy, its membership increased from 2.7 million in 1916 to over 4 million in 1917. Organized labor's wartime gains, however, would prove only temporary.

The war opened up industrial employment opportunities for black men. With four million men in the armed forces and the flow of immigrants interrupted by the war, American manufacturers for the first time hired African Americans in large numbers. In Chicago before the war, only 3,000 black men held factory jobs. In 1920, more than 15,000 did.

Northern labor agents and the railroads actively recruited southern blacks, but the news of jobs in northern cities spread by word of mouth as well. By 1920, more than 300,000 blacks had joined the "great migration" north. This massive movement of people,

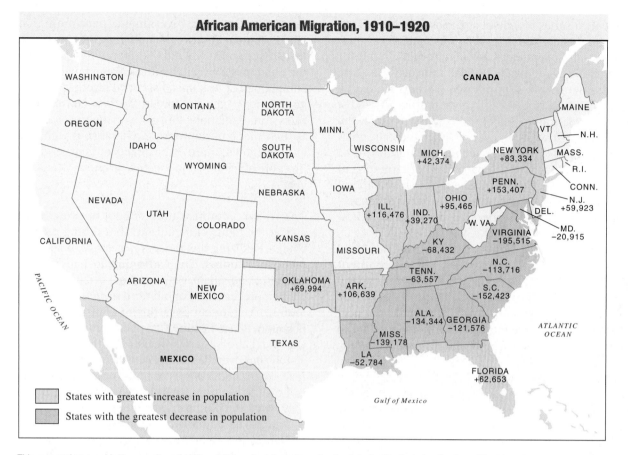

African American Migration, 1910–1920

- States with greatest increase in population
- States with the greatest decrease in population

This map makes graphic the massive migration of African Americans from the South to the North during the Great War. Most moved to find better jobs, but in the process they changed the dynamics of race relations in the country.

which continued into the 1920s, had a permanent impact on the South as well as on the northern cities. As African Americans moved north, thousands of Mexicans crossed into the United States, as immigration officials relaxed the regulations because of the need for labor in the farms and factories of the Southwest.

The war also created new employment opportunities for women. Posters and patriotic speeches urged women to do their duty for the war effort. "NOT JUST HATS OFF TO THE FLAG, BUT SLEEVES UP FOR IT," one poster announced. Another showed a woman at her typewriter, the shadow of a soldier in the background, with the message: "STENOGRAPHERS, WASHINGTON NEEDS YOU."

Women responded to these appeals out of patriotism, as well as out of a need to increase their earnings and to make up for inflation, which diminished real wages. "I used to go to work when my man was sick," one woman reported, "but this is the first time I ever had to go to work to get enough money to feed the kids, when he was working regular." Women went into every kind of industry. They labored in brickyards and in heavy industry, became conductors on the railroad, and turned out shells in munitions plants. They even

organized the Woman's Land Army to mobilize female labor for the farms. They demonstrated that women could do any kind of job, whatever the physical or intellectual demands. "It was not until our men were called overseas," one woman banking executive reported, "that we made any real onslaught on the realm of finance, and became tellers, managers of departments, and junior and senior officers." One black woman who gave up her position as a live-in servant to work in a paperbox factory declared:

> I'll never work in nobody's kitchen but my own any more. No indeed, that's the one thing that makes me stick to this job, but when you're working in anybody's kitchen, well you out of luck. You almost have to eat on the run; you never get any time off.

As black women moved out of domestic service, they took jobs in textile mills or even in the stockyards. Racial discrimination, however, even in the North, prevented them from moving too far up the occupational ladder.

Even though women demonstrated that they could take over jobs once thought suitable only for men, their progress during the war proved tempo-

Women proved during the war that they could do "men's work." These two young women deliver ice, a backbreaking task, but one that was necessary in the days before electric refrigerators. Despite women like these, the war did not change the American ideal that women's proper place was in the home. *(National Archives)*

rary. Only about 5 percent of the women employed during the war were new to the workforce, and almost all of them were unmarried. For most, it meant a shift of occupations or a move up to a better-paying position. Moreover, the war accelerated trends already under way. It increased the need for telephone operators, sales personnel, secretaries, and other white-collar workers, and in these occupations women soon became a majority. Telephone operator, for example, became an almost exclusively female job. There were 15,000 operators in 1900 but 80,000 in 1910, and by 1917, women represented 99 percent of all operators as the telephone network spanned the nation.

In the end, the war did provide limited opportunities for some women, but it did not change the dominant perception that a woman's place was in the home. After the war was over, the men returned, and the gains made by women almost disappeared. There were 8 million women in the workforce in 1910 and only 8.5 million in 1920.

The Climax of Progressivism

Many progressives, especially the social justice progressives, opposed the U.S. entry into the war until a few months before the nation declared war. But after April 1917, many began to see the "social possibilities of war." They deplored the death and destruction, the abridgment of freedom of speech, and the patriotic spirit that accompanied the war. But they praised the social planning stimulated by the conflict. They approved the Wilson administration's support of collective bargaining, the eight-hour day, and protection for women and children in industry. They applauded Secretary of War Baker when he announced, "We cannot afford, when we are losing boys in France, to lose children in the United States at the same time." They welcomed the experiments with government-owned housing projects, woman suffrage, and prohibition. Many endorsed the government takeover of the railroads and control of business during the war.

One of the best examples of the progressives' influence on wartime activities was the Commission on Training Camp Activities, set up early in the war to solve the problem of mobilizing, entertaining, and protecting American servicemen at home and abroad. The chairman of the commission was Raymond Fosdick, a former settlement worker. He appointed a number of experts from the Playground Association, the YMCA, and social work agencies. They set out to organize community singing and baseball, establish post exchanges and theaters, and even provide university extension lectures to educate the servicemen. The overriding assumption was that the military experience would help produce better citizens, people who would be ready to vote for social reform once they returned to civilian life.

The Commission on Training Camp Activities also incorporated the progressive crusades against alcohol and prostitution. The Military Draft Act prohibited the sale of liquor to men in uniform and gave the president power to establish zones around military bases where prostitution and alcohol would be prohibited. Some military commanders protested, and at least one city official argued that prostitutes were "God-provided means for the prevention of the violation of innocent girls, by men who are exercising their 'God-given passions.'" Yet the commission, with the full cooperation of the Wilson administration, set out to wipe out sin, or at least to put it out of the reach of servicemen. "Fit to fight" became the motto. "Men must live straight if they would shoot straight," one official announced. It was a typical progressive effort combining moral indignation with the use of the latest scientific prophylaxis. The commissioners prided themselves on having eliminated by 1918 all the red-light districts near the training camps and producing what one person called "the cleanest army since Cromwell's day." When the boys go to France, the secretary of war remarked, "I want them to have invisible armour to take with them. I want them to have armour made up of a set of social habits replacing those of their homes and communities."

France tested the "invisible armour." The government, despite hundreds of letters of protest from American mothers, decided that it could not prevent the soldiers from drinking wine in France, but it could forbid them to buy or accept as gifts anything but light wine and beer. If Arpin's outfit is typical, the soldiers often ignored the rules.

Sex was even more difficult to regulate in France than liquor. Both the British and the French armies had tried to solve the problem of venereal disease by licensing and inspecting prostitutes. Clemenceau, the French premier, found the American attitude toward prostitution difficult to comprehend. On one occasion, he accused the Americans of spreading disease throughout the French civilian population and graciously offered to provide the Americans with licensed prostitutes. General Pershing considered the letter containing the offer "too hot to handle." So he gave it to Fosdick, who showed it to Baker, who remarked, "For God's sake, Raymond, don't show this to the President or he'll stop the war." The Americans never accepted Clemenceau's offer, and he continued to be baffled by the American progressive mentality.

Suffrage for Women

In the fall of 1918, while American soldiers were mobilizing for the final offensive in France and hundreds of thousands of women were working in factories and serving as Red Cross and Salvation Army volunteers near the army bases, Woodrow Wilson spoke before the Senate to ask its support of woman suffrage, which he maintained was "vital to the winning of the war." Wilson had earlier opposed the vote for women. His positive statement at this late date was not important, but his voice was a welcome addition to a rising chorus of support for an amendment to the Constitution that would permit the female half of the population to vote.

Not everyone favored woman suffrage. Many people still argued that the vote would make women less feminine, more worldly, and less able to perform their primary tasks as wives and mothers. The National Association Opposed to Woman Suffrage argued that it was only radicals who wanted the vote and declared that woman suffrage, socialism, and feminism were "three branches of the same Social Revolution."

Carrie Chapman Catt, an efficient administrator and tireless organizer, devised the strategy that finally secured the vote for women. Catt, who grew up in Iowa, joined the Iowa Woman Suffrage Association at age 28 shortly after her first husband died. Before remarrying, she insisted on a legal agreement giving her four months a year away from her husband to work for the suffrage cause. In 1915, she became president of the National American Woman Suffrage Association (NAWSA), the organization founded in 1890 and based in part on the society organized by Elizabeth Cady Stanton and Susan B. Anthony in 1869.

Catt coordinated the state campaigns with the office in Washington, directing a growing army of dedicated workers. The Washington headquarters sent precise information to the states on ways to pressure congressmen in local districts. In Washington, they maintained a file on each congressman and senator. "There were facts supplied by our members in the states about his personal, political, business and religious affiliations; there were reports of interviews; . . . there was everything that could be discovered about his stand on woman suffrage."

The careful planning began to produce results, but a group of more militant reformers, impatient with the slow progress, broke off from NAWSA to form the National Woman's Party (NWP) in 1916. This group was led by Alice Paul, a Quaker from New Jersey, who had participated in some of the suffrage battles in England. Paul and her group picketed the White House, chained themselves to the fence, and blocked the streets. They carried banners that asked, "MR. PRESIDENT, HOW LONG MUST WOMEN WAIT FOR LIBERTY?" In the summer of 1917, the government arrested more than 200 women and charged them with "obstructing the sidewalk." It was just the kind of publicity the militant group sought, and it made the most of it. Wilson, fearing even more embarrassment, began to cooperate with the more moderate reformers.

The careful organizing of NAWSA and the more militant tactics of the NWP both contributed to the final success of the woman suffrage crusade. The war did not cause the passage of the Nineteenth Amendment, but it did accelerate the process. Fourteen state legislatures petitioned Congress in 1917 and twenty-six in 1919, urging the enactment of the amendment. Early in 1919, the House of Representatives passed the suffrage amendment 304 to 90, and the Senate approved by a vote of 56 to 25. Fourteen months later, the required 36 states had ratified the amendment, and women at last had the vote. "We are no longer petitioners," Catt announced in celebration. "We are not wards of the nation, but free and equal citizens." But the achievement of votes for women would not prove the triumph of feminism, nor the signal for the beginning of a new reform movement, that the women leaders believed at the time.

PLANNING FOR PEACE

Woodrow Wilson turned U.S. participation in the war into a religious crusade to change the nature of international relations. It was a war to make the world safe for democracy—and more. On January 8, 1918, in part to counteract the Bolshevik charge that the war was merely a struggle among imperialist powers, he announced his plan to organize the peace. Called the Fourteen Points, it argued for "open covenants of peace openly arrived at," freedom of the seas, equality of trade, and the self-determination of all peoples. But his most important point, the fourteenth, called for an international organization, a "league of nations," to preserve peace.

The Paris Peace Conference

Late in 1918, Wilson announced that he would head the American delegation in Paris, revealing his belief that he alone could overcome the forces of greed and imperialism in Europe and bring peace to the world. Wilson and his entourage of college professors, technical experts, and advisers set sail for Paris on the *George Washington* on December 4, 1918. Secretary of State Lansing, Edward House, and a number of other advisers were there; conspicuously missing, however, was Henry Cabot Lodge, the most powerful man in the Senate, or any other Republican senator.

This would prove a serious blunder, for the Republican-controlled Senate would have to approve any treaty negotiated in Paris. It is difficult to explain Wilson's lack of political insight, except that he disliked Lodge intensely and hated political bargaining and compromise. Preferring to announce great principles, he had supreme confidence in his ability to persuade and to get his way by appealing to the people.

Wilson's self-confidence grew during a triumphant tour through Europe before the conference. The ordinary people greeted him like a savior who had brought the tragic war to an end. The American president had greater difficulty convincing the political leaders at the peace conference of his genius or his special grace. In Paris, he faced the reality of European power politics and ambitions and the personalities of David Lloyd George of Great Britain, Vittorio Orlando of Italy, and Georges Clemenceau of France.

Though Wilson was more naive and idealistic than his European counterparts, he was a clever negotiator who won many concessions at the peace table, sometimes by threatening to go home if his counterparts would not compromise. The European leaders were determined to punish Germany and enlarge their empires. Wilson, however, believed that he could create a new kind of international relations based on his Fourteen Points. He achieved limited acceptance of the idea of self-determination, his dream that each national group could have its own country and that the people should decide in what country they wanted to live.

The peacemakers carved the new countries of Austria, Hungary, and Yugoslavia out of what had been the Austro-Hungarian Empire. In addition, they created Poland, Czechoslovakia, Finland, Estonia, Latvia, and Lithuania, in part to help contain the threat of bolshevism in eastern Europe. France was to occupy the industrial Saar region of Germany for 15 years with a plebiscite at the end of that time to determine whether the people wanted to become a part of Germany or France. Italy gained the port city of Trieste, but not the neighboring city of Fiume with its largely Italian-speaking population. Dividing up the map of Europe was difficult at best, but perhaps the biggest mistake that Wilson and other major leaders made was to give the small nations little power at the negotiating table and to exclude Soviet Russia entirely.

Wilson won some points at the peace negotiations, but he also had to make major concessions. He was forced to agree that Germany should pay reparations (later set at $56 billion), lose much of its oil- and coal-rich territory, and admit to its war guilt. He accepted a mandate system, to be supervised by the League of Nations, that allowed France and Britain to take over portions of the Middle East and allowed Japan to occupy Germany's colonies in the Pacific. He acquiesced when the Allies turned Germany's African colonies into "mandate possessions" because they did not want to allow the self-determination of blacks in areas they had colonized.

This was not a "peace without victory," and the sense of betrayal the German people felt would later have grave repercussions. Wilson also did not win approval for freedom of the seas or the abolition of trade barriers, but he did gain endorsement for the League of Nations, the organization he hoped would prevent all future wars. The league consisted of a council of the five great powers, elected delegates from the smaller countries, and a World Court to settle disputes. But the key to collective security was contained in Article 10 of the league covenant, which pledged all members "to respect and preserve against external aggression the territorial integrity" of all other members.

Women for Peace

While the statesmen met at Versailles to sign the peace treaty hammered out in Paris and to divide up Europe, a group of prominent and successful women—lawyers, physicians, administrators, and writers from all over the world, including many from the Central Powers—met in Zurich, Switzerland. The American delegation was led by Jane Addams and included Florence Kelley of the National Consumers League; Alice Hamilton, a

Europe and the Near East after World War I

▨ To Great Britain	▨ New states as of 1921
▨ To France	— Border of German Empire in 1914
▨ To Belgium	— Border of Austrian-Hungarian Empire in 1914
▨ To Denmark	— Border of Russian Empire in 1914
▨ To Romania	— Border of Ottoman Empire in 1914
▨ To Greece	— New boundaries as a result of postwar treaties
▨ To Italy	
▨ Became independent	— Boundaries as of 1914

Led in part by President Wilson's goal to promote the self-determination of people and in part by a desire to block the expansion of Germany and the Soviet Union, the diplomats meeting at Versailles reconfigured the map of Europe and the Near East. Redrawing the map, however, was easier than solving the problems of nationalism and ethnic conflict.

professor at Harvard Medical School; and Jeannette Rankin, a congresswoman from Montana (one of the few states where women could vote). They met amid the devastation of war to promote a peace that would last. At their conference, they formed the Women's International League for Peace and Freedom. Electing Addams president of the new organization, they denounced the harsh peace terms, which called for disarmament of only one side and exacted great economic penalties against the Central Powers. Prophetically, they predicted that the peace treaty would result in the

spread of hatred and anarchy and "create all over Europe discords and animosities which can only lead to future wars."

Hate and intolerance were legacies of the war. They were present at the Versailles peace conference, where Clemenceau especially wanted to humiliate Germany for the destruction of French lives and property. Also hanging over the conference was the Bolshevik success in Russia. Lenin's vision of a communist world order, led by workers, conflicted sharply with Wilson's dream of an anti-imperialist, free-trade, capitalist world. The threat of revolution seemed so great that Wilson and the Allies sent American and Japanese troops into Russia in 1919 to attempt to defeat the Bolsheviks and create a moderate republic. But by 1920, the troops had failed in their mission. They withdrew, but Russians never forgot the event, and the threat of bolshevism remained.

Wilson's Failed Dream

Probably most Americans supported the concept of the League of Nations in the summer of 1919. A few, like former senator Albert Beveridge of Indiana, an ardent nationalist, denounced the league as the work of "amiable old male grannies who, over their afternoon tea, are planning to denationalize America and denationalize the nation's manhood." But 33 governors endorsed the plan. Yet in the end, the Senate refused to accept American membership in the league. The League of Nations treaty, one commentator has suggested, was killed by its friends and not by its enemies.

First there was Lodge, who had earlier endorsed the idea of some kind of international peacekeeping organization but who objected to Article 10, claiming that it would force Americans to fight the wars of foreigners. Chairman of the Senate Foreign Relations Committee, Lodge, like Wilson, was a lawyer and a scholar as well as a politician. But in background and personality, he was very different from Wilson. A Republican senator since 1893, he had great faith in the power and prestige of the Senate. He disliked all Democrats, especially Wilson, whose idealism and missionary zeal infuriated him.

Then there was Wilson, whose only hope of passage of the treaty in the Senate was a compromise to bring moderate senators to his side. But Wilson refused to compromise or to modify Article 10 to allow Congress the opportunity to decide whether the United States would support the league in time of crisis. Angry at his opponents, who were exploiting the disagreement for political advantage, he stumped the country to convince the American people of the rightness of his plan. The people did not need to be convinced. They greeted Wilson much the way the people of France had. Traveling by train, he gave 37 speeches in 29 cities in the space of three weeks. When he described the graves of American soldiers in France and announced that American boys would never again die in a foreign war, the people responded with applause.

After one dramatic speech in Pueblo, Colorado, Wilson collapsed. His health had been failing for some months, and the strain of the trip was too much. He was rushed back to Washington, where a few days later he suffered a massive stroke. For the next year and a half, the president was incapable of running the government. Protected by his second wife and his closest advisers, Wilson became irritable and depressed and unable to lead a fight for the league. For a year and a half, the country limped along without a president.

After many votes and much maneuvering, the Senate finally killed the league treaty in March 1920. Had the United States joined the League of Nations, it probably would have made little difference in the international events of the 1920s and 1930s. Nor would American participation have prevented World War II. The United States did not resign from the world of diplomacy or trade, nor did the United States with that

The Big Four in December 1919: Italy's Orlando, Britain's Lloyd George, France's Clemenceau, and the United States' Wilson. (*The Granger Collection, New York*)

single act become isolated from the rest of the world. But the rejection of the league treaty was symbolic of the refusal of many Americans to admit that the world and America's place in it had changed dramatically since 1914.

Timeline

1914	Archduke Ferdinand assassinated; World War I begins
	United States declares neutrality
	American troops invade Mexico and occupy Veracruz
1915	Germany announces submarine blockade of Great Britain
	Lusitania sunk
	Arabic pledge
	Marines land in Haiti
1916	Army Reorganization Bill
	Expedition into Mexico
	Wilson reelected
	Workmen's Compensation Bill
	Keatings-Owen Child Labor Bill
	Federal Farm Loan Act
	National Women's Party founded
1917	Germany resumes unrestricted submarine warfare
	United States breaks relations with Germany

	Zimmermann telegram
	Russian Revolution
	United States declares war on Germany
	War Revenue Act
	Espionage Act
	Committee on Public Information established
	Trading with the Enemy Act
	Selective Service Act
	War Industries Board formed
1918	Sedition Act
	Flu epidemic sweeps nation
	Wilson's Fourteen Points
	American troops intervene in Russian Revolution
1919	Paris peace conference
	Eighteenth Amendment prohibits alcoholic beverages
	Senate rejects Treaty of Versailles
1920	Nineteenth Amendment grants suffrage for women

Conclusion

The Divided Legacy of the Great War

For Edmund Arpin and many of his friends, who left small towns and urban neighborhoods to join the military forces, the war was a great adventure. For the next decades, at American Legion conventions and Armistice Day parades, they continued to celebrate their days of glory. For others who served, the war's results were more tragic. Many died. Some came home injured, disabled by poison gas, or unable to cope with the complex world that had opened up to them.

In a larger sense, the war was both a triumph and a tragedy for the American people. The war created opportunities for blacks who migrated to the North, for women who found more rewarding jobs, and for farmers who suddenly discovered a demand for their products. But much of the promise and the hope proved temporary.

The war provided a certain climax to the progressive movement. The passage of the woman suffrage amendment and the use of federal power in a variety of ways to promote justice and order pleased reformers, who had been working toward these ends for many decades. But the results were often disappointing. Once the war ended, much federal legislation was dismantled or reduced in effectiveness and votes for women had little initial impact on social legislation.

The Great War marked the coming of age of the United States as a world power, but the country seemed reluctant to accept the new responsibility. The war stimulated patriotism and pride in the country, but it also increased intolerance. With this mixed legacy from the war, the country entered the new era of the 1920s.

Recommended Reading

The Early War Years

C. C. Clemenden, *The United States and Pancho Villa* (1961); Charles DeBenedetti, *Origins of the Modern Peace Movement* (1978); Nial Ferguson, *The Pity of War* (1998); Paul Fussell, *The Great War and Modern Memory* (1975); Martin Gilbert, *The First World War: A Complete Account* (1994); C. Roland Marchand, *The American Peace Movement and Social Reform* (1973); Thomas F. O'Brien, *The Revolutionary Mission: American Enterprise in Latin America, 1900–1945* (1996); James Toll, *The Origins of the First World War* (1984); Barbara Tuchman, *The Guns of August* (1962).

The United States Enters the War

C. C. Adams, *The Great Adventure: Male Desire and the Coming of World War I* (1990); Robert H. Ferrell, *Woodrow Wilson and World War I* (1985); Ellis W. Hawley, *The Great War and the Search for Modern Order* (1979); N. Gordon Levin Jr., *Woodrow Wilson and World Politics* (1968); Ernest R. May, *The World War and American Isolation* (1966); Daniel M. Smith, *The Great Departure: The United States and World War I* (1965).

The Military Experience

Arthur D. Barbeau and Florette Henri, *The Unknown Soldiers: Black American Troops in World War I* (1974); Edward M. Coffman, *The War to End All Wars: The American Military Experience in World War I* (1968); John Ellis, *The Social History of the Machine Gun* (1975); Byron Farwell, *Over There: The United States in the Great War* (1999); John Keegan, *The First World War* (1999); Herbert M. Mason, Jr., *The Lafayette Escadrille* (1964); Lawrence Stallings, *The Doughboys: The Story of the A. E. F., 1917–1918* (1963); Russell Weigley, *The American Way of War* (1973).

Domestic Impact of the War

Nancy K. Bristow, *Making Men Moral: Social Engineering During the Great War* (1996); Stanley Cooperman, *World War I and the American Novel* (1970); Alfred W. Crosby, *America's Forgotten Pandemic: The Influenza of 1918* (1989); Leslie Midkiff DeBauche, *Reel Patriotism: The Movies and World War I* (1998); Eric Foner, *The Story of American Freedom* (1998); Lettie Gavin, *American Women in World War I* (1997); Maurine Greenwald, *Women, War and Work* (1980); Carol S. Gruber, *Mars and Minerva: World War I and the Uses of Higher Learning in America* (1975); Florette Henri, *Black Migration: The Movement Northward, 1900–1920* (1975); Donald Johnson, *The Challenge of American Freedoms: World War I and the Rise of the American Civil Liberties Union* (1963); David M. Kennedy, *Over Here: The First World War and American Society* (1980); Gina Kolata, *Flu: The Story of the Great Influenza Pandemic of 1918 and the Search for the Virus that Caused It* (1999); Ronald Schaffer, *America in the Great War: The Rise of the War Welfare State* (1991).

Planning For Peace

John Morton Blum, *Woodrow Wilson and the Politics of Morality* (1956); Peter Filene, *America and the Soviet Experiment* (1967); Lloyd C. Gardner, *Safe for Democracy: The Anglo-American Response to Revolution, 1913–1923* (1984); Warren Kuehl, *Seeking World Order* (1969); Charles L. Mee, Jr., *The End of Order: Versailles, 1919* (1980); Ralph Stone, *The Irreconcilables: The Fight Against the League of Nations* (1970).

Fiction and Film

Erich Maria Remarque highlights the horror of the war in his classic *All Quiet on the Western Front* (1929), which is told from the German point of view; John Dos Passos describes the war as a bitter experience in *Three Soldiers* (1921); and Ernest Hemingway portrays its futility in *A Farewell to Arms* (1929).

   All Quiet on the Western Front was made into a powerful movie (1930) from Remarque's novel. Told from the German point of view, it became an antiwar classic in the 1930s. *Reds* (1981) is a Hollywood film about socialists, feminists, and communists. It tells the story of John Reed, Louise Bryant, and their radical friends in Greenwich Village before the war and their support of the Russian Revolution after 1917.

Suggested Web Sites

http://www.lib.byu.edu/~rdh/wwi/

World War I Document Archive. This archive contains sources about World War I in general, not just on America's involvement.

http://www.pbs.org/wgbh/pages/amex/influenza

The American Experience: Influenza. This PBS site reveals the impact of the great flu epidemic of 1918.

http://scriptorium.lib.duke.edu/wlm/

Documents from the Women's Liberation Movement. Primary documents on-line from the Special Collections Library at Duke University provide firsthand information about the women's liberation movement.

http://www.rochester.edu/SBA/hisindx.html

History of the Suffrage Movement. This site includes a chronology, important texts relating to woman suffrage, and biographical information on Susan B. Anthony and Elizabeth Cady Stanton.

http://www.worldwar1.com/index.html

World War I: Trenches on the Web. This site provides a mass of data concerning the prosecution of the world's first global war.

http://lcweb.loc.gov/exhibits/african/afam011.html

Chicago: Destination for the Great Migration: African-American Mosaic Exhibition. This Library of Congress site looks at the black experience of the great migration through the lens of one prominent destination.

http://www.nationalgeographic.com/society/ngo/explorer/titanic/movie.html

Explorers Hall @ National Geographic. This site offers historical perspective and balanced coverage of the sinking of the *Titanic*, including a 14-minute 3-D tour of the ship's wreckage.

http://www.ushistoryplace.com

 A richly detailed on-line learning environment complete with interactive maps, timelines, history activities, primary source documents, and links to related American history sites.

23

AFFLUENCE *and* ANXIETY

CHAPTER OUTLINE

John and Lizzie Parker were black sharecroppers who lived in a "stubborn, ageless hut squatted on a little hill" in central Alabama. They had two daughters, one age six, the other already married. The whole family worked hard in the cotton fields, but they had little to show for their labor. One day in 1917, Lizzie straightened her shoulders and declared, "I'm through. I've picked my last sack of cotton. I've cleared my last field."

Like many southern African Americans, the Parkers sought opportunity and a better life in the North. World War I cut off the flow of immigrants from Europe, and suddenly there was a shortage of workers. Some companies sent special trains into the South to recruit African Americans. John Parker signed up with a mining company in West Virginia. The company offered free transportation for his family. "You will be allowed to get your food at the company store and there are houses awaiting for you," the agent promised.

The sound of the train whistle seemed to promise better days ahead for her family as Lizzie gathered her possessions and headed north. But it turned out that the houses in the company town in West Virginia were little better than those they left in Alabama. After deducting for rent and for supplies from the company store, almost no money was left at the end of the week. John hated the dirty and dangerous work in the mine and realized that he would never get ahead by staying there. Instead of venting his anger on his white boss, he ran away, leaving his family in West Virginia.

John drifted to Detroit, where he got a job with the American Car and Foundry Company. It was 1918, and the pay was good, more than he had ever made before. After a few weeks, he rented an apartment and sent for his family. For the first time, Lizzie had a gas stove and an indoor toilet, and Sally, who was now seven, started school. It seemed as if their dream had come true. John had always believed that if he worked hard and treated his fellow man fairly, he would succeed.

Detroit was not quite the dream, however. It was crowded with all kinds of migrants, attracted by the wartime jobs at the Ford Motor Company and other factories. The new arrivals increased the racial ten-sion already present in the city. Sally was beaten up by a gang of white youths at school. Even in their neighborhood, which had been solidly Jewish before their arrival, the shopkeeper and the old residents made it clear that they did not like blacks moving into their community. The Ku Klux Klan, which gained many new members in Detroit, also made life uncomfortable for the blacks who had moved north to seek jobs and opportunity. Suddenly the war ended, and almost immediately John lost his job. Then the landlord raised the rent, and the Parkers were forced to leave their apartment for housing in a section just outside the city near Eight Mile Road. The surrounding suburbs had paved streets, wide lawns, and elegant houses, but this black ghetto had dirt streets and shacks that reminded the Parkers of the company town where they had lived in West Virginia. Lizzie had to get along without her bathroom. Here there was no indoor plumbing and no electricity, only a pump in the yard and an outhouse.

The recession winter of 1921–1922 was particularly difficult. The auto industry and the other companies laid off most of their workers. John could find only part-time employment, while Lizzie worked as a domestic servant for white families. Because no bus route connected the black community to surrounding suburbs, she often had to trek miles through the snow. The shack they called home was freezing cold, and it was cramped because their married daughter and her husband had joined them in Detroit.

Lizzie did not give up her dream, however. With strength, determination, and a sense of humor, she kept the family together. In 1924, Sally entered high school. By the end of the decade, Sally had graduated from high school, and the Parkers finally had electricity and indoor plumbing in the house, though the streets were still unpaved. Those unpaved streets stood as a symbol of their unfulfilled dream. The Parkers, like most of the African Americans who moved north in the decade after World War I, had improved their lot, but they still lived outside Detroit—and, in many ways, outside America.

Like most Americans in the 1920s, the Parkers pursued the American dream of success. For them, a comfortable house and a steady job, a new bathroom, and an education for their younger daughter constituted that dream. For others during the decade, the symbol of success was a new automobile, a new suburban house, or perhaps making a killing on the stock market. The 1920s, the decade between the end of World War I and the stock market crash, has often been referred to as the "jazz age,"

The movies, illegal liquor, the stock market, and the new jazz dances all appear in Thomas Hart Benton's painting of the pleasures of urban life in the 1920s. (City Activities with Dance Hall, 1930, *Courtesy Maurice Segoura Gallery, New York*)

a time when the American people had one long party complete with flappers, speakeasies, illegal bathtub gin, and young people doing the Charleston long into the night. This frivolous interpretation has some basis in fact, but most Americans did not share in the party, for they were too busy struggling to make a living.

In this chapter, we will explore some of the conflicting trends of an exciting decade. First, we will examine the currents of intolerance that influenced almost all the events and social movements of the time. We will also look at some developments in technology, especially the automobile, which changed life for almost everyone during the 1920s and created the illusion of prosperity for all. We will then focus on groups—women, blacks, industrial workers, and farmers—who had their hopes raised but not always fulfilled during the decade. We will conclude by looking at the way business, politics, and foreign policy were intertwined during the age of Harding, Coolidge, and Hoover.

POSTWAR PROBLEMS

The enthusiasm for social progress that marked the war years evaporated in 1919. Public housing, social insurance, government ownership of the railroads, and many other experiments quickly ended. The sense of progress and purpose that the war had fostered withered. The year following the end of the war was marked by strikes and violence and by fear that Bolsheviks, blacks, foreigners, and others were destroying the American way of life. Some of the fear and intolerance resulted from wartime patriotism, some from the postwar economic and political turmoil that forced Americans to deal with new and immensely troubling situations.

Red Scare

Americans have often feared radicals and other groups that seem to be conspiring to overthrow the American way of life. In the 1840s, the 1890s, and at other times in the past, Catholics, Mormons, Populists, immigrants, and holders of many political views have all been attacked as dangerous and "un-American." But before 1917, anarchists seemed to pose the worst threat. The Russian Revolution changed that. *Bolshevik* suddenly became the most dangerous and devious radical, while *Communist* was transformed from a member of a utopian community to a dreaded, threatening subversive. For some Americans, Bolshevik and German became somehow mixed together, especially after the Treaty of Brest-Litovsk in 1918 removed the new Soviet state from the war. In the spring of 1919, with the Russian announcement of a policy of worldwide revolution and with Communist uprisings in Hungary and Bavaria, many Americans feared that the Communists planned to take over the United States. There were a few American Communists, but they never really threatened the United States or the American way of life.

Some idealists, like John Reed, found developments in Russia inspiring. Reed, the son of a wealthy businessman, was born in Oregon and went east to private school and then to Harvard. After graduation, he drifted to New York's Greenwich Village, where he joined his classmate Walter Lippmann as well as Max Eastman, Mabel Dodge, and other intellectuals and radicals. This group converted Reed to socialism and made him understand that "my happiness is built on the misery of others."

In Europe shortly after the war began, Reed was appalled by the carnage in what he considered a capitalistic war. The news of the Russian tsar's abdication in 1917 brought him to Russia just in time to witness the bloody Bolshevik takeover. His eyewitness account, *Ten Days That Shook the World,* optimistically predicted a worldwide revolution. However, when he saw how little hope there was for that revolution in postwar America, he returned to the Soviet Union. By the time he died from typhus in 1920, the authoritarian nature of the new Russian regime caused him to become disillusioned.

Working-Class Protest

Reed was one of the romantic American intellectuals who saw great hope for the future in the Russian Revolution. His mentor Lincoln Steffens, the muckraking journalist, remarked after a visit to the Soviet Union a few years later, "I have been over into the future and it works." But relatively few Americans, even among those who had been Socialists, and fewer still among the workers, joined the Communist party. Perhaps in all there were 25,000 to 40,000, and those were split into two groups, the American Communist party and the Communist Labor party. The threat to the American system of government was very slight. But in 1919, the Communists seemed to be a threat, particularly as a series of devastating strikes erupted across the country. Workers in the United States had suffered from wartime inflation, which had almost doubled prices between 1914 and 1919, while most wages remained the same. During 1919, more than four million workers took part in 4,000 strikes. Few wanted to overthrow the government; they demanded higher wages, shorter hours, and in some cases more control over the workplace.

On January 21, 1919, some 35,000 shipyard workers went on strike in Seattle, Washington. Within a few days, a general strike paralyzed the city; transportation and business stopped. The mayor of Seattle called for federal troops. Within five days, using strong-arm tactics, the mayor put down the strike and was hailed across the country as a "red-blooded patriot."

Yet the strikes continued elsewhere. In September 1919, all 343,000 employees of U.S. Steel walked out in an attempt to win an eight-hour day and an "American living wage." The average workweek in the steel industry in 1919 was 68.7 hours; the unskilled worker averaged $1,400 per year, while the minimum subsistence for a family of five that same year was estimated at $1,575. Within days, the strike spread to Bethlehem Steel.

From the beginning, the owners blamed the strikes on the Bolsheviks. They put ads in the newspapers urging workers to "Stand by America, Show Up the Red Agitator." They also imported strikebreakers, provoked riots, broke up union meetings, and finally used police and soldiers to end the strike. Eighteen strikers were killed. Because most people believed the Communists had inspired the strike, the issue of long hours and poor pay got lost, and eventually the union surrendered.

While the steel strike was still in progress, the police in Boston went on strike. Like most other workers, the police were struggling to survive on prewar salaries in inflationary times. The Boston newspapers blamed the strike on Communist influence, but one writer warned that the protest could not succeed because "behind Boston in this skirmish with Bolshevism stands Massachusetts and behind Massachusetts stands America." College students and army veterans volunteered to replace the police and prevent looting in the city. The president of Harvard assured the students that their grades would not suffer. The government quickly broke the strike and fired the policemen. When Samuel Gompers urged Governor Calvin Coolidge to ask the Boston authorities to reinstate them, Coolidge responded with the laconic statement that made him famous and eventually helped him win the presidency: "There is no right to strike against the public safety by anybody, anywhere, anytime."

To many Americans, strikes were bad enough, especially strikes that dangerous radicals seemingly inspired, but bombs were even worse. The "bomb-throwing radical" was almost a cliché, probably stemming from the hysteria over the Haymarket Riot of 1886. On April 28, 1919, a bomb was discovered in a small package delivered to the home of the mayor of Seattle. The next day, the maid of a former senator from Georgia opened a package, and a bomb blew her hands off. Other bombings occurred in June, including one that shattered the front of Attorney General A. Mitchell Palmer's home in Washington. The bombings seem to have been the work of misguided radicals who thought they might spark a genuine revolution in America. But their effect was to provide substantial evidence that revolution was around the corner, even though most American workers wanted only shorter hours, better working conditions, and a chance to realize the American dream.

The strikes and bombs, combined with the general postwar mood of distrust and suspicion, persuaded many people of a real and immediate threat to the nation. No one was more convinced than A. Mitchell Palmer. From a Quaker family in a small Pennsylvania town, the attorney general had graduated from Swarthmore College and had been admitted to the Pennsylvania bar in 1893 at the age of 21. After serving three terms as a congressman, he helped swing the Pennsylvania delegation to Wilson at the 1912 convention.

Wilson offered him the post of secretary of war, but Palmer's pacifism led him to refuse. He did support the United States' entry into the war, however, and served as alien property custodian, a job created by the Trading with the Enemy Act. This position apparently convinced him of the danger of radical subversive activities in America. The bombing of his home intensified his fears, and in the summer of 1919 he determined to find and destroy the Red network. He organized a special antiradical division within the Justice Department and put a young man named J. Edgar Hoover in charge of coordinating information on domestic radical activities.

Obsessed with the "Red Menace," Palmer instituted a series of raids, beginning in November 1919. Simultaneously, in several cities, his men rounded up 250 members of the Union of Russian Workers, many of whom were beaten and roughed up in the process. In December, 249 aliens, including the famous anarchist Emma Goldman, were deported, although very few were Communists and even fewer had any desire to overthrow the government of the United States. Palmer's men arrested 500 people in Detroit and 800 in Boston.

The Palmer raids, one of the most massive violations of civil liberties in American history to this date, found few dangerous radicals but did fan the flames of fear and intolerance in the country. In Indiana, a jury quickly acquitted a man who had killed an alien for yelling, "To hell with the United States." Billy Sunday, a Christian evangelist, suggested that the best solution was to shoot aliens rather than to deport them.

Palmer became a national hero for ferreting out Communists, but Assistant Secretary of State Louis Post insisted that the arrested aliens be given legal rights, and in the end, only about 600 were deported, out of the more than 5,000 arrested. The worst of the "Red Scare" was over by the end of 1920, but the fear of radicals and the emotional patriotism survived throughout the decade to color almost every aspect of politics, daily life, and social legislation.

The Red Scare promoted many patriotic organizations and societies determined to eliminate communism from American life. The best known was the American Legion, but there were also the American Defense Society, the Sentinels of the Republic (whose motto was "Every Citizen a Sentinel, Every Home a Sentry Box"), the United States Flag Association, and the Daughters of the American Revolution. Such groups provided a sense of purpose and a feeling of belonging in a rapidly changing America. But often what united their efforts was an obsessive fear of Communists and radicals.

Some organizations targeted women social reformers. One group attacked the "Hot-House, Hull House Variety of Parlor Bolshevists" and during the 1920s circulated a number of "spider-web charts" that purported to connect liberals and progressives, espe-cially progressive women, to Communist organizations. In one such chart, even the Needlework Guild and the Sunshine Society were accused of being influenced by Communists. The connections were made only through the use of half-truths, innuendo, and outright lies. To protest their charges did little good, for the accusers knew the truth and would not be deflected from their purpose of exterminating dangerous radicals.

Ku Klux Klan

The superpatriotic societies exploited the fear that radicals and Bolsheviks were subverting the American way of life from within. The Ku Klux Klan (KKK) went further. The Klan was organized in Georgia by William J. Simmons, a lay preacher, salesman, and member of many fraternal organizations. He adopted the name and white-sheet uniform of the old antiblack Reconstruction organization that was glorified in 1915 in the immensely popular but racist feature film *Birth of a Nation.* Simmons appointed himself head ("Imperial Wizard") of the new Klan.

Unlike the original organization, which took almost anyone who was white, the new Klan was thoroughly Protestant and explicitly antiforeign, anti-Semitic, and anti-Catholic. As an increasing number of second-

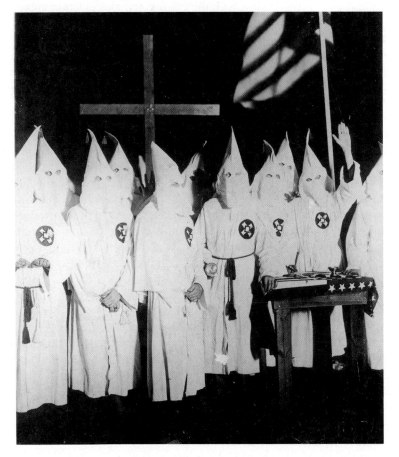

The Klan, with its elaborate rituals and white uniforms, exploited the fear of blacks, Jews, liberals, and Catholics while preaching "traditional" American values. The appeal of the Klan was not limited to the south. This is a photo of a Klan initiation ceremony. *(FPG International)*

and third-generation American Catholics began to achieve some success, even winning elections at the state and municipal level, many Protestants began to worry. The Klan declared that "America is Protestant and so it must remain." It opposed the teaching of evolution; glorified old-time religion; supported immigration restriction; denounced short skirts, petting, and "demon rum"; and upheld patriotism and the purity of women.

The Klan grew slowly until after the war. In some places, returning veterans could join the Klan and the American Legion at the same table. The Klan added over 100,000 new members in 1920 alone. It grew rapidly because of aggressive recruiting but also because of the fear and confusion of the postwar period.

The Klan flourished in small towns and rural areas in the South, where it set out to keep the returning black soldiers in their "proper place," but it soon spread throughout the country, and at least half the members came from urban areas. The Klan was especially strong in the working-class neighborhoods of Detroit, Indianapolis, Atlanta, and Chicago, where the migration of African Americans and other ethnic groups increased fear of everything "un-American." At the peak of its power, the Klan had several million members, many of them from the middle class. In some states, especially Indiana, Oregon, Oklahoma, Louisiana, and Texas, it influenced politics and determined some elections. The Klan's power declined after 1925 because of a series of internal power struggles and several scandals. The most spectacular case involved the head of the Illinois Klan who raped a secretary and then watched her die after she took poison. The Klan survived in some areas into the 1930s, but it had all but disap-peared by the outbreak of World War II. Yet the end of the Klan did not mean the end of prejudice.

The Sacco-Vanzetti Case

One result of the Red Scare and the unreasoned fear of foreigners and radicals, which dragged on through much of the decade, was the conviction and sentencing of two Italian anarchists, Nicola Sacco and Bartolomeo Vanzetti. Arrested in 1920 for allegedly murdering a guard during a robbery of the shoe factory in South Braintree, Massachusetts, the two were convicted and sentenced to die in the summer of 1921 on what many liberals considered circumstantial and flimsy evidence. Indeed, it seemed to many that the two Italians, who spoke in broken English and were admitted anarchists, were punished because of their radicalism and their foreign appearance.

Even now, it is not clear whether Sacco and Vanzetti were guilty, but the case took on symbolic significance as many intellectuals in Europe and America rallied to their defense and to the defense of civil liberties. Appeal after appeal failed, but finally the governor of Massachusetts appointed a commission to reexamine the evidence in the case. The commission reaffirmed the verdict, and the two were executed in the electric chair on August 23, 1927. But the case and the cause would not die. On the fiftieth anniversary of their deaths in 1977, Governor Michael Dukakis of Massachusetts exonerated Sacco and Vanzetti and cleared their names.

Religious Intolerance

The KKK and well-publicized cases like Sacco-Vanzetti touched a relatively small number of people, but a

Bartolomeo Vanzetti and Nicola Sacco, immortalized in paintings by Ben Shahn, became important symbols for liberals fighting prejudice in the 1920s. (*Bartolomeo Vanzetti and Nicola Sacco,* 1931–32. *Tempera on paper over composition board, 10-1/2" by 14-1/2". Gift of Abby Aldrich Rockefeller. Photograph © 1997 The Museum of Modern Art, New York)*

general spirit of intolerance permeated the decade and influenced the lives of millions. In Dearborn, Michigan, Henry Ford published anti-Semitic diatribes in the *Dearborn Independent*, and many country clubs and resort hotels prohibited Jews from even entering the doors. Unable to frequent the fashionable resorts, Jews built their own in the Catskills in New York State, Long Branch in New Jersey, and other areas. Many colleges, private academies, and medical schools had Jewish quotas, some openly and others informally, and many suburbs explicitly limited residents to "Christians." Catholics, too, were prohibited from many fashionable and fraternal organizations as well as many country clubs, but unlike Jews, Catholics created their own schools and colleges. Few Catholics even tried to enroll in the elite colleges where bias against Catholics and Catholicism remained. There had always been a great deal of prejudice and intolerance in the United States, but during the decade of the 1920s, much of that intolerance was made more fixed and formal.

∾ A PROSPERING ECONOMY

Although the decade after World War I was a time of intolerance and anxiety, it was also a time of industrial expansion and widespread prosperity. After recovering from a postwar depression in 1921 and 1922, the economy took off. Fueled by new technology, more efficient planning and management, and innovative advertising, industrial production almost doubled during the decade, and the gross national product rose by an astonishing 40 percent. A construction boom created new suburbs around American cities, and a new generation of skyscrapers transformed the cities themselves. However, the benefits of this prosperity fell unevenly on the many social groups forming American society.

The Rising Standard of Living

Signs of the new prosperity appeared in many forms. Millions of sturdy homes and apartments were built and equipped with the latest conveniences. The number of telephones installed nearly doubled between 1915 and 1930. Plastics, rayon, and cellophane altered the habits of millions of Americans, and new products, such as cigarette lighters, reinforced concrete, dry ice, and Pyrex glass, created new demands unheard of a decade before.

Perhaps the most tangible sign of the new prosperity was the modern American bathroom. For years, the various functions we associate with the bathroom were separated. There was an outhouse or privy, a portable tin bathtub filled with water heated on the kitchen stove, and a pitcher and washbasin in

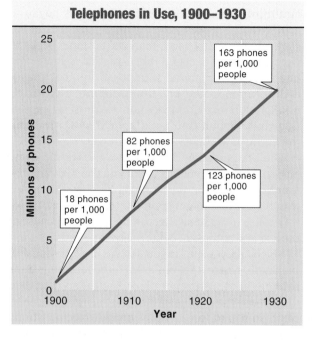

The telephone, though still a primitive instrument in the 1920s, changed business practices, social life, and even dating customs for the middle class. Source: U.S. Bureau of the Census.

the bedroom. Hotels and the urban upper class began to install cast-iron bathtubs and primitive flush toilets in the late nineteenth century, but not until the early 1920s did the enameled tub, toilet, and washbasin become standard. By 1925, American factories turned out five million enameled bathroom fixtures annually. The bathroom, with unlimited hot water, privacy, and clean white fixtures, symbolized American affluence.

In sharp contrast to the nineteenth century, Americans had more leisure time, a shorter work week, and more vacations with pay. The American diet also improved during the decade. Health improved and life expectancy increased. Educational opportunities also expanded. In 1900 only one in ten young people of high school age remained in school; by 1930 that number had increased to six in ten, and much of the improvement came in the 1920s. In 1900, only one college-age person in 33 attended an institution of higher learning; by 1930, the ratio was one in seven, and over a million people were enrolled in the nation's colleges.

The Rise of the Modern Corporation

The structure and practice of American business were transformed in the 1920s. After a crisis created by the economic downturn of 1920–1922, business boomed until the crash of 1929. Mergers increased during the decade at a rate greater than at any time since the end of the 1890s—there were more than 1,200 mergers in 1929 alone—creating such giants as General Electric, General Motors, Sears Roebuck, Du Pont, and U.S. Rubber. These were not monopolies but oligopolies (industry domination spread among a few large firms). By 1930, the 200 largest corporations controlled almost half the corporate wealth in the country. Large businesses also diversified during the decade. GE and Westinghouse began to produce household appliances and radios; Du Pont moved into plastics, paints, dyes, and film. These large corporations also began to spend more money on research and development. This was especially true of the chemical and electrical companies that hired their own scientists and technicians to do pure research as well as to develop new products. During the 1920s the research departments of American corporations became increasingly independent of European scientific expertise.

Perhaps the most important business trend of the decade was the emergence of a new kind of manager. No longer did family entrepreneurs make decisions relating to prices, wages, and output. Alfred P. Sloan, Jr., an engineer who reorganized General Motors, was a prototype of the new kind of manager. He divided the company into components, freeing the top managers to concentrate on planning new products, controlling inventory, and integrating the whole operation. Marketing and advertising became as important as production, and many businesses began to spend more money on research. The new manager often had a large staff but owned no part of the company. He was usually an expert at cost accounting and analyzing data. Increasingly, he was a graduate of one of the new business colleges.

Continuing and extending the trends started by Frederick Taylor before World War I, the new managers tried to keep employees working efficiently, but they used more than the stopwatch and the assembly line. They introduced pensions, recreation facilities, cafeterias, and, in some cases, paid vacations and profit-sharing plans. The managers were not being altruistic, however; "welfare capitalism" was designed to reduce worker discontent and to discourage labor unions.

Planning was the key to the new corporate structure, and planning often meant a continuation of the business–government cooperation that had developed during World War I. Experts from philanthropic foundations, the National Bureau of Economic Research, and the U.S. Department of Commerce worked together hoping that they could provide a middle ground between collectivism and laissez-faire economy. All the planning and the new managerial authority failed to prevent the economic collapse of 1929, but the modern corporation survived the depression to exert a growing influence on American life in the 1930s and after.

Electrification

The 1920s also marked the climax of the "second industrial revolution." During the late nineteenth century, American industry had manufactured goods intended primarily for other producers. In the first quarter of the twentieth century, as industries like coal, textiles, and steel stabilized or declined, new manufacturing concerns that produced rubber, synthetic fabrics, chemicals, and petroleum arose. They focused on goods for consumers, such as silk stockings, washing machines, and cars.

Powering the second industrial revolution was electricity—a form of energy that rapidly replaced steam power after 1900. In the previous two decades, inventors such as Thomas A. Edison and George Westinghouse had developed generators for producing electric current and methods for transmitting it and using it to drive machinery. Edison's illuminating company opened the first commercial power station in New York in 1882; by the end of the century, more than 3,000 stations were supplying businesses and homes with electricity. Meanwhile, Edison's most famous invention, the electric lightbulb, was rapidly replacing gas lanterns in homes and on streets.

Between 1900 and 1920, the replacement of steam power by electricity worked as profound a change as had the substitution of steam power for water power after the Civil War. In 1902, electricity supplied a mere 2 percent of all industrial power; by 1929, fully 80 percent derived from electrical generators. Less than one of every ten American homes was supplied with electricity in 1907, but more than two-thirds were by 1929. Powered by electricity, American industries reached new heights of productivity. By 1929, the workforce was turning out twice as many goods as a similarly sized workforce had ten years before.

Electricity brought dozens of gadgets and labor-saving devices into the home. Washing machines and electric irons gradually reduced the drudgery of washday for women, and vacuum cleaners, electric toasters, and sewing machines lightened housework. But the new machines still needed human direction and did not reduce the time the average housewife spent doing housework. For many poor urban and rural women, the traditional female tasks of carrying, pushing, pulling, and lifting went on as they had for centuries. In many ways, the success of the electric revolution increased the contrast in American life. The "great white ways" of the cities symbolized progress, but they also made the darkness of slums and hamlets seem even more forbidding.

Recovering the Past

ADVERTISING

ave you ever noticed that television commercials can often be more interesting and creative than the programs? One authority has suggested that the best way for a foreign visitor to understand the American character and popular culture is to study television commercials. Television advertising, the thesis goes, appeals to basic cultural assumptions. The nature of advertising not only reveals for historians the prejudices, fears, values, and aspirations of a people but also makes an impact on historical development itself, influencing patterns of taste and purchasing habits. One modern critic calls advertising a "peculiarly American force that now compares with such long-standing institutions as the school and church in the magnitude of its social impact."

As long as manufacturing was local and limited, there was no need to advertise. Before the Civil War, for example, the local area could usually absorb all that was produced; therefore, a simple announcement in a local paper was sufficient to let people know that a particular product was available. But when factories began producing more than the local market could ordinarily consume, advertising came into play to create a larger demand.

Although national advertising began with the emergence of "name brands" in the late nineteenth century, it did not achieve the importance it now holds until the 1920s. In 1918, the total gross advertising revenue in magazines was $58.5 million. By 1920, it had more than doubled to $129.5 million, and by 1929, it was nearly $200 million. These figures should not be surprising in a decade that often equated advertising with religion. The biblical Moses was called the "ad-writer for the Deity," and in a best-selling book, Bruce Barton, a Madison Avenue advertiser, reinterpreted Jesus, the "man nobody knows," as a master salesman. Wrote Barton: "He would be a national advertiser today."

The designers of ads began to study psychology to determine what motives, conscious or unconscious, influenced consumers. One psychologist concluded that the appeal to the human instinct for "gaining social prestige" would sell the most goods. Another way to sell products, many learned, was to create anxiety in the mind of the consumer over body odor, bad breath, oily hair, dandruff, pimples, and other embarrassing ailments.

"...and Jane, dear... Jack just raved about my teeth."

"I just smiled my prettiest smile... and let him rave. I could have said 'Of course I have beautiful teeth... I've used Colgate's all my life'. But I didn't want Jack to think I was a living advertisement for Colgate's tooth paste."

* * * * *

Beautiful teeth glisten gloriously. They compel the admiration of all who see them. And there is health as well as beauty in gleaming teeth; for when they are scrupulously kept clean, germs and poisons of decay can't lurk and breed around them.

Remove Those Causes of Decay

Save yourself the embarrassment so often caused by poor teeth. Fight the germs of tooth decay.

Colgate's will keep your teeth scrupulously clean. It reaches all the hard-to-get-at places between the teeth and around the edges of the gums, and so removes causes of tooth decay. It is the dependable tooth paste for you to use.

Washes—Polishes—Protects

The principal ingredients of Colgate's are mild soap and fine chalk, the two things that dental authorities say a safe dental cream should contain. The combined action of these ingredients washes, polishes and protects the delicate enamel of your teeth.

Use Colgate's Regularly

Just remember that beautiful, healthy teeth are more a matter of good care than of good luck. Use Colgate's after meals and at bedtime. It will keep your teeth clean and gloriously attractive.

And you'll like its taste... even children love to use it regularly.

Priced right too! Large tube 25c.

Colgate's
Established 1806

COLGATE'S
RIBBON DENTAL CREAM

Toothpaste advertisement.

738

In 1921, the Lambert Company used the term *halitosis* for bad breath in an ad for Listerine. Within six years, sales of Listerine had increased from a little over 100,000 bottles a year to more than four million.

The appeal to sex also sold products, advertisers soon found, as did the desire for the latest style or invention. But perhaps the most important thing advertisers marketed was youth. "We are going to sell every artificial thing there is," a cosmetic salesman wrote in 1926, "and above all it is going to be young-young-young! We make women feel young." A great portion of the ads were aimed at women. As one trade journal announced: "The proper study of mankind is man . . . , but the proper study of markets is woman."

Look at the accompanying advertisements carefully. What do they tell you about American culture in the 1920s? What do they suggest about attitudes toward women? Do they reveal any special anxieties? How are they similar to and different from advertising today?

For Clean-up King I Nominate . . .

by LOU GEHRIG

New York Yankees' Clean-up Ace Makes Novel Choice for All-Time Honor

I DON'T need to tell baseball fans how important the "clean-up" (number four) man is in the batting line-up. With three reliable hitters batting ahead of him, it is his wallops that bring in the runs.

In my thirteen years of big league baseball I have watched some of the most famous "clean-up" men in the history of the game. But the other day in Boston I had the pleasure of seeing the "clean-up" king that gets my vote for the "all-time" honors. Strangely enough, this "clean-up" king isn't a slugger at all. Instead of cleaning up the bases, this one's specialty is cleaning up faces.

Here's how it happened. While in Boston playing the Red Sox, I made an inspection trip through the Gillette Safety Razor factory. There I discovered that what is true of baseball is also true of Gillette Blades. In baseball, the pick of the raw material is tried out, tested, and trained for the big league teams. At the Gillette factory I found that they buy only the finest steel, and put it through gruelling tests before it is made into Gillette Blades.

For instance, like a rookie baseball player, Gillette Blade steel has to be hardened and tempered.

To do this, Gillette uses electric furnaces, each one controlled by a device which can tell in an instant if the steel passing through the furnaces requires more heat or less heat. Faster than a speedball, the signal is flashed from the box to a great battery of switches, and the heat is raised or lowered accordingly. Then to make doubly sure that there is no possibility of error, they X-ray the steel with an electro-magnetic tester to detect hidden flaws.

A good ball player has to have precision and accuracy, too . . . and that's where Gillette chalks up a winning score. Grinding machines, adjustable to 1/10,000 of an inch give Gillette Blades shaving edges so keen you can't see them, even with the most powerful microscope.

These are some of the reasons why I nominate the Gillette Blade for all-time Clean-up King. For when it comes to cleaning up on stubborn bristles—with the greatest of ease and comfort—Gillette hits a home run with the bases loaded. Yes, Sir!—if baseball could only train players as accurately and efficiently as Gillette makes razor blades, we'd all find it easy to bat 1000.

With these important facts before you, why let anyone deprive you of shaving comfort by selling you a substitute! Ask for Gillette Blades and be sure to get them.

GILLETTE SAFETY RAZOR COMPANY, BOSTON, MASS.

Razor blade advertisement. *(R. Kravette, Jericho, New York)*

Luxury · The improved Packard Eight is the supremely luxurious car. It is designed and built for those favored few who may and do demand the comfort and ease of their own drawing rooms in motor travel.

Fast or slow, flashing through the maze of metropolitan congestion, or smoothly annihilating distance at almost aircraft speed in the open, Packard passengers know the luxury of truly restful transportation.

The graceful beauty of Packard lines, the roominess of the car's interior, the quiet good taste of its upholstery and appointments, the silent ease of motion, and the sense of security which comes with tremendous power under sure control—all contribute to the mental satisfaction and physical repose of the Packard Eight owner.

Here, the discriminating man or woman finds ideal performance, beauty, distinction and comfort perfectly combined.

PACKARD
ASK THE MAN WHO OWNS ONE

Automobile advertisement (1929). *(Corbis-Bettmann)*

Automobile Culture

Automobile manufacturing, like electrification, underwent spectacular growth in the 1920s. The automobile was one major factor in the postwar economic boom. It stimulated and transformed the petroleum, steel, and rubber industries. The auto forced the construction and improvement of streets and highways and caused the spending of millions of dollars on labor and concrete. In 1925, the secretary of agriculture approved the first uniform numbering system for the nation's highways, but it was still an adventure to drive from one city to another.

The auto created new suburbs and allowed families to live many miles from their work. The filling station, the diner, and the tourist court became familiar and eventually standardized objects on the American scene. Traffic lights, stop signs, billboards, and parking lots appeared. Hitching posts and watering troughs became rarer, and gradually the garage replaced the livery stable. The auto changed the look of the American landscape and threatened the environment as well. Oil and gasoline contaminated streams, and piles of old tires and rusting hulks of discarded cars became a familiar sight along the highways. At the same time, the emissions from thousands and then millions of internal combustion engines polluted the air. The increasing use of nonrenewable fossil fuels was already apparent in the 1920s, and it was a trend that would continue. In 1916, American oil refineries produced 50 million barrels of gasoline; in 1929, production had increased to 425 million barrels. But there was no turning back. The age of the auto had replaced the age of the horse.

The auto changed American life in other ways. It led to the decline of the small crossroads store as well as many small churches because the rural family could now drive to the larger city or town. The tractor changed methods of farming. Trucks replaced the horse and wagon and altered the marketing of farm products. Buses began to eliminate the one-room school, because it was now possible to transport students to larger schools. The automobile allowed young people for the first time to escape the chaperoning of parents. It was hardly the "house of prostitution on wheels" that one judge called it, but it did change courting habits in all parts of the country.

Gradually, as the decade progressed, the automobile became not just transportation but a sign of status. Advertising helped create the impression that it was the symbol of the good life, of sex, freedom, and speed. The auto in turn transformed advertising and design. It even altered the way products were purchased. By 1926, three-fourths of the cars sold were bought on some kind of deferred-payment plan. Installment credit, first tried by a group of business-men in Toledo, Ohio, in 1915 to sell more autos, was soon used to promote sewing machines, refrigerators, and other consumer products. "Buy now, pay later" became the American way.

The United States had a love affair with the auto from the beginning. There were 8,000 motor vehicles registered in the country in 1900, and nearly a million in 1912. But only in the 1920s did the auto come within the reach of middle-class consumers. In 1929, Americans purchased 4.5 million cars, and by the end of that year, nearly 27 million were registered. Automobile culture was a mass movement.

The auto industry, like most American businesses, went through a period of consolidation in the 1920s. In 1908, more than 250 companies were manufacturing automobiles in the United States. By 1929, only 44 remained.

Many men contributed to the development and production of the auto—William Durant organized General Motors; Charles Kettering, an engineering genius, developed the electric self-starter; and Ransom E. Olds built the first mass-produced, moderately priced, light car. Above all the others loomed a name that would become synonymous with the automobile itself—Henry Ford.

Ford had the reputation of being a progressive industrial leader and a champion of the common people. As with all men and women who take on symbolic significance, the truth is less dramatic than the stories. Ford is often credited with inventing the assembly line. In actuality it was the work of a team of engineers. But the Ford Motor Company was the first organization to perfect the moving assembly line and mass-production technology. Introduced in 1913, the new method reduced the time it took to produce a car from 14 hours to an hour and a half. It was the perfect application of Frederick Taylor's system of breaking down each operation into its components, applying careful timing, and integrating the laborer with the machine. The product of the carefully planned system was the Model T, the prototype of the inexpensive family car.

In 1914, Ford startled the country by announcing that he was increasing the minimum pay of the Ford assembly-line worker to $5 a day (almost twice the national average pay for factory workers). Ford was not a humanitarian. He wanted a dependable workforce and understood that skilled workers were less likely to quit if they received good pay. Ford was one of the first to appreciate that workers were consumers as well as producers and that they might buy Model T Fords. But work in the Ford factory had its disadvantages. Work on the assembly line was repetitious and numbing. "You could drop over dead" one worker recalled, "and they wouldn't stop the line." And when

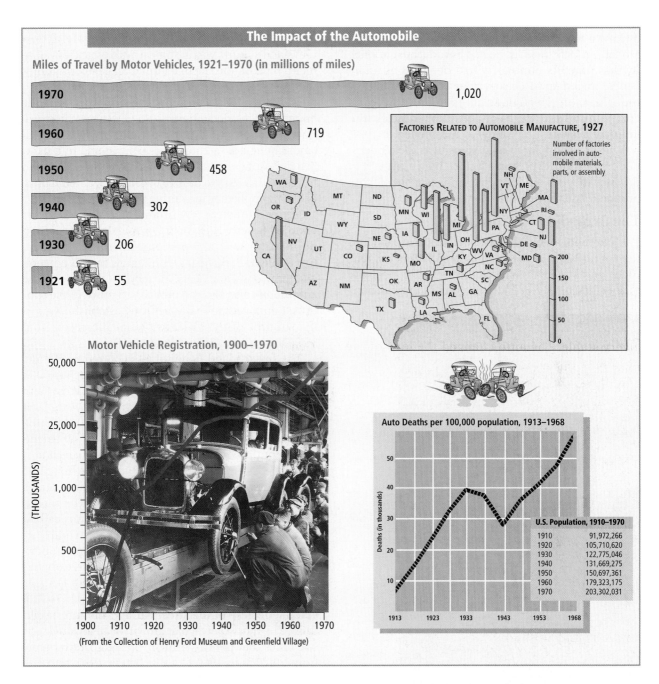

The Impact of the Automobile

Miles of Travel by Motor Vehicles, 1921–1970 (in millions of miles)

Year	Miles
1970	1,020
1960	719
1950	458
1940	302
1930	206
1921	55

FACTORIES RELATED TO AUTOMOBILE MANUFACTURE, 1927

Number of factories involved in automobile materials, parts, or assembly

Motor Vehicle Registration, 1900–1970

(THOUSANDS)

(From the Collection of Henry Ford Museum and Greenfield Village)

Auto Deaths per 100,000 population, 1913–1968

Deaths (in thousands)

U.S. Population, 1910–1970	
1910	91,972,266
1920	105,710,620
1930	122,775,046
1940	131,669,275
1950	150,697,361
1960	179,323,175
1970	203,302,031

the line closed down, as it did periodically, the workers were released without compensation.

Henry Ford was not an easy man for whom to work. One newspaper account in 1928 called him "an industrial fascist—the Mussolini of Detroit." He ruthlessly pressured his dealers and used them to bail him out of difficult financial situations. Instead of borrowing money from a bank, he forced dealers to buy extra cars, trucks, and tractors. He used spies on the assembly lines and fired workers and executives at the least provocation. But he did produce a car that transformed America.

The Model T, which cost $600 in 1912, was reduced gradually in price until it sold for only $290 in 1924. The "Tin Lizzie," as it was affectionately called, was light and easily repaired. Some owners claimed all one needed were a pair of pliers and some baling wire to keep it running. If it got stuck on bad roads, as it often did, it could be lifted out by a reasonably healthy man. Replacement parts were standardized and widely available.

The Model T did not change from year to year, and it did not deviate from its one color, black. Except for adding a self-starter, offering a closed model, and making a few minor face-lift changes, Ford kept the Model T in 1927 much as he had introduced it in 1909. By that time, its popularity had declined as many people traded up to sleeker, more colorful, and, they thought, more prestigious autos put out by Ford's competitors, and wages at Ford dipped below the industry average. The Model A, introduced in 1927, was never as popular or as successful as the Model T, but the gigantic River Rouge factory, built especially to produce the new model, became the symbol of mass production in the new era.

The Exploding Metropolis

The automobile caused American cities to expand into the countryside. In the late nineteenth century, railroads and streetcars had created suburbs near the major cities, but the great expansion of suburban pop-

While some artists and writers in the 1920s looked back nostalgically to a simpler age, others admired the city and the machine. Louis Lozowick, influenced by European modernism, painted geometric portraits of American cities and factories such as this depiction of Pittsburgh. He was part of a group of artists inspired by the inherent beauty of the industrial order in the 1920s. *(Collection of the Whitney Museum of American Art, Gift of Louise and Joe Wissert)*

ulation occurred in the 1920s. Shaker Heights, a Cleveland suburb, was in some ways a typical development. Built on the site of a former Shaker community, the new suburb was planned and developed by two businessmen. They controlled the size and style of the homes and restricted buyers. No blacks were allowed. Curving roads led off the main auto boulevards, and landscaping and natural areas contributed to a park-like atmosphere. The suburb increased in population from 1,700 in 1919 to over 15,000 in 1929, and the price of lots multiplied by ten during the decade.

Other suburbs grew in an equally spectacular manner. Beverly Hills, near Los Angeles, increased in population by 2,485 percent during the decade. Grosse Point Park, near Detroit, grew by 725 percent, and Elmwood Park, near Chicago, by 716 percent. The automobile also allowed industry to move to the suburbs. Employees in manufacturing establishments in the suburbs of the 11 largest cities increased from 365,000 in 1919 to 1.2 million in 1937.

The biggest land boom of all occurred in Florida, where the city of Miami mushroomed from 30,000 in 1920 to 75,000 in 1925. One plot of land in West Palm Beach sold for $800,000 in 1923 and two years later was worth $4 million. A hurricane in 1926 ended the Florida land boom temporarily, but most cities and their suburbs continued to grow during the decade.

The census of 1920 indicated that for the first time, more than half the population of the United States lived in "urban areas" of more than 2,500. The census designation of an urban area was a little misleading because a town of 5,000 could still be more rural than urban. A more significant concept was the metropolitan area of at least 100,000 people. There were only 52 of these areas in 1900, but in 1930 there were 115.

The automobile transformed the city and led to the gradual decline of the street car and the interurban trolly. The most spectacular growth of all took place in two cities that the car virtually created. Detroit grew from 300,000 in 1900 to 1,837,000 in 1930, and Los Angeles expanded from 114,000 in 1900 to 1,778,000 in 1930. With sprawling subdivisions connected by a growing network of roads, Los Angeles was the city of the future.

Cities expanded horizontally during the 1920s, sprawling into the countryside, but city centers grew vertically. A building boom that peaked near the end of the decade created new skylines for most urban centers. Even cities such as Tulsa, Dallas, Kansas City, Memphis, and Syracuse built skyscrapers. By 1929, there were 377 buildings of over 20 stories in American cities. Many were started just before the stock market crash ended the building boom, and the empty offices stood as a stark reminder of the limits of expansion. The most famous skyscraper of all, the Empire State

TEN LARGEST CITIES IN 1900 AND 1930*			
1900		**1930**	
1. New York	4,023,000	1. New York	9,423,000
2. Chicago	1,768,000	2. Chicago	3,870,000
3. Philadelphia	1,458,000	3. Philadelphia	2,399,000
4. Boston	905,000	4. Detroit	1,837,000
5. Pittsburgh	622,000	5. Los Angeles	1,778,000
6. St. Louis	612,000	6. Boston	1,545,000
7. Baltimore	543,000	7. Pittsburgh	1,312,000
8. San Francisco	444,000	8. San Francisco	1,104,000
9. Cincinnati	414,000	9. St. Louis	1,094,000
10. Cleveland	402,000	10. Cleveland	1,048,000

*Figures are for the entire metropolitan areas, including suburbs.
Source: U.S. Bureau of the Census.

Building in New York, which towers 102 stories in the air, was finished in 1931 but not completely occupied until after World War II.

A Communications Revolution

Changing communications altered the way many Americans lived as well as the way they conducted business. The telephone was first demonstrated in 1876. By 1899, more than a million phones were in operation. During the 1920s, the number of homes with phones increased from 9 to 13 million. Still, by the end of the decade, more than half of American homes were without phones.

The radio even more than the telephone symbolized the technological and communicational changes of the 1920s. Department stores quickly began to stock radios, or crystal sets as they were called, but many Americans in the 1920s built their own receivers. The first station to begin commercial broadcasting was WWJ in Detroit in the summer of 1920. When WWJ and KDKA in Pittsburgh broadcast the election returns in 1920, they ushered in a new era in politics. The next year WJZ of Newark, New Jersey, broadcast the World Series, beginning a process that would transform baseball and eventually football and basketball as well. Five hundred stations took to the airwaves in

Department stores opened Radio Departments during the 1920s. This shopper listens to an early model through ear phones. By the end of the decade, the ear phones were no longer necessary, and the number of families owning at least one radio jumped from 60,000 in 1922 to nearly 14,000,000 in 1932. *(Brown Brothers)*

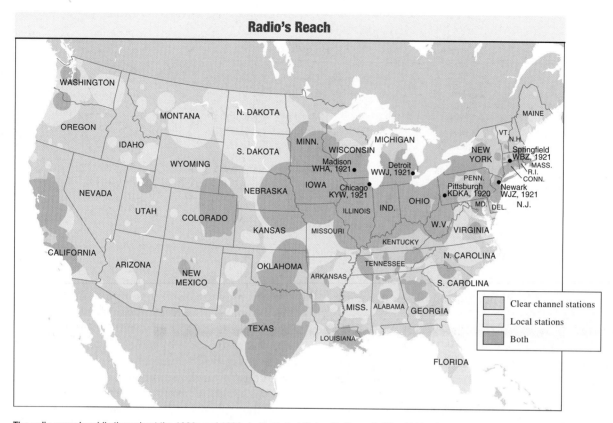

Radio's Reach

The radio spread rapidly throughout the 1920s and 1930s in the United States. By the end of the 1930s almost all Americans could tune in to their favorite programs, although in some rural areas, especially in the West, reception was possible only at night. Static caused by storms made the signal fade in and out everywhere.

1922 alone, many of them sponsored by department stores and others by newspapers and colleges. In the same year, a radio station in New York broadcast the first commercial, an indication that the airways would be used to increase the demand for the goods the factories were producing.

Much early broadcasting consisted of classical music, but soon came news analysis and coverage of presidential inaugurals and important events. Some stations produced live dramas, but it was the serials such as "Amos 'n' Andy" that more than any other programs made radio a national medium. Millions of people scattered across the country could sit in their living rooms (and after 1927, in their cars) listening to the same program. The record industry grew just as rapidly. By the end of the decade, people in all sections of the country were humming the same popular songs. Actors and announcers became celebrities. The music, voice, and sound of the radio, even more than the sound of the automobile, marked the end of silence and, to a certain extent, the end of privacy.

Even more dramatic was the phenomenon of the movies. Forty million viewers a week went to the movies in 1922, and by 1929 that had increased to over 100 million. Men, women, and children flocked to

small theaters in the towns and to movie palaces in the cities, where they could dream of romance or adventure. Charlie Chaplin, Rudolph Valentino, Lillian Gish, and Greta Garbo were more famous and more important to millions of Americans than were most government officials. The motion pictures, which before the war had attracted mostly the working class, now seemed to appeal across class, regional, and generational lines.

The movies had the power to influence attitudes and ideas. In the 1920s, many parents feared that the movies would dictate ideas about sex and life. One young college woman remembered, "One day I went to see Viola Dana in *The Five Dollar Baby*. The scenes which showed her as a baby fascinated me so that I stayed to see it over four times. I forgot home, dinner and everything. About eight o'clock mother came after me." She also admitted that the movies taught her how to smoke, and in some of the movies "there were some lovely scenes which just got me all hot 'n' bothered."

Not only movie stars became celebrities in the 1920s. Sports figures such as Babe Ruth, Bobby Jones, Jack Dempsey, and Red Grange were just as famous. The great spectator sports of the decade owed much to the increase of leisure time and to the automobile,

Opening night, October 6, 1927, at a theater in Times Square, New York. *The Jazz Singer* with Al Jolson, the first commercially successful film with sound, attracted large audiences. The silent film continued to survive for a few years but gradually the sound film took over, forcing theaters to buy new equipment and actors to change their style. Some silent film stars with unattractive voices were forced to retire. *(The Museum of Modern Art, New York, Film Stills Archive)*

the radio, and the mass-circulation newspaper. Thousands drove automobiles to college towns to watch football heroes perform. Millions listened for scores or read about the results the next day. One writer in 1924 called this era "the age of play." He might better have called it "the age of the spectator." The popularity of sports, like the movies and radio, was in part the product of technology.

The year 1927 seemed to mark the beginning of the new age of mechanization and progress. That was the year Henry Ford produced his 15 millionth car and introduced the Model A. During that year, radio-telephone service was established between San Francisco and Manila. The first radio network was organized (CBS), and the first talking movie was released (*The Jazz Singer*). In 1927, the Holland Tunnel, the first underwater vehicular roadway, connected New York and New Jersey. It was also the year that Charles Lindbergh flew from New York to Paris in his single-engine plane in 33½ hours. Lindbergh was not the first to fly the Atlantic, but he was the first to fly it alone, an accomplishment that won him $25,000 in prize money and captured the world's imagination. He was young and handsome, and his feat seemed to represent not only the triumph of an individual but also the triumph of the machine. Lindbergh never talked of his accomplishments in the first person; he always said "we," meaning his airplane as well. He was greeted by four million people when he returned to New York for a triumphant ticker-tape parade. Like many a movie star or sports hero, he had become an instant celebrity. When

Americans cheered Lindbergh, they were reaffirming their belief in the American dream and their faith in individual initiative as well as in technology.

Charles Lindbergh standing next to his plane, "The Spirit of St. Louis." His feat of flying alone from New York to Paris in 1927 and his youthful good looks made him an instant hero. President Coolidge presented him with the Distinguished Flying Cross and called his achievement a shining example of heroic individualism combined with American genius and industry. *(Library of Congress)*

Technology Changes the American People

WIRELESS COMMUNICATION

✶

On the night of April 14, 1912, the *Titanic*, the largest ship ever built, hit an iceberg in the North Atlantic and sank in just over an hour. When the giant ship went down, it took more than 1,500 passengers to their deaths (651 were saved). While the stricken ship settled in the water, wireless operators on board sent out distress signals that were picked up by at least ten ships and a wire-less station in Newfoundland. Only one of the ships was close enough to rescue passengers, but news of the disaster became headlines in the newspapers of Europe and America the next morning. Thanks to the wireless, millions of people received the news almost simultaneously, and they experienced a shared sense of loss.

Ships had been lost at sea almost from the beginning of history, but until the invention of the wireless, they usually just disappeared. A ship would be missing and then presumed lost, and no one would ever know the exact nature of the tragedy, since communication to other ships or shore was impossible. All types of messages traveled slowly. In the eighteenth century, it often took months for letters to cross the Atlantic, and distant events were reported in newspapers many weeks after they happened. The wireless helped to usher in an era of instant news, and it dramatically changed the way people perceived the world. The *New York Times* for April 21, 1912, commenting on the *Titanic* and the magic of the wireless, observed: "Night and day all the year round the millions upon the earth and the thousands upon the sea now reach out and grasp the thin air and use it as a thing more potent for human aid than any strand of wire or cable that was ever spun or woven."

Guglielmo Marconi invented the wireless in 1894, and less than a decade later, U.S. President Theodore Roosevelt and King Edward VII of Great Britain used it to exchange greetings across the Atlantic. By 1912, the wireless was a common, if not always predictable, form of international communication, linking ships to land in a system of instant communication. It joined the telegraph (1844) and the telephone (1876) in transforming communication and in making it possible to seem to be in two places at the same time. Marconi, who, like

A contemporary French drawing of the sinking of the *Titanic*. (*The Granger Collection, New York*)

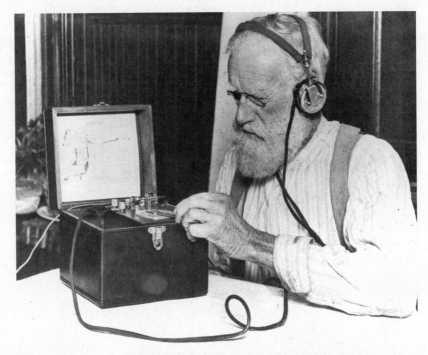

Most farmers did not own a radio until the end of the 1930s when they finally got electricity, but for those living in the cities, the radio altered lives and brought a new magic of sound into 2 or 3 million households in the 1920s. This early radio was battery-powered and had an antenna wire (seen at left) that connected to an outside aerial antenna. Still, even with antenna and headset, the reception was probably poor. *(Corbis-Bettmann)*

all great inventors, built on the work of others, succeeded in sending signals in Morse code over the invisible electromagnetic airwaves. Other experimenters soon successfully transmitted the human voice and music over the same waves. The wireless occupied a midpoint in the rising curve of technology that led to radio, television, the communications satellite, and computers.

The wireless and the radio made ocean travel much safer and war more efficient by improving communications between ships at sea and among army units on the ground. Within a decade after the *Titanic* disaster, technology also transformed American lives in direct and subtle ways. Weather forecasting became more accurate and timely, providing ample warning to farmers and ordinary citizens about approaching storms. News of battles, elections, sporting events, and disasters both domestic and foreign traveled over the airwaves. This instant news could have very practical ramifications, influencing decisions in everything from business matters to whether or not to wear a coat to work. But in a broader sense, it made all Americans citizens of the world. The news of the end of World War I in 1918, the attack on Pearl Harbor in 1941, and the walk on the moon in 1969 united millions of people worldwide and made them participants in the events. The new communications technology and instant news, symbolized by the wireless and its role in spreading the word about the sinking of the *Titanic,* made twentieth-century Americans very different from those who lived before them.

The communication revolution has continued with CNN, e-mail, and the Internet. Can you imagine what life was like before the telegraph, the telephone, and the wireless, let alone e-mail? How has rapid communication and instant news changed the way people live? Has it made your life better or worse than the lives of your great grandparents?

Wireless-telegraphy room of an Atlantic liner, 1912. *(The Granger Collection, New York)*

Stephen Kern, *The Culture of Time and Space* (1983). Tom Lewis, *The Empire of the Air: The Men Who Made Radio* (1996).

HOPES RAISED, PROMISES DEFERRED

The 1920s was a time when all kinds of hopes seemed realizable. "Don't envy successful salesmen—be one!" one advertisement screamed. Buy a car. Build a house. Start a career. Invest in land. Invest in stocks. Make a fortune.

Not all Americans, of course, were intent on making a stock market killing or expected to win a huge fortune. Some merely wished to retain traditional values in a society that seemed to question them. Others wanted a steady job and a little respect. Still others hungered for the new appliances so alluringly described in ads and on the radio. Many discovered, however, that no matter how modest their hopes might be, they lay tantalizingly out of reach.

Clash of Values

During the 1920s, radio, movies, advertising, and mass-circulation magazines promoted a national, secular culture. But this new culture, which emphasized consumption, pleasure, upward mobility, even sex, clashed with traditional values of hard work, thrift, church, family, and home. Although it would be easy to see these cultural differences as a reflection of an urban–rural conflict, in fact, many people clinging to the old ways had moved into the cities. Still, many Americans feared that new cultural values, scientific breakthroughs, and new ideas like bolshevism, relativism, Freudianism, and biblical criticism threatened their familiar way of life. A trial over the teaching of evolutionary ideas in high school in the little town of Dayton, Tennessee, symbolized, even as it exaggerated, the clash of the old versus the new, the traditional versus the modern, the city versus the country.

The scientific community and most educated people had long accepted the basic concepts of evolution, if not all the details of Charles Darwin's theories. But many Christians, especially those from Protestant evangelical churches, accepted the Bible as the literal truth. They believed that faith in the Gospel message was crucial to living a virtuous life on earth and, more important, going to heaven. Many of these faithful saw in the dramatic changes of the 1920s a major spiritual crisis. Resistance to the concept of evolution resulted in legislative efforts in several states to forbid its teaching. The Tennessee law enacted in 1925 became the most famous, for it made it illegal

for any teacher in any of the universities, normal and all other public schools of the state to teach any theory that denies the story of the divine creation of man as taught in the Bible and to teach instead that man has descended from a lower order of animals.

John Scopes, a young biology teacher, broke the law by teaching evolutionary theory to his class, and the state of Tennessee brought him to trial. The American Civil Liberties Union hired Clarence Darrow, perhaps the country's most famous defense lawyer, to defend Scopes; the World Christian Fundamentalist Association engaged William Jennings Bryan, former presidential candidate and secretary of state, to assist the prosecution. Bryan was old and tired (he died only a few days after the trial), but he was still an eloquent and deeply religious man. In cross-examination, Darrow reduced Bryan's statements to intellectual rubble and revealed also that Bryan was at a loss to explain much of the Bible. He could not explain how Eve was created from Adam's rib or where Cain got his wife. Nevertheless, the jury declared Scopes guilty, for he had clearly broken the law.

The press from all over the country covered the trial and upheld science and academic freedom. Journalists like H. L. Mencken had a field day poking fun at Bryan and the fundamentalists. "Heave an egg out a Pullman window," Mencken wrote, "and you will hit a Fundamentalist almost anywhere in the United States today. . . . They are everywhere where learning is too heavy a burden for mortal minds to carry."

Religious Fundamentalism

Some observers, including Mencken, thought that the Scopes trial ended what one writer in 1926 called "the fundamentalist menace." Yet religious fundamentalism continued to survive in a world fast becoming urban, modern, and sophisticated. Fundamentalism cut across many denominations and covered over many differences, but all fundamentalists believed in the literal interpretation and the infallibility of the Bible and that Jesus Christ was the only road to salvation. They rejected secularism, liberal theology, pluralism, the Social Gospel, and any sense that reform on earth could lead to perfection. They had a strong and unshakable belief in what they knew was the truth, and they were willing to stand up and fight for their belief.

Throughout the 1920s and the 1930s, attendance at Christian colleges and the circulation of fundamentalist periodicals and newspapers increased dramatically, and evangelical ministers reached large audiences. One of the most popular and flamboyant of the ministers was Billy Sunday, a former baseball player who jumped about the stage as he pitched his brand of Christianity. For Sunday, Christianity and patriotism were synonymous. Another popular preacher was Aimee Semple McPherson, a faith healer who founded her own church, the International Church of the Four Square Gospel, in Los Angeles in 1927.

Evangelist William Ashley ("Billy") Sunday (1862–1935) was a professional baseball player before experiencing a religious conversion that led him to work with the YMCA. He conducted religious revivals all over the country, captivating listeners with his flamboyant style and converting millions. *(The Granger Collection, New York)*

Dressed as a University of Southern California football player, she ran across the stage "carrying the ball for Christ;" wielding a pitchfork, she drove the devil out of the auditorium.

Sunday and McPherson may have been flamboyant performers, but it was the radio that extended the reach of the fundamentalist preachers even more dramatically. McPherson was the first woman to hold a radio license, and she had the second most popular radio show in Los Angeles in the late 1920s. In the 1930s "The Old Fashioned Revival Hour" was carried on 356 stations and reached an audience of over 20 million people, more than any other prime-time broadcast. For many, the period between the wars was an age of secular humanism, technological marvels, and modernism in all fields, but for many others, it was a time when fundamentalist religion and old-fashioned values not only survived but also prospered. Yet many fundamentalist sects succeeded in winning many converts because their leaders were skilled at using modern technology.

Immigration and Migration

Immigrants and anyone else perceived as "un-American" seemed to threaten the old ways. A movement to restrict immigration had existed for decades. An act passed in 1882 prohibited the entry of criminals, paupers, and the insane, and special agreements between 1880 and 1908 restricted both Chinese and Japanese immigration. But it was the fear and intolerance of the war years and the period right after the war that resulted in major restrictive legislation.

The first strongly restrictive immigration law passed in 1917 over President Wilson's veto. It required a literacy test for the first time (an immigrant had to read a passage in one of a number of languages). The bill also prohibited the immigration of certain political radicals. The literacy test did not stop the more than one million immigrants who poured into the country in 1920 and 1921, however.

In 1921, Congress limited European immigration in any one year to 3 percent of the number of each nationality present in the country in 1910. Congress changed the quota in 1924 to 2 percent of those in the country in 1890, to limit immigration from southern and eastern Europe and ban all immigration from Asia. The National Origins Act of 1927 set an overall limit of 150,000 European immigrants a year, with more than 60 percent coming from Great Britain and Germany, but fewer than 4 percent from Italy.

Ethnicity increasingly became a factor in political alignments during the 1920s. Restrictive immigration laws, sponsored by Republicans, helped attract American Jews, Italians, and Poles to the Democratic party. By 1924, the Democratic party was so evenly divided between northern urban Catholics and southern rural Protestants that the party voted to condemn the Ku Klux Klan, by a very small margin.

The immigration acts of 1921, 1924, and 1927, in sharply limiting European immigration and virtually banning Asian immigrants, cut off the streams of cheap labor that had provided muscle for an industrializing country since the early nineteenth century. At the same time, by exempting immigrants from the Western Hemisphere, the new laws opened the country to Mexican laborers who were eager to escape poverty in their own land and to work in the fields and farms of California and the Southwest.

Though they never matched the flood of eastern and southern Europeans who entered the country before World War I, Mexican immigrants soon became the country's largest first-generation immigrant group. Nearly half a million arrived in the 1920s, in contrast to only 31,000 in the first decade of the century. Mexican farm workers often lived in primitive camps, where conditions were unsanitary and health care was

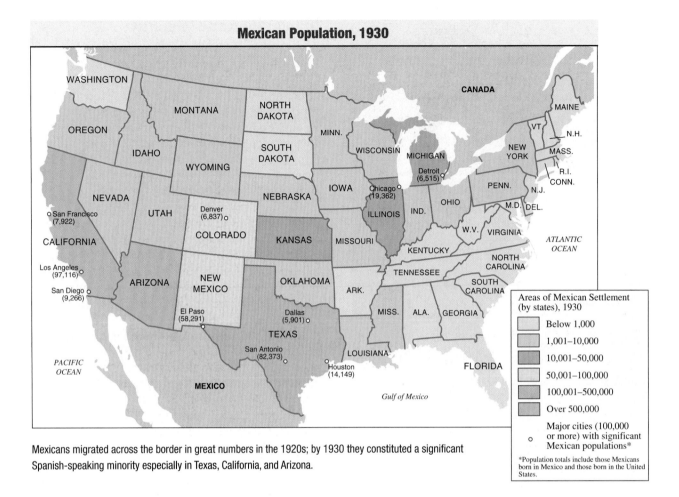

Mexican Population, 1930

Areas of Mexican Settlement (by states), 1930

- Below 1,000
- 1,001–10,000
- 10,001–50,000
- 50,001–100,000
- 100,001–500,000
- Over 500,000

○ Major cities (100,000 or more) with significant Mexican populations*

*Population totals include those Mexicans born in Mexico and those born in the United States.

Mexicans migrated across the border in great numbers in the 1920s; by 1930 they constituted a significant Spanish-speaking minority especially in Texas, California, and Arizona.

nonexistent. "When they have finished harvesting my crops I will kick them out on the country road," one employer announced. "My obligation is ended."

Mexicans also migrated to industrial cities such as Detroit, St. Louis, and Kansas City. Northern companies recruited them and paid their transportation. The Bethlehem Steel Corporation brought 1,000 Mexicans into its Pennsylvania plant in 1923, and U.S. Steel imported 1,500 as strikebreakers to Lorain, Ohio, about the same time. During the 1920s the population of El Paso, Texas, became more than 50 percent Mexican; that of San Antonio, a little less than 50 percent. The Mexican population in California reached 368,000 in 1929, and in Los Angeles the population was about 20 percent Mexican. Like African Americans, the Mexicans found opportunity by migrating, but they did not escape prejudice or hardship.

African Americans migrated north in great numbers from 1915 to 1920. Reduced European immigration and industrial growth caused many northern companies to recruit southern blacks. Trains stopped at the depots in small southern towns, sometimes picking up hundreds of blacks in a single day. Lured by editorials and advertisements placed by industries in

northern black newspapers such as the Chicago *Defender* and driven out of the South by an agricultural depression, many African Americans eagerly headed north.

One young black man wrote to the Chicago *Defender* from Texas that he would prefer to go to Chicago or Philadelphia, but "I don't care where so long as I go where a man is a man." It was the young who tended to move. "Young folks just aren't satisfied to see so little and stay around on the farm all their lives like old folks did," one older man from South Carolina pointed out. Most black migrants were unskilled. They found work in the huge meatpacking plants of Chicago, East St. Louis, Omaha, and Kansas City and in the shipyards and steel mills. Only 50 African Americans worked for the Ford Motor Company in 1916, but there were 2,500 working there in 1920 and 10,000 in 1926. The black population of Chicago increased from 44,000 in 1910 to 234,000 by 1930. Cleveland's black population grew eightfold between 1910 and 1930.

African Americans unquestionably improved their lives by moving north. But most were like the Parkers, their dreams only partly fulfilled. Most crowded into segregated housing and faced prejudice and hate. "Black men stay South," the Chicago *Tribune* advised, and it offered to pay the transportation for any who would return. In one section of Chicago, a group of white residents, fearing the encroachment of blacks, stretched across the street a banner that read: THEY SHALL NOT PASS.

Often the young black men moved first, and only later brought their wives and children, putting great pressure on many black families. Some young men, like John Parker, restrained their anger, but others, like Richard Wright's fictional Bigger Thomas, portrayed movingly in *Native Son* (1940), struck out violently against white society. The presence of more African Americans in the industrial cities of the North led to the development of black ghettos and increased the racial tension that occasionally flared into violence.

One of the worst race riots took place in Chicago in 1919. The riot began at a beach on a hot July day. A black youth drowned in a white swimming area. Blacks claimed he had been hit by stones, but the police refused to arrest any of the white men. A group of African Americans attacked the police, and the riot was on. It lasted four days. White youths drove through the black sections shooting blacks from car windows. Blacks returned the fire. Several dozen were killed, and hundreds were wounded. The tension between the races did not die when the riot was over.

Race riots broke out in other places as well. In the early 1920s, few cities escaped racial tension and violence. Riots exploded in Knoxville, Tennessee; Omaha, Nebraska; and Tulsa, Oklahoma. Racial conflict in Elaine, Arkansas, demonstrated that not even the rural South was immune.

The wave of violence and racism angered and disillusioned W. E. B. Du Bois, who had urged African Americans to close ranks and support the American cause during the war. In an angry editorial for *The Crisis*, he called on blacks to

> fight a sterner, longer, more unbending battle against the forces of hell in our own land. We return. We return from fighting. We return fighting. Make way for Democracy; we saved it in France, and by the Great Jehovah, we will save it in the United States of America, or know the reason why.

Marcus Garvey: Black Messiah

Du Bois was not the only militant black leader in the postwar years. A flamboyant Jamaican fed a growing sense of black pride during that time. Marcus Garvey arrived in New York at the age of 29. Largely self-taught, he was an admirer of Booker T. Washington. Although he never abandoned Washington's philoso-

Marcus Garvey (second from the right), shown dressed in his favorite uniform, became a hero for many black Americans. *(Archive Photos)*

phy of self-help, he thoroughly transformed it. Washington focused on economic betterment through self-help; Garvey saw self-help as a means of political empowerment by which African peoples would reclaim their homelands from European powers.

In Jamaica, Garvey had founded the Universal Negro Improvement Association. By 1919, he had established 30 branches in the United States and the Caribbean. He also set up the newspaper *The Negro World,* the Black Cross Nurses, and a chain of grocery stores, millinery shops, and restaurants. His biggest project was the Black Star Line, a steamship company, to be owned and operated by African Americans. Advocating the return of blacks to Africa, he declared himself the "provisional president of Africa," a title he adopted from Eamon De Valera, the first "provisional president of Ireland." Garvey glorified the African past and preached that God and Jesus were black.

He won converts, mostly among lower-middle-class blacks, through the force of his oratory and the power of his personality, but especially through his message that blacks should be proud of being black. "Up you mighty race, you can accomplish what you will," Garvey thundered. Thousands of blacks cheered as his Universal African Legions, dressed in blue and red uniforms, marched by. They waved the red, black, and green flag and sang "Ethiopia, the Land of Our Fathers," and thousands invested their money in the Black Star Line. The line soon collapsed, however, in part because white entrepreneurs sold Garvey inferior ships and equipment. Garvey was arrested for using the mails to defraud shareholders and was sentenced to five years in prison. President Coolidge commuted the sentence. Ordered deported as an undesirable alien, Garvey left America in 1927. Despite his failures, he convinced thousands of black Americans, especially the poor and discouraged, that they could join together and accomplish something and that they should feel pride in their heritage and their future.

The Harlem Renaissance and the Lost Generation

A group of black writers, artists, and intellectuals who settled in Harlem after the war led a movement related in some ways to Garvey's black nationalism crusade. It was less flamboyant but in the end more important. They studied anthropology, art, history, and music, and they wrote novels and poetry that explored the ambivalent role of blacks in America. Like Garvey, they expressed their pride in being black and sought their African roots and the folk tradition of blacks in America. But unlike Garvey, they had no desire to go back to Africa. They sought a way to be both black and American.

Alain Locke, the first black Rhodes scholar and a dapper professor of philosophy at Howard University, was in one sense the father of the renaissance. His collection of essays and art, *The New Negro* (1925), announced the movement to the outside world and outlined black contributions to American culture and civilization. Langston Hughes, a poet and novelist born in Missouri, went to high school in Cleveland, lived in Mexico, and traveled in Europe and Africa before settling in Harlem. He wrote bitter but laughing poems, using black vernacular to describe the pathos and the pride of African Americans. In *Weary Blues,* he adapted the rhythm and beat of black jazz and the blues to his poetry.

Jazz was an important force in Harlem in the 1920s, and many prosperous whites came from downtown to listen to Louis Armstrong, Fletcher Henderson, Duke Ellington, and other black musicians. The promise of expressing primitive emotions, the erotic atmosphere, the music, and the illegal sex, drugs, and liquor made Harlem an intriguing place for many brought up in Victorian white America.

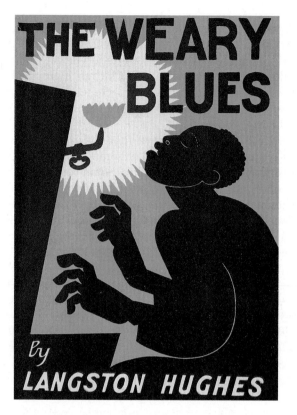

Langston Hughes was one of the most important Harlem Renaissance writers. Like many other African-American writers, he sought out his African roots. But he later wrote: "I was only an American Negro who loved the surface of Africa and the rhythms of Africa, but I was not Africa. I was Chicago and Kansas City and Broadway and Harlem." *(Fales Library/Special Collections, New York University)*

The Jamaican Claude McKay, who came to Harlem by way of Tuskegee and Kansas, wrote about the underside of life in Harlem in *Home to Harlem* (1925), one of the most popular of the "new Negro" novels. McKay portrayed two black men—one, Jake, who has deserted the white man's army and finds a life of simple and erotic pleasure in Harlem's cabarets, the other an intellectual who is unable to make such an easy choice. "My damned white education has robbed me of much of the primitive vitality, the pure stamina, the simple unwaggering strength of the Jakes of the negro race," he laments.

This was the dilemma of many of the Harlem writers: how to be both black and intellectual. They worried that they depended on white patrons, who introduced them to writers and artists in Greenwich Village and made contacts for them at New York publishing houses. Many of the white patrons pressured the black writers to conform to the white elite idea of black authenticity. The black writers resented this intrusion, but it was their only hope to be recognized. Jean Toomer, more self-consciously avant-garde than

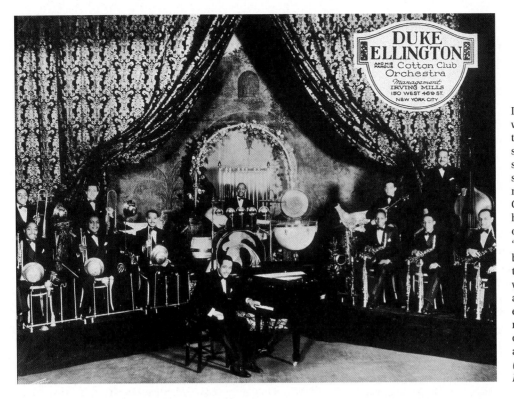

During the 1920s, affluent white Americans flocked to Harlem to see the sensual and flamboyant shows starring black singers, dancers, and musicians at the Cotton Club. They also came to hear the evocative music of Edward Kennedy "Duke" Ellington and his band. Ellington, seated at the piano in this photo, was a talented composer and musician who adapted the rhythms and harmonies of jazz and his own innovations to create a new American music. *(Frank Driggs/Archive Photos)*

many of the other black writers, wrote haunting poems trying to explore the difficulty of black identity, and in a novel, *Cane* (1923), he sketched maladjusted, almost grotesque characters who expressed some of the alienation that many writers felt in the 1920s.

Many African American writers felt alienated from American society. They tried living in Paris or in Greenwich Village, but most felt drawn to Harlem, which in the 1920s was rapidly becoming the center of black population in New York City. Over 117,000 white people left the neighborhood during the decade, while over 87,000 blacks moved in. Countee Cullen, the only writer in the group actually born in New York, remarked, "In spite of myself I find that I am activated by a strong sense of race consciousness." So was Zora Neale Hurston activated—born in Florida, she went to New York to study at Barnard College, earned an advanced degree in anthropology from Columbia University, and used her interest in folklore to write stories of robust and passionate rural blacks. Much of the work of the Harlem writers was read by very small numbers, but another generation of young black intellectuals in the 1960s still struggling with the dilemma of how to be both black and American would rediscover it.

One did not need to be black to be disillusioned with society. Many white intellectuals, writers, and artists also felt alienated from what they perceived as the materialism, conformity, and provincial prejudice that dominated American life. Many writers, including

F. Scott Fitzgerald, Ernest Hemingway, E. E. Cummings, and T. S. Eliot, moved to Europe. They wanted to divorce themselves from the country they pretended to detest, but cheap rents and inexpensive food in Paris also influenced their decisions. Many of those who gathered at European cafés, drinking the wine that was illegal in the United States, wrote novels, plays, and poems about America. Like so many American intellectuals in all periods, they had a love–hate relationship with their country.

For many writers, the disillusionment began with the war itself. Hemingway eagerly volunteered to go to Europe as an ambulance driver. But when he was wounded on the Italian front, he reevaluated the purpose of the war and the meaning of all the slaughter. His novel *The Sun Also Rises* (1926) is the story of the purposeless European wanderings of a group of Americans. But it is also the story of Jake Barnes, made impotent by a war injury. His "unreasonable wound" is a symbol of the futility of life in the postwar period.

F. Scott Fitzgerald, who loved to frequent the cafés and parties in Paris, became a celebrity during the 1920s. He was sometimes confused, even in his own mind, with the dashing heroes about whom he wrote. He epitomized some of the despair of his generation, which had "grown up to find all Gods dead, all wars fought, all faiths in man shaken." His best novel, *The Great Gatsby* (1925), was a critique of the American success myth. The book describes the elaborate parties given by a mysterious businessman, who, it turns out, has made his money illegally as a bootlegger. Gatsby hopes to win back a beautiful woman who has forsaken him for another man. But wealth won't buy happiness, and Gatsby's life ends tragically, as so many lives seemed to end in the novels written during the decade.

Paris was the place to which many American writers flocked, but it was not necessary to live in France to criticize American society. Sherwood Anderson, born in Camden, Ohio, created a fictional midwestern town in *Winesburg, Ohio* (1919), to describe the dull, narrow, warped lives that seemed to provide a metaphor for American culture. Sinclair Lewis, another midwesterner, created scathing parodies of middle-class, small-town life in *Main Street* (1920) and *Babbitt* (1922). The "hero" of the latter novel is a salesman from the town of Zenith. He is a "he-man," a "regular guy" who distrusts "red professors," foreign-born people, and anyone from New York. He lives in a world of gadgets and booster clubs and seems to be the worst product of a standardized civilization.

But no one had more fun laughing at the American middle class than H. L. Mencken, who edited the *American Mercury* in Baltimore and denounced what he called the "booboisie." He labeled Woodrow Wilson a "self-bamboozled Presbyterian" and poked fun at Warren Harding's prose, which he said reminded him of "a string of wet sponges, . . . of stale bean soup, of college yells, of dogs barking idiotically through endless nights."

Ironically, while intellectuals despaired over American society and complained that art could not survive in a business-dominated civilization, literature flourished. The novels of Hemingway, Fitzgerald, Lewis, William Faulkner, and Gertrude Stein; the plays of Eugene O'Neill and Maxwell Anderson; the poetry of T. S. Eliot, Hart Crane, E. E. Cummings, and Marianne Moore; and the work of many black writers, such as Langston Hughes, Claude McKay, and Zora Neale Hurston, marked the 1920s as one of the most creative decades in American literature.

Women Struggle for Equality

Any mention of the role of women in the 1920s brings to mind the image of the flapper—a young woman with a short skirt, bobbed hair, and a boyish figure doing the Charleston, smoking, drinking, and being very casual about sex. F. Scott Fitzgerald's heroines in novels like *This Side of Paradise* (1920) and *The Great Gatsby* (1925) provided the role models for young people to imitate, and movie stars such as Clara Bow and Gloria Swanson, aggressively seductive on the screen, supplied even more dramatic examples of flirtatious and provocative behavior.

Without question, women acquired more sexual freedom in the 1920s. "None of the Victorian mothers

The revolution created by electricity remained out of reach for many rural and working-class women, who continued to use the scrub board rather than the washing machine. (*Culver Pictures*)

had any idea how casually their daughters were accustomed to being kissed," F. Scott Fitzgerald wrote. However, it is difficult, if not impossible, to know how accustomed those daughters (and their mothers) were to kissing and enjoying other sexual activity. Contraceptives, especially the diaphragm, became more readily available during the decade, and Margaret Sanger, who had been indicted for sending birth control information through the mail in 1914, organized the first American birth control conference in 1921. Still, most states made the selling or prescribing of birth control devices illegal, and federal laws prohibited sending literature discussing birth control through the mail.

Family size declined during the decade (from 3.6 children in 1900 to 2.5 in 1930), and young people were apparently more inclined to marry for love than for security. More women expected sexual satisfaction in marriage (nearly 60 percent in one poll) and felt that divorce was the best solution for an unhappy marriage. Nearly 85 percent in another poll approved of sexual intercourse as an expression of love and affection and not simply for procreation. But the polls were hardly scientific and tended to be biased toward the attitudes of the urban middle class. Despite more freedom for women, the double standard persisted. "When lovely woman stoops to folly, she can always find someone to stoop with her," one male writer announced, "but not always someone to lift her up again to the level where she belongs."

Women's lives were shaped by other innovations of the 1920s. Electricity, running water, washing machines, vacuum cleaners, and other labor-saving devices made housework easier for the middle class. Yet these developments did not touch large numbers of rural and urban working-class women. Even middle-class women discovered that new appliances did not reduce time spent doing housework. Standards of cleanliness rose, and women were urged to make their houses more spotless than any nineteenth-century housekeeper would have felt necessary. At the same time, magazines and newspapers bombarded women with advertising urging them to buy products to make themselves better housekeepers, yet still beautiful. It must have been frustrating for those who could not afford the magic new products or whose hands and teeth and skin failed to look youthful despite all their efforts. The ads also promoted new dress styles, shorter skirts, no corsets. The young adopted them quickly, and they also learned to swim (and to display more of their bodies on the beach), to play tennis (but only if they belonged to a tennis club), and to ride a bicycle.

More women worked outside the home. Whereas in 1890 only 17 percent of women were employed, by 1933 some 22 percent were. But their share of manufacturing jobs fell from 19 to 16 percent between 1900 and 1930. The greatest expansion of jobs was in white-collar occupations that were being feminized—secretary, bookkeeper, clerk, telephone operator. In 1930, fully 96 percent of stenographers were women. Although more married women had jobs (an increase of 25 percent during the decade), most of them held low-paying jobs, and most single women assumed that marriage would terminate their employment.

For some working women—secretaries and teachers, for example—marriage often led to dismissal. "A married woman's attitude toward men who come to the office is not the same as that of an unmarried woman," one employment agency decided. Married women are "very unstable in their work; their first claim is to home and children," concluded a businessman. Although women might not be able to work after their weddings (in one poll of college men, only one in nine said he would allow his wife to work after marriage), a job as a secretary could be good preparation for marriage. A business office was a good place to meet eligible men, but more than that, a secretary learned endurance, self-effacement, and obedience, traits that would make her a good wife. Considering these attitudes, it is not surprising that the disparity between male and female wages widened during the decade. By 1930, women earned only 57 percent of what men were paid.

The image of the flapper in the 1920s promised more freedom and equality for women than they actually achieved. The flapper was young, white, slender, and upper class (Fitzgerald fixed her ideal age at 19), and most women did not fit those categories. The flapper was frivolous and daring, not professional and competent. Although the proportion of women lawyers and bankers increased slightly during the decade, the rate of growth declined, and the number of women doctors and scientists dropped. In the 1920s, women acquired some sexual freedom and a limited amount of opportunity outside the home, but the promise of the prewar feminist movement and the hopes that accompanied the suffrage amendment remained unfulfilled.

WOMEN IN THE LABOR FORCE, 1900–1930

Year	Women in Labor Force	Percentage of Women in Total Labor Force	Women in Labor Force Percentage of Total Women of Working Age	Percentage of Women in Labor Force		
				Single	Married	Widowed
1900	4,997,000	18.1	20.6	66.2	15.4	18.4
1910*	7,640,000	NA	25.4	60.2	24.7	15.0
1920	8,347,000	20.4	23.7	77.0†	23.0	—†
1930	10,632,000	21.9	24.8	53.9	28.9	17.2

*Data not comparable with other censuses due to a difference in the basis of enumeration.
†Single includes widowed and divorced.
Source: U.S. Bureau of the Census.

Although the flapper look of short skirts and bobbed hair appeared in the workplace in the 1920s, for most working women of the era, employed in low-paying jobs as file clerks, typists, and telephone operators, the flapper lifestyle of freedom and equality was more illusion than reality. *(Corbis-Bettmann)*

Winning the vote for women did not ensure equality. In most states, a woman's service belonged to her husband. Women could vote, but often they could not serve on juries. In some states, women could not hold office, own a business, or sign a contract without their husbands' permission. Women were usually held responsible for an illegitimate birth, and divorce laws almost always favored men. Many women leaders were disappointed in the small turnout of women in the presidential election of 1920. To educate women in the reality of politics, they organized the National League of Women Voters to "finish the fight." A nonpartisan organization, it became an important educational organization for middle-class women, but it did little to eliminate inequality.

Alice Paul, who had led the militant National Women's Party in 1916, chained herself to the White House fence once again to promote an equal rights amendment to the Constitution. The amendment got support in Wisconsin and several other states, but many women opposed it on the grounds that such an amendment would cancel the special legislation to protect women in industry that had taken so long to enact in the two decades before. Feminists disagreed in the 1920s on the proper way to promote equality and rights for women, but the political and social climate was not conducive to feminist causes.

Rural America in the 1920s

Most farmers did not share in the prosperity of the 1920s. Responding to worldwide demands and rising prices for wheat, cotton, and other products, many farmers invested in more land, tractors, and farm equipment during the war. Then prices tumbled. By 1921, the price of wheat had dropped 40 percent, corn 32 percent, and hogs 50 percent. Total farm income fell from $10 million to $4 million in the postwar depression. Many farmers could not make payments on their tractors. Because the value of land fell, they often lost both mortgage and land and still owed the bank money. One Iowa farmer remembered, "We gave the land back to the mortgage holder, and then we're sued for the remainder—the deficiency judgment—which we have to pay."

The changing nature of farming was part of the problem. The use of chemical fertilizers and new hybrid seeds, some developed by government experiment stations and land-grant colleges, increased the yield per acre. By 1930, some 920,000 tractors and 900,000 trucks were in use on American farms. They not only made farming more efficient, but they also released for cash crops land formerly used to raise feed for horses and mules. Production increased at the very time that worldwide demand for American farm products declined. The United States shipped abroad in 1929 only one-third the wheat it had exported in 1919, and only one-ninth the meat.

Not all farmers suffered. During the 1920s, the farming class separated into those who were getting by barely or not at all and those who earned large profits. Large commercial operations, using mechanized equipment, produced most of the cash crops. At the same time, many small farmers found themselves unable to compete with agribusiness. Some of them, along with many farm laborers, solved the problem of declining rural profitability by leaving the farms. In 1900, fully 40 percent of the labor force worked on farms; by 1930, only 21 percent earned their living from the land.

Few farmers could afford the products of the new technology. Although many middle-class urban families were more prosperous than they had ever been, buying new cars, radios, and bathrooms, only one farm family in ten had electricity in the 1920s. The lot of the farm wife had not changed for centuries. She ran a domestic factory, did all the household chores, and helped on the farm as well.

As they had done in the nineteenth century, farmers tried to act collectively. They sought to influence legislation in the state capital and in Washington. Most of their effort went into the McNary-Haugen Farm Relief Bill, which would have provided government price support for key agricultural products. The bill was introduced a number of times between 1924 and 1928 without success, but farm organizations in all parts of the country learned how to work together to influence Congress. That would have important ramifications for the future.

The 1927 Mississippi Flood

Farmers were particularly vulnerable to the power of nature. Too little or too much rain could ruin their crops and their lives. This vulnerability became apparent in the spring of 1927 when the worst flood in the nation's history devastated the Mississippi valley. Since before the Civil War, the Army Corps of Engineers had been trying unsuccessfully to control flooding caused by the waters of the Mississippi. States and cities along the river constructed levees, but even the experts disagreed on the best way to control the river. Some suggested building levees the length of the river, while others insisted that outlets and reservoirs would help drain off the extra water. But the highest levees could not stop the flood of 1927.

The Mississippi valley received more rain than usual in the fall of 1926, and the next spring the rain continued. More than 30,000 men worked feverishly to strengthen the levees along the Mississippi River and tributaries like the Ohio and the Arkansas that flowed into the Mississippi. But the water continued to rise, and the levees began to collapse. Millions of acres were flooded. To save New Orleans, city authorities dynamited the levees north of the city, flooding even more land. In all, 27,000 square miles of land were inundated (an area the size of Massachusetts, Connecticut, New Hampshire, and Vermont). Nearly a million people were made homeless; 330,000 were rescued from rooftops and trees; 246 died. There was nearly a billion dollars of property damage. Through it all, the black sharecroppers, who often lived close to the river, were hardest hit.

The flood was the biggest news story of the year, even bigger than Lindbergh's flight to Paris. President Calvin Coolidge refused to visit the disaster area, but he appointed Secretary of Commerce Herbert Hoover to coordinate flood relief. Although the federal government did nothing directly to aid the flood victims, Hoover, who believed in volunteerism, secured the assistance of groups like the Red Cross, the American Legion, the Elks, and the Masons. Movie theaters and school children collected donations, and a toothbrush manufacturer provided 4,500 free toothbrushes. The federal government and the states set up emergency camps to house the flood victims, but they quickly became overcrowded and inadequate. Many made homeless by the raging waters suffered from disease and malnutrition. Hardest hit were the black sharecroppers.

Despite the inadequacy of the funds and supplies collected, Hoover became something of a humanitarian hero for his efforts to aid the victims. Like Coolidge, Hoover did not believe the natural disaster was any reason to call a special session of Congress or to have the federal government take direct action. But in 1928

President Coolidge signed a flood control bill that for the first time committed the federal government to build levees to control the Mississippi. Those who favored something more than levees also won support in the new law, which provided several places where the floodwaters could flow into fields and reservoirs.

The flood of 1927 hastened the migration of black sharecroppers north. It also set a precedent for federal involvement in flood control and in local affairs. Although this precedent became important only slowly, it did mark a fundamental change. Meanwhile the debate over the proper technology of flood control continued.

The Workers' Share of Prosperity

Hundreds of thousands of workers improved their standard of living in the 1920s, yet inequality grew. Real wages increased 21 percent between 1923 and 1929, but corporate dividends went up by nearly two-thirds in the same period. The workers did not profit from the increased production they helped to create, and that boded ill for the future. The richest 5 percent of the population increased their share of the wealth from a quarter to a third, and the wealthiest 1 percent controlled a whopping 19 percent of all income.

Even among workers there was great disparity. Those employed on the auto assembly lines or in the new factories producing radios saw their wages go up, and many saw their hours decline. Yet the majority of American working-class families did not earn enough to move them much beyond subsistence level. One study suggested that a family needed $2,000 to $2,400 in 1924 to maintain an "American standard of living." But in that year, 16 million families earned under $2,000. For the chambermaids in New York hotels who worked seven days a week or the itinerant Mexican migrant laborers in the Southwest, labor was so exhausting that at the end of the day it was impossible to take advantage of new consumer products and modern lifestyles, even if they had the money.

Although some workers prospered in the 1920s, organized labor fell on hard times. Labor union membership fell from about 5 million in 1921 to less than 3.5 million in 1929. Although a majority of American workers had never supported unions, unions now faced competition from employers' new policies. A number of large employers lured workers away from unions with promises that seemed to equal union benefits: profit-sharing plans, pensions, and their own company unions. The National Manufacturing Association and individual businesses carried on a vigorous campaign to restore the open shop. The leadership of the AFL became increasingly conservative during the decade and had little interest in launching movements to organize the large industries.

The more aggressive unions like the United Mine Workers, led by the flamboyant John L. Lewis, also encountered difficulties. The union's attempt to organize the mines in West Virginia had led to violent clashes between union members and imported guards. President Harding called out troops in 1921 to put down an "army organized by the strikers." The next year, Lewis called the greatest coal strike in history, and further violence erupted, especially in Williamson County, Illinois. Internal strife also weakened the union, and Lewis had to accept wage reductions in the negotiations of 1927.

Organized labor, like so many other groups, struggled desperately during the decade to take advantage of the prosperity. It won some victories, and it made some progress. But American affluence was beyond the reach of many groups during the decade. Eventually, the inequality would lead to disaster.

THE BUSINESS OF POLITICS

"Among the nations of the earth today America stands for one idea: *Business*," a popular writer announced in 1921. "Through business, properly conceived, managed and conducted, the human race is finally to be redeemed." Bruce Barton, the head of the largest advertising firm in the country, was the author of one of the most popular nonfiction books of the decade. In *The Man Nobody Knows* (1925), he depicted Christ as "the founder of modern business." He took 12 men from the bottom ranks of society and forged them into a successful organization. "All work is worship; all useful service prayer," Barton argued. If the businessman would just copy Christ, he could become a supersalesman.

Business, especially big business, prospered in the 1920s, and the image of businessmen, enhanced by their important role in World War I, rose further. The government reduced regulation, lowered taxes, and cooperated to aid business expansion at home and abroad. Business and politics, always intertwined, were especially allied during the decade. Wealthy financiers such as Andrew Mellon and Charles Dawes played important roles in formulating both domestic and foreign policy. Even more significant, a new kind of businessman was elected president in 1928. Herbert Hoover, international engineer and efficiency expert, was the very symbol of the modern techniques and practices that many people confidently expected to transform the United States and the world.

Harding and Coolidge

The Republicans, almost assured of victory in 1920 because of bitter reaction against Woodrow Wilson, might have preferred nominating their old standard-bearer, Theodore Roosevelt,

Warren G. Harding (left) and Calvin Coolidge were immensely popular in the 1920s, but later historians have criticized them and rated them among the worst of American presidents. *(Library of Congress)*

but he had died the year before. Warren G. Harding, a former newspaper editor from Ohio, captured the nomination after meeting late at night with some of the party's most powerful men in a hotel room in Chicago. What Harding promised no one ever discovered, but the meeting in the "smoke-filled room" became legendary. To balance the ticket, the Republicans chose as their vice presidential candidate Calvin Coolidge of Massachusetts, who had gained attention by his firm stand during the Boston police strike. The Democrats seemed equally unimaginative. After 44 roll calls, they finally nominated Governor James Cox of Ohio and picked Franklin D. Roosevelt, a young politician from New York, to run as vice president. Roosevelt had been the assistant secretary of the navy but otherwise had not distinguished himself.

Harding won in a landslide. His 60.4 percent of the vote was the widest margin yet recorded in a presidential election. More significant, fewer than 50 percent of the eligible voters went to the polls. The newly enfranchised women, especially in working-class neighborhoods, stayed away from the voting booths. So did large numbers of men. To many people, it did not seem to matter who was president.

In contrast to the reform-minded presidents Roosevelt and Wilson, Harding reflected the conservatism of the 1920s. He was a jovial man who brought many Ohio friends to Washington and placed them in positions of power. A visitor to the White House described Harding and his cohorts discussing the problems of the day, with "the air heavy with tobacco smoke, trays with bottles containing every imaginable brand of whiskey" near at hand.

At a little house a few blocks from the White House on K Street, Harry Daugherty, Harding's attorney general and longtime associate, held forth with a group of friends. Amid bootleg liquor and the atmosphere of a brothel, they did a brisk business in selling favors, taking bribes, and organizing illegal schemes. Harding, however, was not personally corrupt, and the nation's leading businessmen approved of his policies of higher tariffs and lower taxes. Nor did Harding spend all his time drinking with his cronies. He called a conference on disarmament and another to deal with the problems of unemployment, and he pardoned Eugene Debs, who had been in prison since the war. Harding once remarked that he could never be considered one of the great presidents, but he thought perhaps he might be "one of the best loved." He was probably right. When he died suddenly in August 1923, the American people genuinely mourned him.

Only after Calvin Coolidge became president did the full extent of the corruption and scandals of the Harding administration come to light. A Senate committee discovered that the secretary of the interior, Albert Fall, had illegally leased government-owned oil reserves in the Teapot Dome section of Wyoming to private business interests in return for over $300,000 in bribes. Illegal activities were also discovered in the Veterans Administration and elsewhere in government. Harding's attorney general resigned in disgrace, the secretary of the Navy barely avoided prison, two of Harding's advisers committed suicide, and the secretary of the interior was sentenced to jail.

Coolidge was dour and taciturn, but honest. No hint of scandal infected his administration or his personal life. Born in a little town in Vermont, he was sworn in as president by his father, a justice of the peace, in a ceremony conducted by the light of kerosene lamps at his ancestral home. To many, Coolidge represented old-fashioned rural values, simple religious faith, and personal integrity—a world fast disappearing in the 1920s. In reality, Coolidge was uncomfortable playing the rural yokel. He was ill at ease posing for photographers holding a pitchfork or sitting on a hay rig; he was much more comfortable around corporate executives.

Coolidge ran for reelection in 1924 with the financier Charles Dawes as his running mate. There was little question that he would win. The Democrats were so equally divided between northern urban Catholics and southern rural Protestants that it took 103 ballots before they nominated John Davis, an affable, corporate lawyer with little national following.

A group of dissidents, mostly representing the farmers and the laborers dissatisfied with both nominees, formed a new Progressive party. They adopted the name, but little else, from Theodore Roosevelt's party of 1912. Nominating Robert La Follette of Wisconsin for president, they drafted a platform call-ing for government ownership of railroads and ratification of the child labor amendment. La Follette attacked the "control of government and industry by private monopoly." He received nearly 5 million votes, only 3.5 million short of Davis's total. But Coolidge and prosperity won easily.

Like Harding, Coolidge was a popular president. Symbolizing his administration was his wealthy secretary of the treasury, Andrew Mellon, who set out to lower individual and corporate taxes. In 1922, Congress, with Mellon's endorsement, repealed the wartime excess profits tax. Although it raised some taxes slightly, it exempted most families from any tax at all by giving everyone a $2,500 exemption, plus $400 for each dependent. In 1926, the rate was lowered to 5 percent and the maximum surtax to 40 percent. Only families with incomes above $3,500 paid any taxes at all. In 1928, Congress reduced taxes further, removed most excise taxes, and lowered the corporate tax rate. The 200 largest corporations increased their assets during the decade from $43 to $81 billion.

"The chief business of the American people is business," Coolidge announced. "The man who builds a factory builds a temple. . . . The man who works there worships there." Coolidge's idea of the proper role of the federal government was to have as little as possible to do with the functioning of business and the lives of the people. Not everyone approved of his policies, or his personality. "No other president in my time slept so much," a White House usher remembered. But most Americans approved of his inactivity.

Herbert Hoover

One bright light in the lackluster Harding and Coolidge administrations was Herbert Hoover, who served as secretary of commerce under both presidents. Hoover had made a fortune as an international mining engineer before 1914 and then earned the reputation as a great humanitarian for his work managing the Belgian Relief Committee and directing the Food Administration. He was mentioned as a candidate for president in 1920, when he had the support of such progressives as Jane Addams, Louis Brandeis, and Walter Lippmann.

Hoover was a dynamo of energy and efficiency. He expanded his department to control and regulate the airlines, radio, and other new industries. By directing the Bureau of Standards to work with the trade associations and with individual businesses, Hoover managed to standardize the size of almost everything manufactured in the United States, from nuts and bolts and bottles to automobile tires, mattresses, and electric fixtures. He supported zoning codes, the eight-hour day in major industries, better nutrition for children, and the conservation of national resources. He pushed through the Pollution Act of 1924, the first attempt to control oil pollution along the American coastline.

While secretary of commerce, Hoover used the force of the federal government to regulate, stimulate, and promote, but he believed first of all in American free enterprise and local volunteer action to solve problems. In 1921, he convinced Harding of the need to do something about unemployment during the postwar recession. The president's conference on unemployment, convened in September 1921, marked the first time the national government had admitted any responsibility to the unemployed. The result of the conference (the first of many on a variety of topics that Hoover was to organize) was a flood of publicity, pamphlets, and advice from experts. Most of all, the conference urged state and local governments and businesses to cooperate on a volunteer basis to solve the problem. The primary responsibility of the federal government, Hoover believed, was to educate and promote. With all his activity and his organizing, Hoover got the reputation during the Harding and Coolidge years as an efficient and progressive administrator, and a humanitarian who could organize flood relief. He became one of the most popular figures in government service.

Foreign Policy in the 1920s

The decade of the 1920s is often remembered as a time of isolation, when the United States rejected the League of Nations treaty and turned its back on the rest of the world. It is true that many Americans had little interest in what was going on in Paris, Moscow, or Rio de Janeiro, and it is also true that a bloc of congressmen was determined that the United States would never again enter another European war. But the United States remained involved—indeed, increased its involvement—in international affairs during the decade. Although the United States never joined the League of Nations, and a few dedicated isolationists, led by Senator William Borah, blocked membership in the World Court, the United States cooperated with many league agencies and conferences and took the lead in trying to reduce naval armaments and to solve the problems of international finance caused in part by the war.

Indeed, business, trade, and finance marked the decade as one of international expansion. With American corporate investments overseas growing sevenfold during the decade, the United States was transformed from a debtor to a creditor nation. The continued involvement of the United States in the affairs of South and Central American countries also indicated that the country had little interest in hiding behind its national boundaries. Yet the United States

took up its role of international power reluctantly and with a number of contradictory and disastrous results.

"We seek no part in directing the destiny of the world," Harding announced in his inaugural address, but even Harding discovered that international problems would not disappear. One that required immediate attention was the naval arms race. Although moderates in Japan and Great Britain wanted to restrict the production of battleships, it was the United States, encouraged by men like William Borah, that took the lead and called the first international conference to discuss disarmament.

At the Washington Conference on Naval Disarmament, which convened in November 1921, Secretary of State Charles Evans Hughes startled the delegates by proposing a ten-year "holiday" on the construction of warships and by offering to sink or scrap 845,000 tons of American ships, including 30 battleships. He urged Britain and Japan to do the same. The delegates greeted Hughes's speech with enthusiastic cheering and applause, and they set about the task of sinking more ships than the admirals of all their countries had managed to do in a century.

The conference participants ultimately agreed to fix the tonnage of capital ships at a ratio of the United States and Great Britain, 5; Japan, 3; and France and Italy, 1.67. Japan agreed only reluctantly, but when the United States promised not to fortify its Pacific Island possessions, Japan yielded. Retrospectively, in light of what happened in 1941, the Washington Naval Conference has often been criticized, but in 1921 it was appropriately hailed as the first time in history that the major nations of the world had agreed to disarm. The conference did not cause World War II; neither, as it turned out, did it prevent it. But it was a creative beginning to reducing tensions and to meeting the challenges of the modern arms race. And it was the United States that took the lead by offering to be the first to scrap its battleships.

American foreign policy in the 1920s tried to reduce the risk of international conflict, resist revolution, and make the world safe for trade and investment. Nobody in the Republican administrations even suggested that the United States should remain isolated from Latin America. American diplomats argued for an open door to trade in China and in Latin America, but the United States had always assumed a special and distinct role. Throughout the decade, American investment in agriculture, minerals, petroleum, and manufacturing increased in the countries to the south. The United States bought nearly 60 percent of Latin America's exports and sold the region nearly 50 percent of its imports. "We are seeking to establish a Pax Americana maintained not by arms but by mutual agreement and good will," Hughes maintained.

Still, the United States continued the process of intervention begun earlier. By the end of the decade, the United States controlled the financial affairs of ten Latin American nations. The marines were withdrawn from the Dominican Republic in 1924, but that country remained a virtual protectorate of the United States until 1941. The government ordered the marines from Nicaragua in 1925 but sent them back the next year when a liberal insurrection threatened the conservative government. But the U.S. Marines, and the Nicaraguan troops they had trained, had a difficult time containing a guerrilla band led by Augusto Sandino, a charismatic leader and one of Latin America's greatest heroes. The Sandinistas, supported by the great majority of peasants, came out of the hills to attack the politicians and their American supporters. One American coffee planter decided in 1931 that the American intervention had been a disaster. "Today we are hated and despised," he announced. "This feeling has been created by employing American Marines to hunt down and kill Nicaraguans in their own country." In 1934, Sandino was murdered by General Anastasio Somoza, a ruthless leader supported by the United States. For more than 40 years, Somoza and his two sons ruled Nicaragua as a private fiefdom, a legacy not yet resolved in that strife-torn country.

Mexico frightened American businessmen in the mid-1920s by beginning to nationalize foreign holdings in oil and mineral rights. Fearing that further military activity would "injure American interests," businessmen and bankers urged Coolidge not to send marines but to negotiate instead. Coolidge appointed Dwight W. Morrow of the J. P. Morgan Company as ambassador, and his conciliatory attitude led to agreements protecting American investments. Throughout the decade, the goal of U.S. policy toward Central and South America, whether in the form of negotiations or intervention, was to maintain a special sphere of influence.

The U.S. policy of promoting peace, stability, and trade was not always consistent or carefully thought out, and this was especially true in its relationships with Europe. At the end of the war, European countries owed the United States over $10 billion, with Great Britain and France responsible for about three-fourths of that amount. Both countries, mired in postwar economic problems, suggested that the United States forgive the debts, arguing that they had paid for the war in lives and property destroyed. But the United States, although adjusting the interest and the payment schedule, refused to forget the debt. "They hired the money, didn't they?" Coolidge supposedly remarked.

International debt was not the same as money borrowed at the neighborhood bank; it influenced trade and investment, which the United States wanted to promote. Practically the only way European nations could repay the United States was by exporting products, but in a series of tariff acts, especially the Fordney-McCumber Tariff of 1922, Congress erected a protective barrier to trade. This act also gave the president power to lower or raise individual rates; both Harding and Coolidge used the power, in almost every case, to raise them. Finally, in 1930, the Hawley-Smoot Tariff raised rates even further, despite the protests of many economists and 35 countries. American policy of high tariffs (a counterproductive policy for a creditor nation) caused retaliation and restrictions on American trade, which American corporations were trying to increase.

The inability of the European countries to export products to the United States and to repay their loans was intertwined with the reparation agreement made with Germany. Germany's economy was in disarray after the war, with inflation raging and its industrial plant throttled by the peace treaty. By 1921, Germany was defaulting on its payments. The United States, which believed a healthy Germany important to the stability of Europe and of world trade, instituted a plan engineered by Charles Dawes whereby the German debt would be renegotiated and spread over a longer period. In the meantime, American bankers and the American government lent Germany hundreds of millions of dollars. In the end, the United States lent money to Germany so it could make payments to Britain and France so that those countries could continue their payments to the United States.

The United States had replaced Great Britain as the dominant force in international finance, but the nation in the 1920s was a reluctant and inconsistent world leader. The United States had stayed out of the League of Nations and was hesitant to get involved in multinational agreements. However, some agreements seemed proper to sign, and the most idealistic of all was the Kellogg-Briand pact to outlaw war. The French foreign minister, Aristide Briand, suggested a treaty between the United States and France in large part to commemorate long years of friendship between the two countries, but Secretary of State Frank B. Kellogg in 1928 expanded the idea to a multinational treaty to outlaw war. Fourteen nations agreed to sign the treaty, and eventually 62 nations signed, but the only power behind the treaty was moral force rather than economic or military sanctions.

The Survival of Progressivism

The decade of the 1920s was a time of reaction against reform, but progressivism did not simply die. It survived in many forms through the period that Jane Addams called a time of "political and social sag." Progressives who sought efficiency and order were perhaps happier during the

1920s than those who tried to promote social justice, but even the fight against poverty and for better housing and the various campaigns to protect children persisted. In a sense, the reformers went underground, but they did not disappear or give up the fight. Child labor reformers worked through the Women's Trade Union League, the Consumers League, and other organizations to promote a child labor amendment to the Constitution after the 1919 law was declared unconstitutional in 1922.

The greatest success of the social justice movement was the 1921 Sheppard-Towner Maternity Act, one of the first pieces of federal social welfare legislation, the product of long progressive agitation. A study conducted by the Children's Bureau discovered that more than 3,000 mothers died in childbirth in 1918 and that more than 250,000 infants also died. The United States ranked 18th out of 20 countries in maternal mortality and 11th in infant deaths. Josephine Baker, the pioneer physician and founder of the American Child Health Association, was not being ironic when she remarked, "It's six times safer to be a soldier in the trenches in France than to be born a baby in the United States."

The maternity bill called for a million dollars a year to assist the states in providing medical aid, consultation centers, and visiting nurses to teach expectant mothers how to care for themselves and their babies. The bill was controversial from the beginning. The American Medical Association, which had supported pure food and drug legislation and laws to protect against health quacks and to enforce standards for medical schools, attacked this bill as leading to socialism and interfering with the relationship between doctor and patient and with the "fee for service" system. Others, especially those who had opposed woman suffrage, argued that it was put forward by extreme feminists, that it was "inspired by foreign experiments in Communism and backed by radical forces in the country," that it "strikes at the heart of American Civilization," and that it would lead to socializing medicine and radicalizing the children.

Despite the opposition, the bill passed Congress and was signed by President Harding in 1921. The appropriation for the bill was only for six years, and the opposition, again raising the specter of a feminist-Socialist-Communist plot, succeeded in repealing the law in 1929. Yet the Sheppard-Towner Act, promoted and fought for by a group of progressive women, indicated that concern for social justice was not dead in the age of Harding and Coolidge.

Temperance Triumphant

For one large group of progressives, prohibition, like child labor reform and maternity benefits, was an important effort to conserve human resources. By 1918,

over three-fourths of the people in the country lived in dry states or counties, but it was the war that allowed the antisaloon advocates to associate prohibition with patriotism. "We have German enemies across the water," one prohibitionist announced. "We have German enemies in this country too. And the worst of all our German enemies, the most treacherous, the most menacing are Pabst, Schlitz, Blatz and Miller." In 1919, Congress passed the Volstead Act, banning the brewing and selling of beverages containing more than $\frac{1}{2}$ percent alcohol. The 36th state ratified the Eighteenth Amendment in June 1919, but the country had, for all practical purposes, been dry since 1917.

The prohibition experiment probably did reduce the total consumption of alcohol in the country, especially in rural areas and urban working-class neighborhoods. Fewer arrests for drunkenness occurred, and deaths from alcoholism declined. But the legislation showed the difficulty of using law to promote moral reform. Most people who wanted to drink during the "noble experiment" found a way. Speakeasies replaced saloons, and people consumed bathtub gin, home brew, and many strange and dangerous concoctions. Bartenders invented the cocktail to disguise the poor quality of liquor, and women, at least middle- and upper-class women, began to drink in public for the first time.

Prohibition also created great bootlegging rings, which were tied to organized crime in many cities. Al Capone of Chicago was the most famous underworld figure whose power and wealth were based on the sale of illegal alcohol. His organization alone is supposed to have grossed over $60 million in 1927; ironically, most of the profit came from distributing beer. Many supporters of prohibition slowly came to favor its repeal, some because it reduced the power of the states, others because it stimulated too much illegal activity and because it did not seem to be worth the social and political costs.

The Election of 1928

On August 2, 1927, President Coolidge announced simply, "I do not choose to run for President in 1928." Hoover immediately became the logical Republican candidate. Hoover and Coolidge were not especially close. Coolidge resented what he considered Hoover's spendthrift ways. "That man has offered me unsolicited advice for six years, all of it bad," Coolidge once remarked. Though lacking an enthusiastic endorsement from the president and opposed by some Republicans who thought him too progressive, Hoover easily won the nomination. In a year when the country was buoyant with optimism and when prosperity seemed as if it would go on forever, few doubted that Hoover would be elected.

Herbert Hoover, one of the most popular politicians of the 1920s and one of the most unpopular after 1929, is seen here campaigning from the platform of his private railway car. Note the hats worn by all the men and the few women in the audience. *(Corbis-Bettmann)*

The Democrats nominated Alfred Smith, a Catholic Irish American from New York. With his New York accent, his opposition to prohibition, and his flamboyant style, he contrasted sharply with the more sedate Hoover. On one level, it was a bitter contest between Catholic "wets" and Protestant "drys," between the urban, ethnic Tammany politician and former governor of New York against the rural-born but sophisticated secretary of commerce. Religious prejudice, especially a persistent anti-Catholicism, played an important role in the campaign. But looked at more closely, the two candidates differed little. Both were self-made men, both were "progressives." Social justice reformers campaigned for each candidate. Both candidates tried to attract women voters, both were favorable to organized labor, both defended cap-

italism, and both had millionaires and corporate executives among their advisers.

Hoover won in a landslide, 444 electoral votes to 76 for Smith, who carried only Massachusetts and Rhode Island outside the Deep South. But the 1928 campaign revitalized the Democratic party. Smith polled nearly twice as many votes as the Democratic candidate in 1924, and for the first time the Democrats carried the 12 largest cities.

Stock Market Crash

Hoover, as it turned out, had only six months to apply his progressive and efficient methods to running the country because in the fall of 1929, the prosperity that seemed endless suddenly came to a halt. In 1928 and 1929, rampant speculation made the stock market

PRESIDENTIAL ELECTIONS, 1920–1928				
Year	Candidate	Party	Popular Vote	Electoral Vote
1920	WARREN G. HARDING	Republican	16,152,200 (60.4%)	404
	James M. Cox	Democratic	9,147,353 (34.2%)	127
	Eugene V. Debs	Socialist	919,799 (3.4%)	0
1924	CALVIN COOLIDGE	Republican	15,725,016 (54.0%)	382
	John W. Davis	Democratic	8,385,586 (28.8%)	136
	Robert M. La Follette	Progressive	4,822,856 (16.6%)	13
1928	HERBERT C. HOOVER	Republican	21,392,190 (58.2%)	444
	Alfred E. Smith	Democratic	15,016,443 (40.9%)	87

Note: Winners' names appear in capital letters.

boom. Money could be made everywhere—in real estate and business ventures, but especially in the stock market. "Everybody ought to be Rich," Al Smith's campaign manager argued in an article in the *Ladies' Home Journal* early in 1929. Just save $15 a month and buy good common stock with it, and that money would turn into $80,000 in 20 years (a considerable fortune in 1929). Good common stock seemed to be easy to find in 1929.

Only a small percentage of the American people invested in the stock market, for many had no way of saving even $15 a month. But a large number got into the game in the late 1920s because it seemed a safe and sure way to make money. For many, the stock market came to represent the American economy, and the economy was booming. The *New York Times* index of 25 industrial stocks reached 100 in 1924, moved up to 181 in 1925, dropped a bit in 1926, and rose again to 245 by the end of 1927.

Then the orgy started. During 1928, the market rose to 331. Many investors and speculators began to buy on margin (borrowing to invest). Businessmen and others began to invest money in the market that would ordinarily have gone into houses, cars, and other goods. Yet even at the peak of the boom, probably only about 1.5 million Americans owned stock.

In early September 1929, the *New York Times* index peaked at 452 and then began to drift downward. On October 23, the market lost 31 points. The next day ("Black Thursday"), it first seemed that everyone was trying to sell, but at the end of the day, the panic appeared over. It was not. By mid-November, the market had plummeted to 224, about half what it had been two months before. This represented a loss on paper of over $26 billion. Still, a month later, the chairman of the board of Bethlehem Steel could announce, "Never before has American business been as firmly entrenched for prosperity as it is today." Some businessmen even got back into the market, thinking that it had reached its low point. But it continued to go down. Tens of thousands of investors lost everything. Those who had bought on margin had to keep coming up with money to pay off their loans as the value of their holdings declined. There was panic and despair, but the legendary stories of executives jumping out of windows were grossly exaggerated.

Timeline

1900–1930	Electricity powers the "second industrial revolution"
1917	Race riot in East Saint Louis, Illinois
1918	World War I ends
1919	Treaty of Versailles
	Strikes in Seattle, Boston, and elsewhere
	Red Scare and Palmer raids
	Race riots in Chicago and other cities
	Marcus Garvey's Universal Negro Improvement Association spreads
1920	Warren Harding elected president
	Women vote in national elections
	First commercial radio broadcast
	Sacco and Vanzetti arrested
	Sinclair Lewis, *Main Street*
1921	Immigration Quota Law
	Naval Disarmament Conference
	First birth control conference
	Sheppard-Towner Maternity Act
1921–1922	Postwar depression
1922	Fordney-McCumber Tariff
	Sinclair Lewis, *Babbitt*
1923	Harding dies; Calvin Coolidge becomes president
	Teapot Dome scandal

1924	Coolidge reelected president
	Peak of Ku Klux Klan activity
	Immigration Quota Law
1925	Scopes trial in Dayton, Tennessee
	F. Scott Fitzgerald, *The Great Gatsby*
	Bruce Barton, *The Man Nobody Knows*
	Alain Locke, *The New Negro*
	Claude McKay, *Home to Harlem*
	Five million enameled bathroom fixtures produced
1926	Ernest Hemingway, *The Sun Also Rises*
1927	National Origins Act
	McNary-Haugen Farm Relief Bill
	Sacco and Vanzetti executed
	Lindbergh flies solo, New York to Paris
	First talking movie, *The Jazz Singer*
	Henry Ford produces 15 millionth car
1928	Herbert Hoover elected president
	Kellogg-Briand Treaty
	Stock market soars
1929	27 million registered cars in country
	10 million households own radios
	100 million people attend movies
	Stock market crash

Conclusion
A New Era of Prosperity and Problems

The stock market crash ended the decade of prosperity. The crash did not cause the depression, but the stock market debacle revealed the weakness of the economy. The fruits of economic expansion had been unevenly distributed. Not enough people could afford to buy the autos, refrigerators, and other products pouring from American factories. Prosperity had been built on a shaky foundation. When that foundation crumbled in 1929, the nation slid into a major depression.

Looking back from the vantage point of the 1930s or later, the 1920s seemed a golden era—an age of flappers, bootleg gin, constant parties, literary masterpieces, sports heroes, and easy wealth. The truth is much more complicated. More than most decades, the 1920s was a time of paradox and contradictions.

The 1920s was a time of prosperity, yet a great many people, including farmers, blacks, and other ordinary Americans, did not prosper. It was a time of modernization, but only about 10 percent of rural families had electricity. It was a time when women achieved more sexual freedom, but the feminist movement declined. It was a time of prohibition, but many Americans increased their consumption of alcohol. It was a time of reaction against reform, yet progressivism survived. It was a time when intellectuals felt disillusioned with America, yet it was one of the most creative and innovative periods for American writers. It was a time of flamboyant heroes, yet the American people elected the lackluster Harding and Coolidge as their presidents. It was a time of progress, when almost every year saw a new technological breakthrough, but it was also a decade of hate and intolerance. The complex and contradictory legacy of the 1920s continues to fascinate and to influence our time.

Recommended Reading

Postwar Problems

David M. Chalmers, *Hooded Americanism: The History of the Ku Klux Klan* (1965); Roberta Strauss Feurlicht, *Justice Crucified: The Story of Sacco and Vanzetti* (1977); Robert L. Friedheim, *The Seattle General Strike* (1965); David J. Goldberg, *Discontented America: The United States in the 1920s* (1998); Kenneth Jackson, *The Ku Klux Klan in the City* (1967); Robert K. Murray, *Red Scare* (1965).

A Prospering Economy

Erik Barnouw, *A Tower of Babel: A History of American Radio to 1933* (1966); Lendal Calder, *Financing the American Dream: A Cultural History of Consumer Credit* (1999); Lizabeth Cohen, *Making a New Deal: Industrial Workers in Chicago, 1919–1939* (1990); James J. Flink, *The Car Culture* (1975); Daniel Horowitz, *The Morality of Spending: Attitudes Toward the Consumer Society in America* (1985); Jackson Lears, *Fables of Abundance: A Cultural History of Advertising in America* (1994); William Leuchtenburg, *The Perils of Prosperity, 1919–1932* (1970); Tom Lewis, *Empire of the Air: The Men who Made Radio* (1991); Margaret Marsh, *Suburban Lives* (1990); Zane Miller, *The Urbanization of America* (1973); David Nye, *Electrifying America* (1991); Roland Marchand, *Advertising the American Dream* (1985); Susan Strasser, *Satisfaction Guaranteed: The Making of the American Mass Market* (1989).

Hopes Raised, Promises Deferred

John M. Barry, *Rising Tide; The Great Mississippi Flood of 1927 and How It Changed America* (1997); William H. Chafe, *The American Woman: Her Changing Social and Political Worlds* (1992); George Chauncey, *Gay New York: Gender, Urban Culture and the Meaning of the Gay World* (1994); Ellen Chesler, *Woman of Valor: Margaret Sanger and the Birth Control Movement* (1992); Nancy F. Cott, *The Grounding of Modern Feminism* (1987); Lyle W. Dorsett, *Billy Sunday and the Redemption of Urban America* (1991); Lynn Dumenil, *Modern Temper: American Culture and Society in the 1920s* (1995); Paula Fass, *The Damned and the Beautiful: American Youth in the 1920s*

(1977); Harvey Green, *The Uncertainty of Everyday Life, 1915–1945* (1992); John Higham, *Strangers in the Land: Patterns of American Nativism, 1860–1925* (1955); Frederick Hoffman, *The Twenties* (1949); Nathan I. Huggins, *Harlem Renaissance* (1971); Alice Kessler-Harris, *Out to Work: A History of Wage Earning Women in America* (1982); Edward Larson, *Summer for the Gods: The Scopes Trial and America's Continuing Debate Over Science and Religion* (1997); J. Stanley Lemons, *The Woman Citizen: Social Feminism in the 1920s* (1973); David Levering Lewis, *When Harlem Was in Vogue* (1981); George M. Marsden, *Fundamentalism and American Culture* (1980); Susan Strasser, *Never Done: A History of American Housework* (1982); Theodore Vincent, *Black Power and the Garvey Movement* (1979).

The Business of Politics

David Burner, *The Politics of Provincialism* (1967); Warren I. Cohen, *Empire Without Tears* (1987); John D. Hicks, *Republican Ascendancy, 1921–1933* (1960); Robert H. Ferrell, *The Presidency of Calvin Coolidge* (1998); John Kenneth Galbraith, *The Great Crash* (1954); Oscar Handlin, *Al Smith and His America* (1958); K. Austin Kerr, *Organized for Prohibition* (1985); David Wilson, *The Presidency of Warren G. Harding* (1977); William Appleman Williams, *The Tragedy of American Diplomacy* (1962); Joan Hoff Wilson, *Herbert Hoover: Forgotten Progressive* (1975).

Fiction and Film

Sinclair Lewis's novel *Babbitt* (1922) depicts the narrowness of small-town life in the Midwest. F. Scott Fitzgerald describes the reckless lives of the very rich in *The Great Gatsby* (1925). Claude McKay's novel *Home to Harlem* (1928) is one of the best fictional works to come out of the Harlem Renaissance.

Front Page (1931) is a movie that depicts the world of corrupt politicians and cynical newspapermen in Chicago during the roaring twenties. The 1974 film version of *The Great Gatsby* is not entirely faithful to the novel, but it still captures some of the opulence and pathos of the lives of the very rich in the 1920s.

Suggested Web Sites

http://mel.lib.mi.us/business/autos-history.html

Automotive History. This site, from the Michigan Electronic Library, has several links to sites about automotive history in America.

http://arts-crafts.com/archive/archive.html

National Arts & Crafts Archives. This site serves as a guide to materials on the Arts & Crafts movement, which lasted roughly from 1890 to 1929.

http://www.si.umich.edu./CHICO/Harlem

Harlem 1900–1940: An African-American Community. The New York Public Library's Schomburg Center for Research in Black Culture hosts this site, which includes a database, a timeline, and an exhibit.

http://memory.loc.gov/ammem/wghtml/wghome.html

Photographs from the Golden Age of Jazz. The Music Division of the Library of Congress offers numerous images, audio elements, and scanned articles from the 1940s.

http://www.negroleaguebaseball.com/

Negro League Baseball Dot Com. Essays about desegregation, baseball, and Jim Crow, as well as images of teams and players, constitute much of this site.

http://www.louisville.edu/~kpray01/1920s.html

The 1920s/Society, Fads, Daily Life. This site, from Kevin Rayburn and the University of Louisville, looks at how the 1920s set the stage for many aspects of modern popular culture.

http://xroads.virginia.edu/~UG97/inherit/1925home.html

The Scopes Trial. This site gives a general description of the "Monkey" trial and the issues surrounding it.

http://www.cohums.ohio-state.edu/history/projects/prohibition/

American Temperance and Prohibition. This site looks at the temperance movement over time and contains many informative links.

http://www.pandorasbox.com/flapper.html

Flapper Culture & Style. This site contains many links to information about the popular culture of the 1920s with special reference to the flapper.

http://www.geocities.com/CapitolHill/4921/

The Coolidge Experience. This site offers an unusual look at one of America's less colorful presidents.

http://www.ushistoryplace.com

A richly detailed on-line learning environment complete with interactive maps, timelines, history activities, primary source documents, and links to related American history sites.

24

The GREAT DEPRESSION *and* *the* NEW DEAL

CHAPTER OUTLINE

Diana Morgan grew up in a small North Carolina town, the daughter of a prosperous cotton merchant. She lived the life of a "southern belle," oblivious to the country's social and political problems, but the Great Depression changed that. She came home from college for Christmas vacation during her junior year to discover that the telephone had been disconnected. Her world suddenly fell apart. Her father's business had failed, her family didn't have a cook or a cleaning woman anymore, and their house was being sold for back taxes. She was confused and embarrassed. Sometimes it was the little things that were the hardest. Friends would come from out of town, and there would be no ice because her family did not own an electric refrigerator and they could not afford to buy ice. "There were those frantic arrangements of running out to the drugstore to get Coca-Cola with crushed ice, and there'd be this embarrassing delay, and I can remember how hot my face was."

Like many Americans, Diana Morgan and her family blamed themselves for what happened during the Great Depression. Americans had been taught to believe that if they worked hard, saved their money, and lived upright and moral lives, they could succeed. Success was an individual matter for Americans. When so many failed during the Depression, they blamed themselves rather than society or larger forces for their plight. The shame and the guilt affected people at all levels of society. The businessman who lost his business, the farmer who watched his farm being sold at auction, the worker who was suddenly unemployed and felt his manhood stripped away because he could not provide for his family were all devastated by the Depression.

Diana Morgan had never intended to get a job; she expected to get married and let her husband support her. But the failure of her father's business forced her to join the growing number of women who worked outside the home in the 1930s. She finally found a position with the Civil Works Administration, a New Deal agency, where at first she had to ask humiliating questions of the people applying for assistance to make sure they were destitute. "Do you own a car?" "Does anyone in the family work?" Diana was appalled at the conditions she saw when she traveled around the county to corroborate their stories. She found dilapidated houses, a dirty, "almost paralyzed-looking mother," and a drunken father, together with malnourished children. She felt helpless that she could do nothing more than write out a food order. One day, a woman who had formerly cooked for her family came in to apply for help. Each was embarrassed to see the other in changed circumstances.

Diana had to defend the New Deal programs to many of her friends, who accused her of being sentimental and told her that the poor, especially poor blacks, did not know any better than to live in squalor. "If you give them coal, they'd put it in the bathtub," was a charge she often heard. But she knew "they didn't have bathtubs to put coal in. So how did anybody know that's what they'd do with coal if they had it?"

Diana Morgan's experience working for a New Deal agency influenced her life and her attitudes; it made her more of a social activist. Her Depression experience gave her a greater appreciation for the struggles of the country's poor and unlucky. Although she prospered in the years after the Depression, the sense of guilt and the fear that the telephone might again be cut off never left her.

The Great Depression changed the lives of all Americans and separated that generation from the one that followed. An exaggerated need for security, the fear of failure, a nagging sense of guilt, and a real sense that it might happen all over again divided the Depression generation from everyone born after 1940. Like Diana Morgan, most Americans never forgot those bleak years.

This chapter explores the causes and consequences of the Great Depression. We will look at Herbert Hoover and his efforts to combat the Depression and then turn to Franklin Roosevelt, the dominant personality of the 1930s. We will examine the New Deal and Roosevelt's program to bring relief, recovery, and reform to the nation. But we will not ignore the other side of the 1930s,

The WPA (Works Progress Administration) hired artists from 1935 to 1943 to create murals for public buildings. The assumption was not only that "artists need to eat too," as Harry Hopkins announced, but also that art was an important part of culture and should be supported by the federal government. Here Moses Soyer, a Philadelphia artist, depicts WPA artists creating a mural. *(Moses Soyer,* Artists on WPA, *1935/National Museum of American Art, Smithsonian Institution, Gift of Mr. and Mrs. Moses Soyer/Art Resource, New York)*

for the decade did not consist only of crippling unemployment and New Deal agencies. It was also a time of great strides in

technology, when innovative developments in radio, movies, and the automobile affected the lives of most Americans.

THE GREAT DEPRESSION

There had been recessions and depressions in American history, notably in the 1830s, 1870s, and 1890s, but nothing compared with the devastating economic collapse of the 1930s. The Great Depression was all the more shocking because it came after a decade of unprecedented prosperity, when most experts assumed that the United States was immune to a downturn in the business cycle. The Great Depression had an impact on all areas of American life; perhaps most important, it destroyed American confidence in the future.

The Depression Begins

Few people anticipated the stock market crash in the fall of 1929. But even after the collapse of the stock market, few expected the entire economy to go into a tailspin. General Electric stock, selling for 396 in 1929, fell to 34 in 1932; U.S. Steel declined from 261 to 21. By 1932, the median income had plunged to half what it had been in 1929. Construction spending fell to one-sixth of the 1929 level. By 1932, at least one of every four American breadwinners was out of work, and industrial production had almost ground to a halt.

Why did the nation sink deeper and deeper into depression? After all, only about 2 percent of the population owned stock of any kind. The answer is complex, but the prosperity of the 1920s, it appears in retrospect, was superficial. Farmers and coal and textile workers had suffered all through the 1920s from low prices, and the farmers were the first group in the 1930s to plunge into depression. But other aspects of the economy also lurched out of balance. Two percent of the population received about 28 percent of the national income, but the lower 60 percent got only 24 percent. Businesses increased profits while holding down wages and the prices of raw materials. This pattern depressed consumer purchasing power. American workers, like American farmers, did not have the money to buy the goods they helped to produce. There was a relative decline in purchasing power in the late 1920s, unemployment was high in some industries, and the housing and automobile industries were already beginning to slacken before the crash.

Well-to-do Americans were speculating a significant portion of their money in the stock market. Their illusion of permanent prosperity helped fire the boom of the 1920s, just as their pessimism and lack of confidence helped exaggerate the depression in 1931 and 1932.

Other factors were also involved. The stock market crash revealed serious structural weaknesses in the financial and banking systems (7,000 banks had failed during the 1920s). The Federal Reserve Board, fearing inflation, tightened credit—exactly the opposite of the action it should have taken to fight a slowdown in purchasing. Economic relations with Europe contributed to deepening depression. High American tariffs during the 1920s had reduced trade. When American investment in Europe declined in 1928 and 1929, European economies declined. As the European financial situation worsened, the American economy spiraled downward.

The federal government might have prevented the stock market crash and the Depression by more careful regulation of business and the stock market. Central planning might have ensured a more equitable distribution of income. But that kind of policy would have taken more foresight than most people had in the 1920s. It certainly would have required different people in power, and it is unlikely that the Democrats, had they been in control, would have altered the government's policies in fundamental ways.

Hoover and the Great Depression

Initial business and government reactions to the stock market crash were optimistic. "All the evidence indicates that the worst effects of the crash upon unemployment will have been passed during the next sixty days," Herbert Hoover reported. Hoover, the great planner and progressive efficiency expert, did not sit idly by and watch the country drift toward disorder. His upbeat first statements were calculated to prevent further panic.

The Agricultural Marketing Act of 1929 set up a $500 million revolving fund to help farmers organize cooperative marketing associations and to establish minimum prices. But as agricultural prices plummeted and banks foreclosed on farm mortgages, the available funds proved inadequate. The Farm Board was helpless to aid the farmer who could not meet mortgage payments because the price of grain had fallen so rapidly. Nor could it help the Arkansas woman who stood weeping in the window as her possessions, including the cows, which all had names, were sold one by one.

One of the New Deal's largest public works projects was actually started during the Hoover administration. Built between 1931 and 1935, the Boulder Dam (renamed the Hoover Dam) was the greatest American construction feat since the Panama Canal. Rising over 726 feet above bedrock and creating Lake Mead, the world's largest reservoir, the Hoover Dam was an engineering marvel. The project employed tens of thousands of men, and 96 lost their lives as they were pushed beyond endurance in 110° heat by companies trying to finish ahead of schedule. The dam provided cheap electricity to Los Angeles and parts of Arizona. And it provided water that turned the imperial valley into one of the most productive agricultural areas in the world. *(Culver Pictures)*

Hoover acted aggressively to stem the economic collapse. More than any president before him, he used the power of the federal government and the office of the president to deal with an economic crisis. Nobody called it a depression for the first year at least, for the economic problems seemed very much like earlier cyclic recessions. Hoover called conferences of businessmen and labor leaders. He met with mayors and governors and encouraged them to speed up public works projects. He created agencies and boards, such as the National Credit Corporation and the Emergency Committee for Employment, to obtain voluntary action to solve the problem. Hoover even supported a tax cut, which Congress enacted in December 1929, but it did little to stimulate spending. Hoover also went on the radio in his effort to convince the American people that the fundamental structure of the economy was sound.

The Collapsing Economy

Voluntary action and psychological campaigns could not stop the Depression. The stock market, after appearing to bottom out in the winter of 1930–1931, continued its decline, responding in part to the European economic collapse that threatened international finance and trade. Of course, not everyone lost money in the market. William Danforth, founder of Ralston Purina, and Joseph Kennedy, film magnate, entrepreneur, and the father of a future president, were among those who made millions of dollars by selling short as the market went down.

More than a collapsing market afflicted the economy. Over 1,300 additional banks failed in 1930.

Despite Hoover's pleas, many factories cut back on production, and some simply closed. U.S. Steel announced a 10 percent wage cut in 1931. As the auto industry laid off workers, the unemployment rate rose to over 40 percent in Detroit. More than 4 million Americans were out of work in 1930, and at least 12 million by 1932. Foreclosures and evictions created thousands of personal tragedies. There were 200,000 evictions in New York City alone in 1930. While the middle class watched in horror as their life savings and their dreams disappeared, the rich were increasingly concerned as the price of government bonds (the symbol of safety and security) dropped. They began to hoard gold and fear revolution.

There was never any real danger of revolution. Some farmers organized to dump their milk to protest low prices, and when a neighbor's farm was sold, they gathered to hold a penny auction, bidding only a few cents for equipment and returning it to their dispossessed neighbor. But everywhere people despaired as the Depression deepened in 1931 and 1932. For unemployed blacks and for many tenant farmers, the Depression had little immediate effect because their lives were already so depressed. Most Americans (the 98 percent who did not own stock) hardly noticed the stock market crash; for them, the Depression meant the loss of a job or a bank foreclosure. For Diana Morgan, it was the discovery that the telephone had been cut off; for some farmers, it was burning corn rather than coal because the price of corn had fallen so low that it was not worth marketing.

For some in the cities, the Depression meant not having enough money to feed the children. "Have you

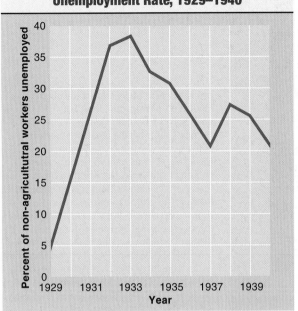

Unemployment Rate, 1929–1940

(Chart: Percent of non-agricultural workers unemployed vs. Year, 1929–1939)

Although the unemployment rate declined during the New Deal years, the number still unemployed remained tragically high until World War II brought full employment. Source: U.S. Bureau of the Census.

ever heard a hungry child cry?" asked Lillian Wald of the Henry Street Settlement. "Have you seen the uncontrollable trembling of parents who have gone half starved for weeks so that the children may have food?" In Chicago, children fought with men and women over the garbage dumped by the city trucks. "We have been eating wild greens," a coal miner wrote from Harlan County, Kentucky, "such as Polk salad, violet tops, wild onions . . . and such weeds as cows eat." In Toledo, when municipal and private charity funds were running low, as they did in all cities, those granted assistance were given only 2.14 cents per meal per person. In another city, a social worker noticed that the children were playing a game called "Eviction." "Sometimes they play 'Relief,'" she remarked, "but 'Eviction' has more action and all of them know how to play."

Not everyone went hungry, stood in breadlines, or lost jobs during the Depression, but almost everyone was affected, and many victims tended to blame themselves. A businessman who lost his job and had to stand in a relief line remembered years later how he would bend his head low so nobody would recognize him. A 28-year-old teacher in New Orleans was released because of a cut in funds, and in desperation she took a job as a domestic servant. "If with all the advantages I've had," she remarked, "I can't make a living, I'm just no good, I guess. I've given up ever amounting to anything. It's no use."

The Depression probably disrupted women's lives less than men's. "When hard times hit, it didn't seem to bother mother as much as it did father," one woman remembered. There were many exceptions, of course, but when men lost their jobs, their identity and sense of purpose as the family breadwinner were shattered. Some helped out with family chores, usually with bitterness and resentment. For women, however, even when money was short, there was still cooking, cleaning, and mending, and women were still in command of their households. Yet many women were forced to do extra work. They took in laundry, found room for a boarder, and made the clothes they formerly would have bought. Women also bore the psychological burden of unemployed husbands, hungry children, and unpaid bills. The Depression altered patterns of family life, and many families were forced to move in with relatives. The marriage rate, the divorce rate, and the birthrate all dropped during the decade. Many of these changes created tension that statistics cannot capture.

Hoover reacted to growing despair by urging more voluntary action. "We are going through a period," he announced in February 1931, "when character and courage are on trial, and where the very faith that is within us is under test." He insisted on maintaining the gold standard, believing it to be the only responsible currency, and a balanced budget, but so did almost everyone else. Congress was nearly unanimous in supporting those ideals, and Governor Franklin Roosevelt of New York accused Hoover of endangering the country by spending too much. Hoover increasingly blamed the Depression on international economic problems, and he was not entirely mistaken. The whole world was gripped by depression, but as it deepened, Americans began to blame Hoover for some of the disaster. The president became isolated and bitter. The shanties that grew near all the large cities were called "Hoovervilles," and the privies "Hoover villas." Unable to admit mistakes and to take a new tack, he could not communicate personal empathy for the poor and the unemployed.

Hoover did try innovative schemes. More public works projects were built during his administration than in the previous 30 years. In the summer of 1931, he attempted to organize a pool of private money to rescue banks and businesses that were near failure. When the private effort failed, he turned reluctantly to Congress, which passed a bill early in 1932 authorizing the Reconstruction Finance Corporation. The RFC was capitalized at $500 million, but a short time later that was increased to $3 billion. It was authorized to make loans to banks, insurance companies, farm mortgage companies, and railroads. Some critics charged that it was simply another trickle-down mea-

The worst result of the Depression was hopelessness and despair. Those emotions are captured in this painting of an unemployment office by Isaac Soyer. (Isaac Soyer, *Employment Agency, 1937, Oil on canvas, 34¼ x 45 in. [87 x 114.3 cm]. Collection of Whitney Museum of American Art, Purchase, 37.44, Photograph © 2000: Whitney Museum of American Art)*

sure whereby businessmen and bankers would be given aid while the unemployed were ignored. Hoover, however, correctly understood the immense costs to individuals and to communities when a bank or mortgage company failed. The RFC did help shore up a number of shaky financial institutions and remained the major government finance agency until World War II. But it became much more effective under Roosevelt because it lent directly to industry.

Hoover also asked Congress for a Home Financing Corporation to make mortgages more readily available. The Federal Home Loan Bank Act of 1932 became the basis for the Federal Housing Administration of the New Deal years. He also pushed the passage of the Glass-Steagall Banking Act of 1932, which expanded credit to make more loans available to businesses and individuals. Hoover failed to suggest any new farm legislation, even though members of the Farm Board insisted that the only answer to the agricultural crisis was for the federal government to step in and restrict production. Hoover believed that was too much federal intervention. He maintained that the federal government should promote cooperation and even create public works. But he firmly believed in loans, not direct subsidies, and he thought it was the responsibility of state and local governments, as well as of private

charity, to provide direct relief to the unemployed and the needy.

The Bonus Army

Many World War I veterans lost their jobs during the Great Depression, and beginning in 1930, they lobbied for the payment of their veterans' bonuses, not due until 1945. A bill passed Congress in 1931, over Hoover's veto, allowing them to borrow up to 50 percent of the bonus due them, but this concession did not satisfy the destitute veterans. In May 1932, about 17,000 veterans marched on Washington. Some took up residence in a shantytown, called Bonus City, in the Anacostia flats outside the city.

In mid-June, the Senate defeated the bonus bill, and most of the veterans, disappointed but resigned, accepted a free railroad ticket home. Several thousand remained, however, along with some wives and children, in the unsanitary shacks during the steaming summer heat. Among them were a small group of committed communists and other radicals. Hoover, who exaggerated the subversive elements among those still camped out in Washington, refused to talk to the leaders and finally called out the U.S. Army.

General Douglas MacArthur, the army chief of staff, ordered the army to disperse the veterans. He described the Bonus marchers as a "mob . . . animated

U.S. soldiers burn the Bonus army shacks within sight of the Capitol in the summer of 1932. This image of the failure of the American dream was published widely around the world. *(National Archives)*

by the essence of revolution." With tanks, guns, and tear gas, the army routed veterans who 15 years before had worn the same uniform as their attackers. Two Bonus marchers were killed, and several others were injured. "What a pitiful spectacle is that of the great American Government, mightiest in the world, chasing unarmed men, women and children with Army tanks," commented a Washington newspaper. "If the Army must be called out to make war on unarmed citizens, this is no longer America." The army was not attacking revolutionaries in the streets of Washington but was routing bewildered, confused, unemployed men who had seen their American dream collapse.

The Bonus army fiasco, breadlines, and Hoovervilles became the symbols of Hoover's presidency. He deserved better because he tried to use the power of the federal government to solve growing and increasingly complex economic problems. But in the end, his personality and background limited him. He could not understand why army veterans marched on Washington to ask for a handout when he thought they should all be back home working hard, practicing self-reliance, and cooperating "to avert the terrible situation in which we are today." He believed that the greatest problem besetting Americans was a lack of confidence. He could not communicate with these people or inspire their confidence. Willing to use the federal government to support business, he could not accept federal aid for the unemployed. He feared an unbalanced budget and a large federal bureaucracy that would interfere with the "American way." Ironically, his actions and his inactions led in the next

years to a massive increase in federal power and in the federal bureaucracy.

ROOSEVELT AND THE FIRST NEW DEAL

The first New Deal, lasting from 1933 to early 1935, focused mainly on recovery from the Depression and relief for the poor and unemployed. Congress passed legislation to aid business, the farmers, and labor and authorized public works projects and massive spending to put Americans back to work. Some of the programs were borrowed from the Hoover administration, and some had their origin in the progressive period. Others were inspired by the nation's experiences in mobilizing for World War I. No single ideological position united all the programs, for Roosevelt was a pragmatist who was willing to try a variety of programs. More than Hoover, however, he believed in economic planning and in government spending to help the poor.

Roosevelt's caution and conservatism shaped the first New Deal. He did not promote socialism or suggest nationalizing the banks. He was even careful in authorizing public works projects to stimulate the economy. The New Deal was based on the assumption that it was possible to create a just society by superimposing a welfare state on the capitalistic system, leaving the profit motive undisturbed. During the first New Deal, Roosevelt believed he would achieve his goals through cooperation with the business community. Later he would move more toward reform, but at first his primary concern was simply relief and recovery.

The Election of 1932

The Republicans nominated Herbert Hoover for a second term, but in the summer of 1932, the Depression and Hoover's unpopularity opened the way for the Democrats. After a shrewd campaign, Franklin D. Roosevelt, governor of New York, emerged from the pack and won the nomination. Journalist Walter Lippmann's comment during the campaign that Roosevelt was a "pleasant man who, without any important qualifications for office, would like very much to be President" was exaggerated at the time and seemed absurd later. Roosevelt, distantly related to Theodore Roosevelt, had served as an assistant secretary of the navy during World War I and had been the Democratic vice presidential candidate in 1920. Crippled by infantile paralysis not long after, he had recovered enough to serve as governor of New York for two terms, though he was not especially well known by the general public in 1932.

Governor Roosevelt had promoted cheaper electric power, conservation, and old-age pensions. Urged on by advisers Frances Perkins and Harry Hopkins, he became the first governor to support state aid for the unemployed, "not as a matter of charity, but as a matter of social duty." But it was difficult to tell during the presidential campaign exactly what he stood for. He did announce that the government must do some-thing for the "forgotten man at the bottom of the economic pyramid," and he struck out at the small group of men who "make huge profits from lending money and the marketing of securities." Yet he also mentioned the need for balancing the budget and maintaining the gold standard. Ambiguity was probably the best strategy in 1932, but the truth was that Roosevelt did not have a master plan to save the country. Yet he won overwhelmingly, carrying more than 57 percent of the popular vote.

During the campaign, Roosevelt had promised a "new deal for the American people." But after his victory, the New Deal had to wait for four months because the Constitution provided that the new president be inaugurated on March 4 (this was changed to January 20 by the Twentieth Amendment, ratified in 1933). During the long interregnum, the state of the nation deteriorated badly. The banking system seemed near collapse, and the hardship increased. Despite his bitter defeat, Hoover tried to cooperate with the president-elect and with a hostile Congress. But he could accomplish little. Everyone waited for the new president to take office and to act.

In his inaugural address, Roosevelt announced confidently, "The only thing we have to fear is fear itself." This, of course, was not true, for the country faced the worst crisis since the Civil War, but Roosevelt's confidence and his ability to communicate with ordinary Americans were obvious early in his presidency. He had clever speech writers, a sense

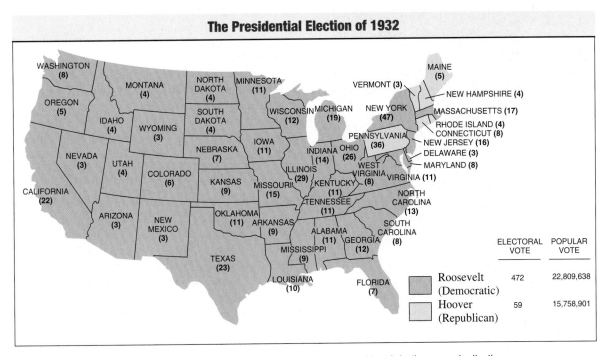

The Presidential Election of 1932

	Electoral Vote	Popular Vote
Roosevelt (Democratic)	472	22,809,638
Hoover (Republican)	59	15,758,901

This map demonstrates the overwhelming extent of Roosevelt's landslide victory, caused largely by the economic situation.

of pace and rhythm in his speeches, and an ability, when he spoke on the radio, to convince listeners that he was speaking directly to them. He instituted a series of radio "fireside chats" to explain to the American people what he was doing to solve the nation's problems. When he said "my friends," millions believed that he meant it, and they wrote letters to him in unprecedented numbers to explain their needs.

The Cabinet and the "Brain Trust"

During the interregnum, Roosevelt surrounded himself with intelligent and innovative advisers. Some, like James A. Farley, a former New York State boxing commissioner with a genius for remembering names, and Louis Howe, Roosevelt's secretary and confidant since 1912, had helped plan his successful campaign. His cabinet was made up of a mixture of people from different backgrounds who often did not agree with one another. Harold Ickes, the secretary of the interior, was a Republican lawyer from Chicago and onetime supporter of Theodore Roosevelt. Another Republican, Henry Wallace of Iowa, a plant geneticist and agricul-

This is a rare photograph of Franklin Roosevelt in his wheelchair taken in a private moment with his dog, Fala, and a young friend. Usually FDR's advisers carefully arranged to have the president photographed only when he was seated or propped up behind a podium. Despite being paralyzed from the waist down, the president until near the end of his life gave the impression of health and vitality. *(Margaret Suckley Collection, Franklin Delano Roosevelt Library)*

tural statistician, became the secretary of agriculture. Frances Perkins, the first woman ever appointed to a cabinet post, became the secretary of labor. A disciple of Jane Addams and Florence Kelley, she had been a settlement resident, secretary of the New York Consumers League, and an adviser to Al Smith.

In addition to the formal cabinet, Roosevelt appointed an informal "Brain Trust," including Adolph Berle, Jr., a young expert on corporation law, and Rexford Tugwell, a Columbia University authority on agricultural economics and a committed national planner. Roosevelt also appointed Raymond Moley, another Columbia professor, who later became one of the president's severest critics, and Harry Hopkins, a nervous, energetic man who loved to bet on horse races and had left Iowa to be a social worker in New York. Hopkins's passionate concern for the poor and unemployed would play a large role in formulating New Deal policy.

Eleanor Roosevelt, the president's wife, was a controversial first lady. She wrote a newspaper column, made radio broadcasts, traveled widely, and was constantly giving speeches and listening to the concerns of women, minorities, and ordinary Americans. Attacked by critics who thought she had too much power and mocked for her protruding front teeth, her awkward ways, and her upper-class accent, she courageously took stands on issues of social justice and civil rights. She helped push the president toward social reform.

Roosevelt proved to be an adept politician. He was not well read, especially on economic matters, but he had the ability to learn from his advisers and yet not be dominated by them. He took ideas, plans, and suggestions from conflicting sources and combined them. He had a "flypaper mind," one of his advisers decided. There was no overall plan, no master strategy. An improviser and an opportunist who once likened himself to a football quarterback who called one play and if it did not work called a different one, Roosevelt was an optimist by nature. And he believed in action.

ONE HUNDRED DAYS

Because Roosevelt took office in the middle of a major crisis, a cooperative Congress was willing to pass almost any legislation that he put before it. Not since Woodrow Wilson's first term had a president orchestrated Congress so effectively. In three months, a bewildering number of bills was rushed through. Some of them were hastily drafted and not well thought out, and some contradicted other legislation. But many of the laws passed during Roosevelt's first 100 days would have far-reaching implications for the relationship of government to society. Roosevelt was an opportunist, but unlike Hoover he was willing to use direct government action to solve the problems of depression and unemployment. As it turned out, none of the bills passed during the first 100 days cured the Depression, but taken together, the legislation constituted one of the most innovative periods in American political history.

The Banking Crisis

The most immediate problem Roosevelt faced was the condition of the banks. Many had closed, and American citizens, no longer trusting the financial institutions, were hoarding money and putting their assets into gold. Using a forgotten provision of a World War I law, Roosevelt immediately declared a four-day bank holiday. Three days later, an emergency session of Congress approved his action and within hours passed the Emergency Banking Relief Act. The bill gave the president broad powers over financial transactions, prohibited the hoarding of gold, and allowed for the reopening of sound banks, sometimes with loans from the Reconstruction Finance Corporation.

Within the next few years, Congress passed additional legislation that gave the federal government more regulatory power over the stock market and over the process by which corporations issued stock. It also passed the Banking Act of 1933, which strengthened the Federal Reserve System, established the Federal Deposit Insurance Corporation (FDIC), and insured individual deposits up to $5,000. Although the American Bankers Association opposed the plan as "unsound, unscientific, unjust and dangerous," banks were soon attracting depositors by advertising that they were protected by government insurance.

The Democratic platform in 1932 called for reduced government spending and an end to prohibition. Roosevelt moved quickly on both. The Economy Act, which passed Congress easily, called for a 15 percent reduction in government salaries as well as a reorganization of federal agencies to save money. The bill also cut veterans' pensions, over their protests. However, the Economy Act's small savings were dwarfed by other bills passed the same week, which called for increased spending. The Beer-Wine Revenue Act legalized 3.2 beer and light wines and levied a tax on both. The Twenty-first Amendment, ratified on December 5, 1933, repealed the Eighteenth Amendment and ended the prohibition experiment. The veterans and the antiliquor forces, two of the strongest lobbying groups in the nation, were both overwhelmed by a Congress that seemed ready to give the president free rein.

Congress granted Roosevelt great power to devalue the dollar and to manipulate inflation. Some members argued for the old Populist solution of free and unlimited coinage of silver, while others called for issuing billions of dollars in paper currency. Bankers and businessmen feared inflation, but farmers and debtors favored an inflationary policy as a way to raise prices and put more money in their pockets. "I have always favored sound money," Roosevelt announced, "and I do now, but it is 'too darned sound' when it takes so much of farm products to buy a dollar." He rejected the more extreme inflationary plans supported by many congressmen from the agricultural states, but he did take the country off the gold standard. No longer would paper currency be redeemable in gold. The action terrified some conservative businessmen, who argued that it would lead to "uncontrolled inflation and complete chaos." Even Roosevelt's director of the budget announced solemnly that going off the gold standard "meant the end of Western Civilization."

Devaluation did not end Western civilization, but neither did it lead to instant recovery. After experimenting with pushing the price of gold up by buying it in the open market, Roosevelt and his advisers fixed the price at $35 an ounce in January 1934 (against the old price of $20.63). This inflated the dollar by about 40 percent. Roosevelt also tried briefly to induce inflation through the purchase of silver, but soon the country settled down to a slightly inflated currency and a dollar based on both gold and silver. Some experts still believed that gold represented fiscal responsibility, even morality, and others still cried for more inflation.

Relief Measures

Roosevelt believed in economy in government and in a balanced budget, but he also wanted to help the unemployed and the homeless. One survey estimated in 1933 that 1.5 million Americans were homeless. One man with a wife and six children from Latrobe, Pennsylvania, who was being evicted wrote, "I have 10 days to get another house, no job, no means of paying rent, can you advise me as to which would be the most humane way to dispose of myself and family, as this is about the only thing that I see left to do."

Roosevelt's answer was the Federal Emergency Relief Administration (FERA), which Congress authorized with an appropriation of $500 million in direct grants to cities and states. A few months later, Roosevelt created a Civil Works Administration (CWA) to put more than four million people to work on various state, municipal, and federal projects. Hopkins, who ran both agencies, had experimented with work relief programs in New York. Like most social workers, he believed it was much better to pay people to work than to give them charity. A woman with two daughters from Houston, Texas, wrote and asked, "Why don't they give us materials and let us make our children's clothes . . . you've no idea how children hate wearing relief clothes." An accountant working on a road project said, "I'd rather stay out here in that ditch the rest of my life than take one cent of direct relief."

The CWA was not always effective, but in just over a year, the agency built or restored a half-million miles of roads and constructed 40,000 schools and 1,000 airports. It hired 50,000 teachers to keep rural schools open and others to teach adult education courses in the cities. The CWA helped millions of people get through the bitterly cold winter of 1933–1934. It also put over a billion dollars of purchasing power into the economy. Roosevelt, who later would be accused of deficit spending, feared that the program was costing too much and might create a permanent class of relief recipients. In the spring of 1934, he ordered the CWA closed down.

The Public Works Administration (PWA), directed by Harold Ickes, in some respects overlapped the work of the CWA, but it lasted longer. Between 1933 and 1939, the PWA built hospitals, courthouses, and school buildings. It helped construct structures as diverse as the port of Brownsville, Texas, a bridge that linked Key West to the Florida mainland, and the library at the University of New Mexico. It built the aircraft carriers *Yorktown* and *Enterprise,* planes for the Army Air Corps, and low-cost housing for slum dwellers.

One purpose of the PWA was economic pump priming—the stimulation of the economy and consumer spending through the investment of government funds. Afraid that there might be scandals in the agency, Ickes spent money slowly and carefully. Thus during the first years, PWA projects, worthwhile as most of them were, did little to stimulate the economy.

Agricultural Adjustment Act

In 1933, most farmers were desperate, as mounting surpluses and falling prices drastically cut their incomes. Some in the Midwest talked of open rebellion, even of revolution. Many observers saw only hopelessness and despair in farmers who had worked hard but were still losing their farms.

Congress passed a number of bills in 1933 and 1934 to deal with the agricultural crisis. They included the Emergency Farm Mortgage Act, designed to prevent more farm foreclosures and evictions. But the New Deal's principal solution to the farm problem was the Agricultural Adjustment Act (AAA), which sought to control the overproduction of basic commodities so that farmers might regain the purchasing power they had enjoyed before World War I. To guarantee these "parity prices" (the average prices in the years 1909–1914), the production of major agricultural staples—wheat, cotton, corn, hogs, rice, tobacco, and milk—would be controlled by paying the farmers to reduce their acreage under cultivation. The AAA levied a tax at the processing stage to pay for the program.

The act aroused great disagreement among farm leaders and economists, but the controversy was nothing compared with the outcry from the public over the initial action of the AAA in the summer of

Margaret Bourke-White, one of the outstanding documentary photographers of the 1930s, captured the disjunction between the ideal and the real in the depression era. This photograph, depicting African-American flood victims lining up for food in Louisville, Kentucky, underneath a propaganda billboard erected by the National Association of Manufacturers, contrasts the American Dream with the reality of racism and poverty. *(Photograph Copyright © 1966: Whitney Museum of American Art, New York, Gift of Sean Callahan)*

1933. To prevent a glut on the cotton and pork markets, the agency ordered 10 million acres of cotton plowed up and six million young pigs slaughtered. It seemed unnatural, even immoral, to kill pigs and plow up cotton when millions of people were underfed and in need of clothes. The story circulated that in the South, mules trained for many years to walk between the rows of cotton now refused to walk on the cotton plants. Some suggested that those mules were more intelligent than the government bureaucrats who had ordered the action.

The Agricultural Adjustment Act did raise the prices of some agricultural products. But it helped the larger farmers more than the small operators, and it was often disastrous for the tenant farmers and sharecroppers, whom crop reduction made expendable. Landowners often discharged tenant families when they reduced the acres under cultivation. There were provisions in the act to help marginal farmers, but little trickled down to them. Many were simply cast out on the road with a few possessions and nowhere to go. As for large farmers, they cultivated their fewer acres more intensely, so that the total crop was little reduced. In the end, the prolonged drought that hit the Southwest in 1934 did more than the AAA to limit production and raise agricultural prices. But the long-range significance of the AAA, which was later declared unconstitutional, was the establishment of the idea that the government should subsidize farmers for limiting production.

Industrial Recovery

The flurry of legislation during the first days of the Roosevelt administration contained something for almost every group. The National Industrial Recovery Act (NIRA) was designed to help business, raise prices, control production, and put people back to work. The act established the National Recovery Administration (NRA), with the power to set fair competition codes in all industries. For a time, everyone forgot about antitrust laws and talked of cooperation and planning rather than competition.

To run the NRA, Roosevelt appointed Hugh Johnson, who had helped organize the World War I draft and served on the War Industries Board. Johnson used his wartime experiences and the enthusiasm of the bond drives to rally the country around the NRA and, implicitly, around all New Deal measures. There were parades and rallies, even a postage stamp, and industries that cooperated could display a blue eagle, the symbol of the NRA. "We Do Our Part," the posters and banners proclaimed, but the results were somewhat less than the promise.

Section 7a of the NIRA, included at the insistence of organized labor, guaranteed labor's right to organize and to bargain collectively and established the National Labor Board to see that their rights were respected. But the board, usually dominated by businessmen, often interpreted the labor provisions of the contracts loosely. In addition, small businessmen complained that the NIRA was unfair to their interests. Any attempt to set prices led to controversy.

Many consumers suspected that the codes and contracts were raising prices, while others feared the return of monopoly in some industries. One woman wrote the president that she was taking down her blue eagle because she had lost her job; another wrote from Tennessee to denounce the NIRA as a joke because it helped only the chain stores. Johnson's booster campaign backfired in the end because anyone with a complaint about a New Deal agency seemed to take it out on the symbol of the blue eagle. When the Supreme Court declared the NIRA unconstitutional in 1935, few people complained. Still, the NIRA was an ambitious attempt to bring some order into a confused business situation, and the labor provisions of the act were picked up later by the National Labor Relations Act.

Civilian Conservation Corps

One of the most popular and successful of the New Deal programs, the Civilian Conservation Corps (CCC), combined work relief with the preservation of natural resources. It put young unemployed men between the ages of 18 and 25 to work on reforestation, road and park construction, flood control, and other projects. The men lived in work camps (there were over 1,500 camps in all) and earned $30 a month, $25 of which had to be sent home to their families. Some complained that the CCC camps, run by the U.S. Army, were too military, and one woman wrote from Minnesota to point out that all the best young men were at CCC camps when they ought to be home looking for real jobs and finding brides. Others complained that the CCC did nothing for unemployed young women, so a few special camps were organized for them, but only 8,000 women took part in a program that by 1941 had included 2.5 million men participants. Overall, the CCC was one of the most successful and least controversial of all the New Deal programs.

Tennessee Valley Authority

Franklin Roosevelt, like his distant Republican relative Theodore, believed in conservation. He promoted flood-control projects and added millions of acres to the country's national forests, wildlife refuges, and fish and game sanctuaries. But the most important New Deal conservation project, the Tennessee Valley Authority (TVA), owed more to Republican George Norris, a progressive senator from Nebraska, than to Roosevelt.

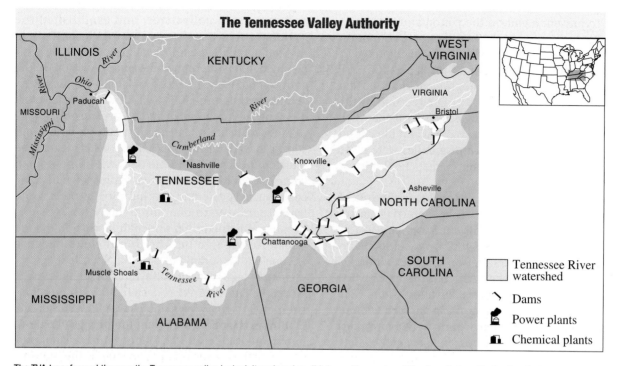

The Tennessee Valley Authority

Legend:
- Tennessee River watershed
- Dams
- Power plants
- Chemical plants

The TVA transformed the way the Tennessee valley looked; it replaced a wild river with a series of flood-control and hydroelectric dams and created a series of lakes behind the dams. It stopped short of the coordinate regional planning that some people wanted, but it was one of the most important New Deal projects.

During World War I, the federal government had built a hydroelectric plant and two munitions factories at Muscle Shoals, on the Tennessee River in Alabama. The government tried unsuccessfully to sell these facilities to private industry, but all through the 1920s, Norris campaigned to have the federal government operate them for the benefit of the valley's residents. Twice Republican presidents vetoed bills that would have allowed federal operation, but Roosevelt endorsed Norris's idea and expanded it into a regional development plan.

Congress authorized the TVA as an independent public corporation with the power to sell electricity and fertilizer and to promote flood control and land reclamation. The TVA built nine major dams and many minor ones between 1933 and 1944, affecting parts of Virginia, North Carolina, Georgia, Alabama, Mississippi, Tennessee, and Kentucky. Some private utility companies claimed that TVA offered unfair competition to private industry, but it was an imaginative experiment in regional planning. It promoted everything from flood control to library bookmobiles. For residents of the valley, it meant cheaper electricity and changed lifestyles. The TVA meant radios, electric irons, washing machines, and other appliances for the first time. The largest federal construction project ever launched, it also created jobs for many thousands who helped build the dams. But government officials and businessmen who feared that the experiment would lead to socialism always curbed the regional planning possibilities of the TVA.

Critics of the New Deal

The furious legislative activity during the first 100 days of the New Deal helped alleviate the pessimism and despair hanging over the country. Stock market prices rose slightly, and industrial production was up 11 percent at the end of 1933. Still, the country remained locked in depression, and nearly 12 million Americans were without jobs. Yet Roosevelt captured the imagination of ordinary Americans everywhere. Hundreds of thousands of letters poured into the White House, so many that eventually 50 people had to be hired to answer them. "If ever there was a saint, he is one," declared a Wisconsin woman.

But conservatives were not so sure that Roosevelt was a savior; in fact, many businessmen, after being impressed with Roosevelt's early economy measures and approving programs such as the NIRA, began to fear that the president was leading the country toward socialism. Appalled by work relief programs, regional planning such as the TVA, and the abandonment of the gold standard, many businessmen were also annoyed by the style of the president, whom they called "that man in the White House."

The conservative revolt against Roosevelt surfaced in the summer of 1934 as the congressional elections approached. A group of disgruntled politicians and businessmen formed the Liberty League. The league supported conservative or at least anti–New Deal candidates for Congress, but it had little influence. In the election of 1934, the Democrats increased their majority from 310 to 319 in the House and from 60 to 69 in the Senate (only the second time in the twentieth century that the party in power had increased its control of Congress in the midterm election). A few people were learning to hate Roosevelt, but it was obvious that most Americans approved of what he was doing.

While some thought the New Deal too radical, others maintained that the government had not done enough to help the poor. One source of criticism was the Communist party. Attracting supporters from all walks of life during a time when capitalism seemed to have failed, the Communist party increased its membership from 7,500 in 1930 to 75,000 in 1938. The Communists organized protest marches and tried to reach out to the oppressed and unemployed. While a majority who joined the party came from the working class, communism had a special appeal to writers, intellectuals, and some college students during a decade when the American dream had turned into a nightmare.

A larger number of Americans, however, was influenced by other movements promising easy solutions to poverty and unemployment. In Minnesota, Governor Floyd Olson, elected on a Farm-Labor ticket, accused capitalism of causing the Depression and startled some listeners when he thundered, "I hope the present system of government goes right to hell." In California, Upton Sinclair, the muckraking socialist and author of *The Jungle,* ran for governor on the platform "End Poverty in California." He promised to pay everyone over 60 years of age a pension of $50 a month using higher income and inheritance taxes to finance the program. He won in the primary but lost the election, and his program collapsed.

California also produced Dr. Francis E. Townsend, who claimed he had a national following of over five million. His supporters backed the Townsend Old Age Revolving Pension Plan, which promised $200 a month to all unemployed citizens over 60 on the condition that they spend it in the same month they received it. Economists laughed at the utopian scheme, but followers organized thousands of Townsend Pension Clubs across the country. As one Minnesota woman wrote to Eleanor Roosevelt, "The old folks who have paid taxes all their lives and built this country up will live in comfort." The plan "will banish crime, give the young a chance to work, pay off the national debt which is mounting every day."

More threatening to Roosevelt and the New Deal than Sinclair and Townsend were the protest movements led by Father Charles E. Coughlin and Senator Huey P. Long. Father Coughlin, a Roman Catholic priest from a Detroit suburb, attracted an audience of 30 to 45 million to his national radio show. At first, he supported Roosevelt's policies, but later he savagely attacked the New Deal as excessively probusiness. Mixing religious commentary with visions of a society operating without bankers and big businessmen, he roused his audience with blatantly anti-Semitic appeals. Most often the "evil" bankers he described were Jewish—the Rothschilds, Warburgs, and Kuhn-Loebs. Anti-Semitism reached a peak in the 1930s, so Jews, rather than Catholics, bore the brunt of nativist fury. Groups like the Silver Shirts and the German-American Bund lashed out against Jews. To members of these groups and others like them, Father Coughlin's attacks made sense.

Huey Long, like Coughlin, had a charisma that won support from the millions still trying to survive in a country where the continuing depression made day-to-day existence a struggle. Elected governor of Louisiana in 1928, Long promoted a "Share the Wealth" program. He taxed the oil refineries and built hospitals, schools, and thousands of miles of new highways. By 1934, he was the virtual dictator of his state, personally controlling the police and the courts. Long talked about a guaranteed $2,000 to $3,000 income for all American families (18.3 million families earned less than $1,000 per year in 1936) and promised pensions for the elderly and college educations for the young. He would pay for these programs by taxing the rich and liquidating the great fortunes. Had not an assassin's bullet cut Long down in September 1935, he might have mounted a third-party challenge to Roosevelt.

THE SECOND NEW DEAL

Responding in part to the discontent of the lower middle class but also to the threat of various utopian schemes, Roosevelt moved his programs in 1935 toward the goals of social reform and social justice. At the same time, he departed from attempts to cooperate with the business community. "We find our population suffering from old inequalities," Roosevelt announced in his annual message to Congress in January 1935. "In spite of our efforts and in spite of our talk, we have not weeded out the overprivileged and we have not effectively lifted up the underprivileged."

Work Relief and Social Security

The Works Progress Administration (WPA), authorized by Congress in April 1935, was the first massive attempt to deal with unemployment and its demoralizing effect on millions of Americans. The WPA employed about three million people a year on a variety of socially useful projects. The WPA workers, who earned wages lower than private industry paid, built bridges, airports, libraries, roads, and golf courses. Nearly 85 percent of the funds went directly into salaries and wages.

A minor but important part of the WPA funding supported writers, artists, actors, and musicians. Richard Wright, Jack Conroy, and Saul Bellow were among the 10,000 writers who were paid less than $100 a month. Experimental theater, innovative and well-written guides to all the states, murals painted in municipal and state buildings, and the Historical Records Survey were among the long-lasting results of these projects.

Only one member of a family could qualify for a WPA job, and first choice always went to the man. A woman could qualify only if she headed the household. But eventually more than 13 percent of the people who worked for the WPA were women, although their most common employment was in the sewing room, where old clothes were made over. "For unskilled men we have the shovel. For unskilled women we have only the needle," one official remarked.

The WPA was controversial from the beginning. Critics charged that the agency had hired Communists to paint murals or work on the state guides. For others, a lazy good-for-nothing leaning on a shovel symbolized the WPA. The initials WPA, some wags charged,

stood for "We Pay for All" or "We Putter Around." Yet for all the criticism, the WPA did useful work; the program built nearly 6,000 schools, more than 2,500 hospitals, and 13,000 playgrounds. More important, it gave millions of unemployed Americans a sense that they were working and bringing in a paycheck to support their families.

The National Youth Administration (NYA) supplemented the work of the WPA and assisted young men and women between the ages of 16 and 25, many of them students. A young law student named Richard Nixon earned 35 cents an hour working for the NYA while he was at Duke University, and Lyndon Johnson began his political career as director of the Texas NYA.

By far the most enduring reform came with the passage of the Social Security Act of 1935. Since the progressive period, social workers and reformers had argued for a national system of health insurance, old-age pensions, and unemployment insurance. By the 1930s, the United States remained the only major industrial country without such programs. Within the Roosevelt circle, Frances Perkins argued most strongly for social insurance, but the popularity of the Townsend Plan and other schemes to aid the elderly helped convince Roosevelt of the need to act. The number of people over 65 in the country increased from 5.7 million in 1925 to 7.8 million in 1935, and that group demanded action.

The WPA (which some wags said stood for "We Putter Around") employed many people for a great variety of jobs. This is an unusual photograph because it is in color. A few photographers who worked for government agencies were beginning to experiment with color film, but most of the photographs that survive from the 1930s are black-and-white. (Corbis-Bettmann)

The Social Security Act of 1935 was a compromise. Congress quickly dropped a plan for federal health insurance because of opposition from the medical profession. The most important provision of the act was old-age and survivor insurance to be paid for by a tax of 1 percent on both employers and employees. The benefits initially ranged from $10 to $85 a month. The act also established a cooperative federal–state system of unemployment compensation. Other provisions authorized federal grants to the states to assist in caring for the disabled and the blind. Finally, the Social Security Act provided some aid to dependent children. This provision would eventually expand to become the largest federal welfare program.

The National Association of Manufacturers denounced social security as a program that would regiment the people and destroy individual self-reliance. In reality, it was a conservative and incomplete system. In no other country was social insurance paid for in part by a regressive tax on the workers' wages. "We put those payroll contributions there so as to give the contributors a legal, moral, and political right to collect their pensions and unemployment benefits," Roosevelt later explained. "With those taxes in there, no damn politician can ever scrap my social security program." But the law also excluded many people, including those who needed it most, such as farm laborers and domestic servants. It discriminated against married women wage earners, and it failed to protect against sickness. Yet for all its weaknesses, it was one of the most important New Deal measures. A landmark in American social legislation, it marked the beginning of the welfare state that would expand significantly after World War II.

Aiding the Farmers

The Social Security Act and the Works Progress Administration were only two signs of Roosevelt's greater concern for social reform. The flurry of legislation in 1935 and early 1936, often called the "second New Deal," also included an effort to help American farmers. Over 1.7 million farm families had incomes of under $500 annually in 1935, and 42 percent of all those who lived on farms were tenants. The Resettlement Administration (RA), motivated in part by a Jeffersonian ideal of yeoman farmers working their own land, set out to relocate tenant farmers on land purchased by the government. Lack of funds and fears that the Roosevelt administration was trying to establish Soviet-style collective farms limited the effectiveness of the RA program.

Much more important in improving the lives of farm families was the Rural Electrification Administration (REA), which was authorized in 1935 to lend money to cooperatives to generate and distribute electricity in isolated rural areas not served by private utilities. Only 10 percent of the nation's farms had electricity in 1936. When the REA's lines were finally attached, they dramatically changed the lives of millions of farm families who had been able only to dream about the radios, washing machines, and farm equipment advertised in magazines.

In the hill country west of Austin, Texas, for example, there was no electricity until the end of the 1930s. Life went on in small towns and on ranches much as it had for decades. Houses were illuminated by kerosene lamps whose wicks had to be trimmed just right or the lamp smoked or went out, but even with perfect adjustment it was difficult to read by them. There were no bathrooms, because bathrooms required running water, and running water depended on an electric pump. "Yes, we had running water," one woman remembered. "I always said we had running water because I grabbed those two buckets up and ran the two hundred yards to the house with them."

Women and children hauled water constantly—for infrequent baths, for continuous canning (because without a refrigerator, fruits and vegetables had to be put up almost immediately or they spoiled), and for washday. Washday, always Monday, meant scrubbing clothes by hand with harsh soap on a washboard; it meant boiling clothes in a large copper vat over a woodstove and stirring them with a wooden fork. It was a hot and backbreaking job, especially in summer. Then the women had to lift the hot, heavy clothes into a rinsing tub. After the clothes were thoroughly mixed with bluing (to make them white), they had to be wrung out by hand, then carried to the lines, where they were hung to dry. Tuesday was for ironing, and even in summer a wood fire was needed to heat the irons. When irons got dirty on the stove, as could easily happen, dirt got on a white shirt or blouse and it had to be washed all over again.

It was memory of life in the hill country and personal knowledge of how hard his mother and grandmother toiled that inspired a young congressman from Texas, Lyndon Johnson, to work to bring rural electrification to the area. In November 1939, the lights finally came on in the hill country, plugging the area into the twentieth century.

The Dust Bowl: An Ecological Disaster

The ultimate goal of the New Deal was to alter and stabilize agriculture through planning and by promoting efficiency. Some farmers profited from the agricultural legislation of the 1930s, but those who tried to farm on the Great Plains fell victim to years of drought and dust storms. Record heat waves and below-average rainfall in the 1930s turned an area from the Oklahoma panhandle to

The Dust Bowl

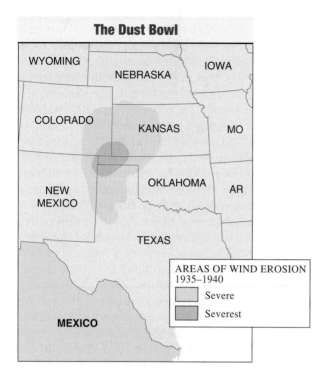

AREAS OF WIND EROSION
1935–1940

- [ ] Severe
- [ ] Severest

This map depicts the wide extent of damage caused by high winds and drought, the worst in the history of the country, according to the U.S. Weather Bureau.

there was an average of 50 storms a year. Cities kept their street lights on for 24 hours a day. Dust covered everything from food to bedspreads and piled up in dunes in city streets and barnyards. Thousands died of "dust pneumonia." One woman remembered what it was like at night: "A trip for water to rinse the grit from our lips, and then back to bed with washcloths over our noses, we try to lie still, because every turn stirs the dust on the blankets."

A 1936 survey of 20 counties in the heart of the dust bowl concluded that 97.6 percent of the land suffered from erosion and more than 50 percent was seriously damaged. By the end of the decade 10,000 farm homes were abandoned to the elements, and 9 million acres of farmland was reduced to a wasteland. By the end of the decade 3.5 million people had abandoned their farms and joined a massive migration to find better lives.

Not all were forced out by the dust storms; some fell victim to large-scale agriculture, and many tenant farmers and hired hands were expendable during the Depression. In most cases they not only lost their jobs, but they also were evicted from their houses. More than 350,000 left Oklahoma during the decade and moved to California, a place that seemed to many like the promised land. But the name *Okie* came to mean any farm migrant. The plight of these wayfarers was immortalized by John Steinbeck in his novel about the Joad family, *The Grapes of Wrath* (1939). The next year John Ford made a powerful movie based on the book,

western Kansas into a giant dust bowl. A single storm on May 11, 1934, removed 300 million tons of topsoil and turned day into night. Between 1932 and 1939

A still from the documentary film *The Plow That Broke the Plains* by Pare Lorentz, a talented filmmaker who also produced *The River* and *The City*. The film depicted the disaster of the dust bowl and the government's response. Some Republicans protested that the last part of the film was propaganda for the New Deal so the ending was cut. *(The Museum of Modern Art, New York, Film Stills Archive)*

starring Henry Fonda as Tom Joad. Many Americans sympathized with the plight of the embattled farm family trying to escape the dust bowl and find a better life in California; others interpreted their defeat as a symbol of the failure of the American dream.

The dust bowl was a natural disaster, but it was aided and exaggerated by human actions and inactions. The semiarid plains west of the 98th meridian were not suitable for intensive agriculture. Overgrazing, too much plowing, and indiscriminate planting over a period of 60 years exposed the thin soil to the elements. When the winds came in the 1930s, much of the land simply blew away. In the end it was a matter of too little government planning and regulation and too many farmers using new technology to exploit natural resources for their own gain.

The Roosevelt administration did try to deal with the problem. The Taylor Grazing Act of 1934 restricted the use of the public range in an attempt to prevent overgrazing, and it also closed 80 million acres of grassland to further settlement. The Civilian Conservation Corps and other New Deal agencies planted trees, and the Soil Conservation Service promoted drought-resistant crops and contour plowing, but it was too little and too late. Even worse, according to some authorities, government measures applied after the disaster of 1930 encouraged farmers to return to raising wheat and other inappropriate crops, leading to more dust bowl crises in the 1950s and 1970s.

The New Deal and the West

The New Deal probably aided the West more than any other region. The CCC, AAA, drought relief measures, and various federal agencies helped the region out of proportion to the people who lived there. In fact, the top 14 states in per capita expenditure by federal agencies during the 1930s were all in the West. Most important were the large-scale water projects. The Boulder Dam (later renamed the Hoover Dam) on the Colorado River not only provided massive amounts of hydroelectric power but, with the construction of a 259-mile aqueduct, also provided the water that caused the city of Los Angeles to boom.

The largest power project of all was the Grand Coulee Dam on the Columbia River northwest of Spokane, Washington. Employing tens of thousands of men and pouring millions of dollars into the economy, the dam, finally completed in 1941, provided cheap electricity for the Pacific Northwest and eventually irrigated over a million acres of arid land.

Despite all the federal aid to the region, many Westerners, holding fast to the myth of frontier individualism, bitterly criticized the regulation and the bureaucracy that went with the grants. The cattlemen in Wyoming, Colorado, and Montana desperately needed the help of the federal government, but even as they accepted the aid they denounced Roosevelt and the New Deal.

Controlling Corporate Power and Taxing the Wealthy

In the summer of 1935, Roosevelt also moved to control the large corporations, and he even toyed with radical plans to tax the well-to-do heavily and redistribute wealth in the United States. The Public Utility Holding Company Act, passed in 1935, attempted to restrict the power of the giant utility companies, the 12 largest of which controlled more than half the country's power. The act gave various government commissions the authority to regulate and control the power companies and included a "death sentence" clause that gave each company five years to demonstrate that its services were efficient. If it could not demonstrate this, the government could dissolve the company. This was one of the most radical attempts to control corporate power in American history.

In his message to Congress in 1935, Roosevelt also pointed out that the federal revenue laws had "done little to prevent an unjust concentration of wealth and economic power." He suggested steeper income taxes for wealthy groups and a much larger inheritance tax. When Congress dropped the inheritance tax provision, however, Roosevelt did not fight to have it restored. Even the weakened bill, increasing estate and gift taxes and raising the income tax rates at the top, angered many in the business community who thought that Roosevelt had sold out to Huey Long's "Share the Wealth" scheme.

The New Deal for Labor

Like many progressive reformers, Roosevelt was more interested in improving the lot of working people by passing social legislation than by strengthening the bargaining position of organized labor. Yet he saw labor as an important balance to the power of industry, and he listened to his advisers, especially Frances Perkins and Senator Robert Wagner of New York, who persistently brought up the needs of organized labor.

After strikes in San Francisco, Minneapolis, and Toledo, Roosevelt supported the Wagner Act, officially called the National Labor Relations Act, which outlawed blacklisting and a number of other practices and reasserted labor's right to organize and to bargain collectively. The act also established a Labor Relations Board with the power to certify a properly elected bargaining unit. The act did not require workers to join unions, but it made the federal government a regulator, or at least a neutral force, in management–labor relations. That alone made the National Labor

Relations Act one of the most important New Deal reform measures.

The Roosevelt administration's friendly attitude toward organized labor helped increase union membership from under 3 million in 1933 to 4.5 million by 1935. Many groups, however, were left out, including farm laborers, unskilled workers, and women. Only about 3 percent of working women belonged to unions, and women earned only about 60 percent of wages paid to men for equivalent work.

Still, many people resented that women were employed at all. The Brotherhood of Railway and Steamship Clerks ruled that no married woman whose husband could support her was eligible for a job. One writer had a perfect solution for the unemployment problem: "Simply fire the women, who shouldn't be working anyway, and hire the men."

The American Federation of Labor (AFL) had little interest in organizing unskilled workers, but a new group of committed and militant labor leaders emerged in the 1930s to take up that task. John L. Lewis, the eloquent head of the United Mine Workers, was the most aggressive. He was joined by David Dubinsky of the International Ladies' Garment Workers and Sidney Hillman, president of the Amalgamated Clothing Workers. Both were socialists who believed in economic planning, but both had worked closely with social justice progressives. These new progressive labor leaders formed the Committee of Industrial Organization

(CIO) within the AFL and set out to organize workers in the steel, auto, and rubber industries. Rather than separating workers by skill or craft as the AFL preferred, they organized everyone into an industrywide union much as the Knights of Labor had done in the 1880s. They also used new and aggressive tactics. When a foreman tried to increase production or enforce discipline, the union leaders would simply pull the switch and declare a spontaneous strike. This "brass knuckle unionism" worked especially well in the auto and rubber industries.

In 1936, the workers at three rubber plants in Akron, Ohio, went on strike without permission from the leaders. Instead of picketing outside the factory, they occupied the buildings and took them over. The "sit-down strike" became a new protest technique. After sit-down strikes against General Motors plants in Atlanta, Georgia, and Flint, Michigan, General Motors finally accepted the United Auto Workers (UAW) as their employees' bargaining agent.

The General Motors strike was the most important event in a critical period of labor upheaval. A group of workers using disorderly but largely nonviolent tactics (as would the civil rights advocates in the mid-1960s) demanded their rights under the law. They helped make labor's voice heard in the decision-making process in major industries where labor had long been denied any role. They also helped raise the status of organized labor in the eyes of many Americans.

"Labor does not seek industrial strife," Lewis announced. "It wants peace, but a peace with justice." As the sit-down tactic spread, violence often accompanied justice. Chrysler capitulated, but the Ford Motor Company used hired gunmen to discourage the strikers. A bloody struggle ensued before Ford agreed to accept the UAW as the bargaining agent. Even U.S. Steel, which had been militantly antiunion, signed an agreement with the Steel Workers Organizing Committee calling for a 40-hour week and an eight-hour day. But other steel companies refused to go along. In Chicago on Memorial Day in 1937, a confrontation between the police and peaceful pickets at the Republic Steel plant resulted in ten deaths. In the "Memorial Day Massacre," as it came to be called, the police fired without provocation into a crowd of workers and their families, who had gathered near the plant in a holiday mood. All ten of the dead were shot in the back.

Despite the violence and management's use of undercover agents within unions, the CIO gained many members. William Green and the leadership of the AFL were horrified at the aggressive tactics of the new labor leaders. They expelled the CIO leaders from the AFL, only to see them form a separate Congress of

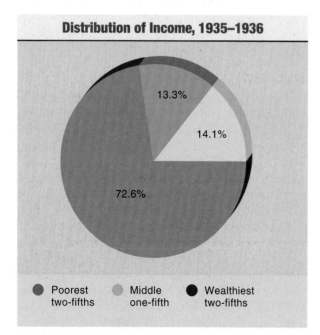

Distribution of Income, 1935–1936

13.3%
14.1%
72.6%

● Poorest two-fifths   ● Middle one-fifth   ● Wealthiest two-fifths

Roosevelt and the New Deal never sought consistently to redistribute wealth in America, and a great disparity in income and assets remained. Source: U.S. Bureau of the Census.

Frances Perkins, FDR's secretary of labor, was an important defender of organized labor within the administration. As the first woman to hold a cabinet position, she was often greeted by surprised stares as she traveled around the country. *(Brown Brothers)*

Industrial Organization (the initials stayed the same). By the end of the decade, the CIO had infused the labor movement with a new spirit. Accepting unskilled workers, African Americans, and others who had never belonged to a union before, the CIO won increased pay, better working conditions, and the right to bargain collectively in most of the basic American industries.

America's Minorities in the 1930s

A half-million African Americans joined unions through the CIO during the 1930s, and many blacks were aided by various New Deal agencies. Yet the familiar pattern of discrimination, low-paying jobs, and intimidation through violence persisted. Lynchings in the South actually increased in the New Deal years, rising from 8 in 1932 to 28 in 1933 and 20 in 1935.

One particular case came to symbolize and dramatize discrimination against African Americans in the 1930s. On March 25, 1931, in Scottsboro, Alabama, two young white women accused nine black men of raping them in a railroad boxcar as they all hitched a free ride. A jury of white men found all nine blacks guilty, and the court sentenced eight to die. The U.S. Supreme Court ordered new trials in 1933, on the grounds that the accused rapists had not received proper legal counsel. The case garnered much publicity in the United States and abroad. The youth of the defendants, their quick trial, and the harsh sentences made the "Scottsboro boys" a popular cause

for many northern liberals and especially the Communist party.

For many southerners, however, it was a matter of defending the honor of white women. As one observer remarked of one of the accusers, she "might be a fallen woman, but by God she is a white woman." However, evidence supporting the alleged rapes was never presented, and eventually one of the women recanted. Yet the case dragged on. In new trials, five of the young men were convicted and given long prison terms. Charges against the other four were dropped in 1937. Four of the remaining five were paroled by 1946, and the fifth escaped to Michigan.

African Americans did not have to be accused of rape to want to flee to the North, however, and the migration of blacks to northern cities, which had accelerated during World War I, continued during the 1930s. The collapse of cotton prices forced black farmers and farm laborers to flee north for survival. But since most were poorly educated, they soon became trapped in northern ghettos, where they were eligible for only the most menial jobs. The black unemployment rate was triple that of whites, and blacks often received less per person in welfare payments.

Black leaders attacked the Roosevelt administration for supporting or allowing segregation in government-sponsored facilities. The TVA model town of Norris, Tennessee, was off limits for blacks, and AAA policies actually drove blacks off the land in the South. The CCC segregated black and white workers, and the PWA financed segregated housing projects. Some charged that NRA stood for "Negroes Rarely Allowed." Many African Americans wrote to the president or the first lady to protest discrimination in New Deal agencies. As one woman from Georgia put it, "I can't sign my name, Mr. President, they will beat me up and run me away from here and this is my home." Blacks ought to realize, a writer in the NAACP journal *The Crisis* warned in 1935, "that the powers-that-be in the Roosevelt administration have nothing for them."

Roosevelt, fearing that he might antagonize southern congressmen whose backing he needed, refused to support the two major civil rights bills of the era, an antilynching bill and a bill to abolish the poll tax. Yet Harold Ickes and Harry Hopkins worked to ensure that blacks were given opportunities in the CCC, the WPA, and other agencies. By 1941, black federal employees totaled 150,000, more than three times the number during the Hoover administration. Most worked in the lower ranks, but some were lawyers, architects, office managers, and engineers.

Partly responsible for the presence of more black employees was the "black cabinet," a group of more than 50 young blacks who had appointments in almost every government department and New Deal agency. The group met on Friday evenings at the home of Mary McLeod Bethune to discuss problems and plan strategy. The daughter of a sharecropper and one of 17 children, Bethune had worked her way through the Moody Bible Institute in Chicago. She had founded a black primary school in Florida and then transformed it into Bethune-Cookman College. In the 1920s, she had organized the National Council of Negro Women. In 1934, Harry Hopkins, following the advice of Eleanor Roosevelt, appointed her to the advisory committee of the National Youth Administration. Bethune had some impact on New Deal policy and on the black cabinet. She spoke out forcefully, she picketed and protested, and she intervened shrewdly to obtain civil rights and more jobs for African Americans, but in the end the gains for blacks during the New Deal were very limited.

W. E. B. Du Bois, in the meantime, had become increasingly discouraged with token appointments and the reform of race relations through integration with white society. In the 1920s, he supported a series of pan-African conferences designed to unite black people from around the world. He resigned from the NAACP and from his position as editor of *The Crisis* in 1934 and devoted his time to promoting "voluntary segregation" and a "Negro Nation within a nation." Eventually, he joined the Communist party and moved to Ghana, where he died in 1963.

Although Roosevelt appointed a number of blacks to government positions, he was never particularly committed to civil rights. That was not true of Eleanor Roosevelt, who was educated in part by Mary McLeod Bethune. In 1939, when the Daughters of the American Revolution refused to allow Marian Anderson, a black concert singer, to use their stage, Mrs. Roosevelt publicly protested and resigned her membership in the DAR. She also arranged for Anderson to sing from the steps of the Lincoln Memorial, where 75,000 people gathered to listen and to support civil rights for all black citizens.

Eleanor Roosevelt meeting in 1937 with the National Youth Administration's executive director, Aubrey Williams, and its director of Negro activities, Mary McLeod Bethune. Eleanor Roosevelt was the most visible and most active of first ladies. She was both praised and attacked for her activities. *(UPI/Corbis-Bettmann)*

Mexican farm workers, eagerly recruited in the 1920s, often found themselves deported back to Mexico in the 1930s. That even the migrants drove cars and trucks, though old and repaired, shocked foreign observers. In much of the rest of the world, autos were still owned only by the wealthy. *(Library of Congress)*

Many Mexicans who had been actively recruited for American farms and businesses in the 1920s discovered that they were not needed in the Depression decade. Hundreds of thousands lost their jobs and drifted from the urban barrios to small towns and farms in the Southwest looking for work. By one estimate, there were 400,000 Mexican migrants in Texas alone. The competition for jobs increased ethnic prejudice. Signs inscribed "Only White Labor Employed" and "No Niggers, Mexicans, or Dogs Allowed" expressed the hate and fear that the Mexicans encountered everywhere.

Some New Deal agencies helped destitute Mexicans. A few worked for the CCC and the WPA, but to be employed, an applicant had to qualify for state relief, and that eliminated most migrants. The primary solution was not to provide aid for Mexicans but to ship them back to Mexico. Both federal and local authorities encouraged and sometimes coerced Mexican aliens into returning to Mexico. In Los Angeles and other cities, the police and immigration authorities rounded up aliens and held them illegally. A trainload of repatriates left Los Angeles every month during 1933, and officials deported thousands from other cities. One estimate placed the number sent back in 1932 at 200,000, including some American citizens.

Not all the Mexicans were repatriated, however, and some who remained adopted militant tactics to obtain fair treatment. Mexican strawberry pickers went on strike in El Monte, California, and 18,000 cotton pickers walked away from their jobs in the San Joaquin valley in 1933. On August 31, 1939, during a record-breaking heat wave, nearly all of the 430 workers, most of them Mexican-American women, staged a massive walkout at one of the largest food processing

plants in Los Angeles. They did not achieve all of their demands, but they won a small raise and recognition of their union. In Gallup, New Mexico, several thousand Mexican coal miners walked out on strike. They constructed a village of shacks and planned to wait out the strike. The miners, who were aided by writers and artists from Santa Fe and Taos, were evicted from their village by the city authorities. Federal agents arrested their leader, Jesus Pallares, and deported him to Mexico.

During the Depression, Native Americans also experienced hunger, disease, and despair, and their plight was compounded by years of exploitation. Since the Dawes Act of 1887 (described in Chapter 17), government policy had sought to make the Indian into a property-owning farmer and to limit tribal rights. Native Americans lost over 60 percent of the 138 million acres granted them in 1887. The government declared some of the land surplus and encouraged individuals to settle on 160 acres and adopt the "habits of civilized life." Few Native Americans profited from this system, but many whites did.

Just as other progressives sought the quick assimilation of immigrants, the progressive era Indian commissioners sped up the allotment process to increase Indian detribalization. But many Native Americans who remained on the reservations were not even citizens. Finally, in 1924, Congress granted citizenship to all Indians born in the United States. The original Americans became U.S. citizens, but that did not end their suffering.

Franklin Roosevelt brought a new spirit to Indian policy by appointing John Collier as commissioner of Indian affairs. Collier had organized the American Indian Defense Association in 1923, but he built on the work of a group of Native American leaders, sometimes called the "Red Progressives." They included Dr. Carlos Montezuma, an Apache physician; Henry Roe Cloud, a Winnebago teacher; and Gertrude Bonnin, a Sioux writer and musician. As commissioner, Collier was responsible primarily for the passage of the Indian Reorganization Act of 1934, which sought to restore the political independence of the tribes and to end the allotment policy of the Dawes Act. "Even where a tribal group is split into factions, where leadership has broken down, where Indians clamor to distribute the tribal property, even there deep forces of cohesion persist and can be evoked," Collier wrote.

The bill also sought to promote the "study of Indian civilization" and to "preserve and develop the special cultural contributions and achievements of such civilization, including Indian arts, crafts, skills and traditions." Not all Indians agreed with the new policies. Some chose to become members of the dominant culture, and the Navajos voted to reject the Reorganization Act. Some Americans charged that the act was inspired by communism. Others argued that its principal result would be to increase government bureaucracy, while missionaries claimed that the government was promoting paganism by allowing the Indians to practice their native religions.

The paradox and contradictions of U.S. policy toward the Indians can be illustrated by Collier's attempt to solve the Navajo problem. Genuinely sympathetic to Native Americans, he was also a modern man who believed in soil conservation, science, and progress. The Navajo lands, like most of the West, were overgrazed, and soil erosion threatened to fill the new lake behind the Hoover Dam with silt. By supporting a policy of reducing the herds of sheep and goats on Indian land and by promoting soil conservation, Collier contributed to the change in the Navajo lifestyle and to the end of their self-sufficiency, something his other policies supported.

Women and the New Deal

Women made some gains during the 1930s, and more women occupied high government positions than in any previous administration. Besides Frances Perkins, the secretary of labor, there was Molly Dewson, a social worker with the Massachusetts Girls Parole Department and the National Consumers League before becoming head of the Women's Division of the Democratic Committee and then an adviser to Roosevelt. Working closely with Eleanor Roosevelt to promote women's causes, she helped achieve a number of firsts: two women appointed ambassadors, a judge on the U.S. Court of Appeals, the director of the mint, and many women in government agencies. Katharine Lenroot, director of the Children's Bureau,

and Mary Anderson, head of the Women's Bureau, selected many other women to serve in their agencies. Some of these women had collaborated as social workers and now joined government bureaus to continue the fight for social justice. But they were usually in offices where they did not threaten male prerogatives. Despite some gains, the early New Deal programs did nothing for an estimated 140,000 homeless women, or the two to four million unemployed women. Married women were often fired from their jobs on the grounds that they should be home caring for their families rather than depriving men of employment. Single, divorced, and widowed women were usually ignored. Eleanor Roosevelt was genuinely concerned over the plight of poor women. She sponsored a White House Conference in November 1933 on the Emergency Needs of Women. She also advocated including more women in the CCC, the WPA, and other programs, but in the end the New Deal did little for poor women.

Although the number of professional women who worked for the government increased in the 1930s, feminism declined. The older feminists died or retired, and younger women did not replace them. Despite some dramatic exceptions, the image of woman's proper role in the 1930s continued to be that of housewife and mother.

THE LAST YEARS OF THE NEW DEAL

The New Deal was not a consistent or well-organized effort to end the Depression and restructure society. Roosevelt was a politician and a pragmatist, unconcerned about ideological or programmatic consistency. The first New Deal in 1933 and 1934 concentrated on relief and recovery, while the legislation passed in 1935 and 1936 was more involved with social reform. In many ways, the election of 1936 marked the high point of Roosevelt's power and influence. After 1937, in part because of the growing threat of war but also because of increasing opposition in Congress, the pace of social legislation slowed. Yet several measures passed in 1937 and 1938 had such far-reaching significance that some historians refer to a third New Deal. Among the new measures were bills that provided for a minimum wage and for housing reform.

The Election of 1936

The Republicans in 1936 nominated a moderate, Governor Alfred Landon of Kansas. Although he attacked the New Deal, charging that new government programs were wasteful and created a dangerous federal bureaucracy, Landon only promised to do the same thing more cheaply and efficiently. Two-thirds

FDR'S SUCCESSFUL PRESIDENTIAL CAMPAIGNS, 1932–1944				
Year	Candidate	Party	Popular Vote	Electoral Vote
1932	FRANKLIN D. ROOSEVELT	Democratic	22,809,638 (57.4%)	472
	Herbert C. Hoover	Republican	15,758,901 (39.7%)	59
	Norman Thomas	Socialist	881,951 (2.2%)	0
1936	FRANKLIN D. ROOSEVELT	Democratic	27,751,612 (60.8%)	523
	Alfred M. Landon	Republican	16,681,913 (36.5%)	8
	William Lemke	Union	891,858 (1.9%)	0
1940	FRANKLIN D. ROOSEVELT	Democratic	27,243,466 (54.8%)	449
	Wendell L. Willkie	Republican	22,304,755 (44.8%)	82
1944	FRANKLIN D. ROOSEVELT	Democratic	25,602,505 (53.5%)	432
	Thomas E. Dewey	Republican	22,006,278 (46.0%)	99

Note: Winners' names appear in capital letters.

of the newspapers in the country supported him, and the *Literary Digest* predicted his victory on the basis of a "scientific" telephone poll.

Roosevelt, helped by signs that the economy was recovering and supported by a coalition of the Democratic South, organized labor, farmers, and urban voters, won easily. A majority of African Americans for the first time deserted the party of Lincoln, not because of Roosevelt's interest in civil rights for blacks but because New Deal relief programs assisted many poor blacks. A viable candidate to the left of the New Deal failed to materialize. In fact, the Socialist party candidate, Norman Thomas, polled fewer than 200,000 votes. Roosevelt won by over ten million votes, carrying every state except Maine and Vermont. Even the traditionally Republican states of Pennsylvania, Delaware, and Connecticut, which had voted Republican in almost every election since 1856, went for Roosevelt. "To some generations much is given," Roosevelt announced in his acceptance speech; "of other generations much is expected. This generation has a rendezvous with destiny." Now he had a mandate to continue his New Deal social and economic reforms.

The Battle of the Supreme Court

"I see one-third of a nation ill-housed, ill-clad, ill-nourished," Roosevelt declared in his second inaugural address, and he vowed to alter that situation. But the president's first action in 1937 did not call for legislation to alleviate poverty. Instead he announced a plan to reform the Supreme Court and the judicial system. The Court had invalidated not only a number of New Deal measures—including the NIRA and the first version of the AAA—but other measures as well.

Increasingly angry at the "nine old men" who seemed to be destroying New Deal initiatives and defying Congress's will, Roosevelt determined to create a more sympathetic Court. He hoped to gain power to appoint an extra justice for each justice over 70 years of age, of whom there were six. His plan also called for modernizing the court system at all levels, but that plan got lost in the public outcry over the Court-packing scheme.

Roosevelt's plan to nullify the influence of the older and more reactionary justices foundered. Republicans accused him of being a dictator and of subverting the Constitution. Many congressmen from his own party refused to support him. Led by Vice President John H. Garner of Texas, a number of southern Democrats broke with the president and formed a coalition with conservative Republicans that lasted for more than 30 years. After months of controversy, Roosevelt withdrew the legislation and admitted defeat. He had perhaps misunderstood his mandate, and he certainly underestimated the respect, even the reverence, that most Americans felt for the Supreme Court. Even in times of economic catastrophe, Americans proved themselves fundamentally conservative toward their institutions, in stark contrast to Europeans, who experimented radically with their governments.

Ironically, though he lost the battle of the Supreme Court, Roosevelt won the war. By the spring of 1937, the Court began to reverse its position and in a 5–4 decision upheld the National Labor Relations Act. When Justice Willis Van Devanter retired, Roosevelt was able to make his first Supreme Court appointment, thus ensuring at least a shaky liberal majority on the Court. But Roosevelt triumphed at great cost. His attempt to reorganize the Court dissipated energy and slowed the momentum of his legislative program. The most unpopular action he took as president, it made him vulnerable to criticism from opponents of the New Deal, and even some of his supporters were dismayed by what they regarded as an attack on the principle of separation of powers.

The economy improved in late 1936 and early 1937, but in August, the fragile prosperity collapsed.

Unemployment shot back up, industrial production fell, and the stock market plummeted. Facing an embarrassing economic slump that evoked charges that the New Deal had failed, Roosevelt resorted to "deficit spending," as recommended by John Maynard Keynes, the British economist.

Keynes argued that to get out of a depression, the government must spend massive amounts of money on goods and services to increase demand and revive production. The economy responded slowly but never fully recovered until wartime expenditures, beginning in 1940, stimulated it, reduced unemployment, and ended the Depression.

The Third New Deal

Despite increasing hostility, Congress passed a number of important bills in 1937 and 1938 that completed the New Deal reform legislation. The Bankhead-Jones Farm Tenancy Act of 1937 created the Farm Security Administration (FSA) to aid tenant farmers, sharecroppers, and farm owners who had lost their farms. The FSA, which provided loans to grain collectives, also set up camps for migratory workers. Some people saw such policies as the first step toward communist collectives, but the FSA in fact never had enough money to make a real difference.

Congress passed a new Agricultural Adjustment Act in 1938 that tried to solve the problem of farm surpluses, which persisted even after hundreds of thousands of farmers had lost their farms. The new act replaced the processing tax, which the Supreme Court had declared unconstitutional, with direct payments from the federal treasury to farmers; added a soil conservation program; and provided for the marketing of surplus crops. Like its predecessor, the new act tried to stabilize farm prices by controlling production. But only the outbreak of World War II would end the problem of farm surplus, and then only temporarily.

In the cities, housing continued to be a problem. Progressive reformers had dreamed of providing better housing for the urban poor. They had campaigned for city ordinances and state laws and had built model tenements, but the first experiment with federal housing occurred during World War I. That brief experience encouraged a number of social reformers, who later became advisers to Roosevelt. They convinced him that federal low-cost housing should be part of New Deal reform.

The Reconstruction Finance Corporation made low-interest loans to housing projects, and the Public Works Administration constructed some apartment buildings. But not until the National Housing Act of 1937 did Roosevelt and his advisers try to develop a comprehensive housing policy for the poor. The act provided federal funds for slum clearance projects

and for the construction of low-cost housing. By 1939, however, only 117,000 units had been built. Most of these housing projects were bleak and boxlike, and many of them soon became problems rather than solutions. Though it made the first effort, the New Deal did not meet the challenge of providing decent housing for millions of American citizens.

In the long run, New Deal housing legislation had a greater impact on middle-class housing policies and patterns. During the first 100 days of the New Deal, at Roosevelt's urging, Congress passed a bill creating the Home Owners Loan Corporation (HOLC), which over the next two years made more than $3 billion in low-interest loans and helped over a million people save their homes from foreclosure. The HOLC also had a strong impact on housing policy by introducing the first long-term fixed-rate mortgages. Formerly, all mortgages were for periods of no more than five years and were subject to frequent renegotiation.

The HOLC also introduced a uniform system of real estate appraisal that tended to undervalue urban property, especially in neighborhoods that were old, crowded, and ethnically mixed. The system gave the highest ratings to suburban developments where, according to the HOLC, there had been no "infiltration of Jews" or other undesirable groups. This was the beginning of the practice later called "redlining" that made it nearly impossible for certain prospective homeowners to obtain a mortgage in many urban areas.

The Federal Housing Administration (FHA), created in 1934 by the National Housing Act, expanded and extended many of these HOLC policies. The FHA insured mortgages, many of them for 25 or 30 years, reduced the down payment required from 30 percent to under 10 percent, and allowed over 11 million families to buy homes between 1934 and 1972. The system, however, tended to favor purchasing new suburban homes rather than repairing older urban residences. New Deal housing policies helped make the suburban home with the long FHA mortgage part of the American way of life, but the policies also contributed to the decline of many urban neighborhoods.

Just as important as housing legislation was the Fair Labor Standards Act, which Congress passed in June 1938. Roosevelt's bill proposed for all industries engaged in interstate commerce a minimum wage of 25 cents an hour, to rise in two years to 40 cents an hour, and a maximum workweek of 44 hours, to be reduced to 40 hours. Congress amended the legislation and exempted many groups, including farm laborers and domestic servants. Nevertheless, when it went into effect, 750,000 workers immediately received raises, and by 1940, some 12 million had had pay increases. The law also prohibited child labor in interstate commerce, making it the first permanent

\multicolumn{3}{c}{KEY 1930S REFORM LEGISLATION}
Year	Legislation	Provisions
1932	Reconstruction Finance Corporation (RFC)	Granted emergency loans to banks, life insurance companies, and railroads (passed during Hoover administration)
1933	Civilian Conservation Corps (CCC)	Employed young men (and a few women) in reforestation, road construction, and flood control projects
1933	Agricultural Adjustment Act (AAA)	Granted farmers direct payments for reducing production of certain products; funds for payments provided by a processing tax, which was later declared unconstitutional
1933	Tennessee Valley Authority (TVA)	Created independent public corporation to construct dams and power projects and to develop the economy of a nine-state area in the Tennessee River valley
1933	National Industrial Recovery Act (NIRA)	Sought to revive business through a series of fair-competition codes; Section 7a guaranteed labor's right to organize (later declared unconstitutional)
1933	Public Works Administration (PWA)	Sought to increase employment and business activity through construction of roads, buildings, and other projects
1934	National Housing Act— created Federal Housing Administration (FHA)	Insured loans made by banks for construction of new homes and repair of old homes
1935	Emergency Relief Appropriation Act— created Works Progress Administration (WPA)	Employed over eight million people to repair roads, build bridges, and work on other projects; also hired artists and writers
1935	Social Security Act	Established unemployment compensation and old-age and survivors' insurance paid for by a joint tax on employers and employees
1935	National Labor Relations Act (Wagner-Connery Act)	Recognized the right of employees to join labor unions and to bargain collectively; created a National Labor Relations Board to supervise elections and to prevent unfair labor practices
1935	Public Utility Holding Act	Outlawed pyramiding of gas and electric companies through the use of holding companies and restricted these companies to activity in one area; a "death sentence" clause gave companies five years to prove local, useful, and efficient operation or be dissolved
1937	National Housing Act (Wagner-Steagall Act)	Authorized low-rent public housing projects
1938	Agricultural Adjustment Act (AAA)	Continued price supports and payments to farmers to limit production, as in 1933 act, but replaced processing tax with direct federal payment
1938	Fair Labor Standards Act	Established minimum wage of 40 cents an hour and maximum workweek of 40 hours in enterprises engaged in interstate commerce

federal law to prohibit youngsters under 16 from working. And without emphasizing the matter, the law made no distinction between men and women, thus diminishing, if not completely ending, the need for special legislation for women.

The New Deal had many weaknesses, but it did dramatically increase government support for the needy. In 1913, local, state, and federal government spent $21 million on public assistance. By 1932, that had risen to $218 million; by 1939, it was $4.9 billion.

THE OTHER SIDE OF THE 1930S

The Great Depression and the New Deal so dominate the history of the 1930s that it is easy to conclude that

nothing else happened, that there were only breadlines and relief agencies. But there is another side of the decade. A communications revolution changed the lives of middle-class Americans. The sale of radios and attendance at movies increased during the 1930s, and literature flourished. Americans were fascinated by technology, especially automobiles. Many people traveled during the decade; they stayed in motor courts and looked ahead to a brighter future dominated by streamlined appliances and gadgets that would mean an easier life.

Taking to the Road

"People give up everything in the world but their car," a banker in Muncie, Indiana, remarked during the

Depression, and that seems to have been true all over the country. Although automobile production dropped off after 1929 and did not recover until the end of the 1930s, the number of motor vehicles registered, which declined from 26.7 million in 1930 to just over 24 million in 1933, increased to over 32 million by 1940. People who could not afford new cars drove used ones. Even the "Okies" fleeing the dust bowl of the Southwest traveled in cars. They were secondhand, run-down cars to be sure, but the fact that even many poor Americans owned cars shocked visitors from Europe, where automobiles were still only for the rich.

The American middle class traveled at an increasing rate after the low point of 1932 and 1933. In 1938, the tourist industry was the third largest in the United States, behind only steel and automobile production. Over four million Americans traveled every year, and four out of five went by car. Many dragged a trailer for sleeping or stopped at the growing number of tourist courts and overnight cabins. In these predecessors of the motel there were no doormen, no bellhops, no register to sign. The tourist court was much more informal than the hotel, and you could park your car next to your cabin.

The Electric Home

If the 1920s was the age of the bathroom, the 1930s was the era of the modern kitchen. The sale of electrical appliances increased throughout the decade, with refrigerators leading the way. In 1930, the number of refrigerators produced exceeded the number of iceboxes for the first time. Refrigerator production continued to rise throughout the decade, reaching a peak of 2.3 million in 1937. At first, the refrigerator was boxy and looked very much like an icebox with a motor sitting on top. In 1935, however, the refrigerator, like most other appliances, became streamlined. Sears, Roebuck advertised "The New 1935 Super Six Coldspot . . . Stunning in Its Streamlined Beauty." The Coldspot, which quickly influenced the look of all other models, was designed by Raymond Loewy, one of a group of industrial designers who emphasized sweeping horizontal lines, rounded corners, and a slick modern look. They hoped modern design would stimulate an optimistic attitude and, of course, increase sales.

Replacing an icebox with an electrical refrigerator, as many middle-class families did in the 1930s, altered more than the appearance of the kitchen. It also changed habits and lifestyles, especially for women. An icebox was part of a culture that included icemen, ice wagons (or ice trucks), picks, tongs, and a pan that had to be emptied continually. The refrigerator required no attention beyond occasional defrosting of the freezer compartment. Like the streamlined auto-

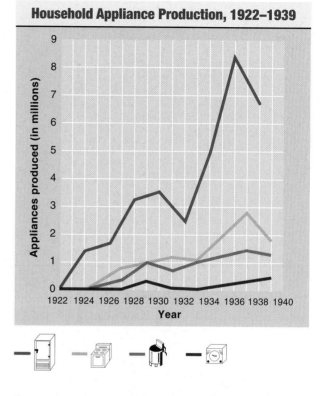

Electric appliances altered the lives of many American middle-class families during the 1930s. The replacement of the icebox with the electric refrigerator was especially dramatic. Source: U.S. Bureau of the Census.

mobile, the sleek refrigerator became a symbol of progress and modern civilization in the 1930s. At the end of the decade, in 1939, the World's Fair in New York glorified the theme of a streamlined future, carefully planned and based on new technology.

This reverence for technological progress contrasted with the economic despair in the 1930s, but people adapted to it selectively. For example, the electric washing machine and electric iron revolutionized washday. Yet even with labor-saving machines, most women continued to do their wash on Monday and their ironing on Tuesday. Packaged and canned goods became more widely available during the decade, and many women discovered that it was easier, and in some cases cheaper, to serve Kellogg's Corn Flakes or Nabisco Shredded Wheat than to make oatmeal, to heat Van Camp's pork and beans or Heinz spaghetti from a can than to prepare a meal, or to use commercially baked bread than to bake their own.

Ironically, despite these new conveniences, a great many middle-class families maintained their standard of living during the 1930s only because the women in the family learned to stretch and save and make do, and most wives spent as much time on housework as before. Some also took jobs outside the home to maintain their level of consumption. The number of mar-

The washing machine dates from the mid-nineteenth century, but it did not end the drudgery of washday. Even the introduction of electric washers did not eliminate the constant wringing and rinsing that made washday (usually Monday) a day to dread. The first automatic washing machines were introduced in the late 1930s but did not become commonplace until after World War II. This advertisement promotes the convenience of a machine that will spin dry as well as wash. Notice the gender roles in the advertisement. The husband appreciates the saving but apparently doesn't put the clothes in the machine. "The Bendix" was a great improvement, but it was not until the 1950s that electric and gas dryers finally ended the task of hanging clothes on the line. (*Bendix Home Appliances, Inc.*)

ried women who worked increased substantially during the decade. At the same time, many rural women, like those in the hill country of Texas and other remote areas, and many wives of the unemployed simply made do. They continued to cook, clean, and sew as their ancestors had for generations.

The Age of Leisure

During the Depression, many middle-class people found themselves with time on their hands and sought out ways of spending it. The 1920s was a time of spectator sports, of football and baseball heroes, of huge crowds that turned out to see boxing matches. Those sports continued during the Depression decade, although attendance suffered. Softball and

miniature golf, which were cheap forms of entertainment and did not require expensive travel, also became popular. But leisure in the 1930s actually grew to be a problem, and professionals published some 450 new books on the subject. Leisure was mechanized; millions put their nickels in a slot and listened to a record played on a jukebox. Millions more played a pinball machine, a mechanized device that had no practical use other than entertainment and could end the game with one word: "Tilt."

Many popular games of the period had elaborate rules and directions. Contract bridge swept the country during the decade, and Monopoly was the most popular game of all. Produced by Parker Brothers, Monopoly was a fantasy of real estate speculation in

Recovering the Past

THE MOVIES

Just as some historians have used fiction to help define the cultural history of a decade, others in the twentieth century have turned to film to describe the "spirit of an age." On an elementary level, the movies help us appreciate changing styles in dress, furniture, and automobiles. We can even get some sense of how a particular time defined a beautiful woman or a handsome man, and we can learn about ethnic and racial stereotypes and assumptions about gender and class.

The decade of the 1930s is sometimes called the "golden age of the movies." Careful selection among the 500 or so feature films Hollywood produced each year during the decade—ranging from gangster and cowboy movies to Marx Brothers comedies, from historical romances to Busby Berkeley musical extravaganzas—could support a number of interpretations about the special myths and assumptions of the era. But one his-

torian has argued that, especially after 1934, "not only did the movies amuse and entertain the nation through its most severe economic and social disorder, holding it together by their capacity to create unifying myths and dreams, but movie culture in the 1930s became a dominant culture for many Americans, providing new values and social ideals to replace shattered old traditions."

The year 1934 was a dividing line for two reasons. The motion picture industry, like all other industries, had suffered during the Depression; 1933 marked the low point in attendance, with more than a third of the theaters in the country shut down. The next year, however, attendance picked up, heralding a revival that lasted until 1946. Also in 1934, the movie industry adopted a code for which the Catholic Legion of Decency and other religious groups had lobbied. The new code prohibited the depiction of "sex perversion, interracial sex, abortion, incest, drugs and profanity." Even married couples could not be shown together in a

A scene from *It Happened One Night*, 1934. *(The Museum of Modern Art Film Stills Archive)*

A scene from *Drums Along the Mohawk*, 1939. *(The Museum of Modern Art Film Stills Archive)*

double bed. Although a movie could depict immoral behavior, sin always had to be punished. "Evil and good should never be confused," the code announced.

Before the code, Hollywood had indeed produced graphic films, such as *The Public Enemy* (1931) and *Scarface* (1932), with a considerable amount of violence; musicals, such as *Gold Diggers of 1933,* filled with scantily clad young women; films featuring prostitutes, such as Jean Harlow in *Red Dust* (1932) and Marlene Dietrich in *Blond Venus* (1930); and other films that confronted the problems of real life. But after 1934, Hollywood concentrated on movies that created a mythical world where evil was always punished, family moral values won out in the end, and patriotism and American democracy were never questioned. Although the code was modified from time to time, it was not abandoned until 1966, when it was replaced by a rating system.

It Happened One Night (1934) and *Drums Along the Mohawk* (1939), two films out of thousands, illustrate some of the myths the movies created and sustained. Frank Capra, one of Hollywood's masters at entertaining without disturbing, directed *It Happened One Night,* a comedy-romance. A rich girl (played by Claudette Colbert) dives from her father's yacht off the coast of Florida and takes a bus for New York. She meets a newspaper reporter (Clark Gable). They have a series of madcap adventures and fall in love. But mix-ups and misunderstandings make it appear that she will marry her old boyfriend. In the end, however, they are reunited and marry in an elaborate outdoor ceremony. Afterward, they presumably live happily ever after. The movie is funny and entertaining and presents a variation on the poor-boy-marries-rich-girl theme. Like so many movies of the time, this one suggests that life is fulfilled for a woman only if she can find the right man to marry.

Claudette Colbert also stars in *Drums Along the Mohawk,* this time with Henry Fonda. Based on a 1936 novel by Walter Edmonds, *Drums* is a sentimental story about a man who builds a house in the wilderness, marries a pretty girl, fights off the Indians, and works with the simple country folk to create a satisfying life in the very year the American colonies rebel against Great Britain. *Drums* was one of a number of films based on historical themes that Hollywood released just before World War II. *The Howards of Virginia* (1940), *Northwest Passage* (1939), and, most popular of all, *Gone with the Wind* (1939) were others in the same genre. Historical themes had been popular before, but with the world on the brink of war, the story of men and women in the wilderness struggling for family and country against the Indians (stereotyped as savages) proved comforting as well as entertaining.

Can a historian use movies to describe the values and myths of a particular time, or are the complexities and exaggerations too great? Are the most popular or most critically acclaimed films more useful than others in getting at the "spirit of an age"? What films popular today tell us most about our time and culture? Is there too much sex and violence in movies today? Should the government control the language, themes, and values depicted in movies? Are movies as important today as they were in the 1930s in defining and influencing the country's myths and values?

While the country was in the grips of the Depression and hovering on the brink of war, industrial designers gave every object from telephones and radios to cars and trains a look of streamlined modernity. *(Minneapolis Institute of Art, Anonymous Loan)*

which chance, luck, and the roll of the dice determined the winner. But one still had to obey the rules: "Go Directly to Jail. Do Not Pass Go. Do Not Collect $200." During a depression brought on in part by frenzied speculation, Americans were fascinated by a game whose purpose was to obtain real estate and utility monopolies and drive one's opponents into bankruptcy.

The 1930s was also a time of fads and instant celebrities, created by radio, newsreels, and businessmen ready to turn almost anything to commercial advantage. The leading box office attraction between 1935 and 1938 was Shirley Temple, a blond and adorable child star. She inspired dolls, dishes, books, and clothes. Even stranger was the excitement created by the birth of five identical girl babies to a couple in northern Ontario in 1934. The Dionne quintuplets appeared on dozens of magazine covers and endorsed every imaginable product. Millions of people waited eagerly for the latest news about the babies, and over three million traveled to see their home in Canada. The crazes over Shirley Temple and the Dionne quintuplets were products of the new technology, especially radio and the movies.

Literary Reflections of the 1930s

Though much of the literature of the 1930s reflected the decade's troubled currents, reading continued to be a popular and cheap entertainment. John Steinbeck, whose later novel *The Grapes of Wrath* (1939) followed the fortunes of the Joad family,

described the plight of Mexican migrant workers in *Tortilla Flat* (1935). His novels expressed his belief that there was in American life a "crime . . . that goes beyond denunciation." "In the eyes of the hungry there is a growing wrath," he warned.

Other writers also questioned the American dream. John Dos Passos's trilogy *U.S.A.* (1930–1936) conveyed a deep pessimism about American capitalism that many other intellectuals shared. Less political were the novels of Thomas Wolfe and William Faulkner, who more sympathetically portrayed Americans caught up in the web of local life and facing the complex problems of the modern era. Faulkner's fictional Yoknapatawpha County, brought to life in *The Sound and the Fury, As I Lay Dying, Sanctuary,* and *Light in August* (1929–1932), documented the South's racial problems and its poverty as well as its stubborn pride. But the book about the South that became one of the decade's best-sellers was far more optimistic and far less complex than Faulkner's work—Margaret Mitchell's *Gone with the Wind* (1936). Its success suggested that many Americans read to escape, not to explore their problems.

Radio's Finest Hour

The number of radio sets purchased increased steadily during the decade. In 1929, slightly more than 10 million households owned radios; by 1939, fully 27.5 million households had radio sets. The radio was not just a source of music and news but a focal point of the living room. In many homes, the top of the radio

Even during the Depression, Americans flocked to the movies. For twenty-five cents(ten cents for children), they could see a double feature as well as a cartoon and a newsreel. Among the most popular films were elaborate musical fantasies, and among the most popular stars were the dance team of Fred Astair and Ginger Rogers. *(Corbis)*

became the symbolic mantel where cherished photos were displayed. Families gathered around the radio at night to listen to and laugh at Jack Benny or Edgar Bergen and Charlie McCarthy or to try to solve a murder mystery with Mr. and Mrs. North. "The Lone Ranger," another popular program, had 20 million listeners by 1939.

During the day there were soap operas. "Between thick slices of advertising," wrote James Thurber, "spread twelve minutes of dialogue, add predicament, villainy, and female suffering in equal measure, throw in a dash of nobility, sprinkle with tears, season with organ music, cover with a rich announcer sauce and serve five times a week." After school, teenagers and younger children argued over whether to listen to "Jack Armstrong, the All-American Boy" and "Captain

Midnight" or "Stella Dallas" and "The Young Widder Brown."

Most families had only one radio, but everyone could join in the contests or send for magic rings or secret decoders. In Chicago's working-class neighborhoods in 1930 there was one radio for every two or three households, but often families and friends gathered to listen to the radio. The reception was sometimes poor, especially in rural areas and small towns. Voices faded in and out and disappeared during storms. But the magic of radio allowed many people to feel connected to distant places and to believe they knew the radio performers personally. Radio was also responsible for one of the most widespread episodes of mass hysteria of all time. On October 31, 1938, Orson Welles broadcast "The War of the Worlds" so realistically that thousands of listeners really believed that Martians had landed in New Jersey. If anyone needed proof, that single program demonstrated the power of the radio.

The Silver Screen

The 1930s were the golden decade of the movies. Between 60 million and 90 million Americans went to the movies every week. The medium was not entirely Depression-proof, but talking films had replaced the silent variety in the late 1920s, and attendance soared.

The radio played an important role in the 1930s. Here a family crowds around a typical floor model to listen to the latest news or a favorite program. *(UPI/Corbis-Bettmann)*

Though it fell off slightly in the early 1930s, by 1934 movie viewing was climbing again. For many families, even in the depth of the Depression, movie money was almost as important as food money.

In the cities, one could go to an elaborate movie palace and live in a fantasy world far removed from the reality of Depression America. In small towns across the country, for 25 cents (10 cents under age 12) one could go to at least four movies during the week. There was a Sunday–Monday feature film (except in communities where the churches had prevented Sunday movies), a different feature of somewhat lesser prominence on Tuesday–Wednesday, and another on Thursday–Friday. On Saturday there was a cowboy or detective movie. Sometimes a double feature played, and always there were short subjects, a cartoon, and a newsreel. On Saturday there was usually a serial that left the heroine or hero in such a dire predicament that one just had to come back the next week to see how she or he survived.

The movies were a place to take a date, to go with friends, or to go as a family. Movies could be talked about for days. Young women tried to speak like Greta Garbo and to hold a cigarette like Joan Crawford. Jean Harlow and Mae West so popularized blonde hair that sales of peroxide shot up. Young men tried to emulate Clark Gable and Cary Grant, and one young man admitted that it was "directly through the movies that I learned to kiss a girl on her ears, neck, and cheeks, as well as on the mouth."

The animated cartoons of Walt Disney, one of the true geniuses of the movie industry, were so popular that Mickey Mouse was more famous and familiar than most human celebrities. In May 1933, halfway into Roosevelt's first 100 days, Disney released *The Three Little Pigs,* whose theme song "Who's Afraid of the Big Bad Wolf?" became a national hit overnight. Some people felt it boosted the nation's morale as much as New Deal legislation. One critic suggested that the moral of the story, as retold by Disney, was that the little pig survived because he was conservative, diligent, and hard-working; others felt that it was the pig who used modern tools and planned ahead who won out.

Timeline

1929	Stock market crashes
	Agricultural Marketing Act
1930	Depression worsens
	Hawley-Smoot Tariff
1932	Reconstruction Finance Corporation established
	Federal Home Loan Bank Act
	Glass-Steagall Banking Act
	Federal Emergency Relief Act
	Bonus march on Washington
	Franklin D. Roosevelt elected president
1933	Emergency Banking Relief Act
	Home Owners Loan Corporation
	Twenty-first Amendment repeals Eighteenth Amendment, ending prohibition
	Agricultural Adjustment Act
	National Industrial Recovery Act
	Civilian Conservation Corps
	Tennessee Valley Authority established
	Public Works Administration established
1934	Unemployment peaks
	Federal Housing Administration established
	Indian Reorganization Act
1935	Second New Deal begins
	Works Progress Administration established
	Social Security Act
	Rural Electrification Act
	National Labor Relations Act
	Public Utility Holding Company Act
	Committee of Industrial Organization (CIO) formed
1936	United Auto Workers hold sit-down strikes against General Motors
	Roosevelt reelected president
	Economy begins to rebound
1937	Attempt to expand the Supreme Court
	Economic collapse
	Farm Security Administration established
	National Housing Act
1938	Fair Labor Standards Act
	Agricultural Adjustment Act
1939	John Steinbeck, *The Grapes of Wrath*
	Margaret Mitchell, *Gone with the Wind*

Conclusion

The Ambivalence of the Great Depression

The New Deal, despite its great variety of legislation, did not end the Depression, nor did it solve the problem of unemployment. For many Americans looking back on the decade of the 1930s, the most vivid memory was the shame and guilt of being unemployed, the despair and fear that came from losing a business or being evicted from a home or an apartment. Parents who lived through the decade urged their children to find a secure job, to get married, and to settle down. "Every time I've encountered the Depression it has been used as a barrier and a club," one daughter of Depression parents remembered; "older people use it to explain to me that I can't understand anything: I didn't live through the Depression."

New Deal legislation did not solve the country's problems, but it did strengthen the federal government, especially the executive branch. Federal agencies like the Federal Deposit Insurance Corporation and programs like social security influenced the daily lives of most Americans, and rural electrification, the WPA, and the CCC changed the lives of millions. The New Deal also established the principle of federal responsibility for the health of the economy, initiated the concept of the welfare state, and dramatically increased government spending to help the poor. Federally subsidized housing, minimum-wage laws, and a policy for paying farmers to limit production, all aspects of these principles, had far-reaching implications.

The New Deal was as important for what it did not do as for what it did. It did not promote socialism or redistribute income or property. It promoted social justice and social reform, but it provided little for people at the bottom of American society. The New Deal did not prevent business consolidation, and, in the end, it probably strengthened corporate capitalism.

Roosevelt, with his colorful personality and his dramatic response to the nation's crisis, dominated his times in a way few presidents have done. Yet for some people who lived through the decade, neither Roosevelt nor breadlines but a new streamlined refrigerator or a Walt Disney movie symbolized the Depression decade.

Recommended Reading

The Great Depression

Ann Banks, ed., *First Person America* (1980); Irving Bernstein, *The Turbulent Years* (1970); Lester Chandler, *America's Greatest Depression* (1970); Andrew J. Dunar and Dennis McBride, *Building Hoover Dam: An Oral History of the Great Depression* (1993); John Kenneth Galbraith, *The Great Crash* (1954); David M. Kennedy, *Freedom From Fear: The American People in Depression and War* (1999); Robert S. McElvain, *The Great Depression* (1984); William Mullins, *The Depression and the Urban West Coast* (1991); Arthur M. Schlesinger, Jr., *The Crisis of the Old Order* (1957); Charles J. Shinto, *Dust Bowl Migrants in the American Imagination* (1997); Kevin Starr, *Endangered Dream: The Great Depression in California* (1996); Studs Terkel, *Hard Times* (1970); T. H. Watkins, *The Hungry Years* (1999); Joan Hoff Wilson, *Herbert Hoover: Forgotten Progressive* (1975); Donald Worster, *Dust Bowl* (1979).

Roosevelt and the First New Deal

Anthony Badger, *The New Deal* (1989); Alan Brinkley, *Voices of Protest: Huey Long, Father Coughlin, and the Great Depression* (1982); James MacGregor Burns, *Roosevelt: The Lion and the Fox* (1956); Paul Conkin, *The New Deal* (1967); Blanche Wiesen Cook, *Eleanor Roosevelt*, Vol. 2 (1999); Frank Freidel, *Launching the New Deal* (1973); Thomas K. McCraw, *TVA and the Power Fight* (1970); James J. Patterson, *America's Struggle Against Poverty, 1900–1980* (1981); Eliot Rosen, *Hoover, Roosevelt and the Brains Trust* (1977).

The Second New Deal

Irving Bernstein, *The Turbulent Years: A History of the American Worker, 1933–1941* (1970); Dan T. Carter, *Scottsboro* (1969); Lizabeth Cohen, *Making a New Deal: Industrial Workers in Chicago, 1919–1939* (1990); Abraham Hoffman, *Unwanted: Mexican Americans and the Great Depression* (1974); Richard Lowitt, *The New Deal and the West* (1984); Roy Lubove, *The Struggle for Social Security* (1968); Richard Pells, *Radical Visions and American Dreams* (1973); Kenneth R. Philip, *John Collier's Crusade for Indian Reform* (1977); Vicki L. Ruiz, *From Out of the Shadows: Mexican Women in Twentieth Century America* (1998); Jordan A. Schwartz, *The New Dealers: Power Politics in the Age of Roosevelt* (1993); Harvard Sitkoff, *A New Deal for Blacks* (1978); Susan Ware, *Holding Their Own: American Women in the 1930s* (1982); Richard White, *The Roots of Dependency: Subsistence, Environment and Social Change Among the Choctaws, Pawnees, and Navajos* (1983).

The Last Years of the New Deal

Alan Brinkley, *The End of Reform: New Deal Liberalism in Recession and War* (1995); Barry Cushman, *Rethinking the New Deal Court* (1998); Steve Fraser and Gary Gertstle, eds., *The Rise and Fall of the New Deal Order* (1989); William E. Leuchtenburg, *The Supreme Court Reborn: The Constitutional Revolution in the Age of Roosevelt* (1995); James T. Patterson, *The New Deal and the States* (1969).

The Other Side of the 1930s

Andrew Bergman, *We're in the Money: Depression America and Its Films* (1971); Terry A. Cooney, *Balancing Acts: American Thought and Culture in the 1930s* (1995); David Gelernter, *1939: The Lost World of the Fair* (1995); Jerre Mangione, *The Dream and the Deal* (1972); Jeffrey L. Meikle, *Twentieth Century Limited: Industrial Design in America, 1925–1939* (1979); Marjorie Rosen, *Popcorn Venus: Women, Movies and the American Dream* (1971); Robert Sklar, *Movie Made America* (1975); William Stott, *Documentary Expression in Thirties America* (1973); Warren Susman, *Culture as History* (1984); Susan Ware, *Amelia Earhart and the Search for Modern Feminism* (1993).

Suggested Web Sites

http://memory.loc.gov/ammem/afctshtml/tshome.html

Voices from the Dust Bowl Home Page. Farm Security Administration (FSA) studies of migrant work camps in central California in 1940 and 1941 compose the bulk of this site. The collection includes audio recordings, photographs, manuscript materials, and publications.

http://newdeal.feri.org/

New Deal Network. This database includes photographs, political cartoons, and texts—including speeches, letters, and other historic documents—from the New Deal period.

http://www.ipl.org/ref/POTUS/fdroosevelt.html

IPL POTUS—Franklin Delano Roosevelt. This site provides information about FDR, the only president to serve more than two terms.

http://www.corbis.com/fdr/fsa/map.html

Picture America. These photographs, from Corbis company and the Library of Congress, reveal the real impact of the Great Depression on American life.

Fiction and Film

James Farrell describes growing up in Depression Chicago in *Studs Lonigan* (1932–1935). John Steinbeck shows Oklahomans trying to escape the dust bowl in his novel *The Grapes of Wrath* (1939). Richard Wright details the trials of a young black man in *Native Son* (1940).

Modern Times (1936) is a classic film that features Charlie Chaplin at his best as he depicts the impersonality of industrial civilization where machines dominate people. *Grapes of Wrath* (1940) is another classic film. Although it doesn't exhibit the despair and anger of the book, it is still a powerful depiction of the human cost of the dust bowl and the Depression.

http://www.nara.gov/exhall/newdeal/newdeal.html

A New Deal for the Arts. Artwork, documents, and photographs recount the federal government's efforts to fund artists in the 1930s in this National Archives site.

http://www.taxhistory.org/CivSite/

The Price of Civilization. This site is part of the Tax History Project at Tax Analysts, an on-line tax information resource. It includes thousands of searchable pages of documents and analysis on tax issues during the Depression and WWII and is part of a larger site that contains a cartoon gallery and WWII-era posters.

http://www.ushistoryplace.com

A richly detailed on-line learning environment complete with interactive maps, timelines, history activities, primary source documents, and links to related American history sites.

25

WORLD WAR II

Reading Right to Left—FIRST ROW: Britain, Canada, Australia, New Zealand, SECOND ROW: Southern Rhodesia, Newfoundland, South Africa, THIRD ROW: India, FOURTH ROW: The Colonial Empire

Reading Left to Right—FIRST ROW: U.S.A., China, U.S.S.R., Yugoslavia, SECOND ROW: Holland, France, Poland, Czechoslovakia, THIRD ROW: Greece, Norway, Belgium

FREEDOM SHALL PREVAIL!

PRINTED IN ENGLAND BY FOSH & CROSS LTD, LONDON.

**N.** Scott Momaday, a Kiowa Indian born at Lawton, Oklahoma, in 1934, grew up on Navajo, Apache, and Pueblo reservations. He was only 11 when World War II ended, yet the war had changed his life. Shortly after the United States entered the war, Momaday's parents moved to New Mexico, where his father got a job with an oil company and his mother worked in the civilian personnel office at an Army Air Force base. Like many couples, they had struggled through the hard times of the Depression. The war meant jobs.

Momaday's best friend was Billy Don Johnson, a "reddish, robust boy of great good humor and intense loyalty." Together they played war, digging trenches and dragging themselves through imaginary minefields. They hurled grenades and fired endless rounds from their imaginary machine guns, pausing only to drink Kool-Aid from their canteens. At school, they were taught history and math and also how to hate the enemy and be proud of America. They recited the Pledge of Allegiance to the flag and sang "God Bless America," "The Star-Spangled Banner," and "Remember Pearl Harbor." Like most Americans, they believed that World War II was a good war fought against evil empires. The United States was always right, the enemy always wrong. It was an attitude that would influence Momaday and his generation for the rest of their lives.

Momaday's only difficulty was that his Native American face was often mistaken for that of an Asian. Almost every day on the playground, someone would yell, "Hi ya, Jap," and a fight was on. Billy Don always came to his friend's defense, but it was disconcerting to be taken for the enemy. His father read old Kiowa tales to Momaday, who was proud to be an Indian but prouder still to be an American. On Saturday, he and his friends would go to the local theater to cheer as they watched a Japanese Zero or a German ME-109 go down in flames. They pretended that they were P-40 pilots. "The whole field of vision shuddered with our fire: the 50-caliber tracers curved out, fixing brilliant arcs upon the span, and

struck; then there was a black burst of smoke, and the target went spinning down to death."

Near the end of the war, his family moved again, as so many families did, so that his father might get a better job. This time they lived right next door to an air force base, and Momaday fell in love with the B-17 "Flying Fortress," the bomber that military strategists thought would win the war in the Pacific and in Europe. He felt a real sense of resentment and loss when the B-17 was replaced by the larger but not nearly so glamorous B-29.

Looking back on his early years, Momaday reflected on the importance of the war in his growing up. "I see now that one experiences easily the ordinary things of life," he decided, "the things which cast familiar shadows upon the sheer, transparent panels of time, and he perceives his experience in the only way he can, according to his age." Though Momaday's life during the war differed from the lives of boys old enough to join the armed forces, the war was no less real for him. Though his youth was affected by the fact that he was male, was an Indian, and lived in the Southwest, the most important influence was that he was an American growing up during the war. Ironically, his parents, made U.S. citizens by an act of Congress in 1924, like all Native Americans living in Arizona and New Mexico were denied the right to vote by state law.

The Momadays fared better than most Native Americans, who found prejudice against them undiminished and jobs, even in wartime, hard to find. Native American servicemen returning from the war discovered that they were still treated like "Indians." They were prohibited from buying liquor in many states, and those who returned to the reservations learned that they were ineligible for veterans' benefits. Still, Momaday thought of himself not so much as an Indian as an American, and that too was a product of his generation. But as he grew to maturity, he became a successful writer and spokesman for his people. In 1969, he won the Pulitzer Prize for his novel *House Made of Dawn*. He also recorded his experiences and memories in a book called *The Names* (1976). In his writing, he stresses the Indian's close identification with the land. Writing about his grandmother, he says: "The immense landscape of the continental interior lay like memory in her blood."

A World War II poster depicting the many nations united in the fight against the Axis powers. In reality there were often disagreements. Notice to the right the American sailor is marching next to Chinese and Soviet soldiers. Within a few years after victory they would be enemies. *(Courtesy The American Legion)*

Although no American cities were bombed and the country was never invaded, World War II influenced almost every aspect of American life. The war ended the Depression. Industrial jobs were plentiful, and even though prejudice and discrimination did not disappear, blacks, Hispanics, women, and other minorities had new opportunities. Like World War I, the second war expanded cooperation between government and industry and increased the influence of government in all areas of American life. The war also ended the last remnants of American isolationism. The United States emerged from the war in 1945 as the most powerful and most prosperous nation in the world.

This chapter traces the gradual involvement of the United States in the international events during the 1930s that finally led to participation in the most devastating war the world had seen. It recounts the diplomatic and military struggles of the war and the search for a secure peace. It also seeks to explain the impact of the war on ordinary people and on American attitudes about the world, as well as its effect on patriotism and the American way of life. The war brought prosperity to some as it brought death to others. It left the American people the most affluent in the world and the United States the most powerful nation.

ᗖ THE TWISTING ROAD TO WAR

Looking back on the events between 1933 and 1941 that eventually led to American involvement in World War II, it is easy either to be critical of decisions made or actions not taken or to see everything that happened during the period as inevitable. Historical events are never inevitable, and leaders who must make decisions never have the advantage of retrospective vision; they have to deal with situations as they find them, and they never have all the facts.

Foreign Policy in the 1930s

In March 1933, Roosevelt faced not only overwhelming domestic difficulties but also international crisis. The worldwide depression had caused near financial disaster in Europe. Germany had defaulted on its reparations installments, and most European countries were unable to keep up the payments on their debts to the United States.

Roosevelt had no master plan in foreign policy, just as he had none in the domestic sphere. In the first days of his administration, he gave conflicting signals as he groped to respond to the international situation. At first, it seemed that the president would cooperate in some kind of international economic agreement on tariffs and currency. But then he undercut the American delegation in London by refusing to go along with any international agreement. Solving the American domestic economic crisis seemed more important to Roosevelt in 1933 than international economic cooperation. His actions signaled a decision to go it alone in foreign policy in the 1930s.

Roosevelt did, however, alter some of the foreign policy decisions of previous administrations. For example, he recognized the Soviet government, hoping to gain a market for surplus American grain. Although the expected trade bonanza never materialized, the Soviet Union agreed to pay the old debts and to extend rights to American citizens living in the Soviet Union. Diplomatic recognition opened communications between the two emerging world powers.

Led by Secretary of State Cordell Hull, Roosevelt's administration also reversed the earlier policy of intervention in South America. The United States continued to support dictators, especially in Central America, because they promised to promote stability and preserve American economic interests. But Roosevelt, extending the Good Neighbor policy Hoover had initiated, completed the removal of American military forces from Haiti and Nicaragua in 1934, and, in a series of pan-American conferences, he joined in pledging that no country in the hemisphere would intervene in the "internal or external affairs" of any other. The United States still had economic and trade interests in Latin America, however, and with many of the Latin American economies in disarray because of the Depression, pressures mounted to resume the policy of military intervention.

The first test case came in Cuba, where a revolution threatened American investments of more than a billion dollars. But the United States did not send troops. Instead Roosevelt dispatched special envoys to work out a conciliatory agreement with the revolutionary government. A short time later, when a coup led by Fulgencio Batista overthrew the revolutionary government, the United States not only recognized the Batista government but also offered a large loan and agreed to abrogate the Platt Amendment (which made Cuba a virtual protectorate of the United States) in return for the rights to a naval base.

The Trade Agreements Act of 1934 gave the president power to lower tariff rates by as much as 50 percent and took the tariff away from the pressure of special-interest groups in Congress. Using this act, the Roosevelt administration negotiated a series of agreements that improved trade. By 1935, half of American cotton exports and a large proportion of other products were going to Latin America. So the Good Neighbor policy was also good business for the United States. But increased trade did not solve the economic problems for either the United States or Latin America.

Another test for Latin American policy came in 1938 when Mexico nationalized the property of a number of American oil companies. Instead of intervening, as many businessmen urged, the State Department patiently worked out an agreement that included some compensation for the companies. The American government might have acted differently, however, if the threat of war in Europe in 1938 had not created a fear that all the Western Hemisphere nations would have to cooperate to resist the growing power of Germany and Italy. At a pan-American conference held that year, the United States and most Latin American countries agreed to resist all foreign intervention in the hemisphere.

Neutrality in Europe

Around the time that Roosevelt was first elected president, Adolf Hitler came to power in Germany. Born in Austria in 1889, Hitler had served as a corporal in the German army during World War I. Like many other Germans, he was angered by the Treaty of Versailles. But he blamed Germany's defeat on the Communists and the Jews.

Hitler had a checkered life after the war. He became the leader of the National Socialist party of the German workers (*Nazi* is short for *National*), and in 1923, after leading an unsuccessful coup, he was sentenced to prison. While in jail he wrote *Mein Kampf* ("My Struggle"), a long, rambling book spelling out his theories of racial purity, his hopes for Germany, and his venomous hatred of the Jews. After his release from prison, Hitler's following grew. He had a charismatic style and a plan. On January 30, 1933, he became chancellor of Germany, and within months the Reichstag (parliament) suspended the constitution, making Hitler Führer (leader) and dictator. His Fascist regime concentrated political and economic power in a centralized state. He intended to conquer Europe and to make the German Third Reich (empire) the center of a new civilization.

In 1934, Hitler announced a program of German rearmament, violating the Versailles Treaty of 1919. Meanwhile, in Italy, a Fascist dictator, Benito Mussolini, was building a powerful military force, and in 1934, he threatened to invade the East African country of Ethiopia. These ominous rumblings in Europe frightened Americans at the very time they were reexamining American entry into the Great War and vowing that they would never again get involved in a European conflict.

Senator Gerald P. Nye of North Dakota, a conscientious and determined man who had helped expose the Teapot Dome scandal in 1924, turned to an investigation of the connection between corporate profits and American participation in World War I. His committee's public hearings revealed that many American businessmen had close relationships with the War Department. Businesses producing war materials had made huge profits. Though the committee failed to prove a conspiracy, it was easy to conclude that the United States had been tricked into going to war by the people who profited most from it.

On many college campuses, students demonstrated against war. On April 13, 1934, a day of protest around the country, students at Smith College placed white crosses on the campus as a memorial to the people killed in the Great War and those who would die in the next one. The next year, even more students went on strike for a day. Students joined organizations

Newsreels and popular magazines such as *Life, Look,* and *Time* made Hitler's image and mannerisms familiar to all Americans. Hitler's picture appeared on the cover of *Time* at least six times between 1931 and 1935. In this 1936 cover he strikes a characteristic pose. *(© 1936/Time Inc.)*

like Veterans of Future Wars and Future Gold Star Mothers and protested the presence of the Reserve Officers Training Corps on their campuses. One college president, who supported the peace movement, announced, "We will be called cowards . . . [but] I say that war must be banished from civilized society if democratic civilization and culture are to be perpetuated." Not all students supported the peace movement, but in the mid-1930s, many young people as well as adults joined peace societies such as the Fellowship of Reconciliation and the Women's International League for Peace and Freedom. They were determined never again to support a foreign war. But in Europe, Asia, and Africa, there were already rumblings of another great international conflict.

Ethiopia and Spain

In May 1935, Italy invaded Ethiopia after rejecting the League of Nations' offer to mediate the difficulties between the two countries. Italian dive bombers and machine guns made quick work of the small and poorly equipped Ethiopian army. The Ethiopian war, remote as it seemed, frightened Congress, which passed a Neutrality Act authorizing the president to prohibit all arms shipments to nations at war and to advise all U.S. citizens not to travel on belligerents' ships except at their own risk. Remembering the process that led the United States into World War I, Congress was determined that it would not happen again.

Though he would have preferred a more flexible bill, Roosevelt used the authority of the Neutrality Act of 1935 to impose an arms embargo. The League of Nations condemned Italy as the aggressor in the war, and Great Britain moved its fleet to the Mediterranean. But neither Britain nor the United States wanted to stop shipments of oil to Italy or to commit its own soldiers to the fight. The embargo on arms had little impact on Italy, but it was disastrous for the poor African nation. Italy quickly defeated Ethiopia, and by 1936, Mussolini had joined forces with Germany to form the Rome-Berlin Axis.

"We shun political commitments which might entangle us in foreign war," Roosevelt announced in 1936. "We are not isolationist except in so far as we seek to isolate ourselves completely from war." But isolation became more difficult when a civil war broke out in Spain in 1936. General Francisco Franco, supported by the Catholic church and large landowners, revolted against the republican government. Germany and Italy aided Franco, sending planes and other weapons, while the Soviet Union came to the support of the anti-Franco Loyalists.

The war in Spain polarized the United States. Most Catholics and many anti-Communists sided with Franco. But many American radicals, even those opposed to all war a few months before, found the Loyalist cause worth fighting and dying for. Over 3,000 Americans joined the Abraham Lincoln Brigade, and hundreds were killed fighting fascism in Spain. "If this were a Spanish matter, I'd let it alone," Sam Levenger, a student at Ohio State, wrote. "But the rebellion would not last a week if it weren't for the Germans and the Italians. And if Hitler and Mussolini can send troops to Spain to attack the government elected by the people, why can't they do so in France? And after France?" Levenger was killed in Spain in 1937 at the age of 20.

Not everyone agreed that the moral issues in Spain were worth dying for. The U.S. government tried to stay neutral and to ship arms and equipment to neither side. The Neutrality Act, extended in 1936, technically did not apply to civil wars, but the State Department imposed a moral embargo. However, when an American businessman disregarded it and attempted to send 400 used airplane engines to the Loyalists, Roosevelt asked Congress to extend the arms embargo to Spain. While the United States, along with Britain and France, carefully protected its neutrality, Franco consolidated his dictatorship with the active aid of Germany and Italy. Meanwhile, Congress in 1937 passed another Neutrality Act, this time making it illegal for American citizens to travel on belligerents' ships. The act extended the embargo on arms and made even nonmilitary items available to belligerents only on a cash-and-carry basis.

In a variety of ways, the United States tried to avoid repeating the mistakes that had led it into World War I. Unfortunately, World War II, which moved closer each day, would be a different kind of war, and the lessons of the first war would be of little use.

War in Europe

Roosevelt had no carefully planned strategy to deal with the rising tide of war in Europe in the late 1930s. He was by no means an isolationist, but he wanted to keep the United States out of the European conflagration. When he announced, "I hate war," he was expressing a deep personal belief that wars solve few problems. Unlike his distant cousin Theodore Roosevelt, he did not view war as a test of one's manhood. In foreign policy, just as in domestic affairs, he responded to events, but he moved reluctantly (and with agonizing slowness, from the point of view of many of his critics) toward more and more American involvement in the war.

In March 1938, Hitler's Germany annexed Austria and then in September, as a result of the Munich Conference, occupied the Sudetenland, a part of Czechoslovakia. Within six months, Hitler's armies had overrun the rest of Czechoslovakia. Little protest came from the United States. Most Americans sympathized with the victims of Hitler's aggression, and eventually some were horrified at rumors of the murder of hundreds of thousands of Jews. But because newspapers avoided intensive coverage of the well-documented but unpleasant stories, many Americans did not learn of the Holocaust of the early 1940s until near the end of the war.

At first, almost everyone hoped that compromises could be worked out and that Europe could settle its own problems. But that notion was destroyed on August 23, 1939, by the news of a Nazi–Soviet pact. Fascism and communism were political philosophies supposedly in deadly opposition. Many Americans had secretly hoped that Nazi Germany and Soviet Russia would fight it out, neutralizing each other. Now they had signed a nonaggression pact. A week later, Hitler's army attacked Poland, marking the official beginning of World War II. Britain and France honored their treaties and came to Poland's defense. "This nation will remain a neutral nation," Roosevelt announced, "but I cannot ask that every American remain neutral in thought as well."

Roosevelt asked for a repeal of the embargo section of the Neutrality Act and for the approval of the sale of arms on a cash-and-carry basis to France and Britain. The United States would help the countries struggling against Hitler, but not at the risk of entering the war or even at the threat of disrupting the civilian economy. Yet Roosevelt did take some secret risks. In August 1939, Albert Einstein, a Jewish refugee from Nazi Germany, and other distinguished scientists warned the president that German researchers were at work on an atomic bomb. Fearing the consequences of a powerful new weapon in Hitler's hands, Roosevelt authorized funds for a top-secret project to build an American bomb first. Only a few advisers and key members of Congress knew of the project, which was officially organized in 1941 and would ultimately change the course of human history.

The war in Poland ended quickly. With Germany attacking from the west and the Soviet Union from the east, the Poles were overwhelmed in a month. The fall of Poland in September 1939 brought a lull in the fighting. A number of Americans, including the American ambassador to Great Britain, Joseph Kennedy, who feared communist Russia more than fascist Germany, urged the United States to take the lead in negotiating a peace settlement that would recognize the German and Russian occupation of Poland. The British and French, however, were not interested in such a solution, and neither was Roosevelt.

Great Britain sent several divisions to aid the French against the expected German attack, but for months nothing happened. This interlude, sometimes called the "phony war," dramatically ended on April 9, 1940, when Germany attacked Norway and Denmark with a furious air and sea assault. A few weeks later, using armored vehicles supported by massive air strikes, the German *Blitzkrieg* ("lightning war") swept through Belgium, Luxembourg, and the Netherlands. A week later, the Germans stormed into France.

The famed Maginot line, a series of fortifications designed to repulse a German invasion, was useless, as German mechanized forces swept around the end of the line and attacked from the rear. The French guns, solidly fixed in concrete and pointing toward Germany, were never fired. The Maginot line, which would have been an effective defensive weapon in World War I, was ineffective in the new mechanized and mobile war of the 1940s. France surrendered in June as the British army fled back across the English Channel from Dunkirk.

How should the United States respond to the new and desperate situation in Europe? William Allen White, journalist and editor, and other concerned Americans organized the Committee to Defend America by Aiding the Allies, but others, including Charles Lindbergh, the hero of the 1920s, supported a group called America First. They argued that the United States should forget about England and concentrate on defending America. Roosevelt steered a cautious course. He approved the shipment to Britain of 50 overage American destroyers. In return, the United States received the right to establish naval and air bases on British territory from Newfoundland to Bermuda and British Guiana.

Winston Churchill, prime minister of Great Britain, asked for much more, but Roosevelt hesitated. In July 1940, the president did sign a measure authorizing $4 billion to increase the number of American naval warships. In September, Congress passed the Selective Service Act, which provided for the first peacetime draft in the history of the United States. Over a million men were to serve in the army for one year, but only in the Western Hemisphere. As the war in Europe reached a crisis in the fall of 1940, the American people were still undecided about the proper response.

The Election of 1940

Part of Roosevelt's reluctance to aid Great Britain more energetically came from his genuine desire to keep the United States out of the war, but it was also related to the presidential campaign waged during the crisis months of the summer and fall of 1940. Roosevelt broke a long tradition by seeking a third term. He marked the increasing support he was drawing from the liberal wing of the Democratic party by selecting liberal farm economist Henry Wallace of Iowa as his running mate.

The Republicans nominated Wendell Willkie of Indiana. Despite his big-business ties, Willkie approved of most New Deal legislation and supported aid to Great Britain. Energetic and attractive, Willkie was the most persuasive and exciting Republican candidate since Theodore Roosevelt, and he appealed to many people who distrusted or disliked Roosevelt. Yet in an atmosphere of international crisis, most voters chose to stay with Roosevelt. He won, 27 million to 22 million, and carried 38 of 48 states.

Lend-Lease

After the election, Roosevelt invented a scheme for sending aid to Britain without demanding payment. He called it "lend-lease." He compared the situation to lending a garden hose to a neighbor whose house was on fire. Senator Robert Taft of Ohio, however, thought the idea of lending military equipment and expecting it back was absurd. He decided it was more like lending chewing gum to a friend: "Once it had been used you did not want it back." Others were even more critical. Senator Burton K. Wheeler, an extreme isolationist, branded lend-lease "Roosevelt's triple A foreign policy" (after the Agricultural Adjustment Act) because it was designed to "plow under every fourth American boy."

The Lend-Lease Act, which Congress passed in March 1941, destroyed the fiction of neutrality. By that time, German submarines were sinking a half-million tons of shipping each month in the Atlantic. In June, Roosevelt proclaimed a national emergency and ordered the closing of German and Italian consulates in the United States. On June 22, Germany suddenly attacked the Soviet Union. It was one of Hitler's biggest blunders of the war, for now his armies had to fight on two fronts.

The surprise attack created a dilemma for the United States. Suddenly the great communist "enemy" had become America's friend and ally. When Roosevelt extended lend-lease aid to Russia in November 1941, many Americans were shocked. But most made a quick transition from viewing the Soviet Union as an enemy to treating it like a friend.

By the autumn of 1941, the United States was virtually at war with Germany in the Atlantic. On September 11, Roosevelt issued a "shoot on sight" order for all American ships operating in the Atlantic, and on October 30, a German submarine sank an American destroyer off the coast of Newfoundland. The war in the Atlantic, however, was undeclared, and many Americans opposed it. Eventually the sinking of enough American ships or another crisis would prob-

ably have provided the excuse for a formal declaration of war against Germany. It was not Germany, however, but Japan that catapulted the United States into World War II.

The Path to Pearl Harbor

Japan, controlled by ambitious military leaders, was the aggressor in the Far East as Hitler's Germany was in Europe. Intent on becoming a major world power yet desperately needing natural resources, especially oil, Japan was willing to risk war with China, the Soviet Union, and even the United States to get those resources. Japan invaded Manchuria in 1931 and launched an all-out assault on China in 1937. The Japanese leaders assumed that at some point the United States would go to war if Japan tried to take the Philippines, but the Japanese attempted to delay that moment as long as possible by diplomatic means. For its part, the United States feared the possibility of a two-front war and was willing to delay the confrontation with Japan until it had dealt with the German threat. Thus between 1938 and 1941, the United States and Japan engaged in a kind of diplomatic shadow boxing.

The United States did exert economic pressure on Japan. In July 1939, the United States gave the required six months' notice regarding cancellation of the 1911 commercial agreement between the two countries. In September 1940, the Roosevelt administration forbade the shipment of airplane fuel and scrap metal to Japan. Other items were added to the embargo until by the spring of 1941, the United States allowed only oil to be shipped to Japan, hoping that the threat of cutting off the important resource would lead to negotiations and avert a crisis. Japan did open negotiations with the United States, but there was little to discuss. Japan would not withdraw from China as the United States demanded. Indeed, Japan, taking advantage of the situation in Europe, occupied French Indochina in 1940 and 1941. In July 1941, Roosevelt froze all Japanese assets in the United States, effectively embargoing trade with Japan.

Roosevelt had an advantage in the negotiations with Japan, for the United States had broken the Japanese secret diplomatic code. But Japanese intentions were hard to decipher from the intercepted messages. The American leaders knew that Japan planned to attack, but they didn't know where. In September 1941, the Japanese decided to strike sometime after November unless the United States offered real concessions. The strike came not in the Philippines but at Pearl Harbor, the main American Pacific naval base, in Hawaii.

On the morning of December 7, 1941, Japanese airplanes launched from aircraft carriers attacked the

U.S. fleet at Pearl Harbor. The surprise attack destroyed or disabled 19 ships (including five battleships) and 150 planes and killed 2,335 soldiers and sailors and 68 civilians. On the same day, the Japanese launched attacks on the Philippines, Guam, and the Midway Islands, as well as on the British colonies of Hong Kong and Malaya. The next day, with only one dissenting vote, Congress declared war on Japan. Jeannette Rankin, a member of Congress from Montana who had voted against the war resolution in 1917, voted no again in 1941. She recalled that in 1917, after a week of tense debate, 50 voted against going to war. "This time I stood alone."

Corporal John J. "Ted" Kohl, a 25-year-old from Springfield, Ohio, was standing guard that Sunday morning near an ammunition warehouse at Hickam Field, near Pearl Harbor. He had joined the army two years before when his marriage failed and he could not find work. A Japanese bomb hit nearby, and Ted Kohl blew up with the warehouse. It was not until Wednesday evening, December 10, that the telegram arrived in Springfield. "The Secretary of War desires to express his deep regrets that your son Cpl. John J. Kohl was killed in action in defense of his country." Ted's younger brothers cried when they heard the news. There would be hundreds of thousands of telegrams and even more tears before the war was over.

December 7, 1941, was a day that "would live in infamy," in the words of Franklin Roosevelt. It was also a day that would have far-reaching implications for American foreign policy and for American attitudes toward the world. The surprise attack united the coun-

try as nothing else could have. Even isolationists and "America first" advocates quickly rallied behind the war effort.

After the shock and anger subsided, Americans searched for a villain. Someone must have blundered, someone must have betrayed the country to have allowed the "inferior" Japanese to have carried out such a successful and devastating attack. A myth persists to this day that the villain was Roosevelt, who, the story goes, knew of the Japanese attack but failed to warn the military commanders so that the American people might unite behind the war effort against Germany. But Roosevelt did not know. There was no specific warning that the attack was coming against Pearl Harbor, and the American ability to read the Japanese coded messages was no help because the fleet kept radio silence.

The irony was that the Americans, partly because of racial prejudice against the Japanese, underestimated their ability. They ignored many warning signals because they did not believe that the Japanese could launch an attack on a target as far away as Hawaii. Most of the experts, including Roosevelt, expected the Japanese to attack the Philippines or perhaps Thailand. Many people blundered, but there was no conspiracy on the part of Roosevelt and his advisers to get the United States into the war.

Even more important in the long run than the way the attack on Pearl Harbor united the American people was its effect on a generation of military and political leaders. Pearl Harbor became the symbol of unpreparedness. For a generation that experienced

An exploding American destroyer at Pearl Harbor, December 7, 1941. The attack on Pearl Harbor united the country and came to symbolize Japanese treachery and American lack of preparedness. Photographs such as this were published throughout the war to inspire Americans to work harder. *(Superstock, Inc.)*

Technology Changes the American People

PLACES

✦

When Nylon stockings were put on sale in February, 1946, 30,000 people "including many brave men," mobbed Gimbel's department store in New York eager to buy an advertised 26,000 pairs of the hose "that would not run." Dupont had actually introduced the Nylon stocking in 1940 but few were able to buy them because the government appropriated the entire supply of the synthetic fiber for use in making parachutes and even tires during the war.

Nylon was only one of many forms of plastic that transformed the way Americans lived in the 20th century. Plastics, usually defined as synthetic materials composed of organic molecules that can be shaped and hardened, have a relatively long history. One of the early pioneers was John Wesley Hyatt, a young printer from Albany, New York, who tried in 1868 to devise a substitute for the ivory billiard ball to win a $10,000 prize. He never succeeded, but he did produce a "transparent slab" as hard as wood, which he called "Celluloid." The new product was used to imitate amber and semiprecious stones. But in 1888 George Eastman used a form of Celluloid to produce a flexible film for his Kodak box camera, and in the process he revolutionized photography. One problem with Celluloid was that it had a tendency to burst into flames. A young Belgian chemist who immigrated to the United States

A woman proudly tries on her new Nylon stockings after waiting in line to purchase them when they were first released to the stores in 1945. (*Hagley Museum and Library*)

solved that problem in 1908 by developing Bakelite, a hard plastic that would not burn, melt, or dissolve. In the 1920s and 1930s the Bakelite Corporation produced door handles, telephones, cases for radios, colorful handles for cooking utensils, and billiard balls superior to those made of ivory.

The plastics industry had to overcome the public's perception that plastics, often used to produce buttons, combs, and knickknacks, were flimsy. The fact that plastics, most often made from petroleum by-products and coal tar, could be made into sheets or poured, shaped, and molded made it a natural product for the streamlined, modern era. The radio industry discovered plastics in the 1930s. A plastic radio case looked bright and colorful, as well as sleek and modern. Just as important, a plastic radio was cheaper to produce than the elaborately carved wooden models. Probably without even recognizing it many Americans accepted plastics when they bought a table model radio in the 1930s.

The Bakelite Corporation was not the only promoter of plastics. Du Pont, known as a manufacturer of explosives, moved into plastics in the 1920s and advertised its products with the slogan: "Better Things for Better Living Through Chemistry." It was in the Du Pont laboratories where a group of young chemists, after many failures, finally produced a synthetic fiber that could be stretched and woven. At first they called it "Fiber 6," then "Exton," and finally "Nylon." The new miracle plastic not only made wonderful stockings but also soon replaced

"And here's what saves that good aroma!"

PROTECTS CIGARS—AND LETS YOU <u>SEE</u> THEIR QUALITY

EVERY cigar has its loyal fans. Add them all together and you have an enthusiastic bunch of rooters for Cellophane wrapping.

Ten years ago, Du Pont chemists discovered how to make a *moistureproof* transparent wrapping. Wise cigar makers quickly appreciated the value of this new Cellophane protection, which keeps cigars

fresher, and prevents pocket breakage—yet still lets smokers *see* the color and quality of the leaf.

Today most cigars come in Cellophane transparent wrapping—so you may be sure of *extra freshness* and *extra pleasure* in the smoking. "Cellophane" Division, E. I. du Pont de Nemours & Co., Inc., Empire State Building, New York City.

Cellophane TRADE MARK DU PONT

"Cellophane" is the trade-mark of E. I. du Pont de Nemours & Co., Inc.

Many Americans were introduced to modern design in the 1930s through tabletop radios made of colorful molded plastic. *(The Granger Collection, New York)* (left) An advertisement for cellophane, the new miracle wrap, demonstrating how it kept cigars fresh. *(Hagley Museum and Library)*

pig bristles in the manufacture of toothbrushes. The same Du Pont laboratories produced Cellophane, a transparent and moisture-resistant plastic that revolutionized the marketing of food and tobacco. Cellophane promised purity and freshness, and soon everything from meat to cookies to cigars were wrapped in the new magic material.

Plastics were important in the 1930s, but it was during World War II and the postwar years that they became commonplace. From disposable pens to Formica tabletops, from Barbie dolls to Styrofoam cups, plastics transformed American life. Yet by the 1960s, for all their innovative uses, plastics had come to seem shoddy and cheap, not modern and sleek. Some called for a return to the use of natural products, such as wool, cotton, and wood, while others worried about the garbage dumps filling up with plastic bottles and bags. Du Pont, perhaps influenced by the bad publicity that chemical companies had received during the Vietnam War for producing Agent Orange and other defoliants, dropped the word *chemistry* from its slogan. The company bragged about how it produced "Better Things for Better Living."

In 1971, ecologist Barry Commoner charged in a crusading book, *The Closing Circle*, that plastics, especially polyvinyl chloride (popularly known as vinyl) was dangerous to the environment. He claimed that plastics contaminated the soil and the water supply and would cause cancer and create problems for generations unborn. But the American people were probably more disturbed by the news that thousands of seals and other wildlife were dying

from becoming entangled with discarded plastic. A photograph of a dead wild duck, strangled on a discarded six-pack holder, summed up the potential evil of plastic. Commoner's book and other reports and articles helped create a series of protests that persuaded McDonald's and other corporations to replace plastic packages with paper or cardboard.

Still, Americans continued to buy Nylons, use plastic computers, and accept plastic products as a natural part of their world. In 1979 the global production of plastics surpassed that of steel. Vinyl, polyester, teflon, silicone, acrylic, and polyurethane have entered our vocabulary and altered our lives. Everyday we encounter plastic bottles and bags and plastic wrappings for food, six-packs, and frozen dinners. We wear plastic glasses and use plastic skis, running shoes, backpacks, and surfboards. Automobiles and airplanes, even missiles, are made, at least in part, of plastics. And credit cards, so much a part of modern life, are often called simply "plastic." The development of plastics, like so many advances in science and technology, has been both a benefit and a menace.

How would your life be different without plastics? How many plastic objects or materials do you use in a day? Can you imagine standing in line to buy nylons? Do you have a different attitude toward plastics than your parents? Have plastics made the world better or worse?

Stephen Fenichell, *Plastic: The Making of a Synthetic Century* (1996). Jeffrey Meikle, *American Plastic* (1995).

the anger and frustration of the attack on Pearl Harbor by an unscrupulous enemy, the lesson was to be prepared and ready to stop an aggressor before it had a chance to strike at the United States. The smoldering remains of the sinking battleships at Pearl Harbor on the morning of December 7, 1941, and the history lesson learned there would influence American policy not only during World War II but also in Korea, Vietnam, and the international confrontations of the 1980s.

THE HOME FRONT

Too often wars are described in terms of presidents and generals, emperors and kings, in terms of grand strategy and elaborate campaigns. But wars affect the lives of all people—the soldiers who fight and the women and children and men who stay home. World War II especially had an impact on all aspects of society—the economy, the movies and radio, even attitudes toward women and blacks. For many people, the war represented opportunity and the end of the Depression. For others, the excitement of faraway places meant that they could never return home again. For still others, the war left lasting scars.

Mobilizing for War

Converting American industry to war production was a complex task. Many corporate executives refused to admit that an emergency existed. Shortly after Pearl Harbor, Roosevelt created the War Production Board (WPB) and appointed Donald Nelson, executive vice president of Sears, Roebuck, to mobilize the nation's resources for an all-out war effort. The WPB offered businesses cost-plus contracts, guaranteeing a fixed and generous profit. Often the government also financed new plants and equipment. Secretary of War Henry Stimson remarked, "If you . . . go to war . . . in a capitalist country, you have to let business make money out of the process or business won't work." Roosevelt seemed to agree.

Even before the United States entered the war Roosevelt had created a National Defense Research Committee to organize scientists to help in the war effort. Later he set up the Office of Scientific Research and Development (OSRD) to perfect new weapons and other products. The most important science and technology project carried on during the war was the development of the atomic bomb, but OSRD also improved radar and developed high-altitude bomb sights, jet engines, pressurized cabins for airplanes, and penicillin and other miracle drugs. Scientists under contract to the government also developed DDT and other effective insecticides, but none of the scientists recognized the dangerous side effects that

DDT would have on the environment. The wartime collaboration of science, industry, and the government would lay the groundwork for massive projects in the postwar years.

The Roosevelt administration leaned over backward to gain the cooperation of businessmen. The president appointed many business executives to key positions, some of whom, like Nelson, served for a dollar a year. He also abandoned antitrust actions in all industries that were remotely war-related. The policy worked. Both industrial production and net corporate profits nearly doubled during the war.

Large commercial farmers also profited. The war years accelerated the mechanization of the farm. Between 1940 and 1945, a million tractors joined those already in use. At the same time, the farm population declined by 17 percent. The consolidation of small farms into large ones and the dramatic increase in the use of fertilizer made farms more productive and farming more profitable for the large operators.

Many government agencies in addition to the War Production Board helped run the war effort efficiently. The Office of Price Administration (OPA) set prices on thousands of items to control inflation. The OPA also

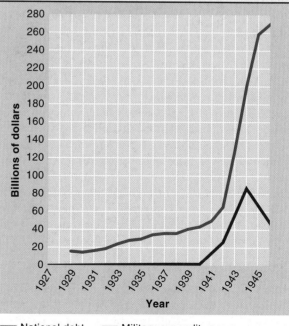

Military Expenditures and the National Debt, 1929–1945

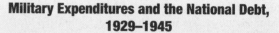
National debt   Military expenditures

Increased taxes, the sale of war bonds, and price controls kept inflation under relative control during the war. Still, the war industry not only stimulated the economy but also increased the national debt.
Source: U.S. Bureau of the Census.

rationed scarce products. Because the OPA's decisions affected what people wore and ate and whether they had gasoline, many regarded it as oppressive. The National War Labor Board (NWLB) had the authority to set wages and hours and to monitor working conditions and could, under the president's wartime emergency powers, seize industrial plants whose owners refused to cooperate.

Membership in labor unions grew rapidly during the war, from a total of 10.5 million in 1941 to 14.7 million in 1945. This increase was aided by government policy. In return for a "no-strike pledge," the NWLB allowed agreements that required workers to retain their union membership through the life of a contract. Labor leaders, however, complained about increased government regulations and argued that wage controls coupled with wartime inflation were unfair. The NWLB finally allowed a 15 percent cost-of-living increase on some contracts, but that did not apply to overtime pay, which helped drive up wages in some industries during the war by about 70 percent.

Labor leaders were often not content with the raises. In the most famous incident, John L. Lewis broke the no-strike pledge of organized labor by calling a nationwide coal strike in 1943. When Roosevelt ordered the secretary of the interior to take over the mines, Lewis called off the strike. But this bold protest did help raise miners' wages.

In addition to wage and price controls and rationing, the government tried to reduce inflation by selling war bonds and by increasing taxes. The Revenue Act of 1942 raised tax rates, broadened the tax base, increased corporate taxes to 40 percent, and raised the excess-profits tax to 90 percent. In addition, the government initiated a payroll deduction for income taxes. The war made the income tax a reality for most Americans for the first time.

Despite some unfairness and much confusion, the American economy responded to the wartime crisis and produced the equipment and supplies that eventually won the war. American industries built 300,000 airplanes, 88,140 tanks, and 3,000 merchant ships. In 1944 alone, American factories produced 800,000 tons of synthetic rubber to replace the supply of natural rubber captured by the Japanese. Although the national debt grew from about $143 billion in 1943 to $260 billion in 1945, the government policy of taxation paid for about 40 percent of the war's cost. At the same time, full employment and the increase in two-income families, together with forced savings, helped provide capital for postwar expansion. In a limited way, the tax policy also tended to redistribute wealth, which the New Deal had failed to do. The top 5 percent income bracket, which controlled 23 percent of the disposable income in 1939, accounted for only 17 percent in 1945.

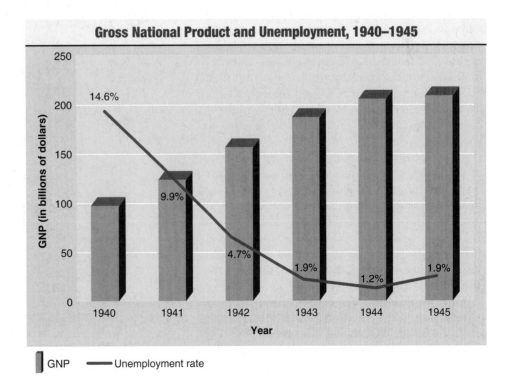

Gross National Product and Unemployment, 1940–1945

The war economy virtually wiped out unemployment and increased production to unprecedented levels.
Source: U.S. Bureau of the Census.

The war stimulated the growth of the federal bureaucracy and accelerated the trend, begun during World War I and extended in the 1920s and 1930s, toward the government's central role in the economy. The war also increased the cooperation between industry and government, creating what would later be called a military-industrial complex. But for most Americans, despite anger at the OPA and the income tax, the war meant the end of the Depression.

Patriotic Fervor

In European and Asian cities, the horror and destruction of war were everywhere. But in the United States, the war was remote. Thousands of American families felt the tragedy of war directly with the arrival of an official telegram telling of a son or husband killed in action. For most Americans, however, it was a foreign war, far removed from the reality of daily life.

The government tried to keep the conflict alive in the minds of Americans and to keep the country united behind the war effort. The Office of War Information, staffed by writers and advertising executives, controlled the news the American public received about the war. It promoted patriotism and presented the American war effort in the best possible light. The government also sold war bonds, not only to help pay for the war and reduce inflation but also to sell the war to the American people. As had been true during World War I, movie stars and other celebrities appeared at war bond rallies. Dorothy Lamour, one of Hollywood's most glamorous actresses, took credit for selling $350 million worth of bonds. Schoolchildren purchased war stamps and faithfully pasted them in an album until they had accumulated stamps worth $18.75, enough to buy a $25 bond (redeemable ten years later). Their bonds, they were told, would purchase bullets or a part for an airplane to kill "Japs" and Germans and defend the American way of life. "For Freedom's Sake, Buy War Bonds," one poster announced. Working men and women purchased bonds through payroll deduction plans and looked forward to spending the money on consumer goods after the war. In the end, the government sold over $135 billion in war bonds. While the bond drives did help control inflation, they were most important in making millions of Americans feel that they were contributing to the war effort.

Those too old or too young to join the armed forces served in other ways. Thousands became air raid wardens or civilian defense and Red Cross volunteers. They raised victory gardens and took part in scrap drives. Even small children could join the war effort by collecting old rubber, wastepaper, and kitchen fats. Boys dived into lakes and rivers to recover old tires and even ripped down iron fences to aid their towns and neighborhoods in meeting their scrap quota. Some items, including gasoline, sugar, butter, and meat, were rationed, but few people complained. Even horsemeat hamburgers seemed edible if they helped win the war. Newspaper and magazine advertising characterized ordinary actions as either speeding victory or impeding the war effort. "Hoarders are the same as spies," one ad announced. "Every time you decide not to buy something you help win the war."

Internment of Japanese Americans

Wartime campaigns not only stimulated patriotism but also promoted hate for the enemy. The Nazis, especially Hitler and his Gestapo, had become synonymous with evil even before 1941. But at the beginning of the war, there was little animosity toward the German people. "You and I don't hate the Nazis because they are Germans. We hate the Germans because they are Nazis," announced a character in one of Helen MacInnes's novels. But before long, most

Japanese-American children on their way to a "relocation center." For many Japanese Americans, but especially for the children, the nightmare of the relocation camp experience would stay with them all their lives. *(Library of Congress)*

Americans ceased to make distinctions. All Germans seemed evil, although the anti-German hysteria that had swept the country during World War I never developed.

The Japanese were easier to hate than the Germans. The attack on Pearl Harbor created a special animosity toward the Japanese, but the depiction of the Japanese as warlike and subhuman owed something to a long tradition of fear of the so-called yellow peril and a distrust of all Asians. The movies, magazine articles, cartoons, and posters added to the image of the Japanese soldier or pilot with a toothy grin murdering innocent women and children or shooting down helpless Americans. Two weeks after Pearl Harbor, *Time* magazine explained to Americans how they could distinguish our Asian friends the Chinese "from the Japs." "Virtually all Japanese are short, Japanese are seldom fat; they often dry up with age," *Time* declared. "Most Chinese avoid horn-rimmed spectacles. Japanese walk stiffly erect, hard-heeled. Chinese, more relaxed, have an easy gait. The Chinese expression is likely to be more kindly, placid, open; the Japanese more positive, dogmatic, arrogant."

The racial stereotype of the Japanese played a role in the treatment of Japanese Americans during the war. Some prejudice was shown against German and Italian Americans, but Japanese Americans were the only group confined in concentration camps, in the greatest mass abridgment of civil liberties in American history.

At the time of Pearl Harbor, about 127,000 Japanese Americans lived in the United States, most on the West Coast. About 80,000 were nisei (Japanese born in the United States and holding American citizenship) and sansei (the sons and daughters of nisei); the rest were issei (aliens born in Japan who were ineligible for U.S. citizenship). The Japanese had long suffered from racial discrimination and prejudice in the United States. They were barred from intermarriage with other groups and excluded from many clubs, restaurants, and recreation facilities. Many worked as tenant farmers, fishermen, and small businessmen. Others made up a small professional class of lawyers, teachers, and doctors and a large number of land-owning farmers.

Although many retained cultural and linguistic ties to Japan, they posed no more threat to the country than did the much larger groups of Italian Americans and German Americans. But their physical characteristics made them stand out as the others did not. After

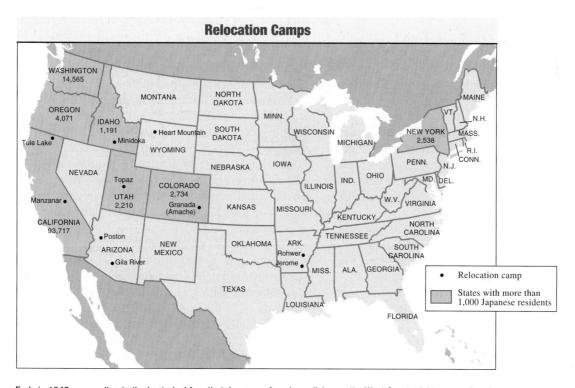

Early in 1942, responding to the hysterical fear that Japanese Americans living on the West Coast might engage in sabotage, the government ordered over 100,000 Japanese Americans (many of them citizens) into relocation camps. A larger group of Japanese Americans living in Hawaii did not have their lives disrupted or their property confiscated.

Pearl Harbor, an anti-Japanese panic seized the West Coast. A Los Angeles newspaper reported that armed Japanese were in Baja, California, ready to attack. Rumors suggested that Japanese fishermen were preparing to sow mines in the harbor, blow up tunnels, and poison the water supply.

West Coast politicians and ordinary citizens urged the War Department and the president to evacuate the Japanese. The president capitulated and issued Executive Order 9066 authorizing the evacuation in February 1942. "The continued pressure of a largely unassimilated, tightly knit racial group, bound to an enemy nation by strong ties of race, culture, custom and religion, constituted a menace which had to be dealt with," General John De Witt argued, justifying the removal on military grounds. But racial fear and animosity, not military necessity, stood behind the order.

Eventually, the government built the "relocation centers" in remote, often arid, sections of the West. "The Japs live like rats, breed like rats, and act like rats. We don't want them," the governor of Idaho announced. The camps were primitive and unattractive. "When I first entered our room, I became sick to my stomach," a Japanese-American woman remembered. "There were seven beds in the room and no furniture nor any partitions to separate the males and the females of the family. I just sat on the bed, staring at the bare wall."

The government evacuated about 110,000 Japanese. Those who were forced to leave their homes, farms, and businesses lost almost all their property and possessions. Farmers left their crops to be harvested by their American neighbors. Store owners sold out for a small percentage of what their goods were worth. No personal items or household goods could be transported. The Japanese Americans lost their worldly possessions, and something more—their pride and respect. One six-year-old kept asking his mother to "take him back to America." He thought his relocation center was in Japan.

The evacuation of the Japanese Americans appears in retrospect to have been unjustified. Even in Hawaii, where a much larger Japanese population existed, the government attempted no evacuation, and no sabotage and little disloyalty occurred. The government allowed Japanese-American men to volunteer for military service, and many served bravely in the European theater. The 442nd Infantry Combat Team, made up entirely of nisei, became the most decorated unit in all the military service—another indication of the loyalty and patriotism of the Japanese Americans. In 1988, Congress belatedly voted limited compensa-

tion for the Japanese Americans relocated during World War II.

African and Hispanic Americans at War

The United States in 1941, even in much of the North, remained a segregated society. African Americans could not live, eat, travel, work, or go to school with the same freedom whites enjoyed. Black Americans profited little from the revival of prosperity and the expansion of jobs early in the war. Those who joined the military were usually assigned to menial jobs as cooks or laborers and were always assigned to segregated units with whites as the high-ranking officers. The myth that black soldiers had failed to perform well in World War I persisted. "Leadership is not embedded in the negro race yet," Secretary of War Henry Stimson wrote, "and to try to make commissioned officers . . . lead men into battle—colored men—is only to work a disaster to both."

Some black leaders found it especially ironic that as the country prepared to fight Hitler and his racist policies, the United States persisted in its own brand of racism. "A jim crow Army cannot fight for a free world," announced *The Crisis*, the journal of the NAACP. A. Philip Randolph decided to act rather than talk. The son of a Methodist minister, Randolph had worked with the first wave of African Americans migrating from the South to the northern cities during and just after World War I. He spent years trying "to carry the gospel of unionism to the colored world." He organized and led the Brotherhood of Sleeping Car Porters, and in 1937, he finally won grudging recognition of the union from the Pullman Company.

Respected and admired by black leaders of all political persuasions, Randolph convinced many of them in 1941 to join him in a march on Washington to demand equal rights. "Dear fellow Negro Americans," Randolph wrote, "be not dismayed in these terrible times. You possess power, great power. Our problem is to harness and hitch it up for action on the broadest, daring and most gigantic scale."

The threat of as many as 100,000 African Americans marching in protest in the nation's capital alarmed Roosevelt. At first, he sent his assistants, including his wife, Eleanor, who was greatly admired in the black community, to dissuade Randolph from such drastic action. Finally, he talked to Randolph in person on June 18, 1941. Randolph and Roosevelt struck a bargain. Roosevelt refused to desegregate the armed forces, but in return for Randolph's calling off the march, the president issued Executive Order 8802, which stated that it was the policy of the United States that "there shall be no discrimination in the employment of workers in defense industries or government because of race, creed, color or national origin." He also established the Fair Employment Practices Commission (FEPC) to enforce the order.

By threatening militant action, the black leaders wrested a major concession from the president. But the executive order did not end prejudice, and the FEPC, which its chairman described as the "most hated agency in Washington," had limited success in erasing the color line. Many black soldiers were angered and humiliated throughout the war by being made to sit in the back of buses and being barred from hotels and restaurants. Years later, one former black soldier recalled being refused service in a restaurant in Salina, Kansas, while the same restaurant served German prisoners from a camp nearby. "We continued to stare," he recalled. "This was really happening. . . . The people of Salina would serve these enemy soldiers and turn away black American G.I.'s."

Many African Americans improved their economic conditions during the war by taking jobs in war industries. Continuing the migration that had begun during World War I, 750,000 southern blacks moved to northern and western cities in search of economic opportunity. Some became skilled workers and a few became professionals, but they did not escape racial prejudice. In Detroit, where a major race riot broke out in the summer of 1943, Polish Americans had protested a public housing development that promised to bring blacks into their neighborhood. In one year, more than 50,000 blacks moved into that city, already overcrowded with many others seeking wartime jobs. The new arrivals increased the pressure on housing and other facilities, and the war accentuated the tension among the various groups.

The riot broke out on a hot, steamy day at a municipal park where a series of incidents led to fights between black and white young people and then to looting in the black community. Before federal and state troops restored order, 34 had been killed (25 blacks and 9 whites) and rioters had destroyed more than $2 million worth of property. Groups of whites roamed the city attacking blacks, overturning cars, setting fires, and sometimes killing wantonly. A group of young men murdered a 58-year-old black "just for the hell of it." "We didn't know him," one of the boys admitted. "He wasn't bothering us. But other people were fighting and killing and we felt like it too." Other riots broke out in Mobile, Los Angeles, New York, and Beaumont, Texas. In all these cities, and in many others where the tension did not lead to open violence, the legacy of bitterness and hate lasted long after the war.

Mexican Americans, like most minority groups, profited during the war from the increased job opportunities provided by wartime industry, but they, too, faced racial prejudice. In California and in many parts of the Southwest, Mexicans could not use public swimming pools. Often lumped together with blacks,

Even before the United States entered the war, black families like this one moved north to look for work and a better life. This massive migration would change the racial mix in northern cities. *(Library of Congress)*

they were excluded from certain restaurants. Usually they were limited to menial jobs and were constantly harassed by the police, picked up for minor offenses, and jailed on the smallest excuse. In Los Angeles, the anti-Mexican prejudice flared into violence. The increased migration of Mexicans into the city and old hatreds created a volatile situation. Most of the hostility and anger focused on Mexican gang members, or pachuchos, especially those wearing zoot suits. The suits consisted of long, loose coats with padded shoulders, ballooned pants pegged at the ankles, and a wide-brimmed hat. A watch chain and a ducktail haircut completed the uniform. The zoot suit had originated in the black sections of northern cities and became a national craze during the war. It was a look some teenage males adopted to call attention to themselves and shock conventional society.

The zoot-suiters especially angered soldiers and sailors who were stationed or on leave in Los Angeles. After a number of provocative incidents, violence broke out between the Mexican-American youths and the servicemen in the spring of 1943. The violence reached a peak on June 7 when gangs of servicemen, often in taxicabs, combed the city, attacking all the young zoot-suiters they could find or anyone who looked Mexican. The servicemen, joined by others, beat up the Mexicans, stripped them of their offensive clothes, and then gave them haircuts. The police, both civilian and military, looked the other way, and when they did move in, they arrested the victims rather than their attackers. The local press and the chamber of commerce hotly denied that race was a factor in the riots, but *Time* magazine was probably closer to the truth when it called the riots the "ugliest brand of mob action since the coolie race riots of the 1870s."

SOCIAL IMPACT OF THE WAR

Modern wars have been incredibly destructive of human lives and property, but they have social results as well. The Civil War ended slavery and ensured the triumph of the industrial North for years to come; in so doing, it left a legacy of bitterness and transformed the race question from a sectional to a national problem. World War I ensured the success of woman suffrage and prohibition, caused a migration of blacks to northern cities, and ushered in a time of intolerance. World War II also had many social results. It altered patterns of work, leisure, education, and family life; caused a massive migration of people; created jobs; and changed lifestyles. It is difficult to overemphasize the impact of the war on the generation that lived through it.

Wartime Opportunities

More than 15 million American civilians moved during the war. Like the Momadays, many left home to find better jobs. In fact, for many Native Americans, wartime opportunities led to a migration from the rural areas and the reservations into the cities. Americans moved off the farms and away from the small towns, flocking to cities, where defense jobs were readily available. They moved west: California alone gained more than two million people during the war. But they also moved out of the South into the northern cities, while a smaller number moved from the North to the South. Late in the war, when a shortage of farm labor developed, some reversed the trend and moved back onto the farms. But a great many people moved somewhere. One observer, noticing the heavily packed cars heading west, decided that it was just like *The Grapes of Wrath,* without the poverty and the hopelessness.

The World War II migrants poured into industrial centers; 200,000 came to the Detroit area, nearly a half-million to Los Angeles, and about 100,000 to Mobile, Alabama. They put pressure on the schools, housing, and other services. Often they had to live in new Hoovervilles, trailer parks, or temporary housing. In San Pablo, California, a family of four adults and seven children lived in an 8-by-10-foot shack. Bill Mauldin, the war cartoonist, showed a young couple with a child buying tickets for a movie with the caption: "Matinee, heck—we want to register for a week."

Nowhere was the change more dramatic than in the West, especially in California, where the wartime boom transformed the region more dramatically than any development since the nineteenth-century economic revolution created by the railroads and mining. The federal government spent over $70 billion in the state (one-tenth of the total for the entire country) to build army bases, shipyards, supply depots, and testing sites. In addition, private industry constructed so many facilities that the region became the center of a growing military-industrial complex. San Diego, for example, was transformed from a sleepy port and naval base into a sprawling metropolis. The population grew by 147 percent between 1941 and 1945, from 202,000 to 380,000. Vallezo, a small city near Oakland, grew from 20,000 to over 100,000 in just two years. The U.S. Navy's Mare Island Shipyard nearby increased its workforce from 5,000 to 45,000. Vanport, just north of Portland, Oregon, was an empty mud flat in 1940; three years later it was a bustling city of more than 40,000. Almost everyone in the new town worked for the Kaiser Ship Yards.

This spectacular growth created problems. There was a housing shortage, schools were overcrowded,

The war caused many quick romances, but also many tearful good-byes. *(Alfred Eisenstadt/LIFE Magazine © Time Inc.)*

ically. The number of marriages also rose sharply. Early in the war, a young man could be deferred if he had a dependent, and a wife qualified as a dependent. Later, many servicemen got married, often to women they barely knew, because they wanted a little excitement and perhaps someone to come home to. The birthrate also began to rise in 1940, as young couples started a family as fast as they could. Some children were "good-bye babies," conceived just before the husband left to join the military or go overseas. The illegitimacy rate also went up, and from the outset of the war, the divorce rate began to climb sharply. Yet most of the wartime marriages survived, and many of the women left at home looked ahead to a time after the war when they could settle down to a normal life.

Women Workers for Victory

Thousands of women took jobs in heavy industry that formerly would have been considered unladylike. They built tanks, airplanes, and ships, but they still earned less than men. At first, women were rarely taken on because as the war in Europe pulled American industry out of its long slump, unemployed men snapped up the newly available positions. In the face of this male labor pool, one government official remarked that we should "give the women something to do to keep their hands busy as we did in the last war, then maybe they won't bother us."

But by 1943, with many men drafted and male unemployment virtually nonexistent, the government was quick to suggest that it was women's patriotic duty to take their place on the assembly line. A government poster showed a woman worker and her uniformed husband standing in front of an American flag with the caption: "I'm proud . . . my husband wants me to do my part." The government tried to convince women that if they could run a vacuum cleaner or a sewing machine or drive a car, they could operate power machinery in a factory. Advertisers in women's magazines joined the campaign by showing fashion models in work clothes. A popular song was "Rosie the Riveter," who was "making history working for victory." She also helped her marine boyfriend by "working overtime on the riveting machine."

At the end of the war, the labor force included 19.5 million women, but three-fourths of them had been working before the conflict, and some of the additional ones might have sought work in normal times. The new women war workers tended to be older, and they were more often married than single. Some worked for patriotic reasons. "Every time I test a batch of rubber, I know it's going to help bring my three sons home quicker," a woman worker in a rubber plant remarked. But others worked for the money or to have something useful to do. Yet in 1944,

and hospitals and municipal services could not keep up with the demand. Crime and prostitution increased as did racial tensions. Some migrants had never lived in a city and were homesick. On one occasion in a Willow Grove, Michigan, school, the children were all instructed to sing "Michigan, My Michigan"; no one knew the words because they all came from other states. One of the most popular country songs of the period, when thousands had left their rural homes to find work in the city, was "I Wanna Go Back to West Virginia."

For the first time in years, many families had money to spend, but they had nothing to spend it on. The last new car rolled off the assembly line in February 1942. There were no washing machines, refrigerators, or radios in the stores, no gasoline and no tires to permit weekend trips. Even when people had time off, they tended to stay at home or in the neighborhood. Some of the new housing developments had the atmosphere of a mining camp, complete with drinking, prostitution, and barroom brawls.

The war required major adjustments in American family life. With several million men in the service and others far away working at defense jobs, the number of households headed by a woman increased dramat-

OURS...to fight for

FREEDOM FROM WANT

The government enlisted artists during the war to help inspire Americans to support the war effort. No one captured the sense of what it meant to be an American as well as Norman Rockwell. He created four paintings to illustrate the four freedoms that Roosevelt had announced in 1941 were the things we were fighting to protect: Freedom of Worship, Freedom of Speech, Freedom from Fear, and Freedom from Want. Commissioned by *The Saturday Evening Post,* these paintings were reproduced as posters in great numbers and used to support war bond drives. *(National Archives)*

women's weekly wages averaged $31.21, compared with $54.65 for men, reflecting women's more menial tasks and their low seniority as well as outright discrimination. Still, many women enjoyed factory work. "Boy have the men been getting away with murder all these years," exclaimed a Pittsburgh housewife. "Why I worked twice as hard selling in a department store and got half the pay."

Black women faced the most difficult situation during the war, and often when they applied for work, they were told, "We have not yet installed separate toilet facilities" or "We can't put a Negro in the front office." Not until 1944 did the telephone company in New York City hire a black telephone operator. Still, some black women moved during the war from domestic jobs to higher-paying factory work. Married women with young children also found it difficult to obtain work. There were few daycare facilities and the women were often informed that they should be home with their children.

Women workers often had to endure catcalls, whistles, and more overt sexual harassment on the job. Still, most persisted, and they tried to look feminine despite the heavy work clothes. In one Boston factory, a woman was hooted at for carrying a lunch box. Only men, it seemed, carried lunch boxes; women brought their lunch in a paper bag.

Many women war workers quickly left their jobs after the war ended. Some left by choice, but dismissals ran twice as high for women as for men. The war had barely shaken the notion that a woman's place was at home. Some women who learned what an extra paycheck meant for the family's standard of living would have preferred to keep working. But most women, and an even larger percentage of men, agreed at the end of the war that women did not deserve an "equal chance with men" for jobs. War work altered individual lives and attitudes, but it did not change dramatically either sex's perception of women's proper role.

Entertaining the People

According to one survey, Americans listened to the radio an average of 4½ hours a day during the war. The major networks increased their news programs from less than 4 percent to nearly 30 percent of broadcasting time. Americans heard Edward R. Murrow broadcasting from London during the German air blitz with the sound of the air raid sirens in the background. They listened to Eric Sevareid cover the battle of Burma and describe the sensation of jumping out of an airplane. Often the signal faded out and the static made listening difficult, but the live broadcasts had drama and authenticity never before possible.

Even more than the reporters, the commentators became celebrities on whom the American people depended to explain what was going on around the world. Millions listened to the clipped, authoritative voice of H. V. Kaltenborn or to Gabriel Heatter, whose trademark was "Ah, there's good news tonight." But the war also intruded on almost all other programming. Even the advertising, which took up more and more air time, reminded listeners of the war. Lucky Strike cigarettes, which changed the color of its package from green to white, presumably because there was a shortage of green pigment, made "Lucky Strike Green Has Gone to War" almost as famous as "Remember Pearl Harbor."

The serials, the standard fare of daytime radio, also adopted wartime themes. Dick Tracy tracked down spies, and Captain Midnight fought against the enemy

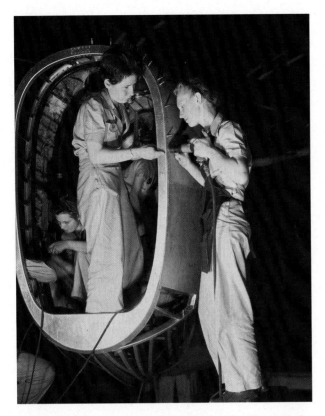

"Rosie the Riveter" became perhaps the most familiar symbol of women's contribution to the war effort during World War II. Here women rivet sections of an aircraft engine compartment. The government recruited women to work in war industries, but after the war ended, it urged women to return to the traditional roles of wife and mother. (*Library of Congress*)

on remote jungle islands. Superman outwitted Nazi agents, and Stella Dallas took a job in a defense plant.

Music, which took up a large proportion of radio programming, also conveyed a war theme. There were "Goodbye, Mama (I'm Off to Yokohama)" and "Praise the Lord and Pass the Ammunition," but more numerous were songs of romance and love, songs about separation and hope for a better time after the war. The danceable tunes of Glenn Miller and Tommy Dorsey became just as much a part of wartime memories as ration books and far-off battlefields.

For many Americans, the motion picture became the most important leisure activity and a part of their fantasy life during the war. Attendance at the movies averaged about 100 million viewers a week. There might not be gasoline for weekend trips or Sunday drives, but the whole family could go to the movies. Even those in the military service could watch American movies on board ship or at a remote outpost. "Pinup" photographs of Hollywood stars decorated the barracks and even tanks and planes wherever American troops were stationed.

Musical comedies, cowboy movies, and historical romances remained popular during the war, but the conflict intruded even on Hollywood. Newsreels that offered a visual synopsis of the war news, always with an upbeat message and a touch of human interest, preceded most movies. Their theme was that the Americans were winning the war, even if early in the conflict there was little evidence to that effect. Many feature films also had a wartime theme, picturing the war in the Pacific complete with grinning, vicious Japanese villains (usually played by Chinese or Korean character actors). In the beginning of these films, the Japanese were always victorious, but in the end, they always got "what they deserved."

The movies set in Europe differed somewhat from those depicting the Far Eastern war. British and Americans, sometimes spies, sometimes downed airmen, could dress up like Germans and get away with it. They outwitted the Germans at every turn, sabotaging important installations and finally escaping in a captured plane.

A number of Hollywood actors went into the service, and some even became heroes. Most, like Ronald Reagan, were employed to produce, narrate, or act in government films. The Office of War Information produced short subjects and documentaries, some of them distinguished, like John Huston's *Battle of San Pietro*, a realistic depiction of war on the Italian front. More typical were propaganda films meant to indoctrinate American soldiers into the reasons they were fighting the war. *Letter from Bataan*, a short film made in 1942, portrayed a wounded GI who wrote home asking his brother-in-law to save his razor blades because "it takes twelve thousand razor blades to make a one-thousand-pound bomb." The film ended with the announcement that the soldier had died in the hospital.

The GIs' War

GI, the abbreviation for *government issue*, became the affectionate designation for the ordinary soldier in World War II. The GIs came from every background and ethnic group. Some served reluctantly, some eagerly. A few became genuine heroes. All were turned into heroes by the press and the public, who seemed to believe that one American could easily defeat at least 20 Japanese or Germans. Ernie Pyle, one of the war correspondents who chronicled the authentic story of the ordinary GI, wrote of soldiers "just toiling from day to day in a world full of insecurity, discomfort, homesickness, and a dulled sense of danger."

Bill Mauldin, another correspondent, told the story of the ordinary soldier in a series of cartoons featuring two tired and resigned infantrymen, Willie and Joe. Joe tries to explain what the war is about, "when they run we try to ketch 'em, when we ketch 'em we try to make 'em run." In another cartoon, Willie says, "Joe, yestiddy ya saved my life an' I swore I'd pay you back. Here's my last pair of dry socks." For the soldier in the front line, the big strategies were irrelevant. The war seemed a constant mix-up; much more important were the little comforts and staying alive.

In the midst of battle, the war was no fun, but only one soldier in eight who served ever saw combat, and even for many of those the war was a great adventure (just as World War I had been). "When World War II broke out I was delighted," Mario Puzo, author of *The Godfather,* remembered. "There is no other word, terrible as it may sound. My country called. I was delivered from my mother, my family, the girl I was loving passionately but did not love. And delivered *without guilt.* Heroically my country called, ordered me to defend it." World War II catapulted young men and women out of their small towns and urban neighborhoods into exotic places where they met new people and did new things.

The war was important for Mexican Americans, who were drafted and volunteered in great numbers. A third of a million served in all branches of the military, a larger percentage than for many other ethnic groups. Although they encountered prejudice, they probably found less in the armed forces than they had at home, and many returned to civilian life with new ambitions and a new sense of self-esteem.

Many Native Americans also served. In fact, many were recruited for special service in the Marine Signal Corps. One group of Navajos completely befuddled the Japanese with a code based on their native language. "Were it not for the Navajos, the Marines would never have taken Iwo Jima," one Signal Corps officer declared. But the Navajo code talkers and all other Native Americans who chose to return to the reservations after the war were ineligible for veterans' loans, hospitalization, and other benefits. They lived on federal land, and that, according to the law, canceled all the advantages that other veterans enjoyed after the war.

For African Americans, who served throughout the war in segregated units and faced prejudice wherever they went, the military experience also had much to teach. Fewer blacks were sent overseas (about 79,000 of 504,000 blacks in the service in 1943), and fewer were in combat outfits, so the percentage of black soldiers killed and wounded was low. Many illiterate blacks, especially from the South, learned to read and write in the service. Blacks who went overseas began to realize that not everyone viewed them as inferior. One black army officer said, "What the hell do we want to fight the Japs for anyhow? They couldn't possibly treat us any worse than these 'crackers' right here

Over 300,000 American servicemen died during the war, but the government tried to protect the American people from learning the real cost of the battles. This photograph, published in 1943, was the first to show dead American soldiers. *(George Strock/LIFE Magazine © 1943 Time Inc.)*

at home." Most realized the paradox of fighting for freedom when they themselves had little freedom; they hoped things would improve after the war.

Because the war lasted longer than World War I, its impact was greater. In all, over 16 million men and women served in some branch of the military service. About 322,000 were killed in the war, and more than 800,000 were wounded. The 12,000 listed as missing just disappeared. The war claimed many more lives than World War I and was the nation's costliest after the Civil War. But because of penicillin, blood plasma, sulfa drugs, and rapid battlefield evacuation, the wounded in World War II were twice as likely to survive as in World War I. Penicillin also minimized the threat of venereal disease, but all men who served saw an anti-VD film, just as their predecessors had in World War I.

Women in Uniform

Women had served in all wars as nurses and cooks and in other support capacities, and during World War II many continued in these traditional roles. A few nurses landed in France just days after the Normandy invasion. Nurses served with the army and the marines in the Pacific. They dug their own foxholes and treated men under enemy fire. Sixty-six nurses spent the entire war in the Philippines as prisoners of the Japanese. Most nurses, however, served far behind the lines tending the sick and wounded. Army nurses who were given officer rank were forbidden to date enlisted men. "Not permitting nurses and enlisted men to be seen together is certainly not American," one soldier decided.

Though nobody objected to women's serving as nurses, not until April 1943 did women physicians win the right to join the Army and Navy Medical Corps. Some people questioned whether it was right for women to serve in other capacities, but Congress authorized full military participation for women (except for combat) because of the military emergency and the argument that women could free men for combat duty. World War II thus became the first war in which women were given regular military status. About 350,000 women joined up, most in the Women's Army Corps (WACS) and the women's branch of the Navy (WAVES), but others served in the coast guard and the marines. Oveta Culp Hobby, wife of a former governor of Texas and the mother of two children, directed the Women's Army Corps.

Many recruiting posters suggested that the services needed women "for the precision work at which women are so adept" or for work in hospitals to comfort and attend to the wounded "as only women can do." Most women served in traditional female roles, doing office work, cooking, and cleaning. But others were engineers and pilots. Still, men and women were not treated equally. Women were explicitly kept out of combat situations and were often underused by male officers who found it difficult to view women in nontraditional roles.

Men were informed about contraceptives and encouraged to use them, but information about birth control was explicitly prohibited for women. Rumors charged many servicewomen with sexual promiscuity. On one occasion, the secretary of war defended the morality and the loyalty of the women in the service, but the rumors continued, spread apparently by men made uncomfortable by women's invasion of the male military domain. One cause for immediate discharge was pregnancy; yet the pregnancy rate for both married and unmarried women remained low.

Thus, despite difficulties, women played important roles during the war, and when they left the service (unlike the women who had served in other wars), they had the same rights and privileges as the male veterans. The women in the service did not permanently alter the military or the public's perception of women's proper role, but they did change a few minds, and many of the women who served had their lives changed and their horizons broadened.

A WAR OF DIPLOMATS AND GENERALS

Pearl Harbor catapulted the country into war with Japan, and on December 11, 1941, Hitler declared war on the United States. Why he did so has never been fully explained; he was perhaps impressed by the apparent weakness of America demonstrated at Pearl Harbor. He was not required by his treaty with Japan to go to war with the United States, and without his declaration, the United States might have concentrated on the war against Japan. But Hitler forced the United States into the war against the Axis powers in both Europe and Asia.

War Aims

Why was the United States fighting the war? What did it hope to accomplish in a peace settlement once the war was over? Roosevelt and the other American leaders never really decided. In a speech before Congress in January 1941, Roosevelt had mentioned the four freedoms: freedom of speech and expression, freedom of worship, freedom from want, and freedom from fear. For many Americans, especially after Norman Rockwell expressed those freedoms in four sentimental paintings, this was what they were fighting for. Roosevelt spoke vaguely of the need to extend democracy and to establish a peacekeeping organization, but in direct contrast to Woodrow Wilson's Fourteen Points, he never spelled out in any detail the political purposes for fighting. The only American policy was to end the war as quickly as possible and to solve the political problems it created when the time came. That policy, or lack of policy, would have important ramifications.

Roosevelt and his advisers, realizing that it would be impossible to mount an all-out war against both Japan and Germany, decided to fight a holding action in the Pacific while concentrating efforts against Hitler in Europe, where the immediate danger seemed greater. But the United States was not fighting alone. It joined the Soviet Union and Great Britain in what became a difficult, but ultimately effective alliance to defeat Nazi Germany. Churchill and Roosevelt got along well, although they often disagreed on strategy and tactics. Roosevelt's relationship with Stalin was much more strained, but often he agreed with the Russian leader about the way to fight the war. Stalin, a ruthless leader who had maintained his position of power only after eliminating hundreds of thousands of opponents, distrusted both the British and the Americans, but he needed them, just as they depended on him. Without the tremendous sacrifices of the Russian army and the Russian people in 1941 and 1942, Germany would have won the war before the vast American military and industrial might could be mobilized.

Year of Disaster, 1942

The first half of 1942 was disastrous for the Allied cause. In the Pacific, the Japanese captured the Dutch East Indies with their vast riches in rubber, oil, and other resources. They swept into Burma, took Wake Island and Guam, and invaded the Aleutian Islands of Alaska. They pushed the American garrison on the Philippines onto the Bataan peninsula and finally onto the tiny island of Corregidor, where U.S. General Jonathan Wainwright surrendered more than 11,000 men to the Japanese. American reporters tried to play down the disasters, concentrating their stories on the few American victories and on tales of American heroism against overwhelming odds. One of the soldiers on a Pacific island picked up an American broadcast one night. "The news commentators in the States had us all winning the war," he discovered, "their buoyant cheerful voices talking of victory. We were out here where we would see these victories. They were all Japanese."

In Europe, the Germans pushed deep into Russia, threatening to capture all the industrial centers and the valuable oil fields. For a time, it appeared that they would even take Moscow. In North Africa, General Erwin Rommel and his mechanized divisions, the Afrika Korps, drove the British forces almost to Cairo in Egypt and threatened the Suez Canal. In contrast to World War I, which had been a war of stalemate, the opening phase of World War II was marked by air strikes and troops supported by trucks and tanks cov-

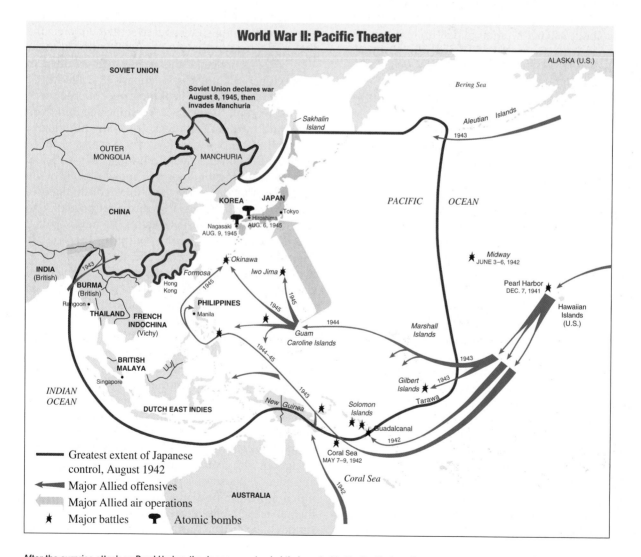

World War II: Pacific Theater

After the surprise attack on Pearl Harbor, the Japanese extended their control in the Pacific from Burma to the Aleutian Islands and almost to Australia. But after American naval and air victories at Coral Sea and Midway in 1942, the Japanese were increasingly on the defensive.

ering many miles a day. In the Atlantic, German submarines sank British and American ships more rapidly than they could be replaced. For a few dark months in 1942, it seemed that the Berlin-Tokyo Axis would win the war before the United States got itself ready to fight.

The Allies could not agree on the proper military strategy in Europe. Churchill advocated tightening the ring around Germany, using bombing raids to weaken the enemy and encouraging resistance among the occupied countries but avoiding any direct assault on the continent until success was ensured. Remembering the vast loss of British lives during World War I, he was determined to avoid similar casualties in this conflict. Stalin demanded a second front, an invasion of Europe in 1942, to relieve the pressure on the Russian army, which faced 200 German divisions along a 2,000-mile front. Roosevelt agreed to an offensive in 1942. But in the end, the invasion in 1942 came not in France but in

North Africa. The decision was probably right from a military point of view, but it taught Russia to distrust Britain and the United States. The delay in opening the second front probably contributed indirectly to the Cold War after 1945.

Attacking in North Africa in November 1942, American and British troops tried to link up with a beleaguered British army. The American army, enthusiastic but inexperienced, met little resistance in the beginning, but at Kasserine Pass in Tunisia, the Germans counterattacked and destroyed a large American force, inflicting 5,000 casualties. Roosevelt, who launched the invasion in part to give the American people a victory to relieve the dreary news from the Far East, learned that victories often came with long casualty lists.

He also learned the necessity of political compromise. To gain a ceasefire in conquered French territory in North Africa, the United States recognized Admiral

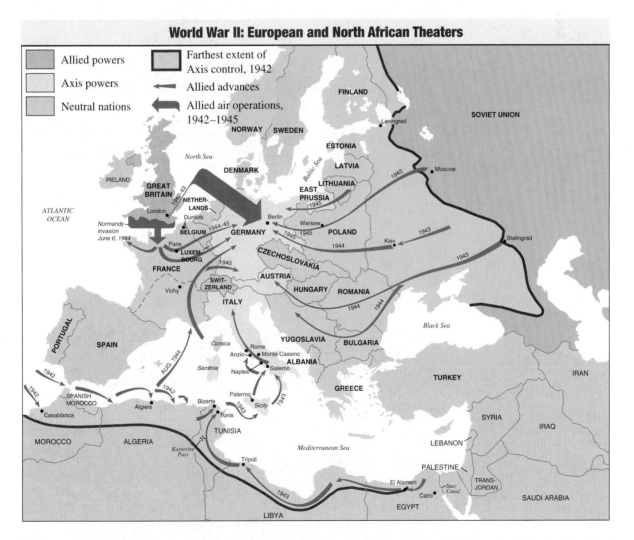

The German war machine swept across Europe and North Africa and almost captured Cairo and Moscow, but after major defeats at Stalingrad and El Alamein in 1943, the Axis powers were in retreat. Many lives were lost on both sides before the Allied victory in 1945.

Jean Darlan as head of its provisional government. Darlan persecuted the Jews, exploited the Arabs, imprisoned his opponents, and collaborated with the Nazis. He seemed diametrically opposed to the principles the Americans said they were fighting for. Did the Darlan deal mean the United States would negotiate with Mussolini? Or with Hitler? The Darlan compromise reinforced Soviet distrust of the Americans and angered many Americans as well.

Roosevelt never compromised or made a deal with Hitler, but he did aid General Francisco Franco, the Fascist dictator in Spain, in return for safe passage of American shipping into the Mediterranean. But the United States did not aid only right-wing dictators. It also supplied arms to the left-wing resistance in France, to the Communist Tito in Yugoslavia, and to Ho Chi Minh, the anti-French resistance leader in Indochina. Roosevelt also authorized large-scale, lend-lease aid to the Soviet Union. Although liberals criticized his support of dictators, Roosevelt was willing to do almost anything to win the war. Military expediency often dictated his political decisions.

Even on one of the most sensitive issues of the war, the plight of the Jews in occupied Europe, Roosevelt's solution was to win the war as quickly as possible. By November 1942, confirmed information had reached the United States that the Nazis were systematically exterminating Jews. Yet the Roosevelt administration did nothing for more than a year, and even then it did scandalously little to rescue European Jews from the

Only at the end of the war did most Americans learn of the horrors of Nazi concentration camps and the gas chambers. These photographs, which appeared in *Life Magazine,* were taken of the dead and dying at Buchenwald in May 1945. They emphasized, more than any words could, the horrors of Nazi Germany. *(George Rodger/Margaret Bourke-White/*LIFE *Magazine © Time, Inc.)*

gas chambers. Only 21,000 refugees were allowed to enter the United States over a period of 3½ years, just 10 percent of those who could have been admitted under immigration quotas. The U.S. War Department rejected suggestions that the Auschwitz gas chambers be bombed, and government officials turned down many rescue schemes. Widespread anti-Semitic feelings in the United States in the 1940s and the fear of massive Jewish immigration help explain the failure of the Roosevelt administration to act. The fact that the mass media, Christian leaders, and even American Jews failed to mount effective pressure on the government does not excuse the president for his shameful indifference to the systematic murder of millions of people. Roosevelt could not have prevented the Holocaust, but vigorous action on his part could have saved many thousands of lives during the war. Roosevelt was not always right, nor was he even consistent, but people who assumed he had a master strategy or a fixed ideological position misunderstood the American president.

A Strategy for Ending the War

The commanding general of the Allied armies in the North African campaign emerged as a genuine leader. Born in Texas, Dwight D. Eisenhower spent his boyhood in Abilene, Kansas. His small-town background made it easy for biographers and newspaper reporters to make him into an American hero. Eisenhower, however, had not come to hero status easily. He saw no action in World War I; he spent that war training soldiers in Texas. Even though he served as assistant to General Douglas MacArthur in the 1930s in the Philippines, he was only a lieutenant colonel when World War II erupted.

General George Marshall had discovered Eisenhower's talents even before the war began. Eisenhower was quickly promoted to general and achieved a reputation as an expert planner and organizer. Gregarious and outgoing, he had a broad smile that made most people like him instantly. He was not a brilliant field commander and made many mistakes in the African campaign, but he had the ability to get diverse people working together, which was crucial where British and American units had to cooperate.

The American army moved slowly across North Africa, linked up with the British, invaded Sicily in July 1943, and finally stormed ashore in Italy in September. The Italian campaign proved long and bitter. Although the Italians overthrew Mussolini and surrendered in September 1943, the Germans occupied the peninsula and gave ground only after bloody fighting. The whole American army seemed to be bogged down for months. One soldier described the "slushy mud that reaches almost up to your knees, . . . making the roads

dangerously slippery." The Allies did not reach Rome until June 1944, and they never controlled all of Italy.

Despite the decision to make the war in Europe the first priority, American ships and planes halted the Japanese advance in the spring of 1942. In the Battle of Coral Sea in May 1942, American carrier-based planes inflicted heavy damage on the Japanese fleet and prevented the invasion of the southern tip of New Guinea and probably of Australia as well. It was the first naval battle in history in which no guns were fired from one surface ship against another; airplanes caused all the damage. In World War II, the aircraft carrier proved more important than the battleship. A month later, at the Battle of Midway, American planes sank four Japanese aircraft carriers and destroyed nearly 300 planes. This was the first major Japanese defeat; it restored some balance of power in the Pacific and ended the threat to Hawaii.

In 1943, the American sea and land forces leapfrogged from island to island, gradually retaking territory from the Japanese and building bases to attack the Philippines and eventually Japan itself. Progress often had terrible costs, however. In November 1943, about 5,000 marines landed on the coral beaches of the tiny island of Tarawa. Despite heavy naval bombardment and the support of hundreds of planes, the marines met heavy opposition. The four-day battle left more than 1,000 Americans dead and over 3,000 wounded. One marine general thought it was all wasted effort. He thought the island should have been bypassed. Others disagreed. No one asked the marines who stormed the beaches. Less than half of the first wave survived.

The Invasion of Europe

Operation Overlord, the code name for the largest amphibious invasion in history, the invasion Stalin had wanted in 1942, began only on June 6, 1944. It was, according to Churchill, "the most difficult and complicated operation that has ever taken place." The initial assault along a 60-mile stretch of the Normandy coast was conducted with 175,000 men supported by 600 warships and 11,000 planes. Within a month, over a million troops and more than 170,000 vehicles had landed. Such an invasion would have been impossible during World War I.

Eisenhower, now bearing the title Supreme Commander of the Allied Expeditionary Force in Western Europe, coordinated and planned the operation. British and American forces, with some units from other countries, worked together, but Overlord was made possible by American industry, which, by the war's end, was turning out an astonishing 50 percent of all the world's goods. During the first few hours of the invasion, there seemed to be too many supplies.

President Roosevelt inspects General Eisenhower's troops in Sicily before returning home from the Cairo-Tehran Conference in 1943. These were two dominant personalities of the war years. *(Department of the Army)*

"Everything was confusing," one soldier remembered. It cost 2,245 killed and 1,670 wounded to secure the beachhead. "It was much lighter than anybody expected," one observer remarked. "But if you saw faces instead of numbers on the casualty list, it wasn't light at all."

For months before the invasion, American and British planes had bombed German transportation lines, industrial plants, and even cities. In all, over 1.5 million tons of bombs were dropped on Europe. The massive bombing raids helped make the invasion a success, but evidence gathered after the war suggests that the bombs did not disrupt German war production as seriously as Allied strategists believed at the time. Often a factory or a rail center would be back in operation within a matter of days, sometimes within hours, after an attack. In the end, the bombing of the cities, rather than destroying morale, may have strengthened the resolve of the German people to fight to the bitter end. And the destruction of German cities did not come cheaply. German fighters and anti-aircraft guns shot down 22 of 60 B-17s on June 23, 1943, and on August 17, the Americans lost 60 bombers.

The most destructive bombing raid of the war, carried out against Dresden on the nights of February 13 and 14, 1945, had no strategic purpose. It was launched by the British and Americans to help demonstrate to Stalin that they were aiding the Russian offensive. Dresden, a city of 630,000, was a communications center. Three waves of 1,200 planes dropped more than 4,000 tons of bombs, causing a firestorm that swept over eight square miles, destroyed everything in its path, and killed an estimated 100,000 civilians. One of the American pilots remarked, "For the first time I felt sorry for the population below."

With the dashing and eccentric General George Patton leading the charge and the more staid General Omar Bradley in command, the American army broke out of the Normandy beachhead in July 1944. Led by the tank battalions, it swept across France. American productive capacity and the ability to supply a mobile and motorized army eventually brought victory. But not all American equipment was superior. The American fighter plane, the P-40, could not compete early in the war with the German ME-109. The United States was also far behind Germany in the development of rockets, but that was not as important in the actual fighting as the inability of the United States, until the end of the war, to develop a tank that could compete in armament or firepower with the German tanks. The American army made up for the deficiency of its tanks in part by having superior artillery. Perhaps even more important, most of the American soldiers had grown up tinkering with cars and radios. Children of the machine age, they managed to make repairs and to keep tanks, trucks, and guns functioning under difficult circumstances. They helped give the American army the superior mobility that eventually led to the defeat of Germany.

By late 1944, the American and British armies had swept across France, while the Russians had pushed the German forces out of much of eastern Europe. The war seemed nearly over. However, just before Christmas in 1944, the Germans launched a massive counterattack along an 80-mile front, much of it held by thinly dispersed and inexperienced American troops. The Germans drove 50 miles inside the American lines before they were checked. During the Battle of the Bulge, as it was called, Eisenhower was so desperate for additional infantry that he offered to pardon any military prisoners in Europe who would take up a rifle and go into battle. Most of the prisoners, who were serving short sentences, declined the opportunity to clear their record. Eisenhower also promised any black soldiers in the service and supply outfits an opportunity to become infantrymen in the white units, though usually with a lower rank. However, Walter Bedell Smith, his chief of staff, pointed out that this was against War Department regulations and was the "most dangerous thing I have seen in regard to race relations." Eisenhower recanted, not wishing to start a social revolution. Black soldiers who did volunteer to join the battle fought in segregated platoons commanded by white officers.

The Politics of Victory

As the American and British armies raced across France into Germany in the winter and spring of 1945, the political and diplomatic aspects of the war began to overshadow military concerns. It became a matter not only of defeating Germany but also of determining who was going to control Germany and the rest of Europe once Hitler fell. The relationship between the Soviet Union and the other Allies had been badly strained during the war; with victory in sight, the tension became even greater. Although the American press pictured Stalin as a wise and democratic leader and the Russian people as quaint and heroic, a number of high-level American diplomats and presidential advisers distrusted the Russians and looked ahead to a confrontation with Soviet communism after the war. These men urged Roosevelt to make military decisions with the postwar political situation in mind.

The main issue in the spring of 1945 concerned who would capture Berlin. The British wanted to beat the Russians to the capital city. Eisenhower, however, fearing that the Germans might barricade themselves in the Austrian Alps and hold out indefinitely, ordered the armies south rather than toward Berlin. He also wanted to avoid unnecessary American casualties,

and he planned to meet the Russian army at an easily marked spot to avoid any unfortunate incidents. The British and American forces could probably not have arrived in Berlin before the Russians in any case, but Eisenhower's decision generated controversy after the war. Russian and American troops met on April 25, 1945, at the Elbe River. On May 2, the Russians took Berlin. Hitler committed suicide. The long war in Europe finally came to an end on May 8, 1945, but political problems remained.

In 1944, the United States continued to tighten the noose on Japan. American long-range B-29 bombers began sustained strikes on the Japanese mainland in June 1944, and by November they were dropping firebombs on Tokyo. In a series of naval and air engagements, especially at the Battle of Leyte Gulf, American planes destroyed most of the remaining Japanese navy. By the end of 1944, an American victory in the Pacific was all but ensured. American forces recaptured the Philippines early the next year, yet the American forces had barely touched Japan itself. It might take years to conquer the Japanese on their home islands.

While the military campaigns reached a critical stage in both Europe and the Pacific, Roosevelt took time off to run for an unprecedented fourth term. To appease members of his own party, he agreed to drop Vice President Henry Wallace from the ticket because some thought him too radical and impetuous. To replace him, the Democratic convention selected a relatively unknown senator from Missouri. Harry S Truman, a World War I veteran, had been a judge in Kansas City before being elected to the Senate in 1934. His only fame came when, as chairman of the Senate Committee to Investigate the National Defense Program, he had insisted on honesty and efficiency in war contracts. He got some publicity for saving the taxpayers' dollars.

The Republicans nominated Thomas Dewey, the colorless and politically moderate governor of New York, who had a difficult time criticizing Roosevelt without appearing unpatriotic. Roosevelt seemed haggard and ill during much of the campaign, but he won the election easily. He would need all his strength to deal with the difficult political problems of ending the war and constructing a peace settlement.

The Big Three at Yalta

Roosevelt, Churchill, and Stalin, together with many of their advisers, met at Yalta in the Crimea in February 1945 to discuss the problems of the peace settlements. Most of the agreements reached at Yalta were secret, and in the atmosphere of the subsequent Cold War, many would become controversial. Roosevelt wanted the help of the Soviet Union in ending the war in the

Recovering the Past

HISTORY, MEMORY, AND MONUMENTS

In recent years historians have been studying collective memory—the stories people tell about the past. Collective memory is closely related to national regional identity and is often associated with patriotism and war. But memory is usually selective and often contested. The generation that lived through World War II is getting older, and often they fear that few remember or care about their war. One veteran of the Italian campaign recently remarked: "Today they don't even know what Anzio was. Most people aren't interested." The collective memory of World War II may include letters, photos, old uniforms, stories told to grandchildren (oral history), but the collective memory of war often includes monuments as well.

Almost every small town and city in the Northeast, the Midwest, and the South has monuments to the soldiers who fought and died in the Civil War; often it is a statue of a common soldier with rifle at rest. In the South a statue of Robert E. Lee on horseback came to symbolize the Lost Cause. Usually monuments to war symbolize triumph or fighting for a just cause, even in defeat.

There is not yet a major monument on the mall in Washington, D.C., to honor those who fought in World War II, but there have been other attempts to honor the World War II generation. The Air and Space Museum of the Smithsonian Institution in Washington, D.C., planned a major exhibit for 1995 to commemorate the 50th anniversary of the dropping of the first atomic bomb on Hiroshima and the end of World War II. The *Enola Gay*, the B-29 that dropped the bomb, was to be the centerpiece of the exhibit, but the historians and curators who organized the exhibit also planned to raise a number of questions that historians had been debating for years. Would the war have ended in days or weeks without the bomb? How was the decision to drop the bomb made? Was there a racial component to the

Dedication of the Iwo Jima Memorial Monument in Washington, D. C., November 10, 1954. *(National Archives)*

decision? Would the United States have dropped the bomb on Germany? Was the bomb dropped more to impress the Soviet Union than to force the Japanese to surrender? What was the impact of the bomb on the ground? What implications did dropping the bomb have on the world after 1945?

The exhibit (except in greatly modified form) never took place. Many veterans of World War II and other Americans denounced it as traitorous and un-American. For these critics the decision to drop the bomb was not something to debate. For them, World War II was a contest between good and evil, and the bomb was simply a way to defeat the evil empire and save American lives. The controversy over the *Enola Gay* exhibit demonstrated that 50 years later memory and history were at odds and that the memory of the war was still contested. The main reason the exhibit did not satisfy those who remembered the war was that it did not commemorate triumph but instead seemed to question the motives of those who fought and died.

The Vietnam Veterans Memorial erected in Washington in 1982 was initially controversial for similar reasons. Designed by Maya Lin, a young artist and sculptor, it consists of a wall of polished granite inscribed with the names of 58,000 dead. There are no soldiers on horseback; in fact, there are no figures at all, not even a flag. Critics called it a "black gash of shame." Even the addition of a sculpture of three "fighting men" did not satisfy many. But to almost everyone's surprise, hundreds of thousands of veterans and friends of veterans found the monument deeply moving, and they left photos, flowers, poems, and other objects. For them, the memorial successfully represented collective memory. Still the critics were dissatisfied; they wanted something more like the Iwo Jima monument.

Iwo Jima was a tiny, desolate island 640 miles from Tokyo, important only because it was a base for Japanese fighters to attack American bombers on their way to the Japanese mainland. The 4th and 5th Marine Divisions invaded the island on February 17, 1945. After bitter fighting, the marines captured Mt. Suribachi, the highest point on the island, on February 23 and completed the conquest of the island on March 17. But it was a costly victory—4,189 Americans were killed, 15,000 wounded, and 419 missing.

Associated Press photographer Joe Rosenthal was one of several journalists who went ashore with the marines and one of three photographers assigned to record the raising of the American flag on top of Mt. Suribachi. A group of marines raised the flag twice so the photographers could get their pictures. It was Rosenthal's photograph of the second flag raising that became famous. On February 25, 1945, his photograph of the six marines raising the flag was on the front pages of Sunday newspapers across the country. "Stars and Stripes on Iwo," "Old Glory over Volcano," the captions read. Within months the image of the flag raising appeared on a War Bond poster with the caption: "Now All Together," and on a postage stamp. Three of the six flag raisers were killed in the battle for Iwo Jima, but those who

Official poster for the 1945 war bond drive using the image of the Iwo Jima flag raising. *(Courtesy of the Virginia War Museum)*

survived became heroes and their images were used to sell war bonds. Clearly, the flag-raising image had touched American emotions and quickly became part of the collective memory of the war, a symbol of the country pulling together to defeat the enemy.

In November 1954 a giant statue of the flag raising, designed by Felix De Weldon, was dedicated as a memorial to the U.S. Marine Corps on the edge of Arlington National Cemetery. Vice President Richard Nixon speaking at the dedication said that the statue symbolized "the hopes and dreams of the American people and the real purpose of our foreign policy." The flag-raising image played important roles in two movies, *The Sands of Iwo Jima* (1949), starring John Wayne, and *The Outsider* (1960), starring Tony Curtis. During the 1988 presidential campaign George Bush chose to make a speech urging a constitutional amendment to ban the desecration of the flag in front of the marine monument. The image of the flag raising in photograph, drawing, film, and cartoon remains part of the collective memory of World War II.

Why did the Iwo Jima monument mean so much to the World War II generation? Was the monument more important than the photograph? What makes a monument meaningful? Is it the size? The accuracy? The ability to arouse emotion? Why do some monuments and symbols become part of collective memory while others become controversial or forgotten? There are over 15,000 outdoor sculptures and monuments in the country, most created since the Civil War. What monuments can you locate in your community? What collective memory do they symbolize?

Pacific to avoid the needless slaughter of American men in an invasion of the Japanese mainland. In return for a promise to enter the war within three months after the war in Europe was over, the Soviet Union was granted the Kurile Islands, the southern half of Sakhalin, and railroads and port facilities in North Korea, Manchuria, and Outer Mongolia. Later that seemed like a heavy price to pay for the promise, but realistically the Soviet Union controlled most of this territory and could not have been dislodged short of going to war.

When the provisions of the secret treaties were revealed much later, many people would accuse Roosevelt of trusting the Russians too much. But Roosevelt wanted to retain a working relationship with the Soviet Union. If the peace was to be preserved, the major powers of the Grand Alliance would have to work together. Moreover, Roosevelt hoped to get the Soviet Union's agreement to cooperate with a new peace-preserving United Nations organization after the war.

The European section of the Yalta agreement proved even more controversial than its Far Eastern provisions. It was decided to partition Germany and to divide the city of Berlin. The Polish agreements were even more difficult to swallow, in part because the invasion of Poland in 1939 had precipitated the war. The Polish government in exile in London was militantly anticommunist and looked forward to returning to Poland after the war. Stalin, however, demanded that the eastern half of Poland be given to the Soviet Union to protect its western border. Churchill and Roosevelt finally agreed to the Russian demands with the proviso that Poland be compensated with German territory on its western border. Stalin also agreed to include some members of the London-based Polish group in the new Polish government. He also promised to carry out "free and unfettered elections as soon as possible."

The Polish settlement would prove divisive after the war, and it quickly became clear that what the British and Americans wanted in eastern Europe contrasted with what the Soviet Union intended. Yet at the time it seemed imperative that Russia enter the war in the Pacific, and the reality was that in 1945 the Soviet army occupied most of eastern Europe.

The most potentially valuable accomplishment at Yalta was agreement on the need to construct a United Nations, an organization for preserving peace and fostering the postwar reconstruction of battered and underdeveloped countries. In 1942, a total of 26 Allied nations had subscribed to the Atlantic Charter, drafted by Churchill and Roosevelt, which laid down several principles for a lasting peace. Discussions among the Allied powers continued during the war,

and Stalin agreed with Roosevelt and Churchill to call a conference in San Francisco in April 1945 to draft a United Nations charter.

Spirited debate occurred in San Francisco when the representatives of 50 nations gathered for this task. As finally accepted, amid optimism about a quick end to the war, the charter provided for a General Assembly in which every member nation had a seat. However, this General Assembly was designed mainly as a forum for discussing international problems. The responsibility for keeping global peace was lodged in the Security Council, composed of five permanent members (the United States, the Soviet Union, Great Britain, France, and China) and six other nations elected for two-year terms. The Security Council's responsibility was to suppress international violence by applying economic, diplomatic, or military sanctions against any nation that all permanent members agreed threatened the peace. In addition, the charter established an International Court of Justice and a number of agencies to promote "collaboration among the nations through education, science, and culture." Among these agencies were the International Monetary Fund, the World Health Organization, and the UN Educational, Scientific, and Cultural Organization (UNESCO).

The Atomic Age Begins

Two months after Yalta, on April 12, 1945, as the United Nations charter was being drafted, Roosevelt died suddenly of a massive cerebral hemorrhage. The nation was shocked. When an industrial worker in Springfield, Ohio, heard the news, he remarked that he was glad that "the old son of a bitch was gone"; another worker punched him in the face. Roosevelt, both hated and loved to the end, was replaced by Harry Truman, who was both more difficult to hate and harder to love. In the beginning, Truman seemed tentative and unsure of himself. Yet it fell to the new president to make some of the most difficult decisions of all time. The most momentous of all was the decision to drop the atomic bomb.

The Manhattan Project, first organized in 1941, was one of the best-kept secrets of the war. The task of the distinguished group of scientists whose work on the project was centered at Los Alamos, New Mexico, was to manufacture an atomic bomb before Germany did. But by the time the bomb was successfully tested in the New Mexico desert on July 16, 1945, the war in Europe had ended.

The scientists working on the bomb assumed that they were perfecting a military weapon. Yet when they saw the ghastly power of that first bomb, remembered J. Robert Oppenheimer, a leading scientist on the project, "some wept, a few cheered. Most stood silently."

The incredible destruction caused by the atomic bomb is graphically shown in this photo of Hiroshima taken a few days after the blast. The decision to use atomic weapons on two Japanese cities is still controversial more than a half century later. *(© Bettmann/Corbis)*

Timeline

1931–1932	Japan seizes Manchuria
1933	Hitler becomes German chancellor
	United States recognizes the Soviet Union
	Roosevelt extends Good Neighbor policy
1934	Germany begins rearmament
1935	Italy invades Ethiopia
	First Neutrality Act
1936	Spanish civil war begins
	Second Neutrality Act
	Roosevelt reelected
1937	Third Neutrality Act
1938	Hitler annexes Austria, occupies Sudetenland
	German persecution of Jews intensifies
1939	Nazi–Soviet Pact
	German invasion of Poland; World War II begins
1940	Roosevelt elected for a third term
	Selective Service Act
1941	FDR's "Four Freedoms" speech
	Proposed black march on Washington
	Executive order outlaws discrimination in defense industries
	Lend-Lease Act
	Germany attacks Russia
	Japanese assets in United States frozen
	Japanese attack Pearl Harbor; United States declares war on Japan
	Germany declares war on United States
1942	Internment of Japanese Americans
	Second Allied front in Africa launched
1943	Invasion of Sicily
	Italian campaign; Italy surrenders
	United Mine Workers strike
	Race riots in Detroit and other cities
1944	Normandy invasion (Operation Overlord)
	Congress passes GI Bill
	Roosevelt elected for a fourth term
1945	Yalta Conference
	Roosevelt dies; Harry Truman becomes president
	Germany surrenders
	Successful test of atomic bomb
	Hiroshima and Nagasaki bombed; Japan surrenders

Some opposed the military use of the bomb. They realized its revolutionary power and worried about the future reputation of the United States if it unleashed this new force. But a presidential committee made up of scientists, military leaders, and politicians recommended that it be used on a military target in Japan as soon as possible.

"The final decision of where and when to use the atomic bomb was up to me," Truman later remembered. "Let there be no doubt about it. I regarded the bomb as a military weapon and never had any doubt that it should be used." But the decision had both military and political ramifications. Even though Japan had lost most of its empire by the summer of 1945, it still had a military force of several million men and thousands of kamikaze planes that had already wreaked havoc on the American fleet. The kamikaze pilots gave up their own lives to make sure that their planes, heavily laden with bombs, crashed on an American ship. There was little defense against such fanaticism.

Even with the Russian promise to enter the war, it appeared that an amphibious landing on the Japanese mainland would be necessary to end the war. The monthlong battle for Iwo Jima, only 750 miles from

Tokyo, had resulted in over 4,000 American dead and 15,000 wounded, and the battle for Okinawa was even more costly. An invasion of the Japanese mainland would presumably be even more expensive in human lives. The bomb, many thought, could end the war without an invasion. But some people involved in the decision wanted to retaliate for Pearl Harbor, and still others needed to justify spending over $2 billion on the project in the first place. The timing of the first bomb, however, indicates to some that the decision was intended to impress the Russians and ensure that they had little to do with the peace settlement in the Far East. One British scientist later charged that the decision to drop the bomb on Hiroshima was the "first major operation of the cold diplomatic war with Russia."

Historians still debate whether the use of the atomic bomb on Japanese cities was necessary to end the war, but for the hundreds of thousands of American troops waiting on board ships and on island bases, even in Europe, to invade the Japanese mainland there was no question about the rightness of the decision. They believed that the bombs ended the war and saved their lives. On August 6, 1945, two days before the Soviet Union had promised to enter the war against Japan, a B-29 bomber, the "Enola Gay," dropped a single atomic bomb over Hiroshima. It killed or severely wounded 160,000 civilians and destroyed four square miles of the city. One of the men on the plane saw the thick cloud of smoke and thought that they had missed their target. "It looked like it had landed on a forest. I didn't see any sign of the city." The Soviet Union entered the war on August 8. When Japan refused to surrender, a second bomb was dropped on Nagasaki on August 9. The Japanese surrendered five days later. The war was finally over, but the problems of the atomic age and the postwar world were just beginning.

Conclusion

Peace, Prosperity, and International Responsibilities

The United States emerged from World War II with an enhanced reputation as the world's most powerful industrial and military nation. The demands of the war had finally ended the Great Depression and brought prosperity to most Americans. The war had also increased the power of the federal government. The payroll deduction of federal income taxes, begun during the war, symbolized the growth of a federal bureaucracy that affected the lives of all Americans. The war had also ended American isolationism and made the United States into the dominant international power. Of all the nations that fought in the war, the United States had suffered the least. No bombs were dropped on American factories, and no cities were destroyed. Although more than 300,000 Americans lost their lives, even this carnage seemed minimal when compared with the more than 20 million Russian soldiers and civilians who died or the 6 million Jews and millions of others systematically exterminated by Hitler.

Americans greeted the end of the war with joy and relief. They looked forward to the peace and prosperity for which they had fought. Yet within two years, the peace would be jeopardized by the Cold War, and the United States would be rearming its former enemies, Japan and Germany, to oppose its former friend, the Soviet Union. The irony of that situation reduced the joy of the hard-won peace and made the American people more suspicious of their government and its foreign policy.

Recommended Reading

The Twisting Road to War

A. Russell Buchanan, *The United States in World War II*, 2 vols. (1964); Robert Dalleck, *Franklin Roosevelt and American Foreign Policy, 1932–1945* (1979); Robert A. Devine, *The Reluctant Belligerent* (1979); Lloyd Gardner, *Economic Aspects of New Deal Diplomacy* (1964); Waldo Heinrichs, *Threshold of War* (1988); Akira Iriye, *The Origins of the Second World War in Asia and the Pacific* (1988); Walter LaFeber, *Inevitable Revolutions: The United States and Central America* (1983); Gordon W. Prange, *At Dawn We Slept* (1981); Gerhard Weinberg, *A Global History of World War II* (1994).

The Home Front

Amy Bentley, *Eating for Victory: Food Rationing and the Politics of Domesticity* (1997); Alison Bernstein, *American Indians and World War II* (1991); John Morton Blum, *V Was for Victory* (1976);

Roger Daniels, *Concentration Camp, USA* (1971); Lewis A. Erenberg and Susan E. Hirsch, eds., *The War in American Culture* (1996); John W. Jeffries, *Wartime America: The World War II Home Front* (1996); Doris Kearns Goodwin, *No Ordinary Time: Franklin and Eleanor Roosevelt, the Home Front in World War II* (1994); Bill Gilbert, *They Also Served: Baseball and the Home Front* (1992); Nicholas Lemann, *The Promised Land: The Great Black Migration and How It Changed America* (1991); Richard R. Lingemann, *Don't You Know There's a War On* (1970); Richard Polenberg, *War and Society* (1972); William Tuttle, *"Daddy's Gone to War"* (1993).

Social Impact of the War

D'Ann Campbell, *Women at War with America* (1984); Richard Dalfiume, *Desegregation of the U. S. Armed Forces* (1975); Sherna

B. Gluck, *Rosie the Riveter Revisited* (1987); Susan Hartmann, *The Home Front and Beyond: American Women in the 1940s* (1982); David M. Kennedy, *Freedom from Fear: The American People in Depression and War* (1999); Ruth Milkman, *Gender at Work* (1987); Stuart Murray and James McCabe, eds., *Norman Rockwell's Four Freedoms* (1993); Gerald D. Nash, *The American West Transformed: The Impact of the Second World War* (1985); George H. Roseder, *The Censored War: American Visual Experience During World War II* (1993); James Tobin, *Ernie Pyle's War* (1997); Alan M. Winkler, *The Politics of Propaganda: The Office of War Information* (1978); Neil A. Wynn, *The Afro-American and the Second World War* (1976).

A War of Diplomats and Generals

Gar Alperovitz, *Atomic Diplomacy* (1965); Stephen Ambrose, *Citizen Soldiers* (1997); Stephen Ambrose, *D-Day* (1994); John Dower, *War Without Mercy* (1986); Paul Fussell, *Wartime* (1989); D. Clayton James, *A Time for Giants: Politics of the American High Command in World War II* (1987); John Keegan, *The Battle for History: Re-Fighting World War II* (1995); Walter LaFeber, *The Clash: U.S. Japanese Relations Throughout History* (1997); Gerald F. Linderman, *The World Within War: America's Combat Experience in World War II* (1997); Karal Ann Marling, *Iwo Jima:*

Monuments, Memories, and the American Hero (1991); Ronald Schaffer, *Wings of Judgement: American Bombing in World War II* (1985); Martin Sherwin, *A World Destroyed* (1975); Gaddis Smith, *American Diplomacy During The Second World War* (1964); Mark A. Stoler, *The Politics of the Second Front* (1977); Russell Weigley, *Eisenhower's Lieutenants: The Campaign of France and Germany, 1944–1945* (1981); David S. Wyman, *The Abandonment of the Jews: America and the Holocaust, 1941–1945* (1984).

Fiction and Film

In *The Dollmaker* (1954), Harriette Arnow tells the fictionalized story of a young woman from Kentucky who finds herself in wartime Detroit. Two powerful novels that tell the story of the battlefield experience are Norman Mailer's *The Naked and the Dead* (1948) and Irwin Shaw's *The Young Lions* (1948).

Tora! Tora! Tora! (1970) is a film that tells the story of the attack on Pearl Harbor from both the American and the Japanese points of view. It is compelling even as it oversimplifies history. *Saving Private Ryan* (1998), a film about one platoon's adventures on D-Day and after, is sentimental and romantic in spots but contains some graphic and violent scenes of the invasion of Normandy.

Suggested Web Sites

http://www.nara.gov/exhall/people/people.html

World War II Exhibit: A People at War. This National Archives exhibit takes a close look at the contributions millions of Americans made to the war effort.

http://www.nara.gov/education/teaching/posters/poster.html

Powers of Persuasion—Poster Art of World War II. These powerful posters at the National Archives were part of the battle for the hearts and minds of the American people during WWII.

http://memory.loc.gov/ammem/fsowhome.html

America from the Great Depression to World War II: Photographs from the FSA-OWI, 1935–1945. These images in the Farm Security Administration-Office of War Information Collection show Americans from all over the nation experiencing everything from despair to triumph in the 1930s and 1940s.

http://www.csi.ad.jp/ABOMB/

A-Bomb WWW Museum. This site offers information about the impact of the first atomic bomb as well as the background and context of weapons of total destruction.

http://www.ushmm.org/index.html

United States Holocaust Memorial Museum. This is the official Web site of the Holocaust Museum in Washington, D.C.

http://wrightmuseum.org/links.html

Links to the War Years. The Wright Museum maintains this page with its many links to information about the World War II era.

http://www.corbis.com/FDR/ww2.html

WWII. This Corbis site houses many pictures about the Second World War and American involvement in the conflict.

http://www.wpafb.af.mil/museum/history/prewwii/ta.htm

Tuskegee Airmen. The Air Force Museum at Wright-Patterson Air Force Base maintains this site about the African-American pilots of World War II.

http://www.alba-valb.org

Abraham Lincoln Brigade Archives. This Brandeis University site has posters and photographs from the Spanish civil war and the unit of American volunteers who fought in it.

http://www.sunsite.unc.edu/pha/index.html

Resource Listing for WWII. This site has a large number of searchable primary texts from all aspects of World War II.

http://www.ushistoryplace.com

 A richly detailed on-line learning environment complete with interactive maps, timelines, history activities, primary source documents, and links to related American history sites.

26

POSTWAR GROWTH *and* SOCIAL CHANGE

Ray Kroc, an ambitious salesman, headed toward San Bernardino, California, on a business trip in 1954. For more than a decade he had been selling "multimixers"—stainless steel machines that could make six milkshakes at once—to restaurants and soda shops around the United States. On this trip, he was particularly interested in checking out a hamburger stand run by Richard and Maurice McDonald, who had bought eight of his "contraptions" and could therefore make 48 shakes at the same time.

Always eager to increase sales, Kroc wanted to see the McDonalds' operation for himself. The 52-year-old son of Slavic parents had sold everything from real estate to radio time to paper cups before peddling the multimixers but had enjoyed no stunning success. Yet he was still on the alert for the key to the fortune that was part of the American dream. As he watched the lines of people at the San Bernardino McDonald's, the answer seemed at hand.

The McDonald brothers sold only standard hamburgers and french fries, but they had developed a system that was fast, efficient, and clean. It drew on the automobile traffic that moved along Route 66. And it was profitable indeed. Sensing the possibilities, Kroc proposed that the two owners open other establishments as well. When they balked, he negotiated a 99-year contract that allowed him to sell the fast-food idea and the name—and their golden arches design—wherever he could.

On April 15, 1955, Kroc opened his first McDonald's in Des Plaines, a suburb of Chicago. Three months later, he sold his first franchise in Fresno, California. Others soon followed. Kroc scouted out new locations, almost always on highway "strips," persuaded people to put up the capital, and provided them with specifications guaranteed to ensure future success. For his efforts, he received a percentage of the gross take.

From the start, Kroc insisted on standardization. Every McDonald's was the same—from the two functional arches supporting the glass enclosure that housed the kitchen and take-out window to the single arch near the road bearing a sign indicating how many 15-cent hamburgers had already been sold. All menus and prices were exactly the same, and Kroc demanded that everything from hamburger size to cooking time be constant. He insisted, too, that the establishments be clean. No pinball games or cigarette machines were permitted; the premium was on a good, inexpensive hamburger, quickly served, at a nice place.

McDonald's, of course, was an enormous success. In 1962, total sales exceeded $76 million. In 1964, before the company had been in operation ten years, it had sold over 400 million hamburgers and 120 million pounds of french fries. By the end of the next year, there were 710 McDonald's stands in 44 states. In 1974, only 20 years after Kroc's vision of the hamburger's future, McDonald's did $2 billion worth of business. When Kroc died in 1984, a total of 45 billion burgers had been sold at 7,500 outlets in 32 countries. Ronald McDonald, the clown who came to represent the company, became known to children around the globe after his Washington, D.C., debut in November 1963. When McDonald's began to advertise, it became the country's first restaurant to buy TV time. Musical slogans like "You deserve a break today" and "We do it all for you" became better known than some popular songs.

The success of McDonald's provides an example of the development of new trends in the United States in the post–World War II years. Kroc capitalized on the changes of the automobile age. He understood that a restaurant had a better chance of success not in the city but along the highways, where it could draw on heavier traffic. The drive-in design, catering to a new and ever-growing clientele, soon became common.

He understood, too, that the franchise notion provided the key to rapid growth. Not prepared to open up thousands of stands himself, he sold the idea to eager entrepreneurs who stood to make sizable profits as long as they remained a part of the larger whole. In numerous other product areas as well as the hamburger business, the franchise method helped create a nationwide web of firms.

Finally, Kroc sensed the importance of standardization and uniformity. He understood the mood of the time, the quiet conformity of Americans searching for success. The McDonald's image may have been monotonous, but that was part of its appeal. Customers always knew what they

The post–World War II years saw tremendous suburban development, which reflected the more general economic growth and economic prosperity of the period. *(Robert Bechtle, '58 Rambler/Sloan Collection, Valparaiso University Museum of Art, gift of Mrs. McCauley Conner in memory of her father, Barklie McK. Henry)*

would get wherever they found the golden arches. If the atmosphere was "bland," that too was deliberate. As Kroc said, "Our theme is kind of synonymous with Sunday school, the Girl Scouts and the YMCA. McDonald's is clean and wholesome." It was a symbol of the age.

This chapter describes the structural changes in American society in the 25 years following World War II. Even as the nation became involved in the Cold War with the Soviet Union (a story taken up in Chapter 27), Americans were preoccupied with the shifts in social and economic patterns that were taking place. This chapter examines how economic growth, spurred by technological advances, transformed the patterns of work and daily life in the United States and provided the context for the development of the liberal state described in Chapter 28. Self-interest triumphed over idealism as most people gained a level of material comfort previously unknown. Working-class Americans shared in

the gains, as the union movement pressed its claims more successfully than it had ever done in the past, and workers entered into a new equilibrium with the world of management. Life for most Americans was more comfortable than it had ever been before. For many of them, this period appeared to promise the possibility of living the American dream.

But even as the nation prospered, it experienced serious social and economic divisions. This chapter also shows the enormous gaps that existed between rich and poor, even in the best of times. It shows the continuing presence of what one critic eloquently called "the other America" and documents the considerable income disparity and persistent prejudice African Americans (like members of other minority groups) encountered in their effort to share in the postwar prosperity. The frustrations they experienced led to the reform movements described in Chapter 29 and highlighted the limits of the postwar American dream.

ECONOMIC BOOM

Despite Cold War anxieties, most Americans were optimistic after 1945. As servicemen returned home, their very presence caused a change in family patterns. A baby boom brought unprecedented population growth. The simultaneous and unexpected economic boom had an even greater impact. Large corporations increasingly dominated the business world, but unions grew as well, and most workers improved their lives. Technology appeared triumphant, with new products flooding the market and finding their way into most American homes. Prosperity convinced the growing middle class that all was well in the United States.

The Thriving Peacetime Economy

The wartime return of prosperity after the Great Depression continued in the postwar years, relieving fears of another depression. The next several decades saw one of the longest sustained economic expansions the country had ever known, as the United States solidified its position as the richest nation in the world.

The statistical evidence of economic success was impressive. The gross national product (GNP) jumped dramatically between 1945 and 1970 (see graph on this page), while per capita personal income likewise rose—from $1,223 in 1945 to $2,987 in 1966 and to $3,945 in 1970. Almost 60 percent of all families in the country were now part of the middle class, a dramatic change from the class structure in the nineteenth and early twentieth centuries.

Personal resources fueled economic growth. During World War II, American consumers had been unable to spend all they earned because factories had concentrated on manufacturing the ships, planes, tanks, and other equipment needed for war. With accumulated savings of $140 billion at war's end, consumers were ready to buy whatever they could.

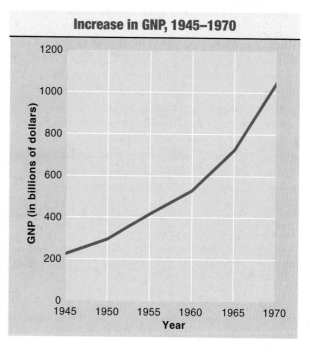

Increase in GNP, 1945–1970

Source: National Income and Product Accounts, 1929–1994.

McDonald's provided a model for other franchisers in the 1950s and the years that followed. The golden arches, shown here in an early version, were virtually the same wherever they appeared. Initially found along highways around the country, they were later built within cities and towns as well. *(Courtesy McDonald's Corporation)*

Equally important was the 22 percent rise in real purchasing power between 1946 and 1960. Families now had far more discretionary income—money to satisfy wants as well as needs—than before. At the end of the Great Depression, fewer than one-quarter of all households had any discretionary income; in 1960, three of every five did.

The United States, which produced half the world's goods, was providing new products that average Americans, unlike their parents, could afford. Higher real wages allowed people across social classes to buy consumer goods, and that consumer power, in contrast to the underconsumption of the 1920s and 1930s, spurred the economy. In the words of one government official, Adolf A. Berle, Jr., Americans were caught up in a spirit of "galloping capitalism."

The automobile industry played a key part in the boom. Just as cars and roads transformed America in the 1920s when mass production came of age, so they contributed to the equally great transformation three decades later. Limited to the production of military vehicles during World War II, the auto industry expanded dramatically in the postwar period. Two million cars were made in 1946; four times as many were built in 1955; and the number rose to over nine million in 1965. Customers now chose from a wide variety of engines, colors, and optional accessories. Fancy grills and tail fins distinguished each year's models.

The automobile became a status symbol. For aspiring members of the middle and upper-middle classes, a fancy car could reflect economic achievement. For younger members of the country, particularly members of the working class, speed was more important.

As Ed Schafer of St. Louis later recalled, "We had a fairly large group of people, 15, 16 guys, and the camaraderie was unbelievable. . . . Your importance in the club increased by your performance on the dragstrip. It didn't matter if you were a nerd; if you had a fast car and could make it down a quarter mile faster than anyone else, you were a big man."

The development of a massive interstate highway system also stimulated auto production and so contributed to prosperity. Rather than encourage the growth of a mass transit system, the Eisenhower administration underscored the American commitment to the car. Through the Interstate Highway Act of 1956 it poured $26 billion, the largest public works expenditure in American history, into building over 40,000 miles of federal highways, linking all parts of the United States.

Though highways added to the problem of pollution and triggered urban flight, enthusiasts hailed the interstate complex as a key to the country's material development. Justified in part on the grounds that it would make evacuation quicker in the event of nuclear attack, the highway system made its proponents proud. President Eisenhower boasted that "the amount of concrete poured to form these roadways would build . . . six sidewalks to the moon. . . . More than any single action by the government since the end of the war, this one would change the face of America." Significantly, this massive effort helped create a nation dependent on a constant supply of cheap and plentiful oil.

A housing boom also fed economic growth. In 1940, 43 percent of all American families owned their

Index of Weekly Wages in Manufacturing, 1945–1970
(1967 = 100)

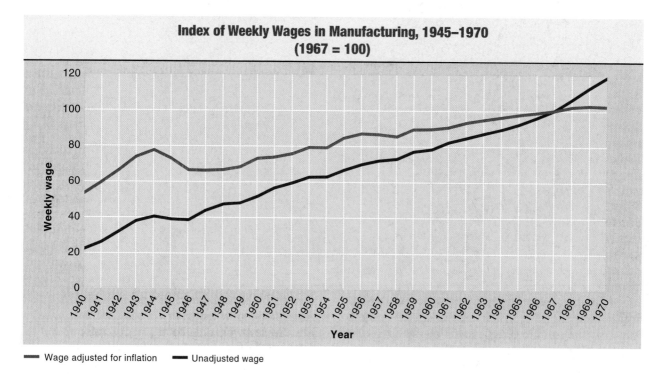

■ Wage adjusted for inflation   ■ Unadjusted wage

Source: U.S. Bureau of Labor Statistics.

own homes; by 1970, 63 percent did. Much of the stimulus came from the GI Bill of 1944. In addition to giving returning servicemen priority for many jobs and providing educational benefits, it offered low-interest home mortgages. Millions of former servicemen from all social classes eagerly purchased their share of the American dream.

The government's increasingly active economic role both stimulated and sustained the expansion. Businesses were allowed to buy almost 80 percent of the factories built by the government during the war for much less than they cost. Even more important was the dramatic rise in defense spending as the Cold War escalated. In 1947, Congress passed the National Security Act creating the Department of Defense and authorized an initial budget of $13 billion. With the onset of the Korean War, the defense budget rose to $22 billion in 1951 and to about $47 billion in 1953. Approximately half of the total federal budget went to the armed forces. This spending, in turn, helped stimulate the aircraft and electronic industries. The government underwrote 90 percent of aviation and space research, 65 percent of electricity and electronics work, and 42 percent of scientific instrument development. Meanwhile, the close business–government ties of World War II grew stronger.

Most citizens welcomed the huge expenditures, not only because they supported the American stance in the struggle against Communism (see Chapter 27) but also because they understood the economic impact of

military spending. Columnist David Lawrence noted in 1950, "Government planners figure they have found the magic formula for almost endless good times. Cold war is an automatic pump primer. Turn a spigot, and the public clamors for more arms spending."

Postwar American growth avoided some of the major problems that often bedevil periods of economic expansion—inflation and the enrichment of a few at the expense of the many. Inflation, a problem in the immediate postwar period, slowed from an average of 7 percent per year in the 1940s to a gentle 2 to 3 percent per year in the 1950s and 1960s. And though the concentration of income remained the same—the bottom half of the population still earned less than the top tenth—the ranks of middle-class Americans grew.

A major economic transformation had occurred in the United States. Peaceful, prosperous, and productive, the nation had become the "affluent society," in economist John Kenneth Galbraith's phrase. Charles Lehman, a veteran from Missouri, later summed up the sentiments of many workers as the postwar era began: "I was a twenty-one-year-old lieutenant with a high school education, and my only prewar experience was as a stock boy in a grocery store. But on V-J day, I knew it was only a matter of time before I was rich—or well-off, anyway."

The Corporate Impact on American Life

After 1945, the major corporations tightened their hold on the American economy. Government policy

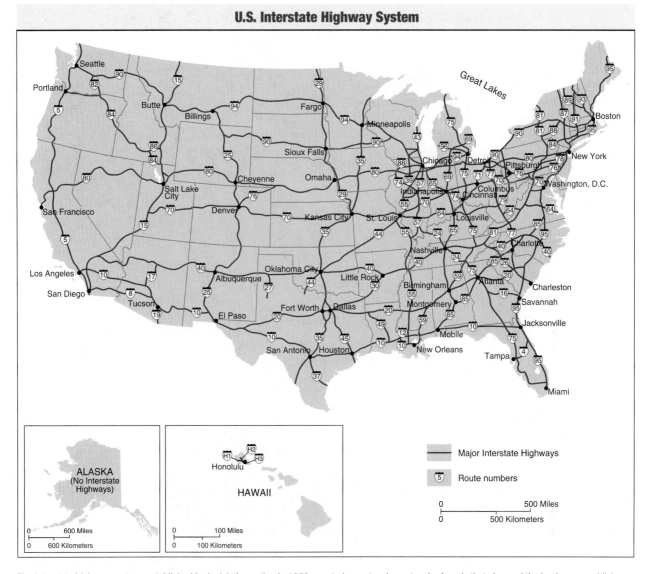

U.S. Interstate Highway System

The interstate highway system, established by legislative action in 1956, created an extensive network of roads that changed the landscape and living patterns of people throughout the United States. While the network was most extensive in the East, it extended throughout the entire country.

in World War II had produced tremendous industrial concentration. The government suspended antitrust actions in the interest of wartime production, while government contracts spurred expansion. During the war, two-thirds of all military contracts were awarded to 100 firms, and half of all contracts went to three dozen giants. Firms such as the Ford Motor Company dominated wartime production. In 1940, some 100 companies accounted for 30 percent of all manufacturing output in the United States. Three years later, those same 100 firms controlled 70 percent of output.

Industrial concentration continued after the war, making oligopoly—domination of a given industry by a few firms—a feature of American capitalism. Several waves of mergers had taken place in the past, including one in the 1890s and another in the 1920s. Still

another occurred in the 1950s. At the same time, the booming economy encouraged the development of conglomerates—firms with holdings in a variety of industries to protect themselves against instability in one particular area. It also led to the further development of finance capitalism to help put the deals together, just as the demands of consolidation in the late nineteenth century had opened the way for bankers like J. P. Morgan (see Chapter 18).

Expansion took other forms as well. Even as the major corporations grew, so did smaller franchise operations like McDonald's, Kentucky Fried Chicken, and Burger King. Ray Kroc, introduced at the start of this chapter, provided a widely imitated pattern.

While expanding at home, large corporations also moved increasingly into foreign markets, as they had

Agricultural and Industrial Employment in the United States in 1950

This map shows the major areas of industrial activity and those regions making the greatest agricultural impact around 1950.

in the 1890s. But at the same time they began to build plants overseas, where labor costs were cheaper. In the decade after 1957, General Electric built 61 plants abroad, and numerous other firms did the same. Corporate planning, meanwhile, developed rapidly, as firms sought managers who could assess information, weigh marketing trends, and make rational decisions. Andrew Carnegie had pioneered such an approach in the late nineteenth century by paying meticulous attention to his costs (see Chapter 18). Now managers, trained in business schools, were even more precise in the effort to maximize profit.

Changing Work Patterns

As corporations changed, so did the world of work. Reversing a 150-year trend after World War II, the United States became less a goods producer and more a service provider. Between 1947 and 1957, the number of factory workers fell by 4 percent, while the number of clerical workers increased 23 percent and the number of salaried middle-class employees rose

61 percent. By 1956, a majority of American workers held white-collar jobs, and the percentage rose in the years that followed. These new white-collar workers, paid by salary rather than by the hour, served as corporate managers, office workers, salespeople, and teachers.

People lived comfortably, enjoying an abundance of leisure time. Experts predicted that a four-day work week loomed ahead. Indeed, the *Harvard Business Review* announced in 1959 that "boredom, which used to bother only aristocrats, has become a common curse." The American Council of Churches met to consider the question of how to deal with spare time. Housewives worried about how to get their work done if their husbands were home for extended weekends on a regular basis.

Yet white-collar employees paid a price for comfort. Work in the huge corporations became ever more impersonal and bureaucratic with white-collar employees seemingly dressing, thinking, and acting the same (as depicted in a popular novel and film of the 1950s, *The Man in the Gray Flannel Suit*). Corporations, preaching that teamwork was all-important, indoctrinated employees with the appropriate standards of conduct. RCA issued company neckties. IBM had training programs to teach employees the company line. Some large firms even set up training programs to show wives how their own behavior could help their husbands' careers. Just as product standardization became increasingly important, individual acceptance of company norms became necessary. "Personal views can cause a lot of trouble," an oil company recruiting pamphlet noted, suggesting that business favored moderate or conservative ideas that would not threaten the system. William H. Whyte, an analyst of organizational behavior, vividly described the lives of young executives whose ultimate goal was "belongingness." Social critic C. Wright Mills observed, "When white-collar people get jobs, they sell not only their time and energy but their personalities as well."

But not all Americans held white-collar jobs. Many were still blue-collar assembly line workers, who made the goods others enjoyed. They too dreamed of owning a suburban home and several cars and providing more for their children than they had enjoyed while growing up. Their lives were now more comfortable than ever before, as the union movement brought substantial gains (see the next section). These were the more fortunate members of the working class. Millions of others, perhaps totaling 40 percent of the workforce, held less appealing and less well-paying positions. More and more worked as taxi drivers, farm laborers, and dime-store sales clerks. For them, jobs were less stable, less secure, and less interesting. Casual employment had involved manual labor in the past; now it consisted of service work, and much of this was done by minorities, teenagers, and women gradually returning to the labor force.

The Union Movement at High Tide

The union movement had come of age during the New Deal (see Chapter 24), and the end of World War II found it even stronger. There were more union members—14.5 million—than ever before. Ten million belonged to the American Federation of Labor (AFL); the other 4.5 million belonged to the Congress of Industrial Organizations (CIO). Having taken a wartime no-strike pledge and given their full support to the war effort, they now looked forward to better pay and a greater voice in workplace management.

The immediate postwar period was difficult. Cancellation of defense orders laid off war workers and prompted fears of a depression, like the one that had followed World War I. Even workers who held their jobs lost the overtime pay they had enjoyed during the war. Many responded by striking. In 1946 alone, 4.6 million workers went out on strike—more than ever before in the history of the United States. There were work stoppages in the automobile, coal, steel, and electrical industries, and a threatened strike by railway workers. These disruptions alienated middle-class Americans who looked for stable employment patterns and provoked the antagonism of conservative Republicans who felt that unionization had gone too far.

In the late 1940s, a new equilibrium emerged. Big business at last recognized the basic rights of industrial workers, and union leaders and members in turn acknowledged the prerogatives of management and accepted the principle of fair profit. Corporations in the same industry agreed to cooperate rather than compete with one another over labor costs. This meant that once a leading firm reached agreement with the union, the other firms in that area would adopt similar terms, and the costs of the new contract would be met by a general increase in prices.

At the same time, companies made material concessions to workers—for example, adjusting their pay to protect them against inflation. In 1948, General Motors offered the United Automobile Workers a contract that included a cost-of-living adjustment (COLA) and a 2 percent "annual improvement factor" wage increase intended to share GM's productivity gains with workers. In 1950, GM again took the lead, this time with a five-year agreement providing pensions along with a cost-of-living adjustment and wage increase. Five years later, automobile workers won a guaranteed annual wage. The merger of the AFL and CIO in 1955 ratified the changes that had occurred in the labor movement, as the new organization, led by building trade unionist George Meany, represented more than 90 percent of the country's now larger group of 17.5 million union members. By the end of the 1950s the COLA principle was built into most union contracts.

Union gains, like middle-class affluence, came at a price. With higher, more predictable incomes, workers were more willing to limit strikes and surrender the last vestiges of workplace autonomy. Co-opted by the materialistic benefits big business provided, workers fell increasingly under the control of middle-level managers and watched anxiously as companies automated at home or expanded abroad, where labor was cheaper. But the agreements they had reached often precluded any response.

The union movement stalled in the 1960s. The heavy industries whose workers gravitated to the union movement stagnated. The unionized percentage of the nonfarm workforce remained stable in the decade and a half following World War II but then began to fall.

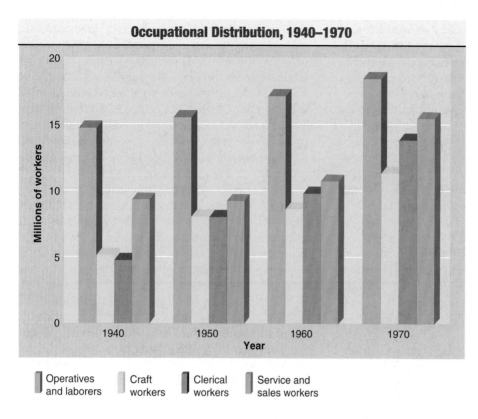

Occupational Distribution, 1940–1970

Millions of workers

Year

■ Operatives and laborers   ■ Craft workers   ■ Clerical workers   ■ Service and sales workers

In the postwar years, the size of the workforce increased considerably. In this graph, observe how all categories grew, particularly the number of clerical workers and service and sales workers in the decades after 1950. Sources: U.S. Department of Labor and *Historical Statistics of the United States.*

Unions tried to expand their base by reaching out to new groups—less skilled minority workers and white-collar, service-oriented employees—but these groups proved difficult to organize.

Agricultural Workers in Trouble

The agricultural world changed even more than the industrial world in the postwar United States. On the eve of World War II, agriculture had supported one of every five Americans. In the course of one generation, mechanization and consolidation forced that figure down to one of every twenty. Altogether, some 15 million rural jobs disappeared.

New technology revolutionized farming. Improved planting and harvesting machines and better fertilizers and pesticides brought massive gains in productivity. Increasing profitability led to agricultural consolidation. In the 25 years after 1945, average farm size almost doubled. Farms specialized more in cash crops, like corn or soybeans, that were more profitable than hay or oats used to feed animals. Demanding large-scale investment, farming became a big business. Family farms often found it difficult to compete with the technologically superior "agribusinesses" and watched their share of the market fall.

In response, farmers left the land in increasing numbers. Some were midwestern whites who generally found jobs in offices and factories. In the South, the upheaval was more disruptive. Many of the uprooted agricultural workers were African Americans, who became part of the huge migration north that had been going on since World War I. Overall, from 1910 to 1970, more than 6.5 million African Americans left the South; of these, 5 million moved north after 1940. Most of them gravitated to cities, where they faced difficulties described later in this chapter. The agricultural life, as it had been known for decades, even centuries, was over.

⟿ DEMOGRAPHIC AND TECHNOLOGICAL TRENDS

The postwar economic boom was interwoven with a series of demographic changes. The population grew dramatically and continued to move west, while at the same time, millions of white Americans left the cities for the suburbs that began to grow exponentially in the postwar years. New patterns, revolving around television and other gadgets provided by the advances of technology, came to characterize the consumer culture that dominated suburban life.

Population Shifts

In post–World War II America, a growing population testified to prosperity's return. During the Great Depression, the birthrate had dropped to an all-time low of 19 births per 1,000, as hard times obliged people to delay marriage and parenthood. As the Second World War boosted the economy, the birthrate began to rise again. Some experts questioned whether the trend was

Birth and Population Rates, 1900–1970

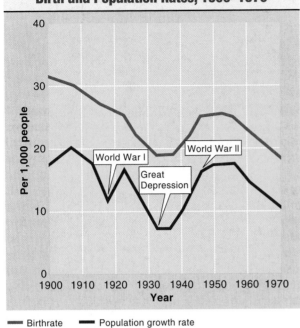

- ▬ Birthrate   ▬ Population growth rate

Both birth and population rates increased dramatically after the difficult years of the Great Depression. Note the baby boom that began at the end of World War II and continued for the next decade. Sources: U.S. Bureau of the Census and *Statistical Abstract of the United States.*

a long-term one. The Census Bureau cautiously claimed that it was at least partly due to "occasional furloughs," but in fact a real shift was under way.

The birthrate soared in the postwar years as millions of Americans began families. The "baby boom" peaked in 1957, with a rate of more than 25 births per 1,000. In that year, 4.3 million babies were born, one every seven seconds. While the population growth of 19 million in the 1940s was double the rise of the decade before, that increase paled against the increase in the 1950s, which totaled 29 million.

The rising birthrate was the dominant factor affecting population growth, but the death rate was also declining. Miracle drugs made a difference. Federal sponsorship of medical research during World War II had spurred the development of penicillin and streptomycin, now widely available. They helped cure strep throat and other bacterial infections, intestinal ailments, and more serious illnesses such as tuberculosis. A polio vaccine introduced a decade after the war virtually eliminated that dreaded disease. Life expectancy rose: midway through the 1950s, the average was 70 years for whites and 64 for blacks, compared with 55 for whites and 45 for blacks in 1920.

The baby boom shaped family and social patterns and material needs. Many women who had taken jobs during the war now left the workforce to rear their children and care for their homes. Their lives changed considerably as they substituted housework for paid work. Demand grew for diaper services and baby foods. Entering school, the baby boom generation strained the educational system. Between 1946 and 1956, enrollment in grades 1 through 8 soared from 20 million to 30 million. Since school construction had slowed during the Depression and had virtually halted during the Second World War, classrooms were needed. Teachers, too, were in short supply.

As Americans became more populous, they also became more mobile. For many generations, working-class Americans had been the most likely to move; now geographic mobility spread to the middle class. Each year in the 1950s, over a million farmers left their farms in search of new employment. Other Americans picked up stakes and headed on as well. Some moved to look for better jobs. Others, like Bob Moses of Baltimore, simply wandered awhile after returning home from the war and then settled down. Moses, traveling in a 1937 Chevrolet with some high school friends, was going "nowhere in particular, just roaming. We'd see a kink in a river on the map, and head there." After regimented military life, it was good to be free.

The war had produced increasing movement, most of it westward. Although the scarcity of water in the West would require massive water projects to support population growth, war workers and their families streamed to western cities where shipyards, airplane factories, and other industrial plants were located. After the war, this migration pattern persisted. The Sun Belt—the region stretching along the southern tier of the United States from Florida to California—attracted new arrivals. Cities like Houston, Albuquerque, Tucson, and Phoenix expanded phenomenally. The population of Phoenix soared from 65,000 in 1940 to 439,000 in 1960. In the 1950s, Los Angeles pulled ahead of Philadelphia as the third-largest city in the United States. One-fifth of all the growth in the period took place in California; even baseball teams—the Brooklyn Dodgers and the New York Giants—left the East Coast for western shores. By 1963, in a dramatic illustration of the importance of the West, California passed New York as the nation's most populous state.

The migration west resulted from a number of reasons. Servicemen who had been stationed in the West liked the scenery, climate, and pace of life. Many returned with their families after the war. With funds from the Federal Housing Administration or Veterans Administration, they could afford to borrow money and buy new homes. That spending, in turn, helped fuel the region's economic growth.

Meanwhile, as noted earlier in this chapter, Cold War spending promoted economic development, and

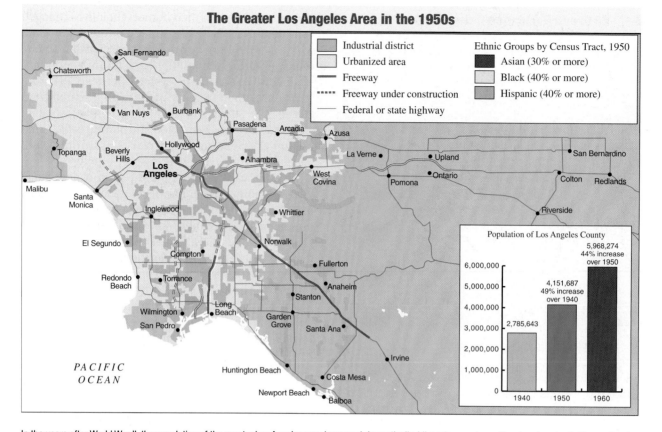

The Greater Los Angeles Area in the 1950s

In the years after World War II, the population of the greater Los Angeles area increased dramatically. Like other western cities, Los Angeles built an extensive freeway system in the metropolitan area that allowed people to live throughout the region. While the population of the city itself increased 31 percent between 1940 and 1950 and another 26 percent between 1950 and 1960, the population of the county, shown in the insert chart, grew even more.

much of that expansion occurred in the West. Once the Korean War sparked increased military expenditures, California's economic growth outpaced that of the country as a whole. Aircraft production in the state accounted for more than 40 percent of the total increase in manufacturing employment there between 1949 and 1953. In the 1950s, rocket research further stimulated the aerospace industry. In 1959, California had nearly a quarter of all prime military contracts in the nation. By 1962, the Pacific Coast as a whole held almost half of all Defense Department research and development contracts.

The West also benefited from the boom in the service economy. Many western workers in postwar America were part of the growing service sector. The percentage of workers in such jobs was higher in virtually all western states than in eastern counterparts. Denver became a major regional center of the federal bureaucracy in the postwar years. From 14,000 people on the payroll in 1951, the number rose to 23,000 in 1961 and to 31,500 in 1975, when it had more such employees than any city other than Washington, D.C. Albuquerque likewise gained numerous federal offices and became known as "little Washington." The old

West of cowboys, farmers, and miners was turning into a new West of bureaucrats, lawyers, and clerks.

The New Suburbs

As the population shifted westward after World War II, another form of movement was taking place. Although the proportion of Americans defined as residents of metropolitan areas increased from 51 to 63 percent between 1940 and 1960, this disguised another shift. Millions of white Americans fled the inner city to suburban fringes, intensifying a movement that had begun before the war. Fourteen of the nation's largest cities, including New York, Boston, Chicago, Philadelphia, and Detroit, actually lost population in the 1950s. As central cities became places where poor nonwhites clustered, new urban and racial problems emerged.

For people of means, cities were places to work in but then to leave at five o'clock. In Manhattan, south of the New York borough's City Hall, the noontime population of 1.5 million dropped to 2,000 overnight. "It was becoming a part-time city," wrote an observer, "tidally swamped with bustling humanity every weekday morning when the cars and commuter trains

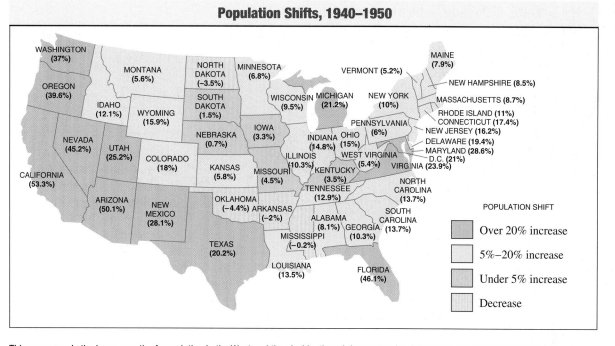

Population Shifts, 1940–1950

WASHINGTON (37%)
OREGON (39.6%)
IDAHO (12.1%)
MONTANA (5.6%)
WYOMING (15.9%)
NEVADA (45.2%)
UTAH (25.2%)
CALIFORNIA (53.3%)
ARIZONA (50.1%)
NEW MEXICO (28.1%)
NORTH DAKOTA (−3.5%)
SOUTH DAKOTA (1.5%)
NEBRASKA (0.7%)
COLORADO (18%)
KANSAS (5.8%)
OKLAHOMA (−4.4%)
TEXAS (20.2%)
MINNESOTA (6.8%)
WISCONSIN (9.5%)
IOWA (3.3%)
MISSOURI (4.5%)
ARKANSAS (−2%)
LOUISIANA (13.5%)
MICHIGAN (21.2%)
INDIANA (14.8%)
ILLINOIS (10.3%)
KENTUCKY (3.5%)
TENNESSEE (12.9%)
MISSISSIPPI (−0.2%)
ALABAMA (8.1%)
OHIO (15%)
WEST VIRGINIA (5.4%)
GEORGIA (10.3%)
FLORIDA (46.1%)
NEW YORK (10%)
PENNSYLVANIA (6%)
VIRGINIA (23.9%)
NORTH CAROLINA (13.7%)
SOUTH CAROLINA (13.7%)
MAINE (7.9%)
VERMONT (5.2%)
NEW HAMPSHIRE (8.5%)
MASSACHUSETTS (8.7%)
RHODE ISLAND (11%)
CONNECTICUT (17.4%)
NEW JERSEY (16.2%)
DELAWARE (19.4%)
MARYLAND (28.6%)
D.C. (21%)

POPULATION SHIFT
Over 20% increase
5%–20% increase
Under 5% increase
Decrease

This map reveals the huge growth of population in the West and the sizable, though less extensive, increase in the Northeast and Southeast between 1940 and 1950.

arrived, and abandoned again at nightfall when the wave sucked back—left pretty much to thieves, policemen, and rats."

As the cities declined, new suburbs blossomed. If the decade after World War I had witnessed a rural-to-urban shift, the decades after World War II saw a reverse shift to the regions outside the central cities, usually accessible only by car. By the end of the 1950s, a third of all Americans resided in suburbs. That figure continued to rise in the next decade, reaching nearly 38 percent in 1970.

Americans moved to the suburbs to buy homes that could accommodate their larger families. Often

GROWTH OF SUN BELT CITIES, 1920–1980 POPULATION (IN THOUSANDS)

	1920	1940	1960	1980
Los Angeles	879	2,916	6,039	7,478
Houston	168	529	1,418	2,905
Dallas	185	527	1,084	2,430
Atlanta	249	559	1,017	2,030
San Diego	74	289	1,033	1,862
Miami	30	268	935	1,626
Phoenix	29	186	664	1,509
New Orleans	398	552	907	1,256
San Antonio	191	338	716	1,072
Tucson	20	37	266	531

Source: U.S. Bureau of the Census.

rapidly constructed, suburban tract houses provided the appearance of comfort and space and the chance to have at least one part of the American dream—a place of one's own. They seemed protected from the growing troubles of the cities, insulated from the difficulties of the world outside.

The pioneer of the postwar suburbanization movement was William J. Levitt, a builder eager to gamble and reap the rewards of a growing demand. Levitt had recognized the advantages of mass production during World War II, when his firm constructed housing for war workers. Aware that the GI Bill made mortgage money readily available, he saw the possibilities of suburban development. But to cash in, Levitt knew he had to use new construction methods.

Mass production was the key. Individually designed houses were a thing of the past, he believed. "The reason we have it so good in this country," he said, "is that we can produce lots of things at low prices through mass production." Houses were among them. Working on a careful schedule, Levitt's team brought precut and preassembled materials to each site, put them together, and then moved on to the next location. As on an assembly line, tasks were broken down into individual steps. Groups of workers performed a single job on each tract.

Levitt proved that his system worked. Construction costs at Levittown, New York, a new community of 17,000 homes built in the late 1940s, were only $10 per square foot, compared with the $12 to $15 common

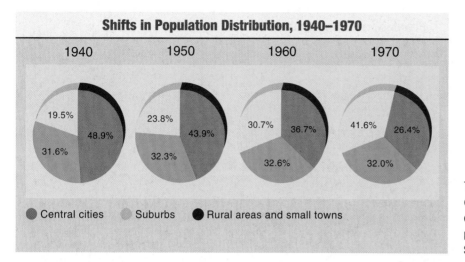

Shifts in Population Distribution, 1940–1970

| 1940 | 1950 | 1960 | 1970 |

1940: 19.5%, 48.9%, 31.6%
1950: 23.8%, 43.9%, 32.3%
1960: 30.7%, 36.7%, 32.6%
1970: 41.6%, 26.4%, 32.0%

● Central cities   ● Suburbs   ● Rural areas and small towns

This graph shows the progressive decline in rural population and the corresponding increase in suburban population between 1940 and 1970. Source: U.S. Bureau of the Census.

elsewhere. The next Levittown appeared in Bucks County, Pennsylvania, several years after the first, and another went up in Willingboro, New Jersey, at the end of the 1950s. Levitt's success provided a model for other developers.

Levitt argued that his homes helped underscore American values. "No man who owns his own house and lot can be a Communist," he once said. "He has too much to do." Levitt also helped perpetuate segregation by refusing to sell homes to blacks. "We can solve a housing problem, or we can try to solve a racial problem but we cannot combine the two," he declared in the early 1950s.

Government-insured mortgages, especially for veterans, fueled the housing boom. So did fairly low postwar interest rates. With many American families vividly remembering the Depression and saving significant parts of their paychecks, the nation had a pool of savings large enough to keep mortgage interest rates in the affordable 5 percent range.

Suburbanization transformed the American landscape. Huge tracts of former fields, pastures, and forests were now divided into standardized squares, each bearing a house with a two-car garage and a manicured lawn. Stands of trees disappeared, for it was cheaper to cut them down than to work around them. Folksinger Malvina Reynolds described the new developments she saw:

Little boxes on the hillside
Little boxes made of ticky tacky
Little boxes on the hillside
Little boxes all the same.
There's a green one and a pink one
And a blue one and a yellow one
And they're all made out of ticky tacky
And they all look just the same.

As suburbs flourished, businesses followed their customers out of the cities. Shopping centers led the

way. At the end of World War II, there were eight, but the number multiplied rapidly in the 1950s. In a single three-month period in 1957, 17 new centers opened; by 1960, there were 3,840 in the United States. Developers like Don M. Casto, who built the Miracle Mile near Columbus, Ohio, understood the impor-

Step-by-step mass production, with units completed in assembly-line fashion, was the key to William Levitt's approach to housing. But the suburban developments he and others created were marked by street after street of houses that all looked the same. The Levittown in this picture was built on 1,200 acres of potato fields on Long Island in New York.
(Cornell Capa/Magnum Photos, Inc.)

tance of location as Americans moved out of the cities. "People have path-habits," he said, "like ants."

Shopping centers catered to the suburban clientele and transformed consumer patterns. They offered easy parking and convenient late hours; if they wished, suburb dwellers could remain entirely insulated from the cities. Their new shopping patterns, however, undermined the downtown department stores and further eroded urban health.

The Environmental Impact

Fast-food restaurants, shopping centers, and suburban housing developments all had environmental consequences. Rapid development often took place without extensive planning and encroached on some of the nation's most attractive rural areas. Before long, virtually every American city was ringed by an ugly highway lined with the eating places, shopping malls, and auto dealerships that catered to the suburban population. Billboard advertisements filled whatever space was not yet developed.

Responding to the increasingly cluttered terrain, architect Peter Blake ruthlessly attacked the practices of the 1950s in his muckraking book *God's Own Junkyard: The Planned Deterioration of America's Landscape,* published in 1964. The largely pictorial account indicted the careless attitudes toward the environment that led to the "uglification" of a once lovely land. After describing breathtaking natural resources, Blake declared, "The only trouble is that we are about to turn this beautiful inheritance into the biggest slum on the face of the earth." Public policy and the pursuit of private profit, coupled with general citizen indifference, he charged, led to the unconscionable desecration of the American landscape:

> Our suburbs are interminable wastelands dotted with millions of monotonous little houses on monotonous little lots and crisscrossed by highways lined with billboards, jazzed-up diners, used-car lots, drive-in movies, beflagged gas stations, and garish motels. Even the relatively unspoiled countryside beyond these suburban fringes has begun to sprout more telephone poles than trees, more trailer camps than national parks.

Despite occasional accounts like Blake's, there was little real consciousness of environmental issues in the early post–World War II years. The term *environment* itself was hardly used prior to the war. Americans had been concerned with conservation earlier in the century and had first focused on efficient use and development of water and forests. Later they turned their attention to the preservation of grasslands, soils, and game.

Yet the very prosperity that created the dismal highway strips in the late 1940s and 1950s was lead-

Highways surrounding cities and towns were filled with commercial establishments advertising their wares with brightly colored, but often tasteless, signs. Here hotels along such a roadway try to entice travelers to come in. *(Photograph by Wallace Litwin)*

ing more and more Americans to appreciate natural environments as treasured parts of their rising standard of living. The shorter workweek provided more free time, and many Americans now had the means for longer vacations. By 1950, most wage laborers worked a 40-hour week, and 60 percent of nonagricultural workers enjoyed paid vacations, whereas few had been able to take regular holidays in 1930. They began to explore mountains and rivers and ocean shores and to ponder how to protect them. In 1958, Congress established the National Outdoor Recreation Review Commission, a first step toward consideration of environmental issues that became far more common in the next decade. In 1964, Congress went still further, passing a National Wilderness Preservation Act, followed by a Wild and Scenic Rivers Act and a National Trails Act in 1968. Americans also began to recognize the need for open space in their communities, to compensate for the urban overdevelopment.

Technology Changes the American People

AIR-CONDITIONING

or much of their history, Americans had little relief from hot weather and heat waves. Many older residents of the United States, especially those living in the South, remember sweltering summer days when it was nearly impossible to work or to relax in the heat. Before the invention of air-conditioning, the federal government sent workers in Washington, D.C., home whenever the temperature/humidity index rose above 90 degrees. People drove their cars with the windows open, hoping for a cooling breeze even if the noise made it difficult to carry on a conversation. Over the course of the twentieth century, the development of successful air-conditioning systems changed residential patterns, altered cultural behavior, and improved the health of the American people. At the same time, technological improvements led to often acrimonious debate about the consequences of the new developments.

Early attempts at controlling the climate in the United States involved forcing air over ice. In the mid-nineteenth century, Florida physician John Gorrie was one of those who envisioned such a refrigeration system to aid feverish patients suffering from malaria and yellow fever. His major accomplishment, however, was to build a refrigeration machine used for the production of ice.

By the 1890s, a number of American cities had central refrigeration systems patterned after those providing electricity, water, and gas. In St. Louis, Missouri, the Ice Palace, a restaurant and beer hall, attached expansion coils containing a refrigerant to a wall and was able to cool the air. "No difficulty is found in maintaining any desired temperature in the room, no matter how crowded it may be or how warm the air outside," a trade magazine reported. But the innovation was expensive and failed to catch on.

During the early years of the twentieth century, several breakthroughs occurred. A scientist writing in the *North American Review* imagined applying mechanical refrigeration systems to businesses and homes and asked, "If they can cool dead hogs in Chicago, why not live 'bulls and bears' in the New York Stock Exchange?" Engineer Alfred R. Wolfe installed such a system in the Stock Exchange that worked by chilling a calcium chlo-

ride brine and circulating it through a cooling coil over which air was circulated by fans. At about the same time, textile manufacturers found they needed to control the amount of moisture in their yarns if they wanted to avoid broken ends and to keep fibers soft. Stuart Cramer, another engineer, found a way to moderate the humidity by forcing air from outside through a fine water spray and a cloth filter and then releasing it inside. He called his procedure "air conditioning," and the name stuck.

Willis H. Carrier, in this same period, devised an even better system. Carrier, who had just received an engineering degree from Cornell, saw the effects of uncontrolled humidity on a printing plant in Brooklyn. The stretching and shrinking of paper made it impossible to print color covers that could be used. Concentrating on the relationship between temperature and humidity, Carrier devised a process using chilled coils that managed to cool air and reduce humidity with remarkable precision. Carrier continued to improve his process in the decades that followed, figuring out ways to push air through the ever-larger buildings that were constructed in the 1920s and 1930s. "Every day a *good* day" was his motto as he promoted the system that carried his name. In these years, air-conditioning worked when institutions or corporations were able to put up the sizable amounts of money to cool large buildings. Central air-conditioning systems reflected the engineers' sense that they could bring the entire inside environment under control.

Industries affected by the heat were among the first to install air-conditioning. Chocolate factories, tobacco factories, bakeries, and printing plants now had an easier time maintaining continuous production in the summer months. An occasional hospital introduced air-conditioning to make doctors and patients more comfortable. The government implemented air-conditioning too, starting in 1928. First the House of Representatives was centrally air-conditioned, then the Senate, the White House, and the Supreme Court.

More and more movie theaters were air-conditioned in the 1920s. A theater in Montgomery, Alabama, had installed a system in 1917, but the real breakthrough came at the Rivoli on Broadway in New York City in 1925. The head of Paramount Pictures appeared for the inauguration of the system and was relieved as cool air circulated and made the show more enjoyable for patrons. Millions of sweltering Americans became accustomed to heading for movie houses on Saturday afternoons where for a dime they could get relief from the hot weather and forget about the mundane patterns of their daily existence.

A major shift in the patterns of air-conditioning occurred with the advent of smaller, less expensive units that could be used in homes. The first home units, such as the Weathermaker in the 1920s, cost about $3,000, a huge amount of money, and followed the centralized structure used in industry. The Great Depression of the 1930s made the market for such systems tighter and encouraged refrigerator manufacturers to experiment with smaller room coolers. By the late 1930s, Frigidaire, Kelvinator, and General Electric were designing less expensive air-conditioners that could cool just one room. Window units came next, and mass production drove costs down still further and made them almost universally accessible in the years following World War II. From 74,000 window units in 1948, the number sold reached 1,045,000 in 1953. In the 1960s, more than three million units were being made each year.

Air-conditioning had an enormous impact. Journalists joked that air-conditioning promoted the huge growth of the Washington bureaucracy, but there was an element of truth in what they said. Air-conditioning was likewise responsible for the tremendous growth of the Sun Belt—that region stretching across the lower tier of the country from east to west—as people discovered they could moderate the effects of the heat. Porches on houses disappeared as people became accustomed to living in the air-conditioned indoors. American culture became more homogenized, as increasingly the patterns of life in one part of the country resembled the patterns in other parts.

Americans moved from one air-conditioned location to another in air-conditioned cars. They shopped in air-conditioned malls, entertained themselves in air-conditioned theme parks, and then returned to their air-conditioned

THE NEW SILHOUETTE *Carrier* ROOM AIR CONDITIONER

BUILT BY THE PEOPLE WHO KNOW AIR CONDITIONING BEST. CARRIER CORPORATION, SYRACUSE, NEW YORK

Window units not only cooled the air but made everything inside more glamorous. *(Courtesy of Carrier)*

homes. With the construction of the Houston Sports Astrodome in 1965, they could now watch a baseball or football game in an entirely enclosed arena, with temperature and humidity carefully controlled.

As the country became air-conditioned, Americans debated desirability of the patterns that became part of daily life. Some complained about sealed rooms in what they considered sterile buildings, where they lost any sense of the world outside. Others objected to the huge amounts of electricity expended in cooling and worried about the environmental impact of the coolants used. Yet air-conditioning remained an inextricable component of American life.

Historians often debate the impact of social change. They attempt to weigh the benefits of development against the consequences of such progress. One recent historian, reflecting on changes in the South and referring back to the Civil War, has written, "General Electric has proved a more devastating invader than General Sherman." Do you agree?

How do you weigh the benefits and consequences of air-conditioning? What advantages do you see in the window units that helped spread air-conditioning? What are some of the disadvantages of such units? What patterns of ordinary life have changed with the advent of air-conditioning? How extensive do you think the impact has been?

Source: Gail Cooper, *Air-conditioning in America: Engineers and the Controlled Environment, 1900–1960* (Baltimore: Johns Hopkins University Press, 1998).

Air-conditioning made movie theaters even more popular than before. *(Corbis)*

853

Technology Supreme

A technological revolution transformed postwar America. Some developments—the use of atomic energy, for example—flowed directly from war research. Federal support for scientific activity increased dramatically, as the pattern of wartime collaboration continued. The government established the National Institutes of Health in 1948 to coordinate medical research and the National Science Foundation in 1950 to fund basic scientific research. Scientists who had created the atomic bomb now found themselves in demand with both politicians and the public. They frequently spoke out about new developments and their impact on American life. Ties with Europe continued as the refugee scientists who had fled the Nazi regime were joined by others uprooted by the war, and men like the German Wernher von Braun played a major role in the development of American rockets.

The advent of the Cold War led to ever greater government involvement. The Atomic Energy Commission, created in 1946, and the Department of Defense, set up in 1947, provided rapidly increasing funding for research and development. Support for the Los Alamos Scientific Laboratory, where the atomic bomb had been assembled, continued, while the government contracted with the University of California to open the new Livermore Laboratory near San Francisco. Money went to other large research universities as well and fueled their growth. Scientists engaged in both basic and applied research and helped develop nuclear weapons, jet planes, satellites, and consumer goods that were often the side products of military research. But not all innovations came from government funding. Others emerged from the research and development activities sponsored by big business.

Computers both reflected and assisted the process of technological development. Prior to World War II, Vannevar Bush, an electrical engineer at the Massachusetts Institute of Technology, had built a machine, filled with gears and shafts, to solve differential equations. His contribution was using electronic tubes that could be turned on and off in place of some mechanical parts to make the machine manipulate numbers.

Wartime advances resulted in large but workable calculators, such as the Mark I electromechanical computer developed by engineer Howard Aiken and installed by IBM at Harvard in 1944. It was huge—55 feet long and 8 feet high—and had a million components. It was noisy, and with various switches clicking, it sounded, according to one scientist, "like a roomful of old ladies knitting."

Even more complicated was the Electronic Numerical Integrator and Calculator, called ENIAC, built in 1946 at the University of Pennsylvania. Like the Mark I, it was huge, containing 18,000 electronic tubes and requiring tremendous amounts of electricity and special cooling procedures. It also needed to be "debugged" to remove insects attracted to the heat and light, giving rise to the term still used today by computer scientists for solving problems they face. In an advertised test conducted soon after installation, operators set out to multiply 97,367 by itself 5,000 times. A reporter pushed the necessary button, and the task was completed in less than half a second. In the years that followed, new machines contained their own internal instructions and memories and were now capable of doing far more.

After the development of the transistor by three scientists at Bell Laboratories in 1948, the computer became faster and more reliable, transforming American society as surely as industrialization had changed it a century before. Airlines, hotels, and other businesses computerized their reservation systems. Business accounting and inventory control began to depend on computers. Computer programmers and operators were in increasing demand as computers contributed dramatically to the centralization and interdependence of the components of American life.

Computers allowed scientists to venture beyond the confines of the earth itself. In the postwar years, increasingly sophisticated forms of space exploration became possible. Rocketry had developed during World War II but really came of age in the postwar years. Rockets could deliver nuclear weapons but

The ENIAC computer, first used in 1946, was a huge machine that took up an entire room. Yet it was far slower and far less powerful than the tiny desktop computers that became popular several decades later. *(Courtesy, Moore School of Engineering)*

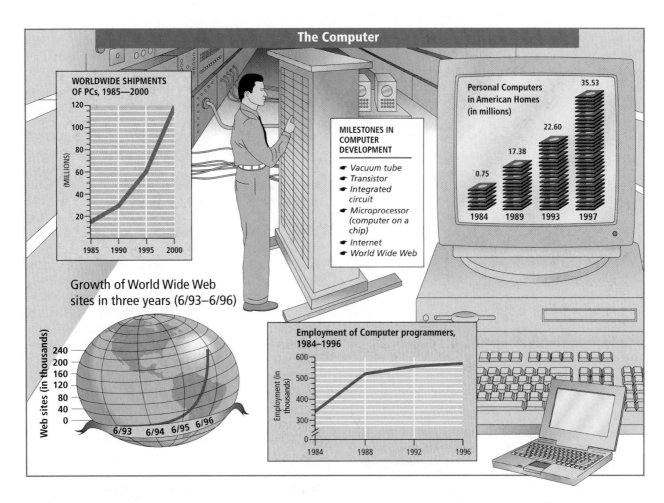

The Computer

WORLDWIDE SHIPMENTS
OF PCs, 1985—2000

(MILLIONS) — 120, 100, 80, 60, 40, 20 — 1985, 1990, 1995, 2000

MILESTONES IN
COMPUTER
DEVELOPMENT

➥ *Vacuum tube*
➥ *Transistor*
➥ *Integrated
circuit*
➥ *Microprocessor
(computer on a
chip)*
➥ *Internet*
➥ *World Wide Web*

Personal Computers
in American Homes
(in millions)

35.53
22.60
17.38
0.75
1984 1989 1993 1997

Growth of World Wide Web
sites in three years (6/93–6/96)

Web sites (in thousands) — 240, 200, 160, 120, 80, 40, 0 — 6/93 6/94 6/95 6/96

Employment of Computer programmers,
1984–1996

Employment (in thousands) — 600, 500, 400, 300, 0 — 1984 1988 1992 1996

could also launch satellites and provide the means to venture millions of miles into outer space.

An ominous technological trend related to computerization was the advent of automation. Mechanization was not new, but now it became far more widespread, threatening both skilled and unskilled workers. In 1952, the Ford Motor Company began using automatic drilling machines in an engine plant and found that 41 workers could do a job 117 had done before. The implications of falling purchasing power as machines replaced workers were serious for an economy dependent on consumer demand.

The Consumer Culture

Tiny transistors powered not only computers but also a wide variety of new appliances and gadgets designed for personal use. A transistorized miniature hearing aid, for example, could fit into the frame of a pair of eyeglasses. Stereophonic high fidelity systems, using new transistor components, provided better sound.

Television, developed in the 1930s, became a major influence on American life after World War II. In 1946, there were fewer than 17,000 TV sets, but by 1960, three-quarters of all American families owned at least one set. In 1955, the average American family tuned in four to five hours each day. Some studies predicted that an American student, on graduating from high school, would have spent 11,000 hours in class and 15,000 hours before the "tube." Young Americans grew up to the strains of "Winky Dink and You," "The Mickey Mouse Club," and "Howdy Doody Time" in the 1950s. Older viewers attended to situation comedies like "I Love Lucy" and "Father Knows Best" and live dramas such as "Playhouse 90." They watched Elvis Presley play his guitar and sing, and they danced to the rock and roll music played on "American Bandstand." Many of the programs aimed at children depicted violence and crime. Hopalong Cassidy was one of America's defenders who became a cult hero in his time. The gunslinging cowboy provided a role model that hundreds of American manufacturing firms capitalized on by making toy guns.

Americans maintained an ardent love affair with the appliances and gadgets produced by modern technology. By the end of the 1950s, most families had at least one automobile, as well as the staple appliances they had begun to purchase before—refrigerator, washing machine, television, and vacuum cleaner. Dozens of less essential items also became popular.

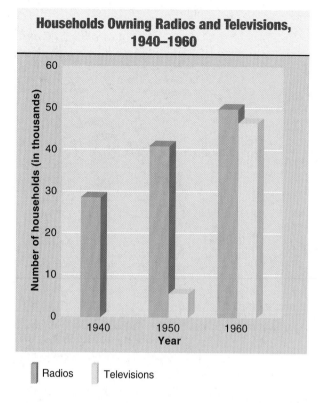

Households Owning Radios and Televisions, 1940–1960

Radio became increasingly popular in the postwar years, but observe the astronomical increase in the number of households owning television sets in the decade after 1950. Source: U.S. Bureau of the Census.

lapsed in the 1930s but began to revive during the war, as firms kept the public aware of consumer goods, even those in short supply. With the postwar boom, advertisers again began to hawk their wares, this time even more aggressively than before.

Motivational research discovered new ways of persuading people to buy. Television played an important part in conveying the spirit of consumption to millions of Americans. Unlike radio, which could only describe new commodities, television could show them. Advertisements featuring the luxury items needed for the good life bombarded TV viewers. Programs such as "The Price Is Right" stressed consumption in direct ways: contestants won goods for quoting their correct retail price. Drawing on a talent honed in shopping centers and department stores, the show encouraged the acquisition of ever more material goods.

If the appeal often seemed overdone, advertisers had their defenders, too. Vance Packard argued in 1957 in his best-selling book *The Hidden Persuaders* that advertisers "fill an important and constructive role in our society. Advertising, for example, not only plays a vital role in promoting our economic growth but [serves] as a colorful, diverting aspect of American life, and many of the creations of admen are tasteful, honest works of artistry." That may have been true of

There were electric can openers, electric pencil sharpeners, and electric toothbrushes. There were push-button phones and aerosol bombs, and automatic transmissions to eliminate the manual shifting of car gears.

Consumption, increasingly a pillar of the American economy, required a vast expansion of consumer credit. Installment plans facilitated buying a new car, while credit cards encouraged the purchase of smaller items such as television sets and household appliances. Eating out became easier when meals could be charged on a card. The first of the consumer credit cards—the Diner's Club card—appeared in 1950, followed at the end of the decade by the American Express card and the BankAmericard. By the end of the 1960s, there were about 50 million credit cards of all kinds in use in the United States. Consumer credit—total private indebtedness—increased from $8.4 billion in 1946 to nearly $45 billion in 1958 and reached $113.2 billion in 1968.

For consumers momentarily unsure about new purchases, a revitalized advertising industry was ready to convince them to go ahead. Advertising had come of age in the 1920s, as businesses persuaded customers that buying new products brought status and satisfaction. Advertising had faltered when the economy col-

"The Mickey Mouse Club" was a popular daily feature on television in the 1950s. Millions of American children were glued to their TV sets each day after school, as they shared a common experience and absorbed the values promoted by the television networks. (*Photofest*)

some ads, but others were garish and conveyed a sense of material wealth run amok.

Having weathered the poverty and unemployment of the 1930s and made sacrifices during a long war, Americans now regarded abundance and leisure as their due, sometimes neglecting to look beyond the immediate objects of their desire. The decade, journalist William Shannon wrote, was one of "self-satisfaction and gross materialism. . . . The loudest sound in the land has been the oink and grunt of private hoggishness. . . . It has been the age of the slob."

CONSENSUS AND CONFORMITY

As the economy expanded, an increasing sense of sameness pervaded American society. Some believed this was the great age of conformity, when members of all social groups learned to emulate those around them rather than strike out on their own. Third- and fourth-generation ethnic Americans became much more alike. As immigration slowed to a trickle after 1924, ties to Europe weakened, assimilation speeded up, and inter-ethnic marriage skyrocketed. Television gave young and old a shared, visually seductive experience. Escaping the homogenizing tendencies was difficult. Sociologist David Riesman pointed out that in the classic nursery rhyme "This Little Pig Went to Market," each pig went his own way. "Today, however, all little pigs go to market; none stay home; all have roast beef, if any do; and all say 'we-we.'"

Conformity in School and Religious Life

The willingness to conform to group norms affected students at all levels. Elementary school children watched the same television shows and coveted the same toys. High school students, always concerned with group norms, dressed in similar ways and shared a common vocabulary that came from television programs and the products featured in advertising jingles. College and university students, while concerned with international affairs, were mostly concerned about business opportunities. "I observe," Yale president A. Whitney Griswold told a graduating class in 1950, "that you share the prevailing mood of the hour, which in your case consists of bargains privately struck with fate—on fate's terms."

Postwar Americans discovered a shared religious sense and returned to their churches in record numbers. By the end of the 1950s, fully 95 percent of all Americans identified with some religious denomination. Church membership doubled between 1945 and 1970.

Part of this upsurge of church attendance grew out of anxieties about "godless Communism" at the height of the Cold War and the threat of nuclear annihilation (see Chapter 27). Clergyman Billy James Hargis founded his Christian Crusade in 1947 and preached the close connection between religion and politics. Hargis claimed: "Patriotism and Christianity are very close to each other. It is impossible to be a true Christian and not be a true patriot." Evangelist Billy Graham was in the forefront of the anti-Communist campaign in the 1950s and 1960s. He preached to millions at his revivals and capitalized on the media, using radio, television, and film to spread his message. "The greatest and most effective weapon against Communism today is to be born again Christian," he thundered in a widely read article. In "Hour of Decision," a regular radio ministry in the 1950s, Graham tried to convert sinners and so save the nation. In one sermon, he declared: "Unless America at this tragic hour is willing to turn to Jesus Christ and be cleansed by the blood of Christ and know the regenerating power of the Holy Spirit, Christ will never save the nation." How could the nation be saved? "When you make your decision for Jesus Christ," Graham said, "it is America making her decision through you."

The religious resurgence had other roots as well. Ecumenical activities—worldwide efforts on the part

Evangelist Billy Graham preached a fiery message to millions of Americans in the 1950s. On the radio, on television, and in huge revivals, he urged sinners to embrace God and so save their nation from the perils of the Communist threat. *(UPI/Corbis-Bettmann)*

of different Christian churches—became more common following a first World Council of Churches meeting in Amsterdam, in The Netherlands, in 1948. These helped draw attention to the place of religion in modern life. Catholicism sought to broaden its appeal in the 1960s, as Pope John XXIII convened the Vatican Ecumenical Council to make the Catholic Church's traditions and practices more accessible—for example, substituting modern languages for Latin in the liturgy. Judaism, likewise, went through important shifts in the postwar years. Second- and third-generation Jews became increasingly affluent, and between 1945 and 1965, a third of all American Jews left cities for the suburbs. There they built new synagogues, most of which adhered to the easier-to-follow patterns of Reform or Conservative, rather than Orthodox, Judaism. In part, this shift reflected an effort by Jews to seek greater acceptance from mainstream American society.

The religious revival resulted to some degree as well from the power of suggestion that led Americans to do what others did. It seemed to reinforce the importance of family life. According to one slogan, "The family that prays together stays together." The renewal of interest in religion also offered an acceptable means of escape from the anxieties of a middle-class executive's life. In the 1950s, the Full Gospel Businessmen's Fellowship not only provided religious camaraderie but also enjoyed access to the White House.

President Dwight Eisenhower reflected the national mood when he observed that "our government makes no sense unless it is founded in a deeply felt religious faith—and I don't care what it is." In 1954, Congress added the words "under God" to the pledge to the flag and the next year voted to require the phrase "In God We Trust" on all U.S. currency. Yet the revival sometimes seemed to rest on a shallow base of religious knowledge. In one public opinion poll, 80 percent of the respondents indicated that the Bible was God's revealed word, but only 35 percent were able to name the four Gospels and over half were unable to name even one.

Traditional Roles for Women

World War II had interrupted traditional patterns of behavior for both men and women. As servicemen went overseas, women left their homes to work. After 1945, there was a period of adjustment as the men returned, and government offices and employers told many working women that they were no longer needed in their jobs. In the 1950s, women faced tremendous pressure to conform to accepted prewar gender patterns, even though, paradoxically, more women entered the workforce than ever before.

Men and women had different postwar expectations. Most men expected to go to school and then find jobs to support their families. Viewing themselves as the primary breadwinners, they wanted their jobs waiting for them after the war. It was fine for women to have worked during the conflict, but now men wanted things the way they had been before. For women, the situation was more complex. While they wanted to resume patterns of family life that had been disrupted by the war, many had enjoyed working in the military plants and were reluctant to retreat to the home, despite pressure to do so.

In 1947, *Life* magazine ran a long photo essay called "The American Woman's Dilemma" that summed up the problem. The essay observed that women were caught in a conflict between the traditional expectation to stay home and the desire to have a paid job. A 1946 *Fortune* magazine poll also captured the discontent of some women. Asked whether they would prefer to be born again as men or women, 25 percent of the women interviewed said they would prefer to be men. That dissatisfaction was strongest among white, well-educated, middle-class women, which was understandable, since family economic circumstances usually required black and lower-class white women to continue working outside the home.

By the 1950s, doubts and questions had largely receded. The baby boom increased average family size and made the decision to remain home easier. The flight to the suburbs gave women more to do, and they settled into the routines of redecorating their homes and gardens and transporting children to and from activities and schools.

In 1956, when *Life* produced a special issue on women, the message differed strikingly from that of nine years before. Profiling Marjorie Sutton, the magazine spoke of the "Busy Wife's Achievements" as "Home Manager, Mother, Hostess, and Useful Civic Worker." Married at 16, Marjorie was now involved with the PTA, Campfire Girls, and charity causes. She cooked and sewed for her family, which included four children, supported her husband by entertaining 1,500 guests a year, and worked out on the trampoline "to keep her size 12 figure."

Marjorie Sutton reflected the widespread social emphasis on marriage and home. Many women went to college to find husbands; if they succeeded, they dropped out. Almost two-thirds of the women in college left before completing a degree, compared with less than half the men. Women were expected to marry young, have children early, and encourage their husbands' careers. An article in *Esquire* magazine in 1954 called working wives a "menace."

The traditional view of women extended throughout American society. Adlai Stevenson, Democratic presidential candidate in 1952 and 1956, defined the female role in politics, telling a group of women that "the assignment for you, as wives and mothers, you can do in the living room with a baby in your lap or in the kitchen with a can opener in your hand." As in much of the nineteenth century, a woman was "to influence man and boy" in her "humble role of housewife" and mother.

Pediatrician Benjamin Spock agreed. In 1946 he published *Baby and Child Care,* the book most responsible for the child-rearing patterns of the postwar generation. In it, he advised mothers to stay at home if they wanted to raise stable and secure youngsters. Working outside the home might jeopardize their children's mental and emotional health.

Popular culture highlighted the stereotype of the woman concerned only about marriage and family. Author Betty Friedan described these patterns in her explosive 1963 critique, *The Feminine Mystique.* Shifting her attention away from working-class and union issues that had concerned her before, she undertook an exhaustive examination of women's magazines and other publications to provide a profile of women in the 1950s and early 1960s. They "could desire no greater destiny than to glory in their own femininity. . . . All they had to do was to devote their lives from earliest girlhood to finding a husband and bearing children." Their role was clear. "It was unquestioned gospel," she wrote, "that women could identify with *nothing* beyond the home—not politics, not art, not science, not events large or small, war or peace, in the United States or the world, unless it could be approached through female experience as a wife or mother or translated into domestic detail."

Movies reinforced conventional images. Doris Day, charming and wholesome, was a favorite heroine. In film after film, she showed how an attractive woman who played her cards right could land her man—the assumed goal of every woman.

The family was all important in this scenario. Fewer than 10 percent of all Americans felt that an unmarried person could be happy. A popular advice book declared: "The family is the center of your living. If it isn't, you've gone far astray." A healthy family strengthened the nation in its Cold War struggle against the Communist menace. In the pattern endlessly reiterated by popular television programs, the family was meant to provide all satisfaction and contentment. The single-story ranch house that became so popular in this period reflected the focus on the family as the source of recreation and fun. No longer were kitchen and den private, as they had been earlier in a reflection of the notion of separate spheres. Now houses, with far more shared and open space, stressed livability and family comfort.

Film star Doris Day was enormously popular in the 1950s. She was pert and pretty, with a winning smile and a captivating charm, and she looked like the special girl next door many men dreamed of marrying. *(Archive Photos)*

Sexuality was a troublesome if compelling postwar concern. In 1948, Alfred C. Kinsey published *Sexual Behavior in the Human Male.* Kinsey was an Indiana University zoologist who had previously studied the gall wasp. When asked to teach a course on marriage problems, he found little published material about human sexual activity and decided to collect his own. He compiled case histories of 5,300 white males, analyzed their personal backgrounds, and recorded patterns of sexual behavior.

Kinsey shocked the country with his statistics on premarital, extramarital, and otherwise illicit sexual acts. Among males who went to college, he concluded, 67 percent had engaged in sexual intercourse before marriage as had 84 percent of those who went to high school but not beyond. Thirty-seven percent of the total male population had experienced some kind of overt homosexual activity. One out of every six farm boys in America, he claimed, had copulated with animals. Five years later, Kinsey published a companion volume, *Sexual Behavior in the Human Female,* which detailed many of the same sexual patterns. Although critics denounced Kinsey for his methodology and his results, both of his books sold widely, for they opened the door to a subject that had previously been considered taboo.

Interest in sexuality was reflected in the fascination with sex goddesses like Marilyn Monroe. With her

Recovering the Past

CLOTHING

Clothing can be an important source of information about the past. The clothes people wear often announce their age, sex, and class and frequently transmit some sense of their origin, occupation, and even their politics. The vocabulary of dress includes more than garments alone: hairstyles, jewelry, and makeup all contribute to the way people choose to present themselves. Clothing can signal strong emotions; a torn, unbuttoned shirt, for example, can indicate that a person who seldom dresses that way is really upset. Bright colors can demonstrate a daring sense and a willingness to make a strong statement. By examining clothing styles in a number of different decades, we can begin to understand something of the changing patterns of people's lives.

In the 1920s, flappers and other women often dressed like children, with loose dresses usually in pastel colors ending just below the knee. Large trimmings, like huge artificial flowers, accentuated the effect. A "boyish" figure

Frances Perkins with laborers in the 1930s. *(Brown Brothers)*

Harlem women in the 1920s. *(Schomburg Collection, New York Public Library)*

was considered most attractive. The clothes conveyed a feeling of playfulness and a willingness to embrace the freedom of the young. Men's suits in the same period were now made out of lighter materials and looked less padded than before. As the tall, stiff collar of an earlier age disappeared and trousers became more high-waisted, men too had a more youthful look.

The Great Depression of the 1930s brought a change in style. Flappers now looked silly, especially as millions of people were starving. Advertisements and films promoted a new maturity and sophistication, more appropriate to hard times. Men's suits became heavier and darker, as if symbolically to provide protection in a breadline. Trousers were wider, and jackets were frequently double-breasted. Overcoats became longer. Women's clothes were likewise made out of heavier fabrics and used darker colors. Skirts fell, almost to the ankles on occasion, and were covered by longer coats. Clothes indicated that there was no place for the playfulness of the decade before.

World War II women at work. *(Oregon Historical Society, Portland)*

A woman and child in the 1950s. *(From the negative by Dorothea Lange, collection of The Oakland Museum, California)*

As conditions improved during and after World War II, styles changed once more. In the 1940s, young teenage girls frequently wore bobby socks, rolled down to their ankles. Working women wore overalls, but with their own adornments to maintain their femininity. Rosie the Riveter, drawn by noted artist Norman Rockwell, wore her overalls proudly as she sat with a riveting gun in her lap and an attractive scarf around her hair. In the postwar years, the Man in the Gray Flannel Suit looked serious, sober, and well-tailored, ready to go work for corporate America. His female partner wanted to look equally worldly and sophisticated and wore carefully tailored adult clothing, with the waist drawn in (often by a girdle) and heels as tall as three inches, when going out. The fashion industry helped define the decorative role women were supposed to play in supporting men as they advanced their business careers.

Then came the 1960s and an entirely new look. Casual clothing became a kind of uniform. The counterculture was a movement of the young, and clothing took on an increasingly youthful look. Skirts rose above the knee in 1963 and a few years later climbed to mid-thigh. Women began to wear pants and trouser suits. Men and women both favored jeans and informal shirts and let their hair grow longer. Men broke away from the gray suits of the preceding decade and indulged themselves in bright colors in what has been called the "peacock revolution."

Look carefully at the pictures on these pages. They show fashions from different periods and can tell us a good deal about how these people defined themselves. Examine first the photo of the three black women from the 1920s. What kinds of adornments do you notice? What impression do these women convey?

Look at the photograph of Frances Perkins, secretary of labor in the 1930s. What kind of dress is she wearing? How do her clothes differ from those of the women in the 1920s? In the picture, she is talking to a number of working men. What do their clothes tell you about the kind of work they might be doing?

In the picture of two drill press operators during World War II, the women are dressed to handle the heavy machinery. Are their clothes different from those of the laborers in the preceding picture? How have the women accommodated themselves to their work, while still maintaining their individuality?

Now look at the picture of a woman in the 1950s. What kind of work might she do? What kind of flexibility do these clothes give her? What do the stylistic touches convey?

Finally, examine the photograph of the man and woman at an outdoor music festival in the 1960s. What does their clothing remind you of? Where might it come from? What impression are these people trying to create by their dress?

Countercultural dress in the 1960s. *(Ken Heyman)*

861

blonde hair, breathy voice, and raw sexuality, she personified the forbidden side of the good life and became one of Hollywood's most popular stars. The images of such film goddesses corresponded to male fantasies of women, visible in *Playboy* magazine, which first appeared in 1953 and soon achieved a huge readership. As for these men's wives, they were expected to manage their suburban homes and to be cheerful and willing objects of their husbands' desire.

Despite reaffirming the old ideology that a woman's place was in the home, the 1950s were years of unnoticed but important change. Because the supply of single women workers was diminished by the low birthrate of the Depression years and by increased schooling and early marriage, older married women continued the pattern begun during the war and entered the labor force in larger numbers than before. In 1940, only 15 percent of American wives had jobs. By 1950, 21 percent were employed, and ten years later, the figure had risen to 30 percent. Moreover, married women now accounted for more than half of all working women, a dramatic reversal of pre–World War II patterns. Although the media hailed those women who primarily tended to their families, some

Sex goddess Marilyn Monroe—shown here in a widely-distributed promotional photo for *The Seven Year Itch*—stirred the fantasies of American males in the 1950s. Despite the family orientation of suburban America, millions were captivated by her seductive appeal. *(Matthew Zimmerman/AP/World Wide Photos)*

magazine articles, in fact, did stress the achievements of women outside the home.

Although many working women were poor, divorced, or widowed, many others worked to acquire the desirable new products that were badges of middle-class status. They stepped into the new jobs created by economic expansion, clustering in office, sales, and service positions, occupations already defined as female. They and their employers considered their work subordinate to their primary role as wives and mothers. The conviction that women's main role was homemaking justified low wages and the denial of promotions. Comparatively few women entered professions where they would have challenged traditional notions of a woman's place. *Life* magazine, in 1956, reflected on the typical female employee: "Household skills take her into the garment trades; neat and personable, she becomes office worker and sales lady; patient and dexterous, she does well on competitive, detailed factory work; compassionate, she becomes teacher and nurse."

African American women worked as always but often lost the jobs they had held during the war. As the percentage of women in the Detroit automobile industry, for example, dropped from 25 to 7.5 in the immediate postwar period, black women who had held some of the jobs were the first to go. Bernice McCannon, an African American employee at a Virginia military base, observed, "I have always done domestic work for families. When war came, I made the same move many domestics did. I took a higher paying job in a government cafeteria as a junior baker. If domestic work offers a good living, I see no reason why most of us will not return to our old jobs. We will have no alternative." These jobs, however, did not pay well at all. In the 1950s, the employment picture improved somewhat. African American women succeeded both in moving into white-collar positions and in increasing their income. By 1960, more than a third of all black women held clerical, sales, service, or professional jobs. The income gap between white women and black women holding similar jobs dropped from about 50 percent in 1940 to about 30 percent in 1960.

Some of these patterns that dominated in the 1950s persisted in the next decade. By the middle of the 1960s, however, the roots of what became a powerful women's movement were visible. Women challenged stereotypical patterns of behavior and patterns of dress. They demanded and seized greater control over their own lives, in a story we will take up in much greater detail in Chapter 29.

Cultural Rebels

Not all Americans fit the 1950s stereotypes. Some were alienated from the culture and rebelled against its values. As young people struggled to meet the standards and expectations of their peers, they were intrigued by Holden Caulfield, the main figure in J. D. Salinger's popular novel *The Catcher in the Rye* (1951). Holden, a boarding school misfit, rebelled against the "phonies" around him who threatened his individuality and independence. Holden's ill-fated effort to preserve his own integrity in the face of pressures to conform aroused readers' sympathy and struck a resonant chord.

Writers of the so-called "beat generation" espoused unconventional values in their stories, poems, and "happenings." Challenging the apathy and conformity of the period, they stressed spontaneity and spirituality and claimed that intuition was more important than reason, Eastern mysticism more valuable than Western faith. The "beats" deliberately outraged respectability by sneering at materialism, flaunting unconventional sex lives, and smoking marijuana.

Their literary work reflected their approach to life. Finding conventional academic forms confining, they rejected them. Jack Kerouac typed his best-selling novel *On the Road* (1957), describing freewheeling trips across country, on a 250-foot roll of paper. Dispensing with conventional punctuation and paragraphing, the book was a song of praise to the free lifestyle the beats espoused.

Poet Allen Ginsberg, like Kerouac a Columbia University dropout, became equally well known for his poem "Howl." Written during a wild weekend in 1955 while Ginsberg was under the influence of drugs, the poem was a scathing critique of modern, mechanized culture and all its effects. Reading the poem to a group of poets in San Francisco, Ginsberg bobbed and wove as he communicated the electric rhythm of his verse. He became a celebrity when "Howl" appeared in print in 1956. The poem, which began with the line "I saw the best minds of my generation destroyed by madness, starving hysterical naked," developed into a cult piece, particularly after the police seized it on the grounds that it was obscene. When the work survived a court test, national acclaim followed for Ginsberg. He and the other beats furnished a model for rebellion in the 1960s, as the counterculture described in Chapter 29 became increasingly powerful.

The popularity of Salinger, Kerouac, and Ginsberg owed much to a revolution in book publishing and to the democratization of education that accompanied the program of GI educational benefits. More Americans than ever before acquired a taste for literature, and they found huge numbers of inexpensive books available because of the "paperback revolution." The paperback, introduced in 1939, dominated the book market after World War II. By 1965, readers could choose among some 25,000 titles, available in bookstores, supermarkets, drugstores, and airplane terminals, and they purchased these cheap volumes at the rate of nearly seven million copies per week.

The signs of cultural rebellion also appeared in popular music. Parents recoiled as their children flocked to hear a young Tennessee singer named Elvis Presley belt out rock and roll songs. Presley's sexy voice, gyrating hips, and other techniques borrowed from black singers made him the undisputed "king of rock and roll." A multimedia blitz of movies, television, and radio helped make songs like "Heartbreak Hotel," "Don't Be Cruel," and "Hound Dog" smash singles. Eighteen Presley hits sold more than a million copies in the last four years of the 1950s. His black leather jacket and ducktail haircut became standard dress for rebellious male teenagers. His music provided a pattern for rock musicians in the 1960s.

American painters, shucking off European influences that had shaped American artists for two centuries, also became a part of the cultural rebellion. Led by Jackson Pollock and the "New York school," some

Allen Ginsberg was one of the most influential "beats" who went out of his way to protest what he considered the stultifying patterns of American life. His poetry (and appearance in later years) challenged more conventional norms. *(Courtesy Mellon)*

Jackson Pollock often stood over the canvas and flung the paint around him as he moved across the painting in progress. Here he is shown in 1951 dripping the paint on the work that became *Autumn Rhythm. (Photo by Hans Namuth/ Courtesy, Center for Creative Photography, The University of Arizona. © 1991 Hans Namuth Estate)*

artists discarded the easel, laid gigantic canvases on the floor, and then used trowels, putty knives, and sticks to apply paint, glass shards, sand, and other materials in wild explosions of color. Known as abstract expressionists, these painters regarded the unconscious as the source of their artistic creations. "I am not aware of what is taking place [as I paint]," Pollock explained; "it is only after that I see what I have done." Like much of the literature of rebellion, abstract expressionism reflected the artist's alienation from a world becoming filled with nuclear threats, computerization, and materialism.

THE OTHER AMERICA

Not all Americans shared postwar middle-class affluence. Although most white Americans were barely conscious of poverty, it clearly existed in inner cities and rural areas. African Americans, uprooted from rural roots and transplanted into urban slums, were among the hardest hit. But members of other minority groups, as well as less fortunate whites, suffered similar dislocations, unknown to the middle class.

Poverty Amid Affluence

Many people in the "affluent society" lived in poverty. Economic growth favored the upper and middle classes. Although the popular "trickle-down" theory argued that economic expansion benefited all classes, little wealth, in fact, reached the citizens at the bottom. In 1960, according to the Federal Bureau of Labor Statistics, a yearly subsistence-level income for a family of four was $3,000 and for a family of six was $4,000. The bureau reported that 40 million people (almost a quarter of the population) lived below those levels, with nearly the same number only marginally above the line. Two million migrant workers labored long hours for a subsistence wage. Many less mobile people were hardly better off. According to the 1960 census, 27 percent of the residential units in the United States were substandard, and even acceptable dwellings were often hopelessly overcrowded in some slums.

Michael Harrington, socialist author and critic, shocked the country with his 1962 study, *The Other America.* The poor, Harrington showed, were everywhere. He described New York City's "economic underworld," where "Puerto Ricans and Negroes, alcoholics, drifters, and disturbed people" haunted employment agencies for temporary positions as "dishwashers and day workers, the fly-by-night jobs." In the afternoon, he continued, "the jobs have all been handed out, yet the people still mill around. Some of them sit on benches in the larger offices. There is no real point to their waiting, yet they have nothing else to do."

Harrington also described the conditions faced by the rural poor living in what songwriter Woody Guthrie had called in an earlier era the "pastures of plenty." Despite the prosperity that surrounded them, the mountain folk of Appalachia, the tenant farmers of Mississippi, and the migrant farmers of Florida, Texas, and California were all caught in poverty's relentless cycle.

Hard Times for African Americans

African Americans were among the postwar nation's least prosperous citizens. They had always known poverty. Now, however, most of them were concentrated in cities rather than on farms. In the South, agricultural workers continued to experience the transformation, mentioned earlier in this chapter, that had been under way for decades. New Deal farm legislation, the popularity of synthetic fabrics, and foreign competition robbed "King Cotton" of world markets. Mechanized cotton picking, first introduced in Mississippi in 1944, wiped out jobs in the Delta. As cotton farmers turned to less labor-intensive crops like soybeans and peanuts, they ousted their tenants, most of whom were African Americans.

The southern agricultural population declined dramatically, as millions of blacks moved to southern cities, where they found better jobs, better schooling, and freedom from landlords. Some achieved middle-class status; many more did not. They remained poor, with even less of a support system than they had known before.

Millions of African Americans also headed for northern cities in the years after 1940. In the 1950s, Detroit's black population increased from 16 to 29 percent, Chicago's from 14 to 23 percent. At one point in this decade, Chicago's black population rose by more than 2,200 people each week. The new arrivals congregated in urban slums, where the growth of facilities and social services failed to keep pace with population growth.

The black ghetto that had begun to develop earlier in the twentieth century became a permanent fixture in the post–World War II years. African Americans attempting to move elsewhere often found the way blocked. In 1951, a black couple purchasing a home in Cicero, Illinois, was driven away when an angry crowd broke the house's windows, defaced the walls, and shouted vile insults. This pattern was repeated throughout the postwar years around the country—in Birmingham, Chicago, Detroit, and countless other cities. Even passage in 1968 of the Fair Housing Act barring racial discrimination in the sale, rental, and financing of housing units failed to end this kind of residential segregation.

The experiences of African Americans in the cities often proved different from what they had expected. As author Claude Brown recalled, blacks were told that in the North, "Negroes lived in houses with bathrooms, electricity, running water, and indoor toilets.

While the 1950s were prosperous years for many Americans in suburban homes, others lived in poverty in urban tenements. Here an apartment building in Harlem rises high above the street, creating a much more crowded and congested community. *(Bruce Davidson/Magnum Photos, Inc.)*

To them, this was the 'promised land' that Mammy had been singing about in the cotton fields for many years." But no one had told them "about one of the most important aspects of the promised land: it was a slum ghetto. . . . There were too many people full of hate and bitterness crowded into a dirty, stinky, uncared-for closet-size section of a great city."

Novelist and essayist James Baldwin likewise described slum conditions and their corrosive effect on American blacks in his 1961 book *Nobody Knows My Name:*

> They work in the white man's world all day and come home in the evening to this fetid block. They struggle to instill in their children some private sense of honor or dignity, which will help the child to survive. This means, of course, that they must struggle, stolidly, incessantly, to keep this sense alive in themselves, in spite of the insults, the indifference, and the cruelty they are certain to encounter in their working day. They patiently browbeat the landlord into fixing the heat, the plaster, the plumbing; this demands prodigious patience, nor is patience usually enough. . . . Such frustration, so long endured, is driving many strong and admirable men and women whose only crime is color to the very gates of paranoia.

Such conditions, and the constant slights that accompanied segregation in both the North and the South, took a toll. African Americans learned how, in the words of a turn-of-the-century poem by Paul Laurence Dunbar, to "wear the mask." Employment opportunities had improved during World War II and later improved still further in the 1960s with the expansion of public programs that were part of the Great Society (see Chapter 28), but cutbacks in the 1970s, when the economy faltered, had a corrosive effect on the stability of African American family life. While the black family managed to hold together until the 1960s, with 70 percent of all units including both husband and wife, in the years that followed, this pattern changed. As a still-smoldering racism erupted into more violent confrontations and drugs became increasingly available, more black men found themselves in trouble with the law. Family stability began to crumble, until by 1983, 50 percent of all black children under 18 lived in households headed by women, and many of these suffered from oppressive poverty, from which there appeared to be no escape.

Still, the larger black community remained intact. Chicago's South Side neighborhood was a vibrant place, replacing New York's Harlem as black America's cultural capital in the 1950s. This section of the city included such figures as boxing champion Joe Louis, gospel singer Mahalia Jackson, and Representative William Dawson, the only African American member of Congress.

Here and elsewhere, the black church played an important role in sustaining African American life. Blacks moving into the cities retained churchgoing habits and commitment to religious institutions from their rural days. Older, established churches assisted newcomers in the transition to urban America, while new religious groups began to form, creating a sense of community for recent arrivals. The churches offered more than religious sustenance alone. Many provided day-care facilities, ran Boy Scout and Girl Scout troops, and sponsored a variety of other social services. These activities gave them a crucial place in the civil rights movement that began to flourish in these years (see Chapter 29).

The growth of the black urban population fostered businesses catering to the African American community. Black newspapers now provided a more regional, rather than a national, focus, but magazines such as *Jet*, a pocket-size weekly with a large countrywide circulation, filled the void. Black-owned and black-operated banks and other financial institutions increased in number.

Yet most African Americans remained second-class citizens. Escape from the slums was difficult for many, impossible for most. Persistent poverty was a dismal fact of life, even as the rest of the United States enjoyed prosperous times.

Minorities on the Fringe

Other groups had similar difficulties in the postwar United States. Latino immigrants from Cuba, Puerto Rico, Mexico, and Central America, often unskilled and illiterate, followed other less fortunate Americans to the cities. The conditions they encountered there were similar to those faced by blacks. Author Piri Thomas, born of Puerto Rican and Cuban parents in New York City's Spanish Harlem, described his neighborhood in his memoir *Down These Mean Streets:*

> Man! How many times have I stood on the
>   rooftop of my broken-down building at night
>   and watched the bulb-lit world below.
> Like somehow it's different at night, this my
>   Harlem.
> There ain't no bright sunlight to reveal the stark
>   naked truth of garbage-lepered streets.
> Gone is the drabness and hurt, covered by a
>   friendly night.
> It makes clean the dirty-faced kids.

In the face of recurring discrimination, these Spanish-speaking groups maintained a strong sense of group identity. The urban *barrios* where they settled preserved a sense of community and close-knit cohesive culture, even in the midst of pervasive poverty. The ties fostered in these communities provided a strong base on which a growing political consciousness could rest as it emerged in the next decade (see Chapter 29).

Chicanos, or Mexican Americans, were the most numerous of the newcomers and faced peculiar difficulties. During World War II, as the country experienced a labor shortage at home, American farmers sought Mexican *braceros* (helping hands) to harvest their crops. A program to encourage the seasonal immigration of farm workers continued after the war when the government signed a Migratory Labor Agreement with Mexico. Between 1948 and 1964, some 4.5 million Mexicans were brought to the United States for temporary work. *Braceros* were expected to return to Mexico at the end of their labor contract, but often they stayed. Joining them were millions more who entered the country illegally.

Conditions were harsh for the *braceros* in the best of times, but in periods of economic difficulty, troubles worsened. During a serious recession in 1953–1954, the government mounted Operation Wetback to deport illegal entrants and *braceros* who had remained in the country illegally and expelled 1.1 million. As immigration officials searched out illegal workers, all Chicanos found themselves vulnerable. They bitterly protested the violations of their rights, to little effect.

Operation Wetback did not end the reliance on poor Mexican farm laborers. A coalition of southern Democrats and conservative Republicans, mostly representing farm states, extended the Migratory Labor Agreement with Mexico, for the legislators wanted to continue to take advantage of the inordinately cheap labor. Two years after the massive deportations of 1954, a record 445,000 *braceros* crossed the border to work on American farms.

Puerto Ricans were numerous in other parts of the country. A steady stream of immigrants had been coming to New York from Puerto Rico since the 1920s. As the island's sugarcane economy became more mechanized, nearly 40 percent of the inhabitants left their homes. By the end of the 1960s, New York City had more Puerto Ricans than San Juan, the island's capital. El Barrio, in East Harlem, became the center of Puerto Rican activity, the home of *salsa* music and small *bodegas*, grocery stores that served the neighborhood. Author Guillermo Cotto-Thorner described the place fondly in his autobiographical novel, *Trópico en Manhattan*, through the words of Antonio, an older resident.

> This . . . is our neighborhood, El Barrio. . . . It's said that we Latins run things here. And that's how we see ourselves. While the American take most of the money that circulates around here, we consider this part of the city to be ours. . . . The stores, barbershops, restaurants, butcher shops, churches, funeral parlors, greasy spoons, pool halls, everything is all Latino. Every now and then you see a business run by a Jew or an Irishman or an Italian, but you'll also see that even these people know a little Spanish.

Mexicans who entered the United States illegally were often arrested and deported. The men in this picture, waiting in a border patrol jail at Calexico, California, in 1951, walked 50 miles across the desert without adequate food and water, only to be apprehended and sent back. *(Loomis Dean/LIFE Magazine © Time Inc.)*

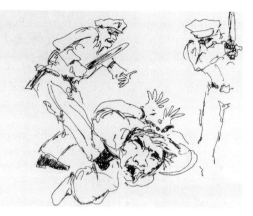

After returning home at the end of World War II, many Indian veterans found it difficult to fit into either Indian or white society. Alcoholism—which sometimes led to confrontations with the law—became a problem, as reflected in these sketches by Indian artist Aaron Yava, who drew what he saw in what he called the "border towns of the Navajo Nation." *(Aaron Yava/Courtesy of the family of Aaron Yava)*

Puerto Ricans, like many other immigrants, hoped to earn money in America and then return home. Some did; others stayed. Like countless Latinos, most failed to enjoy the promise of the American dream.

Native Americans likewise remained outsiders in the postwar years. They faced the consequences of the same technological developments affecting other Americans but often had greater difficulty coping with the changes they faced, given the persistent discrimination they had experienced for generations. As power lines reached their reservations, Indians purchased televisions, refrigerators, washing machines, and automobiles. As they partook of the consumer culture, old patterns inevitably changed. Reservation life lost its cohesiveness, and alcohol became a major problem. With good jobs unavailable on the reservations, more and more Indians gravitated to the cities. Bennie Bearskin, a Winnebago, left home for Chicago in 1947, explaining: "The most important reason was that I could at least feel confident that [I could get] perhaps fifty paychecks a year here. . . . Even though it might be more pleasant to be back home, for instance, Nebraska." But Indians who moved to the cities often had difficulty adjusting to urban life and faced hostility from white Americans, much like that experienced by Latinos and blacks. They too began to protest in a movement that gained strength in succeeding years (see Chapter 29).

Timeline

1946	4.6 million workers on strike
	ENIAC computer built
	Benjamin Spock, *Baby and Child Care*
1947	Defense budget of $13 billion
1948	GM offers UAW cost-of-living adjustment
	Transistor developed at Bell Laboratories
	Kinsey report on male sexuality
1950s	Each year a million farmers leave farms
1950	Diner's Card inaugurated
1951	J. D. Salinger, *The Catcher in the Rye*
1953	Defense budget of $47 billion
	Operation Wetback begins
1954	Congress adds "under God" to pledge to flag
1955	First McDonald's opens in Illinois
	Merger of AFL and CIO
	Congress adds "In God We Trust" to currency

1956	Interstate Highway Act
	Majority of U.S. workers hold white-collar jobs
	Allen Ginsberg, "Howl"
1957	Baby boom peaks
	Vance Packard, *The Hidden Persuaders*
	Jack Kerouac's *On the Road*
1960	Three-quarters of all Americans own a TV set
1962	Michael Harrington, *The Other America*
1963	California passes New York as most populous state
	Betty Friedan, *The Feminine Mystique*
1964	Peter Blake, *God's Own Junkyard*
1970	38 percent of all Americans live in suburbs

Conclusion

Qualms Amid Affluence

In general, the United States during the decade and a half after World War II was stable and secure. Structural adjustments caused occasional moments of friction but were seldom visible in prosperous times. Recessions occurred periodically, but the economy righted itself after short downturns. For the most part, business boomed. The standard of living for many of the nation's citizens reached new heights, especially compared with standards in other parts of the world. Millions of middle-class Americans joined the ranks of suburban property owners, enjoying the benefits of shopping centers, fast-food establishments, and other material manifestations of what they considered the good life. Workers found themselves savoring the materialistic advantages of the era.

Some Americans did not share in the prosperity, but they were not visible in the affluent suburbs. Many African Americans and members of other minority groups were seriously disadvantaged, although they still believed they could share in the American dream and remained confident that deeply rooted patterns of discrimination could be changed. Even when they began to mobilize, their protest was peaceful at first.

Beneath the calm surface, though, there were signs of discontent. The seeds for the protest movements of the 1960s had already been sown. Disquieting signs were likewise evident on other fronts. The divorce rate increased, as a third of all marriages in the 1950s broke apart. Americans increasingly used newly developed tranquilizers in an effort to cope with problems in their lives. Some Americans began to criticize the materialism that seemed to undermine American efforts in the Cold War. Such criticisms in turn legitimized challenges by other groups, in the continuing struggle to make the realities of American life match the nation's ideals.

Criticisms and anxieties notwithstanding, the United States—for most whites and some people of color—continued to develop according to Ray Kroc's dreams as he first envisioned McDonald's establishments across the land. Healthy and comfortable, upper- and middle-class Americans expected prosperity and growth to continue in the years ahead.

Recommended Reading

Economic Boom

American Social History Project, *Who Built America? Working People & the Nation's Economy, Politics, Culture, and Society* (1992); David Brody, *Workers in Industrial America* (1980); James R. Green, *The World of the Worker* (1980); Jacqueline Jones, *American Work: Four Centuries of Black and White Labor* (1998); Juliet B. Schor, *The Overworked American: The Unexpected Decline of Leisure* (1991); Robert H. Zieger, *American Workers, American Unions*, 2nd ed. (1994) and *The CIO, 1935–1955* (1995).

Demographic and Technological Trends

Peter Blake, *God's Own Junkyard: The Planned Deterioration of America's Landscape* (1964); Paul A. Carter, *Another Part of the Fifties* (1983); David Halberstam, *The Fifties* (1993); Samuel P. Hays, *Beauty, Health, and Permanence: Environmental Politics in the United States, 1955–1985* (1987); Daniel Horowitz, ed., *American Social Classes in the 1950s: Selections from Vance Packard's* The Status Seekers (1995); Kenneth T. Jackson, *Crabgrass Frontier: The Suburbanization of the United States* (1985); Zane L. Miller, *The Urbanization of Modern America* (1973); Richard Polenberg, *One Nation Divisible: Class, Race, and Ethnicity in the United States Since 1938* (1980); Richard White, *"It's Your Misfortune and None of My Own": A History of the American West* (1991).

Consensus and Conformity

General Works.   Joel Foreman, ed., *The Other Fifties: Interrogating Midcentury American Icons* (1997); James Howard Jones, *Alfred C. Kinsey: A Public/Private Life* (1997); Alison Lurie, *The Language of Clothes* (1981); C. Wright Mills, *White Collar: The American Middle Classes* (1951); David Riesman, *The Lonely Crowd: A Study of the Changing American Character* (1950).

Religious Developments.   David Chidester, *Patterns of Power: Religion and Politics in American Culture* (1988); Erling Jorstad, *Holding Fast/Pressing On: Religion in America in the 1980s* (1990); R. Laurence Moore, *Selling God: American Religion in the Marketplace of Culture* (1994); Peter W. Williams, *Popular Religion in America: Symbolic Change and the Modernization Process in Historical Perspective* (1980); Garry Wills, *Under God: Religion and American Politics* (1990).

Traditional Roles for Women.   Beth L. Bailey, *From Front Porch to Back Seat: Courtship in Twentieth-Century America* (1988); William H. Chafe, *The American Woman: Her Changing Social, Economic, and Political Roles, 1920–1970* (1972); Stephanie Coontz, *The Way We Never Were: American Families and the Nostalgia Trap* (1992); John D'Emilio and Estelle B. Freedman, *Intimate Matters: A History of Sexuality in America* (1988); Sara Evans, *Born for Liberty: A History of Women in America* (1989); Betty Friedan, *The Feminine Mystique* (1963); Susan M. Hartmann, *The Home Front and Beyond: American Women in the 1940s* (1982); Judith A. Hennessee, *Betty Friedan: Her Life* (1999); Daniel Horowitz, *Betty Friedan and the Making of* The Feminine Mystique: *The American Left, the Cold War and*

Modern Feminism (1998); Eugenia Kaledin, *Mothers and More: American Women in the 1950s* (1984); Elaine Tyler May, *Homeward Bound: American Families in the Cold War Era* (1988); Joanne Meyerowitz, ed., *Not June Cleaver: Women and Gender in Postwar America, 1945–1960* (1994); Gloria Steinem, *Outrageous Acts and Everyday Rebellions*, 2nd ed. (1995).

The Other America

General Works.   Michael Harrington, *The Other America: Poverty in the United States* (1962); James T. Patterson, *America's Struggle Against Poverty, 1900–1994* (1994).

African Americans.   James Baldwin, *Nobody Knows My Name* (1961); Claude Brown, *Manchild in the Promised Land* (1965); Darlene Clark Hine and Kathleen Thompson, *A Shining Thread of Hope: The History of Black Women in America* (1998); Jacqueline Jones, *Labor of Love, Labor of Sorrow: Black Women, Work, and the Family from Slavery to the Present* (1985); Carole Marks, *Farewell, We're Good and Gone: The Great Black Migration* (1989).

Latinos.   Rodolfo Acuña, *Occupied America: A History of Chicanos*, 4th ed. (2000); George J. Sánchez, *Becoming Mexican American: Ethnicity, Culture and Identity in Chicano Los Angeles, 1900–1945* (1993); Peter Skerry, *Mexican Americans: The Ambivalent Minority* (1993); Ronald Takaki, *A Different Mirror: A History of Multicultural America* (1993) and *A Larger Memory: A History of Our Diversity, with Voices* (1998); Piri Thomas, *Down These Mean Streets* (1967).

Native Americans.   Frederick E. Hoxie, ed., *Indians in American History* (1988); Peter Iverson, *"We Are Still Here": American Indians in the Twentieth Century* (1998); Alvin M. Josephy, Jr., *Now That the Buffalo's Gone* (1982); James S. Olson and Raymond Wilson, *Native Americans in the Twentieth Century* (1986).

Fiction and Film

Allen Ginsberg's *Howl and Other Poems* (1956) is a collection of iconoclastic poetry challenging the materialism of contemporary life. Jack Kerouac's *On the Road* (1957) is a stream-of-consciousness novel that questions the values of the 1950s. Arthur Miller's *Death of a Salesman* (1949) is the Pulitzer Prize–winning play about the shallow values of postwar American culture. J. D. Salinger's *Catcher in the Rye* is the story of Holden Caulfield, a troubled adolescent who is overwhelmed by the phoniness of contemporary life (1951). Sloan Wilson's *The Man in the Gray Flannel Suit* (1955) is a novel challenging the conformity of corporate America in the 1950s.

The *Best Years of Our Lives* (1946), a film that tells the story of three servicemen returning home after World War II, captures the values of the immediate postwar era. *The Seven Year Itch* (1955) features Marilyn Monroe as the beautiful and enticing girl next door. *The Man in the Gray Flannel Suit* (1956), a film made from the novel of the same name, critiques the lifestyle of corporate America in the 1950s.

Suggested Web Sites

http://www.fiftiesweb.com/

Fifties Website Home Page. This entertaining site tells about and samples music and television from the 1950s. It also includes a related links page.

http://www.uic.edu/~pbhales/Levittown/

Levittown: Documents of an Ideal American Suburb. The postwar boom in housing made suburban living the cultural norm in America and shaped a generation. The story of the classic suburb, Levittown, is told on this site in pictures and text.

http://vmoc.i.am/

Virtual Museum of Computing. This site relates the history of computing through a series of on-line exhibits.

http://www.ipl.org/ref/POTUS/hstruman.html

Harry S Truman. This site contains basic factual data about Truman's election and presidency, speeches, and on-line biographies.

http://www.trumanlibrary.org

Harry S Truman Library & Museum. This presidential library site has numerous photos and various important primary documents relating to Truman.

http://www.ipl.org/ref/POTUS/ddeisenhower.html

Dwight David Eisenhower. This site contains basic factual data about Eisenhower's election and presidency, including speeches and other materials.

http://www.eisenhower.utexas.edu/

The Dwight D. Eisenhower Library and Museum. This site contains mainly photos of the presidents.

http://www.ushistoryplace.com

A richly detailed on-line learning environment complete with interactive maps, timelines, history activities, primary source documents, and links to related American history sites.

CHILLS *and* FEVER DURING *the* COLD WAR

In November 1950, Val Lorwin learned of the charges against him. A State Department employee, on leave of absence after 16 years of government service, he was in Paris working on a book. Now he had to return to the United States to defend himself against the accusation that he was a member of the Communist party and thus a loyalty and security risk. It seemed to him a tasteless joke. Yet Communism was no laughing matter in the United States. Suspicions of the Soviet Union had escalated after 1945, and a wave of paranoia swept through the United States.

Lorwin was an unlikely candidate to be caught up in the fallout of the Cold War. He had begun to work for the government in 1935, serving in a number of New Deal agencies, then in the Labor Department and on the War Production Board before he was drafted during World War II. While in the army, he was assigned to the Office of Strategic Services, an early intelligence agency, and he was frequently granted security clearances in the United States and abroad.

Lorwin, however, did have a left-wing past as an active Socialist in the 1930s. His social life then had revolved around Socialist party causes, particularly the unionization of southern tenant farmers and the provision of aid to the unemployed. He and his wife, Madge, drafted statements and stuffed envelopes to support their goals. But that activity was wholly open and legal, and Lorwin had from the start been aggressively anti-Communist in political affairs.

Suddenly, Lorwin, like others in the period, faced a nightmare. Despite his spotless record, Lorwin was told that an unnamed accuser had identified him as a Communist. The burden of proof was entirely on him, and the chance of clearing his name was slim. He was entitled to a hearing if he chose, or he could resign.

Lorwin requested a hearing, held late in 1950. Still struck by the absurdity of the situation, he refuted all accusations but made little effort to cite his own positive achievements. At the conclusion, he was informed that the government no longer doubted his loyalty but considered him a security risk, likewise grounds for dismissal from his job.

When he appealed the judgment, Lorwin was again denied access to the identity of his accuser.

The Cold War created a climate of confrontation between East and West and led to wars in Korea and Vietnam that left millions of people injured or dead. (*Edward Keinholz,* O'er the Ramparts We Watched Fascinated/*Courtesy of L.A. Louver Gallery, Venice, CA*)

This time, however, he thoroughly prepared his defense. At the hearing, a total of 97 witnesses either spoke under oath on Lorwin's behalf or left sworn written depositions testifying to his good character and meritorious service.

The issues in the hearings might have been considered comic in view of Lorwin's record, had not a man's reputation been at stake. The accuser had once lived with the Lorwins in Washington, D.C. Fifteen years later, he claimed that in 1935 Lorwin had revealed that he was holding a Communist party meeting in his home and had even shown him a party card.

Lorwin proved all the charges groundless. He also showed that in 1935 the Socialist party card was red, the color the accuser reported seeing, while the Communist party card was black. In March 1952, Lorwin was finally cleared for both loyalty and security.

Lorwin's troubles were not yet over. His name appeared on one of the lists produced by Senator Joseph McCarthy of Wisconsin, the most aggressive anti-Communist of the era, and Lorwin was again victimized. The next year, he was indicted for making false statements to the State Department Loyalty-Security Board. The charges this time proved as specious as before. Finally, in May 1954, admitting that its special prosecutor had deliberately lied to the grand jury and had no legitimate case, the Justice Department asked for dismissal of the indictment. Cleared at last, Lorwin went on to become a distinguished labor historian.

Lorwin was more fortunate than some victims of the anti-Communist crusade. People rallied around him and gave him valuable support. Despite considerable emotional cost, he survived the witch-hunt of the early 1950s, but his case still reflected vividly the ugly domestic consequences of the breakdown in relations between the Soviet Union and the United States.

The Cold War, which unfolded soon after the end of World War II and lasted for nearly 50 years, powerfully affected all aspects of American life. Rejecting for good the isolationist impulse that had governed foreign policy in the 1920s and 1930s, the United States began to play a major role in the world in the postwar years. Doubts about intervention in other lands faded as the nation acknowledged its dominant international position and resolved to do whatever was necessary to maintain it. The same sense of mission that had infused the United States in the

Spanish-American War, World War I, and World War II now committed most Americans to the struggle against Communism at home and abroad.

This chapter explores that continuing sense of mission and its consequences. It examines the roots of the Cold War both in the idealistic aim to keep the world safe for democracy and in the pursuit of economic self-interest that had long fueled American capitalism. It records how the determination to prevent the spread of Communism led American policymakers to consider vast parts of the world as pivotal to American security and to act accordingly, particularly in Korea and Vietnam. It notes the impact on economic development, particularly in the West, where the mighty defense industry flourished. And it considers the tragic consequences of the effort to promote ideological unity within the United States, where excesses threatened the principles of democracy itself.

✍ ORIGINS OF THE COLD WAR

The Cold War developed by degrees. It stemmed from divergent views about the shape of the post–World War II world as the colonial empires in Asia, Africa, and the Middle East began to crumble. The United States, strong and secure, was intent on spreading its vision of freedom and free trade around the world to maintain its economic hegemony. The Soviet Union, concerned about security after a devastating war, demanded politically sympathetic neighbors on its borders to preserve its own autonomy. Suppressed during World War II, these differences now surfaced in a Soviet–American confrontation. As tensions rose, the two nations behaved, according to Senator J. William Fulbright, "like two big dogs, chewing on a bone."

The American Stance

The United States emerged from World War II more powerful than any nation ever before, and it sought to use that might to achieve a world order that could sustain American aims. American policymakers, following in Woodrow Wilson's footsteps, hoped to spread the values—liberty, equality, and democracy—underpinning the American dream. They assumed that they could furnish the stability that postwar reconstruction required. They did not always recognize that what they considered universal truths were rooted in specific historical circumstances in their own country and might not flourish elsewhere.

At the same time, American leaders sought a world where economic enterprise could thrive. Recollections of the Depression decade haunted leaders. With the American economy operating at full speed as a result of the war, world markets were needed once the fighting stopped. Government officials wanted to eliminate trade barriers—imposed by the Soviet Union and other nations—to provide outlets for industrial products and for surplus farm commodities such as wheat, cotton, and tobacco. As the largest source of goods for world markets, with exports totaling $14 billion in 1947, the United States required open channels for growth to continue. Americans assumed that their prosperity would benefit the rest of the world, even when other nations disagreed.

Soviet Aims

The Soviet Union formulated its own goals after World War II. Russia had usually been governed in the past by a strongly centralized, sometimes autocratic, government, and that tradition—as much as Communist ideology, with its stress on class struggle and the inevitable triumph of a proletarian state—guided Soviet policy.

During the war, the Russians had played down talk of world revolution, which they knew their allies found threatening, and had mobilized domestic support with nationalistic appeals. As the struggle drew to a close, the Soviets still said little about world conquest, emphasizing socialism within the nation itself.

Rebuilding was the first priority. Devastated by the war, Soviet agriculture and industry lay in shambles. But revival required internal security. At the same time, the Russians felt vulnerable along their western flank. Such anxieties had a historical basis, for in the early nineteenth century, Napoleon had reached the gates of Moscow. Twice in the twentieth century, invasions had come from the west, most recently when Hitler had attacked in 1941. Haunted by fears of a quick German recovery, the Soviets demanded defensible borders and neighboring regimes sympathetic to Russian aims. They insisted on military and political stability in the regions closest to them.

Early Cold War Leadership

Both the United States and the Soviet Union had strong leadership in the early years of the Cold War. On the American side, presidents Harry Truman and Dwight Eisenhower accepted the centralization of authority Franklin Roosevelt had begun, as the executive branch became increasingly powerful in guiding foreign policy. In the Soviet Union, first Joseph Stalin, then Nikita Khrushchev provided equally forceful direction.

Harry S Truman, America's first postwar president, was an unpretentious man who took a straightforward approach to public affairs. He was, however, ill prepared for the office he assumed in the final months of World War II. His three months as vice president had done little to school him in the complexity of postwar issues. Nor had Franklin Roosevelt confided in Truman. No wonder that the new president felt insecure. To a former colleague in the Senate, he groaned, "I'm not big enough for this job." Critics agreed.

Yet Truman matured rapidly. Impulsive and aggressive, he made a virtue out of rapid response. At his first press conference, reporters could not keep up with his quick replies. A sign on the president's White House desk read "The Buck Stops Here," and he was willing to make quick decisions on issues, even though associates sometimes wondered if he understood all the implications. His rapid-fire decisions had important consequences for the Cold War.

Truman served virtually all of the term to which Roosevelt had been elected in 1944, then won another for himself in 1948. In 1952, war hero Dwight D. Eisenhower, affectionately known as Ike, won the presidency for the Republican party for the first time in 20 years.

Eisenhower stood in stark contrast to Truman. His easy manner and warm smile made him widely popular. As British Field Marshall Bernard Montgomery observed, "He has the power of drawing the hearts of men towards him as a magnet attracts bits of metal."

On occasion, in press conferences or other public gatherings, he gave convoluted and imprecise comments. Yet beneath his casual approach lay real shrewdness. "Don't worry," he once assured his aides briefing him for a press conference, "If that question comes up, I'll just confuse them."

Eisenhower had not taken the typical route to the presidency. After World War II, he served successively as army chief of staff, president of Columbia University, and head of the North Atlantic Treaty Organization (NATO). Despite his lack of formal political background, he had a genuine ability to get people to compromise and work together. Though he remained aloof from party politics, he may have entertained hopes of holding office after the war. General George Patton commented in 1943 that "Ike wants to be President so badly you can taste it," yet Eisenhower made no move in that direction until he sought the Republican nomination in 1952.

Ike's limited experience with everyday politics conditioned his sense of the presidential role. Whereas Truman loved political infighting and wanted to take charge, Eisenhower saw things differently. The presidency for him was no "bully pulpit," as it had been for Theodore Roosevelt and even FDR. "I am not one of those desk-pounding types that likes to stick out his jaw and look like he is bossing the show," he said. "You do not lead by hitting people over the head. Any damn fool can do that, but it's usually called 'assault'—not 'leadership.'" Even so, Ike knew exactly where he

Harry Truman was a simple, unassuming man who became a strong and decisive president when he moved into the White House. Here he is shown in his office with the famous sign "The Buck Stops Here" that sat on his desk and characterized his approach to the presidency. *(Harry S Truman Library)*

Dwight Eisenhower provided a reassuring presence in the White House in the 1950s. His wide smile made Americans feel good about themselves and their country and conveyed the message that everything was going to be all right. *(National Park Service)*

wanted to go and worked behind the scenes to get there.

Though the personal styles of Truman and Eisenhower differed, they both subscribed to traditional American attitudes about self-determination and the superiority of American political institutions and values. Viewing collaboration with the Soviet Union during World War II as a wartime necessity, Truman grew increasingly hostile to Soviet moves as the war neared its end. It was now time, he said, "to stand up to the Russians." Like Truman, Eisenhower saw Communism as a monolithic force struggling for world supremacy and agreed that the Kremlin in Moscow was orchestrating subversive activity around the globe. Like Truman, he saw issues in black and white terms and regarded the Soviet system as a "tyranny that has brought thousands, millions of people into slave camps and is attempting to make all mankind its chattel." Yet Eisenhower was more willing than Truman to practice accommodation when it served his ends.

The Soviet leader at war's end, Joseph Stalin, possessed almost absolute powers. He had presided over ruthless purges against his opponents in the 1930s. Now he was determined to do whatever was necessary to rebuild Soviet society, if possible with Western assistance, and to keep eastern Europe within the Russian sphere of influence.

Stalin's death in March 1953 left a power vacuum in Soviet political affairs that was eventually filled by Nikita Khrushchev, who by 1958 held the offices of both prime minister and party secretary. A crude man, Khrushchev once used his shoe to pound a table at the United Nations while the British prime minister was speaking. During Krushchev's regime, the Cold War continued, but in brief periods Soviet–American relations became less hostile.

Disillusionment with the USSR

American support for the Soviet Union faded quickly after the war. In September 1945, more than half (54 percent) of a national sample trusted the Russians to cooperate with the Americans in the postwar years. Two months later, the figure had dropped to 44 percent, and by February 1946, to 35 percent.

As Americans soured on Russia, they began to equate the Nazi and Soviet systems. Just as they had in the 1930s, authors, journalists, and public officials pointed to similarities, some of them legitimate, between the regimes. Both states, they contended, maintained total control over communications and could eliminate political opposition whenever they chose. Both states used terror to silence dissidents, and Stalin's labor camps in Siberia could be compared with Hitler's concentration camps. After the U.S. publication in 1949 of George Orwell's frightening novel *1984, Life* magazine noted in an editorial that the ominous figure Big Brother was but a "mating" of Hitler and Stalin. Truman spoke for many Americans when he said in 1950 that "there isn't any difference between the totalitarian Russian government and the Hitler government. . . . They are all alike. They are . . . police state governments."

The lingering sense that the nation had not been quick enough to resist totalitarian aggression in the 1930s heightened American fears. Had the United

Joseph Stalin's autocratic approach to foreign and domestic affairs affronted American sensibilities. Here, in this Soviet propaganda poster, the Russian caption reads: "Under the Leadership of the Great Stalin—Forward to Communism!" *(Hoover Institution Archives, Stanford, CA Russian & Soviet Poster Collection)*

Soviet leader Nikita Khrushchev was an aggressive leader who sometimes spoke out belligerently in defense of his country's interests. Here he appears at the podium at the United Nations delivering a speech. *(Archive Photos)*

States stopped the Germans, Italians, or Japanese, it might have prevented the long, devastating war. The free world had not responded quickly enough before and was determined never to repeat the same mistake.

The Troublesome Polish Question

The first clash between East and West came, even before the war ended, over Poland. Soviet demands for a government willing to accept Russian influence clashed with American hopes for a more representative structure patterned after the Western model. The Yalta Conference of February 1945 attempted to resolve the issue (see Chapter 25) with a loosely worded and correspondingly imprecise agreement. When Truman assumed office, the Polish situation remained unresolved. Averell Harriman, the U.S. ambassador to the Soviet Union, warned that the United States faced a "barbarian invasion of Europe" unless the Soviets could be checked and Western-style democracies established. The president agreed.

Truman's unbending stance was clear in an April 1945 meeting with Soviet foreign minister Vyacheslav Molotov on the question of Poland. Concerned that the Russians were breaking the Yalta agreements, imprecise as they were, the American leader demanded a new democratic government there. Though Molotov appeared conciliatory, Truman insisted on Russian acquiescence. Truman later recalled that when Molotov protested, "I have never been talked to like that in my life," he himself retorted bluntly, "Carry out your agreements and you won't get talked to like that." Such bluntness contributed to the deterioration of Soviet–American relations.

Truman and Stalin met face-to-face for the first (and last) time at the Potsdam Conference in July 1945, the final wartime Big Three meeting of the United States, the Soviet Union, and Great Britain. There, outside devastated Berlin, the two leaders sized each other up as they considered the Russian–Polish boundary, the fate of Germany, and the American

CONFLICTING AIMS DURING THE COLD WAR	
United States	**Soviet Union**
Spread ideological values of liberty, equality, democracy	Spread ideological values of class struggle, triumph of the proletariat
Extend the tradition of representative government	Extend the tradition of strong centralized government
Maintain stability around the world	Support revolutionary movements around the world
Fill vacuum created by the end of imperialism with regimes sympathetic to Western ideals	Support regimes sympathetic to the Soviet Union, particularly to avoid attack on its western flank
Maintain a world free for economic enterprise by eliminating trade barriers, providing markets for American exports	Rebuild the devastated Soviet economy by creating preferential trading arrangements in the region of Soviet dominance

desire to obtain an unconditional surrender from Japan. It was Truman's first exposure to international diplomacy at the highest level, and it left him confident of his abilities. When he learned during the meeting of the first successful atomic bomb test in New Mexico, he became even more determined to insist on his positions.

Economic Pressure on the USSR

One major source of controversy in the last stages of World War II was the question of U.S. aid to its allies. Responding to congressional pressure at home to limit foreign assistance as hostilities ended, Truman acted impulsively. Six days after V-E Day signaled the end of the European war in May 1945, he issued an executive order cutting off lend-lease supplies to the Allies. Though the policy affected all nations receiving aid, it hurt the Soviet Union most of all.

The United States intended to use economic pressure in other ways as well. The USSR desperately needed financial assistance to rebuild after the war and, in January 1945, had requested a $6 billion loan. Roosevelt hedged, hoping to win concessions in return. In August, four months after FDR's death, the Russians renewed their application, this time for only $1 billion. Truman dragged his heels, seeking to use the loan as a lever to gain access to markets in areas traditionally dominated by the Soviet Union. The United States first claimed to have lost the Soviet request, then in March 1946 indicated a willingness to consider the matter—but only if Russia pledged "nondiscrimination in world commerce." Stalin refused the offer and launched his own five-year plan instead.

Declaring the Cold War

As Soviet–American relations deteriorated, both sides stepped up their rhetorical attacks. In 1946, Stalin spoke out first, arguing that capitalism and communism were on a collision course, that a series of cataclysmic disturbances would tear the capitalist world apart, and that the Soviet system would triumph. Stalin's speech was a stark and ominous statement that worried the West. Supreme Court Justice William O. Douglas called it the "declaration of World War III."

The response to Stalin's speech came not from an American but from England's former prime minister, Winston Churchill, long suspicious of the Soviet state. Speaking in Fulton, Missouri, in 1946, with Truman on the platform during the address, Churchill declared that "from Stettin in the Baltic to Trieste in the Adriatic, an iron curtain has descended across the Continent." To counter the threat, he urged that a vigilant association of English-speaking peoples work to contain Soviet designs.

CONTAINING THE SOVIET UNION

Containment formed the basis of postwar American policy. Both Democrats and Republicans were determined to check Soviet expansion. In an increasingly contentious world, the American government formulated rigid anti-Soviet policies. The Soviet Union responded in an equally uncompromising way.

Containment Defined

George F. Kennan, chargé d'affaires at the American embassy in the Soviet Union and an expert on Soviet matters, was primarily responsible for defining the new policy. After Stalin's speech in February 1946, Kennan sent an 8,000-word telegram to the State Department. In it he argued that Soviet hostility stemmed from the "Kremlin's neurotic view of world affairs," which in turn came from the "traditional and instinctive Russian sense of insecurity." The stiff Soviet stance was not so much a response to American actions as a reflection of the Russian leaders' own efforts to maintain their autocratic rule. Russian fanaticism would not soften, regardless of how accommodating American policy became. Therefore, it had to be opposed at every turn.

Kennan's "long telegram" struck a resonant chord in Washington. It made his diplomatic reputation and brought him into an influential position in the State Department. Soon he published an extended analysis, under the pseudonym "Mr. X," in the influential journal *Foreign Affairs*. "The whole Soviet governmental machine, including the mechanism of diplomacy," he wrote, "moves inexorably along the prescribed path, like a persistent toy automobile wound up and headed in a given direction, stopping only when it meets with some unanswerable force." Many Americans agreed with Kennan that Soviet pressure had to "be contained by the adroit and vigilant application of counter-force at a series of constantly shifting geographical and political points."

The concept of containment provided the philosophical justification for the hard-line stance that Americans, both in and out of government, adopted. Containment created the framework for military and economic assistance around the globe.

The First Step: The Truman Doctrine

The Truman Doctrine represented the first major application of containment policy. The new policy was devised to respond to conditions in the eastern Mediterranean, an area that Americans had never before considered vital to their national security. The Soviet Union was pressuring Turkey for joint control of the Dardanelles, the passage between the Black Sea and the Mediterranean. Meanwhile, a civil war in

Americans in the early postwar years were afraid that Communism was a contagious disease spreading around the globe. In this picture from the spring of 1946, *Time* magazine pictured the relentless spread of an infection that would need to be contained. (© *1946 TIME Magazine. Reprinted by permission.*)

Greece pitted Communist elements against the ruling English-aided right-wing monarchy. Revolutionary pressures threatened to topple the government.

In February 1947, the British ambassador to the United States informed the State Department that his exhausted country could no longer give Greece and Turkey economic and military aid. Would the United States now move into the void?

Administration officials, who were willing to move forward, knew they needed bipartisan support to accomplish such a major policy shift. A conservative Congress wanted smaller budgets and lower taxes rather than massive and expensive aid programs. Senator Arthur Vandenberg of Michigan, a key Republican, warned that the top policymakers had to begin "scaring hell out of the country" if they were serious about a bold new containment policy.

Undersecretary of State Dean Acheson took the lead. Meeting with congressional leaders, he declared that "like apples in a barrel infected by one rotten one, the corruption of Greece would infect Iran and all to the east." He warned ominously that a Communist victory would "open three continents to Soviet penetration." The major powers were now "met at Armageddon," as the Soviet Union pressed forward. Only the United States had the power to resist.

Truman likewise played on the Soviet threat. On March 12, 1947, he told Congress, in a statement that came to be known as the Truman Doctrine, "I believe that it must be the policy of the United States to support free peoples who are resisting subjugation by armed minorities or by outside pressures." Unless the United States acted, the free world might not survive. "If we falter in our leadership," Truman said, "we may endanger the peace of the world—and we shall surely endanger the welfare of our own Nation." To avert that calamity, he urged Congress to appropriate $400 million for military and economic aid to Turkey and Greece.

Not everyone approved of Truman's request or of his overblown description of the situation. Autocratic regimes controlled Greece and Turkey, some observers pointed out. And where was the proof that Stalin had a hand in the Greek conflict? Others warned that the United States could not by itself stop encroachment in all parts of the world. Nonetheless, Congress passed Truman's foreign aid bill.

In assuming that Americans could police the globe, the Truman Doctrine was a major step in the advent of the Cold War. Truman's address, observed financier Bernard Baruch, "was tantamount to a declaration of . . . an ideological or religious war." Journalist Walter Lippmann was more critical. He termed the new containment policy a "strategic monstrosity" that could embroil the United States in disputes around the world. In the two succeeding decades, Lippmann proved correct.

The Next Steps: The Marshall Plan, NATO, and NSC-68

The next step for American policymakers involved sending extensive economic aid for postwar recovery in Western Europe. At the war's end, most of Europe was economically and politically unstable, thereby offering opportunities to the Communist movement. In France and Italy, large Communist parties grew stronger and refused to cooperate with established governments. In such circumstances, administration officials believed, the Soviet Union might easily intervene. Decisive action was needed, for as the new secretary of state, George Marshall, declared, "The patient is sinking while the doctors deliberate." Another motive for action was to bolster the European economy to provide markets for American goods. Excellent customers earlier, Western Europeans in the aftermath of the war were able to purchase less at a time when the United States was producing much more.

Marshall revealed the administration's willingness to assist European recovery in June 1947. He asked all troubled European nations to draw up an aid program that the United States could support, a program "directed not against any country or doctrine but against hunger, poverty, desperation, and chaos." Soviet-bloc countries were welcome to participate, Marshall announced, aware that their involvement was unlikely since they would have to disclose economic records to join, and Communist nations maintained rigorous secrecy about their internal affairs.

The proposed program would assist the ravaged nations, provide the United States with needed markets, and advance the nation's ideological aims. American aid, Marshall pointed out, would permit the "emergence of political and social conditions in which free institutions can exist." The Marshall Plan and the Truman Doctrine, Truman noted, were "two halves of the same walnut."

Responding quickly to Marshall's invitation, the Western European nations worked out the details of massive requests. In early 1948, Congress committed $17 billion over a period of four years to 16 cooperating nations. Not all Americans supported the Marshall Plan. Henry A. Wallace, former vice president and sec-retary of agriculture, who had broken with the administration, called the scheme the "Martial Plan" and argued that it was another step toward war. Some members of Congress feared spreading American resources too thin. But most legislators approved, and the containment policy moved forward another step.

Closely related to the Marshall Plan was a concerted Western effort to integrate a rebuilt Germany into a reviving Europe. At Yalta, Allied leaders had agreed to divide Germany into four occupation zones (Soviet, American, British, and French) and to force Germany to pay reparations. A year after the end of the war, however, the balance of power in Europe had shifted. With the Soviet Union threatening to dominate eastern Europe, the West moved to fill the vacuum in central Europe. In late 1946, the Americans and British merged their zones for economic purposes and began assigning administrative duties to Germans. By mid-1947, the process of rebuilding West German industry was under way.

Despite French fears, the United States sought to make Germany strong enough to anchor Europe. Secretary Marshall cautiously laid out the connections for Congress:

> The restoration of Europe involves the restoration of Germany. Without a revival of German production there can be no revival of Europe's economy. But we must be very careful to see that a revived Germany cannot again threaten the European community.

An American and British airlift in 1948 brought badly needed supplies to West Berliners isolated by a Soviet blockade of the city. By refusing to allow the Western powers to reach the city, located within the Soviet zone, the Russians hoped to drive them from Berlin, but the airlift broke the blockade. *(Corbis-Bettmann)*

In mid-1948, a crisis erupted when the Soviet Union attempted to force the western powers out of Berlin, which, like Germany itself, was divided into zones after the war. Soviet refusal to allow the other Allies land access to West Berlin, located in the Russian zone of Germany, led to an airlift that broke the Russian blockade.

The next major link in the containment strategy was the creation of a military alliance in Europe in 1949 to complement the economic program. After the Soviets tightened their control of Hungary and Czechoslovakia, the United States took the lead in establishing the North Atlantic Treaty Organization (NATO). Twelve nations formed the alliance, vowing that an attack against any one member would be considered an attack against all, to be met by appropriate armed force.

The Senate, long opposed to such military pacts, approved this time, and the United States established its first military treaty ties with Europe since the American Revolution. Congress also voted military aid for its NATO allies. The Cold War had softened long-standing American reluctance to become closely involved in European affairs.

Two dramatic events in 1949—the Communist victory in the Chinese civil war and the Russian detonation of an atomic device—led the United States to define its aims still more specifically. Responding to Truman's request for a full-fledged review of U.S. foreign and defense policy, the National Security Council, organized in 1947 to provide policy coordination, produced a document called NSC-68, which shaped U.S. policy for the next 20 years.

NSC-68 built on the Cold War rhetoric of the Truman Doctrine, describing challenges facing the United States in cataclysmic terms. "The issues that face us are momentous," the paper said, "involving the fulfillment or destruction not only of this Republic but of civilization itself." Conflict between East and West, the document assumed, was unavoidable, for

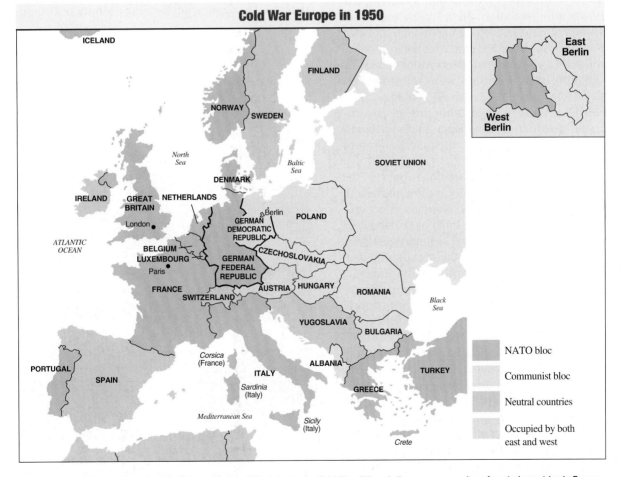

This map shows the rigid demarcation between East and West during the Cold War. Although there were a number of neutral countries in Europe, the other nations found themselves in a standoff, as each side tried to contain the possible advances of the other. The small insert map in the upper-right-hand corner shows the division of Berlin that paralleled the division of Germany itself after World War II.

amoral Soviet objectives ran totally counter to U.S. aims. Negotiation was useless, for the Soviets could never be trusted to bargain in good faith.

NSC-68 then argued that if the United States hoped to meet the Russian challenge, it must increase defense spending from the $13 billion set for 1950 to as much as $50 billion per year and increase the percentage of its budget allotted to defense from 5 to 20 percent. The costs were huge but necessary if the free world was to survive.

Containment in the 1950s

Containment, the keystone of American policy throughout the Truman years, was the rationale for the Truman Doctrine, the Marshall Plan, NATO, and NSC-68. Because this policy required detailed and up-to-date information about Communist moves, the government relied increasingly on the Central Intelligence Agency (CIA). Established by the National Security Act of 1947, which had also created the National Security Council, the CIA conducted espionage in foreign lands, some of it aboveboard and visible, some secret and seldom seen. During the Eisenhower administration, Allen Dulles, brother of the secretary of state, headed the agency and provided close foreign policy coordination. With the president's approval the CIA rearranged its priorities so that by 1957, 80 percent of its budget went toward covert activities. More and more, Eisenhower relied on clandestine CIA actions to undermine foreign governments, subsidize friendly newspapers in distant lands, and assist those who supported the American stance in the Cold War.

At the same time, the administration reassessed the impact of the containment policy itself, especially in light of criticism that it was too cautious to counter the threat of Communism. For most of Eisenhower's two terms, John Foster Dulles was secretary of state. A devout Presbyterian who hated atheistic communism, he sought to move beyond containment. Eager to counter the "Godless terrorism" of communism, Dulles wanted to commit the nation to a holy crusade to promote democracy and to free the countries under Soviet domination. Instead of advocating containment, the United States should make it "publicly known that it wants and expects liberation to occur."

Eisenhower's own rhetoric was equally strong. In his 1953 inaugural address, he declared, "Forces of good and evil are massed and armed and opposed as rarely before in history. Freedom is pitted against slavery, lightness against dark." Yet Eisenhower was more conciliatory, cautious, and realistic than Dulles and recognized the impossibility of changing the governments of the USSR's satellites. In mid-1953, when East Germans mounted anti-Soviet demonstrations, in a

challenge that foreshadowed the revolt against Communism three and a half decades later, the United States maintained its distance. In 1956, when Hungarian "freedom fighters" rose up against Russian domination, the United States again stood back as Soviet forces smashed the rebels and kept control of their satellite. Because Western action could have precipitated a more general conflict, Eisenhower refused to translate rhetoric into action. Throughout the 1950s, the policy of containment, largely as it had been defined earlier, remained in effect.

☜ CONTAINMENT IN ASIA, THE MIDDLE EAST, AND LATIN AMERICA

In a dramatic departure from its history of noninvolvement, the United States extended the policy of containment to meet challenges around the globe. Colonial empires were disintegrating, and countries seeking and attaining their independence now found themselves caught in the middle of the superpower struggle. Decolonization became even more compli-

Secretary of State John Foster Dulles viewed the Cold War as a moral struggle between good and evil. Opposed to "godless Communism," he often appeared as a religious crusader for measures he believed were necessary for the survival of the free world. *(Corbis-Bettmann)*

cated as it became intertwined with the Cold War. Although the containment initiative had resulted from the effort to promote European stability, it now became worldwide. In Asia, the Middle East, and Latin America, the United States discovered the tremendous appeal of Communism as a social and political system in emerging nations and found that ever greater efforts were required to advance American aims.

The Shock of the Chinese Revolution

The U.S. commitment to global containment became stronger with the Communist victory in the Chinese civil war in 1949. An ally during World War II, China had struggled against the Japanese, while simultaneously fighting a bitter civil war deeply rooted in the Chinese past—in widespread poverty, disease, oppression by the landlord class, and national humiliation at the hands of foreign powers. Mao Zedong (Mao Tsetung),* founder of a branch of the Communist party, gathered followers who wished to reshape China in a distinctive Marxist mold. Opposing the Communists were the Nationalists, led by Jiang Jieshi (Chiang Kaishek). By the early 1940s, Jiang Jieshi's regime was exhausted, inefficient, and corrupt. Mao's movement, meanwhile, grew stronger during the Second World War as he opposed the Japanese invaders and won the loyalty of the peasantry. Mao finally prevailed, as Jiang fled in 1949 to the island of Taiwan (Formosa) where he nursed the improbable belief that he was still the rightful ruler of all China and would one day return.

The United States failed to understand the long internal conflict in China or the immense popular support Mao had garnered. As the Communist army moved toward victory, the *New York Times* termed Mao's part as a "nauseous force," a "compact little oligarchy dominated by Moscow's nominees." Mao's proclamation of the People's Republic of China on October 1, 1949, fanned fears of Russian domination, for he had already announced his regime's support for the Soviet Union against the "imperialist" United States.

Events in China caused near hysteria in America. Staunch anti-Communists argued that Truman and the United States were to blame for Jiang's defeat by failing to provide him sufficient support. Secretary of State Dean Acheson briefly considered granting diplomatic recognition to the new government but backed off after the Communists seized American property, harassed American citizens, and openly allied China with the USSR. Like other Americans, Acheson mistakenly viewed the Chinese as Soviet puppets.

*Chinese names are rendered in their modern *pinyin* spelling. At first occurrence, the older but perhaps more familiar spelling (usually Wade-Giles) is given in parentheses.

Mao Zedong, chairman of the Chinese Communist party, was a powerful and popular leader who drove Jiang Jieshi from power in 1949 and established a strong hold over the People's Republic of China he created at that time. *(Corbis-Bettmann)*

Tension with China increased during the Korean War (1950–1953) and again in 1954 when Mao's government began shelling Nationalist positions on the offshore islands of Quemoy and Matsu. Eisenhower, now president, was committed to defending the Nationalists on Taiwan from a Communist attack, but he was unwilling to risk war over the islands. Again he showed an understanding of the need to proceed with caution.

Stalemate in the Korean War

The Korean War, on the other hand, highlighted growing U.S. intervention in Asia. Concern about China and determination to contain Communism led the United States into a bloody foreign struggle. But American objectives were not always clear and were largely unrealized after three years of war.

The conflict in Korea stemmed from tensions lingering after World War II. Korea, long under Japanese control, hoped for independence after Japan's defeat. But the Allies temporarily divided Korea along the 38th parallel when the rapid end to the Pacific struggle allowed Soviet troops to accept Japanese surrender in the north while American forces did the same in the south. The Soviet–American line, initially intended as a matter of military convenience, hardened after 1945, just as a similar division became rigid in Germany. In time, the Soviets set up one Korean government in the north and the Americans another government in the south. Though the major powers left Korea, they continued to support the regimes they had created. Each Korean government hoped to reunify the country on its own terms.

North Korea moved first. On June 25, 1950, North Korean forces crossed the 38th parallel to invade South Korea. Though the North Koreans followed Soviet-built tanks, they operated on their own initiative. Kim Il Sung, the North Korean leader, had visited Moscow earlier and may have gained Soviet acquiescence in the idea of an attack, but both the planning and the implementation occurred in Korea.

North Korea's action took the United States by surprise. Earlier, the nation had seemed reluctant to defend South Korea, but the Communist victory in China had changed the balance of power in Asia. Certain that Russia had masterminded the North Korean offensive and was testing the American policy of containment, Truman responded vigorously. "If this was allowed to go unchallenged," he declared, "it would mean a third world war, just as similar incidents had brought on the second world war."

Truman readied American naval and air forces and directed General Douglas MacArthur in Japan to supply South Korea. The United States also went to the United Nations Security Council. With the Soviet Union absent in protest of the UN's refusal to admit the People's Republic of China, the United States secured a unanimous resolution branding North Korea an aggressor, then another resolution calling on members of the organization to assist South Korea in repelling aggression and restoring peace.

On Truman's orders, American air and naval forces, then American ground forces, went into battle south of the 38th parallel. Following a daring amphibious invasion that pushed the North Koreans back to the former boundary line, UN troops crossed the 38th parallel, hoping to reunify Korea under an American-backed government. Despite Chinese signals that this movement toward their border threatened their security, the United States pressed on. In October, Chinese troops appeared briefly in battle, then disappeared. The next month, the Chinese mounted a full-fledged counterattack, which pushed the UN forces back below the dividing line.

The resulting stalemate provoked a bitter struggle between MacArthur and his civilian commander in chief. The brilliant but arrogant general called for retaliatory air strikes against China, but Truman remained committed to conducting a limited war. MacArthur's statements, issued from the field, finally went too far. In April 1951, he argued that the American approach in

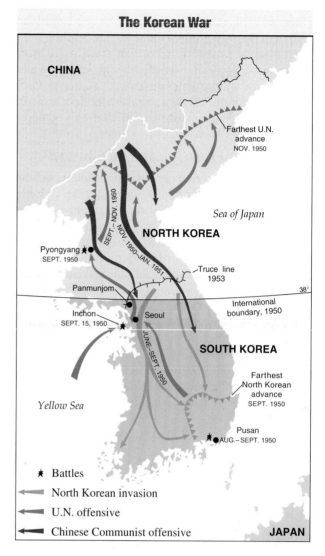

The Korean War

This map shows the ebb and flow of the Korean War. North Korea crossed the 38th parallel first, then the UN offensive drove the North Koreans close to the Chinese border, and finally the Chinese Communists entered the war and drove the UN forces back below the 38th parallel. The armistice signed at Panmunjom in 1953 provided a dividing line very close to the prewar line.

Korea was wrong and asserted publicly that "there is no substitute for victory." Truman had no choice but to relieve the general for insubordination. The decision outraged many Americans. After the stunning victories of World War II, limited war was frustrating and difficult to understand.

The Korean War dragged on into Eisenhower's presidency. Campaigning in 1952, Ike promised to go to Korea, and three weeks after his election, he did so. When truce talks bogged down in May 1953, the new administration privately threatened the Chinese with the use of atomic weapons. This brought about renewed negotiations. Finally, on July 27, 1953, an

General Douglas MacArthur was a superb tactician but a supremely egotistical commander of UN forces in Korea, where this picture was taken in the first year of the Korean War. Eventually his arrogance led him to challenge Truman's policy, whereupon the president relieved him of his command. *(Carl Mydana/LIFE Magazine © Time Inc.)*

armistice was signed. The Republican administration had succeeded where the preceding Democratic administration had failed: after three long years, the unpopular war had ended.

American involvement carried a heavy price: over 33,000 Americans killed in action and many more wounded. But those figures paled beside as many as two million Koreans dead and countless others maimed.

The war significantly changed American attitudes and institutions. For the first time, American forces fought in racially integrated units. As commander in chief, Truman had ordered the integration of the armed forces in 1948, over the opposition of many generals, and African Americans became part of all military units. Their successful performance led to acceptance of military integration.

The Korean War years also saw military expenditures soar from $13 billion in 1950 to about $47 billion three years later as defense spending followed the guidelines proposed in NSC-68. In the process, the United States accepted the demands of permanent mobilization. Whereas the military absorbed less than a third of the federal budget in 1950, a decade later it took half. More than a million military personnel were stationed around the world. At home, an increasingly powerful military establishment became closely tied to corporate and scientific communities and created a military-industrial complex that employed 3.5 million Americans by 1960.

The Korean War had important political effects as well. It led the United States to sign a peace treaty with Japan in September 1951 and to rely on that nation to maintain the balance of power in the Pacific. At the same time, the struggle poisoned relations with the People's Republic of China and ensured a diplomatic standoff that lasted more than 20 years.

Turbulence in the Middle East

Cold War attitudes also influenced American diplomacy in the Middle East. That part of the world had tremendous strategic importance as the supplier of oil for industrialized nations. During World War II, the

The Korean War disrupted numerous families in both the north and south and led them to flee their homes. Here fleeing Korean civilians, with the belongings they could carry with them, pass U.S. soldiers as the bitter struggle dragged on. *(UPI/Corbis-Bettmann)*

major Allied powers (including the Soviet Union) occupied Iran, agreeing that they would leave within six months of the war's end. As of early 1946, both Great Britain and the United States had withdrawn, but the Soviet Union, which bordered on Iran, continued its occupation. Stalin claimed that earlier security agreements had not been honored and demanded oil concessions. Only a threat of vigorous American action forced the Soviets out.

The Eisenhower administration maintained its interest in Iran. In 1953, the CIA helped the Iranian army overthrow the government of Mohammed Mossadegh, which had nationalized oil wells formerly under British control, and placed the shah of Iran securely on the Peacock Throne. After the coup, British and American companies regained command of the wells, and thereafter the U.S. government provided military assistance to the shah.

A far more serious situation emerged in Palestine, which since the end of World War I had been under British rule. With British control set to end in 1948, the United Nations attempted to partition Palestine into an Arab state and a Jewish state. Truman officially recognized the new state of Israel 15 minutes after it was proclaimed. But American recognition could not end bitter animosities between Arabs, who believed they

had been robbed of their territory, and Jews, who felt they had finally regained a homeland after the horrors of the Holocaust. As Americans looked on, Arab forces from Egypt, Trans-Jordan, Syria, Lebanon, and Iraq invaded Israel, but the Israelis won the war and added territory to what the UN had given them.

While cultivating close ties with Israel, the United States also tried to maintain the friendship of oil-rich Arab states or, at the very least, to prevent them from falling into the Soviet orbit. In Egypt, the policy ran into trouble when Arab nationalist General Gamal Abdel Nasser planned a huge dam on the Nile River to produce electric power. Nasser hoped to follow a middle course by proclaiming his country's neutrality in the Cold War. Although Dulles offered U.S. financial support for the Aswan Dam project, Nasser also began discussions with the Soviet Union. Furious, the secretary of state withdrew the American offer. Left without funds for the dam, in July 1956 Nasser seized and nationalized the British-controlled Suez Canal and closed it to Israeli ships. Now Great Britain was enraged. All of Europe feared that Nasser would disrupt the flow of oil from the Middle East.

In the fall, Israeli, British, and French military forces invaded Egypt. Eisenhower, who had not been consulted, was irate. Realizing that the attack might

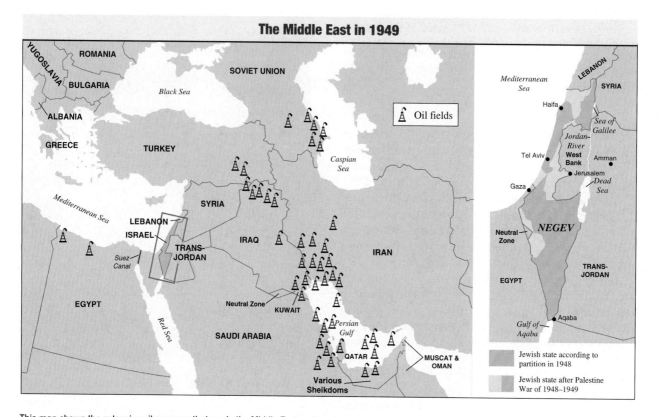

The Middle East in 1949

This map shows the extensive oil reserves that made the Middle East such an important region; it also shows the shifting boundaries of Israel as a result of the war following its independence in 1948. Notice how Israel's size increased after its victory in the first of a series of Middle Eastern conflicts.

push Nasser into Moscow's arms, the United States sponsored a UN resolution condemning the attack and Dulles persuaded other nations not to send petroleum to England and France as long as they remained in Egypt. These actions convinced the invaders to withdraw.

Before long the United States again intervened in the Middle East. Concerned about the region's stability, the president declared in 1957, in what came to be called the Eisenhower Doctrine, that "the existing vacuum in the Middle East must be filled by the United States before it is filled by Russia." A year later, in line with a congressional resolution that committed the United States to stop suspected Communist aggression, he authorized the landing of 14,000 soldiers in Lebanon to prop up a right-wing government challenged from within.

The Middle East remained a battleground. In 1967, Israeli forces defeated the Egyptian army in the Six Day War and seized the West Bank and Jerusalem, the Golan Heights, and the Sinai Peninsula. Then in 1973, the Egyptians seized the initiative in the Yom Kippur War. In each case, the United States used its influence to halt fighting in order to maintain regional stability and uninterrupted supplies of oil.

Restricting Revolt in Latin America

The Cold War also led to intervention in Latin America, the United States' traditional sphere of influence. In 1954, Dulles sniffed Communist activity in Guatemala and Eisenhower ordered CIA support for a coup aimed at ousting the elected government of reform-minded Colonel Jacobo Arbenz Guzmán. It trained and equipped Guatemalans to overthrow the legitimate regime, which had appropriated property of the American-owned United Fruit Company. The right-wing takeover succeeded, established a military dictatorship that responded to U.S. wishes, and restored the property of the United Fruit Company. These actions demonstrated again the shortsighted American commitment to stability and private investment, whatever the internal effect or ultimate cost. The interference in Guatemala fed anti-American feeling throughout Latin America.

In 1959, when Fidel Castro overthrew the dictatorship of Fulgencio Batista in Cuba, the shortsightedness of American policy became even clearer. Nationalism and the thrust for social reform were powerful forces in Latin America, as in the rest of the Third World formerly dominated by European powers. As Milton Eisenhower, Ike's brother and adviser, pointed out: "Revolution is inevitable in Latin America. The people are angry. They are shackled to the past with bonds of ignorance, injustice, and poverty. And they no longer accept as universal or inevitable the oppressive prevail-

ing order." But when Castro confiscated American property in Cuba, the Eisenhower administration cut off exports and severed diplomatic ties. In response, Cuba turned to the Soviet Union for support.

ATOMIC WEAPONS AND THE COLD WAR

Throughout the Cold War, the atomic bomb was a crucial factor that hung over all diplomatic discussions and military initiatives. Atomic weapons were destructive enough, but when the United States and the Soviet Union both developed hydrogen bombs, an age of overkill began.

Sharing the Secret of the Bomb

The United States, with British aid, had built the first atomic bomb and attempted to conceal the project from its wartime ally, the Soviet Union. Soviet spies, however, discovered that the Americans were working on the bomb, and, even before the war was over, the Soviets had initiated a program to create a bomb of their own.

The question of sharing the atomic secret was considered in the immediate postwar years. Just before he retired, Secretary of War Henry L. Stimson favored cooperating with the Soviet Union, rather than acting

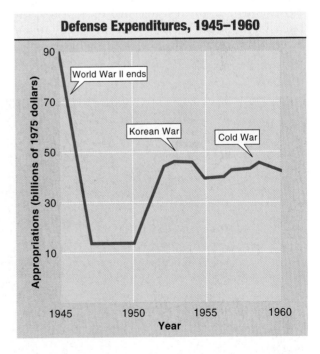

Defense spending plummeted after World War II, only to quadruple with the onset of the Korean War. After that increase, spending levels never dropped dramatically, even after the end of the war. Source: U.S. Bureau of the Census.

unilaterally. Recognizing the futility of trying to cajole the Russians while "having this weapon ostentatiously on our hip," he warned that "their suspicions and their distrust of our purposes and motives will increase." Only mutual accommodation could bring international cooperation.

For a time the administration contemplated a system of international arms control. Realizing by early 1946 that mere possession of the bomb by the United States did not make the Russians more malleable, Truman decided to offer the United Nations a proposal for an international agency to control atomic energy. When the Russians balked at a plan they argued favored the United States, negotiations collapsed.

The United States gave up on the process of sharing atomic secrets. Intent on retaining the technological advantage until the creation of a "foolproof method of control," Truman endorsed the Atomic Energy Act, passed by Congress in 1946. It established the Atomic Energy Commission to supervise all atomic energy development in the United States and, under the tightest security, to authorize all nuclear activity in the nation at large. It also opened the way to a nuclear arms race once Russia developed its own bomb.

Nuclear Proliferation

As the atomic bomb found its way into popular culture, Americans at first showed more excitement than fear. In Los Angeles, the "Atombomb Dancers" wiggled at the Burbank Burlesque Theater. In 1946, the Buchanan Brothers released a record called "Atomic Power," noting the brimstone fire from heaven that was "given by the mighty hand of God."

Anxiety lurked beneath the exuberance, though it did not surface while the United States held a nuclear monopoly. Then, in September 1949, reporters were called to the White House and told: "We have evidence that within recent weeks an atomic explosion occurred in the U.S.S.R." Over the Labor Day weekend, a U.S. Air Force weather reconnaissance plane on a routine mission had picked up air samples showing higher than normal radioactivity counts. Other samples confirmed the reading, and scientists soon concluded that Russia had conducted a nuclear test.

The American public was shocked. Suddenly the security of being the world's only atomic power had vanished. People wondered whether the Soviet test foreshadowed a nuclear attack. Harold C. Urey, a Nobel Prize–winning scientist, summed up the feelings of many Americans: "There is only one thing worse than one nation having the atomic bomb— that's two nations having it."

In early 1950, Truman authorized the development of a new hydrogen superbomb, potentially far more devastating than the atomic bomb. Edward Teller, a physicist on the Manhattan Project, was intrigued with the novelty of the puzzle. During the war, as other scientists struggled with the problem of fission, he had contemplated the possibility that fusion might release energy in even greater amounts. Now he had his chance to prove it.

By 1953, both the United States and the Soviet Union had unlocked the secret of the hydrogen bomb. As kilotons gave way to megatons, the stakes rose. The government remained quiet about MIKE, the first test of a hydrogen device in the Pacific Ocean in 1952, but

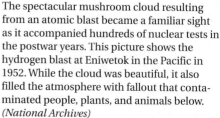

The spectacular mushroom cloud resulting from an atomic blast became a familiar sight as it accompanied hundreds of nuclear tests in the postwar years. This picture shows the hydrogen blast at Eniwetok in the Pacific in 1952. While the cloud was beautiful, it also filled the atmosphere with fallout that contaminated people, plants, and animals below. *(National Archives)*

rumors circulated that it had created a hole in the ocean floor 175 feet deep and a mile wide. Later, after the 1954 BRAVO test, Lewis Strauss, Atomic Energy Commission chairman, admitted that "an H-bomb can be made . . . large enough to take out a city," even New York. Then, in 1957, shortly after the news that the Soviets had successfully tested their first intercontinental ballistic missile (ICBM), Americans learned that the Soviets had lifted the first satellite, *Sputnik,* into outer space—with a rocket that could also deliver a hydrogen bomb.

The discovery of radioactive fallout added another dimension to the nuclear dilemma. Fallout became publicly known after the BRAVO blast in 1954 showered Japanese fishermen 85 miles away with radioactive dust. They became ill with radiation sickness, and several months later, one died. The Japanese, who had been the first to experience the effects of atomic weapons, were outraged and alarmed. But everywhere people began to realize the terrible consequences of the new weapons.

Authors in both the scientific and the popular press focused attention on radioactive fallout. Radiation, physicist Ralph Lapp observed, "cannot be felt and possesses all the terror of the unknown. It is something which evokes revulsion and helplessness—like a bubonic plague." Nevil Shute's best-selling 1957 novel *On the Beach,* and the film that followed, also sparked public awareness and fear. The story described a war that released so much radioactive waste that all life in the Northern Hemisphere disappeared, while the Southern Hemisphere awaited the same deadly fate. In 1959, when *Consumer Reports* warned of the conta-

mination of milk with the radioactive isotope strontium-90, public alarm grew.

The discovery of fallout provoked a shelter craze. Bob Russell, a Michigan sheriff, declared that "to build a new home in this day and age without including such an obvious necessity as a fallout shelter would be like leaving out the bathroom 20 years ago." *Good Housekeeping* magazine carried a full-page editorial in November 1958 urging the construction of family shelters. More and more companies advertised ready-made shelters. A firm in Miami reported numerous inquiries about shelters costing between $1,795 and $3,895, depending on capacity, and planned 900 franchises. *Life* magazine in 1955 featured an "H-Bomb Hideaway" for $3,000. By late 1960, the Office of Civil and Defense Mobilization estimated that a million family shelters had been built.

The Nuclear West

The bomb stimulated more than just shelter building. It sparked an enormous increase in defense spending and created a huge nuclear industry, particularly in the West. Contractors liked the region because of its antiunion attitudes; labor stability, they argued, would make it easier to meet government deadlines.

During World War II, a number of the Manhattan Project's major centers were located in the West. The plant at Hanford, Washington, was one of the most important producers of fissionable material, and the first atomic weapon had been produced at Los Alamos, New Mexico. Development in this area expanded after the war. Hanford continued to produce plutonium, a facility outside Denver made plutonium triggers for

Americans sought protection from fallout in shelters that civil defense authorities told them would be just like home. Here a typical family in 1955 practices in the Kiddie Kokoon, which has beds and supplies of food and water to last for several weeks. (© *J. Edward Bailey/TIME Magazine*)

Nuclear Weapons Facilities in the 1950s

In the post–World War II years, a number of laboratories and plants around the country designed and assembled nuclear weapons, but the greatest concentration, as this map shows, was in the West.

thermonuclear bombs, the new Sandia National Laboratory in Albuquerque provided the production engineering of nuclear bombs, and the Los Alamos laboratory remained a major atomic research center. In 1951, the United States opened the Nevada Test Site, 65 miles north of Las Vegas, to try out nuclear weapons, and the facility had a major impact on the city. The Chamber of Commerce offered schedules of test shots, and the mushroom cloud became the logo for the Southern Nevada telephone directory.

Defense spending promoted other development as well. Naval commands had headquarters in Seattle, San Francisco, San Diego, and Honolulu. Radar sites, aimed at tracking incoming missiles, stretched all the way up to Alaska. The Boeing Company, located in Seattle, stimulated tremendous development in that city, as it produced B-47 and B-52 airplanes that were the U.S. Air Force's main delivery vehicles for nuclear bombs.

"Massive Retaliation"

As Americans grappled with the implications of nuclear weapons, government policy came to depend increasingly on an atomic shield. The Soviet success in

building its own bomb encouraged the conviction that America had to beef up its atomic forces. Truman authorized the development of a nuclear arsenal but also stressed conventional forms of defense. Eisenhower, however, found the effort fragmented and wasteful. Concerned with controlling the budget and cutting taxes, his administration decided to rely on atomic weapons rather than combat forces as the key to American defense.

Secretary of State Dulles developed the policy of threatening "massive retaliation." The United States, he declared, was willing and ready to use nuclear weapons against Communist aggression "at places of our own choosing." The policy allowed troop cutbacks and promised to be cost-effective by giving "more bang for the buck."

Massive retaliation provided for an all-or-nothing response, leaving no middle course, no alternatives between nuclear war and retreat. Still, it reflected Dulles's willingness to threaten direct retaliation to deter Soviet challenges around the world. "The ability to get to the verge without getting into war is the necessary art," he said. "If you cannot master it you inevitably get into war." Critics called the policy "brinkmanship" and wondered what would happen if the line was crossed in the new atomic age. Eisenhower himself was horrified when he saw reports indicating that a coordinated atomic attack could leave a nation "a smoking, radiating ruin at the end of two hours." With characteristic caution, he did his best to ensure that the rhetoric of massive retaliation did not lead to war.

Atomic Protest

As the arms race spiraled, critics demanded that it end. In 1956, Democratic presidential candidate Adlai Stevenson pointed to "the danger of poisoning the atmosphere" and called for a halt to nuclear tests. Eisenhower did not respond but Dulles minimized the hazards of radiation by arguing, "From a health standpoint, there is greater danger from wearing a wrist watch with a luminous dial."

In 1957, activists organized SANE, the National Committee for a Sane Nuclear Policy. One of its most effective advertisements featured internationally known pediatrician Benjamin Spock, looking down at a little girl with a frown on his face. "Dr. Spock is worried," the caption read, and the text below amplified on his concern. "I *am* worried," he said, "not so much about the effect of past tests but at the prospect of endless future ones. As the tests multiply, so will the damage to children—here and around the world."

Several years later, women who had worked with SANE took the protest movement a step further. As one activist later recalled, "This movement was inspired and motivated by mothers' love for children. . . . When they were putting their breakfasts on the table, they saw not only Wheaties and milk, but they also saw Strontium 90 and Iodine 131." To challenge continued testing, which dropped such lethal elements on all inhabitants of the globe, the protesters called on women throughout the country to suspend normal activities for a day and strike for peace. An estimated 50,000 women marched in 60 communities around the nation. Their slogans included "Let the Children Grow" and "End the Arms Race—Not the Human Race."

Pressure from many groups produced a political breakthrough and sustained it for a time. The superpowers began a voluntary moratorium on testing in the fall of 1958. It lasted until the Soviet Union resumed testing in September 1961, the United States the following March.

SANE tried to get the United States, and the rest of the world, to stop testing nuclear weapons and dumping huge amounts of fallout in the atmosphere. This newspaper advertisement, which appeared in 1962, was part of the larger effort to make the world a safer place. (*The Peace Collection, Swarthmore College, PA*)

THE COLD WAR AT HOME

The Cold War also affected domestic affairs and led to the creation of an internal loyalty program that seriously violated civil liberties. Americans had feared radical subversion before and after the Russian Revolution (see Chapters 16, 21, and 22). Now the Soviet Union appeared ever more ominous in confrontations around the globe. Maps showed half the world colored red to dramatize the spread of the monolithic Communist system. As Americans began to suspect Communist infiltration at home, some determined to root out all traces of Communism inside the United States.

Truman's Loyalty Program

When the Truman administration mobilized support for its containment program in the immediate postwar years, its rhetoric became increasingly shrill. Spokesmen contrasted American virtues with diabolical Russian designs. For Truman, the issue confronting the world was one of "tyranny or freedom." Attorney General J. Howard McGrath spoke of "many Communists in America," each bearing the "germ of death for society."

When administration officials perceived an internal threat to security after the discovery of classified documents in the offices of the allegedly pro-Communist *Amerasia* magazine, Truman appointed a Temporary Commission on Employee Loyalty. Republican gains in the midterm elections of 1946 led him to try to head off a congressional loyalty probe that could be used for partisan ends, especially since Republicans had accused the Democrats of being "soft on Communism."

On the basis of the report from his temporary commission, Truman established a new Federal Employee Loyalty Program by executive decree in 1947. In the same week that he announced his containment policy, Truman ordered the FBI to check its files for evidence of subversive activity and to bring suspects before a new Civil Service Commission Loyalty Review Board. Initially, the program included safeguards and assumed that a challenged employee was innocent until proved guilty. But as the Loyalty Review Board assumed more power, it ignored individual rights. Employees about whom there was any doubt, regardless of proof, found themselves under attack, with little chance to fight back. Val Lorwin, met at the start of the chapter, was just one of many victims.

The Truman loyalty program examined several million employees and found grounds for dismissing only several hundred. Nonetheless, it bred the unwarranted fear of subversion, led to the assumption that absolute loyalty could be achieved, and legitimated investigatory tactics that were used irresponsibly to harm innocent individuals.

The Congressional Loyalty Program

While Truman's loyalty probe investigated government employees, Congress launched its own program. In the early years of the Cold War, the law became increasingly explicit about what was illegal in the United States. The Smith Act of 1940 made it a crime to advocate or teach the forcible overthrow of the U.S. government. The McCarran Internal Security Act of 1950, passed over Truman's veto, further circumscribed Communist activity by declaring that it was illegal to conspire to act in a way that would "substantially contribute" to establishing a totalitarian dictatorship in America and by requiring members of Communist organizations to register with the attorney general. The American Communist party, which had never been large, even in the Depression, declined still further. Membership, numbering about 80,000 in 1947, fell to 55,000 in 1950 and 25,000 in 1954.

The investigations of the House Un-American Activities Committee (HUAC) contributed to that decline. Intent on rooting out subversion, HUAC probed the motion picture industry in 1947, claiming that left-wing sympathies were corrupting the

American public. A frequent refrain in congressional hearings was "Are you now or have you ever been a member of the Communist Party?" When 10 Hollywood figures called to testify refused to answer such questions by invoking their constitutional right to remain silent, Congress issued contempt citations, and they went to prison and served sentences ranging from six months to one year. At that point, Hollywood knuckled under and blacklisted anyone with even a marginally questionable past. No one on these lists could find jobs at the studios anymore.

Congress made a greater splash with the Hiss-Chambers case. Whittaker Chambers, a former Communist who had broken with the party in 1938 and had become a successful editor of *Time,* charged that Alger Hiss had been a Communist in the 1930s. Hiss was a distinguished New Dealer who had served in the Agriculture Department before becoming assistant secretary of state. Now out of the government, he was president of the Carnegie Endowment for

Alger Hiss vigorously asserted his innocence but was nonetheless convicted of perjury when evidence indicated he lied under oath about his involvement with the Communist party. His conviction helped heighten American fears of Communism at home. Even after serving time in prison, Hiss continued to proclaim his innocence, but he became an isolated and subdued figure, far different from the prominent government official he had once been. *(AP/World Wide Photos)*

International Peace. He denied Chambers's charge, and the matter might have died there had not freshman congressman Richard Nixon taken up the case. Nixon finally extracted from Hiss an admission that he had once known Chambers. Outside the hearing room, Hiss sued Chambers for libel, whereupon Chambers changed his story and charged that Hiss was a Soviet spy.

Hiss was indicted for perjury for lying under oath about his former relationship with Chambers. The case made front-page news around the nation. Millions of Americans read about the case at about the same time they learned of Russia's first atomic explosion and the final victory of the Communist revolution in China. Chambers appeared unstable and changed his story several times. Yet Hiss, too, seemed contradictory in his testimony and never adequately explained how he had such close ties with members of the Communist party or how some copies of stolen State Department documents had been typed on a typewriter he had once owned. The first trial ended in a hung jury; the second trial, in January 1950, sent Hiss to prison for almost four years.

For many Americans, the Hiss case proved that a Communist threat indeed existed in the United States. It "forcibly demonstrated to the American people that domestic Communism was a real and present danger to the security of the nation," Richard Nixon declared after using the case to win a Senate seat from California and then the Republican vice presidential nomination in 1952. The case also led people to question the Democratic approach to the problem. Critics attacked Dean Acheson for supporting Hiss, his friend. They likewise questioned Truman's own commitment to protect the nation from internal subversion. The dramatic Hiss case helped justify the even worse witch-hunt that followed.

The Second Red Scare

The key anti-Communist warrior in the 1950s was Joseph R. McCarthy. Coming to the Senate from Wisconsin in 1946, McCarthy had an undistinguished career. As he began to contemplate reelection two years hence, he seized on the Communist issue. Truman had carried Wisconsin in 1948, and McCarthy saw in the Communist question a way of mobilizing Republican support. He first gained national attention with a speech before the Wheeling, West Virginia, Women's Club in February 1950, not long after the conviction of Alger Hiss. In that address, McCarthy brandished what he said was a list of 205 known Communists in the State Department. Pressed for details, McCarthy first said that he would release his list only to the president, then reduced the number of names to 57.

Early reactions to McCarthy were mixed. A subcommittee of the Senate Foreign Relations Committee, after investigating, called his charge a "fraud and a hoax." Even other Republicans like Robert Taft and Richard Nixon questioned his effectiveness. As his support grew, however, Republicans realized his partisan value and egged him on. Senator John Bricker of Ohio allegedly told him, "Joe, you're a dirty s.o.b., but there are times when you've got to have an s.o.b. around, and this is one of them."

McCarthy selected assorted targets. In the elections of 1950, he attacked Millard Tydings, the Democrat from Maryland who had chaired the subcommittee that dismissed McCarthy's first accusations. A doctored photograph, showing Tydings with deposed American Communist party head Earl Browder, helped bring about the defeat of Tydings. McCarthy blasted Dean Acheson the "Red Dean of the State Department" and slandered George C. Marshall, the architect of victory in World War II and a powerful figure in formulating Far Eastern policy, as a "man steeped in falsehood . . . who has recourse to the lie whenever it suits his convenience."

A demagogue throughout his career, McCarthy gained visibility through extensive press and television coverage. Playing on his tough reputation, he did not mind appearing disheveled, unshaven, and half sober. He used obscenity and vulgarity freely as he lashed out against his "vile and scurrilous" enemies.

McCarthy's tactics worked because of public alarm about the Communist threat. The Korean War revealed the aggressiveness of Communists in Asia. The arrest in 1950 of Julius and Ethel Rosenberg fed fears of internal subversion. The Rosenbergs, a seemingly ordinary American couple with two small children, were charged with stealing and transmitting atomic secrets to the Russians. To many Americans, it was inconceivable that the Soviets could have developed the bomb on their own. Treachery helped explain the Soviet explosion of an atomic device.

The next year, the Rosenbergs were found guilty of espionage. Judge Irving Kaufman expressed the rage of an insecure nation as he sentenced them to death. "Your conduct in putting into the hands of the Russians the A-bomb," he charged, "has already caused, in my opinion, the Communist aggression in Korea, . . . and who knows but that millions more of innocent people may pay the price of your treason." Their execution in the electric chair reflected a national commitment to respond to the Communist threat.

When the Republicans won control of the Senate in 1952, McCarthy's power grew. He became chairman of the Government Operations Committee and head of its Permanent Investigations Subcommittee. He now had a stronger base and two dedicated assistants, Roy

Senator Joseph McCarthy's spurious charges inflamed anti-Communist sentiment in the 1950s. Here he uses a chart of Communist party organization in the United States to suggest that the nation would be at risk unless subversives were rooted out. *(Corbis-Bettmann)*

Cohn and G. David Schine, who helped keep attention focused on the ostensible Communist threat. The lists of suspects, including Val Lorwin (introduced at the start of this chapter), continued to grow.

As McCarthy's anti-Communist witch-hunt continued, Eisenhower became uneasy. He disliked the senator but, recognizing his popularity, was reluctant to challenge him. At the height of his influence, polls showed that McCarthy had half the public behind him. With the country so inclined, Eisenhower compromised by voicing his disapproval quietly and privately.

With the help of Cohn and Schine, McCarthy pushed on, and finally he pushed too hard. In 1953, the army drafted Schine and then refused to allow the preferential treatment that Cohn insisted his colleague deserved. Angered, McCarthy began to investigate army security and even top-level army leaders. When the army charged that McCarthy was going too far, the Senate investigated the complaint.

The Army–McCarthy hearings began in April 1954 and lasted 36 days. Televised to a fascinated nationwide audience, they demonstrated the power of TV to shape people's opinions. Americans saw McCarthy's savage tactics on screen. He came across to viewers as irresponsible and destructive, particularly in contrast to Boston lawyer Joseph Welch, who argued the army's case with quiet eloquence and asked, "Have you no sense of decency, sir, at long last? Have you left no sense of decency?"

The hearings shattered McCarthy's mystical appeal. In broad daylight, before a national television audience, his ruthless tactics offended millions. The Senate finally summoned the courage to condemn him for his conduct. Even conservatives turned against McCarthy because he was no longer limiting his venom to Democrats and liberals. Although McCarthy remained in office, his influence disappeared. Three years later, at the age of 48, he died a broken man.

Yet for a time he had exerted a powerful hold in the United States. "To many Americans," radio commentator Fulton Lewis, Jr., said, "McCarthyism is Americanism." Seizing upon the frustrations and anxieties of the Cold War, McCarthy struck a resonant chord. As his appeal grew, he put together a following that included both lower-class ethnic groups, who responded to the charges against established elites, and conservative midwestern Republicans. But his real power base was the Senate, where, particularly after 1952, conservative Republicans saw McCarthy as a means of reasserting their own authority. Their support encouraged the vicious crusade.

The Casualties of Fear

The anti-Communist campaign kindled pervasive suspicion in American society. In the late 1940s and early 1950s, dissent no longer seemed safe. Civil servants, government workers, academics, and actors all came under attack and found that the right of due process often evaporated amid the Cold War Red Scare. Seasoned China experts lost their positions in the diplomatic service, and social justice legislation faltered.

This paranoia affected American life in countless ways. In New York, subway workers were fired when they refused to answer questions about their own political actions and beliefs. In Seattle, a fire department officer who denied current membership in the Communist party but refused to speak of his past was dismissed just 40 days before he reached the 25 years of service that would have qualified him for retirement benefits. Navajos in Arizona and New Mexico, facing starvation in the bitter winter of 1947–1948, were denied government relief because of charges that their communal way of life was communistic and therefore un-American. A Senate report branded homosexuals as unfit for government service, claiming they were subject to blackmail and thus a threat to national security. Racism became intertwined with the anti-Communist crusade when African American actor Paul Robeson was accused of Communist leanings for criticizing American foreign policy and denied opportunities to perform. Subsequently the State Department revoked his passport. Black author W. E. B. Du Bois, who actually joined the Communist party, faced even more virulent attacks and likewise lost his passport. Hispanic laborers faced deportation for membership in unions with left-wing sympathies. In 1949, the Congress of Industrial Organizations (CIO) expelled 11 unions with a total membership of more than one million for alleged domination by Communists. Val Lorwin, met at the start of this chapter, weathered the storm of malicious accusations and was finally vindicated, but others were less lucky. They were the unfortunate victims as the United States became consumed by the passions of the Cold War.

CONTINUING CONFRONTATIONS WITH COMMUNISTS

The Cold War continued into the 1960s and 1970s. Presidents John F. Kennedy and Lyndon B. Johnson were both aggressive cold warriors who subscribed to the policies of their predecessors. Their commitment to stopping the spread of Communism kept the nation locked in the same bitter conflict that had dominated foreign policy in the 1950s and led to continuing global confrontations.

John Kennedy and the Bay of Pigs Fiasco

Kennedy, who won the presidency in 1960, was an activist eager to provide bold executive leadership. At 43, he was the youngest man ever elected president, and he hoped to use his youthful vigor to make good on his campaign promise to get the country moving again after the Eisenhower years. The new president was particularly determined to stand firm in the face of Russian power. During the campaign, he had declared: "The enemy is the communist system itself—implacable, insatiable, unceasing in its drive for world domination." In his inaugural address, he eloquently described the dangers and challenges the United States faced. "In the long history of the world," he cried out, "only a few generations have been granted the role of defending freedom in its hour of maximum danger." The United States would "pay any price, bear any burden, meet any hardship, support

Aerial photographs in the fall of 1962 showed the Soviet missile sites in Cuba, and this evidence led President Kennedy to insist on removal of the weapons. The Cuban missile crisis threatened to engulf the world in a nuclear war. *(UPI/Corbis-Bettmann)*

any friend, oppose any foe, to assure the survival and success of liberty."

Kennedy perceived direct challenges from the Soviet Union almost from the beginning of his presidency. The first came at the Bay of Pigs in Cuba in the spring of 1961. Cuban–American relations had been strained since Fidel Castro's revolutionary army had seized power in 1959. A radical regime in Cuba, leaning toward the Soviet Union, could provide a model for upheaval elsewhere in Latin America and threaten the venerable Monroe Doctrine. One initiative to counter the Communist threat was the Alliance for Progress, which provided social and economic assistance to the less-developed nations of the hemisphere. But other, more aggressive, responses were deemed necessary as well.

Just before Kennedy assumed office, the United States broke diplomatic relations with Cuba. The CIA, meanwhile, was covertly training anti-Castro exiles to storm the Cuban coast at the Bay of Pigs. The American planners assumed the invasion would lead to an uprising of the Cuban people against Castro. Told of the plan, Kennedy approved it.

The invasion, on April 17, 1961, was an unmitigated disaster. Cuban forces stopped the invaders on the beach, and there was no popular uprising. The United States stood exposed to the world, attempting to overthrow a sovereign government. It had broken agreements not to interfere in the internal affairs of hemi-

spheric neighbors and had intervened clumsily and unsuccessfully.

Although chastened by the debacle at the Bay of Pigs, Kennedy remained determined to deal sternly with the perceived Communist threat. Following a hostile meeting with Soviet leader Nikita Khrushchev in Vienna in June 1961, where discussion centered on the question of a permanent settlement for the divided city of Berlin, to prevent refugees from fleeing from East Germany to the West, Kennedy reacted aggressively. He asked Congress for $3 billion more in defense appropriations, for more men in the armed forces, and for funds for a civil defense fallout shelter program, explicitly warning of the threat of nuclear war. The crisis eased only when the USSR erected a wall in Berlin to seal off its section.

The Cuban Missile Face-off

The next year, a new crisis arose. Understandably fearful of the American threat to Cuban independence after the Bay of Pigs invasion, Fidel Castro sought and secured Soviet assistance. American aerial photographs taken in October 1962 revealed that the USSR had begun to place what Kennedy considered offensive missiles on Cuban soil, although Cuba insisted they were defensive. The missiles did not change the strategic balance significantly, for the Soviets could still wreak untold damage on American targets from more distant bases. But with

Lyndon Johnson succeeded John Kennedy and sought to emphasize that he would follow in the slain president's footsteps. This photograph, sent to government posts around the world, showed the connection between the two leaders and thereby tried to highlight the continuity of the American government. *(AP/Wide World Photos)*

Russian weapons installed just 90 miles from American shores, appearance was more important than reality. This time Kennedy was determined to win a confrontation with the Soviet Union over Cuba.

Kennedy went on nationwide TV to tell the American people about the missiles and to demand their removal. He declared that the United States would not shrink from the risk of nuclear war and announced a naval "quarantine"—not a blockade, which would have been an act of war—around Cuba to prevent Soviet ships from bringing in additional missiles.

As the Soviet ships steamed toward the blockade and the nations stood "eyeball to eyeball" at the brink, the world held its breath. After several days, the tension broke, but only because Khrushchev called the Soviet ships back. Khrushchev then sent a long letter, transmitted by teletype, to Kennedy pledging to remove the missiles if the United States lifted the quarantine and promised to stay out of Cuba altogether. A second letter demanded that America remove its missiles from Turkey as well. The United States agreed to the first letter, ignored the second, and said nothing about its intention, already voiced, of removing its own missiles from Turkey. With that, the crisis ended.

The Cuban missile crisis was the most terrifying confrontation of the Cold War. Yet the president emerged from it as a hero who had stood firm. His reputation was enhanced, and his party benefited a few weeks later in the congressional elections. As the relief began to fade, however, critics charged that what Kennedy saw as his finest hour was in fact an unnecessary crisis. One consequence of the affair was the installation of a Soviet–American hot line to avoid similar episodes in the future. Another consequence was the USSR's determination to increase its nuclear arsenal so that it would never again be exposed as inferior to the United States. Despite the Limited Test Ban Treaty of 1963, which prohibited atmospheric testing, the nuclear arms race continued.

Confrontation and Containment Under Johnson

After Kennedy's assassination in 1963, Vice President Lyndon Johnson assumed the presidency. An extraordinarily effective legislative leader (see Chapter 28), he had considerably less experience in foreign affairs. Yet he shared many of Kennedy's assumptions about the threat of Communism. His understanding of the past led him to believe that aggressors had to be stopped before they committed more aggression, as had been true in World War II. Like Eisenhower and Kennedy, Johnson believed in the domino theory: if one country in a region fell, others were bound to

follow. He was determined to preserve American power and contain the Communist menace. He assumed he could treat foreign adversaries just as he treated political opponents in the United States.

In 1965, Johnson dispatched over 20,000 troops to the Dominican Republic in the West Indies, believing that "Castro-type elements" might win in a civil war there. In fact, the group Johnson called Communist was led by the former president, Juan Bosch, who had been overthrown by a military junta. Bosch ruefully pointed out that "this was a democratic revolution smashed by the leading democracy of the world." Johnson's credibility suffered badly from the episode.

THE QUAGMIRE OF VIETNAM

The commitment to stopping the spread of Communism led to the massive U.S. involvement in Vietnam. That struggle tore the United States apart, wrought enormous damage in Southeast Asia, and finally forced a reevaluation of America's Cold War policies.

Roots of the Conflict

The roots of the war extended far back in the past. Indochina had been a French colony since the mid-nineteenth century. During World War II, Japan occupied it but allowed French collaborators to administer internal affairs. An independence movement, led by the Communist organizer and revolutionary Ho Chi Minh, sought to expel the Japanese conquerors. In 1945, the Allied powers faced the decision of how to deal with Ho and his nationalist movement.

Franklin Roosevelt, like Woodrow Wilson, believed in self-determination and wanted to end colonialism. But France was determined to regain its colony, and by the time of his death, Roosevelt had backed down. Meanwhile, Ho Chi Minh had established the Democratic Republic of Vietnam in 1945. Although the new government enjoyed widespread support, the United States refused to recognize it.

A long, bitter struggle broke out between French and Vietnamese forces, which became entangled with the larger Cold War. President Truman was less concerned about ending colonialism than with checking Soviet power. He needed France to balance the Soviets in Europe, and that meant cooperating with France in Vietnam.

Although Ho did not have close ties to the Soviet Union and was committed to his independent nationalist crusade, Truman and his advisers, who saw Communism as a monolithic force, assumed wrongly that Ho took orders from Moscow. Hence, in 1950, the United States formally recognized the French puppet government in Vietnam, and by 1954, the United

States was paying over three-quarters of the cost of France's Indochina war.

After Eisenhower took office, France's position in Southeast Asia deteriorated. Secretary of State Dulles was eager to assist the French, and the chairman of the Joint Chiefs of Staff even contemplated using nuclear weapons, but Eisenhower refused to intervene directly. As a French fortress at Dien Bien Phu finally fell to Ho's forces, an international conference in Geneva divided Vietnam along the 17th parallel, with elections promised in 1956 to unify the country and determine its political fate.

The Start of U.S. Involvement in Vietnam

Elections were never held, and two Vietnamese states emerged. Ho Chi Minh held power in the north, while in the south Premier Ngo Dinh Diem, a fierce anti-Communist, formed a separate government. Intent on securing stability in Southeast Asia, the United States supported the Diem government and refused to sign the Geneva pact. In the next few years, American aid increased and military advisers—675 by the time Eisenhower left office—began to assist the South Vietnamese. The United States had taken its first steps toward direct involvement in a ruinous war halfway around the world that would escalate out of control.

John Kennedy's commitment to Cold War victory led him to expand the American role in Vietnam, the country he once called the "cornerstone of the free world in Southeast Asia." Now resolved to resist the spread of Communism, Kennedy and his closest associates were confident of success. As Secretary of Defense Robert McNamara observed, "North Vietnam will never beat us. They can't even make ice cubes." During the Kennedy administration, the number of advisers had risen from 675 to more than 16,000.

Despite American backing, South Vietnamese leader Diem was rapidly losing support in his own country. Buddhist priests burned themselves alive in the capital of Saigon to protest the corruption and arbitrariness of Diem's regime. After receiving assurances that the United States would not object to an internal coup, South Vietnamese military leaders assassinated Diem and seized the government. Kennedy understood the importance of popular support for the South Vietnamese government if that country was to maintain its independence. But he was reluctant to withdraw and let the Vietnamese solve their own problems.

Lyndon Johnson shared the same reservations. After an early briefing, he said he felt like a catfish that had "grabbed a big juicy worm with a right sharp hook in the middle of it." Soon after assuming the presidency, Johnson made a fundamental decision that guided policy for the next four years. South Vietnam was more unstable than ever after the assassination of Diem. Guerrillas, known as Viet Cong, challenged the regime, sometimes covertly, sometimes through the National

In 1963, Buddhist priests in Vietnam burned them-selves to death in Saigon to dramatize their opposi-tion to the Diem govern-ment. Photographs in American newspapers horrified readers and cre-ated suspicion that South Vietnam was led by a cor-rupt and autocratic leader. *(UPI/Corbis-Bettmann)*

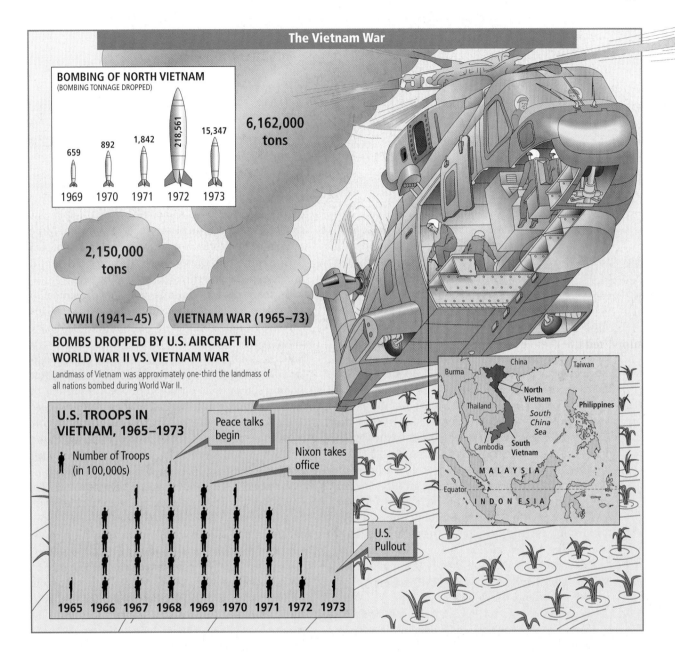

The Vietnam War

BOMBING OF NORTH VIETNAM
(BOMBING TONNAGE DROPPED)

659 — 1969
892 — 1970
1,842 — 1971
218,561 — 1972
15,347 — 1973

6,162,000 tons

2,150,000 tons

WWII (1941–45)   VIETNAM WAR (1965–73)

BOMBS DROPPED BY U.S. AIRCRAFT IN WORLD WAR II VS. VIETNAM WAR

Landmass of Vietnam was approximately one-third the landmass of all nations bombed during World War II.

U.S. TROOPS IN VIETNAM, 1965–1973

Number of Troops (in 100,000s)

Peace talks begin

Nixon takes office

U.S. Pullout

1965 1966 1967 1968 1969 1970 1971 1972 1973

China
Taiwan
Burma
North Vietnam
Thailand
South China Sea
Philippines
Cambodia
South Vietnam
MALAYSIA
Equator
INDONESIA

Liberation Front, their political arm. Aided by Ho Chi Minh and the North Vietnamese, the insurgent Viet Cong slowly gained ground. Henry Cabot Lodge, the American ambassador to South Vietnam, told Johnson that if he wanted to save that country, and indeed the whole region, he had to stand firm. "I am not going to lose Vietnam," Johnson replied. "I am not going to be the President who saw Southeast Asia go the way China went."

In the election campaign of 1964, Johnson posed as a man of peace. "We don't want our American boys to do the fighting for Asian boys," he declared. "We are not going to send American boys nine or ten thousand miles away from home to do what Asian boys ought to be doing for themselves." He criticized

those who suggested moving in with American bombs. But secretly he was planning to escalate the American role.

Escalation

In August 1964, Johnson cleverly obtained congressional authorization for the war by announcing that North Vietnamese torpedo boats had made unprovoked attacks on American destroyers in the international waters of the Gulf of Tonkin, 30 miles from North Vietnam. Only later did it become clear that the American ships had violated the territorial waters of North Vietnam by assisting South Vietnamese commando raids in offshore combat zones. With the details of the attack

Recovering the Past

PUBLIC OPINION POLLS

In recent years, historians have used a new source of evidence: the public opinion poll. People have always been concerned with what others think, and leaders have often sought to frame their behavior according to the preferences of the populace. As techniques of assessing the mind of the public have become more sophisticated, the poll has emerged as an integral part of the analysis of social and political life. Polls now measure opinion on many questions—social, cultural, intellectual, political, and diplomatic. Because of polls' increasing importance, it is useful to know how to use them in an effort to understand and recover the past.

The principle of polling is not new. In 1824 the *Harrisburg Pennsylvanian* sought to predict the winner of that year's presidential race, and in the 1880s, the *Boston Globe* sent reporters to selected precincts on election night to forecast final returns. In 1916, *Literary Digest* began conducting postcard polls to predict political results. By the 1930s, Elmo Roper and George Gallup had further developed the field of market research and public opinion polling. Notwithstanding an embarrassing mistake by *Literary Digest* in predicting a Landon victory over FDR in 1936, polling had by World War II become a scientific enterprise.

According to Gallup, a poll is not magic but "merely an instrument for gauging public opinion," especially the views of those often unheard. As Elmo Roper said, the poll is "one of the few ways through which the so-called common man can be articulate." Polling, therefore, is a valuable way to recover the attitudes, beliefs, and voices of ordinary people.

Yet certain cautions should be observed. Like all instruments of human activity, polls are imperfect and may even be dangerous. Historians using information from polls need to be aware of how large the samples were, when the interviewing was done, and how opinions might have been molded by the form of the poll itself. Questions can be poorly phrased. Some hint at the desirable answer or plant ideas in the minds of those interviewed. Polls sometimes provide ambiguous responses that can be interpreted many ways. More seriously, some critics worry that human freedom itself is threatened by the pollsters' manipulative and increasingly accurate predictive techniques.

Despite these limitations, polls have become an ever-present part of American life. In the late 1940s and early 1950s, Americans were polled frequently about topics ranging from foreign aid, the United Nations, and the occupation of Germany and Japan to labor legislation, child punishment, and whether women should wear slacks in public (39 percent of men said no, as did 49 percent of women). Such topics as the first use of nuclear arms, presidential popularity, national defense, and U.S. troop intervention in a troubled area of the world remain as pertinent today as they were then.

A number of the polls included here deal with foreign policy during the Cold War in the early 1950s. How did people respond to Soviet nuclear capability? How did they regard Russian intentions and the appropriate American response? How do you analyze the results of these polls? What do you think is the significance of rating responses by levels of education? In what ways are the questions "loaded"? How might the results of these polls influence American foreign policy? What do you think is significant about the Indochina poll? These polls show the challenge-and-response nature of the Cold War. How do you think Americans would respond today to these questions?

Polls also shed light on domestic issues. Consider the poll on professions for young men and women taken in 1950. What does it tell us about the attitudes of the pollster on appropriate careers for men and women? Why do you think both men and women had nearly identical views on this subject? How do you think people today would answer these questions? Would they be presented in the same way? Also observe the poll on women in politics. To what extent have attitudes on this issue changed in the intervening years?

Foreign Policy Polls

December 2, 1949—Atom Bomb
Now that Russia has the atom bomb, do you think another war is more likely or less likely?

More likely	45%
Less likely	28%
Will make no difference	17%
No opinion	10%

BY EDUCATION
College

More likely 36%	Will make no difference 23%
Less likely 35%	No opinion 6%

High School

More likely 44%	Will make no difference 19%
Less likely 28%	No opinion 9%

Grade School

More likely 50%	Will make no difference 12%
Less likely 26%	No opinion 12%

May 1, 1950—National Defense
Do you think United States Government spending on national defense should be increased, decreased, or remain about the same?

Increased	63%
Same	24%
Decreased	7%
No opinion	6%

September 18, 1953—Indochina
The United States is now sending war materials to help the French fight the Communists in Indochina. Would you approve or disapprove of sending United States soldiers to take part in the fighting there?

Approve	8%
Disapprove	85%
No opinion	7%

January 11, 1950—Russia
As you hear and read about Russia these days, do you believe Russia is trying to build herself up to be the ruling power of the world—or is Russia just building up protection against being attacked in another war?

Rule the world	70%
Protect herself	18%
No opinion	12%

BY EDUCATION
College

Rule the world	73%
Protect herself	21%
No opinion	6%

High School

Rule the world	72%
Protect herself	18%
No opinion	10%

Grade School

Rule the world	67%
Protect herself	17%
No opinion	16%

February 12, 1951—Atomic Warfare
If the United States gets into an all-out war with Russia, do you think we should drop atom bombs on Russia first—or do you think we should use the atom bomb only if it is used on us?

Drop A-bomb first	66%
Only if used on us	19%
No opinion	15%

The greatest difference was between men and women—72% of the men questioned favored our dropping the bomb first, compared to 61% of the women.

Source: George H. Gallup, *The Gallup Poll: Public Opinion, 1935–1971*, vol. 2 (New York: Random House, 1972). © American Institute of Public Opinion.

Domestic Policy Polls

October 29, 1949—Women in Politics
If the party whose candidate you most often support nominated a woman for President of the United States, would you vote for her if she seemed qualified for the job?

Yes	48%
No	48%
No opinion	4%

BY SEX
Men

Yes	45%
No	50%
No opinion	5%

Women

Yes	51%
No	46%
No opinion	3%

BY POLITICAL AFFILIATION
Democrats

Yes	50%
No	48%
No opinion	2%

Republicans

Yes	46%
No	50%
No opinion	4%

Would you vote for a woman for Vice President of the United States if she seemed qualified for the job?

Yes	53%
No	43%
No opinion	4%

May 5, 1950—Most Important Problem
What do you think is the most important problem facing the entire country today?

War, threat of war	40%
Atomic bomb control	6%
Economic problems, living costs, inflation, taxes	15%
Strikes and labor troubles	4%
Corruption in government	3%
Unemployment	10%
Housing	3%
Communism	8%
Others	11%

July 12, 1950—Professions
Suppose a young man came to you and asked your advice about taking up a profession. Assuming that he was qualified to enter any of these professions, which one of them would you first recommend to him?

Doctor of medicine	29%
Government worker	6%
Engineer, builder	16%
Professor, teacher	5%
Business executive	8%
Banker	4%
Clergyman	8%
Dentist	4%
Lawyer	8%
Veterinarian	3%
None, don't know	9%

July 15, 1950—Professions
Suppose a young girl came to you and asked your advice about taking up a profession. Assuming that she was qualified to enter any of these professions, which one of them would you first recommend?

CHOICE OF WOMEN

Nurse	33%
Teacher	15%
Secretary	8%
Social service worker	8%
Dietitian	7%
Dressmaker	4%
Beautician	4%
Airline stewardess	3%
Actress	3%
Journalist	2%
Musician	2%
Model	2%
Librarian	2%
Medical, dental technician	1%
Others	2%
Don't know	4%

The views of men on this subject were nearly identical with those of women.

Source: George H. Gallup, *The Gallup Poll: Public Opinion, 1935–1971*, vol. 2 (New York: Random House, 1972). © American Institute of Public Opinion.

Napalm, a jellylike chemical dropped by American planes, stuck to people as it burned. In this picture, widely circulated throughout the world, a small girl whose skin was seared off by napalm tries unsuccessfully to escape the ravages of war. *(AP/Wide World Photos)*

still unclear, Johnson used the episode to obtain from Congress a resolution giving him authority to "take all necessary measures to repel any armed attack against the forces of the United States and to prevent further aggression." The Gulf of Tonkin resolution gave Johnson the leverage he sought. As he noted, it was "like grandma's nightshirt—it covered everything."

Military escalation began in earnest in February 1965, after Viet Cong forces killed 7 Americans and wounded 109 in an attack on an American base at Pleiku. Johnson responded by authorizing retaliatory bombing of North Vietnam to cut off the flow of supplies and to ease pressure on South Vietnam. He personally authorized every raid, boasting that the air force "can't even bomb an outhouse without my approval." A few months later, the president sent American ground troops into action. This marked the crucial turning point in the Americanization of the Vietnam War. Only 25,000 American soldiers were in Vietnam at the start of 1965; by the end of the year there were 184,000. The number swelled to 385,000 in 1966, to 485,000 in 1967, and to 543,000 in 1968.

American forces became direct participants in the fight to prop up a dictatorial regime in faraway South Vietnam. Although a somewhat more effective government headed by Nguyen Van Thieu and Nguyen Cao Ky was finally established, the level of violence increased. Saturation bombing of North Vietnam continued. Fragmentation bombs, killing and maiming countless civilians, and napalm, which seared off human flesh, were used extensively. Similar destruction wracked South Vietnam.

Protesting the War

Americans began to protest their involvement in the war. As escalation began, 82 percent of the public felt that American forces should stay in Vietnam until the Communist elements withdrew. Then students began to question basic Cold War assumptions about battling Communism around the globe. The first antiwar teach-in took place in March 1965 at the University of Michigan. Others soon followed. Initially, both supporters and opponents of the war appeared at the teach-ins, but soon the sessions became more like antiwar rallies than instructional affairs. Boxer Muhammad Ali legitimated draft resistance when he declared, "I ain't got no quarrel with them Viet Cong," and refused military induction. Working through Students for a Democratic Society (SDS) and other organizations, radical activists campaigned against the draft, attacked ROTC units on campus, and sought to discredit firms that produced the destructive tools of war (see Chapter 29 for a full discussion of student activism). "Make love, not war," students proclaimed.

The antiwar movement expanded. Women Strike for Peace, the most forceful women's antiwar organization, mobilized support by saying, "Stop! Don't drench the jungles of Asia with the blood of our sons. Don't force our sons to kill women and children whose only crime is to live in a country ripped by civil war." Students became even more shrill. "Hey, hey, LBJ. How many kids did you kill today?" they chanted. In 1967, some 300,000 people marched in New York City. In Washington, D.C., 100,000 tried to close down the Pentagon.

Working-class and middle-class Americans began to sour on the war at the time of the Tet offensive, celebrating the lunar new year in early 1968. The North Vietnamese mounted a massive attack on provincial capitals and district towns in South Vietnam. In Saigon, they struck the American embassy, Tan Son Nhut air base, and the presidential palace. Though beaten back, they won a psychological victory. American audiences watched the fighting on television, as they had for several years, seeing images of burning huts and wounded soldiers each evening. During the Tet offensive, American TV networks showed scenes of a kind never screened before. One such clip, from NBC News, appears here in still photograph form. Viewers who watched the television clip saw the corpse drop to the ground, blood spouting from his head. Gazing at such graphic representations of death and destruction, many Americans wondered about their nation's purposes and actions—indeed, about whether the war could be won.

When Richard Nixon assumed office in 1969, he understood the need to heal the rifts that the war had torn through American society. A lonely, aloof man who had gained political prominence as one of the nation's most aggressive anti-Communists, he now promised to bring the nation together. He gave top priority to extricating the United States from Vietnam while still seeking a way to win the war. To that end, he announced the Nixon Doctrine, which asserted that the United States would aid friends and allies but would not undertake the full burden of troop defense. The policy of Vietnamization entailed removing American forces and replacing them with Vietnamese troops. At the same time, Americans launched ferocious air attacks on North Vietnam. "Let's blow the hell out of them," Nixon instructed the Joint Chiefs of Staff. Between 1968 and 1972, American troop strength dropped from 543,000 to 39,000, and the reduction won political support for Nixon at home. Yet as the transition occurred, the South Vietnamese steadily lost ground to the Viet Cong.

War protests multiplied in 1969 and 1970. In November 1969, as a massive protest demonstration took place in Washington, D.C., stories surfaced about a horrifying massacre of civilians in Vietnam the year before. My Lai, a small village in South Vietnam, was allegedly harboring 250 members of the Viet Cong. An American infantry company was helicoptered in to clear out the village. C Company had already taken heavy combat losses as it prepared to confront the enemy soldiers. Instead of troops, it found women, children, and old men. Perhaps hardened to the random destruction already wrought by the American military, perhaps concerned with the sometimes fuzzy distinction between combatants and civilians in a guerrilla war, the American forces

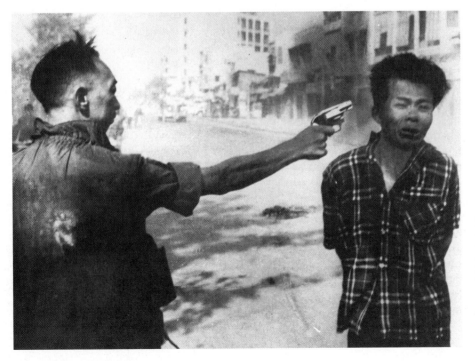

In this picture, General Loan, the chief of the South Vietnamese National Police, looks at a Viet Cong prisoner, lifts his gun, and calmly blows out the captive's brains. This prizewinning photograph captured the horror of the war for many Americans. (AP/Wide World Photos)

lost control and mowed down the civilians in cold blood. Private Paul Meadlo, one of the soldiers involved, later recalled:

> We huddled them up. We made them squat down. . . . I poured about four clips into the group. . . . The mothers was hugging their children. . . . Well, we kept right on firing. They was waving their arms and begging. . . . I still dream about it. About the women and children in my sleep. Some days . . . some nights, I can't even sleep.

Much as Nixon wanted to defuse opposition to the war, he was determined not to lose the struggle either. Realizing that the Vietnamese relied on supplies funneled through Cambodia, Nixon announced in mid-1970 that American and Vietnamese troops were invading that country to clear out Communist enclaves there. The United States, he said, would not stand by as a "pitiful helpless giant" when there were actions it could take to stem the Communist advance.

Nixon's invasion of Cambodia brought renewed demonstrations on college campuses, some with tragic results. At Kent State University in Ohio, the antiwar response was fierce. The day after the president announced his moves, disgruntled students gathered downtown. Worried about the crowd, the local police called in sheriff's deputies to disperse the students. The next evening, groups of students collected on the college grounds. Assembling around the ROTC building, they began throwing firecrackers and rocks at the structure, which had become a hated symbol of the war. Then they set it on fire and watched it burn to the ground.

The governor of Ohio ordered the National Guard to the university. Tension grew, and finally the situation exploded. The Guardsmen watched as students gathered on campus. Though most were so far away they could not have reached the troops, the soldiers reacted by firing without provocation on the students. When the shooting stopped, four students lay dead, nine wounded. Two of the dead had been demonstrators, who were more than 250 feet away when shot. The other two were innocent bystanders, almost 400 feet from the troops.

Students around the country, as well as other Americans, were outraged by the attack. Many were equally disturbed about a similar attack at Jackson State University in Mississippi. As students there returned to their dormitories one evening, they saw police officers and National Guardsmen responding to a bonfire. A few taunted the law officers. The troops responded without warning by firing 460 rounds of automatic weapon fire into a women's dormitory.

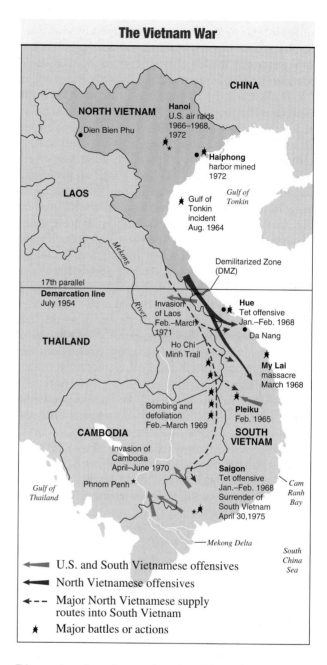

This map shows the major campaigns of the Vietnam War. The North Vietnamese Tet offensive of early 1968, pictured with red arrows, turned the tide against U.S. participation in the war and led to peace talks. The U.S. invasion of Cambodia in 1970, pictured with blue arrows, provoked serious opposition.

When the gunfire ceased, two people were dead, more wounded. The dead, however, were black students at a black institution, and white America paid less attention to this attack.

In 1971, the Vietnam War made major headlines once more when the *New York Times* began publishing a secret Department of Defense account of American involvement. The so-called Pentagon Papers, leaked

When Ohio National Guardsmen fired on a crowd of antiwar demonstrators and killed four students, even prowar Americans were shocked. This photograph shows the grief and outrage of one woman who survived the savage shooting of innocent bystanders. *(Valley Daily News, Tarantum, Pennsylvania)*

by Daniel Ellsberg, a defense analyst, gave Americans a firsthand look at the fabrications and faulty assumptions that had guided the steady expansion of the struggle. Even though the study stopped with the Johnson years, the Nixon administration was furious and tried, without success, to block publication.

Peace and Its Consequences

Vietnam remained a political football as Nixon ran for reelection in 1972. Negotiations aimed at a settlement were under way, and just days before the election, Secretary of State Henry Kissinger announced, "Peace is at hand." When South Vietnam seemed to balk at the proposed settlement, however, the administration responded with the most intensive bombing campaign of the war. Hanoi, the capital of North Vietnam, was hit hard, and North Vietnamese harbors were mined. Only in the new year was a cease-fire finally signed.

The conflict in Vietnam lingered on into the spring of 1975. When at last the North Vietnamese consolidated their control over the entire country, Gerald Ford, Nixon's successor as president, called for another $1 billion in aid, even as the South Vietnamese were abandoning arms and supplies in chaotic retreat. But Congress refused, leaving South Vietnam's crumbling government to fend for itself. Republicans hailed Kissinger for having finally freed the United States from the Southeast Asian quagmire. Antiwar critics condemned him for remaining involved for so long.

The *New Republic* wryly observed that Kissinger brought peace to Vietnam in the same way Napoleon brought peace to Europe: by losing.

The long conflict had enormous consequences. Disillusionment with the war undermined assumptions about America's role in world affairs. In the longest war in its history, the United States lost almost 58,000 men, with far more wounded or maimed. Blacks and Chicanos suffered more than whites, since they were disproportionately represented in combat units. Many minority men saw military service as a means of advancement. In 1965, 24 percent of all soldiers killed in Vietnam were African American—a figure far higher than their percentage of the population as a whole. Financially, the nation spent over $150 billion on the unsuccessful war. Domestic reform slowed, then stopped. Cynicism about the government increased, and American society was deeply divided. Only time would heal the wounds.

Post-Vietnam Détente

If the Republicans' Vietnam policy was a questionable success, accomplishments were impressive in other areas. Nixon, the consummate Red-baiter of the past, dealt imaginatively and successfully with the major Communist powers, reversing the direction of American policy since the Second World War.

Nixon's most dramatic step was establishing better relations with the People's Republic of China. In the two decades since Mao Zedong's victory in the

MAJOR EVENTS OF THE COLD WAR

Year	Event	Effect
1946	Winston Churchill's "Iron Curtain" speech	First Western "declaration" of the Cold War
	George F. Kennan's long telegram	Spoke of Soviet insecurity and the need for containment
1947	George F. Kennan's article signed "Mr. X"	Elaborated on arguments in the telegram
	Truman Doctrine	Provided economic and military aid to Greece and Turkey
	Federal Employee Loyalty Program	Sought to root out subversion in the U.S. government
	HUAC investigation of the motion picture industry	Sought to expose Communist influences in the movies
1948	Marshall Plan	Provided massive American economic aid in rebuilding postwar Europe
	Berlin airlift	Brought in supplies when USSR closed off land access to the divided city
1949	NATO	Created a military alliance to withstand a possible Soviet attack
	First Soviet atomic bomb	Ended the American nuclear monopoly
	Communist victory in China	Made Americans fear the worldwide spread of Communism
1950	Conviction of Alger Hiss	Seemed to bear out Communist danger at home
	Joseph McCarthy's first charges	Launched aggressive anti-Communist campaign in the United States
	NSC-68	Called for vigilance and increased military spending to counter the Communist threat
	Outbreak of the Korean War	North Korean invasion of South Korea viewed as part of Soviet conspiracy
1953	Armistice in Korea	Brought little change after years of bitter fighting
1954	Vietnamese victory over French at Dien Bien Phu	Early triumph for nationalism in Southeast Asia
	Army–McCarthy hearings	Brought downfall of Joseph McCarthy
1961	Invasion at the Bay of Pigs	Showed U.S. efforts to check the spread of Communism in the Americas
1962	Cuban missile crisis	Showed U.S. determination to resist Soviet intrusion in Cuba
1973	Cease-fire in Vietnam	Allowed the United States to withdraw from Vietnam
1975	North Vietnamese victory in Vietnam	Ended the war and allowed for unification of Vietnam

Nixon's policy of détente resulted in improved relations with the Soviet Union. Here he and Soviet leader Leonid Brezhnev toast one another at the signing of the Strategic Arms Limitation Treaty. (*UPI/Corbis-Bettmann*)

Nixon shifted the course of U.S.–China relations by his dramatic visit to the People's Republic. He met Chinese officials for the first time, visited the Great Wall, shown in this picture, and then reported back enthusiastically to the American people. *(Corbis)*

Chinese revolution in 1949, the United States had refused to recognize the Communist government on the mainland, insisting that Jiang Jieshi's rump regime on Taiwan alone was rightful government of the Chinese people. In 1971, with an eye on the upcoming elections, Nixon began softening his administration's rigid stance. After the Chinese invited an American table tennis team to visit the mainland, the United States eased some trading restrictions. Then Nixon announced that he intended to visit China the following year. He suspected that he could use Chinese friendship as a bargaining chip when he dealt with the Soviet Union. He acknowledged what most nations already knew: Communism was not monolithic. He believed that he could open a dialogue with the Chinese Communists without political harm, for he had long ago established his anti-Communist credentials. Finally, he recognized that the press and television coverage of a dramatic trip could boost his image, as indeed it did.

Nixon went to China in February 1972. He met with Chinese leaders Mao Zedong and Zou Enlai (Chou Enlai), talked about international problems, exchanged toasts, and saw some of the major sights. Wherever he went, American television cameras followed, helping introduce to the American public a nation about which it knew little. Though formal diplomatic relations were not yet restored, détente between the two countries had begun.

Seeking to play one Communist state against the other, Nixon also visited Russia, where he was likewise warmly welcomed. At a cordial summit meeting, the president and Soviet premier Leonid Brezhnev signed the first Strategic Arms Limitation Treaty (SALT I). In addition to this move to limit missile stockpiles, the two nations agreed to cooperate in space and to ease long-standing restrictions on trade. Business applauded the new approach, and most Americans approved of détente.

When Gerald Ford assumed office, he followed the policies begun under Nixon, even if he ceased calling the approach détente. He continued the strategic arms limitation talks that provided hope for eventual nuclear disarmament, which culminated in the even more comprehensive SALT II agreement, signed but never ratified during Jimmy Carter's presidency.

Timeline

1945	Yalta Conference
	Roosevelt dies; Harry Truman becomes president
	Potsdam Conference
1946	American plan for control of atomic energy fails
	Atomic Energy Act
	Iran crisis
	Churchill's "Iron Curtain" speech
1947	Truman Doctrine
	Federal Employee Loyalty Program
	House Un-American Activities Committee (HUAC) investigates the movie industry
1948	Marshall Plan launched
	Berlin airlift
	Israel created by the United Nations
	Hiss–Chambers case
	Truman elected president
1949	Soviet Union tests atomic bomb
	North Atlantic Treaty Organization (NATO) established
	George Orwell, *1984*
	Mao Zedong's forces win Chinese civil war; Jiang Jieshi flees to Taiwan
1950	Truman authorizes development of the hydrogen bomb
	Alger Hiss convicted
	Joseph McCarthy's Wheeling (W. Va.) speech on subversion
	NSC-68
	McCarran Internal Security Act
1950–1953	Korean War
1951	Japanese–American treaty
1952	Dwight D. Eisenhower elected president
	McCarthy heads Senate Permanent Investigations Subcommittee
1953	Stalin dies; Khrushchev consolidates power
	East Germans stage anti-Soviet demonstrations
	Shah of Iran returns to power in CIA-supported coup
1954	Fall of Dien Bien Phu ends French control of Indochina
	Geneva Conference
	Guatemalan government overthrown with CIA help
	Mao's forces shell Quemoy and Matsu
	Army–McCarthy hearings

1956	Suez incident
	Hungarian "freedom fighters" suppressed
	Eisenhower reelected
1957	Russians launch *Sputnik* satellite
1958	U.S. troops sent to support Lebanese government
1959	Castro deposes Batista in Cuba
1960	John F. Kennedy elected president
1961	Bay of Pigs invasion fails
	Khrushchev and Kennedy meet in Berlin
	Berlin Wall constructed
1962	Cuban missile crisis
1963	Buddhist demonstrations in Vietnam
	President Diem assassinated in Vietnam
	Kennedy assassinated; Lyndon B. Johnson becomes president
1964	Gulf of Tonkin resolution
	Johnson reelected
1965	Vietnam conflict escalates
	Marines sent to Dominican Republic
1967–1968	Antiwar demonstrations
1968	Tet offensive in Vietnam
	Richard Nixon elected president
	My Lai incident
1969	Nixon Doctrine announced
	Moratorium against the Vietnam War
	SALT talks begin
1970	U.S. invasion of Cambodia
	Shootings at Kent State and Jackson State universities
1971	*New York Times* publishes the Pentagon Papers
1972	Nixon visits People's Republic of China and Soviet Union
	Nixon reelected
	SALT I treaty on nuclear arms
1973	Vietnam cease-fire agreement
1975	South Vietnam falls to the Communists; end of the Vietnam War

Conclusion
The Cold War in Perspective

The Cold War dominated international relations for nearly 50 years. Tensions grew throughout the postwar years as the United States and the Soviet Union found themselves engaged in a bitter standoff that affected all diplomatic exchanges, encouraged an expensive arms race, and limited the resources available for reform at home.

What caused the Cold War? Historians have long argued over the question of where responsibility should be placed. In the early years after the Second World War, policymakers and commentators justified the American stance as a bold and courageous effort to meet the Communist threat. Later, particularly in the 1960s, as the war in Vietnam eroded confidence in American foreign policy, revisionist historians began to argue that American actions were misguided, insensitive to Soviet needs, and at least partially responsible for escalating friction. As with most historical questions, there are no easy answers, but both sides must be weighed.

The Cold War stemmed from a competition for international influence between the two great world powers. After World War II, the U.S. goal was to exercise economic and political leadership in the world and thus to institute capitalist economies and democratic political institutions throughout Europe and in nations emerging from colonial rule. But these goals put the United States on a collision course with nations, such as the Soviet Union, that had a different vision of what the postwar world should be like and with anticolonial movements in emerging countries around the globe. Perceiving threats from the Soviet Union, China, and other Communist countries, the United States clung to its deep-rooted sense of mission and embarked on an increasingly aggressive effort at containment, culminating in the ill-fated war in Vietnam, as the Communist nations of the world defended their own interests with equal force. The Cold War, with its profound effects at home and abroad, was the unfortunate result.

Recommended Reading

Origins of the Cold War

Stephen E. Ambrose, *Rise to Globalism: American Foreign Policy Since 1938*, 3rd rev. ed. (1983); John Lewis Gaddis, *The Long Peace: Inquiries into the History of the Cold War* (1987), *The United States and the Origins of the Cold War, 1941–1947* (1972), and *We Know Now: Rethinking Cold War History* (1997); Walter LaFeber, *America, Russia, and the Cold War, 1945–1996*, 8th ed. (1996); Ralph B. Levering, *The Cold War: A Post–Cold War History* (1994); Thomas J. McCormick, *America's Half Century: United States Foreign Policy in the Cold War* (1992); Ronald A. Powaski, *The Cold War: The United States and the Soviet Union, 1917–1991* (1997); Daniel Yergin, *Shattered Peace: The Origins of the Cold War and the National Security State* (1977).

Containing the Soviet Union

H. W. Brands, Jr., *Cold Warriors: Eisenhower's Generation and American Foreign Policy* (1988); Robert A. Divine, *Eisenhower and the Cold War* (1981) and *The Sputnik Challenge: Eisenhower's Response to the Soviet Satellite* (1993); Michael J. Hogan, *The Marshall Plan: America, Britain, and the Reconstruction of Western Europe* (1987) and *A Cross of Iron: Harry S. Truman and the Origins of the National Security State, 1945–1954* (1998); Townsend Hoopes, *The Devil and John Foster Dulles* (1973); Melvyn P. Leffler, *A Preponderance of Power: National Security, the Truman Administration, and the Cold War* (1992); Thomas G. Patterson, *Meeting the Communist Threat: Truman to Reagan* (1988).

Containment in Asia, the Middle East, and Latin America

Joseph C. Goulden, *Korea: The Untold Story of the War* (1982); Chaim Herzog, *The Arab-Israeli Wars: War and Peace in the Middle East*, rev. ed. (1984); Burton I. Kaufman, *The Korean War: Challenges in Crisis, Credibility, and Command* (1986); Walter LaFeber, *Inevitable Revolutions: The United States in Central America*, 2nd ed. (1993).

Atomic Weapons and the Cold War

Paul Boyer, *By the Bomb's Early Light: American Thought and Culture at the Dawn of the Atomic Age* (1985); McGeorge Bundy, *Danger and Survival: Choices About the Bomb in the First Fifty Years* (1988); Gregg Herken, *Counsels of War* (1985); Bruce Hevly and John M. Findlay, eds., *The Atomic West* (1998); Richard G. Hewlett and Francis Duncan, *Atomic Shield: Volume II: A History of the United States Atomic Energy Commission, 1947–1952* (1972); Richard G. Hewlett and Jack M. Holl, *Atoms for Peace and War: Eisenhower and the Atomic Energy Commission, 1953–1961* (1989); John Newhouse, *War and Peace in the Nuclear Age* (1989); Jessica Wang, *American Scientists in an Age of Anxiety: Scientists, Anti-Communism, and the Cold War* (1999); Spencer R. Weart, *Nuclear Fear: A History of Images* (1988); Allan M. Winkler, *Life Under a Cloud: American Anxiety About the Atom* (1993).

The Cold War at Home

John D'Emilio, "The Homosexual Menace: The Politics of Sexuality in Cold War America," in *Making Trouble: Essays on Gay History, Politics, and the University* (1992); Robert Griffith, *The Politics of Fear: Joseph R. McCarthy and the Senate* (1970); David M. Oshinsky, *A Conspiracy So Immense: The World of Joe McCarthy* (1983); Ronald Radash and Joyce Milton, *The Rosenberg File: A Search for Truth* (1984); Thomas C. Reeves, *The Life and Times of Joe McCarthy: A Biography* (1982); Lisle A. Rose, *The Cold War Comes to Main Street: America in 1950* (1999); Richard H. Rovere, *Senator Joe McCarthy* (1960); Ellen W. Schrecker, *No Ivory Tower: McCarthyism and the Universities* (1986), *The Age of McCarthyism: A Brief History with Documents* (1994), and *Many Are the Crimes: McCarthyism in America* (1998); Allen Weinstein, *Perjury: The Hiss-Chambers Case*, rev. ed. (1997); Allen Weinstein and Alexander Vassiliev, *The Haunted Wood: Soviet Espionage in America—The Stalin Era* (1999).

Continuing Confrontations with Communists

Laurence Chang and Peter Kornbluh, eds., *The Cuban Missile Crisis, 1962: A National Security Archive Documents Reader* (1998); Aleksandr Fursenko and Timothy Naftali, *One Hell of a Gamble: Khrushchev, Castro, and Kennedy* (1997); Ernest R. May and Philip D. Zelikow, eds., *The Kennedy Tapes: Inside the White House During the Cuban Missile Crisis* (1997); Richard J. Walton, *Cold War and Counterrevolution: The Foreign Policy of John F. Kennedy* (1972).

The Quagmire of Vietnam

Christian G. Appy, *Working-Class War: American Combat Soldiers and Vietnam* (1993); Frances FitzGerald, *Fire in the Lake: The Vietnamese and the Americans in Vietnam* (1972); David Halberstam, *The Best and the Brightest* (1972); Le Ly Hayslip, *When Heaven and Earth Changed Places* (1989); George C. Herring, *America's Longest War: The United States and Vietnam, 1950–1975*, 3rd ed. (1996) and *LBJ and Vietnam: A Different Kind of War* (1994); Stanley Karnow, *Vietnam: A History: The First Complete Account of Vietnam at War* (1983); Jeffrey P. Kimball, *Nixon's Vietnam War* (1998); Ron Kovic, *Born on the Fourth of July* (1976); Guenter Lewy, *America in Vietnam* (1978); Robert S. McNamara, *In Retrospect* (1995); George Donelson Moss, *Vietnam: An American Ordeal*, 3rd ed., (1997); Al Santoli,

Everything We Had: An Oral History of the Vietnam War by Thirty-three American Soldiers Who Fought It (1981); Neil Sheehan, *A Bright Shining Lie: John Paul Vann and America in Vietnam* (1988).

Fiction and Film

James A. Michener's *The Bridges at Toko-ri* (1953) is a novel about the frustrations of fighting the Korean War when people at home did not seem to care. Walter M. Miller, Jr.'s *A Canticle for Leibowitz* (1959) is about the devastation following a nuclear war that reduces civilization to a primitive state. Tim O'Brien's *Going After Cacciato* (1978) is a novel about Vietnam in which one soldier simply decides to lay down his gun and walk home. Nevil Shute's *On the Beach* (1957) is a novel about a nuclear war that wiped out most life and created a radioactive cloud that is killing the rest.

The film *Born on the Fourth of July* (1989) tells Ron Kovic's story about being wounded in Vietnam and then returning home. *Dr. Strangelove or: How I Learned to Stop Worrying and Love the Bomb* (1964) is a movie made by Stanley Kubrick about the absurdity of nuclear war. *On the Beach* (1959) is the film from the novel of the same name about a nuclear war that ends all life on earth. *Platoon* (1986) is a film about the soldiers' war in Vietnam. *The Cold War* (1998) is an outstanding multipart series made by CNN and shown on television.

Suggested Web Sites

http:/cnn.com/SPECIALS/cold.war/

Cold War. This is the companion site to the CNN series on the Cold War. It contains a good deal of information about a wide variety of issues.

http://www.koreanwar.org

Korean War Project. This site has information about the Korean War and is a guide to resources on the struggle.

http://www.cnn.com/SPECIALS/1999/nato/

NATO at 50. This site from CNN has an excellent timeline and images telling the history of the North Atlantic Treaty Organization.

http://webcorp.com/mccarthy/

Senator Joe McCarthy—A Multimedia Celebration. This webcorp site includes audio and visual clips of McCarthy's speeches.

http://library.advanced.org/11046/

Fourteen Days in October: The Cuban Missile Crisis. This creative site allows the viewer to explore the Cuban missile crisis.

http://www.pbs.org/wgbh/pages/amex/vietnam/index.html

Vietnam Online. From PBS and the American Experience, this site contains a detailed, interactive timeline of the war, interpretive essays, and autobiographical reflections.

http://www.spartacus.schoolnet.co.uk/vietintro.htm

Investigating the Vietnam War. This site contains narratives, personal accounts, and an excellent list of annotated links to the best Vietnam-related sites.

http://www.law.umkc.edu/faculty/projects/ftrials/mylai/mylai.htm

The My Lai Courts Martial (1970). This site contains chronology, images, and court documents describing the massacre of Vietnamese civilians at My Lai.

http://www.library.kent.edu/exhibits/4may95/index.html

May 4, 1970. This site commemorates the 25th anniversary of the shootings at Kent State University with a detailed chronology and other information.

http://www.ushistoryplace.com

 A richly detailed on-line learning environment complete with interactive maps, timelines, history activities, primary source documents, and links to related American history sites.

HIGH WATER *and* EBB TIDE *of the* LIBERAL STATE

CHAPTER OUTLINE

Paul Cowan was an idealist in the 1960s. Like many students who came of age in these years, he believed in the possibility of social change and plunged into the struggle for liberal reform. He shared the hopes and dreams of other members of his generation, who felt that their government could make a difference in people's lives.

Cowan's commitment had developed slowly. He was a child of the 1950s, when most Americans were caught up in the consumer culture and paid little attention to the problems of people less fortunate than themselves. His grandfather had sold used cement bags in Chicago, but his father had become an executive at CBS television, and Cowan grew up in comfortable surroundings. He graduated from the Choate School (where John Kennedy had gone) in 1958, and then from Harvard University (where Kennedy had also been a student) in 1963.

When he entered college, Cowan was interested in politically conscious writers like John Dos Passos, John Steinbeck, and James Agee and folk singers like Pete Seeger and Woody Guthrie. They offered him entrance, he later recalled, into a "nation that seemed to be filled with energy and decency," one that lurked "beneath the dull, conformist facade of the Eisenhower years." While at Harvard, he was excited by antinuclear campaigns in New England and civil rights demonstrations in the South.

After college, he made good on his commitment to civil rights by going to Mississippi to work in the Freedom Summer Project of 1964. He was inspired by the example of John Kennedy, the liberal president whose administration promised "a new kind of politics" that could make the nation, and the world, a better place. During that summer, he wrote, "it was possible to believe that by changing ourselves we could change, and redeem, our America."

The Peace Corps came next. Paul and his wife, Rachel, were convinced that this organization, the idea of the young president, "really was a unique government agency, permanently protected by the lingering magic of John F. Kennedy's name." They were assigned to the city of Guayaquil, in Ecuador, in South America. Their task was to serve as mediators between administrators of the city hall and residents of the slums. They wanted to try to raise the standard of living by encouraging local governments to provide basic services such as garbage disposal and clean water.

But the work proved more frustrating than they had imagined. They bristled at the restrictions imposed by the Peace Corps bureaucracy. They despaired at the inadequate resources local government officials had to accomplish their aims. They wondered if they were simply new imperialists, trying to impose their values on others who had priorities of their own. "From the day we moved into the *barrio*," Cowan later recalled, "the question we were most frequently asked by the people we were supposed to be organizing was whether we would leave them our clothes when we returned to the States."

Cowan came home disillusioned. "I saw that even the liberals I had wanted to emulate, men who seemed to be devoting their lives to fighting injustice, were unable to accept people from alien cultures on any terms but their own." He called his account of his own odyssey *The Making of an Un-American*.

Paul Cowan's passage through the 1960s mirrored the passage of American society as a whole. Millions of Americans shared his views as the period began. Mostly comfortable and confident, they supported the liberal agenda advanced by the Democratic party of John Kennedy and Lyndon Johnson. They endorsed the proposition that the government had responsibility for the welfare of all its citizens and accepted the need for a more active government role to help those who were unable to help themselves. That commitment lay behind the legislative achievements of the "Great Society," the last wave of twentieth-century reform that built upon the gains of the Progressive era and the New Deal years before.

Then political reaction set in, as the nation was torn apart by the ravages of the Vietnam War. Liberal assumptions eroded, as conservatives argued that an activist approach was responsible for the chaos consuming the country. Republicans who assumed power at the end of the 1960s accepted the basic outlines of the welfare state but rejected many of the liberal initiatives of Democratic administrations as expensive failures. Under Richard Nixon

The United States was comfortable and confident as the 1960s began. The basic consensus about the responsibility of the government to help those who could not help themselves eroded in the turbulent years that followed. *(George Giusti, "Civilization is a method of living, an attitude of equal respect for all men," Jane Addams, 1893. From the series Great Ideas of Western Man, 1955/National Museum of American Art, Washington, DC/Art Resource, New York)*

and Gerald Ford, Republicans capitalized on disillusionment with federal policy and crafted a new consensus that kept them in the White House for most of the next decade and a half. The presidency of Democrat Jimmy Carter was unable to reverse the conservative shift. Liberals despaired as they watched the destruction of their dreams.

This chapter describes both the climax of twentieth-century liberalism and its subsequent decline. It focuses on the effort of the government, begun in the New Deal of Franklin Roosevelt, to help those caught short by the advances of industrial capitalism. It examines first the initiatives in the 1940s and 1950s and early 1960s to provide necessary assistance to the less fortunate members of American society, then the efforts in the late 1960s and 1970s to limit such aid. In pondering the possibilities of reform, this chapter outlines the various attempts to devise an effective political response to the major structural changes in the post–World War II economy outlined in Chapter 26. It explores the debates that took place and the shifts that occurred as the political system struggled to cope with the problems of wholesale economic transformation and to maintain the promise of American life.

✑ THE ORIGINS OF THE WELFARE STATE

The modern American welfare state originated in the New Deal. Roosevelt's efforts to deal with the ravages of the Great Depression and protect Americans from the problems stemming from industrial capitalism (see Chapter 24) provided the basis for subsequent reform. Harry Truman's Fair Deal built squarely on Roosevelt's New Deal, though Truman often found himself stymied by a conservative Congress. His Republican successor, Dwight Eisenhower, sought to scale down spending but made no effort to roll back the most important initiatives of the welfare state. Actions taken in the post–World War II years provided the groundwork for the major reforms of the 1960s.

Truman's Approach

Like Roosevelt, Harry Truman believed that the federal government had the responsibility for ensuring the social welfare of all Americans. He shared his predecessor's commitment to assisting less prosperous inhabitants of the country in a systematic, rational way. Truman wanted his administration to embrace and act upon a series of carefully defined social and economic goals that would extend New Deal initiatives even further.

Immediate problems of reconversion had to be resolved first, to be sure: demands for the return of servicemen, fears of inflation, and labor unrest. But even as he worked (not always successfully) to handle these issues, Truman outlined his larger vision of the welfare state.

As he articulated his goals, Truman took the same feisty approach to public policy that characterized his conduct of foreign affairs (see Chapter 27). He stated his position clearly and simply, often in black-and-white terms. Persuaded that plain speaking was the best approach, he seldom hesitated to let others know exactly where he stood. He attacked his political enemies vigorously when they resisted his initiatives and often took his case to the American people. He was, in many ways, an old-style Democratic politician, schooled and supported by Missouri's Democratic machine, who hoped to use his authority to benefit the middle-class and working-class Americans who made up his political base.

His first articulation of domestic priorities came less than a week after the end of World War II. Truman called on Congress to pass a 21-point program that would produce stability and security in the postwar era by providing full-employment legislation, a higher minimum wage, greater unemployment compensation, and housing assistance. During the next ten weeks, Truman sent blueprints of further proposals to Congress, including health insurance and atomic energy legislation. But this liberal program soon ran into fierce political opposition.

The debate surrounding the Employment Act of 1946 hinted at the fate of Truman's proposals. This measure was a deliberate effort to apply the theory of English economist John Maynard Keynes to preserve economic equilibrium and prevent depression. Keynes had argued a decade earlier that massive spending was necessary to extricate a nation from depression (see Chapter 24). The money spent during World War II caused the economy to respond precisely as Keynes had predicted. Now economists wanted to institutionalize his ideas to forestall further problems. The initial bill, which enjoyed the strong support of labor, committed the government to maintaining full employment by monitoring the economy and taking remedial action in case of decline. Responses to a downturn included tax cuts and spending programs to stimulate the economy and reduce unemployment.

While liberals and labor leaders hailed the measure, business groups such as the National Association of

Truman was a down-to-earth politician who was most comfortable when he could appeal informally to his constituents. His direct approach, however, sometimes got him into trouble. *(UPI/Corbis-Bettmann)*

Manufacturers condemned it. They claimed that government intervention would undermine free enterprise and move the United States one step closer to socialism. Responding to the business community, Congress cut the proposal to bits, and Truman was powerless to respond. As finally passed, the act created a Council of Economic Advisers to make recommendations to the president, who was to report annually to Congress and the nation on the state of the economy. But it stopped short of committing the government to using fiscal tools to maintain full employment when economic indicators turned downward. For all of Truman's rhetoric, the act was only a modest continuation of New Deal attempts at economic planning.

Truman's Struggle with a Conservative Congress

As the midterm elections of 1946 approached, Truman and his supporters knew they were vulnerable. Many Democrats still pined for FDR, and when they questioned what Roosevelt would have done had he been alive, the standard retort was, "I wonder what Truman would do if he were alive." Truman appeared to be a petty, bungling administrator who became the butt of countless political jokes. Opponents observed, "You just sort of forget about Harry until he makes another mistake." As more and more people questioned his competence as president, his support dropped from 87 percent of those polled after he assumed the office to 32 percent in November 1946. Gleeful Republicans asked the voters, "Had enough?"

The voters answered that they had. Republicans won majorities in both houses of Congress for the first time since the 1928 elections and gained a majority of the governorships as well. In Atlantic City, New Jersey, a Republican candidate for justice of the peace who had died a week before the election was victorious in the sweep.

After the 1946 elections, Truman faced an unsympathetic 80th Congress. Republicans and conservative Democrats, dominating both houses, planned to reverse the liberal policies of the Roosevelt years. Hoping to reestablish congressional authority and cut the power of the executive branch, they insisted on less government intervention in the business world and in private life. They demanded tax reduction and curtailment of the privileged position they felt labor had come to enjoy.

When the new Congress met, it slashed federal spending and taxes. Robert A. Taft, one of the Republican leaders in the Senate, believed that $5 to $6 billion could be cut to bring the overall budget down to $30 billion. In 1947, Congress twice passed tax-cut measures, only to watch Truman veto them both times. In 1948, another election year, Congress overrode the veto.

Congress also struck at Democratic labor policies. Angry at the gains won by labor in the 1930s and 1940s, Republicans wanted to check unions and to circumscribe their right to engage in the kind of disruptive strikes that had occurred immediately after the war, when more workers than ever before in the nation's history stayed away from their jobs. Early in Truman's presidency, Congress had passed a bill requiring notice for strikes as well as a cooling-off period if a strike occurred. Truman vetoed it. But in 1947, commanding more votes, the Republicans passed the Taft-Hartley Act, which intended to limit the power of unions by restricting the weapons they could employ. Revising the Wagner Act of 1935, the legislation spelled out unfair labor practices (such as preventing nonunion workers from working if they wished) and outlawed the closed shop, whereby an employee had to join a union before getting a job. The law likewise allowed states to prohibit the union shop, which forced workers to join the union after they had been hired. It also gave the president the right to call for an 80-day cooling-off period in strikes affecting national security and required union officials to sign non-Communist oaths.

Union leaders and members were furious. They called the measure a "slave-labor law" and argued vigorously that it eliminated many of their hard-won rights and left labor–management relations like they had been in pre–New Deal days. Vetoing the measure, Truman claimed that it was unworkable and unfair and went on nationwide radio to seek public approval. This regained him some of the support he had earlier lost when he had sought to force strikers to go back to work in the immediate postwar period. Congress, however, passed the Taft-Hartley measure over Truman's veto.

The Fair Deal and Its Fate

In 1948, Truman wanted a chance to consolidate a liberal program and decided to seek the presidency in his own right. He knew that some people considered him an accidental occupant of the White House. He knew that some Democrats wanted to replace him with Dwight Eisenhower or Supreme Court Justice William O. Douglas or anyone else. That effort failed, but Truman was left with what most people thought was a worthless nomination. Not only was his own popularity waning, but the Democratic party itself seemed to be falling apart.

The civil rights issue—aimed at securing political rights for African Americans—split the Democrats. Truman hoped to straddle it, at least until after the election, to avoid alienating the South. When liberals defeated a moderate platform proposal and pressed for a stronger stand on black civil rights, angry delegates from Mississippi and Alabama stormed out of the convention. They later formed the States' Rights, or Dixiecrat, party. At their own convention, delegates from 13 states nominated Governor J. Strom Thurmond of South Carolina as their presidential candidate and affirmed their support for continued racial segregation.

Meanwhile, Henry A. Wallace, for seven years secretary of agriculture, then vice president during Roosevelt's third term and after that secretary of commerce, mounted his own challenge. Truman had fired Wallace from his cabinet for supporting a more temperate approach to the Soviet Union. Now Wallace became the presidential candidate of the Progressive party. Initially, he attracted widespread liberal interest because of his moderate position on Soviet–American affairs, his promotion of desegregation, and his promise to nationalize the railroads and major industries. But as Communists and "fellow travelers" appeared active in his organization, other support dropped off.

In that fragmented state, facing the first real third-party challenges since 1912, the Democrats took on the Republicans, who coveted the White House after 16 years out of power. Once again the GOP nominated New York Governor Thomas E. Dewey, the unsuccessful candidate in 1944. Stiff and egocentric, Dewey was hardly a charismatic figure. Still, the polls uniformly picked the Republicans to win. Dewey saw little value in brawling with his opponent and campaigned, in the words of one commentator, "with the humorless calculation of a Certified Public Accountant in pursuit of the Holy Grail."

Truman, as the underdog, conducted a two-fisted campaign. He appealed to ordinary Americans as an unpretentious man engaged in an uphill fight. Believing that everyone was against him but the people, he addressed Americans in familiar language. He called the Republicans a "bunch of old mossbacks" out to destroy the New Deal. He attacked the "do nothing" 80th Congress, which he had called into special session in 1948 with instructions to live up to the Republican platform. Predictably, the legislators failed, providing Truman with handy ammunition. Speaking without a prepared text in his choppy, aggressive style, he warmed to crowds, and they warmed to him. "Give 'em hell, Harry," they yelled. "Pour it on." He did.

Though all the polls predicted a Republican victory, the pollsters were wrong. On election day, disproving the bold headline "Dewey Defeats Truman" in the *Chicago Daily Tribune,* the incumbent president scored one of the most unexpected political upsets in American history, winning 303–189 in the Electoral College. Democrats also swept both houses of Congress.

Truman won primarily because he was able to revive the major elements of the Democratic coalition that Franklin Roosevelt had constructed more than a decade before. Despite the rocky days of 1946, Truman managed to hold on to labor, farm, and black votes. Labor's support, in particular, made a major differ-

In one of the nation's most extraordinary political upsets, Harry Truman beat Thomas E. Dewey in 1948. Here an exuberant Truman holds a newspaper headline printed while he slept, before the vote turned his way. *(Corbis-Bettmann)*

ence. Working men and women had been irritated by his response to the strikes in the immediate postwar period but had been buoyed by his veto, even though unsuccessful, of the Taft-Hartley Act. Still, union leaders at first seemed unwilling to support Truman's bid for a second term. Some hoped for a new party, or a new coalition within the Democratic party, that would better support their goals. Henry Wallace, however, worried them, and they feared being tarnished with the Communist label as the Cold War unfolded. They therefore backed Truman.

The fragmentation of the Democratic party, which had threatened to hurt the president severely, helped instead. The splinter parties drew off some votes but allowed Truman to make a more aggressive, direct appeal to the center, and that ultimately accounted for his success.

With the election behind him, Truman pursued his liberal program. In his 1949 State of the Union message, he declared, "Every segment of our population and every individual has a right to expect from our Government a fair deal." Fair Deal became the name for his domestic program, which included the measures he had proposed over and over since 1945.

Parts of Truman's Fair Deal worked; others did not. Lawmakers raised the minimum wage and expanded social security programs. A housing program brought modest gains but did not really meet housing needs. A farm program, aimed at providing income support to farmers if prices fell, never made it through Congress. Although he desegregated the military, other parts of his civil rights program failed to win congressional support (see Chapter 29). The American Medical Association undermined the effort to provide national health insurance, and Congress rejected a measure to provide federal aid to education.

The mixed record was not entirely Truman's fault. Conservative legislators were largely responsible for sabotaging his efforts. At the same time, critics charged correctly that Truman was often unpragmatic and shrill in his struggles with an unsympathetic Congress. They argued that he sometimes seemed to provoke the confrontations that became a hallmark of his presidency. They also claimed that he was most concerned with foreign policy as he strove to secure bipartisan support for Cold War initiatives (see Chapter 27). Committed to checking the perceived Soviet threat, he allowed his domestic program to suffer. As defense expenditures mounted, correspondingly less money was available for projects at home.

Still, Truman had kept the liberal vision alive. The Fair Deal had ratified many of the initiatives begun during the New Deal and had led Americans to take programs like social security for granted. Truman had not achieved everything he wanted—he had not even come close—but the nation had taken another step toward endorsing liberal goals.

The Election of Eisenhower

Acceptance of the liberal state continued in the 1950s, even as the Republicans took control. By 1952, Truman's popularity had plummeted, leaving him with the support of only 23 percent of the American people, and all indicators pointed to a political shift. The Democrats nominated Adlai Stevenson, Illinois's able, articulate, and moderately liberal governor. The Republicans turned to Dwight Eisenhower, the World War II hero Americans knew as Ike.

Stevenson approached political issues in intellectual terms. "Let's talk sense to the American people," he said. "Let's tell them the truth." While liberals loved his approach, Stevenson himself anticipated the probable outcome. How, he wondered, could a man named Adlai beat a soldier called Ike?

The Republicans focused on Communism, corruption, and Korea as major issues. They called the Democrats "soft on communism" and demanded a more aggressive approach at home and abroad. They criticized assorted scandals surrounding Truman's cronies and friends. The president himself was blameless, but some of the people near him were not. The Republicans also promised to end the unpopular Korean War.

Eisenhower proved to be a highly effective campaigner. Though this was his first effort to win political office, he had a natural talent for taking his case to the American people. He spoke in simple, reassuring terms they could understand. Throughout the campaign, he struck a grandfatherly pose, unified the various wings of his party, and went on to victory at the polls. He received 55 percent of the vote and carried 41 states. The new president took office with a Republican Congress as well and had little difficulty gaining a second term four years later.

"Modern Republicanism"

Eisenhower believed firmly in limiting the presidential role. He was uncomfortable with the growth of the executive office that had been taking place for the past 20 years. Like the Republicans in Congress with whom Truman had tangled, he wanted to restore the balance between the branches of government and to reduce the authority of the national government. He recognized, however, that it was impossible to scale back federal power to the limited levels of the 1920s, and he wanted to preserve social gains that even Republicans now accepted. Eisenhower sometimes termed his approach "dynamic conservatism" or "modern Republicanism," which, he explained, meant "conservative when it comes to money, liberal when it comes to human beings." Liberals quipped that his approach meant endorsing social projects and then failing to authorize the funds.

Above all, economic concerns dominated the Eisenhower years. The president and his chief aides wanted desperately to preserve the value of the dollar, pare down levels of funding, cut taxes, and balance the budget after years of deficit spending. To do that, the president appointed George Humphrey, a fiscal conservative, as secretary of the treasury. Humphrey placed a picture of Andrew Mellon, Calvin Coolidge's ultraconservative treasury head, in his office and declared, "We have to cut one-third out of the budget and you can't do that just by eliminating waste. This means, whenever necessary, using a meat axe." His words reflected the administration's approach to economic affairs. In times of economic stagnation, Republican leaders were willing to risk unemployment to keep inflation under control. The business orientation became obvious when Defense Secretary Charles E. Wilson, former president of General Motors, stated his position at confirmation hearings. "What is good for our country is good for General Motors," he declared, "and vice versa."

Eisenhower fulfilled his promise to reduce government's economic role. After Republicans received financial support from oil companies during the campaign, the new Congress, with a strong endorsement

PRESIDENTIAL ELECTIONS, 1948–1956				
Year	Candidate	Party	Popular Vote	Electoral Vote
1948	HARRY S TRUMAN	Democratic	24,105,812 (49.5%)	303
	Thomas E. Dewey	Republican	21,970,065 (45.1%)	189
	J. Strom Thurmond	States' Rights	1,169,063 (12.4%)	39
	Henry A. Wallace	Progressive	1,157,172 (12.4%)	0
1952	DWIGHT D. EISENHOWER	Republican	33,936,234 (55.1%)	442
	Adlai E. Stevenson	Democratic	27,314,992 (44.4%)	89
1956	DWIGHT D. EISENHOWER	Republican	35,590,472 (57.4%)	457
	Adlai E. Stevenson	Democratic	26,022,752 (42.0%)	73

Note: Winners' names appear in capital letters.

Eisenhower was the first president to make extensive use of the new medium of television. Though he took a low-key approach to his office, his intent gaze and wide smile gave Americans a sense of confidence that the country was in good hands, and they listened carefully when he spoke to the nation, as in this televised report on civil defense in 1955. *(AP/World Wide Photos)*

from the president, passed the Submerged Lands Act in 1953. That measure transferred control of about $40 billion worth of oil lands from the federal government to the states. The *New York Times* called it "one of the greatest and surely the most unjustified give-away programs in all the history of the United States."

The administration also sought to reduce federal activity in the electric power field. Eisenhower favored private rather than public development of power. That sentiment came out clearly in a private comment about the Tennessee Valley Authority, the extensive public power and development project begun during the New Deal. "I'd like to see us sell the whole thing," Eisenhower said, "but I suppose we can't go that far." He opposed a TVA proposal for expansion to provide power to the Atomic Energy Commission and instead authorized a private group, the Dixon-Yates syndicate, to build a plant in Arkansas for that purpose. Later, when charges of scandal arose, the administration canceled the agreement, but the basic preference for private development remained.

Committed to supporting business interests, the administration sometimes saw its program backfire. As a result of its reluctance to stimulate the economy too much, the annual rate of economic growth declined from 4.3 percent between 1947 and 1952 to 2.5 percent between 1953 and 1960. The economy was still growing, but more slowly than before. The country also suffered three recessions in Eisenhower's eight

years. During the slumps, tax revenues fell and the deficits that Eisenhower so wanted to avoid increased. Liberal economists argued that Keynesian tools were available to avoid such troubles, but they had to be used to bring results.

Eisenhower's understated approach led to a legislative stalemate, particularly when the Democrats regained control of Congress in 1954. Opponents of the president gibed at Ike's restrained stance and laughed about limited White House leadership. One observed that Eisenhower proved that the country did not "need" a president. Another spoke of the Eisenhower doll—you wound it up, and it did nothing for eight years.

Yet Eisenhower understood just what he was doing and had a better grasp of public policy than his critics realized. He worked quietly to create the consensus that he believed was necessary to make legislative progress and often actively pushed his favorite programs behind the scenes. He practiced what later observers called a "hidden hand" presidency, unobtrusively orchestrating support for his own ends, just as he had done as supreme commander of the Allied forces in World War II.

Even more important was his role in ratifying the welfare state. By 1960, the government had become a major factor in ordinary people's lives. It had grown enormously, employing close to 2.5 million people throughout the 1950s. Federal expenditures, which had stood at $3.1 billion in 1929, rose to $75 billion in 1953 and passed $150 million in the 1960s. The White House was now instrumental in initiating legislation and in steering bills through Congress. Individuals had come to expect old-age pensions, unemployment payments, and a minimum wage. By accepting the fundamental features of the national state the Democrats had created, Eisenhower ensured its survival. Now the debate about social policy broadened, as issues such as educational assistance, federal health care, and increased welfare benefits became part of the political agenda of the 1960s.

For all the jokes at his expense, Eisenhower remained popular with the voters. He accomplished most of the things he had wanted to do. He was one of the few presidents to leave office as highly regarded by the people as when he entered it. He was the kind of leader Americans wanted in prosperous times.

THE HIGH-WATER MARK OF LIBERALISM

The commitment to a welfare state became even stronger in the 1960s. The Democrats who won office in these years wanted to broaden the role of government even further. Dismayed at the problems of

poverty, unemployment, and racism, John F. Kennedy and Lyndon B. Johnson sought to manage the economy more effectively, eradicate poverty, and protect the civil rights of all Americans. Midway through the decade they came close to achieving their goals.

The Election of 1960

In the 1960 campaign, Kennedy argued that the government in general, and the president in particular, had to play an even more active role than they had in the Eisenhower years. He charged that the country had become lazy as it reveled in the prosperity of the 1950s. There were, in fact, problems that needed to be addressed.

Kennedy squared off against Richard Nixon, the Republican nominee, in the first televised presidential debates. Seventy million Americans tuned in to watch the two men in the first contest. The debates made a major difference in the campaign (see the "Recovering the Past" section of this chapter). Kennedy himself admitted, "It was TV more than anything else that turned the tide." From now on, television would play a major role in the political process and reshape its character.

Kennedy overcame seemingly insuperable odds to become the first Catholic in the White House. Yet his

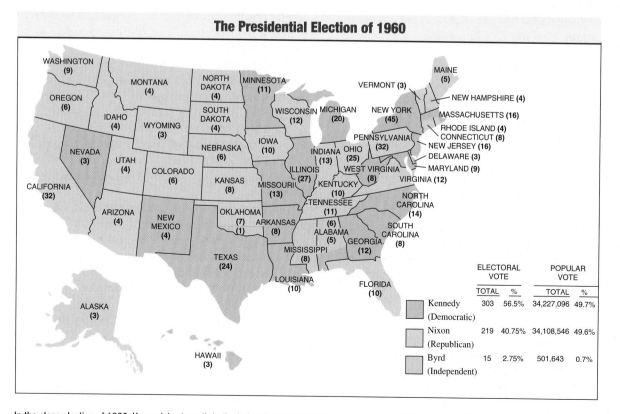

The Presidential Election of 1960

	ELECTORAL VOTE		POPULAR VOTE	
	TOTAL	%	TOTAL	%
Kennedy (Democratic)	303	56.5%	34,227,096	49.7%
Nixon (Republican)	219	40.75%	34,108,546	49.6%
Byrd (Independent)	15	2.75%	501,643	0.7%

In the close election of 1960, Kennedy's strength in the industrial Northeast and the South helped him revive significant elements of the liberal Democratic coalition of the 1930s.

victory was razor-thin. The electoral margin of 303 to 219 concealed the close popular tally, in which he triumphed by fewer than 120,000 of 68 million votes cast. If but a few thousand people had voted differently in Illinois and Texas, the election would have gone to Nixon. While Kennedy had Democratic majorities in Congress, many members of his party came from the South and were less sympathetic to liberal causes.

The new president had a charismatic public presence. He was able to voice his aims in eloquent yet understandable language that motivated his followers. During the campaign, he pointed to "uncharted areas of science and space, unsolved problems of peace and war, unconquered pockets of ignorance and prejudice, unanswered questions of poverty and surplus" that Americans must confront, for "the New Frontier is here whether we seek it or not." He made the same point even more movingly in his inaugural address: "The torch has been passed to a new generation of Americans—born in this century, tempered by war, disciplined by a hard

John Kennedy's energy and enthusiasm captured the imagination of Americans and people around the world, though few were aware of the physical ailments that affected him. He was fond of using this rocking chair in the White House, which he found comfortable for his ailing back. *(Corbis-Bettmann)*

and bitter peace, proud of our ancient heritage." Many, like Paul Cowan met at the start of the chapter, were inspired by Kennedy's concluding call to action: "And so, my fellow Americans: Ask not what your country can do for you—ask what you can do for your country."

For Kennedy, strong leadership was all-important. The president, he believed, "must serve as a catalyst, an energizer." He must be able and willing to perform "in the very thick of the fight." Viewing himself as "tough-minded" and "hard-nosed," he was determined to provide firm direction and play a leading role in creating the national agenda, just as Franklin Roosevelt had done.

Kennedy surrounded himself with talented assistants. On his staff were 15 Rhodes scholars and several famous authors. The secretary of state was Dean Rusk, a former member of the State Department who had then served as president of the Rockefeller Foundation. The secretary of defense was Robert S. McNamara, the highly successful president of the Ford Motor Company, who had proved creative in mobilizing talented assistants—"whiz kids"—and in using computer analysis to turn the company around.

Further contributing to Kennedy's attractive image were his glamorous wife, Jacqueline, and the glittering social occasions the couple hosted. Nobel Prize winners, musicians, and artists attended White House dinners. The Kennedys and their friends played touch football on the White House lawn and charged off on 50-mile hikes. Energy, exuberance, and excitement filled the air. The administration seemed like the Camelot of King Arthur's day, popularized in a Broadway musical in 1960.

The New Frontier

In office, Kennedy was committed to extending the welfare state. He sought to maintain an expanding economic system and to enlarge social welfare programs. As he told one of his advisers in 1962, "I want to go beyond the things that have already been accomplished. Give me facts and figures on things we still have to do." Regarding civil rights, Kennedy espoused liberal goals and social justice, although his policies were limited (see Chapter 29 for a full discussion of civil rights). On the economic front, he tried to end the lingering recession by working with the business community, while controlling price inflation.

These two goals conflicted when, in the spring of 1962, the large steel companies decided on a major price increase after steel unions had accepted a modest wage package. The angry president termed the price increases unjustifiable and on television charged that the firms pursued "private power and profit" rather than the public interest. Determined to force the steel

Recovering the Past

TELEVISION

In the last 50 years, television has played an increasingly important part in American life, providing historians with another source of evidence about American culture and society in the recent past.

Television's popularity by the 1950s was the result of decades of experimentation dating back to the nineteenth century. In the 1930s, NBC installed a television station in the new Empire State Building in New York. With green makeup and purple lipstick to provide better visual contrast, actors began to perform before live cameras in studios. At the end of the decade, "Amos 'n' Andy," a popular radio show, was telecast, and as the 1940s began, Franklin D. Roosevelt became the first president to appear on television. World War II interrupted the development of television, as Americans relied on radio to bring them news. After the war, however, the commercial development of television quickly resumed. Assembly lines that had made electronic implements of war were now converted to consumer production, and thousands of new sets appeared on the market. The opening of Congress could be seen live in 1947; baseball coverage improved that same year owing to the zoom lens; children's shows like "Howdy Doody" made their debut; and "Meet the Press," a radio interview program, made the transition to television.

Although sports programs, variety shows hosted by Ed Sullivan and Milton Berle, TV dramas, and episodic series ("I Love Lucy" and "Gunsmoke," for example) dominated TV broadcasting in the 1950s, television soon became entwined with politics and public affairs. Americans saw Senator Joseph McCarthy for themselves in the televised Army–McCarthy hearings in 1954; his malevolent behavior on camera contributed to his downfall. The 1948 presidential nominating conventions were the first to be televised, but the use of TV to enhance the public image of politicians was most thoroughly developed by the fatherly Dwight D. Eisenhower and the charismatic John F. Kennedy.

In November 1963, people throughout the United States shared the tragedy of John Kennedy's assassination, sitting stunned before their sets trying to under-

The candidates squaring off in their debate. *(AP/Wide World Photos)*

stand the events of his fateful Texas trip. The shock and sorrow of the American people was repeated in the spring of 1968 as they gazed in disbelief at the funerals of Martin Luther King, Jr. and Robert Kennedy. A year later, a quarter of the world's population watched as Neil Armstrong became the first man to set foot on the moon. In that same era, television played an important part in shaping impressions of the war in Vietnam. More and more Americans began to understand the nature and impact of the conflict from what they saw on TV.

This combination of visual entertainment and enlightenment made owning a television set virtually a necessity. By 1970, fully 95 percent of American households owned a TV set, a staggering increase from the 9 percent only 20 years earlier. Fewer families owned refrigerators or indoor toilets.

The implications of the impact of television on American society are of obvious interest to historians. How has television affected other communications and entertainment industries, such as radio, newspapers, and movies? Look at the "Television Tonight" listings shown here. What does the content of TV programming tell us about the values, interests, and tastes of the American people?

Perhaps most significant, what impact has TV had on the course of historical events like presidential campaigns, human relations, and wars? The pictures you see here come from the Kennedy–Nixon debates in the presidential campaign of 1960. The first picture shows the two candidates in the studio. The second picture shows a relaxed and energetic Kennedy staring directly into the TV camera. The third

John Kennedy (left) and Richard Nixon (below). *(AP/Wide World Photos)*

picture shows a taut and tense Nixon challenging the points made by his opponent. Which candidate seems to be speaking directly to the American people? Which candidate makes the better impression? Why? Polls of radio listeners taken after the first debate showed Nixon the winner; surveys of television surveys placed Kennedy in front. How do you account for this discrepancy?

Television Tonight

6:00—WTTV 4: Leave It to Beaver. Beaver tries to help a friend who has run away from home. Repeat.

6:30—WLTW-I 13: Cheyenne has a Laramie adventure in which Slim, Jess, and Jonesy work on a cattle drive. Repeat.

7:30—WTTV 4: The Untouchables. Eliot Ness tries to deal with a late gangster's niece who has a record of the murdered hood's career. Repeat.

7:30—WLW-I 13: Voyage to the Bottom of the Sea presents "Mutiny," in which Admiral Nelson shows signs of a mental breakdown during the search for a giant jellyfish which supposedly consumed a submarine.

7:30—WFBM-TV 6: Members of the Indianapolis Rotary Club discuss the 1965 business outlook with former U.S. Sen. Homer Capehart.

8:00—WFBM-TV 6: The Man from UNCLE is in at a new time and night. Thrush agents try to recapture one of their leaders before Napoleon Solo can deliver him to the Central Intelligence Agency. Ralph Taeger is guest star.

8:00—WISH-TV 8: I've Got a Secret welcomes the panel from To Tell the Truth: Tom Poston, Peggy Cass, Kitty Carlisle, and Orson Bean.

8:30—WLW-I 13: Basketball, I.U. vs. Iowa.

8:30—WISH-TV 8: Andy Griffith's comedy involves Goober's attempts to fill in at the sheriff's office.

9:00—WFBM-TV 6: Andy Williams is visited by composer Henry Mancini, Bobby Darin, and Vic Damone. Musical selections include "Charade," "Hello Dolly," and "Moon River."

9:00—WTTV 4: Lloyd Thaxton welcomes vocal group, Herman's Hermits.

9:30—WISH-TV 8: Many Happy Returns. Walter's plan for currying favor with the store's boss hits a snag.

10:00—WFBM-TV 6: Alfred Hitchcock presents Margaret Leighton as a spinster who goes mad when she cannot cope with the strain of rearing an orphaned niece in "Where the Woodbine Twineth."

10:00—WLW-I 13: Ben Casey gets help in diagnosing a boy's illness from an Australian veterinarian with terminal leukemia. The vet's knowledge of bats provides the key.

10:00—WISH-TV 8: "Viet Nam: How We Got In—Can We Get Out?" is the topic of CBS Reports.

Source: Indianapolis News, January 11, 1965.

Glamour and grace characterized the Kennedy White House, as the President and First Lady invited artists, authors, and other celebrities to official functions. Here they convey a sense of youthful spirit at one of the five inaugural balls in 1961. *(Paul Schutzer/LIFE Magazine © Time Inc.)*

companies to their knees, Kennedy pressed for executive and congressional action. In the end, the large companies capitulated, but they disliked Kennedy's heavy-handed approach and decided that this Democratic administration, like all the others, was hostile to business. In late May, six weeks after the steel crisis, the stock market plunged in the greatest drop since the Great Crash of 1929. Kennedy received the blame. "When Eisenhower had a heart attack," Wall Street analysts joked, "the market broke. If Kennedy would have a heart attack, the market would go up."

It now seemed doubly urgent to end the recession. Earlier a proponent of a balanced budget, Kennedy began to listen to his liberal advisers who proposed a Keynesian approach to economic growth. Budget deficits had promoted prosperity during the Second World War and might work in the same way in peacetime too. By the summer of 1962, the president was convinced. In early 1963, he called for a $13.5 billion cut in corporate taxes over the next three years. While that cut would cause a large deficit, it would also provide capital that business leaders could spend in ways that would stimulate the economy and ultimately increase tax revenues.

Opposition mounted. Conservatives refused to accept the basic premise that deficits would stimulate economic growth and argued, in Eisenhower's words, that "no family, no business, no nation can spend itself into prosperity." Some liberals claimed that it would be better to stimulate the economy by spending money to improve society rather than by cutting taxes and putting money in people's pockets. What good would it do, economist John Kenneth Galbraith wondered, to have "a few more dollars to spend if the air is too dirty to breathe, the water is too polluted to drink, the commuters are losing out in the struggle to get in and out of cities, the streets are filthy, and the schools are so bad that the young, perhaps wisely, stay away?" In Congress, where Democrats had thin majorities but still had to contend with conservative Southerners within the party, opponents pigeonholed the proposal in committee, and there it remained.

On other issues on the liberal agenda, Kennedy met similar resistance. Though he proposed legislation increasing the minimum wage and providing for federal aid for education, medical care for the elderly, housing subsidies, and urban renewal, the results were meager. His new minimum-wage measure passed Congress in pared-down form, but Kennedy did not have the votes in Congress to achieve most of his legislative program.

His inability to win necessary congressional support became even more evident in the struggle to aid public education. Soon after taking office, Kennedy proposed a $2.3 billion program of grants to the states over a three-year period to help build schools and raise teachers' salaries. Immediately, a series of prickly questions emerged. Was it appropriate to spend large sums of money for social goals? Would federal aid bring federal control of school policies and curriculum? Should assistance go to segregated schools? Should it go to parochial schools? The administration proved willing to allow assistance to segregated schools, thereby easing white southern minds. On the Catholic question, however, it stumbled to a halt. Kennedy at first insisted that he would not allow his religion to influence his actions and opposed aid for parochial schools. As Catholic pressure mounted and the administration realized that Catholic votes were necessary for passage, Kennedy began to reconsider. In the end, compromise proved impossible and the school aid measure died in committee.

Kennedy was more successful in securing funding for the exploration of space. As first Alan Shepard, then John Glenn, flew in space, Kennedy proposed that the United States commit itself to landing a man on the moon and returning him to earth before the end of the decade. Congress, caught up in the glamour of the proposal and worried about Soviet achievements in space,

Kennedy's commitment to the space program resulted in an American landing on the moon in 1969. As astronauts headed off into space, they had an altogether different picture of the earth. This photograph was taken by William Anders, one of the astronauts on Apollo 8, the mission that preceded the moon landing. "We'd come 240,000 miles to see the moon," he later wrote, "and it was the earth that was really worth looking at." *(NASA)*

assented and increased funding of the National Aeronautics and Space Administration (NASA).

Kennedy also established the Peace Corps, which sent men and women overseas to assist developing countries. According to Kennedy aide Arthur M. Schlesinger, Jr., the Peace Corps was an effort "to replace protocol-minded, striped-pants officials by reform-minded missionaries of democracy who mixed with the people, spoke the native dialects, ate the food, and involved themselves in local struggles against ignorance and want." Paul Cowan, introduced at the start of this chapter, was one of thousands of volunteers who hoped that they could share their liberal dreams.

If Kennedy's successes were modest, he had at least made commitments that could be broadened later. He had reaffirmed the importance of executive leadership in the effort to extend the boundaries of the welfare state. And he had committed himself to using modern economics to maintain fiscal stability. The nation was poised to achieve liberal goals.

Change of Command

Facing reelection in 1964, Kennedy wanted not only to win the presidency for a second term but also to increase liberal Democratic strength in Congress. In November 1963, he traveled to Texas, where he hoped to unite the state's Democratic party for the upcoming election. Dallas, one of the stops on the trip, was reputed to be hostile to the administration. Four

John Kennedy seemed comfortable and relaxed as he rode in a motorcade through the streets of Dallas. This picture was taken just moments before bullets ended the Camelot dream. *(Corbis-Bettmann)*

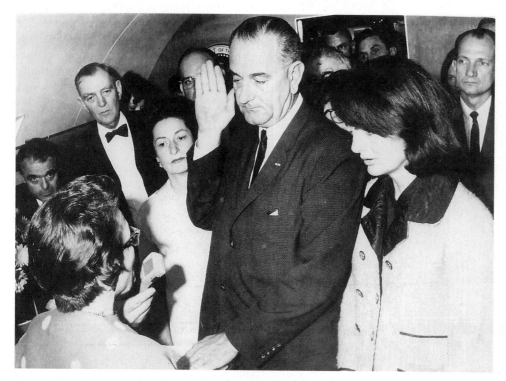

Kennedy's assassination thrust Lyndon Johnson into the presidency in an atmosphere of shocked grief and loss. Here, with Jacqueline Kennedy by his side, he takes the oath of office as he flew back from Dallas to Washington on the presidential plane. *(Corbis-Bettmann)*

weeks before, a conservative mob had abused Adlai Stevenson, ambassador to the United Nations. Now, on November 22, Kennedy had a chance to feel the pulse of the city for himself. Arriving at the airport, Henry González, a congressman accompanying the president in Texas, remarked jokingly, "Well, I'm taking my risks. I haven't got my steel vest yet." As the party entered the city in an open car, the president encountered friendly crowds. Suddenly shots rang out, and Kennedy slumped forward as bullets ripped through his head and throat. Mortally wounded, he died a short time later at a Dallas hospital. Lee Harvey Oswald, the accused assassin, was himself shot and killed a few days later by a minor underworld figure as he was being moved within the jail.

Americans were stunned. For days people stayed at home and watched endless television replays of the assassination and its aftermath. The images of the handsome president felled by bullets, the funeral cortege, the president's young son saluting his father's casket as it rolled by on the way to final burial at Arlington National Cemetery were all imprinted on people's minds. United around the event, members of an entire generation remembered where they had been when Kennedy was shot, just as an earlier generation recalled Pearl Harbor.

Vice President Lyndon Johnson succeeded Kennedy as president. Though less polished, Johnson was a more effective political leader than Kennedy and brought his own special skills and vision to the presidency.

Johnson was a man of elemental force. Always manipulative, he reminded people of a riverboat gambler, according to one White House aide. Though he desperately wanted to be loved, he was, former secretary of state Dean Acheson once told him, "not a very likable man." There was a streak of vulgarity that contributed to his earthy appeal but offended some of his associates. Asked once why he had not responded more sympathetically to a suggestion from Richard Nixon, he said to his friends in Congress, "Boys, I may not know much, but I know the difference between chicken shit and chicken salad."

Those qualities notwithstanding, he was successful in the passion of his life—politics. Schooled in Congress and influenced by FDR, Johnson was the most able legislator of the postwar years. As Senate majority leader, he became famous for his ability to get things done. Ceaseless in his search for information, tireless in his attention to detail, he knew the strengths and weaknesses of everyone he faced. When he approached someone in the hall, one senator remarked, he was like a "great overpowering thunderstorm that consumed you as it closed in on you." He could flatter and cajole, and became famous for what came to be called the "Johnson treatment." He zeroed in, according to columnists Rowland Evans, Jr. and Robert Novak, "his face a scant millimeter from his target, his eyes widening and narrowing, his eyebrows rising and falling." He grabbed people by the lapels, made them listen, and usually got his way.

Lyndon Johnson kept tight control of the Senate in the 1950s and was known for his ability to get his way. Here he is shown giving the famous "Johnson treatment" to Senator Theodore Francis Green in 1957. Note the way Green is bending backwards in his unsuccessful effort to keep his distance from LBJ. *(New York Times Pictures)*

Johnson ran the Senate with tight control and established a credible record for himself and his party during the Eisenhower years. He was the Democrat most responsible for keeping liberal goals alive in a conservative time, as he tried to broaden his own appeal in his quest for the presidency. Unsuccessful in his own bid for the White House in 1960, he agreed to take the second spot under JFK and helped Kennedy win the election, then went into a state of eclipse as vice president. He felt uncomfortable with the Kennedy crowd, useless and stifled in his new role. He told friends that he agreed with John Nance Garner, a vice president under FDR, who once observed that the vice presidency "wasn't worth a pitcher of warm spit."

Despite his own ambivalence about Kennedy, Johnson sensed the profound shock that gripped the United States after the assassination and was determined to utilize Kennedy's memory to achieve legislative success. Even more than Kennedy, he was willing to wield presidential power aggressively and to use the media to shape public opinion in pursuit of his vision of a society in which the comforts of life would be more widely shared and poverty would be eliminated once and for all.

The Great Society in Action

Lyndon Johnson had an expansive vision of the possibilities of reform. Using his considerable political skills, he succeeded in pushing through Congress the most extensive reform program in American history. "Is a new world coming?" the president asked. "We welcome it, and we will bend it to the hopes of man."

Johnson began to develop the support he needed the day he took office. In his first public address, delivered to Congress and televised nationwide, he sought to dispel the image of impostor as he embraced Kennedy's liberal program. He began, in a measured tone, with the words, "All I have, I would have given gladly not to be standing here today." He asked members of Congress to work with him, and he underscored the theme "Let us continue" throughout his speech.

As a first step, Johnson resolved to secure the measures Kennedy had been unable to extract from Congress. Bills to reduce taxes and ensure civil rights were his first and most pressing priorities, but he was interested too in aiding public education, providing medical care for the aged, and eliminating poverty. By the spring of 1964, he began to use the phrase "Great Society" to describe his expansive reform program.

Successful even before the election of 1964, his landslide victory over conservative Republican challenger Barry Goldwater of Arizona validated his approach. LBJ received 61 percent of the popular vote and an electoral tally of 486 to 52 and gained Democratic congressional majorities of 68–32 in the Senate and 295–140 in the House. Despite his defeat, Goldwater's candidacy reflected the growing power of conservatism within the Republican party and the ability of a grassroots group to organize a successful campaign in party primaries. It also drove moderate Republicans to vote for the Democratic party this time and gave Johnson a far more impressive mandate than Kennedy had ever enjoyed.

Johnson knew how to get laws passed. He appointed task forces that included legislators to study problems and suggest solutions, worked with them to draft bills, and maintained close contact with congressional leaders through a sophisticated liaison staff. Not since the FDR years had there been such a coordinated effort.

Civil rights reform was LBJ's first legislative priority and an integral part of the Great Society program (see Chapter 29), but other measures were equally important. Following Kennedy's lead, Johnson pressed for a tax cut. He accepted the Keynesian theory that deficits, properly managed, could promote prosperity. If people had more money to spend, their purchases could stimulate the economy. To gain conservative

PRESIDENTIAL ELECTION OF 1964			
Candidate	**Party**	**Popular Vote**	**Electoral Vote**
LYNDON B. JOHNSON	Democratic	43,126,584 (61.1%)	486
Barry M. Goldwater	Republican	27,177,838 (38.5%)	52

Note: Winner's name appears in capital letters.

support, he agreed to hold down government spending. On one occasion, he applied such pressure that the author of an amendment to provide a tax credit for families with children in college ended up voting against his own proposal. Soon the tax bill passed.

With the tax cut in hand, the president pressed for the antipoverty program that Kennedy had begun to plan. Such an effort was bold and unprecedented. In the Progressive era, at the turn of the century, some legislation had attempted to alleviate conditions associated with poverty. During the New Deal, Franklin Roosevelt had proposed programs to assist the one-third of the nation that could not help itself. Now Johnson took a step that no president had taken before; in his 1964 State of the Union message, he declared an "unconditional war on poverty in America."

The center of this utopian effort to eradicate poverty was the Economic Opportunity Act of 1964. It created an Office of Economic Opportunity (OEO) to provide education and training through programs such as the Job Corps for unskilled young people trapped in the poverty cycle. VISTA (Volunteers in Service to America), patterned after the Peace Corps, offered assistance to the poor at home, while Head Start tried to give disadvantaged children a chance to succeed in school. Assorted community action programs gave the poor themselves a voice in improving housing, health, and education in their own neighborhoods.

Aware of the escalating costs of medical care, Johnson also proposed a medical assistance plan. Both Truman and Kennedy had supported such an initiative but had failed to win congressional approval. Johnson succeeded. To head off conservative attacks, the administration tied the Medicare measure to the social security system and limited the program to the elderly. Medicaid met the needs of those on welfare and certain other groups who could not afford private insurance. The Medicare-Medicaid program was the most important extension of federally directed social benefits since the Social Security Act of 1935. By 1976 the two programs were paying for the medical costs of 20 percent of the American people.

Johnson was similarly successful in his effort to provide aid for elementary and secondary schools.

Kennedy had met defeat when Catholics had insisted on assistance to parochial schools. Johnson, a Protestant, was able to deal with the ticklish religious question without charges of favoritism. His legislation allocated education money to the states based on the number of children from low-income families. Those funds would then be distributed to assist deprived children in public as well as private schools.

In LBJ's expansive vision, the federal government would ensure that everyone shared in the promise of American life. Under his prodding, Congress passed a new housing act to give rent supplements to the poor and created a Cabinet Department of Housing and Urban Development. The federal government provided new forms of aid, such as legal assistance for those who could not afford to pay for it themselves. It moved further in funding higher education, including colleges and universities in its financial grants. Congress

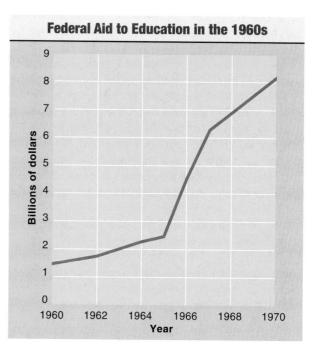

Passage of a bill to provide federal aid to education in 1965 led to rapidly increasing government support at all levels for the remainder of the decade. Source: U.S. Bureau of the Census.

also provided artists and scholars with assistance through the National Endowments for the Arts and Humanities, created in 1965. Not since the Works Progress Administration in the New Deal had such groups been granted government aid.

Johnson's administration also provided much-needed immigration reform. It replaced the restrictive immigration policy, in place since 1924 (which had limited immigration severely and favored northern Europeans), with a measure that vastly increased the ceiling on immigration and opened the door to immigrants from Asia and Latin America. The Immigration Act of 1965 also exempted from the quotas family members of U.S. citizens and political refugees, including at first Cuban and later Indochinese immigrants. By the late 1960s, some 350,000 immigrants were entering the United States annually; in the 1970s, the number exceeded 400,000 a year. This new stream of immigration—largely from Asia and Latin America—created a population more

Immigration from Asia and Latin America brought greater diversity to the United States. Here a Cuban refugee waits to enter the United States at the immigration processing facility at the Miami, Florida, airport in 1974. *(Michael Heron/Woodfin Camp & Associates)*

diverse than it had been since the early decades of the twentieth century. The consequences of this new diversity were far-ranging and affected many areas of American life, from politics, radio programming, and consumer products to street signs and public school classrooms.

The Great Society also reflected the stirring of the environmental movement. In 1962, naturalist Rachel Carson alerted the public to the dangers of pesticide poisoning and environmental pollution in her book *Silent Spring* (see Chapter 29). Though the chemical industry fought Carson and argued that she left readers "unable to sort fact from fancy," a special presidential advisory committee warned against widespread pesticide use.

Johnson recognized the need to go even further. He was determined to deal with caustic fumes in the air, lethal sludge in rivers and streams, and the steady disappearance of wildlife. The National Wilderness Preservation Act of 1964 set aside 9.1 million acres of wilderness, while Lady Bird Johnson, the president's wife, led a beautification campaign to eliminate unsightly billboards and junkyards along the nation's highways, and Congress passed other measures to limit air and water pollution.

A Sympathetic Supreme Court

With the addition of four new liberal justices appointed by Kennedy and Johnson, the Supreme Court supported and promoted the liberal agenda. Under the leadership of Chief Justice Earl Warren, the Court followed the lead it had taken in the 1954 landmark civil rights case *Brown* v. *Board of Education* (see Chapter 29). Several decisions reaffirmed the Court's support of black rights, by moving against Jim Crow practices in other public establishments.

The Court also supported civil liberties. Where earlier judicial decisions had affirmed restrictions on members of the Communist party and radical groups, now the Court began to protect the rights of individuals with radical political views. Similarly, the Court sought to protect accused suspects from police harassment. In *Gideon* v. *Wainwright* (1963), the justices decided that poor defendants in serious cases had the right to free legal counsel. In *Escobedo* v. *Illinois* (1964), they ruled that a suspect had to be given access to an attorney during questioning. In *Miranda* v. *Arizona* (1966), they argued that offenders had to be warned that statements extracted by the police could be used against them and that they could remain silent.

Other decisions similarly broke new ground. *Baker* v. *Carr* (1962) opened the way to reapportionment of state legislative bodies, according to the standard, defined a year later in Justice William O. Douglas's

MAJOR GREAT SOCIETY PROGRAMS

Date of Passage	Program	Effect
January 23, 1964 (ratified)	Twenty-fourth Amendment	Banned poll tax as prerequisite in federal elections
February 26, 1964	Tax Reduction Act	Lowered federal personal tax rates
July 2, 1964	Civil Rights Act	Banned discrimination in public accommodations; gave attorney general right to file suit to desegregate schools or other facilities; banned discrimination in employment on basis of race, color, religion, sex, or national origin
July 9, 1964	Urban Mass Transportation Act	Provided $375 million in financial aid to urban transit systems
August 30, 1964	Economic Opportunity Act	Authorized ten separate programs to be conducted by the Office of Economic Opportunity, including Job Corps and VISTA
September 3, 1964	National Wilderness Preservation Act	Designated 9.1 million acres of land as national forest to be safeguarded permanently against commercial use and construction of permanent roads and buildings
April 11, 1965	Elementary and Secondary Education Act	Provided $1.3 billion in aid to elementary and secondary schools
July 30, 1965	Medicare	Provided medical care for the aged through the social security system
August 6, 1965	Voting Rights Act	Suspended literacy tests and other voter tests; authorized federal supervision of registration in states and districts where few voting-age residents had voted earlier
August 10, 1965	Omnibus Housing Act	Provided rent supplements to low-income families and federal aid to place low-income people in private housing
September 9, 1965	Department of Housing and Urban Development	Provided special programs concerned with housing needs, fair-housing opportunities, and the improvement and development of communities
September 29, 1965	National Endowments for the Arts and Humanities	Provided financial assistance for painters, actors, dancers, musicians, and others in the arts and humanities
October 2, 1965	Water Quality Act	Required states to establish and enforce water quality standards for all interstate waters within their boundaries
October 3, 1965	Immigration Act	Set new quotas
October 20, 1965	Air Quality Act	Amended earlier laws
October 20, 1965	Higher Education Act	Provided federal scholarships to undergraduates and others
September 9, 1966	National Traffic and Motor Vehicle Safety Act	Set federal safety standards
September 9, 1966	Highway Safety Act	Required states to set up federally approved safety programs
September 23, 1966	Minimum wage	Raised minimum wage from $1.25 to $1.40 per hour; extended coverage
October 15, 1966	Department of Transportation	Provided federal agencies to administer policies, in conjunction with state and local officials, regarding highway planning, development, and construction; urban mass transit; railroads; aviation; and safety of waterways, ports, highways, and oil and gas pipelines
November 3, 1966	Model Cities	Encouraged rehabilitation of slums

words, of "one person, one vote." This crucial ruling helped break the political control of lightly populated rural districts in many state assemblies and similarly made the U.S. House of Representatives much more responsive to urban and suburban issues. Meanwhile, the Court outraged conservatives by ruling that prayer could not be required in the public schools and that obscenity laws could no longer restrict allegedly pornographic material that might have some "redeeming social value."

The Great Society Under Attack

Supported by healthy economic growth, the Great Society worked for a few years as Johnson had hoped. The tax cut proved effective, and the consumer and business spending that it promoted led to a steady increase in gross national product (GNP): 7.1 percent in 1964, 8.1 percent in 1965, and 9.5 percent in 1966. As the economy improved, the budget deficit dropped. Unemployment fell, and inflation remained under control. Medical programs provided basic security for the old and the poor. Education flourished as schools were built, and teachers' salaries increased as a result of the influx of federal aid.

Yet Johnson's dream of the Great Society proved illusory. Some programs, like the effort to eliminate poverty, promised too much, and the administration's rhetorical oversell led to disillusionment when problems failed to disappear. Other programs, planned in haste, were simply ill-conceived and did not work. Never were the massive sums allocated to these programs that some argued were necessary to make them successful.

Factionalism also plagued the Great Society. Lyndon Johnson had reconstituted the old Democratic coalition in his triumph in 1964, with urban Catholics and southern whites joining organized labor, the black electorate, and the middle class. But diverse interests within the coalition soon clashed. Conservative white southerners and blue-collar white northerners felt threatened by the government's support of civil rights. Local urban bosses, long the backbone of the Democratic party, objected to grassroots participation of the urban poor, which threatened their own political control.

Criticisms of the Great Society and its liberal underpinnings came from across the political spectrum. There had never been widespread popular enthusiasm for much of the effort. Conservatives disliked the centralization of authority and the government's increased role in defining the national welfare. They also questioned involving the poor themselves in reform programs, arguing that poor people lacked a broad vision of the nation's needs. Even middle-class Americans, generally supportive of liberal goals, sometimes grumbled that the government was paying too much attention to the underprivileged and thereby neglecting their own needs.

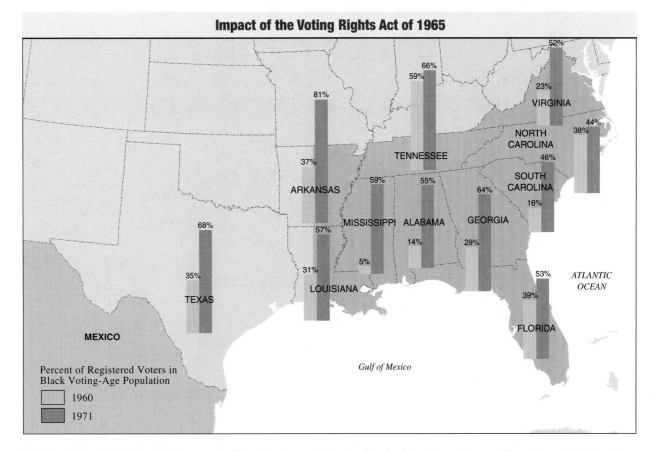

The Voting Rights Act of 1965 greatly increased the African American vote throughout the South but also sparked a reaction on the part of whites who feared the enhanced power of the larger black electorate.

Radicals attacked the Great Society as a warmed-over version of the New Deal. The same middle-class liberal orientation remained, they claimed, with the real intent of programs to provide the working-class poor with middle-class values. "The welfare state is more machinery than substance," activist Tom Hayden declared. Furthermore, radicals charged, the assumption of Great Society programs that the American system was basically sound and that economic growth would finance benefits of the American dream for all meant that no real effort was being made to redistribute income. Only the redistribution of wealth, in their view, could transform American life.

The Vietnam War (discussed in Chapter 27) dealt the Great Society a fatal blow. LBJ wanted to maintain both the war and his treasured domestic reform programs, but his effort to pursue these goals simultaneously produced serious inflation. The economy was already booming as a result of the tax cut and the spending for reform. As military expenditures increased, the productive system of the country could not keep up with demand. When Johnson refused to raise taxes, in an effort to hide the costs of the war, inflation spiraled out of control. Congress finally got into the act and slashed Great Society programs. As hard economic choices became increasingly necessary, many decided the country could no longer afford social reform on the scale Johnson had proposed.

THE DECLINE OF LIBERALISM

After eight years of Democratic rule, many Americans became frustrated with the liberal approach. They questioned the liberal agenda and the government's ability to solve social problems. The war in Vietnam had polarized the country and fragmented the Democratic party. Critics now questioned the entire liberal agenda and argued that the government was trying to do too much. Capitalizing on the alienation sparked by the war, Republicans resolved to scale down the commitment to social change. Like Dwight Eisenhower a decade and a half before, they accepted some social programs as necessary for the well-being of modern America but they resolved to cut spending and the federal bureaucracy. Furthermore, they were determined to pay more attention to white, middle-class Americans who disliked the social disorder they saw as a consequence of rapid social change and resented the government's perceived favoritism toward the poor and dispossessed.

The Election of 1968

Richard Nixon had long dreamed of the nation's highest office. He had failed in his first bid in 1960 and then two years later lost a race for governor of California. His political career seemed over, as he told the press in 1962, "You won't have Nixon to kick

ROOTS OF SELECTED GREAT SOCIETY PROGRAMS

Progressive Period	New Deal	Great Society
Settlement house activity of Jane Addams and others	Relief efforts to ease unemployment (FERA, WPA)	Poverty programs (OEO)
Efforts to clean up slums (tenement house laws)	Housing program	Rehabilitation of slums through Model Cities program
Progressive party platform calling for federal accident, old-age, and unemployment insurance	Social security system providing unemployment compensation and old-age pensions	Medical care for the aged through social security (Medicare)
Activity to break up monopolies and regulate business	Regulation of utility companies	Regulation of highway safety and transportation
Efforts to regulate working conditions and benefits	Establishment of standards for working conditions and minimum wage	Raising of minimum wage
Efforts to increase literacy and spread education at all levels	Efforts to keep college students in school through NYA	Assistance to elementary, secondary, and higher education
Theodore Roosevelt's efforts at wilderness preservation	Conservation efforts (CCC, TVA planning)	Safeguarding of wilderness lands
Establishment of federal income tax	Tax reform to close loopholes and increase taxes for the wealthy	Tax cut to stimulate business activity
Theodore Roosevelt's overtures to Booker T. Washington	Discussion (but not passage) of antilynching legislation	Civil rights measures to ban discrimination in public accommodations and to guarantee right to vote

Urban Uprisings in the 1960s

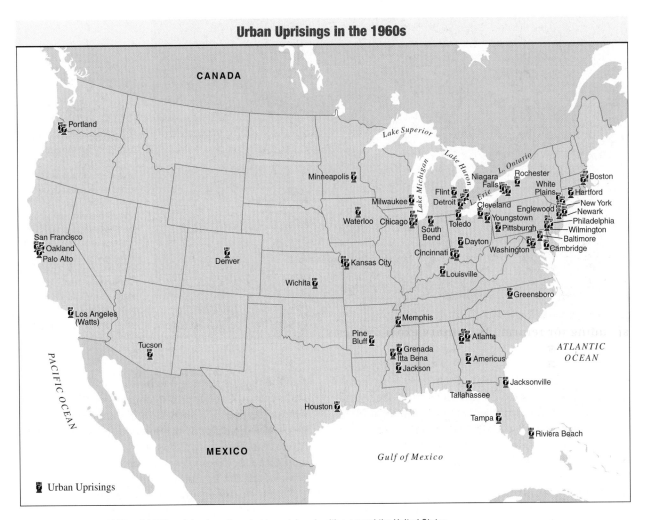

In the years between 1965 and 1968, racial antagonisms led to uprisings in cities around the United States.

around any more because, gentlemen, this is my last press conference." Written off by most politicians, he staged a comeback after the Goldwater disaster of 1964, and by 1968 seemed to have a good shot at the presidency again.

In the election, Nixon faced Vice President Hubert H. Humphrey. The war in Vietnam had fractured the Democratic party and made Johnson so unpopular that he chose not to run for reelection. The turbulent Democratic convention in Chicago, where police ran amok and clubbed demonstrators, reporters, and bystanders, all on nationwide TV, undermined the Democrats' hopes of unification and worked in Nixon's favor. But he faced a serious threat from Governor George C. Wallace of Alabama, a third-party candidate, who exploited social and racial tensions in his campaign. Appealing to northern working-class voters as well as southern whites, Wallace characterized those who wanted to reform American life as "left-wing theoreticians, briefcase-totin' bureaucrats, ivory-tower guideline writers, bearded anarchists,

smart-aleck editorial writers and pointy-headed professors." He hoped to ride into office on blue-collar resentment of social disorder and liberal aims.

Nixon addressed the same constituency, calling it the "silent majority." Capitalizing on the dismay these Americans felt over campus disruptions and inner-city riots and appealing to latent racism, he promised law and order if elected. He also called the Great Society a costly mistake, declaring that it was "time to quit pouring billions of dollars into programs that have failed." Heeding the advice of public-relations advisers, Nixon took the high ground and avoided shrill criticism himself. He gave Governor Spiro Agnew of Maryland, his vice presidential running mate, the task of leading the attack. Agnew, much like the Nixon of old, responded aggressively, calling Hubert Humphrey "squishy soft on communism" and declaring that "if you've seen one city slum, you've seen them all."

Nixon received 43 percent of the popular vote, not quite 1 percent more than Humphrey, with Wallace

Policemen attacked demonstrators and bystanders alike at the turbulent Democratic convention of 1968. The senseless violence, pictured in graphic detail on national television, revealed serious rifts in the Democratic party and underscored the inability of political leaders to bridge the gaps. The horrifying chaos destroyed support for Democratic candidates and helped Nixon win the election. *(UPI/Corbis-Bettmann)*

capturing the rest. But it was enough to give the Republicans a majority in the Electoral College and Nixon the presidency at last. Sixty-two percent of all white voters (but only 12 percent of black voters) had cast their votes for either Nixon or Wallace, suggesting that the covert racial appeal had worked. Because many Americans split their tickets, the Democrats won both houses of Congress.

In and out of office, Nixon was a complex, remote man, who carefully concealed his private self. There was, one of his aides noted, "a mean side to his nature" that he sought to keep from public view. Nixon embraced political life, but never with the exuberance of Lyndon Johnson. Physically awkward and humorless, he was most comfortable alone or with a few wealthy friends. Even at work he insulated himself, preferred written contacts to personal ones, and often retreated to a small room in the executive office building to be alone.

Nixon was keenly aware of the psychology of politics in the electronic age. He believed that "in the modern presidency, concern for image must rank with concern for substance." Thus, he posed in public as the defender of American morality, though in private he was frequently coarse and profane. Earlier in his career he had been labeled "Tricky Dick" for his apparent willingness to do anything to advance his career. In subsequent years, he had tried to create the appearance of a "new Nixon," but to many he still appeared to be a mechanical man, always calculating his next step.

Philosophically, Nixon disagreed with the liberal faith in federal planning and wanted to decentralize social policy. But he agreed with his liberal predecessors that the presidency ought to be the engine of the political system. Faced with a Congress dominated by Democrats and their allocations of money for programs he opposed, he simply impounded (refused to spend) funds authorized by Congress. Later commentators would see the Nixon years as the height of what they came to call the "imperial presidency."

Nixon's cabinet appointees, sworn in with NBC "Today" cameras relaying the ceremony directly to television viewers, were white, male Republicans. For the most part, however, the president worked around his cabinet, relying on other White House staff members. In domestic affairs, Arthur Burns, a former chairman of the Council of Economic Advisers, and Daniel Patrick Moynihan, a Harvard professor of government (and a Democrat) were the most important. In foreign affairs, the talented and ambitious Henry A. Kissinger, another Harvard government professor, directed the National Security Council staff and later became secretary of state.

Another tier of White House officials—none with public policy experience but all intensely loyal to him—insulated the president from the outside world and carried out his commands. Advertising executive H. R. Haldeman, a tireless Nixon campaigner, became chief of staff. Of his relationship with the president, Haldeman remarked, "I get done what he wants done and I take the heat instead of him." Working with Haldeman was lawyer John Ehrlichman. Starting as a legal counselor, he rose to the post of chief domestic adviser. Haldeman and Ehrlichman framed issues and narrowed options for Nixon. They came to be called the "Berlin Wall" for the way they guarded the president's privacy. John Mitchell was known as "El Supremo" by the staff, as the "Big Enchilada" by Ehrlichman. A tough, successful bond lawyer from Nixon's New York law office, he became a fast friend and managed the 1968 campaign. In the new administration, he became attorney general and gave the president daily advice.

The Republican Agenda

Although Nixon had come to political maturity in Republican circles, he understood that it was impossible to roll back the government's expanded role altogether. Accepting the basic contours of the welfare state, he sought to systematize and scale back its programs. Furthermore, he was determined "to reverse the flow of power and resources" away from the federal government to state and local governments, where he believed they belonged.

Despite initial reservations, Nixon proved willing to use economic tools to maintain stability. The economy was faltering when he assumed office. Inflation had risen from 2.2 percent in 1965 to 4.5 percent in 1968, largely as a result of the Vietnam War. Nixon responded by reducing government spending and pressing the Federal Reserve Board to raise interest rates. Although parts of the conservative plan worked, a mild recession occurred in 1969–1970, and inflation continued to rise. Realizing the political dangers of pursuing this policy, Nixon shifted course, imposed wage and price controls to stop inflation, and used monetary and fiscal policies to stimulate the economy. After his reelection in 1972, however, he lifted wage and price controls, and inflation resumed.

A number of factors besides the Vietnam War contributed to the troubling price spiral. Eager to court the farm vote, the administration made a large wheat sale to Russia in 1972. The sale proved to be a major miscalculation. With insufficient wheat left for the American market, grain prices shot up. Twenty-five years of grain surpluses suddenly vanished, and shortages occurred. Other agricultural setbacks like corn blight compounded the problem. Between 1971 and 1974, farm prices rose 66 percent, as agricultural inflation accompanied industrial inflation.

The most critical factor in disrupting the economy, though, was the Arab oil embargo. American economic expansion had rested on cheap energy just as American patterns of life had depended on inexpensive gasoline. Although the Organization of Petroleum Exporting Countries (OPEC) had slowly raised oil prices in the early 1970s, the 1973 Arab-Israeli war led Saudi Arabia to impose an embargo on oil shipped to Israel's ally, the United States. Other OPEC nations continued to supply oil but quadrupled their prices. Dependent on imports for one-third of their energy needs, Americans faced shortages and skyrocketing prices. When the embargo ended in 1974, prices remained high.

The oil crisis affected all aspects of American economic life. Manufacturers, farmers, homeowners—all were touched by high energy prices. A loaf of bread that had cost 28 cents in the early 1970s jumped to 89 cents, and automobiles cost 72 percent more in 1978 than they had in 1973. Accustomed to filling up their cars' tanks for only a few dollars, Americans were shocked at paying 65 cents a gallon. In 1974, inflation reached 11 percent. But then, as higher energy prices encouraged consumers to cut back on their purchases, the nation entered a recession as well. Unemployment climbed to 9 percent for several months in 1975, the highest level since the 1930s.

As economic growth and stability eluded him, Nixon also tried to reorganize rapidly expanding and expensive welfare programs. Changes in welfare during the years of the Great Society had led the government to spend considerably more in this area. Critics claimed that welfare was inefficient and that benefits discouraged people from seeking work. Nixon faced a political dilemma. He recognized the conservative tide growing in the Sun Belt regions of the country from Florida to

Speaking to the "silent majority," Nixon promised to reinstitute traditional values and restore law and order. A private man, Nixon tried to insulate himself from the public and present a carefully crafted image through the national media. *(Hiroji Kubota/Magnum Photos)*

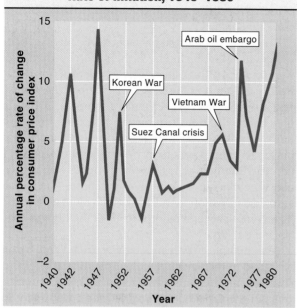

Rate of Inflation, 1940-1980

Annual percentage rate of change in consumer price index

Korean War
Suez Canal crisis
Vietnam War
Arab oil embargo

Year

Inflation often accompanied military spending in the postwar years. In the early 1970s, the Arab oil embargo contributed to an even higher rate. Source: U.S. Bureau of the Census.

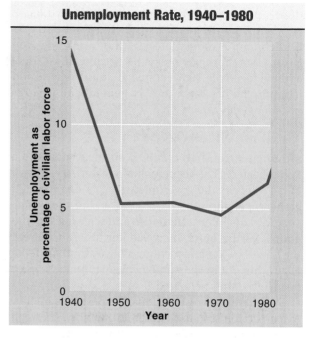

Unemployment Rate, 1940-1980

Unemployment as percentage of civilian labor force

Year

The unemployment rate, which had fallen dramatically during World War II and remained relatively constant in the 1950s and 1960s, rose at the same time inflation increased in the 1970s. Source: U.S. Bureau of Labor Statistics.

Texas to California, where many voters wanted cutbacks in what they viewed as excessive government programs. At the same time, he wanted to create a new Republican coalition by winning over traditionally Democratic blue-collar workers with reassurances that the Republicans would not dismantle the parts of the welfare state on which they relied.

Urged by domestic adviser Daniel Moynihan, Nixon endorsed an expensive but feasible new program. The Family Assistance Plan would have guaranteed a minimum yearly stipend of $1,600 to a family of four, with food stamps providing about $800 more. The program, aiming to cut "welfare cheaters" who took unfair advantage of the system and to encourage recipients to work, required all participants to register for job training and to accept employment when found. Proponents, who doubtless exaggerated the number of cheaters, wanted to make it more profitable to work than to subsist on the public rolls. Though promising, the program was attacked by both liberals, who felt it was too limited, and conservatives, who claimed it tried to do too much. It died in the Senate.

As he struggled with the economy and with what many called the "welfare mess," Nixon irritated liberals still further in his effort to restore "law and order." Political protest, rising crime rates, increased drug use, and more permissive attitudes toward sex all created a growing backlash among working-class

and many middle-class Americans (see Chapter 29 for the development of youth culture). Nixon decided to use government power to silence disruption and thereby strengthen his conservative political constituency.

Part of the administration's campaign involved denouncing disruptive elements. Nixon lashed out at demonstrators, at one point calling student activists "bums." More and more, however, he relied on his vice president to play the part of hatchet man. As he had demonstrated during the 1968 campaign, Agnew had a gift for jugular attack. He branded opposition elements, students in particular, as "ideological eunuchs" who made up an "effete corps of impudent snobs." At the same time, Nixon and Agnew appealed for support to blue-collar youth, whom they described as patriotic supporters of the Vietnam War.

Another part of Nixon's effort to circumscribe the liberal approach involved attacking the communications industry. Although Nixon himself was well aware of the power of the press and used both television and radio effectively, he believed the media represented the opinions of the "Eastern establishment" and viewed him with hostility. After commentators responded negatively to a major address in 1969, he decided to challenge the television networks. Again Agnew spearheaded the pointed attack.

The third and strongest part of Nixon's plan was Attorney General John Mitchell's effort to demonstrate

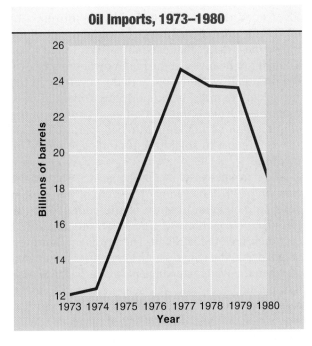

American reliance on foreign oil increased in the mid-1970s, until the United States tried to respond to price increases by reducing reliance on imports. Source: U.S. Energy Information Administration.

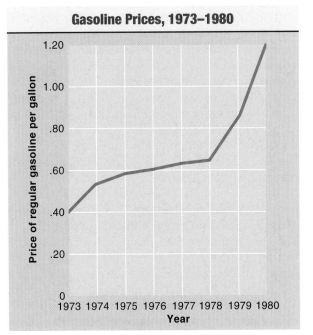

Gasoline prices rose steadily in the years following the Arab oil embargo and affected the entire American economy. Source: U.S. Energy Information Administration.

that the administration supported the values of citizens upset by domestic upheavals. Mitchell sought enhanced powers for a campaign on crime, sometimes at the expense of individuals' constitutional rights. He intended to send a message to the entire country that the new team in the White House would not tolerate certain actions, even if they were protected by the right to free speech.

Mitchell's plan included reshaping the Supreme Court, which had rendered increasingly liberal decisions on the rights of defendants in the past decade and a half. That shift, Republican leaders argued, had resulted in moral and ethical laxity. During his first term, Nixon had the opportunity to name four judges to the Court, and he nominated men who shared his views. His first choice was Warren E. Burger as chief justice to replace the liberal Earl Warren, who was retiring. Burger, a moderate, was confirmed quickly. Other appointments, however, were more partisan and reflected Nixon's aggressively conservative approach. Intent on appealing to white southerners, he first selected Clement Haynesworth of South Carolina, then G. Harold Carswell of Florida. Both men on examination showed such racial biases or limitations that the Senate refused to confirm them. Nixon then appointed Harry Blackmun, Lewis F. Powell, Jr., and William Rehnquist, all able and qualified, and all inclined to tilt the Court in a more conservative direction.

Not surprisingly, the Court gradually shifted to the right. It narrowed defendants' rights in an attempt to ease the burden of the prosecution in its cases and slowed liberalizing of pornography laws. It supported Nixon's assault on the media by ruling that journalists did not have the right to refuse to answer questions for a grand jury, even if they had promised sources confidentiality. On other questions, however, the Court did not always act as the president had hoped. In the controversial 1973 *Roe* v. *Wade* decision, the Court legalized abortion, stating that women's rights included the right to control their own bodies. This decision was one that feminists, a group hardly supported by the president, had ardently sought.

The Watergate Affair

Faced with a solidly Democratic Congress, the Nixon administration found its legislative initiatives blocked. In this situation, Nixon was determined to end the stalemate by winning a second term and sweeping Republican majorities into both houses of Congress in 1972. His efforts to gain a decisive Republican victory at the polls led to excesses that brought his downfall.

Nixon's reelection campaign was even better organized than the effort four years earlier. His fiercely loyal aides were prepared to do anything to win. Special counsel Charles W. Colson described himself as a "flag-waving, kick-'em-in-the-nuts, anti-press, anti-liberal Nixon fanatic." He had earlier played an important part in developing an "enemies list" of prominent figures judged to be unsympathetic to the administration. White House counsel John Dean defined his task as finding a way to "use the available federal machinery to screw our political enemies." Active in carrying out commands were E. Howard Hunt, a former CIA agent and a specialist in "dirty tricks," and G. Gordon Liddy, a onetime member of the FBI, who prided himself on his willingness to do anything without flinching.

The Committee to Re-elect the President (CREEP), headed by John Mitchell, who resigned as attorney general, spared no expense in pursuit of its goal. It launched a massive fund-raising drive, aimed at collecting as much money as it could before the reporting of contributions became necessary under a new campaign-finance law. That money could be used for any purpose, including payments for the performance of dirty tricks aimed at disrupting the opposition's campaign. Other funds financed an intelligence branch within CREEP that had Liddy at its head and included Hunt.

Early in 1972, Liddy and his lieutenants proposed an elaborate scheme to wiretap the phones of various Democrats and to disrupt their nominating convention. Twice Mitchell refused to go along, arguing that the proposal was too risky and expensive. Finally he approved a modified version of the plan to tap the phones of the Democratic National Committee at its headquarters in the Watergate apartment complex in Washington, D.C. Mitchell, formerly the top justice official in the land, had authorized breaking the law.

The wiretapping attempt took place on the evening of June 16, 1972, and ended with the arrest of those involved. Their connection to the Republican party could incriminate the reelection campaign. Top officials of the Nixon reelection team had to decide quickly what to do.

Reelection remained the most pressing priority, so Nixon's aides played the matter down and used federal resources to head off the investigation. When the FBI traced the money carried by the burglars to CREEP, the president authorized the CIA to call off the FBI on the grounds that national security was at stake. Though not involved in the planning of the break-in, the president was now party to the cover-up. In the succeeding months, he authorized payment of hush money to silence Hunt and others. Members of the administration, including Mitchell, perjured themselves in court to shield the top officials who were involved.

Nixon trounced Democrat George McGovern in the election of 1972, receiving 61 percent of the popular vote. In a clear indication of the collapse of the Democratic coalition, 70 percent of southern voters cast their ballots for Nixon. The president, however, failed to gain the congressional majorities he sought.

When the Watergate burglars were brought to trial, they pleaded guilty and were sentenced to jail, but the case refused to die. Judge John Sirica was not satisfied that justice had been done, asserting that the evidence indicated that others had played a part. Meanwhile, two zealous reporters, Bob Woodward and Carl Bernstein of the *Washington Post,* were following a trail of leads on their own. Slowly they recognized who else was involved. On one occasion, when they reached Mitchell and asked him about a story tying him to Watergate, he turned on them in fury. "All that crap you're putting in the paper?" he said. "It's all been denied."

Mitchell's irritation notwithstanding, the unraveling continued. The Senate Select Committee on Presidential Campaign Activities undertook an investigation, and one of the convicted burglars testified that the White House had been involved in the episode. Newspaper stories generated further leads, and the Senate hearings in turn provided new material for the press. Faced with rumors that the White House was actively involved, Nixon decided that he had to release Haldeman and Ehrlichman, his two closest aides, to save his own neck. On nationwide TV he declared that he would take the ultimate responsibility for the mistakes of others, for "there can be no whitewash at the White House."

PRESIDENTIAL ELECTIONS, 1968–1972

Year	Candidate	Party	Popular Vote	Electoral Vote
1968	RICHARD M. NIXON	Republican	31,783,783 (43.4%)	301
	Hubert M. Humphrey	Democratic	31,271,839 (42.7%)	191
	George C. Wallace	American Independent	9,899,557 (13.5%)	46
1972	RICHARD M. NIXON	Republican	45,767,218 (60.7%)	520
	George S. McGovern	Democratic	28,357,668 (37.5%)	17

Note: Winners' names appear in capital letters.

DOONESBURY   by Garry Trudeau

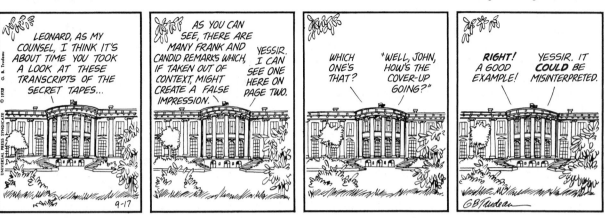

Although Nixon steadfastly denied his complicity in the Watergate affair, his tape recordings of White House conversations told a different story. In this classic "Doonesbury" cartoon from September 17, 1973, Garry Trudeau notes Nixon's efforts to head off the investigation. *(Universal Press Syndicate)*

In May 1973, the Senate committee began televised public hearings, reminiscent of the McCarthy hearings of the 1950s. As millions of Americans watched, the drama built. John Dean, seeking to save himself, testified that Nixon knew about the cover-up, and other staffers revealed a host of illegal activities undertaken at the White House: money had been paid to the burglars to silence them; State Department documents had been forged to smear a previous administration; wiretaps had been used to prevent top-level leaks. The most electrifying moment was the disclosure that the president had installed a secret taping system in his office that recorded all conversations. Tapes could verify or dis-prove the growing rumors that Nixon had in fact been party to the cover-up all along.

To show his own honesty, Nixon appointed Harvard law professor Archibald Cox as a special prosecutor in the Department of Justice. But when Cox tried to gain access to the tapes, Nixon resisted and finally fired him. Nixon's own popularity plummeted, and even the appointment of another special prosecutor, Leon Jaworski, did not help. More and more Americans now believed that the president had played at least some part in the cover-up and should take responsibility for his acts. *Time* magazine ran an editorial headlined "The President Should Resign," and Congress considered impeachment.

The Watergate affair finally brought Nixon down. After resigning the presidency in 1974, Nixon took off for exile in California. Despite leaving Washington in disgrace, Nixon struck an incongruously triumphant pose as he boarded a helicopter on the White House lawn. *(Corbis)*

The first steps, in accordance with constitutional mandate, took place in the House of Representatives. The House Judiciary Committee, made up of 21 Democrats and 17 Republicans, began to debate the impeachment case in late July 1974. By sizable tallies, it voted to impeach the president on the grounds of obstruction of justice, abuse of power, and refusal to obey a congressional subpoena to turn over his tapes. A full House of Representatives vote still had to occur, and the Senate would have to preside over a trial before removal could take place. But for Nixon the handwriting was on the wall.

After a brief delay, on August 5 Nixon obeyed a Supreme Court ruling and released the tapes. Despite a suspicious 18½-minute silence, they contained the "smoking gun"—clear evidence of his complicity in the cover-up. His ultimate resignation became but a matter of time. Four days later, on August 9, 1974, the extraordinary episode came to an end, as Nixon became the first American president ever to resign.

The Watergate affair seemed disturbing evidence that the appropriate balance of power in the federal government had disappeared. As the scandal wound down, many began to question the centralization of power in the American political system and to cite the "imperial presidency" as the cause of recent abuses. Others simply lost faith in the presidency altogether. A 1974 survey showed that trust in the presidency had declined by 50 percent in a two-year period. Coming on the heels of Lyndon Johnson's lying to the American people about involvement in Vietnam, the Watergate affair contributed to the cumulative disillusionment with politics in Washington and to the steady decrease in political participation. Barely half of those eligible to vote bothered to go to the polls in the presidential elections of 1976, 1980, and 1984. Even fewer cast ballots in nonpresidential contests.

Gerald Ford: Caretaker President

When Nixon resigned in disgrace midway through his second term, he was succeeded by Gerald Ford. An unpretentious middle-American Republican who believed in traditional virtues, Ford had been appointed vice president in 1973 when Spiro Agnew resigned in disgrace for accepting bribes. After the appointment, Richard Rovere, a noted journalist, wrote in the *New Yorker:* "That he is thoroughly equipped to serve as Vice President seems unarguable; the office requires only a warm body and occasionally a nimble tongue. However . . . neither Richard Nixon nor anyone else has come forward to explain Gerald Ford's qualifications to serve as Chief Executive." The new president acknowledged his own limitations, declaring, "I am a Ford, not a Lincoln."

More important than his limitations were his views about public policy. Throughout his tenure in Congress, Ford had voted according to the Republican convictions he shared with his Michigan constituents. Over the years he had opposed federal aid to education, the poverty program, and mass transit. He had voted for civil rights measures only when weaker substitutes he had favored had gone down to defeat. Like his predecessor, he was determined to stop the liberal advances promoted by the Democrats in the 1960s.

Ford faced a daunting task. After Watergate, Washington was in turmoil. Americans wondered whether any politician could be trusted to guide public affairs. The new president had to use his authority to restore national confidence at a time when the misuse of presidential power itself had precipitated the crisis.

Ford worked quickly to restore trust in the government. He emphasized conciliation and compromise, and he promised to cooperate both with Congress and with American citizens. The nation responded gratefully. *Time* magazine pointed to a "mood of good feeling and even exhilaration in Washington that the city had not experienced for many years."

The new feeling did not last long. Ford weakened his base of support by pardoning Richard Nixon barely a month after his resignation. Ford's decidedly con-

Gerald Ford, a genial man, sought to reestablish confidence in the government after succeeding Nixon as president. Far different from his predecessor, he served just over two years, as his bid for election to the presidency in 1976 ended in defeat. *(UPI/Corbis-Bettmann)*

servative bent in domestic policy often threw him into confrontation with a Democratic Congress. Economic problems proved most pressing in 1974, as inflation, fueled by oil price increases, hit 11 percent, unemployment reached 6.6 percent at the end of the year, and GNP declined. Home construction slackened and interest rates rose, while stock prices fell. Nixon, preoccupied with the Watergate crisis, had been unable to curb rising inflation and unemployment. Not since Franklin Roosevelt took office in the depths of the Great Depression had a new president faced economic difficulties so severe.

Like Herbert Hoover 45 years before, the conservative Ford hoped to restore confidence and persuade the public that conditions would improve with patience and goodwill. But his campaign to cajole Americans to "Whip Inflation Now" voluntarily failed dismally. At last convinced of the need for strong government action, the administration introduced a tight-money policy as a means of curbing inflation. It led to the most severe recession since the Depression, with unemployment peaking at 9 percent in early 1975. In response, Congress pushed for an antirecession spending program. Recognizing political reality, Ford endorsed a multibillion-dollar tax cut coupled with higher unemployment benefits. The economy made a modest recovery, although inflation and unemployment remained high, and federal budget deficits soared.

Ford's dilemma was that his belief in limited presidential involvement set him against liberals who argued that strong executive leadership was necessary to make the welfare state work. When he failed to take the initiative, Congress intervened, and the two branches of government became embroiled in conflict. Ford vetoed numerous bills, including those creating a consumer protection agency and expanding programs in education, housing, and health. In response, Congress overrode a higher percentage of vetoes than at any time since the presidency of Franklin Pierce more than a century before.

The Carter Interlude

In the election of 1976, the nation's bicentennial year, Ford faced Jimmy Carter, former governor of Georgia.

Carter, appealing to voters distrustful of political leadership, portrayed himself as an outsider. He stressed that he was not from Washington and observed that, unlike many of those mired in recent scandals, he was not a lawyer. Carter's quest for the Democratic nomination benefited from reforms that increased the significance of primary elections in selecting a presidential candidate and decreased the influence of party professionals. Assisted by public relations experts, he effectively utilized the media, especially television, which allowed him to bypass party machines and establish a direct electronic relationship with voters.

In the election, most elements of the old Democratic coalition came together once again, as the Democrats profited from the fallout of the Watergate affair. Carter won a 50 to 48 percent majority of the popular vote and a 297 to 240 tally in the Electoral College. He did well with members of the working class, African Americans, and Catholics. He won most of the South, heartening to the Democrats after Nixon's gains there. Racial voting differences continued, however, as Carter attracted less than half of all white voters but an overwhelming majority of black voters.

Carter stood in stark contrast to his recent predecessors in the White House. Rooted in the rural South, he was a peanut farmer who shared the values of the region. He was also a graduate of the Naval Academy, trained as a manager and an engineer. A modest man, he was uncomfortable with the pomp and incessant political activity in Washington. He hoped to take a more restrained approach to the presidency and thereby defuse its imperial stamp.

Initially, voters saw Carter as a reform Democrat committed to his party's liberal goals. When he had accepted the Democratic nomination, he had called for an end to race and sex discrimination. He had challenged the "political and economic elite" in America and sought a new approach to providing for the poor, old, and weak.

But Carter was hardly the old-line liberal some Democrats had hoped for. Though he called himself a populist, his political philosophy and priorities were never clear. Critics charged that he had no legislative

PRESIDENTIAL ELECTION OF 1976			
Candidate	**Party**	**Popular Vote**	**Electoral Vote**
JIMMY CARTER	Democratic	40,830,763 (50.0%)	297
Gerald R. Ford	Republican	39,147,793 (48.0%)	240

Note: Winner's name appears in capital letters.

Jimmy Carter holds hands with his wife, Rosalyn, as they walk to his inauguration in early 1977. As much as possible, Carter tried to avoid actions that reminded people of the "imperial presidency" of the Nixon years. *(Jimmy Carter Library, Atlanta, Georgia)*

Timeline

1946	Employment Act
1947	Taft-Hartley Act
1948	"Dixiecrat" party formed
	Truman defeats Dewey
1949	Truman launches Fair Deal
1952	Dwight D. Eisenhower elected president
1953	Submerged Lands Act
1956	Eisenhower reelected
1960	John F. Kennedy elected president
1962	JFK confronts steel companies
1963	Kennedy assassinated; Lyndon B. Johnson becomes president
1964	Economic Opportunity Act initiates War on Poverty
	Johnson reelected president
1965	Department of Housing and Urban Development established
	Elementary and Secondary Education Act
1968	Robert F. Kennedy assassinated
	Police and protesters clash at Democratic national convention
	Richard Nixon elected president
1972	Nixon reelected
1973	Watergate hearings in Congress
	Spiro Agnew resigns as vice president
1974	OPEC price increases
	Inflation hits 11 percent
	Unemployment reaches 6.6 percent at end of year
	Nixon resigns; Gerald Ford becomes president
	Ford pardons Nixon
1975	Unemployment reaches 9 percent in early part of year
1976	Jimmy Carter elected president
1977	Carter energy program

strategy. Rather, they said with some truth, he responded to problems in a haphazard way and failed to provide firm direction. His status as an outsider, touted during the campaign, led him to ignore traditional political channels when he assumed power. He also seemed to become mired in detail and to lose sight of larger issues. Like Herbert Hoover, he was a technocrat in the White House when liberals wanted a visionary to help them overcome hard times.

In economic affairs, Carter gave liberals some hope at first as he accepted deficit spending. When the Federal Reserve Board increased the money supply to help meet mounting deficits, which reached peacetime records in these years, inflation rose to about 10 percent a year. Seeking to reduce inflation in 1979, Carter slowed down the economy by reducing spending and cutting the deficit slightly. Contraction of the money supply led to greater unemployment and many small-business failures. Budget cuts fell largely on social programs and distanced Carter from reform-minded Democrats who had supported him three years before. Yet even that effort to arrest growing deficits was not enough. When the budget released in early 1980 still showed high spending levels, the financial community reacted strongly. Bond prices fell, and interest rates rose dramatically.

Similarly, Carter disappointed liberals by failing to construct an effective energy policy. OPEC's increase of oil prices led many Americans to resent their dependence on foreign oil—over 40 percent was being imported by the end of the decade—and to clamor for energy self-sufficiency. Carter responded in April 1977 with a comprehensive energy program, which he called the "moral equivalent of war." Critics seized on the acronym of that expression, MEOW, to ridicule the plan and had a field day attacking the president. Never an effective leader in working with the legislative branch, Carter watched his proposals bog down in Congress for 26 months. Eventually, the program committed the nation to move from oil dependence to reliance on coal, possibly even on sun and wind, and established a new synthetic-fuel corporation. Nuclear power, another alternative, seemed less attractive as costs rose and accidents, like the one at Three Mile Island, occurred.

Carter further upset liberals by beginning deregulation—the removal of government controls in economic life. Arguing that certain restrictions established over the past century stifled competition and increased consumer costs, he supported decontrol of oil and natural gas prices to spur production. He also deregulated the railroad, trucking, and airline industries.

Liberals were disappointed as the 1970s ended. Their hopes for a stronger commitment to a welfare state had been dashed, and conservatives had the upper hand. Despite a tenuous Democratic hold on the presidency at the end of the decade, liberalism was in trouble.

Conclusion

Political Readjustment

The course of public policy shifted significantly in the post–World War II years. In the late 1940s and 1950s, American leaders took the first steps toward consolidating the welfare state that Franklin Roosevelt had begun to create in the decade before. In the 1960s, liberal Democrats went even further, as they pressed for large-scale government intervention to meet the social and economic problems that accompanied the modern industrial age. They were inspired by John Kennedy's rhetoric and saw the triumph of their approach in Lyndon Johnson's Great Society, as the nation strengthened its commitment to a capitalist welfare state. When the Democratic party became impaled on the Vietnam War and lost the presidency, the Republicans began dismantling the Great Society programs. While accepting some provisions of the modern welfare state, they objected to the aggressive liberal effort to make the government the major player in the political game and took exception to many of the programs aimed at the poor.

Most Americans, like Paul Cowan, met at the start of this chapter, embraced the message of John Kennedy and the New Frontier in the 1960s and endorsed the liberal approach. But over time, they began to question the tenets of liberalism as the economy faltered, as hard economic choices had to be made, and as the country became mired in Vietnam. Republicans challenging Democratic priorities gained the upper hand, and disillusioned liberals like Cowan wondered if their approach could ever succeed.

Recommended Reading

The Origins of the Welfare State

General Works. Edward D. Berkowitz and Kim McQuaid, *Creating the Welfare State: The Political Economy of 20th Century Reform* (1994); Robert H. Haveman, ed., *A Decade of Federal Anti-Poverty Programs: Achievements, Failures, and Lessons* (1977); Jacqueline Jones, *The Dispossessed: America's Underclasses from the Civil War to the Present* (1992); Michael B. Katz, *In the Shadow of the Poorhouse: A Social History of Welfare in America*, 10th anniv. ed. (1997) and *The Undeserving Poor: From the War on Poverty to the War on Welfare* (1990); Sar A. Levitan and Robert Taggart, *The Promise of Greatness: The Social Programs of the Last Decade and Their Major Achievements* (1976); Charles Murray, *Losing Ground: American Social Policy, 1950–1980,* 10th anniv. ed. (1995); James T. Patterson, *America's Struggle Against Poverty: 1900–1994* (1995); Frances F. Piven and Richard A. Cloward, eds., *Regulating the Poor: The Functions of Public Welfare*, 2nd ed. (1993); Margaret Weir, Ann Shola Orloff, and Theda Skocpol, *The Politics of Social Policy in the United States* (1988).

Impact of the Media on the Welfare State. Erik Barnouw, *Tube of Plenty: The Evolution of American Television*, 2nd rev. ed. (1990); James L. Baughman, *The Republic of Mass Culture* (1992); Todd Gitlin, *The Whole World Is Watching: Mass Media in the Making and Unmaking of the New Left* (1980); Cecelia Tichi, *Electronic Hearth: Creating an American Television Culture* (1991).

The Truman Years. Robert J. Donovan, *Conflict and Crisis: The Presidency of Harry S Truman, 1945–1948* (1977) and *Tumultuous Years: The Presidency of Harry S Truman* (1982);

Robert H. Ferrell, *Harry S. Truman and the Modern American Presidency* (1998); Alonzo L. Hamby, *Man of the People: A Life of Harry S. Truman* (1995); David McCullough, *Truman* (1992); Harry S Truman, *Memoirs*, 2 vols. (1955, 1956).

The Eisenhower Years. Craig Allen, *Eisenhower and the Mass Media: Peace, Prosperity, and Prime-Time TV* (1993); Stephen E. Ambrose, *Eisenhower: The President* (1984) and *Eisenhower: Soldier and President* (1990); Dwight D. Eisenhower, *Mandate for Change, 1953–1956* (1963) and *Waging Peace* (1965); Fred I. Greenstein, *The Hidden-Hand Presidency: Eisenhower as Leader* (1982); Chester J. Pach, Jr. and Elmo Richardson, *The Presidency of Dwight D. Eisenhower* (1991).

The High-Water Mark of Liberalism

General Works. Terry H. Anderson, *The Movement and the Sixties: Protest in America from Greensboro to Wounded Knee* (1995); David Farber, *The Age of Great Dreams: America in the 1960s* (1994); James J. Farrell, *The Spirit of the Sixties: The Making of Postwar Radicalism* (1997); Todd Gitlin, *The Sixties: Years of Hope, Days of Rage* (1987); Godfrey Hodgson, *America in Our Time* (1976); James L. Sundquist, *Politics and Policy: The Eisenhower, Kennedy, and Johnson Years* (1968).

John F. Kennedy and the New Frontier. James N. Giglio, *The Presidency of John F. Kennedy* (1991); Nigel Hamilton, *JFK: Reckless Youth* (1992); Seymour M. Hersh, *The Dark Side of Camelot* (1997); Herbert S. Parmet, *Jack: The Struggles of John F. Kennedy* (1980) and *JFK: The Presidency of John F. Kennedy* (1983); Richard Reeves, *President Kennedy: Profile of Power*

(1993); Thomas C. Reeves, *A Question of Character: A Life of John F. Kennedy* (1991); Arthur M. Schlesinger, Jr., *A Thousand Days: John F. Kennedy in the White House* (1965); Theodore C. Sorensen, *Kennedy* (1965).

Lyndon B. Johnson and the Great Society.   Michael R. Beschloss, ed., *Taking Charge: The Johnson White House Tapes, 1963–1964* (1997); Vaughn Davis Bornet, *The Presidency of Lyndon B. Johnson* (1983); Robert Dallek, *Lone Star Rising: Lyndon Johnson and His Times* (1990) and *Flawed Giant: Lyndon Johnson and His Times, 1961–1973* (1998); Robert A. Divine, ed., *Exploring the Johnson Years* (1981), *The Johnson Years, Volume Two: Vietnam, the Environment, and Science* (1984), and *The Johnson Years: LBJ at Home and Abroad* (1994); Lyndon Johnson, *The Vantage Point: Perspectives of the Presidency* (1971); Doris Kearns, *Lyndon Johnson and the American Dream* (1976).

The Decline of Liberalism

General Works.   Mary C. Brennan, *Turning Right in the Sixties: The Conservative Capture of the GOP* (1995); Paul Cowan, *The Making of an Un-American: A Dialogue with Experience* (1970); Godfrey Hodgson, *The World Turned Right Side Up: A History of the Conservative Ascendency in America* (1996); Allen J. Matusow, *The Unraveling of America: A History of Liberalism in the 1960s* (1984).

The Nixon Years.   Rowland Evans, Jr., and Robert D. Novak, *Nixon in the White House* (1972); Stanley I. Kutler, *The Wars of Watergate: The Last Crisis of Richard Nixon* (1990); Stanley I. Kutler, ed., *Abuse of Power: The New Nixon Tapes* (1997); J.

Anthony Lukas, *Nightmare: The Underside of the Nixon Years* (1976); Allen J. Matusow, *Nixon's Economy: Booms, Busts, Dollars, and Votes* (1998); Richard Nixon, *RN: The Memoirs of Richard Nixon* (1978); Garry Wills, *Nixon Agonistes: The Crisis of the Self-made Man* (1969); Bob Woodward and Carl Bernstein, *All the President's Men* (1974) and *The Final Days* (1976).

Gerald Ford.   John Robert Greene, *The Limits of Power: The Nixon and Ford Administrations* (1992) and *The Presidency of Gerald R. Ford* (1995); John Hersey, *The President* (1975); Richard Reeves, *A Ford, Not a Lincoln* (1975).

Jimmy Carter.   Jimmy Carter, *Keeping Faith: Memoirs of a President* (1982); Gary M. Fink and Hugh Davis Graham, eds., *The Carter Presidency: Policy Choices in the Post–New Deal Era* (1998); Burton I. Kaufman, *The Presidency of James Earl Carter, Jr.* (1993); Kenneth A. Morris, *Jimmy Carter: American Moralist* (1996).

Fiction and Film

Allen Drury's *Advise and Consent* (1959) is a novel about Washington politics, complete with blackmail and demagoguery. Barbara Garson's *MacBird* (1966), a play patterned loosely after Macbeth, pokes fun at the overarching ambitions of Lyndon Johnson.

All the President's Men (1976) is a film (based on the book of the same name) about the effort by *Washington Post* reporters Bob Woodward and Carl Bernstein to find the truth about the Watergate scandal. *Network* (1976) is a film about the problems and abuses of television journalism.

Suggested Web Sites

http://www.ipl.org/ref/POTUS/jfkennedy.html

John Fitzgerald Kennedy. This site contains basic factual data about Kennedy's election and presidency, speeches, and on-line biographies.

http://mcadams.posc.mu.edu/home.htm

The Kennedy Assassination. This well-organized site has images, essays, and photos on the assassination.

http://ipl.org/ref/POTUS/lbjohnson.html

Lyndon Baines Johnson. This site contains basic factual data about Johnson's election and presidency, speeches, and on-line biographies.

http://www.ipl.org/ref/POTUS/rmnixon.html

Richard Milhous Nixon. This site contains basic factual data about Nixon's election and presidency, speeches, and on-line biographies.

http://www.washingtonpost.com/wp-srv/ national/longterm/watergate/front.htm

Watergate 25. This site features a chronology, images, searchable articles, and a good deal of background information about the burglary and its consequences.

http://www.nara.gov/education/teaching/watergate/ watergat.html

Constitutional Issues: Watergate and the Constitution. From the National Archives teaching materials, this site has a good chronology of Watergate and documents the pros and cons of seeking an indictment against former president Richard Nixon.

http://www.ipl.org/ref/POTUS/grford.html

Gerald Rudolph Ford. This site contains basic factual data about Ford's election and presidency, speeches, and on-line biographies.

http://www.ipl.org/ref/POTUS/jecarter.html

James Earl Carter, Jr. This site contains basic factual data about Carter's election and presidency, speeches, and on-line biographies.

http://cnn.com/TECH/specials/apollo/

Giant Leap. This CNN site commemorates the 30th anniversary of the 1969 moonwalk and tells the story of NASA and the ongoing space program.

http://www.ushistoryplace.com

 A richly detailed on-line learning environment complete with interactive maps, timelines, history activities, primary source documents, and links to related American history sites.

The STRUGGLE *for* SOCIAL REFORM

**A**nn Clarke—as she chooses to call herself now—always wanted to go to college. But girls from Italian families rarely did when she was growing up. Her mother, a Sicilian immigrant and widow, asked her brother for advice: "Should Antonina go to college?" "What's the point?" he replied. "She's just going to get married."

Life had not been easy for Antonina Rose Rumore. As a child in the 1920s, her Italian-speaking grandmother cared for her while her mother worked to support the family, first in the sweatshops, then as a seamstress. Even as she dreamed about the future, Ann accommodated her culture's demands for dutiful daughters. Responsive to family needs, Ann finished the high school commercial course in three years. She struggled with ethnic prejudice as a legal secretary on Wall Street but still believed in the American dream and the Puritan work ethic. She was proud of her ability to bring money home to her family.

When World War II began, Ann wanted to join the WACS. "Better you should be a prostitute," her mother said. Ann went off to California instead, where she worked at a number of resorts. When she left California, she vowed to return to that land of freedom and opportunity.

After the war, Ann married Gerard Clarke, a college man with an English background. Her children would grow up accepted with Anglo-Saxon names. Over the next 15 years, Ann devoted herself to her family. She was a mother first and foremost, and that took all her time. But she still waited for her own chance. "I had this hunger to learn, this curiosity," she later recalled. By the early 1960s, her three children were all in school. Promising her husband to have dinner on the table every night at six, she enrolled at Pasadena City College. It was not easy, for family still came first, but Ann proved creative in finding time to study. When doing dishes or cleaning house, she memorized lists of dates, historical events, and other material for school. Holidays, however, complicated her efforts to complete assignments. Ann occasionally felt compelled to give everything up "to make Christmas." Forgetting about a whole semester's work two weeks before finals one year, she sewed nightgowns instead of writing her art history paper.

Her conflict over her studies was intensified by her position as one of the first older women to go back to college. "Sometimes I felt like I wanted to hide in the woodwork," she admitted. Often her teachers were younger than she was. It took four years to complete the two-year program. But she was not yet done, for she really wanted a bachelor's degree. Back she went, this time to California State College at Los Angeles.

As the years passed and the credits piled up, Ann became an honors student. Her children, now in college themselves, were proud and supportive; dinners became arguments over Faulkner and foreign policy. Even so, Ann still felt caught between her world at home and the world outside. Since she was at the top of her class, graduation should have been a special occasion. But she was only embarrassed when a letter from the school invited her parents to attend the final ceremonies. Ann could not bring herself to go.

With a college degree in hand, Ann returned to school for a teaching credential. Receiving her certificate at age 50, she faced the irony of social change. Once denied opportunities, Italians had assimilated into American society. Now she was just another Anglo in Los Angeles, caught in a changing immigration wave; now the city sought Hispanics and other minorities to teach in the schools. Jobs in education were scarce, and she was close to "retirement age," so she became a substitute in Mexican American areas for the next ten years, specializing in bilingual education.

Meanwhile, Ann was troubled by the Vietnam War. "For every boy that died, one of us should lie down," she told fellow workers. She was not an activist, but rather one of the millions of quieter Americans who ultimately helped bring about change. The social adjustments caused by the war affected her. Her son grew long hair and a beard and attended protest rallies. She worried that he would antagonize the ladies in Pasadena. Her daughter came home from college in boots and a leather miniskirt designed to shock. Ann accepted her children's changes as relatively superficial, confident in their fundamental values; "they were good kids," she knew. She trusted them, even as she worried about them.

Ann Clarke's experience paralleled that of millions of women in the post–World War II years. Caught up in traditional patterns of family life, these women began to recognize their need for something more. Like blacks,

Latinos, Native Americans, and members of other groups, American women struggled to transform the conditions of their lives and the rights they enjoyed within American society. In the process, they changed the nation itself.

This chapter describes the reform impulse that accompanied the effort to define the government's responsibility for economic and social stability described in Chapter 28. Like earlier reform efforts, particularly those during the Progressive era and the New Deal, this modern struggle sought to fulfill the promise of the American past and to provide liberty and equality in racial, gender, and social relations. The third reform cycle of the twenti-

eth century, however, drew more from the militancy of those on the mudsills of society than from the pleas of middle-class activists. It reflected the attempt of often marginalized Americans to make the nation live up to its professed values. This chapter highlights the voices of such "outsiders" as it describes their efforts to square the ideals of American life with the realities many Americans faced. The chapter records the continuing frustrations of integrating diverse groups into American society while acknowledging their integrity and identity. And it notes the still-present tension accompanying the sharp debate over power and its distribution in the United States.

THE BLACK STRUGGLE FOR EQUALITY

The quest for equality by African Americans was central to the postwar struggle for civil rights. It influenced the long-standing protest movements of Native Americans and Latinos noted later in this chapter. It also provided an example for other groups, such as Asian Americans, whose experiences are detailed in the section on changes in immigration patterns in the following chapter. Stemming from an effort dating back to the Civil War and Reconstruction, the black movement had gained momentum by the mid-twentieth century. African Americans, working with churches and other organizations, continued to press for reform through peaceful protest and political pressure. But change came slowly. Despite a number of major victories in the 1950s, the Jim Crow system of rigid segregation of public accommodations remained the rule in the South. In the North, urban ghettos grew, as the influx of southern blacks continued. Crowded public housing, poor schools, and limited economic opportunities fostered serious discontent.

Mid-Twentieth Century Roots

African Americans had increased their demands for change in the 1930s and 1940s and had made significant gains during World War II (see Chapter 25). Black servicemen returning from the war vowed to reject second-class citizenship and helped mobilize a grassroots movement to counter discrimination. In the postwar years, African struggles for independence, such as the Kenyan Mau Mau revolt against the British, inspired African American leaders who now saw the quest for black equality in a broader context. As Adam Clayton Powell, a Harlem preacher (and later congressman), warned, the black man "is ready to

throw himself into the struggle to make the dream of America become flesh and blood, bread and butter, freedom and equality. He walks conscious of the fact that he is no longer alone—no longer a minority."

The racial question was dramatized in 1947 when Jackie Robinson broke the color line and began playing major league baseball with the Brooklyn Dodgers. Sometimes teammates were hostile, sometimes opponents crashed into him with spikes flying high, but Robinson kept his frustrations to himself. A splendid first season helped ease the way and resulted in his selection as Rookie of the Year. African Americans flocked to the ballpark and followed his exploits on the radio. As Charles Jones of Charlotte, North Carolina, noted, "Robinson was knocking a ball everywhere on a *white man's* baseball field. . . . I mean the entire community would be glued to listening, and inevitably Jackie would steal a base or knock a home run, and we'd be rooting." After Robinson's trailblazing effort, other blacks, formerly confined to the old Negro leagues, started to move into the major leagues, then into professional football and basketball.

Many Americans began to respond as the nation's racial problems became entangled with Cold War politics. As leader of the "free world," America appealed for support in Africa and Asia, but discrimination at home was an obvious embarrassment.

A somewhat reluctant Truman supported the civil rights movement. A moderate on questions of race who believed in political, not social, equality, he responded to the growing strength of the African American vote. In 1946, he appointed a Committee on Civil Rights to investigate the problem of lynchings and other brutalities against blacks and recommend remedies. The committee's report, released in October 1947, showed that black Americans remained second-class citizens in every area of American life and set a civil rights agenda for the next two decades.

Jackie Robinson's electrifying play as the first African American in the major leagues led to acceptance of the integration of baseball. A spectacular rookie season in 1947 opened the way for other African Americans who had earlier been limited to the Negro leagues. In this photo, taken at Ebbets Field in Brooklyn during the 1957 World Series, Robinson is about to steal home. *(Ralph Morse/LIFE Magazine © Time Inc.)*

Though Truman hedged at first, in February 1948 he sent a ten-point civil rights program to Congress, the first presidential civil rights plan since Reconstruction. When the southern wing of the Democratic party bolted later that year (see Chapter 28), he moved forward even more aggressively. First he issued an executive order barring discrimination in the federal establishment. Then he ordered equality of treatment in the military services. Manpower needs in the Korean War broke down the last restrictions, particularly when the army found that integrated units performed well.

Elsewhere the administration pushed other reforms. The Justice Department, not previously supportive of litigation from the National Association for the Advancement of Colored People (NAACP) on behalf of equal rights for African Americans, now entered the battle against segregation and filed briefs challenging the constitutionality of restrictions in housing, education, and interstate transportation.

These actions helped build the pressure for change that influenced the Supreme Court. Congress, however, took little action.

Integrating the Schools

As the civil rights struggle gained momentum during the 1950s, the judicial system played a crucial role. The NAACP was determined to overturn the 1896 Supreme Court decision *Plessy* v. *Ferguson,* in which the Court had declared that segregation of the black and white races was constitutional if the facilities used by each were "separate but equal." The decree had been used for generations to sanction rigid segregation, primarily in the South, even though separate facilities were seldom, if ever, equal.

A direct challenge came in 1951. Oliver Brown, the father of eight-year-old Linda Brown, sued the school board of Topeka, Kansas, to allow his daughter to attend a school for white children she passed as she walked to the bus that carried her to a black school farther away. The case reached the Supreme Court, which added other school segregation cases to this one.

On May 17, 1954, the Supreme Court released its bombshell ruling in *Brown* v. *Board of Education.* For more than a decade, Supreme Court decisions had gradually expanded black civil rights. Now the Court unanimously decreed that "separate facilities are inherently unequal" and concluded that the "separate but equal" doctrine had no place in public education. A year later, the Court turned to the question of implementation and declared that local school boards, acting with the guidance of lower courts, should move "with all deliberate speed" to desegregate their facilities.

President Dwight Eisenhower had the ultimate responsibility for executing the law. Doubting that simple changes in the law could improve race relations, he once observed, "I don't believe you can change the hearts of men with laws or decisions." Privately he thought that the *Brown* ruling was wrong, but he knew that it was his constitutional duty to see that the law was carried out. Even while urging sympathy for the South in its period of transition, he acted immediately to desegregate the Washington, D.C., schools as a model for the rest of the country. He also ordered desegregation in navy yards and veterans' hospitals.

The South resisted. In district after district, vicious scenes occurred. The crucial confrontation came in Little Rock, Arkansas, in 1957. A desegregation plan, to begin with the token admission of a few black students to Central High School, was ready to go into effect. Just before the school year began, Governor Orval Faubus declared on television that it would not be possible to maintain order if integration took place. National Guardsmen, posted by the governor to keep

National Guardsmen, under federal command, escorted African American students into Central High School in Little Rock, Arkansas, in 1957. Observe the number of students and the number of soldiers as forcible integration began. *(Burt Glinn/Magnum Photos)*

the peace and armed with bayonets, turned away nine black students as they tried to enter the school. After three weeks, a federal court ordered the troops to leave. When the black children entered the building, the white students, spurred on by their elders, belligerently opposed them, chanting such slogans as "Two, four, six, eight, we ain't gonna integrate." In the face of hostile mobs, the black children left the school.

With the lines drawn, attention focused on the moderate man in the White House, who faced a situation in which Little Rock whites were clearly defying the law. As a former military officer, Ike knew that such resistance could not be tolerated, and he finally took the one action he had earlier called unthinkable. For the first time since the end of Reconstruction, an American president called out federal troops to protect the rights of black citizens. Eisenhower ordered paratroopers to Little Rock and placed National Guardsmen under federal command. The black children entered the school and attended classes with the military protecting their rights. Thus desegregation began.

Black Gains on Other Fronts

Meanwhile, African Americans, encouraged by their churches, began organizing themselves to take direct action, and their efforts significantly advanced the civil rights movement. In the 1930s, some had joined the

"Don't Buy Where You Can't Work" campaign begun in Chicago by itinerant street preacher Sufi Abdul Hamid. During World War II, others had marched under the slogan "We Die Together. Let's Eat Together" in the effort to integrate segregated restaurants. Now they were ready for an even more dramatic confrontation.

The crucial event occurred in Montgomery, Alabama, in December 1955. Rosa Parks, a 42-year-old black seamstress who was also secretary of the Alabama NAACP, sat down in the front of a bus in a section reserved by custom for whites. When ordered to move back, the longtime activist refused to budge. The bus driver called the police at the next stop, and Parks was arrested and ordered to stand trial for violating the segregation laws. Her calculated decision to resist the law marked a new phase in the civil rights struggle. Like Rosa Parks, ordinary black men and women would challenge the racial status quo and force both white and black leaders to respond.

In Montgomery, black civil rights officials seized the issue. E. D. Nixon, state NAACP president, told Parks, "This is the case we've been looking for. We can break this situation on the bus with your case." Fifty black leaders met to discuss the case and decided to organize a massive boycott of the bus system.

Martin Luther King, Jr., the 27-year-old minister of the Baptist church where the meeting was held, soon emerged as the preeminent spokesman of the protest. King was an impressive figure and an inspiring speaker. "There comes a time when people get tired . . . of being kicked about by the brutal feet of oppression," he declared. It was time to be more assertive, to cease being "patient with anything less than freedom and justice."

Although King, like others, was arrested on the trumped-up charge of speeding and jailed, grassroots support bubbled up. In Montgomery, 50,000 African Americans walked or formed car pools to avoid the transit system. Their actions cut gross revenue on city buses by 65 percent. Almost a year later, the Supreme Court ruled that bus segregation, like school segregation, violated the Constitution, and the boycott ended. But the mood it fostered continued, and for many blacks peaceful protest became a way of life.

Meanwhile, a concerted effort developed to guarantee black voting rights. The provisions of the Fifteenth Amendment notwithstanding, many states had circumvented the law for decades (see Chapter 16). Some

Baptist minister Martin Luther King, Jr., emerged as the black spokesman in the Montgomery, Alabama, bus boycott and soon became the most eloquent African American leader of the entire civil rights movement. He was often jailed for his efforts, as shown in this picture of him sharing a cell with Ralph Abernathy, another civil rights leader. *(Corbis)*

states required a poll tax or a literacy test or an examination of constitutional understanding. Blacks often found themselves excluded from the polls.

Largely because of the legislative genius of Senate majority leader Lyndon B. Johnson of Texas, a civil rights bill, the first since Reconstruction, moved toward passage. With his eye on the presidency, Johnson wanted to establish his credentials as a man who could look beyond narrow southern interests. Paring the bill down to the provisions he felt would pass, Johnson pushed the measure through.

The Civil Rights Act of 1957 created a Civil Rights Commission and empowered the Justice Department to go to court in cases where blacks were denied the right to vote. The bill was a compromise measure, yet it was the first successful effort to protect civil rights in 82 years.

Again led by Johnson, Congress passed the Civil Rights Act of 1960. This new measure set stiffer penalties for people who interfered with the right to vote but again stopped short of authorizing federal registrars to register blacks to vote and so, like its predecessor, was generally ineffective.

The civil rights movement made important strides during the Eisenhower years, though little of the progress resulted from the president's leadership. Rather, the efforts of blacks themselves and the rulings of the Supreme Court brought the most significant changes. The period of grassroots civil rights activity, now launched, continued in the 1960s.

Confrontation Continues

A spectrum of organizations, some old, some new, carried the fight forward. The NAACP, founded in 1910, remained committed to overturning the legal bases for segregation. The Congress of Racial Equality (CORE), an interracial group established in 1942, promoted change through peaceful confrontation. In 1957, after their victory in Montgomery, Martin Luther King, Jr., and others formed the Southern Christian Leadership Conference (SCLC), an organization of southern black clergy. The Student Nonviolent Coordinating Committee (SNCC, pronounced "snick") began to operate in 1960 and recruited young Americans who had not been involved in the civil rights struggle. SNCC, an offshoot of SCLC, was far more militant than the older, gradualist organizations.

Confrontations continued in the 1960s. On January 31, 1960, four black college students from the Agricultural and Technical College in Greensboro, North Carolina, sat down at a segregated Woolworth's lunch counter and deliberately violated southern segregation laws by refusing to leave. When a reporter inquired how long they had been planning the protest, the students responded, "All our lives!" The sit-ins captured media attention and soon involved thousands of African Americans. Those protesting often met with a brutal response. John Lewis, an African American activist who participated in a sit-in in Nashville, Tennessee, described his experience:

> A group of young white men came in and they started pulling and beating primarily the young women. They put lighted cigarettes down their backs, in their hair, and they were really beating people. In a short time police officials came in and placed all of us under arrest, and not a single member of the white group, the people that were opposing our sit-in, was arrested.

The following year, sit-ins gave rise to freedom rides, aimed at testing southern transportation facilities, recently desegregated by a Supreme Court decision. Organized initially by CORE and aided by SNCC, the program sent groups of blacks and whites together on buses heading south and stopping at terminals along the way. The riders, peaceful themselves, anticipated confrontations that would publicize their cause and generate political support. In Anniston, Alabama, CORE leader James Farmer depicted the confrontation that occurred as a mob of white men attacked a bus that was preparing to leave:

> Before the bus pulled out . . . members of the mob took their sharp instruments and slashed tires. The bus got to the outskirts of Anniston and the tires blew out and the bus ground to a halt. Members of the mob had boarded cars and followed the bus,

and now with the disabled bus standing there, the members of the mob surrounded it, held the door closed, and a member of the mob threw a firebomb into the bus, breaking a window to do so.

In Birmingham, police made an agreement with the Ku Klux Klan to give Klansmen 15 minutes alone to beat the Freedom Riders. Although the FBI knew about the plan, the federal agency did nothing to stop it.

In North and South alike, consciousness of the need to combat racial discrimination grew. The civil rights movement became the most powerful moral campaign since the abolitionist crusade before the Civil War. Often working together closely, blacks and whites vowed to eliminate racial barriers.

Anne Moody, who grew up in a small town in Mississippi, personified the awakening of black consciousness. As a child, she had watched the murder of friends and acquaintances who had somehow transgressed the limits set for blacks. Overcoming the hardships of growing up poor and black in the rural South, Moody became the first member of her family to go to college, enrolling at Tougaloo College, near Jackson, Mississippi. Once there, she found her own place in the civil rights movement. She joined the NAACP and became involved in the activities of SNCC and CORE. Slowly, she noted, "I could feel myself beginning to change. For the first time I began to think something would be done about whites killing, beating, and misusing Negroes. I knew I was going to be a part of whatever happened." Participating in sit-ins, where she was thrashed and jailed for her activities, she remained deeply involved in the movement.

In violation of southern law, black college students refused to leave a lunch counter, launching a new campaign in the struggle for civil rights. Here the students wait patiently for service, or forcible eviction, as a way of dramatizing their determination to end segregation. *(Bruce Roberts/Photo Researchers)*

Moody was but one of countless black women participating in the struggle. As African American activist Ella Baker observed, "When demonstrations took place and when the community acted, usually it was some woman who came to the fore."

Many whites also joined the movement in the South. Mimi Feingold, a white student at Swarthmore College in Pennsylvania, helped picket Woolworth's in Chester, Pennsylvania, and worked to unionize Swarthmore's black dining hall workers. In 1961, after her sophomore year, she headed south to join the freedom rides sponsored by CORE. Like many others, Feingold found herself in the midst of often-violent confrontations and went to jail as an act of conscience. In Jackson, Mississippi, she spent a month behind bars.

In 1962, the civil rights movement accelerated. James Meredith, a black air force veteran and student at Jackson State College, applied to the all-white University of Mississippi, only to be rejected on racial grounds. Suing to gain admission, he carried his case to the Supreme Court, where Justice Hugo Black affirmed his claim. But then Governor Ross Barnett, an adamant racist, announced defiantly that Meredith

James Meredith refused to be driven from the University of Mississippi, despite the opposition of the governor and a campus riot. His perseverance paid off, as he ultimately earned his degree. *(UPI/Corbis-Bettmann)*

would not be admitted, whatever the Court decision, and on one occasion personally blocked the way. A major riot followed; tear gas covered the university grounds; and by the riot's end, two men lay dead and hundreds were hurt.

Other governors were equally aggressive. In his 1963 inaugural address, George C. Wallace of Alabama declared boldly, "Segregation now! Segregation tomorrow! Segregation forever!" as he voiced his opposition to integration.

Alabama became a national focus that year as a violent confrontation unfolded in Birmingham. Local black leaders encouraged Martin Luther King, Jr., to launch another attack on southern segregation in the city, 40 percent black, which remained rigidly segregated along racial and class lines. "We believed that while a campaign in Birmingham would surely be the toughest fight of our civil rights careers," King later explained, "it could, if successful, break the back of segregation all over the nation."

Though the demonstrations were nonviolent, the responses were not. City officials declared that protest marches violated city regulations against parading without a license, and, over a five-week period, they arrested 2,200 blacks, some of them schoolchildren. Police Commissioner Eugene "Bull" Connor used high-pressure fire hoses, electric cattle prods, and trained police dogs to force the protesters back. As the media recorded the events, Americans watching television and reading newspapers were horrified. The images of violence created mass sympathy for black Americans' civil rights struggle.

Kennedy's Response

John Kennedy claimed to be sickened by the pictures from Birmingham but insisted that he could do nothing, even though he had sought and won black support in 1960. The narrowness of his electoral victory made him reluctant to press white southerners on civil rights when he needed their votes on other issues. Kennedy initially failed to propose any civil rights legislation and likewise ignored a campaign promise to end housing discrimination by presidential order. Not until November 1962, after the midterm elections, did he take a modest action—an executive order ending segregation in federally financed housing.

Events finally forced Kennedy to act more boldly. In the James Meredith confrontation, the president, like his predecessor in the Little Rock crisis, had to send federal troops to restore control and to guarantee Meredith's right to attend. The administration also forced the desegregation of the University of Alabama and helped arrange a compromise providing for desegregation of Birmingham's municipal facilities, implementation of more equitable hiring

In Birmingham, city officials resisted peaceful demonstrators with brutal force. Here city police use trained dogs to drive marchers back. Televised nationally, the police response appalled the American public. As newsman Eric Sevareid observed, "A newspaper or television picture of a snarling police dog set upon a human being is recorded on the permanent photoelectric file of every human brain." *(Charles Moore/Black Star)*

practices, and formation of a biracial committee. And when white bombings aimed at eliminating black leaders in Birmingham caused thousands of blacks to abandon nonviolence and rampage through the streets, Kennedy readied federal troops to intervene.

He also spoke out more forcefully than before. In a nationally televised address, he called the quest for equal rights a "moral issue" and asked, "Are we to say to the world, and, much more importantly, to each other that this is a land of the free except for the Negroes." Just hours after the president spoke, assassins killed Medgar Evers, a black NAACP official, in his own driveway in Jackson, Mississippi.

Kennedy sent Congress a new and stronger civil rights bill, outlawing segregation in public places, banning discrimination wherever federal money was involved, and advancing the process of school integration. Polls showed that 63 percent of the nation supported his stand.

To lobby for passage of this measure, civil rights leaders, pressed from below by black activists, arranged a massive march on Washington in August 1963. More than 200,000 people gathered from across the country and demonstrated enthusiastically. Celebrities present included diplomat Ralph Bunche, writer James Baldwin, entertainers Sammy Davis, Jr.,

Harry Belafonte, and Lena Horne, and former baseball player Jackie Robinson. The folk music artists of the early 1960s were there as well. Joan Baez, Bob Dylan, and Peter, Paul and Mary led the crowd in songs associated with the movement, such as "Blowin' in the Wind" and "We Shall Overcome."

The high point of the day was the address by Martin Luther King, Jr., the nation's preeminent spokesman for civil rights and proponent of nonviolent protest. King proclaimed his faith in the decency of his fellow citizens and in their ability to extend the promises of the Constitution and the Declaration of Independence to every American. With all the power of a southern preacher, he implored his audience to share his faith.

"I have a dream," King declared, "that one day this nation will rise up and live out the true meaning of its creed: 'We hold these truths to be self-evident, that all men are created equal.' I have a dream that one day on the red hills of Georgia, the sons of former slaves and the sons of former slave-owners will be able to sit together at the table of brotherhood." It was a fervent appeal, and one to which the crowd responded. Each time King used the refrain "I have a dream," thousands of blacks and whites roared together. King concluded by quoting from an old hymn: "Free at last! Free at last! Thank God almighty, we are free at last!"

The 1963 march on Washington was a high point in the civil rights movement. Several hundred thousand demonstrators lined the reflecting pool leading out from the Washington Monument and heard Martin Luther King, Jr., shown here, and other black leaders eloquently plead for racial equality. *(AP/Wide World Photos)*

Not all were moved. Anne Moody, who had come up from her activist work in Mississippi to attend the event, sat on the grass by the Lincoln Memorial as the speaker's words rang out. "Martin Luther King went on and on talking about his dream," she said. "I sat there thinking that . . . we never had time to sleep, much less dream." Nor was the Congress prompted to do much. Despite large Democratic majorities, strong white southern resistance to the cause of civil rights continued, and when Kennedy was assassinated in November 1963, his bill was still bottled up in committee.

Legislative Success in the Johnson Years

Lyndon Johnson was more successful than Kennedy in advancing the cause of civil rights. His first priority on assuming office was civil rights reform. Seizing the opportunity provided by Kennedy's assassination, Johnson told Congress, "No memorial oration or eulogy could more eloquently honor President Kennedy's memory than the earliest possible passage of the civil rights bill." He pushed the bill through Congress, heading off a Senate filibuster by persuad-

ing his old colleague, minority leader Everett Dirksen of Illinois, to work for cloture—a two-thirds vote to cut off debate. In June 1964, the Senate for the first time imposed cloture to advance a civil rights measure, and passage soon followed. "No army can withstand the strength of an idea whose time has come," Dirksen explained.

The Civil Rights Act of 1964 outlawed racial discrimination in all public accommodations and authorized the Justice Department to act with greater authority in school and voting matters. In addition, an equal opportunity provision prohibited discriminatory hiring on grounds of race, gender, religion, or national origin in firms with more than 25 employees.

Despite the law being one of the great achievements of the 1960s, Johnson realized that it was only a starting point because widespread discrimination still existed in American society. Even with the voting rights measures of 1957 and 1960, African Americans still found it difficult to vote in large areas of the South. Freedom Summer, sponsored by SNCC and other civil rights groups in 1964, focused attention on the problem by sending black and white students to Mississippi to work for black rights. Early in the summer, two whites, Michael Schwerner and Andrew Goodman, and one black, James Chaney, were murdered. By the end of the summer, 80 workers had been beaten, 1,000 arrests had been made, and 37 churches had been bombed.

Early in 1965, another confrontation made national headlines. Alabama police clubbed and teargassed demonstrators in an aborted march from Selma to the state capital at Montgomery. President Johnson sent the National Guard to protect another march to Montgomery and then asked Congress for a voting bill that would close the loopholes of the previous two acts.

The Voting Rights Act of 1965, perhaps the most important law of the decade, singled out the South for its restrictive practices and authorized the U.S. attorney general to appoint federal examiners to register voters where local officials were obstructing the registration of blacks. In the year after passage of the act, 400,000 blacks registered to vote in the Deep South; by 1968, the number reached a million.

Black Power Challenges Liberal Reform

Despite passage of the Civil Rights Act of 1964 and the Voting Rights Act of 1965, racial discrimination remained in both North and South. Still-segregated schools, wretched housing, and inadequate job opportunities were continuing problems. As the struggle for civil rights moved north, dramatic divisions within the movement emerged.

Fannie Lou Hamer, pictured here, provided eloquent testimony about the discrimination that kept many southern blacks from voting as she lobbied unsuccessfully for seating the delegates of the Mississippi Freedom Democratic party at the Democratic national convention of 1964. *(AP/Wide World Photos)*

Initially, the civil rights campaign had been integrated and nonviolent. Its acknowledged leader was Martin Luther King, Jr. But now tensions between blacks and whites flared within organizations, and younger black leaders began to challenge King's nonviolent approach. They were tired of beatings, jailings, church bombings, and the slow pace of change when dependent on white liberal support and government action. Anne Moody, the stalwart activist in Mississippi, voiced the doubts so many blacks harbored about the possibility of real change. Discouraged after months of struggle, she boarded a bus taking civil rights workers north to testify about the abuses that still remained. As she listened to the others singing the movement's songs, she was overwhelmed by the suffering she had so often seen. "We Shall Overcome" reverberated around her, but all she could think was, "I wonder. I really wonder."

One episode that contributed to many blacks' suspicion of white liberals occurred at the Democratic national convention of 1964 in Atlantic City. SNCC, active in the Freedom Summer project in Mississippi, had founded the Freedom Democratic party as an alternative to the all-white delegation that was to represent the state. Testifying before the credentials committee, black activist Fannie Lou Hamer reported that she had been beaten, jailed, and denied the right to vote. Yet the committee's final compromise, pressed by President Johnson, who worried about losing southern support in the coming election, was that the white delegation would still be seated, with two members of the protest organization offered seats at large. That response hardly satisfied those who had risked their lives and families to try to vote in Mississippi. As

civil rights leader James Forman observed, "Atlantic City was a powerful lesson, not only for the black people from Mississippi, but for all of SNCC. . . . No longer was there any hope . . . that the federal government would change the situation in the Deep South." SNCC, once a religious, integrated organization, began to change into an all-black cadre that could mobilize poor blacks for militant action. "Liberation" replaced civil rights as a goal.

Increasingly, angry blacks argued that the nation must no longer withhold the rights pledged in its founding credo. Black author James Baldwin wrote in one of his eloquent essays that unless change came soon, the worst could be expected: "If we do not now dare everything, the fulfillment of that prophecy, recreated from the Bible in song by a slave, is upon us: God gave Noah the rainbow sign, No more water, the fire next time!"

Even more responsible for channeling black frustration into a new set of goals and tactics was Malcolm X. Born Malcolm Little and reared in ghettos from Detroit to New York, he hustled numbers and prostitutes in the big cities. Arrested and imprisoned, he became a convert to the Nation of Islam and a disciple of black leader

"The day of nonviolence is over," Malcolm X proclaimed, as many African Americans listened enthusiastically. A compelling speaker, Malcolm made a powerful case for a more aggressive campaign for black rights. *(UPI/Corbis-Bettmann)*

THE STRUGGLE FOR EQUAL RIGHTS

Year	Event	Effect
1947	Report of Truman's Committee on Civil Rights	Showed that African Americans remained second-class citizens in the United States
1948	Truman's executive order integrating the armed services	Opened the way for equal opportunity in the armed forces
1954	*Brown* v. *Board of Education* decision	Supreme Court ruled that "separate but equal" schools were unconstitutional; first step in ending school segregation
1955	Montgomery bus boycott	Black solidarity tested local petty segregation laws and customs
1957	Little Rock school integration crisis	White resistance to integration of Little Rock's Central High School resulted in Eisenhower's calling in federal troops
	Civil Rights Act	Created Civil Rights Commission and empowered Justice Department to go to court to guarantee blacks the right to vote
1960	Civil Rights Act	Plugged loopholes in Civil Rights Act of 1957
	Sit-in demonstrations	Gained support for desegregation of public facilities
1961	Freedom rides	Dramatized struggle to desegregate transportation facilities
1962	James Meredith's attempt to attend University of Mississippi	Required federal intervention to uphold blacks' right to attend public institutions
1963	Effort to desegregate Birmingham, Alabama	Brutal response of police televised, sensitizing entire nation to plight of blacks
	March on Washington	Gathered support and inspiration for the civil rights movement; scene of Rev. Martin Luther King, Jr.,'s "I Have a Dream" speech
1964	Civil Rights Act	Outlawed racial discrimination in public accommodations
1965	Voting Rights Act	Allowed federal examiners to register black voters where necessary
1971	Busing decision	Supreme Court ruled that court-ordered desegregation was constitutional, even if it employed busing
1978	*Bakke* decision	Supreme Court ruled that affirmative action was constitutional but that firm racial quotas were not

Elijah Muhammad. He began to preach that the white man was responsible for the black man's condition and that blacks had to help themselves.

Malcolm was impatient with the moderate civil rights movement. He grew tired of hearing "all of this non-violent, begging-the-white-man kind of dying . . . all of this sitting-in, sliding-in, wading-in, eating-in, diving-in, and all the rest." Espousing black separatism and black nationalism for most of his public career, he argued for black control of black communities, preached an international perspective embracing African peoples in diaspora, and appealed to blacks to fight racism "by any means necessary."

Malcolm X became the most dynamic spokesman for poor northern blacks since Marcus Garvey in the 1920s. Though he was assassinated by black antagonists in 1965, his African-centered, uncompromising perspective helped shape the struggle against racism.

One man influenced by Malcolm's message was Stokely Carmichael. Born in Trinidad, he came to the United States at the age of 11, where he grew up with an interest in political affairs and black protest. While at Howard University, he participated in pickets and demonstrations and was beaten and jailed. Frustrated with the strategy of civil disobedience as he became active in SNCC, he urged field-workers to carry weapons for self-defense. It was time for blacks to cease depending on whites, he argued, and to

make SNCC into a black organization. His election as head of the student group reflected SNCC's growing radicalism.

The split in the black movement was dramatized in June 1966 when Carmichael's followers challenged those of Martin Luther King, Jr., during a march in Mississippi. King still adhered to nonviolence and interracial cooperation. Carmichael, just out of jail after arrest for his protest activities, jumped onto a flatbed truck to address the group. "This is the twenty-seventh time I have been arrested—and I ain't going to jail no more!" he shouted. "The only way we gonna stop them white men from whippin' us is to take over. We been saying freedom for six years and we ain't got nothing. What we gonna start saying now is Black Power!" Carmichael had the audience in his hand as he repeated, and the crowd shouted back, "We . . . want . . . Black . . . Power!"

Black Power was a call for a broad-based campaign to build independent institutions in the African American community. It drew on growing demands for an end to the physical and sexual abuse of black women. When Malcolm X heard about a vicious beating Fannie Lou Hamer had received in Winona, Mississippi, he cried, "I ask myself how in the world we can expect to be respected as *men* when we will allow something like this to be done to our women, and we do nothing about it." Black Power fostered a powerful sense of black pride. The movement included a wide variety of different figures: cultural nationalists such as Maulana Ron Karenga, an activist scholar and early authority on Black Studies; advocates of black capitalism such as Nathan Wright, Jr., chairman of the 1967 and 1968 National and International Conferences on Black Power; and revolutionary nationalists such as Huey P. Newton, a proponent of aggressive liberation measures. Its most enduring legacy was political and cultural mobilization at the grassroots level, even if it only partially realized its goals.

Black Power led to demands for more drastic action. The Black Panthers, radical activists who organized first in Oakland, California, and then in other cities, formed a militant organization that vowed to eradicate not only racial discrimination but capitalism as well. H. Rap Brown, who succeeded Carmichael as head of SNCC, became known for his statement that "violence is as American as cherry pie."

Violence accompanied the more militant calls for reform and showed that racial injustice was not a southern problem but an American one. Riots erupted in Rochester, New York City, and several New Jersey cities in 1964. In 1965, in the Watts neighborhood of Los Angeles, a massive uprising lasting five days left 34 dead, more than 1,000 injured, and hundreds of structures burned to the ground. Violence broke out again in other cities in 1966 and 1967. When Martin Luther King, Jr., fell to a white assassin's bullet in April 1968, angry blacks reacted by rioting once more in cities around the country.

"Southern Strategy" and Showdown on Civil Rights

Richard Nixon, elected president in 1968, was less sympathetic to the cause of civil rights than his predecessors. In 1968, the Republicans had won only 12 percent of the black vote, leading Nixon to conclude that any effort to woo the black electorate would endanger his attempt to obtain white southern support.

From the start, the Nixon administration sought to scale back the federal commitment to civil rights. It first moved to reduce appropriations for fair-housing enforcement, then tried to block an extension of the Voting Rights Act of 1965. Although Congress approved the extension, the administration's position on racial issues was clear. When South Carolina Senator Strom Thurmond and others tried to suspend federal school desegregation guidelines, the Justice Department lent support by urging a delay in meeting desegregation deadlines in 33 of Mississippi's school districts. While a unanimous Supreme Court rebuffed the effort, the president disagreed publicly with the decision.

Nixon also faced the growing controversy over busing as a means of desegregation, a highly charged issue in the 1970s. Transporting students from one area to another to attend school was nothing new. By 1970, over 18 million students, almost 40 percent of those in the United States, rode buses to school. Yet when busing became tangled with the question of integration, it inflamed passions.

In the South, before the Supreme Court endorsed integration, busing had long been used to maintain segregated schools. Some black students in Selma, Alabama, for example, traveled 50 miles by bus to an entirely black trade school in Montgomery, even though a similar school for whites stood nearby. Now, however, busing was a means of breaking down racial barriers.

The issue came to a head in North Carolina, in the Charlotte-Mecklenburg school system. A desegregation plan involving voluntary transfer was in effect, but many blacks still attended largely segregated schools. A federal judge ruled that the district was not in compliance with the latest Supreme Court decisions, and in 1971, the Supreme Court ruled that district courts had broad authority to order the desegregation of school systems—by busing, if necessary.

Earlier, Nixon had opposed such busing. Now he proposed a moratorium or even a restriction on busing and went on television to denounce it. Although Congress did not accede to his request, southerners knew where the president stood. So did northerners, for the issue became a national one. Many of the nation's largest northern cities had school segregation as rigid as in the South, largely because of residential patterns. This segregation was called *de facto* to differentiate it from the *de jure*, or legal, segregation that had existed in the South. Mississippi senator John C. Stennis, a bitter foe of busing, hoped to stir up the North by making it subject to the same busing standards as the South. He proposed requiring the government to enforce federal desegregation guidelines uniformly throughout the country or not use them at all. Court decisions subsequently ordered many northern cities to desegregate their schools.

Northern resistance to integration was fiercest in Boston, but the situation there was typical. In 1973, 85 percent of the blacks in the city attended schools that had a black majority. More than half of the African American students were in schools that were 90 percent black. In June 1974, a federal judge ordered busing to begin. The first phase, involving 17,000 pupils, was to start in the fall of that year.

For many younger students, attendance at different elementary schools went smoothly. Reassigned high school students were less fortunate. A white boycott at South Boston High cut attendance from the anticipat-

When busing was mandated to end de facto school segregation in the North, the order frequently prompted fierce resistance. This photograph shows a bitter antibusing demonstration unfolding in Boston in 1976. *(Stanley J. Forman, Pulitzer Prize 1977, "The Soiling of Old Glory")*

ed 1,500 to fewer than 100 on the first day. Buses bringing in black students were stoned, and some children were injured. White working-class South Bostonians felt that they were being asked to carry the burden of middle-class liberals' racial views. Similar resentments triggered racial episodes elsewhere. In many cases, white families either enrolled their children in private schools or fled the city.

The Republicans managed to slow down the school desegregation movement. Nixon openly catered to his conservative constituents and demonstrated he was on their side. His successor, Gerald Ford, never came out squarely against civil rights, but his lukewarm approach to desegregation demonstrated a further weakening of the federal commitment.

The situation was less inflamed at the college level, but the same pattern held. Blacks made significant progress until the Republican administrations in the late 1960s and 1970s slowed the movement for civil rights. Integration at the postsecondary level came easier as federal affirmative action guidelines brought more blacks into colleges and universities. In 1950, only 83,000 black students were enrolled in institutions of higher education. A decade later, more than one million were working for college degrees. Black enrollment in colleges reached 9.3 percent of the college population in 1976, then dropped back slightly to 9.1 percent in 1980, just what it had been in 1973.

As blacks struggled on the educational and occupational fronts, some whites protested that gains came at their expense and amounted to "reverse discrimination." In 1973 and 1974, for example, Allan

Bakke, a white, applied to the medical school at the University of California at Davis. Twice rejected, he sued on the grounds that a racial quota reserving 16 of

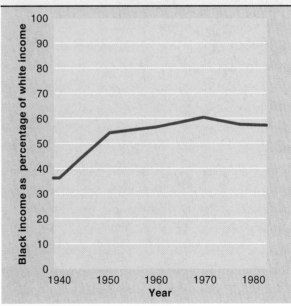

Ratio of Median Black-to-White Family Income, 1940–1980

This chart shows the substantial difference between family income for blacks and whites and reveals that the percentage has risen slowly since World War II. Observe, however, the downturn in the 1970s.
Source: Data from U.S. Department of Labor and *Statistical Abstract of the United States*, 1991.

100 places for minority-group applicants was a form of reverse discrimination that violated the Civil Rights Act of 1964. In 1978, the Supreme Court ordered Bakke's admission to the medical school, but in a complex ruling including six separate opinions, the Court allowed "consideration" of race in admissions policies, but not quotas.

Jimmy Carter, president when the *Bakke* decision was handed down, tried to adopt a more inclusive approach than his Republican predecessors. He brought a large number of blacks into his administration, some of whom, like UN ambassador Andrew Young, were highly visible. But Carter's lack of support for increased social programs for the poor hurt the majority of black citizens and strained their loyalty to the Democratic party.

The civil rights movement underscored the democratic values on which the nation was based, but the gap between rhetoric and reality remained. In an era when industrial and farming employment shrank and rents rose at a highly inflationary rate, most black families remained poor. African American income was substantially lower than white income, as the chart on page 959 shows. After early optimism in the years when the movement made its greatest strides, blacks and sympa-

thetic whites were troubled by the direction of public policy. Given a wavering national commitment to reform in the 1970s, only pressures from reform groups kept the faltering civil rights movement alive.

PRESSURE FROM THE WOMEN'S MOVEMENT

The black struggle for equality in the 1960s and 1970s was accompanied by a women's movement that grew out of the agitation for civil rights but soon developed a life of its own. This struggle, like the struggles by Latinos and Native Americans, employed the confrontational approach and the vocabulary of the civil rights movement to create pressure for change. Using proven strategies, it sometimes proceeded even faster than the black effort.

Attacking the Feminine Mystique

Many white women joined the civil rights movement only to find that they were second-class activists. Men, black and white, held the policy positions and relegated women to menial chores when not actually involved in demonstrations or voter drives. Many women also felt sexually exploited by male leaders. Stokely Carmichael's

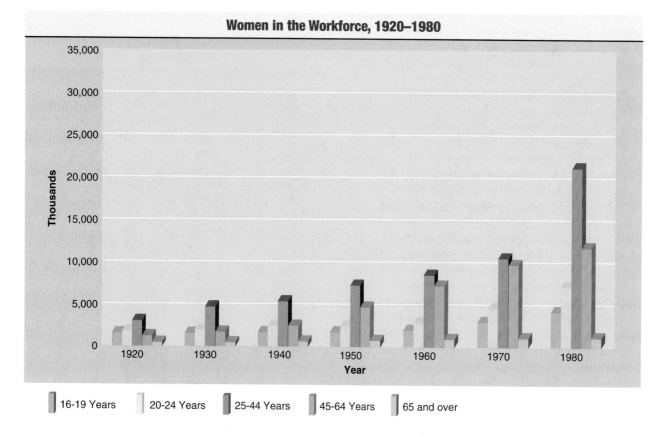

This graph shows the dramatic increase in the number of women in the workforce over the years. Note particularly the rise in the number of working women 25–44 years old in the 1970s. Source: U.S. Bureau of the Census.

comment underscored their point. "The only position for women in SNCC," he said, "is prone."

Although the civil rights movement helped spark the women's movement, broad social changes provided the preconditions. During the 1950s and 1960s, increasing numbers of married women entered the labor force (see Chapter 26). Equally important, many more young women were attending college. By 1970, women earned 41 percent of all B.A. degrees awarded, in comparison with only 25 percent in 1950. These educated young women held high hopes for themselves, even if they still earned substantially less than men.

Just as in the civil rights movement, reform legislation played a part in ending sexual discrimination. Title 7 of the 1964 Civil Rights bill, as originally drafted, prohibited discrimination on the grounds of race. During legislative debate, conservatives opposed to black civil rights seized on an amendment to include discrimination on the basis of gender, in the hope of defeating the entire bill. But the amendment passed, and then the full measure was approved, giving women a legal tool for attacking discrimination. They discovered, however, that the Equal Employment Opportunities Commission regarded women's complaints of discrimination as far less important than those of blacks.

In 1966, a group of 28 professional women, including author Betty Friedan, established the National Organization for Women (NOW) "to take action to bring American women into full participation in the mainstream of American society now." By full participation the founders meant not only fair pay and equal opportunity but a new, more egalitarian form of marriage. NOW also attacked the "false image of women . . . in the media." By 1967, some 1,000 women had joined the organization, and four years later, its membership reached 15,000.

NOW was a pressure group that sought to reform American society by promoting equal opportunity for women. To radical feminists, who had come up through the civil rights movement, NOW's agenda failed to confront adequately the problem of gender discrimination. Jo Freeman, a radical activist, observed, "Women's liberation does not mean equality with men . . . [because] equality in an unjust society is meaningless." These feminists wanted to educate millions of discontented but unpoliticized women about the oppression they faced. They tried, through the technique of consciousness raising, to help women understand the extent of their oppression and to analyze their experience as a political phenomenon. They wanted to demonstrate, in their phrase, that the personal was political.

The radicals gained mass-media attention at the Miss America pageant in Atlantic City, New Jersey, in

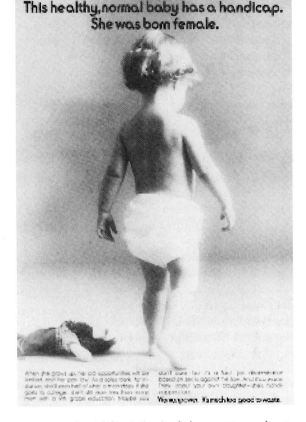

This healthy, normal baby has a handicap. She was born female.

Awareness of racial discrimination led women to speak out against discrimination based on gender, as shown in this pointed advertisement sponsored by the National Organization for Women. *(NOW Legal Defense and Education Fund)*

September 1968. There, in the words of activist author Robin Morgan, they "announced our existence to the world." On the boardwalk, a hundred women nominated a sheep as their candidate for Miss America. They also set up a "freedom trash can" and placed in it "instruments of torture": bras, girdles, hair curlers, high heels, and copies of *Playboy* and *Cosmopolitan* magazines. In the pageant hall, they chanted "Freedom for women" and unfurled banners reading "Women's Liberation."

Feminism at High Tide

In 1971, Helen Reddy expressed the energy of the women's movement in a song called "I Am Woman" that rose to the top of the charts:

I am woman, hear me roar
In numbers too big to ignore
And I know too much to go back and pretend
'Cause I've heard it all before
And I've been down there on the floor,
No one's ever gonna keep me down again.
Oh, yes, I am wise
But it's wisdom born of pain.

Yes, I've paid the price
But look how much I gained
If I have to
I can do anything.
I am strong,
I am invincible,
I am woman.

Reddy's song reflected a new militancy and sense of self-confidence among women.

Real changes were under way. A 1970 survey of first-year college students showed that men interested in such fields as business, medicine, engineering, and law outnumbered women eight to one; by 1975, the ratio had dropped to three to one. The proportion of women beginning law school quadrupled between 1969 and 1973. Women gained access to the military academies and entered senior officer ranks, although they were still restricted from combat command ranks. According to the Census Bureau, 45 percent of mothers with preschool children held jobs outside the home in 1980. That figure was four times greater than it had been 30 years before. To be sure, many employ-

Women marched to mobilize support for ratification of the Equal Rights Amendment, but the campaign failed, as opponents aroused public fears and blocked support in a number of key states. A decade after passage, the ERA was dead. *(J. L. Atlan/Sygma)*

The women's movement spawned a number of publications that attempted to give women greater control over various aspects of their own lives. The book *Our Bodies, Ourselves* and *Ms.* magazine were two important sources in that effort. *(Ms. Magazine)*

ers systematically excluded women from certain positions, and women usually held "female" jobs in the clerical, sales, and service sectors, but the progress was still unmistakable.

Legal changes brought women more benefits and opportunities. Title 9 of the Education Amendments of 1972 broadened the provisions of the Civil Rights Act of 1964. The new legislation, which barred gender bias in federally assisted educational activities and programs, made easier the admission of women to colleges and changed the nature of intercollegiate athletics by requiring schools to fund sports teams for women. By 1980, fully 30 percent of the participants in intercollegiate sports were women, compared with 15 percent before Title 9 became law.

A flurry of publications spread the principles of the women's movement. In 1972, journalist Gloria Steinem and several other women founded a new magazine, *Ms.*, which succeeded beyond their wildest dreams. By 1973, there were almost 200,000 subscribers. *The New Woman's Survival Catalogue* provided useful advice to

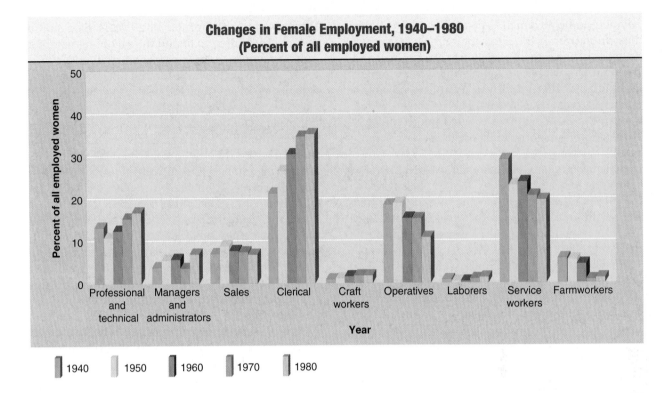

Changes in Female Employment, 1940–1980
(Percent of all employed women)

1940 1950 1960 1970 1980

Sources: Oppenheimer, *The Female Labor Force in the United States* (1976), and *Statistical Abstract of the United States,* 1991.

women readers. *Our Bodies, Ourselves,* a handbook published by a women's health collective, encouraged women to understand and control their bodies; it sold 850,000 copies between 1971 and 1976.

These new books and magazines differed radically from older women's magazines like *Good Housekeeping* and *Ladies' Home Journal,* which focused on domestic interests and needs. *Ms.,* in dramatic contrast, dealt with abortion, employment, discrimination, and other feminist issues, such as the Equal Rights Amendment.

Women both in and out of NOW worked for congressional passage, then ratification, of the Equal Rights Amendment (ERA) to the Constitution. Passed by Congress in 1972, with ratification seemingly assured, it stated simply, "Equality of rights under the law shall not be denied or abridged by the United States or by any State on account of sex."

More radical feminists insisted that legal changes were not sufficient. Traditional gender and family roles would have to be discarded to end social exploitation. Socialist feminists claimed that it was not enough to strike out at male domination, for capitalist society itself was responsible for women's plight. Only through revolution could women be free.

Black women frequently viewed the women's movement with ambivalence. Some, like attorney Pauli Murray, became feminists. She worked closely

with bureaucrats and legislators in Washington on legal measures to end sex discrimination. Others felt that the struggle for racial equality took precedence, and they were reluctant to divert energy and attention from it. Race, more than gender, was the source of their oppression. They were also suspicious of the middle-class orientation of many white feminists. Members of NOW and similar organizations, they claimed, "suffered little more than boredom, gentle repression, and dishpan hands" and were hardly confronting the most important issues when they burned their bras and insisted on using the title Ms. rather than Mrs. or Miss.

Not all women were feminists. Many felt the women's movement was contemptuous of women who stayed at home to perform traditional tasks. Marabel Morgan was one who still insisted that the woman had a place at home by her husband's side. The wife of a Florida attorney, she argued that "it is only when a woman surrenders her life to her husband, reveres and worships him, and is willing to serve him, that she becomes really beautiful to him." In her book *The Total Woman* (1973), she counseled others to follow the 4A approach: accept, admire, adapt, appreciate. As of 1975, some 500,000 copies of the hardcover volume had been sold.

In politics, Phyllis Schlafly headed a nationwide campaign to block ratification of the ERA. "It won't do anything to help women," she said, "and it will take away from women the rights they already have, such as the right of a wife to be supported by her husband, the right of a woman to be exempted from military combat, and the right, if you wanted it, to go to a single-sex college." The ERA, she predicted, would lead to the establishment of coed bathrooms, the elimination of alimony, and the legalization of homosexual marriage.

Schlafly and her allies had their way. Within a few years after passage of the ERA, 35 states had agreed to the measure, but then the momentum disappeared. Even with an extension in the deadline granted in 1979, the amendment could not win support of the necessary 38 states. By mid-1982, the ERA was dead.

Despite the counterattacks, the women's movement flourished in the 1960s and 1970s. In the tenth anniversary issue of *Ms.* magazine, in 1982, founding editor Gloria Steinem noted the differences a decade had made. "Now, we have words like 'sexual harassment' and 'battered women,'" she wrote. "Ten years ago, it was just called 'life.'" She also observed that "now, we are becoming the men we wanted to marry. Ten years ago, we were trained to marry a doctor, not be one."

LATINO MOBILIZATION

Latinos, like women, profited from the example of blacks in the struggle for equality. Long denied equal access to the American dream, they became more vocal and confrontational as their numbers increased dramatically in the postwar years. In 1970, some 9 million residents of the United States declared they were of Spanish origin; in 1980, the figure was 14.6 million. But median household income remained less than three-fourths that of Anglos, and inferior education and political weakness reinforced social and cultural separation. Latinos comprised Puerto Ricans in the Northeast, Cubans in Florida, and Chicanos—Mexican Americans—in the West and Southwest. Chicanos took the lead in the protest struggle, though all groups developed a heightened sense of solidarity and group pride as they began to assert their own rights.

Early Efforts for Equality

The roots of the Latino struggle dated back to the World War II years. Chicanos established the American GI Forum because a Texas funeral home refused to bury a Mexican American casualty of World War II. When the group's protest led to a burial in Arlington National Cemetery, the possibilities of concerted action became clear. In the waning months of the war, a court case challenged Mexican American segregation in the schools. Gonzalo Méndez, an asparagus grower and a U.S. citizen who had lived in

Orange County, California, for 25 years, filed suit to permit his children to attend the school reserved for Anglo-Americans, which was far more attractive than the Mexican one to which they had been assigned. A federal district court upheld his claim in the spring of 1945, and two years later, the circuit court affirmed the original ruling. With the favorable decision, other communities filed similar suits and began to press for integration of their schools. Meanwhile, Mexican Americans returning from wartime service, where they had often been racially invisible, chafed under continuing discrimination at home.

New organizations arose to struggle for equal rights. The Community Service Organization mobilized Chicanos against discrimination, as did the more radical Asociación Nacional México-Americana. And the League of United Latin American Citizens continued efforts to promote educational programs and other reforms.

Advances, however, came slowly. In the late 1940s, many Chicanos sought official classification as Caucasian, hoping that the change would lead to better treatment. But even when the designation changed, their status did not. They still faced discrimination and police brutality, particularly in the cities with the largest Chicano populations.

Los Angeles, with its large number of Chicanos, was the scene of numerous unsavory racial episodes. In mid-1951, on receiving a complaint about a loud record player, police officers raided a baptismal gathering at the home of Simon Fuentes. Breaking into the house without a warrant, they assaulted the members of the party. In the "Bloody Christmas" case at the end of the year, officers removed seven Mexican Americans from jail cells and beat them severely.

Protests continued, yet in the 1950s, Chicano activism was fragmented. Some Mexican Americans considered their situation hopeless. While new and aggressive challenges appeared, fully effective mobilization had to await another day.

César Chávez and the Politics of Confrontation

In the 1960s and 1970s, Mexican Americans became more active politically. In 1960, Chicanos supported Kennedy, helping him win Texas, and began to see the benefits of such support. In 1961, Henry B. González was elected to Congress from San Antonio. Three years later, Elizo ("Kika") de la Garza of Texas won election to the House and Joseph Montoya of New Mexico went to the Senate. Chicanos were gaining a political voice.

More important than political representation, which came only slowly, was direct action. César Chávez, founder of the United Farm Workers, proved what could be done by organizing one of the most

César Chávez organized the United Farm Workers to give migrant Mexican workers representation in their struggle for better wages and working conditions. Here he works with laborers in his tireless campaign for their support. *(Bob Fitch/Black Star)*

exploited and ignored groups of laboring people in the country, the migrant farm workers of the West. Chávez, who came from a family whose members were "the first ones to leave the fields if anyone shouted 'Huelga!'—which is Spanish for 'Strike!'"concentrated on migrant Mexican field hands, who worked long hours for meager pay. By 1965, his organization had recruited 1,700 people and was beginning to attract volunteer help.

Latina women played an important part in the organizing effort. Dolores Huerta, a third-generation Mexican American, who became vice president of the United Farm Workers, observed how entire families were involved:

> Excluding women, protecting them, keeping women at home, that's the middle-class way. Poor people's movements have always had whole families on the line, ready to move at a moment's notice, with more courage because that's all we had. It's a class not an ethnic thing.

Chávez's own wife Helen was equally involved in organizing, bookkeeping, and generating ideas in the movement.

Chávez first took on the grape growers of California. Calling the grape workers out on strike, the union demanded better pay and working conditions as well as recognition of the union. When the growers did not concede, Chávez launched a nationwide consumer boycott of their products. Although the Schenley Corporation and several wine companies came to terms, others held out. In 1966, the DiGiorgio Corporation agreed to permit a union election but then rigged the results. When California governor Edmund G. Brown launched an investigation that resulted in another election, he became the first major political figure to support the long-powerless Chicano field hands. This time, the United Farm Workers won. Similar boycotts of lettuce and other products harvested by exploited labor also ended in success.

In 1975, César Chávez's long struggle for farmworkers won passage in California of a measure that required growers to bargain collectively with the elected representatives of the workers. Farmworkers had never been covered by the National Labor Relations Board. Now they had achieved the legal basis for representation that could help bring higher wages and improved working conditions. And Chávez had become a national figure.

Meanwhile, Mexican Americans pressed for reform in other areas. In the West and Southwest, Mexican American studies programs flourished. In 1969, at least 50 were available in California alone. They offered degrees, built library collections, and gave Chicanos access to their own past. The campuses also provided a network linking students together and mobilizing them for political action.

Beginning in 1968, Mexican American students began to protest conditions in secondary schools. They pointed to overcrowded and run-down institutions and to the 50 percent dropout rate that came from expulsion, transfer, or failure because students had never been taught to read. In March 1968, some 10,000 Chicano students walked out of five high schools in Los Angeles. Their actions inspired other walkouts in Colorado, Texas, and other parts of California and led to successful demands for Latino teachers, counselors, and courses and better facilities.

At the same time, new organizations emerged. Young Citizens for Community Action, founded by teenager David Sánchez and four Chicanos in East Los Angeles, began as a service club to assist the neighborhood. Later the organization adopted a paramilitary stance and evolved into a defensive patrol, now known as Young Chicanos for Community Action, which tried to protect local residents. Its members became identified as the Brown Berets and formed chapters throughout the Midwest and Southwest.

Chicano leaders worked to mobilize their communities behind the campaign for equal rights. This mural in an East Los Angeles housing project helped foster a sense of Chicano pride. *(Craig Aurness/Woodfin Camp & Associates)*

Other Latinos followed a more political path. In Texas, José Angel Gutiérrez formed a citizens' organization that developed into the La Raza Unida political party and successfully promoted Mexican American candidates for political offices. Throughout the 1970s, it gained strength in the West and Southwest.

Among the new Chicano leaders was the charismatic Reis López Tijerina, or "El Tigre." A preacher, he became interested in land-grant issues and argued that the U.S. government had fraudulently deprived Chicanos of village lands. He formed an organization, La Alianza Federal de Mercedes (the Federal Alliance of Land Grants), which marched on the New Mexico state capital and occupied a number of national forests. Arrested, he stood trial and eventually served time in prison, where he became a symbol of political repression.

Rodolfo "Corky" Gonzáles was another such leader. A Golden Gloves boxing champion as a youth, he later served as a district captain for the Democratic party in Denver. He helped direct Denver poverty programs until he was fired for being overly zealous in his support of the Chicano community. Eloquently he described the despair many Chicanos felt:

I am Joaquin,
lost in a world of confusion,
caught up in the whirl of a gringo society,
confused by the rules,
scorned by attitudes,
suppressed by manipulation
and destroyed by modern society.

In 1966, Gonzáles founded the Crusade for Justice to advance the Chicano cause through community organization. Like Tijerina, he was arrested for his part in a demonstration but was subsequently acquitted.

Latinos made a particular point of protesting the Vietnam War. Because the draft drew most heavily from the poorer segments of society, the Latino casualty rate was far higher than that of the population at large. In 1969, the Brown Berets organized the National Chicano Moratorium Committee and demonstrated against what they argued was a racial war, with black and brown Americans being used against their Third World compatriots. Some of the rallies ended in confrontations with the police. News reporter Rubén Salazar, active in exposing questionable police activity, was killed in one such episode in 1970, and his death brought renewed charges of police brutality.

Aware of the growing numbers and growing demands of Latinos, the Nixon administration sought to defuse their anger and win their support. Cuban American refugees, strongly opposed to Communism, shifted toward the Republican party, which they assumed was more likely eventually to intervene against Fidel Castro. Meanwhile, Nixon courted Chicanos by dangling political positions, government jobs, and promises of better programs for Mexican Americans. The effort paid off; Nixon received 31 percent of the Latino vote in 1972. Rather than reward his Latino followers, however, the president moved to cut back the poverty program, begun under Johnson, that assisted many of them.

Despite occasional gains, Latinos from all groups faced continuing problems. Discrimination persisted in housing, education, and employment. Activists had laid the groundwork for a campaign for equal rights, but the struggle had just begun.

⤴ NATIVE AMERICAN PROTEST

Like Latinos, Native Americans continued to suffer second-class status as the 1960s began. But, partly inspired by the confrontational tactics of other groups, they became more aggressive in their efforts to claim their rights and to improve living and working conditions. Their soaring numbers—the census put them at 550,000 in 1960 and 1,480,000 in 1980—gave them greater visibility and political clout.

Origins of the Struggle

Native Americans began the struggle for equality well before the 1960s. They achieved an important victory just after the end of World War II when Congress established the Indian Claims Commission. The commission was mandated to review tribal cases arguing that ancestral lands had been illegally seized and fed-eral treaties violated. Hundreds of tribal suits against the government in federal courts were now possible. Many of them would lead to large settlements of cash—a form of reparation for past injustices—and sometimes the return of long-lost lands.

In the 1950s, federal Indian policy shifted course. As part of its effort to limit the role of the national government, the Eisenhower administration turned away from the New Deal policy of government support for tribal autonomy. In the Indian Reorganization Act of 1934, the government had stepped in to restore lands to tribal ownership and end their loss or sale to outsiders. In 1953, instead of trying to encourage Native American self-government, the administration adopted a new approach, known as the "termination" policy. The government proposed settling all outstanding claims and eliminating reservations as legitimate political entities. To encourage their assimilation into mainstream society, the government offered small subsidies to families who would leave the reservations and relocate in the cities.

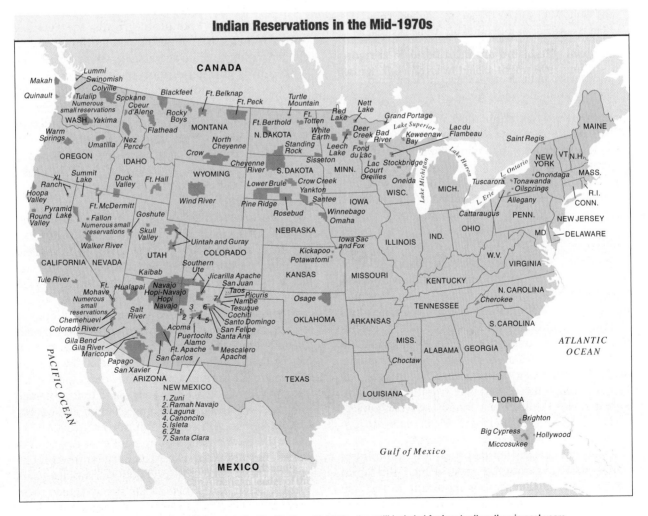

Indian Reservations in the Mid-1970s

While Indian reservations occupied substantial areas in the West in the mid-1970s, they still included far less territory than in past years.

The new policy infuriated American Indians. Earl Old Person, a Blackfoot elder, declared: "It is important to note that in our Indian language the only translation for termination is to 'wipe out' or 'kill off' . . . How can we plan our future when the Indian Bureau threatens to wipe us out as a race? It is like trying to cook a meal in your tipi when someone is standing outside trying to burn the tipi down." With their lands no longer federally protected and their members deprived of treaty rights, many tribes became unwitting victims of people who wanted to seize their land. Though promising more freedom, the new policy caused great disruption as the government terminated tribes like the Klamath in Oregon, the Menominee in Wisconsin, the Alabama and Coushatta in Texas, and bands of Paiute in Utah.

An unintended consequence of the policy was increased Indian activism. The National Congress of American Indians mobilized opposition to the federal program. A Seminole petition to the president in 1954 summed up a general view:

> We do not say that we are superior or inferior to the White Man and we do not say that the White Man is superior or inferior to us. We do say that we are not White Men but Indians, do not wish to become White Men but wish to remain Indians, and have an outlook on all things different from the outlook of the White Man.

Not only did the termination policy foster a sense of Indian identity, but it also sparked a dawning awareness among whites of the Indians' right to maintain their heritage. In 1958, the Eisenhower administration changed the policy of termination so that it required a tribe's consent. The policy continued to have the force of law, but implementation ceased.

Tribal Voices

In the 1960s, Native Americans began to assert themselves even more. Several hundred Indians meeting together in 1961 asked the Kennedy administration for the right to help make decisions about programs and budgets for the tribes. A group of college-educated Indians at the conference formed a National Indian Youth Council aimed at reestablishing Indian national pride. Over the next several decades, the council helped change the attitudes of tribal leaders, who were frequently called Uncle Tomahawks and "apples" (red outside, white inside) for their willingness to sacrifice their people's needs to white demands.

American Indians learned from the examples of protest they saw around them in rising Third World nationalism and, even more important, in the civil rights revolution. They too came to understand the place of interest-group politics in a diverse society.

Finally, they were chastened by the excesses of the Vietnam War. They recognized a pattern of killing people of color that connected Indian–white relations to the excesses in the Philippines at the turn of the century and to atrocities in Korea and Vietnam.

Indians successfully promoted their own values and designs. Native American fashions became more common, museums and galleries displayed Indian art, and Indian jewelry found a new market. The larger culture came to appreciate important work by Native Americans. In 1968, N. Scott Momaday won the Pulitzer Prize for his book *House Made of Dawn*. Vine Deloria, Jr.'s *Custer Died for Your Sins* (1969) had even wider readership. Meanwhile, popular films such as *Little Big Man* (1970) provided sympathetic portrayals of Indian history. Indian studies programs developed in colleges and universities. Organizations like the American Indian Historical Society protested traditional textbook treatment of Indians and demanded more honest portrayals.

Confrontational Tactics

At the same time, Native Americans became more confrontational. Like other groups, they worked through the courts when they could but also challenged authority more aggressively when necessary.

Led by a new generation of leaders, American Indians tried to protect what was left of their tribal lands. Elders reminded young people, "Once we owned all the land." For generations, federal and state governments had steadily encroached on Native American territory. That intrusion had to cease. "Everything is tied to our homeland," D'Arcy McNickle, a Flathead anthropologist, told other Indians in 1961.

The protest spirit was apparent on the Seneca Nation's Allegheny reservation in New York State. Although a 1794 treaty had established the Seneca's right to the land, the federal government had planned since 1928 to build a flood control dam there. In 1956, after hearings to which the Indians were not invited and about which they were not informed, Congress appropriated funds for the project. Court appeals failed to block the scheme, and the dam was eventually built. Although the government belatedly passed a $15 million reparations bill, money did not compensate for the loss of 10,000 acres of land that contained sacred sites, hunting and fishing grounds, and homes.

The Seneca did somewhat better in the 1970s. When New York State tried to condemn a section of Seneca land to build a superhighway to run through part of the Allegheny reservation, the Indians again went to court. In 1981, the state finally agreed to an exchange: state land elsewhere in addition to a cash settlement in return for an easement through the reservation. That decision encouraged tribal efforts in Montana, Wyoming, Utah, New Mexico, and Arizona to resist similar incursions on reservation lands.

Native American leaders found that lawsuits charging violations of treaty rights could give them powerful leverage. In 1967, in the first of many decisions upholding the Indian side, the U.S. Court of Claims ruled that the government in 1823 had forced the Seminole in Florida to cede their land for an unreasonably low price. The court directed the government to pay additional funds 144 years later.

American Indians also vigorously protested a new assault on their long-abused water rights. On the northern plains, large conglomerates, responding to the international oil shortage, vastly extended their coal strip-mining operations. Fierce legal struggles over possession of limited water resources resulted. Litigating tribes gained some legal ammunition when a federal court ruled in 1973, in a landmark case involving the water rights of the Paiute on the Nevada–California border, that the government must carry out its obligation as trustee to protect Indian property.

Another effort involved the reassertion of fishing rights. In various parts of the nation, the Nisqually, Puyallup, Muckleshoot, Chippewa, and other Indian tribes argued that they had treaty rights to fish where they chose, without worrying about the intrusive regulatory efforts of the states. Despite pressure from other fishermen, a series of court cases provided the tribes with some of the protection they claimed by ruling that nineteenth-century treaties allowing Indians fishing rights "in common with" whites meant that Indians could take up to 50 percent of allowable limits.

Still another effort entailed challenging the government's termination policy. The Menominee in Wisconsin were disturbed by the new policy that mandated a policy few wanted. Activist Ada Deer became a major figure in the effort to restore reservation status. She and others organized new protest groups, secured political support from the state's senators, and in 1973 had the satisfaction of seeing President Richard Nixon sign the Menominee Restoration Act.

Urban Indian activism became highly visible in 1968 when George Mitchell and Dennis Banks, Chippewa living in Minneapolis, founded the activist American Indian Movement (AIM). AIM got Office of Economic Opportunity funds channeled to Indian-controlled organizations. It also established patrols to protect drunken Indians from harassment by the police. As its successes became known, chapters formed in other cities.

An incident in November 1969 dramatized Native American militancy. A landing party of 78 Indians seized Alcatraz Island in San Francisco Bay in an effort to protest symbolically the inability of the Bureau of

Indian Affairs to "deal practically" with questions of Indian welfare. The Indians converted the island, with its defunct federal prison, into a cultural and educational center. As author Vine Deloria, Jr., noted, "By making Alcatraz an experimental Indian center operated and planned by Indian people, we would be given a chance to see what we could do toward developing answers to modern social problems. . . . It just seems to a lot of Indians that this continent was a lot better off when we were running it." In 1971 federal officials removed the Indians from Alcatraz.

Similar protests followed. In 1972, militants launched the Broken Treaties Caravan to Washington. For six days, insurgents occupied the Bureau of Indian Affairs. In 1973, AIM took over the South Dakota village of Wounded Knee, where in 1890 the U.S. 7th Cavalry had massacred the Sioux.

The American Indian Movement's armed occupation of Wounded Knee, South Dakota, site of a late-nineteenth-century massacre of the Sioux, resulted in bloodshed that dramatized unfair government treatment of Native Americans. *(AP/Wide World Photos)*

The reservation surrounding the town was mired in poverty. Half the families were on welfare, alcoholism was widespread, and 81 percent of the student population had dropped out of school. The occupation was meant to dramatize these conditions and to draw attention to the 371 treaties AIM leaders claimed the government had broken. Federal officials responded by encircling the area and, when AIM tried to bring in supplies, killed one Indian and wounded another. The confrontation ended with a government agreement to reexamine the treaty rights of the Indians, although little of substance was subsequently done.

At the same time, Native Americans devoted increasing attention to providing education and developing legal skills. Because roughly half of the Indian population continued to live on reservations, many tribal communities founded their own colleges. In 1971, the Oglala Sioux established Oglala Lakota College on the Pine Ridge Reservation in South Dakota. The motto "Wa Wo Ici Ya" ("We can do it ourselves") revealed the college's goal. Nearby Sinte Gleska College on the Rosebud Reservation was the first to offer accredited four-year and graduate programs. The number of Indians in college increased from a few hundred in the early 1960s to tens of thousands by 1980.

Indians themselves studied law and acted as legal advocates for their own people in the court cases they filed. In 1968, funding from the Office of Economic Opportunity helped the University of New Mexico Law School start a Native American scholarship program. Since 1971, that program has graduated 35 to 40 Indian lawyers each year. They have worked for tribes directly and have successfully argued for tribal jurisdiction in conflicts between whites and Indians on the reservations.

Government Response

Indian protest brought results. The outcry against termination in the 1960s led the Kennedy and Johnson administrations to steer a middle course, neither endorsing nor disavowing the policy. Instead they tried to bolster reservation economies and raise standards of living by persuading private industries to locate on reservations and by promoting the leasing of reservation lands to energy and development corporations. In the 1970s, the Navajo, Northern Cheyenne, Crow, and other tribes tried to cancel or renegotiate such leases, fearing "termination by corporation."

In the mid-1960s, the Native American cry for self-determination brought Indian involvement in the poverty program of the Great Society. Two agencies, the Area Redevelopment Administration (later the Economic Development Administration) and the Office of Economic Opportunity, responded to Indian pressure by allowing Indians to devise programs and budgets and administer programs themselves. Indians were similarly involved with Great Society housing, health, and education initiatives.

Finally, in 1975, Congress passed Indian Self-determination and Education Assistance Acts. Five years earlier, Richard Nixon had declared that self-determination had replaced termination as American policy. The self-determination measure was a largely rhetorical statement of that position. The education act involved subcontracting federal services to tribal groups. Though both laws were limited, they nonetheless reflected the government's decision to respond to Indian pressure and created a framework to guide federal policy in the decades ahead.

SOCIAL AND CULTURAL PROTEST

As blacks, Latinos, and American Indians agitated, white middle-class American society experienced an upheaval unlike any it had known before. Young people in particular rejected the stable patterns of affluent life their parents had forged. Some embraced radical political activity; many more renounced old standards of sexual behavior and adopted new kinds of music and dress. In time their actions spawned still other protests as Americans tried to make the political and social world more responsive.

Student Activism

Post–World War II demographic patterns help explain youthful activism and the "generation gap." Members of the baby boom generation came of age in the 1960s, and many of them, especially from the large middle class, moved on to some form of higher education. Between 1950 and 1964, the number of students in college more than doubled. By the end of the 1960s, college enrollment was more than four times what it had been in the 1940s. College served as a training ground for industry and corporate life; more important, it gave students time to experiment and grow before they had to make a living. In college, some students joined the struggle for civil rights. Hopeful at first, they gradually became discouraged by the gap between Kennedy's New Frontier rhetoric and the government's actual commitment.

Out of that disillusionment arose the radical spirit of the New Left. Civil rights activists were among those who in 1960 organized Students for a Democratic Society (SDS). In 1962, SDS issued a manifesto, the Port Huron Statement, written largely by Tom Hayden of the University of Michigan. "We are people of this generation, bred in at least modest comfort, housed now in universities, looking uncomfortably at the world we inherit," it began. It went on to deplore the vast social and economic distances separating people from each other and to condemn the isolation and estrangement of modern life. The document called for a better system, a "democracy of individual participation."

The first blow of the growing student rebellion came at the University of California in Berkeley. There, civil rights activists became involved in a confrontation soon known as the free speech movement. It began in September 1964 when the university refused to allow students to distribute protest material outside the main campus gate. The students, many of whom had worked in the movement in the South, argued that their tables were off campus and therefore not subject to university restrictions on political activity. When police arrested one of the leaders, students surrounded the police car and kept it from moving all night.

The university regents brought charges against the student leaders, and when the regents refused to drop the charges, the students occupied the administration building. Mario Savio, one of the leaders, denounced the university an impersonal machine: "It becomes odious, so we must put our bodies against the gears, against the wheels . . . and make the machine stop until we're free." Folksinger Joan Baez sang "We Shall Overcome," the marching song of the civil rights movement. Then police stormed in and arrested the students in the building. A student strike, with faculty aid, mobilized wider support for the right to free speech.

The free speech movement at Berkeley was basically a plea for traditional liberal reform. Students sought only the reaffirmation of the long-standing right to express themselves as they chose, and they aimed their attacks at the university, not at society as a whole. Later, in other institutions, the attack broadened. Students sought greater involvement in university affairs, argued for curricular reform, and demanded admission of more minority students. Their success in gaining their demands changed the governance of American higher education.

The mounting protest against the escalation of the Vietnam War fueled and refocused the youth movement. Confrontation became the new tactic of radical students, and protest became a way of life. Between January 1 and June 15, 1968, hundreds of thousands of students staged 221 major demonstrations at more than 100 educational institutions.

One of the most dramatic episodes came in April 1968 at Columbia University, where the issues of civil rights and war were tightly intertwined. A strong SDS chapter urged the university to break ties with the Institute of Defense Analysis, which specialized in military research. The Students' Afro-American Society tried to stop the building of a new gymnasium, which it claimed encroached on the Harlem community and disrupted life there. Whites occupied one building, blacks another. Finally, the president of the university called in the police. Hundreds of students were arrested; many were hurt. A student sympathy strike followed, and Columbia closed for the summer several weeks early.

In 1968, the demonstrators pictured here barricaded themselves inside Columbia University's main library to protest U.S. involvement in the Vietnam War and the school's relations with the neighboring African American community. *(Corbis)*

The next year, in October 1969, the Weathermen, a militant fringe group of SDS, sought to show that the revolution had arrived with a frontal attack on Chicago, scene of the violent Democratic convention of 1968. The Weathermen, taking their name from a line in a Bob Dylan song—"You don't need a weatherman to know which way the wind blows"—came from all over the country. Dressed in hard hats, jackboots, work gloves, and other padding, they rampaged through the streets with clubs, pipes, chains, and rocks. They ran into the police, as they had expected and hoped, and continued the attack. Some were arrested, others were shot, and the rest withdrew to regroup. For the next two days, they plotted strategy, engaged in minor skirmishes, and prepared for a final thrust. It came on the fourth day, once again pitting aggressive Weathermen against hostile police.

Why had the Weathermen launched their attack? "The status quo meant to us war, poverty, inequality, ignorance, famine and disease in most of the world," Bo Burlingham, a participant from Ohio, reflected. "To accept it was to condone and help perpetuate it. We felt like miners trapped in a terrible poisonous shaft with no light to guide us out. We resolved to destroy the tunnel even if we risked destroying ourselves in the process." The rationale of the Chicago "national action" may have been clear to the participants, but it convinced few other Americans. Citizens around the country were infuriated at what they saw.

The New Left was, briefly, a powerful force. Although activists never composed a majority, radicals attracted students and other sympathizers to their cause until the movement fragmented. But while it was healthy, the movement focused opposition to the Vietnam War and challenged inequities in American society in a more pointed way than ever before.

The Counterculture

Cultural change accompanied political upheaval. In the 1960s, many Americans, particularly young people, lost faith in the sanctity of the American system. "There was," observed Joseph Heller, the irreverent author of *Catch-22* (1961), "a general feeling that the platitudes of Americanism were horseshit." The protests exposed the emptiness of some of the old patterns, and many Americans—some politically active, some not—found new ways to assert their individuality and independence. As in the political sphere, the young led the way, often drawing on the example of the beats of the 1950s as they sought new means of self-gratification and self-expression.

Surface appearances were most visible and, to older Americans, most troubling. The "hippies" of the 1960s carried themselves in different ways. Men let their hair grow and sprouted beards; men and

Andy Warhol's painting of a Campbell's soup can was one of the best-known examples of "pop" art in the 1960s. Warhol and other artists drew on advertising images, comic strips, and other elements of popular culture in their painting and sculpture. (© *SuperStock, Inc./© 2000 Andy Warhol Foundation for the Visual Arts/ARS, New York.*)

women both donned jeans, muslin shirts, and other simple garments. Stressing spontaneity above all else, some rejected traditional marital customs and gravitated to communal living groups. Their example, shocking to some, soon found its way into the culture at large.

Sexual norms underwent a revolution as more people separated sex from its traditional ties to family life. A generation of young women came of age with access to "the pill"—an oral contraceptive that was effortless to use and freed sexual experimentation from the threat of pregnancy. Margaret Sanger, a pioneer in the birth control movement earlier in the century, had spearheaded the drive to create the pill. She secured financial backing to fund the necessary research and enlisted the support of scientists and doctors to figure out how the female menstrual cycle worked and then to determine how to treat it hormonally so that ovulation—or implantation if ovulation and fertilization accidentally occurred—would not take place. The first tests took place in the 1950s, and then in 1960, the Food and Drug Administration approved Enovid, the first oral contraceptive available on the market. Within three years of its introduction, more than two million women were on the pill, and as the cost dropped, millions more began to use it.

The rock music festival became a popular gathering place for young Americans in the 1960s. Between 1967 and 1971, more than three million people attended 300 festivals around the United States. The largest of these, like the one at Woodstock in 1969 pictured here, brought together hundreds of thousands of members of the baby boom generation, who listened to the live music of rock legends, camped without inhibition in open fields with friends and strangers, and celebrated a sense of liberation from conventional society. *(Jim Marshall/Gamma Liaison)*

In 1961, 14 percent of new patients at Planned Parenthood clinics chose oral contraception. In 1963 the figure jumped to 42 percent, and in 1964 it soared to 62 percent.

Americans of all social classes became more open to exploring, and enjoying, their sexuality. Scholarly findings supported natural inclinations. In 1966, William H. Masters and Virginia E. Johnson published *Human Sexual Response,* based on intensive laboratory observation of couples engaged in sexual activities. Describing the kinds of response that women, as well as men, could experience, they destroyed the myth of the sexually passive woman.

Nora Ephron, author and editor, summed up the sexual changes in the 1960s as she reflected on her own experiences. Initially she had "a hangover from the whole Fifties virgin thing," she recalled. "The first man I went to bed with, I was in love with and wanted to marry. The second one I was in love with, but I didn't have to marry him. With the third one, I thought I might fall in love."

The arts reflected the sexual revolution. Federal courts ruled that books like D. H. Lawrence's *Lady Chatterley's Lover,* earlier considered obscene, could not be banned. Many suppressed works, long available in Europe, now began to appear. Nudity became more common on stage and screen. In *Hair,* a rock musical, one scene featured the disrobing of performers of both sexes in the course of an erotic celebration.

Paintings reflected both the mood of dissent and the urge to innovate, apparent in the larger society. "Op" artists painted sharply defined geometric figures in clear, vibrant colors, starkly different from the flowing, chaotic work of the abstract expressionists. "Pop" artists such as Andy Warhol, Roy Lichtenstein, and Jasper Johns made ironic comments on American materialism and taste with their representations of everyday objects like soup cans, comic strips, and pictures of Marilyn Monroe. Their paintings broke with formal artistic conventions. Some used spray guns and fluorescent paints to gain effect. Others even tried to make their pictures look like giant newspaper photographs.

Hallucinogenic drugs also became a part of the counterculture. One prophet of the "drug scene" was Timothy Leary, a scientific researcher experimenting with LSD at Harvard University. Fired for violating a pledge not to use undergraduates as subjects, Leary aggressively asserted that drugs were necessary to free the mind. Working through his group, the League for Spiritual Discovery, he dressed in long robes and preached his message, "Tune in, turn on, drop out."

Another apostle of life with drugs was Ken Kesey. While writing his first novel, *One Flew Over the Cuckoo's Nest,* he began participating in medical experiments at a hospital where he was introduced to LSD. With the profits from his novel, Kesey established a commune of "Merry Pranksters" near Palo Alto, California. In 1964, the group headed east in a converted school bus painted in psychedelic Day-Glo colors, wired for sound, and stocked with enough orange juice and "acid" (LSD) to sustain the Pranksters across the continent.

Drug use was no longer confined to urban subcultures of musicians, artists, and the streetwise. Soldiers brought experience with drugs back from Vietnam. Young professionals began experimenting with cocaine as a stimulant. Taking a "tab" of LSD became part of the coming-of-age ritual for many middle-class college students. Marijuana became phenomenally popular in the 1960s. "Joints" of "grass" were passed around at high school, neighborhood, and college parties as readily as cans of beer had been in the previous generation.

Music became intimately connected with these cultural changes. The rock and roll of the 1950s and the gentle strains of folk music gave way to a new kind of rock that swept the country—and the world (see the "Recovering the Past" section of this chapter for a discussion of the music of the 1960s).

Rock festivals became popular. On an August weekend in 1969, some 400,000 people gathered in a large pasture in upstate New York for the Woodstock rock festival. This exuberant celebration featuring ear-splitting, around-the-clock entertainment and endlessly available marijuana went off without a hitch and seemed to the young to herald a new era. Another festival four months later at a stock car raceway in Altamont, California, was less fortunate, as a simmering undercurrent of violence resulted in several beatings and a number of deaths.

The underside of the counterculture was most visible in the Haight-Ashbury section of San Francisco, where runaway "flower children" mingled with "burned-out" drug users and radical activists. Joan Didion, a perceptive essayist, wrote of American society in 1967: "Adolescents drifted from city to torn city, sloughing off both the past and the future as snakes shed their skins, children who were never taught and would never now learn the games that had held the society together." For all the spontaneity and exuber-

ance, the counterculture's darker side could not be ignored.

Gay and Lesbian Rights

Closely tied to the revolution in sexual norms that affected sexual relations, marriage, and family life was a fast-growing and increasingly militant gay liberation movement. There had always been people who accepted the "gay" lifestyle, but American society as a whole was unsympathetic, and many homosexuals kept their preferences to themselves. The climate of the 1970s encouraged gays to "come out of the closet." A nightlong riot in 1969, in response to a police raid on the Stonewall Inn, a homosexual bar in Greenwich Village in New York, helped spark a new consciousness and a movement for gay rights. Throughout the 1970s, homosexuals ended the most blatant forms of discrimination against them. In 1973, the American Psychiatric Association ruled that homosexuality should no longer be classified as a mental illness, and that decision was overwhelmingly supported in a vote by the membership the next year. In 1975, the U.S. Civil Service Commission lifted its ban on employment of homosexuals.

In this new climate of acceptance, many gays who had hidden or suppressed their sexuality revealed their darkest secret. Women, too, became more open about their sexual preferences and demanded not to be penalized for choosing other females as partners. A lesbian movement developed, sometimes involving women active in the more radical wing of the women's movement. But many Americans and some churches remained unsympathetic—occasionally vehemently so—to anyone who challenged traditional sexual norms.

Environmental and Consumer Agitation

Although many of the 1960s social movements were defined by race, gender, and sexual preference, one cut across all boundaries. Emerging in the early 1960s, a powerful movement of Americans concerned with the environment began to revive issues raised in the Progressive era and to push them further. In the mid-1960s, a Gallup poll revealed that only 17 percent of the public considered air and water pollution to be one of the three major government problems. By 1970, that figure had risen to 53 percent.

The modern environmental movement stemmed in part from post–World War II yearnings for a better "quality of life." Many Americans began to recognize that clear air, unpolluted waters, and unspoiled wilderness were indispensable to a decent existence (see Chapter 26). They worried about threats to their natural surroundings, particularly after naturalist

The accident at the reactor on Three Mile Island helped spark opposition to nuclear power. For people around the world, the cooling towers pictured here came to represent the horrifying possibilities of a nuclear reaction out of control. *(UPI/Corbis-Bettmann)*

Rachel Carson published her brilliant book *Silent Spring* in 1962. She took aim at chemical pesticides, especially DDT, which had increased crop yields but had disastrous side effects:

> The most alarming of all man's assaults upon the environment is the contamination of air, earth, rivers, and sea with dangerous and even lethal materials. This pollution is for the most part irrecoverable; the chain of evil it initiates not only in the world that must support life but in living tissues is for the most part irreversible. In this now universal contamination of the environment, chemicals are the sinister and little-recognized partners of radiation in changing the very nature of the world—the very nature of its life.

Chemicals entered the food chain and caused a cycle of poisoning and death. As Americans learned of the pollutants surrounding them, they became increasingly worried about pesticides, motor vehicle exhaust, and industrial wastes that filled the air, earth, and water. Earth Day in 1970 celebrated the world's natural resources and warned of continuing threats.

Public concern focused on a variety of targets. Americans were troubled in 1969 to learn how thermal pollution from nuclear power plants was killing fish in both eastern and western rivers. An article in *Sports Illustrated* aroused fishermen, sailors, and other recreational enthusiasts who had not been previously concerned. A massive oil spill off the coast of southern California turned white beaches black and wiped out much of the marine life in the immediate area. Concern about the deterioration of the environment increased as people learned more about substances they had once taken for granted. In 1978, the public became alarmed about the lethal effects of toxic chemicals dumped in the Love Canal neighborhood of Niagara Falls, New York. A few years later, attention focused on dioxin, one of the most deadly substances ever made, which surfaced in the Love Canal and other areas in concentrated form.

Equally frightening was the potential environmental damage from a nuclear accident. Critics of nuclear power had warned for years that regulation of nuclear power was notoriously lax. The Atomic Energy Commission, the agency responsible for promoting the development of nuclear power, was the same agency responsible for regulating the power-producing reactors. Occasional mishaps in the 1960s and mid-1970s raised the specter of an even more serious accident in the future.

Such a calamity occurred at Three Mile Island near Harrisburg, Pennsylvania, in 1979. There, a faulty pressure relief valve led to a loss of coolant. Initially, plant operators refused to believe indicators showing a serious malfunction. Part of the nuclear core became uncovered, part began to disintegrate, and the surrounding steam and water became highly radioactive. An explosion releasing radioactivity into the atmosphere appeared possible, and thousands of residents of the area fled. The scenario of nuclear disaster depicted in the film *The China Syndrome* (1979) seemed frighteningly real. *Mad* magazine's Alfred E. Newman posed in front of the now-famous cooling towers and said, "Yes, me worry!" The worst never occurred and the danger period passed, but the plant remained shut down, filled with radioactive debris, a monument to a form of energy that was once hailed as the wave of the future but now appeared more destructive than any ever known.

The threat of a nuclear catastrophe underscored the arguments of grassroots environmental activists. Groups like the Clamshell Alliance in New Hampshire and the Abalone Alliance in northern

Recovering the Past

POPULAR MUSIC

ne way to recover the past is through music. Popular songs not only provide insight into attitudes and beliefs but also quickly convey the mood and feelings of an era. Through their lyrics, songwriters express the hopes and fears of a people and the emotional tone of an age. Consider, for example, the powerful message conveyed in the Democratic party adoption of "Happy Days Are Here Again" as a campaign theme during the Great Depression. The decline of pop music and the rise of rock and roll in the 1950s tells historians a great deal about the mood of that period. Similarly, the popularity of both folk music and rock in the 1960s provides another way of following social change in that turbulent decade.

The music of the 1960s moved beyond the syrupy ballads of the early 1950s and the rock and roll movement that Elvis Presley helped launch in the middle of the decade. As the United States confronted the challenges of the counterculture and the crosscurrents of political and social reform, new kinds of music began to be played.

Folk music took off at the start of the period. Building on a tradition launched by Woody Guthrie, Pete Seeger, and the Weavers, Joan Baez was one of the first to become popular. Accompanying herself on a guitar as she performed at coffee shops in Harvard Square and at the Newport Folk Festival, she soon overwhelmed audiences with her crystal-clear voice. She sang ballads, laments, and spirituals like "We Shall Overcome" and became caught up in the protest activities of the period.

The Times They Are A-Changin' by Bob Dylan

Come gather 'round people
wherever you roam
And admit that the waters
Around you have grown
And accept it that soon
You'll be drenched to the bone.
If your time to you
Is worth savin'
Then you better start swimmin'
Or you'll sink like a stone
For the times they are a-changin'.

Come writers and critics
Who prophesize with your pen
And keep your eyes wide
The chance won't come again
And don't speak too soon
For the wheel's still in spin
And there's no tellin' who
That it's namin'
For the loser now
Will be later to win
For the times they are a-changin'.

Come senators, congressmen
Please heed the call

Don't stand in the doorway
Don't block up the hall
For he that gets hurt
Will be he who has stalled
There's a battle outside
And it is ragin'.
It'll soon shake your windows
And rattle your walls
For the times they are a-changin'.

Come mothers and fathers
Throughout the land
And don't criticize
What you can't understand
Your sons and your daughters
Are beyond your command
Your old road is
Rapidly agin'.
Please get out of the new one
If you can't lend your hand
For the times they are a-changin'.

The line it is drawn
The curse it is cast
The slow one now
Will later be fast

As the present now
Will later be past
The order is
Rapidly fadin'.
And the first one now
Will later be last
For the times they are a-changin'.

Bob Dylan. (AP/Wide World Photos)

The Beatles. *(Archive Photos)*
The Supremes. *(Brown Brothers)*
Joan Baez. *(John Launois/Black Star)*

Equally active was Bob Dylan, who grew up playing rock and roll in high school, then folk music in college at the University of Minnesota. Disheveled and gravelly voiced, he wrote remarkable songs like "Blowin' in the Wind" that were soon sung by other artists like Peter, Paul and Mary as well. His song "The Times They Are A-Changin'" (printed here) captured the inexorable force of the student protest movement best of all.

But the 1960s were marked by far more than folk music alone. In the early part of the decade, an English group from Liverpool began to build a following in Great Britain. At the start of 1964, the Beatles released "I Want to Hold Your Hand" in the United States and appeared on the popular Ed Sullivan television show. Within weeks, Beatles songs held the first, second, third, fourth, and fifth positions on the *Billboard* singles chart, and *Meet the Beatles* became the best-selling LP record to date. With *Sergeant Pepper's Lonely Hearts Club Band* a few years later, the Beatles branched out in new musical directions and reflected the influence of the counterculture with songs like "Lucy in the Sky with Diamonds" (which some people said referred to the hallucinogenic drug LSD).

Mick Jagger and the Rolling Stones followed at the end of the decade. Another English group that changed the nature of American music, the Stones played a blues-based rock music that proclaimed a commitment to drugs, sex, and a decadent life of social upheaval. Jagger was an aggressive, sometimes violent showman on stage, whose androgynous style showed his contempt for conventional sexual norms. Other artists, such as Jim Morrison of the Doors and Janis Joplin, reflected the same intensity of the new rock world, and both died from drug overdoses.

Meanwhile, other groups were setting off in different directions. On the pop scene, Motown Records in Detroit popularized a new kind of black rhythm and blues. By 1960, the gospel-pop-soul fusion was gaining followers. By the late 1960s, Motown Records was one of the largest black-owned companies in America and one of the most successful independent recording ventures in the business. Stevie Wonder, the Temptations, and the Supremes were among the groups who became enormously popular. The Supremes, led by Diana Ross, epitomized the Motown sound with such hits as "Where Did Our Love Go."

What songs come to your mind when you think of the 1960s? How is the music different from that of the 1950s? What do the lyrics tell you about the period?

Look at the lyrics for "The Times They Are A-Changin'" reprinted here. What do they tell you about the social upheaval of the 1960s? What, if anything, does the song imply can be done about the changes in the air? What other songs can you think of that give you a similar handle on the decade?

California campaigned aggressively against licensing new nuclear plants at Seabrook, New Hampshire, and Diablo Canyon, California. While activist tactics did not always succeed in their immediate goals, they mobilized opinion sufficiently that no new plants were authorized after 1978.

Western environmentalists were particularly worried about excessive use of water. The American West, one critic observed, had become "the greatest hydraulic society ever built in history." Massive irrigation systems had boosted the nation's use of water from 40 billion gallons a day in 1900 to 393 billion gallons by 1975, though the population had only tripled. Americans used three times as much water per capita as the world's average, and far more than other industrialized societies.

One serious source of concern was the Ogallala aquifer in the Great Plains. The drawing of enormous amounts of water in the 1950s and 1960s to make arid areas productive for farming had by the mid-1970s dramatically depleted the water stored in the aquifer. Conservation measures might delay, but not prevent, the day of reckoning.

The situation was similar in California. Because the state was naturally dry, its prosperity rested on massive irrigation projects, and in the late 1970s, it had 1,251 major reservoirs. Virtually every large river had at least one dam. Almost as much water was pumped from the ground, with little natural replenishment and even less regulation. Pointing to the destruction of the nation's rivers and streams and the severe lowering of the water table in many areas, environmentalists argued that something needed to

be done before it was too late. Slowly, they made themselves heard. Critic Marc Reisner later noted, "Forty years ago, only a handful of heretics, howling at wilderness, challenged the notion that the West needed hundreds of new dams. Today they are almost vindicated."

Environmental agitation produced legislative results in the 1960s and 1970s. Lyndon Johnson, whose vision of the Great Society included an "environment that is pleasing to the senses and healthy to live in," won basic legislation to halt the depletion of the country's natural resources (see Chapter 28). In the next few years, environmentalists went further, pressuring legislative and administrative bodies to regulate polluters. During Richard Nixon's presidency, Congress passed the Clean Air Act, the Water Quality Improvement Act, and the Resource Recovery Act and mandated a new Environmental Protection Agency (EPA) to spearhead the effort to control abuses. Initially, these measures aimed at controlling the toxic by-products of the modern industrial order. In subsequent years, environmentalists broadened the effort to include occupational health and social justice issues.

One such effort developed into an extraordinarily bitter economic and ecological debate. The Endangered Species Act of 1973 prohibited the federal government from supporting any projects that might jeopardize species threatened with extinction. It ran into direct conflict with commercial imperatives in the Pacific Northwest. Loggers in the Olympic Peninsula had long exploited the land by clearcutting (cutting down all trees in a region, without leaving any stand-

Antinuclear activists protested the proliferation of both atomic weapons and atomic power plants. Here members of the Clamshell Alliance agitate in 1977 against construction of a nuclear power plant in Seabrook, New Hampshire. *(AP/Wide World Photos)*

ing). Environmentalists claimed that the forests they cut provided the last refuge for the spotted owl. Scientists and members of the U.S. Forest Service pushed to set aside timberland so that the owl could survive. Loggers protested that this action jeopardized their livelihood. As the issue wound its way through the courts, logging fell off drastically.

Another protest against regulation in the late 1970s and early 1980s came to be called the Sagebrush Rebellion. Critics argued that large federal landholdings in the West put that region at a disadvantage in economic competition with the East. They demanded that the national government cede the lands to states, which could sell or lease them for local gain. Conservative state legislatures in the Rocky Mountain states supported the scheme. Ranchers applauded the

notion. In the end, it went nowhere, though the agitation did persuade federal authorities to endorse a less restrictive policy on grazing.

Related to the environmental movement was a consumer movement. As Americans bought fashionable clothes, house furnishings, and electrical and electronic gadgets, they began to worry about unscrupulous sellers, just as they had earlier in the twentieth century. Over the years, Congress had established a variety of regulatory efforts as it started to safeguard citizens from marketplace abuse. In the 1970s, a stronger consumer movement developed, aimed at protecting the interests of the purchasing public and making business more responsible to consumers.

Ralph Nader led the movement. He had become interested in the issue of automobile safety while

Timeline

1947	Jackie Robinson breaks the color line in major league baseball
1950	Asociación Nacional México-Americana formed
1954	*Brown* v. *Board of Education*
1955	Montgomery, Alabama, bus boycott begins
1957	Little Rock, Arkansas, school integration crisis
	Civil Rights Act
1960	Civil Rights Act
	Birth control pill becomes available
	Sit-ins begin
	Students for a Democratic Society (SDS) founded
1961	Freedom rides
	Joseph Heller, *Catch-22*
	Ken Kesey, *One Flew Over the Cuckoo's Nest*
1962	James Meredith crisis at the University of Mississippi
	SDS's Port Huron Statement
	Rachel Carson, *Silent Spring*
1963	Birmingham demonstration
	Civil rights march on Washington
	Betty Friedan's *The Feminine Mystique*
1964	Civil Rights Act
	Free speech movement, Berkeley
1965	Martin Luther King, Jr., leads march from Selma to Montgomery
	Voting Rights Act
	United Farm Workers grape boycott
	Malcolm X assassinated

	Riot in Watts section of Los Angeles
	Ralph Nader, *Unsafe at Any Speed*
1966	Stokely Carmichael becomes head of SNCC and calls for "black power"
	Black Panthers founded
	NOW founded
	Masters and Johnson, *Human Sexual Response*
1967	Urban riots in 22 cities
1968	Martin Luther King, Jr., assassinated
	Student demonstrations at Columbia University and elsewhere
	Chicano student walkouts
	American Indian Movement (AIM) founded
1969	Woodstock and Altamont rock festivals
	Weathermen's "Days of Rage" in Chicago
	Native Americans seize Alcatraz
	La Raza Unida founded
1971–1975	School busing controversies in North and South
1972	*Ms.* magazine founded
	Congress passes Equal Rights Amendment
1973	AIM occupies Wounded Knee, South Dakota
1975	Farmworkers win right to bargain collectively with growers
	Indian Self-determination and Education Assistance Acts
1978	*Bakke* v. *Regents of the University of California*
1979	Accident at Three Mile Island nuclear power plant
1982	Ratification of ERA fails

studying law at Harvard and had pursued that interest as a consultant to the Department of Labor. His book *Unsafe at Any Speed: The Designed-in Dangers of the American Automobile* (1965) argued that many cars were coffins on wheels. Head-on collisions, even at low speeds, could easily kill, for cosmetic bumpers could not withstand modest shocks. He termed the Chevrolet Corvair "one of the nastiest-handling cars ever built" because of its tendency to roll over in certain situations. His efforts paved the way for the National Traffic and Motor Vehicle Safety Act of 1966, which set minimum safety standards for vehicles on public highways, provided for inspection to ensure compliance, and created a National Motor Vehicle Safety Advisory Council.

Nader's efforts attracted scores of volunteers, called "Nader's Raiders." They turned out critiques and reports and, more important, inspired consumer activists at all levels of government—city, state, and national. Consumer protection offices began to monitor a flood of complaints as ordinary citizens became more vocal in defending their rights.

Conclusion
Extending the American Dream

The 1960s and 1970s were turbulent years. Yet this third major reform era of the twentieth century accomplished a good deal for the groups fighting to expand the meaning of equality. African Americans now enjoyed greater access to the rights and privileges enjoyed by mainstream American society, despite the backlash the movement brought. Women, like Ann Clarke, introduced at the start of the chapter, returned to school in ever-increasing numbers and found jobs and sometimes independence after years of being told that their place was at home. Native Americans and Latinos mobilized too and could see the stirrings of change. Environmentalists created a new awareness of the global dangers the nation and the world faced. Slowly, reformers succeeded in pressuring the government to help the nation fulfill its promise and ensure the realization of the ideals of American life.

But the course of change was ragged. The reform effort reached its high-water mark during Lyndon Johnson's Great Society and in the years immediately following, then faltered with the rise of conservatism and disillusionment with liberalism (see Chapter 28). Some movements were circumscribed by the changing political climate; others simply ran out of steam. Still, the various efforts left a legacy of ferment that could help spark further change in future years.

Recommended Reading

The Black Struggle for Equality

James Baldwin, *The Fire Next Time* (1962); Taylor Branch, *Parting the Waters: America in the King Years, 1954–1963* (1988) and *Pillar of Fire: America in the King Years, 1963–1965* (1998); Clayborne Carson, *In Struggle: SNCC and the Black Awakening of the 1960s* (1981); William H. Chafe, *Civilities and Civil Rights: Greensboro, North Carolina, and the Black Struggle for Freedom* (1980); John Dittmer, *Local People: The Struggle for Civil Rights in Mississippi* (1994); Eric Foner, *The Story of American Freedom* (1998); David J. Garrow, *Bearing the Cross: Martin Luther King, Jr., and the Southern Christian Leadership Conference* (1986); Joanne Grant, *Ella Baker: Freedom Bound* (1998); Martin Luther King, Jr., *Why We Can't Wait*, reissue ed. (1991); Richard Kluger, *Simple Justice: The History of Brown v. Board of Education and Black America's Struggle for Equality* (1975); John Lewis with Michael D'Orso, *Walking with the Wind: A Memoir of the Movement* (1998); Malcolm X (with Alex Haley), *The Autobiography of Malcolm X* (1966); August Meier and Elliott Rudwick, *CORE: A Study in the Civil Rights Movement, 1942–1968* (1973); Anne Moody, *Coming of Age in Mississippi* (1968); Arnold Rampersad, *Jackie Robinson: A Biography* (1997);Harvard Sitkoff, *The Struggle for Black Equality, 1954–1992*, rev. ed. (1993).

Pressure from the Women's Movement

William H. Chafe, *The American Woman: Her Changing Social, Political, and Economic Roles, 1920–1970* (1972); Sara Evans, *Personal Politics: The Roots of Women's Liberation in the Civil Rights Movements and the New Left* (1979); Peter Gabriel Filene, *Him/Her/Self: Gender Identities in Modern America*, 3rd ed. (1998); Shulamith Firestone, *The Dialectic of Sex: The Case for Feminist Revolution* (1970); Susan M. Hartmann, *The Other Feminists: Activists in the Liberal Establishment* (1998); Jacqueline Jones, *Labor of Love, Labor of Sorrow: Black Women, Work, and the Family from Slavery to the Present* (1985); Alice Kessler-Harris, *Out to Work: A History of Wage-earning Women in the United States* (1982); Blanche Linden-Ward, *Changing the Future: American Women in the 1960s* (1993); Gloria Steinem, *Outrageous Acts and Everyday Rebellions*, 2nd ed. (1995); Winifred D. Wandersee, *On the Move: American Women in the 1970s* (1988).

Latino Mobilization

Rodolfo Acuña, *Occupied America: A History of Chicanos*, 4th ed. (2000); Mario T. García, *Memories of Chicano History: The Life and Narrative of Bert Corona* (1994) and *Mexican Americans: Leadership, Ideology, and Identity, 1930–1960* (1989); Ed Ludwig and James Santibañez, eds., *The Chicanos: Mexican American Voices* (1971); Beatrice Rodriguez Owsley, *The Hispanic-American Entrepreneur: An Oral History of the American Dream* (1992); Peter Skerry, *Mexican Americans: The Ambivalent Minority* (1993).

Native American Protest

Dee Brown, *Bury My Heart at Wounded Knee: An Indian History of the American West* (1971); Stephen Cornell, *The Return of the*

Native: American Indian Political Resurgence (1988); Vine Deloria, Jr., *Custer Died for Your Sins: An Indian Manifesto* (1969); Frederick E. Hoxie, ed., *Indians in American History* (1988); Peter Iverson, *"We Are Still Here": American Indians in the Twentieth Century* (1998); Alvin M. Josephy, Jr., *Now That the Buffalo's Gone* (1982); James S. Olson and Raymond Wilson, *Native Americans in the Twentieth Century* (1984).

Social and Cultural Protest

Student Activism and the Counterculture. Terry H. Anderson, *The Movement and the Sixties: Protest in America from Greensboro to Wounded Knee* (1995) and *The Sixties* (1999); David Burner, *Making Peace with the Sixties* (1996); David Chalmers, *And the Crooked Places Made Straight: The Struggle for Social Change in the 1960s* (1991); Joan Didion, *Slouching Towards Bethlehem* (1968); Barbara Epstein, *Political Protest and Cultural Revolution: Nonviolent Direct Action in the 1970s and 1980s* (1991); David Farber, *The Age of Great Dreams: America in the 1960s* (1994); Todd Gitlin, *The Sixties: Years of Hope, Days of Rage* (1987); Neil A. Hamilton, *The ABC-CLIO Companion to the 1960s Counterculture in America* (1997); Charles A. Reich, *The Greening of America* (1978); W. J. Rorabaugh, *Berkeley at War: The 1960s* (1989); Theodore Roszak, *The Making of a Counter Culture* (1969); Jules Witcover, *The Year the Dream Died: Revisiting 1968 in America* (1998); Tom Wolfe, *The Electric Kool-Aid Acid Test* (1968).

Sexuality and Gay and Lesbian Rights. Beth L. Bailey, *From Front Porch to Back Seat: Courtship in Twentieth Century America* (1988); Dudley Clendinen and Adam Nagourney, *Out for Good: The Struggle to Build a Gay Rights Movement in America* (1999); John D'Emilio and Estelle B. Freedman, *Intimate Matters: A History of Sexuality in America* (1988); John Loughery, *The Other Side of Silence: Men's Lives and Gay Identities: A Twentieth Century History* (1998).

The Environmental Movement

Rachel Carson, *Silent Spring* (1962); William Dietrich, *The Final Forest: The Battle for the Last Great Trees of the Pacific Northwest* (1992); Robert Gottlieb, *Forcing the Spring: The Transformation of the American Environmental Movement* (1993); Samuel P. Hays, *Beauty, Health, and Permanence: Environmental Politics in the United States, 1955–1985* (1987); Patricia Nelson Limerick, *The Legacy of Conquest: The Unbroken Past of the American West* (1987); John Opie, *The Law of the Land: Two Hundred Years of American Farmland Policy* (1987); Marc Reisner, *Cadillac Desert: The American West and Its Disappearing Water*, rev. and updated ed. (1993); Kirkpatrick Sale, *The Green Revolution: The American Environmental Movement, 1962–1992* (1993); Charles F. Wilkinson, *Crossing the Next Meridian: Land, Water, and the Future of the West* (1992); Donald Worster, *Rivers of Empire: Water, Aridity and the Growth of the American West* (1985).

Fiction and Film

Sara Davidson's *Loose Change* (1977) is a novel about the lives of three young women at the University of California at Berkeley. Richard Fariña's, *Been Down So Long It Looks Like Up to Me* (1966) is a novel about hallucinatory life in the 1960s. Marilyn French's *The Women's Room* (1977) is a novel about the impact of the women's movement on a circle of women. *House Made of Dawn* (1968) is N. Scott Momaday's Pulitzer Prize–winning novel about a young Indian living in both the white and Indian worlds. Alix Kates Shulman's *Memoirs of an Ex-Prom Queen* (1972) is the story of a young midwestern woman and her awakening during and after college.

Annie Hall (1977) is Woody Allen's film about the problems of relationships. *Easy Rider* (1969) is a low-budget movie about two motorcyclists looking for freedom in a world of conformity. *The Graduate* (1967) became a cult film as it challenged the values of the 1950s and mocked the priorities of the world in which "plastics" were most important. *In the Heat of the Night* (1967) is about a black man in Mississippi accused of murder solely because of his color. *To Kill a Mockingbird* (1962) is a film based on Harper Lee's novel by the same title about children learning about racism—and about how to deal with it—in the South. *The Times of Horvey Milk* (1984), which won the Academy Award for best documentary feature, tells the story of California's first openly gay politician who was assassinated in 1978.

Suggested Web Sites

http://www.wmich.edu/politics/mlk/

Timeline of the American Civil Rights Movement. This site contains a timeline of events in the 1950s and 1960s with pictures and documents.

http://webcorp.com/civilrights/index.htm

Historical Audio Archives: Voices of the Civil Rights Era. This site provides audio clips about the civil rights movement from Martin Luther King, Jr., and Malcom X.

http://www.stanford.edu/group/King/

Martin Luther King, Jr., Papers Project at Stanford University. This site has links and selected digital documents by and about Martin Luther King, Jr.

http://xroads.virginia.edu/~YP/ethnic.html

American Identities. This site suggests resources for studying America's multiple ethnic identities.

http://www.lib.berkeley.edu/BANC/FSM/

Free Speech Movement: Student Protest—U.C. Berkeley, 1964–65. This site describes student protest through oral histories, documents, and a chronology.

http://lists.village.virginia.edu/sixties/

The Sixties Project. This site has extensive exhibits, documents, and personal narratives from the 1960s.

http://www.diggers.org/

The Digger Archives. This site provides information about the San Francisco Diggers, who became one of the legendary groups in Haight-Ashbury during the years 1966–1968.

http://www.woodstock69.com/index.htm

1969 Woodstock Festival and Concert. This site provides pictures and lists of songs from the famous rock festival.

http://www.pbs.org/wgbh/amex/three/

Meltdown at Three Mile Island. This site provides a chronology and description of the frightening nuclear accident in 1979.

http://www.ushistoryplace.com

 A richly detailed on-line learning environment complete with interactive maps, timelines, history activities, primary source documents, and links to related American history sites.

The REVIVAL *of* CONSERVATISM

Every morning at 5 A.M. in 1997, Marlene Garrett bundled up her three sleepy children—aged four, three, and one—and took them to the baby sitter's home. "Mama has to go to work so she can buy you shoes," she told them as she left for a job behind the counter at a bagel café in Fort Lauderdale, Florida, that began at 6 A.M. This was a new position, and she did not want to be late.

Marlene had come to the United States from Jamaica eight years before. She and her husband Rod had high hopes for a better life in the United States and were fortunate enough to be employed. But both held entry-level jobs and had to struggle to make ends meet. Rod worked in a factory making hospital curtains and brought home about $250 a week. Marlene had just left a $5.25-an-hour job selling sneakers for her $6-an-hour job at the bagel café. It was a small improvement, but the $200 she earned made it possible to pay the monthly rent of $400 and buy groceries. With luck, they could repair or replace the car that had recently died and perhaps begin to pay off their $5,000 debt from medical bills. They had no health insurance and could only hope that no one got sick.

Marlene was not happy about her baby-sitting arrangements. Her real preference was to stay at home. "Who's a better caretaker than Mom?" she asked. But remaining at home was out of the question. Welfare might have been a possibility in the past, but the United States was in the process of cutting back drastically on its welfare rolls, and, in any event, Marlene was not comfortable with that alternative. "I don't want to plant that seed in my children," she said. "I want to work."

Marlene had few day-care options. She would have liked to have taken Scherrod, Angelique, and Hasia to the Holy Temple Christian Academy—her church day care center and preschool—but it cost $180 a week for three children and was beyond reach. Several months before, when she had been earning $8 an hour as a home health aide for the elderly, she had thought the church center would work, and she even put money down for school uniforms for the kids. Then her car gave out and made it impossible to continue that job.

Instead of the Holy Temple Christian Academy, Marlene took the children to the home of Vivienne, a woman from the Bahamas who worked nights at the self-service laundry where Marlene did her wash. Vivienne's apartment was simple and clean, but it had no toys or books anywhere in sight. Most days the children spent the ten hours Marlene was away watching television.

The Garretts knew how important it was to stimulate the kids. Reflecting longingly on the church center and what it offered, Marlene said, "The children play games. They go on field trips. They teach them, they train them. My children are bright. You would be amazed at what they would acquire in a year." But instead of a stimulating center, the Garretts had to settle for a place that was simply safe.

Florida, like many states, budgeted most of its child care money for families moving off welfare to jobs. People who had never been on welfare found themselves left out. As the executive director of a Florida child care referral agency observed, "Many of these parents have no choice but to leave their children in substandard arrangements that are rotting their brains, and jeopardizing their futures."

Marlene refused to give up hope. Her children were on a waiting list for help from the state that might make the Holy Temple Christian Academy accessible. Meanwhile, she took a second job working nights at the local Marriott Hotel. She had to pay Vivienne more money for the extra hours, and she worried even more about the additional time away from the children, but she felt she had no choice. "It is temporary," she said. "I am doing what I have to do."

Marlene and Rod Garrett were like millions of poor Americans who found themselves left out of the prosperity that returned to the United States in the mid-1990s. Despite rosy economic indicators, more than 35 million Americans still lived below the federally defined poverty line. Life was hardly easy for the Garretts or for other families who found themselves on the bottom side of the line.

American society became more and more aware of its multicultural past and present in the 1980s and 1990s. Different groups competed with each other for positions in the marketplace and other public spaces as the gap between rich and poor grew greater in these years. (*Billy Morrow Jackson, Station, 1981–82, Courtesy of the Artist*)

The Garretts' struggle to care for their children—and for themselves—unfolded against the backdrop of a conservative era that was marked by extravagance and a widening gap between rich and poor. As a deep recession in the early 1990s lifted, the economy went on a tear and enjoyed the longest expansion in the nation's history. With inflation low, the Federal Reserve Board kept interest rates down, and that easy availability of money encouraged middle- and upper-class Americans to invest in the stock market and mutual funds and to realize large gains. The unemployment level dropped, yet for Americans at the bottom of the economic ladder, many of the jobs now available as a result of the relentless shift toward a service economy paid little more than the minimum wage. People like the Garretts still found themselves struggling to survive.

As it relished the return of prosperity, the nation continued to struggle with questions about the government's responsibility for those who could not help themselves. Republican administrations in the 1980s and early 1990s argued that the government was trying to do too much and demanded that the welfare system be cut back. Democrats, who won the White House in 1992, proved willing to cut welfare as well in their efforts to preempt the issue for their own political ends.

At the same time, cataclysmic events shook Communist governments in the USSR and Eastern Europe, ending nearly a half century of Cold War and requiring the United States to redefine its international role. This led to substantial debate, as first Republicans and then Democrats voiced reservations about playing an activist, and potentially expensive, role abroad.

This chapter describes the enormous changes that occurred in the 1980s and 1990s. It highlights the economic and technological shifts that affected the daily lives of millions of Americans. It then notes the social, political, and diplomatic adjustments that affected the lives of millions of Americans in these years.

THE CONSERVATIVE TRANSFORMATION

In the 1980s and 1990s, the Republican party again became the dominant force in national politics. The Republican ascendancy that had begun in the Nixon era was now largely complete. The liberal agenda that had governed national affairs ever since the New Deal gave way to a new Republican coalition determined to scale back the social welfare state and prevent what its proponents perceived as the erosion of the nation's moral values. Firmly in control of the presidency, sometimes in control of the Senate and later the whole Congress, the Republican party directed the new national agenda.

The New Politics

Conservatism gained new respect in the 1980s. It attracted countless new adherents after the turbulence of the 1960s and the backlash of the Vietnam War. Innovative advertising and fund-raising techniques capitalized on national disaffection with liberal solutions to continuing social problems and made the conservative movement almost unstoppable.

Conservatives seized on Thomas Jefferson's maxim "That government is best which governs least." They argued that the United States in the 1980s had entered an era of limits, as international competition made resources scarcer than before. The dramatic economic growth of the 1960s and 1970s, they believed, left a legacy of rising inflation, falling productivity, enormous waste, and out-of-control entitlements. The liberal solution of "throwing money at social problems" no longer worked, argued conservatives. They therefore sought to downsize government, reduce taxes, and roll back the regulations they claimed hampered business competition. In the process, they would restore individual initiative and private enterprise that they believed had made the nation strong.

The conservative philosophy had tremendous appeal. It promised profitability to those who worked hard and showed initiative in the economic arena. It attracted middle-class Americans who were troubled that they were being forgotten in the commitment to assist minorities and the poor. And it offered hope for the revival of basic social and religious values that many citizens worried had been eaten away by rising divorce rates, legalized abortion, homosexuality, and media preoccupation with violence and sex.

The new conservative coalition covered a broad spectrum. Some followers embraced the economic doctrines of the University of Chicago's Milton Friedman, who advocated freeing market forces and sharply restricting government activism in regulating the economy. Others applauded the social and political conservatism of North Carolina Senator Jesse Helms, a tireless foe of any forms of expression he deemed pornographic and a fervent campaigner for a more limited federal role. Still others flocked to the Republican fold because of their conviction that civil rights activists and "bleeding heart liberals" practiced "reverse racism" with their programs of affirmative action, job quotas, and school busing to promote equal opportunity.

The conservative coalition also drew deeply from religious fundamentalists who advocated a literal interpretation of Scriptures. Millions, ranging from devout Catholics to orthodox Jews to evangelical Protestants, demanded stricter morality. Muslims, relying on the Koran, took an equally fundamentalist

Islam became increasingly popular in the United States in the 1980s and 1990s. This picture shows girls at the Al Iman School in Queens, New York City, wearing the long shapeless robes and head scarves traditional in the Muslim world. Boys and girls are separated, but all study Arabic and English and learn Muslim rituals and prayers. *(William Lopez/New York Times Picture Collection)*

approach. All groups worried about sexual permissiveness and gay rights and were disturbed at the increase of women working outside the home, a practice they believed eroded family life. They were bothered by rising crime and drug use. Marijuana was not simply a youthful fad but a recreational drug for a broad segment of society. Cocaine use was increasingly common. In short, fundamentalists objected to what they viewed as the liberalizing tendencies of American life and sought to refashion society by reaffirming biblical morality and the centrality of religion in American life.

Many of these activists belonged to the Moral Majority. The Reverend Jerry Falwell of Virginia and other television evangelists who focused the concerns of religious fundamentalism attracted large followings in the 1980s. Emulating Father Charles E. Coughlin, the radio priest of the 1930s, they appealed to audiences who knew them only on the airwaves. Using electronic means to preach fiery sermons to enormous audiences, they focused their television congregations on specific political ends. They also used their fund-raising ability to support sympathetic candidates. Moral Majority money began to fund politicians who demanded reinstituting school prayer, ending legalized abortion, and defeating the Equal Rights Amendment. Later a group calling itself the Christian Coalition became even more powerful in supporting—and electing—conservative candidates.

Conservatives from all camps capitalized on changing political techniques more successfully than their liberal opponents. They understood the importance of television in providing instant access to the

American public. Politicians became increasingly adept at using brief "sound bites," often lasting no more than 15 or 30 seconds, to state their views. They also relied on new electronic systems, such as e-mail, the Internet, and fax, to mobilize their followers.

Moreover, conservatives outdid liberals in using negative political advertising. Mudslinging has always been a part of the American political tradition, but now carefully crafted television ads concentrated not so much on conveying a positive image of a candidate's platform but on destroying an opponent's character. That effort was visible in both presidential and congressional campaigns.

Conservatives led the way in refining their appeal to voters. Polls, sometimes taken daily, showed which part of a candidate's image needed polishing most or where one's opponent was most vulnerable. "Spin doctors" moved into action after a candidate made a public statement to put the best possible gloss on what politicians had said. Small wonder that Americans became increasingly cynical about politics and stayed away from the voting booth in record numbers as the twentieth century drew to a close.

Conservatives also were most successful in raising unprecedented sums of money for their campaigns. Richard Viguerie, the New Right mastermind, understood how to tap the huge conservative constituency for political ends. A young Houston activist who later moved to Washington, he developed direct-mail appeals that assisted conservative candidates around the country.

Conservatives understood as well the need to provide an intellectual grounding for their positions.

The Reverend Jerry Falwell, founder of the Moral Majority, called for a crusade to revive moral values in the United States. His constituency was an important part of the new conservative movement. *(UPI/Corbis-Bettmann)*

Conservative scholars worked in think tanks and other research organizations—such as the Hoover Institution at Stanford University and the American Enterprise Institute in Washington, D.C.—that gave conservatism a solid institutional base. Their books, articles, and reports helped elect Ronald Reagan and other conservative politicians.

Conservative Leadership

More than any other Republican, Ronald Reagan was responsible for the success of the conservative cause.

An actor turned politician, he had been a radio broadcaster in his native Midwest before launching a movie career. His success affected his political inclinations, and he changed his affiliation from Democrat to Republican. His visibility and ability to articulate corporate values as a TV spokesman for General Electric attracted the attention of conservatives who recognized his political potential and helped him win election as governor of California in 1966. He failed in his first bid for the presidency in 1976 but gathered strength over the next four years. By 1980, he had the firm support of the growing right, which applauded his promise to reduce the size of the federal government but bolster military might.

Running against incumbent Jimmy Carter in 1980, Reagan scored a landslide victory—a popular vote of 51 to 41 percent and a 489 to 49 in the Electoral College. He also led the Republican party to control of the Senate for the first time since 1955. In 1984, he was reelected by an even larger margin. He received 59 percent of the popular vote and swamped Democratic candidate Walter Mondale in the Electoral College 525 to 13, losing only Minnesota, Mondale's home state, and the District of Columbia. The Democrats, however, netted two additional seats in the Senate and held the House of Representatives.

Reagan had a pleasing manner and a special skill as a media communicator. Relying on lessons learned in his acting days, he used television as Franklin D. Roosevelt had used radio in the 1930s. He was a gifted storyteller, who loved using anecdotes or one-liners to make his point. In 1980, for example, he quibbled playfully with Carter over definitions of economic doldrums. "I'm talking in human terms and he is hiding

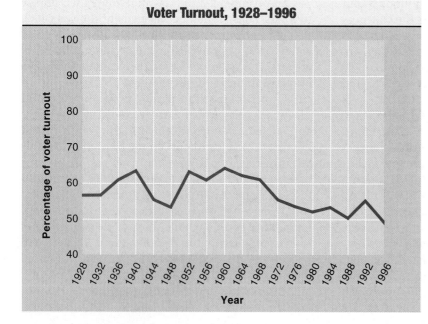

Voter turnout was far lower in the twentieth century than it had been in the nineteenth century. The fact that barely 50 percent of the electorate voted in the last decade reflects a pervasive sense of disillusionment with the political process. Source: Data from *Historical Statistics of the United States* and *Statistical Abstract of the United States.*

general escaped indictment but nonetheless resigned after severe criticism for improprieties.

In 1988, Republican George Bush, who served eight years as Reagan's vice president, sought the presidency. Though a New Englander, he had prospered in the oil industry in Texas, then served in Congress, as ambassador to China, and as head of the CIA. Sneered at by the press as a preppy wimp, he became a pit bull who ran a mudslinging campaign against his Democratic opponent, Michael Dukakis, governor of Massachusetts. On election day, Bush won 54 to 46 percent in popular votes, with a 40-state 426–112 Electoral College victory. But he did not have the kind of mandate Reagan had enjoyed eight years earlier, and Democrats controlled both houses of Congress.

Bush quickly put his own imprint on the presidency. Despite his upper-crust background, he was an unpretentious man, who made a point of trying to appear down-to-earth. He also maintained his own network of friends and political contacts through handwritten notes, telephone calls, and personal visits. More than a year and a half into his term, he was still on his political honeymoon, with a personal approval rating of 67 percent. Support grew even stronger as he presided over the Persian Gulf War in 1991. Then, as the economy faltered and the results of the war seemed suspect, approval levels began to drop.

Richard Viguerie pioneered direct-mail, fund-raising techniques that raised huge amounts of money for conservative political campaigns. Viguerie's large lists of donors helped candidates around the country as the conservative movement gained momentum. *(AP/Wide World Photos)*

behind a dictionary," Reagan said. "If he wants a definition, I'll give him one. A recession is when your neighbor loses his job. A depression is when you lose yours. A recovery is when Jimmy Carter loses his."

Reagan enjoyed enormous popularity. People talked about a "Teflon" presidency, making a comparison with nonstick frying pans, for even serious criticisms failed to stick and disagreements over policy never diminished his personal approval ratings. When he left the White House, an overwhelming 68 percent of the American public approved of his performance over the past eight years.

But Reagan had a number of liabilities that surfaced over time. As the oldest president the nation had ever had, his attention often drifted, and he occasionally fell asleep during meetings. In press conferences, he was frequently unsure about what was being asked. Uninterested in governing, he delegated much authority, leaving him unclear about policy decisions.

Worst of all, he suffered from charges of "sleaze" in his administration. In a period of several months during his last year in office, one former aide was convicted of lying under oath to conceal episodes of influence peddling. Another was convicted of illegally lobbying former government colleagues. His attorney

Ronald Reagan drew on his experience in the movies to project an appealing, if old-fashioned, image. Though he was the nation's oldest president, he gave the appearance of vitality. Here he is pictured with his wife, Nancy, who was one of his most influential advisers. *(Diana Walker/Gamma Liaison)*

Though the Democrats won the presidency in 1992, the Republicans won control of both houses of Congress in the midterm elections of 1994. Legislative leaders were now responsible for promoting the Republican cause. Robert Dole of Kansas became the Majority Leader of the Senate. Newt Gingrich, a brash, aggressive, and outspoken Georgia congressman, became Speaker of the House and the most visible advocate of the conservative Republican agenda.

Republican Policies at Home

Republicans in the 1980s aimed to reverse the stagnation of the Carter years and to provide new opportunities for business to prosper. To that end Reagan proposed and implemented an economic recovery program that rested on the theory of supply-side economics. According to this much-criticized theory, reduction of taxes would encourage business expansion, which in turn would lead to a larger supply of goods to help stimulate the system as a whole. Even George Bush, during his brief run for the Republican nomination in 1980, called Reagan's program "voodoo economics." Despite these criticisms, Republicans endorsed "Reaganomics" with its promise of a revitalized economy.

One early initiative involved tax reductions. A 5 percent cut in the tax rate went into effect on October 1, 1981, followed by 10 percent cuts in 1982 and 1983. Although all taxpayers enjoyed tax relief, the rich gained far more than middle- and lower-income Americans. Poverty-level Americans did not benefit at all. Tax cuts and enormous defense expenditures increased the budget deficit. From $74 billion in 1980, it rose to $208 billion in 1983 and then jumped to $290 billion in 1992. Such massive deficits drove the gross federal debt—the total national indebtedness—upward from $909 billion in 1980 to $4.4 trillion in 1992. When Reagan assumed office, the per capita national debt was $4,035; ten years later, in 1990, it was about $12,400.

Faced with the need to raise more money and to rectify the increasingly skewed tax code, in 1986 Congress passed and Reagan signed the most sweeping tax reform revision since the federal income tax began in 1913. It lowered rates, simplified brackets, and closed loopholes to expand the tax base. Though it ended up neither increasing nor decreasing the government's tax take, the measure was an important step toward treating low-income Americans more equitably. Still, most of the benefits went to the richest

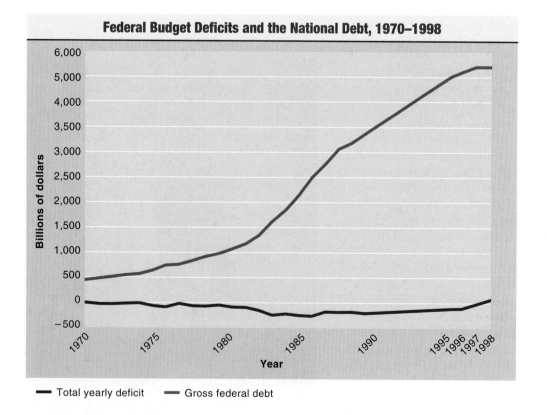

Federal Budget Deficits and the National Debt, 1970–1998

In the 1970s, 1980s, and early 1990s, the yearly federal deficit grew steadily larger, and the gross federal debt skyrocketed. Although the deficit began to decline after 1992 and the government announced a budget surplus in 1998, the gross federal debt continued to climb, moving over $5 trillion. Source: Data from *Statistical Abstract of the United States.*

5 percent of Americans, whose tax rate dropped from 50 to 38 percent.

At the same time, Reagan embarked on a major program of deregulation. In a campaign more comprehensive than President Carter's, he focused on agencies of the 1970s such as the Environmental Protection Agency, the Consumer Product Safety Commission, and the Occupational Safety and Health Administration. The Republican administration argued that regulations pertaining to the consumer, the workplace, and the environment were inefficient, paternalistic, and excessively expensive. They impeded business growth and needed to be eliminated.

Meanwhile, Reagan challenged the consensus fostered by the New Deal that the federal government should monitor the economy and assist the least fortunate. He had played by the rules of the system and had won fame and fortune. Others could do the same. He charged that government intruded too deeply into American life and declared it was time to eliminate "waste, fraud, and abuse" by cutting unnecessary programs.

Reagan needed to curtail social programs, both because of sizable tax cuts and because of enormous military expenditures. Committed to a massive arms buildup, over a five-year period, the administration sought an unprecedented military budget of $1.5 trillion. By 1985, with an allocation of $300 billion, the United States was spending half a million dollars a minute on defense and four times as much as at the height of the Vietnam War.

The huge cuts in social programs reversed the approach of liberals over the past 50 years. Republicans in the 1970s had begun to question the social policy goals of Lyndon Johnson's Great Society (see Chapter 28). Now, in the 1980s, they attacked those liberal aims head-on. They eliminated public service jobs, mandated under the Comprehensive Employment and Training Act, and reduced other aid to the cities, where the poor congregated. They cut back unemployment compensation and required Medicare patients to pay more. They lowered welfare benefits and reduced food stamp allocations. They slashed the Legal Services Corporation, which provided legal services to the poor. They replaced grants for college students with loans. Spending on human resources fell by $101 billion between 1980 and 1982. The process continued even after Reagan left office. Between 1981 and 1992, U.S. spending, after adjustment for inflation, fell 82 percent for subsidized housing, 63 percent for job training and employment services, and 40 percent for community services. Middle-class Americans, benefiting from the tax cuts, were not hurt by the slashes in social programs. But

for millions of the nation's poorest citizens, the administration's approach caused real suffering.

As a political conservative distrustful of central government, Reagan wanted to place more power in the hands of state and local governments and to reduce the involvement of the federal government in people's lives. His "New Federalism" attempted to shift responsibilities from the federal to the state level. By eliminating federal funding and instead making grants to the states, which could spend the money as they saw fit, he hoped to fortify local initiative. Critics charged, with some justification, that the proposal was merely a backhanded way of moving programs from one place to another, while eliminating federal funding. When a prolonged recession began in 1990, the policy contributed to the near-bankruptcy of a number of states and municipalities, which now bore responsibility for programs formerly funded in Washington.

Reagan took a conservative approach to social issues as well. Accepting the support of the New Right, he strongly endorsed conservative social goals. To avoid compromising his economic program, however, he provided only symbolic support at first. He spoke out for public prayer in the schools without expending political capital in Congress to support the issue. In the same way, he showed his opposition to abortion by making sure that the first nongovernmental group to receive an audience at the White House was an antiabortion March for Life contingent.

George Bush followed directly in his predecessor's footsteps. Having forsworn his objection to "voodoo economics" as soon as he received the vice presidential nomination, Bush faithfully backed Reagan's general economic policy even after he became president. In the 1988 campaign, he admonished voters to "read my lips" and promised "no new taxes." Though he backed down from that pledge in a bipartisan effort to bring the budget deficit under control, he later renounced his own agreement to modest tax increases when he went back on the campaign trail in 1992.

Like Reagan, Bush wanted deep cuts in social programs. Tireless in his criticism of the Democratic majorities in the Senate and House of Representatives, he vetoed measure after measure to assist those caught in the ravages of a troubling recession that sent unemployment rates up to 8 percent and left one of every four urban children living in poverty.

Bush was more outspoken than Reagan in supporting conservative social goals. At the start of the 1980s, conservatives had questioned Bush's commitment to their social agenda, and, indeed, Bush had been sympathetic to a woman's right to choice in the abortion issue. As president, however, he firmly opposed abortion, and his Supreme Court appointments, like

In 1988, and again in 1992, George Bush and the Republicans emphasized traditional family values as a way of healing the social ills of the nation. In this campaign picture, Bush poses with his family at their home in Maine as a way of showing that he was a good family man. *(Sipa Press)*

Reagan's, guaranteed that the effort to roll back or overturn *Roe* v. *Wade* would continue.

The Republican philosophy under Reagan and Bush dramatically reversed the nation's domestic agenda. Liberalism in the 1960s had reached a high-water mark in a time of steady growth, when hard choices about where to spend money had been less necessary. As limits began to loom, decisions about social programs became more difficult, and millions of Americans came to believe that most of the Great Society programs had failed to conquer poverty and in fact had created lifelong welfare dependency. Conservatism offered a more attractive answer, particularly to comfortable Americans in the middle and upper classes.

But the transformation was accompanied by a number of serious problems that emerged in the early 1990s. Bush faced a crisis in the long-mismanaged savings and loan industry. The Republican deregulation policy had allowed owners of savings and loan institutions to operate without previous restrictions. Many, paying themselves lavish salaries, made unwise high-risk investments that proved profitable for a while but then produced tremendous losses. To protect depositors whose assets had been lost by these questionable lending practices, Congress approved a $166 billion rescue plan (which soon reached more

than $250 billion) committing taxpayers to bail out the industry.

Republican policy also widened the gap between rich and poor. Tax breaks for the wealthy, deregulation initiatives, high interest rates for investors, permissiveness toward mergers, and an enormous growth in the salaries of business executives all contributed to the disparity. So did more lenient antitrust enforcement and a general sympathy for speculative finance.

The results of the 1980s were clear. This was "a decade of money fever," according to author Tom Wolfe. It reflected "the triumph of upper America," political analyst Kevin Phillips observed, "an ostentatious celebration of wealth, the political ascendancy of the rich and a glorification of capitalism, free markets and finance." The concentration of capital increased, and the sums involved took what Phillips termed a "megaleap" forward. Now there was an extraordinary amassing of wealth at the top levels, among the dekamillionaires, centmillionaires, half-billionaires, and billionaires. "Garden-variety millionaires," Phillips noted, "had become so common that there were about 1.5 million of them by 1989." According to one study, the share of national wealth of the richest 1 percent of the nation rose from about 18 percent in 1976 to 36 percent in 1989. The net worth of the *Forbes*

The Wealthiest Americans

During the 1980s, the percentage of national wealth held by the richest 1 percent of Americans reached the highest level since the 1930s.
Source: *New York Times*, August 16, 1992.

magazine 400 richest Americans nearly tripled between 1981 and 1989.

Meanwhile, less fortunate Americans suffered more than they had since the Great Depression of the 1930s. Financial expert Felix Rohatyn decried the "huge transfer of wealth from lower-skilled, middle-class American workers to owners of capital assets and a new technological aristocracy." Millions of people,

ranging from foreclosed farmers to laid-off industrial workers, were struggling to make ends meet.

Liberal Interlude

In 1992, the Democratic party mounted an aggressive challenge to Republican rule. After a fierce primary campaign, Governor Bill Clinton of Arkansas triumphed over a crowded field of candidates. Overcoming allegations of marital instability, marijuana use, and draft evasion, he argued that it was time for a new generation to take command. Forty-six years old, he had reached maturity in the 1960s and stood in stark contrast to George Bush, now running for reelection, who was a World War II veteran. The third candidate in a three-way race was H. Ross Perot, a billionaire businessman from Texas who declared that he alone could provide the leadership the nation needed.

This campaign, more than any in the past, was fought on television. In addition to three televised presidential debates, the candidates appeared on talk shows and interview programs. Perot energized his campaign with appearances on "Larry King Live." Bill Clinton used a post–Super Bowl appearance on "60 Minutes" to answer charges questioning his character and later played his saxophone on the "Arsenio Hall Show" and appeared on MTV. This reliance on the electronic marketplace reoriented American campaign politics.

On election day, Clinton won 43 percent of the popular vote to 38 percent for Bush and 19 percent for Perot. The electoral vote margin was even larger: 357 for Clinton, 168 for Bush, 0 for Perot. The Democrats

Bill Clinton was an exuberant campaigner who used his musical talent to attract support as he ran for president in 1992. Here he plays his saxophone on nationwide television on "The Arsenio Hall Show" in Los Angeles. (*AP/Wide World Photos*)

PRESIDENTIAL ELECTIONS, 1980–1996

Year	Candidate	Party	Popular Vote	Electoral Vote
1980	RONALD REAGAN	Republican	43,899,248 (50.8%)	489
	Jimmy Carter	Democratic	36,481,435 (41.0%)	49
	John B. Anderson	Independent	5,719,437 (6.6%)	0
1984	RONALD REAGAN	Republican	53,428,357 (58.7%)	525
	Walter F. Mondale	Democratic	36,930,923 (40.6%)	13
1988	GEORGE BUSH	Republican	47,946,422 (53.9%)	426
	Michael Dukakis	Democratic	41,016,429 (46.1%)	112
1992	BILL CLINTON	Democratic	43,728,275 (43.2%)	357
	George Bush	Republican	38,167,416 (37.7%)	168
	H. Ross Perot	Independent	19,237,245 (19.0%)	0
1996	BILL CLINTON	Democratic	47,401,185 (49.2%)	379
	Robert Dole	Republican	39,197,469 (40.7%)	159
	H. Ross Perot	Reform	8,085,294 (8.4%)	0

Note: Winners' names appear in capital letters.

retained control of both houses of Congress, with more women and minority members than ever before.

The president-elect wanted to check the cynicism that was poisoning political life. In 1964, three-quarters of the American public trusted the government to do the right thing most of the time. Three decades later, the number was closer to one-quarter. Clinton sought to shift the nation's course after 12 years of Republican rule with Cabinet nominations that included four women, four African Americans, and two Latinos. He held a televised "economic summit" to explore national options and demonstrated a keen grasp of the details of policy. In his inaugural address, Clinton declared that "a new season of American renewal has begun."

Clinton soon found his hands full at home. Although the economy finally began to improve, the public gave the president little credit for the upturn. He gained Senate ratification of the North American Free Trade Agreement (NAFTA)—aimed at promoting free trade among Canada, Mexico, and the United States—in November 1993 after a bitter battle. He secured passage of a crime bill banning manufacture, sale, or possession of 19 different assault weapons (though not of a much larger number of semiautomatic guns). But he failed to win approval of his major legislative initiative: health care reform. "This health-care system of ours is badly broken," he said in September 1993, "and it's time to fix it." Particularly troublesome were escalating costs and the lack of universal medical care, which left 35 million Americans with no medical insurance. Clinton's complicated proposal for a system of health alliances in each state provoked intense opposition from the health care and insurance industries and from politicians with plans of their own. In the end he was unable to persuade Congress either to accept his approach or adopt a workable alternative.

Conservative Resurgence

Voters demonstrated their dissatisfaction in the midterm elections of 1994. Republicans swept control of both the Senate and the House for the first time in over 40 years, winning over 50 races against Democratic incumbents. Some of the strongest and most senior Representatives, including Speaker Thomas Foley, lost their seats. At the state level, Republicans picked up 12 governorships and took control in seven of the eight largest states.

The election marked the end of the commitment to the welfare state. The 104th Congress moved aggressively to make good on its promises—outlined during the campaign in the Republicans' "Contract with America"—to scale back the role of the federal government, eliminate environmental regulations, cut funding for educational programs like Head Start, reduce taxes, and balance the budget. Newt Gingrich, the new Speaker of the House of Representatives, pushed through changes in the House rules that provided him with far greater power in appointing committee members and moving legislation along. Under his leadership, Congress launched a frontal attack on the budget, proposing massive cuts in virtually all social services. It demanded the elimination of three Cabinet departments and insisted on gutting the National Endowment for the Humanities, the National Endowment for the Arts, and the Public Broadcasting System. When, at the end of 1995 the president and the Speaker tangled with one another on the size of the cuts and refused to compromise on a budget, the government shut down and 800,000 federal employees found themselves temporarily "furloughed."

While the House of Representatives passed many of the measures proposed in the "Contract with America," only a few of them became law. The Senate balked at some; the president vetoed others. As the election of 1996 approached, Newt Gingrich found himself out of favor as millions of Americans began to realize that they would suffer from the cuts more aggressive Republicans sought.

A Second Term for Clinton

As Bill Clinton sought a second term in 1996, the Republicans nominated Senate Minority Leader Robert Dole as their presidential candidate. The 73-year-old Dole ran a lackluster campaign. His pledge to push through a sweeping 15 percent tax reduction failed to excite voter interest. Even supporters wondered how he would balance the budget at the same time. Stung by Democratic congressional defeats two years before, Clinton reshaped his own image and announced that the "era of big government is over." He coopted Republican issues, pledging to balance the budget himself and enraging liberal supporters by signing a welfare reform bill that slashed benefits and removed millions of people from the rolls. At the same time, he posed as the protector of Medicare and other programs that were threatened by proposed Republican cuts.

Clinton's strategy worked. On election day, he won a resounding victory: 49 percent of the popular vote to 41 percent for Dole and 8 percent for Perot, who ran again. In the electoral tally, Clinton received 379 votes to 159 for Dole. Yet the Republicans kept control of Congress. In the House of Representatives, they lost a number of seats but retained a majority. In the Senate, they added two seats to what they had won in 1994. Around the country, voters seemed willing to support Clinton but not to give him the blanket mandate he sought.

Partisan Politics and Impeachment

Democrats made small gains in the midterm elections of 1998. They worried about their prospects as election day approached, for Clinton had been accused by an independent prosecutor, appointed by the Justice Department, of having engaged in an improper sexual relationship with Monica Lewinsky, a White House intern. While Clinton denied the relationship at first, the lengthy report presented to Congress left little doubt that such a connection existed, and Clinton finally admitted to the relationship in a nationally televised address.

As Congress began to consider impeachment, Americans outside Washington felt differently. Disturbed at what Clinton had done in his personal life, they nonetheless approved overwhelmingly of the job he was doing as president, and his approval rat-

Bill Clinton's relationship with Monica Lewinsky affected both the country and his own family. Here he heads off for vacation with wife, Hillary, and daughter, Chelsea, after the painful acknowledgment of the relationship to the nation. *(Brad Markel/Liaison Agency, Inc.)*

ings were higher than any of his presidential predecessors in the recent past.

Those sentiments were reflected in the 1998 vote. Republicans, who had hoped to score sizable gains in both house of Congress, maintained their 55–45 margin in the Senate but lost 5 seats in the House of Representatives, ending up with a 223–211 margin that made it even more difficult to pursue their own agenda.

Despite that clear signal from the voters, House Republicans continued their efforts to remove the president. Just weeks after the election, a majority impeached him on counts of perjury and obstruction of justice. At the start of 1999, the case moved to the Senate for a trial, where Clinton fought to retain his office, just as Andrew Johnson had done 131 years before. In the Senate, presided over by the Chief Justice of the Supreme Court, a two-thirds vote was necessary to find the president guilty and remove him from office. After weeks of testimony, despite universal condemnation of Clinton's personal behavior, the Senate voted for acquittal. Democrats, joined by a number of Republicans, stood by the president, and with that coalition, neither charge managed to muster even a majority. The count of perjury was decided by a 45–55 vote, while the count of obstruction of justice failed on 50–50 vote. At long last, the nightmare was over, and the country could deal with more pressing issues again.

AN END TO SOCIAL REFORM

The Republican attack on the welfare state included an effort to limit commitments to social reform. Enough had been done, conservatives argued, and gains for less fortunate Americans came at the expense of the middle class. It was time to end federal "intrusion."

Slowdown in the Struggle for Civil Rights

Republican policies slowed the civil rights movement. Ronald Reagan opposed busing to achieve racial balance, and his attorney general worked to dismantle affirmative action programs. Initially reluctant to support extension of the enormously successful Voting Rights Act of 1965, Reagan relented only under severe criticism from Republicans, as well as Democrats. He directed the Internal Revenue Service to cease banning tax exemptions for private schools that discriminated against blacks, only to see that move overturned by the Supreme Court in 1983. He also launched an assault on the Civil Rights Commission and hampered its effectiveness by appointing members who did not support its main goals.

The courts similarly weakened the commitment to equal rights. As a result of Reagan's and Bush's judicial appointments, federal courts stopped pushing for school integration and in some cases actively encouraged the pattern of separation. The Supreme Court's *Freeman* v. *Pitts* decision in 1992 granted a suburban Atlanta school board relief from a desegregation order on the grounds that it was not possible to counteract massive demographic shifts. In 1995, the Court let stand a lower court ruling prohibiting colleges and universities from awarding special scholarships to African Americans and other minorities. Then, in 1996, the Supreme Court declined to hear an appeal of a U.S. District Court decision two years before in *Hopwood* v. *Texas*, which prohibited the use of affirmative action in higher education.

These latter two decisions were part of a larger backlash against the policy of affirmative action that began at the state level and spread around the nation. Energized by their political victories in 1994, conservatives launched a powerful attack on the policy of giving preferential treatment to groups that had suffered discrimination in the past. Arguing that government leaders had never intended affirmative action to be a permanent policy, they pushed ballot initiatives and pressured public agencies to halt the practice. The most visible of those was Proposition 209 in California, approved by voters in the election of 1996, which prohibited using gender or race in awarding state government contracts or admitting students to state colleges and universities. After victory in California, businessman Ward Connerly, who had spearheaded the effort, established an organization called, ironically, the American Civil Rights Institute to help other states enact similar bans on preferences. When he declared that he wanted to create the kind of color-blind society Martin Luther King, Jr. had sought, black lawmakers and civil rights leaders blasted him for "spitting on the grave" of King's legacy.

The court rulings and ballot initiatives had a chilling effect on the number of minority candidates seek-

Jesse Jackson demonstrated that an African American could attract a substantial level of support as he ran for president in 1984 and 1988. Here he is shown on the campaign trail in Chicago in 1988. *(Marc Pokempner/ Impact Visuals)*

ing admission to colleges and universities. At the University of California, Berkeley, the number of first-year African American students arriving in 1998 dropped by about 60 percent.

Despite significant progress in the electoral arena—where African Americans won mayoral elections in major cities, captured the governor's office in Virginia, and helped the Reverend Jesse Jackson mount two impressive presidential campaigns in 1984 and 1988—black–white relations remained tense in the mid-1990s. As Joseph Lattimore, an African American from Chicago, observed, "As far as integrating with you—we have sang 'We Shall Overcome,' we have prayed at the courthouse steps, we have made all these gestures, and the door is not open." Sylvia Matthews, from the same city, noted, "Today it seems more acceptable to be racist. Just in the kinds of things you hear people say." African American historian John Hope Franklin, looking back in 1995 at the eight decades of his life, said, "Just about the time you sit down or sit back and say, 'Oh, yes, we're really moving,' you get slapped back down."

In an effort to promote racial harmony, President Clinton launched a nationwide dialogue on race in 1997. He appointed a multiracial advisory panel, headed by John Hope Franklin, to convene discussions around the country to try to get all Americans to talk frankly about race.

Conversation was a first step in fostering better relations. Even more helpful was a booming job market in the late 1990s that provided new opportunities for people who had been unemployed. A survey in 1999 reported that young black men in particular were moving back into the economic mainstream at a faster rate than their white counterparts, and crime levels were falling in areas where joblessness was declining. The jobless rate for young black men was still twice that for young white men, but the improvement was encouraging.

Obstacles to Women's Rights

Women had a similar experience in the 1980s and 1990s. They too made significant electoral gains at the local, state, and national levels. In 1981, President Ronald Reagan appointed Sandra Day O'Connor as the first woman Supreme Court justice, and in 1984, Geraldine Ferraro, a Democratic member of Congress, became the first woman vice presidential candidate for a major party.

Yet women still faced serious problems that were compounded by conservative social policies. Access to new positions did not change their concentration in lower-paying jobs. In 1985, most women still served as secretaries, cashiers, bookkeepers, registered nurses, and waitresses—the same jobs most frequently held ten years before. Even when women moved into positions traditionally held by men, their progress often stopped at the lower and middle levels. Interruptions of work—to bear children or assume family responsibilities—impeded advancement. A "glass ceiling" seemed to prevent them from moving up.

Wage differentials between women and men continued to exist. In 1985, full-time working women still earned only 63.6 cents for every dollar earned by men. Their concentration in the so-called pink-collar positions—traditional women's jobs—made further improvement difficult. Comparable-worth cases—arguing that women should receive equal pay for different jobs of similar value—met with conservative resistance.

Conservative activists also waged a dedicated campaign against the right to legal abortion. Despite the 1973 Supreme Court decision legalizing abortion, the issue remained very much alive. The number of abortions increased dramatically in the decade after the decision and reached nearly 30 million by the 25th anniversary of the ruling. In response, "pro-life" forces mobilized. Opponents lobbied to cut off federal funds that allowed the poor to obtain the abortions the better-off could pay for themselves; they insisted that abortions should be performed in hospitals and not in less expensive clinics; and they worked to reverse the original decision itself.

Though the Supreme Court underscored its judgment in 1983, the pro-life movement was not deterred. In 1989, a solidifying conservative majority on the Court ruled in *Webster* v. *Reproductive Health Services* that while women's right to abortion remained intact, state legislatures could impose limitations if they chose. With that judgment, a major legislative debate over the issue began, and numerous states began to mandate restrictions.

In 1992, in *Planned Parenthood* v. *Casey*, the Supreme Court reaffirmed what it termed the essence of the right to abortion, while permitting further state restrictions. It declared that a 24-hour waiting period for women seeking abortions was acceptable and required teenage girls to secure the permission of a parent (or a judge) before ending a pregnancy. The ruling clearly gave states greater latitude in the overall restrictive effort and made an abortion harder to obtain, particularly for poor women and young women.

While imposing restrictions, antiabortion activists also sought to disrupt abortion clinics. They launched around-the-clock pickets, aimed at frightening away women seeking abortions. Physicians performing abortions found their lives at risk, and Barnet Slepian, a Buffalo doctor, became the latest casualty when he was killed in 1998 in his own home by a sniper shooting through a window.

Sandra Day O'Connor became the first woman justice to sit on the U.S. Supreme Court. Her pre-Court career was similar to that of many other women, as she was denied numerous jobs when she emerged from law school. A decade later, Ruth Bader Ginsburg joined O'Connor on the nation's highest Court. *(Tom Zimberoff/Sygma)*

The backlash had an impact on the larger women's liberation movement. After two decades in which the gap in wages between men and women gradually narrowed, reaching 77 percent in 1993, it fell back to 75 percent in 1997. In 1998, only 26 percent of working women said, "To me, a career is as important as being a wife and mother," down from 36 percent in 1979. While young women took for granted the gains fought for and won by their mothers and grandmothers, fewer wanted to call themselves feminists.

Yet the movement persisted and brought continued improvements in the lives of women. The glass ceiling began to crumble in the 1990s, as women gained top managerial positions in some industries. The movement also became more inclusive and more sensitive to issues of race. Black women still had their own concerns but now found more common ground. Although black women in the early 1990s still earned less, on a weekly basis, than white men and white women, that situation began to improve.

Women and men became more sensitive to the issue of sexual harassment. The dramatic confrontation between Supreme Court nominee Clarence Thomas and lawyer Anita Hill during confirmation hearings in 1991 dramatized both racial questions and the prob-

lem of sexual harassment. In the aftermath, Americans in Congress, in the business community, and in the larger workplace all became more aware of inappropriate behavior that could no longer be tolerated.

The Limited Commitment to Latino Rights

Latinos from all groups likewise faced continuing problems in the 1980s and 1990s as commitments to reform eroded. Spanish-speaking students often found it difficult to move through the educational system. In 1987, fully 40 percent of all Latino high school students did not graduate. Only 31 percent of the Latino seniors were enrolled in college-preparatory courses, and those who were in such classes frequently received little help from guidance counselors. Anel Albarran, a Mexican immigrant who arrived in East Los Angeles when she was 11, applied to UCLA when a special high school teacher encouraged her and made sure that she received help in choosing the necessary courses. By contrast, her regular counselor asked her two months before graduation whether she had considered college: "All he had wanted to do during high school was give me my classes and get me out of the room."

College itself was another problem. Of those Latinos who went to college in the early 1990s, 56 percent attended community colleges. Graduation often proved difficult; fewer than 7 percent completed a course of study. When forced to take courses that had little connection to their background and less relevance to their lives, many students became frustrated and dropped out. Affirmative action brought significant gains, but the passage of Proposition 209 hurt Latinos as much as blacks. At the University of California, Berkeley, the percentage of Latino students in the first-year class dropped from 13 in 1997 to 7 in 1998.

Like other groups, Latinos slowly extended their political gains. In the 1980s, Henry Cisneros became mayor of San Antonio and Colorado state legislator Federico Peña was elected mayor of Denver. In New Mexico, Governor Toney Anaya called himself the nation's highest elected Hispanic. The number of Latino public officials nationwide increased 73 percent between 1985 and 1994. Lauro Cavazos became the first Latino Cabinet official when he was appointed secretary of Education in 1988, and then Henry Cisneros became secretary of Housing and Urban Development and Federico Peña secretary of Transportation in 1993. At the end of the decade, with Latinos projected to become the nation's largest minority by 2005, Latino political figures became even more numerous and visible. In California, for example, both the lieutenant governor and the speaker of the Assembly were Chicano, as was the mayor of San

Spanish-speaking students often faced serious problems in U.S. schools. Bilingual classrooms, like the one pictured here, made learning easier for Latino pupils, although some critics argued that such classes slowed assimilation, and in 1998 California banned bilingual education. *(Dan F. Connolly/ Gamma Liaison)*

Jose. Democrat Loretta Sanchez, who defeated eight-term congressman Robert Dornan in Orange County, served in the U.S. House of Representatives.

As the nation's overall unemployment rate dropped in the mid-1990s, the rate for the 12 million Latino workers likewise fell—from 9.8 percent in 1992 to 7.3 percent in 1997. Despite that drop, the rate remained higher than the rate for white workers. Meanwhile, median household income fell, even as it rose for every other ethnic and racial group. Many Latinos, like Marlene Garrett, met at the start of the chapter, found it difficult to make ends meet.

Continuing Problems for Native Americans

Native Americans likewise experienced the waning commitment to reform. Gains achieved came as a result of their own efforts. Some tribal communities developed business skills, although traditional Indian attitudes hardly fostered the capitalist perspective. As Dale Old Horn, an MIT graduate and department head at Little Big Horn College in Crow Agency, Montana, explained:

> The Crow Indian child is taught that he is part of a harmonious circle of kin relations, clans and nature. The white child is taught that he is the center of the circle. The Crow believe in sharing wealth, and whites believe in accumulating wealth.

Even so, some Indian groups adapted to the capitalist ethos. "Now we're beginning to realize that, if we want to be self-sufficient, we're going to have to become entrepreneurs ourselves," observed Iola

Hayden, the Comanche executive director of Oklahomans for Indian Opportunity. The Choctaw in Mississippi were among the most successful. Before they began a drive toward self-sufficiency in 1979, their unemployment rate was 50 percent. By the middle of the 1980s, Choctaws owned all or part of three businesses on the reservation, employed 1,000 people, generated $30 million in work annually, and cut the unemployment rate in half. After Congress approved Native American gambling in 1988, an increasing number of tribes became involved in this industry. The Pequot in Connecticut built a casino in the southeastern part of the state that became the most profitable casino in the nation, grossing more than $800 million in 1994. Three years later, 183 tribes ran 273 gaming operations in 26 states in what was a $27 billion tax-exempt industry. Additional income helped ease the poverty that had a corrosive effect on reservation life.

Indians continued their legal efforts to regain lost land. In 1999, the federal government joined the Oneida Indians in a lawsuit arguing that state and local governments in central New York illegally acquired 270,000 acres of land from the Indians in the late eighteenth and early nineteenth centuries. Now it was the turn of 20,000 landowners to be worried about the fate of their property.

Indians also pressed successfully for the return of Indian remains, removed by white scientists and museum officials over the course of the last century. Ever since passage of the Native American Graves Protection and Repatriation Act of 1990, skeletons and sacred objects flowed back to the tribes where they

Native Americans became more politically active in the 1990s. In the election of 1992, Ben Nighthorse Campbell was elected to the Senate from his home state of Colorado. *(AP/Wide World Photos)*

belonged. In 1997, Harvard's Peabody Museum sent back the bones of nearly 2,000 Pueblo Indians in the largest single return of these remains.

Native American women became increasingly active in the reform effort. Ada Deer, who had successfully fought the government's termination policy in the 1970s (see Chapter 29) served as Assistant Secretary of the Interior for Indian Affairs in the 1990s. Winona LaDuke, an environmental activist, directed the Honor the Earth Fund and the White Earth Land Recovery Project, fought needless hydroelectric development, and was singled out by *Time* magazine as one of the nation's 50 most promising leaders under 40 years of age.

Despite entrepreneurial gains and legal advances, Indians remained the nation's poorest group. As Ben Nighthorse Campbell, Republican Senator from Colorado, noted in 1995, average Indian household income fell by 5 percent in the 1980s, while it rose for all other ethnic and racial groups. Median Indian household income, according to the 1990 census, was less than $20,000 a year. Many Indians still felt a sense of dislocation, captured in words by novelist Sherman Alexie in 1993. Asked what it was like to return from

the city to the reservation, he responded through the narrator in one of the stories in *The Lone Ranger and Tonto Fistfight in Heaven:*

> "It's like a bad dream you never wake up from," I said, and it's true. Sometimes I still feel like half of me is lost in the city, with its foot wedged into a steam grate or something. Stuck in one of those revolving doors, going round and round while all the white people are laughing. Standing completely still on an escalator that will not move, but I didn't have the courage to climb the stairs by myself.

Pressures on the Environmental Movement

Environmentalists too were often discouraged by the direction of public policy in the 1980s and 1990s. Activists found that they faced fierce opposition, particularly in the Republican years. Ronald Reagan systematically restrained the EPA in his avowed effort to promote economic growth. The Department of the Interior opened forest lands, wilderness areas, and coastal waters to economic development, with little concern for preserving the natural environment. George Bush initially proved more sympathetic to environmental causes and delighted environmentalists by signing new clean air legislation. Later, as the economy faltered, he was less willing to support environmental action that he claimed might slow economic growth. In 1992, he accommodated business by easing clean air restrictions. That same year, at a United Nations–sponsored Earth Summit in Rio de Janeiro, Brazil, with 100 other heads of state, Bush stood alone in his refusal to sign a biological diversity treaty framed to conserve plant and animal species.

Bill Clinton seemed to promise a new approach for the 1990s. Vice President Al Gore and Secretary of the Interior Bruce Babbitt, who had gained environmental support during his tenure as governor of Arizona, were staunch environmentalists. The Clinton administration tried to take the middle ground in the still-continuing spotted owl controversy, by protecting substantial stretches of forest yet permitting more logging than had been done in recent years. In 1999, the National Marine Fisheries Service placed nine wild salmon populations in the Northwest on the endangered species list, opening the way for further controversy like that in the spotted owl case. Meanwhile, state and federal regulators pressed the city of Los Angeles to return some of the water drawn for the past 85 years from the Owens Valley, on the grounds that it created a parched patch of dry land—and polluting dust—in what was once a fertile farming region. The city resisted the demand in what promised to be a drawn out and difficult-to-settle controversy. Environmental issues seldom could be easily resolved in a conservative age.

THE POSTINDUSTRIAL ECONOMY

Republicans sought to reorganize the government against the backdrop of an economy that was volatile in the 1980s and then improved dramatically in the 1990s. Under Republican supply-side economics, the business cycle moved from recession to boom and back to recession again. When Reagan took office in 1980, the economy was reeling under the impact of declining productivity, galloping inflation, oil shortages, and high unemployment. It revived in the early 1980s but faltered in the last years of the decade and gave way to a deep recession that lasted from 1990 to 1992. Then, in the Clinton years, the economy surged in what Alan Greenspan, chairman of the Federal Reserve Board, called the longest sustained boom in American history. As patterns of employment in an increasingly mechanized workplace changed, however, millions of

workers were able to find jobs but, like Marlene Garrett, met at the start of the chapter, still had trouble making ends meet.

The Changing Nature of Work

Automation and other technological advances had a powerful impact on the American workplace and caused a shift in the occupational structure of the working class. Formerly profitable jobs disappeared. Reporting on the industrial Midwest, the *New York Times* described how "some factories look as if they have been hit by a kind of economic neutron bomb, which left assembly lines running at full speed but eliminated most of the people who worked on them." One pulp mill worker voiced gloom about the future: "I think the country has a problem. The managers want everything run by computers. But if no one has a job, no one will know how to do anything anymore. Who will pay the taxes? What kind of society will it be when people have lost their knowledge and depend on computers for everything?"

The introduction of the computer had other consequences. Now workers sat for hours before their

In the 1990s, computer chips could be found in virtually every household appliance Americans used. Microprocessors were necessary not just for computers, but for telephones, washers and dryers, refrigerators, microwave ovens, televisions, and watches, to mention a few. Patterns of daily life changed, and Americans relied more and more on these computer-based devices, just as they had come to rely on new mechanical devices decades before.

screens. Some described the feeling of "floating in space" as they worked, or of being "lost behind the screen." Others worried about radiation from the monitor or muscular fatigue from sitting at a keyboard all day. Still others complained that they could no longer touch their work. People who did not work with computers or use them in their homes complained about a growing "digital divide" that further increased the gap between rich and poor. Members of the middle and upper classes could surf the Internet whenever they chose, while less fortunate individuals, many of whom belonged to minority groups, found themselves left behind.

Even as the nature of work changed, people seemed to be working more. In past decades leisure time had seemed to expand. By the late 1950s, people spoke of the four-day workweek, which seemed to "loom on the immediate horizon." In the last 20 years, however, the amount of time Americans worked has steadily risen. In the mid-1990s, American employees worked 320 hours more each year than their counterparts in Germany or France. Meanwhile, they experienced more stress, as they attempted to juggle the pressures between employment and family life. Problems were particularly severe for women, still trying to cope with the pressures of maintaining the home while working outside. Marriages came under significant strain. One 26-year-old legal secretary in California spoke for many as she summed up her frustration. Her husband, she noted, "does no cooking, no washing, no anything else. How do I feel? Furious. If our marriage ends, it will be on this issue."

The Shift to a Service Economy

The scarcity of good jobs stemmed in part from the restructuring of the economy that occurred in the 1980s. In a trend under way for more than half a century, the United States continued the shift from an industrial base, where most workers produced tangible things, to a service base, where most provided expertise or service to others in the workforce. By the mid-1980s, three-fourths of the 113 million employees in the country worked in the service sector—as fast-food workers, clerks, computer programmers, doctors, lawyers, bankers, teachers, and public employees.

That shift, in turn, had its roots in the decline of the country's industrial sector. The United States had been the world's industrial leader since the late nineteenth century. By the 1970s, however, the nation began to lose that predominant position. After 1973, productivity slowed in virtually all American industries and remained lower than it had been in the past in the 1980s and 1990s.

The causes of this decline in productivity were complex. The most important factor was a widespread

and systematic failure on the part of the United States to invest sufficiently in its basic productive capacity. During the Reagan years, capital investment in real plants and equipment within the United States gave way to speculation, mergers, and spending abroad. Gross private domestic investment in national industries rose modestly during the boom years, though many companies became caught up in an acquisition mania continuing through the 1990s that consumed even more resources. At the end of the 1980s, domestic investment was down—5.7 percent in 1990 and 9.5 percent in 1991. The oil crisis and rising oil prices (see Chapter 28) also contributed to the industrial decline. Finally, the war in Vietnam diverted federal funds from support for research and development.

While American industry became less productive, other industrial nations moved forward. German and Japanese industries, rebuilt after World War II with U.S. aid and aggressively modernized thereafter, reached new heights of efficiency. As a result, the United States began to lose its share of the world market for industrial goods. In 1946, the country had provided 60 percent of the world's iron and steel. In 1978, it provided a mere 16 percent. So efficient and cost-effective were foreign steel producers that the United States found itself importing a fifth of its iron and steel. By 1980, Japanese car manufacturers had also captured nearly a quarter of the American automobile market, and they continued to hold a substantial share in the 1990s. The auto industry, which had been a mainstay of economic growth for much of the twentieth century, suffered plant shutdowns and massive layoffs. In 1991, its worst year ever, Ford lost a staggering $2.3 billion.

Workers in Transition

In the 1980s and 1990s, American labor struggled to hold on to the gains realized by the post–World War II generation of blue-collar workers. The largest problems involved adjusting to the nation's changing economic needs. The shift to a service economy, while providing new jobs, was problematic for many American workers. Millions of men and women who had lost positions as a result of mergers, plant closings, and permanent economic contractions now found themselves in low-paying jobs with few opportunities for advancement. Entry-level posts were seldom located in the central cities, where most of the poor lived. Even when new jobs were created in the cities, minority residents often lacked the skills to acquire or hold them.

Meanwhile, the trade union movement faltered as the economy moved from an industrial to a service base. Unions had been most successful in organizing the nation's industrial workers in the years since the

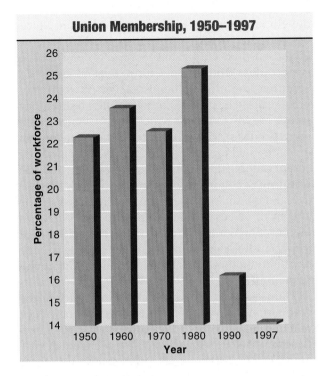

Union Membership, 1950–1997

The percentage of workers belonging to unions dropped dramatically after 1980 and continued to fall in the 1990s. Source: U.S. Bureau of Labor Statistics.

1930s, and the United States emerged from World War II with unions strong. In the years that followed, the percentage of workers belonging to unions dropped. As the chart shows, it was just over 25 percent in 1980, barely 14 percent in 1997. As the total number of wage and salary workers rose substantially between 1983 and 1997, the overall number of union members dropped from 17.7 to 16.1 million.

The pattern was visible in the example of U.S. Steel. It had once relied on a unionized workforce of 200,000 employees. In the early 1980s, it reconstituted itself as USX Corporation and shut many of its steel mills, while branching out into the more profitable oil business. The union—the United Steelworkers of America—lost half of its members in the process.

Union membership declined for several reasons. One was the shift from blue-collar to white-collar work. The increase in the numbers of women and young people in the workforce (groups that have historically been difficult to organize) was a second factor. A third was the more forceful opposition to unions by managers applying the provisions of the Taft-Hartley Act of 1947, which restricted the tactics labor leaders could use. Union organizing efforts fell off significantly. One study showed a drop in spending to organize from $1.03 per nonunion member in 1953 to $0.71 in 1974. At the same time, managerial opposi-

tion to unions increased. A 1994 report presented to the Secretaries of Labor and Commerce found that "there is a dismal side to American labor relations in which the rights of some individual workers are violated by some employers who resist the right to organize." Such unfair labor practices, the report noted, were on the rise.

Union vulnerability was visible early in Ronald Reagan's first term, when the Professional Air Traffic Controllers Organization (PATCO) went out on strike. Charging that the strike violated the law, the president fired the strikers, decertified the union, and ordered the training of new air controllers at a cost of $1.3 billion. The message was clear: government employees could not challenge the public interest.

Antiunion sentiments reverberated throughout the nongovernment sector as well. The management of Phelps Dodge, one of the world's largest copper producers, was beset by falling prices and company losses. It decided to end the cost-of-living allowance that enabled workers, many of them Mexican Americans, to earn $12 an hour. When negotiations failed, Arizona miners struck, only to find that the company, working with antiunion experts at the University of Pennsylvania's Wharton School of Business, had hired permanent replacement workers. The company president later acknowledged, "I had decided to break the union." In 1984, the United Auto Workers ended a strike at General Motors by trading a pledge that GM would guarantee up to 70 percent of the production workers' lifetime jobs for a smaller wage increase than the union sought and a modification of the cost-of-living allowance that had been a part of UAW contracts since 1948. In 1988, General Electric workers in the Midwest accepted a pay cut to save their jobs and keep GE from relying on foreign labor.

Workers took heart with a successful strike by the Teamsters against the United Parcel Service in 1997. In the most successful labor action in a decade, 185,000 workers won gains after a 15-day work stoppage that led the union leader to call the settlement "a victory over corporate greed." But the overall union movement still remained in trouble.

Farmers also had to adjust as the larger workforce was reconstituted. Continuing a trend that began in

WORK STOPPAGES, 1960–1997	
Year	Number of Stoppages
1960	222
1970	381
1980	187
1990	44
1997	29

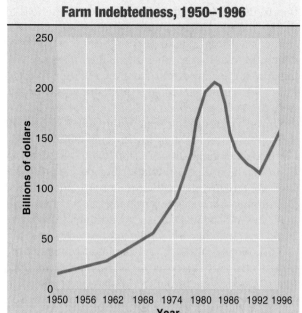

Farm Indebtedness, 1950–1996

Farm indebtedness was a continuing problem in the postwar years. Even modest improvement in the mid-1980s and early 1990s did not change the overall picture. Source: U.S. Department of Agriculture.

the early twentieth century, the number of farms and farmers declined steadily. When Franklin Roosevelt took office in 1933, some 6.7 million farms covered the American landscape. Sixty years later, there were fewer than 2 million. In 1980, farm residents made up 2.7 percent of the total population; by 1989, that figure had fallen to 1.9 percent. As family farms disappeared, farming income became more concentrated in the hands of the largest operators. In 1983, the largest 1 percent of the nation's farmers produced 30 percent of all farm products; the top 12 percent generated 90 percent of all farm income. The top 1 percent of the growers in the United States had average annual incomes of $572,000, but the small and medium-size farmers who were being forced off the land frequently had incomes below the official government poverty line. Several surveys reported in 1997 that farm workers' wages, after accounting for inflation, had fallen substantially in the past 20 years, often leaving them without adequate housing and other necessities.

The extraordinary productivity of the most successful American farmers derived in part from the use of chemical fertilizers, irrigation, pesticides, and scientific agricultural management. Equally important were the government's price support programs, initiated during the New Deal to shield struggling farmers from unstable prices and continued thereafter.

Yet that very productivity caused unexpected setbacks in the 1980s. In the 1970s, as food shortages developed in many countries, the United States became the "breadbasket of the world." Farmers increased their output to meet multibillion-bushel grain orders from India, China, Russia, and other countries and profited handsomely from high grain prices caused by global shortages. Often farmers borrowed heavily to increase production, sometimes at interest rates reaching 18 percent. Then, the fourfold increase in oil prices beginning in 1973 drove up the cost of running the modern mechanized farm. When a worldwide economic slump began in 1980, overseas demand for American farm products declined sharply and farm prices fell. Farmers who had borrowed money at high interest rates, when corn sold at $3 to $4 per bushel, now found themselves trying to meet payments on these loans with corn that brought only $2 per bushel.

Thousands of farmers, caught in the cycle of overproduction, heavy indebtedness, and falling prices, watched helplessly as banks and federal agencies foreclosed on their mortgages and drove them out of business. Dale Christensen, an Iowa corn grower, faced foreclosure in 1983 when the Farmers Home Administration called in his overdue payments on debts totaling $300,000. "I am 58 years old," he said. "My whole life has gone into this farm." He was one of many struggling farmers, who, in spite of government crop support programs that cost more in 1982 than all welfare programs for the poor, could not make ends meet.

Conditions changed little in the next decade and a half. Family farms continued to disappear. A drought in the Southeast in 1986 led to burned and stunted fields. An even worse drought in 1988 stretched across most of the Midwest, and still another in 1996 devastated the Southwest. A massive flood in 1993 wrought further damage. An economic crisis in Asia in the late 1990s reduced demand overseas and increased stockpiles of American wheat that could not be sold.

The Roller Coaster Economy

The economy shifted back and forth during the 1980s and 1990s. The Reagan years began with a recession that lasted for several years. An economic boom between 1983 and 1990 gave way to a punishing recession as the new decade began. It was followed, in turn, by a period of sustained growth and expansion that was marked by low interest, unemployment, and inflation rates, and a dramatic surge in the stock market.

The recession of 1980–1982 began during Jimmy Carter's administration when the Federal Reserve Board tried to deal with mounting deficits by increasing the money supply. Program cuts to counter inflation brought substantial unemployment in the workforce. During Reagan's first year, the job situation deteriorated further, and by the end of 1982, the unemployment rate had climbed to 10.8 percent, with joblessness among African Americans exceeding 20 percent. Nearly a third of the nation's industrial capacity lay idle, and 12 million Americans were out of work. The inflation rate, which reached 12.4 percent a year under Carter in 1980, fell after Reagan assumed office, to 8.9 percent in his first year and to about 5 percent during the remainder of his first term. But even the lower rate eroded the purchasing power of people already in difficulty.

The recession afflicted every region of the country. Business failures proliferated in every city and state, as large and small businesses closed their doors and fired their employees. In 1982, business bankruptcies rose 50 percent from the previous year. In one week in June 1982, a total of 548 businesses failed, close to the 1932 weekly record of 612.

Detroit was one of the hardest-hit areas in the United States. An industrial city revolving around automobile manufacturing, it suffered both from Japanese competition and from the high interest rates that made car sales plummet. The Detroit unemployment rate rose to more than 19 percent and affected the entire city.

Even the Sun Belt—the vast southern region stretching from coast to coast—showed the effects of the recession. It had enjoyed economic growth fostered by the availability of cheap, nonunion labor, tax advantages that state governments offered corporations willing to locate plants there, and a favorable climate. Now it too began to suffer economic problems, and large areas began to stagnate. Overexpansion in the oil industry led to a collapse in prices that disrupted the economy in Texas, Oklahoma, Louisiana, and other oil-producing regions. Worldwide gluts of some minerals, copper for example, added to unemployment elsewhere in the Southwest.

Economic conditions improved in late 1983 and early 1984, particularly for Americans in the middle and upper income ranges. The federal tax cut Reagan pushed through encouraged consumer spending, and huge defense expenditures had a stimulating effect. The Republican effort to reduce restrictions and cut waste sparked business confidence. A voluntary Japanese quota on car exports assisted the ailing automobile industry. The stock market climbed as it reflected the optimistic buying spree. Inflation remained low, about 3 to 4 percent annually from 1982 to 1988. Interest rates likewise fell, from 16.5 percent in 1982 to 10.5 percent in the same period and remained thereafter under 11 percent. The unemployment rate at the end of the 1980s fell to below 6 percent nationally (though many of the new jobs created paid less than $13,000 per year).

Between the start of the recovery and 1988, real GNP grew at an annual rate of 4.2 percent.

But the upswing masked a number of problems. Millions of Americans remained poor. Many families continued to earn a middle-class income, but only by having two full-time income earners. They also went deeply into debt. To buy homes, young people accepted vastly higher mortgage interest rates than their parents had. Stiff credit card debts, often at 20 percent interest, were common. Under such circumstances, some young families struggled to remain in the middle class. Single mothers were hit hardest of all.

The huge and growing budget deficits reflected the fundamental economic instability. Those deficits provoked doubts that resulted in the stock market crash of 1987. Six weeks of falling prices ended with a 22.6 percent drop on Monday, October 19, almost double the plunge of "Black Tuesday," October 29, 1929. The deficits, negative trade balances, and exposures of Wall Street fraud all combined to puncture the bubble. Later the market revived, but problems remained.

Those problems surfaced in the early 1990s, as the country experienced another recession. The combination of extravagant military spending, the uncontrolled growth of entitlements—programs such as Medicare and Medicaid, which provided benefits for millions of Americans on the basis of need—and the tax cut sent budget deficits skyward. As bond traders in the 1980s speculated recklessly and pocketed huge profits, the basic productive structure of the country continued to decline. The huge increase in the national debt eroded business confidence, and this time the effects were felt not simply in the stock market but in the economy as a whole.

American firms suffered a serious decline as corporate profits fell from $327 billion in 1989 to $315.5 billion in 1991. In an effort to cope with declining profits and decreased consumer demand, companies scaled back dramatically. In late 1991, General Motors announced that it would close 21 plants, lay off 9,000 white-collar employees the next year, and eliminate more than 70,000 jobs in the next several years. Hundreds of other companies did the same thing, trimming corporate fat but also cutting thousands of jobs.

The unemployment rate rose once again. In mid-1991, it reached 7 percent, the highest level in nearly five years. About 8.7 million Americans were without jobs, up 2 million in the year since the recession began.

Around the nation, state governments found it impossible to balance their budgets without resorting to massive spending cuts. Reagan's efforts to move programs from the federal to the state level worked as long as funding lasted, but as national support dropped and state tax revenues declined, states found themselves in a budgetary gridlock.

Most had constitutional prohibitions against running deficits, and so they had to slash spending for social services and education, even after yearly budgets had been approved.

After a number of false starts, the economy began to recover in mid-1992. The lowering of interest rates by the Federal Reserve Board revived confidence and promoted significant consumer spending. Productivity rose steadily throughout the decade, though not quite as quickly as it had in the 1950s and 1960s. Similarly, the national economic growth rate began to rise again, reaching 3.9 percent in 1997, while averaging 3 percent in the years since the recovery began. Growth, like productivity, was not as dramatic as it had sometimes been in the golden years of industrial development, but it was steady and sustained and gave no signs of flagging. In 2000, the expansion became the longest such growth period in the nation's history. Inflation fell, and in 1998 stood at the lowest rate since 1965. The unemployment rate also declined, dropping from 7.4 percent in 1992 to 4.9 percent in 1997, with monthly rates occasionally even lower in the next several years. Taking credit for the recovery, President Clinton declared that the drop in unemployment was "the latest evidence that our economy is growing, steady and strong, that the American dream is in fact alive and well."

One reflection of the return of prosperity was the soaring stock market. A willingness to invest in the market is often a good indicator of confidence in the nation's economic health. In the 1990s, Americans became emboldened by the positive economic indicators and invested billions of dollars in mutual funds and stocks. The market, which had inched upward in years past, now began a dramatic rise. The Dow Jones average topped the once-unimaginable 10,000 barrier in 1999 and quickly moved on past the 11,000 mark. Investors, most from the middle and upper classes, made considerable amounts of money in the market. Even when corrections occurred, the market indices remained high.

An even more important sign of economic health was the steady reduction in the budget deficit. Bill Clinton's effort to preempt a Republican issue and hold down spending paid off, particularly as low interest rates encourage economic expansion. In 1998, the United States finished with a budget surplus for the first time in 29 years. With $70 billion—the largest surplus ever—left over at the end of the fiscal year, Democrats and Republicans began arguing with one another about how the money should be used. The president and most Democrats favored using funds to bolster the social security system, which seemed likely to run out of money, while Republicans, who controlled Congress, preferred a politically attractive tax cut. Ignored in the euphoria was the fact that the national debt—the total of all past deficits—remained over $5.4 trillion.

In these prosperous times, American companies embarked upon a wave of mergers like those around the turn of the century that created the great oil and steel corporations. In the defense industry, for example, Lockheed and Martin Marietta merged in 1994, while Boeing merged with McDonnell Douglas in 1996. In 1997, a record $1 trillion in mergers involving American companies took place as huge conglomerates swallowed up smaller competitors in the interests of efficiency and ever larger profits. One consequence of the mergers, however, was layoffs of workers who duplicated tasks and seemed superfluous. The jobs available as they looked for other work were often positions like those held by Marlene Garrett and her husband, met earlier in the chapter, which paid far less.

DEMOGRAPHIC AND REGIONAL CHANGE

As the American people dealt with the swings of the economy, demographic patterns changed significantly. The nation's population increased from 228 million to approximately 250 million between 1980 and 1990—a rise of 9.6 percent (as opposed to 11.5 percent in the 1970s), one of the lowest rates of growth in American history. At the same time, the complexion of the country changed. As a result of increased immigration and minority birthrates significantly higher than the rate for whites, an all-time high of 25 percent of the population in 1992 was black, Latino, Asian, or Native American, and that figure continued to rise. The population shifted as well. Suburban growth continued, leaving ever larger minority populations in the cities. In the West, a pattern of urban and regional development under way since World War II continued and provided a model for the rest of the country.

Urban and Suburban Shifts

American cities became concentrations of minorities. White families continued to leave for the steadily growing suburbs, which by 1990 contained almost half the population, more than ever before. In 15 of the nation's 28 largest cities—New York, Chicago, and Houston among them—minorities made up at least half the population. Minority representation varied by urban region. In Detroit, Washington, New Orleans, and Chicago, blacks were the largest minority; in Phoenix, El Paso, San Antonio, and Los Angeles, Latinos held that position; in San Francisco, Asians outnumbered other groups.

The cities also grew steadily poorer. In Houston, for example, although increasing numbers of blacks, Latinos, and Asians lived in the suburbs, most of the poorest minority families concentrated in the city itself. As had been the case since World War II, commuters from the suburbs took the better-paying jobs, while people living in the cities held lower-paying positions. Mario Perez, a 27-year-old Latino immigrant, noted in 1991 that the increase in the number of Spanish-speaking immigrants in the nine years since he arrived in Houston made it easier to find a job but harder to secure well-paying work. Perez himself worked seven days a week sweeping streets downtown and tending plants for $5.50 an hour.

Western Development

At the same time, the population was moving west. In 1900, the region consisting of the Mountain and Pacific states contained about 5 percent of the nation's population. By 1990 that figure stood at 21 percent. The population of the nation as a whole rose by less than 10 percent in the 1980s, but the population of the West increased by 22 percent.

That population was becoming much more urbanized. In the 50 years following 1940, the six largest metropolitan areas in the West grew by 380 percent; the six largest in the East expanded by only 64 percent. While the West remained the nation's emptiest region, it was nonetheless the most urbanized. By 1990, 80 percent of all Westerners lived in metropolitan areas (compared with 76 percent of the people in the rest of the United States). Writer Wallace Stegner observed that the West "*is* urban; it's an oasis civilization."

With its urban development, the West became a pacesetter for the rest of the country. If the New England village had been a representative symbol of the eighteenth century, and the midwestern town a similar symbol of the nineteenth century, now in the late twentieth century the western metropolis was singled out for special symbolic attention. The Stanford Industrial Park, established in California in 1951, focused on research-oriented manufacturing and became a model for other high-tech centers. Western cities were often unbounded, open-ended, sprawling in all directions. They seemed capable of expanding indefinitely. Horizontal, low-slung homes made western neighborhoods look very different from those in the Northeast. Tourism became a dynamic industry, with the West in the forefront. The motel, a western invention, made automobile travel easier. Western cities were among the most popular tourist destinations, catering to visitors from both the Pacific Basin and the rest of the world.

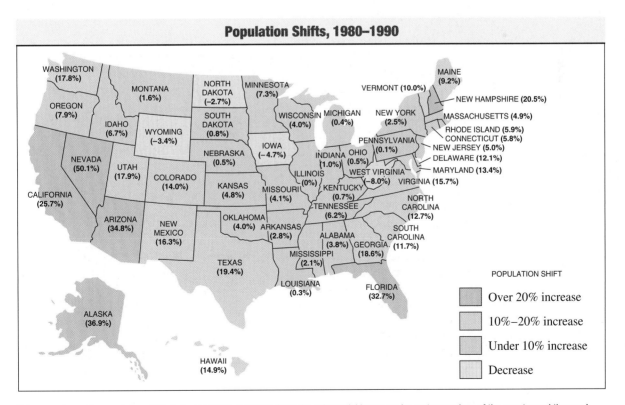

Population Shifts, 1980–1990

POPULATION SHIFT

- Over 20% increase
- 10%–20% increase
- Under 10% increase
- Decrease

This map shows the population shifts between 1980 and 1990. Note the substantial increases in western regions of the country and the much smaller increases along the Atlantic seaboard.

California was the nation's fastest growing state, its population increasing in the 1980s by nearly 26 percent. Responding to a question about California's impact on the rest of the country, Wallace Stegner said, "We *are* the national culture, at its most energetic end."

Within the state, Los Angeles became the most dynamic example of American vitality and creativity. The motion picture industry exerted a worldwide impact. The city became a capital of consumption. Novelist Thomas Pynchon caught the energy of Los Angeles in his 1990 novel, *Vineland.* In the following passage, he described the city as seen at night from the freeway. There were

> screaming black motorcades that could have carried any of several office seekers, cruisers heading for treed and more gently roaring boulevards, huge double and triple trailer rigs that loved to find Volkswagens laboring up grades and go sashaying around them gracefully and at gnat's-ass tolerances, plus flirters, deserters, wimps and pimps, speeding like bullets, grinning like chimps, above the heads of the TV watchers, lovers under the overpasses, movies at the mall letting out, bright gas-station oases in the pure fluorescent spill, . . . the adobe air, the smell of distant fireworks, the spilled, the broken world.

The New Pilgrims

The second great wave of immigrants in the twentieth century brought about another demographic shift. The number of immigrants has risen dramatically in the past 30 years. In the 1970s, the number averaged 450,000 a year, far higher than in the decade before. In the 1980s, it averaged 730,000. In the 1990s, it averaged approximately 1,000,000, and in 1991, as the chart shows, more people arrived than in any single year in this century. Altogether, a fifth of the population growth in the 1980s stemmed from immigration.

The influx was spurred by the Immigration Act of 1965 (see Chapter 28). Part of Lyndon Johnson's Great Society program, this act authorized the acceptance of immigrants impartially from all parts of the world. The result in the 1980s, as in the 1970s, was far greater numbers of Asians and Latin Americans. In this latter decade, 37 percent came from Asia, and 47 percent came from Mexico, the Caribbean, and Latin America. Always a nation of immigrants, the United States was once again receiving new, and very different, ethnic infusions.

As has long been true, the desire for jobs fostered immigration. But foreign crises also fueled the influx. After 1975, the United States accepted more than a half million Vietnamese refugees, uprooted by the war

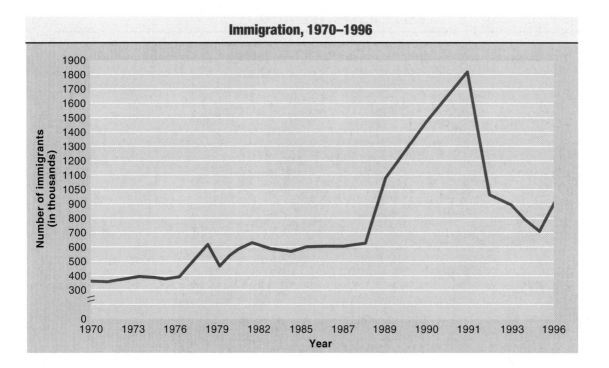

This chart shows the significant rise in immigration after 1970, as the tightly restricted quotas in force from the 1920s to 1965 were liberalized. Note the most rapid rise in the 1980s and early 1990s, as Asians and Latin Americans came in ever larger numbers. Source: Data from *Statistical Abstract of the United States.*

that had finally come to an end. In 1980, more than 160,000 arrived. That same year, the nation admitted 125,000 Cuban and Haitian refugees.

Millions more arrived illegally. As the populations of Latin American nations soared and as economic conditions deteriorated, more and more people looked to the United States for relief. In the mid-1970s, Leonard Chapman, commissioner of the Immigration and Naturalization Service, estimated that there might be 12 million foreigners in the nation illegally. While official estimates were lower, Attorney General William French Smith declared in 1983, "Simply put, we've lost control of our own borders."

Several legislative measures sought to rationalize the immigration process. In 1986, Congress passed the Immigration Reform and Control Act, aimed at curbing illegal immigration while offering amnesty to aliens who had lived in the United States since 1982. As the mid-1988 deadline approached, 50,000 per week applied to stay. The Immigration Act of 1990 revised the level and preference system for admission of immigrants to the United States and refined administrative procedures for naturalization. Raising immigration quotas by 40 percent per year, the act cut back on restrictions based on ideology or sexual orientation that had been used to deny entry in the past. It also set aside a substantial number of visas for large investors and provided for swift deportation of aliens who committed crimes. "This act recognizes the fundamental importance and historic contributions of immigrants to our country," President Bush said in signing the measure.

The more than 10 million immigrants who arrived between 1976 and 1990 belonged to two very different economic classes. In the 1970s and early 1980s, almost a quarter were professionals, and even more were white-collar employees. Many of these immigrants brought skills, funds, and family support networks that could assist in business ventures in America. At the same time, the United States absorbed a large group of less skilled workers. In this decade and a half, about 46 percent of all employed immigrants were laborers, service sector workers, and semiskilled employees. The flow of this group increased in the 1980s and 1990s.

This new wave of immigration changed the complexion of the United States, as it had in decades past. Once again, as before 1924, the nation was a refuge for people from very different parts of the world. The Sun Belt in particular, from Florida to California, felt the impact of the new Asians and Hispanics. In Los Angeles, Samoans, Taiwanese, Koreans, Vietnamese, Filipinos, and Cambodians competed for jobs and apartments with Mexicans, African Americans, and Anglos, just as newcomers from different countries had contended with one another in New York City a

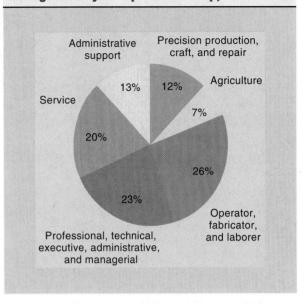

Immigration by Occupational Group, 1976–1990

Administrative support — 13%
Precision production, craft, and repair — 12%
Agriculture — 7%
Operator, fabricator, and laborer — 26%
Professional, technical, executive, administrative, and managerial — 23%
Service — 20%

This graph shows the large fraction of immigrants in 1976–1990 who were white-collar and professional workers. Source: *1990 Statistical Yearbook of the Immigration and Naturalization Service.*

century before. Throughout the country, in Miami, in Houston, in Brooklyn, the languages heard in the schools and on the streets changed.

These groups left a new imprint on the United States. As African Americans and Latinos became major figures in the urban equation, the number of Asians in the country doubled in the 1980s, and they made up nearly half of all immigrants by the end of the decade. Immigrants from India, the Philippines, China, and Korea often brought skills and professional expertise, although Southeast Asian refugees were frequently less well off when they arrived. Many of these unskilled immigrants provided the labor for the rapidly expanding West Coast electronics industry. The Asian immigrants, following a pattern established decades before, sought better and better opportunities for their children, and in California they became the largest group of entering students at a number of college campuses.

Sometimes the media highlighted the successes of Asian immigrants, particularly in contrast to the problems encountered by other groups. In 1986, *U.S. News & World Report* noted Asian American advances in a cover story, while *Newsweek* ran a lead article on "Asian Americans: A 'Model Minority,'" and *Fortune* called them "America's Super Minority." Asian Americans were proud of the exposure but pointed out that many members of the working class still struggled for a foothold. In the Chinatowns of San Francisco and Los Angeles, 40 to 50 percent of the

Asian workers often found themselves trapped in low-paying jobs with little hope of advancement. Here women work at sewing machines in a cluttered factory in Queens, New York, in 1993, in conditions similar to those earlier in the twentieth century. *(Donna Binder/Impact Visuals)*

workers were employed in the ill-paid service sector or garment industry; in New York's Chinatown the figure was close to 70 percent. Chinese immigrant women, in particular, often had little choice but to work as seamstresses, just as women from other nationalities had earlier in the century.

Each group, each family, had its own story. Nguyen Ninh and Nguyen Viet, two brothers who remained in Vietnam after the victory of the North Vietnamese in 1975, were among the many who finally fled their war-torn country by boat. The boat sank, but they were rescued, only to be shuttled to Kuwait, then Greece, and finally to the United States, where another brother had arrived a few years before. Though they spoke no English, they immediately began to look for work. One became a carpenter's helper; the other, an attendant at a valet parking firm. With the money they earned, they helped other members of their family emigrate. Slowly they learned English, obtained better jobs, and saved enough money to purchase a home.

Professionals often had a hard time. Frequently, training in their country of birth had little bearing in the United States. One Vietnamese physician who resettled in Oklahoma noted, "When I come here, I am told that I must be a beginner again and serve like an apprentice for two years. I have no choice, so I will do it, but I have been wronged to be asked to do this."

In the 1970s and 1980s, America's efforts to help immigrants coincided with still-intact social assistance programs of the liberal welfare state. Affirmative action programs, in particular, provided aid for both legal and illegal arrivals. Bilingual classrooms became more common, and multiculturalism, stressing the different values that made up a larger American identity, became a dominant theme in many schools.

Yet those efforts brought increasing resistance from Americans already here. That opposition, which echoed anti-immigrant feelings of the past, included strenuous efforts to restrict illegal immigration and to lower annual quotas for new arrivals. A new law, passed in 1996, restricted the number of people immigrating and made it easier for the government to deport illegal entrants on instructions from a single immigration agent, without a hearing or review by a judge. Meanwhile, in the midterm elections of 1994, immigration opponents in California pushed through Proposition 187, which required teachers and clinic doctors to deny assistance to illegal aliens and to report them to police. While the courts declared most of the measure unconstitutional and it was never implemented, it still had a chilling effect on new arrivals, who suffered as well from the cutbacks in welfare and the efforts to end affirmative action noted earlier in the chapter. Still another referendum in California in 1998 banned bilingual education.

Growing Up

In the mid-1970s, the birthrate began to rise slowly after a decade and a half of decline. The baby boom, which had created a population explosion in the years after World War II, peaked in 1960 with a rate of 24 births per 1,000 people. In 1981, the rate stood at 16, then rose to nearly 17 in 1990, as demographers viewed the new increase in births as part of a long-term trend.

But children less frequently lived in traditional homes. The Labor Department estimated that by the

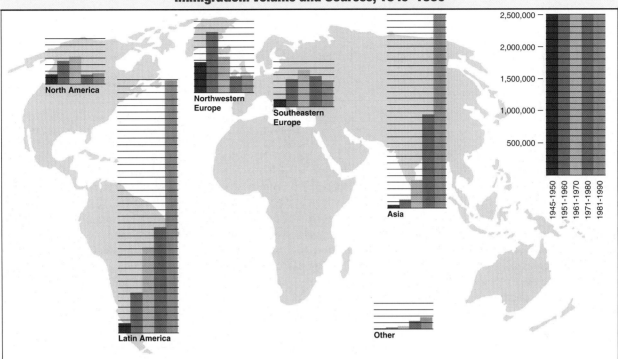

Immigration: Volume and Sources, 1945–1990

This map shows the shifting patterns of American immigration in the postwar years. In particular, note the large increase in Asian and Latin American immigration from the 1970s to 1990.

late 1970s only 7 percent of the nation's families matched the stereotypical pattern of the breadwinner father, the homemaker mother, and two children. Divorce shattered the mold. In 1980, the courts granted nearly 1.2 million divorces, the highest total in the nation's history. In 1990, the figure of 1.175 million was almost as high. For each 1,000 marriages there were 480 divorces, down slightly from 490 in 1980 but significantly higher than 328 per 1,000 in 1970 and 258 per 1,000 in 1960. The social stigma once attached to divorce disappeared; Reagan was the first divorced person to be elected president. "Nonfamily households" became increasingly common. Between 1980 and 1990, such households, led by either a man or a woman, increased from 26 to 29 percent of the total number, while the percentage of family households declined. Single-parent families, particularly those headed by women, were now common. In 1960, 11 percent of all children lived in such homes; by 1990, the figure had reached 25 percent. For African Americans, the proportion of families headed by women was three times as great as for whites.

During hard times, particularly for members of the working class, new children could pose problems. An extra mouth to feed could make a difference to a family on the fringe. New children also required women of all classes to consider the relationship between family and career. Women entering the workforce faced the daunting problem of juggling work and home schedules and finding adequate child care facilities.

The rising death rate among the young was disturbing. The Public Health Service reported in 1982 that the death rate for most Americans had dropped significantly over a 30-year period, and it continued to drop throughout the decade, but the rate for those between 15 and 24 rose steadily after 1976. Automobile accidents, murders, and suicides accounted for three out of four deaths for this group. A wave of school shootings in the late-1990s, such as the tragedy at Columbine High School in Littleton, Colorado, made it clear that childhood and adolescence could be troubling times.

The discovery of AIDS (acquired immune deficiency syndrome) in 1981 complicated the process of growing up. The sexual revolution of the 1960s had brought a major change in sexual patterns, particularly among the young, but sexual experimentation now involved facing a deadly threat. Although it seemed to strike intravenous drug users and homosexuals with numerous partners more than other groups at first, it soon spread to the heterosexual population as well. Babies with AIDS were born to mothers with the illness. AIDS became the leading cause of death in Americans between the ages of 25 and 44.

Recovering the Past

AUTOBIOGRAPHY

s we reach our own time, the historical past most worth recovering, perhaps, is our own. Our own story is as valid a part of the story of American history as the tale of Revolutionary War soldiers, frontier women, reform politicians, and immigrant grandparents. In this increasingly computerized and depersonalized age, the person we need to recover and know is ourself, a self that has been formed, at least in part, by the entire American experience we have been studying.

Autobiography is the form of writing in which people tell their own life's history. Although written autobiographies are at least as old as the literature of the early Christians—for example, *The Confessions of St. Augustine*—the word *autobiography* dates from the late eighteenth century, around the time of the French and American Revolutions. That is no accident. These

Autobiographical Memoirs

Benjamin Franklin

DEAR SON,

I have ever had a pleasure in obtaining any little anecdotes of my ancestors. You may remember the enquiries I made among the remains of my relations when you were with me in England and the journey I undertook for that purpose. Imagining it may be equally agreeable to you to know the circumstances of my life—many of which you are yet unacquainted with—and expecting a week's uninterrupted leisure in my present country retirement, I sit down to write them for you. Besides, there are some other inducements that excite me to this undertaking. From the poverty and obscurity in which I was born and in which I passed my earliest years, I have raised myself to a state of affluence and some degree of celebrity in the world. As constant good fortune has accompanied me even to an advanced period of life, my posterity will perhaps be desirous of learning the means, which I employed, and which, thanks to Providence, so well succeeded with me. They may also deem them fit to be imitated, should any of them find themselves in similar circumstances.

Source: *The Autobiography of Benjamin Franklin* (1771).

Elizabeth Cady Stanton

Elizabeth Cady Stanton

It was 'mid such exhilarating scenes that Miss Anthony and I wrote addresses for temperance, anti-slavery, educational and woman's rights conventions. Here we forged resolutions, protests, appeals, petitions, agricultural reports, and constitutional arguments; for we made it a matter of conscience to accept every invitation to speak on every question, in order to maintain woman's right to do so. To this end we took turns on the domestic watchtowers, directing amusements, settling disputes, protecting the weak against the strong, and trying to secure equal rights to all in the home as well as the nation.

It is often said, by those who know Miss Anthony best, that she has been my good angel, always pushing and goading me to work, and that but for her pertinacity I should never have accomplished the little I have. On the other hand it has been said that I forged the thunderbolts and she fired them. Perhaps all this is, in a measure, true. With the cares of a large family I might, in time, like too many women, have become wholly absorbed in a narrow family selfishness, had not my friend been continually exploring new fields for missionary labors. Her description of a body of men on any platform, complacently deciding questions in which women had an equal interest, without an equal voice, readily aroused me to a determination to throw a firebrand into the midst of their assembly.

Source: Elizabeth Cady Stanton, *Eighty Years and More: Reminiscences, 1815–1897* (1898).

Confessional Autobiographies

Black Elk

And so it was all over.

I did not know then how much was ended. When I look back now from this high hill of my old age, I can still see the butchered women and children lying heaped and scattered all along the crooked gulch as plain as when I saw them with eyes still young. And I can see that something else died there in the bloody mud, and was buried in the blizzard. A people's dream died there. It was a beautiful dream.

And I, to whom so great a vision was given in my youth,—you see me now a pitiful old man who has done nothing, for the nation's hoop is broken and scattered. There is no center any longer, and the sacred tree is dead.

Source: *Black Elk Speaks*, as told through John G. Neihardt (1932).

Malcolm X

I want to say before I go on that I have never previously told anyone my sordid past in detail. I haven't done it now to sound as though I might be proud of how bad, how evil, I was.

But people are always speculating—why am I as I am? To understand that of any person, his whole life, from birth, must be reviewed. All of our experiences fuse into our personality. Everything that ever happened to us is an ingredient.

Today, when everything that I do has an urgency, I would not spend one hour in the preparation of a book which has the ambition to perhaps titillate some readers. But I am spending many hours because the full story is the best way that I know to have it seen, and understood, that I had sunk to the very bottom of the American white man's society when—soon now, in prison—I found Allah and the religion of Islam and it completely transformed my life.

Source: *The Autobiography of Malcolm X*, with the assistance of Alex Haley (1964).

---

momentous events represented the triumph of individual liberty and the sovereignty of the self. *The Autobiography of Benjamin Franklin,* written between 1771 and his death in 1790, and excerpted here, is a classic celebration of the American success story. Franklin's work set the standard for one autobiographical form, the memoir of one's public achievements and success. The other brief autobiographical memoir, from the reminiscences of Elizabeth Cady Stanton, also reflects the tone and range of this tradition.

Not all autobiographies are written late in life to celebrate one's accomplishments. The confessional autobiography, unlike most memoirs, explores the author's interior life, acknowledging flaws and failures as well as successes; it may be written at any age. The purpose of this type of autobiography is not just to reconstruct one's past to preserve it for posterity but to find from one's past an identity to know better how to live one's future. The story of religious confessions and conversions is an obvious example. This form also includes secular self-examinations such as those by Maxine Hong Kingston in *The Woman Warrior* (1976), Piri Thomas in *Down These Mean Streets* (1967), and Maya Angelou in a series of five autobiographical sketches beginning with *I Know Why the Caged Bird Sings* (1969). The other two excerpts presented here are among the finest examples of confessional autobiography and suggest its variety.

These examples hardly convey the full range of the autobiographical form or how available to all people is the opportunity to tell the story of one's life. In 1909, William

Dean Howells called autobiography the "most democratic province in the republic of letters." A recent critic agrees, pointing out:

> To this genre have been drawn public and private figures: poets, philosophers, prizefighters; actresses, artists, political activists; statesmen and penitentiary prisoners; financiers and football players; Quakers and Black Muslims; immigrants and Indians. The range of personality, experience, and profession reflected in the forms of American autobiography is as varied as American life itself.

Your story, too, is a legitimate part of American history. But writing an autobiography, while open to all, is deceptively difficult. Like historians, autobiographers face problems of sources, selection, interpretation, and style. As in the writing of any history, the account of one's past must be objective, not only in the verifiable accuracy of details but also in the honest selection of representative events to be described. Moreover, as in fiction as well as history, the autobiographer must provide a structured form, an organizing principle, literary merit, and thematic coherence to the story. Many other challenges face the would-be autobiographer, such as finding a balance between one's public life and the private self and handling problems of memory, ego (should one, for example, use the first or third person?), and death.

To get an idea of the difficulties of writing an autobiography, try writing your own. Limit yourself to 1,000 words. Good luck.

As the AIDS epidemic caused more and more deaths, family members and friends began a huge quilt to celebrate the lives of those who had died. Each panel represented a different person. The quilt, shown here in Washington, D.C., was on display around the country and drew millions of viewers who came to remember those lost to the disease. *(Lisa Quinones/ Black Star)*

The growing number of deaths—more than 250,000 by 1995—suggested that the disease would reach epic proportions. New drugs, taken in combination, extended the life-span of those with the HIV virus and reduced the death rate at the end of the decade, but AIDS remained a lethal, and ultimately fatal, disease. Advertisements in the national media advised the use of condoms, and the U.S. surgeon general mailed a brochure, "Understanding AIDS," to every household in the United States.

Growing Old

As concern with the problems of the young increased, awareness of the plight of the old also grew. Between 1900 and 1980, when the population of the country tripled, the number of people over 65 rose eightfold and continued to rise in the next decade. In the 1980s, the number of Americans over 75 grew by more than 27 percent. Underlying the rapid increase was the

steady advance in medical care, which in the twentieth century had increased life expectancy from 47 to 74 years. Americans became aware of the "aging revolution," which promised to become the most lasting of all twentieth-century social changes.

One component of that revolution was Viagra, a new drug designed to help men suffering from impotence. Whether sexual dysfunction was a result of prostate illness, common among older males, or emotional distress, Viagra helped ailing men enjoy normal sex lives. Bob Dole, the defeated presidential candidate in 1996 when he was in his 70s, participated in a national advertising campaign extolling the benefits of Viagra in his own life. Americans, including the elderly, now talked frankly about erectile dysfunction, just as they had talked openly about birth control when the birth control pill was introduced three and a half decades before. *Newsweek* magazine noted in 1998 that Viagra was the fastest-selling drug in history.

The elderly raised new issues in a nation suffering periodic recession. Many wanted to continue working and opposed mandatory retirement rules that drove them from their jobs. Legislation in 1978 that raised the mandatory retirement age from 65 to 70 helped older workers but cut employment opportunities for younger workers seeking jobs, a pattern that became even more problematic in the 1990s.

Generational resentment over jobs was compounded by the knotty problems faced by the social security system established a half century before. As more and more Americans retired, the system could not generate sufficient revenue to make the payments due without assistance from the general government fund. In the early 1980s, it appeared that the entire system might collapse. A government solution involving higher taxes for those still employed and a later age for qualifying for benefits rescued the fund for a time, but many Americans in the 1990s wondered whether social security would survive.

As Americans lived longer, they suffered increasingly from Alzheimer's disease, an affliction that gradually destroyed a patient's memory and brought on infantile behavior. Diagnosis was difficult, and there was no treatment to reverse the ailment's course. The illness gained exposure in 1995 when the family of Ronald Reagan disclosed that the former president was suffering from the incurable disease.

American families faced difficult decisions about caring for older parents. In the past, the elderly often came into their children's homes, but attitudes and family patterns had changed. As women entered the paid workforce, they were less able to assist in the home care of an elderly parent. Retirement villages and nursing homes provided two alternatives, but the

The homeless became far more visible in the 1990s. Here a man lies sleeping under a thin sheet of plastic serving as a blanket right in front of the White House in Washington, D.C. *(UPI/Corbis-Bettmann)*

decision to place a parent under institutional care was often excruciating.

Growing Poor

Meanwhile, despite the increase in wealth enjoyed by the already-rich, many Americans were growing poorer. The Census Bureau reported in 1997 that 35.6 million people in the United States still lived below what was defined as the poverty line of about $16,000 a year for a family of four. The percentage—13.3 percent—had fallen slightly in each of the past few years but was still sizable, especially considering that it included one out of every three *working* Americans. As always, minorities fared worse than whites. The net worth of a typical white household at the beginning of the decade was 12 times greater than the net worth of a typical black household and 8 times greater than the net worth of a typical Latino household. Minorities and women continued to lose ground faster than the rest of the population.

Just as the United States rediscovered its poor in the 1960s, so it rediscovered its homeless in the 1980s and 1990s. Even as unemployment dropped in the 1980s, the number of homeless quadrupled during that time. Numbers were hard to ascertain, for the homeless had no fixed addresses, but one estimate in 1990 calculated that 6 or 7 million people had been homeless at some point in the past 5 years. A more careful study in 1994 scaled that figure down to 500,000, still a huge number in the richest nation on earth. Still another study noted that family homelessness in New York had risen between 1990 and 1995, with the largest increase coming among children nine years old and younger.

People became homeless for a variety of reasons. Some started life in seriously disturbed families. Others fell prey to alcohol and drugs. Still others had health or learning problems that eroded the possibility of a stable life. For millions of working Americans, homelessness was just a serious and unaffordable illness away. Though many Americans initially regarded the homeless as "bag ladies, winos, and junkies," they gradually came to realize that the underclass category included others as well.

One homeless single mother described the plight so many people faced. Deborah M., interviewed on television in 1991, observed, "This could happen to anyone. As for me, I finished high school. I've done a year and a half of college. I'm a certified nurse's aid and a bank teller, and I'm homeless." Her four children suffered most of all. "From the little timid children that they were," Deborah noted, "they're not that anymore." She was lucky; a city agency found an affordable apartment for her family. Others were less fortunate.

The growing disparity in wealth, and the neglect of the urban poor and resurgent racism noted earlier in this chapter, became horrifyingly visible in the terrible rioting that engulfed Los Angeles in the spring of 1992. The year before, Americans had watched a videotaped savage beating of black motorist Rodney King by white police officers, the most dramatic of a long string of incidents involving police brutality. When a California jury, which contained no African Americans, acquitted the policemen, many people throughout the country became convinced that people of color could not obtain equal justice under the law. In Los Angeles thousands reacted with uncontrolled fury. As widespread arson and looting swept through many neighborhoods, the police proved unable to control the mayhem. Much of it was led by gang members but involved as well hundreds of ordinary citizens who acted irresponsibly yet with a sense that the social contract had been broken by politicians and the rich, who were unresponsive to their plight. Several days later, after the riot had run its course, 51 people (most of them black and Hispanic) lay dead, 2,000 were injured, and $1 billion in damage had been done to the city. It was the worst riot in decades, more deadly even than the Watts riot 27 years before. Political candidates from both parties scurried around trying to define an urban policy, as the upheaval served notice that racial injustice, social inequality, and poverty could no longer be ignored.

THE UNITED STATES IN A CHANGED WORLD

In the 1980s and 1990s, the United States emerged triumphant in the Cold War that had dominated world politics since the end of World War II. In one of the most momentous developments in modern world history, Communism collapsed in Eastern Europe and in the Soviet Union, and the various republics in the Soviet orbit embraced both capitalism and democracy. Other regions—the Middle East and Africa—experienced equally breathtaking change.

This international tumult forced the United States to examine its own assumptions about its role in the world. What kind of leadership would the United States exert as the one remaining superpower on the globe? How involved would it become in peacekeeping missions in troubled lands? What kind of assistance would it extend to developing nations once the competition with the Soviet Union that had fueled foreign aid was over? These questions, asked in different forms over the course of past centuries, helped shape foreign policy in transitional times.

Triumph in the Cold War

The Cold War was very much alive when Reagan assumed the presidency in 1981. The new president asserted U.S. overseas interests far more aggressively than had President Carter. Like most of his contemporaries, Reagan believed in large defense budgets and a militant approach toward the Soviet Union. He wanted to cripple the Russians

economically by forcing them to spend more than they could afford on defense.

Viewing the Soviet Union as an "evil empire" in his first term, Reagan promoted an increased atomic arsenal by arguing that a nuclear war could be fought and won. The administration abandoned Senate ratification of SALT II, the arms reduction plan negotiated under Carter, although it observed the pact's restrictions. Then Reagan proposed the enormously expensive and bitterly criticized Strategic Defense Initiative, popularly known as "Star Wars" after a 1977 movie, to intercept Soviet missiles by means of a shield in outer space.

In his second term, however, Reagan softened his belligerence. Mikhail Gorbachev, the new Soviet leader, watching his own economy collapse under the pressure of the superheated arms race, realized the need for greater accommodation with the West. He understood that the only way the Soviet Union could survive was through arms negotiations with the United States that would help reduce his overextended budget. He therefore proposed a policy of *perestroika* (restructuring the economy) and *glasnost* (political openness to encourage personal initiative). His overtures opened the way to better relations with the United States.

Mikhail Gorbachev was the Soviet leader who initiated the process that helped ease tensions with the United States and ultimately ended the Cold War. Gorbachev's policies provided for major readjustments in Soviet society, but those eventually tore the Soviet Union apart. (*AP/Wide World Photos*)

Concerned with his own place in history, Reagan met with Gorbachev, and the two heads of state developed a close working relationship. Summit meetings led to an Intermediate Range Nuclear Forces Treaty in 1987 that provided for withdrawal and destruction of 2,500 Soviet and American nuclear missiles in Europe.

George Bush maintained Reagan's comfortable relationship with Gorbachev. At several summit meetings in 1989 and 1990, the two leaders signed agreements reducing the number of long-range nuclear weapons to a maximum of 1,600 rockets and 6,000 warheads, ending manufacture of chemical weapons, and easing trade restrictions between the two nations. The Strategic Arms Reduction Treaty (START) signed in 1991 dramatically decreased the stockpiles of long-range weapons.

Hailed around the world for his part in easing tensions, Gorbachev encountered trouble at home. In mid-1991, he faced an old-guard Communist coup, led by those who opposed *glasnost* and *perestroika* and wanted to slow the process of change. He survived this right-wing challenge, but he could not resist those who wanted to go even further to establish democracy and capitalism. The forces he had unleashed within the Soviet Union finally tore the USSR apart.

Boris Yeltsin, president of Russia, the strongest and most populous of the Soviet republics, emerged as the dominant leader, but even he could not contain the forces of disintegration. Independence movements in the tiny Baltic republics began the dismantling of the Soviet Union, and other republics likewise went their own way. The once-powerful superpower was now a collection of separate states. Although the republics coalesced loosely in a Commonwealth of Independent States, led by Russia, they retained their autonomy—and independent leadership—in domestic and foreign affairs.

Early in 1992, Bush and Yeltsin proclaimed a new era of "friendship and partnership" and formally declared an end to the Cold War. After half a century of conflict, the United States had won. Yeltsin abandoned the notion of nuclear parity—maintaining an arsenal similar to that of the United States—and agreed to cut back conventional Russian forces to complement nuclear cuts. The United States then extended aid to the former Soviet republics, which needed help in reorganizing their economies as free enterprise systems. Relations became strained in 1994, when Russia sought to prevent further fragmentation and moved aggressively to squelch a rebellion in the republic of Chechnya. The brutal nature of Yeltsin's response led allies to question both his democratic values and his ability to govern, yet the West continued to support him for lack of a better alternative.

Boris Yeltsin, president of Russia, the largest of the republics in what had been the Soviet Union, became the most influential leader after Gorbachev's fall. But Yeltsin's efforts at economic reform met with serious opposition and led to his resignation as the century came to an end. *(Corbis-Bettmann)*

Meanwhile, Communist regimes throughout Europe collapsed. In a series of remarkable developments that occurred at the same time and intertwined with the turbulence in the Soviet Union, many of the Communist satellites broke loose, rejected Communism, and proclaimed a new commitment to democracy.

The most dramatic episodes unfolded in Germany in November 1989. Responding to Gorbachev's softening stance toward the West, East Germany's Communist party boss announced unexpectedly that citizens of his country were free to leave East Germany. Within hours, thousands of people gathered on both sides of the 28-mile Berlin Wall—the symbol of the Cold War that divided Berlin into east and west sectors. As border guards stepped aside, East Germans flooded into West Berlin amidst dancing, shouting, and fireworks. All through the night noisy celebrators reveled in what one observer called the "greatest street party in the history of the world." Within days, sledgehammer-wielding Germans pulverized the Berlin Wall, and soon the Communist government itself came tumbling down. By October 1990, less than a year after the free movement of East Germans across their borders began, the two Germanys were reunited.

The fall of the Berlin Wall reverberated all over Eastern Europe. Everywhere it brought the pell-mell overthrow of Communist regimes. In Poland, the ten-year-old Solidarity movement led by Lech Walesa triumphed in its long struggle against Soviet domination

Technology Changes the American People

THE INTERNET AND THE WORLD WIDE WEB

Today, the Internet is an integral part of our daily lives. More and more people use e-mail to communicate quickly with friends and colleagues around the world. Many Americans use the World Wide Web to make purchases ranging from books to automobiles. Others buy stocks on-line and rely on the Web to manage their portfolios. Historians and other scholars have come to depend on huge databases on the Web that are accessible from computers anywhere at the click of a mouse.

But the Internet is not new. Its roots extend back 30 years, to the mid-1960s, when Americans were worried about the nuclear arms race with the Soviet Union at the height of the Cold War. After the Russians launched their *Sputnik* satellite in 1957, with a rocket that demonstrated the ability to send atomic weapons from one continent to another, American scientists dedicated themselves to catching up and surpassing the Soviets in space. Proud of their technological achievements in the past, including the creation of the world's first atomic bomb, they wanted to regain the scientific lead. But if they were to launch satellites of their own, and eventually put a man on the moon, they needed to develop their computer technology.

Scientists were also interested in figuring out how to maintain communication in the aftermath of a nuclear attack. As both the United States and the Soviet Union developed bigger and better atomic bombs, and then in the 1950s began to create even more potent hydrogen weapons, it became clear that a full-scale nuclear war could wipe out a nation's ability to communicate with its distant military bases. The Department of Defense wanted to create a communications link that could withstand any such disaster. It envisioned a decentralized system that could continue to function even if part of it was wiped out.

A number of developments in the fledgling computer world were the first steps in creating an extended communications network. In the early 1960s, scientists at the Massachusetts Institute of Technology developed the concept of timesharing, whereby different users at widely separated sites could use the same central computer at the same time. Another step forward came in the mid-1960s, with the development of "packet-switching" technology, which broke down data into small, discrete packets that could be transmitted over telephone lines, using modems to connect the computers to the phone lines, and then reassembled when received by another computer at the other end.

Building on those steps, the Department of Defense established the Advanced Research Projects Agency Network, known as the ARPANET, in 1969. It linked together the computers of four institutions—the University of California campuses at Los Angeles and Santa Barbara, the Stanford Research Institute, and the University of Utah. Two years later, the system had expanded to include 23 universities and research centers around the country. This early system was a remarkable achievement, since each computer had a unique operating system. The first task, finally accomplished, was to develop ways of allowing the different machines to communicate with one another.

The system was hardly user-friendly in these early days. In an age before the advent of personal computers at home, or even office computers at work, only computer professionals, engineers, and other scientists mastered the intricacies of what were very complex systems. Once they did, however, they were able to join computerized discussion groups, which allowed them to exchange research articles and to communicate with one another through what became known as electronic mail, or e-mail.

By 1981, the ARPANET connected 213 different institutions, with a new one joining the system approximately every three weeks. The term *Internet* was first used to describe this decentralized network in 1982, and in 1986 the National Science Foundation created a network called the NSFNET that created a better organized backbone for the entire system. In this new infrastructure, there were different domains, each marked by a different suffix at the end of an e-mail address, such as "edu" for educational establishments, "com" for commercial enterprises, and "gov" for government offices. With the

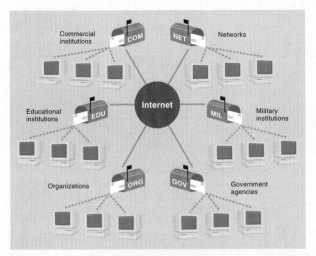

Internet and World Wide Web addresses are organized into domains, each indicated by a different three-letter suffix. Colleges and universities, for example, all use the "edu" designation.

development of the personal computer—IBM released its first PC in 1981—the system continued to grow.

But even with improvements, the Internet remained hard to use. While computer experts could find all kinds of information, others found it difficult to access what they wanted. Then, in 1991, the University of Minnesota developed a system for finding information by accessing a huge number of databases and named it after the university mascot—the golden gopher. Such gopher systems multiplied, until within a few years there were over 10,000 around the world. These provided menus for computer users to select items they wanted to see and made the Internet far more useful for people who had been stymied in the past. The University of Minnesota gopher served as a central clearinghouse to provide access to other gophers.

At about the same time, another development made an even greater impact on Internet use. In 1989, Tim Berners-Lee and others at the European Laboratory for Particle Physics (known as CERN) in Geneva, Switzerland, developed a new system for information distribution. It was based on the concept of hypertext, which involved embedding links to other documents or pieces of information in the text of a document itself. While reading an article or essay on the computer, you could simply move to another document by

The World Wide Web links numerous Web pages together. By clicking the computer mouse on a highlighted item, a user can move easily from one linked page to another.

selecting the appropriate link. This system became the basis for what came to be called the World Wide Web in 1991, and over the next few years it supplanted the gophers as the easiest way to maneuver the masses of information in cyberspace. In 1993, Mark Andreessen and others at the National Center for Superconducting Applications at the University of Illinois at Champaign-Urbana went a step further when they developed what they called Mosaic, which was a graphical Web browser. It was an easy-to-use piece of computer software that allowed you to click your mouse on graphics or icons as well as text in a document to move to another document or Web site. Andreessen and others then formed the Netscape Navigation Corporation, a private company, which marketed the Netscape Navigator to browse the Web. It continues to be widely used today, though it faces challenges from Microsoft's Internet Explorer.

Today, though the ARPANET and the NSFNET have been discontinued, the World Wide Web is more accessible than ever to computer users all over the world. In 1997, according to one estimate, one in six adult Americans regularly used the system, and that number has risen steadily since then. Children use the Web as well, and their ability to obtain pornographic and sexually explicit material has troubled parents and teachers who wish to have more control over what is available to the young. Legal issues remain to be resolved. What kinds of censorship are acceptable on the Web? How can writers, artists, and musicians maintain copyright protection for their work when the materials they produce are frequently instantly accessible on the Web? How can technology improve access to the Web, as telephone lines become choked with Internet traffic? How can we protect systems from "hackers" who use their ingenuity to break into commercial or government computer systems and disrupt the flow of information?

How do you use the Web? What advantages does it provide you in your daily life? How has it helped you at school? What patterns in your own family's existence has it changed? What problems with the Web seem most important to you?

Sources: Linda Ericksen and Emily Kim, *Projects for the Internet* (New York: Addison Wesley Longman, 1998); Walt Howe, "A Brief History of the Internet," available on the World Wide Web at http://wwwo.delphi.com/navnet/faq/history.html.

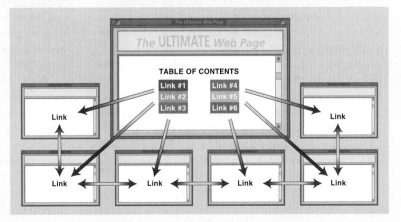

The Fall of Communism

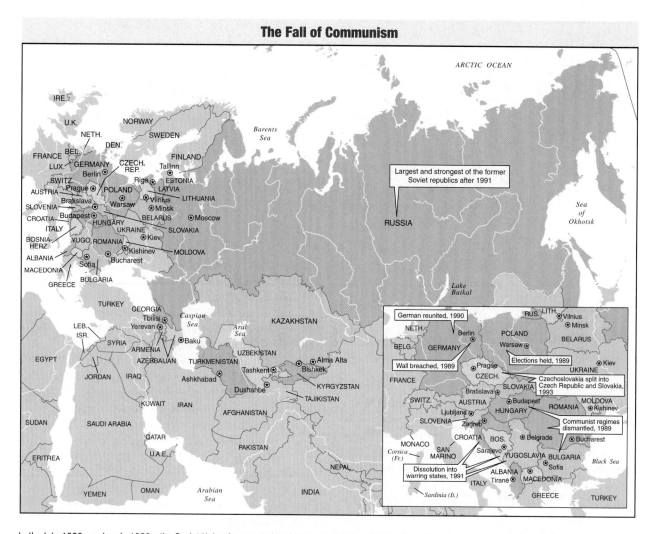

In the late 1980s and early 1990s, the Soviet Union fragmented and lost control of its satellites in eastern Europe. As many countries shown above declared their independence, Czechoslovakia broke into two nations, while Yugoslavia ruptured into a group of feuding states.

and found itself in power, with Walesa as president. Governing, however, sometimes proved more difficult than leading the revolt. The nation faced enormous economic problems, and Americans had to decide just how much help they could afford to give.

In Czechoslovakia, two decades after Soviet tanks had rolled into the streets of Prague to suppress a policy of liberalization, the forces of freedom were victorious. A month after the Berlin Wall dismantlement, playwright Vaclav Havel was elected president. Like Walesa, he sought and received aid from the United States. But not even economic assistance could keep the nation intact, as turbulence led to the creation of separate and independent Czech and Slovak republics. The same forces that culminated in the independence of Czechoslovakia brought new, post-Communist regimes in Bulgaria, Hungary, Romania, and Albania.

Former Yugoslavia proved to be the extreme case of resurgent ethnic hostility in the face of collapsing

central authority. The Balkan region had long been a powder keg—a spark there had set off World War I—and only dictatorship had held the diverse republics together. When two of these states declared their independence in 1991, the fragile nation fell apart. The decision of the Muslim and Croatian majority in Bosnia to secede from Serbian-dominated Yugoslavia led Bosnian Serbs, backed by the Serbian republic, to embark upon a brutal siege of the city of Sarajevo and an even more ruthless "ethnic cleansing" campaign to liquidate opponents in newly independent Bosnia and Herzegovina. In the mid-1990s, ethnic and religious violence worsened. Brutal killing escalated out of control; rape became commonplace; and civilians suffered most from the uncurbed violence. The United States stayed out of the conflict, while the United Nations proved unable to bring about peace. In mid-1995, a NATO bombing campaign forced the Bosnian Serbs into negotiations, and a peace conference held in Dayton, Ohio, led to the commitment of American

The destruction of the Berlin Wall in November 1989 was a symbolic blow to the entire Cold War structure that had grown up in Europe in the postwar years. People grabbed hammers and joined together in tearing down the hated wall. Joyous celebrations marked the reunification of a city that had been divided for decades. *(Alexandria Avakian/ Woodfin Camp & Associates)*

troops, along with soldiers from other countries, to stabilize the region.

In 1999, a smoldering conflict in Kosovo, one of the provinces of Yugoslavia, led to war. In an effort to stop Slobodan Milosevic, the Serbian leader responsible for the devastation of Bosnia, from squelching a movement for autonomy in Kosovo, the North Atlantic Treaty Organization (NATO), now 50 years old, launched an American-led bombing campaign. Milosevic responded with an even more violent "ethnic cleansing" campaign that drove hundreds of thousands of Kosovars from their homes. Even without the introduction of ground troops, this ultimately

successful air assault was the largest allied operation in Europe since World War II.

Steps Toward Peace in the Middle East

Americans were equally involved with events in the Middle East. Here too they were concerned with preserving stability as the Cold War drew to an end. During President Bush's term, the United States went to war in the region. When Saddam Hussein, ruler of Iraq, invaded neighboring Kuwait in August 1990 and annexed the territory, the United States reacted strongly. Saddam seemed intent on unifying Arab nations, thereby threatening

A multinational coalition freed Kuwait after Iraqi leader Saddam Hussein—whose image appears on the signs at the anti-American demonstration in Baghdad— annexed the oil-rich land in 1990. The Persian Gulf War gave George Bush a quick victory, but the long-range results of U.S. involvement were more questionable. *(Chris Morris/Black Star)*

The Gulf War

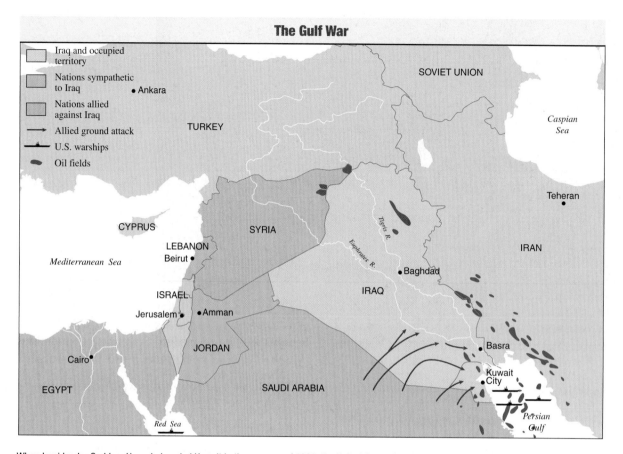

☐	Iraq and occupied territory
◼	Nations sympathetic to Iraq
◼	Nations allied against Iraq
→	Allied ground attack
⚓	U.S. warships
◗	Oil fields

When Iraqi leader Saddam Hussein invaded Kuwait in the summer of 1990, the United States formed a coalition to drive Iraq out. Operation Desert Storm began in early 1991 and routed Iraqi forces, while leaving Kuwait's extensive oil fields in flames.

President Bill Clinton helped orchestrate this famous handshake between Israeli Prime Minister Yitzhak Rabin and Palestine Liberation Organization Chairman Yasir Arafat in 1993. Though the two men had long been adversaries, they now began to work together to settle the bitter conflicts in the Middle East. *(AP/Wide World Photos)*

Israel and dominating the region's production of oil on which the United States relied.

Working through the United Nations, as Truman had done in Korea, the United States persuaded the Security Council to vote unanimously to condemn the attack and impose an embargo on Iraq. In mid-January 1991, a 28-nation coalition struck at Iraq in Operation Desert Storm with a multinational army of nearly half a million troops.

The coalition forces, with their sophisticated missiles, airplanes, and tanks, overwhelmed the Iraqis. Americans were initially enthusiastic about their victory. Then the mood of euphoria in the United States soured as Saddam used his remaining military power against minorities in Iraq. Bush's unwillingness to become bogged down in an Iraqi civil war and his eagerness to return U.S. troops home left the conflict unfinished. A year after his defeat, Saddam was as strongly entrenched as ever.

Meanwhile, the United States was involved in a larger, and ultimately more important, effort to bring peace to the Middle East. In the early 1990s, Secretary of State James Baker finally secured agreement from the major parties in the region to speak to one another face-to-face. Though intense squabbling continued, the discussions themselves were a step forward. A victory in the Israeli parliamentary elections in mid-1992 for Yitzhak Rabin, a soldier who recognized the need for peace and was ready to compromise, offered further hope for the talks.

During his first year in office, Clinton played the part of peacemaker, just as Jimmy Carter had done 15 years before. On September 13, 1993, in a dramatic ceremony on the White House lawn, Palestine Liberation Organization leader Yasir Arafat and Israeli prime minister Rabin signed an agreement that promised the Palestinians a step-by-step progression toward self-rule. In 1995, Israel and the PLO signed a further agreement and the Israelis handed over control of the West Bank of the Jordan River to the Palestinians. A treaty between Jordan and Israel brought peace on still another border. While extremists tried to destroy the peace process by continued violence and assassinated Rabin in a move deplored worldwide, the effort to heal old animosities continued. In 1998, Clinton once again played the role of mediator, this time facilitating an agreement between Arafat and Israeli leader Benjamin Netanyahu that moved the peace process along.

Turbulence in Latin America

The United States intervened frequently in Latin American affairs, as it had in the past, hoping to impose stability in this volatile region. Viewing Central America as a Cold War battlefield, Reagan openly opposed left-wing guerrillas in El Salvador who fought to overthrow a repressive right-wing regime. He was fearful that still another nation might follow the Marxist examples of Cuba and Nicaragua. The United States increased its assistance to the antirevolutionary Salvadoran government, heedless of a similar course followed years before in Vietnam. Efforts to destroy the radical forces failed, despite the expenditure of about $1 million a day. Then in 1989, a far-right faction won Salvadoran elections and polarized the country. As fighting continued, U.S. officials despaired of finding a solution.

Nicaragua became an even bloodier battleground. In 1979, revolutionaries calling themselves Sandinistas (after César Sandino, who fought in the 1920s against U.S. occupation troops) overthrew the repressive Somoza family, which had ruled for three decades. President Carter initially extended aid to the Sandinistas and recognized the new regime, then cut off support to show his disapproval of their curbs on civil liberties and their alleged efforts to assist rebels in El Salvador. Reagan took a far tougher stand. The 1980 Republican platform pledged to replace the Sandinistas with a "free and independent" government. Once in office, Reagan circumvented congressional opposition to his efforts to defeat the revolutionary reformers and signed a National Security directive in November 1981 authorizing the CIA to arm and train counterrevolutionaries, known as *contras*.

The *contras* began to attack from bases outside the country, and Nicaragua became enmeshed in a bitter civil war. When the war went badly for the *contras*, the CIA secretly mined Nicaraguan harbors, violating international law. Upon discovering these secret missions, Congress cut off military aid to the *contras*. Peaceful elections in early 1990 finally drove out the Sandinistas and brought the fighting to an end. Though the economy remained in desperate straits, the new regime seemed to offer the best hope of healing the wounds of the bloody conflict.

Middle Eastern and Central American concerns became entangled in the Iran-*contra* affair. In 1987, Congress learned that the National Security Council had launched an effort to free American hostages in the Middle East by selling arms to Iran and then using the funds to aid the *contras*, in direct violation of both the law and congressional will. The trial of Oliver North, the National Security Council official responsible for the policy, focused on his distortions and falsifications before congressional committees and on his destruction of official documents that could have substantiated charges of wrongdoing by top officials. Convicted in 1989, North received a light sentence requiring no time in prison from a judge who recognized that North was not acting entirely on his own.

Reagan was more successful in maintaining stability on the tiny Caribbean island of Grenada. The

Oliver North, shown here testifying before a congressional committee, flouted the law in the Iran-*contra* affair. Convicted for his cavalier distortions and fabrications, North was not the only one involved in the illegal government program. *(Fred Ward/Black Star)*

president ordered marines there in October 1983, after a military coup installed a government sympathetic to Fidel Castro's Cuba. Concerned about the construction of a large airfield on the island, 2,000 marines invaded the island, rescued a number of American medical students, and claimed triumph. Though the United Nations condemned the incursion, Americans still cheered what the administration called its "rescue mission."

George Bush took credit for a similar incursion in Panama, ostensibly to protect American lives. Invoking memories of past imperialism, the United States invaded Panama, it said, to protect the Panama Canal, defend American citizens following a number of attacks, and stop drug traffic. The campaign resulted in the capture of military leader Manuel Noriega, notorious for his involvement in the drug trade. Noriega was brought to the United States, tried, and, after a lengthy trial, convicted of drug-trafficking charges.

Stabilization efforts enjoyed more success in the mid-1990s, in the aftermath of the Cold War. El Salvador and Nicaragua seemed to emerge from the turbulence of the preceding decade. In Haiti, after seeking for several years to restore deposed president Jean Bertrand Aristide to power, Clinton authorized an invasion of the island. A last-minute visit by an American delegation, including former president Jimmy Carter and former chairman of the Joint Chiefs of Staff Colin Powell, forced Haiti's military dictatorship to relinquish power.

Upheaval in Africa

The United States likewise found itself drawn into turbulent African affairs. In South Africa, the United States supported the long and ultimately successful struggle against apartheid. This policy, whereby the white minority (only 15 percent of the population) segregated, suppressed, and denied basic human rights to the black majority, was part of South African law. While the United States had long expressed its dislike of this ruthless system of segregation, in past years it had refused to go further. Large investments, naval ports, and a reluctance to oppose allies who still controlled African territory tempered U.S. resistance. Then the ferment within the United States, sparked by the civil rights movement and opposition to dictatorships in Central America, brought pressure to take a stronger stand. Over Reagan's objections, in 1986 Congress imposed sanctions, including a rule prohibiting new American investments. The economic pressure damaged the South African economy and persuaded more than half of the 300 American firms in business there to leave.

The final blow to apartheid was dealt by Nelson Mandela, South Africa's leading black activist who had become a symbol of resistance during 27 years in prison. In 1990, Prime Minister Frederik W. De Klerk succumbed to pressure from the United States and the rest of the world. He freed Mandela and announced plans gradually to overturn apartheid. Talks in South Africa between the white government and the African National Congress that Mandela led laid the groundwork for a smooth transition to a biracial democracy. Mandela and De Klerk worked together to ensure peaceful elections in 1994, in which blacks voted for the first time. After years of struggle, the African National Congress assumed power and dismantled the apartheid system. Mandela himself became president of this nation that was building itself anew. American aid provided support in transitional times. When Mandela finally retired at the end of the decade, South Africa remained stable and ready to move ahead.

Elsewhere in Africa, U.S. policymakers had greater difficulty in maintaining the post–Cold War stability they sought. Somalia, in East Africa, suffered from a devastating famine, compounded by the struggles of local warlords that led to almost total disintegration of public order. In 1992, President Bush sent U.S. troops to assist a United Nations effort to provide relief and

Nelson Mandela served as a source of inspiration to black South Africans, as the long struggle against apartheid finally brought that system of rigid segregation to an end and led to the setting up of a biracial democracy with Mandela himself as president. *(AP/Wide World Photos)*

stabilize the country. Six months after Clinton became president, a firefight with one Somali faction resulted in several dozen American casualties. The shooting prompted some Americans, still haunted by the memory of Vietnam, to demand withdrawal. Reluctant to back down as he groped to define his policy, Clinton first increased the number of U.S. troops, then in 1993 recalled the soldiers without having restored order.

The United States was similarly baffled by a crisis in Rwanda, in Central Africa. There a fragile balance of power between two ethnic groups—the Tutsis and the Hutus—broke down. When the Hutu president died in a suspicious plane crash, hard-line Hutus blamed Tutsi rebels and embarked on a massive genocidal campaign that resulted in the slaughter of hundreds of thousands of innocent Tutsis and moderate Hutus. As the world followed the carnage on television, the United States, like many European nations, debated the possibility of intervention on humanitarian grounds but decided to do nothing. Eventually the

Timeline

1980	Ronald Reagan elected president
1980–1982	Recession
1981	Reagan breaks air controllers' strike
	AIDS (acquired immune deficiency syndrome) discovered
1981–1983	Tax cuts; deficit spending increases
1982	U.S. invasion of Lebanon
1983	Reagan proposes Strategic Defense Initiative ("Star Wars")
1984	Reagan reelected
1986	Tax reform measure passed
	Immigration Reform and Control Act
1987	Iran-*contra* affair becomes public
	Stock market crashes
	Intermediate Range Nuclear Forces Treaty signed
1988	George Bush elected president
1989	Federal bailout of savings and loan industry
	Fall of the Berlin Wall
1990	National debt reaches $3.1 trillion
	Immigration Act of 1990
	Sandinistas driven from power in Nicaragua
	Nelson Mandela freed in South Africa
	U.S. population reaches 250 million
1990–1992	Recession
1991	Persian Gulf War

	Failed coup in Soviet Union
	Disintegration of the Soviet Union
	Strategic Arms Reduction Treaty (START) signed
1991–1999	Ethnic turbulence in fragmented former Yugoslavia
1992	Bill Clinton elected president
	Czechoslovakia splits into separate Czech and Slovak Republics
	Riots erupt in Los Angeles
1993	North American Free Trade Agreement (NAFTA) ratified
	Palestine Liberation Organization and Israel sign peace treaty
1994	Nelson Mandela elected president of South Africa
1996	Bill Clinton reelected president
1998	Budget surplus announced
	National debt reaches $5.5 trillion
	Bill Clinton impeached by the House of Representatives
1999	Bill Clinton acquitted by the Senate in an impeachment trial
	Stock market soars as Dow Jones average passes 10,000 and then 11,000
2000	Nation sets record for longest economic expansion in U.S. history
	U.S. weathers Y2K computer glitch at start of new millennium

killing stopped, although the friction between the rival groups remained.

The post–Cold War world remained an unsettled and uncertain place. While the United States was committed to nourishing democracy and protecting its economic interests, Americans remained wary of foreign intervention, even to prevent genocide or massive violations of human rights. They continued to be haunted by the specter of Vietnam, 20 years after the war's end. Yet powerful political, military, and economic interests still required attention, just as they had for the past 50 years, and the United States remained deeply involved in the effort to promote international stability. Despite hopes that money formerly allocated for defense could be used for domestic needs, the military budget remained huge. Even though the Cold War was over, global responsibilities remained.

Conclusion
The Recent Past in Perspective

In the 1980s and 1990s, the United States witnessed the resurgence of conservatism. The assault on the welfare state, dubbed the "Reagan Revolution," created a less regulated economy, whatever the implications for less fortunate Americans. The policies of Ronald Reagan and George Bush continued the trend begun by Richard Nixon in the 1970s. They reshaped the political agenda and reversed the liberal approach that had held sway since the New Deal of Franklin Roosevelt in the 1930s. Bill Clinton's brief effort to revive the liberal welfare state failed to reverse the conservative trend. In foreign affairs, Republican administrations likewise shifted course. Reagan first assumed a steel-ribbed posture toward the Soviet Union, then moved toward détente, and watched as his successor declared victory in the Cold War. When Democrats were in charge, they followed much the same approach. Yet leaders of both parties still had to struggle with resistance to taking an aggressive role abroad, particularly in time of economic distress at home.

To be sure, there were limits to the transformation. Such fundamental programs as Social Security and Medicare remained securely in place, accepted by all but the most implacable splinter groups. Even the most conservative presidents of the past half century could not return to an imagined era of unbridled individualism and puny federal government. On the international front, despite the end of the Cold War, the nation's defense budget remained far higher than many Americans wished, and the nuclear arsenal continued to pose a threat to the human race.

Nor was the transformation beneficial to everyone. Periods of deep recession wrought havoc on the lives of blue-collar and white-collar workers alike. Working-class Americans like Marlene Garrett, introduced at the start of the chapter, often had a hard time even in periods of prosperity. Countless Americans fretted about the growing gaps between rich and poor. They fought with one another, sometimes viciously, over what rules should govern a woman's right to an abortion. For the first time in American history, many children could not hope to do better than their parents had done. Reluctantly they tried to prepare themselves to accept a scaled-down vision of the future.

In the 1980s and 1990s, the United States sought a new stability, at home and abroad. In the process, the nation struggled to adhere to its historic values in a complex and changing world. Despite shifts in policy during the Republican resurgence, those basic values still governed, as the American people continued their centuries-old effort to live up to the promise of the American dream.

Recommended Reading

Historians have not yet had a chance to deal in detail with the developments of the immediate past, so full descriptions must be found in other sources. Much good writing about the years in this chapter appears in the newspapers and magazines of the popular press. But a number of useful treatments about selected topics provide good starting points in various areas.

The Conservative Transformation

General and Statistical Works. Stephanie Coontz, *The Way We Really Are: Coming to Terms with America's Changing Families* (1997); Samuel G. Freedman, *The Inheritance: How Three Families*

and America Moved from Roosevelt to Reagan and Beyond (1996); Susan J. Tolchin, *The Angry American: How Voter Rage Is Changing the Nation*, 2nd ed. (1999); U.S. Bureau of the Census, *Statistical Abstract of the United States: 1994 & 1998;* U.S. Bureau of the Census, *U.S. Census of Population, 1990;* Vincent Virga, *The Eighties: Images of America* (1992); Alan Wolfe, *One Nation, After All: What Middle-Class Americans Really Think About: God, Country, Family, Racism, Welfare, Immigration, Homosexuality, Work, the Right, the Left, and Each Other* (1998).

Religious Developments. David Chidester, *Patterns of Power: Religion and Politics in American Culture* (1988); Yvonne Yazbeck

Haddad and Jane Idleman Smith, *Muslim Communities in North America* (1994); Erling Jorstad, *Holding Fast/Pressing On: Religion in America in the 1980s* (1990); R. Laurence Moore, *Selling God: American Religion in the Marketplace of Culture* (1994); Richard Brent Turner, *Islam in the African American Experience* (1997); Garry Wills, *Under God: Religion and American Politics* (1990).

The Reagan Presidency.   Paul Boyer, ed., *Reagan as President: Contemporary Views of the Man, His Politics, and His Policies* (1990); Lou Cannon, *President Reagan: A Role of a Lifetime* (1991); Ronnie Dugger, *On Reagan: The Man and His Presidency* (1983); Fred I. Greenstein, ed., *The Reagan Presidency: An Early Assessment* (1983); Godfrey Hodgson, *The World Turned Right Side Up: A History of the Conservative Ascendancy in America* (1997); Haynes Johnson, *Sleepwalking Through History: America Through the Reagan Years* (1991); William E. Pemberton, *Exit with Honor: The Life and Presidency of Ronald Reagan* (1998); Garry Wills, *Reagan's America: Innocents at Home* (1985).

The Bush Presidency.   Colin Campbell, S.J., and Bert A. Rockman, eds., *The Bush Presidency: First Appraisals* (1991); Herbert S. Parmet, *George Bush: The Life of a Lone Star Yankee* (1997).

The Clinton Presidency.   Christopher Hitchens, *No One Left to Lie To: The Triangulations of William Jefferson Clinton* (1999); David Maraniss, *First in His Class: A Biography of Bill Clinton* (1995); George Stephanopoulos, *All Too Human: A Political Education* (1999).

An End to Social Reform

Rodolfo Acuña, *Occupied America: A History of Chicanos*, 4th ed. (2000) and *Sometimes There Is No Other Side: Chicanos and the Myth of Equality* (1998); Stephen Cornell, *The Return of the Native: American Indian Political Resurgence* (1988); Susan Faludi, *Backlash: The Undeclared War Against American Women* (1991); John Hope Franklin and Alfred A. Moss, Jr., *From Slavery to Freedom: A History of African Americans*, 7th ed. (1994); David G. Gutiérrez, *Walls and Mirrors: Mexican Americans, Mexican Immigrants, and the Politics of Identity* (1995); Jacqueline Jones, *Labor of Love, Labor of Sorrow: Black Women, Work, and the Family from Slavery to the Present* (1985); Peter Skerry, *Mexican Americans: The Ambivalent Minority* (1993); Studs Terkel, *Race: How Blacks and Whites Think and Feel About the American Obsession* (1992); Stephan Thernstrom and Abigail Thernstrom, *America in Black and White: One Nation, Indivisible* (1997); David Hurst Thomas, Jay Miller, Richard White, Peter Nabokov, Philip J. Deloria, *The Native Americans: An Illustrated History* (1993).

The Postindustrial Economy

Work and Industrial Life.   William Bamberger and Cathy N. Davidson, *Closing: The Life and Death of an American Factory* (1998); Kathryn Marie Dudley, *The End of the Line: Lost Jobs, New Lives in Postindustrial America* (1994); Arlie Russell Hochschild, *The Time Bind: When Work Becomes Home and Home Becomes Work* (1997); Christopher Jencks, *The Homeless* (1994); Jacqueline Jones, *American Work: Four Centuries of Black and White Labor* (1998) and *The Dispossessed: America's Underclasses from the Civil War to the Present* (1992); Michael B. Katz, *The Undeserving Poor: From the War on Poverty to the War on Welfare* (1990); Katherine S. Newman, *Falling from Grace: The Experience of Downward Mobility in the American Middle Class* (1988); James T. Patterson, *America's Struggle Against Poverty: 1900–1994* (1995); Kevin P. Phillips, *The Politics of Rich and Poor: Wealth and the American Electorate in the Reagan Aftermath* (1990); Juliet B. Schor, *The Overworked American: The Unexpected Decline of Leisure* (1991);

John C. Teaford, *Cities of the Heartland: The Rise and Fall of the Industrial Midwest* (1993); William Julius Wilson, *When Work Disappears: The World of the New Urban Poor* (1996).

Unionization.   Richard B. Freeman and James L. Medoff, *What Do Unions Do?* (1984); Arthur B. Shostak, *Robust Unionism: Innovations in the Labor Movement* (1991).

Demographic and Regional Change

The West.   Carl Abbott, *The Metropolitan Frontier: Cities in the Modern American West* (1993); Timothy Egan, *Lasso the Wind: Away to the New West* (1998); John M. Findlay, *Magic Lands: Western Cityscapes and American Culture After 1940* (1992); William G. Robbins, *Colony and Empire: The Capitalist Transformation of the American West* (1994); Richard White, *"It's Your Misfortune and None of My Own": A New History of the American West* (1991).

Immigration.   Roger Daniels, *Coming to America: A History of Immigration and Ethnicity in American Life* (1990); Alejandro Portes and Rubén G. Rumbaut, *Immigrant America: A Portrait*, 2nd ed. (1996); David M. Reimers, *Still the Golden Door: The Third World Comes to America* (1985); Paul James Rutledge, *The Vietnamese Experience in America* (1992); Al Santoli, *New Americans: An Oral History: Immigrants and Refugees in the U.S. Today* (1988); Ronald Takaki, *A Different Mirror: A History of Multicultural America* (1993) and *A Larger Memory: A History of Our Diversity, With Voices* (1998); Reed Ueda, *Postwar Immigrant America: A Social History* (1994); Roger Waldinger and Mehdi Bozorgmehr, eds., *Ethnic Los Angeles* (1996).

The United States in a Changed World

George Bush and Brent Scowcroft, *A World Transformed* (1998); Paul Kennedy, *The Rise and Fall of the Great Powers: Economic Change and Military Conflict from 1500 to 2000* (1987); Walter LaFeber, *America, Russia, and the Cold War, 1945–1992*, 7th ed. (1993) and *Inevitable Revolutions: The United States in Central America* (1983); Robert Scheer, *With Enough Shovels: Reagan, Bush & Nuclear War* (1982); Laura Silber and Alan Little, *Yugoslavia: Death of a Nation* (1996); Ronald Steel, *Temptations of a Superpower* (1995); Strobe Talbott, *The Russians and Reagan* (1984).

Fiction and Film

Sherman Alexie's *The Lone Ranger and Tonto Fistfight in Heaven* (1993) is a collection of stories about contemporary Indian life. Julia Alvarez's *How the Garcia Girls Lost Their Accents* (1992) is the fictional account of four young women from the Dominican Republic and their transition to American life. Alice Mattison's *Men Giving Money, Women Yelling* (1997) is a series of intersecting stories about the complexities of people's lives and relationships. Lorrie Moore's *Birds of America: Stories* is another collection of stories about modern culture and life, including one about a nuclear family involved in a meltdown (1998). Tom Wolfe's *The Bonfire of the Vanities* (1987) is a novel about the arrogance of the upper class in New York—the masters of the universe—and the consequences suffered by people who assume they can do no wrong when an accident occurs.

Philadelphia (1993) is a movie about a lawyer who contracts AIDS. *When Harry Met Sally* (1989) is a film about the difficulties of relationships between men and women. *Thelma and Louise* (1994) is a movie about two women taking their lives into their own hands and traveling across the country together. *American Beauty* (1999) is a corrosive film about the problems of life in the affluent suburbs.

Suggested Web Sites

http://www.ipl.org/ref/POTUS/rwreagan.html

Ronald Wilson Reagan. This site contains basic factual data about Reagan's election and presidency, speeches, and on-line biographies.

http://www.ipl.org/ref/POTUS/ghwbush.html

George Herbert Walker Bush. This site contains basic factual data about Bush's election and presidency, speeches, and on-line biographies.

http://www.ipl.org/ref/POTUS/wjclinton.html

William Jefferson Clinton. This site contains basic factual data about Clinton's election and presidency, speeches and on-line biographies.

http://www.cnn.com/ALLPOLITICS/resources/1998/ lewinsky/

Investigating the President: The Trial. This site from CNN provides information and documents about the scandals surrounding President Clinton and his impeachment.

http://www.pbs.org/pages/frontline/gulf/index.html

The Gulf War. This PBS site combines personal accounts with a chronology and general information about the war.

http://www.umi.com/hp/Support/K12/GreatEvents/

Resources for Schools: Great Events Study Guides. This site provides descriptions of a number of important events, such as the Iran-*contra* hearings in the late 1980s and the fall of Communism in Eastern Europe at the end of the 1980s and start of the 1990s.

http://www.policy.com/reports/dojvsms/

Special Report: U.S. *v.* Microsoft. This site provides background information and documents on the antitrust case unfolding as this book went to press.

http://www.ushistoryplace.com

A richly detailed on-line learning environment complete with interactive maps, timelines, history activities, primary source documents, and links to related American history sites.

Appendix

THE DECLARATION OF INDEPENDENCE IN CONGRESS, JULY 4, 1776

The Unanimous Declaration of the Thirteen United States of America

When, in the course of human events, it becomes necessary for one people to dissolve the political bonds which have connected them with another, and to assume, among the powers of the earth, the separate and equal station to which the laws of nature and of nature's God entitle them, a decent respect to the opinions of mankind requires that they should declare the causes which impel them to the separation.

We hold these truths to be self-evident: That all men are created equal; that they are endowed by their Creator with certain unalienable rights; that among these are life, liberty, and the pursuit of happiness; that, to secure these rights, governments are instituted among men, deriving their just powers from the consent of the governed; that whenever any form of government becomes destructive of these ends, it is the right of the people to alter or to abolish it, and to institute new government, laying its foundation on such principles, and organizing its powers in such form, as to them shall seem most likely to effect their safety and happiness. Prudence, indeed, will dictate that governments long established should not be changed for light and transient causes; and accordingly all experience hath shown that mankind are more disposed to suffer, while evils are sufferable, than to right themselves by abolishing the forms to which they are accustomed. But when a long train of abuses and usurpations, pursuing invariably the same object, evinces a design to reduce them under absolute despotism, it is their right, it is their duty, to throw off such government, and to provide new guards for their future security. Such has been the patient sufferance of these colonies; and such is now the necessity which constrains them to alter their former systems of government. The history of the present King of Great Britain is a history of repeated injuries and usurpations, all having in direct object the establishment of an absolute tyranny over these states. To prove this, let facts be submitted to a candid world.

He has refused his assent to laws, the most wholesome and necessary for the public good.

He has forbidden his governors to pass laws of immediate and pressing importance, unless suspended in their operation till his assent should be obtained; and, when so suspended, he has utterly neglected to attend to them.

He has refused to pass other laws for the accommodation of large districts of people, unless those people would relinquish the right of representation in the legislature, a right inestimable to them, and formidable to tyrants only.

He has called together legislative bodies at places unusual, uncomfortable, and distant from the depository of their public records, for the sole purpose of fatiguing them into compliance with his measures.

He has dissolved representative houses repeatedly, for opposing, with manly firmness, his invasions on the rights of the people.

He has refused for a long time, after such dissolutions, to cause others to be elected; whereby the legislative powers, incapable of annihilation, have returned to the people at large for their exercise; the state remaining, in the mean time, exposed to all the dangers of invasions from without and convulsions within.

He has endeavored to prevent the population of these states; for that purpose obstructing the laws for naturalization of foreigners; refusing to pass others to encourage their migration hither, and raising the conditions of new appropriations of lands.

He has obstructed the administration of justice, by refusing his assent to laws for establishing judiciary powers.

He has made judges dependent on his will alone, for the tenure of their offices, and the amount and payment of their salaries.

He has erected a multitude of new offices, and sent hither swarms of officers to harass our people and eat out their substance.

He has kept among us, in times of peace, standing armies, without the consent of our legislatures.

He has affected to render the military independent of, and superior to, the civil power.

He has combined with others to subject us to a jurisdiction foreign to our constitution, and unacknowledged by our laws, giving his assent to their acts of pretended legislation:

For quartering large bodies of armed troops among us;

For protecting them, by a mock trial, from punishment for any murder which they should commit on the inhabitants of these states;

For cutting off our trade with all parts of the world;

For imposing taxes on us without our consent;

For depriving us, in many cases, of the benefits of trial by jury;

For transporting us beyond seas, to be tried for pretended offenses;

For abolishing the free system of English laws in a neighboring province, establishing therein an arbitrary government, and enlarging its boundaries, so as to render it at once an example and fit instrument for introducing the same absolute rule into these colonies;

For taking away our charters abolishing our most valuable laws, and altering fundamentally the forms of our governments;

For suspending our own legislatures, and declaring themselves invested with power to legislate for us in all cases whatsoever.

He has abdicated government here, by declaring us out of his protection and waging war against us.

He has plundered our seas, ravaged our coasts, burned our towns, and destroyed the lives of our people.

He is at this time transporting large armies of foreign mercenaries to complete the works of death, desolation, and tyranny already begun with circumstances of cruelty and perfidy scarcely paralleled in the most barbarous ages, and totally unworthy the head of a civilized nation.

He has constrained our fellow-citizens, taken captive on the high seas, to bear arms against their country, to become the executioners of their friends and brethren, or to fall themselves by their hands.

He has excited domestic insurrection among us, and has endeavored to bring on the inhabitants of our frontiers the merciless Indian savages, whose known rule of warfare is an undistinguished destruction of all ages, sexes, and conditions.

In every stage of these oppressions we have petitioned for redress in the most humble terms; our repeated petitions have been answered only by repeated injury. A prince, whose character is thus marked by every act which may define a tyrant, is unfit to be the ruler of a free people.

Nor have we been wanting in our attentions to our British brethren. We have warned them, from time to time, of attempts by their legislature to extend an unwarrantable jurisdiction over us. We have reminded them of the circumstances of our emigration and settlement here. We have appealed to their native justice and magnanimity; and we have conjured them, by the ties of our common kindred, to disavow these usurpations, which would inevitably interrupt our connections and correspondence. They, too, have been deaf to the voice of justice and of consanguinity. We must, therefore, acquiesce in the necessity which denounces our separation, and hold them, as we hold the rest of mankind, enemies in war, in peace friends.

We, therefore, the representatives of the United States of America, in General Congress assembled, appealing to the Supreme Judge of the world for the rectitude of our intentions, do, in the name and by the authority of the good people of these colonies, solemnly publish and declare, that these United Colonies are, and of right, ought to be, FREE AND INDEPENDENT STATES; that they are absolved from all allegiance to the British crown, and that all political connection between them and the state of Great Britain is, and ought to be, totally dissolved; and that, as free and independent states, they have full power to levy war, conclude peace, contract alliances, establish commerce, and do all other acts and things which independent states may of right do. And for the support of this declaration, with a firm reliance on the protection of Devine Providence, we mutually pledge to each other our lives, our fortunes, and our sacred honor.

JOHN HANCOCK

BUTTON GWENNETT	THS. NELSON, JR.	RICHD. STOCKTON
LYMAN HALL	FRANCIS LIGHTFOOT LEE	JNO. WITHERSPOON
GEO. WALTON	CARTER BRAXTON	FRAS. HOPKINSON
WM. HOOPER	ROBT. MORRIS	JOHN HART
JOSEPH HEWES	BENJAMIN RUSH	ABRA. CLARK
JOHN PENN	BENJA. FRANKLIN	JOSIAH BARTLETT
EDWARD RUTLEDGE	JOHN MORTON	WM. WHIPPLE
THOS. HEYWARD, JUNR.	GEO. CLYMER	SAML. ADAMS
THOMAS LYNCH, JUNR.	JAS. SMITH	JOHN ADAMS
ARTHUR MIDDLETON	GEO. TAYLOR	ROBT. TREAT PAINE
SAMUEL CHASE	JAMES WILSON	ELBRIDGE GERRY
WM. PACA	GEO. ROSS	STEP. HOPKINS
THOS. STONE	CAESAR RODNEY	WILLIAM ELLERY
CHARLES CARROLL OF CARROLLTON	GEO. READ	ROGER SHERMAN
GEORGE WYTHE	THO. MíKEAN	SAMíEL. HUNTINGTON
RICHARD HENRY LEE	WM. FLOYD	WM. WILLIAMS
TH. JEFFERSON	PHIL. LIVINGSTON	OLIVER WOLCOTT
BENJA. HARRISON	FRANS. LEWIS	MATHEW THORNTON
	LEWIS MORRIS	

THE CONSTITUTION OF THE UNITED STATES OF AMERICA*

PREAMBLE

We the People of the United States, in Order to form a more perfect Union, establish Justice, insure domestic Tranquility, provide for the common defence, promote the general Welfare, and secure the Blessings of Liberty to ourselves and our Posterity, do ordain and establish this Constitution for the United States of America.

ARTICLE I.

Section 1   All legislative Powers herein granted shall be vested in a Congress of the United States, which shall consist of a Senate and House of Representatives.

Section 2   The House of Representatives shall be composed of Members chosen every second Year by the People of the several States, and the Electors in each State shall have the Qualifications requisite for Electors of the most numerous Branch of the State Legislature.

No Person shall be a Representative who shall not have attained to the Age of twenty five Years, and been seven Years a Citizen of the United States, and who shall not, when elected, be an Inhabitant of that State in which he shall be chosen.

Representatives and direct Taxes shall be apportioned among the several States which may be included within this Union, according to their respective Numbers, *which shall be determined by adding to the whole Number of free Persons, including those bound to Service for a Term of Years, and excluding Indians not taxed, three fifths of all other Persons.* The actual Enumeration shall be made within three Years after the first Meeting of the Congress of the United States, and within every subsequent Term of ten Years, in such Manner as they shall by Law direct. The Number of Representatives shall not exceed one for every thirty Thousand, but each State shall have at Least one Representative; *and until such enumeration shall be made, the State of New Hampshire shall be entitled to chuse three, Massachusetts eight, Rhode-Island and Providence Plantations one, Connecticut five, New-York six, New Jersey four, Pennsylvania eight, Delaware one, Maryland six, Virginia ten, North Carolina five, South Carolina five, and Georgia three.*

When vacancies happen in the Representation from any State, the Executive Authority thereof shall issue Writs of Election to fill such Vacancies.

The House of Representatives shall chuse their Speaker and other Officers; and shall have the sole Power of Impeachment.

Section 3   The Senate of the United States shall be composed of two Senators from each State, chosen by the Legislature thereof, for six Years; and each Senator shall have one Vote.

Immediately after they shall be assembled in Consequence of the first Election, they shall be divided as equally as may be into three Classes. The Seats of the Senators of the first Class shall be vacated at the Expiration of the second Year, of the second Class at the Expiration of the fourth Year, and of the third Class at the Expiration of the sixth Year, so that one third may be chosen every second Year; and if Vacancies happen by Resignation, or otherwise, during the Recess of the Legislature of any State, the Executive thereof may make temporary Appointments until the next Meeting of the Legislature, which shall then fill such Vacancies.

No Person shall be a Senator who shall not have attained to the Age of thirty Years, and been nine Years a Citizen of the United States, and who shall not, when elected, be an Inhabitant of that State for which he shall be chosen.

The Vice President of the United States shall be President of the Senate, but shall have no Vote, unless they be equally divided.

The Senate shall choose their other Officers, and also a President *pro tempore,* in the Absence of the Vice President, or when he shall exercise the Office of President of the United States.

The Senate shall have the sole Power to try all Impeachments. When sitting for that Purpose, they shall be on Oath or Affirmation. When the President of the United States is tried the Chief Justice shall preside: And no Person shall be convicted without the Concurrence of two thirds of the Members present.

Judgment in Cases of Impeachment shall not extend further than to removal from Office, and disqualification to hold and enjoy any Office of honor, Trust or Profit under the United States: but the Party convicted shall nevertheless be liable and subject to Indictment, Trial, Judgment and Punishment, according to Law.

Section 4   The Times, Places and Manner of holding Elections for Senators and Representatives, shall be prescribed in each State by the Legislature thereof; but the Congress may at any time by Law make or alter such Regulations, except as to the Places of chusing Senators.

The Congress shall assemble at least once in every Year, and such Meeting *shall be on the first Monday in December, unless they shall by Law appoint a different Day.*

Section 5   Each House shall be the Judge of the Elections, Returns and Qualifications of its own Members, and a Majority of each shall constitute a Quorum to do Business; but a smaller Number may adjourn from day to day, and may be authorized to compel the Attendance of absent Members, in such Manner, and under such Penalties as each House may provide.

Each House may determine the Rules of its Proceedings, punish its Members for disorderly Behaviour, and, with the Concurrence of two thirds, expel a Member.

Each House shall keep a Journal of its Proceedings, and from time to time publish the same, excepting such Parts as may in their Judgment require Secrecy; and the Yeas and Nays of the Members of either House on any question shall, at the Desire of one fifth of those Present, be entered on the Journal.

Neither House, during the Session of Congress, shall, without the Consent of the other, adjourn for more than

---

*The Constitution became effective March 4, 1789. Any portion of the text that has been amended is printed in italics.

three days, nor to any other Place than that in which the two Houses shall be sitting.

Section 6   The Senators and Representatives shall receive a Compensation for their Services, to be ascertained by Law, and paid out of the Treasury of the United States. They shall in all Cases, except Treason, Felony and Breach of the Peace, be privileged from Arrest during their Attendance at the Session of their respective Houses, and in going to and returning from the same; and for any Speech or Debate in either House, they shall not be questioned in any other Place.

No Senator or Representative shall, during the Time for which he was elected, be appointed to any civil Office under the Authority of the United States, which shall have been created, or the Emoluments whereof shall have been encreased during such time; and no Person holding any Office under the United States, shall be a Member of either House during his Continuance in Office.

Section 7   All Bills for raising Revenue shall originate in the House of Representatives; but the Senate may propose or concur with Amendments as on other Bills.

Every Bill which shall have passed the House of Representatives and the Senate, shall, before it become a Law, be presented to the President of the United States; If he approve he shall sign it, but if not he shall return it, with his Objections to that House in which it shall have originated, who shall enter the Objections at large on their Journal, and proceed to reconsider it. If after such Reconsideration two thirds of that House shall agree to pass the Bill, it shall be sent, together with the Objections, to the other House, by which it shall likewise be reconsidered, and if approved by two thirds of that House, it shall become a Law. But in all such Cases the Votes of both Houses shall be determined by yeas and Nays, and the Names of the Persons voting for and against the Bill shall be entered on the Journal of each House respectively. If any Bill shall not be returned by the President within ten Days (Sundays excepted) after it shall have been presented to him, the Same shall be a Law, in like Manner as if he had signed it, unless the Congress by their Adjournment prevent its Return, in which Case it shall not be a Law.

Every Order, Resolution, or Vote to which the Concurrence of the Senate and House of Representatives may be necessary (except on a question of Adjournment) shall be presented to the President of the United States; and before the Same shall take Effect, shall be approved by him, or being disapproved by him, shall be repassed by two thirds of the Senate and House of Representatives, according to the Rules and Limitations prescribed in the Case of a Bill.

Section 8   The Congress shall have Power:

To lay and collect Taxes, Duties, Imposts and Excises, to pay the Debts and provide for the common Defence and general Welfare of the United States; but all Duties, Imposts and Excises shall be uniform throughout the United States;

To borrow Money on the credit of the United States;

To regulate Commerce with foreign Nations, and among the several States, and with the Indian Tribes;

To establish an uniform Rule of Naturalization, and uniform Laws on the subject of Bankruptcies throughout the United States;

To coin Money, regulate the Value thereof, and of foreign Coin, and fix the Standard of Weights and Measures;

To provide for the Punishment of counterfeiting the Securities and current Coin of the United States;

To establish Post Offices and post Roads;

To promote the Progress of Science and useful Arts, by securing for limited Times to Authors and Inventors the exclusive Right to their respective Writings and Discoveries;

To constitute Tribunals inferior to the supreme Court;

To define and punish Piracies and Felonies committed on the high Seas, and Offences against the Law of Nations;

To declare War, grant Letters of Marque and Reprisal, and make Rules concerning Captures on Land and Water;

To raise and support Armies, but no Appropriation of Money to that Use shall be for a longer Term than two Years;

To provide and maintain a Navy;

To make Rules for the Government and Regulation of the land and naval Forces;

To provide for calling forth the Militia to execute the Laws of the Union, suppress Insurrections and repel Invasions;

To provide for organizing, arming, and disciplining, the Militia, and for governing such Part of them as may be employed in the Service of the United States, reserving to the States respectively, the Appointment of the Officers, and the Authority of training the Militia according to the discipline prescribed by Congress;

To exercise exclusive Legislation in all Cases whatsoever, over such District (not exceeding ten Miles square) as may, by Cession of particular States, and the Acceptance of Congress, become the Seat of the Government of the United States, and to exercise like Authority over all Places purchased by the Consent of the Legislature of the State in which the Same shall be, for the Erection of Forts, Magazines, Arsenals, dock-Yards, and other needful Buildings;-And

To make all Laws which shall be necessary and proper for carrying into Execution the foregoing Powers, and all other Powers vested by this Constitution in the Government of the United States, or in any Department or Officer thereof.

Section 9   *The Migration or Importation of such Persons as any of the States now existing shall think proper to admit, shall not be prohibited by the Congress prior to the Year one thousand eight hundred and eight, but a Tax or duty may be imposed on such Importation, not exceeding ten dollars for each Person.*

The Privilege of the Writ of Habeas Corpus shall not be suspended, unless when in Cases of Rebellion or Invasion the public Safety may require it.

No Bill of Attainder or ex post facto Law shall be passed.

No Capitation, or other direct, Tax shall be laid, unless in Proportion to the Census or Enumeration herein before directed to be taken.

No Tax or Duty shall be laid on Articles exported from any State.

No Preference shall be given by any Regulation of Commerce or Revenue to the Ports of one State over those of another: nor shall Vessels bound to, or from, one State, be obliged to enter, clear, or pay Duties in another.

No Money shall be drawn from the Treasury, but in Consequence of Appropriations made by Law; and a regular Statement and Account of the Receipts and Expenditures of all public Money shall be published from time to time.

No Title of Nobility shall be granted by the United States: And no Person holding any Office of Profit or Trust under them, shall, without the Consent of the Congress, accept of any present, Emolument, Office, or Title, of any kind whatever, from any King, Prince, or foreign State.

Section 10   No State shall enter into any Treaty, Alliance, or Confederation; grant Letters of Marque and Reprisal; coin Money; emit Bills of Credit; make any Thing but gold and silver Coin a Tender in Payment of Debts; pass any Bill of Attainder, ex post facto Law, or Law impairing the Obligation of Contracts, or grant any Title of Nobility.

No State shall, without the Consent of the Congress, lay any Imposts or Duties on Imports or Exports, except what may be absolutely necessary for executing it's inspection Laws: and the net Produce of all Duties and Imposts, laid by any State on Imports or Exports, shall be for the Use of the Treasury of the United States; and all such Laws shall be subject to the Revision and Controul of the Congress.

No State shall, without the Consent of Congress, lay any Duty of Tonnage, keep Troops, or Ships of War in time of Peace, enter into any Agreement or Compact with another State, or with a foreign Power, or engage in War, unless actually invaded, or in such imminent Danger as will not admit of delay.

ARTICLE II.

Section 1   The executive Power shall be vested in a President of the United States of America. He shall hold his Office during the Term of four Years, and, together with the Vice President, chosen for the same Term, be elected, as follows

Each State shall appoint, in such Manner as the Legislature thereof may direct, a Number of Electors, equal to the whole Number of Senators and Representatives to which the State may be entitled in the Congress: but no Senator or Representative, or Person holding an Office of Trust or Profit under the United States, shall be appointed an Elector.

The Electors shall meet in their respective States, and vote by Ballot for two Persons, of whom one at least shall not be an Inhabitant of the same State with themselves. And they shall make a List of all the Persons voted for, and of the Number of Votes for each; which List they shall sign and certify, and transmit sealed to the Seat of Government of the United States, directed to the President of the Senate. The President of the Senate shall, in the Presence of the Senate and House of Representatives, open all the Certificates, and the Votes shall then be counted. The Person having the greatest Number of Votes shall be the President, if such Number be a Majority of the whole Number of Electors appointed; and if there be more than one who have such Majority, and have an equal Number of Votes, then the House of Representatives shall immediately chuse by Ballot one of

them for President; and if no Person have a Majority, then from the five highest on the List the said House shall in like Manner chuse the President. But in chusing the President, the Votes shall be taken by States, the Representation from each State having one Vote; A quorum for this Purpose shall consist of a Member or Members from two thirds of the States, and a Majority of all the States shall be necessary to a Choice. In every Case, after the Choice of the President, the Person having the greatest Number of Votes of the Electors shall be the Vice President. But if there should remain two or more who have equal Votes, the Senate shall chuse from them by Ballot the Vice President. The Congress may determine the Time of chusing the Electors, and the Day on which they shall give their Votes; which Day shall be the same throughout the United States.

No Person except a natural born Citizen, *or a Citizen of the United States, at the time of the Adoption of this Constitution,* shall be eligible to the Office of President; neither shall any Person be eligible to that Office who shall not have attained to the Age of thirty five Years, and been fourteen Years a Resident within the United States.

In Case of the Removal of the President from Office, or of his Death, Resignation, or Inability to discharge the Powers and Duties of the said Office, the Same shall devolve on the Vice President, and the Congress may by Law provide for the Case of Removal, Death, Resignation or Inability, both of the President and Vice President declaring what Officer shall then act as President, and such Officer shall act accordingly, until the Disability be removed, or a President shall be elected.

The President shall, at stated Times, receive for his Services, a Compensation, which shall neither be encreased nor diminished during the Period for which he shall have been elected, and he shall not receive within that Period any other Emolument from the United States, or any of them.

Before he enter on the Execution of his Office, he shall take the following Oath or Affirmation: "I do solemnly swear (or affirm) that I will faithfully execute the Office of President of the United States, and will to the best of my Ability, preserve, protect and defend the Constitution of the United States."

Section 2   The President shall be Commander in Chief of the Army and Navy of the United States, and of the Militia of the several States, when called into the actual Service of the United States; he may require the Opinion, in writing, of the principal Officer in each of the executive Departments, upon any Subject relating to the Duties of their respective Offices, and he shall have Power to grant Reprieves and Pardons for Offences against the United States, except in Cases of Impeachment.

He shall have Power, by and with the Advice and Consent of the Senate, to make Treaties, provided two thirds of the Senators present concur; and he shall nominate, and by and with the Advice and Consent of the Senate, shall appoint Ambassadors, other public Ministers and Consuls, Judges of the supreme Court, and all other Officers of the United States, whose Appointments are not herein otherwise provided for, and which shall be established by Law: but the Congress may by Law vest the Appointment of such inferior

Officers, as they think proper, in the President alone, in the Courts of Law, or in the Heads of Departments.

The President shall have Power to fill up all Vacancies that may happen during the Recess of the Senate, by granting Commissions which shall expire at the End of their next Session.

Section 3 He shall from time to time give to the Congress Information of the State of the Union, and recommend to their Consideration such Measures as he shall judge necessary and expedient; he may, on extraordinary Occasions, convene both Houses, or either of them, and in Case of Disagreement between them, with Respect to the Time of Adjournment, he may adjourn them to such Time as he shall think proper; he shall receive Ambassadors and other public Ministers; he shall take Care that the Laws be faithfully executed, and shall Commission all the Officers of the United States.

Section 4 The President, Vice President and all civil Officers of the United States, shall be removed from Office on Impeachment for, and Conviction of, Treason, Bribery, or other high Crimes and Misdemeanors.

ARTICLE III.

Section 1 The judicial Power of the United States, shall be vested in one supreme Court, and in such inferior Courts as the Congress may from time to time ordain and establish. The Judges, both of the supreme and inferior Courts, shall hold their Offices during good Behaviour, and shall, at stated Times, receive for their Services, a Compensation which shall not be diminished during their Continuance in Office.

Section 2 The judicial Power shall extend to all Cases, in Law and Equity, arising under this Constitution, the Laws of the United States, and Treaties made, or which shall be made, under their Authority;—to all Cases affecting Ambassadors, other public Ministers and Consuls;—to all Cases of admiralty and maritime Jurisdiction;—to Controversies to which the United States shall be a Party;—to Controversies between two or more States;—*between a State and Citizens of another State;*—between Citizens of different States;—between Citizens of the same State claiming Lands under Grants of different States, and between a State, or the Citizens thereof, and foreign States, Citizens or Subjects.

In all Cases affecting Ambassadors, other public Ministers and Consuls, and those in which a State shall be Party, the supreme Court shall have original Jurisdiction. In all the other Cases before mentioned, the supreme Court shall have appellate Jurisdiction, both as to Law and Fact, with such Exceptions, and under such Regulations as the Congress shall make.

The Trial of all Crimes, except in Cases of Impeachment, shall be by Jury; and such Trial shall be held in the State where the said Crimes shall have been committed; but when not committed within any State, the Trial shall be at such Place or Places as the Congress may by Law have directed.

Section 3 Treason against the United States, shall consist only in levying War against them, or in adhering to their Enemies, giving them Aid and Comfort. No Person shall be convicted of Treason unless on the Testimony of two Witnesses to the same overt Act, or on Confession in open Court.

The Congress shall have Power to declare the Punishment of Treason, but no Attainder of Treason shall work Corruption of Blood, or Forfeiture except during the Life of the Person attainted.

ARTICLE IV.

Section 1 Full Faith and Credit shall be given in each State to the public Acts, Records, and judicial Proceedings of every other State. And the Congress may by general Laws prescribe the Manner in which such Acts, Records and Proceedings shall be proved, and the Effect thereof.

Section 2 The Citizens of each State shall be entitled to all Privileges and Immunities of Citizens in the several States.

A Person charged in any State with Treason, Felony, or other Crime, who shall flee from Justice, and be found in another State, shall on Demand of the executive Authority of the State from which he fled, be delivered up, to be removed to the State having Jurisdiction of the Crime.

No Person held to Service or Labour in one State, under the Laws thereof, escaping into another, shall, in Consequence of any Law or Regulation therein, be discharged from such Service or Labour, but shall be delivered up on Claim of the Party to whom such Service or Labour may be due.

Section 3 New States may be admitted by the Congress into this Union; but no new State shall be formed or erected within the Jurisdiction of any other State; nor any State be formed by the Junction of two or more States, or Parts of States, without the Consent of the Legislatures of the States concerned as well as of the Congress.

The Congress shall have Power to dispose of and make all needful Rules and Regulations respecting the Territory or other Property belonging to the United States; and nothing in this Constitution shall be so construed as to Prejudice any Claims of the United States, or of any particular State.

Section 4 The United States shall guarantee to every State in this Union a Republican Form of Government, and shall protect each of them against Invasion; and on Application of the Legislature, or of the Executive (when the Legislature cannot be convened) against domestic Violence.

ARTICLE V.

The Congress, whenever two thirds of both Houses shall deem it necessary, shall propose Amendments to this Constitution, or, on the Application of the Legislatures of two thirds of the several States, shall call a Convention for proposing Amendments, which, in either Case, shall be valid to all Intents and Purposes, as Part of this Constitution, when ratified by the Legislatures of three fourths of the several States, or by Conventions in three fourths thereof, as the one or the other Mode of Ratification may be proposed by the Congress; Provided *that no Amendment which may be made prior to the Year One thousand eight hundred and eight shall in any Manner affect the first and fourth Clauses in the Ninth Section of the first Article; and* that no State, without its Consent, shall be deprived of its equal Suffrage in the Senate.

ARTICLE VI.

All Debts contracted and Engagements entered into, before the Adoption of this Constitution, shall be as valid against the United States under this Constitution, as under the Confederation.

This Constitution, and the Laws of the United States which shall be made in Pursuance thereof; and all Treaties made or which shall be made, under the Authority of the United States, shall be the supreme Law of the Land; and the Judges in every State shall be bound thereby, any Thing in the Constitution or Laws of any State to the Contrary notwithstanding.

The Senators and Representatives before mentioned, and the Members of the several State Legislatures, and all executive and judicial Officers, both of the United States and of the several States, shall be bound by Oath or Affirmation, to support this Constitution; but no religious Test shall ever be required as a Qualification to any Office or public Trust under the United States.

ARTICLE VII.

The Ratification of the Conventions of nine States, shall be sufficient for the Establishment of this Constitution between the States so ratifying the Same.

Done in Convention by the Unanimous Consent of the States present the Seventeenth Day of September in the Year of our Lord one thousand seven hundred and Eighty seven and of the Independence of the United States of America the Twelfth IN WITNESS whereof We have hereunto subscribed our Names,

GEORGE WASHINGTON,
President and Deputy from Virginia

North Carolina
WILLIAM BLOUNT
RICHARD DOBBS SPRAIGHT
HU WILLIAMSON

Pennsylvania
BENJAMIN FRANKLIN
THOMAS MIFFLIN
ROBERT MORRIS
GEORGE CLYMER
THOMAS FITZSIMONS
JARED INGERSOLL
JAMES WILSON
GOUVERNEUR MORRIS

Delaware
GEORGE READ
GUNNING BEDFORD, JR.
JOHN DICKINSON
RICHARD BASSETT
JACOB BROOM

South Carolina
J. RUTLEDGE
CHARLES C. PINCKNEY
PIERCE BUTLER

Virginia
JOHN BLAIR
JAMES MADISON, JR.

New Jersey
WILLIAM LIVINGSTON
DAVID BREARLEY
WILLIAM PATERSON
JONATHAN DAYTON

Maryland
JAMES MCHENRY
DANIEL OF ST. THOMAS JENIFER
DANIEL CARROLL

Massachusetts
NATHANIEL GORHAM
RUFUS KING

Connecticut
WILLIAM S. JOHNSON
ROGER SHERMAN

New York
ALEXANDER HAMILTON

New Hampshire
JOHN LANGDON
NICHOLAS GILMAN

Georgia
WILLIAM FEW
ABRAHAM BALDWIN

Amendments to the Constitution*

Amendment I
Congress shall make no law respecting an establishment of religion, or prohibiting the free exercise thereof; or abridging the freedom of speech, or of the press; or the right of the people peaceably to assemble, and to petition the Government for a redress of grievances.

Amendment II
A well regulated Militia, being necessary to the security of a free State, the right of the people to keep and bear Arms, shall not be infringed.

Amendment III
No Soldier shall, in time of peace be quartered in any house, without the consent of the Owner, nor in time of war, but in a manner to be prescribed by law.

Amendment IV
The right of the people to be secure in their persons, houses, papers, and effects, against unreasonable searches and seizures, shall not be violated, and no Warrants shall issue, but upon probable cause, supported by Oath or affirmation, and particularly describing the place to be searched, and the persons or things to be seized.

Amendment V
No person shall be held to answer for a capital, or otherwise infamous crime, unless on a presentment or indictment of a Grand Jury, except in cases arising in the land or naval forces, or in the Militia, when in actual service in time of War or public danger; nor shall any person be subject for the same offence to be twice put in jeopardy of life or limb; nor shall be compelled in any criminal case to be a witness against himself, nor be deprived of life, liberty, or property, without due process of law; nor shall private property be taken for public use, without just compensation.

Amendment VI
In all criminal prosecutions, the accused shall enjoy the right to a speedy and public trial, by an impartial jury of the State and district wherein the crime shall have been committed, which district shall have been previously ascertained by law, and to be informed of the nature and cause of the accusation; to be confronted with the witnesses against him; to have compulsory process for obtaining witnesses in his favor, and to have the Assistance of Counsel for his defence.

*The first ten amendments (the Bill of Rights) were adopted in 1791.

Amendment VII

In Suits at common law, where the value in controversy shall exceed twenty dollars, the right of trial by jury shall be preserved, and no fact tried by a jury, shall be otherwise re-examined in any Court of the United States, than according to the rules of the common law.

Amendment VIII

Excessive bail shall not be required, nor excessive fines imposed, nor cruel and unusual punishments inflicted.

Amendment IX

The enumeration in the Constitution, of certain rights, shall not be construed to deny or disparage others retained by the people.

Amendment X

The powers not delegated to the United States by the Constitution, nor prohibited by it to the States, are reserved to the States respectively, or to the people.

Amendment XI [Adopted 1798]

The Judicial power of the United States shall not be construed to extend to any suit in law or equity, commenced or prosecuted against one of the United States by Citizens of another State, or by Citizens or Subjects of any Foreign State.

Amendment XII [Adopted 1804]

The Electors shall meet in their respective states, and vote by ballot for President and Vice-President, one of whom, at least, shall not be an inhabitant of the same state with themselves; they shall name in their ballots the person voted for as President, and in distinct ballots the person voted for as Vice-President, and they shall make distinct lists of all persons voted for as President, and of all persons voted for as Vice-President, and of the number of votes for each, which list they shall sign and certify, and transmit sealed to the seat of the government of the United States, directed to the President of the Senate;—The President of the Senate shall, in the presence of the Senate and House of Representatives, open all the certificates and the votes shall then be counted;—The person having the greatest number of votes for President, shall be the President, if such number be a majority of the whole number of Electors appointed; and if no person have such majority, then from the persons having the highest numbers not exceeding three on the list of those voted for as President, the House of Representatives shall choose immediately, by ballot, the President. But in choosing the President, the votes shall be taken by states, the representation from each state having one vote; a quorum for this purpose shall consist of a member or members from two thirds of the states, and a majority of all the states shall be necessary to a choice. And if the House of Representatives shall not choose a President whenever the right of choice shall devolve upon them, before the *fourth day of March* next following, then the Vice-President shall act as President, as in the case of the death or other constitutional disability of the President.

The person having the greatest number of votes as Vice-President, shall be the Vice-President, if such number be a majority of the whole number of Electors appointed, and if no person have a majority, then from the two highest numbers on the list, the Senate shall choose the Vice-President; a quorum for the purpose shall consist of two thirds of the whole number of Senators, and a majority of the whole number shall be necessary to a choice. But no person constitutionally ineligible to the office of President shall be eligible to that of Vice-President of the United States.

Amendment XIII [Adopted 1865]

Section 1 Neither slavery nor involuntary servitude, except as a punishment for crime whereof the party shall have been duly convicted, shall exist within the United States, or any place subject to their jurisdiction.

Section 2 Congress shall have power to enforce this article by appropriate legislation.

Amendment XIV [Adopted 1868]

Section 1 All persons born or naturalized in the United States, and subject to the jurisdiction thereof, are citizens of the United States and of the State wherein they reside. No State shall make or enforce any law which shall abridge the privileges or immunities of citizens of the United States; nor shall any State deprive any person of life, liberty, or property, without due process of law; nor deny to any person within its jurisdiction the equal protection of the laws.

Section 2 Representatives shall be apportioned among the several States according to their respective numbers, counting the whole number of persons in each State, excluding Indians not taxed. But when the right to vote at any election for the choice of electors for President and Vice-President of the United States, Representatives in Congress, the Executive and Judicial officers of a State, or the members of the Legislature thereof, is denied to any of the male inhabitants of such State, being twenty-one years of age, and citizens of the United States, or in any way abridged, except for participation in rebellion, or other crime, the basis of representation therein shall be reduced in the proportion which the number of such male citizens shall bear to the whole number of male citizens twenty-one years of age in such State.

Section 3 No person shall be a Senator or Representative in Congress, or elector of President and Vice-President, or hold any office, civil or military, under the United States, or under any State, who, having previously taken an oath, as a member of Congress, or as an officer of the United States, or as a member of any State legislature, or as an executive or judicial officer of any State, to support the Constitution of the United States, shall have engaged in insurrection or rebellion against the same, or given aid or comfort to the enemies thereof. But Congress may by a vote of two thirds of each House, remove such disability.

Section 4 The validity of the public debt of the United States, authorized by law, including debts incurred for payment of pensions and bounties for services in suppressing insurrection or rebellion, shall not be questioned. But neither the United States nor any State shall assume or pay any debt or obligation incurred in aid of insurrection or rebellion against the United States, or any claim for the loss or emancipation of any slave; but all such debts, obligations and claims shall be held illegal and void.

Section 5 The Congress shall have power to enforce, by appropriate legislation, the provisions of this article.

Amendment XV [Adopted 1870]

Section 1 The right of citizens of the United States to vote shall not be denied or abridged by the United States or by any State on account of race, color, or previous condition of servitude

Section 2 The Congress shall have power to enforce this article by appropriate legislation.

Amendment XVI [Adopted 1913]

The Congress shall have power to lay and collect taxes on incomes, from whatever source derived, without apportionment among the several States, and without regard to any census or enumeration.

Amendment XVII [Adopted 1913]

The Senate of the United States shall be composed of two Senators from each State, elected by the people thereof, for six years; and each Senator shall have one vote. The electors in each State shall have the qualifications requisite for electors of the most numerous branch of the State legislatures.

When vacancies happen in the representation of any State in the Senate, the executive authority of such State shall issue writs of election to fill such vacancies: *Provided,* That the legislature of any State may empower the executive thereof to make temporary appointments until the people fill the vacancies by election as the legislature may direct.

This amendment shall not be so construed as to affect the election or term of any Senator chosen before it becomes valid as part of the Constitution.

Amendment XVIII [Adopted 1919; Repealed 1933]

Section 1 After one year from the ratification of this article the manufacture, sale, or transportation of intoxicating liquors within, the importation thereof into, or the exportation thereof from the United States and all territory subject to the jurisdiction thereof for beverage purposes is hereby prohibited.

Section 2 The Congress and the several States shall have concurrent power to enforce this article by appropriate legislation.

Section 3 This article shall be inoperative unless it shall have been ratified as an amendment to the Constitution by the legislatures of the several States, as provided in the Constitution, within seven years from the date of the submission hereof to the States by the Congress.

Amendment XIX [Adopted 1920]

Section 1 The right of citizens of the United States to vote shall not be denied or abridged by the United States or by any State on account of sex.

Section 2 Congress shall have power to enforce this article by appropriate legislation.

Amendment XX [Adopted 1933]

Section 1 The terms of the President and Vice-President shall end at noon on the 20th day of January, and the terms of Senators and Representatives at noon on the third day of January, of the years in which such terms would have ended if this article had not been ratified; and the terms of their successors shall then begin.

Section 2 The Congress shall assemble at least once in every year, and such meeting shall begin at noon on the third day of January, unless they shall by law appoint a different day.

Section 3 If, at the time fixed for the beginning of the term of the President, the President elect shall have died, the Vice-President elect shall become President. If a President shall not have been chosen before the time fixed for the beginning of his term, or if the President elect shall have failed to qualify, then the Vice-President elect shall act as President until a President shall have qualified; and the Congress may by law provide for the case wherein neither a President elect nor a Vice-President elect shall have qualified, declaring who shall then act as President, or the manner in which one who is to act shall be selected, and such person shall act accordingly until a President or Vice-President shall have qualified.

Section 4 The Congress may by law provide for the case of the death of any of the persons from whom the House of Representatives may choose a President whenever the right of choice shall have devolved upon them, and for the case of the death of any of the persons from whom the Senate may choose a Vice-President whenever the right of choice shall have devolved upon them.

Section 5 Sections 1 and 2 shall take effect on the 15th day of October following the ratification of this article.

Section 6 This article shall be inoperative unless it shall have been ratified as an amendment to the Constitution by the legislatures of three fourths of the several States within seven years from the date of its submission.

Amendment XXI [Adopted 1933]

Section 1 The eighteenth article of amendment to the Constitution of the United States is hereby repealed.

Section 2 The transportation or importation into any State, Territory, or possession of the United States for delivery or use therein of intoxicating liquors, in violation of the laws thereof, is hereby prohibited.

Section 3 This article shall be inoperative unless it shall have been ratified as an amendment to the Constitution by conventions in the several States, as provided in the Constitution, within seven years from the date of the submission hereof to the States by the Congress.

Amendment XXII [Adopted 1951]

Section 1 No person shall be elected to the office of the President more than twice, and no person who has held the office of President, or acted as President, for more than two years of a term to which some other person was elected President shall be elected to the office of the President more than once. But this Article shall not apply to any person holding the office of President when this Article was proposed by the Congress, and shall not prevent any person who may be holding the office of President, or acting as President, during the term within which this Article becomes operative from holding the office of President or acting as President during the remainder of such term.

Section 2 This article shall be inoperative unless it shall have been ratified as an amendment to the

Constitution by the legislatures of three fourths of the several States within seven years from the date of its submission to the States by the Congress.

Amendment XXIII [Adopted 1961]

Section 1   The District constituting the seat of Government of the United States shall appoint in such manner as the Congress may direct:

A number of electors of President and Vice-President equal to the whole number of Senators and Representatives in Congress to which the District would be entitled if it were a State, but in no event more than the least populous State; they shall be in addition to those appointed by the States, but they shall be considered, for the purposes of the election of President and Vice-President, to be electors appointed by a State; and they shall meet in the District and perform such duties as provided by the twelfth article of amendment.

Section 2   The Congress shall have power to enforce this article by appropriate legislation.

Amendment XXIV [Adopted 1944]

Section 1   The right of citizens of the United States to vote in any primary or other election for President or Vice-President, for electors for President or Vice-President, or for Senator or Representative in Congress, shall not be denied or abridged by the United States or any State by reason of failure to pay any poll tax or other tax.

Section 2   The Congress shall have power to enforce this article by appropriate legislation.

Amendment XXV [Adopted 1967]

Section 1   In case of the removal of the President from office or his death or resignation, the Vice-President shall become President.

Section 2   Whenever there is a vacancy in the office of the Vice-President, the President shall nominate a Vice-President who shall take the office upon confirmation by a majority vote of both houses of Congress.

Section 3   Whenever the President transmits to the President pro tempore of the Senate and the Speaker of the House of Representatives his written declaration that he is unable to discharge the powers and duties of his office, and until he transmits to them a written dec-

laration to the contrary, such powers and duties shall be discharged by the Vice-President as Acting President.

Section 4   Whenever the Vice-President and a majority of either the principal officers of the executive departments, or of such other body as Congress may by law provide, transmit to the President pro tempore of the Senate and the Speaker of the House of Representatives their written declaration that the President is unable to discharge the powers and duties of his office, the Vice-President shall immediately assume the powers and duties of the office as Acting President.

Thereafter, when the President transmits to the President pro tempore of the Senate and the Speaker of the House of Representatives his written declaration that no inability exists, he shall resume the powers and duties of his office unless the Vice-President and a majority of either the principal officers of the executive department, or of such other body as Congress may by law provide, transmit within four days to the President pro tempore of the Senate and the Speaker of the House of Representatives their written declaration that the President is unable to discharge the powers and duties of his office. Thereupon Congress shall decide the issue, assembling within 48 hours for that purpose if not in session. If the Congress, within 21 days after receipt of the latter written declaration, or, if Congress is not in session, within 21 days after Congress is required to assemble, determines by two-thirds vote of both houses that the President is unable to discharge the powers and duties of his office, the Vice-President shall continue to discharge the same as Acting President; otherwise, the President shall resume the powers and duties of his office.

Amendment XXVI [Adopted 1971]

Section 1   The right of citizens of the United States, who are eighteen years of age or older, to vote shall not be denied or abridged by the United States or any state on account of age.

Section 2   The Congress shall have power to enforce this article by appropriate legislation.

Amendent XXVII [Adopted 1992]

No law, varying the compensation for the services of Senators and Representatives, shall take effect until an election of Representatives have intervened.

PRESIDENTIAL ELECTIONS

Year	Candidates	Parties	Popular Vote	Electoral Vote	Voter Participation
1789	GEORGE WASHINGTON		*	69	
	John Adams			34	
	Others			35	
1792	GEORGE WASHINGTON		*	132	
	John Adams			77	
	George Clinton			50	
	Others			5	
1796	JOHN ADAMS	Federalist	*	71	
	Thomas Jefferson	Democratic-Republican		68	
	Thomas Pinckney	Federalist		59	
	Aaron Burr	Dem.-Rep.		30	
	Others			48	
1800	THOMAS JEFFERSON	Dem.-Rep.	*	73	
	Aaron Burr	Dem.-Rep.		73	
	C. C. Pinckney	Federalist		64	
	John Jay	Federalist		1	
1804	THOMAS JEFFERSON	Dem.-Rep.	*	122	
	C. C. Pinckney	Federalist		14	
1808	JAMES MADISON	Dem.-Rep.	*	122	
	C. C. Pinckney	Federalist		47	
	George Clinton	Dem.-Rep.		6	
1812	JAMES MADISON	Dem.-Rep.	*	128	
	De Witt Clinton	Federalist		89	
1816	JAMES MONROE	Dem.-Rep.	*	183	
	Rufus King	Federalist		34	
1820	JAMES MONROE	Dem.-Rep.	*	231	
	John Quincy Adams	Dem.-Rep.		1	
1824	JOHN Q. ADAMS	Dem.-Rep.	108,740 (10.5%)	84	26.9%
	Andrew Jackson	Dem.-Rep.	153,544 (43.1%)	99	
	William H. Crawford	Dem.-Rep.	46,618 (13.1%)	41	
	Henry Clay	Dem.-Rep.	47,136 (13.2%)	37	
1828	ANDREW JACKSON	Democratic	647,286 (56.0%)	178	57.6%
	John Quincy Adams	National Republican	508,064 (44.0%)	83	
1832	ANDREW JACKSON	Democratic	687,502 (55.0%)	219	55.4%
	Henry Clay	National Republican	530,189 (42.4%)	49	
	John Floyd	Independent		11	
	William Wirt	Anti-Mason	33,108 (2.6%)	7	
1836	MARTIN VAN BUREN	Democratic	765,483 (50.9%)	170	57.8%
	W. H. Harrison	Whig		73	
	Hugh L. White	Whig	739,795 (49.1%)	26	
	Daniel Webster	Whig		14	
	W. P. Magnum	Independent		11	
1840	WILLIAM H. HARRISON	Whig	1,274,624 (53.1%)	234	80.2%
	Martin Van Buren	Democratic	1,127,781 (46.9%)	60	
	J. G. Birney	Liberty	7069	—	
1844	JAMES K. POLK	Democratic	1,338,464 (49.6%)	170	78.9%
	Henry Clay	Whig	1,300,097 (48.1%)	105	
	J. G. Birney	Liberty	62,300 (2.3%)	—	
1848	ZACHARY TAYLOR	Whig	1,360,967 (47.4%)	163	72.7%
	Lewis Cass	Democratic	1,222,342 (42.5%)	127	
	Martin Van Buren	Free-Soil	291,263 (10.1%)	—	
1852	FRANKLIN PIERCE	Democratic	1,601,117 (50.9%)	254	69.6%
	Winfield Scott	Whig	1,385,453 (44.1%)	42	
	John P. Hale	Free-Soil	155,825 (5.0%)	—	
1856	JAMES BUCHANAN	Democratic	1,832,955 (45.3%)	174	78.9%
	John C. Fremont	Republican	1,339,932 (33.1%)	114	
	Millard Fillmore	American	871,731 (21.6%)	8	

Year	Candidates	Parties	Popular Vote	Electoral Vote	Voter Participation
1860	ABRAHAM LINCOLN	Republican	1,865,593 (39.8%)	180	81.2%
	Stephen A. Douglas	Democratic	1,382,713 (29.5%)	12	
	John C. Breckinridge	Democratic	848,356 (18.1%)	72	
	John Bell	Union	592,906 (12.6%)	39	
1864	ABRAHAM LINCOLN	Republican	2,213,655 (55.0%)	212	73.8%
	George B. McClellan	Democratic	1,805,237 (45.0%)	21	
1868	ULYSSES S. GRANT	Republican	3,012,833 (52.7%)	214	78.1%
	Horatio Seymour	Democratic	2,703,249 (47.3%)	80	
1872	ULYSSES S. GRANT	Republican	3,597,132 (55.6%)	286	71.3%
	Horace Greeley	Democratic; Liberal Republican	2,834,125 (43.9%)	66	
1876	RUTHERFORD B. HAYES	Republican	4,036,298 (48.0%)	185	81.8%
	Samuel J. Tilden	Democratic	4,300,590 (51.0%)	184	
1880	JAMES A. GARFIELD	Republican	4,454,416 (48.5%)	214	79.4%
	Winfield S. Hancock	Democratic	4,444,952 (48.1%)	155	
1884	GROVER CLEVELAND	Democratic	4,874,986 (48.5%)	219	77.5%
	James G. Blaine	Republican	4,851,981 (48.2%)	182	
1888	BENJAMIN HARRISON	Republican	5,439,853 (47.9%)	233	79.3%
	Grover Cleveland	Democratic	5,540,309 (48.6%)	168	
1892	GROVER CLEVELAND	Democratic	5,556,918 (46.1%)	277	74.7%
	Benjamin Harrison	Republican	5,176,108 (43.0%)	145	
	James B. Weaver	People's	1,041,028 (8.5%)	22	
1896	WILLIAM McKINLEY	Republican	7,104,779 (51.1%)	271	79.3%
	William J. Bryan	Democratic People's	6,502,925 (47.7%)	176	
1900	WILLIAM McKINLEY	Republican	7,207,923 (51.7%)	292	73.2%
	William J. Bryan	Dem.-Populist	6,358,133 (45.5%)	155	
1904	THEODORE ROOSEVELT	Republican	7,623,486 (57.9%)	336	65.2%
	Alton B. Parker	Democratic	5,077,911 (37.6%)	140	
	Eugene V. Debs	Socialist	402,283 (3.0%)	—	
1908	WILLIAM H. TAFT	Republican	7,678,908 (51.6%)	321	65.4%
	William J. Bryan	Democratic	6,409,104 (43.1%)	162	
	Eugene V. Debs	Socialist	420,793 (2.8%)	—	
1912	WOODROW WILSON	Democratic	6,293,454 (41.9%)	435	58.8%
	Theodore Roosevelt	Progressive	4,119,538 (27.4%)	88	
	William H. Taft	Republican	3,484,980 (23.2%)	8	
	Eugene V. Debs	Socialist	900,672 (6.0%)	—	
1916	WOODROW WILSON	Democratic	9,129,606 (49.4%)	277	61.6%
	Charles E. Hughes	Republican	8,538,221 (46.2%)	254	
	A. L. Benson	Socialist	585,113 (3.2%)	—	
1920	WARREN G. HARDING	Republican	16,152,200 (60.4%)	404	49.2%
	James M. Cox	Democratic	9,147,353 (34.2%)	127	
	Eugene V. Debs	Socialist	919,799 (3.4%)	—	
1924	CALVIN COOLIDGE	Republican	15,725,016 (54.0%)	382	48.9%
	John W. Davis	Democratic	8,386,503 (28.8%)	136	
	Robert M. La Follette	Progressive	4,822,856 (16.6%)	13	
1928	HERBERT HOOVER	Republican	21,391,381 (58.2%)	444	56.9%
	Alfred E. Smith	Democratic	15,016,443 (40.9%)	87	
	Normal Thomas	Socialist	267,835 (0.7%)	—	
1932	FRANKLIN D. ROOSEVELT	Democratic	22,821,857 (57.4%)	472	56.9%
	Herbert Hoover	Republican	15,761,841 (39.7%)	59	
	Norman Thomas	Socialist	881,951 (2.2%)	—	
1936	FRANKLIN D. ROOSEVELT	Democratic	27,751,597 (60.8%)	523	61.0%
	Alfred M. Landon	Republican	16,679,583 (36.5%)	8	
	William Lemke	Union	882,479 (1.9%)	—	
1940	FRANKLIN D. ROOSEVELT	Democratic	27,244,160 (54.8%)	449	62.5%
	Wendell L. Willkie	Republican	22,305,198 (44.8%)	82	

Year	Candidates	Parties	Popular Vote	Electoral Vote	Voter Participation
1944	FRANKLIN D. ROOSEVELT	Democrat	25,602,504 (53.5%)	432	55.9%
	Thomas E. Dewey	Republican	22,006,285 (46.0%)	99	
1948	HARRY S TRUMAN	Democratic	24,105,695 (49.5%)	304	53.0%
	Thomas E. Dewey	Republican	21,969,170 (45.1%)	189	
	J. Strom Thurmond	State-Rights Democratic	1,169,021 (2.4%)	38	
	Henry A. Wallace	Progressive	1,156,103 (2.4%)	—	
1952	DWIGHT D. EISENHOWER	Republican	33,936,252 (55.1%)	442	63.3%
	Adlai E. Stevenson	Democratic	27,314,992 (44.4%)	89	
1956	DWIGHT D. EISENHOWER	Republican	35,575,420 (57.6%)	457	60.5%
	Adlai E. Stevenson	Democratic	26,033,066 (42.1%)	73	
	Other	—	—	1	
1960	JOHN F. KENNEDY	Democratic	34,227,096 (49.9%)	303	62.8%
	Richard M. Nixon	Republican	34,108,546 (49.6%)	219	
	Other	—	—	15	
1964	LYNDON B. JOHNSON	Democratic	43,126,506 (61.1%)	486	61.7%
	Barry M. Goldwater	Republican	27,176,799 (38.5%)	52	
1968	RICHARD M. NIXON	Republican	31,770,237 (43.4%)	301	60.6%
	Hubert H. Humphrey	Democratic	31,270,633 (42.7%)	191	
	George Wallace	American Indep.	9,906,141 (13.5%)	46	
1972	RICHARD M. NIXON	Republican	47,169,911 (60.7%)	520	55.2%
	George S. McGovern	Democratic	29,170,383 (37.5%)	17	
	Other	—	—	1	
1976	JIMMY CARTER	Democratic	40,828,587 (50.0%)	297	53.5%
	Gerald R. Ford	Republican	39,147,613 (47.9%)	241	
	Other	—	1,575,459 92.1%)	—	
1980	RONALD REAGAN	Republican	43,901,812 (50.7%)	489	52.6%
	Jimmy Carter	Democratic	35,483,820 (41.0%)	49	
	John B. Anderson	Independent	5,719,722 (6.6%)	—	
	Ed Clark	Libertarian	921,188 (1.1%)	—	
1984	RONALD REAGAN	Republican	54,455,075 (59.0%)	525	53.3%
	Walter Mondale	Democratic	37,577,185 (41.0%)	13	
1988	GEORGE H. W. BUSH	Republican	48,886,000 (45.6%)	426	57.4%
	Michael S. Dukakis	Democratic	41,809,000 (45.6%)	111	
1992	WILLIAM J. CLINTON	Democratic	43,728,375 (43%)	370	55.0%
	George H. W. Bush	Republican	38,167,416 (38%)	168	
	Ross Perot	—	19,237,247 (19%)	—	
1996	WILLIAM J. CLINTON	Democratic	45,590,703 (50%)	379	48.8%
	Robert Dole	Republican	37,816,307 (41%)	159	
	Ross Perot	Independent	7,866,284 (9%)		

SUPREME COURT JUSTICES

Name	Service	Appointed by	Name	Service	Appointed by
John Jay*	1789–1795	Washington	Oliver W. Holmes	1902–1932	T. Roosevelt
James Wilson	1789–1798	Washington	William R. Day	1903–1922	T. Roosevelt
John Blair	1789–1796	Washington	William H. Moody	1906–1910	T. Roosevelt
John Rutledge	1790–1791	Washington	Horace H. Lurton	1910–1914	Taft
William Cushing	1790–1810	Washington	Charles E. Hughes	1910–1916	Taft
James Iredell	1790–1799	Washington	Willis Van Devanter	1910–1937	Taft
Thomas Johnson	1791–1793	Washington	Joseph R. Lamar	1911–1916	Taft
William Paterson	1793–1806	Washington	**Edward D. White**	1910–1921	Taft
John Rutledge†	1795	Washington	Mahlon Pitney	1912–1922	Taft
Samuel Chase	1796–1811	Washington	James C. McReynolds	1914–1941	Wilson
Oliver Ellsworth	1796–1799	Washington	Louis D. Brandeis	1916–1939	Wilson
Bushrod Washington	1798–1829	J. Adams	John H. Clarke	1916–1922	Wilson
Alfred Moore	1799–1804	J. Adams	**William H. Taft**	1921–1930	Harding
John Marshall	1801–1835	J. Adams	George Sutherland	1922–1938	Harding
William Johnson	1804–1834	Jefferson	Pierce Butler	1923–1939	Harding
Henry B. Livingston	1806–1823	Jefferson	Edward T. Sanford	1923–1930	Harding
Thomas Todd	1807–1826	Jefferson	Harlan F. Stone	1925–1941	Coolidge
Gabriel Duval	1811–1836	Madison	**Charles E. Hughes**	1930–1941	Hoover
Joseph Story	1811–1845	Madison	Owen J. Roberts	1930–1945	Hoover
Smith Thompson	1823–1843	Monroe	Benjamin N. Cardozo	1932–1938	Hoover
Robert Trimble	1826–1828	J.Q. Adams	Hugo L. Black	1937–1971	F. Roosevelt
John McLean	1829–1861	Jackson	Stanley F. Reed	1938–1957	F. Roosevelt
Henry Baldwin	1830–1844	Jackson	Felix Frankfurter	1939–1962	F. Roosevelt
James M. Wayne	1835–1867	Jackson	William O. Douglas	1939–1975	F. Roosevelt
Roger B. Taney	1836–1864	Jackson	Frank Murphy	1940–1949	F. Roosevelt
Philip P. Barbour	1836–1841	Jackson	**Harlan F. Stone**	1941–1946	F. Roosevelt
John Catron	1837–1865	Van Buren	James F. Byrnes	1941–1942	F. Roosevelt
John McKinley	1837–1852	Van Buren	Robert H. Jackson	1941–1954	F. Roosevelt
Peter V. Daniel	1841–1860	Van Buren	Wiley B. Rutledge	1943–1949	F. Roosevelt
Samuel Nelson	1845–1872	Tyler	Harold H. Burton	1945–1958	Truman
Levi Woodbury	1845–1851	Polk	**Frederick M. Vinson**	1946–1953	Truman
Robert C. Grier	1846–1870	Polk	Tom C. Clark	1949–1967	Truman
Benjamin R. Curtis	1851–1857	Fillmore	Sherman Minton	1949–1956	Truman
John A. Campbell	1853–1861	Pierce	**Earl Warren**	1953–1969	Eisenhower
Nathan Clifford	1858–1881	Buchanan	John Marshall Harlan	1955–1971	Eisenhower
Noah H. Swayne	1862–1881	Lincoln	William J. Brennan, Jr.	1956–1990	Eisenhower
Samuel F. Miller	1862–1890	Lincoln	Charles E. Whittaker	1957–1962	Eisenhower
David Davis	1862–1877	Lincoln	Potter Stewart	1958–1981	Eisenhower
Stephen J. Field	1863–1897	Lincoln	Byron R. White	1962–1993	Kennedy
Salmon P. Chase	1864–1873	Lincoln	Arthur J. Goldberg	1962–1965	Kennedy
William Strong	1870–1880	Grant	Abe Fortas	1965–1969	Johnson
Joseph P. Bradley	1870–1892	Grant	Thurgood Marshall	1967–1991	Johnson
Ward Hunt	1873–1882	Grant	**Warren E. Burger**	1969–1986	Nixon
Morrison R. Waite	1874–1888	Grant	Harry A. Blackmun	1970–1994	Nixon
John M. Harlan	1877–1911	Hayes	Lewis F. Powell, Jr.	1972–1988	Nixon
William B. Woods	1880–1887	Hayes	William H. Rehnquist	1972–1986	Nixon
Stanley Matthews	1881–1889	Garfield	John Paul Stevens	1975–	Ford
Horace Gray	1882–1902	Arthur	Sandra Day O'Connor	1981–	Reagan
Samuel Blatchford	1882–1893	Arthur	**William H. Rehnquist**	1986–	Reagan
Lucious Q. C. Lamar	1888–1893	Cleveland	Antonin Scalia	1986–	Reagan
Melville W. Fuller	1888–1910	Cleveland	Anthony M. Kennedy	1988–	Reagan
David J. Brewer	1889–1910	B. Harrison	David H. Souter	1990–	Bush
Henry B. Brown	1890–1906	B. Harrison	Clarence Thomas	1991–	Bush
George Shiras	1892–1903	B. Harrison	Ruth Bader Ginsberg	1993–	Clinton
Howell E. Jackson	1893–1895	B. Harrison	Stephen Breyer	1994–	Clinton
Edward D. White	1894–1910	Cleveland			
Rufus W. Peckham	1896–1909	Cleveland	*Chief Justices appear in bold type.		
Joseph McKenna	1898–1925	McKinley	†Acting Chief Justice; Senate refused to confirm appointment.		

STATES OF THE UNITED STATES

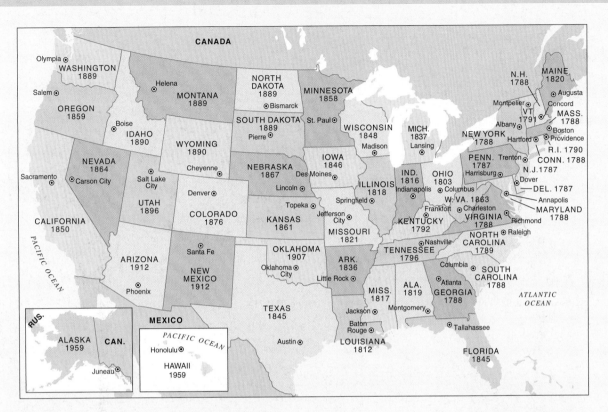

State	Date of Admission	State	Date of Admission
Delaware	December 7, 1787	Michigan	January 16, 1837
Pennsylvania	December 12, 1787	Florida	March 3, 1845
New Jersey	December 18, 1787	Texas	December 29, 1845
Georgia	January 2, 1788	Iowa	December 28, 1846
Connecticut	January 9, 1788	Wisconsin	May 29, 1848
Massachusetts	February 6, 1788	California	September 9, 1850
Maryland	April 28, 1788	Minnesota	May 11, 1858
South Carolina	May 23, 1788	Oregon	February 14, 1859
New Hampshire	June 21, 1788	Kansas	January 29, 1861
Virginia	June 25, 1788	West Virginia	June 19, 1863
New York	July 26, 1788	Nevada	October 31, 1864
North Carolina	November 21, 1789	Nebraska	March 1, 1867
Rhode Island	May 29, 1790	Colorado	August 1, 1876
Vermont	March 4, 1791	North Dakota	November 2, 1889
Kentucky	June 1, 1792	South Dakota	November 2, 1889
Tennessee	June 1, 1796	Montana	November 8, 1889
Ohio	March 1, 1803	Washington	November 11, 1889
Louisiana	April 30, 1812	Idaho	July 3, 1890
Indiana	December 11, 1816	Wyoming	July 10, 1890
Mississippi	December 10, 1817	Utah	January 4, 1896
Illinois	December 3, 1818	Oklahoma	November 16, 1907
Alabama	December 14, 1819	New Mexico	January 6, 1912
Maine	March 15, 1820	Arizona	February 14, 1912
Missouri	August 10, 1821	Alaska	January 3, 1959
Arkansas	June 15, 1836	Hawaii	August 21, 1959

TERRITORIAL EXPANSION OF THE UNITED STATES

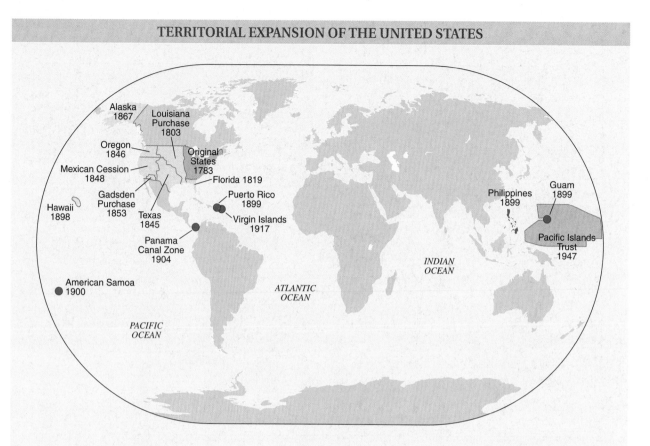

Date	Territory	Area (sq. mi.)	Cumulative Total (sq.mi.)
1793	Original states	888,685	888,685
1803	Louisiana Purchase	827,192	1,715,877
1819	Florida	72,003	1,787,880
1845	Texas	390,143	2,178,023
1846	Oregon	285,580	2,463,603
1848	Mexican Cession	529,017	2,992,620
1853	Gadsden Purchase	29,640	3,022,260
1867	Alaska	589,757	3,612,017
1898	Hawaii	6,450	3,618,467
1899	Philippines	115,600	3,734,067
1899	Puerto Rico	3,435	3,737,502
1899	Guam	212	3,737,714
1900	American Samoa	76	3,737,790
1904	Panama Canal Zone	553	3,738,343
1917	Virgin Islands	133	3,738,476
1947	Pacific Islands Trust	8,489	3,746,965
	All others	46	3,747,011

POPULATION OF THE UNITED STATES

Year	Number of States	Population	Percent Increase	Population per Square Mile
1790	13	3,929,214		4.5
1800	16	5,308,483	35.1	6.1
1810	17	7,239,881	36.4	4.3
1820	23	9,638,453	33.1	5.5
1830	24	12,866,020	33.5	7.4
1840	26	17,069,453	32.7	9.8
1850	31	23,191,876	35.9	7.9
1860	33	31,443,321	35.6	10.6
1870	37	39,818,449	26.6	13.4
1880	38	50,155,783	26.0	16.9
1890	44	62,947,714	25.5	21.2
1900	45	75,994,575	20.7	25.6
1910	46	91,972,266	21.0	31.0
1920	48	105,710,620	14.9	35.6
1930	48	122,775,046	16.1	41.2
1940	48	131,669,275	7.2	44.2
1950	48	150,697,361	14.5	50.7
1960	50	179,323,175	19.0	50.6
1970	50	203,235,298	13.3	57.5
1980	50	226,545,805	11.5	64.1
1990	50	248,709,873	9.8	70.3

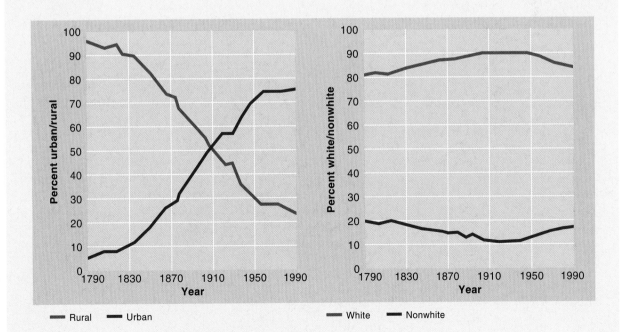

Source: U.S. Bureau of the Census estimates.

Index

Art(s). See also Architecture; Artifacts;
    Artisans; Literature; Music; Painting
  Armory Show and, 692 (illus.)
  colonial artisans and, 110
  Harlem Renaissance and, 752–753
  industrial design, 798 (illus.)
  National Endowment for, 929
  Native American, 968
  of Niger River region, 13 (illus.)
  "Op" art, 973
  "Pop" art, 972, 973
  progressives and, 665
  rebellion in, 862–864
  Revere and, 146 (illus.)
  sexual revolution and, 973
  in Twenties, 742 (illus.)
  World War II war effort and, 822 (illus.)
  WPA and, 768 (illus.), 782
Arthur, Chester, 605, 607
Arthur's Home Magazine, 586
Articles of Confederation, 166–168
  inadequacies of, 208
Artifacts, of ancient Indians, 8–9, 8 (illus.)
Artisans
  colonial, 110
  factory work and, 307
  labor and, 676
  in Philadelphia, 154–155
  after Revolution, 203
  slave, 71
ARU. See American Railway Union (ARU)
Ash can school, of painting, 664 (illus.)
Ashley, William, 298
Asia. See also Immigrants and immigra-
    tion; specific countries
  ancient migrations from, 4, 4 (map)
  balance of power in, 655–656
  China and, 655–656
  Chinese Revolution in, 883
  immigration from, 749, 929, 1006
  investments in, 638
  Japan and balance of power in, 656–657
  Korean War in, 883–885
  markets in, 638
  Portuguese trade and, 17
  U.S. involvement in, 656 (map)
Asians, 1008 (illus.)
  in cities, 1004
  progressivism and, 688
  proportion of, 1007
As I Lay Dying (Faulkner), 798
Asociación Nacional México-Americana,
    964
Assassination
  of Franz Ferdinand, 702
  of Kennedy, John F., 897, 922–923, 926
  of Kennedy, Robert, 923
  of King, Martin Luther, Jr., 923, 958
  of Lincoln, 490
  of Malcolm X, 957
  of McKinley, 648, 683
Assemblies. See also Legislatures
  in Carolinas, 54
  colonial, 123, 149
  composition of revolutionary, 187 (illus.)
  political power of, 125
  right to, 125
  after Seven Years' War, 140
Assembly line, 676
  at Ford, 740–741
Assimilation, of Indians, 267, 967–968
Associations
  in cities, 575

professional, 581
Astaire, Fred, 799 (illus.)
Astor, John Jacob, 266, 291
Aswan Dam Project, 886
Asylums, 272
  reform of, 381–382
Atchison, David, 446, 447, 447 (illus.)
Atlanta
  black draftees in, 716
  Sherman's capture of, 486
Atlanta Constitution, 547
Atlanta Monthly, on blacks, 551
Atlanta University, 512
Atlantic Charter, 834
Atlantic magazine, 665
Atlantic Monthly, 614
Atlantic Ocean region
  Portuguese exploration of, 16–17
  slave trade in, 64–67
  in World War II, 810
Atlantic trading system, colonies in, 109
Atomic age, 834–836
Atomic energy, 854
Atomic Energy Act (1946), 888
Atomic Energy Commission, 854, 888,
    919, 975
Atomic weapons, 834–836. See also
    Nuclear power
  Cold War and, 887–891
  Einstein and, 809
  facilities in 1950s, 890 (map)
  fallout shelters and, 889, 889 (illus.)
  hydrogen bomb and, 888
  protests against, 891
  Russia and, 881
  SANE and, 891, 891 (illus.)
  Soviet Union and, 888
  testing of, 888 (illus.), 891
  Truman and, 878
Auburn prison, 381
Auctions, of slaves, 95–96
Audiotapes, Nixon and, 939, 940
Audubon, John, 322
Augusta, Georgia, 548
Auld, Sophia, 327
Auschwitz, gas chambers at, 829
Austin, Stephen F., 400, 401
Australia, 829
Austria
  German annexation of, 808
  after World War I, 725
Austria-Hungary
  as Central Power, 702
  immigrants from, 675
Austrian Americans, 705
Authority. See also Federal government;
    Government
  of government, 225
  in Pennsylvania, 58
  in Puritan settlements, 49
Autobiography
  of Douglass, 357
  as historical documentation, 1010–1011
Autobiography of Benjamin Franklin, The,
    1010, 1011
Automation, 855
Automobiles, 855
  cities and, 742
  culture of, 740–742
  economic decline in, 1000
  Ford and, 740–741
  impact of, 741 (illus.)
  McDonald's and, 839
  in 1930s, 793–794

recession and, 1003
  safety of, 979–980
  suburban growth and, 849
  after World War II, 841
Awakeners, 121
Awakening, The (Chopin), 618
Axis powers, 804 (illus.), 808
Aztec empire, 10, 20, 21 (illus.)
  Spanish conquest of, 20–21

Babbitt (Lewis), 754
Babbitt, Bruce, 998
Baby and Child Care (Spock), 859
Baby boom, 847, 858
Backcountry, 107–108
  marriage and family life in, 108–109
"Back-to-nature" movement, 688
Backus, Isaac, 199
Backus, John, 272
Backward integration, 568
Bacon, Nathaniel, 75–76
Bacon's Rebellion, 75–77
Badlands, Roosevelt, Theodore, and, 649
Baer, George, 685
Baez, Joan, 954, 971, 976
Bahamas, Columbus and, 17
Bailey, Mary Stuart, journal of, 410, 411
Bakelite Corporation, 812, 813
Baker, Ella, 953
Baker, James, 1021
Baker, Josephine, 762
Baker, Newton D., 681, 712, 723
  city beautiful movement and, 682
Baker, Ray Stannard, 665, 683
Baker v. Carr, 929
Bakke, Allan, 959–960
Balance of power
  in Asia, 655–656
  Japan and, 656–657
  before World War I, 702
Baldwin, James, 866, 954, 956
Baldwin, Luther, 237–238
Baldwin, Roger, 713
Balkan region
  after communism, 1018–1019
  World War I and, 702
Ballinger, Richard A., 690
Balloon frame construction, 309 (illus.)
Ballou, Adin, 377
Ballou, Mary, 417
Baltimore, 465
  black Catholics in, 355–356
  riot in, 278–279
Baltimore (Lord). See Calvert family
Bandidos, 426
Bankhead-Jones Farm Tenancy Act (1937),
    792
Bank holiday, 777
Banking Act (1933), 777
Bank of North America, 197
Bank of the United States, 282
  Second, 370–372
Banks, Dennis, 969
Banks and banking. See also Bank of the
    United States
  Civil War and, 482
  failures in, 771
  Federal Farm Loan banks, 709
  Federal Reserve and, 694
  investments and, 295, 568
  Madison and, 282
  reform of, 694
  Roosevelt, Franklin D., and, 777

homesteading in, 529–530
settlement of, 533–536
Great Society, 927–932
attacks on, 931–932
Indians and, 970
major programs of, 930
reversal of, 989
roots of programs in, 932
Great Valley of California, 540
Great War. See World War I
Great War for Empire. See Seven Years' War
"Great White Fleet," 657
Greece, 878–879
Greeley, Horace, 474
election of 1872 and, 522
Green, Theodore Francis, 927 (illus.)
Green, William, 786
Greenbacks, 472, 606
Green Corn Rebellion, 712–713
Greene, Asa, 258
Greene, Nathanael, 169, 174
Green Mountain Boys, 150
Greensboro, North Carolina
black workers in, 551
Woolworth's lunch counter sit-in and, 951–952
Greenspan, Alan, 999
Greenville, Treaty of, 268
Greenwich Village, 752
Grenada, invasion of, 1021–1022
Grenville, George, 140, 141
Grid patterns, in cities, 310 (illus.)
Griffith, D. W., 520, 672–673
Grifs, 67
Grimké sisters
Angelina, 388, 389
Sarah, 388, 389, 393
Griswold, A. Whitney, 857
Griswold, Roger, 237, 237 (illus.)
Grosse Point Park, 742
Gross national product (GNP)
under Johnson, Lyndon, 931
unemployment and (1940-1945), 815 (illus.)
after World War II, 840, 840 (illus.)
Grund, Francis, 232
Grundy, Felix, 278
Guadalupe Hidalgo, Treaty of, 425
Utah and, 419–420
Guadeloupe, 86
Guam, 644, 826
Japan and, 811
Guanajuato, 23
Guantanamo Bay, 651
Guatemala, 21, 887
intervention in, 654
Guendalos, 493
Guiana, England and, 27–28
Gulf Coast
Spain and, 197
in War of 1812, 278, 280 (map)
Gulf of Guinea, 12
Gulf of Mexico
France and, 97, 98
Spain and, 25
Gulf of Tonkin, 899–902
Gulf of Tonkin resolution, 902
Gulf War. See Persian Gulf War
Gullah language, 70
Guns, Spanish conquests and, 20
Guthrie, Woody, 864, 913, 976
Gutiérrez, José Angel, 966
Guy, Francis, 259 (illus.)
Gwinn Land Law, 425

Habsburgs, 85
Haggerty, Rose, 587
Hague conference on disarmament (190), 659
Haight-Ashbury district, 974
Hair (rock musical), 973
Haiti, 17
black rebellion against, 253
Clinton and, 1022
Douglass and, 456
intervention in, 707
refugees from, 1007
slave rebellion in, 273
Hakluyts, Richard (uncle and nephew), 27
Haldeman, H. R., 934–935
Hale, Sarah, 313
Half-Way Covenant, 117
Hall, Prince, 276
Hallucinogenic drugs, 973–974
Hamer, Fannie Lou, 956, 956 (illus.), 957
Hamid, Sufi Abdul, 950
Hamilton (ship), 216 (illus.)
Hamilton, Alexander
army and, 236
criticisms of, 225, 226
economic policy of, 224–226
as Federalist, 208
Federalist Papers and, 213
at Grand Convention, 209, 210
national bank and, 225
national policy and, 224 (illus.)
Revolution of 1800 and, 238–239
Whiskey Rebellion and, 227–228, 227 (illus.)
Hamilton, Alice, World War I peace and, 725–726
Hamilton, Andrew
Zenger case and, 127
Hammond, James, 335–336
Hancock, John, 111, 131, 145, 147, 164
ratification and, 214
at Second Continental Congress, 150
Hancock, Thomas, 111, 137
Hancock, Winfield, 605
Handsome Lake, 267
Hanford, Washington, 889
Hanna, Mark, 629, 648
Harassment. See Sexual harassment
Harding, Warren G., 758–759, 758 (illus.)
death of, 759
foreign policy of, 760
Hard-money interests, 606
Hargis, Billy James, 857
Harlan, John, 619
Harlem, women in, 860 (illus.)
Harlem Renaissance, 138, 752–753
Cotton Club and, 753 (illus.)
Harlow, Jean, 800
Harmonists, 377
Harmony (ship), 148
Harper, Frances Ellen Watkins, 550
Harpers Ferry, Brown's attack at, 453–454, 453 (illus.), 454 (illus.)
Harper's Weekly, 544, 545 (illus.), 595 (illus.)
Harriman, Averell, 877
Harrington, Michael, 864
Harris, Emily and David, 484–485
Harrisburg Pennsylvanian, public opinion poll and, 900
Harrison, Benjamin, 540, 557, 605, 636
anti-imperialism of, 645
black voting rights and, 621
election of 1888 and, 607

election of 1892 and, 558
environment and, 569
Harrison, William Henry, 268, 402
election of 1840 and, 374–375, 374 (illus.)
Harrod, Mary and James, 247, 264
Hartford, 46
Hartford Convention, 279
Harvard Business Review, 844
Harvard University, 122, 581
Harvesting, 319–320
"Harvest of Death, Gettysburg, Pennsylvania. . . ." (O'Sullivan), 479 (illus.)
Harvey, William, 625
Hastings, Lansford, 399
Havana, 642
Spain and, 136
Havel, Vaclav, 1018
Hawaii
annexation of, 637, 655
Pearl Harbor attack and, 810–814
rights of, 647
Roosevelt, Theodore, on, 642
U.S. expansionism and, 636–637
as U.S. territory, 636 (illus.), 636 (map)
Hawkins, Joe, 400
Hawley-Smoot Tariff, 761
Hawthorne, Nathaniel, 364
Hay, John, 651, 655
Hay-Bunau Varilla Treaty, 651
Hayden, Iola, 997
Hayden, Lewis, 387
Hayden, Tom, 970–971
Hayes, Rutherford B., 522, 523, 605, 636
Haymarket Riot, 593, 733
Hayne, Robert, 368
Haynesworth, Clement, 937
Haywood, "Big Bill," 679–680
Haywood, Felix, 511
H-bomb. See Hydrogen bomb
Head Start, 928
Health. See also Diseases; Medicine
in New England, 49
of North American environment, 70
in North Carolina, 55
of revolutionary soldiers, 176
sexuality and, 380–381
of slaves, 341–343
smallpox inoculation and, 157
in West, 409
Health care. See also Medicaid; Medicare
Clinton and reform of, 992
Health insurance. See also Insurance
social security and, 782, 783
Hearings. See Congressional hearings
Hearst, William Randolph, 640, 652
"Heathens," 10
Heating fuel, forest depletion and, 258
Heatter, Gabriel, 822
Hecker, Isaac, 444
Heller, Joseph, 972
Helms, Jesse, 984
Hemingway, Ernest, 703, 713, 753, 754
Hemmings, Sally, 282
Henderson, Fletcher, 752
Henry III (France), 15
Henry IV (France), 51
Henry VII (England), 15
Henry VIII (England), 20
Henry, Fort, 469
Henry, Patrick, 140, 141, 142 (illus.), 149, 153, 225
Continental Congress and, 149

European North American holdings
and, 198
Indian opposition to, 171–172
for Philippines, 647
statue of George III and, 184 (illus.)
Independence Day, celebration of,
283 (illus.)
Independence movements, in Africa, 948
Independent Whig, 126–127
India, immigrants from, 1007
Indiana, 285
blacks and, 318
election of 1852 and, 440
settlement of, 320, 321
Indian Claims Commission, 967
Indian policy, 265–267. See also Native
Americans
Dawes Act and, 543–546
Fort Laramie Council and, 424–425
Indian perspective on, 541–542
of Jackson, 369–370
removal to Oklahoma, 541–542
of Roosevelt, Franklin D., 789–790
self-determination and, 970
termination policy, 967–968
white perspective on, 541–542
Indian Reorganization Act (1934), 790
Indians. See Native Americans
Indian Self-determination and Education
Assistance Acts, 970
Indian territory, 370, 370 (map),
371 (illus.)
Indies, sailing to, 17
Indigenous peoples. See Native
Americans
Indigo, 107
Individualism, 248
of workers, 596
Individual salvation, 363
Indochina. See Vietnam War
Indulgences, Luther and, 19
Industrial design, 798 (illus.)
Industrialization, 290 (illus.), 292,
298–301, 562 (illus.)
in Cincinnati, 308
cities and, 574–576
economic cycle and, 568–569
economic growth and, 292
English working class and, 15
environmental impacts of, 300–301
financing of, 568
living standards and, 577
manufacturing and, 301–302
pollution and, 569
railroads and, 565–567
in South, 547–548
steel industry and, 566 (illus.)
technology and, 564–565
in textile, metal, and machinery industries, 567–568
urban manufacturing and, 259
Industrial Relations Commission, 679
Industrial Revolution, 300 (illus.)
Industrial technology, 240–241,
240 (illus.), 241 (illus.)
Industrial Workers of the World (IWW),
679, 679 (illus.), 721
Industry. See also Manufacturing
accidents in, 584
air conditioning in, 853
artists inspired by, 742 (illus.)
black workers in, 551, 721
Civil War and, 463, 482, 486
decline of, 1000

electric power in, 737
employment in (1950), 844 (map)
labor and, 675–677
in mining, 416–417
overseas markets and, 638
recovery in Great Depression, 779
service economy and, 1000–1001
size of, 569
in South, 548
women in, 821
working class and, 582–590
World War II and, 814, 820
Infantile paralysis, of Roosevelt, Franklin
D., 775, 776 (illus.)
Infant mortality, 762
Inflation
in Civil War, 483–484
Ford and, 941
1982–1988, 1003
rate of (1940–1980), 936 (illus.)
Roosevelt, Franklin D., and, 777
World War II and, 814–815, 842
Influenza
epidemic, 157
pandemic (1918), 719, 720 (illus.)
Inheritance
of land, 101
taxes, 785
In His Steps (Sheldon), 613
Inner city, white flight from, 848
Innovations. See also Inventions and
inventors
American, 296
Inoculation, against smallpox, 156–157,
157 (illus.)
Insane asylums. See Asylums
Insecticides, 814
Installment plans, 856
Institute of Defense Analysis, 971
Institutions, in cities, 575
Insular cases, 647
Insurance. See also Old-age insurance;
Social Security
disability, 586
health, 782, 783
unemployment, 586
Integration. See also Desegregation
of armed forces, 884, 949
of baseball, 948
of defense industries, 819
at postsecondary level, 959
of schools, 946 (illus.), 949–950
Intellectual thought
black intellectuals and, 576
Enlightenment and, 115–116
Harlem Renaissance and, 752–753
Lost Generation and, 753–754
in postwar period, 732
Transcendentalism and, 363–364
Intelligence agency. See Central
Intelligence Agency (CIA); Office of
Strategic Services
Interchangeable parts, 264
bicycle and, 614
Interest rates, 1004
farm products and, 1002
Interior, expansion into, 96–100, 98 (map)
Intermarriage, white fear of, 500
Intermediate Range Nuclear Forces Treaty
(1987), 1015
Internal improvements, 282
by CWA, 778
government loans for, 296
Hamilton and, 225–226

Jackson and, 367–368
Old Northwest and, 320–321
PWA and, 778
in Reconstruction South, 514
Internal Revenue Service, 994
International Church of the Four Square
Gospel, 748
International Congress of Women (The
Hague, 1915), 704 (illus.)
International Ladies' Garment Workers
Union (ILGWU), 594, 677, 786
International Migration Society, 553
International Monetary Fund, 834
Internet, 747, 1016–1017
Internment, of Japanese Americans,
816–818
Interracial relationships
coercion of slave women and, 73
of French and Indians, 97–98
in New Spain, 100
Interstate commerce, workday for railway
workers and, 709
Interstate Commerce Act (1887), 554–555
Interstate Commerce Commission (ICC),
554–555, 685, 690
Interstate Highway Act (1956), 841
Interstate highway system, 843 (map)
Intervention
in Central America and Caribbean,
651–655, 654 (map)
in Cold War Latin America, 887
in Cuba, 641, 643–644, 651–654
in Dominican Republic, 707, 897
Good Neighbor Policy and, 806–807
in Grenada, 1021–1022
in Haiti, 707
in Mexico, 707–708, 708 (illus.)
in Middle East, 886, 887
in Nicaragua, 707, 761
in Panama, 1022
in Somalia, 1022–1023
in Twenties, 761
Intolerable Acts, 148
Continental Congress and, 148–149
Philadelphia and, 155
Intolerance, religious, 735–736
Inventions and inventors, 296, 569
barbed wire as, 533–534
cotton gin and, 260, 262–263
Edison and, 565
Franklin and, 116
Fulton and, 240
sewing machine and, 307, 390–391,
390 (illus.)
standard of living and, 736, 736 (illus.)
World War I and, 721
Investigative commission, progressive
reformers and, 678–679
Investment
capital, 292, 294–296, 1000
foreign, 638
Investment banking, 568
Inward light, among Quakers, 55, 56
Iolani Palace (Hawaii), 636 (illus.)
Iowa, settlement of, 320
Iran, 886
Iran-contra affair, 1021
Iraq, Persian Gulf War and, 1019–1021,
1019 (illus.), 1020 (map)
Ireland
England and, 27
immigrant labor support and, 597
immigrants from, 92, 236, 294, 305, 308,
317, 444, 571, 572, 574, 575, 587

in Haiti, 707
  Latin American interventions by, 654–655
  in Nicaragua, 707, 761
Maritime trade
  Dutch and, 52
  England and, 52–53
Market, for industrial goods, 1000
Marketing, 577, 737
  strategies for, 536 (illus.)
Markets
  Anglo-French wars and, 87
  development of, 298–299
  foreign, 843–844
  overseas, 637–638
Mark I computer, 854
Marne, Battle of the, 704
Maroons (runaways), 350
Marquette, Jacques, 84
Marriage. See also Divorce
  in Chesapeake region, 39
  in colonies, 103
  dismissal of women employees and, 755
  divorce and, 869, 1009
  of freedmen, 496–497
  French-Indian, 97–98
  of indentured servants, 37
  Mormon, 420
  property rights and, 577
  sex and, 754
  of slaves, 72, 344
  in South, 108
  stress in, 1000
  women and, 587, 590, 858
  women's rights and, 388 (illus.), 618
  in World War II, 821
Married women, in workforce, 313
Marshall, George C., 829, 879–880
  McCarthy and, 893
Marshall, John, 248, 250–251, 250 (illus.), 369, 372
  XYZ Affair and, 235
Marshall Plan, 880, 882
Martin, Luther, 210
Martineau, Harriet, 232
Martinique, 86, 136
Martin Marietta, 1004
Marx, Karl, 612, 710
Marx Brothers, 796
Mary II (England), William of Orange and, 80
Maryland, 38–39
  Calvert family in, 32 (illus.)
  Civil War and, 462, 464, 477
  Glorious Revolution and, 81
  manufacturing in, 300
  ratification in, 214
  rebellion in, 77, 207–208
  slavery in, 67, 202
  tobacco in, 106
  workers' compensation law in, 682
Mason, Arthur and Joanna, 50 (illus.)
Mason, George, 208
Mason, James, 434
Mason, John, 33, 47
Masons
  African Americans and, 275
  Jackson and, 372
Massachusetts. See also Boston
  Anglo-French wars and, 86
  constitutional convention in, 185–186, 186 (illus.)
  constitution of, 187–188
  Dominion of New England and, 80

election of 1852 and, 440
Intolerable Acts and, 148
ratification in, 214
redress of grievances in, 206 (illus.)
schools in, 297
separation of church and state in, 199
settlement of, 40–51
Shays's Rebellion and, 206–208, 207 (illus.)
taxation and, 204
Townshend Acts and, 144
voting requirements in, 124
working-class families in, 575
Massachusetts Bay Colony, 33, 44. See also Massachusetts
  success of, 50
Massachusetts Bay Company, 44, 45, 46–47
Massachusetts Emigrant Aid Society, 446
Massachusetts Institute of Technology, 1017
Massachusetts Society for Promoting Agriculture, 257
Massacres. See specific massacres
Massasoit, 74
Masses, The, 711
Massive retaliation policy, 890–891
Mass media, 744–745
Mass production
  bicycle and, 614–615
  Ford and, 740
  Levittowns and, 849, 850, 850 (illus.)
  railroads and, 565
Mass transit. See also Public transportation; Transportation
  automobiles and, 841
Masters. See also Planters and plantations; Slaves and slavery
  of indentured servants, 37
Masters, William H., 973
Masturbation, 381
Matagorda Bay, 84
Materialism
  consumer culture and, 855–857
  criticisms of, 869
Material possessions, of urban middle class, 312
"Maternal Instruction," 313 (illus.)
Maternity bill, 761
Mather, Cotton, 101, 103, 156
Matlack, Timothy, 155, 186
Matrilineal society
  in Africa, 13
  of Indians, 10
Matsu, 883
Matthews, Sylvia, 995
Mauldin, Bill, 820, 823–824
Mau Mau movement, 948
Maxim, Hiram Percy, 615
Mayan people, Spanish and, 21
Mayflower (ship), 41
Mayham, Hezekiah, 208
Mayor-council government, in cities, 681
Maysville Road bill, 368
McAdoo, William, 720
McCallum, Daniel, 567
McCannon, Bernice, 862
McCarran Internal Security Act (1950), 892
McCarthy, Joseph R., 893–894, 894 (illus.)
  McCarthyism, 873
  on television, 922
McClellan, George, 467–468, 477
  election of 1864 and, 486
McClure's magazine, 665

McCormick reaper, 296, 320 (illus.)
McCormick Reaper Works, Haymarket Riot and, 593
McCulloch v. Maryland, 251
McDonald's, 839–840, 841 (illus.)
McDonnell Douglas, 1004
McDougall, Alexander, 144, 146
McDowell, Irwin, 466, 467
McDuffie, George, 287
McGee, W. J., 614, 615
McGovern, George, election of 1972 and, 938
McGrath, J. Howard, 891
McGuffey readers, 301
McKay, Claude, 752, 754
McKinley, William, 620–621
  assassination of, 648, 683
  Cuba and, 640, 641, 642, 643
  economy and, 630
  election of 1896 and, 625, 625 (illus.), 626–628, 626 (illus.), 627 (illus.), 628 (map), 629
  election of 1900 and, 647, 648 (illus.)
  on Hawaii, 636 (illus.)
  Philippine annexation and, 645
  Spanish-American War and, 644
McKinley Tariff, 620–621
McNamara, Robert S., 898, 921
McNary-Haugen Farm Relief Bill, 756
McNickle, D'Arcy, 968
McPherson, Aimee Semple, 748–749
McPherson, William, 227
Meade, George, 477, 478
Meadlo, Paul, 904
Meany, George, 845
Measles, 22
Meat inspection, 686–687
Meat Inspection Act (1906), 686, 687
Meatpacking industry, 537
  Jungle, The, and, 686
Mechanization, 676, 855. See also Machinery
Media. See also specific media
  conservatives and, 985
Medicaid, 928, 1003
Medical assistance plan, 928
Medical schools, 581
  women and, 580
Medicare, 928, 930, 1003
Medicine. See also Diseases
  aging and, 1012
  miracle drugs and, 824, 847
  during Revolutionary War, 176
  smallpox inoculation and, 156
Mediterranean region, 878
  Barbary States and, 277
  slavery in, 64
Meetinghouse, Puritan, 48
Megafauna, 4–5
Mein Kampf (Hitler), 807
Mekras, John, 675
Mellon, Andrew, 758, 759, 918
Melville, Herman, 364
Membership, in Knights of Labor, 593
Memminger, Christopher G., 465
Memorial Day Massacre, 786
Memory, collective, 832
Memphis, 548, 742
  race riot in, 502–503, 503 (illus.)
Men. See Families and family life; Immigrants; Marriage; Soldiers; Sports; Workers
Men and Religion Forward movement, 682

popular, 976–977, 976 (illus.), 977 (illus.)
rock concerts and, 973 (illus.), 974
rock musicals and, 973
of slaves, 72, 347–348
in World War II, 823
Music festivals, 973 (illus.)
Muslims, 985 (illus.). See also Islam
in Balkans, 1018
fundamentalist, 984–985
North Africa and, 12
Spanish conquest of, 15
trade, exploration, and, 15–16
West Africa and, 13
Musschenbroek, Pieter van, 118
Mussolini, Benito, 807. See also Italy and
Italians
overthrow of, 829
Mutual-protection treaty, English-
Japanese, 658
My Lai massacre, 903–904
Mystic River, Pequot massacre at, 33

NAACP, 688–689, 951
Afro-American League and, 552
Du Bois and, 788
Justice Department and, 949
Montgomery and, 950
Niagara movement and, 690
school integration and, 949
Nader, Ralph, 979–980
NAFTA. See North American Free Trade
Agreement (NAFTA)
Nagasaki, atomic bombing of, 836
Nalil, Charles, 415 (illus.)
NAM. See National Association of
Manufacturers (NAM)
Name brands, 737
Names, The (Momaday), 805
Names and naming practices
among slaves, 348
surnames of freedmen, 497
Napalm, in Vietnam War, 902 (illus.)
Napoleon I (Bonaparte), 253, 277
Narragansett Bay region, 45, 147
Narragansett Indians, 33, 47, 73
Narrative of the Life of Frederick Douglass,
The (Douglass), 357
NASA, 925
Nasser, Gamal Abdel, 886–887
Nast, Thomas, 523 (illus.), 544, 652
Natchez Indians, 10, 99
Nation, The, 544
National Advisory Committee on
Aeronautics, 721
National Aeronautics and Space
Administration. See NASA
National Alliance, Ocala Platform and,
556–557
National American Woman Suffrage
Association (NAWSA), 618, 619, 724
National Association for the
Advancement of Colored People. See
NAACP
National Association of Manufacturers
(NAM), 638, 677, 778 (illus.)
on social security, 783
Truman and, 914–915
National Association Opposed to Woman
Suffrage, 724
National bank. See also Bank of the
United States
Hamilton and, 225

National Bureau of Economic Research,
737
National Chicano Moratorium
Committee, 966
National Child Labor Committee, 666
National Committee for a Sane Nuclear
Policy. See SANE
National Committee for Immigrants in
America, 663
National Congress of American Indians,
968
National Conservation Commission, 688
National Consumers League, 666
women's workday and, 667
National Credit Corporation, 771
National debt, 988 (illus.)
military expenditures and, 814 (illus.)
Reagan and, 988
after Revolution, 197–198
National Defense Research Committee,
814
National Economist, 556
National Endowment for the Arts, 929,
930, 992
National Endowment for the Humanities,
930, 992
National Gazette, 226
National government. See Federal govern-
ment; Government
National Grange, 554
National Guard
at Kent State, 904, 905 (illus.)
school desegregation and, 949–950,
950 (illus.)
Selma-Montgomery march and, 955
World War I and, 707
National health insurance, 917
National Housing Act (1937), 792
National Indian Youth Council, 968
National Industrial Recovery Act (NIRA),
779
National Institutes of Health, 157, 854
Nationalism, 603
Filipino-American War and, 647
Indian, 268
sectionalism and, 282–284
before World War I, 702
Nationalist Chinese, 883
National Labor Board, 779
National Labor Relations Act. See Wagner
Act (1935)
National Labor Relations Board, farm-
workers and, 965
National Labor Union (NLU), 519,
592–593
National League of Women Voters, 752
National Liberation Front, 898–899
National Magazine, 544
National Manufacturing Association, 757
National Marine Fisheries Service, 998
National Motor Vehicle Safety Advisory
Council, 980
National Negro Convention movement,
356, 387
National Organization for Women (NOW),
961, 961 (illus.)
National Origins Act (1927), 749
National Outdoor Recreation Review
Commission, 851
National parks and forests, 687 (map)
conservation movement and, 688
Roosevelt, Franklin D., and, 779
Yosemite and, 540

National Reclamation Act. See Newlands
Act
National Recovery Administration (NRA),
779
National Republicans, 282, 366
as Whigs, 372
National Research Council, 721
National Road, 252
National Science Foundation, Internet
and, 1017
National Security Act (1947), 842, 882
National Security Council (NSC), 881, 882
Iran-contra and, 1021
National Security League, 707
National Traffic and Motor Vehicle Safety
Act (1966), 930, 980
National Trails Act (1968), 851
National War Labor Board (NWLB), 815
in World War I, 721
National Wilderness Preservation Act
(1964), 851, 929, 930
National Woman's Party (NWP), 724, 756
National Youth Administration (NYA),
782, 788 (illus.)
Bethune and, 788, 788 (illus.)
Nation of Islam, Malcolm X and, 956
Native American Graves Protection and
Repatriation Act (1990), 997–998
Native Americans, 396 (illus.). See also
Land; Treaties; specific groups
African slaves and, 67
artifacts of, 8–9
assimilation of, 267
battles (1775-1783), 170 (map)
Cahokia and, 8–9
Carolinas and, 54
Cherokee survival and, 267–268
"civilizing" and Christianizing of,
266–267
Civil War and, 470
in college, 970
Columbus and, 18
conflict with Anglos in West, 422–425
conquest strategy toward, 196
creation myths of, 138
cultures of, 7–10
Dawes Act and, 543–546
diversity of, 4
domestication of plants by, 5
1850-1896, 543 (map)
European cultural regions and, 86 (map)
European settlement and, 3
expansionism of U.S. and, 634
former slaves of, 499
Fort Laramie Council and, 424–425
as French allies, 84
French-Indian marriages and, 97–98
Ghost Dance and, 546–547
during Great Depression, 789–790
Harper's Weekly story on, 544,
545 (illus.)
hatred for, 76
image of, 29
interior tribes of, 96–97
Iroquois survival and, 267–268
Jackson and, 369–370
Jamestown colonists and, 34–35
land cessions by, 166 (map), 196, 266
(map), 268, 269, 369, 423 (map)
land of, 73–77
Lewis and Clark expedition and, 253
marriages with fur trappers, 398
migration to cities, 820
mining frontier and, 418

homesteading and, 529
Indians and, 195–197, 422–425
land clearing and, 264 (illus.)
Manifest Destiny and, 399
Mexican War and, 403–404
migrants and, 407–409
Mississippi River region and, 197
Oregon and, 406–407
after Revolution, 194–197
sea route and, 409
into trans-Mississippi West, 253–256,
 397–407
after World War II, 847
Weyler, "Butcher," 641
Wheat, 530–531
 in California, 539
 harvesting, 536 (illus.)
 price of, 532, 532 (illus.)
Wheatley, John, 138
Wheatley, Phillis, 138, 139 (illus.)
Wheatley, Susannah, 139 (illus.)
Wheel, Indians and, 7–10
Wheeler, Burton K., 810
Wheeless, Zenobia, 556
Whetten, Harriet, 485
Whigs, 368 (illus.)
 and election of 1848, 433–436
 ideology of, 126–127
 National Republicans as, 372
 in second American party system,
  373, 374–375
"Whip Inflation Now" campaign, 941
Whipping, of slaves, 343
Whiskey Rebellion, 226–228
Whiskey Ring affair, 519
Whiskey Tax, 225
Whisper to a Bride, 312
White, John, 28 (illus.)
White, William Allen, 692, 809
White City, at Chicago World's Fair, 623,
 682
White-collar jobs and workers, 844–845
 immigrants and, 1007
 shift to, 1001
White Earth Land Recovery Project, 998
Whitefield, George, 91, 117–120,
 120 (illus.), 122
White flight, in Civil War, 484
White House, naming of, 278
White House Conference on Emergency
 Needs of Women (1933), 790
White House Conservation Conference,
 687–688
White League, 516 (illus.)
"White Man's Burden" (Kipling), 640,
 647
Whites. See also Anglos
 as abolitionists, 387
 in civil rights movement, 953
 after Civil War, 497 (illus.)
 Democratic party and, 523 (illus.)
 education for blacks and, 512–513
 education of, 296–297
 fear of slave revolts, 327
 flight from inner city, 848
 free blacks "passing" as, 354
 Freedom Summer and, 954
 income of, 959 (illus.), 960
 Indian perspective of, 541–542
 land during Reconstruction and,
  505–506
 lynchings by, 556
 Native American relations with,
  265–269

progressivism for, 688–690
race riots and, 316–317
racism of, 274–275
 in Reconstruction South, 509,
  510–511, 517
 reverse discrimination and, 959–960
 Scottsboro case and, 787
 secondary school enrollment of,
  297 (illus.)
 in South, 332 (map)
 as southern farmers, 549
 World War I soldiers and, 717
"White trash," 335
Whitman, Marcus and Narcissa, 398
Whitman, Walt, 448, 612
Whitney, Eli, 260, 262–263, 262 (illus.),
 263 (illus.), 328
Wholesale price index, 204 (illus.)
Why America Fights Germany, 714
Whyte, William H., 845
Wichita Indians, 422
Wide, Wide World, The (Warner), 291,
 301
Widows and widowers, 111
 in Chesapeake region, 39
 after Seven Years' War, 137
Wigglesworth, Michael, 78, 79, 138
Wild and Scenic Rivers Act, 851
Wilderness, Battle of the, 486
Wilderness, preservation of, 687–688,
 687 (illus.), 974–975
Wildlife refuges, Roosevelt, Franklin D.,
 and, 779
Wilhelm II (Germany), 658–659, 705
 abdication of, 718
Wilkerson, Eliza, 189
Wilkes, John, 174
Willard, Frances, 609–610, 618
William and Mary, College of, 122
William of Orange, 80
Williams, Abigail, 83
Williams, Aubrey, 788 (illus.)
Williams, George Washington, 576
Williams, John Skelton, 548
Williams, Roger, 45, 50
Williams, Rose, 345
Williamson County, Illinois, labor vio-
 lence in, 758
Willkie, Wendell, 810
Willow Grove, Michigan, 821
Wills, 112
Wilmington, 309
Wilmington Committee of Safety, 193
Wilmot, David, 433
Wilmot Proviso, 433, 436
Wilson, Charles E., 918
Wilson, Ellen Axson, 703
Wilson, James, 209
Wilson, Luzena, 417
Wilson, Woodrow, 727 (illus.)
 Allied sympathies of, 705
 collapse of, 727
 declaration of war by, 710
 election of 1912 and, 690–693,
  691 (map)
 election of 1916 and, 709
 federal power and, 720–721
 Fourteen Points and, 725
 on Gilded Age politics, 605
 Latin American intervention by, 655,
  707–709
 League of Nations and, 727–728
 negotiated war settlement and,
  709–710

neutrality policy of, 702, 705
New Freedom and, 692, 693–696
 as New Jersey governor, 683
 Paris Peace Conference and, 725
 tariff and banking reform of, 693–694
 woman suffrage and, 724
 World War I and, 659, 720
Wind, on Great Plains, 536
Windmills, 534
Windsor, 33
Winesburg, Ohio (Anderson), 754
Winter Scene in Brooklyn (Guy),
 259 (illus.)
Winthrop, John, 44, 45, 47, 50, 102, 634
Winthrop, John III, 116
Wireless communication, 746–747,
 746 (illus.)
Wirt, William, 372
Wisconsin
 La Follette in, 683
 settlement of, 320
"Wisconsin idea," 683
Witchcraft, Salem and, 83–84, 83 (illus.)
Witch-hunt, McCarthyism and, 893–894
Wives, 312. See also Families and family
 life; Women
WJZ (Newark), 743
Wobblies. See Industrial Workers of the
 World (IWW)
Wolfe, Alfred R., 852
Wolfe, James, 135 (illus.)
 at Quebec, 136
Wolfe, Thomas, 798
Wolfe, Tom, 990
Woman, in cabinet post, 776
Woman Rebel, The (Sanger), 668
Woman's Bible (Stanton), 618–619
Woman's Land Army, 722
Woman's Loyal League, 506
Woman suffrage, 617, 618–619, 693
 (illus.), 724
 in movies, 673
 before 19th Amendment, 669 (map)
 social justice movement and, 667
 Wilson and, 694
Woman Warrior, The (Kingston), 1011
Women. See also Abortion; Professions;
 Woman suffrage; specific issues
 abolitionism and, 386
 AFL and, 594
 anti-tea agreement and, 158 (illus.)
 black, 550, 963
 black Catholics and, 356
 in cabinet, 992
 CCC and, 779
 changing role of Native American, 97
 citizenship of, 188–190
 Civil War and, 485–486
 as Civil War nurse, 469 (illus.)
 college education for, 947
 as consumers, 721
 in cotton mills, 548
 cult of domesticity and, 388
 in domestic service, 587, 590 (illus.)
 earnings of, 586
 education for, 272, 273 (illus.),
  298 (illus.), 580
 electricity and, 754 (illus.)
 as emigrants to West, 410, 411, 412
 employment of, 786, 794–795,
  963 (illus.), 995
 equality for, 754–756
 European, 10
 evangelicalism and, 272–273